W9-CMO-898

Dictionary

OF THE Later New Testament

& Its Developments

Editors:

Ralph P. Martin

Peter H. Davids

INTERVARSITY PRESS

DOWNERS GROVE, ILLINOIS 60515

LEICESTER, ENGLAND

InterVarsity Press
P.O. Box 1400
Downers Grove, IL 60515 USA
World Wide Web: www.ivpress.com
E-mail: mail@ivpress.com

Inter-Varsity Press
38 De Montfort Street,
Leicester LE1 7GP, England

InterVarsity Press® is the book-publishing division of InterVarsity Christian Fellowship/USA, a student movement active on campus at hundreds of universities, colleges and schools of nursing in the United States of America, and a member movement of the International Fellowship of Evangelical Students. For information about local and regional activities, write Public Relations Dept., InterVarsity Christian Fellowship/USA, 6400 Schroeder Rd., P.O. Box 7895, Madison, WI 53707-7895.

Inter-Varsity Press, England, is the book-publishing division of the Universities and Colleges Christian Fellowship (formerly the Inter-Varsity Fellowship), a student movement linking Christian Unions in universities and colleges throughout the United Kingdom and the Republic of Ireland, and a member movement of the International Fellowship of Evangelical Students. For information about local and national activities write to UCCF, 38 De Montfort Street, Leicester LE1 7GP.

All Scripture quotations, unless otherwise indicated, are the authors' own translations. Those identified NIV are taken from the Holy Bible, New International Version®. NIV® Copyright ©1973, 1978, 1984 by International Bible Society. Used by permission of Zondervan Publishing House and published in Great Britain by Hodder and Stoughton Ltd. All rights reserved. Those identified RSV are from the Revised Standard Version of the Bible, copyright 1946, 1952, 1971 by the Division of Christian Education of the National Council of the Churches of Christ in the U.S.A., and used by permission. Those identified NRSV are from the New Revised Standard Version of the Bible, copyright 1989 by the Division of Christian Education of the National Council of the Churches of Christ in the U.S.A., and used by permission.

Cover photograph: Scala/Art Resource, NY. Rublev, Andrei. Saint Peter. Russian state Museum, St. Petersburg, Russia.

USA: ISBN 0-8308-1779-4

UK: ISBN 0-85111-751-1

Printed in the United States of America

Library of Congress Cataloging-in-Publication Data

Dictionary of the later New Testament and its developments/editors:
  Ralph P. Martin, Peter H. Davids.
    p.   cm.
    Includes bibliographical references and index.
    ISBN 0-8308-1779-4 (alk. paper)
    1. Bible   N.T. Acts—Encyclopedias.   2. Bible. N.T. Hebrews—
  Encyclopedias.   3. Bible. N.T. Catholic Epistles—Encyclopedias.
  4. Bible. N.T. Revelation—Encyclopedias.   5. Church history—
  Primitive and early church, ca. 30-600—Encyclopedias.   I. Martin,
  Ralph P.   II. Davids, Peter H.
  BS2625.5.D53   1997
  225.3—dc21   97-36095
                                                       CIP

British Library Cataloguing in Publication Data

A catalogue entry for this book is available from the British Library.

17	16	15	14	13	12	11	10	9	8	7	6	5	4	3
10	09	08	07	06	05	04	03	02	01	00				

InterVarsity Press

Executive Director
Robert Fryling

Editorial Staff

Editorial Director
Andrew T. Le Peau

Managing Editor
James Hoover

Reference Book Editor
Daniel G. Reid

Editorial Assistants
Gloria Duncan-Bevilacqua
Melinda Syens

Proofreaders
Drew Blankman
David Zimmerman

Production Staff

Production Manager
Nancy Fox

Production Coordinator
Don Frye

Design
Kathy Lay Burrows

Design Assistant
Andrew Craft

Typesetters
Gail Munroe
Audrey Smith
Marjorie Sire

Programming Consultant
Andy Shermer

Contents

Preface _____ *ix*

How to Use This Dictionary _____ *xi*

Abbreviations _____ *xiii*

Transliterations _____ *xxvi*

List of Contributors _____ *xxvii*

Dictionary Articles _____ *1*

Scripture Index _____ *1243*

Subject Index _____ *1266*

Articles Index _____ *1288*

Preface

In the previous two companion volumes, dedicated to the parts of the New Testament called "Gospels" and "Pauline Epistles," an attempt was made to introduce readers to those documents with which the readers would be familiar. Hence the respective prefaces acknowledged the foundational character of what the early church called "the Gospel" and "the Apostle."

A different kind of introduction is called for in this third yet complementary reference work. Here—in the remaining books of the New Testament canon—the reader is more than likely to be on a *terra incognita*. Features such as the complex arguments of the letter to the Hebrews, the moralizing tendency of James the Just, the fierce denunciations sounded in the epistle of Jude as well as the more accessible First Peter and the Acts of the Apostles will come to mind as representing books which cry out for elucidation. And who has not felt the need for scholarly and sympathetic guidance while patiently, if with puzzlement, reading the final book, called the Revelation? This *Dictionary* will, we hope, be among the first resources a student, teacher and communicator will turn to when seeking assistance.

It is to offer such help that the contributions to the present full-scale *Dictionary of the Later New Testament and Its Developments* were conceived, assembled, composed—and now are offered to the public. The editors are bold to surmise that this volume, perhaps more than the two earlier dictionaries, will fill a perceived gap in the field of reference books on the New Testament. It is designed to come to the aid of preachers, ministers, Christian laypeople and hard-pressed students of theology no less than the editors' colleagues in the academy when called on to teach these often neglected books of the canon.

Mention of the New Testament canon calls to mind a recent (1983, 1995) pronouncement of the doyen scholar C. K. Barrett. Writing on "The Centre of the New Testament and the Canon" (in his collected essays *Jesus and the Word* [Edinburgh: T & T Clark, 1995] 259-76), he states in support of his position that the *norma normans* of New Testament theology, the means of testing theological propositions (or better, he would say, the church's proclamation), is a nuanced version of the slogans *sola fide, solus Christus,* the "claim that *in practice* no harm but good results [follow] if we look at all the literary products of the apostolic and subapostolic ages" (his emphasis). To respond to this remark would involve a discussion of the ongoing debate regarding the "center of the New Testament" and the limits and definition of canonical authority. It is sufficient here to note that the coverage in this *Dictionary* will, we trust, put the readers in a position to see the ways the formulation of the Christian message developed from the Synoptic Gospels and Paul to the remaining New Testament books and then up to about the middle of the second century. Commitment to a determinative canon (embracing the twenty-seven books in our New Testament) should make room for (1) a frank admission that books often thought to be peripheral to the alleged "center" are still held to be normative, for as Dr. Barrett remarks, "there cannot be degrees of canonicity"; and (2) an equally frank acknowledgment that Christian thinking did not cease with the last New Testament book, and it developed in those writings usually called the apostolic fathers.

The decision to take the lines of development up to A.D. 150 was a matter of convenience, since a cut-off point was clearly needed if the volume was to be of manageable size. A certain editorial latitude, however, was granted to contributors who felt it needful to include material from the later patristic period. One reason for this inclusion is to allow developments that come to fuller fruition in the late second and subsequent early centuries to cast their light backward on the obscurities of the period A.D. 100-150. To change the metaphor, germination and flowering of a Christian truth often requires a considerable length of time to appear.

The editors and publisher struggled to find a suitable title for this volume that would do justice to its diverse subject matter and yet stand in continuity with the *Dictionary of Jesus and the Gospels* and the *Dictionary of Paul and His Letters*. No prejudicial judgment should be read into the part-title, *The Later New Testament*. As will be clear, the case for dating Jude or James anterior to the Pauline letters still continues to be made, even if the tendency is to place these letters in a subsequent decade. By general consensus, however, the bulk of the literature covered in this volume was written chronologically after the Pauline chief letters and, in some cases, after the publication of the Synoptics. Again, the adjective "later" is one of convenience, just as the term *Developments* is in no way intended to blur the line of demarcation the church has accepted (since Athanasius) between canonical and noncanonical, even if the story of the canonization of the New Testament has the ragged edges admitted by Eusebius.

Once more the editors are quick to recognize their debts and pay tribute to all who have made this volume possible. Secretarial help in the production processes and the ready cooperation of our team of contributors, drawn from around the world and across the boundaries of church affiliation, ethnicity and gender, are gratefully acknowledged.

It remains to send out the third member of this ambitious series (which will eventually include a *Dictionary of New Testament Background* and four volumes on the Old Testament) in the hope that it may, with its partners, serve the interests of readers. It is designed to assist those who seek to understand the remaining books of the New Testament in their historical, literary and religious setting and to observe the flow of church life, thought and history across a diverse spectrum of geography and culture, from Paul and the Synoptic Gospels to Justin in Rome.

Ralph P. Martin
Peter H. Davids

How to Use This Dictionary

Abbreviations

Comprehensive tables of abbreviations for general matters as well as for scholarly, biblical and ancient literature may found on pages xiii-xxv.

Authorship of Articles

The authors of articles are indicated by their first initials and last name at the end of each article. A full list of contributors may be found on pages xxvii-xxx, in alphabetical order of their last name. The contribution of each author is listed alphabetically.

Bibliographies

A bibliography has been appended to each article. The bibliographies include works cited in the articles and other significant related works. Bibliographical entries are listed in alphabetical order by the author's last name, and where an author has more than one work cited, they are listed alphabetically by title. In some types of articles (e.g., articles on specific NT literature and apostolic fathers) the bibliographies are divided into categories. Abbreviations used in the bibliographies appear in the tables of abbreviations.

Cross-references

The *Dictionary* has been extensively cross-referenced in order to aid readers in making the most of material appearing throughout the volume. Five types of cross-referencing will be found:

1. One-line entries appearing in alphabetical order throughout the *Dictionary* direct readers to articles where a topic is discussed:

Abba. *See* God; Son of God.

2. An asterisk after a single word in the body of an article indicates that an article by that title appears in the *Dictionary*. For example, "Christ*" directs the reader to an article entitled **Christ.**

3. A cross-reference appearing within parentheses in the body of an article also directs the reader to an article by that title. For example, (*see* Church Order) directs the reader to an article entitled **Church Order, Government.** Such cross-references are used either to prevent the confusion an asterisk might introduce (i.e., Son of God* could refer to either an article on "God" or "Son of God") or to direct the readers attention to an article of related interest.

4. Cross-references have been appended to the end of articles, immediately preceding the bibliography, to direct readers to articles significantly related to the subject:

See also HYMNS; LITURGICAL ELEMENTS; WORSHIP, LITURGY.

5. Where appropriate, references are made to articles in the companion volumes, the *Dictionary of Jesus and the Gospels* and the *Dictionary of Paul and His Letters*. These references are found within the body of the text of articles and never in bibliographies. For example, a reference such as (*see DJG*, Gentiles) refers to the article on "Gentiles" in the *Dictionary of Jesus and the Gospels*, and a reference such as (*see DPL*, Righteousness of God §2.4) refers to a specific section within the article on "Righteousness of God" found in the *Dictionary of Paul and His Letters*. The purpose of these references is both to assist readers in exploring related topics in Jesus and Paul as well as to provide contrasting or alternative points of view.

Indexes

Since most of the *Dictionary* articles cover broad topics in some depth, the *Subject Index* is intended to assist readers in finding relevant information on narrower topics that might, for instance, appear in a standard Bible dictionary. For example, while there is no article entitled "Nazoreans," the subject index might direct the reader to pages where the Nazoreans are discussed in the articles on "Jewish Christianity," "Ebionites" or elsewhere.

A *Scripture Index* is provided to assist readers in gaining quick access to the Scriptures referred to throughout the *Dictionary*.

An *Articles Index* found at the end of the *Dictionary* allows readers quickly to review the breadth of topics covered and select the ones most apt to serve their interests or needs. For those who wish to identify the articles written by specific contributors, they are listed with the name of the contributors in the list of contributors.

Transliteration

Hebrew and Greek words have been transliterated according to a system set out in the front matter. Greek verbs appear in their lexical form (rather than infinitive) in order to assist those with little or no knowledge of the language in using other reference works.

Abbreviations

General Abbreviations

§ or §§	section or paragraph number(s) (frequently to indicate Loeb Classical Library numbering system for Josephus)		mg.	margin
			MS or MSS	manuscript or manuscripts
			MT	Masoretic Text (standard Hebrew text of the Old Testament)
א	Codex Sinaiticus		n.d.	no date
κτλ	etc. (Greek)		n.s.	new series
2d ed.	second edition		NT	New Testament
3d ed.	third edition		o.s.	old series
A	Codex Alexandrinus		OT	Old Testament
B	Codex Vaticanus		p. or pp.	page or pages
C	Codex Ephraemi Syri		*pace*	with due respect to, but differing from
c.	circa, about (with dates); column		par.	parallel passage in another/other Gospel(s)
cent.	century			
cf.	compare		passim	throughout
chap(s).	chapter(s)		pl.	plural
D	Codex Bezae		presc.	prescript
DSS	Dead Sea Scrolls		Q	Quelle ("sayings" source for Synoptic Gospels)
e.g.	*exempli gratia,* for example			
ed.	edition; editor(s), edited by		repr.	reprint
esp.	especially		rev.	revised (edition)
ET	English translation		sy	Syriac
EVV	English versions of the Bible		Symm.	Symmachus's Greek translation of the Old Testament
exp.	expanded (edition)			
Frag.	Fragment (of document)		Tg.	Targum
Gk	Greek		Theod.	Theodotian's Greek translation of the Old Testament
Heb	Hebrew			
i.e.	*id est,* that is		v. or vv.	verse or verses
km.	kilometer		v.l.	*vario lectio* ("variant reading")
Lat	Latin		vol.	volume
LXX	Septuagint (Greek translation of the Old Testament)		x	times (2x = two times, etc.)
m	meter			

Translations of the Bible

ASV	American Standard Version (1901)		NIV	New International Version
AV	Authorized Version (Use KJV)		NRSV	New Revised Standard Version
JB	Jerusalem Bible		REB	Revised English Bible
KJV	King James Version (same as AV)		RSV	Revised Standard Version
NASB	New American Standard Bible		RV	Revised Version (1881-85)
NEB	New English Bible			

Books of the Bible

Old Testament

Gen	Ps	Nahum	Gal
Ex	Prov	Hab	Eph
Lev	Eccles	Zeph	Phil
Num	Song	Hag	Col
Deut	Is	Zech	1-2 Thess
Josh	Jer	Mal	1-2 Tim
Judg	Lam		Tit
Ruth	Ezek	*New Testament*	Philem
1-2 Sam	Dan	Mt	Heb
1-2 Kings	Hos	Mk	Jas
1-2 Chron	Joel	Lk	1-2 Peter
Ezra	Amos	Jn	1-2-3 Jn
Neh	Obad	Acts	Jude
Esther	Jon	Rom	Rev
Job	Mic	1-2 Cor	

The Apocrypha and Septuagint

1-2-3-4 Kgdms	1-2-3-4 Kingdoms	1-2-3-4 Macc	1-2-3-4 Maccabees
Add Esth	Additions to Esther	Pr Azar	Prayer of Azariah
Bar	Baruch	Pr Man	Prayer of Manasseh
Bel	Bel and the Dragon	Sir	Sirach (or Ecclesiasticus)
1-2 Esdr	1-2 Esdras	Sus	Susanna
4 Ezra	4 Ezra	Tob	Tobit
Jdt	Judith	Wis	Wisdom of Solomon
Ep Jer	Epistle of Jeremiah		

The Old Testament Pseudepigrapha

Adam and Eve	*Life of Adam and Eve*	*Mart. Isa.*	*Martyrdom of Isaiah*
Ahiq.	*Ahiqar*	*Pss. Sol.*	*Psalms of Solomon*
Apoc. Abr.	*Apocalypse of Abraham*	*Pseud.-Phoc.*	*Pseudo-Phocylides*
2-3 Apoc. Bar.	*Syriac, Greek Apocalypse of Baruch*	*Sib. Or.*	*Sibylline Oracles*
Apoc. Mos.	*Apocalypse of Moses*	*T. 12 Patr.*	*Testaments of the Twelve Patriarchs*
Apoc. Elijah	*Apocalypse of Elijah*	*T. Reub.*	*Testament of Reuben*
Apoc. Zeph.	*Apocalypse of Zephaniah*	*T. Sim.*	*Testament of Simeon*
Apoc. Sed.	*Apocalypse of Sedrach*	*T. Levi*	*Testament of Levi*
As. Mos.	*Assumption of Moses* (or	*T. Jud.*	*Testament of Judah*
	Testament of Moses)	*T. Iss.*	*Testament of Issachar*
Asc. Isa.	*Ascension of Isaiah*	*T. Zeb.*	*Testament of Zebulon*
Bib. Ant.	*Biblical Antiquities* of	*T. Dan.*	*Testament of Dan*
	Pseudo-Philo	*T. Naph.*	*Testament of Naphthali*
1-2-3 Enoch	*Ethiopic, Slavonic, Hebrew*	*T. Gad.*	*Testament of Gad*
	Enoch	*T. Asher*	*Testament of Asher*
Ep. Arist.	*Epistle of Aristeas*	*T. Jos.*	*Testament of Joseph*
Jos. and As.	*Joseph and Asenath*	*T. Benj.*	*Testament of Benjamin*
Jub.	*Jubilees*	*T. Abr.*	*Testament of Abraham*
Liv. Proph.	*Lives of the Prophets* (fol-	*T. Job*	*Testament of Job*
	lowed by prophet's name)	*T. Mos.*	*Testament of Moses*

Apostolic Fathers

Barn.	Epistle of Barnabas	
1 Clem.	1 Clement	
2 Clem.	2 Clement	
Did.	Didache	
Diogn.	Epistle to Diognetus	
Herm. Man.	Shepherd of Hermas, Mandate(s)	
Herm. Sim.	Shepherd of Hermas, Similitude(s)	
Herm. Vis.	Shepherd of Hermas, Vision(s)	
Ign. Eph.	Ignatius Letter to the Ephesians	

Ign.	Magm.	Ignatius Letter to the Magnesians
Ign.	Phld.	Ignatius Letter to the Philadelphians
Ign.	Pol.	Ignatius Letter to Polycarp
Ign.	Rom.	Ignatius Letter to the Romans
Ign.	Smyrn.	Ignatius Letter to the Smyrneans
Ign.	Trall.	Ignatius Letter to the Trallians
Mart. Pol.		Martyrdom of Polycarp
Pol. Phil.		Polycarp Letter to the Philippians

Other Early Christian Literature

Acts
Acts Apoll.	Acts of Apollonius
Acts Pil.	Acts of Pilate
Acts Paul & Thec.	Acts of Paul and Thecla
Acts Thom.	Acts of Thomas

Ambrose
Abr.	De Abrahamo
Exp. Ev. Luc.	Expositio Evangelii Secundum Lucam
Ps.	In Psalmos
Virg.	De Virginibus

Ap. Jas	Apocryphon of James

Aphrahat (or Aphraates)
Dem.	Demonstrations

Apocalypses
Apoc. Paul	Apocalypse of Paul
Apoc. Peter	Apocalypse of Peter

Aristides
Apol.	Apologia

Athanasius
Ar.	Adversus Arianos
Ep. Fest.	Festal Epistles
Fug.	Apologia pro Fuga Sua

Athenagoras
Leg.	Legatio pro Christianis
Suppl.	Supplicatio pro Christianis

Augustine
Civ. D.	De Civitate Dei
Conf.	Confessiones
De Cons.	De Consensu Evangelistarum
Doctr. Christ.	De Doctrina Christiana
Ep.	Epistulae
Haer.	De Haeresibus
Hom.	Homilia
Quaest. Evan.	Quaestiones Evangeliorum

BG	Berlin Gnostic Codex
CG	Nag Hammadi Gnostic Codices

Chrysostom
Hom. Gen.	Homilies on Genesis
Hom. Mt.	Homilies on Matthew
Regno	De Regno

Clement of Alexandria
Ecl. Proph.	Eclogae Propheticae
Excerpta	Excerpta ex Theodoto
Frag. Adum.	Fragmente in Adumbrationes
Frag. Ep. Jude	Fragmente in Epistle of Jude
Paed.	Paedagogus
Protr.	Protreptikos
Quis Div.	Quis Dives Salvetur
Strom.	Stromateis
Theod.	Letter to Theodore

Cyprian
Dom. Or.	De Dominica Oratione
Ep.	Epistulae
Laps.	De Lapsis

Cyril of Jerusalem
Myst. Cat.	Mystagogical Catecheses

Ep. Apos.	Epistola Apostolorum

Epiphanius
Haer.	Haereses
Weights	Weights and Measures

Eusebius
Eccl. Theol.	De Ecclesiastica Theologia
Hist. Eccl.	Historia Ecclesiastica
Dem. Ev.	Demonstratio Evangelica
In Ps	Commentary on the Psalms
Praep. Ev.	Praeparatio Evangelica

Gospels
Gos. Bar.	Gospel of Bartholomew
Gos. Eb.	Gospel of the Ebionites
Gos. Eg.	Gospel of the Egyptians
Gos. Heb.	Gospel of the Hebrews
Gos. Mary	Gospel of Mary
Gos. Naass.	Gospel of the Naassenes
Gos. Phil.	Gospel of Philip
Gos. Pet.	Gospel of Peter
Gos. Thom.	Gospel of Thomas

Hilary of Poitiers
Trin.	De trinitate

Hippolytus
Apos. Trad.	Apostolic Tradition
Dem. Chr.	Demonstratio de Christo et Antichristo
Haer.	De Haeresibus

Refut.	*Refutation of All Heresies,* or *Philosophumena*	*Pap. Frag.*	*Fragments of Papias*
		PBerol	*Papyrus Berolinensis*
Irenaeus		PG	*Patrologia Graeca,* ed. J. P. Migne
Haer.	*Adversus Haereses*		
Jerome		*Protev. Jas.*	*Protevangelium of James*
Comm. Gal.	*Commentary on Galatians*	Pseudo-Clementines	
Comm. Matt.	*Commentary on Matthew*	*Hom.*	*Homilies*
Comm. Mic.	*Commentary on Micah*	*Recogn.*	*Recognitions*
Ep.	*Epistulae*	Rufinus	
Vir.	*De Viris Illustribus*	*Hist. Eccl.*	*Historia Ecclesiastica*
Prol. in Matt.	*Prologue to Matthew*	Tatian	
Praef. in Quat. Ev.	*Preface to the Four Gospels*	*Or. Graec.*	*Oratio ad Graecos*
Justin Martyr		Tertullian	
Apol. I, II	*Apology I, II*	*Adv. Jud.*	*Adversus Judaeos*
Cohor. Graec.	*Cohortatio ad Graecos*	*Ad Nat.*	*Ad Nationes*
Dial. Tryph.	*Dialogue with Trypho the Jew*	*Ad Ux.*	*Ad Uxorem*
Or. Gr.	*Oratio ad Graecos*	*Apol.*	*Apologeticus*
Resurrec.	*On the Resurrection*	*De Anim.*	*De Anima*
Lactantius		*De Carn.*	*De Carne Christi*
Div. Inst.	*Divinae Institutiones*	*De Praescr.*	*De Praescriptione Haereticorum*
Mart. Justin	*The Martyrdom of Justin and Companions*	*De Bapt.*	*De Baptismo*
		De Cor.	*De Corona*
Mur. Frag.	*Muratorian Fragment*	*De Cult. Fem.*	*De Cultu Feminarum*
Odes Sol.	*Odes of Solomon*	*De Idol.*	*De Idololatria*
Origen		*De. Jejun.*	*De Jejunio Adversus Psychicos*
Comm. Joh.	*Commentary on John*	*De Orat.*	*De Oratione*
Comm. Mt.	*Commentary on Matthew*	*De Pud.*	*De Pudicitia*
Cont. Cels.	*Contra Celsum*	*De Resur.*	*De Resurrectione Carnis*
De Princ.	*De Principiis*	*De Spect.*	*De Spectaculis*
Exhort. Mart.	*Exhortatio ad Martyrium*	*Marc.*	*Adversus Marcionem*
Hom. Ez.	*Homilies on Ezekiel*	*Pud.*	*De Pudicitia*
Hom. Jos	*Homilies on Joshua*	*Prax.*	*Adversus Praxeas*
Hom. Luc.	*Homilies on Luke*	*Scorp.*	*Scorpiace*
Pass. Perp. Fel.	*Passion of Perpetua and Felicitas*	Theophilus of Antioch	
Peri Arch.	*Peri Archon*	*Autol.*	*Ad Autolycum*
Selec. Ps.	*Selecta in Psalmos*		

Classical and Hellenistic Writers and Sources

Aelian		Aratus	
De Nat. Anim.	*De Natura Animalum*	*Phaen.*	*Phaenomena*
Aeschylus		Aristophanes	
Pers.	*Persae*	*Thes.*	*Thesmophorizousai*
Sept. c. Theb.	*Septem contra Thebas*	*Acharn.*	*Acharnenses*
Suppl.	*Supplices*	Aristotle	
Ammonius		*Cael.*	*De Caelo*
Adfin. Vocab. Diff.	*De Adfinium Vocabulorum Differentia*	*Eth. Nic.*	*Ethica Nicomachea*
		Pol.	*Politica*
Anacharsis		*Prob.*	*Problemata*
Ep.	*Epistle to Tereus*	Artemidorus	
Antipater		*Oneir.*	*Oneirocriticon*
Anth. Pal.	*Anthologia Palatina*	Aulus Gellius	
Appian		*Noc. Att.*	*Noctes Atticae*
Mith. W.	*Mithridatic Wars*	Callimachus	
Civ. W.	*Civil Wars*	*Epigr.*	*Epigrammata*
Apuleius		Chariton	
Met.	*Metamorphoses*	*Chaer.*	*Chaereas and Callirhoe*

Cicero			Life	Life of Flavius Josephus
De Div.	De Divinatione		Ag. Ap.	Against Apion
De Leg.	De Legibus		Justinian	
De Offic.	De Officiis		Digest	Digest of Roman Law
De Orat.	De Oratore		Juvenal	
De Repub.	De Republica		Sat.	Satirae
Phil.	Orationes Philippicae		Livy	
Rab. Perd.	Rabirio Perduellionis		Epit.	Epitomae
Tusc.	Tusculanae Disputationes		Hist.	History of Rome
Code Just.	Code of Justinian		Lucian of Samosata	
Corp. Herm.	Corpus Hermeticum		Alex.	Alexander the False Prophet
Demosthenes			Herm.	Hermotimus
Ag. Conon	Against Conon		Peregr.	De Morte Peregrini
Lacrit.	Against Lacritus		Philops.	Philopseudes
Dig. Just.	Digest of Justinian		Tox.	Toxaris
Dio Cassius			Marcus Aurelius	
Epit.	Roman History		Med.	Meditations
Hist.	Roman History		Martial	
Dio Chrysostom			Epigr.	Epigrams
De Homero	De Homero et Socrate		Muson. Ruf.	Musonius Rufus
Disc.	Discourses		Nicolaus of Damascus	
Or.	Orationes		Vit. Caes.	Vita Caesaris
Diodorus Siculus			Orosius	
Bib. Hist.	Bibliotheca Historica		Pag.	Adversus Paganos
Diogenes Laertius			Orph. Frag.	Orphic Fragments
Vit.	Vitae		Ovid	
Clit.	Clitomachus		Met.	Metamorphoses
Dion. Hal.	Dionysius of Halicarnassus		P Cair. Zen.	Zenon Papyri, ed. C. C.
Epictetus				Edgar, Zenon Payri, vols. 1-4
Disc.	Discourses			(Le Caire, 1925-31; Cata-
Diss.	Dissertationes			logue générale des antiquités
Ench.	Enchiridion			égyptiennes du Musée du
Euripides				Caire).
Hipp.	Hippolytus		Pausanius	
Galen			Descr.	Description of Greece
De Placitis	De Placitis Hippocratis et		Petronius	
	Platonis		Sat.	Satyricon
Grk. Anth.	Greek Anthology		PGM	Papyri-Graecae Magicae
Hesiod			Philo	
Op.	Opera et Dies		Abr.	De Abrahamo
Theog.	Theogonia		Aet. Mund.	De Aeternitate Mundi
Homer			Agric.	De Agricultura
Il.	Iliad		Cher.	De Cherubim
Odys.	Odyssey		Conf. Ling.	De Confusione Linguarum
Horace			Congr.	De Congressu Eruditionis Gratia
Sat.	Satires		Decal.	De Decalogo
Iamblichus			Det. Pot. Ins.	Quod Deterius Potiori Insidiari
De Myst.	De Mysteriis			Soleat
Inscr. Cos	The Inscriptions of Cos, ed.		Deus Imm.	Quod Deus Sit Immutabilis
	W. R. Paton and E. L. Hicks		Ebr.	De Ebrietate
	(1891)		Flacc.	In Flaccum
Isocrates			Fug.	De Fuga et Inventione
Dem.	Demonicus		Gig.	De Gigantibus
Panath.	Panathenaicus		Jos.	De Josepho
Paneg.	Panegyricus		Leg. All.	Legum Allegoriae
Josephus			Leg. Gai.	Legatio ad Gaium
Ant.	Antiquities of the Jews		Migr. Abr.	De Migratione Abrahami
J.W.	Jewish Wars		Mut. Nom.	De Mutatione Nominum

Omn. Prob. Lib.	Quod Omnis Probus Liber Sit
Op. Mund.	De Opificio Mundi
Plant.	De Plantatione
Poster. C.	De Posteritate Caini
Praem. Poen.	De Praemiis et Poenis
Prov.	De Providentia
Quaest. in Ex.	Quaestiones in Exodum
Quaest. in Gen.	Quaestiones in Genesin
Rer. Div. Her.	Quis Rerum Divinarum Heres Sit.
Sacr.	De Sacrificiis Abelis et Caini
Som.	De Somnis
Spec. Leg.	De Specialibus Legibus
Virt.	De Virtibus
Vit. Cont.	De Vita Contemplativa
Vit. Mos.	De Vita Mosis

Philostratus
Vit. Ap.	Vita Apollonii

Pindar
Isth.	Isthmia

Plato
Alc.	Alcibiades
Apol.	Apologia
Crat.	Cratylus
Gorg.	Gorgias
Leg.	Leges
Phaedr.	Phaedrus
Protag.	Protagoras
Rep.	Res Publica
Soph.	Sophista
Symp.	Symposion
Tim.	Timaeus

Pliny (the elder)
Nat. Hist.	Naturalis Historia
Panegyr.	Panegyricus

Pliny (the younger)
Ep.	Epistles

Plutarch
Mor.	Moralia
Adulat.	De Adulatore et Amico
Colot.	Adversus Colotem
Con. Praec.	Coniugalia Praecepta
Conv.	Quaestiones Convivales
Def. Orac.	De Defectu Oraculorum
Fac. Lun.	De Facie in Orbe Lunae
Fort. Rom.	De Fortuna Romanorum
Gen. Socr.	De Genio Socratis
Iside	De Iside et Osiride
Lib. Educ.	De Liberis Educandis
Mul. Virt.	Mulierum Virtutes
Non Posse Suav.	Non Posse Suaviter Vivi Secundum Epicurum
Praec. Ger. Reipub.	Praecepta Gerendae Reipublicae
Rom.	Quaestiones Romanae
Ser. Num. Vind.	De Sera Numinis Vindicta

Vit.	Vitae
Alex.	De Alexandro
Anton.	De Antonio
Caesar	De Caesar
Numa	De Numa
Pomp.	De Pompeio

Polybius
Hist.	Histories

Proclus
In Tim.	In Platonis Timaeum Commentarius

Quintilian
Inst. Orat.	Institutio Oratoria

Seneca
Ben.	De Beneficius
Brev. Vit.	De Brevitate Vitae
De Clem.	De Clementia
Ep. Lucil.	Epistles to Lucilius
Ep. Mor.	Epistulae Morales

Sophocles
Elec.	Electra
Oed. Tyr.	Oedipus Tyrannus

Stobaeus
Ecl.	Ecloge

Strabo
Geog.	Geography

Suetonius
Claudius	from The Twelve Caesars
Domitian	from The Twelve Caesars
Galba	from The Twelve Caesars
Julius	from The Twelve Caesars
Nero	from The Twelve Caesars
Tiberius	from The Twelve Caesars
Titus	from The Twelve Caesars
Vespasian	from The Twelve Caesars

Tacitus
Ann.	Annales ab Excessu Divi Augusti
Hist.	Historiae

Theon
Progymn.	Progymnasmata

Thucydides
Hist.	History of the Peloponnesian War

Valerius Maximus
Fact. ac Dict.	Factorum ac Dictorum Memorabilium Libri

Vegetius Renatus
Epit. Rei Milit.	Epitoma Rei Militaris

Vergil
Georg.	Georgics

Xenophon
Hist. Gr.	Historia Graeca
Mem.	Memorabilia Socratis

Dead Sea Scrolls and Related Texts

CD	Cairo (Genizah text of the) *Damascus (Document/Rule)*
P	Pesher (commentary)
Q	Qumran
1Q, 3Q, 4Q etc.	Numbered caves of Qumran, yielding written material; followed by abbreviation or number of document
1QapGen	*Genesis Apocryphon* from Qumran Cave 1 (1Q20)
1QH	*Hôdāyôt* or *Thanksgiving Hymns* from Qumran Cave 1
1QIsa^a,b	First or second copy of Isaiah from Qumran Cave 1
1QM	*Milḥāmāh* or *War Scroll* from Qumran Cave 1
1QMyst	Mysteries (1Q27)
1QpHab	*Pesher on Habakkuk* from Qumran Cave 1
1QPsa^a	Fragmentary copy of Psalms (1Q10)
1QS	*Serek hayyaḥad* or *Rule of the Community, Manual of Discipline* from Qumran Cave 1
1QSa	Appendix A, *Messianic Rule*, to 1QS from Qumran Cave 1 (1Q28a)
1QSb	Appendix B, *Rule of the Blessings*, to 1QS from Qumran Cave 1 (1Q28b)
3Q15	*Copper Scroll* from Qumran Cave 3
4Q139	Ordinances or commentaries on biblical laws from Qumran Cave 4
4Q169	Pesher on Nahum from Qumran Cave 4
4Q171	Pesher on Psalms from Qumran Cave 4
4Q176	*Tanhumim* or *Consolations* from Qumran Cave 4
4Q186	(see 4QMess ar)
4Q246	(see 4QPsDanA^a)
4Q400-407	(see 4QShirShabb)
4Q504	*Words of the Luminaries* from Qumran Cave 4
4Q513-14	Ordinances or commentaries on biblical laws from Qumran Cave 4
4QDibHam^a	*Words of the Luminaries*^a (4Q504)
4QEnGiants	*1 Enoch* fragments from Book of Giants from Qumran Cave 4 (4Q203)
4QEn^a-g	*1 Enoch* fragments from Qumran Cave 4 (4Q201-212)
4QEnastr^a-g	*1 Enoch* fragments from Astronomical Book from Qumran Cave 4 (4Q208-211)
4QFlor	*Florilegium* or *Eschatological Midrashim* from Qumran Cave 4 (4Q174)
4QMess ar	Aramaic "Messianic" text from Qumran Cave 4 (4Q534)
4QMMT	*Miqsat Maiaseh Torah* from Qumran Cave 4 (4Q394-399)
4QpNah	Nahum Pesher from Qumran Cave 4 (4Q169)
4QPhyl	Phylacteries from Qumran Cave 4 (4Q128-148)
4QPrNab	*Prayer of Nabonidus* from Qumran Cave 4 (4Q242)
4QPsDanA^a	Pseudo-Danielic Writings from Qumran Cave 4 (4Q246)
4QPssJosh	*Psalms of Joshua* from Qumran Cave 4 (4Q379)
4QShirShabb	*Songs of Sabbath Sacrifice* or *Angelic Liturgy* from Qumran Cave 4 (4Q400-407)
4QTestim	*Testimonia* text from Qumran Cave 4 (4Q175)
4QtgJob	*Targum of Job* from Qumran Cave 4 (4Q157)
4QtgLev	*Targum of Leviticus* from Qumran Cave 4 (4Q156)
5Q15	*New Jerusalem* from Qumran Cave 5 (5Q15)
11QH	*Hymns* (11Q15-16)
11QMelch	*Melchizedek* from Qumran Cave 11 (11Q13)
11QpaleoLev	Copy of Leviticus in paleo-Hebrew script from Qumran Cave 11 (11Q1)
11QPs^a	*Psalms Scroll* from Qumran Cave 11 (11Q5)
11QTemple	*Temple Scroll* from Qumran Cave 11 (11Q19)
11QtgJob	*Targum of Job* from Qumran Cave 11 (11Q10)

Targumic Material

Frg. Tg.	*Fragmentary Targum*
Sam. Tg.	*Samaritan Targum*
Tg. Cant.	*Targum of Canticles* (Song of Solomon)
Tg. Esth I, II	*First or Second Targum of Esther*
Tg. Isa.	*Targum of Isaiah*
Tg. Ket.	*Targum of the Writings*
Tg. Neb.	*Targum of the Prophets*
Tg. Neof.	*Targum Neofiti I*
Tg. Onq.	*Targum Onqelos*
Tg. Ps.-J.	*Targum Pseudo-Jonathan*
Tg. Yer. I	*Targum Yerušalmi I*
Tg. Yer. II	*Targum Yerušalmi II*
Yem. Tg.	*Yemenite Targum*

Orders and Tractates in the Mishnah, Tosefta and Talmud

Same-named tractates in the Mishnah, Tosefta, Babylonian Talmud and Jerusalem Talmud are distinguished by *m.*, *t.*, *b.* and *y.* respectively.

'Abot	*'Abot*	Nazir	*Nazir*
'Arak.	*'Arakin*	Ned.	*Nedarim*
'Abod. Zar.	*'Aboda Zara*	Neg.	*Nega'im*
B. Bat.	*Baba Batra*	Nez.	*Neziqin*
Bek.	*Bekorot*	Nid.	*Niddah*
Ber.	*Berakot*	Ohol.	*Oholot*
Beṣa	*Beṣa* (= Yom Ṭob)	'Or.	*'Orla*
Bik.	*Bikkurim*	Para	*Para*
B. Meṣ.	*Baba Meṣi'a*	Pe'a	*Pe'a*
B. Qam.	*Baba Qamma*	Pesaḥ.	*Pesaḥim*
Dem.	*Demai*	Qinnim	*Qinnim*
'Erub.	*'Erubin*	Qidd.	*Qiddušin*
'Ed.	*'Eduyyot*	Qod.	*Qodašin*
Giṭ.	*Giṭṭin*	Roš Haš.	*Roš Haššana*
Ḥag.	*Ḥagiga*	Sanh.	*Sanhedrin*
Ḥal.	*Ḥalla*	Šabb.	*Šabbat*
Hor.	*Horayot*	Šeb.	*Šebi'it*
Ḥul.	*Ḥullin*	Šebu.	*Šebu'ot*
Kelim	*Kelim*	Šeqal.	*Šeqalim*
Ker.	*Keritot*	Soṭa	*Soṭa*
Ketub.	*Ketubot*	Sukk.	*Sukka*
Kil.	*Kil'ayim*	Ta'an.	*Ta'anit*
Ma'aś.	*Ma'aśerot*	Tamid	*Tamid*
Mak.	*Makkot*	Tem.	*Temura*
Makš.	*Makširin* (=Mašqin)	Ter.	*Terumot*
Meg.	*Megilla*	Ṭohar.	*Ṭoharot*
Me'il.	*Me'ila*	Ṭ. Yom	*Ṭebul Yom*
Menaḥ.	*Menaḥot*	'Uq.	*'Uqṣin*
Mid.	*Middot*	Yad.	*Yadayim*
Miqw.	*Miqwa'ot*	Yebam.	*Yebamot*
Mo'ed	*Mo'ed*	Yoma	*Yoma* (= Kippurim)
Mo'ed Qaṭ.	*Mo'ed Qatan*	Zabim	*Zabim*
Ma'aś. Šeni	*Ma'aśer Šeni*	Zebaḥ.	*Zebaḥim*
Našim	*Naši m*	Zer.	*Zera'im*

Other Rabbinic Works

		Pesiq. R.	*Pesiqta Rabbati*
'Abot R. Nat.	*'Abot de Rabbi Nathan*	*Pesiq. Rab Kah.*	*Pesiqta de Rab Kahana*
'Ag. Ber	*'Aggadat Berešit*	*Pirqe R. El.*	*Pirqe Rabbi Eliezer*
Bab.	*Babylonian*	*Rab.*	*Rabbah* (following abbreviation for biblical book: *Gen. Rab.* = *Genesis Rabbah*)
Bar	*Baraita*		
Der Er Rab.	*Derek Ereṣ Rabba*		
Der Er Zu.	*Derek Ereṣ Zuṭa*	*Ṣem.*	*Ṣemaḥot*
Gem.	*Gemara*	*Sipra*	*Sipra*
Kalla	*Kalla*	*Sipre*	*Sipre*
Mek.	*Mekilta*	*Sop.*	*Soperim*
Midr	*Midraš* (cited with abbreviation for biblical book)	*S. 'Olam Rab.*	*Seder 'Olam Rabbah*
		Talm.	*Talmud*
Pal.	*Palestinian*	*Yal.*	*Yalquṭ*

Nag Hammadi Tractates

Acts Pet. 12 Apost.	*The Acts of Peter and the Twelve Apostles*	*Marsanes*	*Marsanes*
		Melch.	*Melchizedek*
Allogenes	*Allogenes*	*Norea*	*The Thought of Norea*
Ap. Jas.	*The Apocryphon of James*	*On Anoint.*	*On the Anointing*
Ap. John	*The Apocryphon of John*	*On Bapt. A*	*On Baptism A*
Apoc. Adam	*The Apocalypse of Adam*	*On Bapt. B*	*On Baptism B*
1 Apoc. Jas.	*The (First) Apocalypse of James*	*On Bapt. C*	*On Baptism C*
2 Apoc. Jas.	*The (Second) Apocalypse of James*	*On Euch. A*	*On the Eucharist A*
Apoc. Paul	*The Apocalypse of Paul*	*On Euch. B*	*On the Eucharist B*
Apoc. Peter	*Apocalypse of Peter*	*Orig. World*	*On the Origin of the World*
Asclepius	*Asclepius 21-29*	*Paraph. Shem*	*The Paraphrase of Shem*
Auth. Teach.	*Authoritative Teaching*	*Pr Paul*	*The Prayer of the Apostle Paul*
Dial. Sau	*The Dialogue of the Savior*	*Pr Thanks.*	*The Prayer of Thanksgiving*
Disc. 8-9	*The Discourse on the Eighth and Ninth*	*Sent. Sextus*	*The Sentences of Sextus*
		Soph. Jes. Chr	*The Sophia of Jesus Christ*
Ep. Pet. Phil.	*The Letter of Peter to Philip*	*Steles Seth*	*The Three Steles of Seth*
Eugnostos	*Eugnostos the Blessed*	*Teach. Silu*	*The Teachings of Silvanus*
Exeg. Soul	*The Exegesis on the Soul*	*Testim. Truth*	*The Testimony of Truth*
Gos. Eg.	*The Gospel of the Egyptians*	*Thom. Cont.*	*The Book of Thomas the Contender*
Gos. Phil.	*The Gospel of Philip*	*Thund.*	*The Thunder: Perfect Mind*
Gos. Thom.	*The Gospel of Thomas*	*Treat. Res.*	*The Treatise on the Resurrection*
Gos. Truth	*The Gospel of Truth*	*Treat. Seth*	*The Second Treatise of the Great Seth*
Great Pow	*The Concept of Our Great Power*	*Tri. Trac.*	*The Tripartite Tractate*
Hyp. Arch.	*The Hypostasis of the Archons*	*Trim. Prot.*	*Trimorphic Protennoia*
Hypsiph.	*Hypsiphrone*	*Val. Exp.*	*A Valentinian Exposition*
Interp. Know	*The Interpretation of Knowledge*	*Zost.*	*Zostrianos*

Periodicals, Reference Works and Serials

AARAS	American Academy of Religion Academy Series	*AbrN*	*Abr-Nahrain*
		ACNT	The Augsburg Commentary on the New Testament
AARSR	American Academy of Religion Studies in Religion		
		ACW	Ancient Christian Writers
AB	Anchor Bible	*AER*	*American Ecclesiastical Review*
ABD	*Anchor Bible Dictionary*, ed. D. N. Freedman	AGJU	Arbeiten zur Geschichte des antiken Judentums und des Urchristentums
ABQ	*American Baptist Quarterly*		
ABR	*Australian Biblical Review*	AGSU	Arbeiten zur Geschichte des Spätjudentums und Urchristentums
ABRL	Anchor Bible Reference Library		

AJA	*American Journal of Archaeology*	BR	*Biblical Research*
AJBI	*Annual of the Japanese Biblical Institute*	BRev	*Bible Review*
AJT	*American Journal of Theology*	BS	Bollingen Series
AK	Arbeiten zur Kirchengeschichte	BSac	*Biblioteca Sacra*
ALGHJ	Arbeiten zur Literatur und Geschichte des hellenistischen Judentums	BT	*The Bible Translator*
		BTB	*Biblical Theology Bulletin*
ALUOS	*Annual of Leeds University Oriental Society*	BTS	Biblisch-Theologische Studien
AnBib	Analecta Biblica	BU	Biblische Untersuchungen
AnBoll	*Analecta Bollandiana*	BZ	*Biblische Zeitschrift*
ANF	Ante-Nicene Fathers, ed. A. Roberts and J. Donaldson (10 vols.; 1890 [repr. 1951])	BZNW	*Beihefte zur Zeitschrift für die Neutestamentliche Wissenschaft*
ANRW	Aufstieg und Niedergang der römischen Welt	CAH	*Cambridge Ancient History*
APOT	*The Apocrypha and Pseudepigrapha of the Old Testament in English*, ed., R. H. Charles (2 vols., 1913).	CahTheol	Cahiers Théologiques
		CBC	Cambridge Bible Commentary
		CBQ	*Catholic Biblical Quarterly*
ARWAW	Abhandlungen der Rheinisch-Westfälischen Akademie der Wissenschaften	CBQMS	*Catholic Biblical Quarterly* Monograph Series
		CCWJCW	Cambridge Commentaries on Writings of the Jewish and Christian World 200 B.C. to A.D. 200
ASNU	Acta seminarii neotestamentici upsaliensis		
ATANT	Abhandllungen zur Theologie des Alten und Neuen Testaments	CD	*Church Dogmatics*, Karl Barth
ATLABibS	ATLA Bibliography Series	CEB	Commentaire Evangélique de la Bible
ATR	*Anglican Theological Review*	CGTC	Cambridge Greek Testament Commentary
AusBR	*Australian Biblical Review*		
AUSS	*Andrews University Seminary Studies*	CH	*Church History*
BA	*Biblical Archaeologist*	CIG	*Corpus Inscriptionum Graecarum* I-IV (1828-1877)
BAFCS	The Book of Acts in Its First Century Setting		
BAGD	W. Bauer, W. F. Arndt, F. W. Gingrich and F. W. Danker, *Greek-English Lexicon of the NT*	CII	*Corpus inscriptionum iudaicarum* I-II, J. B. Frey (1936-1952)
		CIL	*Corpus Inscriptionum Latinarum* I-XI (1862-1943, 2d ed. 1893-)
BBB	Bonner biblische Beiträge		
BBR	*Bulletin for Biblical Research*	CJT	*Canadian Journal of Theology*
BCJ	Brown Classics in Judaica	CNT	Commentaire du Nouveau Testament
BDB	Brown, Driver and Briggs, *Hebrew and English Lexicon of the Old Testament*	ConB	Coniectanea biblica
		ConBNT	Coniectanea biblica Neotestamentica
BDF	F. Blass, A. Debrunner and R. W. Funk, *A Greek Grammar of the New Testament and Other Early Christian Literature* (Chicago: University of Chicago Press, 1961)	ConNT	Coniectanea neotestamentica
		CPG	*Clavis Patrum Graecorum*, ed. M. Geerard, 5 vols. (Turnhout: Brepols, 1974-87)
		CPJ	*Corpus Papyrorum Judaicarum*
BET	Beitrage zur evangelischen Theologie	CQ	*Classical Quarterly*
BETL	Bibliotheca ephemeridum theologicarum lovaniensium	CQR	*Church Quarterly Review*
		CRB	Cahiers de la Revue Biblique
BF	Beiträge zur Forschung	CRINT	Compendia rerum iudaicarum ad novum testamentum
BG	Berlin Gnostic Codex		
BGU	Ägyptische Urkunden aus den Museen zu Berlin: Griech. Urkunden I-VIII (1895-1933)	CSCO	Corpus Scriptorum Christianorum Orientalium
		CSEL	Corpus Scriptorum Ecclesiasticorum Latinorum
BHT	Beiträge zur historischen Theologie		
BI	*Biblical Interpretation*	CSHJ	Chicago Studies in the History of Judaism
Bib	*Biblica*	CTJ	*Calvin Theological Journal*
BibO	Biblica et Orientica	CTM	*Concordia Theological Monthly*
BibRes	*Biblical Research*	CTR	*Criswell Theological Review*
BibS(F)	Biblische Studien (Freiburg, 1895-)	CurTM	*Currents in Theology and Mission*
BibS(N)	Biblische Studien (Neukirchen, 1951-)	CV	*Communio Viatorum*
BibTh	*Biblical Theology*	DCB	*Dictionary of Christian Biography*, ed. W. Smith and H. Wace, 4 vols. (London, 1877-87)
BJRL	*Bulletin of the John Rylands University Library of Manchester*		
BJS	Brown Judaic Studies	DHL	Dissertationes humanarum litterarum
BMI	The Bible and its Modern Interpreters	DJD	Discoveries in the Judaean Desert

DJG	*Dictionary of Jesus and the Gospels,* ed. J. B. Green and S. McKnight	*HeyJ*	*The Heythrop Journal*
DPL	*Dictionary of Paul and His Letters,* ed. R. P. Martin and G. F. Hawthorne	HNT	Handbuch zum Neuen Testament
		HNTC	Harper's New Testament Commentaries
DRev	*Downside Review*	*HR*	*History of Religions*
DSB	Daily Study Bible	HSMS	Harvard Semitic Monograph Series
DTT	*Dansk teologisk tidsskrift*	HSS	Harvard Semitic Studies
EB	Études bibliques	HTKNT	Herders theologischer Kommentar zum Neuen Testament
EBC	The Expositor's Bible Commentary		
EBT	*Encyclopedia of Biblical Theology,* ed. J. B. Bauer	HTS	Harvard Theological Studies
EDNT	*Exegetical Dictionary of the New Testament,* ed., H. Balz and G. Schneider	HUT	Hermeneutische Untersuchungen zur Theologie
		HZ	*Historische Zeitschrift*
EGT	Expositor's Greek Testament	*IBS*	*Irish Biblical Studies*
EH	Europäische Hochschulschriften	ICC	International Critical Commentary
EKK	Evangelisch-katholischer Kommentar zum Neuen Testament	*IDB*	*Interpreter's Dictionary of the Bible*
		IDBSup	*Interpreter's Dictionary of the Bible, Supplementary Volume*
ELS	*Enchiridion Locorum Sanctorum. Documenta S. Evangelii Loca Respicientia*		
		IEJ	*Israel Exploration Journal*
EncJud	*Encyclopaedia Judaica*	*ILS*	*Inscriptiones Latinae Selectae* (Berlin, 1892)
EP	Études Bibliques	*Int*	*Interpretation*
EPTA Bulletin	*European Pentecostal Theological Association Bulletin*	IntC	Interpretation Commentaries
		IRT	Issues in Religion and Theology
ER	*The Encyclopedia of Religion,* ed. M. Eliade	*ISBE*	*International Standard Bible Encyclopedia* (rev. ed.)
ERev	*Ecumenical Review*		
ESEC	Emory Studies in Early Christianity	IVPNTC	InterVarsity Press New Testament Commentary
ESW	Ecumenical Studies in Worship		
ETS	Erfurter Theologische Schriften	*JAC*	*Jahrbuch für Antike und Christentum*
EvJ	*Evangelical Journal*	*JAOS*	*Journal of the American Oriental Society*
EvQ	*Evangelical Quarterly*	*JBL*	*Journal of Biblical Literature*
EvT	*Evangelische Theologie*	*JBR*	*Journal of Bible and Religion*
EWNT	*Exegetisches Wörterbuch zum Neuen Testament,* ed., H. Balz and G. Schneider (ET, *Exegetical Dictionary of the New Testament*)	*JCBRF*	*Journal of the Christian Brethren Research Fellowship*
		JCR	*The Journal of Communication and Religion*
		JCSR	*Journal of Comparative Sociology and Religion*
Exp	*Expositor*	*JECS*	*Journal of Early Christian Studies*
ExpT	*Expository Times*	*JEH*	*Journal of Ecclesiastical History*
FB	Facet Books	*JES*	*Journal of Ecumenical Studies*
FBib	Forschung zur Bibel	*JETS*	*Journal of the Evangelical Theological Society*
FCCGRW	First-Century Christians in the Greco-Roman World	*JFSR*	*Journal of Feminist Studies in Religion*
FF	Foundations and Facets	*JJS*	*Journal of Jewish Studies*
FIRA	Fontes Iuris Romani Antejustiniani	*JPT*	*Journal of Pentecostal Theology*
FJ	The Foundation of Judaism	JPTSup	Journal of Pentecostal Theology Supplement Series
FKD	Forschungen zur Kirchen- und Dogmengeschichte		
		JQR	*Jewish Quarterly Review*
FN	*Filologia Neotestamentaria*	*JR*	*Journal of Religion*
FRLANT	Forschungen zur Religion und Literatur des Alten und Neuen Testaments	*JRE*	*Journal of Religious Ethics*
		JRH	*Journal of Religious History*
GBL	*Das Große Bibellexikon*	*JRS*	*Journal of Roman Studies*
GBS	Guides to Biblical Scholarship	*JSJ*	*Journal for the Study of Judaism in the Persian, Hellenistic and Roman Period*
GLS	Grove Liturgical Studies		
GNS	Good News Studies	*JSNT*	*Journal for the Study of the New Testament*
GNTE	Guides to New Testament Exegesis	*JSNTSup*	*Journal for the Study of the New Testament Supplement Series*
GTJ	*Grace Theological Journal*		
HBD	*Harper's Bible Dictionary*	*JSOT*	*Journal for the Study of the Old Testament*
HBT	*Horizons in Biblical Theology*	*JSOTSup*	*Journal for the Study of the Old Testament Supplement Series*
HDBA	*Dictionary of the Bible* (ed. J. Hastings)		
HDR	Harvard Dissertations in Religion	*JSPSup*	*Journal for the Study of the Pseudepigrapha and Related Literature* Supplement Series
Herm	Hermeneia		

JSS	Journal of Semitic Studies		on the New Testament
JTC	Journal for Theology and the Church	NIDNTT	New International Dictionary of New
JTS	Journal of Theological Studies		Testament Theology
JTS(n.s.)	Journal of Theological Studies (new series)	NIGTC	New International Greek Testament
JTSA	Journal of Theology for Southern Africa		Commentary
KAV	Kommentar zu den Apostolischen Vätern	NLC	New London Commentary
KNT	Kommentar zum Neuen Testament	NovT	Novum Testamentum
KP	Der Kleine Pauly, ed. K. Ziegler	NovTSup	Supplement to Novum Testamentum
LAE	Light from the Ancient East, A. Deissmann	NRT	La nouvelle revue théologique
LB	Linguistica Biblica	NTAbh	Neutestamentliche Abhandlungen
LBS	Library of Biblical Studies	NTC	TPI New Testament Commentaries
LCC	Library of Christian Classics	NTCom	New Testament Commentary (Baker)
LEC	Library of Early Christianity	NTD	DasNeue Testament Deutsch
Lightfoot/	The Apostolic Fathers, trans. J. B. Lightfoot	NTG	New Testament Guides
Harmer	and J. R. Harmer, ed. and rev. M. W.	NTOA	Novum Testamentum et Orbis Antiquus
	Holmes (2d ed.; Grand Rapids: Baker,	NTR	New Theology Review
	1992)	NTS	New Testament Studies
Louw-Nida	Greek-English Lexicon, ed. J. P. Louw and	NTT	New Testament Theology, ed. J. D. G.
	E. A. Nida		Dunn
LPGL	G. W. H. Lampe, Patristic Greek Lexicon	NTTS	New Testament Tools and Studies
LSJ	Liddell-Scott-Jones, Greek-English Lexicon	OBO	Orbis Biblicus et Orientalis
LTJ	Lutheran Theological Journal	OBT	Overtures to Biblical Theology
LW	Luther's Works, ed. J. Pelikan and H. T.	OCA	Orientalia Christiana analecta
	Lehmann	OCD	Oxford Classical Dictionary
MBPAR	Münchener Beiträge zur Papyrusfor-	OGIS	Orientis Graeci Inscriptiones Selectae
	schung und Antiken Rechtsgeschichte	OPTAT	Occasional Papers in Translation and
MBTh	Münsterische Beiträge zur Theologie		Textlinguistics
MeyerK	Meyer Kommentar	OTP	The Old Testament Pseudepigrapha, ed.
MFC	Message of the Fathers of the Church		J. H. Charlesworth
MM	J. H. Moulton and G. Milligan, The	PC	Proclamation Commentaries
	Vocabulary of the Greek Testament, Illus-	PEQ	Palestine Exploration Quarterly
	trated from the Papyri and Other Non-	PG	Patrologiae Graeca, ed. J.-P. Migne. 162 vols.
	Literary Sources (1930)	PGL	Patristic Greek Lexicon, ed. G. W. H. Lampe
MNTC	Moffatt New Testament Commentary	PL	Patrologia Latina, ed. J.-P. Migne. 217 vols.
MPAT	A Manual of Palestinian Aramaic Texts	PRS	Perspectives in Religious Studies
MSB	Monographic Series of Benedictina	PSBFMi	Publications of the Studium Biblicum
MTh	Melita Theologica		Franciscanum. Collectio minor
MTS	Münchener theologische Studien	PTMS	Pittsburgh Theological Monograph Series
Mus	Le Muséon	QD	Quaestiones Disputatae
NA²⁶	Nestlé-Aland Novum Testamentum Graece	QJS	Quarterly Journal of Speech
	26th ed.	RAC	Reallexikon für Antike und Christentum
NABPRSS	National Association of Baptist Professors	RB	Revue biblique
	of Religion Special Studies	RE	Real-Encyclopädie der classischen Altertums-
NAC	The New American Commentary		wissenschaft, ed. Pauly-Wissowa
NCB	New Century Bible	RelSRev	Religious Studies Review
NCIB	New Clarendon Bible	RevExp	Review and Expositor
NedTTs	Nederlands theologisch tijdschrift	RevQ	Revue de Qumran
Neot	Neotestamentica	RGG	Religion in Geschichte und Gegenwart
NewDocs	New Documents Illustrating Early Christian-	RGRW	Religions in the Graeco-Roman World
	ity, ed. G. H. R. Horsley	RHE	Revue d'Histoire Ecclésiastique
NGS	New Gospel Studies	RHPR	Revue d'histoire et de philosophie religieuses
NHC	Nag Hammadi Codices	RHR	Revue de l'histoire des religions
NHMS	Nag Hammadi and Manichaean Studies	RICP	Revue de l'Institut Catholique de Paris
NHS	Nag Hammadi Studies	RQ	Restoration Quarterly
NIB	New Interpreter's Bible	RSR	Recherches des science religieuse
NIBC	The New International Biblical Com-	RST	Regensburger Studien zur Theologie
	mentary	RTR	Reformed Theological Review
NICNT	The New International Commentary	SA	Studia Antiqua

SacP	Sacra Pagina		graph Series
SAJ	Studies in Ancient Judaism	SNTU	Studien zum Neuen Testament und
SAM	Studies in Ancient Medicine		seiner Umwelt
SANT	Studien zum Alten und Neuen Testament	SO	*Symbolae osloenses*
SB	Sources bibliques	SOTBT	Studies in Old Testament Biblical
SBEC	Studies in the Bible and Early Christianity		Theology
SBFLA	*Studii biblici franciscani liber annuus*	*SP*	*Studia Patristica*
SBLASP	Society of Biblical Literature Abstracts	*SPB*	*Studia Post-Biblica*
	and Seminar Papers	SPP	Studien zur Palaeographie und Papyrus-
SBLDS	Society of Biblical Literature Dissertation		kunde
	Series	*SR*	*Studies in Religion*
SBLMS	Society of Biblical Literature Monograph	SS	Symposium Series
	Series	SSEJC	Studies in Scripture in Early Judaism and
SBLRBS	Society of Biblical Literature Resources		Christianity
	for Biblical Studies	SSRH	Sociological Studies in Roman History
SBLSBS	Society of Biblical Literature Sources for	*ST*	*Studia theologica*
	Biblical Study	*StBT*	*Studia Biblica et Theologica*
SBLSP	*Society of Biblical Literature Seminar Papers*	STL	Studia theologica Lundensia
SBS	Stuttgart Bibelstudien	Str-B	Strack and Billerbeck, *Kommentar zum*
SBT	Studies in Biblical Theology		*Neuen Testament*
SC	Sources chrétiennes	*StudLit*	*Studia Liturgica*
ScrHier	*Scripta hierosolymitana*	*StudNeot*	*Studia Neotestamentica*
SCJ	Studies in Christianity and Judaism	SUNT	Studien zur Umwelt des Neuen Testa-
Schürer	E. Schürer, *The History of the Jewish People*		ments
	in the Age of Jesus Christ (175 B.C.—A.D.	*SWJT*	*Southwestern Journal of Theology*
	135), rev. and ed. G. Vermes et al. (3	TB	Theologische Bücherei
	vols.; Edinburgh: 1973-87)	TBC	Torch Bible Commentaries
SE	*Studia Evangelica*	*TBl*	*Theologische Blätter*
SEÅ	*Svensk Exegetisk Årsbok*	*TBT*	*The Bible Today*
SecCent	*Second Century*	*TD*	*Theology Digest*
SECT	Sources of Early Christian Thought	*TDGR*	*Translated Documents of Greece and Rome,*
SEG	Supplementum Epigraphicum Graecum		ed. R. K. Sherk
	(Leiden, 1923-)	*TDNT*	*Theological Dictionary of the New Testament,*
SESJ	Suomen Ekseegeettisen Seuran Julkaisuja		ed. G. Kittel and G. Friedrich
SFEG	Schriften der Finnischen Exegetischen	TEH	Theologische Existenz heute, new series
	Gesellschaft	THKNT	Theologische Handkommentar zum
SFSHJ	South Florida Studies in the History of		Neuen Testament
	Judaism	TI	Theological Inquiries
SFSMD	Studia Francisci Scholten memoriae	*TJ* (n.s.)	*Trinity Journal* (new series)
	dicata	*TLG*	*Thesaurus Linguae Graecae*
SH	Studia Hellenistica	*TLZ*	*Theologische Literaturzeitung*
SHT	Studies in Historical Theology	TNTC	Tyndale New Testament Commentary
SIG³	*Sylloge Inscriptionum Graecarum* (3d ed.	TOP	*Theology Occasional Papers*
	Leipzig, 1915-24)	TPINTC	Trinity Press International New Testa-
SJ	Studia Judaica		ment Commentaries
SJLA	Studies in Judaism in Late Antiquity	*TQ*	*Theologische Quartalschrift*
SJSJ	Supplements to the Journal for the	*TRE*	*Theologische Realenzydlopädie*
	Study of Judaism	*TRu*	*Theologische Rundschau*
SJT	*Scottish Journal of Theology*	*TS*	*Theological Studies*
SJTOP	*Scottish Journal of Theology* Occasional	*TSFBul*	*TSF Bulletin*
	Papers	*TToday*	*Theology Today*
SKKNT	R. Hoppe, *Jakobusbrief* Stuttgart: Katho-	TU	Texte und Untersuchungen
	lisches Bibelwerk, 1989)	*TWOT*	*Theological Wordbook of the Old Testament*
SL	*Studia Liturgica*	*TynB*	*Tyndale Bulletin*
SM	*Sacramentum Mundi*	*TZ*	*Theologische Zeitschrift*
SNTW	Studies in the New Testament and Its	UBSGNT	United Bible Societies *Greek New Testament*
	World	UCOS	University of Cambridge Oriental Studies
SNTSMS	Society for New Testament Studies Mono-	*USQR*	*Union Seminary Quarterly Review*

VC	*Vigiliae Christianae*	ZBNT	Züricher Bibelkommentare: Neues Testament
VCSup	Supplements to *Vigiliae Christianae*	*ZKG*	*Zeitschrift fur Kirchengeschicte*
VoxEv	*Vox Evangelica*	*ZLTK*	*Zeitschrift für lutherische Theologie und Kirche*
VT	*Vetus Testamentum*	ZNW	*Zeitschrift für die neutestamentliche Wissenschaft*
VTSup	*Vetus Testamentum* Supplements		
WA	Weimar Ausgabe		
WBC	Word Biblical Commentary	*ZPEB*	*Zondervan Pictorial Encyclopedia of the Bible*, ed. M. C. Tenney
WTJ	*Wesleyan Theological Journal*		
WMANT	Wissenschaftliche Monographien zum Alten und Neuen Testament	*ZPE*	*Zeitschrift für Papyrologie und Epigraphik*
		ZRG	*Zeitschrift für Religions- und Geistesgeschichte*
WPC	Westminster Pelican Commentary	ZS:NT	Zacchaeus Studies: New Testament
WTJ	*Westminster Theological Journal*	*ZSTh*	*Zeitschrift für Systematische Theologie*
WUNT	Wissenschaftliche Untersuchungen zum Neuen Testament	*ZTK*	*Zeitschrift für Theologie und Kirche*
		ZWT	*Zeitschrift für wissenschaftliche Theologie*

Transliteration of Hebrew and Greek

HEBREW

Consonants

Hebrew	Translit.	Hebrew	Translit.
א	= '	י	= y
ב	= b	כ	= k
בּ	= ḇ	כ	= ḵ
ג	= g	ל	= l
ג	= ḡ	מ	= m
ד	= d	נ	= n
ד	= ḏ	ס	= s
ה	= h	ע	= '
ו	= w	פ	= p
ז	= z	פ	= p̄
ח	= ḥ	צ	= ṣ
ט	= ṭ	ק	= q
		ר	= r
		שׁ	= ś

Hebrew	Translit.
שׁ	= š
ת	= t
ת	= t̲

Long Vowels

Hebrew	Translit.
(ה) ָ	= â
ֵ	= ê
ִ	= î
וֹ	= ô
ו	= û
ָ	= ā
ֵ	= ē
	= ō

Short Vowels

Hebrew	Translit.
ַ	= a
ֶ	= e
	= i
ָ	= o
	= u

Very Short Vowels

Hebrew	Translit.
ֲ	= a
ֱ	= e
ְ	= e (if vocal)
ֳ	= o

GREEK

Greek	Translit.	Greek	Translit.	Greek	Translit.	Greek	Translit.
A	= A	Θ	= Th	o	= o	Ψ	= Ps
α	= a	θ	= th	Π	= P	ψ	= ps
B	= B	I	= I	π	= p	Ω	= Ō
β	= b	ι	= i	P	= R	ω	= ō
Γ	= G	K	= K	ρ	= r	'Ρ	= Rh
γ	= g	κ	= k	Σ	= S	ῥ	= rh
Δ	= D	Λ	= L	σ/ς	= s	'	= h
δ	= d	λ	= l	T	= T	γξ	= nx
E	= E	M	= M	τ	= t	γγ	= ng
ε	= e	μ	= m	Υ	= Y	αυ	= au
Z	= Z	N	= N	υ	= y	ευ	= eu
ζ	= z	ν	= n	Φ	= Ph	ου	= ou
H	= Ē	Ξ	= X	φ	= ph	υι	= yi
η	= ē	ξ	= x	X	= Ch		
		O	= O	χ	= ch		

Contributors

Allison, Dale C., Jr., Ph.D. Associate Professor, Pittsburgh Theological Seminary, Pittsburgh, Pennsylvania, USA: **Land in Early Christianity; Melchizedek; Moses.**

Arnold, Clinton E., Ph.D. Professor of New Testament, Talbot School of Theology, La Mirada, California, USA: **Centers of Christianity; Magic and Astrology; Power; Satan, Devil; Syncretism.**

Baker, William R., Ph.D. Professor of New Testament and Greek and Biblical Division Chair, Saint Louis Christian College, Florissant, Missouri, USA: **Endurance, Perseverance; Temptation.**

Barnett, Paul W., Ph.D. Bishop of North Sydney, Anglican Church, Diocese of Sydney, Sydney, New South Wales, Australia: **Apostasy; Salvation.**

Bartchy, S. Scott, Ph.D. Director, UCLA Center for the Study of Religion and Adjunct Professor of Christian Origins and History of Religions, Department of History, University of California, Los Angeles, Los Angeles, California, USA: **Narrative Criticism; Slave, Slavery.**

Barton, Stephen C., Ph.D. Lecturer in New Testament, University of Durham, Durham, UK: **Hospitality; Social Setting of Early Non-Pauline Christianity.**

Bauckham, Richard J., Ph.D. Professor of New Testament Studies, University of St. Andrews, St. Andrews, UK: **Apocryphal and Pseudepigraphal Writings; 2 Peter; Relatives of Jesus.**

Beagley, Alan J., Ph.D. Pastor, Williston Park Reformed Church, Williston Park, New York, USA: **Babylon; Beasts, Dragon, Sea, Conflict Motif; Bowls; Scrolls, Seals; Trumpets.**

Beale, Gregory K., Ph.D. Professor of New Testament and Director of the Th.M. in Biblical Theology Program, Gordon-Conwell Theological Seminary, South Hamilton, Massachusetts, USA: **Eschatology.**

Beasley-Murray, George R., D.D., Ph.D. Professor of New Testament Emeritus, The Southern Baptist Theological Seminary, Louisville, Kentucky, USA: **Revelation, Book of.**

Blackburn, Barry L., Ph.D. Professor, Atlanta Christian College, East Point, Georgia, USA: **Stephen.**

Blue, Bradley B., Ph.D. Instructor in Aerospace, Marcy Open, Minneapolis, Minnesota, USA: **Architecture, Early Church; Food, Food Laws, Table Fellowship.**

Bock, Darrell L., Ph.D. Research Professor for New Testament Studies, Dallas Theological Seminary, Dallas, Texas, USA: **Old Testament in Acts.**

Burge, Gary M., Ph.D. Professor of New Testament, Wheaton College, Wheaton, Illinois, USA: **John, Letters of.**

Calvert-Koyzis, Nancy, Ph.D. Professor of New Testament, Ontario Theological Seminary, North York, Ontario, Canada. **Ancestors; Abraham.**

Campbell, William S., Ph.D. Reader in Religious and Theological Studies, Westhill College, University of Birmingham, Birmingham, UK: **Church as Israel, People of God.**

Canales, Isaac J., Ph.D. Assistant Professor of New Testament and Director of Hispanic Church Studies, Fuller Theological Seminary, Pasadena, California, USA: **Mercy.**

Capes, David B., Ph.D. Associate Professor, Houston Baptist University, Houston, Texas, USA: **Preexistence.**

Caragounis, Chrys C., Th.D. Associate Professor of New Testament Exegesis, Department of Theology, Lund University, Lund, Sweden: **Reveal, Revelation; Stone, Cornerstone.**

Carson, D. A., Ph.D. Research Professor of New Testament, Trinity Evangelical Divinity School, Deerfield, Illinois, USA: **New Testament Theology.**

Casurella, Anthony, Ph.D. Associate Professor, George Fox University, Portland, Oregon, USA: **Fellowship; Gospel; Grace; Israel, Twelve Tribes.**

Charles, J. Daryl, Ph.D. Assistant Professor of Religion, Taylor University, Upland, Indiana, USA: **Noncanonical Writings, Citations in the General Epistles; Old Testament in General Epistles.**

Chilton, Bruce D., Ph.D. Bernard Id-

dings Bell Professor of Religion and Chaplain of the College, Bard College, Annandale-on-Hudson, New York, USA: **Purity and Impurity; Synagogue; Temple.**

Comfort, Philip W., Ph.D., D. Litt. et Phil. Senior Editor, Tyndale House Publishers, and Adjunct Professor, Trinity Episcopal Seminary, Pawleys Island, South Carolina, USA: **Textual Criticism.**

Davids, Peter H., Ph.D. Director of Studies, Schloss Mittersill Study Center, Mittersill, Austria: **Anointing; Faith and Works; Healing, Illness; Miracles in Acts; Tongues; Signs and Wonders.**

Davies, Glenn N., Ph.D. Rector, St. Luke's Anglican Church, Miranda, Sydney, New South Wales, Australia: **Sacrifice, Offerings, Gifts; Tabernacle, Sanctuary.**

De Lacey, Douglas R., Ph.D. Faculties of Divinity and Oriental Studies, University of Cambridge, Cambridge, UK: **Circumcision.**

deSilva, David A., Ph.D. Assistant Professor of New Testament, Ashland Theological Seminary, Ashland, Ohio, USA: **Exaltation, Enthronement; Heaven, New Heaven; Repentance, Second Repentance; Visions, Ecstatic Experience.**

Dodd, Brian J., Ph.D. Assistant Professor of Leadership, and Associate Director, Doctor of Ministry Program, Asbury Theological Seminary, Wilmore, Kentucky, USA: **Millennium; Universalism; World.**

Drane, John W., D.D. Directory, Centre for the Study of Christianity and Contemporary Society, University of Stirling, Stirling, UK: **Son of God; Sonship, Child, Children.**

Dunn, James D. G., D.D. Lightfoot Professor of Divinity, University of Durham, Durham, UK: **Pseudepigraphy; Pauline Legacy and School.**

Eastman, Brad J., Ph.D. Instructor, Regent College, Vancouver, British Columbia, Canada: **Faith, Faithfulness; Hope; Name.**

Evans, Craig A., Ph.D. Director of Graduate Program in Biblical Studies and the Dead Sea Scrolls Institute, Trinity Western University, Langley, British Columbia, Canada: **Christianity and Judaism: Partings** of the Ways; Judaism, Post-A.D. 70; Thomas, Gospel of.

Ferguson, Everett, Ph.D. Professor Emeritus, Abilene Christian University, Abilene, Texas, USA: **Old Testament in Apostolic Fathers; Religions, Greco-Roman.**

Fowl, Stephen E., Ph.D. Associate Professor of Theology, Loyola College in Baltimore, Baltimore, Maryland, USA: **Paul and Paulinisms in Acts.**

Fuller, Ruth M., Ph.D. Adjunct Professor, Azusa Pacific University, Azusa, California, USA: **Rewards.**

Giles, Kevin N., Th.D. Vicar, St. Michael's Church, North Carlton, Victoria, Australia: **Church; Church Order, Government; Prophecy, Prophets, False Prophets.**

Graham, David J., Ph.D. Lecturer in New Testament and Greek, Glasgow Bible College, and Honorary Lecturer in Theology and Religious Studies, The University of Glasgow, Glasgow, UK: **Watchfulness; Witness.**

Green, Joel B., Ph.D. Professor of New Testament Interpretation, Asbury Theological Seminary, Wilmore, Kentucky, USA: **Acts of the Apostles; Cornelius; Peter, Gospel of.**

Guthrie, George H., Ph.D. Associate Professor of Christian Studies, Union University, Jackson, Tennessee, USA: **Old Testament in Hebrews; Promise.**

Hagner, Donald A., Ph.D. George Eldon Ladd Professor of New Testament, Fuller Theological Seminary, Pasadena, California, USA: **Apostolic Fathers; Jewish Christianity.**

Hansen, G. Walter, Th.D. Director of the Global Research Institute and Associate Professor of New Testament, Fuller Theological Seminary, Pasadena, California, USA: **Authority.**

Hawthorne, Gerald F., Ph.D. Emeritus Professor of Greek, Wheaton College, Wheaton, Illinois, USA: **Holy, Holiness; Holy Spirit; Joy; Melito of Sardis.**

Hertig, Paul A., Ph.D. Instructor in New Testament and Mission, Azusa Pacific University, Azusa, California, USA: **Galilean Christianity.**

Hill, Craig C., D.Phil. Associate Professor of New Testament, Wesley Theological Seminary, Washington, D.C., USA: **Hellenists, Hellenistic and Hellenistic-Jewish Christianity.**

Holmes, Michael W., Ph.D. Professor of Biblical Studies and Early Christi-

anity, Bethel College, St. Paul, Minnesota, USA: **Barnabas, Epistle of; Clement of Rome; Didache; Hermas, Shepherd of; Ignatius of Antioch; Polycarp of Smyrna.**

Hunt, Steven A., M.C.S., Ph.D. Cand. Adjunct Professor of Biblical Studies, Bethel College, St. Paul, Minnesota, USA: **Light and Darkness.**

Hurst, Lincoln D., Ph.D. Associate Professor of Religious Studies, University of California, Davis, California, USA: **Priest, High Priest; Qumran.**

Hurtado, L. W., Ph.D. Professor of New Testament Language, Literature and Theology, The University of Edinburgh, Edinburgh, UK: **Christology.**

Johnson, David H., Ph.D. Professor of New Testament, Providence Theological Seminary, Otterburne, Manitoba, Canada: **Assurance; Blessing; Flesh.**

Keener, Craig S., Ph.D. Visiting Professor of New Testament, Eastern Baptist Theological Seminary, Philadelphia, Pennsylvania, USA: **Lamb; Marriage, Divorce, Adultery; Shepherd, Flock; Woman and Man.**

Kim, Seyoon, Ph.D. Professor of New Testament, Fuller Theological Seminary, Pasadena, California, USA: **Kingdom of God.**

Klein, William W., Ph.D. Professor of New Testament and Associate Academic Dean, Denver Seminary, Denver, Colorado, USA: **Election.**

Knight, Jonathan M., Ph.D. Research Assistant to the Bishop of Ely, Ely, Cambs, UK: **Alexandria, Alexandrian Christianity.**

Kreitzer, Larry J., Ph.D. Tutor of New Testament, Regent's Park College, University of Oxford, Oxford, UK: **Apocalyptic, Apocalypticism; Parousia.**

Kroeger, Catherine C., Adjunct Associate Professor of Classical and Ministry Studies, Gordon-Conwell Theological Seminary, South Hamilton, Massachusetts, USA: **Women in the Early Church.**

Kruse, Colin G., Ph.D. Lecturer in New Testament, Bible College of Victoria, Lilydale, Victoria, Australia: **Apostle, Apostleship; Ministry; Servant, Service.**

Laansma, Jon C., Ph.D. Assistant Professor of Bible, Moody Bible Institute, Chicago, Illinois, USA: **Lord's Day; Peace.**

Lane, William L., Th.D. Paul T. Walls Professor of Biblical Studies, Seattle

Pacific University, Seattle, Washington, USA: **Hebrews.**

Larkin, William J., Jr., Ph.D. Professor of New Testament and Greek, Columbia Biblical Seminary and Graduate School of Missions, Columbia, South Carolina, USA: **Ascension.**

Lim, David S., Ph.D. Executive Director, China Ministries International—Philippines, Quezon City, Metro-Manila, Philippines: **Evangelism in the Early Church.**

Lincoln, Andrew T., Ph.D. Senior Professor of New Testament, Wycliffe College, University of Toronto, Toronto, Ontario, Canada: **Pentecost.**

Losie, Lynn A., Ph.D. Associate Professor of New Testament, Haggard Graduate School of Theology, Azusa Pacific University, Azusa, California, USA: **Mark, Secret Gospel of.**

Luter, A. Boyd, Jr., Th.D. Associate Professor of Bible, Cedarville College, Cedarville, Ohio, USA: **Martyrdom; Savior.**

Maier, Paul L., Ph.D. Professor of History, Western Michigan University, Kalamazoo, Michigan, USA: **Chronology.**

Marshall, I. Howard, D.D. Professor of New Testament Exegesis, University of Aberdeen, Aberdeen, UK: **Redemption.**

Martin, D. Michael, Ph.D. Professor of New Testament Studies, Golden Gate Baptist Theological Seminary, Mill Valley, California, USA: **Philo.**

Martin, Ralph P., Ph.D. Distinguished Scholar in Residence at Fuller Theological Seminary, Pasadena, California; Haggard Graduate School of Theology, Azusa Pacific University, Azusa, California; and Logos Evangelical Seminary, El Monte, California, USA: **Early Catholicism; Worship and Liturgy.**

Maynard-Reid, Pedrito U., Th.D. Professor of Biblical Studies and Missiology, Walla Walla College, College Place, Washington, USA: **Forgiveness; Samaria.**

McCartney, Dan G., Ph.D. Associate Professor of New Testament, Westminster Theological Seminary, Philadelphia, Pennsylvania, USA: **Conscience; House, Spiritual House; Household, Family.**

McDonald, Lee M., Ph.D. Senior Pastor, First Baptist Church, Alhambra, California, and Adjunct Professor of New Testament Studies, Fuller

Theological Seminary, Pasadena, California, USA: **Canon.**

McKnight, Scot, Ph.D. Karl A. Olsson Professor in Religious Studies, North Park University, Chicago, Illinois, USA: **Gentiles, Gentile Mission; Matthean Community.**

Michaels, J. Ramsey, Th.D. Professor Emeritus, Southwest Missouri State University, Springfield, Missouri, USA: **Old Testament in Revelation; 1 Peter.**

Morris, Leon L., Ph.D. Retired, Melbourne, Victoria, Australia: **Love.**

Mott, Stephen C., Ph.D. Pastor, Cochesett United Methodist Church, West Bridgewater, Massachusetts, USA: **Civil Authority.**

Motyer, Stephen, Ph.D. Lecturer, London Bible College, London, UK: **Cross, Theology of the.**

Newman, Carey C., Ph.D. Research Professor of New Testament, The Southern Baptist Theological Seminary, Louisville, Kentucky, USA: **Covenant, New Covenant; Glory; God; Jerusalem, Zion, Holy City; Righteousness.**

Noll, Stephen F., Ph.D. Associate Dean for Academic Affairs and Professor of Biblical Studies, Trinity Episcopal School for Ministry, Ambridge, Pennsylvania, USA: **Angels, Heavenly Beings, Angel Christology.**

Nystrom, David P., Ph.D. Chair, Department of Biblical and Theological Studies, North Park University, Director of Institute for Christian Studies, Chicago, Illinois, USA: **Josephus.**

Osborne, Grant R., Ph.D. Professor of New Testament, Trinity Evangelical Divinity School, Deerfield, Illinois, USA: **Hermeneutics.**

Padgett, Alan G., D.Phil. Professor of Religion and Philosophy, Azusa Pacific University, Azusa, California, USA: **Marcion.**

Paige, Terence P., Ph.D. Associate Professor of New Testament, Houghton College, Houghton, New York, USA: **Spirits.**

Painter, John, Ph.D., FAHA. Professor of Theology, St. Mark's National Theological Centre, Charles Sturt University, Canberra, Australian Capital Territory, Australia: **Creation, Cosmology.**

Patzia, Arthur G., Ph.D. Associate Professor of New Testament and Area Director, Fuller Seminary in Northern California, Menlo Park, California, USA: **Knowledge; Mystery; Wisdom.**

Pearson, Sharon Clark, Ph.D. Associate Professor of New Testament, Azusa Pacific University, Azusa, California, USA: **Hymns, Songs.**

Polhill, John B., Ph.D. J. B. Harrison Professor of New Testament, Southern Baptist Theological Seminary, Louisville, Kentucky, USA: **Kerygma and Didache; Pride and Humility.**

Porter, Stanley E., Ph.D. Professor of Theology and Head of the Department of Theology and Religious Studies, Roehampton Institute London, London, UK: **Eternity, Eternal; Fear; Sin, Wickedness; Tribulation, Messianic Woes; Wrath, Destruction.**

Rainbow, Paul A., D.Phil. Professor of New Testament, North American Baptist Seminary, Sioux Falls, South Dakota, USA: **Idolatry; Logos Christology.**

Rapske, Brian M., Ph.D. Assistant Professor of New Testament, Northwest Baptist College and Seminary, Langley, British Columbia, Canada: **Roman Empire, Christians and the; Rome and Roman Christianity.**

Reasoner, Mark, Ph.D. Associate Professor of Biblical Studies, Bethel College, St. Paul, Minnesota, USA: **Emperor, Emperor Cult; Persecution.**

Reed, Jeffrey T., Ph.D. Redmond, Washington, USA: **Truth.**

Reid, Daniel G., Ph.D. Senior Editor, Reference and Academic Books, InterVarsity Press, Downers Grove, Illinois, USA: **Pella, Flight to; Virtues and Vices.**

Reimer, Andy M., M.C.S., Ph.D. Cand. Adjunct Lecturer, Canadian Bible College, Regina, Saskatchewan, Canada: **Freedom, Liberty.**

Schmidt, Thomas E., Ph.D. Santa Barbara, California, USA: **Discipline; Riches and Poverty.**

Schnabel, Eckhard J., Ph.D. Dozent, Head of New Testament Department, Giessen Theological Seminary, Giessen, Germany: **Mission, Early Non-Pauline.**

Scholer, David M., Th.D. Professor of New Testament, and Associate Dean for the Center for Advanced Theological Studies, Fuller Theological Seminary, Pasadena, California, USA: **Gnosis, Gnosticism.**

Schreiner, Thomas R., Ph.D. Professor of New Testament, The Southern Baptist Theological Seminary, Louisville, Kentucky, USA: **Commandments; Law; Obedience and Lawlessness.**

Seifrid, Mark A., Ph.D. Associate Professor of New Testament, The Southern Baptist Theological Seminary, Louisville, Kentucky, USA: **Death of Christ; Judgment.**

Shogren, Gary S., Ph.D. Associate Professor of New Testament, Biblical Theological Seminary, Hatfield, Pennsylvania, USA: **Hell, Abyss, Eternal Punishment; Life and Death; Mortality and Immortality.**

Shuster, Marguerite, Ph.D. Associate Professor of Preaching, Fuller Theological Seminary, Pasadena, California, USA: **Preaching from Acts, Hebrews, General Epistles and Revelation.**

Spencer, F. Scott, Ph.D. Associate Professor of Religion, Wingate College, Wingate, North Carolina, USA: **Philip the Evangelist.**

Stanton, Graham N., Ph.D. Professor of New Testament Studies, King's College, University of London, London, UK: **Jesus Traditions.**

Sumney, Jerry L., Ph.D. Associate Professor of Bible, Lexington Theological Seminary, Lexington, Kentucky, USA: **Adversaries; Imitation.**

Sunquist, Scott W., Ph.D. Associate Professor of World Mission and Evangelism, Pittsburgh Theological Seminary, Pitts-burgh, Pennsylvania, USA: **Syria, Syrian Christianity.**

Swartley, Willard M., Ph.D. Academic Dean and Professor of New Testament, Associated Mennonite Biblical Seminary, Elkhart, Indiana, USA: **Intertextuality in Early Christian Literature.**

Towner, Philip H., Ph.D. Translation Consultant, United Bible Societies, and Adjunct Professor, Regent College, Vancouver, British Columbia, Canada: **Household Codes.**

Travis, Stephen H., Ph.D. Vice-Principal, St. John's College, Nottingham, Nottingham, UK: **Psychology; Resurrection.**

Trebilco, Paul R., Ph.D. Associate Professor of New Testament, Department of Theology and Religious Studies, University of Otago, Dunedin, New Zealand: **Diaspora Judaism.**

Verhey, Allen D., Ph.D. Evert J. and Hattie E. Blekkink Professor of Religion, Hope College, Holland, Michigan, USA: **Ethics.**

Wainwright, Geoffrey, Dr. Théol., D.D. Cushman Professor of Christian Theology, Duke University,

Durham, North Carolina, USA: **Baptism, Baptismal Rites; Lord's Supper, Love Feast.**

Wall, Robert W., Th.D. Professor of Biblical Studies, Seattle Pacific University, Seattle, Washington, USA: **James, Letter of.**

Watson, Duane F., Ph.D. Professor of New Testament and Chair of Department of Religion and Philosophy, Malone College, Canton, Ohio, USA: **Antichrist; Letter, Letter Form; Rhetoric, Rhetorical Criticism; Structuralism and Discourse Analysis.**

Webb, Robert L., Ph.D. Lecturer, Luther College, University of Regina, Regina, Saskatchewan, Canada: **Day of the Lord; Jude.**

Webb, William J., Ph.D. Professor of New Testament, Heritage Theological Seminary, Cambridge, Ontario, Canada: **Suffering.**

Weima, Jeffrey A. D., Ph.D. Associate Professor of New Testament, Calvin Theological Seminary, Grand Rapids, Michigan, USA: **Diognetus, Epistle to.**

Wilkins, Michael J., Ph.D. Professor of New Testament Language and Literature and Dean of the Faculty, Talbot School of Theology, Biola University, La Mirada, California, USA: **Milk, Solid Food; New Birth; Pastoral Theology; Prayer; Teaching, Paraenesis**

Williams, David John, Ph.D. Vice Principal, Ridley College, Parkville,

Victoria, Australia: **Antioch on the Orontes.**

Witherington, Ben, III, Ph.D. Professor of New Testament, Asbury Theological Seminary, Wilmore, Kentucky, USA: **Christ; Lord.**

Wright, David F., M.A. Senior Lecturer in Ecclesiastical History, The University of Edinburgh, Edinburgh, UK: **Creeds, Confessional Forms; Docetism; Ebionites; Sexuality, Sexual Ethics.**

Wu, Julie L., Ph.D. Associate Professor of New Testament, Logos Evangelical Seminary, El Monte, California, USA: **Hymns, Songs; Liturgical Elements; Mary.**

ABBA. *See* LITURGICAL ELEMENTS.

ABRAHAM
A key figure in early Jewish literature, Abraham played a central part in the letters to the Galatians and the Romans (*see DPL*, Abraham). Later NT authors continue to employ Abraham in significant ways in Acts* (Acts 3:13, 25; 7:2, 8, 16-17, 32; 13:26) and Hebrews* (Heb 2:16; 6:13; 7:1, 2, 4-6, 9; 11:8, 17) and to a lesser degree in James* (Jas 2:21, 23) and 1 Peter* (1 Pet 3:6). References to Abraham are found in numerous documents of the early church, a fact that suggests that the patriarch held continued importance for early Christian self-understanding.

1. Abraham the Exemplary Jew
2. Acts: Abraham the Father of the Jews in Continuity with Believers
3. Hebrews: Abraham the Prototype of Faith for Believers
4. James and 1 Peter: The Patriarchal Couple as Examples of Obedient Behavior
5. Apostolic Fathers: Adopted Christians and Disinherited Jews

1. Abraham the Exemplary Jew.
For those Jews who returned from exile in Babylon, Abraham often exemplified the characteristics of the ideal Jew. While authors of early Jewish literature often based their writings upon the OT accounts of Abraham (Gen 11:27—25:11), they also elaborated them in order to speak to the readers of their day.

Four primary themes emerge about Abraham in early Jewish literature. He is a tenacious monotheist and the first proselyte to Judaism (*Jub.* 11:6-17; 12:1-5, 16-21; 20:6-9; Ps.-Philo *Bib. Ant.* 6.4; Josephus *Ant.* 1.7.1 §§154-57; Philo *Abr.* 68-71; *Apoc. Ab.* 1-8). God established a covenant* with Abraham through which his descendants are blessed (*Jub.* 15:9-10; Ps.-Philo *Bib. Ant.* 7.4; 1QapGen 21:8-14), although one must

obey the stipulations of the covenant in order to remain within it (*Jub.* 15:26-27). Abraham's character is often extolled as righteous (*T. Abr.* 1:1A), hospitable (*T. Abr.* 1:1-3A; Philo *Abr.* 107-110; Josephus *Ant.* 1.11.2 §196), virtuous (Josephus *Ant.* 1.7.1 §154; Philo *Abr.* 68), faithful (Sir 44:20; 1 Macc 2:52; *Jub.* 17:17-18), a lover of God (*Jub.* 17:18) and a friend of God (CD 3:2-4). Abraham lived according to the Mosaic law* (*Jub.* 15:1-2; 16:20; Sir 44:20) or the natural/philosophical law (Philo *Abr.* 3-6), and he praises those who die for keeping the law (4 Macc 13:13-18).

2. Acts: Abraham the Father of the Jews in Continuity with Believers.
In Acts Abraham is used not so much as a prototype for Christians to be emulated as he is in the Pauline epistles, but he remains the father of the Jews. Using Abraham exclusively in his sermons, Luke establishes a connection and continuity between Abraham and the events about which he is writing (Dahl, 140).

2.1. Acts 3. Peter uses the figure of Abraham during his speech in Solomon's portico to identify the God of Abraham, Isaac and Jacob (Acts 3:13, 25; cf. Acts 7:32; Ex 3:6) as the God whose "servant" Jesus was (*see* Service) and through whose name* Peter had just healed the lame beggar (Acts 3:6, 16). The usage of the uncommon and early title *servant* (cf. Acts 3:26) for Jesus here may indicate that an allusion is being made to the Suffering Servant of Isaiah (Is 52:13—53:12). By using this appellation Peter clearly implicates the Jews as those who killed Jesus, the chosen servant of their own God (Acts 3:15).

Yet in Acts 3:25 Peter invokes the blessing* to Abraham that through his seed all the families of the earth would be blessed (Gen 22:18; cf. Gen 12:3; 18:18; Gal 3:8). The Septuagint has "nations" (*ethnē*), which could be interpreted to mean Gentiles.* Peter instead uses the ambiguous "families" *(patria),* which probably refers first to Jews (cf. Acts 3:26) and implicitly to Gentiles. Thus Peter tells his listeners that they are the descendants of the prophets and the covenant that foretold the Messiah, Jesus (Acts 3:22-23), who himself was the fulfillment of the covenant with Abraham through whom the Jews and other families may be blessed.

2.2. Acts 7. Stephen's* speech provides the framework for several allusions to Abraham (Acts 7:2-8, 16-17, 32) in which he appears as the recipient of promises* by which his descendants later benefit.

Luke's affinity with Hellenistic Judaism* is seen most clearly in Acts 7:2-8 (Dahl, 142). In Acts 7:2 Stephen places God's call to Abraham in Ur rather than in Haran (Gen 12:1). Luke's tradition could be drawn from OT texts (Gen 15:7; Neh 9:7) that suggest the call from Ur. Philo* assumes that a divine call came to Abraham in both places (Philo *Abr.* 62, 85), while Josephus* sees the two migrations as a single exodus (Josephus *Ant.* 1.7.1 §154). Luke further remarks (Acts 7:4) that Abraham left the country of the "Chaldeans," a term that often referred to astrologers and the interpreters of dreams (*Jub.* 11:8; Philo *Abr.* 69, 71), traditions connected with Abraham before his call (*Jub.* 12:16; Philo *Abr.* 70; Josephus *Ant.* 1.7.1 §156; *Apoc. Abr.* 7:9; cf. Josh 24:2).

In a free rendering of Genesis 17:7 Stephen remains true to the Genesis account in which Abraham possessed no land* but received only a promise of land (Acts 7:5; cf. Gen 12:7; 13:15; 48:4) for himself and his offspring. Abraham followed God although he neither took ownership of any part of the land (cf. Deut 2:5) nor yet had his descendants who would eventually inherit the land. While authors sometimes magnify Abraham's taking ownership of the land (1QapGen 21:15-19), Stephen instead magnifies Abraham's trust in God (cf. Rom 4:16-22).

By including references to the prophecy to Abraham about his descendants' four-hundred-year (Acts 7:6; cf. Ex 12:40; Gal 3:17) bondage in Egypt (Gen 15:13-14; cf. Ex 2:22) Luke emphasizes God's faithfulness (*see* Faith) to his people in the midst of crisis. In an expansion of Exodus 3:12 (Acts 7:7) Luke modifies the term *mountain (horos),* used for Sinai in the Septuagint, using instead "place" *(topos),* referring to Jerusalem* or the temple* itself (cf. Acts 6:13-

14). God's faithfulness to his promise to Abraham is demonstrated in that Stephen and his Jewish contemporaries in Jerusalem could worship God in that very "place."

Stephen then refers to the "covenant of circumcision" *(diathēkē peritomēs;* Acts 7:8) established with Abraham (Gen 17:10, 12), a covenant that confirmed God's promise to grant him descendants (Gen 21:1-4), who include his listeners.

Stephen returns to Abraham when he suggests that Jacob, Joseph and his relatives were buried at the cave Abraham bought near Shechem (Acts 7:16). In Genesis Abraham bought the cave of Machpelah near Hebron (Gen 23), not Shechem. Jacob is reportedly buried in the cave Abraham bought near Hebron (Gen 49:29-32; 50:13), while Joseph was buried at Shechem (Josh 24:32) in land that Jacob had bought (Gen 33:18-20). Stephen may have telescoped the two accounts of purchases of land in Canaan as he telescoped earlier events (see Acts 7:2, 7) and has attributed the purchase of the grave in Shechem to Abraham.

2.3. Acts 13. During his speech in the synagogue* of Antioch of Pisidia on his first missionary journey, Paul refers to his Jewish listeners as "Abraham's family," to whom the message of salvation* was sent (Acts 13:26). Paul calls upon them to be different from the residents of Jerusalem who rejected the Messiah, Jesus, and fulfilled the message of the prophets (e.g., Isa 52:13—53:12) by condemning him to death (Acts 13:27-29). It was through David's people, those chosen in Abraham, that their Messiah had come (Acts 13:22-25). The Jews tragically would later reject the message of salvation (Acts 13:45).

3. Hebrews: Abraham the Prototype of Faith for Believers.
Abraham functions in the letter to the Hebrews as the prototype of faithful endurance* that the believing readers are to emulate.

3.1. Hebrews 2:14-16. In the context of showing how the Son of God has solidarity with the human family by virtue of having become one of them (Heb 2:14), the author of Hebrews first uses the figure of Abraham to identify those whom Jesus Christ came to liberate (Heb 2:15-16). Those who are now called descendants of Abraham are those who are of the faithful remnant (cf. Is 41:8-10), oppressed men and women of whom Jesus takes hold to deliver from the bondage to Satan* and to bring them under the authority* of the exalted Son (see Exaltation).

3.2. Hebrews 6:13-20. In this passage God's promise of descendants to Abraham (Heb 6:13-15; Gen 12:2-3; 15:5; 17:5) is brought to the fore. The author repeats a phrase from the sacrifice* of Isaac concerning an oath God swore "by himself" (Heb 6:13; Gen 22:16) because there was no one greater by whom God could swear (Heb 6:16-17) in order to guarantee the promise. The author reminds the readers of the popular tradition of the *Aqedah,* or binding of Isaac, reinforcing the portrayal of Abraham as the prototype of faithful endurance (Heb 6:15) who in obedience* was willing to sacrifice his only son, thereby receiving God's promises. The exposition provides an example for the addressees to emulate in the expectation that they will receive what God has promised them because their own high priest,* Jesus Christ, has already obtained the promises and is a forerunner on their behalf (Heb 6:19-20).

3.3. Hebrews 7:1-10. Within his broader goal of proving that Jesus' priestly office is greater than the levitical priesthood, the writer interprets the account of Abraham and Melchizedek* (Gen 14:17-20; cf. Ps 110:4) in order to show how Melchizedek is greater than Abraham and the levitical priests (Heb 7:7). His proof lies in the account of Abraham the exalted patriarch (Heb 7:4) giving Melchizedek a tenth of the spoils of war (Gen 14:20). Because the levitical priests received tithes (cf. Lev 18:21; Num 18:26-28; Neh 10:38-39; Josephus *Ant.* 20.9.8 §181; 20.9.2 §206-7; Josephus *Life* 15 §80) and because Abraham represented the Levites as the progenitor of Israel,* this fact signifies that Levi was actually tithing to Melchizedek (Acts 7:5-6, 8-10), who is thereby even greater than Israel's progenitor. It is not clear in Genesis who gave tithes to whom, but the author of Hebrews reflects the tradition that Abraham was the one who tithed (cf. 1QapGen 22:17; Josephus *Ant.* 1.10.2 §181). The author further provides a contrast between Abraham, who received promises (Acts 7:6), and the Levites, who received their office according to the law (Acts 7:5). For the author promise connotes something effective and certain (see Acts 6:13), while the law implied that which was ineffective. Thus the contrast between Melchizedek and the levitical priests heightens Melchizedek's priest-

hood because the levitical priests collected tithes according to law while Melchizedek received tithes from and blessed the one to whom God had made promises (Acts 7:6) and to whom he is superior (Acts 7:7).

3.4. Hebrews 11:8-12, 17-19. In this chapter the author employs Abraham more than any other figure as an example of faith. Abraham first exemplifies his faith by his obedience to God's call (Heb 11:8; Gen 12:1-2; cf. Gen 15:7; Neh 9:7; Acts 7:2-8; Philo *Abr.* 60, 62, 85, 88).

Abraham's sojourn as an alien indicates his unsettled status as a foreigner, without native and civil rights, "living in tents" (Heb 11:9; Gen 12:8; 13:3; 18:1) as a nomad. His obedience brought not immediate settlement in the promised land but a life of sojourning for himself and his descendants (Heb 11:9) as he looked toward the ultimate goal. For the author of Hebrews that goal was not Canaan but the firmly established city of God (Heb 11:10; cf. Heb 11:1; Ps 48:8; 87:1-3; Is 14:32). Jewish apocalyptic* tradition affirms that Abraham saw the heavenly* city (*2 Apoc. Bar.* 4:2-5; cf. 4 Ezra 3:13-14).

Abraham further exemplifies faith through his trust that God would give him a son, even though he and his wife had never produced children and were no longer physically capable of doing so (Heb 11:11-12; cf. Rom 4:19-21; Gen 15:1-6; 17:15-22; 18:9-15). The reliability of God is heightened in the contrast between the singular Abraham and the multitude of his descendants (Heb 11:12 cf. Heb 11:11) in accordance with the promise (Gen 15:5; 22:17; cf. Heb 6:13-15).

Finally Abraham exemplifies faith through his willingness to sacrifice his only son and fulfillment of promise, Isaac (Heb 11:17-19). This event of Abraham's testing (Sir 44:20; 1 Macc 2:52; see 3.2 above) became central to the Jewish exegetical imagination in postbiblical Judaism (*Jub.* 17:15—18:19; Philo *Abr.* 167-297; 4 Macc 7:11-14; 13:12; 16:18-20; Josephus *Ant.* 1.13.1-4 §222-36; Ps.-Philo *Bib. Ant.* 18.5; 23.8; 32.1-4; 40.2-3). Abraham's action was celebrated as a model of faithfulness and obedience to God in the literary tradition of Jewish models of faith (Sir 44:20; Jdt 8:25-26; 1 Macc 2:52; 4 Macc 16:20; cf. Jas 2:21-24; *1 Clem.* 10.7). Details in the presentation in Hebrews suggest that the author was influenced by this tradition.

The tense and sacrificial nuance of the verb *offered (prosphero;* Heb 11:17) suggests that in

3

some sense the sacrifice was an accomplished event because of Abraham's intention (Philo *Abr.* 177; Ps.-Philo *Bib. Ant.* 32.4; Swetnam, 122) while the second use of the verb (Heb 11:17, the second part of the verse) indicates that Abraham did not make the sacrifice but was interrupted by God's intervention. Jewish tradition refers to blood that was shed during the sacrifice; because of this God chose Abraham and his family (Ps.-Philo *Bib. Ant.* 18.5-6), perhaps implying that the blood had some kind of atoning value.

The author's reference to Genesis 21:12 (Heb 11:18) and subsequent reference to God raising "someone from the dead" (Heb 11:19; cf. *Pirqe R. El.* 31) simultaneously refers to Hebrews 11:12, where Abraham is said to be as "good as dead" in reference to procreation. The implication is that Abraham had faith that God was able to raise someone from the dead—namely, Isaac—through both procreation and his salvation from sacrifice. The Christian readers would also see the sacrifice of Isaac as a foreshadowing of God's raising Jesus from the dead. From this they could derive faith in the God who is faithful to his promises (Swetnam, 122-23, 128).

3.5. Hebrews 13:1-2. The author reminds his readers that they are to have the attitude of welcoming fellow Christians who are strangers. Hospitality* was a mark not only of one who was cultured but also of Christians, who met in the homes of others. Hospitality was necessary especially in regard to itinerant preachers. In the Christian community the guest/host relationship attained an almost sacramental quality as they expected that God would play a significant role in the exchange between guests and hosts (Lane, 512). Abraham, who was known for his hospitality (*1 Clem.* 31; *T. Abr.* 1:1-3A; Philo *Abr.* 107-10; Josephus *Ant.* 1.11.2 §196), is alluded to in reference to his meeting with the three visitors to his tent at Mamre when he and his wife received the promise of the birth of their son Isaac (Heb 13:1-2; Gen 18:1-21; *1 Clem.* 10.7).

4. James and 1 Peter: The Patriarchal Couple as Examples of Obedient Behavior.

4.1. James 2:21-24. Abraham, known for his exemplary faith (see 3.4 above), was also revered for his obedience to God for his willingness to sacrifice Isaac (the *Aqedah;* see 3.2 above) which was a story popular in Jewish circles (see

3.4 above). James 2:21-24 brings these two traditions together; Abraham becomes the example of one who completes his faith by his works (*see* Faith and Works).

Because James 2:21 implies that Abraham was justified (*dikaioō*) by works and that sounds as if it contradicts statements by Paul about justification (*dikaioō;* cf. Gal 2:15-16; Rom 3:22) by faith alone, a few observations must be made. First, the sense in which *dikaioō* is used in James is in reference to Abraham's demonstrated faithfulness, perhaps in reference to the theme of testings (Jas 1:2, 12). Thus God declares Abraham "righteous" or "faithful." The sense in which Paul uses *dikaioō* refers to the eschatological* act in which God declares sinners rightly related to himself. Paul then can say that Abraham was made righteous by faith (Gal 3:6-9; Rom 4:22). Furthermore, the sense of "works" in the two letters is different: in James it refers to acts of obedience and compassion that should arise out of faith in Christ* (Jas 2:14-17) and that complete faith. The works (as in "works of the law") against which Paul builds his polemic of Abraham's becoming righteous by faith alone are those acts that formerly identified the people of God and that are still being used by some to identify the people of God in Christ. Paul uses Abraham as an example of righteousness* by faith because he is contending with those who would undermine the foundation of his gospel.*

4.2. 1 Peter 3:4-5. Within the context of a household code* the focus is on Sarah, whose example the readers are to emulate. It is surprising that the author did not reflect the situation of the OT account, in which Sarah laughs at the promise of a son, saying that her "lord" is too old (Gen 18:12; *see* Lord).

Many of the women reading the letter (*see* 1 Peter) would have had unbelieving husbands. It is through their demeanor that they are to bring their husbands to the gospel (1 Pet 3:1-2). The principle is that one influences a spouse by modest behavior worthy of respect. In the culture of the time this meant that wives were to defer to the authority of their husbands.

5. Apostolic Fathers: Adopted Christians and Disinherited Jews.

While Paul employed Abraham in order to include Gentile believers within the people of God, Abraham's function changed in the writings of the early church (*see* Apostolic Fathers). As J. Siker has shown, Justin Martyr reverses the function of Abraham when he "claims the Abrahamic heritage for the Christians and denies it to the Jews" (Siker, 145).

5.1. The Revised Promises to Abraham. Early noncanonical Christian authors revise God's promises to Abraham in such a way that Christians alone become the inheritors of those promises. For example, the author of the *Epistle of Barnabas* (*see* Barnabas, Epistle of) appeals to Abraham regarding God's promise of the land (*Barn.* 6.8; cf. *Barn.* 8.4; 9.7-8; 13.7; cf. Ex 33:1, 3) to Abraham and his descendants. Christians become heirs of the promised land of milk and honey (*Barn.* 6.8, 10, 17) through the new creation* in their hearts (*Barn.* 6.14-15) through Christ.

Justin Martyr sees Hadrian's banning the Jews from the city of Jerusalem (A.D. 135) as God's punishment for their disobedience and disbelief (Justin *Dial. Tryph.* 16.2; cf. 40.1; 92.2; 25.5). It is the Gentiles, along with the Hebrew ancestors, who will receive the inheritance of land, particularly as symbolized by Jerusalem (Justin *Dial. Tryph.* 26.1). Through Christ, the land promised to Abraham's descendants is given to Gentiles (Justin *Dial. Tryph.* 119.5-6) and will be established eternally at Christ's Second Coming (Justin *Dial. Tryph.* 85.7; cf. 80.5, 81.4; *see* Parousia).

For Justin, Christians additionally are the fulfillment of God's promise to Abraham of descendants by virtue of their faith in Christ (Justin *Dial. Tryph.* 11.5). The Jews are merely physical descendants of Abraham (Justin *Dial. Tryph.* 47.4; 80.4), which counts for nothing (Justin *Dial. Tryph.* 25.1; 26.1; 44.1; cf. Mt 3:9 par. Lk 3:8). Further, in *Barnabas* 13.7 we find that the author has reinterpreted the account in Genesis 17:4-5, in which God promises Abraham that he will be the "father of nations," to mean that Abraham is the father exclusively of the Gentiles.

Gentiles furthermore become the fruit of God's promise to Abraham that through him the nations would be blessed (Justin *Dial. Tryph.* 11.5; 119.3-6). Abraham's descendants become a blessing to the nations by becoming the nations (i.e., Gentiles) themselves. Thus the promise to Abraham that his progeny would be a blessing to the nations is fulfilled.

5.2. Circumcision Recast. In these texts circumcision* is also given a new meaning. For example, in the *Epistle of Barnabas* Abraham points to Christ through his circumcision, which was solely a "spiritual witness of the grace to come, through the death of Jesus, not as a seal of a grace already given" (*Barn.* 9.3-4, 7-9; Siker, 150; cf. Gal 3:8; *see* Grace). The circumcision of the Jews in the flesh* is even seen to be the misleading of an evil angel* (*Barn.* 9.4).

Like Paul, Justin emphasizes Abraham's justification by faith apart from circumcision (Justin *Dial. Tryph.* 11.5; 23.3-4; cf. Rom 4:9-10). Not only does physical circumcision fail to bring righteousness, but only the spiritual circumcision of the heart has positive significance (Justin *Dial. Tryph.* 11.3; 24.1; 34.1; 43.1; 67.9; 118.2), which Christians receive through baptism.*

Justin further states that circumcision was given to Abraham because God foreknew that the Jews would be disobedient, particularly by virtue of their responsibility for Jesus' death (*see* Death of Jesus). Circumcision was a mark of those designated for punishment (Justin *Dial. Tryph.* 16.2-4; 19.2-5; 92.2-3).

5.3. Continuity Between Abraham and Christ. In *Barnabas* Abraham also points forward to Christ, first through his casting of Abraham as one who sprinkles the people for purification from sin (*Barn.* 8.3-4; cf. Num 19), which means that he was one who preached the gospel of forgiveness* of sin and purification of the heart (*Barn.* 8.3).

By using the account of the angels who visit Abraham at Mamre (Gen 18) and the eschatological banquet at which Abraham is present (Mt 8:11-12), Justin argues that as Christ was with Abraham at Mamre, so Abraham will be with Christ at the eschatological banquet (Justin *Dial. Tryph.* 55-59).

In a response to Trypho's challenge that Justin prove the existence of another God besides the Creator, in *Dialogue* 56 Justin uses a number of biblical citations to prove that it was Christ who, with the two angels, appeared to Abraham under the oak at Mamre, not God the Father and Creator. In fact it was Jesus who appeared to Moses, Abraham and other Jewish ancestors (Justin *Dial. Tryph.* 113.4). The unbelieving Jews are not children of Abraham, for they fail to believe in the very Christ to whom Abraham bore witness.

5.4. Father Abraham. Marcion* sought to exclude Abraham from God's promised inheritance (Irenaeus *Haer.* 4.8.1); given Marcion's antipathy toward all things Jewish, this is not surprising. Irenaeus responded by reasoning that those who disallow the salvation of Abraham and assume that it was another God who made promises to Abraham, presumably as Marcion did, are themselves outside of the kingdom of God (*see* Kingdom of God) because it is Abraham's seed who receive the adoption and inheritance promised to Abraham. By the time of Irenaeus, proof-texts from the NT were being offered to show Abraham as the father of the Christian faith (Rom 4:3; Mt 8:11; Lk 13:28).

5.5. Abraham and the Afterlife. Irenaeus alludes to a passage in which Marcion states that the unbelieving souls of Abraham's progeny and implicitly also of Abraham remained in Hades (Irenaeus *Haer.* 1.27.3). Marcion further separates Abraham from inheritance in Christ by placing him in Hades as one who refused salvation.

In the *Apocalypse of Peter,* Peter takes a detour from hell* and proceeds to the mount of the transfiguration. Abraham is one of the righteous fathers who are in a heavenly plane described as a garden that was "full of fair trees and blessed fruits" (*Apoc. Peter,* Ethiopic Recension, 16). This description resembles the description of the garden of Eden (Gen 1:29; 2:8-9).

In citing Matthew 8:11-12, relating to the patriarchal eschatological banquet, Justin emphasizes the judgment* of the Jews who are no longer the children of God but are cast out into darkness (Justin *Dial. Tryph.* 76; *see* Light and Darkness) because of their unbelief. The Gentiles who believe in Christ and who repent will receive the inheritance with the patriarchs (Justin *Dial. Tryph.* 26.1; cf. 130.2).

Thus the Jews will be damned by God at the end of time, while the believing Gentiles will share in the eschatological banquet with Abraham, other patriarchs and the prophets. Siker states, "There is no clearer indication of the Jews' status as a disinherited people than Justin's appeal to Matthew 8:11-12" (Siker, 183).

5.6. The Virtuous Abraham. Clement (*see* Clement of Rome) uses Abraham, who is often called "father," as an example of faith and piety. In *1 Clement* 10 Abraham is called "the friend" of God (cf. *1 Clem.* 17), and Clement also states that Abraham rendered obedience to God by leaving his country and family in order to in-

herit God's promises. It was on account of his faith and hospitality that a son was given to him in his old age and also that in exercising his obedience Abraham offered Isaac as a sacrifice to God (*1 Clem.* 31).

See also ANCESTORS; CIRCUMCISION; HEBREWS; MOSES; PROMISE; STEPHEN.

BIBLIOGRAPHY. H. W. Attridge, *Hebrews* (Herm; Philadelphia: Fortress, 1989); W. Baird, "Abraham in the New Testament: Tradition and the New Identity," *Int* 42 (1988) 367-79; N. L. Calvert, *Early Jewish Traditions of Abraham: Implications for Pauline Texts* (JSNTS; Sheffield: Sheffield Academic Press, forthcoming); H. Conzelmann, *The Acts of the Apostles* (Herm; Philadelphia: Fortress, 1987); N. A. Dahl, "The Story of Abraham in Luke-Acts" in *Studies in Luke-Acts,* ed. L. E. Keck and J. L. Martyn (Nashville: Abingdon, 1966) 139-59; M. Dibelius, *James: A Commentary on the Epistle of James* (Herm; Philadelphia: Fortress, 1975); E. Ferguson, ed., *Encyclopedia of Early Christianity* (New York: Garland, 1990); D. Harrington, "Pseudo-Philo: A New Translation and Introduction" in *The Old Testament Pseudepigrapha,* ed. J. H. Charlesworth (2 vols.; Garden City, N.Y.: Doubleday, 1983); W. L. Lane, *Hebrews* (2 vols.; WBC; Dallas: Word, 1991); I. H. Marshall, *The Acts of the Apostles* (TNTC; Grand Rapids: Eerdmans, 1980); R. P. Martin, *James* (WBC; Dallas: Word, 1988); J. B. Polhill, *Acts: An Exegetical and Theological Exposition of Holy Scripture* (NAC; Nashville: Broadman, 1992); W. Schneemelcher, ed., *New Testament Apocrypha* (2 vols.; Louisville, KY: Westminster/John Knox, 1989); J. S. Siker, *Disinheriting the Jews: Abraham in Early Christian Controversy* (Louisville, KY: Westminster/John Knox, 1991); J. Swetnam, *Jesus and Isaac: A Study of the Epistle to the Hebrews in Light of the Aqedah* (Rome: Biblical Institute Press, 1981); A. L. Williams, *Justin Martyr: The Dialogue with Trypho* (New York: SPCK, 1930).   N. Calvert-Koyzis

ABYSS. *See* HELL, ABYSS, ETERNAL PUNISHMENT

ACTS OF ANDREW. *See* APOCRYPHAL AND PSEUDEPIGRAPHAL WRITINGS.

ACTS OF JOHN. *See* APOCRYPHAL AND PSEUDEPIGRAPHAL WRITINGS.

ACTS OF PETER. *See* APOCRYPHAL AND PSEUDEPIGRAPHAL WRITINGS.

ACTS OF PETER AND THE TWELVE APOS-TLES. See APOCRYPHAL AND PSEUDEPIGRAPHAL WRITINGS.

ACTS OF THE APOSTLES

The Acts of the Apostles is the fifth book in the NT canon,* located between collections of Gospels and letters.* Although it is not the first Christian or NT document to have incorporated an interest in narrative history, together with the Gospel of Luke it is the earliest example of Christian historiography.

1. The Genre of Acts
2. The Text of Acts
3. The Speeches in Acts
4. The Narrative Unity of Luke-Acts
5. The Theology and Purpose of Acts

1. The Genre of Acts.
Particularly because of the content of Acts as well as the nature of the prefaces to Luke-Acts (Lk 1:1-4; Acts 1:1-3; cf. Josephus *Ag. Ap.* 1.1 §§1-5; 2.1 §§1-2), Acts has long been understood as the first example of Christian historiography. Following the influential work of H. J. Cadbury early in the twentieth century, study of Acts has until recently identified the work within the genre of ancient historiography. Questions about the historical veracity of the narrative of Acts, combined with ongoing reassessments of Acts within the context of the literature of Jewish and Greco-Roman antiquity, have opened to a lively discussion the problem of the genre of Acts. Consequently Acts has been located within each of the three primary genres of the Roman world—historiography, the novel and biography.

1.1. Acts: Novel? Biography? Scientific Treatise? Ancient Historiography? Those scholars with doubts about the classification of Acts as historiography have tended to maximize the formal discrepancies between the Lukan prefaces and those of Hellenistic historiography, contended that the preface to the Third Gospel does not intend the narrative of Acts and/or argued that because Acts is not reliable as a historical account it should not be seen as an example of the genre of ancient historiography.

R. I. Pervo, for example, maintains that Acts is an ancient historical novel written with the purpose of entertaining and edifying its readers. In making his case Pervo caricatures some of the more radical studies of Acts (e.g.,

Haenchen) as demonstrating that Luke was a "bumbling and incompetent" historian but a "brilliant and creative" writer. The problem with this characterization of Luke, according to Pervo, is that it wrongly assumes that Acts is intended as history. If one recognizes Acts as historical fiction, he observes, then the impasse is breached and Acts can be read for what it is rather than what it fails to achieve. Pervo correctly acknowledges the humor and wit of Acts but is unable to squeeze all of Acts into the mold demanded by esthetic delight. Even those formal features that Acts shares with the novel are not peculiar to ancient novels; in his second-century treatise on *How to Write History*, Lucian advised historians to give their audiences "what will interest and instruct them" (§53).

Potentially more useful is the identification of (Luke-)Acts as "biography," since ancient biographers, like historians, dealt with people who actually lived and events that actually took place. However, the narrative of Acts is manifestly not focused on the performance of one person, so it can hardly be pressed into the biographical genre. C. H. Talbert has tried to overcome this obstacle in his proposal that Luke-Acts is a biographical "succession narrative," analogous to Diogenes Laertius's *Lives of the Philosophers* (mid-third century A.D.). These biographies, he proposes, more or less conform to a threefold format: the life of the founder, a description of the community of his followers and a précis of the teachings* of the community in its contemporary form. Accordingly Luke's first volume, the Third Gospel, highlights the life of Jesus (founder), with Acts concentrating on the deeds and teachings of his followers. D. E. Aune has criticized this approach, questioning the existence of any such genre and noting the significant discrepancies between the respective functions of Laertius's *Lives* and Acts (Aune, 78-79). Moreover, Luke signals his interest not so much in particular people as in "events" (Lk 1:1-4); and the two parts of Luke's work are held together more basically by the overarching redemptive purpose (*see* Redemption) of God* than by the life* of one or more individuals, as would be expected in a biography. That Luke has been influenced in his writing by features of the genre of biography is clear (cf. Barr and Wentling), even if Acts cannot simply be identified as a specimen of the ancient biographical genre.

A different approach has been followed by L. C. A. Alexander, who draws attention to the formal differences between Luke's preface (Lk 1:1-4) and those of the Greek historiographers. Luke's preface seems too brief, consisting of only one sentence, as compared with the more elaborate openings of Greek historians; the transition from Luke's preface to the narrative itself is surprisingly abrupt; unlike others, Luke does not engage in explicit criticism of his predecessors; Luke's preface exhibits such a personal style, with its first-person pronouns and dedication, that it has seemed inappropriate for inclusion in the genre of "dispassionate and timeless historiography"; and Luke's opening offers no general moral reflections, common among Greek historians. Such problems led Alexander to a reassessment of the literary map of Greek preface writing, with the result that she finds the closest analogues to Luke 1:1-4 and Acts 1:1 in the "scientific tradition"—that is, technical and professional writing on medicine, mathematics, engineering, and the like. Alexander proposes that Luke's narrative presentation of Jesus and the early Christian movement is scientific in the sense that it is concerned to pass on the tradition of accumulated teaching on this subject.

The affinities between Luke and the scientific tradition do not negate the identification of Luke 1:1-4 and Luke-Acts with historiography, however. First, that Luke-Acts does not match in every instance the formal features of Greco-Roman historiography presents no immediate problem, for the genre itself was easily manipulated. What is more, Luke has been influenced as well by OT and Jewish historiography, especially with respect to the use of historical sequences to shape a narrative theology (see, e.g., Hall, Soards, Sterling), and Luke's predecessors in Israelite and Jewish historiography did not reflect on their aims and procedures within the context of the writing itself. Moreover, in describing his work as *diēgēsis* ("narrative," Lk 1:1), Luke identifies his project as a long narrative account of many events, for which the chief prototypes were the early Greek histories of Herodotus and Thucydides (cf. Hermogenes *Progymnasmata* 2; Lucian *How to Write History* §55). Further, numerous components of Luke's work—symposia, travel narratives, letters, speeches—support a positive comparison of Luke's work with Greco-Roman historiography.

A number of recent studies have strengthened the earlier consensus that Acts is an example of the genre of ancient historiography. For example, viewing Acts in the context of descriptions of Hellenistic, Israelite and Hellenistic Jewish historiography, Aune concludes that "Luke was an eclectic Hellenistic Christian who narrated the early history of Christianity from its origins in Judaism with Jesus of Nazareth through its emergence as a relatively independent religious movement open to all ethnic groups" (Aune, 138-39); this qualifies Luke-Acts as belonging to the genre of "general history." G. L. Sterling, however, argues that Acts belongs to a type of history whose narratives "relate the story of a particular people by deliberately hellenizing their native traditions" (Sterling, 374). Other subgenres (e.g., historical monograph and political history) have also been proposed. Critical work in historiography has begun to underscore the apologetic role of all historiography (see 1.2 below), and this is the case with Acts, written to defend the unfolding of the divine purpose, from Israel* to the life and ministry* of Jesus to the early church* with its inclusion of Gentile* believers as full participants, and thus to legitimate the Christian movement of which Luke himself was a part.

1.2. Historiography and Historicism. In what sense, though, is it appropriate to refer to the narrative of Acts as history? What are we to make of the denial of Acts as historiography on the basis of its alleged duplicity in historical matters? Two points merit reflection. First, an attempt to present material in the generic framework of historiography is no guarantee of historical veracity; choice of genre and quality of performance are separate issues. Hence, even if more radical critics are correct in their indictments of Acts as poor history, this would not be tantamount to excluding a generic identification of Acts as historiography.

At the same time it must be admitted that such indictments against Luke as a historian are not so firmly based as is sometimes claimed. (1) Although study of Acts as history continues to be plagued by a relative dearth of corroborative evidence, whether literary or physical, recent examination of that evidence by C. J. Hemer has encouraged a much more positive assessment of the historical reliability of Acts (see also Hengel). (2) The sometimes spectacular accounts of healing in Acts (e.g., Acts 5:15; 19:11-12) have given some scholars pause in accepting the whole as an historically faithful account. However, in the wake of postmodern epistemology and in light of increasing criticism of the biomedical paradigm for making sense of non-Western accounts of healing (see, e.g., Hahn), such miraculous phenomena—previously understood as expressions of duplicity, mental pathology, superstition, fantasy and/or a prescientific worldview—are not so easily dismissed and have begun to be reexamined for their sociohistorical significance.

Second, Acts has too often been and continues in some quarters to be evaluated as historiography on the basis of modernist, positivistic canons—that is, on the basis of criteria that have themselves been made problematic and are anachronistic with reference to Luke as historiographer (see, e.g., Green 1996, Krieger, White, Stock). The central problem on which the debate on Luke the historian has typically turned has had much less to do with the nature of Luke-Acts than with modern, problematic conceptions of the historian's enterprise and with the concomitant, absurd divorce of event from interpretation. The view of the last two centuries, that historical inquiry is interested in establishing that certain events took place and in objectively reporting those facts, is being eclipsed by a conception of the historiographical project in which Luke would have found himself more at home. The primary question is not, How can the past be accurately captured? or What methods will allow the recovery of what actually happened? for it is increasingly recognized that historiography is always teleological. It imposes significance on the past by its choice of events to record and to order as well as by its inherent efforts to postulate for those events an end and/or origin. The emphasis thus shifts from validation to signification, so the issue is, How is the past being represented? Luke's concern with truth or certainty (see Lk 1:4) resides in his narrative interpretation of the past.

Identification of Acts as ancient historiography adds to the expectations we may bring to the narrative. Alongside those raised by Luke's professed intentions (Lk 1:1-4), we may anticipate a narrative in which recent history is given prominence, issues of both causation and teleology are accorded privilege and determined research is placed in the service* of persuasive and engaging instruction.

2. The Text of Acts.

Textual criticism of Acts presents a special quandary because of the existence of two primary and disparate textual types, the Alexandrian (A B C 81) and the Western (esp. Codex Bezae Cantabrigiensis [D]). The book of Acts in the Western tradition is almost 10 percent longer than the Alexandrian, and the character of each of these two textual types is distinctive. The essential question is, Whence the Western text? Is it the product of a studied recension of Acts? If so, can this effort be assigned a particular provenance? Or does the Western text bear witness* to an ongoing process of emendation? Is the Western text thoroughly secondary to the Alexandrian textual type? Can it be traced back to the hand of the Third Evangelist himself? Or does it display an amalgam of more or less original and secondary readings that must be considered (according to the eclectic method of textual criticism) on a case-by-case basis? In the history of research on the text of Acts, several related proposals have continued to surface (see the surveys in Strange, 1-34; Barrett, 2-29).

As early as the late seventeenth century it was suggested that Luke was responsible for two recensions of Acts and that this explains the existence of the two major text types. This view has gained new momentum since the onset of redaction criticism in the twentieth century as a result of the detection of alleged Lukanisms in the Western versions. It is represented today by M.-É. Boismard and A. Lamouille, who postulate two authentically Lukan versions of Acts, of which Codex Bezae (D) and Codex Vaticanus (B) are the best, though not unsullied, representatives; in their view the Western text type stems from the first edition of Acts while the Alexandrian reflects Luke's later, revised perspective. With this view one may compare the work of W. A. Strange; he believes that Acts was published posthumously by editors who left two versions of Acts now represented by the two manuscript types.

In spite of theories of this nature, most scholars continue to contend that the witnesses of the so-called Western tradition do not contain something approximating the original text of Acts and to deny that with the Western tradition we have access to a revision, primary or secondary, from the hand of the Third Evangelist. Agreeing with such earlier work as that of Martin Dibelius (84-92), they assume that while the Western text has no claim to originality, it may contain superior readings at some points.

Although there remains little agreement on the nature of the original text of Acts, it remains true that most study of Acts continues to proceed on the basis of the relative superiority of the Alexandrian text type. In some cases the Western text type is neglected, on the supposition that it represents a deliberate and sustained revision of the book of Acts; in others Western-type readings are considered on a case-by-case basis. Given this unsettled state of affairs, we may hope that calls for the production of a critical edition of the text of Acts will be heeded (Osburn).

3. The Speeches in Acts.

Among the narrative elements that abound in Acts, the speeches are especially conspicuous, both in the narrative itself as well as on the landscape of the past century of scholarly work on Acts. Many of these are missionary speeches, delivered to both Jewish and Gentile audiences. These would include such important sermons as those delivered by Peter at Pentecost* (Acts 2:14-40) and by Paul at Pisidian Antioch* (Acts 13:16-41); these speeches play programmatic roles within their narrative cotexts. This category of speeches, the missionary sermons, has been at the center of scholarly debate: How accurately has Luke reproduced early Christian missionary discourse? Other speeches have important roles within the narrative, however, including Stephen's* defense speech to the Jerusalem council (Acts 7:2-53), Paul's farewell address to the Ephesian elders (Acts 20:18-35), Paul's forensic addresses before Roman officials (e.g., Acts 24:10-21; 26:2-23), addresses by Peter and James at the Jerusalem council (Acts 15:7-11, 13-21), and so on. Of approximately 1,000 verses in Acts, 365 are found in major and minor speeches and dialogues (Soards, 1), with direct address responsible for more than half of the book.

3.1. The Debate over Sources and Tradition.

The agenda for the modern study of the speeches in Acts was set by the work of Dibelius, first published in 1949 (ET 1956). He sought to locate the speeches of Acts within the matrix of ancient historiography, where, he insisted, the speech was "the natural complement of the deed" (Dibelius, 139). Accordingly the chief question was not the transcription of a particular address but the aim of a speech in the hands of the historiographer—that is, within the historical writing as a whole. A speech might impart to the reader insight into the total situation of the narrative, interpretive insight into the historical moment, insight into the character of a speaker, and/or insight into general ideas that might explain situation. Additionally a speech might advance the action of the account (Dibelius, 139-40). But the inclusion of speeches in historical writing would not constitute any claim for the historicity of the address itself. In his examination of the speeches in Acts, Dibelius was concerned with its function in the book as a whole.

With the hegemony of diachronic approaches to NT study in general, subsequent study of the speeches of Acts remembered Dibelius mostly for his view that the speeches were Lukan compositions (see esp. Haenchen). Even though practically no one would claim that the addresses in Acts are verbatim representations of what was said, it is with reference to just such categories that the debate on their historicity has typically been framed. On the basis of what have now been shown to be largely specious arguments, scholars have referred to consistency of language and style from speech to speech and from indirect to direct discourse, and consistency of content from speech to speech, in order to deny their historicity.

Viewed primarily as a traditio-historical problem, the speeches of Acts have been studied for their historicity. With few exceptions (e.g., Bruce 1942), such examinations have led to largely negative conclusions, even if on matters of detail the handprint of apostolic tradition might be discerned here and there (e.g., Acts 13:38-39; 20:28, where Pauline-type categories are found). Most scholars have concluded that the speeches in Acts are Lukan in composition, typically with little if any traditional basis, and that they serve primarily as instruments of discourse from the author of Acts to his audience (see esp. Wilckens).

Until recently scholarship has not taken as seriously as it might that by "composition" Dibelius pointed not only to "Lukan invention" but also and fundamentally to Lukan artistry. With the rise of interest in narrative* and rhetorical* criticisms, however, some interpreters have begun largely to disregard questions of tradition and history and to examine how the setting and elements of each speech are deployed so as to portend the importance of each speech as an action in the unfolding narrative (see Neyrey 1984, Tannehill 1991, Soards).

An important reexamination of speech writing in ancient historiography by C. H. Gempf has surfaced a via media that moves beyond the impasse of these conflicting paradigms of study. Gempf insists that the principal question relevant to ancient historiography is not, Is it accurate or inaccurate in its representation of this speech? thus producing a false either-or choice or a continuum concerned primarily with faithfulness to an alleged source. Instead ancient writers sought to achieve a twofold balance between artistic and historical appropriateness. This is because speeches are included in narrative representations of history not to provide a transcript of what was spoken on a given occasion but to document the speech event itself. Historiographers (like Luke) would be concerned, therefore, with composing speeches that would cohere with the work as a whole in terms of language, style and content (the literary dimension) and that would not be regarded as anachronistic or out of character with what was known of the person to whom the speech was attributed (the socio-historical dimension).

In other words, contra the modern consensus in the discussion on tradition and sources in the speeches of Acts, literary aspirations do not preclude historical value, and the presence of Lukan style and theology in the speeches of Acts does not lead necessarily to the inference that these speeches are Lukan in origin. With respect to historical appropriateness the issue is not narrowly defined in terms of accuracy; instead the writer would compose a speech in keeping with what could be known of the historical data available to him.

3.2. The Role of the Speeches.

3.2.1. A Unified Worldview. As has often been demonstrated, one can discern a pattern in the missionary speeches of Acts: appeal for hearing, including a connection between the situation and the speech; christological* kerygma* supported with scriptural proof; the offer of salvation*; and often the interruption of the sermon by the audience or by the narrator himself. Taken as a whole the speeches in Acts by followers of Jesus evidence a kerygma that is over-whelmingly christocentric but that also features a medley of reoccurring motifs, including the centrality of Jesus' exaltation* (i.e., resurrection* and/or ascension*), together with its salvific effect; repentance* and/or forgiveness* of sins; the universal offer of salvation; the Holy Spirit*; and, frequently through scriptural interpretation, the assurance* that the message of this salvation is the manifestation of the divine will.

As we would expect, each of these motifs is integral to Luke's theology (see 5 below), but this does not render the speeches in Acts as simply a collective deposit of Lukan thought. Where comparative material is available, close examination will indicate how the speeches of Acts have struggled to hold in tension the sometimes competing aims of speech writing in historiography, literary and socio-historical faithfulness. These instances of repetition within the narrative of Acts demonstrate more particularly Luke's concern to advance through these speeches a distinct (though not at all points distinctive) view of God's purpose. This perspective is then propagated by each of the major figures who serve as witnesses to redemption in Acts.

3.2.2. Performative Utterances. It would not be appropriate in every case to catalog these addresses as commentary, even if, as deliberate pauses in the action, they possess an interpretive function. Instead the speeches often have performative roles; they advance the action of the narrative as they provide the logic and impetus for further developments in the realization of the narrative aim of Luke-Acts. The speeches of Stephen and Peter in Acts 7:2-53 and Acts 10:34-43 (and Acts 11:5-17), for example, appear at crucial junctures, pushing the narrative beyond Jerusalem* and Judea to Samaria* and to "the end of the earth" (Acts 1:8).

3.2.3. "Revealed History." Paul's sermon at Pisidian Antioch (Acts 13:16-41) exemplifies a common concern of the speeches in Acts to locate historical events in an interpretive web by splicing together in one narrative thread the past, present and future of God's salvific activity. In this perspective the meaning of historical data is not self-evident but must be interpreted, and legitimate interpretation is a product of divine revelation* (cf. Hall). Paul's speech moves deliberately and naturally from divine activity in the OT to the work of John and Jesus to the need for present response, thus providing christological interpretations of the Scriptures and of history.

3.2.4. Acts as Witness. The sheer amount of the narrative given over to speeches when compared with other exemplars of ancient historiography (or biography or novel) is suggestive of another narrative role for the speeches in Acts. Combined with the fact that in Acts speeches are typically given by witnesses or for or against the witness, this suggests that via the speeches Luke himself is giving witness, relating "all that God had done with them" (Acts 14:27). "In Luke-Acts, speeches are an essential feature of the action itself, which is the spread of the word of God" (Aune, 125).

4. The Narrative Unity of Luke-Acts.

4.1. Luke-Acts, or Luke and Acts. Since Cadbury fixed the hyphen between Luke and Acts early in the twentieth century, the relationship between these two books has been more assumed than explored. The canonical separation of the two notwithstanding, until recently most scholars have assumed that the Third Gospel and Acts shared the same author, genre and a common theological perspective and that the narrative of Acts was written as the calculated continuation of the narrative of the Gospel. Such assumptions have been called into question by M. C. Parsons and Pervo (1993), among others. Although they agree that Luke and Acts share authorship, they question whether these two books belong to the same genre, are theologically harmonious and together embody one continuous narrative.

The issues raised by Parsons and Pervo are important if only because their central observation is correct: the unity of Luke-Acts has been more assumed than justified and explored. But their arguments are difficult to sustain.

Because scholarship has not reached a consensus on the generic identification of Luke and Acts, Parsons and Pervo conclude that Luke and Acts do not share unity at the level of genre. This discussion begs important questions: Given the fluidity of generic forms in antiquity, why must one work for the high level of precision on which this rejection of generic unity depends? With respect to the Third Gospel, why must we assume Luke worked with constraints related to an evolving Gospel genre? Could Luke not be setting out to do something for which previous models or forms proved inadequate? And the possible analogues for serial volumes using multiple genres posed by the authors (e.g., 1-4 Kingdoms and 1-2 Maccabees) are hardly material, given our understanding of the composition and unity of those books.

Further, Parsons and Pervo deny narrative unity by positing the potential identification of two different (textually constructed) narrators, one for Luke, the other for Acts—this in spite of the fact that the application of narratology to even one of these books surfaces multiple narrators and levels of narration (Kurz). Nor do the authors deal constructively with the possible claim of the narrator of Luke 1:1-4 to have been of the circle of those ("us") among whom (some of) these events "have been fulfilled" (cf. the "we passages" in Acts, 4.5 below). Nor do they raise the possibility that Luke and Acts share a single narrative purpose and that in this lies their essential narrative unity.

Along more constructive lines it is important to note that the division of Luke-Acts into two volumes does not signify that one account had ended and a new one begun or that volume 2 would turn to a different subject matter. Rather, as a matter of physical expediency ancient authors divided their lengthy works into "books," each of which fit on one papyrus roll. The maximum length of a papyrus roll extended to thirty-five feet, and Luke's two volumes, the two longest books in the NT, would have each required a full papyrus roll.

Moreover, in size the two are roughly equivalent—the Gospel with about 19,400 words, Acts with approximately 18,400 words—so that they would have required papyrus rolls of about the same length. Thus the division between Luke and Acts conformed to the desire of contemporary writers to keep the size of their books symmetrical (cf. Diodorus 1.29.6; 1.41.10; Josephus *Ag. Ap.* 1.35 §320). In other ways too the plan of Luke and Acts suggests a purposeful proportionality. Both narratives begin in Jerusalem; the Gospel ends and Acts begins with commission narratives associated with reports of Jesus' ascension; the time span covered by each volume is approximately thirty years; Luke's narration of Jesus' last days in Jerusalem (Lk 19:28—24:53) and of Paul's arrest, trials and arrival in Rome* (Acts 21:27—28:31) each occupy 25 percent of their respective books; and Luke has regularly developed parallels between

Jesus in the Gospel of Luke and his disciples in the Acts of the Apostles.

Further, though Parsons and Pervo do not consider this question in their 1993 work, Luke 1:1-4 serves as a prologue for the whole of Luke's work, two volumes, Luke-Acts. This is suggested by the parallel between the primary and recapitulatory prefaces in Luke-Acts and Josephus's *Against Apion*. In addition Acts 1:1 not only refers to a "first book" but also denotes as the subject of that first book "all that Jesus began to do and to teach." This is a transparent summary of the Third Gospel, which continues the characteristic Lukan emphasis on the inseparable connection of word and deed. With the term *began*, this summary suggests a continuation of the mission of Jesus, an expectation that is not disappointed, for Jesus' followers "call on his name" (e.g., Acts 2:21; 9:21; 15:17; 18:15; 22:16)—a name* that signifies the continuing presence of Jesus to bring wholeness of life (e.g., Acts 3:6, 16; 4:7, 10, 12, 17, 30; 8:12; 9:15, 34; 10:43; 16:18). The Gospel of Luke and the Acts of the Apostles narrate one continuous story (see Augustine *De Cons.* 4.8), therefore, and the phrase "the events that have been fulfilled among us" (Lk 1:1-4) refers both to the story of Jesus and to the activity of the early church.

The Gospel of Luke thus anticipates the Acts of the Apostles, and it also authorizes the narrative of the Acts, with Acts both continuing the narrative of God's mighty acts of salvation begun with the births of John and Jesus (Lk 1—2) and at the same time showing how the significance of the Jesus story might be worked out and articulated for changing times (Korn). Acts thus builds on the foundation established in Luke, demonstrating the ongoing relation of the church to the Jesus event by interpreting the significance of Jesus for a new day.

The narrative unity of Luke-Acts has important implications for our reading of Luke's work. Most significantly it requires that our understanding of Luke's purpose in writing and thus our understanding of the need(s) and audience he addressed account for all the evidence, both the Gospel and Acts. Similarly it is critical that we understand that incidents in the Gospel anticipate aspects of the story narrated only (finally) in Acts. Notably, in Luke 2:25-35 Simeon realizes that in this child Jesus a salvation has come that will be experienced as "a light for revelation to the Gentiles" (Lk 2:32),

but during his ministry as recorded in the Gospel of Luke, Jesus interacts only rarely with non-Jews. One must wait for Acts to see how the Gentile mission is begun, legitimated and takes firm shape at the behest of God and as guided and empowered by the Holy Spirit. The last chapter of the Gospel closes off significant aspects of the story's plot, but there is a more overarching intent at work, the redemptive purpose of God for all people. Seen against this purpose, the Gospel of Luke is incomplete in itself, for it opens up possibilities in the narrative cycle that go unrealized in the Gospel but materialize in the Acts of the Apostles.

4.2. Luke, Acts and the New Testament Canon. The unity of Luke-Acts—two volumes, one story—easily escapes the modern reader in large part due to the canonical placement of these two books in the NT. Although the Gospel and Acts may have been completed and made available to the wider public separately, in the second century A.D. the Gospel of Luke came to be located with the other Gospels so as to form the fourfold Gospel. Not surprisingly, then, Luke's first volume has come to be thought of primarily as a Gospel. It is worth reflecting on the probability that in Luke's day no such literary form existed, however, so that we would be amiss to think either that Luke set out to write a Gospel or that his readership would have understood his work within this category. Luke refers to his predecessors as "narratives," not as "Gospels," and there is no a priori reason to imagine that Luke's purpose was to write a story of Jesus to which he later appended an account of the early church. Rather, the narrative he wished to relate developed naturally and purposefully from the story of Jesus' earthly ministry to that of the continuation of Jesus' mission through the early church.

Nevertheless, according to the logic of the canonical placement of Acts, Luke's second volume rests in an interpretive relationship with the Pauline letters. In fact early lists of NT books usually situated Acts sometimes before, sometimes after the Pauline corpus. Presumably as a bridge from the story of Jesus to the ministry of Paul, Acts was eventually located in its present position between the Gospels and the letters. The consequence of its location in the canon is that Acts came to provide a sequential, biographical and missionary framework within which to fit the Pauline letters—a framework that is presumed in most biblical study even though critical scholarship has surfaced important tensions between the portraits of Paul and his mission available to us in Acts and in his letters.

4.3. Luke-Acts: One Narrative Aim. A conclusion for the unity of Luke-Acts has as its immediate consequence the rejection of any proposed purpose for Luke's writing that does not account for the evidence of both volumes. Although the primary purpose of Acts may have as its corollary, for example, a defense of Paul (as has been argued), this formulation does not grapple fully with the whole of Luke-Acts. A conclusion for the narrative unity of Luke-Acts would presuppose that the whole could be examined as the unfolding of one continuous narrative cycle moving from anticipation to narrative possibilities to probabilities to actualities to consequences and serving one primary narrative aim.

If we view Luke-Acts on the large canvas of narrative analysis, it is possible to see in its entirety one narrative aim unfolding in a simple narrative cycle. In it we see the working out of one aim: God's purpose to bring salvation in all of its fullness to all (Green 1994, 62-63). This aim is anticipated by the angelic* and prophetic* voices that speak on God's behalf (Lk 1:5—2:52). It is made possible by the birth and growth of John and Jesus in households that honor God. According to the Lukan birth narrative, though, this is not an aim that will be reached easily or without opposition. Not all will respond favorably to God's agent of salvation, Jesus, resulting in antagonism, division and conflict. The realization of God's aim is made probable through the preparatory mission of John and the life, death and exaltation of Jesus, with its concomitant commissioning and promised empowering of Jesus' followers to extend the message to all people (Lk 3—Acts 1). Jesus himself prepares the way for this universal mission by systematically dissolving the barriers that predetermine and have as their consequence division between ethnic groups, men and women, adults and children, rich and poor, righteous and sinner, and so on. In his ministry even conflict is understood within the bounds of God's salvific purpose, Jesus' death as a divine necessity, his exaltation a vindication of his ministry and powerful act of God making possible the extension of salvation to Jew and Gentile alike.

The subsequent story in Acts consists of a narration of the realization of God's purpose, particularly in Acts 2—15, as the Christian mission is directed by God to take the necessary steps to achieve a community of God's people composed of Jews, Samaritans and Gentiles. The results of this narrative aim (Acts 16—28) highlight more and more Jewish antagonism to the Christian movement, and the church appears more and more to be Gentile in makeup. This too is God's purpose, according to the narrator, speaking above all through his spokesperson Paul (and through Paul, the Scriptures), even if efforts among the Jewish people at interpreting Moses* and the prophets as showing the Messiah is Jesus should continue.

4.4. Acts 1:8 and the Outline of the Book of Acts. The story related in Acts begins in Jerusalem and ends in Rome, with the plan of the book thus giving form to the centrifugal shape of the mission it recounts. It would not be unusual for a Hellenistic writer of sequential books to provide in a second or subsequent book a preface that includes a summary of the former and outline of the present book. Many readers of Acts have found in Jesus' words in Acts 1:8— "Rather, you will receive power when the Holy Spirit comes upon you, and you will be my witnesses in Jerusalem, in all Judea and Samaria, and to the end of the earth"—a summary outline of Acts. Many who see an outline of the book in Acts 1:8 further identify "the end of the earth" as Rome. Although Jesus' words may be taken as the outline of Acts, albeit in a superficial sense, this identification of Rome as "the end of the earth" is almost certainly mistaken.

Acts 1:8 relates Jesus' response to the disciples' question about the restoration of the kingdom* to Israel. Jesus does not replace a parochial, nationalistic hope* for the restoration of Israel's dominion with a universal mission as much as he sets the future of Israel within the now more widely defined plan of God. Jesus' references to a mission in Jerusalem, Judea (i.e., "the land of the Jews"—cf. Lk 4:44; Acts 10:37; *see* Land) and Samaria represent significant progress in this direction and portend the development of the mission in Acts 2—8.

Beyond Samaria the Spirit-endowed mission was to continue to "the end of the earth." Various options have been championed for making sense of the phrase *heōs eschatou tēs gēs*. Some regard it as a geographical location: Ethiopia,

Spain, Rome, or even the "Land [of Israel]." Others find in it a more symbolic reference to a universal mission including the Gentiles— that is, a mission to the whole world.*

That Luke must have had in view in Acts 1:8 a purely geographical connotation (as is often emphasized) can hardly be sustained, for space is never measured in purely geographical terms but is always imbued with symbolic power. Geography—and especially such geographical markers as "Judea" and "Samaria"—is not a "naively given container" but rather a social production that both reflects and configures being in the world. Note, for example, the identification of "Jerusalem" as the location of the temple* and abode of God in Jewish and Lukan perspective and the religious sensibilities that would have been transgressed by this juxtaposition of "Judea" (land of the Jews) and "Samaria" (land of the Samaritans; cf. Lk 10:30-37; 17:11-19). Nor is it necessary to restrict the referent of this phrase to a location within the narrative of Acts; other possibilities generated within the narrative are left unfulfilled at its close (other examples of external prolepsis include Paul's execution and Jesus' Parousia*).

Nor does Luke ever identify Rome as the mission's final point; Rome may serve as nothing more than a new point of departure for the mission, like Jerusalem and Antioch earlier in the story. Moreover, even in Acts "witnesses" precede Paul to Rome, so that Acts 27—28 brings Paul, not the gospel, to Rome.

Although in the literature of Greco-Roman antiquity the meaning of the phrase "the end of the earth" was used to refer to Spain, Ethiopia, and so on, one must inquire into how this phrase functions in this cotext. At this juncture in Acts, the meaning of "the end of the earth" is polysemous—that is, we have been given almost nothing by way of interpretive guidelines for identifying the referent of this phrase. As a result one may read through the narrative inquiring at multiple points, Is this "the end"? (And if so, will God's dominion now be realized?) Greek usage elsewhere allows for such open-endedness (cf. Strabo *Geog.*). But these various interpretive possibilities are narrowed considerably upon reading Acts 13:47, with its citation of Isaiah 49:6, where the phrase "the end of the earth" is again found but with the sense more transparent: "everywhere," "among all peoples," "across all boundaries." Luke's evi-dent dependence on the Isaianic eschatological* vision* elsewhere provides corroborative evidence for the conclusion that the narrative encourages an identification of "the end of the earth" with a mission to all peoples, Jew and Gentile. This underscores the redemptive-historical continuity between this text and its Isaianic pre-text (also Is 8:9; 45:22; 48:20; 62:11; cf. Deut 28:49; Ps 134:6-7; Jer 10:12; 16:19; 1 Macc 3:9).

In only a very limited sense might one take Acts 1:8 as an outline of Acts. Much more significant is the way it identifies God's aim within the narrative (and, one may presume, for the story as it extends beyond the narrative of Acts). As it clarifies God's purpose, it also gives us a measure by which to ascertain what persons within the narrative have oriented themselves fully around serving God's design. That is, those who obey the missionary program of Acts 1:8 are shown to be operating under the guidance and power* of the Spirit and thus following God's plan; they are shown to be authentic witnesses.

The importance of Acts 1:8 is not diminished if it is not regarded as framing the outline of Acts, for its statement of God's aim within the narrative has certainly left its imprint on the form of the narrative itself. One can easily follow the centrifugal shape of the mission, though sometimes the progression of the mission is less geographical and more theological, as when Jesus' witnesses return to Jerusalem in order to work out further the theological rationale for a mission that includes those "at the end of the earth" (Acts 11:1-18; 15; 21:1—26:32). Moreover, our identification of "the end of the earth" as a reference to the universal scope and not the geographical goal of the mission suggests that the story of Acts does not end with the close of the narrative in Acts 28:31. Rather, the challenge to mission reaches beyond the narrative to Luke's subsequent readers.

4.5. The Author and the Narrator of Acts. Examining Acts as a narrative raises the question of the voice through whom the story is told— that is, the identity of the narrator. An author might choose to adopt some voice other than his or her own, and in narrative theory narrators differ in how much they choose to tell, the degree of their reliability and how willing they are to intrude into the narrative itself. Narrative critics agree that the narrators of the Gospels and Acts are knowledgeable and are willing to alert their audiences to realities other than those on the surface of recounted events—e.g., the motivations of characters within the story (e.g., Acts 24:27; 25:3); that they are so reliable that their points of view are consistent with those expressed by God and God's agents within the narratives; and that they are generally unobtrusive in telling their stories. At the same time the narrator of Acts might on occasion provide an explanatory comment to his reader (e.g., Acts 9:36 [Tabitha's name in Greek is Dorcas]; 12:9 [Peter's inner thoughts]), and in Acts 16:10-17; 20:5-15; 21:1-18; 27:1—28:16 (i.e., in the "we" passages) he steps into the story as a character. Today, when many scholars speak of "Luke" with reference to the hand behind Luke-Acts, they have reference to Luke as narrator, often without any necessary inference regarding the identification of the actual author of this work.

Luke-Acts, like the Gospels of Matthew, Mark and John, are anonymous documents (though see John 21:24-25), and the we passages do nothing at a literary level to alter this state of affairs. That is, even when involved in first-person narration, the narrator of Acts identifies himself not as an individual with a name but as one of a group. He is present, sometimes as a participant, other times as an observer, at some events, but his focus is not his individual identity; rather, the "we" of his narration contributes to the vividness of his account and invites his audience into active participation in the narrative. That first-person narration happens in only selected portions of the account underscores that the narrator makes no claim to being a constant companion of Paul and his circle. It also suggests, however, that first-person narration is more than a literary device calculated to enliven the narrative.

Long before the onset of narrative criticism, this last set of observations led readers of Acts to an identification of the author of Acts as Luke, Paul's fellow worker (Philem 24) and sometime companion, a physician (Col 4:11, 14; 2 Tim 4:11). Eusebius, for example, identifies the author of Acts as Luke, an Antiochene, a physician and frequent companion of Paul (Eusebius Hist. Eccl. 3.4.1), as do Jerome (Vir. 7) and many others (see Barrett, 30-48; Fitzmyer, 1-26).

In the second century, Irenaeus identified Luke, the companion of Paul, as the author of Acts, though he also goes further, to speak of the relationship between Luke and Paul as "inseparable" (Haer. 3.1.1, 4). This latter inference lies behind critical rejection of Luke as the author of Acts since, it is alleged, the author of Acts has distorted the message of Paul and so could not have been his regular companion. But the inseparability of Luke and Paul is not a necessary inference from Acts; indeed, it is contradicted by Acts, wherein we are informed repeatedly that the narrator was part of a company whose traveling agenda overlapped with that of Paul but that did not join Paul's entourage regularly, permanently or even for lengthy periods of time.

When it is further remembered that the portrait of Paul available to us via his letters is itself tendentious, shaped by sometimes tension-filled relations with his audiences; that discussions of the incongruity between the Paul of Acts and the Paul of the Pauline correspondence have sometimes suffered from critical hyperbole; that in any case the narrator of Acts is more concerned with telling the story of the realization of God's salvific aim than with developing personalities; and that characters within Acts are more important for what they add to that story than with reference to their own stories (cf. Schwartz), then the critical concerns that have led to the denial of the identity of Luke as the author of Acts dissipate considerably.

Nevertheless, it is worth inquiring into what is at stake in the identification of the real author of Acts. That, for example, C. K. Barrett can engage in a critical reading of Acts without first deciding the issue of authorship is surely suggestive. This is all the more true when it is recalled that Luke makes no apparent attempt to assert himself into the narrative in order to serve concerns of historical veracity. Final resolution of the question of authorship would not table questions of historical accuracy, and, as we know almost nothing of the background of the historical Luke, our insisting that he is responsible for Acts adds almost nothing to our understanding of his narrative. As with the canonical Gospels, then, so with Acts: our reading proceeds best on the basis of what we are able to discern about its narrator from within the narrative itself.

5. The Theology and Purpose of Acts.

Numerous proposals for the purpose of Acts

have been defended in recent scholarship, including the following:

1. Acts is a defense of the Christian church to Rome (e.g., Bruce).

2. Acts is a defense of Rome to the Christian church (Walaskay).

3. Acts is an apology for Paul against Judaizers who have sided with non-Christian Jews against Paul's notion that Christianity is the true successor to Judaism* (see Mattill and Mattill).

4. Acts is a work of edification designed to provide an eschatological corrective for a church in crisis (Conzelmann).

5. Acts is written to reassure believers struggling with the reliability of the kerygma—either with regard to its truth and relevance (e.g., van Unnik) or with respect to its firm foundation in the story of God's people (e.g., Maddox).

6. Acts was intended to assist the Christian movement in its attempts to legitimate itself over against Judaism (Esler).

7. Acts is written to encourage among Christians a fundamental allegiance to Jesus that called for a basic social and political stance within the empire (Cassidy).

In light of our earlier comments on the narrative unity of Luke-Acts, some of these can be excluded from the outset—namely, those centering on aims particular to Acts and/or Paul (i.e., 1-3)—since these do not account for the whole of the Lukan narrative. This is not immediately to deny that Luke may have had such concerns, however, for the Evangelist may have been motivated by multiple aims that might not lay a claim on the narrative as a whole.

Our understanding of the aim of (Luke-) Acts flows from our understanding of its genre and narrative aim. We have seen that the genre of Acts suggests Luke's concern with legitimation and apologetic. Our discussion of the narrative aim of Acts highlighted the centrality of God's purpose to bring salvation to all. In the conflicted world of the first-century Mediterranean, not least within the larger Jewish world, it is not difficult to see how this understanding of God's purpose and its embodiment in the Christian movement would have been the source of controversy and uncertainty. We may then propose that the purpose of Luke-Acts would have been to strengthen the Christian movement in the face of opposition by ensuring them in their interpretation and experience of the redemptive purpose of God and by calling them to

continued faithfulness and witness in God's salvific project. The purpose of Luke-Acts would thus be primarily ecclesiological, centered on the invitation to participate in God's project.

Our understanding of the aim of (Luke-) Acts must also account for its primary theological emphases. Recent scholarship has repeatedly identified salvation as the primary theme of Luke-Acts, theme being understood as that which unifies other textual elements within the narrative. In order to make sense of the theme of salvation and to show the degree to which it is integrated into the overall purpose of strengthening the church (as we have just described), we must develop it within what can only be an outline of key theological motifs.

5.1. God's Purpose. The purpose or plan of God is of signal importance for Acts, and its presence behind and in the narrative is paraded in a variety of ways. This motif is present especially through a constellation of terms expressive of God's design (e.g., *boulē/boulomai* ["purpose/to purpose"—Acts 2:23; 4:28; 13:36; 20:27], *dei* ["it is necessary"—Acts 1:16, 21; 3:21; 4:12; 5:29; 9:16; 14:22; 16:30; 17:3; 19:21; 20:35; 23:11; 27:24, 26], *horizō* ["to determine"—Acts 2:23; 10:42; 17:26, 31]); through angels, visions and prophecies; through instances of divine choreography of events; through the employment of the Scriptures of Israel; and through the activity of the Holy Spirit.

This pronounced emphasis on the divine will is present in Acts to certify that the direction of the Christian mission is legitimate but not to eclipse human decision making and involvement in the mission. Indeed, the dramatic quality of the narrative is noticeably enhanced by the conflict engendered as some people choose to oppose the divine aim. God does not coerce people into serving his will, but neither will God's plan ultimately be derailed by opposition to it. The communication of his purpose comes as an invitation for people to align themselves with that purpose; some may refuse to do so, but others (and the invitation is to all) will embrace his will, receive the gift of salvation and join in his redemptive activity (see further Squires; Green, 1995, 22-49).

5.1.1. The Divine Purpose. Although God never enters the narrative of Acts as a character, his presence is everywhere apparent through the activity of the Holy Spirit (see 5.1.3 below) and angels and through visions and prophecies.

Through these agents and agencies, God both choreographs human encounters and events and verifies that the mission to the Gentiles is consonant with his will.

Two case studies in divine choreography (Philip and the Ethiopian eunuch, Peter and Cornelius) accompany the narration of the beginnings of the mission to the Gentiles. There is no socio-historical or narratological reason to suspect that the Ethiopian eunuch is anything but a Gentile (Acts 8:26-40). Philip's* encounter with him on the road to Gaza comes at the intersection of (1) the Ethiopian's having made pilgrimage, like many Gentiles in the ancient Mediterranean, to worship in Jerusalem; (2) his reading of a text (Is 53:7-8) that highlights the humility of the Isaianic servant and so declares the solidarity of Yahweh's servant with the eunuch in his own humble status (even though he went to worship* in Jerusalem, as a eunuch he would have been excluded from the Lord's assembly; cf. Deut 23:1; Is 56:3-5); (3) Philip's being directed by an angel of the Lord to travel on the same road, then instructed by the Spirit to join the entourage of the Ethiopian court official; (5) his being able to serve as interpreter of the Scriptures. Following the eunuch's baptism,* Philip is snatched away by the Spirit of the Lord; this divine encounter has reached its conclusion.

Philip's appointment with the eunuch may have initiated the Gentile mission, but this innovation is unknown to anyone within the narrative; Philip does not report what has happened to Jerusalem, and presumably the eunuch journeys home. Hence the encounter between Peter and Cornelius* (Acts 10:1—11:18) initiates the Gentile mission in its own way, particularly since in this case the believers in Jerusalem are included in the account. As with Philip, so with Peter, this novelty comes at God's behest, through the careful staging of visionary and angelic messages to communicate the divine purpose (Acts 10:1-16).

In both cases, but more explicitly in the latter, the importance of human volition is not diminished. Cornelius and Peter have separate divine directives, neither of which is complete in itself. According to this choreography, both persons must obey what disclosure they have received in order to understand more fully what God is working to accomplish in their encounter. As if to underscore again that the Gentile mission is God's doing, when they do follow through on God's purpose, the Holy Spirit breaks into their gathering, falling upon "all who heard the word" (Acts 10:44). This work of the autonomous Spirit is taken as the proof that the Gentile mission, together with full fellowship* between Jewish and Gentile believers, was God's purpose (Acts 11:17-18).

Angels are active elsewhere too (cf. Acts 5:19, 21; 12:7-11, 23; 18:9-20; 27:23-24), indicating the ongoing direction and providential care of God, as do visions (Acts 10:10-16; 16:6-10; 22:17-21).

5.1.2. The Scriptures of Israel. By the Scriptures of Israel, we mean the Septuagint, and especially Deuteronomy, the Psalms and Isaiah, for these are the authoritative texts that appear most in Acts. Two factors characterize the use of the Scriptures by God's spokespersons in Acts. First, characters within Acts are concerned to show that what has happened with Jesus and what is happening with the movement of those who name him as Lord* are continuous with the Scriptures. Second and inseparably related, however, is an important proviso—namely, it is not the Scriptures per se that speak authoritatively but the Scriptures as they bear witness to God's purpose, an interpretation accessible only in light of the mission, death and exaltation of Jesus of Nazareth. Hence, even if it is vital that the actions of the Christian community be grounded in Scripture, that their christological formulations be shaped in dialogue with Scripture, and that they understand the rejection of the message by some Jews and the mission to the Gentiles via scriptural precedent, the Scriptures speak authoritatively only when they are legitimately interpreted.

This suggests that the primary significance of the Scriptures in Acts is ecclesiological and hermeneutical, as the Christian community struggles with its own identity, not least over against those who also read the Scriptures but who refuse faith* in Christ. In Luke's view it is through the Scriptures that Jesus' followers should be able to confirm their status as the heirs of the Scriptures, God's people serving God's mission. The struggle with the Jewish people and with Jewish institutions in Acts is essentially hermeneutical: Who interprets the Scriptures faithfully? Or, to put it more starkly, Whose interpretation has the divine imprimatur? Whose receives divine legitimation? In Acts the answer is simple: Jesus has been accredited by God (Acts 2:22) and vindicated in his resurrection and ascension (e.g., Acts 2:23-36; 3:13-26). Those whose form of life is like his serve as his witnesses, and their charismatic preaching* includes authorized scriptural interpretation (e.g., Acts 4:8-13). The validity of their message is further validated by the signs* and wonders God does through them (Acts 14:3).

5.1.3. The Holy Spirit. If God does not explicitly appear within the narrative of Acts, his virtual stand-in is the Holy Spirit, and it is by means of the activity of the Spirit that God's purpose is known, the mission is directed and the universality of the gospel is legitimated. This is not because the Holy Spirit is for Luke the immanence of God, as is often suggested, but because the Spirit highlights God's transcendence, his freedom of purpose. Throughout Acts, the Lord's witnesses never control or possess the Spirit but attempt to catch up with the Spirit's work whose activity is often serendipitous.

Just as the Spirit had been active in and through the whole of Jesus' ministry (cf. Lk 3:21-22; 4:1, 14-15, 18-19; et al.), so the Spirit would empower the mission of the Lord's witnesses in Acts (esp. Acts 1:8). The Spirit directs the mission (e.g., Acts 13:1-4; 16:6-7) and empowers witness in word and deed. Within Acts, signs and wonders certify the presence of God in the ministry of his witnesses, legitimating the universal reach of salvation as they authenticate the message among the Gentiles (Acts 14:3; 15:12; cf. Acts 2:19, 22, 43; 4:30; 5:12; 6:8; 7:36; 8:6, 13).

One of the primary purposes of Luke's portrayal of the Spirit's activity is legitimation for the breaching of barriers that separate Jew and Gentile. The gift of the Spirit is one of the primary ways in which Luke articulates the content of salvation (see 5.2.2 below), and in Luke's economy of salvation those on whom the Spirit has been poured out are believers. The Spirit thus clarifies the status of believers, especially Gentiles (Acts 10:45-47; 11:15-18; 15:8).

This authorizing role of the Spirit reaches further, however. It is through the Spirit that prophets prophesy in Acts, and this verifies that their messages are grounded in the divine will. The plot of the narrative itself, behind and through which the Spirit is active, is thereby shown to be a faithful interpretation of the early Christian mission. Moreover, because Luke's presentation of the Spirit is in its essence continuous with the understanding of the Spirit in Second Temple Judaism, he portrays the Christian mission, which proceeds with the direction and empowerment of the Spirit, as the fulfillment of Israel. This is true even if in the Lukan conception the activity of the Spirit has been recast along christological lines: Spirit-empowered witness focuses on Christ, and it is through the agency of the exalted Messiah that the Spirit is poured out (Acts 2:33). As a consequence Luke's pneumatology can be viewed as providing an apologetic for God; the Spirit substantiates the direction God's purpose takes in Acts: from Israel to the life and ministry of Jesus to the early church with its inclusion of Gentile believers as full participants.

5.2. Salvation. Salvation is the principal theme of Acts, its narrative centrally concerned with the realization of God's purpose to bring salvation in all of its fullness to all people. Conflict within the narrative arises as a consequence of the division between those who embrace and serve that aim, who join the community of God's people who bear witness to God's salvific work, and those who refuse to do so (cf. Lk 2:34; on 5.2 see Green 1997).

5.2.1. God as Savior, Jesus as Savior. For Luke salvation is first and always from God. God initiates salvation, and even in the salvific activity of Jesus, God is the often silent but nonetheless primary actor. Jesus' powerful deeds are repeatedly attributed to God (Acts 2:22; 10:38). God appointed him Lord and Messiah; God glorified him, sent him, raised him and so on. Luke's soteriology is christocentric, but above all it is theocentric. (Given the strength of this emphasis, it is not surprising [contra those who find in Acts a "divine man" portrayal of the apostles and Paul] that those who align themselves with God's salvific aim in Acts are never credited with possessing the power to minister salvation. The signs and wonders that partially constitute their missionary activity are effected by God, granted by the Lord [cf., e.g., Acts 3:12, 16; 4:10, 29-30; 5:12, 38-39; 8:18-24; 14:3, 14-15; et al.].)

Nevertheless, Jesus is God's agent of salvation, the Savior (Lk 2:11; Acts 5:30-31); as Lord, Jesus is the one on whom people call for salvation. How did Jesus achieve this status? For Luke, a corollary of Jesus' being raised up is that he now administers the promise* of the Father (cf. Lk 11:13; 24:49; Acts 1:4), the gift of the

Spirit—that is, salvation (Acts 2:29-36). Similarly in Acts 5:30-31 we find a straightforward affirmation that Jesus' confirmation as Savior, as the one who "gives" repentance and forgiveness, is grounded in his resurrection and ascension. As the enthroned one (Messiah), as the Benefactor of the people (Lord), the exalted Jesus now reigns as Savior, pouring out the blessings* of salvation, including the Spirit with whom he was anointed at the outset of his ministry, to all.

What then of the crucifixion of Jesus? The sheer frequency of times that we read in Acts of the divine necessity (dei) of the suffering of Jesus is warning enough that salvation has not come in spite of the crucifixion of Jesus. What is more, the specifically covenantal* language employed in Acts 20:28 (peripoieomai, "to acquire"; cf. Ex 19:5; Is 43:21) and Acts 20:32; 26:18 (hagiazō, "to sanctify"; cf. Deut 33:3) reminds us of Luke's record of Jesus' last meal with his disciples, wherein he grounds the "new covenant" in his own death (Lk 22:19-20). Although sparsely mentioned, the salvific effect of the cross* is not absent from Luke, even if it is not woven fully into the fabric of Luke's theology of the cross.

Luke's broader perspective on the suffering* of the Messiah can be outlined along three interrelated lines.

First, the rejection of Jesus by the Jewish leaders in Jerusalem leads to the widening of the mission to embrace all peoples, Jew and Gentile. Indeed, suffering and rejection foster the propagation of the word (cf. Lk 21:13-19; Acts 13:44-49; 14:1-18; 18:2-6; 28:17-29). As Luke is fond of narrating, struggle and opposition do not impede but seem to promote the progress of the gospel: "It is through many persecutions that we must enter the kingdom of God" (Acts 14:22; cf., e.g., Acts 6:1, 7; 8:1-3, 4).

Second, the passion of Jesus is paradigmatic for all of those who follow Jesus (cf. Lk 9:23; Acts 9:16). For Luke the theologia crucis is rooted not so much in a theory of the atonement but in a narrative portrayal of the life of faithful discipleship as the way of the cross.

Third, in describing Jesus' crucifixion, Acts echoes the words of Deuteronomy 21:22-23: Jesus was "hung on a tree" (Acts 5:30; 10:39; 13:29). The narrative thus signals the disgrace of Jesus' execution while at the same time it locates Jesus' death firmly in the necessity of God's purpose. The ultimate disgrace, the curse from God, is antecedent to exaltation. Thus in his suffering and resurrection Jesus embodied the fullness of salvation interpreted as status reversal; his death was the center point of the divine-human struggle over how life is to be lived, in humility or self-glorification. Though anointed by God, though righteous before God, though innocent, he is put to death. Rejected by people, he is raised up by God—and with him the least, the lost, the left out are also raised. In his death, and in consequence of his resurrection by God, the way of salvation is exemplified and made accessible to all those who will follow.

5.2.2. The Message of Salvation. Luke develops the content of salvation along five related lines.

First, salvation entails incorporation and participation in the christocentric community of God's people. These are people whose unity is emphatic in the narrative (e.g., Acts 1:14-15, 24; 14:1; cf. Acts 2:44-45; 4:32—5:11; Plato *Rep.* 5.46.2c; Cicero *De Offic.* 1.16.51; Aristotle *Eth. Nic.* 9.8.1168b; Josephus *J.W.* 2.8.3 §§122-23), who together "call on the name of the Lord [Jesus]" and are baptized in his name (Acts 2:21-22, 38; 8:16; 9:14, 21; 10:48; 19:5; 22:16); who heal* (Acts 3:6, 16; 4:10, 30; 19:13) and preach (Acts 4:12; 5:28, 40) in his name; and who suffer for his name (Acts 5:41; 9:16; 21:13).

What may be surprising is the identification of those who belong to this community. The invitation is for everyone, for "you, your children and all who are far off" (Acts 2:39; cf. Is 57:19; Acts 1:8; 2:5, 9-11, 17, 21; 10:1—11:18; et al.). By pouring upon them the blessing of forgiveness and the gift of the Spirit, God both testifies to the authenticity of the membership of Gentiles in the number of God's people and confirms that "he has made no distinction between them and us" (Acts 15:7-8; cf. 11:15-18). Jesus is Lord of all (Acts 10:43). Also "saved" are those set apart from normal social discourse by sickness and demon possession (e.g., Acts 3:1—4:12; 5:12-16; 8:7; 14:8-10). This reminds us that the Lukan soteriology knows no distinction between the physical, spiritual and social; that in the larger Greco-Roman world "salvation" would be recognized in the healing of physical disorders; and that physical restoration had as one of its ramifications restoration to social intercourse.

Second, salvation entails "rescue from our enemies" (cf. Lk 1:68-79). Salvation as divine rescue does not appear to be prominent in Acts, but there are important hints in this direction. For example, the use of Joel 2:28-32 in Acts 2 brings onto the stage apocalyptic* connotations reminding us that the coming of God signifies the downfall of those who oppose God's purpose, and elsewhere Luke employs exodus typology to characterize salvation (Acts 3:17-26; 7:25). Salvation as rescue from peril takes on concrete form elsewhere when the language of salvation is used to signify safe travel in spite of the threat of ambush (Acts 23:16-24) or storms at sea (Acts 27:31, 43—28:6) or escape from prison and mob action (cf. Acts 5:17-21; 12:1-19; 16:19-40; 19:23-41).

What of salvation from foreign domination (as anticipated in Zechariah's song)? First, although Luke does not report the dismantling of Roman overlordship, he does narrate the relativizing of the sovereignty Rome wielded, as R. J. Cassidy has suggested. More importantly for Luke, the real enemy from which deliverance is needed is not Rome but the cosmic power of evil resident and active behind all forms of opposition to God and God's people. This form of salvation—from the power of darkness, of Satan*—is prominent in Acts (e.g., Acts 26:17-18; 5:16; 13:4-12; 16:16-18; 19:8-20).

Third, salvation is forgiveness of sins. In Acts, Luke continues an emphasis on forgiveness firmly rooted in Jesus' mission according to the Third Gospel (see Acts 2:38; 3:19; 5:31; 10:43; 13:38; 15:9; 22:16; 26:18). This signals a renewed or new relationship with God but also with God's people: as sin is the means by which persons exclude themselves or are excluded from the community of God's people, so forgiveness marks their restoration to the community.

Fourth, salvation is the reception of the Holy Spirit. Peter also promises those who respond to the message that they will receive "the gift of the Holy Spirit" (Acts 2:38), an emphasis that will resurface repeatedly (Acts 9:17; 10:43-44; 11:15-17; 15:8). The gift of the Spirit marks persons, whether Gentile or Jew, as members of the community of God's people and thus clarifies the status of those, especially Gentiles, who believe.

Finally, the offer of salvation calls for response. The necessity of response is set forth programmatically in the narration of the Pentecost address, where Peter is interrupted by his audience: "What shall we do?" (Acts 2:37; cf. 16:30-34). What is the appropriate response to the good news of salvation? Luke addresses this question with an arsenal of possibilities—calls to believe (Acts 2:44; 3:16; 11:17; 13:39; 14:9; 15:7; 16:30-31; 18:8), to be baptized (Acts 2:41; 8:12, 36; 9:18; 10:47-48; 16:15) and to turn to God or to repent (Acts 2:38; 3:19; 5:31; 11:18; 17:30; 20:21; 26:20); and other potential responses, including some that employ metaphors of illumination (e.g., Acts 26:17-18)—but singles out no particular pattern of response as paradigmatic. God has acted graciously in Christ to bring salvation to all humanity. All humanity is called to welcome the good news, to respond with receptivity and thus to share in that salvation not only as recipients but also as those who serve God's redemptive aim.

5.2.3. Eschatology. Students of Acts have long noticed that eschatological hope has not been developed within the narrative. Although the future of salvation is not missing (e.g., Acts 3:21; 7:31; 10:42), the focus has moved from the eschaton to the present. In Acts 1:6-8 Jesus reorients concerns about the restoration of the kingdom to Israel, an eschatological concern, to the importance of faithful witness in the present. This should not be taken as an attempt on Luke's part to diminish the importance of the Parousia (as Conzelmann argued); in counseling agnosticism about "the times and seasons" established by the Father (Acts 1:7), Jesus emphasizes the unpredictability of the Parousia. "Luke sought to reinforce living eschatological faith, all the while summoning his readers to vigilant, faithful service" (Carroll, 166). That is, Luke employs eschatology as a motivation for mission.

5.2.4. Judaism. The question of Luke's relationship to Jewish institutions and Jewish people is one of the most debated in Lukan studies, with some scholars arguing that Luke's theology is irretrievably anti-Jewish, others insisting that Lukan thought derives from a lively Jewish Christian church and many viewpoints falling between these poles. (For representative views see Tyson.) How does the Lukan treatment of people and things Jewish point toward Luke's overall purpose? Without engaging fully this larger debate, two observations are possible.

First, the centrality of the temple and the synagogue,* the continuous use of Israel's Scriptures, the primacy of the mission to the

Jewish people—these and related phenomena within the narrative of Acts suggest the degree to which the story of the Christian community is continuous with the ancient story of God's people.

Second, however, the critical perspective on the temple and the synagogue, for example, and the contested nature of the relationship between the Christian movement and Jewish structures suggests the degree to which the Judaism with which Luke is interested is an interpreted Judaism. That is, "the religion of Israel—its institutions, practices, and so on—is to be embraced fully when understood *vis-à-vis* the redemptive purpose of God. But in order to be understood thus, Israel's religion must cohere with the purpose of God as articulated by God's own authorized interpretive agent, God's Son, Jesus of Nazareth" and in Acts by the Lord's witnesses who thus serve as interpretive agents (Green 1995, 75). This perspective on the question of Judaism within Acts underscores the nature of the fundamental struggle between the Christian movement and its representatives on the one hand, Judaism on the other, just as it also provides a rationale for the opposition faced by that movement.

5.3. Discipleship. The interdependence of the Gospel of Luke and Acts is perhaps nowhere more evident than in the Lukan perspective on discipleship. Especially when compared with the other Synoptic Gospels, the Third Gospel is noteworthy for how little it has the disciples participating in Jesus' ministry. This is easily explained, since the Third Gospel can provide instruction and models for discipleship while allowing Acts to document more fully how the disciples came to serve actively in the missionary work of Jesus. Among the motifs that might be developed, two are of particular importance: economic koinonia and witness and allegiance.

5.3.1. Economic Koinonia. Throughout the Third Gospel, Jesus' message has returned again and again to undercut the determination of social relations on the basis of widespread canons of status and to affirm the redefinition of economic relations within the community of his followers. These two points address the same set of issues, since economic exchange is a function and representation of social relations. Patrons, for example, have higher status than their clients, and in their acts of benefaction they obligate others to supply them with loyalty, rec-

ognition, venerated status. Among friends and within kinship groups, however, giving and receiving need not have stipulations carried over from the patronal ethic that pervaded the empire. In these cases giving is a function not of obligations and debt but of mutuality, generosity, solidarity and need. Economic koinonia would thus grow out of, as well as symbolize, kinship.

What Jesus had called for in his Sermon on the Plain (Lk 6:27-38, esp. Lk 6:35)—dispositions of kinship giving rise to practices of material generosity—the early church is reported to practice (Acts 2:44-45; 4:32—5:11; see also Acts 6:1-6; 11:27-30). What Luke describes in the summary statements of Acts 2:44-45 and Acts 4:32-35, however, is not communitarianism, either as a requisite for belonging to the people of God or as an ideal. Instead he outlines a disposition of kinship and generosity, an orientation toward the needs of others and toward the generosity of God that characterizes the Christian community outside the normal constraints of reciprocity and the gift-obligation cycle. Accordingly Barnabas is introduced as an exemplary figure who embodied the ideal of kinship that was to characterize the whole community (Acts 4:32, 36-37). Similarly Ananias and Sapphira demonstrate by their falsehood and their choice of private ownership that they have not refused the way of patronage and status-seeking of the larger empire and so that they are not members of this new community of God's people (Acts 5:1-11).

5.3.2. Witness and Allegiance. One of the hallmarks of Luke's narrative is the consistency with which faithful witnesses attract opposition and with which opposition leads to the spread of the gospel. Exemplars include Jesus, Peter and John (e.g., Acts 4:23-31; 5:41-42), Stephen (Acts 8:1-4) and Paul (e.g., Acts 13:45-49). The conflict surrounding these key characters, whose faithfulness is underscored repeatedly by the narrator (e.g., Acts 3:14-15; 5:38-39; 6:8-10; 7:55; 25:25; 26:32; 28:17-22), portends the opposition that faithful witnesses outside the narrative, including those among Luke's audience, may also encounter in the course of the mission.

That is, opposition in the course of the church's mission should not necessarily be interpreted as a sign of misapprehension of the divine purpose. Faithfulness calls for a fundamental allegiance to Jesus as Lord, which calls for a basic social and political stance within the empire (Cassidy), and this may well generate opposition. Peter, John, Stephen and Paul may thus serve as models for Christians who in the course of the church's mission face similar struggles.

See also CORNELIUS; EVANGELISM IN THE EARLY CHURCH; GENTILES, GENTILE MISSION; HELLENISTS; MIRACLES IN ACTS; MISSION, EARLY NONPAULINE; NARRATIVE CRITICISM; OLD TESTAMENT IN ACTS; PAUL AND PAULINISMS IN ACTS; PENTECOST; PHILIP THE EVANGELIST; SAMARIA; SIGNS AND WONDERS; STEPHEN; TONGUES.

BIBLIOGRAPHY. **Bibliographies:** F. Bovon, *Luke the Theologian: Thirty-Three Years of Research (1950-83)* (PTMS 12; Allison Park, PA: Pickwick, 1987); J. B. Green and M. C. McKeever, *Luke-Acts and New Testament Historiography* (IBRB 8; Grand Rapids: Baker, 1994); A. J. Mattill Jr. and M. B. Mattill, *A Classified Bibliography of Literature on the Acts of the Apostles* (NTTS 7; Leiden: E. J. Brill, 1966); W. E. Mills, *A Bibliography of the Periodical Literature on the Acts of the Apostles 1962-1984* (NovTSup 58; Leiden: E. J. Brill, 1986); P. F. Stuehrenberg, "The Study of Acts before the Reformation: A Bibliographic Introduction," *NovT* 29 (1987) 100-36. **Commentaries:** C. K. Barrett, *The Acts of the Apostles* (2 vols.; ICC; Edinburgh: T & T Clark, 1994-); F. F. Bruce, *The Acts of the Apostles: The Greek Text with Introduction and Commentary* (3d ed.; Leicester: Inter-Varsity (Apollos)/Grand Rapids: Eerdmans, 1990); idem, *The Book of the Acts* (NICNT; rev. ed.; Grand Rapids: Eerdmans, 1988); H. Conzelmann, *The Acts of the Apostles: A Commentary on the Acts of the Apostles* (Herm; Philadelphia: Fortress, 1987); E. Haenchen, *The Acts of the Apostles: A Commentary* (Oxford: Blackwell; Philadelphia: Westminster, 1971); L. T. Johnson, *The Acts of the Apostles* (SP 5; Collegeville, MN: Liturgical Press, 1992); I. H. Marshall, *The Acts of the Apostles: An Introduction and Commentary* (TNTC; Leicester: Inter-Varsity; Grand Rapids: Eerdmans, 1980); R. Pesch, *Die Apostelgeschichte* (2 vols.; EKK 5; Zürich: Benziger; Neukirchen-Vluyn: Neukirchener, 1986); J. B. Polhill, *Acts* (NAC; Nashville: Broadman, 1992); G. Schneider, *Die Apostelgeschichte* (2 vols.; HTKNT 5; Freiburg: Herder, 1980, 1982); R. C. Tannehill, *The Narrative Unity of Luke-Acts: A Literary Interpretation, 2: The Acts of the Apostles* (Minneapolis: Fortress, 1990); B. Witherington III, *The Acts of the Apostles: A Socio-Rhetorical Commentary* (Grand Rapids: Eerdmans, 1977). **Studies:** L. C. A. Alexander, *The Preface to Luke's Gospel: Literary Convention and Social Context in Luke 1:1-4 and Acts 1:1* (SNTSMS 78; Cambridge: Cambridge University Press, 1993); D. E. Aune, *The New Testament in Its Literary Environment* (LEC 8; Philadelphia: Westminster, 1987) esp. 77-157; D. L. Barr and J. L. Wentling, "The Convention of Classical Biography and the Genre of Luke-Acts: A Preliminary Study" in *Luke-Acts: New Perspectives from the Society of Biblical Literature Seminar,* ed. C. H. Talbert (New York: Crossroad, 1984) 63-88; M.-É. Boismard and A. Lamouille, *Le Texte Occidental des Actes des Apôtres: Reconstitution et Réhabitaliation* (2 vols.; Paris: Recherche sur les Civilisations, 1984); F. F. Bruce, *The Speeches in the Acts of the Apostles* (London: Tyndale, 1942); H. J. Cadbury, "Commentary on the Preface of Luke" in *The Beginnings of Christianity,* pt. 1: *The Acts of the Apostles,* ed. F. J. Foakes Jackson and K. Lake (5 vols.; London: Macmillan, 1922; Grand Rapids: Baker, 1979 repr.) 2:489-510; idem, *The Making of Luke-Acts* (2d ed.; London: SPCK, 1958); J. T. Carroll, *Response to the End of History: Eschatology and Situation in Luke-Acts* (SBLDS 92; Atlanta: Scholars Press, 1988); R. J. Cassidy, *Society and Politics in the Acts of the Apostles* (Maryknoll, NY: Orbis, 1987); M. Dibelius, *Studies in the Acts of the Apostles* (London: SCM; New York: Scribner's, 1956); P. F. Esler, *Community and Gospel in Luke-Acts: The Social and Political Motivations of Lukan Theology* (SNTSMS 57; Cambridge: Cambridge University Press, 1987); J. A. Fitzmyer, *Luke the Theologian: Aspects of His Teaching* (Mahwah, NJ: Paulist, 1989); S. R. Garrett, *The Demise of the Devil: Magic and the Demonic in Luke's Writings* (Minneapolis: Fortress, 1989); C. H. Gempf, "Public Speaking and Published Accounts" in *The Book of Acts in Its Ancient Literary Setting,* ed. B. W. Winter and A. D. Clarke (BAFCS 1; Grand Rapids: Eerdmans, 1993) 259-303; J. B. Green, "Internal Repetition in Luke-Acts: Contemporary Narratology and Lukan Historiography" in *History, Literature and Society in the Book of Acts,* ed. Ben Witherington III (Cambridge: Cambridge University Press, 1996) 283-99; idem, "The Problem of a Beginning: Israel's Scriptures in Luke 1-2," *BBR* 4 (1994) 61-85; idem, "'Salvation to the End of the Earth' (Acts 13:47): God as Savior in the Acts of the Apostles" in *The Book of Acts and Its Theology,* ed. I. H. Marshall and D. Peterson (BAFCS 6; Grand Rapids: Eerdmans, 1997) 83-106; idem,

The Theology of the Gospel of Luke (NTT; Cambridge: Cambridge University Press, 1995); R. A. Hahn, *Sickness and Healing: An Anthropological Perspective* (New Haven, CT: Yale University Press, 1995); R. G. Hall, *Revealed Histories: Techniques for Ancient Jewish and Christian Historiography* (JSPSup 6; Sheffield: JSOT, 1991); C. J. Hemer, *The Book of Acts in the Setting of Hellenistic History,* ed. C. H. Gempf (WUNT 49; Tübingen: J. C. B. Mohr [Paul Siebeck], 1989); M. Hengel, *Acts and the History of Earliest Christianity* (London: SCM; Philadelphia: Fortress, 1979); F. J. Foakes Jackson and K. Lake, eds., *The Beginnings of Christianity,* pt. 1: *The Acts of the Apostles* (5 vols.; London: Macmillan, 1920-33; Grand Rapids: Baker, 1979, repr.); J. Jervell, *The Theology of the Acts of the Apostles* (NTT; Cambridge: Cambridge University Press, 1996); M. Korn, *Die Geschichte Jesu in veränderter Zeit: Studien zur bleibenden Bedeutung Jesu im lukanischen Doppelwerk* (WUNT 2.51; Tübingen: J. C. B. Mohr [Paul Siebeck], 1993); M. Krieger, ed., *The Aims of Representation: Subject/Text/History* (New York: Columbia University Press, 1987; Palo Alto, CA: Stanford University Press, 1993, repr.); W. S. Kurz, *Reading Luke-Acts: Dynamics of Biblical Narrative* (Louisville, KY: Westminster/John Knox, 1993); R. Maddox, *The Purpose of Luke-Acts* (FRLANT 126; Göttingen: Vandenhoeck & Ruprecht, 1982); I. H. Marshall, *The Acts of the Apostles* (NTG; Sheffield: JSOT, 1992); J. H. Neyrey, "The Forensic Defense Speech and Paul's Trial Speeches in Acts 22-26: Form and Function" in *Luke-Acts: New Perspectives from the Society of Biblical Literature Seminar,* ed. C. H. Talbert (New York: Crossroad, 1984) 210-24; idem, ed., *The Social World of Luke-Acts: Models for Interpretation* (Peabody, MA: Hendrickson, 1991); C. D. Osburn, "The Search for the Original Text of Acts: The International Project on the Text of Acts," *JSNT* 44 (1991) 39-55; M. C. Parsons and R. I. Pervo, *Rethinking the Unity of Luke and Acts* (Minneapolis: Fortress, 1993); R. I. Pervo, *Profit with Delight: The Literary Genre of the Acts of the Apostles* (Philadelphia: Fortress, 1987); M. A. Powell, *What Are They Saying About Acts?* (Mahwah, NJ: Paulist, 1991); D. Schwartz, "The End of the Line: Paul in the Canonical Book of Acts" in *Paul and the Legacies of Paul,* ed. W. S. Babcock (Dallas: Southern Methodist University Press, 1990) 3-24; M. L. Soards, *The Speeches in Acts: Their Content, Context, and Concerns* (Louisville, KY: Westminster/John Knox, 1994); J. T.

Squires, *The Plan of God in Luke-Acts* (SNTSMS 76; Cambridge: Cambridge University Press, 1993); G. L. Sterling, *Historiography and Self-Definition: Josephus, Luke-Acts and Apologetic Historiography* (NovTSup 64; Leiden: E. J. Brill, 1992); B. Stock, *Listening for the Text: On the Uses of the Past* (Baltimore: Johns Hopkins University Press, 1990); W. A. Strange, *The Problem of the Text of Acts* (SNTSMS 71; Cambridge: Cambridge University Press, 1992); C. H. Talbert, *Literary Patterns, Theological Themes and the Genre of Luke-Acts* (SBLMS 20; Missoula, MT: Scholars Press, 1974); R. C. Tannehill, "The Functions of Peter's Mission Speeches in the Narrative of Acts," *NTS* 37 (1991) 400-14; M. Turner, *Power from on High: The Spirit in Israel's Restoration and Witness in Luke-Acts* (JPTSup 9; Sheffield: Sheffield Academic Press, 1996); J. B. Tyson, ed., *Luke-Acts and the Jewish People: Eight Critical Perspectives* (Minneapolis: Augsburg, 1988); W. C. van Unnik, *Sparsa Collecta: The Collected Essays of W. C. van Unnik,* pt. 1: *Evangelia—Paulina—Acta* (NovTSup 29; Leiden: E. J. Brill, 1973) esp. 6-15, 340-73; P. W. Walaskay, *'And So We Came to Rome': The Political Perspective of St. Luke* (SNTSMS 49; Cambridge: Cambridge University Press, 1983); R. W. Wall, "The Acts of the Apostles in Canonical Context," *BTB* 18 (1988) 16-24; H. White, *The Content of the Form: Narrative Discourse and Historical Representation* (Baltimore: Johns Hopkins University Press, 1987); U. Wilckens, *Die Missionsreden der Apostelgeschichte: Form- und traditionsgeschichtliche Untersuchungen* (3d ed.; WMANT 5; NeukirchenVluyn: Neukirchener, 1974); B. W. Winter, ed., *The Book of Acts in Its First-Century Setting* (6 vols.; Grand Rapids: Eerdmans, 1993-97); B. Witherington III, ed., *History, Literature and Society in the Book of Acts* (Cambridge: Cambridge University Press, 1996). J. B. Green

ACTS OF THOMAS. *See* APOCRYPHAL AND PSEUDEPIGRAPHAL WRITINGS.

ADOPTIONISM. *See* CHRISTOLOGY; DOCETISM; JEWISH CHRISTIANITY.

ADULTERY. *See* MARRIAGE, DIVORCE AND ADULTERY.

ADVERSARIES

Several later NT writings combat what their authors view as unacceptable beliefs and practices. As they do, they are setting limits to the diversity of earliest Christianity. Interpreters have usually identified the adversaries of most of these writings as Gnostics* of some description. This identification was based on a reconstruction of the late first and early second century which envisioned Gnosticism as the primary heresy Christians faced. Thus it was simply assumed that since these writings come from that period, their adversaries were probably Gnostic and could be identified as such with very little evidence. More recent scholarship has recognized diversity among those rejected by the developing orthodoxy of this period and so less often simply assumes a particular type of adversary for these writings.

1. Defining Adversaries
2. Revelation
3. Johannine Epistles
4. Jude
5. 2 Peter
6. Pastoral Epistles
7. Ignatius of Antioch
8. Ebionites
9. Gnostics

1. Defining Adversaries.

Adversaries, understood as those who identify themselves as Christians (hinted at in Paul's* farewell discourse in Acts 20:29-30) but who are rejected and opposed by a particular author, are not part of the occasion of all late NT writings. 1 Peter,* for example, addresses Christians troubled by persecution,* offering encouragement to help them interpret and endure persecution, but has no Christian adversaries in view. Other writings mention unacceptable views while not having the defeat of those who hold these views as their primary goal. For example, the central purpose of James* is to pass on ethical instructions, but it alludes to some use of Pauline teaching* which it rejects (2:18-26). This view is opposed in passing, but opposing its proponents is not central to the purpose of James.

It is also necessary to distinguish between correcting dangerous or unacceptable tendencies or views and opposing adversaries. Not every person who held views our authors thought needed correction was viewed as an adversary. Hebrews* opposes some attraction to cultic practices associated with the Jerusalem temple or its replacement. Those with such inclinations are not, however, treated as heretics or adversaries, but rather as Christians in need of instruction.

When the primary goal is the defeat of adversaries, later NT writings often take up a polemical tone, which means that many of their accusations and charges cannot be straightforwardly attributed to their adversaries. In both early Christian and earlier non-Christian writings, polemics often involved stock charges of immorality applied to whatever opposition one encountered. Often this was done in the belief that deviation from the acceptable inevitably led to such behavior. Thus we must be cautious when such charges appear.

2. Revelation.

Revelation* is a special case. Its primary purpose is to encourage those enduring persecution, but the opening section (Rev 1—3) treats some within the communities addressed as adversaries. The seven "letters" to the churches* are often thought to address a single type of adversary. But some interpreters resist this assumption and examine them individually before making connections. The adversaries repudiated in Revelation 1—3 have been identified as Gnostic libertines or libertines with gnostic tendencies. A few interpreters find a dispute between moderate and conservative Jewish Christians (*see* Jewish Christianity), with John taking the more conservative position. Many interpreters identify these adversaries as Christians willing to accommodate themselves to the culture by participating in trade guild meetings which were held in temples and included a meal in which sacrificed* food* was eaten.

Only the letters to Ephesus, Pergamum and Thyatira deal with adversaries within the church. The Nicolaitans are mentioned in the messages to both Ephesus and Pergamum. John commends the Ephesians for hating the Nicolaitans and for rejecting some who claim to be apostles.* If, as seems probable, these apostles were Nicolaitans, this brand of teaching was brought to Ephesus by teachers claiming some authority.* But it seems they were unsuccessful there. There is no hint of the content of their teaching. John rebukes the church at Pergamum for having within its congregation Nicolaitans and those who hold the teachings of Balaam. While it initially appears that these are separate groups, the name Balaam is probably used metaphorically for the Nicolaitans, because the two names have similar meanings. Again, no teachings are ascribed to the Nicolaitans. The Balaamites are accused of eating food sacrificed to idols* and of fornication. The charge of fornication is probably figurative, standing for religious infidelity. This is its usual meaning in Revelation. Additionally, fornication had long been associated with idolatry (see Num 25:1-2, which immediately follows the Balaam story, and the apostolic decree in Acts 15:23-29). Since this accusation is a polemically charged metaphor, these Balaamites are not libertines. The only other charge leveled against them is that they eat idol meat. Such conduct was viewed as an unacceptable accommodation to the surrounding culture.

John condemns the Thyatirans for tolerating Jezebel, who is accused of teaching and practicing fornication and eating sacrificed meat. This Jezebel, who claimed to be a prophet, must have been an influential member of this church. The charge of fornication is again metaphorical. So the only practice Jezebel is condemned for is eating idol meat, the same accusation made against the Nicolaitans/Balaamites. However, the Seer adds that those who follow Jezebel call their teaching "the deep things of Satan."* It is doubtful that the followers of Jezebel attribute their teachings to Satan, but they must claim some insight that reconciles their eating of idol meat and Christian conduct.

In the end, all the adversaries mentioned are accused only of eating idol meat, and thus of being unfaithful. So John's opposition to them is based on their accommodation to the surrounding culture and whatever reasons they give for allowing it. There is no evidence that allows us to associate any tendency of these adversaries, whether taken individually or as a group, with any other known group.

3. Johannine Epistles.
The adversaries of 1 and 2 John (*see* John, Letters of) are usually discussed together, and 3 John is often included within the same broad situation as well. The opponents of both 1 and 2 John are recognized as former members of the Johannine community who have split off from that group. Nearly all interpreters understand the debate to be over the proper interpretation of the traditions* now found in John. Throughout the first half of the twentieth century most

interpreters identified these separatists as docetic,* libertine Gnostics. However, many recent interpreters deny that these adversaries were Gnostic, libertine or fully docetic. Several (e.g., Brown) argue that these opponents deny only the salvific significance of Jesus' earthly life, not the reality of his material existence. Some interpreters also find 1 John opposing an adoptionist christology* and argue that the separatists see the life of Jesus as one phase of the work of the "divine word." Similarly, Painter identifies them as pneumatics who see Jesus as merely an example of the spiritual person's life.

3.1. 1 John. 1 John yields clear evidence that its adversaries have seceded from the addressed community and are now viewed as enemies; they are even identified as antichrists* (1 Jn 2:18-19). Two issues dominate 1 John: keeping the commandments (particularly the love commandment) and christology.

1 John frames the christological debate so that denying that Jesus is the Christ* is equivalent to denying "the Son" (1 Jn 2:22-23), and these are further synonymous with denying "Jesus" and not confessing that "Jesus Christ is come in flesh"* (1 Jn 4:2-3). These carefully worded statements indicate that the adversaries separate the earthly Jesus from the Son in some way unacceptable to 1 John, perhaps denying that the heavenly Christ is to be fully identified with the human Jesus. 1 John's prologue (1 Jn 1:1-4) supports the notion that these adversaries have a docetic tendency, as does 1 John 4:3, where the issue is cast as denying Jesus. If they are docetists, they are not necessarily Gnostics. One needs only the common Hellenistic* devaluing of the material world* to find docetism attractive. However, the question may not be whether Jesus had a material body, but rather whether Jesus is to be fully identified with the Son of God (*see* Son of God), or for how long such an identification is envisioned. The opponents may have an adoptionist christology that has the Son come upon Jesus at his baptism. This could be based in part on their interpretation of the first chapter of the Gospel of John.

But this part of the adversaries' christology may not be at issue; the dispute may concern when or whether the Son separated himself from Jesus. Most interpreters see the reference to blood in 1 John 5:5-6 as an allusion to the crucifixion. The antithetical structure of these verses suggests that this mention of blood opposes some teaching advocated by the separatists. If it does, they seem to deny that the Son (or the Christ) was crucified and only allow that Jesus was. This—in 1 John's view—premature departure of the Son was unacceptable because it at least implicitly denied the importance of that death* for the forgiveness of sins, a function 1 John affirms as central (1 Jn 1:7; 2:1-2, 12; 4:9-10). This understanding of 1 John 5:5-6 also fits if the separatists are docetists.

Thus the most we can say with relative certainty is that these separatists advocated a christology that does not affirm a sufficient identification of Jesus with the Son of God. That insufficiency may involve some form of docetism, or alternatively an adoptionist christology that does not identify Jesus completely enough with the Son and has the Son leave Jesus before the crucifixion. Neither of these positions requires a gnostic theology, but only a descending/ascending redeemer schema, a schema that the Johannine community affirmed.

Beyond the broad indictment that they do not keep the commandments, the sole recurring accusation about the adversaries' ethics* is that they lack love for fellow Christians. This charge probably stems from their separation from the Johannine community. Their lack of love is demonstrated by their absence from the assembly of the remaining community. So this accusation reveals little about the separatists' ethical conduct and certainly does not indicate that they were libertines.

It appears from 1 John 1:8, 10 that the secessionists claim to be sinless. Based on the presence of the perfect tense in 1 John 1:18 ("we have not sinned"), some interpreters discern a perfectionism, based on gnostic beliefs, which claims either that material existence is so unimportant that sin* does not affect them or that their spiritual nature has made them "intrinsically sinless" (Bogart, 33). However, these statements are probably 1 John's interpretation of the adversaries' views, not quotations of their claims. Still, they must advocate a type of perfectionism that the author of 1 John rejects, even as he embraces a perfectionism of another type in 1 John 3:4-9.

The rejected perfectionism may be a correlate of the separatists' denial of the expiatory function of the crucifixion: if they claimed never to have sinned, atonement would be superfluous (*see* Death of Christ). But their position on Jesus' death may be based on a different understanding of the means of salvation* rather than a gnostic-like anthropology. They may argue that the vital element is that the Son brought down eternal life from God,* an act that has nothing to do with Jesus' death (cf. Brown 1979). Since 1 John rejects their assertions of sinlessness in 1 John 1:8, 10 with comments on the atoning function of Jesus' death in 1 John 1:7, 9; 2:1-2, these two points are either related in the adversaries' teachings or inseparable from 1 John's perspective. While these adversaries seem to claim an advanced spiritual status that includes sinlessness, there is insufficient evidence to tie this claim to any system of thought (e.g., Gnosticism or a realized eschatology*). Perhaps 1 John denies them this status because of their christology and their secession from his community—after all, he expects sinlessness from those "born of God" (1 Jn 3:9).

Our understanding of these separatists must remain vague. We can establish that they refuse to identify the Son of God with Jesus as completely as 1 John demands and that they deny the expiatory significance of the death of Jesus. Furthermore, they claim a spiritual status that probably includes the assertion that they are beyond sin. There is no good evidence that they are libertines or Gnostics or that they belong to any other known group.

3.2. 2 John. The adversaries of 2 John are described in essentially identical ways to those of 1 John. Again in 2 John these adversaries are perceived as secessionists (2 Jn 7) who have not remained "in the teaching of Christ" (2 Jn 9). The Elder warns his readers to beware of the antichrist who does not confess that "Jesus Christ is come in flesh" (2 Jn 7-8). This shorthand for the adversaries' teaching gives more weight to the view that they are docetists, but in light of its use in 1 John, this phrase remains too ambiguous to be decisive. This letter* may represent a later stage in the dispute than 1 John because now there are "many" deceivers (2 Jn 7). Unfortunately, even though we can see that 1 John and 2 John address the same adversaries, 2 John does not appreciably clarify our understanding of them.

3.3. 3 John. 3 John identifies the adversary by name, Diotrephes. The Elder writes that Diotrephes is fond of holding a position of leadership, does not acknowledge the Elder's authority, makes false charges against the Elder and does not welcome itinerant preachers associated with the Elder's community. Some interpreters find here a further disintegration of the Johannine community at the hands of the adversaries of 1 and 2 John. On this reading, the adversaries can now claim an adherent from among those with institutional authority. Others identify Diotrephes as one of the first monarchical bishops and locate the dispute between him and the Elder in issues of ecclesial structure (*see* Church Order). Käsemann argues that Diotrephes legitimately holds the office that was soon to develop into the monarchical episcopacy. Occupying this position, Diotrephes has, Käsemann asserts, excommunicated the Presbyter for being an enthusiast who valued the immediate encounter of the presence of Christ above the tradition.

Third John serves a dual purpose: it is a commendation for Gaius and a letter of recommendation for Demetrius as he travels to the area where both Gaius and Diotrephes are church leaders, probably the leading members of separate house churches in the same immediate area. The main issue of 3 John is Diotrephes' refusal of hospitality for itinerant preachers sent by the Elder. The Elder interprets this action as an affront to his honor, a primary value in Greco-Roman culture, and thus as both a personal matter and a matter that affects his standing in the broader Christian community in that area.

While this action by Diotrephes may have been due to doctrinal disputes, any such dispute remains veiled. If the false charges brought against the Elder involve some doctrinal issue, the text gives no indication that this is the case. There is no evidence to support Käsemann's claim that the Presbyter has been excommunicated as a heretic. The Elder approaches this problem as he does (i.e., he seems to be on the defensive according to Käsemann) because of Diotrephes' position in the church, not because he has been excommunicated. The dispute could involve ecclesial structure, but again there is no evidence to support this view; it could equally concern Diotrephes' exercise of a recognized office. Thus while we can identify this single adversary by name, we cannot identify (or assume the presence of) any doctrinal, ecclesial or ethical issues beyond inhospitality for itinerants as the root of this struggle for control of a

segment of the Johannine community.

4. Jude.

The adversaries of Jude* and 2 Peter* have often been identified together and assumed to be the same because 2 Peter borrows so heavily from Jude. But methodologically this is a mistake. Even though 2 Peter uses much of Jude's polemic, he may well apply this stereotyped material to a different group. Thus, as with all NT writings, adversaries must be identified solely on the basis of the text under consideration.

Most interpreters find some sort of Gnostics or proto-Gnostics as the target of Jude's attack. But this identification can be supported only by reading far more into Jude than his statements reasonably permit. Most interpreters also fail to take the thoroughly polemical nature of Jude into account and so accept at face value his often exaggerated charges and accusations. Consequently they identify his adversaries as libertines. Wisse has shown that such charges were typical of polemics in both Christian anti-heretical writings and the broader Hellenistic milieu.

Jude's adversaries were traveling, perhaps charismatic, teachers (Jude 4, 8) who participated in the churches' worship services (Jude 12). Their presence and teaching were causing divisions, as some accepted their teaching and others did not (Jude 18-19). This much is clear. Even though Jude constantly charges these adversaries with being immoral, the level of polemic makes it doubtful that we should see them as libertines. Such charges probably do indicate that Jude and these teachers disagree about some aspect of Christian behavior. But it is difficult to imagine that Jude's rather broad audience (basically all Christians, Jude 1) needed special instructions to reject the kind of sexually profligate teachers many interpreters find opposed. Charges of "defiling the flesh" (Jude 8) or even of being licentious (Jude 4) do not necessarily indicate that these adversaries were without any moral code. At most, such charges show only that they allowed something(s) the author does not.

Given that Jude is totally immersed in Jewish traditions, it seems likely that both the author and audience were Christian Jews. It seems most likely that Jude represents a more law-observant perspective than that advocated by the itinerant teachers. If the "glories" of Jude 8 are the angels* involved with giving the law* (as many interpreters assert), the "insult" of the adversaries is that they do not keep part of the law. They need not be devoid of morality to insult the law and its mediators, they need only to ignore one aspect of it. In addition, if the traditional archenemies of God's people cited in Jude 11-12 are intended to portray Jude's adversaries in any specific way, the inclusion of Korah may be significant. In Jewish tradition he is known not only for rebellion but also for not keeping the law properly—though with no hint of antinomianism. We are left with almost no clues about the aspect of the law the teachers fail to keep. Jude's characterization of them as problematic at fellowship meals (Jude 12) may indicate that their nonobservance involves food laws (or some other purity* regulation that complicated association at table), but this is far from certain.

So Jude's adversaries are itinerant teachers whose primary offense involves their understanding of the responsibilities of Christians with respect to the law. They may cite visionary experiences as evidence of their authority. Taking a more law-observant stance, Jude rejects them as the false teachers of the last days and characterizes them as ungodly, lawless and haughty. They undoubtedly had a different picture of themselves.

5. 2 Peter.

Many interpreters also identify the adversaries of 2 Peter* as Gnostics or proto-Gnostics, in large part because they deny the Parousia.* But this is insufficient evidence to make a connection with Gnosticism, for no beliefs central to Gnosticism are combated in 2 Peter. Rejecting a gnostic connection, Neyrey identifies these adversaries as teachers who draw on Epicurean ideas that had filtered out into the broader culture. Specifically, their denial of the parousia is a manifestation of popular doubts about the reality of divine judgment.* Bauckham (1983) also finds eschatological skepticism to be their central tenet but does not connect their teaching with Epicurean beliefs. Based on their denial of the judgment, Bauckham argues that they advocate antinomianism.

Like Jude, 2 Peter is a thoroughly polemical document. Once again, such direct and fierce polemic must be read carefully, taking into account that stock accusations served to discredit, not accurately describe, adversaries. All of 2 Peter 1:16—3:13 is intended to refute, accuse and denounce the adversaries, not objectively describe them.

The clearest point about these adversaries, who were formerly part of the communities 2 Peter addresses (2 Pet 2:1, 15), is that they deny the Parousia (2 Pet 3:3-4). They based their rejection of it on two things: the passing of the first-generation Christians who thought the Parousia would occur in their lifetime (2 Pet 3:8-10) and the absence of God's action against evil in the world (2 Pet 3:4-6). References to the reality of the Parousia at the beginning and end of the polemical section (2 Pet 1:16—3:13) show that this is the central issue. In 2 Peter 1:16 the author asserts that the Parousia is not a myth and interprets the denial of the Parousia as a rejection of the apostolic testimony. While it is possible that the adversaries explicitly rejected apostolic teaching, it seems unlikely. Even though 2 Peter interprets their view in this way, it is difficult to see how they could have gained influence (2 Pet 2:2) in a community that reveres apostles (as the attribution of this letter to Peter indicates) if they rejected apostolic testimony. Instead they probably argued that the apostles had been misunderstood. 2 Peter 1:16-19 intends to make this claim untenable.

It seems that these adversaries expect no future judgment, but this may only be 2 Peter's interpretation of what it means to deny the Parousia. Some interpreters combine the adversaries' rejection of the judgment with 2 Peter's accusations about their licentiousness to argue that they are libertines. However, this section's sharp polemic prohibits us from reading such charges literally. These denunciations were intended to damage the adversaries' ethos, not accurately describe them. The writer of 2 Peter has no doubt that the adversaries' beliefs lead to moral corruptness, but these polemical denunciations are insufficient evidence that they, for example, "revel in the daytime" (2 Pet 2:13)—a stock polemical accusation.

2 Peter also says that these adversaries revile "glories" (2 Pet 2:10). This expression is taken from Jude but given new meaning here. 2 Peter 2:11 indicates that these "glories" are spiritual beings subject to God's judgment. The charge of reviling may be 2 Peter's interpretation of the adversaries' rejection of the Parousia and its

attending judgment. If these "glories" are involved with the judgment, as Neyrey contends, they may be beings who accuse humans before God at judgment. Thus the adversaries' reviling consists in their disbelief that such judging and accusing takes place.

These teachers also "promise freedom" to those who accept their views. Although 2 Peter gives no clear indication of what this freedom* involves, many see it as freedom from moral constraint, perhaps because it is juxtaposed to the charge that the adversaries are "slaves of corruption." But again, such polemical accusations are primarily denunciation. If the "glories" of 2 Peter 2:10 are accusers at the judgment, the freedom of 2 Peter 2:19 may be freedom from fear of such beings. This fits well with the adversaries' denial of the Parousia, but no interpretation of this freedom is certain. 2 Peter also accuses these adversaries of despising authority* or lordship. This is a polemical implication the author draws from their denial of the Parousia.

These adversaries are further accused of "twisting" the Scriptures (2 Pet 3:15-16; cf. 1:20-21). 2 Peter mentions Paul as an authority who agrees that the delay of the Parousia is a sign of God's patience (2 Pet 3:15), but then adds that some misuse Paul's writings and other Scriptures. This is no basis for identifying these teachers as hyper-Paulinists or for asserting that they claim him as their primary authority. He may be simply one apostle they call on. However important Paul is, the reference to him shows that the adversaries do not reject apostolic testimony. Their "twisting" of the prophets shows that particular interpretations of Scripture contribute significantly to their arguments for their teaching.

2 Peter, then, opposes teachers who previously held the same beliefs about the Parousia as the author but now deny its reality and use Scripture to support their position. They do not reject apostolic authority, but 2 Peter interprets their denial of the Parousia as implying such a rejection. Their denial of the Parousia may include a rejection of a final divine judgment; at least 2 Peter presents the two as necessarily related. Denial of a final judgment need not entail the removal of all moral constraints (consider the Sadducees), but the writer of 2 Peter is certain it will lead to licentiousness. Their beliefs about the Parousia and judgment seem

to allow them to claim freedom from the fear of certain spirit* beings, perhaps accusers at judgment. Clearly, the primary issue for the writer of 2 Peter is the adversaries' rejection of the Parousia, which he sees as a rejection of Scripture, apostolic authority and morality. So all questions and accusations stem from this one central concern.

6. Pastoral Epistles.
Although the authorship and dating of the Pastorals are debated (*see DPL,* Pastoral Letters), the majority opinion of scholarship is that the Pastorals are pseudepigraphic* and date from the post-Pauline era. However, those who maintain the Pauline authorship of the Pastorals frequently date these letters in the mid-60s, at the close of Paul's life and ministry, and regard them as reflective of a changing situation. Whether Pauline or post-Pauline, the identity of the adversaries depicted in the Pastorals has long been at issue in reconstructions of early Christianity and the study of the texts under review in this volume.

Most scholars have assumed that the three Pastoral Epistles address a single type of adversary. This single front is usually identified as a type of Jewish Gnosticism or proto-Gnosticism. A few interpreters, however, identify these adversaries as Judaizing Christians with an ascetic regime and a realized eschatology, or alternatively as Jewish Christians who engage in rabbinic exegesis and emphasize keeping the Torah and ascetic practices. Others identify them as Hellenistic-Jewish legalists, and still others see the main problem to be that these teachers are perceived as a threat by those in authority. Barrett comments that the Pastorals seem to mention every heresy that comes to the author's mind and so are directed at no single, specific adversary. Fiore finds these adversaries to be largely indefinite and described in ways contemporary paraenetic writings typically describe rejected teachers.

6.1. 1 Timothy. A growing number of scholars identify the adversaries of these letters individually. Among types of opponents interpreters have proposed for 1 Timothy we find proto-Gnostics, libertines, elitists from within, some who hold a fully realized eschatology, Jewish Christians who keep the food* laws of Judaism, and a circle of Torah-observing Jewish Christians who included the author of Revelation in their number. Interpreters have identified the opponents of 2 Timothy as Gnostics, proto-Gnostics and enthusiastic Paulinists with a realized eschatology. For Titus scholars have found proto-Gnostics, Judaizers and perhaps Marcionites,* rival Jewish missionaries, and the same two types of law-observant Jewish Christians proposed for 1 Timothy.

First Timothy, like the other Pastorals, yields little specific information about its adversaries. Its primary concern is not to describe and oppose some false teaching but to encourage a particular type of behavior by placing it in antithesis with a different type. Consistent with this purpose, its polemic is rather stylized, drawing on stock accusations and denunciations. Still, some things are discernible about these adversaries. First, the author's assertion in 1 Timothy 1:6-7 that they want to be teachers of the law implies that they require more Torah observance than 1 Timothy does. This may be corroborated by 1 Timothy 4:3, where we find that they demand abstinence from certain unspecified foods. This food prohibition is usually taken to signify that these adversaries have an ascetic tendency, especially since it is combined with a proscription against marriage.* But the marriage prohibition could be also associated with an expectation that the Parousia was near (see Paul's comments in 1 Cor 7) or any number of rationales, including some relationship between prophecy and celibacy or the emancipation of women. Still, they may have had some ascetic tendency. Even if they did, their food regulations probably originated with the food laws of Judaism, since other passages allude to questions about the law. One of these is 1 Timothy 1:8-11, where 1 Timothy distinguishes between proper and improper uses of the law. 1 Timothy 2:5-7 may include a passing defense of Paul's mission to Gentiles* and so intimate that observance of the law is an issue.

1 Timothy also accuses the adversaries of propagating myths, genealogies and old wives' tales (1 Tim 1:3-4; 4:7-8). Modern interpreters have often used these characterizations to identify these adversaries as Gnostics. But such accusations were commonly employed as a polemical device designed to disparage one's adversaries, no matter what their teaching was. That seems to be their function here. Even if these statements have specific teachings in view, there is no clear information about their con-

tent. Not even the reference to their teaching as *gnōsis* (knowledge*) in 1 Timothy 6:20 is sufficient to attribute gnostic tendencies to these adversaries, for many groups used this language to designate their teachings in this period.

There is, then, insufficient evidence to connect the teachings of these adversaries with Gnostic or proto-Gnostic beliefs. They do advocate adherence to more of the law than the author of 1 Timothy allows. Their urging of food and marriage prohibitions may indicate that they have some ascetic tendencies. 1 Timothy's comments about these adversaries give us no further information about them.

6.2. 2 Timothy. The adversaries of 2 Timothy are identified by name and by problematic teaching in 2 Timothy 2:17-18; they are Hymenaeus and Philetus, and they claim that the resurrection* has already taken place. 2 Timothy 2:17-18 is probably a polemical recasting of their teaching which makes it as unacceptable as possible to the readers. But it still shows that they advocate an eschatology which asserts that Christians now participate (or at least can participate) in blessings that the author believes are reserved for the Parousia. Their teaching surely excludes a future bodily resurrection but may not deny every sort of afterlife with God. Though some interpreters use this more fully realized eschatology to identify these adversaries as Gnostics, this is not sufficient evidence of such a tendency. Not only are there other bases for a more fully realized eschatology, but no other Gnostic teachings are opposed in this letter.

These opponents are also identified as the predicted eschatological false teachers (2 Tim 3:1-9). The licentiousness attributed to them in this role is again part of the stock polemic against one's adversaries and so is not to be taken at face value without corroborating evidence. The function of this characterization is twofold in 2 Timothy: it makes them odious to the readers, and it is a foil against which to describe and recommend the proper manner of life (e.g., 2 Tim 3:10-15). The remaining references to adversaries in 2 Timothy charge them only with engaging in worthless and harmful disputations (2 Tim 2:14-17, 23-26), an accusation that fits nearly any adversary.

2 Timothy 1:15 may indicate that these teachers who advocated a more fully realized escha-

tology were fairly successful, because it says that everyone in Asia had deserted Paul. Some interpreters use this as evidence that 2 Timothy represents a later stage in the battle with the same adversaries found in 1 Timothy. However, 2 Timothy 2:24-26 not only encourages Timothy to correct these adversaries gently but also grants the possibility that they may repent.* That hardly sounds like a later stage of the controversy that provoked the accusations in 1 Timothy. More important, nothing in 2 Timothy links its adversaries with those of 1 Timothy beyond the broad and stock rejection of their teaching as worthless disputing. Thus the adversaries of 1 and 2 Timothy do not seem to be related.

6.3. Titus. Titus identifies its adversaries as "the circumcision,"* a group actively propagating a message that included "Jewish myths and commands of those who turn away from the truth"* (Tit 1:10-14). This same passage also indicates that they are native Cretans. The mention of "myths" here is, again, an insufficient basis on which to support the idea that they are Gnostics. These adversaries are Jewish Christians who have begun to demand observance of parts of the law beyond those this author allows. Confirmation that the adversaries' commands involve the law comes from Titus 3:9-11, where Titus is exhorted not to engage in arguments about the law and to exclude from the community anyone who presses such discussions. Further confirmation of this origin of their commands and perhaps more specification of them is found in Titus 1:15. Immediately following the condemnatory description of the adversaries' commands in Titus 1:14, the author turns to the question of what is "clean" and "unclean" for Christians. Thus the adversaries probably urged some purity laws of the Torah. In addition to holding these views, the accusation that these adversaries teach for "dishonorable profit" (Tit 1:11) indicates that they are active teachers who accept pay from their followers.

While these adversaries do seem intent on spreading their message, there is no sign that they are part of a traveling band of missionaries. While they may possibly belong to such a group, any such group must be composed of native Cretans. This makes a direct connection between these adversaries and those of 1 Timothy unlikely, even though the two groups have similar tendencies.

When examined individually, the evidence shows that the Pastorals do not all address the same adversaries. 1 Timothy and Titus do address adversaries with similar tendencies, but we have no evidence that they are part of the same larger Jewish-Christian, law-observant movement. The discussion about the law, particularly among Jewish Christians, continued well into the fourth century and beyond. Any Jews who joined the Christian fellowship would be confronted by questions about their (and Christian Gentiles') observance of the law and could arrive at a more law-observant view than 1 Timothy and Titus deemed acceptable. Thus the adversaries of these two letters need not be part of a large or organized movement. Unlike those of 1 Timothy and Titus, the adversaries of 2 Timothy do not seem interested in Torah observance. Rather, the primary charge against them is that they hold a faulty and harmful eschatology, a more fully realized eschatology than 2 Timothy can accept. Our finding that these letters address significantly different types of adversaries requires future study of these letters to begin by treating them individually rather than simply viewing them as part of the Pastoral Epistles.

7. Ignatius of Antioch.

On his way to martyrdom in Rome, Ignatius* of Antioch (d. 107/110) wrote letters to churches in Asia Minor and Europe. Some of these letters oppose adversaries he encountered on visits to individual churches and perhaps in his home church. In his letter to the Smyrneans he rejects docetists,* who denied that Christ had a physical body and that he suffered in the passion. Furthermore, they probably did not participate in the bishop's Eucharist but celebrated their own in a way consistent with their christology. In Philadelphia, Ignatius finds a very different group which he treats as adversaries. These Christians understood differently and granted more authority to the Hebrew Scriptures than Ignatius did. Additionally, they proposed a sort of continuity with Judaism, a relationship between Judaism and Christianity, that he rejects. But they do not advocate observance of any part of the law that Ignatius does not require. While other letters of Ignatius discuss many issues (including the continually raised matter of the monarchical bishop), he treats no other Christian groups he encounters as adversaries.

8. Ebionites.

Looking beyond the canonical writings and Ignatius, we find that the place of the law continued to be a debated issue into and beyond the second century. In addition to the adversaries of Jude, 1 Timothy, Titus and Ignatius, this matter was crucial in the rejection of the Ebionites* and the Gnostics—though for opposite reasons. The Ebionites originated in Palestine, perhaps as a remnant of the original Jerusalem church. They were Christian Jews who kept the law (including circumcision* and the sabbath) and used only the Gospel of Matthew. It is possible that they also possessed a *Gospel of the Hebrews,* though this is reported only in later sources. Justin and Origen knew some Ebionites who required Gentiles to keep the law and others who did not. They rejected the former group but accepted the latter group as Christians, albeit weak ones. It is possible that this accepted group is known in other writers as Nazoreans or Nazarenes.

Epiphanius (*Haer.* 29.9.1-4) labels Nazoreans a group that differs from the orthodox only in that they keep the Mosaic law. However, a wider gap had developed between most Ebionites and the emerging orthodoxy, so that they denied Paul's apostleship (Origen *Cont. Cels.* 5.66; Eusebius *Hist. Eccl.* 3.27.17-4), seeing him as an apostate from the law. Some also held an adoptionist christology that usually entailed denial of the virgin birth, though others accepted it (Origen *Cont. Cels.* 5.61). It is not surprising that Eusebius (*Hist. Eccl.* 3.27.1.6) asserts that all Ebionites have an aberrant christology. Among the adoptionists there were differing views on the nature of the Christ who descended on Jesus. Some saw the Christ as an archangel, while others believed him to be a being created in heaven* who had intermittently descended on Adam (Epiphanius *Haer.* 2.30.1). By the fourth century, the heresiologists charged that Ebionites require marriage, allow divorce, eat no meat, reject the Prophets, use water instead of wine in the Eucharist and use multiple baptisms for sanctification (Epiphanius *Haer.* 30.17.6-18.8). There is no indication in pre-fourth-century sources that these practices were found among the Ebionites at earlier times.

9. Gnostics.

The developed Gnostic systems of the second through the fourth centuries held a view of the law opposite to the Ebionites' (*see* Gnosis, Gnosticism). Some Gnostics rejected completely the authority of the Hebrew Scriptures, disparaging them as the work of an inferior, and often evil, god who also created the material world. Most Gnostics viewed matter, and so the material world, as evil. They believed that humans, at least some of them, possess within themselves a piece of divine substance which descended to earth after a catastrophe within the divine realm. That divine spark remained trapped in the world of matter until it learned its true nature and how to escape. For Christian Gnostics, Christ came to reveal this saving knowledge, which enables the ascent of the soul to its true home.

Gnostic christology was usually either docetic to some degree or a radical adoptionism. Though the heresiologists usually portrayed Gnostics as licentious or antinomian, the writings of Nag Hammadi reveal that most of them were somewhat ascetic. Their challenge to emerging Christianity's interpretation of the world, Christ and God was strong, widespread and of significant endurance.

See also ANTICHRIST; CHRISTOLOGY; DOCETISM; EBIONITES; GNOSIS, GNOSTICISM; JEWISH CHRISTIANITY; PROPHECY, PROPHETS, FALSE PROPHETS.

BIBLIOGRAPHY. C. K. Barrett, "Pauline Controversies in the Post-Pauline Period," *NTS* 20 (1973-74) 229-45; R. J. Bauckham, *Jude and the Relatives of Jesus in the Early Church* (Edinburgh: T & T Clark, 1990); idem, *Jude, 2 Peter* (WBC; Waco, TX: Word, 1983); J. Bogart, *Orthodox and Heretical Perfectionism in the Johannine Community as Evident in the First Epistle of John* (SBLDS 33; Missoula, MT: Scholars Press, 1973); R. E. Brown, *The Community of the Beloved Disciple* (New York: Paulist, 1979); idem, *The Epistles of John* (AB; Garden City, NY: Doubleday, 1982); R. Bultmann, *The Johannine Epistles* (Herm; Philadelphia: Fortress, 1973); H. C. C. Cavallin, "The False Teachers of 2 Peter as Pseudo-Prophets," *NovT* 21 (1979) 263-70; B. Fiore, *The Function of Personal Example in the Socratic and Pastoral Epistles* (AnBib 105; Rome: Biblical Institute Press, 1986); T. Fornberg, *An Early Church in a Pluralistic Society: A Study of 2 Peter* (CBNTS 9; Lund: C. W. K. Gleerup, 1977); R. M. Grant, *Heresy and Criticism: The Search for Authority in Early Christian Literature* (Louisville, KY: Westminster/John Knox, 1993); G. Haufe, "Gnostische Irrlehre und ihre Abwehr in den Pastoralbriefen" in

Gnosis und Neues Testament: Studien aus Religionswissenschaft und Theologie, ed. K.-W. Tröger (Gütersloher: Mohn, 1980) 325-39; R. Heiligenthal, "Wer waren die 'Nikolaiten'? Ein Beitrag zur Theologiegeschichte des frühen Christentums," *ZNW* 82 (1991) 133-37; R. J. Hoffmann, *Marcion: On the Restitution of Christianity* (AAR Academic Series 46; Chico, CA: Scholars Press, 1984); L. T. Johnson, "2 Timothy and the Polemic Against False Teachers: A Re-examination," *JRS* 6-7 (1978-79) 1-26; R. J. Karris, "The Background and Significance of the Polemic of the Pastoral Epistles," *JBL* 92 (1973) 549-64; E. Käsemann, "Ketzer und Zeuge: Zum johanneischen Verfasserproblem," *ZTK* 48 (1951) 292-311; A. F. J. Klijn and G. J. Reinink, *Patristic Evidence for Jewish-Christian Sects* (NovTSup 36; Leiden: E. J. Brill, 1973); G. W. Knight III, *The Pastoral Epistles: A Commentary on the Greek Text* (NIGTC; Grand Rapids, MI: Eerdmans, 1992); J. Lieu, *The Second and Third Epistles of John: History and Background,* ed. J. Riches (Edinburgh: T & T Clark, 1986); A. J. Malherbe, *Social Aspects of Early Christianity* (2d ed.; Philadelphia: Fortress, 1983); I. H. Marshall, *The Epistles of John* (NICNT; Grand Rapids, MI: Eerdmans, 1978); J. Murphy-O'Connor, "2 Timothy Contrasted with 1 Timothy and Titus," *RB* 98 (1991) 403-18; J. H. Neyrey, *2 Peter, Jude* (AB; New York: Doubleday, 1993); J. Painter, "The 'Opponents' of 1 John," *NTS* 32 (1986) 48-71; A. F. Segal, "Jewish Christianity" in *Eusebius, Christianity and Judaism,* ed. H. W. Attridge and G. Hata (SPB 42; Leiden: E. J. Brill, 1992) 326-51; T. V. Smith, *Petrine Controversies in Early Christianity: Attitudes Towards Peter in Christian Writings of the First Two Centuries* (WUNT 15; Tübingen: J. C. B. Mohr-Siebeck, 1985); J. L. Sumney, "Those Who 'Ignorantly Deny Him': The Opponents of Ignatius of Antioch," *JECS* 1 (1993) 345-65; C. H. Talbert, "II Peter and the Delay of the Parousia," *VC* 20 (1966) 137-45; D. C. Verner, *The Household of God: The Social World of the Pastoral Epistles* (SBLDS 71; Chico, CA: Scholars Press, 1983); D. F. Watson, "Amplification Techniques in 1 John: The Interaction of Rhetorical Style and Invention," *JSNT* 51 (1993) 99-123; idem, *Invention, Arrangement and Style: Rhetorical Criticism of Jude and 2 Peter* (SBLDS; Atlanta: Scholars Press, 1986); R. A. Whitacre, *Johannine Polemic: The Role of Tradition and Theology* (SBLDS 104; Chico, CA: Scholars Press, 1980); F. Wisse, "The Epistle of Jude in the History of Heresiology" in *Essays on the Nag Hammadi Texts in Honour of Alexander Böhlig,* ed. M. Krause (NHS 3; Leiden: E. J. Brill, 1972) 133-43.   J. L. Sumney

AGAPE, THE. *See* LORD'S SUPPER, LOVE FEAST.

ALEXANDRIA, ALEXANDRIAN CHRISTIANITY

Because of the scarcity of evidence for the origins and early development of Christianity in Alexandria, our subject is best viewed from the broader perspective of the first three centuries of Christianity. Although this takes us beyond the primary historical focus of this dictionary, the late second and third centuries present vital evidence for the transmission of biblical material by Christians in Alexandria.

    1. Historical and Geographical Considerations
    2. Philo
    3. Hebrews
    4. The Catechetical School

1. Historical and Geographical Considerations. Alexandria was the chief seaport of Egypt, situated 129 miles northwest of Cairo. The city was founded by Alexander the Great in 331 B.C. on the site of an earlier Egyptian hamlet called Rhakotis. Under Ptolemy I (Soter) the city became the capital of Egypt, a status that it enjoyed for more than a thousand years. Alexandria prospered under the Ptolemaic dynasty and acquired importance as a cultural and intellectual center for Jews and Greeks alike. It was the home of the Septuagint and witnessed Julius Caesar's and then Antony's interest in Cleopatra. In Christian history it was a major center of the Arian controversy, home to both protagonists and orthodox in it.

Jewish immigration into Egypt goes back as early as the sixth century B.C. (see Josephus *J.W.* 2 §487). Archaeological excavations have uncovered Jewish tombs from the late fourth century B.C. The Jews were known as a separate community in Alexandria (*Ep. Arist.* 310), and by the first century the Egyptian Jewish community numbered more than a million people (see Philo *Flacc.* 43). Judaism* prospered under the Ptolemaic dynasty, but the situation evidently changed under Roman rule after 30 B.C. There was a persecution* of the Jews in Alexandria, and a delegation, led by Philo,* made an unsuccessful appeal to the emperor in A.D. 39. Jewish unrest continued sporadically in the first and second centuries, notably in A.D. 66 and 115. The Jewish rebellion of A.D. 115 resulted in the virtual annihilation of the Alexandrian Jewish community (see Eusebius *Hist. Eccl.* 4.2). It was not substantially restored until the fourth century A.D. The Jewish community was once again destroyed by the Christian bishop Cyril in A.D. 415.

The origins of the Christian presence in Alexandria are difficult to discover, but Christianity was probably brought there by Jewish emigrés from Palestine, evidently before the fall of Jerusalem* in A.D. 70. The Gospels reveal considerable movement between Palestine and Egypt in the first century (Mt 2:13-19; cf. Acts 2:10). Eusebius (*Hist. Eccl.* 2.16.1; 2.4.1) says that John Mark the Evangelist founded the church in Alexandria, but the reliability of this report is difficult to assess. The letter to the Hebrews,* which comes from the late first century A.D., is sometimes associated with Alexandria. If this is so, it would show the presence of a Christian community there and the intellectual ability of some of its members. Church buildings existed in Alexandria before the fourth century, for Eusebius reports the destruction of many of them during the Diocletian persecution of 303-11 (Eusebius *Hist. Eccl.* 8.2). The city was home to the famous catechetical school over which both Clement and Origen in turn presided.

2. Philo.

The strength of Jewish intellectual life in Alexandria is best illustrated by the numerous writings of the biblical philosopher Philo (c. 15 B.C.—A.D. 50). Philo's writings fall into two distinct categories: exposition of the law* of Moses* and exegetical commentaries. Philo's significance for the NT (especially for John and Hebrews) lies in his approach to scriptural exegesis. He accepted the literal meaning of a text (see Philo *Migr. Abr.* 89-93) but also thought that Scripture contains an allegorical meaning that the exegete must disclose. This double meaning determines his exegetical method: Philo was critical of those who were exclusively literal or allegorical in their work. For him God* is a transcendent spirit who had created the world* by means of his Word, or *Logos,* which for Philo denoted God's mental activity and which he sometimes presented as an exalted angel* (Philo *Conf. Ling.* 146). Philo established an attitude toward the Hebrew Scriptures in Alexandria that was both rigorous in its attention to the meaning of the text but also willing to engage in reflection about the religious understanding that the Scriptures conveyed. Early Christianity benefited from this intelligent reflection; the Alexandrian school imitated and developed it.

3. Hebrews.

No NT document, including Hebrews, can be proved to have been written in Alexandria. However, we must acknowledge that Philonic exegesis exercised an important influence on this document. Hebrews shares several exegetical concerns with Philo. The comment about the high priest* in Hebrews 7:27 is often compared with Philo's *De Specialibus Legibus* 1.131, and there is a certain affinity between the use of cultic imagery in Hebrews 8—10 and Philonic material. The relation between the two must not be over-pressed, however. Philo lacks the emphasis that Hebrews, in company with all other Christian literature, places on eschatology.* Nevertheless, the approach that Philo adopted was more widely disseminated, which explains why Hebrews rather obviously has affinities with the so-called Alexandrian method of exegesis.

Hebrews was written to persuade Christians of the dangers of a return to Judaism. Despite the strongly Jewish character of the language and imagery, it seems unlikely that the recipient church (which has never been identified with certainty) would have been composed of Jewish Christians alone. It was more likely a mixed community, so that Gentiles* are also addressed in the letter. We are perhaps entitled to assume that the author was writing for people who were familiar with the conventions of Alexandrian exegesis and who knew their Bibles well. They would have realized that OT institutions like the sabbath and the tabernacle* had an inner meaning that the letter discloses. This debt to Philonic exegesis must be acknowledged even when it is recognized that early Christianity in general believed that it could interpret the Scriptures with confidence because of its convictions about Jesus and about the imminent eschatological climax (2 Cor 3:16-17).

Hebrews is by no means an easy text to read. The center of its argument is the premise that Jewish institutions had received their fulfillment in the final age that the death of Jesus had inaugurated (see Death of Christ). This is exemplified in the opening chapter, where the ephemeral ministry* of the prophets* (Heb 1:1) and angels (Heb 1:5-14) is contrasted with the permanent achievement of the Son of God (Heb 1:3-4). It was through the Son's offering himself, priest and victim, in the heavenly sanctuary that the decisive reconciliation of humanity to God had been achieved. To desert Christianity, so the author argues, was to negate the achievement of Christ and thus to spurn the redemption* that God had instigated. This central theme accounts for the different methods of argument that are used in Hebrews.

In Hebrews 3 the idea of the divine rest is introduced for the first time. The context is the citation and elucidation of Psalm 95:7-11 (Heb 3:8-11): the passage that says of the rebellious Israelites that they would never enter God's rest. Rest is interpreted as the eschatological sabbath that the author of Hebrews apparently understands in connection with the earthly kingdom* of Christ. This promise of rest could be negated only by disobedience (see Obedience) on the part of the readers (Heb 3:11).

The theme of rest leads to major christological* teaching in the letter. The linchpin of the author's view of Jesus is the mediator's journey from earth to heaven,* a journey that allowed him to make his unique act of atonement in the heavenly sanctuary (Heb 4:14; cf. Heb 10:19-20). In this sense the high-priestly ministry is presented as an antitype of the achievement of Jesus. The author's exegesis of the OT ritual leads him to find reasons why Jesus was different from his earlier counterparts. Jesus was a priest after the order of Melchizedek* (Heb 7:17); he was himself both priest and victim (Heb 9:11-12); and he ministered in the heavenly sanctuary of which the earthly was merely a copy (Heb 8:5). The christology presented in this way has an exegetical foundation. Its key is the recognition that, in the author's view, the OT ritual anticipated the sacrifice* of Jesus, which brought its precursor to its fruition and end.

The eschatological difference between Hebrews and Philo must not be minimized. Philo was essentially a Platonist whose understanding of the soul's destiny was that it would return to its true home in heaven. The background of Hebrews's eschatology has been disputed in twentieth-century scholarship, but there are reasons for questioning the view that its author

thought in the same terms. The goal of Hebrews's eschatology is not the heavenly salvation* of the elect* but the appearance on earth of the kingdom of Christ. This is the theme of Hebrews 11, where the author praises the heroes of faith* who anticipated a city that they did not live to see. Christians, by contrast, were on the very threshold of Mount Zion, the heavenly Jerusalem, which the author thought would be revealed on earth (Heb 12:22; cf. Heb 13:14). This eschatology has much in common with that of other NT literature, especially the view expressed by Paul (Gal 4:26) and the author of the Apocalypse (Rev 21—22; see Revelation, Book of). It would be wrong to read Hebrews without acknowledging this central eschatological core. The basis of Hebrews's outlook is its apocalyptic* belief that the city that was currently in heaven would soon be revealed on earth, when the promises* of God would finally be realized.

One must also therefore acknowledge the different uses to which so-called Alexandrian methods of exegesis were put in the ancient Jewish world. Philo was by no means the only example of this method, even if he is the best documented. Hebrews is an interesting glimpse at what may have been a prevalent exegetical method in early Christianity. The distinction between the literal and the allegorical meaning was to exercise an important influence on Alexandrian Christianity in the patristic period.

4. The Catechetical School.
By the late second century A.D. there had emerged in Alexandria the so-called catechetical school, over which both Clement and Origen presided. Clement of Alexandria (c. 150-215) studied at the school under its founder, Pantaenus, whom he succeeded in 190. Clement, who had fled the city in the persecution of 202, is rightly regarded as the first Christian scholar. He knew the Bible and much Christian literature and also classical and philosophical texts. The latter helped Clement to form his distinctive understanding of revelation,* according to which pagan literature contained the seeds of truth that came to full fruit in the Christian faith. Clement opposed the Gnostics, who had taken root in Alexandria by the second century (see Gnosis, Gnosticism), in his insistence that faith is more important than knowledge* (Clement Strom. 6.18.114) and that the earthly life has significance in its own right

(Clement *Strom.* 7.70.6-8). The fact that Clement provides us with the earliest witness to the *Epistle of Barnabas** has led many scholars to locate the origin of this late first- or second-century document in Alexandria, though this provenance for the letter is disputed.

Clement was succeeded as head of the school by Origen, who assumed his responsibilities when peace was restored after the persecution. (During the persecution Origen was preserved from martyrdom* only by the foresight of his mother, who hid all his clothes.) Origen too was a learned man. He brought to Alexandrian Christianity a depth of knowledge and a substantial intellectual and reflective ability. Origen remained in Alexandria until 230, when he was deposed from his chair by Bishop Demetrius on the grounds of his supposedly irregular ordination by the bishops of Caesarea and Aelia. Origen's approach to the Bible, which looks back to Philo's, distinguished three senses of the text: the literal, the moral and the allegorical, of which Origen held the third the most important. Corresponding to this distinction was a distinction between different grades of Christians: Origen acknowledged both simple believers and the more able, who could contemplate the Word as he dwelt with the Father.

Origen is noteworthy for his teaching about Christ. He asserts the ultimate transcendence of the Father over the Son and in consequence the Son's subordination to the Father, whom he mediates to the angels and to humanity. He identified the Son with the platonic Logos who had assumed a body and whom, in consequence, Origen called the God-Man (Origen *Hom. Ez.* 3.3). Origen's understanding of the Holy Spirit* is both imprecise and unsystematic. This is a sobering reminder of the difficulties that attended trinitarian belief in the third century, and that would be resolved only by later conciliar decisions.

In this way Origen exercised a profound importance on later Alexandrian theologians and typified both a method and a christology that came to be associated with that city (as opposed to Antiochene christology). In later times, however, the importance of Alexandria as a Christian center (which ranked second only to Rome at the Council of Nicea in 325) was overshadowed by the emergence of Constantinople as the new imperial capital.

See also CENTERS OF CHRISTIANITY; GNOSIS, GNOSTICISM; HEBREWS; PHILO.

BIBLIOGRAPHY. H. Attridge, *Hebrews* (Herm; Philadelphia: Fortress, 1988); C. Bigg, *The Christian Platonists of Alexandria* (Oxford: Clarendon, 1913); P. Borgen, "Philo of Alexandria" in *Jewish Writings of the Second Temple Period,* ed. M. Stone (CRINT 2; Philadelphia: Fortress, 1984); J. Daniélou, *Origen* (New York: Sheed & Ward, 1955); L. K. K. Dey, *The Intermediary World and Patterns of Perfection in Philo and Hebrews* (SBLDS 26; Missoula, MT: Scholars Press, 1975); E. de Faye, *Origène: Sa vie, son oeuvre, sa pensée* (3 vols.; Paris, 1923-28); P. M. Fraser, *Ptolemaic Alexandria* (3 vols.; Oxford: Clarendon, 1972) 2.2:233-82; E. R. Goodenough, *An Introduction to Philo Judaeus* (New Haven, CT: Yale University Press, 1940); O. Hofius, *Katapausis: Die Vorstellung vom endzeitlichen Ruheort im Hebräerbrief* (WUNT 11; Tübingen: J. C. B. Mohr, 1972); B. A. Pearson, "Earliest Christianity in Egypt" in *The Roots of Egyptian Christianity,* ed. B. A. Pearson and J. E. Goehring (Philadelphia: Fortress, 1986); D. Peterson, *Hebrews and Perfection* (SNTSMS 47; Cambridge: Cambridge University Press, 1982); S. Sandmel, *Philo of Alexandria: An Introduction* (New York: Oxford University Press, 1979); J. W. Trigg, *Origen: The Bible and Philosophy in the Third-Century Church* (Atlanta: John Knox, 1983); R. Williamson, *Philo and the Epistle to the Hebrews* (Leiden: E. J. Brill, 1970); H. A. Wolfson, *Philo* (2 vols.; Cambridge, MA: Harvard University Press, 1947).   J. M. Knight

ALLEGORY. *See* OLD TESTAMENT IN THE APOSTOLIC FATHERS.

ALLUSIONS, OLD TESTAMENT. *See* OLD TESTAMENT.

AMEN. *See* LITURGICAL ELEMENTS.

AMORAIM. *See* JUDAISM, POST-A.D. 70.

ANCESTORS

Ancestors play an important role in the later NT documents. God* purposed the new covenant* in Christ* in fulfillment of the promises* made to ancestors. Authors depict ancestors as models of behavior to be both emulated and avoided. While both male and female ancestors are noted, the majority of examples are male.

1. Ancestors as Receivers of Promise and

Covenant
2. Ancestors as Revered Figures
3. Negative Examples of Ancestors
4. Ethnic and Spiritual Descent from
   Ancestors
5. The Name of God Specified Using
   Ancestors' Names

1. Ancestors as Receivers of Promise and Covenant.

Early Jewish and Christian authors speak of how God chose the nation of Israel* for his own from all of the nations. Often this chosen status was related to the reputation of ancestors such as Abraham* or Jacob (*Jub.* 15:30-32; *1 Clem.* 29.2-3; cf. Deut 4:34; 14:2).

The ancestors are often grouped together with the concept of Israel's covenants with God. For example, in the *Epistle of Barnabas* the covenant given to Moses* on Mount Sinai is highlighted (*Barn.* 14.1-5; *see* Barnabas, Epistle of; cf. 2 Cor 3:7-18).

In Acts* ancient covenants are usually shown to be pointers to God's work in Christ. For example, Peter mentions the covenant that God gave to the ancestors (*patēr;* Acts 3:25; cf. Acts 13:32-33; 26:6-7; Rom 11:28; *Barn.* 14.1; cf. *Barn.* 6.8) in order to show that this covenant was realized in Jesus Christ (cf. Lk 1:55; *Barn.* 14.5).

Stephen* refers to the "covenant of circumcision" (*diathēkē peritomēs;* Acts 7:8) established with Abraham (Gen 17:10, 12), which confirmed God's promise to grant him descendants (Gen 21:1-4) such as Isaac, Jacob and the twelve patriarchs (Acts 7:8). Abraham's submission to the command of circumcision* (Gen 17:10-14) in turn illustrates his obedience* to God.

In Hebrews* aspects of the old covenant are inferior to the new covenant in Christ. For example, using Jeremiah 31:31-34, the author of Hebrews shows how the new covenant is superior to the old covenant that God made with the people of Israel when he delivered them from Egypt (Heb 8:8-13) but that their forebears (*patēr*) forsook (Heb 8:9).

God's promise of descendants to Abraham (Gen 12:2-3; 15:5; 17:5; cf. *1 Clem.* 10.3, 5-6) is brought to the fore in Hebrews 6:13-15. The author repeats a phrase from the sacrifice* of Isaac concerning an oath God swore "by himself" (Heb 6:13; Gen 22:16) because there was no one greater by whom God could swear (Heb 6:16-17) in order to guarantee the promise.

2. Ancestors as Revered Figures.

2.1. Hebrews 11. Ancestors are sometimes held up as figures deserving reverence and emulation (e.g., 2 Tim 1:3). Abraham, Isaac and Jacob are treated with particularly high regard (*Barn.* 8.4; cf. Ign. *Phld.* 9.1). In Hebrews 11 the author "brings before his audience a long series of exemplary witnesses to an enduring faith," who act upon God's promises even though the fulfillment of those promises is not in sight (Lane, 315; cf. Heb 11:2, *presbyteroi,* "ancestors"). These figures include Abel, whose sacrifice was more acceptable than Cain's (Heb 11:4; cf. Heb 12:24; 1 Jn 3:12; Jude 11). Abel's death at the hand of his brother did not silence his example of faith.*

Enoch, who did not experience death (Heb 11:5; cf. Jude 14; *1 Clem.* 9.3) because he "pleased" God (cf. Gen. 5:22, 24 [LXX]; Sir 44:16; Wis 4:10, 14), was often seen in Jewish literature as a figure of repentance* (Sir 44:16) or as a preacher of righteousness* (*Jub.* 4:22-24). Because of the author's interest in providing examples of faith for his readers, whose confidence in God has been shaken (Heb 10:35), resulting in the defection of some of them (Heb 10:25), he has cast Enoch as an exemplar of obedience.

Noah heeded God's warnings (cf. 1 Pet 3:20; 2 Pet 2:5; 2.4 below) and saved his household,* yet condemned the world (cf. *1 Clem.* 7.6; 9.4). Noah endured the contempt of his contemporaries and persevered under God's direction (Gen 6:9-21). He personifies the description of the faithful (Heb 11:6), providing an example to the readers of Hebrews, who are also enduring contempt from their peers. Noah's reward was to be made "heir of righteousness" (Heb 11:7; cf. Gen 6:9; 7:1; Ezek 14:14, 20; *2 Clem.* 6.8-9) in accordance with his faith (cf. Heb 10:38; Hab 2:4), a reward* that the persevering reader can also expect (*see* Endurance).

In Hebrews 11 the author employs Abraham as an example of faith more often than he does than any other figure (cf. *1 Clem.* 31.2). Abraham first exemplifies his faith by his obedience to God's call (Heb 11:8; Gen 12:1-2; cf. Gen 15:7; Neh 9:7; Acts 7:2-8; *1 Clem.* 10.1-3). His obedience did not bring immediate settlement in the promised land* (Gen 13:14-16; *1 Clem.* 10.4); instead it brought a life of pilgrimage for himself and his descendants (Heb 11:9) as he looked toward the ultimate goal, the firmly established city of God (Heb 11:10; cf. Heb 11:1; Ps 48:8; 87:1-3; Is 14:32). Abraham's trust that God would give him a son, even though he and Sarah (cf. 1 Pet 3:6; Gal 4:21-31; Rom 9:9; *1 Clem.* 10.5-6) had never produced children and were no longer physically capable of doing so (Heb 11:11; cf. Rom 4:19-21; Gen 15:1-6; 17:15-22; 18:9-15), is eventually rewarded through the birth of his son Isaac (*1 Clem.* 10.7) and a multitude of descendants (Heb 11:12).

Finally, Abraham exemplifies faith through his willingness to sacrifice his only son and fulfillment of promise, Isaac (Heb 11:17-19; *1 Clem.* 10.7). As in other Jewish literature of the time, Abraham's action is celebrated as a model of faithfulness and obedience to God (Sir 44:20; Jdt 8:25-26; 1 Macc 2:52; 4 Macc 16:20; cf. Jas 2:21-24; *1 Clem.* 10:7). The readers may see the "sacrifice" of Isaac as a foreshadowing of God's raising Jesus from the dead. From this they could derive faith in the God who is faithful to his promises (Swetnam, 122-23, 128).

Isaac manifests his faith not only in his life of pilgrimage (Heb 11:9; cf. Heb 11:18; Acts 7:8) but also as he confers blessing* upon his sons, Jacob and Esau (Gen 27:1-40; cf. Heb 12:16; Rom 9:13), an action through which he continued to look for the fulfillment of promises yet unseen (Heb 11:20). Similarly Jacob (cf. Heb 11:9; Acts 7:12-15; Gen 47:29-31) blesses Ephraim and Manasseh (Gen 48:1-22) while he was still sojourning. This fact is attested to by his use of a staff (Heb 11:21), which for the Jews was a sign of pilgrimage. God's faithfulness in spite of human folly is exemplified in that in both cases of blessing strict observance of birth order is not observed. In Isaac's case Jacob received Esau's blessing (Gen 27:1-40; cf. *1 Clem.* 31.4; Rebekah's insight, *Barn.* 13.2-3), while in the case of Jacob his right hand rested on the head of the youngest (Ephraim) rather than the oldest (Manasseh; Gen 48:12-20; cf. *Barn.* 13.4-5). Even in the face of death Joseph (cf. Acts 7:9, 13-14, 18) saw the as yet unseen fulfillment of the promise (Heb 11:22; cf. Heb 11:1) of inheriting the land in which he directed that his body should be buried rather than in Egypt (Gen 50:24-25; cf. Acts 7:15-16).

In disobedience to the edict to kill all male babies (Ex 1:15-22; 2:1-2), Moses' (cf. Acts 7:20-44) parents saw a sign of God's favor in his appearance (Heb 11:23; cf. Acts 7:20; Ex 2:2 [LXX]; Josephus *Ant.* 2.9.5 §225; 2.9.6 §230-31)

and hid him, because their faith in God's purposes overcame their fear of Pharaoh. Moses' renunciation of temporary power and privilege (Ex 2:11-12; D'Angelo, 43-45), perhaps even as a successor to Pharaoh (Heb 11:24; D'Angelo, 42-43), to join the ill-treated Hebrew people (Heb 11:25) marks him as a man of faith, who focuses on the reward that the unseen God (Heb 11:27; on Moses' humility see *1 Clem.* 17.5-6) grants those who please him (Heb 11:26). As God's work through Moses' suffering* eventually resulted in the coming of the Messiah (Heb 11:26), so God's purposes will be realized through the readers who persevere in the midst of suffering for Christ. The author emphasizes Moses' observance of God's directions for Passover (Heb 11:28; Ex 11:1-12:28; cf. Heb 3:5; *1 Clem.* 17.5; 43.1), which spared their firstborn children and livestock from the plague of death that devastated the Egyptians and was the final, critical event in the deliverance of God's people from enslavement.

God's power on behalf of his people is demonstrated by the passage of the Israelites through the Red Sea (Heb 11:29; cf. Rom 10:1-4) and the fall of Jericho (Heb 11:29-30). Further specific ancestors include Rahab (Heb 11:31; cf. Mt 1:5) the prostitute, who is often seen as an example of faith and good works (cf. Jas 2:25; *1 Clem.* 12.1-8; *see* Faith and Works) because of her assistance to Joshua's spies and her faith in the God of Israel (Josh 2:1-15).

Six figures are mentioned as if in passing (Heb 11:32). These are intended to remind us of Gideon's victory over the Midianites (Judg 6:33—8:21), Sisera's defeat under the command of Barak as supported by Deborah (Judg 4:4-16), Samson's victories over the Philistines (Judg 13:1—16:31) and Jephthah's devotion to God in the face of the Ammonites (Judg 10:6—11:32). David (cf. Rev 22:16) is a popular figure in the exemplary tradition (Sir 45:25; 47:2-11; *1 Clem.* 18.1-17; cf. 4.13), particularly in view of his conviction of God's providence and faithfulness (1 Sam 17:26, 32, 34-37, 45-47). The judge (1 Sam 7:15-17) and prophet (1 Sam 3:19-20; cf. Acts 3:24; 13:20) Samuel is remembered particularly for his intercession on behalf of Israel at Mizpah, when Israel defeated the Philistines (1 Sam 7:5-14). Further deeds by exemplary forebears are listed without using particular names (Heb 11:33-38), but the discussion presupposes a detailed knowledge of Israelite history (drawn from 1-2 Macc) that would enable one to recognize the situations mentioned and the faith exemplified.

2.2. Acts 7. Stephen's* speech contains another major catalogue of revered ancestors. The speech provides the framework for several allusions to Abraham (Acts 7:2-8, 16-17, 32) in which he appears as the recipient of promises by which his descendants benefit.

Stephen speaks of Abraham's departing from his homeland in obedience to God's call (Acts 7:2-4; see 2.1 above; Gen 12:1; Gen 15:7; Neh 9:7). He magnifies Abraham's trust in God when he shows that Abraham possessed no land but received only a promise of land (Acts 7:5; cf. Gen 12:7; 13:15; 17:7-8; 48:4; *1 Clem.* 10.4) for himself and his offspring.

By including references to the prophecy to Abraham about his descendants' four-hundred-year (Acts 7:6-7; cf. Ex 12:40; Gal 3:17) bondage in Egypt (Gen 15:13-14; cf. Ex 2:22) Luke emphasizes God's faithfulness to his people in the midst of crisis. In an expansion of Exodus 3:12 (Acts 7:7) Luke modifies the term *mountain (horos),* used for Sinai in the Septuagint; he substitutes "place" *(topos),* referring to Jerusalem* or the temple* itself (cf. Acts 6:13-14). God's faithfulness to his promise to Abraham is demonstrated in that his descendants could worship* God in that very "place."

The story of Joseph (Acts 7:9-16; Heb 11:21-22; Rev 7:8) illustrates God's continued care for his people as exemplified by Joseph's wisdom* (Acts 7:10), which won him a ruling position in Egypt (Gen 41:41). Wisdom is a particular sign of God's favor to his faithful disciples (cf. Acts 7:22) and could include a variety of manifestations, including Joseph's divinely inspired skill in the reading of dreams (Gen 40:1-41:36).

Stephen then shows how Jacob (cf. Heb 11:9, 21; 2.1 above) and his family came to Egypt: because of severe famine (Acts 7:11-12; Gen 41:57). The severity of famine in Canaan may have been a result of divine retribution for the actions of Joseph's brothers (Acts 7:9; cf. *1 Clem.* 4.9), which was later instrumental in bringing about God's purposes (Marshall, 138; cf. Acts 7:15-16; Heb 11:22).

Moses' life (Acts 7:20-44) is treated in three parts, each part corresponding to forty years (Acts 7:23, 30). Moses is born "beautiful" before God (Acts 7:20; Philo *Vit. Mos.* 1.9, 18; cf. 2.1 above; Heb. 11:23) and is brought up in Phar-

aoh's house, instructed in wisdom (cf. Acts 7:10). In contrast to the account in Exodus, Stephen states that Moses' concern for his kins-people is manifested when he kills an Egyptian who was oppressing an Israelite (Acts 7:24-25; Ex 2:11-15). Moses may have hoped that as a result of his actions the Israelites would recognize that they had a type of savior* in the form of one who was influential. This is not the case (Acts 7:26-28; cf. *1 Clem.* 4.11), and Moses flees to Midian, where he has a family (Acts 7:29; Ex 2:21-22; 18:1-5). Stephen's addition probably points to an intentional parallel between Moses and Christ, intended to show the reader the continuity of God's faithful actions in history on behalf of his people and their continued rejection of his emissaries (cf. Acts 7:52).

God appears to Moses in a burning bush with the promise of the deliverance of the Israelites from Egypt (Acts 7:30-34; Ex 3:1-12). Stephen reverses the order of the statements in Exodus (Ex 3:5-6; cf. Acts 7:32-33) which address Moses removing his sandals and the declaration of God's identity as the God of his fathers, so that "it is the God of Moses' ancestors who is revealing himself" (Marshall, 141; see 5 below). God's faithfulness to his promises to earlier forebears continues (Acts 7:6-7; cf. Acts 13:17-18) through his revelation* to Moses.

Stephen further depicts Moses as having qualities similar to those Christ had that would be recognized by the Christian reader (Acts 7:35-36). Moses is called "ruler" (cf. *1 Clem.* 43). Ruler is a term that was also applied to Christ *(archēgos;* cf. Acts 5:31). Moses is also "redeemer" *(lytrōtēs;* cf. *1 Clem.* 53), which is descriptive of Christ's activity (Lk 2:38; 24:21) as well *(see* Redemption). Moses was further responsible for a prophecy (Deut 18:15; Heb 1:1-2; cf. *Barn.* 6.8-19) about the coming of a prophet like himself, "which the early Christians had already begun to see fulfilled in the coming of Jesus" (Marshall, 142; cf. Acts 3:22; *Barn.* 12). Yet those who followed Moses did not obey him and turned back to Egypt "in their hearts" (Acts 7:38), turning to idolatry* (Acts 7:40-41; Ex 32:1; cf. Acts 7:52).

Finally, Stephen speaks of Moses receiving the pattern of the tabernacle* in the wilderness (Acts 7:44; Ex 25:40; cf. Heb 8:5-6; Jude 9). While they are not specifically mentioned, the law* or customs of the Israelites are attributed to Moses (Heb 10:28; Acts 13:39; 15:1, 5, 21;

21:21; 28:23; *Barn.* 10.9, 11).

Joshua (cf. Heb. 4:8) took with him the tabernacle when the Israelites took possession of their promised land (Acts 7:45). According to Stephen, David found favor with God (Acts 7:46), which most likely refers to his being the ruler of a united kingdom and enjoying possession of the land. But it was also David (cf. Acts 2:29; 4:25; Mt 1:17), a man who was said to carry out God's wishes (Acts 13:22), who desired to build a place for God to dwell with his people (Ps 132:4-5; cf. 2 Sam 6:17). Solomon (cf. Mt 6:29; 12:42; Lk 11:31; 12:27) is noted for actually building the first temple (Acts 7:47; cf. 2 Sam 7:5-16).

2.3. James. James* uses the figures of Abraham (Jas 2:21-24) and Rahab (Jas 2:25) in order to show how faith without works is dead (Jas 2:26). Abraham, known for his exemplary faith (see 2.1 above), was also revered for his obedience to God because of his willingness to sacrifice Isaac, another popular story in Jewish circles. James 2:21-24 brings these two traditions together in order to show how Abraham's faith was brought to completion (Jas 2:22) through his willingness to sacrifice Isaac.

Abraham is also known as the "friend of God" (Jas 2:23), which is a popular description for him (*1 Clem.* 10.1; 12.2; CD 3:2-4), and as one who exhibits exemplary hospitality* (*1 Clem.* 10.7; *T. Abr.* 1:1-3A; Philo *Abr.* 107-10; Josephus *Ant.* 1.11.2 §196).

Rahab (Jas 2:25), one of the few women mentioned, is praised in traditions of the time (Mt 1:5; Heb. 11:31) and is lauded for her provision of hospitality to Joshua's spies (Josh 2:1-15; *1 Clem.* 12.1, 3). Her actions also fulfill the earlier command to provide food and shelter for those in need (Jas 2:14-17).

In the context of exhorting his readers to patient endurance, James uses Job as an example of one who was steadfast in his faith (Jas 5:11; cf. *2 Clem.* 6.8-9). This endurance leads to blessing (Jas 5:11). The readers have apparently heard of Job's endurance already. Whether they considered Job to have been steadfast even though he complained to God (Job 7:11-16; 10:18; 23:2; 30:20-23) or whether they had been influenced by the *Testament of Job,* which casts Job's wife as the complainer (e.g., *Test. Job* 24:1-4), is not clear. The point is that even in the midst of dire circumstances Job did not lose his faith in God and that God seemed to have a purpose in such suffering—Job's understanding of God's faithful nature (Job 42:5). The readers should emulate Job's example in the midst of their own trials.

James characterizes Elijah as a man who was a "human being with a nature like ours" (*anthrōpos ēn homoiopathēs hēmin;* Jas 5:17; cf. Acts 14:15), meaning that he had the same limitations as do all human beings. Yet Elijah was able to offer fervent prayer* that was so effective that he could control the rain (Jas 5:17-18; cf. 1 Kings 18:41-45; 4 Ezra 7:109; rabbinic legend calls him the "Key of Rain"; see commentaries). James is informing his readers that they have access to the same divine assistance as Elijah did.

2.4. Miscellaneous Figures. Noah (1 Pet 3:20; 2 Pet 2:5; cf. Heb 11:6; see 2.1 above) heeded God's warnings about the flood and saved his household (Gen 6—9; cf. *1 Clem.* 9.4), yet the world was condemned (2 Pet 2:5). God patiently waited for generations for humanity to turn from evil (Gen 6:3-7), even through the building of the ark (1 Pet 3:20). Noah, who was believed to have preached righteousness* (2 Pet 2:5; cf. *Sib. Or.* 1:148-98; *1 Clem.* 7.6), is contrasted with the ungodly (2 Pet 2:5). A fate similar to that of those who did not believe in the time of Noah will befall the false teachers.* In 1 Peter* the flood prefigured baptism* (1 Pet 3:21) because the readers have also experienced salvation* by passing through the water to safety. Just as a believing remnant remained in the time of Noah (1 Pet 3:20), so the persecuted readers will be delivered.

Lot (2 Pet 2:7-8; cf. Lk 17:28-29) is heralded as a righteous man who is helpless to prevent the blatant evil that surrounds him (Gen 18:22-32; cf. Gen 19:1-11). Clement (*see* Clement of Rome) praises Lot for his hospitality and piety, for which he was saved from the destruction of Sodom (*1 Clem.* 11.1). The readers of 2 Peter may identify with this man who not only is saved by God from evil (Gen 19:12-22; 29) but also is distressed by the evil around him, desiring that righteousness be done in the world.*

In early Jewish and Christian literature Isaac is sometimes seen as a revered figure because he was willing to allow himself to be sacrificed (*1 Clem.* 31.3; Ps.-Philo *Bib. Ant.* 32.3-4; 40.2). Clement reports that it was Jacob's meekness in leaving behind his country after gaining Isaac's blessing (Gen 27:41-45) that gained Jacob the scepter of the twelve tribes of Israel (*1 Clem.* 31.4). It is also from Jacob that the Levites, kings and the Messiah came (*1 Clem.* 32.2).

Figures whom Clement praises but who are not found in the NT include Esther, who is lauded for facing danger so that she might rescue Israel through her humble seeking of God (*1 Clem.* 55.6; cf. Esther 4:9-17); Ezekiel (*1 Clem.* 17.1), who is known as a prophet who heralded the coming of Christ; Daniel, who is known for his righteousness (*2 Clem.* 6.8-9; cf. *1 Clem.* 45.6); and Jonah, who is a messenger of repentance* and the forgiveness* of God (*1 Clem.* 7.7).

3. Negative Examples of Ancestors.
While many of Israel's ancestors were revered, some are recalled in order to caution readers against the kind of behavior exhibited by them (cf. Lk 6:23; 6:26; 11:47-48). For example, while Hebrews contains accounts of several exemplary ancestors, it also contains a warning against the readers acting as those who wandered in the wilderness. In Hebrews 3:7-11 the author cites Psalm 95:7-11, which contains the warning that the hardness of heart exhibited by those in the wilderness must not be emulated (cf. Ex 17:1-7; Num 14:20-23; 28-35; 20:2-13; Heb 4:2, 6, 8; 1 Cor 10:5; *Barn.* 2.7-9; *1 Clem.* 51.3-5). In early Christian literature even Aaron and Miriam are portrayed negatively for their jealousy of Moses' prophetic gifts (*1 Clem.* 4.11; cf. Num 12:1-15). The readers of Hebrews are warned not to become like those who wandered in the wilderness and did not enter the promised land because of their unbelief (Heb 3:12-19). For those who persevere in their faith, the promised rest of God remains (Heb 4:9-10).

The writer of Hebrews also portrays Esau in a negative light (Heb 12:16; cf. Rom 9:13) because he sold his birthright for a pot of lentil stew (Gen 25:34). Esau is called "godless" (*bebēlos*) because he was concerned foremost with personal gratification and relinquished his status as firstborn for the sake of momentary satisfaction. In a pointed reading of the account in Genesis (Heb 12:16; Gen 27:30-40) the author refers to the birthright which Esau rejected, and notes that he, through Isaac, later would not receive the blessing even though he sought it with tears. The example speaks to those in the persecuted community who are tempted to apostatize, or to leave behind their own birthright in the new covenant in Christ. The result of such apostasy* is inescapable judgment* and rejection by God.

While some ancestors are revered in Stephen's speech (e.g., Acts 7:1-4 and 2.2 above), others serve as negative examples. The patriarchs are jealous of Joseph (Acts 7:9; Gen 37:11), selling him into slavery (Gen 37:28; 45:4) from which God rescues him (Acts 7:9-10). Other ancestors did not see that God had appointed Moses as their salvation from oppression in Egypt (Acts 7:27, 35; Ex 2:14; cf. *1 Clem.* 4.10). Nor did they obey him in the wilderness (Acts 7:39; Num 14); they turned to idolatry (Acts 7:40-41; Ex 32:1,4), resulting in God's turning away from them and handing them over to worship the host of heaven* (Deut 4:19).

In Stephen's final scathing words to his Jewish listeners, he attacks them for sharing the attitudes shown by their ancestors (cf. Acts 28:25-28; 1 Pet 1:18, *patroparadotos*). They are obstinate ("stiff-necked"; cf. Ex 33:3) and uncircumcised in heart and ears, which refers to their being proud and sinful and resisting the Holy Spirit* (cf. Lev 26:41; Deut 10:16; Jer 4:4; 6:10; Is 63:10). Those listening also fit the established tradition that the Jewish people had been responsible for the deaths of the prophets (1 Kings 19:10, 14; Neh 9:26; Jer 26:20-24; Lk 6:23; 11:49; 13:34; 1 Thess 2:15; Heb 11:36-38) because they murdered the "Righteous One" (Acts 7:52; cf. Jas 5:6), Jesus, who was the Messiah or "coming" one (Acts 7:52).

Cain was known not only for murder and hatred for his brother (*T. Benj.* 7:5; *1 Clem.* 4.6-7) but also as the archetypal sinner and the one who instructed others in sin (Josephus *Ant.* 1.2.1-2 §§52-66). In the context of 1 John (*see* John, Letters of), in which the person who sins belongs to the devil (1 Jn 3:8; cf. Jn 8:44), Cain, who was mastered by sin when he murdered his brother (Gen 4:7-8), is said to be "from the evil one" (1 Jn 3:12; cf. Heb 11:4). For the readers of 1 John, Cain stands for those who are children of the devil (1 Jn 3:12; *see* Satan), perhaps secessionists from the believing community. They are in stark contrast to those who are adherents to the faith, or the children of God (1 Jn 3:1, 7; *see* Sonship). In Jude* those false teachers who "go the way of Cain" (Jude 11) have conducted themselves in a manner similar to Cain in that they taught immorality (*see* Purity) and also enticed others into sin.

Although in the biblical account Balaam refused to be persuaded to curse Israel for the sake of monetary reward (Num 22:18; 24:13; cf. Deut 23:4; Neh 13:2), later Jewish exegetes portray him as accepting Balak's invitation out of greed for the promised reward (Philo *Vit. Mos.* 1.266-68; Philo *Mig.* 114). Jewish texts also portray Balaam as advising Balak how to entice Israel into sexual immorality and idolatry (Ps.-Philo *Bib. Ant.* 18.13; Num 31:16), so Balaam was regarded as responsible for Israel's apostasy (Num 25:1-3) and the divine judgment that resulted (Num 25:9). In the General Epistles Balaam represents those false teachers who are disobedient to God for the sake of financial reward (Jude 11; 2 Pet 2:15). In Revelation following the example of Balaam means that some of those in Pergamum influence others, either literally or metaphorically, to compromise with idolatrous practices (Rev 2:14).

Korah, who led a rebellion against Moses and Aaron (Num 16:1-35; 26:9-10) and ultimately against God, was a classic example of a lawless schismatic (*1 Clem.* 51.3-4; 4.12). Because Korah was believed to have persuaded others to follow him against Moses and Aaron (cf. *1 Clem.* 4.12), he was a natural prototype for heretical teachers in the church (cf. 2 Tim 2:19; Num 16:5).

Saul is mentioned negatively in the early church texts as one who persecuted David because of jealousy (*1 Clem.* 4.13).

4. Ethnic and Spiritual Descent from Ancestors.
Adam is of course the ancestor of the entire human race (Acts 17:26; Lk 3:38; *1 Clem.* 6.3, "father" Adam). Eve is usually portrayed negatively, as the one responsible for the Fall (2 Cor 11:3; *Barn.* 12.5; cf. 1 Tim 2:13; *Diogn.* 12.8; *Adam and Eve*). Enoch is said to have been born in the seventh generation from Adam (Jude 14; Lk 3:37).

Abraham is the patriarch (Heb 7:4) from whom descent is necessary if one is to be considered ethnically Jewish (Heb 7:5; Mt 1:2, 17; Rom 4:1, *propatōr;* cf. Rom 4:11-12; "daughter of Abraham," Lk 13:16). This is reflected in the NT documents, as believers often appeal to this descent when speaking to Jews (Acts 7:2) or when Jews (Mt 3:9; Lk 3:8; Jn 8:33) or Jewish Christians speak of themselves (Jas 2:21; Rom 11:1; cf. Heb 7:10).

It is through Isaac that descent from Abra-ham comes (Heb 11:18; cf. Rom 9:10). David is often invoked as one of the premier ancestors of the Jewish people who also represents royalty (Acts 2:29, *patriarchēs;* Acts 4:25; Mk 11:10; Lk 1:32, 73). He is known for his great humility, specifically because he is a man after God's own heart (*1 Clem.* 18.1), and for his prophetic gifts, especially in view of his calling Jesus "Lord" (Ps 110:1), thus proving that Christ was not David's son but Lord* (*Barn.* 12.10-11; cf. 10.10).

Jesus Christ is said to be a descendant of David (Mt 1:6, 17; Lk 3:31; Jn 7:42; Rom 1:3; 2 Tim. 2:8; Rev 5:5; 22:16; Ign. *Eph.* 18.2; 20.2; Ign. *Trall.* 9.1; Ign. *Rom.* 7.3; Ign. *Smyrn.* 1.1; *Did.* 9.2) and Abraham (Mt 1:2, 17; Lk 3:34) as well as scores of other ancient Israelites (Mt 1:2-17; Lk 3:23-38).

Although references to spiritual descent from Israel's ancestors are not often found outside of Paul's letters (e.g., Rom 4:9-13, 16; Gal 3:6-7; 4:28), Jesus is also said to have come to help the descendants of Abraham (Heb 2:16), to take hold of the persevering believing community to deliver them from the fear of death (Heb 2:15). Early Christian authors depict Abraham as one who is no longer father of Jews alone or of Jews and Christians but father of Gentiles alone (*Barn.* 13.7).

5. The Name of God Specified Using Ancestors' Names.
During his speech in Solomon's portico, Peter identifies the God of the people of Israel, using the names of his ancestors (*patēr*), Abraham, Isaac and Jacob (Acts 3:13; cf. Ex 3:6; Mt 22:32; 12:26), as the God whose "servant" Jesus was. As is the case elsewhere in Acts (cf. 5:30; 7:32, 52; 22:14; 24:14, *patrōos*) this identification serves to remind the Jews that this is the God with whom they had a covenant and demonstrates continuity between that covenant and God's work through Jesus Christ.

Early church fathers (*see* Apostolic Fathers) similarly use the names of ancestors to identify God as the God of the Jews. For example, in the *Didache** God is identified as the "God of David" (*Did.* 10.6).

See also ABRAHAM; MOSES.

BIBLIOGRAPHY. R. J. Bauckham, *Jude, 2 Peter* (WBC; Waco, TX: Word, 1983); R. E. Brown, *The Epistles of John* (AB; Garden City, NY: Doubleday, 1982); F. F. Bruce, *The Epistle to the Hebrews* (NICNT; Grand Rapids: Eerdmans, 1990);

M. R. D'Angelo, *Moses in the Letter to the Hebrews* (SBLDS 42; Missoula, MT: Scholars Press, 1979); P. H. Davids, *The First Epistle of Peter* (NICNT; Grand Rapids: Eerdmans, 1990); M. Dibelius, *James: A Commentary on the Epistle of James*, reissued by H. Greeven (Herm; Philadelphia: Fortress, 1975); E. Haenchen, *The Acts of the Apostles: A Commentary* (Oxford: Blackwell, 1971); W. L. Lane, *Hebrews* (2 vols.; WBC; Dallas: Word, 1991); I. H. Marshall, *The Acts of the Apostles* (Leicester: Inter-Varsity Press, 1980); R. P. Martin, *James* (WBC; Waco, TX: Word, 1988); J. B. Polhill, *Acts: An Exegetical and Theological Exposition of Holy Scripture* (NAC; Nashville: Broadman, 1992); J. Swetnam, *Jesus and Isaac: A Study of the Epistle to the Hebrews in Light of the Aqedah* (Rome: Biblical Institute Press, 1981).

N. Calvert-Koyzis

ANGELS, HEAVENLY BEINGS, ANGEL CHRISTOLOGY

Angels as spiritual beings and powers are found throughout the canonical and extracanonical biblical literature, and they feature especially in the late NT and early Christian writings.

1. Background
2. Acts of the Apostles
3. Hebrews and General Epistles
4. The Book of Revelation
5. Early Christian Literature
6. Angels and Christology

1. Background.

1.1. Terms for Angels. While the Bible employs the term *angel* (Heb *māl'ak;* Gk *angelos*) most frequently for spiritual beings, it can also speak of them as "gods" or "sons of God" *([bᵉnê] 'ēlîm),* "holy ones," "spirits," "princes," "host" or "watchers." The only named holy angels in the Bible are Gabriel and Michael (and Raphael in the book of Tobit); however, angelic names and titles proliferate in early Jewish apocalyptic (e.g., 4QShirShabb; *1 Enoch* 6:7-8; 20; *3 Enoch* 14—29).

1.2. Angels in the Old Testament. The two most important themes of OT angelology are angels in the "divine council" (1 Kings 22:19-23; Job 1—2) and the "angel of the LORD," who is a singular messenger closely identified with Yahweh himself (Judg 13:8-23; cf. Gen 18—19). There are holy angels (Ps 148:2), fallen angels (Gen 6:1-4) and corrupt angels (Ps 82). Angels can be seen as presiding over the nations (Deut 32:8-9) or, in the case of Michael, over Israel (Dan 10:13).

1.3. Angels in Jewish Apocalyptic. Angels are increasingly prominent in the book of Daniel and in the apocrypha and pseudepigrapha of the OT (*see* Apocryphal and Pseudepigraphal Writings). Apocalyptic* involves the unveiling of secrets of the end time and heavenly world, and angels frequently function as guides and interpreters in these realms (*T. Levi* 2—5). The myth of the fallen Watchers and their demonic offspring (*1 Enoch* 6—11; cf. Gen 6:1-4) becomes a popular theme among apocalyptically minded Jews and Christians. The Dead Sea Scrolls have provided a new store of angelology contemporaneous with the NT. Qumran* angelology combines a marvelous sense of fellowship between angels and humans with the conviction of participating in spiritual warfare between the Belial, the "prince of darkness," and Michael, the angel of light (1QS 3:22-23; 1QM 13). The close identification of a principal angel with God* reappears in figures like Michael (Dan 12:1), the angel Melchizedek at Qumran and Yahoel in the *Apocalypse of Abraham.*

1.4. Angels in the New Testament. The NT reflects the apocalyptic milieu of early Judaism.* Angels are particularly present at the boundaries of this world and heaven.* They are party to the birth, resurrection* and ascension* of Jesus; they rejoice over one sinner who repents; and they will accompany Christ* at his Parousia.* In Paul's letters angels figure particularly as intermediary "principalities and powers" (Rom 8:38-39; *see DPL*, Principalities and Powers). The powers, like the OT angels of the nations, exercise a necessary though frequently corrupt authority* in this age, but they are superseded by Christ and his people in the heavenly places (Eph 1:17-23).

2. Acts of the Apostles.

2.1. The Acts of Angels. Considering the prominence of the Holy Spirit* in the book of Acts,* the continued activity of angels in salvation history, equally distributed in Luke and Acts, is noteworthy. At times an angel and the Spirit operate interchangeably (Acts 8:26, 29, 39 [cf. Acts 8:39, Western text]). Angels are perceived in a vision,* as when Peter is freed from jail or possibly when Paul sees a "Macedonian man" summoning him to help (Acts 12:6-11; 16:9-10). In Luke's recital of salvation history, angels continue to punctuate key moments: Jesus' ascension (Acts 1:10), the miraculous exodus of the apostles* and Peter from prison (Acts 5:19; 12:11), the conversion of the Ethiopian eunuch and the Gentile* Cornelius* (Acts 8:26; 10:3, 7, 22; 11:13), the death of Herod (Acts 12:23) and the comforting of the shipwrecked Paul (Acts 27:23). So while Luke-Acts recounts the "demise of the devil" and magic* through the preaching of the gospel, it continues to see a place for angelic helpers in the history of the church.

2.2. Episodes Involving Angels. Acts touches on several peculiar beliefs about angels. Stephen,* who has been described as "full of faith and the Holy Spirit" and "full of grace and power," is brought before the Sanhedrin, and even his opponents cannot but notice that "his face was like the face of an angel" (Acts 6:15; cf. Rev 10:1; Esther 15:13 Vulgate; Dan 3:25[92] LXX). Later, when Peter is freed from prison and Rhoda leaves him standing at the gate, the believers scoff at her, saying "It is his angel!" (Acts 12:15). It is unclear whether they mean by this his angelic double (Mt 18:10; Tob 5:22; *Herm. Vis.* 5.2; *T. Jacob* 2:5) or they believe he has died and his spirit hovers near (Lk 24:37; Mt 22:30). Finally Luke's claim that "the Sadducees say that there is no resurrection or angel or spirit" (Acts 23:8) would seem to require some qualification in that the Sadducees accepted the authority of the Pentateuch, in which angels are prominent. Perhaps they differed from the Pharisees and Paul in assigning angels to a past dispensation (cf. Acts 23:9).

3. Hebrews and General Epistles.
The General Epistles mention angels with the purpose of confirming basic teaching on the person and work of Christ (Hebrews,* 1 Peter*) or of warning against moral and eschatological* laxity (Jude,* 2 Peter*). In referring to "angels" and "glorious ones," the writers do not necessarily mean the holy angels but may include the lower principalities and powers, including custodians of the Law* (Heb 2:2).

3.1. Hebrews. The comparison of Christ with the angels in Hebrews 1—2 belongs apparently to the "elementary doctrine of Christ," which the author now reiterates by means of a series of proof-texts. God's preparatory word in the OT had already indicated a fundamental distinction between the Son* and the angels. The

angels are always "sons of God" (plural), whereas Christ is the firstborn Son, worshiped by angels (Heb 1:5-6). The angels are fellow inhabitants of heaven, but the Son rules in God's name, and the angels serve him (Heb 1:7-9). The angels are creatures, while the Son is the agent of creation* (Heb 1:10-12). The Son is also the agent of salvation,* whereas the angels merely serve those who are being saved (Heb 1:13-14).

Having established the deity of Christ, the author continues comparing Christ and the angels to establish his full humanity. He interprets Psalm 8:6-8 christologically,* pointing up the paradox that the "man" and "son of man" is "made 'for a time' lower than the angels" but is now crowned with glory* and dominion (Heb 2:9). The psalmist marveled at the mystery of God's overreaching the angels to choose human covenant* partners. Thus "it is fitting," the author says, that the Son should partake of the same nature and be perfected through suffering* (Heb 2:10). Because Christians live in the interim age when they do not see Jesus crowned with glory (as they might see a vision of angels), they may inherit the promised sonship only by faith* and endurance* (Heb 2:8-9; 6:12). The eschatological vision of heaven in Hebrews 12:22-24 reflects this same cosmic reordering, where the perfected human saints are brought into proximity to God and Christ, and the angels form the outer circle.

In the more advanced teaching in Hebrews 7, the author speaks of Melchizedek* as a type of Christ. The publication of the Melchizedek scroll from Qumran has raised the possibility that, in addition to its use of Psalm 110:4 and Genesis 14:18-20, Hebrews is addressing Essene converts who thought of Melchizedek as the archangel Michael, who redeems Israel* in the end of days. Hebrews, however, seems to involve a separate exegetical tradition, focused on the OT personage as a type of Christ.

3.2. 1 Peter. In Peter's attempt to assure his congregations that Christ's death (*see* Death of Christ) and resurrection have procured them an "inheritance kept for them in heaven" (1 Pet 1:4), he makes several allusions to angelic intermediaries as representing inferior or evil dispensations in salvation history. Neither the OT prophets nor the angels were able to discern the mystery of the apostolic gospel (1 Pet 1:10-12). Furthermore, Christ, being made alive in the spirit, "preached to the spirits in prison" from the days of Noah (1 Pet 3:19). This difficult verse probably is to be seen as parallel with 1 Peter 3:22: by his resurrection and ascension Christ manifested his victory over the principalities and powers of the present world order (Eph 1:20-23; Col 2:15; 1 Tim 3:16).

3.3. Jude and 2 Peter. Jude, probably followed by 2 Peter, makes specific reference to the sin and imprisonment of the Watchers (Jude 6; 2 Pet 2:4; cf. *1 Enoch* 6—11) as an OT warning against libertinism. Similarly these writings contrast the arrogance of those teachers who "insult the glorious ones," the upholders of the present world order, when even strong angels like the archangel Michael (in an early Jewish tradition about Moses*) refuse to pronounce judgment on the devil himself (Jude 8; 2 Pet 2:10-11; *see* Satan). By contrast believers will wait patiently for "the Lord"* (i.e., Christ, not Michael) to come with his holy ones to judge the world (Jude 14-15; cf. 2 Pet 3:10-13).

4. The Book of Revelation.

The final book of the canon* is a unique Christian prophecy* that draws from OT apocalyptic sources (especially Ezekiel, Zechariah and Daniel) in which angels serve as divine courtiers, guardians and guides of God's people and agents of judgment (*see* Revelation, Book of).

4.1. Revelation Through an Angel. Despite the ubiquity of angels in the Apocalypse, they play an ancillary role in revelation* itself. John's prophecy comes from God through Jesus Christ, who sent his angel to John (Rev 1:1-3; 22:6). However, the agents of revelation in Revelation 1—10 are the exalted Christ and the Spirit. R. J. Bauckham (1993, 254) argues that the core prophecy of the two cities in Revelation 12:1—22:5 is contained in the scroll* (Rev 5:1), which is unsealed by the Lamb* and delivered to John by the strong angel in Revelation 10. At the end of this vision of the cities, the angel forbids John from worshiping him, declaring that he is a fellow servant of the prophets and those who study the book as God's word (Rev 19:10; 22:8-9).

4.2. Angels of the Churches. In his initial vision John sees Christ, holding in his right hand seven stars, which represent "the angels of the seven churches" (Rev 1:12-16, 20). Each of the seven letters is then addressed to the "angel of the church in . . . " (Rev 2—3). The nearly unani-

mous view today is that these angels are not elders or bishops but spiritual entities like the angelic princes of the nations. Each angel is so closely identified with the congregation that John occasionally addresses it in the second person plural (Rev 2:10, 13). The angels are not necessarily holy (cf. the twenty-four elders). Indeed, Christ calls them to repentance.* W. Wink (1986, 73) argues that they are the corporate personality and vocation of each congregation.

4.3. Angels and the Triune God. In the vision of the divine throne (Rev 4—5), angels serve to highlight the transcendence of God and the Lamb. The throne is encircled by heavenly representatives of the mysteries of creation (four living creatures) and election* (twenty-four elders). As in the OT, this divine council contributes little counsel to God (cf. 1 Kings 22:20; Is 40:13). Even the "strong angel" can merely announce the sealed scroll of God's plan, but no creature can open it or look into it (Rev 5:2-3). When the Lamb proceeds to take the scroll, he is hailed with similar acclamations as the Lord God (Rev 4:1; 5:9). The revelation of God and the Lamb calls forth praise* from all the angels and from every creature (Rev 5:11-14). Throughout the book, Christ as the Lamb is consistently placed on the divine side of the distinction between God and creature. Similarly the sevenfold Spirit is differentiated from the traditional archangels of Jewish apocalyptic (Rev 1:4; 4:6; 5:6; 8:2).

4.4. Angels and Saints. The heavenly beings in Revelation, in a manner reminiscent of Qumran angelology, share special fellowship* with and concern for God's people. The twenty-four elders offer bowls* of incense, "which are the prayers of the saints" (Rev 5:8). At a critical moment an angel interrupts the flow of judgment* in order to seal the elect, and the angel host joins with him in acclaiming God's salvation (Rev 7:2-4, 10-12). In a climactic pause in the heavenly liturgy, an angel presents the prayers* of the full complement of saints, which leads to convulsions on earth (Rev 8:1-5).

4.5. Angels and Spiritual Warfare. The holy angels announce and carry out God's judgment of the world. The judgment of Babylon* is initiated by Michael and his angels and completed by Christ, the rider on the white horse and his angels (Rev 12:7-8; 19:11-16). The secondary role of Michael stands in contrast with the Qumran War Scroll and Melchizedek text, in which the archangel is the final deliverer of God's people (cf. 1 Thess 4:16).

4.6. Angels and the Parousia. With the coming of Christ, angels bow out of the picture. The millennial "thrones" are occupied by the martyrs (Rev 20:4; cf. Rev 3:21; Dan 7:9). An angel displays the new Jerusalem* as having "angelic" dimensions (Rev 21:17), and its portals are guarded by angelic representatives of the new people of God. But the city itself is made for human occupation, not identical to the heavenly world. The Lord's Prayer is now fulfilled, as God's kingdom has come, on earth as in heaven (cf. Rev 11:15; *see* Kingdom of God).

5. Early Christian Literature.
The early Christians are responsible for preserving many of the Jewish apocalyptic writings featuring angels. In some cases they kept the works as written (e.g., *1-2 Enoch, Apoc. Zeph.*), edited them *(T. 12 Patr.)* or modeled independent Christian apocalypses after them. For our purposes the most important of the subapostolic apocalypses (pre-A.D. 150) are the *Martyrdom and Ascension of Isaiah,* the *Shepherd of Hermas** and the *Apocalypse of Peter.*

5.1. Christology. In the pseudepigraphal *Ascension of Isaiah* 6—11, the prophet Isaiah is taken on tour to the seventh heaven, passing through the realm of Satan and his angels in the firmament, then through five heavens, each occupied by angels of ascending rank and by a crowned angelic gatekeeper. In the seventh heaven he sees myriads of angels and the souls of the OT righteous, who have exchanged their robes of flesh* for angelic robes. Finally he sees the preincarnate Christ and the "angel of the Holy Spirit," standing on the right and left hand of the great Glory. As he watches, Isaiah sees the drama of salvation unfold: Christ descends through the heavens, masking himself in angelic form until he has completed his work on earth. As he ascends, even Satan worships, and the angels of the lower heavens marvel at how they failed to recognize him in his descent.

In Hermas's visions, he describes the Son of God (*see* Son of God) in the constant company of six archangels who are God's counselors and guardians of the church (*Herm. Sim.* 5.5.3; 9.6.2; 9.12.8). While Hermas's christology is probably adoptionist (cf. *Herm. Sim.* 5.6.), he identifies a principal angel more strongly with the Spirit than with Christ (*Herm. Man.* 11.9).

5.2. The Two Ways Tradition. The existence of a Two Ways tradition in early Judaism and Christianity has been confirmed by the striking catechism in the Qumran *Rule of the Community* (1QS 3:13—4:26). While it is based on OT types of moral instruction (Deut 30:15-20; Ps 1) and Jewish notions of good and evil inclinations (Sir 33:7-15; *T. Asher* 1:3-9), the tradition includes both a cosmic antithesis of good and evil angels and an eschatological meting out of rewards* and punishments. A truncated version of this tradition may be present in Paul's catalogue of works of the flesh and fruits of the Spirit (Gal 5:17-24), but a much fuller account is found in the *Epistle of Barnabas* 18 and *Hermas Mandates* 6.2 (cf. *Did.* 1.1—2.7 and *Doctrina Apostolorum*).

5.3. Eschatology. While the idea of angels administering eternal punishment is implicit in NT eschatology (Mt 25:31, 46; Rev 20:2, 15), the *Apocalypse of Peter* depicts graphically the last judgment of humans and spirits carried out by four angels, Uriel, Esrael, Tartarouchos and Temelouchos (*Apoc. Pet.* 6—13). The angels show no mercy to the damned; but the righteous victims are permitted to intercede for the wicked after a period of purgation, and some will be saved (*Apoc. Pet.* 14.1).

6. Angels and Christology.
The canonical materials surveyed here give no indication that Christ is to be understood to have an angelic nature (angel christology) or role (angelomorphic christology). Whether in the development of christology the divine agency of a principal angel like the OT "angel of the Lord" or Michael provided a conceptuality by which Christians could reconcile monotheistic belief with worship of Jesus is an open question (note the tradition of angelic refusal of worship in Tob 12:16-22; Rev 19:10; 22:9; *Apoc. Zeph.* 6:11-15; *Asc. Isa.* 7:18-23; 8:5).

See also APOCALYPTIC, APOCALYPTICISM; CHRISTOLOGY; ESCHATOLOGY; HEAVEN, NEW HEAVEN; MELCHIZEDEK; SATAN, DEVIL; SPIRITS.

BIBLIOGRAPHY. R. J. Bauckham, "The Apocalypse of Peter: A Jewish-Christian Apocalypse from the Time of Bar Kokhba," *Apocrypha* 5 (1994) 7-111; idem, *The Climax of Prophecy: Studies on the Book of Revelation* (Edinburgh: T & T Clark, 1993); idem, *Jude and the Relatives of Jesus in the Early Church* (Edinburgh: T & T Clark, 1990); P. M. Casey, *From Jewish Prophet to Gentile God: The Origins and Development of New Testament*

Christology (Louisville, KY: Westminster/John Knox, 1991); W. J. Dalton, *Christ's Proclamation to the Spirits: A Study of 1 Peter 3:18—4:6* (2d ed.; AnBib 23; Rome: Pontifical Biblical Institute, 1989); J. Daniélou, *The Theology of Jewish Christianity* (Philadelphia: Westminster, 1964); S. R. Garrett, *The Demise of the Devil: Magic and the Demonic in Luke's Writings* (Minneapolis: Fortress, 1989); F. L. Horton, *The Melchizedek Tradition: A Critical Examination of the Sources to the Fifth Century* A.D. *and in the Epistle to the Hebrews* (SNTSMS 30; Cambridge: Cambridge University Press, 1976); L. W. Hurtado, *One God, One Lord: Early Christian Devotion and Ancient Jewish Monotheism* (Philadelphia: Fortress, 1988); C. Newsom, *Songs of the Sabbath Sacrifice: A Critical Edition* (HSS 27; Atlanta: Scholars Press, 1985); P. A. Rainbow, "Jewish Monotheism as the Matrix for New Testament Christology: A Review Article" [of Hurtado], *NovT* 33 (1991) 78-91; C. C. Rowland, *The Open Heaven: A Study of Apocalyptic in Judaism and Early Christianity* (New York: Crossroad, 1982); M. J. Suggs, "The Christian Two Ways Tradition: Its Antiquity, Form and Function" in *Studies in New Testament and Early Christian Literature: Essays in Honor of Allen P. Wikgren,* ed. D. E. Aune (NovTSup 33; Leiden: E. J. Brill, 1972) 60-74; W. Wink, *Naming the Powers: The Language of Power in the New Testament* (Philadelphia: Fortress, 1984); idem, *Unmasking the Powers: The Invisible Forces That Determine Human Existence* (Philadelphia: Fortress, 1986).

S. F. Noll

ANOINTING

In ancient Mediterranean cultures anointing was the act of pouring or smearing an oil or cream on a person for cosmetic, medical, magical,* honorific or ritual purposes. Literary references to anointing make use of both its literal sense and an extended figurative sense, as one would expect in literature coming from cultures in which anointing for various purposes was a common practice.

    1. The Background of Anointing
    2. Anointing in Later New Testament Documents
    3. Anointing in the Apostolic Fathers

1. The Background of Anointing.

The practice of pouring or smearing olive oil on people and objects is well documented in the OT. Genesis 28:18 is the earliest reference, where Jacob anoints a rock to signify its sacredness. Later we find that not only objects but also priests (Ex 30:26-32), kings (1 Sam 10:1) and prophets (1 Kings 19:16) were ritually set apart for sacred service by ritual anointing (anointing of persons is usually translated in the LXX by the verb *chriō*). So significant was this act in the case of the king that he could be referred to simply as "the Lord's anointed" (e.g., 2 Sam 1:14; Ps 89:38). However, nonritual anointing was also commonly used for cosmetic reasons (2 Sam 12:20; Ruth 3:3; Ps 104:15; Amos 6:6; cf. Add Esth 2:12; Sus 17), its absence indicating mourning (Deut 10:3; 2 Sam 14:2). Because of this cosmetic use, "anointing" was also used as a metaphor for honor, joy* and abundance (Ps 23:5; 45:7; 92:10; Is 61:3). Medicinal anointing is also known in Jewish literature (e.g., Tob 6:9; 11:8, 11; the anointing is with a fish's gall), and oil was used in some medicine (Is 1:6; Jer 51:8; perhaps Ezek 16:9), but we have no use of oil with verbs for anointing in a healing* context until the NT (for Jewish post-NT magical* anointing for healing, see Kee, 136; cf. 134, 138). These various OT uses of anointing continued into later Judaism and were also common in Mediterranean cultures from Egypt to Rome.

2. Anointing in Later New Testament Documents.

Literal anointing (always using *aleiphō*) occurs in our literature only in James 5:14, which likely picks up the practice referred to in Mark 6:13. While the act of anointing is not medicinal, for it is associated with prayer* (*see* Healing) and does not change according to the diagnosis (for a contrast see Kee, 42-43, 50-52), its meaning is unclear. While some view it as exorcistic (Brunotte), this fits Mark better than James,* where casting out demons is not an issue. Even in Mark it could be viewed as an acted prayer or as connecting the sick person to Jesus (since Jesus is never said to use oil, but the disciples do, presumably at his direction).

    Without knowing how James's community understood the Synoptic narrative (assuming that they knew it and that this is not an accidental parallel), we cannot tell the exact meaning that they attached to the action. What is clear is that James attributes healing power not to the oil but to the "prayer of faith" and the action of God.* This removes the activity from the arena of magic and places it squarely in that of prayer and miracle. Thus the anointing is done either because Christians believe that is how Jesus taught the disciples to pray for the sick or because it is itself a form of prayer (see Davids, Martin). The "in the name of the Lord," if it is attached to the anointing rather than the whole action, could indicate that it was an invocation of Jesus' authority,* which could also be the meaning in Mark 6.

The metaphorical sense of anointing (picking up on the use of *chriō* in the LXX) appears more often in the NT. It appears first of all with respect to Jesus (*see DJG*, Anointing, for its use in the Gospel narratives themselves). In Acts 4:27 Jesus is God's "servant whom you anointed," which is probably a reference to his Davidic messianic role (*see* Christology). In Acts 10:38 Peter describes Jesus as anointed by God with the Holy Spirit. Here the anointing refers to the designation of Jesus as Messiah and his empowering for that task. In both passages the anointing is christological* in that it prepares or inaugurates Jesus in his office. (Hebrews 1:9 also refers to "the Son" as anointed, but the metaphorical anointing is taken over from Psalm 45 and refers, as in the psalm context, to the exaltation of the king over his companions; the author of Hebrews makes no special point of the anointing.)

Secondarily, metaphorical anointing appears in the Johannine tradition with respect to the believer. In Revelation 3:18 it is prophylactic, a cure for spiritual blindness which can be "bought" from Jesus. It is also an obvious play on the ophthalmic school and the making of eye salve from "Phrygian stone" in Laodicea (Hemer).

In 1 John 2:20, 27 the anointing *(chrisma)* is probably the Holy Spirit (*see* Holy Spirit; Smalley, 105-7; Marshall, 153-55). While a century later this would be signified by the anointing of the person with oil at baptism* (Tertullian *De Bapt.* 7), there is no evidence for that practice at this early date. Because the believers have "an anointing from the Holy One [i.e., God]," they know all, so the author explains that he is not trying to give them an awareness they do not have. A similar caveat appears at the end of the discussion, where he notes that they do not need instruction because the anointing they have received from "him" (probably Jesus) "remains in you." Thus in pointing out the charac-

teristics of the false, the author takes pains to point out that his readers have a spiritual awareness of the true, which is given to them through the Holy Spirit (the author strengthens this connection in 4:13, where he describes the Spirit as a gift and connects it to knowing). In this 1 John is similar to Acts 10, for both describe the Spirit as a form of anointing, although in quite different contexts.

3. Anointing in the Apostolic Fathers.
Other than the citations of Psalm 89:20 in *1 Clement* 18.1 and Isaiah 61:1 in *Barnabas* 14.9, there are only a few references to anointing in the apostolic fathers. Ignatius in *Ephesians* 17.1 instructs, "For this end did the Lord receive ointment *[myron]* on his head that he might breathe immortality on the Church.* Be not anointed *[aleiphō]* with the evil odor of the doctrine of the Prince of this world, lest he lead you away captive from the life which is set before you." The initial reference is to the anointing of Jesus in Bethany, which the Gospel accounts interpret in terms of his burial or death.* Ignatius uses this image to point out that through Jesus' death life comes to the church. He then shifts the image from the literal anointing of Jesus to the "anointing" that is the false teaching of those whom he opposes in chapters 16—20. Likewise *1 Clement* 56.5 cites Psalm 141:5 in terms of the "oil of sinners" anointing *(lipanatō)* one's head (here with reference to honor bestowed by sinners). Thus in Ignatius anointing takes on a soteriological sense, but in both Ignatius and *1 Clement* the use is secondary: in Ignatius we have a spiritualizing of a narrative about Jesus, as a means to warn against false teaching, while in *1 Clement* the reference to anointing is incidental to the use of the longer citation from the psalm.

See also Healing, Illness; Holy Spirit.

Bibliography. W. Brunotte, "Anoint," *NIDNTT* 1:119-21; P. Davids, *The Epistle of James* (NIGTC; Grand Rapids: Eerdmans, 1982); C. Hemer, *The Letters to the Seven Churches of Asia in Their Local Settings* (JSNTSup 11; Sheffield: JSOT, 1986); H. C. Kee, *Medicine, Miracle and Magic in New Testament Times* (SNTSMS 55; Cambridge: Cambridge University Press, 1986); G. W. H. Lampe, *The Seal of the Spirit* (London: SPCK, 1971); D. Lys, *L'onction dans la Bible* (Paris: Presses Universitaires, 1954); I. H. Marshall, *The Epistles of John* (NICNT; Grand Rapids:

MI: Eerdmans, 1978); R. P. Martin, *James* (WBC; Waco, TX: Word, 1988); W. Michaelis, "μύρον," *TDNT* 4:800-801; D. Mueller, "Anoint," *NIDNTT* 1:121-23; H. Schlier, "ἀλείφω," *TDNT* 1:229-32; S. S. Smalley, *1, 2, 3 John* (WBC; Waco, TX: Word, 1984). P. H. Davids

ANTICHRIST

As eventually defined in Christian tradition, the antichrist is a mythical-historical figure controlled by Satan* who opposes Christ* and usurps his place among humankind. He deceives humanity with false teaching and signs and wonders (*see* Signs) in order to obtain allegiance that only Christ deserves. He opposes Christ and persecutes* Christians who maintain their proper allegiance to Christ alone. At his return Christ will defeat the antichrist and his followers, thus establishing his divine authority* without challenge. Christ's victory over the antichrist is central to the final battle of the cosmic struggle between God* and Satan linked with the forces of evil.

1. Historical and Theological Origins
2. Antichrist in the New Testament
3. Antichrist in the Early Church

1. Historical and Theological Origins.
The early Christian conception of the antichrist is multifaceted, and its origins are obscure. The concept is rooted in the apocalyptic* and messianic traditions of late Second Temple Judaism (third century B.C. to A.D. 70) and Christian interpretation of the OT in light of these traditions. In turn, these traditions are often rooted in the mythology of the ancient Near East and in Persian dualism. Jewish apocalyptic adapted the ancient Near Eastern combat myth of a great primeval battle at creation* between a powerful god and a chaos monster or dragon (*see* Beasts, Dragon). It also adapted the Persian dualism that taught that the world is engaged in a fierce battle between the powers of good and evil. In Jewish thought, battles between the wicked and the faithful, good and evil angels,* and the dragon of chaos and the Creator God are all parts of this struggle. The present age is controlled by evil but will be followed by a new age controlled by good.

Typically Jewish apocalyptic molded this mythology and dualism into prophecy that explained the struggles of the righteous in this world in terms of the contemporary struggle of God and the righteous against adversaries who are agents of the powers of evil. These adversaries include oppressive foreign rulers who persecute the righteous, as well as false teachers and prophets* who deceive them. The end of the struggle is the victorious coming of the Messiah to defeat the adversaries and establish the kingdom of God (Dan 11:36; Ezek 28:2; *2 Apoc. Bar.* 36-40; *T. Mos.* 8; *see* Kingdom of God). The most powerful adversary emerging within Jewish apocalyptic was Satan, or Beliar (or Belial). Satan has roots in the dragon of chaos that opposed God in creation mythology. In the *Testaments of the Twelve Patriarchs*, Beliar, a demonic figure from the tribe of Dan, entices Israel to turn from worshiping God to live in error. A messiah of the tribe of Levi binds him and casts him into everlasting fire (*T. Dan.* 5:10-11; *T. Levi* 18:12; *T. Judah* 25:3).

Actual historical events often shaped the adaptation of mythology and dualism by Jewish apocalyptic. The rule of the Seleucid king Antiochus IV Epiphanes of Syria (175-164 B.C.) did the most to sharpen the depiction of tyrannical opposition to God focused in an individual. He desecrated the Jerusalem temple by dedicating the altar to Zeus and sacrificing a pig on it; this act was called the "abomination of desolation." In the book of Daniel the Greek empire is portrayed as a beast with ten horns and a little horn (Antiochus) speaking arrogantly and waging war against the righteous, only to be destroyed by the Ancient of Days, who gives his kingdom to a "son of man" (Dan 7; cf. 8:5-25; 9:26-27; 11:21-45). *Testament of Moses* 6—10 (first century A.D.) combines traits of Antiochus Epiphanes and Herod the Great to form an anti-God figure of the last day whose influence, along with the devil, is destroyed by God.

In A.D. 68 Emperor Nero committed suicide by stabbing himself in the throat with a sword. There were rumors that he did not die but had escaped to Rome's enemy, the Parthian Empire. Others thought that he had died and been resurrected. The myth is called *Nero redivivus*. Either scenario depicted him as planning to invade the Roman Empire (*see* Roman Empire). In one scheme he was to attack Jerusalem only to be stopped by the Messiah (*Sib. Or.* 5:93-110), and in another he was Beliar incarnate (*Sib. Or.* 3:63-74).

2. Antichrist in the New Testament.

The word *antichrist (antichristos)* appears only in the Johannine epistles (1 Jn 2:18, 22; 4:3; 2 Jn 7), although the concept occurs elsewhere. In the NT and early Christian sources the antichrist appears in apocalyptic contexts expressing the hope* that God will intervene in history to destroy God's enemies and the enemies of God's people and usher in a new era under God's undisputed command. Within this dualism, the antichrist is the enemy and evil substitute for Christ. As God, angels and the righteous have evil counterparts in Satan,* demons and the wicked respectively, so Christ has his counterpart in the antichrist.

It is anachronistic to speak of an antichrist before the early Christians identified Jesus as the Messiah and modified Jewish traditions accordingly. The antichrist tradition results from the converging of separate streams of Jewish tradition within early Christian eschatology. It has two forms, based on the Jewish traditions used. One is a nonpolitical, deceptive religious figure from within the community. It may be rooted in the Jewish tradition of the prophet like Moses and a false prophet who opposes the true prophet and misleads the righteous with signs and wonders (Deut 18:18-22). The second form is a tyrannical ruler from outside the community who oppresses the faithful in the end times. It may be rooted in the Jewish tradition of end-time tyrants. Both traditions are reflected in the prefix *anti-* (Greek *anti,* not Latin *anti*), which means "acting in place of" as well as "opposed to." These Jewish traditions themselves are hard to trace, as is the path of their convergence into the antichrist tradition, a convergence from which the NT picture of the antichrist emerges unfocused.

These traditions of the false prophet and end-time tyrant were used by NT and early Christian writers as the situations they addressed dictated. The end-time tyrant tradition was used in light of the anti-Jewish and Christian activities of the emperors* Caligula and Nero, as well as Rome's destruction of Jerusalem, which was reminiscent of the actions of Antiochus IV Epiphanes (2 Thess; Rev). The false prophet tradition was used when the church was threatened by false teaching (Mk 13 and par.; 2 Thess; 1-3 Jn).

2.1. The Synoptic Apocalypse. The Synoptic Apocalypse (Mk 13 par. Mt 24 and Lk 21) contains Jesus' prophecy of the appearance in the last days of such false prophets and false Christs, who will perform signs and wonders, deceive the faithful and lead many astray (Mk 13:6 par. Mt 24:5 and Lk 21:8; Mk 13:21-22 par. Mt 24:23-24). These false prophets and false Christs are closely associated with the concept of the antichrist but are not equivalent. They do not demand worship, nor are they the cause of the suffering* of those days; they only accompany the appearance of the desolating sacrilege mentioned (perhaps Zealot activity in the temple during the war of A.D. 66-73).

2.2. 2 Thessalonians. Paul gives us the earliest Christian prophecy of the antichrist in 2 Thessalonians 2:1-12, written about A.D. 52 (*see DPL,* Man of Lawlessness). Paul asserts that in the last days a great rebellion against God will be led by a man of lawlessness. He will usurp the place of God, placing himself in the temple of God and demanding to be worshiped. He will perform all kinds of signs and wonders under the power and plan of Satan. Paul combines the false prophet and the end-time tyrant traditions in a single figure, perhaps in part because of the contemporary actions of Emperor Caligula, who wanted to be worshiped as a god and demanded that his statue be set up in the temple at Jerusalem (A.D. 40).

2.3. Johannine Epistles. In the Johannine epistles the antichrist is portrayed as a spirit* (1 Jn 4:3) or collective force for evil in the last days (1 Jn 2:18). The antichrist is plural, representing all those who held erroneous views of the person of Christ and were already manifest in the church* at the time of the writing (1 Jn 2:22; 4:3; 2 Jn 7). In this case the antichrists are docetists* who did not confess that Jesus the man was the divine Christ come in the flesh.* This portrayal of the antichrist as a collective of deceptive false teachers (*see* Adversaries) already present in the Johannine community relies on the false prophet tradition. This portrayal is an expression of Johannine realized eschatology,* in which the age to come is already present (*see* John, Letters of).

2.4. Revelation. The most developed treatment of the antichrist is found in the book of Revelation,* written at the end of the reign of Emperor Domitian, who was persecuting Christians (A.D. 96). John uses the emperor to symbolize the Roman imperial system as evil and empowered by Satan, in part because the emperor* demanded worship as God and persecuted Christians who refused to do so. John combines the traditions of the false prophet and the end-time tyrant, specifically *Nero redivivus* traditions, with the chaos dragon of ancient Near Eastern mythology.

John portrays the evil Roman Empire using the images of two beasts.* The first beast, from the sea, is modeled on Daniel's fourth beast (Dan 7:7-8, 23-27). It has ten horns and seven heads, with one of the heads having a fatal wound that has been healed (Rev 11:7; 13:1-10; 16:12-16; 17; 19:20-21). This beast is given power by the dragon (Satan; Rev 12:3, 9), blasphemes God and demands that people worship it. As the symbolism of Revelation 17 makes clear, the first beast is the antichrist and symbolizes the Roman Empire; its heads are various emperors who demanded worship, with the healed head representing Nero—all empowered by Satan. Nero became a focus for the antichrist because he was the first official persecutor of God's people, the church, and was rumored to have been resurrected from the dead like Christ.

The second beast has two horns like a lamb* and speaks like the dragon. It performs miracles and compels the worship of the first beast under threat of death (13:11-18; 16:13; 19:20-21). This beast represents the emperor cult, whose priests enforced the worship of the emperor throughout the Roman Empire. In the consummation of all things Christ throws both beasts into the lake of fire as part of the eradication of evil from creation (19:20-21).

3. Antichrist in the Early Church.
The antichrist tradition was popular among the early Christians, and both false prophet and end-time tyrant traditions continued. One Christian source from the end of the first century is the "Testament of Hezekiah" (3:13—4:22 of the *Martyrdom and Ascension of Isaiah*). It blends the false Christ, Beliar and end-time tyrant traditions into a mature concept of antichrist. Here the antichrist is Beliar (Satan) incarnate in *Nero redivivus*. He presents himself as Christ, performs miracles and sets up his image in every city for people to worship. At the Second Coming, Christ throws Beliar and his followers into Gehenna.

In the *Epistle of Barnabas* 4.1-5 (late first century A.D.) the beast of the fourth kingdom of Daniel 7:7-8 is the Roman Empire of the author's time. The beast is part of the wickedness and lawlessness of the last days and is probably to be identified as the antichrist. *Didache* 16 (second century A.D.) predicts that in the last days there will arise false prophets as well as the Deceiver, who will claim to be a Son of God, perform miracles and persecute the righteous.

Quoting 1 John 4:2-3 and 2 John 7, Polycarp* (early second century A.D.) agrees with the Johannine epistles that the antichrist is the spirit of heresy. Everyone who denies the actual Incarnation is an antichrist (docetism), and everyone who denies the resurrection* and judgment* is the firstborn of Satan (Pol. *Phil.* 7.1). In deciphering the number of the antichrist, 666, Irenaeus (second century A.D.) identifies the antichrist with *Lateinos*, the Roman Empire, or *Teitan*, the ancient name of royal dignity belonging to a tyrant (*Haer.* 5.25, 30). Hippolytus (third century) wrote that the antichrist would arise from a revived Roman Empire to become the accepted Messiah of the Jews who persecutes the church, combining political tyrant with false prophet or messiah traditions (Hippolytus *Dem. Chr.*).

Although the NT and the early church identified contemporary heresies or political persons and systems as the antichrist, for both the antichrist in his fullness remains a future eschatological reality. His appearance is part of the final conflagration in which the forces of evil make their greatest and final effort to deceive the people of God, divert their allegiance and defeat the powers of good only to be completely and ultimately defeated.

See also BEASTS, DRAGON, SEA, CONFLICT MOTIF; EMPEROR, EMPEROR CULT; ESCHATOLOGY; JOHN, LETTERS OF; PROPHECY, PROPHETS, FALSE PROPHETS; REVELATION, BOOK OF; SATAN, DEVIL.

BIBLIOGRAPHY. W. Bousset, *The Antichrist Legend,* London: Hutchinson, 1896); F. Bruce, *1 & 2 Thessalonians* (WBC; Waco, TX: Word, 1982); D. Ford, *The Abomination of Desolation in Biblical Eschatology* (Washington, D.C.: University Press of America, 1979); J. Ernst, *Die eschatologischen Gegenspieler in den Schriften des Neuen Testaments* (Regensburg, Germany: Friedrich Pustet, 1967); R. Fuller, *Naming the Antichrist: The History of an American Obsession* (New York: Oxford University Press, 1995); C. H. Giblin, *The Threat to Faith: An Exegetical and Theological Re-examination of 2 Thessalonians 2* (AnBib 31; Rome: Pontifical Biblical Institute, 1967); G. C. Jenks, *The*

Origins and Early Development of the Antichrist Myth (BZNW 59; Berlin: Walter de Gruyter, 1991); H.-J. Klauck, "Der Antichrist und das johanneische Schisma: Zu 1 Joh 2,18-19" in *Christus bezeugen: Festschrift für Wolfgang Trilling zum 65 Geburtstag,* ed. K. Kertlege et al. (ETS 59; Leipzig: St. Benno, 1989) 237-48; L. J. Lietaert Peerbolte, *The Antecedents of Antichrist: A Traditio-Historical Study of the Earliest Christian Views on Eschatological Opponents* (SJSJ 49; Leiden: E. J. Brill, 1996); V. Maag, "The Antichrist as a Symbol of Evil" in *Evil,* ed. Curatorium of the C. G. Jung Institute (Evanston, IL: Northwestern University Press, 1967) 57-82; B. McGinn, *Antichrist: Two Thousand Years of the Human Fascination with Evil* (San Francisco: HarperCollins, 1994); B. Rigaux, *L'antéchrist et l'opposition au royaume messianique dans l'ancien et le Nouveau Testament* (Gembloux: J. Duculot, 1932); R. Schippers, *Mythologie en Eschatologie in 2 Thessalonicenzen 2,1-17* (Assen: Van Gorcum, 1961); H. Schlier, "Vom Antichrist: Zum 13. Kapitel der Offenbarung Johannes" in his *Die Zeit der Kirche* (Freiburg: Herder, 1956) 16-29; L. Sirard, "La parousie de l'antéchrist: 2 Thess 2,3-9" in *Studiorum Paulinorum Congressus II 1961* (AnBib 17-18; Rome: Pontifical Biblical Institute, 1963) 2:89-100; G. Strecker, "Der Antichrist: Zum religionsgeschichtlichen Hintergrund von 1 Joh 2,18.22; 4,3 und 2 Joh 7" in *Text and Testimony: Essays on New Testament and Apocryphal Literature in Honour of A. J. J. Klijn,* ed. T. Baarda et al. (Kampen: Uitgeversmaatsschappij: J. H. Kok, 1988) 247-54.   D. F. Watson

ANTIOCH ON THE ORONTES

This city, a melting pot of peoples and cultures, on the evidence of the book of Acts became the second center (Jerusalem* was the first) from which the Christian faith journeyed "to the ends of the earth" (Acts 1:8). The church, as described in Acts, appears to have reflected its milieu in the racial mix of its congregation and, under God, this fitted it well, first to nurture the nascent apostle to the Gentiles and then to sponsor his missionary journeys. Of the names associated with the church in Antioch, two in particular stand out: Paul's in the first century and Ignatius's* in the second. Each may be said to have left his stamp on Antiochene Christianity.

1. Antioch in the Mediterranean World
2. The Antiochene Church in the New Testament
3. The Antiochene Church of Ignatius's Day

1. Antioch in the Mediterranean World.

Situated on the Orontes some fifteen miles from its mouth, Antioch was founded c. 300 B.C. as his capital by Seleucus I Nicator (312-281 B.C.). It was one of sixteen cities similarly named by him in honor of his father Antiochus (the "Antioch in Pisidia" of Acts 13:14 was another).

With the collapse of the Seleucid dynasty and the Roman occupation of Syria, Antioch became the capital and military headquarters of the new province and a free (i.e., self-governing) city. Under Augustus and Tiberius, aided by Herod the Great, the city was enlarged and beautified in the Roman manner, the road systems extending from it were improved, and its seaport of Seleucia Piera was further developed (for more detail *see DPL,* Antioch on the Orontes). Thus the communications of Antioch with the Levant and indeed with the whole of the Mediterranean world were made far more rapid and secure than they had ever been before. This was soon to prove useful for the Christian mission.

From the first the city had a mixed population, which in the first century A.D. numbered about 300,000 (Strabo *Geog.* 16.2.5) and by the third century possibly twice that number. At the beginning of the Christian era the Jews of Antioch may have numbered about 25,000 (see Josephus *Ant.* 12.3.1 §119-24; 2 Macc 4). Josephus calls it the third city of the empire after Rome* and Alexandria* (*Josephus J.W.* 3.29 §276-82); others are not so sure, regarding it as the second. It has been described as "a bastion of Hellenism in the Syriac lands . . . the inevitable meeting point of the two worlds" (Dix, 33). This mix of cultures had good and bad results. It gave rise, on the one hand, to the literature and art that won Antioch the praise of Cicero (see *Pro Archia* 4), but, on the other, it led to the luxury and immorality that made it as infamous as it was famous. Five miles from the city lay the renowned sanctuary of Daphne, where orgiastic rites were practiced in the name of religion. These gave rise to the so-called *Daphinici mores,* which Juvenal blamed for the disintegration of Roman morality when, as he put it, "the waters of Syrian Orontes flowed into the Tiber" (Juvenal *Sat.* 3.62). And yet for all that, and perhaps because of the kind of city it was, Antioch was to play an important role in the history of Christianity. For with its mix of race and culture, it was ready-made for the breaking down of "the dividing wall of hostility" between Jews (*see* Jewish Christianity) and Gentiles* and the forming both into the "one body of Christ" (Eph 2:14-16). Something of this mix is reflected in the early leadership of the church* (see Acts 13:1; Williams, 220-21).

2. The Antiochene Church in the New Testament.
Christians first came to Antioch probably in the 40s of the first century A.D., having been driven out of Jerusalem by the persecution* that arose over Stephen (Acts 8:1; 11:19-30). To begin with, they confined their preaching to the Jews. But in Antioch, where the prevailing moral climate drove many to seek something better, the Jews had attracted large numbers of Gentiles to their synagogues.* Many became proselytes (see Josephus *J.W.* 7.3.3 §43; cf. Acts 6:5), but many more (as we suppose) remained as "God-fearers"; and before long this group in particular was targeted by the Christian preachers (as may be understood by Acts 11:20) with good results. The juxtaposition of verses implies that the "great number of people [who] believed and turned to the Lord" in Acts 11:21 were largely the God-fearing Gentiles of the previous verse. It would appear, moreover, from the ease with which the Christians were able to order their affairs that they had soon separated from the synagogues.

Given then that it was an independent and perhaps predominantly Gentile body, it is not surprising that before long the church's polity (*see* Church Order) could be described as "doing as the Gentiles did" as far as circumcision* and the Jewish dietary laws (*see* Food, Food Laws) were concerned (cf. Acts 15:1; Gal 2:11-14). Paul, who had been brought to Antioch by Barnabas (himself sent there to make contact with the Antiochene believers by the church in Jerusalem), may have first glimpsed here the real scope of his calling to be "an apostle to the Gentiles" (Gal 2:8; see Acts 11:22-26). It was from this church that he and Barnabas, and later Silas, were sent out as missionaries (Acts 13:3; 15:40) and to this church that they returned from time to time with a report on their work (Acts 14:27; 18:22).

While the church in Antioch may soon have been independent of the synagogues in an organizational sense, it remained within the ambit of Jewish influence both from within its own ranks and from outside. Inevitably, then, there were tensions as the transition was made from Jewish to Gentile practice and thought—the more so as this was a period of heightened and intensifying Jewish nationalism, which eventually erupted in the war against Rome in A.D. 66-70. Controversy arose early over the initiation of Gentiles and the extent to which Gentile Christians should be subject to Jewish dietary laws (Acts 15:1-35; Gal 2:11-13). The latter issue is also reflected in the Antiochene sources of 4 Maccabees and, possibly, the Gospel according to Matthew and the *Didache*.

Paul himself insists that he never accepted any compromise of his "freedom"* on either issue, and according to Acts 15 his, and what might be called the Antiochene, position with regard to the initiation of Gentiles was vindicated by a council held in Jerusalem. However, the battle fought by Paul on this occasion had to be fought again and again, as his letters bear witness, and may have been subsequently lost by him in Antioch, at least in terms of complete freedom from the dietary laws, in the so-called incident at Antioch referred to in Galatians 2:11-14. (See Dunn, who further suggests that as a consequence of his defeat Paul was severed from his connection with Antioch, while the victory of the more conservative Jewish Christians may have inspired their later inroads into the sphere of the Pauline mission.)

3. The Antiochene Church of Ignatius's Day.
From this point on the history of the church in Antioch fades into obscurity. In defiance of the biblical evidence, it was later claimed that Peter was "the founder" and "first bishop" of this church (probably to counter the Roman claim to primacy). He was succeeded, it was said, by Euodius and then Ignatius* (see Eusebius *Hist. Eccl.* 3.22; 3.36.2). Of the latter we know a little from his seven letters, written from Smyrna and Troas as he was being taken a prisoner to Rome during the reign of the emperor Trajan (A.D. 98-117). They evidence two dominant concerns. One was his approaching martyrdom*; see especially his letter to the church in Rome, in which he urges the Christians not to interfere and prevent his death by winning a reprieve for him. His other concern was for the unity of the church. In unity, he said, believers would find their union with Christ* (Ign. *Trall.* 3.1.; cf. Ign. *Magn.* 6.1; Ign. *Trall.* 13; Ign. *Smyrn.* 8.1). To the same end (their

union with Christ), Ignatius stressed the importance of the Eucharist (Ign. *Phld.* 4.; cf. also Ign. *Smyrn.* 7.1; Ign. *Eph.* 13.1; 20.1).

This concern for unity is reflected also in Ignatius's perception of the bishop as the focal point of church affairs (*see* Church Order). In earlier writers the titles and offices of "bishops" and "presbyters" are not clearly distinguished, but in Ignatius's letters there is a clear separation. The bishop is supreme. Without his approval no service can be held or other action taken. "Nobody must do anything that has to do with the church without the bishop's approval" (Ign. *Smyrn.* 8.1-2). Nevertheless, it should be noted that Ignatius does not yet enunciate a doctrine of apostolic succession. "For him the authority of the church officers is not derived from a chain of teaching chairs (as in Irenaeus) or from a succession of ordinations (as in Augustine), but from the fact that their offices are the earthly antitype of a heavenly pattern" (Richardson, 76).

In all of this it may be possible to identify a number of factors as shaping Ignatius's thought. His stress on the unity of the church and its unity with Christ may owe something to the influence of the mystery religions.* The influence of Gnosticism (*see* Gnosis) may possibly be seen positively in his emphasis on Christ's work of revelation* (Ign. *Magn.* 8.1; Ign. *Eph.* 19.1; see Corwin, 116-53), negatively in his insistence on the historical reality of the Incarnation (Ign. *Smyrn.* 1; 2; 3.1; Ign. *Trall.* 10.1). On another front, Ignatius may have been contending with the continuing influence of Judaism (in some form: Essene? Ebionite*?), and hence his stress on the divinity of Christ (Ign. *Magn.* 9-10; Ign. *Phld.* 6.1; Ign. *Eph. salut.;* 15.3; 18.2; Ign. *Rom.* 3.3; Ign. *Pol.* 8.3). (In Ign. *Rom.* 6.3, Ignatius calls Christ "my God." The title "God"* without the definite article is applied to Christ in Ign. *Eph.* 1.1; 7.2; 19.3; Ign. *Trall.* 7.1; Ign. *Smyrn.* 10.1.) The threat of false teaching generally may have pushed Ignatius in the direction of a stronger episcopate.

We see in Ignatius the seeds of what was to become a distinctive Antiochene theology whose methodology was characteristically rational, historical and literal. He died in the Roman arena c. A.D. 110.

See also ACTS OF THE APOSTLES; CENTERS OF CHRISTIANITY; IGNATIUS.

BIBLIOGRAPHY. R. E. Brown and J. P. Meier, *Antioch and Rome: New Testament Cradles of Catholic Christianity* (New York: Paulist, 1983); V. Corwin, *St. Ignatius and Christianity in Antioch* (New Haven, CN: Yale University Press, 1960); G. Dix, *Jew and Greek: A Study in the Primitive Church* (London: Dacre, 1953); G. Downey, *A History of Antioch in Syria from Seleucus to the Arab Conquest* (Princeton, NJ: Princeton University Press, 1961); idem, *Ancient Antioch* (Princeton, NJ: Princeton University Press, 1963); J. D. G. Dunn, "The Incident at Antioch (Gal. 2.11-18)" in *Jesus, Paul and the Law* (Louisville, KY: Westminster/John Knox, 1990) 129-82; H. W. G. Liebeschuetz, *Antioch: City and Imperial Administration in the Later Roman Empire* (Oxford: Clarendon, 1972); W. Meeks and R. Wilken, *Jews and Christians in Antioch in the First Four Centuries of the Common Era* (SBLSBS 13; Missoula, MT: Scholars Press, 1978); C. C. Richardson, *The Christianity of Ignatius of Antioch* (New York: Columbia University Press, 1935); J. Stambaugh and D. Balch, *The Social World of the First Christians* (Philadelphia: Westminster, 1986); D. S. Wallace-Hadrill, *Christian Antioch: A Study of Early Christian Thought in the East* (Cambridge: Cambridge University Press, 1982); D. J. Williams, *Acts* (Peabody, MA: Hendrickson, 1990).

D. J. Williams

APOCALYPSE, THE. *See* REVELATION, BOOK OF.

APOCALYPSE OF PETER. See APOCRYPHAL AND PSEUDEPIGRAPHAL WRITINGS.

APOCALYPSE OF THOMAS. See APOCRYPHAL AND PSEUDEPIGRAPHAL WRITINGS.

APOCALYPTIC, APOCALYPTICISM

The use of the term *apocalyptic* is so widespread within scholarly studies of both the OT and the NT that its meaning is often taken for granted. Yet there is a great deal of imprecision in the use of the word as well as generalized confusion about the meaning of the related terms *apocalypticism* and *apocalypse*. Terminological definition has been a long time in the making, although something of a working consensus has now been arrived at within the scholarly community. However, the question of how much *eschatology** and *apocalyptic* overlap as conceptual categories of biblical theology is not quite so clear-cut, and debate on this question is still on-going with phrases like "apocalyptic eschatology" appearing frequently. *Apocalypse* is now generally taken to refer to a particular style or genre of writing or to a work which exhibits the distinctive characteristics of that genre; *apocalyptic* is generally taken to be an adjective used with reference to either the literary genre or the religious perspective underlying it; *apocalypticism* refers to either the social movement or religious idealogy which produced such apocalyptic writings; and *apocalyptic eschatology* is understood to refer to a particular type of eschatology, a perspective about how God's future purposes are worked out, which is mainly expressed in, though not restricted to, apocalypses (*see DJG*, Apocalyptic; *DPL*, Apocalypticism).

In the main, we see the all-important question about the correspondence between form and content being worked out within these terminological distinctions. For the purposes of our discussion the terms apocalyptic and apocalypticism are associated with select Jewish and Christian writings produced between 250 B.C. and A.D. 150, of which Daniel and Revelation* are the two canonical examples, although apocalypses from other religious traditions of this time period are also known. It is hard to exaggerate the importance of apocalyptic as a conceptual category and equally as difficult to delimit its significance as a theological idea, so determinative has it been for NT studies over the past 150 years.

The phenomenon of apocalypticism is one of the most extensively discussed areas of biblical studies and the secondary literature on the subject is vast. Many have viewed Christianity as nothing less than an apocalyptic movement, at least as far as its origins are concerned. However, there has been something of a love-hate relationship between apocalyptic and NT scholarship over the years. Opinions about the possibility of using apocalypticism as a hermeneutical key to unlock the meaning of the NT documents have varied greatly. Some interpreters see it as absolutely indispensable, others as completely unusable. In 1960 E. Käsemann argued in a celebrated article (first published in *ZTK* and reprinted in English in *JThC* in 1969) that apocalyptic is the source of all NT theology, an opinion which has been a veritable Archimedean point within NT studies ever since. All of which stands as testimony to the importance of both apocalyptic literature and apocalypticism in any serious investigation of the NT materials.

1. Terminological Considerations: The Relationship between Apocalyptic and Eschatology
2. The Origins of Apocalyptic Eschatology
3. Some Key Features of Apocalyptic Eschatology

1. Terminological Considerations: The Relationship between Apocalyptic and Eschatology.
Both apocalyptic and eschatology are such loaded terms that it is difficult to use them with any precision; both are, in the delightful phrase used by the *Expository Times*, "slippery words" which are frequently used interchangeably to refer to "the last things" or "the things that will happen in the future" (see the articles by Marshall, Barker and Webb). In particular, the word *apocalyptic* has been so problematic that there have been serious calls for the abandonment of it altogether as a term of any value or meaning (see Carmignac, Glasson and Barton for recent arguments).

Three preliminary points need to be made when considering the matter. First, it must be recognized that the term *apocalyptic* has undergone a significant evolution in usage and has taken on a whole new range of meanings in which the traditional association with the events of the future is dissolved or effaced. A good example of this is the way in which it is applied to an astonishing range of literary and artistic works spanning several centuries. Most of these literary and artistic works are ultimately dependent upon the book of Revelation for their imagery or thematic content; in the words of N. Frye, Revelation is "our grammar of apocalyptic imagery" (Frye, 141). In short, the fact that the author uses the term *apokalypsis* in Revelation 1:1 to describe his work (the only time out of the 18 instances where the noun appears in the NT that it is so used) means that the subsequent literary works which rely upon the biblical book for their imagery, whether of final judgment, or ultimate catastrophe, or the coming of a new heaven and a new earth, inevitably find that the term *apocalyptic* is also applied to them. Even Theodotion's application of the term *apokalypsis* to chapters of Daniel is probably dependent upon its use as a title for Revelation. In any event, we need to recognize that apocalyptic is a term widely used in popular culture, often with little acknowledgment of the biblical basis for it, a fact which in itself stands as a testimony to the enduring influence of Revelation.

Our second point concerns the connection apocalyptic has with eschatology. Far too often the casual assumption is that apocalyptic is to be equated with eschatology; that to speak of the one is to mean the other. To a certain degree we may attribute the casual identification of the two terms to J. Weiss whose *Die Predigt Jesu vom Reich Gottes* (1892) was among the first works to bring them together. Moreover, the abiding impact of the *konsequente eschatologie* school of J. Weiss and A. Schweitzer upon biblical studies has led to the situation where many NT interpreters speak of eschatology as if it were simply the contents of apocalyptic. Occasionally this gives rise to potential confusion as can be seen in the classic statement by E. Käsemann that "Apocalyptic was the mother of all Christian theology" (Käsemann, 102), when it is quite clear that what Käsemann meant was that "an eschatological framework of thought was the source of all subsequent Christian theological development." (See Rollins for a helpful critique of Käsemann's imprecise use of terminology and a challenge to his central thesis; also worth noting on this is Laws's essay).

One of the most important things to be remembered when we consider the meaning of the term *apocalyptic* is that in terms of grammar it is an adjective and not a noun. That is to say that it defines a form of literature and does not exist in its own right. There is no such thing as "Jewish apocalyptic" or "Christian apocalyptic" as such; there is, for example, only Jewish apocalyptic literature or a Christian apocalyptic perspective. Thus the call has been for a more precise definition of apocalyptic literature (assuming that the literature reflects the perspective). This has resulted in some fruitful clarifications of how terms are used as part of the larger definition of the literary genre of an apocalypse.

Our third point follows on directly from the last one and concerns the core meaning of the term *apocalyptic* itself. In terms of NT studies it is important to keep in mind the etymological meaning of both the noun *apokalypsis* and its cognate verb *apokalyptō* and not allow our definition of their meaning to stray too far (see

Smith for a history of the use of the two terms). While etymological considerations cannot be made determinative, neither can they be completely ignored. The basic meaning is "an unveiling/to unveil" with the corresponding Latin translation of the noun and verb being *revelatio/revelare* (from which our term *revelation* comes). Recognition of this key point has been one of the main impetuses for scholarly investigations concerned with defining the genre of apocalyptic literature.

1.1. Apocalypse: The Difficulties of Defining a Literary Genre. It is extremely important that some sort of distinction between form and content be maintained whenever we speak of Jewish or Christian "apocalyptic literature." We must be careful not to confuse what is revealed with the form of literature through which it is revealed. This is particularly true when it comes to discussing the subject of eschatology since, as we have noted, the tendency has been to use the two terms (apocalyptic and eschatology) as if they were interchangeable. To put the critical point another way, we could say that apocalyptic literature may or may not speak about eschatological matters; what is revealed within an apocalypse may be knowledge about the future, but then again it may not be. The substance of the heavenly revelation might be knowledge about astronomy, or the creation,* or celestial worlds, or matters concerning the heavenly Jerusalem,* for example, and not knowledge of eschatological matters and what is going to happen in the future (the important article by Stone is a convenient place to begin to explore this point; see also Rowland 1982).

In recent years the most frequently cited definition is that offered by J. J. Collins as part of the SBL Genres Project:

> Apocalypse is a genre of revelatory literature with a narrative framework, in which a revelation is mediated by an otherworldly being to a human recipient, disclosing a transcendent reality which is both temporal, insofar as it envisages eschatological salvation, and spatial, insofar as it involves another, supernatural world. (J. J. Collins 1979, 9)

In terms of this formal definition, within the biblical materials it is only Daniel 7—12 and Revelation which might properly be described as apocalypses (although, strangely, some NT scholars have argued against regarding Revelation as an apocalyptic work; see Kallas on this point). Moreover, a total of fourteen other Jewish and twenty-three other Christian documents from the period of 250 B.C. to A.D. 150 are now usually catalogued under the definition, including the composite work known as *1 (Ethiopic) Enoch*, a text central to any scholarly discussion of apocalyptic literature and thought by many to embody the earliest examples of apocalyptic writing (as VanderKam suggests). Several other documents are discussed in addition to these more well-known texts, on the basis that they are similar in terms of form or detail (debate still continues whether *Jubilees* and *Sibylline Oracles* technically should be classified as apocalypses). These thirty-seven apocalypses are then subdivided into various types and groups depending on whether or not they have an otherworldly journey, whether or not they express a cosmic or political eschatology, and whether or not they contain an historical review as a part of the revelation afforded to the seer (see the contributions by J. J. Collins and A. Y. Collins to *Semeia* 14 for full details of the criteria; similarly, Bauckham, 17, helpfully suggests on the basis of a study of *1 Enoch* that a distinction be made between eschatological and cosmological apocalypses).

More recently members of the SBL Seminar on Early Christian Apocalypticism applied themselves to examining the function of apocalyptic literature within its own social setting, something which had been somewhat neglected within the deliberations of the SBL Apocalypse Group. The result of this thorough investigation is that a fairly detailed picture of what constitutes an apocalypse has now been arrived at and something of a working definition agreed. Nevertheless, there is still a tendency among some experts in the subject, such as P. D. Hanson, to resist the imposition of a rigid genre definition upon apocalyptic literature if it means that attention to the wider considerations of the phenomenon of apocalypticism is thereby compromised.

Moreover, Rowland, who may be taken to be largely sympathetic to the use of a literary form as a means of defining an apocalypse and getting to the heart of what apocalyptic writings are all about, interjects an important qualification which must be kept ever in mind. He suggests that it is not simply conformity to a common literary form which defines a work as apocalyptic, but conformity to a common mode of religious experience which is expressed through that form which does so. That is to say that a work may be classified as apocalyptic when it asserts that the hidden things of God may be made known through direct communication with the heavenly. The key here is the stress laid upon the essential meaning of the Greek words *apokalypsis* and *apokalyptō* as "revelation"/"to reveal."* Apocalyptic literature is concerned above all with the knowledge of divine mysteries* through revelation (*see* Reveal, Revelation). Rowland cites *Mishna Ḥagiga* 2:1 as a means to discussing the contents of apocalyptic literature under four headings: it reveals knowledge about what is above, what is below, what was before and what will be. This corresponds nicely with the distinction J. J. Collins makes about a spatial axis and a temporal axis within apocalyptic writing (more on this below).

Herein we see aspects of the dilemma that characterizes much modern research into apocalyptic literature: the relationship which exists between literary form and the contents of a given document. Striking the right balance between form and content becomes especially acute when we compare apocalypses with other types of literature which either have a similar message or claim to be revelatory in nature (such as ecstatic visions* like Paul's experience related in 2 Cor 12:1-6). For example, many of the ideas and expressions contained in Mark 13 are similar to those contained in *4 Ezra* and *2 Baruch*, yet it is, strictly speaking, improper to describe the Gospel chapter as "the little apocalypse" since it does not conform to the literary characteristics of the genre (it contains no heavenly visitation or angelic revealer, for example). The way in which we perceive how the form of an apocalypse and the contents (expressed by means of that form) combine often depends not so much upon our opinion about the literary-genre question as upon our understanding of related matters. These include our understanding of the phenomenon of apocalypticism which is responsible for producing the literature, and the place that we accord apocalypticism within the religious history of the Judeo-Christian world.

1.2. Apocalypticism: The Definition of a Social Movement or an Ideology? Apocalypticism is frequently defined as a social movement which arises out of a context of persecution in which a minority group within society feels alienated and seeks to express their hopes for the future in terms of an alternative symbolic universe. The key here is that apocalypticism is viewed primarily as a social phenomenon, and that the writings produced within apocalypticism have an identifiable *Sitz im Leben* (Hanson 1979 and Sanders offer good discussions on this). On the other hand, some have sought to define apocalypticism not so much in terms of its being a sociological phenomenon as an ideology which is embodied in the literary works from an apocalyptically minded group whose writings have managed to survive, all the while recognizing that the connection between the literary remains of a movement and its social realities is a difficult one to establish with precision and that a simple equation of the two cannot be asserted (Webb offers a correction to Hanson and Sanders along these lines).

Is apocalypticism then to be defined as a social movement or as an ideology? It may well be that in attempting to phrase the question in such an either/or fashion we are forcing too fine a distinction between the two: a social phenomenon is invariably going to be recognized, at least in part, by the ideology, the belief structures, which are contained within it. While the connections between belief and social practice may be difficult to prove, some sort of relationship between them seems even more difficult, even foolish, to deny. Thankfully, some initial explorations into the social dimensions of apocalypticism have been offered in recent years (such as those by M. Hengel 1974, G. W. E. Nickelsburg 1983, P. R. Davies 1989, and J. J. Collins 1991). However, further investigation of the sociological and cultural factors within a given society which give rise to the production of apocalyptic literature stands as one of the most promising areas of research today. At the same time, a word of caution should prevail here.

We must not presume that apocalyptic literature is something that arises only out of the marginalized segments of society, for there is ample evidence to suggest that the phenomenon we describe as apocalypticism does not recognize the rigid socio-religious boundaries we so often impose upon it (see Rowland 1988 on this point). In short, it is methodologically unsound to assume that all apocalyptic literature was produced by a single, socially-identifiable group in response to one particular concern. A definitive social setting for apocalyp-

tic literature is not to be inferred from the literary genre alone, and the oft-asserted declaration that all apocalyptic literature arises out of a crisis situation needs to be revised; more often than not it does arise in such historical settings, but it need not do so as a matter of course. Most agree that much apocalyptic writing is in some way crisis literature, that it is born out of a situation of social upheaval and political turmoil, that it addresses real concerns about the future fate of human beings in the face of great uncertainty and attempts to offer hope* and assurance in the midst of such despair.

I. Gruenwald (1979, 89) describes Jewish apocalyptic writing as a "literature of protest" insofar as it expresses strong feelings of resentment against oppressive worldly regimes, notably Rome (*see* Roman Empire). However, precision about exactly where apocalypticism is to be traced and how it develops, and exactly what social or literary pedigree it has, or indeed what the precise relationship it has to the prophecy and wisdom traditions, remain matters of considerable debate. P. D. Hanson is surely correct when, at the conclusion of his survey of study of apocalyptic literature since the Second World War, he says: "Apocalyptic is a complex and many-faceted phenomenon, and matters are not simplified by the restless development that characterizes its passage through time" (Hanson 1985, 483).

2. The Origins of Apocalyptic Eschatology.
The historical origins of apocalypticism have also been the subject of considerable scholarly investigation. Is it correct (as is often asserted) to view apocalyptic eschatology as the "bridge between the Old and New Testaments"? A connection between apocalyptic writings and the OT prophetic tradition is, in the main, accepted by many, particularly in the English-speaking world, as a given (see Nicholson). Many believe that Jewish apocalypticism has an historical link with the priestly circle of the Hasidim of the second century B.C. and view it essentially as a religious phenomenon characteristic of the Hellenistic period (see Hengel, 175-218). However, precisely what the relationship was between what we now describe as apocalypticism and the earlier periods of Israel's history has been hotly debated; virtually every conceivable group within Judaism has been suggested by someone as responsible for the rise of apocalyp-

ticism (P. R. Davies 1977 critiques the Hasidim hypothesis).

P. D. Hanson, who offers one of the most extensive treatments of the subject, suggests (Hanson 1979) that Jewish apocalyptic eschatology gradually develops out of the prophetic movement as it confronts national crisis and religious disintegration beginning early in the post-exilic period. Hanson's work is perhaps the most thorough treatment of the topic and remains the standard from which much subsequent discussion proceeds (see R. P. Carroll 1979, J. D. Thomas 1980, M. Knibb 1982, P. R. Davies 1989 and D. S. Russell 1992 for critical evaluations of Hanson).

There is much to be said for seeing a close connection between apocalypticism and early Christian prophecy* (as Fiorenza suggests). Indeed, it should not be overlooked that the only example of an apocalypse in the NT, the book of Revelation,* describes itself not only as an apocalypse but also as a prophecy (the word *propheteia* is so used five times in Rev 1:3; 22:7, 10, 18, 19). However, such a close association between prophecy and apocalyptic as has been suggested is something which many notable OT commentators such as G. von Rad dismiss out of hand, arguing instead that the wisdom tradition (as opposed to the prophetic tradition) within Israel is responsible for giving birth to apocalypticism.

Others have similarly addressed the question of the relationship between prophecy, wisdom and apocalyptic literature. J. J. Collins, for example, argues that there is a closer connection between wisdom and prophecy as religious traditions within Judaism than is often appreciated and suggests that both need to be investigated against the larger backdrop of the ancient Near East (see also Betz). The tendency to locate the phenomenon of apocalypticism within Palestinian Judaism also must be checked with due attention being given to Babylonian Judaism and Egyptian Judaism (to cite but two further provenances) as possible locations for the production of apocalyptic literature. One further consideration of this widening of the field of study is the recognition that apocalyptic literature was written in a wide variety of languages, including Hebrew, Aramaic, Greek and Latin. Further, Collins argues that apocalyptic literature not only contains elements of both prophetic and wisdom traditions, but also

contributes to the further development of them in subsequent writings, notably through the pervasive influence of Daniel, which combines earlier mantic wisdom traditions in Daniel 1—6 with the later apocalyptic passages of Daniel 7—12 (see Collins's articles from 1974, 1975 and 1977-78, and his books from 1977 and 1984 where the matter is further discussed). Thus, R. Bauckham goes some way in bringing the two traditions (prophecy and wisdom) together when he says: "The continuity between prophecy and apocalyptic occurred when the apocalyptists assumed the role of interpreters of prophecy" (Bauckham, 17).

In summary we could say that the phenomenon often described as apocalypticism is an exceedingly complex one. It has established connections with the prophetic tradition as well as with the wisdom tradition of the religious world of the ancient Near East in which Judaism had a key role to play. Any attempt to stress one of these traditions at the expense of the other runs the risk of misunderstanding and misinterpreting apocalyptic literature as a whole; both prophetic and wisdom features are to be found in apocalyptic writings.

One final consideration concerns the connection between apocalypticism and the Qumran* community. This is particularly important given the number of close parallels in thought and expression between many of the classic apocalypses and some of the sectarian works of the community, notably 1QS, 1QM, 1QH and 11QTemple. The book of Daniel and *1 Enoch* were clearly favorites within the community and are well represented among the manuscripts recovered from the various caves (the oldest fragments known of Daniel come from Qumran). Some have even suggested that the origins of the community itself can be traced back to the Hasidim of the Maccabean period, a group commonly suggested as the source of the phenomenon we now describe as apocalypticism (see Freedman on this; P. R. Davies 1989 disagrees). Thus, it is not unusual to find the Essenes of Qumran described as "an apocalyptic community" and find them prominently figuring in discussions about early Christian apocalypticism. This is the case even though many of the same problems about genre definition and the relationship between apocalyptic literature and the communities producing it or preserving it (which we noted in connection with the

Hasidic origins of apocalypticism) also surface in connection with discussions of the Dead Sea materials. Given the extraordinary opportunity that the Qumran community affords for insight into the first-century world, it is understandable that any study of apocalypticism gives due attention to it despite these difficulties (see N. A. Dahl 1971; F. F. Bruce 1975; H. Stegemann 1983; P. R. Davies 1985; 1990; J. J. Collins 1989, 1990; C. A. Newsom 1990 and M. O. Wise 1990 for further discussion of Qumran and apocalypticism).

3. Some Key Features of Apocalyptic Eschatology.

We now turn to consider some of the characteristic features of apocalyptic eschatology as it is found in both Judaism and early Christianity. Most scholarly studies of the subject which predate the detailed discussions of an apocalyptic genre, such as those by H. H. Rowley (1944), D. S. Russell (1964) and P. Vielhauer (1965), discuss the contents of apocalyptic eschatology by organizing their discussion around common themes or ideas. There is a great deal of overlap between these scholarly assessments, although no two scholars use exactly the same themes or identify the same ideas as characteristic of the apocalyptic mindset. For example, Vielhauer's discussion, which has been adopted by many, identifies a number of key themes, including: a doctrine of two ages, an attitude of pessimism about the present and hope in the beyond, a concern for universalism and individualism, a concern for determinism and imminent expectation, and a lack of uniformity. An added problem is that not every work which is described as apocalyptic contains each and every theme.

In any event, all such attempts to characterize apocalyptic eschatology are but the tip of an interpretative iceberg, concealing much more below the surface than we might at first think is there. Throughout we can detect the creative tension between the form and the content of apocalyptic writings being played out, a tension which has an important bearing on assessing the apocalyptic eschatology contained in the NT. While it may be true that within the Bible only Daniel 7—12 and Revelation formally fit the definition of apocalypse (and thus might be properly described as apocalyptic literature), does that mean that other NT passages have no contribution to make when it comes to

the matter? Are we to rule them out of bounds on the grounds of not conforming to the formal pattern of an apocalypse? Such a move may be the inevitable result of the detailed genre studies that have taken place in recent years, but does it necessarily follow that other NT passages containing motifs of an apocalyptic eschatology are to be excluded from helping to form an understanding of a theology of apocalypticism? Should not images and ideas occurring in the NT which are closely related to those found in apocalyptic literature also be employed in our investigations, despite the fact that the authors expressing them did not choose to express themselves in the literary form of an apocalypse? When put this baldly, the answer seems obvious, although it must not be allowed to undermine the important studies into the nature of the genre of apocalyptic literature.

We thus need to recognize that it is possible to have a religious perspective, a point of view or a way of thinking, which flows out of, or is at least influenced by, an apocalyptic eschatology which is not necessarily contained within the literary framework of an apocalypse (as Russell 1992 rightly notes). Even if we wished to stress the idea of revelation as central to Jewish apocalyptic writing and thought, this does not require that our understanding of the rise of Christian thinking is on this point somehow incompatible with it. Indeed, it is possible to view that most distinctive, even foundational, Christian claim, the resurrection* of Jesus Christ from the dead, as essentially a revelation from heaven. As J. J. Collins puts it: "The importance of apocalypticism for Christian origins centers on the most basic of all Christian beliefs, the resurrection of Jesus from the dead. The resurrection was never viewed as an isolated miracle but rather as a revelatory event that provided a new perspective on life and history" (J. J. Collins 1989, 207).

An attempt to integrate the insights of a number of scholars who have cataloged the contents of apocalyptic literature may be of some use and will be offered here under five headings. We shall first consider two of the formal features which have to do with how the revelation contained is expressed and communicated within apocalyptic literature. Then we shall turn to consider matters of content and note how apocalypses deal with three perceptual axes of thought. These three axes could be seen as expressive of the dualism which is inherent within apocalyptic writings, although it is important to remember that the overlap between the three is often extensive (the description of the first two axes comes from J. J. Collins 1979, who uses them to intimate what he feels is the essence of apocalyptic literature, the idea of transcendence which bridges both the form and the content of the revelation).

The first axis concerns how time is perceived, where the present is juxtaposed to the future. The second concerns how space is perceived, where the earthly is juxtaposed to the heavenly. The third concerns how human beings are perceived, where the evil are juxtaposed to the good. In each instance we shall endeavor to provide one or two examples from Jewish and Christian writings which express these facets of apocalyptic eschatology, although given the limits of space it is not possible to offer a comprehensive discussion (the secondary literature cited may be turned to for a more detailed study).

3.1. The Essence of Heavenly Communication: the Hidden is Revealed. We noted above in our discussion of scholarly attempts to define the genre of apocalyptic literature how important it is to remember the central idea of the word *apokalypsis* as "revelation" (*see* Reveal, Revelation). Of all of the variety of features of apocalyptic literature addressed by interpreters over the past thirty years or so, this is perhaps the only one which might gain a general agreement as essential to any definition of the literature as a whole. Nowhere is this better seen than in the opening verse of Revelation where the *apokalypsis* is described in terms of God, through Jesus Christ, granting heavenly mysteries* to his servant John: "The revelation of Jesus Christ, which God gave him to show to his servants what must soon take place; and he made it known by sending his angel to his servant John" (RSV). At the same time, heavenly revelation appears in a number of other passages in the NT, occasionally using the same key terms *apokalypsis* or *apokalyptō* (the noun and the verb appear three times each in 1 Pet in connection with the Parousia of Jesus Christ). Perhaps the most striking example of divine revelation in Acts is found in Acts 7:55-56 where Stephen* has a vision of heaven opening and the Son of Man standing at the right hand of God.

In many apocalypses one of the key means

whereby the contents of heavenly revelation is communicated is by the extensive use of symbols. Thus a bewildering variety of figures and images, both animals and beasts,* dragons (see Beasts, Dragon) and angels,* symbolic bowls* and trumpets* appear regularly within apocalyptic writings. The meaning of these figures and symbolic images is ever adaptable and constantly changing, leading to a situation which Rowland describes as "a happy hunting-ground for many conflicting opinions" (Rowland 1990, 34). The use of complex and unusual symbols, often involving bizarre animals and mythological beasts, is one of the most striking features of apocalyptic literature and the one that has occasioned all sorts of interpretations over the years. However, such symbolism does have a basis in the OT prophetic literature as both Ezekiel and Zechariah 1—8 testify.

It is perhaps the visions of Daniel 2 and 7 which are most influential as the basis for the use of symbolism within subsequent apocalyptic writings, largely due to the fact that the symbols which appear in these visions stand for hostile nations and thus focus the political message of the work (see Rowland 1988 for a discussion of the influence of Daniel upon the NT). In the NT the clearest example of this occurs in Revelation where similar symbols are applied to the Roman Empire,* notably the red dragon (Rev 12), the beast rising from the sea (Rev 13; *see* Beasts, Dragon, Sea) and the great harlot (Rev 17). These symbols are immediately recognizable to the readership of the book and serve to dehumanize the opposition while allowing God's judgment* to be pronounced upon them. G. B. Caird's suggestion (1962-63, 103) that such symbols functioned as the political cartoons of the day is a good one to keep in mind (Beasley-Murray extends this suggestion, offering some specific examples).

3.2. The Medium of Communication: Angelic Messengers and Heavenly Ascents. Angelic messengers (*see* Angels) have an important place in the NT, particularly in Acts where they serve as witnesses to God's actions in the past, as agents of his deliverance and as revealers of the divine will. Thus the apostles are released from jail by means of an angel of the Lord (Acts 5:19-20), and Peter's deliverance from prison is effected through angelic mediation (Acts 12:6-11). Meanwhile, angels also communicate God's will and purposes to responsive human beings, as evidenced by Cornelius's* instruction by a holy angel to seek out Peter* (Acts 10:22-33). Even the Pharisees are made to express belief in the possibility that Paul could have been the recipient of a visitation by an angel (Acts 23:9).

A fairly developed angelology can also be seen in several NT passages which speak of the judgment of Satan* and the punishment of his wicked angels, themes which are commonplace in many Jewish apocalypses. Thus in 1 Peter 3:19 the reference to the "spirits in prison" builds upon an interpretation of Genesis 6:1-4 which is common within apocalyptic writings, including *1 Enoch* 16:3-4 where the disobedient angels who foment a heavenly revolt are punished. Similar allusions to the punishment of disobedient angels are found in 2 Peter 2:4 and Jude 6 (it should not be overlooked that Jude 14-15 contains the only explicit quotation from *1 Enoch* in the NT).

However, we noted above how central the idea of the revelation of divine mysteries is in scholarly attempts to define the literary genre of apocalyptic literature. Typically in apocalypses revelation is communicated to earthly figures through angelic messengers who are responsible for the transportation of the chosen seer to the heavenly realms where the divine plans and intentions are revealed. The place of heavenly ascents within the larger Hellenistic world has been the subject of considerable investigation (see Segal 1980, Himmelfarb 1983 and Dean-Otting 1984, for example). It has been linked to investigations into the so-called merkabah mysticism strand of thought within rabbinic Judaism, and may stand as an important point of contact between wisdom traditions and apocalyptic writings of the Second Temple period and later rabbinic speculations of mysticism (as Gruenwald 1978, Rowland 1979 and others suggest).

Moreover, the idea of a heavenly ascent wherein revelation is communicated is contained in the NT as well. In Revelation we are given an opening declaration that John is sent an angelic messenger who reveals news of what is soon to take place (Rev 1:1). In Revelation 4:1 this heavenly revelation is continued, and is cast within the framework of a heavenly journey by John: "After this I looked, and lo, in heaven an open door! And the first voice, which I had heard speaking to me like a trumpet, said, "Come up hither, and I will show you what must

take place after this" (RSV). This heavenly journey is also described in spiritual terms, wherein John says that he was "in the spirit" (*egenomēn en pneumati*, the exact same phrase is used in Rev 1:10 in introducing the book); further angelic guidance is also mentioned in Revelation 17:7. Most importantly, the throne vision of Revelation 4—5 stands as the most extensive description of the heavenly realm found in the NT. This vision of heavenly ascent is so similar to passages in other Jewish apocalypses that severe doubts have been raised as to its being Christian in origin; many suggest that it was a Jewish apocalypse which has been incorporated into a Christian work (see Rowland 1979 and Hurtado for a debate over this point). Finally, it should be noted that some have taken the description of the ascension* of Jesus Christ recorded in Acts 1:9-11 (cf. Lk 24:50-51) to be based upon the apocalyptic motif of a heavenly ascent.

3.3. The Temporal Axis: The Present Versus the Future. We turn now to consider a number of perceptual axes of thought, beginning with one which addresses the question of time and history. Concentration on this axis within apocalyptic literature lends itself to seeing a connection with the prophetic traditions of Judaism in that a key motif within the prophetic writings is the future Day of the Lord when human history is brought to its fulfillment. It is often said that much apocalyptic literature is characterized by a deterministic view of history and that it frequently employs a periodization of both the past and the future which places the author and his readership at the final critical juncture of history (see Grabbe for an introductory discussion). Foundational to this view of history is a contrast between two ages, the present and the age to come. Daniel 9:24-27 stands as one of the most frequently cited Jewish sources for such a periodization of history.

The oft-repeated assertion that apocalyptic literature rejects history, whereas the prophetic writers see God as working within history, was axiomatic in early scholarly discussions on the relationship between the prophetic and apocalyptic traditions (Frost is a classic statement of this). However, not all have been as dismissive of the importance that earthly history has within apocalyptic literature and many would go so far as to insist that earthly, human history has a very important place within apocalyptic writings. E. F. Scott, for example, although in many ways quite critical of the religious value of apocalyptic literature as a whole, usefully suggests that within the writings of the apocalypticists we have the first Jewish attempts at a philosophy of history. Others have attempted to solve the question of the meaning of history within apocalyptic writings by a careful consideration of the language used within them. G. B. Caird's distinction between *Das Ende* and *Die Endzeit* is a useful one to keep in mind at this point (Caird 1976, 84-85): "to expect an End is not the same as to expect an End-time. The one is an event beyond which nothing can conceivably happen. The other is a period of indefinite duration in which much is expected to happen." Caird's differentiation between the two is used to support his understanding of the nature of eschatological language as concerned not so much with the future that is beyond history as it is with the future which will be revealed within history (see Caird 1980 for a fuller treatment). Nevertheless, this distinction is not without its limitations as D. S. Russell rightly notes: "I myself would prefer to define *das Ende* in terms of the transcendental and the end of history, and *die Endzeit* in terms of the temporal and the continuity of history and to say that in apocalyptic thought there is a fluctuation between the one and the other and, at times, a mingling and merging of these two concepts" (Russell 1978, 24).

Many different expressions are used to describe the juxtaposition of present and future within the Jewish and Christian apocalyptic writings. At times it is a straightforward opposition between "the present age" and "the age to come" (a distinction explicitly made in *t. Pe'a* 4.18). However, within the apocalyptic literature of the Judeo-Christian world there is perhaps no better example of the juxtaposition of present and future than 4 Ezra, generally dated around the end of the first century A.D. Several classic statements of this are contained in 4 Ezra: "The Most High has made not one age but two" (4 Ezra 7:50); "The day of judgment shall be the end of this age and the beginning of the eternal age that is to come" (4 Ezra 7:113); "This age the Most High has made for many, but the age to come for the few" (4 Ezra 8:1). It is clear within 4 Ezra that the author is writing to give his Jewish audience a message of hope following the traumatic events of A.D. 70. In effect the apocalypse addresses the theological problem of theodicy (see Thompson and Willett).

This prompts the question of what it is that generates the juxtaposition of present and future within so many works, such as 4 Ezra, which express apocalyptic eschatology. Is this, as is often asserted, a straightforward temporal dualism which solves the tension in a simple, almost cavalier, fashion, which sees the temporal dualism almost as an extension of a deeper cosmological dualism? Or can the juxtaposition between present and future be anchored more firmly in the experience of the Jewish nation following the destruction of the temple in Jerusalem in 587 B.C. and in A.D. 70 (*see* Judaism), and the resulting crisis of theology that arose as the questions about theodicy had to be faced? Do hopes for a better future gain currency precisely because of the agonies within society over the offense of a present situation? Was the problem faced by postexilic Judaism so acute that it generated the temporal dualism so characteristic of apocalyptic literature? Was the situation for the Jewish nation one in which, as R. Bauckham puts it, "the experience of God"s absence from their own history might become the dogma of his absence from all history" (Bauckham, 21)? However we may seek to answer these complicated questions, it seems certain that a sensitivity to the sociological dimensions of the people of Israel needs to be kept ever in mind.

In this regard it is perhaps no accident that the production of Jewish apocalyptic writings seems associated with two of the most traumatic episodes in the life of the people, the struggle for national survival against the Seleucid Empire in the form of Antiochus Epiphanes (175-163 B.C.) and against the Roman Empire in the form of Titus and his legions (A.D. 66-70), both of which led ultimately to the destruction of the temple in Jerusalem. At the same time, the belief of the apocalyptists in God as the one who has acted in the past must also be remembered and given its due place, including the implication that he will act again decisively in future history (G. I. Davies rightly argues that many apocalyptic texts demonstrate an interest in past history and that it is a mistake to assume that they are concerned with eschatological matters alone). Herein is contained the theological paradox which lies at the heart of matter: on the one hand, the place that the events of human history have within apocalyptic eschatology; and on the other, how that history itself is to be transformed by the actions of God in the future.

Moreover, it is now almost universally accepted that the creative tension between the present and the future was a feature of the teaching of Jesus himself and that it has characterized Christian thought from the very beginning. Indeed, every work within the NT either makes an explicit declaration along these lines, or implies it. A good example is Hebrews 6:5 which speaks of the Christian life in terms of the believer tasting the "powers of the age to come."

3.4. The Spatial Axis: The Earthly Versus the Heavenly. The image of a military headquarters in which the campaign moves for a battle are being enacted which G. B. Caird uses (1962-63) to portray the relationship between heavenly and earthly events is a useful one to illustrate the complex nature of eschatological language. In Caird's image the moving of various flags (representing military units) is both determinative and descriptive, both establishing movements to be made and reflecting those that have taken place; the same principle holds, Caird argues, for the symbolic language that is being employed in eschatology. At the same time, while Caird's illustration does help us see the complexity of eschatological language, it also begs the question of how such "military moves" (to continue the image for a moment) are played out in history and what relationship they have to the temporal axis discussed above.

We might at times be tempted to view the emphasis on the spatial axis in apocalyptic literature as a reaction to the disappointments of history. However, Bauckham (19) rightly questions the commonly held assumption that the apocalyptists abandoned faith in God's action within history in favor of a transcendent eschatology. In fact the temporal axis and the spatial axis are intricately connected within much Jewish and Christian apocalyptic literature; at times one or the other may come to the fore, as the temporal axis does in 4 Ezra and the spatial does in *2 Baruch*, for example, but we must avoid setting up a false dichotomy here. Indeed, the importance of the spatial axis within apocalyptic literature invites one to see a connection with the wisdom traditions of Judaism in precisely the same way that the temporal axis invites one to see a connection to the prophetic traditions. At the same time it is unfair to suggest that wisdom literature as a whole is uninterested in temporal history. The Hellenistic Book of Wisdom stands against any attempt at such a simplistic division between wisdom and apocalyptic on this point, particularly when it comes to the way in which the cosmic order is presented in both. As J. J. Collins (1977-78, 138) remarks: "The conviction that the experience of God and even eschatology is mediated through the cosmic order constitutes the common ground of wisdom and apocalyptic."

Given the fact that the difference between apocalyptic literature and prophetic literature cannot be reduced to a simple difference between their respective views about future history, what can we say about how each stresses the relationship between the temporal axis and the spatial axis? Might we attempt to draw some distinction between them on the basis of how they handle the horizontal and vertical axes? A key question is how this spatial axis of perception is expressed; what gives it substance? J. J. Collins (1974) suggests that one distinctive characteristic that is found in apocalyptic literature, as over against prophetic literature, is the former's concentration on the transcendence of death (he here cites Dan, 1 *Enoch, Jub., As. Mos.* and select Qumran materials as evidence; Russell 1992 offers an assessment of Collins's distinction). This focal point leads inevitably to a consideration of the idea of the resurrection of the body (as hinted at in Dan 12:2-3), a subject of considerable debate in its own right.

One of the most significant ways that the spatial axis is expressed within apocalyptic eschatology is through the idea of a cosmic transformation and the establishment of a new heaven* and a new earth (*see* Creation, Cosmology). Perhaps the most explicit description of the cosmic transformation in the NT is found in 2 Peter 3:10-14, while Hebrews 12:18-24 and 13:14 speak of the future heavenly city of Jerusalem.* In any event, the most extensive discussion of the new heaven and the new earth is found in Revelation 21—22, a passage of immense importance as far as Christian millennialism is concerned (*see* Millennium). In all of these examples the establishment of a new order is closely associated with the imminent Parousia* of a Messianic Deliverer. Indeed, the idea of an imminent Parousia of Jesus Christ has long been seen as one of the premiere features of Christian apocalypticism. E. Käsemann (100) went so far as to define apocalyptic as belief in the imminent Parousia, virtually equating the two.

3.5. The Anthropological Axis: The Wicked Versus the Righteous.
As we noted above, the periodical reviews of history which are found in so many of the apocalyptic writings generally place the author (and his readership) in the last crucial moments of human history. This placement is not simply to suggest the ability to predict the future with crystal ball-like accuracy, but is designed to evoke a decision, to elicit a response on the part of the readership. In other words, apocalyptic literature has an ethical dimension which lies at the heart of much of its message, however that may be formally presented and whatever its contents might be.

Many of the apocalyptic texts of both Judaism and Christianity contain explicit declarations about the fate of human beings, dividing them up into two opposing groups, the wicked and the righteous, the evil and the good. Generally this dualism is viewed as an expression of the ethical dimension of apocalyptic literature, a feature which invites a comparison between apocalyptic texts and the wisdom traditions of both Judaism and Christianity and suggests that something of an overlap occurs between the two on this very point (see Gammie). A number of NT passages speak of future eschatological judgment,* particularly associated with the Parousia of Jesus Christ (including Heb 2:2; 4:1, 12-13; 6:2, 4-8; 9:27; 10:25-27, 30-31; 12:5-11, 18-19, 23, 25, 29; 13:4, 17; Jas 1:12; 4:11-12; 5:1-11; 1 Pet 4:5-7; 2 Pet 2:3, 9-12; 3:5-7; 1 Jn 2:28; 4:17; Jude 9, 14-16, 22; Rev 6—19).

Moreover, some of the sectarian documents from Qumran also contain material which speaks of human beings in starkly dualistic terms, effectively equating membership within the community with righteousness and contrasting that with those who are outside and hence wicked. This is most clearly seen in 1QS 3:13—4:26 and 1QM, a scroll sometimes provocatively titled "The War of the Sons of Light against the Sons of Darkness" (see Charlesworth and Yadin). The larger question of how the eschatological perspective of the Qumran community might shed light upon the NT documents is one which has engendered considerable interest. One only need call attention to James* to see how tightly interwoven ethical teaching and eschatological ideas can be within the NT, a fact which has invited comparison with the Qumran materials, notably 1QM (see, e.g., Eisenman).

See also CREATION, COSMOLOGY; ESCHATOLOGY; HEAVEN, NEW HEAVEN; MILLENNIUM; MYSTERY; PAROUSIA; QUMRAN; REVEAL, REVELATION; REVELATION, BOOK OF; VISIONS, ECSTATIC EXPERIENCE.

BIBLIOGRAPHY. D. Aune, "The Apocalypse of John and the Problem of Genre" in *Semeia* 36: *Early Christian Apocalypticism: Genre and Social Setting*, ed. A. Y. Collins (Decatur, GA: Scholars, 1986) 65-96; M. Barker, "Slippery Words: III. Apocalyptic," *ExpT* 89 (1977-78) 324-29; J. Barr, "Jewish Apocalyptic in Recent Scholarly Study," *BJRL* 58 (1975-76) 9-35; J. Barton, *Oracles of God* (London: Darton, Longman & Todd, 1986); R. Bauckham, "The Rise of Apocalyptic," *Themelios* 3 (1977-78) 10-23; G. R. Beasley-Murray, *Highlights of the Book of Revelation* (Nashville: Broadman, 1972); H. D. Betz, "On the Problem of the Religio-Historical Understanding of Apocalypticism" in *JThC* 6 (1969) 134-56; F. F. Bruce, "A Reappraisal of Jewish Apocalyptic Literature," *RevExp* 72 (1975) 305-15; G. B. Caird, "On Deciphering the Book of Revelation," *ExpT* 74 (1962-63) 13-15, 51-53, 82-84, 103-5; idem, "Eschatology and Politics: Some Misconception" in *Biblical Studies: Essays in Honour of William Barclay*, ed. J. R. McKay and J. F. Miller (London: Collins, 1976) 72-86; idem, *The Language and Imagery of the Bible* (London: Duckworth, 1980) 243-27; J. Carmignac, "Qu'est-ce que l'apocalyptique?," *RevQ* 10 (1979-80) 3-33; R. P. Carroll, "Twilight of Prophecy or Dawn of Apocalyptic?," *JSOT* 14 (1979) 3-35; J. H. Charlesworth, "A Critical Comparison of the Dualism in 1QS III, 13-IV, 26 and the 'Dualism' Contained in the Fourth Gospel," *NTS* 15 (1968-69) 389-418; N. Cohn, *Cosmos, Chaos and the World to Come: The Ancient Roots of Apocalyptic Faith* (London: Yale University Press, 1994); A. Y. Collins "Early Christian Apocalypses," *Semeia* 14 (1979) 61-121; idem, ed. *Semeia* 36: *Early Christian Apocalypticism: Genre and Social Setting* (Decatur, GA: Scholars, 1986); J. J. Collins, "Apocalyptic Eschatology as the Transcendence of Death," *CBQ* 36 (1974) 21-43; idem, "Jewish Apocalyptic Against its Hellenistic Near Eastern Environment," *BASOR* 220 (1975) 27-36; idem, "The Court Tales in Daniel and the Development of Apocalyptic," *JBL* 94 (1975) 218-34; idem, *The Apocalyptic Vision of the Book of Daniel* (Missoula: Scholars, 1977); idem, "Cosmos and History: Jewish Wisdom and Apocalyptic in the Hellenistic Age," *HR* 17 (1977-78) 121-42; idem, "The

Jewish Apocalypses," *Semeia* 14 (1979) 21-59; idem, ed., *Semeia* 14: *Apocalypse: The Morphology of a Genre* (Missoula: Scholars, 1979); idem, *Daniel, with an Introduction to Apocalyptic Literature* (FOTL 20; Grand Rapids: Eerdmans, 1984); idem, "Apocalyptic Literature" in *Early Judaism and Its Modern Interpreters*, ed. R. A. Kraft and G. W. E. Nickelsburg, (Philadelphia: Fortress, 1986) 345-70; idem, *The Apocalyptic Imagination* (New York: Crossroads, 1989); idem, "Was the Dead Sea Sect an Apocalyptic Community?" in *Archeology and History in the Dead Sea Scrolls*, ed. L. Schiffman (JSPSup 8; Sheffield: Sheffield Academic Press, 1990) 25-51; idem, "Genre, Ideology and Social Movements in Jewish Apocalypticism," in *Mysteries and Revelations: Apocalyptic Studies since the Uppsala Colloquium*, ed. J. J. Collins and J. H. Charlesworth (JSPSup 9; Sheffield: Sheffield Academic Press, 1991) 11-32; N. A. Dahl, "Eschatology and History in the Light of the Dead Sea Scrolls," in *The Future of Our Religious Past: Essays in Honour of Rudolf Bultmann*, ed. J. M. Robinson (London: SCM, 1971) 9-28; G. I. Davies, "Apocalyptic and Historiography," *JSOT* 5 (1978) 15-28; P. R. Davies, "Hasidim in the Maccabean Period," *JJS* 28 (1977) 127-40; idem, "Eschatology at Qumran," *JBL* 104 (1985) 39-55; idem, "The Social World of Apocalyptic Writings" in *The World of Ancient Israel*, ed. R. E. Clements (Cambridge: Cambridge University Press, 1989) 251-71; idem, "Qumran and Apocalyptic or *Obscurum Per Obscurius*," *JNES* 49 (1990) 127-34; M. Dean-Otting, *Heavenly Journeys: A Study of the Motif in Hellenistic Jewish Literature* (Frankfurt: Peter Lang, 1984); R. Eisenman, "Eschatological 'Rain' Imagery in the War Scroll from Qumran and in the Letter of James," *JNES* 49 (1990) 173-84; E. S. Fiorenza, "The Phenomenon of Early Christian Apocalyptic: Some Reflections on Method" in *Apocalypticism in the Mediterranean World and the Near East*, ed. D. Hellholm (Tübingen: J. C. B. Mohr [Paul Siebeck], 1983) 295-316; D. N. Freedman, "The Flowering of Apocalyptic," *JThC* 6 (1969) 166-74; S. B. Frost, "Apocalyptic and History" in *The Bible in Modern Scholarship*, ed. J. P. Hyatt (Nashville: Abingdon, 1965) 98-113; N. Frye, *Anatomy of Criticism* (Princeton: Princeton University Press, 1957); J. G. Gammie, "Spatial and Ethical Dualism in Jewish Wisdom and Apocalyptic Literature," *JBL* 93 (1974) 356-85; T. F. Glasson, "What is Apocalyptic?," *NTS* 27 (1980) 98-105; L. L. Grabbe, "Chronography in Hellenistic Jewish Historiography," *SBLSP* (1979) 43-68; I. Gruenwald, *Apocalyptic and Merkavah Mysticism* (Leiden: E. J. Brill, 1978); idem, "Jewish Apocalyptic Literature," *ANRW* 2.19.1 (1979) 89-118; P. D. Hanson, "Jewish Apocalyptic Against Its Near Eastern Environment," *RB* 78 (1971) 31-58; idem, "Apocalypticism" in *IDBSup* 28-34; idem, "Prolegomena to the Study of Jewish Apocalyptic" in *Magnalia Dei: The Mighty Acts of God*, ed. F. M. Cross, W. E. Lemke and P. D. Miller (Garden City, NY: Doubleday, 1976) 389-413; idem, *The Dawn of Apocalyptic* (rev. ed.; Philadelphia: Fortress, 1979); idem, "Apocalyptic Literature" in *The Hebrew Bible and Its Modern Interpreters*, ed. D. A. Knight and G. M. Tucker (Philadelphia: Fortress, 1985) 465-88; idem, "Apocalypses and Apocalypticism: The Genre," *ABD* 1:279-80; D. Hellholm, ed., *Apocalypticism in the Mediterranean World and the Near East: Proceedings of the International Colloquium on Apocalypticism, August 12-17, 1979* (Tübingen: J. C. B. Mohr [Paul Siebeck], 1983); idem, "The Problem of Apocalyptic Genre and the Apocalypse of John" in *Semeia* 36: *Early Christian Apocalypticism: Genre and Social Setting*, ed. A. Y. Collins (Decatur, GA: Scholars, 1986) 13-64; M. Hengel, *Judaism and Hellenism* (Philadelphia: Fortress, 1974); M. Himmelfarb, *Tours of Hell: An Apocalyptic Form in Jewish and Christian Literature* (Philadelphia: Fortress, 1983); L. W. Hurtado, "Revelation 4-5 in the Light of Jewish Apocalyptic Analoges," *JSNT* 25 (1985) 105-24; J. Kallas, "The Apocalypse—An Apocalyptic Book?," JBL 86 (1967) 69-80; E. Käsemann, *New Testament Questions of Today* (London: SCM, 1969); M. Knibb, "Prophecy and the Emergence of the Jewish Apocalypses" in *Israel's Prophetic Tradition: Essays in Honour of Peter Ackroyd*, ed. R. Coggins, A. Phillips and M. Knibb (Cambridge: Cambridge University Press, 1982): K. Koch, *The Rediscovery of Apocalyptic* (London: SCM, 1972); S. Laws, "Can Apocalyptic Be Relevant?" in *What About the New Testament? Essays for Christopher Evans*, ed. M. D. Hooker and C. J. A. Hickling (London: SCM, 1975) 89-102; I. H. Marshall, "Slippery Words: I. Eschatology," ExpT 89 (1977-78) 264-69; H.-P. Müller, "Mantische Weisheit und Apokalyptik," VT Supp 22, (Leiden: E. J. Brill, 1972) 268-93; C. A. Newsom, "Apocalyptic and the Discourse of the Qumran Community," JNES 49 (1990) 135-44; E. W. Nicholson, "Apocalyptic" in *Tradition and Interpretation*, ed. G. W. Anderson (Oxford: Oxford University Press, 1979) 189-213; G. W. E.

Nickelsburg, "Social Aspects of Palestinian Apocalypticism" in *Apocalypticism in the Mediterranean World and the Near East*, ed. D. Hellholm (Tübingen: J. C. B. Mohr [Paul Siebeck], 1983) 641-54; O. Plöger, *Theocracy and Eschatology* (Oxford: Blackwell, 1964); G. von Rad, *Wisdom in Israel* (London: SCM, 1972); W. G. Rollins, "The New Testament and Apocalyptic," *NTS* 17 (1970-71) 454-76; C. C. Rowland, "The Visions of God in Apocalyptic Literature," *JSJ* 10 (1979) 137-54; idem, *The Open Heaven* (London: SPCK, 1982); idem, "Apocalyptic Literature" in *It Is Written: Scripture Citing Scripture: Essays in Honour of Barnabas Lindars*, ed. D. A. Carson and H. G. M. Williamson (Cambridge: Cambridge University Press, 1988) 170-89; idem, "Apocalyptic" in *A Dictionary of Biblical Interpretation*, ed. R. J. Coggins and J. L. Houlden (London: SCM, 1990) 34-36; H. H. Rowley, *The Relevance of Apocalyptic* (London: Lutterworth, 1944); D. S. Russell, *The Method and Message of Jewish Apocalyptic* (London: SCM, 1964); idem, *Apocalyptic: Ancient and Modern* (Philadelphia: Fortress, 1978); idem, *Divine Disclosure: An Introduction to Jewish Apocalyptic* (London: SCM, 1992); E. P. Sanders, "The Genre of Palestinian Apocalypses" in *Apocalypticism in the Mediterranean World and the Near East*, ed. D. Hellholm (Tübingen: J.C.B. Mohr [Paul Siebeck], 1983) 447-59; E. F. Scott, "The Natural Language of Religion: Apocalyptic and the Christian Message," *Int* 2 (1948) 419-29; A. F. Segal, "Heavenly Ascent in Hellenistic Judaism, Early Christianity and their Environments," *ANRW* 2.23.2 (1980) 1333-94; M. Smith, "On the History of *Apokalyptō* and *Apokalypsis*" in *Apocalypticism in the Mediterranean World and the Near East*, ed. D. Hellholm (Tübingen: J.C.B. Mohr [Paul Siebeck], 1983) 9-19; H. Stegemann, "Die Bedeutung der Qumranfunde für die Erforschung der Apokalyptik" in *Apocalypticism in the Mediterranean World and the Near East*, ed. D. Hellholm (Tübingen: J. C. B. Mohr [Paul Siebeck], 1983) 495-530; M. E. Stone, "Lists of Revealed Things in the Apocalyptic Literature" in *Magnalia Dei: The Mighty Acts of God*, ed. F. M. Cross, W. E. Lemke and P. D. Miller (Garden City, NY: Doubleday, 1976) 414-52; R. E. Sturm, "Defining the Word 'Apocalyptic': A Problem in Biblical Criticism" in *Apocalyptic and the New Testament: Essays in Honor of J. Louis Martyn*, ed. J. Marcus and M. L. Soards (JSNTSup 24; Sheffield: JSOT, 1989) 17-48; J. T. Thomas, "Jewish Apocalyptic and the Comparative Method" in *Scripture in Context:*

Essays on Comparative Method, ed. C. D. Evans, W. W. Hallo and J. B. White (Pittsburgh, PA: Pickwick, 1980) 245-62; A. T. Thompson, *Responsibility for Evil in the Theodicy of IV Ezra* (SBLDS 29; Missoula: Scholars, 1977); J. C. VanderKam, *Enoch and the Growth of an Apocalyptic Tradition* (CBQMS 16; Washington, DC: The Catholic Biblical Association of America, 1984); P. Vielhauer, "Apocalypses and Related Subjects" in *New Testament Apocrypha II*, ed. R. McL. Wilson (London: Lutterworth, 1965) 581-607; R. L. Webb, " 'Apocalyptic': Observations on a Slippery Term," *JNES* 49 (1990) 115-26; T. W. Willett, *Eschatology in the Theodicies of 2 Baruch and 4 Ezra* (JSP 4; Sheffield: Sheffield Academic Press, 1989); M. O. Wise, "The Eschatological Vision of the Temple Scroll," *JNES* 49 (1990) 155-72; Y. Yadin, *The Message of the Scrolls* (New York: Simon & Schuster, 1957). L. J. Kreitzer

APOCALYPTIC ESCHATOLOGY. *See* APOCALYPTIC, APOCALYPTICISM.

APOCALYPTICISM. *See* APOCALYPTIC, APOCALYPTICISM.

APOCRYPHAL AND PSEUDEPIGRAPHAL WRITINGS

This article covers extracanonical Christian literature that is either attributed to biblical persons as authors or recounts narratives about biblical persons that parallel or supplement the biblical narratives. In most early Christian literature of this kind the biblical persons are NT characters, but in some cases they are OT characters. Christian apocryphal literature (so defined) continued to be written for many centuries, in many Christian traditions, and so the whole corpus of such literature is vast. Modern collections of such literature in translation (see especially Schneemelcher 1991-92; Elliott 1993) are only selections, usually including the earliest such literature, but often also including later works that have been particularly influential in Christian history. Only occasionally do they include Christian works written under OT pseudonyms, which can often be found, along with Jewish works of this kind, in collections of the OT Pseudepigrapha. The present article is restricted to literature that can plausibly be dated before the mid-third century, but excludes apocryphal Gospels (treated in DJG) and apocryphal Pauline literature (treated in *DPL*).

1. Apocalyptic and Prophetic Literature
2. Apostolic Acts
3. Other Apostolic Pseudepigrapha
4. Wisdom Literature
5. Hymnic Literature

1. Apocalyptic and Prophetic Literature.

An apocalypse* is a work in which a seer receives from a supernatural revealer (usually God, Christ or an angel; *see* Reveal, Revelation) a revelation (auditory or visionary) of heavenly secrets, which are often, though not always, eschatological* in nature. Many such Jewish works were attributed to biblical figures, such as Enoch or Ezra, and Christian writers continued this Jewish literary tradition, attributing their apocalypses sometimes to OT figures, sometimes to NT figures.

Early Christian apocalypses were not modeled on the NT Apocalypse of John; they form a Christian continuation of the Jewish apocalyptic tradition. But there are two distinctive (and overlapping) developments of the apocalyptic genre. First, revelations made by Jesus Christ to his disciples in the period between his resurrection* and his ascension* form a large category of early Christian works. Many, but not all, of these are Gnostic (*see* Gnosis). Many of them are often classified as Gospels. One non-Gnostic example (the *Apoc. Peter*) is treated below (1.1), because its content is eschatological and closely related to Jewish apocalyptic traditions. One Gnostic example is also discussed below (1.6). (Other such works, both Gnostic and non-Gnostic, are discussed in *DJG*, Gospels [Apocryphal], §9). Second, many Gnostic works, including those just mentioned but also others attributed to biblical pseudonyms, record revelations of otherworldly secrets and must be classified as apocalypses in a broad sense (see 1.7 below). Finally, it should be noted that although apocalypses were the major literary vehicle for prophecy in this period (*see* Hermas, Shepherd of), there are also some other kinds of prophetic works among the Christian apocrypha (see 1.4-5 below).

1.1. Apocalypse of Peter. Of all the Christian apocrypha, this one came closest to being accepted into the NT canon.* In the second to fourth centuries it was widely read and was treated as Scripture by some. Its popularity was no doubt due to the detailed information it gives as to the postmortem fate of human beings in paradise or hell.* It comprises revelations made to the disciples by the risen Christ about the persecutions and downfall of antichrist,* the Parousia,* the resurrection of the dead and the last judgment,* the punishments of the wicked in hell, and the rewards of the righteous in paradise. Peter receives a revelation of his own future life up to his martyrdom,* and the work ends with an account of Christ's ascension to heaven.* The longest section of the work, the description of hell, in which twenty-one different types of sinners are seen each undergoing a punishment appropriate to their sin, is in the tradition of Jewish apocalyptic "tours of hell."

A good case can be made that the apocalypse was written in Palestinian Jewish Christian (*see* Jewish Christianity) circles during the Bar Kokhba revolt (A.D. 132-35). It reflects the difficult circumstances of Jewish Christians who refused to join the revolt, since they could not accept the messiahship of Bar Kokhba, portrayed here as the false messiah (antichrist), or support his aim of rebuilding the temple.* In this case the apocalypse is of great historical importance as rare evidence for the history of Jewish Christianity in Palestine after 70.

1.2. Ascension of Isaiah. Though this work has sometimes been treated as a Christian redaction of pre-Christian Jewish sources, it should probably be seen as an originally Christian apocalypse, employing some Jewish traditions about the martyrdom of the prophet Isaiah but largely inspired by the strong early Christian tradition of interpreting the prophecies of Isaiah as prophetic of Jesus Christ. Like the book of Daniel and some other Jewish apocalypses, it comprises a largely narrative section (*Asc. Isa.* 1—5) and a largely visionary section (*Asc. Isa.* 6—11). These contain two complementary accounts of Isaiah's vision. The first (*Asc. Isa.* 3:13—4:18) takes the form of a prophecy of events from the incarnation of Christ (known in this work as "the Beloved") to the Parousia and the end of history. The second narrates Isaiah's visionary ascent through the seven heavens to the throne of God, where he sees in prophetic vision the descent of the Beloved from the seventh heaven to earth, his incarnation, life, death* and descent to Hades, followed by his reascent through the heavens to enthronement at God's right hand. The Jewish apocalyptic idea of a visionary's ascent through the seven heavens to receive revelation from God in the highest heaven is thus adapted to a Christian purpose.

The *Ascension of Isaiah* seems to derive from a circle of early Christian prophets, whose own corporate visionary experience is strikingly described in the narrative of Isaiah's experience (*Asc. Isa.* 6). This, along with its distinctive forms of trinitarian and christological* expression, make it interesting evidence that is not easy to place on the map of early Christianity. It has been plausibly dated between the late first and mid-second centuries.

1.3. Apocalypse of Thomas. This revelation of Christ to the apostle* Thomas predicts the signs that over the course of seven days will precede the end of this world. Though difficult to date, it may well be relatively early; it certainly depends closely on Jewish apocalyptic tradition.

1.4. Sibylline Oracles. The Sibyls were pagan prophetesses to whom Jewish writers from the third century B.C. onward had already attributed prophetic oracles in poetic form and enigmatic style. These works, which espouse monotheism, denounce idolatry,* prophesy events of world history and predict judgments, were presumably meant to appeal to pagan readers who did not know their Jewish authorship. Early Christians continued this Jewish tradition by expanding originally Jewish Sibylline oracles with Christian additions and by writing fresh Christian compositions of the same kind.

1.5. 5 Ezra and 6 Ezra. These terms are used for, respectively, chapters 1-2 and chapters 15-16 of the composite work known as 2 Esdras or 4 Ezra, whose core (chaps. 3-14) is a Jewish apocalypse. 5 Ezra, a series of prophecies and visions attributed to Ezra, is a Christian work of the second century, portraying the church as the true people of God who replace disobedient and faithless Israel (*see* Church as Israel). Prefaced to the Jewish apocalypse of Ezra, it provides a Christian perspective for the reading of the latter. 6 Ezra is a prophecy usually regarded as Christian and of a later date.

1.6. Coptic Apocalypse of Peter (CG VII, 3). This Gnostic work, found in the Nag Hammadi library and dating probably from the late second or early third century, has no connection with the *Apocalypse of Peter* described above (1.1). The unusual setting of this apocalypse, in the temple before the crucifixion of Jesus, is appropriate to the unusual contents of the visionary revelation which "the Savior"* gives to Peter. Its climax is the disclosure that only the physical Jesus suffers and dies on the cross,* while the spiritual, immortal Savior stands aside, laughing with joy. This revelation provides the basis for polemic against those blind Christians who can recognize only the physical Christ they think died and rose bodily, and who therefore have only a mortal destiny themselves. Thus the apocalyptic form of revelation of the true reality behind the appearances of history in this world serves here the purposes of a strongly dualistic, Gnostic understanding of christology and human destiny.

1.7. Other Gnostic Apocalypses. Gnostic works that do not take the form of postresurrection dialogues between Christ and the apostles, but that do recount revelations made by heavenly revealers to biblical figures, include the *Paraphrase of Shem* (CG VII, 1), the *Three Steles of Seth* (CG VII, 5) and *Melchizedek* (CG IX, 1).

2. Apostolic Acts.

The five oldest apocryphal Acts are those of Andrew, John, Paul, Peter and Thomas (see 2.1-4 below; the *Acts of Paul* are discussed in *DPL*). These all date from the second or early third century. (Many other apocryphal Acts were composed in subsequent centuries.) More precise dates are difficult to determine, partly because they depend on the literary relationships between these five works. That there are such literary relationships is clear, but what the relationships are, with implications for the chronological order in which the five works were written, remains debatable. The tendency of recent scholarship has been to date the *Acts of Thomas* in the first half of the third century but the other four Acts in the second half of the second century or even somewhat earlier.

Though there are considerable differences among these five works, they all belong to a common literary subgenre, which can be defined as a narrative of the missionary activity of a single apostle subsequent to the resurrection of Jesus and concluding with the martyrdom (or, in John's case, death) of the apostle. The Lukan Acts* clearly had some influence on the development of this genre, though the extent of indebtedness to the Lukan Acts varies among the apocryphal Acts and is probably not direct in every case. The Lukan Acts provided the model for an episodic travel narrative that is characteristic, to a greater or lesser extent, of these apocryphal Acts—with the exception of the *Acts of Peter* in its surviving form—as well as for some, but by no means all, of the contents (such as miracles and preaching) of the various episodes in the apostle's missionary career. In this respect the *Acts of Paul* is closer to Acts than any other of the oldest apocryphal Acts.

But even the second half of the Lukan Acts, with its concentration on Paul, does not provide a model for a narrative ending with the apostle's death. Here, as in some other respects also, the apocryphal Acts show a more biographical interest in their subjects than the Lukan Acts shows even in Paul. They can be located within the growing interest in biographical literature in the period in which they were written. More specifically, they resemble the novelistic biographies of the period, which combine a genuine interest in history with a freedom for historical imagination, such that the line between fact and fiction is not easily drawn. The extent to which their authors drew on existing legends or even traditions of some historical value in their accounts of the apostles is rarely possible to determine, but to a large extent they are works of historical imagination. But the resemblances to the Greek romantic novels which have often been observed do not place them in the genre of the novel. The resemblances result from the fact that the semifictional biographies to which the apocryphal Acts are most akin themselves have features in common with or borrowed from the novels. The apocryphal Acts were written to engage and entertain readers who might well be familiar with novels and novelistic biographies, but they also convey the Christian message and invite to the Christian lifestyle as their authors understood these.

None of these five apocryphal Acts can properly be called Gnostic (but see 2.2 below), but some of them have clear affinities with aspects of the religious milieu of the period in which Gnosticism flourished, and all show some tendency to favor sexual abstinence and other forms of detachment from material or worldly life. Similarly, the tendencies to docetism* and modalism in the christology of several of the Acts should not, for the most part, be attributed specifically to Gnosticism; instead they reflect the christological piety of the period. However, despite some important affinities, each of the five Acts has its own theological distinctiveness.

2.1. Acts of Andrew. This work survives only in a variety of incomplete and often adapted later forms which allow a partial reconstruction of the original text and contents. They recounted Andrew's travels and missionary successes in various parts of northern Asia Minor and Greece, ending with his death by crucifixion in Patras. (It is uncertain whether the *Acts of Andrew and Matthias*, which tells of Andrew's adventures in the city of the cannibals, belonged originally to the *Acts of Andrew*.) Salvation, which is the central concern of the work, is understood as the detachment and liberation of the soul, which is akin to God, from the body, in which it is imprisoned in this life, and from the material world.

2.2. Acts of John. Though some of the contents of the original *Acts of John* have to be conjectured, much of the text has survived. It recounts the apostle John's journey to Ephesus, where much of the narrative takes place, a missionary journey through the province of Asia (perhaps in the original text to all seven churches of the Apocalypse of John), John's return to Ephesus and his death. The most distinctive section is John's preaching of the gospel* in chapters 87-102, in which he recounts episodes from the ministry of Jesus. These include revelations to the apostles of the polymorphous and elusive nature of Christ's bodily appearance, the famous hymn* of Christ in which he dances with the apostles, and a revelation of the esoteric meaning of the cross. These chapters, uniquely in the five apocryphal Acts, express a clearly Gnostic theology, with special affinities with Valentinian Gnosticism. The special character of chapters 94-102 (and the related chapter 109) suggests that they existed independently and were incorporated in the *Acts of John* either originally or subsequently. While this does not make the *Acts of John* as a whole a Gnostic composition, it does indicate that in this work the line between Gnostic and non-Gnostic interpretations of Christianity is thin.

2.3. Acts of Peter. The *Acts of Peter* survives in a secondary edited form (the Vercelli Acts), which, after an introduction describing Paul's departure from Rome for Spain, recounts the arrival of Simon Magus in Rome, Peter's journey from Jerusalem to Rome and his ministry there, largely in the form of a contest with Simon Magus, in both miracles and argument, concluding with Simon's spectacular defeat. Finally Peter dies by crucifixion and appears after his death. Two other surviving stories about Peter's miracles suggest that the original form of the *Acts of Peter* was longer and may have recounted his ministry in Jerusalem. Along with the *Acts of Paul*, the *Acts of Peter* is the least unorthodox of the five apocryphal Acts, though here too the christology and the sexual asceticism reflect popular piety and preaching.

2.4. Acts of Thomas. This is the only one of the five major apocryphal Acts of which the original form has survived intact, though it is uncertain whether the Syriac (*see* Syria) or the Greek version preserves the language of composition. It certainly derives from east Syrian Christianity, in which the apostle Thomas was celebrated and (since Thomas means "twin") understood as the spiritual twin of Jesus, and in which radical asceticism (encratism), more extreme in this Acts than in the others, flourished. While the *Acts of Thomas* is not strictly Gnostic, its understanding of salvation as awareness of one's true self once again shows the affinities of the apocryphal Acts with some aspects of Gnosticism. The *Acts of Thomas* recounts Thomas's missionary activity in India, but despite some historically accurate information about first-century India, his mission there is likely to be entirely legendary. The "Hymn of the Pearl" (chaps. 108-13), an allegorical myth, has been variously interpreted but probably tells of the heavenly origin and destiny of the soul.

2.5. Acts of the Peter and the Twelve Apostles (CG VI, 1). Though found in the Nag Hammadi library, it is not clear whether this fragmentary text, which has nothing to do with the five major apocryphal Acts, is Gnostic or not. It tells of the apostles' encounter with Lithargoel, a pearl merchant, who turns out to be Christ in disguise.

3. Other Apostolic Pseudepigrapha.
Works included here have some affinities with the apocryphal Acts but cannot strictly be classified as such. Apocryphal apostolic letters are rare (see 3.2 below; *see also DPL*, Apocryphal Pauline Literature). The *Epistle of the Apostles*, though written in the form of a letter by the apostles, belongs otherwise to the genre of revelatory dialogues with the risen Christ (see sec. 1 above).

3.1. Preaching of Peter. This work, probably of the early second century, survives only in a small number of quotations. These suggest that it was a collection of missionary sermons attributed to Peter.

3.2. Letter of Peter to Philip (CG VIII, 2). Only the first half of this Gnostic work consists of Peter's letter to Philip; the rest is one of the revelatory dialogues between the risen Christ and the apostles which are the favorite literary genre of the Gnostic literature.

3.3. Second Apocalypse of James (CG V, 4). This work, though it could be classified as a Gnostic apocalypse, is included here because it recounts a sermon by James of Jerusalem, in which he reports the revelations made to him by the risen Jesus, followed by the martyrdom of James. The account of the martyrdom is closely related to that derived by Hegesippus from Palestinian Jewish Christian tradition (Eusebius *Hist. Eccl.* 2.23).

3.4. Pseudo-Clementine Literature. The Pseudo-Clementine *Recognitions* and *Homilies* are attributed to Clement* of Rome, portrayed as a disciple and companion of Peter. Since they recount Peter's travels, preaching and conflict with Simon Magus, they bear some resemblance to the apocryphal Acts. They date from the fourth century but are mentioned here because numerous attempts have been made to discern much earlier Jewish Christian sources incorporated in them.

4. Wisdom Literature.
The *Teachings of Silvanus (CG VII, 4)*, though preserved in the Nag Hammadi Library, is not a Gnostic work but a Christian work in the genre of wisdom* instruction. It has affinities both with Jewish wisdom literature and with the Alexandrian* tradition of philosophically influenced Christian theology. Since wisdom literature is usually attributed to authoritative teachers of the past, it is likely that the name Silvanus refers to the companion of Paul, but this cannot be certain.

5. Hymnic Literature.
The only Christian apocryphal work in this category is the *Odes of Solomon*, a collection of forty-two odes. The author was a Christian prophet. Whether he himself associated his work with Solomon is uncertain. The ascription to Solomon results from the association of his work with the Jewish *Psalms of Solomon*, whether by the

author himself or at a subsequent but early date. The complete collection is extant only in Syriac, and this may have been the language of composition, though some have argued for Greek as the original language. In any case, affinities with the Qumran* literature and with Ignatius indicate an origin in Syrian Christianity under strong Jewish influence. The *Odes* have been dated as early as the end of the first century and as late as the third century.

See also MARK, SECRET GOSPEL OF; PETER, GOSPEL OF; THOMAS, GOSPEL OF.

BIBLIOGRAPHY. J. K. Elliott, *The Apocryphal New Testament* (Oxford: Clarendon, 1993; contains translations and very full bibliographies); J. M. Robinson, ed., *The Nag Hammadi Library in English* (Leiden: E. J. Brill, 1977); W. Schneemelcher, ed., *New Testament Apocrypha* (2 vols.; rev. ed.; Louisville: Westminster/John Knox, 1991-92). The most important new editions of the Christian apocryphal literature are those appearing in the *Corpus Christianorum Series Apocryphorum* (Turnhout: Brepols, 8 vols. published so far). See J.-D. Dubois, "The New Series Apocryphorum of the Corpus Christianorum," *Second Century* 4 (1984) 29-36. The series *Apocryphes en Poche* (Turnhout: Brepols, 8 vols. published so far) provides accessible French translations and introductions of individual apocryphal works. (Brepols also publishes an annual *Bulletin* of the Association pour l'Etude de la Littérature Apocryphe Chrétienne [AELAC], which is responsible for these and other projects in the field.)

R. J. Bauckham

APOSTASY

Apostasy is the antonym of conversion; it is deconversion. In the literature covered by this volume, the word *apostasy (apostasia)* occurs only in a context of Jews falling away from the teachings* of Moses,* for which Paul was being blamed (Acts 21:21; cf. 2 Thess 2:3; *see DPL,* Apostasy, Falling Away, Perseverance).

1. Apostasy Foreseen by Jesus
2. Apostasy in Acts
3. Apostasy in Hebrews
4. Apostasy in the General Epistles
5. Apostasy in Revelation
6. Occasions of Apostasy
7. Means of Resistance
8. Apostasy in the Postapostolic Literature

1. Apostasy Foreseen by Jesus.

Jesus foresaw the fact of apostasy and warned both those who would fall into sin as well as those who would cause others to fall (see, e.g., Mk 9:42-49). He knew that his disciples would "all fall away" and that Peter in particular would deny him (Mk 14:27-31). There are hints that Jesus foresaw a significant falling away as a prelude to the Parousia* (Mk 13:20-23; Rev 20:3; cf. 2 Thess 2:3-12). Judas, one of the Twelve,* was an apostate (Jn 6:70-71).

2. Apostasy in Acts.

Acts* describes a number of those who fell away under the ministry* of the apostle Peter. Early in the history of the Jerusalem* church,* Ananias and Sapphira died for the sin of lying to the apostles* (Acts 5:1-11; 1 Cor 11:30). In Samaria* a sorcerer, Simon, who had "believed" the message of Philip* and had been baptized,* was rebuked by Peter (and excommunicated?) for the sin of seeking to buy the power* of God* evident in the coming of the Spirit to the Samaritans (Acts 8:9-24; *see* Holy Spirit).

Notwithstanding the remarkable impact of his ministry in Ephesus, Paul foresaw that after he would leave "wolves" from outside would ravage the flock and that false teachers would arise from within the church and draw many away from his teaching (Acts 20:29-30). Doubtless Paul was proved right in his prophecy* (cf. 2 Tim 1:15).

Examples of the language of apostasy in Acts includes "draw away" (*aphistēmi,* Acts 20:30; cf. Acts 5:37) and "apostasy" (*apostasia,* Acts 21:21). Ananias and Sapphira "fall down" (*piptō,* Acts 5:5, 10), but that word has a literal meaning here and a metaphorical meaning elsewhere.

3. Apostasy in Hebrews.

The letter to the Hebrews* is the *locus classicus* of the subject of apostasy in the NT. The writer and the readers of the letter, who appear to have been Jewish believers, had been evangelized by the original disciples of Jesus (Heb 2:3). At the time they suffered persecution* (Heb 10:32-34), though in the meantime they have become "dull of hearing" (Heb 5:11-14). At the time of writing they are again facing persecution, though not yet "to the point of shedding blood" (Heb 12:4). The anonymous writer is well aware of their spiritual danger, that they are under the pressure of total apostasy; that is, of deliberately rejecting Christ (Heb 10:36-41; 6:6). The latter text has been the occasion of exegetical debate, with some scholars taking seriously the possibility of rejection and others pointing to Hebrews 6:9 as indicating the author's more optimistic attitude to his readers. To be noted is the vocabulary of apostasy: "fall away" (*aphistēmi*, Heb 3:12), "fall" (*piptō*, Heb 4:11), "commit apostasy" (*parapiptō*, Heb 6:6) and "throw away" (*apoballō*, Heb 10:35).

Against the possibility of committing apostasy, the writer urges his readers not to "drift" from the gospel or "neglect" their salvation,* not to harden their hearts to the word of promise* that they had received but with faithfulness to "hold fast" their "confession" (Heb 3:7-13). He calls on them to persevere in hope,* not deflected by the suffering* of that present time (Heb 2:14-3:6; 5:7; 11:1—12:2).

How are the readers to be helped to resist this temptation* to apostatize from Christ? The writer is clear. Throughout the letter he builds for them a superb view of Christ: as God, not to be compared with angels* (Heb 1:1—2:4); as an exalted but compassionate high priest* (Heb 7:26-28; 2:17-18; 4:14-16) whose sacrifice* is "once for all" (Heb 10:9-18; 9:11-14), superseding the old covenant* (Heb 8:24-28), who has entered the sanctuary of heaven* where he intercedes for his people (Heb 9:24-28). Thus he powerfully encourages them to "enter" that sanctuary, since the way has been opened for them to do so by the death of Christ.* Let them hold fast their confession* (Heb 10:19-25), running the race with perseverance (*see* Endurance, Perseverance), looking to Jesus who has gone on before them, through suffering, to the right hand of God (Heb 12:1-2).

4. Apostasy in the General Epistles.

James* warns of the possibility of temptation. The person is not tempted by God but is "lured and enticed by his own desires" (Jas 1:13-15). This letter has in mind a "way" (*hodos*, Jas 5:20) of belief and behavior, from which one may be "led astray" (*planasthe*, Jas 1:16; i.e., by the influence of others) or "stray from" (*planēthē*, Jas 5:19; i.e., by one's own decision). Either way the one who is away from the true path is in jeopardy in regard to his or her personal salvation (Jas 5:20). James also uses the language of "falling"; to misuse one's words is "to fall (*piptō,*) under condemnation" (Jas 5:12).

1 Peter* warns the readers about the pressure that will come to them through persecution (1 Pet 4:12-19), which ultimately originates in Satan* (1 Pet 5:8). Against such, Peter encourages, "have no fear of them . . . but in your hearts reverence Christ as Lord. Always be prepared to make a defense (*apologia*) . . . for the hope that is in you" (1 Pet 3:13-17). The example and saving effects of Christ's sufferings are held up before the readers (1 Pet 2:22-25).

2 Peter* addresses the grim situation of apostasy expressed by immorality (2 Pet 2:2-3, 14-16), under the influence of false teachers who have "denied the master who bought them" (2 Pet 2:1, 17-22). This letter serves as a warning given to the readers "beforehand . . . lest you be carried away with the error of lawless men" (2 Pet 3:17). Like James, Peter has in mind a straight path of truth,* from which the readers are admonished not to "go astray" (*planē; ekplanō,* 2 Pet 2:15; 3:17). Against this, Peter encourages patient hope, a zeal for purity* and growth in the grace* and knowledge* of Jesus Christ (2 Pet 3:14-18).

Like 2 Peter, Jude* warns the readers, notwithstanding having been "once for all fully informed" (Jude 5-7), of the danger to them of "ungodly persons who pervert the grace of our God into licentiousness and deny our only master" (Jude 4, 8-16). Their erroneous teaching is called "the way (*hodos*) of Cain" and the error (*planē*) of Balaam," implying departure from "the faith once for all delivered to the saints" (Jude 3). Jude encourages the readers to build themselves up in their "most holy faith" (Jude 20) and to "keep" themselves in the love* of God (Jude 21), in the knowledge that God is "able to keep" them "unfallen" (*aptaistous,* Jude 24). It is noted that both 2 Peter 2:1 and Jude 4 refer to those who have "denied" Christ (*arneomai*).

The letters of John (*see* John, Letters of) see that the current presence of "antichrists" is evidence of the appearance of the antichrist* (1 Jn 4:3; 2 Jn 7-11). ("Antichrist" [Gk *antichristos*] means a spurious substitute for the true Messiah, Jesus.) This signals that it is the "last hour" (1 Jn 2:18). These "antichrists," who have "gone out from us," have denied that Jesus is the Christ and the Son of God, his Father (1 Jn 2:22). Thus John warns, "let no one deceive you" (*planatō,* 1 Jn 3:7). Once again is implied a straight path of truth from which one should not deviate. The readers are to continue to believe what they have been taught (1 Jn 2:24) and to do what is right (1 Jn 3:7). The world* listens to the deceivers because they are "of" the world. But believers have been "born of God" (1 Jn 4:4-6) and have overcome these teachers; greater is he who is in them (Christ) than he who is in the world (Satan).

5. Apostasy in Revelation.
In the Revelation (*see* Revelation, Book of) it is clear that the churches of Asia are subject to persecution and its accompanying pressure to apostatize that arise from a Jewish quarter in Smyrna and Philadelphia (Rev 2:9) and from the emperor* cult in Pergamum (Rev 2:13). At the same time various false teachings are touching the churches of Ephesus (Rev 2:6), Pergamum (Rev 2:14-15) and Thyatira (Rev 2:20). The language of "deception," that is, of being "led astray," is applied to the false prophetess, Jezebel (Rev 2:20). Satan, the source of all these persecutions and false teachings, is also "the deceiver of the whole world" (Rev 12:9). The metaphor, "deception" *(planaō)*, implies a path of truth from which one might be "turned aside." Against these Satan-inspired obstacles the readers are called upon to "conquer," that is, to overcome these problems. Here the example and saving power of Christ's death are constantly appealed to (Rev 7:14; 12:11; 14:4). The church of Ephesus is said to have "fallen" *(piptō,* Rev 2:5); however, this does not mean apostasy but having "fallen" from its "first love" (i.e., Christ).

6. Occasions of Apostasy.
A review of this literature suggests the following occasions of apostasy: (1) moral or spiritual failure (Acts 5:1-11; 8:9-24); (2) persecution (Heb 10:32-39; 1 Pet 3:13-17; 4:12-19; 5:8; Rev 2:9, 13; 3:9); (3) false teaching (Acts 20:30; Jas 1:16; 2 Pet 2:1; Jude 4; 1 Jn 2:18-19; 2 Jn 7-11; Rev 2:6, 14-15, 20); (4) self-choice (Jas 1:13-15; 5:19).

7. Means of Resistance.
While many warnings are given of the dangers of falling away, there are also encouragements about the mercy* of God shown in these situations (e.g., Heb 4:14-16) as well as the strength and faithfulness of God to "keep" his children (*see* Sonship, Child, Children) from falling away from the true path of faith* (e.g., 1 Pet 1:5; 2 Peter 2:9; 1 Jn 4:4; Jude 24; Rev 3:10).

8. Apostasy in the Postapostolic Literature.
Believers in the era following that of the apostles probably suffered a greater intensity to turn aside from Christ than did their predecessors. They were known to be separate from the Jews and were vulnerable to Jewish reprisals as well as action from the state. Details of the pressure applied to Christians to apostatize is given from both Christian and non-Christian sources (*Mart. Pol.* 9-11; Pliny *Ep.* 10). Pliny reports that Christians in Bithynia had abandoned their faith as long ago as twenty years. It is understandable, therefore, that the postapostolic literature should contain many warnings not to apostatize. Appeal is made, however, on the basis of human effort; little is said about the power of God to "keep" the Christian. It is a matter of the human will rather than the power of God.

1 Clement is not addressing the matter of "apostasy" so much as disorder within the Corinthian church (*see* Clement of Rome; Church Order). Nonetheless there is a warning against "changing the mind" (*1 Clem.* 11.2) and an encouragement to persevere to the end (*1 Clem.* 45). But let those who are disobedient to Clement's words know that they are in "no little danger" (*1 Clem.* 59.1; *see* Obedience). *2 Clement* also warns that failure to do the will of Christ will incur the eternal punishment* (*2 Clem.* 6.7). *2 Clement* repeatedly calls for genuine repentance* (e.g., *2 Clem.* 9.8).

For the most part Ignatius's* warnings are applied to heretical teachers, who are like "ravening dogs" (Ign. *Eph.* 7; cf. Ign. *Eph.* 16). Judaism* and Docetism* are among the false teachings abroad at that time. Ignatius commends the church, which resists the influence of the false teacher (e.g., Ign. *Eph.* 9.1). For his part Ignatius was painfully aware of the temptation he faced to deny Christ (Ign. *Rom.* 7).

Polycarp* warns of failure to acknowledge Jesus Christ (Pol. *Phil.* 7) but strongly encourages perseverance among believers (Pol. *Phil.* 8), appealing to the example of martyrs like Ignatius. Barnabas makes a powerful appeal: "flee from all works of lawlessness lest the works of lawlessness overcome us" (*Barn.* 4.1; *see* Barnabas, Epistle of; Law). He warns, "The day is at hand when all things shall perish with the evil one" (*Barn.* 21.3).

The *Shepherd of Hermas** makes a number of references to the matter of apostasy. The noun apostate (apostatēs), appearing in Hermas (*Herm. Sim.* 8.6.2-6), indicates the reality of a pastoral problem at the time. "Apostates" are in effect deconverted, doing "the deeds of the heathen" (*Herm. Sim.* 8.9.3). Hermas's admonition against a servant* denying his Lord* (*Herm. Sim.* 9.28.4) is a probable echo from 2 Peter 2:1, Jude 4 and 1 John 2:2. To do so is to "deny" one's own life* (*Herm. Vis.* 2.2.7-8). The impulse for such denial is fear* of persecution and a desire to hold on to one's wealth (*Herm. Vis.* 3.6.5; *Herm. Sim.* 8.8.5; *see* Riches). For the "apostate" (i.e., the denier), unlike the lesser sinners (hypocrites and false teachers who may find repentance if it is speedily sought), there is no repentance but only death (*Herm. Sim.* 9.19.1).

See also ADVERSARIES; ANTICHRIST; ENDURANCE, PERSEVERANCE; REPENTANCE, SECOND REPENTANCE.

BIBLIOGRAPHY. W. Bauder, "Fall, Fall Away," *NIDNTT* 1:606-11; G. C. Berkouwer, *Studies in Dogmatics: Faith and Perseverance* (Grand Rapids: Eerdmans, 1973); M. Eaton, *No Condemnation: A New Theology of Assurance* (Downers Grove, IL: InterVarsity Press, 1997); I. H. Marshall, *Kept by the Power of God* (Minneapolis: Bethany, 1975); idem, "The Problem of Apostasy in New Testament Theology" in *Jesus the Savior: Studies in New Testament Theology* (Downers Grove, IL: InterVarsity Press, 1990) 306-24; H. Schlier, "ἀφίστημι κτλ," *TDNT* 1:512-14.   P. W. Barnett

APOSTLE, APOSTLESHIP

The term *apostle* refers, for the most part, to the Twelve plus Paul (and Barnabas) in the literature covered by this dictionary. The *Didache** and 1-3 John* provide some evidence of itinerants other than these who could be called apostles, some orthodox and some heterodox. The main function of apostles is to preach the gospel* and teach* the Christian community. In some places they are held up as examples of endurance under persecution.* In other places they are regarded as those who, by appointing bishops and deacons, provided for a continuation of their ministry* in the church.* In Hebrews the term *apostle* is applied to Christ.*

1. The Acts of the Apostles
2. Hebrews to Revelation
3. Apostolic Fathers.

1. The Acts of the Apostles.

1.1. The Twelve Apostles. The primary use of the word *apostle* in Acts is to denote the Twelve. In this respect Acts follows the Gospel of Luke, where *apostle* nearly always refers to the twelve disciples whom Jesus called (Lk 6:13, cf. 9:1, 10; 22:14, 30), but following the defection of Judas it is used of the eleven (Lk 24:9-10).

It was to the eleven that Christ gave instructions following his resurrection* (Acts 1:2). It was to their number that another person was added following Christ's ascension* to replace Judas and so reconstitute the Twelve (Acts 1:15-22). Only those who had accompanied the Eleven during the whole time the Lord Jesus was among them (from his baptism to his ascension) were eligible for selection (Acts 1:21-22). The final choice was left to the Lord, to whom prayer* was offered; then lots were cast, resulting in the selection of Matthias (Acts 1:24-26). It is to this reconstituted group of Twelve that the majority of references to apostles apply (Acts 1:26; 2:37, 42, 43; 4:33, 35, 36, 37; 5:2, 12, 18, 29, 40; 6:6; 8:1, 14, 18; 9:27; 11:1). The importance of completing again the full number of the Twelve is probably best understood in the light of Jesus' promise that the Twelve would sit on thrones judging the twelve tribes of Israel* (Lk 22:30). Rengstorf says that "the re-establishment of the apostolate of the Twelve proves that the risen Lord, like the historical Jesus, has not given up his claim to incorporate the twelve tribes of Israel into his kingdom" (Rengstorf 1962, 192).

The ministry of the Twelve consisted essentially of preaching and bearing witness to the resurrection of Christ (Acts 1:22; 4:33), teaching* (Acts 2:42) and prayer (Acts 6:2-4). Their preaching was often accompanied by signs and wonders (Acts 2:43; 5:12; *see* Signs). They felt a special responsibility to continue preaching in Jerusalem,* so they remained there even when many of the believers fled the city because of the persecution (Acts 8:1). They felt a responsibility also for new groups of believers that sprang up as the message of Christ was carried abroad by those who were scattered (Acts 8:4-17; 11:19-26). It was through the laying on of the apostles' hands that the Samaritan believers received the Holy Spirit (Acts 8:14-17; *see* Holy Spirit). In Acts 15—16 the apostles, together with the elders, form the group with whom Paul and Barnabas, being sent by the Antioch* church, discussed the need or otherwise for Gentile* believers to submit to circumcision.*

The Twelve provide an important link between the ministry of Jesus (in Luke's Gospel) and the ministry of the early church (in Acts). When Acts 1:2 speaks of the apostles whom Jesus chose *(exelexato)*, it recalls Luke 6:13, which relates how Jesus called his disciples and chose *(eklexamenos)* twelve of them. The Twelve provided the foundational testimony to the resurrection of Christ (Acts 2:14; 4:33; 5:29-32) and legitimized the Samaritan and Gentile missions* (Acts 8:14; 11:1-18). Having accomplished these purposes, they fade from view in Acts. It is noteworthy that no attempt was made to reconstitute the group of twelve by choosing another replacement when the apostle James was put to death by Herod (Acts 12:1-2). When the Twelve as a group fade from view, the focus of attention in Acts shifts to the parts played by Peter, James (the brother of the Lord, who was not one of the Twelve) and most of all Paul.

1.2. The Origin of the Concept of Twelve Apostles. Luke's Gospel ascribes to Jesus himself the naming of the Twelve as apostles (Lk 6:13). However, this has been regarded by some scholars as an anachronistic application of the term by Luke (so, e.g., Barrett, Campenhausen, Mosbech, Munck, Schmithals), one that he carries over into Acts. A number of alternative explanations for the emergence of the concept of twelve apostles have been suggested.

Schmithals argues that the concept of the Christian apostolate arose with Paul, who was (unconsciously) dependent on gnostic categories for his understanding of what it meant to be an apostle. What Acts says about the Twelve is legend. Following the resurrection appearance of Jesus to Peter, the core group that gathered around him came to be known as the Twelve; they were later given the designation "apostles," but they themselves had no historical connection with Jesus.

Barrett, while insisting that "the Twelve" is not an after-Easter phenomenon read back into the time of Jesus, argues that the use of the term *apostle* in connection with the Twelve is. Barrett points out that within the post-Easter church there were a number of overlapping applications of the word *apostle*. These included the Twelve, the "pillars" of the Jerusalem church, representatives appointed by the Jerusalem church, Paul, subordinate apostles appointed by Paul, and delegates appointed by the churches.

Mosbech argues that the Christian use of *apostle* originated in Antioch, where it was applied to missionaries sent out by congregations. Its narrower application to the Twelve (and then to Paul) arose as a result of Paul's conflict with the Judaizers (*see* Circumcision). Paul's opponents, wanting to deny Paul the right to call himself an apostle, claimed that only those who had accompanied Jesus during his earthly ministry, and been sent out by Jesus, could be called apostles. According to this reconstruction, it was Paul's opponents who first applied the term *apostles* to the Twelve.

Munck argues that originally the Twelve constituted a "college" with its seat in Jerusalem. They were not thought of as itinerant missionaries but were respected as those called by Christ. It was only later, when the battle over the legitimacy of Paul's apostolate for the Gentiles* erupted, that the designation *apostle* was applied to the Twelve and they too came to be regarded as apostles to the Gentiles (Mt 28:18-20). Munck says, "For what has happened is nothing less than that the Church of the Gentiles has taken over the Twelve disciples, sent out by Jesus to Israel, and made them apostles of the Gentiles like Paul" (Munck, 110).

These alternative suggestions all assume that the concept of the apostolate of the Twelve could not have originated with Jesus. However, strong arguments can be advanced in favor of the view that it can be traced back to Jesus (*see DJG,* Apostle). If this is the case (as Lk 6:13 and Mk 3:14 assert that it was), it is unnecessary to seek alternative explanations.

1.3. The Apostleship of Peter. The activities of Peter dominate the first twelve chapters of Acts (as the activities of Paul dominate the last sixteen). Peter takes the leading role in the church in Jerusalem in the earliest years. He takes the initiative in seeking a replacement for Judas Iscariot (Acts 1:15-26). Peter is the main spokesperson: he speaks on behalf of the Twelve on the Day of Pentecost* (Acts 2:14-40), addresses the crowd following the healing* of the lame beggar (Acts 3:11-26), replies on behalf of himself and John when called to account by the Jewish leaders (Act 4:5-22), and replies on behalf of the Twelve when they are interrogated by the Sanhedrin (Acts 5:27-32). He deals with the deception of Ananias and Sapphira (Acts 5:1-10) and the wickedness of Simon the sorcerer (Acts 8:18-24). Peter features in nearly all the healing stories of the first twelve chapters (Acts 3:1-10; 5:15; 9:32-43). He is involved in the expansion of the church into Samaria (Acts 8:14-25) and the conversion of the Gentile God-fearer Cornelius* (Acts 10:1-48). Peter also defends the inclusion of Gentiles among the people of God without circumcision in respect of both Cornelius (Acts 11:1-18) and those converted through Paul's missionary work (Acts 15:7-11).

One thing that emerges from all this is that Peter's apostolate was no more restricted solely to Jews than Paul's was to Gentiles. While Peter's main area of responsibility was to the circumcision (cf. Gal 2:7-9), he was also involved to a certain extent in the Gentile mission. This is consistent with what we find in 1 Peter (see 2.2 below) and with hints about Peter's ministry among Gentiles found in Paul's letters (cf. 1 Cor 1:12; 3:22; 9:5; Gal 2:11, 14).

1.4. The Joint Ministry of Barnabas and Paul. Paul and Barnabas were not included among the Twelve, nor were they eligible to be included, not having accompanied the Eleven from the time of Jesus' baptism to his ascension. The first hint of some special ministry for Barnabas is found in Acts 11:22, where he is sent by the Jerusalem apostles to Antioch in response to news of a great turning to the Lord among Greeks there. Barnabas and Paul were later sent as emissaries of the church in Antioch bearing gifts to the saints in Jerusalem (Acts 11:27-30).

In Acts 13:1-3 the prophets* and teachers* in the church at Antioch were directed by the Holy Spirit to set apart Barnabas and Paul for the work to which he had called them. The prophets and teachers released them for this ministry (Acts 13:3), and being sent out by the Holy Spirit, Barnabas and Paul made their way to Cyprus (Acts 13:4-12). In Acts it is only after being set apart for missionary work that Barnabas and Paul are referred to as apostles (Acts 14:4, 14).

It is worth noting that the sending agent in this context is not the church, as is often assumed, but the Holy Spirit. He directs the prophets and teachers to set apart *(aphorisate)* Barnabas and Paul to the work to which he had called them (Acts 13:2). The prophets and teachers lay their hands on Barnabas and Paul, pray for them and then release *(apelysan)* them (Acts 13:3). Being sent out *(ekpemphthentes)* by

the Holy Spirit, Barnabas and Paul then make their way to Cyprus (13:4). It was the Holy Spirit who called Barnabas and Paul, it was the Holy Spirit who directed the prophets and teachers to set them apart, and it was the Holy Spirit who sent them out. The role of the prophets and teachers was to pray for them and to release them.

The mission that Barnabas and Paul carried out was initially one of proclaiming the Word of God among Jews in the synagogues* of Cyprus (Acts 13:4-5). It was widened to include Gentiles when Barnabas and Paul were sent for by the proconsul in Paphos, who also wanted to hear the Word of God (Acts 13:6-12). However, when their message was later rejected by many of the Jews in Pisidian Antioch, they deliberately turned to the Gentiles, believing they had been commanded by God to do so (Acts 13:46-47). This decision was confirmed by God when he enabled them to perform signs* and wonders (Acts 13:8-12; 14:1-3, 8-10).

1.5. The Apostleship of Paul. In Acts 13:2 the Holy Spirit directs the prophets and teachers to set aside Barnabas and Paul for the work to which he had called them. Paul's calling predates this and may be traced back to his encounter with the risen Christ on the Damascus road (Acts 9:3-6; 22:6-11; 26:12-18). It was on this occasion, and through Ananias, that Paul was initially given details of his commission (Acts 9:10-19; 22:12-16). He was to make known what he had seen and heard to all peoples—to the Gentiles and their kings and to the people of Israel—so that they might repent and turn to God (Acts 9:15; 22:14-15, 21; 26:16-20). The comprehensive nature of this commission (involving preaching to both Gentiles and the people of Israel) is reflected in the accounts of Paul's missionary work in Acts. In town after town he preached first in the Jewish synagogue and afterward to the Gentiles. Acts indicates that it was Paul's practice to appoint elders in the churches that he founded (Acts 14:23, cf. 20:17).

Sometimes this presentation of Paul's missionary work is rejected as an invention of the writer of Acts. It is rejected because of Paul's own statements in Galatians 2:6-9 (that he was commissioned as the apostle to Gentiles and Peter as the apostle to the Jews). While this certainly represents the broad distinction between the apostolic ministries of Paul and Peter, it should not be read in such a way as to mean that Peter had no ministry to Gentiles or that Paul had none to Jews. That Paul ministered among Jews as well as Gentiles is confirmed by his own account of his persecutions at the hands of the Jews (2 Cor 11:24, 26) which were occasioned in part by his refusal to preach circumcision (Gal 5:11).

1.6. Apostles and the Spirit in Acts. Probably the most outstanding feature of apostleship as it is portrayed in Acts is the involvement of the Holy Spirit in apostolic ministry. The risen Jesus promised the apostles that they would receive power* and be his witnesses when the Holy Spirit came upon them (Acts 1:5, 8). Having been filled with the Spirit on the Day of Pentecost, they proceeded to give their witness to the resurrection (Acts 2:4; 4:8; 5:32). It was through the laying on of the apostles' hands that Samaritan believers received the Holy Spirit (Acts 8:14-17). When Paul was called and commissioned to be an apostle, he too was filled with the Holy Spirit (Acts 9:17). It was the Holy Spirit who prepared Peter to preach the gospel to the Gentile God-fearer Cornelius, and it was through Peter's ministry that Cornelius's household* received the Spirit (Acts 10:19, 44-48; 11:12-17).

Barnabas, who (along with Paul) is described as an apostle in Acts 14:4, 14, is described as a good man who was full of the Holy Spirit (Acts 11:24). It was the Holy Spirit who told the prophets and teachers at Antioch to set apart Paul and Barnabas for the missionary work to which he had called them, and who sent them out on what was to be Paul's first missionary journey (Acts 13:1-4). On Paul's second missionary journey, the Holy Spirit prevented him and his companions from undertaking work in the regions of Asia and Bithynia (Acts 16:6-7), so that they would cross over into Macedonia following Paul's vision in Troas (Acts 16:8-10). The Spirit came upon the Ephesian believers when Paul laid his hands on them (Acts 19:6). Finally, it was the compulsion of the Holy Spirit that led Paul to continue on his way to Jerusalem, despite dire warnings of what awaited him there (Acts 20:22-23).

In Acts it is the Holy Spirit who impels the apostles into ever-widening circles of ministry and who provides authentication for the Gentile mission. The promise and bestowal of the Holy Spirit by Christ constitutes an important link between the ministry of the historical Jesus and that of the apostles.

2. Hebrews to Revelation.

2.1. Hebrews. There is in Hebrews* only one reference to apostleship, and this is related to the commission given by God to Christ himself. The readers are urged to consider Jesus, the apostle and high priest* of their confession, who was faithful to the One who appointed him (Heb 3:1-6). This forms the basis for an exhortation to the readers to be faithful as Jesus was and not to repeat the faithlessness of the exodus generation (Heb 3:7—4:11). In the context of Hebrews, Jesus' role (which reflects the nature of his apostleship) includes proclaiming the Word of God and enduring suffering* and death* so that he might become both high priest on behalf of God's people and the atoning sacrifice* for their sins,* in order that through his ministry God's children might be brought to glory.*

2.2. 1 Peter. In 1 Peter* the author introduces himself as an apostle of Jesus Christ and addresses his readers as exiles of the Dispersion in Pontus, Galatia, Cappadocia, Asia and Bithynia (1 Pet 1:1). On first reading this would appear to be in line with the view that Peter restricted himself to a ministry among Jews (in this case his ministry among Jews of the Diaspora*). We have already seen that Acts depicts Peter working among Gentiles (as well as Jews), and a close reading of 1 Peter discloses the same thing. In fact, 1 Peter itself is written to Gentiles. The preconversion period of the lives of the readers is described as a time when they did "what the Gentiles like to do, living in licentiousness, passions, drunkenness, revels, carousing, and lawless idolatry" (1 Pet 4:3-4). The readers were clearly Gentiles, and therefore Peter's address to them as "exiles of the Dispersion" is metaphorical. It refers to their status as Christian aliens and exiles in a hostile world.

2.3. 2 Peter and Jude. In 2 Peter* the author introduces himself as an apostle of Jesus Christ (2 Pet 1:1). He exhorts his readers to remember the command of the Lord and Savior spoken in advance through the holy prophets and "your" apostles (2 Pet 3:2), and warns them about those who twist the teaching of Paul's letters to their own destruction, as they do other Scriptures (2 Pet 3:15-16). In the epistle of Jude* the readers are exhorted to remember the words spoken beforehand (about the last days) by the apostles of the Lord Jesus Christ (Jude 17). In these two epistles, then, the function of the apostles that is stressed is teaching, and in particular handing on the teaching of Jesus. The mention of "your" apostles in 2 Peter 3:2 would seem to refer not to the Twelve but to those missionaries through whom the readers first heard the gospel,* presumably including the apostle Paul (cf. 2 Pet 3:15-16).

2.4. 1-3 John. In 3 John the Elder commends Gaius for providing hospitality* for itinerant preachers who were traveling about "for the sake of the name," and urges him to continue doing so (3 Jn 5-8). On the other hand he criticizes a certain Diotrephes, apparently a leading figure in the Christian community in the town where Gaius lived, because he refused to provide them with hospitality (3 Jn 9-10). In 2 John the Elder warns the "Elect Lady" concerning certain deceivers who have gone out into the world—people who deny that Jesus Christ has come in the flesh.* He urges the "Elect Lady" not to provide such itinerants with hospitality, for that would be to participate in their evil deeds (2 Jn 7-11). In 1 John the author warns his readers about certain people who had seceded from his community and were traveling about propagating false teaching concerning the person of Christ, and so leading people astray (1 Jn 2:18-19, 22-23, 26).

While the letters of 1-3 John do not use the word *apostle,* they do reflect the fact that toward the end of the first century itinerant preachers, some orthodox and some heretical, were moving around among the churches, at least in the area in which these letters were written. These people could not command the recognition enjoyed by either the Twelve or Paul, and congregations had to exercise discernment before providing them with hospitality and so supporting their work. (A similar situation is reflected in the *Didache.*) 1 John provides ethical* and doctrinal criteria by which the readers should test the claims of itinerant preachers (*see* John, Letters of).

2.5. Revelation. The book of Revelation* makes reference to those who claim to be apostles but are not (Rev 2:2), and to true apostles who are urged to join with saints and prophets in rejoicing over the downfall of "Babylon"* (Rev 18:2). It also speaks of the names of the twelve apostles being written on the twelve foun-

dations of the wall of the heavenly Jerusalem,* a symbol of the church (Rev 21:9-14). From this last reference it may be inferred that the author of Revelation believed that the ministry of the twelve apostles was fundamental to the building of the church. Their preaching of the gospel laid the church's foundation.

3. Apostolic Fathers.

3.1. The Epistle of Barnabas. Possibly written between A.D. 70 and 79, the *Epistle of Barnabas,* * in the one place where it mentions apostles, says that when Christ "chose out his own apostles who were to preach his gospel, he chose those who were iniquitous above all sin to show that 'he came not to call the righteous but sinners' " (*Barn.* 5.9). From this it may be inferred that Barnabas knew of apostles chosen by Christ (i.e., the Twelve), and that their essential role was to proclaim the gospel. The reference to "his own apostles" perhaps reflects that Barnabas knew of other apostles beside the Twelve.

3.2. The Epistle of St. Clement to the Corinthians. Generally agreed to have been written around A.D. 95, this letter contains several references to apostles (*see* Clement). The apostles Peter and Paul are held up as examples of patient endurance in the midst of persecution (*1 Clem.* 5.2-7). The apostles are said to have been sent from Christ, as Christ himself was sent from God. They received the gospel from Christ and preached it everywhere, and from among their first converts they appointed bishops and deacons (*1 Clem.* 42.1-5). The apostles of Christ are attributed with foreknowledge concerning the controversy that would later surround the office of bishop (*see* Church Order, Government). For this reason they not only appointed bishops but also provided for the continuance of their office. Those appointed by the apostles were to appoint other approved men to succeed to their ministry (*1 Clem.* 44.1-2), men of repute who were to be appointed with the consent of the whole church (*1 Clem.* 44.3).

3.3. The Didache. As noted above, the *Didache* * reflects a situation similar to that in 1-3 John, a situation in which many itinerant preachers, both orthodox and heretical, were seeking to influence Christian congregations. The *Didache,* written in the late first or early second century, provides very practical criteria by which people may distinguish between true and false traveling apostles (and prophets):

And concerning the Apostles and Prophets, act thus according to the ordinance of the Gospel. Let every Apostle who comes to you be received as the Lord, but let him not stay more than one day, or if need be a second as well; but if he stay three days, he is a false prophet. And when an Apostle goes forth let him accept nothing but bread till he reach his night's lodging; but if he ask for money, he is a false prophet (*Did.* 11.3-6).

A number of matters worthy of note emerge from this statement. First, true apostles were held in high esteem. They were to "be received as the Lord." This reflects the *shaliach* background to the notion of the apostle, according to which the one sent is as the one who sent him (*see DJG*, Apostle). Second, the readers were expected to act in accordance with the teaching of Jesus: they were to offer hospitality to the apostles who ministered to them. Third, this gospel ordinance had been abused by those who were not true apostles, so that the *Didache* provides guidelines for distinguishing true apostles from false apostles. Fourth, the fact that at the end of the first or the beginning of the second century the author can still speak of itinerant apostles shows that the term *apostle* was being used to denote a group much wider than the Twelve and Paul and his colleagues. The apostles in the *Didache* seem scarcely to be distinguished from traveling prophets* (an *apostle* who asks for money is a false *prophet*).

3.4. The Epistles of Ignatius. In letters written early in the second century, Ignatius* makes several references to apostles, among whom he includes Paul (Ign. *Rom.* 4.3). When referring to the apostles, he appears to be looking back to a past era (Ign. *Magn.* 13.1-2). He distinguishes himself from the apostles by disclaiming the sort of authority they bore (Ign. *Rom.* 4.3; Ign. *Trall.* 3.3). By far his most frequent references to the apostles are those that compare God and the apostles on the one hand to the bishop and the presbyters on the other. He does this to enhance the authority of bishops and presbyters in the eyes of church members (Ign. *Magn.* 6.1; 7.1; 13.1-2; Ign. *Phld.* 5.1; Ign. *Smyrn.* 8.1; Ign. *Trall.* 2.2; 3.1; 7.1). Ignatius makes a number of allusions to the function of the apostles: they gave directions that must be heeded (Ign. *Rom.* 4.3; Ign. *Smyrn.* 8.1; Ign. *Magn.* 13.1; Ign. *Trall.* 7.1); they provided an example to

follow, so that to be of one mind with the apostles (Ign. *Eph.* 11.2) and to follow in their footsteps (Ign. *Eph.* 12.2) is praiseworthy; and they presided over the church, a role taken over later by the presbyters (Ign. *Magn.* 6.1).

3.5. The Epistle of Polycarp to the Philippians. From this letter, written in the early part of the second century, it seems that for Polycarp* Paul was the most illustrious of the apostles. Polycarp speaks of him as "the blessed and glorious Paul" (Pol. *Phil.* 3.2) and describes the apostolic group as "Paul himself, and . . . the other apostles" (Pol. *Phil.* 9.1). The function of the apostles was to preach the gospel (Pol. *Phil.* 6.3). From the study of Paul's letters people can build themselves up in the faith (Pol. *Phil.* 3.2). The apostles also provided examples of the way in which believers should be obedient to the "word of righteousness" (Pol. *Phil.* 9.1), a term used to refer to teaching about enduring persecution and martyrdom.*

3.6. 2 Clement. This homily, written by an unknown author and generally known as *2 Clement*, is dated to around A.D. 120-40. It contains but one relevant reference, in which the teaching of the apostles is appealed to as an authoritative guide about the nature of the church (*2 Clem.* 14.2).

3.7. The Shepherd of Hermas. This document, written possibly about A.D. 140-45, consists of preliminary visions seen by Hermas* and mandates and similitudes conveyed to Hermas by a glorious figure in the garb of a shepherd.* It is in the third vision and the ninth similitude that references to apostles are found.

In the third vision Hermas sees a tower, which represents the church, being built with stones squared and white, representing the apostles, bishops, teachers and deacons (*Herm. Vis.* 3.5.1). In the ninth similitude forty stones are identified as "apostles and teachers of the preaching of the Son of God" (*Herm. Sim.* 9.15.4). The apostles are described as those who preached to the twelve nations who inhabit the whole world (*Herm. Sim.* 9.17.1; 9.25.2). The apostles and teachers, having fallen asleep themselves, are said to have preached to them that had fallen asleep before them (*Herm. Sim.* 9.16.5). In this document, then, it is the preaching of the gospel that is seen as the main function of the apostles, whether that be thought of in terms of preaching to all the inhabitants of the world during their lifetime or to the dead when the apostles themselves joined their ranks.

In light of all of the above, it may be said in very general terms that within the NT literature under consideration, the emphasis falls upon the function of apostles as witnesses of the resurrection and preachers of the gospel of Jesus Christ. In one place the Twelve are portrayed as the foundations upon which the church is built and in another as the authoritative transmitters of the tradition. In the writings of the apostolic fathers the emphasis upon apostles as preachers is also found, but this is supplemented variously by emphases upon their role as examples in the matter of godly living and perseverance in face of persecution, upon ways in which true and false apostles/prophets may be distinguished, and upon the apostles' role in appointing bishops and presbyters in the church, all of which reflect the concerns of the post-apostolic church.

See also ACTS OF THE APOSTLES; APOSTOLIC FATHERS; AUTHORITY; CHURCH ORDER, GOVERNMENT; MISSION, EARLY NON-PAULINE.

BIBLIOGRAPHY. C. K. Barrett, *The Signs of an Apostle* (London: Epworth, 1970); S. Brown, "Apostleship in the New Testament as an Historical and Theological Problem," *NTS* 30 (1984) 474-80; H. von Campenhausen, "Der urchristliche Apostelbegriff," *ST* 1 (1948) 96-130; A. C. Clark, "Apostleship: Evidence from the New Testament and Early Christian Literature," *VoxEv* 19 (1989) 49-82; idem, "The Role of the Apostles" in *The Book of Acts and Its Theology,* ed. I. H. Marshall and D. Peterson (BAFCS 6; Grand Rapids: Eerdmans; Carlisle: Paternoster, forthcoming); K. Giles, "Apostles Before and After Paul," *Churchman* 99 (1985) 241-56; J. A. Kirk, "Apostleship Since Rengstorf: Towards a Synthesis," *NTS* 21 (1975) 249-64; C. G. Kruse, *New Testament Foundations for Ministry* (London: Marshall, Morgan & Scott, 1983); M. Lohmeyer, *Der Apostelbegriff im Neuen Testament: Eine Untersuchung auf dem Hintergrund der synoptischen Aussendungsreden* (Stuttgart: Katholisches Bibelwerk, 1995); H. Mosbech, "*Apostolos* in the New Testament," *ST* 2 (1948) 166-200; J. Munck, "Paul, the Apostles and the Twelve," *ST* 3 (1950-51) 96-110; V. C. Pfitzner, " 'Pneumatic' Apostleship? Apostle and Spirit in the Acts of the Apostles" in *Wort in der Zeit: Neutestamentliche Studien,* FS K. H. Rengstorf, ed. W. Haubeck, M. Bachmann (Leiden: E. J. Brill, 1980) 210-35; K. H. Rengstorf, "ἀπόστολος," *TDNT* 1:398-447; idem, "The Election of Matthias: Acts 1.15 ff." in *Current Issues in New Testament Interpretation: Essays in Honor of Otto A. Piper,* ed. W. Klassen, G. F. Snyder (London: SCM, 1962) 178-92; B. Rigaux, "Die 'Zwölf' in Geschichte und Kerygma" in *Das kirchliche Amt im Neuen Testament,* ed. K. Kertelge (Darmstadt: Wissenschaftliche Buchgesellschaft, 1977) 279-304; W. Schmithals, *The Office of Apostle in the Early Church* (London: SPCK, 1971); C. Zettner, *Amt, Gemeinde und kirchliche Einheit in der Apostelgeschichte des Lukas* (Frankfurt am Main: Peter Lang, 1991).   C. G. Kruse

APOSTLE'S CREED. *See* CREEDS, CONFESSIONAL FORMS.

APOSTOLIC FATHERS

The apostolic fathers is a somewhat arbitrary group of Christian writings that follows immediately upon the NT writings, spanning approximately fifty years, beginning with Clement* of Rome (A.D. 96) up until the middle of the second century. These writings are to be distinguished from the NT Apocrypha* in two important regards: they are rooted in actual historical situations of the church and they are generally orthodox, rather than gnostic,* in doctrine.

1. The Name "Apostolic Fathers"
2. The Study of the Apostolic Fathers
3. The Literary Genre of the Apostolic Fathers
4. The Life Setting of Early Second-Century Christianity
5. The Canon in the Apostolic Fathers
6. The Theology of the Apostolic Fathers
7. The Significance of the Apostolic Fathers

1. The Name "Apostolic Fathers."

The name "apostolical fathers" has been traced back as early as 1693, to William Wake, who published in London a translation of the epistles of Barnabas,* Clement,* Ignatius* and Polycarp,* as well as the *Shepherd of Hermas** and the Martyrdoms of Ignatius and Polycarp. R. M. Grant notes that the equivalent term was used by Severus of Antioch in the sixth century. In the "Preliminary Discourse" to his volume, Wake described these writings as coming from "the contemporaries of the Holy Apostles; some of them bred up under our Saviour Christ himself, and the rest instructed by those great men whom he commissioned to go forth and preach to all the world." Consequently, Wake continues "we cannot doubt but that what they deliver to us, must be, without controverse, the pure doctrine of the Gospel; what Christ and the Apostles taught, and what they had themselves received from their own mouths" (quoted from de Jonge, 505).

The name soon became the commonly used one from the late seventeenth century onwards. As can be seen from Wake's comment, the word "apostolic" was not meant to imply that these writers possessed the authority* of the apostles, but rather that their writings perpetuate apostolic doctrine. The idea that they were contemporaries of the apostles, however, or that any of them had been directly instructed by Jesus or the apostles is improbable, although Polycarp is reputed to have been a disciple of John (Irenaeus *Adv. Haer.* 3.3.4; cf. Eusebius *Hist. Eccl.* 3.36.1; 5.20.6).

It has always been a question as to what writings belong in the category of the apostolic fathers. The authors in Wake's volume, namely Barnabas, Clement of Rome, Ignatius, Polycarp and Hermas, have held a place in the group from the earliest time. Even this grouping, however, is not without its problems. Barnabas is really pseudo-Barnabas, that is, not the companion of Paul; only the first of the two letters of Clement is authentic, *2 Clement** being a document from the mid-second century; and the letters of Ignatius come down to us in no less than three recensions, one of which has thirteen letters, one seven (now regarded in unabridged form as the authentic corpus) and the third three. Also included in the earliest collections is the *Martyrdom of Polycarp,** in the form of a letter written to the church of Philomelium from the church of Smyrna. (The other martyrdom in Wake's collection, that of Ignatius, is late and spurious.)

By late in the eighteenth century it became customary to include the fragments of Papias (drawn from Ireneaus [*Adv. Haer.* v. 33-45] and Eusebius [*Hist. Eccl.* 3.39]), the *Epistle to Diognetus** (probably rather later than the apostolic fathers, and in content more readily classifiable among the apologists), and in the twentieth century even the fragment of Quadratus (again drawn from Eusebius [*Hist. Eccl.* 4.3.2], and again an apologist).

The latest universally accepted addition to the corpus of apostolic fathers was the *Didache.**

Although this work seems to have been referred to by early Christian writers (Eusebius *Hist. Eccl.* 3.25.4; Athanasius *Ep. Fest.* 39), the document itself was first published in 1883, having been discovered in 1875 (see 2.3 below). Although it cannot have come from the twelve apostles, as the proem alleges, it is nevertheless an early document and it immediately became a part of the corpus of the apostolic fathers.

2. The Study of the Apostolic Fathers.

The early use of the apostolic fathers has been examined by R. M. Grant. He shows the relatively constant popularity of Ignatius and Clement of Rome through the first thousand years, and the general neglect of the other writings.

2.1. Seventeenth-Century British Studies. While there was considerable attention given in continental Europe to the apostolic fathers during the Reformation period, in Britain the apostolic fathers were virtually unknown until the publication of Codex Alexandrinus in the 1630s by Patrick Young, the librarian of Charles I. At the end of this manuscript were the letters known as *1* and *2 Clement* (the latter only partially). A decade later (1644) James Ussher published a thirteenth-century Latin translation of the seven-letter corpus of Ignatius which he had discovered in the library of Gaius College, Cambridge. This he carefully compared with earlier interpolated editions of Ignatius' letters. Ussher had also been at work on *Barnabas,* but his manuscript was destroyed in a fire at Oxford. These publications stirred up a new interest in the apostolic fathers, and Grant can conclude of this seventeenth-century British work that it "produced a genuine revolution in patristic studies and for the first time made possible a valid historical and theological picture of earliest Christianity outside the New Testament" (Grant 1967, 5).

2.2. Nineteenth-Century Controversy. The apostolic fathers assumed great importance in the modern period when F. C. Baur made his reconstruction of early Christianity dependent largely upon the late (i.e., mid-second century) dating of *1 Clement* and the Ignatian Epistles. Since these documents display none of the conflict between Jewish (*see* Jewish Christianity) and Gentile Christianity that Baur posited prior to the middle of the second century, they could not be genuine, that is, from the end of the first and early in the second century. Thus Baur concluded that the Ignatian letters had been forged in Rome* and that *1 Clement* was not by Clement, bishop of Rome (an invented person according to Baur), but by the Clement of Philippians 4:3 who was located in the eastern part of the empire.

Not long after Baur, however, Th. Zahn and J. B. Lightfoot demonstrated beyond question the authenticity of the seven Ignatian letters. Lightfoot's vindication of *1 Clement* as coming from the Roman church of the nineties remains relatively unchallenged. This more responsible dating of the letters of Ignatius and Clement overturned Baur's hypothesis in a definitive manner.

2.3. Discovery of the Didache. Toward the end of the nineteenth century a most astonishing discovery again brought new excitement to the study of the apostolic fathers. In a Greek manuscript (Codex Constantinopolitanus), dated exactly at 1056, Philotheos Bryennios found in addition to *1* and *2 Clement, Barnabas* and the interpolated Ignatian epistles, a document entitled the *Didache* ("Teaching") *of the Twelve Apostles.* Bryennios published the manuscript in 1885. Grant likens the excitement first caused by this event to that caused by the discovery of the Dead Sea Scrolls in the twentieth century.

3. The Literary Genre of the Apostolic Fathers.
It is no surprise that a corpus of writings as diverse in origin as the apostolic fathers should also reveal a variety of literary types. It is in fact possible to speak of no fewer than seven representative genres among these writings.

3.1. Epistle. The largest number of writings are true epistles (*see* Letters): *1 Clement,* the seven epistles of Ignatius (six to churches [Ephesus; Magnesia; Tralles; Rome; Philadelphia; Smyrna], one to an individual [Polycarp]); and Polycarp to the Philippians. *1 Clement,* to be sure, has somewhat the character of a treatise, because of its length and content, but it is an authentic letter from the church at Rome to the church at Corinth. *Barnabas,* on the other hand, while ending like an epistle, is more of a treatise. Both *1 Clement* and *Barnabas* are anonymous documents.

3.2. Homily. The so-called *Second Epistle of Clement* is neither by Clement nor a letter, but in reality a homily (cf. *2 Clem.* 17.3; 19.1). The final two chapters of the *Epistle to Diognetus* (see 3.5 below) also qualify for inclusion here since they form an independent homily.

3.3. Apocalypse. Although apocalyptic in genre, the *Shepherd of Hermas* is unlike other apocalypses known to us (*see* Apocalyptic). Its division into the three major parts, *Visions, Mandates* and *Similitudes* (Parables), points to its uniqueness. In addition to the clear apocalyptic* elements (i.e., those focusing on divine revelation of truth concerning the world to come), Hermas is presented in the framework of a captivating story filled with allegorical elements and practical applications. The *Mandates* become in effect like instructions of a church manual, similar to the genre of the Didache.

3.4. Church Manual. Quite distinctive among the apostolic fathers is the *Didache* ("*Teaching*") *of the Twelve Apostles.* This document was apparently a catechetical manual, perhaps used in connection with candidates for baptism* (*Did.* 7.1-4). A host of practical injunctions are given in this handbook addressed to the Gentiles (according to the proem).

3.5. Treatise. The pseudonymous *Barnabas* belongs here. Barnabas presents a comparison and contrast between Judaism and Christianity in which it is argued, often by means of allegorical exegesis (e.g., *Barn.* 9.7-9), that the latter is the fulfillment and, indeed, displacement of the former (*Barn.* 4.7). The length of *1 Clement* together with much of its content also gives it a treatise-like character.

3.6. Apology. The so-called *Epistle to Diognetus* is in fact a defense of the truth of Christianity against other religions. The final two chapters, however, appear to be a separate homily. The fragment of Quadratus, if included among the apostolic fathers, is to be classified here.

3.7. Martyrdom. The account of the *Martyrdom of Polycarp* is the oldest example of a genre that would become popular in the church. The martyrdom of Ignatius, so prominent an expectation in Ignatius's letters, does not exist as a separate document but is recorded in Eusebius (*Hist. Eccl.* 3.36).

4. The Life Setting of Early Second-Century Christianity.
It is no easier to reconstruct the life setting of the documents immediately following the NT than it is for many of the NT writings themselves. Here too one must do so mainly from the individual writings themselves, and thus there is the danger of a certain circularity in argument.

Clearly the two main backgrounds of the apostolic fathers are Judaism and Hellenism (in this regard *1 Clement* is a perfect example of the combination of both in one author). Because, however, of the importance of Hellenistic Judaism in the Roman world—and hence of Hellenistic-Jewish Christianity—the lines between the two are often necessarily blurred (*see* Hellenists).

4.1. The Jewish Milieu. At the end of the first century and into the first half of the second, the Christianity we encounter in the apostolic fathers often has a remarkably Jewish cast. This can be seen in several ways. Of very great importance is the dependence upon Jewish writings, canonical and extracanonical. The extent of the quotation from the OT and the Apocrypha and Pseudepigrapha is impressive (see 5 below; *see* Noncanonical Writings, Citations of). Beyond that are the allusions (cf. *1 Clem.* 9—12; 45) and the frequent Jewish imagery of these writings (e.g., *1 Clem.* 64; Ign. *Trall.* 7.2; *Barn.* 6—8). The influence of Jewish liturgy is also occasionally evident (e.g., *1 Clem.* 40; and the great prayer of *1 Clem.* 59.3—61.3). Furthermore, the ethical exhortation we encounter here is frequently Jewish in character (cf. the "two ways" pattern in *Did.* 1—6; and *Barn.* 18—20). The apocalyptic cast of *Hermas* reflects a Jewish background.

Even those documents that clearly reveal a polemic against Judaism may well reflect the background of a Jewish Christianity* (*see* Jewish Christianity) attempting to establish itself over against non-Christian Judaism. Thus Ignatius and *Barnabas* (cf. *Barn.* 2), generally related to a Gentile Christianity, may nevertheless point to the context of a Jewish Christianity (*pace* Grant).

4.2. The Hellenistic World. The Christianity of the apostolic fathers was lived in a thoroughly Hellenized Roman world. These writers all wrote in Greek, but in addition many of them reveal a significant dependence upon Greek thought. They can on occasion appeal to Hellenistic virtues and perspectives, Hellenistic philosophy, and to ethics that resemble the best in Hellenism (e.g., Stoicism). Clement of Rome uses Hellenistic motifs frequently, as for example in the comparison of the church* with the Roman army in *1 Clement* 37.1-3, in the reference to the peace* and harmony of the universe in *1 Clement* 20.1-4, and in his famous reference to the phoenix bird as a proof of the resurrection* from the dead in *1 Clement* 25.1—26.1. He

can furthermore appeal to "examples from the Gentiles" in his exhortation to the Corinthians (*1 Clem.* 55.1-3) and make use of numerous Stoic metaphors (e.g., peace and concord; voluntary exile). Ignatius employed Hellenistic rhetoric* in his use of medical, musical, nautical and athletic images (see Ign. *Eph.* 4.1-2; 7.2; 10.2 and Ign. *Pol.* 1.3; 2.1-3; 3.1). *2 Clement's* use of the imagery of the athletic games in *2 Clement* 7.1-5 reflects a similar background. Hellenistic influence upon *Hermas*, on the other hand, is only encountered at a relatively superficial level (see Grant 1964, 106).

4.3. Polemical Contexts. While it is relatively infrequently that we find polemic against the pagan religion of their environment (cf. *Diogn.* 2), it is evident that a number of the apostolic fathers had to confront an incipient gnosticism* of growing importance. When Ignatius uses gnostic-laden language, he is indirectly polemicizing against them (e.g., Ign. *Trall.* 5.2). When he stresses the humanity of Christ and argues against docetism's view that Christ only seemed to suffer, he probably has gnostics in view (Ign. *Trall.* 10; cf. 9.1; Ign. *Smyrn.* 2—3; 5.2). Similarly, Polycarp's antidocetic (*see* Docetism) polemic in *Philippians* 7.1 is apparently directed against the gnostics. The author of *2 Clement* seems to provide an anti-gnostic interpretation of a passage from the gnostically tinged *Gospel of the Egyptians* (*2 Clem.* 12.2). Hermas too probably opposes gnostics in *Similitudes* 5.7.2 and 9.22, arguing against those who falsely claim knowledge.

5. The Canon in the Apostolic Fathers.

Because the apostolic fathers quote frequently from the OT and also from the NT writings, they are particularly important witnesses to the state of formation of both canons up to the middle of the second century.

5.1. Old Testament and Other Jewish Writings. Although the Jews decisively closed the canon of their scriptures toward the end of the first century at Yavneh, the Christian church did not conform its "Old" Testament to that decision until the late fourth and early fifth centuries. Before that time the church continued to use a larger collection of writings than it eventually took up into its OT canon.

Among the apostolic fathers, *Barnabas* and *1 Clement* quote the OT far more often than the others. *Barnabas* has nearly a hundred quotations prefaced by introductory formulae. *1 Clement* quotes the OT frequently (approximately seventy times) and at greater length than any other apostolic father or any NT writer (e.g., the whole of Is 53 is found in *1 Clem.* 16; nearly the whole of Ps 51 in *1 Clem.* 18). The only other apostolic father who quotes the OT substantially is *2 Clement* (approximately fifteen times). The others have only a few quotations or allusions, and Hermas, the longest of the apostolic fathers by far, has no OT quotations (*see* Old Testament in apostolic fathers).

The presence of quotations from the Apocrypha and Pseudepigrapha, given with introductory formulae, in the apostolic fathers points to the fact of an OT canon not yet closed. The situation is not different from that obtaining within the NT itself, where, for example, *1 Enoch* is quoted in Jude 14-15 and unknown writings are probably or possibly quoted in James 4:5, Luke 11:49, John 7:38 and 1 Corinthians 2:9 (*see* Noncanonical Citations). *Barnabas* cites *1 Enoch* with introductory formulae in *Barnabas* 4.3 and 16.5. *1 Clement* alludes to *Judith* (*1 Clem.* 55.4-5), quotes from Wisdom (*1 Clem.* 3.4; 27.5) and from such diverse writings as (probably) *Eldad and Modad* (23.3-4), *Apocryphal Ezekiel* (*1 Clem.* 8.3; 29.3), *Assumption of Moses* (*1 Clem.* 17.6) and one quite unknown writing (*1 Clem.* 46.2). *2 Clement* quotes possibly from *Eldad and Modad* (*2 Clem.* 11.2). *Hermas* explicitly cites *Eldad and Modad* (*Herm. Vis.* 2.3.4). Early second-century Christianity thus freely made use of a larger collection of Jewish writings than would be the case later (*see* Canon).

5.2. Gospels. The apostolic fathers do not cite (i.e., with introductory formulae) the NT writings with anything like the frequency of the OT and other Jewish writings just examined, but a number of clear allusions do exist. In the earliest of the apostolic fathers, it is the oral tradition underlying or parallel to the Synoptic Gospels, rather than those writings themselves, that is cited (hence by memory; *see* Jesus Traditions). This appears to be the case in *1 Clement* 13.2 and 46.8, as probably also such instances as Ignatius *Smyrnaeans* 3.2 and Ignatius *Polycarp* 2.2; Polycarp *Philippians* 2.3, 7.2; *Didache* 9.5; 8.1; 1.2; etc.; *Barnabas* 4.14 (despite the introductory formula); 5.9; and Hermas *Similitudes* 9.20.2; 9.29.1-3; 5.6.4; *Mandates* 9.8; 4.1.1; 4.1.6; *Visions* 4.2.6. *2 Clement*, on the other hand, probably reflects knowledge of the written Gospels, but the author does not cite the texts exactly (cf. *2 Clem.* 2.4; 8.5; 9.11; 6.1-2; 5.2-4—all of which have introductory formulae), making the final determination of source very difficult.

5.3. Pauline Epistles. Since the contents of the Pauline epistles were not handed on by oral tradition, the allusions we encounter in the apostolic fathers must point at least indirectly to the actual documents themselves, which apparently were nevertheless often quoted from memory. The pattern and frequency of quotation is such that we may conclude that the apostolic fathers, even as early as Clement of Rome, probably made use of a collection of Paul's letters, perhaps already in codex form. Thus *1 Clement* evinces a probable knowledge of the following Pauline letters: Romans, 1 Corinthians, Galatians, Ephesians, Philippians, 1 Timothy and Titus. Ignatius shows evidence of a knowledge of Romans, 1 Corinthians, Ephesians and Colossians, and probably also 2 Corinthians, Galatians, Philippians and the Pastorals. Polycarp also alludes to most of Paul's letters. 1 Corinthians is best attested, but also well attested are Romans, 2 Corinthians, Galatians, Ephesians, Philippians, the Thessalonian letters and the Pastorals.

Because the remaining apostolic fathers do not quote the Pauline letters with the same frequency as Clement, Ignatius and Polycarp, some (e.g., Barnett) have argued that in the first part of the second century Paul's letters fell into a period of neglect, perhaps because of the popularity of the letters among the Gnostics. This hypothesis can hardly be substantiated from the apostolic fathers however. One may well expect less quotation of Paul in documents of the special character of the *Didache, Barnabas* and *Hermas*. Furthermore, among the remaining apostolic fathers there are allusions to Paul's letters. Thus the *Didache* possibly alludes to 1 Corinthians, Romans and 1 Thessalonians; *Barnabas* clearly alludes to Romans and Ephesians, and also possibly to 1 and 2 Corinthians, Colossians and the Pastorals. The unique character of *Hermas* is indicated from the start by the fact that there are no OT quotations in the whole of this long document. Nevertheless, *Hermas* does allude to 1 Corinthians and Ephesians, and there are possible echoes of Romans, 2 Corinthians, Philippians, Colossians and 1 Thessalonians. *2 Clement* does have relatively few allusions to the Pauline letters for its size and character, yet there are clear allusions to 1 Corinthians and Ephesians and possibly also to Romans and Galatians. The *Martyrdom of Polycarp* alludes to 1 Corinthians and Philippians, and possibly to Romans, 2 Corinthians and 1 Thessalonians. The *Epistle to Diognetus* alludes clearly to 1 and 2 Corinthians and possibly Galatians, Philippians and Romans (*see* Pauline Legacy and School).

5.4. The Remainder of the New Testament. The apostolic fathers do not allude as frequently to the remaining writings of the NT. The Gospel of John is most clearly alluded to by Ignatius, probably by Polycarp, and only possibly by *Hermas*. Acts is probably alluded to in *1 Clement* and Polycarp, and possibly in Ignatius and *Hermas*. Hebrews and 1 Peter are clearly alluded to in *1 Clement*, and appear to be attested in the other apostolic fathers except the *Didache*. By contrast, James is alluded to only in *1 Clement*, *Hermas* and *2 Clement*. The only allusion to the Johannine letters is to 1 John in Polycarp, and there are no convincing allusions to the Apocalypse in the apostolic fathers.

5.5. The Emerging Shape of the Christian Canon. In summary, the apostolic fathers provide a unique glimpse of the state of the OT and NT canons during the fifty-year period beginning toward the end of the first century. As for the former, it is clear that the church during this period had a rather wider OT canon than it would have later when it eventually conformed its canon to the Jewish decision made at Yavneh. As for the latter, we can already see the NT canon taking shape. While it is clear that the Gospels are already around in the early second century, it seems that there was a preference to quote the words of Jesus from an ongoing oral tradition. With this comes an impressive substantiation of the importance and stability of the Gospel tradition. The majority of the Pauline letters are alluded to in these writers, suggesting that they had access to an established collection of Pauline letters, quite possibly a corpus that already included the Pastorals. The pattern of allusion to the other writings of the NT fits well with what we know of the later history of the development of the canon. That is, solid evidence exists to show the use of Acts,* Hebrews,* 1 Peter* and 1 John,* but James* is only weakly attested and there is no evidence of the use of 2 Peter,* 2 and 3 John, Jude* or Revelation* (*see* Canon).

5.6. The Authority of "Scripture." There remains a difference between the way the apostolic fathers use the OT and the NT. The OT is in fact quoted more formally, even though at times apparently from memory. The result is that these quotations can be useful for their contribution to our knowledge of the LXX text used by the apostolic fathers. On the other hand, the NT material is used in such an allusory manner that it cannot readily be used for text-critical purposes. It has not yet acquired the full status of "Scripture." The authority of the NT writings, however, is implied by the frequent allusion to them. Clearly, the words of Jesus are treasured as of supreme authority parallel to, and indeed exceeding, the authority of the OT Scriptures themselves (cf. the introductory formula to the quoted words of Jesus in *1 Clem.* 13.2; *see* Jesus Traditions). The apostles share in the authority of Jesus (cf. *1 Clem.* 42.1; Ign. *Magn.* 13.1), they are paralleled with the OT prophets (Ign. *Phld.* 6.3; Pol. *Phil.* 6.3), and the apostolic fathers can indicate their consciousness that their own authority is not on a par with that of the apostles (Ign. *Rom.* 4.3; Ign. *Trall.* 3.3; cf. Pol. *Phil.* 3.2). By the time we reach *2 Clement* (14.2) we encounter the parallel authority of the OT writings and the apostles (*ta biblia kai hoi apostoloi*; cf. 2 Pet 3:2, 15-16). Thus while it may be strictly true to conclude that prior to the middle of the second century the NT writings were not regarded as "Scripture," it must also be admitted that the apostolic fathers grant them an authority that amounts to such a designation and is fully consonant with it.

6. The Theology of the Apostolic Fathers.

While the theology of the apostolic fathers builds upon that of the NT writings and is clearly continuous with the theology of the early church that preceded them, the apostolic fathers by no means simply repeat that theology. Because these writings are so different in purpose and content, it is difficult to generalize, and the best we can do is to call attention to some of the emphases of the individual writers. We can see here several examples of the apostolic fathers going somewhat beyond the positions held in the NT writings of the first century.

6.1. Christology. The apostolic fathers share with the entire church the faith that the one God who exists and who is Creator and Lord of all, has sent to the world his unique Son Jesus

Christ* (see Christology). Clement of Rome describes Christ as the Son of God (1 Clem. 36.4), as superior to the angels (1 Clem. 36.2-5, alluding to Heb 1) and as the one who spoke through the OT (1 Clem. 22.1). Clement can refer to Christ as the "scepter of the majesty of God" (1 Clem. 16.2). A triadic form referring to God,* the Lord* Jesus Christ* and the Holy Spirit* is found in 1 Clement 58.2.

For Hermas, Christ was instrumental in the creation (Herm. Sim. 9.12.2; in Sim. 5.6.5 the pre-existent* Christ as Holy Spirit "created all creation") and sustains it (Herm. Sim. 9.14.5). Hermas also can write: "the gate is the Son of God, this is the only entrance to the Lord. No man can enter into him otherwise than through his Son" (Herm. Sim. 9.12.6 [cf. 4-5]). Hermas also refers to Christ as superior to the angels* (Herm. Sim. 5.6.2).

The letters of Ignatius are known for the freedom with which they can refer to Christ as God (e.g., Ign. Eph. presc.; 1.1; 15.3; 17.2; 18.2; Ign. Rom. presc.; 3.3; Ign. Smyrn. 1.1; Ign. Pol. 8.3). Ignatius refers to Jesus Christ as the Son of God (Ign. Eph. 20.2), Lord (e.g., Ign. Eph. 7.2) and one "who was from eternity with the Father" (Ign. Magn. 6.1) and as God's "Word (logos) proceeding from silence" (Ign. Magn. 8.2). A trinitarian-like formula occurs in Magnesians 13.1, "in the Son and the Father and the Spirit." For Ignatius, Jesus is God become man (cf. Ign. Eph. 7.2; 19.1-3). Polycarp not only repeatedly refers to Christ as "Lord" (e.g., Pol. Phil. 1.1-2; 2.1) and as "the Son of God" (Pol. Phil. 12.1), but he also refers to Jesus Christ as "our God" (Pol. Phil. 12.2, although some MSS omit these words).

The Didache refers to Christ as "the Lord" (e.g., Did. 6.2; 8.2; 9.5; 11.8; 14.1; 16.8) and "the Holy Vine of David thy child" (i.e., pais, possibly "servant," Did. 9.2-3; 10.2-3). Also to be noted is the threefold baptismal name, "of the Son, of the Father and of the Holy Spirit" (Did. 7.1-3).

Barnabas holds to a high Christology, putting Christ at the beginning of creation (Barn. 5.5, in reference to Gen 1:26), referring to him as "the Son of God" (e.g., Barn. 5.9; 7.9; 12.10) who will be the eschatological judge (Barn. 15.5).

The high christology of 2 Clement is indicated from the very opening sentence: "We must think of Jesus Christ as of God, as of the Judge of the living and the dead" (2 Clem. 1.1). The preexistence of Christ is clear from the reference to his being "originally spirit" before he became flesh (2 Clem. 9.5). The church, however, also exists from the beginning, and the implication seems to be that God created both at the beginning (2 Clem. 14.2).

6.2. Soteriology. Although it has been argued by some (e.g., Torrance) that the apostolic fathers no longer knew or valued the Pauline doctrine of justification by faith* (cf. 1 Clem. 30.3 with James 2:14-26), there is evidence to the contrary (see Righteousness). To begin with, there is a frequent emphasis on the importance of the cross* for our salvation. The death of Jesus by the will of God was on our behalf (1 Clem. 49.6; "whose blood was given for us," 1 Clem. 21.6; cf. 7.4, "poured out for our salvation"). Clement can write: "all who believe and hope on God shall have redemption* (lytrōsis) through the blood of the Lord" (1 Clem. 12.7). Hermas refers to Christ as the one who "cleansed the sins of the people" through much painful labor and toil (Herm. Sim. 5.6.2-3). Ignatius traces the Christian's life back to the death of Christ (see Death of Christ): "Our life sprang up through him and his death" (Ign. Magn. 9.1). Indeed, for Ignatius the suffering of Christ was for our salvation* (e.g., Ign. Smyrn. 2.1; 7.1; Ign. Trall. 2.1). Polycarp understands the death of Christ in the same way (e.g., "for our sins," Poly. Phil. 1.2; "for our sakes," Pol. Phil. 8.1). Barnabas also speaks of the blood of Christ as the means of the remission of sins* (Barn. 5.1; 6.11; 8.3; cf. 16.8) and of his death as "a sacrifice for our sins" (Barn. 7.3). 2 Clement refers to the sufferings* endured by Christ as "for our sake" (2 Clem. 1.2) but otherwise does not indicate an understanding of the cross.

As for the specific Pauline doctrine of justification by faith, we occasionally find in the apostolic fathers an argument against the efficacy of righteous works (e.g., 1 Clem. 32), and indeed Clement can quote Genesis 15:6 (1 Clem. 10.6) in the same sense as Paul in Romans 4:3 and Galatians 3:6. A strong Pauline-sounding statement can be found in 1 Clement 32.4: "we who by his will have been called in Jesus Christ, are not made righteous by ourselves, or by our wisdom or understanding or piety or the deeds which we have wrought in holiness of heart, but through faith, by which Almighty God has justified all men from the beginning of the world" (see Räisänen). Such an emphasis did not however weaken the strength of ethical exhortation. In that sense the apostolic fathers are more like Paul than the antinomian Paulinists.

If it is true that *Hermas* tends to become moralistic, that is no doubt due to his preoccupation with repentance after post-baptismal sins. But even in *Hermas*, faith is not without its importance (*Herm. Sim.* 6.1.2). *Hermas* is told by the Lady (the church*) that he escaped the destroying beast "because you cast your care upon God, and opened your heart to the Lord, believing that salvation can be found through nothing save through the great and glorious name*" (*Herm. Vis.* 4.2.4; cf. *Herm. Sim.* 8.3.2).

Polycarp is very clear on the matter of justification by faith: "by grace you are saved, not by works, but by the will of God through Jesus Christ" (Pol. *Phil.* 1.3). True to form, Polycarp follows this statement with an urgent appeal to the importance of good works (Pol. *Phil.* 2.1-3; cf. 4.1; 5.1).

Barnabas, in articulating the grace of God, goes so far as to say that when God chose the apostles, "he chose those who were iniquitous above all sin to show that he came not to call the righteous but sinners" (*Barn.* 5.9). Faith for *Barnabas* is the means of appropriation of eternal life* (*Barn.* 11.11). *Barnabas* can allude to Genesis 15:6, where Abraham's* faith is counted as righteousness* (*Barn.* 13.7). Again, however, *Barnabas* stresses righteousness (*Barn.* 4.12; 5.4; and in the two-ways section with which the book ends, *Barn.* 19—20). In the two-ways tradition stands a statement that makes forgiveness* of sins dependent upon the work of one's hands. It is found both in *Didache* 4.6 and *Barnabas* 19.10. It stands in conspicuous tension with other statements in Barnabas, and is probably originally a piece of Jewish paraenesis that is uncritically included as part of the larger tradition being used.

2 Clement indicates the supreme importance of "confessing Christ" before others, but then goes on to define this in terms of righteous deeds (*2 Clem.* 3.2-5) and can advocate what amounts to a works-based salvation (*2 Clem.* 6.7, 9; 13.1; 17.4). In this regard, *2 Clement* has moved away from the apostolic gospel.

6.3. Church Order. The crisis at Corinth to which *1 Clement* is addressed required an emphasis on order and discipline.* It is therefore no surprise to find that Clement refers to "strife for the title of bishop" (*1 Clem.* 44.1) and the consequent importance of proper succession in the leadership of the church. Elder and bishop seem still to be interchangeable (*1 Clem.* 44.5), as in the Pastorals. Subjection to the leadership remains a high priority (*1 Clem.* 21.6). The church, presented under a variety of metaphors, is exceptionally important in *Hermas*, but church order itself receives no attention.

It is in Ignatius that we get the strongest emphasis on church order in the apostolic fathers. For Ignatius what the Father, Christ and the apostles are to the universal church, the bishop, deacons and presbyters respectively are to the local church. He adds that "Without these the name of 'Church' is not given" (Ign. *Trall.* 3.1; Ign. *Magn.* 6.1). Elsewhere it is the bishop who is paralleled to Christ (Ign. *Trall.* 2.1-2). Ignatius is tireless in his exhortation to the churches to be in subordination to the bishop, and this is an often repeated emphasis in most of his letters (e.g., Ign. *Eph.* 4.1; Ign. *Magn.* 4.1; Ign. *Trall.* 7.1; Ign. *Phld.* presc.; Ign. *Smyrn.* 8.1; Ign. *Pol.* 6.1). The reason for this emphasis upon the bishop is not only for the preservation of authority and order in the church, but also for the maintenance of ethics and orthodoxy in the face of heretical teaching, in particular that of gnosticism. The bishop is also necessary for the proper administration of the sacraments of baptism* and Eucharist (Ign. *Smyrn.* 8.2; see Lord's Supper). Ignatius is also the first to speak of the "catholic church" (*katholikē ekklēsia*), by which is meant the universal church (Ign. *Smyrn.* 8.2; so too the *Martyrdom of Polycarp*, presc., 8.1; 16.2; 19.2). The *Didache* makes only a brief reference to the importance of appointing worthy bishops and deacons who are to be honored (*Did.* 15.1-2). *Barnabas* and *2 Clement* make no contribution on the subject (*see* Church Order, Government; Early Catholicism).

6.4. View of Judaism. Although *1 Clement* and *Hermas* present a Christianity that must be described as Jewish in much of its character, no attitude to Judaism is indicated. The *Didache*, Polycarp and *2 Clement* also provide very little on this subject. By contrast, however, Ignatius gives us a distinct anti-Judaism. The law* of Judaism and the grace* of Christ stand in opposition to each other (Ign. *Magn.* 8.1). Ignatius writes: "It is improper to talk of Jesus Christ and to practice Judaism. For Christianity did not base its faith on [believe in] Judaism, but Judaism on Christianity" (Ign. *Magn.* 10.3). *Barnabas* is well known for his polemic against Judaism. Illustrative are his remarks about the end of the Jewish law and its displacement by "the new law of our Lord Jesus Christ, which is without the yoke of necessity" (*Barn.* 2.6; cf. 3.6). *Barnabas* strongly denies that the covenant* can belong both to the Jews and the Christians: "It is ours" and the Jews have lost it (*Barn.* 4.7; *see* Christianity and Judaism).

6.5. Christian Life. It can hardly be doubted that the apostolic fathers put a great stress on the importance of righteousness.* This is of course particularly true of *Hermas* with its persistent stress on proper conduct after repentance.* *1 Clement* is emphatic on proper deeds (e.g., *1 Clem.* 21). Ignatius speaks of the divine combination of faith and love,* and concludes that "all other noble things follow after them," adding that "No one who professes faith sins, nor does one hate who has obtained love" (Ign. *Eph.* 14.1-2). For Ignatius the indwelling Christ, "our true life" (Ign. *Smyrn.* 4.1), is of great importance for the living of the Christian life (Ign. *Magn.* 12.1). The presence of the "two ways" tradition in the *Didache* (1—5) and *Barnabas* (19—20) give these documents a particular ethical emphasis. Furthermore the very nature of the *Didache* as a church manual gives it a more practical character than other of the apostolic fathers. *2 Clement* also is emphatic about the importance of righteousness in the believer; indeed, it is a kind of recompense for what Christ has done (*2 Clem.* 1.3; 9.7; 15.2).

6.6. Eschatology. Clement provides a clear argument for a future resurrection* of the body in *1 Clement* 24—26. The nature of the Christian's future hope is so wonderful that only God truly knows its greatness and beauty (*1 Clem.* 34.3—35.3). The final judgment* of the wicked (e.g., *Herm. Sim.* 9.18.2) and the blessing of the righteous (e.g., *Herm. Sim.* 9.18.4; 4.2-3) are important motifs in *Hermas.* Ignatius notes that Jesus "was made manifest at the end of time" (Ign. *Magn.* 6.1) and he can also write: "These are the last times" (Ign. *Eph.* 11.1), while anticipating the future resurrection (Ign. *Pol.* 7.1). Polycarp anticipates the future resurrection of the dead and the reign of the righteous with Christ (Pol. *Phil.* 5.2; cf. 7.1). Papias is notorious for his millennialism (cf. Irenaeus *Adv. Haer.* 5.33.3; Eusebius *Hist. Eccl.* 3.39.12; *see* Millennium). The *Didache* maintains an eschatological

hope* (*Did.* 10.5) and in the concluding chapter articulates an imminent expectation of the end of the age (*Did.* 16). An expectation of the imminent end of the world can also be found in *Barnabas* (*Barn.* 21.3; cf. "the final cause of stumbling is at hand" in *Barn.* 4.3). Indeed, *Barnabas* can speculate about the time of the world as being six thousand years, the day of the Lord as another thousand years, and a new beginning marked by an eighth such period (*Barn.* 15.4-9). *2 Clement* too thinks of the day of the Lord as "already approaching" (*2 Clem.* 16.3) and argues for the reality of the future bodily resurrection (*2 Clem.* 9.1-5) and a literal final judgment (*2 Clem.* 17.4-7). Given their distance in time from the gospel events, the continuing—and even urgent—eschatology of the apostolic fathers is impressive (*see* Eschatology).

7. The Significance of the apostolic fathers.

These documents are invaluable for the view they give us of the church just after the NT period. They are, to be sure, like the NT writings, occasional documents often written with quite specific purposes and they reflect partial viewpoints rather than full-orbed expressions of their faith and theology. Any assessment of their significance must take this into consideration.

Several of these writings were regarded very highly in the second-century church and beyond. A sign of the value attributed to them is the fact that *Barnabas* and *Hermas* fill in the extra pages of the fourth-century MS known as *Sinaiticus*, and *1* and *2 Clement* fill out the fifth-century *Alexandrinus*. We know, furthermore, that Polycarp made use of *1 Clement* and the letters of Ignatius, and that apparently *1 Clement* was read in the church of Corinth (Dionysius, quoted by Eusebius *Hist. Eccl.* 4.23.11). Irenaeus quotes from *1 Clement*, Ignatius, Polycarp and *Hermas*, as well as possibly *2 Clement* and *Barnabas*. Clement of Alexandria quotes as authoritative *1 Clement, Barnabas, Didache* and *Hermas.* Eusebius in Book Three of his *Ecclesiastical History* gives an account of the apostolic fathers in the fourth century. Eusebius specifically places *Hermas, Barnabas* and the *Didache* in the category of books "not genuine" and thus not qualifying for canonicity (*Hist. Eccl.* 3.25.4). It may fairly be said that although these writings were recognized as subordinate and inferior to what was emerging as the NT canon, they were nevertheless regarded as significant and valuable.

The apostolic fathers provide a bridge between the NT and the later fathers of the church. We see in them a diversity of viewpoint but at the same time evidence of a common and uniting faith. Without question there is theological development on some issues from the NT writings with the result that we find both continuity and at times a degree of discontinuity with the views of the NT writers. The apostolic fathers neither simply repeat the theology of the NT, nor do they depart radically from it by creating a new theology. Rather than being creators they are supreme adapters of the theology they received. These writings, in short, throw light upon the church of the late first century to the middle of the second, a church faced with a variety of difficult problems. These they address by means of the frequent quotation of OT Scripture, the sayings of Jesus and the tradition of the apostles. Using these materials and others, they consolidate the faith and practice of the church in an era of increasing challenges. In so doing they remain remarkably faithful to what they had received.

See also BARNABAS, EPISTLE OF; CANON; CLEMENT OF ROME; DIDACHE; DIOGNETUS, EPISTLE TO; HERMAS, SHEPHERD OF; IGNATIUS; MARCION; MELITO OF SARDIS; OLD TESTAMENT IN THE APOSTOLIC FATHERS; POLYCARP.

BIBLIOGRAPHY. J. N. Bakhuizen van den Brink, "Reconciliation in the Early Fathers," *SP* 13 (1975) 90-106; L. W. Barnard, *Studies in the Apostolic Fathers and their Background* (Oxford: Blackwell, 1966); idem, "Bishop Lightfoot and the Apostolic Fathers," *CQR* 161 (1960) 423-35; A. E. Barnett, *Paul Becomes a Literary Influence* (Chicago: University of Chicago Press, 1941); F. F. Bruce, "Eschatology in the Apostolic Fathers" in *The Heritage of the Early Church*, FS G. V. Florovsky, ed. D. Neiman and M. Schatkin (Rome: Pont. Institutum Studiorum Orientalium, 1973) 77-89; A Committee of the Oxford Society of Historical Theology, *The New Testament in the Apostolic Fathers* (Oxford: Clarendon, 1905); F. L. Cross, *The Early Christian Fathers* (London: Duckworth, 1960) 7-28; F. W. Danker, "Bridging St. Paul and the Apostolic Fathers: A Study in Reciprocity," *CurTM* 15 (1988) 84-94; H. J. de Jonge, "On the Origin of the Term 'Apostolic Fathers,' " *JTS* 29 (1978) 503-5; R. M. Grant, *After the New Testament* (Philadelphia: Fortress, 1967); idem, *The Apostolic Fathers,* 1: *An Introduction* (New York: Thomas Nelson, 1964); idem, "The Apostolic Fathers' First Thousand Years," *CH* 31 (1962) 421-29; D. A. Hagner, "The Sayings of Jesus in the Apostolic Fathers and Justin Martyr" in *Gospel Perspectives* 5: *The Jesus Tradition Outside the Gospels*, ed. R. T. France and D. Wenham (Sheffield: JSOT, 1985) 233-68; idem, *The Use of the Old and New Testaments in Clement of Rome* (NovTSup 34, Leiden: E. J. Brill, 1973); J. N. D. Kelly, *Early Christian Doctrines* (3d ed.; London: Adam and Charles Black, 1965); J. Lawson, *A Theological and Historical Introduction to the Apostolic Fathers* (New York: Macmillan, 1961); J. Liébaert, *Les enseignements moraux des Pères apostoliques* (Gembloux: Duculot, 1970); H. Räisänen, " 'Righteousness by Works': An Early Catholic Doctrine? Thoughts on *1 Clement*" in *Jesus, Paul and Torah: Collected Essays* (JSNTSup 43; Sheffield: JSOT, 1992) 203-24; W. R. Schoedel, "The Apostolic Fathers" in *The New Testament and its Modern Interpeters*, ed. E. J. Epp and G. W. MacRae (Philadelphia: Fortress; Atlanta: Scholars Press, 1989) 457-98; A. C. Sundberg Jr., *The Old Testament of the Early Church* (Cambridge: Harvard University, 1964); T. F. Torrance, *The Doctrine of Grace in the Apostolic Fathers* (Edinburgh: Oliver & Boyd, 1948); S. C. Walke, "The Use of *Ecclesia* in the Apostolic Fathers," *ATR* 32 (1950) 39-53.

D. A. Hagner

APOSTOLIC TRADITION. *See* CREEDS, CONFESSIONAL FORMS.

ARCHITECTURE, EARLY CHURCH

Both literary and nonliterary evidence points to the domestic residence as the venue for early Christian gatherings. This pattern is affirmed in Acts,* where we read that the first believers met together in private homes, and in Paul's letters we find that the new communities that the apostle* established were centered in homes. The gathering of Christian believers in private homes continued to be the norm until the early decades of the fourth century, when Constantine began erecting the first Christian basilicas. For almost three hundred years the believers met in homes, not in synagogues* or edifices constructed for the sole purpose of religious assembly.

1. The Need for and Development of House Churches

2. The House Church, 50-150

3. The *Domus Ecclesiae*, 150-250

4. The *Aula Ecclesiae*, 250-313

1. The Need for and Development of House Churches.

The assembly of Christians in house churches was not fortuitous. Four reasons suggest themselves for the choice of the house as a meeting place. First, the "upper rooms" and domestic residences were immediately available. Second, the domestic structure provided a relatively inconspicuous meeting place. Although the house setting was not a guarantee against persecution* (see Acts 8:3), in the early years when persecution was a threat, Christians used discretion in their choice of meeting place. Third, the Jews in Palestine and the Diaspora (*see* Diaspora Judaism) assembled in house synagogues. Since most of the early believers were Jews and God-fearers, it is not difficult to envisage the Christian communities adopting Jewish patterns, particularly since many of the activities in the house church resembled those of the house synagogue. Fourth, the "house" provided the necessities of a Christian gathering, most importantly, the facilities needed for the preparation, serving and eating of the Lord's Supper.*

The early Christian period of 50-313 can be divided roughly into three stages of development (Krautheimer). During the first stage (c. 50-150), Christians would have met in the private homes belonging to individual members, or benefactors, of the community. The appellation "house church" is most appropriately applied to this period. The house church by definition is a domestic residence that is architecturally unaltered for the purpose of Christian assembly and is used at least occasionally by the local Christian community or a part of it.

During the second stage (c. 150-250), private domestic residences were renovated for the exclusive use of the assembled Christian communities. In some instances these renovated homes had been used formerly as a meeting place for believers during the earlier period. These architectural alterations and change of function are the two characteristics of the so-called *domus ecclesiae*, appropriately rendered in English as "community center" or "meeting house."

During the third and final stage (c. 250-313), larger buildings and halls, both private and public, were used. These larger buildings preceded the basilical architecture of Constantine's era, and some of them may have previously functioned as *domus ecclesiae*. They were rectangular in shape and had none of the formal features of later basilical architecture.

Recent archaeological discoveries have allowed a reconstruction of the history of Christian architecture. The following discussion surveys the broad developments of pre-Constantinian church architecture and provides some illustrative examples.

2. The House Church, 50-150.

Acts gives us the picture of early believers regularly gathering in homes and "upper rooms" (Acts 2:46; 5:42; cf. Acts 1:13, 15-16; 20:7-8). Two possibilities present themselves: that the early community rented a room that was part of a domestic residence (cf. P.Oxy 1129, 1036, 1037, 1038, 2190 and P. Mich. Inventory 319) or that a Christian benefactor and homeowner set aside a room, or an entire level of rooms, for the early community's use. There is evidence from Second-Temple Pharisaism confirming that second-floor halls and dining rooms (*triclinium*) were used as a place of study and *haburoth*, or meetings of the "brotherhood" (e.g., *m. Šabb.* 1:4).

In Acts 12:12 Peter, having been delivered from prison, goes to the house of Mary mother of John Mark, where many of the believers were gathered praying.* Presumably this was a house regularly made available to the community. The incidental details suggest that this house was not part of an *insulae*, or "apartment" complex, but was a large house with a gateway that acted as a buffer between the street and the inner courtyard and rooms.

Luke never portrays the entire post-Pentecost* community gathered in one place. If we are to understand the number three thousand as in any sense an accurate count of these believers (Acts 2:41; cf. Acts 4:4; 5:14; 6:7), they obviously could not have gathered under one roof. Peter's own instruction to the group assembled in Mary's house suggests the reality of multiple places of meeting: they were to report his release to James and "the brethren" (Acts 12:17), who were presumably meeting elsewhere.

The problem of the early Christian community in securing a sufficient number of houses for their assemblies may find its solution in contemporary Judaism.* Most synagogues were single rooms in houses. The majority of early believers residing in Jerusalem* were Jews, and their number included individuals who had financial means. It is plausible that some of these Jewish Christians* had formerly opened their houses or parts of them to the synagogue community. It would have been natural for these patrons, having now become followers of Jesus, to use the same facilities as a gathering place for the Christian community.

Archaeologists have uncovered the remains of domestic residences in Jerusalem that allow us a glimpse of the conditions under which these early Christians may have met. Excavations in one area on the Western Hill (the Upper City) revealed a residential district that included some very large houses. The individual dwelling units were extensive, with inner courtyards characteristic of luxurious villas built in the style of the Hellenistic-Roman period (Avigad). This was where the noble families of Jerusalem lived.

The so-called Palatial Mansion is an example of an ostentatious residence that could easily have accommodated the sorts of activities described in Acts. The house covered more than six hundred square meters and included an upper level for dwelling and a lower basement for water installations (pools, baths and cisterns). The structure probably included a second level, an upper story of rooms, but the destruction of Jerusalem in 70 has made a reconstruction of this level impossible.

The numerous rooms of this spacious mansion were arranged around a courtyard. The ornate frescoes in many of the rooms testify to strong Hellenistic influences such as may be observed at Pompeii. Two prominent features are worth mentioning: first, the large reception hall measuring 6.5 meters wide and 11 meters long (71.5 square meters). Access from the courtyard was through a buffer room through which other areas were also reached. In our estimation this reception hall could have accommodated seventy-five people. Access to three other, smaller rooms was gained only by passing through this room. The ornamental frescoes (Ionic columns bearing a schematic Doric frieze) in these rooms suggest a public character. Taken together, the hall and the smaller adjoining rooms would have accommodated about one hundred people quite comfortably.

The second feature is the water installations on the lower level. In addition to a small, tastefully decorated bathroom, there were two large ritual baths, each with a double entrance. N. Avigad suggests that the emphasis on ritual cleanliness in this household borders on "a cult of immersion."

Acts speaks of a significant number of priests* responding in faith to the apostle's preaching (Acts 6:7). Although Acts does not draw a correlation between these priests and the house assemblies, we find a consistent pattern of converts who could have been significant benefactors, including the provision of homes for the community to gather. Water installations such as those in the Palatial Mansion could have functioned for Christian baptisms.*

Various places in Acts 13—28 and in the Pauline epistles refer to private domestic residences that were used as venues for Christians to gather and where the traveling apostle found hospitality* (see 1 Cor 16:19; Col 4:15; Philem 2; Rom 16:5).

In Luke's selective recounting of Paul's mission and establishment of churches throughout the Roman Empire,* we find Paul consistently converting a homeowner who is capable of benefaction, including the provision of a house for Christian assembly (e.g., Lydia, Acts 16, and Titius Justus, Acts 18). This was important, for the predominant domicile in urban areas was the insula, or apartment complex: only 3 percent of the population lived in a *domus,* or house. The disproportionate number of *insulae* is probably evidence of the relatively high cost of housing (*see* Rome, Roman Christianity). Owning a fine house and property was one of the leading indicators of wealth and status. Thus the conversion of a household* or householder was a strategic means of establishing the new cult in unfamiliar surroundings, and the household remained the soundest basis for the meetings of Christians.

We should reasonably assume that at Corinth, for example, Aquila and Priscilla would have opened their house to the Christian community. When they move on with Paul to Ephesus (Acts 18:18), we find them with a "church in their house" (1 Cor 16:19 and apocryphal* attestation), and when they later reestablish their residency in Rome (Acts 18:1-2), they again have a "church in their house" (Rom 16:3-5).

Since house churches did not demand architectural alterations, their archaeological remains are undetectable unless they were subsequently incorporated into a *domus ecclesiae* and/or an *aula ecclesiae*. At Corinth the excavated remains of the Roman villa in the vicinity of the Sicyonian Gate, the house in the vicinity of Temple E and the sumptuous villa at Anaploga are examples of residences in which the early community could have gathered (see Blue 1994, 152-61).

3. The *Domus Ecclesiae*, 150-250.

Radical change in the social position and composition of Christian communities necessitated changes in meeting places. To be sure, poorer communities continued to meet in domestic residences, but in many areas the Christians began to own property, perhaps by proxy through a member or the bishop (Krautheimer).

3.1. Capernaum, Galilee. The archaeological excavations at Capernaum suggest that the former house of Peter was later transformed into a *domus ecclesiae* and may well be the most ancient evidence of an original house church. Unlike the remains at Dura-Europos, the remains at Capernaum do not allow an unambiguous reconstruction of the original building and its history of structural development. This is due to the fifth-century construction of an octagonal Byzantine church on the same site and the subsequent invasion by the Persians in 614, which resulted in the end of Byzantine Christian rule and the demolition of Christian places. But with renewed interest in Galilee and detailed archaeological field reports, a satisfying reconstruction is possible.

Beneath the octagonal Byzantine church lie the remains of two earlier building campaigns. The earliest remains testify to a common *insula,* or joined buildings, which were domestic habitations characteristic of the small fishing community at Capernaum. Within this complex, dating to the first century A.D., is a large hall (7.0 meters by 6.5 meters = c. 45.5 square meters) that was venerated by Christians as the house of Peter. This hall was likely used by the local community of Jewish Christians while the other rooms of the insula continued to function as part of the domestic residence. This partial adaptation of a house, with the surrounding rooms continuing to throb with daily life, continued into the late Roman period when the community enlarged the primitive house church by adding to the hall an atrium on the east and dependencies on the north and by enclosing the entire small insula of the house of Peter within a sacred precinct in order to serve the needs of the community and pilgrims. Subsequently this entire complex was superseded by the octagonal church of the fifth century (for floor plans and isometric reconstructions see Blue 1994, 193-96).

3.2. Dura-Europos, Syria. The evidence from Dura-Europos, a third-century garrison town in Syria,* provides the most convincing archaeological testimony to an early Christian *domus ecclesiae.* It is conservatively estimated that the private house was constructed in 232/33 and renovated (in one campaign) in about 240/41. Although it is somewhat larger than most private dwellings in Dura, its outward appearance would not have suggested anything other than a private dwelling.

The remains were discovered in a relatively good state of preservation in 1931, and the Christian building was excavated from 1932 to 1933. The quality of the remains are due to the fact that Dura was destroyed in 256 by the Sassanians and was not reinhabited.

When the house was renovated by the Christians, three major changes were introduced. First, the wall dividing the diwan and the adjoining room was removed, thereby creating a large assembly hall measuring 12.9 meters by 5.15 meters (c. 66.5 square meters). At the east end of the room there was a small platform, or dais, which was likely used during the reading and teaching. A smaller room was transformed into a baptistry. This appears to be the earliest evidence for a structural adaptation in order to build a baptismal font. A canopy was also installed, and the walls were decorated with frescoes. The central courtyard was tiled and benches (.50 meters wide and .42 meters high) were built around the walls. All of these renovations suggest a developed and organized Christian community. It is difficult to determine, however, whether communal meals were eaten in this particular *domus ecclesiae.*

Among the reasons for the transition from the house church to the *domus ecclesiae* were the size of the community and diversification of activities. By 250, for example, the believers in Rome numbered approximately thirty thousand. Growth such as this necessitated the remodeling of existing structures. The need to accommodate a diversity of activities left its impact on architectural features. For example, the separation of Eucharist from the agape meal meant that dining setting and culinary facilities were no longer needed. Instead, a formal seating was implemented (including a "throne," *Didascalia Apostolorum* 12) with the orientation toward the dais. A distinction was made between the catechumens and full members, and particular features, such as baptismal fonts, were added. In this way the transition was made from the house church to the *domus ecclesiae*.

4. The *Aula Ecclesiae, 250-313.*

A number of remains are preserved beneath some of the churches at Rome that intimate earlier structures used by Christian communities. Many of these ancient *tituli* (a legal term related to the establishment of ownership, or title) of Rome became the sites of the basilicas, thereby preserving a tradition of a "sacred place" *(loca sancta)*. Basilica S. Crisogono *(Titulus Chrysogoni)* is an indisputable example of an *aula ecclesiae* in Rome. It is located on the ancient *Via Aurelia,* and the basilica was constructed by incorporating a large, preexisting rectangular hall (29.50 meters by 17.25 meters). This particular hall dates to the beginning of the fourth century (c. 310).

This pre-Constantinian structure was used as a church building, but the hall was not distinguishable as such. It is a common Roman type of assembly hall found in administrative and other buildings (Krautheimer). The only recognizable indications of its use by Christians were choir screens and side rooms that could have been reserved for the catechumens.

Although the *domus ecclesiae* continued to be used well into the fourth century, early in that same century Christians began to use public buildings as places of assembly. This change accompanied the collapse of the periodic persecutions (e.g., Diocletian's in 303-5) and the recognition of Christianity by Constantine, culminating in the Edict of Milan in 313.

See also CENTERS OF CHRISTIANITY; HOUSEHOLD, FAMILY.

BIBLIOGRAPHY. N. Avigad, *Discovering Jerusalem: Recent Archaeological Excavations in the Upper City* (Oxford: Blackwell, 1984); B. B. Blue, "Acts and the House Church" in *The Book of Acts in Its First-Century Setting,* 2: *Greco-Roman Setting,* ed. D. W. J. Gill and C. Gempf (BAFCS 2; Grand Rapids: Eerdmans, 1994) 119-22; idem, "The Influence of Jewish Worship on Luke's Presentation of the Early Church" in *The Theology of Acts,* ed. I. H. Marshall and D. Peterson (Grand Rapids: Eerdmans, 1997); idem, *Secure the Well-Being of the Family: Christians as Householders and Servants* (FCCGRW; Grand Rapids: Eerdmans, forthcoming); V. Corbo, *The House of Saint Peter at Capernaum: A Preliminary Report of the First Two Campaigns of Excavations, 1968* (PSBFMi 5; Jerusalem: Franciscan Printing Press, 1969); H-J. Klauck, *Hausgemeinde und Hauskirche im frühen Christentum* (SBS 103; Stuttgart: Katholisches Bibelwerk, 1981); C. H. Kraeling, *The Excavations at Dura-Europos: Final Report,* 8.2: *The Christian Building* (New Haven, CT: Dura-Europos Publications, 1967); R. Krautheimer, *Early Christian and Byzantine Architecture* (3d ed.; Pelican History of Art; New York: Penguin, 1979); R. Krautheimer et al., *Corpus Basilicarum Christianarum Romae* (5 vols.; Pontificio Istituto di Archeologia Christiana; Vatican City: Pontifical Gregorian Institute, 1937-77); L. M. White, *Building God's House in the Roman World: Architectural Adaptation among Pagans, Jews and Christians* (The ASOR Library of Biblical and Near Eastern Archaeology; Baltimore: Johns Hopkins University Press, 1990).   B. B. Blue

ARMY, ROMAN. *See* ROMAN EMPIRE, CHRISTIANS AND THE.

ASCENSION

The ascension is the second stage of Jesus Christ's three-stage exaltation,* in which after his bodily resurrection* (the first stage) he visibly departed earth and entered the presence of God* in heaven* to be crowned at his right hand with glory,* honor and authority.* The third stage, his enthronement, or session at God's right hand, commences his perpetual reign and intercession for his people.

In NT usage Jesus' triumph after his death, his exaltation, refers to either the whole of a three-stage process (resurrection, ascension and session); to stages two and three (ascension and session) taken together; or to stage two, the ascension. Acts gives the most detail about the ascension. It brings out its decisive role for christology,* the coming of salvation* blessings,* the church's* mission,* and eschatology.* The book of Hebrews teaches that the ascension was essential to the completion of Christ's high-priestly work and to his continuing intercessory work. 1 Peter and Revelation pursue the theme of ascension as victory over hostile spiritual powers. In the apostolic fathers the ascension undergirds the Christian calendar and, since it culminates in Christ's universal reign, it provides a rationale for virtue.

    1. Exaltation, Resurrection and Ascension
    2. Acts
    3. Hebrews
    4. 1 Peter and Revelation
    5. Apostolic Fathers

1. Exaltation, Resurrection and Ascension.
The normal method of investigation has been to separate kerygmatic statements that allude to the ascension without narrating it from the few narrative accounts in Luke-Acts (Parsons, 149). The kerygmatic statements contain a variety of ways of referring to Jesus' triumph after his death. It is (a) an "exaltation" presented with no explicit reference to the resurrection or ascension (Lk 24:26; Acts 5:31; Eph 4:8-10; Phil 2:6-11; Heb 1:3, 5; 2:9; 5:5; 12:2; note Rev 3:21; 12:5, which do not mention Christ's* death; *see* Death of Christ). Or it is (b) a resurrection followed by an exaltation, stated in either general terms (1 Pet 1:21) or in the specific terms of its result: session at God's right hand (Rom 8:34; Eph 1:20; 2:5-6; Col 3:1). And it is (c) a resurrection followed by an ascension (1 Pet 3:18, 22; Acts 2:32-34; 1 Tim 3:16). The writer to the Hebrews will also refer to (d) the ascension alone: Hebrews 4:14; 6:20; 9:12; 9:24; and (e) the session at God's right hand alone: Hebrews 7:26; 8:1; 10:12.

    This profile of kerygmatic statements, especially the interplay between exaltation and resurrection, has led many scholars to conclude that fundamental to NT thought is the fact that resurrection and exaltation refer to the same spiritual reality (Court and Kasper describe the consensus; Lohfink, Segal and Jones model it). Any presentation of the ascension as a separate event is a secondary development, often traced to Luke. A careful perusal of the vocabulary of category (b) shows, however, that this is not the case. The kerygmatic statements concerning Jesus' triumph do distinguish the resurrection from the exaltation, especially in terms of a subsequent session at God's right hand (Harris, 85). Further, category (c) contains non-Lukan

material; hence G. Lohfink must qualify his assessment of it so that he may maintain his resurrection-exaltation identification (Lohfink, 95). He admits 1 Peter sets resurrection and ascension over against each other, but he says they are also in visible unity; the contrast is only a relative one because of the development of cosmic christology.

    NT kerygmatic statements, then, do not see exaltation as the same event as resurrection. But they do apply the concept to the whole process of triumph: resurrection, ascension, session (*hyperypsoō*, "highly exalt," Phil 2:9; *hypsoō*, "exalt," Acts 5:31; cf. Heb 2:9) or to the ascension (*hypsoō*, "exalt," Acts 2:33; cf. 1 Pet 1:21). When these are combined with other kerygmatic statements that use the language of literal ascension (*eiserchomai*, "enter into," Heb 9:24; *poreuomai*, "go," 1 Pet 3:21-22; cf. Acts 1:11; *anabainō*, "go up," Acts 2:34; cf. Eph 4:8-10), a profile of ascension in NT kerygmatic statements emerges. This profile is congruent with the narratives of the ascension as a distinct, visible event (Acts 1:9-11).

    If the resurrection is not Jesus' exaltation, many interpreters conclude then that "Jesus' resurrection and ascension seem to form one continuous movement" (Bruce, 37). When Jesus arose on that first Easter he did so in a glorified, spiritual body that immediately ascended into the presence of God. All of his postresurrection appearances were appearances from heaven, and the visible ascension forty days later was his final but not his first departure from earth and entry into God's presence. It visually dramatized "as an acted parable of the raising up of Jesus to cosmic dominion" (Harris, 84). According to this view, there were two ascensions: an invisible one on Easter, integrally united with the resurrection, and a visible one after the period of resurrection appearances (*see DJG*, Ascension, 49).

    The evidence for this view, however, should be understood otherwise. Luke 24:26 views the triumph, the exaltation, as a whole, without demanding that the ascension be an invisible, spiritual one at the resurrection (contrast *DJG*, Ascension §4). Acts 2:22-36 is in a chiastic pattern. The kerygma, Scripture proof (Ps 16:8-11), Scripture interpretation, and witness* about the resurrection (Acts 2:22-24, 25-28, 29-31, 32) are then mirrored in the witness, Scripture interpretation, Scripture proof (Ps 110:1), and the kerygma about Jesus' ascension (Acts

2:33, 34-35, 36; Krodel, 83; Barrett, 149). Given the close link between Jesus' exaltation and the outpouring of the Holy Spirit* and the presence of ascension vocabulary (Acts 2:34, *anebē*, "ascended"; cf. Acts 1:9-11), it is better to conclude that Acts 2:33-34 refers to the visible ascension after the period of postresurrection appearances (contrast *DJG*, Ascension §4). Luke's use of the ascension vocabulary in chronological statements tied to the visible ascent of Acts 1:9-11 further confirms that he knows only one ascension (Acts 1:2, 11, 22; *analambanō*, "to take up").

K. Giles's (*see DJG*, Ascension, 49) scriptural evidence does not support the contention that the speeches in Acts do not allow for an intermediate state between the resurrection and exaltation. In fact the references cited do not consistently place the resurrection and exaltation side by side in such a way that their essential unity is asserted. Further, the case cannot be convincingly made from elsewhere in the NT (Harris, 83, cites passages that have been categorized otherwise above; he also appeals to Mt 28:18-20, which may or may not imply that the exaltation has already taken place).

What was the nature of the resurrection body if it were not at the resurrection raised a glorified, spiritual body, exalted immediately into God's presence? Where was Jesus located during the postresurrection period, when he was not appearing to his disciples? These questions, found in W. Milligan's classic work, where he attributes them to D. F. Strauss, continue to be a key part of the discussion (Milligan, 15, 20). Scripture does not help us to answer these questions directly. It does, however, give us evidence that Jesus as he appeared in a physical body after the resurrection was not yet glorified. His body did not display all the attributes of the glorified, spiritual body Christians are promised (Erickson, 574-75). If we allow for stages of exaltation, then, the view that there was one visible departure and ascension continues to be the most congruent with Scripture's witness.

2. Acts.

Giles (*see DJG*, Ascension) provides an overview of the pre-Christian ascension tradition and a balanced assessment of what may have influenced Luke (see O'Toole for a somewhat dated but still valuable history of recent interpretation; Segal provides further enrichment). Giles makes a solid case for Luke 24 and Acts 1 containing two accounts of the same visible ascension event after the period of postresurrection appearances.

Giles's discussion of the origin of the account in Acts* is that of a redaction based on tradition or Lukan inventive composition; he makes a strong case for the former. He does, however, express uncertainty about whether the timing of the ascension, "forty days," should be taken literally. Since, however, Luke's other references to the postresurrection period do not use this number, it is probably to be taken literally, not symbolically (Acts 10:40-41; 13:31). Further, the various events of the postresurrection period, together with preparation for Pentecost,* can be fit together well within the forty-day boundary (Moule).

In the current discussion of Acts, further refinements on the issue of redaction and composition have occurred. One approach of literary analysis explains the origin and importance of all details in the narrative, so that the historical questions become irrelevant, even wrongheaded. For example, C. L. Stockhausen sees the difference between the timing of ascension in Luke 24 and Acts 1 (assuming that Luke 24 presents an Easter evening ascension) as a function of renarration. Luke describes the ascension through two renarrations of the account about Elijah (2 Kings 2:1-12). She also ties Luke's distinct presentation of ascension as visible, observable event to Lukan literary concerns as he renarrates the account from 2 Kings. Such analysis, however, displaces the text's intended sense by importing meaning from the renarrated passage.

The current scientific historical approach does not find the "stuff of scientific history" in the account in Acts 1 (Johnson, 28). According to C. K. Barrett, Acts 1:9-11 may be based on tradition, but it is the tradition spawned by the theological conviction, expressed in terms of Psalm 110:1, that Jesus after his death now reigns at God's right hand in heaven (Barrett, 62). This plus the physical problem of the disappearance of Jesus' body gave rise to the belief that on a certain day Jesus went up to heaven.

This approach's historical reconstruction reveals more about the constraints of its antisupernaturalist presuppositions than it does about what occurred (cf. Court, 40). The details—Jesus' being lifted upward off the ground and a cloud enveloping him, hiding him from the witnesses' eyes—are told in a straightforward fashion from the standpoint of human observation of empirical phenomena. Luke does not describe, so much as assert, the second part of the ascension: Christ's being taken into the presence of God. No ancient cosmology is essential to Luke's narrative (Gooding, 113; Dunn, 23-25, disagrees).

Giles gives a fine exposition of the significance of the ascension for Luke's theology in matters of christology, coming of salvation blessings, church's mission, and eschatology. It does play a central role in Luke's thought. Luke indicates this by the placement of the accounts of the visible ascent at the transition between the two volumes (Lk 24:51; Acts 1:9-11), together with references to it (Acts 1:2, 22) and kerygmatic statements about it (Acts 2:33-35; 3:21) or the whole exaltation in triumph (Acts 5:31).

Luke wrote Acts in order to evangelize pagan Romans by showing them the truth of the salvation-applied portion of the gospel. "Thus it stands written . . . that repentance and the forgiveness of sins is to be proclaimed in his name among all the nations" (Lk 24:46-47; see Forgiveness; Name; Repentance). That gospel cannot be applied with saving effect until after the ascension, since only then can the exalted Jesus pour out the Spirit. The ascension, then, becomes for Luke the pivotal event (the second stage of exaltation) for God achieving his saving purposes now.

3. Hebrews.

More than any other book in the NT, Hebrews* brings out the theological significance of the ascension. At the beginning and the end of his word of exhortation the writer presents the ascension as part of Christ's triumphant exaltation, which manifests his true nature and position, at God's right hand, and the completion of his saving work (Heb 1:3; 2:9; 12:2; cf. Heb 5:5). At the heart of his argument for Christ's superiority to the Aaronic priesthood and the OT sacrificial system is the writer's claim that Jesus' ascension is an entry with his sacrifice* into the true sanctuary (see Tabernacle) in heaven (Heb 6:20; 9:12; 9:24); his session is as high priest* at God's right hand perpetually (Heb 7:26; 8:1; 10:12).

3.1. Ascension as a Part of Exaltation. Though the writer does affirm the resurrection once

(Heb 13:20), his normal practice is to concentrate on the goal of Jesus' triumph: session at God's right hand. This he does by referring to it immediately after pointing to Christ's death (Heb 1:3; 2:9; 12:2; cf. Heb 5:5) or by focusing solely on it (Heb 7:26; 8:1; 10:12). Sitting at God's right hand means that the saving work is complete and that one has received a place of divine honor and authority (Hughes, 21). As the OT quotations in Hebrews indicate, Jesus' exaltation is a fulfillment of Psalm 110:1 (Heb 1:13), Psalm 2:7 (Heb 1:5; 5:5) and Psalm 8:5 (Heb 2:7; see Old Testament in Hebrews). If Psalm 110:1 and Psalm 2:7 can point to his exalted position above the angels* as son* at God's right hand, Psalm 110:4 and Psalm 2:7 point to Christ's glorification to become son and priest according to Melchizedek's* order (Heb 5:5-6; cf. Acts 2:36). Psalm 8:5 introduces Jesus as the "captain of salvation," who when crowned with glory and honor leads many sons to glory (Heb 2:9-10). L. D. Hurst's contention that Hebrews 1—2 are more about Jesus as glorified humanity than as deity incarnate, humbled and exalted, can be maintained only through a selective use of the text.

In Hebrews the theological benefits of the exaltation, which includes the ascension, focus on Jesus' nature and position, his saving work as completed and pioneering for humanity, and the paraenetic encouragement his triumph after death in sitting (*kekathiken*, "has sat down"; perfect tense, completed action; Heb 12:2) at the right hand will have for those who must endure suffering* for his sake (see Endurance).

3.2. Ascension as an Essential Part of Christ's Atoning Work. The writer unfolds for us in Hebrews 4, 6 and 9 a view of Christ's saving work that begins on earth and is completed in heaven. He introduces Christ as a great high priest who has "passed through (*dielēlythota*) the heavens" to the presence of God (Heb 4:14). This expresses strongly God's transcendence above his creation.* In Hebrews 6 we learn that the ascension is an entry "within the veil" to the most holy place (Rice's contention that the veil is at the entrance to the sanctuary and not to the holy of holies does not square with whole presentation of Hebrews). Jesus enters as a precursor on our behalf, since he has become a high priest forever according to the order of Melchizedek (Heb 6:19-20). This passage then teaches that Jesus' priestly office and the ascension are intimately tied together (Lane, 154) and brings into clearer focus that as precursor he takes our humanity to heaven (Hughes, 26).

Hebrews 9 teaches that by a once-for-all sacrifice "through his own blood" Jesus entered the holy place, having found eternal salvation (Heb 9:12). Later the writer reveals that he "entered into" heaven itself to appear before God on our behalf, which he styles as the "true" holy place (Heb 9:24; cf. Heb 9:11). The actions of the high priest on the Day of Atonement, especially in their relation to the holy precincts (Lev 16:14-19), is a pattern (Heb 8:5) that corresponds to the "reality," the "true" in heaven (Heb 9:24). Jesus fulfills the pattern and enters the reality by his sacrificial death and his ascension into God's presence. The writer's presentation of the accomplishment of salvation as a two-step process, death and ascension, does not imply that Christ's sacrificial death is incomplete. Rather, since the sacrifice is "once for all" and needs no repetition or renewal, the ascension "completes" the death in that it "consecrates the eternal validity of his redemptive ministry" (Lane, 239).

3.3. Session as Perpetual Intercession. In addition to the opening and closing references to Jesus' triumphant exaltation as "sitting" or "having sat down" at God's right hand (Heb 1:3; 12:2), references to his session are so interspersed with ascension references that they bring out clearly the completed yet continuing priestly work of Christ. Just as he passed "through the heavens" to the presence of God, who is transcendent above creation (Heb 4:14), so his position is "higher than the heavens" (Heb 7:26). And it is a posture of completion. He is a high priest who offered himself once for all and now sits (Heb 7:27; 8:1). He sits continually in a place of highest honor at God's right hand, awaiting the time of complete triumph when all enemies will be put under his feet (Heb 10:12-13). The writer brings together the representations of Jesus' sacrificial work's effectiveness as completed sacrifice and perpetual priestly labor through the concept of continual high-priestly intercession for us with the Father (Heb 7:25; Mealand, 186 n. 13). In his climactic statement of Jesus' triumph ("endured the cross, despising the shame, and has sat down" [kekathiken, "has sat down," perfect tense, as noted above]; Heb 12:2), the writer provides paraenetic encouragement to a church suffering trials by pointing them to Christ's fidelity and reward.*

4. 1 Peter and Revelation.
Written to encourage Christians undergoing persecution,* both works present the ascension in its cosmic spiritual dimensions as an event in which Christ displays his conquest of hostile spiritual forces (1 Pet 1:21; 3:18-22; Rev 3:21; 12:5).

4.1. 1 Peter.
4.1.1. Profile. 1 Peter 1:21 is an example of a category (b) kerygmatic statement (resurrection and exaltation). For some interpreters the exaltation statement "and gave him glory" is an elaboration of what Jesus' resurrection means; that is, the beginning of a new and transcendent existence (Michaels, 69), and may even be used, though not without qualification, for the claim that the fundamental NT teaching is that Jesus' resurrection is his exaltation (Lohfink, 89). Others remain unconvinced of the proposed equivalence (Achtemeier, 133). Peter (see 1 Peter), in the light of his theme of suffering and glory, is giving "enthronement in glory" center stage but sets it next to the resurrection (Richard, 132).

Christ's death, resurrection, ascension and session are clearly distinguished by Peter in 1 Peter 3:18-22. Through a series of participles (*thanatōtheis,* "having been put to death"; *zōpoiētheis,* "having been made alive"; *poreutheis,* "having gone"; cf. Acts 1:10-11), often seen as evidence of creedal* or hymnic* material (Sanders, 17; Shimada), Peter presents the ascension as the third essential component of Christ's saving work (cf. 1 Tim 3:16). J. R. Michaels (199) suggests that Peter may have given us a relatively early, possibly the earliest, stage of such a three-part traditional summary: death, resurrection, ascension (cf. Rom 8:34; and see the development by Paul in applying it to sanctification via the concept of the Christians' identification with Christ, Eph 2:5-6; Col 2:11-13; Rom 6:8; 8:17; 2 Tim 2:11).

The participle *poreutheis* ("having gone," 1 Pet 3:19; 3:22) refers to the ascension. *Zōopoiētheis* ("having been made alive"), which precedes it in a distinct sequence, refers to the resurrection (Dalton, 126). The phrase "into heaven" qualifies *poreutheis* in 1 Peter 3:22.

First Peter 3:18-22 describes Jesus' activity during his ascension not only in terms of having gone into heaven but also in terms of "having preached to spirits in prison." Some scholars are content to say that this latter activity is an aspect of Jesus' postresurrection activity and is not directly linked to the ascension (Michaels, 205). W. J. Dalton (chap. five) and P. J. Achtemeier (256), with the aid of Jewish apocalyptic* reflection, make their cases for the "preaching to spirits in prison" as proclaiming victory or confirming condemnation to fallen angels, the sons of God (Gen 6:1-6) now in bondage in one of the heavens Jesus passes through on his ascent to the Father's presence (2 Enoch 7:1-3; 18:3-6; T. Levi 3:2; 1 Enoch 12:4-6; 13:3; 14:3-6; 16:3). It is difficult to distinguish between Michaels's "domestication" purpose and a proclamation of victory or condemnation. A. T. Hanson's (102) claim that it is a preaching of salvation that fits neither the audience nor Jesus' conquering relation to them. Dalton (185-86) claims that this is an "invisible ascent" at the resurrection since no time interval is supposed But each stage of exaltation is distinguished, though there is no explicit mention of intervals between them. Nothing in Peter's presentation prevents identifying the ascension, including the declaration of victory, with the visible ascension.

4.1.2. Theological and Practical Significance. 1 Peter 1:21 declares the exaltation "gave him glory" (ascension implied) as part of a description of God, the one in whom faith* and hope* for salvation are placed. Since God already has given the same glory to Jesus that the Christians are waiting for in the end (1 Pet 1:11; 4:13; 5:1, 4, 10), they can be confident, even in the midst of persecution for Christ's name, that their hope is not misplaced.

Christ's ascension in 1 Peter 3:18-22 included the declaration of victory or confirming of condemnation to hostile spiritual powers so that the result, enthronement at God's right hand, also means that all spiritual powers are already subordinate to Christ. Such a message would encourage the Christian to remain faithful despite persecution since Christ's present victory over the forces behind such hostility also ensures the Christian's final victory (Achtemeier, 261).

4.2. Revelation. The ascension is assumed by the multiple references of the present heavenly reign of the risen Christ as the Lamb* who reveals the future, receives worship,* administers history, leads his own in salvation blessing and is the coming warrior-king and judge (Rev 1:1, 5, 12-18; 5:6, 11-13; 6:1-7, 9-17; 7:17; 14:1-5; 21:22-23; 22:1, 3; Milligan, 8). In Revelation 3:21 the ascension is implied in an exaltation-session statement. Christ has conquered and sits with his Father on his throne. This pattern is an encouragement to those who themselves will conquer in the midst of trials. As Christ conquered and received a place of honor, so he promises the same for them.

In the cosmic battle of Satan* and his forces with God and his anointed, graphically portrayed in Revelation 12, the ascension plays a decisive role. Christ's saving mission occurs in the context of Satan's opposition (Rev 12:4-5). At the incarnation the dragon* stands ready to devour the child. But the child is snatched up to God and to his throne. The triumph of Christ's saving work is dramatically portrayed as a divine rescue. To do so the writer moves directly from Christ's birth to his ascension and session on God's heavenly throne. He assumes Jesus' life and ministry,* his death and his resurrection. "The Dragon's vigilance was futile; his failure was manifested by the Ascension" (Swete, 151). And it was a bodily assumption or ascension to heaven; the incarnate Son of God took our humanity with him there.

5. Apostolic Fathers.

These writings assume the ascension when they present Christ as high priest, even heavenly high priest (*Mart. Pol.* 14.3), through whom prayers* are offered to God (*1 Clem.* 61.3; 64.3; Pol. *Phil.* 12.2). Clement (*see* Clement of Rome) has an extended comment, which relies on Hebrews 1:3-5, 7, 13 and the OT background, Psalm 104:4; 2:7-8; 110:1. In it he portrays Christ's present glory as high priest and defender and helper of our weakness (*1 Clem.* 36; see also Ign. *Phld.* 9). The apostolic fathers* also assume the ascension when they point to Christ's return (*Barn.* 21.3; *Did.* 16.7-8; *1 Clem.* 23.5; cf. *2 Clem.* 17.4; Ign. *Pol.* 3; *Diogn.* 7.6; Pol. *Phil.* 5.2-3; 6.2).

The apostolic fathers in their appropriation of the NT teaching about ascension employ modes of expression that are both faithful to the NT understanding and shaped to meet the needs of their audiences. Ignatius* and Quadratus approximate category (a) when they use *chōreō* and *apallassō* (both meaning "to depart") to describe the whole of Jesus' exaltation beginning with his death (Ign. *Magn.* 7.2; Quadratus cited in Eusebius *Hist. Eccl.* 4.3.2). Though the vocabulary is not Johannine, the thought pattern seems to be (Jn 13:3; 14:28; 16:10, 28; Schoedel, 117). J. G. Davies sees Ignatius referring to the ascension, but Lohfink finds here evidence for his "exaltation kerygma" thesis (Davies, 69; Lohfink, 101). The verb is too general, however, and the context is too sweeping to draw a firm conclusion in either direction.

Barnabas 12.10 also sets the incarnation next to the exaltation, though this time the writer represents the latter in the form of prophecy: Psalm 110:1. Jesus' deity is proven by an appeal to the prophecy of his post-Easter exaltation (Hay, 118).

By bringing together an allusion to 1 Peter 1:21 and the imagery of Psalm 110:1, Polycarp in his letter to the Philadelphians creates an elaboration of the exaltation that slightly reconfigures category (b) (Pol. *Phil.* 2.1). Jesus is raised from the dead and given glory and a throne on God's right hand. Here the beginning and ending points of the exaltation (resurrection and session) are explicit, and consequently "and gave him glory" could well be a reference to the ascension (Davies, 69; contrast Lohfink, 104, who views it as evidence for his "exaltation kerygma"). Polycarp* uses this description of Jesus as a rationale for virtue,* for he ties it directly to Christ's present reign and his second coming as judge.

The clearest reference to the ascension in the apostolic fathers is *Barnabas* 15.9, an example of category (c). In making a case for worship on the Lord's day,* termed the "eighth day," the writer argues that on it "Jesus also rose from the dead and was made manifest *(phanerōtheis)* and ascended into heaven" *(anebē eis ouranous)*. Because of the difference in vocabulary, M. C. Parsons (147) says Barnabas (*see* Barnabas, Epistle of) does not depend on Luke-Acts but rather provides an independent witness to an early church tradition about a distinct, visible ascension. At the least it is evidence of an ascension tradition on which both the authors of Acts and *Barnabas* may have relied (Lohfink, 125, must concede as much).

Lohfink contends that if the ascension were a distinct event in the early church's thinking (i.e., thinking uninfluenced by Luke-Acts), there are several places in the apostolic fathers where its absence is surprising (Lohfink, 99-

102). *1 Clement* 42.3, in describing the church's firm apostolic foundation, speaks of the apostles' assurance* by Jesus' resurrection, their faith confirmed by the word of God and their going forth preaching in the assurance of the Holy Spirit. But there is no mention of ascension. This may be because the assurance the apostles* received on earth to do their task does not require reference to the ascension.

Ignatius, in combatting Docetism,* points out Jesus' "true death" and "true resurrection," but he does not mention the ascension (Ign. *Trall.* 9). Since he is countering a heresy that professed an ascension of the "Christ" to heaven from the cross* before death, reference to the ascension might have been confusing. Further, the reality of the death and resurrection as events fundamental to salvation is what Ignatius is trying to establish. The ascension is implied in the promise* that at the last day God will raise up "in Christ" those who believe in him. Ignatius in his letter to the Smyrneans describes Christ's resurrection in the flesh* by alluding to details of the resurrection appearances also found in Luke 24 (Ign. *Smyrn.* 3.3). Again there is no reference to the ascension, and again it is unnecessary to Ignatius's argument. Further, the phrase "united with the Father" does not support Lohfink's exaltation kerygma understanding of the resurrection. This phrase is a favorite Ignatian theological theme that he uses for various purposes (Schoedel, 227; note Schoedel, 88-92, corrects H. Schlier's claim that Ign. *Eph.* 19.2-3 and Ign. *Magn.* 9.2 speak of the ascension).

See also ACTS OF THE APOSTLES; CHRISTOLOGY; EXALTATION, ENTHRONEMENT; GLORY; HOLY SPIRIT; PAROUSIA; RESURRECTION.

BIBLIOGRAPHY. P. J. Achtemeier, *1 Peter* (Herm; Minneapolis: Fortress, 1996); C. K. Barrett, *Acts 1-14* (ICC; rev. ed.; Edinburgh: T & T Clark, 1994); F. F. Bruce, *The Book of Acts* (rev. ed.; Grand Rapids: Eerdmans, 1988); J. M. Court, "Risen, Ascended, Glorified," *King's Theological Review* 6 (autumn 1983) 39-42; W. J. Dalton, *Christ's Proclamation to the Spirits: A Study of First Peter 3:18—4:6* (AnBib 23; Rome: Pontifical Biblical Institute, 1965); J. G. Davies, *He Ascended into Heaven: A Study in the History of Doctrine* (London: Lutterworth, 1958); J. D. G. Dunn, "Demythologizing the Ascension—A Reply to Professor Gooding," *IBS* 3 (1981) 15-27; M. J. Erickson, *The Word Became Flesh* (Grand

Rapids: Baker, 1991); D. W. Gooding, "Demythologizing Old and New, and Luke's Description of the Ascension: A Layman's Appraisal," *IBS* 2 (1980) 95-119; A. T. Hanson, "Salvation Proclaimed I. 1 Peter 3:18-22," *ExpT* 93 (1981) 100-105; M. J. Harris, *Raised Immortal: Resurrection and Immortality in the New Testament* (Grand Rapids: Eerdmans, 1983); D. M. Hay, *Glory at the Right Hand: Psalm 110 in Early Christianity* (SBLMS 18; Nashville: Abingdon, 1973); P. E. Hughes, "The Christology of Hebrews," *SWJT* 28 (1985) 19-27; L. D. Hurst, "The Christology of Hebrews 1 and 2" in *The Glory of Christ in the New Testament,* ed. N. T. Wright and L. D. Hurst (Oxford: Clarendon, 1987) 151-64; L. T. Johnson, *The Acts of the Apostles* (SacP; Collegeville, MN: Liturgical Press, 1992); E. Jones, "The Origins of 'Ascension' Terminology," *Churchman* 104 (1990) 156-61; W. Kasper, "Christi Himmelfahrt—Geschichte und Theologische Bedeutung," *Internationale Katholische Zeitschrift—"Communio"* 12 (1983) 205-13; G. A. Krodel, *Acts* (ACNT; Minneapolis: Augsburg, 1986); W. L. Lane, *Hebrews* (2 vols.; WBC; Waco, TX: Word, 1991); G. Lohfink, *Die Himmelfahrt Jesu* (Munich: Kösel, 1971); D. L. Mealand, "The Christology of the Epistle to the Hebrews," *Modern Churchman* n.s. 22 (1979) 180-87; J. R. Michaels, *1 Peter* (WBC; Waco, TX: Word, 1988); W. Milligan, *The Ascension and Heavenly Priesthood of Our Lord* (London: Macmillan, 1908); C. F. D. Moule, "Expository Problems: The Ascension—Acts 1:9," *ExpT* 68 (1957) 205-9; R. F. O'Toole, "Luke's Understanding of Jesus' Resurrection-Ascension-Exaltation," *BTB* 9 (1979) 106-14; M. C. Parsons, *The Departure of Jesus in Luke-Acts* (JSOTSup 21; Sheffield: Sheffield Academic Press, 1987); G. E. Rice, "Hebrews 6:19: Analysis of Some Assumptions concerning *KATAPETASMA,*" *AUSS* 25 (1987) 65-71; E. Richard, "The Functional Christology of First Peter" in *Perspectives on First Peter,* ed. C. H. Talbert (Macon, GA: Mercer University Press, 1986) 121-39; J. T. Sanders, *The New Testament Christological Hymns* (SNTSMS 15; Cambridge: Cambridge University Press, 1971); W. R. Schoedel, *Ignatius of Antioch: A Commentary on the Letters of Ignatius of Antioch* (Herm; Philadelphia: Fortress, 1985); A. F. Segal, "Heavenly Ascent in Hellenistic Judaism, Early Christianity and their Environment," *ANRW* 2.23.2 (1980) 1334-94; K. Shimada, "The Christological Creedal Formula in 1 Peter 3:18-22—Reconsidered," *AJBI* 5 (1979) 154-76; C. L. Stockhausen, "Luke's Stories of the Ascension: The Background and Function of a Dual Narrative" in *Proceedings of the Eastern Great Lakes and Midwest Biblical Societies,* ed. T. Callan (vol. 10; Cincinnati: EGLMBS, 1990) 251-63; H. B. Swete, *The Apocalypse of Saint John* (Grand Rapids: Eerdmans, 1951 [1909]).   W. J. Larkin Jr.

ASCENSION OF ISAIAH. *See* APOCRYPHAL AND PSEUDEPIGRAPHAL WRITINGS.

ASSURANCE

Assurance is a concept that is not encompassed by a single word in the Greek NT. It falls within the same semantic domain as faith,* hope,* peace,* confidence, boldness, firmness, certainty, knowledge* and courage (cf. Louw and Nida). So instead of offering a word study, this article defines the concept and then discusses it in the various contexts in which it occurs in the General Writings, Revelation and the apostolic fathers.

1. Definition
2. Spheres of Assurance
3. Assurance in the Apostolic Fathers

1. Definition.

In the broadest sense assurance is confidence. It is the opposite of doubt. But rather than thinking of the two ideas as polar opposites, it is best to think of assurance and doubt as opposite ends of a continuum. One can be more or less confident of particular truths or realities.

Christian assurance is confidence in what God* has said regarding the past, present or future or regarding his own character. The concept of assurance is especially prominent in discussions of things that cannot be seen. Hence assurance means holding as true and firm the declarations and actions of God.

2. Spheres of Assurance.

2.1. Prayer. James 1:5-8 encourages the one who needs wisdom* for the trials of life to ask for it. The one who asks can have assurance that God will answer because of the character of God, who is generous and kind (cf. Jas 1:17). Asking without assurance or faith is described as doubting and being double-minded in James 1:6-8. The context does not advocate never praying* without absolute assurance. In that case few would ever venture to pray. Rather, doubting or double-mindedness refers to when one receives the answer of what to do in the trial but then hesitates to do it. As the chapter moves on, it is the Word of God that supplies wisdom for life (Jas 1:20-25), and the person who looks into that Word is warned not to go away unchanged (Jas 1:24). So assurance in prayer is not so much a confidence that God will answer, but rather enough confidence in the Word that God has revealed to put it into practice. The mark of assurance is obedience.*

1 John 3:21-22 and 5:14-15 also speak of assurance in prayer. The former passage ties assurance in prayer closely to obedience to the love* command (1 Jn 3:11-18), which is a sign of an intimate relationship with God (1 Jn 3:21, "the boldness [assurance] we have before him"). This latter phrase is repeated in 1 John 5:14-15, which also leads to assurance of answered prayer: "Whatever we ask according to his will he hears, and we know that if he hears, we have the requests made of him." So assurance in prayer is based on intimacy with God demonstrated by obedience to his commands (see Prayer).

Assurance in prayer is not a major theme in the apostolic fathers, probably because it is assumed. *1 Clement* 2.3 describes the Corinthians as praying with godly confidence for mercy toward unwilling sin.*

2.2. Faith. "Faith is the assurance of things hoped for, the conviction of things not seen" (Heb 11:1). Every translation of Hebrews 11:1, including this one, is ambiguous in defining faith. The problem arises because the Greek words behind assurance *(hypostasis)* and conviction *(elenchos)* are multivalent. Many scholars have attempted word studies of these many-faceted words, with varying results. A different approach to the problem seems to be called for.

Perhaps the best way to understand the meaning of the assurance of faith in Hebrews 11:1 is to examine what the author himself wrote in defining faith in the rest of the chapter (cf. Goppelt, 2:263-65). Faith is defined by OT examples more than by didactic propositions because stories often make a greater impact than logical propositions. Faith goes forward without knowing where the journey will end (Heb 11:8-16); faith trusts in God's promise of the future, including eternity (Heb 11:17-22); faith involves a changed set of values (Heb 11:23-31). So faith is a confidence (assurance)

and conviction by which people act without seeing immediate results. An assured faith does not involve cognitive or demonstrable certainty. Rather, it causes Christians to act in ways that are inexplicable to those without faith.

2.3. Salvation. Assurance of salvation* is a dominant theme in Hebrews, James, 1 John and Revelation, and is assumed in 1 Peter. Hebrews and James are written to bolster assurance by causing readers to examine their faith. In Hebrews salvation is pictured as a journey. This is in keeping with the idea that from a human point of view conversion is a process (Carson, 18-20). This "word of exhortation" (Heb 13:22) is addressed to Christians who, because of discouragement, are tempted to leave off their journey in faith and regress to what they were before beginning the Christian pilgrimage. Hebrews leads them to assurance by telling them not to neglect their salvation lest they imperil it (Heb 2:1-4). The loss of salvation is more a stopping of the journey or a losing of one's way than a losing of something that had already been gained. Assurance of final salvation is based on continuing the journey of faith which Jesus has already taken (in spite of its difficulty; Heb 12:1-3), and on the character of God (Heb 6:13-20) and the reliability of his Word (Heb 2:2; 3:6 v.l.; 6:19; 9:17; 13:9).

James attempts to give assurance by telling Christians to examine their faith to make sure it works. "Faith if it has no works is dead by itself" (Jas 2:17). James defines works as acts of kindness to the needy and just dealings. In the final judgment* the rotting wealth of the rich will stand as a testimony against them. They have no assurance that they will be saved, if their wealth is not being used for good deeds (Jas 5:1-6). So assurance of salvation comes as Christians see their faith produce works of kindness and love: "I will show you my faith by works" (Jas 2:18).

Hebrews and James function to the same end (assurance) but in different ways. They both call Christians to examine their faith. Hebrews calls them to examine the perseverance of their faith; James calls them to examine the genuineness of their faith.

1 John and Revelation are written to encourage those who lack assurance. 1 John seems to address people who were left wondering about their status in the larger church after an exodus of members from their Christian community (1 Jn 2:19). This tract tells Christians that their

doctrine and their practice assure them that their faith is genuine (Carson, 27). They can have assurance of eternal life (1 Jn 4:17; 5:13; *see* Eternity) because of their rightful confession of Jesus (1 Jn 4:2-3, 6, 13-16) and because they keep the command to love their Christian brothers and sisters (1 Jn 3:22-23; 4:7-8, 20-21). Although they may sin, God is faithful to forgive* their sin and cleanse them from all unrighteousness (1 Jn 1:9).

Revelation assures Christian witnesses living in an anti-Christian world that they are on the victorious side of the battle even though now the world is dominated by evil. Although the book is filled with visions of apocalyptic* battles between good and evil, it never gives the impression that God has lost control; in fact, evil is a tool in God's hand. The breaking of the seven seals unleashes devastation on the earth; nevertheless, the Lamb is in control. He is the one who breaks the seals (Rev 6); and the scroll itself is God's last will and testament for the creation. So the martyrs* who have suffered* and will suffer under the various empires of the present world (including those who are presently suffering under the persecutions* of Domitian) are told to wait with patience for the final victory of the kingdom of God (*see* Kingdom of God) over the kingdoms of the world (Rev 6:10-11). Final salvation is guaranteed for the people of God, because God is sovereign (Rev 21:7).

Assurance of salvation is a growing confidence that God will deliver the believer from final judgment and bless him or her with eternal life. Assurance grows through constant exposure to the promises and program of God revealed in the Scriptures and through the application of God's Word to life.

3. Assurance in the Apostolic Fathers.
The apostolic fathers follow the NT in its views of Christian assurance. *1 Clement* speaks of confidence in prayer and service (*1 Clem.* 2.3; 26.1; 34.5). This confident faith is a gift of God to those who strive "to be found among the number of those who wait" (*1 Clem.* 35.1-4). In the fathers, to be found among that number, one must submit to the steps leading to baptism.* This often involved an extensive training program of two to three years (Hall, 16-17). This training was mainly in morality and ritual, as evidenced in the early part of the *Didache*. It probably also included instruction in the Bible, although evidence for this

is somewhat later (e.g., Origen's homilies). After baptism a believer was allowed to remain with the faithful for the Eucharistic service (*Did.* 9.5; Justin Martyr *Apol. I.* 65). In this way a believer was assured of salvation.

But what about a person who sinned after baptism? This issue is taken up in the *Shepherd of Hermas, Mandate* 4.3.1-7 (cf. 1.8; Hippolytus *Haer.* 9.12.20-26). Hermas is told that there is no repentance after baptism (*Herm. Man.* 4.3.2). The passage is rather confusing after this, but at its end Hermas is given assurance of his salvation, as are all who practice these things (*Herm. Man.* 4.3.7). The Shepherd gives his instruction in such a way as not to give an excuse (*aphormē*) to present or future believers (*Herm. Man.* 4.3.3, 6). At the same time he points out the weakness of humanity and the wiles of the devil as causes for sin (*Herm. Man.* 4.3.4). For his main answer to the question, the Shepherd seems to rely on the foreknowledge and mercy of God in the granting of repentance,* the Shepherd himself being given the authority* over this repentance (*Herm. Man.* 4.3.5). It seems, then, that the Shepherd does not say it is impossible for a person to be saved if they sin after baptism, but that they will be saved only with difficulty (*dyskolōs;* cf. *Herm. Sim.* 9.23.3; *Herm. Man.* 9.6), akin to 1 Peter 4:18 and Jude 22-23.

See also APOSTASY; BAPTISM, BAPTISMAL RITES; ENDURANCE, PERSEVERANCE; FAITH, FAITHFULNESS; FAITH AND WORKS; FORGIVENESS; JUDGMENT; REPENTANCE, SECOND REPENTANCE; SALVATION.

BIBLIOGRAPHY. G. Braumann and G. Harder, "Form, Substance," *NIDNTT* 1:703-14; D. A. Carson, "Reflections on Christian Assurance," *WTJ* 54 (1992) 1-29; L. Goppelt, *Theology of the New Testament* (2 vols.; Grand Rapids: Eerdmans, 1981-*82); S. G. Hall, *Doctrine and Practice in the Early Church* (Grand Rapids: Eerdmans, 1992); J. P. Louw and E. A. Nida, ed., "25 N, Courage, Boldness," "31 I, Trust, Rely," *Greek-English Lexicon of the New Testament Based on Semantic Domains* (2d ed.; New York: United Bible Societies, 1989); H. Schönweiss et al., "Firm, Foundation, Certainty, Confirm," *NIDNTT* 1:658-64.

D. H. Johnson

ASTROLOGY. *See* MAGIC AND ASTROLOGY.

ATONEMENT. *See* DEATH OF CHRIST.

AUTHORITY

Christian writers in the late first century and early second century expressed divergent views on authority in the church.* While a discernible trend toward hierarchical structure can be found in some of their works, other authors clearly reacted against such a trend. The NT documents covered in this article are arranged in a rough succession from those advocating institutionalized forms of authority to those protesting hierarchical organization. A brief survey of selected writings of the apostolic fathers* traces trajectories from the NT into the second century.

1. Pastorals
2. Acts
3. James
4. 1 Peter
5. Hebrews
6. Revelation
7. Letters of John
8. Apostolic Fathers

1. Pastorals.

The Pastorals present the most highly developed structure of authority in the NT. We can almost draw a chart of the ecclesiastical organization. At the top of the pyramid is the apostle* Paul. Repeatedly the letters point to the divine appointment of Paul to his apostolic office (1 Tim 1:11-16; 2:7; 2 Tim 1:11; 4:17; Tit 1:3). Church order* is maintained by those who faithfully guard Paul's apostolic teaching* (1 Tim 6:20; 2 Tim 1:13-14; 2:1-2; Tit 1:9). Apostolic authority is limited to Paul alone; there is no mention of other apostles or of any successors to the apostle. Authority is tied not to succession but to transmission of Pauline doctrine.

Timothy and Titus exercised authority as Paul's emissaries. Their responsibilities were the faithful transmission of the tradition of Paul's teaching (1 Tim 4:6, 16; 2 Tim 2:15; Tit 2:7) and the careful installation of church officers (1 Tim 3:1-15; 5:17-22; 2 Tim 2:1-2; Tit 1:5). They were constantly reminded that their use of authority had to be accompanied and authenticated by their blameless conduct (1 Tim 4:12; Tit 2:7-8). Timothy was ordained to his authoritative role by receiving a gift *(charisma)* through the laying on of hands by the elders (1 Tim 4:14; 2 Tim 1:6). The exercise of charismatic authority depended on rekindling the gift of God* *(to charisma tou theou)* within. In the Pastoral Epis-

tles we do not find the teaching that spiritual gifts *(charismata)* for ministry* are distributed universally by the Spirit *(see* Holy Spirit) to all in the church, as we do in 1 Corinthians 12, but only the narrower concept that a single gift is given in the course of ordination to a special office.

The only reference to elders *(presbyteros)* in the Pauline corpus is found in the Pastorals. In some cases the word denotes old men (1 Tim 5:1; Tit 2:2), but a more technical use refers to appointed leaders in the church (1 Tim 5:17; Tit 1:5). Elders have the authority to rule and teach and deserve to be compensated when they exercise their authority well. Accusations against them are not to be accepted unless there is substantial evidence (1 Tim 5:19).

The list of qualifications for a bishop (or overseer *[episkopos],* 1 Tim 3:1-7; Tit 1:7-9) and deacons (1 Tim 3:8-13) indicates the high regard given to these offices in the church. Aspiration to the office of bishop is encouraged (1 Tim 3:1). The use of the singular form of "bishop" in the Pastorals leads some scholars to suggest that there was monarchical episcopate in view, but the singular "bishop" is probably a generic reference to overseers and serves as a designation for a leadership role carried out by one or a few of the elders within the local church, "elders who rule well" (1 Tim 5:17). The sequence of 1 Timothy 3 is usually taken as a signal that deacons were subordinate to bishops and elders, but the exact relation of these various offices is not described. The reference to women* in 1 Timothy 3:11 appears to indicate that women were involved in the work of deacons, but their official status is not clearly defined. Their inclusion in the leadership group of the church means that the perplexing prohibition in 1 Timothy 2:12 ("I permit no woman to teach or to have authority over a man") should be taken as a safeguard against abuse of authority rather than an exclusion from any leadership function.

The emphasis in the Pastoral Letters on church offices, hierarchical organization and the restriction of a divine charisma to the ordained leader seems to be in contrast to the other letters in the Pauline corpus and leads some scholars to deny the Pauline authorship of the Pastorals. Others defend Pauline authorship of the Pastorals on the basis of their unique historical circumstances: they were written to individuals (not to churches) who were instructed by Paul to establish church order in a time of crisis caused by influential false teachers.

2. Acts.

Acts* is viewed by some interpreters as an expression of early catholicism.* According to this perspective, Luke wrote the history of the first-generation church to legitimize the fixed forms and hierarchical structures of the second- or third-generation church. He replaced the authority of the direct guidance of the Spirit with the authority of a well-defined organization. This interpretation claims to find a three-level structure of ministry: the twelve apostles (Acts 1:15-26; 2:42; 4:33-37; 6:2, 6; 8:1, 14; 15:22), elders (Acts 11:30; 15:2, 4, 6, 22) and deacons (Acts 6:1-6). Though the names of the offices were later changed to bishops (the successors to apostles), priests* (who carry on the role of the elders) and deacons, this hierarchical structure was supposedly the same as that of the second-century church.

Examination of the text does not support this view that Acts presents the structures of early catholicism. Luke's view of the church as the restored Israel* is indicated by the election of Matthias to close the gap in the circle of the Twelve. But the authority of the twelve apostles over the restored Israel was primarily a prophetic authority (see Old Testament in Acts; Prophecy) fulfilled by their Spirit-empowered proclamation of the resurrection* (Acts 1:2-3, 22; 2:14, 36, 42; 4:33). Financial resources were brought to the apostles for distribution (Acts 4:35, 37), but they asserted that their ministry did not involve administrative functions, since they were devoted to "prayer and the ministry of the word" (Acts 6:2, 4; see Prayer). They did not exercise an ongoing role of leadership in the administration of the church. Once they fulfilled their role as eyewitnesses to the resurrection, for the most part they disappeared from the scene (The exceptions are Peter and occasionally John and James.) After the council in Jerusalem* the apostles are never mentioned again. Acts emphasizes Peter's role as the star witness* to the risen and exalted Lord.* But even Peter's authority was not absolute. When he returned to Jerusalem after his mission to Cornelius,* the believers criticized him (Acts 11:8). Only the irrefutable evidence of the Holy Spirit's sanction of Peter's mission silenced their objections (Acts 11:18).

There is no evidence in Acts for the theory of succession from the apostles. Indeed, their unique function described by Luke as eyewitnesses to the risen Lord could not be repeated. Although the Twelve were involved in the appointment of the Seven (Acts 6:1-6), the Seven already exercised charismatic authority by the evident presence of the Spirit before their election (Acts 6:3). Luke gives no explanation of any ongoing relation between the Twelve and the Seven. The latter have often been regarded as deacons because they were called to table service,* but the text never refers to them as deacons. Though they were appointed to an administrative task, they functioned as prophets and evangelists.* In any case they cannot have provided a line of successors from the apostles, since Stephen* was quickly martyred,* five immediately and completely disappeared, and Philip's* only successors were four virgin daughters (Acts 21:8-9).

Luke gives no clues about the origin of the elders in Jerusalem. There is no mention of their appointment by the apostles and no clarification of their relation to the apostles. The elders of the Jerusalem church received gifts (Acts 11:30), participated in the council (Acts 15:2, 4, 6, 22, 23; 16:4) and ruled over the Jerusalem church with James (Acts 21:18). Many scholars regard James* as the one who instituted the pattern of synagogue* government by ruling the church with a board of elders.

James was the key leader at the Jerusalem council (Acts 15:13-21), but his decision is portrayed by Luke as a reflection of the Spirit-led consensus of the entire council (Acts 15:22-28). James also appears to be the leader and spokesperson for the elders at the time of Paul's return to Jerusalem (Acts 21:18), but the directions given to Paul to observe the Mosaic sacrificial law* came from the united leadership group (Acts 21:23: "do what we tell you"). Authority was more collegiate than hierarchical.

It is clear that the Twelve had no part in the appointment of Paul; if it had not been for Barnabas's intervention, they would not even have accepted him as a genuine Christian (Acts 9:26-28). Paul was brought into a teaching role in the church of Antioch* by Barnabas. Apparently "prophets and teachers" were the leaders of that church (Acts 13:1-3). Directed by the Holy Spirit, they laid hands on Barnabas and Paul to commission them for an evangelistic mission. Luke grants the title *apostle* to them (Acts 14:4, 14), since their prophetic mission bears witness to the resurrection. But in their case the title has the secondary meaning of "missionary." Even though Luke establishes the authority of Paul's prophetic mission in a roughly parallel way to Peter's, he does not present Paul as link in a chain of apostolic succession.

Acts 14:23 reports that Paul and Barnabas appointed elders in the churches they had started. In his address to the Ephesian elders (Acts 20:17-35), Paul instructs them in their responsibility as overseers *(episkopoi)* to shepherd* the church of God (Acts 20:28). So the terms "bishops" *(episkopoi),* "elders" and "pastors" all seem to apply to the same group of leaders. There is no differentiation or hierarchy implied in the use of these alternative terms. There is no indication that Paul appointed the Ephesian elders, and no instruction is given about appointing others to succeed them.

What is most pervasive in Luke's account of the exercise of authority in the early church is his conviction that the leaders of the church were directed by the risen Lord and guided by the Holy Spirit. The Spirit empowered Peter to speak to the rulers of Israel (Acts 4:8) and directed him to go the house of Cornelius (Acts 10:19). The Lord commanded Ananias to speak to Saul (Acts 9:10-16). Stephen and Philip were leaders guided by the Spirit (Acts 6:10; 7:55; 8:29, 39). The church of Antioch was directed by the Spirit to send out Barnabas and Paul (Acts 13:2-4). Paul was guided on his mission by the Spirit (Acts 16:6, 7). Far from presenting a church restricted by institutional structures, Luke describes the way leaders exercised authority under the immediate mandate of the Spirit without direction from other leaders, any local church or the mother church in Jerusalem.

3. James.
Those who are sick are instructed to call the elders of the church for prayer* and anointing* (Jas 5:14). This instruction assumes the appointment of elders, but it says nothing else about their duties or position beyond this basic description of their pastoral care for the sick (*see* Healing).

James discourages the ambition to be a teacher on the grounds that teachers will be judged with greater strictness (Jas 3:1).

4. 1 Peter.
In the striking image of the church as a spiritual house* constructed of living stones that are built upon Christ the living stone* (1 Pet 2:4-10), all members serve together in this new, living temple* as "a royal priesthood" (1 Pet 2:9). This concept of the "priesthood of all believers" is augmented by the teaching that all are stewards of the manifold grace* of God and that "each" individual serves with the gift *(charisma)* that each has received. Although speaking and serving are the only two kinds of charismatic ministry mentioned (1 Pet 4:11), these two probably serve as a summary of the many different ways that the "manifold grace of God" is displayed.

This emphasis on the ministry of all is combined with a recognition of the authority of elders over the "flock of God" (1 Pet 5:1-2). Yet the exhortation to elders is aimed against an abuse of authority: elders should not exercise their oversight for "sordid gain" and by "lording it over" others but willingly and by example (1 Pet 5:2-3). Humility* in leadership is encouraged by the recognition that Jesus alone is the "chief shepherd" (1 Pet 5:4; 2:25) and bishop *(episkopos,* 1 Pet 2:25) of the church. 1 Peter* presents a church in which the authority of elders does not inhibit but inspires the priestly and charismatic ministry of all the members of the church.

5. Hebrews.
The ministry of Jesus is the central focus and major theme of Hebrews.* The emphasis that all the ministries of priests under the Mosaic law are fulfilled in the high-priestly work of Jesus Christ effectively removes any basis for extending those old covenant* ministries in the new covenant church. All believers are repeatedly encouraged to "draw near" to the throne of the high priest without depending on any human priesthood (Heb 4:14-16; 9:22). All believers ought to be teachers not by appointment to any office but on the basis of spiritual maturity (Heb 5:11-14). All members are responsible to serve and exhort one another (Heb 6:10; 10:25).

In the postscript the author encourages his readers to remember and imitate the good example of their previous leaders (Heb 13:7) and to obey their present leaders (Heb 13:17). Leaders worthy of imitation* and respect are characterized by their proclamation of the word of God, their faithful lives and their careful watch over the lives of God's people. Submission to them is motivated by the prospect that they "will give an account" of their ministry.

So leaders are defined by their pastoral functions and held accountable for their use of authority. There is no reference to church offices or hierarchical organization. All offices and hierarchical positions are held only by Jesus: the Son exalted to the right hand of the Majesty on high (see Exaltation), the high priest according to the order of Melchizedek,* the apostle, the mediator of the new covenant, the pioneer of salvation* and the great shepherd of the sheep.

This transference of all titles and offices to Christ leads some interpreters to see a protest in Hebrews against the increasing institutionalization of the church.

6. Revelation.

Diverse interpretations of Revelation (see Revelation, Book of) offer different perspectives on authority in the church. For example, the relation of the church to Israel is a major subject of debate. If on the one hand the church and Israel are kept separate, then some or all of the titles of Israel apply only to Israel and not to the church. In that case most of the book, except for the seven letters, has little to say about the church. If on the other hand the church is seen as the true Israel, then the church is the heir to all the titles of Israel: the church is identified with 144,000 witnesses sealed from the twelve tribes of Israel (Rev 7:1-8; 14:1-5), the temple of God and the holy city (Rev 11:1-2), the two witnesses (Rev 11:3), the woman in the wilderness (Rev 12:1-17) and the saints ruling as priests of God on thrones with Christ for a thousand years (Rev 20:1-6). These images of the church do not point to a hierarchy within the church but to the authority of the church as God's prophetic witness in the world.*

A number of signals seem to point to the second interpretation. The book opens with praise to Jesus Christ for what he has done for the church: "to him who loves us and freed us from our sins by his blood and made us to be a kingdom, priests serving his God and Father"

(Rev 1:5-6). The letter to the church of Laodicea promises all faithful members a place on Christ's throne. And the book closes with a vision* of the heavenly Jerusalem, the home of God for all his people (see Heaven). So in the sections clearly addressed to the church, the role of Israel as God's authoritative witness is given to the church.

Positions of authority in the church are held either by all members or by the founders. All believers are kings and priests (Rev 1:6; 5:10; 20:6). Twenty-four elders are seen in the throne room of God (Rev 4:4, 10; 5:8; 11:16; 19:4). They are sitting on thrones, wearing golden crowns, casting their crowns before the throne and falling on their faces to worship* God. They seem to represent the whole people of God: twelve for the old Israel and twelve for the new Israel, the church. The names of the apostles of the Lamb* are written on the foundations of the heavenly city (Rev 21:14).

The letters to the seven churches are addressed to the angels* of the churches. Though some scholars have interpreted the term angel as a reference to the ruling official (bishop) of the congregation, the use of this term in Revelation supports identifying these angels as heavenly beings or as personifications of the prevailing spirits of the churches.

In Revelation the authority of the Messiah is demonstrated in the lives of believers who conquer Satan* "by the blood of the Lamb and by the word of their testimony" (Rev 12:10-12).

7. Letters of John.

The "beloved children" (see Sonship) of the author are protected against the deceptive influence of false teachers in the church by the assurance that they do not need anyone to teach them (see John, Letters of). They have been anointed by the Holy One and have all knowledge* (1 Jn 2:20; but cf. variant reading). Since that anointing teaches them all things, they can discern on their own what is true and what is false (1 Jn 2:18-27). This radical understanding of authority in the church removes the need for any offices or special leadership ministries. Each believer is taught by the inner witness of the Spirit and is called to test all spirits by the apostolic proclamation that "Jesus Christ has come in the flesh" (1 Jn 4:1-3).

The only reference to a position of authority in the church is a negative one (in 3 Jn). Diotrephes refused to welcome some Christians into the church (*see* Hospitality) and had expelled others from the church. The author strongly censures the ambition of Diotrephes, who "put himself first," and his unwarranted assumption of the role of a monarchical bishop in the church. The letters of John present a strong check to a development of institutionalized authority in the church.

8. Apostolic Fathers.

In the *Didache** there is instruction to appoint bishops and deacons (there is no reference to elders), who are to be honored, "for they too carry out the ministry of prophets and teachers" (*Did.* 15.1). Yet the prophets and teachers are a distinct class of leaders in the church (*Did.* 13.1; 15.2). Their ministry of teaching must be examined to see if it is true or false (*Did.* 11.8-12). But the "prophet who speaks in the spirit" should not be tested (*Did.* 11.7). It appears that the highest honor of all is to be given to prophets who experience ecstasy in the Spirit. So the *Didache* presents several classes of church members, including ordinary members and those who speak in the Spirit.

The letter of *1 Clement* (*see* Clement of Rome) was written from Rome* to stop a rebellion against the established leadership in the Corinthian church. In fact the opposition had removed certain presbyters from office (*1 Clem.* 44.3-6). The arguments in *1 Clement* for submission to bishops and elders indicate that the development of hierarchical church structures was strongly opposed by a segment of the church. The author points to the way that all the elements of nature move in their orbits given to them by God: "the sun and the moon and the choir of stars circle in harmony within the courses assigned to them" (*1 Clem.* 20.3). The author calls the readers to consider how soldiers are placed in higher and lower ranks: "not all are prefects or tribunes or centurions or captains of fifty and so forth, but each in his own rank executes the orders given by the emperor and the commanders" (*1 Clem.* 37.3). These arguments from the structure of nature and the army for the appointment of higher and lower ranks in the church hierarchy were not made simply in defense of the reputation of individual presbyters but primarily in defense of the legitimacy of the hierarchical organization itself.

The "good order" of the church was a straight line of authority: "Christ is from God, and the apostles are from Christ. . . . They appointed their first fruits . . . to be bishops and deacons for the future believers" (*1 Clem.* 42.1-5). Presbyters held the office of bishop (*1 Clem.* 44.4-5); deacons were ranked lower than the bishops (*1 Clem.* 42.4-5). The apostles who set up this structure "gave the offices a permanent character" (*1 Clem.* 44.2). When individuals who held offices died (probably a reference to the death of bishops, not apostles, though this is disputed), approved successors were to be appointed to fill the established offices (*1 Clem.* 44.2).

The letter of *1 Clement* leaves no room for opposition to hierarchical structure in the church; the duty of all members is to "submit to the presbyters and accept discipline leading to repentance, bending the knees of your heart" (*1 Clem.* 57.1; *see* Repentance).

The development of hierarchical structure in the church takes another momentous change in the letters of Ignatius* of Antioch. Whereas the bishops and presbyters were the same in *1 Clement,* Ignatius viewed "the bishop presiding in the place of God and the presbyters in the place of the council of the apostles" and the deacons doing Jesus Christ's service (Ign. *Magn.* 6.1). Bishops served as monarchical leaders in local churches and over all the churches in a city or a region. The authority of the bishop was absolute: members "must follow the bishop as Jesus Christ followed the Father" (Ign. *Smyrn.* 8.1); they "must regard the bishop as the Lord himself" (Ign. *Eph.* 6.1); they should be "subject to the bishop as to Jesus Christ" (Ign. *Trall.* 2.1); they should "do nothing without the bishop" (Ign. *Trall.* 2.2), "for the one who does anything without the bishop's knowledge serves the devil" (Ign. *Smyrn.* 9.1). Only the Eucharist served under the authority of the bishop was to be considered valid (Ign. *Smyrn.* 8.1).

The authority of the bishop was not the result of his ministry, such as his preaching, "for the more anyone observes that the bishop is silent, the more one should fear him" (Ign. *Eph.* 6.1). His position in the place of God over the church rather than his function gave him his authority.

The emphasis of Ignatius on the gradation of authority—presbyters subject to the bishop and deacons to the bishop and the presbyters—and on the absolute authority of the bishop places his letters at the extreme end of the trajectory toward the development of hierarchical authority in the church.

See also APOSTLE, APOSTLESHIP; CHURCH ORDER, GOVERNMENT; CIVIL AUTHORITY; SERVANT, SERVICE.

BIBLIOGRAPHY. C. K. Barrett, *Church, Ministry and Sacraments in the New Testament* (Exeter: Paternoster, 1985); B. E. Bowe, *A Church in Crisis: Ecclesiology and Paraenesis in Clement of Rome* (Minneapolis: Fortress, 1988); A. Campbell, *The Elder in the New Testament* (Edinburgh: T & T Clark, 1995); H. von Campenhausen, *Ecclesiastical Authority and Spiritual Power in the Church of the First Three Centuries* (Palo Alto, CA: Stanford University Press, 1969); L. Coenen, "Bishop," *NIDNTT* 1:188-201; J. D. G. Dunn, *Unity and Diversity in the New Testament* (Philadelphia: Westminster, 1977); J. S. Jeffery, *Conflict at Rome: Social Order and Hierarchy in Early Christianity* (Minneapolis: Fortress, 1991); I. H. Marshall, " 'Early Catholicism' in the New Testament" in *New Dimensions in New Testament Study,* ed. R. N. Longenecker and M. C. Tenney (Grand Rapids: Zondervan, 1974) 217-31; E. Schweizer, *Church Order in the New Testament* (London: SCM, 1961); P. H. Towner, *The Goal of Our Instruction: The Structure of Theology and Ethics in the Pastoral Epistles* (JSNTSup 34; Sheffield: JSOT, 1989). G. W. Hansen

B

BABYLON

Apart from Acts 7:43, where Babylon refers to the geographical location to which Jews were deported, references to Babylon in our NT literature are limited to 1 Peter* and Revelation (see Revelation, Book of), where a symbolic sense seems to be employed. There are no references to Babylon in the apostolic fathers.*

1. 1 Peter
2. Revelation

1. 1 Peter.

In 1 Peter 5:13 "Babylon" probably does not refer to the literal city of Babylon on the Euphrates; although it had a significant Jewish population, the only apostle* associated by tradition with that city is Thomas. It is still less likely to refer to the Roman colony of the same name in Egypt. It is commonly held that "Babylon" refers to Rome,* as it does (or so it is widely believed) in Revelation, so that "she who is in Babylon, chosen together with you" would refer to the Christian community in Rome (so NRSV: "your sister church in Babylon"). This interpretation is in harmony with the ancient tradition that associates Peter's ministry* with Rome. Yet the only certain references to Rome as "Babylon" are found in later works, such as Sibylline Oracles 5.143, 159 (dated by most scholars after A.D. 80 but before 130). Such a usage probably originated in Jewish circles after the fall of Jerusalem* in A.D. 70, Rome being seen as a "second Babylon" because, like the first Babylon, it was responsible for the destruction of Jerusalem.

Moreover, nothing in 1 Peter could raise suspicions about the loyalty of either the writer or the recipients of the letter,* so there was no reason to refer to Rome by any cryptic term. The name Babylon probably refers, therefore, not to any specific place but merely to "the place of exile" (Moule, 9), indicating the Christian community's situation as "strangers and exiles" (1 Pet 2:11) in the world.*

2. Revelation.

The six references in Revelation (Rev 14:8; 16:19; 17:5; 18:2, 10, 21) are all to an entity that falls under the judgment* of God* and whose destruction brings hope* and rejoicing for the people of God (see Church; Church as Israel). In Revelation 14:8 the fall of "Babylon the Great" is announced without a word of explanation as to the city's identity. No more is said by way of identification in Revelation 16:19, when it is said that "God remembered Babylon the Great and gave her the cup filled with the wine of the fury of his wrath." The main clues to the identity of Babylon are found in Revelation 17—18, where the Seer is shown a woman clothed in scarlet and purple and bedecked with jewelry, seated on a beast* with seven heads and ten horns. On her forehead is the title "Babylon the great, the mother of prostitutes and of the abominations of the earth" (Rev 17:5).

2.1. Babylon as Rome. Although the interpreting angel's* explanation of this vision* introduces problems of its own, most interpreters see in the explanation of the beast's seven heads as "seven hills on which the woman is seated" (Rev 17:9) a reference to Rome as the City of the Seven Hills. When the seven heads are explained as also signifying "seven kings, of whom five have fallen, one is alive" and one whose brief reign is future (Rev 17:9-10), this is commonly seen as a reference to a sequence of seven Roman emperors,* although there is little agreement about which seven are in mind. Thus "Babylon" is seen as a reference to pagan Rome, the city, while the beast on which she rides represents the Roman Empire, on which the city depends.

The further explanation that the woman is "the great city that rules over the kings of the earth" (Rev 17:18) is alleged to point to Rome's political dominance; the lament of the merchants over her fall "because no one buys their cargoes any more" (Rev 18:11) to her position as a trading power; and the charge that "in her was found the blood of prophets and of saints, and of all who have been killed on the earth" (Rev 18:24), together with the rejoicing of the multitude in heaven* because God "has avenged on her the blood of his servants" (Rev 19:2) to her unenviable reputation as a persecutor of Christians.

2.2. Babylon as Jerusalem. Yet none of these claims is immune to challenge. Rome was by no means the only city situated on seven hills; seven notable hills can be pointed out in Jerusalem also. And if the mention of seven hills pointed so clearly to Rome, how would the use of this image save the writer or those found with copies of the book in their possession from a charge of treason against the Roman Empire? Nor was Rome the only city whose fall would bring ruin to her trading partners; Jerusalem was also a substantial importer of just the kinds of goods that are named in Revelation 18:12-13. Much of what is said about "Babylon" applies better to Jerusalem than it does to Rome. The designation *prostitute* and the charge of "adultery" are more appropriately used of Jerusalem and the Jewish people, who were called to be the wife of Yahweh and whom OT prophets* accused of unfaithfulness, fornication and adultery (Ezek 16).

Moreover, although some Christians did meet their death at the hands of Roman officials, such persecution* was sporadic and local, not the result of an official policy of persecuting Christians. Thus one recent writer, while maintaining the view that "Babylon" symbolizes Rome, views the Apocalypse as a response by the Christian community to the perceived (but unreal) threat of repression by Rome (Thompson, 27-28). It is Jerusalem that Jesus is said to have accused of being guilty of the blood of the prophets (Mt 23:35). It should also be noted that the "great city" where the corpses of the "two witnesses" lie (Rev 11:8) is identified as the place "where their Lord was crucified," that is, Jerusalem.

Finally, it has been argued that just as the seven churches of Revelation 2-3 have their celestial counterparts in the "angels" of the churches and since Jerusalem is the only "sky city" in Revelation, its earthly counterpart must be the historical Jerusalem (Malina, 219-23).

See also JERUSALEM, ZION, HOLY CITY; 1 PETER; REVELATION, BOOK OF; ROMAN EMPIRE, CHRISTIANS AND THE.

BIBLIOGRAPHY. R. J. Bauckham, *The Climax of Prophecy: Studies on the Book of Revelation* (Edinburgh: T & T Clark, 1993); A. J. Beagley, *The 'Sitz im Leben' of the Apocalypse with Particular Reference to the Role of the Church's Enemies* (BZNW 50; Berlin and New York: Walter de Gruyter, 1987); M. E. Boring, *Revelation* (IntC; Louisville, KY: Westminster/John Knox, 1989); J. M. Court, *Myth and History in the Book of Revelation* (London: SPCK, 1979); idem, *Revelation* (NTG; Sheffield: JSOT, 1994); C.-H. Hunzinger, "Babylon als Deckname für Rom und die Datierung des I Petrusbriefes" in *Gottes Wort und Gottes Land: Festschrift W. Hertzberg*, ed. H. G. Reventlow (Göttingen: Vandenhoeck & Ruprecht, 1965) 67-77; K. G. Kuhn, "Βαβυλών," *TDNT* 1:514-17; B. J. Malina, *On the Genre and Message of Revelation: Star Visions and Sky Journeys* (Peabody, MA: Hendrickson, 1995); C. F. D. Moule, "The Nature and Purpose of I Peter," *NTS* 3 (1956-57) 1-11; R. H. Mounce, *The Book of Revelation* (NICNT; Grand Rapids: Eerdmans, 1977); I. Provan, "Foul Spirits, Fornication and Finance: Revelation 18 from an Old Testament Perspective," *JSNT* 64 (1996) 81-100; S. Safrai et al., *The Jewish People in the First Century; Historical Geography, Political History, Social, Cultural and Religious Institutions* (2 vols.; CRINT 1; Philadelphia: Fortress, 1976); E. Schüssler Fiorenza, *Revelation: Vision of a Just World* (PC; Minneapolis: Augsburg Fortress, 1991); L. L. Thompson, *The Book of Revelation: Apocalypse and Empire* (New York: Oxford University Press, 1990); R. W. Wall, *Revelation* (NIBC; Peabody, MA: Hendrickson, 1991).

A. J. Beagley

BAPTISM, BAPTISMAL RITES

The apostle Paul could presuppose that the addressees of his letters had received baptism: in Romans 6 he showed the absurdity of their continuing in sin since it contradicted their having died to sin when they had been baptized into Christ's death*; in 1 Corinthians 12:12-13 it was their baptism by the one Spirit into the one body of Christ which meant that the various gifts of the Corinthians were to serve the common good; in Galatians 3:27-28 baptism into Christ is seen as effecting a unity that overrides differences between Jew and Greek, slave and free, male and female (*see DPL*, Baptism). Matthew records the command of the risen Lord to "make disciples of all nations, baptizing them in the name of the Father and of the Son and of the Holy Spirit" (Mt 28:19; *see DJG*, Baptism). Here, then, are indications from the Epistles and the Gospels that baptism was from a very early date the universal rite of admission to the church.

The Acts* of the Apostles relate that practice episodically in narrative form. Elsewhere in the later writings of the NT there are a few clear references to baptism and several more possible allusions to it. The detection of the latter can be controversial among scholars, since it involves hints toward rites surrounding the water bath that find their first direct attestation only in the second or third centuries.

The early postscriptural writings add some details to our knowledge about baptismal understanding and practice in their day, but it is not until Justin Martyr, in the middle of the second century, that we find a relatively full ritual description of baptismal practice, and not until the late second century that we find sustained theological reflection in Tertullian's treatise *De Baptismo*. The early patristic evidence concerning Christian initiation is completed by the ancient church order which most twentieth-century scholarship has identified with *The Apostolic Tradition* of Hippolytus. Tertullian and Hippolytus also provide the first uncontested evidence of the baptism of young children.

Confronted with the fragmentary and allusive material in the NT concerning baptism (in the Gospels and in the Pauline letters as well as in other writings), the historian and exegete has to make decisions concerning its relation to understandings and practices attested only in (say) Justin, Tertullian and Hippolytus. Do these latter illuminate directly what was believed, said and done concerning baptism in NT times? Or do the patristic texts rather represent additions or alterations to the apostolic rites and doctrines? Or is it possible (in something like a middle way) that the second century witnessed liturgical developments that elaborated what was embryonically present in the first century, or brought to concrete expression what existed at the level of theological statement in the apostolic writings? Any serious treatment of baptism according to the NT has to

remain aware of such issues.

1. Water and the Spirit in the Acts of the Apostles
2. The Non-Pauline Epistles and Revelation
3. The Early Postapostolic Period
4. The Later Second Century
5 The Baptism of Young Children

1. Water and the Spirit in the Acts of the Apostles.

1.1. The Day of Pentecost. According to Acts 1:4-5, the risen Lord ordered his apostles to wait in Jerusalem for "the promise of the Father" (cf. Lk 24:49; Jn 14:26; 15:26), the fulfillment of Jesus' own word that "John baptized with water, but before many days you shall be baptized with (the) Holy Spirit" (cf. Acts 11:16; also Mt 3:11; Mk 1:8; Lk 3:16). Acts 2 then relates the story of the first Christian Pentecost.* With a sound like the rush of a mighty wind and the appearance as of tongues of fire resting on each recipient, the Holy Spirit* came from heaven and filled the apostles and their associates, so that they "began to speak in other tongues, as the Spirit gave them utterance" (Acts 2:4; *see* Tongues). To the crowd which gathers, Peter interprets this event in terms of Joel's prophecy: "And in the last days it shall be, God declares, that I will pour out my Spirit upon all flesh . . . and it shall be that whoever calls on the name of the Lord shall be saved" (Acts 2:17-21; cf. Joel 2:28-32 [LXX 3:1-5]). The apostle then rehearses to the "men of Israel" the life, death and resurrection* of Jesus, whom "you crucified and killed by the hands of lawless men, but God raised him up" (Acts 2:23-24). Having now been "exalted to the right hand of God" (Acts 2:33) as "Lord and Christ" (Acts 2:36), and "having received from the Father the promise of the Holy Spirit," Jesus "has poured out this which you see and hear" (Acts 2:33). Cut to the heart, the hearers ask what they should do, and Peter replies: "Repent, and be baptized every one of you in the name of Jesus Christ for the forgiveness of your sins, and you shall receive the gift of the Holy Spirit" (Acts 2:38). The result was striking: "Those who received his word were baptized, and there were added that day about three thousand souls" (Acts 2:41).

Several points need to be noted from that narrative which are of significance for the practice and understanding of baptism in the church. First, Peter's listeners are summoned to repentance* for their part in the death of Jesus, with the promise that their sins will be forgiven. Christian baptism will be understood as the seal of both human repentance and divine forgiveness* in reference to the weight of all that Jesus redemptively bore on the cross as the suffering servant (cf. Lk 3:22; 24:25-27; Acts 3:12-21; 10:43; 13:38-39).

Second, baptism takes place precisely "in the name of Jesus Christ." Much ink has been spilled on the phrase (cf. Acts 8:16; 10:48; 19:5; *see* Name). It seems sufficient to take "in the name of" as indicating Jesus as "the fundamental reference of the rite": L. Hartman suggests it was an application of a familiar Semitic phrase by the Palestinian church (*lešēm* in Hebrew, or *lešûm* in Aramaic), with Luke letting Peter express himself in prepositional forms familiar in the biblical style of the LXX at Acts 2:38 (*epi tō onomati*) and Acts 10:48 (*en tō onomati*), while the narrative at Acts 8:16 and 19:5 uses *eis to onoma* as the form that Luke himself had learned, with *eis* being the preposition that Paul employs in connection with baptism (Rom 6:3; 1 Cor 1:13, 15; Gal 3:27). It has been suggested that the beginnings of Christian baptism go hand in hand with the recognition of Jesus' resurrection and of his status as Christ* and Lord* (Pokorný). We do not know whether the phrase "in the name of (the Lord) Jesus (Christ)" was ritually pronounced by the minister at baptisms in the earliest times (cf. Jas 2:7 for a possible allusion). Third- and fourth-century evidence suggests that the earliest "form" by which the divine name was invoked at baptism was that of a question or questions to the candidate, "Do you believe in . . . ?" (Whitaker 1965). In the NT "Jesus is Lord" may have been a confession of faith on the part of the candidate at baptism (cf. Rom 10:9, 13; 1 Cor 12:3).

Third, there is no indication that the apostles* themselves had been baptized with water (perhaps they had received John's baptism) when they received the Holy Spirit; but the immediate message of Peter calls others to baptism "in the name of Jesus Christ" with the promise that they, too, will "receive the Holy Spirit." From this passage the expected post-Pentecostal sequence appears to be water baptism resulting in the reception of the Spirit: the Spirit, like the forgiveness of sins, remains God's to give; water baptism will be the occasion, or the means, of God's giving the Spirit.

In fact, however, the narrative episodes in Acts* are complicated, as we shall see; and the varying sequence of events in them makes it difficult to draw theological conclusions regarding the relation between water baptism and the giving of the Spirit. In light of the various episodes in Acts, Dunn, for instance, will allow no more than that water baptism is for Luke a "vehicle of faith," a means whereby believers "reach out to God" (Dunn, 90-102). By contrast, a sacramental reading takes Acts 2:38 to establish water baptism as a divinely provided rite whereby God will regularly bestow the Holy Spirit when it is approached with right disposition. Somewhat mediatingly, G. Barth sees Acts 2:38 as stating a "normal" connection between water baptism and the reception of the Spirit, even though the narrative episodes in Acts show the Spirit to be free also to come before or after water baptism (Barth, 60-72).

Fourth, the baptized are thereby "added" to the company of those who "devoted themselves to the apostles' teaching and fellowship, to the breaking of bread and the prayers" (Acts 2:41-42). Baptism brings entry into the church, which is marked by a common faith,* common worship* and a common life (*see* Lord's Supper). Speaking "in other tongues" (cf. Acts 2:4) is not mentioned again of the Spirit-filled apostolic community, but boldness in witness* is (Acts 4:23-33).

1.2. Samaria. The next baptismal episode occurs in Acts 8:1-25 with the spread of the gospel throughout Judea and Samaria* (cf. Acts 1:8). Philip* in particular went to a city in Samaria and preached the "good news about the kingdom of God and the name of Jesus Christ" (Acts 8:12; cf. Acts 8:4-5). Many "believed" and "were baptized, both men and women" (Acts 8:12), including Simon "who had previously practiced magic in the city and amazed the nation of Samaria" (Acts 8:9, 12). This new stage in the mission* apparently called for supervision from Jerusalem, for the apostles sent Peter and John down to Samaria (Acts 8:14). Peter and John "prayed" for the Samaritan believers "that they might receive the Holy Spirit, for it had not yet fallen on any of them, but they had only been baptized in the name of the Lord Jesus" (Acts 8:15-16): "Then they laid their hands on them and they received the Holy Spirit" (Acts 8:17).

This passage raises a number of issues. How

could the Samaritans have come to believe the gospel* and be baptized in the name of Christ *without* receiving the Holy Spirit? The impression which the result of the action by Peter and John made on Simon the magician* suggests that what had been lacking was a spectacular manifestation of the Holy Spirit: "Now when Simon saw that the Spirit was given through the laying on of the apostles' hands, he offered them money, saying, 'Give me also this power, that any one on whom I lay my hands may receive the Holy Spirit' " (Acts 8:18-19). At another level, the passage has traditionally been invoked as an apostolic basis for "confirmation," or the imposition of episcopal hands, in ritual completion of water baptism.

1.3. The Ethiopian Eunuch. The gospel continues its spread to "all nations" (Lk 24:47; cf. Mt 28:19; Acts 1:8) in the story of the baptism of the Ethiopian eunuch (Acts 8:26-39). On the basis of a passage from Isaiah 53 concerning the Suffering Servant, Philip proclaims to the African courtier the gospel of Jesus and instructs him in the faith. His hearer's response is rapid: "See, here is water! What is to prevent my being baptized?" (Acts 8:36). The Western text at Acts 8:37 then continues the dialogue between the evangelist and the eunuch: "Philip said, 'If you believe with all your heart, you may.' And he replied, 'I believe that Jesus Christ is the Son of God.' " Philip and the eunuch "went down into the water," and "he baptized him" (Acts 8:38). The eunuch "went on his way rejoicing" (Acts 8:39): "joy"* is a characteristic of the primitive Christian community, where it is associated with their common meals (Acts 2:46; cf. 16:34; Rom 14:17).

1.4. Paul. The next baptism, in Acts 9:18, is that of Paul,* apostle to the Gentiles.* In this first account, Ananias lays hands on Saul/Paul, so that he may "regain his sight" (Acts 9:12, 17-18) after the blinding vision on the road to Damascus. Then Paul rose "and was baptized, and took food and was strengthened" (Acts 9:18-19). It is not specified by which action Paul was "filled with the Holy Spirit" (Acts 9:17), although he immediately began preaching Jesus (Acts 9:20). As Paul recounts the events in his speech before the crowd in Jerusalem at Acts 22:16, Ananias after healing him had said: "Rise and *be baptized,* and *wash away* your sins, calling on his name." The imperatives, *baptisai* and *apolousai,* are in the middle voice ("Get yourself

baptized, and get your sins washed away") but need not imply that the baptism was self-administered; unlike Jewish proselyte baptism (*see DJG,* Baptism), Christian baptism appears always to have been administered by another (the story of the martyr Thecla is the exception that proves the rule). It is, however, Paul himself who is to call on the Lord's name (cf. Acts 4:12; Rom 10:9, 13). Paul's sins clearly include having persecuted Jesus in his followers (Acts 9:4-5; 22:7-8).

The final account of Paul's conversion comes in his speech before King Agrippa in Acts 26:2-23. This speech contains baptismal allusions. Paul's mission as an apostle is "to open their eyes, that they may turn from darkness to light and from the power of Satan to God, that they may receive forgiveness of sins and a place among those who are sanctified by faith in me [i.e., the Lord Jesus]" (Acts 26:18). Apart from the themes of belief in Christ and the forgiveness of sins, already encountered in connection with baptism, the turn from darkness to light, from the power of Satan to God, will find expression in the patristically attested rites of renunciation of the devil and profession of faith, and most dramatically in the Eastern ceremonies of the *apotaxis* and *syntaxis,* where the candidate faces west, the place of darkness, to renounce Satan (and even to spit on him in some rites!), and then is turned east, toward the rising sun, to enlist with Christ and the Holy Trinity. Being "sanctified" (*hēgiasmenois*) is mentioned in connection with baptism also at 1 Corinthians 6:11 ("You were washed, you were sanctified, you were justified in the name of the Lord Jesus Christ and in the Spirit of our God"). Finally in Acts 26:23 Paul refers to the now fulfilled prophecies "that the Christ must suffer, and that, by being the first to rise from the dead, he would proclaim light both to the people and to the Gentiles." Death and resurrection are baptismal themes in the Pauline writings (especially Rom 6:1-23), and "enlightenment," or "illumination," was from at least the second century onward, as we shall see, a term for baptism (cf. already perhaps in Eph 5:14).

1.5. Cornelius. The next incident (Acts 10:1—11:17) is the case of the God-fearing centurion of the Italian Cohort, Cornelius,* and thereby marks an important stage in the spread of the gospel to the Gentiles (Acts 10:44; 11:1, 18) and toward Rome.* When Peter recounts in Cornelius's house the story of Jesus Christ, the apostle concludes with the promise that "every one who believes in him receives forgiveness of sins through his name" (Acts 10:43), which can also be described as the gift of "repentance unto life" (Acts 11:18). Immediately "the Holy Spirit fell on all who heard the word" (Acts 10:44), and they began "speaking in tongues and extolling God" (Acts 10:46). Peter's conclusion is that "these people have received the Holy Spirit just as we have" (Acts 10:47), "God gave the same gift to them as he gave to us when we believed in the Lord Jesus Christ" (Acts 11:17). Peter could not "withstand God" (Acts 11:17), so no one should "forbid water" (Acts 10:47). Therefore, Peter "commanded them to be baptized in the name of Jesus Christ" (Acts 10:48). Baptized with Cornelius, apparently, were "his relatives and close friends" (Acts 10:24).

The primary significance of the episode clearly resides, in Luke's historiography, in the extension of the mission—in God's footsteps, as it were—to the Gentiles. While the story undoubtedly shows God's freedom of action in giving the Spirit, and even the manifestation of the gift in glossolalia, it is debatable how far the manner of the Spirit's gift in this case may properly be claimed as a regular part of a more general doctrine of (say) "prevenient grace." It is to be noted that Cornelius and "his household" were already God fearers (Acts 10:2) and in some way knew the story of Jesus (Acts 10:36). It was Peter's preaching which provoked their faith in Christ (as Acts 10:43 and 11:17 imply), and their baptism thus sealed their faith in Christ and God's forgiveness of their sin (Acts 10:43, 48) and, in their case, the gift of the Holy Spirit *already (just) received.*

1.6. The Philippian Jailor. When a nocturnal earthquake opened the doors of the prison at Philippi in which Paul and Silas were being kept, the terrified jailer asked them, "Men, what must I do to be saved?" (Acts 16:30). Taking their cue from the ambiguity of the verb *sōzō* ("to save"), the evangelists replied: "Believe in the Lord Jesus, and you will be saved, you and your household" (Acts 16:24). They then unfolded "the word of the Lord" to those present, by which the narrator means (as we know from similar cases) "the gospel of Jesus Christ." The preaching was successful, and the jailor "was baptized at once, with all his family" (Acts 16:33). He "set a table

for them," and "he rejoiced with all his household that he had believed in God" (Acts 16:34). The table and the rejoicing suggest the common meal of Christians (*see* Lord's Supper). Certainly it was later the practice, as Justin Martyr testifies, for the newly baptized to share at once in the Holy Communion.

1.7. Ephesus. The most puzzling feature in Acts 19:1-7 is why those dozen whom Paul encountered at Ephesus are said from the start to be "disciples" who "believed" (Acts 19:1-2). It seems that they were disciples of *John the Baptist.* They had been baptized "into John's baptism" (Acts 19:3). They had never so much as heard "that there is a Holy Spirit," let alone "received the Holy Spirit" (Acts 19:2-3). Thus they appear to have caught only part of John's message (perhaps the "baptism of repentance"), to which Paul has to add that John himself told the people "to believe in the one who was to come after him, that is, Jesus" (Acts 19:4). Immediately on hearing this, "they were baptized in the name of the Lord Jesus" (Acts 19:5). Such was clearly not a repetition of *Christian* baptism. Paul next "laid his hands upon them," and the result was that "the Holy Spirit came upon them, and they spoke with tongues and prophesied" (Acts 19:6). That sequence of water baptism and imposition of apostolic hands has traditionally been invoked in favor of episcopal "confirmation" after baptism; more recently, the story has been used among Pentecostals and others in support of "Spirit baptism," even marked by glossolalia, as a second stage after water baptism in the making of Christians.

1.8. Conclusions. It is hard to put together from Acts a systematic understanding of baptism or a consistent ritual of Christian initiation. There are differences in the circumstances of the episodes recounted and in the sequences of events within each story, and Luke is in any case chiefly concerned with the larger picture of the gospel's first spread. It is probably sufficient and wise to limit ourselves to noticing a cluster of recurrent themes that will appear in various configurations in the later theological and liturgical history: proclamation of the gospel, repentance, faith, the name of the Lord Jesus Christ, washing in water, the forgiveness of sin, imposition of hands, the reception of the Holy Spirit, glossolalia, life and salvation, entrance into the Christian community.

2. The Non-Pauline Epistles and Revelation.

2.1. Hebrews. This epistle (*see* Hebrews) contains two passages that demand consideration: Hebrews 5:11—6:6 and Hebrews 10:19-25. The first passage recalls to the addressees certain features from their first admission to Christianity that should not need repeating and perhaps cannot be repeated: learning "the first principles of God's word," "the elementary doctrine of Christ," which are likened to the milk that is succeeded by solid food (*see* Milk, Solid Food); a "foundation of repentance from dead works and of faith toward God"; "instruction about ablutions *[baptismoi]*, the laying on of hands, the resurrection of the dead and eternal judgment." So far the reference appears to be to the evangelism which elicits repentance and faith, and to the catechesis which instructs the recipients in basic Christian beliefs and in the significance of the rites of baptism in water and the imposition of hands which seal their entrance into the Christian community (the plural *baptismoi* may be due to the need for baptizands to be taught the difference between Christian baptism and other religious ablutions current at the time).

Then the text proceeds to mention in the aorist tense certain events, or a complex of events, that took place only once for each participant: they have "been enlightened," have "tasted the heavenly gift," have "become partakers of the Holy Spirit" and have "tasted the goodness of the word of God and the powers of the age to come." These could describe different facets of the entry into the realm of salvation* and/or the corresponding parts of a complex ritual process of initiation: "enlightenment" became a synonym for baptism; the gift of the Holy Spirit was associated with both water and the imposition of hands; "tasting the goodness of the Lord," in the phrase borrowed from Psalm 34:8, was applied by the early church to receiving the Holy Communion. In the context of Hebrews, all this is part of an exhortation to press on and a warning against backsliding, for it is "impossible to restore again to repentance" any who should go so far as to "commit apostasy" (*see* Apostasy). Gradually the church would later develop a system of penance for the readmission of grave sinners, but a second baptism has always been excluded (such would be tantamount to crucifying Christ afresh, said John of Damascus in an application of Heb 6:6; cf. John of Damascus *On the Orthodox Faith* 4.9).

In the other passage (Heb 10:19-25), against a background of Levitical ritual (Lev 8 and 16), the writer appears to recall to the already baptized the meaning and effect of their baptism: it is an assurance of current access to God through Christ and a stimulus to mutual encouragement and love within the Christian community. The summons to present action is based on the enduring reality, spoken of by perfect participles, of having "our hearts sprinkled clean from an evil conscience and our bodies washed with pure water" (Heb 10:22). That phrase, which does not set up an antithesis between the internal and the external but rather in a positive "rhetorical parallelism" joins the inner and the outer in "one indivisible reality" (Beasley-Murray), suggests a view of baptism as "an outward and visible sign of an inward and spiritual grace" (to speak with the traditional Anglican Catechism). The rite enacts a meeting between the faithful God of promise and the believers who confess their hope (Heb 10:23; the noun *homologia*, "confession," became a technical term for the baptismal confession, and the Byzantine exegete Theophylact echoed the eschatological orientation of the baptismal creed when he wrote: "We confessed, when we made the covenants of faith, to believe in the resurrection of the dead and in the life eternal"). The original ground of baptism is "the blood of Jesus" (Heb 10:19), and its ultimate outlook is "the Day drawing near" (Heb 10:25). The verbs of "sprinkling" and "washing" have been invoked in favor of aspersion and affusion as modes of baptism.

2.2. 1 Peter. Baptism is directly mentioned at 1 Peter 3:20, where it is said that "baptism now saves you, not as a removal of dirt from the body but as an appeal to God for [or: a pledge to God from] a clear conscience, through the resurrection of Jesus Christ." Baptism's power derives from the resurrection of Christ, which is made available to believers for the sake of a life of righteousness* in Christ (cf. 1 Pet 3:8-18; 4:1-19). The outward act of baptism has an inner significance: the saving gift of God is there met by the resolve of faith. The term *eperōtēma*, variously translated "appeal" or "pledge," appears to be contractual language and may refer to the baptizand's ethical commitment (Justin *Apology* I.61: the candidates "undertake to live accordingly") or the *responsio*, "response," to the questions put in baptism (Tertullian *De Resur.* 48; *De Cor.* 3). The passage sees Christian baptism as having been prefigured by God's saving of Noah and his family in the days of the Flood, a theme which along with other OT "types" (such as the Exodus through the Red Sea; cf. 1 Cor 10:1-2) will be sounded in later baptismal prayers and commentaries (*see* Old Testament).

The entire epistle of 1 Peter* has according to much recent scholarship a baptismal cast (*see* Worship). Within an epistolary framework, some have seen the bulk of it structured on the pattern of an entire rite of initiation, with the frequently repeated "now" constituting a trace of actual performance. The German Protestant H. Preisker found in the epistle the "deposit" (*Niederschlag*) of a baptismal service composed of hymns,* sermons and prayers: a prayer psalm (*Gebetspsalm*) as introit (1 Pet 1:3-12); an instructional address (*belehrende Rede*) echoing confessional and liturgical formulae (1 Pet 1:13-21; *see* Liturgical Elements); the baptism itself (between 1 Pet 1:21 and 1:22), followed by a brief charge to the baptized (*Taufvotum*), who have now "purified [their] souls" and "been born anew" (1 Pet 1:22-25); a festal hymn (*Festlied*; *see* Hymns) in three verses from a Spirit-inspired individual (1 Pet 2:1-10); an exhortation (*Paränese*) from another preacher (1 Pet 2:11—3:12), interrupted by a traditional Christ-hymn (*Christuslied*) from the congregation (1 Pet 2:21-24; *see* Hymns); an eschatological* discourse (*Offenbarungsrede*) from an apocalyptist* seer (1 Pet 3:13—4:7a); a concluding prayer (*Schlussgebet*) and sung doxology, bringing the baptismal service proper to an end (1 Pet 4:7b-11); a closing service for the whole church (*Schlussgottesdienst der Gesamtgemeinde*), consisting of an eschatological revelation (1 Pet 4:12-19), an exhortation (*Mahnrede*) to the presbyters, younger church members and the entire company (1 Pet 5:1-9), a blessing (*Segenspruch*) uttered by a presbyter (1 Pet 5:10) and a doxology by the entire congregation (1 Pet 5:11).

The Anglo-Catholic F. L. Cross saw even more precisely in 1 Peter the celebrant's part in the baptismal liturgy of a Paschal Vigil. The bishop's script ran as follows: solemn opening prayer (1 Pet 1:3-12); charge to the candidates, based on the Exodus theme as a "type" of baptism (1 Pet 1:13-21); [baptism, followed by] welcome of the newly baptized into the redeemed community (1 Pet 1:22-25); address on

the fundamentals of the sacramental life, i.e., baptism, Eucharist, sanctification, priesthood of God's people (1 Pet 2:1-10); [eucharistic consecration and communion, followed by] address on the duties of Christian discipleship, comprising the moral responsibilities of Christians in their several callings (1 Pet 2:11—3:12) and the Christian's vocation to the "paschal life," i.e., the life of mystical suffering in Christ (1 Pet 3:13—4:6); final admonitions and doxology (1 Pet 4:7-11). The epistle's twelvefold use of *paschō* for "to suffer" encouraged Cross to locate the presumed liturgy in the Easter Vigil, for such early patristic homilists as Melito* of Sardis and Hippolytus of Rome make a (fanciful) linguistic connection between that verb and *ta pascha* (Passover), and we know from Tertullian (*De Bapt.* 19) that the Christian version of that feast was the favored time for the administration of baptism at least by the late second century (and so the likely season of the baptismal liturgy described in the ancient church order that much twentieth-century scholarship has identified with the otherwise lost *Apostolic Tradition* of Hippolytus).

Most exegetes have considered that Preisker and Cross were too ambitious in their respective reconstructions of a baptismal liturgy in 1 Peter, but there is widespread agreement that the language of the epistle does indeed bear many baptismal associations. Whether or not such terms allude to existing rites of initiation, they certainly helped to establish the thematic repertoire of Christian baptism and thus also presage what may only later have found detailed ritual embodiment. Within the repeatedly recalled context of the preaching of the gospel and the response of faith, the following items deserve particular attention in connection with the understanding and practice of baptism: God's regenerative activity manifested in the resurrection of Christ (1 Pet 1:3) and the preached word (1 Pet 1:23), with the recipients being addressed as "new born babes" (1 Pet 2:2), remembering that John 3:3-7 speaks of being born again (*see* New Birth) of water and the Spirit and Titus 3:5-7 refers to baptism as "the washing of regeneration and renewal in the Holy Spirit"; the outline recital of Christ's saving work in 1 Peter 3:18 and 22 that echoes the apostolic kerygma of Paul and Acts and anticipates the confession of faith in baptismal creeds; the move from darkness into God's "marvelous light" (1 Pet 2:9), noting that "enlightenment" is found in Justin Martyr c.150 as a term for baptism; the mention of "spiritual milk" and "tasting the goodness of the Lord" in 1 Peter 2:2-3, which may suggest the practice of joining a cup of milk and honey to the eucharistic communion of neophytes as alluded to by Tertullian (*De Cor.* 3) and described in *The Apostolic Tradition* of Hippolytus.

2.3. 1 John. Two passages in this letter (*see* John, Letters of) come into consideration. 1 John 5:6-8 speaks of Jesus Christ as having come "with the water and the blood," and of "three witnesses: the Spirit, the water and the blood." The primary reference may be to the baptism of Christ ("the water") and to his death ("the blood"), the Spirit having rested on him throughout his ministry (Jn 1:32-34); or it may be to the "blood and water" which sprang from the pierced side of the crucified Christ (Jn 19:34), and in which patristic writers such as Ambrose (*De Virg.* 3.5.22) and Chrysostom (e.g., *Homily 85 on John,* 3) found an origin of baptism and the Eucharist, and to the Spirit which became available to believers once Jesus was "glorified" on the Cross (Jn 7:37-39). In either case, there will then be a secondary reference to the rites of Christian initiation, which bear a derivative witness to Christ dependent on the primary events of his life, death and resurrection.

It has been suggested (G. Dix) that this passage in the epistle matches an early Syrian* pattern of Christian initiation in the sequence of the gift of the Spirit (which Dix equated with "confirmation" but which may have been either "pentecostal" or exorcistic), water baptism (which in Syrian understanding was chiefly associated with the filial adoption of the Christian) and first communion (Whitaker 1970, 12-23). While it may be dangerous to find such detailed correspondences between theological statements in the Scriptures and ritual practices that are securely attested only later, there can be no doubt that the Scriptures nourished subsequent liturgical understanding even if not all the liturgical elements were present in scriptural times. Similar considerations apply in the case of the other passage in 1 John: twice in quick succession the epistle speaks of Christians having received an "anointing"* by the Holy One (1 Jn 2:20, 27), which brings truth and life. Did an unction with oil, as in the chrismation found in patristic liturgies of initiation (attested from Tertullian on), already in the apostolic period convey the sealing by the Spirit (cf. 2 Cor 1:21-22; Eph 1:13-14; 4:30)?

2.4. Revelation. M. H. Shepherd proposed that the structure of the Apocalypse (*see* Revelation, Book of) reflects an already existing paschal liturgy (*see* Worship), although admitting that elements in the scriptural book may rather have served as "a source of inspiration and suggestion for embellishments of the Church's liturgy that were developed in later times" (in which case, the charge could be made against Shepherd's thesis that "a paschal liturgy of a later age has been read into the Apocalypse, not read out of it"). The seven letters of Revelation 1—3 would correspond to the "scrutinies" or final screening of the candidates before baptism. Chapters 4—6 place the assembly before God in vigil. The "pause" of Revelation 7 houses "the initiation ceremony of washing and sealing." Revelation 8—19 matches the eucharistic synaxis, with prayers, readings from the Law, the Prophets and the Gospels, and the singing of the Hallel psalms (cf. Rev 19:1-8). The "marriage supper of the Lamb" (Rev 19:9) refers to the Eucharist itself, "a participation in and anticipation of the worship of heaven," "the earnest of the final consummation of the age to come" (Rev 20—22). What is certain is that the vision of the martyrs in Revelation 7 contains features that *sooner or later* were associated with baptism: the "washing" in the blood of the Lamb, or immersion in the saving death of Christ; the "sealing" of the foreheads, whether with a cross as a sign of belonging to the crucified Lord (cf. Tertullian *Marc.* 3.22) or with the name of God (cf. Rev 14:1) that was invoked over the initiands at several points in the baptismal process; the "clothing in white robes," whether as having "put on Christ" (cf. Gal 3:27; Col 3:9-10) or the "garment of righteousness" (as in the Byzantine rite); the allusions in Revelation 7:15-17 to Psalms 23 and 42, whose imagery of shepherd,* waters and deer occurs in ancient baptistries. If martyrdom* as viewed by the biblical Seer reflected or inspired the rites of baptism, conversely baptism supplied a category for describing martyrdom—the "baptism of blood" (as when *The Apostolic Tradition* speaks of a martyred catechumen's salvation being made secure through "baptism in his own blood").

3. The Early Postapostolic Period.

3.1. The Didache. This document, which may encode Syrian* practice around the turn of the first century, presents in its first six chapters what looks like catechetical material as it expounds the "Two Ways" of "life" and "death" (*see* Didache). Then in chapter 7 the document prescribes: "Baptize in the name of the Father and of the Son and of the Holy Spirit, in running water." No more than in Matthew 28:19 is it specified how the threefold divine name was invoked: it may have been covered by the exchange of questions and answers between minister and candidate concerning the latter's faith (as in *The Apostolic Tradition* of Hippolytus), for we have no evidence before the fourth century of a declaratory pronouncement "I baptize you in the name of. . . ." "Running water" is literally "living water" (*hydōr zōn*), which has biblical associations with divine grace (e.g., Jer 2:13; 17:13). While running water is preferred, it is not indispensable: "If you do not have running water, baptize in other water; and if you cannot in cold, then in warm." Some form of immersion is envisaged, although affusion is allowed if running or standing water is lacking: "If you do not have either, pour water three times on the head." Both the minister and the candidate should come to the event fasting, together with "such others as are able"; the candidate's fast should be of one or two days. *Didache* 9.5 stipulates that none but those baptized in the name of the Lord may eat or drink at the community's thanksgiving meals, in accordance with the Lord's injunction not to give what is holy to the dogs (*see* Lord's Supper).

3.2. Ignatius of Antioch. Early in the second century Ignatius* states that "without the bishop it is not lawful either to baptize or to hold a lovefeast" (Ign. *Smyrn.* 8.2). Later history will show the chief pastor's oversight of admission to the community maintained in various ways when the water rite is performed by other ministers: the Western churches will characteristically reserve to the bishop a postbaptismal imposition of hand and/or anointing signifying the gift of the Holy Spirit (eventually called "confirmation"); the Eastern churches will allow presbyters both to baptize and to "chrismate," but always with the use of episcopally consecrated *myron* (lit. "ointment").

4. The Later Second Century.

4.1. Justin Martyr. In his *First Apology* written in Rome around the middle of the second century and addressed to the Emperor Antoninus Pius, Justin Martyr offers the earliest direct and deliberate description of the process of Christian initiation, which he calls "the manner in which we dedicated ourselves to God when we were made new through Christ." Chapter 61 relates:

As many as are persuaded and believe that these things which we teach and describe are true, and undertake to live accordingly, are taught to pray and ask God, while fasting, for the forgiveness of their sins: and we pray and fast with them. Then they are led by us to a place where there is water, and they are reborn after the manner of rebirth by which we also were reborn: for they are then washed in the water in the name of the Father and Lord God of all things, and of our Savior Jesus Christ, and of the Holy Spirit. . . . Over him that now chooses to be reborn and repents of his sins is named the Father and Lord God of all things. . . . This washing is called enlightenment, because those that are experiencing these things have their minds enlightened. And he that is being enlightened is washed in the name of Jesus Christ who was crucified under Pontius Pilate, and in the name of the Holy Spirit, which through the prophets foretold all things concerning Jesus.

Chapter 65 continues:

After we have thus washed him that is persuaded and declares his assent, we lead him to those who are called brethren, where they are assembled, and make common prayer for ourselves, for him that has been enlightened, and for all people everywhere, that, embracing the truth, we may be found in our lives good and obedient citizens, and also attain to everlasting salvation. When we have ended the prayers we greet one another with a kiss.

A brief account of the Eucharist follows, in which the newly baptized will have participated for the first time ("for no one may partake of it unless he is convinced of the truth of our teaching, and has been cleansed with the washing for forgiveness of sins and regeneration, and lives as Christ handed down").

The following features of a process of Christian initiation are stated or clearly implied by Justin: those who respond to the church's message are put through an unspecified time of learning (the technical term will be "catechumenate"), which includes doctrinal and moral instruction as well as prayer and fasting; they must express their repentance, faith and commitment; their baptism takes place away from the congregation; forgiveness of sins and rebirth are both associated with baptism in the threefold name, and this baptism appears to play an instrumental role in the conveying of these divine gifts; baptism is also termed a washing and an enlightenment; the newly baptized are brought into the liturgical assembly, where prayer is made for them (some scholars have seen this as the location of some kind of "confirmation," which is otherwise lacking), and they join for the first time in the kiss of peace and the eucharistic communion.

4.2. Tertullian. Another, slightly later, description of the rites of initiation, together with fuller theological reflection on their meaning and effect, can be pieced together from the writings of the North African, Tertullian. His treatise "On Baptism" (*De Baptismo*) may be supplemented from passages in several other writings. The immediate preparation for the rite is thus: "Those who are at the point of entering upon baptism ought to pray, with frequent prayers, fastings, bendings of the knee, and all-night vigils, along with the confession of all their sins, so as to make a copy of the baptism of John [i.e., in its aspect of repentance]" (*De Bapt.* 20). The baptismal water is blessed in a prayer of invocation (technically called an epiclesis): "All waters, when God is invoked, acquire the sacred significance of conveying sanctity: for at once the Spirit comes down from heaven and stays upon the waters, sanctifying them from within himself, and when thus sanctified they absorb the power of sanctifying" (*De Bapt.* 4). At the edge of the water, the candidates make a renunciation of the devil, and once in the water "make profession of the Christian faith in the words of its rule" (*De Spect.* 4): "When on the point of coming to the water, we then and there as somewhat earlier in church under the bishop's hand affirm that we renounce the devil and his pomp and his angels. After this we are thrice immersed, while we answer interrogations rather more extensive than our Lord has prescribed in the gospel" (*De Cor.* 3). (As *De*

Bapt. 13 reveals, the reference is to the command to baptize in the threefold name of Mt 28:19, and *Adversus Praxean* 26 makes explicit that "not once only, but thrice are we dipped *[tinguimur]*, into each of the three persons at each of the several names." Tertullian's phraseology is consonant with the practice in *The Apostolic Tradition* of Hippolytus, where the minister of baptism put questions to the baptizands in the form of a threefold "interrogatory creed" and "baptized" them at each affirmative reply.) Then "we come up from the washing and are anointed with the blessed unction," which is linked with Moses' anointing of Aaron to the priesthood and with Christ's own anointing by the Father with the Spirit (*De Bapt.* 7). "Next follows the imposition of the hand in benediction, inviting and welcoming the Holy Spirit," and here the OT type is Jacob's blessing of Ephraim and Manasseh with "crossed hands" (cf. Gen 48:12-14) in prefiguration of "the blessing that was to be in Christ" (*De Bapt.* 8). Welcomed into the whole assembly, the neophytes receive at communion also from a cup of milk and honey (*De Cor.* 3; cf. *Marc.* I.14).

As to the minister of baptism: "The supreme right of giving it belongs to the high priest, which is the bishop; after him, to the presbyters and deacons, yet not without commission from the bishop, on account of the church's dignity; for when this is safe, peace is safe. Except for that, even laymen have the right" (*De Bapt.* 17). As to the time of baptism: "The Passover [i.e., Easter] provides the day of most solemnity for baptism, for then was accomplished our Lord's passion, and into it we are baptized. . . . After that, [the fifty days of] Pentecost is a most auspicious period for arranging baptisms, for during it our Lord's resurrection was several times made known among the disciples, and the grace of the Holy Spirit first given. . . . For all that, every day is a Lord's day; any hour, any season, is suitable for baptism. If there is a difference of solemnity, it makes no difference to the grace" (*De Bapt.* 19). The special appropriateness of Passover and Pentecost for baptism matches the Pauline themes of baptism as participation in the death and resurrection of Christ (Rom 6), and of baptism by the one Spirit into the one body of Christ (1 Cor 12:12-13).

As to the significance and effect of baptism, God's powerful work is accomplished by incredibly simple means: "A person is sent down into the water, is washed to the accompaniment of very few words, and comes up little or no cleaner than he was"—and yet he has been "granted eternity" (*De Bapt.* 2). Tertullian describes the sacramental operation thus: "The spirit is in those waters corporally washed, while the flesh is in those same waters spiritually cleansed" (*De Bapt.* 4). Or, with a distribution of effect among the various elements in the rite, and bringing out Tertullian's belief that "the flesh (*caro*) is the hinge (*cardo*) of salvation": "The flesh is washed that the soul may be made spotless; the flesh is anointed that the soul may be consecrated; the flesh is signed [with the cross] that the soul too may be protected; the flesh is overshadowed by the imposition of the hand that the soul also may be illumined by the Spirit; the flesh feeds on the body and blood of Christ so that the soul as well may be replete with God" (*De Resur.* 8).

4.3. The Apostolic Tradition. If the ancient church order that twentieth-century scholarship has pieced together is correctly identified with the otherwise lost *Apostolic Tradition* of Hippolytus, then it bears witness to the practice of Christian initiation in the church of Rome around the turn of the second century into the third. This testimony is of vital importance for the two-way reading between the evidence of the NT and the early patristic writings.

According to Hippolytus, inquirers are to be examined by the church's teachers as to their motives for wanting to "hear the word," and their admittance to instruction depends on their readiness to forsake evil ways and forbidden occupations. The catechumenate normally lasts three years, but the time may be shortened "if a person be earnest and persevere, because it is not the time that is judged but the conduct." Teaching is accompanied by prayer. When the catechumens are "chosen" to receive baptism (they will be called "*electi*" in the Roman tradition for the weeks of their proximate preparation before a baptism that typically takes place at Easter), their lives are examined for good works and then they may "hear the gospel" (this probably refers to a ceremony more fully described later, whereby the ears of the candidates were opened to all four Gospels). Thenceforth they are exorcised daily, and at last by the bishop. On the final Thursday, they bathe, and on the Friday and Saturday they fast. On the Saturday (typically Easter Eve), the bishop assembles the candidates and gives them a definitive exorcism. The night is spent in vigil, with Scripture reading and instruction.

At cockcrow, a prayer is said over the water, which is to be "pure and flowing." The candidates divest, ready for baptism. First it is the children's turn, "and if they can answer for themselves, let them answer; but if they cannot, let their parents answer or someone from their family." Then come the adult males, and finally the women, "who shall have loosed their hair and laid aside their gold ornaments." A presbyter bids the candidates say "I renounce thee, Satan, and all thy service and all thy works," anointing them with "the oil of exorcism" already prepared by the bishop. Then another presbyter takes over, assisted by a deacon; and in the water the baptizer lays hand on the baptizand and asks "Do you believe in God the Father Almighty?" On the response "I believe," the candidate is "baptized (*baptizatur*)" by the minister once. And similarly twice more, after creedal questions concerning "Christ Jesus, the Son of God" and "the Holy Spirit in the Holy Church, and the resurrection of the flesh." On coming up from the water, the baptized is anointed with "the oil of thanksgiving" already blessed by the bishop, the presbyter saying "I anoint you with holy oil in the name of Jesus Christ."

The newly baptized dry themselves and dress, and then enter the main assembly. There the bishop lays hand on them, praying "O Lord God, who didst grant these the forgiveness of sins by the bath of regeneration of the Holy Spirit, send upon them thy grace, that they may serve thee according to thy will" (Latin version) or "O Lord God, who didst grant these the forgiveness of sins by the bath of regeneration, fill them now with thy Holy Spirit and send upon them thy grace . . ." (Oriental versions). (The different versions have been deemed significant in debates over "confirmation" and the moment of the Spirit's gift.) Then the bishop pours consecrated oil on each head and, resting his hand there, says "I anoint you with holy oil in God the Father Almighty and Christ Jesus and the Holy Spirit." (The *double* post-baptismal anointing, by presbyter and by bishop, is a peculiarity of the Roman rite.) The bishop "seals" each forehead with the sign of the cross, kissing the neophyte and saying "The Lord be with you" and getting the response "And with your spirit."

Then for the first time the newly baptized

pray with the whole congregation and exchange the kiss of peace. The Eucharist ensues, at which the neophytes not only receive the bread ("the antitype of the body of Christ," delivered with the words "The bread of heaven in Christ Jesus") but also taste of three cups: of water ("to signify the washing, that the inner man also, which is the soul, may receive the same things as the body"), of milk and honey ("in fulfillment of the promise made to the fathers," and now in Christ giving believers nourishment "like little children, making the bitterness of the heart sweet by the gentleness of his word"), and of mixed wine ("the antitype of the blood which was shed for all who have believed in him").

5. The Baptism of Young Children.

From the earliest documents certain facts about baptism emerge. On the divine side, baptism is an occasion, or even a means, but certainly a testimony, of God's saving activity toward a person on the basis of the redemptive work of Christ. But nowhere is faith in Christ dispensed with on the human side. In the most clearly attested cases in the apostolic period and the early centuries, baptism is administered upon a confession of faith on the part of the recipient. The question, however, arises whether baptism was also given to some—particularly children—who were in a way "covered" by the faith of others or could at least be "spoken for" by them, as we see ritually encoded for the first time in *The Apostolic Tradition* of Hippolytus ("If [the children] cannot [answer for themselves], let their parents answer, or someone from their family"). Historians and exegetes often have a heavy ecclesial and ecclesiological investment here, for the answer affects, even if it does not finally settle, the contested issue of the impropriety, legitimacy or necessity of infant baptism.

Third and fourth-century writers speak of the baptism of infants as an apostolic custom. The only piece of potentially hard evidence extant from apostolic times is the reference to the baptism of "households"* in Acts (up to four cases) and in Paul (once). According to Acts 10:2, Cornelius feared God "with all his household *[syn panti tō oikō autou]*," and Peter was sent to declare to him "a message by which you will be saved, you and all your household *[kai pas ho oikos sou]*" (Acts 11:14); for Peter's visit, Cornelius called together "his relatives and close friends" (Acts 10:24), and when "the Holy Spirit

fell on all who heard the word" spoken by Peter (Acts 10:44), the apostle commanded them to be baptized (Acts 10:48). According to Acts 16:14-15, Lydia, whose heart the Lord had opened to Paul's message, "was baptized, and her household *[kai ho oikos autēs]*." According to Acts 16:31-32, Paul and Silas told the Philippian jailor "Believe in the Lord Jesus, and you will be saved, you and your household *[su kai ho oikos sou]*," and they "spoke the word of the Lord to him and to all that were in his house *[pasin tois en tē oikia autou]*"; at once the jailor "was baptized, and all those belonging to him [*kai hoi autou hapantes*]" (Acts 16:33), and "he rejoiced with all his household *[panoikei]* that he had believed in God" (Acts 16:34). According to Acts 18:8, "Crispus, the ruler of the synagogue, believed in the Lord, together with all his household *[syn holō tō oikō autou]*; and many of the Corinthians hearing Paul believed and were baptized." In 1 Corinthians 1:16 Paul writes that he "baptized the household of Stephen *[ton Stephana oikon]*," "the firstfruits of Achaia," who "have devoted themselves to the service of the saints" (1 Cor 16:15). As the story is told in some of these cases, it may be possible to equate the baptized with those who heard the word and believed, but in others the "household" that was "saved" may have been more extensive. In particular, those looking for apostolic evidence of infant baptism argue that the "households" which were "saved" *and* "baptized" will have included infants. In the estimation of those opposed to infant baptism, infants can hardly be said to have heard the word and believed and so will *not* have been baptized.

The classic modern debate on the *early history* of infant baptism is that between J. Jeremias and K. Aland. While Jeremias, against an OT background, holds that a quasi-ritual "*oikos*-formula" includes children, and even especially so, Aland considers that the reference of the common word "household" in any given case depends on the context and notes that small children are nowhere mentioned in the relevant NT passages. Aland is equally unimpressed by Jeremias's appeal to indirect literary evidence from the early or middle second century (such as the martyr Polycarp's confession of Christ, "Eighty-six years I have been his slave") or the data of funerary inscriptions, which in any case belong to the third century. Aland finds the clue to the beginnings of infant baptism in

Tertullian's treatise *On Baptism*. There Tertullian opposes what sounds to Aland like a new practice of bringing young children to baptism. Granting that the Lord said "Forbid them not to come to me," Tertullian draws the conclusion: "So let them come when they are growing up, when they are learning, when they are being taught what they are coming to; let them be made Christians when they have become competent to know Christ" (*De Bapt.* 18). For Tertullian, childhood remains an age of innocency (*innocens aetas*): "Why should innocent infancy come with haste to the remission of sins?" Infant baptism will have arisen, according to Aland, with the shift toward the view of original sin finally represented in Cyprian: a new-born child "has not sinned, except that, being born after the flesh according to Adam, he has contracted the contagion of the ancient death at its earliest birth; yet on this very account he approaches more easily to the reception of the forgiveness of sins, because it is not his own sins that are forgiven him but the sins of another" (Cyprian *Epistle* 64; Aland adduces similar passages from Origen). Later, Augustine of Hippo would appeal to the church's practice of baptizing infants—when baptism is "for the remission of sins"—as liturgical proof of the doctrine of original sin (e.g., Augustine *Sermon 174*, Migne PL 38.944-45; *Epistle* 194, Migne PL 33.889-91).

On the *theological* plane, proponents of infant baptism offer various accounts, severally or in combination, of the relation between faith and such baptism: a child may have faith (like, in Luther's example, the embryonic John who leapt in Elizabeth's womb when confronted by the Word in Mary's womb); a child may be given faith through baptism; sponsors may stand in for the faith of the child; the community of faith may "supply" the faith of one being aggregated to it; the child may be baptized with a view to its future faith. Moreover, the practice of infant baptism is considered warranted, or even necessitated, by its congruity with a variety of themes in biblical soteriology and anthropology: fallen humanity's need for redemption; the unity of God's covenant (with baptism as the Christian circumcision); the prevenience of grace; the universality of the gospel offer; unmerited justification; the intercessory power of others; the solidarity of the family. Those who reject the baptism of infants in favor of baptism solely upon profession of faith by the candidate argue that faith includes a measure of understanding and is personally unsubstitutable. Moreover, the "new" covenant requires circumcision* "of the heart"; the prevenience of grace and the universality of the gospel are properly and sufficiently embodied in the preaching of the word to all; original sin does not imply personal guilt in each human being from birth; justification may be "by faith alone," but it does not occur "without faith"; parents, guardians and the church properly exercise their responsibilities and privileges toward children by prayer and teaching, as towards catechumens in preparation for baptism; even then, there is the prospect, according to the Lord's teaching in the Gospels, that the eschatological crisis will actually divide families (see Wainwright 1980, 139-42).

See also HOLY SPIRIT; HYMNS; LITURGICAL ELEMENTS; LORD'S SUPPER, LOVE FEAST; PENTECOST; TONGUES; WORSHIP AND LITURGY.

BIBLIOGRAPHY. K. Aland, *Did the Early Church Baptize Infants?* (London: SCM, 1963); idem, *Die Stellung der Kinder in den frühen christlichen Gemeinden—und ihre Taufe* (TEH 138; Munich: Kaiser, 1967); G. Barth, *Die Taufe in frühchristlicher Zeit* (BTS 4; Neukirchen-Vluyn: Neukirchener Verlag, 1981); G. R. Beasley-Murray, *Baptism in the New Testament* (London: Macmillan, 1962); P. F. Bradshaw, *The Search for the Origins of Christian Worship: Sources and Methods for the Study of Early Liturgy* (New York: Oxford University Press, 1992); F. L. Cross, *I. Peter: A Paschal Liturgy* (London: Mowbray, 1954); O. Cullmann, *Baptism in the New Testament* (SBT 1; London: SCM, 1950); G. J. Cuming, *Hippolytus: A Text for Students* (GLS 8; Bramcote, Notts: Grove Books, 1976); G. Dix, *Confirmation or Laying on of Hands?* (TOP 5; London: SPCK, 1936); J. D. G. Dunn, *Baptism in the Holy Spirit: A Re-examination of the New Testament Teaching on the Gift of the Spirit in Relation to Pentecostalism Today* (SBT 2d ser. 15; London: SCM, 1970); E. Evans, ed. and trans., *Tertullian's Homily on Baptism* (London: SPCK, 1964); W. F. Flemington, *The New Testament Doctrine of Baptism* (London: SPCK, 1948); L. Hartman, "Into the Name of Jesus," *NTS* 20 (1973-74) 432-40; J. Jeremias, *Infant Baptism in the First Four Centuries* (London: SCM, 1960); J. Jeremias, *The Origins of Infant Baptism: A Further Study in Reply to Kurt Aland* (SHT 1; London: SCM, 1963); G. W. H. Lampe, *The Seal of the Spirit: A Study in the Doctrine of Baptism and Confirmation in the New Testament and the Fathers*

(2d ed.; London: SPCK, 1967); P. Pokorný, "Christologie et baptême à l'époque du christianisme primitif," *NTS* 27 (1980-81) 368-80; H. Preisker, *Die Katholischen Briefe* (HNT 15; 3d rev. ed. of H. Windisch's work; Tübingen: J. C. B. Mohr, 1951); M. H. Shepherd, *The Paschal Liturgy and the Apocalypse* (ESW 6; London: Lutterworth, 1960); G. Wainwright, *Doxology: The Praise of God in Worship, Doctrine, and Life* (New York: Oxford University Press, 1980); idem, "The Rites and Ceremonies of Christian Initiation: Developments in the Past," *SL* 10 (1974) 2-24; E. C. Whitaker, *Documents of the Baptismal Liturgy* (2d ed.; London: SPCK, 1970); idem, "The History of the Baptismal Formula," *JEH* 16 (1965) 1-12.

G. Wainwright

BAR KOKHBA. *See* JUDAISM, POST-A.D. 70.

BARNABAS, EPISTLE OF

An anonymous late first- or early second-century Christian writing that seeks to show by means of an allegorical interpretation of Scripture that Christians are the true heirs of God's covenant.*

1. Form and Structure
2. Central Concerns
3. The Interpretation of Scripture
4. Author, Date and Place

1. Form and Structure.
Though cast in the form of a letter,* the epistolary framework (*Barn.* 1.1-8; 21.1-9) is largely a literary device. The bulk of the document (*Barn.* 2.1—17.2) is something of a "tract for the times" (Barnard 1993, 172), a polemical essay that seeks to persuade and convince. In it the author shares with his readers *gnōsis*, "knowledge"* (*Barn.* 1.5b; cf. *Barn.* 6.9; 9.8; 10.10; 13.7; 18.1; 19.1; also *Barn.* 2.3; 5.4; 11.4; 12.3; 21.5) that he himself has received (*Barn.* 1.5a), that is, traditional material. The following outline (cf. Kraft) offers some indication of the topics addressed.
A. What the Lord requires (*Barn.* 2.1—3.6)
B. Readiness in the face of impending judgment (*Barn.* 4.1-14)
C. The Lord's suffering (*Barn.* 5.1—8.7)
  1. Why the Lord endured suffering in the flesh (*Barn.* 5.1—6.19)
  2. The Lord's suffering foreshadowed (*Barn.* 7.1—8.7)
D. Concerning "circumcised" understanding (*Barn.* 9.1—10.12)
  1. The "true meaning" of circumcision* (*Barn.* 9.1-9)
  2. The correct understanding of the Mosaic laws (*Barn.* 10.1-12)
E. Baptism and the Cross foreshadowed (*Barn.* 11.1—12.11)
F. The Covenant and its true recipients (*Barn.* 13.1—14.9)
G. Concerning the Sabbath (*Barn.* 15.1-9)
H. Concerning the Temple (*Barn.* 16.1-10)
I. Conclusion (*Barn.* 17.1-2)

In *Barnabas* 18.1—20.2 the author presents, as "another kind of knowledge [*gnōsis*] and teaching" (*Barn.* 18.1), a version of the "Two Ways," one of light (*Barn.* 19.1-12) and one of darkness (*Barn.* 20.1-2). The former is comprised almost entirely of "do's and don't's," while the latter is a description of evil actions and persons. This represents a Christian application of a common Jewish form of moral instruction. Similar material is found in a number of other Christian writings from the first through about fifth centuries, including the *Didache.** The complex connections between the "Two Ways" sections of the *Didache* and *Barnabas* have been closely examined. Rather than either one being directly dependent upon the other, it seems much more likely that both are dependent, perhaps indirectly, on a common source (Kraft; Barnard 1993, 194-95), and thus they are examples of what Kraft has termed "evolved literature." Similar material may be utilized quite differently in the two documents (Draper, 96-99).

2. Central Concerns.
2.1. Ethics and Eschatology. Tying together the two major sections of the document and the epistolary framework is a pervasive ethical concern set within an apocalyptic* eschatological* perspective. The struggle between good and evil in the "present evil age" (*Barn.* 2.1; 4.1; 4.9) will soon (*Barn.* 4.9b; 21.3) come to an end with the arrival of the "age to come" (*Barn.* 4.1) and its accompanying judgment* (*Barn.* 4.12; 5.7; 15.5; 21.6), for which Christians must be prepared. This conviction lends a note of urgency to the exhortations found everywhere in the document (*see* Ethics); Christians should take nothing for granted (e.g., *Barn.* 2.1; 4.9b; 4.13), unlike Israel (e.g., *Barn.* 4.13-14), who stands as a negative example throughout.

2.2. Church and Israel. Written at a time when the level of antagonism between church and synagogue (and perhaps also Jewish Messianic speculations [Lowy]) still ran high (*see* Christianity and Judaism), Barnabas represents one of the earliest contributions outside the NT to the discussion of a set of questions that has confronted the followers of Jesus since the earliest days of his ministry: how do the followers of Jesus relate to Israel's covenant and Scriptures? With respect to the first point, the author of *Barnabas* asserts that Christians are the true and intended heirs of God's covenant* (*Barn.* 4.8; 6.19; 13.6; 14.4b-5), that is, the covenant is "ours," not "theirs"; Israel forfeited it, according to the author, due to idolatry* (*Barn.* 4.8; cf. *Barn.* 16.1-2), disobedience (*Barn.* 8.7; 9.4; 14.1-4a) and ignorance (they interpreted the Mosaic laws literally, rather than "spiritually," as intended, *Barn.* 10.2, 9). As for the second point, the author presents a Christian reading of the Mosaic law* and prophets by means of an allegorical method of exegesis (*see* Church as Israel).

3. The Interpretation of Scripture.
In utilizing an allegorical approach the author is following an ancient and well-respected tradition of interpretation (*see* Old Testament in the Apostolic Fathers). Developed by the Greeks, the allegorical method assumes the existence of and seeks to uncover the hidden spiritual meaning of a text, which may be quite different from the apparent meaning. This method of interpretation played a role in all known forms of first-century Judaism, and particularly in the numerous writings of Philo,* an Alexandrian Jew contemporary with Paul, who himself offers a nice example in Galatians 4:21-31. An allegorical approach enables the author of Barnabas to offer a "Christian" interpretation of biblical texts that at first glance appear to have nothing to do with Jesus (cf. *Barn.* 9.7-8), and to claim that only Christians understand the true meaning of the Scriptures (cf. *Barn.* 10.12).

4. Author, Date and Place.
The document is the work of an anonymous teacher (*Barn.* 6.5, 9, 10b; 9.7; 13.1; 14.4; 16.1; 17.1) who, though he makes the customary declarations of modesty and self-deprecation (e.g., *Barn.* 1.8; 4.6, 9; 21.1), nonetheless considers his efforts to explain the meaning of the Scripture to be of no small significance, since they include his choicest insights (*Barn.* 9.9). Any connection with the historical Barnabas, though sometimes alleged, is generally held to be extremely unlikely if not impossible. Apart from possibly *Barnabas* 4.14 (which is susceptible of other explanations), the author offers no evidence of any use of documents that came to comprise the NT.

The document appears to have been written after the destruction of the temple in Jerusalem in A.D. 70 (cf. *Barn.* 16.3-5) but before the city was rebuilt by Hadrian (117-138) in 132-135. Within these limits greater precision is difficult to achieve (*see* Chronology). Interesting cases have recently been made for the time of Nerva (96-98; Richardson and Shukster) or the early years of Hadrian (Barnard 1993, 173-180).

A lack of information renders difficult a confident determination regarding location. In view of its numerous affinities in hermeneutical approach and style with Alexandrian Judaism and Christianity, and the fact that its earliest witness is Clement of Alexandria (who accorded it the same authority as the Catholic epistles), most scholars have located it there (*see* Alexandria), although Syria* (Prigent) and western Asia Minor (Wengst) have been suggested.

See also APOSTOLIC FATHERS; DIDACHE.

BIBLIOGRAPHY. **Text and Translation:** J. B. Lightfoot and J. R. Harmer, *The Apostolic Fathers: Greek Texts and English Translations of Their Writings*, ed. and rev. M. W. Holmes (2d ed.; Grand Rapids: Baker, 1992). **Commentaries and/or Editions:** R. A. Kraft, *Barnabas and the Didache* (AF 3; New York: Nelson, 1965); P. Prigent and R. A. Kraft, *Épître de Barnabé* (SC 172; Paris: Cerf, 1971); H. Windisch, *Der Barnabasbrief* (Tübingen: J. C. B. Mohr, 1920). **Studies:** L. W. Barnard, "The 'Epistle of Barnabas' and its Contemporary Setting," *ANRW* 2.27.1 (1993) 159-207; idem, *Studies in the Apostolic Fathers and their Background* (Oxford: Blackwell, 1966); J. A. Draper, "Barnabas and the Riddle of the Didache Revisited," *JSNT* 58 (1995) 89-113; R. Hvalvik, *The Struggle for Scripture and Covenant: The Purpose of the* Epistle of Barnabas *and Jewish-Christian Competition in the Second Century* (Tübingen: J. C. B. Mohr, 1995); S. Lowy, "The Confutation of Judaism in the Epistle of Barnabas," *JJS* 11 (1960) 1-33; E. Massaux, *The Influence of the Gospel of Saint Matthew on Christian Literature before Saint Irenaeus, Book 1: The First Ecclesiastical Writers*, ed. A. J. Bellinzoni (NGS 5/1; Macon, GA: Mercer University Press, 1990); J. N. B. Carleton Paget, "Barnabas 9:4: A Peculiar Verse on Circumcision," *VC* 45 (1991) 242-54; P. Prigent, *Les Testimonia dans le Christianisme primitif: L'Épître de Barnabé I-XVI et Ses Sources* (Paris: Librairie Lecoffre, 1961); P. Richardson and M. B. Shukster, "Barnabas, Nerva and the Yavnean Rabbis," *JTS* 34 (1983) 31-55; K. Wengst, *Tradition und Theologie des Barnabasbriefes* (Berlin/New York: De Gruyter, 1971).   M. W. Holmes

BASILIDES. *See* GNOSIS, GNOSTICISM.

BEASTS, DRAGON, SEA, CONFLICT MOTIF

The dragon, the beasts and the sea in Revelation (*see* Revelation, Book of) constitute a complex of evil powers that war against God* and Christ* and instigate conflict between humans.

1. Revelation as the Product of Conflict
2. Conflict Between Humans
3. Conflict Between Christ and Disloyal Christians
4. Conflict with the Dragon and the Beasts
5. The Fate of the Forces of Evil

1. Revelation as the Product of Conflict.
Revelation as a whole is a work permeated by conflict, especially the conflict between those who follow Christ and those who oppose Christ and his followers. The book was written in circumstances that sprang directly from the conflict of which the writer was a victim—his exile on the island of Patmos as punishment by the Roman authorities (*see* Civil Authority) for proclaiming the Word of God (Rev 1:9).

2. Conflict Between Humans.
Conflict exists between Christians at Smyrna and those who claim falsely to be Jews (Rev 2:9), although there is no evidence that this conflict reached the point of physical violence. Again, even though the word *conflict* is not used, violent conflict results from the release of the second horseman, the rider on the red horse, who receives power* to deprive the earth of peace,* with the result that people slaughter one another (Rev 6:3-4).

3. Conflict Between Christ and Disloyal Christians.
Even where the word is not used, there are warnings of imminent conflict between Christ and the disloyal members of the seven churches.* And there is an explicit warning of conflict with those members of the Christian community at Pergamum who hold the teaching of Balaam and of the Nicolaitans (Rev 2:14-16).

4. Conflict with the Dragon and the Beasts.
Although the locusts (Rev 9:1-11) and the horses (Rev 9:17-19) fall within the scope of the Greek word for "beast" (Foerster, *TDNT* 3:135), the most prominent examples of conflict in Revelation are those associated with the trinity of evil (the dragon and the two beasts) and its opposition to God and his people (Rev 12—13). God's "two witnesses" who, with their characteristics reminiscent of Moses* and of Elijah (Rev 11:16), must be seen as representatives of the Law* and the Prophets,* are caught up in this conflict. Until their prophetic task is complete, they are immune from danger (Rev 11:5), but when their witness* is complete, they meet their death at the hands of the "beast that ascends from the bottomless pit" (Rev 11:7). Yet they are vindicated when they are raised to life* again and taken up to heaven* (Rev 11:11-12).

The "great red dragon, with seven heads and ten horns and seven diadems on his heads" (Rev 12:3), who is identified also as "that ancient serpent, who is called the Devil and Satan, the deceiver of the whole world" (Rev 12:9), appears first as the opponent of the woman whom he pursues in an attempt to devour her son at birth. The attack is unsuccessful, for the woman is granted refuge in the wilderness while her child is taken to safety in the presence of God (Rev 12:5-6). This imagery probably owes much to a widely known myth, according to which the dragon (Python) pursues Leto, the mother of Apollo, at the time of his birth but then is killed by Apollo.

Although the son* undoubtedly represents Christ, the woman probably symbolizes the people of God as a whole, rather than any specific individual, such as Mary.* The deliverance of the child is therefore probably to be seen as a reference to the resurrection* and ascension* of Christ, while the deliverance of the woman may represent the flight of the Christian community across the Jordan to Pella (*see* Pella, Flight to), just before the siege of Jerusalem* by the Romans.

The dragon suffers defeat at the hands of Michael and his angels and is cast down from heaven to earth, where he wages war on "the rest of [the woman's] children, those who keep the commandments of God and hold the testimony of Jesus" (Rev 12:17), that is, the Christian community. The form this war takes is seen in Revelation 13, where there arises from the sea a beast who is inspired and authorized by the dragon. Like the dragon, the beast has seven heads and ten horns. Like the dragon, this beast is crowned with diadems, but whereas the dragon has one diadem for each of its seven heads, the beast has a diadem for each of its ten horns (Rev 13:1). In describing the beast as coming from the sea, the Seer is drawing on the ancient Canaanite mythology that is found in the OT as well: the sea is the special abode and domain of Leviathan (or *Lōtān*), the serpent that opposes God, and creation* involves the victory of God over the sea, the serpent and the forces of evil (Gen 1:9-10; Job 41:1-11; Ps 74:13-14; *see* Old Testament in Revelation).

As with the dragon from which the beast gets its authority,* the description of the beast borrows from the description of the four beasts in Daniel 7:2-7. This beast parodies the Lamb*: the horned Lamb appeared to have been killed (Rev 5:6); although the horned beast received an apparently fatal blow to one of its heads, the beast recovered. Again, the worship* ascribed to the beast by its followers, those whose names have not been written in the Lamb's book of life—"Who is like the beast, and who can fight against it?" (Rev 13:4)—is a conscious parody on the acknowledgment of God's greatness in such passages as Exodus 15:11. Many scholars believe that the historical referent of this image is the Roman emperors,* many of whom laid claim to divinity and demanded the worship of their subjects—specifically the emperor Nero, whose death and (so it is alleged by many) expected return at the head of a Parthian army are seen as equivalent to a death and resurrection.

Just as in Canaanite mythology the sea creature Leviathan is often accompanied by the oxlike land creature Behemoth, so in Revelation the beast from the sea has as its partner a second beast, one that arises from the earth (as distinct from the sea—or perhaps "the land" [i.e., Judah]). This second beast is a demonic counterpart to the Holy Spirit,* a "false prophet" (Rev 20:10) who directs the worship of the "earth-dwellers" to the antichrist,* just as the Holy Spirit directs attention to Christ. This second beast performs miracles that convince the "earth-dwellers" to worship an image of the beast from the sea and to wear the beast's mark (that is, its name or number of its name) on right hand or forehead.

Death is the penalty for failure to worship the beast, exclusion from commercial life the penalty for refusing the beast's mark. The Seer does not name the beast but says that the "number of its name" is "the number of a human being" (or "a human number"), that number being "six hundred and sixty-six" (Rev 13:18). Most scholars believe that the Seer is following a practice, common in his day, of using a number to signify a word, the numerical values of whose letters add up to that number (since in both Greek and Hebrew letters did double duty as numbers), and hold that the reference is to either Nero or Domitian, both of whose names and titles can with a little ingenuity be written in a form whose letters yield the sum of 666 (or, spelled differently, the "six hundred and sixteen" that is found in some manuscripts). It seems more likely, however, that the Seer intends to indicate not a specific individual but rather the merely human status of the beast: "six hundred and sixty-six" falls short in each digit of the perfect number, seven; in contrast, as *Sibylline Oracles* 1.326-30 points out, the name *Jesus* has a numerical value of 888 (that is, exceeding in each digit the perfect number). If, as seems likely, the first beast represents the Roman political power, the second beast may represent the religious officials who were responsible for conducting the ceremonies demanded by the state (*see* Religions, Greco-Roman).

The beast appears also as the willing ally of the great prostitute Babylon* (Rev 17:1-6) but later turns against her (Rev 17:16). This vision* provides further details concerning the beast, its heads being interpreted both as seven hills on which the prostitute sits and as seven kings, one of whom is still alive at the time of the vision (Rev 17:9-10). Its ten horns are interpreted as ten kings who have yet to receive authority (Rev 17:12-13). Of the beast it is said that "it was, and is not, and is about to ascend from the Abyss and go to destruction" and that it "was, and is not, and is to come"(Rev 17:8)—the latter a claim that can be made rightly only by God or Christ (Rev 1:18; 2:8). These features also suggest to most interpreters that the beast symbolizes Rome's political aspect, although there are many opinions about which specific rulers the heads and horns represent.

5. The Fate of the Forces of Evil.
The beast and its followers are not immune from retribution. Its kingdom is plunged into darkness (*see* Light) and its followers suffer great torments, yet they fail to repent (*see* Repentance), preferring instead to curse God (Rev 16:10-11). The dragon, the beast and the false prophet mount yet another attack, as and demonic spirits proceeding from their mouths inspire the kings of the earth to gather for battle at "Armageddon" (probably a reference to Jerusalem; Rev 16:12-16). A similar assault occurs after the "thousand years," when Satan* is released from his prison and induces the nations to gather together against "the camp of the saints and the beloved city." The final doom of the dragon, the beast and the false prophet is to be cast alive into the lake of burning sulphur (Rev 19:20; 20:10). The sea, the domain of the beast, will finally be destroyed as well—not merely pushed back but dried up (Rev 21:1).

See also ANTICHRIST; REVELATION, BOOK OF; SATAN, DEVIL.

BIBLIOGRAPHY. R. J. Bauckham, *The Climax of Prophecy: Studies on the Book of Revelation* (Edinburgh: T & T Clark, 1993); O. Bauernfeind, "πόλεμος, πολεμέω," *TDNT* 6:502-15; A. J. Beagley, *The 'Sitz im Leben' of the Apocalypse with Particular Reference to the Role of the Enemies of the Church* (BZNW 50; Berlin: Walter de Gruyter, 1987); G. R. Beasley-Murray, *The Book of Revelation* (NCB; London: Oliphants, 1978); G. B. Caird, *The Revelation of St. John the Divine* (HNTC; New York and Evanston: Harper & Row, 1966); P. Carrington, *The Meaning of the Revelation* (London: SPCK, 1931); R. H. Charles, *A Critical and Exegetical Commentary on the Revelation of St. John* (ICC; Edinburgh: T & T Clark, 1920); A. Y. Collins, *The Combat Myth in the Book of Revelation* (HDR 9; Missoula, MT: Scholars Press, 1976); J. M. Court, *Myth and History in the Book of Revelation* (London: SPCK, 1979); J. Day, *God's Conflict with the Dragon and the Sea: Echoes of a Canaanite Myth in the Old Testament* (UCOS 35; Cambridge: Cambridge University Press, 1985); W. Foerster, "δράκων," *TDNT* 2:281-83; idem, "θηρίον," *TDNT* 3:133-35; C. Kloos, *Yhwh's Combat with the Sea: A Canaanite Tradition in the Religion of Ancient Israel* (Leiden: E. J. Brill, 1986); R. H. Mounce, *The Book of Revelation* (NICNT 17; Grand Rapids: Eerdmans, 1977); H. B. Swete, *The Apocalypse of St. John: The Greek Text with Introduction, Notes and Indices* (Grand Rapids: Eerdmans, 1968 repr.); C. van der Waal, *Openbaring van Jezus Christus: Inleiding en Vertaling* (Groningen: De Vuurbaak, 1971); idem, *Openbaring van Jezus Christus II: Verklaring* (Oudkarspel: De Neverheid, 1981); M. K. Wakeman, *God's Battle with the Monster: A Study in Biblical Imagery* (Leiden: E. J. Brill, 1973). A. J. Beagley

BENEDICTIONS. *See* LITURGICAL ELEMENTS.

BENEFACTORS. *See* SOCIAL SETTING OF EARLY NON-PAULINE CHRISTIANITY.

BIBLICAL THEOLOGY. *See* NEW TESTAMENT THEOLOGY.

BISHOPS. *See* CHURCH ORDER, GOVERNMENT; MINISTRY.

BLESSING

The English word *blessing* is used in two ways in the literature under review. These two ways are represented by two different Greek word groups, *eulogia* and *makarismos*. The difference between the two word groups is clarified when one compares their opposites. The opposite of *eulogia* is cursing. This kind of blessing seeks an effect. It refers to an act of bestowing praise or favor. The opposite of *makarios* is woe. This kind of blessing makes a statement of value. It refers to a state of well-being, usually as a result of fulfilling some stipulation (*see DPL*, Benediction, Blessing).

    1. Effective Blessing (*eulogia*)
    2. Evaluative Blessing (*makarismos*)

1. Effective Blessing (*eulogia*).
Blessing is a prominent OT theme. For example, Isaac's blessing of the firstborn is stolen by Jacob from his brother Esau (Gen 27). Jacob blesses Joseph's two sons in reverse order (Gen 48). And the pagan prophet Balaam blesses Israel (Num 23—24). In many cases such as these, the OT sees the blessing as effecting some sort of outcome, as if it were an official last will and testament. But the power* of the blessings was not in the words nor in the speaker, but in the God* who was invoked.

    Blessing God was the classic form of prayer*

in Second Temple Judaism, as it is in modern Judaism (Bradshaw, 12). Evidence for this can be seen in the benedictions incorporated in the final form of the Psalter (Ps 41:14; 72:18-19; 89:53; 106:48), in a text from Qumran (Weinfeld), and in the fact that the first tractate of the Mishnah (c. 200 B.C.), called *Berakot* (Benedictions), is devoted to discussions among the rabbis about the formal blessings that were recited at various religious functions, especially at mealtimes, and during the normal routines of life. In these cases the blessing was essentially a declaration of praise: "Blessed is the Lord, the God of Israel," or "Blessed are you, O Lord our God, King of the Universe." The change from third to second person took place at the end of the OT period (Bradshaw, 16). One of the most common Jewish blessings was the *qiddûš*, said over the cup of wine at the onset of the sabbath to "keep it holy" (Ex 20:8). Another common blessing was the *'āmidāh*, a set of eighteen benedictions that were to be recited "standing up" at the daily service of the synagogue (cf. *m. Ber.* 4:3). The theme of effective blessing carries over to the NT but not with the same prominence, being replaced by a secondary form of Jewish prayer, the *hôdāyah*, or "thanksgiving" (for the distinction between *eulog-* and *eucharist-* form see Bradshaw).

Acts and Hebrews use the word *blessing* for various purposes in contexts with OT citations of patriarchal blessings. Acts 3:25 cites the divine blessing of Abraham,* "in your seed all the families of the earth shall be blessed," to affirm Israel's* election.* Acts 3:26 applies the verse to the Jewish listeners: the Abrahamic blessing comes through the gospel,* which they accept when they turn from their wicked ways (which in this case constitute the rejection of the Messiah). Hebrews 6:14 cites the blessing on Abraham after the offering of Isaac (Gen 22:17) to affirm the faithfulness* of God, so that the community might emulate Abraham's perseverance (Heb 6:12). The blessing of Abraham by Melchizedek* is cited in Hebrews 7:1. This blessing is given a commentary in Hebrews 7:6-7. The lesser, Abraham (one of the greatest men in Israelite history), is blessed by the greater, Melchizedek. Thus the priesthood* of the order of Melchizedek is greater than the levitical order that comes from Abraham via Aaron. Hebrews 11:20-21 also mentions the blessings of Isaac on his two sons and Jacob's blessing of

Joseph's two sons. The final mention of ancestral blessing is in Hebrews 12:17, where Esau could not inherit Jacob's blessing even though he sought for it with tears. Acts and Hebrews treat these ancestral blessings as part of God's salvific plan rather than as intimate personal communications between relatives or friends. Humans are vehicles for God's acts of blessing.

The notion of effective blessing occurs in 1 Peter 3:9: "Bless because you were called to inherit a blessing." This saying may have derived from the gospel tradition (Lk 6:28; cf. Rom 12:14). The point is that Christians, having been or about to be blessed by God, should bless their enemies. The inherited blessing is not defined in this verse, but it is probably the blessing of salvation* mentioned in 1 Peter 1:3-5. The citation of Psalm 34:13-17 in 1 Peter 3:10-12 outlines the blessing believers are to give: to do good and to seek peace* and pursue it. So the blessing is bestowed not so much through effective speech as through actions. It is not a pronouncement of blessing as much as it is being an instrument of blessing. This blessing is not without salvation-historical ramifications, since it is based on the blessing that Christians inherit by belonging to Christ.*

Christians also bless God. James 3:9-10 notes the inconsistency of human speech, blessing God and cursing people with the same tongue. *Blessing* here may refer to various Jewish liturgical benedictions referred to above, which may have been commonplace in James's church. The thrust of a large part of the letter of James is illustrated here: people can be religious without practicing true religion. The Godhead is also blessed in the opening eulogy of 1 Peter 1:3-5 and in the worship of heaven in Revelation 5:12, 13; 7:12. These blessings show the Jewish context in which the church was born.

The use of effective blessings continues in much the same vein in the apostolic fathers (*see* Apostolic Fathers). People are blessed as when Ignatius calls the Ephesian and Magnesian churches to whom he writes blessed by God (Ign. *Eph.* presc.; Ign. *Magn.* presc.; cf. *Herm. Vis.* 1.3.4.). Polycarp blesses God for allowing him to suffer martyrdom (*Mart. Pol.* 14.2-3). In contrast to developments in Judaism, the blessing of God seems to have been replaced by thanksgiving in the early church (Bradshaw, 31). Nevertheless, "the structure of prayer inherited from Judaism was still preserved—praise and thanksgiving leading to petition and intercession and concluding with a doxology" (Bradshaw, 63).

A special blessing developed among the apostolic fathers which may have roots in the practices of early Judaism. This blessing was actually a thanksgiving and was said in conjunction with the Lord's Supper (*see* Lord's Supper). *Didache** 9.1 begins, "Concerning the Eucharist, celebrate Eucharist thus . . . " The *Didache* uses the Greek verb *eucharisteō,* "to give thanks," and the noun *eucharistia,* meaning "thanksgiving" as an act. So the prayers said before the cup and the bread begin with the phrase "We give thanks to you, our Father" (*Did.* 9.2, 3), and the prayer after the supper begins, "We give thanks to you, Holy Father" (*Did.* 10.2). This prayer parallels early Jewish prayers (Weinfeld, 436-37). Justin Martyr echoes Jewish *qiddûsîm* in his description of the prayer said at the Eucharist when he notes that the president gives praise and glory to the Father of the universe, but the actual words of the prayer are not recorded (Justin Martyr *Apol. I* 66).

2. Evaluative Blessing (*makarismos*).

The adjective *makarios* in Acts (except Acts 26:2), the General Epistles and Revelation is linked with the values and ideals of Christian subcultures. Those who live according to these values will experience well-being—if not now, in the future. Acts 20:35 is a dominical saying, "It is more blessed to give than to receive." James 1:12; 5:11; 1 Peter 3:14; 4:14 note that the person who endures trials (*see* Persecution, Suffering) is blessed. In James 1:25 it is the one who hears and does the law* who will be blessed, not the one who hears and forgets. The blessing here is most likely eschatological,* since the verb is future and because there is probably a verbal link with James 1:12. The chief value highlighted in these macarisms is an enduring obedience* in the face of trials and persecutions. It is this enduring obedience that will be rewarded with life in the end as well as maturity in the present.

There are seven benedictions in the book of Revelation, five of them spoken from heaven.* Each highlights a value of the early Christian community. The reader and the listeners of the prophecy* are blessed as they keep the things written (Rev 1:3). This blessing is repeated as a sort of framing device in the penultimate benediction of the book, "Blessed is the one who keeps the words of the prophecy of this book"

(Rev 22:7). This value of hearing and doing also stands behind the blessing in Revelation 14:13, where those who die in the Lord are blessed because their works follow them.

In Revelation 19:9 those invited to the marriage supper of the Lamb are pronounced blessed. In Revelation 19:7 these are called the bride of Christ and are given clean white linen to make themselves ready. According to Revelation 19:8, the linen represents the righteous* acts of the saints. So again, the blessing is connected to the works of those who follow Christ.* These saints are also those who eagerly anticipate the coming of the Lord* (Rev 16:15). His sudden coming motivates them to keep their garments ready and available. This benediction is for those who remain faithful* in difficult times of waiting.

These same saints are blessed because they have a part in the first resurrection* (Rev 20:6). This benediction is slightly different in that these saints are both blessed and holy.* And they are blessed because they already have a part in the resurrection. Their blessedness here is not dependent on faithfulness but on participation in resurrection.

The final benediction (Rev 22:14) is directed to those who wash their garments. In the context of the book this can be nothing other than a symbol for conversion (Rev 7:14). These persons are blessed because they have the right to enter the heavenly city and partake of the tree of life.* This benediction "complete[s] a ring around the entire Christian Bible by reversing the prohibition of Genesis (3:22) and alluding to the solemn warning and invitation of Deuteronomy (4:2; 30:19)" (Urbrock, 760).

If all these benedictions are read together (and perhaps the number seven indicates that they should be), one can see that those who remain faithful in their actions in the face of persecution while waiting for the Lord are blessed. Faithfulness in persecution is one of the highest virtues* of the NT church. That faithfulness flows from "washing in the blood of the Lamb"—that is, cleansing from sin as a precondition to membership in the elect community.

The use of *makarios,* along with its verbal form, to denote evaluative blessing continues in the apostolic fathers. The Corinthians are blessed for their character and actions (*1 Clem.* 1.2-3), and the deacon who proves worthy is also blessed (Ign. *Phld.* 10.2). In two places Paul is called "blessed," presumably because of his special place in the church (Ign. *Eph.* 12.2; Ign. *Pol.* 3.2); here the term is an equivalent of "saintly" in the later sense.

See also PRAYER; WORSHIP AND LITURGY.

BIBLIOGRAPHY. "Amidah," "Benedictions," "Kiddush," *EncJud;* D. E. Aune, *Prophecy in Early Christianity and the Ancient Mediterranean World* (Grand Rapids: Eerdmans, 1983); P. F. Bradshaw, *Daily Prayer in the Early Church: A Study of the Origin and Early Development of the Divine Office* (New York: Oxford University Press, 1982); F. Hauck and G. Bertram, "μακάριος," *TDNT* 4:362-70; H.-G. Link and U. Becker, "Blessing," *NIDNTT* 1:206-18; W. J. Urbrock, "Blessings and Curses," *ABD* 1:755-61; M. Weinfeld, "Grace After Meals in Qumran," *JBL* 111 (1992) 427-40.

D. H. Johnson

BODY. *See* PSYCHOLOGY.

BORN AGAIN. *See* NEW BIRTH

BOWLS

The Apocalypse (*see* Revelation, Book of) depicts a series of seven visions* in which seven bowls containing the seven last plagues ("last" because they bring to completion the wrath* of God* [Rev 15:1]) are given to seven angels* who are then summoned by a loud voice from the temple* to pour out their bowls on the earth (Rev 16:1).

1. The Context of the Bowls
2. The Seven Bowls

1. The Context of the Bowls.

The "bowls" constitute the third and climactic series of seven explicitly numbered judgments* in the book of Revelation. There are clear parallels between each member of this series and its like-numbered counterpart in the second series (the visions of the trumpets). Some of these judgments are also parallel to the plagues leading up to Israel's* exodus from Egypt (Ex 7:14—12:32). Unlike the preceding judgments, in which only a portion of the target group— one fourth in the case of the seals* (Rev 6:1—8:1); one third in the case of the trumpets (Rev 8:2—11:19)—is affected by the judgments, each of the plagues poured from the bowls affects the whole of the target group. Moreover, whereas in the judgments of the trumpets humans are not affected directly until the fifth judgment,

humans are affected directly from the beginning of the judgments of the bowls.

The "earth" upon which the bowls are poured out could refer to earth as distinguished from heaven* or more probably "the land" (i.e., the land* of Israel). In both Greek and Hebrew the same word may denote earth as distinct from heaven, land as distinct from sea and land as a territorial or political entity, with the phrase "the land" often referring specifically to the land of Israel. The meaning in any specific text has to be determined from the context.

2. The Seven Bowls.

The first bowl is poured on the earth—the dry land as distinct from the bodies of water (cf. Rev 16:3-4)—afflicting with sores all those who had received the mark of the fearsome dragon-inspired beast* (Rev 13) and worshiped its image. This parallels the sixth plague on Egypt, in which the Egyptians were afflicted with boils (Ex 9:8-12).

The second and third bowls are poured out on the sea, the rivers and the sources of water, turning them to blood. All forms of aquatic life die, while humans who had been responsible for shedding the blood of God's servants* ("saints and prophets," Rev 16:6) find that they have no choice but to drink blood themselves. This parallels the first plague on Egypt, in which the Egyptian water sources were turned to blood (Ex 7:14-21).

As with the seven seals and the seven trumpets, the series of seven bowls is divided into subgroups. In this case the divisions occur between the third and fourth visions (the angel of the waters, together with the altar, acclaim God's justice in meting out appropriate punishment* on the enemies of his people, Rev 16:5-7) and between the sixth and seventh visions (the call to wakefulness in view of the impending coming of the Lord,* Rev 16:15), resulting in a 3+3+1 structure.

The pouring out of the fourth bowl on the sun results in scorching heat (Rev 16:8-9), a reversal of the promise* to the new people of God who are sealed in Revelation 7:16 as protection from the coming tribulation,* a reversal also of the promise to those Israelites who would return from captivity among the nations (Is 49:10) and of the promise of protection for those making the pilgrimage to Jerusalem* (Ps 121:5-6; *see* Old Testament in Revelation).

The fifth bowl is poured on the throne of the

beast, resulting in darkness (Rev 16:10-11), as in the ninth plague on Egypt (Ex 10:21-23).

When the sixth angel pours his bowl on the river Euphrates, its waters dry up (Rev 16:12), thus eliminating the barrier that afforded protection to Israel from invasion by its enemies to the north. Demonic spirits gather "the kings of the whole world" to battle at "Armageddon," perhaps meaning "his fruitful mountain," "the desirable city" or "the mount of assembly" (cf. Is 14:13), all of which terms could refer to Jerusalem. If the traditional understanding, Mount Megiddo, is accepted, this is another instance of the reversal-of-the-exodus motif that occurs throughout the book. Megiddo was the site of a major victory in Israel's conquest of Canaan (Judg 5:19) but also, later, of a major defeat for Judah, when King Josiah met his death at the hands of the Egyptians under Pharaoh Neco (2 Kings 23:29-30; 2 Chron 35:20-24). This reversal of the exodus forms a parallel to the Seer's presentation of Jerusalem as the Egypt on which the plagues now fall (cf. Rev 11:8).

When the final bowl is poured into the air, thunder, lightning and a great earthquake result. The "great city" is split into three parts, and the "cities of the nations" fall. "Great Babylon" is given the wine of the fury of God's wrath to drink, and massive hailstones fall on people. The thunder and lightning, together with the hail, are parallel to the seventh plague on Egypt but probably allude also to Ezekiel 13:8-16, which prophesies that "great hailstones" will be a feature of the storm that will beat upon Jerusalem and break down its walls despite the "visions of peace" that the false prophets had proclaimed for the city (cf. Carrington, 65, 273).

Even more significant than the parallels between individual visions of bowls and particular OT passages is the overall picture portrayed by this series. The use of the term *plague* is significant because of its use in OT passages such as Exodus 23:30-33, Deuteronomy 28 and Leviticus 17-26. Leviticus 26:1-2 warns the Israelites against idolatry,* and that chapter also threatens the nation with "sevenfold punishment" for rejecting God's commandments* (Lev 26:18, 21, 23-24, 28). The targum on Isaiah 51:17, 22 uses an Aramaic loan word closely related to the Greek *phialē* ("bowl"; Sweet, 241). In the first of these texts Jerusalem is said to have "drunk at the hand of Yahweh the cup of his wrath, drunk to the dregs the bowl of stag-

gering"; in Isaiah 51:22-23 Yahweh declares that the cup has been taken from his people and has instead been put into the hand of their tormentors.

B. J. Malina suggests that what the Seer saw, which then prompted his meditation on OT Scripture and its earlier interpretations, were bowl-shaped comets (Malina, 196).

See also REVELATION, BOOK OF.

BIBLIOGRAPHY. A. J. Beagley, *The 'Sitz im Leben' of the Apocalypse with Particular Reference to the Role of the Enemies of the Church* (BZNW 50; Berlin: Walter de Gruyter, 1987); G. R. Beasley-Murray, *The Book of Revelation* (NCB; London: Oliphants, 1978); I. T. Beckwith, *The Apocalypse of John: Studies in Introduction with a Critical and Exegetical Commentary* (Grand Rapids: Baker, 1979 [1919]); G. B. Caird, *The Revelation of St. John the Divine* (HNTC; New York and Evanston: Harper & Row, 1966); P. Carrington, *The Meaning of the Revelation* (London: SPCK, 1931); R. H. Charles, *A Critical and Exegetical Commentary on the Revelation of St. John* (ICC; Edinburgh: T & T Clark, 1920); J. M. Court, *Myth and History in the Book of Revelation* (London: SPCK, 1979); A. M. Farrer, *The Revelation of St. John the Divine: Commentary on the English Text* (New York and London: Oxford University Press, 1964); J. M. Ford, *Revelation; Introduction, Translation and Commentary* (AB; Garden City, NY: Doubleday, 1975); H. W. Günther, *Der Nah- und Enderwartungshorizont in der Apokalypse des heiligen Johannes* (FBib 41; n.p.: Echter, 1980); J. Jeremias, "'Αρ Μαγεδών," *TDNT* 1:468; G. E. Ladd, *A Commentary on the Revelation of John* (Grand Rapids: Eerdmans, 1972); E. Lohmeyer, *Die Offenbarung des Johannes* (3d. ed.; HNT 16; Tübingen: J. C. B. Mohr, 1970); B. J. Malina, *On the Genre and Message of Revelation: Star Visions and Sky Journeys* (Peabody, MA: Hendrickson, 1995); R. H. Mounce, *The Book of Revelation* (NICNT; Grand Rapids: Eerdmans, 1977); J. Sweet, *Revelation* (WPC; Philadelphia: Westminster, 1979); H. B. Swete, *The Apocalypse of St. John: The Greek Text with Introduction, Notes and Indices* (Grand Rapids: Eerdmans, 1968 repr.); C. van der Waal, *Openbaring van Jezus Christus: Inleiding en Vertaling* (Groningen: De Vuurbaak, 1971); idem, *Openbaring van Jezus Christus II: Verklaring* (Oudkarspel: De Neverheid, 1981). A. J. Beagley

BROTHERS OF JESUS. *See* RELATIVES OF JESUS.

C

CAIN. *See* ANCESTORS.

CANON

When speaking of canon in reference to the NT literature, the focus is specifically on that limited collection of Christian writings that was recognized by the church to be inspired by God and consequently to have divine authority in the church's life and ministry. As such these writings were also believed to reveal the truth and will of God for the Christian community. It is certain that the NT writings were not recognized as Scripture at the same time for all of the churches everywhere or even by churches in the same geographic location. The literature that was first acknowledged in the churches as Scripture and eventually formed the core of the biblical canon included the four Gospels (*see DJG*, Canon), the epistles of Paul (*see DPL*, Canon) and Acts, but there were differences even at the beginning between those (Ebionites*) who believed that Matthew better represented who Jesus was than did Paul (Hellenistic* Christians). The literature that took the longest to gain near universal approval in the churches as canonical was Hebrews,* the General Epistles—except 1 Peter* and 1 John*—and Revelation.* The following discussion will focus especially on the early use and recognition of the authority of Acts, Hebrews, the General Epistles and Revelation.

    1. The Canonization Process
    2. The Use and Authority of NT Writings
    3. The Muratorian Fragment
    4. Summary

1. The Canonization Process.

The recognition of the sacred and canonical status of the NT writings in the church was a long and complicated process beginning in the early part of the second century when some of these writings began to be used by the apostolic fathers* to support their teachings. The process was largely completed by the end of the fourth century, but never fully so. The NT writings were seldom directly mentioned by name in the second century and generally not called Scripture or any other similar terminology, though there were some notable exceptions (see McDonald 1995, chap. 6). Later in the second century, many of these writings were employed in arguments against heresies and heretics in the church such as the Marcionites,* Gnostics* and Montanists.

The final stages of the closing of the NT canon came in the early part of the fourth century during the empire-wide Diocletian persecutions* in the years 303-313. This included the forcing of Christians to hand over their sacred writings to the Romans to be burned (see Eusebius *Hist. Eccl.* 8.2.1-5 for a description). When the persecution began, churches had to decide, if they had not done so already, which books were sacred to them and which could be handed over to the authorities. They tried to preserve the sacred Scriptures often by handing over to the authorities only the writings of lesser importance. At that time there was no universal agreement on the books of the Christian canon nor had any church councils taken place to decide the matter. As the various lists of Christian Scriptures began to appear in the fourth and fifth centuries, there was no unanimous or simultaneous agreement on what comprised these collections, but in the first third of the fourth century there was general agreement about accepting the four Gospels, Acts, the epistles of Paul (numbering thirteen or fourteen letters depending on whether Hebrews was included as a letter of Paul), 1 Peter and 1 John. Some doubts persisted, however, in regard to the status of Hebrews, the remaining five of the General (Catholic) Epistles, and Revelation. Acts was received rather early because of its association with the Gospel of Luke, but by the early second century it was circulating separately from the Gospel and, though often cited, it was not yet called Scripture in the second century. On the other hand, some noncanonical writings were also contenders for inclusion, for instance, the *Shepherd of Hermas,* * 1 Clement,* * the letters of Ignatius* and even the pseudepigraphal *Wisdom of Solomon*, which showed up in some NT collections in the fourth century.

The generally accepted criteria for canonicity, however unevenly applied by the early church, included: (1) *apostolicity*, that is, whether a writing was written by an apostle (Eusebius *Hist. Eccl.* 3.25.4-7); (2) *orthodoxy*, whether the writing conformed to a widely accepted canon of faith, or *regula fidei* (Eusebius *Hist. Eccl.* 3.25.6-7 and also Serapion's criteria for his rejection of the use and reading of the *Gospel of Peter* in his churches [c. 195] discussed in Eusebius *Hist. Eccl.* 6.12.1-6); (3) *antiquity*, whether it was written during the apostolic period (see the *Muratorian Fragment*, lines 73-74); and (4) *usage*, whether it was generally accepted in prominent or large numbers of churches and used in their worship and catechetical programs (Eusebius *Hist. Eccl.* 3.24.18 and 3.25.6). The recognition of the inspiration of a writing was not so much a criterion for inclusion as it was a corollary of its acceptance in the church's scriptural canon.

The earliest extant list, or catalogue, of the Christian writings as a sacred collection comes to us from Eusebius of Caesarea (c. 320-30), who made a list of "canonical" (he calls them *endiathēkē*, "encovenanted") books. Even though he reported that some lists preceded his, including lists supposedly from Clement of Alexandria and Origen (Eusebius *Hist. Eccl.* 6.14.5-7 and 6.25.3-14 respectively), these lists were more likely inventions of Eusebius which he constructed from *his own* tabulation of the references to the NT Scriptures that Clement and Origen cited. No such lists or discussions of canon collections are to be found in the extant writings of either Clement or Origen (see argument of Kalin, 274-82). Thus Eusebius seems to have presented the church with its first list of *Christian* Scriptures along with a brief categorization listing the NT books either as "recognized" *(homologoumena)*, "disputed" *(antilegomena)* or "spurious" *(notha)* (see Eusebius *Hist. Eccl.* 3.25.1-7, but see also 3.3.1-2, 6).

In the second century the NT writings were not *generally* called Scripture (*graphē*), even though there were a number of writers who already had begun to designate some of them by that and other similar terms (e.g., "it is written," "the Scripture says," "that which is written," etc.) at various times throughout that century (see, e.g., 2 Pet 3:15-16, Pol. *Phil.* 12.1; *1 Clem.* 2.4; *Barn.* 4.14; Justin *Dial. Tryph.* 100-103; and Apollinarius at the end of the second century in Eusebius *Hist. Eccl.* 5.16.3).

As the church faced major threats from what it considered heretical groups (the Marcionites, Gnostics and Montanists), writers often referred to or cited the NT writings (especially Matthew and the letters of Paul) to answer these challenges. Although some scholars insist that the church responded to these concerns with a canon of Scripture in the second century, there is no evidence to support that claim. Rather, it responded with a *canon of truth* (*regula fidei*) that it believed was transmitted by the earliest witnesses themselves (the apostles). This canon of truth, a summary of the essence of the Christian faith that was believed to have been transmitted or handed down from the apostles to a succession of bishops in the churches, was most clearly set forth by Irenaeus (*Haer.* 1.10.1; 3.4.2) and was illustrated or supported by the writings that the church believed had come from persons in the earliest period of the church.

By the fourth century, however, there was a certain move toward a standardization of the contents of the biblical collection of Scriptures in various churches. The literature that was questioned, or "doubted," in Eusebius's collection (Eusebius *Hist. Eccl.* 3.25.4-7) in the early fourth century eventually found a secure place in most of the biblical canons by the end of that century, even though unanimity was never found. For example, in the East the Syriac Peshitta and other Syrian translations of the NT writings for centuries regularly excluded 2 Peter, 2 and 3 John, Jude and Revelation. A number of writings that held a high place in the esteem of some churches in the fourth and fifth centuries—for example, *1 Clement, Hermas* and *Barnabas*—were listed with other Christian Scriptures of the NT in the primary codexes Sinaiticus, Alexandrinus and Claromontanus. Eventually these and other writings were eliminated from the canonical lists of most of the later churches, while the canonical Gospels,

Acts and the letters of Paul obtained a prominent place in all such lists, even though their sequence varied within the collections. At the beginning of this standardization, or canonization, period, however, several writings—Hebrews, the General Epistles (except 1 Peter and 1 John) and Revelation—often found a troubled reception in the churches. They were finally admitted into the canons after several centuries of debate, but not unanimously or without suspicion.

After Eusebius numerous collections or lists of sacred Scriptures appeared in the churches and were discussed at various church councils in the late fourth and fifth centuries, for example, the council of Rome in 382 and especially those councils at Laodicea in 397 and 419. The varied acceptance of this literature as Scripture and ultimately as canonical had much to do with the prior experiences and beliefs of those communities that so acknowledged them. For example, in the first century the church was divided over whether Paul, reflecting Gentile Christianity and freedom from the law, or Matthew and James, exhibiting Jewish Christianity (*see* Jewish Christianity), better represented the essence of Christian faith. In the middle- to late-second century, the Gospel of John was more highly prized in Asia Minor than were the other Gospels, not only by the Montanists but also by others (e.g., Irenaeus who came from Asia Minor and relocated in Gaul), whereas the Gospel of Matthew was by far the more popular Gospel in most of the Eastern churches. After the major canonization period (fourth through the sixth centuries), there were still many differences of opinion in the churches over some books of the canon. The various lists of NT Scriptures that were produced in that period demonstrate the lack of unanimity regarding the "fringe" areas of the biblical canon. (For a survey of the variations in the Scripture canons, see the lists reproduced in Souter 1917, Grosheide 1948, Bruce 1987, Metzger 1987, McDonald [1988] 1995, Hahneman 1992, and Patzia 1995.)

The primary factors leading to a focus on a closed canon of Scripture is never spelled out in the church fathers, but it appears that the persecutions of Christians and the consequent burning of books in the early fourth century may have initiated that process for at least some of the churches. More important for the final stages of canonization, however, was Constantine's call for unity in the churches (see McDonald 1995, chap. 7). Added to this was Constantine's ordering (or requesting) that some fifty copies of the Scriptures be produced by Eusebius to be used in the churches of the new Rome (Constantinople). These copies received the emperor's approval and support, and must therefore have had some importance in the churches of that region, if not in the whole of the Empire. Therefore, both Eusebius's role in the selection and production of these Scriptures and Constantine's acceptance of them probably influenced many churches in the final stages of their selection process, especially those churches in the eastern part of the Empire.

The notion of a standard, or canon, by which other things can be measured was present long before the Christian community, but the notion of a fixed biblical canon emerged during a time when the Empire was focusing on religious uniformity, accompanied by demands on all subjects to return to the ancient pagan religion. That focus began with the Diocletian persecutions (303-310) and continued in a different form in the church during the reign of Constantine, who did not hesitate to impose religious norms on the church in order to establish such unity (McDonald 1995, chap. 7). It is interesting that in this context of religious conformity, the impulse to define a canon emerged.

2. The Use and Authority of New Testament Writings.

With regard to the canonization of Acts, Hebrews, the General Epistles and Revelation, it is important to remember that citations of these writings in the early church fathers does not necessarily mean that they were accepted as Scripture by the writers that used them. Further, even when these books were referred to as Scripture by an ancient writer, not all Christians of the same location or era drew the same conclusions about them. The following is a brief survey of the use, acceptance and recognition of these Scriptures in the ancient churches. Inferences of this for the formation of the NT canon must be drawn with care, keeping the above qualifications in mind. Once their authority was established or recognized, their inclusion into a fixed canon generally followed. This process began, however, by the early church's use of these writings.

2.1. Acts. References to the Book of Acts* are rather vague until the time of Justin Martyr (155-60). It has been argued that the Pastoral Epistles made use of Acts, but that is highly unlikely and few scholars make a direct connection. The similarities between Acts and the Pastorals include references to ordination, to the laying on of hands (Acts 13:3), the association of the institution of elders with the Apostle Paul (Acts 14:23; 15:22-23; cf. 1 Tim 5:17-19), the reference to the mother of Timothy (Acts 16:1; cf. 2 Tim 1:5) and an allusion to Paul's ministry in Lystra, Iconium and Derbe (Acts 14:1-7; cf. 2 Tim 3:11). These examples do not necessarily involve dependence. They could easily be the result of oral or written tradition common to both, and since there are no exact word parallels, the strength of the case for dependence is not convincing.

There are a number of similarities in content between Acts and other late first- and early to middle second-century documents, but again, a clear dependence is difficult to establish. What may better explain the parallels is that the ancient sources shared a common oral or written tradition (see other parallels of substance: *1 Clem.* 2:2, cf. Acts 2:17; *1 Clem.* 5.4, 7, cf. Acts 1:25; Pol. *Phil.* 2.3, cf. Acts 20:35; Pol. *Phil.* 6.3, cf. Acts 7:52; Pol. *Phil.* 12.2, cf. Acts 2:5 and 4:12; allusions in Pol. *Phil.* 12.2, cf. Acts 8:31 and 20:32; *2 Clem.* 20.5, cf. Acts 3:15 and 5:31; *2 Clem.* 4.4, cf. Acts 4:19; *Herm. Sim.* 9.28.2, cf. Acts 5:41, 9:16, 15:26; *1 Clem.* 59.2, cf. Acts 26:18; *Barn.* 7:2, cf. Acts 10:42; Pol. *Phil.* 1.2, cf. Acts 2:24; *Barn.* 19.8 and *Did.* 4.8, cf. Acts 4:32; *1 Clem.* 18.1, cf. Acts 13:22; *1 Clem.* 2.1 and *Did.* 1.5, cf. Acts 20:35).

Justin shows awareness of Acts as a written source (Justin *Apol. I* 50.12, cf. Lk 23:49; 24:25; and 24:44-45), but he omits referring to Acts either as Scripture or as an authoritative source (see also Justin *Apol. I* 39.3, cf. Acts 4:13; *Apol.* I.49.5 cf. Acts 13:48; *Apol. II* 10.6, cf. Acts 17:23 for other but less obvious parallels). His argument with Trypho regarding foods* (*Dial. Tryph.* 20:3ff.) could have been considerably enhanced had he appealed to Acts 10:14 or 15:29. The *Martyrs of Lyons* (preserved in Eusebius *Hist. Eccl.* 5.2.5) also have impressive word parallels with Acts, which strongly suggests dependence. Irenaeus is the first to use Acts in an authoritative manner and is the first of the church fathers to quote the book by name and at length (see, e.g., his *Haer.* 1.6.3; 1.23.1, 2, 3; 2.23.3; 3.1.1; 3.12.1, etc.; cf. also *Haer.* 1.26.3 with Acts 6:1-6; 3.12.1 with Acts 1:16-17; the story of the Ethiopian eunuch in Acts 8 is recounted in *Haer.* 4.23.2). In numerous cases there is clear dependence, and Irenaeus views Acts as a valuable source for substantiating his arguments against heresy in the church.

In the second century Acts was not yet cited as "Scripture," nor was it found in any collections of sacred literature. The appeals to the book, however, continued on in the third century and even increased. Tertullian made considerable use of Acts in his arguments against what he considered heresy (*Marc.* 5.1-2 and *De Praesc.* 22). There are also word parallels to Acts in the *Anti-Marcionite Gospel Prologues* (c. late second century). In the fourth century Eusebius had no hesitation in placing the book among the collection of "recognized" (*homologoumena*) writings (see Eusebius *Hist. Eccl.* 3.25.1; but also *Hist. Eccl.* 3.4.1 where he acknowledges that Luke, the companion of Paul, is also the author of the Acts). He cites Acts as a historical text (Eusebius *Hist. Eccl.* 2.22.1, 6, 7) and is the earliest writer to include it in a list of Scriptures (see Eusebius *Hist. Eccl.* 3.4.6).

Normally in the lists of canonical books, Acts served as a bridge between the Gospels and Paul's letters, but often this was not the case (see lists by Mommsen/Cheltenham where Acts stands just before Revelation; Clermont, where Acts follows Revelation; Cyril of Jerusalem in his *Cat.* 4.33 and Athanasius in his thirty-ninth *Festal Letter*, who place Acts between the Gospels and the General Epistles, which are then followed by the Pauline epistles). In Epiphanius, Acts comes after the Pauline epistles and before the Catholic epistles (Epiphanius *Haer.* 76.5). Pope Innocent placed Acts after all of the epistles and just before Revelation.

Barrett has suggested that rather than use Acts, Marcion may have substituted his own *Antitheses* (see Barrett 1:47), but what is clear is that Luke and Acts were separated by the time of Marcion (c. 140) (Barrett, 1:47). There apparently was no time in the second-century church or later when Luke and Acts were circulated together and, consequently, it may be concluded that they probably circulated separately by the end of the first century if not sooner. The early acceptance of Acts probably has more to do with its association with Luke's Gospel than with any other single factor.

2.2. Hebrews. The canonical status of Hebrews* was ensured when a second-century editor (possibly Pantaenus, the director of a theological school in Alexandria c. 170) incorporated this writing into the Pauline corpus. After that, Hebrews' authoritative status was never questioned in Alexandria. Eventually the Syrian* churches also agreed that Hebrews was written by Paul, and they eventually received it into their Scripture canon. The book was both known and quoted in the east and west, but that did not mean that the churches in the west accepted it as Scripture. Clement* of Rome, for example, made obvious use of Hebrews and incorporated its words into his letter without referring to it as Scripture or making any direct reference to the letter or its author (see *1 Clem.* 9.3, cf. Heb 11:5; *1 Clem.* 10.7, cf. Heb 11:17; *1 Clem.* 17.1, cf. Heb 11:37; *1 Clem.* 21.1, cf. Heb 12:1, and esp. *1 Clem.* 36.1-5, cf. Heb 2:18; 3:1; 1:3-4, 7, 13). Other parallels appear in Justin Martyr (c. 160) who, like the author of Hebrews 3:1, strangely refers to Christ as an "apostle" (*Apol. I* 1.12, 63; other parallels are found in his *Dial. Tryph.* 34, cf. Heb 8:7; *Dial. Tryph. 13*, cf. Heb 9:13-14; *Dial. Tryph.* 67, cf. Heb 12:18-19).

When Eusebius concluded that it was "obvious and plain" that Hebrews was one of fourteen letters by Paul, he conceded that others questioned that view, noting that even the church in Rome had denied its Pauline authorship (Eusebius *Hist. Eccl.* 3.3.4-5). It is clear that authorship of the book was central to its acceptance in the churches.

Clement of Alexandria was evidently the first of the fathers to maintain that Paul had written Hebrews, but he also claimed that it was originally written in Hebrew and that Luke translated it into Greek, leaving off Paul's name so as not to offend the Jewish Christians who were prejudiced against him (Eusebius *Hist. Eccl.* 6.14.2-4). Although Origen acknowledged that others "with good reason" accepted Hebrews as Paul's letter, he admits that "who wrote the epistle, in truth God knows," but notes that some of his contemporaries believed that Clement of Rome wrote it while others thought that it was Luke (Eusebius *Hist. Eccl.* 6.25.11-14). Tertullian later claimed that Barnabas wrote Hebrews (Tertullian *De Pud.* 20). In all of these cases, authorship was the basis for acceptance into the canon, quite apart from the basis for

acceptance today, which is essentially the value of the message for the life and ministry of the Christian community.

Hebrews had a questionable position in the Syriac Peshitta and was placed after the epistles of Paul, not unlike in the current biblical canon where its position is somewhat equivocal. Later, Augustine and Jerome had doubts about the authorship of Hebrews, but they nevertheless accepted it as Paul's so as to ensure its inclusion in the biblical canon. Jerome observed that the churches to his west (the "Latins") "do not receive it among the canonical Scriptures as St. Paul's" (Jerome *Ep. ad Dard.* 129). Eventually in the fourth and fifth centuries, the book was included in many of the Scripture canons of the west, at first by the Synod of Hippo in 393, and then by the Third and Sixth Synods of Carthage in 397 and 419 respectively.

2.3. The General Epistles. This collection of seven letters (James, 1-2 Peter, 1-2-3 John, Jude) are called "catholic" or "general" because of their encyclical nature; namely, they were intended for a wider or more general audience rather than for a specific church or individual as in the case of the letters of Paul. The term *catholic* appears to have originated in the latter part of the second century when it was used by Apollonius (died c. 185) to describe a letter (*katholikē epistolē*) composed by a Montanist named Themiso (Eusebius *Hist. Eccl.* 5.18.5). Clement of Alexandria called the letter that came from the council in Jerusalem in Acts 15:22-29 a "catholic epistle," written by all of the apostles. In the early third century Origen also designated the *Epistle of Barnabas* (c. 140) as a "catholic epistle" (Origen *Cont. Cels.* 1.63). The term had nothing to do with the canonical nature of the letters, but rather their general appeal. It was later used of the seven letters that are now called the General or Catholic Epistles by Eusebius in the fourth century (*Hist. Eccl.* 2.23.24-25 and 6.14.1) and later by Athanasius who in his thirty-ninth *Festal Letter* (39.5) called this collection the "seven catholic epistles."

2.3.1. James. This small book had a mixed reception in early Christianity as a result of its apparent contradiction of Paul's teaching on faith and works (*see* Faith and Works). In Eusebius James* was classified as one of the disputed writings (*antilegomena*; *Hist. Eccl.* 3.25.3), and it is missing from several of the fourth-century lists of NT books. Earlier, Clement* of Rome (c. 95) knew of James, and without mentioning it by name he used it to balance the teaching of Paul on the issue of works and the law versus faith (see *1 Clem.* 3, 5, 17, and especially 21, but also 30, 33, 35, 38, 40, 46, 53). Clement did not neglect the need for faith but like James also insisted on the importance of good works. There are further parallels of thought with the *Didache** (see *Did.* 2.4, cf. Jas 3:6-10; *Did.* 4.3, cf. Jas 1:8, 4:8; and *Did.* 4.14, cf. Jas 5:16). Mayor has noted numerous parallels in thought (but not always with clear dependence upon James) in the writings of Ignatius, Barnabas, Polycarp, Hermas, Diognetus and Justin (Mayor, lxxiii-lxxix).

Eusebius says that Clement of Alexandria commented on all of the canonical [lit., "en-covenanted"] Scriptures, not passing over even the disputed writings, namely, Jude and the rest of the "catholic epistles" (Eusebius *Hist. Eccl.* 6.14.1-3). It is not clear, however, what books he had in mind, and he nowhere mentions the epistle of James by name. Origen, who was the first person to refer to the letter as Scripture, claimed that it was written by James the brother of Jesus (*Comm. Joh.* 19.6; compare *Sel. in Exod.* 15.25). Later the same view emerges in Dionysius of Alexandria (c. 250-65) where he cites James 1:17 (*Comm. in Lucam*) and refers to God speaking. A similar reference is found in Gregory Thaumaturgus (c. 250-65) whose *Fragment* is cited in *Catena.* James's inclusion in the NT canon was widespread at the end of the fourth century, but it was not universal. Even in the sixteenth century it was held in suspicion by Martin Luther. (For a detailed examination of the use and citations of James in the early church fathers, see Mayor, lxvi-lxxxiv.)

2.3.2. 1 Peter. Although there are several parallel phrases in *Barnabas** and 1 Peter* (e.g., *Barn.* 5.6, cf. 1 Pet. 1:20), it is only with Polycarp* that direct use is first found among the apostolic fathers (see, e.g., *Phil.* 1.3, cf. 1 Pet. 1:8; *Phil.* 10.2, cf. 1 Pet. 2:12). The author of 2 Peter (*see* 2 Peter) refers to the existence of an earlier letter by Peter (2 Pet 3:1) and, depending on the dating of 2 Peter,* this may be the oldest reference to 1 Peter. Eusebius claimed that Papias (c. 100-150) knew and used 1 Peter (Eusebius *Hist. Eccl* 3.39.17) and added it to his own recognized books (in Eusebius *Hist. Eccl.* 3.3.1; 3.25.1-2). Irenaeus appears to have been the first to refer to 1 Peter by name (*Haer.* 4.9.2;

4.16.5; 5.7.2), and thereafter many references were made to the book by the early church fathers. There is a very strong early witness to the usefulness of the letter in various Christian communities, and it does not appear to have been seriously questioned in the fourth century even though it is absent from the Muratorian Fragment. One explanation for this may be that the Fragment is incomplete, that is, it is a *fragment,* and its original form may have incorporated it, but this is all supposition. Eusebius claims that only one letter from Peter was admitted to the recognized collection, even though he was aware of another having been written in Peter's name (Eusebius *Hist. Eccl.* 3.3.1-4).

2.3.3. 2 Peter. Essentially 2 Peter* was under suspicion in much of the church until the time of Athanasius's publication of his thirty-ninth *Festal Letter* in 367. Eusebius rejected it (Eusebius *Hist. Eccl.* 3.25.3) and was aware of widespread doubts about its authenticity (Eusebius *Hist. Eccl.* 3.3.1-4), and the Syrian churches held it in question until the sixth century. It is missing from the recension of Lucian of Antioch and the most prominent church fathers from Antioch. John Chrysostom and Theodore of Mopsuestia never refer to it even though it is almost certain that they knew of it. Athanasius of Alexandria apparently set the stage for the acceptance of both 2 Peter and Jude into the Christian NT canon, but their witness was being questioned even as late as the Reformation when Martin Luther concluded that the Christian message did not shine well through them. The use of 2 Peter in the early Christian churches was limited and mixed at best.

2.3.4. 1 John. This was one of the earliest books apart from the Gospels and Epistles of Paul to be acknowledged as Scripture and subsequently to be included as part of the Christian canon (*see* John, Letters of). Both Eusebius (*Hist. Eccl.* 3.24.17) and Origen, according to Eusebius (*Hist. Eccl.* 6.25.10), accepted this book as a part of their sacred collection of Christian Scriptures. It was cited in an authoritative manner by Irenaeus (*Haer.* 3.17.5, 8), Clement of Alexandria (*Frag. Adum.*) and Tertullian *Prax.* 15; *Marc.* 5.16; *Scorp.* 12). Apart from the Alogoi from Asia Minor in the last third of the second century, who rejected the Gospel of John, Acts and Revelation (see Irenaeus' report in *Haer.* 3.11.12), and probably 1 John as well, few others were opposed to the authenticity of this letter and most writers of antiquity agreed that John had written it. Eusebius in the fourth century states that very few leaders of the church ever questioned its authenticity (*Hist. Eccl.* 3.3.1-5 and 3.25.1-3). It appears that it was accepted into the Syriac Peshitta version no later than the fifth century, but it was evidently not included in the early stages of its formation.

The first clear citation of the letter appears in Polycarp (Pol. *Phil.* 7) and Justin (*Dial. Tryph.* 123.9, see also the possible reference in Ign. *Eph.* 7.2; *Diogn.* 10.3). The gnostic *Gospel of Truth* may allude to 1 John (see *Gos. Truth* 27.24 and 31.4-5), but that is not certain. Again, allusions and citations in themselves do not necessarily imply that a writing was accepted as Scripture *or* that it was a part of some fixed biblical canon, but the *kind* of use that this letter received in the early church shows clearly that there was widespread acknowledgment of its authority, and its use is abundant in the church fathers. When canon lists of Christian scriptures first appeared in the fourth century, 1 John was regularly included.

2.3.5. 2 and 3 John. These two small letters (*see* John, Letters of) have very little attestation prior to the fourth century, and both Eusebius (*Hist. Eccl.* 3.25.3) and Origen (*Comm. Joh.* 5.3, see the quote in Eusebius *Hist. Eccl.* 6.25.10, which is probably a Eusebian invention) omit them from the recognized (*homologoumena*) writings. Prior to that time there is very little ancient testimony that speaks either to the existence or the authority of these letters. There are possible parallels in content in the apostolic fathers, but they are not conclusive (see, e.g., Pol. *Phil.* 7.2, cf. 2 John 7 and 1 Jn 4:2; Ign. *Smyrn.* 4.1, cf. 2 Jn 10-11; cf. also Tertullian, *De Car.* 24). Better information is available on the use of 2 John from the time of Clement of Alexandria (*Strom.* 2.15.66), but references to 3 John are missing (Irenaeus quotes 2 Jn 11 and 7 in *Haer.* 3.17.8). According to Eusebius, Dionysius of Alexandria knew of all three epistles of John (Eusebius *Hist. Eccl.* 7.25.11), but in regard to authorship he concludes "that the writer of these words, therefore, was John, one must believe since he says it. But what John, is not clear" (Eusebius *Hist. Eccl.* 7.25.12, LCL trans.).

Irenaeus and Tertullian do not mention 3 John and even the fourth-century Muratorian Fragment (lines 68-69) knew of only two letters

of John. Cyprian (fl. c. 240-50) frequently referred to 1 John, but also cited 2 John 10-11 in his *Sententiae Episcoporum* 81. Elsewhere in the fourth century the three epistles were known, but the second and third were not yet generally accepted among the churches as Scripture or placed in a collection of Scriptures. They were included in lists from Athanasius's thirty-ninth *Festal Letter* (c. 367), Cyril of Jerusalem (*Cat.* 4.36) and the Mommsen Catalogue (c. 360 in North Africa), but doubts continued to be expressed about their canonicity by Jerome in his *De Viris Illustribus* 9, 18 (c. 420). There apparently was a time when only two epistles of John were accepted in the west and also in Alexandria. Churches under the leadership of Antioch generally accepted only James, 1 Peter and 1 John of the seven General Epistles. Chrysostom, who moved from Antioch to Constantinople in 398, refers only to those three General Epistles. This was also true of the Cappadocian Fathers, Basil, Gregory of Nazianzus and Gregory of Nyssa, at the end of the fourth century. Outside of appearances in canonical lists, there appear to have been no certain references to 3 John until the time of Jerome and Augustine. Both 2 and 3 John had a slim history of use in the church until the fifth century, even though they both appear in lists of canonical Scriptures (e.g., Athanasius) generally dated earlier than the treatises which appeal to their authority and reception. Churches that followed the Syriac Peshitta did not include 2 and 3 John until the production of the Philoxenian version in 508.

Although some scholars have argued that 2 and 3 John were circulated at first as one epistle, hence their common designation under one name, and consequently there were only two epistles mentioned in some lists, the evidence for this is not at all convincing. Others, with admittedly even less evidence to support their thesis, have tried to change the meaning of the Muratorian Fragment from two to one catholic epistle (1 Jn) and two others (*see* Schnackenburg, 274).

2.3.6. Jude. The use and citation of Jude in the ancient church was common, and numerous parallels exist in the second and third centuries. But there is a mixed reception in the fourth century because of Jude's use of *1 Enoch* (for early parallels of thought and possible use, see Pol. *Phil.* 3.2, cf. Jude 3, 20; Pol. *Phil.* 11.4, cf. Jude 20, 23; *Barn.* 2.10, cf. Jude 3, 4; as well as Athenagoras, *Suppl.* 24-25; Theophilus of Antioch, *Autol.* 2.15; and *Clement of Alexandria in his Paed.* 3.8.44, who quotes Jude 5, 6 by name and later in 3.8.45 quotes Jude 11). Clement of Alexandria quotes Jude 8-16 and mentions Jude by name (*Strom.* 3.2.11), and Eusebius claims that Clement accepted "even the disputed writings," including Hebrews, *Barnabas, 1 Clement* and Jude (Eusebius *Hist. Eccl.* 6.13.6 and 6.14.1). Tertullian implies that Jude was known in Latin translation to his readers (*De Cult. Fem.* 1.3), but later Eusebius suggests that Jude came under suspicion after the time of Clement, possibly even by Origen (see Eusebius *Hist. Eccl.* 6.13.6 and 6.14.1).

Origen knew of questions about Jude, but he does not appear to have expressed them himself and variously cites the book (see *Comm. Mt.* 17.30 where he quotes Jude 6 and again in 10.17 where he refers to Jude as a servant of "our Lord Jesus Christ and a brother of James." See also *Comm. Joh.* 13.37, cf. Jude 6; *Hom. Ez.* 4.1, cf. Jude. 8-9; and in *De Princ.* 3.2.1, where he shows awareness of the book). In the case of 2 Peter, Origen was aware of doubts about the book, but that did not deter him from using it. He may have been attracted to 2 Peter and Jude because of their angelology.*

The widely acknowledged use of Jude in 2 Peter gives further witness to the widespread use of the epistle. The book was fully accepted as canon by Athanasius, however, in his canon of 367. The stormy reception of Jude in the fourth and fifth centuries came primarily as a result of its use of *1 Enoch* (Jude 14). In the early part of the second century, but generally throughout the first two centuries, the *Book of Enoch* was accepted as an inspired writing and therefore was considered sacred in many Christian communities (*see* Non-Canonical Citations).

Jude's appeal to *Enoch*, therefore, was not a problem in the Christian communities in the beginning of the church. Only in the third century and later do we find doubts expressed about the canonicity of *Enoch*, mostly because of its attributing carnal lust to heavenly beings. Consequently in the fourth century and later, Jude's use of *Enoch* led to questions about its own place in the Scripture canon. *Enoch* was used by the author of the *Assumption of Moses,* the apocryphal book of *Jubilees,* the *Apocalypse of*

Baruch (c. A.D. 70), and even by the author of the *Testaments of the Twelve Patriarchs.* In the Christian era, the author of *Epistle of Barnabas* cites the book some three times, and in two of those instances he refers to *Enoch* as Scripture (see *Barn.* 4.3 which begins, "it was written as Enoch says," and *Barn.* 16.5 citing *Enoch* 89.55, 66, 67, beginning with the words, "For the Scripture says"). Eusebius lists Jude among the "doubted" (*antilegomena*) writings in the church (Eusebius *Hist. Eccl.* 3.25.3, see also *Hist. Eccl.* 2.23.25), and even Jerome, who accepted its authenticity, felt obligated to deal with the issue of Jude's use of Enoch (*Vir.* 4). Didymus of Alexandria (c. 395) defended Jude against those who attacked its use of Enoch (Migne, PG 39.1811-18). Interestingly, Bigg suggests that the offense leveled against Jude in the fourth century was not that Jude made use of Enoch, as other Christian writers had done, but that he referred to the writing specifically by *name* (309-10)! He also claims that 1 and 2 Peter, along with Jude, made use of Jewish apocalypses in much the same manner, and that they exhibited characteristics that were common to their Jewish education. Although Jude goes further than the other two epistles when he cites *Enoch* by name, Bigg claims that Jude is nonetheless within the context of the practice of the writers of his age and within the bounds of acceptable "spiritual perception which distinguishes the Church from the sectarians" (Bigg, 310).

Except for James, 1 Peter and 1 John, the General Epistles were not widely known in the churches throughout the second century, and they were variously disputed in the fourth and fifth centuries and even later. Further, the literature that informed the life and ministry of the churches in the second century was, in some notable cases (*1 Enoch, Eldad and Modad, 1 Clement,* letters of Ignatius, *Shepherd of Hermas* and others) somewhat different from that which informed the churches in the fourth to the sixth centuries, the period of canonization.

2.4. Revelation. There are a number of parallels but no certain traces of the Revelation,* or Apocalypse, in the apostolic fathers. The closest parallels, of course, come from the *Visions* of the *Shepherd of Hermas,** where some of the same imagery is used (*Herm. Vis.* 2.4, cf. Rev 12:1; *Herm. Vis.* 4.6-10, cf. Rev 13; *Herm. Vis.* 4.1, 6, cf. Rev 9:3). In Revelation 21:14 the names of the apostles are on the foundation stones of the

New Jerusalem (*see* Jerusalem), and in *Hermas, Vision* 5.5.1, the apostles and other teachers of the church form the foundation stones. Also, the faithful in Revelation and in *Hermas* are given white robes and crowns to wear (Rev 2:10; 3:11; 6:11, cf. *Herm. Sim.* 8.2.1, 3; notice also that *Herm. Vis.* 2.2.7; 4.2.5; 4.3.6 are similar to Rev 7:14 and close to Rev 3:10; *Herm. Vis.* 1.1.3 is similar also to Rev 17:3). Along with this, there appear to be several parallels in words and thoughts between Revelation and other of the apostolic fathers, for example, *Barnabas* 21.3 probably depends on Revelation 22:10, and *Barnabas* 7.9 is close to Revelation 1:7, 13. Again, however, the work is not cited by name in the apostolic fathers.

Charles claims that Revelation was all but universally accepted (and consequently used in an authoritative manner) in Asia Minor, western Syria, Africa, Rome and southern Gaul in the second century (Charles, I.xcvii-ciii). Justin appears to have been the first to say that Revelation was written by John the apostle of Christ (Justin *Dial. Tryph.* 81:15, cf. also *Apol. I* 28, which refers to Rev 12:9). According to Eusebius, Apollonius used Revelation in the second century to write against the Montanists (Eusebius *Hist. Eccl. 5.18.14*). Clement of Alexandria (*Paed.* 2.119) cites Revelation as Scripture and as the work of John the Apostle (see *Quis Div.* 42 and *Strom.* 6.106-107).

At various periods Revelation also had a mixed reception in the church, especially in the eastern churches. The Alogoi of the second century rejected the writing altogether and, according to Eusebius, Dionysius of Alexandria wrote a critical appraisal of the authorship of the book (Eusebius *Hist. Eccl.* 7.24-25) concluding that it was not written by John the Apostle. Eusebius himself placed Revelation among the doubtful books in his own collection of Christian writings (Eusebius *Hist. Eccl.* 3.24.18; 3.25.4). Later, Cyril of Jerusalem rejected the book altogether and forbade its use in public or private (*Cat.* 4.36). Around 360, Revelation did not get included in the canon list of the Council of Laodicea nor in Canon 85 of the *Apostolic Constitutions*.

Most scholars have contended, as Charles has shown (Charles, 1:ci-ciii), that Revelation was ignored or largely rejected in the Eastern churches. On the other hand, some Eastern writers both accepted and referred to Revela-

tion (see Andreas Caesariensis, *Apoc.* 34, *Serm.* 12 Oecumenius and Arethas, *Comm. in Apoc.* 12.7), including Melito* of Sardis who, according to Eusebius (*Hist. Eccl.* 4.26.2), wrote a book on it. Both Jerome (*Vir.* 24) and Theophilus of Antioch (*Autol.* 2.28) alluded to it, and the latter used its testimonies in a lost work against Hermogenes (see Eusebius *Hist. Eccl.* 5.24.1 for details here). Apollonius of Hierapolis (c. 186) used its testimonies (Eusebius *Hist. Eccl.* 5.18.13), Clement of Alexandria quoted it approvingly (*Paed.* 1.6; 2.11; *Strom.* 6.13, 25), and Origen frequently cited the book of Revelation (*De Princ.* 1.2.10; 4.1.25; *Comm. Joh.* 1.1, 2, 14, 23, 42). Although citation does not prove the acceptance of this book as Scripture, it does show favor toward the work. All of these church fathers are from the East in the second and third centuries, and the most significant rejection of Revelation in the East did not occur until the end of the fourth century. Cyril of Jerusalem, for instance, appears to be the first to exclude Revelation without comment (*Cat.* 4.36), but Epiphanius of Salamis (*Haer.* 76.5) still included it at the end of the fourth century, as did Jerome (*Ad Paul. Ep.* 53) and Codex Alexandrinus (c. 425). The work was cited in an authoritative manner in many of the church fathers and on occasion even called "Scripture" when lists or canons of Scripture began to appear in the fourth century.

3. The Muratorian Fragment.

It is quite common today to speak of the Muratorian Fragment as if it were a late second-century document that expressed what the general understanding was regarding the extent of the biblical canon at that time. If it were a second century writing, however, it was without parallel until the fourth century and had no observable bearing on how others viewed the biblical canon in the second century. There are in fact no other discussions of a biblical canon in the second century nor of what form such a canon might take. The only parallels of a descriptive list of sacred Christian writings are found in the fourth century (esp. Eusebius *Hist. Eccl.* 3.25.1-7), and thus far no one has produced a parallel in the second century.

Interestingly, its author included the *Wisdom of Solomon*, a pseudepigraphal OT writing, in a NT canon (see the Murat. Frag. lines 69-70). The same writing was placed earlier in an OT list of Scriptures (Melito includes *Wisdom* in his OT Scripture list according to Eusebius, *Hist. Eccl.* 4.26.12-14). It logically belongs with OT collections since it was written *before* the time of Christ. The only parallels to the Muratorian Fragment's reference to *Wisdom* in a NT list are found in fourth-century lists from the East (Eusebius *Hist. Eccl.* 5.8.1-8 and Epiphanius *Haer.* 76.5). Further, the listing of the four canonical Gospels (the document is missing the opening section, but Luke is listed as the third Gospel) is strangely quiet about the discussions in the second-century churches over which gospel to use. If the Muratorian Fragment comes from the second century, why is there no defense of the four Gospels such as we see in Irenaeus (*Haer.* 3.11.8, 9), but also in Tertullian, as noted above, who distinguishes Matthew and John from Mark and Luke on apostolic grounds? For the many arguments against a second-century date and the western provenance of the Muratorian Fragment, see Hahneman, Sundberg and McDonald (1995, chap. 8). For opposing views, see Ferguson, Metzger and Bruce.

4. Summary.
The recognition of the literature of the NT as authoritative and useful in the life and worship of the church came earlier than its recognition as Scripture. In general the NT writings were not called Scripture in the second century even though they often functioned in that capacity for some Christians. By the end of the second century, the principle of a Christian Scriptures had already been recognized by vast segments of the Christian community. Acts appears to have been included in that sacred collection early as a result of its relation to the Gospel of Luke and eventually, when collections began to be made of Christian Scriptures, some churches began to place Acts between the Gospels and the Epistles of Paul as a bridge to the letters that reflected the growth and development of the early church. In other collections Acts appears later in the collection.

The reception of the General Epistles was always mixed in the early church. 1 Peter and 1 John were cited early by the major writers of the second century, but 2 Peter had a more difficult reception. James was a highly disputed book throughout the history of the church because of its supposed differences from the Apostle Paul on the issue of justification by faith. 2 John, 3 John and Jude likewise had something of a mixed reception in the churches until late in the fourth century even though some churches had recognized their authority earlier. The mere fact that these books survived the burning of books in the Diocletian persecution (303-310) attests to their acceptance in many churches.

Revelation was more generally accepted in the Western churches in the second and third centuries, and eventually also in the East in the fourth and fifth centuries as the surviving lists of NT writings show, even though it was favorably received in some sectors in the eastern churches but not in others. Today there are still Christian communities of the East (the Eastern Orthodox and the Nestorians) who either reject the canonicity of Revelation or neglect its use in their liturgies.

See also ACTS OF THE APOSTLES; APOSTOLIC FATHERS; HEBREWS; JAMES; JOHN, LETTERS OF; JUDE; MARCION; OLD TESTAMENT IN APOSTOLIC FATHERS; 1 PETER; 2 PETER; PSEUDEPIGRAPHY; REVELATION, BOOK OF.

BIBLIOGRAPHY. K. Aland, *The Problem of the New Testament Canon* (Oxford: Mowbray, 1962); J. Barr, *Holy Scripture: Canon, Authority, Criticism* (Philadelphia: Westminster, 1983); C. K. Barrett, *A Critical and Exegetical Commentary on the Book of Acts 1-14* (ICC; Edinburgh: T & T Clark, 1994); D. Barthélemy, "La Critique Canonique," *RICP* 36 (1991) 191-220; C. Bigg, *A Critical and Exegetical Commentary on the Epistles of St. Peter and St. Jude* (ICC; Edinburgh: T & T Clark, 1902); F. F. Bruce, *The Canon of Scripture* (Downers Grove, IL: InterVarsity, 1988); H. von Campenhausen, *The Formation of the Christian Bible* (Philadelphia: Fortress, 1972); R. H. Charles, *The Revelation of St. John* (ICC; 2 vols.; Edinburgh: T & T Clark, 1920); H. Conzelmann, *Acts of the Apostles* (Herm; Philadelphia: Fortress, 1987); W. R. Farmer, *Jesus and the Gospel: Tradition, Scripture and Canon* (Philadelphia: Fortress, 1982); W. R. Farmer and D. M. Farkasfalvy, *The Formation of the New Testament Canon* (New York: Paulist, 1983); E. Ferguson, "Canon Muratori: Date and Provenance," *SP* 18 (1982) 677-83; H. Y. Gamble, "Canon: New Testament," *ABD* 1:852-61; idem, "The Canon of the New Testament" in *The New Testament and Its Modern Interpreters*, ed. E. J. Epp and G. W. MacRae (Atlanta: Scholars Press, 1989) 201-43; idem, *The New Testament Canon: Its Making and Meaning*

(GBS; Philadelphia: Fortress, 1985); R. M. Grant, *The Formation of the New Testament* (New York: Harper & Row, 1965); F. W. Grosheide, ed., *Some Early Lists of the Books of the New Testament.* 1: *Textus Minores* (Leiden: E. J. Brill, 1948); G. M. Hahneman, *The Muratorian Fragment and the Development of the Canon.* (Oxford: Clarendon, 1992); D. J. Harrington, "Introduction to the Canon," *NIB* 1:7-21; E. R. Kalin, "Re-examining New Testament Canon History: 1. The Canon of Origen," *CTM* 17 (1990) 274-82; J. T. Lienhard, *The Bible The Church, and Authority: The Canon of the Christian Bible in History and Theology* (Collegeville, MN: Liturgical Press/Michael Glazier, 1995); L. M. McDonald, *The Formation of the Christian Biblical Canon* (rev. and exp. ed.; Peabody, MA: Hendrickson, 1995); idem, "The Integrity of the Biblical Canon in Light of Its Historical Development," *BBR* 6 (1996) 95-132; J. B. Mayor, *The Epistle of James: The Greek Text with Introduction, Notes, Comments and Further Studies in the Epistle of James* (3d ed.; New York: Macmillan, 1913); B. M. Metzger, The *Canon of the New Testament: Its Origin, Development, and Significance.* (Oxford: Clarendon, 1987); A. G. Patzia, *The Making of the New Testament: Origin, Collection, Text and Canon* (Downers Grove, IL: InterVarsity, 1995); G. A. Robbins, "Muratorian Fragment," *ABD* IV:928-29; R. Schnackenburg, *The Johannine Epistles: Introduction and Commentary* (New York: Crossroad, 1992); A. Souter, *The Text and Canon of the New Testament* (New York: Charles Scribners, 1917); A. C. Sundberg Jr., "Canon Muratori: A Fourth-Century List," *HTR* 66 (1973) 1-41.

L. M. McDonald

CATECHETICAL SCHOOL OF ALEXANDRIA. *See* ALEXANDRIAN CHRISTIANITY.

CELIBACY. *See* MARRIAGE, DIVORCE AND ADULTERY; SEXUALITY, SEXUAL ETHICS.

CENTERS OF CHRISTIANITY

Christianity spread from Jerusalem throughout the entire Mediterranean world. Cities in Syria, Asia Minor, Greece, Egypt and Italy became important centers for the extension and ongoing development of Christianity (for one illustration of this development, *see* Worship). This essay will explore the contribution of these key cities in the early Christian movement through the middle of the second century.

1. Jerusalem
2. Antioch (Syria)
3. Ephesus (Asia Minor)
4. Corinth (Greece)
5. Alexandria (Egypt)
6. Rome (Italy)

1. Jerusalem.

Jerusalem* was not only the center of Jewish religion, it was also the cradle for the birth of Christianity. It was in this city that Jesus taught, died on the cross, rose from his tomb, and from where he ascended to the right hand of the Father. It was in this city that Jesus instructed his disciples to stay and receive the promised new-covenant outpouring of the Holy Spirit. And it was in this city that the first new community of Christians was formed when thousands believed in Jesus as Messiah and Lord in response to the Spirit-empowered message of Peter. Ironically (if we credit the tradition of the Christian's flight from Jerusalem to Pella) for a period of time less than forty years after the beginning of the Jerusalem church, no Christians remained in the city (see below). Nevertheless, the extensive movement that began in Jerusalem was stronger than ever.

For the first generation of Christianity, the city of Jerusalem was the hub of this new movement that was advancing in every direction. According to Luke, Jesus himself had intended that the gospel spread from this city to the entire then-known world (Acts 1:8). This happened right from the beginning when Jews from all over the Mediterranean world and the East were present for the Pentecost celebration and many became participants in the new movement (see Acts 2:5-12, 41). Although recorded history is silent about what happened to these people, we may assume that they returned to their various cities in the diaspora,* proclaimed Jesus as Messiah in their synagogues,* and started churches. This may explain the beginnings of Christian communities in places such as Damascus, Rome* and Alexandria.* Persecution also played a role in scattering Jerusalem Christians to various regions where they proclaimed the gospel of Christ. This resulted, for example, in Samaria* and Antioch* hearing the gospel (see Acts 8; 11:19-21).

The church of Jerusalem naturally assumed a leadership role in clarifying the beliefs and practices of this new movement. Luke represents "the teaching of the apostles" as foundational (Acts 2:42), out of which stemmed a set of oral traditions that spread beyond the city walls of Jerusalem. The inner group who had been with Jesus during his public ministry thus shaped the self understanding and beliefs of early Christianity at the beginning. Luke focuses primarily on the leadership of Peter, John and the two James. After the death of James the son of Zebedee (c. A.D. 44; Acts 12:1-2), James* the brother of the Lord (see Relatives of Jesus) emerged as a principal figure in the Jerusalem church (Acts 12:17; 15:13; Paul speaks of him, together with Peter and John, as one of the "pillar" apostles; cf. Gal 2:9).

Churches throughout the Mediterranean world developed to a large degree independently from Jerusalem. There is no evidence in Luke's account, for example, of embassies from Alexandria or Rome consulting the Jerusalem apostles. In spite of the absence of a networked institutionalization of authority, there appears to have been widespread and universal agreement among the churches in affirming that Christ* is the Son* of God and Messiah, that his death is an atoning sacrifice* for sins, that he died and rose from the dead, and that he will return (though variations on these themes were inevitable, e.g., see Christology; Eschatology). This was likely facilitated by apostolic traditions in oral form circulating widely from Jerusalem. The common experience of the Holy Spirit,* the empowering and unifying presence of Christ with his people, also served to constitute and establish these new communities.

The only hint we have of Jerusalem attempting to assert its authority over other churches is in the so-called Jerusalem Council (Acts 15). Luke reveals that a serious dispute arose in Antioch concerning the way and conditions of entry into the new community. He says that "certain people" (tines) came from Jerusalem teaching the necessity of circumcision* for salvation* (Acts 15:1). Luke implies to the reader that they were not explicitly commissioned by the leadership of the Jerusalem church. The Antioch church subsequently initiated a meeting in Jerusalem between Paul and Barnabas and the apostles to clarify this central issue. The interpretation of the so-called "Jerusalem Council" and its relationship to Galatians 1 and 2 has been widely discussed (see DPL, Jerusalem,

Galatians). What is important for us to note here is that there was agreement between the Antiochian and Jerusalem representatives affirming salvation apart from circumcision and by grace* alone (Acts 15:11, 19, 28). There are no compelling reasons to think that Luke was merely trying to paper over an unbridgeable chasm that separated Jewish Christianity from Gentile Christianity (contra F. C. Baur; see Jewish Christianity). Although the Jerusalem church filled no institutional and authoritative role with respect to the Pauline mission to the Gentiles, this agreement was certainly a positive step in fostering the unity of the Jewish and Gentile* segments of the church and a significant affirmation of the Gentile mission.

The Jerusalem church faced persecution from the earliest stages and throughout its brief history (Acts 4:3-21; 5:17-42; 6:11-14; 7:54—8:3; 9:1-2; 11:19-20; 12:1-19). According to Eusebius, when the Jewish revolt broke out in A.D. 66, the Jerusalem Christians fled the city and migrated to Pella* in Perea (Eusebius Hist. Eccl. 3.5.3-4). Some did return to Jerusalem after the war, but the city was no longer the "center" for Christianity that it once was. Hadrian's edict prohibiting any Jews from living in Jerusalem after the Bar Kokhba revolt of A.D. 132-35 had a drastic impact upon the Jerusalem church (see Christianity and Judaism).

Despite its status as the earliest center for Christianity, Jerusalem's literary output was meager. The letter of James* (and possibly Jude*) is the only Christian document stemming from the city (see Jewish Christianity). Here we need to be reminded of the predominance of oral traditions* of various sorts—hymns,* creeds,* stories* and other forms—that were passed on from Jerusalem (e.g., 1 Cor 15:3-5). Jerusalem fell into demise, but the apostolic traditions nurtured communities all over the world.

2. Antioch (Syria).

Nearly 300 miles to the north of Jerusalem in the province of Syria was a city that became a major center for Christianity as it spread to the Gentile world—Antioch on the Orontes (see Antioch; DPL, Antioch). The third largest city in the Roman empire with a population between one-quarter and a half-million people (Strabo Geog. 16.2.5; cf. Diodorus Siculus 17.52 and Pliny Nat. Hist. 6.122), Antioch was quite naturally a strategic location for the propagation of the gospel. The city lay in a fertile plain near the foot of Mt. Silpius, with the Orontes River flowing through the city and continuing on for a distance of fifteen miles to the Mediterranean Sea. Antioch was a major junction for roads coming from the east (Aleppo), the south (the Lebanon, Damascus and Palestine) and the north (Tarsus and the whole of Anatolia).

Very early on, a great number of Gentiles became Christians in Antioch. Luke suggests that this happened as a result of the proclamation of Jewish Christians who came to Antioch while fleeing from the outbreak of persecution in Jerusalem associated with Stephen (Acts 11:19-21). Luke does not tell us if these Gentiles were predominantly god fearers linked to the synagogues of the sizeable Jewish population (between twenty and forty thousand people) in Antioch. It was only a matter of time, however, until more Gentiles—friends, family members and neighbors of the initial wave—responded to the gospel. Most of these people would have turned to Christ from adherence to Apollo, Artemis, Zeus, Tyche or the Syrian cults of Baal and the mother goddess Cybele—some of the popular deities of the city (*see* Religions). We can safely assume that a good number of the Jews in the city also turned to Christ. From Acts we learn that the initial leadership of the church actually consisted of primarily Jewish Christians from outside Antioch (see Acts 13:1).

The growth of the Christian community in the city forced outsiders to reckon with their presence. The local population identified the followers of Jesus as a sect distinct from Judaism and dubbed them *christianoi* (Acts 11:26). It is likely that these Antiochian Christians gathered in several different house groups rather than meeting all in one place (Downey, 277). We do know that Luke could speak of Antioch as one unified church with a common leadership (Acts 13:1).

The church clearly agreed, under the guiding impulse of the Holy Spirit, to commission Paul and Barnabas to continue the mission to the Gentiles in regions beyond Syria (Acts 13:2-3). Antioch thus became a "missionary sending" church and the initial base of operations for the Pauline mission (*see* Mission; *DPL*, Mission).

There are no explicit indications that any canonical literature was produced at Antioch. If one accepts the South Galatia hypothesis (*see*

DPL, Galatians), Paul's letter to the Galatians, however, would have been written in Antioch. Many contemporary scholars have argued that Matthew's Gospel (or at least the earlier traditions embedded in the Gospel) was composed at Antioch to address concerns of the Antiochian church in the 80s or 90s (e.g., Meier; Hann). This hypothesis, however, is quite speculative and some have questioned its viability (*see* Matthean Community). The literature that does have a clear connection with Antioch is the collection of letters written by Ignatius,* the bishop (*episkopos*) of Antioch at the beginning of the second century. Although none of the letters address the church at Antioch, they do provide some insight into the nature and structure of the church at that time. Most significantly, Ignatius bears witness to the threat of a rising docetism* in the churches (e.g., Ign. *Trall.* 10.1) and assumes a widespread acceptance of a threefold ministry (bishop, presbyters and deacons; e.g., Ign. *Magn.* 13.1; Ign. *Trall.* 7.2; *see* Church Order). Unfortunately, Ignatius leaves us in the dark regarding many of the specific issues confronting the Antiochian church as well as the circumstances of his arrest.

About the time of Ignatius or shortly after, Antioch became known as a center for the spread of Gnosticism.* Saturninus, a native of Antioch, began teaching that Christ was not truly incarnated and that he merely appeared as a man (Irenaeus *Haer.* 1.24.1-2; cf. Eusebius *Hist. Eccl.* 4.7.3). Basilides was another teacher in the city propagating a docetic christology. According to Irenaeus, both studied under a man named Menander who allegedly was a follower of Simon Magus. Basilides later returned to his native Alexandria and began disseminating his Gnostic teaching there during the time of Hadrian (A.D. 117-38) (Irenaeus *Haer.* 1.24.3ff).

3. Ephesus (Asia Minor).

From Ephesus, "all the Jews and Greeks who lived in the province of Asia heard the word of the Lord" (Acts 19:10). In the early 50s, Ephesus became the famed center for Christianity in Asia Minor (*see DPL*, Ephesus). From the NT and Ignatius, we know that churches were established in the territories of Phrygia (Colossae, Laodicea and Hierapolis), Lydia (Smyrna, Philadelphia, Thyatira, Sardis), Ionia (Magnesia, Tralles) and Mysia (Pergamum). New communities presumably formed in numerous other villages and cities throughout Asia Minor.

The church in Ephesus began with the ministry of Paul and his colleagues (Acts 19). Starting with a nucleus of twelve men whom he led into a full Christian experience of the Spirit (Acts 19:1-7), Paul reached many more people with the gospel of Christ, first through the local synagogue and then through regular teaching in a local lecture hall (Acts 19:8-10). As in Antioch (Acts 13:1-3) and other cities of the Pauline mission, it is probable that these new believers met regularly in homes for teaching, fellowship,* worship* and prayer.* We have no way of determining how many such home groups existed. It is likely that many new house churches were added year by year as the movement experienced significant growth.

During his Gentile mission Paul spent more time in Ephesus than in any other city. This was due in large part to the strategic importance of Ephesus as a base of operations for spreading the gospel throughout Asia Minor. Ephesus was the principal Aegean port city for Asia Minor. Consequently roads from Ephesus radiated in every direction along the coast and through the interior of the province. Since 133 B.C. when Attalus III bequeathed the Pergameme kingdom to Rome, Ephesus had served as the seat of the Roman proconsul. This prosperous "metropolis of Asia," with a population of at least 250,000 was home to a multi-ethnic and religiously diverse set of people. Ionians, Lydians, Phrygians and Carians lived in the city together with Greeks, Persians, Italians and Egyptians. There was also a sizeable Jewish population.

Epigraphic, numismatic and literary evidence reveals that the people of Ephesus worshiped up to fifty different gods and goddesses. Primacy of place, however, went to Artemis of Ephesus (Diana Ephesia) who enjoyed an official covenant bond with the city. Ephesus was also famous in antiquity as a center for the practice and dissemination of the magical arts (see Magic). Certain magical formulas were even referred to as "the Ephesian letters." Not surprisingly, then, Luke records two incidents portraying the impact Christianity had on the local magical practices and the cult of Artemis (Acts 19:13-20, 23-41).

There is significant Christian literary activity associated with Ephesus. Of the letters attributed to Paul, two were probably written to Ephe-

sus (1 Timothy and Ephesians [even if Ephesians was a circular letter]) and one was written from Ephesus (1 Corinthians; see DPL, Ephesus). There is a strong historical tradition that the Apostle John lived in Ephesus toward the end of the first century. Eusebius and other patristic writers report that John the son of Zebedee spent the latter years of his life in Ephesus where he served as a key leader among the churches (Eusebius Hist. Eccl. 3.1, 23, 28, 31). A considerable body of ancient traditions affirm that the Apostle wrote the Fourth Gospel from Ephesus (e.g., Irenaeus Haer. 3.1.1; cf. Eusebius Hist. Eccl. 5.8.4; et al.). The same writers also link John the Apostle with John the author of the Apocalypse (Rev 1:9; see Revelation), which was composed on the island of Patmos, roughly sixty miles southeast of Ephesus. Although the Johannine letters are anonymous, many scholars have followed the church fathers by also arguing for their Johannine authorship (see John, Letters of). The tradition is muddied to some degree by Eusebius's report of the presence of another John (the elder) in Ephesus (Eusebius Hist. Eccl. 7.25.6-16; 3.39.6) who may have served as the author of one or more of these documents. All five of these writings, however, have very close ties with Ephesus and reflect the situation of the churches there at the time of their composition.

The message to the church of Ephesus in the Apocalypse (Rev 2:1-7) commends these believers for their hard work, perseverance and spiritual discernment, but it calls them back to their "first love." Their focus on detecting and rooting out dangerous teachings (such as that of the "Nicolaitans") unfortunately appears to have taken precedence over the maintenance of a personal love for God and a deep love for one another in the Christian community.

In the early second century, Ignatius wrote a letter to the church in Ephesus as he was on his way to martyrdom* in Rome. The letter assumes the presence of a three-tiered ecclesiastical structure in Ephesus. Ignatius even refers to a certain Onesimus as their bishop (episkopos; Ign. Eph. 1.3). He also confirms the positive report of the Apocalypse regarding their intolerance of heresy (Ign. Eph. 6.2; 9.1) but makes no specific mention of the Nicolaitans.

4. Corinth (Greece).

Because of the cultural and historical importance of Athens to the Greek world, one would have expected this city to take on a prominent role as the center of Christianity for Macedonia and Achaia. Rather, the Peloponnesian city of Corinth became the focal point of the Christian movement. As the westward missionary expansion of the gospel of Christ continued in the early 50s through the preaching of Paul, some in Athens heard the gospel with interest, though only a few responded to his message (Acts 17:16-34). For this and perhaps other reasons that Luke does not disclose, Paul spent little time in Athens and immediately went to Corinth where he stayed for a year and a half (Acts 18:1-18).

Paul may have turned his attention to Corinth because of its strategic location for reaching many people with the gospel. Corinth had become the economic, political and trade center for Greece. This was due in part to its location overlooking the narrow isthmus connecting the Peloponnese to the mainland. Much of the shipping between east and west passed by Corinth as boats were hauled across the four-mile wide isthmus on the special road built for this purpose. Corinth was also served by two harbors: Lechaeum on the west, giving access to the Adriatic, and Cenchraea on the east, serving the Aegean. The 1900-foot hill adjacent to the city, the Acrocorinth, provided the city with an important defensive acropolis.

From the time the city was established as a Roman colony in 44 B.C. nearly a hundred years after its destruction, it grew and prospered. The amount of building that took place during the reigns of Augustus (31 B.C.—A.D. 14) and Tiberius (A.D. 14-37) well illustrates how the city was thriving when Christianity was introduced by Paul in A.D. 51.

Aside from the strategic importance of the city, Luke clearly depicts Paul's extended stay as determined by the providential leading of God (Acts 18:9-11). Many people, both Jews and Gentiles, turned to Christ during Paul's time of ministry there. Some of these included prominent people in the city. In Romans 16:23 Paul mentions a certain Erastus whom he calls the "steward" (*oikonomos*) of the city. This may indicate that he was one of the two city managers (an *aedile*). It is likely that this is the same Erastus named on a civic inscription dating to the mid-first century (Murphy-O'Connor 1983, 37-38). Luke also tells us that the ruler of the syna-

gogue, Crispus, and his household became Christians (Acts 18:8).

Stringent Jewish opposition to Paul's preaching in the city resulted in Paul's making a forced appearance before the *bēma*, or magistrate's bench of the Roman proconsul of Achaia, Gallio (Acts 18:12-17). After listening to their complaints, Gallio summarily dismissed the case, ruling that it was an internal Jewish squabble and not a matter appropriate for him to decide. By determining that this nascent Christian movement came under the umbrella of Judaism, Gallio effectively insured that Christianity would be under the same legal protection as Judaism.* This set an important precedent for Paul and the Corinthian Christians that made possible the legally unhindered proclamation of the gospel in Achaia, at least for the immediate future.

From a careful reading of Paul's two letters to Corinth, we can infer that he and his companions experienced great success in sharing the gospel and building a Christian community there. As in other cities, the church at Corinth likely came to be comprised of a network of house churches (see Blue, 153-61, 172-77). The various divisions in the church reflected in 1 Corinthians 1—4 may very well have been schisms between house churches. Some of the difficulties faced by Christians in Corinth stemmed from their cultural and religious background in the city, such as the controversy over food* sacrificed to idols* (1 Cor 8-10). Much more can be learned about the Corinthian church through an analysis of the Corinthian correspondence (*see DPL* Corinthians). Paul wrote his letter to the Romans at some point during his stay in this city.

At the end of the first century, the church at Corinth was once again splintered by an unhealthy divisiveness. It appears that younger members of the congregation had a conflict with the elders and eventually gained enough support to foment a change of leadership (*1 Clem.* 3.3; 44.6; 47.6). A prominent leader in the church at Rome, Clement,* wrote a lengthy letter to the Corinthian community with the hope of restoring unity within the church.

Little else is known about this important church in the first century of its existence. It is likely that through the ministry and outreach of the Corinthian church, many new communities were established throughout the Peloponnese and to the north.

5. Alexandria (Egypt).

Although no mention is made of the beginnings of Egyptian Christianity in the NT, other material and literary evidence suggests that Christianity started there early and became well established. The most important city for the rise of Christianity in Egypt was Alexandria.*

Egyptian Jews who heard the gospel on the day of Pentecost in Jerusalem (Acts 2:10) were probably the first to introduce Christianity to Alexandria. Eusebius passes on a tradition, obtained by hearsay, purporting that Mark was the first to found churches in Alexandria and that he remained and functioned in a leadership capacity until the eighth year of Nero (Eusebius *Hist. Eccl.* 2.16; 2.24.1). Most scholars discount the viability of this tradition because of the better attested accounts of Mark accompanying Peter as his interpreter and composing his Gospel in Rome (Papias *Frag.* 3.15; Eusebius *Hist. Eccl.* 3.39; Metzger, 100; *see DJG*, Mark).

Alexandria was a natural place for the spread of the gospel to the rest of Egypt and to the (north) African continent. The city was a key commercial center, possessing the busiest port in the empire. Strabo, who spent five years in the city working on his *Geography,* remarked that Alexandria is "the greatest emporium of the inhabited world" (Strabo *Geog.* 17.1.13). With a population of up to a half-million people, Alexandria was the second largest city of the Roman world. Among this population was the largest Jewish settlement in the diaspora.*

It is doubtful that Apollos provides us with insight into the early Christian community in Alexandria (Acts 18:24-28) in spite of the testimony of the Western text that he had been instructed in the way of the Lord "in his native place [*en tē patridi*]." Apollos was only familiar with the OT and the baptism of John, not the gospel of Jesus Christ. We can only speculate as to where he came into contact with the John-the-Baptist tradition.

The *Epistle of Barnabas** is the oldest Christian document from Alexandria that we possess. This document was written after some monumental events in the Alexandrian Jewish community: a horrific massacre of Jews under Tiberius Julius Alexander in A.D. 66, the reverberations from the destruction of the Jerusalem temple in A.D. 70 and the decimation of the

Jewish community in Alexandria after they revolted during the reign of Trajan (A.D. 115-17; *see* Judaism, Post-A.D. 70). The content of *Barnabas* reflects some significant similarities to Stephen's* speech as recorded in Acts 7. In both, there is an emphasis on the demise of the temple cult, an appeal to the golden-calf episode of the exodus, and a similar christology,* including the use of the title, "the Righteous One." B. Pearson suggests that, "this type of Christianity was introduced to Alexandria soon after the death of Stephen and the scattering of the 'Hellenists' from Jerusalem" (Pearson 1986, 213). Since Alexandrian Jews already tended toward a spiritual interpretation of the temple* and its observances, the ground was well prepared for the reception of Christianity along the lines expressed by Stephen (*see* Hellenists).

Perhaps some of the most significant discoveries illustrating the spread of Christianity into various parts of Egypt have been the fragments of NT and LXX biblical texts on papyri. The earliest of these, the John Rylands fragment of the Gospel of John (P^{52}), dates to the first half of the second century. Another fragment of the Gospel of John dating to the second century was published in 1983 and has been designated (P^{90}). Further analysis of P^{64} has recently led C. Thiede to suggest a late first-century date (in *ZPE* 105 [1994] 13-20), though this is debated. A fragment from an unknown Gospel (Egerton Pap. 2) dates to the middle of the second century. We could also add to this a number of early fragments of the Greek OT that have been found scattered throughout Egypt which show signs of being Christian copies. Metzger observes that for every papyrus fragment discovered in Egypt, scores have perished or still lie hidden in the sand (Metzger, 101-3). All this points to a thriving Christianity in Egypt that has radiated from its origin in Alexandria to various parts of the hinterland.

At a very early date, it appears that forms of Christianity began to emerge that deviated significantly from the apostolic brand of Christianity represented in the NT documents. From the second century on, Alexandria became a noted center for Gnosticism through a variety of famous teachers such as Basilides and Valentinus. The discovery of the Nag Hammadi documents in the late 1940s has given us a much better understanding of the varieties of Gnosis present in the city at a very early stage (*see* Gnosticism).

6. Rome (Italy).

Christianity spread to Rome* at the very beginning and, by the end of the first century, Rome was a major center for Christianity. This capital city of the Empire was soon to become the most important city for the development of Western Christianity (*see DPL*, Rome).

The start of the church in Rome is shrouded in some obscurity. As with Alexandria, the best hypothesis is that Jewish pilgrims who were present at Pentecost* returned home proclaiming in their synagogues that Jesus is the Messiah (Acts 2:10). This would mean that Christianity took root first in the Jewish sector of the city. The largest group of Jews occupied a region known as the Trastevere ("across the Tiber"), where there were as many as thirteen synagogues. The best estimates for the Jewish population of Rome at this time place it at 40,000-50,000 (Brown, 94) within the total city population of about one million. Many of these families had originally come to Rome as captives after Pompey had taken Jerusalem (60 B.C.) and were subsequently sold as slaves. By the first century, many were freedmen, but most were probably poor and not well educated.

Presumably a number of house churches formed in the Trastevere area were composed of Jews and Gentile god-fearers. From there the gospel spread to other parts of the city and to the Gentile population.

A major crisis confronted the church during Claudius's reign (*see* Chronology; Emperor) when, according to Suetonius, the emperor expelled the Jews from the city around A.D. 49 because they "caused continuous disturbances at the instigation of *Chrestus*" (Suetonius *Claudius* 25). Most scholars interpret *Chrestus* as a reference to Christ and see this as evidence of internal tension in the Jewish community resulting from the preaching of the gospel by Jewish Christians and the formation of Christian communities. This harsh decree would have had a major impact on the church by depleting it of all its Jewish members and forcing Gentiles to assume places of leadership. When Jewish Christians began returning to Rome after Nero became emperor, the situation would have been ripe for conflict between the new leadership and the old.

The Apostle Paul wrote to the Roman church in the mid-50s, about twenty years after its founding. Evidence from the last chapter of his letter suggests that Roman Christianity consisted of a network of house churches and that these people came from a cross-section of social classes, both slave and freed. There is much in Paul's letter that reflects the situation and issues of the Roman church at this time (*see DPL*, Romans).

There is no historical substance to the tradition that Peter was the founder and first bishop of the church at Rome. Roman Catholic scholar Raymond Brown dispels this legend:

> We have no knowledge at all of when he came to Rome and what he did there before he was martyred. Certainly he was *not* the original missionary who brought Christianity to Rome (and therefore *not* the founder of the church at Rome in that sense). There is no serious proof that he was the bishop (or local ecclesiastical officer) of the Roman church—a claim not made till the third century. (Brown, 98)

It is certainly possible, however, that Peter came to Rome at some point and perhaps even ministered there together with Paul for a brief time (see Eusebius *Hist. Eccl.* 2.25.8).

The burning of Rome in A.D. 64 and the subsequent persecution of Christians by Nero marked a very dark period for Roman Christianity (Tacitus *Ann.* 15.44). The maniacally deranged Nero executed Christians by crucifying them, burning them as a spectacle or dressing them in wild animals' skins and letting dogs tear them to pieces.

It is likely that Paul was released from (or possibly exiled after) his Roman imprisonment recorded by Luke and engaged in further missionary activity before the great fire of Rome in July 64, for which the Nero blamed the Christians. The plight of Roman Christianity after the fire may have been what drew Paul back to the city. Many scholars accept Clement's testimony that both Peter and Paul were martyred in the city (*1 Clem.* 5—6). He intimates that Peter "endured not one or two but many trials" before his death (*1 Clem.* 5.4). This evidence would suggest that both of the Apostles died around A.D. 65-67.

Sometime before his death, Peter wrote a letter from Rome to churches scattered around the northern and western regions of Asia Minor (this, of course, assumes the authenticity of 1 Peter; *see* 1 Peter). The theme of suffering is prominent in this letter reflecting not only the situation in the Roman church, but especially the local outbreaks of persecution in Asia Minor during this period. It is quite likely that 2 Peter* also originated from Rome.

Although the Apocalypse was written from Asia Minor (specifically, Patmos), Rome is designated as the recipient of a visitation of the wrath of God spoken of in the imagery and symbolism of the book. By the end of the first century, Rome came to be compared with the ancient city of Babylon because of its antagonism to the purposes of God and for spilling the blood of his people (*Sib. Or.* 5.137-44, 159-60, 434-46). Rome is the city sitting on seven mountains (Rev 17:9), ruling over the kings of the earth (Rev 17:18) and serving as the luxurious center of commerce for the world market (Rev 18:2-3; 19:2). The message of the Apocalypse is that "Babylon"* would fall and be judged through the direct intervention of God (Rev 14:8; 18:2, 10, 21). While there is much in the Apocalypse that has the historical city of Rome in view, there appears to be the anticipation of judgment on a future city (or, possibly, some future manifestation symbolized by the city) that possesses all the ungodly and evil characteristics of ancient Rome and Babylon.

At a time not too far removed from the writing of the Apocalypse, Clement,* a famous leader of the church at Rome, wrote his letter to the church at Corinth. He was earnestly attempting to mediate in a leadership crisis of the Corinthian church that had disrupted the peace and order of the whole Christian community. It cannot be inferred from this, however, that the bishop of Rome exercised sovereignty over the churches of the Empire.

The *Shepherd of Hermas* gives us a fascinating glimpse into a segment of Christianity at Rome that appears, in many ways, quite different from that represented in *1 Clement* (*see* Hermas). This early second-century book may give us some perspective on a form of folk Christianity popular among the lower classes in Rome at this time (see Jeffers). The book attests to the ongoing experience of visions, prophecies and struggle with the devil and his powers. The "Two Ways" theology of *Hermas,* in fact, depicts life as a struggle between the opposing influences of two powers. The christology* can be described as adoptionist in that the Son is said to have been taken by God as a partner because of his blamelessness and the complete dwelling of the Spirit in his life (*Herm. Sim.* 5.6).

Rome had clearly become a literary center for the Christian movement. In addition to the documents we have already discussed that have a connection to Rome, we might also add the Gospel of Mark (Eusebius *Hist. Eccl.* 2.14; 6.14.16). Based on an assortment of traditions, C.-J. Thornton has suggested that by the middle of the second century the Roman church had a central library where they made available to believers in the city an archive of Christian documents that they had collected from the very beginning (Thornton, 47-55).

See also ALEXANDRIA, ALEXANDRIAN CHRISTIANITY; ANTIOCH; DIASPORA JUDAISM; GALILEAN CHRISTIANITY; JERUSALEM, ZION, HOLY CITY; JEWISH CHRISTIANITY; MATTHEAN COMMUNITY; MISSION, EARLY NON-PAULINE; ROME, ROMAN CHRISTIANITY; SAMARIA; SOCIAL SETTING OF EARLY NONPAULINE CHRISTIANITY; SYRIA, SYRIAN CHRISTIANITY.

BIBLIOGRAPHY. **Jerusalem:** M. Hengel, *The 'Hellenization' of Judaea in the First Century after Christ* (Philadelphia: Trinity Press International, 1989); J. Jeremias, *Jerusalem in the Time of Jesus* (Philadelphia: Fortress, 1969); T. Wright, "Jerusalem in the New Testament" in *Jerusalem: Past and Present in the Purposes of God,* ed. P. W. L. Walker (Cambridge: Tyndale House, 1992) 53-77. **Antioch:** R. E. Brown and J. P. Meier, *Antioch and Rome* (New York: Paulist Press, 1983); G. Downey, *A History of Antioch in Syria from Seleucus to the Arab Conquest* (Princeton: Princeton University Press, 1961); R. R. Hann, "Judaism and Jewish Christianity in Antioch: Charisma and Conflict in the First Century," *JRH* 14 (1987) 341-60; S. E. Johnson, "Antioch, The Base of Operations," *LTQ* 18 (1983) 64-73; W. A. Meeks and R. L. Wilken, *Jews and Christians In Antioch In the First Four Centuries of the Common Era* (SBS 13; Missoula: Scholar's Press, 1978). **Ephesus:** W. Elliger, *Ephesos: Geschichte einer antiken Weltstadt* (Stuttgart: Kohlhammer, 1985); E. E. Lemcio, "Ephesus and the New Testament Canon," *BJRL* 69 (1986) 210-34; R. E. Oster, "Christianity in Asia Minor," *ABD* 1:938-54; idem, "Ephesus," *ABD* 2:542-49; P. Trebilco, "Asia" in *The Book of Acts in its Graeco-Roman Setting,* ed. D. W. J. Gill and C. Gempf (BAFCS; Grand Rapids: Eerdmans, 1994) 291-362. **Corinth:** B. Blue, "Acts and the House Church" in *The Book of Acts in its Graeco-Roman Setting,* ed. D. W. J. Gill and C. Gempf (BAFCS; Grand Rapids: Eerdmans, 1994) 119-222; D. W. J. Gill,

"Achaia" in *The Book of Acts in its Graeco-Roman Setting*, ed. D. W. J. Gill and C. Gempf (BAFCS; Grand Rapids: Eerdmans, 1994) 433-53; W. A. Meeks, *The First Urban Christians* (New Haven: Yale University Press, 1983); J. Murphy-O'Connor, *St. Paul's Corinth* (GNS 6; Collegeville, MN: The Liturgical Press, 1983); idem, "Corinth," *ABD* 1:1134-39; J. Wiseman, "Corinth and Rome I: 228 BC—AD 267," *ANRW* 2.7.1 (1979) 438-548. **Alexandria:** B. A. Pearson, "Christians and Jews in First-Century Alexandria," *HTR* 79 (1986) 206-16; idem, "Christianity in Egypt," *ABD* 1:954-60; idem, "Alexandria," *ABD* 2.152-57; B. M. Metzger, *The Early Versions of the New Testament* (Oxford: Clarendon, 1977); J. A. Thompson, "Alexandria," *ISBE* 1:89-94. **Rome:** R. E. Brown and J. P. Meier, *Antioch and Rome* (New York: Paulist Press, 1983); A. D. Clarke, "Rome and Italy" in *The Book of Acts in its Graeco-Roman Setting*, ed. D. W. J. Gill and C. Gempf (BAFCS; Grand Rapids: Eerdmans, 1994) 455-81; J. Jeffers, *Conflict at Rome: Social Order and Hierarchy in Early Christianity* (Minneapolis: Fortress, 1991); S. E. Johnson, "Jews and Christians in Rome," *LTQ* 17 (1982) 51-58; P. Lampe, *Die stadtrömischen Christen in den ersten beiden Jahrhunderten* (WUNT 2/18; Tübingen: J. C. B. Mohr, 1989); G. F. Snyder, "Christianity in Rome," *ABD* 1:968-70; idem, *Ante Pacem: Archaeological Evidence of Church Life Before Constantine* (Macon, GA: Mercer University Press, 1985); C.-J. Thornton, *Der Zeuge des Zeugen* (WUNT 56; Tübingen: J. C. B. Mohr, 1991).   C. E. Arnold

CERINTHUS. *See* DOCETISM; JOHN, LETTERS OF.

CHILDREN, CHILDREN OF GOD. *See* SONSHIP, CHILD, CHILDREN.

CHRIST

The term *Christos*, transliterated as "Christ" in English, is used in Jewish and Christian contexts as the equivalent of the Hebrew term *māšîaḥ* When they are used as nouns both the Hebrew and the Greek terms refer to an anointed person (*see DJG*, Christ), though originally *Christos* was an adjective. Jews sometimes used the term *māšîaḥ* to refer to an individual anointed by God, a king (Ps. 18:50; 89:20) or a priest* (CD 12.23-24; 14.19), and sometimes they saw this person as one who would come to restore or renew Israel.* The evidence that *māšîaḥ*, much

less *Christos*, was a technical term for "messiah" before NT times is slim (de Jonge 1986).

Nevertheless the use of the term *Christos* in early Christian literature presupposes and draws on Jewish hopes for an anointed one, especially one in the line of David (*see* Judaism). We find in the Gospels and in Paul the use of *Christos* as a title or a term referring to this longed-for figure, but we also find it used as a second name for Jesus. For example, Mark's Gospel begins with the heading that he will relate good news about Jesus Christ, not Jesus "the Christ," though clearly Mark knows that the term began as a title (Mk 13:21-22). This duality is also found in Paul's writings, where most often the term is used as a name for Jesus, especially at the beginning of letters* (e.g., Rom 1:1; 1 Cor 1:1). Equally clearly Paul knows the Jewish background of the term. For example, he does not juxtapose the term *Christ* with the term *Lord*, * for that would be putting two titles together, and it appears his usage is primarily indebted to his reflection on the narrative about the end of Jesus' life (1 Cor 1:23; *see DPL*, Christ §4).

The use of the term *Christos* outside the Gospels and the Pauline corpus also falls into certain definite patterns, some of which support the notion that "Christ" was frequently used as another name for Jesus of Nazareth and sometimes also was used to describe a role, function or position he assumed at some point in his career. The fact that on various occasions the same document, such as Acts* or 1 Peter,* can reflect both the titular and nominal use of *Christos* shows the flexibility with which the term could be used.

1. Acts
2. Hebrews
3. James and Jude
4. 1 and 2 Peter
5. Johannine Letters and Revelation
6. Apostolic Fathers and Justin Martyr
7. Conclusions

1. Acts.

The twenty-six references to *Christos* in Acts refer to Jesus. The term occurs only rarely in conjunction with an OT citation, no doubt because it is rather rare in the Greek OT (*see* Old Testament in Acts). Nevertheless Acts 4:26 does contain a citation of some form of Psalm 2:2, in which God as Lord is distinguished from "his anointed one" (in Acts *tou Christou autou*). Texts such as this one and others where the qualifier *his* occurs (cf. Acts 3:18) make clear that the author knows the root meaning of the word *Christos* and understands its relational character. If one is the Christ, one must be anointed by someone else, in this case the Father. Hence when we find the phrase "our Lord, Jesus Christ" in Acts (Acts 15:26; 20:21) we see the two relationships that are implied—Jesus is the anointed one of God* and the believer's Lord.

The author of Acts makes explicit that essential to being a Christian is confessing Jesus to be "the Christ" (*ho Christos*, Acts 9:22; 17:22). In the witness* to Jews in the synagogue* this issue is pressed; precisely this point had to be demonstrated from the Scriptures if Jews were to be followers of Jesus. In Acts it appears that "Christ" functions mainly as a name when the audience is Gentile* but can serve as a functional description or title when the audience is Jewish. The phrase "in/by the name of Jesus Christ" or a variant (Acts 2:38; 4:10; 8:12; 10:48; 15:26; 16:18) shows, however, not only that *Christos* could be used as part of a name even in a Jewish context (Acts 4:18, noting the Jewish authorities leave out "Christ") but also that it was believed that confessing, invoking, proclaiming, praying* or exorcising in this name produced miraculous events (*see* Miracles), including conversions and healings.* Baptism* "in the name of Jesus Christ" is seen as the characteristic entrance rite into the Christian community for both Jews and Gentiles (Acts 2:38; 10:48; see Jones 1970).

Luke stresses the necessity of Jesus' sufferings* and resurrection* (Lk 24:26-27), and in this context he asserts that it was God's plan revealed in Scripture for "the Christ" to suffer (Acts 17:2-3) and to be raised (Acts 2:31, citing Ps 16:10; see Moessner 1995). The fulfillment of Scripture in these matters is stressed in the context of the synagogue or where the audience is Jewish. When the audience is solely or almost solely Gentiles who are not synagogue adherents or connected with Jews the term *Christ* as a title or description does not arise, and in various cases it does not arise even as a name in such contexts (see Paul's speech to the Lystrans in Acts 14:15-17 and to the Athenians in Acts 17:22-31). For a Jewish audience it was critical to confess was that Jesus is the Christ (Acts 5:22;

17:3), while for a Gentile audience it was paramount to confess that the person called Jesus Christ is Lord (cf. Acts 15:23 with Acts 15:26). The community of Christian Jews and Gentiles shared the confession of Jesus as "our Lord" (Acts 15:26; 20:21). One was to have faith* in him (Acts 24:24; 20:21).

One should probably not make too much of Acts 2:36, for while this text does speak of God "making" Jesus the Messiah (presumably after his crucifixion; *see* Death of Christ) elsewhere he is spoken of as suffering as messiah (Acts 17:3). At most Acts 2:36 suggested to the author that Jesus entered a new stage of his messianic roles and duties after his death. What we find notably lacking in Acts is the Pauline idea of being "in Christ" or being participants in his body (*see* DPL, Christ §5) or the notion of Christ's preexistence.* The author's christology has sometimes been dubbed "absentee christology," since Luke stresses that Christ ascended and rules from heaven* (cf. Acts 3:11-26; Robinson 1962; Moule 1966).

2. Hebrews.

By contrast with Acts the references to Christ in Hebrews* appear much closer to Pauline usage (see Witherington 1991) not only in the frequency with which Christ seems to be a name rather than a description or title but also in the use of the idea of sharing in or being partners of Christ (Heb 3:14). Again and again, however, "Christ" seems to be a name (Heb 5:5; 6:1; 9:11, 24, 28) for a human being who is flesh and blood (Heb 9:14; 10:10) yet is also much more than that, since "Jesus Christ is the same yesterday and today and forever" (Heb 13:8) and is one for whom Moses* could suffer in advance (Heb 11:26).

One of the distinctive notes in Hebrews is relating the idea of sonship* to the term *Christ* (cf. Hurst 1987). At Hebrews 3:6 we hear of Christ being faithful over God's house* as a son, and at Hebrews 5:5 it is Christ who is glorified and royally appointed by God, who said to him, "You are my Son, today I have begotten you" (using the language of Ps 2:7, part of a coronation ode). Notably missing in all the rich christological discussion in Hebrews is any discussion or explanation about Jesus being the Christ, the anointed one, unless we count the sonship language as a surrogate for such. The author is much more interested in the role of Jesus as both sacrifice* and sacrificer—the heavenly high priest. The Pauline influence on this document makes unlikely the suggestion of J. D. G. Dunn that in Hebrews 1-2 the author is talking about the preexistence of an idea rather than the personal preexistence of the Son/Christ (cf. Dunn 1980 to Craddock 1968 and Schweizer 1982).

3. James and Jude.

Little needs to be said about the use of *Christos* in James,* since it appears twice (Jas 1:1; 2:1). In both cases it appears in one long appellation, "the [our] Lord Jesus Christ," with "Christ" used as a name. There are six references to Christ in Jude,* all of the same variety as we find in James (Jude 4, 17, 21, 25) or even briefer ("Jesus Christ," Jude 1 [twice]). James, Jude and Hebrews show little reflection on Jesus as the Christ even though they appear to be directed to an audience that includes a goodly number of Jews or Jewish Christians. Perhaps the explanation lies in the fact that these documents are not apologetic or evangelistic documents but are meant for those who are already convinced Jesus is the Christ. By contrast, Luke-Acts, which is often thought to be the only document in the NT clearly written by a Gentile, shows considerable interest in this subject.

4. 1 and 2 Peter.

1 Peter and 2 Peter* reflect a variety of uses of the term *Christ,* and since the two letters manifest distinct tendencies they deserve to be treated separately. For example, in 1 Peter we find the formula *en Christō* (1 Pet 3:16; 5:14), while in 2 Peter we find the phrase "our Lord and Savior Jesus Christ" (2 Pet 1:11; 2:20; 3:18) (Richard 1986, 380-96).

In 1 Peter there is a major stress on the suffering and resurrection of Christ (1 Pet 1:2, 3, 11, 19; 2:21; 3:18, 21; 4:1; 5:1). The author also emphasizes in Pauline fashion that the believer may share in these sufferings or ones of a similar nature (1 Pet 4:13; cf. Phil 3:10). The author of 1 Peter is also not reluctant to refer to Christ's return, in this case called "the revelation of Christ" (1 Pet 1:7, *en apokalypsei Iēsou Christou;* 1 Pet 1:13). There is also the reference in 1 Peter 1:11 to the spirit of Christ who inspired and illuminated the OT prophets. The author appears to subscribe to Christ's preexistence, but he does not discourse on the matter

(cf. 1 Pet 1:20; 2:4; Hanson 1965; Craddock 1968; contrast Dunn 1980). He also uses the phrase "the name of Christ," which one may be reviled for bearing or bearing witness to (1 Pet 4:14), and one is to hallow Christ in one's heart as Lord (1 Pet 3:15). The author seems to understand the relational character of the term *Christ,* for he refers to "the Father of . . . Jesus Christ" (1 Pet 1:3).

In 2 Peter the usage is less varied with the most intriguing passage being the reference to "our God and Savior, Jesus Christ" (2 Pet 1:1). This appears to be a clear example of Jesus being called God in the NT (cf. Harris 1992). This letter stresses the connection of the term *Christ* with the term *savior (sōtēr).* Of the eight references to Christ in this letter, half of them (2 Pet 1:1, 11; 2:20; 3:18) connect these two terms. There is a special stress on the knowledge* of Jesus Christ (2 Pet 1:16; 2:20; 3:18). The author clearly uses the term *Christ* as part of a name (e.g., 2 Pet 1:1) throughout, as is the case in 1 Peter. In 2 Peter, Jesus Christ is not seen as merely a hero of antiquity, for in 2 Peter 1:14 he reveals to the author in the present that his time of death is near. It is possible that there is a Petrine source in 2 Peter 1:16—2:4, as this section shares much vocabulary and ideas with 1 Peter, including the manner of the use of the term *Christ* in this subsection (cf. 1 Pet 3:1 with 2 Pet 1:16; see Witherington 1985).

5. Johannine Letters and Revelation.

Like the author of Hebrews, the writer of the Johannine epistles (*see* John, Letters of) has a penchant for combining ideas about sonship with the name *Jesus Christ.* We hear repeatedly of "his Son, Jesus Christ" (1 Jn 1:3; 3:23; 5:20; 2 Jn 3). There is also a special emphasis on the need for the true believer to confess "Jesus Christ has come in the flesh" (1 Jn 4:2; 2 Jn 7), probably reflecting the need to combat Docetic* or proto-gnostic (*see* Gnosis, Gnosticism) teachings offered by some false teachers who had frequented the Johannine community (*see* Adversaries). 1 John 2:22 shows that confessing Jesus to be the Christ is also seen as critical for his community.

The special concern with confession in these letters should not be overlooked, and the incarnational character of what is to be confessed is striking. Deceivers and antichrists* are those who do not confess that the Christ has come in the flesh,* in the person of Jesus (2 Jn 7). In view of the content of the confession, the crucial text (1 Jn 5:6) refers not to the sacraments but to the birth (water) and death (blood) of Jesus Christ—the two means by which he comes to the believer (see Witherington 1989). The author of these letters also knows of the idea of *koinonia* (*see* Fellowship) in and with Jesus Christ (1 Jn 1:3) and in 1 John 5:20 refers to the believer being not only in the truth* but also "in his Son Jesus Christ." Abiding in Christ involves abiding in the teaching of Christ (2 Jn 9), which likely means the teaching about Christ referred to in the confessional statements. Jesus Christ is seen as so closely associated with the Father that the divine blessings* of grace,* mercy* and peace* come to the believer from them both (2 Jn 3).

The term *Christos* does not appear in 3 John.

Despite the plethora of images of Christ in Revelation (*see* Revelation, Book of), the term *Christ* appears there only eight times, and half of these are in the opening and closing verses of the document. The seer John receives a revelation* from or about Jesus Christ (Rev 1:1; probably the former is being emphasized), which is also a testimony *(martyrian)* about Jesus Christ (Rev 1:2) that encompasses all that follows in the Apocalypse. Jesus Christ is the faithful witness who reveals and testifies to all these things.

The author knows that *Christos* is more than a name, as is clear from the allusion to OT ideas referring to God as Lord and to God's Christ (Rev 11:15, drawing on a host of texts, including Ps 10:16; 22:28; Dan 7:14; Zech 14:9; *see* OT in Revelation). It is also clear from Revelation 12:10, which speaks of the power or authority* of God's Messiah. The martyrs* in Revelation 20:4 are seen as those who will rise and reign with the Christ for one thousand years, indicating that the roles of Christ were not completed by what Jesus accomplished during his earthly ministry.* These martyrs are said to be priests not only of God but also of Christ (Rev 20:6). The author has no difficulty distinguishing God from Christ, but he also clearly defines Christ in divine terms, roles and functions (Rev 19:16). Christ is the one who dispenses grace from heaven to God's people (Rev 22:21). Thus both the titular sense and "Christ" as a name are evident in this work, though the use as a name is notable only at the beginning of the document. Perhaps the intent is to orient the hearer

or reader, who is about to be introduced to a multitude of apocalyptic* images (cf. Grundmann 1974). Revelation shows that the original messianic meaning of *Christos* was still known in the last decade of the first century (cf. de Jonge 1992).

6. Apostolic Fathers and Justin Martyr.

The use of the name Jesus Christ or phrases such as "the [our] Lord Jesus Christ" in early Christian literature are too numerous to list and add little to our perspective of how the authors understood these phrases. We will instead concentrate on some of the important usages carried over from the NT period as well as some of the new and distinctive ways the term *Christ* is used.

In some early Christian documents the term *Christos* appears hardly at all. In the *Epistle to Barnabas** Jesus is frequently referred to, but the term *Christ* appears only three times, twice in *Barnabas* 12.10-11, where the discussion is about the meaning of Psalm 110:1 as it had been interpreted in the Jesus tradition* (cf. Mk 12:35-37 and par.), and also the meaning of Isaiah 45:1. The author refers to Jesus as the Christ about whom David has prophesied and who is David's son. Isaiah 45:1 is the famous passage in which Cyrus is said to be God's anointed, but our author clearly uses it in a christological manner. The other reference is found in *Barnabas* 2.6, where the author speaks of the new law* of "our Lord Jesus Christ," which is to be contrasted with the OT law.

In the *Didache** as well the name *Jesus* comes up at various points, but the term *Christ* is rare. Once it is found in the eucharistic prayer (*Did.* 9.4, where it occurs in the form *Jesus Christ* as a name), and once it is found as part of a compound word apparently coined by the author (*christemporos, Did.* 12.5, which seems to mean "making traffic of Christ"). Neither of these references tells us much about the author's understanding of the term *Christ* other than that it refers to the person Jesus.

The *Shepherd of Hermas** contains no references to Christ, the author preferring to use either the term *Lord* or the phrase "Son of God." A possible exception is a reference in *Visions* 2.2.8, but this is doubtful; only one manuscript has *christon*, while a variety of others have *kyrion*.

Barnabas, the *Didache* and *Hermas* are Jewish-Christian documents, and yet the term *Christos* and the idea of Jesus as Messiah are rarely found, much as we saw in James and Jude (see 3 above and Grundmann 1974).

In the letter of Polycarp to the Philippians we find the familiar phrase "our Lord Jesus Christ" (Pol. *Phil.* 1.1), the one whom God raised from the dead (Pol. *Phil.* 2.1). We also find the use of "Christ" as a name (Pol. *Phil.* 3.3) and a reference to the future judgment* seat of Christ before which all must appear (Pol. *Phil.* 6.2, no doubt quoting 2 Cor 5:10). Christ Jesus is said to be "our righteousness" (Pol. *Phil.* 8.1, possibly alluding to 1 Cor 1:30). Perhaps most interesting is the quoting of 2 John 4-7 at the *Letter to the Philippians* 8.1. Jesus Christ is also said to be "our Lord and God" (Pol. *Phil.* 12.2), and yet the author speaks of "the God and Father of our Lord Jesus Christ," who in the same sentence is also called the Son of God and the "eternal priest."

In the *Martyrdom of Polycarp* we find a variety of references to Christ, frequently as a personal name (*Mart. Pol.* 2.1-3; 14.3; 17.2; 20.2). We also find the familiar phrase "the [our] Lord, Jesus Christ" more than once (*Mart. Pol.* presc.; 19.2; 22.3). Of more significance in this document, which comes at the earliest from the late second century A.D., is the probable reference to "your Christ" (though there is some textual evidence for omitting *sou; Mart. Pol.* 14.2), showing that the author understands the original meaning of the term and its relational content. *Martyrdom of Polycarp* 9.3 also reflects awareness of the messiahship of Jesus (Grundmann 1974). Christ is also said to be one who has a kingdom* (*Mart. Pol.* 22.1), though whether this is envisioned as in heaven or on earth at the eschaton* is not clear (*Mart. Pol.* 22.2, God's heavenly kingdom; other manuscripts have "eternal kingdom"; *Epilogus Alius* 6).

By far the most important and varied early postcanonical uses of the term *Christos* are to be found in the letters of Clement (*see* Clement of Rome) and the letters of Ignatius.*

We can summarize first the evidence for the Clementine literature. References to "the [our] Lord, Jesus Christ" are very common (*1 Clem.* presc.; 16.2; 20.11; 21.6; 24.1; 42.1, 3; 44.1; 58.2; 65.2), and the reverse, "Jesus Christ, our Lord," is also found (*1 Clem.* 49.6; 50.7). The simple name *Jesus Christ* is used infrequently (*1 Clem.* 59.2; 62.3; 64.1). "Christ" can also be used as a personal name (*1 Clem.* 46.7, the members of

Christ; *1 Clem.* 2.1), but we do not find (with one possible exception) the juxtaposition of two titles (e.g., "the Lord Christ").

The Pauline formula *en Christō* appears, which reflects the great debt of especially *1 Clement* to the Pauline corpus (*1 Clem.* 22.1, *en Christō pistis; 1 Clem.* 38.1, "in Christ Jesus"; *1 Clem.* 43.1, those who were "in Christ"; cf. *1 Clem.* 46.5; 48.4; 49.1; 54.3).

Clement can refer to Jesus as "the Christ" (*1 Clem.* 42:1-2) and asserts that the Christ is from God and the apostles* from the Christ. In Clement's view Jesus came to earth as the Christ and remained such throughout his career; hence he can speak of "heralding the coming of Christ" (*1 Clem.* 17.1), the giving of the gospel* to the apostles by Christ (*1 Clem.* 42.1), the blood of Christ (*1 Clem.* 7.4), the raising of the Lord Jesus Christ (*1 Clem.* 24.1), Jesus Christ as high priest in heaven (*1 Clem.* 36.1) and the flock of Christ now on earth (*1 Clem.* 44.3). Clement refers to a future kingdom of Christ that will appear on earth (*1 Clem.* 50.3).

Like Paul, Clement sees Christ as the elect one and the election* of believers happening only in and through him (*1 Clem.* 64.1).

The material in *2 Clement* adds little to this, where "Christ" is almost always used as a part of a simple name (*2 Clem.* 1.1, 2; 2.7; 5.5), so much so that in the phrase "Christ, the Lord" the former is seen as a name and the latter as a title (*2 Clem.* 9.5).

The material found in the Ignatian letters is rich and deserves close scrutiny, but again we can only summarize the salient aspects of the data. Ignatius uses "Christ" as part of Jesus' name frequently (e.g., Ign. *Eph.* 3.1-2; 6.2; 9.2; 14.1; 16.2). We find the phrase "in Jesus Christ" or "in Christ Jesus" (Ign. *Eph.* 9.2; 10.3; Ign. *Magn.* 6.2; Ign. *Trall.* 9.2, 13.2; Ign. *Rom.* 1.1; 6.1), which Ignatius seems to prefer to the shorter "in Christ." Ignatius also speaks of being "of Christ" (Ign. *Eph.* 14.2) and uses the phrase "Jesus Christ, our Lord" (Ign. *Eph.* 7.2).

He is emphatic about calling Jesus Christ "God" or "our God" to a degree and in a manner not found in the canonical literature. There are six explicit references and five more references where the identification of Christ and God is probably implicit, though the name or title *Christ* does not always occur in such texts (cf. Ign. *Eph.* presc.; Ign. *Eph.* 1.1; 7.2; 15.3; 17.2; 18.2; 19.3; Ign. *Rom.* presc.; Ign. *Rom.* 3.3; Ign. *Smyrn.* 1.1; Ign.

Pol. 8.3; and see Trakatellis 1991).

Like Clement, Ignatius sees Jesus as the Christ throughout his earthly career and beyond; hence he can speak of Christ currently granting permission through prayer (Ign. *Eph.* 20.1) but also can refer to "the new human being Jesus Christ, which I have begun to discuss, dealing with his faith and his love, his suffering and his resurrection" (Ign. *Eph.* 20.1; cf. Ign. *Trall.* presc.). He emphasizes both the human and divine natures of Christ.

As a further development Ignatius uses the phrase *christophoroi,* paralleling it with *theophoroi* (Ign. *Eph.* 9.2)—Christians are both God-bearers and Christ-bearers in the world. This high christology was not invented by Ignatius but rather "can very well be seen as echoes of John 1 and 1 Corinthians 15" (Trakatellis 1991, 430). Ignatius follows the lead of earlier Christian traditions and more strongly emphasizes the divine side of the christological equation. The effect of this is that it pushes the idea of "the Christ" as a proxy and representative for God on earth somewhat into the background (Grundmann 1974, p. 574).

Ignatius frequently couples the appellation "Christ Jesus" or the reverse with the description "our savior" (Ign. *Eph.* 1.1; Ign. *Magn.* presc.; Ign. *Phld.* 9.2). He uses the phrase "the faith of Jesus Christ," in the sense of the faith about Jesus (Ign. *Magn.* 1.1), and the phrase "the law of Jesus Christ" occurs (Ign. *Magn.* 2.1). Jesus Christ is also called "the new leaven" (Ign. *Magn.* 10.2).

God the Father is said to operate and manifest himself through *(dia)* Jesus Christ (Ign. *Magn.* 5.2; 8.2). There is stress on there being only one Christ who came forth from the one Father (Ign. *Magn.* 7.2) as God's only Son (Ign. *Rom.* presc.).

As part of his theory that the Jewish faith derives from Christianity and not vice versa (Ign. *Magn.* 10.3; *see* Christianity and Judaism) Ignatius also claims that the divine (OT) prophets lived according to Jesus Christ (Ign. *Magn.* 8.2). This is part of his polemic to warn off Christians from Jewish practices.

Ignatius speaks of exhorting "in the name of Jesus Christ," apparently as a solemn sanction to make sure something is done (Ign. *Pol.* 5.1).

Unlike all the other authors mentioned in this article, Ignatius uses language about Christ that foreshadows the eucharistic developments of the early Middle Ages. Thus he says he desires "the bread of God which is the flesh of Jesus Christ. . . . And for drink I desire his blood, which is incorruptible agape" (Ign. *Rom.* 7.3). He urges, "Be careful . . . to use one Eucharist (for there is one flesh of our Lord Jesus Christ and one cup for union with his blood)" (Ign. *Phld.* 4.1).

Justin Martyr, even though he wrote in the middle of the second century, shows that the titular sense of *Christos* was not forgotten by Christians even 120 or more years after Jesus' death. The majority of times when *Christos* occurs in the probably authentic writings of Justin (*Apology I, Apology II* and the *Dialogue with Trypho*) it is used as a part of a name for Jesus ("Jesus Christ"; Justin *Apol. I* 12, 21, 23 et al.) or occasionally the reverse ("Christ Jesus," *Dial. Tryph.* 35) or alone as his name ("We have learned from Christ," Justin *Apol. I* 8, 41, 49). Justin also speaks of "our Christ" (Justin *Apol. I* 11, 31; *Apol. II* 10). He even combines two titles in the phrase "our Christ and Lord" (Justin *Dial. Tryph.* 133).

Justin is also fond of combinations such as "our master Jesus Christ" (Justin *Apol. I* 19) or "our Savior Jesus Christ" (Justin *Apol. I* 33). More significant are the references to "the Christ" (Justin *Apol. I* 49; *Dial. Tryph.* 32), "the Christ of God" (Justin *Dial. Tryph.* 8) or "God's Christ" (Justin *Dial. Tryph.* 136). He evens refer to "the knowledge of God and of his Christ" (Justin *Dial. Tryph.* 28, 133). If we ask what accounts for the prevalent use of *Christos* in its proper sense as a title rather than as a name, this may perhaps be accounted for by the fact that Justin was born in Samaria* (Nablus), seems to have grown up in a Semitic environment and was well acquainted with the OT. Yet he is also capable of going beyond the Jewish sense of the term and refers to Christ as an inclusive divine person in striking fashion: "As therefore Christ is the Israel and the Jacob, even so we, who have been quarried out from the bowels of Christ, are the true Israelite race" (Justin *Dial. Tryph.* 135). There is greater variety in Justin's use of *Christos* than in most of the other authors we have surveyed.

7. Conclusions.

We have endeavored to show the rich and varied use of the term *Christos* in the literature under survey. One could say a good deal more, but the following conclusions seem to be warranted.

There do not seem to be any clear distinctions to be made between Hellenistic and Jewish Christian handling of the "Christ" concept. Some of the more Jewish documents use "Christ" as a simple name, and some of those documents assumed to be less Jewish reflect knowledge of the Jewish background of the concept.

While it is not true that one cannot find references to Christ as divine in the canon,* especially in some of its later documents (e.g., 2 Pet), it is true to say that the use of such language escalated in the second century A.D., especially in the case of Ignatius, in part because of the rise of christological controversies within the Christian community and disputes with opponents.

The term *Christ* is sometimes used indiscriminately of any and all phases of the career of Christ, including apparently his preincarnate and postincarnate existence. There is little or no evidence of adoptionist tendencies unless Acts 2:36 provides such evidence (see 1 above).

"Christ" is frequently used as a name and sometimes as a title but also as a description of a relationship. Jesus is God's anointed but the believer's Lord.

The Pauline concept of being "in Christ" seems to have influenced a wide range of Christians, including especially Ignatius and Clement and to a lesser degree the author of 1 Peter.

The general avoidance of juxtaposing the two titles "Lord Christ" is notable and suggests that the early Christian writers knew the background of the term *Christ* and knew it was not merely a name, even when they do not make this explicit by calling Jesus "the Christ."

The eucharistic use of *Christos* language clearly appears only in Ignatius in the data we analyzed, and in this regard he stands out not only from his predecessors but also from his contemporaries and near contemporaries in the second century. His usage is a harbinger of things to come.

Our authors seem to understand that the term *Christ* refers to a human being, one anointed by God, and in some cases, such as we find in Ignatius, this is made clear when Christ is called "the new human being." Yet many authors also refer to Jesus Christ as God.

Notably absent in all this material is any attempt to explain the term *Christ* by using the phrase "the Son of Man."

To judge from Acts it appears that demonstrating Jesus to be the Christ was an exercise undertaken by Jewish Christian preachers and teachers on behalf of a largely Jewish audience.

The royal or messianic background of the term *Christos* is not emphasized in most of the sources considered in this article, but it can be argued to be determinative of how the term is used in most cases (cf. Hahn).

It has also been argued that the parting of the ways between Judaism and early Christianity in the late first century accelerated the process whereby Jesus was called God openly and frequently, and this may be so, but it is notable that some early Jews did use exalted language to speak of various agents, both supernatural (angelic)* and human, between God and humankind (cf. Hurtado 1988). My suggestion is that the high christological language used by early Christians ultimately goes back to some of the sapiential language Jesus and early Jewish Christians used to portray the man from Nazareth as God's Wisdom* come in the flesh (Witherington, *Sage* 1994). Jesus and his self-presentation stand as the middle term between the particularization of Wisdom as residing on earth in Torah (Sir) and the hypostasization of Wisdom (Wis) and the use of the term *theos* of Christ (in the NT and in Pliny).

See also CHRISTOLOGY; DOCETISM; LAMB; LOGOS CHRISTOLOGY; LORD; PREEXISTENCE; SHEPHERD, FLOCK; SON OF GOD; STONE, CORNERSTONE; WISDOM.

BIBLIOGRAPHY. M. Black, "The Christological Use of the Old Testament in the New Testament," *NTS* 18 (1971-72) 1-14; F. Büchsel, *Die Christologie des Hebräerbriefs* (Gütersloh: Bertelmann, 1922); V. Burch, "Factors in the Christology of the Letter to the Hebrews," *Exp* 47 (1921) 68-79; R. P. Casey, "The Earliest Christologies," *JTS* 10 (1959) 253-77; N. Cleary, "Jesus, Pioneer and Source of Salvation: The Christology of Hebrews 1-6," *TBT* 67 (1973) 1242-48; F. B. Craddock, *The Preexistence of Christ in the New Testament* (Nashville: Abingdon, 1968); O. Cullmann, *The Christology of the New Testament* (Philadelphia: Westminster, 1963); N. A. Dahl, *Jesus the Christ: The Historical Origins of Christological Doctrine* (Minneapolis: Augsburg, 1991); W. J. Dalton, *Christ's Proclamation to the Spirits: A Study of 1 Peter 3:18—4:6* (Rome: Pontifical Institute Press, 1965); P. E. Davies, "Primitive Christology in 1 Peter" in *Festschrift to Honor F. W. Gingrich,* ed. E. H. Barth and R. E. Cocraft (Leiden: E. J. Brill, 1972) 115-22; S. Duffy, "The Early Church Fathers and the Great Councils: The Emergence of Classical Christology" in *Jesus, One and Many: The Christological Concept of New Testament Authors,* ed. E. Richard (Wilmington, DE: Michael Glazier, 1988) 435-86; J. D. G. Dunn, *Christology in the Making* (Philadelphia: Westminster, 1980) 51-56; idem, "Christology (NT)," *ABD* 1:979-91; E. J. Goodspeed, "First Clement Called Forth by Hebrews," *JBL* 30 (1911) 157-60; W. Grundmann, "χρίω, χριστός κτλ," *TDNT* 9:527-80; F. Hahn, "χριστός," *EDNT* 3:478-86; A. T. Hanson, *Jesus Christ in the Old Testament* (London: SPCK, 1965); M. J. Harris, *Jesus as God: The New Testament Use of* Theos *in Reference to Jesus* (Grand Rapids: Baker, 1992); M. Hengel, *Between Jesus and Paul* (Philadelphia: Fortress, 1983); A. J. B. Higgins, "The Priestly Messiah," *NTS* 13 (1967) 211-39; P. E. Hughes, "The Christology of Hebrews," *SWJT* 28 (1985) 19-27; L. D. Hurst, "The Christology of Hebrews 1 and 2" in *The Glory of Christ in the New Testament,* ed. L. D. Hurst and N. T. Wright (Oxford: Oxford University Press, 1987) 151-64; L. Hurtado, *One God, One Lord* (Philadelphia: Fortress, 1988); D. Jones, "The Title *Christos* in Luke-Acts," *CBQ* 32 (1970) 69-76; M. de Jonge, "Christ," *ABD* (1992) 1:914-21; idem, "The Earliest Christian Use of Christos," *NTS* 32 (1986) 321-43; idem, "The Use of the Expression *ho Christos* in the Apocalypse of John" in *L'Apocalypse johannique et l'apocalyptique dan le Nouveau Testament,* ed. J. Lambrecht (BETL 53; Gembloux: Duculot; Louvain: Leuven University, 1980); J. Macquarrie, "The Rise of Classical Christology" in *Jesus Christ in Modern Thought* (Philadelphia: Trinity Press International, 1990) 147-72; I. H. Marshall, *Jesus the Savior: Studies in New Testament Theology* (Downers Grove, IL: InterVarsity Press, 1990); D. Moessner, "The Script of the Scriptures: Suffering and the Cross in Acts" in *History, Literature and Society in the Book of Acts,* ed. B. Witherington III (Cambridge: Cambridge University Press, 1996); C. F. D. Moule, "The Christology of Acts" in *Studies in Luke-Acts,* ed. L. E. Keck and J. L. Martyn (Nashville: Abingdon, 1966) 159-85; C. D. Osburn, "The Christological Use of 1 Enoch 1.9 in Jude 14, 15," *NTS* 23 (1976-77) 334-41; T. E. Pollard, *Johannine Christology and the Early Church* (Cambridge: Cambridge University Press, 1970); E. Richard, "The Functional Christology of First Peter" in *Perspectives on First Peter,* ed. C. H. Talbert (Macon, GA: Mercer University Press, 1986) 121-39; idem, *Jesus One and Many: The Christological Concept of New Testament Authors* (Wilmington, DE: Michael Glazier, 1988); J. A. T. Robinson, "The Most Primitive Christology of All?" in *Twelve New Testament Studies* (London: SCM, 1962) 139-52; S. S. Smalley, "The Christology of Acts Again" in *Christ and Spirit in the New Testament,* ed. B. Lindars and S. S. Smalley (Cambridge: Cambridge University Press, 1973) 79-94; E. Schweizer, "Paul's Christology and Gnosticism" in *Paul and Paulinism: Essays in Honour of C. K. Barrett,* ed. M. D. Hooker and S. G. Wilson (London: SPCK, 1982) 115-23; D. Trakellis, "God Language in Ignatius of Antioch" in *The Future of Early Christianity: Essays in Honor of Helmut Koester,* ed. B. A. Pearson et al. (Minneapolis: Fortress, 1991) 422-430; B. Witherington III, "The Influence of Galatians on Hebrews," *NTS* 37 (1991) 146-52; idem, *Jesus the Sage: the Pilgrimage of Wisdom* (Minneapolis: Fortress, 1994); idem, *Paul's Narrative Thought World: The Tapestry of Tragedy and Triumph* (Louisville, KY: Westminster/John Knox, 1994); idem, "A Petrine Source in 2nd Peter?" *SBLSP* (1985) 187-92; idem, "The Waters of Birth—John 3:5 and 1 John 5:6-8," *NTS* 35 (1989) 155-60; F. M. Young, "Christological Ideas in the Greek Commentaries on Hebrews," *JTS* 20 (1969) 150-63.

B. Witherington III

CHRISTIANITY AND JUDAISM: PARTINGS OF THE WAYS

In recent years the factors involved in the separation of Christianity from Judaism have stimulated much discussion and are themselves a byproduct of a healthy Jewish-Christian dialogue that has been under way for some time. Review of these factors helps explain why Judaism and Christianity moved so far apart, even though both religions sprang from common roots, and helps in part to explain the origin of anti-Semitism. Critical study of these religions' common roots and the causes of their separation is important, and its continuation should be encouraged.

Christian and Jewish separation has often in recent years been referred to in terms of the "partings of the ways" (see Dunn 1992). This more or less neutral language may, however, mask aspects of the bitterly opposed perspectives of early Jews and Christians themselves (see Lieu). Some of these perspectives will be considered below.

1. Jesus, the Apostles and the New Testament Writings
2. Christianity's Gentile Mission
3. The Divinization of Jesus
4. Historical Factors
5. Jewish and Christian Polemic

1. Jesus, the Apostles and the New Testament Writings.

The roots of early Christianity's separation from Judaism are found in the teachings of Jesus, the apostles* and the NT writings; that is, the roots of the separation are found in the earliest forms of Christianity. But this is not to say that Jesus and his earliest followers intended to found a new religion, one that would break away from the mother faith. Jesus and his earliest followers variously sought renewal and/or proclaimed eschatological* fulfillment *within the context of Jewish faith*. However, their liberal summons to sinners to enter the community of the redeemed and their criticisms of Torah-observant Jews who opposed this summons sowed the seeds of separation, which in the wake of political and social events and theological developments would later bear fruit.

1.1. The Message of Jesus. However the kingdom* that Jesus preached is to be understood, it seems clear that he envisioned it as open to a great many. We see this inclusiveness not only in his words but also in his actions. Jesus associated with "sinners" and other marginalized members of Jewish society and even showed consideration for Gentiles.* Jesus' inclusiveness paved the way for the later inclusion of Gentiles and other non-Torah-observant persons that marked Christian mission* and evangelism.*

But the message of Jesus was in no sense un-Jewish or anti-Jewish. Every aspect of Jesus' social and religious life and activities was thoroughly Jewish. Jesus frequented the synagogue,* visited the temple,* may very well have had concerns with matters of purity,* never challenged the authority of Torah (though he openly disagreed with the interpretation of Torah held by many of the religious teachers of his day; *see* Law) and evidently spoke of the fulfillment of Scripture. His proclamation of the kingdom should be understood

within the context of a theology of restoration. In short, Jesus anticipated through God's* intervention the restoration of Israel.* In every sense Jesus' message affirmed historic Israel and answered Jewish eschatological hopes,* as Jesus understood them.

1.2. The Apostolic Kerygma. Another factor that paved the way for the separation of Christianity and Judaism was the former's exclusivistic doctrine of salvation.* Early Christians proclaimed Jesus as the only way of salvation (Acts 4:12; Jn 14:6). This exclusivism stood somewhat in tension with Christianity's inclusivism. The gospel* was available to all; anyone could repent and be saved (see the use of Joel 2:32 in Acts 2:21 and Rom 10:13). But this repentance had to be combined with faith* in Jesus as the only Savior of humanity.

Like non-Christian Jews who believed that redemption lay in holding fast to certain beliefs and behaviors, early Christian Jews (*see* Jewish Christianity) also held fast to certain beliefs and behaviors. The principal point of disagreement lay in *which* beliefs and behaviors should be regarded as normative. Christian Jews understood the content of faith to revolve around Jesus' teaching, his life, his death* and his resurrection,* while their behavior increasingly revolved around the acceptance and inclusion of persons many Torah-observant Jews regarded as outside the community of the redeemed or redeemable.

The apostolic kerygma also implied that Israel's religious leaders seriously erred in opposing Jesus and in having participated in the events that led to his execution at the hands of the Romans. This criticism is underscored emphatically in the passion narratives (see esp. Mt 27:25) and reiterated elsewhere (Acts 2:23; 4:8-12; 5:17-42; 1 Cor 1—2; 1 Thess 4:14-16). Although the Jewish people as a whole are not condemned, the sharp condemnation of the religious leaders, including criticism leveled at the more popular Pharisees, probably deepened the growing rift between Christian Jews and proselytes on the one side and non-Christian Jews on the other.

1.3. The New Testament Writings. The polemic of the NT, though in-house criticism, paved the way for later anti-Judaistic and eventually anti-Semitic expressions that would drive a wedge between Jews and Christians. Paul's discussion of Jewish-Gentile relations in Romans 9—11 is especially important. Paul believed that owing to a lack of faith, Israel has "stumbled" (Rom 9:32-33, quoting parts of Is 28:16 and 8:14-15). Israel has attempted to establish its own righteousness,* the apostle avers, not knowing that God bestows it and that it is received through faith (Rom 10:1-17). Israel has rejected the proclamation of the gospel and instead has behaved as a "disobedient and contrary people" (Rom 10:21, quoting Is 65:2). Paul adds that only the elect* have obtained God's grace,* but "the rest (of Israel) were hardened" (Rom 11:7, with Rom 11:8-10 quoting Is 29:10 and Ps 69:22-23 as scriptural explanation and confirmation). With respect to the gospel, these fallen Israelites are "enemies of God" (Rom 11:28).

But Paul is not in any sense un-Jewish or anti-Jewish (as is sometimes alleged), any more than were the Essenes, who harshly criticized fellow Jews for not observing the law according to their interpretation (see 1QS 2:4-9; 5:10-13; 1QH 4:9-14). As Romans 11 (see esp. Rom 11:1-2, 26-32) makes clear, Paul firmly believed that the Jewish people, his own people, remained the people of God, even if estranged through their unbelief in the gospel. In Galatians 1 and Philippians 3 Paul speaks of his achievements in his "former life in Judaism" (Gal 1:13). But though he regarded these achievements as "refuse" (Phil 3:8), this does not mean that the Jewish people or Judaism as the faith of the OT had been abandoned. Paul regarded his pre-Christian life, in which he strove to attain to a righteousness outside of the provision of Christ and in which he persecuted* the Christian faith, as completely wrongheaded and therefore completely worthless. But the coming of Christ and the accomplishment of the cross* are part of the Jewish heritage, the fulfillment of Jewish Scripture and the true essence of Judaism (Rom 9:1-5).

Some of the criticisms found in the Gospels themselves also contributed to the later polemic that drove Christianity out of and away from Judaism. One thinks of the sharp diatribe directed against the Pharisees in Matthew 23. Especially noteworthy is the angry exchange between Jesus and the Pharisees depicted in John 8 (Jn 8:44: "you are of your father the devil"). As forthright as this material is, in its original setting and composition it gave expression to in-house debate and polemic, not anti-Semitism. This polemical material, however, did provide an increasingly gentilizing church* a significant corpus of authoritative tradition* out of which anti-Semitic ideas and expressions could be fashioned (see Evans and Hagner; Gager).

1.4. Jewish and Christian Interpretation of the "Four Pillars." Dunn identifies four important pillars of Second Temple Jewish faith: (1) monotheism (the affirmation that God* is one), (2) election* (the affirmation of Israel as the chosen people of God), (3) covenant* (as affirmed and described in Torah) and (4) the land* of Israel (including Jerusalem* and the temple*). Dunn explores in what ways Jews and Christians understood these pillars and finds in their differing understandings the seeds of separation. This important work deserves special consideration.

Dunn observes that Christians became increasingly critical not only of the temple establishment (a criticism that had roots in Jesus' ministry) but even of the temple itself. The temple came to be viewed as "made with human hands" (Acts 7:48), implying that it had taken on idolatrous connotations (see Hellenists; Stephen). God no longer resided in the temple, but in the Christian community. Sacrifice* was no longer needed, because Christ had died once for all. Even Christians themselves fulfilled the priestly* function of reconciliation (2 Cor 5:18; 1 Pet 2:5, 9; Rev 1:6; 5:10; 20:6).

Although Jesus disputed with his contemporaries the requirements of Torah and the question of election—on what grounds human beings receive forgiveness* and how they might qualify for admission into the kingdom—he accepted the basic concept of Israel's election. In comparison to Pharisees, Jesus was more inclusive, and he symbolized this inclusiveness by his table fellowship with persons some regarded as sinful and neglectful of Torah. Paul advanced Jesus' inclusiveness still further by teaching that Gentiles did not need to observe the fundamentals of Jewish identity, such as circumcision,* observance of the sabbath and food* laws.

Dunn finds that Jesus held to Jewish monotheism and that although he saw himself as a prophet empowered with God's Spirit (see Holy Spirit) and as having a close relationship with God, he did not understand himself as a divine figure. Dunn believes that in response to the resurrection* and the emergence of a theology of exaltation,* whereby Jesus was envisioned as seated in heaven* at God's right hand, Jesus came increasingly to be viewed as sharing in divine functions. This christology* in time grew into expressions of deification, which in non-Jewish Christian circles led to assertions of Jesus' equality, even identity, with God.

Dunn's arguments with respect to land, election and Torah are well taken, but his arguments with respect to monotheism and christology require some qualification. It can be plausibly argued that the recognition of Jesus' divinity began during his ministry,* not in the early church in response to the resurrection. Such an argument would appeal to messianic traditions* that imply a divine status for the Messiah (1 Chron 17:13; Ps 2:2, 7; Dan 7:9-14; 1QSa 2:11-12; 4Q521 1 ii 1; 4Q246 2:1), traditions that would have tempered messianic hopes* associated with Jesus, and Jesus' own tendency to assume divine prerogatives in his words and deeds (Mt 11:25-30; Mk 2:7; 2:27-28; 14:61-64; Lk 7:49; 11:21-22). Of course this is not to say that the trinitarian monotheism and christology of the fourth and fifth centuries represent no significant advancement of Jesus' teachings and activities. The contribution to the Jewish-Christian rift that the deification of Jesus made will be explored further in section 3 below.

2. Christianity's Gentile Mission.
Christian evangelization* of Gentiles* was out of step with Jewish proselytism. Jewish proselytes were to take on the yoke of the Torah (*m. 'Abot* 3:5), which involved scrupulous observation of sabbath and food laws. But early Christian proselytism seemed, in the eyes of its Jewish critics, bent on removing the yoke of the Torah. The councils depicted in Acts 11 and 15 exemplify the nature of the problems brought on by early Christianity's aggressive Gentile mission.* Pauline polemic against the "Judaizers" (as esp. seen in Gal) offers firsthand evidence of how divisive this issue was.

Although profoundly theologically and programmatic, the account in Acts 8—15 reflects a very real struggle in the life of the early church. The criticisms against the Gentile mission, portrayed as within the early church itself, raised the fundamental question of whether Gentiles were fit for the gospel of Messiah Jesus. The council described in Acts 15 convened to explore the question whether Christian Jews could "eat with" Christian Gentiles. The council decided that they could, because God had given his Holy Spirit to the Gentiles. The indwelling of the Holy Spirit provides divine warranty that in Christ the Gentiles are pure. As such, Christian Jews should have no qualms about fellowshipping with them.

The council described in Acts 15 treated more directly the question of salvation. Christian Pharisees asserted that "it is necessary to circumcise" the Gentile converts "and to charge them to keep the law of Moses*" if they are to be saved (Acts 15:1, 5). But the council decided it was not necessary to require that the "yoke of Torah" be placed on the Christian Gentiles. They were instead to be urged to "abstain from the pollutions of idols* and from unchastity and from what is strangled and from blood" (Acts 15:20, 29). These instructions evidently echo the Mosaic legislation that applies to "strangers" who reside among the Jews (cf. Lev 17:8-13; 18:26) and perhaps the Noachic covenant (Gen 9:3-4). In other words, Christian Gentiles are under no obligation to observe the Israelite covenant itself, as commanded in the written Torah and explicated in oral Torah (the oral traditions), but they are obligated to live godly lives. They cannot simply live as the heathen do.

Because the early church imposed on Gentile converts only the laws that applied to the nations and the sojourners among Israel, conflict with non-Christian Jews, whose faith in the post-70 era increasingly was defined by rabbinic halakoth, was unavoidable. (Halakoth are exegetically derived legal opinions; *halākôt* coming from *halāk*, i.e., "how one should walk.") Christian Halakoth and rabbinic Halakoth could hardly have been in sharper disagreement. On this score alone, separation was inevitable.

3. The Divinization of Jesus.
The tendency of the Greco-Roman church to deify Jesus in the absolute sense, that is, to intensify Johannine and Pauline christology in terms of Jesus as God (in contrast to Ebionite* christology), only made Christianity all the more unacceptable to Jews. The divinization of Jesus stood in tension with strict Jewish monotheism, and in its extremest form of presentation it appeared to be a direct violation of the First Commandment (Ex 20:3; Deut 5:7).

As has been suggested above, the roots of deification are probably to be found in Jesus' teaching and activities. But at best the sense of divine identity is implicit and only hinted at. It is in the theologies of Paul and the Fourth Evangelist that the divinization of Jesus became explicit and then paved the way for the absolute deification that would later characterize Greco-Roman Christianity.

3.1. Pauline Christology. Paul routinely refers to Jesus as "Christ"* and as "Lord"* (Rom 1:3, 7; 5:1, 11, *passim*). The first title gives expression to the Jewish hope for the appearance of an anointed* descendant of David through whom Israel would be restored and the kingdom of God be established (Rom 1:3-4; *see* Kingdom of God). The second title normally functions as a title of respect and does not necessarily denote deity (as though "Lord" necessarily referred to Yahweh). But there is one instance that is of special interest.

In Romans 10:9 Paul tells his readers, "If you confess with your lips that Jesus is Lord and believe in your heart that God raised him from the dead, you will be saved." The apostle then digresses (Rom 10:10-12), explaining aspects of faith and confession and how it is that all people—Jew and Gentile alike—must make this confession. He concludes his argument—and here is the interesting point—by quoting from Joel 2:32: "For 'everyone who calls upon the name of the Lord will be saved' " (Rom 10:13). The close association of Jesus, who is "Lord," with the "name of the Lord" in the quotation from Joel is remarkable. At the very least Paul seems to presuppose a very close relationship between the Lord Jesus and the Lord God.

The "name" of the Lord also plays an important role in the Christ hymn* of Philippians 2:6-11, in which we are told that Jesus has received the "name which is above every name" and will be confessed by all as "Lord." The exaltation of Jesus in this hymn (note especially the assertion in Phil 2:6 that Jesus possessed "equality with God") clearly implies that Paul thought of Jesus in terms of divinity, probably as God's coregent.

After cataloging Israel's rich heritage (Rom 9:1-5), Paul concludes with a eulogy (Rom 9:5) that bears an uncertain syntactical relationship to what precedes. The RSV renders the relevant portion of the verse thus: "and of their race, according to the flesh, is the Christ. God who is over all be blessed for ever. Amen." The original Greek, of course, had no punctuation. The NASB translates: "and from whom is the Christ according to the flesh, who is over all, God blessed forever. Amen." Some scholars have argued that in this one place Paul has confessed Jesus to be God. Such a confession would put a serious strain on the monotheism of Judaism.

In the Pastoral Epistles, whose Pauline authorship many dispute, there may be further examples of the divinization of Jesus. Of special interest is the affirmation in Titus 2:13, which may be rendered literally "awaiting the blessed hope and appearance of the glory of our great God and Savior Jesus Christ." Some have insisted that the verse be translated "awaiting the blessed hope and appearance of the glory of our great God and of our Savior Jesus Christ." The use of the definite article, however, supports the first translation, as opposed to the second, which would distinguish "great God" from "Savior Jesus Christ." An affirmation such as this would have been viewed by most first- and second-century Jews as clearly in violation of monotheistic faith.

3.2. Johannine Christology. Johannine christology appears to have been fashioned from Jewish wisdom* ideas and the related concept of the *shaliach* (lit. "one who is sent" from heaven; *šāliaḥ* in Hebrew, *apostolos* in Greek). *Shaliach* and wisdom ideas were easily exploited by first-century Christians who were trying to explain to themselves and to others who Jesus was and what the nature of his relationship to God. In the Fourth Gospel Jesus is presented as the Word that became flesh* (Jn 1:1, 14). The function of the Johannine "Word" (*logos*) approximates that of Wisdom, which in biblical and postbiblical traditions is sometimes personified (Prov 8:1—9:6; Sir 24:1-34; one should note that in Sir 24:3, Wisdom is identified as the word that proceeds from God's mouth). As God's *shaliach* (see Jn 13:16; 17:3; cf. Mt 15:24; Lk 4:18, 43; Heb 3:1) Jesus is able to reveal the Father (Jn 14:9: "He who has seen me has seen the father") and complete his "work" on earth (Jn 17:4: "I have accomplished the work which you gave me to do"). The theme of Jesus being sent from heaven finds frequent expression in the Johannine writings (Jn 3:16-17, 34; 5:36-38; 6:29, 57; 7:29; 10:36; 11:42; 17:3, 8, 18, 21, 23, 25; 20:21; 1 Jn 4:9, 10, 14). As the one who had been sent from heaven, Jesus now sends his disciples into the world to continue his ministry (Jn 4:38; 17:18; 20:21).

In three passages Jesus is accused of blaspheming for claiming divine privilege and prerogatives. In the first passage Jesus supposedly breaks the sabbath by healing* a man and then intensifies the ensuing controversy by referring to God as his Father (Jn 5:16-18). Jesus' critics infer from this claim that Jesus has made himself "equal with God." The second passage is similar. In it Jesus affirms, "I and the Father are one" (Jn 10:30). His critics take up stones to stone him, because, athough only a human, Jesus has made himself God. But the meaning here is probably not that Jesus has literally claimed to be God. The claim to be one with God probably relates to the *shaliach* concept. As God's representative, sent to do God's work, Jesus can claim that he is "one" with the Father.

But a third passage, in which Jesus states, "Before Abraham was, I am" (Jn 8:58), probably does imply a divine identity of Jesus. The Greek is somewhat ambiguous. The words "I am" (*egō eimi*) may very well be a conscious allusion to God, who in the Scriptures of Israel reveals himself as the God "who is" (LXX Is 43:10: "that you should know and believe and understand that I am [*egō eimi]"*). That these words in John should be understood in an epiphanic sense is strongly supported by the description of the arrest scene: "When he said to them, 'I am,' they drew back and fell to the ground" (Jn 18:6). If John's use of *egō eimi* in these two passages was intended to imply that in some sense Jesus was the manifestation of Israel's God, then Jewish offense becomes understandable.

John's exaltation of Jesus appears to have been directly challenged by Rabbi Abahu (third century), who is reported to have said, "If a man says to you, 'I am God,' he is a liar; [or] 'I am the son of man,' in the end he will regret it; [or] 'I will go up to heaven'—he that says it will not perform it" (*y. Ta'an.* 2.1). Elsewhere Abahu adds, "[God] says . . . 'I am the first'—I have no father; 'I am the last'—I have no son" (*Ex. Rab.* 29.5 [on Ex 20:2]). Similarly Rabbi Aha (fourth century) declares: "There is One that is alone, and he has not a second; indeed, he has neither son nor brother—but: 'Hear O Israel, the Lord our God, the Lord is One' " (*Deut. Rab.* 2.33 [on Deut 6:4]). An anonymous saying offers further illustration: "There was a man, the son of a woman, who would rise up and seek to make

himself God, and cause the entire world to err. . . . If he says that he is God, he lies; and in the future he will cause to err—that he departs and returns in the end. He says, but will not do. . . . Alas, who shall live of that people that listens to that man who makes himself God?" (*Yal. Šim.* on Num 23:7).

3.3. Patristic Christology. Justin Martyr (c. A.D. 110-65) tried to convince Trypho the Jew that in the Scriptures "Christ is called both God and Lord of hosts" (*Dial. Tryph.* 36, 85). Elsewhere Justin argued that Jesus is "God and Lord," the very same who appeared to Abraham and who with God the Father created the heavens and the earth (*Dial. Tryph.* 55–63). Justin's exegesis and theology represented logical extensions of what is for the most part only implied in the NT writings. The primary confession of the early church—that Jesus died for our sins, was raised on the third day and is now the Lord of the church—was becoming more oriented to ontological aspects of christology.

The Apostles' Creed (earliest form dating to c. A.D. 150) reflects the primitive elements of NT christology; part of it reads: "I believe in God the Father Almighty, Maker of heaven and earth, and in Jesus Christ his only Son our Lord, who was conceived by the Holy Spirit, born of the virgin Mary, suffered under Pontius Pilate, was crucified, dead, and buried. He descended into hell. The third day he rose again from the dead. He ascended into heaven and sits at the right hand of God the Father Almighty; from there he shall come to judge the living and the dead." The antiquity of this creed is witnessed by the early baptismal catechism, dating from the time of Hippolytus (170?–235), in which the convert is asked: "Do you believe in Jesus Christ the Son of God, who was born of the Holy Spirit and the virgin Mary, who was crucified under Pontius Pilate and died, and rose the third day living from the dead, and ascended into heaven and sat down at the right hand of the Father, and will come to judge the living and the dead?"

But the Nicene Creed (A.D. 325) reflects the growing interest in the question of Jesus' divine essence. Part of this creed reads: "I believe in . . . one Lord Jesus Christ, the only begotten Son of God, begotten of his Father before all worlds; God of God, Light of Light, very God of very God, begotten, not made, being of one substance with the Father."

Church theologians became consumed with

the difficult questions of Christ's divine nature—was he in essence similar *(homoiousios)* to God or the same *(homoousios)* as God? How can there be a God the Son and a God the Father, if there is only one God, as the OT and Jesus himself affirm? Orthodoxy answered this question with the concept of the triune Godhead (see the Athanasian Creed, which reads in part: "But the Godhead of the Father and of the Son, and of the Holy Spirit is all one; the glory equal, the majesty co-eternal . . . yet there are not three Gods, but one God . . . not three Lords, but one Lord"). All of this to Jewish ears sounded foreign and blasphemous and was answered in polemical treatments of the "two powers in heaven" heresy (i.e., the belief, especially in reference to Gnosticism,* that there were two or more gods; see Segal).

4. Historical Factors.

Several historical events played a part in Jewish and Christian separation. Some of these events did not directly reflect the growing Jewish-Christian dispute, but they did have an impact on it. Other events directly reflected the dispute and contributed significantly to Jewish-Christian antipathy.

4.1. The Jewish Wars. A major catalyst that led to the partings of the ways was the destruction of Jerusalem* and the temple in A.D. 70 and the later Bar Kokhba defeat (A.D. 135), which resulted in the loss of Jerusalem as a Jewish city and the loss of Israel as a state. Prior to the destruction of Jerusalem, the temple remained important to Christian Jews. We see this in Acts especially (Acts 2:46; 3:1; 5:20, 42; 21:26; 22:17). The destruction of the temple proved to be a significant loss of common ground.

The Bar Kokhba war also intensified hostilities between Christian and non-Christian Jews. According to patristic sources, Christians were persecuted by Simon ben Kosiba, who evidently had been dubbed "bar kokhba" (Aramaic for "son of the star"). Justin Martyr, a contemporary of Simon, relates that the Jews "count us foes and enemies; and, like yourselves, they kill and punish us whenever they have the power, as you can well believe. For in the Jewish war which lately raged, Bar Kokhba, the leader of the revolt of the Jews, gave orders that Christians alone should be led away to cruel punishments, unless they should deny [that] Jesus [is] the Christ and blaspheme" (Justin *Apol. I* 31.5-6).

Eusebius, possibly dependent on Justin, similarly states that "Kokhba, prince of the Jewish sect, killed the Christians with all kinds of persecutions, when they refused to help him against the Roman troops" (*Hadrian Year 17*).

Why did the Christians refuse to support Simon's bid for freedom? The most probable reason is that Simon was regarded as the Messiah, as both Jewish and Christian sources relate (Eusebius *Hist. Eccl.* 4.6.1–4; *y. Ta'an.* 4.5; *b. Sanh.* 93b). Christian allegiance to Jesus as the Messiah contradicted Simon's claims and undermined his authority. Christians "alone" were dealt with severely, because among the Jews they alone regarded someone else as Israel's Messiah.

4.2. The Jewish Hope of Rebuilding the Temple. Horbury draws our attention to *Barnabas* 16.1-4, a polemical passage that expresses criticism of the Jews for placing their confidence in the temple and, after it had been destroyed, hoping to rebuild it (see Horbury, in Dunn 1992, 315-45). Horbury thinks the author of *Barnabas* was alluding to the Jewish hope to rebuild the temple, perhaps at some time near the end of the Flavian dynasty. The author of *Barnabas,* as well as other Christians, may have feared a Jewish resurgence that would have undermined Christianity. In fact, such a resurgence was in some sense under way, and many Christian Jews were abandoning Christian teaching in order to remain loyal to the synagogue. Pressure to do so was greatly increased by the introduction of the *Birkat ha-Minim* (lit. "the blessing [or cursing] of the heretics"). Jews willing to utter this "benediction" tended to abandon Christianity, while Jews or proselytes unwilling to utter it were put out of the synagogue. (The revision of this benediction is treated in 5.1 below.)

4.3. The Demise of Jewish Membership in the Church. The demise of Jewish membership in the Christian church was hastened by punishment and persecution of Christian Jews within the synagogue, eventually followed by expulsions from the synagogue. The evidence for the former is found in the Gospels, Acts, Paul's letters and the book of Revelation. According to Mark 13:9, Jesus warns his disciples that "they will deliver you up to councils; and you will be beaten in synagogues." This material is carried over into Matthew (10:17) and Luke (21:12), perhaps with parallel material drawn from Q (Mt 10:19 par. Lk 12:11). A similar saying is also found in Matthew 23:34, which may have been drawn from the Evangelist's special source: "Therefore I send you prophets and wise men and scribes, some of whom you will kill and crucify, and some you will scourge in your synagogues and persecute from town to town." Similar traditions are related in the Acts of the Apostles, where we read of Paul and various traveling companions being persecuted and driven out of town (Acts 13:50-51; 14:2-6, 19-20; 17:5-9, 13-14; 18:6, 12-17). Indeed, prior to his conversion Paul is portrayed as a persecutor of the young church (Acts 7:58; 8:1-3; 9:1-9, 21; 22:4-5). That this portrait is not a self-serving and imaginative retelling of history is seen in Paul's own letters, where he admits with shame his role in trying to destroy the church ("I persecuted the church of God," 1 Cor 15:9; "you have heard of my former life in Judaism, how I persecuted the church of God violently and tried to destroy it," Gal 1:13, 23; "a persecutor of the church," Phil 3:6).

From the reference to the "synagogue of Satan" in Revelation 3:9 we should probably infer persecution, as the fuller context suggests: "I know that you have but little power, and yet you have kept my word and have not denied my name. Behold, I will make those of the synagogue of Satan who say that they are Jews and are not, but lie—behold, I will make them come and bow down before your feet, and learn that I have loved you" (Rev 3:8-9). This assurance strongly implies that the Christians understood themselves as the true Jews. What we have here is an intramural controversy involving Christian Jews and non-Christian Jews, with the former claiming to be the righteous remnant, the twelve thousand preserved from each of the twelve tribes (Rev 7:4-8; 14:1-3). The non-Christian Jews were stronger (probably in social and political standing, as well as in numbers) and were persecuting those who had believed the Christian message. These Christian Jews, who "have but little power," regarded their persecutors as not really Jews but apostates.

Similar polemic is found in the Fourth Gospel. In three passages we find explicit reference to Christian expulsion from the synagogue (Jn 9:22; 12:42; 16:2). Although it is possible that such actions were taken in the time of Jesus, it is probable that these threats reflected the experience of the Johannine community sometime late in the first century, perhaps in the wake of the revision of the twelfth benediction of the *Amidah* (*'āmidāh,* a set of eighteen benedictions that were to be recited "standing up" at the daily service of the synagogue) as part of concerted effort to drive Christians out of the synagogue. If anyone confessed Jesus as the Messiah, he was to be cast out of the synagogue. If such actions were indeed taking place in the late first century, then the decline in Jewish membership in the church is all the more understandable.

According to Eusebius, in the aftermath of the Bar Kokhba war the Jewish presence in the Christian church of Palestine was diminished still further. "I have not found any written statement of the dates of the bishops in Jerusalem, for tradition says that they were extremely short-lived, but I have gathered from documents this much—that up to the siege of the Jews by Hadrian the successions of bishops were fifteen in number. It is said that they were all Hebrews by origin who had nobly accepted the knowledge* of Christ, so that they were counted worthy even of the episcopal ministry by those who had the power to judge such questions. For their whole church at that time consisted of Hebrews who had continued Christian from the Apostles down to the siege at the time when the Jews again rebelled from the Romans and were beaten in a great war" (Eusebius *Hist. Eccl.* 4.4.1-2). Eusebius goes on to list the names and lengths of tenure of the Jewish bishops. He then comments that when the Bar Kokhba war ended, the church in Judea was no longer Jewish but was "composed of Gentiles," over whom a Gentile named Marcus was appointed bishop (Eusebius *Hist. Eccl.* 4.5.4). As a result of this war Christianity had begun to evolve into a predominantly Gentile religion. As such, it is not surprising that Christian writers became increasingly ignorant and critical of their Jewish heritage.

4.4. The Use of Different Versions of Scripture. Hengel has pointed out the significance of the use of different versions of the OT (see Hengel, in Dunn 1992, 39-84). The synagogue continued to read and study the Scriptures in Hebrew as well as provide commentary on them in Aramaic. But Christians came to use the Greek translation, the Septuagint, almost exclusively. Most Christian Gentiles could read the Scriptures only in Greek (or in Latin), while there is some evidence that non-Christian Jews (and perhaps Christian Jews as well) were discouraged from reading the Septuagint. Hengel even suggests that Aquila's recension of the Septuagint may have been intended as a targum for Greek-speaking Jews, perhaps to counter Christian interpretation of the Greek version.

The use of different versions of Scripture worked as a wedge, further dividing Christians from Jews. As the church became increasingly dominated by Gentiles, it became increasingly Greek and non-Hebrew. The church's use of the Septuagint reflected this ethnic shift and at the same time contributed to it.

5. Jewish and Christian Polemic.

From the second century on Jewish and Christian polemics not only intensified but took on a new character. The polemics were no longer those of squabbling siblings but those of largely ethnically distinct peoples who viewed one another as foreign. Jews began to regard Christianity as idolatry* and heresy; Christians began to view Judaism in terms of apostasy* and obduracy.

5.1. Jewish Polemic and Rejection of Christianity. Jewish polemic directed against Christianity could be just as harsh and ugly as was Christian polemic, though with the ascendancy of Christianity, Jewish polemic came to be muted and sometimes was even edited out of texts. Some of the Jewish polemic is preserved in "dialogues" composed by Christians. The best known is Justin Martyr's *Dialogue with Trypho the Jew.* Although these dialogues are artificial and routinely portray the Christian apologists as refuting, even silencing, their Jewish opponents, the nature of the objections raised by the Jews in all probability accurately reflects the arguments and polemic that Jews directed against Christians.

Justin's Trypho found it difficult to accept that Jesus could really have been the fulfillment of the Jewish Scriptures. How could Jesus have been the Messiah, since he had been defeated and put to death by the Romans in such a shameful manner? Trypho declares: "Be assured that all our nation awaits the Messiah; and we admit that all the Scriptures which you have quoted refer to him. . . . But we are in doubt about whether the Messiah should be so shamefully crucified. For whoever is crucified is said in the Law to be accursed, so that I am very skeptical on this point. It is quite clear, to be sure, the Scriptures announce that the Messiah had to suffer; but we wish to learn if you

can prove it to us whether by suffering* he was cursed . . . Prove to us whether he must also be crucified and die such a disgraceful and dishonorable death, cursed by the Law. For we cannot bring ourselves even to consider this" (*Dial. Tryph.* 89–90).

With the passage of time the polemic became much sharper, even hateful. Civil arguments, such as we find in Justin's *Dialogue,* gave way to vituperation and slurs. The polemic found in the Talmud and Midrashim document some of this nastier polemic. In reference to Jesus' birth we find: "She who was the descendant of princes and governors [= Mary] played the harlot with carpenters [= Joseph]" (*b. Sanh.* 106a). Jesus is accused of idolatry: "When king Jannai [104-78 B.C.] slew our rabbis, R. Joshua and Jesus fled to Alexandria of Egypt. On the resumption of peace . . . he arose, went, and found himself in a certain inn, where great honor was shown him. 'How beautiful is this innkeeper!' Thereupon Jesus observed, 'Rabbi, her eyes are narrow.' 'Wretch,' he rebuked him, 'do you engage yourself thus?' He sounded four hundred trumpets and excommunicated him. He [Jesus] came before him many times pleading, 'Receive me!' But he would pay no heed to him. One day he [R. Joshua] was reciting the Shema, when Jesus came before him. He intended to receive him and made a sign to him. He [Jesus], thinking that it was to repel him, went, put up a brick, and worshipped it. 'Repent,' said he [R. Joshua] to him. He replied, 'I have thus learned from you: "He who sins and causes others to sin is not afforded the means of repentance"'" (*b. Sanh.* 107b; cf. *b. Soṭa* 47a). We are told that Jesus had five disciples and that their names imply a variety of evils and misfortunes (*b. Sanh.* 107b). In various places Jesus is accused of having practiced magic* and having led Israel astray (*b. Sanh.* 43a; *t. Šab.* 11.15; *b. Šab.* 104b). Indeed, Jesus can be raised through incantation (*b. Giṭ.* 57a, MS M).

As early as the end of the first century the liturgy of the synagogue was modified to discourage Christian Jews. It was apparently at this time that the twelfth benediction of the ancient Jewish prayer, called the *Amidah* (or *Shemoneh Esreh*), was expanded: "Can anyone among you frame a benediction relating to the heretics? Samuel the Lesser arose and composed it" (*b. Ber.* 28b). Samuel the Lesser's composition may have something to do with the revision of the twelfth benediction: "For apostates let there be no hope, and the kingdom of arrogance quickly uproot. [In a moment let the Nazarenes and the heretics be destroyed; let them be blotted from the Book of Life, and with the righteous not be inscribed.] Blessed are you, O Lord, who loves judgment!" (*Amidah* §12). The bracketed words are thought to be the later inserted material. It was probably to this malediction (often referred as the *Birkat ha-Minim,* lit. "blessing of the heretics") that Justin alluded when he told Trypho, "You curse in your synagogues all those who are called from him Christians" (Justin *Dial. Tryph.* 96).

Note also the comment made by the author of the *Epistle to Diognetus,* who claims that Christians "are warred upon by the Jews as foreigners" (*Diogn.* 5.17). Horbury (1982) has argued that the expanded twelfth benediction was an attempt to strengthen older expulsion mechanisms. Kimelman's argument (1980-82) that there never was an anti-Christian "blessing" in the synagogue is not persuasive.

In the end, to the Jewish mind, to convert to the Christian faith was to abandon one's Jewish identity. In Jewish thinking, Christianity was not simply wrong, it was idolatry and apostasy. Judaism and Christianity had moved from fraternal debate to a completely antithetical relationship. To become one was to cease being the other. This thinking, which with the demise of Jewish (Ebionite*) Christianity came to dominate sometime in the fifth century, marked a stage in the development of Jewish and Christian self-understanding that was far removed from the lively proclamations and in-house disputes of the first century.

5.2. Christian Polemic and Condemnation of Judaism. Judaism and Christianity were driven further apart by Christian polemic, which became increasingly ugly. According to Ignatius* of Antioch (early second century), "if we continue to live according to Judaism, we are admitting that we have not received grace" (Ign. *Magn.* 8.1). More sharply, Ignatius later says that "it is monstrous to talk of Jesus Christ and to practice Judaism" (Ign. *Magn.* 10.3). According to *Barnabas* 13—14 God's covenant with Israel ended when the people committed idolatry at Sinai; God's covenant is now with the Christian church alone. The author of the *Epistle to Diognetus* ridicules circumcision and the Jewish food laws (*Diogn.* 4.1-6). Opposition to Jewish practices contributed to Christian condemnation of the Jewish Christians called Nazoreans (Epiphanius *Haer.* 29; Augustine *Haer.* 9).

Later Christian polemic (third to fifth centuries) becomes noticeably more bitter. According to Chrysostom, "the synagogue is a temple of idolatry. . . . A synagogue is less honorable than any inn. For it is not simply a gathering place for thieves and hucksters, but also of demons. Indeed, not only the synagogue, but the soul of the Jews are also the dwelling places of demons" (Chrysostom *Discourse* 1.3.3—4.2). Christians accused Jews of apostasy and rebellion against God. And with respect to the execution of Jesus, the Jews were even accused of deicide, that is, of killing God. In the words of Melito* of Sardis: "And you killed the Lord at the great feast . . . O lawless Israel, what is this unprecedented crime that you committed, thrusting your Lord among unprecedented sufferings, your Sovereign, who formed you, who made you, who honored you, who called you 'Israel'? . . . And who has been murdered? Who is the murderer? I am ashamed to say and I am obliged to tell. . . . The Sovereign has been insulted; the God has been murdered; the King of Israel has been put to death by an Israelite right hand!" (*Peri Pascha* 567-84, 693-716).

Because of their rejection of Jesus and their ongoing unbelief in the Christian proclamation, God had abandoned the Jews to their doom. Cyprian asks, "Did not the Jews perish on this account, since they preferred to envy rather than to believe in Christ? Disparaging the great things that he did, they were deceived by a blinding jealousy and they were unable to open the eyes of their hearts so as to recognize his divine works" (*Jealousy and Envy* 5). Some patristic writers believed that there was no longer any hope for the redemption* of Israel (Chrysostom *Hom. 1 Thess.* 3 [on 1 Thess 2:14-16]; Eusebius *Dem. Ev.* 1.1; Augustine *Civ. D.* 18.46; 20.29; Aphrahat *Dem.* 23.20). (For a convenient assembly and summary of the primary documents that relate to Jewish-Christian polemic, see Callan. For bibliography of relevant secondary sources, see Siker in Charlesworth, ed., 242-48.)

These factors largely account for the disappearance of Jewish Christianity. This disappearance only widened the gap between Christianity (now almost exclusively non-Jewish) and the Jewish people (now almost without any Christians among its population). By the time the church reached its determinative period (fourth and fifth centuries) there was virtually no Jewish input. At about this same time, the rabbinic tradition, which was very critical of Jesus and Christianity, prevailed in defining Judaism. The shape of the NT canon and the definition of several important doctrines, such as the Trinity and the deity of Jesus, were settled without Jewish input. The final shape of Christianity therefore was increasingly non-Jewish, thus making Christianity less attractive and so widening further the gap between Jews and Christians.

See also APOSTOLIC FATHERS; BARNABAS; CHURCH AS ISRAEL, PEOPLE OF GOD; CIRCUMCISION; DIASPORA JUDAISM; GENTILES, GENTILE MISSION; JEWISH CHRISTIANITY; JUDAISM, POST-A.D. 70; SYNAGOGUE.

BIBLIOGRAPHY. C. K. Barrett, "Jews and Judaizers in the Epistles of Ignatius" in *Jews, Greeks and Christians: Religious Cultures in Late Antiquity,* ed. R. Hammerton-Kelly and R. Scroggs (SJLA 21; Leiden: E. J. Brill, 1976) 220-44; T. Callan, *Forgetting the Root: The Emergence of Christianity from Judaism* (New York: Paulist, 1986); J. H. Charlesworth, ed., *Jews and Christians: Exploring the Past, Present and Future* (New York: Crossroad, 1990); P. Donahue, "Jewish Christianity in the Letters of Ignatius of Antioch," *VC* 32 (1978) 81-93; J. D. G. Dunn, *The Partings of the Ways* (London: SCM; Philadelphia: Trinity Press International, 1991); idem, ed., *Jews and Christians: The Partings of the Ways A.D. 70 to 135* (WUNT 66; Tübingen: J. C. B. Mohr/Siebeck, 1992); C. A. Evans and D. A. Hagner, eds., *Anti-Semitism and Early Christianity: Issues of Polemic and Faith* (Minneapolis: Fortress, 1993); J. G. Gager, *The Origins of Anti-Semitism: Attitudes Toward Judaism in Pagan and Christian Antiquity* (New York: Oxford University Press, 1985); L. Goppelt, *Christentum und Judentum in ersten und zweiten Jahrhundert* (Gütersloh: Bertelsmann, 1955); W. Horbury, "The Benediction of the Minim and Early Jewish-Christian Controversy," *JTS* 33 (1982) 19-61; J. Jocz, *The Jewish People and Jesus Christ: A Study in the Relationship Between the Jewish People and Jesus Christ* (London: SPCK, 1949); S. T. Katz, "The Separation of Judaism and Christianity After 70 C.E.: A Reconsideration," *JBL* 103 (1984) 43-76; H. C. Kee, "The Transformation of the Synagogue After 70 C.E.: Its Import for Early Christianity," *NTS* 36 (1990) 1-24; R. Kimelman, "*Birkat Ha-Minim* and the Lack of Evidence for an Anti-Christian Jewish Prayer in Late Antiquity" in *Jewish and Christian Self-Definition,* ed. E. P. Sanders et al. (3 vols.; Philadelphia: Fortress, 1980-82) 2:226-44, 391-403; A. J. F. Klijn and G. J. Reinink, *Patristic Evidence for Jewish-Christian Sects* (NovTSup 36; Leiden: E. J. Brill, 1973); N. de Lange, *Origen and the Jews: Studies in Jewish-Christian Relations in Third-century Palestine* (Cambridge: Cambridge University Press, 1976); E. Lerle, "Liturgische Reformen des Synagogengottesdienstes als Antwort auf die judenchristliche Mission des ersten Jahrhunderts," *NovT* 10 (1968) 31-42; J. Lieu, " 'The Parting of the Ways': Theological Construct or Historical Reality?" *JSNT* 56 (1994) 101-19; G. Lindeskog, "Anfänge des jüdisch-christlichen Problems: Ein programmatischer Entwurf" in *Donum Gentilicium: New Testament Studies in Honour of David Daube,* ed. C. K. Barrett et al. (Oxford: Clarendon, 1978) 255-75; G. Lüdemann, Opposition to Paul in Jewish Christianity (Philadelphia: Fortress, 1989); S. McKnight, *A Light Among the Gentiles: Jewish Missionary Activity in the Second Temple Period* (Minneapolis: Fortress, 1991); W. A. Meeks and R. L. Wilken, *Jews and Christians in Antioch in the First Four Centuries of the Common Era* (SBLSBS 13; Missoula, MT: Scholars Press, 1978); J. Parkes, *The Conflict of the Church and the Synagogue: A Study of the Origins of Anti-Semitism* (London: Soncino, 1934); H. G. Perelmuter, *Siblings: Rabbinic Judaism and Early Christianity at their Beginnings* (New York: Paulist, 1989); L. Schiffman, "At the Crossroads: Tannaitic Perspectives on the Jewish-Christian Schism" in *Jewish and Christian Self-Definition,* ed. E. P. Sanders et al., (3 vols. Philadelphia: Fortress, 1980-82) 2:115-56; idem, *Who Was a Jew? Rabbinic and Halakhic Perspectives on the Jewish-Christian Schism* (Hoboken, NJ: Ktav, 1985); H. J. Schoeps, *Jewish Christianity: Factional Disputes in the Early Church* (Philadelphia: Fortress, 1969); E. Schüssler Fiorenza, ed., *Aspects of Religious Propaganda in Judaism and Early Christianity* (University of Notre Dame Center for the Study of Judaism and Christianity in Antiquity 2; Notre Dame, IN: University of Notre Dame Press, 1976); A. F. Segal, *Two Powers in Heaven: Early Rabbinic Reports About Christianity and Gnosticism* (SJLA 25; Leiden: E. J. Brill, 1977); J. S. Siker, *Disinheriting the Jews: Abraham in Early Christian Controversy* (Louisville, KY: Westminster/John Knox, 1991); M. Simon, *Verus Israel: A Study of the Relations Between Christians and Jews in the Roman*

Empire (135–425) (Oxford: Oxford University Press, 1986); G. N. Stanton, *A Gospel for a New People: Studies in Matthew* (Edinburgh: T & T Clark, 1992); G. Strecker, *Das Judenchristen in den Pseudoclementinen* (Berlin: Akademie, 1958); R. Wilde, *The Treatment of the Jews in the Greek Christian Writers of the First Three Centuries* (Washington, DC: Catholic University of America Press, 1949); S. G. Wilson, ed., *Anti-Judaism in Early Christianity*, vol. 2, *Separation and Polemic* (Studies in Early Judaism and Christianity 2; Waterloo, ON: Wilfrid Laurier University Press, 1986).   C. A. Evans

CHRISTOLOGY

A great deal of scholarly effort has been devoted to analyzing the christological statements of early Christian texts as to how they reflect Jewish Christian or Hellenistic influences. The effort reflects an understanding of the formation of earliest christology as a historical process that was conditioned by the cultural, linguistic and religious environment of nascent Christianity. This standpoint can be accepted, whatever one's belief about the transcendent causes and significance behind the historical process.

The complexity of the issues and the diversity of the evidence make this investigation demanding. However, this work has also been hindered by such problems as a lack of agreement among scholars as to what the terms *Jewish Christian* and *Hellenistic* signify, overly simplified notions of the interaction between Jewish and non-Jewish culture in the Greco-Roman period and, sometimes, insufficiently examined assumptions and personal agendas of the scholars participating in the investigation. In this article the aims are to clarify the issues and categories involved in the modern discussion, survey relevant Christian texts as to their christological emphases and offer some basic conclusions about the christological developments and diversification evident in NT writings comprising Hebrews—Revelation and important extracanonical Christian writings down to approximately A.D. 150.

    1. Terminology
    2. New Testament Sources: Acts 1—11, Hebrews—Revelation
    3. Early Extracanonical Texts

1. Terminology.

In one sense the christological expressions of all NT documents and of many early extracanonical Christian writings are Jewish in that they reflect terms, concepts and values that are indebted to the OT and to Jewish tradition (*see* Judaism). But all earliest Christian literature is also Hellenistic, reflecting the impact of Hellenistic culture in the language (Koine Greek), rhetorical and literary conventions, and some of the conceptual categories and themes they exhibit. Also, the Jewish tradition, which served as the immediate matrix of earliest Christianity, had been in direct interaction with Hellenistic culture for more than three hundred years (since the time of Alexander the Great), variously reacting against and absorbing this or that feature of the larger cultural environment, both in the Diaspora* and in Palestine. Consequently distinguishing between Jewish and Hellenistic factors or elements in earliest christology, though not impossible, is more difficult than some have supposed.

It further complicates matters, however, that the labels *Jewish Christian* and *Hellenistic* have been used by scholars in varying ways. In some cases it appears that Jewish Christian christology is limited to beliefs that reflect what a given scholar imagines Christian Jews would have found congenial as belief, usually a low christology in which Jesus is seen as a human Messiah or teacher and is not given divine honor. But such an approach is apt to tell us more about the assumptions of the scholar than about the actual beliefs of ancient Christian Jews.

In other cases the label *Jewish Christian* is restricted to Christian Jews who rejected Gentile* Christians and their beliefs (e.g., the Ebionites*). But, given that the ancient sources indicate a variety of Christian Jewish groups and beliefs, restricting Jewish Christian to one type is misleading.

At the other extreme the term *Jewish Christian* has sometimes been used for all forms of early Christianity that used any language, symbols and categories drawn from the Jewish tradition. But this definition applies to a wide spectrum of early Christianity, and used this way "Jewish Christian" merely functions to emphasize the Jewish religious and intellectual roots of the early Christian movement.

In this article, therefore, we shall classify as Jewish Christian the christological beliefs and practices of Christian Jews who understood themselves and articulated their faith* and piety in terms and categories drawn from their Jewish religious tradition. Their faith, however, was usually not simply Judaism but was redefined in some major ways by the figure of Jesus and the consequences and implications of acknowledging him as uniquely authoritative divine agent. We shall also have to reckon with texts that may not have Jewish Christian authors but that show interest in and respect for Jewish Christian figures, beliefs and traditions, thereby giving us some further though perhaps indirect access to these beliefs and traditions.

It also has to be acknowledged that the question of what was Jewish and what was Hellenistic in early Christianity has often been dealt with in the service of agendas larger than historical inquiry. Alleging much Hellenistic syncretistic influence upon early Christian beliefs was often a useful way of downplaying the continuing validity of these beliefs for those engaged in an avowedly liberalizing and revisionist agenda for modern Christianity. Countering this agenda but accepting the notions of Hellenistic influences as indicative of corruption of early Christianity, conservative scholars often emphasized the Jewish roots of early Christianity and its beliefs, especially in the NT. In both camps, however, historical analysis has often been skewed under the influence of theological polemics.

Few can credibly claim to be disinterested in the question of the continuing validity of early christology. But it is important to try to prevent exegetical and historical judgments from being determined by theological agendas, whether of a revisionist or a traditionalist leaning. Also, it would be facile either to portray the development of christology as religious syncretism or to deny that early Christians interacted with and were shaped by the larger Greco-Roman religious and cultural environment. Moreover, the religious validity of a christological expression does not depend upon whether it appropriates Jewish or non-Jewish terms, concepts and cultural background. Consequently we shall attempt to characterize the christology of the texts considered so far as possible with a view to accurate historical knowledge of developments and diversification in early Christian beliefs.

2. New Testament Sources: Acts 1—11, Hebrews—Revelation.

2.1. Acts 1—11. The early chapters of Acts give us narratives describing the Jerusalem* church, which was composed of Jews. These narratives include speeches and prayers* as well as the author's summaries of the preaching* and activities of these Christian Jews. Although scholars debate the source(s) and historical reliability of specific events in the narratives, Acts* 1—11 contains a good deal of christological material that looks to be both early and of Jewish Christian derivation.

In these materials Jesus' death (*see* Death of Christ) is presented both as a misguided act of the Jewish leaders (Acts 3:14, 17; 4:10; 5:30; 7:52) and as a fulfillment of the divine redemptive plan (Acts 2:23-31; 3:18; 4:28; 10:39-43). There is no explanation of how Jesus' death is redemptive (no theory of atonement), only the firm proclamation that his death was essential and foreordained. There is a strong emphasis on Jesus' resurrection*: the key event to which the apostles* are to bear witness* (Acts 1:22; 2:32; 4:33; 5:32) and the act of God* by which Jesus is designated a unique position of salvific importance as "Lord and Christ" (Acts 2:36), "Leader and Savior" (Acts 5:31) and eschatological* judge through whom forgiveness* is given (Acts 10:42-43). This idea of Jesus being installed by God in a uniquely lofty position as a consequence of his resurrection (esp. Acts 2:36; 3:20) seems particularly reflective of early, Jewish Christian christological conceptions (cf. Rom 1:3-4, also often thought to reflect Jewish Christian tradition). Jesus is the exclusive medium of salvation* for all (Acts 4:10-12) and is now "Lord of all" (Acts 10:36). But by linking Jesus' exalted status to the act of God the traditional Jewish/biblical monotheistic concern seems reflected, so that Jesus' uniquely lofty role does not reduce God's status or importance.

The frequent references to Jesus as God's Messiah appear particularly in passages mentioning proclamation to Jews (*Christos,* Acts 2:36; 3:18-21; 5:42; 9:22; and in Acts 8:5 to Samaritans*). "Son of God" in Acts 9:20 seems to be intended as a synonymous (royal) messianic title. Other honorific terms applied to Jesus reflect the Jewish tradition: a prophet like Moses* (Acts 3:22), "the Righteous One" (Acts 7:52) and "servant" (*pais,* Acts 3:13, 26; 4:27, 30; *see* Servant). This last term (applied also to David, Acts 4:25) is used as a (royal?) christological title only here in the NT and outside the NT only in texts showing strong Jewish Christian influence and a traditional (liturgical) flavor (e.g., *1 Clem.* 59.2-4; *Did.* 9.3; 10.2-3; *Mart. Pol.* 14.1, 3). The emphasis upon the name* (of Jesus, Acts 4:10-12, 18; 5:28, 40-41; 8:12) may also reflect ancient Jewish culture with its high reverence for the name of God.

2.2. Hebrews. Several of the specific historical questions about the epistle to the Hebrews* remain without satisfactory answers: author, date, destination. Though we cannot be sure that the original recipients were Hebrews (i.e., Christian Jews), it is widely agreed that the document shows an elaborate effort to articulate Christ's significance in terms and categories drawn from Jewish tradition. In this sense Hebrews reflects Jewish Christian christological expression. In Hebrews 1, after appropriating Jewish wisdom* tradition to describe Christ's glorious relationship to God (Heb 1:1-4; cf. Wis 7:22—8:1), the author goes into a more lengthy statement of Christ's superiority to God's angels,* using a seven-link catena of OT quotations to make his points (Heb 1:5-14; *see* OT in Hebrews). This contrast continues in Hebrews 2, with additional OT passages used as evidence, here emphasizing Christ's superiority to angels as Redeemer on account of his participation in human nature. The rhetorical force of this contrast with angels depends upon a sympathetic familiarity with OT material and with ancient Jewish reverence for angels. Although "sons of God" is one of the ancient terms for angels (e.g., Job 1:6; 2:1; 38:7), the author here draws upon royal Davidic references to God's son to make a strong contrast between the status of angels as servants (esp. Heb 1:7, 14) and Christ's status as unique Son.*

Next the author asserts Christ's superiority to Moses (Heb 3:1—4:13), again emphasizing Jesus' sonship in comparison with Moses as faithful servant (esp. Heb 3:1-6). By reference to the rebellious generation of Israelites the author warns readers against disobedience to or abandonment of the Christian profession (Heb 3:7—4:13). As with the discussion of Christ and the angels, the force of this contrast of Christ with Moses depends upon an acquaintance with Jewish tradition, in this case the revered place it gives to Moses.

The author continues to argue for Christ's exalted significance by portraying his superiority as high priest* over the Aaronic priesthood of the OT (Heb 4:14—7:28). The divine

sonship of Christ resurfaces as an important christological category (Heb 5:5-10; 7:28); the superiority of Christ's high priesthood is connected with his being divine Son. In addition the author introduces the theme of Christ's priesthood "according to the order of Melchizedek" (Heb 5:6; *see* Melchizedek). The extended discussion of Christ's high priesthood by reference to this figure in Hebrews 7:1-28 is a unique christological emphasis of Hebrews (although there are brief references to Christ as heavenly intercessor in Rom 8:34; 1 Jn 2:1; *see* Heaven), and it too suggests an author and readers appreciative of Jewish traditions. Unlike the Aaronic priests, Christ is personally "a priest forever" (Heb 5:6; 7:15-17, 21), because he now "always lives" and is able "for all time to save those who approach God through him" (Heb 7:23-28, esp. Heb 7:25).

In the following chapters of Hebrews Christ is shown to be the mediator of a new covenant* better than that represented by the OT law* (Heb 8:1-13); Christ's death establishes this new covenant (Heb 9:15-22) by providing for it the superior and permanently effective sacrifice* (Heb 9:23—10:18). The author returns to this theme in Hebrews 12:18-29, where he contrasts phenomena of the revelation* at Sinai (Heb 12:18-21) with the blessings* of this new covenant (Heb 12:22-24), the climactic position of Jesus and his "sprinkled blood" indicating his importance.

In Hebrews 12:1-4 Jesus is referred to as the "pioneer and perfector of our faith" whose patient endurance* of his sufferings* can provide the encouraging precedent for Christians in their trials (Heb 12:5-13). The exemplary significance of Christ's sufferings is easily combined with reference to their redemptive effect in Hebrews 13:10-15.

Throughout the book the author is primarily concerned to emphasize two christological themes: Jesus' salvific death in imagery and language drawn from OT cultic traditions and Jesus' exalted status in imagery drawn from OT royal tradition. From the reference in Hebrews 1:3 to Christ having made "purification for sins" (priestly image) and having "sat down at the right hand" of God (royal image), through to the benediction in Hebrews 13:20-21 with its reference to Jesus as the resurrected "great shepherd" (a common royal image in the OT and the ancient Near East generally; *see* Shepherd) and his "blood of the eternal covenant" (cultic imagery), this author focuses on Christ's death, resurrection and exaltation.*

Also striking is the author's dual emphasis upon Christ as exalted divine Son and as full partaker in the human nature of those he redeems to God. This dialectic is particularly profound in Hebrews 1—2. After having affirmed Christ's vast superiority to the angels, the author then makes Christ's participation in human nature ("for a little while . . . lower than the angels," Heb 2:9) both evidence that humans are the object of God's redemptive purposes and precisely the strategic step that enables Christ to carry out that redemptive purpose effectively (Heb 2:14-18). In Hebrews 5:7-10 the author makes much of Jesus' humanity, Jesus being pictured as having "learned obedience through what he suffered."

The author of Hebrews produced one of the most developed treatments of Christ in the NT. He illustrates the early Christian appropriation and adaptation of Jewish categories in the effort to understand and communicate the significance of Christ.

2.3. James. The Epistle of James* is mainly concerned with exhortation about right behavior; its christology is implicit and largely a reflection of what the author and first readers held as traditional. Whatever one's view of the question of authorship, the attribution of the document to James the brother of Jesus (*see* Relatives of Jesus), the description of the addressees as "the twelve tribes in the Dispersion" (Jas 1:1) and other factors, including the strongly eschatological outlook (e.g., Jas 5:1-9), combine to give the document a Jewish Christian flavor. It is therefore interesting to note what the author and readers (who either were Jewish Christians or revered Jewish Christian traditions) must have regarded as traditional and uncontroversial christology.

Jesus bears the titles *Christ* and *Lord (kyrios)* in formulaic expressions (Jas 1:1; 2:1). Indeed in James 2:1 we have mention of "the glorious Lord Jesus Christ" *(tou kyriou hēmōn Iesou Christou tēs doxēs),* giving a particularly sonorous and honorific expression. In several other cases Jesus is probably intended in references to "the Lord." This holds for James 4:15, for example, where the will of "the Lord" is to govern Christian decisions. In James 5:7-11 it is also probable that Jesus is the "Lord" whose coming is awaited

(Jas 5:7-8) and the judge standing at the door (Jas 5:9), in whose name the OT prophets spoke (Jas 5:10) and whose mercy* and compassion are applauded (Jas 5:11). In all these cases it is noteworthy that Jesus is referred to in roles associated with God in the OT (*see* OT in General Epistles).

Jesus is likewise probably the "Lord" in whose name the sick are to be anointed* and who will raise the sick and forgive their sins* (Jas 5:13-15). There is probably a reference to Jesus' name in James 2:7 as "invoked [in baptism?] over you" and blasphemed by opponents. This emphasis upon the sacred significance of Jesus' name accords with references in Acts 1—11 and other evidence of Jewish Christian attitudes.

In addition many commentators have noted that this epistle is full of allusions to sayings of Jesus preserved in the Synoptic Gospels. This indicates both a familiarity with the Jesus tradition* and a practical acceptance of Jesus' authority* as Lord* of Christian behavior. We may say that James emphasizes the practical and ethical* consequences of the christological convictions shared by the author and intended readers.

2.4. 1 Peter. Scholars remain divided as to whether 1 Peter* stems from the apostle Peter or is a pseudonymous attempt to address the intended readers in his voice. Whatever one's view of this issue, 1 Peter is an important window on Christian beliefs and concerns from sometime in the latter part of the first century and is particularly rich in christological material. As is James, 1 Peter is addressed to readers described in Judaic terms, "the exiles of the Dispersion" (1 Pet 1:1), which along with other data suggests Christians who revere Jewish Christian traditions.

The high status of Christ is set within God the Father's supremacy. For example, Christians have been "chosen and destined by God the Father" for obedience* to Jesus Christ (1 Pet 1:2). "The God and Father of our Lord Jesus Christ" has given new birth* through Christ's resurrection (1 Pet 1:3), which is explicitly an act of God (1 Pet 1:21). Readers are to come to Christ because he is "precious in God's sight" and the one through whom acceptable "spiritual sacrifices" are now offered to God (1 Pet 2:4-5). It is God's will that Christians are to heed (1 Pet 2:15; 4:19). 1 Peter 1:20 places Christ's redemptive work within the context of God's precosmic plan ("destined before the foundation of the world"; cf. 1 Pet 1:11, where "sufferings destined for Christ" are predicted by OT prophets). The liturgical-sounding benediction and doxologies are all directed to God the Father (1 Pet 1:3; 5:11; even 1 Pet 4:11, though slightly ambiguous, is probably directed to God, who is glorified "through Jesus Christ"; *see* Liturgical Elements).

There can be no question, however, as to the author's high and richly textured view of Christ. One of the dominant emphases is the redemptive effect of Christ's death, expressed in sacrificial terms. Christians are "sprinkled with his blood" (1 Pet 1:2), alluding to the OT practice of sprinkling the blood of animal victims for dedication and ritual cleansing of people and cultic items (e.g., Exod 29:19-21; Lev 4:3-6, 13-17; 14:5-7). In 1 Peter 1:18-21 Christians are ransomed *(lytroō)* with the "precious blood of Christ, like that of a lamb without defect or blemish," likely alluding to the Passover lamb* of Exodus 12:5 (cf. 1 Cor 5:7 for another echo of Passover imagery for Christ's death). 1 Peter 2:21-25 lifts wording from Isaiah 53:4-12 to reveal the significance of Christ's sufferings, emphasizing both his exemplary behavior (1 Pet 2:21-23) and the vicarious nature of his death ("he himself bore our sins in his body") on the "tree" *(xylon,* 1 Pet 2:24, a probable allusion to Deut 27:6, which seems early to have become a key OT text used to interpret the significance of Christ's crucifixion). In 1 Peter 3:18 the author refers to Christ's undeserved sufferings as both exemplary for Christian behavior and vicariously redemptive ("the righteous for the unrighteous . . . to bring you to God").

The author's reference to "the Spirit of Christ within them" as the inspiring power of OT prophets (1 Pet 1:11) reflects a remarkably exalted view of Christ, perhaps implying some kind of preexistence* conviction and certainly associating Christ with the divine Spirit (*see* Holy Spirit). The exhortation in 1 Peter 3:14-15 alludes directly to Isaiah 8:12-13 (LXX), and the command to "sanctify Christ as Lord" thus applies and extends to Christ an imperative there concerned with reverence to Yahweh, another direct and striking association of Christ with God. 1 Peter 3:22 explicitly proclaims Christ's unique exaltation* above all heavenly ranks, using OT royal imagery in placing Christ "at the right hand of God" (cf. Ps 110:1). The references to Christ as shepherd and "chief shepherd" (1 Pet 2:25; 5:4) also probably draw upon OT royal imagery.

The exalted position of Christ in the author's beliefs is matched by the crucial place of Christ in practical living. As the chosen stone,* Christ becomes the basis of the redeemed community (1 Pet 2:4-10), to which a variety of OT images are applied (temple* and priesthood [1 Pet 2:5], chosen race and holy nation [1 Pet 2:9], God's people [1 Pet 2:10]). "For the Lord's sake" (i.e., out of reverence for Christ) Christians are to show respect for legitimate earthly authorities (1 Pet 2:13-17; *see* Civil Authority). Christians are to face unjust abuse looking to Christ's example and following "in his steps" (1 Pet 2:21; *see* Imitation). If they are persecuted* on account of their Christian faith, they are to take inspiration from Christ's sufferings and subsequent exaltation (1 Pet 3:13-22). They are to take joy in "sharing Christ's sufferings," in being "reviled for the name of Christ," suffering "as a Christian" and glorifying God "because you bear this name" (1 Pet 4:12-16).

2.5. 2 Peter and Jude. Scholars commonly see a direct literary relationship linking Jude* and 2 Peter,* 2 Peter probably being dependent upon Jude. The authorship of these texts is disputed. But whatever one's view of this question, both documents are attributed to figures associated with Jewish Christian groups, especially Jude, which is attributed to the "brother of James" (Jude 1:1), making him also a brother of Jesus. Both documents evidence an exalted view of Christ and share specific christological terms and convictions. But there are also variations.

In addition to more familiar formulaic expressions ("our Lord Jesus Christ" and variations: Jude 17, 21, 25; 2 Pet 1:8, 14, 16), in Jude 4 there is reference to those who "deny our only Master *[despotēs]* and Lord *[kyrios],* Jesus Christ." This formula is echoed in 2 Peter 2:1, which condemns heretics who "deny the Master *[despotēs]* who bought them." Both "Master" and "Lord" are applied to God in other NT writings (e.g., *despotēs* in prayer to God: Lk 2:29; Acts 4:24; Rev 6:10) and in Jude and 2 Peter are to be taken as titles connoting divine honor extended to Christ. In 2 Peter we repeatedly find the distinctive expression "our Lord *[kyrios]* and Savior *[sōtēr]* Jesus Christ" (2 Pet 1:11; 2:20; 3:2, 18). The only occurrence of "Savior" in Jude, however, is with reference to God ("the only God our Savior," Jude 25). In the NT as a whole *sōtēr* refers to God in eight of its twenty-four uses and is otherwise applied to Christ (e.g., Phil 3:20; Lk 2:11; Jn 4:42).

This tendency to attribute divine titles to Christ occasionally results in some ambiguous passages in which it is difficult to tell whether God or Christ is intended. In Jude 5-16 there are references to "the Lord" who saved Israel* from Egypt (Jude 5), Michael's invocation of "the Lord" against Satan* (Jude 9) and Enoch's prophecy of the coming of "the Lord" with thousands of angels (Jude 14-15). Given that the author otherwise consistently uses "Lord" as a title for Christ and that he appears to expect Christ to come bringing eschatological judgment* and mercy (Jude 17-21), it is probable that Jude 14-15 refers to Christ. But it is difficult to be sure who the "Lord" is in Jude 5 and Jude 9 (the textual variants, Jude 5 *[kyrios/Iēsous/christos/theos]* and Jude 9 *[kyrios/theos]*, indicate that ancient readers and scribes shared our difficulty). It seems likely that Christ is the "Lord" in this whole passage in Jude, indicating a rather far-reaching association of Christ with the God of the OT. In 2 Peter 3:8-10 it is also likely that Christ is the "Lord" whose promised coming is delayed but sure.

But 2 Peter 1:1 presents a particularly difficult case. The more likely Greek reading *(tou theou hēmōn kai sōteros Iēsou Christou)* could easily be taken as "our God and Savior Jesus Christ," although it is possible that the phrase refers to God and Christ (cf. 2 Pet 1:2, where the best reading is probably "knowledge of God and of Jesus our Lord"). The textual variation here, substituting *kyriou* ("Lord") for *theou* ("God"), shows ancient scribes saw the ambiguity as well.

In addition to the honorific terms and divine roles applied to Christ, there is also evidence of cultic devotion offered to Christ. The elaborate doxology in Jude 24-25 is directed to God "through Jesus Christ our Lord," and the phrase "before all time and now and forever" implicitly seems to extend to Christ the eternal qualities of God. The concluding doxology in 2 Peter 3:18 is directed to Christ, extending to him liturgical expressions connoting divine status and probably reflecting liturgical practices of the readers.

In both documents there is a strong eschatological tone to the christology. In Jude Christians are being "kept safe for/by Jesus Christ" (Jude 1), and Christians are told "keep [themselves] in the love of God" while they await the eschatological mercy of Christ that "leads to eternal life" (Jude 21). In 2 Peter 1:11 readers are offered the hope* of "entry into the eternal kingdom of our Lord and Savior Jesus Christ." Against the scoffing of some, 2 Peter 3:1-18 is devoted to asserting the reality of the eschatological coming of Christ and the present ethical consequences of this hope. In 2 Peter 1:16-19 the author refers to the transfiguration story (Mk 9:2-8) as indicating that Christ "received honor and glory from God the Father" and urges readers to take encouragement from this to live in the light* of Christ's "power and coming" until his eschatological appearance as "the morning star" (*see* Glory; Power).

2.6. Johannine Epistles. Although the Johannine epistles are thought to derive from the same early Christian group from which the Gospel of John came, it is widely recognized that there are differences in christological emphases (*see* John, Letters of). The Gospel of John asserts Jesus' divine significance over against Jewish refusal to recognize him as Christ and Son of God. In 1 John (the other Johannine epistles contain little christological material and nothing not found in 1 John), however, the author asserts his christology over against other Christians whose beliefs he regards as heretical. Because of this doctrinal conflict, 1 John is particularly rich in christological material. It is also commonly accepted that the Johannine community was originally a Jewish Christian group that suffered a severe rupture in relations with the larger Jewish community and at some point included Gentile converts. 1 John seems to reflect this later stage of the Johannine community but still shows the influence of the Jewish Christian heritage of the group.

The major christological emphasis is that the corporal, historical figure Jesus is "the Son" of God. It appears that the opponents in some way distinguished between Jesus and the divine Son, perhaps holding a docetic* (*dokēsis,* "appearance") christology in which the divine Christ only seemed to be a human. A few decades later Ignatius* of Antioch attacked the same or similar views (see 3.5 below). In 1 John 2:18-27 the opponents are referred to directly as schismatics (1 Jn 2:19) who have left the Johannine group and appear to have sought to win other

Johannine Christians over to their views, for which they claimed the authority of a superior enlightenment (1 Jn 2:26-27).

The opening statements of 1 John (1 Jn 1:1-4) emphasize the tangible, historical nature of the revelation witnessed to in the foundational ("from the beginning") gospel* message and explicitly link fellowship* with God and with "his Son Jesus Christ." The heretical alternative to "confessing the Son" (1 Jn 2:23b) is described as denying that Jesus is the Christ (1 Jn 2:22), denying "the Son" and thus "the Father" (1 Jn 2:23). The heresy is described more specifically perhaps in 1 John 4:1-3, where in contrast to the genuine divine Spirit who "confesses that Jesus Christ has come in the flesh," the ungodly spirit "does not confess Jesus is from God" (1 Jn 4:3; this is probably the best reading among the textual variants). The implication is that the heretics hesitate to identify the man Jesus with the divine Son.

Repeatedly the author emphasizes this confessional link: the historical manifestation of the Son is affirmed (1 Jn 3:5, 8); the required confession* is "Jesus is the Son of God" (1 Jn 4:15); the one born of God believes in Jesus as the Christ (1 Jn 5:1); in 1 John 3:23 God's command is to believe in the name of his Son Jesus Christ (probably alluding to the ritual use of Jesus' name in confession, healing* and baptism*), which makes precise the historical identification of the divine Son. Such a faith in the true, divine Son acknowledges thereby the Father also and brings eternal life (e.g., 1 Jn 5:11-12).

Unlike some later, Gentile Christian writers, this author does not try to define Jesus' sonship in metaphysical or philosophical terms; his main concern is to insist upon the direct identification of Jesus as divine Son. Nevertheless the reference to Jesus as "the eternal life that was with the Father and was revealed/manifested to us" (1 Jn 1:2) at least suggests some notion of an "incarnation" of the divine in Jesus, all the more likely given the familiar prologue to John (Jn 1:1-18), which stems from the same community. In light of this it is difficult to be sure whether the referent in 1 John 5:20, "This *[houtos]* is the true God and eternal life," is Jesus (the immediate antecedent) or God the Father. In light of the close link between the Son and the Father in this document, it may be that the author did not intend a mutually exclusive choice, for in his view one cannot be in right relation to God the Father without reverencing the Son.

The author also repeatedly affirms the soteriological significance of Christ. The efficaciousness of Jesus' death is described in sacrificial terms: the blood of Jesus "cleanses us from all sin" (1 Jn 1:7); Jesus is the "atoning sacrifice" *(hilasmos)* for our sins (1 Jn 2:2; 4:10). He is now "advocate" *(paraklētos)* for Christians "with the Father" (1 Jn 2:1). Jesus "was revealed to take away sins" (1 Jn 3:5) and "to destroy the works of the devil" (1 Jn 3:8). Christians hope to be made like Jesus when he appears again in future glory (1 Jn 3:2) and in the present time identify themselves with him as their model (1 Jn 4:17).

2.7. Revelation. The Jewish elements in Revelation (*see* Revelation, Book of) are so plentiful that some scholars have offered the unlikely suggestion that the book is a Christian revision of an originally Jewish apocalypse,* and some theologians (e.g., Luther, Bultmann) have erroneously regarded the book as deficient in the Christian beliefs reflected in it. Revelation presents a highly exalted view of Christ, perhaps unsurpassed in the NT. It is thus noteworthy that the author was in all likelihood a Christian Jew (e.g., John, apparently the author's actual name, is Jewish, only much later taken over as a Christian given name). Moreover, he seems to have had decidedly conservative attitudes (e.g., his condemnations of various Christian innovations, the Nicolaitans [Rev 2:6, 14-16] and the teachings of "Jezebel" [Rev 2:20-25]). Consequently his christological views and practices are unlikely to be innovative and probably reflect much earlier Jewish Christian circles. The prophet John sought to respond to what he saw as immediate pressing concerns, both internal problems and the looming pressure from the larger society. In his references to the emperor cult (worship of the "beast"; *see* Emperor) he was interacting with pagan religious phenomena and practices (*see* Religions), and these must be considered in understanding the book. But John responds to these influences negatively. Although he shows some acquaintance with pagan myth (e.g., the dragon and Leto analogy to Rev 12), his christology seems mainly expressed in terms from his biblical and Jewish tradition.

As with the Johannine Gospel and epistles, so in Revelation we see a dialectical combination of concern for the supremacy of the one

God together with a high christology. The most direct manifestation of this is with regard to worship,* which is a major theme of the book. The revelation claimed by the author is set on "the Lord's day" (the special weekly occasion of early Christian gathered worship; *see* Lord's Day). The vision* of heavenly worship in Revelation 4—5 seems intended to overshadow the remainder of the book, in which there are repeated calls and references to worship of God (e.g., Rev 7:11-12, 15; 11:16-17) and repeated warnings against worshiping any other (e.g., Rev 9:20-21; 13:4; 14:9-11). In Revelation 19:10 and Revelation 22:9 the angel interpreter sent from God twice forbids John to worship him, insisting that worship may be directed to God alone. The author clearly pictures the exalted Christ receiving worship with God (Rev 5:8-14; 7:10), which must indicate for this author the highest imaginable status for Christ. If later Christian thinkers speak of Christ and God sharing a common substance, John seems to offer something like a functional approximation in portraying idealized heavenly worship as directed jointly to God and Christ.

The scenes of ideal worship must have been intended both to reflect and inspire worship patterns among Christians, and in Revelation 22:20 we probably have a fragment of early liturgical practice in which the Lord Jesus is invoked in the gathered worship setting (cf. 1 Cor 16:22, "maranatha," which suggests that this practice derived from very early Aramaic-speaking circles of Jewish Christians).

This close association of Christ with God is reflected in other ways too. The eschatological kingdom* belongs jointly to "our Lord [or God] and his Christ" (Rev 11:15; 12:10). Christians hold both to the word of God and the testimony of Jesus (Rev 1:2, 9; cf. Rev 12:17). The august self-designation "Alpha and the Omega" appears in the mouth of God in Revelation 1:8, but in Revelation 22:12-13 it seems likely that we are to take the voice as Christ, designating himself with the same title. The opening greeting (Rev 1:4-5) comes jointly from God, the "seven spirits" and Jesus Christ, "the faithful witness [role model for the readers], the firstborn of the dead [assurance* of resurrection of believers] and the ruler of the kings of the earth [against the blasphemous claims of the Roman emperor]."

Although there is a subordination of Christ to God (e.g., Rev 1:1, where God gives Jesus the revelation to be shown to his servants), the opening vision, which functions like the OT call-visions, is a christophany (Rev 1:10-20) in which the glorious Christ is described with features taken from OT theophanies and angelophanies (e.g., Dan 7:9-10, 13-14; 10:5-6; Ezek 1:24-28). Moreover, in Revelation 2—3 it is Christ's assessment of the seven churches that is to be written to them, Christ's words voiced by the Spirit in prophecy through John (e.g., Rev 2:7, 11) and Christ who determines future reward* or judgment (e.g., Rev 2:7, 10, 17, 22-23, 26-28). Also, the divine plan of redemption and judgment cannot proceed until the Lamb has conquered and is then alone qualified to open the heavenly book and execute its contents (Rev 5:1-5). Yet at the same time this exalted Christ positions his role under the supremacy of God (e.g., Rev 2:28; 3:4, 12, 21).

The image of Christ as the Lamb reflects another christological belief important to this author—the redemptive significance of Jesus' death. The initial doxology (Rev 1:5-6; again probably reflecting the binitarian liturgical patterns of his readers) is directed to Christ, "who loves us and freed us from our sins by his blood," thereby constituting believers as "a kingdom, priests to his God and Father." In the initial, christophanic vision Christ's self-identification includes the crucial reference to his death (Rev 1:18), as a result of which he now has "the keys of Death and Hades" (*see* Hell). The Lamb's conquest is accomplished through being slaughtered (Rev 1:9-10), and through his "blood" he has "ransomed" (*agorazō*) saints of all nations. References to Jesus' "blood" (sacrificial imagery) appear also in Revelation 7:14 (the elect* have "washed their robes and made them white in the blood of the Lamb," a riveting image) and in Revelation 12:11 (believers conquer the great dragon "by the blood of the Lamb and by the word of their testimony," linking Jesus' death and the faithfulness of the saints; *see* Beasts). In the context of a highly symbolic passage the author drops this sacrificial imagery and makes direct reference to the crucifixion of the "Lord" in Revelation 11:8, making Jesus' death and its consequences the model for the witnesses* who are killed and rise again (Rev 11:11).

2.8. Summary. The NT documents considered all were written either by Christian Jews or by Christians with a good acquaintance with

Jewish Christian traditions who sought to express their faith in Christ in categories and terms adapted from the biblical and Jewish tradition. The dominant mode of christological reflection and expression in the first century seems to have been constituted out of Jewish tradition, mediated through Jewish Christian circles and adapted under the impact of Jesus' ministry and subsequent early Christian experience. The Jewish matrix, from which basic terms and categories were derived and adapted, was Jewish tradition of the Greco-Roman period, a robust religious tradition that for several centuries had confidently interacted with the larger cultural environment, appropriating whatever seemed useful and compatible with its fundamental convictions. Thus it should occasion no surprise to find terms or concepts that may have originated much earlier in Greek tradition. Such interaction is the sign of a healthy cultural and religious tradition, not an indication of something negative, certainly not a betrayal or uncritical assimilation of pagan influences.

There can be little question, however, that the christological affirmations and the pattern of binitarian religious devotion reflected in these NT documents exceed both in degree and kind the reverence characteristically shown toward divine agents in Jewish evidence relevant to the first century. In ancient Jewish sources amazingly honorific language can be applied to principal angels and also to revered human figures (esp. Moses or Enoch). Speculations about divine Wisdom or divine Logos* make for interesting comparison with and may have contributed to Christian attempts to define plurality in God, leading to the doctrine of the Trinity in the centuries after the NT. But the exalted status of Christ reflected in the documents surveyed seems to represent a distinctive development in comparison with the pre-Christian Jewish tradition. This is especially so when we take account of the accommodation of the glorified Christ alongside God in the worship setting and practices of first-century Christians.

In the older history-of-religions school (e.g., Bousset), the distinctively exalted status of Christ was often portrayed as the unconscious and deliberate assimilation of a supposedly original and low christology (nondivine Jesus) to pagan-influenced beliefs in demigods, divine sons and lords. More recent research (e.g., Hurtado) indicates that the mutation or innovation

represented in early Christian Christ-devotion had its decisive beginnings among Jewish Christian circles within the earliest years of the Christian movement. Moreover, the development in question was almost explosively rapid in the first few years, and elaborate theories of identifiable stages of christological development leading up to a divine status accorded to Christ are refuted by the evidence.

Not only in the texts surveyed but even in earliest NT writings (Paul's letters; *see DPL,* Christology) Christ is associated with God in astonishing ways, is accorded divine titles (esp. "Lord," informed by OT passages referring to Yahweh), functions in divine roles (e.g., as eschatological judge and as the divine source of prophetic oracles) and is formally reverenced in specific ways otherwise reserved for God. Such Christ-devotion is not readily compatible with the Judaism familiar to us and was apparently an exception in Jewish practice as reflected in ancient Jewish sources. At least in the second century it appears that there were Jewish Christian groups whose reverence of Christ was significantly more modest (the so-called Ebionites,* about whom, however, far too many overconfident claims have been made by scholars). But it is also clear that at least some Jewish Christian groups affirmed the sorts of exalted christological claims and binitarian devotional patterns surveyed.

The main features of Jewish Christian christology apparent to us in the NT and earliest Christian sources are the following. Jesus is proclaimed as the Messiah (Christ) promised by God in the OT, royal Davidic OT texts in particular interpreted as messianic predictions. One of the terms applied to Jesus in Greek-speaking circles of Jewish Christians is *pais* ("child" or "servant"), which appears to have carried royal Davidic connotations. It is likewise probably earliest Jewish Christian circles who felt required and empowered to interpret Jesus' death so as to see God acting through it in fulfilment of previously unrecognized prophecies of Messiah's sufferings. References to Jesus' death in terms taken from Jewish Passover and from OT sacrificial vocabulary (e.g., "blood," "lamb") probably began among Jewish Christian circles as well.

Jesus was also likely presented as the eschatological prophet like Moses, with consequent authority over the believing community to define obedience to God (reflected, e.g., in Matthew). Early Jewish Christian circles may therefore have begun early to organize and transmit in writing teachings or sayings of Jesus (as reflected in sayings collections thought to lie behind the Synoptics and James).

From Aramaic-speaking Jewish Christian circles of the earliest years of the Christian movement, the exalted Jesus was referred to as the "Lord" *(Marê)* of the community, a practice carried over into Greek-speaking circles in the common use of *Kyrios* for Jesus. Already by Paul's time this had generated a collection of Christian terms: Lord's day, Lord's Supper (1 Cor 11:20), Lord's brothers (1 Cor 9:5), which are used as terms familiar in Christian circles. Even more importantly the exalted Jesus was invoked in corporate worship as "Lord" and, in other ways as well, functioned with God as the object of devotion.

Particulary noteworthy is the ritual use of Jesus' name, for example, in the initiatory rite of baptism ("into the name of Jesus"), indicating the exalted Jesus as the one through whom exclusively the elect community is constituted. Especially in the context of the larger Jewish community, sharply conflicting judgments about Jesus appear to have been formulated and expressed: "Jesus is Lord" versus "Jesus is Anathema" (1 Cor 12:3, "cursed," a use of the term suggesting Jewish provenance).

It is also particularly to Jewish Christian circles that we can trace the concern to avoid making the exalted Jesus a second god in any way diminishing the supremacy of the Creator God of the OT. Thus, especially in texts showing Jewish Christian influence, we have Jesus' resurrection more characteristically portrayed as God raising Jesus, Jesus' exalted status as conferred or declared by God and Jesus' redemptive work as bringing the elect into relationship with God the Father. As we move farther from the influence of Jewish Christian christology, this concern to maintain a kind of functional subordination of Christ to God the Father is not always maintained, particularly in the apocryphal* Christian writings from Gentile Christian circles of the late second century and thereafter.

3. Early Extracanonical Texts.

The traditional Christian distinction between canonical and extracanonical Christian writings reflects ecclesiastical judgments about the proper relative theological and liturgical role of the writings. But in date, general circumstances and beliefs reflected there are varying degrees of overlap, especially with reference to extracanonical texts from the late first and early second centuries. Along with the NT these documents provide us invaluable historical resources for tracing the early diversification and development of belief in Christ. In particular these early texts show variously a continuing Jewish Christian tradition, the appropriation of it in wider Christian circles and the beginnings of a more deliberate attempt to express christological convictions in terms and categories drawn directly from the non-Jewish intellectual and religious environment.

Given the chronological limit for this article (approx. A.D. 150) and the varying dates proposed for some early Christian writings, it is difficult to decide what to include. Our purpose is to illustrate the sorts of christological developments of the early second century. We shall therefore concentrate on a few documents whose early dates are widely supported.

3.1. 1 Clement. Among the most securely dated extracanonical Christian texts is the lengthy letter sent A.D. 95-96 from the church at Rome* to the Corinthian church. *1 Clement* is rich in christological material but except for a few features repeats themes we have already encountered. The author (*see* Clement of Rome) does not seek to develop any new christological idea but instead urges obedience to what are for him traditional Christian beliefs and values. This aim is reflected in the frequent use of expressions derived from liturgical usage. Given that liturgy is characteristically the most conservative aspect of a religious tradition, the liturgical expressions in *1 Clement* probably reflect beliefs and practices in place for some considerable time. The christological rhetoric of *1 Clement* seems almost entirely formed of terms and categories from Jewish tradition (see Bumpus 1972) and probably thus has been taken over from Jewish Christian discourse of earlier decades of the Roman churches.

From the reference to the addressees and the opening grace-and-peace wish onward, *1 Clement* joins Christ with God as uniquely defining the Christian communities and as objects of religious devotion. The many doxologies show an interesting pattern, with some directly expressed to God (*1 Clem.* 38.4; 43.6; 45.7), some expressed through Christ (*1 Clem.* 58.2; 61.3; 64; 65.2) and two that are ambiguous as to whether God or Christ is the object of the praise (*1 Clem.* 20.12; 50.7; in my judgment God "the Father" is probably to be understood as the intended object). In this placing of God as supreme and Christ as unique agent, *1 Clement* follows the characteristic conceptual scheme and worship* dynamics reflected in the NT. Even the implicitly trinitarian expressions in *1 Clement* 46.6 and *1 Clement* 58.2 do not take us beyond equivalent expressions in earlier Christian texts in the NT (e.g., 2 Cor 13:13; Eph 4:4-6).

The dominant christological titles *Christ* and *Lord (kyrios)* are likewise traditional, the latter clearly a divine title used also for God (e.g., *1 Clem.* 59.3). *1 Clement* restricts *despotēs,* however, for God as "Lord" or "Master" (e.g., *1 Clem.* 7.5; 8.2; 9.4; 20.11-12). In *1 Clement* 16.2 there is an apparently unique christological metaphor, "the sceptre of the majesty of God, our Lord Jesus Christ" (possibly an allusion to Num 24:17; cf. CD 7:20), which both directly associates Christ with God and pictures his role as agent of the divine purpose. The lengthy liturgical prayer in *1 Clement* 59 applies the term "beloved servant" or "child" *(pais)* to Christ (*1 Clem.* 59.2-4), another indication of a traditional christological expression probably derived from Jewish Christian circles. The several references to Jesus as "High Priest" (*1 Clem.* 36.1; 61.3; 64) are analogous to (dependent on?) the christological use of the term in Hebrews, although in *1 Clement* the term is consistently combined with the term *guardian (prostatēs),* not otherwise used as a christological title in early Christian sources and possibly derived from non-Jewish religious or secular usage. Overall, however, *1 Clement* uses a more restricted number of christological titles than do the NT authors.

The traditional character of the christology is further demonstrated in the rather formulaic references to Jesus' salvific death. There are references to Jesus' blood as "poured out" (*1 Clem.* 7.4), "given for us" (*1 Clem.* 21.6; cf. *1 Clem.* 49.6), through which redemption has come (*1 Clem.* 12.7). In *1 Clement* 16.3-17 there is an extended appropriation of Isaiah 53:1-12, explicitly taking the suffering servant of the latter passage as Christ suffering for the sins of the redeemed. Characteristic of this author, however, is the emphasis placed on Christ's sufferings as ethical example for Christian life (*1 Clem*

16.17). Christ's resurrection is treated mainly as proof ("first fruit"; cf. 1 Cor 15:20) of the coming resurrection of the elect (*1 Clem.* 24.1).

1 Clement shows a traditionally minded handling of christological emphases already familiar in the NT. Though the Roman church at this time is probably mainly non-Jewish in composition, the beliefs and terms used seem largely derived from Jewish Christian circles and from biblical and Jewish extracanonical sources. There is little evidence here of any serious attempt to redefine christology using non-Jewish categories.

3.2. 2 Clement. Though the date and provenance of this anonymous homily are not agreed upon, a number of scholars accept a date of A.D. 100 or shortly thereafter. As the opening words indicate ("Brothers, we ought to think of Jesus Christ, as of God, as 'Judge of the living and the dead'"), this author too urges an exalted view of Christ and links him with God as extension and manifestation of God's purposes, not at all as rival or threat to God. Note the concluding doxology to the Father through "the Savior and Founder of immortality" sent by God (*2 Clem.* 20.5). In this document as well the christology is traditional and the emphasis is more on right behavior than doctrinal development.

Christ's redemptive work, including his sufferings, is celebrated in *2 Clement* 1—2 in lyrical terms as the divine overture to which Christian obedience is to be offered in gratitude. Christ's redemptive sufferings could never be repaid (*2 Clem.* 1.2-3), for "as a father he has called us sons" (*2 Clem.* 1.4, an unusual paternal image for Christ), he "saved us when we were perishing," banished the former pagan blindness of Gentile Christians (*2 Clem.* 1.4-7) and has created a people *ex nihilo* (*2 Clem.* 1.8).

Perhaps the dominant christological emphasis, however, is on the authoritative words of Jesus "the Lord," which are cited a number of times (e.g., *2 Clem.* 3.2; 4.2, 5.2-4; 6.1; 9.11; 12.2; 15.4; 17.4). Some of these sayings attributed to Jesus are not otherwise attested (at least in the form they have in *2 Clement)* and are thought to derive from now lost sources such as the *Gospel of the Egyptians* (e.g., *2 Clem.* 4.5). Nevertheless this emphasis on Christ's authoritative words echoes the sort of interest reflected in the sayings material gathered in the Gospels (*see* Jesus Traditions). In keeping with this, note how the author refers almost interchangeably to doing "the will of Christ/God/the Father" (cf. *2 Clem.* 6.7; 8.4; 14.1), and in *2 Clement* 8.4 he links directly doing the "will of the Father" and observing "the commandments of the Lord." The interest in Jesus' authoritative sayings probably stems from Jewish Christian circles but obviously carried over into Gentile Christian circles as well. The *Gospel of Thomas* (c. A.D. 150?), an early gnosticizing* appropriation and collection of Jesus' sayings, shows how widely shared this interest in dominical sayings became.

3.3. Didache. This probably composite document is variously dated, but many favor placing it in the early decades of the second century. At least some of the traditions must be considerably earlier. It exhibits christological reinterpretation and adaptation of Jewish material.

In the Two Ways portion (*Did.* 1.1—6.2) we have a profoundly christological recasting of ethical exhortation derived from Jewish tradition. The opening words (*Did.* 1.1) attribute the teaching to "the Lord," and the concluding words (*Did.* 6.2) describe the obligations as "the whole yoke of the Lord," bracketing the entire section as Jesus' instruction. The specific teachings in this section make use of sayings of Jesus as authoritative (e.g., *Did.* 1.3-6). Here Jesus' sayings and interpretation of divine commandments* are placed at the center of what it means to follow God's way.

In *Didache* 6.3—16.8 we have the earliest surviving manual of church order* and practice, rich in early Christian liturgical traditions. There is both a trinitarian baptismal formula in *Didache* 7.1-3 and later a reference to baptism* "into the name of the Lord" (*Did.* 9.5). Prayer is to be "as the Lord commanded in his Gospel," with a version of the Lord's Prayer prescribed (*Did.* 8.2; cf. Mt 6:9-13). The sacred meal is the Eucharist (*see* Lord's Supper), and we have set prayers associated with the cup and the bread (*Did.* 9.1-4) that are directed to the "Father" through Jesus, who is God's "servant" (*pais*). Through Jesus God "made known to us" life, knowledge* and "the holy vine of David your servant." In the prescribed prayer after Eucharist, God is thanked for the indwelling of his holy name and for knowledge, faith and immortality made known through Jesus "your servant" (*pais, Did.* 10.1-4). But in *Didache* 10.5 the prayer may well address Christ as "Lord" (*kyrios*), who is implored to "remember your church" and gather it "into your kingdom." Among the following liturgical exclamations is the "maranatha," attested also in 1 Corinthians 16:22 and probably deriving originally from earliest Jewish Christian practice, an invocation directed to Jesus.

In this material Jesus is clearly the one mediator of revelation from and the relationship to God. Jesus' sayings are treated with scriptural authority (e.g., *Did.* 9.5), and in *Didache* 14.3 Jesus may well be presented as the "Lord" speaking through OT passages (here Mal 1:11, 14). "The Lord's ways" are the behavioral standard for testing prophets (*Did.* 11.8). In the concluding apocalyptic section there is repeated emphasis on the eschatological coming of the "Lord," another christological theme preserved from earliest Christian traditions.

3.4. Odes of Solomon. Many scholars believe this collection of early Christian hymns* may stem from the early second or late first century. The imagery and themes suggest Jewish Christian provenance, and this makes the christological affirmations reflected all the more interesting.

The terms used include "the Beloved" (e.g., *Odes Sol.* 3.7; 7.1; 8.21), "Messiah" (e.g., *Odes Sol.* 9.3; 17.17), "the Son" (e.g., *Odes Sol.* 3.7; 7.15; 19.2), "Son of Man" and "Son of God" (*Odes Sol.* 36.3). There is also the intriguing *Odes of Solomon* 19.1-5, in which the Son is "the cup" from which believers drink the milk* from the breasts of "the Father," milked by the Holy Spirit. In *Odes of Solomon* 29.6 the author says, "I believed in the Lord's Messiah and considered that he is the Lord" (the same Syriac term in both cases). In *Odes of Solomon* 23.22 we have a trinitarian reference to Father, Son and Holy Spirit.

One feature of this collection is that in several odes it appears that Christ speaks in first-person form, celebrating his redemptive victory (e.g., *Odes Sol.* 17.6-16; 22.1-12) and giving us the unique image of the singing Christ. The theme of Christ's incarnation/humbling and exaltation found in Philippians 2:5-11 appears here also (e.g., *Odes Sol.* 7.3-6; 41.11-12), as does Christ's preexistence (e.g., *Odes Sol.* 41.15). Though the doxologies are usually directed to the Father (*Odes Sol.* 11.24; 16.20; 18.16; 20.10), we have one to Christ: "Glory to you, our Head, O Lord Messiah" (*Odes Sol.* 17.17). And in several odes there is reference to the Christian posture of outspread hands (in prayer and/or creedal confession) as the "sign" that represents

Christ's cross* (*Odes Sol.* 27.1-3; 42.1-2; cf. 35.7; 37.1), which suggests a specifically Christian liturgical practice well developed. In several features (e.g., the highly realized eschatology and some of the christological terms) *Odes of Solomon* resembles the Gospel of John.

3.5. Ignatius. To a large degree Ignatius* (letters written c. A.D. 107-15) reflects traditional christological affirmations (e.g., Christ's preexistence, redemptive sufferings, the Virgin Birth, Incarnation). But in the particular emphases he chooses and in some of his phrasing, Ignatius adds interesting features.

Against docetic ideas Ignatius emphasizes the reality of Christ's birth, sufferings and resurrection (e.g., Ign. *Magn.* 11.1; Ign. *Smyrn.* 2.1; 4.2; Ign. *Trall.* 10). In this he echoes an emphasis in 1 John but probably because the issue continues a live one in his own time. This docetic christology is the innovation, although in response to what he regards as an unacceptable christology Ignatius may have contributed to what became a developing orthodox view of Christ, giving an early form of two-natures christology. Ignatius seems to like confessional statements in which contrasting affirmations appear, such as Jesus' humanity and divinity (e.g., Ign. *Eph.* 7.2; Ign. *Pol.* 3.2). He also gives lists of salvation events connected to Jesus (birth, death, resurrection; Ign. *Eph.* 18.2; Ign. *Trall.* 9; Ign. *Smyrn.* 1.1-2).

Another remarkable feature is Ignatius's resolute alignment of his looming martyrdom* with Christ. He is "in chains for the sake of the Name" (Ign. *Eph.* 3.1). He and other martyrs "voluntarily choose to die into his [Christ's] suffering" (*eis to autou pathos;* Ign. *Magn.* 5.2). As "God's wheat" to be ground by the teeth of the Roman beasts in the arena, he sees his coming death as his chance to be "truly a disciple of Jesus Christ" (Ign. *Rom.* 4.1-2) and as the means by which "I may reach Jesus Christ" (Ign. *Rom.* 5.3) and become "an imitator of the sufferings of my God" (Ign. *Rom.* 6.3). In this Ignatius both develops a christology of martyrdom begun in Revelation and anticipates the flowering of this theme in Christian martyrdom literature of the second and third centuries.

But perhaps the most striking feature in Ignatius's christological expressions are the references to Jesus Christ as "God" (*theos*): "our God" (Ign. *Eph.* presc.; 18.2; Ign. *Rom.* presc.; 3.3; Ign. *Smyrn.* 1.1), "the blood of God" (Ign. *Eph.* 1.1) and "the sufferings of my God" (Ign. *Rom.* 6.3). These expressions appear in only three of his seven genuine letters (*Ephesians, Romans, Smyrneans),* the same letters in which he seems to be tackling docetic ideas, and so the expressions may well be rhetorically and pugnaciously framed to assert the divine identity and significance of the human Jesus. In *Ephesians* 19.3 Ignatius refers to the birth of Jesus as "when God appeared in human form."

Yet it is clear that the divinity of Jesus in no way reduces the primacy of God the Father. The openings of all seven letters mention both God and Christ in traditional terms, and even in the letters where the term *theos* is applied to Christ there are many references indicating a traditional subordination of Christ to the Father (e.g., Ign. *Eph.* 2.1; 4.2; 5.2; Ign. *Rom.* presc.; 2.2; 8.2, "Jesus Christ, the unerring mouth by whom the Father has spoken truly"). In the other letters there is a consistent pattern linking Christ with the Father's purposes (e.g., Ign. *Magn.* 7.1, "the Lord did nothing without the Father"; Ign. *Eph.* 8.2, "one God revealed in Jesus Christ his Son"; Ign. *Phld.* 9.1, Jesus "the door of the Father").

Though essentially traditional in his christology, Ignatius also shows an early and modest experimentation with christological expressions and emphases that were intended to speak to a mainly non-Jewish Christian audience. He was probably indebted to Hellenistic-Jewish traditions, but he also attempted to make his letters meaningful in analogies and categories drawn from the larger Greco-Roman culture.

3.6. Justin Martyr. In the writings of Justin (d. A.D. 162-66) we have the earliest major example of a serious effort to reflect upon Christian faith by someone with training in Greek philosophy. For the most part Justin articulates and defends traditional Christian christology, a good deal of which stems from Jewish Christian circles. Even in his *Apology I* to the emperor, his christology is expressed mainly in these traditional terms and categories, and he develops and defends his christology through use of OT proof-texts. There is an abundance of christological titles taken from the OT (e.g., Justin *Dial. Tryph.* 126.1: Son, Logos, Angel, Man, Stone,* Star, Firstborn, Day, Rising, Only begotten, Captain, to cite only a few). To serve his apologetic aims Justin probably gathers up the results of a long tradition of early christological exegesis and reflection.

But there are some new features as well. For example, Justin explicitly distinguishes the miraculous conception of Christ from pagan myths of demigods (e.g., Justin *Apol. I* 33), showing an attempt to set christological claims within the larger religious environment. Much more significant is his notion of the "spermatic Word" (*spermatikos logos*), the universal mode in which Christ has illumined and taught humankind throughout history, accounting for pre-Christian and non-Christian truths yet making them all truths from Christ (e.g., Justin *Apol. II* 13.3-4). This idea allows Justin to engage Greek philosophy both critically and appreciatively, yet he also insists upon the superiority and greater fullness of divine truth now revealed in Christ.

Justin also shows an early attempt to reflect philosophically on the divine unity and plurality involved in traditional Christian views of God and Christ. Christ is "numerically distinct" from the Father and was "begotten from the Father by his power and will" (Justin *Dial. Tryph.* 128.4; 129.4), yet the "essence" (*ousia*) of the Father is not thereby reduced. Another of Justin's ways of distinguishing Father and Son is that although the Son can be called "God" he is "begotten," whereas the Father is the "unbegotten" God (*agennētos;* e.g., Justin *Dial. Tryph.* 114.3; 126.2). This begetting of the Son/Logos is before all creation* and is unique (e.g., Justin *Dial. Tryph.* 105.1), but it is not clear that this is the same as the later idea of the Son's eternal sonship. Justin also distinguishes between the "person" (*prosōpon*) of the Father and Son as he sees them referred to in the OT (e.g., Justin *Apol. I* 36-38).

Justin takes all the theophanies in the OT as manifestations of the Son/Logos (e.g., Justin *Dial. Tryph.* 59; 126), even arguing that "Jesus" was the divine name revealed to Moses (Justin *Dial. Tryph.* 75; cf. Exod 23:20). A number of times Justin insists upon the propriety of worshiping Christ as well as the Father (e.g., Justin *Dial. Tryph.* 63.5; 68.3; Justin *Apol. I* 6.1-2; 13.3), and in one exegesis he manages to make Isaiah 42:8 a proof-text that Christ shares the glory of the Father (Justin *Dial. Tryph.* 65).

These all amount to a creative attempt to reflect upon and justify Christian convictions about monotheism and the divinity of Christ. Only in Paul and the Johannine writings do we

have comparable theological effort. Justin is distinctive, however, in giving us the first extended example of theological effort informed by and consciously intended to engage Greek philosophy.

3.7. Summary. The early extracanonical Christian texts show the continued life and development of christological traditions attested earlier in the NT. If one were to consider also such documents as *Gospel of Peter** and *Gospel of Thomas,** both of which may incorporate Christian traditions of the early second century, the range of christological expression and piety would be extended even further. Clearly Jewish Christian circles are reflected in *Didache* and *Odes of Solomon.* In *1 Clement* and *2 Clement* we see largely traditional christological affirmations, showing a strong conceptual indebtedness to Jewish Christian tradition, taken up in Gentile Christian groups and put to the service of ethical exhortation. In Ignatius and even more in Justin we have Gentile Christians ready to engage heresy (Ignatius) and non-Christian religious and philosophical options (Justin) with an obvious indebtedness and a firm commitment to earlier Christian tradition yet also exhibiting a somewhat creative development of this tradition. Both these figures, especially Justin, are early examples of one type of reindiginization of Christian beliefs in terms and categories adapted from non-Jewish traditions (e.g., Ignatius's use of the image of a pagan religious procession in Ign. *Eph.* 9.2), a process that continues in later christological and trinitarian debates. Christian gnostic texts show other, perhaps more radical, experiments in Christian thought and practice that proved too incautiously innovative for the developing orthodox (more traditional) Christians.

See also Christ; Docetism; Lamb; Logos Christology; Lord; Preexistence; Shepherd, Flock; Son of God; Stone, Cornerstone; Wisdom; Worship and Liturgy.

Bibliography. L. W. Barnard, *Justin Martyr: His Life and Thought* (Cambridge: Cambridge University Press, 1967); R. J. Bauckham, "The Worship of Jesus," in *The Climax of Prophecy* (Edinburgh: T & T Clark, 1993); idem, *The Theology of the Book of Revelation* (Cambridge: Cambridge University Press, 1993); W. Bousset, *Kyrios Christos,* (Nashville: Abingdon, 1970 [1921]); W. F. Bunge, "The Christology of Ignatius of Antioch" (unpublished Ph.D. dissertation, Harvard University, 1966); H. B. Bumpus, *The Christological Awareness of Clement of Rome and Its Sources* (Cambridge, MA: University Press of Cambridge, 1972); O. Cullmann, *The Christology of the New Testament* (rev. ed.; London: SCM, 1963); J. Daniélou, *Gospel Message and Hellenistic Culture* (London: Darton, Longman & Todd; Philadelphia: Westminster, 1973); idem, *The Theology of Jewish Christianity* (London: Darton, Longman & Todd, 1964); J. A. Draper, "A Commentary on the Didache in the Light of the Dead Sea Scrolls and Related Documents" (unpublished Ph.D. dissertation, Cambridge University, 1983); R. M. Grant, *The Christ of the Second Century* (Louisville, KY: Westminster/John Knox, 1990); L. W. Hurtado, *One God, One Lord: Early Christian Devotion and Ancient Jewish Monotheism* (Philadelphia: Fortress, 1988); B. Lindars, *The Theology of the Letter to the Hebrews* (Cambridge: Cambridge University Press, 1991); V. A. Spence Little, *The Christology of the Apologists* (London: Duckworth, 1934); R. N. Longenecker, *The Christology of Early Jewish Christianity* (SBT 2d series 17; London: SCM, 1970); E. Osborn, *The Emergence of Christian Theology* (Cambridge: Cambridge University Press, 1993); G. N. Stanton, "Aspects of Early Christian-Jewish Polemic and Apologetics," *NTS* 31 (1985) 377-92; D. C. Trakatellis, "God Language in Ignatius of Antioch" in *The Future of Early Christianity: Essays in Honor of Helmut Koester,* ed. B. A. Pearson (Minneapolis: Fortress, 1991), 422-30; idem, *The Preexistence of Christ in Justin Martyr* (HDR 6; Missoula, MT: Scholars Press, 1976). L. W. Hurtado

CHRONOLOGY

Chronology here concerns the datings and sequence of significant events and personalities—aside from Jesus (*see DJG,* Chronology) and Paul (*see DPL,* Chronology of Paul)—mentioned in the canonical books of the NT and the apostolic fathers (*see* Apostolic Fathers), as well as the attendant literature. The chronology for this period—approximately A.D. 60 to 150—is a matter of synchronizing three principal time lines: (1) the reliable chronology of Roman imperial history, (2) its interaction with Jewish history and (3) NT history, as integrated into these time grids.

1. The Roman Historical Framework
2. Jewish History
3. New Testament Personalities
4. New Testament Literature
5. The Apostolic Fathers
6. Early Apologists
7. Early Heretics

1. The Roman Historical Framework.
Throughout this period the Roman Empire (*see* Roman Empire) had final authority in Palestine and all the other biblical lands. The regnal years of the various emperors* are undisputed, and in most cases specific dates of accession and death are known. The relation of each to Judaism and Christianity (if any) is sketched in what follows, with corresponding detail later in this article.

1.1. Nero (54-68). His empress, Poppaea, was interested in Judaism. After the Great Fire of Rome in July 64, Nero blunted suspicion that he himself had set the fire by blaming the Christians, resulting in the first Roman persecution* (Tacitus *Ann.* 15.44), which seems to have been local in character rather than empirewide. Probably in some association with this, both Peter and Paul were martyred. Nero dispatched Vespasian to put down the Jewish rebellion, which had erupted about May 66.

1.2. Galba (68-69), Otho (69) and Vitellius (69). These transition emperors ruled only months, not years, during the later phases of the Jewish War.

1.3. Vespasian (69-79). The founder of the Flavian dynasty was summoned to the imperial purple while fighting the Jewish War. Neither he nor Titus resumed a persecution of the Christians.

1.4. Titus (79-81). Vespasian had left his son Titus to pursue the Jewish War in Palestine, which he concluded with the destruction of Jerusalem* in 70. Titus had a love affair with the Jewish princess Bernice, sister of Agrippa II (Acts 25:13, 23), whom he subsequently abandoned for political reasons.

1.5. Domitian (81-96). After Titus's brief reign, his brother Domitian may have instigated a Christian persecution that affected the Roman nobility, with his relatives Clemens and Domitilla as victims as well as Acilius Glabrio. *1 Clement* (c. 95) may well reflect this persecution of Roman Christians.

1.6. Nerva (96-98). The elderly jurist who succeeded the assassinated Domitian abolished defamations resulting from Jewish proselytism and the *fiscus Iudaicus*. He did not resume a persecution against Christians and was the first of the so-called Five Good Emperors, the next four of which follow.

1.7. Trajan (98-117). His conquests in Dacia and Mesopotamia expanded the boundaries of the Roman Empire to their greatest extent. A so-called Second Jewish War broke out in Egypt, Cyrene and Mesopotamia (115-17), which Trajan subdued. His moderate policy vis-à-vis Christians surfaces in his celebrated correspondence with Pliny the Younger, governor of Bithynia c. 112, in which he advises him not to seek out the Christians even if the law had to take its course in the case of those properly indicted (*Ep.* 10.97). Still, Ignatius,* bishop of Antioch, was arrested in Antioch and martyred in Rome under Trajan's administration c. 114, probably during Hadrian's governorship in Antioch (Ign. *Eph.* 1.2).

1.8. Hadrian (117-38). The Third Jewish War, or the Bar-Kokhba revolt (132-35), erupted under Hadrian's administration and ended with the exclusion of Jews from Jerusalem, which was rebuilt as a Gentile* Roman *colonia* named Aelia Capitolina (Eusebius *Hist. Eccl.* 4.6). Hadrian's rescript to Fundanus, governor of Asia c. 125, continued Trajan's moderate policy regarding the Christians: they were illegal, but not to be sought out via illegal methods. Quadratus (see 6.1 below) addressed the earliest Christian apology to Hadrian.

1.9. Antoninus Pius (138-61). During his administration, but not at his instigation, the aged Polycarp, bishop of Smyrna, was martyred in the stadium at Smyrna, although some scholars still share the traditional view of Eusebius that this occurred later in the reign of Marcus Aurelius. Aristides (see 6.2 below) addressed his *Apology* to Antoninus Pius.

1.10. Marcus Aurelius (161-80, with Lucius Verus 161-69). The great apologist Justin (see 6.3 below) was martyred at Rome c. 165 under his administration. A terrible local persecution of Christians broke out at Vienne and Lugdunum (Lyons) in Gaul in 177, as well as at Scillium in Africa c. 180.

For a general integration of Roman, Jewish and early Christian chronology, see the chart at the end of this article.

2. Jewish History.

This period was marked by three major Jewish rebellions against Roman control, far more serious than the periodic imbroglios that had cluttered previous decades. Several famous Jewish figures also lived at this time.

2.1. Events in Jewish History. The great Jewish War was touched off by a riot between Greeks and Jews at Caesarea in the spring of 66. Due to the criminal folly of the Roman procurator Gessius Florus, Zealot elements in the Jerusalem populace were able to escalate hostilities into a major rebellion against Rome. To meet this challenge, Nero dispatched Flavius Vespasian with three Roman legions, and he conquered Galilee and Samaria by 69, leaving his son Titus to conquer Jerusalem and end the war. After an excruciating siege, the temple* was torched on August 30, A.D. 70, and Jerusalem itself was destroyed by September 26. When Herod's great fortress at Masada fell three years later on May 2, the last Jewish resistance was crushed. Considerable precision in dates and details are provided by an eyewitness and participant in the struggle, Flavius Josephus (see 2.2.4 below). After Jerusalem's destruction, Jamnia became the home of the Great Sanhedrin. Around 100, a council of rabbis there established the final canon* of the OT.

The Second Jewish War (115-17) broke out in Cyrene and Egypt, where Zealot unrest had already erupted in 72, following the great Jewish War. This spread to Mesopotamia, where there was hope of Parthian support in opposition to Trajan. But Hadrian, the commander in Syria, subdued the rebellion with great loss of Jewish life (Eusebius *Hist. Eccl.* 4.2; Dio Cassius *Hist.* 68.32).

In the Third Jewish War (132-35), Zealot rebellion in Palestine was provoked by Hadrian's plan to rebuild the desolate site of Jerusalem as a Gentile Roman colony to be called Aelia Capitolina. Having been proclaimed Messiah by Rabbi Akiba, Simeon bar Kosiba led the revolt under the name Bar Kokhba ("son of the star"). After savage guerrilla warfare, Palestine was ruined and Jews were excluded from Jerusalem, which became a Gentile city for the next two centuries (Eusebius *Hist. Eccl.* 4.6; Spartianus *Hadrian* 14).

2.2. Personalities in Jewish History. Major Jewish figures in this era include Philo of Alexandria (*see* Alexandria), Gamaliel the Elder, Johanan Ben-Zakkai and Flavius Josephus.

2.2.1. Philo of Alexandria. Also called Philo

185

Judaeus, he lived just prior to the period covered by this volume, but he strongly influenced both Jews and Christians (particularly Origen) during the first three centuries A.D. through his blending of Greek philosophy and Hebrew Scriptures, which he often interpreted allegorically. The one sure date in his life is A.D. 40, when he led a delegation of Jews to Rome in order to defend his people before the emperor Gaius Caligula after anti-Jewish rioting in Alexandria (*Leg. Gai.* 299-305). Approximate dates of his life are usually set at 20 B.C. to A.D. 50.

2.2.2. Gamaliel I ("the Elder"). This Sanhedral Pharisee, who advised moderation in the case of the apostles* (Acts 5:34-39) and whom Paul boasts as his teacher (Acts 22:3), was a grandson of the great Hillel. Continuing in the liberalizing tradition of his grandfather, he was an authority on Jewish law* and the first to be honored with the title Rabban ("our Master") rather than the ordinary Rabbi ("my master"). His dates are unknown, but his prime might be assumed at c. A.D. 55.

2.2.3. Johanan Ben-Zakkai. This most important expounder of Jewish law in the A.D. 60s is supposed to have spent forty years in business, forty in study and forty in teaching (*Sanh.* 41a), a 120-year life span that too closely mirrors that of Moses* for full credibility. In 68, during the first Jewish War with Rome, he outwitted the extremists and made his way to Vespasian's camp, where he successfully asked the Roman general to spare Jamnia and its sages. There he founded the famous Jewish academy, served as its first president and worked for the continuation of Judaism before his death in the 80s.

2.2.4. Flavius Josephus. This Jewish historian was born in Jerusalem in 37, only four years after Jesus' crucifixion. In 66 he was commander of the Jewish forces in Galilee before his capture by Vespasian. Subsequently he served as interpreter in negotiations between the Roman and Jewish forces, and finally he emigrated to Rome, where he was patronized by the Flavians. There he published his *Jewish War* in 77-78 and his *Jewish Antiquities* in 93-94. The latter provides extraordinary detail about the intertestamental and especially NT era. Josephus* is our most copious source for extrabiblical information in the first century A.D.

3. New Testament Personalities.

Christian figures in the later NT era may be placed with varying degrees of precision. The subsequent career and fate of many are unknown, and if no chronological benchmarks have survived to provide relevant data, their names are not included in this listing.

3.1. Simon Peter. The date of his birth is unknown. His prominent role in the book of Acts fades with his imprisonment by Herod Agrippa I and subsequent deliverance, after which "he departed and went to another place" (Acts 12:17), which is never specified in the NT. Since his arrest and deliverance occurred near the Passover and Agrippa died shortly thereafter in A.D. 44, Peter's deliverance and departure must have occurred in the spring of 44. Five years later he resurfaces at the apostolic council in Jerusalem defending Paul's ministry (Acts 15), after which he is in Antioch, reprimanded by Paul for withdrawing from table fellowship with Christian Gentiles (Gal 2:11-14).

Whether Peter subsequently visited Rome has been debated for centuries. The evidence that he did not rests on an argument from silence: the absence of any mention in Acts, the Pauline corpus or the writings of Justin Martyr, who lived in Rome. The evidence supporting his presence there is larger. If, as seems probable, *Babylon* was a cryptic name for Rome, then 1 Peter was addressed from Rome (1 Pet 5:13), though there is some debate over the authorship of this epistle. The *Letter to the Corinthians* by Clement* of Rome (A.D. 95) links the martyrdoms of Peter and Paul with those of the Roman Christians who endured the Neronian persecution (*1 Clem.* 5.6). A short time later (c. 107) Ignatius of Antioch's *Letter to the Romans* contains the revealing phrase "Not like Peter and Paul do I give you [Roman Christians] commands" (Ign. *Rom.* 4.3).

In the second century there are numerous references in Christian writings to the martyrdoms* of Peter and Paul in Rome, particularly the testimony of the presbyter Gaius, whom Eusebius quotes as stating, "I can point out the monuments [or trophies] of the apostles: for if you will go to the Vatican Hill or the Ostian Way, you will find the monuments of those who founded this church* [Peter and Paul]" (Eusebius *Hist. Eccl.* 2.25). The monuments marked the traditional sites of their martyrdoms and probably their places of burial as well, since Gaius was countering the claim that there were apostolic tombs in Asia. Constantine would later erect the basilicas of St. Peter and St. Paul, respectively, at these locations. The evidence, then, inclines heavily toward Peter's presence in Rome, though it does not support the tradition that he conducted a lengthy, twenty-five-year ministry there.

Nero's persecution of the Christians—to which Peter has always been linked—followed the Great Fire of Rome in 64, as noted earlier. How much later is not known, but the fall of 64, or the winter or early spring of 65 most likely marks the first Roman persecution of Christians and the martyrdom of Peter.

3.2. James the Just. Despite those who claim that Mary* the mother of Jesus was "ever virgin," the most natural interpretation of all texts concerned is that the man whom Paul and the early church called "the Lord's brother" (Gal 1:19) was indeed Jesus' half-brother, the son of Joseph and Mary born next after Jesus, since he is always mentioned first among Jesus' four brothers (Mt 13:55; Mk 6:3; *see* Relatives of Jesus). Skeptical of Jesus before the resurrection* but a believer after, James presided in A.D. 49 at the apostolic council of Jerusalem (Acts 15), which approved the mission* and theology of Paul and Barnabas. Apparently James was still in a leadership role at the time of Paul's arrest in Jerusalem c. 57 (Acts 21:18) and working on behalf of the Jewish Christians there. (For his authorship of the epistle of James, see 4.1.8 below.) At this point all evidence on James fades from the NT except for Jude's identifying himself as "brother of James" (Jude 1).

Interestingly enough, information about the death of James comes not from biblical sources but from Josephus, who reports that James "the brother of Jesus who was called the Christ*" was stoned to death by sentence of the high priest* Ananus and the Sanhedrin in the absence of the Roman governor Albinus, who had not yet arrived in Palestine (Josephus *Ant.* 20.9.1 §200). This occurred in 62—information of great importance not only because it is Josephus's second reference to Jesus of Nazareth but also because it is evidence that closely parallels the events of Good Friday (*contra* revisionists who discount Jewish involvement in Jesus' trial before Pilate). A further version of James's death appears in Hegesippus (as cited by Eusebius *Hist. Eccl.* 2.23), who also states that James was stoned to death.

3.3. Jude. Brother of the above, and called Judas in the Gospels, Jude was the probable author of the NT epistle bearing his name (see 4.1.13 below). His placement last among the four brothers of Jesus (Mt 13:55) may imply that he was the youngest, although Mark places him second to last (Mk 6:3). His letter, the penultimate book in the NT, suggests that he outlived his brother James. According to Hegesippus, Jude's grandsons were brought before Domitian as belonging to the royal line of David, but their hands, rough from agricultural labor, convinced him that they were not a threat. Subsequently they became leaders in the church, according to Eusebius (*Hist. Eccl.* 3.20).

3.4. John. As with all the apostles, John's birth date is unknown. Although the NT is silent on his later life, earliest traditions are quite vocal in associating him with Ephesus in Asia Minor. Eusebius states that John was exiled to the island of Patmos during the reign of Domitian, then returned to Ephesus after the emperor's death (A.D. 96) and remained there for the rest of his life, dying a natural death at an advanced age in the time of Trajan—that is, post-A.D. 98 (Eusebius *Hist. Eccl.* 3.1, 18, 20, 23, 31). Irenaeus documents John's Ephesian residence through Polycarp, whom he claims to have heard as a boy (Irenaeus *Haer.* 2.33; 3.3; 5.33; Eusebius *Hist. Eccl.* 5.20). Several less-attested traditions report an early martyrdom for John, but this may be due to confusion with John the Baptist. Estimating John's death c. A.D. 100 would not fall wide of the mark. For writings ascribed to John and their datings, see below.

4. New Testament Literature.
Aside from the Pauline corpus (see *DPL*, Chronology of Paul), the dating of the Gospels and General Epistles usually hinges on the destruction of Jerusalem in A.D. 70. Some critics argue that Jesus' prediction of this event is a *vaticinium ex eventu* (a "prophecy after the fact") on the part of the Gospel writers, hence these documents must have been written *after* 70. Traditionalist scholars generally insist, to the contrary, that the Synoptics must have been written *before* that event, which is the plain reading of the texts, especially since Matthew—with his penchant for prophecy-fulfillment couplets—could hardly have resisted reporting the fulfillment of Jesus' prophecy regarding Jerusalem's destruction had it already occurred.

4.1. The Synoptic Gospels. Early church traditions place the authorship of Matthew, Mark and Luke within an A.D. 60-70 time frame. Modern critics, on the other hand, claim that they reflect elements of postbellum Judaism *after* the 70s.

4.1.1. Matthew. According to Irenaeus (*Haer.* 3.1, and cited by Eusebius *Hist. Eccl.* 5.8), Matthew was composed "while Peter and Paul were preaching the gospel in Rome and founding the church there," hence c. 60-67. Origen accepted it as the first written Gospel, followed, in order, by Mark, Luke and John (Origen *Comm. Mt.,* as cited by Eusebius *Hist. Eccl.* 6.24). Modern critics point to Matthew 26:52—Jesus' reprimand to Peter at Gethsemane—as the author's refusal of a supposedly revived Zealotism *after* the Jewish War, but this could just as easily apply to that *before* the conflict. Jesus' famous statement to Peter (Mt 16:19) using the term *church (ekklēsia)* is similarly presumed to reflect a more established ecclesiology and thus a later date. The term *ekklēsia,* however, appears already in the Pauline corpus that preceded the Gospels, as well as in Acts.

Dating Matthew depends on a resolution of the Synoptic problem: how to interpret the fact, for example, that 91 percent of Mark is contained in Matthew. If the Griesbach hypothesis is true (Matthew wrote first, and his Gospel was condensed by Mark), then Matthew and its Jewish focus may well reflect an early period of the church, even the A.D. 50s. But if the more commonly held priority of Mark is assumed, and its authorship is assigned to the 50s or 60s, Matthew would date to the later 50s or 60s. Other scholarship, however, has generally inclined toward a date after the 70s. In the absence of new evidence, no firm date is possible beyond such ranges.

4.1.2. Mark. Irenaeus (*Haer.* 3.1) claims that after the death of Peter and Paul, Mark, as Peter's disciple and interpreter, wrote his Gospel. Clement of Alexandria, however, states that Mark wrote it during Peter's lifetime (as cited by Eusebius *Hist. Eccl.* 6.14), as does Eusebius himself (*Hist. Eccl.* 2.15), hence sometime pre-A.D. 65. Again the Synoptic problem intrudes (see 4.1.1 above). If Markan priority (the majority opinion) is assumed and Clement is correct, the Gospel could have been composed any time in the 50s or early 60s. But if Mark condensed the other Synoptics, then a date in the later 60s—but before the destruction of Jerusalem in

70—would apply. Again, however, most modern scholars generally opt for a dating after Jerusalem's fall.

4.1.3. Luke-Acts. Eusebius (*Hist. Eccl.* 2.22) assumes that Luke's second treatise, Acts, was written prior to Paul's trial at Rome, since it is not reported in Acts, which concludes with the statement at 28:30 that Paul lived in Rome "two whole years at his own expense" before any hearing or trial. If Acts were written at the close of this two-year period, the composition would date to c. 61-62. Luke's Gospel, accordingly, would necessarily have preceded it. This view, propounded by Jerome (*Vir.* 7) and A. von Harnack (*Neue Untersuchungen zur Apostelgeschichte* [1911]), is often supported by traditionalist scholars, whereas others date Luke, Acts and the other Synoptics later into the 70s and 80s, as indicated.

4.1.4. John. According to all traditions of the earliest church, the Fourth Gospel was written last, the apostle John knowing that the other three had provided external details and therefore writing a spiritual Gospel, according to Clement of Alexandria (cited by Eusebius *Hist. Eccl.* 6.14). Similarly, Eusebius writes that John knew the other three Gospels and provided necessary addenda (Eusebius *Hist. Eccl.* 3.24). According to the traditional view, the more developed theology in John also argues for a later origination. Irenaeus (*Haer.* 3:1) writes that John wrote his Gospel "while residing at Ephesus in Asia." If true, this would likely have been before his reported exile to Patmos in connection with Domitian's persecution c. 95. Accordingly, a date between A.D. 85 and the 90s is often posited by scholars of various stripes.

Recently, however, some writers have urged an earlier dating for John. Paul's letter to the Romans, written much earlier, shows high theological development, and the contrast couplets in John (light vs. darkness, love vs. hate, etc.) that were presumed to reflect later Hellenistic influence occur already in the Dead Sea Scrolls. Furthermore, John 5:2 states, "Now there *is* in Jerusalem near the Sheep Gate a pool . . . called Bethesda," a present tense of the verb that would have been less likely after the destruction of Jerusalem in 70. Moreover, geographical specifics in the Fourth Gospel, early locutions and other considerations lead some scholars to place it before 70 like the Synoptics, or even preceding them (see Robinson).

4.1.5. Acts. (See 4.1.3 above). No event or personality cited in Acts is datable to a time post-A.D. 61/62 (*see* Acts).

4.1.6. The Pauline Corpus. (See *DPL*, Chronology of Paul.)

As above, the following NT writings are listed in canonical—not necessarily chronological—order.

4.1.7. Hebrews. Many scholars suggest a date in the A.D. 80s. Hebrews 10:32-34 seems to refer to a persecution (assumed to be Nero's in 64-65) that took place in "the former days." Hebrews 12:4, however—"You have not yet resisted to the point of shedding your blood"—would seem to militate against this identification, and the suffering mentioned in Hebrews 10:32 could refer instead to the first persecution of Christians by Jews described in the early chapters of Acts. The absence of any reference to the destruction of the temple* or Jerusalem in 70 (and thus the end of the Jewish sacrificial system), the mention of Timothy (Heb 13:23), the primitive condition of the church, and the author's use of the present tense in referring to temple activities all suggest an earlier dating, likely in the 60s (*see* Hebrews).

4.1.8. James. This NT epistle contains no references to people or events that might assist in dating it, which has resulted in a wide variety of scholarly opinion. Early tradition names James the Just, Jesus' half-brother, as author, although Eusebius reports that some doubted this because, as in the case of Jude, few early writers referred to it. Still, he concluded, both epistles were used regularly in a great many churches (Eusebius *Hist. Eccl.* 2.23; *see* Canon). If James was indeed the author, the epistle would obviously have to have been written prior to his martyrdom in A.D. 62.

Internal evidence, in any case, favors an even earlier date. W. P. Armstrong and J. Finegan point out that since the epistle does not reflect debate on any of the questions raised in the Pauline corpus, particularly Gentile circumcision, "it is possibly the earliest book of the NT, written before the Apostolic Council [in A.D. 49]" (Armstrong and Finegan 1:692). Other considerations also favor an early date, at least for the traditions contained in the document. The social climate in the epistle in which the rich oppress the poor characterizes the era before the Jewish War, not after, while the imminent expectation of the parousia,* loose church

organization and Jewish focus all bespeak an early authorship (*see* James).

4.1.9. 1 Peter. The first general epistle of Peter was accepted as the work of the apostle by early church tradition. Papias of Hierapolis (c. 125) used this letter, according to Eusebius (*Hist. Eccl.* 3.39), as did the primitive elders of Asia (*Hist. Eccl.* 3.1), Polycarp (*Hist. Eccl.* 4.14), Irenaeus (*Haer.* 4.9) and other early authorities. Eusebius himself regarded 1 Peter as authentic and part of the undisputed canon (Eusebius *Hist. Eccl.* 3.25). If the apostle Peter was indeed the author, the letter must obviously have been written prior to his martyrdom in A.D. 64-65. However, scholars who claim the work was only attributed to Peter have offered later datings.

Since this is apparently a persecution document (1 Pet 1:6-7; 4:12; 5:9), the Neronian persecution of 64-65, that of Domitian c. 95, and even that implied in Pliny the Younger's famous letter from Asia Minor to Trajan c. 112 (Pliny *Ep.* 10.96-97) have all been suggested. 1 Peter 5:9, however, refers to suffering ("throughout the world") from spiritual warfare rather than persecution by the state. There was no empire-wide persecution until the third century. Still, this does not prove that earlier references in the epistle to suffering might not have been the result of persecution, present or threatened. If so, the persecution in Asia reported in Pliny's letter seems too late for attestation of 1 Peter by Papias only fifteen years later, and the Domitianic persecution, if it occurred, appeared targeted to select members of the nobility. The most workable conclusion, accordingly, is authorship just before or during the Neronian persecution, probably c. 64. In terms of outer limits, it cannot be placed earlier than 59, since it shows some familiarity with the Pauline prison letters, nor later than 68, the death of Nero (*see* 1 Peter).

4.1.10. 2 Peter. Unlike 1 Peter, the second letter attributed to the apostle has the weakest credentials of any book in the NT, and Eusebius lists it among the disputed writings, "though familiar to most" (Eusebius *Hist. Eccl.* 3.25). The first explicit reference to 2 Peter in patristic writings does not come until c. A.D. 240 with Origen (*Comm. Joh.* 5.3). Most modern interpreters conclude that Peter the apostle cannot have written it, since it is too obviously a later work dealing with the problem of a delayed Parousia (2 Pet 3:4), it presents a style much different from that of 1 Peter, and it incorporates an abstract of Jude. Some claim that 2 Peter reflects conditions in the church of the second century and place its authorship there, while, at the other extreme, some conservative scholars either insist that Peter himself wrote it or suggest that a coworker of Peter, perhaps John Mark, put into writing Peter's final thoughts as a posthumous testament. The latter supposition, however, is far from proven (*see* 2 Peter). Accordingly, no firm dating is possible for 2 Peter, whose canonicity was not fully accepted until the fourth century (*see* Canon).

4.1.11. 1 John. This document, more a treatise than a letter, is quoted by Polycarp of Smyrna (Pol. *Phil.* 7) and Justin Martyr (*Dial. Tryph.* 123.9), was known to Papias of Hierapolis (Eusebius *Hist. Eccl.* 3.39) and Irenaeus (*Haer.* 3.16), and is regarded as undisputed and therefore canonical by Eusebius himself (*Hist. Eccl.* 3.25). He states that both present and past scholars accepted it as the apostle's without question (Eusebius *Hist. Eccl.* 3.24). Its dating, of course, depends on its authorship: John the apostle for 1 John, according to Jerome, and John the presbyter for 2 and 3 John. Other scholars argue that John the presbyter wrote all three letters. The time and place of authorship, however, are hardly affected if either John the apostle or John the presbyter was the author, since they were near contemporaries in Asia Minor, a setting that is further supported if the teaching opposed in 1 John is the Gnosticism (*see* Gnosis, Gnosticism) of Cerinthus (fl. c. 90). The development of such heresy militates against any considerably earlier dating, and an origination of 1 John sometime in the decade 85-95 is posited by most scholars (*see* John, Letters of).

4.1.12. 2 John and 3 John. The second and third Johannine epistles have diminishing canonical authority in that order. Irenaeus quotes the second (*Haer.* 1.16), and Eusebius lists both letters under the works "disputed, yet familiar to most" (Eusebius *Hist. Eccl.* 3.25). Their content reflects a provenance similar to that of 1 John in terms of place and time, but with a sharpened specificity as to authorship—John the presbyter—and recipients—"the elect lady" (2 Jn) and "Gaius" (3 Jn). Furthermore, a keener opposition to heresy in 2 John and internal challenge to the elder's authority on the part of a Diotrephes in 3 John suggest a somewhat later date for the last two Johannines.

Accordingly, an authorship in the last decade of the first century should not fall wide of the mark (*see* John, Letters of).

4.1.13. Jude. Since the author does not claim apostleship but identifies himself as "a brother of James," the apostle Jude or Judas of Luke 6:16 would seem ruled out in favor of one of the four half-brothers of Jesus and the full brother of James the Just of Jerusalem (Mt 13:55; Mk 6:3). As to the date of Jude's letter, nothing in it requires a postapostolic origin, and Jude 17-18 implies that his readers had personally heard the apostles speak. Since 2 Peter uses Jude, Jude must be earlier, and its probable use by Clement* of Rome suggests a date between 65 and 80. Eusebius, however, lists it among the books "disputed, yet familiar to most" (Eusebius *Hist. Eccl.* 3.35) (*See* Jude).

4.1.14. Revelation. Probably used by Hermas (c. 100), known by Papias of Hierapolis and Melito of Sardis, and used by Justin and Irenaeus among the early fathers, Revelation enjoyed considerable canonical* authority in the church. Eusebius, however, includes it among both the undisputed and the spurious books, according it something of an intermediate status, for at the end of the canonical book list he writes, "To these may be added, if deemed appropriate, the Revelation of John, the arguments about which I shall discuss at the proper time" (Eusebius *Hist. Eccl.* 3.25). The earliest identification of its author was John the apostle. In the third century, however, Bishop Dionysius of Alexandria* found so many differences between the Fourth Gospel and Revelation that he suggested John the presbyter as author of the latter (Eusebius *Hist. Eccl.* 7.25), a view shared widely today. As above, however, either identification hardly affects the dating. Since Revelation was written when persecution in Asia was thought imminent—and Nero's was limited to Rome—the latter part of Domitian's reign comes into focus, probably c. 95, a date favored by most scholars.

5. The Apostolic Fathers.

This earliest group of Christian writers was once thought to have been in direct contact with the apostles, although this could possibly apply only to Clement, Ignatius and Polycarp. This section will cover the earliest noncanonical writers and writings from the late first century through the mid-second century.

5.1. Clement of Rome. Clement was the early presbyter and third "bishop" at Rome who wrote his *Letter to the Corinthians (1 Clement)* shortly after "sudden misfortunes and calamities" had overtaken the Roman Christians. Most scholars attribute this persecution to that presumed under Domitian, thus c. A.D. 95-96. As such, this is among the earliest of the noncanonical Christian writings, probably sharing this position with Hermas's *Shepherd* (which also mentions a Clement, who, unlike the one cited in Philippians 4:3, is probably the same as this Clement). Clement accordingly flourished during the period c. 90-100. The homily *2 Clement* was attributed to Clement but written later—probably 130-150—since it incorporates citations from apocryphal Gospels (*see* Clement of Rome).

5.2. Hermas. The author of the *Shepherd*, which had near-canonical status in some sectors of the early church (e.g., Irenaeus, according to Eusebius *Hist. Eccl.* 5.8), refers to Clement as his contemporary, which would place him in a late first-century time frame. The Muratorian Canon, however, identifies Hermas as a brother of Pius, bishop of Rome c. 140-54, and states that he wrote the *Shepherd* during his reign, which would require a later date. The chronological difference has not been resolved, and it is possible that the *Shepherd* was composed in stages incorporating both time slots, possibly by several authors (*see* Hermas, Shepherd of).

5.3. Ignatius. The bishop of Antioch who was arrested and sent to Rome, where he was martyred in the reign of Trajan, must thus have died in a time frame 98 to 117, probably c. 107-10. En route to his execution he wrote seven letters: four from Smyrna to the churches of Ephesus, Magnesia, Tralles and Rome, three from Troas to the churches at Smyrna and Philadelphia, and to Polycarp, bishop of Smyrna, personally. Polycarp (Pol. *Phil.* 9.2), Origen (*Hom. Luc.* 6) and Eusebius (*Hist. Eccl.* 3.36) tell of his martyrdom as he was thrown to the beasts (*see* Ignatius).

5.4. Papias. This bishop of Hierapolis in Asia Minor wrote five books entitled *Exposition of Dominical Oracles*. Fragmentary quotations from these preserved primarily in Irenaeus and Eusebius reveal intriguing data about the authors of three of the Gospels. Irenaeus claims that Papias lived "at a very early date," listened to the apostle John and was "later a companion of Polycarp" (Irenaeus *Haer.* 5.33). Eusebius, however, claims the John referred to was not the apostle but John the presbyter (Eusebius *Hist. Eccl.* 3.39), and he has a low opinion of Papias primarily due to his millennialism. Since Papias claims to have learned information about the apostolic age from the daughters of Philip the evangelist (Acts 21:8-9) who later settled in Hierapolis, scholars are prone to assign him a time frame somewhat earlier than that of Polycarp: c. A.D. 60 to c. 130.

5.5. Polycarp. This bishop of Smyrna, as a disciple of the apostle John, was revered as a living witness of the apostolic age. Arrested in Smyrna, he claimed at his trial to have served Christ for eighty-six years (*Martyrdom of Polycarp* 9) and, refusing to recant, was martyred. When he was over eighty he journeyed to Rome to settle a controversy on the date of Easter with Anicetus, bishop of Rome c. 155-66. Eusebius states that the martyrdom occurred under the reign of Marcus Aurelius (Eusebius *Hist. Eccl.* 4.14-15), and specifically in 166 according to his *Chronicon*. This date was unchallenged until 1867, when Waddington's *Mémoire sur la chronologie de la vie du rhéteur Aelius Aristide* appeared, in which he demonstrated that the Quadratus cited in the *Martyrdom of Polycarp* was proconsul of Asia in 155-56, during the administration of Antoninus Pius. Accordingly, many scholars prefer 156 as the year of Polycarp's martyrdom, with his birth thus in 70 if, as seems likely, Polycarp was referring to his own baptism as an infant when he claimed to have served Christ for eighty-six years. Of the numerous letters Polycarp is known to have written, only his *Letter to the Philippians* has survived, most probably written c. 140-50.

5.6. The Epistle of Barnabas. Of anonymous authorship, this treatise had scriptural authority in the church at Alexandria and is found in the Codex Sinaiticus, which accounts for its traditional inclusion among the apostolic fathers. Its penchant for allegorization had much less influence elsewhere in the early church. An allusion in *Barnabas* 16.3 to the destruction and rebuilding of the temple at Jerusalem by enemies seems to reflect on what Hadrian did to Jerusalem, thus suggesting a provenance c. 135-45 (*see* Barnabas).

5.7. The Didache. The full title of this document is *The Teaching of the Lord to the Gentiles Through the Twelve Apostles*. It was lost until a manuscript dated in 1056 was discovered by P. Bryennios at Constantinople in 1875. The *Didache*, which reflects church order and liturgy in the Christian East, was included among the disputed or spurious books by Eusebius (*Hist.*

Eccl. 3.25), and it clearly is not the work of an apostolic father. Dating this document is fraught with uncertainty, and suggestions have ranged from the close of the first century to a writer archaizing in the third century. Since the *Didache* shows a close relationship to the *Epistle of Barnabas,* a similar origin somewhere in the first half of the second century would seem appropriate (*see* Didache).

6. The Early Apologists.
Earliest defenders of the faith before the Greco-Roman world, who continued the effort begun by St. Paul at the Areopagus (Acts 17), include Quadratus, Aristides and Justin Martyr.

6.1. Quadratus. His is the earliest known apology, but it is lost except for a brief fragment preserved by Eusebius (*Hist. Eccl.* 4.3), which states that some of the people Jesus cured survived up to his (Quadratus's) own time. He addressed his apology to the emperor Hadrian, perhaps during the emperor's visit to Athens during the winter of 124-25. A child whom Jesus cured in his last year of ministry would have been ninety-one years old at that time, or as young as eighty-four if Quadratus presented his apology to Hadrian at his accession in 117. Subsequently, a Quadratus became the third bishop of Athens after the martyrdom of Publius, and he is likely the same person (Eusebius *Hist. Eccl.* 4.23).

6.2. Aristides. Mentioning him in the same context with Quadratus, Eusebius states that Aristides also addressed an *Apology* to Hadrian (Eusebius *Hist. Eccl.* 4.3), but he does not quote from it. Most scholars, however, claim on internal evidence that the Athenian philosopher addressed it instead to Antoninus Pius early in his administration, c. 140. Aristides' is the earliest extant Christian apology. In the nineteenth century a partial Armenian version was discovered, then a complete Syriac translation. A short time later J. A. Robinson found that the Greek version of the *Apology* had almost entirely been incorporated in a Greek medieval novel, *Barlaam and Josaphat.*

6.3. Justin Martyr. Justin is the most important of the early Christian apologists. Born of pagan parentage at Flavia Neapolis (the modern Nablus) in biblical Samaria c. 100, he moved to Ephesus, where he converted to Christianity c. 132. Teaching in various cities, he later spent a longer time lecturing in Rome, where he addressed his *Apology,* written c. 150, to Antoninus

Pius. His so-called *Second Apology,* a shorter work against persecution of Christians, appeared c. 153, and his *Dialogue with Trypho the Jew* derives from this period also. According to the *Acta SS Justini et sociorum,* Justin was martyred under the prefect Rusticus between 163 and 167.

7. Early Heretics.
Challenges to the theology of the Christian mainstream arose during late apostolic and postapostolic times, principally from Jewish Christian and Gnostic errorists.

7.1. Jewish Christian Errorists. The Ebionites* rejected the Pauline epistles and regarded Jesus as the natural son of Joseph and Mary who was elected Son of God at his baptism.* Probably originating both from the Judaizers opposed to Paul and survivors from Qumran after the destruction of Jerusalem in 70, the Ebionites suffered during the Bar Kokhba revolt (132-35) because they refused to accept him as Messiah (*see* Jewish Christianity). Their numbers dwindled thereafter, and their remnant was inundated in the Muslim tide that swept over Syria* in the seventh century.

7.2. Gnostic Errorists. Gnosticism, a hydra-headed mélange of various recondite teachings often based on (or spawning) apocryphal* and pseudepigraphic* writings, alarmed church fathers of the second and third centuries. Its roots, however, are in the purview of the later NT era (*see* Gnosis, Gnosticism). Only the most prominent Gnostics are listed here.

7.2.1. Simon Magus. He is not described as a Gnostic in Acts 8:9 ff., but patristic accounts all deem him the very source of this and all other heresies. The Samaritan magician (*see* Magic) who tried to buy the power of miracles from Peter (and thus gave rise to the term *simony*) arrived in Rome during the reign of Claudius (41-54), where he was defeated by Peter, according to Justin Martyr (cited by Eusebius *Hist. Eccl.* 2.13-14). A fellow Samaritan, Menander, followed Simon as head of the Simonians, teaching at Antioch* near the close of the first century.

7.2.2. Saturninus. An ascetic disciple of Menander, Saturninus taught at Antioch early in the second century. He claimed that seven angels* created the world and man, although a docetic* Christ was the redeemer.

7.2.3. Basilides. Another disciple of Menander, Basilides, taught at Alexandria during the reign of Hadrian. He claimed archon-gods had power over the universe but were ignorant of the "nonexistent" God until the Gospel of Light descended on them. Another Gnostic, Carpocrates, taught a syncretistic theology at Alexandria a little later, c. 135.

7.2.4. Cerinthus. A heresiarch at Ephesus c. 100 who was both Gnostic and Ebionite, according to Irenaeus (*Haer.* 1.3), Cerinthus was also a sensual chiliast, according to Eusebius (*Hist. Eccl.* 3.28). In patristic writings he appears as the archenemy of Johannine Christianity.

7.2.5. Marcion. A native of Pontus, Marcion* taught at Rome from 137 to 144, when he was excommunicated. Like the Gnostics, he had a docetic Christology and a negative attitude toward the material world, which he thought was created by the demiurge, the god of the OT. He rejected the OT and included only an edited version of Luke and the Pauline corpus in his canon.

7.2.6. Valentinus. The most influential Gnostic, founder of the Valentinian sect, Valentinus taught at Alexandria and then at Rome c. 136-65. His esoteric theology posited a hierarchy of aeon pairs and a visible world resulting from the fall of Sophia, the last of the aeons. Jesus, as redeemer, saved people by imparting to them saving knowledge *(gnōsis)*.

See also APOSTOLIC FATHERS; EMPEROR, EMPEROR CULT; ROMAN EMPIRE, CHRISTIANS AND THE.

BIBLIOGRAPHY. W. R. Armstrong and J. Finegan, "Chronology of the NT" *ISBE* 1:686-93; F. F. Bruce, *The Acts of the Apostles*, (3rd ed., Grand Rapids: Eerdmans, 1990); idem, *New Testament History* (Garden City, NY: Doubleday, 1972); G. B. Caird, "Chronology of the NT," *IDB* 1:599-607; K. P. Donfried, "Chronology: New Testament" in *ABD* 1:1011-22; J. Finegan, *Handbook of Biblical Chronology* (Princeton: Princeton University Press, 1964); R. Jewett, *A Chronology of Paul's Life* (Philadelphia: Fortress, 1979); G. Ogg, *The Chronology of the Life of Paul* (London: Epworth, 1968); B. Reicke, *The New Testament Era* (Philadelphia: Fortress, 1968); J. A. T. Robinson, *Redating the New Testament* (Philadelphia: Westminster, 1976); E. M. Smallwood, *The Jews Under Roman Rule* (Leiden: E. J. Brill, 1976).

P. L. Maier

CHRONOLOGICAL TABLE

(Years in parentheses are significant dates within the reigns of Roman emperors appearing in the Roman & General History column.)

Dates	Roman & General History	Christian History	Jewish History
27 B.C.-A.D. 14	Augustus		
(c. 5 B.C.)		Birth of Jesus	
A.D. 14-37	Tiberius		
(26-36)	Administration of Pontius Pilate as Prefect of Judea		
(c. 29-33)		Jesus' public ministry	
(c. 33)		Crucifixion of Jesus	
37-41	Caligula	Simon Magus at Samaria	Exile of Herod Antipas; Philo's delegation to Rome
41-54	Claudius	Paul's mission journeys	Death of Philo; death of Herod Agrippa I
(49)		Apostolic Council at Jerusalem	
(51-52)	Gallio Proconsul of Acaia	Paul in Corinth	
54-68	Nero	*James* written? *1 Peter* written? Much of the Pauline corpus written; Synoptics	Gamaliel; Outbreak of the Jewish War with Rome

193

		and *Acts* written (early view) *Gospel of John* written (early view).	
(62)		Death of James the Just at Jerusalem	Albinus succeeds Festus as procurator of Judea
(64)	Great Fire of Rome	First Roman persecution; Peter martyred; Paul, subsequently	
68-69	Galba, Otho, Vitellius	*Hebrews* written?	Johanan Ben-Zakkai at Jamnia
69-79	Vespasian	*Synoptic Gospels* written (later view); *Jude* written?	Josephus publishes the *Jewish War*
(70)	Titus conquers Jerusalem		Fall of Jerusalem, burning of the temple
79-81	Titus		
(79)	Mt. Vesuvius destroys Herculaneum, Pompeii		
81-96	Domitian	*Revelation* written? Second Roman persecution of Christians; *Gospel of John* written? (later view); John the Seer on Patmos; *1 John* written; *1 Clement* written.	Josephus publishes *Jewish Antiquities*
96-98	Nerva	*2 and 3 John* written?	
98-117	Trajan	Ignatius martyred at Rome; Pliny asks about Christians; Gnostics Cerinthus, Saturn- inus, and Basilides	Council at Jamnia fixes OT canon; Second Jewish War
(c. 100)		Death of John?	Death of Josephus?
117-138	Hadrian	Letter to Fundanus; Quadra- tus writes *Apology* to Hadrian; Papias at Hierapolis	Third Jewish War (Bar Kokhba revolt); exclusion of Jews from Jerusalem.
138-161	Antoninus Pius	Polycarp martyred; Aristides writes *Apology* to Antoninus Pius; Marcion excommun- icated at Rome; of Gnostic teacher Valentinus	
161-180	Marcus Aurelius	Justin martyred at Rome; per- secutions at Lyons and Scillium.	

CHURCH

The book of Acts* ends with Paul in Rome.* By this time the church is well established in Palestine, Syria, Asia Minor, Greece and Italy (*see DPL,* Church). When Justin Martyr concludes his *Dialogue with Trypho* (A.D. 160) the Christian church has spread around the Mediterranean basin and beyond. With this geographical dispersion the early Christian communities could have easily thought of themselves as self-contained groups, but their profound consciousness that they belonged to the one Christian community, the church, did not allow this. In this period we see a widening gulf between Christians and Jews as each comes to recognize the separate identity of the other (*see* Christianity and Judaism).

1. Presuppositions
2. Acts
3. Hebrews
4. James
5. 1 Peter
6. The Johannine Epistles
7. The Book of Revelation
8. Apostolic Fathers

1. Presuppositions.

In seeking to discover how early Christian writers understood the church, a number of basic presuppositions must be spelled out.

In this article the idea that a doctrine of the church can be achieved solely by focusing on and determining a fixed meaning of the Greek word *ekklēsia* ("church") is rejected. Words are used with different meanings in different contexts and usually represent a concept that can be denoted by other words, metaphors or expressions. In what follows the focus is on the church concept, defined as the Christian community. One word used frequently to designate this concept is *ekklēsia*, but as we will see many virtual synonyms, descriptive phrases and metaphors are also used. Furthermore, the concept can be in mind even when this one word is not present.

The church is to be thought of as "the Christian community" because the early Christians were one in understanding that while men and women individually came to faith* in Christ,* this involved by definition becoming part of the family of God* open to all people everywhere. The goal of the Christian mission* was not to save individuals, though it involved this, but to call out a people for God's name.* All the apostolic and postapostolic writers see this new community emerging out of historic Israel.* It is therefore, like Israel, a corporate entity. The local gathering of Christians was important because this was where communal life in Christ was most personally realized; but for the early Christians, belonging to the one community established by Christ was the primary reality. The modern Western individualistic spectacles through which we read the early Christian writings all too often blind us to seeing the profound communalism of early Christianity.

How each author understood the relationship between this community and the one from which it had emerged, namely, Israel, is one of the key issues to be worked out in any study of ecclesiology. As this was a difficult matter for the early Christians to resolve and as it was conditioned historically by an ever-widening breach between Jews and Christians, we would anticipate finding differing answers. The two stark alternatives were restoration or replacement. The church was a purified and renewed Israel into which Gentiles* were welcomed, or the church was a breakaway from Israel, a new work of God. In the first case continuity is to the fore; in the second, discontinuity.

In seeking to conceptualize the form of the church in this early period, we recognize that Christians normally met in relatively small groups in a home. The largest home would hold no more than fifty people. Most homes would have accommodated fewer than this number. Thus our modern experience of church must be put to one side as we try to visualize church life in the first and second centuries.

2. Acts.

Lukan ecclesiology has a number of distinctive features.

2.1. Spirit and Church. In Acts Luke has the new Christian community coming into existence on the day of Pentecost,* when the Holy Spirit* is poured out on those who confess Jesus as Lord* and Christ. In Luke's thinking the Holy Spirit institutes and empowers the church. He sees the coming of the Holy Spirit as the fulfillment of the words of the prophet Joel, who along with other OT prophets had predicted a universal outpouring of the Holy Spirit on God's people in the age of final redemption* (Joel 2:28-32; cf. Ezek 36:27; 37:14; Is 32:15; Zech 12:10; *see* Old Testament in Acts). In quoting Joel's prophecy Luke adds as an introduction the words "in the last days" (Acts 2:17) to show he understood that this mighty giving of the Spirit indicated that the eschatological* age had dawned. In pouring out the Spirit, God was restoring Israel and inaugurating the new covenant* (cf. Ezek 36:27 and Jer 31:33). The word *ekklēsia* does not appear in Acts until Acts 5:11. Immediately after the giving of the Holy Spirit Luke is content to use a number of descriptive designations of the newly created, Spirit-filled community: "those who received the word" (Acts 2:41), "those who believed" (Acts 2:44), those who are being saved (Acts 2:47) and "the community" (*epi to auto,* Acts 2:47; see Giles 1995, 261 n. 9). Nevertheless we can correctly speak of this event as the birth of the church. In Luke's mind this is when the post-Easter Christian community came into existence.

Having made the Holy Spirit foundational to the establishment of the new community, Luke has an abiding preoccupation with the Holy Spirit. Some seventy times the word *pneuma* ("Spirit") appears in Acts. R. E. Brown concludes, "the distinguishing feature of Lucan ecclesiology is the overshadowing presence of the Holy Spirit" (Brown, 65).

2.2. Church and Israel. A protracted debate has taken place as to how Luke views the relationship between historic Israel and the new Christian community. What seems to be the case is that Luke's distinctive ecclesiology depicts those Jews who recognize Jesus as the long-awaited Messiah and are empowered by the Holy Spirit as restored Israel. Gentiles who believe are included in this restored Israel, as the prophets had predicted (Acts 15:12-18). Jews who reject Christ are "rooted out" and lose their status as the people of God (Acts 3:23). In telling his story in historical sequence, Luke allows that the realization only gradually dawned on the first believers that historic Israel as such had ceased to be the people of God (for a different perspective on Israel's status *see* Covenant).

This new community, Luke insists, is, like historic Israel, very much on earth. A heavenly church would have been a contradiction in terms for him. Christ has ascended into heaven* to rule in power* and glory* (Acts 1:6-11; 2:33), and the church is on earth "passing through many tribulations" (Acts 14:22).

2.3. Names for the Church. Luke gives a large number of names to the one reality we call the church. H. J. Cadbury lists and discusses nineteen collective titles. A few of these are doubtful, but even leaving two or three aside, a large number remain.

2.3.1. "Those Who. . . ." Some titles are descriptive and may have been developed by Luke or taken over from common usage. The designations "those who believe" (several participial forms are used; see Acts 2:44; 4:32; 15:5; 16:34; 18:27); "those who call on the name" (Acts 9:14, 21; 22:16); "those who received the word" (Acts 2:41) and "those who are being saved" (Acts 2:47; cf. Lk 13:23) fall into this category.

2.3.2. Early Titles Preserved. Another group of titles seem to be almost historical fossils. They reflect very early Palestinian terminology. "Galileans" (Acts 1:11; 2:7) is one possible example. Others include "the Nazarenes" (Acts 24:5) and "the Way" (*ho hodos;* Acts 9:2; 19:9, 23; 24:14, 22), to which we can add Acts 22:4 ("this way"). In the OT and at Qumran* the word *way* is often used figuratively of living in a manner pleasing or not pleasing to God (Ps 101:2; 119:1-3; Is 53:6; 57:17). Besides using the word absolutely, Luke also speaks of "the way of the Lord"

(Acts 18:25), "the way of God" (Acts 18:26) and "the way of salvation" (Acts 16:17). Possibly the absolute usage is but an abbreviation. Both titles, "the Nazarenes" and "the Way," can designate what Jewish opponents call a "sect" or "party" *(hairesis).* This word is not yet another title for Christians but a Jewish way of viewing the early believers as a sect within Israel. Luke uses this word of the Pharisees (Acts 15:15) and of the Sadducees (Acts 5:17), but he does not think it is appropriate to use it of the disciples of Christ. They are more than this. In the three instances (Acts 24:5, 14; 28:22) where this term is used of believers, it is on the tongue of opponents.

Another very early title used first by the enemies of the new community (this time from a Gentile setting) is "the Christians." The Greek transliteration of a Latin ending *(-ianos)* means "belonging to." In Acts 11:26 Luke says, "At Antioch the disciples were first called Christians." Here and in the second usage (Acts 26:28) Luke has others calling Christians by this name. It was at this stage not a self-designation, and this is still the case when the title appears in 1 Peter 4:16. On a number of occasions Luke also calls Christians collectively *to plēthos.* He can use this word of any group of people ("a crowd"; Acts 14:1; 17:4; 21:22), but sometimes he allows it to have an almost technical meaning so that it can be translated "the [Christian] community" (Acts 6:2, 5; 15:12, 30; possibly Acts 21:22). Twice in the Septuagint *to plēthosis* is used to render into Greek the Hebrew word *qāhāl* ("assembly/the Jewish covenant community"), which is usually translated by the word *ekklēsia* (Ex 12:6; 2 Chron 31:18).

2.3.3. Saints. The collective titles "the saints" *(hoi hagioi)* and "the people [of God]" *(ho laos)* may be grouped together. These two terms are given weighty theological content by their use in the Septuagint to designate Israel. Four times Luke calls Christians collectively "the saints" (Acts 9:13, 32, 41; 26:10), and twice he speaks of them as being "sanctified," using the participial form of the word (Acts 20:32; 26:18). In establishing the covenant with Israel God sets them apart as a holy nation (Ex 19:6; Lev 11:44-45). It is on this basis that the Jews became God's holy people, the saints (Num 16:13; Deut 33:3; Ps 16:3; 34:9; 89:5; Is 4:3). In calling Christians "the saints" Luke identifies them with restored Israel. Similarly, by twice designating Christians *ho laos,* "the people of God" (Acts 15:14; 18:10; cf. Acts 3:23), Luke makes the same point. In the Septuagint this term is a distinctive and theologically weighted designation of Israel.

2.3.4. Disciples and Brethren. It is, however, the titles "the disciples," "the brethren" and "the church" that Luke uses most commonly. The title "the brethren" *(hoi adelphoi),* a gender-inclusive term, is interesting because Luke uses it for both Jews and Christians, which suggests the relationship between these two groups was still relatively fluid. Even as late as Acts 28:21 Luke can speak of fellow Jews as brethren. Nevertheless, without any apology he calls Christians "the brethren" twenty-five times (Acts 9:30; 10:23; 11:1; 12:17). This term underlines the familial nature of being a believer. The title "the disciples" *(hoi mathētai)* is almost as common, being used twenty-three times of Christians (Acts 6:7; 9:26; 11:26; 15:10). In this case this title is a reminder that believers are followers of Christ.

2.3.5. Church. Finally we come to the word *ekklēsia,* which Luke uses nineteen times of Christians (Acts 5:11; 8:1; 9:31; 11:26), three times of an unruly assembly of citizens in the theater at Ephesus (Acts 19:32, 39, 41) and once of the Jews assembled at Mount Sinai to receive the law* (Acts 7:38). In classical Greek this word referred to people actually assembled, and Luke uses the word in this sense to denote the crowd at Ephesus. To argue on this basis that this is the meaning of the term in all the other uses in Acts is absurd. It would be like arguing that because Luke uses the verb "to save" of the rescue of Paul and the ship's crew (in Acts 27:20, 31) he believed salvation* is only a this-worldly rescue. Elsewhere (excepting Acts 7:38) Luke uses the word *ekklēsia* in a specifically Christian sense to speak of Christians as a theologically defined community, restored Israel. In this sense it carries the content of the more developed meaning of this word in the Septuagint (see Giles 1995, 230-40).

Luke uses the one word to designate both a local community of Christians (Acts 5:11; 8:1; 11:26; 13:1) and the Christian community in its entirety (Acts 20:28). The addition of the genitive "of God" in this last reference adds nothing. In the Gospels "the kingdom of God" means the same as "the kingdom" (*see* Kingdom of God). When Luke wishes to speak of local Christian communities in more than one place he uses the plural (Acts 15:41; 16:5). Acts 9:31 is prob-

lematic, as both the word *ekklēsia* and the verbs and participles that follow are found in the singular and the plural in different manuscripts. Luke makes it clear that the church in Jerusalem,* numbering many thousands, met in homes (Acts 2:46; 5:42; 10:2; 11:14; 12:12-17), but he never uses the word *ekklēsia* for a house church. For him the Christians in one geographical spot are "the" local church.

2.3.6. Synonymity of Titles. What is important to note is that while each of these collective titles has its own nuance, they are virtual synonyms that can be used interchangeably. Acts 9 is instructive, as Luke uses five collective titles for stylistic variation in this chapter. In Acts 9:1 he speaks of "the disciples" and repeats this term in Acts 9:25, 26 and 38. Next comes the title those "who belong to the way" (Acts 9:2). In Acts 9:30 he uses the title "the brethren"; in Acts 9:13 and 32 "the saints"; in Acts 9:14 and 21 "those who call on the name." Elsewhere in Acts the most common titles—"the disciples," "the brethren" and "the church"—are frequently interchanged. For example, Luke speaks of the disciples of a city or of the church of a city (Acts 8:1; cf. Acts 9:19). He can speak of Paul strengthening the churches or the disciples (Acts 14:22; 15:41; 18:23). The overlapping but not identical meaning of each of these collective titles can be diagrammatically illustrated by using a selection of the terms.

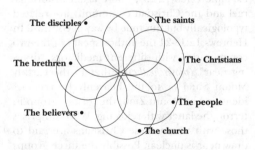

One reality, the Christian community, designated by different terms

3. Hebrews.

On reading Hebrews* one is immediately struck by the distinctive language, christology* and use of the OT (*see* Old Testament in Hebrews). It is not surprising therefore to discover that this epistle also has a distinctive ecclesiology. Although Hebrews appeals primarily to the OT to make its case, it envisages a radical breach with Israel. The old covenant has been replaced by the new (Heb 8:6-13); the Jewish priesthood* and the office and work of the High Priest have come to an end (Heb 7:11-14, 23-28); and Jesus in offering himself has made obsolete the old sacrificial* system (Heb 9:25-28; 10:11-15). As a consequence the author views the Christian community as new Israel in all but name. The Christians have taken the place of the historic people of God, assuming their distinctive titles and privileges. Thus in Hebrews 3—4 the author can typologically identify the Christian family with Israel. How God dealt with Israel and what he said to them in the past now, one for one, applies to the Christian community.

The author of Hebrews uses a number of terms to designate this new community. They are "the people of God" (*ho laos,* Heb 2:17; 4:9; 8:10; 10:30; 11:25; 13:12); "the children of God" (Heb 2:10; 12:5, 6, 7); "the saints" (Heb 6:10; 13:24) and "God's house" (Heb 3:6). All these titles were originally the prerogative of historic Israel. By implication Christians are also understood to be the new covenant community (Heb 8:8-12; 10:16-17).

The word *ekklēsia,* is used only twice. It appears first in Hebrews 2:12 in a quote from Psalm 22:22, in which God's people are depicted as a worshiping community (*see* Worship). This same thought appears in the second example (Heb 12:23), where again historic Israel and the Christian community are related typologically but this time by way of contrast. In Hebrews 12:18-24 the author speaks of the two communities, with different mediators, "drawing near" *(proserchesthai)* either to the earthly Mount Sinai or to the heavenly Jerusalem,* identified as Mount Zion, the former group in terror, the latter with rejoicing. Who comprises those with whom these Christians are said to draw near is unclear. Possibly the three groups are angels* (Heb 12:22); Christian believers who have died ("the *ekklēsia*/assembly of the firstborn") and whose names are enrolled in heaven (Heb 12:23); and OT believers described as "just men made perfect" (Heb 12:23).

If we ask, How did the author envisage the Christian community on earth drawing near in Hebrews 12:22, the best answer is, in worship. In Hebrews 2:12 the church is described as a worshiping community, and the key verb *proser-*

chesthai ("to draw near") is a cultic term drawn from the OT alluding to what takes place in worship (see Giles 1995, 155-56). At this point we should also add that the argument does not stand that because the word *ekklēsia* in Hebrews 12:23 is used of a heavenly assembly, all universal uses of the word *ekklēsia* in the NT refer exclusively to a heavenly gathering. The language and thought of the epistle to the Hebrews is distinctive, and all the writer seems to be suggesting is that in worship Christians come near to God *along with* a great heavenly company.

4. James.
The epistle of James* is a pastoral epistle, not a theological treatise. Most commentators think James is addressing Jewish Christians* when he calls them "the twelve tribes of the dispersion" (Jas 1:1; *see* Diaspora Judaism). This title is strongly communal and bears witness to a belief that the Christian community is dispersed throughout the world, but it is probably not a claim that Christians are the new Israel. In James 2:2 the writer calls a Christian gathering a synagogue* (cf. Heb 10:25; Ign. *Pol.* 5.2; *Herm. Man.* 11.9; Justin *Dial. Tryph.* 63.5). In James 5:14 he speaks of "the elders of the church" *(ekklēsia).* This suggests that the Christian community addressed, called an *ekklēsia,* was a structured one with appointed office bearers (*see* Church Order). This means then that the two terms are used differently. In James 2:2 the Greek word *synagogē* refers to an assembly, to people as they are gathered; the word *ekklēsia,* in James 5:14 refers to a community of Christians with an ongoing existence and an ordered life.

5. 1 Peter.
First Peter* is important, for although it does not use the word *ekklēsia,* it is more interested in theologically defining the Christian community, the church, than is any other NT writing. It seems certain that the epistle is addressed to predominantly Gentile Christians living in northern Asia Minor, who are suffering* for their faith.

In the opening address these Christians are explicitly identified as Israel. They are the "exiles of the dispersion," "chosen and destined by God," "sanctified by the Spirit and . . . sprinkled with his blood" (1 Pet 1:1-2). Three times elsewhere Peter speaks of the Christian community as being "chosen" or elect* (1 Pet 2:4, 6, 9), a way of designating Israel (1 Chron 16:13; Ps 105:6; Is 65:9). The mention of them being sprinkled with blood marks them out as the new covenant community, for these words reflect the enactment of the Sinai covenant, which constituted Israel as God's elect and destined people (Ex 24:3-8; cf. 1 Pet 1:18-21).

But the most theologically pregnant comment about the Christian community is found in 1 Peter 2:4-10. The author begins by exhorting individual Christians to come to Jesus the "living stone" (cf. Is 8:4; 28:16; Ps 117:22; *see* Stone). He then moves to corporate imagery by speaking of a building process that creates a "spiritual house" (1 Pet 2:5; *see* House), a community, which may be understood because of the associated cultic language to be the new temple* of Jewish apocalyptic* hope* (cf. 1 Cor 3:16; Eph 2:19-22). It is "spiritual" in the sense that it is not a literal house or temple, being constituted by the Spirit, built up as believers are added. Collectively they are "a holy priesthood" *(hierateuma)*. This designation reflects Exodus 19:6, where it is applied to the whole people of Israel.

Finally in 1 Peter 2:9 an overlapping series of theologically weighted collective titles are given to the Christian community. Peter declares: "But you [plural] are a chosen race, a royal priesthood, a holy nation, a people *(laos)* belonging to God." The four titles are drawn from Exodus 19:6 and Isaiah 43:20-1, where they denote Israel as the covenant people of God. In applying them to the Christian community Peter is emphatically saying the church is now Israel. The corporate identity of those belonging to the church is so profound that Peter calls them a chosen "race" *(genos)*. On this basis later Christian writers would speak of the Christian community as "a third race," neither Jew nor Gentile *(Preaching of Peter;* Tertullian *Ad Nat.* 1.8).

Another characteristic of the ecclesiology of 1 Peter is a very strong sense of the separation between the believing community and the society in which the church finds itself. Believers are described as "exiles" (1 Pet 1:1, 17) and "aliens and exiles" (1 Pet 2:11); they are exhorted to be holy* (1 Pet 1:15-16) and morally distinct (1 Pet 1:17-18; 3:1-2, 11-12, 18-25; 3:1-7; 8-17; 4:1-6, 12-19). They are to expect to suffer as Christ

suffered (1 Pet 1:6-7; 2:19-25; 3:13-22; 4:1-6, 12-19; 5:9-10).

Peter, like most other NT writers, recognizes that the Christian community has both a localized and a universal expression. He designates the whole Christian community as God's "flock" (1 Pet 5:2), who have returned to their "shepherd and guardian" (1 Pet 2:25; *see* Shepherd). The elders, however, as local leaders are exhorted to "tend the flock of God in your charge" (1 Pet 5:20); that is, the Christians whom they lead in one place. This same contrast appears in the concluding words of the epistle, in which the author distinguishes between those to whom he writes, a localized group of Christians, and "your brothers and sisters *(adelphotēs)* in all the world" (1 Pet 5:9).

6. The Johannine Epistles.
One of the special characteristics of the three epistles of John *(see* John, Letters of) is their concern to differentiate the "true church" from those who have broken away (1 Jn 2:19), whom the author thinks are the enemies of Christ (1 Jn 2:18-19; 4:3; 2 Jn 7). This means his main ecclesiological concern is the boundaries of the Christian community (what are the marks of the true church), not the church's relationship with Israel, a matter not alluded to in these epistles.

The true Christian community is made up of believers who are in fellowship* "with us" (those representing the views of John the apostle), who confess that Jesus is the Christ (1 Jn 5:1), the Son of God (1 Jn 1:3, 7; 3:8, 23) who came in the flesh (1 Jn 4:2; 2 Jn 7); and love* others who are in this restricted company (1 Jn 2:10; 3:11). Those who have broken with "us" are to be shown no welcome: they are to be turned away if they seek contact (2 Jn 10-11). The true church is to be separate from the wider society in which it finds itself. Members are "not to love the world" (1 Jn 2:15), for the "the whole world lies under the power of the evil one" (1 Jn 5:19; *see* Satan). In return the world hates them (1 Jn 3:13). This restricted understanding of love and hostility to unbelievers is less than the Christian ideal and must be explained as part of the damage control of a church under extreme pressure from schism and external threat.

In 3 John the word *ekklēsia* is used three times (3 Jn 6, 9, 10) of a circumscribed local group of believers, but otherwise these epistles do not use this word or other theologically significant communal terms such as "the saints" or "the people of God." Instead the author addresses his readers as "beloved," "children" (*see* Sonship) or "brothers." Some scholars have suggested on this basis and other evidence that we see here an individualistic view of the Christian life, but nothing could be further from the truth. The author underlines the distinctiveness and separation from the world of these believers as a community. They owe their communal identity to the fact that they have been "born of God" (1 Jn 2:29; 5:1); they are God's children (1 Jn 3:1, 10) in whom God abides and they in him (1 Jn 2:24, 27; 3:9).

Very little is said in these epistles about congregational life, and what can be deduced comes mainly from 2 John and 3 John. These epistles seem to reflect a situation in which Christians are meeting in a number of house churches. If this is so then 2 John is a letter from one house church leader to another house church leader in the near vicinity. He calls those to whom he writes "the elect lady and her children" (2 Jn 1). His advice is that anyone who does not make the true confession* of Christ should not be "received into the house or welcomed" (2 Jn 10), which almost certainly means not into "your" house church. In 3 John such house churches are three times designated by the word *ekklēsia* (3 Jn 6, 9, 10).

7. The Book of Revelation.

The final book of the Bible is addressed to "the seven churches" (Rev 1:4, 11) in Asia Minor. As the number seven is always the number of completeness for this author, the implication is that the whole church is being addressed, of which these seven churches are representative. This is made clear in the refrain at the end of each individual letter, "Let anyone who has an ear listen to what the Spirit is saying to the churches." This means "Listen well, for these words have a message for every believer, the universal church."

In Revelation (*see* Revelation, Book of) the universal church on earth is Israel. The author makes this transfer of identity even more emphatically than does the author of the epistle to the Hebrews or 1 Peter. The Jewish people are allied with the forces of the beast* and doomed to destruction (Rev 2:9; 3:9; 13:1, 5, 6; 17:3). Jerusalem, representing Israel, is identified with "Sodom and Egypt" (Rev 11:8). Conversely the Christian community is true Israel who inherit all the promises* once made to the Jewish people. Twice the author applies the foundational OT covenant passage, Exodus 19:6, to Christians, declaring that they have been made "a kingdom of priests to God" (Rev 1:6; 5:10; cf. Rev 20:6). This is the text applied to Christians collectively in 1 Peter 2:9 ("you are a royal priesthood"). But whereas in 1 Peter the collective term *hierateuma* ("priesthood") is used, in Revelation the individual title *hiereus* ("priest") is found. Every believer is a priest in his or her own right, but collectively they are a kingdom. Christ is the king (Rev 9:11; 15:3; 17:4; 19:16), and the people over whom he rules are a kingdom of priests (Rev 1:6, 9; 5:10; 11:15; 12:10). Revelation also depicts the Christian community as a temple (*naos*, Rev 3:12; 11:1-2) and as a city (*polis*, Rev 3:12; 11:3; 20:9; 21:2, 22; 22:19)—a city that is opposed by another city, the embodiment of evil (Rev 11:8; 14:8; 16:19).

As is true in Hebrews, the author of Revelation identifies the Christian community typologically with historic Israel. It is the Christian community who is taking part in the second exodus, who have been redeemed from slavery* by the death of the Lamb* and are now enjoying the blessings of the new covenant; and it is the enemies of this community who fall under the judgment* of God as he sends plagues on them (Rev 12:1—14:20). In Revelation 7 the Christian community is equated symbolically with historic Israel, having assumed its identity. In the first vision* (Rev 7:1-8) the 144,000, identified as "the servants of our God" (Rev 7:3), are God's new covenant people, the suffering church of the first century. In the second vision (Rev 7:9-17) the "great multitude that no one could number" are the same group at the climax of world history.

Particularly important for determining the ecclesiology of the John the Seer is the final vision given in Revelation 21:1—22:22. This speaks amid a confusing number of visual images of the future that is promised to the church. It is described as the new creation* (Rev 21:1), the new Jerusalem (Rev 21:2), the new temple (Rev 21:3a), the new covenant community (Rev 21:3b) and the new Israel (Rev 21:4). This vision proclaims that what is true now will be perfected and revealed for all to see when the Lamb returns in victory. At present the church is the believing community on earth, which has a triumphant counterpart in heaven made up of angels and those who have been martyred (Rev 8:3-4; *see* Martyrdom). The final vision speaks of the merging into one of these two worshiping communities.

Viewing the church as a worshiping community is another special characteristic of the ecclesiology of Revelation. The term *worship** *(proskyneō)* is used twenty-four times; word pictures of worship in heaven are common and vivid (cf. Rev 4), and liturgical refrains appear frequently (Rev 4:11; 5:9-13; 7:9-17; 11:15-18; 12:10-12; 15:3-4; 16:5-7; 19:1-8). On earth there are two options. One can either "worship" the beast (Rev 9:20; 13:4, 8, 12, 15; 16:2; 19:20) or worship God and the Lamb (Rev 11:1; 14:7; 15:4).

8. Apostolic Fathers.

8.1. The Didache.
In the *Didache** the church is primarily the whole Christian community on earth. The attributes "one" and "holy" are particularly stressed. In *Didache* 9 the coming together of believers to celebrate the Eucharist is seen as pointing to the unity of all Christians. As one of the prayers* puts it: "As the broken bread was scattered on the mountains, and then when gathered, became one, so let your church be gathered from the ends of the earth into your kingdom" (*Did.* 9.4). And similarly: "Remember, Lord, your church, deliver it from all evil and make it perfect in your love, and from the four winds gather it together in holiness to your kingdom which you have prepared for it" (*Did.* 10.5). Besides using the word *ekklēsia* of all Christians the author also uses it once of believers "in assembly" (*Did.* 4.14; cf. 1 Cor 11:18; 14:19, 28, 34, 35). He says confession of sin is to be made "in church."

8.2. 1 Clement.
The inscription of this epistle immediately reveals that Clement (*see* Clement of Rome) saw the church as a universal reality that was located in specific places such as Rome and Corinth. He writes from "The church *(ekklēsia)* of God which sojourns in Rome to the church of God which sojourns in Corinth." The latter is equated with "those who are called and sanctified by the will of God." In both cases the church *(ekklēsia)* refers to all the Christians in each of these two cities (*1 Clem.* 44.3) who would have met in a number of homes as separate congregations (see Maier). H. O. Maier argues that the divisions at Corinth may have origi-

nated in disputes between house church groups.

One of Clement's favored designations for the whole Christian community is "the elect of God" (*1 Clem.* 2.4; 6.1; 6.3, 4, 8; 49.5). He also calls them "the flock of Christ" (*1 Clem.* 16.1; 44.3; 54.2; 57.2), "the whole brotherhood" *(pasēs tēs adelphotētos, 1 Clem.* 2.4; cf. 1 Pet 2:17; 5:9) and "the people" of God (*ho laos, 1 Clem.* 59.4; 64.1). Clement clearly considers Christians to be the new Israel (*1 Clem.* 29.1-3) and therefore consistently sees the OT typologically addressing the church. However, as it is the matter of "order" (*taxis;* the *tax-* word group is found forty-two times) that concerns Clement the most, titles and metaphors that emphasise the structured nature of the Christian community are to the fore.

Clement uses the metaphor of the city-state in a distinctive way in defining the church. He calls Christians "citizens *(politeia)* of the city of God" (*1 Clem.* 54.4), and he views disturbances in the church as a political uprising (*statis, 1 Clem.* 1.1; 2.6; 3.2). Thus he praises the Corinthians for being "virtuous and honorable citizens" (*1 Clem.* 2.8) before "the worthless rose up against those who were in honor," thereby undermining "their citizenship" (*1 Clem.* 3.4; cf. *1 Clem.* 6.1; 21.1). Clement also likens the church to an army, calling those who lead "our generals" (*1 Clem.* 37.1-3).

It is within this framework of thought that Clement's two passages outlining the traditional household order (*see* Household Codes) and his concern that appointed office bearers be recognized and obeyed should be understood. In the extended household communities that constituted the basis of the individual congregations, respect for the traditional order is to prevail (*1 Clem.* 1.3; 21.6-8). Those who have been appointed as leaders should be the ones who rule (*1 Clem.* 1.3; 21.6; 42.4; 54.2). In his zeal to uphold order Clement introduces the idea that church leaders are the counterpart of the OT priests and Levites, who may be contrasted with ordinary church members, whom he calls "the laity" (*ho laikos, 1 Clem.* 40.5). For the first time the one people of God is divided into two distinct groups. The clergy-laity distinction, which has had such fateful consequences on the life of the church, developed on this basis. Finally we mention that unity in the Christian community is of fundamental importance to Clement. He writes primarily to restore and to foster "peace and concord" in the community at Corinth (*1 Clem.* 63.2; 65.1) and in the whole Christian community on earth (*1 Clem.* 64).

8.3. Ignatius. Ignatius* develops the doctrine of the church in three ways in advance of anything seen so far. He exalts the church by viewing it as an entity above world history, makes the order of the church essential to its being and insists on unity centred in the bishop. Ignatius is completely negative about Israel. For him the teachings and myths of Judaism* are "old" (Ign. *Magn.* 9.1; 10.2), a term he uses to describe what is opposed to God (Ign. *Eph.* 19.3). Writing to the Magnesians, he sets in opposition living "according to Judaism" and living according to grace (Ign. *Magn.* 8.1; cf. Ign. *Magn.* 9.1). The OT prophets are radically Christianized being depicted as believers in and proclaimers of Christ who were persecuted by the Jews for this reason (Ign. *Magn.* 8.2; 9.2; Ign. *Phld.* 5.2; 9.1-2).

In the opening paragraph of his epistle to the Ephesians Ignatius describes the church (*ekklēsia*) as "being foreordained before the ages, to be ever destined for enduring and unchanging glory." The language is close to that of Paul's epistle to the Ephesians, in which Christians collectively are said to be chosen in Christ before the foundation of the world* (Eph 1:4). But Ignatius goes beyond Paul in making the church a reality apart from its historical manifestation. Later Ignatius speaks of God "breathing incorruptibility on the church" (Ign. *Eph.* 17.1). This also is something with no parallel in the NT.

It is in the Ignatian epistles that the threefold order of bishop, presbyters and deacons is found for the first time, although all three titles appear in the Pastoral Epistles. But it is not just that the threefold order appears. Ignatius insists that without these three there is no church. He says emphatically, "Nothing can be called a church without these" (Ign. *Trall.* 3.1). In this order the bishop is to be "regarded as the Lord himself" (Ign. *Eph.* 6.1; Ign. *Trall.* 2.1); "nothing is to be done without the bishop" (Ign. *Trall.* 2.2; Ign. *Smyrn.* 8.1; 9.1); and especially no Eucharist is to be celebrated without him (Ign. *Smyrn.* 8.2; Ign. *Phld.* 4.1) or his appointed representative if he is not present (Ign. *Smyrn.* 8.2). It is, however, to be noted that the modern threefold order (known, for example, in the Roman Catholic and Anglican churches) does not parallel the Ignatian order. For Ignatius the bishop is the leader of a citywide church, the presbyters are a pastoral council that advises the bishop, and the deacons (also in the plural) assist the bishop. Neither the bishop nor the presbyters are considered to be priests, and there is no mention of the ordination of anyone in these letters.

Many scholars consider the concern for the unity of the church to be the most important theme in the Ignatian letters. The words *unity* (*henotēs*) and *union* (*henōsis*) are used repeatedly to describe the given solidarity of the Christian community (the indicative) for which it must strive (the imperative) (Ign. *Eph.* 4.2; 5.1; Ign. *Phld.* 2.2; 3.2; 8.1; Ign. *Magn.* 1.2). In the context of speaking about the unity of all Christians on earth, Ignatius says believers, whether Jews or Gentiles, are united "in one body of his church" (Ign. *Smyrn.* 1.2). The body metaphor hovers in the background in two other passages, *Ephesians* 4.2 and *Trallians* 11.2.

Like Luke and Paul, Ignatius uses the word *ekklēsia* of a localized community of believers (e.g., the church in Smyrna or the church in Magnesia) and in the plural when he speaks of more than one of these communities (Ign. *Magn.* 1.2; Ign. *Phld.* 10.2; Ign. *Pol.* 8.1) or of the entire Christian community on earth (Ign. *Eph.* inscr 5.1; 17.1; Ign. *Smyrn.* 1.2; Ign. *Pol.* 5.1). In this last category Ignatius uses for the first time the expression "the catholic church" (*hē katholikē ekklēsia,* Ign. *Smyrn.* 8.2). This is contrasted with any particular congregation (*to plēthos*), probably to be understood as a group that met in a particular home. Following W. R. Schoedel (243), the word *katholikē* ("catholic") is taken here to mean the whole church, which cannot be divided. Just once Ignatius uses the word *synagōgē* for a gathering of Christians (Ign. *Pol.* 4.2).

8.4. Epistle of Barnabas. This theological treatise is divided into two parts. In *Barnabas* 1—17 (*see* Barnabas, Epistle of) the author argues that the Christian community has now replaced Israel as the people of God. In *Barnabas* 18—21 he outlines what he thinks his readers need to know of the Christian ethic. He reads the OT allegorically and typologically as a book intended for Christians from the beginning. In a hitherto unused expression he calls the Christian community "the new people of God" (*ton laon ton kainon, Barn.* 5.7; 7.5). He also speaks of the covenant offered to the historic people of God, Israel, now being given to the church, the new people of God (*Barn.* 13.6; 14.1-9). But it is not just that Christians have inherited the promises once given to Israel. Judaism is rejected. A strong anti-Jewish tone pervades this work. The word *ekklēsia* is used twice (*Barn.* 6.16; 7.11). In the second instance it clearly alludes to all Christians on earth who are the beneficiaries of the atoning work of Christ, and this probably is so also in the first instance, where it is found in a quote from Psalm 22:22. The most important metaphor for the church in the epistle of Barnabas is the "spiritual temple," which is understood to replace the old temple made with hands (*Barn.* 4.11; 6.15; 16.1-10).

8.5. Shepherd of Hermas. In this speculative and difficult treatise (*see* Hermas, Shepherd of) the church is depicted as the primal creation of God, hence seen as an old woman (*Herm. Vis.* 2.4.1; cf. *Herm. Vis.* 1.1.4-6). Everything was created for her. The background of this thought is the Jewish apocalyptic tradition in which eschatological realities are assumed to be preexistent in heaven (*see* Preexistence). In 4 Esdras everything is created for Israel, who is seen as an old woman (4 Esdr 7:11; 9:45—10:1). In subsequent visions the old woman becomes progressively younger, until she is radiant with beauty (*Herm Vis.* 3.10-13). In a later vision she is presented as a bride dressed in white (*Herm. Vis.* 4.2.1-2).

More common, however, is the image of the church as a tower (*Herm. Vis.* 3.3.3—4.1; *Herm. Sim.* 8.7.5; 8.8.2; 9.1.2; 9.13.1). In using this image the thought of the church being built (*oikodomein*) naturally follows. This Greek word and the related words *oikodomē* ("building") and *oikos* ("house") are repeatedly applied to the Christian community. Three times Hermas calls the church "the house of God" (*Herm. Sim.* 9.13.9; 9.14.1). The frequency of this terminology probably reflects the house setting of congregational life lying behind Hermas's comments. Hermas also speaks of "his [God's] holy church" (*Herm. Vis.* 1.1.6; 1.3.6; 4.1.3; cf. *Herm. Sim.* 9.18.3). This church is gathered from all the peoples of the world to become "one body" (*Herm. Sim.* 9.17.5; cf. *Herm. Sim.* 9.13.5; 9.18.4). It is the people of God designated as *ho laos* (*Herm. Sim.* 5.5.2-3; 5.6.2-3; 8.1.2, 5).

8.6. 2 Clement, the Epistle to Diognetus and Justin Martyr. 2 Clement also depicts the church as preexistent (*2 Clem.* 14.1-3; cf. *2 Clem.* 2.1) but adds a number of elements to this idea. Only those who are obedient (*see* Obedience) to the Father belong to this transcendent church, called "the first church, the spiritual one," "the church of life" (*2 Clem.* 14.1) and "the living church, the body of Christ" (*2 Clem.* 14.2). This is contrasted with "my house," the empirical church, which has become "a den of robbers" (*2 Clem.* 14.1). The concept of a visible and invisible church appears in this language. Following these comments, 2 Clement then declares that "the male is Christ and the female is the church" (*2 Clem.* 14.2). In suggesting a preexistent marriage of Christ and the church, *2 Clement* closely parallels Valentinian Gnosticism (Irenaeus *Adv. Haer.* 1.18.2). Like the *Epistle of Barnabas*, 2 Clement consistently takes the OT to speak of the church. It is a Christian book. Thus he says the prophets spoke "of us" and of "our church" (*2 Clem.* 2.1).

The *Epistle to Diognetus* likens "Christians in the world" to "what the soul is to the body" (*Diogn.* 6.1), calling them a "new race" (*kainos genos*) distinct from Jews and Gentiles (*Diogn.* 1.1). The author is dismissive of Judaism, arguing that Jewish worship, sabbath keeping and food* restrictions are "quite wrong" (*Diogn.* 3—4). In the *Preaching of Peter* and in subsequent texts (e.g., Tertullian *Ad Nat.* 1.8) this "new race" becomes "a third race" (*tritos genos*), or in Latin a *tertium genus.*

In his *Dialogue with Trypho,* a Jew, Justin Martyr argues that the old covenant and its precepts have been fulfilled and superseded in Christ; Jesus as the Logos is God's "firstborn" who appeared in OT times in theophanies; the church, now made up mostly of Gentiles, has become Israel. The thought that Christians are the new Israel is definitive for Justin's ecclesiology. The Jewish law is abrogated (Justin *Dial. Tryph.* 11; 12); Jews need "a second circumcision" (Justin *Dial. Tryph.* 12.3; *see* Circumcision); the prophetic ministry has been "transferred" to the church (Justin *Dial. Tryph.* 82.1) and Christian sacrifices are "better" than Jewish sacrifices (Justin *Dial. Tryph.* 29.1; 117.1). The covenant that was once "theirs" is now "ours" (Justin *Dial. Tryph.* 4.4-8; cf. *Dial. Tryph.* 6.9).

When eventually Trypho asks, "Are you [Christians] Israel?" (Justin *Dial. Tryph.* 123.7) Justin answers, "we . . . are . . . both called and in fact are Jacob and Israel and Judah and

Joseph and David, and true children of God" (Justin *Dial. Tryph.* 123.9). A little later he argues that as Isaiah calls Christ "Israel and Jacob," we Christians coming from "the bowels of Christ" are "the true Israelite race" (*Israēlitikon to alēthinon esmen genos,* Justin *Dial. Tryph.* 135.3). For Justin spiritual descent from Jacob is more significant than from Abraham.* Christians are a "race" that has taken the place of the Jewish "race." In the context of this argument Justin introduces a new usage of the words *ekklēsia* and *synagoge.* In *Dialogue* 134.3 these words stand for Christianity and Judaism respectively. In Justin we see the starkest expression of the thought that Christianity has taken the place of Israel.

See also CHURCH AS ISRAEL, PEOPLE OF GOD; CHURCH ORDER, GOVERNMENT; WORSHIP AND LITURGY.

BIBLIOGRAPHY. B. Blue, "Acts and the House Church" in *The Book of Acts in Its First-Century Setting,* 2: *Graeco-Roman Setting,* ed. D. W. J. Gill and C. Gempf (Grand Rapids: Eerdmans, 1994) 119-89; B. Bowe, *A Church in Crisis: Ecclesiology and Paraenesis in Clement of Rome* (Minneapolis: Fortress, 1988); R. E. Brown, *The Churches the Apostles Left Behind* (London: Chapman, 1984); N. Brox, *Der Hirt des Hermas* (Gottingen: Vandenhoeck & Ruprecht, 1991); H. J. Cadbury, "Names for Christianity and Christians in Acts" in *The Beginnings of Christianity,* ed. F. J. Foakes-Jackson and K. Lake (5 vols.; London: Macmillan, 1927) 5:375-92; J. Daniélou, *The Theology of Jewish Christianity* (London: Darton, Longman & Todd, 1964); K. P. Donfried, *The Setting of Second Clement in Early Christianity* (Leiden: E. J. Brill, 1974); K. N. Giles, *Patterns of Ministry Among the First Christians* (Australia: Collins-Dove, 1989); idem, *What on Earth Is the Church? A Biblical and Theological Inquiry* (Melbourne, Australia: Harper-Collins; London: SPCK; Downers Grove, IL: InterVarsity Press, 1995); A. von Harnack, "The Names of Christian Believers" in *The Mission and Expansion of Christianity* (Gloucester, MA: Peter Smith, 1972 repr.) 399-418; E. G. Jay, *The Church: Its Changing Image Through Twenty Centuries,* 1: *The First Seventeen Centuries* (London: SPCK, 1977); H. C. Kee, *Who Are the People of God? Early Christian Models of Community* (New Haven, CT: Yale University Press, 1995); M. Leutzsch, *Die Wahrnehmung Sozialer Wirklichkeit im Hirten des Hermas* (Göttingen: Vandenhoeck & Ruprecht, 1989); H. O. Maier,

The Social Setting of the Ministry as Reflected in the Writings of Hermas, Clement and Ignatius (Waterloo, ON: Wilfrid Laurier University Press, 1991); L. Pernveden, *The Concept of the Church in the Shepherd of Hermas* (Lund: Gleerup, 1966); D. Ravens, *Luke and the Restoration of Israel* (Sheffield: Sheffield Academic Press, 1995); W. R. Schoedel, *Ignatius of Antioch* (Herm; Philadelphia: Fortress, 1985); M. Turner, *Power from on High: The Spirit of Prophecy in Luke-Acts* (JPTSup 9; Sheffield: Sheffield Academic Press, 1996).

K. N. Giles

CHURCH AS ISRAEL, PEOPLE OF GOD

1. *Ekklēsia* and Synagōgē, Church and Synagogue, in the New Testament
2. The Relation of the Church to Israel
3. Membership in the *Ekklēsia* and Abrahamic Descent
4. *Ekklēsia* and *Laos:* Church as People of God
5. Christ, Church and Israel
6. The Church as Israel, People of God in the Post-New Testament Period
7. Christ, Church and Israel Today: Theological Reflections

1. *Ekklēsia* and *Synagōgē,* Church and Synagogue, in the New Testament.
The Greek term *ekklēsia* is primarily a political term and refers to any assembly of citizens duly summoned by the herald. It is also used along with a number of other Greek terms, such as *synagōgē* and *syllogos,* for the meetings of various Greek voluntary associations. These groups often met in private houses, as did Jewish assemblies (synagogues) and early Christian assemblies (*ekklēsiai*). Matthew is the only Gospel writer to use the term *ekklēsia.* If Matthew has drawn the term from the Septuagint (where it is used of the assembly of Israelites, e.g., Deut 31:30, and very often translates the Hebrew *qāhāl*), he has used a familiar Greek term for the people of Israel, and this may indicate that he sees his and Jesus' group not as a new or different assembly. However, *ekklēsia* is frequently thought of as a Christian technical term for a clearly Christian institution (*see* Church), sharply differentiated from Judaism.*

This understanding possibly derives from the frequent use of the term by Paul as a designation of the Christian assembly. Since Paul's communities are in the Diaspora* regions outside of Israel and are socially distinct from though not unrelated to the Jewish assemblies, being comprised primarily of Gentiles,* it is easy to see how the Pauline pattern has tended to be the lens through which other more ambiguous evidence is viewed, usually in strong contrast to the synagogue.* Thus there is much debate as to whether Luke in Acts* intends the *ekklēsia* to be polemically contrasted with the Jewish synagogue, as also in relation to whether or not he holds a positive outlook on Israel's future. When Luke wishes to refer to the Jewish assembly of believers in Jerusalem,* he uses *ekklēsia* (Acts 5:11; 8:1), and the same term is also used for the Jewish/Gentile group in Antioch* (Acts 13:1) and Paul's Gentile communities in the Diaspora (Acts 14:23; 16:5). A. J. Saldarini says that "at a minimum, the author of Luke-Acts sees the *ekklēsiai* as different from and in tension with Jewish communities, yet also as outgrowths of that same group" (Saldarini, 118). It would seem legitimate to hold that an element of continuity with Israel is being maintained while simultaneously avoiding the closer identification that synagogue might imply.

Paul can refer to "all the churches of the Gentiles" (Rom 16:4) and also to "the churches of Christ in Judea" (Gal 1:22). Even the reference to a "synagogue of Satan" (Rev 2:9) need not imply a polemical contrast between church and synagogue as such. It would be wrong to assume that all *ekklēsiai* everywhere have no links with and no connection whatsoever with Judaism. "All the assemblies of the Gentiles" (Rom 16:4) is an interesting reference, suggesting that Paul recognizes the existence of assemblies that were non-Gentile. When this is set alongside the address to the seven *ekklēsiai* in Revelation 2—3, a more diverse picture emerges. Those whom John perceives as deviants in the churches at Smyrna and Philadelphia are apparently calling themselves Jews but are not. These deviants among the true church members are designated "a synagogue of Satan." However, it would be erroneous to see here simply an implied contrast between a Jewish synagogue and a Christian *ekklēsia*, since the charge that the Jewish communities are not truly Jewish implies the corresponding claim that the *ekklēsiai* themselves truly affirm Judaism. In any case *ekklēsia* and *synagōgē* are both Greek words for an assembly and cannot be naively contrasted as if one were exclusively

Christian and the other exclusively Jewish. Luke can still use *ekklēsia* in a completely profane sense (Acts 19:32-41).

In the first century in both Jewish and Christian literature both words were used to describe a variety of gatherings. Saldarini concludes that "neither Christian nor Jewish meaning nor any fixed content can be assigned to the word *ekklēsia* without detailed argument from context" (Saldarini, 118). This is borne out by the fact that James* uses *ekklēsia* and *synagōgē* interchangeably (Jas 2:2; 5:14) and by Ignatius's designation of a Christian gathering as a synagogue (Ign. *Pol.* 4.2).

An example of the fluid situation we have described is found in Matthew's use of *ekklēsia* in Matthew 16 and Matthew 18, instances unique to this Gospel. It might have been expected that Matthew, being a very Jewish Gospel, would have used the word *synagōgē*. But since he chose *ekklēsia*, was he thus distancing and distinguishing his group from the wider community of Jews who rejected the message of Jesus? Even if it is accepted that Matthew deliberately avoided using the term *synagōgē*, this must not be taken to mean that he was rejecting Judaism or that he no longer regarded his group as Jewish. He must have known of the existence of other groups, such as the Pauline congregations, who were already using the term *ekklēsia*, and that these, despite the common terminology, were demonstrably different from his group of *ekklēsiai*. This underlines the need to avoid giving a fixed content to *ekklēsia*, especially in the earlier period.

2. The Relation of the Church to Israel.

2.1. Ephesians. It will be useful at this point to outline Paul's view of Israel (*see DPL*, Israel). Paul was deeply conscious of Israel's unique heritage. Yet this presented him with a real dilemma because Israel, beloved of God* because of the patriarchs (*see* Ancestors), is presently rejecting the gospel. Paul is clearly aware that the Israel of God is not coextensive with empirical Israel. Yet he does not seek a solution in which Israel's privileges are transferred to Gentiles. The latter are included not by displacing Israel but by being allowed to share in the richness of Israel's "olive tree." They will thus contribute in some degree to the future salvation* of "all Israel" (Rom 11:25-26). Paul does not designate the new entity as Israel; the term retains its reference to empirical Israel.

There is much disagreement among scholars as to the authorship of Ephesians but not on its designation as part of the Pauline school (see Pauline Legacy and School; Pseudepigraphy). As such it will provide a fitting link between the Pauline letters and the post-Pauline era. M. Barth regarded Ephesians 2 as the climax of a development in Paul's theology moving away from the ideas of Galatians through Romans and culminating in Ephesians. For Barth Ephesians 2 is crucial as it prevents scholars from playing Romans and Galatians off against one another. Barth's laudable intention was to secure Paul's teaching in Romans and Ephesians as the firm ground from which to oppose all anti-Semitism in the church. Barth maintained that Ephesians speaks of a single people of God, of the citizenship of Israel into which Gentiles have been accepted by their being grafted into the people of Israel.

A. T. Lincoln has responded to the preceding view of the relation of the church to Israel, maintaining that in Ephesians the church is decisively new, and he proposes a reversal of Pauline development as Barth had conceived it. He proposes a movement from the stress on discontinuity in Galatians, through a greater stress on continuity and a future role for Israel in the context of pressing contemporary issues about the relation of Jews and Gentiles in Romans, to a return to more stress on discontinuity in Ephesians. There are valid insights in the views of both scholars, but rather than opt for one monochrome view of the relation of the church to Israel throughout the NT, the discussion should remind us that the NT writers were addressing widely varying contexts and that this diversity must be reflected in their understanding of the relation of the new communities to the old in any specific location at a particular time. Primarily we should be ascertaining the perspective of each individual letter before proceeding to the subsequent theological task of investigating their relation to one another and whether or not it may be possible to discover or develop a coherent understanding from them.

2.2. Matthew's Community. In regard to the decades that saw the publication of the Synoptic Gospels, Matthew's references to Israel are mainly what we would expect of a Jewish-oriented group in conflict with fellow Jews about the nature and identity of their common inheritance (see Matthean Community). Of the twelve explicit references, none are pejorative and most are neutral or positive concerning the historic people or the land.* Two references in Matthew 8—9 stress the exceptional nature of individual Gentiles' faith, beyond that to be found in Israel. This is clearly pointing to present or envisaged Gentile members in Matthew's group of churches, but we should not read too much into it as if Gentile inclusion necessitates Jewish exclusion.

It is significant, however, that the imagery of shepherd* and sheep occurs three times (Mt 2:6; 10:6; 15:24) and that in the latter two of these the emphasis upon a mission to the lost sheep of the house of Israel is reiterated. It cannot be said of Matthew that he was unaware of the unique place of Israel in salvation history. The story of the Canaanite woman lends added support (Mt 15:21-28). Jesus says, "It is not fair to take the children's food and throw it to the dogs" (Mt 15:26). It would appear therefore that Matthew is very aware that the mission of Jesus had its starting point with Israel and that a Gentile mission* is both subsequent to and dependant upon a prior mission to Israel.

But despite his severely critical stance against the Pharisees and the leaders of the people, Matthew is not entirely pessimistic. The crowds are still seen as potential converts, and a mission to Israel will continue. Gundry (194-95) suggests this will continue "until the Son of Man comes" (Mt 10:23). There seems to be no clear evidence in Matthew that asserts that Israel is beyond redemption.* Almost all claims to the contrary are heavily dependant on parables, the interpretation of which is by definition flexible, and their interpretation is frequently controlled by the assumptions one brings to the text. Saldarini offers a useful summary of Matthew in this respect. He maintains that when we look closely at Matthew's terms for the people of Israel and their narrative role in relationship to Jesus (and the Matthean community), it seems clear that he sees himself and his group as still part of Israel and that he hopes to attract members of the larger Jewish community to his form of Judaism, just as Jesus did (Saldarini, 195).

The reasons why Matthew's attitude to Israel has been seen to be more hostile (than we think is warranted) are several. First, interpreters have failed to distinguish between the leaders and the people in general. The definitive rejection of Jesus by the former merits extreme condemnation, but Matthew never states or implies that the nation as a whole has rejected Jesus. Second, the presentation of various non-Jews and the Great Commission to disciple all nations (Mt 28:19) have erroneously suggested to some that Matthew's interest in Gentile mission requires the cessation of mission to Jews. Third, the clear statement in Matthew 21:43 that the leaders of the Jews will be replaced by a new group (ethnos) who will produce the fruits of the kingdom (see Kingdom of God) has led to theories of the Jews being displaced by the Gentile nations. But it should be noted that Matthew uses ethnos rather than laos, the normal word to designate God's people, and that we should not read theology into general terms that cannot sustain this imposition. At most what can be claimed in this instance is the displacement of a corrupt leadership that was to a great extent responsible for the disaster soon to befall the nation in the advent of the Jewish-Roman war.

The extreme forms of denunciation Matthew employs are frequently viewed as clear evidence of Matthew's permanent alienation from pharisaic Judaism. Sociological insights, however, enable a differing understanding of such language. The sharpest denunciation is often used within the family; family conflicts are often the most extreme, and the closer the relationship has previously been, the greater the distancing that results. But this outcome may not be final, nor need it imply that all future contact is rendered either futile or impossible. It seems best therefore to regard Matthew's groups as perceived deviants who are not content with this portrayal but who hope to win the majority of Jews to their convictions.

2.3. Luke-Acts. Although Luke never uses the term *ekklēsia* in his Gospel, it occurs very frequently in Acts. It is to be expected that Luke knew and appreciated Paul's view of Israel, and a comparison between the two may enable us to identify those significant elements they held in common. Like Paul, Luke is careful to limit the use of the term *Israel* to empirical Israel: there remains a clear and abiding distinction between the historic people of God and even believing Gentiles. In Acts, Israel continues to refer to the Jewish people, whether repentant or rejecting the gospel. In Luke's presentation the gospel message has divided the nation (cf. Acts 28:24-25), but both the whole and the two resultant parts can still singly or together be described by the privileged title. While "Israel" can refer to the repentant part of empirical Israel, it does not refer to a church of Jews and Gentiles; nor is the early-catholic view of the church as a *tertium genus*, a third race, present in Luke (see Early Catholicism). Even the references to "seed of Abraham" and its equivalents do not refer to Christ or the church but only to Israel and to Israelites (Lk 1:55; Acts 7:5-6; 13:23). What is even more surprising is that in Acts, Christian missionaries continue to address Jews as "brothers," and "men of Israel" are addressed separately from "you that fear God" (Acts 13:16). Gentiles are not addressed as brothers (Acts 2:28; 3:7; 7:2; 13:26; 22:1).

Luke's intention seems to be to secure the advent of salvation for Gentiles by demonstrating that the nation of Israel has truly heard the gospel and that a substantial number of the most devout have accepted it (e.g., Lk 1:54, 68; 2:41; 4:4). Only in this way is there good news for Gentiles; for the first time, as Gentiles, through the operation of the Holy Spirit* they are called to share in the salvation that was promised through Israel (Acts 10:47). Initially the gospel must come to Gentiles via Israel and not just via Christ, because the continuity of salvation history does not lie exclusively in the history of Jesus but also in the people who represent Israel. Thus Luke insists that it is in and through the Jewish Christians,* who formed the nucleus of the apostolic church, that the unity and continuity of salvation history are maintained and the gospel guaranteed to Gentiles (Lk 13:16-17). Only when the gospel had been accepted by the earliest Jewish believers, the *Urgemeinde* in Jerusalem, could the transition take place via these believing Jews to a predominantly Gentile church. Moreover, it is important for Luke to show that the Christian church is part of Israel, since it is in and through them that the unity and continuity of salvation history are maintained (Jervell 1972, 68).

2.4. Other New Testament Witnesses. In Mark's Gospel we find only two references to Israel, and in John's Gospel we find four. Of the three references in Hebrews,* two are citations of the new covenant* text of Jeremiah 31:31, and the other looks back to the exodus. Of the three occurrences of Israel in Revelation (see Revelation, Book of), two relate to the twelve tribes of Israel and one to the people of Israel. Although the terminology refers to the tribes of Israel, it is likely that it is the church from every tribe and nation that the writer has primarily in view. In Revelation 10:11, peoples, nations and tongues are not clearly distinguished, making it difficult to maintain that there was a clear-cut distinction between *laos* and *ethnos*. In the case of the Gospel of John, the infrequency of reference to the term *Israel* may be due to the fact that he refers to "the Jews" more than seventy times.

It is not possible to discuss this issue adequately here, but as we have already noted in relation to Abrahamic descent, there developed an increasing alienation between the new Christian groups and the Jewish people, especially their leaders. This was accentuated by the fact that Jewish believers were expelled or at least forced from the synagogues. They felt bereft, like orphans (cf. Jn 14:18), and John responded by arguing that such actions proved that "the Jews" were no longer God's children. It is clear from the Gospel itself that John is aware of and capable of making distinctions among "the Jews." John can refer to believing Jews (Jn 8:31; 11:45; 12:11), Jesus does not object to being called a Jew (Jn 4:9), and salvation is "of the Jews" (*ek tōn Ioudaiōn,* Jn 4:22). But there is no doubt that his undifferentiated use of the description has contributed greatly to the common Christian tendency to dismiss the Jews as unworthy of any future role in the divine purpose.

It seems that for John the distinction between Israelite and Jew was not significant. John does not appear to have developed any precise understanding of believers as the new people of God, in place of the Jews. Painter (108-9) suggests that the reason for this is that John's attention is focused elsewhere: his emphasis is christocentric*; it is Jesus who is the true vine; and by implication Israel is the false vine. But John does not equate the Jewish believers with the new or true Israel, since Christ himself is the vine, and those who abide in him share his status. There is now the possibility for all to share in the vine through faith, but unlike Paul, John does not give us an image of an olive with some branches broken off and some abiding. There is little self-conscious ecclesiology in John, and when he does refer to the community, it is in relation to Jesus. Nothing is indicated about the status of believers by John's use of *laos* or Israel. If there is a word symbol for the believing community in John, it would be *poimē* ("flock") under the guidance of the shepherd whose word they obey.

The changes we have noted in John's Gospel demonstrate that in later NT times, in some areas at least, a growing rift was developing between the followers of Jesus and Jews who were hostile to the gospel; this was beginning to produce opposing self-definitions and frequent recriminations. It is in such circumstances that the stereotyping of the Jews in toto as reprobate had its genesis (*see* Christianity and Judaism).

3. Membership in the *Ekklēsia* and Abrahamic Descent.

By way of introduction to this section, it will be useful to recall Paul's stress on this theme in Galatians and Romans. In Galatians Paul argues that Gentiles are blessed with Abraham* through Christ, the one seed (*sperma*) of Abraham, and not on the basis of circumcision* or any form of judaization. In Romans Paul presents Abraham as the inclusive "father of all the faithful" of the two peoples, Jews and Gentiles. Abraham is the unique recipient of the promise,* which included Gentiles, and the prototype of all believers who hear with faith.* Paul distinguishes three kinds of descendants of Abraham: those who are descendants both according to flesh* and according to faith; those who are descendants according to faith alone; and those who are descendants according to flesh alone (Siker, 60-61). What is new in Romans is Paul's assertion that Gentile inclusion does not come at the expense of Jewish exclusion and of God's faithfulness. In the analogy of the olive tree, the Gentiles are represented not as self-supporting branches but as dependent on the stem of Abraham.

3.1. Matthew's Community. Abraham, somewhat surprisingly, plays a rather limited role in Matthew, appearing in only four passages corresponding to the Lukan parallels. Luke, by comparison, refers to Abraham more frequently, having five passages not paralleled in Matthew. The first reference in Matthew comes in the first verse, where Jesus' genealogy starts by designating him a "son of Abraham" (*hyios Abraam*), denoting at the outset Jesus' continuity with the bearer of the promise. Descent from Abraham alone, however, is not stressed so much as descent from David, and a favorite title for Jesus in Matthew is the messianic "Son of David."

The second reference to Abraham is from John the Baptist, who warns the Pharisees and Sadducees to produce fruit that befits repentance* rather than saying "we have Abraham as our father." The warning is that it is not enough to rely on one's Jewish ancestry; descent from Abraham is of itself not sufficient, since God is able to raise up children to Abraham *(tekna tō Abraam)* from stones (Mt 3:7-10). Thus the reference to Abraham somewhat relativizes Jewish birth and at the same time hints that God is not tied exclusively to his historic people.

In the story of Jesus and the Gentile centurion (Mt 8:5-13), Matthew has Jesus express surprise at the great faith of this Gentile and then contrast it with the response of Jews: "Not even in Israel have I found such faith" (Mt 8:10). This is followed by a saying to the effect that many from the east and the west (probably Gentiles) will come to sit down at table with Abraham, Isaac and Jacob in the kingdom of heaven. In this story Matthew retains his Jewish tradition to some extent: there is surprise at Gentile faith, and the guests sit at table with the patriarchs. Significantly, however, both Jesus and Abraham are associated with Gentiles and not with "the sons of the kingdom" (Mt 8:12).

In his fourth section on Abraham, Matthew has Jesus in dispute with the Sadducees about resurrection.* What is noteworthy here is that Abraham is associated with the resurrection of the dead, as was already implied in Matthew 8 (Siker, 86).

3.2. Hebrews. The author of Hebrews refers to Abraham no fewer than ten times. In the most well-known passage (Heb 11:8-19), real continuity with Jewish traditions is predominant in the depiction of Abraham as the model of steadfast faith. He persevered and thus obtained a promise (Heb 3:13-20). The only other significant passage for our purposes is Hebrews 7, in which Abraham enters the stage in a somewhat subsidiary role to the figure of Melchizedek,* on whom attention centers as a type of Christ. In the Genesis narrative Melchizedek blessed Abraham, and the patriarch gave him tithes of all his spoils from his victory over the kings. In Hebrews 7 Abraham is used to assist in elevating the high priesthood* of Jesus, but there is no obvious attempt to decrease his own significance. Abraham was subjected to Melchizedek, whose priestly line Jesus triumphantly fulfills (Wilson, 122). The interest is not so much in

Abraham himself as in his role in the salvation history that culminated in Jesus. But this factor alone is significant in that it implies that Abrahamic descent is not now the crucial indicator it once was. Although Abraham is referred to in James, the use made of the reference is entirely traditional, stressing the unity of faith and works (*see* Faith and Works), with no explicit evidence of Jewish Christian controversy.

3.3. Luke-Acts. Abraham appears in the Magnificat in Luke's first chapter in connection with God's mercy*: "as he spoke to our fathers, to Abraham and to his descendants (*tō spermati autou*) forever" (Lk 1:54-55). The text recalls Isaiah 41:8-9, which refers to "Israel, my servant Jacob whom I chose, seed of Abraham, whom I have helped." God's mercy in the covenant with Abraham has been realized in the birth of Jesus, so that the humble poor may rejoice; similarly in the Benedictus, there is a reference to the "oath which he swore to our father Abraham" (Lk 1:73). Luke thus links the birth of Jesus with the Abrahamic covenant in a very specific way, emphasizing continuity with the bearer of the promise.

In two other passages Abrahamic descent is explicitly discussed. As in the case of Matthew, Luke uses the Q tradition in which Jewish claims to Abrahamic descent are attacked. Luke does not dismiss the significance of such ancestry, but he qualifies the claims that may legitimately be based upon it (Lk 3:8) and further limits Abraham's importance by tracing Jesus' genealogy back to Adam (Lk 3:34). The patriarch is thus given a more universal significance, and Jesus likewise. In Luke 13:10-11 a crippled woman who is healed by Jesus is called by him "a daughter of Abraham," and in Luke 19:9 Zacchaeus is termed "a son of Abraham" (*hyios Abraam*). In these stories as in those previously, the patriarch is associated with the needy and now also with the repentant sinner who makes restitution and gives half of his goods to the poor. In two other stories, Abraham is further associated with the poor: in God's kingdom, (Lk 13:28) with the rich man and Lazarus (Lk 16:19-31) and with the sons of God or of the resurrection (Lk 20:38).

The association of Abraham with the needy and Gentile sinners is fully developed in Acts, where the healing of a blind man happens through the God of Abraham, Isaac and Jacob (Acts 3:1-10); where the Jews, though not the only ones, are the first to be blessed as sons of the covenant (*hyioi tēs diathēkēs,* Acts 3:25). But the covenant with Abraham, far from being a symbol of Jewish exclusivism, becomes in Acts the charter for the inclusion of the Gentiles. For Gentiles, faith in Christ—mediated to them through the blessing of the seed of Abraham (Acts 3:25)—enables the realization of the promise that all the families of the earth would be blessed. It is possible to interpret "in your seed" *(en tō spermati sou)* in Acts 3:25 as referring to Christ, so that Gentiles would be blessed not through and in association with Israel but directly in relation to Christ, without any necessary connection with Israel. The general tenor of Acts, however, gives little support for such a view. The crucial significance of Jerusalem and of the earliest Christian community for Luke go hand in hand with his christological perspective in which Christ is both the fulfillment of the Jewish heritage and simultaneously the mediator of the promises to Gentiles.

3.4. Gospel of John. Only one passage of John's Gospel deals explicitly with Abrahamic descent (Jn 8:31-39). In it, however, there are no fewer than eleven references to him. In John 8:39 some Jews claim in dispute with Jesus that they are descendants of Abraham *(sperma Abraam).* While acknowledging to some extent the validity of the claim, Jesus does not give it the significance his opponents desired because he later denies that God is their father. It is apparent then that John is drawing a distinction between genetic descent and divine paternity. He achieves this by changing the terminology from "descendants" to "children" (of Abraham). He maintains that while the Jews are descendants of Abraham, they are not his children *(tekna Abraam)* but only his seed *(sperma Abraam).* In this way John equates children of Abraham *(tekna Abraam)* with children of God, thus relativizing Abrahamic descent and distinguishing it from children of God *(tekna theou).*

In John's view the works that people do identify their true paternity, and the opposition of the Jews to Jesus demonstrates that Abraham is not their father since they do not do his works. Despite the genetic link, they are in fact children of their father, the devil *(tekna diabolou,* Jn 8:39; *see* Satan). John does give some recognition to physical descent, but he qualifies it to such an extent that he comes close to saying that it is of no real significance. And as for Abraham

himself, not only is he not greater than Jesus, but he becomes instead a witness to Jesus (Jn 8:53). Abraham lived and died, but Jesus claims "before Abraham was, I am." Thus Abraham, like Moses* (Jn 5:46) and Isaiah (Jn 12:41), is subordinated to Jesus, and instead of being Jesus' judge, his greatest virtue is that "he rejoiced to see my day" (Jn 8:56).

4. *Ekklēsia* and *Laos:* Church as People of God.

4.1. Luke-Acts. The term *laos* ("people") occurs more than 140 times in the NT. Although it is used by Matthew, Paul, and the authors of Hebrews and Revelation and appears only occasionally in Mark, John and 1 Peter* (with single examples in Titus, 2 Peter* and Jude*), by far the greatest number of instances are to be found in Luke-Acts, in which Luke uses it more than 80 times. In several places Luke seems to be quite explicitly claiming that the Gentile believers are the new people of God, as for example in Acts 18:10, where he speaks of a great group of people *(laos polys)* in Corinth, or Acts 15:14, where it is asserted that God has planned to take a people out of the Gentile nations and make them his own. In a study of the phrase "a people for his name," N. A. Dahl has noted that it is in these two passages alone that *laos* is apparently used to refer to non-Israelites—the people of Corinth are most likely Gentiles, but here they are being described as potential people of God.

However, when these texts are considered carefully, it becomes clear that neither of them claims that believing Gentiles will be *the* people of God but rather people of God, because the status of Israel as people of God is not questioned. This is in keeping with texts such as Zechariah 2:10-11, where the Gentiles join themselves to a renewed Israel. Luke states only that in addition to those to whom the promises were first entrusted, God has also taken from Gentiles people for his name. The collective "people" without the article is likely to be less misleading because there is no idea here of a people in the sense of a nation or a cultural unit, as if God would choose one nation in preference to another or displace one by the other en bloc.

This does not mean, however, that for Luke *laos* has always the full theological meaning of "the people of God"; he frequently uses it as a synonym for *ochlos,* a crowd of people. On closer inspection, however, this usage is limited to contexts in which the crowd specified is a crowd of Israelites, even if they happen to live among Gentiles (cf. Lk 6:17). It would appear that Luke was careful to limit *laos* only to Israelites and to the land where the *laos* dwell. It never occurs in those narratives that are located outside Palestine if it is not in direct speech and referring to Jews (this includes texts such as Acts 21:30, where the people who rushed together were most likely the Jews from Asia referred to a few verses earlier). The word is missing from the central section of Luke 9:51—18:14, where Jesus is supposed to travel in Samaria.* Luke's usage of *laos* is derived from the Septuagint, both in the specific sense and the more general; he never uses *laos* in a completely profane sense. This is in accordance with his limitation of Israel to the Israelite people and *ethnē* ("nations") to non-Israelites. Luke, despite his emphasis on the influx of believing Gentiles who have become heirs of Israel's hope,* is careful to retain a special understanding of Israel, and though he comes close to it, he never asserts that the church is Israel—he never absolutely identifies the two.

4.2. Other New Testament Witnesses. In many of the places in the NT where *laos* is found, especially in scriptural citations, it refers to empirical Israel or its leaders, whether in the past or the present, without making any comparison or link with the nascent church. Many such examples are to be found in Matthew or Hebrews. In other instances a continuity between Israel and the church is implicit because texts originally relating to Israel are applied to the church for instruction and guidance (e.g., 1 Cor 10:7-8). But in a number of places in the NT, scriptural texts foundational to Israel's election* from among the nations, to become a people dedicated exclusively to Yahweh, are reiterated to confirm the identity of the emergent church (e.g., 1 Pet 2:1-10; Tit 2:14). It would appear that two main functions are being served in this process.

Preeminent is the stress upon the call of God as the creator of his people in accordance with his merciful purposes for the world* (e.g., Rom 9:25-26). This emphasis is designed to denote both continuity with God's previous activity in Israel and confidence in his continuing presence with the communities of believers (e.g., Heb 4:9). Second, the assured destiny of the believing community in times of severe persecution* was strengthened by the use of such texts that offered a secure foundation for hope when earthly realities manifestly denied it (e.g., Rev 1:6; 1 Pet 2:9; both are based upon Exod 19:5-6). In such later NT texts the redemption in Christ* is seen as the eschatological* exodus and the church as the new covenant people of God; this differs somewhat from Paul, despite certain similarities.

Less frequently a resort to texts significant for Israel's origins may indicate fierce competition with Jews who denied the basis of the new communities, who claimed exclusive access to the divine presence and who thus precipitated a comparable response from believers in Jesus. In any discussion of the use of such scriptural texts in the NT, it is essential to consider carefully each citation in the context in which it has been introduced rather than proceed on the basis of a general assumption, such as that the mere use of the OT denotes conflict with Jews and signals their rejection. Jews were not the only opponents or persecutors of the Christian communities. Moreover, these new communities were by no means always looking outward; their attention had necessarily at times to focus on their own identity in order to forge for themselves an appropriate self-understanding. Scriptural texts descriptive of Israel's own origins proved particularly appropriate for the self-definition of an emergent community.

It is also important to recognize development in the ways in which the same texts were used over a period of time as extended as that between Paul's writing his first NT letter and the appearance of a much later text such as the book of Revelation. It is not surprising to discover that polemical intensity increases as the Jewish and Christian communities gradually acquire and even deliberately forge their own distinctive identities. However this later development must not be read back anachronistically into the earliest period when relations were much more fluid and a certain openness and optimism as regards Israel were still feasible.

5. Christ, Church and Israel.

For the majority of the NT writers, the church and Israel are two related but still individually distinguishable entities. Most of them are careful and precise in their use of terminology. Paul and Luke in particular are careful to distinguish Israel from Gentiles even as believers, and they are concerned about how and on what terms Gentile believers are admitted to faith. For them the continuity of salvation history is of great significance; it is secured not by Gentile believers linking with Christ alone but via the believing people in Israel. The continuity in salvation history does not lie exclusively in the history of Jesus but also in the history of the people who represent Israel (Jervell 1972, 53). However, it cannot be argued that John fits into this picture; for him to be linked by faith to the true vine is what counts.

There are also differing emphases on the value of physical descent from Abraham. It is severely qualified to a great extent by Paul and to such an extent by John as to render it almost worthless. But despite the warning that God is able to raise up children from stones, descent from Abraham is never rendered entirely superfluous, nor is Israel desacralized to become like the Gentiles, except possibly in John, and even here we cannot be certain. As we noted, discussion of Abrahamic descent may arise from two directions—the issue of Gentile inclusion as well as the warning against Jewish exclusion; it is not always slanted against Jews. What should be recognized is that this entire discussion had to do with the question of the continuity of the church with Israel. Again, when 1 Peter takes over the imagery of Israel to affirm the self-identity of believers (1 Pet 2:1-10), we must realize that this primarily denotes continuity in the people of God.

We need also to consider what kind of continuity is intended. Is it the continuity of one people of God being succeeded by another (i.e., displacement), or is it the continuity that the majority of the NT writers adhere to, of extension of the privileges of Israel to Gentiles? There is, however, more than one way in which this inclusion of Gentiles may be understood. In order to emphasize the roots of the church in Israel, Barth argued for a model of a single people of God, in preference to a remnant theory, in which continuity between the old and new peoples is maintained by believing Jews, and also in strong opposition to all theories involving the displacement of Israel by the church. It could well be argued that in differing circumstances the contemporary church chooses whichever of these NT models of the

relationship is most productive for its own self-understanding and mission. But one must ask whether any models are to be excluded or whether all are equally acceptable for this purpose. Many people today would not regard the displacement model as a legitimate option. The disastrous consequences to which this perspective contributed, to some extent at least, in the Holocaust, is seen as sufficient grounds to merit its exclusion.

What is essential is that we recognize that there are differing emphases related to the circumstances of the audience and that perhaps we are wrong to expect a uniform pattern throughout the NT. We certainly ought not to try to force the texts into the pattern of our preference. As in Judaism, so too in the church, there is an abiding diversity rooted in differing models of community, as H. C. Kee has recently argued.

6. The Church as Israel, People of God in the Post-New Testament Period.

Until the time of Paul's death, most believers in Christ were Jews or former God-fearers. These were probably in the majority until the end of the first century; but even after the time when Gentile believers were in the majority, Jews and Christians often retained close contact if only to dispute over legitimacy or status. In the East, Jewish Christian groups persisted, often overlapping the Jewish communities, and to outsiders at least were often indistinguishable (Saldarini, 195). The period when rabbinic Judaism and nascent Christianity were both in a formative state was an era of great fluidity that allowed the coexistence and interaction of diverse groups of believers in ways that subsequent developments would render impossible. It is essential for scholars who know only a period of history in which church and synagogue are distinct and mutually exclusive communities with developed and divergent theological traditions not to retroject later classical forms of the two religions into the earlier period. The inevitable outcome of such anachronistic thinking is a neglect of traditions held in common prior to the deliberate development and accentuation of separate identities.

Saldarini has stressed this danger in relation to the question of whether or not Matthew's group is perceived as still being part of Judaism, but we believe the same risks face interpreters of documents relevant to Christian-Jewish relations in the second century. Our duty as historians is to try to understand the complex relationships without imposing presupposed or familiar patterns upon our material. Only thus can the variety and diversity of opinion and practice be uncovered. For this reason we will consider separately the relevant thinkers and their distinctive contribution rather than follow thematic studies on selected topics.

6.1. Ignatius. In the last book of the NT we find a reference to the Nicolaitans, those who say they are Jews but are not (Rev 2:9-10; 3:9). Most likely we have here a reference to Gentile Christian judaizers who, in order to escape persecution or for other reasons, called themselves Jews. The only inference we draw from this at this point is that it demonstrates that a certain overlap still exists in certain regions between the church and Judaism. The two entities are still not completely distinct.

In the letters of Ignatius,* which were written shortly after the book of Revelation (in the reign of Trajan, 98-117) and to churches in the same region, we find indications of a similar phenomenon. Ignatius refers to Gentile Christians "who expound Judaism": "it is better to hear Christianity from a man who is circumcised than Judaism from a man who is uncircumcised" (Ign. *Phld.* 6.1). It is the latter that troubles Ignatius. He is aware that former God-fearers had brought with them into the church their propensity for observing Jewish customs and have continued to live a Jewish lifestyle. "If we continue to live until now according to Judaism, we confess that we have not received grace" (Ign. *Magn.* 8.1). Ignatius wants to resolve what he sees as the dilemma of conflicting loyalties: Christians should henceforth follow a new norm and "live according to Jesus Christ." In his single reference to Abraham, Ignatius accords the patriarch some christological significance, but both Abraham and the other patriarchs come to God through Christ, "the door of the Father" (Ign. *Phld.* 9.1).

Ignatius is thus drawn to stress the distinctiveness of Christianity (Ign. *Phld.* 8.2; 9.1-2) over against Gentile judaizers who had previously attempted to combine Jewish practices and a Christian profession, a position he now regards as untenable. This blurring of boundaries, Ignatius had come to recognize, was a dangerous practice—the Christians concerned probably observed sabbath instead of Sunday (Ign. *Magn.* 9.1) and may also have had a distinctive view and separate celebration of the Eucharist (Ign. *Phld.* 4.1).

Ignatius challenged the judaizers to an exclusive commitment: to live according to Jesus Christ. "It is ridiculous to confess Jesus Christ and to judaize," for "Christianity did not believe in Judaism but Judaism in Christianity" (Ign. *Magn.* 10.2). It is significant that in this, the first known reference to Christianity in literature, we have evidence of existing tensions between the new movement and its Jewish roots, with the call to an exclusive commitment to Christ as the only viable solution.

6.2. The Epistle of Barnabas. Although the Jewish war and the subsequent destruction of the temple* strengthened that Christian opinion which saw in these events proof of Israel's rejection and punishment, there is some evidence that suggests that hopes for a rebuilt temple were not dead. In the reign of the Nerva (96-98) this hope may have been rekindled.

The *Epistle of Barnabas** was probably written during this period (i.e., between the reign of Nerva and the outbreak of the Bar Kokhba revolt in 132). Whether it was ever a real possibility or merely a pious hope, *Barnabas* takes seriously the report that "those who tore down this temple will rebuild it" (*Barn.* 16.2). Even the rumor of a rebuilt temple and hence the possibility of a revived Judaism posed a real threat to *Barnabas.* Moreover, internal problems in the Christian movement were also threatening. Some Gentile Christians were claiming that "the covenant is both ours and theirs" (*Barn.* 4.6-8). *Barnabas* represents a strong reaction to this suggestion of one covenant shared by both Christians and Jews.

So the author set out to distinguish Christians from Jews. Christians are another type of people (*allon typon, Barn.* 6.1), a new creation, a new people (*Barn.* 2.6; 5.7; 7.5), and they will inherit the promise. As for the Jews, their supreme failure is that they alone were responsible for the death of Jesus (*Barn.* 5.11). The wretched Jews, like their pagan neighbors, failed to realize that the Most High does not dwell in temples made with hands. So there is no future hope for them or their temple; their rituals such as sacrifice* and circumcision have been replaced.

Barnabas refers to Abraham seven times,

three of these in OT citations. J. S. Siker notes that this is more than in any other writing between John's Gospel and Justin Martyr (Siker, 148). But the real significance of Abraham is that he bore witness* to the salvific meaning of the death of Jesus (*Barn.* 8.1-2; *see* Death of Christ). Again, the only virtue in the circumcision that Abraham practiced was that it pointed toward Christ, but an evil angel "enlightened" the Jews and caused them to misinterpret its significance (*Barn.* 9.4). God did give the covenant to the Israelites, but their sin led to its immediate withdrawal. From this *Barnabas* concludes that the covenant was never theirs and that it was always ours in God's intention. Moses had received the covenant on behalf of the Jews, but "they were not worthy." So the Lord "gave it to us, as the people of his inheritance" (*Barn.* 13.6-7; 14.4), and by "us" it is clear that *Barnabas* means Gentile Christians. Abraham is really the father of the Gentiles.

The sectarian use in *Barnabas* of pronouns such as "ours" and "theirs" denotes the basic tendency to contrast rather than compare and to stress discontinuity rather than continuity in relating Christianity and Judaism. The author does not use the term *Jews;* most of his references to Israel are to the distant past (*Barn.* 5.2; 6.7; 9.2; etc) or to the time of Jesus (e.g., *Barn.* 5.8). Inevitably Jewish observances are, whether by allegory, typology or ethical argument, unfavorably contrasted with Christianity and finally discarded.

What we can see here is the development of a process of counter self-definition. Themes like a new law* and a new people (i.e., a people other than the Jews) are used to distinguish and distance the new movement from its Jewish counterpart and thus to prevent any blurring of the boundaries between the two. Christianity, as a new religious movement, needs to assert its own identity over and against the parent body.

6.3. 5 Ezra and the Apocalypse of Peter. An early Christian apocalypse, 5 Ezra, which has come down to us as chapters 1—2 of the Jewish apocalypse 4 Ezra, reveals a continuous concern with the concept of the replacement of Israel by another people, the church, described here as "the coming people" (5 Ezra 2:23-32). Jerusalem is compared to a mother who has lost one son but gains another (5 Ezra 2:10-14). The mother is brought to ruin and the people dispersed among the nations (5 Ezra 2:6-7). This could refer quite precisely to the events of the Bar Kokhba revolt, the destruction of Jerusalem, the banning of Jews from the city and the transfer of leadership of the church there to Gentile bishops in 135.

The *Apocalypse of Peter* may relate to this same period. S. G. Wilson draws attention to the close association of three themes in its first two chapters: the appearance of false messiahs, the persecution and martyrdom* of Christians and their eternal reward* and the fate of Israel (Wilson, 91-92).

In these last days Israel, the fig tree, is cut down and rejected. There is intense interest in and stress upon a radical rejection of Israel as the apparent prerequisite for the transfer of the divine affection to a "new people." Only a historical crisis of great significance can explain the concentration of these associated themes. The Bar Kokhba revolt, particularly in the light of its messianic expectations, provides the most fitting historical context for their emergence. From the content of writings such as 5 Ezra and *Apocalypse of Peter*, it becomes clear that although the fall of Jerusalem in A.D. 70 was a most significant event, its lasting influence was not nearly as decisive as the events associated with the Bar Kokhba rebellion. Doubtless the persecution of some Christians at a moment of high messianic fervor, the replacement of the temple by a pagan building and the abolition of the Jews from Jerusalem with the concomitant transfer of leadership of the church to Gentiles had a profound influence upon the Christian perception of reality. For an emergent movement involved in developing its own independent identity and drawing up boundaries between itself and other Jews and Gentiles, the outcome of Bar Kokhba for Judaism must have denoted an aspect of finality and provided the catalyst that encouraged the hardening of the concept of the transfer of divine affection to a new entity, "the coming people."

6.4. Marcionites and Gnostics. Gnostics and Marcionites were by no means identical, since it is clear that the former may have originated among disillusioned Jews. Yet for the purposes of this study, their combined influence cannot be underestimated.

Gnostics,* like Marcion, had an intense interest in the problem of evil within a divinely created world. Their myths posit a decline from an upper and perfect world inhabited by the ultimate, absolute God and heavenly beings that emanate from him. But a fall from this world of perfection, associated with one of the lower emanations, precipitated the creation* of the world. This is the work of the Demiurge, an inferior deity, and therefore this cosmos is corrupt and evil, as are the humans who reside there, apart from a residual spark infused in them from the transcendent deity. Only by receiving the enlightenment of gnosis can humans be reunited with the supreme God and their true destiny. In the *Gospel of Philip* Abraham's circumcision is interpreted as demonstrating that the fleshly must give way to the spiritual in order that true gnosis may be attained.

In many Gnostic myths the Demiurge, the creator of this world and of human beings, is identified with the God of Israel. Heracleon, a student of Valentinus, did not include Abraham among the true Gnostics. The Jewish law also is associated with this lesser creator god, and its adherents are essentially in a state of enslavement. There emerged thus in Gnosticism the potential for a radical anti-Judaism which, when transferred in the second century into Christian communities, contributed strongly to an adverse estimate of Judaism itself and in this way assisted the developing separation between the two faiths.

Marcion,* arriving in Rome* within a decade of the Bar Kokhba revolt, espoused a hyper-Paulinism that stressed divine revelation* as eruption into history rather than as a gradual development within history. His predisposition was not to read the Jewish Scriptures in a christological fashion but to see them rather as law in contrast to the Christian message of the gospel. These two contrasting entities corresponded respectively to the inferior creator god of the Jewish Bible and the redeemer God, wholly unknown until revealed by Jesus. Human beings are sinful and belong wholly to the inferior creator god. Not surprisingly, therefore, Marcion demanded complete asceticism from his followers. For him, Luke and the Pauline writings constituted the one gospel of his hero Paul and therefore for all who like Marcion wished to live like their favorite apostle.*

Marcion's stress on the radical newness of Christianity unavoidably reflected adversely upon Judaism and its Scriptures as inevitably old. Yet Marcion's interest was not in opposing Judaism as such but in opposing Christian judaizers who, in his opinion, had lost the true understanding of Paul's gospel. For him Judaism and Christianity are not related as promise is to fulfillment but are two separate entities. Even the figure of Abraham, frequently representing some element of positive continuity, is excluded by Marcion from the inheritance (rather than entering the kingdom through Christ). So instead of taking over, as did most of his contemporary Christians, the Jewish God, the patriarchs, the Jewish Scriptures and the privileged inheritance of Israel, Marcion conceded to the Jews their God, their founders and Scriptures and even their Messiah (the Jewish Messiah is yet to appear) and chose what to him was an entirely superior and novel revelation. Marcion's solution to the problem of continuity with Israel was to posit a radical separation that solved some problems but also created certain others.

The catholic church reacted strongly to both Marcion and the Gnostics and chose the solutions of neither of them. While it is difficult to be precise as to the influence of either Gnostics or Marcionites, it is clear that they supplied ideas and options previously unavailable that to a greater or lesser extent were utilized by those who for one reason or another wished to stress their difference from or superiority over Judaism. The analogy of the free availability of dangerous weapons in a society, whether they be guns or knives, suggests that where serious conflict arises, every available weapon in the arsenal is likely to be utilized. The denigration of Judaism, so plainly visible in both Marcion and Gnostic ideas, was to become a useful weapon for Christian polemicists in their struggle with opponents both from within and from outside their own faith.

6.5. Justin Martyr. That the church is in some sense the true Israel is implied in earlier Christian writings, but Justin, writing in Rome shortly after 150, is the first openly to express and defend the claim with explicit arguments. Justin denies continuing theological validity to a Judaism apart from Jesus: Judaism had been superseded.

The universal promises of the Scriptures refer to Christ and to Christians, not to Diaspora Jews and proselytes. While the Scriptures contain both promises and threats, Justin tends to apply the former to Christians and the latter to

Jews. If once there was one people of God, now there are two, a physical and a spiritual. "So, also we . . . are . . . both called and in fact are Jacob and Israel and Judah and Joseph and David, the true children of God" (Justin *Dial. Tryph.* 123.9). He does allow a place in God's true people for persons who confess Jesus Christ but practice traditional Jewish practices, provided they do not seek to compel nonobservant Christians to do the same (Justin *Dial. Tryph.* 47.2-4). Even so, he characterizes Jewish Christians as uncomprehending (Justin *Dial. Tryph.* 7.3; 12.2).

Justin was able to turn the destruction of the temple to good advantage by claiming it was not only a punishment for the wickedness of the Jews but also clear proof that the Mosaic law was a temporary dispensation since it could now no longer be fulfilled. The only useful function he adduces for circumcision is that it could be used to identify Jews illegally returning to Jerusalem after 135. Nevertheless he is aware of and does try to take seriously contemporary Jewish objections to Christianity. It is also probable that he still holds out some hope for the eventual conversion of Israel, whether by direct action of God or through Christ.

In the end, however, Justin gives the impression that Gentiles are the true and possibly the sole inheritors of God's promises, thereby showing signs of falling into the typically Jewish sin of exclusiveness, this time in a Gentile version.

Siker has drawn attention to the way in which Justin uses Abraham in the gentilization of Christianity in the paradoxical continuity of inversion (Siker, 184). In relation to circumcision, Abraham is a Gentile since Justin dissociates him from the carnal circumcision of the Jews. As regards God's promises to Abraham, Justin reinterprets them all as applying to Gentile Christians; even the concept of the chosen people and the nations is inverted so that the chosen people become no people. For Justin this inversion of the status of Jews and Gentiles stands in continuity with God's purposes in Christ from the beginning, since the Christ existed from the beginning.

It is not surprising that Trypho and Justin, with their competing and conflicting claims, arrive at an impasse. It becomes clear that Justin regards baptism* as an enlightenment that only Christians enjoy. Justin perceived what John Chrysostom was to express more explicitly at a later date: "Don't you realize, if the Jewish rites are holy and venerable, our way of life must be false." To ensure the survival and success of Christianity, Justin felt compelled to demolish the rival claims of Judaism.

6.6. Conclusion. The evolution of the Christian movement from its origins as a Jewish faction in Palestine involved in internal disputes within Judaism to its emergence as a rival religion, with large numbers of Gentile adherents throughout the Gentile world and laying exclusive claim to the heritage of Israel, was marked by intense conflicts. In the earliest period, especially in Palestine itself or in areas with a strong concentration of Jews, the first Christians were probably perceived as deviants by the traditional majority, as a faction within Judaism (see Elliott). Conflicts were no less serious in the Diaspora world, but here most of them are best understood as characteristic of a new religious movement (Sanders 1993, 255-56). From this vantage point we may note that there were several influential factors that help to explain why Christians sought to regard themselves as the "true Israel."

First, there were social reasons. Christians needed to express their own sense of identity over and against both Jews and pagans. Sometimes this took the form of counter self-definition (i.e., defining oneself over and against the other and stressing the divergence, especially in times of conflict). In conflicts with Judaism, the negative continuity of inversion may be seen as an extreme form of defining oneself over against the other.

Second, there were powerful theological reasons. It was necessary and beneficial for Christians, especially Gentiles, to locate themselves in the grand divine plan of salvation history. Here Abraham often played a significant role especially in conflicts with Jews. But even where this was not the case, a writing such as *1 Clement* calls Abraham "our father" and holds him up as an example of virtue and piety (*see* Clement of Rome). In general, however, it is true to state that Abraham is not so frequently discussed in the second-century writings as he is in the NT.

Third, for political reasons it was expedient, in order to avert the charge of being a new and novel religion, to lay claim to an ancient heritage and thus avoid persecution. Despite this, it is also necessary to recognize that there may well have been other occasions when Christians felt it was advantageous for them to dissociate themselves, for example in the collection by the Romans of the *fiscus Judaicus.*

For many and varied reasons the church felt obligated to challenge the very foundation of Israel and to claim to be the people of the new covenant. But there is no doubt that both the greatest impulse towards this displacement theology, as well as the greatest threat to its credibility, was the existence of a surviving and at times thriving Judaism. The shape and the substance of much early Christian theology were in fact shaped by the proximity, both geographically and theologically, between Christianity and Judaism.

7. Christ, Church and Israel Today: Theological Reflections.

To understand how and why history evolved as it did is not to hold that all developments were good and that all change was necessarily beneficial. Christianity did not develop in a vacuum, and many developments were forced upon it by the mighty power of Rome (*see* Roman Empire) or other circumstances. Our final exercise therefore is one of theological reflection.

The abiding truth in the church's claim to be the true Israel is that there exists an inalienable connection between the historic people of God, the Jews, and the new entity, the Christian church. The church's Lord* must necessarily be identified as the Messiah of Israel as promised in their Scriptures. Gentiles who trust in Christ are therefore not trusting in an isolated individual whom God has apparently arbitrarily chosen. They are linked through Christ, as part of the faithful remnant, to the people of Israel from whom he came by human descent. If Jesus as a human being, as part of the faithful remnant of believing Israelites, is ignored or forgotten, he becomes unreal, because his family upbringing and personal devotion are disregarded as if it would not have mattered what kind of community he had been born into. But the Gospels, especially Luke, witness otherwise. Jesus was nurtured among faithful believers who were longing and hoping for Israel's restoration.

Christ cannot therefore be decontextualized to become the exclusive property of the Christian church; otherwise he becomes a meaningless cipher or a theological abstraction. He is the Lord of the church and the Messiah of Israel.

This leads us to a further christological assertion. Although we do acknowledge Jesus as the true Israelite, the ideal servant* of God, we must not totally identify him with Israel. We cannot claim that Christ is Israel. While Christian doctrine affirms that Christ is the only mediator between God and humanity, this confession* does not negate the fact that historically the righteous remnant in Israel was an essential vehicle in the extension of the covenant faith to Gentiles (not everyone could expect a personal appearance of Christ as in the case of Paul).

Nor is it legitimate to claim that Christ displaces or becomes Israel. In such a theology, the humanity of Christ is obliterated with Israel, and the outcome is that we are left with a theological docetism (*see* Docetism) that manifests itself as individualism. In order to avoid such an outcome, some recognition has to be given to the fact that the church is called to share in the salvation promised to Israel, as Paul describes in the analogy of the olive tree in Romans 11:13-14. In other words, it must be recognized, as we have already asserted, that there exists an inalienable connection between the church and Israel, one that cannot be subsumed under the notion of believers having a connection with Christ, as if he were an isolated individual and as if Israel could be ignored.

The church's roots in Israel is not merely a historical fact of purely historical significance. It is also of great theological significance. The roots of both Jesus and of the church in Israel are important theologically because this is part of the identity of both the church and of Jesus. As such, this is much more than a temporary stage in their history; it remains a part of their ongoing identity.

Although the NT writers and their immediate successors did not all equally emphasize the aspect of the church as people of God, it is a useful and a valuable title. It stresses the continuity in God's purposes for humanity. It draws attention to the faithfulness of God throughout history, despite the faithlessness of humans. It reminds us of the oneness of God and of the corporate nature of the people of faith. As such it is a healthy deterrent against all forms of extreme individualism. But above all, it reveals to us something of the sovereignty of God in salvation, since it is God who alone determines the membership of his people.

See also BARNABAS, EPISTLE OF; CHRISTIANITY

217

AND JUDAISM: PARTINGS OF THE WAYS; CHURCH; COVENANT AND NEW COVENANT; ESCHATOLOGY; ISRAEL; JERUSALEM, ZION, HOLY CITY; LAND IN EARLY CHRISTIANITY; MATTHEAN COMMUNITY; NEW TESTAMENT THEOLOGY; SYNAGOGUE; TEMPLE.

BIBLIOGRAPHY. M. Barth, "The Faith of the Messiah," *HeyJ* 10 (1969) 36-70; idem, *The People of God* (JSNTSup 5; Sheffield: JSOT, 1983); S. C. Barton, "The Communal Dimension of Earliest Christianity: A Critical Survey of the Field," *JTS* 43 (1992) 399-427; J. C. Beker, "The Faithfulness of God and the Priority of Israel in Paul's Letter to the Romans" in *Christians Among Jews and Gentiles,* ed. G. W. E. Nicklesburg with G. W. MacRae (Philadelphia: Fortress, 1986) 10-16; D. G. Bloesch, " 'All Israel Will Be Saved': Supercessionism and the Biblical Witness," *Int* 43 (1989) 130-42; W. S. Campbell, *Paul's Gospel in an Intercultural Context: Jew and Gentile in the Letter to the Romans* (Frankfurt, NY: Peter Lang, 1992); L. Coenen, "Church, Synagogue," *NIDNTT* 1:291-307; N. A. Dahl, "A People for His Name," *NTS* 4 (1957-58) 319-27; idem, "The Story of Abraham in Luke-Acts" in *Jesus in the Memory of the Early Church* (Minneapolis: Augsburg, 1976) 66-86; W. D. Davies, "Paul and the People of Israel" in *Jewish and Pauline Studies* (Philadelphia: Fortress, 1984) 123-52; W. D. Davies and D. C. Allison, *The Gospel According to Saint Matthew* (Edinburgh: T & T Clark, 1988), vol. 1; J. D. G. Dunn, *The Partings of the Ways Between Christianity and Judaism and Their Significance for the Character of Christianity* (Philadelphia: Trinity Press International, 1991); J. H. Elliott, "The Jewish Messianic Movement: From Faction to Sect" in *Modeling Early Christianity: Social-Scientific Studies of the New Testament in Its Context,* ed. P. F. Esler (New York: Routledge, 1995) 75-95; E. J. Epp, "Jewish-Gentile Continuity in Paul: Torah and/or Faith? (Romans 9:1-5)" in *Christians Among Jews and Gentiles,* ed. G. W. E. Nicklesburg with G. W. MacRae (Philadelphia: Fortress, 1986) 80-90; P. F. Esler, *The First Christians in Their Social Worlds: Social-Scientific Approaches to New Testament Interpretation* (New York: Routledge, 1994); idem, *Modeling Early Christianity: Social-Scientific Studies of the New Testament in Its Context* (New York: Routledge, 1995); F. O. Fearghail, "Israel in Luke-Acts," *Proceedings of the Irish Biblical Association* 11 (1988) 23-43; R. H. Gundry, *Matthew: A Commentary on His Handbook for a Mixed Church Under Persecution* (Grand Rapids: Eerdmans, 1994); R. B. Hays, " 'Have We Found Abraham to Be Our Forefather According to the Flesh?' A Reconsideration of Rom. 4:1," *NovT* 27 (1985) 76-98; N. B. Huffmon, "The Israel of God," *Int* 23 (1969) 66-77; J. Jervell, *Luke and the People of God* (Minneapolis: Augsburg, 1972); idem, "Das Volk des Geistes" in *God's Christ and His People,* ed. J. Jervell and W. A. Meeks (Oslo: Universitetsforlaget, 1977) 87-106; H. C. Kee, *Who Are the People of God? Early Christian Models of Community* (New Haven, CT: Yale University Press, 1995); W. L. Lane, *Hebrews* (2 vols.; WBC; Dallas: Word, 1991); A. T. Lincoln, "The Church and Israel in Ephesians 2," *CBQ* 49 (1987) 605-24; R. P. Martin, *2 Corinthians* (WBC; Waco, TX: Word, 1986); W. A. Meeks, "Breaking Away: Three New Testament Pictures of Christianity's Separation from the Jewish Communities" in *Essential Papers on Judaism and Christianity in Conflict,* ed. J. Cohen (New York: New York University Press, 1991) 89-113; idem, *The First Urban Christians: The Social World of the Apostle Paul* (New Haven, CT: Yale University Press, 1983); J. A. Overman, *Matthew's Gospel and Formative Judaism: The Social World of the Matthean Community* (Minneapolis: Fortress, 1990); J. Painter, "The Church and Israel in the Gospel of John: A Response," *NTS* 25 (1979) 103-12; P. Richardson, *Israel in the Apostolic Church* (Cambridge: Cambridge University Press, 1968); A. J. Saldarini, *Matthew's Christian-Jewish Community* (CSHJ; Chicago: University of Chicago Press, 1994); J. T. Sanders, *The Jews in Luke-Acts* (Philadelphia: Fortress, 1987); idem, *Sectarians, Schismatics, Dissidents, Deviants: The First One Hundred Years of Jewish-Christian Relations* (London: SCM, 1993); K. L. Schmidt, "καλέω κτλ," *TDNT* 3:487-536; W. Schrage, "*Ekklēsia* und Synagogue, Zum Ursprung des Urchristlichen Kirchenbegriffs," *ZTK* 60 (1963) 178-202; J. S. Siker, *Disinheriting the Jews: Abraham in Early Christian Controversy* (Louisville, KY: Westminster/John Knox, 1991); R. K. Soulen, *The God of Israel and Christian Theology* (Minneapolis: Augsburg Fortress, 1996); G. N. Stanton, *A Gospel for a New People* (Edinburgh: T & T Clark, 1992); W. M. Swartley, *Israel's Scripture Traditions and the Synoptic Gospels: Story Shaping Story* (Peabody, MA: Hendrickson, 1994); K. Tagawa, "People and Community in the Gospel of Matthew," *NTS* 16 (1969-70) 149-211; J. B. Tyson, ed., *Luke-Acts and the Jewish People: Eight Critical Perspectives* (Minneapolis: Augsburg, 1988); U. C. von Wahlde, "The Gospel of John and the Presentation of Jews and Judaism" in *Within Context: Essays on Jews and Judaism in the New Testament,* ed. M. C. Boys et al. (Collegeville, MN: Liturgical Press, 1993) 67-84; S. K. Williams, "Again *Pistis Christou,*" *CBQ* 49 (1987) 431-47; S. G. Wilson, *Related Strangers: Jews and Christians 70-170 C.E.* (Minneapolis: Fortress, 1995); N. T. Wright, *The New Testament and the People of God* (Minneapolis: Fortress, 1992).   W. S. Campbell

CHURCH ORDER, GOVERNMENT

How the earliest Christians organized their communal life, who provided the leadership, and the relationship between the whole community of Christians and local congregations has been for centuries a topic of debate. Many issues, however, have become clearer in recent times because a more critical methodology has been adopted. The consensus is that Jesus did not lay down a given pattern for the organization and government of the church, but this slowly evolved as the early Christians took over and modified Jewish communal structures, which were also evolving in the first century A.D.

1. Methodology and Presuppositions
2. Jewish Communal Organization
3. Church Order and Government in the Apostolic Age
4. Church Order and Government in the Postapostolic Age
5. Conclusion

1. Methodology and Presuppositions.
The question of how the earliest churches were organized and governed has been fiercely debated from the time of the Reformation. The diverse interpretations are due partly to the scarcity of information available and partly to the deficiencies in the methodology adopted. The limited and divergent data have all too often been read ahistorically and uncritically, and as a result the same texts have been made to substantiate opposing positions. In what follows the importance of an appropriate critical methodology in gaining an accurate picture of the ordering of the earliest churches is taken as the fundamental issue in resolving the debates over ecclesiology and polity.

1.1. Critical Methodology. Modern critical scholarship demands that ancient texts be read in their historical and cultural context. When

we come to the text the primary question must be, What is presupposed by these words and ideas as far as the writer and his readers were concerned? This approach demands that contemporary cultural experience and ecclesial commitments be laid to one side, as far as possible, as the text is studied. It means that we recognize there are profound differences between the social and ecclesial world of the early Christians and those we take for granted. It also means that in coming to the text our concern is not to prove or substantiate any viewpoint already held but to hear the text itself. This leads to a second principle basic to a critical theological methodology, namely, that dogma or doctrine must not be allowed to determine in advance the conclusions reached. The possibility must be accepted that the earliest Christian texts reflect a diversity of opinion and ideas that do not correspond to later dogmatic formulations.

1.2. False Presuppositions. Many of those who have sought to outline the early Christian view of ministerial leadership and church government have assumed a number of viewpoints that we now see as alien to the world of the first Christians.

1.2.1. Individualism. Far too commonly the NT has been and is read as if it reflects and endorses modern individualism and therefore radical congregationalism. In contemporary Western culture the individual is thought of as the primary unit of society. We moderns see ourselves as free agents who may rightly pursue our own interests and self-development, with or without the endorsement of the collective groupings (family [*see* Household, Family], church,* nation) with which we are associated. But in premodern times and in many undeveloped countries today the individual finds his or her identity and meaning for living not as an individual but as a member of one or more communities of which the individual is but a part. The extended family, the village, the state and the religious community are the primary categories. It is this viewpoint that both the OT and NT writers presuppose. When this is not recognized it is easy for modern Christians to conclude mistakenly that the NT reflects a congregational understanding of the church. The apostolic church was an association of individual believers who freely choose to assemble together: a kind of voluntary club based on faith* in Christ.* There is truth in this, as people did freely choose to meet, but as far as the NT writers are concerned the individual response of faith led inexorably to membership in a new community. This community was the whole company of those who were united with Christ, the elect,* the saints, the (new or true) people of God. The particular congregation of which one was a member was but the arena in which this communal membership was expressed most personally. This means that a strictly congregational understanding of the church is seriously flawed.

Belonging to the one worldwide Christian community brought into existence by Christ was always the primary reality as far as the earliest believers were concerned. This community is designated in many ways by the NT writers, but the most favored term in the writings of Paul and Luke is the word *ekklēsia,* which in most cases has lost the meaning "assembly" and has come to mean specifically the Christian community (see Giles 1995). In Paul this word is sometimes used of the Christian community that meets in a particular home (Rom 16:5; 16:22; Col 4:15), sometimes of the Christian community in one geographical location, which may or may not assemble in totality (1 Cor 1:2; 2 Cor 1:1), and of all Christians on earth (1 Cor 10:32; 12:28; 15:9). But to reject a radically congregational understanding of the church does not imply that the early believers saw themselves as belonging to a national or worldwide *institution* that linked them together. Their unity was understood in familial terms (*see* Households, Family). To conceive of the worldwide community of Christians in the first centuries of Christian history as the hierarchically ordered Roman Catholic Church in embryo is also a mistaken presupposition.

1.2.2. One Defined Ecclesiology. Many Christians still believe that the NT exclusively supports their ecclesiology. All too many Presbyterians, Roman Catholics, Anglicans and Pentecostals, just to take four examples, find their church order and no other endorsed by the NT. Aspects of each ecclesiology are present in the Scriptures but not as one given pattern and not in any set form. The NT exhibits diversity and development in church order and in patterns of leadership.

1.2.3. Charismatic versus Institutional. Another presupposition that too often has determined the outcome of supposedly critical discussions of polity in the early church, especially since World War II, has been the view that we see in our earliest sources two opposing orders, the charismatic and the institutional. According to this thesis the earliest letters of Paul and the Johannine writings (*see* John, Letters of) bear witness to an entirely Spirit-initiated ministry* given by prophets,* tongues* speakers and others as the Spirit empowers (*see* Holy Spirit); Luke, James,* 1 Peter* and the Pastoral Epistles, in contrast, bear witness to an institutional order in which office bearers, notably elders, rule the church. While it is true that the more charismatic forms of leadership such as seen at Corinth did give way to more ordered institutional leadership with the passing of time, the data suggest that the charismatic and the institutional existed side by side from the beginning (see esp. Holmberg). There never were two diametrically opposed patterns but differing degrees of emphasis and a tendency for the process of institutionalization to become more pronounced.

1.3. The Starting Point. Because so little is said about leadership and church order in the early Christian writings and because what is said is by no means self-explanatory or consistent, a common practice, especially among Roman Catholic and Anglo-Catholic writers, has been to start with what is clear, the church order of the fourth century and later, and then use this as the key to interpret the NT and postapostolic writings. With some ingenuity Catholic order is found from earliest times, and the old dogma that Jesus himself ordained this order is established. A critical methodology must reject this approach, insisting that the starting point must be the NT understood in the context of its first-century social and historical context.

As the Christian church began as a Jewish renewal movement, what is said in the NT, often in passing, about Christian leadership should be read in the light of what we known about the ordering of Jewish communal life in the first century (see esp. Burtchaell). It may be presupposed that at first the early believers took over Jewish forms, modifying them only as the need arose and as the Holy Spirit bestowed new life and vitality. Beginning with this assumption we may take it that the earliest Christian congregations were the counterparts of Jewish synagogues,* albeit of a more charismatic nature, the first Christian leaders had Jewish antecedents and the linkages that developed between Christians in a given area or in different locations followed patterns the Jews had developed (*see* Worship).

2. Jewish Communal Organization.

Before studying the limited and varied data in the NT and postapostolic writings on church order and government, we turn to a brief outline of what we know about Jewish communal organization and leadership in the century before the fall of Jerusalem in A.D. 70 (*see* Judaism). What can be discovered from Jewish texts is also limited and not always uniform, but a broad picture of typical thinking and structures can be outlined.

2.1. Jewish Communal Identity. The Jews had a strong sense of themselves as a distinct people in the world. Circumcision,* law* keeping and sabbath observance were the primary visible identity markers, but their inner belief that they were the elect people of God was foundational to their communal identity. This communal self-awareness was universal in scope, but of necessity it took localized expression wherever Jews found themselves. Because the Jews insisted so strongly on being seen as a distinct people, the Roman authorities allowed the numerous Jewish communities in the Mediterranean world to be self-governing *politeumata,* a term used of an organized body of citizens. They themselves, however, more characteristically called their local communities a synagogue, literally an assembly. In the Septuagint *synagōgē* was used of all Israel as God's elect people, but in the Second Temple period it came to be used of specific communities of Jews and then secondarily in the first century A.D. of the building where Jews assembled together.

2.2. Jewish Communal Government. Self-governing Jewish communities usually had a ruling council, the *gerousia,* to direct their affairs. The *gerousia* was made up of respected older men who were generally called *presbyteroi* ("elders"). One elder was usually recognized as the presiding elder, sometimes called a *gerousiarchēs* ("ruling council member") and sometimes an *archōn* ("ruler"), but some texts and inscriptions mention three ruling *archōntes.* The oft-mentioned *archisynagōgos* ("ruler of the synagogue") was also a significant communal figure, but his special domain was the sabbath assemblies where he presided. He was assisted by a one or more officers who were designated individually *ḥāzzān* (Heb), *hyperetēs* (Gk) and in English translation, servant.

2.3. Sabbath Assemblies. Meeting together for Scripture reading, exposition, prayer* and common meals was very much part of localized Jewish communal life in the first century. Although special buildings were known, the most common venue was a home setting. In any location where there was a Jewish community of some size there were usually several meeting places. One tradition has it that there were 394 synagogues in Jerusalem* when the city was destroyed by Titus in A.D. 70; another tradition has it that there were 480. It may be conjectured that the owner of the home, as the host of those meeting in his house,* usually assumed the office of *archisynagōgos.* Philo* and Josephus* usually called these buildings *proseuchai* ("a house of prayer"). Once Josephus calls them *sabbateion* ("sabbath meeting place"). Later Jewish texts also use the title "house of prayer" as well as "house of study" and "house of assembly." It was only late in the Second Temple era and first in Palestine that the name for the local community of Jews in their complete number, *synagōgos,* became the name for a specific meeting place, a usage often seen in the NT.

3. Church Order and Government in the Apostolic Age.

As there is no evidence to suggest that Jesus laid down a blueprint for the ordering of the church, and as leadership structures and titles seem to have slowly evolved, our task must be to trace this development rather than seek out one pattern. In doing this we take as our starting point Jewish models of local self-government and Jewish weekly assemblies. The other determining factor assumed is the home setting for the earliest congregations. In the apostolic and postapostolic period Christians usually met in the home of one of their number. Men and women are mentioned as hosts of house churches, and in both cases it seems they were people of some social standing whose home was somewhat larger than average. Meeting numbers were limited, since only the very largest of homes could accommodate fifty people. This means that once the number of believers multiplied in any one place several house churches must have existed.

3.1. The Book of Acts. In Acts* Luke sets out his account of how the Christian community came into being in Jerusalem and then how Christianity spread throughout the Roman Empire.* He presents the twelve apostles* as the earliest communal leaders. They are recognized as leaders by the early Christians because they have been chosen by Christ himself (Acts 1:2, 24) and then filled with the Holy Spirit (Acts 2:1-4). In other words they are legitimated as leaders both institutionally and charismatically.

But the evangelistic* work of the Twelve, Luke suggests, soon demanded that communal leadership be taken over by others. Luke maintains that the first step took place when the Greek-speaking Jewish believers demanded better care for their widows (Acts 6:1-6). The seven men appointed are not given any title, but they are drawn as communal elders, set apart to oversee the Greek-speaking section of the Jerusalem Christian community.

Later when the Christians in Antioch* send relief for the poor believers in Jerusalem their gifts are received by the elders (Acts 11:30). Luke speaks of Jewish elders earlier and later and so no significant difference, besides the fact that they are Christian elders, can be allowed. They were not teaching* or liturgical functionaries who presided at sabbath assemblies. On one occasion Luke aptly describes their ministry as that of *episkopos,* oversight, or supervision (Acts 20:28). This Greek noun and its verbal form *(episkopein)* were commonly used of supervisors or supervision in any endeavor, and in the first instance, as in this example, Christians used these words in a nontechnical and functional way (cf. 1 Pet 2:25; 5:2; Heb 12:15). Luke presents Paul and Barnabas appointing elders in the cities of Iconium, Lystra and Derbe on a return visit to these places (Acts 14:23). In Acts 21:18 Luke depicts James as the president of a group of elders to whom Paul and his missionary coworkers report. In this scene James appears as a typical Jewish *archōn* or *gerousiarchēs,* the prototype of the later monarchical bishop—a bishop who rules over a geographically circumscribed community. This use of the word *episkopos* is first found in the writings of Ignatius* (see 4.3 below).

But alongside the apostles and later the elders Luke has charismatically endowed ministers of the word active in preaching* and teaching, whom he generally calls prophets. (These leaders were legitimated solely on the basis of their Spirit-filled ministries.) They are associated with particular places, but from time to time as the need arose they would travel (Acts 11:27; 15:22, 32). The meeting place for Christians is usually said to be a home (Acts 2:46; 8:3; 12:12-17; 16:15, 34; 18:7). Neither apostles, elders nor prophets are drawn as leaders of house churches. It seems rather that the owner of the home presided when believers assembled, as did the "ruler of the synagogue," and people present contributed freely as the Spirit led. Luke has Crispus, the ruler of a synagogue in Corinth, become a believer and then start a house church (Acts 18:8).

Luke never suggests that particular congregations were autonomous. The *ekklēsia* for Luke is the Christian community in one given location (Acts 8:1; 13:1) or the whole community of Christians on earth (Acts 20:28). The word when used of Christians means the Christian community, not assembly or congregation. Collective titles like "the brethren," "the disciples," "the saints" or "the believers" are for Luke synonyms of the word *ekklēsia.* After the initial period elders become the pastoral supervisors of these local Christian communities, or churches, which are subdivided into groups meeting in particular homes that had their own leaders. But besides this locally based oversight Luke insists that the Jerusalem leaders exercised a wider oversight. When the apostles hear of the work beginning at Antioch they send Barnabas to take charge (Acts 11:22); when a doctrinal dispute arises over the question of whether Gentiles* should keep the law a delegation comes from Antioch to Jerusalem for a decision (Acts 15:1-21), and when Paul and his missionary coworkers return to Jerusalem at the end of the third missionary journey they report to James and the other elders (Acts 21:18). Luke also sets Paul and his coworkers over the churches founded by their missionary activity. They appoint the communal elders (Acts 14:23) and return to instruct further these early believers.

3.2. Paul. The Pauline understanding of ministry is outlined in some detail by C. Kruse (*see DPL,* Ministry) and Paul's views on church order and government by R. Banks (*see DPL,* Church Order and Government), but a brief additional comment may help. The early Paul is often thought to have endorsed only a charismatic, congregational order, but this is not so.

In his earliest epistles he tells his readers to respect and obey those set over them (1 Thess 5:12-13; 1 Cor 16:15-18), and in his epistle to the Philippians he singles out the bishops and deacons, who it would seem were Christian office bearers. In these three texts Paul is probably alluding to the leaders of the individual house churches (Giles 1989). These were the first designated leaders, or to use the technical terminology, the first institutional leaders. The charismatic ministries took place under their supervision. In Philippians we find for the first time these leaders being given titles, namely, *episkopoi* and *diakonoi*. The terminology differs, but their Jewish counterparts would seem to be the ruler of the synagogue and the servant.

In Paul's thinking, like Luke's, Christians belong to a worldwide community, the new people of God. Becoming a Christian is an individual decision, but it involves in Paul's mind a transfer from one community to another. The two communities are variously described by the apostle, but possibly the most fundamental contrast he adopts is when he distinguishes between those in Adam and thus in the flesh* and those in Christ and thus in the Spirit (Rom 8:1-17; 1 Cor 15:12-58).

Although Paul uses the word *ekklēsia* for the whole redeemed community on earth (1 Cor 10:32, 12:28 etc.), all those "in Christ," he also uses this word of all the Christians in one city (1 Cor 1:2; 2 Cor 1:1) and of a congregation that meets in the home of a particular believer (Rom 16:5, 23). To suggest that Paul uses the word *ekklēsia* only of either specific assemblies of believers on earth or all Christians in heaven is mistaken (*see DPL*, Church). It would have been alien to Paul's thinking as a Jew and for him as a Christian to imagine each of the house churches as but atomistic units in no way bound together in one community in Christ (see Giles 1995). Paul consistently holds that there is but one Christian community, and in any given place the communal identity of believers was an axiom. That by necessity they needed to assemble in small groups in no way breached their unity in Christ. Paul's fully corporate understanding of Christian existence is illustrated by his own conception of his work and mission. He is convinced that God had set him over all believers in the Gentile world, and they are subject to his pastoral care and apostolic rule.

In the Pastoral Epistles, which come from a later period, some major differences can be noted. Because of changed circumstances and the progress in the process of institutionalization more ordered forms of ministry are to the fore. In Ephesus "a council of elders" (1 Tim 4:14) is firmly in charge of the local communities of Christians, and as Titus goes to Crete he is told to correct what is lacking and appoint elders "in every town" (Tit 1:5). The bishops and deacons (1 Tim 3:1-13), who are specific office bearers, are probably house church leaders and their assistants, as we suggested they were at Philippi (Giles 1989). The overall superintendence of the believers on a wider than congregational basis is in the hands of Timothy and Titus, Paul's delegates. This suggests that the Pauline tradition envisages a continuing oversight of believers at a congregational level and a transcongregational level.

3.3. Matthew and John. Matthew's Gospel (*see* Matthean Community) and the Johannine tradition also have a distinctive ecclesiology. Matthew 16:18-19 is of particular importance. Here Jesus, in a passage found only in the First Gospel, says to Simon Peter, "You are Peter, and on this rock I will build my church, and the gates of hades will not prevail against it. I will give you the keys of the kingdom of heaven." The term *ekklēsia* in this context must allude to the new people of God that Jesus has come to gather, of which Peter is to be the leader. Rather than choosing to equate either Peter or his confession as "the rock" on which the Christian community is built, it is best to see Peter as the founding rock (*see* Stone) because he is the first openly to confess Jesus as Messiah and Son* of the living God.* The gift to Peter of the keys, almost certainly a symbolic way of speaking of his responsibility to decide on matters of faith and discipline, also suggests that Matthew understood that Peter was the leader of the first Christians.

In Acts Peter is depicted as the leader of the earliest believers, but nowhere in the NT do we see him exercising the ministry of the keys. Luke and Paul suggest that Peter's leadership was restricted mainly to the Jewish mission.* But despite these caveats the point to be noted is that Matthew gives to Peter a leadership over the church that is wider than a congregational ministry. He is drawn as the leader of the new Israel.* In regard to congregational gatherings Matthew sees the local *ekklēsia* as the counterpart of the local Jewish synagogue (Mt 18:15, 17), and he allows that this body also can exercise the keys (Mt 18:18), thereby disallowing this to be a ministry restricted to Peter. Nowhere does Matthew say anything explicit about office bearers. He does nevertheless suggest that in the churches known to him Christian teachers and prophets played an important role (Mt 7:15-20; 13:17; 23:34). In the epistle of James, which is often thought to come from the same milieu as Matthew's Gospel, a Christian congregation is called a synagogue (Jas 2:2), and those who lead it are designated "the elders" (Jas 5:14).

The Johannine tradition exhibits no interest in church office bearers. The emphasis falls on the direct leading of the Holy Spirit, but that virtually nothing is said about church officers should not lead us to dogmatic conclusions one way or the other. In regard to the leadership on a wider canvas, than the congregation the tendency in John's Gospel is to exalt "the beloved disciple" over Peter (see e.g. Jn 20:1-10). This is thought to indicate that in the dispersed communities that saw John as their founder and teacher he was considered in some ways more important than Peter. Some have thought that perhaps Diotrephes, "who likes to put himself first" (2 Jn 9), was an early pretender to the office of the bishop, but this is conjecture. It is more likely that Diotrephes was a house church leader who, John thought, had too big an ego.

3.4. Other New Testament Writers. 1 Peter* is noted for its bold affirmation that Christians are now God's own people, the inheritors of all the promises* bestowed on Israel of old (1 Pet 1:1-2; 2:4-10). The Christian community, the church, is the whole company of believers dispersed throughout the world* (1 Pet 5:10). Peter sees himself as having authority* over those to whom he writes, but when he comes to speak of local leadership he, like Luke, has the elders as the overseers of the geographically circumscribed flock (1 Pet 5:1-5; *see* Shepherd) and those who are charismatically inspired as the providers of the teaching and serving ministries (1 Pet 4:11-12; *see* Service). In other words 1 Peter allows that charismatic and institutional forms of leadership could exist side by side.

The book of Revelation (*see* Revelation, Book of) also emphatically makes the whole company of Christians the heirs and successors of the promises once the preserve of historic Israel (Rev 1:6; 5:9-10; 7:1-17). As far as the author of this book is concerned, the followers of Christ are one community on earth united in faith and suffering.* It is only when addressing the seven churches of Asia minor (Rev 2—3) that particular believing communities come into focus. Nothing is said directly about the leadership of these churches, but as prophets are given prominence in Revelation, we may assume they played an important part in community gatherings (Rev 10:7; 11:18; 16:6; 18:20, 24; 22:6, 9). John addresses "the angel" of each of the seven churches to which he writes. The suggestion has been made that this was a title for a church office bearer, possibly a bishop, but this is unlikely. In Revelation, angels* are heavenly figures. Probably John thought that each congregation had a guardian angel.

4. Church Order and Government in the Postapostolic Age.
Besides the passing comments about church order and church government to be found in the canonical writings we have additional historical data in the limited body of Christian literature coming from the late first and early second century A.D.

4.1. 1 Clement. The occasion for this letter is the removal from office of certain presbyters set over the Christian community in Corinth by a group of young men who seem to have been claiming charismatic authority for their ministry (*1 Clem.* 21.5; 48.5; 57.2). *1 Clement* is introduced as a letter "from the church of God in Rome to the church in Corinth" (*1 Clem.* 1.10). The name of the author is not given, but later tradition ascribes it to Clement, the supposed third or fourth bishop of Rome (*see* Clement of Rome; Rome). The author, however, does not claim this title for himself and in fact makes no mention of monarchical episcopacy. When he does come to use the word *episkopos* he uses it in the plural of "bishops and deacons" (*1 Clem.* 42.4-5; cf. Phil 1:1; *Did.* 15.1). This may suggest that in Rome at this time the word *episkopos* was still used only of house church leaders. As in the Pastorals, all bishops were elders (*1 Clem.* 44.5), but not all elders were bishops. In both writings the titles *bishop* and *deacon* probably refer to particular ministries exercised in relation to specific congregations, whereas the elders are the general overseers of the city-wide community of Christians (cf. *1 Clem.* 44.5; 47.6; 54.2;

57.1). Elders are always mentioned in the plural, and their right to give authoritative direction to the Corinthian believers is consistently upheld (*1 Clem.* 1.3; 3.3; 21.6; 47.6; 54.2; 57.1).

4.2. The Didache. The *Didache* (or to give it its full title, The *Teaching of the Twelve Apostles)* is almost certainly a composite document coming from the early second century A.D. but incorporating earlier material. Elders are not mentioned and monarchical episcopacy is not envisaged, but prophets and teachers are prominent, with the former having the honor of presiding at the Eucharist (*Did.* 11.7). In *Didache* 15.1 the bishops and deacons are seen as the successors to the prophets and teachers. These two office bearers, the author says, you are "to appoint for yourselves" (*Did.* 15.1).

4.3. Ignatius. The seven epistles of Ignatius, the bishop of Antioch, written in about A.D. 108 as he travels to Rome to face martyrdom,* introduce us to something hitherto unseen. We read of a clearly defined threefold church order in which monarchical episcopacy is the most important element. Center stage stands the bishop, the unquestioned leader of the Christian community in a given city, who presides over a council of elders and is assisted by a group of deacons. A constant refrain in these epistles is that the bishop must be obeyed. Ignatius insists that "we must regard the bishop as the Lord himself" (Ign. *Eph.* 6.1; cf. Ign. *Trall.* 3.1; Ign. *Eph.* 13.2; Ign. *Symrn.* 9.2). This use of the term *episkopos* is a new development. In the NT the word is first used functionally to refer to anyone who gives oversight, and then it becomes a title for a house church leader. Here it is used of the leader of a localized community of Christians. Like James in Jerusalem, Ignatius appears as the counterpart of a Jewish communal *archōn;* he is not called by this term but by a virtual synonym, *episkopos.*

Closely allied with the bishop are the deacons. They complement his work by serving the community and are regarded by Ignatius as "his fellow servants" (Ign. *Eph.* 2.1; Ign. *Magn.* 2.1; Ign. *Phld.* 4.1; Ign. *Smyrn.* 12.2). The elders are a council of older men "after the likeness of the council of the apostles," who assist and advise the bishop in his rule over the local Christian community. They are not drawn as ministers of the word and sacrament. Ignatius's epistles assume this particular form of the threefold order was well established in Asia Minor but possibly not in Rome, as he makes no claims about the Christian leadership in his epistle to the Romans.

4.4. Other Evidence. Other early Christian writings such as the *Shepherd of Hermas,** an apocalypse (*see* Apocalyptic) emanating from the church in Rome; the *Epistle of Barnabas,* from an unknown origin; and the writings of Justin Martyr, also coming from Rome, and all written around the middle of the first century A.D., make no mention of the threefold order or of monarchical episcopacy, but from this time on this polity becomes common, and by the end of the century it is well nigh universal. It is to be noted, however, that this particular form of the threefold order is quite different from that which prevails in Roman Catholic and Anglican churches. The monarchical bishop in the second century and for many centuries to follow was the leader of a local community of Christians, the deacons in some number were his assistants and the elders were a patriarchal governing council. In none of these postapostolic writings are any of these office bearers thought of as priests* offering sacrifices* to God, and no mention is made of ordination. Ignatius based his authority solely on his claim to be Spirit-possessed (he repeatedly introduces himself as *theophorus,* which means "God-inspired"). It was not until the sixth century, in the Frankish reordering of the church, that individual presbyters, thought of as priests, became the leaders of local congregations set under a diocesan bishop (Osborne).

5. Conclusion.
In the period studied a number of changes can be seen taking place. Both institutional and charismatic forms of ministry were present from the beginning, but gradually the more institutional forms came to prevail. Jewish communal and organizational ideas were taken over by the early Christians but changed along the way. For example, terminology was often altered. The word *synagōgē* was replaced by *ekklēsia,* although both words by the first century bore much the same meaning. Likewise it seems the title *archisynagōgos* became *episkopos* when used of a house church leader, and their assistants were called not *hypēretai* but *diakonoi,* while later *archōn* was replaced by a new usage of the term *episkopos.* But the dynamic presence of the Holy Spirit also brought other changes, notably

a renewed outbreak of the prophetic ministry, which flowered for a while and then waned. Christians and Jews met in small groups, but for both their collective and universal communal identity as those obedient* to the law, or those subject to Christ, was always to the fore. For this reason early Christianity always allowed for transcongregational leadership of differing kinds.

See also AUTHORITY; CHURCH; EARLY CATHOLICISM; WORSHIP AND LITURGY.

BIBLIOGRAPHY. V. Branick, *The House Church in the Writings of Paul* (Wilmington, DE: Michael Glazier, 1989); J. T. Burtchaell, *From Synagogue to Church: Public Services and Offices in the Earliest Christian Communities* (Cambridge: Cambridge University Press, 1992); K. N. Giles, *Patterns of Ministry Among the First Christians* (Melbourne: Collins-Dove, 1989); idem, *What on Earth Is the Church?* (Downers Grove, IL: InterVarsity Press, 1995); B. Holmberg, *Paul and Power: Authority in the Primitive Church as Reflected in the Pauline Epistles* (Lund: Gleerup, 1978); M. Y. MacDonald, *The Pauline Churches: A Sociohistorical Study of Institutionalization in the Pauline and Deutero-Pauline Churches* (SNTSMS 60; Cambridge: Cambridge University Press, 1988); H. O. Maier, *The Social Setting of the Ministry as Reflected in the Writings of Hermas, Clement and Ignatius* (Waterloo, ON: Wilfred Laurier University Press, 1991); K. Osborne, *Priesthood: A History of the Ordained Ministry in the Roman Catholic Church* (New York: Paulist, 1988); S. Safrai and M. Stern et al., ed., *The Jewish People of the First Century: Historical Geography, Political History, Social, Cultural and Religious Life and Institutions* (2 vols.; CRINT 1.1, 1.2; Philadelphia: Fortress, 1974, 1976). K. N. Giles

CIRCUMCISION

Although it was also practiced by other groups, circumcision was widely regarded in antiquity as a specific and defining mark of Jewishness. While the practice was quickly abandoned by the Pauline church, it remained an issue to other Christian groups well beyond the second century. This article explores the NT and other early Christian writings for evidence of the authors' attitudes and attempts to plot the debate through the first century of the church's existence. Since Judaism* never practiced any form of female circumcision, the status of Jewish women* and female converts is outside the scope of this article.

1. Circumcision in Judaism
2. Paul: The Gospel of Uncircumcision
3. The Churches of the Evangelists
4. The Rest of the New Testament
5. The *Epistle of Barnabas*
6. Other Writings
7. The Flow of the Debate

1. Circumcision in Judaism.

It was well known in antiquity that the Jews were not the only group that circumcised, though it is not clear how widespread the practice was. Ancient authors include Arabs, Egyptians and some pagan priests (see, e.g., Herodotus *Hist.* 2.104; Strabo *Geog.* 17.2.5; Josephus *Ant.* 8.260-63; Josephus *Ag. Ap.* 1.168-171; Philo *Spec. Leg.* 1.2; *Barn.* 9). Such evidence may be inaccurate. Yet it is equally clear that male circumcision was generally seen as one of the practices (others included food* laws and sabbath observance) that served to distinguish Jews so sharply from all around them (see Strabo *Geog.* 16.2.37; Horace *Sermones* 1.9.69-70; Petronius *Sat.* 102.13-14; *Frag.* 37; Martial *Epig.* 7.30, 35; Tacitus *Hist.* 5.5.2; Juvenal *Sat.* 14.96, 99, 101; Diodorus *Bib. Hist.* 1.28.3; Ptolemy *Hist.*; Josephus *Ag. Ap.* 2.137).

For the Gentile* male who wanted to ally himself to Judaism there was a range of options, from mere interested outsider, through being a God-fearer who would adhere to various halakic regulations but not be circumcised, to full conversion as proselyte. For this last, circumcision was obligatory except in very special circumstances (Josephus *Ant.* 20.38).

It is clear, however, that many Jewish groups conceived of an eschatological* inclusion of Gentiles (Is 2:2-4 = Mic 4:1-3; Is 25:6) that they distinguished from conversion and hence without circumcision (see Fredriksen). Even before the eschaton, the category of "the righteous Gentile" under the so-called Noahic covenant* provided for the participation of the uncircumcised, to at least some extent, in the divine blessings* in the present age and in the age to come (details in de Lacey). It is noteworthy that two God-fearers (together with three proselytes) appear to have been members of the *decany* of the Jewish soup kitchen at Aphrodisias.

2. Paul: The Gospel of Uncircumcision.

When Gentiles first became accepted within the church, their status appears to have been left undefined. Luke suggests that the question of circumcision was not raised (Acts 10:47-48; 11:18); the later controversy indicates both that Gentile converts were in the main not circumcised and that no definitive decision had been taken on the question. Paul, working largely in isolation from Jerusalem, appears by the time of his second visit there to have worked out a definitive position on the issue (Gal 2:2: note the present tense of *kēryssō,* "I proclaim"). To him it is no longer a matter of indifference how Gentile converts are viewed: they are full members of the new Israel* of God* by which God is fulfilling his promises* (Rom 9—11). Hence any attempt to join the old alliance through circumcision is a betrayal (Gal 5:2-6). Whatever occurred at the first visit (Gal 1:18-19), it is clear that nothing Peter said can have excluded the development of such a theology.

Although Paul does seem at one point to deny the continuing validity of Torah observance even for Jewish Christians (Gal 3:23-28), he stops short of suggesting they should not continue to circumcise their children. His affirmation of the existence of two gospels (Gal 2:7) suggests he could have been happy with a Jewish church that continued to circumcise, provided that it never threatened the status of uncircumcised Gentile Christians. Nothing in the later statements on the law* in Romans suggests any change in this area of his thinking.

The details of the incident at Antioch* (Gal 2) are puzzlingly unclear. If the men from James* had been insisting on the circumcision of the Gentile Christians, we would expect Paul either to proclaim in triumph that their demand was rejected or to explain why it should have been fulfilled in Antioch but not in Galatia. Hence the "compulsion" (Gal 2:14) probably does not go so far as full proselyte conversion; it may have extended only to food laws or to a rigid apartheid between the circumcised and the uncircumcised. Paul carefully does not attribute to James a demand for the circumcision of Gentile converts. Nor does he categorize the debate as one between the strict and the lax or the weak and the strong: the point at issue is the proper interpretation of the plan of God and his Torah (*see DPL,* Circumcision).

3. The Churches of the Evangelists.
If traditions about Jesus (*see* Jesus Traditions) were preserved because among other things they were useful in establishing the self-identity of the Christian community, it is remarkable that no discussion about circumcision is found in the Gospels other than the brief reference in John 7:22-23, which hardly suggests that John's community was troubled about the issue. The negative attitude displayed in this Gospel to "the Jews" and their law (Jn 8:17; 10:34; 15:25) most naturally suggests that the Johannine church did not observe Torah and did not circumcise; but if so, these are no longer live issues. The schism that appears to have rent the Johannine church and that the three Johannine epistles address seems to have been unrelated to questions of Torah observance (*see* John, Letters of).

Matthew and Mark have no references to circumcision; Luke records the circumcision of John and Jesus but without comment. In Acts,* however, the issue is raised at several key points. Stephen* identifies the Abrahamic covenant as a "covenant of circumcision" (Acts 7:8; *see* Abraham); but when Cornelius* receives the Holy Spirit* the community rejoices that God has given even to the Gentiles the "repentance that leads to life" (Acts 11:18; *see* Repentance). There is no suggestion of a debate over whether they should be circumcised into the Abrahamic covenant.

Hence even before Acts 15 it is clear that for Luke the apostolic church acknowledged a circumcision-free gospel to Gentiles. All of the language of Acts 15 indicates that Luke himself has little sympathy for the circumcision party. He gives no indication of their arguments, still less a refutation of them. He describes the proponents of this position as being "of the sect of the Pharisees," a group that in general is given a bad press by Luke and people who are certainly not seen as leading lights in the church. We may conclude that for his church any debates over the issue of the circumcision of Gentiles had been long since won. The existence of a circumcision party, however, and also Paul's letters indicate that this was not universally so. To persuade even Barnabas to change his theology (Gal 2:13), the opponents must clearly have had some weighty arguments in their armory.

In Acts 16:1-3 Paul circumcises Timothy "because of the Jews." Luke does not give enough detail for us to decide whether he expects us to think of Timothy as essentially Jewish (Acts 16:1) or essentially Gentile (Acts 16:3); his status was at least ambivalent. The only reason for including this cameo, however, is to show that Paul did not reject circumcision outright; and this links with the final reference (Acts 21:21). Luke clearly wishes the reader to perceive that the report is false (Acts 21:24); his Paul lives in observance of the Torah. The model of the church that Luke intends to portray (cf. Brawley) is one in which Jewish and Gentile practice are clearly distinguished, even in Diaspora* churches. This seems very close to Paul's own position.

4. The Rest of the New Testament.

No other part of the NT refers directly to circumcision, and negative statements about Jews (e.g., Rev 2:9; 3:9) cannot safely be extrapolated to specific areas of belief or praxis. If the letter of James is a polemic against any form of Paulinism (whether true to Paul himself or not), it is remarkable that the issue of the status of circumcision is not even considered. This would seem to confirm the Lukan picture that, whatever their other differences, on this issue Paul was not perceived as rocking the Jewish Christian boat (see Jewish Christianity).

For all its interpretation of other parts of the Jewish liturgy, the epistle to the Hebrews* makes no attempt to spiritualize the act of circumcision, even when speaking of "baptisms" (Heb 6:2; 9:10), and the same is true of 1 Peter.* There cannot be said, therefore, to be any grounds in these writings for the later replacement theology by which apologists sought to explain the church's repudiation of the physical act in favor of baptism.*

5. The *Epistle of Barnabas.*

The *Epistle of Barnabas**is important both for the exalted, perhaps canonical, status it enjoyed in parts of the early church and also for its unusual perspective on the rite of circumcision. The author denies emphatically in *Barnabas* 9 that physical circumcision was ever required by God and offers two arguments for his thesis. First, the only valid OT commands relate to the metaphorical circumcision of the ears or heart (he quotes Ps 18:44; Is 33:13; Jer 4:4; 7:2; Ps 34:11-12; Is 1:2, 10; 40:3; Jer 4:3; Deut 10:16; Jer 9:26). Second, physical circumcision is practiced by people manifestly outside the covenant of grace* (*Barn.* 9.6, though the evidence he gives is inaccurate). Only in the case of Abraham was

physical circumcision of any value and then only to provide a "spiritual prevision" of Jesus. In the church that preserved and venerated this epistle, there was clearly no place for any continued act of circumcision, even for Jewish Christians. A similar attitude to the Jewish rite can also be found in the anonymous *Epistle to Diognetus** (*Diogn.* 4.4). A Gentile, Pauline church is likely to have found this perspective attractive, though it is not Paul's.

6. Other Writings.

6.1. Polemical Opposition. Historical factors, in particular the Jewish wars of 66-73 and 135 and resulting imperial attitudes to Judaism, led quickly to the separation of the Jewish and Gentile churches.

To many in the latter, by the turn of the century Judaism and Christianity are already regarded as totally separate religions (see Christianity and Judaism), as may be seen from Aristides' *Apologia* and asides in Ignatius's* letters (e.g., Ign. *Magn.* 10.3; Ign. *Phld.* 6.1). At about the same time Justin Martyr in his *Dialogue with Trypho,* provides the first link in a chain of development from Colossians 2:11 to the identification of baptism as "Christian circumcision," only for Justin the circumcision by which Gentiles are circumcised from their errors is achieved primarily by the words of the apostles* (*Dial. Tryph.* 114.4; cf. *Dial. Tryph.* 19.2-3; only in *Dial. Tryph.* 43.2 is it said to be "through" *[dia]* baptism).

There is a large body of Christian writing generically designated as *Adversus Judaeos,* "Against the Jews." It was important for the early apologists to indicate to their readers how Christianity differed from both Judaism and paganism, and it was necessary for Christians to wrestle with the status of Scriptures whose commands were no longer obeyed. But the rhetoric used in much of this material suggests another reason too: that for a long period church leaders perceived a real danger that their flocks might judaize. To such writers the approach of *Barnabas* provided one obvious weapon, though few went as far as he did in denying any validity of circumcision even under the old covenant. The link with baptism quickly becomes a truism; it is found particularly in John Chrysostom, whose constant warnings against circumcision, Jewish festivals and visits to the synagogue* suggest that the threat remained a real one well into the fifth century. The quartodeciman controversy over the date of Easter also indicates long-held Jewish attitudes.

The reason is not hard to seek; the church historians and apologists indicate the continuing existence of Christian groups that both affirmed the validity of literal circumcision and practiced it. Such groups are regarded by the writers as heretics and often as fools, and hence they have become effectively invisible to later historians. But their continued existence (to this day in the case of the Ethiopian church) indicates a viable form of Christianity that should not be ignored.

6.2. Judeo-Christianity. Shortly before A.D. 70, at the time of the Jewish war, the Jerusalem church emigrated to Pella (Eusebius *Hist. Eccl.* 3.5.3; Epiphanius *Haer.* 1.330, 335), but after the dust had settled they returned (Epiphanius *Weights* 393-401; *see* Pella, Flight to). It was not until the Hadrianic ban (135) on Jews in the Holy City that the Jerusalem church had a Gentile bishop and presumably a Gentile constituency. However, it appears that a Jewish Christian group remained or perhaps subsequently returned and based itself on the original Christian center on Mount Zion. Even in the fourth century Gregory of Nyssa describes a city rent by sectarianism.

Syrian Christianity kept such traditions alive, and Bardesanes (c. 180-223) distinguishes his group from "the Christians of Judea" by the facts that they keep Sunday rather than sabbath (*see* Lord's Day) and do not circumcise (*Dialogue of Destiny, Patrologia Syriaca* 2.605). Ebionite* and Nazarene Christian groups (the latter of which Epiphanius locates in Pella, with the expatriate Jerusalemites) are also said to circumcise. Such groups were, however, quickly driven to the fringes by reason of their small size and geographical location (and possibly also their theological views: the heresiologists always attribute to them a very low christology,* though that may be mere rhetoric). It must have become increasingly difficult in this situation for Jewish Christians within what became the later orthodoxy to maintain their Jewish customs.

7. The Flow of the Debate.

It is clear that at the earliest stage of Gentile conversion to Christianity, uncircumcised Gentiles could be comfortably accommodated within a Torah-observant church, either on the model of the God-fearers in the synagogue or on that of the eschatological inclusion of Gentiles. It is equally clear that no definitive decision was made as to their status. This was, however, an essentially temporary state of affairs.

The incident at Antioch (Gal 2) indicates a clash of ideologies between Paul, working in relative isolation in predominantly Gentile churches, and the Jerusalem-based Jewish church, and it hints at differences within the latter. It is intrinsically likely that some members (Luke's "Pharisees") pressed for complete conformity to Torah by all Christians and that few Jewish Christians would see any grounds for ceasing their own observance. Eusebius (*Hist. Eccl.* 3.32) attributes to relatives of the Lord* himself (descendants of Jude, the Lord's brother; *see* Relatives of Jesus) presidency "of every church" in Trajan's reign, and if this is so they are likely to have encouraged Torah observance among Jewish Christians (see Bauckham). As the proportion of Gentiles increased, however, it is likely that the Jewish Christians increasingly saw their own position threatened. The social disruption and identity crisis caused by the war of 135 and the accompanying anti-Jewish atmosphere would have served further to isolate Jewish Christian communities that wished to maintain their traditional rites. With circumcision proscribed by the emperor* and the majority of the church opposing it, the development of a doctrine that saw it replaced by the church's own initiatory rite of baptism is not surprising.

See also CHRISTIANITY AND JUDAISM: PARTINGS OF THE WAYS; CHURCH AS ISRAEL, PEOPLE OF GOD; EBIONITES; GENTILES, GENTILE MISSION; JEWISH CHRISTIANITY.

BIBLIOGRAPHY. B. Bagatti, *The Church from the Circumcision: History and Archaeology of the Judeo-Christians* (Jerusalem: Studium Biblicum Franciscanum, 1971); R. J. Bauckham, *Jude and the Relatives of Jesus in the Early Church* (Edinburgh: T & T Clark, 1990); R. L. Brawley, *Luke-Acts and the Jews* (Atlanta: Scholars Press, 1987); D. de Lacey, "The Law and the Gentiles: A Rationale for Paul," *TynB* 48 (1997); P. Fredriksen, "Judaism, the Circumcision of Gentiles and Apocalyptic Hope: Another Look at Galatians 1 and 2," *JTS* 42 (1991) 532-64; L. L. Grabbe, *Judaism from Cyrus to Hadrian*, 2: *The Roman Period* (Minneapolis: Fortress, 1992); A. F. J. Klijn and G. J.

Reinink, *Patristic Evidence for Jewish-Christian Sects* (Leiden: E. J. Brill, 1973); G. Lüdemann, *Opposition to Paul in Jewish Christianity* (Philadelphia: Fortress, 1989); F. Manns, *Bibliographie de Judeo-Christianisme* (Jerusalem: Franciscan Printing Press, 1979); W. A. Meeks and R. L. Wilken, *Jews and Christians in Antioch in the First Four Centuries of the Common Era* (Missoula, MT: Scholars Press, 1978); S. Pines, *The Jewish Christians of the Early Centuries of Christianity According to a New Source* (Jerusalem: Central Press, 1966); R. A. Pritz, *Nazarene Jewish Christianity: From the End of the New Testament Period Until its Disappearance in the Fourth Century* (Jerusalem: Magnes, 1988); J. Reynolds and R. F. Tannenbaum, *Jews and God-fearers at Aphrodisias: Greek Inscriptions with Commentary* (Cambridge: Cambridge Philological Society, 1987); H. Schreckenberg, *Die Christlichen Adversus Judaeos-Texte und ihr Literarisches und Historisches Umfeld (1.-11. Jh)* (3d ed.; Frankfurt: Peter Lang, 1995); M. Stern, *Greek and Latin Authors on Jews and Judaism* (3 vols.; Jerusalem: Israel Academy of Science and Humanities, 1980-84); J. E. Taylor, *Christians and the Holy Places: The Myth of Jewish Christian Origins* (Oxford: Clarendon, 1993).   D. R. de Lacey

CITY. *See* HEAVEN.

CIVIC CULT. *See* RELIGIONS, GRECO-ROMAN.

CIVIL AUTHORITY

Civil authority is the centralized and recognized control in human society with the power* to formulate and enforce the basic, formal rules of that society. The early church manifested the extreme range of attitudes toward government found in Hellenistic Judaism,* namely, from flattery to hatred of the ruler (e.g., Philo *Jos.* 243; Philo *Som.* 2.91-2). The affirmation of the order required by government is grounded in a distinction of the church from the world,* which provides a potential basis for critical judgment of government.

1. Responsibility to Social Institutions
2. The Freedom of Belonging Elsewhere
3. The Ordering of Evil

1. Responsibility to Social Institutions.

First Peter* presents respect for civil authority as an aspect of a general recognition of the positive claims of society. "Be subordinate to 'every fundamental social institution'" (1 Pet 2:13, translation by Selwyn). In the context, as in Romans 13 (with which it likely shared a common tradition), this is not a grudging coexistence with evil but a recognition that the basic structures of society function as instruments for good (although this is not stated as strongly as in Rom 13:3-4). The emperor* is to be "honored" (1 Pet 2:17). Civil authorities at all levels are included in this command; 1 Peter specifically mentions the governor as representing the emperor. The authorities' function, stated through an ancient Greco-Roman formula for the essence of authority, is the maintenance of order and the securing of justice in society by punishment of those who do evil and praise of those who do good (1 Pet 2:14; cf. Rom 13:4).

The local authorities are significant in Acts.* The role of government in the persecution* of Paul came from them (Acts 24:1-8; 16:22-24; cf. 1 Thess 2:2). The severe punishments in 2 Corinthians 11:25 may be cases of civil authorities disregarding the limits of their authority.* Paul, however, is shown more commonly to have found civil authority as a source of deliverance (Acts 23:10). He appeals to his rights as a Roman citizen (Acts 16:37; 21:39; 22:25; 25:10-12, 25). Similarly the persecutions referred to in 1 Peter (1 Pet 1:6; 3:13-14; 4:4, 12-16; 5:9-10) appear to be initiated less by official condemnation than by social groups threatened by the separate and peculiar behavior of the Christians.

The call in 1 Peter 2:13 to responsibility within the institutions of society is represented by the initial imperative, "be subordinate." *Hypotassō*, an important term in 1 Peter's instructions for the basic relationships of the household* (1 Pet 2:18; 3:1, 5; 5:5), should be distinguished from a blanket command of unthinking obedience.* Rather it is a call to order, a call to responsibility within the basic arrangements of social life—in this case those of the institution of government. Diognetus (*see* Diognetus, Epistle to) interprets the Christians' participation in the broader society as God's* having placed them in their posts (*taxis, Diogn.* 6.10).

In these types of texts the early church is an expression of the aspect of Hellenistic Judaism, which was friendly to Roman authority. *1 Clement* 60.4—61.2 is part of a prayer* that shows strongly Jewish origins (*see* Clement of Rome).

Even more than Romans 13, it presents the civil authorities as lieutenants of God.

2. The Freedom of Belonging Elsewhere.

In contrast to Romans 13 and *1 Clement* 60—61, 1 Peter does not present the civil authorities as subordinate officers representing God. God is carefully distinguished from the emperor. One "loves" the family of believers, one "fears" God, but one only "honors" the emperor, the same response that is due "everyone" (1 Pet 2:17). This appears to be a modification of Proverbs 24:21, where God and the king appear to be on a similar level of authority: both are to be feared. The motivation is that Christ* may be honored in the pure conduct of believers' lives and that criticism may be dispelled (1 Pet 2:12-13, 15). One should note that in *1 Clement,* the strongest statement in this literature of the rulers' relationship to God, there still is a qualifier: in nothing are they to resist God's will (*1 Clem.* 61.1). The *Martyrdom of Polycarp,* while restating the obligation to honor rulers as instituted by God, qualifies the honor: "as is fitting" (*prosēkon, Mart. Pol.* 10.2).

For Ignatius* (Ign. *Smyrn.* 4.2), Polycarp* (Pol. *Phil.* 8.2—9.2) and Diognetus (*Diogn.* 5.11-17) persecution is part of normal Christian experience. Ignatius wrote his letters as he traveled to meet death, condemned by Roman authority. His passion for martyrdom* and fear of its being prevented (Ign. *Rom.*) preserved the motif of discipleship of the earliest Christian faith. It provides a reserve of independence from the state in the context of submission to it. Polycarp also refused to flee (*Mart. Pol.* 5.1; 6.1; 7.1). The prayers for the persecuting authorities (Ign. *Eph.* 10.1-2; Ign. *Rom.* 5.1; Pol. *Phil.* 12.3) and readiness to appear in court, answer questions and plead their cause (e.g., *Mart. Pol.* 10.2) manifest a freedom* even in submission.

1 Peter places the tradition that it shares with Romans 13 in the context of the church as a separate people. The sojourning character of the priestly and royal people chosen by God does not mean a separation from a morally praiseworthy life in the context of social institutions (1 Pet 2:9-17). The tradition that Paul used to ward off an antinomian pulling out from social responsibilities is used in 1 Peter to prevent irresponsible applications of the image of being strangers. "[Subordinate yourselves] as free persons—not to use your freedom as a covering for vice but as slaves of God" (1 Pet 2:16). Believers are free as sojourners, but as slaves* of God they are sent back into the community as different persons. Those who belong to God must bear their share of community responsibility.

Diognetus used the motif of the church's sojourning existence to note the contribution Christians made to their host communities. They obey the laws of every foreign country; but as those who have another homeland, they "outdo the laws" in loving and forgiving acts, despite the persecutions, which also are the marks of their foreign distinctiveness (*Diogn.* 5). *Hermas Similitudes* 1, however, played heavily upon the separate character of the Christian's sojourning (*see* Hermas, Shepherd of). The law of the Christian's city ("your city") differs from that of the city ("this city") of the strange country in which he or she lives. The Christians will be rejected for following their own law; thus to be consistent they should avoid the accumulation of many possessions.

When Peter and the apostles* claim, "It is necessary to obey God rather than people" (Acts 5:29), they are resisting a civil authority, even if they are doing it openly, thereby accepting the consequences. The civil authority faced by the early church included local magistrates to whom Rome delegated responsibility for internal legal affairs (*see* Roman Empire). The Sanhedrin was not, as has been frequently claimed, only a religious versus a civil authority. The local rule in Judea included the high priest* and the Sanhedrin. The high priests' legal authority had been affirmed by Julius Caesar (Josephus *Ant.* 14.10.6 §208; cf. 1 Macc 15:21). Acts describes the Sanhedrin as "the senate (*gerousia*) of the children of Israel" (Acts 5:21), and Peter addresses it as "the rulers [*archontes;* cf. Acts 23:5] of the people" (Acts 4:8).

Peter's words literally read, "To obey God is more of an obligation than to obey people." The basic duty to submit to human authority is acknowledged, but also recognized is the authorities' capacity of rebellion against God (see also Acts 5:30-33; 7:51-53). Peter brings a new element to the tension by asserting concrete claims of God that transcend the demands of civil authority.

3. The Ordering of Evil.

The Revelation of John (*see* Revelation, Book

of) reflects vividly the critical alternative in the evaluation of government in Hellenistic Judaism. By means of apocalyptic* imagery, Roman government is presented in the most negative theological perspective. The dragon (see Beasts), which is Satan* (Rev 12:9), bestows its power and authority upon the beast (an imperial priesthood), which comes out of the sea, indicating its own demonic character (cf. Dan 7:3; Rev 11:7; *Barn.* 4.4-5). It functions as an imperial power, attacking the church and receiving universal worship* (Rev 13:7-8). This demonic power is also visualized as Babylon,* and its seven heads represent seven mountains, identifying it with Rome,* which for centuries had been described and celebrated as the city of seven hills (Rev 17:5, 9; cf., e.g., Vergil *Georg.* 2.535; Suetonius *Domitian* 4.5). Nothing is said of political loyalty or submission.

The book of Revelation confronts a situation in which a distorted theology encouraged some people in the churches to think that they could rise above their social world through privileged knowledge and advanced powers (Rev 2:24). Without moral consequences they now could eat meat offered to idols (see Idolatry), ignore moral restrictions (Rev 2:14, 20) and acknowledge the ruler as an object of worship (Rev 2:13; 13:16).

This accommodating spirit is addressed forcefully by the dualistic imagery of apocalyptic thought. Life is sharply divided between allegiance to God or Satan. A cosmic battle is being waged that involves idols, sexual conduct, economic trade and political rule. The cosmic powers are unmasked to reveal the battle being waged between Satan and Christ, which incorporates human political and moral choices. The Revelation of John is more explicit than Paul on the political aspects of the cosmic powers (see *DPL,* Civil Authority, Ethics, Principalities and Powers).

Ethical* and political struggles thus have a universal dimension, opening the door for a more radical, more sweeping solution. Rome combines in itself all four beasts of Daniel 7:3-8 (Rev 13:1-2). It is a paradigm of the whole history of human organized evil—political, religious and economic—including Rome's predecessors and its successors. The answer is tied to the outcome of human history itself and to salvation* in its most comprehensive sense, in another reign whose coming is the source of the believers' hopes.*

Some interpreters would discount the opposition to government in Revelation as prompted only by religious persecution. This objection misses the economic critique of the authorities as well as the interlocking of the religious, moral and economic aspects of the state's power. Economic exploitation, particularly through accumulation of luxury items, is characteristic of the whole system of imperial power, which is about to be doomed under the judgment of God (Rev 18:3, 7, 9). The lavish commerce is described as "engaging in prostitution" with Rome (Rev 18:3, 9), quoting Isaiah 23:17, where prostitution is a metaphor for economic rather than sexual activity. Addressing a rural situation, James* also connects economic oppression (*katadynasteuō,* common in this regard in LXX) with legal persecution (Jas 2:6). The Two Ways tradition in *Didache* 5.2 and *Barnabas* 20.2 condemns judges of the poor who disobey the law and are advocates for the rich (see Riches; *Didache; Barnabas, Epistle of*).

The deepest theological issue in the book of Revelation is power. In contrast to the false claims of human authorities, the most prominent title of God is *pantokratōr,* "Almighty" (Rev 1:8 and nine other uses). God's throne, symbolic of God's rule, appears in all but five chapters. Against the oppressive power of the state there exists God's power. Christ is already "ruler of the monarchs of the earth" (Rev 1:9). The revelation* about the beast is not to identify the oppressors but to disclose what is going to happen to them in God's anticipated action. The beast will pass away and go into perdition (Rev 17:8, 11). The apocalyptic dualism not only calls forth moral, political and religious seriousness; it also provides ultimate hope to those suffering* because of their faithful response.

The tension regarding civil authority in the NT was important for the succeeding generations. When the church from Justin Martyr onward had to take on itself new political and social tasks, its identity was preserved because of the NT. The church was able to engage in political tasks even as it pointed to a transcending loyalty and destiny grounded in the reign of God rather than the kingdoms of this world (see Kingdom of God).

See also AUTHORITY; EMPEROR, EMPEROR CULT; ETHICS; PERSECUTION; ROMAN EMPIRE, CHRISTIANS AND THE.

BIBLIOGRAPHY. R. J. Bauckham, "The Fallen City: Revelation 18" in *The Bible in Politics* (Louisville: Westminster, 1989) 85-102; A. A. Boesak, *Comfort and Protest: Reflections on the Apocalypse of John of Patmos* (Philadelphia: Westminster, 1987); N. Brox, "Hinnahme des Bestehenden: Zur 'Stattstheologie' des Neuen Testaments," *BK* 26 (1971) 47-50; C. J. Cadoux, *The Early Church and the World: A History of the Christian Attitude to Pagan Society and the State Down to the Time of Constantinus* (Edinburgh: T & T Clark, 1925); H. von Campenhausen, "Church and State in the Light of the New Testament" in *Biblical Authority for Today*, ed. A. Richardson and W. Schweitzer (London: SCM, 1951) 293-309; N. Larn, "The Church of the Apostles and Secular Authority," *AER* 112 (1945) 110-18; S. Légasse, "La soumission aux autorités d'après 1 Pierre 2:13-17: Version spécifique d'une parénèse traditionelle," *NTS* 34 (1988) 378-96; A. Lindemann, "Christliche Gemeinden und das römische Reich im ersten und zweiten Jahrhundert," *WD* 18 (1985) 105-33; R. Lugo Rodríguez, "El verbo *hypotassein* y la parénesis social de 1 Pet 2:11-17," *Efemerides Mexicana* 9 (1991) 557-70; P. U. Maynard-Reid, *Poverty and Wealth in James* (Maryknoll, NY: Orbis, 1987); E. Schüssler Fiorenza, "Apocalyptic and Gnosis in Revelation and in Paul," *JBL* 92 (1973) 565-81; idem, *Revelation: Vision of a Just World* (PC; Philadelphia: Fortress, 1992); E. G. Selwyn, *The First Epistle of St. Peter* (2d ed.; Grand Rapids: Baker, 1981 [1947]); C. R. Smith, "Reclaiming the Social Justice Message of Revelation: Materialism, Imperialism and Divine Judgment in Revelation 18," *Transformation* 7,4 (October/December 1990) 28-33; W. C. van Unnik, "Lob und Strafe durch die Obrigkeit: Hellenistisches zu Röm 13:3-4" in *Jesus und Paulus*, ed. E. E. Ellis and E. Grässer (Göttingen: Vandenhoeck & Ruprecht, 1975) 334-43.

S. C. Mott

CLAUDIUS, EDICT OF. See HEBREWS.

CLEAN AND UNCLEAN. See PURITY AND IMPURITY.

1 CLEMENT. See CLEMENT OF ROME.

2 CLEMENT. See CLEMENT OF ROME.

CLEMENT OF ROME

A late first-century Roman Christian leader, likely responsible for the document known as *1 Clement*, to whom also are (wrongly) attributed several other documents.

1. Clement of Rome
2. 1 Clement
3. 2 Clement
4. Other Clementine Writings

1. Clement of Rome.

Clement of Rome was a key leader of the Roman* church during the last decade of the first century. A late romance (the Pseudo-Clementines) describing him as a noble Roman citizen connected with the family of the Caesars who was baptized and discipled by Peter is wholly legendary. On the basis of literary and archeological evidence, Lightfoot hypothesizes that he was a freedman of the household of the emperor's cousin, the consul Titus Flavius Clemens (Lightfoot, 1.25-63). The claim by Irenaeus (*Haer.* 3.3.3) that Clement was the third bishop of Rome after Peter may be correct with regard to the sequence, but misleading with regard to the office, because the position of monarchical bishop, in the sense intended by Irenaeus, does not appear to have existed in Rome at this time. Instead, leadership seems to have been entrusted to a group of presbyters or bishops (the two terms appear to be synonymous in *1 Clement*; see *1 Clem.* 44.1-6), among whom Clement almost certainly was a (if not the) leading figure (*see* Church Order, Government). It is possible that he is the Clement mentioned in the *Shepherd of Hermas*￼* (*Vis.* 2.4.3 [8.3]), in which case he functioned as the corresponding secretary of the Roman church. Origen's claim that he is the Clement mentioned in Philippians 4:3 (*Commentary on John* 6.36; cf. Eusebius *Hist. Eccl.* 3.4.9; 3.15.1) is an unlikely conjecture at best. Nothing is known about his background (Jewish? pagan?) or age.

2. 1 Clement.

The document known as *1 Clement* is a late first-century A.D. letter sent from the church in Rome to the church in Corinth.

2.1. Occasion and Purpose. The letter was written in response to a report (*1 Clem.* 47.7) of trouble in Corinth. Apparently some of the younger men in the congregation had provoked a revolt (this is the Roman view; the younger men no doubt defended their action in different and more positive terms) and succeeded in deposing the established leadership of the church (*1 Clem.* 3.3; 44.6; 47.6). When news of this reached Rome (*1 Clem.* 47.7), the leaders of the congregation there were sufficiently distressed by this breach of proper conduct and order and the damage it inflicted upon the reputation of the Corinthian church (*1 Clem.* 1.1; cf. 39.1) that they took it upon themselves to write this letter and to dispatch mediators (*1 Clem.* 63.3; 65.1) in an effort to restore peace and harmony to the Corinthian congregation. Because details regarding the uprising are unavailable or not clear (due to restrictions imposed by the genre; cf. 2.4 below), the real point of the dispute cannot be discerned; suggestions—for example, that it was a struggle between "Spirit and Order" (Campenhausen, 86), or heresy and orthodoxy (Bauer, 96-104), or involved finances (Welborn 1992, 1059) or a conflict between house churches (Maier)—must remain hypotheses.

The motivation of those responsible ("the 'social elite' of the Roman congregations" [Jeffers, 195]) in acting on their own initiative is much debated. Is the document an expression of disinterested fraternal authority (Jaubert), or of a will to power (Bauer, 97; Welborn 1992, 1059), or a service of love in the interest of the unity of the church (Lietzmann, in Bauer, 96)? The answer often appears to depend on the modern reader's ecclesiastical sympathies and estimation of human nature. Analysis from a sociological perspective, which suggests that Clement was attempting to legitimate a certain pattern of institutional leadership (Maier), though still tentative, is promising.

2.2. Date. Reading the "misfortunes and reversals" (*1 Clem.* 1.1) of the Roman church as an allusion to recent persecution,* most date the letter c. 95-97, the last years of Domitian or the first of Nerva. Suggestions of 69 or 70 (e.g., Wilhelm-Hooijbergh) have not proven persuasive; the Neronian persecutions are an event of the past (*1 Clem.* 5—6) and passages like *1 Clem.* 44.3-5 and 63.3 seem to require a date subsequent to the late 60s. Correctly noting that the rhetorical language of *1 Clement* 1.1 may not in fact refer to persecution, Welborn (1984, 37-40; 1992, 1060) would not allow greater precision than sometime between 80 and 140, but the use of the letter by Polycarp* of Smyrna establishes an upper limit of c. 120. If Clement is the writer,

the range may be narrowed to the 90s.

2.3. Authorship. The letter does not identify who wrote it. While it was sent on behalf of the entire church (so the subscription in the Coptic version), the unity of style suggests a single writer (Jaubert, 90), whom the earliest witnesses, Dionysius and Hegesippus (Eusebius *Hist. Eccl.* 4.23.11; 3.16; 4.22.1), and most manuscripts identify as Clement of Rome.

2.4. Literary and Rhetorical Aspects. In *1 Clement* 58.2 the readers are asked to "accept our advice" (*symboulē*), indicating that the document was intended as a symbouleutic (i.e., advisory), or deliberative letter, a category widely discussed by ancient rhetoricians and to which *1 Clement* closely conforms (van Unnik 1975, 11; Welborn 1984, 44-48; 1992, 1058; *see* Letters). The "appeal for peace and concord" (*1 Clem.* 63.2) indicates the theme of the letter, one very much in keeping with contemporary examples, which often sought to resolve *stasis*, "revolt" or "dissension" (*1 Clem.* 1.1, 63.1; the term is used a total of nine times) by an appeal to *homonoia*, "concord" (used fourteen times in the letter). Since the purpose of such a work was to persuade or advise about a future course of action, narrative was intentionally kept to a minimum (this accounts for sparsity of details about the specific problems in Corinth). As in secular examples, the writer assigns blame (jealousy is a key problem, *1 Clem.* 3.4—6.4), warns about the consequences of wrong behavior (e.g., *1 Clem.* 46.7-9), extols the benefits of the recommended course of action (e.g., *1 Clem.* 48.1-4), and makes extensive use of examples (some of which, such as the phoenix [*1 Clem.* 25] or the theme of cosmic harmony [*1 Clem.* 20], are the standard stuff of secular rhetoric*).

2.5. Principal Sources. It seems clear that secular concepts and forms have deeply imbued the letter. Before we draw any conclusions regarding the extent or depth of such influence, it will be useful to survey the question of sources more thoroughly.

2.5.1. Old Testament. The "Scriptures, which are true, which were given by the Holy Spirit" (*1 Clem.* 45.2) are a major authority for Clement; in functional terms, this means the Septuagint (including the deutero-canonical books; pseudepigraphal and/or unidentified sources [*1 Clem.* 8.3; 17.6; 23.3-4; 46.2; 29.3?] are also quoted.). In particular Clement finds in the Scriptures rules and models for conduct, to the extent that

Christian behavior is in many respects indistinguishable from traditional Jewish piety (Hagner, 125). There are also prophecies about Jesus (e.g., *1 Clem.* 16.2b-17; 36.3-5) and typological predictions, not only of Jesus (e.g., *1 Clem.* 12.7) but also early church order and offices (*1 Clem.* 42.5, citing Is 60:17 [LXX]; *see* Old Testament in the Apostolic Fathers).

2.5.2. Words of Jesus. Sayings of Jesus comprise a second source of authority. Interestingly, Clement considers parts of the OT to have been spoken by Jesus (e.g., *1 Clem.* 22.1-8; 16.15-16). At least as important, however, are the teachings of Jesus during his earthly ministry, which Clement can quote at length (e.g., *1 Clem.* 13.1b-2; 46.7b-8; *see* Jesus Traditions). He seems to have known them via collections (either oral or written) shaped by catechetical interests; dependence on written Gospels cannot be demonstrated (Hagner; Koester, 291).

2.5.3. Early Christian Writings and Traditions. Early Christian tradition, in a variety of forms, was a third source of authority. Clement, who makes explicit reference to 1 Corinthians (*1 Clem.* 47.1-4), probably had a collection of Pauline letters (estimates of its size range from four to ten); he also knew Hebrews, and possibly Acts, James and/or 1 Peter (there is no indication that he viewed any of the above as "Scripture"; *see* Canon). The lives of the apostles* and others, especially Peter and Paul (*1 Clem.* 5.3-7), offer paradigmatic examples of proper Christian behavior and endurance. Traditional paraenetic material, including catalogs of virtues* (*1 Clem.* 62.2; 64) or vices (*1 Clem.* 30.1; 35.5b) and "household codes"* (*1 Clem.* 1.3; 21.6-8) have also been utilized freely, and liturgical* elements, including trinitarian formulae (*1 Clem.* 46.6; 58.2), doxologies (e.g., *1 Clem.* 20.12; 43.6b; 45.7b-8; 64) and prayers* (see especially *1 Clem.* 59.2—61.3), have been incorporated.

2.5.4. Secular. In addition to scriptural and Christian sources of authority, Clement in the same manner also utilizes secular sources. The legend of the phoenix (*1 Clem.* 25.1-5) is a source of divine revelation (*1 Clem.* 26.1); the portrait of cosmic harmony (*1 Clem.* 20.1-12) is largely of Stoic origins; and in *1 Clement* 37.1-3 the Roman army (a favorite topic of the Stoics) offers, no less than OT heroes or an earlier generation of believers, a model of proper Christian behavior. Moreover, the points drawn from this last example—the mutual dependency of great and small, and the advantages of *synkrasis*, "blending" (*1 Clem.* 37.4)—are commonplaces of Greek philosophy. Even the metaphor of the body (*1 Clem.* 37.5), which Paul also uses, leads to a conclusion—"everything breathes [*synpnei*] together"—that reflects a Stoic cosmology* (Sanders, 82-91; Jaeger, 19-23), and the portrait of Peter* and Paul* (*1 Clem.* 5.3-7) is shaped in light of the ideal of the philosopher-athlete (Sanders, 30-31).

2.6. The Christianity of Clement and Greco-Roman Culture. The extent to which Clement draws upon secular sources and the level of authority with which he invests them raises a fundamental question: are these elements part of the circumstantial means by which he expressed or illustrated his understanding of Christianity (van Unnik 1975, 11; cf. Jaubert), or have they been shaped on a deeper level and become part of that understanding (Welborn 1992, 1057)?

At times it seems to be a matter of the former. The phoenix, for example, is largely used as an apologetic device on behalf of a fundamentally Christian understanding of the resurrection,* and the military imagery is not without OT and Jewish parallels (Jaubert, 79-80). Moreover, however Stoic the context of *1 Clement* 20, it is not without Jewish parallels, and more importantly, whereas in Stoic use it is employed from an anthropocentric perspective, Clement's point of view is fundamentally theocentric (van Unnik 1950, 184).

But at other points it appears that Clement's Christianity is not merely illustrated but fundamentally shaped by Greco-Roman categories and conceptions. His central theme of "concord," for example, was a popular but non-scriptural norm which, moreover, closely coincided with the imperial interests of the Roman* state (and Corinth, it will be remembered, was a Roman colony). Whereas Paul had mocked the imperial slogan of "peace and security" (1 Thess 5:3), Clement makes it his central concern; indeed, he has been charged with buying wholesale into the imperial ideology and propaganda (Welborn 1992, 1059; *see* Roman Empire).

One may also note instances where Clement imports his agenda into scriptural texts (Derrett, 670). He finds "concord" in the Ark (*1 Clem.* 9.4), while Lot's wife became salt because she lacked "concord" (*1 Clem.* 11.2). At *1 Clement* 48.2-4 a key point, "without confusion," is not in the text quoted, while in *1 Clement* 60.2 there is the significant addition, "and in the sight of our rulers." The scriptural citation in *1 Clement* 50.6 does mention forgiveness,* but not forgiveness "through love" (*1 Clem.* 50.5), which Clement has just defined as the opposite of factionalism (*1 Clem.* 50.2, 49.5 [a tendentious expansion of 1 Cor 13]).

It is difficult to avoid the conclusion that at some points Clement has shaped his Christianity to fit his cultural values. This is not at all to say that he is not deeply Christian, for he is, and his Christianity shines throughout the letter. But it is a Christianity of a specific sort. The largely undeveloped christology, utilizing intertestamental categories more than NT ones, presents the ministry and death* of Jesus more as confirmation of God's constancy than as signs of an inbreaking kingdom*; resurrection* is a future event, not a present reality (Bumpus, 173-83). There is little mention of the inbreaking of a new age, which might threaten the present one; in short, it is a largely non-apocalyptic* Christianity that poses no threat to the present Roman social order and its values. It is hard to imagine Clement coming into conflict with the Roman authorities as did Jesus, or getting arrested with Paul; he seems far more comfortable with 1 Corinthians 14:40 (whose wording he cites) than 1 Thessalonians 5:19 (*see* Civil Authority; Worship).

2.7. Later Influence. *1 Clement* was still being read in Corinth a half century later, and, according to Eusebius, was read in many churches in his day (Eusebius *Hist. Eccl.* 4.23; 3.16). It was held in high regard by later writers (Polycarp of Smyrna used it extensively as early as c. 120), and Clement of Alexandria cites it as Scripture. It is found in some copies of the NT: in the fifth-century Codex Alexandrinus it stands (with *2 Clement*) right after Revelation, and in a Syriac manuscript the two letters are found after the catholic letters (which is how *1 Clement* is explicitly described) and before the Pauline letters. A Latin translation was made early on, and later Syriac and Coptic versions appeared. A late fourth-century Syrian work, the *Apostolic Canons*, lists *1 Clement* and *2 Clement* as part of the NT, and at about the same time in Alexandria Didymus the Blind appears to have counted *1 Clement* as part of his canon. But despite the popularity of this document in antiquity, only two Greek manuscripts have survived, the only

complete one not being discovered until 1873.

Modern discussion has often been shaped by questions extrinsic to the document. Arguments about Roman primacy on the basis of the letter, for example, are undercut by the document itself: Rome's uninvited intervention in Corinth's affairs and its strong disciplinary recommendations (e.g., exile, *1 Clem.* 54.2) notwithstanding, the letter does not command, but can only attempt to persuade. And while the letter does offer apparently the earliest reference to the laity as a distinct and separate category (*1 Clem.* 40.5), it offers no evidence of a monarchical episcopate, let alone one to which other churches deferred.

3. 2 Clement.

The so-called second letter of Clement is not a letter, nor is it by Clement. It is, in fact, a mid-second century sermon or "word of exhortation" by an anonymous presbyter (*2 Clem.* 17.3), the oldest complete Christian sermon that has survived. Based upon a text from Isaiah (Is 54:1; see *2 Clem.* 2.1), it presents an exhortation to repentance, purity and steadfastness in the face of persecution. The reader (*2 Clem.* 19.1), addressing a primarily Gentile congregation (*2 Clem.* 1.6; 3.1), may be reacting to gnostic* influences (*2 Clem.* 10.5; cf. the stress on the deity of Jesus [*2 Clem.* 1.1] and the resurrection and judgment* [*2 Clem.* 9.1-5]). It is often characterized as displaying a domesticated Synoptic Gospels type of piety.

3.1. Use of Early Christian Writings. The author makes use of a wide range of writings in seeking to persuade his listeners. In addition to the Scriptures, which he occasionally cites by name (Isaiah, *2 Clem.* 3.5; Ezekiel, *2 Clem.* 6.8), and an apocryphal book (*2 Clem.* 11.2-4), he certainly knew and used Matthew, Luke, 1 Corinthians and Ephesians, and may have known Hebrews, James and 1 Peter. *2 Clement* 2.4 appears to be the earliest instance of a NT passage being quoted as "Scripture." At least four of the quoted sayings of Jesus (out of a total of at least nine) do not occur in the canonical Gospels; one of these (*2 Clem.* 12.2) best preserves a saying also found in the *Gospel of Thomas** (saying 22) and the *Gospel of the Egyptians* (Baarda; *see* Jesus Traditions).

3.2. Occasion and Date. It is puzzling that although the sermon was deemed worthy of preservation, nothing is known with any certainty about its author, date or occasion. Suggestions regarding its date and place of origin include the following: (1) From Rome,* perhaps around A.D. 100; (2) the lost letter of Bishop Soter of Rome mentioned by Bishop Dionysius of Corinth (c. 170; Eusebius *Hist. Eccl.* 4.23.9-11); (3) Alexandria* sometime before the middle of the second century "fits the temper and tone" of the sermon, particularly in light of its "semi-gnostic phrases" and its use of the *Gospel of the Egyptians* (Richardson, 186-87); (4) *2 Clement* 7.1, people "coming to enter the contests," without any reference to location, implies that the speaker was near the location of the contests, in this case Corinth, the site of the well-known Isthmian games, perhaps c. 120-140 (Lightfoot, 2.194-208); (5) a hortatory address preached to the Corinthian congregation by one of the previously deposed but now re-instated elders on the occasion of the successful resolution of its crisis following the arrival of *1 Clement*, c. 98-100 (Donfried, 1-48); (6) an anti-Gnostic* sermon from Egypt prior to the middle of the second century, possibly "the first tangible evidence for the existence of anti-gnostic Christianity in Egypt before the middle of II CE" (Koester). It is clear that the date and occasion of *2 Clement* remain open questions.

4. Other Clementine Writings.

A number of writings falsely attributed to Clement of Rome have survived. These include, in addition to *2 Clement*, two letters on virginity and the *Apostolic Constitutions*. Clement is the subject of a third-century romance, known as the *Pseudo-Clementines* (extant in two forms: the *Clementine Homilies* and the *Clementine Recognitions*), and a fourth-century martyrdom.

See also APOSTOLIC FATHERS; ROME, ROMAN CHRISTIANITY.

BIBLIOGRAPHY. **Texts and Translations:** J. B. Lightfoot and J. R. Harmer, *The Apostolic Fathers: Greek Texts and English Translations of Their Writings*, ed. and rev. M. W. Holmes (2d ed.; Grand Rapids: Baker, 1992). **Commentaries and/or Editions:** M. Grant and H. H. Graham, *First and Second Clement* (The Apostolic Fathers 2; New York: Nelson, 1965); A. Jaubert, *Clément de Rome: Epître aux Corinthiens* (SC 167; Paris: Cerf, 1971); J. B. Lightfoot, *The Apostolic Fathers, Part I: S. Clement of Rome* (2d ed.; 2 vols.; London: Macmillan, 1890); A. Lindemann, *Die Clemensbriefe* (HNT 17; Die Apostolischen Väter 1; Tübingen:

J. C. B. Mohr [Siebeck], 1992). **Studies in 1 Clement:** W. Bauer, *Orthodoxy and Heresy in Earliest Christianity*, ed. R. A. Kraft and G. Krodel (Philadelphia: Fortress, 1971); H. B. Bumpus, *The Christological Awareness of Clement of Rome and Its Sources* (Cambridge, MA: University Press of Cambridge, 1972); H. von Campenhausen, *Ecclesiastical Authority and Spiritual Power in the Church of the First Three Centuries* (Stanford, CA: Stanford University Press, 1969); J. D. M. Derrett, "Scripture and Norms in the Apostolic Fathers," *ANRW* 2.27.1 (1993) 649-99; J. Fuellenbach, *Ecclesiastical Office and the Primacy of Rome: An Evaluation of Recent Theological Discussion of First Clement* (Washington, D.C.: Catholic University of America Press, 1980); D. A. Hagner, *The Use of the Old and New Testaments in Clement of Rome* (NovTSup 34; Leiden: E. J. Brill, 1973); W. Jaeger, *Early Christianity and Greek Paideia* (Cambridge, MA: Belknap, 1961); J. S. Jeffers, *Conflict at Rome: Social Order and Hierarchy in Early Christianity* (Minneapolis: Fortress, 1991); O. B. Knoch, "Im Namen des Petrus und Paulus: Der brief des Clemens Romanus und die Eigenart des römischen Christentums," *ANRW* II.27.1 (1993) 3-54; H. Koester, *Introduction to the New Testament*, Vol. 2: *History and Literature of Early Christianity* (Philadelphia: Fortress, 1982); H. O. Maier, *The Social Setting of the Ministry as Reflected in the Writings of Hermas, Clement and Ignatius* (Waterloo, Ont.: Wilfrid Laurier University Press, 1991); E. Massaux, *The Influence of the Gospel of Saint Matthew on Christian Literature before Saint Irenaeus*, Book 1: *The First Ecclesiastical Writers* (NGS 5/1; Macon, GA: Mercer University Press, 1990); L. Sanders, *L'Hellénisme de Saint Clément de Rome et le Paulinisme* (SH 2; Louvain, 1943); W. C. van Unnik, "First Century A.D. Literary Culture and Early Christian Literature" in *Center for Hermeneutical Studies in Hellenistic and Modern Culture Protocol Series 1* (Berkeley, CA: Center for Hermeneutical Studies in Hellenistic and Modern Culture, 1975); W. C. van Unnik, "Is 1 Clement 20 Purely Stoic?," *VC* 4 (1950) 181-89 (= *Sparsa Collecta*, vol. 3 [Leiden: E. J. Brill, 1983] 52-58); L. L. Welborn, "Clement, First Epistle of," *ABD* 1:1055-60; idem, "On the Date of First Clement, *BR* 29 (1984) 35-53; A. E. Wilhelm-Hooijberg, "A Different View of Clemens Romanus," *HeyJ* 16 (1975) 266-88. **Studies in 2 Clement:** T. Baarda, "2 Clement 12 and the Sayings of Jesus" in *Logia; Les Paroles de Jésus—The Sayings of Jesus*, ed. J. Delobel (BETL

59; Leuven: Leuven University Press and Peeters, 1982) 529-56; E. Baasland, "Der 2. Klemensbrief und frühchristliche Rhetorik: 'Die erste christliche Predigt' im Lichte der neueren Forschung," *ANRW* 2.27.1 (1993) 78-157; K. P. Donfried, *The Setting of Second Clement in Early Christianity* (NovTSup 38; Leiden: E. J. Brill, 1974); H. Koester, *Introduction to the New Testament*, Vol. 2: *History and Literature of Early Christianity* (Philadelphia: Fortress, 1982); E. Massaux, *The Influence of the Gospel of Saint Matthew on Christian Literature before Saint Irenaeus*, Book 2: *The Later Christian Writings* (NGS 5/2; Macon, GA: Mercer University Press, 1990); C. C. Richardson, "An Anonymous Sermon, Commonly Called Clement's Second Letter" in *Early Christian Fathers*, ed. C. C. Richardson (Philadelphia: Westminster, 1953; repr. Macmillan, 1970) 183-202. **Studies in Other Clementine Writings:** O. Cullmann, *Le Problème littéraire et historique du roman pseudo-clémentin: Étude sur le rapport entre le gnosticisme et le judéo-christianisme* (EHPhR 23; Paris: Librairie Félix Alcan, 1930); F. Stanley Jones, "Clementines, Pseudo-," *ABD* 1.1061-62.

M. W. Holmes

CLEMENTINE LITERATURE. *See* CLEMENT OF ROME.

COMMANDMENTS

This article will focus upon the word *commandment* or *commandments* (sing. *entolē*) in 1 and 2 John (*see* John, Letters of). A few texts in which the term is found elsewhere in Hebrews—Revelation and the apostolic fathers* will also be noted. Texts in which a commandment from the OT law* is cited will also be consulted.

1. 1 and 2 John
2. Revelation and Other Epistles
3. Apostolic Fathers

1. 1 and 2 John.

1.1. The Importance of Commandments. The word *commandment* (*entolē*) is featured prominently in both 1 John and 2 John (1 Jn 2:3, 4, 7, 8; 3:22, 23, 24; 4:21; 5:2-3; 2 Jn 4, 5, 6), and in every case it appears that the commandments of God* rather than Jesus are intended (see esp. 1 Jn 5:2-3; 2 Jn 4). John teaches that those who truly know God keep his commandments (1 Jn 2:3-4). Another way of articulating the same thought is that those who abide in God keep his commands (1 Jn 3:24; cf. Jn 15:10). Because

believers keep his commandments, God answers their prayers* (1 Jn 3:23). This does not mean that believers keep God's commands perfectly, for John has already stated that all believers still sin* (1 Jn 1:6—2:2). John's absolute language about believers not sinning is difficult to interpret (see 1 Jn 3:4-10), presumably because his words are a response to proto-gnostic* secessionists (cf. 1 Jn 2:19) who claimed to be free from sin. Our partial knowledge of the secessionists' teaching prevents us from fully understanding John's teaching on sin. Most likely John's intention is to say that believers are no longer under the domination and tyranny of sin, even though they still sin (1 Jn 1:6—2:2).

1.2. The Content of the Commandments. What is the content of the commandments in 1 and 2 John? John notes that the command (*entolē*) is not a new one but an old commandment that they have had from the beginning (1 Jn 2:7; 2 Jn 5). Given the parallels in 1 John 2:24 and 1 John 3:11, "from the beginning" (*ap' archēs*) likely refers to the time when the readers first heard the Christian gospel.* The old commandment is the "message" (*logos,* so 1 Jn 2:7) that was communicated when their faith* commenced. By stressing the historic continuity of the message, the error of the secessionists' deviation from the gospel vouchsafed by John (cf. 1 Jn 1:1-4) is suggested. Even though the commandment is old it is also "new" (1 Jn 2:8). The newness of the command hearkens back to John 13:34, where Jesus enunciates the new commandment to "love one another as I have loved you" (cf. Jn 15:12). The new commandment is specifically identified in 2 John 5 in terms of loving one another (*see* Love), and the same is inferred in 1 John 2, for 1 John 2:9-11, which immediately follows the reference to the "new commandment," emphasizes the importance of loving brothers and sisters (cf. 1 Jn 3:23; 4:21).

The commandment in 1 John is not exhausted by the call to love one another, for in 1 John 3:23 it is also defined as believing "in the name of his Son, Jesus Christ." R. E. Brown suggests that the "commandment" in 1 John 3:23 is parallel to the "message" (*angelia*) in 1 John 3:11, for the command to believe in Jesus and to love one another is a shorthand summary of the gospel John proclaimed. 2 John 4 seems to enunciate a strikingly similar point. John rejoices greatly that some of his children (*see* Sonship) are walking in the "truth" (*alētheia*) "just as we received commandment from the Father." The words "just as" *(kathōs)* forge a connection between walking in truth* and observing the commandment of the Father, leading to the conclusion that the commandment here is nothing other than walking in the truth. And the "truth" is centered in the gospel of Jesus Christ who truly came in the flesh* (2 Jn 7-11). John probably counters the theology of the secessionists, who were docetic in their christology* (*see* Docetism).

The relationship between the singular "commandment" (1 Jn 2:7 [3x], 8; 3:23 [2x]; 4:21; 2 Jn 4, 5, 6) and the plural "commandments" (1 Jn 2:3, 4; 3:22, 24; 5:2, 3 [2x]; 2 Jn 6) also needs to be investigated. Are the two interchangeable, or should they be distinguished in some way?

Probably the best way to sort this out is to examine briefly 2 John 4-6. The commandment is defined in terms of loving one another (2 Jn 5). 2 John 6 proceeds to say that "this is love that we should walk according to his commandments." If the plural "commandments" has the same definition as the singular "commandment" in 2 John 5, then John would be saying love exists when we walk in love. Such a tautology is certainly possible for John, but I. H. Marshall is probably correct in seeing a distinction between the singular command to love and the detailed requirements that summarize the nature of love. The moral norms of the law encapsulate love akin to Paul's statement in Romans 13:8-10. John concludes by saying (2 Jn 6), "This is the command . . . that you should walk in it." The reference to "it" *(autē)* is disputed. Brown suggests that "commandment" is understood, and this fits nicely with the observation (2 Jn 5) that love can never be separated from keeping commandments. But most commentators argue that "love" is the antecedent to *autē*, and the singular use of *entolē* in this sentence would support this interpretation. John circles back to love here because he wants to emphasize that love is the central feature in keeping the commandments. Love can never be separated from observing moral norms, for one can never claim to be loving and jettison moral absolutes. Nonetheless moral norms should not be exalted above love, for the latter is the heart and soul of the Christian ethic.*

The flow of thought in 1 John 3:22-24 could be explained similarly. Keeping commandments is one indication that one abides in God (1 Jn 3:24), and answers to prayer are given to those who observe his commandments and do what pleases him (1 Jn 3:22). But the center of the commandments is located in the singular command to believe in Jesus as Messiah and love the brothers and sisters (1 Jn 3:23).

The role of the commandments (i.e., moral norms) in guarding against deception comes to the forefront in 1 John 5:3. A claim to love God must be measured by the extent to which his commandments are observed. This recalls 1 John 2:3-4, where a similar observation is made. Brown has shown that there is a close connection between "word" *(logos)* and "commandment" *(entolē)* in Johannine writings. This is borne out by 1 John 2:3-6, where knowing God is described in terms of keeping "his commandments" (1 Jn 2:3-4) and also as "keeping his word" (1 Jn 2:5; cf. 2:7). The "commandments" and the "word" probably hearken back to the "ten words" (Ex 34:28) Moses* inscribed upon the stone tablets. Yet John's letters never explicitly refer to the OT commands and thus certainly eludes us. To sum up, John's claim that the commandment is new in Jesus Christ (1 Jn 2:7-9) perhaps indicates that the commandments of the OT were interpreted in the light of the Christ event.

1.3. Interpreting 1 John 5:2. 1 John 5:2 poses problems, for it sits awkwardly with what John wrote previously. He says that we know we love God's children "when we love God and observe his commandments" (1 Jn 5:2). But earlier John insisted that the claim to love God is negated if believers do not love their brothers or sisters (1 Jn 4:20). 1 John 5:2 seems to say that love for God's children is validated by love for God, whereas 1 John 4:19 avers that love for God is substantiated by loving brothers and sisters. The paradoxical character of John's thought is well known, but Brown suggests a promising solution to this paradox. He says that 1 John 5:2 is directed against the secessionists who claim to love brothers and sisters, although in their case it is the so-called brothers and sisters who seceded from the community. What John wants to establish, therefore, is what it truly means to love God's children. Those who love the true children of God are those who love God and keep his commands. The secessionists' declaration that they love fellow believers is contradicted by their failure to keep the moral norms contained in the commandments (cf. 1 Jn 1:6-10).

1.4. Power for Obedience. An emphasis on keeping commandments may seem onerous, but John comments that "his commandments are not burdensome" (1 Jn 5:3). The reason given (1 Jn 5:4—note the "because" *[hoti]*) is that whatever is born of God overcomes the world.* God himself has provided the life* and power* so that believers can observe the commandments (*see* Obedience), not as a burden but as a joy.* The victory that enables believers to overcome the world is faith, and faith trusts that Jesus is the Christ (1 Jn 5:4-5) and that he has provided the ability to conquer sin.

2. Revelation and Other Epistles.

2.1. Revelation. Twice Revelation (*see* Revelation, Book of) refers to keeping commands (Rev 12:17; 14:12), and in both cases the context is one in which persecution* is envisioned. Satan* in the form of Roman imperial power tries to destroy those who "keep the commandments of God and hold to the testimony of Jesus" (Rev 12:17; *see* Roman Empire). Believers were placed under severe pressure to submit to Roman authority* and offer worship* to the emperor* (Rev 14:9-12). Those who capitulate will be punished forever, but those who endure are "those who keep the commandments of God and faith in Jesus" (Rev 14:12). Obedience and endurance* are the marks of those who will enjoy the new heavens* and earth.

2.2. 2 Peter. 2 Peter* speaks of "the holy commandment delivered to them" (2 Pet 2:21) and of "the commandment of your apostles" (2 Pet 3:2; *see* Apostles). In the former text "the holy commandment" is parallel to "the way of righteousness" that was abandoned by the disobedient. R. J. Bauckham observes that in both of these verses the Christian gospel is conceived of ethically, predominantly in response to the false teachers who had disturbed the community with their advocacy of antinomianism.

2.3. The Citation of Old Testament Commandments. The only clear reference to an OT commandment in 1 Peter* is the injunction "to be holy because I am holy" in 1 Peter 1:16. Peter cites from either Leviticus 19:2 or Leviticus 11:44 or both. If the citation is from the latter text, it is instructive that the charge to be holy* is retained while the food* laws that undergird that injunction are not mentioned (*see* Old Testament in General Epistles).

James* appeals to three OT commandments: loving one's neighbor as oneself (Jas 2:8 from Lev 19:18) and the prohibitions against adultery and murder (Jas 2:11 from Ex 20:13-14 and Deut 15:17-18). This text is discussed more fully elsewhere (*see* Law). It should be noted that James betrays no concern with sabbath, circumcision* or food* laws—all of which were central for most Jews and naturally so, since the OT commanded them. Instead James only cites some moral norms from the law as authoritative (*see* Old Testament in General Epistles).

The author of Hebrews* uses the word *commandment* occasionally (Heb 7:5, 16, 18; 9:19). All of these references when considered in context (*see* Law) indicate that the Mosaic law was no longer considered to be in force, for the Levitical priesthood* and sacrifices* have been superseded by the priesthood and sacrifice of Christ (*see* Death of Christ). There may be an allusion to the moral requirements of the law being placed on the heart of believers, for the author quotes approvingly Jeremiah 31:31-34 in Hebrews 10:16, where it is said that God will write his laws on human hearts (*see* Old Testament in Hebrews).

3. Apostolic Fathers.

A full discussion of the teaching of the apostolic fathers* on commandments is not possible here, since they often use the word *entolē*, and a number of texts cite or allude to commands from the OT. The apostolic fathers have some strong statements against observing the ceremonial law, but they speak positively about keeping the Lord's commandments where observance of moral norms is commended (*Did.* 2.1-3; 4.13; 6.1-2; *Herm. Sim.* 54.5; 56.2-3, 5; *2 Clem.* 3.4; 4.5; 6.7; 8.4; 17.1, 3, 6). Ignatius,* in line with his desire to strengthen the authority of the monarchial episcopate, says God's command is to submit to the authority of the bishop and deacons (Ign. *Trall.* 13.2; Ign. *Magn.* 4.1; Ign. *Smyrn.* 8.1). *Barnabas* (*see* Barnabas, Epistle of) reinterprets OT commands and applies them to the church*: circumcision relates to the circumcision of the heart (*Barn.* 9.1-9; 10.12), the sabbath points to the eschatological* rest and has been superseded by the eighth day in which Jesus arose from the dead (*Barn.* 15.1-9), and food laws should be understood spiritually (*Barn.* 10.1-12). For instance, the permission to eat animals that chew the cud and divide the hoof should not be understood literally. Those who fear* the Lord* and meditate and ruminate on his word "chew the cud," whereas those who live righteously in this age and anticipate the coming one "divide the hoof" (*Barn.* 10.11).

The author of *Barnabas* sees the new law of Jesus Christ as binding and warns his readers against becoming "proselytes to the law," the Mosaic Torah (*Barn.* 2.6; 3.6). Other writers also suggest that the words of Jesus Christ and his gospel constitute the new law for believers (*Herm. Sim.* 59.3; 69.1-8; *1 Clem.* 13.2-3; Pol. *Phil.* 2.1-3). Polycarp, for instance, says that love for God and Christ fulfills the commandment (Pol. *Phil.* 3.3). God's law is identified as the preaching of the gospel of the Son of God throughout the world (*Barn.* 69.2). This accords with the *Epistle to Diognetus* 11.6, where the acknowledgment of Christ is understood as the fulfillment of the law. And in the *Didache* normative commandments are cited from the Jesus tradition,* especially from the Sermon on the Mount (*Did.* 1.2-5). The idea that the words of Christ are normative seems to continue in the apostolic fathers.

But it is also the case that some of the moral norms from the OT law are cited as authoritative. In the *Didache* some of the commandments hail from the Decalogue (e.g., *Did.* 2.1-5). The entire Two Ways section of the *Didache* is filled with moral instruction and exhortations, and some of the material stems from the OT (*Did.* 1.1—6.2; see also the Two Ways material in *Barn.* 18.1—21.1). In both the *Didache* and *Barnabas* moral righteousness* is necessary to experience eternal life, for the way of evil leads to death (*Did.* 1.1; *Barn.* 18.1-2; 19.1; 20.1; 21.1; cf. *2 Clem.* 4.1-5; 6.7, 9; 8.4; 14.1; 17.6; 19.3). The *Shepherd of Hermas** emphasizes repeatedly that obedience to the commands is necessary for participation in the future kingdom,* and that the commandments are not impossible to obey, since believers have the Lord in their heart (*Herm. Vis.* 25.5-7; *Herm. Man.* 30.4; 37.4-5; 38.12; 46.2-6; 47.1-6; 48.1-2; 49.3-5; *Herm. Sim.* 54.5; 56.2; 61.1-4; 72.6; 73.6; 74.2; 77.2-4; 106.2). When the commandments required are specified, they focus upon moral norms. Believers should visit orphans and widows, abstain from sexual sin (*see* Purity) and refrain from pride, slander, lying and greed (*Herm. Man.* 27.1-7; 28.2, 5; 38.1-12; *Herm. Sim.* 50.4-6, 7-9). The apostolic fathers appear to follow the same gen-

eral stream of tradition found in the NT. The law of Christ is authoritative for believers and the Mosaic Torah is no longer binding. Nonetheless the moral norms of the OT law seem to be included in the law of Christ.

See also AUTHORITY; ETHICS; LAW; LOVE; OBEDIENCE AND LAWLESSNESS.

BIBLIOGRAPHY. R. J. Bauckham, *Jude, 2 Peter* (WBC; Waco, TX: Word, 1983); R. E. Brown, *The Epistles of John* (AB; Garden City, NY: Doubleday, 1982); P. H. Davids, *The Epistle of James* (NIGTC; Grand Rapids: Eerdmans, 1982); I. H. Marshall, *The Epistles of John* (NICNT; Grand Rapids, 1978); R. P. Martin, *James* (WBC; Waco, TX: Word, 1988); D. J. Moo, *The Letter of James* (TNTC; Grand Rapids: Eerdmans, 1985); S. S. Smalley, *1, 2, 3 John* (WBC; Waco, TX: Word, 1984).   T. R. Schreiner

CONFESSIONAL FORMS. See CREEDS, CONFESSIONAL FORMS.

CONFLICT MOTIF. See BEASTS, DRAGON, SEA, CONFLICT MOTIF.

CONSCIENCE

The biblical term *syneidēsis,* usually translated "conscience," means the faculty of a human being that is aware of the ethical* quality of one's actions and that internally condemns one's own wrongdoing. By the first century *syneidēsis* and its cognate *syneidos* usually referred to an awareness of guilt (Pierce 1955, 54), although Josephus uses the word in the positive sense of an awareness of righteousness* (Josephus *Ag. Ap.* 2.218). Although the NT use of the term is derived from this Greek ethical terminology, it is also related to the OT concept of the heart, since in the Bible ethical awareness is always tied up with the knowledge* of God* and the concomitant orientation of one's life.

1. Acts
2. Hebrews and 1 Peter
3. Apostolic Fathers

1. Acts.
The only occurrences of "conscience" in Acts are both in speeches of Paul (Acts 23:1; 24:16). In these cases Paul refers to his "blameless" or "good" conscience, in a way similar to the usage found in the Pastoral Epistles (1 Tim 1:5, 19; 3:9; 2 Tim 1:3; *see DPL,* Conscience). A good or clear conscience is the result of behavior in conform-

ity with God's demands and appears to have not just a subjective element but a quasi-objective character. That is, the good conscience reflects an actual state of affairs with God, not just a lack of guilty feelings.

2. Hebrews and 1 Peter.

In the General Epistles the term occurs only in Hebrews* (Heb 9:9, 14; 10:2, 22; 13:8) and 1 Peter* (1 Pet 2:19; 3:16, 21). As in the Pastorals, a conscience can be either bad or evil (convicting a person of his or her sin, e.g., Heb 10:22) or good (testifying to the absence of guilt, e.g., 1 Pet 3:16), with a semi-objective character. This use is sometimes contrasted with Paul's major letters, but there too conscience "accuses" or "excuses" a person (Rom 2:15), signifying either a guilty or a clear conscience.

Hebrews is concerned with the fact that, as people have done evil and have a consciousness of their unacceptability to God, the conscience needs to be cleansed, because the defiled conscience is an obstacle to worship.* In Hebrews 9:9 the old sacrificial system is defective because, among other things, it cannot perfect the worshiper in conscience; that is, it cannot enable him or her to come to God in a cleared state. If it could, there would have been no need for the sacrifices* to continue, "for the worshipers would have been cleansed once for all, and would no longer have felt guilty for their sins" (Heb 10:2, NIV; lit., "would no longer have conscience of sins").

For the author of Hebrews this need for cleansing of the conscience is one of the factors that indicate the superiority of the new covenant* over the old. The old covenant sacrifices not only did not cleanse the conscience but also served as a continual reminder of sin (Heb 10:3), keeping the conscience aware of its guilt. The new covenant blood of Jesus does cleanse the conscience from works that lead to death (Heb 9:14) and so deals with sin once and for all (Heb 9:12). Such cleansing makes believers free to serve the living God (Heb 10:22; see Servant), their hearts having been "sprinkled from a conscience of evil" (i.e., cleansed from guilt). Thus both objective guilt before God and subjective awareness of that guilt in the conscience have been dealt with. A conscience that has been so cleansed can call itself "good" or "clear" (Heb 13:8).

1 Peter emphasizes this "good" conscience as a requisite for Christians so that their testimony (see Witness) in suffering* might shame their slanderers (1 Pet 3:16). A good conscience is the result of good behavior (1 Pet 3:17). Such a good conscience can even be called a "godly conscience" (1 Pet 2:19; literally, a "conscience of God"). Although most translations render *dia syneidēsin theou* as "because of an awareness of God" or the like, E. G. Selwyn points out that the term is consistently used elsewhere in the NT, including 1 Peter, to mean "conscience" and thus argues that *dia syneidēsin theou* should bear the meaning "for conscience' sake before God" (Selwyn 1947, pp. 176-77). However, Selwyn also points out that the distinction should not be too sharply drawn, since in the NT the conscience is bound up with a consciousness of God's presence and will. Suffering that occurs because of doing good (1 Pet 2:20), which both stems from and results in a godly conscience, is a "gift" or "sign of favor" with God (cf. 1 Pet 3:14 and Mt 5:10-11).

First Peter 3:21 refers to baptism* as "not the removal of dirt from the body but the pledge of a good conscience toward God." This is an enigmatic verse within an enigmatic paragraph. The verse could mean either that baptism is the act of asking God to cleanse the conscience, that baptism is a promise* to keep the conscience clear in the future (by not sinning) or that it is the confirming act that proceeds from a conscience that has been cleansed. Given that baptism is here typologically connected to the judgment* of God in the Noahic flood and that suffering in Christ is an aspect of the judgment of God (1 Pet 4:17), the best conclusion is that baptism is not a request to clear the conscience but a covenant sign of the objective conscience cleansing that God has applied to the believer by virtue of the resurrection* of Christ.

Hebrews also connects the cleansing of conscience with baptism. Hebrews 10:22 indicates that drawing near to God requires having the heart sprinkled to cleanse the conscience and the body washed in pure water. In both Hebrews and 1 Peter baptism serves as the symbolic marker of the change of condition of conscience brought about by God in the redemptive act of Jesus Christ. Thus the good state of the conscience is a distinguishing mark of the Christian.

3. Apostolic Fathers.

In the apostolic fathers* the use of "conscience"

mostly echoes that of the NT. Both the *Epistle of Barnabas** (*Barn.* 19.12) and the *Didache** (*Did.* 4.14) exhort Christians to confess sins because it is forbidden to come to prayer* with an evil conscience (cf. *2 Clem.* 16.4). It appears the evil conscience is not just a subjective problem but an objective hindrance to prayer. Ignatius* (Ign. *Trall.* 7.2) argues that noncooperation with church officers makes a person impure in conscience (*see* Church Order). This could hardly be simply a subjective feeling. Likewise the *Shepherd of Hermas** indicates that an evil conscience cannot coexist with the Spirit of truth* (*Herm.* 28.4; *see* Holy Spirit). The "good" or "pure" conscience also has an objective character (*1 Clem.* 1.3; 41.1; 45.7). Clement (*see* Clement of Rome) reminds his readers that "you were struggling day and night for all the brotherhood, in order that the number of his elect might be saved with mercy [v.l., fear] and conscience" (*1 Clem.* 2.4). The Lightfoot-Harmer translation suggests "conscientiousness," but it is probably better to understand *syneidēsis* in this case not as a sense of carrying through on responsibilities but a knowledge of purity* or cleansing that accompanies salvation.* The unusual use in *1 Clement* 34.7 to mean a commonality of awareness makes it clear, however, that the subjective function of the human perceiver has not been lost sight of.

Thus in our literature as in Paul, "conscience" is a function of the mind, but, like true knowledge (as opposed to false opinion), it has an objective character. The "evil conscience" is the reflection of an objective state of guilt; the "good conscience" is an accurate awareness of an objective state of purity before God and thus a mark of the Christian.

See also ETHICS; PSYCHOLOGY.

BIBLIOGRAPHY. W. D. Davies, "Conscience," *IDB* 1:671-76; J. Dupont, "Syneidesis. Aux origines de la notion chrétienne de conscience morale," *Studia Hellenistica* 5 (1948) 119-53; C. Maurer, "σύνοιδα, συνείδησις," *TDNT* 7:918-19; H. Osborn, "Συνείδησις, *JTS* 32 (1931) 167-79; A. Pelletier, "Deux expressions de la notion de conscience dans le judaïsme hellénistique et le christianisme naissant," *Revue des études grecques* 80 (1967) 363-71; C. A. Pierce, *Conscience in the New Testament* (Chicago: Allenson, 1955); G. S. Selby, "The Meaning and Function of συνείδησις in Hebrews 9 and 10," *RQ* 28 (1985-86) 145-54; E. G. Selwyn, *The First Epistle of St. Peter* (London: Macmillan, 1947) 176-78; C. Spicq, "La conscience dans le Nouveau Testament," *RB* 47 (1938) 50-80.   D. G. McCartney

CONVERSION. *See* NEW BIRTH.

COPTIC APOCALYPSE OF PETER. See APOCRYPHAL AND PSEUDEPIGRAPHAL WRITINGS.

CORINTH. *See* CENTERS OF CHRISTIANITY.

CORNELIUS

Cornelius is a pious centurion whose Christian conversion is recounted in Acts 10:1—11:18 (cf. Acts 15:6-11). The circumstances of the encounter of Cornelius and his household* with the gospel mark a key turning point in Luke's narration of the spread of the gospel to "the end of the earth" (Acts 1:8). Historical and source-critical study of the account in Acts has recently been supplemented by more literary-theological and sociological concerns.

1. The Characterization of Cornelius
2. The Cornelius Episode

1. The Characterization of Cornelius.
Acts 10:1 portrays Cornelius as one of probably six centurions, a commander of one hundred men, within the Italian Cohort. Six hundred men made up a cohort; archaeological evidence demonstrates the presence of such a cohort in Syria before A.D. 69 (*Cohors II. Militaria Italica Civium Romanorum Voluntariorum quae est in Syria; ILS* 9168; *CIL* 6.3528; 11.6117; see Broughton, 441-3]). This would mark Cornelius as a Gentile* (see Acts 10:28; 11:1-3; cf. Josephus *J.W.* 18.3.5 §84) and a Roman citizen of considerable social standing. Within the Lukan narrative it would also locate him at least provisionally in the good company of those soldiers who respond positively to the good news (Lk 3:10-14) and the two (Gentile) centurions already mentioned by Luke—one who is an example of faith* even to Israel* (Lk 7:1-10), the other who praises God* and affirms Jesus as "the righteous one" (*ho dikaios,* Lk 23:47; cf. Acts 3:13-15).

This positive characterization is furthered by the links Luke has drawn between the account about Cornelius and earlier material in the Third Gospel. Like the earlier episodes involving Zechariah and Mary* (Lk 1:8-56) and Saul and Ananias (Acts 9:1-19), the account of Cornelius and Peter (Acts 10) relates a complementary vision—complementary in the sense that visionary experiences are juxtaposed, with the successful completion of the one act of God through a human agent related to the faithful response of the other.

More particularly the far-reaching linguistic and conceptual points of contact between the stories of Zechariah and Cornelius (Lk 1:5-13, 29, 39, 41; Acts 10:1-4, 17, 23) underscore the piety of Cornelius—comparing, surprisingly, the devotion of a Gentile with that of a priest.* They also highlight the reality and nature of God's ongoing intervention. Even if historical events are proceeding under divine guidance, this working out of the divine will is not a fait accompli in the narrow sense (contra Pervo, 73-74); God thus reveals his objective, according to Luke, but its fulfillment involves the partnership of human agents. Cornelius, like Mary and Ananias before him, proves himself to be such a partner (see Green).

2. The Cornelius Episode.

The three most noticeable characteristics of the account are its sheer length, the initial intertwining of the visions of Cornelius and Peter and the retelling of parts or all of the narrative by Luke, by Cornelius and by Peter. These first and last literary devices help to mark the significance of this episode in the Lukan narrative. Acts 10 reaches its climax in the speech of Peter, with its universalizing proclamation of the gospel, declaring Jesus as "Lord of all" (Acts 10:36); it finds its denouement in the coming of the Holy Spirit* on these Gentiles, Cornelius and his household (Acts 10:44-48). Acts 11:1-18, following the protests of the circumcised believers, finds its climax in Peter's interpretation of the whole affair as God's doing, analogous to the outpouring of the Spirit on the first believers at Pentecost* (Acts 2:1-4); it finds its denouement in the acceptance of God's work among Gentiles (Acts 11:18).

Such a brief summary masks the apparent incongruity within the narrative, debated by scholars since Martin Dibelius. He argued that Luke has recontextualized an account about the distinction between clean and animals so as to apply it to clean and people. Subsequent source-critical studies suggested modifications to Dibelius's position, positing various ways in which the vision* of Peter might be recognized as integral to the Cornelius story (e.g., Haacker, Löning).

Source-critical analysis has proceeded, though, on the assumption that the narrative of Acts 10:1—11:18 was a narrative about Cornelius, with the consequence that the Petrine material, presumed to have independent existence, must somehow be made to fit into the material about Cornelius. Beverly R. Gaventa has urged the opposite view, noting first that dreams or visions in Greco-Roman antiquity might occur at the beginning of an account with their significance becoming clear only as the episode unfolds; and second that the conversion Luke narrates in Acts 10:1—11:18 may be that of Cornelius and his household but it is also, and more so, that of the church (see also along related lines, Esler, 93-97; Plunkett).

That Acts 10:1—11:18 is fundamentally concerned with Peter and the Jerusalem* church* and especially with the issue of ethnocentric practices is also highlighted by its reverberations with the story of Jonah: continuity of location, Joppa (Jon 1:3; Acts 9:43), to which God directs his messengers; God's intervention to overcome the messengers' reluctance, together with the symbolically important use of the number three (Jon 1:17; Acts 10:16); the divine commission to "arise . . . and go" (Jon 3:2; Acts 10:20) in order to deliver the message to the Gentiles; a report of the Gentiles' faith (Jon 3:5; Acts 10:43) and being forgiven; a subsequent, hostile response (Jon 4:1; Acts 10:14; 11:2); God's rejoinder to human animosity (Jon 4:2-11; Acts 11:17-18; cf. Acts 15:13-21). Luke's inscription of the Cornelius narrative into scriptural tradition highlights the message that Jonah's God (who extends grace* even to the Gentiles) is Peter's God: "Against this Scripture-scape, the 'theo-logic' of the Gentile mission is painted by Luke: the Cornelius conversion is legitimized as the continuation of God's merciful work at Nineveh, Simon-Peter is the bar Jonah who is called by his ancestor's God to convert the Gentiles, and the people of God should do nothing but praise God and say, 'God has granted the Gentiles repentance unto life' (Acts 11.18)" (Wall, 140).

Luke's narration of the episode brims with confirmation of the divine hand at work. This is seen best in the presence of an angel* and the complementary visions (Acts 10:3-16), the prayer* motif (and consequent anticipation of divine revelation* [Acts 10:3, 4, 9]; on this motif in Luke-Acts see Crump), the aforementioned use of the OT and the spontaneous outpouring of the Spirit (Acts 10:44-47). Indeed, Peter's recounting of the episode underscores the initiative and activity of God in the whole affair (Acts 11:1-18; cf. Maloney). This emphasis does not serve the legitimation of the communication of the good news to Gentiles (contra, e.g., Wilson), which has already been mandated by the risen Lord* (Acts 1:8) and performed by Philip* (Acts 8:26-40). After all, hospitality,* not preaching* or baptism,* was at stake in the protestations of the circumcised in the Jerusalem church (Acts 11:2-3; cf. Acts 10:28). Rather, it serves to legitimate full fellowship* between Jewish and Gentile believers.

See also ACTS OF THE APOSTLES; GENTILES, GENTILE MISSION.

BIBLIOGRAPHY. F. Bovon, "Tradition et rédaction en Actes 10:1-11, 18," *TZ* 26 (1970) 22-45; T. R. S. Broughton, "The Roman Army" in *The Beginnings of Christianity*, pt. 1: *The Acts of the Apostles*, ed. F. J. Foakes Jackson and K. Lake, 5: *Additional Notes to the Commentary*, ed. K. Lake and H. J. Cadbury (5 vols.; Grand Rapids: Baker, 1979 [1933]) 427-45; D. Crump, *Jesus the Intercessor: Prayer and Christology in Luke-Acts* (WUNT 2:49; Tübingen: J. C. B. Mohr [Paul Siebeck], 1992); M. Dibelius, "The Conversion of Cornelius" in *Studies in the Acts of the Apostles*, ed. H. Greeven (New York: Scribner's, 1956) 109-22; P. F. Esler, *Community and Gospel in Luke-Acts: The Social and Political Motivations of Lukan Theology* (SNTSMS 57; Cambridge: Cambridge University Press, 1987) esp. 93-97; B. R. Gaventa, *Aspects of Conversion in the New Testament* (OBT; Philadelphia: Fortress, 1986) 107-22; J. B. Green, "Internal Repetition in Luke-Acts: Contemporary Narratology and Lukan Historiography" in *History, Literature and Society in the Book of Acts*, ed. B. Witherington III (Cambridge: Cambridge University Press, 1996) 283-99; K. Haacker, "Dibelius und Cornelius: Ein Beispiel formgeschichtlicher Überlieferungskritik," *BZ* 24 (1980) 234-51; K. Löning, "Die Korneliustradition," *BZ* 18 (1974) 1-19; L. M. Maloney, *"All That God Had Done with Them": The Narration of the Works of God in the Early Christian Community as Described in the Acts of the Apostles* (AUS 7, Theology and Religion 91; New York: Peter Lang, 1991) 67-100; R. I. Pervo, *Profit with Delight: The Literary Genre of the Acts of the Apostles* (Philadelphia: Fortress, 1987); M. A. Plunkett,

"Ethnocentricity and Salvation History in the Cornelius Episode (Acts 10:1-11:18)" in *SBLSP* (1985) 465-79; R. W. Wall, "Peter, 'Son' of Jonah: The Conversion of Cornelius in the Context of the Canon" in *The New Testament as Canon: A Reader in Canonical Criticism*, ed. R. W. Wall and E. Lemcio (JSNTSup 76; Sheffield: JSOT, 1992) 129-40; S. G. Wilson, *The Gentiles and the Gentile Mission* (SNTSMS 23; Cambridge: Cambridge University Press, 1973) 171-78; R. D. Witherup, "Cornelius Over and Over and Over Again: 'Functional Redundancy' in the Acts of the Apostles," *JSNT* 49 (1993) 45-66.

J. B. Green

CORNERSTONE. *See* STONE, CORNERSTONE.

COSMOLOGY. *See* CREATION, COSMOLOGY.

COVENANT, NEW COVENANT

"Covenant" implies relationship, promise* and expectation. Within the biblical tradition the covenant points to the unique relationship Yahweh established with the world through Israel, Yahweh's immutable and sacred pledge of faithfulness to this special relationship and Yahweh's legitimate expectation for his people to respond appropriately (i.e., to live as covenant people). The covenant thus plays a central, if not controlling, role in understanding Israel's identity, history and place within God's purposes.

Early Christianity also understood its relationship to God* in covenantal terms. In and through the sacrificial death of Jesus (*see* Death of Christ), God had once and for all demonstrated his covenant faithfulness. For Christians to commemorate ritually Jesus' death as the beginning of a "new covenant" (1 Cor 11:25; cf. Mt 26:28; Mk 14:24; Lk 22:20) raises many questions about the historical and theological relationship between Judaism* and Christianity (*see* Christianity and Judaism).

    1. Lexical Observations
    2. Old Testament Background
    3. Covenant in Acts
    4. New Covenant in Hebrews
    5. Covenant in *Barnabas*
    6. Summary

1. Lexical Observations.

The word *covenant (diathēkē)* appears only a

handful of times in the later NT writings and the apostolic fathers*—twice in Acts* (Acts 3:25; 7:8), seventeen times in Hebrews* (Heb 7:22; 8:6, 9 [2x], 10; 9:4 [2x], 15 [2x], 16, 17, 20; 10:16, 29; 12:24; 13:20), once in Revelation (Rev 11:19; *see* Revelation, Book of), twice in *1 Clement* (*1 Clem.* 15.4; 35.7; *see* Clement of Rome) and eight times in *Barnabas* (*Barn.* 4.6, 8; 6.19; 9.6; 13.1, 6; 14.1, 3; *see* Barnabas, Epistle of). The phrase "new covenant" *(kainē diathēkē; nea diathēkē* appears even less frequently—three times in Hebrews (Heb 8:8 [quoting Jer 38:31 LXX; Jer 31:31 MT]; 9:15; 12:24). The numbers hardly swell when the constructions that bear the same semantic weight are added—"better covenant" *(kreitton diathēkē,* Heb 7:22; 8:6), "eternal covenant" *(diathēkē aiōniou,* Heb 13:20), "the covenant of the beloved Jesus" *(hē [diathēkē] tou ēgapēmenou Iesou, Barn.* 4.8), "Lord's covenant" *(diathēkē kyriou, Barn.* 6.19; 14.3) and the reference to the "first covenant" *(prōtē [diathēkē], Heb* 9:15; cf. Heb 9:1:) *hē prōtē [dikaiōmata],* which implies a second or new covenant.

This relative lack of usage may come as a surprise, especially since the Christian Bible is divided into two "testaments" (Lat *testamentum,* "covenant") and since covenant is the "root metaphor" for Judaism (Segal, 4). However, the absence of extensive and explicit covenant language in early Christian writings could be due to several factors. (1) The identity and deeds of Jesus as a mediator eclipsed that which he mediated, the new covenant. The resultant contrast was not between an old Jewish covenant and a new Christian one but between the first covenant and Jesus. For earliest Christianity, christology* thus became a way of speaking about the new covenant. (2) The identification of Jesus with the new covenant could have operated at such a deep level of shared Christian conviction that it rarely needed and consequently did not receive far-reaching elaboration in Christian writings. (3) At the same time that Christians attempted to show the theological inadequacy of their Jewish contemporaries, they also sought to ground their identity within the Jewish Scriptures. The drive to demonstrate historical and theological continuity with Jewish predecessors may well have tempered the Christian appropriation of new covenant language. Given these factors, what may surprise us most is that Christianity employed covenant language at all.

2. Old Testament Background.

The Hebrew word *bᵉrît* is most often translated as "covenant," although *bᵉrît* possesses a much wider semantic range (see Barr). Of particular importance is the use of *bᵉrît* to describe Yahweh's special relationship with his people.

Four covenants in particular take on a special importance for the OT and Jewish tradition: God's unconditional covenant with the world through Noah (Gen 6:18; 9:8-16); the promise of land* and posterity to Abraham* (Gen 12:1-3; 15:18-19; 17:1-4), which was repeated to the ancestors* Isaac, Jacob and Joseph (Gen 26:1-5; 28:13-15; 48—50 passim); the royal and eventually messianic covenant with David and his descendants (2 Sam 7:1-17; Ps 89; Is 9:2-7; *Pss. Sol.* 18—19); and the conditional covenant formed between God and Israel at Sinai (Ex 19—24, 34; Deut 5—28). Despite the multiplicity of covenants and any tension that may have existed between them, the Mosaic covenant is the one by which and through which all others should be understood (Childs, 419).

At the heart of the Mosaic covenant is Yahweh's choice of Israel to be his people and his promise to be Israel's God. For their part Israel was to respond through obedience to the Law. Election and law thus gave shape to Jewish religious practice. Jews believed that they were elected by grace, that they were to respond to the historical expressions of Yahweh's mercy* through obedience to the law, that Yahweh's blessing would follow obedience, that his judgment would follow their disobedience and that forgiveness for their transgressions could be found through repentance and sacrifice. As E. P. Sanders has shown, this "pattern of religion" (what he terms "covenantal nomism") was a unifying feature of various Jewish groups from Deuteronomy onward.

The covenant is also a common thread running through the OT. Much of the Pentateuch seeks to elaborate and detail the covenant established through Moses. The historical books explain Israel's persistent difficulties as disobedience to the covenant. The prophets too see Israel's covenantal indiscretions as the chief reason for the punishment of exile. The prophets also describe the future in covenantal terms. God is going to reestablish the Mosaic covenant, variously depicted as a covenant of love (Hos 2:16-20) or peace (Ezek 34:25; 37:26) or as "everlasting" (Is 61:8; Jer 32:40; 50:5). The prophet Jeremiah even speaks of a "new covenant" that entails unprecedented forgiveness, reconciliation and re-creation (Jer 31:31-33). The prophets also universalize the particular covenant given to Israel: the future covenant includes the whole world (Is 42:6; 49:6-8). This eschatological and universal covenantal vision—a vision that authentically reflects the covenants God forged with David, Israel, Abraham and Noah—provides the conceptual framework for understanding new covenant language in the NT.

3. Covenant in Acts.

On several occasions Acts appeals to Israel's covenant history to identify the followers of the risen Jesus as the genuine heirs of the covenant. Acts accomplishes this without extensive reference to the word *diathēkē* (which appears only twice: Acts 3:25; 7:8), using instead the word "promise" *(epangelia)* to show how Christianity identified itself as God's covenant people (Acts 1:4; 2:33, 39; 7:17; 13:23; 37; 23:21; 26:6).

Peter's sermons in Acts 2—3 illustrate this identification. Peter proclaims that the resurrection* of Jesus fulfills the "oath" *(horkos)* God swore to David (that one of David's descendants would inherit the throne, Acts 2:30; cf. Ps 132:11) and the promise made to Moses (that God would raise a prophet like him, Acts 3:22; cf. Deut 18:15-16; *see* Old Testament in Acts). Further, repentance, baptism,* forgiveness and the reception of the Holy Spirit* confirm God's "promise" (Acts 2:39) and make believers "children of the prophets and of the covenant" (Acts 3:22-26).

Stephen's* sermon points to how God's covenant with Abraham (Acts 7:2-8) epitomizes the history of Israel and thus of Christianity. God's covenant with Abraham is seen as a beginning in which partial realizations are interconnected with new beginnings; stories containing new promises are embedded within older, foundational narratives (Dahl). For example, Moses' prediction of a new prophet lies within the story of Abraham (Acts 7:37). Jesus, as the prophet like Moses, is thus placed squarely in Abrahamic covenant. The rhetorical force of this narrative suturing reaches a climax in the final appeal. Stephen derides his Jewish audience for being "stiff-necked" and "uncircumcised in the heart," a people who "always resist the Holy Spirit" (Acts 7:51; *see* Circumci-

sion). He does this precisely because they have failed to see the connection between Jesus and their own covenant history (Acts 7:52-53). The programmatic appeal to Abraham within the sermon thus locates those who follow Jesus as true Israel (*see* Church as Israel).

Paul's sermon at Pisidian Antioch explicitly links the message about Jesus with the covenant history of Israel. Israel's covenant history includes election, exodus, wilderness wanderings, conquest, the promise of land, the judges, the prophets and the office of the king (Acts 13:17-21). This covenant now includes another, for out of David's posterity "God has brought to Israel a Savior, Jesus, as he promised" (Acts 13:24; cf. Acts 26:6). Indeed, Paul's gospel is that all of God's covenantal promises find their fulfillment in Jesus (Acts 13:33). Paul's sermon thus echoes the themes already heard in Peter's and Stephen's, namely, Christianity is the true heir of the Jewish covenant promises.

If Israel's covenant history could show that Jewish followers of Jesus were the genuine heirs, then an appeal to the covenant could also show that Gentiles,* people traditionally thought to be outside the covenant, are (and always were?) also a part of it. This is best seen in the accounts of Cornelius's* conversion (Acts 10:1—11:18) and the apostolic council (Acts 15:1-29). It took a heavenly vision and a thrice-repeated heavenly command to convince Peter too that it was not a covenantal breach to "associate or to visit with any one of another nation" (Acts 10:28). The dramatic coming of the Spirit (Acts 10:44-48), not unlike that at Pentecost,* confirmed to him and the Jerusalem* church that God's promise of forgiveness and salvation* through Jesus was for everyone (Acts 11:17-18). The apostolic council (Acts 15) not only officially sanctioned Gentile inclusion but also clarified the role of circumcision and the law of Moses in salvation. Peter argued that God makes no distinction: all are saved "through the grace of the Lord Jesus" (Acts 15:11). James links Gentile inclusion with the covenant by citing a string of prophetic texts (Amos 9:11-12; Jer 12:15; Is 45:21). Not only are Christians the true covenant people, but also the covenant is seen now to include Gentiles.

In Acts the covenant promises given to Israel are never withdrawn. Israel is not rejected (Acts 13:46; 28:25-28 notwithstanding). It is better to speak of a separation within Israel, with the church (described within Acts as "believers," "brethren," "saints" or "disciples"; but *see* Church §2.2 for a different reading of Luke's ecclesiology) as carrying on the unbroken line stemming from Abraham. There is no "new" Israel. The church is true Israel, the true covenant people of God. Acts does not emphasize the inadequacy of the Mosaic covenant (but cf. Acts 13:39; 15:10) but only the disobedience of the people. Indeed, Acts underscores the prophetic character of the covenant: its narrative and promissory linkages with the message and movement surrounding Jesus. Acts consistently portrays the community and the message as the intended destiny of Israel.

4. New Covenant in Hebrews.
No NT document so extensively reflects upon the new covenant as does Hebrews. Although the book is full of covenantal imagery and terminology, it is Hebrews's central section (Heb 4:14—10:15) that highlights the relationship between the old and new covenants.

Hebrews's central section can be broken into two halves: the first half argues that Jesus was appointed a superior, eternal high priest* after the order of Melchizedek* (Heb 5:1-10; 7:1-28), while the second half (Heb 8:1—10:16) examines the character of Jesus' high-priestly ministry (Heb 8:1-6), the nature of the new covenant that he mediates (Heb 8:7-13) and the new covenant offering that his ministry includes (Heb 9:1—10:16). The author begins and ends this second section by quoting the new covenant prophecy of Jeremiah 31 (Heb 8:8-12; 10:16-17). Thus, against the backdrop of the OT priestly sacrificial system and within the horizon of hope generated by biblical prophecy, Hebrews presents a sustained, expositional argument that identifies Jesus as the superior, heavenly and sinless high priest, the mediator of a new and better covenant (*see* Old Testament in Hebrews).

Numerous contrasts can be detected within the second half of this central section. The old covenant was earthly; the new covenant is heavenly (Heb 8:1; 9:1). The old covenant ministry was a copy and shadow (Heb 8:5; 9:23; 10:1); the new covenant is real (Heb 9:24) and true (Heb 8:2; 10:1). The old covenant featured human priests who were destined to die; the new covenant possesses a high priest who lives forever (Heb 9:28). The administration of a priest under the old covenant occurred according to the dictates of the law (Heb 8:4); the new covenant is directly and divinely administered (Heb 8:1-2). A priest under the old covenant had to offer sacrifice for his own sins (Heb 9:7); Jesus' sinlessness means that he did not offer sacrifice for himself (Heb 9:7). Under the old covenant multiple priests had to enter repeatedly the sanctuary to offer numerous sacrifices (Heb 9:6-7, 25; 10:11); under the new covenant a single high priest, Jesus, enters the heavenly sanctuary once (through his death and resurrection) and offers a singular sacrifice once and for all time (Heb 9:12, 26; 10:10, 12). The old covenant contained the sacrificial blood of animals (Heb 9:18-22); under the new covenant Jesus offers his own blood (Heb 9:12, 26). The efficacy of the old covenant offerings was limited (Heb 10:1-2); the efficacy of the new covenant sacrifice was definitive—there are no more offerings for sins. Under the old covenant the worshiper could not be perfected (Heb 9:9); under the new covenant a process of moral transformation has been enacted that will completely purify (Heb 9:14; 10:14).

S. G. Wilson reads these and other contrasts in Hebrews as a pointed effort to "denigrate" the old covenant and thus Judaism—an inference not necessarily demanded by the evidence. Wilson points to the pejorative connotation of such language as "weak and ineffectual," "shadow," "abolished" and "annulled" (see Wilson, 117-21). While the comparative character of much of Hebrews, especially of Hebrews 8:1—10:16, should not be denied, neither should the positive role of the first covenant be ignored. After all, the new covenant Jesus established was "concerned with the descendants of Abraham" (Heb 2:16).

Hebrews's valuation of the new covenant over the old was not a calculated anti-Jewish polemic (as Wilson would have us believe) but a natural consequence of the new covenant's eschatological* character. The old covenant, tied to this "present age" (Heb 9:9), was seen as "growing old" and "passing away" (Heb 8:13); the new covenant excels because it is founded on "better promises" (Heb 8:6), those of resurrection life.* The resulting contrast is not between something evil (old covenant/Judaism) and something good (new covenant/Christianity) but between something good (old covenant) and something better (new covenant). This is a very Jewish way of reasoning known as

Qal wahomer, the argument from the lesser to the greater: if the old covenant was good, then how much better will the new be? The argument of Hebrews about the relationship between the old and new covenants at this point is thus very similar to Paul's argument (2 Cor 3) about the two covenants.

The author of Hebrews uses both spatial and temporal imagery to demonstrate the comparable yet provisionary character of the Sinai covenant. The elaborate analogies between the earthly and heavenly elements of the old and new covenants work to show similarity, while the strategic citations of Jeremiah 31 demonstrate that a new day in salvation history has dawned.

5. Covenant in *Barnabas*.

In the *Epistle of Barnabas* we first meet what surely can be termed an anti-Jewish polemic. Barnabas's disdain for the practice of Judaism is obvious.

The litany of covenantal critiques begins early on. Barnabas warns his readers about overconfidence. They should not be like a "certain people" who "pile up sins" while claiming that the covenant was "irrevocably" theirs (*Barn.* 4.6). In fact, Jews "lost it completely" (*Barn.* 4.6) when they "turned to idols" and "broke the law" (*Barn.* 4.8; cf. *Barn.* 14.3, "the Lord's covenant was shattered"). Even Moses understood this as a forfeiture: "he hurled the two tablets from his hands, and their covenant was broken in pieces" (*Barn.* 4.8) All this occurred in order that the "covenant of the beloved Jesus" might be sealed in believers' hearts (*Barn.* 4.8). According to *Barnabas*, God gave the covenant, Moses received it and the Jewish people rejected it, a rejection that made them "unworthy" (*Barn.* 14.1, 4) and thus opened the way for another people (*Barn.* 6.11).

Barnabas also appeals to the history of election to demonstrate God's covenantal preference for Christians over Jews. "Let us see if this people [i.e., Christians] or the first people [i.e., Jews] receive the inheritance and if the covenant is ours or theirs" (*Barn.* 13.1). Barnabas then marshals the OT to show that Jacob was preferred over Esau (*Barn.* 13.2-3) and Ephraim over Manasseh (*Barn.* 13.3-5). The choice of the younger over the older prefigures God's choice of Christians as his people and therefore as the only legitimate "heir of the covenant" (*Barn.* 13.6).

But what happened to the covenant the Jews rejected? Barnabas argues that it passed on to Christians through Jesus. Jesus was both the mediator of the covenant (*Barn.* 14.5) and the covenant itself (*Barn.* 14.7). The covenant is the "Lord's covenant" (*Barn.* 6.19), the "covenant of the beloved Jesus" (*Barn.* 4.8). Nowhere does Barnabas speak of a completely "new" covenant. Indeed, the Mosaic covenant is Jesus' covenant (*Barn.* 14.3). For Barnabas the covenant remained the same; only the people changed.

Unlike Hebrews, which links the old and new covenants through an eschatological reading of Jeremiah 31, Barnabas allegorizes covenant imagery to speak of Jesus. The covenant, when properly read with special gnosis,* leads to the truth. For example, the circumcision of Abraham in reality preaches Jesus (*Barn.* 9.7-9). This different hermeneutic yields a completely different theological relationship between Judaism and Christianity.

6. Summary.

Acts, Hebrews and Barnabas agree that God has demonstrated covenantal faithfulness in the death of his Son.* However, each takes a different position on this new covenant's relationship to the old. Acts consistently presents those who follow Jesus as the true Israel, the genuine covenant people of God, a covenant newly shaped by the death and resurrection of Jesus. Working with a proof from prophecy/proclamation hermeneutic, Acts emphasizes continuity. At the other end of the spectrum is *Barnabas*, which espouses a throughgoing supersessionist position. The church replaces Israel in the covenant. Indeed, the covenant was never Israel's at all. Standing in the middle is Hebrews. Hebrews recognizes the legitimacy and efficacy of the first covenant; however, Hebrews argues that the "old" or "first" covenant pales in comparison with eschatological power of the new covenant.

See also BARNABAS, EPISTLE OF; CHRISTIANITY AND JUDAISM: PARTINGS OF THE WAYS; CHURCH AS ISRAEL, PEOPLE OF GOD; HEBREWS; LAW; MOSES; OLD TESTAMENT IN HEBREWS.

BIBLIOGRAPHY. J. Barr, "Some Semantic Notes on the Covenant" in *Beiträge zur Alttestamentlichen Theologie: Festschrift für Walther Zimmerli*, ed. H. Donner (Göttingen: Vandenhoeck & Ruprecht, 1977) 23-38; R. T. Beckwith,

"The Unity and Diversity of God's Covenants," *TynB* 38 (1987) 93-118; F. F. Bruce, "The People of God" in *New Testament Development of Old Testament Themes* (Grand Rapids: Eerdmans, 1968) 51-67; B. S. Childs, *Biblical Theology of the Old and New Testaments: Theological Reflection on the Christian Bible* (Philadelphia: Fortress, 1993); N. A. Dahl, "The Story of Abraham in Luke-Acts" in *Studies in Luke-Acts,* ed. L. E. Keck and J. L. Martyn (London: SPCK, 1966) 139-58; J. D. G. Dunn, *The Partings of the Ways: Between Christianity and Judaism and Their Significance for the Character of Christianity* (London: SCM; Philadelphia: Trinity Press International, 1991); E. Ferguson, "The Covenant Idea in the Second Century" in *Texts and Testaments: Critical Essays on the Bible and Early Church Fathers,* ed. W. E. March (San Antonio, TX: Trinity University Press, 1980) 135-62; W. Horbury, "Jewish-Christian Relations in Barnabas and Justin Martyr" in *Jews and Christians: The Parting of the Ways* A.D. *70-135,* ed. J. D. G. Dunn (WUNT 1.66; Tübingen: J. C. B. Mohr, 1992); W. Kanzig, "Καινή διαθήκη: The Title of the New Testament in the Second and Third Centuries," *JTS* 45 (1994) 519-44; E. P. Sanders, *Paul and Palestinian Judaism: A Comparison of Patterns of Religions* (Philadelphia: Fortress, 1977); A. F. Segal, *Rebecca's Children: Judaism and Christianity in the Roman World* (Cambridge, MA: Harvard University Press, 1986); S. G. Wilson, *Related Strangers: Jews and Christians 70-170 C.E.* (Minneapolis: Fortress, 1995).

C. C. Newman

CREATION, COSMOLOGY

Because the world* and its origin, structure and destiny (cosmology) are not treated systematically in the works under consideration, gaps must be filled in from what we suppose was commonly known. Several words impinge on this semantic area: *kosmos* ("world"), *aiōn* ("age"), *gē* ("earth"), *oikoumenē* ("inhabited world"). *Kairos* ("time") sometimes overlaps temporal aspects of *aiōn,* and the creation (*ktisis;* cf. *ktizō*) is also called *ta panta* ("all things") and is referred to as the "foundation of the world" (*katabolē kosmou*).

This rich fund of language derives from both the Jewish and Greek traditions. The Jewish teaching of creation, especially in Genesis, made use of a variety of mythical traditions and, because the early Christians did not find this area to be in dispute with Judaism,* scholars sometimes suggest that the NT writers thought of the earth as a disk upon which the heavens rest like a dome, under which the waters of the deep form the sea. It could however be a mistake to interpret such imagery as scientific description rather than as poetic portrayal. From the time of Aristotle the Greeks understood the world to be a sphere (Aristotle *Cael.* 2.2, 285a, 32), and perceptive attempts were made to calculate the circumference of the earth, though the debate persisted concerning whether the earth or the sun circled the other. Only in dialogue with the wider Hellenistic* world did certain aspects of this teaching become disputed. These were then dealt with in some detail in the second century.

1. Terminology
2. Perspectives of Later New Testament Works
3. Beyond the New Testament

1. Terminology.

In the works under consideration various terms are prominent, depending on the influence of Jewish (*'ereṣ/gē; tēbēl/oikoumenē* and *'ōlām/aiōn*) or Greek (*kosmos* and probably *ta panta*) traditions as well as whether the focus is upon temporal or spatial aspects. Apart from 1 John (*see* John, Letters of), where *kosmos* is used twenty-three times, this term is rarely used in the books under consideration. "Earth" (*gē*) is the most frequently used term in Acts* (thirty-two times, almost one-third of which come in OT quotations; *see* OT in Acts) and Revelation (eighty-two times; *see* Revelation, Book of). Of the fifteen uses of *oikoumenē* in the NT, five are to be found in Acts, three in Luke and three in Revelation, two of which are in parallelism to *gē.* In Hebrews* the most frequently used term is *aiōn* (fifteen times); it is used only twice in Acts and twenty-seven times times in Revelation, of which twenty-six are used in the expression "to the age of the ages," commonly translated "forever and ever," though *gē* is used eleven times and *oikoumenē* twice. God is spoken of as Creator and the world as creation (*ktizō, ktisis, ktisma*) in Hebrews, James,* 1 Peter,* 2 Peter* and Revelation.

1.1. The World of Space. While "land" (*gē*) may be used in a local sense, so that it is possible to leave one's land* and go to another (Acts 7:3, 4, 6, 29; 13:17, 19), or even in the more local sense of "holy ground" or other specific pieces of ground (Acts 7:33; cf. 9:4, 8; 10:11; 26:14), it can also be used in formulae incorporating the total creation in terms of heaven,* earth, sea and all that is in them (Acts 4:24; 7:49; Rev 5:13). In this sense the *oikoumenē* is roughly the equivalent of the earth (Acts 11:28; 17:26; Rev 3:10; 12:9). The extensiveness of the earth is also in view in the expressions "the four corners of the earth" and "the four winds of the earth" (Rev 7:1).

1.2. The Temporal World. The temporal nature of the world is expressed first in the affirmation of creation. God created the world *(kosmos)*, the heaven, the earth, the sea and all that is in them. Thus the world has a beginning (*archē,* Heb 1:10) and a foundation (*katabolē,* Heb 4:3; 9:26; Rev 13:8; 17:8). The world begins with creation and ends or passes away (Rev 21:1), or at least the last word about the world concerns the judgment* brought about by God* through Jesus, the person chosen by him to perform this task (Acts 17:31). For the author of Hebrews the last days were ushered in by the ministry* of Jesus (Heb 1:2), but the last word concerns the judgment of the world at the Second Coming of Jesus (*see* Parousia). In Revelation 20:11—21:8 the end of the present world and the judgment are closely associated. But there the end of the present world signals the dawning of the new and ideal world.

2. Perspective of Later New Testament Works. Generally, the various works are oriented to either a spatial or a temporal view of the world. Most make some contribution to each of these perspectives while concentrating on one of them. In Hebrews, James, 1 Peter and Revelation the world is seen as a place of testing, in which endurance* produces positive results but sin* produces death. Because of the testing in one's present life,* these works all look to a final day of visitation or judgment when the righteous and the wicked receive their just reward* or punishment.

2.1. Acts. Acts 4:24 makes explicit the Jewish understanding of creation and does so in strongly Jewish idiom, addressing God as "Sovereign Lord*" *(despota)* and confessing, "you who made *[sy ho poiēsas]* the heaven and the earth and the sea and all that is in them" (cf. Acts 14:15). The created world *(kosmos)* can also be spoken of in terms of heaven and earth (Acts 17:24). In Acts 17:26 Paul says that God "made

[epoiēsen] from one [person] (Adam) every nation of people to dwell upon the face of the earth." Thus Acts affirms the unity of humanity based in creation, the importance of which is revealed in Acts 1:8. Whereas the Gospel of Luke portrayed the purpose of God in Jesus coming to its fulfillment in Jerusalem,* Acts announces the mission* of the witnesses* to the risen Jesus going out from Jerusalem to Judea and Samaria* and to the uttermost parts of the earth *(heōs eschatou tēs gēs,* an expression repeated in Acts 13:47, where it occurs in the quotation of Isaiah 49:6 (LXX). In both places in Acts the focus is on the extensive nature of the inhabited earth *(oikoumenē)* and the inclusive scope of the mission (cf. Acts 17:6; 24:5). The mission involved the proclamation that God had fixed a day on which he will judge the inhabited world *(oikoumenē]* in righteousness* by the man he has designated by raising him from the dead (Acts 17:31; *see* Resurrection).

Although there are but two uses of *aiōn* (Acts 3:21; 15:18), the temporal nature of the world is not without importance and finds expression in Acts 1:7. According to Acts, the risen Jesus spoke to the disciples about the kingdom* of God and called on them to stay in Jerusalem until they were baptized (*see* Baptism) with the Holy Spirit.* In response the disciples asked if at this time he would restore the kingdom to Israel,* to which Jesus responded, "It is not for you to know the times *[chronous]* or the opportune moments *[kairous]* which the Father has placed in his own authority." By implication it seems that the disciples associated the kingdom of God with the baptism of the Spirit and the restoring of the kingdom to Israel. Neither of these associations is confirmed by the Jesus of Acts, though such eschatological* fulfillment is implied by Acts 2:17 and Acts 3:20, 25.

Acts depicts the world as God's creation, a creation, however, on the way to fulfillment. That fulfillment involved the historic mission of Jesus and the ongoing mission of the followers of Jesus to the inhabited world. The consummation of the purpose of God in creation, however, lay in the future, awaiting the coming of Jesus, God's appointed judge of all the inhabited earth. Thus the fulfillment of the creation is perceived in terms of the relationship of the purpose of God to human history.

2.2. Hebrews. The orientation of Hebrews (see Heb 1:2) is to the eschatological nature *(ep'* eschatou tōn hēmerōn toutōn) of the ministry of Jesus. Hebrews asserts the entry (eisagagē) of the Son,* spoken of as prōtotokos, into the world of humanity (oikoumenē, Heb 1:6), while Hebrews 10:5 speaks of Christ's coming into the world (eiserchomenos eis ton kosmon). His ministry is given its due significance (thus Heb 2:1-4) by revealing that Jesus (spoken of as "son") was appointed heir of all things and was the one through whom (di' hou) God made (epoiēsen) the worlds (tous aiōnas, Heb 1:2). Here as in Acts 4:24 the act of creation is signified using the verb poiein rather than the more specific ktizein. The debate about whether the world was created ex nihilo or from already existent formless matter was not yet an issue.

While Acts continues in the tradition of Genesis 1:1 in affirming that God made the heaven and the earth (cf. Heb 1.10), interpretatively adding the sea and all that is in them, Hebrews asserts that God made the ages (tous aiōnas). This is a favorite term in Hebrews, being used fifteen times with important connections between Hebrews 1:2 and Hebrews 11:3. The verb used in the latter is katetisthai, again confirming that no single technical term was used exclusively to describe the act of creation. The idea of the world, understood as the "ages," is dependent on the Hebrew 'ōlām (Eccles 3:11) and the plural 'ōlāmiym (Wis 13:9). The use of the plural (tous aiōnous) refers to all periods of time and what is manifest in and through them, emphasizing the temporal character of creation.

The purpose of this reference to Jesus as "son" (Heb 1:2-3) is to compare him favorably with the prophets* and the angels* (angeloi, "messengers"). Several points are made to demonstrate the superiority of the Son: God appointed him heir of "all things" (pantōn; and see ta panta in Heb 1:3), a reference to the totality of the creation; God made the "ages" through him; and the Son maintains (pherōn) the creation (ta panta) by his powerful word (tō rhēmati tēs dynameōs autou).

Further, the Son is described as "being" the visible revelation* of the invisible God (apaugasma tēs doxēs kai charaktēr tēs hypostaseōs autou; cf. Paul in Col 1:15-20 and Philo Vit. Mos. 2.65; Philo Leg. All. 1.43; Philo Conf. Ling. 97, 147). At the same time the use of Psalm 2:7 ("You are my son, today I have begotten you") in Hebrews 1:5 and Hebrews 5:5-6 suggests that Jesus became son at some point of time. The exaltation* of the Son to the right hand of God (Heb 1:3) is also made consequent to his having made purification for sin. It is unclear whether the appointment of the Son as heir of all things was based on his "being" or his agency in creation or was made effective in his exaltation to the right hand of God (see Heb 1:3,13; 10:12-13). The latter could be said to presuppose his being, his agency in creation as well as his work of purification. Alternatively, we may think that a number of independent traditions are being piled up to emphasize the superiority of the Son. The creation is seen to be directed toward him as the one who established its underlying purpose and also as the one who reestablished that purpose in purification (redemption*). Hebrews adopts the christological* perspective found in Colossians 1:16, 20 rather than the theocentric perspective of Romans 11:36. This apparent conflict is reconciled in the declaration that the Son is the image of the invisible God.

The author ascribes references to God in the Septuagint (Deut 32:43) to the Son, asserting that his throne is eternal (eis ton aiōna tou aiōnos) although his created works were temporal and would perish (Heb 1:8, 10). The temporal and temporary nature of the creation finds expression in reference to the foundation of the creation, which was laid in the beginning (Heb 1:10; cf. 4:3; 9:26) by the one who is. Though laid by him, the creation will pass away and perish in due course. Thus the Son is contrasted not only with the prophets and messengers but with the whole creation. While he remains, the creation established (ethemeliōsas) by him will pass away (Heb 1:10-12; 13:8). By contrast Abraham,* one of those with faith,* is said not to have set his hope* on any earthly city but to have "looked forward to the city which has foundations [tous themelious] whose builder [technitēs] and maker [dēmiourgos] is God" (Heb 11:10; cf. 11:16; 12:22-24; 13:14). Hebrews 9:26-28 (cf. Heb 10:25, 37) is oriented to the completion of the age (epi synteleia tōn aiōnōn) and the second appearance of Christ.

2.3. James. "Every good and perfect gift is from above coming down from the Father of lights" (Jas 1:17). This Jewish characterization of God (see T. Abr. 7:6 and the ascription "the prince of lights" in CD 5:17-18; 1QS 3:20) crystallizes the recognition of the sovereign power of God, especially in control of the heavenly lights. James is one of the least apocalyptic* or dualistic books in the NT. In the Genesis tradition the creation is perceived as good, and James (Jas 1:5, 17) affirms its ongoing goodness. Nevertheless, James is not untouched by the apocalyptic perspective and acknowledges the hostility of the world to God (Jas 1:27; 4:4) and the adversarial role of the devil (*see* Adversaries, Satan).

At the same time James teaches that it is possible to resist the devil, who flees from those who resist (Jas 4:7-8). The notion that temptation* and testing come from God or the devil is rejected by James, who asserts that temptation arises from evil desire, which when it is satisfied brings forth sin and death (Jas 1:13-16). This looks much like the rabbinic teaching of the "evil inclination" that is balanced by the "good inclination." The good inclination (good desire) is strengthened by the appropriate teaching, which is the role of the law* in Judaism. Thus armed, a person can act appropriately, resisting the devil and performing good works. James thus has an optimistic view of human life in the world.

Even so a two-stage understanding of creation seems to be presupposed in that the author claims to be one of those begotten by the word of truth* (the gospel*?) to be a kind of first fruits of God's creation (*aparchēn tina tōn autou ktismatōn*, Jas 1:18). What is in view appears to be the beginning of the harvest of the creation, which presupposes the judgment in the last days when the wicked will be punished while those who practice good will be rewarded (Jas 5:1-9). James affirms the imminence of judgment and the coming of the Lord as judge at the end of history. Thus this epistle also reflects an apocalyptic worldview, but it lacks the characteristic pessimistic evaluation of the present age. The "world" (*kosmos*), however, is viewed with suspicion (Jas 1:27; 4:4).

2.4. 1 and 2 Peter. The worldview of 1 Peter deals with the beginning of creation in terms of the "foundation of the world" (*katabolēs kosmou*, 1 Pet 1:20). Nevertheless the faithful are strangers and pilgrims (1 Pet 2:11) who must endure testing (1 Pet 4:12-19; 5:6-11), and the devil roams about like a roaring lion (1 Pet 5:8). Meanwhile, salvation* is hidden in heaven waiting to be revealed (1 Pet 1:4), where the risen Jesus Christ is at the right hand of God until

angels, authorities and powers* are made subject to him (1 Pet 3:21-22). That apparently is to be at the last time (*en kairō eschatō*, 1 Pet 1:5), when salvation will be revealed. Nevertheless, Christ was destined before the foundation of the world but revealed (*phanerōthentos*) at the end of times (*ep' eschatou tōn chronōn*, 1 Pet 1:20). At the same time it is asserted that the end (ultimate fulfillment) of all things is at hand (*to telos ēngiken*, 1 Pet 4:7). The coming of Jesus ushered in the last days. The author imminently awaits final fulfillment at the revelation of Jesus Christ (1 Pet 1:20) as judge of the living and the dead (1 Pet 4:5, 17-19).

In response to the assertion that since creation all has continued without change, 2 Peter 3:5-6 echoes the Genesis tradition, according to which the heavens were created in the beginning by the word of God. This reference shows that the earth, formed out of the water, was deluged at the flood (see 2 Pet 2:4-9). Judgments within history are made a basis for affirming the reality of the coming judgment of the last day, which, like the creation, is to be by the word of the Lord (2 Pet 3:7). The delay is explained in terms of the compassion of the Lord, who does not will that any should perish. Nevertheless, the day of the Lord* (judgment) will come suddenly and unexpectedly, when heaven and earth will be dissolved cataclysmically with fire (2 Pet 3:10, 12). The fire of judgment purifies a creation beyond redemption, though there are those to be saved out of it who await the promise of new heaven and new earth in which righteousness dwells (2 Pet 3:13; cf. Rev 21:1). Meanwhile the faithful are granted divine aid to escape from the corruption that is in the world (*kosmos*) and to become partakers of the divine nature (2 Pet 1:3-4). In this context the message of judgment is used to reinforce the exhortation to live a life of godliness (2 Pet 3:11-13).

2.5. 1, 2 and 3 John. The Johannine epistles are dominated by the use of *kosmos*. 1 John stands with the Gospel of John (where *kosmos* is used seventy-eight times) in its understanding of the world. While there is no explicit teaching on creation, the teaching of the Gospel, which seems to underpin that of the Epistles, should be presupposed. The outcome is a hostile world that shows hatred toward believers (Jn 15:18-25; 1 Jn 3:13; 4:1-6). Consequently, believers are exhorted not to love* the world, which is passing away (1 Jn 2:15-17). The world lies in the power of "the evil one" (1 Jn 5:19) and is characterized as being in darkness, apart from God's light (1 Jn 1:7) and in death (1 Jn 3:14).

People are divided into children of God and children of the devil (1 Jn 3:10; 5:18-19), who sinned in the beginning (1 Jn 3:8). The transition from the darkness to the light and from death to life is manifest in love for one another. Jesus Christ died to deal with the sins of the whole world (1 Jn 2:2); he was manifest to take away sins (1 Jn 3:5; 4:9-10) and to destroy the works of the devil (1 Jn 3:8); he was sent to be the savior of the world (1 Jn 4:14). The present time is characterized as the last hour when many antichrists* and false prophets have appeared in the world (1 Jn 2:18; 4:1). Yet everyone born of God conquers the world (1 Jn 5:4), and the young men have conquered the evil one (1 Jn 2:13-14).

There is also expectation of the day of judgment (1 Jn 4:17) at the manifestation or Parousia of Jesus (1 Jn 2:28). Thus 1 John portrays a threefold assault on the world and the devil: the historic mission of Jesus, the triumphant faith of believers (1 Jn 5:4) and the Parousia of Jesus in judgment. 2 John also affirms that many deceivers have gone out into the world and that the person who refuses to confess Jesus Christ coming in the flesh* is the deceiver and the antichrist (2 Jn 7).

2.6. Jude. Jude* may have been used by the author of 2 Peter, but the two works have different purposes. The scoffers of Jude 18, however, are those who deny the coming day of judgment (2 Pet 3:3-4). Jude presupposes a world under the influence of the devil, with whom Michael struggled (Jude 9; see Rev 12:7-12). For those who serve the devil's purposes, the nether gloom of darkness has been reserved forever (Jude 13). The punishment is also described in alternative imagery of fire from which those who are saved are snatched (Jude 23). Jude affirms the certainty of judgment, appealing to the salvation of the people out of Egypt and the judgment of those who did not believe; the judgment of the angels who did not keep their appointed place, who are now kept in eternal chains until the judgment day; and the punishment of Sodom and Gomorrah with eternal fire. Thus the judgment of those who troubled the addressees of Jude is assured.

2.7. The Apocalypse of John. The linguistic evidence of this book is distinct from the rest of the Johannine literature. In the Apocalypse *gē* ("earth") is used eighty-two times, while *kosmos* ("world") is used only three times, two of which (Rev 13:8; 17:8) occur in reference to those whose names were written in the book of life from the foundation of the world *(apo katabolēs kosmou)*. In the third (Rev 11:15) a great voice in heaven announces that "the kingdom of the world has become the kingdom of our Lord and of his Christ, and he will reign forever and ever," indicating the opposition of the "world" to God. Nevertheless, the world, spoken of as "all things" *(ta panta)*, is God's creation (Rev 4:11) and comprises every creature in heaven, on earth, under the earth, in the sea and all therein (Rev 5:13). In this formulation "the earth" is more or less the equivalent of "the inhabited earth" *(oikoumenē]*, a description with which it appears in parallelism (Rev 3:10; 12:9). This usage is common in the poetic works of the Septuagint, where *oikoumenē* was used to translate *tēbēl* and *gē* was used to translate *'ereṣ*.

God is characterized as eternal, "the one who is and who was and who is to come" (*ho ōn kai ho ēn kai ho erchomenos*, Rev 1:4, 8; 4:8; 11:17; 16:5). The future is characterized in terms of the coming of God, and the phrase "forever and ever" is appropriately used of God. But the creation has a beginning, and the heaven and earth and sea will become obsolete and pass away (Rev 21:1). The temporality of the creation is stressed.

Further, the world, though created by God, is dominantly evil; Rome,* characterized as great Babylon,* epitomizes the powers of evil (Rev 17-18). The faithful witnesses to Jesus must pass through great afflictions and endure suffering.* The struggle on earth has as a counterpart a war in heaven between Michael and his angels and the dragon (the ancient serpent, the devil, Satan; *see* Beasts) and his angels (Rev 12:7-12). Although the devil and his angels are cast out of heaven, they come down to earth to wreak havoc. This is apparently the great trial coming on all who dwell on the earth (Rev 3:10). Nevertheless, heaven is called to rejoice because, although the event signals coming trouble on earth, it also signals the imminent end of the devil's reign and of his role as the accuser of the faithful. The prospective period appears to be three and a half years, or 1,260 days (Rev 11:2-3; 12:6; 13:5).

Thus Revelation is oriented to the end of

history and the final judgment. The righteous call out to God "How long?" before he judges and avenges his faithful servants (Rev 6:10). The prospect of cataclysmic judgment is depicted (Rev 6:12-17), and the fate of the faithful and the wicked at the judgment is set out (Rev 7:13-17; 21:3-8). There is, however, an apparent conflict in the account of the prospects for the future of the world. There is the assertion that the kingdom of the world has become the kingdom of our Lord and of his Christ who will reign forever (Rev 11:15). Alternatively, the first heaven and earth pass away, to be replaced by a new heaven and a new earth (Rev 21:1). This is a warning against treating the imagery as factual information that can be added together like pieces of a jigsaw puzzle to make up a complete picture. Rather it seems that alternative sets of imagery are used to enrich the reader's perception of reality. Thus both views (Rev 11:15; 21:1) depict a radically transformed order and make the reader aware that the present world does not yet conform to the loving purposes of God.

3. Beyond the New Testament.
In the second century the understanding of the world and creation became a battleground. Aided by those works that depicted the alienation of the world from God (esp. Paul, the Gospel and epistles of John and Revelation) and recognizing the chaos of life and the breakdown of values in the Roman Empire,* the Jewish and Christian teaching about creation was challenged by Marcion* and the early gnostic* teachers such as Valentinus. Marcion apparently taught that the Creator of the world, worshiped by the Jews and spoken of in their Scriptures, was not the God and Father of Jesus. Jesus was not the Jewish Messiah but had been sent by his Father to set right the mess caused by the morally and creatively inferior creator god. Valentinus taught that the world is a kind of accident caused by a lack within the divine pleroma that produced error, and from the error the world was born. Thus both Marcion and Valentinus took further the recognition of the hostility of the world to God, which is to be found in Jewish apocalyptic works, by denying any positive connection between God and the world. In response to this challenge Justin Martyr, Irenaeus, Clement of Alexandria and Origen were challenged to deal with the problem of

theodicy in new and more effective ways that enabled them to affirm the goodness of the creation without ignoring the problem of human and natural evil.

See also APOCALYPTIC, APOCALYPTICISM; ESCHATOLOGY; GNOSIS, GNOSTICISM; HEAVEN, NEW HEAVEN; WORLD.

BIBLIOGRAPHY. R. Bultmann, *Theology of the New Testament* (London: SCM, 1951, 1955); idem, "The Understanding of Man and the World in the New Testament and in the Greek World" in *Essays Philosophical and Theological* (London: SCM, 1955) 67-89; C. H. Dodd, *The Interpretation of the Fourth Gospel* (Cambridge: Cambridge University Press, 1953); idem, *The Johannine Epistles* (London: Hodder & Stoughton, 1946); J. G. Gibbs, *Creation and Redemption* (Leiden: E. J. Brill, 1971); G. Gloege, "Welt," RGG^3 6:1595 ff.; G. Johnston, "*Oikoumene* and *kosmos* in the New Testament," *NTS* 10 (1963-64) 352-60; O. Michel, "ἡ οἰκουμένη," *TDNT* 5:157-59; R. A. Norris, *God and World in Early Christian Theology: A Study in Justin Martyr, Irenaeus, Tertullian and Origen* (London: A & C Black, 1966); E. F. Osborn, *The Beginning of Christian Philosophy* (Cambridge: Cambridge University Press, 1981) chap. 5; H. Sasse, "αἰών, αἰώνιος," *TDNT* 1:197-209; idem, "γῆ, ἐπίγειος," *TDNT* 1:677-81; idem, "κόσμος," *TDNT* 3:868-95; R. Schnackenburg, *Christliche Existenz nach dem Neuen Testament: Abhandlungen und Vorträge* (2 vols.; München: Kösel, 1967, 1968). J. Painter

CREEDS, CONFESSIONAL FORMS
It has become common to distinguish between creeds, such as the Apostles' Creed and the Nicene Creed (conventional titles that, as with the Athanasian Creed, give a misleading account of their origins), and confessions, such as the Augsburg Confession (1530), the Scots Confession (1560) and the Westminster Confession (1647), normally to the detriment of the latter. Yet the contrast is usually overdrawn. No sharp differentiation between them can be sustained, apart from the rather obvious one that the three creeds were produced in a still largely united church and in the case of the Nicene Creed as a basis for safeguarding unity.

But no creed, however venerable, is free of the limitations of its original context or can be interpreted without regard for it. Thus in the

Apostles' Creed, "Father" almost certainly denotes God's* role as Creator, while in the Nicene Creed, "one baptism for the remission of sins" cannot originally have covered infant baptism* since the responsible church fathers did not believe that infants had sins to be remitted (Wright). In the case of all the three early creeds, historical exegesis must include attention to the teachings each seeks to condemn or exclude. Hence one may understand the extraordinary fact that Pontius Pilate gets a mention in the Apostles' Creed, originally for antidocetic reasons (*see* Docetism).

Although no formal creeds or confessions appear in the NT, the identification and analysis of creedal elements and formulae, especially in the Pauline epistles, have engaged much scholarly energy in recent decades (*see DPL*, Creed). Telltale stylistic features have been enumerated and different settings, such as baptism and confession under persecution,* recognized and patterns of development discerned. Such study has emphasized that Christianity, in its earliest phase as the Jesus movement, was distinguished from the rest of Judaism* by its beliefs about Jesus of Nazareth. It was constituted confessionally. Recent translations of the NT often draw attention to creedal and confessional formulations by laying them out in stanza form (see for example 1 Tim 3:16). With the exception of 1 Peter,* the NT writings other than the Gospels and the Pauline epistles do not contain a great deal of relevant material bearing on creedal developments.

1. Acts of the Apostles
2. 1 Peter
2. 1 John
4. Other New Testament Writings
5. The Apostolic Fathers
6. Justin Martyr
7. The Rule of Faith
8. Toward the Apostles' Creed

1. Acts of the Apostles.

In the primitive mission* preaching to their fellow Jews, the apostles* and others repeatedly affirmed that Jesus was the Messiah. This basic homologia appears as a formulaic summary in Acts 9:22 and Acts 17:3 (introduced by *hoti recitativum* to denote a quotation) and elsewhere is frequent (cf. Acts 5:42; 18:5, 28), whereas the confession of Jesus as Lord* or as Son* of God is rare (for the latter see Acts 8:36 [Codex Bezae] and Acts 9:20; for the former see

Acts 10:36 and Acts 11:20, both to Gentile* audiences).

In addition a two-part pattern is common in Acts,* comprising the antithesis of "you/they crucified Jesus" but "God raised him up" (Acts 2:22-24, 36; 3:15; 4:10; 5:30-31; 10:39-40; 17:2-3; 26:23). The first limb of this summary declaration varies considerably in wording. A shift is observable from the polemical directness of "you" (put to death) to "they," as is another transposition into the necessity for the Messiah to suffer (*see* Suffering). The context for most of the confessional forms in Acts is missionary proclamation. Exorcism is another context (cf. Acts 4:10), but both exorcism (or healing*) and baptism regularly include only the invocation of the name* of Jesus Christ* (cf. Acts 2:38; 3:6; 8:16; 10:48; 19:5; 22:16).

2. 1 Peter.

A long succession of scholars has found in 1 Peter a baptismal homily, or liturgy (*see* Liturgical Elements), or at least a pattern of catechesis that had baptism as a focal point (*see* Worship). Since baptism was indubitably a central context for the development of creeds in primitive Christianity, creedal fragments are recognizable in 1 Peter, most obviously at 1 Peter 3:18, with the death and resurrection* of Christ as the subject matter (*see* Death of Christ), formulaic phrasing ("the just for the unjust") and contrasting parallelism in the final clause ("put to death in the body, brought to life in the spirit"). The baptismal setting of 1 Peter 3:18-22 is obvious, and echoes of baptismal confession or doxology may well be present also in 1 Peter 3:21-22.

Other formulae in the epistle focus on either the resurrection (1 Pet 1:21) or the passion of Christ but not both at the same time. The sufferings of Christ are prominent throughout, partly because of the experiences of the intended readers, and the traditional catechetical resource of Isaiah 53 informs 1 Peter 2:21-24 in its recognizably stylized presentation of Christ's passion as both vicarious ("Christ suffered for you," 1 Pet 2:21; "he bore our sins in his body," 1 Pet 2:24) and yet exemplary (1 Pet 2:21).

3. 1 John.

The background in 1 John (*see* John, Letters of) is not baptism and Christian demeanor in persecution* but division and conflict over false teaching* (1 Jn 2:19). Short creedal criteria are cited throughout the letter: "Jesus is the Christ" (1 Jn 2:22; 5:1), "Jesus is the Son of God" (1 Jn 4:15; 5:5) and "Jesus Christ has come in the flesh" (1 Jn 4:2; cf. 2 Jn 7). They serve to debar one of the versions of Docetism that split the human Jesus from the divine Christ.

In addition to these christological formulae, others occur that confess the significance of the death of Christ, especially the repeated "propitiation for our sins" (1 Jn 2:2; 4:10; cf. 1 Jn 3:16, "Jesus Christ laid down his life for us"). The literary style of 1 John, with its penchant for short, lapidary clauses and sentences in a declarative rather than an argumentative or expository mode, makes it harder to isolate certain creedal or confessional elements. Yet the letter illustrates with sharp clarity how the core content of Christian teaching was summarized in situations of dispute to draw unambiguous lines between what would later be called heresy and orthodoxy ("the teaching of Christ," 2 Jn 9).

4. Other New Testament Writings.

The writer to the Hebrews* more than once appeals to "the confession" to which his readers must adhere (Heb 4:14; 10:23; cf. Heb 3:1), but little clue is given to its content (but cf. "Jesus the Son of God" in Heb 4:14). The summary of heads of elementary teachings about Christ found in Hebrews 6:1-2 reflects an extensive catechesis without echoing formulations of any degree of fixity.

In James* the only creedal-type affirmations are of the oneness of God (Jas 2:19; 4:12). Jude* ends with a formal doxology (Jude 24-25), and the Apocalypse of John (see Revelation, Book of) includes a number of verses that must belong to the worship of the congregations known to the author (cf. Rev 4:8, 11; 5:9-10, 12, 13; 7:12; 11:15, etc.). They reflect a Jewish Christian* milieu, but although they and other shorter formulae (e.g., "I am the Alpha and the Omega," Rev 1:8) are by no means bereft of creedal substance, they are best regarded from the perspective of the liturgical sources of the book. Various theories have been advanced, viewing it in terms of a lectionary framework or the celebration of the Christian pascha, for example. John's prophecy* stands within the line of development of early Christian worship rather than of creedal formulation.

5. The Apostolic Fathers.

The formation of creedal statements is one of those subjects (like, for example, attitudes to sabbath and Sunday and observance of the pascha) on which recognition of the continuity between the NT and the earliest post-NT or non-NT writings is particularly helpful. Even if no historical credit can be attached to the delightful legend (found in Rufinus of Aquileia's *Commentary on the Apostles' Creed* 2, written early in the fifth century) that after Pentecost* the apostles composed the creed known by their name at one sitting, each contributing a clause, nevertheless the development of creeds in general may be deemed in a less precise sense apostolic. This is so because the practice of using formalized summaries of central Christian beliefs goes back to the apostles themselves, and also the faith thus summarized more extensively in later generations derived from apostolic teaching and writing.

Ignatius* is the one of the apostolic fathers* in whose letters creed-like statements most obviously occur, usually with antiheretical import. The following is perhaps hymnodic in its antithetical rhythms:

> One alone is Physician,
> Both fleshly and spiritual.
> Born and unborn,
> God come in the flesh,
> True life in death,
> From both Mary and God,
> At first passible and then impassible,
> Jesus Christ our Lord.
> (Ign. *Eph.* 7.2)

Others more prosaic in style are found in Ignatius *Ephesians* 18.2 and in *Letter to Polycarp* 3.2. Of particular interest is the appearance of "in the time of Pontius Pilate" in three of these formulations (Ign. *Magn.* 11; Ign. *Trall.* 9; Ign. *Smyrn.* 1.2), illustrating, along with Ignatius's repeated use of the adverb "actually/really" *(alēthōs)*, the strongly historical character of his christological confession against docetic denial. These embryonic creeds in Ignatius reflect the tendency of oft-repeated teaching to assume a standardized pattern. At this early stage it is unlikely that they echo an already elaborated baptismal confession in use at Antioch.* They bear more explicit connection with the Lord's Supper,* which Ignatius speaks of in realist terms, possessing significance only as the true flesh* and blood of the Christ who was truly flesh and truly died.

The quasi-creedal fragments in the other apostolic fathers are briefer and more varied. "Have we not one God and one Christ and one Spirit of grace who was poured upon us?" (*1 Clem.* 46.6) is at once trinitarian, baptismal and interrogatory, a combination prophetic of later developments. Elsewhere Clement (*see* Clement of Rome) uses phrases more reminiscent of the kerygma focused on Christ (e.g., "Jesus Christ, our Lord by the will of God, gave his blood on our behalf," *1 Clem.* 49.6). Formulae of different kinds—triadic, binitarian (naming God the Father and Christ but not the Spirit) and confessing Christ alone—were already attested in the NT. The *Didache** instructs baptism "in the name of the Father and of the Son and of the Holy Spirit" (*Did.* 7.1; cf. Mt 28:19), confirming evidence that a trinitarian confession was normal at baptism probably by the end of the first century.

6. Justin Martyr.

Among the second-century writers before Irenaeus and Tertullian, Justin Martyr, who came from Palestine but taught and died (c. 165) in Rome,* is the most informative on creedal developments. In the first case he gives the fullest account of baptism to date: "There is pronounced over the one who elects to be born again and has repented of his sins *the name of God the Father and Lord of the universe,* the person who leads the one to be washed to the water calling him by this name alone. . . . Also *in the name of Jesus Christ, who was crucified under Pontius Pilate,* and *in the name of the Holy Spirit, who through the prophets foretold everything about Jesus,* the one to be enlightened is washed" (Justin Martyr *Apol. I* 61.10). The italicized clauses must be fairly close to the wording used by the minister of baptism (not by the candidate) in the Roman church.

Second, Justin's writings furnish several creedal-like summaries of Christian beliefs, whose open elucidation is one of his chief apologetic purposes. Some of these statements are in threefold form (the most developed at *Apol. I* 13), but more of them focus on Christ alone. Of the latter the *Dialogue with Trypho* 85.2 provides an instructive example: "In the name of this very one, the Son of God and first-born of all creation, and born through the virgin and become a passible human being, and crucified under Pontius Pilate by your people and dead, and

risen from the dead and ascended to heaven, every demon that is exorcised is conquered and subdued." This passage reminds us of another context of creedal declaration; exorcism is by far the most frequently recorded miracle* in pre-Constantinian Christianity. Here and elsewhere in Justin (e.g., *Apol. I* 21.1; 46.5; *Dial. Tryph.* 63.1; 132.1) we meet a christological confession more elaborate than the second baptismal clause. Other settings than exorcism, particularly of teaching and preaching,* seem to have nurtured the increasingly standardized christological statements. In Justin they remain close to the apostolic kerygma, scarcely reflecting at all the apologetically slanted logos theology his writings promote (*see* Christology; Logos).

7. The Rule of Faith.

Christian writers of the late second and early third centuries, especially Irenaeus, Tertullian and Origen, present statements of what Irenaeus calls "the faith [which] the church, though dispersed throughout the whole world . . . , has received from the apostles and their disciples" (Irenaeus *Haer.* 1.2) and what Origen calls "the proclamation of the church . . . preserved unaltered handed down in unbroken succession from the apostles and existing to this day in the churches" (Origen *De Princ.* 1. presc. 2). These summaries are usually termed the rule (Gk *kanōn;* Lat *regula*) of faith* or truth.* They are trinitarian in structure, considerably longer than any formula noted so far and not verbally fixed, as is evident from different texts of the rule within a single writer.

The apostolic fathers' common conviction is that the rule comprised the teaching handed on by the apostles (no claim is made for the apostolic authorship of its wording) and was everywhere uniform; a fragment of Hegesippus records that on a journey from Palestine to Rome he found very many bishops teaching the same faith: "in every succession and in every city what the law and the prophets and the Lord preach is faithfully followed" (Eusebius *Hist. Eccl.* 4.22.1, 3). In reality it represented the sum and substance of the public faith of the local church in question, filtered through the particular theological lens of the apostolic father in question. Thus Irenaeus's rule touches on his distinctive notion of recapitulation, while Origen's includes paragraphs on the soul and free will.

Again, while the rule is advanced as the essence of the church's teaching voice ever since its apostolic foundation, it is not set over against the apostolic writings. From one perspective it may be viewed as what the teaching mind of the church receives from the apostolic Scriptures. From another perspective the rule consists of one of three or four strands woven inextricably together in mainstream second-century Christianity's vindication of its apostolic credentials, in rejection of Gnosticism* and other, lesser false claimants to apostolic descent. Within churches of demonstrable apostolic foundation or close association, the rule of faith stands for the unbroken continuity of public (not secret or esoteric) teaching from the time of the apostles onward (not latter-day novelties), carried by a historically recognizable succession of teachers (presbyters or bishops) and by an openly transmitted corpus of apostolic writings (a canon* larger than Marcion's but exclusive of many gnostic gospels, etc.). As such the appeal to the rule of faith had validity for only a limited period of living memory (Irenaeus, c. 200, believed he knew the apostle John through Polycarp*; Eusebius *Hist. Eccl.* 5.4-8); by Origen's time it is losing obvious contact with the apostolic kerygma.

Since the diverse gnostic platforms chiefly stimulated the elaboration of the rule of faith but always in continuity with earlier trends toward more stereotypical summaries of church teaching seen in Ignatius and Justin, so its content reflected anti-gnostic emphases on the goodness of Creator and creation,* the historical reality of the incarnation of the Son, the unity of old and new covenants* and the concreteness of the last things.

8. Toward the Apostles' Creed.

The rule of faith is not to be confused with a fixed creed, but it cannot be separated from the development of the latter. For if baptism was the locus of the creed, prebaptismal instruction embodied the elements of the rule of faith. In turn the formulation of the rule may have influenced the wording of the creed at critical points.

Just as the rule of faith varied from church to church, so all creeds were originally local (there was no one Apostles' Creed). Yet not only is the development of a verbally fixed creed most easily traced for Rome, but also what happened at Rome in this respect as in others proved normative for elsewhere in the West. The Old Roman creed (as scholars call it; see the masterly work by Kelly) of c. 200 was in essence not far short of what was first called "the Apostles' Creed" *(Symbolon)* in the later fourth century and had received its definitive form by the eighth. The chief witness for the Old Roman creed is the *Apostolic Tradition,* commonly attributed to Hippolytus of Rome c. 215 but increasingly viewed as a compilation of traditions over a longer period.

The main surprise for modern readers is the form of the baptismal creed in Hippolytus: not declaratory ("I believe in God . . . ") but interrogatory. The baptizing minister asked the candidate "Do you believe . . . ?" three times, baptizing him or her after each response of "I believe." The structure is trinitarian, the first question is very brief ("Do you believe in God, the Father Almighty?") and the third not much longer ("Do you believe in the Holy Spirit, in the holy church and the resurrection of the flesh?"; the text is not wholly certain). The second in length and emphasis sums up the development that this article has traced: "Do you believe in Christ Jesus, the Son of God, who was born by the Holy Spirit of the virgin Mary, and was crucified under Pontius Pilate, and was dead [and buried], and rose the third day alive from the dead, and ascended into heaven and was seated at the right hand of the Father, and will come to judge the living and the dead?" (Hippolytus *Apos. Trad.* 21).

Scholars agree that this interrogatory form goes back to earliest creedal beginnings. The expansion of Hippolytus's second clause compared with Justin's version less than a half-century earlier at Rome probably points to the impact of the gnostic crisis and the influence, or symbiosis, of the rule of faith. By the of the second century both rule and creed bear eloquent testimony to the christological and historical heart of the church's faith.

See also CHRISTOLOGY; GOSPEL; LITURGICAL ELEMENTS; TRUTH; WORSHIP AND LITURGY.

BIBLIOGRAPHY. R. Bultmann, "Bekenntnis- und Liedfragmente im ersten Petrusbrief," *ConNT* 11 (1949) 1-14; P. Carrington, *The Primitive Christian Catechism: A Study in the Epistles* (Cambridge: Cambridge University Press,

1940); L. W. Countryman, "Tertullian and the *Regula Fidei,*" *SecCent* 2 (1982) 208-27; J. Crehan, *Early Christian Baptism and the Creed: A Study in Ante-Nicene Theology* (London: Burns, Oates & Washbourne, 1950); O. Cullmann, *The Earliest Christian Confessions* (London: Lutterworth, 1949); C. H. Dodd, *The Apostolic Preaching and Its Developments* (London: Hodder & Stoughton, 1936); W. R. Farmer, "Galatians and the Second-Century Development of the *Regula Fidei,*" *SecCent* 4 (1984) 143-70; R. P. C. Hanson, *Tradition in the Early Church* (London: SCM, 1962); J. N. D. Kelly, *Early Christian Creeds* (2d ed.; London: Longmans, 1960); V. H. Neufeld, *The Earliest Christian Confessions* (Leiden: E. J. Brill, 1963); A. M. Ritter, "Glaubensbekenntnis(se), V. Alte Kirche," *TRE* 13 (1984) 399-412; J. Stevenson, ed., W. H. C. Frend, rev. ed., *A New Eusebius: Documents Illustrating the History of the Church to A.D. 337* (rev. ed.; London: SPCK, 1987); D. van den Eynde, *Les normes de l'enseignement chrétien dans la littérature patristique des trois premiers siècles* (Gembloux: Duculot, 1933); K. Wengst, "Glaubensbeken-ntnis(se), IV. Neues Testament," *TRE* 13 (1984) 392-99; D. F. Wright, "The Meaning and Reference of 'One Baptism for the Remission of Sins' in the Niceno-Constantinopolitan Creed," *SP* 19 (1989) 281-85.　　　　　D. F. Wright

CROSS, THEOLOGY OF THE

For Christianity generally, the "theology of the cross" (or *theologia crucis*) has been the criterion by which all Christian thinking and living are tested. The cross is seen as the sole ground of salvation,* the starting point of all authentic Christian thought and the indispensable center of the theological enterprise. But we do not find a uniform *theologia crucis* in the NT, and indeed considerable differences may be observed between the NT and the writings of the post-apostolic period. Some of the latter abandon it altogether (see comments on the *Shepherd of Hermas** below), but generally we will survey a variety of authors for whom the cross was central to their theology but who gave different expression to their convictions because of the differing circumstances they faced. They thus point contemporary theology to differing ways in which the cross addresses human needs (*see DPL,* Cross, Theology of the).

　　1. Later New Testament Writings
　　2. Post-New Testament Writings

1. Later New Testament Writings.

1.1. Acts. Older scholarship held that "Luke fails to attach special significance to the crucifixion and death of Jesus. . . . There is no Passion-mysticism such as is found in Paul, no appreciation of the paradox of the crucified Messiah presented as the burning centre of the Christian message" (Hanson, 43-44). Instead, Luke's focus rests on the resurrection* and ascension* of Christ,* which releases the outpouring of the Holy Spirit* and the universal offer of forgiveness* through repentance,* faith* and baptism* (Acts 2:32-33, 38; 3:14-16; 13:32-39). The death of Jesus features chiefly as the sin that reveals the culpability of Israel's* leaders (Acts 3:14, 5:30; *see* Death of Christ), even if God* had also planned it (Acts 2:23).

More recently the picture has been balanced. First, C. K. Barrett argued that a *theologia crucis* involves more than just a theory about what was achieved on the cross. It also concerns "a pattern of daily life, in which the believer practices the daily discipline (in the strictest sense of the term) of cross-bearing" (Barrett, 77). And he does not find it hard to show that this is the case in Acts.* The apostles are anything but triumphant figures. They are persecuted, suffer great reversals and "through many tribulations . . . enter the kingdom of God" (Acts 14:22; cf. Acts 9:16). They thus live out the death-resurrection pattern of their Lord, which is exactly what we find in Paul (2 Cor 4:7-12).

Second, R. H. Fuller has pointed to Luke's connection between the passion and "the forgiveness of sins" (see Lk 24:46-47; Acts 2:38, 3:18-19, 5:31, 10:43; 13:38-39). "Luke accepted and transmitted a tradition which identified with the belief that the passion effected remission of sins and that this salvific event was made available through baptism" (Fuller, 217). Implicitly, therefore, the death of Christ is treated as salvific, even if Luke does not spell it out (though cf. Acts 20:28).

Third, J. B. Green has shown that from the start Jesus' death was interpreted through the traditions of the "Suffering Righteous" and the "Servant of the Lord." Since Luke employs both terms in his opening speeches (Acts 3:13-14, 26; 4:27, 30; 7:52), since the "Servant of the Lord" traditions clearly enabled the first Christians to explain the death of the Messiah as salvific, and since the apologetic context of early preaching* would inevitably have laid emphasis on God's vindication of the crucified Messiah, a good case can be made that Luke does not reject a salvific understanding of the cross in Acts but rather presupposes and defends it by emphasizing the resurrection.

1.2. Hebrews. In Hebrews* the picture is very different. The cross takes center stage as the author draws heavily on OT cultic and sacrificial language to explain Christ. "Without the shedding of blood forgiveness cannot happen" (Heb 9:22) is a fundamental presupposition, not just a comment about the OT cult. Christ's blood is different from that of the animal victims: it is effective. The blood of animals could provide ritual purity* (Heb 9:13) but not forgiveness (Heb 10:4). But the blood of Christ cleanses the conscience* (Heb 9:14; 10:11-14, 22).

Why is this? The language of Hebrews is stirring, but we cannot help pressing to find the theological rationale for this emphasis on the effectiveness of the cross. E. Grässer finds it in the gnostic* idea of the preincarnate unity of Christ and his "children"; Hebrews 2:14 implies that Christ's children were already such before they "shared flesh and blood," and their "incarnation" is then made the reason for Christ's. Grässer suggests, then, that in Hebrews the cross works because of that existing family relationship between Christ and his children, so that automatically his death has an effect on them.

Apart from wider questions about the possibility of such gnostic influence on the NT, Grässer's explanation tends to undermine Hebrews's emphasis on faith as the vital means of obtaining the salvation won on the cross (Heb 11:1—12:3) and also undermines the possibility of apostasy.* The passionate warning passages (e.g., Heb 2:2-3; 3:12; 4:11) lose their force if salvation happens quasi-automatically on the basis of a relationship that exists apart from faith. But Grässer rightly points to the unique connection in Hebrews between salvation and incarnation—not only in Hebrews 2:14-18 but also in Hebrews 5:7-10 and Hebrews 10:5-10. The cross is the climax of a process of sacrifice* that embraces the whole incarnation of the Son,* through which he unites himself to flesh* and blood, so that he might then truly represent us as our high priest* in offering himself for us and entering the presence of God.

1.3. The Other General Letters. James* uniquely contains no reference to the death or resurrection of Christ. But if we employ Bar-

rett's point about the *theologia crucis* in Acts, we understand that James pictures the Christian life on a death-resurrection pattern that must presuppose that a message about the cross formed part of the "word of truth" by which "he brought us to birth" (Jas 1:18). But his strongly pastoral and ethical* purpose does not require him to make this explicit.

We find the opposite in 1 Peter.* Here the purpose is also pastoral and ethical—the encouragement and instruction of scattered and potentially persecuted believers—but an explicit *theologia crucis* is germane. "The theme of Christian suffering dominates the whole letter, and . . . it is one of the writer's chief aims to bring this suffering into relationship with the suffering of Christ" (Dalton, 123; *see* Persecution; Suffering). This the author does by underlining the example of Christ (1 Pet 2:21-25) but also and chiefly by pointing to his victory, through the cross, over all the unbelieving powers arrayed against his readers (this is Dalton's persuasive interpretation of 1 Peter 3:17-22).

Similarly in 1 John (*see* John, Letters of) the purpose is clearly pastoral. An explicit *theologia crucis* has an important role to play in giving confidence about the forgiveness of sins (1 Jn 2:1-2), in providing a role model of Christian love* (1 Jn 3:16-18) and as a vital doctrinal test distinguishing the Spirit of God from that of antichrist.* The view that it was not God's Son who died on the cross but a mere human being from whom the Son of God had just departed denies the heart of the gospel: the cross as a demonstration of God's love in sending his Son as "the atoning sacrifice for our sins" (1 Jn 4:10 NRSV).

1.4. Revelation. The vision* of "the Lamb, standing as slain" (Rev 5:6) is central to the book (*see* Revelation, Book of). Death and resurrection are incorporated into a remarkably high christology,* with divine titles, attributes and functions being applied without hesitation to Christ. As R. J. Bauckham puts it (55-56), Christ "as 'the living one' ([Rev] 1:18) shares God's eternal livingness," but "his eternal livingness was interrupted by the experience of a human death, and he shares the eternal life of God through triumph over death." This triumph is displayed in Revelation 5:5-6, where John first hears that "the Lion of the tribe of Judah has conquered" but then sees the slain Lamb* on the throne. The Lion's victory has been achieved through innocence, weakness and death.

This then becomes the pattern for the church*: "They too have conquered him by the blood of the Lamb and by the word of their testimony *(martyria)*; they did not prefer their own lives to death" (Rev 12:11). Here it seems clear that "the blood of the Lamb" connotes their blood as well as Jesus' (Bauckham). In Revelation, martyrdom* is of the essence of discipleship, not because every follower of Christ will be martyred but because "testimony" means an association with Christ that may not stop short of it, if necessary.

2. Post-New Testament Writings.

2.1. Clement of Rome. A *theologia crucis* is barely visible in Clement (*see* Clement of Rome), which is particularly surprising in view of his clear love of Hebrews. As in the case of James, however, the limitations of his aim may explain this. The blood of Christ brings "the grace of repentance" to the world in this generation, parallel to other generations called to repentance by Noah and Jonah (*1 Clem.* 7.4-7). Clement frequently uses the cross to reinforce his moral appeal to love and humility (e.g., *1 Clem.* 16; 21; 49.6).

2.2. Ignatius. Ignatius* is very different. Facing martyrdom, he says, "My spirit is now all humble devotion to the cross, which is a stumbling block to unbelievers but to us salvation and eternal life" (Ign. *Eph.* 18.1). For him martyrdom was something to be sought actively as a means of union with Christ. "I seek him, who died for us! I want him, who rose for us! Birth pangs are upon me" (Ign. *Rom.* 6.1). His own forthcoming physical death underlines for him the importance of the real, physical death of Christ; hence his passionate opposition to the Docetists,* who "deny his death—but it is the mystery through which we have received the gift of faith; and because of it we endure, so that we may be found as disciples of Jesus Christ, our only teacher" (Ign. *Magn.* 9.2).

A mystical, personal union with Christ is at the heart of Ignatius's vision, and its physical component, related to his own death, produces for him his twin emphases on the physical unity of the Christian community around the symbolic person of the bishop and on the Eucharist as a real participation in the body and blood of Christ.

There is much in Ignatius that reexpresses

the authentic Pauline *theologia crucis*, but there are new thoughts as well: particularly the desire for martyrdom and the emphasis on the Eucharist both as a real participation in the death of Christ and as a focus of the unity of the church around bishop and clergy.

2.3. Lesser Works. The *Epistle to Diognetus** reaches a rhetorical climax with the presentation of the love of God displayed in the gift of his Son to be our ransom from sin (*Diogn.* 9). The author does not say that the ransom was effected through Christ's death, a strange oversight in an evangelistic tract directed at unbelievers. The *Epistle of Barnabas** has a strongly polemical edge to its presentation of the incarnation and death of Christ (chiefly in *Barn.* 5—6 but also later). The aim is to show that the Scriptures prophesy his death for us, so that they do not belong to Israel but to the church. The result is that "the Lord conferred [the covenant] on us, making us the People of the Inheritance by His sufferings on our behalf. Though the purpose of the incarnation was partly to allow them to put the final seal on their sins, it was also that we might receive the covenant of the Lord Jesus from its rightful heir" (*Barn.* 14.4-5, Staniforth).

It is sobering to reflect on the enormous popularity of the *Shepherd of Hermas** in the second and third centuries—often it is treated on a par with the NT. In its first two parts, the *Vision* and the *Mandates,* Christ is not mentioned. He appears in several passages of the *Similitudes* (*Herm. Sim.* 5.6; 8.3; 9.12), where an adoptionist christology is espoused and he is presented as the giver of new law. In only one passage are his sufferings mentioned. This work represents a marginalization of authentic Christian faith in favor of a visionary romanticism and moralism.

2.4. Justin Martyr. Justin's remarkable *theologia crucis* is hard to analyze. On the one hand the cross was clearly central for him: he refers to it repeatedly and is no runner-up to Ignatius in attacking Docetists who deny Christ's sufferings (e.g., *Apol. I* 63.10; *Dial. Tryph.* 103.8). He finds the cross foreshadowed throughout the OT (*Dial. Tryph.* 86) and in nature (*Apol. I* 55.2-7). In *Dialogue with Trypho* 94—96 he draws heavily on Galatians 3 in presenting Christ as the one who bears our curse, although, as E. R. Goodenough notes (259-60), he leaves vital parts of the argument to be inferred (i.e., it was our curse that Christ bore, and Christ bore away the curse by his death).

On the other hand it is clear that the essential elements of Justin's soteriology lie elsewhere. His doctrine of the "spermatic Logos" (his belief, drawn from middle Platonism, that every human being already possesses a "seed" of the Logos* of God, which is Christ) led him to emphasize the revelation* of the truth* as the vital center of Christ's ministry.* "He is his Logos, his firstborn and his power, and by his will he became man so that he might teach us these things, in order to turn and lift the human race" (*Dial. Tryph.* 23.2). And he believed that all truly rational human beings would respond to the patient explanation of the truth revealed by Christ: this is the evangelistic theory on which his chief writings rest, his two *Apologies* and his *Dialogue with Trypho*.

So why then the cross? Justin's answer would doubtless relate to the demons. The devil (*see* Satan) and demons are the chief enemies of truth and instigators of persecution and martyrdom. The heart of the atonement is the destruction of their power, so that they may no longer deceive (e.g., *Dial. Tryph.* 45.4; 76.6; 121.2-3). Justin proves the truth of Christianity by pointing to successful exorcisms by the name* of Christ (*Apol. II* 6.6).

However, Justin never explains how the cross achieves this victory over the demons—a puzzling gap in his thinking, for he emphasizes Christ's power over the demons during his ministry by virtue just of his incarnation. So we should probably agree with L. W. Barnard (125) that Justin's belief in the cross as the heart of the atonement attests the teaching of the church that he joined. He took it up as a central article of the faith but never managed to integrate it into his Platonist presentation of it.

See also DEATH OF CHRIST.

BIBLIOGRAPHY. J. B. Adamson, *James: The Man and His Message* (Grand Rapids: Eerdmans, 1989); L. W. Barnard, *Justin Martyr: His Life and Thought* (Cambridge: Cambridge University Press, 1967); C. K. Barrett, "Theologia Crucis—in Acts?" in *Theologia Crucis—Signum Crucis*, ed. C. Andresen and G. Klein (Tübingen: J. C. B. Mohr, 1979) 72-84; R. J. Bauckham, *The Theology of the Book of Revelation* (Cambridge: Cambridge University Press, 1993); C. B. Cousar, *A Theology of the Cross* (Minneapolis: Fortress, 1990); W. J. Dalton, *Christ's Proclamation to the Spirits: A Study of 1 Peter 3:18—4:6* (AnBib 23; Rome: Pontifical Biblical Institute, 1989); R. H. Fuller, "Luke and the Theologia Crucis" in *Sin, Salvation and the Spirit*, ed. D. Durken (Collegeville, MN: Liturgical Press, 1979) 214-20; E. R. Goodenough, *The Theology of Justin Martyr* (Amsterdam: Philo Press, 1968 [1923]); E. Grässer, "Die Heilsbedeutung des Todes Jesu in Hebräer 2:14-18" in *Theologia Crucis—Signum Crucis*, ed. C. Andresen and G. Klein (Tübingen: J. C. B. Mohr, 1979) 165-84; J. B. Green, *The Death of Jesus: Tradition and Interpretation in the Passion Narrative* (WUNT 2.33; Tübingen: J. C. B. Mohr, 1988); R. P. C. Hanson, *The Acts* (NClB; Oxford: Clarendon, 1967); E. F. Osborn, *Justin Martyr* (BHT 47; Tübingen: J. C. B. Mohr, 1973); C. C. Richardson, *The Christianity of Ignatius of Antioch* (New York: AMS Press, 1967 [1935]); A. Roberts and J. Donaldson, eds., *Ante-Nicene Christian Library* (Edinburgh: T & T Clark, 1867) vols. 1-2; J. A. Robinson, *Barnabas, Hermas and the Didache* (London: SPCK, 1920); W. R. Schoedel, *Ignatius of Antioch* (Herm; Philadelphia: Fortress, 1985); M. Staniforth, *Early Christian Writings: The Apostolic Fathers* (Penguin Classics; Harmondsworth: Penguin, 1968). S. Motyer

CULT, EMPEROR. *See* EMPEROR, EMPEROR CULT.

CURSE. *See* COVENANT, NEW COVENANT.

D

DARKNESS. *See* Light and Darkness.

DAVID. *See* Ancestors.

DAY OF THE LORD

The NT expression "the day of the Lord" is derived from similar expressions in the OT and extracanonical Jewish literature where it developed an eschatological orientation. It refers to the expectation of God's final judgment on the ungodly and the liberation and restoration of his people in the age to come. In the NT it developed a specifically Christian orientation in which the term *Lord* in the expression was understood as a reference to Jesus at his Parousia.

1. Origins in the Old Testament
2. Use in Extra-Canonical Jewish Literature
3. Use in Hebrews, the General Epistles and Revelation
4. Use in the Apostolic Fathers

1. Origins in the Old Testament.

The expression "day of the Lord" (Gk *hēmera kyriou*) is derived from the expression "day of Yahweh" (Heb *yôm yhwh*) which is found in certain OT prophetic books (e.g., Is 13:6, 9; Joel 1:15; 2:1, 11; 2:31 [MT 3:4]; 3:14 [MT 4:14]; Zeph 1:7, 14; Mal 3:23). Related expressions use "day" in similar ways, such as "the day of the wrath of Yahweh" (e.g., Ezek 7:19) or simply "the/that/your day" (e.g., Jer 50:31; Joel 3:18).

The earliest use of the expression in the OT, Amos 5:18-20, suggests that the term already existed in popular belief as a reference to the time when Yahweh would come to judge the foreign nations and, at the same time, to deliver and bless his people Israel (for a discussion of its origins, see von Rad 1959; Cathcart and the literature cited there). Amos countered this belief by portraying the day of Yahweh as his judgment upon Israel for unfaithfulness. Similar usage is found in other pre-exilic prophets

(e.g., Zeph 1:7, 14; Joel 2:1). In some cases the prophetic oracles used the day of Yahweh to warn about the impending exile (e.g., Ezek 7:7-12), and later the exile was interpreted as the day of Yahweh having arrived (e.g., Ezek 34:12; Lam 1:12; 2:1, 22). The term "day of judgment" became an equivalent expression which emphasized this aspect of the "day of Yahweh."

In post-exilic contexts the day of Yahweh developed an eschatological orientation, with the expectation that Israel's enemies would be judged and the faithful remnant experience God's salvation* in a future age (e.g., Is 61:1-2; Zech 12—14; Mal 4:1-6).

2. Use in Extra-Canonical Jewish Literature.

Jewish apocalyptic* literature further developed the eschatological orientation of the later prophets by exploring questions of timing, signs and events surrounding the day of final judgment* and the age to come, and often expressing it in vivid, mythological terms (Russell, 92-96). In Greek versions of Jewish literature the term "day of Yahweh" became the "day of the Lord" (e.g., *Pss. Sol.* 15:12), probably under influence of the LXX which translated *yôm yhwh* as *hēmera kyriou* (e.g., Is 13:6, 9 LXX). Similar expressions such as the "day of the Mighty One" were also used (*2 Apoc. Bar.* 55:6). In addition, the expression "day of judgment" developed as an equivalent (e.g., 2 Esdr 7:38, 102, 104, 113; 12:34; Jdt 16:17; Add Esth 10:11; *1 Enoch* 10:12; 22:11, 13; 27:3-4; 98:10; 99:15; 100:4; 104:5; *T. Levi* 1:1; 3:2-3; *Adam and Eve* 12:1; 26:4; cf. Is 34:8 LXX; *Pss. Sol.* 15:12; 1QS 10:19-20; 1QM 7:5; 13:14; 15:2-3), and the use of the simple expression "the/that/your day" continued (*2 Apoc. Bar.* 48:47; 49:2). Though the term itself is not used frequently, the concept of a day when God would judge and save pervades this literature (e.g., *Apoc. Abr.* 29:14-21; *1 Enoch* 1:3-9; 100:1-6;

2 Apoc. Bar. 24:1-2; 83:1-7). In some instances an agent of judgment and restoration works on behalf of God, and so the day may be designated by some appropriate expression such as the "day of the Elect One" (*1 Enoch* 61:5; on agents of judgment and restoration, see Webb 1991, 219-60). This day is understood as bringing to an end the present age and to usher in the glorious age to come (e.g., 2 Esdr 7:112-114; *2 Enoch* 65:5-11).

3. Use in Hebrews, the General Epistles and Revelation.

The Gospels and the letters of Paul use the terms "day of the Lord" and "day of judgment" in continuity with the emphases of Jewish apocalyptic* literature (e.g., Mt 10:15; 11:22, 24; 12:36; 1 Thess 5:2; 2 Thess 2:2). They do, of course, understand the "Lord"* in the "day of the Lord" to be a reference to Jesus Christ and his role as judge at the Parousia* (e.g., 1 Cor 1:8; 5:5; 2 Cor 1:14). Also in continuity with Jewish literature, Paul uses the expression "day of Christ" to identify explicitly Jesus Christ as the agent of judgment (Phil 1:10; 2:16; cf. Phil 1:6; 1 Cor 1:8; 5:5; 2 Cor 1:14; see *DJG, DPL,* Eschatology).

3.1. Hebrews and James. While both Hebrews* and James* do have an eschatological orientation (e.g., Heb 1:2; Jas 1:12; 2:5) and allude to the Parousia and coming judgment (e.g., Heb 4:13; 9:27; 10:12-13, 27, 30-31, 37; 12:23; Jas 4:12; 5:7-9), the day of the Lord is not a major focus of these books. The one allusion is in Hebrews 10:25 which exhorts the readers to encourage one another, being motivated "as you see the day approaching" (cf. Heb 3:13).

3.2. 1 Peter. In 1 Peter* the eschatological orientation is more pronounced than in Hebrews and James (e.g., 1 Pet 4:7). In light of the readers' suffering,* the author encourages them to have hope in the eschatological salvation to be brought at the Parousia (e.g., 1 Pet 1:4-5; 4:13; 5:1, 4, 10). Eschatological judgment is a concomitant theme, reassuring the readers that the ungodly will be judged (1 Pet 4:5-6) and encouraging their own continued godliness and faithfulness (1 Pet 1:17; 4:17-18).

While these eschatological themes are prominent, the specific terminology of the day of the Lord is found only in 1 Peter 2:12 which refers to God's "day of visitation." This expression is derived from the OT which used it to refer to that "day" when God would "visit" his people in judgment (e.g., Is 10:3; Hos 9:7; Jer 6:15; cf. Sir 16:18; 1QS 4:18-19). The verb is also used for God "visiting" his people for their vindication and blessing (e.g., Gen 50:24; Wis 3:7; *Pss. Sol.* 11:1).

3.3. 2 Peter. In 2 Peter* the day of the Lord is a significant element, for the opponents against whom the letter is addressed are eschatological skeptics (*see* Adversaries). The Parousia of Jesus Christ, expected during the lifetime of the first generation of Christians, had not happened (2 Pet 3:4, 9), and so these scoffers rejected the notion of the Parousia (2 Pet 3:4) and a final judgment (2 Pet 2:3; 3:9).

While the delay of the Parousia was a problem for these scoffers, the author does not agree with them. Rather, he denounces these scoffers, affirming and arguing that the Parousia hope* and eschatological judgment are true. In so doing, the author uses the day of the Lord to support the argument. Rejecting the opponents' denial of coming judgment, the author affirms in 2 Peter 2:9 that God will "rescue the godly" but the unrighteous will be kept for "punishment at the day of judgment" (cf. 2 Pet 3:7). Having explained the Parousia's delay by affirming that God's timetable is different and that judgment may be delayed from a human point of view (2 Pet 3:8-9), the author states that, nevertheless "the day of the Lord will come like a thief" (2 Pet 3:10). In so doing the author draws imagery from early Christian, apocalyptic tradition (Mt 24:43-44 par. Lk 12:39-40; 1 Thess 5:2; Rev 3:3; 16:15) which stresses the unexpected nature of the Parousia and judgment. In 2 Peter 3:12, 18 the author uses two somewhat unusual expressions, the "day of God" and the "day of eternity." These terms probably are not intended to be distinguished from the "day of the Lord," but rather stress a particular element of expectation associated with that day.

3.4. 1, 2, 3 John. Eschatology is not a major concern in the Johannine letters,* but the orientation is present (1 Jn 2:17-18; 2:28; 3:2). The language of the day of judgment appears only in 1 John 4:17 where "confidence on the day of judgment" expresses the result of believers showing love for one another.

3.5. Jude. In contrast with 2 Peter (see above), eschatology is not one of the issues being debated between Jude* and his opponents. Rather, eschatology and eschatological judgment in particular are used by Jude as part of his rhetorical response to the threat posed to the community by the opponents. Thus Jude refers to examples of past judgment (Jude 5-7, 11) and the promise of future judgment (Jude 14-15, 17-18) to convince his readers that the opponents are under present judgment (Jude 4, 8, 13, 16, 19; cf. Webb 1996).

Jude's argument is steeped in the traditions of Jewish eschatology, and his understanding of judgment involves motifs of the day of the Lord (e.g., Jude 14-15, citing *1 Enoch* 1:9, which begins in 1:1 by calling this the "day of tribulation"). But Jude uses the language explicitly in Jude 6, in which the evil angels* are kept by God "in perpetual chains under darkness for the judgment of the great day." While eschatological judgment is the predominant motif, Jude does allude to eschatological salvation, though he does not use "day of the Lord" terminology to do so (Jude 24-25; cf. Jude 1).

3.6. Revelation. Eschatological judgment and salvation are dominant themes in Revelation.* The author makes extensive use of Jewish and early Christian apocalyptic motifs to express these themes, including that of the day of the Lord. The precise term "day of the Lord" is not used (the expression, "Lord's day" in Rev 1:10 is not associated with this theme), but similar language does appear.

In Revelation 6:17, those who are fleeing from the One on the throne and the Lamb* describe their judgment as "the great day of their wrath has come, and who is able to stand?" And in Revelation 16:14 the demonic spirits* gather the kings of the world "for battle on the great day of God the Almighty." A parenthetical word from Jesus in the following verse (Rev 16:15) states, "Behold I am coming like a thief!" which associates this image with the day of the Lord as found elsewhere in early Christian thought (cf. Rev 3:3; Mt 24:43-44 par. Lk 12:39-40; 1 Thess 5:2; 2 Pet 3:10). Though the term "day of judgment" does not appear, the expression "hour of judgment" is used in a synonymous way (Rev 14:7; 18:10; cf. 3:3, 10; 14:15; Mt 24:36 par. Mk 13:32; Mt 24:44 par. Lk 12:40).

The emphasis in Revelation's use of the day of the Lord is upon the judgment of the ungodly which has as its corollary the liberation and vindication of the righteous (e.g., Rev 6:10; 11:18; 16:6-7; 19:1-2). But in the letters to the seven churches in Revelation 2—3 language associated with the day of the Lord is used in at least one letter as a warning to the people of God themselves (Rev 3:3).

4. Use in the Apostolic Fathers.

Eschatological concerns of judgment and deliverance are not prominent in the apostolic fathers, but eschatological references are frequently made in passing (e.g., *1 Clem.* 50.3-4; *Did.* 16.1-8; *Herm. Vis.* 2.2.5; 3.8.9; 3.9.5; 4.1—3; Ign. *Eph.* 11.1; Ign. *Smyrn.* 6.1; *Mart. Poly.* 2.1-2; 5.2; cf. Bruce). In most works of the apostolic fathers, references to eschatological matters do not use motifs associated with the day of the Lord. The two exceptions are the *Epistle of Barnabas** and *2 Clement** where ethical concerns are linked to eschatologically oriented motivation.

The *Epistle of Barnabas* refers to eschatological judgment (e.g., *Barn.* 4.12-13; 7.2), eschatological salvation (e.g., *Barn.* 1.6-7; 4.1; 21.1) as well as other eschatological themes (e.g., *Barn.* 4.3-5; 6.13; 18.2). With respect to motifs associated with the day of the Lord, *Barnabas* 15.4, alluding to 2 Peter 3:8, states, "behold the day of the Lord will be as a thousand years." Linking this with the six days of creation (Gen 2:2), the author calculates the eschaton to begin after six thousand years, and then proceeds with a brief description of the Parousia and the final judgment (*Barn.* 15.5). Later, in the midst of describing the ethical teaching of "the way of light," the author exhorts his readers in *Barnabas* 19.10 to "remember the day of judgment day and night." Finally, in the conclusion to the letter the author exhorts his readers to faithfulness, motivating them with references to eschatological judgment and salvation (*Barn.* 21.1-2) and then asserts that "the day is at hand when all things shall perish with the evil one; the Lord and his reward is at hand" (*Barn.* 21.3). Thus, his readers should seek to "be found faithful in the day of judgment" (*Barn.* 21.6).

In *2 Clement* 12.1, Clement exhorts his readers to manifest continually love* and righteousness* while waiting for the kingdom* of God. The motivation expressed is that "we do not know the day of the appearing of God." Similarly, *2 Clement* 16.1-2 exhorts the readers to repentance and abstinence from worldly enjoyments with the motivation being the imminence of the day of judgment: "And you know that the day of judgment is already coming as a burning oven, . . . and then the hidden and visible deeds of humankind will be revealed" (*2 Clem.* 16.3; alluding to Mal 4:1). Finally, *2 Clement* 17.4 refers to the Parousia as "the day of his appearing" at which the unbelievers as well as "the ungodly who are among us" will be judged, while the righteous will be rewarded* (*2 Clem.* 17.5-7).

See also APOCALYPTIC, APOCALYPTICISM; ESCHATOLOGY; JUDGMENT; SALVATION; WRATH, DESTRUCTION.

BIBLIOGRAPHY. G. Braumann, and C. Brown, "Present, etc.," *NIDNTT* 2:887-95; F. F. Bruce, "Eschatology in the Apostolic Fathers," in *The Heritage of the Early Church: Essays in Honor of the Very Reverend Georges Vasilievich Florovsky*, ed. D. Neiman and M. Schatkin (OCA 195; Rome: Pont. Institutum Studiorum Orientalium, 1973) 77-89; K. J. Cathcart, "Day of Yahweh," *ABD* 2:84-85; R. H. Hiers, "Day of Judgment," *ABD* 2:79-82; idem, "Day of the Lord," *ABD* 2:82-83; Y. Hoffmann, "The Day of the Lord as a Concept and a Term in the Prophetic Literature," *ZAW* 93 (1987) 37-50; J. H. le Roux, "The 'Last Days' in Apocalyptic Perspective," *Neot* 12 (1981) 41-74; R. L. Mayhue, "The Prophet's Watchword: Day of the Lord" *GTJ* 6 (1985) 231-46; H. H. Rowley, "The Day of the Lord" in *The Faith of Israel: Aspects of Old Testament Thought* (London, SCM, 1956) 177-201; D. S. Russell, *The Method and Message of Jewish Apocalyptic: 200 BC—AD 100* (OTL; Philadelphia: Westminster, 1964); D. Stuart, "The Sovereign's Day of Conquest," *BASOR* 221 (1976) 159-64; G. von Rad, "The Origin of the Concept of the Day of Yahweh," *JSS* 4 (1959) 97-108; G. von Rad and G. Delling, "ἡμέρα," *TDNT* 2:943-53; R. L. Webb, *John the Baptizer and Prophet: A Socio-Historical Study* (JSNTSup 62; Sheffield: Sheffield Academic Press, 1991); idem, "The Eschatology of the Epistle of Jude and Its Rhetorical and Social Functions," *BBR* 6 (1996) 139-51; M. Weiss, "The Origin of the 'Day of the Lord'—Reconsidered," *HUCA* 37 (1966) 29-71.

R. L. Webb

DEACONS. *See* CHURCH ORDER, GOVERNMENT; MINISTRY.

DEAD SEA SCROLLS. *See* QUMRAN.

DEATH. *See* LIFE AND DEATH.

DEATH OF CHRIST

The writings of the NT interpret the death of Christ fundamentally in sacrificial* terms as a vicarious atonement that secures the forgiveness* of sins. That is not to say that this understanding of the cross or the death of Christ itself always receives emphasis, although it frequently does. Rather, in the NT writings salvation* is conceived in such a way that it has its basis and completion in the forgiveness secured by the death of Christ on behalf of sinners (though the theme is assumed rather than explicit in James,* 2 Peter,* 2—3 John [*see* John, Letters of], Jude*). This category of thought clearly does not exclude others. The cross is also viewed as a divine victory, a deliverance of humanity from sin and evil, a revelation* of God* and his love* and a pattern of obedience.* No one form of description is exhaustive. The innermost aspects of God's working in the cross necessarily lie beyond human language, as the metaphorical language of the NT and the multiplicity of its images indicate.

Yet it is obviously not the case that nothing can be known or said about the saving effects of Christ's death. Characteristically the NT writers place objective guilt and radical, eschatological* forgiveness at the center of the structure of salvation, deriving all other aspects of the cross from it. The victory at the cross is victory because it secures the forgiveness of sins. Deliverance from sin's power issues from the release from objective guilt. The cross reveals God's love in that God gave his Son* for our sins. This conception of salvation as full forgiveness distinguishes the NT writings from those of the postapostolic period. The various images of salvation and the OT texts used to derive them are taken up in early Christianity of the second century. But the framework of thought shifts, so that salvation is conceived as the attainment of incorruption and becomes contingent upon the obedience of the believer.

1. Acts
2. Hebrews
3. 1 Peter
4. 1 John
5. Revelation
6. Apostolic Fathers

1. Acts.

The understanding of the death of Christ in Luke-Acts has been a center of scholarly interest in recent years. Early redaction-critical studies, particularly those by P. Vielhauer, Hans Conzelmann and Ernst Haenchen, regarded the author of Luke-Acts as lacking any interest in Jesus' death as an atonement and concomitantly charged him with embracing a theology of glory* that measured divine favor by the outward success of the church. Newer studies have moved in various directions: a number have called for an appreciation for a distinctively Lukan understanding of the death of Christ primarily as a pattern for Christian obedience (e.g., Green, Carroll, Garrett), a few have argued that the understanding of Jesus' death as an atonement holds a larger place in Lukan thought than is generally recognized (Moessner), and still others have reasserted the claim that Luke rejects such an understanding of Jesus' death (Ehrman).

When all the evidence has been taken into account, it becomes clear that Luke does understand Jesus' death as a vicarious atonement and that this understanding is foundational to the message of Luke-Acts. Luke obviously emphasizes the salvific nature of Jesus' resurrection,* yet in doing so he undergirds rather than diminishes the atoning significance of Jesus' death. Jesus' death is also paradigmatic and exemplary for Luke. Yet despite its current attractiveness as a category for understanding the death of Jesus in Luke-Acts, it is no more prominent than Luke's interpretation of the cross as an atonement. Finally, the Lukan emphasis on the divine purpose behind Jesus' death does not reduce the human responsibility for it.

1.1. Jesus' Death as an Atonement.

1.1.1. Text-Critical Considerations in Luke 22:19-20. Although twentieth-century textual criticism has been increasingly inclined to regard the longer version of the words of institution in Luke as original, B. D. Ehrman (198-209) has argued forcefully in favor of the judgment of Westcott and Hort that the shorter version is more likely authentic. The shorter text, one of Westcott and Hort's so-called Western noninterpolations, is preserved in Codex Bezae and various Old Latin manuscripts and omits the italicized material:

[19]And taking bread, having given thanks he broke it and gave it to them, saying, "This is my body *which is given for you. Do this in memory of me.* [20]*And the cup likewise, after they had eaten, saying, "This cup is the new covenant in my blood,*

which is poured out for you." [21]But the hand of my betrayer is on the table.

Ehrman argues as follows: the external evidence for both readings runs back to the second century and cannot resolve the question; in cases such as this in which the Western witness is shorter it must be taken seriously; the usual explanations for an omission are inadequate (viz., that scribes were motivated by the desire either to harmonize Luke's account with Matthew and Mark or to keep the eucharistic words a secret); the vocabulary and more importantly the theology of the additional material are contrary to Lukan usage and thought.

Despite Ehrman's appeal to the significance of the shorter Western reading, its restriction to some Western witnesses at the very least raises some question about its originality, even if it does not decide the matter. And while Ehrman has rightly pointed out the inadequacy of the usual explanations for a scribal abbreviation of the text, an additional, persuasive possibility suggests itself. Although Luke undoubtedly intends the reader to understand Jesus to say that after this supper he will no longer eat and drink with his disciples, the tradition represented in Codex Bezae seems to have taken Jesus' words to mean that he would not participate in that very Passover (the Greek column of Bezae at Lk 22:15 divides *touto* to read *epethymēsa [tou to] to pascha phagein,* the genitive and accusative articles thereby created suggesting that Jesus' desire to eat the Passover with the apostles remained unfulfilled [cf. the genitive following *epithymeō* in 1 Tim 3:1; Ex 34:24 LXX; Prov 23:3, 6 LXX; Sir 16:1]; moreover Bezae at Lk 22:16 reads: "I certainly will no longer eat *[ouketi mē phagomai; iam non manducabo]* of it until it is eaten *(brōthē; edatur)* new in the kingdom of God"). The scribal omission of Luke 22:19-20 removes the troublesome reference to Jesus' eating (Lk 22:20) and the words of institution. Given the parallels in the other Synoptics and Paul, these words of institution nearly require the subsequent mention of the second cup, which in Luke is necessarily distinguished from the first by the reference to Jesus' having eaten. Once emended in this way, the passage also harmonizes nicely with the Matthean and Markan wording concerning the bread, breaking off precisely where they do and leaving Luke with one cup, even if it is out of the usual order (see, however, *Did.* 9.1-5). The only problem that the emendation failed to overcome is the adversative *plēn,* which begins Luke 22:21. In the shorter version the statement "the hand of my betrayer on the table" stands in contrast to Jesus' words "this is my body," an impossible juxtaposition, since the hand of the betrayer is not opposed to but is precisely the means of Jesus' death (i.e., his "body"). It appears then that the shorter version in Bezae and probably in the Western tradition in general represents an attempt to smooth out a perceived difficulty in the Lukan text and to remove Jesus' participation in the Passover.

The intrinsic probabilities of vocabulary do not weaken and may strengthen this judgment. Words unique to Luke appear in the longer text, in particular the references to the "remembrance" of Jesus and the new covenant. Yet this phenomenon is not different from the speeches of Acts, each of which contains distinctive vocabulary. Moreover a number of vocabulary items link the longer text to the surrounding material. The second person language ("on behalf of you" [twice]) corresponds to the Lukan context quite closely, including Jesus' desire to eat the Passover "with you" and his instruction regarding the first cup: to "take this and divide it among yourselves" (Lk 22:17-18). "Blood poured out on behalf of you" (Lk 22:20) varies from the Markan and Matthean "poured out on behalf of many" and corresponds to references to martyrdom elsewhere in Luke-Acts (Lk 11:50; Acts 22:20). Furthermore, like Mark, Luke indicates that Jesus gave the bread to his disciples (Lk 22:19; Mk 14:22). And in distinction to the Pauline version (1 Cor 11:24), Jesus indicates (Lk 22:19) that his body is "given for you." It is conceivable that a copyist artistically interwove the Markan ("giving") and Pauline ("for you"), but it is more likely that it is a Lukan composition, linking Luke 22:19 with its context (see also Green 1988, 28-42).

Intrinsic theological probabilities, because of the room they allow for subjective judgments, must be accorded the least weight in assessing the authenticity of any reading. The validity of Ehrman's claim that Luke nowhere else in the Gospel or Acts* portrays Jesus' death as an atonement depends on three considerations: the interpretation of Acts 20:28, to which we will turn shortly; the absence of explicit development of the theme of Jesus' death as an atonement for sin, despite numerous allusions to the

Isaianic Servant* that suggest such an understanding (see 1.1.4.1 below); Luke's decision not to include the ransom saying from Mark 10:45. The last two observations provide only arguments from silence, which are fragile, particularly in this case.

It is of considerable importance that Luke transposes the disciples' dispute over greatness from the Markan position immediately following the third passion prediction (Mk 10:41-45) to its place in his Gospel following the Last Supper (Lk 22:24-27). The distinctively Lukan material in the longer version of the words of institution ("given for you," "new covenant in my blood") may serve as Luke's replacement for the saying he chose to omit. Luke's shifting of the material (or use of an alternative tradition; Green 1988, 44-46) adds considerable pathos and irony to the narrative. As Jesus speaks of his affection and self-giving, the disciples are caught up in self-seeking and quarrels. While in Mark greatness is described in terms of doing, in Luke it consists in what one is. The greatest is to be as the youngest and as one who serves, just as Jesus is one who serves. This emphasis corresponds to Luke's presentation of Jesus as the obedient Servant of God (see 1.1.3.1 below) and may therefore explain why Luke left out the ransom saying. He prefers to focus on Jesus' humility and submission to the divine will rather than on Jesus' own intent.

1.1.2. Summary of Luke 22:19-20. We may safely say that the weight of both external and internal evidence favors the originality of Luke 22:19-20 (for further discussion see Green 1988, 35-42). In this case Luke clearly attaches atoning significance to Jesus' death, especially in his allusion to Jeremiah 31:31-34. Jesus' body is given and his blood is poured out "on behalf of you," securing the new covenant* in which sins and transgressions are forgiven. This passage is pivotal to Luke-Acts, supplying for the reader the reason John's baptism* of repentance* for forgiveness is inadequate and faith* in Jesus is necessary (cf. Lk 3:3; 24:47; Acts 19:4). Luke does not want the reader to forget these words and intends the entire subsequent narrative of Acts to be read in light of them, as Acts 20:28 makes clear.

1.1.3. Acts 20:28. The second explicit reference to Christ's death as an atoning sacrifice appears in Acts 20:28, where text-critical and interpretive issues are again intertwined. Although the external evidence is evenly balanced, it is probable that the original text referred to "the church of God" rather than the variant "the church of the Lord." The latter reading most likely represents a scribal amelioration of the difficult wording, "the church of God that he acquired with his own blood," which suggests patripassianism (i.e., the Father is said to suffer) to modern ears, as it probably did to scribes of the third century and onward. Like the NRSV, most commentators opt for reading the passage as speaking of "the church of God, which he obtained with the blood of his own [Son]," for which the word *Son* is supplied. This is grammatically possible but unlikely. Luke frequently places adjectival modifiers in the form in question. Had he intended to speak of "God's own Son," he most likely would have included the final noun (cf. Rom 8:32). We are left with his striking language to describe the death of Christ. But how are we to understand it?

Ehrman's claim (202-3) that Luke regards Jesus' blood not as an atonement but as saving because it brings a recognition of guilt is unconvincing. The charge of guilt for Jesus' death is present only within the Jerusalem speeches and disappears after Acts 7. Moreover, in Acts it is not Jesus' death but the proclamation of his resurrection that brings repentance.

Statements that speak of the "suffering of God," "the crucified God" or even "the blood of God" are common in Christian writers until the end of the second century, when (monarchialist) conceptions of God existing in sequential modes forced further definition to avoid connotations of patripassianism (e.g., Ign. *Eph.* 1.1; see Elert, Ehrman, 87-88). We therefore should not be surprised to find such forms of expression in NT writers. The antecedent reference to Jesus' blood (Lk 22:19-20) makes it clear that when Luke uses the expression "God's own blood," he is thinking of Christ's blood and that as with the Christian writers of the second century, this statement represents a bold ascription of deity to Christ. The directness of Luke's statement is not unanticipated, since elsewhere he stresses that Jesus is Lord* with overtones of deity (e.g., Acts 2:21). And Paul, in whose mouth these words appear, is quite capable of making such a statement (Rom 9:5; 1 Cor 8:6).

We should not overlook the biblical allusions conveyed by Luke's language. The word that the NRSV renders "obtained" (*peripoieō,* cf. *peripoiēsis*) carries salvific overtones and might better be rendered "spared for himself" or "delivered for himself" (see Lk 17:33; Mal 3:17 LXX; Num 22:33 LXX; Ps 78:11 LXX; Jdt 11:9). Yet the word also conveys the sense of possession and therefore recalls the exodus in which God savingly acquired a people for himself. They are his "special possession" (*s^egulâh;* LXX *periousios;* Ex 19:5; Deut 7:6; 14:2; 26:18; cf. 1 Pet 2:9; Ps 73:2 LXX). Likewise the description of the people of God as a flock has its basis in the exodus (Ps 78:52; cf. Num 27:15-17). The reference to "God's own blood" therefore likely recalls the Passover and suggests a typology in which Christ transcends the original Passover. The striking Lukan wording then signals a contrast between the original Passover and the cross. If this reading of the text is correct, we have in Paul's speech at Miletus a powerful recollection of the words of institution in Luke 22:19-20, where Luke reports Jesus' interpretation of his death (precisely, his blood) as a new covenant. Notions of fulfillment are present in both passages. And the striking ascription of deity to Christ marks Acts 20:28 as a pivotal text.

In narrative, as opposed to direct theological discourse, the character of the speaker and the placement of speech count a great deal. The frequency of appearance of a thought or an expression is far less important than who says it and when it is said. It therefore must not escape our notice that this single explicit reference in Acts to the death of Jesus as an atonement appears at a crucial point, in the mouth of the one whom Luke presents as Christ's chosen vessel, the apostolic witness* in whom the promise of Acts 1:8 is fulfilled. Without diminishing the continuing witness of Paul, Luke presents his Miletus speech as the closure of his ministry* to the churches. That is apparent everywhere in the discourse, from Paul's prediction that he would not see the Ephesian elders again (Acts 20:25) to the potent christology* that we have noticed. The elders are in a sense responsible not merely for the Ephesian church but also for the "church of God." Therefore when Paul says that God has "delivered the church for himself with his own blood," Luke is indicating that Jesus' atoning death stands behind all that he has worked among Jews and Gentiles* since the cross (Lk 22:19-20). Rather than serving an insignificant role, the two explicit references to

Jesus' atoning death bracket and inform the entire intervening narrative.

1.1.4. Allusions to Jesus' Death as an Atonement. How is it that Luke employs numerous biblical allusions to Jesus' death as a substitutionary atonement yet does not develop them? The answer lies partly in his emphasis on Jesus' resurrection and partly in the bracketing we have just observed. The words of institution and the subsequent statement of Paul provide the interpretation of Jesus' death as an atonement, which Luke reinforces by repeated allusions to the Isaianic Servant, the breaking of bread and the divine necessity of Jesus' death.

1.1.4.1. Jesus as the Isaianic Servant. The most prominent of these allusions is the section of Isaiah 53 that Philip* finds the Ethiopian eunuch reading (Acts 8:32-33; Is 53:7-8). Luke focuses on the unjust death of the Servant of God, yet notions of atonement lie tantalizingly close (Is 53:6) and come to mind for anyone who knows Jesus' words at the Last Supper and the larger Isaianic context.

This citation of Isaiah 53:7-8 does not stand alone in Luke-Acts. References to Jesus' identity as the Isaianic Servant extend back to Jesus' own definition of his ministry (Lk 4:18-19; Is 61:1-2) and into his passion (Lk 22:37; Is 53:12). As J. B. Green observes, the latter is the only instance of the Servant material found on Jesus' lips in the NT (Green 1990, 22). And only in Luke's account of Jesus' death is there a suggestion that the watching centurion unwittingly acknowledges Jesus as the "Righteous One," the Servant (Lk 23:47; Is 53:11, see Karris). Indeed, Luke regards the Servant passages of Isaiah as reflecting a larger biblical understanding of the role of the Messiah (Lk 24:25-27, 44-49), including his mission* to the Gentiles (Acts 13:47; *see DJG* Death of Jesus §6.3).

Jesus' role as the Servant clearly informs the speeches of Acts, where the running theme of reversal draws upon the biblical motif of the vindication of the suffering* righteous, which is central to the Servant passage of Isaiah 52:13—53:12. When Peter proclaims that God has "glorified his servant *(pais),* Jesus" and that the people rejected the "holy and righteous one" he uses the language of Isaiah 52:13 and Isaiah 53:11. The distinctive element of the Servant image that distinguishes it from the larger category of the righteous sufferer is the idea that forgiveness is given through him (Is 53:4-6, 10-

11). This theme characterizes Luke's narrative. The offer of salvation to the thief on the cross and the omission of the words of dereliction tilts the Lukan passion narrative away from the Markan presentation of Jesus as a righteous sufferer and toward the Isaianic background (cf. Green 1990, 23). Likewise, the offer of forgiveness is central to the proclamation of the Christ in Acts (Acts 2:38-39; 3:18-20; 10:43; 13:38-39).

Luke therefore does not regard Jesus' death as that of a martyr or a hero, or even that of a biblical, righteous sufferer, but as that of the suffering Servant-Messiah through whom God offers the forgiveness of sins. This conception of Jesus and the Isaianic background that serves as its source reinforce the two Lukan references to Jesus' atoning death, and these references inform the entire presentation. Given Luke's abundant allusions to the Isaianic Servant, it is overwhelmingly likely that he intends his readers to draw this connection.

1.1.4.2. The Breaking of Bread. Luke also intends his readers to understand the believing community's "breaking bread" as an expression of faith and obedience to Jesus' injunction to "do this in remembrance of me" (Lk 22:19). As D. P. Moessner (182) observes, the misunderstanding and disappointment of the disciples on the way to Emmaus is reversed not simply by instruction from the unrecognized Jesus but in Jesus' breaking of the bread, suggesting that Jesus' words at the Last Supper represent the culmination of the biblical witness and the focal point of revelation (Lk 24:30-32). Moreover, as is the case with Luke's references to Jesus' atoning death, his references to the communal "breaking bread" bracket his presentation of the spread of the gospel. He includes it in his sketch of the piety of the infant church (Acts 2:42, 46) and mentions it again in Paul's closing meeting with the church at Troas (Acts 20:7, 11). Believers "break bread" along with instruction, fellowship* and prayer (Acts 2:42) and gather together for it on the first day of the week (Acts 20:7). Given their placement in the narrative, these descriptions are intended to show that the practices were typical of the churches. Luke thus indicates that the first disciples have followed Jesus' command to remember his atoning death. He expects his readers to do so as well.

1.1.4.3. Jesus' Death as a Divine Necessity. As

with Matthew, Mark and John, in Luke-Acts Jesus' death is not simply the result of human ignorance and wrongdoing that God subsequently corrects by the resurrection. Rather the suffering of the Messiah is the will and plan of God, which must come to fulfillment. This theme appears not only in the passion predictions (Lk 9:22, 43; 18:31) and in the prediction of betrayal (Lk 22:21) but also in Jesus' reference to his role as the Isaianic Servant (Lk 22:37; Is 53:12). The divine necessity of Jesus' death consists in that which is written about him (Lk 24:26-27, 44-47; Acts 3:18; 10:43; 13:27; 17:3; 26:23). As the Messiah, Jesus is destined to fulfill the role prescribed for him as the Suffering Servant. This recurring motif subtly underscores Jesus' interpretation of his death as an atonement (Lk 22:19-20), since in it we have the one point in Luke-Acts at which the divine purpose for the cross is disclosed. Luke does not merely assert that the Messiah died because God willed it but supplies Jesus' own interpretation of that death.

Yet the theme of the necessity of the suffering of the Messiah also serves a larger, apologetic end in Acts. Far from disqualifying Jesus as the promised Messiah, his unjust death fulfills the words of the prophets* (e.g., Acts 13:27). This apology for the cross and Luke's interpretation of Jesus' death as an atonement are bound up with one another, as is his emphasis on the resurrection.

1.1.5. Jesus' Atoning Death and His Saving Resurrection. Luke presents the resurrection of Jesus as the central saving event in Acts in order to undergird the exclusive claims of the gospel. The resurrection not only confirms Jesus as the Servant Messiah but also elevates him into the role of risen Lord. The saving promises* of God for Israel* and the nations have now been fulfilled in him. Having poured out the Spirit (*see* Holy Spirit), he is now at work in the world sending the message of salvation to the ends of the earth (*see* Creation). He therefore is the sole mediator of salvation for humanity. He is not only the prophet like Moses,* whom all Israel must obey (Acts 3:22-26), but also the one who will judge the living and the dead and to whom all the world is accountable (Acts 10:42; 17:31). Salvation is given in his name alone (Acts 4:12).

As the fulfillment of promise, the resurrection also serves as an apology for the cross, vindicating Jesus as Messiah and Lord. This concern is especially apparent in Luke's references to Jesus' death "on the tree" (Acts 5:30; 10:39-40; 13:28-30), which reflect an early Jewish interpretation of Deuteronomy 21:22-23 as speaking of crucifixion as a punishment to be inflicted on those guilty of serious offenses (Wilcox; cf. 11QTemple 64:7-9). Questions of guilt and innocence are present in all three occurrences of this description of Jesus' death. In each case the speaker points to the resurrection as the exculpation of Jesus and confirmation of the divine favor resting on him. Luke's emphasis upon God's action suggests that he is aware of the divine curse that Deuteronomy 21:22-23 was regarded as pronouncing on the guilty, yet he does not develop the idea of Jesus' bearing a curse for others (cf. Gal 3:13). His focus is fixed on removing any doubts about God's vindication of Jesus.

Here we are brought back to one of the most pressing current questions about Luke's understanding of salvation. The tendency has been to suppose that since Luke leaves the theme of Jesus' death as an atonement undeveloped and places his main emphasis on the resurrection, he lacks such an understanding of Jesus' death (Vielhauer, Conzelmann) or rejects it, or, although he is aware of it, he has not appropriated it himself (*see DJG* Death of Jesus §6.2.1; Marshall 1970, 169-75).

But these judgments overlook the character of Acts as a narrative and the function of Luke's emphasis on the resurrection. As we noted, the infrequency of reference to Jesus' death as an atonement is not important. In narrative the character of the speaker and the occasion of the utterance counts far more. Moreover, Luke wishes to provide assurance to a circle of readers who already have received basic Christian instruction (Lk 1:1-4), assurance that necessarily entails a confirmation of the events upon which such instruction was based. In focusing on Jesus' resurrection and exaltation* Luke provides an apology for the claims of the gospel, supporting rather than diminishing the understanding of Jesus' death as a vicarious atonement. Furthermore, the central role of Jesus' exaltation in Acts is indicative of a salvation-historical perspective that is essential for understanding Jesus' death as an atonement. From Luke's point of view, unless the crucified Jesus was raised from the dead it makes no sense to speak of his death in this way. And unless there is a judgment* to come, it makes no sense to speak of the forgiveness of sins. Luke does not confront a diminution of the atoning work of the cross, as do Paul and the author of Hebrews,* but he does defend it in his own circumstances by providing at length the framework and basis for its acceptance.

Two final observations help to confirm this conclusion. First, while it is true that the resurrection receives primary attention in Acts and that Luke does not directly connect forgiveness to the death of Jesus, it is nevertheless also true that Jesus' exaltation and the forgiveness of sins are not independent of the cross. The resurrection and exaltation are not viewed in the abstract but as God's act upon the crucified Servant of God (e.g., Acts 2:33; 5:30-31). Forgiveness is not proclaimed apart from Jesus' death (Acts 2:38; 3:18-21; 5:30-31; 10:40-43; 13:38-39; 26:18, 23). Second and more importantly, NT writers characteristically attach saving significance to both the cross and the resurrection without suggesting that the significance of one eclipses the other (e.g., Rom 4:25). Both are essential elements of the saving work of God in Christ. If that is true elsewhere, we should not be surprised to find it in Luke-Acts (cf. Bovon 177-78).

1.2. Jesus' Suffering as a Pattern for Believers. Luke also provides indications that he regards Jesus' suffering and death as a paradigm for those who believe in him. The call to discipleship in Luke's Gospel includes a general application. Those who follow Jesus must take up their cross "daily" (Lk 9:23). The one who does not bear a cross cannot be Jesus' disciple (Lk 14:27). Moreover, the apostles* are those who have stood with Jesus in his trials and upon whom he confers a kingdom just as the Father has upon him (Lk 22:28-30; *see* Kingdom of God). Something more than following Jesus' example is operative. Just as it is necessary for the Messiah to suffer, it is necessary for those who believe in him to "enter the kingdom through many tribulations" (Acts 14:22; *see* Tribulation). This instruction by Paul to the churches of Lystra, Iconium and Pisidian Antioch amounts to the only explicit statement of the matter in Acts. Yet Luke signals his expectation of suffering to his readers through his description of the experiences of the early church (Acts 8:1-3) and its leaders (Acts 5:41), the first martyr, Stephen* (Acts 6—7), and Paul,

"the chosen vessel" of the Lord, to whom Jesus himself promises to reveal "all that he must suffer on account of my name" (Acts 9:16).

The parallelism to Luke's treatment of Jesus' death as an atonement is striking. Again we have numerous allusions alongside a single clarifying pronouncement, which is to be understood as typical. And in this case Luke provides even less information as to the workings of this experience. He obviously regards the people of God as identified with the Messiah. That is clear from the dying Stephen's vision* of the Son of Man standing at the right hand of God (Acts 7:55) and from the words of the risen Jesus to the thunderstruck Saul ("Why are you persecuting me?"; Acts 9:4 et al.). And just as Christ is identified with them, Luke implies that they are identified with him. The will of God was accomplished in the case of his Servant *(pais),* and his servants *(douloi)* pray that it will be worked out in them as well (Acts 4:23-31). Yet Luke does not spell out the nature and basis of this relation. From one perspective the persecution* of believers is due to the witness they bear to the name* of Jesus (Acts 5:41; 9:16; 15:17; 26:9). Luke also gently hints at the Messiah's role as a second Adam (Acts 26:13). Whatever its basis in Luke-Acts, this theme of conformation to Christ's death (which is quite different from the idea of imitation*) reappears in the Pauline letters, Hebrews, 1 Peter,* 1 John, and Revelation (*see* Revelation, Book of) alongside the interpretation of Jesus' death as an atonement for sin.

1.3. Human Responsibility for Jesus' Death. Despite Luke's considerable emphasis upon the divine purpose behind the death of the Messiah, he does not diminish human responsibility for Jesus' crucifixion. Indeed, here the biblical tension between divine sovereignty and human responsibility reaches its peak. The cross is not a tragedy from which God somehow retrieves some good but is part of his own plan foretold by the prophets. Yet those who perpetrated the deed are not relieved of responsibility but are called to repent.

Unlike Christian writers of the second century, Luke also finely differentiates the guilt for Jesus' death. He regards as responsible for Jesus' death all who participated in his trials and execution: Herod and Pilate, the Gentiles and the people of Israel (Acts 4:23-28; cf. 7:51-53). Yet the Jews of Jerusalem* especially are charged with guilt, since Luke understands Pilate to have decided to release Jesus, only to be opposed by the crowd (Lk 23:13-25; Acts 2:23; 3:13; 10:39; 13:27-28). Within Jerusalem the leaders are singled out as being especially culpable (Lk 22:66—23:5; Acts 3:17; 5:30-31).

Nevertheless, this guilt does not exclude any from salvation. Both leaders and people acted in ignorance and are called to repent, believe and be baptized, so that they may receive the promises God made to Israel (Acts 2:38-39; 3:17-21; 5:31). Luke regards the door to salvation as remaining open to Israel. Paul's concluding words in the book of Acts do not indicate otherwise (Acts 28:25-28). The hardening of Israel's heart does not mean that no Jews have believed or yet will do so but that the time at which the whole nation will turn to the Messiah is still to come (Acts 3:19-21).

2. Hebrews.

Coupled with his exaltation, the death of Christ is the focal point and basis of the sermonic exhortation of Hebrews. The author derives his framework for interpreting the cross primarily from the OT cult, in particular from the high-priestly service on the Day of Atonement (Lev 16). Christ's death works purification from sin and enables approach to a gracious God (Heb 4:14-16). The levitical priesthood, the wilderness tabernacle* and its sacrifices anticipated the saving significance of Christ's death, providing an earthly pattern or type of the heavenly benefits that Christ secured (*hypodeigma,* Heb 8:5; 9:23; *typos,* Heb 8:5). Christ's sacrifice is superior to those enjoined by the Law, since they are mere copies and shadows of the eternal realities achieved in the cross (Heb 8:5; 9:23; 10:1). While the OT cult has been superseded, its conceptual world is firmly retained as the basis for understanding the death of Christ (contra Tuckett, 1:521). This is evident in the concise, introductory description of the saving work of the Son as his "making purification for sins" (Heb 1:3), which both interprets the cross in sacrificial terms and anticipates the subsequent theme of forgiveness as the surpassing effect of the cross. Other ways of interpreting Christ's death supplement and expand this idea. By death Christ divested the devil of the power of death (*see* Satan). Moreover, he blazed a trail to the divine presence for all the children of God (Heb 2:10, 14-16).

2.1. The Great High Priest. The author introduces the motif of Christ as high priest* as a summary of the purpose of the Incarnation, a theme that figures prominently in the first part of the material (Heb 2:1-18; 4:14—5:10). Jesus had to share in "flesh and blood," including the suffering of death, so that he might become "a merciful and faithful high priest." This thought recurs and reaches a dramatic closure in Hebrews 5:7-9, where the author, recalling early Christian tradition of the prayer in Gethsemane, describes Jesus' fully human experience in facing the ordeal of the cross: "He offered up supplications and petitions with loud crying and tears to the one able to save him from death." Even the Son learned obedience in suffering and was "perfected" in his role as high priest. This attribute sets him apart from the earthly priesthood and qualifies him for an eternal one (Heb 4:15; 5:2-3; 7:26-28; Peterson, 104-25). His own suffering enables him to have compassion toward our moral weakness (*astheneia,* cf. Heb 5:2; 7:28) and to help us (Heb 5:16).

The Son became not only a merciful and faithful high priest (Heb 2:17) but also the great high priest who has passed through the heavens* (Heb 4:14). This becomes the dominating theme of Hebrews 7—10, where the author presents Christ's superiority in both the effectual character of the sacrifice he made "once for all" and in his eternal status as high priest, a juxtaposition that raises the question as to what Christ's eternal ministry might be.

2.2. The Sacrifice.

2.2.1. Blood. Central to the author's argument is his claim that Christ's blood provides cleansing from sin (Heb 9:14; 9:22-23; 10:22). In such contexts "blood" signifies a sacrificial death and not, as has sometimes been argued, the life of the victim (see especially Heb 9:15-22; cf. Heb 10:5, 10, where the parallel term *body* appears). The author does not make use of every aspect of the atoning ritual in explicating Christ's work and in particular makes no mention of a presentation of blood in the heavenly sanctuary (cf. Lev 16:15-19). Christ enters into heaven not *with* his blood but *through* his blood; that is, through his death on the cross (Heb 9:12; see Laub). Moreover, the finality of Christ's offering distinguishes his ministry from that of earthly priests (Heb 7:26-28). Christ's entrance into heaven, which itself is associated with his cross (Heb 9:12), is followed by his session at the right hand of God, as the author stresses (Heb 1:3; 8:1; 10:11-13). These considerations weigh heavily against interpreting Christ's ministry in Hebrews as including an application of his blood in the heavenly sanctuary subsequent to his death. Rather, the whole of Christ's work is accomplished at the cross, once for all (Heb 7:27; 9:28; 10:10). His ministry as high priest entails not a perpetual offering but his presence before God on our behalf (Heb 4:14-16; 6:19-20; 7:26-28; 9:23-28).

This heavenly ministry has two interrelated aspects. First, Christ serves as mediator, eternally interceding for those drawing near to God through him, providing grace* and mercy* (Heb 2:18; 4:16; 7:25). Second, his entrance into the presence of God *for us* is an entrance *before us*. By his struggles, suffering and death, he has established the pilgrimage of his brothers and sisters into the presence of God (Heb 6:19-20). In Jesus' humanity, humanity has been "perfected," having passed obediently through suffering and into heaven itself. By virtue of God's saving purpose for the human race (and not some material conception as in Ignatius* or Irenaeus), the high-priestly language flows over into the imagery of progress and conquest. Christ is the champion (*archēgos*) of salvation (Heb 2:10; 12:2) and its perfecter (Heb 12:2). He has entered into the presence of God as a forerunner for us (Heb 6:20). Yet Christ's unique high-priestly role is not set aside by these additional conceptions. He alone is the sinless mediator who deals mercifully with sinners (Heb 2:17; 7:26-28). The way into God's presence has its basis in the forgiveness secured at the cross, not in a divinization of humanity. And the forgiveness once and for all secured has its application in the essential help it provides to "the children" on the difficult path to glory.

2.2.2. Offering. In expounding the relation between the sacrifices of the old covenant and the death of Christ, the author generally employs the familiar language of "offering." Significantly, however, at the outset and the conclusion of the main argument, interpretive theological terms appear.

The author introduces Jesus' high-priestly role by describing its purpose as "making propitiation with respect to the sins of the people" (*eis to hilaskesthai tas hamartias tou laou*, Heb 2:17). There has been extensive discussion as to

whether the biblical usage of the Greek verb *hilaskesthai* signifies the propitiation of divine wrath,* as in secular Greek, or the expiation of sin. Yet once it is acknowledged that the removal of sin averts divine wrath, as is the case here, one arrives at the idea of propitiation. The only distinction that might remain is a dubious insistence that the removal of sin from persons does not entail the appeasing of divine wrath against persons. However, to exclude the idea of punitive divine action is to give the cult an absolute, quasi-magical status and an impersonal character. In the biblical writings the personal, covenantal understanding of the divine-human relation remains decisive, as is evidenced by the close association between sacrifice and forgiveness (e.g., Ex 30:30-32; Lev 4:20, 26, 31, 35).

In the passage at hand it is clear that the author understands Jesus' death to avert the wrath of God. It is of the greatest significance that he shifts without discussion from speaking of the forgiveness of the sins to the removal of sin and back again, all in the context of sacrificial language (Heb 9:22, 26; 10:4, 18). If covenantal provisions are rejected, divine wrath will be directed against the disobedient and unbelieving (Heb 2:1-4; 3:7-19; 4:7-8; 9:26-31; 12:25-29). The syntax of this clause is paralleled in the Septuagint by only a few passages in Sirach, where atonement is closely connected to the avoidance of God's anger (see especially Sir 3:30; 28:5). Moreover, the author stresses that the capacity for mercy is a central duty of a high priest (Heb 2:17; 5:2), implying that strict judgment is the alternative to mediation.

The second passage in which the author interprets the language of "offering" corroborates this reading of Hebrews 2:17. As the author brings to a close his presentation of the death of Christ as a superior sacrifice, he describes the cross as Christ's "being offered up in order to bear the sins of many" (Heb 9:28). Here he obviously recalls the substitutionary suffering of the Isaianic Servant (Is 53:4-12). Bearing the sins "of many," the Christ bore their punishment. It is not simply that at the cross he represented them but that the punishment that was theirs became his, so that they now await salvation rather than condemning judgment (contra Hooker). As he does with the entire sacrificial structure, the author assumes the reality and validity of this substitutionary act (on this topic see Hill, Morris 1965).

2.2.3. Atonement. As is the case with other NT contexts in which Christ's death is interpreted as an atonement, God is not only the object of Christ's sacrifice (Heb 2:17) but also its subject (Heb 9:28), as is apparent from the covenantal framework of Hebrews (e.g., Heb 8:6-13). It is God who ordains all high-priestly ministry and who chose Christ as an eternal high priest (Heb 5:1-6). He offered Christ up to bear sin (Heb 9:28), and by God's will Christ offered up his body for the sanctification of the people of God (Heb 10:10). God not only required a death for the forgiveness of sins but also provided it in the Son.

2.3. The Effect of Christ's Death. Like the sacrifices of the Law, Christ's death "atones," "cleanses" and "sanctifies." Yet the cross alone, not the former sacrifices, secures forgiveness (Heb 10:4, 11). And once sins have been removed and forgiven, no need for sacrifice remains (Heb 8:12; 9:26; 10:18). Likewise, Christ's sacrifice and priesthood bring "perfection," in distinction from the sacrifices of the Law.

2.3.1. Forgiveness. "To sanctify," in Hebrews, generally signifies not the effecting of progressive moral improvement but forgiveness (Heb 2:11; 9:13; 10:10, 29; 13:29; cf., however, Heb 12:14). Those who believe have been sanctified "once for all" through the offering of the body of Jesus Christ (Heb 10:10). This sanctification is nothing other than the forgiveness of sins (see Heb 10:2, 18). As James Denney (126) commented,

> In the Epistle to the Hebrews, the word ἁγιάζειν, corresponds as nearly as possible to the Pauline δικαιοῦν. The sanctification of the one writer is the justification of the other; and the προσαγωγή or access to God, which Paul emphasizes as the primary blessing* of justification, appears everywhere in Hebrews as the primary religious act of 'drawing near' to God through the great High Priest.

2.3.2. Perfection. The "perfection" of believers signifies their participation in the saving blessings of the age to come through the forgiveness won at the cross. "Perfection" could not be achieved through the levitical priesthood, since the law made nothing "perfect" and was not able "to perfect" those who offered sacrifices (Heb 7:11, 19; 10:1). In contrast, with one sacrifice Christ "perfected forever" those being sanctified (Heb 10:14). The provisions of the law were

temporary and had only outward effects, cleansing "the flesh" and the copies of the heavenly things. Christ by his death, in contrast, achieved redemption and cleanses the conscience.* Now exalted, he appears before God "for us" (Heb 9:1-15, 23-28).

As an eschatological term, "perfection" involves a fundamental distinction between material and spiritual orders, but not an unconditioned dualism. It is misleading, therefore, to interpret Hebrews on the basis of Platonism or Gnosticism (as was once common), despite its obvious coloring with Hellenistic religious terminology. The "vertical" opposition is not absolute, but appears as an element, albeit a pivotal one, in a salvation-historical framework.

In Hebrews, hope* is not fixed on a disembodied eternity but on a transformation of the creation that has been subverted by sin and death into an eternal dwelling place for God and his people. The author speaks of the tent through which Christ entered as high priest as being not of *this* creation (Heb 9:11), implying that Christ entered into a *new* creation. Heavenly realities, then, are eschatological realities. Similarly, in a striking figure, he symbolically equates Jesus' (material) flesh* with the veil before the holy place, making it plain that the "undecayed" *(prosphatos)* and "living way" into the divine presence is none other than the once crucified and now resurrected Jesus (Heb 9:11; cf. Heb 6:19-20). The world to come is a physical one, as is evidenced by the hope for a "better" resurrection of the dead (Heb 11:35). God will "yet once shake" the structure of the present creation, heaven and earth (Heb 12:26). Created things will then be subjected not to "removal" (wrongly NRSV, NIV) but to a radical "transposition" *(metathesis:* Heb 7:12; 11:5, cf. Heb 1:10-12). Salvation in Hebrews therefore does not involve a journey from the material into the immaterial but from the present world into the age to come.

Correspondingly, although it is varied in nuance, the language of "perfection" bears an eschatological thrust. The contrast between the earthly tent and the "more perfect" heavenly tent through which Christ entered in offering his sacrifice is strictly eschatological (Heb 9:11). The author's language of perfection therefore is essentially salvation-historical, underscoring the completion of the divine saving purposes.

By virtue of the plan of God, eternal and complete salvation comes only in these last days through the Son (Heb 11:40; Heb 1:2; cf. Heb 9:10).

The perfection of believers is won at the expense of the perfection of the Son through suffering (Heb 2:10; 5:9; 7:28). Here too the eschatological sense is primary. Christ's sinlessness is never in question in Hebrews and in fact receives emphasis (Heb 4:15; 7:26-28; 9:14). His "perfection" represents his progress into his full role as mediator of salvation (Heb 7:26-28). In being perfected, the Son reaches his eschatological station and awaits the subjection of all things under his feet (Heb 1:13; 10:13).

Above all else, the perfection of believers signifies their access to God and participation in the heavenly Jerusalem (Heb 7:19; 12:22-24). *Perfection* also takes a cognitive sense in Hebrews 5:11—6:3, where maturity involves the capacity to comprehend "the word of righteousness." Yet this perfection of the mind and heart is also obviously bound up with eschatology, since it represents, among other things, "tasting" the heavenly gift and the powers of the age to come (Heb 6:4-8).

As with the language of sanctification in Hebrews, the "perfection" of believers that Christ wrought by his sacrifice entails in the first place the remission of sins (Heb 7:11, 19; 9:9; 11:40; and especially Heb 10:14-18). This corresponds to our earlier observation that the author's fundamental category for interpreting Christ's death lies in its effecting forgiveness. The "perfection" of believers implies the surpassing eschatological cleansing accomplished at the cross (Heb 10:14). In this way the difference between the perfection of the Son and the perfection of believers becomes understandable. He was perfected through suffering; they are perfected by his suffering. They are not thereby spared the difficult path to glory (Heb 2:10; 12:1-13), but through Jesus they participate in their destination already. He is the perfector of faith, since his arrival at his eschatological station ensures their arrival as well (Heb 12:2).

2.3.3. Human Transformation. This eternal redemption effected by Christ is reflected in the experience of the believer. In contrast to the sacrifices offered under the Law, Christ's death cleanses the conscience and not merely the "flesh" from sin and guilt (Heb 9:9, 14; 10:2, 22).

There is to be a subjective appreciation of the objective and external reality. The sense of forgiveness does not come about automatically, however. The access to God that Christ's death has achieved must be grasped and held by faith. Indeed, the path of testing on which believers walk requires that they avail themselves of divine assistance. Unbelief, not faith, is passive and sluggish. The primary exhortation of the letter is the call to maintain confidence in the forgiveness that the cross has won (Heb 3:6; 4:16; 10:35).

In a pattern similar to Paul's letters, in Hebrews the forgiveness of sins is not an isolated gift but issues in service to God. The "indicative" of forgiveness forms the basis of the "imperative." This is apparent in the author's understanding of suffering. Believers endure adversity not in order to become "sons" but because they are "sons" already. If they do not receive "discipline," they are not "sons" at all. As a loving father, God works righteousness* within them, which will bear peaceful fruit (Heb 12:4-11). Likewise, believers are pilgrims and wanderers because they have their true home already in the heavenly city (Heb 3:6; 12:18-24). Their progress is assured by virtue of Christ alone, who as a great high priest supplies the gracious help that they need (Heb 2:16-18; 4:16; 7:25).

In Hebrews, then, the transformation of the human heart has its basis in the forgiveness of sins. This is especially apparent in the repeated references to the promise of a new covenant from the book of Jeremiah (Jer 31:31-34). In Hebrews 8:7-12 the author cites the passage in order to establish the inadequacy of the Law, "the first, antiquated covenant." The inscription of the Law of God on the heart is summarized in Jeremiah as "knowing God," and this knowledge* of God in turn is based on the forgiveness of sins (Jer 31:34; Heb 8:12). In his second recollection of the Jeremianic text (Heb 10:15-18) the author underscores the finality of Christ's sacrifice, which, by providing forgiveness of sins, sets aside the provisions of the Law. The author's inclusion in his citation of God's promise to implant his laws in the hearts of his people serves as a reminder of the inability of the Law to do so and implicitly presents inward renewal as result of the forgiveness of sins.

It is important to observe, too, that for Hebrews the church, "the communion of the saints," derives from the forgiveness that each person individually has received, since forgiveness means common access to the throne of grace, participation in the heavenly city and a common sojourn (Heb 3:12-14; 10:24-25; 12:22-23).

2.3.4. Deliverance. Just as Christ's high-priestly role overflows into that of champion, the author portrays his work on the cross as deliverance from the devil, who held the power of death (Heb 2:14-15). Although he leaves the source of the devil's power unexplained, he no doubt assumes a biblical background, in which the devil incites human beings to sin (Gen 3; 1 Chron 21:1) and accuses them before God (Zech 3:1-5). The immediate context suggests that the devil's power derives from his accusations too, since the help that Christ extends to his brothers and sisters consists in his making propitiation for their sins (Heb 2:17-18; cf. Rev 12:9-10). It is likewise highly probable that the author assumes an inner connection between a guilty conscience and the fear* of death, which subjected human beings all their lives to slavery (Heb 2:14-15; *see* Slave). The "fear of death" in Hebrews has in view the judgment of God that follows (Heb 9:27; 10:27, 31; cf. Heb 12:21). Christ's sacrifice cleanses the conscience from "dead works"; that is, from "works that bring the judgment of death," so that believers may serve the living God (Heb 9:14). Just as forgiveness, both as an objective reality and subjectively grasped, brings the freedom to serve, guilt in both respects makes one a slave.

2.3.5. Covenant Ratification. J. J. Hughes (27-66) has persuasively argued that in Hebrews 9:16-17 *diathēkē* retains the usual biblical sense of "covenant" (rather than the usual rendering as "testament") and that the proper background for the imagery is the sacrificial covenant ritual reflected in the OT (e.g., Gen 15:9-21). The verses then would be rendered:

> For where there is a covenant, it is necessary for the death of the one who ratifies it to be attested [or represented], for a covenant is confirmed over dead animals, since it is not valid while the ratifier still lives [i.e., has not undergone representative death].

Christ's death provides the ratifying sacrifice prerequisite to the establishment of the new, eternal covenant (Heb 9:15-22), as well as redeeming from the transgressions committed under the "first covenant," the law.

But why would the author characterize Christ's death in this way? The ritual splitting of the carcasses of animals signified the fate that awaited the ratifying party should he or she violate the terms of the covenant. Therefore the mention of Christ's blood as a ratification almost certainly anticipates the warnings of the terrifying judgment that will come upon those who knowingly reject the new covenant, to which the author turns in Hebrews 10. In doing so he takes up the very formula for covenant ratification he has used in Hebrews 9:20—the one who regards "the blood of the covenant by which he was cleansed as will receive the severest of punishments" (Heb 10:26-30). There is therefore an implicit reference to divine wrath in Hebrews 9:16-17, which corresponds to the author's usual method of presentation: he introduces an idea prior to developing it (cf. the description of Jesus as high priest in Heb 2:17-18, which is then followed by his exposition beginning Heb 5).

3. 1 Peter.

Viewed from the perspective of its supreme moral beauty and inestimable value, the death of Christ, or in the language of the letter, Christ's "suffering," serves as the leitmotif of 1 Peter. Elsewhere Christ's death is often described as his suffering (particularly in the Gospels, Acts and Hebrews; see Ign. *Eph.* 7.2; Ign. *Trall.* presc.; Ign. *Phld.* 9.2; *2 Clem.* 1.2), but 1 Peter does so exclusively, even altering traditional formulas (see 1 Pet 2:21; 3:18, where variant readings attest scribal tendencies to "correct" the wording).

Peter develops the theme of the excellence of Christ's innocence and humility in three ways. In language suggestive of a common confession, he reminds his readers of the undeserved favor that has come to them by Christ's suffering on their behalf. The sinless Christ accomplished redemption through his meek endurance* of injustice, a redemption that therefore is worthy of highest esteem. A second prominent theme is regularly attached to this idea: in his suffering and death Christ freed believers from their empty past for conduct like his, thereby pleasing God. Finally Peter points to the eschatological "glories" that follow the cross. Christ, although rejected by the disobedient, is precious to God who has now raised him from the dead and exalted him. Believers wait in faith and hope for the revelation of Christ's glory in which they themselves shall be delivered and vindicated. The letter therefore serves as an encouragement to Gentile Christians under pressure and the threat of persecution to persevere in faith and in excellence of conduct.

These three themes characterize each of the three confessions of Christ's cross that appear in the letter (1 Pet 1:18-21; 2:21-25; 3:18). The cross is simultaneously the source of forgiveness, the basis for conduct and the ground of eschatological hope. Moreover, in the course of the letter a certain progression unfolds. In 1 Peter 1:18-21 emphasis falls on the contrast between the vanity of the past conduct of the readers and the exceeding value of Christ's redeeming death. In 1 Peter 2:21-25, while the same elements are retained, the focus shifts to the pattern of life that Christ's meekness set for believers to follow. And in the third passage (1 Pet 3:18 and its context) Peter stresses Christ's vindicating resurrection and the eschatological salvation of those who believe in him.

These passages may represent hymns* or confessions of which the author made use (*see* Worship). Nevertheless, in each case the phrasing bears the distinct vocabulary of the author, reflects his particular interests and (as we are arguing) contains material integral to his argument in the letter, so that while the passages reflect early Christian traditions, they do not lend themselves to the reconstruction of underlying strata of thought. They are confessional in nature and form as they stand in the letter and may well have been constructed with catechesis in mind.

It is necessary to mention briefly the debate as to whether 1 Peter 3:18-22 includes a description of a postmortem or postresurrection descent of Christ to the dead. Despite its current disfavor, some form of the Augustinian interpretation of the passage is the most satisfactory interpretation (Feinberg, Grudem, cf. Dalton), since it best accounts for the particularity of reference to Noah and the evangelization of the dead in 1 Peter 4:6. This interpretation also receives considerable support from the mention of the presence of the Spirit of Christ in the prophets (1 Pet 1:11), which among the NT writings is unique. In this reading Christ did not descend into hell or the underworld but was present by the Spirit in the preaching of Noah.

The "spirits in prison" are those of persons who were then disobedient (1 Pet 3:20; cf. Heb 12:23).

3.1. The Suffering of Christ as an Atonement. In contrast to Hebrews, the theme of forgiveness remains undeveloped in 1 Peter. Yet it is clearly foundational, an essential element of the confession of Christ that Peter and his readers share and upon which he builds. This significance of the cross as a means of forgiveness is apparent in the opening greeting, which describes the ultimate saving aim of God for his people as "obedience and sprinkling with the blood of Jesus Christ."

The first element of the divine aim, "obedience," serves as a pregnant description of faith (see 1 Pet 1:22), which is thereby represented as the primary act of obedience (1 Pet 1:7-9; contra Garlington), with the underlying suggestion that faith is to issue in holy conduct (1 Pet 1:14). This language may represent Pauline influence, since the term *obedience* is infrequent apart from his letters. And the usage of "obedience" in the sense of "faith" is mistakably Paul's. At the outset of the letter a pattern appears, which is prominent in letters of Paul and common to the NT generally. The forgiveness given by the cross is not an isolated gift but is joined to the new obedience. The focus of the letter is upon the new obedience, but its basis lies in the forgiveness worked by Christ's death.

The second phrase, which bears overtones of the covenantal ceremony described in Exodus 24 (cf. Heb 9:13; 10:22; 12:24), conveys assurance to the Gentile readers that they have now become the people of God and that they are so on the basis of the death of Christ. Notions of cleansing and forgiveness are also implicit (cf. *Barn.* 5.1), since the sprinkling of blood recalls the Day of Atonement as well (Lev 16; see too the red heifer ceremony, Num 19).

In the first christological confession (1 Pet 1:18-21) the reference to the blood of Christ as that of a "lamb unblemished and spotless" (1 Pet 1:19) recalls the sacrificial system (e.g., Lev 9:3), and in its personal and moral aspect it bears associations with the Suffering Servant of Isaiah 53. The understanding of Christ's death as a substitutionary atonement lies just under the surface in the biblical imagery that the passage evokes. The focal point of the confession is found in the contrast between the worthless conduct of the pagan world and the "precious blood of Christ."

The soteriology is profound. As L. Goppelt (117) observes, the "ancestral inheritance of empty conduct" (1 Pet 1:18) describes sociologically what the Adam-Christ typology (Rom 5:12-21) says theologically. There is something more here than a bad example that might be either followed or disregarded. Humanity is entrapped in an empty and reprehensible pattern of life. Yet God's redeeming work in Christ has overcome the fallen human condition. Before the foundation of the world Christ and his saving work were determined *(proginōskein)*, and this inestimable sacrifice was made for those whose deeds were worthless. Since God's impartial judgment yet stands before Christians, they are to conduct themselves in reverential fear, knowing both the incalculable cost of redemption and the efficacy which that cost implies. The "imperative" springs from the "indicative" here in the same paradoxical manner that it does for Paul. The exhortation has faith, not mere gratitude, as its sustaining force (1 Pet 1:21), just as faith (which rightly treasures and loves Christ) is introduced in the letter as the prime virtue of Christians (1 Pet 1:5-9).

The theme of Christ's death as a substitutionary atonement appears again, explicitly, in the second, lengthier confession (1 Pet 2:21-25). "Christ suffered on behalf of you," the readers are told (1 Pet 2:21), a thought that is then expanded in the following confession. This confession is built around Isaiah 53 and represents the most extensive use of that passage in the NT. Thematically it is similar to the citation of Isaiah 53:7-8 in Acts 8:32-33 but goes beyond it precisely in its reference to the substitutionary nature of Christ's death and its saving benefits: "[Christ] who bore our sins in his body on the tree" (1 Pet 2:24; Is 53:12). The phrase "on the tree" reflects the biblical terminology used by early Christians for the shame associated with the cross, reflecting in particular the curse of Deuteronomy 21:23 (see Acts 5:30; 10:39; Gal 3:13; cf. Josh 8:29 LXX, Esther 7:9 LXX).

The underlying thought of 1 Peter 1:2 and 1 Peter 1:19 now becomes explicit. Christ, the sinless Servant of Isaiah 53, has borne the sins of believers upon the cross. Even more than in the earlier confession, attention is concentrated upon the new pattern of conduct that Christ's cross has secured for his people. Yet, as before, the substitutionary and unique character of

Christ's death provides the basis for exhortation, so that Christ's suffering is not merely exemplary. The "indicative" of forgiveness that appears in 1 Peter 2:21, 24 is extended to transformed life and gathered up together with the "imperative" in the summary statements. He bore our sins, that "having [by death] departed from sin, we might live to righteousness" (1 Pet 2:24). With remarkable similarity to Paul, Peter understands Christ's death for sin to include the death of believers to sin, which issues in a new life. In the words of N. Dahl, this is not imitation but conformation. Goppelt's claim (206-7) that the interpretation of Christ's death in terms of mere *imitatio* does not emerge until the second century is substantiated here.

A third succinct description of Christ's death as a vicarious atonement appears in the brief confession found in 1 Peter 3:18. The phrasing "Christ suffered concerning sins *[peri hamartiōn]*" again reflects sacrificial language (e.g., Lev 16:3, 5, 9 LXX). The following reference to "the righteous one on behalf of the unrighteous" (cf. Is 53:11) completes the substitutionary idea. As in the previous confessions, Peter interprets the cross in sacrificial terms, as an atoning act that brings grace and forgiveness. The stark moral contrast between Christ and those he redeemed reinforces the continuing theme of the virtue of Christ's suffering.

3.2. The Suffering of Christ as a Pattern for Christian Conduct. We have already observed that in 1 Peter Christ's death is interpreted as an atonement for sin in connection with and as the basis for the new obedience of believers and that the interest of the letter lies primarily in exhortation, as is indicated by the frequency of reference to "conduct" (the noun and verb appear seven times).

In the first confession this idea appears in a straightforward but undeveloped way. Christ's death has provided redemption (1 Pet 1:18) and release from slavery, which in context recalls not only contemporary practices of securing manumission but more particularly the exodus from Egypt. Associations not only of the sacrificial system (and the Suffering Servant of Is 53) but also of the Passover lamb* (Ex 12) are present. Bondage is bondage to sinful conduct, from which the "blood" of Christ secures release.

As we have noted, in the progression of emphases the second confession (1 Pet 2:21-25)

makes the pattern of Christ's suffering its primary theme. With perhaps a backward glance to the corrupt ancestral inheritance (1 Pet 1:18), Peter indicates that in his patient suffering Christ left behind a model that believers are to follow, tracing his steps (1 Pet 2:21). The following description of Christ's meekness in the face of suffering makes it clear that discipleship consists in conformity to Christ's character. Peter does not suppose that all Christians will suffer crucifixion or even that they all will face persecution (1 Pet 1:6; 3:14; 4:14-16). He expects them to avoid it if possible and does not encourage them to seek abuse or martyrdom* as, for example, Ignatius did. He assumes, however, that they cannot escape all suffering, and what they are called to endure they are called to face in the same manner as Christ did. The extensive reference to the Suffering Servant in Isaiah 53 has its basis here and is expanded with Christ's refusing verbal retaliation: "being railed at, he did not rail in return; while suffering, he did not threaten." Instead he entrusted himself to God the righteous judge (1 Pet 2:23).

In this extraordinary virtue Christ provided a example for believers (cf. 1 Pet 3:9-10; 4:19). Yet, as we observed, Peter does not call for mere imitation. Rather, salvation itself is understood as conformation to Christ's character: "the wounding of Christ has brought our healing" (1 Pet 2:24). Christ remains active in guarding and guiding his people, "for as wandering sheep you have now returned to your Shepherd and Guardian" (1 Pet 2:25). Christ by his cross has secured the wholeness of his people, and that wholeness consists in conformity to his character as righteous (see 1 Pet 2:20).

3.3. The Suffering of Christ and Eschatological Glory. In a manner reminiscent of Luke-Acts (see, e.g., Lk 24:26, 46) Peter describes the interest of the prophets in the "sufferings of Christ and the subsequent glories" (1 Pet 1:11). Christ's rejection by human beings was overruled by God's delight in him and his virtue (1 Pet 2:4, 2:19; 3:4, 3:12). Although put to death in the flesh, he was made alive by the Spirit (1 Pet 3:18) and exalted to the right hand of God (1 Pet 3:22). Christians who share in his sufferings therefore are to rejoice, since such hardship portends eschatological blessing for them at the revelation of Christ's glory (1 Pet 4:13; 1:7). Just as Christ's moral excellence was met with divine reward,* so too those who share

in his suffering will share in his glory.

4. 1 John.

The death of Christ in its sacrificial, atoning significance is again basic to the message of this letter. The author writes to a confused and battered believing community, which has been fractured by some form of Docetism.* The claims of the wayward group and the status of the remaining community are to be tested against the apostolic witness to the incarnation and atoning death of the Christ. The cross constitutes the eschatological revelation of God's love, which is to determine the confession and the conduct of those who belong to him. Faith and obedience are inherently bound up with one another, not merely by an ethic* of obligation to Jesus' pattern of behavior but more fundamentally in the divine "begetting" of believers and the gift of the Spirit (1 Jn 2:29; 3:24). The world and the works of the devil have been overcome in the cross of Jesus (1 Jn 3:8; 5:4).

4.1. The Death of Christ as a Propitiatory Sacrifice. The opponents deny that "the Christ is Jesus" (1 Jn 2:22; 5:1, 5) and that "Jesus Christ has come in the flesh" (1 Jn 4:2). This implicit denial of the need for the cross is coupled with the errant group's claim that they were without guilt or sin (1 Jn 1:8-10). The author in response insists not only on the confession that Jesus is the Christ but also on the fundamental role Christ's death plays in securing salvation. Particularly the initial and final references to the cross in 1 John address this error, specifying the "blood" of Jesus the Christ as essential to the Christian confession (1 Jn 1:7; 5:6, 8). This language includes a certain stress upon the physical reality of the death of Christ and highlights its saving effect by presenting it in terms of an atoning sacrifice.

The placement of the first of these references to Christ's atoning death at the beginning of the letter (in 1 Jn 1:7—2:2) signals the importance of this topic to the whole discourse. Cultic language appears immediately, which carries associations of the violent death of Christ. "The blood of Jesus cleanses us from all sin" (cf. Lev 8:15; 16:30). The author most likely has in view the forgiveness of sins and not the transformation of the person (contra Brown, Marshall 1978, Smalley), as is suggested not only by the cultic and hence legal background of this expression but also by its counterpart in the denial of guilt (1 Jn 1:8, "to have no sin"; see Brown), in the parallel promise of forgiveness (1 Jn 1:9) and in the elaboration in 1 John 2:1-2, where again sin, forgiveness and cultic-legal ideas are present.

The sacrificial interpretation of Christ's death concludes by the description of it as a *hilasmos* for sin, around which there has been considerable debate (as with the related term *hilaskesthai* in Heb 2:17, see 2.2.2 above). Does the expression merely convey the idea of expiation of sin or also that of propitiation of divine wrath? Although notions of wrath remain in the background, in this letter death is not an impersonal effect but the result of divine judgment (1 Jn 2:28; 4:17-18), the consequence of disobedience and unbelief (1 Jn 2:17; 3:14). Correspondingly in this context forgiveness is clearly covenantal and juridical. Christ is our advocate (*parakletos*) with the Father (1 Jn 2:1), and this advocacy implicitly derives from his being the *hilasmos* for sin (1 Jn 2:2). Consequently it is best to understand the term as including the sense of propitiation along with the idea of cleansing, which is obviously present (1 Jn 1:7, 9).

Again, as with all other NT writings, God is both subject and object of Christ's atoning death. He is faithful and righteous to forgive our sins and cleanse us, even as Christ is our advocate before him (1 Jn 1:9; 2:1). He sent his Son as a propitiation (*hilasmos*) for our sins (1 Jn 4:10).

The concluding reference to Christ's death again uses the term *blood*, recalling the initial interpretation of his death as an atoning sacrifice and thus carrying salvific associations. These implicitly reinforce the author's assertion that Jesus Christ came not "through water only but through water and blood" (1 Jn 5:6), which here and in 1 John 5:8 most likely refer to Jesus' baptism and death on the cross (see Smalley). Jesus was attested as the Christ not only at his baptism but also in his crucifixion. His death, far from disqualifying him as the Christ, is essential to the divine witness to him.

Christ's death is an atoning sacrifice not only for believers but also for "the world." The "world" is probably not a neutral usage but has in view the hostility of fallen humanity to God and his purposes (e.g., 1 Jn 2:15-17; 3:1, 13; 4:4). The scope of the atonement stands in contrast to the apparent exclusiveness of the group that had departed from the church. Yet 1 John is decidedly exclusive itself in its insistence on faith in Jesus and the belief that the entire world lies in the power of the evil one (1 Jn 5:19). Coupled with this belief are clear statements of divine ultimacy in salvation (e.g., 1 Jn 3:9; 4:4). The author shows no embarrassment at this juxtaposition. The God revealed in the offer of forgiveness in the cross is nevertheless the God who freely and sovereignly gives new birth.

4.2. The Death of Christ as Eschatological Revelation. The cross is centrally and predominantly interpreted as a revelation in 1 John, as is apparent from the emphasis of the prescript (1 Jn 1:1-4) and the running themes of truth,* knowledge and revelation. This perspective does not diminish its status as an atoning event. As a sacrifice for sins, Jesus' death on the cross is the decisive revelatory event, the eschatological manifestation of God and his love and of eternal life.

A historical dimension is attached to this interpretation of the cross as revelation. The author is distinct from the audience. He has seen the "eternal life" (1 Jn 1:2-3), but they have not. They have only heard from him (1 Jn 1:5). Even his vision is only proleptic. He has seen neither God nor Christ "as he is" in his eschatological glory (1 Jn 3:2; 4:12). Yet he has seen and has borne witness that the Father sent the Son as Savior of the world (1 Jn 4:14). And in sending his only Son that "the world" might live, God has manifest his love (1 Jn 4:9). Revelation in 1 John, therefore, is objective in character rather than a matter of inner illumination. "Seeing" comes about only in so far as the testimony is heard, believed and obeyed (1 Jn 2:7-11, 24; 4:6; 5:5-12). The reception of this revelation is not ultimately a matter of human capacities but a divine work: a being begotten of God (1 Jn 5:1), anointed by him (1 Jn 2:20, 27), given the Spirit (1 Jn 4:13).

The cross is the revelation of the love of God and of love itself. And it reveals this love specifically as a death in our place, for our sins. We know love only through Christ's yielding his life for us on the cross (1 Jn 3:16; cf. Mk 10:45: Is 53:10). God manifest his love in sending his only (*monogenes*) Son as a propitiation sacrifice (*hilasmos*) for our sins (1 Jn 4:9-10). The radical nature of this claim derives on the one hand from the author's view that "the world" is filled with hatred (1 Jn 3:11-12) and on the other that Christ gave his life for that world, which hates him (1 Jn 2:2). Love as a reality among believers derives not from our love for God but his love for us manifest in Christ's atoning death for our sins (1 Jn 4:10). Apart from the cross, love of this nature would remain unknown. Through the cross, it has dawned on the world as an eschatological reality (1 Jn 2:8-11).

The love of God revealed in the cross places believers under a moral obligation. "If God so loved us, we ought to love one another" (1 Jn 4:11). Yet the ethic of 1 John derives ultimately from the eschatological realities that the cross has introduced. Conduct reveals whether one knows God, whether one is "in him." God is active in the revelation of his love, so that love has its perfection in the transformation of the human being (1 Jn 2:5; 4:17-18).

The eschatological character of the cross is apparent in other references (1 Jn 3:14; 5:4) and provides the essential structure for the seemingly conflicting statements regarding the relation of believers to sin. As we have seen, the opening declaration of the letter makes continuing confession of sins the mark of true spirituality (1 Jn 1:9-10). Yet the author claims that it is not possible for believers to sin (1 Jn 3:6, 9) and derives this assertion in part from the cross: "That one appeared that he might take away sins, and 'in him' there is no sin" (1 Jn 3:5). The following reference to "abiding in him" (1 Jn 3:6) suggests that the expression "in him there is no sin" refers to the eschatological state that Christ has brought.

Parallel references indicate that the "taking away" sins most likely signifies the provision of forgiveness, not transformation of life (cf. the juridical contexts in Deut 17:12; 19:19; 21:9 LXX, etc.; and see Jn 1:29; 1 Sam 15:25; 25:28 LXX; Sir 16:9; Tob 12:9; *Pss. Sol.* 3:7-8). With the forgiveness won at the cross the eschatological state has arrived, in which the power of sin has been abolished by the forgiveness which has been granted. This corresponds to 1 John 3:8, where the purpose of the Incarnation is said to be the "destruction of the works of the devil." Believers are now said to have the seed of God abiding within them (1 Jn 3:9), just as they abide in him (1 Jn 3:6). From the eschatological perspective, the perspective of the effects of the cross, the "inability to sin" has been granted. Yet this state of affairs is clearly proleptic. Believers live between the times. They therefore must continue to confess their sins. But they also must

live in the light of the eschaton and purify themselves, as Christ is pure (1 Jn 3:3). As the reference to the divine seed implies, eschatological realities have entered the present and indelibly mark the conduct of the believer.

As an eschatological reality the death of Christ represents a triumph over the devil and destruction of his works (1 Jn 3:8), a triumph in which believers share (1 Jn 2:12, 14; 4:5). Moreover, victory consists in the confession of Jesus as the Son of God, including his "coming through water and blood," so that the forgiveness worked through the cross stands behind the triumph, a connection that is suggested by the parallel between 1 John 3:5 and 1 John 3:8 as well.

5. Revelation.
Paradoxically in the Revelation to John, the cross of Christ is the path to his lordship and the reign of those who belong to him. Moreover, as we have seen in the other NT writings, it is as an atoning sacrifice that the death of Christ achieves the divine triumph. Not only death and life, apparent defeat and overwhelming victory are juxtaposed in the letter, but also the deity and humanity of Christ. The paradox therefore is deeper than a mere reversal of fortune. Christ died as both God and human.

5.1. Christ's Death as the Death of God. Although Christ's deity and his death are not paired elsewhere in Revelation, the appearance of this juxtaposition in the opening vision and in the message to the church in Smyrna (Rev 2:8) significantly informs the unfolding drama, particularly the adoration of the Lamb (Rev 5:8-14). The worthiness of the Lamb to receive worship derives not only from his redeeming death but also, subtly and implicitly, from his very being. Christ is "the first and the last" (Rev 1:17; 2:8; 22:13), an ascription of divine self-sufficiency and uniqueness (cf. Is 43:10; 44:6; 48:12). He is "the Living One," the expression used to describe the one sitting on the throne (Rev 4:9-10; cf. Rev 10:6; Sir 18:1). Nevertheless this very one died and lived again (Rev 1:18; 2:8) and now lives forever with authority* over death itself (Rev 1:18), with which he grants encouragement to the suffering church (Rev 2:9-11). The paradoxical relation focuses attention on his death, which is explicable only as a redemptive act.

5.2. Christ's Death as Redemption and Triumph.

Most often in Revelation, Christ's death is presented in its saving significance and in sacrificial language. As elsewhere, Christ's death is his "blood" that redeems from sin (Rev 1:5; 7:14) and purchases a people for God (Rev 5:9; cf. Rev 14:3, 4). This language of purchase, drawn from the field of slavery, expresses God's claim upon the redeemed. The cross frees them for their divinely appointed role as rulers and as priests (Rev 1:6; 5:10). The image of Christ as "the Lamb who was slain" further links the language of redemption and purchase with the Passover and exodus (Ex 12-13; cf. 1 Cor 5:7) and with the Suffering Servant of Isaiah (Is 53:7; cf. Acts 8:32; 1 Pet 1:19; Jn 1:29).

The frequent depiction of Christ as the Lamb underscores the centrality of his saving death in Revelation (Rev 5:6; passim). In an ironic juxtaposition this Lamb is first introduced as the conquering Lion of the tribe of Judah (Rev 5:5). God has achieved victory not through force but through weakness in the death of Christ. The violence and oppression of the world and the devil have only caused his purposes to succeed.

These purposes consist in the working of the forgiveness of sins. This idea is inherent to the sacrificial language of Revelation and appears strikingly in the proleptic announcement of triumph in Revelation 12:10-12. The kingdom of God has come, because the "accuser of the brothers and sisters" has been thrown down from heaven (Rev 12:10; cf. Job 1:9-11). The devil, who opposes the divine saving purpose by bringing charges against the people of God for their sins, has been overcome by "the blood of the Lamb" and by faithful testimony to this Lamb. Those who do not believe will be subject to the wrath of God and of the Lamb (Rev 6:16-17; 14:9-11).

The Lamb is supremely worthy of praise because of his sacrificial death (Rev 5:9-12). The moral excellence of his act distinguishes it from the beast's cheap imitation of it in a mortal wound (Rev 13:3, 12).

5.3. Christ's Death as the Destiny of Believers. A stark division between belief and unbelief emerges in Revelation. One is either a follower of the beast (Rev 13:3-4) or a follower of the Lamb (Rev 14:4), subject to the hostility he faced (Rev 12:17). The churches stand in the relation to the risen Lord that he stood to the Father in his earthly ministry (Rev 2:26-28; 3:21-

22). They are martyred for their witness (Rev 6:9-11; 12:10), just as he was for his (Rev 1:5). And they likewise share in his triumph (Rev 7:17; 15:3-5; 19:1—20:15).

6. Apostolic Fathers.

The saving significance of the death of Christ is widely assumed but nowhere defined in the Christian writings of the second century. Writers such as Ignatius and Irenaeus were concerned to stress the physical reality of Christ's death in opposition to docetic and gnostic opponents (respectively), but the meaning of Christ's death is not otherwise the subject of debate. The work of Christ did not become the center of contention as the person of Christ did in this period. That is not to say that the salvific nature of Christ's death was unimportant to these writers or that Christian thinking on this matter did not undergo development. New concerns obviously did emerge, particularly those arising from the Hellenistic presupposition of an antithesis between spirit and matter, which were bound to shape the understanding of salvation itself. And the threat of martyrdom clearly influenced, although it did not determine, Christian thinking on the death of Christ (cf. Pagels). Such assumptions and concerns shaped the reception of the apostolic witness. The various understandings of Christ's death found in the NT writings reappear here, along with the OT passages by which his death was interpreted. Christ's death is an atoning sacrifice that secures forgiveness, a pattern for believers to follow and a triumph over the powers of evil. Yet the structure of thought shows a marked shift, so that the traditional concepts are weighed differently and given new connections over against the apostolic witness.

Particularly with Irenaeus, there are developments in soteriology that are to be appreciated. Yet the restructuring that takes place in the second century represents a serious loss of understanding of the gospel. This loss in most instances is not immediately apparent, since traditional formulations of Christ's death found in the NT are often preserved. But the larger framework in which these statements appear reflects a soteriology that is noticeably impoverished. As T. F. Torrance has commented, "It was not that they [the apostolic fathers] were opposed to them [i.e., such statements], but that they did not grasp them properly" (Torrance,

137). In the fathers (*see* Apostolic Fathers) of the second century, the cross no longer works the whole of salvation. It merely provides the basis for it.

It is not possible here to trace all the various interpretations of Christ's death that appear in early Christian writings of this period, let alone gnostic writings or those showing gnostic tendencies (for whom the death of Christ, when treated, served to display the triumph of spirit over matter; *Gos. Pet.* 4.10; *Apoc. Pet.* 81.15-24; see van Voorst, Pagels). The most we can hope to do is briefly touch upon some basic conceptions that characterize many of the writers and to highlight the differences between them and the writings of the NT.

6.1. Deliverance. Christ's death and resurrection freed human beings from the power of the devil. Taking Irenaeus as his starting point, G. Aulén claimed this theme of Christus Victor as the "classic theory" of the atonement and offered it as an alternative to theories of substitution and moral influence. The idea appears in Justin Martyr as well (see Goodenough, 250-52) and incipiently in other writers, who tend to focus upon deliverance from death (Melito,* *Homily on the Passion* 11-27, 51-56, 100-102; Ign. *Eph.* 17.1; 19.3; *Barn.* 14.5). In the Christian writings of the second century, however, in distinction from the NT, this deliverance involves the forgiveness of past sins and moral transformation, not ultimate salvation. Eschatological redemption is yet to be accomplished, with divine assistance, by the works of one's hands (e.g., *Barn.* 19.10; *Did.* 4.6; *see* Barnabas, Epistle of; Didache). Forgiveness is no longer absolute and eschatological but only the remission of past sins that opens the way to salvation. The Christian life is no longer based on a conformation to Christ worked ultimately by God alone but on an imitation of him by the believer aided by grace.

6.2. Revelation. Viewed as an event on the path from the Incarnation to the resurrection, the death of Christ also serves as a revelation of the divine will. The antecedents to Irenaeus's theory of recapitulation, the "restoration" of humanity through the obedient "repetition" of the human life in Christ (Irenaeus *Haer.* 4.38.1), seem to lie here, particularly in Ignatius (Ign. *Eph.* 19.1—20.2). Christ has provided a pattern by which disciples may attain to incorruption. Ignatius longs for martyrdom precisely for this

reason (Ign. *Magn.* 1.2; Ign. *Rom.* 4.1-2; 6.1-3). Christ's humility in suffering also provides a pattern for believers (*1 Clem.* 2.1; 1.16; *Mart. Pol.; see* Clement of Rome). Here, however, the shift we noted has taken place. No longer, as in the NT writings, does obedience spring from an absolute, completed "indicative." Imitation takes place by divine grace, not by human resources (see *Diogn.* 9.6; *see* Diognetes, Epistle to), but the arrival at salvation is now fully contingent upon one's own efforts.

For most second-century writers, as a divine revelation, the cross marks the supersession of Judaism* by Christianity. This idea is present in Ignatius and prominent in *Barnabas*, the *Epistle to Diognetus* and Melito, among others. Christ brings a new law and a new covenant for Christians, since by disobedience Israel long ago had forfeited the old covenant. Generally this new covenant represents a spiritualization of the sacrificial system of the law. Borrowing on the prophetic critique, cultic practices are replaced by Christian obedience. Despite some similarities to the NT writings, fundamental differences again appear. The cross is not central, except as a means of charging Israel collectively with guilt for the death of the Lord. Instead of Christ, it is the church, its institutions and practices that transcends the nation of Israel. Consequently the clear hope for Israel characteristic of the NT writings has disappeared.

6.3. Impartation of Incorruptibility. The impartation of salvation takes on a quasi-physical nature, first in Ignatius and later in Irenaeus. The "breaking of one bread," the celebration of the Lord's Supper,* becomes for Ignatius "the medicine of immortality" (Ign. *Eph.* 20.2), the means for obtaining life (Ign. *Phld.* 4). The resurrected flesh of Christ becomes the means by which the church attains to incorruption. Believers are joined to the tree of the cross in an organic way, as branches, and thereby to God (Ign. *Trall.* 11). In all of this there is an emphasis on the real death of the Lord, which brings the possibility of the salvation of the whole human being. The fronts against Docetism and Gnosticism are apparent, as is the wrestling with the relation of material flesh to immaterial spirit. The death of Christ is understood primarily as a solution to the problem of mortality and corruption rather than that of guilt.

6.4. Forgiveness of Sins. The language of forgiveness and atonement often bears striking similarities to that of the NT but with the marked departure in meaning that we have noted. Rather than having a juridical sense as in Paul, "justification" seems to signify moral transformation (*1 Clem.* 30-33; *Diogn.* 9-10; Ign. *Rom.* 5; Ign. *Phld.* 8; *Herm. Vis.* 3.9; *Herm. Sim.* 5.7; *see* Hermas, Shepherd of). The atoning death of Christ brings forgiveness (Ign. *Smyrn.* 6) but only as prerequisite for obtaining salvation (Ign. *Eph.* 9). As Torrance (94-95) observes, for Polycarp Christ is the "down payment" *(arrabōn)* of our righteousness (Pol. *Phil.* 8.1), a down payment that must be supplemented by obedience (Pol. *Phil.* 2.2).

See also CHRISTOLOGY; CROSS, THEOLOGY OF THE; FORGIVENESS; LAMB; LORD'S SUPPER, LOVE FEAST; REDEMPTION; RESURRECTION; SACRIFICE, OFFERINGS, GIFTS; SALVATION; SUFFERING.

BIBLIOGRAPHY. G. Aulén, *Christus Victor: A Historical Study of the Three Main Types of the Idea of Atonement* (New York: Macmillan, 1969); F. Bovon, *Luc le Théologien: Vingt-cinq Ans de Recherches* (1950-75) (Le Monde de la Bible; Neuchâtel: Delachaux & Niestlé, 1978); R. E. Brown, *The Epistles of John* (AB; Garden City, NY: Doubleday, 1982); J. T. Carroll and J. B. Green, *The Death of Jesus in Early Christianity* (Peabody, MA: Hendrickson, 1995); H. Conzelmann, *The Theology of Luke* (New York: Harper & Row, 1961); O. Cullmann, *The Christology of the New Testament* (rev. ed.; Philadelphia: Westminster, 1959); W. J. Dalton, *Christ's Proclamation to the Spirits: A Study of 1 Peter 3:18—4:6* (2d ed.; AnBib 23; Rome: Pontifical Biblical Institute, 1989); P. H. Davids, *The First Epistle of Peter* (NICNT; Grand Rapids: Eerdmans, 1990); J. Denney, *The Death of Christ*, ed. R. V. G. Tasker (London: Tyndale, 1951); B. D. Ehrman, *The Orthodox Corruption of Scripture: The Effects of Early Christological Controversies on the Text of the New Testament* (Oxford: Oxford University Press, 1993); W. Elert, "Die Theopaschitische Formel," *TLZ* 56 (1931) 195-204; J. S. Feinberg, "1 Peter 3:18-20, Ancient Mythology and the Intermediate State," *WTJ* 48 (1986) 303-36; D. Garlington, *The Obedience of Faith* (WUNT 38; Tübingen: J. C. B. Mohr, 1991); S. R. Garrett, "The Meaning of Jesus' Death in Luke," *Word & World* (1992) 11-16; E. R. Goodenough, *The Theology of Justin Martyr: An Investigation into the Conceptions of Early Christian Literature and Its Hellenistic and Judaistic Influences* (Amsterdam: Philo, 1968); L. Goppelt, *A Commentary on I Peter*, ed. F. Hahn (Grand Rapids: Eerdmans, 1993); K. Grayston, *Dying, We Live: A New Enquiry into the Death of Christ in the New Testament* (New York: Oxford University Press, 1990); J. B. Green, "The Death of Jesus, God's Servant" in *Reimaging the Death of the Lukan Jesus,* ed. D. D. Sylva (Athenum Monographien/Theologie: BBB 73; Frankfurt: Hain, 1990) 1-28; idem, *The Death of Jesus* (WUNT 33; Tübingen: J. C. B. Mohr, 1988); W. Grudem, "Christ Preaching Through Noah: 1 Peter 3:19-20 in the Light of Dominant Themes in Jewish Literature," *TJ* 7 (1986) 3-31; E. Haenchen, *The Acts of the Apostles: A Commentary* (Philadelphia: Westminster, 1971); D. Hill, *Greek Words and Hebrew Meanings: Studies in the Semantics of Soteriological Terms* (SNTSMS 5; London: Cambridge University Press, 1967); M. D. Hooker, *Not Ashamed of the Gospel: New Testament Interpretations of the Death of Christ* (Grand Rapids: Eerdmans, 1995); J. J. Hughes, "Hebrews 9:15ff. and Galatians 3:15ff.: A Study in Covenant Practice and Procedure," *NovT* 21 (1979) 27-96; R. J. Karris, "Luke 23:47 and the Lukan View of Jesus' Death" in *Reimaging the Death of the Lukan Jesus,* ed. D. D. Sylva (Athenum Monographien/Theologie: BBB 73; Frankfurt: Hain, 1990) 68-78; J. Kodell, "Luke's Theology of the Death of Jesus" in *Sin, Salvation and the Spirit,* ed. D. Durken (Collegeville, MN: Liturgical Press, 1979) 221-30; F. Laub, " 'Ein für Allemal Hineingegangen in das Allerheiligste' (Hebr 9,12) zum Verständnis des Kreuzestodes im Hebräerbrief," *BZ* 35 (1991) 65-85; I. H. Marshall, *The Epistles of John* (NICNT: Grand Rapids: Eerdmans, 1978); idem, *Luke: Historian and Theologian* (Exeter: Paternoster, 1970); D. P. Moessner, " 'The Christ Must Suffer,' The Church Must Suffer: Rethinking the Theology of the Cross in Luke-Acts" in *SBLSP* 29 (1990) 165-95; L. L. Morris, *The Apostolic Preaching of the Cross* (Grand Rapids: Eerdmans, 1965); idem, *The Atonement: Its Meaning and Significance* (Downers Grove, IL: InterVarsity Press, 1983); J. H. Neyrey, *The Passion According to Luke* (New York: Paulist, 1985); E. H. Pagels, "Gnostic and Orthodox Views of Christ's Passion: Paradigms for the Christian's Response to Persecution?" in *The Rediscovery of Gnosticism,* ed. B. Layton (SHR 41; Leiden: E. J. Brill, 1980) 1:262-88; D. Peterson, *Hebrews and Perfection: An Examination of the Concept of Perfection in the "Epistle to the Hebrews"* (SNTSMS 47; Cambridge: Cambridge University Press, 1982); S. S. Smalley, *1, 2, 3 John* (WBC;

Waco, TX: Word, 1984); J. R. W. Stott, *The Cross of Christ* (Downers Grove, IL: InterVarsity Press, 1986); V. Taylor, *The Atonement in the New Testament Teaching* (London: Epworth, 1958); T. F. Torrance, *The Doctrine of Grace in the Apostolic Fathers* (Grand Rapids: Eerdmans, 1959); C. M. Tuckett, "Atonement in the NT," *ABD* 1:518-22; J. B. Tyson, *The Death of Jesus in Luke-Acts* (Columbia, SC: University of South Carolina Press, 1986); R. E. van Voorst, "Extracanonical Passion Narratives" in *The Death of Jesus in Early Christianity*, ed. J. T. Carroll and J. B. Green (Peabody, MA: Hendrickson, 1995) 148-61; P. Vielhauer, "On the 'Paulinism' of Acts" in *Studies in Luke-Acts*, ed. L. E. Keck and J. L. Martyn (Nashville: Abingdon, 1966) 33-50; R. S. Wallace, *The Atoning Death of Christ* (Westchester, IL: Crossway, 1981); M. Wilcox, " 'Upon the Tree'—Deut 21:22-23 in the New Testament," *JBL* 96 (1977) 85-99.   M. A. Seifrid

DECONSTRUCTION. *See* HERMENEUTICS.

DELAY OF PAROUSIA. *See* PAROUSIA.

DEMONS. *See* RELIGIONS, GRECO-ROMAN; SPIRITS.

DESPOSYNOI. *See* RELATIVES OF JESUS.

DESTRUCTION. *See* WRATH, DESTRUCTION.

DEVIL. *See* SATAN, DEVIL.

DIASPORA JUDAISM

By the first century A.D. Jewish communities had become established in almost every part of the then civilized world. Our period of investigation will be from the foundation of the various Diaspora communities until the second century A.D., although material relating to later periods will be discussed occasionally.

    1. Definitions
    2. Sources
    3. A Geographical Survey of Diaspora Communities
    4. Population
    5. Economic Situation
    6. The Diaspora Synagogue
    7. Community Leadership
    8. Diaspora Communities in the Greek City
    9. The Assimilation, Acculturation and Accommodation of Diaspora Communities
    10. Facets of Jewish Identity in the Diaspora
    11. Conclusions

1. Definitions.

Scholars of earlier generations categorized Judaism* as either Palestinian Judaism or Hellenistic Judaism. The former was regarded as "uncontaminated" and "normative" and, as the name suggests, restricted to Palestine. The latter was an adulterated, Hellenized form of Judaism found in the Diaspora. However, recent scholarship has noted how inadequate such a distinction is since strong hellenizing influences were at work in Palestine, and Diaspora communities continued to regard themselves as Jewish and can in no way be thought of as somehow less genuine.

Therefore, the primary distinction made in the study of Judaism is a geographical one between Judaism in Palestine and that in the Diaspora. Further, it is generally acknowledged that there was much diversity in Judaism in both geographical areas and that the development of Jewish life was influenced by the social and political context of each community.

2. Sources.

Often it is difficult to determine which Jewish texts from our period come from the Diaspora, but the following certainly or almost certainly do: Artapanus, Aristobulus, Demetrius, Ezekiel, *Joseph and Aseneth*, Josephus,* the *Epistle of Aristeas*, 3 and 4 Maccabees, Philo,* Pseudo-Philo, *Pseudo-Phocylides*, the Septuagint, some of the *Sibylline Oracles*, *Testament of Abraham* and Wisdom of Solomon. We have a significant number of papyri and inscriptions that shed valuable light on Diaspora Jewish life, although their preservation and discovery is haphazard, and it is often difficult to determine their dating and whether they are Jewish. In addition six Diaspora synagogues have been excavated. Further information about Diaspora Judaism comes from texts written by non-Jewish authors who provide us with insight into how Jews and Judaism were perceived by others. Overall our evidence is sufficient for us to construct a coherent account of Jewish life in only a very few places.

3. A Geographical Survey of Diaspora Communities.

By the first century A.D. there were significant Jewish communities throughout the Greco-Roman world, so that there were probably few major cities or regions that were without a community of resident Jews (see Philo *Leg. Gai.* 214, 281-83; *Flacc.* 45-46; *Vit. Mos.* 2.232; Josephus *Ant.* 14.7.2 §115; *J.W.* 7.3.3 §43; 1 Macc 15:23-24; *Sib. Or.* 3.271-72; Acts 2:9-11). There were two main reasons for the development of communities in the Diaspora. First, on occasions conquerors forcibly deported Jews; for example, the Babylonians carried numerous Jews to Babylonia (*see* Babylon), and Pompey took hundreds of Jews to Rome* as prisoners of war. Second, voluntary migration from Palestine to the Diaspora, arising from diverse motives, was highly significant.

The origins of the Jewish communities in Babylonia lie in the exile, since many Jews chose to remain in Babylonia when Cyrus allowed them to return to Jerusalem* (2 Chron 36:22-23; Ezra 1:1-4). Josephus wrote of the size of the Jewish population beyond the Euphrates in his time (Josephus *Ant.* 15.8.2.2 §14; cf. Philo *Leg. Gai.* 216, 282); there were significant Jewish settlements in Nehardea, Nisibis (Josephus *Ant.* 18.9.1 §311-12) and Seleucia (Josephus *Ant.* 18.9.8-9 §372-79). Queen Helena of Adiabene and her son Izates were converted to Judaism in the middle of the first century A.D. (Josephus *Ant.* 20.2.1-5 §17-53). During the Jewish war of A.D. 66-70 Jews in Palestine attempted to arouse hostility against the Romans among their fellow Jews beyond the Euphrates (Josephus *J.W.* 6.6.2 §343). The synagogue* in Dura-Europos, which was a modified house, was decorated with the most elaborate frescoes to survive from the ancient Jewish world.

The Jewish community in Antioch,* which was the largest in Syria, probably began in the third century B.C. (Josephus *Ant.* 12.3.1 §119). Under the Romans the Jewish community continued to grow, and Josephus notes its size, wealth and success in gaining sympathizers and proselytes (Josephus *J.W.* 7.3.3 §45). However, Jewish-Gentile tensions grew in the first century A.D., particularly among the lower social classes, and during the Jewish war of 66-70 the Jewish communities in many Syrian cities suffered on several occasions at the hands of the Gentile majority (Josephus *J.W.* 2.18.1 §457-60; 2.18.5 §477-79; 7.3.1-4 §40-62). After the war the inhabitants of Antioch asked Titus to expel the Jews from the city, but Titus refused to do so and confirmed the Jews' former rights (Josephus

J.W. 7.5.2 §100-111). We also know of other Jewish communities in Syria in Apamea, Damascus, Caesarea and elsewhere.

Between 210-205 B.C. Antiochus III transferred two thousand Jewish families from Mesopotamia and Babylonia to Lydia and Phrygia as military settlers; this provides us with the first unambiguous evidence of Jewish communities in Asia Minor (Josephus *Ant.* 12.3.4 §147-53). In *Pro Flacco* 28.67-68 Cicero writes of significant amounts of temple tax that had been seized in Asia in 62 B.C. by the Roman governor, Flaccus, giving evidence of the size and prosperity of some Jewish communities. A series of probably generally authentic documents preserved by Josephus and to be dated from 49 B.C. to A.D. 2/3 provide evidence for a number of Jewish communities in Asia Minor (Josephus *Ant.* 12.3.2 §125-28; 14.10.1-26 §185-267; 16.2.3-5 §27-61; 16.6.1-8 §160-78; Philo *Leg. Gai.* 315). They indicate these Jewish communities experienced ongoing tension in their local cities with respect to their social and religious privileges. The evidence suggests the Jewish communities were a significant and influential presence in the cities concerned and some Jews were of social and economic importance, but their limited participation in the main currents of city life led to their being a considerable irritant as far as the local cities were concerned.

By the beginning of the first century A.D., however, hostility toward the Jewish communities seems to have abated. An inscription from Acmonia shows that Julia Severa, a high priestess of the imperial cult in the time of Nero (*see* Emperor), built the Jewish community a synagogue (*CII* 766). She was thus a Gentile benefactor of the local Jewish community, a fact that shows Jews had friends in the highest social circles. Luke indicates that Jews were able to influence the local Gentile population in some places, which suggests that the Jews were respected in their cities (Acts 13:50; 14:2, 5). The presence of God-fearers of some social standing also suggests Jews were a respected group (e.g., Acts 13:16, 48-50; 14:1). Revelation 2:9 and Revelation 3:9 suggest that around A.D. 95 the Jewish communities in Smyrna and Philadelphia actively opposed Christians (*see* Revelation, Book of). Asian Christians addressed by Ignatius* clearly were tempted to go to the synagogue and adopt Jewish customs (Ign. *Phld.* 6.1-2; Ign. *Magn.* 8.1; 9.1-2; 10.3), a circumstance that points to the impact of some Jewish communities on local Christians.

From the second century A.D. onward it seems clear that some Jewish communities and individuals in Asia played a prominent part in their cities (e.g., *CII* 745, 748, 770; *Monumenta Asiae Minoris Antiqua* 6, 335a; Trebilco, 37-103). The size and prominence of the Sardis synagogue points to the social integration and civic prestige of this Jewish community. It seems that at least some of these communities were able to become acculturated and integrated into their cities while remaining faithfully Jewish. They seem to have belonged in their cities, where they were respected and made significant social contributions without compromising their Jewish identity.

We know that Jews lived in at least three towns in the kingdom of Bosporus. An almost certainly Jewish inscription from Gorgippia, dated A.D. 41, refers to the manumission of a female slave,* which was carried out in a synagogue (*CII* 690; cf. *CII* 683-84, 683a-b from Panticapaeum).

We are best informed about the Jewish communities in Egypt, which were the largest Diaspora communities in our period. At the time of the Babylonian conquest some Jews fled to Egypt (Jer 43:6-7; 44:1; 46:14); Aramaic papyri of the fifth century B.C. give evidence of a Jewish military colony at Elephantine, a colony that included a Jewish temple.

Jewish immigration into Egypt, both forced and voluntary, was significant from the third century B.C., with the result that Jews came to be settled throughout Egypt. The Ptolemaic era was a period when the Jews in Egypt encountered little hostility (although there were some notable exceptions) and came to fill a significant and prominent role in the economic, political, military and social life of Egypt. They generally flourished as Jews who retained their ethnic identity while also being strongly attracted to Hellenistic culture. However, their position was also precarious, since they had become alienated from significant sections of the wider populace.

At Leontopolis there was another significant Jewish community, formed by Jewish military settlers around 160 B.C. and including the Temple of Onias, which served the needs of the military colony (Tcherikover and Fuks, hereafter *CPJ*, 3:145-63; Josephus *Ant.* 13.3.1-3 §62-73).

In Philo's day Jews lived throughout Alexandria* but were particularly concentrated in two of its five quarters (Philo *Flacc.* 55; Josephus *J.W.* 2.18.8 §495). Synagogues were to be found throughout the city (Philo *Leg. Gai.* 132).

Octavian reaffirmed the privileges of the Jewish community in Egypt when he annexed that country in 30 B.C. The Romans also redefined the various classes of the population and emphasized the distinctions Romans, citizens of Greek cities and "foreigners." The Jews seem to have been relegated en bloc to the same category as the Egyptians and thus were compelled to pay the poll tax *(laographia);* Romans and citizens of Greek cities were exempted from paying this tax or paid at a lower rate. This was not only a financial burden; to be grouped with the native Egyptians was also a grave cultural affront, particularly to the upper classes of the Jewish population. Hence the matter of civic status became an increasingly important one for some Jews. Thus began a period of decline for the Jews in Egypt.

Jewish-Greek tension erupted in A.D. 38, when the Greeks destroyed synagogues or put up images of Gaius inside them. Flaccus, the Roman governor, declared the Jews to be "foreigners and aliens" in Alexandria and ordered them all to live in one section of the city (Philo *Flacc.* 25-57; *Leg. Gai.* 120-35). Murder of Jews and widespread looting also occurred. Flaccus was subsequently dismissed from office, and both sides sent delegations to Caligula, who died in A.D. 41 before giving his decision on the matter of Jewish communal privileges, which Flaccus had annulled.

Further trouble erupted in A.D. 41, which led to hearings before Claudius. He wrote a letter to the city (*CPJ* 153; cf. Josephus *Ant.* 19.5.2 §280-85) in which he called upon the Alexandrians to allow the Jews to keep their customs and ordered the Jews not to seek any privileges beyond those they had enjoyed for a long period. He also forbade the Jews from participating in the gymnasium and told them to be satisfied with the benefits they were enjoying in "a city not their own." Both these last factors support the view that the Jews had never possessed citizenship rights as a body in the city (Smallwood, 235-55). However, it seems clear that some Jews had become citizens individually. Claudius's letter halted the social and cultural integration of such Jews and their children.

The conflict between Jews and Greeks erupted again in A.D. 66 and resulted in the slaughter of a large number of Jews (Josephus *J.W.* 2.18.7-8 §487-98). After the Jewish war some of the most zealous insurgents escaped to Egypt, where they endeavored to stir up the Jewish population against the Romans, although they met strong opposition from the leaders of the Jewish community (Josephus *J.W.* 7.10.1 §409-19). In A.D. 115-17 Jews in Egypt, Cyrenaica, Cyprus and Mesopotamia attacked their Greek neighbors and launched a revolt. The loss of life was huge, and the Diaspora communities concerned were decimated as a result. Messianic expectation, resentment against the local population and radical social disaffection seem to have been factors behind this revolt.

Jewish settlement in Cyrenaica probably dates from near the beginning of Ptolemaic rule in the area (Josephus *Ag. Ap.* 2.4 §44), with numerous inscriptions testifying to a large Jewish population (see Lüderitz). In Cyrene the Jews formed a well-established and independent body, since Strabo notes that the population of the city was made up of citizens, farmers, resident aliens and Jews (Josephus *Ant.* 14.7.2 §115). Inscriptions show that in the first century A.D. some Jews were taking part in the life of the city and had attained considerable standing politically and culturally. The city also produced the Jewish historian Jason, who wrote a history of the Hasmonean revolt that was abbreviated in 2 Maccabees. He indicates the high cultural level attained by some Jews in Cyrene.

Three inscriptions suggest that some Jews in Berenice had been successful in their social and cultural integration into city life and that other Jews considered this to be legitimate (Lüderitz, nos. 70-72). The community seems to have called a building it owned an amphitheater. We also know of Jewish communities in Teuchira, Apollonia and Ptolemais and in Latin-speaking North Africa.

Philo (*Leg. Gai.* 281-82) gives evidence for a number of Jewish communities in Macedonia and Greece; he lists Thessaly, Boetia, Macedonia, Aetolia, Attica, Argos, Corinth, most of the Peloponnese and the islands of Euboea and Crete. In Paul's time there were Jews in Philippi, Thessalonica, Berea, Athens and Corinth (Acts 16:13; 17:1, 10, 17; 18:4). The Jewish communi-

ties in these areas were probably never large, and the epigraphical data for them are limited. One inscription from Corinth, to be dated after the NT period, speaks of a "synagogue of the Hebrews" (*CII* 718). An inscription from Stobi (*CII* 694) records the grant of part of a private house for use as a synagogue. The Jews of Cyprus participated in the revolt under Trajan; clearly they were numerically strong. We have some information about Jews living on Cos, Rhodes and Samos, and a synagogue, built in the first century B.C., has been discovered on Delos.

A significant number of Jews lived in Rome. We do not know when Jews first settled there, but given the significance of Rome and the contacts between the Romans and Hasmonean Judea it was probably in the second century B.C. Some Jews were probably expelled from the city in 139 B.C. (see Valerius Maximus 1.3.3; Goodman in Lieu, North and Rajak, 69-70). A number of Jews were brought to Rome as prisoners of war by Pompey in 63 B.C. (Josephus *Ant.* 14.4.4-5 §70-71, 79), and in 59 B.C. Cicero suggests that they were securely established in the city (*Pro Flacco* 28.66-67). Josephus reports that eight thousand Roman Jews supported an embassy from Judea in 4 B.C. (Josephus *Ant.* 17.11.1 §300). The community flourished in the Augustan era while maintaining its Jewish identity; a number of Roman authors commented on the presence and practices of Jews in Rome in this period (e.g., Horace *Sermones* 1.4.139-43; 1.5.96-104; 1.9.60-78; Ovid *Ars amatoria* 1.75-80, 413-16).

In A.D. 19 the Jews were expelled from Rome because of their burgeoning influence (Josephus *Ant.* 18.3.4-5 §65-84; Tacitus *Ann.* 2.85); however, it is doubtful that all the Jews living in Rome left the city. There was further trouble in the 40s, although the evidence is problematic. Two events probably occurred: first, a prohibition of assemblies in A.D. 41 referred to by Dio Cassius (60.6.6), and second, an expulsion mentioned by Suetonius (*Claudius* 25.4), Acts 18:2 and Orosius (*Adv. Pag.* 7.6.15-16), which the latter dates to A.D. 49. According to Suetonius, the Jews were expelled since "they were constantly rioting at the instigation of Chrestus." This probably refers to troubles resulting from Jewish Christian missionaries'* preaching about Christ among Jews in Rome; it seems likely that only known troublemakers were expelled (e.g., Acts 18:2: Priscilla and Aquila).

For the rest of the first century A.D. the Jews in Rome were in an ambiguous position; they thrived, were able to maintain their identity through faithfulness to their traditions and won admirers and imitators from Romans belonging to a range of social classes. They were also subject to criticism from some quarters, mainly because they were seen as a threat to Roman traditions.

Inscriptions from the Roman Jewish catacombs, mostly to be dated in the second to fourth centuries A.D., show that there was a significant number of Jews spread over several parts of the city in this period. From these inscriptions we learn the names of eleven synagogues in Rome, including "the synagogue of the Hebrews" and synagogues named after Augustus and probably Marcus Agrippa. *1 Clement,* written from Rome in the A.D. 90s (*see* Clement of Rome), tells us nothing about Jews in the city.

A synagogue has been discovered in Ostia, the port of Rome. Part of the building was erected toward the end of the first century A.D.; it was expanded in the second and third centuries and received its final form in the fourth century A.D. We also know of Jews in other cities in Italy, including Puteoli, Pompeii, Venosa and Naples.

4. Population.

Although we lack sufficient data to ascertain accurately the number of Jews in the Diaspora, our sources give some information. Some ancient authors emphasize the large numbers of Jews in Egypt and elsewhere (Strabo *Geog.* 16.2.28; Philo *Vit. Mos.* 2.232; *Leg. Gai.* 214, 245; *Flacc.* 43; Josephus *Ant.* 11.5.2 §133; 17.11.1 §300; 18.3.4-5 §65-84; *J.W.* 7.9.2 §445), and the amount of temple tax seized by Flaccus in four Asian cities suggests a considerable Jewish population in these areas (Cicero *Pro Flacco* 66-69). That the Jews of Egypt, Cyrenaica, Cyprus and Mesopotamia fought a protracted war in the time of Trajan suggests that the total population of the Jews in these areas of the Diaspora was considerable, although again we are unable to give estimates. It does seem clear, however, that the total Jewish population of the Diaspora considerably exceeded the Jewish population in

Palestine (Tcherikover, 292-95) and that Diaspora Jews constituted a group of significant size. Scholars often suggest that five to six million Jews were living in the Diaspora in the first century, but such figures can be only speculative.

5. Economic Situation.

Diaspora Jews participated in a variety of branches of economic life. We know, for example, of Jews who were soldiers, land-owning farmers, agricultural laborers, shepherds, artisans, manual workers, traders, merchants, bankers, government officials and slaves. In some Roman writers Jewish poverty was a byword (e.g., Juvenal *Sat.* 3.14-16; 6.542-47), but we also know of some very wealthy Jews (Josephus *Ant.* 20.7.3 §147; *J.W.* 7.11.1-2 §442-45; *see* Riches). Diaspora Jews, then, were found in almost all socioeconomic strata of the period (Safrai and Stern, 701-27).

6. The Diaspora Synagogue.

6.1. Synagogue Buildings. Synagogues have been discovered at Delos, Ostia, Sardis, Dura-Europos, Stobi and Priene. The existence of many others is clear from inscriptions or literary evidence. There would have been more than one synagogue in a large city; eleven are attested for Rome, and Philo says that there were many synagogues in Alexandria (Philo *Leg. Gai.* 132; cf. *Spec. Leg.* 2.62). Acts shows that there were many synagogues throughout the regions where Paul traveled (Acts 9:2; 13:5, 14; 14:1; 17:1, 10, 17; 18:4-7, 19-26; 19:8). Small communities would meet in a house* belonging to a member. The earliest synagogue buildings were probably originally private houses modified for use by the community (e.g., Delos and Priene).

The earliest references to a Diaspora synagogue building are dated between 246-221 B.C. and come from Egypt (Horbury and Noy, nos. 22, 117). At first the building seems to have been called a *proseuchē*, or place of prayer (see *CPJ* 129, 134, 138, 432; Horbury and Noy, nos. 9, 13, 22, 25, 27, 125-26; 3 Macc 7:20; Philo *Flacc.* 41, 45, 122; Josephus *Life* 280; *CII* 682-84, 690, 726); sometimes the congregation that gathered in the building is called *synagōgē*, which means "assembly." However, later the building in which they assembled is more often called the *synagōgē*.

There was no uniform architectural design

for Diaspora synagogues, and the very different plans of the six known buildings are clearly influenced by local factors; however, they do share some common features. They generally contain an architectural feature for keeping the biblical scrolls and sometimes had a platform for a reader and benches. Often there were also guest rooms or a dining hall adjoining the assembly room. The Dura-Europos synagogue contains an outstanding set of frescoes that provide our most important evidence for the existence of Jewish figurative art in this period. The Sardis synagogue, which was one part of a complex of buildings including a bathhouse and gymnasium in the center of the city, is the largest synagogue known from antiquity. The synagogue reveals a confident Jewish community that was also integrated to some extent into the wider city (see Kraabel in Urman and Flesher, 95-126).

6.2. The Synagogue as an Institution. The synagogue was the focus of community life for Diaspora Jews and was organized by the community for the community. Not only was it the center of religious life where the sabbath service was held, but also it was the focus for the educational, political, economic, social and judicial life of the community; communal meals were also often held there. It was thus a crucial institution for the maintenance of Jewish identity and played a central role in Jewish life.

Sources describe synagogue services primarily in terms of the reading and study of Scripture (Philo *Vit. Mos.* 2.215-16; Josephus *Ag. Ap.* 2.17 §175). That some of the buildings were called "prayer houses" indicates that prayer was also an important feature.

6.3. God-fearers. A recently discovered inscription from Aphrodisias lists, along with a number of Jews, fifty-four Gentiles who are called *theosebis* or "God-fearers" (see Reynolds and Tannenbaum). Although some scholars argue that the title *God-fearer* here means the Gentiles concerned have simply expressed their support for the Jews as fellow townspeople, it seems much more likely that the term indicates that these Gentiles were linked in some formal way to the Jewish community, without being proselytes. This and other inscriptions, and some literary sources, strongly suggest that there were a number of Gentile "God-fearers" who were formally associated with the Jewish community, were involved in at least some facets of synagogue life and kept some of the commandments without becoming proselytes who joined the community (see Trebilco, 145-66; Juvenal *Sat.* 14.96-99; Josephus *Ant.* 14.7.2 §110; *J.W.* 7.3.3 §45).

Although Diaspora Jews do not seem to have been involved in an organized active mission to convert Gentiles (see Goodman in Lieu, North and Rajak, 53-78), they do seem to have welcomed Gentiles who were attracted to the Jewish community either as God-fearers or proselytes. The role of the Jews here then was passively to bear witness through their existence and life. It also seems likely that at least some Diaspora synagogues were visible and open to outsiders. It is also noteworthy that we know of some proselytes (see Juvenal *Sat.* 14.96-106; Josephus *J.W.* 2.19.2 §520; 2.20.2 §559-61; Acts 6:5 and some inscriptions), although their numbers are quite small.

We can also note the fairly widespread adoption of some Jewish customs such as lighting of lamps (Josephus *Ag. Ap.* 2.38 §282; Persius *Sat.* 5.179-84) and not working on the sabbath (Ovid *Ars amatoria* 1.413-16) by Gentiles who did not come into the more formal category of God-fearers. Clearly Gentiles were attracted to Judaism to varying degrees throughout our period.

7. Community Leadership.

The names and functions of community leaders probably varied from place to place. In the third century B.C. a *gerousia* represented the Jews of the whole city of Alexandria (*Ep. Arist.* 310). At the time of Strabo an *ethnarchēs* stood at the head of the Jews (Josephus *Ant.* 14.7.2 §117 quoting Strabo), but in A.D. 11 Augustus modified the situation by either reintroducing the *gerousia* or giving it the power previously vested in the *ethnarchēs* (Philo *Flacc.* 74, 117).

The position of *archōn* or ruler was widespread among Diaspora Jews, although the title may have meant different things in different places. In some communities the *archontes* were elected, formed the executive committee of the *gerousia* and looked after all the affairs of the community. The title of *presbyteros* or elder is found in some places (e.g., *CII* 663, 735, 739; *Ep. Arist.* 310). The relation of *archōn* and *presbyteros* is unclear; they may have been alternative titles, or the members of the *gerousia* who were not members of the executive committee (the archons) may have been called *presbyteroi*. In some places a *gerousiarchēs* was head of the gerousia. The *archisynagōgos* or ruler of the synagogue had a role in making arrangements for the services of the synagogue (Acts 13:15) and probably also had some responsibility for maintaining Jewish life and teaching (Acts 18:17). They were often wealthy people of influence and standing in the community, who were benefactors and patrons.

Other titles found in inscriptions include *phrontistēs* ("overseer"), *grammateus* ("clerk"), *prostatēs* ("patron"), father or mother of the synagogue, rabbi and priest. It is often difficult to determine what these titles meant (see van der Horst, 89-98).

We know of more than twenty women who held titles such as "ruler of the synagogue," "mother of the synagogue," "elder," "leader" or "priestess." If holding the equivalent title involved a man in active leadership (as opposed to being an honorary title), then it seems likely that when a woman held the title she too was involved in active leadership in the synagogue. There is a continuing debate, however, about whether some of these positions were essentially honorific for all holders of the posts, in which case those who held the titles would have benefited the Jewish community through their munificence or patronage (see Rajak in Lieu, North and Rajak, 22-24). We have no evidence that women were segregated in Diaspora synagogues, and no ancient text calls for segregation.

8. Diaspora Communities in the Greek City.

We do not have any clear evidence that in the Hellenistic and early Roman periods Jews possessed citizenship as a body in any Greek city. Josephus's statements that suggest that they did have citizenship (e.g., Josephus *Ant.* 12.3.1 §119; 12.3.2 §125-26; *Ag. Ap.* 2.4 §37-39) are all historically dubious or ambiguous (see Safrai and Stern, 440-8l). Clearly, however, some individuals did obtain citizenship in their cities (e.g., Paul in Acts 21:39; Philo *Leg. Gai.* 155-57; Trebilco, 172).

Diaspora Jews generally organized themselves into communities, although the constitutional position of these communities varied from place to place and over time. The position of the Jewish community within any city probably depended on local factors such as when, how and for what purpose the Jewish community became established in that particular local-

ity. In some cities, such as Alexandria, they seem to have formed self-governing groups. It is often suggested that the Jews there were officially recognized as a *politeuma*, that is, a formally constituted, semiautonomous civic body within a city whose members were not citizens but possessed some important rights. However, the term *politeuma* is found only once in Jewish literature from Alexandria (*Ep. Arist.* 310). Since it is unclear to whom it refers there (see Lüderitz in van Henten and van der Horst, 183-225), it is precarious to base far-reaching theories on this one reference. In Berenice we have evidence for a Jewish *politeuma*, but it was probably a kind of council of the Jews of the city rather than an organization for the whole Jewish community. In other cities the position of the Jews is best compared with that of other associations of immigrants who lived as foreign people in a city. The actual form of communal life probably varied from place to place, as is shown by the variety of terms used to express the notion of community, including the terms "the Jews," "the people," *synodos, politeuma, katoikia,* the *ethnos* and the *synagōgē.*

A crucial matter in relations between the Jewish Diaspora communities and the cities in which they lived was being granted certain privileges that enabled them to live as Jews in accordance with their law and maintain their identity as communities. The support of the Roman authorities for these privileges was crucial in the face of periodic challenges from individual cities, with Julius Caesar and Augustus being particularly noteworthy in their support for Jewish privileges (*see* Civil Authority). These included being able to meet regularly, organize their own community life and have internal jurisdiction; to own buildings; to have their "ancestral" food; to collect and send the temple tax to Jerusalem; and to live according to their customs and laws, such as observing the sabbath. Privileges connected with observing the sabbath included being free from appearing in court on the sabbath and an exemption from serving in the Roman army. That they enjoyed these privileges, without being citizens and participating fully in a city's life and cults, often led to friction between the Jews and the city authorities.

The status of Diaspora Jewish communities was not greatly affected after the revolt of A.D. 66-70, in which Diaspora Jews were little involved. Titus resisted demands for the abolition of Jewish communal privileges in Antioch and Alexandria (Josephus *J.W.* 7.5.2 §100-111), and generally privileges remained unmodified outside Judea. The diversion of the temple tax to the *fiscus Judaicus* in order to support the temple of Jupiter Capitolinus was the one important change that affected the Diaspora after A.D. 70. Domitian exacted the tax with special severity; Nerva prohibited the accusations to officials that had resulted from Domitian's policy.

9. The Assimilation, Acculturation and Accommodation of Diaspora Communities.

We have noted that the old distinction between "pure" Palestinian Judaism and "Hellenized" Diaspora Judaism is no longer viable. We cannot analyze Diaspora Judaism by simple measurement against Palestinian Judaism; we must find appropriate criteria for the analysis of Diaspora Judaism and in particular the ways Jews reacted to their environment.

In this regard J. M. G. Barclay notes that we can distinguish among different kinds of Hellenization, such as political, social, linguistic, educational, ideological, religious and material Hellenization. Further, engagement with Hellenism could occur to a different degree in each of these areas, which were not all equally significant. Barclay has devised three scales to depict these different kinds of Hellenization (92-102).

First is an assimilation scale, which refers to the level of social integration and concerns social contacts, interaction and practices. Someone at the top of the assimilation scale had abandoned the social distinctives fundamental to Jewish identity; someone at the bottom confined his or her social life entirely to the Jewish community. Second is an acculturation scale, which refers to the linguistic, educational and ideological aspects of a cultural matrix. Someone at the top of the acculturation scale had scholarly expertise in Hellenistic scholarship; someone at the bottom knew no Greek. Third is an accommodation scale, which refers to the use to which acculturation is put. Here Barclay distinguishes between integrative trends, which involved the imitation of Hellenistic culture and its use in reinterpreting the Jewish traditions and could lead to the submersion of Jewish cultural uniqueness, and oppositional trends, which involved the use of Hellenistic weapons in polemic against Hellenism itself and could lead to antagonism to Greco-Roman culture.

Thus "acculturation could be used to construct either bridges or fences between Jews and their surrounding cultures" (Barclay, 98). Although our evidence only rarely enables us to plot Diaspora Jews on these three scales, their use allows us to distinguish among the many different ways Diaspora Jews interacted with their environment. (For the following see in particular Barclay, 103-228, 320-80.)

9.1. Assimilation. There was an enormous range in the degree of assimilation of Diaspora Jews into non-Jewish society. Those who were highly assimilated, to the degree of losing their Jewish distinctiveness and abandoning Jewish practices, included Jews who were fully integrated into political and/or religious affairs of state (e.g., Tiberius Julius Alexander [see Barclay, 105-6]; *CII* 749; Josephus *J.W.* 7.3.3 §50); those who abandoned some aspects of Jewish customs in order to be socially successful or to gain some other benefit (Philo *Vit. Mos.* 1.31; Josephus *Ant.* 12.4.6 §186-89; 18.5.4 §141); those who married Gentiles and did not rear their children as Jews (e.g., Philo *Spec. Leg.* 3.29); those who had become critics of their own traditions (Philo *Abr.* 178-93; *Conf. Ling.* 2-13); those whose allegorical interpretations of the law led them to abandon key Jewish practices (Philo *Migr. Abr.* 89-93); and those whose isolated social circumstances necessitated a high level of assimilation (e.g., *CPJ* 7, 148).

The category of medium assimilation includes those who had significant social ties with the non-Jewish environment but who also preserved their Jewish identity. Again types of assimilation can be discerned. First were those who were well-educated and participated in the social and cultural life of a city or had significant social ties to the non-Jewish world but remained faithful to Jewish tradition (e.g., Alexander the Alabarch [Josephus *J.W.* 5.5.3 §205]; the author of the *Epistle to Aristeas;* Philo; Jewish ephebes, city magistrates and citizens [*CII* 755; Acts 21:39; citizenship did not necessarily entail loss of Jewish distinctiveness]). Many Jews were well integrated into civic life (e.g., Lüderitz, no. 36; *CII* 748), attained influential positions within their cities and adopted many local customs; yet "a degree of integration did not mean the abandonment of an active attention to Jewish tradition or of Jewish distinctiveness. It was as Jews that they were involved in, and a part of, the life of the cities in which they lived" (Trebilco, 187).

Second were those who were in various forms of employment with or for non-Jews (e.,g. in the Ptolemaic army). Third were those who were associated with non-Jews in legal matters. Fourth were those who gained patrons, supporters or converts among non-Jews, which suggests there was considerable social interaction between these Jews and non-Jews.

Barclay (329) concludes that "the patterns of life we have observed in the Mediterranean Diaspora suggest that Jews were neither socially and culturally isolated nor simply blended into some social amalgam. While their boundaries may have been defined variously in differing circumstances, it was precisely the ability to maintain these boundaries while continuing everyday social contacts with non-Jews that was the peculiar achievement of the successful Diaspora communities."

In the category of low assimilation are Jews whose social contact with non-Jews was minimal. Factors leading to low assimilation include the existence of Jewish residential districts (e.g., *CPJ* 423, 468; Josephus *Ant.* 14.10.24 §259-61); the isolation of some communities such as the Therapeutae, a group found throughout Egypt that in some ways resembled the Essenes (Philo *Vit. Cont.* 2-90); and social conflict with non-Jews (e.g., in Alexandria in A.D. 38), which expressed and encouraged social alienation.

This range in levels from high assimilation to careful preservation of Jewish distinction means that we cannot rule out in advance what was or was not possible for Jews in their assimilation.

9.2. Acculturation and Accommodation. Clearly there was a range in the levels of acculturation of Diaspora Jews, from those authors with expertly utilized different genres of Hellenistic literature to Jews who had no capacity in Greek, although the latter must have been rare, since papyri and inscriptions show us that Greek was used for nearly all communication in virtually all Diaspora communities. In general the involvement of Diaspora Jews in the life, ways and thought forms of the Greek city helps to explain the flourishing of Diaspora Jewish literature written in Greek in this period. But what use did Diaspora Jews make of their acculturation? This leads to the question of what sort of accommodation was effected by Diaspora Jews with their social and cultural environments. Barclay (125-228, 336-80) divides the written texts that can be assigned to the Diaspora with some confidence into those that embrace cultural convergence (while normally retaining some form of Jewish distinction) by integrating Jewish practices with the norms and values of their cultural context and those that emphasize cultural antagonism.

9.2.1. Cultural Convergence. A number of texts exhibit cultural convergence and show the ability of Diaspora Jews to express their traditions within a Hellenistic moral, historical, philosophical and theological framework. The following examples are representative. First, Artapanus was self-consciously Jewish while also being supportive of the Hellenized Egyptian culture he clearly appreciated. Artapanus claims biblical characters brought culture and philosophy to Egypt, thus claiming national superiority for the Jews; yet his work also has a pro-Egyptian tone, for example, when it is asserted that Moses established the annual flooding of the Nile. In order to boost Moses' and his people's reputation further, Artapanus gives a positive evaluation of Egypt and its religion. Clearly the author is very much at home in Egypt, whose culture, temples, priests and cults he eulogizes. Artapanus represents a cultural synthesis, an Egyptianized Judaism, and shows that some Jews stood for an important measure of synthesis with Egyptian culture, including Egyptian religion. Barclay (132) notes that "he indicates the possibility of being both a proud Egyptian and a self-conscious Jew." Artapanus is a clear example of cultural convergence.

Second, Ezekiel the Tragedian rewrote the exodus in the form of a Greek tragedy and thus represents a synthesis with Greek literary tradition. He has an enthusiastic appreciation of Greek education and is another example of acculturation. The drama is thoroughly Jewish in character, but the form and cultural framework of the classical Greek tradition has made it comprehensible and attractive to Greeks. The work seems to be an attempt to align Jews with Greeks in the common environment in Egypt, without weakening Jewish ethnic loyalty. Ezekiel was Greek and Jewish at the same time, being skilled in Greek poetry, literature and history and committed to the Jewish tradition.

Third, Philo represents the climax of a Jewish philosophical tradition that was deeply engaged with Hellenistic culture. He received a thorough Hellenistic education and participated in Alexandrian cultural life. He also received an intensive Jewish education and was intimately acquainted with the life and traditions of the Jewish community in Alexandria, to which he was deeply loyal. He does not give any indication of a tension between Greek and Jewish values. As Barclay (91) puts it, Philo was both "Jewish to the core and Hellenized to the same core."

For Philo the most sublime expression of philosophy was found in the Pentateuch. However, his debt to Plato was just as great, since his thought was structured by Platonic dualism. Philo tried to show the profound philosophical truths found in the Pentateuch by means of allegorical exegesis. An effect of his allegorization was to dehistoricize the text and to shift from the particular to the universal. Hence the exodus was about the escape of the soul from the confines of the body to the virtues (Philo *Som.* 2.255). His philosophy thus led away from Jewish particularity; Jewish laws were of universal significance. In this way he sought to build bridges between his Mosaic text and Hellenistic culture and to understand Judaism in the light of the themes, motifs and intellectual horizons of his Hellenistic environment. However, "ultimately his allegorical reading of Scripture functions not to submerge Moses' authority in the sea of Hellenism nor to parallel Moses with Plato as equal sources of truth. Rather the whole gamut of Hellenistic culture is subordinated to Moses, pressed into service to endorse *his* original achievement. As Dawson observes, Philonic allegory 'is an effort to make Greek culture Jewish rather than to dissolve Jewish identity into Greek culture'" (Barclay, 173). Thus Greek culture is subordinated to Jewish cultural and religious identity.

Overall Philo's erudition in Greek ways of thought was used in the service of his Judaism. In his reaction to extreme allegorizers (Philo *Migr. Abr.* 89-93) Philo shows that his identity was ultimately defined by the Jewish community; his leadership of the embassy to Gaius showed that this was where his social and political commitments lay. With Philo the integration of Judaism into Hellenistic culture was exceptionally profound, but he ultimately used that synthesis for the Jewish community and remained loyal to his Jewish heritage.

Other examples of cultural convergence include the *Epistle of Aristeas*, Aristobulus and *Pseudo-Phocylides*.

9.2.2. Cultural Antagonism. In some other Diaspora texts acculturation is used in the service of a sociocultural stance that is predominantly oppositional and antagonistic to Judaism's social and cultural environment. In these cases acculturation results in a religious and social critique of other peoples and a call to resist the cultural pressures of the wider society. Again some representative examples can be noted.

First, the author of the Wisdom of Solomon clearly had a thoroughgoing Greek education, and there is a strong universalist strand in the work. However, the predominant theme is social and cultural antagonism between Jews and non-Jews. The author's Greek education and acculturation serve not to integrate his Judaism with his environment but rather to construct a sophisticated attack upon the latter. It is a deeply Hellenized exercise in cultural aggression and a vigorous defense of Jewish particularity.

Second, the author of *Joseph and Aseneth* uses the Hellenistic form of the romance to launch an attack on Hellenistic religion (*see* Religions, Greco-Roman). A sense of cultural antagonism and alienation between Jews and non-Jews is the predominant tone of the book. The work may be thought to show an open attitude to outsiders, but such outsiders can be welcomed only if they have been totally changed by conversion.

Third, *Sibylline Oracles* 3 and 5 speak of the moral and religious superiority of Israel and the author's cultural antagonism toward non-Jews. They also reveal a cultural and social alienation between Jews and non-Jews. The oracles emphasize the Jews' national greatness, centered on temple and law. The acculturation revealed by the use of the Sibylline genre is thus used to express antagonism toward that culture.

Other examples of cultural antagonism include 3 and 4 Maccabees.

10. Facets of Jewish Identity in the Diaspora.

Despite the evident diversity of Diaspora Judaism, we can also identify elements that enabled Jewish communities to endure as coherent entities and that made the difference between a Jew and a non-Jew clear to Jews themselves and to others. We should note that we are looking at Diaspora Judaism as a social as well as a religious and intellectual phenomenon. The following facets were integral to the identity of Diaspora Jews; they were bonds that held Diaspora Jews together and enabled their communities to survive as coherent entities over time (for what follows see in particular Barclay, 399-444; Trebilco, 12-19).

10.1. Ethnicity. At the core of Diaspora Jewish identity was ethnicity or the ethnic bond; that is, the combination of ancestry and customs that could be voluntarily adopted or abandoned. The importance of ethnicity is demonstrated by the following evidence. First, Diaspora literature emphasizes the significance of the "nation," "race" or "people" as the bearer of the Jewish tradition, with Jews being seen as "people of the same race," bound together by a common ethnicity (e.g., Philo *Vit. Mos.* 2.43-44; Ezekiel 12, 35, 43; Noy 1995, no. 240). Second, non-Jewish authors consistently refer to Judaism as an ethnic entity. Thus the Romans allowed the Jews to follow their "ancestral customs," or time-honored ethnic practices, which points to the combination of kinship and custom that defines ethnicity. Third, proselytes who joined the Jewish community underwent a thorough resocialization, so that they acquired a new ethnicity. The conversion process meant that they were transferred to the Jewish nation (Philo *Spec. Leg.* 1.51-52; *Jos. and As.*), which points to the significance of ethnicity. Fourth, the recognition of the importance of endogamy by Diaspora Jews underlines the significance of ethnicity (e.g., Demetrius in Eusebius *Praep. Ev.* 9.29.1; Philo *Spec. Leg.* 3.29). Finally, the emphasis on the training of children in the Jewish way of life was to ensure that Judaism continued as an ethnic phenomenon (e.g., 4 Macc 18:10-19; Philo *Leg. Gai.* 115, 195). The evidence thus suggests that ethnicity constituted the core of Jewish identity.

10.2. The Local Community. A crucial factor in affirming the identity of Diaspora Jews was the life of the local community. As we have indicated, the nature of the local Diaspora Jewish community varied from place to place and over time, with some owning prayer houses or synagogues, others meeting in private houses, some communities having a range of officials, operating their own courts, voting their own decrees and negotiating with civic authorities, while other communities were less institutionalized. Clearly a strong local community of Jews would have provided invaluable support for the retention of Jewish identity by individuals.

Some elements of communal life were particularly important in binding Jews together.

First, festivals and fasts (Passover [Ezekiel 184-92; *CII* 777]; Tabernacles [*CPJ* 452a; Lüderitz, no. 71]; the Day of Atonement [*CII* 725]; see also Philo *Vit. Mos.* 2.42; Josephus *Ag. Ap.* 2.5 §55) meant Diaspora Jews could express their solidarity with one another. Second, the weekly sabbath gathering at the synagogue was of immense social significance and was a crucial feature of Diaspora Jewish life (Philo *Leg. Gai.* 156-57; *Spec. Leg.* 2.62-63). These gatherings and the instruction that occurred during them bound the community together in loyalty to their distinctive way of life. Third, Diaspora communities generally paid the temple tax (Philo *Spec. Leg.* 1.77-78; *Leg. Gai.* 156-57, 311-16; Josephus *Ant.* 14.10.1-26 §185-267; 16.6.17 §162-73; 18.9.1 §312-13; Cicero *Pro Flacco* 28.67-68); its payment reinforced the individual's sense of belonging to the local community.

10.3. Links with Jerusalem and Other Diaspora Communities. Diaspora Jewish communities were connected with Jerusalem and "the homeland" by payment of the temple tax and other gifts for the temple. Through the tax, Diaspora communities were linked to and participated in the temple's life and worship. Diaspora literature shows a deep respect for the holiness of the temple (*Ep. Arist.* 83-120; Philo *Leg. Gai.* 184f). Diaspora Jews also went on pilgrimage to the temple, probably in considerable numbers (Philo *Spec. Leg.* 1.69; Josephus *Ant.* 18.9.1 §310-13; *J.W.* 6.9.3 §425; *CII* 1404), indicating that the temple's symbolic power was considerable even if its impact on daily life was less significant. Pilgrimage to Jerusalem probably provided significant contact for the Diaspora communities with developments in Jerusalem and Palestine in general and further consolidated the bond between the Diaspora and Palestine. On pilgrimage and in other ways Diaspora Jews would have come into contact with others from the Diaspora and thus forged important connections.

There were also strong social and political links between the Diaspora and Palestine (e.g., 2 Macc 1:1-9; Josephus *Ant.* 12.3.2 §125-26; 17.12.1 §324-31), and some Diaspora literature expresses a strong attachment to the land of Palestine and a sense of solidarity between the Diaspora and Jews in Judea (Artapanus 27.21; *Sib. Or.* 5:281, 328-32; Wis 12:3, 7; 3 Macc). However, an attachment to Palestine did not necessarily weaken a strong sense of being at home in the Diaspora (Philo *Flacc.* 45-46). In general, Palestine retained some significance as the holy land,* and the continuing relationship between Diaspora communities and Palestine was an important facet of Jewish identity, but the strength of attachment to Palestine probably varied from community to community.

10.4. The Torah. The Torah was clearly the key text for Diaspora Jews (Josephus *Ag. Ap.* 2.32 §232-35; *Sib. Or.* 3:584-85, 768-69; 4 Macc 5:16-21). The existence of the Septuagint, a translation begun in the third century B.C. probably in Alexandria, shows that at this time Egyptian Jews regarded the Torah as their key text. This is also illustrated by synagogue architecture in which some piece of furniture for the Law was prominent (e.g., Ostia; see Noy 1993, 22-26). The dependence of Diaspora authors on the Scriptures is clear (e.g., *Pseud.-Phoc.*), and the allegorical method used by Aristobulus and Philo presupposes the supreme authority of the Scriptures. "Whether as legislation, mystery, constitution, philosophy, founding legend or moral guide, the Jewish Scriptures were integral to all the social and intellectual achievements of Diaspora Judaism" (Barclay, 425).

Instruction in the law formed a key element in Diaspora synagogue life and laid the foundation for Jewish identity (Josephus *Ag. Ap.* 2.16-18 §171-8; Philo *Leg. Gai.* 156-57). Devotion to the law is regularly noted in the inscriptions from Rome (Noy 1995, nos. 103, 212, 281, 576). In general Diaspora Jewish communities preserved the distinctive customs that were laid down in the law. That Jewish communities took the initiative in the defense of their customs in the face of difficulties with the civic authorities in, for example, Asia and Cyrenaica, and the consistency with which the distinctive traits prescribed by the law were noted as characteristics of Diaspora Jews by outsiders indicate the continuing loyalty of Diaspora Jews to the law and their conviction that their way of life should be ruled by God's law.

Moses, as the person most prominent in the Torah, was also a key figure for Jewish identity. He was seen by Diaspora Jews as a skillful lawgiver, a profound philosopher, a noble king, a supreme military commander, miracle worker and priest (e.g., Philo *Vit. Mos.*; Josephus *Ag. Ap.* 2.15 §151-172).

10.5. Jewish Practices and Beliefs. Four features of Jewish practice and belief visibly marked off Diaspora Jews from their neighbors and thus were key boundary markers of Jewish identity, with great social significance.

First, Diaspora Jews generally worshiped the one God of Israel (3 Macc 5:13; *Jos. and As.* 11:10) and rejected other alien and iconic cults (Wis 13:1—15:17; *Ep. Arist.* 134-39; Josephus *Ant.* 12.3.2 §126; Philo *Conf. Ling.* 168-73). It seems that Jews were generally exempt from the obligation to worship local gods; we have no documentary evidence for this (and it is unlikely that such an exemption was ever officially expressed), but the outrage expressed when the customary exemption was in danger of being suspended suggests it was a privilege with some consistency (Philo *Leg. Gai.* 117, 134).

Second, the evidence suggests that Jewish dietary laws were generally kept in the Diaspora (e.g., 3 Macc 3:3-7; 7:11). These customs and the consequent separatism at meals would have bound the Jewish communities together and created a consistent social distinction between Jews and non-Jews (Philo *Leg. Gai.* 361-62; *Ep. Arist.* 139-42).

Third, although circumcision* was practiced by some other groups, it seems to have constituted a strong affirmation of Jewish identity for men (Philo *Migr. Abr.* 89-93; Josephus *Ant.* 1.10.5 §192).

Fourth, sabbath observance was well-known by non-Jews as a characteristic feature that marked off Jewish communal life from that of other peoples (e.g., Horace *Satires* 1.9.69-70). The evidence suggests that Diaspora Jews generally observed the sabbath and abstained from work on this day (Philo *Som.* 2.123-24; *Leg. Gai.* 158; Josephus *Ant.* 14.10.12 §225-27; 14.10.25 §262-64; *CPJ* 10). The vigor with which Asian Jews, for example, defended the sabbath indicates the depth of their commitment to its observance (e.g., Josephus *Ant.* 16.2.3 §27; 16.6.2-4 §163-68). It was a highly visible sign of their unique identity as a people.

Each of these strands of Jewish identity—ethnicity, the local community, links with Jerusalem and other Diaspora communities, the Torah, and specifically Jewish practices and beliefs—was interwoven with the others. Together they enabled Diaspora communities to survive in very diverse circumstances.

That Diaspora Jewish identity was reinforced by this combination of factors meant that Diaspora Jews could interpret their traditions in many different ways. "It was not necessary, for instance, to interpret the ethnic bond only in terms of 'election' and 'covenant.' Other metaphors, derived from historical (Ezekiel) or political (Aristeas) spheres, could serve equally well so long as they fulfilled the requisite social functions" (Barclay, 443; *see* Covenant; Election). This led to diversity in interpretations of Judaism in the Diaspora; unanimity was unnecessary, provided the various customs were preserved intact. This meant that Diaspora communities endured and flourished not by being isolated from their environment but by having clearly differentiated boundary markers at key points. This very strength meant Diaspora communities suffered hostility at times, precisely because they were considered a social and political offense as communities that remained unassimilated.

11. Conclusions.
One feature to emerge from recent study of Diaspora Judaism is its diversity. Diversity within and among Diaspora communities is clearly apparent in a number of areas, including social status and conditions, wealth, size, community organization, assimilation, acculturation and accommodation. We must investigate each community and period as well as the particular circumstances of Jewish individuals and communities in each environment. Clearly factors such as when the Jews settled in a given city and under what conditions, how the community developed, ongoing relations with other groups and the number of new Jewish settlers over time were all crucial factors in the development of particular communities and their religious traditions, and these factors led to diversity among communities. This means that there were no typical Diaspora conditions; nor can we speak of a Diaspora Jew or a Diaspora community as typical.

It is also to be noted that Diaspora communities in the imperial period seem to have developed largely outside rabbinic control and influence, so these communities were not directed by any central authority and should probably be thought of as nonrabbinic (see Rajak in Lieu, North and Rajak, 9-28). Without an authority to impose uniformity, great variety could develop in Diaspora Judaism, which became a complex and variegated phenomenon. We should also note that at least for a time Jewish Christian communities in the Diaspora

would have been seen as one more dimension of this diversity.

Some earlier scholars thought that in order to remain as faithful Jews, it was necessary for Diaspora communities to live in social isolation. It is now recognized that although some Diaspora Jews probably did form tightly enclosed communities with relatively closed boundaries, many other Diaspora communities showed a higher degree of openness to their political, social and cultural environment. Yet clearly different Diaspora communities, with different sociocultural stances, continued to regard themselves as Jewish and maintained their identity as Jews over time while often expressing that Judaism in a particular way that varied from the practices of other Jewish communities. Thus we have been able to draw attention to a number of facets of Diaspora Jewish identity that enabled Jewish communities to endure as coherent entities over time and that meant that there was some commonality between different communities. We also have no evidence that Diaspora Jews were significantly involved in syncretism.*

Literary and inscriptional sources indicate that some Jewish communities in the Diaspora continued to flourish until the end of antiquity. The presence of local Diaspora Jewish communities was often a real factor in the life of the early Christian churches.

See also CHRISTIANITY AND JUDAISM: PARTINGS OF THE WAYS; GENTILES, GENTILE MISSION; JEWISH CHRISTIANITY; JUDAISM, POST-A.D. 70; MISSION, EARLY NON-PAULINE; PHILO; SYNCRETISM; SYNAGOGUE.

BIBLIOGRAPHY. J. M. G. Barclay, *Jews in the Mediterranean Diaspora from Alexander to Trajan (323 BCE–117 CE)* (Edinburgh: T & T Clark, 1996); B. J. Brooten, *Women Leaders in the Ancient Synagogues: Inscriptional Evidence and Background Issues* (BJS 36; Chico, CA: Scholars Press, 1982); S. J. D. Cohen and E. S. Frerichs, eds., *Diasporas in Antiquity* (BJS 288; Atlanta: Scholars Press, 1993); J. J. Collins, *Between Athens and Jerusalem: Jewish Identity in the Hellenistic Diaspora* (New York: Crossroad, 1986); L. H. Feldman, *Jew and Gentile in the Ancient World: Attitudes and Interactions from Alexander to Justinian* (Princeton, NJ: Princeton University Press, 1993); J. B. Frey, *Corpus Inscriptionum Iudaicarum* (2 vols.; vol 1. [1936], rev. B. Lifshitz, New York: Ktav, 1975; vol. 2, Rome: Pontificio istituto di archeologia christiana, 1952); I. M. Gafri, *Land, Centre and*

Diaspora: Jewish Perceptions of National Dispersion and Land Centrality in Late Antiquity (JSPSup 21; Sheffield: Sheffield Academic Press, 1997); W. Horbury and D. Noy, eds., *Jewish Inscriptions of Graeco-Roman Egypt* (Cambridge: Cambridge University Press, 1992); H. J. Leon, *The Jews of Ancient Rome* (updated ed., with new introduction by C. A. Osiek; Peabody, MA: Hendrickson, 1995); I. Levinskaya, *The Book of Acts in Its Diaspora Setting* (BAFCS 5; Grand Rapids: Eerdmans, 1996); J. Lieu, J. North, and T. Rajak, eds., *The Jews Among Pagans and Christians in the Roman Empire* (London: Routledge, 1992); G. Lüderitz, *Corpus jüdischer Zeugnisse aus der Cyrenaika. Mit einem Anhang von J. M. Reynolds* (Beihefte zum Tübinger Atlas des Vorderen Orients, Reihe B, Nr. 53; Wiesbaden: Dr Ludwig Reichert, 1983); J. M. Modrzejewski, *The Jews of Egypt from Rameses II to Emperor Hadrian* (Philadelphia and Jerusalem: Jewish Publication Society, 1995); J. Neusner, ed., *Judaism in Late Antiquity*. Pt. 1: *The Literary and Archaeological Sources*. Pt. 2: *Historical Synthesis* (Handbuch der Orientalistik Abt 1, Band 16-17; Leiden: E. J. Brill, 1995); D. Noy, *Jewish Inscriptions of Western Europe* 1: *Italy (Excluding the City of Rome), Spain and Gaul*; 2: *The City of Rome* (Cambridge: Cambridge University Press, 1993; 1995); J. A. Overman and R. S. MacLennan, *Diaspora Jews and Judaism: Essays in Honor of and in Dialogue with A. Thomas Kraabel* (SFSHJ 41; Atlanta: Scholars Press, 1992); J. Reynolds and R. Tannenbaum, *Jews and God-fearers at Aphrodisias* (Cambridge Philological Society Supplementary vol. 12; Cambridge: Cambridge Philological Society, 1987); S. Safrai and M. Stern, eds., *The Jewish People in the First Century* (2 vols.; CRINT 1; Assen: Van Gorcum; Philadelphia: Fortress, 1974-76); E. Schürer, *The History of the Jewish People in the Age of Jesus Christ (175 B.C.-A.D. 135)* rev. and ed. G. Vermes et al. (3 vols.; Edinburgh: T & T Clark, 1973-87); E. M. Smallwood, *The Jews Under Roman Rule: From Pompey to Diocletian* (2d ed.; Leiden: E. J. Brill, 1981); M. Stern, *Greek and Latin Authors on Jews and Judaism* (3 vols.; Jerusalem: The Israel Academy of Sciences and Humanities, 1974, 1981, 1984); M. E. Stone, ed., *Jewish Writings of the Second Temple Period* (CRINT 2.2; Assen: Van Gorcum; Philadelphia: Fortress, 1984); V. Tcherikover, *Hellenistic Civilization and the Jews* (Philadelphia: Jewish Publication Society of America, 1961); V. Tcherikover and A. Fuks, *Corpus Papyrorum Judaicarum* (3 vols.; with M. Stern and D. M. Lewis; Jerusalem: Magnes; Cambridge, MA: Harvard University Press, 1957, 1960, 1964) vol. 3; P. R. Trebilco, *Jewish Communities in Asia Minor* (SNTSMS 69; Cambridge: Cambridge University Press, 1991); D. Urman and P. V. M. Flesher, *Ancient Synagogues: Historical Analysis and Archaeological Discovery* (2 vols.; SPB 47; Leiden: E. J. Brill, 1995); P. W. van der Horst, *Ancient Jewish Epitaphs* (Kampen: Kok Pharos, 1991); J. W. van Henten and P. W. van der Horst, eds., *Studies in Early Jewish Epigraphy* (AGJU 21; Leiden: E. J. Brill, 1994).

P. R. Trebilco

DIDACHE, THE

The Teaching of the Lord to the Gentiles by the Twelve Apostles, or *The Teaching of the (Twelve) Apostles*, as it was known in ancient times, or simply the *Didache* ("The Teaching"), as it is usually known today, is a "handbook," or manual of Christian ethical instruction and church order. Although the title was known from references to it by ancient writers, some of whom (e.g., Clement of Alexandria, Origen and Didymus the Blind) used it as Scripture, no copy was known to exist until the 1873 recovery of a manuscript containing, among other things, a complete text of the *Didache* (published in 1883).

1. Contents
2. The Didache as "Evolved" Literature
3. Date and Place

1. Contents.
The anonymous document is composed of three parts: (1) instruction about the Two Ways (the "way of life" and the "way of death"; *Did.* 1.1—6.2); (2) a manual of church order and practice (*Did.* 6.3—15.4); and (3) an apocalyptic section (*Did.* 16.1-8).

1.1 Two Ways. The Two Ways material appears to have been intended, in light of *Didache* 7.1, as a summary of basic instruction about the Christian life to be taught to those who were preparing for baptism.* The "way of life" (*Did.* 1.2—4.14), which opens with the "love command" and the "golden rule," is comprised almost entirely of "do's and don't's," while the "way of death" (*Did.* 5.1-2) is a description of evil actions and persons.

1.2. Church Order. The second part resembles a "how to" booklet of instructions about food* (*Did.* 6.3), baptism* (*Did.* 7.1-4), fasting (*Did.* 7.4—8.1), prayer* (*Did.* 8.2-3), the Lord's Supper* (*Did.* 9.1—10.7), and various practical issues (e.g., almsgiving) and offices and positions of leadership (*Did.* 11.1—15.4; *see* Church Order; Worship). In addition to providing the earliest evidence of a mode of baptism other than immersion, it records the oldest known eucharistic and/or *agapē* prayers and a form of the Lord's Prayer quite similar to that found in Matthew. There is a concern to differentiate Christian practice from Jewish piety (cf. Did. 8.1-2), and to prevent abuses of the church's hospitality (*Did.* 11.3-6; cf. Lucian *Peregrinus* 13).

1.3. Apocalyptic. The document closes with a brief apocalyptic* section that has much in common with the so-called "Synoptic Apocalypse" (cf. Mk 13; Mt 24—25; Lk 24).

2. The Didache as "Evolved" Literature.
In its present form the Two Ways section represents the Christianization (by means of, e.g., the insertion of collections of Gospel sayings and related admonitions, such as *Did.* 1.3—2.1) of a common Jewish form of moral instruction. Similar material is found in a number of other Christian writings from the first through about the fifth centuries, including the *Epistle of Barnabas,* the *Didascalia*, the *Apostolic Church Ordinances*, the *Summary of Doctrine*, the *Apostolic Constitutions*, the *Life of Schnudi* and *On the Teaching of the Apostles* (or *Doctrina*), some of which are dependent on the *Didache*. The inter-relationships between these various documents are quite complex and while much remains to be worked out, there is clearly a post-history as well as a pre-history to the Two Ways section of the *Didache*.

The connections between the *Didache* and *Barnabas** have been closely examined. Similar material may be utilized quite differently in the two documents (Draper 1995, 96-99). Rather than either one being directly dependent upon the other, it seems much more likely that both are dependent, perhaps indirectly, on a common source (Kraft 1965).

The "church order" section also bears evidence of change over time (e.g., cf. *Did.* 11.4 with *Did.* 12.1, or note the intrusive character of *Did.* 14.1-3). But the "evolved" nature of this part of the document is at least in part due to its origin in a Christian community that is itself evolving: a transition from (more charismatic?) itinerant ministers to (less glamorous?) resident leadership (*Did.* 15.2) is evident, as is tension

between the ideal and the actual (*Did.* 6.2).

3. Date and Place.
Dating the *Didache* is made difficult by (1) a lack of hard evidence and (2) the fact that it is a composite document. Thus the date when the final form was compiled must be differentiated from the time represented by the pre-existing materials incorporated into it.

Some of the materials from which it was composed reflect the state of the church at a fairly early time. The relative simplicity of the prayers, for example, and the form of church organization—note the two-fold structure of bishops and deacons (*Did.* 15.1; cf. Phil 1:1) and the continued existence of traveling apostles* and prophets* (*Did.* 11.1-7; 13.1) alongside a resident ministry* (*Did.* 15.2)—appear to reflect a time closer to that of Paul or James (who died in the 60s) than Ignatius* (who died sometime after 110).

A remarkably wide range of dates, extending from the mid-first century (e.g., Audet) to the early third century (Vokes 1938) or later, has been proposed for the final form of the *Didache*. The greatest part of it, however, likely reached its present form by c. 150, though a date considerably closer to the beginning of the second century is not improbable.

Syria (e.g., Audet, Rordorf and Tuilier), the Syro-Palestine region (e.g., Niederwimmer) and Egypt (e.g., Kraft 1965) are the places mentioned most often as the place of origin of the *Didache*. The evidence is indirect and circumstantial (and, as with the date, complicated by the document's composite nature). An urban origin, perhaps Antioch (Draper, 310, in Jeffords 1995), has recently been asserted against a widely assumed rural setting. The reference to mountains in *Didache* 9.4 suggests to some a Syrian* or Syro-Palestinian provenance; the final editing, however, may well have occurred elsewhere. The strongest (but not only) ancient testimony to the document comes from Egypt.

See also APOSTOLIC FATHERS; BAPTISM; BARNABAS, EPISTLE OF; CHURCH ORDER, GOVERNMENT; KERYGMA AND DIDACHE; LORD'S SUPPER; WORSHIP AND LITURGY.

BIBLIOGRAPHY. **Text and Translation:** J. B. Lightfoot and J. R. Harmer, *The Apostolic Fathers: Greek Texts and English Translations of Their Writings*, ed. and rev. M. W. Holmes (2d ed.; Grand Rapids: Baker, 1992). **Commentaries and/or**

Editions: R. A. Kraft, *Barnabas and the Didache* (AF 3; New York: Nelson, 1965); K. Niederwimmer, *Die Didache* (KAV 1; Göttingen: Vandenhoeck & Ruprecht, 1989); W. Rordorf and A. Tuilier, *La Doctrine des douze apôtres (Didache): Introduction, Texte, Traduction* (SC 248; Paris: Cerf, 1978). **Studies:** J. P. Audet, *La Didachè: Instructions des Apôtres* (EB; Paris: Gabalda, 1958); J. A. Draper, "Barnabas and the Riddle of the Didache Revisited," *JSNT* 58 (1995) 89-113; idem, "The Jesus Tradition in the Didache" in *Gospel Perspectives* 5: *The Jesus Tradition Outside the Gospels*, ed. D. Wenham (Sheffield: JSOT, 1985) 269-87; C. N. Jeffords, *The Sayings of Jesus in the Teaching of the Twelve Apostles* (VCSup 11; Leiden: E. J. Brill, 1989); idem, ed., *The Didache in Context: Essays on Its Text, History, & Transmission* (NovTSup 77; Leiden: E. J. Brill, 1995); R. A. Kraft, "Didache," *ABD* 2:197-98; E. Massaux, *The Influence of the Gospel of Saint Matthew on Christian Literature before Saint Irenaeus*, 3: *The Apologists and the Didache*, ed. A. J. Bellinzoni (NGS 5/3; Macon, GA: Mercer University Press, 1993); F. E. Vokes, "The Didache—Still Debated," *CQ* 3 (1970) 57-62; idem, "Life and Order in an Early Church: the Didache," *ANRW* 2.27.1 (1993) 209-33; idem, *The Riddle of the Didache: Fact or Fiction, Heresy or Catholicism?* (London: SPCK, 1938).

M. W. Holmes

DIDACHE. *See* KERYGMA AND DIDACHE.

DIOGNETUS, EPISTLE TO

The *Epistle to Diognetus* is a relatively brief (698 words, excluding articles, proper names and pronouns) apologetic treatise for Christianity presented in an epistolary form (*see* Letters). It claims to be written to a pagan of high social or political rank in response to certain questions about the Christian religion. This short document is one of the more enigmatic writings belonging to the patristic period. Not only is it impossible to determine with certainty its authorship, date, recipient and provenance, but also it is composite in character and seemingly unknown to any ancient author. Furthermore, its only textual source is a single medieval manuscript, which has itself perished. Nevertheless the *Epistle to Diognetus*, with its skillful rhetoric* and elegant style, has elicited high praise from both classical and Christian scholars. It has been justly called the "pearl of the Patristic age" (Bar-

nard), "the noblest of early Christian writings" (Lightfoot) and "one of the most brilliant things ever written by Christians in the Greek language" (Norden).

1. Text
2. Literary Form
3. Authorship
4. Date
5. Recipient
6. Contents and Outline

1. Text.

The text of the *Epistle to Diognetus* was preserved in only one manuscript, Codex Argentoratensis Graec. ix, which dates from the thirteenth or fourteenth century. This manuscript contained five treatises (the last of which was the *Epistle to Diognetus*) that were ascribed to the early church theologian Justin Martyr. What is known about the history of this manuscript is as follows. Although privately owned during the early sixteenth century, by 1560 it was housed in the Alsatian monastery of Maursmünster. At the end of the eighteenth century the manuscript was moved to the municipal library of Strasbourg, where it was destroyed by fire on August 24, 1870, during the Franco-Prussian War. However, at least five copies, three of which date from the late sixteenth century, had been made by competent scholars, so that the text of this important document has been preserved. Nevertheless, it is clear from these copies that Codex Argentoratensis Graec. ix was itself defective in a number of places. The document thus contains several conjectural readings arising from attempts to make sense of the text.

2. Literary Form.

The identification of the literary form of the *Epistle to Diognetus* is complicated by the fact that it likely is a compilation of two distinct documents: *Diognetus* 1-10, which ostensibly is a letter but in reality is an apologetic treatise for the Christian faith, and *Diognetus* 11-12, which is probably a fragment of an early Christian homily. Among the various reasons for separating chapters 11-12 from the rest of the document, the following two are the most significant. First, Codex Argentoratensis had a gap at the end of chapter 10 with a marginal note that read "and here the copy had a break." This gap suggests that the original conclusion to the letter (or, more accurately, the apologetic treatise) was lost or perhaps deleted when chapters 11-12 were added. Since the argument of the first part of the document reaches its logical conclusion by the end of chapter 10, the size of this lost or deleted material must not have been very great. Second, there are significant differences in content, vocabulary and style between chapters 1-10 and chapters 11-12. For example, whereas chapters 1-10 have a strongly apologetic focus and are clearly addressed to pagan readers, chapters 11-12 appear to be a homily that has Christians in view.

A few scholars have argued for the literary unity of the document in its present form. The consensus, however, is that the *Epistle to Diognetus* consists of two distinct sources—an apologetic treatise and a homily—that have been brought together. Although it is frequently classified with the works of the apostolic fathers,* this composite document more properly belongs to the works of the apologists.

3. Authorship.

The text contains no reference to its author. External evidence is likewise lacking, since there is no reference to the *Epistle to Diognetus* in all ancient Christian literature. The identification of its author, therefore, can be made only on the basis of comparing its vocabulary, style and content with those other documents whose authorship is known. As a result the door of speculation stands wide open on this issue, and many scholars have not hesitated to walk boldly through. Among the numerous names that have been proposed, the more plausible candidates include Hippolytus of Rome, Theophilus of Antioch and Pantaenus of Alexandria.

The most intriguing and carefully argued proposal is that the *Epistle to Diognetus* is the supposedly lost *Apology of Quadratus* (Andriessen). Quadratus, a missionary bishop who had come to Athens, presented this document (a short fragment of which is preserved by Eusebius) in A.D. 125 to Hadrian, who was known to his contemporaries by the name Diognetus. This theory, however, like all other claims about the authorship of this document, cannot be established with any degree of certainty. The most that can be said with confidence is that the author of the *Epistle to Diognetus* was a Christian who was classically trained and who possessed considerable literary skill and style. The strong argument against Judaism* (*Diogn.* 3) and in particular the ridicule of its practices (*Diogn.* 4) also suggest that the author was not Jewish.

What has been stated thus far about authorship applies only to *Diognetus* 1-10 and not to *Diognetus* 11-12. The brevity of these chapters make the authorship of this document even more a matter of conjecture. This distinction between chapters 1-10 and chapters 11-12, although it is justifiable with respect to content and form, might be irrelevant with respect to authorship, since it is possible that the same person wrote both documents on different occasions (Barnard).

4. Date.

Like the issue of authorship, the question of date cannot be determined with any degree of certainty. Although the range of realistic possibilities for *Diognetus* 1-10 spans the period A.D. 117-310, the prevailing view is that this material belongs to the middle or latter half of the second century. A relatively early date is supported by the following general considerations: the common condemnation of paganism and Judaism; the relatively simple christology,* which seems unaware of any formulated heresies; the absence of any reference to the Holy Spirit*; the lack of the tendency to identify the ideal of Christian excellence with asceticism; the absence of sacerdotalism; the depiction of the Christian faith as a new phenomenon; and parallels with the *Epistle of Barnabas.* * The date of chapters 11-12 is even harder to determine, although most scholars locate it a short time after the material of chapters 1-10.

5. Recipient.

It is likewise impossible to identify definitively the recipient of this document. The text claims to have been written to a specific individual named Diognetus, whose title, "most excellent," was a common one in ancient writings for a figure of high social or political status. It may well be, however, that Diognetus is a fictional character, created to ask the questions that the anonymous author wanted to address. That the document was intended for a larger audience is indicated by its use of the plural pronoun *you* and the absence of any personal references to its readers.

6. Contents and Outline.

The opening chapter depicts Diognetus as wrestling with three questions about the Christian faith: (1) Who is the God* in whom the Christians trust and what is the nature of the worship* they offer him such that they refuse to recognize the gods believed by the Greeks (*see* Religions, Greco-Roman) and refrain from the practices of the Jews? (2) What is the secret of the strong affection that Christians have for each other? (3) Why has this new race or people entered the world now and not formerly?

The remaining chapters answer these questions, following in a rather general way the same order. Chapter 2 highlights the folly of pagan practices and so answers the first part of question 1. Chapters 3 and 4 emphasize the folly of Jewish practices, both its worship (*Diogn.* 3) and its rites and customs (*Diogn.* 4) and so answer the second part of question 1. Chapters 5-7 portray in an attractive manner the distinctiveness of the Christian life and so answer in a general way question 2. Chapters 8 and 9 present the Son* of God as the revealer of the true knowledge* of God (*Diogn.* 8) and as the agent of salvation* for humankind (*Diogn.* 9) and in so doing answer question 3. Chapter 10 concludes the work with an invitation for the reader to accept the Christian faith and thus become an imitator of God. The final two chapters, almost certainly a separate document and probably written by another hand, is a two-part homily. The first section focuses on the Logos*: his preexistence,* his being sent into the world,* his work of revelation* and his blessing* both in the church and the individual (*Diogn.* 11). The second section uses the story of the Garden of Eden to emphasize how only true knowledge leads to true life (*Diogn.* 12).

Thus the *Epistle to Diognetus* exhibits the following outline:

Introduction: The Questions of Diognetus (*Diogn.* 1)

Pagans: The Folly of Their Worship (*Diogn.* 2)

Jews: The Folly of Their Worship and Practices (*Diogn.* 3-4)

Christians: The Distinctiveness of Their Faith and Practices (*Diogn.* 5-7)

The Son: Revealer of God and Agent of Salvation (*Diogn.* 8-9)

Conclusion: Imitation of God (*Diogn.* 10)

Appendix: Homily on the Logos and Union of Knowledge and Life (*Diogn.* 11-12)

See also APOSTOLIC FATHERS.

BIBLIOGRAPHY. D. P. Andriessen, "The Authorship of the Epistula ad Diognetum," *VC* 1 (1947) 129-36; L. W. Barnard, "The Epistle ad Diognetum: Two Units from One Author?" *ZNW* 56 (1965) 130-37; R. Brändle, *Die Ethik der "Schrift an Diognet": Eine Wideraufnahme paulinischer und johanneischer Theologie am Ausgang des zweiten Jahrhunderts* (Zurich: Theologischer Verlag, 1975); R. H. Connolly, "The Date and Authorship of the Epistle to Diognetus," *JTS* 36 (1935) 347-53; idem, "Ad Diognetum xi-xii," *JTS* 37 (1936) 2-15; R. M. Grant, "The Epistle to Diognetus" in *Greek Apologists of the Second Century* (Philadephia: Westminster, 1988) 178-79; C. N. Jefford, "The Letter to Diognetus" in *Reading the Apostolic Fathers: An Introduction* (Peabody, MA: Hendrickson, 1996) 159-69; J. T. Lienhard, "The Christology of the Epistle to Diognetus," *VC* 24 (1970) 280-89; H. G. Meecham, *The Epistle to Diognetus* (Manchester: Manchester University Press, 1949); J. G. O'Neill, "The Epistle to Diognetus," *Irish Ecclesiastical Record* 85 (1956) 92-106; J. J. Thierry, "The Logos as Teacher in ad Diognetum XI, 1," *VC* 20 (1966) 146-49; A. L. Townsley, "Notes for an Interpretation of the Epistle to Diognetus," *Rivista di studi classici* 24 (1976) 5-20.

J. A. D. Weima

DISCIPLINE

Early church practices of community discipline for immorality or heresy were adapted from Judaism with a Christian flavor exhibited most fully in the writings of Paul. There is surprisingly little attention given to discipline in late first- and early second-century Christian writings. The few references appear to signal a shift of interest from immorality to heresy.

1. Discipline in Judaism and Early Christianity

2. Discipline in Later New Testament and Noncanonical Christian Writings

1. Discipline in Judaism and Early Christianity.
The Qumran* sectarians discouraged misbehavior by means of an elaborate system designed to ensure the purity* of the community. Penalties were usually administered by community leaders following progressive reproof procedures (1 QS 5:24-26; *CD* 9:16-20). Discipline included exclusion from ritual meals (1 QS 7:20) and permanent expulsion from the community (1 QS 8:20—9:2).

Pharisees in the NT era imposed a form of social isolation known as a "ban" to punish violation of ritual purity laws or doctrinal aberrations (*m. 'Ed.* 5:6; *Mid.* 2:2; *Mo'ed Qaṭ.* 3:1; *b. B. Meṣ.* 59b; *Mo'ed Qaṭ.* 16a; *t. Dem.* 2:9). The offender was required to exhibit signs of mourning and establish his repentance* during the period of the ban in order to qualify for full restoration to the community.

Development during the NT period is impossible to trace, but it appears that an approach similar to that of the Jews was in effect from the start. Community leaders had primary responsibility for discipline (Mt 18:17-20; Acts 5:1-11; 8:20-24); attempts to persuade or warn offenders preceded disciplinary measures (Mt 18:15-16; 2 Cor 13:1-2; Gal 6:1; 2 Thess 3:15), and disciplinary measures might involve food* (2 Thess 3:11; 1 Cor 5:11, the latter perhaps denoting exclusion from the Eucharist) or expulsion from the community (Rom 16:17; 1 Cor 5:1-13; 16:22).

It is apparent that expulsion was a last resort. Furthermore, when it was enforced, it was intended not as a punitive measure and not to denote damnation but to persuade a believer to repent (1 Cor 5:5; 2 Thess 3:14-15). A different stress distinguished early Christian practice from that of the Qumran sectarians and the Pharisees: that is, the deprivation of the loving community of believers would constitute a persuasive force to lead deviants to reformation and restoration.

2. Discipline in Later New Testament and Noncanonical Christian Writings.

The focus in the earliest Christian texts is almost exclusively on aberrant behavior rather than false teaching as the reason for discipline. A distinction between immorality and false teaching as a reason for church discipline may be a false distinction, since some later texts are ambiguous and others suggest a link between false teaching and immorality (e.g., 2 Tim 3:1-13; Tit 3:10-11; 2 Pet 2; Jude 18-19; Rev 2:19-23). Nevertheless, the Pastoral Epistles signal an increasing interest in doctrinal over against behavioral concerns.

The Pastorals recommend discipline for Hymenaeus and Alexander in order that "they might learn not to blaspheme" (1 Tim 1:20 NRSV). Timothy is exhorted to correct his opponents (2 Tim 2:24-26); Titus is admonished

to avoid the schismatic (Tit 3:10-11). The last passage is the only NT occurrence of *hairetikon,* but it is better to translate this as "divisive person" rather than "heretic" to avoid the connotations that became attached to the word in later Christian history. Both 2 John 10-11 and 3 John 9-11 address discipline for false teaching, as does Revelation 2:19-23. In the case of the elder and his friends in 3 John, it is Diotrephes who exercises discipline by expelling John's group from the church. To this action the elder raises a protest. Clement* (*1 Clem.* 54.1-4), Ignatius* (Ign. *Eph.* 5.3; Ign. *Phld.* 3.1-3; Ign. *Smyrn.* 7.2), Polycarp (Pol. *Phil.* 6.3) and the *Didache** (*Did.* 4.3; 14.2) all warn against schism and association with schismatics.

Discipline is not limited to false teachers, however. The "root of bitterness" warned against in Hebrews 12:15 may well involve immorality that corrupts the community (see Deut 29:18 for background). James 5:19-20 enjoins persuasion of "sinners," and 1 John 5:16 recommends prayer for the restoration of those who have committed certain sins. ("Mortal sin" probably involves behavior deserving death in the OT and is not the "unforgivable sin" against the Spirit of Mk 3:28-29.) Clement (*1 Clem.* 56.1-2; 57.1-2; *2 Clem.* 17.1-3), Polycarp (Pol. *Phil.* 6.1) and the *Didache* (*Did.* 14.2; 15.3) all recommend discipline for immorality.

The texts reveal a wide range of disciplinary measures. Many texts are limited to recommendations of persuasion (2 Tim 2:24-26; Jas 5:19-20; *1 Clem.* 56.1-2; 57.1-2; *2 Clem.* 17.1-3; Pol. *Phil.* 6.1). Other texts enjoin avoidance of offenders, presumably or explicitly until they repent (Tit 3:10-11; 2 Jn 10-11; Rev 2:20; 18:4; Ign. *Eph.* 5.3; Ign. *Smyrn.* 7.2; *Did.* 14.2; 15.3). 1 Timothy 1:20 recommends that Hymenaeus and Alexander be "delivered to Satan" (cf. 1 Cor 5:5), which denotes expulsion from the Christian fellowship—possibly for life—but not damnation. Titus 3:10-11 suggests that expulsion should occur only "after a first and second admonition" (NRSV; cf. Mt 18:15-17). Hebrews 6:4-6 and 10:26-31 (cf. *Herm. Sim.* 6.2.3) imply a more final pronouncement against the apostate,* but it is not clear that this is a matter of church discipline rather than a statement of the offender's status before God.

Perhaps surprisingly, given the increasing problem of heterodoxy in the late first and early second centuries, Christian writers of the period do not indulge in or recommend final pronouncements against moral or doctrinal miscreants. Clement is gentle enough to promise heavenly reward for schismatics who voluntarily remove themselves (*1 Clem.* 54.1-4), and the *Shepherd of Hermas* suggests that discernment of true from false disciples is an eschatological* rather than temporal matter (*Herm. Vis.* 3.5.1-7; *Herm. Sim.* 9.13-14). The shift to (or at least addition of) concern about doctrinal deviation appears to have been accomplished by the early church without abandoning the pastoral, redemptive discipline characteristic of incipient Christianity.

See also ADVERSARIES; APOSTASY; AUTHORITY; CHURCH ORDER, GOVERNMENT; PROPHECY, PROPHETS, FALSE PROPHETS; REPENTANCE, SECOND REPENTANCE.

BIBLIOGRAPHY. P. Davids, *The Epistle of James* (Grand Rapids: Eerdmans, 1982); G. Forkman, *The Limits of the Religious Community* (Lund: C. W. K. Gleerup, 1972); L. Goppelt, *Apostolic and Post-apostolic Times* (New York: Harper & Row, 1970); G. W. Knight III, *The Pastoral Epistles* (NIGTC; Grand Rapids: Eerdmans, 1992); G. W. H. Lampe, "Church Discipline and the Interpretation of the Epistles to the Corinthians" in *Christian History and Interpretation: Studies Presented to John Knox*, ed. W. R. Farmer, C. F. D. Moule and R. R. Niebuhr (Cambridge: Cambridge University Press, 1967) 337-61; W. L. Lane, *Hebrews 9-13* (WBC; Dallas: Word, 1991); C. J. Roetzel, *Judgment in the Community* (Leiden: E. J. Brill, 1972); R. Schnackenburg, *The Johannine Epistles* (New York: Crossroad, 1992); W. Telfer, *The Forgiveness of Sins* (London: SCM, 1959). T. E. Schmidt

DISCOURSE ANALYSIS. *See* HERMENEUTICS; STRUCTURALISM AND DISCOURSE ANALYSIS.

DIVINE PRESENCE. *See* GLORY.

DIVORCE. *See* MARRIAGE, DIVORCE AND ADULTRY.

DOCETISM

"Docetic" derives from the common Greek verb *dokein* ("seem, appear"). This verb and the nouns *dokēsis* and *dokētai* in the plural are used in early Christian literature of a variety of teachings about Jesus Christ that are united perhaps solely in denying that the divine Redeemer, by whatever name or title he is identified, was the subject of all the human experiences attributed to Jesus in the canonical Gospels.

1. Definition
2. The Sect of the Docetists
3. The *Gospel of Peter*
4. The Heretics in Ignatius's Letters
5. The Docetism of Marcionites and Gnostics
6. Docetism in the New Testament?

1. Definition.
The proper application of the term *Docetism* is a matter of dispute among patristic scholars (see Slusser). Some wish to restrict its usage exclusively to those presentations in which the human life of Jesus in all its aspects was mere illusion; though visible, it was no more than semblance, devoid of flesh-and-blood reality (Weigandt, Brox). This limitation of the label would certainly confine its use far more narrowly than is found in the sources. Since the latter employ it much less rigidly and furnish nothing akin to an official or agreed definition, most modern writers have sought to pinpoint some common element that might unify the diverse historical references. This can be found, it seems, only in what Docetists of whatever kind denied and probably also in the presuppositions that informed this denial.

The Docetists of primitive Christianity were united in being unable to affirm inseparable lifelong identity between the heavenly or divine One (often distinguished as Christ*) and the human Jesus. But they differed widely in their christological* accounts. Some believed that Jesus was born and lived like other human beings but was indwelt by the Christ only temporarily, from his baptism to the eve of the crucifixion, thus avoiding implicating the divine power* or agent in the processes of human birth and death. This strand of Docetism has obvious affinities with adoptionism.

Others at the opposite end of the docetic spectrum regarded the figure of the Gospels literally as ghostlike, a phantom, an optical illusion. (One wonders how widespread was such a viewpoint.) Between these two extremes cluster a number of versions that attribute to the divine or heavenly Savior while on earth an abnormal human nature of some sort but falling decisively short of an insubstantial specter. The body of Jesus was variously portrayed as composed of a different substance from that of other human bodies, originating perhaps through Mary* but not by normal processes of human birth, capable of some range of human functions but not such as to entangle the Christ himself in the suffering* of death.* Most of these varieties of Docetism deployed not only a distinction between divine and human natures (a phrase that does not here imply the categories of Chalcedonian debate) but also a belief in their essential incompatibility, so that whatever humanity might be predicted of Christ must have been of a special kind, tailor-made for the purpose (except in the temporary union of quasi-adoptionist Docetism).

Underlying all docetic christologies in the early centuries was a conviction, whether of philosophical or theological inspiration, of the impropriety or even impossibility of real incarnation of divinity in human matter. Some flavor of dualism of spirit and flesh* was nearly always operative, but the precise nuance of that dualism, varying from gut-level revulsion against the very thought of God in the womb or the tomb to high-minded notions of divine transcendence, must be observed in each case.

J. G. Davies distinguishes between four primary springs of Docetism: theology (doctrine of the Godhead), cosmology, anthropology and christology. But they easily flow into one another. Although Hellenistic preconceptions inform most Docetism, a Jewish contribution may sometimes be noted. For Jewish faith, theophany was wholly preferable to incarnation.

The imprecision of the content of Docetism in the early church fathers may be partly responsible for the loose use of the label in modern theological debate. Docetism is perhaps the only ancient heresy that recent scholarship has not attempted to rehabilitate, for in an age in which no other creedal* affirmation has been safe from assault, late-twentieth-century believers are sure of nothing so much as (and sometimes nothing more than) that Jesus was one of us. The docetic tag lies ready to affix on the lapels of those for whom virginal conception, sinlessness or knowledge beyond first-century Palestinian norms—or miracle-working power,* resurrection* or even incarnation itself—is incongruent with belief in the humanity of Christ. The antidocetic early-Christian writers held all these credenda together.

2. The Sect of the Docetists.

"Docetist" as the name of a specific group or sect is rare in patristic sources. Hippolytus of Rome, whose authorship is not certain, records the beliefs of the self-styled *Dokētai* (Hippolytus *Refut.* 8.8.2; 8.11.1), who were patently of a highly syncretistic mold (Hippolytus *Refut.* 8.2, 8.8.1—11.2, 10.16.1-6). Hippolytus seems unaware why they assumed this name, which he sarcastically links with the *dokos* ("beam") of Matthew 7:3. His account of their teachings does not emphasize a docetic strain, which on this evidence was no longer the defining focus of their identity.

Clement of Alexandria names the obscure Julius Cassianus (*CPG* 1290-91) as *ho tēs dokēseōs exarchōn* (Clement *Strom.* 3.13), normally translated "the founder of Docetism" but perhaps meaning, as elsewhere in Clement, "inculcator of Docetism" (Le Boulluec, 348-49). Elsewhere Clement cites the *Dokētai* as an example of a heretical sect that derives its name not from geography or practice but from "peculiar dogma" (Clement *Strom.* 7.17). Julius Cassianus, who should be placed in the later second century in Egypt or perhaps Syria, wrote on encratism, for which his Docetism may have been a basis or post factum defense.

3. The *Gospel of Peter*.

A fragment of a lost work by Serapion, bishop of Antioch (in Eusebius *Hist. Eccl.* 6.12.6), introduces us to the difficulty of characterizing a text as docetic. Serapion, who flourished c. 200, came across the *Gospel of Peter** in use in the church of Rhossus and was drawn into scrutinizing it by the discovery that the Christians of Rhossus were entangled in heresy. (Its nature is not clarified, and the name Marcianus is no help, unless we should discern here Marcion,* which would be appropriate in both location and *Tendenz.)* Serapion got some help from the successors of those who began the gospel, "whom we call *Dokētai.* " He found most of it authentic and proceeded to list the additions, which were presumably divergent. But at this point the fragment breaks off.

A sizeable section generally recognized as belonging to this apocryphal* *Gospel of Peter* was discovered in the 1880s (and more recently two tiny papyri). Its supposed Docetism is no longer so obvious. Discussion has focused chiefly on Jesus' silence on the cross (*hōs mēden ponon echōn,* "as having no pain" [*Gos. Pet.* 4.10]; the text does not settle whether he did or did not suffer pain) and the gospel's version of the cry of dereliction, with its distinctive sequel " 'My power, O power you have forsaken me!' And having said this he was taken up" (*Gos. Pet.* 5.19). In addition the narrative displays heightened apocalyptic* and miraculous elements. The evidence probably does not warrant an endorsement of Serapion's judgment on its docetic origin, but its hypersupernatural christology at least makes its use by Docetists comprehensible, even if it barely squeezes into the moderate end of the docetic spectrum.

4. The Heretics in Ignatius's Letters.

The letters written by Ignatius,* bishop of Antioch,* early in the second century to churches in western Asia Minor attack a denial of the reality of Christ's sufferings. He does not name the heretics but uses the verb *dokein* in reporting their teaching (Ign. *Smyrn.* 2.1; 4.2; Ign. *Trall.* 10.1). But their precise understanding, in terms of their position on the spectrum plotted above, remains elusive, nor are scholars agreed whether they or some other group propagated the judaizing errors Ignatius also attacked. Yet the implications of their Docetism emerge unmistakably: the Eucharist was no longer "the flesh of our Savior Jesus Christ which suffered for our sins" (Ign. *Smyrn.* 7.1), and the afflictions and death of the martyrs likewise lost their significance (*see* Martyrdom). In response Ignatius weaves together with wonderful suggestiveness the mutually authenticating threefold reality of Christ's humanity and passion, of the eucharistic flesh and blood and of the death of martyrdom. "Under Pontius Pilate" (Ign. *Trall.* 9.1; cf. 1 Tim 6:13; Apostles' Creed) makes its appearance in a confessional context.

5. The Docetism of Marcionites and Gnostics.

The testimony of anti-gnostic writers like Irenaeus to the Docetism of the unholy succession of Gnostics* and gnosticizing teachers in the second century (beginning for Irenaeus with Cerinthus and in this respect including Marcion and his followers) is broadly confirmed by the Nag Hammadi gnostic texts (Rudolph, 157-71, Tröger). Thus the *Acts of John* 97-104 portray Christ, already risen from his temporary body, watching the crucifixion of Jesus taking place (*see* Death of Jesus). The common christological core of these writings presupposes a Christ who cannot suffer, but their variety encompasses commendation of others' martyr-

dom (e.g., *1 Apoc. Jas.*), metaphorical transpositions of "crucifixion" ("Jesus came to crucify the world," *Gos. Phil.* 63) and texts such as the *Gospel of Truth* in which docetizing elements coexist with nondocetic motifs. Nor should we forget that one or two more mainstream teachers, especially Clement of Alexandria, evinced patent docetic strains in their christology.

6. Docetism in the New Testament?

John's Gospel has been characterized by a few interpreters as docetic but is more plausibly viewed as antidocetic. Certainly the Johannine Epistles (*see* John, Letters of) identify a schismatic group who denied that Jesus Christ had come in the flesh (1 Jn 4:2-3; 2 Jn 7). Some commentators (e.g., Brown) ascribe this to an ultrahigh christology that was en route to Docetism proper; others (e.g., Strecker) more confidently align it with recognizably docetic currents, especially of a Cerinthian kind. According to Epiphanius (*Haer.* 28.1), Cerinthus, who flourished in Asia Minor in the early second century, taught an adoptionist-style Docetism whereby Christ and Jesus were not identical (*see* John, Letters of). Given the appeal of the varieties of Docetism, at the latest from the early second century onward, we should not be surprised to detect it as part of the backdrop against which other, later NT writings should be understood.

See also CHRISTOLOGY; GNOSIS, GNOSTICISM; JOHN, LETTERS OF.

BIBLIOGRAPHY. R. E. Brown, *The Epistles of John* (AB; Garden City, NY: Doubleday, 1982); N. Brox, "Doketismus. Eine Problemanzeige," *ZKG* 95 (1984) 301-14; J. G. Davies, "The Origins of Docetism," *SP* 6 (TU 81; 1962) 13-35; P. M. Head, "On the Christology of the Gospel of Peter," *VC* 46 (1992) 209-24; A. Le Boulluec, *La notion d'hérésie dans la littérature grecque II*-III* siècles* (2 vols.; Paris: Etudes Augustiniennes, 1985); J. W. McCant, "The Gospel of Peter: Docetism Reconsidered," *NTS* 30 (1984) 258-73; C. Maurer and W. Schneemelcher, "The Gospel of Peter" in *New Testament Apocrypha*, ed. W. Schneemelcher (2 vols.; Louisville, KY: Westminster/John Knox, 1989) 1:216-27; K. Rudolph, *Gnosis* (San Francisco: Harper & Row, 1987); G. Salmon, "Cassianus, Julius," *DCB* 1:412-13; idem, "Docetae," *DCB* 1:865-7; M. Slusser, "Docetism: A Historical Definition," *SecCent* 1 (1981) 163-72; G. Strecker, *Die Johannesbriefe*

(Göttingen: Vandenhoeck & Ruprecht, 1989); K. W. Tröger, "Doketistische Christologie in Nag-Hammadi-Texten. Ein Beitrag zum Doketismus in frühchristlicher Zeit," *Kairos* 19 (1977) 45-52; P. Weigandt, "Der Doketismus im Urchristentum und in der theologischen Entwicklung des zweiten Jahrhunderts," (2 vols.; unpublished Ph.D. dissertation, Heidelberg, 1961); K. Wengst, *Häresie und Orthodoxie in Spiegel des ersten Johannesbriefes* (Gütersloh:

Mohn, 1976).

D. F. Wright

DOXOLOGY. *See* GLORY; LITURGICAL ELEMENTS

DRAGON. *See* BEASTS, DRAGON, SEA, CONFLICT MOTIF.

DUALISM. *See* GNOSIS, GNOSTICISM; SYNCRETISM.

E

EARLY CATHOLICISM

The term *early catholicism* (German *Frühkatholizismus*) has taken on a special nuance in contemporary discussion, chiefly because of its employment in 1950 by Ph. Vielhauer (see *DPL*, "Early Catholicism"). In general the term "refers to a situation in which primitive apocalyptic expectation has been weakened, and the Church as an institution with an organized ministry and sacraments has begun to replace the Word as the means of salvation" (Marshall, 222-23).

1. Definition
2. Features
3. Assessment

1. Definition.

The boundary lines between Paul's letters generally claimed as authentic and those labeled Deutero-Pauline (2 Thess, Pastorals, Col—Eph) are contested and difficult to draw, and even Käsemann hesitated about the direct authorship of Colossians (Käsemann *RGG*, 1727-28; see Dunn 1996, 35-39). Yet it remains true that from the witness of the *Hauptbriefe* (Paul's capital epistles of Gal, 1—2 Cor, Rom) a fairly consistent picture of Pauline Christianity can be assembled, in which God's gracious action in saving his people and reconciling the world through Christ alone, is made available to faith, evidenced by love and obedience in the community, is paramount (*see DPL*, Center of Paul's Theology).

Within the evidence of the NT, however, other witnesses add their distinctive voices, offering variations and emphases not apparent in Paul's situational and contingently driven theology. It was the observation that certain (later) parts of the NT offered some views divergent from Paul's that led Ph. Vielhauer in his investigation of Luke-Acts to conclude that in this two-volumed work we are in touch with "the

nascent early catholic church" (Vielhauer, 49). This conclusion formed the basis of H. Conzelmann's influential work on early and later Christianity when he distinguished between (1) the epoch of Israel ending with John the Baptist; (2) the time of Jesus, forming the "center of time" (hence the title of his study of Luke's Gospel, *Die Mitte der Zeit*; and (3) the era of the church* extending into Christian history which he saw as represented in Luke's historiographical writing of both Gospel and Acts. Traces of "early catholic" influences were sought in Conzelmann's segment (3) as the church became domesticated in its earthly existence, lost much of its apocalyptic* fervor, and saw its life as reaching into the unknown future on earth.

More importantly, on theological grounds, E. Käsemann proposed that non-Pauline parts of the NT not only express their message in idioms and ideas that have no counterpart in Paul; they are in conflict with the Pauline insistence on God's justifying the godless (the Pauline center, according to Käsemann, based on his understanding of the twin themes of God's righteousness and Christ's lordly control of the world and the church: see Way; Ehler); and they promote a version of Christianity at odds with Paul. Since the signs of these rival kerygmata have links with the shape Christianity took in becoming institutionalized under clergy and demarcated by its creedal fixities, with a loss of eschatological* verve as the apocalyptic hope of the Parousia* waned, Käsemann found it natural to brand these movements away from Pauline soteriology as "early catholic" (*frühkatholische*), or less questionably, "incipient catholic." "Emergent catholicism" is one such modification of terms (Perrin, 61), which again might better be expressed as "emerging catholicism," since no NT document says exactly that "where Jesus Christ is, there is the catholic church" with a full-blown sacramental, hierarchical system in place (Ign. *Smyrn.* 8) and where faith is replaced by moralism (as some of the apostolic fathers have been said to teach; see Torrance).

2. Features.

The data often appealed to in support of the contention of the presence of "early catholic" elements in the NT may now be passed under review.

2.1. Church Order. The Pauline model (based on 1 Cor 12—14) of a responsible congregational life with all the members playing their role (albeit under some leadership; see 1 Cor 11:19; 16:15-18) takes on new configuration in the Pastoral Letters, often regarded as setting down directions for an organized, regulated and structured life, with the spontaneity and freedom under the Spirit's immediate afflatus checked (Dunn 1975; 1 Tim 3:1-13; 4:14; Tit 1:5-9; 2 Tim 1:13-14). Church life and order evolved, partly under pressure from encroaching deviant ideas, partly due to the onset of a *bürglich-liche*-Hellenistic (i.e., bourgeois) mentality into a hierarchical, bishop-directed institution of ministry, emanating from the closed circle of the apostles* and their successors (heralded, it may be, in Eph 2:20; 4:16-20; *see* Worship; further evidence in Ign. *Phld.* 3.4; *Did.* 15.1-2; *1 Clement* 40—44). Hints of this development are seen in 1 Peter 5:1-5; Hebrews 13:7; and 3 John (rivalry between the Johannine elder and Diotrephes is held to reflect ecclesiastical tensions over power; von Campenhausen, Käsemann 1960; *see* Adversaries; Church Order and Government).

2.2. Faith. Faith* that in the early literature retains its value as salvific and a response in obedience to the kerygma's call now becomes transformed into a belief in articles of religion (*fides quae creditur*, "what is believed"; cf. Eph 4:5; Jude 3, 20), regarded as a treasured possession to be adhered to and preserved inviolate, then handed on (1 Tim 6:20; 2 Tim 1:14) and thereby losing its personal character in that it is subsumed under a generalized Christian attitude as one virtue* among several (2 Pet 1:5-7).

2.3. Canonical Authority. The limits of the canon,* the list of authoritative writings, are determined by the church's acting in collecting such writings, especially Paul's letters (2 Pet 3:15-16), and erecting a "formal principle" of canonical authority (Käsemann; Ehler, 35-70)

which is fixed (cf. Rev 22:18-19 for this idea of a "closed book"). The church in its later self-awareness takes on the role of a "saved community" protected as the "bulwark of the truth" (1 Tim 3:15) by the normative Scripture (*sola scriptura*) it is called to safeguard rather than live by or under.

2.4. Gospel. Perhaps the most serious index of an alleged decline from pristine, Pauline standards is seen in the way the gospel* message is said to have degenerated into "orthodoxy," with right belief replacing saving faith, leading to a moralistic way of fulfilling the commandments (evident in the "Two Ways" teaching underlying *Barnabas* and *Didache;* see Kirk, 111-39) and a transmutation of Christian living as dependent on a sacramental observance (clear in Ignatius) with clergy and laity separated (*1 Clement*). The notes of God's sovereign, unfettered grace, displayed in putting the world into right relationship by a gracious act-of-power and suspending the Christians' response on obedience to the lordship of Christ (Käsemann; Way) are muted. Hence, it is said, the Pauline kerygma is eclipsed.

3. Assessments.

A serviceable paradigm of the way critics who favor this reading of NT Christianity in its obvious multiform variety support their case may now be considered. And it will provide an opportunity to assess its strength and weakness.

E. Käsemann (1964) has launched an attack on 2 Peter* by dubbing it an "early catholic" work. As we noted above, in Käsemann's terminology it is a book that fails to articulate and champion the heart of the (Pauline) message and represents an accommodation of Christianity to Hellenistic culture and categories. Marks of "early catholic" influence in 2 Peter are, first, a fading of the parousial hope as part of a general reordering of eschatological conviction in which Christ's coming is sidelined in favor of a stoic idea of cosmic renewal (2 Pet 3:3-14). Second, moralistic ideas stemming from an understanding of salvation as a divinization of human nature (2 Pet 1:4) are part of the (late) author's approach to making the practice of Christian living a cultivation of a basket of virtues (2 Pet 1:5-9). Third, appeal to apostolic authority* in the person of venerated church leaders of the past (Paul and Peter in Rome) seen in 2 Peter 1:16-18 and 3:15-16 replaces reliance on the immediacy of the Spirit's guidance in the community (links with *1 Clem.* 5 and Ign. *Rom.* 4.3 are evident). Fourth, the way in which the faith is codified in set forms and fixed formulas leads to the setting up of canonical authority as a bulwark against gnosticizing heresy. Church members are encouraged to remain committed to the apostolic teaching (2 Pet 3:1; for the "recall" formula and technique, see Talbert, cited in Martin, 134-35) in a way that differs from earlier Pauline charismatic groups who retain a fresh awareness of living "between the times" as a harbinger of receiving the Spirit's final salvation.

Judged by these criteria, Käsemann avers, 2 Peter shows clear signs of its second-century setting. He argues that it wrestles with the problem of the Parousia's delay by recasting eschatology to fit in with the world's continued existence; and he further maintains that the church's role as a bastion of orthodoxy to counter "false teachers" (2 Pet 2:1) shows a distinct shift from Paul's ecclesiology of a church charismatically moved and led. The church as guardian of Scripture (2 Pet 1:12-21; 3:16) is said to betoken a teaching office held in veneration as opposed to Paul's view (1 Cor 12) that all the Spirit-gifted members of the congregation can offer teaching and revelation.*

The upshot is that in 2 Peter the essential gospel (what Käsemann called its "material principle," i.e., justification by faith) has been overlaid and corrupted. The witness of 2 Peter is not to the gospel as "event" but to its transmutation to "doctrine."

There is, in our review of Käsemann's estimate, the need to recognize both truth and exaggeration. He has overstated the case in several ways, chiefly in ignoring the fact that the denial of imminence in the Parousia is the sectarians' position, not the author's. The latter has a strongly held belief in Christ's coming to judgment* in apocalyptic glory* (2 Pet 1:19; 2:12; 3:10-14). True, he expresses salvation in a way that sets a gulf between God's nature (as divine) and human existence (as mortal). The remedy is found in divine power (2 Pet 1:3) that intervenes to promise incorruption (2 Pet 1:4) and moral power (2 Pet 2:19-20). Yet this idea of divinization is still a long way from the later church doctrine seen in the Cappadocian fathers' expression that humans may become as

God (Gk *theopoiēsis;* Kelly, 348-52) in a way that turns the church into a sacramental system offering to transform (Gk *metaballein*) the human condition into gaining a share of the divine life by osmosis.

The author of 2 Peter does have recourse to apostolic traditions as the ground of appeal—here Käsemann's point is well taken—and this feature marks the normative character assigned to "apostolic words" (2 Pet 2:21; 3:2) as well as their "ways" (2 Pet 2:1, 15, 21), a trait seen in Jude 17 and the Johannine letters. Yet the apostolic office is not exalted as indispensable, and all the addressees are expected to interpret Scripture for themselves much as among the Pauline congregants (2 Pet 1:19-21; 3:14-18; see also Heb 5:12-14; 1 Jn 2:20, 27). The author is building his case on apostolic testimony inherited from Peter, as the writer of Ephesians may well be doing in regard to Paul's legacy—and adapting it to post-apostolic situations (cf. Beker). As Bauckham (153) remarks, this is the key to the author's conception of the task at hand. Finally, while "faith" does have a nuance of "what is believed"—and this usage is not without parallel in the early Paul—both "faith" and "knowledge"* retain a meaning understood as a living relationship to Christ, implied in personal conversion, again much as Paul does (see Reumann, 291-92, who argues that "faith" is the cement that binds together the various parts of the NT's pluriform witness, and that convictional faith [*fides qua creditur*] can never be understood without or separated from the content of faith [*fides quae*]).

In sum, we should be alert to the developments of the kerygma as new situations arose in the post-apostolic era, but these enrichments are a deeper explication and application of the central core themes (Best, 87-113) rather than a distortion or contradiction of them. Moreover, with Best (46) we should recognize the need to have in the NT's witness *both* what he calls "existentialist" interpretations of Christ *and* the "non-existentialist" interpretations; both emphases are required, he avers, for the church's continued existence (see also Fuller).

See also CHURCH ORDER AND GOVERNMENT; ESCHATOLOGY; NEW TESTAMENT THEOLOGY; PAROUSIA; PAULINE LEGACY AND SCHOOL; 2 PETER.

BIBLIOGRAPHY. R. J. Bauckham, *Jude, 2 Peter* (WBC; Waco: Word, 1983); J. C. Beker, *Heirs of Paul: Paul's Legacy in the New Testament and in the*

Church Today (Minneapolis: Fortress, 1991);
E. Best, *Interpreting Christ* (Edinburgh: T & T
Clark, 1993); H. Conzelmann, *The Theology of St
Luke* (New York: Harper & Row, 1960); J. D. G.
Dunn, *The Epistles to the Colossians and to Philemon*
(NIGTC; Grand Rapids: Eerdmans, 1996);
idem, *Jesus and the Spirit* (Philadelphia: West-
minster, 1975); B. Ehler, *Die Herrschaft des Gek-
reuzigten* (Berlin: de Gruyter, 1986); R. H. Fuller,
"Early Catholicism: An Anglican Reaction to a
German Debate" in *Die Mitte des Neuen Testaments*,
ed. U. Luz & H. Weder (Göttingen: Vandenhoeck
& Ruprecht, 1983) 34-41; E. Käsemann, "An Apologia for Primitive Christian Eschatology" in *Essays on New Testament Themes* (Philadelphia:
Fortress 1964) 169-95; idem, "Ketzer und
Zeuge," *Exegetische Versuche und Besinnungen*, Erster Band (Göttingen: Vandenhoeck & Ruprecht, 1960) 168-87; idem, "Kolosserbrief," *RGG*
(3d ed.) 1727-28; idem, "Paul and Early Catholicism" in *New Testament Questions of Today* (Philadelphia: Fortress, 1969) 236-51; J. N. D. Kelly, *Early
Christian Doctrines* (New York: Harper, 1958);
K. E. Kirk, *The Vision of God* (London: Longmans, 1931); R. P. Martin, "The Theology of
Jude, 1 Peter, and 2 Peter" in A. Chester and R.
P. Martin, *The Theology of the Letters of James, Peter
and Jude* (NTT; Cambridge: Cambridge University Press, 1994); I. H. Marshall, " 'Early Catholicism' in the New Testament" in *New Dimensions
in New Testament Study*, ed. R. N. Longenecker
and M. C. Tenney (Grand Rapids: Zondervan,
1974); N. Perrin, *The New Testament: An Introduction* (New York: Harcourt Brace, Javonovich,
1974); J. Reumann, *Variety and Unity in New
Testament Thought* (Oxford: Oxford University
Press, 1991); T. F. Torrance, *The Doctrine of Grace
in the Apostolic Fathers* (Edinburgh: Oliver &
Boyd, 1948); Ph. Vielhauer, "On the 'Paulinism'
in Acts" in *Studies in Luke-Acts*, ed. L. E. Keck and
J. L. Martyn (New York: Abingdon, 1966) 33-56;
H. F. von Campenhausen, *Ecclesiastical Authority
and Spiritual Power in the Church of the First Three
Centuries* (Stanford, CA: Stanford University
Press, 1969); D. V. Way, *The Lordship of Christ:
Ernst Käsemann's Interpretation of Paul's Theology*
(Oxford: Clarendon, 1991). R. P. Martin

EBIONITES

"Ebionites" is one of the names given by the
early church fathers to a leading group of Jewish
Christians or to Jewish Christians in general.
The name, which originally meant "the poor,"

may reflect NT usage (cf. Rom 15:26), but on
this and other questions, such as the Ebionites'
differentiation from the Nazarenes (Nazoreans), no agreement exists among scholars.

1. Patristic Testimonies
2. Modern Discussion

1. Patristic Testimonies.

1.1. Irenaeus. "Ebionites" first appears among
the names given to groups of Jewish Christians
in the writings of Irenaeus (c. 180). The Greek
Ebionaioi (Ebionaei in Latin, in the sole extant
version of Irenaeus's text) is a transliteration of
the Hebrew or Aramaic for "poor," but there is
no agreement on the origins of the name.
Irenaeus's report, sandwiched between his accounts of Cerinthus and of the Nicolaitans,
Cerdo and Marcion,* provides no explanation:
"Those who are called Ebionites allow that the
world was made by God but as concerns the
Lord hold the same opinions as Cerinthus and
Carpocrates [omitting a negative, with most
editors; for the contrary case see Klijn and Reinink, 19-20]. They use only the Gospel according to Matthew and reject the apostle Paul,
calling him an apostate from the law. They strive
to expound the prophecies too punctiliously.
They circumcise themselves and persist in customs based on the law and in a Jewish lifestyle,
such that they even venerate Jerusalem as
though it were the home of God" (Irenaeus
Haer. 1.26.2).

Elsewhere Irenaeus adds that the Ebionites'
use of only Matthew's Gospel misled them in
their beliefs about the Lord (Irenaeus *Haer.*
3.11.7); that they rejected the virginal conception of Jesus, following Theodotion and Aquila
in interpreting Isaiah 7:14 ("of a young woman,"
Gk *neanis;* Lat *adulescentula*), thereby dissolving
the divine plan and nullifying the God-given
witness of the prophets (Irenaeus *Haer.* 3.21.2);
and that consequently they denied the incarnate union of God* and humanity, failing to
discern the parallel with the creation of Adam
in which God-breathed life united with and
vivified the human substance (Irenaeus *Haer.*
5.1.3; cf. 4.33.4).

1.2. Tertullian. To Irenaeus's account Tertullian added little except to introduce Ebion, the
successor of Cerinthus, as the exponent of the
heresy (Tertullian *De Praescr.* 33; cf. the slightly
later Ps-Tertullian's *Against All Heresies* 3). Tertullian cited the variant text of John 1:13 (sin-

gular *natus*) against Ebion's rejection of the virginal conception (Tertullian *De Carn.* 24) and alluded to Ebion's teaching that, though he was no more than a Solomon or a Jonah, Jesus was indwelt by an angel (Tertullian *De Carn.* 14, 18). Tertullian never mentions the Ebionites but only Ebion, reflecting the custom Justin Martyr attributes to heretics, like philosophers, of tracing their beliefs back to an eponymous founder (Justin Martyr *Dial. Tryph.* 35).

1.3. Hippolytus. Hippolytus's chapter on the Ebionites is heavily indebted to Irenaeus. Hippolytus adds that Jesus was named Christ only for his perfect observance of the Jewish law and that others after him are able likewise to become Christs if they fulfill the law (Hippolytus *Refut.* 7.34; cf. 10.22.1).

1.4. Origen. Origen's several references to the Ebionites (and once to Ebion) repeat the main points found in Irenaeus and supply other details in agreement with them: as Jews the Ebionites cited Jesus' statement that he was sent only to the lost sheep of Israel (Origen *De Princ.* 4.3.8); like Christ they celebrated pascha on the same day as the Jews and with unleavened bread (Origen *Comm. Mt.* ser. 79). Origen is the first to claim that the Ebionites were so called because of the poverty of their understanding (Origen *De Princ.* 4.3.8) or the poverty of the law to which they clung (Origen *Cont. Cels.* 2.1). He also distinguishes between two kinds of Ebionites, some who confess the virginal conception of Jesus and others who ascribe to him a normal birth (Origen *Cont. Cels.* 5.61; cf. *Comm. Mt.* 16.12). Such a distinction among Jewish followers of Jesus is indicated by Justin Martyr (*Dial. Tryph.* 48), but he never names the Ebionites. The distinction may reflect divergent texts of Irenaeus (see 1.1 above): Hippolytus had one without the negative, Eusebius probably one with it.

1.5. Eusebius. Eusebius's main account of the Ebionites combines traditions derived from Irenaeus, Hippolytus and Origen (Eusebius *Hist. Eccl.* 3.27). "Ebionites" was the name appropriately given them from the first because of their poor and base opinions about Christ, who, as an ordinary human being, was "justified" solely by moral achievement. Other Ebionites did not deny the birth from the virgin, yet they too rejected Christ's preexistence* as the divine Word and Wisdom.* To this second group Eusebius attributes the use of the Gospel of the

Hebrews to the contempt of other Gospels. He also says that they, like other Christians, worship* on the Lord's Day* in commemoration of the Savior's resurrection* but alongside their continuing observance of the sabbath. It seems that Eusebius had no independent information about the Ebionites but sought to reconcile his sources. Hence he differentiates the two groups more fully than before and disagrees with Irenaeus (who has the Ebionites using Matthew's Gospel) probably in preference for Origen, who several times mentions the Gospel of the Hebrews without linking it with the Ebionites.

Elsewhere, in his account of Origen's work on the text of the OT, Eusebius is the first writer to describe Symmachus as an Ebionite (Eusebius *Hist. Eccl.* 6.17; cf. *Dem. Ev.* 7.1). In his *Onomasticon* he asserts that there are Ebionites living in Choba "to the left of Damascus," probably identical with the Kochaba mentioned, along with Nazareth, as the home of the relatives of the Savior (Eusebius *Hist. Eccl.* 1.7.14; *see* Relatives of Jesus).

1.6. Epiphanius. Epiphanius's *Haereses [Panarion]* was written in the mid-370s while he was bishop of Salamis in Cyprus. Although it provides by far the longest patristic report on the Ebionites, with apparently much fresh information, the extent of Epiphanius's access to independent sources remains uncertain. In the *Haereses* the Ebionites follow the Nazoreans, with whom Ebion began before developing his distinctive teaching (Epiphanius *Haer.* 30.1.1). Both groups originated among the Christian Jews who fled eastward into Transjordan before A.D. 70 (Epiphanius *Haer.* 30.2.7).

Unlike most earlier writers, Epiphanius does not link the Ebionites with Cerinthus, whom he places in Asia Minor. The Ebionites settled in Kochaba and other named towns in the Basanitis region (Epiphanius *Haer.* 30.2.8), but Ebion also taught in Asia (where he, not Cerinthus, met the apostle John in the Ephesian baths, Epiphanius *Haer.* 30.24.1-5), Rome and Cyprus (Epiphanius *Haer.* 30.18.1—did Epiphanius draw on local traditions or experience?). Like the Cerinthians, the Ebionites use only Matthew's Gospel, which they call the Gospel according to the Hebrews (Epiphanius *Haer.* 30.3.7), but in a version incomplete and corrupted (Ephiphanius *Haer.* 30.13.2); the corruptions Epiphanius cites reflect particularly a rejection of eating meat (Epiphanius *Haer.* 30.14.4; 30.22.4). This Hebrew Gospel began with the baptizing by John (Epiphanius *Haer.* 30.13.6-8) and omitted the genealogy of Jesus.

Epiphanius highlights development as well as diversity in Ebionite teaching. Ebion viewed Jesus Christ as the natural son of Joseph (Epiphanius *Haer.* 30.2.2; 30.3.1), but through the influence of Elxai (Epiphanius *Haer.* 19.1.4—19.6.5), Ebion's followers adopted variant christologies,* chiefly based on the notion of a heavenly Christ (Epiphanius *Haer.* 30.3.1-6; cf. 30.14.4-6). So Epiphanius can depict the Ebionites as observing Ebion's Jewish practice and adhering to Elxai's fantasies about Christ (Epiphanius *Haer.* 30.17.5-7).

The Ebionites originally commended virginity because of James the brother of Jesus but later repudiated celibacy and continence (Epiphanius *Haer.* 30.2.6; 30.18.2-3 makes marriage* compulsory). This comment should probably be linked with another distinctive feature of Epiphanius's record: the Ebionites' use of the *Peregrinations (Periodoi) of Peter* attributed to Clement* of Rome, although this too they corrupted. Clement taught celibacy (Epiphanius no doubt regards Ps-Clement's *Letter to Virgins* as authentic), but the adulterated Ebionite version of the *Peregrinations* overturned this. It also depicted Peter's daily baptisms* and abstinence from meat (Epiphanius *Haer.* 30.15.1-3). Epiphanius has been widely held to have had access to one of the sources, perhaps the Grundschrift, of the Pseudo-Clementine *Homilies* and *Recognitions.* He also speaks of the Ebionites' *Ascents (Anabathmoi) of James,* with its polemic against sacrifices and the temple* (Epiphanius *Haer.* 30.16.7)—another possible source of the Pseudo-Clementines. Epiphanius ascribes to the heresy the production or use of other works falsely named from apostles (John is mentioned as well as James and Matthew), but identification is impossible (Epiphanius *Haer.* 30.16.6; 30.23.1-2).

Epiphanius may well have had first-hand acquaintance with Ebionites and their books, but his attempt to reconcile his divergent sources of information about them by introducing the diverting impact of Elxai is unconvincing if only because it explains the obscure by the more obscure. The Elkesaites (from Elxai or Elkesai) have, however, attracted renewed interest through the recent publication of the Cologne Mani codex, showing that the founder of Manichaeism grew up in this syncretistic Jewish Christian baptizing sect.

1.7. Jerome. Other writers contemporaneous with or later than Epiphanius contribute nothing more of significance, except possibly for Jerome. But he appears to confuse Ebionites and Nazoreans (Jerome *Ep.* 112.13) and perhaps Ebion and Symmachus, the allegedly Ebionite translator of the Hebrew Bible (Jerome *Comm. Gal.* 3.13-14). His most intriguing claim is to have recently translated from Hebrew (Aramaic) into Greek and Latin the Gospel according to the Hebrews, which is used by the Nazoreans and Ebionites (Jerome *Comm. Matt.* 12.13; *Comm. Mic.* 7.6; *Vir.* 2).

2. Modern Discussion.

Making consistent and historically plausible sense of patristic testimonies to the Ebionites (translated and reviewed in Klijn and Reinink) is a taxing assignment. Among the attendant difficulties is that of differentiating them from other Jewish Christian groups, especially the Nazoreans (Nazareans, Nazarenes).

2.1. Origin of the Name. The tradition first found in Tertullian of a historical founder named Ebion is almost entirely discounted (but note Fitzmyer, 210). The etiology first found in Origen of their pejorative naming for their "poverty" of belief or practice is even less credible. Epiphanius rejects their own claim that "they are poor because they sold their possessions in the apostles' time . . . and have gone over to poverty and renunciation; and thus, they say, they are called 'poor' by everyone" (Epiphanius *Haer.* 30.17.2).

This origination of the name in "the poor" as a designation of the primitive Jesus people, with probably a double reference to economic and spiritual poverty (cf. Rom 15:26; Mt 5:3; Bammel, 909, 912-14; *see* Riches), has not won universal acceptance. Scholars who deny that "the poor" was used in this sense (e.g., Keck) cannot entertain it. Yet, whether self-adopted or applied by others, it remains the most likely possibility. It appeals especially to those who discern in the Ebionites a continuity with the earliest Jewish Christianity* of Jerusalem.* M. Goulder relies on Ebionite writings to reconstruct "The Pre-Marcan Gospel."

2.2. Emergence of Ebionism. H.-J. Schoeps's influential interpretation accepts that both

Ebionites and Nazoreans derive from the first community in Jerusalem but prefers to use both names only of separate groups that formed after the fall of Jerusalem, settled east of Jordan and came to be viewed as heretical by the mainstream church. Joseph Thomas, following Jerome, identifies "the orthodox Ebionites" with the Nazoreans; by the time of Irenaeus some had become heretical, some would even become Gnostic,* and eventually, through Elkesaite influence, some became baptist Ebionites. In this presentation "Ebionite" is near to an all-inclusive category for all distinctively Jewish Christian groups. More recently R. A. Pritz discerns a split in the ranks of the Nazarenes (who stand in direct descent from the first Jerusalem believers) around the end of the first century, probably over christology, out of which Ebionitism emerged. In terms of continuing adherence to Judaism and in geography, Nazarenes and Ebionites are scarcely distinguishable. The former are less well documented than the latter (Fitzmyer, 292-93 tabulates the features attributed to each), but the Nazarenes (Nazoreans) are generally credited with orthodox beliefs about Christ.

2.3. Ebionites and Qumran. J. L. Teicher held the Qumran* sect to be Ebionite. A number of scholars have seen the conversion of Essene Jews as the source or one source of the Ebionites, before or more likely after A.D. 70 (Bammel, 913; Daniélou, 63, following Oscar Cullmann). J. A. Fitzmyer cautiously concludes that the Essenes did not become Christians but undoubtedly influenced Ebionite teachings and practices.

2.4. An Ebionite Gospel. Sorting out one Jewish Christian Gospel from another is made difficult by the scantiness of the remains. According to G. Howard, from the seven fragments given by Epiphanius, the Ebionites' Gospel presupposed the three Synoptics, was harmonistic (following Bertrand) and was written in Greek, not Hebrew, as Epiphanius supposed. This writer also wrongly identified it with the Gospel of the Hebrews (which clearly contained syncretistic and gnostic elements). The Ebionite Gospel cannot be dated more precisely than the pre-Irenaean second century. Its *Tendenz* reflects Ebionite christology and antipathy to meat-eating (see 1.6 above; text in Vielhauer and Strecker, 169-70).

2.5. Other Ebionite Literature. Following Epiphanius on the *Periodoi Petrou,* modern study has widely accepted the *Kerygmata Petrou (Preachings of Peter)* as a major Ebionite source of the Pseudo-Clementines (Jones, 84-96 for review of research). G. Strecker's analysis (in Bauer, 257-71) locates its Jewish Christianity (anti-Pauline, dependent on the four Gospels but ignorant of the Catholic Epistles and the Apocalypse, with a high regard for James of Jerusalem, repeated baptisms) on the borderlands of Greek Syria and Edessa around the turn of the second and third centuries.

Although Symmachus is identified by some Fathers as Ebionite, a recent monograph finds "no traces of any Ebionite belief in his Pentateuch translations" (Salvesen, 297). Other patristic evidence identifies a Jewish Christian group of Symmachians (Klijn and Reinink, 52-54) but does not link it with the tradition of Symmachus's Ebionitism. Epiphanius makes him a Samaritan who became a Jewish proselyte (*Weights* 16). Symmachus's alleged Ebionitism contributes nothing to any understanding of this strand of Jewish Christianity.

See also JEWISH CHRISTIANITY.

BIBLIOGRAPHY. E. Bammel, "πτωχός κτλ" in *TDNT* 6:885-915; W. Bauer, *Orthodoxy and Heresy in Earliest Christianity* (Philadelphia: Fortress, 1971); D. Bertrand, "L'Évangile des Ebionites et problème synoptique: Mc 1.2-6 et par.," *NTS* 26 (1980) 548-63; J. Daniélou, *The Theology of Jewish Christianity* (London: Darton, Longman & Todd, 1964); J. A. Fitzmyer, "The Qumran Scrolls, the Ebionites and Their Literature" in *The Scrolls and the New Testament,* ed. K. Stendahl (New York: Harper, 1957) 208-31, 291-98; M. Goulder, "The Pre-Marcan Gospel," *SJT* 47 (1994) 453-71; G. Howard, "The Gospel of the Ebionites," *ANRW* 2.25.5 (1988) 4034-53; F. S. Jones, "The Pseudo-Clementines: A History of Research, Part II," *SecCent* 2 (1982) 63-96; L. E. Keck, "The Poor Among the Saints in Jewish Christianity and Qumran," *ZNTW* 57 (1966) 54-78; A. F. J. Klijn and G. J. Reinink, *Patristic Evidence for Jewish Christian Sects* (NovTSup 36; Leiden: E. J. Brill, 1973); R. A. Pritz, *Nazarene Jewish Christianity* (SPB 37; Leiden: E. J. Brill, 1988); A. Salvesen, *Symmachus in the Pentateuch* (JSSM 15; Manchester: University of Manchester, 1991); H.-J. Schoeps, *Jewish Christianity* (Philadelphia: Fortress, 1964); M. Simon, *Verus Israel* (Oxford: Oxford University Press, 1986); G. Strecker, "Ebioniten," *RAC* 4 (1959) 487-500;

J. Thomas, *Le mouvement baptiste en Palestine et Syrie (150 av. J.-C.-300 ap. J.-C.)* (Gembloux: J. Duculot, 1935); P. Vielhauer and G. Strecker, "Jewish-Christian Gospels" in *New Testament Apocrypha*, ed. W. Schneemelcher (2 vols.; rev. ed.; Louisville: Westminster/John Knox, 1991-92) 1:134-78.   D. F. Wright

ECSTATIC EXPERIENCE. *See* VISIONS, ECSTATIC EXPERIENCE.

EDESSA. *See* SYRIA, SYRIAN CHRISTIANITY.

ELDERS. *See* CHURCH ORDER, GOVERNMENT; MINISTRY.

ELECTION
The presentation of the concept of election mostly parallels what we find in the Gospels and the Pauline literature (*see DPL*, Election and Predestination). This is understandable, given the formative influence of Jesus and Paul on the development of the theology of the early church. At the same time the topic occupies less space overall in view of the unique purposes for the writings that constitute the remaining books of the NT.

    1. God Determines Events and Dates
    2. God Elects or Appoints Individuals
    3. God Chooses or Appoints Christ
    4. God Elects People to Salvation
    5. Conclusion and Early Christian
       Developments

1. God Determines Events and Dates.
This represents a minor element of the topic to be sure, but the authors of Acts and Hebrews assert God's role in the occurrence of certain events and dates that we could consider elective in nature. God decides the timing of the future kingdom* (Acts 1:7). God has "determined" (*horizō*) the times and locations of the nations on planet earth (Acts 17:26). Using the same verb, the writer of Hebrews affirms that God has appointed a certain day to be "Today" (Heb 4:7). God chose that the Gentiles*—not merely Jews—would hear and believe the word of salvation* through Peter's mouth (Acts 15:7). God's elective will can overturn or determine human plans (Acts 18:21; 21:14).

2. God Elects or Appoints Individuals.
Reserving God's appointment of Christ for the next section, we find in Acts the confirmation that Jesus chose the Twelve* to be apostles* (Acts 1:2, 24; 10:41-42), parallel to God's choice of the ancestors of Israel* (Acts 13:17) or his appointment of the high priest* (Heb 5:4). Beyond that, the use of *dei* ("it is necessary") plays an important role here: "Claimed by the divine will, they [Christ's disciples] are shaped and determined by it down to the smallest details of their lives (Lk 12:12; Acts 9:6, 16; 14:22; 19:21; 23:11; 27:24)" [Grundmann, 22-23]. The writer of Acts confirms that God's Spirit (*see* Holy Spirit) *called* Barnabas and Saul to their missionary endeavors (Acts 13:2; 16:10). In Paul's words, the Holy Spirit appointed those who served as elders/overseers of the church of Ephesus (Acts 20:28). Paul, Luke's hero, is a special specimen of God's electing activity: Paul owes his role as an apostle to God's appointment (Acts 9:15—Paul is a *chosen* instrument; 13:47; 22:10, 14; 26:16). In Acts 26:19 Paul affirms that he responded positively to God's appointment of him to be a servant and witness.*

3. God Chooses or Appoints Christ.
Parallel to statements in the Gospels, the author of Acts asserts that Jesus was a man under divine appointment. In one of Peter's speeches he affirms that Christ's* career as Messiah was appointed by God (Acts 3:20). The verb *dei* has elective significance again. It expresses divine lordship* that determines Christ's activity and leads to his suffering,* death* and glory* (Acts 1:16; 3:21; 17:3).

    In his first epistle Peter asserts that Christ was foreknown before the foundation of the world (1 Pet 1:20). Scholars debate whether this refers only to prescience or to predestination. In either case, though salvation* may have been a mystery that the prophets* announced and into which angels* longed to look, God knew all along precisely how he would accomplish redemption*—through Christ's death. Indeed, Jesus' crucifixion, though perpetrated by evil people, took place "according to the definite plan and foreknowledge of God" (Acts 2:23 NRSV; see also 4:28; 13:29). Though people rejected Christ, he is God's *chosen* and precious Stone, the cornerstone of the building that constitutes God's people (1 Pet 2:4, 6; quoting Is 28:16).

    With virtual quotations of the transfiguration narratives (see Mt 17:5; Mk 9:7), 2 Peter affirms that Jesus enjoys God's appointment to his messianic role because he is God's beloved Son upon whom his divine pleasure rests (2 Pet 1:17). R. J. Bauckham agrees that this pleasure "carries the special sense of God's *electing* good pleasure" (220).

The writer of Hebrews echoes the same thought (Heb 10:9-10). God has also appointed Jesus to his future role as judge* of people (Acts 10:42; 17:31). Beyond this the writer of Hebrews contends that God appointed the Son to be heir of all things (Heb 1:2). The author defends this divine appointment by citing texts from Psalm 2:7 and 2 Samuel 7:14 (Heb 1:5; 5:5). Christ's role in the Melchizedekian* priesthood stems from definitive divine selection (Heb 5:10; 7:28; 8:3).

4. God Elects People to Salvation.

As we would expect, this final category comprises the largest number of texts. Preeminently, election is the action of a loving and gracious God to secure salvation for sinful people. God chose Christ as his "elect one" in order that people might enter into his elect body, the church. Theological debate has centered on how we should understand the relationship between individuals' election to salvation and the corporate election of the church in Christ. Peter certainly applies corporate categories when he speaks of the church as Christ's elect body. He says, "But you are a chosen race, a royal priesthood, a holy nation, God's own people. . . . Once you were not a people, but now you are God's people" (1 Pet 2:9-10 NRSV; cf. Hos 2:23; Ex 19:6). Yet the debate throughout the church's history has often hinged on whether or not this corporate reality implies that God chose specific individuals to be in the elect body. First we must survey the biblical evidence.

Most scholars acknowledge the importance of "calling" language in the biblical authors' discussion of election (*see*, e.g., *DPL*, Call, Calling). The author of Acts asserts that God calls people to salvation; his name is called upon them (Acts 2:39; 15:17), though it may not be precisely certain that election themes are in view. Likewise, James identifies believers as those upon whom Christ's name is called (Jas 2:7). At the same time, people must call upon the name of the Lord to be saved (Acts 2:21). People are appointed to eternal* life (Acts 13:48), though the ambiguity of the middle or passive voice in the Greek construction here makes it unclear whether the author wants to stress God's specific appointment or the hearers' decision to believe (MacDonald, 226-28). Certainly these appointed ones believe.

The elder refers to the recipient of his letter as a "chosen lady," an appellation most commentators believe refers to a local church congregation; the corporate body is elect (2 Jn 1, 13). John piles up collective substantives to describe Jesus' followers: they are the "called," "chosen" and "faithful" (Rev 17:14). Using a metaphor that appears to have elective connotations—"book of life"—John describes believers as ones whose names appear in the book while unbelievers' names are absent from the book. This becomes the criterion for habitation in the New Jerusalem* (Rev 20:12, 15; 21:27). The picture is strange, though, for on one hand names appear to be written from the creation* of the world (Rev 17:8; cf. 13:8), but on the other hand those who remain faithful to Jesus avoid having their names erased from the book (Rev. 3:5; cf. Ex 32:32-33). It is best not to press this metaphor too much for elective significance. It may point to God's foreknowledge of his people, while the possibility of erasure highlights the requirement for human response to God's grace.*

James asks a perplexing question: "Has not God chosen the poor in the world to be rich in faith and to be heirs of the kingdom that he has promised to those who love him?" (Jas 2:5). Can James mean that all economically poor people will attain God's salvation due to his pretemporal choice? Surely that cannot be James's meaning; not *all* poor people are elect, and certainly *some* rich people are (arguably, those in Jas 1:10-11 and possibly those in Jas 4:13-17). The phrase "to those who love him" certainly specifies the intent of James's words. Most likely, following the pervasive biblical avowal of God's care for the poor (e.g., Deut 15:7-9; Ps 41:1; 69:33; 82:3-4; 140:12; Prov 14:31), the common OT link of poor with pious (Hebrew *'anawim*), and given the historical reality that the early church included those classified as "poor" people, James's question describes the real state of the church. This shows why Christians ought not show favoritism to the rich: the church consists primarily of "poor"—that is, humble—people who are God's chosen ones. Election terminology here describes the status of believers: they are God's chosen ones.

The author of 1 Peter employs the concept of "call" (using the verb *kalein*) five times to affirm that Christians are the objects of God's action of calling (1 Pet 1:15; 2:9; 2:21; 3:9; 5:10). In the second letter similar language occurs—both the verb *kalein* and the noun *klēsis* ("calling": 2 Pet 1:3, 10; see also Jude 1). Christians bear the standing or status of God's "called ones," a virtual synonym for "those whom God has named as his own" (Klein 1984). It is impossible, on the basis of these texts alone, to make any of the distinctions systematic theologians attempt between "verbal" and "effectual" calling. That is beside Peter's point. However, 2 Peter 1:10 presents a fascinating juxtaposition: "Therefore, brothers and sisters, be all the more eager to confirm your call and election" (NRSV). The apparently definitive divine acts of "calling" and "election" necessitate human actions if they are to be confirmed or made sure *(bebaios)*. Peter abhors the emptiness of a mere profession that produces no fruit in a believer's life. Not that one's acts earn salvation, but the confirmation of calling and election exists in a life of faithfulness.* Peter's paraenesis (*see* Teaching, Paraenesis) is appropriate: unless the Christian virtues* of 2 Peter 1:5-9 now characterize a person's life, one has no evidence that the calling or election is authentic.

Peter employs the adjective *eklektos* ("elect") as a substantive to identify his Christian readers (1 Pet 1:1-2): they are the elect. According to these verses, Peter's apostolic ministry on behalf of God's dispersed elect is based on or grounded in God's foreknowledge, accomplished through the Spirit's work of sanctification, with the goal of obedience* to Jesus and the sprinkling of his blood. As mentioned above, Peter goes on to describe this elect body in corporate terms, applying to the church terms and categories that once described Israel, God's chosen nation (1 Pet 2:9-10). He ends his letter with a reference (presumably) to his own local fellowship of Christians using the term *syneklektos* ("she who is chosen with you"). The local church is an elect body.

Have some been predetermined *not* to believe? Some draw this conclusion from 1 Peter 2:8. However, most commentators agree that this was not Peter's intention here. He defines "unbelief" as disobedience to the message of salvation. Such unbelief leads, inevitably, to stumbling. God does not predestine some to reject Christ. But God has ordained that for such unbelievers Christ becomes a stumbling block, because no salvation exists apart from him. The failure to believe and obey accounts for their stumbling. This is God's predestined plan.

5. Conclusion and Early Christian Developments.

Does God choose individuals? In the realm of ministry, clearly he does. God chose people to perform certain tasks, functions or ministries for him. The clearest instance is his appointment of Christ for his redemptive career. Beyond that, Israel's ancestors and high priests and the church's missionaries and apostles are said to have their role as the result of God's elective activity. In the realm of salvation, the church is God's chosen people; once not a people, it is now the people of God—a nation chosen to declare God's mighty acts to an unbelieving world.

Has God specifically chosen certain ones to believe and be saved? This controversial question cannot be solved solely on the basis of the texts examined here. Apparently the earliest Christians following the age of the apostles did not understand that God chose some to be saved and others to be damned. The emphasis in the next century or so clearly resides with human free will to choose either for or against God. We find only a little evidence of divine determination of the elect. We can display only a small sample of evidence.

In a section of exhortation in *1 Clement* the writer urges prayer* and the keeping of God's commandments in the harmony of love,* "that through love our sins* may be forgiven* us." Then after quoting the pronouncement of blessing* from Psalm 32:1-2, he affirms, "This blessedness cometh upon those who have been chosen by God through Jesus Christ our Lord; to whom be glory for ever and ever" (*1 Clem.* 50.7). The kind of people one associates with demonstrates one's character and status. So "with a harmless man thou shalt prove thyself harmless, and with an elect man thou shalt be elect, and with a perverse man thou shalt show thyself perverse" (*1 Clem.* 46.3). The innocent and righteous prove themselves therefore to be the elect of God (*1 Clem.* 46.4). David is simply described as "the elect David" (*1 Clem.* 52.2).

In his praise of love the author affirms: "By love, have all the elect of God been made perfect; without love nothing is well-pleasing to God" (*1 Clem.* 49.5). At the book's outset the author, in praising the Corinthians, commends their concern for other believers, adding, "Day and night ye were anxious for the whole brotherhood, that the number of God's elect might be saved with mercy and a good conscience" (*1 Clem.* 2.4).

Because of the worthy example of the martyrs,* a great multitude was added to the number of the elect (*1 Clem.* 6.1). The author warns against causing others to sin, saying—reminiscent of Jesus—that it were better for a person not to have been born than for him to throw a stumbling block before one of the elect (*1 Clem.* 46.8). Praising God, the author affirms that God chose Jesus, and us through him to be a peculiar people (*1 Clem.* 58.2). The author appeals to the readers to draw near to God, the One who has made them an elect portion (*eklogēs meros*) for himself (*1 Clem.* 29.1).

In the introduction to his letter to the Ephesians, Ignatius* affirms that the Ephesians were predestined before the ages and elected through the true passion by the will of God (Ign. *Eph.* presc.). Likewise, in the introduction to the letter to the Trallians, Ignatius affirms that they are elect and worthy of God (Ign. *Trall.* presc.). Ignatius calls an individual named Agathopus "an elect man" (Ign. *Phld.* 11.1).

In the account of the martyrdom of Polycarp,* bishop of Smyrna, he is reported to have shown no ill effects when enveloped by flames and then pierced by a dagger. The onlookers expressed amazement that the elect, like Polycarp, were so different from unbelievers (*Mart. Pol.* 16.1). Those whom God saves are called his holy elect (*Mart. Pol.* 22.1).

In his *Dialogue with Trypho the Jew,* Justin Martyr (c. A.D. 100-65) writes, "But if the word of God foretells that some angels and men shall certainly be punished, it did so because it foreknew that they would be unchangeably [wicked], but not because God created them so. So if they repent,* all who wish for it can obtain mercy from God" ("Free-will in Men and Angels," chap. 141). Foreknowledge did not determine destiny.

Mathetes of Diognetus* (c. A.D. 130) includes a passage in which he ridicules the Jews who thought that circumcision* of the flesh* could be a proof of election (*Diogn.* 4.4).

The *Shepherd of Hermas* was probably composed between c. A.D. 90 and 150, possibly in stages. In his visions Hermas speaks of people as the elect of the Lord (*Herm. Vis.* 3.9.10; 4.2.5), his elect (e.g., *Herm. Vis.* 1.3.4), the elect of God (e.g., *Herm. Vis.* 2.1.3; 3.5.1) or simply the elect (e.g., *Herm. Vis.* 2.4.2). He sees that the elect of God will inhabit the age to come, "since those elected by God to eternal life will be spotless and pure" (*Herm. Vis.* 4.3.5). In the course of his vision the seer observes a tower surrounded by seven women. The explanation comes: the tower is supported by the women. The first woman is called Faith. "Through her the elect of God are saved" (*Herm. Vis.* 3.8.3). Salvation derives from repentance, for "if they will repent with all their heart, they will be enrolled in the Books of Life with the saints" (*Herm. Vis.* 1.3). With a severe warning it was revealed to Hermas that "the Lord has sworn by His glory, in regard to His elect, that if any one of them sin after a certain day which has been fixed, he shall not be saved. For the repentance of the righteous has limits" (*Herm. Vis.* 2.2.5). Clearly the concept of election departs from any rigid understanding of a fixed number that God has determined will be saved.

Barnabas (c. A.D. 100) refers to Christ as the elect one, the precious cornerstone (*Barn.* 6.2). In another section, after an extended appeal to obedience, the writer affirms that the Lord will judge the world and each person will receive "as he has done: if he is righteous, his righteousness will precede him; if he is wicked, the reward of wickedness is before him." He calls for faithfulness, and for his readers not to make the same mistake as the Jews before them who abandoned the Lord. The section concludes with a quotation from Matthew 20:16 introduced by "as it is written": "Many are called, but few are chosen" (*Barn.* 4.14).

Tatian (A.D. 110-72), the composer of the *Diatessaron,* a harmony of the Gospels, wrote in his *Address to the Greeks* 11, "Live to God, and by apprehending him lay aside your old nature. We were not created to die, but we die by our own fault. Our free will has destroyed us; we who were free have become slaves; we have been sold through sin. Nothing evil has been created by God; we ourselves have manifested wickedness; but we, who have manifested it, are able again to reject it." Free will to choose or reject God's provision determines one's eternal fate.

See also APOSTASY; CHRISTOLOGY; ENDURANCE, PERSEVERANCE; GRACE; SALVATION.

BIBLIOGRAPHY. D. Basinger and R. Basinger, eds., *Predestination and Free Will* (Downers Grove, IL: InterVarsity Press, 1986); R. J. Bauckham, *Jude, 2 Peter* (WBC; Waco, TX: Word, 1983); E. Best, *One Body in Christ* (London: SPCK, 1955); D. A. Carson, *Divine Sovereignty and Human Responsibility* (Atlanta: John Knox, 1981); L. Coenen, "Elect, Choose," *NIDNTT* 1:536-43; J. Daane, *The Freedom of God* (Grand Rapids: Eerdmans, 1973); J. H. Elliott, *The Elect and the Holy: An Exegetical Examination of 1 Peter 2:4-10* (NovTSupp 12; Leiden: E. J. Brill, 1966); R. Forster and V. P. Marston, *God's Strategy in Human History* (Wheaton, IL: Tyndale House, 1974); W. Grundmann, "δεῖ κτλ," *TDNT* 2:21-25; J. Jocz, *A Theology of Election* (London: SPCK, 1958); W. W. Klein, *The New Chosen People: A Corporate View of Election* (Grand Rapids: Zondervan, 1990); idem, "Paul's Use of *kalein*: A Proposal," *JETS* 27 (1984) 53-64; W. G. MacDonald, "The Biblical Doctrine of Election" in *The Grace of God, the Will of Man,* ed. C. Pinnock (Grand Rapids: Zondervan, 1988) 207-30; C. Pinnock, ed., *The Grace of God, the Will of Man: A Case for Arminianism* (Grand Rapids: Zondervan, 1988); A. Roberts and J. Donaldson, ed., *The Ante-Nicene Fathers* (10 vols.; Grand Rapids: Eerdmans, 1950-51 repr.); T. R. Schreiner and B. A. Ware, eds., *The Grace of God, the Bondage of the Will* (2 vols.; Grand Rapids: Baker, 1995); R. Shank, *Elect in the Son* (Springfield, MO: Westcott, 1970); R. P. Shedd, *Man in Community* (London: Epworth, 1958); C. S. Storms, *Chosen for Life: An Introductory Guide to the Doctrine of Divine Election* (Grand Rapids: Baker, 1987).

W. W. Klein

ELKESAITES. *See* JEWISH CHRISTIANITY.

EMPEROR, EMPEROR CULT

The office of Roman emperor was significant for Jews in the land and those in the Diaspora, as well as for the emerging group we now know as Christians. The command to pray for emperors (1 Tim 2:1-2) is tacit recognition of the power that this ruler held over Christians.

    1. A Survey of the Emperors
    2. The Emperor Cult

1. A Survey of the Emperors.

The vicissitudes of imperial rule and their implications for Jews and Christians are highlighted in the following survey, which concludes with a statement on the significance of the emperor.

1.1. Year of the Four Emperors. The year following Nero's death was one of civil unrest, as four men were acclaimed as emperor and sought to establish uncontested rule. The players in this tumultuous year were Galba, Otho, Vitellius and Vespasian.

Galba was governor of Tarragonian Spain in A.D. 68, when Vindex, the governor of Aquitaine who was rebelling against Nero, asked him to become the next emperor. Galba acceded to the request, encouraged by some favorable signs (Suetonius *Galba* 10).

The governor of Lusitania, Nero's close friend Otho, soon joined Galba in the coalition against Nero. But Galba's army turned against him when he refused to pay a promised donative. Otho also was particularly upset, since Galba named someone else as his successor. Otho therefore arranged a plot among the Praetorians, who killed Galba in Rome on January 15, 69, and proclaimed Otho emperor.

Meanwhile in lower Germany Vitellius was acclaimed "Emperor!" by his troops on January 2, 69. Immediately receiving the support of the troops in Gaul, Britain and Spain, he headed toward Italy. After he had begun this campaign, news of Galba's death reached him. Before he had left Germany's borders, his men had already marched on Otho in northern Italy, where the latter committed suicide. Thus Vitellius marched on Rome as a triumphant conqueror.

In the East, however, the general Vespasian was also contemplating the imperial office. After years of receiving signs of being a future emperor, then receiving Josephus's prophecy and having a favorable result from consulting "the God of Carmel" (Suetonius *Vespasian* 5; Josephus *J.W.* 3.8.9 §399-403), Vespasian gathered legions to support him and began a civil war. In July of 69 the legions of Egypt and Judea swore allegiance to Vespasian, and he was in Egypt when he heard of the assassination of Vitellius that occurred on December 20 that year.

1.2. Vespasian. Supported as emperor by the Roman legions of Egypt, Syria and Judea, Titus Flavius Vespasian (A.D. 9-79) gained an upper hand when the armies of the Danube joined his cause in August 69. Vespasian was formally recognized as emperor by the Senate soon after Vitellius's death. His reign therefore is dated 69-79. His accession is significant in that it marks the rise of an unexpected family to hold imperial power and to begin the Flavian dynasty (Vespasian, Titus, Domitian). To support this rise to power, Vespasian announced certain portents that he thought heralded his accession. He repeatedly made clear that his sons would follow him as emperor, an idea of succession that was not necessarily accepted by everyone in the Senate.

During Vespasian's reign Jerusalem* fell to Rome. Viewed not as a minor battle in a corner of the empire, this victory was celebrated with the minting of coins bearing the phrase *IUDAEA CAPTA* ("Judea is captured"). Since there was no longer a temple* in Jerusalem to which Jews could contribute, Vespasian decreed that each Jew in the empire was to be taxed two *denarii* annually, to go toward rebuilding the temple of Capitoline Jupiter in Rome.

Though he took stiff and unpopular measures to increase revenue, Vespasian's rule was generally looked on by the Romans as a good one, not least since he restored the Roman peace, another accomplishment celebrated on Vespasian's coins. Tacitus writes that he was the first emperor who improved in character while emperor (Tacitus *Hist.* 1.50). Tacitus also describes how a hesitant Vespasian healed a blind man and a man with a paralyzed hand in Alexandria,* both of whom had been told by the god Serapis to seek Vespasian for healing (Tacitus *Hist.* 4.8; cf. Suetonius *Vespasian* 7). He is reported to have remarked on his deathbed: "Alas, I think I am becoming a god" (*vae, puto deus fio*—Suetonius *Vespasian* 23).

1.3. Titus. Titus Flavius Vespasianus (A.D. 39-81) took an active part in helping his father jockey for power during the year of the four emperors. Half a year after Vespasian was acclaimed emperor by the Senate, Titus captured Jerusalem and oversaw the destruction of the temple (August 70). While he was in Judea he fell in love with Berenice, the daughter of Agrippa I. When she and her brother, Agrippa II, traveled to Rome around 75, Titus lived with her and perhaps promised to marry her, but this promise was not fulfilled (Suetonius *Titus* 7).

During his short reign (79-81) Titus was popular for his friendly personality and his generous use of funds for the people of Rome. He spent money to allay the destruction caused by Vesuvius in 79, and in the next year he released funds to offset the effects of the plague and fire in Rome. He also finished the Colosseum and constructed the public baths that are named after him. As Titus lay dying prematurely (about age 42), he complained that he did not deserve to die, since only one sin bothered his conscience. After giving this description Suetonius goes on to wonder whether that sin might have been incest between Titus and his sister-in-law, Domitia Longina (Suetonius *Titus* 10). Jewish tradition interprets this unspecified sin as being Titus's entry into the holy of holies in 70, before the destruction of the temple (*Sipre* Deut 328; *'Abot R. Nat.* B 7; *b. Git* 56b).

1.4. Domitian. Titus Flavius Domitianus (A.D. 51-96) was perhaps more unpopular than his brother, Titus, had been popular as emperor. He controlled the membership of the Senate and consulted the Senate only as a formality. Although his rule of the empire (81-96) was marked by efficiency and some good appointments, it also was marred by his personality. Suetonius tells us that in the beginning of his reign Domitian's virtues balanced his vices, but later this emperor changed his virtues into vices. His greed came from lack of funds and his cruelty from fear of assassination (Suetonius *Domitian* 3). Domitian's steps against Christians (*see* Persecution) were only a part of the generally pro-Roman, conservative morality he sought to enforce on the public. In 83 he sentenced three vestal virgins to be executed for immorality; in 90 he sentenced Cornelia, the chief vestal virgin, to be buried alive. He banished the philosophers from Italy twice (perhaps in 89 and 95). Suetonius tells us that Domitian levied the Jewish tax (see 1.2 above) very harshly (Suetonius *Domitian* 12.2). Instead of deifying him, as it had done with his brother and father, the Senate officially damned his memory and took legal action to remove his name from every monument or building. His death marked the end of the Flavian dynasty and the beginning of the era of the "five good emperors."

1.5. Nerva. The reign of Marcus Cocceius Nerva (A.D. 30?-98), chosen for his pro-Senate stance and peaceful demeanor, marks the start of a period in which the Senate's voice was heard and emperors were chosen for their ability rather than their popularity with the legions. Though they passed without scandal, Nerva's sixteen months of rule (96-98) were marred by his weak leadership, the lack of support from the army and direct opposition from the Praetorian Guard. He and his successor, Trajan, are thought to be the first emperors to use public funds for the support of poor children in Italian towns. (This marks the start of the *alimenta* system.) Nerva sought to distinguish himself from his predecessors by using moderation in the collection of the *fiscus Judaicus.* Coins minted during his short reign have the slogan *fisci Judaici calumnia sublata* ("malicious prosecution of the Jewish fund is removed"). It is likely that ethnic Jews who were not practicing their religion were now exempted from the tax. With this change Rome took a big step toward identifying Jews as a religious group rather than an ethnic people.

1.6. Trajan. Marcus Ulpius Traianus (A.D. 53-117) was adopted by Nerva in order to please the Praetorians and the armies of Rome, since the former had extensive military experience. But he nevertheless confirmed the Senate's privileges early in his reign, which is dated 98-117. He was a popular leader, and as the closing line of his letter to Pliny about the Christians illustrates, he was concerned to be tolerant (Pliny *Ep.* 10.97; *see* Persecution). Harried by two Dacian wars in Europe (101-2; 105-6), the Parthian war (113-17) and Jewish revolts in Cyrene, Egypt, Cyprus and Roman-held Mesopotamia (115-17), his reign was filled not only with enforcing the Roman peace internationally but also with building and welfare projects at home and abroad. His title *Optimus* seems well-earned.

1.7. Hadrian. Publius Aelius Hadrianus (A.D. 76-138), Spanish-born and appreciative of Greek culture and learning, represents an early step in an imperial succession that would see other foreign-born, non-Italian emperors. In his response to the question raised (c. 121-22) by the proconsul Silvanus Granianus, Hadrian affirmed Trajan's policy toward Christians (*see* Persecution).

For our purposes Hadrian is most notorious for building a temple to Jupiter Capitolinus on the site of the Jerusalem temple and forbidding Jews to circumcise their male children (*see* Circumcision). The Second Jewish Revolt (also called Bar Kokhba, after its Jewish leader) re-

sulted in 132-35. Christians in Judea did not side with the militant Jews in this uprising. The result was tragic persecution for the Jews and more lenient treatment of Christians. Though it was not the only cause of the separation of Christianity from its spiritual mother, this war certainly is a major factor (*see* Christianity and Judaism). Though it is difficult to conceive of anything as demoralizing as the loss of the temple that occurred in 70, Rome's conquest in this war was perhaps equally tragic, for Rome no longer recognized Judea; it became *Syria Palaestina,* no longer to be ruled by a local king as in the previous centuries but now under a consular legate with two legions to stifle any thought of questioning Rome's power.

In foreign policy Hadrian was more defensive than his predecessor had been. Hadrian's wall in England illustrates his strategy of choosing defensible borders and holding them. Hadrian is also known for touring the empire with his young male lover, Antinous. When the latter drowned in the Nile River in 130, he was immediately deified at Hadrian's insistence. This is the background to Justin's stinging attack on Antinous's deification (*Apol. I* 29). It has been suggested that Hadrian's homosexuality is in the background of 2 Peter 2:7 (cf. Jude 6-7, where the problem is human-angelic intercourse), but this cannot be proven. If so, it would only strengthen the obvious historical datum that as in the Judaisms* of the Hellenistic age, so in the early church: homosexuality was continuously regarded as immoral.

1.8. Antoninus Pius. Titus Aurelius Fulvus Boionius Antoninus (A.D. 86-161), known for his integrity and his firm belief in Rome's mission in the world, was given the title *Pius* ("devout one") by the Senate, with whom he had a harmonious relationship all during his reign (137-61). An Italian who believed in Rome's past and treasured this heritage, Antoninus may never have left Italy while he was emperor. Proconsul of Asia for three years (133-36), as emperor Antoninus kept his legates and officials in domestic and foreign posts in office for longer periods of time. This was part of a tendency to centralize government control and to encourage the development of the bureaucracy. Aelius Aristides's oration "To Rome" pictures the peaceful and beneficent Roman Empire under this emperor. While there were some foreign revolts during his tenure, Antoninus experienced nothing of the foreign threats that later emperors, including Marcus Aurelius, would.

1.9. Marcus Aurelius. Born Marcus Annius Verus (A.D. 121-80), this man was known better by his imperial name, Marcus Aurelius Antoninus. His reign (161-80) marks the end of the era of the five good emperors. Conservative in Roman values and committed to Stoicism, this man was preoccupied with fighting wars to keep Rome's borders strong. There was instability in Mesopotamia, Syria, Egypt and Britain during his reign, but most familiar are the Roman battles north of the Danube, where Marcus Aurelius personally led his troops in battle and died. His letters to Fronto, written in Latin, still survive, but he is best known for his *Meditations (Ta eis heauton),* a sort of philosophical diary written in Greek. The latter work contains some veiled references to Christians (identified by C. R. Haines—1.6; 3.16.1; 7.68; 8.48; 8.51.2; 11.3), whom Marcus Aurelius persecuted. Though he was a conscientious ruler, his wars and public spending depleted the treasury, and the economic crises of the third century were not unrelated to trends already in motion during his reign.

1.10. The Significance of the Emperor. The Roman emperors, especially the five good emperors, were convinced that they were prime agents for the welfare of humanity *(salus generis humani).* Part of this responsibility involved maintaining moral and social order, as Paul notes in Romans 13:3-4. In addition, generosity *(liberalitas)* was an expected virtue for emperors. We might think Gaius Caligula's habit of throwing coins to his people from the top of the Basilica Iulia to be odd (Suetonius *Caligula* 37.1; Josephus *Ant.* 19.1.11 §71; Dio Cassius 59.25.5), but his practice of throwing out tokens for gifts (*missilia;* Suetonius *Caligula* 18.2) was followed by several other emperors (Suetonius *Nero* 11; Suetonius *Domitian* 4.5; Dio Cassius 61.18.1-2; 66.25.5; 67.4.4; 69.8.2). Titus's famous exclamation that he had wasted a day—upon realizing that he had given no favors to anyone that day—illustrates how seriously at least this emperor took the expectations of generosity that accompanied his office (Suetonius *Titus* 8).

The office included the weighty responsibility of hearing many petitions and being expected to answer them, as well as returning gifts received with even more bountiful favors. Sometimes emperors refused gifts from municipalities when they were not ready to reciprocate with favors valued at the expected fourfold or more of the embassy's gift to the emperor. Indeed, J. A. Overman thinks that Matthew's presentation of the magi bringing gifts to Jesus does not represent an act of pure worship*; he sees it rather as an embassy that expected a return favor.

In general the NT authors (except the author of Revelation) and probably most Christians living outside of direct persecution had more positive views of the emperors than do modern readers. The angel's words to Paul, "You must stand before Caesar!" (Acts 27:24), as well as the line from his conversion story that he would be stand before "kings of the sons of Israel" (Acts 9:15), illustrate the importance that monarchs had in the first-century person's mind. Romans 13:1-7, 1 Peter 2:13-14 and the famous "render to Caesar" logion (Mt 22:21; Mk 12:17; Lk 20:25; *Gos. Thom.* 100; Justin *Apol. I* 17.2) expect obedience* to the emperor. The NT also includes commands to pray for the emperor (1 Tim 2:1-2) and to honor him (1 Pet 2:17), commands that are predicated on God's establishment of emperors to office, even Nero (Rom 13:1—written c. 56-58).

2. The Emperor Cult.

In the East the worship of kings as divine beings had precedents in the practices of the Hittites and the Egyptians, whose rulers (including the Ptolemies) were worshiped as divine while they reigned. It is more difficult to detect an official cult for the living king in other kingdoms such as the neo-Babylonian, Assyrian and Persian. In the Persian case we know that Cyrus was deified after his death, and a continuous cult was established for him that lasted presumably even into the Principate, when Rome experienced the burgeoning of its own imperial cult. The material that follows is general in nature; investigators of the imperial cult in a given city or province must consult studies explicitly focused on those areas, since the evidence points to a significant variety in cult practice throughout the empire.

2.1. Roman Imperial Cult. In NT and second-century times the imperial cult was primarily of the latter type mentioned; that is, the deification of a deceased ruler and the establishment of a worship regimen to that newly acclaimed deity. In our time period the following rulers were deified after their deaths: Julius Caesar, Augustus (and later his wife Livia—renamed Julia Augusta), Claudius, Vespasian, Titus, Hadrian and Antoninus Pius. Though the apotheosis of Claudius was satirized by Seneca in his *Apocolocyntosis* ("The Pumpkinification"), it is inaccurate to say that the elite of society were skeptical of the imperial cult as an institution. It continued to be a part of Roman life that was seriously followed, even under Christian emperors.

One discernible change in the cult is that it moved from being a religious act to a political stamp of approval. In the first century or so, the Senate would decide to apotheosize an emperor after his funeral if a witness had seen the soul of the deceased emperor rise to heaven. Later evidence shows that the Senate's decision to deify someone could occur before the funeral, motivated presumably by the political sentiment toward the deceased emperor and pressure from the next emperor to deify his predecessor.

2.2. The Significance of the Imperial Cult. Besides official deification that occurred by an act of the Senate after an emperor's death, sacrifices* were already performed to the *genius* ("spirit") of living emperors. This practice often was demanded of Christians; refusal to perform such worship constituted legal grounds for the execution of Christians in some later periods of persecution.

Though there is no clear evidence that Christian emperors promoted the cult, they did allow it to continue. Constantine granted one city's wish to construct its own temple for the imperial cult and allowed the imperial cult games to continue, with only the stipulation that sacrifices be discontinued (*ILS* 705).

The NT is clearly against the imperial cult, though there is some intratestamental tension in picturing the emperor. Acts 12:20-23 illustrates how the ruler cult was used by people petitioning a monarch. Its description of the death of Herod Agrippa I also reveals a decidedly monotheistic disapproval of such cult worship. Revelation (*see* Revelation, Book of) is clearly against the imperial cult as well, with its caricatures of the cult (Rev 13:4-8, 12-17) and judgments* directly linked to one's involvement with the cult (Rev 14:9-12; 20:4). The specter of the imperial cult certainly makes Revelation's portraits of the emperor(s) the most negative among the NT books. The Roman emperors are pictured as evil beasts* (Rev 13; 17:3-12), and it is unimaginable that the author of Revelation could accept Romans 13:2, since Revelation describes the imperial establishment as directly hostile to God, far different from the picture in Paul's mind during the quiet years of Nero's early reign. Whatever a given author's perspective on the imperial system, however, they remain united in expectation for the enthronement of the coming King (*see* Exaltation) and can even use imperial language to describe him (Phil 2:9-11; Col 1:16-17; 2 Pet 1:11; Rev 11:15; 17:14; 19:6-8).

See also CIVIL AUTHORITY; PERSECUTION; RELIGIONS, GRECO-ROMAN; REVELATION, BOOK OF; ROMAN EMPIRE, CHRISTIANS AND THE.

BIBLIOGRAPHY. J. Béranger, *Recherches sur l'aspect idéologique du principat* (Basel: F. Reinhardt, 1953); H. C. Boren, *Roman Society* (2d ed.; Lexington, MA: D. C. Heath, 1992); G. F. Chestnut, "The Ruler and the Logos in Neopythagorean, Middle Platonic, and Late Stoic Political Philosophy," *ANRW* 17.2 (1978) 1310-32; R. Combès, *Imperator* (Paris: Presses universitaires de France, 1966); E. Faust, *Pax Christ et Pax Caesaris* (Freiburg: Universitätsverlag; Göttingen: Vandenhoeck & Ruprecht, 1993); J. R. Fears, "Rome: The Ideology of Imperial Power," *Thought* 55 (March 1980) 98-109; D. Fishwick, *The Imperial Cult in the Latin West* (Leiden: E. J. Brill, 1987); E. R. Goodenough, "The Political Philosophy of Hellenistic Kingship," *YCS* 1 (1928) 55-102; M. Goodman, "Nerva, the *Fiscus Judaicus* and Jewish Identity," *JRS* 79 (1989) 40-44; R. M. Grant, *Augustus to Constantine* (New York: Harper & Row, 1970); C. R. Haines, ed., *Marcus Aurelius* (LCL; Cambridge, MA: Harvard University Press; London: Heinemann, 1979 [1916]); F. Millar, *The Emperor in the Roman World* (Ithaca, NY: Cornell University Press, 1977); J. A. Overman, "Matthew's Parables and Roman Politics" in *SBLSP* (1995) 425-39; *Oxford Classical Dictionary* (2d ed.; Oxford: Oxford University Press, 1970) passim; B. Parsi, *Désignation et investiture de l'empereur romain* (Paris: Sirey, 1963); S. R. F. Price, "From Noble Funerals to Divine Cult" in *Rituals of Royalty,* ed. D. Cannadine and S. R. F. Price (Cambridge: Cambridge University Press, 1987) 56-105; idem, *Rituals and Power* (Cambridge: Cambridge University Press, 1984); G. E. M. de Ste Croix, "Why Were the Early Christians Persecuted?" in *Studies in An-*

cient Society, ed. M. I. Finley (London: Routledge & Kegan Paul, 1974) 210-49; L. R. Taylor, *The Divinity of the Roman Emperor* (Middletown, CT: American Philological Association, 1931); K. Wengst, *Pax Romana and the Peace of Jesus Christ* (Philadelphia: Fortress, 1987).

M. Reasoner

END TIMES. *See* ESCHATOLOGY.

ENDURANCE, PERSEVERANCE

Endurance is a characteristic mark of a Christian in the NT. The key Greek word that conveys this point is *hypomenō* or *hypomonē*. This word presumes that the Christian life garners opposition that must be met by spiritual resistance. The opposition may come from formal or informal persecution* or from the general difficulties of life. Although it is natural to view the suffering* this brings as a negative, the NT encourages Christians to contemplate the long-range blessing* of successfully overcoming hardship for Christ* and enduring to the end. Endurance is a virtue* needed for the Christian's transition from suffering to blessing.

A second word, *makrothymeō* or *makrothymia,* also encourages endurance as a characteristic mark of a Christian but in a different sense. This word, most often translated "patience," views endurance as a quality of personal relationships. It is not a response to opposition as much as a voluntary act of love* for difficult and irritating people. As opposed to becoming angry and upset with others, Christians who endure in this sense control themselves and are able to do so indefinitely.

Both *hypomenō* and *makrothymeō* describe Christians waiting for the return of Christ. Both qualities appear in lists of virtues, although *makrothyme* appears more often. However, *makrothyme* is used to describe God's attitude toward humanity, both in the NT and in the OT, but *hypomen* is never used to refer to God.* Despite this fact, the word is used to pinpoint the quality of Christ that Christians can and should imitate in their own lives.

1. The Greek and Jewish Background
2. Acts, the General Epistles and Revelation
3. Early Church Fathers

1. The Greek and Jewish Background.

1.1. Suffering as God's Discipline. J. A. Sanders identifies Jeremiah as the hub in the Jewish understanding of hardship as a positive value within God's activity. Acquaintance with the idea that God expects his people to learn at least repentance* through hardship comes as early as Amos 4:6-11. However, it is in Jeremiah, beginning with Jeremiah 2:30, that the concept is established. There the people of Judah are told that their ancestors* failed to respond to God's correcting punishment *(mûsar).* The tenor of instruction that follows is that they must do so in order for a new covenant* relationship with God to occur (Jer 5:3; 6:8; 7:28; 30:14; 35:13). Other passages that reflect the concept but without elaboration include Isaiah 9:12; 42:25; 57:17; Ezekiel 16:27-28; 23:18-20; Amos 4:6-11; Zephaniah 3:2; Haggai 2:17; and Zechariah 1:6. On an individual, as opposed to a corporate national, basis the concept can be seen in Job 5:17; 13:10; 22:4; 33:19; 42:1-6; Psalm 6:2; 22:1-21; 38:2; 39:12; 51:9-10; 73:14; 94:12; 119:25-26; Proverbs 3:11-12; 15:10.

C. H. Talbert has distinguished between Jewish and Greco-Roman perspectives on suffering. Besides the obvious differences conditioned by a pagan, pantheistic concept of the divine and a personal, monotheistic concept, he perceives in Jewish writings the purpose for suffering to be correction of misdirection. Key texts cited in support include Deuteronomy 8:5; Proverbs 15:32; Malachi 3:3; Wisdom of Solomon 3:5-6; 11:9; Sirach 2:1-6; 4:17; 18:13; 2 Maccabees 6:12-17; 7:33; 10:4; *Psalms of Solomon* 13:7-10; 18:4-5; *2 Apoc. Bar.* 13:10; Philo *Congr.* 160, 175; *The Words of the Heavenly Lights* III; 1QH 8; *b. Sanh.* 101a; *b. Ber.* 5a, b; *Sipre* 32.

In Greco-Roman literature the purpose of suffering, Talbert observes, focuses on strengthening and improving character. Chief support for this comes from Aeschylus (*Agamemnon* 177), Sophocles (*Oedipus at Colonus* 7), Herodotus (*History* 1.207), Plato (*Rep.* 380b), Dio Chrysostom (*Or.* 8), Seneca (*On Providence* 1.5; 2.5-6; 4.5-7) and Epictetus (*Disc.* 1.24.1-3; 3.10.7-8).

Talbert holds that the Jewish and Greco-Roman perspectives on suffering merge in 4 Maccabees 11:12, 20, 27; 16:24-25; 17:2, 11, 12, 18. He proceeds to show how both the Greco-Roman and Jewish concepts of suffering reside in James,* 1 Peter,* Hebrews* and Luke-Acts (*see* Acts).

1.2. Endurance in the Testament of Job. C. Haas traces the vocabulary of endurance in the *Testament of Job,* viewed by many scholars as the document behind the comments of James 5:11 rather than the biblical book of Job because of the former's more positive characterization of Job. From this work Haas recognizes endurance *(hypomenō)* to mean "to stand firm" (in battle; *T. Job* 4:6; 5:1). He further suggests that *karteria* means "stubbornness" or "toughness" *(T. Job* 4:10; 27:4) and that that patience *(makrothymia)* implies waiting for God's saving intervention *(T. Job* 24:1; 26:5).

2. Acts, the General Epistles and Revelation.

2.1. Mark of Christian Maturity. Endurance turns the cycle of Christian maturity (Jas 1:2-4). James* was possibly written in the early days of the church to Christians who had fled Jerusalem* because of vicious persecution following Stephen's* martyrdom* (Acts 8:1). The letter addresses the immaturity of Christians who face humiliation (Jas 2:5-8) and injustice (Jas 5:1-6) from nonbelievers as well as jealousy and enmity from fellow believers (Jas 4:1-3; 5:8-9).

From the outset (Jas 1:2-4) the letter calls on its readers to meet the variety of trials life offers not with uncertainty and failure (Jas 1:6-8), which seems to have characterized their experience thus far, but with confidence that stems from a growing, substantial faith* and trust in God who provides insight and success (Jas 1:5). James 1:2-4 teaches that anything which tests Christian faith requires determined endurance in order to pass the test and to gain maturity. This is a continuous cycle that builds from one success to the next. Perseverance and maturity from one trial prepares one for ever greater challenges to Christian faith that result in yet greater maturity as the Christian moves toward full potential or "complete maturity." Endurance is the key to this cycle of growth.

2.2. Mark of God's Blessing. Endurance pleases God and draws out his blessing. James 1:12, continuing under the banner of James 1:2-4 (repeating the three key words: "endure," "trial," "test"), makes "endurance under trial" the primary goal of the Christian. By enduring a lifetime of difficulty but remaining faithful, Christians demonstrate their love for God and receive his blessing. James calls this the "crown of life," perhaps having in mind a royal crown (Rev 4:4; 6:2; 12:1) but more likely a bay or an olive wreath for the victor in an athletic contest (1 Cor 9:25; 2 Tim 2:5). The metaphor indicates

that God is watching and judging the performance of Christians. In any case the reward* is eternal life (Rev 2:10). James intends to motivate his readers beyond their immature failures toward a Christian life of endurance by reminding them of the reality of this eternal blessing. James 5:10-11 offers Job as one of numerous OT examples that provide proof that God indeed blesses those who endure life's difficulties.

Like James, Hebrews* is also written to a Christian community (heavily Jewish), probably in Rome,* that has withstood the hardship of persecution in the past. At the brink of a new wave of persecution, however, it seems the second generation of believers is faltering (Heb 12:4; 13:13-14). Waning confidence in their beliefs makes them susceptible not only to persecution but also to renegade doctrine (Heb 3:12-14; 10:35; 13:9). The writer of Hebrews endeavors to renew their confidence in the superiority of their faith and motivate them to endure these difficult days and to regain their boldness for Christ.

Like James 1:12, Hebrews 6:12 explains that God's eternal blessing is at stake when it emphasizes that such lifelong endurance, teamed with faith, enables believers "to inherit what has been promised." Hebrews 10:32-39 reminds its readers of the great sacrifices they have already made for their Christian faith and pleads with them not to turn back. In order to "receive what he has promised," the believer must not "shrink back." Hebrews 12:7-13 explains that the struggles of Christians, especially against sin, are part of God's fatherly discipline to make them holy* like God himself and that successful endurance will bring about his delight.

Like James 5:10-11, Hebrews 6:13-15 offers documentation of God's surety in the life of Abraham,* whose endurance enabled him to receive "what was promised." Hebrews 12:1 reminds Christians, following the great examples of faithfulness chronicled in Hebrews 11 (Moses* is said to endure: *ekarterēsen,* Heb 11:27), that they are not alone in this struggle. A host of others are cheering Christians on to endure successfully "the race marked out for us." Hope* in receiving God's promised blessing, as they have, should provide motivation to endure also.

2.3. Mark of Identity with Christ. The most pervasive concept of endurance in this literature views every vital facet of endurance to be embodied in the person and work of Christ. He is placed before Christians as the ultimate model and strength for a Christian's endurance.

Employing a stirring athletic metaphor (as does Jas 1:12), Hebrews 12:1-3 challenges its readers who contemplate quitting the Christian life under the pressure of persecution instead to renew the vigor of their convictions by listening to the cheering crowd ("cloud of witnesses") but mostly by looking ahead to the one who stands waiting and encouraging at the finish line. Having completed the rigorous course successfully, Christ now looks back, eager for Christian runners to lock onto his eyes and "run with perseverance" to complete the course. Christ is not only a model and encourager, as "author and perfecter of our faith," but also teams up with the believer to supply the additional spiritual resources required for endurance. The passage encourages its readers to do their part by stripping off any worldly impediments that weigh them down and by laying aside their own sin that trips them up.

In Hebrews 12:3 the readers are told to look to Jesus not only as the model for victory but also as a model of suffering. Sinful people, blind to his sinlessness, tortured him on the cross. He suffered physically and spiritually beyond anything the believer can imagine. Yet even death did not defeat him. So the believers, like Christ, must endure the hardship confronting them and not "become discouraged" and give up, if necessary even shedding their blood (Heb 12:4).

The believer's identification with Christ culminates in the joy* and blessing of Christ's enthronement to the right hand of God (Heb 12:2; see Exaltation). Blessing awaits Christians who endure as well.

First Peter* is written to Gentile* Christians (1 Pet 1:14, 18, 21; 2:11) in Asia Minor who are experiencing persecution in their social contexts, possibly around the time of Nero, who accused Christians of setting fire to Rome in A.D. 64. Distrusted by their neighbors because of their beliefs, Christians are being treated like criminals and outcasts in their own communities (1 Pet 4:12-19). They suffer specifically because they bear the name* of Christ (1 Pet 2:16). The letter attempts to dissipate their fears* (1 Pet 3:14) and lead them to trust God (1 Pet 4:19) no matter the level of suffering they must endure.

Like Hebrews, 1 Peter views identification with Christ as the crucial principle to motivate these suffering Christians to the highest planes of endurance. The key passage, 1 Peter 2:19-25, focuses on the problem of the Christians who are suffering unjustly. They are asked to contemplate the alternative: receiving punishment for just cause. Which is the preferable way for Christians to witness* to their misunderstanding neighbors as well as identify the Christian most closely with Christ? The passage elaborates the injustice yet the necessity of Christ's torture and death on the cross despite his sinlessness (see Death of Christ). Therefore identification with Christ is accomplished not by enduring a beating for wrongdoing but by suffering "for doing good" and enduring it (1 Pet 2:20). Christians must trust themselves to God's judgment and not allow human judgments to affect them.

1 John (see John, Letters of) seeks to sustain the loyalty of believers, probably in and around Ephesus, who are barraged by heretical (probably pre-gnostic; see Gnosis, Gnosticism), second-generation challenges to apostolic christology* concerning the real humanity of Christ and enticements to worldly practices (1 Jn 2:22; 4:2; 5:1, 5, 6). Substantial numbers of people have broken away from the orthodox church* and are soliciting many others to join them (1 Jn 2:19; 4:5). Suffering comes in the form of "believers" haranguing other believers, the former having been affected, says the epistle, by worldly ambitions. Those who endure the onslaught from the evil world* are called "overcomers" (from nikaō; 1 Jn 2:13, 14; 4:4; 5:4, 5) and can achieve this status only because of their faith in Christ.

Revelation (see Revelation, Book of), written to solidify the faith of believers faced with severe persecution, possibly from the government, clarifies "overcomer" as a term of identification with Christ when it uses the term both for Christians who endure (Rev 2:7, 11, 17, 26; 3:5, 12, 21; 11:7; 21:7) and for Christ himself persisting against the evil of the world (Rev 5:5; 6:2; 12:11; 17:14; also Jn 16:33). Revelation 3:21 sets out this identification when it states that the one who "overcomes," like the one who "overcame," will receiving the blessing of a throne.

2.4. Mark of the True Church. John opens Revelation by presenting himself as representing the church in the suffering he has endured on Patmos as a result of preaching the Word of God and sharing his testimony of Jesus Christ (Rev 1:9). The letters to the seven churches that soon follow proceed to evaluate these churches, among other criteria, as to whether they have endured persecution successfully. He compliments Ephesus, Thyatira and Philadelphia for their endurance (Rev 2:2, 3, 19; 3:10) and assumes that idea with regard to Smyrna and Pergamum (Rev 2:10; 2:13). For Sardis and Laodicea the compliment notably is lacking.

2.5. Mark of Martyrdom. Martyrdom for those who endure extends from their identification with Christ. His suffering and endurance led to death and so it could for enduring Christians (Heb 12:4; 1 Pet 2:24; 3:18). The emergence of the beast out of the sea and the beast out of the earth in Revelation signal the call for the ultimate choice for Christians: remain true to the Lamb* or worship the beast.* For the "saints" to endure (Rev 13:9-10; 14:12-13) could well mean death, or martyrdom. "Blessed are the dead who die in the Lord from now on."

2.6. Mark of Christian Virtue. In 2 Peter 1:6 endurance *(hypomonē)* appears between self-control and godliness in a list of Christian virtues. It is synonymous here with patience *(makrothymia)*, which is much more common in these lists, especially in Paul's letters (2 Cor 6:4; Gal 5:2; Eph 4:2; Col 3:12; 2 Tim 3:10). In this sense the idea has to do with controlling anger toward others out of love for them (1 Cor 13:4). Patient endurance, among other Christian virtues, reflects the nature of God renewing the Christian into his own character (1 Pet 1:3-4).

2.7. Mark of God's Character. Since patient endurance in the Christian reflects the nature of God, it stands to reason that God's own character is said to exemplify this trait. 2 Peter,* which defends God's character from the attack of second-generation teachers who mock God's promise* that he will return to judge and condemn this sinful world, extols the enduring patience of God (2 Pet 3:9, 15) to explain why God might seem "slow in keeping his promise" to come in judgment upon humanity. God's patient endurance provides for many more people the opportunity for salvation.* This is consistent with Paul's use of "endurance" *(makrothymia)* in Romans 2:4 and Romans 9:22. God's long-suffering nature toward Israel* and humanity is a major OT theme.

2.8. Mark of Expecting the Lord's Return. Enduring patience is not only a characteristic of

God concerning his coming in judgment. It also is to characterize Christians awaiting the Lord's coming. The beleaguered Christians who are addressed in James long for the Lord* to come soon to relieve them from their situation (Jas 5:1-6). James 5:7-8 encourages them to wait patiently *(makrothymeō)* for the Lord's return (probably meaning Christ's), being as convinced of its coming as the farmer who relies on the certainty of changing seasons. In Hebrews endurance is also in the context of preparing for the approaching day of the Lord (Heb 10:25; *see* Day of the Lord).

3. Early Church Fathers.

3.1. Continuity. For the most part the vocabulary of endurance lined out in Acts, the General Epistles, Revelation and in the NT as a whole remains unchanged in the writings of the apostolic fathers.* Both patience *(makrothymia)* and endurance *(hypomenē)* continue as synonyms for putting up with the irritations of others and appear on numerous lists of positive Christian traits, sometimes together *(Barn.* 2.2; Ign. *Smyrn.* 12.2; Ign. *Pol.* 6.2; Ign. *Eph.* 3.1), sometimes separately *(Barn.* 20.2; *Herm. Man.* 5.1.1-2; 8:9-10; *Did.* 3.8; 5.2; Pol. *Phil.* 9.1; 13.2; *Herm. Sim.* 8.7.6; *Herm. Vis.* 1.2.3; *1 Clem.* 49.5). According to *Hermas Mandate* 5.1.6, anger cannot be "mingled" with patience without patience being "polluted."

Endurance typifies identification with the sufferings of Christ (Ign. *Smyrn.* 4.2; *Barn.* 5.1-12). Enduring torments is the mark of the true church (*2 Clem.* 16.7; *Herm. Vis.* 2.2.7). Endurance is associated with waiting for the Lord's return (*1 Clem.* 35.3).

3.2. Martyrdom, Completion and Miscellaneous Meanings. Association of endurance with martyrdom strengthens in works of the early church fathers. Both Peter and Paul are noted as enduring to the point of suffering martyrdom (*1 Clem.* 5.5, 7), as are Ignatius,* Zosimus and Rufus (Pol. *Phil.* 9.1). Polycarp* rejects being nailed to his funeral pyre, contending that God who "gives me strength to endure the fire" will also keep him from "moving in the pile" (*Mart. Pol.* 13.3). The *Martyrdom of Polycarp* 2 stresses that "all the martyrdoms" must be admired for the awful tortures they "endured": wild beasts, beds of spikes, scourgings that exposed veins and arteries (also *Diogn.* 10.8).

Endurance continues to be a mark of God's

blessing (Ign. *Magn.* 1.3; 9.2; Ign. *Pol.* 3.1; *Diogn.* 5.5; *2 Clem.* 11.5; *Mart. Pol.* 2.3; Pol. *Phil.* 8.2). However, reward does not hinge necessarily on enduring suffering. It may be completion of life with its various hardships without relinquishing Christian faith (Pol. *Phil.* 1.2) or baptism* (Ign. *Pol.* 6.2). Ignatius's *Letter to the Smyrneans* 9.2 is typical: "May God recompense you for whose sake you endure all things."

The role of endurance in spiritual maturity does not seem to continue past the epistle of James. Patience *(makrothymia)* remains a characteristic of God (*Herm. Man.* 5.2.3; *Herm. Sim.* 8.11; *1 Clem.* 19.3; *Barn.* 3.6; *Diogn.* 8.7; 9.2). Exhibited in a person, it is a mark of the indwelling Holy Spirit* (*Herm. Man.* 5.1.1-2). However, "endurance" *(hypomonē)* is used once in reference to God, but that reference is negative: *Barnabas* 2.5 says God cannot endure new moons and sabbaths.*

See also FAITH; HOPE; MARTYRDOM; PERSECUTION; SUFFERING.

BIBLIOGRAPHY. D. R. Denton, "Hope and Perseverance," *SJT* 34 (1981) 313-20; U. Falkenroth and C. Brown, "Patience," *NIDNTT* 3:765-76; C. Haas, "Job's Perseverance in the Testament of Job" in *Studies in the Testament of Job,* ed. M. A. Knibb and P. W. van der Horst (New York: Cambridge University Press, 1989); F. Hauch, "ὑπομένω," *TDNT* 4:582-88; D. Hill, "On Suffering and Baptism in 1 Peter," *NovT* 18 (1976) 181-89; D. Johnson, "Fire in God's House: Imagery from Malachi in Peter's Theology of Suffering (1 Pet 4:12-19)," *JETS* 29 (1986) 285-94; A. R. C. Leaney, "Eschatological Significance of Human Suffering in the Old Testament and the Dead Sea Scrolls," *SJT* 16 (1963) 286-96; S. McKnight, "The Warning Passages of Hebrews: A Formal Analysis and Theological Conclusions," *TJ* 13 (1992) 21-59; I. H. Marshall, *Kept by the Power of God* (Minneapolis: Bethany House, 1975); idem, "The Problem of Apostasy in the New Testament" in *Jesus the Savior: Studies in New Testament Theology* (Downers Grove, IL: InterVarsity Press, 1990) 306-24; T. Oberholtzer, "The Warning Passages in Hebrews," *BSac* 145 (1988) 83-97, 319-28, 410-19; *BSac* 146 (1989) 67-75; T. Osborne, "Guidelines for Christian Suffering: A Source-Critical and Theological Study of 1 Peter 2:21-25," *Bib* 64 (1983) 381-408; R. Peterson, "The Perseverance of the Saints: A Theological Exegesis of Four Key New Testament Passages," *Presbyterion* 17 (1991) 95-112; J. E.

Rosscup, "The Overcomer of the Apocalypse," *GTJ* 3 (1982) 261-86; J. A. Sanders, *Suffering as Divine Discipline in the Old Testament and Post-Biblical Judaism* (Rochester, NY: Colgate Rochester Divinity School, 1955); J. P. M. Sweet, "Maintaining the Testimony of Jesus: The Suffering of Christians in the Revelation of John" in *Suffering and Martyrdom in the New Testament,* ed. W. Horburg and B. McNeil (New York: Cambridge University Press, 1981) 101-17; C. H. Talbert, *Learning Through Suffering: The Educational Value of Suffering in the New Testament and Its Milieu* (Collegeville, MN: Liturgical Press, 1991); J. Wolmarans, "Making Sense out of Suffering: James 1:2-4," *Hervormde Teologiese Studies* 47 (1991) 1109-21.   W. R. Baker

ENTHRONEMENT. *See* EXALTATION, ENTHRONEMENT.

EPHESUS. *See* CENTERS OF CHRISTIANITY.

EPISTLES. *See* LETTER, LETTER FORM.

ESAU. *See* ANCESTORS.

ESCHATOLOGY

In order to understand NT theology it is necessary to grasp how the NT authors viewed eschatology, or the "end times" (see Marshall 1978 "Slippery Words"). For them the end times were not a period coming only at the final phase of history. This can be illustrated by the phrase "latter days" (or similar expressions), which occurs numerous times in the NT and rarely refers exclusively to the end of history as we think of it. Without exception it is used to describe the end times as beginning in the events associated with the life, death and resurrection* of Jesus Christ* (*see* Death of Christ).

1. Background
2. Eschatology of Acts, Hebrews, the General Epistles and Revelation
3. Special Problems of Eschatology in Revelation
4. Eschatology of the Apostolic Fathers

1. Background.

1.1. Eschatology of the Old Testament. NT phrases such as "latter days" allude to or echo phrases in the OT, where this wording appears in prophetic contexts referring to a future series of events: (1) Israel* will undergo tribulation consisting of exile (Jer 23:20; cf. Jer 30:24), subsequent oppression (Ezek 38:14-17), persecution* (Dan 10:14; 11:27—12:10), false teaching, deception and apostasy* (Dan 10:14ff.; 11:27-35). (2) After the tribulation Israel will seek the Lord (Hos 3:4-5) and will be delivered (Ezek 38:14-16; Dan 10:14; 12:1-13) while their enemies will be judged (Ezek 38:14-16; Dan 10:14; 11:40-45; 12:2). (3) This deliverance and judgment* will occur because a leader (Messiah) from Israel will finally conquer all of its Gentile* enemies (Gen 49:1, 8-12; Num 24:14-19; Is 2:2-4; Mic 4:1-3; Dan 2:28-45; 10:14—12:10). (4) The saints of Israel will be raised from the dead (Dan 12:2). (5) God will establish a new covenant* with Israel (cf. Jer 31:31-34 with Jer 30:24). (6) God will establish a kingdom on the earth and rule over it (Is 2:2-4; Dan 2:28-45; Mic 4:1-3) together with a Davidic king (Hos 3:4-5). (7) Some of Israel's Gentile enemies will experience deliverance during these eschatological days (Jer 47:48; 49:39; cf. Is 19:19-25).

The OT does not always employ the technical terminology of "latter days" when it addresses eschatological themes. For example, Isaiah's prophecy of the new creation* is overtly eschatological, but no eschatological formula introduces the prophecy (cf. Is 65:17; 66:22). Joel's prophecy of the Holy Spirit* is introduced by "after this" (for further discussion of OT eschatology, see Pryor, Gowan).

1.2. Eschatology of Judaism. The writings of intertestamental Judaism* express a hope in and an expectation of God's bringing history to consummation through a final, great tribulation (on which see Allison, 5-25), followed by judgment* of the wicked and salvation* of the faithful. Jewish apocalyptic* literature usually views the end as imminent, though there are examples of something approaching an "inaugurated eschatology" (see Lincoln 1981, 177-78). The notion that the latter days have begun to be fulfilled on earth is found in the Dead Sea Scrolls of Qumran* (see Carmignac; for further discussion of eschatology in postbiblical Jewish literature, see Howard).

1.3. Eschatology of the Gospels and Paul. The NT repeatedly uses the phrase "latter days" precisely as it is found in the OT prophecies. The meaning of the phrase is identical to that of the OT except that in the NT the end days are seen as beginning their fulfillment in Christ's first coming. All that the OT spoke of occurring in the end times has begun in the first century and continues until the final coming of Christ. The OT expectations of the great tribulation,* God's domination of the Gentiles, deliverance of Israel from oppressors, Israel's resurrection, the new covenant, the new creation and the establishment of God's kingdom (*see* Kingdom of God) have been set in motion by Christ's death and resurrection and in the emergence of the Christian church.* Christ's first coming marked the beginning of his messianic reign, which was underscored by the presence of the Holy Spirit in his ministry (e.g., at his baptism* [Mt 3:13-17] and in the casting out of demons [Mt 12:22-32]). The resurrection marked a heightened level of Jesus' inaugurated reign. Persecution of Jesus and his followers indicated the beginning of the final tribulation. What the OT did not foresee so clearly was that the kingdom and the tribulation could coexist simultaneously (e.g., Rev 1:6-9). Thus for the NT the latter days do not take place only at a point in the future but occur throughout the church age.

Paul says that the OT was written to instruct Christians about how to live in the end times, since upon them "the ends of the ages have come" (1 Cor 10:11). He refers to Jesus' birth as occurring "when the fullness of the time came" in fulfillment of the messianic prophecies (Gal 4:4). Likewise "the fullness of the times" alludes to when believers were delivered from Satan* and sin through Christ's death and resurrection (Eph 1:7-10; 1:20—2:6), which commenced his own rule over the created order (Eph 1:19-23). Christ's death and resurrection launched the beginning of the latter-day new creation prophesied by Isaiah (cf. 2 Cor 5:17 with Is 43; 65—66). The end-time prophecies of Israel's restoration from exile begin to find fulfillment in Christ's, the true Israel's, resurrection and in believers who identify by faith with him (e.g., 2 Cor 6:16-18; see Beale 1989). Tribulation in the form of false teaching* is also one of the signs that the latter days had arrived (1 Tim 4; 2 Tim 3:1-9). Since 1 Timothy and 2 Timothy speak of the Ephesian church as already experiencing this tribulation of deceptive teaching and apostasy* (see 1 Tim 1:3-4, 6, 7, 19-20; 4:7; 5:13-15; 6:20-21; 2 Tim 1:15; 2:16-19; 2:25-26; 3:2-9), it is evident that a distant, future time is not in view.

Other NT texts speak of the future consummation of the latter days. Many eschatological events will not be fulfilled until Christ returns, including the bodily resurrection of all people, the destruction of the present cosmos, the creation of a new heavens and earth, and the final judgment.

Until this consummation, Christ's followers experience only a part of the eschatological blessings* that will be fulfilled in the new heavens and earth. This is the already/not yet dimension of NT eschatology. O. Cullmann has described this tension by using the World War II analogy of D-day and V-Day. Jesus' first coming (the "already") is D-Day, since it marks the battle in which Satan* is decisively defeated. The Second Coming of Christ is V-Day, when Jesus' enemies will surrender and bow down to him (*see* Parousia). (See Moule 1964; Lincoln 1981, 181-84, on how NT authors developed aspects of eschatological thought in response to a variety of situations. For further discussion of already/not yet, *see DJG*, Eschatology; *DPL*, Eschatology. See also Allison; Caird 1980, 241-71; Hoekema; König; Ladd; Pate; Vos.)

2. Eschatology of Acts, Hebrews, the General Epistles and Revelation.

The eschatological pattern found in the Gospels and Paul is also found in the rest of the NT literature. The discussion of eschatology in this literature may be organized under the headings of "past and present" (the already) and "future" (the not yet).

2.1. Acts.

2.1.1. Past and Present. In Acts 2:17, the first place the words "last days" appear in the canonically ordered NT literature, Peter understands that the tongues* being spoken at Pentecost* begin to fulfill Joel's prophecy that a day would come when God's Spirit would gift not merely prophets,* priests* and kings but all of God's people (Acts 2:15-17; cf. Joel 2:28). The resurrection marked the beginning of Jesus' messianic reign, and the giving of the Holy Spirit* signaled the inauguration of his rule through the church (Acts 1:6-8; 2:1-43). Subsequent outpourings of the Spirit mark significant transitional points in Acts,* where the gospel is extended to new regions or ethnic groups. These later outpourings demonstrate Christ's exalted reign and that Gentiles as well as Jews are included by their faith* as subjects in the Messiah's new kingdom. This is implied in Acts

2, where we read that Jews representing all parts of the known Gentile world were present at Pentecost. The clearest example of a subsequent outpouring of the Spirit modeled on Pentecost is Acts 10:34-47, where the Roman soldier Cornelius* and his Gentile associates believed in Christ.

Some scholars have identified in Acts* a de-eschatologizing perspective in which a history of the church is substituted for a near expectation of the end (see, e.g., Sabourin). But Luke sees the outpouring of the Spirit as a further stage of eschatological fulfillment, which makes the time of the church an eschatological era (for both sides of the debate see Gaventa; on the purported delay of the end, *see* Parousia).

In the OT (see 1.1 above) and Judaism, as well as elsewhere in the NT (e.g., Rom 1:3-4, 1 Tim 3:16; see Vos 1980), the Spirit was linked with the hope of resurrection life. As a consequence of Jesus' resurrection, the eschatological center of gravity had shifted from Jesus' ministry* on earth to his reign in heaven.* The notion that Jesus had been raised from the dead was charged with eschatological significance, with roots in the OT (Is 25:7-8; 26:18-19; Ezek 37:1-14; Dan 12:1-2) and postbiblical Judaism (e.g., 2 Macc 7:9, 14; 1QH 11.12; *1 Enoch* 51:1; *2 Apoc. Bar.* 30:1-3; 50:1-4; *T. Judah* 25:1; *Adam and Eve* [Apoc.] 41:3). In Acts other references to Jesus' resurrection, though they are not formally linked with eschatological terminology (as in Acts 2), are still eschatological in nature, especially since they are often associated with OT hopes and promises (see Acts 1:3-11, 22; 3:15, 26; 4:2, 10, 33; 5:30-31; 7:55-56; 9:3-6; 10:40-41; 13:30-37; 17:31-32; 22:6-11; 25:19; 26:6-18, 22-23). Likewise the resurrection of some Christians was probably viewed as the corollary of Jesus' eschatological resurrection (Acts 9:37-41; 20:9-12; cf. Mt 27:52-53).

The fulfillment of other latter-day OT prophecies were indications that the last times had begun (Acts 3:18, 22-26; 4:25-28; 13:27-29, 46-48; 15:14-18; 26:22-23). Possibly even the mention of entering the kingdom of God after enduring tribulation is an allusion not merely to an event at the end of history but also to the inaugurated messianic, heavenly realm that one enters at death (Acts 14:22; cf. Stephen's* vision,* just prior to his death, of Christ as the presently reigning "Son of Man" [Acts 7:55-56]).

The idea of a new creation is arguably the best encompassing term for the eschatology of Acts and the NT as a whole, for it ties together all the various thematic strands linked to NT eschatology. For example, the resurrection is an act of new creation (the creation of new life) that is brought about by the life-giving agency of the Spirit. Even the healings* in Acts (Acts 3:1-16; 5:16; 9:33-34; 14:8-11; 19:11-12) and in the Gospels are best understood within the larger redemptive framework of new creation wherein the curses of the fallen creation begin to be reversed.

2.1.2. Future. In Acts 1:6 the disciples ask the resurrected Jesus if it is "at this time that you are restoring the kingdom to Israel." Jesus replies that "It is not for you to know times or epochs which the Father has fixed by his own authority" (Acts 1:7). He then promises (Acts 1:8) that the Spirit will come upon them and will empower them to witness.* Some commentators understand Acts 1:7-8 to mean that there will be an indefinite delay of the coming of Israel's restored kingdom in its consummated form but that during the interim period the Spirit will maintain the witness of Jesus' followers (see Buzzard). Accordingly, the restoration of the kingdom is equated with the time of Jesus' second coming to conclude history (Acts 1:11). From this point of view, Acts 3:19-21 continues the theme of the future kingdom, with the "times of refreshing" and the "times of restoration of all things" occurring when Jesus returns to conclude history, apparently in the same way as he left at the ascension* (Acts 1:11).

Another interpretation of Acts 1:6-8 is plausible, if not more probable. In Acts 1:7-8 Jesus responds to three misunderstandings inherent in the apostles' question (Acts 1:6). First, Acts 1:7 is a response to their mistaken assumption that it was proper for them to know the precise time (cf. 1 Thess 5:1-3) when the kingdom would be restored to Israel. Such knowledge is reserved for the Father alone.

Second, Acts 1:8 appears to be a response to an implicit assumption that future stages of the kingdom would be exclusively physical in expression. Although some interpreters understand Acts 1:8 to refer to a parenthetical period characterized by the Spirit, rather than a part of the messianic kingdom, it is more likely that the verse asserts that a future form of the kingdom is to be "spiritual" in nature ("you will receive power [of the kingdom] when the Holy *Spirit* has come"). This promise* begins its fulfillment at Pentecost, which Peter understands to be an escalation of the "latter days" inaugurated when Jesus received the Spirit at his baptism. In the OT and Judaism "the latter days" was the time of the expected outpouring of God's Spirit; the OT inextricably links the "latter days" with the prophesied kingdom, so that Peter's reference to the "latter days" in Acts 2:17 alludes to the fulfillment of the foreseen kingdom (e.g., see the OT references in 1.1 above).

Third, Acts 1:8 appears to be a reply to an apparent ethnocentric presupposition expressed by the disciples: that the nature of the kingdom would be Israelite. Jesus' reply is that the kingdom would encompass subjects who lived even "unto to the end of the earth" (in partial allusion to Is 49:6; cf. Acts 13:47, which refers to the conclusion of Acts 1:8 and where the OT reference is explicit). Hence Acts 1:8 affirms an ongoing, progressive and nonconsummative fulfillment of the prophecy of the OT kingdom, which had already begun to be established in Jesus' earthly ministry (see Hill, though he denies that Luke has an inaugurated eschatological perspective; see Bruce for a balanced view of Acts 1:6-8 and of eschatology in Acts).

Acts 3:20-21 refers to a future consummation when Christ comes and achieves "the restoration of all things." Acts 3:19, however, may include an already and not yet notion, especially because of its placement directly following an assertion that God had already fulfilled the OT prophecy of Christ's suffering: "Repent therefore and return, that your sins may be wiped away, in order that times of refreshing may come from the presence of the Lord" (which may be parallel to Acts 2:38: "Repent, and . . . be baptized . . . for the forgiveness of your sins, and you will receive the gift of the Holy Spirit"). Likewise Acts 3:22-26 refers to beginning fulfillments of OT messianic prophecy (for further argument in support of this analysis, see Kurz and sources cited; see also Bayer). Even the reference "until the times of restoration of all things" in Acts 3:21 has an already and not yet element, since the restoration had likely begun with Jesus' coming, resurrection and giving of the Spirit (Bayer).

An incontestably future reference to judgment is found in Acts 17:30-31, where Paul affirms that people should repent in the present because God has determined a specific day at the end of history when "he will judge the world in righteousness" through Jesus Christ (also Acts 24:25).

Paul also affirms a "hope of the promise" of the final resurrection for the nation Israel in Acts 26:6-7. Yet even this has been inaugurated when Christ, the true Israel, was resurrected from the dead (as is clear from Acts 13:32-33; 23:6-7; 26:22-24). (On futurist aspects of eschatology in Acts see Nielsen; on the already and not yet, see Cadbury; Carroll, 121-67; Giles; Francis; Franklin; Gaventa; Smith; cf. also Mattill.)

2.2. Hebrews.

2.2.1. Past and Present. In the opening sentence of Hebrews* we read that God "in these last days has spoken to us in his son, whom he appointed heir of all things" (Heb 1:2). As with the Gospels, Acts and Paul, Christ's first coming commences the beginning of the end times. In this vein Hebrews 1:5-13 cites OT texts primarily concerning the messianic son's* kingship which have begun their fulfillment in Jesus' first advent (se also Heb 5:5; 8:1; 10:12-13; 12:2). Likewise the ideal Adam's reign as "the Son of Man" portrayed in Psalm 8, never completely realized in the OT period, is applied to Christ as the one who has started to fill the shoes of this exemplary human figure (Heb 2:6-9). Christ has done what the first Adam and Israel, the corporate Adam, failed to achieve (for the notion of Israel as a corporate Adam, see Wright, 21-26). In this sense of Christ's "fulfillment" of end-time prophecy, he is a "son" who was "made [eschatologically] complete" *(teleioō)* and who has begun to lead and will finish leading his people to their eschatologically completed salvation (see also Heb 2:10; 5:8-9, 14; 6:1; 7:11, 19, 28; 9:9; 10:1, 14; 11:40; 12:2; see, e.g., Silva).

The work of Christ is viewed as eschatological fulfillment. Christ has decisively defeated the power of the devil and of death (Heb 2:14), a reality not expected to occur until the eschatological new creation. And Christ's mission "to put away sin by the sacrifice of himself" is an event taking place at the "consummation of the ages" (Heb 9:26; cf. Heb 10:10, 12, 14). Thus Jeremiah's prophecy of a new covenant is beginning to be fulfilled, a point underscored as Hebrews quotes Jeremiah 31:31-34 with the concluding words, "I will be merciful to their iniqui-

ties, and their sin I will remember no more" (Heb 8:8-12; cf. Heb 10:16-17). The eschatological tone of Hebrews 9:26 is true to the setting of Jeremiah's prophecy of a new covenant, which was inextricably linked to latter-day events (cf. Jer. 30:24; 31:31, 33). Finally, the author of Hebrews mentions another hallmark of the arrival of the last age, the resurrection of Christ (Heb 13:20).

Jesus' followers have also "tasted the powers of the age to come" (Heb 6:5), among which is "the heavenly gift . . . of the Holy Spirit" (Heb 6:4; cf. Ellingworth, 320). This is the closest the NT comes to formally identifying the Holy Spirit as a mark of the inbreaking eschatological age (though cf. Rom 8:23; 2 Cor 2:20-22; Eph 1:13-14). The Christians' hope of a future, consummated salvation is rooted in Christ's having already begun to realize that hope (Heb 6:17-20; see Robinson). Christians have already "come to Mount Zion and to the city of the living God, the heavenly city" (the new Jerusalem; cf. Heb 12:22); the latter-day city of God has invisibly invaded the present age so that saints might participate in its life. In a related image, Hebrews speaks of Christ's priestly work of sacrificing himself as inaugurating the eschatological temple* (Heb 9:8, 23; see Hurst). Those who spurn Christ's "once for all" sacrifice at the "consummation of the ages" (Heb 9:26) are not able to be "renewed to repentance," since no other sacrifice will be offered other than the one they have despised (Heb 6:4-6; 10:26-29; see Carlston).

The two-dimensional nature of Hebrews's eschatology (though it is found elsewhere in the NT, e.g. Ephesians) is striking: a vertical, or spatial, dimension is developed in addition to a horizontal, or temporal, dimension. The preceding discussion has focused on the temporal aspect. Yet from a spatial perspective, the end-time temple, for example, is viewed both as a reality in present time and as having a spatial dimension other than that of the material, earthly dimension (Heb 9:1—10:26).

2.2.2. Future. In Hebrews 3—4 there are repeated references to a "rest" that believers may "enter." Interpreters debate whether this "rest" has been inaugurated with Christ's first coming (so Barrett, 366-73; Lincoln 1982) or will transpire at the final consummation (Gaffin). Both views are supported by viable arguments, though the futuristic view is perhaps more likely.

The emphasis throughout Hebrews 3—4, as well as the entire epistle, is upon persevering until the end when the final reward is to be received (Heb 3:6, 14). Furthermore, the "rest" is referred to as "a promise" that "remains," one that has not yet been fulfilled (Heb 4:1, 6, 9). While it is true that the "rest" is spoken of as being present (Heb 4:3) and even past (Heb 4:10), these expressions are best understood as being spoken from a future vantage point (e.g., Heb 4:10 can be understood in the sense of a Hebrew prophetic perfect, referring to the certainty of a future event by speaking of it as if it had already happened). The dominant theme of Hebrews 3—4 is that, in contrast with Israel's failure to enter the "rest" of the promised land after its wilderness sojourn, the Hebrew Christians are exhorted to persevere in their earthly sojourn so that they will enter the "rest" of the "heavenly country" (Heb 11:16), which the land of Canaan typologically foreshadowed. Only then will the intended sabbath rest of the new creation be enjoyed (*see* Land).

The coming judgment of unbelievers and apostates at the end of the age is a repeated theme in Hebrews (Heb 6:2; 9:27), especially as a warning and an encouragement to persevere (Heb 10:27-31, 36-38; 12:25-29; 13:4; cf. Toussaint). Those who heed the warnings of judgment and the exhortations to persevere will receive at the consummation of history full salvation (Heb 9:28), their reward* (Heb 10:35; 11:26) and the complete inheritance that was promised (Heb 6:11-12, 17-18; 9:15; 10:23, 34-35; 11:39). The inheritance of the promised land of the new earth is the author's irreducible summary of what true believers will receive at the eschaton (Heb 11:9-16; 13:14). God will raise them from the dead in order that they might participate in the inheritance (Heb 11:35; cf. Heb 6:20). This final inheritance will be indestructible (Heb 12:27-28) and eternal. There God's presence can be more fully experienced (cf. Heb 12:14). The readers should not be lax about these exhortations because the final "day" is "near" (Heb 10:25; for further discussion see Barrett, MacRae, Woods).

2.3. General Epistles.

2.3.1. Past and Present. James 1:18 speaks of the incipient emergence of the new creation. Later, James* alludes to the true nature of the time in which his audience is living as he chastises people for living in ungodly ways and not

redeeming opportunities for doing righteousness: "It is in the last days that you have stored up your treasure" (Jas 5:3). Because it is already the last period of history, the final "coming of the Lord" and the time of judgment for the unrighteous is imminent (cf. Jas 5:7-9; on the problem of imminence, *see* Parousia).

First Peter* commences by mentioning that the latter-day new creation of believers has taken place: God has "caused us to be born again, unto a living hope, by means of the resurrection of Jesus Christ from the dead." The new birth and consequent "living hope" are linked to Christ's resurrection. This notion is developed further in 1 Peter 1:20-21, where Christ's resurrection is portrayed as part of "the end of the times." Through the resurrected Christ the readers have become believers possessing hope.* Through this same resurrection Jesus has been exalted to God's right hand to begin ruling (1 Pet 3:18-19, 21-22). The latter-day Spirit is the agent who brings about the resurrection of Christ (1 Pet 3:18) as well as the resurrection life of his followers (1 Pet 4:6) and their ongoing conduct in that life (1 Pet 1:2). Like the author of Hebrews, Peter speaks of Christ's death for sins as "once for all" (1 Pet 3:18), an expression that evokes the turning of the ages. Not only this, but the final judgment has been set in motion with the divinely ordained sufferings* that serve to test the faith of the Christian community (1 Pet 4:12-19).

Second Peter* makes the most far-reaching reference to Christ's kingship by observing that it commenced at the beginning of his earthly ministry, when he was baptized (2 Pet 1:16-17). Christ and the apostles* prophesied that false teachers would infiltrate the church in "the last days" (2 Pet 3:3; Jude has "last time"). Both 2 Peter and Jude* contend that this expected latter-day tribulation of apostate teaching has come to expression through the appearance of false teachers who are attempting to pervert the truth* in the Christian community (cf. 2 Pet. 3:2-3 with 2 Pet 2:1-22; 3:16-17; cf. Jude 17-18 with Jude 4, 8, 10-13).

The Johannine epistles (*see* John, Letters of) reveal an acute awareness that the eschaton has already broken into history. The most notable expression of this is the repeated references to the Antichrist,* especially in 1 John 2:18. There are false teachers, little antichrists, from within the community, who have departed but still threaten to deceive Christians about the nature of Christ's person and his commandments* (cf. 1 Jn 2:22-23, 26; 4:1-6; 2 Jn 7-11). These deceivers (*see* Adversaries) are the corporate embodiment of the beginning fulfillment of the prophecy of Daniel 7—12 that an eschatological opponent of God's people would deceive and arouse covenant disloyalty within the community of faith (see also Mk 13; Mt 24; Lk 21; 2 Thess 2). 1 John 3:4 even labels these false teachers with the covenantal "lawlessness" that Daniel prophesied would characterize the deceivers who would arise from within the ranks of the faithful (cf. Dan 12:10 [esp. cf. LXX with Theod.]): "Everyone who does the sin also does the lawlessness, and the sin is the lawlessness" (see Marshall 1978 *John*, 176-77; Smalley, 155; R. E. Brown, 399-400). In this respect, the notion of lawlessness is to be identified with the end-time sin of the "lawless one" of 2 Thessalonians 2:3-12.

The readers of 1 John are made aware that they are living in the midst of the "great tribulation," which they are experiencing in the form of false teachers. They must not be taken off guard and deceived. In fact, "the sin to death" in 1 John 5:16 is best understood in light of this latter-day context of apostasy within the covenant community. Those who deceive others or allow themselves to be deceived by the false teachers are regarded as never having belonged truly to the community of faith and experiencing spiritual death (cf. 1 Jn 2:19; see Scholer, who argues that "the sin to death" is committed only by pseudo-believers).

From another perspective, Christ's life and death have such a cosmic impact that it can be said that the old, fallen world of darkness "is passing away" (cf. 1 Jn 2:2, 8, 12-14, 17). Christ's redemptive work has dealt a mortal blow to the evil ruler of the old age (1 Jn 3:8), and those who identify with Christ's redemptive work also participate in his victory over the devil (1 Jn 2:13-14).

Although the old world has begun to disintegrate spiritually, Christ's death and resurrection have also set in motion a new creation. There is an overlap of the old with the new: "the darkness is passing away and the true light is already shining" (1 Jn 2:8). The resurrection life of the eternal age to come has begun in Jesus' resurrection and in the spiritual resurrection of his followers who identify with his death and resurrection (1 Jn 1:2; 2:17, 25; 3:14; 4:9; 5:11-13, 20, especially in the light of Jn 5:21-29). The Spirit, prophesied to be poured out in the eschatological age (see 2.1.1 above), gives assurance* to believers that they have entered into the divine presence characterizing the new age (1 Jn 3:24; 4:13).

2.3.2. Future. Judgment is also a significant theme in James (Jas 2:13; 3:1). People will be judged because of their selfishness, greed and persecution of the righteous* (Jas 5:1-9). The day of the final judgment is near (Jas 5:7-9). However, those who demonstrate true faith through good works will receive a reward at the last day (Jas 1:12; 5:7-9; *see* Faith and Works).

First Peter affirms that a day will come when God will impartially judge everyone by their works, whether or not they have lived lives of godly obedience (1 Pet 1:17; cf. 1 Pet 4:17-18). Even now God "is ready to judge the living and the dead" (1 Pet 4:5), since "the end of all things has come near" (1 Pet 4:7). In view of such an imminent judgment, believers are advised to live circumspectly. Those who are able to persevere in faithfulness will receive definitive "salvation ready to be revealed in the last time" (1 Pet 1:5; cf. 1 Pet 1:9) when Christ returns again (1 Pet 1:13), and his followers can fully rejoice in the greater manifestation of his glory* (1 Pet 4:13; cf. 1 Pet 5:1). At this "proper time" (1 Pet 5:6) believers "will receive the unfading crown of glory" (1 Pet 5:4), and God will "perfect, confirm, strengthen and establish" for all time those who have persevered (1 Pet 5:10; cf. 1 Pet 5:6). Another image of this final reward is that of receiving an "inheritance" that "will not fade away" (1 Pet 1:4; cf. 1 Pet 3:9). The believers' "hope" is focused on this goal (1 Pet 3:15). When the final day comes, God's "dominion" will be decisively manifested as being "forever and ever" (1 Pet 5:11; cf. 1 Pet 4:11). Both the already and the not yet aspects of the latter days provide a theological framework in which 1 Peter's readers might better understand their ethical* obligations (see Russell; Selwyn).

The notion of the coming final judgment is developed in 2 Peter (2 Pet 2:3, 9; 3:7; see Michaels 1967b) and Jude (Jude 6, 14-15). At the time of this judgment, "the earth and its works will be burned up" (2 Pet 3:7-13). This is likely a literal expectation on the part of the author, though some commentators interpret it figuratively as a picture of an ethical purification of the earth.

A figurative view of the fiery judgment is affirmed by some who favor the textual reading in 2 Peter 3:10 of "the earth and its works will be found [or, discovered]." If this is the original reading, it probably does not refer to the earth and what people have done as literally surviving a judgment but to the works of the wicked which will be laid bare, so that the ungodly will not be able to escape judgment (cf. Bauckham 1983, 301, 316-21; cf. Wenham).

The purpose of reflecting on the cosmic conflagration is pastoral and ethical: to encourage saints to be holy* in order that they should "be found" faithful when the expected judgment day occurs (cf. 2 Pet 3:11-12, 14). In contrast to the ungodly, they will find mercy* on this dreadful day (Jude 21). The old creation, which is to be destroyed, will be replaced by "a new heavens and a new earth" (2 Pet 3:13; see Rev 21:1; both passages are based on the prophecy of Is 65:17; 66:22). The kingdom that was inaugurated at Jesus' first coming will be established in its completeness (2 Pet 1:11), and God's people will stand in the immediate presence of his glory* (Jude 24).

1 John 2:28 and 1 John 4:17 speak of the possibility of Christ's final Parousia* occurring at any time. Readers should therefore persevere in their faith, so that they will obtain salvation and not be ashamed as ones who deserve wrath on the day of judgment. Such perseverance until Christ's coming will result in their becoming fully conformed to his likeness, for the faithful will finally be able "to see him just as he is" (1 Jn 3:2). Those who maintain this hope will be motivated in the present to begin to resemble his holy image (1 Jn 3:3; similarly 1 Jn 4:17).

2.4. Revelation.

2.4.1. Past and Present. The technical vocabulary for the eschatological period is not to be found in John's Apocalypse. Nevertheless other kinds of terminology are used, and the concepts of inaugurated and consummated eschatology are part of the fabric of the book.

The book opens with mention that Christ's resurrection has inaugurated the fulfillment of the prophesied resurrection of the saints (Rev 1:5, "Jesus Christ . . . the firstborn from among the dead"). This resurrection places Christ in the position of "ruler of the kings of the earth" (Rev 1:5) and as the one who now possesses the "keys of death and Hades" (Rev 1:18). The resurrection described in Revelation 1:5 is later

explained to be none other than "the beginning of the [new] creation of God" (Rev 3:14; see Beale 1996). By virtue of his resurrection Christ has also continued to fulfill Daniel's prophecy of the eschatological, worldwide reign of the Son of Man (cf. Dan 7:13-14 with Rev 1:13) as well as the Son of God's* rule predicted in Psalm 2 (cf. Rev 2:26-27; 12:5). Through the resurrection Christ likewise has been declared openly as God (e.g., "I am the first and the last" [Rev 1:17; 2:8; 22:13], based on the self-attribution of Yahweh in Is 41:4, 44:6; 48:12).

Christ's followers are also identified with him in the present age as subjects in his newly established messianic kingdom and as those who rule with him (Rev 1:6, 9; 5:10; see Beale 1994; Bandstra 1992). The predominantly Gentile church has also begun to fulfill the prophecies of Israel's latter-day restoration (cf. OT allusions of Rev 3:9 with Is 43:4; 45:14; 49:23; 60:14; as well as the LXX of Is 41:8; 44:2; etc.).

2.4.2. Future. Revelation expects the final coming of Christ to occur in the near future (e.g., Rev 16:15; 22:7, 12, 17, 20). The visions* of the book also express parabolically an expectation of his coming, especially to judge the ungodly (e.g., Rev 6:12-17; 11:15-19; 14:14-20; 17:14; 19:11-21; or where either Christ or God is the agent of judgment [Rev 6:10-11; 11:11-13; 14:8-11; 16:17-21; 20:9-15; 21:8]). Nevertheless Christ will come also to reward and finally bless his people (Rev 11:18; 19:7-9; 21:1—22:5, 12, 14; possibly Rev 7:9-17). He then will establish his kingdom in its final, complete and eternal form (Rev 11:15-17; 19:1; 22:5; possibly Rev 7:9-17). A tribulation of deception and persecution for God's people will directly precede the last judgment and the full coming of the kingdom (e.g., Rev 11:7-10; 16:12-14; 20:7-9; possibly Rev 3:10; 6:11; 7:14; 13:5-18), as well as a final period of torment for their persecutors (e.g., Rev 16:21; 17:16-17; cf. Rev 3:10).

3. Special Problems of Eschatology in Revelation.

A variety of exegetical problems in Revelation pertain to whether passages speak of inaugurated eschatological realities or eschatological fulfillment at the end of the present age (for discussion of the problem in general, see Bandstra 1970; for the question of the thousand-year reign of Christ, *see* Millennium; for the problem of the delay of Christ's coming, *see* Parousia).

3.1. Christ's Comings in Revelation 1—3 and 22.
Some of the references to Christ's "coming" in the letters to the churches (Rev 1—3) appear to refer to a conditional coming of Christ in judgment. If there is no repentance* in response to the present warning, then Christ will come in a pre-Parousia judgment on that particular church (so Rev 2:5, 16; 3:3; cf. Rev 3:20, referring to a conditional blessing). Some interpreters, however, argue that Christ's judgment or reward at the end of history, rather than his coming, is conditional on the response of the churches (cf. Bauckham 1977, 173-74; Holtz, 207; Satake, 153; Krodel, 109; Thomas 1992, 143-47, 154). Although this interpretation is possible, it rests on a grammatical exception. In NT usages outside of Revelation of the conditional *ei de mē* ("if not") the whole of what follows is always conditional. Thus in Revelation 2:5, without contextual indications that would suggest the contrary, Christ's activity of "removing" and *"coming"* are probably conditional (with the same principle holding for Rev 2:16; 3:3; 3:20; see, e.g., Caird, 27-28; Roloff, 45). The references to Christ's coming in Revelation 2:25 and Revelation 3:11 could well refer to the final Parousia, but they are not in the form of conditional statements.

Furthermore, in Revelation 2:5 the removal of the lampstand "from its place" indicates the removal of the church as a light of witness* to the world. Since the witness of the churches is an activity that takes place prior to the final advent of Christ, the removal of the lampstand must take place prior to Christ's final coming, not afterward (cf. Thomas 1992, 146-47). Part of the "witness" of the churches is to the promise that Christ will return to judge and to redeem (Rev 19:7-21; 22:7-20; see Bauckham 1993, 166-67). This also suits the visionary context of Christ walking in the midst of the lampstands as their priestly custodian who repairs or removes them according to their function (Mounce, 89).

It is probably best to see the conditional and nonconditional comings as not precisely identical but to view the conditional comings as local interventions during the church age and the nonconditional ones as referring to the final Parousia. There may be an intended ambiguity in these sayings as they express the tension between the already and not yet.

Other interpreters have proposed that the dual theme of promise and judgment is woven throughout the letters and that in part the imagery is drawn from a eucharistic background (cf. most prominently Rev 2:17, 20). In the Eucharist believers repeatedly anticipate the present judicial and salvific effects of Christ's final coming (see Moule 1956). The identification of the Spirit with Christ in the conclusion of each letter suggests that Christ's salvific presence with the churches is through the Spirit, and his threatened judgment will occur also through the Spirit's visitation.

The repeated affirmations of Christ's "comings" leads us to consider Revelation 1:7, which some interpreters understand as introducing the main idea of the book: "Behold, he is coming with the clouds, and every eye will see him, even those who pierced him, and all the tribes of the earth will mourn over him." The verse is composed of two OT citations, Daniel 7:13 and Zechariah 12:10. In its OT context Daniel 7:13 speaks of the enthronement of the Son of Man over all the nations following God's judgment of the evil empires (Dan 7:9-12, 14). Applied to Jesus, it indicates the fulfillment of his eschatological kingship (Rev 1:5). In its original context Zechariah 12:10 pertains to God's eschatological defeat of the enemy nations surrounding Israel and his redemption of Israel after the nation has repented of sinfully rejecting God and his messenger (i.e., "the one they have pierced"; cf. Mt 24:30; *Midr. Wayosa'*; Justin Martyr *Dial. Tryph.* 14.8).

In Revelation 1:7 the text from Zechariah has been altered in two significant ways. The phrases *pas ophthalmos* ("every eye") and *tēs gēs* ("of the earth") have been added to universalize its original meaning, which was specific to Israel. Repentant Gentiles are viewed as fulfilling the prophecy at the second coming of Christ. However, the reference from Daniel 7 ("Behold he is coming with the clouds") may include the whole course of the church age during which Christ guides the events of history in judgment and blessing. (Note how the Son of Man allusion in Rev 1:13 is given a present application; see also Rev 1:5-6, 14-20; but cf. Rev 14:14.) Precedent may be found in the use of Daniel 7:13 in Mark 13:26 and Mark 14:62, both of which may refer not to the Second Coming but to the Son of Man's coming in judgment of Jerusalem in A.D. 70 (cf. Mt 24:30; see France, 140-42, 227-39).

Christ's coming in the letters to the churches

appears to refer to his conditional visitation in judgment of the churches (though an allusion to his second coming is not excluded). Therefore, Christ's coming in Revelation 1:7 and elsewhere in the Apocalypse is understood better as a process occurring throughout history so that his second coming concludes the whole process (so also Brütsch, 31).

3.2. The Promises and the "Overcomers" in the Letters of Revelation. Each of the letters to the churches concludes with a reference to "the one who overcomes" or "conquers" *(nikaō)*. This is then followed by a promise. In the letters to Smyrna and Philadelphia, persecution is to be overcome. In the letters to the other five churches, particular sins are to be overcome. But it is clear that overcoming these problematic sins that compromise the witness of the churches will lead to persecution. The church that perseveres in its witnessing faith will win a victory on earth prior to the consummation of history, even though it suffers earthly defeat.

The use of *nikaō* (Rev 12:11; 15:2; Rom 8:35-37) confirms that "overcoming" is best understood individually, ironically, and as an inaugurated event, not merely as a future reality on a corporate level. The ironic, or paradoxical, meaning of *nikaō* is modeled after that of Christ's eschatological "conquest" (Rev 3:21). In Revelation 5:5-6 and John 16:33 Christ's conquering is understood as his death on the cross* (cf. also Rom 8:36-37 with Rev 5:5-6). Elsewhere in Revelation we find that the beast* "overcomes" the saints (Rev 11:7; 13:7), and in turn Christ and the saints "overcome" the beast by maintaining their faithful testimony in the midst of suffering (Rev 5:5-6; 12:11; 15:2; 17:14). The origin of this ironic application of *nikaō* to the beast and to Christ and his saints may lie in Daniel 7:21, which speaks of the eschatological opponent overcoming the saints. John quotes this contextually in Revelation 11:7; 12:7; and 13:7 but then ironically applies it to Jesus and the saints in Revelation 17:14 and to the angels* in Revelation 12:7-8 (see Beale 1997, 1998). But the image of conquering may also owe something to the Jewish interpretation of martyrs who were said to have "conquered the tyrant" (4 Macc 1:11; 6:10; 7:3; 9:6, 30; 11:20-21; 16:14; 17:12-18) because they maintained their faith and obedience* to God's law.

The eschatological promises to the overcomers are intended not only for those who suffer martyrdom* (e.g., Charles 1:54; Caird, 27-28, 33-34, 58; Kiddle, 61-65) but also for all true believers (Beale 1998, excursus on Rev 2:28). Overcoming refers to the victory of one's whole life of faith. A parallel may be observed in 1 John (1 Jn 5:4-5; cf. 1 Jn 2:13-14), where *nikaō* always refers to not succumbing to false teaching from within the community, a theme underscored in the letters to Pergamum and Thyatira.

The eschatological promises to overcomers in Revelation pertain to the salvific blessing of communion with God and are focused on the essentials of life. All of these promises are described in the final vision of the book (Rev 21:1—22:5) and generally refer to participation in the eternal kingdom of God. They include protection from judgment (Rev 2:10; 3:5), an inheritance in the city of God (Rev 3:12), participation in Christ's reign (Rev 2:26-28; 3:21) and eternal life (Rev 2:7; 3:5). Those who overcome are promised that they will begin to partake of the blessings of the age to come prior to the final consummation.

3.3. Temporal References in Revelation 1:19 and 4:1. Many commentators see Revelation 1:19 ("Write what you have seen, the things which are and the things about to take place after these things") as denoting a straightforward, threefold, chronological division of Revelation (and of the history of the church in relation to the world: e.g., Lohse, 19; Thomas 1967). In this view, the three clauses of Revelation 1:19 describe consecutive, mutually exclusive periods of the entire history of the church age; they do not overlap:

(1) "What you have seen" refers to the previous vision of Revelation 1, which concerns the events of the first century;

(2) "The things which are" relates to Revelation 2—3 and describes the condition of the churches in Asia Minor (and the world) during the church age, the time extending from the first century until the commencement of the "great tribulation";

(3) "The things about to take place after these things" applies exclusively to Revelation 4:1—22:5 and narrates the final tribulation, which will begin directly before the end of history and will continue for a brief period until Christ's final coming to conclude history.

Though the chronological perspective is a popular understanding of Revelation 1:19, making Revelation 4—22 come alive with tantalizing insight into future events, there are weighty objections to this interpretation. In general it interprets Revelation without sufficient sensitivity to its literary form, giving a straightforward, literal reading of the book rather than using a figurative approach that is more appropriate to its symbolic genre.

The principal argument against the chronological understanding of Revelation 1:19 is that since both Revelation 2—3 and Revelation 4—22 contain repeated references both to the past (cf. Rev 2—3; 12:1-5) and future, neither Revelation 2—3 nor Revelation 4—22 can be understood as *strictly* chronological. Since these chapters are described in some sense by Revelation 1:19, if Revelation 2—3 and 4—22 are not strictly chronological, neither is Revelation 1:19 likely to be chronological.

Not only does Revelation 4—22 describe events of past, present and future, but also its subsections recapitulate the same events in different ways (see Beale 1998). There is no reason to assume that the past and future references are tangential allusions to past or future events. Too often it seems that an a priori assumption that the events of Revelation must be understood as a chronological ordering of the future impedes interpreters from seeing their recapitulatory nature.

The concluding phrase of Revelation 1:19 ("what must take place after these things") is probably a conscious allusion to Daniel 2:28 29, 45, which in the original context refers to the eschatological scope of the vision of God's kingdom being established throughout the earth. In Daniel 2:28, 45 the phrase "latter days" is used synonymously with "after these things." If "after these things" refers to the general eschatological age, then Revelation 1:19 cannot express such a tidy chronological formula. It would refer to the eschatological period that includes inauguration in the past, present and future (see Beale 1992).

The initial phrase of Revelation 1:19 ("what things you have seen") probably refers to the entire vision of the book. The section in which it stands, Revelation 1:9-20, is best viewed as a commissioning narrative, with Revelation 1:19 as a repetition of the initial command in Revelation 1:11 to record all of the visions of the book. The second phrase ("what things are") probably does not refer to the present time only of Revelation 2—3 but the present-time seg-

ments scattered throughout the book. Alternatively, it may not be a temporal reference but rather an allusion to the figurative nature of the book, which needs to be interpreted accordingly (i.e., Rev 1:19 could be rendered "what they mean"; Stuart, 54; Alford, 559; Johnson, 429; Gundry, 66; Chilton, 78; Michaels 1991).

W. C. van Unnik maintains that the entire formula of Revelation 1:19 refers to all of Revelation and explains that John is commissioned to prophesy about the totality and meaning of history, whose truths apply not only within history but transcend any one historical period. He is able to adduce numerous examples of comparable threefold prophetic formulae in pagan religious contexts, ranging from the time of Homer to the fourth century A.D. (van Unnik 1962-63, 1980; Sweet, 73).

Whereas the majority of these views understand the three clauses of Revelation 1:19 as in some way temporal designations of past, present and future, an alternative view is that they are primarily statements about the genre of the book. The threefold structure describes the literary nature of the visions, not when they will take place. Revelation 1:19 is thus an elaboration of the threefold hermeneutical nature or genre of the entire Apocalypse: (1) because the vision is apocalyptic (visionary), (2) the whole book is to be interpreted both figuratively (cf. Rev 1:12-18 with Rev 1:20) and (3) eschatologically (Rev 1:19; Dan 2:28-29, 45). The phrases "what you have seen" and "the things which are" are not to be limited to the vision of Revelation 1:12-20 but include the whole book (see Beale 1992).

Revelation 4:1 ("I will show you what must come to pass after these things"), which repeats most of the last clause of Revelation 1:19, is likely to be understood in the same way, and not as a reference to visions pertaining exclusively to the future great tribulation, as some futuristically oriented commentators argue.

3.4. The Temporal Scope of the Sevenfold Series of Seals, Trumpets and Bowls, and the Unnumbered Visions of Revelation 12—14. Are the discernible sections within Revelation 4—16 related to one another chronologically, thematically or both? The main lines of debate revolve around whether Revelation 4—16 represents a forecast of events to happen sequentially or whether some segments overlap temporally and thematically. Typically the former interpretation views

Revelation 4—16 as a panorama of events to happen only in the period immediately preceding and culminating with the final coming of Christ, whereas the latter see a threefold temporal reference to events associated with (1) the redemptive work of Christ's first coming, (2) the course of the inaugurated latter-day church age and (3) the Second Coming of Christ and consummation of cosmic history. An exception to this is G. R. Beasley-Murray, who is both a futurist and a recapitulationist, understanding the parallel sections to cover exclusively different aspects of the eschatological future (*see* Revelation, Book of).

4. Eschatology of the Apostolic Fathers.

4.1. The Past and Present. Like the writers of the NT, the apostolic fathers* understand that the blessings of the age to come have begun but have not yet reached their consummation. These writers can speak of the age in which they are living as the last days (e.g., *2 Clem.* 14.2; *Barn.* 12.9; 16.5). For example, we read that "these are the last times" (Ign. *Eph.* 11.1), that "Christ appeared at the end of time" (Ign. *Magn.* 6.1; *Herm. Sim.* 9.12.3) and that Christians have a "foretaste of things to come" (*Barn.* 1.7).

Much like the NT writers, the early fathers held so intensely to the inaugurated aspect of the end times that they believed that the promised new creation had been set in motion. *Barnabas* 6.13 says that "He made a second creation in the last days," which was modeled on the first creation: "Behold, I make the last things as the first." Christians had become "new, created again from the beginning" (*Barn.* 16.8; also 6.11, 14), a statement likely based on the fact that their progenitor, Jesus Christ, was the representative from whom they received their identity (Ign. *Eph.* 20). Such thinking motivated some writers to liken the present experience of believers to the blessings of the Garden of Eden (*Diogn.* 12). Such a heightened notion of inaugurated eschatology is apparently the basis for the seer's misguided question in the *Shepherd of Hermas* concerning whether "the consummation had already arrived" (*Herm. Vis.* 3.8.9).

Again, following the lead of NT writers, the apostolic fathers see an inextricable link between the beginning phase of the eschatological new creation and the resurrection of saints. Resurrection is the means by which believers become a part of the new creation, first spiritu-

ally at conversion, then physically in the final resurrection of the dead. Christ brought "the newness of eternal life" (Ign. *Eph.* 19.3) by himself becoming a "new man" (Ign. *Eph.* 20.1) as a result of his own resurrection. The inaugurated and consummated resurrection of Christians occurs because of their identification with Christ's resurrection (Ign. *Magn.* 9; Ign. *Trall.* 9.2; cf. *1 Clem.* 24.1; Pol. *Phil.* 2.2; *Barn.* 5.6-7).

Those who believe in Jesus "will live forever" (*Barn.* 11.11). Conversely, God has also commenced with the destruction of the old creation "for his elect" (*Herm. Vis.* 1.3.4), which is best understood as beginning with Christ's own death (i.e., destruction of his old body) and resurrection; the resurrection put an end to the curse of death for God's people (Ign. *Eph.* 19.3; *Barn.* 5.6), so that even when believers die physically, they enter into an escalated phase of their new birth and of their immortality (*Mart. Pol.* 19.2). Christ's resurrection is the decisive blow in defeating the devil (Papias Frag. 24), and those who remain faithful to Christ participate with him in completing this defeat (Ign. *Eph.* 13.1; Ign. *Trall.* 4.2). In this respect Christ's resurrection is also the basis of his messianic reign (Pol. *Phil.* 2.1). Those who trust in Christ also enter into the kingdom during the present age (*Herm. Sim.* 9.16.2-4).

There is a link not only between the eschatological new creation and resurrection but also between the new creation and the notion that the church has become the "temple" of God (Ign. *Eph.* 15.3; Ign. *Trall.* 7.2; Ign. *Phil.* 7.2; *Barn.* 4.11), though this connection is explicitly made only in *Barnabas* 6.8-19 and *Barnabas* 16.1-10. The likely reason for associating the two concepts is that the Garden of Eden of the first creation was identified by later OT writers as being like a sanctuary (see Kline, 35-56), and it became natural for NT writers and the early fathers to make the same connection. John's Apocalypse and *Barnabas* draw a parallel between the first creation when Adam and Eve were placed in Eden and the second creation of Christians as a temple (Rev 21:1—22:5; *Barn.* 6.8-19). The same passage from *Barnabas* draws a parallel between Israel's promised land and the new-creation temple of the church because the OT depicts that land as "Eden" (Gen 13:10; Is 51:3; Ezek 36:35; Joel 2:3) and Israel as a corporate Adam, who was chosen ideally to succeed where the first Adam failed (see Wright, 21-26).

Presumably these writers also view the gift of the Holy Spirit as among the eschatological blessings (*1 Clem.* 2.2; 46.6), though this connection seems to be drawn only in Barnabas (cf. *Barn.* 1.3 with *Barn.* 1.7; see Heb 6:4-5).

In the OT the apparent chronology of predicted eschatological events placed the final tribulation prior to the resurrection of the dead and the new creation (e.g., Dan 11:35—12:12). The Fathers follow the NT in placing the beginning of the final tribulation at the same time as the inaugurated new creation and its attendant blessings (as, e.g., Rev 1:9). *Barnabas* understands that he is living in the "last days," the "age of lawlessness" (*Barn.* 4.9) and "the deception of the present age" (*Barn.* 4.1; cf. 18.2), which is the inception and harbinger of the soon to be fulfilled prophecy from Daniel 7:7-8, 24 (*Barn.* 4.4-6; likewise cf. 2 Thess 2:3-7 and 1 Jn 2:18-27, where "lawlessness" is also used and is rooted in Dan 12:10 [Theod.]). That prophecy was apparently to commence its more concrete fulfillment imminently, though not necessarily consummately, through the infiltration of false teachers in the church (cf. *Barn.* 4.1, 9-11; 18.1-2). Similarly the *Shepherd of Hermas* contends that "great tribulations" have already been suffered (*Herm. Vis.* 2.7.1) which apparently prepare saints for "the coming great tribulation" (*Herm. Vis.* 2.6.7; cf. *Herm. Vis.* 7.4; cf. Rev 2:22; 7:14). Likewise, Hermas "escaped a great tribulation" from a satanic beast which was "a foreshadowing of the great tribulation that is coming" (*Herm. Vis.* 4.2.4-5).

4.2. The Future. The consummation of all things will be in the "age to come" (*Herm. Vis.* 4.3.5; *2 Clem.* 6.3). *Barnabas* states that at this concluding temporal point there will be a creation (*Barn.* 15.7); the "renewed creation" will be exceedingly fertile (Papias Frag. 14). A Jewish apocalyptic work, *2 Enoch* 25—33, on the basis of the scriptural testimony that "a thousand years is like one day" (Ps 90:4), appeals to the seven days of creation in Genesis 1 and affirms that history will follow the same sevenfold pattern. The historical age will be seven thousand years and a following "eighth day," referring apparently to eternity (see Wikenhauser). In the same tradition, *Barnabas* 15 reckons history to last six thousand years, at the conclusion of which the Lord will bring everything to an end, for with him a day signifies a thousand years . . . in six thousand years everything will be brought to

an end . . . it is not the present sabbaths that are acceptable to me, but the one [the sabbath of the last thousand years] that I have made; on that sabbath, after I have set everything at rest, I will create the beginning of an eighth day, which is the beginning of another world" (*Barn.* 15.4-8).

The sabbath of the last thousand years merges into the eternity of the eighth day, "the day on which Jesus both arose from the dead and . . . ascended into heaven" (*Barn.* 15.9). The last thousand years is figurative for the saints' eternal sabbath rest, and the eighth day of Christ's resurrection becomes figurative not merely for eternity but for the age of the saints' resurrection, which commences eternal rejoicing; hence the seventh and eighth day for Barnabas overlap and are virtually identical (Daniélou, 396-401; Kromminga, 29-40; Ferguson; for other viewpoints on *Barnabas* see Mealy, 48). Irenaeus (Irenaeus *Adv. Haer.* 5.28.3; 5.33-36) may follow the same line of thought as in *Barnabas* 15, though his view seems inconsistent and the consensus is that Irenaeus was a premillennialist.

Just as there is a link between the inauguration of the new creation and the resurrection inaugurated in Christ, so there is a connection between the final phase of both: "when the righteous will rise from the dead and reign, when creation, too, [is] renewed" (Papias Frag. 14). This will be the time of the consummated resurrection (*1 Clem.* 50.4; *2 Clem.* 19.3-4; Pol. *Phil.* 2.2; *Mart. Pol.* 14.2), eternal life (*Herm. Vis.* 4.3.5; cf. *Barn.* 11.11) and immortality (*1 Clem.* 35.1-4; *2 Clem.* 14.5). The tradition purportedly stemming from Papias associates the final resurrection of the righteous with the commencement of the millennial reign of the saints (Papias Frag. 3.12; 16).

Believers will enter the final form of God's kingdom at this time (*2 Clem.* 5.5; 11.7; 12.1-2, 6; *Herm. Sim.* 9.12.5, 8) and will reign with the Lord (Pol. *Phil.* 5.2). Before this occurs, however, Christians must pass through a final tribulation of deception and persecution that is greater than any earlier trials (*Did.* 16.3-5; cf. also the notion of "the coming great tribulation" in *Herm. Vis.* 2.2.7; cf. 2.3.4; on "great tribulation" in Hermas, see Bauckham 1974).

Therefore the full reward of the true saint lies in the future and must be awaited in the present (*2 Clem.* 20.2-4). This reward will be given by the Son of God when he comes to draw the present age to its conclusion (*Did.* 16.7-8; *Herm. Sim.* 5.5.3), though no one knows the time that this is to occur (*Did.* 16.1). Consequently, one must be constantly ready for his coming (*Did.* 16.1; cf. *Herm. Sim.* 10.4.4).

There will be a final judgment for God's enemies and the unfaithful who are not prepared for Christ's coming (*2 Clem.* 18.2; Ign. *Eph.* 16.2; *Mart. Pol.* 11.2; *Barn.* 19.10); this judgment is imminent and is already on the way (*2 Clem.* 16.3). Continued awareness of the coming judgment serves as the basis of motivation for a believer's upright conduct (*2 Clem.* 18.2; *Barn.* 19.10). Christ himself will execute this judgment (Pol. *Phil.* 2.1; 6.2).

There will be both salvific reward and judgment at the conclusion of history (*2 Clem.* 10.3-5; *Barn.* 4.12-14; 21.2-3, 6; *Herm. Sim.* 4; for further sources discussing patristic eschatology, see McRay; Cunningham; Daley).

See also ANTICHRIST; APOCALYPTIC, APOCALYPTICISM; ASCENSION; CREATION, COSMOLOGY; DAY OF THE LORD; GLORY; HEAVEN, NEW HEAVEN; HOLY SPIRIT; HOPE; JUDGMENT; KINGDOM OF GOD; MILLENNIUM; MORTALITY AND IMMORTALITY; MYSTERY; PAROUSIA; RESURRECTION; REVELATION, BOOK OF; REWARDS; TRIBULATION, MESSIANIC WOES; UNIVERSALISM; WRATH, DESTRUCTION.

BIBLIOGRAPHY. H. Alford, *The Greek Testament* (Cambridge: Deighton, Bell & Co., 1866), vol. 4; D. C. Allison, *The End of the Ages Has Come* (Philadelphia: Fortress, 1985); A. J. Bandstra, "History and Eschatology in the Apocalypse," *CTJ* 5 (1970) 180-83; idem, " 'A Kingship and Priests': Inaugurated Eschatology in the Apocalypse," *CTJ* 27 (1992) 10-25; C. K. Barrett, "The Eschatology of the Epistle to the Hebrews" in *The Background of the New Testament and Its Eschatology: Studies in Honour of C. H. Dodd*, ed. W. D. Davies and D. Daube (Cambridge: Cambridge University Press, 1956) 363-93; R. J. Bauckham, *The Climax of Prophecy: Studies in the Book of Revelation* (Edinburgh: T & T Clark, 1993); idem, "The Great Tribulation in the Shepherd of Hermas," *JTS* 25 (1974) 27-40; idem, *Jude, 2 Peter* (WBC; Waco, TX: Word, 1983); idem, "Synoptic Parousia Parables and the Apocalypse," *NTS* 23 (1977) 162-76; H. F. Bayer, "Christ-Centered Eschatology in Acts 3:17-26" in *Jesus of Nazareth: Lord and Christ*, ed. J. B. Green and M. Turner (Grand Rapids: Eerdmans, 1994) 236-50; G. K. Beale, *The Book of Revelation* (NIGTC; Grand Rapids: Eerdmans; Carlisle: Paternoster, 1998); idem, "The Formula 'He Who Has Ears Let Him Hear What the Spirit Says to the Churches' in Rev. 2—3" in *A Vision for the Church: Essays in Honour of J. P. M. Sweet*, ed. M. Bockmuehl and M. Thompson (Edinburgh: T & T Clark, 1997); idem, "The Interpretative Problem of Rev. 1:19," *NovT* 34 (1992) 360-87; idem, "The Old Testament Background of Reconciliation in 2 Corinthians 5—7 and Its Bearing on the Literary Problem of 2 Corinthians 6:14-18," *NTS* (1989) 550-81; idem, "The Old Testament Background of Rev. 3:14," *NTS* 42 (1996) 133-52; idem, "Review Article: J. W. Mealy, *After the Thousand Years*," *EvQ* 66 (1994) 242-45; idem, "The Use of the Old Testament in Revelation" in *It Is Written: Scripture Citing Scripture: Essays in Honour of B. Lindars*, ed. D. A. Carson and H. G. M. Williamson (Cambridge: University Press, 1988) 318-36; C. Brown, "The Parousia and Eschatology in the New Testament," *NIDNTT* 2:901-35; R. E. Brown, *The Epistles of John* (AB; Garden City, NY: Doubleday, 1982); F. F. Bruce, "Eschatology in Acts" in *Eschatology and the New Testament: Essays in Honor of G. R. Beasley-Murray*, ed. W. H. Gloer (Peabody, MA: Hendriksen, 1988) 51-63; C. Brütsch, *Clarte de l'Apocalypse* (Geneva: Labor et Fides, 1955); A. Buzzard, "Acts 1:6 and the Eclipse of the Biblical Kingdom," *EvQ* 66 (1994) 197-215; H. J. Cadbury, "Acts and Eschatology" in *The Background of the New Testament and Its Eschatology: Studies in Honour of C. H. Dodd*, ed. W. D. Davies and D. Daube (Cambridge: Cambridge University Press, 1956) 300-321; G. B. Caird, *A Commentary on the Revelation of St. John the Divine* (London: A & C Black; New York: Harper & Row, 1966); idem, *The Language and Imagery of the Bible* (Philadelphia: Westminster, 1980); C. E. Carlston, "Eschatology and Repentance in the Epistle to the Hebrews," *JBL* 78 (1959) 296-302; J. Carmignac, "La notion d'eschatologie dans la Bible et 'a Qumran," *Revue de Qumran* 7 (1969) 17-31; J. T. Carroll, *Response to the End of History: Eschatology and Situation in Luke-Acts* (Atlanta: Scholars Press, 1988); R. H. Charles, *A Critical and Exegetical Commentary on the Revelation of St. John* (2 vols.; ICC; Edinburgh: T & T Clark, 1920); D. C. Chilton, *The Days of Vengeance* (Ft. Worth, TX: Dominion, 1987); O. Cullmann, *Christ and Time* (Philadelphia: Westminster, 1964); A. Cunningham, "From Strangers to Citizens: Eschatology in the Patristic Era," *Ex Auditu* 6 (1990) 73-85;

B. E. Daley, "Eschatology" in *Encyclopedia of Early Christianity* (New York: Garland, 1990) 309-14; J. Daniélou, *The Theology of Jewish Christianity: The Development of Christian Doctrine Before the Council of Nicea* (Chicago: Regnery, 1964), vol. 1; W. J. Dumbrell, *The Search for Order: Biblical Eschatology in Focus* (Grand Rapids: Baker, 1994); P. Ellingworth, *The Epistle to the Hebrews* (NIGTC; Grand Rapids: Eerdmans, 1993); E. E. Ellis, "Present and Future Eschatology in Luke," *NTS* 12 (1965) 27-41; A. Farrer, *The Revelation of St. John the Divine* (Oxford: Clarendon, 1964); E. Ferguson, "Was Barnabas a Chiliast? An Example of Hellenistic Number Symbolism in Barnabas and Clement of Alexandria" in *Greeks, Romans, and Christians: Essays in Honor of A. J. Malherbe,* ed. D. L. Balch, E. Ferguson and W. A. Meeks (Minneapolis: Fortress, 1990) 157-67; R. T. France, *Jesus and the Old Testament* (London: Tyndale, 1971); F. O. Francis, "Eschatology and History in Luke-Acts, *JAAR* 37 (1969) 49-63; E. Franklin, "The Ascension and the Eschatology of Luke-Acts" *SJT* 23 (1970) 191-200; R. B. Gaffin, "A Sabbath Rest Still Awaits the People of God" in *Pressing Toward the Mark,* ed. C. G. Dennison and R. C. Gamble (Philadelphia: The Committee for the Historian of the Orthodox Presbyterian Church, 1986) 33-51; B. R. Gaventa, "The Eschatology of Luke-Acts Revisited," *Encounter* 43 (1982) 27-42; K. Giles, "Present-Future Eschatology in the Book of Acts (I)," *RTR* 40 (1981) 65-71; idem, "Present-Future Eschatology in the Book of Acts (II)," *RTR* 41 (1982) 11-18; D. E. Gowan, *Eschatology in the Old Testament* (Philadelphia: Fortress, 1986); R. H. Gundry, *The Church and the Tribulation* (Grand Rapids: Zondervan, 1973); D. Hill, "The Spirit and the Church's Witness: Observations on Acts 1:6-8," *IBS* 6 (1984) 16-26; A. A. Hoekema, *The Bible and the Future* (Grand Rapids: Eerdmans, 1979); T. Holtz, *Die Christologie der Apokalypse des Johannes* (TU 85; Berlin: Akademie Verlag, 1971); G. Howard, "Eschatology in the Period Between the Testaments" in *The Last Things: Essays Presented to W. B. West Jr.,* ed. J. P. Lewis (Austin, TX: Sweet, 1972) 60-73; L. D. Hurst, "Eschatology and 'Platonism' in the Epistle to the Hebrews," *SBLSP* (1984) 41-74; A. Johnson, *Revelation* (EBC; Grand Rapids: Zondervan, 1981) 397-603; M. Kiddle, *The Revelation of St. John* (MNTC; New York: Harper, 1940); M. G. Kline, *Images of the Spirit* (Grand Rapids: Baker, 1980); A. König, *The Eclipse of Christ in Eschatology* (Grand Rapids: Eerdmans; London: Marshall, Morgan, & Scott, 1980); G. A. Krodel, *Revelation* (ACNT; Minneapolis: Augsburg, 1989); D. H. Kromminga, *The Millennium in the Church* (Grand Rapids: Eerdmans, 1945); W. S. Kurz, "Acts 3:19-26 as a Test of the Role of Eschatology in Lukan Christology," *SBLSP* (1977) 309-23; G. E. Ladd, "Eschatology and the Unity of New Testament Theology," *ExpT* 68 (1957) 268-78; idem, *The Presence of the Future* (Grand Rapids: Eerdmans, 1974); H. K. LaRondelle, *The Israel of God in Prophecy* (Berrien Springs, MI: Andrews University Press, 1983); A. T. Lincoln, *Paradise Now and Not Yet* (SNTSMS 43; Cambridge: Cambridge University Press, 1981); idem, "Sabbath, Rest and Eschatology in the New Testament" in *From Sabbath to Lord's Day,* ed. D. A. Carson (Grand Rapids: Zondervan, 1982), 197-220; E. Lohse, *Die Offenbarung des Johannes* (Göttingen: Vandenhoek & Ruprecht, 1960); G. W. MacRae, "Heavenly Temple and Eschatology in the Letter to the Hebrews," *Semeia* 12 (1978) 179-99; J. McRay, "Charismata in Second-Century Eschatology" in *The Last Things: Essays Presented to W. B. West Jr.,* ed. J. P. Lewis (Austin, TX: Sweet, 1972) 151-68; I. H. Marshall, *The Epistles of John* (NICNT; Grand Rapids: Eerdmans, 1978); idem, "Slippery Words," *ExpT* 89 (1978) 264-69; A. J. Mattill, *Luke and the Last Things* (Dillsboro, NC: Western North Carolina University Press, 1979); J. W. Mealy, *After the Thousand Years* (JSNTSup 70; Sheffield: JSOT, 1992); J. R. Michaels, "The Centurion's Confession and the Spear Thrust," *CBQ* 29 (1967) 102-9; idem, "Eschatology in 1 Peter 3:17," *NTS* 13 (1967) 394-401; idem, "Revelation 1:19 and The Narrative Voices of the Apocalypse," *NTS* 37 (1991) 604-20; P. S. Minear, *I Saw a New Earth: An Introduction to the Visions of the Apocalypse* (Washington. DC: Corpus, 1969); C. F. D. Moule, "Influence of Circumstances on the Use of Eschatological Terms," *JTS* 15 (1964) 1-15; idem, "The Judgment Theme in the Sacraments" in *The Background of the New Testament and Its Eschatology: Studies in Honour of C. H. Dodd,* ed. W. D. Davies and D. Daube (Cambridge: Cambridge University Press, 1956) 464-81; A. E. Nielsen, "The Purpose of the Lukan Writings with Particular Reference to Eschatology" in *Luke-Acts,* ed. P. Luomanen (Helsinki: The Finnish Exegetical Society, 1991) 76-93; C. M. Pate, *The End of the Ages Has Come: The Theology of Paul* (Grand Rapids: Zondervan, 1995); P. Prigent, *Apocalypse et Liturgie* (CahThéol 52; Paris: Delachaux & Niestlé, 1964); N. Pryor, "Eschatological Expectations in the Old Testament Prophets" in *The Last Things: Essays Presented to W. B. West Jr.,* ed. J. P. Lewis (Austin, TX: Sweet, 1972), 32-59; W. C. Robinson, "Eschatology of the Epistle to the Hebrews: A Study in the Christian Doctrine of Hope," *Encounter* 22 (1961) 37-51; J. Roloff, *Revelation* (Minneapolis: Fortress, 1993); R. Russell, "Eschatology and Ethics in 1 Peter," *EvQ* 47 (1975) 78-84; L. Sabourin, "The Eschatology of Luke," *BTB* 12 (1982) 73-76; A. Satake, *Gemeindeordnung in der Johannesapokalypse* (Neukirchen: Neukirchener Verlag, 1966); D. M. Scholer, "Sins Within and Sins Without: An Interpretation of 1 John 5:16-17" in *Current Issues in Biblical and Patristic Interpretation,* ed. G. F. Hawthorne (Grand Rapids: Eerdmans, 1975) 230-46; E. F. Scott, *The Book of Revelation* (London: SCM, 1939); E. G. Selwyn, "Eschatology in 1 Peter" in *The Background of the New Testament and Its Eschatology: Studies in Honour of C. H. Dodd,* ed. W. D. Davies and D. Daube (Cambridge: Cambridge University Press, 1956) 394-401; M. Silva, "Perfection and Eschatology in Hebrews," *WTJ* 39 (1976) 60-71; S. S. Smalley, *1, 2, 3 John* (WBC; Waco, TX: Word, 1984); R. H. Smith, "The Eschatology of Acts and Contemporary Exegesis," *CTM* 29 (1958) 641-63; idem, "History and Eschatology in Luke-Acts," *CTM* 29 (1958) 881-901; M. Stuart, *Commentary on the Apocalypse* (New York: M. H. Newman, 1845), vol. 2; J. P. M. Sweet, *Revelation* (SCM Pelican Series; London: SCM, 1979); R. L. Thomas, "The Chronological Interpretation of Revelation 2—3," *BSac* 124 (1967) 321-31; idem, *Revelation 1—7: An Exegetical Commentary* (Chicago: Moody, 1992); S. D. Toussaint, "The Eschatology of the Warning Passages in the Book of Hebrews," *GTJ* 3 (1982) 67-80; W. C. van Unnik, "A Formula Describing Prophecy," *NTS* 9 (1962-63) 86-94; idem, *Sparsa Collecta* 2 (NovTSup 30; Leiden: E. J. Brill, 1980) 183-93; G. Vos, "The Eschatological Aspect of the Pauline Conception of the Spirit" in *Redemptive History and Biblical Interpretation: The Shorter Writings of Geerhardus Vos,* ed. R. B. Gaffin (Phillipsburg, NJ: Presbyterian & Reformed, 1980) 91-125; idem, *The Pauline Eschatology* (Grand Rapids: Baker, 1979); D. Wenham, "Being 'Found' on the Last Day: New Light on 2 Peter 3:10 and 2 Corinthians 5.3," *NTS* 33 (1987) 477-79; A. Wikenhauser, "Weltwoche und tausendjähriges Reich," *Tübinger Theologische Quartalschrift* 127 (1947) 399-417; C. Woods, "Eschatological Motifs in the Epistle to the Hebrews" in *The Last Things: Essays Presented to W. B. West Jr.,* ed. J. P. Lewis (Austin, TX: Sweet, 1972) 140-51; N. T. Wright, *Climax of the Covenant* (Minneapolis: Fortress, 1991).   G. K. Beale

ESSENES. *See* QUMRAN.

ETERNAL LIFE. *See* ETERNITY, ETERNAL; LIFE AND DEATH.

ETERNITY, ETERNAL

The concept of eternity or eternal existence is ambiguous in the NT and the apostolic fathers,* referring to two different temporal schemes: one that something exists for the totality of time; the other for the totality of a set period of time, often in terms of beginning from a particular point. Time is an important concept in apocalyptic* literature, and this concern is shared by several of the biblical and early church writers, in which reference to eternity is a way of designating passage from one temporal age to another.

The concept of eternity is not expressed by a single word in the Greek of the NT or the apostolic fathers (the concept is infrequent in extrabiblical Greek; cf. 4 Macc 17:18); there is always some syntactical structure, usually involving a form of the noun *aiōn* (which also indicates a fixed period of time). The adjective *aiōnios* also requires definition along the lines suggested. In these writings, reference to eternity is virtually always with the phrase *eis ton aiōna* or a variant of it, with either the singular or the plural form of the noun. The distinction in usage seems to be not conceptual but authorial. For example, in the NT the author of Hebrews* uses the singular phrase in all instances but one, while the Johannine writings (1 John, 2 John and Revelation; *see* John, Letters of; Revelation, Book of) use the plural form in all instances but one. In the other authors who use the phrase (1 Peter* and Jude*), there are four instances of the singular phrase and one of the plural.

Few words have caused as much longstanding dispute as temporal words in the Bible. Some of these misunderstandings continue to be found in current biblical studies. For example, on the basis of the temporal vocabulary in the languages involved (Greek and Hebrew), some scholars have wished to argue that the Greek of the NT expresses only a single view of time (as unlimited) and that this reflects a Hebraic form of thought, one out of character with extrabiblical Greek language and thought. J. Barr has shown that this is a clear misunderstanding of the lexical and syntactical evidence. When it is reassessed, the linguistic evidence makes it difficult to sustain this conclusion, even from a theological standpoint.

One of the major difficulties of this topic is that we are discussing a concept obfuscated by unsupported preconceptions and only loosely attached to particular Greek wording. Nevertheless there are three concepts in this biblical and early church literature worth discussing.

1. Eternity Unlimited
2. Eternity Circumscribed
3. Eternal Life
4. Conclusion

1. Eternity Unlimited.
The concept of eternity unlimited refers to instances in which eternity is an open-ended and unbounded concept, not restricted by parameters of temporal limitation. There are surprisingly few instances of this kind of usage in this body of NT writings. These contexts often speak of God* and his existence. For example, God's throne and kingdom are eternal (Heb 1:8; Rev 4:9, 10; 5:13, where Christ is included; 7:12; and with the adjective 2 Pet 1:11), and God and his word are eternal (1 Pet 1:25; Rev 10:6; 15:7). Typical here are doxological passages to God (Heb 13:21; 1 Pet 4:11; 5:11) and references to the Holy Spirit* (Heb 9:14). God is seen to have worked through an eternal covenant* (Heb 13:20).

In the writings of the apostolic fathers the usage is similar, with God and his dominion said to be eternal in most instances (e.g., *1 Clem.* 35.3; 55.6; 61.2) but with Christ* also mentioned (e.g., *Mart. Pol.* 14.3). Doxological passages speak of eternity unlimited with reference to both God (e.g., *1 Clem.* 32.4; 50.7; 58.2; 61.3) and especially Christ (e.g., *Did.* 9.2, 3; *1 Clem.* 64; *2 Clem.* 20.5; *Diogn.* 12.9).

2. Eternity Circumscribed.
The concept of eternity circumscribed refers to continued existence from a point in time, perhaps extending into a new temporal age.

Although most instances of this usage look forward, two NT passages in these NT writings reflect the concept of eternity past: Acts 3:21 and Acts 15:18. Although some scholars have argued that these refer to a period of limitless time, this does not appear to be the way that the author is using the phrase *ap' aiōnos*. In Acts 3:21 Peter is quoted as saying that God promised to restore everything through his holy prophets "from long ago." Three points are worth noting. The first is that the phrase "long ago" describes the prophets and therefore cannot mean that they were prophesying from before creation.* The second is that the context has apocalyptic overtones; these are not connected to the phrase "long ago" but to God's restoring actions. The third is that this phrase is found in extrabiblical Greek authors, including the apostolic fathers, with this sense (e.g., *1 Clem.* 32.4; *Barn.* 18.2; cf. *Did.* 16.4; Hesiod *Theog.* 609; cf. Lk 1:70). The same interpretation applies to Acts 15:18, where in wording that perhaps reflects Isaiah 45:21 James adds to the quotation of Amos 9:11-12 a phrase referring to the Lord's* actions being known "from long ago," that is, from a time when it was possible to know them. (Cf. Jude 25, where the sense is of existence probably before any temporal age.)

The second usage speaks of continued existence for the entirety of a set period of time, often with reference to the future. These contexts often speak of Christ and his having been established in a particular role or function. For example, he has become a priest* in the order of Melchizedek* or the living ruler of the earth (Heb 5:6; 6:20; 7:17, 21, 24, 28; Rev 1:6, 18; 11:15), having obtained a special enduring status (Heb 9:1). Hebrews 13:8 illustrates this usage when it states that Jesus Christ is the same yesterday, today and forever (*eis tous aiōnas*), indicating a third temporal sphere extending into the future (see also 2 Pet 3:18; 2 Jn 2). The same sense applies to humans who have something marked out for them from a particular time on into the future. For example, the one who does the will of God abides forever (1 Jn 2:17; Rev 22:5; and with the adjective Heb 9:15; 1 Pet 5:10), and the one who does not incurs a similarly long-lasting punishment (Jude 13; Rev 14:11; 19:3; 20:10; and with the adjective Heb 6:2; Jude 7).

Although this usage is not as frequent in the apostolic fathers as is the first category (see 1 above), there is discussion of eternity circumscribed in several passages especially concerning punishment. For example, *Hermas Visions* 2.3.3 speaks of the righteous* not being punished forever (see also *Herm. Vis.* 6.2.4; *Herm. Sim.* 9.24.4; 9.18.2; but cf. *2 Clem.* 6.7, which speaks of nothing saving the unrighteous from eternal punishment; cf. *Barn.* 20.1). Several of the passages in the apostolic fathers are invocations of the OT regarding eternity (e.g., *Barn.* 6.3; 9.2; 11.10, 11). One important passage (*Barn.* 18.2, in the Two Ways section) speaks of Christ enduring from age to age (cf. Ign. *Smyrn.* 1.2).

3. Eternal Life.
The concept of eternal life is one linked to a phrase created by use of the adjective *aiōnios* and a noun, usually the word for life, *zōē*. The attributive use of the adjective follows standard Greek usage, and the phrase is not Semitic as some have thought (where it would have been more typical to use a genitive structure with a noun). Although strictly speaking this usage could be categorized as a specific instance of eternity circumscribed, since eternal life is seen as having a beginning, the usage is listed separately here. The language of "eternal life" is especially frequent in the Johannine writings, although it appears in all literary strata of the NT. Apart from 1 John 1:2 (cf. 1 Jn 5:20), where it is used to characterize the word of life, it is used of the condition of a present and/or futuristic relationship with God based on the redemptive work of the Son* (*see* Redemption). Eternal life is spoken of in 1 John 2:25; 3:15; 5:11, 13, 20. The only other instances are Jude 21 and Acts 13:46, 48. In Hebrews 5:9 the phrase "eternal salvation" is used, with similar sense. The same usage is found in the apostolic fathers. Although there are more occurrences of the concept in the Fathers than in the NT, the frequency of usage is less due to the larger size of the corpus (see *Herm. Vis.* 2.3.2; 3.8.4; 4.3.5; *Did.* 10.3; Ign. *Eph.* 18.1; *2 Clem.* 5.5; 8.4, 6; *Mart. Pol.* 14.2; 2.3).

4. Conclusion.
The distinction between eternity as a period of time with at least one fixed point and as a boundless concept reveals two different temporal frames of reference. Discussion of eternality is important not only for debunking unnecessary false distinctions regarding Hebrew and Greek mindsets but also for illustrating the importance of interpretation rather than simply translation. Though the same words are used, their spheres of reference are significantly different. Eternality as bounded is a temporal concept that can be readily used of a new or transferred state of the believer, such that, for example, that person enters into eternal life. Eternity as unbounded is a timeless concept that is suitably used of God and his existence.

See also CREATION, COSMOLOGY; ESCHATOLOGY; GOD; HEAVEN, NEW HEAVEN; HELL, ABYSS, ETERNAL PUNISHMENT; LIFE AND DEATH; MILLENNIUM; MORTALITY AND IMMORTALITY.

BIBLIOGRAPHY. J. Barr, *Biblical Words for Time* (rev. ed.; SBT 33; London: SCM, 1969); J. Guhrt, "Time," *NIDNTT* 3:826-33; J. Lawson, *A Theological and Historical Introduction to the Apostolic Fathers* (New York: Macmillan, 1961).

S. E. Porter

ETHICS
The equivalent of the term *ethics* is not found in the later NT writings—or in the Gospels or in the Pauline epistles—but there is ethics (*see DJG*, Ethics of Jesus; *DPL*, Ethics). There is reflection and instruction concerning the character and conduct worthy of the gospel, rich reflection and inspired instruction, but the ethical teaching of the later NT resists any simple summary.

The voices in the later NT are "many and various," to use the words of Hebrews 1:1 concerning the prophets.* To be sure, the voices all proclaim that "in these last days" God has "spoken to us by a Son," the final and definitive revelation, the One from whom and unto whom are "all things" (Heb 1:2); and to be sure, the story of God's Son* is the foundation for reflection and instruction concerning fitting human deeds and dispositions not only in Hebrews but also in all these writings of the later NT. Even so, there are distinct voices in this literature, using different genres and addressing diverse communities in disparate circumstances.

1. Life in Light of the End: Revelation
2. Life in Accord with the Tradition: 1 Peter, Hebrews, Jude, 2 Peter
3. Life with Wisdom from Above: James
4. Life in Mutual Love: The Epistles of John
5. Developments in the Apostolic Fathers

1. Life in Light of the End: Revelation.

The later NT writings see the moral life in the light of the end. The proclamation of Jesus and the earliest proclamation about Jesus, of course, had announced the end. The final judgment* and the good future of God were "at hand." The end of the whole cosmic story had been anticipated in Jesus' works and words and in the gift of the Holy Spirit.* Moreover, the end had been already established when God raised the crucified Jesus of Nazareth from the dead. When the later NT writings appropriated the Christian tradition, they appropriated certain convictions about the end. They knew the end of the story, and when they thought about the conduct and character appropriate to Christians, they thought about conduct and character in the light of the end.

Nowhere is the link between ethics and eschatology* more obvious than in the Revelation (see Revelation, Book of). As apocalyptic* literature, Revelation is an unveiling of the secrets of the end. It and other such literature was not, however, written for the sake of divining the future. Revelation was written to console and to encourage the churches* of Asia Minor suffering the emperor's* oppression (see Persecution). It called for patience, not computation; for courage, not calculation.

Instruction in the moral life did not here take the shape of traditional admonitions and sage advice; rather the author constructed a symbolic universe that made intelligible both the readers' faith* that Christ* is Lord* and their daily experience of injustice and suffering* at the hands of Caesar. The rock on which that universe was built and on which the author would have his readers build their lives was the confidence that God* has acted, is acting and will act eschatologically in Jesus Christ (Rev 1:3-8). There are sovereignties in conflict; on the one side are God, the Christ of God and those who worship them; on the other are Satan,* his viceregents, the beasts* and "the kings of the earth" and those who prostrate themselves before them. The victory has been won by Christ, the final triumph is assured, but Satan and his minions still battle and threaten Christ's people on earth. That conflict is the background of intelligibility for their suffering and for their obligations.

The seer, exiled on Patmos, was keen to be a part of the battle and anxious about the churches on the mainland where some tried to avoid the conflict, accommodating Caesar and the standards of this age. "On the Lord's day" (Rev 1:10), taken to be the day the victory of Christ was celebrated (see Lord's Day), he saw and communicated his apocalyptic visions* of the end and called the churches to share "in Jesus the tribulation and the kingdom and the patient endurance" (Rev 1:9; see Kingdom of God; Tribulation).

Life in the light of the end was here first of all "patient endurance." In the letters to the churches (Rev 2:1—3:22) the patient endurance* John commended and called for took the shape of faithfulness in spite of the persecution by the emperor (Rev 2:3, 10, 13; 3:10), the harassment by the synagogues* that had cast them out (Rev 2:9; 3:9) and the accommodation urged and practiced by the false teachers (Rev 2:2, 6, 14, 15, 20). Patient endurance required fidelity in their devotion to God (Rev 2:4, 3:15, 16) and in their love* of and service* to one another (Rev 2:19) and resistance to the temptations to immorality (Rev 2:14, 20; 3:4) and the seductions of ease (Rev 2:9; 3:17).

The vision of the enthronement of the Lamb* that was slain (Rev 4:1—5:14) was at once political and liturgical (see Exaltation; Liturgical Elements). The churches already participated in hymnic* acclaim given the Lamb in their worship.* They were heralds of God's reign and a token of its realization; they were the voice in their time of the whole creation,* of all that was abused and oppressed by the false sovereign, of all that will be liberated by the Lamb that was slain. They were in Domitian's empire a counterempire. The promise that they shall reign (Rev 5:10) stood under the standard of the Lamb that was slain, not of Domitian's pomp and privilege; their reign might thus, like that of the Lamb, be found through death but at least through "patient endurance."

The subsequent visions unveiled both God's judgment against aspects of imperial culture and God's good future, and that good future included the vindication of the counterempire and the renewal of the creation. In the four horsemen the empire of Domitian rides upon the earth with military expansionism, civil strife and war, the inflation that robs the poor of sustenance, and death (Rev 6:1-8), but the victory of God answers the plea of the martyrs* (Rev 6:10) and brings in its train not strife and hunger and death but complete well-being (Rev 7:15-17). The beasts use political power (Rev 13:5-7) and economic power (Rev 13:16-17) to persecute and oppress, but the victory of God brings the fall of Babylon/Rome and the unveiling of a new Jerusalem.*

The vision of Babylon* and its fall (Rev 17:1—19:10) portrays the great splendor of Rome (see Roman Empire), but its wealth and power cannot hide the immorality, idolatry,* oppression and murder that prompt God's judgment (Rev 18:2-8, 21-24). The fall of Babylon/Rome is lamented by those who are powerful and wealthy according to its standards and with its aid ("the kings of the earth," "the merchants" and "the shipmasters" [Rev 18:9-19]), but their dirge is overwhelmed by the rejoicing of those who heed the call for a spiritual exodus (Rev 18:4) and by the heavenly "hallelujah" (Rev 19:1, 3, 6). Such a spiritual exodus from the demonic values of Rome, the pride of power (Rev 18:3, 9-10) and the greed (Rev 18:3, 11-19; see Generosity and Greed) that marked Rome's life and justified its doom can be and must be undertaken in the light of the end, the victory of the "King of kings and Lord of lords" (Rev 19:16) and the gift of a new world* and a new city where God dwells and reigns and blesses and where God's people and God's creation flourish (Rev 21:1-5).

Watchfulness is hardly calculation. "Patient endurance" is not passivity. To be sure, the Christian communities in Asia Minor were not called to take up arms to achieve power; this counterempire was not to plot a coup to seize economic and political control. But they were called to be a resistance movement, to defend God's claim to a world corrupted and abused by the spiritual and political powers. They were called to live courageously and faithfully, resisting the pollutions of the cult of the emperor, including its murder, sorcery, idolatry and the lie that Caesar is Lord (see the vice lists in Rev 9:20-21; 21:8; 22:15; see Virtues).

The exhortation to ethics in light of the end is found not only in Revelation but also in "many and various" ways throughout this literature. 1 Peter, for example, saw the moral life in the light of the "living hope" and "inheritance" secured by the resurrection* (1 Pet 1:3-5), reminding readers that "the end of all things is near" (1 Pet 4:7), warning them of the judgment (1 Pet 1:17; 4:17) and urging them to attend to

Christ's glory* (1 Pet 4:13; 5:1). Life in the light of the end is in 1 Peter, no less than in Revelation, patient endurance of suffering, "sharing Christ's suffering" (1 Pet 4:13) and his glory (1 Pet 5:1).

2. Life in Accord with the Tradition: 1 Peter, Hebrews, Jude, 2 Peter.

1 Peter,* however, is not an example of apocalyptic literature, though it reflects a church setting in a hostile world. It is a "baptismal anamnesis," to use the phrase of N. A. Dahl. Readers of 1 Peter are reminded of their baptism,* of their initiation into the death and resurrection of Christ (see Death of Christ) and into the Christian community—and of the moral instruction that was part of that initiation. Life in the light of the end was to be lived with fidelity to the identity given in baptism and in accord with the moral instruction that traditionally accompanied it. The use of these traditions is common in the later NT writings and in the apostolic fathers,* but 1 Peter is a particularly rich account of the moral life as life in accord with the tradition.

The traditional elements utilized in 1 Peter include what E. G. Selwyn called an early Christian "holiness code," the instruction to "put off" vices and to "put on" virtues (here "rid yourselves" and "arm yourselves," 1 Pet 2:1; 4:1), the tradition concerning joy* in suffering (1 Pet 1:6-7; 4:13; cf. Rom 5:35; Jas 1:2-4), the tradition of nonretaliation (1 Pet 3:9-12; cf. 1 Thess 5:12-22; Rom 12:3-20) and a Haustafel (1 Pet 2:13—3:8).

The holiness code instructed Gentile* converts to "abstain" from pagan immorality (1 Pet 2:11; see also Acts 15:20, 29; 21:25; 1 Thess 4:3; 5:22; Pol. Phil. 2.2; 5.3) and called them to "be holy" (1 Pet 1:15-16; cf. 1 Thess 4:3, 7; see Holy) and to love one another (1 Pet 1:22; 1 Thess 4:9). It evidently related the Christian life to the end, to the revelation* of Christ as judge and avenger (1 Pet 1:13, 17, 20; 1 Thess 4:6), and it construed the Christian life as testimony to those still in ignorance (1 Pet 2:12; 1 Thess 4:12).

The Haustafeln, or tables of rules for the household (see Household Codes), instruct Christians to "be subject" (1 Pet 2:13—3:8; cf. Col 3:18—4:1; Eph 5:21—6:9; 1 Tim 2:1-15; Tit 2:4-10; Did. 4; Barn. 19; 1 Clem. 21; Ign. Pol. 4—5; Pol. Phil. 4—5; 10, which called for mutual subjection). The *Haustafeln* take up conventional role responsibilities; it is God's will that while Christians wait for the end they should live lives beyond any reasonable reproach. Such lives will silence their detractors and serve the mission* of the church (1 Pet 2:12, 15; 3:1-2, 16).

The redaction of this tradition in 1 Peter puts submission to government first (*see* Civil Authority). One may contrast this with Revelation, but 1 Peter knows that Christians are not merely subjects but "aliens" and "exiles" (1 Pet 2:11). Their submission is a free submission, not a constrained one, and it is balanced by the recognition of God's greater authority* and finally set in context of a series of other obligations, obligations that may override duties to the emperor (1 Pet 2:17). The exhortation to slaves* to be submissive (1 Pet 2:18-25) is not based on requirements of the role but on the example of Christ (1 Pet 2:21-23), and just as Christ's suffering led to his vindication and glory, so slaves may, like Jesus, trust the One who "judges justly." The admonition that wives be submissive (1 Pet 3:1-6) is given a missionary motive and is balanced by a reciprocal admonition that husbands "likewise" treat their wives with consideration and honor, recognizing "the weaker sex" as "joint heirs" (1 Pet 3:7) of life. "Finally" the duty of submission is the duty of all (1 Pet 3:8; 5:5). 1 Peter and the early Christian tradition of *Haustafeln* generally did not disown civic and domestic role responsibilities; however, by placing them in the context of the Christian identity and community and in the light of the end, it subtly relativized and qualified them.

Hebrews* describes itself as a "word of exhortation" (Heb 13:22). There is little concrete moral instruction in Hebrews. The concern is not that the church does not know what it ought to do; it is that the church does not do what it knows it ought to. The Christian moral tradition has already informed the consciences* of these people; the task the author undertakes is to exhort them against inattention to what they know (Heb 2:1), against disobedience (Heb 4:11), against becoming dull of hearing (Heb 5:11), against being "sluggish" (Heb 6:12), against weariness in their "struggle against sin" (Heb 12:4).

The theological basis for this "word of exhortation" is the covenant,* more explicitly, the "second" (Heb 8:7), "new" (Heb 8:8, 13; 9:15: 12:24) and "better" (Heb 7:22; 8:6) covenant, the covenant that cannot be reduced to a written code (Heb 8:10; 10:16). Keeping this covenant is not a matter of obedience* to the law* of Moses*; it is a matter of living in accord with the Christian tradition, in accord with the set of precepts that are exemplified rather than codified in the list in Hebrews 13: mutual love, hospitality,* care for prisoners, respect for marriage. "Do not neglect to do good and to share what you have, for such sacrifices are pleasing to God" (Heb 13:16; *see* Sacrifice).

The failure to keep covenant evokes judgment no less in the new covenant than in the old. Hebrews warns against apostasy* and deliberate sin with rigorous severity (Heb 6:4-6; cf. Heb 10:26-31; 12:16-17), and some early commentators took the letter to be introducing a system of penitential discipline in which there is no possibility of a second repentance* (cf. *Herm. Man.* 4.3). The author, however, provides not a ruling in canon law but a warning, a "word of exhortation," lest the church become "sluggish" (Heb 6:12).

The letters* of Jude* and 2 Peter* defend a life in accord with the tradition against the heretics who "promise freedom" (2 Pet 2:19) but "pervert the gospel of God into licentiousness" (Jude 4; cf. 2 Pet 2:2). Against those who "scoff" at the promise of Christ's return (Jude 18; 2 Pet 3:3-4), they remind their readers to live "lives of holiness and godliness" while they wait for the end (2 Pet 3:11). Here 2 Peter adds a new note: such lives in accord with the tradition can "hasten" the end (2 Pet 3:12).

2 Peter also adds a carefully wrought catalog of virtues (2 Pet 1:5-8), noteworthy for the prominence of Hellenistic vocabulary in it and for its concern for moral development and progress.

3. Life with Wisdom from Above: James.
The letter of James* is really a paraenesis, a didactic text that gathers moral instruction from a variety of sources, including Jewish and Greek, as well as Christian, traditions. As such it surely represents the moral life as living in accord with tradition, but it tests tradition and behavior by "the wisdom from above" (Jas 3:17). This wisdom* is not simply based on experience; it is wisdom in light of the end. In the light of "the coming of the Lord" readers are advised

to "be patient" (Jas 5:7-8). Such patience entails both the endurance of hardship (Jas 1:2-4; utilizing the tradition of joy in suffering [cf. 1 Pet 1:6-7; Rom 5:3-5]) and withstanding temptation* (Jas 1:12-16, in the form of a beatitude, a wisdom form). Moreover, in the light of the coming great reversal (Jas 2:5; 4:6-10; 5:1), the rich are urged to repent. Such repentance entails rejecting the conventional reliance on wealth that passes for wisdom (Jas 1:9-11; 4:13—5:3), and it requires hospitality to the poor (Jas 2:2-6), justice (Jas 5:4) and tangible charity (Jas 1:27; 2:15-17; *see* Riches and Poverty).

The "wisdom from above" is not a human achievement but a gift "from above" (cf. Jas 1:5, 17-18). It is not an esoteric knowledge* or gnostic* enlightenment; it results in virtue, in community-forming and community-preserving traits of character (Jas 3:17), so that Christians become "firstfruits of his creatures" (Jas 1:18), firstfruits of "a harvest of righteousness" (Jas 3:18; *see* Righteousness).

This wisdom must govern all things and not least for James that recalcitrant bit of human flesh, the tongue (Jas 1:19, 26; 3:1-12; 4:11; 5:9, 12). The tongue can be used to bless* or to curse, to speak evil or to make peace,* to deceive or to speak the truth in love; every time we open our mouths and let loose our tongues there is a struggle between the rule of wisdom and the reign of evil.

The "law" was obviously important to James (Jas 1:25; 2:8-12; 4:11), but it cannot be identified with the 613 commandments of the Torah or simply with the love commandment* (Jas 2:10). It is the whole of morality as morality is known through Scripture and tradition and tested by the "wisdom from above" in the light of the end.

James's famous polemic against "justification by faith alone" (Jas 2:14-26) was hardly interested in defending an alternative theology of justification or a new concept of faith. It was not Pauline theology that was opposed so much as the use of a Pauline slogan to justify libertine conduct (cf. 2 Pet 3:14-17). For Paul a faith that does not issue in good dispositions and deeds was incomprehensible; for James it was reprehensible. Both writers wanted a faith that acts (Jas 2:22; cf. Gal 5:6; *see* Faith and Works).

4. Life in Mutual Love: The Epistles of John.
The epistles of John (*see* John, Letters of) concentrate the Christian life into the duty of mutual love. Life in the light of the end in this "last hour" (1 Jn 2:18) is marked by mutual love, for it is love that marks the (already but awaited) good future of God: "We know we have passed out of death into life, because we love the brethren" (1 Jn 3:14). Life in accord with the tradition is marked by keeping "the commandments" of God (1 Jn 2:3,4), but John never identifies "the commandments," except to say, "This is his commandment, that we should believe in the name of his Son Jesus Christ and love one another" (1 Jn 3:23; cf. 4:21; 2 Jn 6).

This "new commandment" (1 Jn 2:8) is not novel; it is really an "old" commandment (1 Jn 2:7; 2 Jn. 5). It stands in continuity not only with the beginning of Christian preaching* and with Jesus' proclamation (1 Jn 2:7, 24; 2 Jn 5, 6) but also with God's intention from the beginning, so that the devil's sin (1 Jn 3:8) and Cain's were precisely their violation of the unity and love that mark the heavenly reign of God. Love is the primal will of God, who "is love" (1 Jn 4:8, 16), the original and fundamental commandment, now "perfected" in Christ and in his community. To believe in this Christ is to stand under the obligation to love; his death on the cross* is the way in which "we know love" (1 Jn 3:16; cf. 1 Jn 4:1-21). The faith that God sent Jesus in the flesh,* that Jesus died on the cross and that the Spirit has been given expresses itself in love.

John's epistles, like his Gospel, focus on the community as the place love must be put into practice, but this focus should not be understood as a limit or a restriction. If we know love from the death of Christ, and if Christ's death is not only for us but also for the whole world (1 Jn 2:1, 2), then it would be quite unreasonable for the author to restrict love to members of the community.

5. Developments in the Apostolic Fathers.
The literature of the early church reprised these themes, but the Christian life was more and more regarded as life in accord with the tradition. The *Didache,* * for example, began with moral instruction following the traditional pattern of Two Ways, "one of life and one of death" (*Did.* 1—5; see also *Barn.* 18—20), utilizing not only the tradition of Jesus' teachings (*Did.* 1) and the decalogue (*Did.* 2) but also the tradition of the *Haustafeln* (*Did.* 4). Then, after providing instruction concerning baptism (*Did.* 7), fasting

and prayer* (*Did.* 8), Eucharist (*Did.* 9, 10) and duties of hospitality to itinerant preachers (*Did.* 11—13), it concluded with attention to the end and the admonition to "be watchful" (*Did.* 16). Along the way it made use of certain wisdom forms, such as the address to "my child" (*Did.* 3), and emphasized the duty to love (*Did.* 1). The *Didache* is noteworthy for its prohibition of abortion and infanticide (*Did.* 2; see also *Barn.* 19.5; *Diogn.* 5, 6), for its introduction of a double standard (*Did.* 6) and for its appreciation for the church as a community of moral discourse and mutual admonition (*Did.* 4, 15).

Not only was the Christian life more and more focused on life in accord with the tradition, but also the tradition was more and more regarded as properly interpreted by ecclesiastical officers and takes on the role of a "new law" (*lex nova*) to be obeyed (*see* Church Government). So, for example, *1 Clement* (*see* Clement of Rome) rebukes the Corinthian church for deposing its lawful leaders. Such sedition puts them in great moral peril; they should rather be obedient to God and to the leaders who have been appointed by God (*1 Clem.* 14; 21; 30; 41—44; 57; 63). Similarly the epistles of Ignatius* are full of admonitions to live in harmony with the bishop. Harmony with God and with the will of God is found in harmony with the bishop; the unity in the spirit is formed by unity under the leadership of proper ecclesiastical officers; the holiness of participation in the Spirit is domesticated into obedience to church leaders who stand in succession to the apostles.*

The Christian life continued to be regarded in the light of the end, even if eschatology did not shape life as directly or force the revision of conventional assumptions as deliberately as it did in Revelation. The *Shepherd of Hermas*, for example, although apocalyptic in form, is really a moral treatise. The apocalyptic visions, which constitute the first part of the work, include a vision of the terrors of judgment (*Herm. Vis.* 4), but they function to make repentance, the practice of the "mandates" and the performance of "good works" urgent (*Herm. Sim.* 10.4). The mandates (the second part of the work) and the moral instruction of the similitudes (the third part) conform to the conventions of apocalyptic literature by being given by a heavenly figure, "the shepherd, the angel of repentance" (*Herm. Vis.* 5), but in content they rely on the traditions of baptismal instruction and moral wisdom

within the church, contrasting the Two Ways (*Herm. Man.* 6), for example, and urging Christians to "abstain" from wickedness (*Herm. Man.* 8).

The sense of being "aliens and exiles" (1 Pet 2:11; cf. Heb 11:13-14; 13:14; *Herm. Sim.* 1) remained in the light of the end, but the counter-cultural emphasis of Revelation existed alongside and in tension with an appreciation of the best of the Hellenistic morality and culture. Perhaps the *Epistle to Diognetus** captured this tension and its fruitfulness best in its series of paradoxes:

> Christians . . . dwell in their own countries but only as sojourners; they bear their share in all things as citizens, and they endure all hardships as strangers. Every foreign country is a fatherland to them, and every fatherland is foreign. They marry like all other men, and they beget children; but they do not cast away their offspring. They have their meals in common but not their wives. They find themselves in the flesh, and yet they live not after the flesh. Their existence is on earth, but their citizenship is in heaven. They obey the established laws, and they surpass the laws in their own lives. (*Diogn.* 5.5-10)

See also Civil Authority; Commandments; Conscience; Faith and Works; Freedom, Liberty; Hospitality; Household Codes; Imitation; James; Marriage, Divorce, Adultery; Obedience, Lawlessness; Pastoral Theology; Repentance, Second Repentance; Rewards; Riches and Poverty; Sexuality, Sexual Ethics; Virtues and Vices.

Bibliography. W. R. Baker, *Personal Speech-Ethics in the Epistle of James* (WUNT 2.65; Tübingen: J. C. B. Mohr, 1995); N. A. Dahl, "Anamnesis: Memory and Commemoration in Early Christianity" in *Jesus in the Memory of the Early Church* (Minneapolis: Augsburg, 1964) 11-29; R. B. Hays, *The Moral Vision of the New Testament* (San Francisco: HarperCollins, 1996); J. B. Lightfoot, ed., *The Apostolic Fathers* (Grand Rapids: Baker, 1965 [1891]); W. A. Meeks, *The Origins of Christian Morality: The First Two Centuries* (New Haven, CT: Yale University Press, 1993); F. X. Murphy, *Moral Teaching in the Primitive Church* (Glen Rock, NJ: Paulist, 1968); W. Schrage, *The Ethics of the New Testament* (Philadelphia: Fortress, 1988); E. G. Selwyn, *The First Epistle of St. Peter* (London: Macmillan, 1947); A. Verhey, *The Great Reversal: Ethics and the New Testament*

(Grand Rapids: Eerdmans, 1984).

A. Verhey

ETHIOPIAN EUNUCH. *See* PHILIP THE EVANGELIST.

EUCHARIST. *See* LORD'S SUPPER, LOVE FEAST.

EVANGELISM IN THE EARLY CHURCH

Evangelism is defined here in the narrow sense of the verbal proclamation of the good news of salvation* with a view of leading people to a right relationship with God* through faith* in Jesus Christ.* But it touches on other aspects of "mission,"* which also includes the nonverbal aspects of Christian witness* to non-Christians.

Two works stand out as classics on this subject: A. von Harnack's *The Mission and Expansion of Christianity in the First Three Centuries* (ET 1905) and M. Green's *Evangelism in the Early Church* (1970). Where the two disagree, the latter often gives the better reconstruction.

Three Greek word-groups were commonly used to denote evangelism: *euangelizō* ("to share good news"), *kēryssō* ("to preach") and *martyreō* ("to bear witness"). In reference to the act and/or process of telling others about Jesus Christ, the first is used most frequently in its verbal form accompanied by a word or phrase that describes the content of the news, such as "the kingdom of God" (Acts 8:12; *see* Kingdom of God) or "Jesus" (Acts 11:20), hence emphasizing the message's content. The second highlights the method of public proclamation, as it originally denoted what a *kēryx* ("herald") did. The third emphasizes the veracity and credibility of both the message and the messenger, for it was a legal term that referred to the attestation to facts and events based on the personal experience of the testifier.

1. The Message
2. The Motives
3. The Objective
4. The Context
5. The Strategy
6. The Methods
7. Postapostolic Developments

1. The Message.

The *euangelion* ("gospel"* or "good news") or *kērygma** ("preaching") centers on the person and work of Jesus Christ, its sole subject and focus (as in Acts 5:42; 8:35; 28:31). To the Jews it was the joyful announcement that God had finally acted to fulfill the promise* of messianic *sōtēria* ("salvation") which they had long been hoping for (as in Acts 2:22-36; 3:13-25). To those not familiar with the OT, it was the victorious proclamation that a new order of peace* had dawned on the world with the defeat of the evil forces through Jesus' resurrection* (as in Acts 17:18), though the term ran the risk of being misunderstood, since *euangelion* was used in a political sense in the imperial cult (cf. Acts 17:7).

Euangelion and *kērygma* are used by Paul and most other NT writers as technical terms to refer to both the content of what is proclaimed and the act, process and execution of the proclamation. Content and process belong together, for in the very act of preaching its content becomes reality and brings about the salvation that it proclaims. The gospel is not a human word but the word of God (1 Pet 1:12) which produces new birth and new life (1 Pet 1:23-25; cf. 2 Tim 1:10). Clear warnings are given against diverting from "the truth" into false teachings* (Acts 20:28-32; 1 Jn 4:1-6; 2 Jn 7-11; 2 Pet 2; Jude 3-4; cf. Rev 2:2, 14-16).

NT scholars have raised three issues about the *kērygma*. The first interacts with C. H. Dodd's claim that it had a fixed form and structure that were recognizably different from the *didachē* ("teaching"). The present consensus is that there were indeed a definite form and content centered on the lordship of Jesus, but there were also varied presentations of his relevance to the different needs of the hearers, which were not necessarily different from the teaching materials for new believers.

The second question centers on how reliable are the recorded evangelistic sermons in Acts. It seems clear now that they reflect very old strata of tradition,* with Lukan translation and modifications, which were intended to serve as patterns for the creative exposition of the key points of the gospel.

The third issue has been raised by the Bultmannian school that affirmed only the theological significance of Jesus and denied the significance of his historical reality in early Christian preaching. It seems that the contents of the four Gospels, the sermons in Acts (especially Acts 10:36-38) and the anti-(proto)Gnostic warnings in the Johannine epistles all point to the importance of the historicity and life of Jesus in the *kērygma*.

2. The Motives.

What motivated the evangelistic efforts of the early Christians? The NT texts show that it was their overwhelming sense of gratitude to God for his love* revealed in Jesus' life and death,* which they had actually experienced (1 Jn 4:10-12, 14, 19; cf. 2 Cor 5:14; Eph 3:7-8). Perhaps this served as the strongest impulse for most of them to share what they had received from the Lord.

There was also a keen sense of responsibility to do what God required them to do, as faithful stewards of the gospel that had been graciously given to them (1 Pet 4:11; 5:2-4; cf. Eph 3:2-3). Paul, for example, felt under obligation to fulfill a commission entrusted to him (Acts 20:24; cf. 1 Cor 4:1-2; 9:16-17; Rom 1:14-15), constantly conscious of the eternal consequences in the final judgment* (2 Cor 5:9-11; cf. 2 Tim 4:8).

Another motivation was the early believers' concern for the state of unbelievers (1 Pet 3:1-6): they believed that those without Christ were lost and condemned (Rev 20:11-15; cf. Rom 3:19, 23; Eph 2:1-3, 12-13; 2 Pet 3:7).

3. The Objective.

The early church aimed to lead all peoples to conversion. For pagans conversion was a complete change of one's religion to be exclusively attached to that of the Christians (cf. 2 Pet 3:9). Except for Jews, for whom conversion was within the faith in which they were nourished (Christ is the end or fulfillment of the OT), this demand to change one's faith, ethic and cult entirely was totally new to the peoples in the Greco-Roman world, since they did not regard a belief system, a moral code and exclusive commitment as necessary for religion (see Stark). Though Judaism was specially protected by law and was open to Gentile* adherents (called "God-fearers"), it generally failed to gain significant conversions.

The early Christians were not shy about the uniqueness (not just superiority) of their faith, for they believed that they had *the* good news for their families, friends, communities and nations. They knew that the *kērygma* was in essence a definitive call that demanded a response. They expected results and succeeded; they even counted the number of converts (Acts 2:41; 4:4; 17:4).

To them conversion meant three things: repentance,* faith and baptism.* To do "deeds that showed repentance" (Acts 26:20; cf. 3:26; 17:30) toward God, who had generously supplied all their needs (Acts 14:17; cf. 17:25-28) but whom they had offended through neglect or rejection of his righteous rule over their lives (cf. 2 Pet 2; Jude 4-16; Rev 18), meant forsaking idols* for the Lystran religionists (Acts 14:15), washing Paul's wounds for the Philippian jailer (Acts 16:33) and burning precious scrolls for the Ephesian occultists (Acts 19:18-19).

"Faith toward Jesus Christ" (Acts 20:21; cf. 10:43; 11:17; 16:31) was more than assent to spiritual facts; it included also commitment to a personal God revealed in Jesus Christ, not without basis in certain propositional truths about him (hence the severe warnings against heresies or false teachers), not without evidence of good works (cf., e.g., Jas 1:21-27; 2:14-26; 1 Jn 2:28—3:24) and not without persistence of hope* (cf. Heb 11—13; 2 Pet 3:17-18; Rev 2:10, 19).

Converts were also required to receive water baptism* immediately upon their profession of faith (Acts 8:37; 9:18; 16:33; cf. 1 Cor 1:14-15). Baptism was viewed as the mark of cleansing from old sins* (2 Pet 1:19; cf. Tit 3:5), union with Christ (1 Pet 3:21—4:3; cf. Rom 6:1-4) and incorporation into the church* (1 Cor 12:13). The instances of household* baptisms (Acts 10:24, 27, 48; 16:15, 33; cf. 18:8) suggest that it was also viewed as a parallel to OT circumcision* (cf. Rom 4:1-12; Col 2:11). Both Jews and Gentiles were baptized into the church, as into a third race (1 Pet 2:9-10; cf. 1 Cor 10:32; Eph 2:11-22).

4. The Context.

It seems clear that the first century providentially gave the early church some good conditions to succeed in rapidly propagating the new faith. Though maintained by military force, the *pax Romana* ("Roman peace"; *see* Roman Empire) provided an atmosphere of order, plenty and well-being. A network of roads was kept in good condition for fast and relatively safe travel and communication. The Greek language with its developed philosophical vocabulary was widely used in the Mediterranean region, thus facilitating communication across various ethnic groups.

Theologically there was a movement among the intelligentsia, except for the Epicureans and

Skeptics, away from the traditional worship* of mythological gods toward some sort of monism. More important, monotheism and simple worship services had spread throughout the Empire through the Jewish diaspora.* Though the Jews were often not popular, they were influential, sometimes even among the social elite. They also set the precedent for the practice of conversion to an exclusive religion.

There were some apparent disadvantages: the early Christians were accused of being atheistic (nonworship of the gods), antisocial (attending secret meetings), traitors (refusal to confess "Caesar is Lord") and depraved (rumored to have practiced sexual* immorality and cannibalism). But up to the later NT era and until Domitian, c. A.D. 95, the persecutions* and hostilities were sporadic and largely in limited regions. Luke sees them as mostly instigated by the Jews (Acts 4:1-31; 5:17-41; 14:2; 17:5-9; 21:27—26:32; cf. Jas 5:10-11; 1 Pet 4:12-19; Rev 2:9). Though they seemed to be setbacks, these "trials" presumably helped to keep the church pure* and members' commitment level high.

To the Jews the first evangelizers were nobodies: they had no formal rabbinic training (hence "untrained laity," Acts 4:13) and were trying to correct centuries-old traditions of the Torah taught and practiced by qualified religious leaders. Worse, they worshiped* a crucified criminal as Messiah and a second God (Heb. *Adonai*, "Lord"), which was blatant blasphemy (*see* God).

The polytheistic peoples in the Roman Empire had complete tolerance of private religious beliefs (Lat. *superstitiones*) as long as they did not disturb public decency and order. In societies where low morals prevailed, Christian conversion required major changes in values, ethical standards and behavior. Moreover, the early Christians were despised for sociocultural inferiority: most of them belonged to the lower classes (cf. 1 Cor 1:26; 2 Cor 8:1-4; Rev 2:9). Nevertheless, the populace soon took notice that the new movement was "turning the world upside down" (cf. Acts 17:6 KJV).

5. The Strategy.

Was there a general plan of action to evangelize the world? In terms of geographical expansion, it was spontaneous via the existing networks of sea and land trade routes, perhaps even to India

and Armenia. Like Paul, most evangelizers settled in cities of Roman governance, Greek culture, Jewish influence and commercial importance, such as Antioch, Philippi, Corinth, Paphos, Ephesus, Rome. Paul chose to set up churches in only a couple of urban centers in each province (cf. Acts 19:10; Rom 15:19-23; *see* Centers of Christianity) to serve as outreach centers in their respective regions. The neat schema of outward expansion "to the ends of the earth" from Jerusalem (summed up in Acts 1:8) is most probably Lukan.

5.1. Total Mobilization. The prime agents in evangelism were the ordinary believers (Acts 8:4; 11:19-21), called "informal missionaries" (Harnack; Green). Wherever they lived or migrated, the good news spread by word of mouth through their natural relationships of families, friends and acquaintances (cf. 1 Pet 3:15). As they "gossiped the gospel" with conviction and enthusiasm, people were converted and added to the church and its evangelistic force. Those who were gifted with special endowments to preach were encouraged to use them faithfully (1 Pet 4:10-11; cf. 1 Cor 12—14; Rom 12:6-8).

These evangelizers were "equipped" (cf. Eph 4:11-13) by two kinds of church leaders: the itinerant *apostoloi* ("apostles"* or "missionaries") and the resident *presbyteroi* ("elders"). Besides the Twelve* and Paul, there were "missionaries of the churches" commissioned and supported by the house churches (2 Cor 8:23; Phil 2:25; 3 Jn 6-7; Rev 2:2; cf. 1 Cor 9:4; 1 Thess 2:7; etc.). They went from place to place, appointed local leaders and then proceeded to preach in other areas where people had yet to be evangelized (cf. Acts 14:23-28).

Though the main task of the elders (also called *episkopoi*, "overseers" or "bishops," and *diakonoi*, "deacons," as in Phil 1:1) was to build up the Christian community so that all members discovered and used their spiritual gifts; they also served as exemplars in doing evangelism (2 Tim 4:5; cf. 1 Pet 5:3), just as Paul set this evangelistic concern as a model for the Ephesian elders (Acts 20:18-28). One of their qualifications for church "office" was a good reputation before unbelievers (1 Tim 3:1-7).

5.2. Simple Structures. Total mobilization was maintained for a couple of centuries, because the early Christians met in homes and ministered "from house to house" (Acts 20:20; cf. 2:46; 5:42; Rom 16). With no buildings to maintain, they used their limited resources to support the itinerant ministers and the poor among them. This was most probably done consciously, not just by force of circumstance (frequent poverty and persecution), for they were not without resources (cf. Acts 2:44-45; 4:34—5:11; 1 Cor 16:1-4; 2 Cor 8:1-5) and faced no prohibition against building temples, synagogues* or shrines for religious purposes.

The conversion of a husband led usually to the baptism of the entire household,* which included relatives, friends, slaves or freedmen, and even clients. Though the process was very difficult, converted wives were exhorted to win their husbands to Christ through godly behavior (1 Pet 3:1-6; cf. 1 Cor 7:14). Such homes then served as centers for prayer* and worship* (Acts 1:13-14; 2:46; 12:12), pastoral care and fellowship* (Acts 16:40; 18:26; 20:20-21; 21:7), hospitality* (Acts 16:15, 32-34; 17:5-7; 18:7; 21:8) and especially evangelism (Acts 5:42; 10:22; 16:32; 28:17-18).

Moreover, they were not dependent on a priestly class or a few professional religious leaders. Each house church was led by mature adults who, though new in the faith, were capable to take charge of the prayers and study of the Word in weekly gatherings and in fellowship with neighboring house churches.

5.3. High Morality. Living in immoral societies, Christians prized their witness of righteous living. As the gospel called for repentance from sins, the converts were urged to shun ungodliness and put on holiness (Heb 13:4-5; Jas 1:19—4:12; 1 Pet 1:13—2:25; 2 Pet 2; Jude 4-23; *see* Holy, Holiness). They were expected to live transformed lives and exhibit a self-sacrificial love* that would transcend race (cf. Acts 13:1-3), social class (Jas 2:1-9) and gender (Gal 3:28), as shown in their *agapē* feasts (cf. Jude 12; 2 Pet 2:13 NRSV mg.; *see* Lord's Supper).

5.4. Joy in Persecution. Also significant was the witness of courage, endurance* and even joy in the midst of persecution* for the sake of the gospel (cf. Acts 4:23-31; 5:41; 13:50-52; Jas 1:2-4; 1 Pet 1:6-8; Rev 2:3), as when Paul and Silas sang in prison (Acts 16:25). Such serenity and joy in the face of death was viewed as an expression of one's faith (Phil 1:29; Rev 2:10; cf. Heb 10:34) and was exemplified by the Lord Jesus himself (Heb 12:2).

5.5. Contextualized Message. Although the focus of the *euangelion* was clearly Jesus Christ, it was expressed flexibly according to the Christians' own spiritual and intellectual understanding as well as on their audience's backgrounds. To the Jews, Jesus was presented as the Messiah in fulfillment of the high expectations in first-century Judaism. Jesus was introduced as the second Moses* (Deut 18:15, 18-19; as in Acts 3:22; 7:37; Heb 7:4-11), the eternal son of David (2 Sam 7:1-16; as in Acts 2:25-36; 1 Pet 2:21-25), the Son of Man (Dan 7:14; as in Acts 7:56) and the suffering* servant (Is 53; as in Acts 3:18; 8:34). Jesus was also fitted into the Primal Man philosophy of intellectual Hellenistic* Judaism (cf. Rom 5:12-19; Heb 5:7-10; Rev 1:13; 14:14) and the Wisdom-Logos ideology of liberal Judaism (cf. Jn 1:1-18; Heb 1:1-12; *see* Logos). As opportunities arose, the evangelizers appealed to the OT (such as Acts 2:16; 26:23) and used the different types of Jewish exegesis (such as Acts 2:17-26; 1 Pet 1:10-12; Rev 5:5), to highlight the importance and relevance of their Lord.

In preaching to non-Jews, they drew on Greek literature and Stoic and Epicurean philosophies when needed (Acts 17:27-28). When speaking to the religious, especially in the mystery cults, they used words like *mystērion, plērōma* ("fullness") and *zōē aiōnios* ("eternal life"); God was the Creator and provider of all and not dependent on people's idolatrous offerings (Acts 14:15-17). To others they offered God's forgiveness* (Acts 17:31; 24:25) and freedom from demons, magic* and Fate (Acts 16:16-18; 27:13—28:10; cf. 1 Pet 3:22; Rev 5; 18—19).

5.6. Healings and Miracles. In a world filled with fears of diseases, demons, Destiny and magic, the impact of "power evangelism" was very significant. Acts mentions the "signs and wonders"* performed by Peter (Acts 5:15-19) and John (Acts 3:1-9), Stephen (Acts 6:8), Philip (Acts 8:6-7), Paul (Acts 19:11-12; cf. Rom 15:18-19) and the apostles in general (Acts 2:43; 4:33; 5:12; cf. Heb 2:4; *see* Miracles; Signs and Wonders). Some believers were specially endowed with spiritual gifts of healing* and miraculous powers (1 Cor 12:9-10; cf. Jas 5:14-16). Such phenomena done in Jesus' name proved to be superior to the cures and exorcisms of pagan physicians and magicians.

5.7. Prayer. Above all, the early Christians prayed together (cf. Acts 1:13-14; 4:24-31; 12:12). They recognized that their desire, strength and boldness to evangelize came from a divine source: the Holy Spirit was God's gift par excellence (Lk 11:13; *see* Holy Spirit), given to empower them to bear witness to Jesus (Acts 1:8; 5:29-31, 33; cf. Jn 15:26-27). He was the Evangelizer who equipped individuals, like Peter (Acts 2:4, 33; 4:8), Stephen (Acts 6:10), Philip (Acts 8:29), and Paul (Acts 9:17; 16:6), as well as churches, like Antioch (Acts 13:2), to witness for Christ.

All important decisions in the church were marked by prayer* (Acts 1:14, 24-25; 6:6; 9:11; 10:9; 13:3). James 5:13-18 shows that for the early believers prayer was both an ongoing conversation with God (cf. 1 Thess 5:16-18; Phil 6:18; Eph 6:18-20; Col 4:2) and a special activity when people were sick—not just for evangelistic value.

6. The Methods.

The primary methods used in evangelism in the early church included the following.

6.1. Witnessing. As seen above, the primary means was the spontaneous sharing of the gospel* by all believers, including prominent leaders like Peter and John (Acts 3:1-8), Philip (Acts 8), Ananias (Acts 9:10-18) and Paul (Acts 13:6-12; 16:29-32), even before authorities (Acts 24:10-25; 26:1-29). Converted heads of households had their constituencies baptized at the same time with themselves.

6.2. Preaching. For the first twenty years (c. A.D. 35-55) before the break with Judaism, preaching in the synagogues* was done commonly (Acts 6:10; 9:22; 13:44; 18:28). Open-air preaching was done where people naturally passed or assembled (e.g., Acts 2; 8; 14); this was not uniquely Christian, for Jews and Cynics also used courtyards, open fields, riverbanks and even markets. Some preaching was "prophetic" in the sense of "ecstatic," i.e., speaking directly in Christ's name and coherently "in the Spirit" (Acts 11:28; 1 Cor 14:24-25; cf. Rev 19:10).

6.3. Testimonials. Evangelism both in private and in public included persuasive testimonies (*diamartyresthai,* "testify forcefully," as in Acts 2:40; 8:25; 18:5; 23:11; 28:23, cf. 10:42). These consisted of one's personal experience of salvation, especially the power behind one's transformed and/or exemplary life (cf. 1 Pet 3:15).

6.4. Teaching. Most prominent here is Paul's use of the school of Tyrannus in Ephesus to explicate the faith to inquirers (Acts 19:8-9). From the beginning, evangelistic teaching* in public to explain the faith* was already practiced (Acts 5:21, 25, 28, 42).

Included in this category is "dialogue," which used intellectual discussion, careful study of Scripture and patient argumentation, usually in small groups (Acts 17:2-3, 17; 18:4, 19; 19:8-9; 24:25; 28:23). Some dialogues were quite intense and were considered public debates (cf. Acts 9:22, 29; 17:3; 18:28).

6.5. Literature. The OT texts were used to bring Timothy and many Jews to the faith (2 Tim 3:15; Acts 17:2-3). The four Gospels were a new literary form in the first-century world; three of them (except Matthew) were written with the clear intent to challenge their readers to respond in faith to the person whose story they record (see esp. Jn 20:30-31).

7. Postapostolic Developments.

Evangelism in the first half of the second century may be summarized as follows.

The message remained focused on the historical Jesus as the kerygmatic Christ and called for absolute allegiance to him (e.g., *Diogn.* 8—9). There were warnings against false teachers or false teachings (e.g., Ign. *Eph.;* Ign. *Smyrn.;* Ign. *Magn.* 8, 10; Pol. *Phil.* 7) as well as nominal faith (Ign. *Rom.* 3.2; Ign. *Magn.* 4.1; Pol. *Phil.* 2.2; Justin Martyr *Apol. I* 4.7-8; 16.8).

Though love* for God remained as a motive for evangelism, the main motivation soon shifted to obedience* to a mandate, often with meritorious connotations such as the desire to be rewarded with eternal* life (Justin Martyr *Apol. I* 8) or the fear of being punished on judgment* day (*Barn.* 19, 21; Pol. *Phil.* 2, 5; Justin Martyr *Apol. II* 12). There are a few instances of gloating over the tragic fate of the heathen (*Apol. I* 19; *Apol. II* 9; *Mart. Pol.* 11), but what prevailed was the concern to win them to Christ, even pleading for repentance* (*1 Clem.* 7—8; Justin Martyr *Apol. II* 13—15; Justin Martyr *Dial. Tryph.* 7).

Concerning conversions, the apostolic fathers remained wary of superficial faith even after baptism* (as in the NT case of Simon Magus, Acts 8:23). Some started to regard baptism as unrepeatable (*see* Repentance, Second Repentance), thus needing to be administered by a bishop (Ign. *Smyrn.* 8.2), and as an amulet to ward off evil forces (Ign. *Pol.* 6.2). The most obvious change was the delay in administering baptism, which was done only after a period of instruction on the doctrinal and especially ethical aspects of the faith (cf. "the Two Ways" in *Did., Barn.* and *Herm.*) and a time of prayer and fasting (*Apol. I* 61).

A relatively nonrepressive context for evangelism continued to prevail from A.D. 100 to 150. Except for Trajan's reign, the persecution* of Christians remained sporadic and localized until A.D. 170. Most converts were still from the lower or middle classes (*Diogn.* 5-7; cf. *Barn.* 5), with some notable exceptions. The spontaneous expansion geographically to the whole world (*1 Clem.* 59; Justin Martyr *Dial. Tryph.* 42; cf. *Apol. I* 39) continued to be through the existing road networks and trade routes; by 150 there were thriving churches in France, Spain, Germany, Gaul and Africa Proconsularis (from Alexandria and extending up the Nile).

The gospel continued to spread through the spontaneous witness of ordinary believers (Ign. *Trall.* 8). The tradition of roving evangelists and evangelizing bishops/elders also continued (*Did.* 4, 11, 13; *Herm. Vis.* 3.5.1; *Herm. Sim.* 9.15.4; 16.5). Ignatius* urged Polycarp,* a bishop like himself, to "exhort all people that they may be saved" (Ign. *Pol.* 1; cf. *Mart. Pol.* 12).

Without following von Harnack's extreme claim that the second-century church's* "incipient Catholicism" (*see* Early Catholicism) was a "corrupt synthesis" of Hellenism and apostolic Christianity, we must acknowledge that there were indeed departures from the simplicity of NT concepts to a more institutionalized view of church order (e.g., *Did.* 12-13; *1 Clem.* 40—41; Ign. *Eph.* 12, 20; Ign. *Phld.* 9; *Herm. Sim.* 9.16).

Though the hope* for an imminent parousia* was less intense, no one thought of erecting religious buildings (*see* Architecture, Early Church). Homes continued to be the main venue for church meetings. The presence of many children in the house churches (Pliny *Ep.* 10.96; cf. Justin Martyr *Apol. I* 15) indicates that the admonitions for parents to raise their children in the faith (*Barn.* 19.10; *1 Clem.* 21.6-8; Pol. *Phil.* 4.2; cf. Eph 6:1-4) were heeded.

Evangelists preached against immorality, pleaded for repentance and the holy option of the "Two Ways" (*Did.; Barn.;* Justin Martyr *Apol. I* 14), and criticized faults among the believers (*1-2 Clem.; Herm.*). Pliny the Younger found out for himself that Christians did hold to high morals (Pliny *Ep.* 10.96), in contrast to those of

pagan associations (*Apol. I* 9). Their exemplary lives caused people to say, "This does not look like the work of humans: this is the power of God" (*Diogn.* 7; cf. 10).

Those who suffered* and faced martyrdom* considered it a privilege and an opportunity to bear witness* to Christ; *1 Clement* 5 attests to the courage and endurance* Peter and Paul had when they bore witness to Jesus. Ignatius (d. 117) showed an extreme form of confidence and eagerness to face martyrdom. This emphasis on the witness's death in the conception of *martyrein* (cf. Justin Martyr *Apol. II* 12) is a marked development from the NT emphasis on the witness's faithfulness to the role of representing Jesus (Rev 2:13; 6:19; 11:3, 7; 11:6).

The gospel* continued to be contextualized to address the different needs and understandings of both Jews and non-Jews. For instance, Justin Martyr discussed Jesus as the Logos* with intellectual Jews (*Apol. I* 5; *Dial. Tryph.* 1, 8) and offered freedom from fear (*Dial. Tryph.* 30) and God's forgiveness* to others (*Apol. I* 68; *Apol. II* 2, 11, 14). Ignatius showed Jesus to be the *pantocratōr* who is sovereign over all rivals (Ign. *Eph.* 19; cf. *Barn.* 2.6), and *1 Clement* 25 used the phoenix to prove the resurrection.*

After the break with official Judaism, Christians were considered "impious blasphemers" who believed in two Gods and that God had union with a woman (cf. *Dial. Tryph.* 16, 96). Especially after the A.D. 135 Bar Kokhba revolt, there was no longer any known attempt to win Jews to the faith.

The postapostolic period continued to see the gifts of miracles and healings* in the name of Jesus as powerful evidences of the reality of the message. Quadratus was cited as saying that some of the people whom Jesus healed or raised from the dead were still alive when he wrote (Eusebius *Hist. Eccl.* 4.3.2). Justin Martyr also referred to such healings among the Christians (Justin Martyr *Dial. Tryph.* 30, 85), saying that Jesus was made man "for the destruction of demons" (Justin *Martyr Apol. II* 6). As in the NT, no magic formula or training program was needed for such ministry.

Fervent prayer* continued to be a vital part of the early second-century church: Ignatius taught, "Pray without ceasing, on behalf of others" (Ign. *Eph.* 10, cf. Justin Martyr *Dial. Tryph.* 7).

Public preaching, including prophetic preaching, was still practiced (*Did.* 11; Ign. *Phld.* 7.1). But except for the *Epistle to Diognetus* and Justin *Apology II*, section 15, there seems to be no second-century Christian literature aiming to win the goodwill of and positive response from nonbelieving readers. A development was the rise of philosopher-evangelists who founded their own "schools," like Justin Martyr in Rome (cf. *Apol. II*) and Pantaenus in Alexandria (Eusebius *Hist. Eccl.* 5.10).

See also ACTS OF THE APOSTLES; CENTERS OF CHRISTIANITY; GENTILES, GENTILE MISSION; GOSPEL; KERYGMA AND DIDACHE; MISSION, EARLY NON-PAULINE; UNIVERSALISM.

BIBLIOGRAPHY. U. Becker, "Gospel, Evangelize, Evangelist," *NIDNNT* 2:107-15; U. Becker et al., "Proclamation, Preach, Kerygma," *NIDNNT* 3:44-68; F. F. Bruce, *The Defense of the Gospel in the New Testament* (rev. ed.; Grand Rapids: Eerdmans, 1977); L. Coenen, A. A. Trites, "Witness, Testimony," *NIDNNT* 3:1038-50; C. H. Dodd, *The Apostolic Preaching and Its Developments* (London: Hodder & Stoughton, 1936); J. D. Dunn, ed., *Jews and Christians: The Partings of the Ways, A.D. 70 to 135* (Tübingen: J. C. B. Mohr, 1992); W. H. C. Frend, *Martyrdom and Persecution in the Early Church* (Grand Rapids: Baker, 1981); G. Friedrich, "εὐαγγελίζομαι κτλ," *TDNT* 2:707-37; M. Green, *Evangelism in the Early Church* (Grand Rapids: Eerdmans, 1970); F. Hahn, *Mission in the New Testament* (Naperville, IL: Allenson, 1965); A. von Harnack, *Mission and Expansion of Christianity in the First Three Centuries* (2 vols; London: Williams and Norgate, 1905); E. A. Judge, *The Social Pattern of Christian Groups in the First Century* (London: Tyndale, 1960); J. A. Kirk, "Apostleship After Rengstorf: Towards a Synthesis," *NTS* 21 (1975) 249-64; A. D. Nock, *Conversion* (New York: Oxford University Press, 1961); W. H. Ramsay, *The Church in the Roman Empire Before A.D. 170* (London: Hodder & Stoughton, 1893); H. Shanks, ed., *Christianity and Rabbinic Judaism: A Parallel History of Their Origins and Early Development* (Washington, D.C.: Biblical Archaeology Society, 1992); R. Stark, *The Rise of Christianity* (Princeton: Princeton University Press, 1996); R. C. Worley, *Preaching and Teaching in the Earliest Church* (Philadelphia: Westminster, 1967).

D. S. Lim

EVIL ONE. *See* SATAN, DEVIL.

EVIL SPIRITS. *See* SPIRITS.

EXALTATION, ENTHRONEMENT

The exaltation of Jesus, a concept that embraces Jesus' ascension,* session at God's* right hand and return in triumph, expresses God's approval of Jesus' life and acceptance of Jesus' sacrificial death (*see* Death of Christ). It expresses the conviction that Jesus is the agent of God's reign and judgment*: loyalty to him and obedience* to his example and teaching would mean a share in his honor and authority* as well as vindication at his coming in power (*see DPL*, Exaltation, Enthronement). Even though following Christ brought one into disrepute in the eyes of the world, Jesus' exaltation assured his followers that they too would be honored before God's eternal court. Jesus' exaltation signified that Jesus now exists in the presence of God, forever able to intercede on behalf of his followers as their high priest,* assuring them of their perpetual access to God's favor and timely help. Jesus encounters his church* as Lord,* the one who rules the church and claims the complete allegiance of believers, and Savior, the one who is able to bring his followers to their promised inheritance; Jesus will encounter the world as Judge, whose coming will bring terror to all who resist his rule but whose appearing will mean the consummation of God's purposes for God's faithful people. In such ways Jesus' exaltation became a powerful source of encouragement to the churches of the first and second centuries.

1. Jewish Background
2. Acts
3. Hebrews
4. General Epistles
5. Revelation
6. Apostolic Fathers

1. Jewish Background.
The NT authors share the Jewish conviction that God is exalted over creation* and enthroned as king (a frequent theme of the Psalms, for example), but through their experience of the risen Jesus and through their reading of certain OT texts they now see that exaltation shared by God's agent, the Son.* Especially important for this process are the "royal psalms" such as Psalms 2, 45 and 110, which are read as indications of Jesus' voca-

tion and activity after his resurrection* and ascension. The Danielic vision of the Son of Man (Dan 7:13-14) is also now read as God's giving eternal royal authority to Jesus: what he now possesses by right will be actualized at his Parousia.* The hope* formerly expressed in prayers* for God's intervention in human affairs to set things right, establish justice and vindicate the righteous (cf. Is 64:1) is now expressed in prayers for Jesus' return as exalted Lord and Judge to effect these ends.

2. Acts.

Acts* begins with the story of Jesus' ascension, after which the apostles* speak of Jesus being "exalted at the right hand of God" (Acts 2:33-36, referring explicitly to Ps 110:1; cf. Acts 5:30-31) and the martyr Stephen* can see the heavens open to reveal Jesus in this highly exalted station (Acts 7:55-56). Jesus' vindication and exaltation by God necessitate that all who participated in his rejection repent (*see* Repentance) and respond to Jesus not as the crucified criminal but the one on whom God has set the highest seal of approval (Acts 2:36-38). Jesus' exaltation imposes a similar mandate on the Gentiles*: Jesus has made possible their turning away from idols (*see* Idolatry) to the one God and their inclusion in the people of God; he is returning as Judge of those who refuse to repent (Acts 17:31).

Jesus' exaltation is explicated in Acts by a number of titles denoting the rank Jesus has attained: God has made Jesus "Lord and Christ" (Acts 2:36) and "Author and Savior" (Acts 5:30-31). "Lord" represents the attribution of the divine title *kyrios* to the exalted Jesus, such that Jesus now shares in God's dominion over creation and history. He is Lord actively of the church, receiving its worship* (Acts 7:59; 13:2), directing it from his exalted position (Acts 9:10-16; 16:7-8) and supplying it with the Holy Spirit* (Acts 1:5; 2:32-33). D. L. Tiede is thus correct to note that Acts does not express an "absentee Christology"*—even though he "must remain in heaven" for this interim period (Acts 3:21), the exalted Lord is still present for his people. Jesus' lordship will become absolute when he returns to judge the world (Acts 17:31). As "Christ," it is Jesus who has been appointed by God to bring the "times of refreshing" for his people at the time set beforehand by God (Acts 3:19-21). As "Author" or Founder, Jesus has

initiated God's purpose for Israel's* repentance and laid the foundation for its restoration, and as "Savior" he has been empowered by God to deliver his followers.

3. Hebrews.

Hebrews* opens with a vivid presentation of Jesus' exaltation and enthronement. Following Jesus' suffering* of death on behalf of all (Heb 2:9) and making purification for sins (Heb 1:3), God seats Jesus at God's right hand (Heb 1:3, 13; 8:1; 10:12; 12:2). Hebrews's extensive use of this image of session shows the importance of Psalm 110:1 for this author, as for NT reflection on Christ's status generally (Cullmann). He is exalted above the angels* to the extent that a "Son"* is greater than "servants"* (Heb 1:4-7, 9). God's own self is Jesus' eternal throne—Jesus' authority and reign are embedded in God's authority and reign, and Jesus rules with a scepter of righteousness* (Heb 1:8-9; cf. Ps. 45:6-7). Seated at God's right hand, Jesus awaits the final subjection of all his enemies (Heb 1:13; 10:13; cf. Ps. 110:1).

The author of Hebrews did not stop reading Psalm 110 at the first verse, however. Hebrews finds in this psalm that Jesus' exaltation was an appointment to an eternal priesthood "after the order of Melchizedek" (Heb 5:6, 10; 7:17, 21; Ps 110:4; *see* Melchizedek). At his exaltation Jesus "passed through the heavens" (Heb 4:14) and stands "above the heavens" (Heb 7:26) so that he has entered the heavenly tabernacle,* the "true" sanctuary "not made with hands" (Heb 8:2; 9:24), which stands in the permanent, unshakable realm of the divine (*see* Heaven). There Jesus, possessing an "indestructible life" (Heb 7:16, 25), lives forever to make intercession for his followers (Heb 7:25; cf. Rom 8:34).

Jesus has become the believers' "great high priest" (Heb 4:14; 5:5-6, 10; 8:1-2), whose mediation assures believers of God's favor. Jesus' death becomes the one sacrifice* that is able to remove sins and cleanse the heavenly sanctuary of defilement (Heb 9:23-26; 10:11-14) so that the believers can approach God with the anticipation of favor rather than judgment (Heb 4:14-16; 10:19-22). Jesus enjoys face-to-face access to God (Heb 9:12, 24) and enjoys the closest possible relationship to God in God's household* ("Son"): he is the one mediator whose mediation would be assured success (Heb 7:26-28). It is also in this priestly aspect of Christ's ministry* that the author of Hebrews draws the closest connections between Jesus' earthly activity and his activity as exalted Son (Heb 5:7-10). Jesus' session at God's right hand demonstrates the completeness and efficacy of Jesus' one high-priestly sacrifice (Heb 10:11-14). Psalm 110:1 signifies therefore not so much Jesus' active rule for the author of Hebrews (Hay, Saucy) as God's approval of Jesus' work and the completion of the priestly task of restoring favor between God and the people who approach God through Jesus.

The author's development of Jesus' exaltation and priestly mediation serves an intense pastoral interest. First, Jesus' exaltation assists believers, who are Christ's "partners" (*metochoi*, Heb 3:6, 14) and "brothers and sisters" (Heb 2:10-12), to rise above society's attempts to shame them back into conformity. As Jesus steered the course of obedience to God, despising the world's negative opinion and hostility, and came thus to enjoy the place of highest honor in the cosmos, so believers are called to look to God's reward* of approval and honor (Heb 12:1-3), if they hold fast to the confession and continue in service to fellow believers (Heb 3:14; 6:10; 10:35-36). As Jesus has been "crowned with glory and honor" after his incarnation and suffering of death on behalf of all (Heb 2:6-9; cf. Ps 8:4-6), so the believers have the sure hope* that they will also share in Jesus' exaltation at the consummation (Heb 2:10; cf. Hurst).

Second, Jesus' exaltation to the priesthood* of the heavenly tabernacle means that Jesus' loyal clients also enjoy face-to-face access with God through Jesus' mediation. Unlike earthly high priests, Jesus does not leave his people standing outside the Holy Place but allows them also to "approach with boldness the throne of favor," so that they may "receive mercy and find favor for timely help" (Heb 4:16). The believers may "enter the sanctuary" and go "through the curtain" (Heb 10:19-22) and so receive from the Fount of favor the resources they require to endure in loyalty to Jesus. Moreover, when Jesus entered the abiding realm he did so as a forerunner (Heb 6:20; cf. Maclean): the believers too will be brought into their heavenly homeland and permanent city that they purchased with the price of disenfranchisement in the world (Heb 10:34; 11:13-16; 13:13-14). This is the salvation* that believers may anticipate at Jesus' return (Heb 9:28).

Third, Jesus' exaltation to the place of highest honor and his embeddedness in God's honor as Son make the consequences of breaking faith* with him all the more severe. Those who enjoy the benefits that the Son's death and present mediation have made possible and then reject these costly favors for the sake of peace with the unbelieving society have shown contempt for the One whose honor God will uphold and avenge at the judgment (Heb 10:26-31; cf. Heb 2:1-4; 6:4-8). Christ's exaltation is thus part of a carefully orchestrated rhetorical strategy designed to encourage believers to persevere in their Christian commitment.

4. General Epistles.

1 Peter* speaks frequently of Jesus' exaltation, often in close connection with his suffering (1 Pet 1:11, 21). This no doubt stems from one pastoral intent of the epistle, namely, to encourage Christians to face trial, reproach and suffering now so as to share in the glory* and vindication that also followed Jesus' suffering on account of obedience to God (1 Pet 4:13-14). The exaltation of Jesus is present also in the architectural metaphor of the cornerstone (1 Pet 2:4, 6-8; *see* Stone). God's exaltation of Jesus, the "stone" rejected by human beings, to the place of "cornerstone" shows the fallibility of human evaluation, encouraging believers to disregard society's negative evaluation of the followers of Jesus (1 Pet 2:12; 3:13-17; 4:4) now in hope of future exaltation by God with Christ, to whom they are being joined as "living stones." The promise of sharing in Christ's glory is also used to encourage submission and humility* toward one another within the church (1 Pet 5:6): because God exalts the humble, there is no need or place for competition and self-advancement within the group (which erodes group cohesion and solidarity).

Jesus' exaltation by God shows God's approval of and public identification with Jesus, such that the believers may be assured that their hope and confidence in Jesus are well-placed—they are in fact placed in God's own self (1 Pet 1:21). The efficacy of baptism* is also linked with Christ's exaltation to the right hand of God, above angels and authorities and powers (1 Pet 3:21-22). In the context of the discussion of Jesus' suffering "for sins once for all . . . in order to bring" believers "to God" (1 Pet 3:18), the resurrection shows God's acceptance of Jesus' sacrifice and thus also of the believers who have identified themselves as Christ's clients through baptism. Jesus as exalted Christ remains our mediator, through whom we may "offer spiritual sacrifices to God" (1 Pet 2:5; cf. Heb 13:15-16).

References to Jesus' exaltation in the other General Epistles are scant. 2 Peter 1:16-18 refers to the transfiguration of Jesus as a revelation of his true honor, a prefiguration of the glory Jesus now enjoys and prophetic vision of the Parousia (*see* 2 Peter). This vision of Jesus' power and majesty assures the genuineness of the apostolic teaching: it does not consist in humanly devised myths but is a revelation* from the divine Son. James* refers once to the "glorious Lord Jesus Christ" (Jas 2:1; see commentaries for variant translations, one linking Jesus to the "glory" [*šᵉkînâh*]) in the context of an exhortation to show no partiality toward the rich or contempt for the poor, for the well-to-do are the ones who fail to honor the "excellent name" of Jesus (Jas 2:7). 1 John 2:2 speaks of Jesus' ongoing role as advocate before God on our behalf, but the Johannine epistles focus much more on the incarnation and its effects rather than its sequel (*see* John, Letters of).

5. Revelation.

In Revelation (*see* Revelation, Book of) Jesus is presented at the outset as the "ruler of the kings of the earth" (Rev 1:5). Jesus as God's Messiah has been exalted to share in God's kingship: Jesus' reign has been confirmed in God's court (Rev 5:12-14; 11:15) and will soon be actualized in the human and demonic realms. John's initial vision depicts Jesus as he now exists, in his exalted, glorified, resurrected body (Rev 1:12-17). He is the male child who was caught up into heaven, whence he awaits reception of universal rule (Rev 12:5); he has sat down on his "Father's throne" and thus shares in God's kingly rule (Rev 3:21). Jesus is the Lamb* who enjoys unique privilege and authority in light of what he accomplished by his voluntary death: the right to open the seven-sealed scroll* and thus authority over the setting in motion of the end (Rev 5:2-3, 6-10, 11-12). Jesus has received authority from his Father (Rev 2:28), and the heavenly hosts celebrate the initial realization of this authority in the casting down of Satan* from heaven to earth (Rev 12:10).

Revelation's primary movement is toward the realization of the kingship of God and God's Messiah, specifically through their destruction of their spiritual and human opponents, their judgment of the world and their vindication of the faithful (Rev 11:15-18). Liturgical expressions of the enthronement of God and Jesus in Revelation are, like the liturgical expressions of the same in Christian worship, anticipations of fulfillment—the reign is consistently celebrated before it is consummated (Rev 11:15-18; 19:6; *see* Worship; Liturgical Elements). Christ's victory over all his enemies is, however, assured. As "Lord of lords and King of kings," his rule and exaltation are ultimate and his authority irresistible (Rev 17:13-14). In John's second vision of the glorified Christ, Jesus now takes his royal authority and makes his reign secure by destroying his enemies (Rev 19:11-16). The symbols of multiple crowns express the coming monarch's rule over the "kingdoms of this world." The promise of Psalm 2:9 that "he will rule them with a rod of iron" is finally fulfilled, as Christ's enthronement is actualized at last.

Again Christ's enthronement and the assurance of his victory serve an important pastoral purpose. Christ's exaltation and enthronement are made a motivation for believers' steadfastness as they are given the hope of sharing in Christ's reign (Rev 2:25-28; 3:21). This is vividly portrayed in the vision of those believers who were shamefully executed for their loyalty to Jesus but who will be rewarded with a share in Christ's reign, seated upon thrones themselves (Rev 20:4-6). Christ's ultimate triumph as "Lord of lords and King of kings" (Rev 17:13-14) also serves to orient believers toward the antienthronement of the emperor* by the dragon (Rev 13:2, 4, 7-8; *see* Beasts) and toward Roman imperial ideology as a whole. Those who participate in the exaltation of God's enemy fall prey to dire consequences when the true Lord judges the world (Rev 14:9-11; 16:2), whereas those who revere Christ as Lord by not giving reverence to a usurper will enjoy God's presence and favor eternally (Rev 15:2-4; 20:4-6; 22:3-5).

6. Apostolic Fathers.

The successors of the apostles shared the conviction that Jesus was exalted to a throne at God's right hand and given authority and dominion following his resurrection (Pol. *Phil.* 2.1). These writers (*see* Apostolic Fathers) wrestled as well with the nature of that dominion and its significance for believers. Jesus the incarnate One is the preexistent Son (*see* Preexistence), "Lord over all the earth" already by virtue of his agency in creation (*Barn.* 5.5; 12.10). The *Shepherd of Hermas** also underscores this identification (*Herm. Sim.* 9.12.2-3), although his parabolic language threatens the unity of the Son and Jesus at one point (*Herm. Sim.* 5.2, 6). Here Hermas distinguishes Jesus, the embodied "servant" who obeys God's command and exceeds it, from the Son of God, who is Spirit, with whom he is made coheir by God. Hermas's point, however, is that Jesus has been exalted now in his human nature as well as his divine nature and aims thus at arousing hope in his followers, who are depicted in the parable as Jesus' fellow servants and who share in the bounty to which Jesus as "servant" has attained.

Jesus now reigns over the church as "the bishop of all" (Ign. *Magn.* 3.1-2; Ign. *Rom.* 9.1), the "lord of the whole tower" which is the church (*Herm. Sim.* 9.7.1). All believers owe Jesus complete allegiance and obedience "from the heart." Jesus, who now shares God's status (*2 Clem.* 1.1-2; Ign. *Pol.* 8.3), is the "helper" and "protector" of the believers (*1 Clem.* 36.1; 61.3; 64.1). His exalted status assures the believers that they will be well taken care of and makes Jesus a patron par excellence: if believers think of him as they ought, they will know him as the source of outstanding benefactions (*2 Clem.* 1.1-2). The impact of Hebrews's portrayal of the exalted Jesus as high priest, through whom prayer become efficacious and through whom believers offer their gratitude to God, is widespread in this literature (*1 Clem.* 36.1; 61.3; 64.1; Ign. *Phld.* 9.1; Pol. *Phil.* 12.2; *Mart. Pol.* 14.3).

Jesus' enthronement now as "ruling monarch" (*Mart. Pol.* 21.1) once again looks to the future for the full realization of his authority and reign, when Christ will return upon the clouds of heaven as "Lord" (*Did.* 16.6-8). The believers therefore pray for this consummation, a petition that dominates the celebration of the Eucharist (*Did.* 10.5-6), when the "future Judge of living and dead alike" (*Barn.* 7.2; *2 Clem.* 1.1-2) will receive the "kingdom of this world" to the amazement of unbelievers (*2 Clem.* 17.5-7). Once more one finds that discussion of Christ's exaltation now and at the Parousia serves a hortatory function. Exaltation as the outcome of Jesus' endurance* of suffering helps believers endure in the hope of sharing in Christ's vindication by God (*Barn.* 7.11). Those who remain loyal even unto death, God will exalt to honor and renown above (*1 Clem.* 45.7-8). Believers are confirmed in their doing of God's will as revealed by Jesus by the hope that Jesus' own exaltation provides (Pol. *Phil.* 2.1-2; Ign. *Trall.* 9.2). As they live with a view to the day of Jesus' return as Judge and King, they are enabled to endure in the discipline of the Christian life and not to deny Jesus by word or deed (*2 Clem.* 17.5-7).

See also ASCENSION; CHRISTOLOGY; DEATH OF CHRIST; GLORY; HEAVEN, NEW HEAVEN; RESURRECTION.

BIBLIOGRAPHY. H. Bietenhard, "Lord, Master," *NIDNTT* 2:508-20; O. Cullmann, *The Christology of the New Testament* (Philadelphia: Westminster, 1959); J. G. Davies, *He Ascended into Heaven* (London: Lutterworth, 1958); D. A. deSilva, *Despising Shame: Honor Discourse and Community Maintenance in the Epistle to the Hebrews* (SBLDS 152; Atlanta: Scholars Press, 1996); J. D. G. Dunn, *Christology in the Making* (Philadelphia: Westminster, 1980); M. Gourgues, *A la droite de Dieu: Résurrection de Jésus et actualisation du Psaume 110:1 dans le Nouveau Testament* (Paris: Gabalda, 1978); D. M. Hay, *Glory at the Right Hand: Psalm 110 in Early Christianity* (SBLMS 18; Nashville: Abingdon, 1973); L. D. Hurst, "The Christology of Hebrews 1 and 2" in *The Glory of Christ in the New Testament: Studies in Christology,* ed. L. D. Hurst and N. T. Wright (Oxford: Clarendon, 1987); W. R. G. Loader, "Christ at the Right Hand—Ps. 110:1 in the New Testament," *NTS* 24 (1977-78) 199-217; A. J. Maclean, "Ascension" in *Dictionary of the Apostolic Church,* ed. J. Hastings (New York: Charles Scribner's Sons, 1916) 1:95-99; W. Milligan, *The Ascension and Heavenly Priesthood of Our Lord* (London: Macmillan, 1891); C. F. D. Moule, *The Origins of Christology* (Cambridge: Cambridge University Press, 1977); M. C. Parsons, "Son and High Priest: A Study in the Christology of Hebrews," *EvQ* 60 (1988) 195-215; M. Saucy, "Exaltation Christology in Hebrews: What Kind of Reign?" *TJ* (n.s.) 14 (1993) 41-62; E. Schweizer, *Lordship and Discipleship* (London: SCM, 1960); D. L. Tiede, "The Exaltation of Jesus and the Restoration of Israel in Acts 1," *HTR* 79 (1986) 178-286.   D. A. deSilva

5 EZRA AND 6 EZRA. *See* APOCRYPHAL AND PSEUDEPIGRAPHAL WRITINGS.

F

FAITH, FAITHFULNESS

Faith is one of the most important theological concepts of the NT. Although the Pauline corpus most readily comes to mind when one speaks of faith, the concept is no less important in the later NT. One need only read Hebrews 11 to be reminded of that fact. "Faith" and its cognates are used in a variety of ways in the later NT; the word group is used to refer to religious faith (belief and trust in God* or Christ*) or trust, to the Christian faith itself, to something that functions as a proof, to those who are faithful and to that which is certain or unfailing.

1. Acts
2. Hebrews
3. James
4. Petrine Letters
5. Johannine Letters
6. Revelation
7. Apostolic Fathers

1. Acts.

Acts* uses *pisteuō* ("to believe") to refer to conversion to the Christian faith. When it is said in Acts 13:12 that the proconsul "began to believe," it means that upon seeing the blinding of Bar-Jesus, he became a believer, that is, that he was converted to the Christian faith. It is interesting to note that his baptism* is not mentioned, although it is almost always connected with conversion (Acts 8:12, 13; 11:16, 17; 16:15, 31-33; 18:8; 19:4, 5; cf. Acts 2:38, 41; 22:16). However, this does not mean that Sergius Paulus was not truly converted (cf. the discussion in Bruce, 299).

Acts very closely connects faith in Christ (or "in his name" [Acts 3:16, 11:17; 16:31; 20:21]) with repentance.* This is not surprising, since in Acts the call to repentance is an essential element in proclaiming the gospel (cf. Barrett, 154). Thus after we read in Acts 11:17 that the Gentiles* believed in God, in the next verse we

learn that it is through Christ that the Gentiles were "granted repentance that leads to life." Acts 6:7 says that those who became believers become "obedient to the faith" (where "faith" refers to the content of Christian belief and life), highlighting that for Luke faith is always more than mental assent to a set of doctrines; having faith means that one begins to live as God would have one to live.

The important theme that Gentiles are to believe in Christ and thus become part of the people of God (*see* Church as Israel) surfaces in various places in Acts, such as Acts 14:27 (see also Acts 13:8, 12, 39, 41, 48; 14:1, 9, 22, 23), which says that God opened a "door of faith" to the Gentiles. We are not to assume that for the first time in Acts, Gentiles have become believers (see the conversion of the eunuch in Acts 8 and of Cornelius* in Acts 10). It is rather a summary statement of what has happened. The phrase "door of faith" is ambiguous; "faith" here most likely means not "true piety" (against Haenchen, 437) but the act of believing and the subsequent lifestyle. Though it is impossible to be precise, the expression implies that a way into faith has been made possible for the Gentiles through Christ.

2. Hebrews.

As we would expect, Hebrews* emphasizes the idea that merely hearing the gospel message without responding in faith will benefit the hearers nothing (Heb 4:2). One must respond to the message with faith and must persevere in that faith.

The Christians to which Hebrews is addressed are not threatened by a specific false teaching but seem to be afflicted with a fear of suffering* that is crippling their faith (cf. the discussion in Ellingworth). Thus the author encourages them to "hold firmly to Jesus Christ, who is the initiator and the perfecter of faith."

Faith, they must realize, is of divine origin. Moreover, since it is not a mere human invention, they must understand that "faith is the assurance of things hoped for, the conviction of things not seen" (Heb 11:1). This is not a definition of faith (against Michel and Attridge) but a description of what it can accomplish in the life of the believer; properly understood and lived, faith ties believers to that which they do not yet see, but hope for. It is a dynamic, not static, response to God that allows one to live life in light of what one does not see (cf. the discussion in Lane).

In Hebrews, to have faith is to be faithful to God and to the gospel. There is an important difference between Hebrews's and Paul's use of Habakkuk 2:3-4. Galatians 3:12 makes it clear that Paul sees the law* as operating on a different principle than that of the faith enunciated in Habakkuk 2:4. For Paul "the law is not based on faith." The just live "by faith," but the law is based on "doing," a point Paul buttresses by citing Leviticus 18:5: "whoever does the works of the law will live by them" (though Paul does not mean to imply that those who live by faith are not required to live in obedience* to God).

For the author of Hebrews, perseverance is the point of the affirmation of Habakkuk 2:3-4 (which he adapts much more freely than Paul does): "but my righteous one will live by faith" (Heb 10:38). It provides the starting point for the lengthy list of OT heroes of perseverance in faith in Hebrews 11:1-40. Faced with the possibility of destruction such as Israel* faced in the wilderness (Heb 10:38-39), the readers of Hebrews are encouraged to remain faithful and to live by faith (Heb 10:38-39; 4:2-3). The OT heroes were faithful, as Habakkuk 2:3-4 says one must be. "My righteous one shall live by faith" is seen by Hebrews as a call to perseverance, a perseverance that is possible only because one can trust God. Faith in Hebrews involves both elements of obedience (manifested in endurance*) and trust in a God who is himself faithful (Fitzmyer).

3. James.

James* emphasizes that faith must be accompanied by works (see Faith and Works). Whereas Paul says that one is saved by faith apart from works (cf. Rom 9:32), James says that faith without works is dead (Jas 2:17). However, contrary to J. T. Sanders, James has not misunderstood

Paul. Sanders, who compares James to Romans 3—4, fails to take into account not only other Pauline letters but even the evidence of Romans itself. James is arguing that faith without works is not authentic faith. True faith calls for works, that is, doing the will of God, which includes kindness to the poor. A person, he says, is justified by works and not by faith alone (Jas 2:24). Yet there is no dichotomy between James and Paul. It is a matter of different but mutually compatible perspectives. Paul insists on the necessity of works in the believer's life (cf. Gal 5:6; 6:40), but because of his focus on justification by faith he emphasizes that it is faith that saves. For James the works that must accompany faith are in focus. James's emphasis can easily be accounted for by positing that some people were saying that belief was enough, and they did not want to be concerned about such things as charity or that the church was courting the rich by not insisting on good works from them (Davids).

There is also a significant point of contact between James and Paul that should not be ignored. Throughout the Pauline corpus we see that Paul believes that God makes possible the good works that believers do. This, although it is not emphasized, also appears in James. In James 1:5 he says that if anyone desires wisdom* from God, God will give it him or her. In James 3:17 the wisdom that comes from above is said to consist of, among other things, "mercy and good fruits." The works that are to accompany faith thus find their ultimate origin in God (see also Jas 4:6: "he gives more grace"). Thus for both James and Paul the demand for Christian works is predicated upon one's experience of grace* (see DPL, James and Paul).

4. Petrine Letters.

In 1 Peter 1:21 Christ is spoken of as the agent of faith in God. It is "through him you have confidence in God . . . so that your faith and hope are in God." This verse highlights that in 1 Peter* faith and hope* are virtual synonyms (cf. Davids), but more importantly they show that for Peter, as for much of the NT, God has taken the initiative in Christ in his death (see Death of Christ) and resurrection,* and this makes possible the human response of faith.

In 1 Peter perseverance in the face of severe suffering is a central theme. The Gentile believers to whom the letter is addressed must realize that they must be ready to suffer as Jesus did (cf. 1 Pet 1:6; 2:21-23). They must expect their faith to be tested, and they must realize that this is the norm for believers. Believers must remain "strong in [their] faith" (1 Pet 5:9), knowing that they can look forward to the last day when God will "restore, establish and strengthen" the suffering church.*

2 Peter 1:5-7 urges believers to "make every effort to supplement your faith with virtue" (and other positive behaviors and qualities; *see* 2 Peter). Virtue* (moral excellence) is but one of the necessary components of the believer's life. As we also see in James and Paul, for Peter complete trust in God must be accompanied by works (cf. 2 Pet 1:8). That this should be so is here predicated on the fact that Christ's divine power has granted believers "everything that pertains to life and godliness." That the ability to live an authentic life of faith has already been granted them is what lies behind 1 Peter 2:24-25, the importance of which is not always recognized by interpreters. It provides the theological underpinning for all of Peter's paraenesis. Believers can do as God asks of them (which includes remaining faithful while suffering) because Christ has died so that believers "might live to righteousness."

5. Johannine Letters.

In the Johannine letters (*see* John, Letters of) as in the Gospel of John, faith does not represent a retreat from the world but rather signals the ultimate defeat of the world,* that is, the forces that are arrayed against God (1 Jn 5:4). In 1 John we read that one cannot love God (and to love God is to have faith in God) and not love fellow believers. Faith then must be evidenced by action; to see a brother or a sister in need and not to meet their needs is to fail in love of God and therefore in faith (1 Jn 3:17).

In the Johannine letters "to believe" involves nothing less than total commitment to Christ, his commandments* and one's fellow believers. Although the ideas of faith as receptivity and belief and of faithfulness are present throughout the Johannine letters, the verb occurs only in 1 John 5:1 and the noun occurs only once in the Johannine letters. 1 John 5:1 states that "the one who believes that Jesus is the Christ is a child of God." With R. Bultmann we must note that for John *pisteuō* and *homologeō* are practically synonyms (cf. 1 Jn 2:23; 4:2, 3, 15) with right

belief leading to new birth.* 1 John 5:4 reads, "For whatever is born of God overcomes the world; and this is the victory that overcomes the world, our faith." Faith refers not just to belief itself; in light of the context, which emphasizes belief in what is true about Christ, it must have christological* content (cf. 1 Jn 5:6; cf. the discussion in Smalley). It is fidelity to the confession* that Christ has come in the flesh* that will enable believers to have victory over the world and its false prophets* (1 Jn 4:1-3).

6. Revelation.

In Revelation (*see* Revelation, Book of) persevering in faith is of paramount importance. The Revelation to John is to be written down (Rev 1:19) so that the oppressed elect* might know what is and what is to come and thereby be challenged, comforted and ultimately remain faithful to Christ. Revelation 13:10 calls the believers to walk the same path as did Christ— one of suffering. Thus comes the "call for the endurance and faith of the saints." Unwavering trust in the face of persecution* is called for on the part of believers. In Revelation 2:10 John reveals his understanding of the nature of the persecution; although the Roman government (*see* Roman Empire) is the earthly agent of the church's trials, the trials are diabolical in origin (*see* Satan). Thus he says that it is "the devil" who "is about to throw some of you into prison." In this text, as we see throughout the NT, exhortations to faithfulness are complemented by assurances* or the certainty of the future consummation of salvation* (the "crown of life" in Rev 2:10).

7. Apostolic Fathers.

H. Chadwick observes that as time passed and as the church spread "the faith," that is, "that which is believed," was crucial for giving scattered communities a sense of belonging to a larger whole. The unity of early Christian communities depended on the things they had in common: modes of worship* and more importantly their allegiance to Jesus and to his teaching. Despite this commonality, however, we do find different emphases (cf. De Simone).

In Hermas it is stated explicitly that faith should lead to living righteously and that this combination leads to "life." *Pistis* is the means by which "the elect of God are saved" (*Herm. Vis.* 3.8.2-3), and such faith gives birth to "self-control" and a host of other virtues.* When one evidences these, then one can be sure that one will live (see also *Herm. Man.* 4.3.7). Knowing the truth is not enough: "if you bear the name but do not bear his power, you bear his name in vain" (*Herm. Sim.* 9.13.2). It is interesting to note that Hermas (like Jas 1:6) connects faith with the granting of prayer* requests (cf. *Herm. Man.* 9.6). For *1 Clement* faith and knowledge* go hand in hand. "Let a man be faithful, let him have the power to speak deep [or secret] knowledge (*1 Clem.* 48.5; *see* Clement of Rome). Faith and knowledge are partners, for it is through faith in Christ that "our foolish and darkened understanding blossoms toward the light" and that "we should taste the immortal knowledge" (*1 Clem.* 36.2).

For Ignatius* of Antioch, as for the other apostolic fathers,* the object and ground of faith is Christ, crucified and raised from the dead (Ign. *Trall.* 9.2; cf. Ign. *Phld.* 8.2). The Christian life begins with belief in Christ and this very early summary of the essentials of "the faith," but it must end in "love." "They who proclaim to be of Christ shall be seen through their deeds" (Ign. *Eph.* 14.1-2).

By the time of John Chrysostom, Christians are speaking about the difference between faith and the knowledge that can be gotten by human reason alone. Chrysostom, in *Homily* 22.1.3, comments on Hebrews 11:3-4, saying that "faith needs a generous and vigorous soul, and one rising above all things of sense and passing beyond the weakness of human reasonings. For it is not possible to become a believer otherwise than by raising one's self above the common customs [of the world]." Faith, according to Chrysostom, cannot depend on human reason. It must rise above it; one must be open to enlightenment, which comes from God.

See also ASSURANCE; BAPTISM, BAPTISMAL RITES; ENDURANCE, PERSEVERANCE; FAITH AND WORKS; FORGIVENESS; GRACE; HOPE; LOVE; REPENTANCE, SECOND REPENTANCE.

BIBLIOGRAPHY. H. Attridge, *The Epistle to the Hebrews* (Herm; Philadelphia: Fortress, 1989); C. K. Barrett, *The Acts of the Apostles* (2 vols.; ICC; Edinburgh: T & T Clark, 1994-); G. Barth, "πίστις," *EDNT* 3:91-98; G. R. Beasley-Murray, *The Book of Revelation* (NCB; Grand Rapids: Eerdmans, 1974); R. E. Brown, *The Epistles of John* (AB; Garden City, NY: Doubleday, 1982); F. F. Bruce, *The Acts of the Apostles* (3d ed.; Grand Rapids: Eerdmans, 1990); R. Bultmann, *The Johannine Epistles* (Philadelphia: Fortress, 1973); idem, "πιστεύω κτλ," *TDNT* 6:174-228; G. B. Caird, *The Revelation of St. John the Divine* (HNTC; New York: Harper & Row, 1966); H. Chadwick, *The Early Church* (Harmondsworth: Penguin, 1967); P. H. Davids, *The Epistle of James* (NIGTC; Grand Rapids: Eerdmans, 1982); idem, *The First Epistle of Peter* (NICNT; Grand Rapids: Eerdmans, 1990); M. Dibelius, *The Epistle of James* (Herm; Philadelphia: Fortress, 1975); R. J. De Simone, "Faith" in *Encyclopedia of the Early Church,* ed. A. Di Berardino (2 vols.; New York: Oxford University Press, 1992) 1:315-17; P. Ellingworth, *The Epistle to the Hebrews* (Grand Rapids: Eerdmans, 1993); J. A. Fitzmyer, "Habakkuk 2:3-4 and the New Testament" in *To Advance the Gospel* (New York: Crossroad, 1981) 236-46; L. Goppelt, *A Commentary on 1 Peter* (Grand Rapids: Eerdmans, 1993); E. Haenchen, *The Acts of the Apostles* (Philadelphia: Westminster, 1971); R. P. C. Hanson, *Tradition in the Early Church* (London: SCM, 1962); J. N. D. Kelly, *The Epistles of Peter and of Jude* (London: A. & C. Black, 1969); W. L. Lane, *Hebrews* (2 vols.; WBC; Dallas: Word, 1991); D. R. Lindsay, "The Roots and Development of the *pist-*Word Group as Faith Terminology," *JSNT* 49 (1993) 103-18; D. Lührmann, "Faith," *ABD* 2:752-58; O. Michel, "Faith," *NIDNTT* 1:587-605; R. H. Mounce, *The Book of Revelation* (NICNT; Grand Rapids; Eerdmans, 1977); J. T. Sanders, *Ethics in the New Testament* (Philadelphia: Fortress, 1975); S. S. Smalley, *1, 2, 3 John* (WBC; Waco, TX: Word, 1984); C. Spicq, "πίστις," *TLNT* 3:110-16.   B. Eastman

FAITH AND WORKS

While the issue of the relationship of faith and works has focused on Paul's controversies with Judaizers and his relationship to the epistle of James* (*see DPL*, James and Paul), several works in our literature make a contribution to this discussion. Each work in the later NT literature makes a situationally appropriate application of a position not unlike Paul's (even if he might not have chosen the wording used or the emphasis of an individual author). In the apostolic fathers* the balance shifts decidedly in favor of works to give evidence of faith.*

1. Later New Testament Writings
2. Apostolic Fathers

1. Later New Testament Writings.

1.1. Acts. Acts* reflects an evangelistic orientation. In Acts 3:16 it is through faith in Jesus that the lame man is healed, not through any merit or skill residing in Peter and John. Likewise, in Acts 14:9 Paul sees faith, not claim, in another beggar. Therefore his conclusion at the end of his missionary journey is that a door of faith had been opened to the Gentiles* (Acts 14:27). While there is a pairing of repentance* and faith in Acts (Acts 20:21), it is clear that the primary interest is in faith (Acts 24:24; 26:18).

At the same time Acts does not ignore works, for Tabitha is praised for her good works (Acts 9:36), and although they are not called works, Cornelius's* deeds are "remembered" by God* (Acts 10:4). Likewise, when people repent and turn to God they should do deeds worthy of repentance (Acts 26:20).

Therefore faith and works remain in creative tension in Acts. It is clear that faith, the human response to God's call, is what brings one salvation* or physical healing* and that the primary deed is to remain in "the faith" (Acts 13:8; 14:22). Yet it is expected that appropriate deeds will flow from faith, and in this light the author of Acts probably views Cornelius as expressing true faith in God as a "righteous Gentile" (in the rabbinic phrase) even before he hears about Jesus.

1.2. Hebrews. In Hebrews* the core issue is whether the group being addressed has already departed or may in the future depart from Christian commitment. Thus in Hebrews 4:2 a message comes from God but does not help since it is not united with the recipients' faith. However, those who "inherit the promises" are characterized by faith and endurance* (Heb 6:12). Thus in Hebrews, while faith does indicate confident trust in God (especially in Heb 11), it carries with it strong overtones of faithfulness and far more than in Paul it is a human response rather than a divine gift (e.g., Heb 10:39; Rose, 349).

Works therefore are not ignored in this context, since even faith takes effort; God will not forget the deeds of the addressees, which is one reason the writer is confident of their salvation (Heb 6:10). In Hebrews 10:24 the author exhorts his readers to practice good deeds, although in Hebrews 13:21 it is Jesus who will work in them to produce God's will. Finally, in Hebrews 11 the virtue of faith, akin to endur-ance, normally produces some clear action in the person, even if the action is not called a work. In Hebrews salvation clearly is through faith in Jesus, but this is a faith that calls for persevering faithfulness. And a mark of this faithfulness is the good deeds that are produced in the believers.

1.3. James. The Jacobean community knows nothing of the tension with the Mosaic law* (seen as salvific Torah) that animated Paul, nor is it concerned about either possible apostasy* or evangelistic outreach. The issue in James is about conflict in the community and sharing among its members. The question is whether faith will move beyond mere words. Thus the teacher shows which "wisdom" animates him or her by deeds, not orthodox teaching (Jas 3:13). It is the doer of deeds, not the mere auditor, who is blessed (Jas 1:25). And faith (here defined as nominal, orthodox belief, not commitment to Christ) that lacks works (defined in context as deeds of charity) is useless (Jas 2:14, 17, 26).

It is not that James ignores faith. Believers are characterized by faith (Jas 1:3; 2:1) and can even be said to be "rich in faith" (Jas 2:5). It takes faith (trust in God) to approach God fruitfully in prayer* (Jas 1:6; 5:15; Davids 1996, 231-32). If faith divorced from works cannot save, James never contemplates the idea that works could exist without faith. For James the ideal is faith working with and being completed by one's deed (Jas 2:22), for as a result of this a person will be declared (proved) righteous (Jas 2:21, 24; *see* Righteousness). James asserts that a mere confession of faith is not enough; true commitment to God shows in one's deeds (*see* DPL, James and Paul).

1.4. 1 Peter. In 1 Peter* one finds an author encouraging a group of communities in the face of unofficial persecution.* The stress therefore is on faith as commitment to God. It is faith that brings divine protection and receives a reward* (1 Pet 1:5, 9). This faith is connected to hope* and is fixed upon God with an effect reaching beyond death (1 Pet 1:21; Michaels, 22-24). Persecution and the devil (*see* Satan) test this faith and thus must be endured and resisted (1 Pet 1:7; 5:9). Works are also relevant, for the Father will judge each person's works, which should mean that despite the security of faith, the believer's lifestyle will be one lived in the light of a healthy respect of judgment* (1 Pet

1:17). When it comes to the situation of persecution, the good works of the Christian should be such that God will be glorified by the persecutors concerning the areas of life about which slander commonly circulated in the pagan community.

1.5. 2 Peter and Jude. Turning to 2 Peter* and Jude,* we discover that in a context in which the communities are threatened by heterodox groups (whether originating within or without the community), faith is presented as something received from God (2 Pet 1:1) which needs to be protected or supported by appropriate character and works (2 Pet 1:5; Reumann, 257, 265-66). The faith must be actively maintained ("fought for," Jude 3), and one should exert effort to build oneself up in it (Jude 20). Works are significant, for in the end of the age all deeds will be exposed and judged (2 Pet 3:10; Jude 15). The emphasis in this literature is clearly on works (*see* Early Catholicism for the debate on the nature of such "works"), for it is effort that must be expended to protect "the faith" and maintain one's relationship with God. Antinomians are rebutted by such a call in both letters.

1.6. 1-3 John. The Johannine epistles (*see* John, Letters of) mention the noun *faith* only once (1 Jn 5:4), and there it is an active agent that conquers "the world" (1 Jn 5:5). The author clearly prefers the verbal form *believe (pisteuō)* to the noun *faith (pistis),* for it is through believing in Jesus that one knows that he or she has eternal life* (1 Jn 5:1, 10, 13). Believing is also an act of obedience* in response to a command (1 Jn 3:23; Reumann, 215-16). All three letters are full of commands, particularly the command to love* one another and the warning that sinning is a mark of not knowing God. Thus there is no sense in the Johannine epistles that one could believe correctly (or "walk in the truth") and consistently act wrongly ("continue in sin" or do evil deeds or hate one's fellow believer). The two are so intertwined that to do right is to show that one has life or knows God (1 Jn 3:7, 10, 14), which the elder also attributes to right belief.

1.7. Revelation. In Revelation (*see* Revelation, Book of) various levels of persecution confront the church, so the emphasis is on works, especially on endurance in those works. "I know your deeds," says Jesus (Rev 2:2). And the appropriate deeds must be done (Rev 2:5, a command

to return to their former deeds), for judgment will be according to one's deeds (Rev 20:13; 22:12). While there is no reference to believing (*pisteuō,* "believe," does not occur), there are references to "the faith," and this is something to be guarded (Rev 2:13; although usually where *pistis* occurs it means "faithfulness"—e.g., Rev 2:19; 13:10; Reumann, 245).

In the NT literature under consideration, commitment to God (faith) and obedience to God (works) occur in a dynamic tension. The stress in the various pieces of literature could be arranged on a continuum according to the situation of the author and the church or churches addressed. The more evangelistic the document is, the more the emphasis is on faith. The more pressure the community is experiencing (whether as outside persecution or internal factionalism caused by false teachers who advocate a relaxed morality, in turn stemming from a notion of nominal faith), the more the emphasis is on works with faith being reduced to "keeping the faith," which is itself an activity of the individual. Yet in no place in the NT is faith eclipsed as the core of what it means to be Christian (Reumann, 290-92).

2. Apostolic Fathers.
In the post-NT world the emphasis falls increasingly on works. Examples of this are the Two Ways sections of the *Epistle of Barnabas** and the *Didache,** for there it is clearly how one lives that determines one's ultimate fate. For example, it is through generous charity that one gives "a ransom for your sins" (*Did.* 4.6). In a parallel in *Barnabas* we read, "You shall remember the day of judgment day and night . . . [then comes a list of deeds to be performed] or working with your hands for the ransom of your sins" (*Barn.* 19.10). While *2 Clement* does not have a two-ways section, the author does mention "the day of [the Lord's] appearing when he will come and ransom each of us according to his or her deeds" (*2 Clem.* 17.4). Indeed, "Your faith shall not profit except you be found perfect at the last time" (*Did.* 16.2; *see* Redemption).

Faith is important in this literature, but it is often paired with works. *1 Clement* 12 states that "For her faith and hospitality Rahab the harlot was saved" (cf. *1 Clem.* 10.7, which asserts the same of Abraham*), and later "the faith which is in Christ" is defined in terms of virtues* (*1 Clem.* 22.1; Ign. *Eph.* 8.2; *Herm. Man.* 8.8-11; cf.

Pancovski). Faith at times becomes the hope of future reward (*1 Clem.* 58.2; cf. *1 Clem.* 35.2; *Barn.* 1.4) or confident trust in God when one prays (*Herm. Man.* 9). While it is clear that salvation is through believing "on the blood of Jesus" (Ign. *Smyrn.* 6.1; cf. *Herm. Sim.* 9.17.4; *Did.* 16.2, although here faith is virtually synonymous with knowledge*) and thus without appropriate belief one will not receive salvation, the emphasis is strongly on the works that flow from faith.

Therefore, although faith is mentioned in this literature of the second century, the emphasis is on works, reflecting moralistic strains and the reformulation of Christianity as "new law" (*lex nova;* Torrance, 105; the term is specifically mentioned in *Barnabas*). In some places one starts with faith and then must produce the appropriate virtue in order to remain with a hope of salvation. In others the important issue is holding onto the faith itself. In still others faith is itself defined in terms of or paired with virtue. In general, faith is spoken of in terms of right belief rather than personal commitment, as "the faith" rather than faith in Jesus (cf. Schwartz). The balance has shifted to works more strongly than in any of our NT literature, which tendency will characterize the church through the following centuries. Although T. F. Torrance (133-41) argues that it is Judaism* plus Hellenism (especially the Stoic ethic) that created the change within Christianity, it may as likely have been caused by the cultural move into the Roman world, with the church increasingly adopting a Roman legal mentality seen later in Tertullian.

See also ENDURANCE, PERSEVERANCE; ETHICS; FAITH, FAITHFULNESS; JAMES; OBEDIENCE.

BIBLIOGRAPHY. P. H. Davids, "Controlling the Tongue and the Wallet: Discipleship in the Epistle of James" in *Patterns of Discipleship in the Epistle of James,* ed. R. N. Longenecker (Grand Rapids: Eerdmans, 1996) 220-39; idem, *The Epistle of James* (NIGTC; Grand Rapids: Eerdmans, 1982) 19-21, 120-34; idem, *The First Epistle of Peter* (NICNT; Grand Rapids: Eerdmans, 1990); M. Dibelius, *James* (Herm; Philadelphia: Fortress, 1976); H. P. Hamann, "Faith and Works: Paul and James," *LTJ* 9 (1975) 33-41; M. Hengel, "Der Jakobusbrief als antipaulinische Polemik" in *Tradition and Interpretation in the New Testament,* ed. G. F. Hawthorne and O. Betz (Grand Rapids: Eerdmans, 1987) 248-78; J. Jeremias, "Paul and James," *ExpT* 66 (1954-55) 368-71; W. L. Lane, *Hebrews* (WBC; Dallas: Word, 1991); J. G. Lodge, "James and Paul at Cross-Purposes? James 2:22," *Bib* 62 (1981) 195-213; R. P. Martin, *James* (WBC; Waco, TX: Word, 1988) 75-101; J. R. Michaels, *1 Peter* (WBC; Waco, TX: Word, 1988); I. Pancovski, "Tugend: Weg zum Heil," *Ostkirchlichen Studien* 32 (1983) 105-16; W. Pratscher, *Der Herrenbruder Jakobus und die Jakobustradition* (Göttingen: Vandenhoeck & Ruprecht, 1987); C. Rose, *Die Wolke der Zeugen* (WUNT 2.60; Tübingen: J. C. B. Mohr, 1994); J. Reumann, *Variety and Unity in New Testament Thought* (Oxford: Oxford University Press, 1991); D. Schwartz, "Paul in the Writings of the Apostolic Fathers" in *Paul and the Legacies of Paul,* ed. W. S. Babcock (Dallas: Southern Methodist University Press, 1990); T. F. Torrance, *The Doctrine of Grace in the Apostolic Fathers* (Grand Rapids: Eerdmans, 1959); A. E. Travis, "James and Paul: A Comparative Study," *SWJT* 12 (1969) 57-70; R. B. Ward, "James and Paul: A Critical Review," *RQ* 7 (1963) 159-64. P. H. Davids

FALSE PROPHETS. *See* ADVERSARIES; PROPHECY, PROPHETS, FALSE PROPHETS.

FALSE TEACHERS. *See* ADVERSARIES; PROPHECY, PROPHETS, FALSE PROPHETS.

FAMILY. *See* HOUSEHOLD, FAMILY.

FASTING. See PRAYER; WORSHIP AND LITURGY.

FEAR

The language of fear is pronounced in this portion of the NT and is fairly frequent in the apostolic fathers. As in the other portions of the NT (*see DPL,* Fear, Reverence), fear usually refers to an appropriate level of respect and honor to be shown to another, often in the light of fulfilling one's service to God,* and also implies terror at the prospect of failing to fulfill one's obligations. In keeping with the possible composition of a number of these writings in the light of rising persecution of the early church, a two-sided approach to fear is evident. On the one hand there is suitable fear of God, other people and things, fear that in some contexts appropriately represents respect and provides a suitable basis for Christian conduct. On the other hand there is admonition not to have a craven fear of God, humans or things such as suffering in the light of God's larger plan and purpose. The primary words used to speak of fear are *phobos* and *phobeomai*, although Acts uses *sebomai* as well (see 4 below on God-fearers).

1. Fear of Things
2. Fear of Others
3. Fear of God
4. The God-fearers

1. Fear of Things.

Whereas most references in these writings are to the fear of animate beings, a number of usages refer to fear of inanimate things. These reflect a number of kinds of fear, from simple fear of inauspicious circumstances (Acts 27:17, 24, 29; Heb 12:21; *Herm. Sim.* 9.20.2) to the natural human fear of the unknown. For example, in Hebrews 2:15 the author speaks of Jesus as having freed those who were in slavery to fear of death. *Diognetus* 10.7 speaks similarly of the fear of death, and *1 Clement* 12.5 speaks of dread. Several passages tend to emerge from adversarial relationships, probably reflecting persecution* in the early church.* For example, in Revelation 2:10 Christ* says to the Smyrneans not to fear what they are to suffer*; Ignatius* (Ign. *Eph.* 11.1) says not to fear the wrath* to come but to love the grace* present; and in 1 Peter 3:6, 14 Christians are encouraged not to fear for doing right (cf. 1 Pet 3:15). *1 Clement* 56.10 speaks of not fearing evil. In an extended discussion, *Hermas Mandate* 7.1, 3 implores Christians to fear the Lord and keep his commandments* and thereby resist the devil (*see* Satan). For those who are followers of Christ, there is to be no cowardly fear for proper behavior.

2. Fear of Others.

It is much more common for the NT writings to instruct Christians regarding fear or respect of other people, often linked to motivating human conduct, while there are a relatively smaller number in the apostolic fathers.* At least two classes of people are mentioned, including those in family and societal relations and those outside the church. The majority of references in the apostolic fathers have to do with fearing or not fearing the devil (see *Herm. Man.* 7.2, 3; 12.4.6, 7; 12.5.2, 3; 12.6.1, 2).

Regarding family and societal relations, wives are told in 1 Peter 3:2 that unbelieving husbands may be won over by the respect (*phobos*) of their wives. Likewise in 1 Peter 2:18

slaves* are told to submit to their masters with appropriate respect (*phobos;* cf. Heb 11:23, 27, where Moses' parents are said to have feared Pharaoh's edict; *Did.* 4.11, which includes a description of household duties; *see* Household Codes). Ignatius (Ign. *Eph.* 6.1) tells the readers to fear or respect the bishop if he is silent (*see* Church Order). Regarding those outside the church, 1 Peter 3:16 implores Christians to have an explanation for their faith,* doing this with gentleness and respect (*phobos*). In a quotation of Psalm 118:6-7, the author of Hebrews (Heb 13:6) states the situation bluntly: with God as their helper believers do not need to be afraid, since humans can do nothing to them when they are protected or aided by God.

These last two examples, when compared with examples of merely human fear, that is, where humans are said to fear circumstances or others (e.g., Acts 16:38; 22:29; 23:10; 27:17), well illustrate that the fear of Christians is one grounded in their faith and their desire to please God and that this is related to but should take priority over their other relations. 1 Peter 2:17, reflecting a balanced Hellenistic ethical* position with regard to social structures, puts fear of God in proper perspective when it says to honor all people: love the Christian "brethren" (*adelphotēs*), fear God and honor the king (= emperor*).

3. Fear of God.

The fear of God is the most important motivating factor for Christian conduct in these writings, and it is what distinguishes Christian behavior from that of others. There are two sides to this fear or reverence for God in this body of NT writings. The first is seen in 1 John 4:18, where after saying that God is love* the author says that believers will be confident on the day of judgment,* because there is no fear in love. Perfect loves casts out fear. The second is a more pronounced emphasis on fear of God. For example, in Acts 9:31 it is fear of the Lord that distinguishes the church in Palestine as it grew in strength and numbers.

It is to a large extent the distinguishing mark of believers in these writings that they fear God (cf. Acts 2:43). For example, Peter says in Acts 10:35 that God accepts people from all nations who fear him, and similarly 1 Peter 1:17 implores its readers to live lives of fear before the God who judges. This God is one into whose hands it is a fearful thing to fall (Heb 10:27, 31). This is the image of God and Christ that one is impressed with in Revelation (*see* Revelation, Book of), where it becomes clear that fear of God or Christ, which includes reverence and awe before his overpowering presence, is the only motivation needed for the writer's response and behavior. For example, in Revelation 1:17, the author is told not to be afraid, having fallen at the feet of Christ. God's ultimate apocalyptic triumph in judgment will come against those who do not fear God (Rev 11:18; 14:7; 15:4; 19:5).

The apostolic fathers speak of the fear of God far more than they speak of any other type of fear, reverence or awe. The fear of God is seen to be the key to Christian behavior (e.g., *Herm. Man.* 7.4; *Barn.* 19.5) and includes humility* before him (Ign. *Trall.* 4.1).

4. The God-Fearers.

Although it might be possible to discuss the God-fearers under the preceding categories, the special usage in Acts* requires separate comment. There are several issues to discuss. The first is the two separate phrases used in Acts to distinguish what appears to be one or possibly two groups. The first phrase is "the ones fearing (*phobeomai*) God," and it appears at Acts 10:2, 22, 35; 13:16, 26. The second phrase is "the ones revering (*sebomai*) God," and it appears at Acts 13:43, 50; 16:14; 17:4, 17; 18:7 (cf. Acts 18:13; 19:27). The first phrase essentially appears in the first half of Acts and the second in the second half. This has raised a number of questions regarding why the author changes terminology midway through his account, especially if the phrasing constitutes technical terminology to label a particular group. Several of the possible explanations for the change are that the author was using different sources, although the language does seem very Lukan; that it reflects standard terminology in use for this kind of group; or that the author uses a more Hellenistic term when the Christian mission* becomes more Hellenistic.

The second issue, however, is the meaning of the phrase in Acts. The switch in the terminology and apparent parallels with some rabbinic literature, combined with the supposed failure to find any extrabiblical parallels in Hellenistic Greek, have led some scholars to posit this phrasing as a Lukan creation or to maintain that

the reference was to any highly pious person, including pious Jews. This would account for several instances in which reference is made to "Israelites [or a similar phrase] and those fearing God" (e.g., Acts 13:16, 26, 43; 17:17), with the second a devout subgroup of the first. Nevertheless, the most widely accepted understanding of the phrase is that these people were Gentiles* who were attracted to the piety and theology of Diaspora Judaism* but who were not willing to become full proselytes. Without being willing to submit to circumcision,* they feared the God of the Jews.

The third issue is the attestation of the phrase. A number of scholars have maintained that there was no outside attestation for such phrasing, but it has been shown recently that although there is no exact parallel, there is sufficient inscriptional evidence to suggest that the terminology of Luke-Acts would have been recognizable to a Hellenistic audience.

The fourth issue is the meaning of the phrase in the light of the topic of this essay. The use in Acts is consonant with what this essay has described as the general tenor of discussion in this group of NT writings with regard to fear of God. It constitutes the major motivational force for behavior, so much so that it attracts those from beyond the ethnic and racial boundaries of the Jewish people and distinguishes a group known by fear of or reverence for God.

See also GOD; JUDGMENT; WORSHIP AND LITURGY.

BIBLIOGRAPHY. M. C. de Boer, "God-Fearers in Luke-Acts" in *Luke's Literary Achievement: Collected Essays,* ed. C. M. Tuckett (JSNTSup 116; Sheffield: Sheffield Academic Press, 1995) 50-71; L. Goppelt, *A Commentary on 1 Peter* (Grand Rapids: Eerdmans, 1993); P. van der Horst, "A New Altar of a Godfearer?" in *Hellenism—Judaism—Christianity: Essays on Their Interaction* (Kampen: Kok Pharos, 1994) 65-72; J. Lawson, *A Theological and Historical Introduction to the Apostolic Fathers* (New York: Macmillan, 1961); I. Levinskaya, *The Book of Acts in its Diaspora Setting* (BAFCS; Grand Rapids: Eerdmans, 1996); J. M. Lieu, "Do God-Fearers Make Good Christians?" in *Crossing the Boundaries: Essays in Biblical Interpretation in Honor of Michael D. Goulder,* ed. S. E. Porter et al. (Leiden: E. J. Brill, 1994) 329-45; G. Lüdemann, *Early Christianity According to the Traditions in Acts: A Commentary* (Minneapolis: Fortress, 1989); S. Snyder, "1 Peter 2:17: A Reconsideration," *FN* 4.8 (1991) 211-15; M. Wilcox, "The 'God-Fearers' in Acts— A Reconsideration," *JSNT* 13 (1981) 102-22.

S. E. Porter

FELLOWSHIP

In the later NT and other early Christian literature, fellowship is not described predominantly by the *koinōnia* ("fellowship") group of words; rather it is approached mainly through descriptions of Christians giving and receiving mutual love or through commandments that they should involve themselves by obedience* (*see DPL,* Fellowship). Early Christian teaching about this can be organized into three categories.

1. Fellowship and *Koinōneō*
2. Receiving and Giving Fellowship
3. Mutual Love

1. Fellowship and *Koinōneō*.

It has become commonplace in the Western church to speak of Christian fellowship in terms of *koinōnia* ("community," "fellowship," "participation"). Fellowship does comprise part of the semantic range of the NT Greek verb *koinōneō* and its cognates, including *koinōnia*. In 1 John 1:3, 6-10, for example, fellowship with the author is based on partaking of what the author knows, and fellowship with God* and other Christians is predicated on living righteously. This word group, however, does not exhaust the idea of Christian fellowship and is insufficient to develop this theme fully in the literature of the later NT and the apostolic fathers.*

1.1. Insufficiency of Focusing on the Koinōneō Word Group.
In this Greek word group there are pejorative meanings. In Acts 11:4-10 Peter reports his vision* in the house of Simon the tanner in which a heavenly voice exhorted him three times not to call common or profane *(koinos)* what God reckons to be allowable. The word group is also used with meanings that lie beyond what is owed by Christians to all Christians as a result of salvation* and the new community in Christ. In Hebrews 2:14, for example, the verb *(koinōneō)* is employed to speak of the physical flesh and blood shared by all humans. In 2 John 11 the same verb is used not of Christian fellowship but of taking part in the evil deeds of a heretic.

In short the *koinōneō* word group is not often used in the later NT literature and apostolic

fathers, and when it is, it has a semantic range that goes beyond the concept of Christian fellowship. But the concept of fellowship or communion is strongly present in the literature, and it is to this that we turn.

1.2. Community of Goods.
On two occasions one of the words from the *koinōnia* word group is used in the literature of the NT to refer to an aspect of early Christian fellowship. In the summary passages of Acts 2:43-47 and Acts 4:32-37, which conclude stages of development of the formation of nascent Christianity, the adjective *koinos* ("common," Acts 2:44; 4:32) refers to the community of ownership practiced by the young church.* A third passage (Acts 6:1-7), however, lacks the adjective *koinos* and describes a situation in which part of the church was not experiencing the full fellowship expected (certainly not the community of goods, which is not mentioned) but also was not receiving the needed portions at the common meals. This third passage mentions a negative case, though also the good that flowed from it; but even this negative statement assumes the positive meaning that the church at that period gave to the concept *fellowship* (for further details on these three passages see Barrett, 1:158-73, 251-60, 302-17).

2. Receiving and Giving Fellowship.
A similar positive view of the hospitality* and communion to be shown to Christians by Christians is encountered in Acts* in descriptions of the way the central characters of that book are treated by believers. It is apparent in the way that Ananias and the Damascus Christians respond to Paul in his need (Acts 9:17-19, 25) and in the way Barnabas endorses him to the suspicious Jerusalem Christians (Acts 9:26-27). We catch glimpses of it in the hospitality shown Peter by the household of Simon the tanner (Acts 9:43) and in that shown to the missionaries Paul and Barnabas by disciples in Antioch* (Acts 14:26-28), Jerusalem* (Acts 15:4), Philippi (Acts 16:15), Tyre (Acts 21:4-6) and the environs of Rome* (Acts 28:14-15).

It is not a matter solely, however, of believers giving loving attention to functionaries of the church like Peter, Paul and Barnabas. Paul also works at encouraging his converts (Acts 14:22-23; 18:23) and also others who come under his care, such as those who are with him on the ill-fated voyage to Rome on the ship from Adramyttium (Acts 27:33-38). The latter passage exemplifies this whether or not it is to be interpreted eucharistically (see Barrett and the major commentaries listed by him, 1:xiii-xiv), but the connection of communion with fellowship would give further cause for thought if the passage is to be understood that way. There are other such descriptions.

3. Mutual Love.
Taken by themselves, such passages descriptive of demonstrated love* need not necessarily be understood as showing anything more than the actions of amiable people, whether they are responding to evangelists who brought them the good news or are themselves concerned with the care of converts. But there are passages in the later NT that enjoin or praise deeds of love, as did Jesus and Paul after him, and demonstrate that such behavior was thought to be normative. In fact it is expected of believers that the graciousness of God in granting them a new and purified life should result in mutual love (1 Pet 1:22—2:3) expressed in practical ways (1 Pet 4:8-11, but see 1 Pet more widely).

Expressions of love like this are not to be limited to known and familiar believers but are commended and encouraged when they are demonstrated toward strangers (traveling missionaries) too (3 Jn 5-8; see Smalley, 348-53). A related encouragement to sharing and to the expression of love and hospitality to strangers also occurs at Hebrews 13:1-3, though with a special expression of concern for any mistreated in prison (see Lane, 2:509-15), and Hebrews 13:16, where the noun koinōnia is to be found. Similar acceptance and treatment of all who come into the church, without social judging and positioning, is expected by James* of the church to which he writes (Jas 2:1-9; see Martin, 67-68).

Though the tone changes and mutual love is subordinated to other themes, the apostolic fathers may also be found urging Christians to unity and love. In 1 Clement 37—38 and 1 Clement 47—49 purity* of the redeemed life is in primary view, but harmony and mutual love in the church are also to be desired. Ignatius* also demands love and harmony in the body of believers, but the way to achieve this is to be in harmony with the bishop and presbyters (Ign. Eph. 3—5; Ign. Magn. 6—7; see Church Order). Other postapostolic literature touches on the theme of fellowship but only tangentially; other

concerns and themes predominate.

See also CHURCH; GOD; HOSPITALITY; HOUSEHOLDS, FAMILY; LOVE; SOCIAL SETTING OF EARLY NON-PAULINE CHRISTIANITY; WORSHIP AND LITURGY.

BIBLIOGRAPHY. C. K. Barrett, A Critical and Exegetical Commentary on the Acts of the Apostles (2 vols.; ICC; Edinburgh: T & T Clark, 1994); J. Y. Campbell, "Koinōnia and Its Cognates in the New Testament" in Three New Testament Studies (Leiden: E. J. Brill, 1965) 1-28; J. Hainz, "κοινωνία κτλ," EDNT 2:303-5; F. Hauck, "κοινός κτλ," TDNT 3:789-809; W. L. Lane, Hebrews (2 vols.; WBC; Dallas: Word, 1991); J. M. McDermott, "The Biblical Doctrine of KOINONIA," BZ 19 (1975) 64-77, 219-33; R. P. Martin, James (WBC; Waco, TX: Word, 1988); G. Panikulam, Koinonia in the New Testament: A Dynamic Expression of Christian Life (AnBib 85; Rome: Pontifical Biblical Institute, 1979); H. Seesemann, Der Begriff KOINΩNIA im Neuen Testament (BZNW 14; Giessen: A. Töpelmann, 1933); S. S. Smalley, 1, 2, 3 John (WBC; Waco, TX: Word, 1984).
A. Casurella

FLESH
In the NT the corporeal aspect of human earthly existence is sometimes called sarx (flesh). In Acts, the General Writings and Revelation, sarx and two derived adjectives, sarkinos and sarkikos, occur thirty-four times. As with the Hebrew bāśār, sarx is used figuratively as well as to refer to literal flesh. Trying to categorize uses into literal and figurative is difficult. It is best to see the two types of use as ends of a continuum rather than as hard and fast classes.

1. Literal Uses
2. Figurative Uses

1. Literal Uses.
To refer to the physical parts of the human body, sarx is used in the plural five times in Revelation 19:18 and once each in Revelation 17:16 and 19:21. In Revelation 17:16 the flesh of the harlot (a symbol for a city, Rev 17:18) is consumed by the beast* (cf. Rev 19:18, 21). The plural in James 5:3 once more paints a vivid picture, this time of those whose hoards of wealth are found rusting. These occurrences of the plural in James and Revelation lend graphic detail to the portrayal of the eschatological fate* of those who are the enemies of God. The Epistle of Barnabas uses the plural of the flesh of Christ*

nailed to the cross* (*Barn.* 5.13).

Sarx in the singular can refer to earthly human form. In Hebrews 2:14 *sarx* is used in the combination "blood and flesh" to refer to the physical being of people and of the Son who shares in this. In Hebrews 5:7 *sarx* occurs in the phrase "in the days of his flesh," which again refers to the time of the Messiah's physical life on earth in its weakness as truly human. The same way of using *sarx* is found in Hebrews 12:9 with reference to our earthly fathers. *Sarx* in Acts 2:26, 31 might also refer to the physical body of Jesus; it cites Psalm 16:9, "Moreover, my flesh will dwell in hope." Acts 2:31 combines this notion of flesh with the notion of corruption in Acts 2:27 to say that the flesh of the Messiah will not decay (cf. Gundry, 210; Harris, 109).

Because it was supposed that humans are made up of a material part (flesh) and an immaterial part (spirit, soul or conscience*), *flesh* referring to the physical body occurs in later debates between docetic* and antidocetic sects, especially with regard to the pre- and postresurrection natures of Christ and of believers (e.g., *2 Clem.* 9.1-6; Ign. *Smyrn.* 2—3, 5.2; *Barn.* 5.10-11). Perhaps this sort of debate stands behind the Apostles' Creed, which uses "the resurrection* of the flesh" rather than the NT term, "the resurrection of the dead." Likewise, the baptismal* confession in Hippolytus (*Apos. Trad.* 20-21, c. A.D. 200, cited in Hall, 20-21) admits the resurrection of the flesh. Hippolytus also writes against Sabellianism, which says that the flesh is one mode of God's existence (Hippolytus *Haer.* 9.12.15-19).

2. Figurative Uses.

2.1. Flesh as a Morally Neutral Term. The phrase "all flesh" occurs twice in NT citations of the OT (Acts 2:17 cites Joel 3:1 [MT]; 1 Pet 1:24 cites Is 40:6). In both cases the phrase refers to all of humanity. In 1 Peter 1:24 the emphasis seems to be on the temporality of humankind when compared with the eternal word of God (cf. Bratsiotis).

Sometimes the term *flesh* is neutral but qualified by an adjective or phrase that gives the concept negative nuances, e.g., 1 John 2:16, "the lust of the flesh," or 2 Peter 2:10, "those who go after other flesh," or 2:18, "the sensual desires of the flesh" (cf. Jude 7, 8, 23).

Three times *sarx* is used of the Messiah. In 1 John 4:2 and 2 John 7 *flesh* speaks of the incarnation: "every spirit that confesses that Jesus has come in the flesh." But here it refers more to a realm of existence than to having human flesh. According to John, an orthodox confession says that Jesus' salvific coming was into the real world of flesh and blood (Brown, 493). Hebrews 10:20 also refers to the flesh of the Messiah. Here "his flesh" occurs as the interpretation (*tout' estin*, "this is") of the "veil" (since both *veil* and *flesh* are in the genitive case in Greek). *Flesh*, by metonymy, refers to the offering of his flesh, i.e., his death (cf. Lane, 275-76). This death inaugurates the new and living way as opposed to the dead way of the old covenant.* These uses of *sarx* in Hebrews and 1 John prepare us for its use in other texts as a salvation-historical term.

2.2. Flesh as a Salvation-Historical Term. In the NT *flesh* is often used in contrast to other terms such as *conscience* and *spirit*. The earliest uses of this dualistic language in the church fathers are often Neo-Platonic or Hellenistic (e.g., *Diogn.* 6.5-10; cf. Davies, 448, 455). In Neo-Platonism the flesh-spirit dualism was considered ontological (see above under literal uses). In gnostic and some patristic literature, taking over some aspects of Neo-Platonism, the flesh is wicked, the spirit is pure. This dualism has been used as an interpretive grid for many NT texts. The validity of this grid has recently been questioned based on the eschatological nature of both the OT and the NT. In passages referring to flesh and spirit or flesh and conscience, an eschatological dualism seems more in keeping with the biblical context than an ontological dualism. *Flesh*, in some of these passages, refers to the old or present age, while *spirit* (or a clean conscience) belongs to the future age, which has broken into the present with the coming of the Messiah.

In Hebrews 7:16 the Mosaic covenant is called a law of fleshly *(sarkinos)* commandment and is opposed to the power of an indestructible life. In Hebrews 9:9-10 regulations of flesh (the worship of the Mosaic order) are in force until the time of the new order, in which worshipers will be perfected in conscience. In Hebrews 9:13-14 the blood of goats and bulls and the sprinkled ashes of a heifer sanctified the participants for the cleansing of the flesh (preparing them for worship*; the *pros* phrase translated "for" is added to qualify the sanctification), but the blood of Christ cleanses the conscience.

Flesh in these passages is a characteristic of the Mosaic as opposed to the new covenant. Flesh is not morally negative; rather it is a part of the old age.

As in Romans 8 and Galatians 5—6, flesh-spirit dualism forms the dominant conceptual grid in the notoriously difficult 1 Peter 3:18—4:6. A full exegesis of the passage is not possible here, but perhaps a recognition of the meaning of flesh can shed some light on the passage. The eschatological point is clear in its conclusion, "The end of all things is near" (1 Pet 4:7), followed by moral exhortation.

According to 1 Peter 3:18, Christ "was put to death in the flesh but made alive in the spirit" (perhaps a pre-Petrine traditional phrase). The contrast here is between two spheres or modes of existence (Michaels, 204; Davids, 137). Christ died to the old realm (flesh) but was made alive to the new realm of existence (spirit). These could be ontological realms of existence, but perhaps it is best to view them as eschatological. Christ is the first to live in the new age into which all Christians will enter via resurrection. 1 Peter 3:19 says that it was in this sphere of the new age beyond death that Jesus preached to spirits* in prison (perhaps via the Spirit; *see* Holy Spirit).

The next occurrence of *flesh* is in 1 Peter 3:21, which asserts that baptism* is not the cleansing of the flesh. Flesh here could refer to the physical body (Beare, 175), but it is more likely that moral filth is in view (Michaels, 216). But if flesh retains its contrast to spirit as a realm of existence, the intention is that baptism does not cause a person to move from the old realm to the new; that was accomplished by Christ, who cleanses (forgives*) us (1 Pet 1:3-7). Rather, baptism is a pledge to live the moral life of the new realm, a pledge that comes from a conscience made clean through forgiveness from the resurrected Christ (Michaels, 217).

1 Peter 4:1 picks up the train of thought from 1 Peter 3:18. The flesh is the sphere in which Christ suffered.* And those who follow Christ must adopt his attitude toward the old world, because the one who suffers in this life (the flesh) has ceased from sin.* Suffering in the preresurrection age is an imitation of Messiah, and as the Messiah has ceased from sin because he has entered the new age, so too will his followers. Life in the flesh is life of the old age. Although we must still do battle with sin in this old age (cf. 1 Pet 2:11), we must not allow the old age to determine our lives (1 Pet 4:2).

Finally, flesh is used in 1 Peter 4:6, again in opposition to spirit. The datives "in flesh" and "in spirit" here are similiar to those in 1 Peter 3:18. Those who have been converted (evangelized) in the old sphere of Christ's suffering (whether they are now dead or alive) will be judged in the new sphere of life—that is, they will be resurrected. As J. N. D. Kelly concludes, "Christ's experience of 'being put to death in the flesh but made alive in the spirit' becomes through baptism the experience of all Christians, not excluding those who have already undergone physical death" (176).

Perhaps *2 Clement* 14.3-5 recognizes this eschatological dualism when it discusses the present form of the church as being the flesh of Christ (an antitype), while the future form of the church will be the Spirit.

See also Holy Spirit; Mortality and Immortality; Psychology; Purity and Impurity; Resurrection; Sin, Wickedness.

BIBLIOGRAPHY. F. W. Beare, *The First Epistle of Peter* (Oxford: Blackwell, 1970); N. P. Bratsiotis, "בָּשָׂר," *TDOT* 2:317-32; Raymond E. Brown, *The Epistles of John* (AB; Garden City, NY: Doubleday, 1982); P. H. Davids, *The First Epistle of Peter* (NICNT; Grand Rapids: Eerdmans, 1990); J. G. Davies, "Factors Leading to the Emergence of Belief in the Resurrection of the Flesh," *JTS* 23 (1972) 448-55; R. Gundry, "The Essential Physicality of Jesus' Resurrection" in *Jesus of Nazareth: Lord and Christ*, ed. J. B. Green and M. Turner (Grand Rapids: Eerdmans, 1994) 204-19; S. G. Hall, *Doctrine and Practice in the Early Church* (Grand Rapids: Eerdmans, 1992); M. Harris, *Raised Immortal* (Grand Rapids: Eerdmans, 1983); J. N. D. Kelly, *A Commentary on the Epistles of Peter and Jude* (London: Black, 1969); W. L. Lane, *Hebrews 9-13* (WBC; Dallas: Word, 1991); J. R. Michaels, *1 Peter* (WBC; Waco, TX: Word, 1988); E. Schweizer, R. Meyer, F. Baumgärtel, "σάρξ κτλ," *TDNT* 7:981 1; H. Seebass and A. C. Thiselton, "Flesh," *NIDNTT* 1:671-82. D. H. Johnson

FLOCK. *See* Shepherd, Flock.

FOOD, FOOD LAWS, TABLE FELLOWSHIP

The early Christians gathered in house churches (1 Cor 16:19; Rom 16:5; Philem 2; Col 4:15) for a variety of reasons, not least because the house provided the necessary means of preparing the Lord's Supper (see Architecture). Like the house synagogue communities of this period, the early Christian gatherings included communal meals. In reference to Christianity the willingness of Jewish and Gentile believers to extend hospitality to one another, and specifically to partake of a meal together, was the litmus test in determining the validity of the gospel message. In this respect the house became the testing ground, and within the confines of the domestic setting the early believers were forced to define how the gospel message stood in relation to its Jewish heritage, its society and the pagan world (on meat or food offered to idols, see Idolatry).

1. Christian Table Fellowship and Jewish Food Laws
2. Jewish and Pagan Attitudes Toward Jewish-Gentile Table Fellowship
3. Early Christian Practices and Paradigms

1. Christian Table Fellowship and Jewish Food Laws.

One of the earliest disputes within Christianity arose over the question of the inclusion of Gentiles* in the new community. Fundamentally two problems faced the early Christians: (1) Is circumcision* a requirement for inclusion into the new community, and (2) to what degree, if any, must Gentile believers adhere to the Mosaic law* so that a Jewish Christian would be able to associate with a Gentile believer? The latter question involves the issue of Jewish purity laws and their place in the lives of Christian believers, and in particular the question of Jewish-Gentile table fellowship. The limits of acceptable table fellowship between a Jew and a Gentile were for Jews determined by two authoritative sources: (1) the laws in Leviticus 11:1-23 and Deuteronomy 14:3-21 and (2) the various Halakoth of the oral tradition. For the most part, these laws and traditions primarily concerned the production and consumption of food and the appropriate venue for eating.

Table fellowship is the central issue in Acts 10:1—11:18, and the offense is stated explicitly in Acts 11:3. It was Peter's willingness to enter Cornelius's home, to eat at his table and to live with him that alarmed the Jewish Christians in Jerusalem.* For Luke the obstacle of a Jew associating with the "unclean" was overcome by Peter's vision* at Joppa. For the Jewish Chris-

tians in Jerusalem, however, the issue was not so clear.

The Cornelius* incident, as much as Luke intends it to be paradigmatic, is only the beginning of the problem of defining appropriate social relations between Jewish and Gentile Christians. The conflicts reflected in Galatians 2 and Acts 15 were intense and the opinions varied, and more often than not, the diverse opinions and friction caused inconsistent behavior among the leaders. It is obvious from reading these accounts that the failure to reconcile differences would have nullified the possibility of fellowship,* and Christianity might have become as segmented as first-century Judaism.* The Jerusalem council (Acts 15) decreed that the Gentile Christians abstain from eating food that was sacrificed to idols, from what was strangled, from blood and from fornication (see DPL, Jerusalem §4).

2. Jewish and Pagan Attitudes Toward Jewish-Gentile Table Fellowship.

Both Jewish and pagan writers comment on the tendency for the Jews to separate themselves from the Gentiles. This separation was based on the fundamental differences of custom. Maintaining their customs and traditions was often a costly enterprise for the Jews, both in Palestine and in the Diaspora.* Circumcision and laws of ritual purity* served as boundary markers defining who was in and who was outside the community. And the maintenance of these boundaries ensured group identity.

Obedience* (or disobedience) to the laws pertaining to foods was a telltale indicator of Jew's faithfulness (or unfaithfulness). Many Jews observed the laws and "were resolved in their hearts not to eat food. They chose to die rather than to be defiled by food or to profane the holy covenant" (1 Macc 1:62-63; cf. 2 Macc 6, 7; 3 Macc 3:4; Jub. 22; Jos. and As. 7; 11:9, 16; 12:5; Dan 1:8 LXX; Jdt 12; Esther 4:17 LXX; Tob 1:10-12; Ep. Arist. 151).

Pagan writers also discuss the Jewish attitude of separation and the reluctance to associate with non-Jews. Diodorus Siculus is the earliest (extant) pagan author to mention the Jewish reluctance to engage in table fellowship with a Gentile. In his Bibliotheca Historica he comments that the Jews "had made their hatred of humankind into a tradition, and on this account had introduced utterly outlandish laws: not to break bread with any other race, nor to show them any good will at all" (Diodorus Siculus *Bib. Hist.* 63.2).

Dio Cassius says of the Jewish people, "They are distinguished from the rest of humankind in practically every detail of life" (Dio Cassius *Hist.* 37.15.2). And in Philostratus's *Life of Apollonius of Tyana,* the Jewish people are described as "a race that has made its own a life apart and irreconcilable; that cannot share with the rest of humankind in the pleasures of the table" (Philostratus *Vit. Ap.* 5.33). These examples are representative of the catalog of opinions from pagan writers.

3. Early Christian Practices and Paradigms.

Like the Cornelius incident of Acts 10—11, Jewish and pagan texts indicate that in the mind of a pious Jew there was a correlation between what was and who was : the Gentile consumption of foods meant that the Gentiles themselves were . But for the early church,* forgiveness* and inclusion within the community were not predicated on the observance of the ritual laws of dietary purity. Evidence of this is recorded by the Evangelists, who address the nascent misunderstanding of the early church.

The Gospels are not silent on the subject of table fellowship in reference to forgiveness (*see DJG,* Table Fellowship). On more than one occasion Jesus is accused of eating with tax collectors and sinners in their homes and is condemned for his willingness to associate with the unrighteous (see Hofius). Often in these conflicts we can see evidence of the struggles of the early church. While Mark, commenting on Jesus' saying regarding what defiles a person, can confidently comment, "thus he declared all foods clean" (Mk 7:19), Matthew, writing later and probably reflecting the mind of a Jewish Christian community (*see* Matthean Community), does not echo Mark's assessment (Mt 15:17-18; note also Luke's redaction of another incident in Lk 5:27-32).

The Pauline mission to Gentiles and the willingness to engage in table fellowship with Gentile converts was seen as a threat to the church in Jerusalem, especially among the strong judaizing constituency (so Acts 13—14; Gal 2 and Acts 15). In Acts 16:11-15 Luke records the second conversion incident in which table fellowship becomes the test for the validity of the gospel message. The narrative involves

the conversion of Lydia who, like Cornelius, was a God-fearer. Following the baptism* of Lydia and her household,* she strongly urged and insisted that Paul and his companions lodge in her home and, presumably, enjoy table fellowship. Luke strategically places Lydia's invitation after her conversion as a way of confirming the legitimacy of the gospel in Philippi. For Luke the invitation is more than mere protocol, and Paul's acceptance of the invitation is a clear indication of the Gentiles' having received the gospel.

Acts 16:25-34 is consonant with the Cornelius and Lydia episodes. Following the Philippian jailor's conversion, Paul and his companions enjoy the hospitality* of this new convert. On this occasion, however, Luke is explicit: the jailor brought them into his home and enjoyed table fellowship with them before returning them to the prison. Subsequently, Paul visits Lydia at her home, which became the meeting place for the believers in Philippi.

Paul's experience at Corinth (Acts 18) was the same in kind: rejected by the Jews and forced from the synagogue, Paul went to another venue for Christian assembly, the house of Titius Justus. A similar relationship existed between Paul and the husband-wife team of Priscilla and Aquila (1 Cor 16:19; Rom 16:3-5), for their home also provided a suitable venue for gathering and for preparing table fellowship. Such convivial fellowship at meal times derives from Jewish practice (e.g., the *ḥābûra* meals of Pharisees and Qumran* sectaries as well as the Therapeutae, described by Philo*) and is in evidence among Luke's descriptions of early Jewish Christianity* in Jerusalem (Acts 2:44-46). The precise relation of such meals to the gatherings, for example, at Troas (Acts 20:7, 11) and at Corinth (1 Cor 11:20-34) is not clear, though it would be straining the evidence to find (following Lietzmann) two distinctive types of meal, one essentially social, the other sacrificial-sacramental. The connection between the meals in *Didache* 9—10 and 14 is sometimes appealed to in order to establish such a dichotomy (*see* Worship), but with equal lack of cogency.

Thus for the early church the move away from the synagogue* and from Jewish laws and expectations of ritual purity was only the first stage in a complicated development. It is not clear what the author of Hebrews* has in mind when in Hebrews 13:9 he writes: "Do not be carried away by all kinds of strange teachings; for it is well for the heart to be strengthened by grace, not by regulations about food, which have not benefited those who observe them" (cf. Heb 9:9-10). This may be a reference to partaking in Jewish cultic meals. It seems clear that new notions of purity were to be applied to Christian table fellowship, particularly the Lord's Supper.* In Jude 12 we read of ungodly persons who are "blots and blemishes on your love feasts" (*agapais hymōn,* cf. 2 Pet 2:13 v.l.). The practice of common meals among Christians persisted into the second century (Ign. *Smyrn.* 8.2; *Ep. Ap.* 15; *Acts Paul & Thec.* 25), though it was open to abuse, exposed by Tertullian (*Apol.* 39; *De Jejun.* 17—18) and died out. And the Jewish Christian and Pauline concern and instruction regarding food offered to idols resurfaces in Revelation 2:14, where some within the church at Pergamum have followed the way of Balaam and "eat food sacrificed to idols and practice fornication" (*see* Idolatry).

The evidence from the apostolic fathers* suggests that if the Pauline view had eventually won the battle and carved out a broad place for the church to stand, the issue was not a dead one in the late first century and into the second century. Ignatius* may have had in mind certain Jewish Christians when in his letter to the Magnesians he writes, "It is monstrous to speak of Jesus Christ and to practice Judaism *[Ioudaizein]*" (Ign. *Magn.* 10.3; cf. 8.1). The *Epistle to Diognetus,** an apologetic document addressed to a Gentile audience, refers to Jewish timidity over food and other such "superstitions" as "ridiculous and not worth discussing" (*Diogn.* 4.1). Justin Martyr, writing around the mid-second century, knows of Jewish Christians who fellowship and eat with *(koinōnein homilias ē hestias)* Gentile Christians only on the grounds that the Gentile Christians adopt the Jewish way of life (Justin *Dial. Tryph.* 47.2-3).

In a bid to claim the OT for Christians, *Barnabas** takes an interest in the subject as he argues that the Jews had misinterpreted the OT by seeking a literal sense rather than the intended spiritual sense. Thus in *Barnabas* 10 we read that animals such as the pig, eagle, cuttlefish, hyena, rabbit and weasel have their counterparts in humans and their character traits and vices. The righteous should avoid associating with or becoming like the "swine," who "when they have plenty, forget the Lord" (*Barn.*

10.3). On the positive side, the commandment to "eat of every animal that is cloven hoofed and ruminant" means to associate with those who "meditate in their heart on the meaning of the word they have received" and who both walk "in this world and look forward to the age to come" (*Barn.* 10.11).

See also CHRISTIANITY AND JUDAISM: PARTINGS OF THE WAYS; CIRCUMCISION; IDOLATRY; JEWISH CHRISTIANITY; LORD'S SUPPER, LOVE FEAST; PURITY AND IMPURITY.

BIBLIOGRAPHY. S. C. Barton, "The Communal Dimension of Earliest Christianity," *JTS* 43 (1992) 399-427; idem, "Paul's Sense of Place: An Anthropological Approach to Community Formation in Corinth," *NTS* 32 (1986) 225-46; B. B. Blue, "The Influence of Jewish Worship on Luke's Presentation of the Early Church" in *The Book of Acts in Its Theological Setting,* ed. I. H. Marshall (BAFCS 6; Grand Rapids: Eerdmans, 1997); M. Douglas, "Deciphering a Meal," *Daedalus* 101 (1972) 61-81; idem, "The Idea of Purity in Mark's Gospel," *Semeia* 35 (1986) 91-128; O. Hofius, *Jesu Tischgemeinschaft mit den Sündern* (Stuttgart: Calwer, 1967); J. Jeremias, *New Testament Theology: The Proclamation of Jesus* (New York: Scribner's, 1971); H. Lietzmann, *Mass and Lord's Supper: A Study in the History of the Liturgy* (Leiden: E. J. Brill, 1953-78); J. Neusner, "Two Pictures of the Pharisees: Philosophical Circle or Eating Club," *ATR* 64 (1982) 525-57; J. H. Neyrey, "Ceremonies in Luke-Acts: The Case of Meals and Table-Fellowship" in *The Social World of Luke-Acts: Models for Interpretation,* ed. J. H. Neyrey (Peabody, MA: Hendrickson, 1991) 361-87; G. Theissen, *The Social Setting of Pauline Christianity* (Edinburgh: T & T Clark, 1982); M. J. Townsend, "Exit the Agape?" *ExpT* 90 (1978-79) 356-61; W. L. Willis, *Idol Meat at Corinth: The Pauline Argument in 1 Corinthians 8 and 10* (SBLDS; Chico, CA: Scholars Press, 1985); A. C. Wire, *The Corinthian Women Prophets* (Minneapolis: Fortress, 1990).

B. B. Blue

FORGIVENESS

For the most part "forgiveness" in the NT and the apostolic fathers* is a translation of the Greek word *aphesis,* the basic idea of which is "release." Although emphasis is given to the release or remission of sin and punishment— thus, forgiveness—this is not always the case. In Hebrews 9:22 and Hebrews 10:18 the argument is cultic. In these verses the rendering of *aphesis* as "forgiveness of sins" is unwarranted in its immediate context. "Release" or "cultic blood purification" is more appropriate.

Aphiēmi is the word used most frequently to express the concept of forgiveness of sin. This word occurs 142 times in the NT with a wide range of meanings, including "let go," "cancel," "remit," "leave," "set aside," "suffer," "forsake" and "let alone." Approximately 45 of these times it has the sense of "forgive."

1. Forgiveness and the Conversion Experience
2. Forgiveness and Healing
3. Forgiveness in the Paul of Acts

1. Forgiveness and the Conversion Experience. In Acts,* the non-Pauline documents and the writings of the apostolic fathers, the idea of forgiveness is usually linked with the conversion experience. Repentance,* baptism* and forgiveness of sin were included in the standard call by the evangelists in Acts at the conclusion of their preaching. The first Johannine epistle, while not highlighting directly those conventional ingredients of conversion, focuses on the necessity of confession. Hebrews* and later writings, however, are more concerned with the postconversion possibility of forgiveness.

1.1. Forgiveness and Repentance. Peter's speeches on the day of Pentecost* and before the Jewish council are almost programmatic in their combination of repentance and forgiveness (Acts 2:38; 5:31). The speech at Pentecost makes it clear that repentance is a condition of forgiveness (Acts 2:38). The defense before the council, however, does not assign any specific order. Rather, repentance and forgiveness are both equally regarded as a dual gift given by the exalted Christ.*

In the case of Simon Magus, repentance and prayer* were presented as possible means of forgiveness. But the inclusion of "if" raises questions of full assurance* of that gift in Simon Magus's case (Acts 8:22) even if those conditions were met.

It is significant that nothing is mentioned regarding the repentance or conversion of Cornelius* in Acts 10. Yet at the conclusion of his sermon, Peter declares simply that everyone who believes in Christ receives forgiveness through his name* (Acts 10:43). A possible explanation for this omission is that Peter's sermon was not to bring about the conversion of Cornelius and his people or to offer them forgiveness. They were already saved and received the gift. It seems, however, that in the early church* repentance is a basic requirement for conversion and the gift of forgiveness (Ign. *Eph.* 10.1).

1.2. Forgiveness and Baptism. Although forgiveness and repentance are often linked in Acts, the connection with baptism is found only in Peter's speech at Pentecost (Acts 2:38; cf., however, Acts 22:16, where "wash away *[apolyō]* your sins" is linked with baptism). This connection is more common in the Gospels (*see DJG,* Forgiveness of Sins). Yet intense controversy surrounds this linking of baptism to forgiveness. The disputed word is the Greek preposition *eis.* Does the word indicate purpose, and thus should it be translated "for"; that is, baptism is the prerequisite for the forgiveness of sins? Or should it be interpreted causally: "be baptized because your sins are forgiven"? Forgiveness in this case would then be the ground of or basis for baptism.

In the past the causal interpretation has been more accepted. However, recently the purposive translation has become common. *Barnabas* 11 speaks of baptism that leads to remission of sin—something that Israel* did not receive (cf. *Barn.* 16; *Herm. Man.* 4.3). In Justin Martyr's *Apology I,* we find that initiates pray and fast for the remission of their past sins, and then they are baptized (Justin *Apol. I* 61).

1.3. Forgiveness and Confession. Twice in his first epistle, John alludes to forgiveness of sins (*see* John, Letters of). In 1 John 2:12 he tells his readers that their sins are forgiven. He uses the Greek perfect tense, which indicates that they have been and remain forgiven. Here he is thinking of the initial conversion experience. In 1 John 1:19, however, the call is for confession of sins in order to receive forgiveness (cf. *1 Clem.* 61—62). This confession, it seems, is a postbaptismal experience. Forgiveness of the confessed sins is assured because God is "faithful and just."

James* also calls for confession of sins, but he does so in the context of healing* (Jas 5:15-16). He promises the sick that their sins will be forgiven. But healing will take place only if they confess their sins to one another.

1.4. Forgiveness and Postbaptismal Sins. In Acts 8:22 we find the possibility of repentance and forgiveness of a postbaptismal sin being open to

Simon Magus. The same is true in the first Johannine epistle, where it is clear that Christians do sin. All they need to do is confess, and they will receive forgiveness (1 Jn 1:9). However, some people in the apostolic and postapostolic church would not allow that sins after baptism would be forgiven. Three passages in Hebrews (Heb 6:4-6; 10:26-31; 12:15-17) seem to posit this position.

These passages are complex and difficult to interpret. It is clear that they all deny the possibility of repentance. But Hebrews 6:4-6 seems to indicate that the sin that cannot be forgiven is apostasy* ("it is impossible to restore again to repentance those who have once been enlightened . . . and then have fallen away," NRSV). The apostates cannot be forgiven because they have crucified the Son of God again (Heb 6:6; *see* Son of God). It is widely held by commentators that the context for this statement is the persecution* the church began to undergo at that time. To make a deliberate, intelligent and planned denial of Christ in order to be released would be like crucifying Christ again. For such persons there is no coming back.

Although Hebrews 6:4-6 seems not to take a position on postbaptismal sins in general but only on apostasy, some commentators feel that in Hebrews 10:26-31 the door is opened a bit to exclude forgiveness to any willful postbaptismal sin: "For if we willfully persist in sin after having received the knowledge of the truth, there no longer remains a sacrifice for sins. . . . Anyone who has violated the law of Moses dies without mercy" (NRSV). Yet even in this passage it is possible that the primary concern is with apostasy.

In the final passage (Heb 12:15-17) Esau is used as a stark example of one who "found no chance to repent *(metanoia),* even though he sought the blessing with tears" (Heb 10:17 NRSV). There are those who would translate *metanoia* as "change of mind." But in light of the earlier passages (Heb 6:4-6; 10:26-31), we should read this passage just as rigorously and recognize that for the author of Hebrews a second repentance is objectively not possible. However, it seems that the sin he is concerned with here is also apostasy in the face of persecution.

Because of verses like these, the practice of putting off baptism until one's deathbed became widespread. In reaction to this practice, the *Shepherd of Hermas** modified the idea to admit a second repentance after baptism. He is convinced that a Christian who at baptism received forgiveness of sins ought never to sin again but will live blamelessly. However, he feels called by a revelation* from an angel* to preach that if after baptism a person sins, he or she has one more opportunity for repentance, but only one (*Herm. Man.* 4.3; see *Barn.* 6.11, 8).

As in Hebrews it is possible that the rigor of the *Shepherd of Hermas* is a result of a certain aspect of the severe persecution the church was facing at the time. Up to the fourth century, Christians had no legal standing in the Roman Empire.* Persecution was accompanied by a test—emperor* worship. Some Christians publicly renounced Christ and offered incense to Caesar as God. Such apostates were seen as in the dominion of Satan* and outside the realm of reacceptance by God.

Other voices were not as strident. *Didache* 11.7 advises that if a prophet* speaks in ecstasy, one should not test him or entertain doubt. Such a sin cannot be forgiven; but any other sin may be forgiven (*see DJG,* Holy Spirit §2.4.1). And in *1 Clement* 51, readers are admonished to acknowledge and ask forgiveness for sins that have been committed. We must admit, however, that Clement (*see* Clement of Rome) could be referring to the recollection of prebaptismal sins. The context is not clear.

2. Forgiveness and Healing.

James is unique in the Epistles or Acts when he juxtaposes healing with forgiveness of sin. There is not a strict equation of sickness and sinfulness. But James gives the impression that at least some illness is connected with sin when he writes: "The prayer of faith will save the sick, and the Lord will raise them up; and anyone who has committed sins will be forgiven. Therefore confess your sins to one another, and pray for one another, so that you may be healed" (Jas 5:15-16 NRSV).

James is expressing a thought that was common to one degree or another in the ancient world: Sin and sickness went hand in hand. The case of Job, who was accused by his friend of committing sin, causing his illness, illustrates that view (Job 4:1—5:27); and the question of the disciples ("who sinned, this man or his parents, that he was born blind?" Jn 9:2 NRSV), also highlights the equation in the minds of many. Jesus' assurance to the paralytic that his sins were forgiven (Mk 2:5) demonstrates that Jesus also made the connection, though not as the Jews did (Jn 9).

James, like Jesus and his world, makes the connection and seems to imply that if sin caused the illness, there needs to be confession and forgiveness.

3. Forgiveness in the Paul of Acts.

The word for forgiveness, *aphesis,* is absent in the Pauline epistles except for Ephesians 1:7 and Colossians 1:14. Yet in Paul's speeches in Acts (at Pisidian Antioch and before Agrippa), the climax to which all things lead is the forgiveness of sins (Acts 13:38; 26:18). It seems clear that the "forgiveness" expression is Lukan rather than Pauline. The words and the sermons overall parallel those of Peter (Acts 2:38-40; 10:43).

In his epistles Paul focuses on justification (*see* Righteousness) and other such parallel concepts rather than forgiveness (*see DPL,* Forgiveness). The death of Christ is also highlighted in Paul's writings (*see* Death of Christ). However, in Acts forgiveness is not directly linked with the death of Christ. There is an indirect link. But the emphasis is on the risen and exalted Christ (see Acts 5:30-31; *see* Exaltation). These differences can be easily explained by the different theological foci of Luke and the Johannine epistles on the one hand and of Paul on the other. In Acts the overwhelming theme is that of resurrection,* and thus forgiveness is the gift of the risen Lord.* Paul in his epistles for the most part presents justification as the gift of the crucified Christ.

See also Apostasy; Assurance; Baptism, Baptismal Rites; Grace; Repentance, Second Repentance; Righteousness; Sin, Wickedness.

BIBLIOGRAPHY. F. L. Arrington, *The Acts of the Apostles* (Peabody, MA: Hendrickson, 1988); R. Bultmann, "ἀφίημι κτλ," *TDNT* 1:509-12; J. C. Davis, "Another Look at the Relationship Between Baptism and Forgiveness of Sins in Acts 2:38," *RQ* 24 (1981) 80-88; W. G. Johnsson, *Hebrews* (Boise, ID: Pacific Press, 1994); W. L. Lane, *Hebrews 9—13* (WBC; Dallas: Word, 1991); H. Leroy, "ἀφίημι, ἄφεσις," *EDNT* 1:181-83; V. N. Olsen, "The Doctrine of Forgiveness in the Light of the Hebrew and Greek Languages" in *The Statue of Christ,* ed. V. Carner and G. Stanhiser (Loma Linda, CA: published privately, 1970); J. B. Polhill, *Acts* (NAC; Nashville:

Broadman, 1992); E. B. Redlich, *The Forgiveness of Sins* (Edinburgh: T & T Clark, 1937); V. Taylor, *Forgiveness and Reconciliation* (London: Macmillan, 1948); W. Telfer, *The Forgiveness of Sins* (Philadelphia: Muhlenberg, 1960); H. Verländer, "Forgiveness," *NIDNTT* 1:699-703.

P. U. Maynard-Reid

FREEDOM, LIBERTY

The most common terminology for freedom (*eleutheria* and its cognates) occurs only eight times in Acts, the General Epistles and Revelation out of a total of forty-one NT usages. If one adds to these eight specific usages a comparison of freedom-related topics in both these and other early Christian texts with the Gospels and the Pauline epistles, three broad patterns emerge. Freedom from self-servitude, satanic oppression, sin, death and OT legal requirements are embraced in certain texts; warnings of the abuse of freedom are expressed in others; and occasionally notions of Christian freedom appear to be forgotten.

1. Freedom Embraced: Acts, Hebrews and 1 Peter
2. Freedom Abused: 2 Peter, Jude and Revelation
3. Freedom as Law: James
4. Freedom Obscured: The Early Fathers
5. Freedom and Context

1. Freedom Embraced: Acts, Hebrews and 1 Peter.

1.1. Acts. Acts* provides a demonstration of the freedom that comes through Christ* and his kingdom first introduced in the Gospels. There is liberation from demonic oppression (Acts 5:16; 8:7; 16:18; 19:12) and a demonstration of freedom from self-interest expressed in the early community of goods and other acts of generosity (Acts 2:44-45; 4:36-37; 11:29). In Acts 13:38-39 Paul's speech approximates Pauline teachings on liberation from sin, and freedom from sin and death are demonstrated in incidents such as the Ephesians burning their magic* books (Acts 19:18-19) and the apostle's bold speech (*parrēsia*) in the face of deadly persecution* (Acts 4:13, 31; 7:2-56; 9:27-29; 13:46; Schlier, 490).

More debatable is whether Acts and Paul are at odds over the issue of liberty from OT law.* While Acts does not proclaim freedom from the law in the same bold terminology as Paul uses (Acts 10:1—11:18; 15:1-29), in practical terms the compromise on legal requirements at the Jerusalem council, the circumcision* of Timothy or taking Jewish vows do not contradict Paul's own pragmatism on these matters (Rom 14:20-21; 1 Cor 8:13; 9:20; 10:32-33; Longenecker, 245-63).

1.2. Hebrews. Hebrews* matches certain Pauline attitudes toward the law, particularly its passing and replacement by a new covenant* (Heb 7:18-19; 8:6-13; 10:16-18). However, since the writer of Hebrews is not facing Paul's struggles with legalism but rather Christians failing to mature and abandoning their faith* in the midst of persecution, this theme remains undeveloped. The only clear reference to any sort of freedom comes in Hebrews 2:14-15, where humans are described as delivered *(apallassō)* from a lifelong bondage that resulted from the fear of death.

1.3. 1 Peter. 1 Peter 2:16 exhorts its readers to live as free persons while not using that freedom as a "pretext for evil." This encapsulates two larger themes of the epistle: the believers' identity as sojourners on earth and therefore free from the evil passions that lead to "Gentile" behavior (1 Pet 2:11; 4:1-5); and the call to social behavior that is beyond reproach, so that any suffering* will be undeserved persecution (1 Pet 3:13-17; 4:13-16). This warning, however, implies the possibility of using teaching about freedom from the present earthly order as a justification for immoral and antisocial behavior.

2. Freedom Abused: 2 Peter, Jude and Revelation.

2.1. 2 Peter and Jude. In 2 Peter* freedom is the misleading promise of the false teachers, who appear to promote or permit a hedonistic lifestyle of some sort (2 Pet 2:1-22, esp. 2 Pet 2:19; Bauckham 1990, 67-77). Jude* matches 2 Peter's concern for a group within the church* who have turned teachings about God's grace* into a permit for licentious behavior *(aselgeia,* Jude 4). The irony is that while freedom was the promise of these teachers, the final state was one of reenslavement to "worldly passions" (2 Pet 2:19-20). These false teachers are among those whom the writer of 2 Peter describes as twisting the "hard to understand" Pauline epistles (2 Pet 3:15-16). It is likely these teachers distorted Pauline teachings on freedom that were well suited to their permissive

doctrines (Bauckham 1983, 332).

2.2. Revelation. With the exception of Revelation 1:5, where Christ is described as the one who has "freed us from our sins by his blood" (a theme also expressed in the Johannine epistles, e.g., 1 Jn 1:9; 5:18; *see* John, Letters of), Revelation (*see* Revelation, Book of) matches 2 Peter and Jude with its concern over groups abusing Christian freedom. Sexual immorality and the eating of food sacrificed to idols are singled out as characteristics of these groups (Rev 2:14, 20). It is possible that the groups denounced in Revelation had lost the spirit of Pauline teaching on meat offered to idols (i.e., food is a matter of indifference); like the "strong" of Paul's churches, these groups perhaps had made the flaunting of sexual mores and public eating of meat sacrificed to idols a critical expression of Christian freedom (1 Cor 8:4-13; 10:23-33; Rom 14:14-23).

3. Freedom as Law: James.
Some scholars suggest that James's* expression "the law of freedom" in James 1:25 and James 2:12 contradicts Pauline teachings on freedom and the law (Bultmann, 162-63). E. Käsemann suggests its origins lie in the Jewish identification of "the divine law [with] what the Stoics called cosmic reason" and their assertion "that one can live in thorough harmony with the order of things only if one knows and follows the law" (86; Käsemann, 493-96). Even if this is the origin of the expression, in James the "law of freedom" is linked with "the implanted word" that offers salvation* (Jas 1:21). This suggests a strongly Christian connotation to the phrase (Martin, 51). According to James, the freedom offered by this law is a liberty from self-serving behavior in order to do the works of true faith— acts of charity, self-restraint and harmonious living (Jas 1:27; 2:15-17; 3:9-10, 17-18; 4:11; *see* Faith and Works). In this regard James echoes the Gospels' theme of freedom from self-servitude as well as freedom from external powers of evil (Jas 3:6; 4:7; Davids, 47-50). Whatever the apparent differences between James and Paul on faith and works, in practice both make the love of neighbor the fulfillment of the law (Rom 13:8-10; Jas 2:8-10).

4. Freedom Obscured: The Early Fathers.
R. Bultmann bemoans the loss of Pauline teaching of freedom in both the preceding texts as

well as the apostolic fathers* (Bultmann, 162-202). Certainly the latter offer little to counter this claim. The *Didache** commends strict rather than libertine views on diet (*Did.* 6.3; 8.1), while *1 Clement* and the epistles of Ignatius,* with their strong emphasis on leadership, hardly promote individual expressions of liberty. The *Shepherd of Hermas, 2 Clement* and early apocryphal* acts stress repentance,* purity* and perseverance (*see* Endurance) in the face of persecution. Perhaps most pessimistic on the Christian's ability to live in freedom is Ignatius, who recommends that slaves* should not seek manumission at the church's expense on the grounds that they may become "slaves of lust" (Ign. *Pol.* 4.3).

Despite the missing message of freedom in the apostolic fathers, apocryphal gospels and other early Christian texts, the picture is not as dark as Bultmann and Käsemann suggest. The *Epistle of Barnabas** stands within the Gospel and Pauline tradition of freedom from the law and its food* regulations as well as freedom from the effects of sin, including death and demonic oppression (*Barn.* 3.6; 10.9; 16.9; 18.1-2 [coupled with *Barn.* 3.3; 14.7-9]). Justin Martyr indicates that freedom from demonic oppression was still demonstrated through exorcism (Justin *Apol. II* 6), and even the *Didache* demonstrates a spirit of freedom in its prophetic* ministry* (*Did.* 10.7; 11—13).

5. Freedom and Context.
As one shifts from early Christian communities, particularly those under Pauline influence, to the communities represented in the General Epistles (both early and late), Revelation and the apostolic fathers, there is a shift in context that alters the debate over the believer's freedom. Paul fought for the believers' right to live free from the constraints of OT nomism over against those within the early church who demanded strict adherence to the law. In other contexts, particularly as one moves to the latter part of the first century and beyond, calls for perseverance under more widespread Gentile persecution was a more pressing issue than liberation from legalism. Teaching on a believer's freedom from the law was marginalized in favor of speaking of freedom from the cares, concerns and desires of earthly existence that were a constant distraction to an increasingly oppressed group whose identity and existence were threatened by external persecution and internal schisms.

See also ETHICS; FORGIVENESS; LAW; REDEMPTION; SLAVE, SLAVERY.

BIBLIOGRAPHY. R. J. Bauckham, *Jude, 2 Peter* (WBC; Waco, TX: Word, 1983); idem, *Word Biblical Themes: Jude, 2 Peter* (WBT; Dallas: Word, 1990); R. Bultmann, *Theology of the New Testament* (2 vols.; New York: Scribners, 1955) vol. 2; P. H. Davids, *The Epistle of James: A Commentary on the Greek Text* (NIGTC; Grand Rapids: Eerdmans, 1982); E. Käsemann, *Jesus Means Freedom* (3d rev. ed.; Philadelphia: Fortress, 1969); R. N. Longenecker, *Paul: Apostle of Liberty* (New York: Harper & Row, 1964); R. P. Martin, *James* (WBC; Waco, TX: Word, 1988); H. Schlier, "ἐλεύθερος κτλ," *TDNT* 2:487-502. A. M. Reimer

FULFILLMENT. *See* PROMISE.

G

GALILEAN CHRISTIANITY

The Gospels depict Galilee as the region in which Jesus carried out most of his ministry and found his greatest following. It has long been assumed that the Jesus movement continued in Galilee and developed into Jewish Christianity (*see* Jewish Christianity). Although there is a limited amount of direct evidence for Galilean Christianity, the Gospels themselves are potentially rich resources of the Galilean Christianity which originated with Jesus' Galilean ministry. E. Lohmeyer pointed to Mark's emphasis on Galilee as the central motif for divine revelation and for the Parousia* (Mk 14:28; 16:7). Galilee is portrayed as the land of salvation; Jerusalem as the land of Jesus' rejection. Written sometime between 60-70, Mark depicts Jesus' widespread popularity largely within the boundaries of Galilee (i.e., the area around the Sea of Galilee). For these reasons, Marxsen nicknamed Mark the Galilean Gospel (Marxsen, 92), and others have developed the thesis of its Galilean provenance (e.g., Kelber). But it is Matthew, even more than Mark, that offers promise of shedding light on Galilean Christianity.

1. Matthew: The Gospel of Galilean Christianity
2. First-Century Terms for Galilean Christianity
3. Later Galilean Christianity and the Pella Tradition
4. The Nazarenes and the Gospel of Matthew

1. Matthew: The Gospel of Galilean Christianity

Matthew, written sometime in the period A.D. 80-90, builds upon and expands Mark's Galilean motif. An exploration of Matthew's emphasis on Galilee will suggest possible lines along which the First Gospel both reflects and addresses Galilean Christianity of the late first century.

Matthew introduces Jesus by authenticating his activity in Galilee (Mt 4:12-16), particularly Nazareth and Capernaum, through OT promises. Matthew also concludes Jesus' ministry with a long-anticipated meeting in Galilee during which he commissions his disciples to the nations (Mt 26:32; 28:7; 28:10; 28:16-20). In addition Matthew uniquely reverses the traditional understanding of Galilee: The land of peril (Mt 4:12-16) becomes the land of safety when Jesus twice "withdraws" *(anechōrēsen)* into Galilee in the face of imminent danger (Mt 2:22-23; 4:12). The light of salvation prophetically dawns upon the Galilean people who are sitting in darkness and in the shadow of death (Mt 4:16). And the death of Jesus in Jerusalem suddenly is transformed into a celebration of the resurrection on a mountain in Galilee where Jesus declares his authority among his disciples (see Donaldson). Why did Matthew meticulously reverse negative nuances of Galilee? And how might this reflect Galilean Christianity of the late first century?

1.1. The Social-Historical Setting of Galilee. Galilee had a gloomy history. Gentile nations periodically raided this richly fertile land, sometimes killing, imprisoning or exiling its people. Matthew sought to justify the birth of Christianity and the presence of the Messiah in a land with a dark history set far away from the religious center of Jerusalem.

The first-century form of oppression included Roman occupation and domination of Galilee through client-rulers, multiple levels of taxation, massive building projects which advertised and glorified Rome, and Roman military presence. The land and people of Galilee were used as an economic base, but the client rulers allowed no channel for indigenous Galileans to voice their concerns. The only known expressions of the populace were through popular insurrections and a peasant strike (Horsley, 126).

Galilee of the Gentiles was at a crossroads of cultures and empires. International trade routes gave Galileans contact with various people groups (Mt 4:15). As indicated in the Gospels and other historical sources, first-century Galilee was likely populated by Jews, Romans, Greeks, Syrians, Phoenicians, Samaritans, Arabians and Egyptians. Early rabbinic case laws refer to Jews and Gentiles living beside one another, sharing a courtyard or working together in the fields.

Tolerant and open minded due to their contact with Gentiles, Galilean Jews were often at odds with Jerusalem Temple authorities. Galileans resented their oppressive intrusions and rigid interpretations of the law. Matthew's unique phrase "Galilee of the Gentiles," quoted from Isaiah 9:1, most likely refers to the Gentile cities surrounding Galilee. "Galilee of the Gentiles" has been appropriately translated, "heathen Galilee."

For the above reasons, there are indications of widespread prejudice against Galileans in the first century. Galileans were known to slur their gutturals, and were therefore sometimes prohibited from reciting public prayers in the synagogues. The Gospel of John records Nathaniel saying, "Can anything good come out of Nazareth?" (Jn 1:46), and others saying, "a prophet does not arise from Galilee" (Jn 7:52).

1.2. Galilean Christianity and Rabbinic Judaism. At the time Matthew wrote his Gospel, Jewish Christians were likely expelled from the synagogues.* This is probably reflected in Matthew's unique phrase, "their synagogues" (Mt 4:23; 9:35; 10:17; 12:9; 13:54; cf. the "cursing of the heretics," or *birkaṯ hā mînîm* in Jewish synagogue prayers; see Di Sante, 107-10). This situation was due to the underlying tension between Jewish Christianity and rabbinic Judaism which originated after the destruction of the Jerusalem temple (*see* Christianity and Judaism). In comparison to the other Synoptic writers, Matthew highlights the conflicts between Jesus and the Jewish leaders (e.g., Mt 23). Jewish Christianity's separation from the synagogues implies increased Gentile* involvement in Matthew's Jewish Christian community. It is no coincidence, therefore, that woven among the strongly Jewish overtones in Matthew's Gospel are unique Gentile affirmations: the four Gentile women found in the opening genealogy, the magi from the east who are the first to worship

Jesus, the phrase "Galilee of the Gentiles" which introduces Jesus' ministry location (Mt 4:15), and dual climactic mission mandates to all nations (Mt 24:14; 28:19).

If Matthew was addressing Galilean Christians, we may surmise that they had to struggle daily with the above issues as they lived their faith within intense social conditions that dominated their lives. Galilean Christianity found itself immersed in issues of multiculturalism, oppression and conflict with religious and political authorities.

1.3. A Case for the Galilean Provenance of Matthew. A. Overman has suggested that the Gospel of Matthew was composed in or around Galilee, and he cites two reasons: (1) Matthew's Gospel fundamentally limits the Jesus movement to the general region of Galilee; (2) Galilee was the center of the development of early rabbinic Judaism. Its dominant figures were primarily Galileans. The term "rabbi" appears to have originated in Galilee and so did rabbinic Judaism's first authoritative writing, the Mishnah (Overman 1996, 17-18). To these may be added the Council of Jabneh (Jamnia) in Galilee and modern archaeological evidence of synagogues in Galilee (see Levine; *see* Judaism, Post-A.D. 70).

The issues dominating the period following the destruction of the Jerusalem temple, such as interpretations of the law,* ritual purity,* authority and community structure, are found both in Matthew and early rabbinic Judaism. Early rabbinic Judaism and Matthew's community (*see* Matthean Community) appear to have understood and defined one another through mutual engagement and conflict. The Pharisees in Matthew are basically limited to Galilee, giving Overman the impression that the Galilean Pharisees of early rabbinic Judaism represented the main contenders of Matthew's community (Overman 1996, 15-18; Overman 1990, 156). The Gospel of Matthew may be viewed as an informed response to the very tensions found in the writings of early rabbinic Judaism which emerged in the period A.D. 70-100 and apparently prevailed over Galilean Christianity. Matthew reads like a treatise to persuade the Jew to accept the kind of Jewish Christianity that would have been incorporating Gentiles into its fellowship.

Overman suggests that Matthew's Gospel was written in or near a Galilean city large enough to have been located on a major trade route and to have had an imperial presence, a nearby court and diverse forms of Judaism. The location would require a multicultural setting outside of Palestine among Gentile Greek-speakers. Overman concludes that the most plausible location of the Matthean community is Capernaum, Jesus' home and ministry base (Mt 4:13) near the city of Tiberias. Interestingly, Jesus called Matthew from his tax collector's booth in Capernaum. Other possibilities include regions in or around the thriving first-century Galilean cities of Sepphoris or Tiberias (Overman 1996, 17-18).

2. First-Century Terms for Galilean Christianity
The name "Galilean" may have been an early term for the followers of Jesus. The apostles were addressed as "People of Galilee" in Acts 1:11. Peter, upon denying Jesus, was reprimanded: "Certainly you are one of them, for you are a Galilean" (Mk 14:70; cf. Mt 26:73). Although lacking details, Acts acknowledges a church in Galilee: "the church throughout Judea, Galilee and Samaria had peace and was built up" (Acts 9:31). After the death of Stephen* Christians "scattered throughout the countryside of Judea and Samaria" (Acts 8:1). They likely fled to Galilee as well since Luke often utilizes Judea as a broadly inclusive reference. While Christianity originated in Galilee, the center of the movement eventually shifted to Jerusalem,* and therefore we have little information of the Galilean community apart from what can be gleaned from the Gospels. Once Gentiles flooded into the movement, the non-Jewish term Christians (Christianoi) replaced Galileans (Acts 11:26).

The early use of Nazarene appears to be a derogatory allusion to Galilean Christianity. Tertullus accused Paul of being "an agitator among all the Jews" and "a ringleader of the sect of the Nazarenes" (Acts 24:5). This derogatory reference appears to give deliberate precedence of Jerusalem over Galilee (cf. Acts 2:7). Matthew also felt the need to justify Jesus' presence in Nazareth as a fulfillment of the prophecy, "He shall be called a Nazarene" (2:23).

3. Later Galilean Christianity and the Pella Tradition.
Eusebius and Epiphanius report that prior to the First Jewish revolt (A.D. 66-70), Jerusalem Christians migrated to Pella.* Eusebius also mentions the relatives of the Lord (desposynoi) who traveled extensively from the Jewish villages of Cochaba and Nazareth (see Relatives of Jesus). Cochaba was located east of the Sea of Galilee in the Transjordan, just north of the Decapolis. Therefore some of Jesus' relatives may have resided in the Transjordan during the first two centuries.

Pella was in the Transjordan region near the border of the Decapolis and Peraea. There were three known Jewish Christian sects located in Pella: the Ebionites,* Jacobites and Nazarenes. All three sects utilized and favored the Gospel of Matthew. They zealously interpreted Scripture and observed Jewish law. But all three had differences, revealing a diversity among Jewish Christians. The Ebionites rejected the virgin birth, accused Paul of breaking the law and strictly followed Jewish law, including circumcision.* The Jacobites legalistically observed Jewish law but also supported Gentile mission. The Nazarenes knew Hebrew, had a Hebrew version of Matthew and endorsed the mission of Paul to the Gentiles. They were the more progressive of the three and were cursed and hated by Jews for their messianic beliefs. According to Epiphanius, the Nazarenes were located in Pella, Cochaba and Coele-Syria.

Although they kept the law like other Jewish Christians, the Nazarenes have been compared to a mainstream Christian group (Wilson, 156). Their long history dates prior to the A.D. 70 destruction of Jerusalem. In fact Matthew's Gospel uniquely describes Jesus as a Nazarene who appears in fulfillment of prophecy (Mt 2:23). This and Matthew's Jewish perspective may explain the Nazarenes' affinity to Matthew. NT and later Jewish use of the term "Nazarenes" for Christians reveals the deep and enduring historical roots of the term. The Nazarenes flourished at Pella after the pre-70 influx of Jewish Christians from Jerusalem, and they endured on into the fourth century when they were condemned as heretical. The use of the name Nazarenes for Christians in Transjordan likely indicates the presence of people who originally came from Nazareth.

The Transjordan is mentioned in the key geographical passage of Matthew 4:15: "Land of Zebulun, land of Naphtali, on the way to the sea, beyond the Jordan, Galilee of the Gentiles." This phrase appears to broaden the scope of Galilee to include Gentile regions, since "beyond the Jordan" usually referred to the land east of the Jordan, the Transjordan. This would include the Decapolis and possibly Peraea to the southeast. Matthew's summary verses, "So the news about him spread throughout all Syria" and "Many crowds of people followed him from Galilee, the Decapolis, Jerusalem, Judea, and from beyond the Jordan" (Mt 4:24,25), strengthen this interpretation. Furthermore the Synoptics indicate activity of Jesus southeast of the Sea of Galilee, which could have left a lasting impact in the Decapolis region of the Transjordan (e.g., Mt 8:28).

4. The Nazarenes and the Gospel of Matthew.
Internal and external evidence strongly suggest that Matthew is the Gospel of Galilean Christianity. Both the Matthean and Nazarene communities reveal underlying renewal movements within Judaism which extended their mission outward to the Gentiles and incorporated them into their respective communities. Both communities, though representing differing times and places, were condemned for their inclusiveness of Gentiles. Both appear to be rooted in the earliest Jewish Christian movement of Galilee (cf. Mt 2:23; Mk 14:67; 16:6).

Matthew best represents Galilean Jewish Christianity in the later first century, and Pella represents Jewish Christianity's migration to the Transjordan beginning in the same time period and continuing on into the fourth century.

The remains of the *Gospel of the Nazaraeans* (c. A.D. 100-150) and the *Gospel of the Ebionites* (c. A.D. 100-175; *see DJG*, Gospels [Apocryphal] §4), as well as the lost works of Ariston of Pella, reveal a flurry of activity in the Jewish Christian communities of the Transjordan, Decapolis and Syria (Van Elderen, 113). This activity appears to have at least some roots in Galilean Christianity.

Indications that Jesus' own family members were active in both Galilee and the Transjordan are further strengthened by the traditions concerning James's family. Since Galilee was linked to Damascus, we may also surmise that Galilean Christians spread the gospel to Damascus, after which the movement experienced persecution from Saul. A few decades later Jewish Christians migrated to the Transjordan, and many second-century Jewish Christian movements flourished there. In the third and fourth centuries, Jewish Christianity waned when it was scorned by both Christians and Jews.

See also CHRISTIANITY AND JUDAISM: PARTINGS OF THE WAYS; EBIONITES; JEWISH CHRISTIANITY; MATTHEAN COMMUNITY; PELLA, FLIGHT TO.

BIBLIOGRAPHY: C. Di Sante, *Jewish Prayer: The Origins of the Christian Liturgy* (New York: Paulist, 1991); T. L. Donaldson, *Jesus on the Mountain: A Study in Matthean Theology* (JSNTSup 8; Sheffield: JSOT, 1985); L. E. Elliott-Binns, *Galilean Christianity* (SBT; Chicago: Alec R. Allenson, 1956); S. Freyne, *Galilee, Jesus and the Gospels* (Philadelphia: Fortress, 1988); P. Hertig, "The Galilee Theme in Matthew: Transforming Mission through Marginality," *Missiology* 25 (1997) 155-63; R. A. Horsley, *Galilee: History, Politics, People* (Valley Forge: Trinity Press International, 1995); E. Lohmeyer, *Galiläa und Jerusalem* (Göttingen: Vandenhoeck & Ruprecht, 1936); W. H. Kelber, *The Kingdom in Mark: A New Place and a New Time* (Philadelphia: Fortress, 1974); W. Marxsen, *Mark the Evangelist: Studies in the Redaction History of the Gospels* (Nashville: Abingdon, 1969); G. Stemberger, "Galilee—Land of Salvation?" in W. D. Davies, *The Gospel and the Land* (Berkeley: University of California Press, 1974) 409-38; J. A. Overman, *Church and Community in Crisis: The Gospel According to Matthew* (Valley Forge: Trinity Press International, 1996); idem, *Matthew's Gospel and Formative Judaism* (Minneapolis: Fortress, 1990); A. J. Saldarini, "The Gospel of Matthew and Jewish-Christian Conflict in the Galilee" in *The Galilee in Late Antiquity*, ed. L. I. Levine (Cambridge: Harvard University Press, 1992) 23-38; B. Van Elderen, "Early Christianity in Transjordan," *TynB* 45 (1994) 97-117; S. G. Wilson, *Related Strangers: Jews and Christians, 70-170 C.E.* (Minneapolis: Fortress, 1995).
P. A. Hertig

GENTILES, GENTILE MISSION

Gentiles (usually Gk *ethnē*) is a term used by Jews to describe non-Israelites, a distinction made with many other terms (Bietenhard, 788-95; Porton, *gôyîm*; *see DPL*, Gentiles, §1). However, the early church* increasingly was composed of Gentiles, and because often it appropriated terms previously used of Israel,* the term *Gentiles* sometimes refers to "unbelieving, non-Christian gentiles" (e.g., 1 Pet 2:12; 4:3). The "Gentile mission," on the other hand, characterized earliest Christianity in that it aggressively sought out converts to Christianity from any people group all over the Roman Empire (*see* Roman Empire) and beyond. Accordingly, the

"Gentile mission" assumes an early Christian self-identity as it formed itself into a self-conscious group (church) and a desire to recruit members to this church by actively evangelizing* non-Israelites. This mission characterized and shaped earliest Christianity. "In short, the history and theology of earliest Christianity are 'mission* history' and 'mission theology'" (Hengel, 64).

The relationship of Jews to Gentiles was diverse, showing signs of both integration and resistance, and this diversity varied considerably with respect to time and place. What Jews did in Alexandria* at one time could be considerably at variance with what they did later (or earlier), and what Jews did there could be significantly contrasted with what Jews did in the land of Israel or in, say, Sardis or Rome.* It should be observed that Jews of all times believed that Yahweh, their God, was the King of the whole world (Ps 96:4-5, 10), that all people had been created by Yahweh and there was really only one God (Sir 13:15; Philo *Decal.* 64), that all people could join Judaism through conversion (exceptions to this permission were rare), that it was wise to get along with Gentiles in the diaspora* (Philo *Flacc.* 94; Josephus records numerous treaties Jews established with Gentiles) and that Jews ought to show general friendliness with their neighbors (the Good Samaritan story of Jesus concerns a religious boundary; cf. Josephus *J.W.* 2.412-16).

However, despite this integrative tendency there were almost always limits to what Jews were willing to do with Gentiles: they were opposed to intermarriage (Ezra 9—10; *T. Levi* 9:10; 14:6), religious idolatry* (1 Macc) and permission for Gentiles to penetrate into the central courts of the temple* (Acts 21:28). A fairly standardized hope* of Judaism was a massive conversion of Gentiles to worship* of Yahweh at the last day (Tob 13:11; *1 Enoch* 48:7-10; 63:1-12; Mt 8:11-12). This was the context for early Christians, since most were Jewish (*see DJG,* Gentiles).

1. Origins of the Gentile Mission
2. Nature of the Gentile Mission in Earliest Christianity
3. Two Later Developments

1. Origins of the Gentile Mission.
Evangelizing Gentiles was not natural to the people of Israel, neither in the land of Israel nor in the diaspora. Because of the holiness* laws

and their effective, practical implementation in Jewish culture by the first century A.D., concerns were raised not only about the influence of paganism through contact with idolaters but also about the practical impact that regular relations with Gentiles would have on purity* and personal holiness. Thus when the first Christians, who were nearly all Jewish, began to extend the message about Jesus Messiah to non-Israelites, there would have been considerable consternation and conflict among both Christian Jews and non-Christian Jews (cf. Acts 1—15).

We need then to ask how the Gentile mission began. With Paul this mission found its principal spokesman, and the evidence for his understanding of the mission is significant (cf. Acts; Gal 2:1-10; Rom 15:14-29; *see DPL,* Mission). But one thing is clear: it is inaccurate to argue that it would have been "natural" for Jewish Christians to share their newfound religious ideals realized in Jesus with any pagan who happened to be in their company.

1.1. Jewish Proselytism. It has been argued by very influential scholars (e.g., J. Jeremias, E. Schürer, A. von Harnack, D. Georgi; on this scholarship see McKnight 1991, 1-10) that early Christianity simply adopted the missionary nature and practices of contemporary Judaism and extended them along Christian lines, eventually eclipsing the Jewish mission altogether with a decisive victory: Christians won over the Roman Empire, while Jews, so it is argued, caved in and withdrew from missionary work completely. However, the recent consensus of scholarship is that this picture is not only exaggerated but wrong-headed in its essential arguments. A majority of current scholars working on Jewish missionary activity agree that Judaism was not a missionary movement, did not have a missionary theology and only rarely involved itself in what may be called "universal proselytization" (see McKnight 1991, Goodman, Cohen, Taylor, Porton).

If this conclusion is sound, earliest Christianity did not adopt or adapt the Jewish missionary activity of its contemporaries. Earliest Christianity did not get its missionary impulse from Judaism; the two religions diverge here. "Christianity was committed to encountering the world in its universal mission to convert it; Judaism was committed to keeping the holiness of the people sacrosanct" (Segal, 177).

1.2. Jesus. The closing words of Jesus to his disciples were to make disciples of all nations (Mt 28:16-20), and in Acts 1:8 the resurrected Christ informs the disciples that they are to be "witnesses"* throughout the world, beginning in Jerusalem* and its environs. Thus the Gentile mission, however indirectly, begins with Jesus (Hengel, 61-63; *See DJG*, Gentiles, §2). However important these words have been in the development of the Christian conception of a mission to the whole world, they apparently fell on deaf ears among the apostolic cadre. For as the text of Acts unfolds and as any reader of the NT can see, the apostles did not appeal to Jesus to explain their mission, nor did they use his words to urge others to evangelize the world. The issue was not the *importance* of the Gentile misson but rather the *manner of accepting Gentile converts.*

Even Paul's early missions were designed, in the first level, to be evangelism of Jews in synagogues,* and it was only after rejection by Jews and acceptance by Gentiles that the Gentile mission came into focus (e.g., Acts 13:44-52). In spite of the foundational nature of the Great Commission words of Jesus, and even if these words did have some generative effects, the origins of the early Christian Gentile mission must be largely sought elsewhere.

1.3. Sociological Explanations. M. Goodman has argued that the Christian mission was a sociologically explicable phenomenon (Goodman, 160-74). The eschaton did not arrive as expected, and when we factor in the powerful personality of Paul and his theology, we are led to the view that something new was on the horizon. Paul's ministry, and that of several other early Christians, led to the conversion of some Gentiles, and this led to conflict among early Christians and Jews. Such a conflict forced rationalization and legitimation on the part of the early Christians, and this legitimation led to an overreactive defense of a Gentile, universal mission. Permission was always granted to convert to Judaism; now such activity was not only permitted but positively desired. Thus an initial defensiveness led to what was the distinguishing and defining characteristic of much early Christianity: evangelism of the Gentiles.

However attractive this explanation might be—and arguably it clarifies what inevitably did take place—it falls short of a fully adequate explanation for the origins of the Gentile mission. To be sure, the Gentile mission was in part stumbled upon; but that act of stumbling had greater momentum than a curious, heated interchange arising from a defensive overreaction.

1.4. Divine Providence. If we factor in (1) an ancient Jewish, and pagan, willingness to declare one's religious views in public, (2) a minimal impact of both the example (cf. Mt 8:5-13; 15:21-28) and words of Jesus (Mt 28:16-20; Acts 1:8), (3) the historical accidents of early Christians bumping into pagans and evangelizing them, along with the accompanying debate and legitimation (Dunn; Hengel, 54-58), (4) the presence of a ready-made audience of some Gentiles in Jewish synagogues, and therefore their preparedness for examining the Christian gospel,* and (5) the impact of persecution,* driving early Jewish Christians away from the land of Israel to other places where they would necessarily have to explain their new views, we are led to see the origins of the Gentile mission in a constellation of factors.

Not to be discounted here either is the importance of scriptural exegesis: success would have led Jewish Christians to their Scriptures to find wisdom and guidance for Gentile converts. At least the apostle Paul saw justification for the early Christian mission in the Abrahamic covenant* and its promise that Abraham would be the father of many nations (cf. Gen 12:1-3; 17:5; Gal 2:1-10, 15-21; 3:6-9, 28). Furthermore, the powerful experience of the Holy Spirit among early Christians (Acts 1:5, 8; 2:1-4, 17-18; 4:31; 9:31; 10:19, 44-48; *see* Holy Spirit) contributed to their developing confidence in a universal missionary outreach.

One might argue, then, that the mission began with accidents: successes among the Gentiles and consequent debates. But these accidents, according to the earliest Christian evidence, were generated by God's guidance through the Spirit and were continued through the divinely permitted driving of Christians away from the land of Israel. The early Christians' appeal to the universal dimensions of God's activity in the history of Israel is solidly based.

2. Nature of the Gentile Mission in Earliest Christianity.

Early Christian literature that survives is not written for the purpose of evangelizing unbelievers. Consequently, the information we do have comes to us indirectly, for it is found in contexts embedded in other concerns. However, one book, the Acts of the Apostles, describes the "development of the church" from Jerusalem to Rome. Every study of the Gentile mission must begin there.

2.1. Acts. Several features of Acts are notable. First, Luke emphasizes the sovereign prompting of the Holy Spirit (Kee, 28-41). The mission of the early church was generated, directed and sustained by the Holy Spirit. Thus it received its decisive impetus from the Spirit's descent at Pentecost* (Acts 2, esp. Acts 2:1-4, 17-18, 33, 38), and its effectiveness is attributed to the Spirit (Acts 4:31; 5:32). When Philip, who became the first "Gentile missonary," had success with the Samaritans, fulfilling the programmatic design of Acts 1:8, it was because the Spirit was at work (Acts 8:14-25); he furthered his ministry by evangelizing the Ethiopian eunuch as a result of Spirit-directed work (Acts 8:29, 39). Paul's conversion was a filling of the Spirit (Acts 9:17), and the Spirit brought about his calling to Gentile missionary work (Acts 13:2, 4), not to mention its actual operation (Acts 13:9, 52; 16:6-7; 19:1-7, 21; 20:22-23, 28; 21:4, 11; 28:25). Peter had to receive revelation from the Spirit before he could comprehend that this same Spirit would also fill Gentiles (Acts 10:19, 44-48; 11:12, 15-17), and similar things are said of others (e.g., Acts 11:24, 28).

Second, Luke intends to record the geographical spread of the gospel from Jerusalem to Rome along with its encounter of different cultures and religions (Kee, 42-69). For each of these, Luke records the establishment of local churches where this faith and practice could be centered and nurtured (*see* Centers of Christianity). After an initial statement to this effect (Acts 1:8), Luke is careful to record the spread of the gospel: from Jerusalem (Acts 2), to Samaria (Acts 8:4-25), to an Ethiopian traveler (Acts 8:26-40), to Caesarea and the Gentile Cornelius (Acts 10—11), to Antioch (Acts 11:19-30), throughout Cyprus and Asia Minor (Acts 13:4—14:21), to Europe through the evangelization of some of Greece with its different cultural, philosophical, political and religious orientations (Acts 16:6—18:17), and then on to Rome (Acts 27:1—28:16), where once again Paul evangelized both Jews and Gentiles from prison (Acts 28:17-31). Along the way Luke records controversies about this mission and their

various solutions (see esp. Acts 11:1-18; 15:1-35). In particular, the Gentile mission was endorsed by the apostles (Acts 11:1-18), but minimal ethical requirements were expected of pagan converts to the gospel (Acts 15:1-35).

Third, Luke shows a Paul who begins with the Jews and only extends that Jewish offer to the Gentiles. At the very end of his account, Luke has Paul warning the Jews that though he has evangelized them, God has appointed this same message to go out to the Gentiles as well (Acts 28:28). This theme (to the Jews first) is a foundational method for Paul's missionary preaching: the same occurs in Pisidian Antioch (Acts 13:46), Corinth (Acts 18:6) and Ephesus (Acts 19:8-10). Jewish privilege is affirmed, as is found deeply embedded in the early Christian Bible (Gen 12:1-3), but it is not an exclusive privilege: Gentiles who believe will be grafted into the vine, and Jews who do not believe will be snipped from the vine (cf. Rom 9—11). Along this line of evidence, it is Luke who records the presence of the so-called God-fearers in the Jewish synagogues, who, so it seems, were especially attracted to the gospel of universal salvation,* apart from joining the nation of Israel (McKnight 1991, 108-14).

2.2. The Theology of the Evangelists. We can begin with Luke by observing that the theology Luke expounds in Acts is quite similar to his approach to the life of Jesus of Nazareth. He affirms that the Gentile mission begins with the preaching of repentance in Jerusalem (Lk 24:47), but this motif begins in the infancy narratives of Luke and continues throughout: Luke 2:14, 32; 3:4-6; 4:26-27; 7:1-10; 10:29-37; 13:29; 17:11-19. The gospel of the kingdom,* of the salvation of God, is offered to all, but this "all" is subsequent to the offer to Jews. Luke emphasizes the future salvation* of Gentiles in his Gospel (Lk 13:28-29; 14:15-24; 24:47-48), as well as the piety of specific Gentiles (Lk 7:1-10; 19:2-10).

Much of Mark's content is picked up by either Luke or Matthew, but several points regarding Mark deserve mention. Like Paul, Mark affirms the priority of the Jews (Mk 7:27). In addition, Mark emphasizes, along with the rest of the Synoptic tradition, the positive response of Gentiles, including the Roman centurion (Mk 15:39). Mark suggests that Gentiles respond in agreement with the Jews (cf. Mk 1:21-28 and 5:1-20; 5:18-20 and 7:29-30).

On most accounts Matthew's Gospel is the most Jewish of the Gospels, yet it is also marked by a heavy accent on universalism,* leading most scholars today to think that Matthew was seeking to lead his community to greater involvement in the Gentile mission. While Jesus is King of Israel (Mt 2:1-12) and has come for the salvation of his (read "Jewish") people (Mt 1:21), and while he demands that his disciples evangelize only Jews (Mt 10:5-6; cf. 10:23) and he himself restricts himself in some sense to Jews (cf. 15:24), this same Jesus is bent on a more universal scope to the mission of God's kingdom.* Thus the first to worship are the magi (Mt 2:1-12), who become descendants of Abraham (Mt 1:1); Jesus' dwelling in Galilee fulfills the dream of the light of Israel shining on all nations (Mt 4:12-16). The birds of the air (read "Gentiles") will nest in Israel's tree (Mt 13:31-32; cf. 21:33-46; 22:1-14; 24:14), just as Jesus himself evangelizes some Gentiles (Mt 8:5-13; 15:21-28). The centurion at the cross is the first to confess Jesus as Son of God without being rebuked, and he is a Gentile (Mt 27:54). So it is Matthew's design to show that from the very beginning, though the Jews are the privileged people and remain so (this is probably why Matthew retains sayings like 10:5-6 and 15:24), the gospel moves from them to the whole world (Mt 28:16-20). Like Paul's very practice, Matthew, Mark and Luke each see a particularism (to the Jews first) that leads to a universalism (and also to the Gentiles; see DJG, Gentiles, §§3-6).

2.3. 1 Peter. Peter's first letter is addressed to Christians who most probably were former Gentile unbelievers (cf. 1 Pet 1:18; 4:1-6) but who were now members of the family of God. These Christians now see Gentiles as "the other," as those who do not believe in Jesus Messiah and do not live in this new society (cf. 1 Pet 2:12). But Peter's concept of the Gentile mission, if we can judge from his letter (and we have to admit our limitations here), is that Christians are to live in the midst of a disobedient society in such a way that Gentiles can see their holy,* loving* manner of life and, through their observation, be led to glorify God (1 Pet 2:11-12, 15; 3:1-2). These "strangers and temporary residents" (1 Pet 1:1; 2:11) are to be prepared to defend their faith* and hope* (1 Pet 3:15), but this seems to be an action done in the midst of persecution* rather than in some public forum. What we see in 1 Peter, then, is a group of churches

in Asia Minor (1 Pet 1:1-2) who have settled into a lifestyle of obedience* but are questioning why they must undergo suffering.* Peter's response is that (1) God uses this suffering to purify their character (1 Pet 1:3-12) and (2) they are to live in such a way as to influence those who persecute them.

In Peter's list of spiritual gifts (1 Pet 4:7-11) there is no mention of evangelism, though it is remotely possible that this could be involved in the "if anyone speaks, let the words be the oracles of God" (1 Pet 4:11). Nor is evangelism a part of the instructions given to the elders (1 Pet 5:1-4). Peter, then, appears to have a different concept of the Gentile mission, one hammered out on the anvil of life experience over the heat of persecution. Peter's perception of the Gentile mission is that it advances as a result of Christian lifestyle, rather than along the lines of a Pauline concept of geographical growth through missonary evangelism. (2 Pet is even more concerned with internal doctrinal and moral questions.)

2.4. Johannine Literature. The complex of writings under the name of John witness to some common themes about Gentiles and the Gentile mission. First, whether in anticipation of a work to be accomplished (Jn 1:9; 3:17; 4:42; 6:33, 51; 11:27; 12:20-23; 16:8-10; 20:21-23) or in apocalyptic imagery for a heavenly reality (Rev 5:1-14; 19:1—20:15), John witnesses to Jesus as Savior of the whole world because he has provided a sacrifice* for the sins* of the whole world (1 Jn 2:2; 4:14). Second, the ministry of Jesus was directed toward Jews, and Gentiles were only exceptionally included (Jn 4:1-42, 46-54; 12:20-22). Thus as for Paul and the Synoptics, Gentile salvation is secondary to the preaching to Jews (Jn 4:22). Third, like Luke, John emphasizes the Spirit's role in mission (Jn 14:25-26; 16:8-11; 20:19-23). However, John's Gospel has little trace of a uniquely Gentile mission, and apart from John 11:52, the only statement along these lines is a misunderstanding on the part of John's enemies, the Jews (Jn 7:35-36). Though we cannot be sure, it is possible that the travelers of 3 John are missionaries (3 Jn 5-8); it is also possible that they are prophets* or teachers* who are not primarily concerned with evangelism.

One might assume that John has this concern for evangelism of Gentiles in view in mission statements cited above, but his concerns lie elsewhere, especially in doctrinal controversies about Jesus and in the fundamental importance of faith in this Word of God and how that faith separates believers from the world (Hahn, 152-63). While John envisions a day when people from all the world will sing praises to the Lamb* on the throne, John does not spell out how it is that all those people got there. Missionary activity must be assumed.

For John there is an absolute contrast between the followers of Jesus and the world; the difference is effected by faith, by believing in Jesus, but John does not expound the role humans play in this gathering of people of faith.

2.5. Miscellaneous. Regardless of how difficult it is to explain the origins of the early Christian mission to the Gentiles, it is a fact that by the time of Constantine the Roman Empire had been "conquered" by the Christian messengers and message. Christianity was found from India to England and throughout the Mediterranean basin. Remarkable success like this deserves careful, sympathetic and analytical explanation.

There was something about Christianity that made it appealing to the Roman world and therefore in some sense superior to all other options available in that day. It must have seemed satisfying and attractive; by the end of the fourth century A.D. it was even advantageous to become Christian in most parts of the Roman Empire (Macmullen). Even if Christianity had many martyrs* in its history, and even if the apologists of the second century worked hard to defend the faith, the blood of the martyrs and the arguments of the apologists outlasted the opponents.

In spite of the inherited traditions of pagans and Jews, the unease of Rome with respect to the legal status of Christianity (especially under Nero, Domitian, Trajan and Hadrian, not to mention the later Decius), the establishment of other religious orientations and the fractious nature of much Christian development, Christianity did gain control of the religious beliefs and worship* of the Roman world. The full story can never be completely recovered, but at least the following contributed to the success of the Christian mission: a unified Roman Empire with an intricate, largely safe system for travel; the widespread use of the Greek language; the foundation that had been laid through the presence of Judaism throughout the Hellenistic* world; the sterling testimony of martyrs; the

attractive wholesomeness of pure, loving lives; the effective counterarguments of the apologists; and the longing for religion throughout the Mediterranean (Green; Grant; Neill, 26-60; Ferguson, 571-82; Stark).

However, alongside this noteworthy development is the near absence of records of missionary efforts. We do not know the names of mission centers or of missionaries (but see Green, 166-93); we have no records of missionary endeavors; and we have little reflection by early Christians on the importance, urgency or necessity of missionary work to the definition of what Christianity was (Goodman, 91-108). This absence of information is most readily explained as an accident of history, probably generated largely because early Christian writers were concerned with other issues (like apologetical debates). While early Christians were engaging in apologetics in their writing, a world mission was under way; however unorganized it may have been, this sect of Judaism became a worldwide religion.

2.6. Summary. Christianity, understood here to be the message both of and about Jesus Christ, and then later in its more doctrinal and theological forms, had within it a missionary impulse that was not to be denied. Wherever it got its genesis, its effectiveness is well-known: Rome eventually became the head of a Christian empire.

3. Two Later Developments.

3.1. Conflict with Judaism. Scholarship is split on the nature of early Christian and Jewish relations. Some have argued that Christianity and Judaism were in a competition for pagan souls (e.g., Simon), while others argue that Judaism was never really in competition with Christianity at all. In fact, some more recent scholarship argues that the battle was an imagined battle, really only a theological construct: Christianity's battle with Judaism (as seen in some early Christian literature) was the use of older biblical themes (especially the prophets) for current issues that had almost nothing to do with Judaism (Taylor). It will take a generation to follow up this debate with some definitive conclusions, but for now it must be said that Christianity's conflict with Judaism for the conversion of pagans in the first three centuries of the common era may very well have not been a battle at all; it may be theological argumentation (*see* Christianity and Judaism).

3.2. Decreasing Centrality of Mission. Goals, once achieved, usually recede in importance and give way to other concerns. In early Christianity, in many areas, this seems to have been the case with missionary efforts to convert pagans. Settled communities, achieved often with considerable effort, soon found other issues dominating their concern. Doctrinal controversies and practical issues may well have sapped many early Christian communities of their interest in evangelizing harder to reach people groups. For whatever reasons, it is clear that evangelistic energies waned and went through local ups and downs for many of the early Christian communities (Goodman).

Christianity gained the confidence of the Roman Empire, but this was not achieved by some central strategy, nor was it the result of increasing momentum. Rather, Christian goals and Roman goals were conflated, and this conflation dominated the Western world for centuries.

See also CIRCUMCISION; DIASPORA JUDAISM; EVANGELISM IN THE EARLY CHURCH; MISSION, EARLY NON-PAULINE.

BIBLIOGRAPHY. H. Bietenhard, "People, Nation, Gentiles, Crowd, City," *NIDNTT* 2:788-805; S. J. D. Cohen, "Was Judaism in Antiquity a Missionary Religion?" in *Jewish Assimilation, Acculturation and Accommodation: Past Traditions, Current Issues and Future Prospects,* ed. M. Mor (SJC 2; Lanham, MD: University Press of America, 1992); J. D. G. Dunn, "The Incident at Antioch (Gal. 2.11-18)" in *Jesus, Paul and the Law: Studies in Mark and Galatians* (Louisville, KY: Westminster/John Knox, 1990) 129-82; E. Ferguson, *Backgrounds of Early Christianity* (2d ed.; Grand Rapids: Eerdmans, 1993); M. Goodman, *Mission and Conversion: Proselytizing in the Religious History of the Roman Empire* (Oxford: Clarendon, 1994); R. M. Grant, *Greek Apologists of the Second Century* (Philadelphia: Westminster, 1988); M. Green, *Evangelism in the Early Church* (Grand Rapids: Eerdmans, 1970); F. Hahn, *Mission in the New Testament* (London: SCM, 1965); A. von Harnack, *The Mission and Expansion of Christianity in the First Three Centuries* (Gloucester, MA: Peter Smith, 1972 [1908]); M. Hengel, *Between Jesus and Paul: Studies in the Earliest History of Christianity* (Minneapolis: Fortress, 1983); H. C. Kee, *Good News to the Ends of the Earth: The Theology of Acts* (Philadelphia: Trin-

ity Press International, 1990); R. Macmullen, *Christianizing the Roman Empire* A.D. *100-400* (New Haven: Yale University Press, 1984); S. McKnight, *A Light Among the Gentiles: Jewish Missionary Activity in the Second Temple Period* (Minneapolis: Fortress, 1991); S. Neill, *Christian Missions* (Pelican History of the Church 6; Baltimore: Penguin, 1964); G. Porton, *The Stranger Within Your Gates: Converts and Conversion in Rabbinic Literature* (Chicago: University of Chicago Press, 1994); A. Segal, *Rebecca's Children: Judaism and Christianity in the Roman World* (Cambridge, MA: Harvard University Press, 1986); M. Simon, *Verus Israel: A Study of Relations Between Christians and Jews in the Roman Empire (135-425)* (Oxford: Oxford University Press, 1986); R. Stark, *The Rise of Chrisianity* (Princeton: Princeton University Press, 1996); M. S. Taylor, *Anti-Judaism and Early Christian Identity: A Critique of the Scholarly Consensus* (SPB 46; Leiden: E. J. Brill, 1995).   S. McKnight

GEONIM. *See* JUDAISM, POST-A.D. 70.

GIFTS. *See* SACRIFICE, OFFERINGS, GIFTS.

GLORY

The English words *glory* and *glorify* are the principal translations for the Greek noun *doxa* ("glory") and the verb *doxazō* ("glorify"). However, the translation and significance of *doxa* and *doxazō* should not be limited to one English word apiece. In the later writings of the NT and the apostolic fathers,* both the noun and the verb possess wide ranges of meaning. *Doxa* designates either a person's favorable status, reputation or position (e.g., Heb 3:3; *1 Clem.* 32.2; *Barn.* 19.3; *Herm. Vis.* 1.1.8; *Herm. Man.* 4.4.2; *Herm. Sim.* 5.3.3; 8.7.4, 6; cf. *1 Clem.* 61.2) or their vanity and conceit (*Barn.* 8.2). *Doxa* is used as a term of measurement; that is, the "brightness" (*doxa*) of a light (Acts 22:11), the "beauty" (*doxa*) of a flower (1 Pet 1:24) or the "wealth" (*doxa*) of the nations (Rev 21:24, 26). *Doxa* can even refer to heavenly, angelic* figures (Jude 8; cf. Rev 18:1; Ign. *Smyrn.* 6.1; Szewc, 129-40). The verb *doxazō* means "appoint" (Heb 5:5), "exalt" (*Barn.* 6.16; *Herm. Vis.* 1.1.3), "honor" (*1 Clem.* 17.5; 32.3; *Diogn.* 5.14), "bless" (Ign. *Pol.* 7.2) and "boast" (Rev 18:7). By far, however, the two most frequent and theologically important uses of *doxa* and *doxazō* are as terms that denote worship and refer to God's* revealed presence.

1. Glory as Doxology
2. Glory as Divine Presence
3. Summary

1. Glory as Doxology.

1.1. Glory to God. The use of the noun *doxa* to mean "praise" or "adoration" falls into two basic patterns (but cf. Rev 4:9; 5:12). The first pattern employs *doxa* in the nominative case, an understood verb, a dative or a genitive that refers to God and a reference to time: "glory [be] to God forever and ever" is an example. This construction appears with some variation twenty-seven times in the literature (Heb 13:21; 1 Pet 4:11; 2 Pet 3:18; Jude 25; Rev 1:6; 5:13; 7:12; 19:1; *1 Clem.* 20.12; 32.4; 38.4; 43.6; 45.7; 50.7; 58.2; 61.3; 64; *2 Clem.* 20.5; *Mart. Pol.* 20.2; 21.2; cf. 22.1; *Did.* 8.2; 9.2, 3; 10.2, 4, 5; *Diogn.* 12.9). The second noun pattern uses a form of *didōmi* and *doxa* in the accusative with a dative referring to God: for example, "give glory to God." This construction, again with some variation, appears eight times (Acts 12:23; 1 Pet 1:7; Rev 4:9; 11:13; 14:7; 16:9; 19:7; *2 Clem.* 17.7).

In these passages *doxa* is contextually coordinated with other nouns used in the veneration of God; "honor" (*timē*, 1 Pet 1:7; Rev 4:9, 11; 5:12, 13; 7:12; *1 Clem.* 64; 65.2; *Mart. Pol.* 20.2; 21.2), "power" (*dynamis*, Rev 4:11; 5:12; 7:12; 19:1; *Did.* 8.2; 9.4, 5), "might" (*kratos*, 1 Pet 4:11; Rev 1:6; 5:13; *1 Clem.* 64; 65.2; *Mart. Pol.* 20.2), "majesty" (*megalōsynē, 1 Clem.* 20.12; 61.3; 64; 65.2; *Mart. Pol.* 20.2; 21.2), "blessing" (*eulogia*, Rev 5:12, 13; 7:12), "thanksgiving" (*eucharistos*, Rev 4:9; 7:12), "wisdom" (*sophia*, Rev 5:12; 7:12), "strength" (*ischys*, Rev 5:12; 7:12), "eternal dominion" (*thronos aiōnios, 1 Clem.* 65.2; *Mart. Pol.* 21.2), "salvation" (*sōtēria*, Rev 19:1), "praise" (*epainos*, 1 Pet 1:7) and "riches" (*ploutos*, Rev 5:12).

1.2. Glorify God. When *theos* or its semantic equivalent is the object of the verb *doxazō* or when *theos* or its semantic equivalent is the subject of *doxazō* in the passive voice, then *doxazō* without fail means to "praise," "worship" or "venerate": "glorify God" or "God be glorified." These constructions occur twenty-eight times (Acts 4:21; 11:18; 13:48; 21:20; 1 Pet 2:12; 4:11, 16; Rev 15:4; 18:7; *1 Clem.* 35.12; 43.6; 52.3; Ign. *Trall.* 1.2; Ign. *Phld.* 10.1; *Barn.* 2.10; 19.2; *Herm. Vis.* 2.1.2; 3.4.2; 4.1.3; 4.1.4; *Herm. Man.* 3.1; 5.2.3; *Herm. Sim.* 6.1.1; 6.3.6 [2x]; 8.6.3; 9.18.5; 9.28.5).

Doxazō is thus coordinated with other verbs for worship such as "fear" (*phobeō*, Rev 5:14; *Barn.* 19.2), "love" (*agapaō, Barn.* 19.2), "praise" (*aineō, Mart. Pol.* 14.3), "bless" (*eulogeō, Mart. Pol.* 14.3; 19.2), "pray" (*proseucheō, Herm. Vis.* 2.1.2) and "rejoice" (*agalliaomai, Mart. Poly.* 19.2; *euphrainō, Herm. Vis.* 3.4.2).

1.3. The Rhetoric of Glory Doxologies. The consistent syntactic patterns, the circumscribed range of meaning associated with both *doxa* and *doxazō* within these patterns, and the words contextually coordinated with *doxa* and *doxazō* all point to a specific historical setting—the worship experiences of the early church.* Repeated liturgical use accounts for the syntactic and semantic uniformity (*see* Worship; Liturgical Elements). *Doxa* and *doxazō* formed part of the church's rich vocabulary of doxology.

The glory doxologies perform similar functions in their literary context as they did in their original liturgical setting. Although most of the noun patterns imply action, sometimes the verb appears in the indicative (Acts 12:23; 1 Pet 4:11; Rev 4:9; 11:13; 19:7; *1 Clem.* 58.2; *2 Clem.* 17.7; *Mart. Pol.* 20.2; *Did.* 8.2; 9.4; 10.5), subjunctive (1 Pet 1:7) or imperative moods (Rev 14:7; *1 Clem.* 32.4). *Doxa* and *doxazō* therefore continue to elicit, exemplify and command worship.

The glory doxologies also explicitly identify God as the object of worship. This is underscored when God is directly addressed (Rev 4:9; *1 Clem.* 61.3; *Did.* 9.2, 3; 10.2, 4; *Mart. Pol.* 14.3). The glory doxologies thus underline early Christianity's continued commitment to Jewish monotheism.

In addition the doxologies demonstrate the liturgical significance of the risen Jesus. Jesus is singled out as the agent through whom glory is offered to God (Jude 25; *1 Clem.* 58.2; 61.3; 64; 65.2; *Mart. Pol.* 14.3; *Did.* 9.4). In some cases Jesus even replaces God as the object of worship (2 Pet 3:18; Ign. *Eph.* 2.2; Ign. *Smyrn.* 1.1; Ign. *Pol.* 8.2; *Mart. Pol.* 22.3), anticipating later trinitarian developments. The doxologies indicate that Jesus was and should be venerated as God.

Finally, the repeated references to time— "now and for ever more"; "for ever and ever" (Heb 13:21; 1 Pet 1:7; 4:11; 2 Pet 3:18; Jude 25; Rev 1:6; 5:13; 7:12; *1 Clem.* 20.12; 32.4; 38.4; 43.6, 7; 50.7; 58.2; 61.3; 64; 65.2; *2 Clem.* 20.5; *Mart. Pol.* 14.3; 20.2; 21.2; 22.3; *Did.* 8.2; 9.2, 3; 10.2, 4, 5; *Diogn.* 12.9)—place the glory doxologies within an eschatological* context: the church's worship anticipates that of the coming kingdom. In short the glory doxologies collapse the boundaries between heaven* and earth, present and future, and model the worship of God for the readers.

2. Glory as Divine Presence.

Glory language not only refers to the act of worship; it also indicates who is worshiped, God. Along with "wisdom" *(sophia)*, "spirit" *(pneuma)*, "image" *(eikōn)*, "word" *(logos)*, "name" *(onoma)* and "power" *(dynamis)*, "glory" formed part of the semantic-filled words that could sign God's revealed presence.

2.1. Background. While the "glory of the Lord" *(K°bôd YHWH/doxa tou kyriou)* indicates God's visible, movable presence in the OT and Jewish tradition, it does so in a variety of ways. The "glory of the Lord" was intimately tied up with theophany—the mighty and ominous arrival of God, an arrival that dramatically subdues evil. God's glory "thunders" upon the waters and defeats the powers of chaos (Ps 29:3); its arrival "shakes" the world (1QH 11:34). The revelation of glory to Moses* on Mount Sinai (Ex 24:16) legitimized him as a sacred mediator and thus established his experience as an archetype for other disclosures (e.g., *Jub.* 1:2-4; 2 Macc 2:8; 1Q34 frag. 3 col. 2; Sir 45:1-5).

Glory connoted the unqualified blessing of God during the Davidic monarchy. Hailed as the cosmic "king of glory" (Ps 24:7-10), Yahweh "fills the earth with his glory" (Ps 72:19; Is 6:3; 1QH 9:10). From this web of royal associations sprang speculation about a messiah figure who uniquely bears God's glory (*Pss. Sol.* 17:30-32; 4Q504/4QDibHam[a] 4:1-9). In the hands of the prophets* glory became a sign of hope: Yahweh will one day manifest himself, his glory, in an unprecedented way and gather together the nations, forgive and transform humanity and recreate the world (e.g., Is 40:5; 58:8; 60:1-3).

Ezekiel's dramatic inaugural vision* of God's human-shaped glory (Ezek 1:28) profoundly influenced the throne visionary accounts of Jewish apocalypses. Glory signified the anthropomorphic depictions of God, defined certain angelic figures as God's specially chosen agents and demonstrated the exalted status of translated heroes (*1 Enoch* 14:20; *T. Levi* 3:4; *2 Enoch* 22:1-4, 7). Specifically the "one like a son of man" (Dan 7:13-14) became exegetically equated with the human-shaped "glory of the

Lord" (Ezek 1:28), and it was this strand of the tradition that Jesus employed to define his own future role as the Son of Man "in" or "with" glory (Mk 8:28 par. Mt 16:27, Lk 9:26; Mt 19:28; Mk 13:26 par. Mt 24:30, Lk 21:27; Mt 25:31).

2.2. The Glory of God. The later NT documents and the apostolic fathers depend directly upon the variegated glory tradition stemming from the OT. For example, when Acts* records that Stephen* looked into heaven and saw the "glory of God and Jesus standing at his right hand" (Acts 7:55), the echoes of Jesus' Son of Man sayings and the throne vision tradition of Ezekiel 1 and Daniel 7 can be clearly heard. Hebrews's* description of the ark also mentions the "cherubim of glory" positioned over the mercy seat (Heb 9:5). The cherubim, together with the seat, had always been associated with tabernacle* and temple* theophanies (Ex 25:22; Deut 33:26; Num 12:89; 1 Sam 4:4; Ps 18:10; Ezek 9:3; 10:4). 2 Peter's* description of Jesus' transfiguration stands squarely in prophetic-call/throne theophany tradition (Hubbard). God is the "majestic glory" *(megaloprepous doxēs)* who spoke to Jesus (2 Pet 1:17). *1 Clement* (*1 Clem.* 34.6) creatively places the seraphim's confession of Isaiah 6:3 ("Holy, Holy, Holy is the Lord of Hosts; all creation is full of his glory") in the mouth of the angelic hosts of Daniel 7:13 to speak of God's presence. This quotation is a historical precursor to the liturgical *Sanctus* of the third century (*see* Liturgical Elements).

These same documents take an additional step: any past appearance of God could be legitimately construed as an appearance of his glory. *1 Clement* states that Abraham* "looked intently at the glory of God" (1 Clem. 17.2; *atenizōn*, a technical term for a throne vision; cf. *Adam and Eve* 33:2; *T. Abr.* [B] 8:4; 12:6). Genesis, however, never records such a glory theophany. Although Acts has Stephen proclaiming that the "God of glory" *(theos tēs doxēs)* "appeared" *(ōphthē)*, the technical word for the appearance of God "to our fathers" (Acts 7:2), the patriarchal narratives are silent about such an appearance of glory. The *Shepherd of Hermas** (*Herm. Vis.* 1.3.3) can adjure the readers to "pay attention and hear about the glories of God" *(tas doxas tou theou)*, precisely because *doxas* can refer to any or all of God's past appearances, whether glory was specifically referenced (cf. Rom 9:3). Glory became shorthand for speaking about the manifestation of God's presence.

The later NT documents and the apostolic fathers also press the ethical dimensions of God's glory. Because God has called Christians "by his own glory" (2 Pet 1:3; cf. *1 Clem.* 59.2), they should "make every effort" to cultivate the appropriate virtues* (2 Pet 1:5-9). The Christian life includes the disciplines of "seeing" (*Barn.* 11.5), "knowing" (*Herm. Vis.* 3.11.1; *Herm. Man.* 12.4.2), "understanding" (*Herm. Man.* 12.4.2), "remembering" (*Herm. Vis.* 3.9.5) and "meditating" (*1 Clem.* 27.7) upon God's glory. Others who have "served his magnificent glory" provide a model of faithfulness (*1 Clem.* 9.2). All anxiety should be cast aside because God is a "nurse, father, teacher, counselor, healer, mind, light, honor, glory, strength, life" (*Diogn.* 9.6; cf. *Barn.* 3.4). In sum, Christians are to "live in a manner that is worthy of his commandment and glory" (Pol. *Phil.* 5.1).

2.3. Glory as Eschatological Divine Presence. Early Christianity laid claim to the mantle of the prophets. Thus God's glory figures prominently in the description of the future.

2.3.1. God's Glory and the Future. Even though all believers will undergo judgment* at the throne of God, Jude* assures its readers of God's commitment and ability to make them "stand in the presence of his glory" (*stēsai katenōpion tēs doxēs autou,* Jude 24; cf. 11QH 12:29-30; Rom 3:23; Pr Man 5). Revelation (*see* Revelation, Book of) combines theophanic, royal and prophetic imagery in the description of the eschatological, heavenly temple that will be filled with the smoke "from the glory of God and from his power" (*ek tēs doxēs tou theou kai ek tēs dynameōs autou,* Rev 15:8).

Glory also describes the new, creative powers God unleashes. On that great day a new city will descend from heaven awash in the glory of God (*echousan tēn doxan tou theou,* Rev 21:11). In that new city there will be no need for sun or moon, "for the glory of God will be its light" (*hē gar doxa tou theou ephōtisen autēn,* Rev 21:23). Christians themselves can expect transformation into glory in the eschatological age. God leads believers "to glory" (*eis doxan,* Heb 2:10). Those who endure will receive the promised "crown of glory" (*tēs doxēs stephanon,* 1 Pet 5:4; cf. 1 Cor 9:25; 2 Tim 2:4; Jas 1:12). Indeed, unjust suffering for the name* of Jesus ensures a "certain glory" (*doxan tina*) for the faithful (*Herm. Vis.* 3.2.1; cf. 2.6.6). These texts demonstrate that Christians, like the prophets, continued to hope

for an age ushered in and defined by Yahweh's glory.

2.3.2. Jesus' Glory and the Future. Evidence of a profound and controversial referential shift can be detected in a few of the eschatological glory texts. The apocalypse that ushers in the eschatological age is no longer described as a theophany of Yahweh's glory; it is the advent of Jesus and his glory.

1 Peter* states that believers should joyfully share in Christ's sufferings* in this life so that they may also rejoice "at the revelation of his glory" (*en tēs apokalypsei tēs doxēs autou,* 1 Pet. 4:13; cf. 2 Thess 1:7). Christians are "blessed," even if charged with blasphemy, for holding to the "name of Christ," because "the spirit of glory and of God" (*to tēs doxēs kai to tou theou pneuma*) rests upon them (1 Pet 4:14). Suffering certifies the hope of sharing in the "glory that is about to be revealed" (*tēs mellousēs apokalyptesthai doxēs*) at the Parousia* of Jesus (1 Pet 5:1; cf. Rom 8:18). For 1 Peter the apocalypse is not defined by the revelation* of the Father's glory, nor does Jesus simply share it with the Father; glory here belongs to Jesus alone. Further, the present suffering/future glory shape of these passages probably reflects the cross*/resurrection* shape of early Christian preaching and the life of the Jesus tradition.* Suffering was a messianic necessity for the experience of eschatological glory (1 Pet 1:11; cf. Lk 24:26).

2 Clement quotes Isaiah 66:18 to describe the return of Jesus: "And the unbelievers will see his glory" (*kai opsontai tēn doxan autou* [Is 66:18 LXX]) and will be "astonished" because this apocalypse will demonstrate "that the kingdom of the world belongs to Jesus" (*2 Clem.* 17.5). In Isaiah the promised theophany is that of Yahweh; in *2 Clement* it is that of Jesus. That Jesus can substitute for Yahweh in an overtly monotheistic quotation demonstrates early Christianity's tacit redefinition of the Godhead via an eschatological christology* (or a christocentric eschatology).

2.4. A Glory Christology. The depiction of the final day as an apocalypse of Jesus' glory (and not only Yahweh's) implicitly witnesses to early Christianity's belief in the divinity of Jesus. What was implicit in the eschatological appropriation of glory becomes explicit when glory is deployed in a decidedly christological way.

2.4.1. Hebrews 1:3. The hymnic/confessional fragment preserved in Hebrews 1:1-4 describes

Jesus as the "radiance of his glory" *(apaugasma tēs doxēs)* and the "exact representation of his very being" *(charaktēr tēs hypostaseōs,* Heb 1:3). The juxtaposition of *doxa* with *hypostasis* in the ontological characterization of Jesus clearly articulates Jesus' status. Jesus is God's glory, God's very being. This hymn*/confession* formed part of the author's strategy to distinguish between Jesus and angels, as the catena of OT texts and the sustained midrash on these texts proves (see Heb 1:5—2:18). The binatarian shape and content of the hymn/confession—its focus upon Jesus and God and Jesus as God—alleviates potential confusion between Jesus and powerful angelic figures. Jesus is ontologically superior to any and all angelic agents; Jesus is equal with God; Jesus is God. The performative force of singing this hymn (or reciting, if a confession) was to strengthen community identity. No less powerful than the Lord's Supper* or baptism,* the ritual of confessing "Jesus as the glory of Yahweh" created and reinforced the boundary lines between Christianity and Judaism.*

2.4.2. James 2:1. James* also directly connects Jesus with glory but does so in a passage beset with grammatical ambiguity. James 2:1 warns the Christian community about showing partiality in expressing their "faith in our Lord Jesus Christ of glory" *(tēn pistin tou kyriou hēmōn Iēsou Christou tēs doxēs).* The awkward separation of "of glory" *(tēs doxēs)* from "in the Lord" *(tou kyriou)* by the words "our Jesus Christ" *(hēmōn Iēsou Christou)* has led some interpreters to suppose a later interpolation. However, there is no manuscript evidence to justify such a theory.

Instead one should try to make sense of the text as it stands. "Of glory" *(tēs doxēs)* could modify "faith" *(pistin),* yielding the translation "faith in the glory of our Lord Jesus Christ." The content of faith* would be belief in the divinity (glory) of the Lord Jesus Christ. Or "of glory *(tēs doxēs)* and the personal pronoun "our" *(hēmōn)* could be understood as both directly modifying "Lord" *(kyriou),* yielding the translation "faith of our Lord Jesus Christ, the Lord of glory" (KJV; RSV). "The Lord of glory" would function as a technical title and "Jesus Christ" as an appositional proper name. A third option treats *tēs doxēs* with adjectival force that modifies "Lord Jesus Christ." The resultant translation would be faith "in our glorious Lord Jesus Christ" (NASB; NRSV). Glory thus becomes a way of

referring to the resurrection of Jesus (Johnson, 221; see 2.5 below). A fourth option, favored here, is to understand *tēs doxēs* in apposition to the phrase "Lord Jesus Christ," that is, "faith in our Lord Jesus Christ, [who is] the glory." Regardless of which option is chosen, James identifies Jesus as God's glory.

2.4.3. Barnabas 21.9. In the closing benediction Barnabas prays, "May the Lord of glory *(ho kyrios tēs doxēs)* and all grace be with your spirit" *(Barn.* 21.9). The phrase "Lord of glory" is quite rare, occurring only in Paul (1 Cor 2:8) and in *1 Enoch* *(1 Enoch* 22:14; 25:3; 63:3). That *Barnabas* can use this phrase without the apocalyptic overtones and context that appear in 1 Corinthians and *1 Enoch* witnesses to the fact that it had become a technical title for Jesus. Jesus is the "Lord of glory."

2.5. Resurrection as Glory. The question then becomes, Why and how did early Christianity begin to make the provocative redeployment of glory from Yahweh to Jesus? The resurrection of Jesus can be singled out as the historical and theological trigger for the identification of Jesus as the glory of God.

2.5.1. Acts 3:20. Acts 3:1-26 records Peter's and John's healing* of a cripple and the subsequent crowd reaction. Disavowing any substantive participation, Peter identifies to those gathered at Solomon's portico the "power" behind the miracle*: Peter asserts that it was the God of the Jewish Scriptures—"the God of Abraham, Isaac and Jacob, the God of the fathers" (Acts 3:13)—who had healed the man. This God, Peter further declares, is none other than the God who had "glorified his servant Jesus" *(edoxasen ton paida autou Iēsoun,* Acts 3:13).

God's glorification of Jesus here must be a reference to the resurrection (cf. Haenchen, 205). (1) The "glorification" of Jesus (i.e., his being raised from the dead) is set in the context of major events of Jesus' life, specifically his betrayal and death. (2) Acts 3:15 forms the best commentary on Acts 3:12 (Polhill, 134), where the death and resurrection of Jesus are specifically mentioned (*see* Death of Christ). Like "raised" *(egertheis,* Rom 8:34 and *passim),* "designated" *(horisthentos,* Rom 1:4), "exalted" *(hyperypsōsen,* Phil 2:9), "sat down at the right hand" *(ekathisen en dexia,* Heb 1:3 and *passim)* and "taken up in glory" *(anelēmphthē en doxē,* 1 Tim 3:16), "glorified" *(edoxasen)* is thus one of several constructions used to denote the resurrection of Jesus. God's glorification of Jesus (the resurrection) should be construed as an inauguration of eschatological glory (God's end-of-time presence).

2.5.2. Hebrews 2:7-9. The expositional material of Hebrews 1:5—2:18 presents a sustained contrast of the Son* with angelic figures. Through a series of OT quotations the author asserts the Son's relational, functional and ontological superiority (Heb 1:5-9), even though the author must concede the Son's death (Heb 2:10-18). In Hebrews 2:5-9 the author effects a crucial textual and theological transition. The quotation (vv. 6-8) and exposition (vv. 8-9) of Psalm 8:5-7 (LXX) provide the key textual hinge, while the theological transition occurs through repeated references to the life of Jesus: his incarnation (Heb 2:9), death (Heb 2:9) and resurrection (Heb 2:5, 8), all set in an eschatological context (Heb 2:5, 9).

The narrative architecture of this passage therefore defines "crowned with glory and honor" (*doxē kai timē estephanōmenon,* Heb 2:9) as a reference to Jesus' resurrection and therefore a homologation for "subject" *(hypotassō)* of Hebrews 2:9. To be "crowned with glory" is to be raised from the dead, an act that commences eschatological subjection. The "crowning with glory and honor" parallels the twofold conferral of "glory and honor" in the hymnic fragment of Revelation 5:12-13 and the "receiving of the name above every name" (i.e., the name *kyrios,* the Lord, Yahweh) in the hymn of Philippians 2:6-11.

2.5.3. 1 Peter 1:21 and Polycarp 2.1. Two other confessional passages textually and theologically juxtapose *doxa* and resurrection. 1 Peter 1:21 assures its readers about the wisdom of placing faith in God. God is "the one who raised him [Jesus] from the dead and gave him glory" *(ton egeiranta auton ek nekrōn kai doxan autō donta).* This saying is repeated by Polycarp* (Pol. *Phil.* 2.1), who also encourages his readers to believe "in him who raised our Lord Jesus Christ from and the dead and gave him glory" *(ton egeiranta ton kyrion hēmōn Iēsoun Christon ek nekrōn kai donta autō doxan).* There can be no doubt that "the one who raised him out of the dead" *(ton egeiranta auton ek nekrōn)* formed part of early Christianity's confession of faith (see, e.g., Acts 3:15; 4:10; 5:30; 13:30; Rom 4:24; 8:11; 10:9; Gal 1:1; Eph 1:20; 1 Thess 1:10 and passim). The addition of "and gave him glory" is unique in early Christian literature. The addition of the phrase could be part of the earliest confessional formulae (which do not appear elsewhere) or Peter's own addition (which is then followed by Polycarp).

In either case the phrase structurally parallels "crowned with glory and honor" of Psalm 8:7 (LXX) and Hebrews 2:9 and isolates the resurrection as the moment of Jesus' investiture with eschatological glory. Notably, then, Jesus as a bearer of eschatological divine presence is tied to believers' faith and hope. It is not just that God raised Jesus (as crucial for Christian theology as that is) but that in his resurrection the divine character of Jesus, his glory, becomes an essential confessional element. "To believe in Christ's glory is to believe in God, who gave it to him" (Hay, 77).

3. Summary.
In the later NT writings and apostolic fathers, glory language is what G. B. Caird called "bivocal" (Caird 28). That is, glory possess both a subjective and an objective field of meaning. On the subjective side glory refers to the act of worship (i.e., "give glory to God"; "glorify God"). On the objective side glory denotes the object of worship (i.e., God's presence). Glory in both its subjective and objective senses evidences the development of the church's faith and practice. When glory began to be ascribed to Jesus within the church's liturgy and when Jesus was identified as God's glory in the church's confession, Christianity was well on the way toward Nicea and Chalcedon. Glory language was an important vehicle for conveying the Christian redefinition of God.

See also CHRISTOLOGY; ESCHATOLOGY; GOD; REVEAL, REVELATION; RESURRECTION; WORSHIP.

BIBLIOGRAPHY. I. Abrahams, *The Glory of God: Three Lectures* (London: Oxford University Press, 1925); G. B. Caird, *The Language and Imagery of the Bible* (Philadelphia: Westminster, 1980); P. H. Davids, *The Epistle of James* (NIGTC; Grand Rapids: Eerdmans, 1982); G. Dix, *The Shape of the Liturgy* (Westminster: Dace, 1945); E. Haen-chen, *The Acts of the Apostles* (Philadelphia: Westminster, 1971); D. M. Hay, *Glory at the Right Hand: Psalm 110 in Early Christianity* (SBLMS 18; Nashville: Abingdon, 1973); B. J. Hubbard, *The Matthean Redaction of a Primitive Apostolic Commissioning: An Exegesis of Matthew 28:16-20* (SBLDS 19; Missoula, MT:

SBL/Scholars Press, 1974); L. T. Johnson, *The Letter of James* (AB; Garden City, NY: Doubleday, 1995); H. Kittel, *Die Herrlichkeit Gottes: Studien zu Geschichte und Wesen eines neutestamentlichen Begriffs* (BZNW 16; Giessen: Töpelmann, 1934); C. C. Newman, *Paul's Glory-Christology: Tradition and Rhetoric* (NovTSup 69; Leiden: E. J. Brill, 1992); idem, "Resurrection as Glory: Divine Presence and Christian Origins" in *Resurrection at 2000*, ed. S. T. Davis, D. Kendall and G. O'Collins (Oxford: Oxford University Press, 1997); J. B. Polhill, *Acts* (NAC; Nashville: Broadman, 1992); A. M. Ramsey, *The Glory of God and the Transfiguration of Christ* (London: Darton, Longman & Todd, 1949); C. Rowland, *The Open Heaven: A Study of Apocalyptic in Judaism and Early Christianity* (New York: Crossroad, 1982); M. Steinheimer, *Die ΔΟΞΑ ΤΟΥ ΘΕΟΥ in der römischen Liturgie* (Münchener Theologische Studien 2.4; Munich: Karl Zink, 1951); E. Szewc, " 'Doxai' in den katholischen Briefen und die Qumranische Literatur," *Folia Orientalia* 21 (1980) 129-40; G. Wainwright, *Doxology* (Oxford: Oxford University Press, 1980).

C. C. Newman

GLOSSOLALIA. *See* TONGUES.

GNOSIS, GNOSTICISM

Gnosticism is the modern term used to refer to a religious and philosophical movement that originated in the first or second century A.D., that was especially strong in the second and third centuries A.D. and that was considered heretical by the majority of Christians at that time as well as the majority of the pagan bearers of the Platonic philosophical traditions (i.e., Neo-Platonists). The ancients often referred to the people of this movement as Gnostics (*gnōstikoi*). The movement, which was not a single, monolithic social-theological reality, emphasized at its core a special claim to special gnosis (*gnōsis,* knowledge); thus the terms *Gnostics* and *Gnosticism*. Until the discovery in 1945 of a large group of texts near Nag Hammadi, Egypt, most of our knowledge* of the ancient Gnostics came from their opponents. With the Nag Hammadi texts (usually designated NHC, Nag Hammadi Codices [Books]), which were made available to the public between 1956 and 1977 and most of which can be identified as gnostic writings, we have for the first time in our modern period the opportunity to understand

the Gnostics on their own terms.

1. Definitions and Characteristics
2. Origins and History
3. Sources and Literature

1. Definitions and Characteristics.

1.1. Definitions. Gnosticism is the modern term used to describe a religious movement or complex of movements from the Mediterranean world in the first to the fourth centuries A.D. The term *Gnosticism* was evidently first used by the Protestant Englishman Henry More in his 1669 work on Revelation 1—3 (*An Exposition of the Seven Epistles to the Seven Churches . . .* , 99, in reference to the teachings of Jezebel in Rev 2:20; see Layton, 1995).

The religious movement(s) meant to be identified by the modern term *Gnosticism* were variously named by the ancient sources, but the most common designation was to identify those of the movement as Gnostics (*gnōstikoi*), a term evidently first used by Irenaeus in the late second century. This term was used by both the church fathers and the pagan Neo-Platonic opponents of the Gnostics. The church fathers also referred to the Gnostics by the names of their leaders or teachers (e.g., Basilides; Valentinus) and by group designations based on names (e.g., Nicolaitans) or concepts (e.g., Ophites, based on the Greek term for serpent). None of the surviving primary gnostic texts shows any use of the term *Gnostics* as a self-designation. This should be seen, however, as no more unusual than the lack within and among the NT writings of a single self-designation (such as Christians). The Gnostics describe themselves with a host of terms and phrases drawn from their theological self-understandings (e.g., offspring of Seth; elect; enlightened ones; immovable race; the perfect).

The term *Gnostics* as Irenaeus's designation for a movement arises from the place of the concept of *gnōsis* in the movement. Knowledge was a claim made by virtually all religious groups and movements at the time, but the Gnostics appeared to give it a major, central and distinctive role in their understanding of reality and salvation.* Irenaeus and others considered the Gnostics' *gnōsis* a "falsely called knowledge," alluding to the phrase known from 1 Timothy 6:20 (*pseudōnymos gnōsis*).

Modern debates concerning the origin of Gnosticism (see 2.1 below) have led to the development of various other subterms to refer to the gnostic phenomena, movements or tendencies in the first century, such as pre-Gnosticism, proto-Gnosticism, incipient Gnosticism or gnosticizing tendencies, as well as the use of the term *gnōsis* (especially in German scholarship) to refer to the larger intellectual-spiritual milieu out of which Gnosticism, as known in the second-century gnostic systems (described by the church fathers or reflected in gnostic texts), emerges.

1.2. Characteristics. The characteristic beliefs of the Gnostics are difficult to summarize both because of the varieties among the different gnostic systems and groups that existed in the early church and because no one surviving primary gnostic text contains all of the alleged basic characteristic beliefs. It is possible to find in some clearly gnostic texts ideas that appear to contradict or significantly differ from the standard description of gnostic beliefs. Nevertheless, it is possible to identify the fundamental belief system that is reflected in most gnostic sources (both in the Gnostics' own writings and in the works of their opponents).

Probably the foundational conviction of the Gnostics is the commitment to a radical anticosmic dualism in which all that is material—the world and the body—is seen as evil and as the creation* of a lesser, inferior god. In some ways all ancient Mediterranean belief systems involved some type of dualism (shown by Jonas), but gnostic dualism is distinctive in terms of its absolute radicalism between matter and spirit and in terms of its proactive descriptions of the status and role of the inferior god(s) who created matter.

The inferior god arose through a mysterious tragic split within the deity within the ultimate realm (usually the "Pleroma") of the ultimate, true God (often called Father-Mother or Father of All). Often this is expressed as the ultimate God's Sophia (Wisdom) engaging in independent reflection that results in producing an illegitimate offspring, who is the inferior creator god or the progenitor of that inferior god. Elements of this understanding are indebted to the Platonic traditions and to the Hellenistic-Jewish wisdom* traditions. Further, in Christian gnostic texts from the second century, the inferior god is usually identified with the creator god of Genesis, who then clearly is not the ultimate, true God.*

In addition most gnostic texts and systems reflect a belief in a proliferated array of intermediary beings (archons, powers, principalities, and the like, many of whom are given names and who often exist in pairs) who inhabit the cosmos between the Pleroma and the earthly realm of humanity. Often the description of the intermediary beings draws much on Greek mythology as well as on wordplays with various Hebrew names and terms. These intermediary beings add to the distance between the ultimate God and humanity.

Given their radical and complex anticosmic dualism and its consequences for understanding material reality, the Gnostics understood humanity to be trapped within the physical body. Yet the human spirit is understood to be part of the ultimate spiritual reality (the Pleroma and/or part of the ultimate God). This entrapment is usually understood as ignorance or sleep but not as sin. In order for the human spirit to find salvation, it would need to be awakened and delivered from its ignorance by recovering the knowledge *(gnōsis)* of its true self or character as part of the Pleroma or ultimate God.

In order for humanity to be saved, the ultimate God sent a redeemer *(see* Redemption) from the Pleroma to bring knowledge *(gnōsis)* to the entrapped human spirits that would bring illumination and salvation. The redeemer figure had to descend from the Pleroma to earth, successfully navigating through the cosmic territory of all the intermediary beings opposed to the ultimate God. Although this redeemer figure can be variously described in gnostic texts (e.g., as Seth), the majority of the Christian gnostic texts identify the redeemer figure with the Christ.* Because they understood the human body to be evil, the Gnostics were generally docetic in their thinking about the appearance of Christ in an alleged human form (Docetism* was the first- and second-century Christian belief, considered false teaching by the majority church, that Jesus Christ appeared to be human but that he was actually and only divine). The redeemer figure, Christ, is thus often portrayed in gnostic texts as delivering special discourses of revelation (the true *gnōsis*) to his true followers. Further, the Christ is usually portrayed in gnostic texts and sources as not actually dying on the cross; a substitute person (a deluded human) dies at the hands of the inferior god and its intermediary powers.

As noted, many gnostic texts identify the creator god of Genesis as the inferior, evil god. In this context Adam and Eve are often seen as paradigmatic representatives of humanity who are on the verge of contact with the ultimate God. Thus the serpent, in directing Adam and Eve to the tree of knowledge *(gnōsis),* is actually a servant of the ultimate God; it is the inferior god who does not want them to discover the value of this tree. This is why some gnostic groups are identified with the serpent (the Naassenes = the Ophites, names the church fathers give gnostic groups; the names are based on Hebrew and Greek words for serpent). This is also why Eve is a heroic figure in some gnostic texts as well as Seth, the replacement offspring for Abel, both of whom were understood in some sense to be representatives of the ultimate God. It is evident in these gnostic systems that a significant part of the theological understanding is based on a midrash of Genesis, albeit what is often called an inverted interpretation of Genesis 1—3.

The Gnostics, according to their own writings, given their radical anticosmic dualism, tended strongly to a docetic, ascetic lifestyle—the denial of the reality and importance of the human body, considered the appropriate response for those who knew the true character of salvation and the Pleroma. This is such a strong motif that it may be the most common denominator of all primary gnostic texts. The Gnostics identified themselves as the Pneumatics (the spiritual ones) over against the Psychics (the soulish ones enslaved to and in the flesh*/human body), a view that was sometimes accompanied by a strong election consciousness. This emphasis on the spiritual quality of reality led the Gnostics also to hold to either the immortality of the soul or a spiritual concept of resurrection* or some combination of both. Many church fathers, especially Irenaeus and Epiphanius, portrayed the Gnostics as immoral libertines, who indulged the body and its passions (*see* Purity). Many scholars doubt the accuracy of these portrayals, since none of the primary texts written by the Gnostics themselves indicate any tendency toward or approval of that type of lifestyle. Yet the church fathers may well have described what was a social reality for some Gnostics, and it is logically possible to understand that an ideology that believes that the body is fundamentally evil could lead not only to asceticism but also to indulgence of the body, since it is of no relevance for religion or morality.

The Gnostics believed that the cosmic order would eventually be dissolved and that the divine sparks within humanity would return to the Light (the Pleroma).

2. Origins and History.

Probably the most disputed questions among scholars, and those for which the sources do not provide adequate information for resolutions with strong consensus, are the issues of the origins of the gnostic movement and the course and details of its historical developments.

2.1. Origins. The view of the church fathers, which prevailed into the nineteenth century, is that the gnostic movement was a second-century heresy within the Christian church that had its ultimate roots in Simon Magus (see Acts 8), who was understood as the father of all heretics in the church. The modern debate, now fueled by the Nag Hammadi discoveries, has involved opening the issue of origins. Thus some scholars argue that the gnostic movement began in the first century as a non-Christian and pre-Christian movement (see especially Filoramo, Jonas, Perkins, Robinson, Rudolph), while others maintain that the gnostic movement is a second-century Christian deviation (see especially Logan, Nock in Scholer 1993, Pétrement, Yamauchi, Yamauchi in Scholer 1993; for a type of mediating position see Wilson). One of the main debated implications of these alternate views has been whether the NT texts could be indebted to and/or reflect in any way the gnostic movement.

In favor of the traditional view is the fact that all extant primary gnostic texts were written in the second or third centuries A.D.; there are no known gnostic texts from the first century. Further, the church fathers' presentation of the Gnostics is completely on the side of understanding the movement as a second-century Christian heresy. Adolf von Harnack defined Gnosticism as "the acute Hellenization of Christianity," a view that affirms the church fathers' allegations and descriptions of gnostic systems clearly indebted to pagan mythologies and Platonic philosophical traditions.

In addition no known first-century texts (pagan, Jewish or Christian) refer clearly to what can be established as a gnostic movement, text or system of ideas. All alleged first-century references to the gnostic movement, especially those in the NT, remain part of the debate on the origins of Gnosticism.

Further, the late nineteenth- and early twentieth-century understandings of Philo,* the prolific first-century A.D. Jewish philosopher from Alexandria,* and of the *Corpus Hermeticum* (seventeen tractates reflecting a Hellenized pagan amalgam of Greek and Egyptian religious traditions) as first-century A.D. evidences of Gnosticism seem no longer possible to be used to support this view (see 3.4.4.2 below for the evidence that three Hermetic writings were found in the Nag Hammadi collection). The *Corpus Hermeticum,* especially the first tractate *Poimandres,* and the writings of Philo do contain some clear parallels to certain gnostic emphases, especially related to issues of *gnōsis* and alleged dualism. But these texts do not reflect the radical anticosmic dualism and many of its accompanying traits so well documented in known gnostic texts.

There is, however, substantial indirect evidence that the gnostic movement was formulated in the first century as an amalgam of a deviant Hellenistic Judaism* and certain forms of the Platonic tradition and that this movement eventually attached itself to and found its truest home within the Christian church. This view should not be equated, however, with Hans Jonas's inclusive view in which much of Hellenistic thought is designated as gnosis.

This view takes with some seriousness the first-century tradition of the Simon Magus material (not necessarily its historicity but its location in time). Further, this view argues that it is hardly possible to think that the gnostic movements as described by the church fathers sprang so suddenly into existence; they betray evidence of a much longer period of development. This development, it is argued, can be seen in the extensive Jewish elements (inverted and deviant though they may be) in the gnostic movement, the development of which would make better historical sense in the first century than in the second century. It is further argued that many Nag Hammadi texts (e.g., *The Apocalypse of Adam, The Three Steles of Seth, The Paraphrase of Shem, Eugnostos the Blessed, The Thought of Norea, The Thunder: Perfect Mind*) reflect a only a slight Christian redaction (or none at all) of what were

originally non-Christian and likely pre-Christian writings, a claim the traditional point of view denies.

The modern debate between these two points of view has led to the emergence of terminology such as incipient Gnosticism, proto-Gnosticism and the like to describe in a mediating way the first-century evidence for the gnostic movement. In this sense part of the debate is a terminological one, but it is also a substantive one about the ideological and historical origin of a movement, whatever it is called.

The role of the NT writings in this debate is both important and interesting. Those who argue that the gnostic movement is a second-century Christian heresy in origin either argue that alleged gnostic influences upon or alleged gnostic opponents of NT texts do not exist or grant that these features may be categorized as evidences of incipient Gnosticism. Those who argue for a first-century origin of the gnostic movement see certain NT texts (e.g., 1 Corinthians, Colossians, 1 John [*see* John, Letters of], the prologue of the Gospel of John, the Pastoral Epistles, Jude* and 2 Peter*—which texts are involved varies among the scholars of this point of view) as additional evidence for their hypothesis.

The debate over gnostic origins and their relationship to various NT texts continues and will not be easily resolved and perhaps cannot be resolved unless additional evidence would be found. The analysis of the Nag Hammadi texts and its consequent reevaluation of the Jewish elements within gnostic ideology and of the possible anti-gnostic polemics in certain NT writings suggest that first-century origins for the gnostic movement is a more likely position. If the term *Gnosticism* should be limited only to the evidence of identifiable gnostic texts, then perhaps the first-century history of the gnostic movement should be called something like incipient Gnosticism, as problematic as the terminological issues remain.

2.2. History. The history of the gnostic movement is difficult to reconstruct for various reasons: the uncertainty about the origins of the gnostic movement; the virtually complete lack of historical or social data in the primary gnostic texts; and the polemical character of the church fathers' (and others') attack on the Gnostics. Assuming some type of origin for the gnostic movement in the first century and a certain degree of reliability in the historical notices in the church fathers about the Gnostics, the following historical outline can be reconstructed.

Sometime early in the first century A.D., probably within a sophisticated circle of Hellenistic Jewish scholars likely located in Alexandria, gnostic speculations about the nature of reality, the problem of evil, the character of God and the possibility of salvation emerged. These reflections combined a reinterpretation of Jewish Scripture and certain Platonic and Greek mythological traditions in such a way as to create a deviant (from a Jewish point of view) Hellenistic religious movement, which in retrospect can be called incipient Gnosticism. Virtually nothing is known about the historical or social character of this movement, but it would appear that very early in its history it attached itself to the church and found in the church's reflections on Jesus Christ its perfect redeemer figure. Already certain leaders within the church found this incipient Gnosticism problematic, in particular Paul and the Pauline school (see Pauline Legacy and School) as found in Colossians and the Pastoral Epistles, the authors of 1 John, Jude and 2 Peter,* and John in Revelation (see Revelation, Book of) with respect to the Nicolaitans.

According to the church fathers, the figure of Simon Magus (first century A.D.) became a focal point for the development of the gnostic movement. To whatever degree that might be the case, the tradition suggests the importance of Syria* as a second location for the early development of incipient Gnosticism. According to the patristic sources, Simon's prime disciple was Menander, who in turn influenced Saturninus and Basilides. Basilides, presumably from Syria, subsequently moved to Alexandria.

As speculative as the preceding historical reconstruction might be, it can be more safely assumed that at least some patristic information about the two primary gnostic teachers of the mid-second century A.D. is reasonably reliable.

Basilides emerged as a teacher in Alexandria before A.D. 150. The details of his teaching provided by Hippolytus and Irenaeus are in conflict, so it is very difficult to reconstruct his gnostic construction of reality. Basilides apparently had a series of 365 heavens that emanated from the ultimate God; the powers of the 365th heaven were those that created the material world. Basilides was docetic in his christology; it

was Simon of Cyrene, not Jesus, who died on the cross (this tradition seems to be attested also in the Nag Hammadi text *The Second Treatise of the Great Seth* [VII,2]). Basilides evidently wrote several books, including a Gospel, but none of these is extant. Basilides' main disciple was Isidore, who wrote books as well (which are not extant), including one on ethics.

The other major gnostic teacher, who also emerged in Alexandria, was Valentinus, who later went to Rome (about A.D. 140) and to other places in the East. Valentinus was considered a brilliant thinker and apparently was even a candidate for a time for bishop of Rome. Valentinus evidently wrote many books; a few fragments of them have been preserved within the writings of the church fathers. Some scholars believe that the Nag Hammadi text *The Gospel of Truth* (I,3) was written by Valentinus. This clearly Valentinian work reflects on Jesus as the revealer of knowledge and argues that the revelation delivers its recipients from ignorance and reunites them with the Father of All. According to patristic sources, Valentinus's construction of reality involved a series of thirty eons emanating from the Pleroma, the last of which was Sophia, who in error produced the Demiurge who is equated with the creator god of Genesis. Valentinus was very influential; among his famous followers were Marcus, Heracleon (some of whose comments on the Gospel of John are preserved by Origen), Ptolemy and Flora (see the *Letter to Flora*, 3.3.1 below), and Theodotus (see the *Excerpta ex Theodoto*, 3.3.2 below). In the patristic sources it is often difficult to distinguish between the ideas of Valentinus himself and those of his disciples (Valentinianism).

There apparently was another school of gnostic thought known as Sethianism, described by various church fathers and apparently attested by the unity of various texts from Nag Hammadi (see 3.4.4.2. below). It is not clear how independent this alleged group might have been and what its relationship to the Valentinians or other groups might have been. The Sethians ("the seed of Seth") understood Seth to be a representative, through a primal or heavenly Adam, of the ultimate God (there is a divine triad of Father [Invisible Spirit], Mother [Barbelo] and Son). The inferior god, Yaldabaoth, created the world and humanity (led by a false Adam). Seth was the revealer/redeemer figure, who in Christian Sethian texts can be identified with and/or augmented by Christ.

The patristic sources list other gnostic teachers and movements as well: the Archontici, Audians, Barbelo-Gnostics, Borborians, Cainites, Carpocrates, Epiphanes, Florinus, Justin, Marcosians, Melchizedekians, Naassenes, Nicolaitans, Ophites (the same group as the Naassenes), Peratae and Phibionites. Scholars tend to be very skeptical about the social and historical identity of these teachers and groups as distinct gnostic movements. Rather, they may be designations and categories projected by the church fathers upon the gnostic movements in their attempts to combat and identify them as false teachers.

Marcion* (an important mid-second-century Christian leader) has often been classified as a Gnostic, but that is now generally considered an inappropriate designation. To be sure, Marcion shared to a significant degree in the same thought world of the Gnostics. Marcion was strongly dualistic in his theology and held that the god of the Jewish Scripture was a false, inferior god. But Marcion's analysis of the human condition and the nature of salvation, as well as his social location, distinguishes him from the gnostic movement.

One of the most difficult aspects of understanding the ancient gnostic movement has to do with the problems of attempting to reconstruct the social history of the movement. Both the primary gnostic texts and the attacks of the church fathers on the Gnostics focus almost exclusively on the ideological structures and theological details of gnostic thought; very little is reported about the social reality of gnostic groups and believers. The primary gnostic texts themselves do indicate the deep gnostic commitments to ascetic lifestyles. It is not known, however, how this was practiced in detail.

Virtually nothing is known about the community organization of gnostic churches. One Nag Hammadi text, *Apocalypse of Peter* (VII,3), refers to "those who are outside our number who name themselves bishop and also deacons, as if they have received their authority from God. . . . Those people are dry canals" (from Robinson). Whether this indicates anything about structures within the gnostic communities is not clear, but it is evident—as virtually all the evidence suggests—that the Gnostics and their opponents were deeply involved in competing claims of authority.*

There is some indication both in the gnostic primary texts and in the accounts of the church fathers that at least some gnostic communities practiced certain liturgical rituals, including baptism* and the Eucharist. The Nag Hammadi text *The Gospel of Philip* (II,3) refers to five mysteries: baptism, chrism, Eucharist, redemption and the bridal chamber. It is not clear what all of this meant, but it probably indicates a process of gnostic ritual initiation in which the bridal chamber symbolizes the return of the true self to the Pleroma and union with the ultimate God.

There has been considerable discussion of the place of women* in the gnostic movement. Due to the great number of female figures in the presentation of the structures of deity and due to the prominent role of women, particularly Mary Magdalene, in many of the gnostic texts, it has often been assumed that the Gnostics were more open to the participation of women in their religious life than were the majority of the orthodox, central churches. This, however, is difficult to establish with any certainty.

The mainstream church consistently opposed the gnostic movement, particularly with reference to its understandings of God, creation, Jesus Christ and the nature of salvation. The great church emphasized the proper interpretation of Scripture, which was guided by their sense of the public apostolic tradition (the Gnostics often claimed that the revelations of the risen Jesus Christ were secretly communicated through the gnostic apostolic chain). The great church also vested church officials with the authority to protect and guard the tradition and to identify deviant persons and positions. Clearly the great church overwhelmed the gnostic movement with its strong sense of unity, internal connections and common links of biblical interpretation. It is impossible to know how strong the gnostic movement was at any given time and place, but it is known that the church fathers considered it a major threat and that it had the learning and leadership to produce powerful teachers and an extensive literature.

The gnostic movement lasted to the fourth and fifth centuries A.D. at least. Some of the post-second-century/early-third-century forms of the gnostic movement are undoubtedly reflected in some of the descriptions of the church father Epiphanius and in the late gnostic works *Pistis Sophia* and the *Two Books of Jeu* (see 3.3.7 and 3.3.8 below).

Other forms of the gnostic movement may be found in the Mandeans and especially in Mani and the Manicheans, but those movements have their own distinct histories and are usually treated separately. Some scholars find gnostic survivals and/or revivals in various medieval groups, such as the Catharists or the Bogomiles, in some forms of medieval Jewish mysticism and in some forms of Islamic mysticism. Various nineteenth- and twentieth-century groups too have claimed the ancient gnostic movement as their spiritual heritage to one degree or another.

3. Sources and Literature.

Prior to the discovery of the gnostic writings near Nag Hammadi, most of what was known about the ancient Gnostics was derived from attacks on them by Christian church fathers and by Neo-Platonic philosophers. Some information was known from a few gnostic texts quoted by the church fathers or that had otherwise survived. (For much of the important bibliography see the volumes of D. M. Scholer; for primary source readers of the church fathers, the Neo-Platonic philosophers and the pre-Nag Hammadi gnostic texts, see the volumes of W. Foerster and R. M. Grant; for the Nag Hammadi texts, see the volumes of B. Layton and J. M. Robinson.)

3.1. The Church Fathers. The two most important writings against the Gnostics from church fathers, often called heresiologists in this connection, are Irenaeus (second century), *Adversus Haereses* (Against Heresies; Book 1 is especially important), and Epiphanius (fourth century), *Haereses* or *Panarion* (Medicine Chest [to protect against the heresies]; sections 21-40 are especially important). Probably the most important patristic text for the study of Gnosticism is Irenaeus (*Haer.* 1.29), in which he summarizes an unnamed work that he claims belongs to the Gnostics. With the discovery of the Nag Hammadi texts, it is now known that this text is *The Apocryphon of John* (NHC II,1; III,1; IV,1; also the second work in the Berlin Gnostic Codex). Other church fathers, notably Justin Martyr (second century), Tertullian, Clement of Alexandria and Hippolytus (all early third century), and Origen (third century) also opposed the heretical Gnostics (Clement, it

should be noted, also used the term *gnostic* to describe the "ideal Christian").

3.2. Neo-Platonic Philosophers. Pagan Neo-Platonic philosophers also opposed the Gnostics, because they saw them as perverting the Platonic tradition. Especially important are Celsus (second century; preserved only in Origen's work against him: *Contra Celsum*), Plotinus (third century; see especially his *Enneads* 2.9) and Porphyry (third century; see especially his *Life of Plotinus* 16). Porphyry mentions some gnostic texts by name, two of which can now be identified as part of the Nag Hammadi group: *Zostrianos* (NHC VIII,1) and *Allogenes* (NHC XI,3).

3.3. Pre-Nag Hammadi Gnostic Texts. A few texts, apart from brief quotations and summaries by the church fathers, known before the discovery of the Nag Hammadi manuscripts were identified as gnostic texts and provided a partial, primary source basis for the understanding of the Gnostics.

3.3.1. Ptolemy, Letter to Flora. Ptolemy was a prominent second-century Valentinian Gnostic. His letter to an unknown Flora is preserved by Epiphanius (*Haer.* 33.3-7). The letter is an analysis of the Mosaic law, which is understood to have been given by the imperfect god, the Demiurge, creator of the world.

3.3.2. Theodotus, Excerpta ex Theodoto. Theodotus was a second-century Valentinian Gnostic whose *Excerpts* are preserved at the conclusion of Clement of Alexandria's *Stromateis* (Miscellanies). This collection of excerpts from Theodotus and other Gnostics may be Clement's attempt to provide a summary of their fundamental beliefs.

3.3.3. Justin, Book of Baruch. Justin, an otherwise unknown second-century Gnostic, is the alleged author of the *Book of Baruch* (who is the revealer of gnosis), preserved in Hippolytus (*Refutation of Heresies* 5.26-27). It is an amalgam of Genesis and pagan myths on the creation of the world by the "second god" (Elohim). The ultimate power beyond the world, whom Baruch reveals, is "the good."

3.3.4. The Naassene Hymn. The Naassenes were a Gnostic group mentioned only by Hippolytus. The name comes from the Greek word *naas,* for the Hebrew word for serpent. The hymn is preserved in Hippolytus (*Refutations of Heresies* 5.10).

3.3.5. The Apophasis Megale (Great Exposition).

This work represents mature Simonian Gnostic thought and is preserved in Hippolytus (*Refutation of Heresies* 6.9-18).

3.3.6. The Hymn of the Pearl. Although its gnostic identification has been debated, this probably second-century hymn reflects the gnostic story of the descent of the redeemer. It is preserved in the NT apocryphal* *Acts of Thomas* 108-13.

3.3.7. The Two Books of Jeu. This third-century work reflects later gnostic thought. It is preserved in Coptic in the Codex Brucianus (at Oxford), named after James Bruce, who acquired the manuscript in the eighteenth century.

3.3.8. Pistis Sophia. This third-century work consists primarily of postresurrection dialogues, allegedly over a twelve-year period, between Jesus and his disciples, especially Mary Magdalene. It is preserved in Coptic in the Codex Askewianus (in London), named after A. Askew, who acquired the manuscript in the eighteenth century. This work cites five of the *Odes of Solomon,* a second-century Syriac non-gnostic collection of Christian hymns* (*see* John, Letters of; Liturgical Elements).

3.3.9. The Berolinensis Gnosticus Codex (the Berlin Gnostic Codex; known also as Papyrus Berolinensis 8502 [and as BG 8502]). This manuscript was discovered in 1896 and housed in Berlin but, due to various circumstances, including the two world wars, was not published until 1955, after the Nag Hammadi texts were known to exist. It contains four gnostic works in Coptic, two of which appear also in the Nag Hammadi texts (*The Apocryphon of John* [BG 8502,2; see NHC II,1; III,1; IV,1]; and *The Sophia of Jesus Christ* [BG 8502,3; see NHC III,4]). The two works not found at Nag Hammadi are *The Gospel of Mary* [Magdalene] (BG 8502,1) and *The Acts of Peter* (BG 8502,4).

3.4. The Nag Hammadi Texts. This group of fifty-two papyrus texts was discovered in a jar near Nag Hammadi (for the intriguing and complex story of the finds and their early history see Pearson and Robinson). These texts are contained in twelve codices (books) plus some leaves from another codex (now numbered Codex XIII). Thus the Nag Hammadi texts, known as tractates, are numbered within each of the thirteen codices (e.g., the first tractate in the first codex is I,1). This collection is sometimes designated by the symbol CG (Cairensis Gnosticus; all the manuscripts are in the Coptic Museum in Old Cairo). Codex I is sometimes known as the Jung Codex, since it was originally purchased by the C. G. Jung Institute in Zürich.

3.4.1. General Background. The Nag Hammadi manuscripts are written in Coptic (in two major dialects: Sahidic and Lycopolitan = Subakhmimic) and in at least fourteen different scribal hands. The manuscripts were produced in the fourth century, but all of the texts are clearly translations from Greek originals. The original Greek compositions date most likely from the second century and the early third century, although there are debates over whether some texts might have originated in the first century (e.g., II,2 *The Gospel of Thomas*).

The fifty-two Nag Hammadi texts contain six internal duplicates, albeit with variations (I,3 = XII,2 *The Gospel of Truth;* II,1 = III,1 = IV,1 *The Apocryphon of John;* II,5 = XIII,2 *On the Origin of the World;* III,2 = IV,2 *The Gospel of the Egyptians;* III,3 = V,1 *Eugnostos the Blessed);* thus forty-six works are represented. Six of the Nag Hammadi texts were texts already known to exist (II,1 *The Apocryphon of John* and III,4 *The Sophia of Jesus Christ,* both in BG 8502; VI,5 *Plato, Republic 588a-589b;* VI,7 *The Prayer of Thanksgiving* and VI,8 *Asclepius,* known from the Hermetic tradition; and XII,1 *The Sentences of Sextus,* a collection of moral aphorisms popular in the early church); thus the Nag Hammadi find yields forty new texts. As it turned out, Greek fragments of one of these texts were known to exist, but only with the Nag Hammadi find was it possible for the first time to identify them (*Oxyrhynchus Papyri* 1, 654 and 655 are part of *The Gospel of Thomas* [II,2]; previously known Coptic fragments were also found to be from *On the Origin of the World* [II,5] and from *The Teachings of Silvanus* [VII,4]). Codex VII is the best preserved manuscript. Many of the tractates have missing pages (and parts of pages) in their extant forms.

3.4.2. The Origin of the Collection. The origin and nature of the Nag Hammadi texts is not known, and attempts to posit answers to these questions are debated. The Nag Hammadi texts are often called a gnostic library, a designation that can be misleading. Not all of the texts are gnostic texts, although there may be reasons to think that the non-gnostic texts may well have had appeal to Gnostics. It is not clear that a gnostic group put the texts in the jar and buried them; the group that probably collected and later buried these texts was probably quite orthodox. It is unclear whether this group collected these texts in order to refute them (possible) or in order to use them for various kinds of spiritual and theological edification (more likely).

There is some meaningful evidence that the Nag Hammadi collection was assembled, used and buried by orthodox Pachomian monks, a debated hypothesis to be sure. The site of the Nag Hammadi manuscript discovery is only about five-and-a-half miles from the ancient headquarters of the monastic movement of Pachomius (the Basilica of St. Pachomius at Faw Qibli [ancient Pabau]) and only about three miles from the third Pachomian monastery at Chenoboskia, where Pachomius himself had studied. The cartonnage (stuffing in the binding of a codex) of Codex VII contains documents that are virtually certain to have come from the Pachomian movement. Some of the manuscripts contain scribal notes that are pious Christian prayers.*

A possible scenario for the burial of the manuscripts (in a jar for safekeeping) would be the response of Pachomius's successor, Theodore, to Bishop Athanasius's A.D. 367 *Easter Letter*, in which he condemned heretical and noncanonical books and listed for the first time the exact list of the twenty-seven books in our common NT (*see* Canon). Thus it may be that at least some Pachomian monks collected and read the literature now known as the Nag Hammadi texts for their own spiritual and theological purposes but had to hide them once Athanasius's order was put into effect (see especially Pearson and Robinson for this hypothesis). Further, it has now come to light in the wake of the Nag Hammadi discoveries that the Bodmer Papyri (known also as the Dishna Papers) were found only about three miles from the site of the Nag Hammadi discovery. The Bodmer Papyri (now in the Bodmer Library in Geneva) contain not only very important NT texts but also other apocryphal, spiritual and theological writings. Presumably these texts too were buried by Pachomian monks.

3.4.3. Contents of Collection. The adjoining chart lists the official codex and tractate number, title and abbreviation for each of the fifty-two Nag Hammadi texts (see Robinson). Many of the titles come from the works themselves; others have been given to them by scholars.

3.4.4. Classifications of the Tractates. Any classification of the Nag Hammadi texts will be open for discussion among scholars, but it is possible to gain some understanding of the collection by noting both the literary genres and forms and the religious and theological character of the texts, some of which could fit into more than one category in each division. Not categorized here are *Plato, Republic 588a-589b* (VI,5), one of the clear reminders that although the collection is basically one of gnostic works, not every text in the collection is a gnostic one, and *Fragments* (XII,3).

3.4.4.1. Literary Genres and Forms. About half of the Nag Hammadi texts (twenty-five of the fifty-two) can be classified as apocalypses and/or revelation discourses of some kind, not surprising for what is a collection of gnostic texts that stress the special character of the secret and/or revealed special knowledge that belongs to the Gnostics. These texts include (listed through this section in codex/tractate order): *The Apocryphon of John* (three copies), *The Hypostasis of the Archons, The Book of Thomas the Contender, The Sophia of Jesus Christ, The Dialogue of the Savior, The Apocalypse of Paul, The (First) Apocalypse of James, The (Second) Apocalypse of James, The Apocalypse of Adam, The Thunder: Perfect Mind, The Concept of Our Great Power, The Discourse on the Eighth and Ninth, Asclepius 21-29, The Paraphrase of Shem, The Second Treatise of the Great Seth, Apocalypse of Peter, Zostrianos, The Letter of Peter to Philip, Melchizedek, Marsanes, Allogenes, Hypsiphrone,* and *Trimorphic Protennoia.*

Other tractates may be classified according to the somewhat traditional canonical categories of gospels, epistles and acts. Six texts are called gospels: *The Gospel of Truth* (two copies), *The Gospel of Thomas, The Gospel of Philip,* and *The Gospel of the Egyptians* (two copies). None of them is in form close to the canonical gospels. *The Gospel of Thomas* is a collection of 114 sayings of the risen Jesus; the other three are various styles of theological discourses. *The Gospel of Truth* probably uses the term *gospel* as in the Pauline literature (gospel = message about Jesus Christ) and intends to claim that it presents the true gospel. Six texts may be considered, at least to some degree, epistles (letters*), although they too are theological tracts: *The Apocryphon of James, The Treatise on the Resurrection, The Hypostasis of the Archons, Eugnostos the Blessed* (two cop-

Table of Nag Hammadi Texts

I, 1	The Prayer of the Apostle Paul	Pr. Paul		Power	Great Pow.
I, 2	The Apocryphon of James	Ap. Jas.	VI, 5	Plato, Republic 588a-589b	Plato Rep.
I, 3	The Gospel of Truth	Gos. Truth	VI, 6	The Discourse on the Eighth	
I, 4	The Treatise on the Resurrec-			and Ninth	Disc. 8-9
	tion	Treat. Res.	VI, 7	The Prayer of Thanksgiving	Pr. Thanks.
I, 5	The Tripartite Tractate	Tri. Trac.	VI, 8	Asclepius 21-29	Asclepius
II, 1	The Apocryphon of John	Ap. John	VII, 1	The Paraphrase of Shem	Paraph. Shem
II, 2	The Gospel of Thomas	Gos. Thom.	VII, 2	The Second Treatise of the	
II, 3	The Gospel of Philip	Gos. Phil.		Great Seth	Treat. Seth
II, 4	The Hypostasis of the		VII, 3	Apocalypse of Peter	Apoc. Peter
	Archons	Hyp. Arch.	VII, 4	The Teachings of Silvanus	Teach. Silv.
II, 5	On the Origin of the World	Orig. World	VII, 5	The Three Steles of Seth	Steles Seth
II, 6	The Exegesis on the Soul	Exeg. Soul	VIII, 1	Zostrianos	Zost.
II, 7	The Book of Thomas the		VIII, 2	The Letter of Peter to Philip	Ep. Pet. Phil.
	Contender	Thom. Cont.	IX, 1	Melchizedek	Melch.
III, 1	The Apocryphon of John	Ap. John	IX, 2	The Thought of Norea	Norea
III, 2	The Gospel of the Egyptians	Gos. Eg.	IX, 3	The Testimony of Truth	Testim. Truth
III, 3	Eugnostos the Blessed	Eugnostos	X	Marsanes	Marsanes
III, 4	The Sophia of Jesus Christ	Soph. Jes. Chr.	XI, 1	The Interpretation of	
III, 5	The Dialogue of the Savior	Dial. Sav.		Knowledge	Interp. Know.
IV, 1	The Apocryphon of John	Ap. John	XI, 2	A Valentinian Exposition	Val. Exp.
IV, 2	The Gospel of the Egyptians	Gos. Eg.	XI, 2a	On the Anointing	On Anoint.
V, 1	Eugnostos the Blessed	Eugnostos	XI, 2b	On Baptism A	On Bapt. A
V, 2	The Apocalypse of Paul	Apoc. Paul	XI, 2c	On Baptism B	On Bapt. B
V, 3	The (First) Apocalypse of James	1 Apoc. Jas.	XI, 2d	On the Eucharist A	On Euch. A
V, 4	The (Second) Apocalypse of		XI, 2e	On the Eucharist B	On Euch. B
	James	2 Apoc. Jas.	XI,3	Allogenes	Allogenes
V, 5	The Apocalypse of Adam	Apoc. Adam	XI,4	Hypsiphrone	Hypsiph.
VI, 1	The Acts of Peter and the	Acts Pet. 12	XII,1	The Sentences of Sextus	Sent. Sextus
	Twelve Apostles	Apost.	XII,2	The Gospel of Truth	Gos. Truth
VI, 2	The Thunder: Perfect Mind	Thund.	XII,3	Fragments	Frm.
VI, 3	Authoritative Teaching	Auth. Teach.	XIII,1	Trimorphic Protennoia	Trim. Prot.
VI, 4	The Concept of Our Great		XIII,2	On the Origin of the World	Orig. World

ies), and *The Letter of Peter to Philip.* One text falls in the acts genre: *The Acts of Peter and the Twelve Apostles.*

Other literary categories could include the following: wisdom texts, neither of which is a gnostic text *(The Teachings of Silvanus, The Sentences of Sextus);* texts that "rewrite" the Bible, especially the early chapters of Genesis *(The Apocryphon of John, The Hypostasis of the Archons, On the Origin of the World,* and *The Testimony of Truth);* doctrinal and homiletical treatises (recall that many of the gospels and epistles also fit here; *The Tripartite Tractate, On the Origin of the World, The Exegesis on the Soul, The Book of Thomas the Contender, Authoritative Teaching, The Testimony of Truth, The Interpretation of Knowledge,* and *A Valentinian Exposition);* and prayers and hymns (apart from such embedded in larger works; *The Prayer of the Apostle Paul, The Discourse on the Eighth and the Ninth, The Prayer of Thanksgiving, The Three Steles of Seth,* and *The Thought of Norea).*

3.4.4.2. Religious-Theological Character. The religious-theological classification of Nag Hammadi texts are judgments made primarily on the basis of data known from other sources, especially the church fathers, and on inferences from the content of the texts themselves. Many of these judgments are debated among scholars, and some of them reflect hypotheses various persons have about the origins and development of the gnostic movement. Most of the texts are clearly gnostic in character; thus their enormous value as primary sources for understanding the ancient gnostic movement. However, the most pervasive factor of unity among all the texts is the reflection of an ascetic lifestyle, which is often a result of the gnostic devaluation of the material world and the physical body. Even those texts that are clearly gnostic in character show that there was considerable diversity within the gnostic movement, which serves as a caution against simplistic descrip-

409

tions of gnostic beliefs.

The texts show clearly the influences of the pagan context (both pagan mythologies and Platonic philosophical traditions), the Jewish environment (e.g., the OT figures of Adam, Seth and Shem; the extensive use of the early chapters of Genesis; the critique of Moses* and other OT figures (e.g., *The Apocryphon of John; The Second Treatise of the Great Seth*) and the Christian church (e.g., the obvious centrality of Jesus Christ in many texts); the apostolic figures of Paul, James, John, Thomas, Philip, Peter, Mary Magdelene and Silvanus; critique of the main church (e.g., *Apocalypse of Peter*). The history and redaction of the various texts are difficult to determine and are much debated among scholars. Some of them seem clearly to be non-Christian in origin with, often, a rather thin overlay of Christian redaction. There have already emerged in scholarship an abundance of commentaries and articles on the individual texts (see Scholer's bibliographies; *Bibliothèque Copte de Nag Hammadi, Section "Textes"; The Coptic Gnostic Library edited with English Translation, Introduction and Notes*).

The largest group of gnostic texts in the Nag Hammadi collection are those that can be identified as Sethian in character. These texts present Seth as a revealer/redeemer figure, have a similar cosmic system and fit at least to some degree into patristic descriptions of Sethian beliefs. Although some identifications are clearer than others, the following texts are generally considered to represent the Sethian group of Gnostics: *The Apocryphon of John, The Hypostasis of the Archons, On the Origin of the World, The Gospel of the Egyptians, Eugnostos the Blessed, The Sophia of Jesus Christ, The Apocalypse of Adam, The Paraphrase of Shem, The Second Treatise of the Great Seth, The Three Steles of Seth, Zostrianos, Melchizedek, The Thought of Norea, Marsanes, Allogenes,* and *Trimorphic Protennoia.*

Another large group of texts within the Nag Hammadi collection are the Valentianian writings. Valentinus and his followers constituted an important movement among Christian Gnostics. These texts are identified by criteria similar to those for identifying Sethian texts. Some scholars have even suggested that one or more of the Valentinian texts might have been written by Valentinus himself, a hypothesis beyond any possible verification (e.g., *The Gospel of Truth*). The following texts, with varying degrees of certainty,

are generally considered representatives of the Valentinian school: *The Prayer of the Apostle Paul, The Apocryphon of James, The Gospel of Truth, The Treatise on the Resurrection, The Tripartite Tractate* (it should be noted that all of the texts in Codex I are probably Valentinian), *The Gospel of Philip, The Exegesis on the Soul, The Interpretation of Knowledge,* and *A Valentinian Exposition (On the Origin of the World* and *The Thought of Norea,* both considered Sethian works to some degree, are also often thought to reflect Valentinian ideas as well). *The Testimony of Truth* may be an anti-Valentinian work by a former Valentinian.

Three Nag Hammadi texts reflect the pagan Hermetic tradition: *The Discourse on the Eighth and Ninth, The Prayer of Thanksgiving,* and *Asclepius 21-29* (it will be recalled that the latter two of these were previously known Hermetic texts). This provides the occasion to note that some scholars consider the *Corpus Hermeticum,* especially its first tractate known as *Poimandres,* to be examples of pagan gnostic literature. This judgment, however, is not widely shared and reflects the difficulties of defining the gnostic movement and identifying its history.

Two Nag Hammadi texts, *The Gospel of Thomas* and *The Book of Thomas the Contender,* reflect an early church Thomas tradition, which was not likely gnostic in its earlier forms, although it reflected asceticism. The Nag Hammadi Thomas works exhibit the gnosticizing of the Thomas tradition. Without doubt *The Gospel of Thomas* has become the most famous and most controversial Nag Hammadi text, on which more has been published than any other Nag Hammadi writing. *The Gospel of Thomas* consists of 114 sayings of the risen Jesus, approximately half of which have a significant parallel in the canonical Synoptic Gospels. The differences between the Synoptic Gospels and *The Gospel of Thomas* in the parallel sayings often show a so-called gnosticizing tendency in the latter.

The major debates over *The Gospel of Thomas* are whether its traditions parallel to the Synoptic Gospels, are dependent or independent of them (or some combination thereof), and to what degree it is appropriate to identify *The Gospel of Thomas* as a gnostic work at the various stages of its redaction. Some scholars have strongly argued that at least some of the parallel sayings in *The Gospel of Thomas* are independent first-century witnesses to Jesus traditions* of competing value with the traditions contained in the Synoptic Gospels (and that such also constitute an indirect witness for the existence of a text such as *Q,* the alleged sayings source for words of Jesus common to Luke and Matthew). Others have argued just as strongly that all *The Gospel of Thomas* parallel sayings are second-century forms dependent upon the Synoptic Gospels. This remains an unresolved debate, with the reality likely to be found somewhere in between the two extremes.

Three Nag Hammadi texts are clearly non-gnostic in character: *Plato, Republic 588a-589b, The Teachings of Silvanus* and *The Sentences of Sextus* (the first and last of these are previously known texts).

The remaining Nag Hammadi texts not named in this section (about twelve tractates) are gnostic works that have defied classification and are additional witnesses to the varieties among the Gnostics.

3.4.5. The Importance of the Nag Hammadi Texts. The Nag Hammadi find ranks with the Dead Sea Scrolls (*see* Qumran) as the most significant finds of this century for the reevaluation of our knowledge of the religious movements of the Greco-Roman period (*see* Religions, Greco-Roman), including Judaism and the early church. The foremost contribution of the Nag Hammadi texts is that they provide primary source documents for the study of ancient gnostic movements, through which it is possible to understand better the variety and theological nuances of those movements. Much traditional literature on the gnostic movement has stressed its heretical and/or fanciful or irrational character. The primary gnostic texts should document that the Christian Gnostics, even if deviant from "orthodox" Christianity, were attempting to provide serious answers to the problem of evil and to provide a hope for salvation, as complex as it may seem. Further, the Nag Hammadi texts, by virtue of their sources, have contributed to our understandings of early church history, ancient Judaism and the Middle Platonic and Neo-Platonic traditions. With reference to early church history, these texts show how complex the issues were in the second century with reference to what in retrospect we consider "orthodox" and "heretical."

The Nag Hammadi texts are also important for NT studies. They contribute to the discussion of the alleged anti-gnostic character of certain NT texts (e.g., compare 1 John with the "we have not sinned" litany in *The Second Treatise of the Great Seth).* As already indicated, *The Gospel of Thomas* contributes to the discussion of the tradition of Jesus' sayings in the Synoptic Gospels, as do *The Apocryphon of James* and *The Dialogue of the Savior. Trimorphic Protennoia* has been widely discussed as related to the prologue of the Gospel of John. Many of the Nag Hammadi texts were composed in the second century and indirectly give witness to the authority of many of the texts that were in the process of constituting the canonical NT at that time.

The Nag Hammadi texts have also made significant contributions to the knowledge of the Coptic language and the disciplines of codicology (the study of the production of the codex) and papyrology.

3.5. A Suggested Reading Program of Ancient Gnostic Texts. As a suggestion for those who have not read the ancient sources on the gnostic movement, the following ten items (seven from Nag Hammadi) would be an excellent way to begin: *The Gospel of Truth, The Treatise on the Resurrection, The Tripartite Tractate, The Apocryphon of John, The Hypostasis of the Archons, The Second Treatise of the Great Seth, Apocalypse of Peter,* Ptolemy's *Letter to Flora,* the *Excerpta ex Theodoto* and the major selections on the Gnostics from Irenaeus (see Robinson; Foerster; or Grant).

See also ADVERSARIES; DOCETISM; MARCION; RELIGIONS, GRECO-ROMAN; SYNCRETISM; THOMAS, GOSPEL OF.

BIBLIOGRAPY. **Texts and Bibliographies:** *Bibliothèque Copte de Nag Hammadi, Section "Textes"* (22 vols., not yet complete; Québec: Les Presses de Université Laval/Louvain: Peeters, 1977-95); *The Coptic Gnostic Library edited with English Translation, Introduction and Notes* (13 vols., complete; NHS 4, 11, 15, 20-23, 26-28, 31; NHMS 30, 33; Leiden: E. J. Brill, 1975-96); C. A. Evans, R. L. Webb and R. A. Wiebe, *Nag Hammadi Texts and the Bible: A Synopsis and Index* (NTTS 18; Leiden: E. J. Brill, 1993); *The Facsimile Edition of the Nag Hammadi Codices* (12 vols.; Leiden: E. J. Brill, 1972-84); W. Foerster, *Gnosis: A Selection of Gnostic Texts* (2 vols.; Oxford: Clarendon, 1972); R. M. Grant, *Gnosticism: A Source Book of Heretical Writings from the Early Christian Period* (New York: Harper & Brothers, 1961); B. Layton, *The Gnos-*

tic Scriptures: A New Translation with Annotations and Introductions (ABRL; New York: Doubleday, 1987, 1995); J. M. Robinson, ed., *The Nag Hammadi Library in English* (San Francisco: HarperSanFrancisco, 1988); D. M. Scholer, *Nag Hammadi Bibliography 1948-69* (NHS 1; Leiden: E. J. Brill, 1971); idem, *Nag Hammadi Bibliography 1970-94* (NHMS 32; Leiden: E. J. Brill, 1997). **Studies:** G. Filoramo, *A History of Gnosticism* (Oxford: Blackwell, 1990); C. W. Hedrick and R. Hodgson Jr., eds., *Nag Hammadi, Gnosticism and Early Christianity* (Peabody, MA: Hendrickson, 1986); H. Jonas, *The Gnostic Religion: The Message of the Alien God and the Beginnings of Christianity* (2d ed.; Boston: Beacon, 1970); B. Layton, "Prolegomena to the Study of Ancient Gnosticism" in *The Social World of the First Christians: Essays in Honor of Wayne A. Meeks*, ed. L. M. White and O. L. Yarbrough (Minneapolis: Fortress, 1995) 334-50; idem, ed., *The Rediscovery of Gnosticism: Proceedings of the International Conference on Gnosticism at Yale, New Haven, Connecticut, March 28-31, 1978* (2 vols.; Supplements to Numen 41; Leiden: E. J. Brill, 1980, 1981); A. H. B. Logan, *Gnostic Truth and Christian Heresy: A Study in the History of Gnosticism* (Peabody, MA: Hendrickson; Edinburgh: T & T Clark, 1996); E. H. Pagels, *The Gnostic Gospels* (New York: Random House, 1979); B. A. Pearson, *Gnosticism, Judaism and Egyptian Christianity* (SAC; Minneapolis: Fortress, 1990); idem, "Nag Hammadi Codices," *ABD* (1992) 4:984-91; P. Perkins, *Gnosticism and the New Testament* (Minneapolis: Fortress, 1993); S. Pétrement, *A Separate God: The Christian Origins of Gnosticism* (San Francisco: HarperSanFrancisco, 1990); K. Rudolph, *Gnosis: The Nature and History of Gnosticism* (San Francisco: Harper & Row, 1983); D. M. Scholer, ed., *Gnosticism in the Early Church* (SEC 5; New York & London: Garland, 1993); R. McL. Wilson, *Gnosis and the New Testament* (Philadelphia: Fortress, 1968); idem, *The Gnostic Problem: A Study of the Relations Between Hellenistic Judaism and the Gnostic Heresy* (London: A. R. Mowbray, 1958); E. M. Yamauchi, *Pre-Christian Gnosticism: A Survey of the Proposed Evidences* (2d ed.; Grand Rapids: Baker, 1983).   D. M. Scholer

GNOSTICISM. *See* GNOSIS, GNOSTICISM.

GOD

"God" *(theos)* in the later NT documents continues to denote the unique deity of Israel's* Scripture and tradition. Most every use of *theos* (or its semantic or pronominal substitutes) consequently carried with it the explicit commitment to an exclusive brand of Jewish monotheism—i.e., that there is only one God, Israel's God, Yahweh. These same later NT documents, however, demonstrate that the identity of this God underwent a profound redefinition. The identity of Israel's one true God was enlarged to include Jesus of Nazareth.

Given such revision, it was not a foregone conclusion that Christianity would stay within the constraints dictated by Jewish monotheism (Harvey, 154-73). The temptations to entertain a whole host of other arrangements—from a full-fledged ditheism to supplanting Yahweh with Jesus—were ever present. The various christological* debates and controversies of the first four centuries of the church can be read as a sustained struggle to bind the theological energy unleashed by the juxtaposition of Yahweh and Jesus within the worship of the church.* Remarkably, Christianity did remain within the bounds of monotheism. Just as an unwavering commitment to an exclusive brand of monotheism provided the theological context for the Jewish way of living *(Halakah)*, so too a christologically reformatted monotheism fueled the communal identity and eschatological* ethics* of the new Christian movement. Monotheism proved to be as essential to Christianity's various conciliar confessions as it had been to Israel's *Shema* (Deut 6:4).

The crucial historical, theological and philosophical question then becomes, How did Christianity successfully effect the transition from "there is but one God" of Deuteronomy 6 to the Nicene affirmation of the three, "Father," "Son" and "Spirit," all within the bounds of monotheism? Although it was not until the second, third and particularly the fourth centuries that Christian trinitarian reflection gathered momentum, the NT sets the trajectory for the course of Jewish monotheism in the Christian tradition. It is here that the later NT writers and the authors of the early second century take on a special significance, for they were the first to delineate the identity and mission of Jesus within Jewish monotheism. Moreover, the NT and early second-century documents inscripturate how the first Christians revised what they knew to be true about their God in light of Jesus. These documents are thus crucial for the theological trajectory that began to wrestle with Jesus' identity within the context of Jewish monotheism and God's identity in light of the veneration of Jesus.

1. Background
2. Acts
3. Hebrews
4. James
5. 1 Peter
6. 2 Peter and Jude
7. 1, 2 and 3 John
8. Revelation
9. Apostolic Fathers
10. Summary

1. Background.
Jewish monotheism formed the primary conceptual matrix for Christianity's understanding of God. In particular two aspects of Jewish monotheism were important for Christianity—the singularity of God (i.e., that there are no other gods aside from Yahweh) and the unity of the Jewish God (that there is no division within Yahweh).

1.1. The Shape of Jewish Monotheism. One way to approach the study of a deity is through a careful examination of the god's attributes (e.g., mercy, love, righteousness). However, the character, nature and attributes of Yahweh are primarily inferred only from the shape and tenor of his past and promised deeds. In turn Yahweh's actions, and thus by extension Yahweh's attributes, have meaning only when framed by the larger narration of Israel's story. It is the emplotment of all of Yahweh's deeds that imbues any individual event with revelatory and hermeneutical* power. Monotheism thus becomes a necessary presupposition for and consequence of the narration of Israel's history: it is the same God who is responsible for all, from beginning to end. Jewish reflection upon its unique history implied and demanded one and only one God.

The OT repeatedly affirms the singularity of God and simultaneously opposes the multideity worldview of idolatrous paganism. The Decalogue states, "You shall have no other gods before me" (Ex 20:3 RSV; cf. Deut 5:6-7); the *Shema* declares, "Hear, O Israel: The LORD our God is one LORD"* (Deut 6:4 RSV); and the prophet proclaims that "Before me no god was formed, nor shall there be any after me. . . . I am the LORD, and besides me there is no savior" (Is 43:10b-11 RSV; cf. Is 40:28-31; 44:6; *see* Savior).

Israel openly asserted that this one God made the world and everything in it, that this one God had elected a people, and that this one God providentially cared for them. That Yahweh had decisively and consistently acted on their behalf in the past emboldened Jews, even in the face of a historical crisis like the exile, to envision a new and better day. Jewish monotheism can be characterized as creational (it was Yahweh who created the world), covenantal* (it was Yahweh who had given the promises) and providential (it was Yahweh who was directing the course of history), an exclusive monotheism that forged a dogged eschatological hope* (Wright, 248-52).

1.2. Divine Agency Within the Matrix of Jewish Monotheism. The documents of Second Temple Judaism* demonstrate a proliferation of "divine agents" (Hurtado, 17-92). These heavenly figures can be divided into three sometimes overlapping categories: agents who are depicted as personified attributes of God (e.g., Wisdom, Word), as exalted patriarchs/matriarchs (e.g., Enoch, Moses,* Jacob) or as principal angels* (e.g., Michael, Melchizedek, Yaoel). Similar to other figures, these divine agents either originated in or were exalted to heaven*; however, unlike other figures, these divine agents were depicted as bearing the marks and properties of divinity in unprecedented ways. In some cases these divine agents were described as performing deeds typically reserved for Israel's God—i.e., creating the world and/or executing eschatological judgment* and redemption.*

The phenomenon of divine agency undermines any claim that Jewish monotheism had weakened during the Second-Temple period. Instead of indicating transcendence and distance (Bousset), these divine agents actually demonstrate God's immanence and immediacy (Hurtado). Despite the exalted ways in which these figures could be described, divine agency did not compromise the piety of Jewish monotheism. Divine agents were never worshiped as god(s). Although the extravagant epiphanies could well have confused the line of demarcation between one of these powerful agents and the one true God, the angelic refusal tradition (in which angelic figures refuse to be worshiped) safeguarded Jewish monotheism by legitimating the veneration of the one true God alone (Stuckenbruck; *see* Worship).

If the monotheism of the biblical writings emphasized the singularity of the one true God (there is only one God, Yahweh; all others are mere idols), the writings of Second Temple Judaism preserved the unity of the one true God (despite the presence of powerful agents that share the marks of divinity, Yahweh is one). The singularity and unity of the creating, covenanting and purposeful God formed the conceptual matrix for early Christian theological reflection.

2. Acts.

The Book of Acts* demonstrates that the supreme deity of the earliest followers of Jesus was none other than the God of Israel, that the identity of this God underwent a profound change and that belief in a Christian-style monotheism should not be confused with other theistic claims.

2.1. Lexical Observations. Acts (*see* OT in Acts) employs six different constructions to denote the traditional deity of Jewish piety. The list includes "God" (*theos*, 159 times), "Lord"* (*kyrios*, at least 31 times; see Mowery 1995, 89 and fn. 32-35), "Father" (*patēr*, 3 times), *"Most High"* (*hypsistos*, 2 times), "Sovereign" (*despotēs*, 1 time); "Deity" (*theios*, 1 time). Occasionally the terms are combined—e.g., "Sovereign Lord" (Acts 4:24), "Lord God" (Acts 2:39; 3:32).

Acts distinguishes between this God (i.e., the one worshiped by Jews and Christians) and other "gods" in the Greco-Roman world (Grant 1966). The list of other gods (*see* Religions) includes the god "called Great" (*hē kaloumenē Megalē*, Acts 8:10), "the gods" (*hoi theoi*) Hermes and Zeus (Acts 14:11-12), "the great goddess Artemis" (*megalēs theas Artemidos*, Acts 19:27) and the god "Justice" (*hē dikē*, Acts 28:4) as well as unofficial or unsanctioned (demonic) deities—i.e., "host of heaven" (*stratia tou ouranou*, Acts 7:42), " spirits" (*pneumata akatharta*, Acts 5:16; 8:7), or "Satan"* (*ho satanas*, Acts 5:2; 26:20). While adamant about its brand of exclusive monotheism, Acts does demonstrate an awareness of competing and opposing claims.

2.2. Christian Monotheism as a Continuation of Jewish Monotheism. Acts assumes that its readers will identify its references to *theos* as Israel's singular deity. There is not even the slightest hint otherwise. Repeated references to the "kingdom of God"* (Acts 1:8; 8:12; 14:22; 19:8; 28:23; 28:34) not only link the story Acts narrates with the "first word" (Acts 1:1) told in the Gospel of Luke but also situates the narrative of Acts within the horizon of the Israel's story. The kingdom must belong to the one God about whom both the prophets and Jesus preached. That Acts can summarize the preaching and teaching* of the early church as "the word of God" (Acts 4:11; 6:2, 7; 8:14; 11:1; 12:24; 13:5, 7; 13:46; 17:13; 18:11), without pausing to identify which god only reinforces this presupposed continuity. The "word of God" consists in a message about the one true God of Israel.

The disciples' continued veneration of the God of Israel also clearly documents the strength of early Christianity's unequivocal monotheistic commitment. This religious devotion included praising God (Acts 2:47; 3:8-9), glorifying God (Acts 4:21; 11:18; 21:20), magnifying God (Acts 10:46), lifting voices to God (Acts 4:24), singing hymns to God (Acts 16:25), giving thanks to God (Acts 27:35; 28:15) and offering prayer to God (Acts 12:5). The terms "God-fearer" (Acts 10:2, 22; 13:16, 26) and "worshiper of God" (Acts 16:14; 18:7, 13), while probably not technical, do refer to the worship of Israel's God. Acts consistently depicts the object of the disciples' preaching and worship as the God of Israel.

2.3. Images of God in Acts. Since the unstated theological assumption of Acts is that Israel's God is the God of early Christianity, it is not surprising to find God's picture painted with very traditional Jewish colors.

2.3.1. God as Creator. Acts several times depicts God as the creator of the world (*see* Creation) and in each case echoes Genesis 1. The community of disciples addressed their prayer to the "Sovereign Lord, who made the heaven and the earth, the sea, and everything in them" (Acts 4:24, NRSV). Stephen's* quotation of Isaiah 66:1-2 highlights the creative power of Israel's God (Acts 7:50). At Lystra Paul* encourages his hearers to turn from idols to "the living God who made the heaven and earth and the sea and all that is in them" (Acts 14:15 RSV), while at Athens he begins his sermon by identifying the God of his preaching as "the God who made the world and everything in it" (Acts 17:24 RSV). The God of the earliest disciples is the God who made the world.

2.3.2. The Faithfulness of God. Acts repeatedly underscores God's covenant-keeping faithfulness.* Peter, Stephen and Paul all clearly invoke the covenant promises made by Israel's God to

Abraham* (Acts 3:25; 7:3, 5-7) by identifying the God they both preach and serve as the "God of Abraham, and of Isaac, and of Jacob, the God of our fathers" (Acts 3:13; 5:30; 7:32; 24:14; 26:6). The speeches of Acts specify the occasions when God demonstrably reaffirmed this covenant promise (Mowery 1990, 198). God rescued Joseph (Acts 7:9-10), secured Israel's release from Egyptian bondage (Acts 7:17; 13:17), promised a future deliverer like Moses (Acts 3:22; 7:37), endured Israel's rebellion during the wilderness wanderings (Acts 7:42; 13:18), led Israel in conquest over the nations (Acts 7:45; 13:19), swore an oath to David (Acts 2:30; 13:23) and reaffirmed his covenant promises to the prophets (Acts 3:18; 26:22). Even the risen Jesus charges his disciples to wait patiently for the complete fulfillment of God's covenant (Acts 1:4). The narrative force of these affirmations serves to characterize God as faithful to his covenant.

But Acts presses further. The events of Jesus' life should also be understood as an act of God's covenant faithfulness. It is the "God of our fathers" who has now "raised" and "glorified" Jesus (Acts 3:13; 5:30); from David's posterity "God brought a Savior, Jesus"—just as was promised (Acts 13:23); the good news of Jesus' resurrection fulfills what was "promised to the fathers" (Acts 13:32-33). More than just another faithful act, the death (see Death of Christ) and resurrection* of Jesus should be read as God's supreme act of covenant faithfulness.

2.3.3. God, the Sovereign Lord of History. God's resolute commitment to the covenant bespeaks a larger plan and purpose for the world. Acts portrays God as controlling all of history (Conzelmann, 149-63; Cosgrove). It was God who determined the temporal and geographical boundaries for the nations of the world (Acts 17:26). While past generations were permitted "to walk in their own ways" (Acts 14:16), God now requires undivided allegiance (Acts 17:31). God's sovereign control of history even includes the foreknowledge of the future (Acts 1:7).

Acts also portrays God as choreographing Jesus' life. God is the one who "sent" (Acts 3:26) or "brought" (Acts 13:23) Jesus to Israel. God is the one who "anointed" Jesus with the Spirit at his baptism* (Acts 10:38; cf. 4:26-27); who, through signs and wonders,* "attested" to Jesus' ministry (Acts 2:22); and who was "with him" (Acts 10:38). Even Jesus' death occurred in

accordance with the definite plan *(boulē)* and foreknowledge *(prognōsis)* of God (Acts 2:23; see also 3:18; 4:27-28; 20:28). God is the one who "ordained" Jesus to be the eschatological judge (Acts 10:42; 17:31). God is consistently pictured as controlling the life of Jesus from beginning to end.

Acts also sees providence at work in the community's mission* (*see* Evangelism) to the Gentiles.* Peter's Pentecost sermon (Acts 2:39), Paul's conversion (Acts 9:15; 21:21) and missionary endeavors (Acts 13:46; 18:6; 28:28 [quoting Is 49:6]) and the apostolic councils of the Jerusalem church (Acts 11:18; 15:7; 15:16-18 [quoting Amos 9:11-12, Jer 12:15 and Is 45:21]) all show how the events of Jesus' life, death and resurrection have empowered the church to fulfill the task originally assigned to Israel. God's sovereign control of history and his covenant promises to Israel coalesce in the predestined events of Jesus' life to bring about his intention to bless the nations with salvation* (Acts 26:22-23).

The adventuresome character of Acts is due in large measure to the dramatic ways in which God intervenes on behalf of the community of followers within the story (see the extensive list provided by Pervo, 14-17). The external hazards of persecution,* mob violence, imprisonment, punishment and travel, along with the internal threats of strife, deceit and prejudice, receive decisive resolution in God's many and multifaceted divine interventions. Through visions,* miracles,* sermons, angelophanies, christophanies and theophanies God consistently transforms both external and internal threats into further growth and expansion (Newman). Acts depicts God as in control of every aspect of history.

2.3.4. God as Judge. The image of God as judge would be familiar to Jews, and thus the assertion in Acts that God had judged Egypt (Acts 7:7), the nations of Canaan (Acts 13:19) and even Israel (Acts 7:42) would not have surprised them. Neither would the portrayal in Acts of characters within the narrative as being aware of God's oversight (Acts 3:23; 4:19; 8:21; 10:4, 31, 33; 23:1; 24:16), for surely the God of Israel "knows the heart of all persons" (Acts 15:8). Acts portrays those outside of Christian circles as conscientiously avoiding being found "opposing God" (Acts 5:39) and records the rather severe judgment received by unsavory characters (e.g., Acts 5:5; 12:23). That God has "fixed a day in which he will judge the world in righteousness" (Acts 17:31) continues the OT's "day of the Lord"* tradition. Acts states that God's eschatological, universal and impartial judgment will be executed "by a man who he has appointed" (cf. Acts 10:42), namely, Jesus of Nazareth, thus demonstrating how the tradition of divine agency was appropriated within Christianity.

2.4. Christian Monotheism as a Redefinition of Jewish Monotheism. The images enumerated meld the identity of God in Acts to that presupposed and evoked by the Jewish Scriptures. Acts, however, engages in a scandalous redefinition of God's identity.

2.4.1. The God of Israel Is the God Who Raised Jesus. The persistent refrain that it was God (i.e., the one true God of Israel) who raised, exalted and glorified Jesus (Acts 2:24, 32, 36; 3:13, 15, 26; 4:10; 5:30, 31; 7:37; 10:38, 40; 13:23, 30, 33, 37; 17:18, 31; 24:21; 26:8) rhetorically and theologically punctuates the narrative. By supplying the newest (and ultimately most important) bit of information about the God of Israel, these confessional fragments represent a determined effort by the early church, as depicted in Acts, to retrofit God's identity. The God of Israel is the God who raised the crucified Jesus. The historical implications of this claim are matched only by its hermeneutical ones: the resurrection unlocks the enigma of crucifixion; the cross* and resurrection reveal the true significance of the earthly ministry and message of Jesus; the life of Jesus, rightly understood through the cross and resurrection, divulges the true intentions of Israel's God for the world. The resurrection of Jesus thus becomes the best commentary on God and his purposes for his people and the world.

2.4.2. Jesus as God. The resurrection of Jesus not only disclosed something new about the God of Israel but also simultaneously revealed the true stature of Jesus. The resurrection undeniably revealed Jesus' true identity as the divine Lord, the *kyrios* (Acts 2:36; Marshall, 161-69). Numerous times within the narrative does Acts specifically identify Jesus as the "Lord" (Acts 1:6, 21; 4:33; 7:59; 8:16; 9:5-6; 11:17, 20; 15:11, 26; 16:30; 19:5, 13; 20:21, 24; 21:13; 22:8; 26:15; in many others it is implied). By employing the same word used by the Septuagint to translate the divine name (i.e., Yahweh) as a title

for Jesus, Acts comes close to binitarianism.

While it is true that Acts never applies *theos* to Jesus (unless the *kai* at Acts 7:55 is construed epexegetically—i.e., Stephen saw the "glory of God, even *[kai]* Jesus"), Acts does position Jesus as a divine being alongside Yahweh. First, Acts explicitly substitutes "Jesus" for "Yahweh" in several OT quotations (Joel 2:32 at Acts 2:21; Ps 110:1 at Acts 3:34; Ps 118:22 at Acts 4:11-12; and Amos 9:11-12, Jer 12:15 and Is 45:21 at Acts 15:16-18). Second, official, public, corporate religious acts are done "in the [divine] name of Jesus," including public repentance, conversion and baptism (Acts 2:38; 4:12; 8:16; 10:43; 10:48; 19:15; 22:16); religious healings and exorcisms (Acts 3:6; 16; 4:7, 10, 30); preaching* and teaching (Acts 4:17, 18; 5:28, 40; 8:12; 9:27, 29); being appointed an official representative of the community (Acts 9:15); and suffering religious persecution (Acts 5:41; 9:16; 15:26; 21:13). Most importantly, religious devotion, the true test of monotheism, is directed to the name of Jesus (Acts 9:14, 21; 19:17; 22:16) or directly offered to the risen Jesus (Acts 1:24; 7:59-60; 13:2; 19:17; see Bauckham 1992). The divine title *Lord*, the OT quotations, the use of the name of Jesus and religious devotion offered to Jesus all function to identify Jesus as participating in Yahweh's divinity.

2.5. Christian Monotheism in Opposition to Paganism. The geographical expansion of the Christian movement necessarily brought it into contact with other official and some unsanctioned competitors. Acts gives seven snapshots of Christianity's encounter with other religious construals: Philip's* evangelistic efforts in Samaria* (Acts 8:4-24) entangled both him and Peter with the powers of magic*; in his missionary activities on Cyprus, Paul had an encounter with magical powers (Acts 13:6-12); after healing a cripple at Lystra (Acts 14:8-20), Paul and Barnabas were confused with the pagan gods Hermes and Zeus; Paul's exorcism of a demon-possessed girl at Philippi (Acts 16:16-24) brought him into conflict with her owners; at Athens (Acts 17:16-34) Paul debated monotheism and resurrection with the philosophers gathered at the Areopagus; the success of Paul's apostolic ministry at Ephesus (Acts 19:1-40) undermined the cultic practices associated with Artemis; and at Malta (Acts 28:3-6) observers concluded that the god Justice had taken revenge upon Paul when he was bitten by a viper.

In each of these episodes Acts pits Christian monotheism against the surrounding paganism, graphically demonstrating that idols are not real (there is only one true God); that there are magical or demonic forces at work in the world (in direct opposition to the God of Christianity); that this magical world is intimately connected to economic gain by the practitioners (which contrasts with the benevolence associated with the new community); that Christianity's exclusive monotheism threatened devotion to other ethnic and nationalistic deities; and that Jesus should not be confused with other divine agents, be they pneumatic or human. Christianity, like Judaism, ardently and scandalously proclaimed monotheism to its pagan environment.

3. Hebrews.

The theological sophistication of Hebrews* is matched by its literary elegance. The author's ability to refer to the theological language of levitical sacrifice* balances a text thickly plotted with inventive scriptural interpretations, interlaced with elaborate analogies and structured by alternating genres of exposition and exhortation. At the same time that Hebrews presents a sustained theological argument about Jesus as Son and high priest,* it also issues persuasive appeals to a community for repentance. The blended structural components of exposition and admonition yield complementary yet integrated pictures of God. While the expositional material focuses upon God in relationship to Jesus, the admonitions highlight God in relationship to the community. The literary and theological artistry in Hebrews unite in its intricate depiction of God.

3.1. Lexical Observations. God is the referent in all but one of the sixty-eight occurrences of *theos* (God) and twelve of the fifteen occurrences of *kyrios* (Lord). That Jesus also bears both appellations (*theos*, Heb 1:8; *kyrios*, Heb 2:3; 7:14; 13:20) within the text of Hebrews confirms at the semantic level the kind of theological vitality that existed within the earliest church; both God and Jesus enjoyed the same status as divine beings (Heb 1:3, 8-9; see Harris, 205-28).

The titles "Majesty on High" (*megalōsynē en hypsēlois,* Heb 1:3), the "Majesty in Heaven" (*megalōsynē en tois ouranois,* Heb 8:1), the "God Most High" (*theos tou hypsistou,* Heb 7:1) and the

"Father of Spirits" (*patri tōn pneumatōn,* Heb 12:9) all emphasize that God sits atop a hierarchy of heavenly/angelic/pneumatic beings. The formulations "God of peace" (*ho theos tēs eirēnēs,* Heb 13:20) and "living God" (*theou zōntos,* Heb 3:12; 9:14; 10:31; 12:22), while characteristic of Christianity (e.g., Mt 16:16; Jn 7:38; Rom 9:26; 15:33; 16:20; 2 Cor 3:3; Phil 4:9; 1 Thess 5:23; 1 Pet 1:23; Rev 7:2), locate both author and readers in the broad stream of Jewish tradition. The circumlocutions "heaven" (Heb 3:1; 12:25) and "grace"* ("throne of grace," Heb 4:16; "Spirit of grace," Heb 10:29) appear where "God" may be expected. Hebrews thus employs a rich and varied vocabulary in referring to God.

3.2. The God Who (Still) Speaks. Hebrews presents the reader with some thirty-eight OT quotations (following the list printed in the UBS GNT) and thereby confronts the reader with a God who continues to speak in and through these citations (*see* OT in Hebrews). God is the grammatical subject in twenty-two of these quotations (Heb 1:5a, 5b, 6, 7, 8-9, 10-12, 13; 4:3, 4, 7; 5:5, 6; 6:14; 7:17, 21; 8:5, 8-12; 10:30a, 30b, 37-38; 12:26; 13:5; see Lane, cxvii), with the verb *legō,* in the present tense, active voice, being employed ten times (Heb 1:6, 7; 4:7; 5:6; 6:14; 8:8a, 8b, 9, 10; 12:26). Even a text that Hebrews ascribes to the Holy Spirit* in its introductory formula (Heb 10:15) has God speaking in the quotation (Heb 10:16-17 [using Jer 31:33-34]), and one that is patently about God (Gen 2:2 quoted at Heb 4:4) Hebrews attributes to God. These OT citations position God as the ultimate authority* of all Scripture, bestow a dynamic quality upon the text of the OT and bolster the community's awareness of the presence and nearness of God.

3.2.1. Hebrews 1:1-4. The opening hymnic/confessional exordium (Heb 1:1-4) parallels what God spoke to the ancestors* through the prophets (in the past) with what God speaks to the community through the Son (in the author's present). Hebrews situates this new word as God's final eschatological revelation by setting it within the prophetic sequence. The author also contrasts the Son (Heb 1:1-4) with the angels (Heb 1:5-14). The disparity between the Son and angels not only works on an ontological axis (Jesus is divine; angels are not) but also pivots on the eschatologically superior revelation delivered by the Son. The word God speaks through the Son is much preferred to that spoken through angels (Heb 2:2). God speaks his final word to the community through (the message about) his Son.

3.2.2. Hebrews 4:11-13. When at Hebrews 4:11 the readers are admonished not to fall into disobedience, the author grounds this admonition in the character and power of God's word (Heb 4:12-13). Like God (Heb 3:12; 9:14; 10:31; 12:22) the word is "living" *(zōn),* "active" *(energēs)* and "sharper than any two-edged sword" (Heb 4:12a; cf. Eph 6:17; Rev 1:16; 2:12). The author predicates divine qualities to the word through the use of physiognomic imagery: God's word pierces the division of the soul and spirit, of joints and marrow; it discerns the thoughts and intentions of the heart (Heb 4:12b). The distinction between God and the "word" finally vanishes: to stand before God's word is to stand before "him" (Heb 4:13).

3.2.3. Hebrews 5:11-14. In Hebrews 5:11-14 the author employs four binary opposites to chastise the community. Instead of teaching others, the community has become dull of hearing; instead of exhibiting competency in the "word of righteousness" *(logou dikaiosynēs,* Heb 5:13), they are in need of instruction in the "elementary principles of [God's] words" *(ta stoicheia tēs archēs tōn logiōn,* Heb 5:12); instead of feasting on solid food, they can only stomach milk*; instead of experiencing maturity, they languish in adolescence. While the rhetoric is intended to shame the community, the passage also highlights the efficacy inherent in the divine message. Like God, the word demands attention and discipline* and nurtures spiritual growth.

3.3. God in the Expositional Material. While it is common practice to divide Hebrews into expositional and hortatory sections (although the precise lines of division are often disputed), it has not been the norm to employ these divisions for theological ends. Recent work into the structure of Hebrews, however, advocates the separate treatment, at least initially, for the purpose of gaining a more precise theological profile (Guthrie).

The expositional material develops a spatial argument about Jesus that traces his journey from heaven to earth and back to heaven. The argument is logical in that each expositional unit depends directly upon the one that precedes it. This spatial and logical argument dis-

closes two pictures of Jesus, as Son and as high priest (see Parsons), and consequently two corresponding pictures of God, as Father and as heavenly beneficiary.

3.3.1. God as Father. Although only explicitly used twice of God in the entire epistle (Heb 1:5; 12:9), "Father" *(patēr)* is one of the primary images for God. By frequently calling Jesus the "Son" (Heb 1:2, 5a [quoting Ps 2:7], 5b [quoting 2 Sam 7:14], 8 [in the introductory formula for Ps 45]; 2:6 [quoting Ps 8:4]; 3:6; 4:14; 5:5 [quoting Ps 2:7], 8; 6:6; 7:28; 10:29), Hebrews implicitly identifies God as "Father." The importance of "Father" for Hebrews can be seen in one of the epistle's opening OT citations in which God declares: "I will be a father to him [referring to Jesus], and he shall be a Son to me" (Heb 1:5b [quoting 2 Sam 7:14]).

God, as "Father," actively participates in the crucial events of Jesus' life. God "begot" (Heb 1:5) and "anointed" (Heb 2:9; cf. 1:2) Jesus, making him "a little lower than the angels" (Heb 2:7, 9; cf. 2:17). "Only by God's grace" did Jesus taste death for everyone (Heb 2:9; cf. 9:28). God "completed"/"perfected" *(teleiōsai)* Jesus though suffering (Heb 2:10). God heard Jesus' cries in the garden and from the cross and always possessed the power to save him from death (Heb 5:7). God "enthroned"/ "crowned"/"appointed"/"exalted"/"designated" Jesus (Heb 1:13; 2:9; 3:2; 5:5, 10; 7:26, 28; 8:1)—all references to the events of resurrection, which is only once (Heb 13:20) referred to explicitly—where he awaits God to make all enemies a footstool (Heb 10:13). God as "Father" and Jesus as "Son" help structure the expositional argument in Hebrews.

3.3.2. God as Heavenly Beneficiary. A second set of expositional texts, organized by the rubric of Jesus as high priest, picture God as the recipient of Jesus' activity. Jesus' life was one of faithful "obedience" and "service"* to God (Heb 2:17; 3:2, 6; 5:8; 10:5-10; 12:2). In his death Jesus "offered" himself up as a sacrifice to God, "once for all" (Heb 2:17; 7:28; 9:14; 10:12). Jesus "passed through the heavens" (Heb 4:14) to "enter the true sanctuary" and "appear" before God (Heb 9:24). Jesus intercedes with God for those who "draw near" (Heb 7:25), being the mediator of God's new covenant with humanity (Heb 8:6; 9:15). As the "Father," God is actively involved in the course of Jesus' life; as the divine beneficiary, God passively receives the liturgical offerings and sacrifices rendered by his high priest, Jesus.

3.4. God in the Exhortations. The hortatory sections also contain two depictions of God— one emphasizing God's distance and one stressing God's accessibility.

3.4.1. The God Who Warns and Punishes. On five separate occasions Hebrews sternly cautions its readers about the divine consequences of persisting in sin.

If disobedience to the (eschatologically) inferior words delivered by angels received God's judgment, how can those who "drift away" from the message by the Son hope to escape (Heb 2:1-4)? Disobedience cannot be hidden from the "eyes of him" who knows and sees all (Heb 4:11-12). For those who finally apostatize there is nothing but judgment, because God "curses" the life that produces only "thorns and thistles" (Heb 6:4-8). Those who persist in sin should harbor no hope for forgiveness* (Heb 10:26-31). They face a "terrifying prospect of judgment," "a raging fire," ready to fall upon God's "adversaries"* (Heb 10:27). They should be forewarned: "It is a fearful thing to fall into the hands of the living God" (Heb 10:31). Hebrews 12:25-29 also cautions about rejecting "him who warns from heaven" (Heb 12:25). Theophanic imagery underscores the severity and certainty of impending divine judgment: "Yet once more I will shake not only the earth, but also the heaven" (Heb 12:26 [quoting Hag 2:6 LXX]). The readers are encouraged to respond with "worship," "reverence" and "awe" (Heb 12:28b), because God is a "consuming fire" (Heb 10:29; cf. Deut 4:24). Standing behind all five of the warning passages is a God who is holy* and righteous and vows judgment for those who refuse him. Volatility and distance dominate when Hebrews pictures God as Judge.

3.4.2. The God Who Promises, Disciplines and Rewards. Hebrews also emphasizes the predictability and nearness of God. He is a God who promises, disciplines and rewards.* God's promises provide the warranting basis for many of the author's exhortations. The admonition to "strive to enter that rest" (Heb 4:11) depends directly upon a God who promises a "rest" (Heb 4:1, 3, 4-5, 7, 9). The exhortations to "draw near" (Heb 10:22), "hold fast" (Heb 10:23) and "to stir up" (Heb 10:24) all acquire their rhetorical power from a God who is faithful to do all that he promises (Heb 10:23). Abel, Enoch, Noah, Abraham, Sarah, Isaac, Jacob, Joseph, Moses, and Rahab (as well as many others!) are examples of those who, even through they did not receive in their earthly life all that was promised (Heb 11:13-14, 39), were still faithful to God. Like this "great cloud of witnesses" the community should also "run the race with perseverance" (Heb 12:1-2). God promises; the community should persevere.

Discipline, like promises, should spur the readers on. In order to gain a perspective upon their own difficulties, the author invites the readers to consider those experienced by Jesus (Heb 12:3-4). The midrash on Proverbs 3:11-12 that follows (Heb 12:5b-6) identifies the community as God's children and God as their heavenly Father. It also interprets the difficulties they face as God's discipline. The community should not be dismayed when God treats them "as children," because discipline is a normal aspect of the parent-child relationship (Heb 12:7). The absence of discipline denotes illegitimacy (12:8). Since earthly fathers are held in respect for disciplining their children (Heb 12:9), the chastisement received from "the Father of spirits" should only inspire confidence, respect and holiness (Heb 12:10-11).

If the God of Hebrews promises and disciplines, this God also rewards.* Those who seek to draw near should not think God "so unjust" so as to overlook their work and love (Heb 6:10). The author exhorts the community not to throw away their confidence, "which has a great reward" (Heb 10:35), but instead to develop endurance,* so that they might "do the will of God and receive what has been promised" (Heb 10:36). Believing in a God who rewards is essential for moral transformation: "For whoever would draw near to God must believe that he exists and that he rewards those who seek him" (Heb 11:6 RSV). The hortatory material in Hebrews profiles both God's volatility and his nearness, images strategically deployed to elicit the same response: repentance.

3.5. God, the Architect and Builder. Hebrews affirms that God designed and created this world. God founded the earth in the beginning, and the heavens are the work of his hands (Heb 1:10 [quoting Ps 102:25]). God is the one "through whom and for whom all things exist" (Heb 2:10), which is doubtless a monotheistic confession of the early church (cf. Rom 11:36; 1 Cor 8:6; 15:27-28; Col 1:16; Rev 4:11). God's "works were finished from the foundation of the world" (Heb 4:3b; cf. 9:26), a fact understood only "by faith" (Heb 11:3). Such language pictures creation as a divine enterprise stretching back to eternity (cf. Mt 13:35; 25:34; Jn 17:24; Eph 1:4) and God as its architect.

Hebrews baptizes this building imagery to describe God's eschatological act of new creation. Abraham looked forward to an eschatological city "whose builder and maker is God" (Heb 11:10). The OT heroes died in faith, not having received what was promised, not having entered that heavenly "better country," the "city" that God prepared for them (Heb 11:13-16). Here on earth believers have no lasting city but seek the city "which is to come" (Heb 13:14). Remarkably, however, in salvation believers have already come to the eschatological Mount Zion (see Jerusalem), the "city of the living God, the heavenly Jerusalem" (Heb 12:22). God designed and founded this world and is in the process of rebuilding it.

4. James.

More than any other NT document James* has been subject to the shifting opinions of its interpreters. This may largely be due to the unfortunate (and inordinate) influence wielded by Luther's negative evaluation of James as a "strawy epistle." While Luther's hesitation was based upon a perceived fall from Paul's doctrine of justification by faith, the absence (again, perceived) of an explicitly developed christology accounts for more recent uncertainty as to its point. So damning are the kerygmatic* omissions that some consider James to be "wholly Jewish in language and thought" (Dunn, 212). Such an observation unfairly pits James's theocentrism against the christocentrism of other NT documents.

The charges of theological irregularities in James levied by some tell us more about the singular lack of information about the setting of the letter than they do about James's theology. James both knows and employs the common core of apostolic theology (Sloan, 3-14) and, while admittedly more indirect, James is not entirely lacking direct and explicit christological claims (Mussner 1970, 111-17). James calls Jesus the "Lord" (kyrios, Jas 1:1; 2:1) and identifies him with God's divine presence, his

Glory* (tou kyriou . . . tēs doxēs, Jas 2:1; cf. 1 Cor 2:8). Despite the claims of some, James admirably illustrates a profoundly theocentric perspective that is genuinely Christian.

4.1. Lexical Observations. All sixteen occurrences of *theos* ("God") in James refer to the one God of Judaism (Jas 1:1, 5, 13 [2x], 20, 27; 2:5, 19, 23 [2x]; 3:9; 4:4 [2x], 6, 7, 8). *Kyrios* ("Lord") appears fourteen times, and in five occurrences God is the clear referent (Jas 1:7; 3:9; 4:10, 15; 5:4). In two others Jesus is the clear referent (Jas 1:1; 2:1). The referent in the other seven occurrences of *kyrios* is uncertain, though the three occurrences in James 5:10-11 probably refer to God and on balance the other four (Jas 5:7, 8, 14, 15) refer to Jesus (Mussner 1981, 97). Three times James uses *patēr* ("Father") to refer to God, always in conjunction with or as part of other titles—i.e., "Father of Lights" (*patros tōn phōtōn,* Jas 1:17), "God and Father" (*tō theō kai patri,* Jas 1:27), "Lord and Father" (*kyrion kai patera,* Jas 3:9). Additionally, James uses the Isaiah's "Lord of Hosts" (*kyriou Sabaōth,* Jas 5:4; cf. Rom 9:29; it is used sixty-one times in Isaiah and only nine others in the entire OT) to refer to God. James also uses circumlocutions— "from above (*anōthen,* Jas 1:17; 3:15, 17) and "heaven" (*ouranos,* Jas 5:12) for God. If God and not Jesus (cf. Rev 3:20) is the referent, then James refers to God as "the Judge" (*ho kritēs,* Jas 5:9; cf. 5:12; Heb 12:23). James's multiple references to God endow his work with a powerful theocentrism.

4.2. A Wisdom Pneumatology? "Wisdom"* (*sophia*) figures prominently in two important passages (Jas 1:5-8; 3:13-18), while echoes of it may be heard in two others (Jas 1:16-18; 2:1-3). James explicitly quotes Proverbs 3:34 at 4:6 and implicitly alludes to other wisdom literature (Chester and Martin, 9 n. 8). Further, the parallels between wisdom in James and the Holy Spirit in other parts of the NT are also striking. Specific verbal connections can be made between the virtues of "wisdom" in James 3:13, 17 and those of the "Spirit" in Galatians 5:22-23—i.e., "meekness" (*praÿtēs*), "peaceableness"/peace (*eirēnikos/eirēnē*) and "fruit" (*karpos*). This has led some (e.g., Davids, 56) to suppose James betrays a "wisdom pneumatology" that forms the major conceptual matrix and organizing principle of the text.

However, the connections between these two passages may be due to common dependence upon Jesus traditions* rather than to an independent wisdom pneumatology. Further, James explicitly subordinates wisdom to God: Wisdom comes "from above" (Jas 1:17; 2:15). Thus a wisdom pneumatology does not run parallel with or control James's theological perspective; rather, James's reflection upon the one true God is the larger conceptual category into which specific comments about wisdom fit.

4.3. The Constancy of the One God. James no doubt approves of and accepts the exclusive monotheism of the Jewish Scriptures. Twice he plainly states that God is "one" (*heis*, Jas 2:19; 4:12). However, James's interest in the one God of Jewish piety is of a different sort. His monotheistic exploration seeks to map the unchanging character of the one true God.

James describes God as the "Father of lights with whom there is not any variation or shadow of change" (Jas 1:17b). "Lights" (*phōtōn*, i.e., the "stars") and "change" (*tropēs*, i.e., "solstice")— and possibly even "shadow" (*aposkisma*, i.e., "eclipse"; see Dibelius-Greeven, 102-4)—are technical cosmological terms. James invokes the solar system to contrast the permanence of the Creator God with the instability of the creation. The heavenly bodies are subject to change; God is not. James applies this to the faith of the community. The constancy of God means that he is the author only of "good and perfect gifts" (Jas 1:17a).

God's unaltering, equitable character can be seen in other of James's statements. God gives "freely" and "generously" to anyone who asks (Jas 1:5, 9, 17, 21). God will give the "crown of life" to anyone who endures (Jas 1:12). God neither tempts with nor is tempted by evil (Jas 1:13). God blesses anyone who is both a hearer and a doer of the word (Jas 1:22-25). God's promises about the kingdom are inclusive, regardless of social or economic status (Jas 2:5). God applies the same law* to everyone (Jas 2:8-13). God is jealous over anyone in whom his Spirit dwells (Jas 4:5; see commentaries on this problem text). God will draw near to anyone who seeks to draw near to him (Jas 4:8). God expects the same responses from all—submission (Jas 4:6), humility (Jas 4:10), patience (Jas 5:8). God hears the prayer of the oppressed and the righteous (Jas 5:5, 16).

The one God's immutable character dramatically contrasts with humanity's duplicitous nature. Although created in God's likeness (Jas 3:9) to be "a kind of first fruit of his creatures" (Jas 1:18)—i.e., to be like God—a double-mindedness (*dipsychoi*, Jas 1:8; 4:8) plagues humanity. Humanity doubts (Jas 1:6-8), denies (Jas 1:13-15), deceives (Jas 1:16-18, 26-27), forgets (Jas 1:22-25), discriminates (Jas 2:1-13; cf. 1:9-11), and slanders (Jas 3:6-12; 4:11-13); humanity is impetuous (Jas 1:19-21), controlled by selfish ambition (Jas 3:13-18; 4:1-10), arrogant (Jas 4:13-16), short-sighted (Jas 5:1-6) and impatient (Jas 5:7-11). Mired in fickleness, capriciousness and inconsistency, humanity fails to mime God's constant, true character.

4.4. Monotheism and Ethics. James offers a simple solution: believers should become as consistent as God. Word must always be matched by deed. But James does not simply preside over the marriage of monotheism to ethics (as if monotheism and ethics could legitimately exist independent of each other); for James a commitment to the one true God is at its core, and at the same time, a commitment to ethics.

By quoting the *Shema* (Deut 6:4) James demonstrates Christianity's continued confessional allegiance to Jewish monotheism. "You believe that 'God is one'; you do well" (Jas 2:19). While this text can be read as affirming God's singularity (there is no other god) or unity (there is no division with God) or both, James pursues another rhetorical goal. A monotheistic confession, while necessary, is not sufficient for Christian identity. There has to be more. Christianity moves beyond intellectual recognition and verbal confession—for even the demonic world does this in fear (Jas 2:19)—to a specific ethical program. The character of this one true God demands a certain relationship between confession and living. Believers' works should no more be separated from their faith than God's deeds are from his nature (*see* Faith and Works). Since there is no variance between God's nature and deeds, there should be none between a believer's faith (confession) and works (Jas 2:14, 16, 18b), a point amply illustrated by Abraham and Rahab (Jas 2:21-25). If there is separation, faith is "dead" (Jas 2:17, 20, 26).

James repeatedly illustrates the ethical obligation inherent in a monotheistic commitment. Genuine faith in God produces faithfulness, maturity and completeness in the believer (Jas 1:3). Embracing "the righteousness of God" outlaws the expression of human anger (Jas

1:20). Devotion to the one true God is to care for those who cannot care for themselves and to demonstrate moral purity* (Jas 1:27). Christian "faith" (Jas 2:1) does not discriminate (Jas 2:1-13). Since God's wisdom is peaceable (Jas 3:17), those who are wise should make peace* (Jas 3:18). That there is but one Lawgiver and Judge means that believers are not to judge each other (Jas 4:11-12). In imitation of God, the yes of a believer's life needs to remain a yes and the no a no (Jas 5:12). The singularity and constancy of the one true God elicits and demands a singular ethical resolve from those who would commit themselves to this God. Christian monotheism obligates the believer to the same relationship between faith and works that exists between God's nature and his deeds.

5. 1 Peter

1 Peter* identifies its readers as "visiting strangers" (1 Pet 1:1; 2:11) and "resident aliens" (1 Pet 2:11; cf. 1:17). Both terms imply that the recipients were experiencing political and social displacement (see Elliott). The ever-increasing friction with and ever-growing estrangement from the surrounding culture prompts the author to intertwine two themes in one letter, both of which are firmly anchored in the author's understanding of the one true God. 1 Peter preaches patience and endurance to those undergoing hardship because of their Christian identity. Support for this message is found in the christological shape of God's providence. 1 Peter also strongly advocates the maintenance of Christian distinctiveness in the face of a strong temptation to assimilate to the surrounding culture. The community is to be as holy as God is (based on Lev 17—26). God's providence and holiness are thus crucial for 1 Peter.

5.1. Lexical Observations. 1 Peter employs a closely circumscribed number of words for God. *Theos* (God) appears thirty-nine times and each refers to the one God of the Scriptures. "Father" (*patēr*) is used of God three times (1 Pet 1:2, 3, 17). *Kyrios* (Lord) appears seven times; four of the references are to God (1 Pet 1:25, 2:3; 3:12 [2x]), all in OT quotations. Twice Jesus bears the title "Lord" (1 Pet 1:3; 3:15), and once the precise referent is unclear (1 Pet 2:13). 1 Peter also refers to God as the "faithful Creator" (*pistos ktistēs,* 1 Pet 4:19). Despite employing a small range of vocabulary for God, 1 Peter does possess a distinct image of God.

5.2. The Providence of God.

5.2.1. God's Election of Believers. 1 Peter applies God's providential care as a balm for the wounds inflicted by a world hostile to Christian faith. 1 Peter identifies its readers as God's "called" (*eklektois,* 1 Pet 1:1); they are God's "chosen race" (*genos eklekton,* 1 Pet 2:9). This calling occurred "according to God's foreknowledge" (*kata prognōsin theou,* 1 Pet 1:2a) and unites the readers with other Christian communities—specifically the one in Babylon* (Rome?)—as the "co-called" (*syneklētos,* 1 Pet 5:12). God's electing purposes help to locate and give self-identity to the estranged communities.

Election* entails the experience of God's "mercy" in "new birth" (1 Pet 1:3a, 23), the possession of a "living hope" (1 Pet 1:3b; cf. 1:13, 21; 3:15), the promise of an "inheritance" no less magnificent than God himself (1 Pet 1:4; 3:9) and the constant protection of God's "power" (1 Pet 1:5). The effectual work of God's call commences with conversion, determines the shape of the Christian life and ensures final transformation (1 Pet 1:15; 5:10). For Peter, God's electing purposes embrace the beginning, middle and end of Christian experience.

5.2.2. God's Election of Jesus. What is true of every Christian is especially true of Jesus. His appearance on the stage of history was "destined" by God "before the foundation of the world" (*proegnōsmenou pro katabolēs kosmou,* 1 Pet 1:20). 1 Peter's exegesis of Isaiah 28:16 identifies Jesus as the "living stone," "the chief cornerstone" and the stone "specially chosen by God" (*para theō eklekton entimon,* 1 Pet 2:4, 6; *see* OT in 1 Peter). God's electing purposes for Jesus included his death (1 Pet 1:2, 19; 2:21; 3:18), resurrection (1 Pet 1:21; cf. 1:3; 2:1; 3:18), exaltation (1 Pet 3:22) and future apocalypse (1 Pet 1:7, 13; 4:13; 5:1). Jesus is God's Elect One par excellence.

5.2.3. Election and Suffering. The juxtaposition of Jesus' election with that of believers implicitly suggests a connection between the two. The connection becomes explicit when the issue of suffering* is raised. God's providential purposes worked through Jesus serve as both a model and a guarantee of his providential care for all Christians.

Peter acknowledges that the community was undergoing a period of intense suffering (1 Pet

4:12; cf. 1:6-7; 3:14). Though probably not "official" persecution, the anguish was nonetheless real. Peter states, incredibly, that such difficulties are a natural consequence of God's calling (1 Pet 2:21); they are a "necessary" (1 Pet 1:6) and "required" (1 Pet 5:9) part of his "will" (1 Pet 3:17; 4:1-2, 19). What justification could there be for these extraordinary statements? Unlike Paul (who primarily uses physiomorphic eschatology) or Hebrews (whose author uses a journey motif), 1 Peter answers christologically the question that suffering puts to God's providence.

5.2.3.1. 1 Peter 2:18-25. 1 Peter admonishes servants to persist in respectful service to their masters despite the harsh treatment they receive (1 Pet 2:18), for anyone who patiently endures unjust suffering will find God's approval (1 Pet 2:19-20). Such moral stamina is required precisely because of the christological shape of the God's call: Christians "have been called to this [suffering], because Christ also suffered" (1 Pet 2:21). Jesus blazed the trail by not responding in kind but by completely trusting the "one who judges justly" (1 Pet 2:21). Jesus' response to unjust suffering (detailed in 1 Pet 2:22-24, based on Is 53) serves as a model for God's elect to follow.

5.2.3.2. 1 Peter 3:13-22. 1 Peter 3:13-22 also demonstrates that the interconnectedness of Jesus' election and that of believers is most apparent at the point of suffering. The passage opens with the rhetorical question about the ability of anyone to harm a Christian "zealous for the good" (1 Pet 3:13). But even if believers should suffer harm for the sake of righteousness, they will certainly enjoy God's blessing* (1 Pet 3:14). 1 Peter then details what a proper response to suffering looks like—reverence, preparedness, gentleness and a clear conscious (1 Pet 3:15-16). Finally, Peter lays down his guiding principle: it is better for Christians to suffer for doing right than for wrong (1 Pet 3:17). This is so precisely "because Christ also died for sins once for all, the righteous for the unrighteous" (1 Pet 3:18a). Peter's confessional justification (3:18b-22) for patient endurance of unjust suffering (1) makes plain his christological belief, (2) promotes confidence in God's providential care and (3) celebrates God's victory over the demonic powers. Not only is unjust suffering a natural consequence of belonging to Christ* but also the prospect of receiving God's blessing is no less certain than Jesus' resurrection.

5.2.3.3. 1 Peter 4:12-19. The christological shape of Christian suffering is most clear, however, in 1 Peter 4:12-19. Here Peter plainly states that a Christian shares in Christ's sufferings (*koinōneite tois tou Christou pathēmasin*, 1 Pet 4:13a) and that sharing in Christ's suffering determines future joy* (*hina kai en tē apokalypsei tēs doxēs autou charēte agalliōmenoi*, 1 Pet 4:13b; cf. Rom 8:18). The present suffering/future glory shape of the passage follows the cross*/resurrection* shape of early Christian preaching and thereby confirms 1 Peter's theological indebtedness to the paradigmatic influence of the life of Jesus.

Peter's treatment of unjust suffering demonstrates that the destiny of believers lies within the destiny of Jesus. The prophetic predictions (1 Pet 1:11) and historical reality (1 Pet 2:21; 4:1, 13; 5:1) of messianic suffering become paradigmatic for all who follow in the steps of the Messiah. 1 Peter resolves the question that unjust Christian suffering puts to God's providence by pointing to the life of Jesus. Jesus is the divine exemplar (Christians should respond as Jesus did) and the guarantor (those who suffer unjustly yet patiently will enjoy the same eschatological blessings). God works his purposes in Christians in and through Jesus the Christ.

5.3. The Holiness of God. The emphasis upon suffering in 1 Peter encourages an adversarial picture of society, but that is not the whole story. Paradoxically running alongside the threat of persecution is the danger of assimilation (to avoid hardship?). Christians were tempted to return to or adopt a secular lifestyle. Peter insists that the boundary between the Christian community and society must remain distinct and recognizable. Crossing the line pollutes the purity* of the community, a purity that is defined by and grounded in God's holiness.*

1 Peter systematically employs purity language to define community identity. The readers are to abandon their former life (1 Pet 1:14) and to pursue holiness in all their conduct (1 Pet 1:15). This 1 Peter justifies by quoting Leviticus 11:44-45, where God declares: "Be holy for I am holy" (1 Pet 1:16). In 1 Peter 2:11-12 Peter instructs the community "to abstain from passions of the flesh" and instead "to maintain good conduct among the Gentiles" in order that the outsiders might see the purity of

their "good deeds." Christians are to submit "for the Lord's sake" to every human institution in order to silence detractors (1 Pet 2:13-17). Peter instructs the community to refrain from living as the Gentiles do (1 Pet 4:3), because the Christians will one day have to give an account of their life to God (1 Pet 4:5). God's holiness defines what it means to be inside or outside the community.

God's holiness also builds cohesion within the community. Christians are to express "love" to one another (1 Pet 1:22), precisely because they have experienced God's "new birth" (1 Pet 1:23). Mutual submission (1 Pet 3:1, 7) should characterize marital relations because it is God who knows "the inner self" (1 Pet 3:4) and "hears" prayers* (1 Pet 3:7). Love,* hospitality* and sacrificial service* should guide the use of spiritual gifts (1 Pet 4:9-10) because it is God who gives, supplies and strengthens (1 Pet 4:11). Leaders are to tend the flock of God in a Christlike humility (1 Pet 5:1-5) because "God opposes the proud but gives grace to the humble" (1 Pet 5:6). The whole community should always be humble, sober, watchful and resistant (1 Pet 5:6-11), because the "God of all grace" will himself restore, establish and strengthen (1 Pet 5:10). To imitate God not only becomes a way of defining the boundary lines of the community but also strengthens bonds within it.

6. 2 Peter and Jude.

That 2 Peter* and Jude* bear a literary relationship with each other is hard to doubt (cf. Jude 4-13 and 16-18 with 2 Pet 2:1-18 and 3:1-3). In all probability 2 Peter was dependent upon Jude. Further, both documents employ common topoi of Jewish apocalypticism* and address a similar situations, i.e., problems with false teachers and teaching. Not surprisingly, then, both documents emphasize God's forbearance and judgment and do so in very similar ways.

6.1. Lexical Observations. 2 Peter uses only four words to refer to God—"God" (*theos*), "Lord" (*kyrios*), "glory" (*doxa*) and "Father" (*patēr*). Six of the seven uses of *theos* are applied to God (2 Pet 1:2, 17, 21; 2:4; 3:5, 12). The other occurrence of *theos* refers to Jesus (2 Pet 1:1; see Harris, 229-38). Six of the fourteen occurrences of *kyrios* refer to God (2 Pet 2:9, 11; 3:8, 9; 3:10, 15), while the other eight refer to Jesus (2 Pet

1:2, 8, 11, 14, 16; 2:20; 3:2, 18). Once 2 Peter refers to God as the "majestic Glory" (*megalōprepous doxēs*, 2 Pet 1:17) and as "Father" (*para theou patros*, 2 Pet 1:17). The identical lexical situation prevails in Jude. All four occurrences of *theos* refer to God (Jude 1, 4, 21, 25). *Kyrios* is used seven times with two, possibly three, occurrences referring to God (Jude 5, 9, 14). Jude identifies God as "Father" (*patēr*) once (Jude 1) and, like 2 Peter, makes reference to God's glory (Jude 24).

6.2. God's Forbearance in 2 Peter. False teachers had undermined the stability of the church by calling into question the certainty of the Parousia.* The answer 2 Peter provides moves well beyond just reaffirming the certainty of the Parousia; it addresses the issue of the delay, in light of the forbearance of God.

2 Peter begins by emphasizing God's beneficence. From the bounty of his "divine power" God gave "all" (*panta*) that could be given (2 Pet 1:3). The call includes "life and godliness" and a share in God's own "glory and excellence" (2 Pet 1:3). He has provided an "escape" from the corrupting powers of this world and promised a share in his "divine nature" (2 Pet 1:4). All of this is mediated through the "knowledge"* of him (2 Pet 1:3). The certainty and efficacy of God's gifts should never be doubted.

It is not what God has done but what he has apparently failed to do that has given an opportunity to the false teachers (2 Pet 2:1). Specifically, the fact that the end had not yet come allowed the false teachers to conclude that it would not come at all.

To counteract the appraisal of the Parousia as simply a "cleverly devised myth" (2 Pet 1:16), 2 Peter points to Jesus' transfiguration. In that event the "majestic Glory" gave voice to his divine approval of Jesus (2 Pet 1:17). 2 Peter interprets the transfiguration as a prolepsis of God's eschatological presence—Jesus received "honor and glory" from God—and thus a sure sign of the future apocalypse (2 Pet 1:19). This is a testimony still heard in the apostolic community (2 Pet 1:18) and verified by God's Spirit-inspired prophets* (2 Pet 1:20-21). The transfiguration and the subsequent testimony mean that the Parousia can hardly be described as a myth.

The false teachers also asserted that a day of judgment would never come. 2 Peter rehearses past examples when God, despite the passage of time, judged the unrighteous and vindicated the faithful (2 Pet 2:1-10). God did not spare the disobedient angels (2 Pet 2:4); those who sinned during Noah's day (2 Pet 2:5); or the ungodly of Sodom and Gomorrah (2 Pet 2:6). However, God did rescue Noah out of the flood (2 Pet 2:4) and honored the endurance of Lot (2 Pet 2:7-8). Delay does not invalidate divine judgment, as the false prophets claimed; delay only witnesses to God's forbearance. God knows how both to rescue and to punish (2 Pet 2:9), and thus to indulge one's passions (2 Pet 2:1-3, 10), as the false teachers encouraged, is not only eschatologically perilous but openly sneers at God's patience.

When the scoffers taunt, "Where is the promise of his coming?" (2 Pet 3:4a) and "All has remained the same since the beginning of creation!" (2 Pet 3:4b), they call into question God's intention and power to intervene in history. Such mockery deliberately ignores what is common knowledge: God's ability to create confirms his ability to judge (2 Pet 3:5-6).

Since the passage of time in no way undermines the certainty of God's promises—"with the Lord one day is as a thousand years, and a thousand years as one day" (2 Pet 3:8 [quoting Ps 90:6])—any perceived delay should be construed as an expression of God's mercy. God wishes that all should repent and that none should perish (2 Pet 3:9). God's forbearance is thus an expression of his saving purposes (2 Pet 3:15). The day of the Lord* will come quickly enough, like a thief (2 Pet 3:10), and thus holiness and Godliness should be the order of the day (2 Pet 3:11, 14).

6.3. The Judgment of God in Jude. Jude also seeks to contradict false teaching. The opponents advocate licentiousness—words denoting "ungodliness" are listed: *asebeia* (Jude 15, 18), *asebēs* (Jude 4, 15) *asebōs* (Jude 15), *aselgeia* (Jude 4)—apparently grounded in an overly realized eschatology. Jude instead mandates doctrinal purity (Jude 3) and moral sobriety (Jude 20-23) in the face of God's imminent judgment.

Jude begins by describing the readers as those having been "beloved by God the Father" (Jude 1b). Jude follows this with another reference to the goodness of God (Jude 3-4). But God's grace* does not legitimate any sort of behavior (as the false teachers apparently taught). God's grace has limits. To appeal to God's grace as a cover for "licentiousness" is to "pervert" it and to "deny" the lordship of Jesus (Jude 4). Judgment awaits the ungodly, as it did for the disobedient of Israel (Jude 5), the disobedient angels (Jude 6) and the immoral of Sodom and Gomorrah (Jude 7). The Lord's rebuke will most surely come upon those who reject and revile authority (Jude 8-10). "Woe to them!" (Jude 11), for the Lord will certainly come to judge (Jude 14; cf. *1 Enoch* 1:9). Jude even asserts that the ungodly false teachers are a sure sign of the end (Jude 17-18). The cure for such moral laxity is to stay within the "love of God" (Jude 21), for God is able to keep believers from falling and to finishing the process of eschatological transformation (Jude 24).

7. 1, 2 and 3 John.
The letters of 1, 2 and 3 John (*see* John, Letters of) seek to close social fissures opened by an amalgamation of erroneous teaching and practice of the gnosticizing kind. The letters encourage right belief and praxis, both of which are tied to the nature of the one true God.

7.1. Lexical Observations. Theos ("God") appears in 1 John sixty-two times, in 2 John twice (2 Jn 2, 9) and in 3 John three times (3 Jn 6, 11 [2x]). 1 John explicitly calls God "Father" *(patēr)* twelve times (1 Jn 1:2; 1:3; 2:1, 14, 15, 16, 22, 23 [2x], 24; 3:1, 14) and implies it in twenty-two other instances by identifying Jesus as the or his "Son." 2 John refers to God as "Father" four times (2 Jn 3 [2x], 4, 9). Additionally, 1 John twice calls God the "One [who is] from the beginning (*ton ap' archēs,* 1 Jn 2:13; 14).

7.2. God as Light. "God is light and in him there is no darkness at all" (1 Jn 1:5). By juxtaposing "light"* *(phōs)* and "darkness" *(skotia)* 1 John divides the world and human existence into two mutually exclusive domains. Specifically, 1 John allies "light" with "truth" (1 Jn 1:6), "love" (1 Jn 1:7; 2:10) and "forgiveness" (1 Jn 1:7). "Darkness" keeps company with lying (1 Jn 1:6), disobedience (1 Jn 1:6), ignorance (1 Jn 2:11) and spiritual blindness (1 Jn 2:11). Light invokes all the images associated with God and salvation; darkness, of sin and death.

John's Gospel identifies Jesus as the light that shines in a dark world (1 Jn 1:5), an illumination that bestows life upon all who are willing to identify with him (Jn 1:4, 9; 9:5; 12:46). 1 John also marks the transition from "darkness" to "light" at the advent of Jesus. "The darkness is (already) passing and the true light is already shining" (1 Jn 2:8). The "message" that the church first "heard" and continues to "preach" (1 Jn 1:5), the "word" that they had "from the beginning" (1 Jn 2:7), is the narration of Jesus' life, death and resurrection. Adherence to this message of light demands spiritual transformation. The community is to "walk in the light as God is in the light" (1 Jn 1:7). Adherence to the message of light also requires confession (1 Jn 1:8), one that is not exhausted by words. To "hate" a fellow Christian is to betray the confession and demonstrates solidarity with darkness (1 Jn 2:9; cf. 2:1). To walk in God's light is to be forgiven, cleansed and unencumbered by the powers of evil (1 Jn 1:8; 2:10). The community is created and sustained by God's light.

7.3. God as Love. "God is love" (1 Jn 4:8, 16), God gives love (1 Jn 3:1; 4:7, 16), and God initiates love (1 Jn 4:10, 19; cf. Rom 5:8). God demonstrated his love in the sending of his Son (1 Jn 4:9) and most particularly in the Son's sacrificial death (1 Jn 3:16; 4:10). God's love permits knowledge of him (1 Jn 4:16), inspires belief and confidence (1 Jn 4:17) and conquers all fear* (1 Jn 4:18).

God's love requires and enables love for one another (1 Jn 3:11, 16, 17, 23; 4:11, 19, 21; cf. 2 Jn 6; 3 Jn 11). Confession should be matched with compassion. "And this is his commandment: that we should believe in the name of his Son Jesus Christ and love one another" (1 Jn 3:23). To love authenticates the claim to saving knowledge of God (1 Jn 3:14; 4:8). To love demonstrates God's perfecting presence within (1 Jn 2:5, 10; 3:1; 4:12, 16; 5:1; cf. 2:14; 2 Jn 7, 9). "The one who does not love remains in the grip of death" (1 Jn 3:14; cf. 3:10). To love anything other than God (e.g., the "world") illustrates the absence of God's love (1 Jn 2:15; 3:17-18). To confess love for God and yet to hate others transforms the confession into a lie (1 Jn 4:20).

8. Revelation.

Revelation* forms a fitting conclusion to the Christian canon: it narrates the final disposition of all things. Revelation's depiction of God equally satisfies: God faces opponents of great power—the dragon, the sea and earth beasts,* Babylon—and soundly defeats them.

8.1. Lexical Observations. Revelation employs the most varied terminology in the NT to refer to the one true God. Standing at the head of the list are ninety-six occurrences of *theos* (God), *kyrios* (Lord), which appears twenty-three times (of which seventeen refer to God; the other occurrences refer to the risen Jesus (Rev 11:8; 14:13; 17:14; 19:16; 22:20, 21) and *patēr* (Father), which is used of God five times (Rev 1:6, 2:28; 3:5, 21; 14:1; cf. 21:7).

The list widens to include constructions rarely or never used in other NT writings. "Almighty" *(pantokratōr)* is used only once outside of Revelation (2 Cor 6:18), but within Revelation it is used of God nine times (Rev 1:8, 4:8; 11:17; 15:3; 16:7, 14; 19:6, 15; 21:23). Revelation uniquely entitles God "The King of the Nations"/"Ages" (*ho basileus tōn ethnōn/aiōnōn,* Rev 15:3—depending on the textual reading), "The Sovereign [One]" (*ho despotēs,* Rev 6:10; but cf. Lk 2:19; Acts 4:24), "The Holy and True [One]" (*ho hagios kai alēthinos,* Rev 6:10), "The Lord of the Earth" (*tou kyriou tēs gēs,* Rev 11:4), "The One who was, is and comes" (*ho ōn kai ho ēn kai ho erchomenos,* Rev 1:4, 8; 4:8; 11:17; 16:5), "The Alpha and the Omega" (*egō eimi to Alpha kai to Ō,* Rev 1:8, 21:6; 22:13), "The Beginning and the End" (*hē archē kai to telos,* Rev 21:6; 22:13) and "The First and the Last" (*ho prōtos kai ho eschatos,* Rev 22:13). On numerous occasions Revelation refers to God as "the One who sits/is seated upon the throne" (Rev 4:2, 3, 9, 10; 5:1, 7, 13; 6:16; 7:10, 15; 12:5; 14:3; 19:4; 20:11; 21:5). The unique ways in which Revelation refers to God corresponds to the singular importance of Revelation's message.

8.2. The Unseen Revealer. As a literary hybrid (the combination of letter,* prophecy and narrative), Revelation communicates on several levels simultaneously. As a letter, Revelation addresses the situation and needs of specific congregations; as a prophetic work, Revelation dialogues with major historical events, albeit obliquely; and as a narrative, characters within Revelation's narrative (e.g., the angelic mediators, the Lamb,* the unnamed voices or even the scroll) communicate with each other and the author. Revelation is something of a literary symphony.

Revelation wraps this complex enterprise within an apocalyptic disclosure. The book opens with the self-descriptive line "the revelation of Jesus Christ" (*apokalypsis Iēsou Christou,* Rev 1:1), a phrase that should be read both objectively (i.e., "a revelation about Jesus Christ") and subjectively (i.e., "a revelation from Jesus Christ"). Jesus is both the author and the content of the apocalyptic visions given to John.

Revelation envelops Jesus' disclosure to John within yet another disclosure. The text stresses that what Jesus makes known to John is what "God gave him" (Rev 1:1). It was God who gave this revelation to Jesus (who in turn gave it to John, who then obediently wrote it up for the communities where it should be read aloud). God therefore is the ultimate source of revelation—but, curiously, a source who is only rarely seen or heard.

While various heavenly beings are described in detail, including the risen Jesus (Rev 1:12-16) and the four living creatures (Rev 4:6b-8a), the only sort of descriptive accounting of God occurs when John likens his vision of the "One seated upon the throne" (Rev 4:2) to "jasper and carnelian" (Rev 4:3). John's approximation moves from the known (jasper and carnelian) to the unknown (God). Further, God only speaks twice within the entire narrative—the self-predication of Revelation 1:8 and the promises of Revelation 22:1-5. Thus even though God is the ultimate source (and therefore positioned as the most powerful agent in Revelation's story-world) and even though Revelation is putatively the most revelatory of all NT documents, the text never finally diminishes the mystery of God. What Revelation does make clear is that God is the all-powerful King who will judge evil and vindicate the righteous.

8.3. The Omnipotence of God. Simply naming God the "Almighty" (Rev 1:8, 4:8; 11:17; 15:3; 16:7, 14; 19:6, 15; 21:23) was not enough. The greatness of God's all-embracing power to be unleashed during the final days demanded elaboration.

8.3.1. God's Temporal Omnipotence. God is the One "who was, is and is to come" (Rev 1:4, 8; 4:8; 11:17; 16:5). God "lives for ever and ever" (Rev 4:9, 10; 10:6; 15:7; cf. 1:6; 5:13; 7:2, 12). God is "The Alpha and the Omega" (Rev 1:8, 21:6; 22:13), "The Beginning and the End" (Rev 21:6; 22:13) and "The First and the Last" (Rev 22:13). While these sorts of declarations position God above and beyond time, Revelation also makes clear once and for all that the one God of the Scriptures intervenes within the flow of history to direct its course to a final and proper conclusion. The God who is beyond time controls time.

8.3.2. God's Cosmic Omnipotence. Revelation augments the picture of God's temporal power by linking it with his cosmic power. God created this world and everything in it (Rev 4:11; 10:6; 14:7). It is by his will that the world exists (Rev 4:11). He is the "Lord of the earth" (11:4). But God's powers do not end there. The risen Jesus, "The Amen, the Faithful and True Witness," is the "beginning of God's [new] creation" (*hē archēs ktiseōs tou theou*, Rev 3:14; cf. 1:5; Col 1:15, 18), and those who obediently follow this Lamb are its "first fruits" (*aparchē*, Rev 14:4; cf. 11:11). God culminates his re-creation by refashioning a new heaven, a new earth and a new Jerusalem (Rev 21:1-2, 10). God's omnipotence includes his ability to create and recreate. God rules both chronos (time) and cosmos (the universe).

8.3.3. God's Theophanic Omnipotence. Revelation also strategically employs theophanic imagery to accentuate the God's power. John's initial vision included God's throne from which spewed "flashes of lightning and voices and peals of thunder" (Rev 4:5). The unsealing of the seventh seal resulted in "peals of thunder, voices, flashes of lightning, and an earthquake" (Rev 8:5). The blowing of the seventh trumpet* triggered "flashes of lightning, voices, peals of thunder, an earthquake and heavy hail" (Rev 11:19). The emptying of the seventh bowl of God was followed by "flashes of lighting, voices, peals of thunder, and a great earthquake such as had never been since men were on the earth, so great was that earthquake" (Rev 16:8). Not only does such rhetoric graphically depict God's power but the sequential intensification of theophanic imagery—at the very place where one might expect a detailed description of the Parousia—moves the narrative forward toward the final theophany (cf. Rev 19:11-16).

8.3.4. God's Royal Omnipotence. Revelation explicitly identifies God as King only once (Rev 15:3) and makes reference to God's "kingdom" only twice (Rev 11:15; 12:10). However, Revelation refers to God's "throne" forty-two times. The throne thus becomes Revelation's major symbol for conveying God's royal power and authority.

God is explicitly identified as the One who sits/is seated upon the "throne" (Rev 3:21; 4:2, 3, 9, 10; 5:1, 7, 13; 6:16; 7:10, 15; 12:5; 14:3; 19:4; 20:11; 21:5). The throne is surrounded by a rainbow (Rev 4:3), seven torches of fire (Rev 4:5), a sea of glass (Rev 4:6) and a golden altar

(Rev 8:3). From the throne spew flashes of lightning and fire (Rev 4:5), come unidentified voices (Rev 16:17; 19:5; 21:3) and flows a river (Rev 22:1). Revelation pictures all sorts of heavenly beings and angelic creatures as gathered around God's throne—i.e., the seven spirits/angels (Rev 1:4; 8:2), twenty-four elders (Rev 4:4; 5:11; 7:11; 11:16; 19:4), four living creatures (Rev 4:6; 5:11; 7:11; 19:4), the Lamb (Rev 5:6; 7:17), myriads of angels (Rev 5:11; 7:11), great multitudes from all the tribes of the earth (Rev 7:9; cf. 19:1), innumerable people in white robes (Rev 7:15), the male child brought forth by a woman (Rev 12:5), the 144,000 (Rev 14:3) and all the dead, both great and small (Rev 20:12). At the throne these heavenly beings sing (Rev 4:6; 14:3), give thanks and praise (Rev 4:9), fall prostrate (Rev 4:10), worship (Rev 4:10; 5:13; 7:10, 11) and utter confessions/acclamations (Rev 7:10, 11; cf. 19:1). This extravagant imagery positions God as the most majestic, commanding and potent being in Revelation's hierarchy of beings.

8.3.5. God's Juridical Omnipotence. God's complete control is nowhere more evident than in the expression of his judgment. While Revelation makes explicit reference to God's judgments (Rev 6:10; 14:7; 15:4; 17:1; 19:8) or "plagues" (Rev 9:18, 20; 11:6; 15:1, 6, 8, 9; 16:21; 18:4, 8; 21:9), it is the complex of events unfolding from the seven "seals" (Rev 4:1—6:17; 8:1-5), "trumpets"* (Rev 8:2—9:21; 11:15-19) and "bowls"* (Rev 15:1—19:10)—culminating in the judgment of the great harlot Babylon (Rev 18:1-24) and the great white throne (Rev 20:11-15)—that dramatically illustrate God's omnipotence. The all-powerful God of Revelation denies the evil powers of this world the final say: there is only one God powerful enough to render judgment.

Divine judgment is an expression of God's "anger" *(thymos)* and "wrath" *(orgē)*. No one will be able to stand the great day of God's wrath (Rev 6:17). God will answer the unrepentant nations with his wrath (Rev 11:18). Whoever worships the beast and opposes God will certainly "drink the wine of God's anger, poured unmixed into the cup of his wrath" (Rev 14:10; 16:19) and thereby experience eternal torment (Rev 14:11). God's judgment is nothing short of a "wine press" of his anger (Rev 14:19). The seven bowls are full of God's anger (Rev 15:7; 16:1), and only when the bowls are emptied shall God's anger cease (Rev 15:1). God's anger and wrath, however, should never be construed as indiscriminate vengeance. Revelation asserts that God's judgments are always "just and true" (Rev 16:5; 19:2).

8.4. The Worship of the Omnipotent God and the Crucified Lamb. Revelation weaves together the various images of God in the twelve songs/confessions that punctuate the narrative (Rev 4:8, 11; 5:13; 7:10, 12; 11:15, 17-18; 15:3-4, 5-6; 16:7; 19:1-3, 4). These songs/confessions celebrate God's "worthiness" (Rev 4:11) to receive "glory" (Rev 4:11; 5:13; 7:12; 19:1), "honor" (Rev 4:11; 5:13; 7:12), "power" (Rev 4:11; 7:12; 19:1), "blessing" (Rev 5:13; 7:12), "might" (Rev 5:13; 12), "wisdom" (Rev 7:12) and "thanksgiving" (Rev 7:12; 11:17). The songs/confessions affirm that "salvation" (Rev 7:10; 19:1) and "power" (Rev 11:17) belong only to God. The hymns* extol God as the one who "reigns" (Rev 11:15, 17), "judges" (Rev 11:18; 15:4; 16:5; 19:2) and "rewards" (Rev 11:18; 19:2). God is "holy" (Rev 4:8; 15:4; 16:5), "just" and "true" (Rev 15:3; 16:5, 7; 19:2). In no other place in the NT are so many images for God brought together with such power.

Thus, in a book that venerates God's omnipotence in unprecedented ways, it is surprising to find that Revelation also openly encourages and models the worship* of the enthroned Jesus. The opening doxology honors the risen Jesus as the one "who loves us and has freed us from our sins by his blood and made us a kingdom, priests to his God and Father, to him [i.e., to Jesus] be glory and dominion for ever and ever" (Rev 1:6). The new song sung by the elders and the creatures hallows the worthiness of Jesus (Rev 5:9). When the angelic hosts join the chorus, Jesus is again reckoned worthy to "receive power and wealth and wisdom and might and honor and glory and blessing" (Rev 5:12). The final song sung by every creature on earth culminates in worship being simultaneously given "to him who sits upon the throne and to the Lamb" (Rev 5:15; cf. 7:10; 12:10). Revelation legitimates and promotes the worship of Jesus and God—and the worship of Jesus as God—and it does so at the very places where God is worshiped and with the very language that is used to venerate God. Revelation shows how the revision of Jewish monotheism occurred in context of Christian worship where OT psalms originally addressed to God, under the inspiration of the Spirit, were redirected to Jesus (Hengel, 81-83). The omnipotence of the only God was fully shared with the only one worthy enough to open the scroll.

9. Apostolic Fathers.
The apostolic fathers* continue in the conceptual trajectory of the NT, even if some of the language and imagery is borrowed from Hellenistic philosophy.

9.1. Lexical Observations. The apostolic fathers refer to God in similar ways as the NT. This list includes God *(theos)*, "Lord" *(kyrios)*, "Father" *(patēr)*, "Most High" *(hypsistos)*, "Majesty" *(megalōsynē)*, "Almighty" *(pantokratōr)*, "Master" *(despotēs)* and "the Holy One" *(ho hagios)*. Additionally, the apostolic fathers employ some constructions not found in the NT. For example, "The Great Demiurge" *(ho megas dēmiourgos*, e.g., *1 Clem.* 20.11; *Diogn.* 8.7), "All Holy One" *(panagios*, e.g., *1 Clem.* 35.3; cf. 58.1), "Father of Truth" *(patri tēs alētheias*, e.g., *2 Clem.* 20.5), "God of the Powers" *(ho theos tōn dynameōn, Herm. Vis.* 1.3.4), "All Creating God" *(ho pantoktistēs . . . theos, Diogn.* 7.2).

9.2. Oneness of God. The apostolic fathers preserve the commitment to monotheism. The "Jews rightly claim to worship the one God of the universe" *(Diogn.* 3.2). God is the "true and only God" *(1 Clem.* 43.6 [or "Lord," depending on the textual reading]; 59.4). The beginning of faith is to "believe that God is one, who created all things and set them in order, and made out of what did not exist everything that is, and who contains all but is himself alone uncontained" *(Herm. Man.* 1.1; *1 Clem.* 46.6; *2 Clem.* 20.5). Further, this one God has revealed himself in and through Jesus his Son (Ign. *Magn.* 7.2; 8.2), and it is God alone who is able to do the good things through Jesus *(1 Clem.* 61.3). Ignatius* extends the exclusiveness to Jesus: Just as there is but one God, there is also only "one physician . . . God in man, one Jesus Christ" (Ign. *Magn.* 7.2; cf. Pol. *Phil.* 4.1).

9.3. God as Creator. The apostolic fathers also affirm the creatorship of this one God. God is the "Father and Creator of the whole universe" *(1 Clem.* 19.2; 60.1; *Diogn.* 7.2). He is the "Demiurge and Master of all" *(1 Clem.* 20.11; *Diogn.* 8.7). "By the word of his majesty he established everything" *(1 Clem.* 27.4). Everything in the world owes its order to him *(1 Clem.* 23.1). Barnabas makes explicit reference to the crea-

tion in seven days *(Barn.* 15.3). 2 Clement applies the creation of male and female to relationship between Christ and the church *(2 Clem.* 14.2). God is the one who "made humanity" *(1 Clem.* 7.3; *Did.* 1.2; *Barn.* 16.8; 19.2) and "created the world for humanity" *(Herm. Man.* 12.4.2; cf. *Did.* 10.3). God is the God of the "angels, the power and of all creation" *(Mart. Pol.* 14.1). God "created out of nothing the things that are" *(Herm. Man.* 1.1; *Herm. Sim.* 1.1.6). God created the world through Christ *(Barn.* 5.5; *Diogn.* 7). Both 1 Clement and Hermas describe in detail God's creative work (see *1 Clem.* 33; *Herm. Vis.* 1.3.4).

9.4. God as Ruler. God's ability to create and his sovereign power are closely related. Nothing is impossible for him to do *(1 Clem.* 27.2). He hears and sees everything *(1 Clem.* 28.1; Ign. *Magn.* 3.2). He wills creation into being (Ign. *Rom.* presc.). He needs nothing and asks for nothing *(1 Clem.* 52.1). God has a purpose (Ign. *Eph.* 3.2; Ign. *Rom.* 8.3; Ign. *Smyrn.* 6.2; Ign. *Pol.* 8.1) and will (Ign. *Eph.* presc. 20.1; Ign. *Trall.* 1.1) and exercises providence *(1 Clem.* 24.5). Resurrection was part of his providential plan and well within his creative powers *(1 Clem.* 24). He is Master of the universe *(1 Clem.* 8.2; 20.11). God rules the whole world *(Barn.* 21.5; cf. 5.5).

9.5. God as Judge. God's power extends to judgment. God has judged in the past *(1 Clem.* 17.5), judges in the present (e.g., *1 Clem.* 11.2; 21.1), and will execute judgment in the future *(Barn.* 5.7; 7.2; 15.5; *Did.* 11.11; Pol. *Phil.* 2.1; 6.2; *Herm. Man.* 1.7; 12.6.3; *Diogn.* 7.6). God opposes the proud (Ign. *Eph.* 5.3), and those who disobey will find eternal punishment *(2 Clem.* 6.7), the "dreadful torments of an unquenchable fire" *(2 Clem.* 17.7). Sinners will be burned *(Herm. Sim.* 4.1.2; 4.4.4).

9.6. The Grace and Mercy of God. God is also the source of grace (e.g., *1 Clem.* 1.1; 30.2; 65.2; Ign. *Smyrn.* 11.1; *Mart. Pol.* 20.3). God is compassionate *(1 Clem.* 23.1), merciful* (Ign. *Trall.* 12.3; *Barn.* 14.3), long-suffering (Ign. *Eph.* 11.1) and patient (Pol. *Phil.* 6.2). He has been and always will be kind, good, without anger and true *(1 Clem.* 19.3; *Diogn.* 8.8). "Who can describe the bond of God's love" *(1 Clem.* 49.2)? God hears the prayers of the righteous *(Barn.* 5.3) and rewards the righteous *(2 Clem.* 20.4). If anyone does what is right in God's sight he or she will enter the kingdom *(2 Clem.* 11.7).

10. Summary.

The NT and the apostolic fathers employ a wide range of vocabulary to refer to the one true God. All the later NT authors and many of the apostolic fathers employ *theos, kyrios* and *patēr* to designate God. But any common lexical pattern ends there. Of the other twenty-eight separate titles noted here, only four titles appear in two or more authors—*hypsistos* in Acts, Hebrews and *1 Clement; despotēs* in Acts, Revelation, *1 Clement, Barnabas,* Hermas,* Didache** and *Diognetus*; pantokratōr* in Revelation, *1 Clement, Martyrdom of Polycarp, Diognetus,* and *Hermas;* and *ho hagios* in Revelation and *1 Clement.* When the NT and the apostolic fathers speak, they tell of God's faithfulness, sovereignty, holiness, constancy, providence, forbearance, mercy, grace, love, anger and omnipotence; they explain God as Father, love and light; they write of a God who creates, builds, reveals, promises, saves, redeems, justifies, warns, disciplines, judges, vindicates and rewards.

Despite such wide-ranging vocabulary and imagery, the NT and apostolic fathers hold certain features of God in common (see Dahl, Bassler)—there is only one God who is the Creator and Giver of life, who rules, judges and mercifully redeems.

	Oneness	Creator of the World and the Giver of Life	Sovereign Ruler of the World	Righteous Judge	Gracious Merciful Redeemer
Acts	X	X	X	X	X
Hebrews	X	X	X	X	X
James	X		X	X	X
1 Peter		X	X	X	X
2 Peter		X		X	X
1, 2, 3 John				X	X
Jude	X			X	X
Revelation		X	X	X	X
Apostolic Fathers	X	X	X	X	X

The chart not only demonstrates commonality among the NT and apostolic fathers but also indicates the indebtedness of early Christianity to Jewish monotheism. The Jewish scriptures, the Christian OT, bequeathed to Christianity the identity of the one true God.

Christianity did, however, recast Jewish monotheism in light of Jesus' death, resurrection and installation to God's right hand (*see* Exaltation). Early on, Christians recognized the divine status of the risen Jesus, despite the high threshold that Jewish monotheism had established. Christians offered worship and prayers to Jesus (e.g., Acts, Revelation). Christians also began to call Jesus *theos* (e.g., Heb 1:8; 2 Pet 1:1; *2 Clem.* 1.1; 12.1; Ign. *Eph.* presc. 1.1; 7.2; 15.3; 17.2; 18.2; 19.3; Ign. *Trall.* 7.1; Ign. *Rom.* presc. [2x]; 3.3; 6.3; Ign. *Smyrn.* 1.1; Ign. *Pol.* 8.3). The trinitarian seeds planted within the later NT documents and the apostolic fathers (Acts 2:33; *1 Clem.* 46.6; 58.2; Ign. *Eph.* 9.1; 18.2; Ign. *Magn.* 8.2; 13.1, 2; Ign. *Trall.* 9; Ign. *Smyrn.* 1.1; *Mart. Pol.* 14.3; Pol. *Phil.* 3; *Did.* 7.1, 3) were destined to flower into the great confessions of the church. The later NT documents and the apostolic fathers demonstrate that the office of the one true God had been enlarged to include Jesus as worthy of worship and service.

See also CHRISTIANITY AND JUDAISM: PARTINGS OF THE WAYS; CHRISTOLOGY; HOLY SPIRIT; LORD; WORSHIP AND LITURGY.

BIBLIOGRAPHY. J. M. Bassler, "God (NT)," *ABD* (1992) 2:1049-55; R. J. Bauckham, "Jesus, Worship of," *ADB* (1992) 3:812-19; idem, "The Worship of Jesus in Apocalyptic Christianity," *NTS* 27 (1981) 323-31; W. Bousset, *Kyrios Christos* (Nashville: Abingdon, 1970); A. Chester and R. P. Martin, *The Theology of the Letters of James, Peter and Jude* (Cambridge: Cambridge University Press, 1994); H. Conzelmann, *The Theology of St. Luke* (Philadelphia: Fortress, 1961); C. H. Cosgrove, "The Divine *Dei* in Luke-Acts," *NovT* 26 (1984) 168-90; N. A. Dahl, "The Neglected Factor in New Testament Theology," in *Jesus the Christ: The Historical Origins of Christological Doctrine,* ed. D. H. Juel (Minneapolis: Fortress, 1991) 153-63; N. A. Dahl and A. F. Segal, "Philo and the Rabbis on the Name of God," *JSJ* 9 (1978) 1-28; J. Daniélou, *The Theology of Jewish Christianity* (London: Darton, Longman & Todd, 1964); P. H. Davids, *The Epistle of James* (NIGTC; Grand Rapids: Eerdmans, 1982); C. J. Davis, *The Name and Way of the Lord: Old Testament Themes; New Testament Christology* (JSNTSup 129; Sheffield: Sheffeld Academic Press, 1996); M. Dibelius and H. Greeven, *James* (Herm; Philadephia: Fortress, 1976); J. D. G. Dunn, *The Partings of the Ways* (Philadelphia: Trinity Press International, 1991); J. H. Elliott, *A Home for the Homeless: A Sociological Exegesis of 1 Peter* (Philadelphia: Fortress, 1981); R. M. Grant, *The Early Christian Doctrine of God* (Charlottesville, VA: University of Virginia Press, 1966); idem, *Gods and the One God* (Philadelphia: Westminster, 1986); G. Guthrie, *The Structure of Hebrews: A Text-Linguistic Analysis* (NovTSup 73:

Leiden: E. J. Brill, 1994); M. J. Harris, *Jesus as God: The New Testament Use of Theos in Reference to Jesus* (Grand Rapids: Eerdmans, 1992); A. E. Harvey, *Jesus and the Constraints of History* (Philadelphia: Westminster, 1982); M. Hengel, "Hymns and Christology" in *Between Jesus and Paul: Studies in the History of Earliest Christianity* (Philadelphia: Fortress, 1983) 78-96; L. W. Hurtado, *One God, One Lord: Early Christian Devotion and Ancient Jewish Monotheism* (Philadelphia: Fortress, 1988); J. N. D. Kelly, *Early Christian Doctrines* (rev. ed.; New York: Harper & Row, 1978); W. L. Lane, *Hebrews* (WBC; Dallas: Word, 1991); R. MacMullen, *Christianizing the Roman Empire* A.D. *100-400* (New Haven, CT: Yale University Press, 1984); A. C. McGiffert, *The God of the Early Christians* (New York: Charles Scribner's Sons, 1924); I. H. Marshall, *Luke: Historian and Theologian* (Grand Rapids: Zondervan, 1970); T. N. D. Mettinger, *In Search of God: The Meaning and Message of the Everlasting Names* (Philadelphia: Fortress, 1988); R. L. Mowery, "Direct Statements Concerning God's Activity in Acts," *SBLSP* (1990) 196-211; idem, "Lord, God, and Father: Theological Language in Luke-Acts," *SBLSP* (1995) 82-101; F. Mussner, " 'Direkte' und 'Indirekte' Christologie im Jakobusbrief," *Catholica* 24 (1970) 111-16; idem, *Jakobusbrief* (4th ed.; HTKNT; Freiburg: Herders, 1981); V. H. Neufeld, *The Earliest Christian Confessions* (NTTS 5; Leiden: E. J. Brill, 1963); C. C. Newman, "Acts" in *A Complete Literary Guide to the Bible,* ed. L. Ryken and T. Longman III (Grand Rapids: Zondervan, 1993) 436-44; M. C. Parsons, "Son and High Priest: A Study in the Christology of Hebrews," *EvQ* 60 (1988) 195-218; R. I. Pervo, *Profit with Delight: The Literary Genre of the Acts of the Apostles* (Philadelphia: Fortress, 1987); P. Rainbow, "Jewish Monotheism as the Matrix for New Testament Christology," *NovT* 33 (1991) 78-91; A. F. Segal, *Two Powers in Heaven* (SJLA 25; Leiden: E. J. Brill, 1978); R. B. Sloan, "The Christology of James," *Criswell Theological Review* 1 (1986) 2-29; E. Stauffer, "θεό," *TDNT* 3:65-122; L. Stuckenbruck, *"Do Not Worship Me, Worship God!": The Problem of Angel Veneration in Early Judaism and Angelmorphic Aspects in the Christology of the Apocalypse of John* (WUNT; Tübingen: Mohr-Siebeck, 1995); A. W. Wainwright, *The Trinity in the New Testament* (London: SPCK, 1962); N. T. Wright, *The New Testament and the People of God* (Minneapolis: Fortress, 1992).   C. C. Newman

GOD-FEARERS. *See* DIASPORA JUDAISM; FEAR.

GOSPEL

The *euangelizomai* ("I proclaim") word group refers in the apostolic and subapostolic literature to the good news of salvation* in Jesus, not to a written gospel (*see DPL,* Gospel). It is not until Marcion* and Justin Martyr that *euangelion* ("gospel, good news") is used to refer to a written Gospel, though there are hints of such usage in the *Didache.**

1. The *Euangel-* Word Group
2. The Verb *Euangelizō*
3. The Noun *Euangelion*
4. The Noun *Euangelistēs*
5. The Verb *Proeuangelizomai*

1. The *Euangel-* Word Group.

Neither any single member of the *euangel-* word group nor all its members taken together can represent what the early NT and other early Christian literature meant by "the gospel."

An examination of the *euangel-* word group gives an idea of what Christians until about A.D. 150 understood by the term *gospel.* Where they occur in the later NT and the writings of the apostolic fathers,* the words belonging to this group refer to the grace* of God* in Christ* rather than to a written gospel (for helpful summaries see Friedrich; Strecker).

2. The Verb *Euangelizō.*

The verb *euangelizō* ("proclaim [glad tidings]"), with the thing proclaimed expressed, is used thirteen times in the later NT: ten times in Acts,* twice in 1 Peter* and once in Revelation (*see* Revelation, Book of). Yet on every occasion, although the explicit wording varies, some aspect of the Christian message is being proclaimed. In Acts Jesus is proclaimed as Messiah by Peter and the apostles* (Acts 5:42; see Barrett, 1:301) in spite of rough treatment and orders from the Sanhedrin to refrain from doing so. Similar messages are attributed to those who proclaimed the good news about Jesus (the Lord,* Christ) and his fulfillment of what God had promised (Acts 8:12, 35; 10:36; 11:20; 13:32; 17:18). When Acts portrays Christians proclaiming "the word," whether or not (Acts 8:4; 15:35) the expression is further modified by a Greek defining genitive such as in the phrase "the word of the Lord," it means that they were expounding the good news of what God had done in Christ. The contents of the proclamations in 1 Peter (1 Pet 1:12, 25) and Revelation (Rev 10:7) are not made as precise, but their meaning is clear enough (though the sense of 1 Pet 4:6 is still uncertain; see commentaries). The grace of God in Christ is at issue.

Euangelizō also appears in absolute form— that is, without an express indication of the thing proclaimed—five times in Acts (Acts 8:25, 40; 14:7, 15, 21; 16:10), twice in Hebrews (Heb 4:2, 6), once in 1 Peter (1 Pet 4:6) and once in Revelation (Rev 14:6). The passage in Revelation is a special case; there is present an accusative object of the thing to be proclaimed, but it does not in itself clarify the passage further (see 3.1 below). In all these cases context makes it plain that what is being proclaimed is the grace of God in Jesus. It is apparent that *euangelizō* refers to proclamation of the Christian message whether or not the content of the proclamation is expressed explicitly.

Although this verb occurs twenty-two times in the later NT, it is found only twice in the postapostolic writings and then only in *1 Clement*. Where it does occur it appears in proximity, the first time with the content of the proclamation indicated and the second time with it excluded. We are told that the apostles were evangelized or received the gospel from the Lord Jesus Christ (with no express indication of the content of the proclamation; *1 Clem.* 42.1) and that, fully in line with the will of God, they then proclaimed that the kingdom of God was imminent (*1 Clem.* 42.3; *see* Kingdom of God). The grammatical possibilities for the verb *euangelizō* have not here changed from what was available to the NT writers. In the postapostolic period the word still refers to the Christian glad tidings.

3. The Noun *Euangelion*.

The spread of occurrences of the noun *euangelion* ("gospel, good tidings") is different from that of the verb *euangelizō*. The noun is found only four times in the later NT, in Acts (twice), 1 Peter (once) and Revelation (once); but it appears six times (in more than one gender) in Josephus* and several times in a variety of writings of the apostolic fathers.

3.1. Later New Testament. Each time the noun occurs in the NT it is accompanied by another word or words that modify its meaning slightly. In his speech to the Jerusalem council Peter

remembers that in the early days he had been divinely appointed to carry "the word of the gospel [good news] to the Gentiles" (Acts 15:7; *see* Gentiles). Paul tells the Ephesian elders that he values above his own life the ministry* he had from the Lord to bear witness to "the gospel [good news] of God's grace" (Acts 20:24). At 1 Peter 4:17 the author wonders about the heaviness of the judgment* that will rest on those who do not obey the "gospel of God," with a more favorable response indicated in 1 Peter 4:6 (see commentaries). John the revelator speaks of the "eternal gospel" that the angel* flying in the sky had to proclaim (Rev 14:6). *Euangelion* in 1 Peter 4:17 probably stresses the demands of the gospel (see Davids, 171-72), as opposed to its delights ("good news"), and in Revelation 14:6 judgment is again in view, a fact that also colors the meaning of "gospel." In the two passages from Acts, however, there is every reason for allowing the word its usual meaning in Acts of "good news."

3.2. Josephus. The substantive occurs four times in Josephus (usually given the feminine form *hē euangelia;* Josephus *Ant.* 18.6.10 §229; Josephus *J.W.* 2.17.4 §420; 4.10.6 §618; 4.11.5 §656), all in the sense of "good [welcome] news." Josephus uses it ironically in the phrase *deinon euangelion* ("terrible tidings") in one place (Josephus *J.W.* 2.17.4 §420), but the ironic insertion of the adjective adapts *euangelion* to its context, though it does not alter its basic sense.

3.3. Apostolic Fathers. Subapostolic usage, in contrast to earlier (NT) Christian literature, requires a more lengthy discussion. It is frequently acknowledged that Marcion was the first to have used *euangelion* to designate a written Gospel. That is how he identified the purified and harmonized account of the life and ministry of Jesus that he promulgated.

Was this use of *euangelion* prepared for gradually in the literature that went before it, or did it appear all at once? H. Koester has insisted on the latter because neither the NT nor postapostolic literature before Marcion can be construed as using it for anything like a written gospel. The usage of the later NT has been discussed; in the apostolic fathers, when the word is singular and where context suggests nothing else, it is clear that postapostolic usage is continuous with NT usage. That is, "gospel" evokes what was proclaimed rather than any canonical or otherwise written Gospel (Ign.

Phld. 5.1, 2 [twice]; 9.2; *Mart. Pol.* 4.1; 19.1; 22.1). Similarly, in the difficult passage (Ign. *Phld.* 8.2) in which Ignatius* refers to the "charters *(archeioi)* of the gospel," there is no indication that the written gospel is being referred to.

But though several passages from the apostolic fathers have been adduced to disprove Koester's assertion, R. H. Gundry rightly asserts that they are all patient of explanations that do not contradict Koester. Instead they point to the modified contention that while "subapostolic literature borrows from books that became canonical" (*2 Clem.* 8.5; Ign. *Smyrn.* 5.1; 7.2; *Did.* 8.2; 11.3; 15.3, 4), they do not refer to any of these books by the appellation *euangelion* (Gundry, 322-25). Except for *2 Clement* 8.5, which may have been written somewhat after Marcion, and *Didache* 11.3, Gundry is persuasive. These two passages, however, are not proved conclusively to be referring to an oral gospel, though the usage elsewhere in the *Didache* does suggest that is the case in the second of the two passages.

4. The Noun *Euangelistēs*.

Euangelistēs ("proclaimer [of the Christian message]," "evangelist") does not occur often outside of Christian writing and appears in our literature only once. It refers to one who carries out the ministry of a Christian preacher (cf. 2 Tim 4:5). Acts 21:8 speaks of Philip* the *euangelistēs,* one of the seven "deacons" (Acts 6:5) who at that time lived in Caesarea and entertained Paul and his companions on their way from Antioch* to Jerusalem.* Philip had done missionary work at the time of the great persecution* (Acts 8:4-8, 26-40), and repeated activity in propagation of the Christian tidings may have prompted the designation *euangelistēs*.

5. The Verb *Proeuangelizomai*.

The verb *proeuangelizomai* ("proclaim the gospel [good news] in advance") occurs only once in the NT, in Galatians 3:8, and it does not appear in the apostolic fathers.

See also EVANGELISM IN THE EARLY CHURCH; GRACE; KERYGMA AND DIDACHE; REDEMPTION; SALVATION.

BIBLIOGRAPHY. C. K. Barrett, *A Critical and Exegetical Commentary on the Acts of the Apostles* (2 vols.; ICC; Edinburgh: T & T Clark, 1994); P. H. Davids, *The First Epistle of Peter* (NICNT; Grand Rapids: Eerdmans, 1990); G. Friedrich,

"εὐαγγελίζομαι κτλ," *TDNT* 2:707-37; R. H. Gundry, "*EUANGELION:* How Soon A Book?" *JBL* 115 (1996) 321-25; H. Koester, "From the Kerygma-Gospel to Written Gospels," *NTS* 35 (1989) 361-81; F. R. McCurley and J. Reumann, *Witness of the Word: A Biblical Theology of the Gospel* (Philadelphia: Fortress, 1986); G. Strecker, "εὐαγγελίζω, εὐαγγελιστής," *EDNT* 2:69-70; idem, "εὐαγγέλιον," *EDNT* 2:70-74.

A. Casurella

GOSPEL OF PETER. *See* PETER, GOSPEL OF.

GOSPEL OF THOMAS. *See* THOMAS, GOSPEL OF.

GRACE

Grace, often described as the unmerited favor of God,* is spoken of and alluded to in the earliest Christian literature by the word *charis* ("grace"). It is difficult to discourse on all the aspects of grace in early Christian literature, because there is a sense in which the entire NT and much early Christian writing is about the grace of God in Christ* and its outworking in the believer. This is so whether or not the Greek word *charis* is employed in a particular passage. Nevertheless *charis* does mean "grace," and with the preceding caveat this article explores this English concept as represented by that Greek word (see helpful summaries in Berger; Conzelmann).

1. Heavenly Grace
2. Miscellaneous Uses

1. Heavenly Grace.

Charis is most often used to refer to some form of heavenly favor shown to the human race, and this use of the word *charis* is considered first.

1.1. Grace **(Charis Unmodified).** On occasion *charis* appears undefined and without a modifier to indicate the heavenly grace from God that incorporates people into the community of the redeemed and empowers them. This is probably the way it should be interpreted in Acts 4:33 (cf. Barrett, 1:254). It is surely the understanding behind the descriptions of Stephen* as "full of grace" (Acts 6:8) and the Christians in Achaia who had become believers "through grace" (Acts 18:27). Grace, rather than dietary laws (*see* Food, Food Laws), is also laid down by the author of Hebrews* as the appropriate strengthener of the heart (Heb 13:9). Usually, however, when the NT speaks of this sort of heavenly grace, *charis* is explicitly defined as God's grace or the grace of the Lord Jesus Christ.

In the post-NT period *charis* assumes a slightly different nuance. It is still possible to speak of the grace by which God can bring us to his kingdom (*Mart. Pol.* 20.2) and to speak of individuals as filled with some aspect of grace (Polycarp* in *Mart. Pol.* 12.1). But there is a different feel about the word, so that one begins to understand grace to comprise an aspect of the present Christian order of salvation.* Thus the way of Judaism* is contrasted with grace (Ign. *Magn.* 8.1), and the prophets* are portrayed as having been in tune with Jesus, from whom they received inspiration, rather than with their own Israelite people (Ign. *Magn.* 8.2; *Barn.* 5.6). Christians are exhorted to be in love with the present order of grace (Ign. *Eph.* 11.1) and to advance in this grace (Ign. *Pol.* 1.2). It is an extension of this use of the word that takes grace to represent something like the whole economy of heaven* and opposes it to this undesirable world* (*Did.* 10.6).

1.2. Grace of God. The phrase "grace of God" becomes in Acts* a way of referring to the merciful action of God in Christ by which people become believers. Barnabas, for instance, pursues a fact-finding mission to Syrian Antioch* for the Jerusalem* church* and discovers that Gentiles* are also recipients of this grace (Acts 11:23). It is in this sense that the Christians of Pisidian Antioch are admonished to continue in the grace of God (Acts 13:43; cf. Acts 20:32) and Paul was set apart to testify to God's grace (Acts 20:24). The phrase is also used to refer to the loving favor of God (Acts 14:3, 26; 15:40). *Charis,* as the kind and salvific action of God in redeeming and strengthening people, also occurs in the General Epistles (Heb 2:9; 12:15; Jas 4:6; 1 Pet 5:5, 10, 12). Grace motivates the gifts of God, which believers are admonished to use to serve each other (1 Pet 4:10; Goppelt, 301-2). The grace of God is also behind the encouragement offered by 1 Peter* to the Christians of Asia Minor in their straitened circumstances (1 Pet 5:12; Davids, 197-201).

For the apostolic fathers* as for the NT writers, the originator of grace is God; therefore the phrase "grace of God" occurs from time to time. Those who share the faith* with others are known as the ministers of the grace of God (*1 Clem.* 8.1), and those to whom God has given grace are holy* and sanctified (*1 Clem.* 30.3). From this grace come love* (*1 Clem.* 50.3) and at the necessary times power (*1 Clem.* 55.3), steadfastness (Ign. *Rom.* greeting) and endurance* (Ign. *Smyrn.* 11.1).

1.3. Grace of the Lord Jesus Christ. Twice the NT refers specifically to the grace of Jesus (Acts 15:11; 2 Pet 3:18). The former reference is part of Peter's address to the Jerusalem council and argues against an imposition of law* on Gentile believers because all, Jew and Gentile alike, have access to salvation "through the grace of the Lord Jesus." The latter reference is part of the closing greeting of 2 Peter* and exhorts the recipients to grow in what R. J. Bauckham (337-38) refers to as "the need for progress in the Christian life."

The apostolic fathers speak of salvation and redemption* as by the grace of our Lord Jesus Christ, using some form of that name and title (Ign. *Phld.* 8.1; 11.1; *Ep. Apos.* 6). This grace enables those who have it to endure tortures (*Mart. Pol.* 2.3). But those who have erroneous notions about the grace of Jesus Christ are opposed to the mind of God and deficient in love (Ign. *Smyrn.* 6.2).

1.4. Related Uses. So far we have spoken of occurrences of *charis* that refer directly to some form of heavenly grace. Now we turn to instances that adapt or modify this use or make the heavenly connection less direct. Several times (Heb 13:25; 1 Pet 1:2; 2 Pet 1:2; 2 Jn 3; Rev 1:4) the word occurs in salutations and benedictions in which it refers to the gracious action of God himself (see Lane, 2:571 on Heb 13:25 and Brown, 681-82 on the assertion of 2 Jn 3). This use continues in the postbiblical period (*1 Clem.* 65.2; Ign. *Smyrn.* 9.2; 12.2; 13.2; *Mart. Pol.* 22.2; *Barn.* 21.9; *Ep. Apos. 1; cf. Ign. Smyrn.* 12.1). In these passages it is akin to usage in the greetings of the Pauline epistles.

Hebrews 4:16 uses *charis* twice. Once it is used absolutely and represents the practical application of the mercy* that it defines and renames. The other time it is in the phrase "throne of grace" and denominates the source of the mercy and grace that come from God; in this sense it is an almost Jewish way of referring to God without mentioning God by name.

Hebrews 10:29 denounces the apostate* who has, among other things, insulted "the Spirit of grace," the Spirit who conveys grace (cf. Lane, 2:293-95).

In the postapostolic period the phrase "grace of" is completed by other things than "God" and "Lord Jesus Christ," but the citations tend to relate to one or more aspects of the order of salvation. As a result *Diognetus* * refers to the faith as the "grace of the church" (*Diogn.* 11.6; 11.7); Clement (*see* Clement of Rome) speaks of the "grace of repentance" (*1 Clem.* 7.4) and, in resisting schisms, of the "Spirit of grace" (*1 Clem.* 46.6); and the *Epistle of Barnabas** mentions the "grace of the gift of the Spirit" (*Barn.* 1.2). In *Diognetus* there is also mentioned a "grace of the Prophets," which the author distinguishes from the Law (*Diogn.* 11.6).

2. Miscellaneous Uses.

A few times *charis* carries a sense best translated into English with some word other than "grace." It is not that the Greek word is inappropriate in the original; it is that *charis* and *grace* do not coincide exactly in semantic range. Thus it is appropriate to understand this word in 1 Peter 2:19-20 to refer to it being creditworthy for a slave* to endure beating for right behavior but not creditworthy to endure it for doing wrong. Similarly, while it is not wrong to understand 1 Peter 3:7 to speak of husband and wife as sharing the grace of life, it is better to understand them as sharing the gift of eternal life, that is, the life of heaven (Davids, 123; Goppelt, 227-28). In Hebrews 12:28 the phrase that includes *charis* is best translated "let us be thankful" or "let us give thanks" (cf. Lane, 2:483-84).

Frequently, however, *charis* is used of goodwill or favor. This takes place where it is a matter of people seeking and granting favors to each other, as in the cases of Felix or Festus and the Jews (Acts 24:27; 25:3, 9), or of one person having the goodwill of another, as in the case of Joseph and Pharaoh (Acts 7:10). *Charis* is also used of David winning God's favor (Acts 7:46). There is some discussion over the proper translation of Acts 2:47, but T. D. Andersen argues persuasively that the verse ought to be translated "praising God and having goodwill towards all the people."

See also DEATH OF CHRIST; GOD; GOSPEL; LOVE; MERCY; REDEMPTION; RIGHTEOUSNESS; SALVATION.

BIBLIOGRAPHY. T. D. Andersen, "The Meaning of ἔχοντες χάριν πρός in Acts 2:47," *NTS* 34 (1988) 604-10; C. K. Barrett, *A Critical and Exegetical Commentary on the Acts of the Apostles* (2 vols.; ICC; Edinburgh: T & T Clark, 1994) vol. 1; R. J. Bauckham, *Jude, 2 Peter* (WBC; Waco, TX: Word, 1983); K. Berger, "χάρις," *EDNT* 3:457-60; R. E. Brown, *The Epistles of John* (AB; Garden City, NY: Doubleday, 1982); H. Conzelmann, "χάρις κτλ," *TDNT* 9:387-402; P. H. Davids, *The First Epistle of Peter* (NICNT; Grand Rapids: Eerdmans, 1990); L. Goppelt, *A Commentary on 1 Peter,* ed. F. Hahn (Grand Rapids: Eerdmans, 1993); W. L. Lane, *Hebrews* (2 vols.; WBC; Dallas: Word, 1991); J. Moffatt, *Grace in the New Testament* (New York: Long & Smith, 1932); T. F. Torrance, *The Doctrine of Grace in the Apostolic Fathers* (Grand Rapids: Eerdmans, 1959). A. Casurella

GUESTS. *See* HOSPITALITY.

H

HALLELUJAH. *See* LITURGICAL ELEMENTS.

HAUSTAFEL. *See* HOUSEHOLD CODES.

HEALING, ILLNESS

Various forms of healing practices were widely used in the ancient Mediterranean world. The distinctive item in our literature is that healing is principally through the name of or faith in Jesus. The references are concentrated in Acts* but also occur in James,* 1 John and Revelation (*see* John, Letters of; Revelation, Book of), as well as the largely metaphorical references to healing in the apostolic fathers.*

1. Healing in the Ancient Mediterranean World
2. Healing in the New Testament
3. Healing in the Second Century

1. Healing in the Ancient Mediterranean World.
In the ancient Mediterranean world in which the NT was born, there were multiple means of seeking healing. First, there were a number of healing cults with their shrines, such as those of Asclepsis (Asklepios) and Isis. Second, there were various magical means that one could use individually or in combination, such as spells, amulets, special oils and sacred inscriptions. Third, there were the various physicians, trained to some degree in a combination of the healing arts of the Greek (e.g., Hippocrates) or Roman (Celsus *De medicina*) type. While this typology of miracle* (involving the gods), magic* and medicine (Kee 1986) is descriptively helpful, in practice the lines were blurred, with practitioners using a variety of means and ill individuals selecting eclectically from whatever practitioners were available (e.g., Pliny *Nat. Hist.* 25; 27-28). Among these practitioners were, on occasion, charismatic wandering miracle workers, such as Apollonius of Tyana (Philostratus *Vit. Ap.*), who taught philosophical or religious reform along with working healing through a variety of medicinal or magical means. They related their abilities to their relationship with the gods (Apollonius started out in the temple of Asclepsis; *see* Religions) rather than to wisdom* derived from other sources. In certain cases they were themselves viewed as in some sense divine.

Although the sources we have cited are all from the non-Judaic world, a similar pattern would hold true in Second Temple and rabbinic Judaisms.* The major difference is that of a strong underlying monotheism in Jewish practices. This means that, drawing on the OT traditions of Elijah and Elisha and a growing tradition about Solomon and his wonder-working wisdom, in Judaism charismatic miracle workers are either prophets* or sages such as Honi the Circle-Drawer or Hannina ben Dosa, who lived in the first centuries B.C. and A.D. respectively. While these two used mainly prayer,* others in all branches of Judaism used medicine and magic as well, with the understanding that the effectiveness of both was due to the action of God.*

2. Healing in the New Testament.
While healing is mentioned in all types of NT literature (*see* DJG, Healing; DPL, Healing, Illness), we will focus on three types of NT literature within the scope of this volume, each of which has a significant contribution to make.

2.1. Acts. The pattern of Acts is that of "the miracle-working messenger" much in the fashion of the OT prophet (Reimer, 54). The general pattern is that the messenger is called for or shows up and heals through a word of command or prayer, with or without touch. In two instances healing is apparently worked through intermediate means (Peter's shadow, Acts 5:15; Paul's handkerchiefs or aprons, Acts 19:11-12). Other than these examples (where the objects serve as a means of contact with the messenger), there is no use of medical or magical means. Given the close connection between healing (i.e., signs and wonders*) and the Spirit (*see* Holy Spirit) in Acts (2:43; 5:12, both of which follow passages that speak of Spirit-filling), the basic model appears to be that of the OT wonder-working prophet, such as Elisha, for the stress in Acts 2 is that the Spirit of prophecy* has been poured out.

This pattern is emphasized by the fact that in Acts alone in the NT (with the possible exception of 1 Cor 11:30) there is some divine causation of illness. Most illnesses are mentioned without any reference to their ultimate causation (e.g., when in Acts 20:7-12 Eutychus falls, only natural causes such as lamps and the length of the discourse are mentioned). The people are simply sick or dead (in the case of Dorcas, Acts 9:36-43). However, in three cases illness or death is caused by God or his agent (Acts 5:1-11; 12:20-23; 13:6-12; cf. Davids 1990, 218-20). One of these uses an angel and two use divine messengers, functioning much as Elijah and Elisha do in the OT (*see* OT in Acts).

In Acts, then, healing is a function of prophetic miracle-working messengers (the Twelve, the Seven, Paul*). The messengers make it clear that they act "in the name of" Jesus and thus that his power* and authority* accomplish the healing. Given the presence of charismatic miracle workers in the Mediterranean world, this explanation was absolutely necessary. In giving it they separate themselves from magic and the possible attribution of the deed to another god or even their own divinity (Acts 14:8-18). The miracles* serve primarily to give divine attestation to the messenger and his message.

2.2. James and 1 John. In both James* and 1 John* instructions about healing prayer appear in the closing of the letter where a Hellenistic reader would expect a health wish (Jas 5:13-18; 1 Jn 5:14-17). In both there is one named cause of illness, for in James some but not all illness is traced to sin* (Jas 5:15-16; note the conditional clause), while in 1 John only illness caused by sin is in view. The issue there is the nature of the sin: whether it is mortal (i.e., leading to death) or not (1 Jn 5:17). At this point the two epistles diverge.

In 1 John the illness is never mentioned, so it is not clear whether physical or spiritual death is in view, although in view of the use of "life" and "death" in the rest of the letter (e.g., 1 Jn 3:14; 5:11-12) the latter is more likely (Marshall, Scholer, Smalley). The passage starts with a general exhortation on prayer, which is then applied to praying for a fellow believer who sins a nonmortal sin. In the case of a mortal sin, prayer is not required (although perhaps not prohibited either), since it will not be effective. Furthermore, whether this healing is spiritual or physical, all readers of the letter are addressed with the command to pray for appropriate healing.

The passage in 1 John is paralleled in reverse order in James 5:16-18, where all community members are addressed and instructed to confess their sins to one another and pray for one another; then a general exhortation on prayer is given. The example of Elijah, the basis of this exhortation, rests not on his being a prophet but on his being a human "just like us" who prayed and suffered* for his faith. Prayer for healing is a communal activity.

James 5:14-15, however, adds a new dimension to healing in that in at least some cases (perhaps when the person is too ill to come to community meetings, if there is any intention to differentiate this from Jas 5:16) the sick person calls the leaders of the community, the elders, to him or her. They use a specific means, anointing with oil (also mentioned in Mark 6:13; *see* Anointing). The focus of the rite, however, is not on the oil but on "the name of the Lord." This is confirmed in the following verse where it is "the prayer of faith" which heals and specifically "the Lord" who "raises [the sick person] up." In the process of this prayer the responsible sins, if there are any, will be forgiven.

As in Acts the focus is on the divine source of healing, with the human agent serving as an intermediary. Yet now the picture is not that of a miracle-working messenger coming to town, but that of the mutual care of the whole Christian community or a specific authority vested in the leaders of that community. In either case healing is viewed as an ongoing internal activity of the church,* not as something that attests the messengers of the gospel* to outsiders.

2.3. Revelation. In Revelation no one is described as ill and then healed. However, the book contains several references to eschatological* healing. In Revelation 3:17-18 illness and anointing with salve are used as a metaphor for the lukewarm state of the church and its remedy in Christ.* In Revelation 22:2 the leaves of the tree of life bring "healing to the nations," although what this healing consists of is never described. It is only in Revelation 7:16-17 (with reference to those coming out of the great tribulation*) and Revelation 21:4 (with reference to the inhabitants of the new Jerusalem*) that physical healing is clearly included in the description of heavenly existence. Believers may have suffered pain and gone through sickness on earth, but in the resurrection "God will wipe away every tear" from them; pain and death will have been banished. There is no human agent of this healing; God (and possibly the Lamb* in Rev 7) is its only agent, reminding the readers that ultimate healing awaits the eschaton.

3. Healing in the Second Century.
By the time of the apostolic fathers, healing imagery is usually applied only to spiritual sickness. Thus Hermas frequently refers to the "healing of the former sins" (e.g., *Herm. Sim.* 8.11.1). Likewise sickness is a metaphor for spiritual weakness (*Herm. Vis.* 3.11.4). *Barnabas* and *2 Clement* both accepted medical practice (e.g., *Barn.* 9.6), but the OT references to healing are interpreted as metaphors for repentance or other spiritual healing (*2 Clem.* 9.7). When Jesus is referred to as a physician, it is with reference to these spiritual ills (Ign. *Eph.* 7.2; *Diogn.* 9.6).

In Hermas* there is a close relationship between illness and sin. On the one hand those who wander away from God are punished with, among other things, illness (*Herm. Sim.* 6.3.4), while on the other physical suffering heals sins (*Herm. Sim.* 9.28.5; cf. *Herm. Sim.* 7.4, which refers to penance). On a more prosaic level Hermas notes that some get ill due to eating too much, while others get ill due to their lack of food; therefore people should share (*Herm. Vis.* 3.9.3).

In this literature we never see examples of specific prayers for the sick, but there is concern for them. In the final prayer of *1 Clement* (*1 Clem.* 59.4) we read, "We beseech you, Master, to . . . heal the sick." Although the prayer recognizes that God does heal the sick, we have no idea whether Clement's* community did more than pray such general prayers nor how, assuming that they did do more, their belief was reflected in pastoral practice.

Later, in Justin and other apologists, we find references to prayers for healing, although often the healing is exorcistic: "We do continually beseech God by Jesus Christ to preserve us from the demons which are hostile to the worship of God, and whom we of old time served, in order that, after our conversion by him to God, we may be blameless" (Justin *Dial. Tryph.* 30; cf. 85; *Apol. II* 2.6). There is, however, an awareness of gifts of healing, which appear to be separate from exorcism (Justin *Dial. Tryph.* 39).

See also ANOINTING; MIRACLES IN ACTS; SIGNS AND WONDERS.

BIBLIOGRAPHY. D. E. Aune, "Magic in Early Christianity," *ANRW* 2.23.2 (1980) 1510-16; E. Buck, "Healing in the New Testament," *Consensus* 17 no. 2 (1991) 63-77; P. H. Davids, *The Epistle of James* (NIGTC; Grand Rapids: Eerdmans, 1982); idem, "Sickness and Suffering in the New Testament" in *Wrestling with Dark Angels*, ed. C. P. Wagner, F. D. Pennoyer (Ventura, CA: Regal, 1990) 213-37; H. C. Kee, *Medicine, Miracle and Magic in New Testament Times* (Cambridge: Cambridge University Press, 1986); idem, *Miracle in the Early Christian World* (New Haven, CT: Yale University Press, 1983); I. Jacob and W. Jacob, eds., *The Healing Past: Pharmaceuticals in the Biblical and Rabbinic World* (SAM 7; Leiden: E. J. Brill, 1993); I. H. Marshall, *The Epistles of John* (NICNT; Grand Rapids: Eerdmans, 1978); R. P. Martin, *James* (WBC; Waco, TX: Word, 1988); R. E. A. Palmer, "Paean and Paenists of Serapis and the Flavian Emperors," in *Nomodeiktes: Greek Studies in Honor of Martin Ostwald*, ed. R. M. Rosen and J. Farrell (Ann Arbor, MI: University of Michigan Press, 1993) 355-65; C. Pickar, "Is Anyone Sick Among You?" *CBQ* 7 (1945) 165-74; J. J. Pilch, "Sickness and Healing in Luke-Acts," in *The Social World of Luke-Acts*, ed. J. H. Neyrey (Peabody, MA: Hendrickson, 1991); idem, "Understanding Healing in the Social World of Early Christianity," *BTB* 22 (1992) 26-33; A. Reimer, *Divine Healing Rites in the New Testament: Diversity and Unity* (Vancouver, BC: unpublished M.C.S. thesis, Regent College, 1994); D. M. Scholer, "Sins Within and Sins Without: An Interpretation of 1 John 5:16-17" in *Current Issues in Biblical and Patristic Interpretation*, ed. G. F. Hawthorne (Grand Rapids: Eerdmans, 1975) 230-46; S. S. Smalley, *1, 2, 3 John* (WBC; Waco, TX: Word, 1984); D. L. Tiede, *The Charismatic*

Figure as Miracle Worker (Missoula, MT: Scholars Press, 1972); M. F. Unger, "Divine Healing," *BSac* 128 (1971) 234-44; K. Warrington, "Anointing with Oil and Healing," *EPTA Bulletin* 12 (1993) 5-22; idem, "Some Observations on James 5:13-18," *EPTA Bulletin* 8 (1989) 160-77.

P. H. Davids

HEART. *See* PSYCHOLOGY.

HEAVEN, NEW HEAVENS

Heaven signifies both the visible realm of sun, moon and stars as well as the invisible realm of God's dwelling to which Christ has ascended. In this second sense heaven is also an expression of the believer's hope for an enduring homeland and inheritance in the presence of God. Both this awareness of God's realm as the site of eternal reward (showing the value of worldly gains to be inferior) and the hope for a "new heaven and new earth" (showing the duration of worldly benefits to be short-lived) assisted early Christians to accept the temporal costs and self-denial of following the way of Jesus for the sake of eternal gain.

1. Jewish and Greco-Roman Background
2. Hebrews
3. Acts and the General Epistles
4. Revelation
5. Apostolic Fathers

1. Jewish and Greco-Roman Background.

1.1. Jewish Background. The Jewish Scriptures speak of God* as Creator of the heavens (Gen 1:1; Ps 33:6). Authors began to differentiate between heaven as the visible firmament of the stars and celestial bodies and a higher heaven that was the dwelling of God, referred to as the "heaven of heavens" (Deut 10:14; 1 Kings 8:27; Ps 148:4; 3 Macc. 2:15). God dwells "above the firmament"; as early as Exodus 24:9-12 God appears only beyond the "sapphire pavement" that is the firmament (Bietenhard; *pace* Gaster). Psalm 148:4 speaks of a threefold division of heaven into the heavens, the waters above the heavens and the highest heavens (the dwelling of God and God's closely related agents, such as Wisdom in Sir 24:4). Heaven as the dwelling of God is frequently conceived as a temple,* an image that goes back to *1 Enoch* 14:8—15:2 (Himmelfarb) and to early exegesis of Exodus 25:9, 40, stressing the correspondence between the earthly and heavenly (Bietenhard). The activity of the earthly tabernacle* and cultus is a reflection and an extension of a heavenly temple and cultus where angels* worship the one God.

The Septuagint translation of the Hebrew dual *šamayim* ("heavens") as the Greek plural *ouranoi* facilitates the development during the intertestamental period of widespread speculation on the number of the heavens and the beings associated with each. The *Testament of Levi* 2:6—5:1 speaks of the seven heavens and their inhabitants and functions: the lower three are the "gloomier" heavens, which witness human unrighteousness and in which are stored the materials for judgment* (rain, hail, fire; cf. Job 37:9; 38:22, 37 on the "storehouses" of heaven). The higher four are the dwelling places of lower spiritual beings, angels, the seven archangels and finally God. During this period many interpreters were convinced that the heavens are accessible to the seer and a source of revelation.* Apocalypticists regularly peered into the activity of the heavenly realm with the conviction that it would provide a much-needed perspective on their mundane circumstances (Rowland, Russell, deSilva). The cosmos, moreover, was not regarded as absolute: the later prophetic* and apocalyptic* literature expresses the conviction that God would dissolve the present cosmos and bring into being a "new creation" (Is 65:17; 66:22). Only such a radical renewal could allow the fulfillment of God's promises.*

The NT authors engage in no speculation of number of heavens (save for 2 Cor 12:2-4), but the more general conception of the realm of God's activity lying beyond the visible heaven (cf. Is 64:1) is important for Hebrews,* Revelation (*see* Revelation, Book of) and the *Shepherd of Hermas.* * Only if the visible heavens open or part can the latter authors, who share with other apocalypticists the conviction that the heavens are accessible to visionaries, witness the activity in the divine realm (celestial phenomena require no such parting of the firmament). The concept of new heavens is a pillar in the arguments of 2 Peter* and Revelation. Hebrews and Revelation share the conviction that a heavenly temple exists in the realm of God, of which the earthly temple is but a copy.

1.2. Greco-Roman Background. The Greeks tended to refer to heaven in the singular as the dwelling place of God (Plato *Phaedr.* 246E; Dio Chrysostom *Or.* 19.22) and sometimes of the righteous dead (Dio Chrysostom *Or.* 23.35). Even this single heaven, however, contained a multitiered system of concentric spheres (Aristotle *Cael.*). For Plato the term *heavenly (ouranios)* denoted what "really is and what is truly coming to be" (Bietenhard). This axiological sense of "heavenly" appears again in Aristotle's cosmology—the further out one moves from the earthly into the heavenly, the more permanent, divine and valuable things become. This conception appears also to be at work in the mind of the author of Hebrews, for whom the "heavenly," in the sense not of what belongs to the visible "heavens" but to the realm of the divine, is what is "abiding" and "better."

2. Hebrews.

The author of Hebrews uses the term *heaven* to refer to two different realities in his cosmos. There are the "heavens" that are part of the changing, temporary creation. These will "perish" and "wear out like clothing," in stark contrast to the unchangeableness and constancy of the Son* (Heb 1:10-12). This image is attested in Hellenistic Judaism,* notably in the Septuagint translation of Job 14:12. The translator gives a different vocalization to the Hebrew "will be no more" so that it reads "will become unstitched," bringing the verse in line with the image of heaven as a garment (Gaster). The earth and these heavens will be shaken and removed at the end, so that the invisible and unshakable kingdom that the believers are inheriting will remain (Heb 12:26-28; Hooke, Bietenhard).

Hebrews also speaks of "heaven itself" (Heb 9:24), the place that Jesus entered after he "passed through the heavens" (Heb 4:14) and from which vantage point he stands "exalted above the heavens" (Heb 7:26). This is the eternal and abiding realm, beyond the material and visible creation,* where Jesus serves as high priest* in the "greater and perfect tabernacle not made with hands, that is, not of this creation" (Heb 9:11). The impermanent heavens are what Jesus must pass through in order to get to the true and real tabernacle (Hooke). This is the realm of the believers' "better and lasting possessions" (Heb 10:34), their "better" because "heavenly" homeland (Heb 11:16) and the "unshakable kingdom" that they are receiving (Heb 12:28) in which is their "abiding" city (Heb 13:13-14). The concept of "abiding" and

"permanent" enjoyment of enfranchisement in a city and homeland is especially important to the recipients of this epistle, who have lost their status and sense of belonging in their own city (Heb 10:32-34) and continue to live as "aliens and foreigners" (Heb 11:13). That this homeland exists now and stands prepared for them encourages the believers to remain loyal to their Christian commitments even in the face of continued dishonor and marginalization in the world. Since earthly cities and homelands will not survive the eschatological "shaking," believers may the more easily invest themselves in the pursuit that will grant them entrance into the one homeland that will remain intact through the shaking (Heb 12:26-28).

This heaven beyond the material heavens is portrayed as a temple (cf. Rev 11:19; 15:5-8), of which the earthly one is but a shadow and copy (Heb 8:2, 5; 9:24). Jesus' exaltation* to God's right hand is specifically his entrance into the Holy Place of the heavenly sanctuary, the dwelling place of God (Heb 8:1-6), in whose presence Jesus intercedes on behalf of believers. Through Jesus, Christians also have access to the throne of God and are able to go behind the curtain and enter in a spiritual sense this ultimate "heaven" that is God's presence (Heb 10:19-22; 4:14-16). They have in this way a foretaste now of their final entrance into that unshakable heaven and divine rest (Heb 4:1, 11; 6:19-20). The believers have already drawn near to the "heavenly Jerusalem," in which are found the angels performing their celebratory liturgy, the souls of the righteous people, Jesus and God's own self (Heb 12:22-24), and they have only to persevere until the time of God's visitation.

3. Acts and the General Epistles.

Acts* refers to heaven as the place that has received Jesus until the appointed time (Acts 3:20-21; cf. 1 Pet 3:22), whence Jesus continues to direct his church (Acts 9:10-16; 16:7-8). This author also distinguishes between the visible heavens and the heaven that contains God and now Jesus, for the former must part or open in order for the latter to be visible (Acts 7:55-56). 1 Peter* speaks of heaven as the locus of the believers' inheritance, on which they are to set their hopes (1 Pet 1:4). The certainty of this imperishable inheritance should be a source of joy* that helps the addressees to endure the "various trials" to which they have been and continue to be subject (1 Pet 1:6).

2 Peter* contains the most well-developed discussion of the origin and future of the heavens (2 Pet 3:5-14). The same divine word that brought the heavens into being (2 Pet 3:5) has decreed that the "present heavens and earth" will be dissolved in an eschatological* conflagration (2 Pet 3:7, 10). This conception has a certain affinity with the Stoic doctrine of the *ekpyrōsis* ("conflagration"), which holds that each age ends in a fire that renews the elements and returns to the beginning, to play out the same history again and again. 2 Peter rejects this cyclical component in favor of the apocalyptic conception of two and only two ages. The first age is prey to unrighteousness, but the second age with its "new heavens and a new earth" will be an age in which "righteousness has its home" (2 Pet 3:13). This expectation of the dissolution of the created order (earth and heavens) and the arrival of the coming "new heavens and new earth" is used to shape and motivate certain behaviors (2 Pet 3:11-14, 17-18). The addressees' knowledge of the end of this age should give them stability and steadfastness in their pursuit of holiness,* godliness and unity within the church, as they wait for the fulfillment of God's promise.

4. Revelation.

John shares with other apocalypticists the conviction that the heavens are accessible to the visionary and that the events of heavenly spheres place the everyday experience of the community in an important and informative perspective. John passed through a "door standing open in heaven" (Rev 1:1) in order to witness the events of the court of God, which stands in John's cosmology beyond the visible firmament (hence the need for an open door). He sees the throne of God surrounded by a variety of angelic beings (four fantastic beings resembling the seraphim of Isaiah 6:2-3, seven archangels, twenty-four elders on their "thrones" and myriads of angels), all arranged concentrically around the throne of God and giving worship, together with "every creature in heaven and on earth and under the earth," to the one God and the Lamb (Rev 4:1—5:14; *see* Worship; Liturgical Elements). This window into the heavenly realm lends an essential perspective to the commitment made by Christians in Asia Minor to worship the one God and withdraw

from the worship of idols (*see* Idolatry). In their everyday experience they form a minority, a small group standing apart from the majority of people who still worship the Greco-Roman pantheon (*see* Religions, Greco-Roman), and are thus susceptible to accept the larger society's labeling of them as deviant. John's vision,* however, assures them that they are in touch with the true order of the cosmos and that from this cosmic perspective those who center themselves around the worship of idols or the emperor* are really the deviants standing in need of correction (deSilva).

The heaven of God's court has ultimate authority* over the earthly realm. It is in heaven that the seals (*see* Scrolls) that set the end in motion are broken (Rev 6:1-17); it is from heaven that judgments and agents of judgment are released upon the earth (Rev 8:6; 14:14, 17; 16:1); it is from heaven that final destruction falls upon God's enemies (Rev 20:9). Heaven's inhabitants, whether the righteous martyrs under the altar (Rev 6:9-11; 16:7) or the angels themselves (Rev 16:4-6), encourage God's judgment of those who resist God's justice and harm God's servants* on the earth, rejoicing when the righteous are finally vindicated and the oppressors punished (Rev 18:20; 19:1-4). The faithful on earth are also assured of vital connections between their sphere and the realm of God, for the "prayers of the saints" rise up before God's throne and result in the vindication that they seek (Rev 8:3-6).

Revelation's window into the heavenly realm provides the encouragement believers needed to continue to resist Roman imperial ideology and the pressure to conform to their Greco-Roman neighbors' definitions of piety. As their eyes are opened to this invisible realm, they are enabled to hold fast their allegiance to Christ,* assured that they are acting wisely in light of heaven's authority over the earth. They are encouraged by the promise of a place in the new Jerusalem* that belongs to the new heavens and new earth (Rev 3:12) and by the hope* of dwelling eternally under the protection and care of God and the Lamb* (Rev 7:9-17; 22:1-5).

In the present age heaven and earth remain two separate realms. God and humanity remain apart in the visions of Revelation 4—20: only the righteous dead now enjoy the full presence of God. Revelation looks forward, however, to the joining of these two realms in the new heavens and new earth (Rev 22:1-5), where God finally dwells with humanity as the new Jerusalem descends to the new earth, bringing with it the dwelling of God and the Lamb. After the passing away of the first creation, the dwelling of God and the dwelling of people become one and the same, and the longstanding promise of God is fulfilled (Rev 21:3-4, 22; 22:3-5; cf. Ezek 37:27).

5. Apostolic Fathers.

For the successors of the apostles* heaven remains the place of God's throne (*Barn.* 16.2; *Herm. Vis.* 1.1.6) and the abode of diverse orders of angelic beings (Ign. *Trall.* 5.2; Ign. *Smyrn.* 6.1). Within this literature too there is some awareness of different levels of heaven. *2 Clement*, for example, expects the dissolution of the earth and only "certain of the heavens" at the judgment (*2 Clem.* 16.3), suggesting that the higher heaven of God's realm will persist. The visible heavens must still open or part in order for a revelation from beyond the material creation to be imparted (*Herm. Vis.* 1.1.4; 1.2.1) or for the triumphant Christ to appear to the inhabitants of the earth at the Parousia* (*Did.* 16.6-8).

Most frequently heaven appears in the literature as the ultimate goal that believers seek to attain, toward which they shape their lives in the present, mundane realm. The righteous who die in Christ, like Peter and Paul, enter the "place of glory" at their death (*1 Clem.* 5.4, 7; 50.3; Ign. *Rom.* 4.3; 6.2; *Mart. Pol.* 19.2; so Hooke). Believers set their minds fully on being received by Christ into the eternal, heavenly kingdom (*Mart. Pol.* 20.2; 22.3; *Diogn.* 6.7-8; 10.2; *Did.* 10.5-6). This hope is to shape their actions now, so that they walk in holiness and righteousness,* not indulging the love for temporary things that might distract the believers from attaining eternal treasures (*2 Clem.* 5.5-6) and bravely persevering in the face of hostility and reproach (*2 Clem.* 19.3-4). Knowing that "true life" belongs to "heaven" shows up the deceitfulness of the world and allows one to commend the choices of the Christian martyrs rather than despise them, for they are despising a temporary death in order not to fall victim to eternal loss (*Diogn.* 10.7). For the author of the *Epistle to Diognetus,* however, the life of heaven is not merely a future possession of the believer; it is experienced as one begins in discipleship,

for the believers themselves become "a paradise of delight" through the knowledge of God and the experience of God's favor (*Diogn.* 12.1). A righteous person's honor and reputation are already established in heaven: the believer is to preserve his or her reputation in that sphere unblemished, which also assures the believer of the Lord's assistance (*Herm. Vis.* 1.1.8). Heaven encourages the martyr to persevere and serves as the court to which the martyr appeals for justice and vindication (*Mart. Pol.* 9.1-2).

Clement (*see* Clement of Rome) shows an interest in the visible heavens as a source of moral instruction. As the heavens move in complete harmony in submission to God's will, so the divided Corinthians must return to concord through each person's submission to God (*1 Clem.* 20.1-3). As the heavens declare God's glory* without words or speech, so also there is nothing unseen or unknown to God, be it spoken or kept in silence: the believers therefore are to leave off their rebelliousness, so as to be safe at the judgment (*1 Clem.* 27.6—28.1). Finally, just as the orderly heavens bear witness to God's delight in working what is noble, so those who are created in God's image are to delight in well-doing (*1 Clem.* 33.1-3).

While the eschatology of this corpus is not uniform, a number of authors look forward to some change in the heavenly realm at the time of God's visitation. The *Didache**reproduces the widespread expectation of the rending of the heavens and the descent of the conquering Christ at the Parousia (*Did.* 16.6-8). *2 Clement* 16.3 resonates with 2 Peter 3:5-14 in its expectation of the melting of the earth and certain of the heavens, after which shall be uncovered all the works done by people, whether secretly or openly. For both authors the eschatological expectation should lead to readiness through repentance* and holy living. The *Shepherd of Hermas** extends the image of Isaiah 40:1-3, namely, that the way for the Lord's deliverance shall be made smooth, to include the heavens as well. God will remove heaven and all natural barriers that stand between the righteous and God's promises for the righteous, so that their way into their eternal possessions will be "made level" (*Herm. Vis.* 1.3.4).

See also ANGELS, HEAVENLY BEINGS, ANGEL CHRISTOLOGY; APOCALYPTIC, APOCALYPTICISM; ASCENSION; CREATION, COSMOLOGY; ESCHATOLOGY; EXALTATION, ENTHRONEMENT.

BIBLIOGRAPHY. H. Bietenhard, "οὐρανός," *NIDNTT* 2:188-96; D. A. deSilva, "The Construction and Social Function of a Counter-Cosmos in the Revelation of John," *Forum* 9:1-2 (1993) 47-61; P. Ellingworth, "Jesus and the Universe in Hebrews," *EvQ* 58 (1986) 337-50; T. H. Gaster, "Heaven," *IDB* 2:551-52; M. Himmelfarb, "Apocalyptic Ascent and the Heavenly Temple," *SBLSP* 26 (1987) 210-18; S. H. Hooke, "Heaven" in *Dictionary of the Apostolic Church,* ed. J. Hastings (New York: Scribner's, 1916) 1:530-33; C. Rowland, *The Open Heaven: A Study of Apocalyptic in Judaism and Early Christianity* (New York: Crossroad, 1982); D. S. Russell, *Divine Disclosure: An Introduction to Jewish Apocalyptic* (Minneapolis: Fortress, 1992); J. W. Thompson, " 'That Which Abides': Some Metaphysical Assumptions in the Epistle to the Hebrews" (unpublished Ph.D. dissertation, Vanderbilt University, 1974); H. Traub and G. von Rad, "οὐρανός," *TDNT* 5:497-543; D. F. Watson, "New Earth, New Heaven," *ABD* 4:1094-95.   D. A. deSilva

HEAVENLY ASCENT. *See* APOCALYPTIC, APOCALYPTICISM.

HEAVENLY BEINGS. See ANGELS, HEAVENLY BEINGS, ANGEL CHRISTOLOGY.

HEBREWS

Hebrews is a richly textured discourse addressed to a group of Christians who were experiencing a crisis of faith and a failure of nerve. The intended audience was almost certainly the members of a house church with a history of fidelity to Christ (Heb 10:32-34). These facts may be gleaned from the surface of the text. Although the character and location of the community addressed, the precise nature of the crisis to which Hebrews is a response, the circumstances and date of its composition, the literary genre of the discourse, and the purpose and plan of the work continue to be debated vigorously, no broad consensus has been reached.

All texts pose the challenge of reconstructing history from them. The only rational means by which this can be achieved is historical methodology, in which the historian's intuition is an essential component. This is particularly true in the case of Hebrews, which is distinctive in form and complex in literary structure. The early tradition concerning its authorship, purpose and intended audience is conflicting and unreliable. The evidence provided by the text lends itself to divergent interpretations. Any historical reconstruction must be proposed as tentative and exploratory in nature.

Patient interaction with the text and with the discussion it has prompted, especially during recent decades, supports the opinion that Hebrews is a sermon in response to circumstances in the life of the audience. The sermon throbs with an awareness of the privilege and the cost of Christian discipleship. It proves to be a sensitive pastoral response to the sagging faith* of seasoned and weary individuals who were in danger of abandoning their Christian commitments. The writer sought to strengthen them in the face of a new crisis so that they would hold fast to their confession* and stand firm in their faith. He warned them of the judgment* of God* they would incur if they were to falter in their commitments. His exhortations to covenant* faithfulness and unwavering perseverance were grounded in a fresh presentation of the significance of Jesus and his sacrificial death. As high priest and Son of God in solidarity with the human family, he is the supreme exemplar of faithfulness to God and of endurance, whose death on the cross secured for his people unlimited access to God and the assurance of divine help that arrives at the appropriate time.

 1. Authorship
 2. Audience
 3. Circumstances and Date of
  Composition
 4. Integrity
 5. Genre
 6. Literary Structural Devices
 7. Purpose and Plan
 8. Structural Function of Old Testament
  Texts
 9. Canonical Recognition
 10. Concluding Observations

1. Authorship.

Hebrews is anonymous, and the identity of the author has been veiled from the earliest period of the church.* Although it has been suggested that the author was Priscilla or some other woman (*see* Women), we are well advised to refer to the author as "he" in light of the masculine ending of the participle *diēgoumenon* in Hebrews 11:32. The writer was known to the community he addressed (Heb 13:19), but the brief personal notes in Hebrews 13 are not specific enough to reveal his identity.

The author clearly was not Paul, though presumably he moved within the Pauline circle (*see* Pauline Legacy and School) and expected to travel with Timothy (Heb 13:23). He classed himself as one who had not heard the Lord* deliver the message of salvation* (Heb 2:3-4). He was capable of writing some of the finest Greek in the NT, far superior in vocabulary and sentence construction to that of Paul. He also employs a distinctive range of images that are not found in Paul (Heb 2:1; 4:12, 13; 6:7-8, 19) and moves easily within the conceptual world of priesthood* and sacrifice,* emphases that are foreign to Paul's letters.

Among early church traditions we find the author of Hebrews identified as Paul, Barnabas, Luke or Clement of Rome.* Contemporary scholars have suggested Apollos, Silvanus, the deacon Philip,* Priscilla and Aquila, Jude, Aristion and others (see Moffatt). This variety of opinion shows that the limits of our historical knowledge preclude any certainty regarding the writer's identity. We are left to conclude that Hebrews was composed by a creative theologian, one well trained in the art of expounding the Greek Scriptures, whose thought world was shaped by, and whose vocabulary, traditions and theological conceptions were indebted to Hellenistic Judaism* and the early Hellenistic church.

We may draw a number of plausible inferences regarding the author from the composition of Hebrews. He was structured in his thought patterns, stating a thesis and then developing it through analysis. His reasoning powers were exceptional, as illustrated by the majestic opening sentence (Heb 1:1-4) that sets the program for the entire discourse. He was evidently trained in rhetoric* and understood speech as a medium of power to be used in the service of the gospel. He was able to deploy a rich vocabulary (169 of his 1,038 different words are found in the NT only in Hebrews) and a cultured diction. He had confidence in the persuasive power of oral speech as it is committed to the written text.

The writer's educational level may be compared with that of Philo* of Alexandria* and probably reflects training in a gymnasium or a private rhetorical school. Luke's description of Apollos as "an eloquent man" (Acts 18:24), a designation associated with formal rhetorical training and so used by Philo (see Philo *Poster. C.* 53; *Leg. Gai.* 142, 237, 310; *Vit. Mos.* 1.2), has suggested to many scholars that Apollos was the author of Hebrews.

The writer was an intensely devout man whose subconscious mind was steeped in the cultic categories and language of the Septuagint. He was also a pastoral theologian (*see* Pastoral Theology) who shaped early Christian tradition into an urgent appeal to a community in crisis. He was a gifted preacher and interpreter of salvation, a covenant theologian whose spiritual insight, scriptural exegesis and situational discernment provided encouragement, admonition and pastoral direction. He presents himself as a charismatic leader whose effectiveness did not depend on office or title. He at best wrote reluctantly, shaping his "word of exhortation" (Heb 13:22) as an effective substitute for his personal presence and immediate address. Our encounter with his discourse is fragmentary, for he does not present himself to us as he would have to his contemporaries.

2. Audience.

The attempt to establish a social and historical context for Hebrews is important for understanding its place within the life of an early Christian congregation. We must first sketch a profile of the audience on the basis of the evidence of the text itself.

2.1. The Audience in Profile. Hebrews was written with a specific local assembly in mind. The author is able to distinguish this assembly from its leaders and from other congregations in their social setting (Heb 13:17, 24), which was almost certainly an urban center (cf. Heb 13:14). This is borne out by the paraenetic concerns expressed in Hebrews 13:1-6, all of which are appropriate within an urban setting: hospitality* to Christian "strangers" (Heb 13:2), empathetic "remembering" of Christians imprisoned or suffering ill treatment (Heb 13:3), concern for the sanctity of marriage* and for sexual purity (Heb 13:4), and caution against greed and crass materialism (Heb 13:5-6).

The assembly was probably a house church (note "house" or "household" of God in Heb 3:6; 10:21) meeting in an ordinary room in a private home or apartment complex (*insula; see* Architecture). The group was small, perhaps numbering no more than fifteen or twenty persons, though it was probably part of a larger network of local assemblies scattered throughout the city. Their numbers had recently been depleted through defections (Heb 10:25).

The roots of the congregation may be traced to a Hellenistic synagogue* in the Jewish quarters of the city. Their primary source of authority* is the Hebrew Bible in an old Greek version. Their familiarity with the biblical narratives makes it possible for the writer to refer to the story of Esau without elaboration (Heb 12:17). In the opening lines of Hebrews the writer can presume to establish contact by presenting the transcendent Son of God (*see* Son of God; Sonship) in the distinctive vocabulary associated with divine Wisdom in the traditions of Hellenistic Judaism of the Diaspora (cf. Wis 7:24-27; *see* Diaspora Judaism).

Their spiritual, intellectual and social nurture in the Hellenistic synagogue is further borne out by the allusion to angels* as the heavenly mediators of the old revelation* (Heb 2:2). This notion, absent from Exodus 19—20 but hinted at in Deuteronomy 33:2 (cf. Ps 68:17), gained acceptance sometime prior to the first century and spread among Hellenistic Jews (cf. Acts 7:38, 53; Gal. 3:19; Josephus *Ant.* 15.5.3 §136). The centrality of the figure of Moses* in Hebrews corresponds with the veneration of Moses in Hellenistic Judaism (see *The Exodus* by the Hellenistic Jewish writer Ezekiel the Tragedian, preserved by Eusebius *Praep. Ev.* 9.29; and Philo *Vit. Mos.* 2.66-186; *Rer. Div. Her.* 182; *Praem. Poen.* 53, 56). In the Hellenistic Jewish tradition, Moses is the supreme exemplar of perfection because of his unique access to the unmediated presence of God, a feature that would explain Hebrews's sustained comparison of Moses and Jesus (see, e.g., Heb 3:1-6; 8:3-5; 12:18-29; 13:20).

2.2. Their Past Commitment and Present Crisis.

The writer is well acquainted with the previous experience of his readers (see Heb 2:2-4; 5:11-14; 6:9-11; 10:32-34; 12:4; 13:7). They had been brought to faith through the preaching of some who had direct access to Jesus' ministry (Heb 2:3), and the testimony of these witnesses* had been endorsed by the tangible evidence of "signs and wonders," "various miracles" and "gifts of the Holy Spirit" (Heb 2:4). The community's reception of the spoken word and their experience of the "powers of the age to come" (Heb 6:5) had confirmed that, as with Israel,* God had constituted this Christian community by an act of revelation.

Those who first proclaimed the gospel to the community had become its first leaders (Heb 13:7). And although these first charismatic leaders were now deceased, the community's present response to their original proclamation is of utmost concern: "We must pay the closest attention, therefore, to what we have heard, so that we do not drift off course" (Heb 2:1).

Hebrews 2:1-4 is the first in a series of sections that addresses the audience in the light of their current situation (see Heb 3:7—4:13; 5:11—6:12; 10:19-39; 12:14-29). These sections form pauses in the discourse and are characterized by stern warning or urgent appeal. As such they also provide a window on the social and historical setting of Hebrews (*see* Social Setting). The admonition in Hebrews 2:1-4, for example, implies that the readers had grown lax in their commitment to the basic Christian message of salvation, a situation that severely threatened the stability and integrity of the community. They are summoned to recognize the solemn import of the message and reaffirm their allegiance to it.

Throughout Hebrews the writer is pastorally concerned that the community might falter in its response to the claim of God upon their lives, a concern that extends to individual members (Heb 3:12, 13; 4:1, 11; 6:11; 12:15). The congregation was most likely varied in its experience, disposition and maturity (cf. Heb 12:13, 15), and the admonition to "encourage one another every day" (Heb 3:13) may presuppose a daily gathering of the household* fellowship* as the occasion for mutual encouragement.

The paraenetic unity of Hebrews 5:11—6:12 sheds further light on the circumstances. In Hebrews 5:11 the group is charged with spiritual lethargy ("you have become sluggish in understanding" [or, "hard of hearing"]), and this becomes the occasion for a resumed stress on the importance of listening to the voice of God (cf. Heb 2:1; 3:7-8, 15; 4:1-2, 7). This spiritual inertia and apathy must be checked before it undercuts their faith, hope* and obedience.*

The indictment of Hebrews 5:12, "You are at the stage of needing milk and not solid food," is probably ironical (*see* Milk). Although interpreters often understand this as the author's considered estimation of his readers' current condition, this is difficult to reconcile with his determination to respond to them as mature believers (Heb 6:1, 3). It is more likely that he is employing biting irony to call them to acknowledge their maturity and thus reckon with their ethical,* theological and social responsibilities as Christians in an urban society.

In Hebrews 5:13 the community is described as "unskilled in the word of righteousness." The meaning of this expression is unlocked by Polycarp's* use of this precise expression in *Letter to the Philippians* 9.1, where, as in Hebrews, it is associated with a call to endurance.* For Polycarp the "word of righteousness" is the paramount lesson in holiness* that Christians must be prepared for the cost of discipleship, even if that cost extends to martyrdom.* The use of the phrase in Hebrews 5:13 suggests that the threat of renewed suffering,* perhaps even of martyrdom, has brought about a crisis of faith and a failure of nerve. In Hebrews 10:32-34 the writer appeals to their past and valiant commitment to Christ and to one another under the pressure of public abuse as a paradigm for their responding to renewed perils. But the indelible memory of past suffering and loss may account for some now deserting the assembly (Heb 10:25) and a general inclination to avoid contact with outsiders (Heb 5:12).

The likelihood of this threat of persecution* is enhanced by the catalog of martyrs in Hebrews 11:35-38, crowned with the reference to Jesus, who endured a cross,* disregarding the shame of crucifixion (Heb 12:2-3; 13:12). The use of agonistic (i.e., conflict-oriented) vocabulary is intentional (Heb 12:4), for it prepares readers to risk public identification with Jesus, bearing the shame he bore (Heb 13:12-13).

2.3. Their Social Location. Proposals for locating the audience have ranged from Jerusalem* in the East to Spain in the West. But there are good reasons for placing them in or around Rome.* The only NT parallel to "Those from Italy greet you" (Heb 13:24) is found in Acts 18:2. There the phrase "from Italy" is used of Aquila and Priscilla, who were currently in Corinth and had departed "from Italy," namely, Rome, because of the Claudian expulsion (see 3.3 below). Thus the most natural way of reading Hebrews 13:24 is as a greeting from certain Italian Christians who are currently absent from their homeland that is being communicated by the author to the members of the house church in or near Rome.

This judgment is supported by several additional lines of evidence: the allusions to the readers' generosity (Heb 6:10-11; 10:33-34) comport with the known character of Roman Christianity (cf. Ign. *Rom.* salutation; Eusebius *Hist. Eccl.* 4.23.10); the sufferings endured by the believers shortly after they came to faith (Heb 10:32-34) suggest the events surrounding the Claudian expulsion of A.D. 49 (Acts 18:2; Suetonius *Claudius* 25.4); the use of the term *hēgoumenoi* for leaders in the community (Heb 13:7, 17, 24) is found in early Christian documents associated with Rome (e.g., *1 Clem.* 21.6; *Herm. Vis.* 2.2.6; 3.9.7); and the first evidence of Hebrews' recognized authority comes to us from Clement of Rome, who throughout his letter produces striking parallels to Hebrews and is literarily dependent upon Hebrews in *1 Clement* 36.1-6.

This construction of social location cannot be proven, yet it provides a concreteness to Hebrews that other hypotheses lack, and it offers a plausible destination that may be tested exegetically. We may also fill out the picture by invoking what is known concerning the Jewish community and the early house churches in Rome. There is little doubt that Roman Christianity was originally Jewish. It is striking that the fourth-century commentator on Romans, Ambrosiaster, attests to Gentile* Christians in Rome who came to faith through the evangelistic outreach of the original Jewish converts of the earliest Roman community (*Exposition of Romans,* prologue, 2 [CSEL 81.1.5-6]). By the time Paul wrote his letter to the Romans, there had been a significant influx of Gentile Christians in Rome, and the balance of power had shifted to Gentile leadership. In Romans 16:3-15 Paul gives us evidence for the existence of several house churches in Rome (see Rom 16:3-5, 10, 11, 14, 15).

Archaeological investigation has uncovered the remains of apartment complexes *(insulae)* several stories high that date to the second and third centuries. Incorporated into the walls or preserved below the floors of at least three of the existing titular churches in Rome are the remnants of large tenement houses (*see* Architecture; Rome, Roman Christianity). The ground floors would have been occupied by shops and the upper levels by prosperous families. Craftsmen and artisans such as Aquila and

Priscilla might well have lived in such quarters, which served as workshop, residence and meeting place. From Paul's greetings in Romans 16:3-15 we may picture a number of relatively small household fellowships only loosely related to one another. Evidence indicates that even in the early second century the congregations of Rome were not centrally organized under the administrative authority of a single bishop. Ignatius* insists on the importance of the office of bishop in six of his seven letters to churches (*see* Church Order), but he is silent on this matter in his letter to the Romans (Ign. *Rom.*, c. 110), presumably because there was no monarchical bishop in Rome. Shortly thereafter the *Shepherd of Hermas** refers only to "the elders who preside over the church" at Rome (*Herm. Vis.* 2.4.3; 3.9.7).

The setting we have sketched suggests why the Roman church may have been troubled by problems of diversity, disunity and a tendency toward independence. In Hebrews we see evidence of tension between the intended audience and the recognized leaders (Heb 13:17-18) and a pastoral concern to bring the two groups together (Heb 13:24). The members of the house church are not to regard themselves as an autonomous assembly or to isolate themselves from other household groups within the city, and as a countermeasure the writer asks them to convey his greetings "to all the saints" throughout the city (Heb 13:24).

3. Circumstances and Date of Composition.

3.1. Circumstances of Composition. In reconstructing the circumstances surrounding the composition of Hebrews, we are left to rely on the document itself. What is the precise relationship of the writer to his audience? The answer is difficult to discern, but in Hebrews 13:17-19 the writer identifies himself with the "leaders" of the community. He considers his pastoral responsibility, epitomized in his "word of exhortation" (Heb 13:22), to extend to the congregation. And his desire to be "restored to you sooner" (Heb 13:19) implies his personal acquaintance with them. His discourse (Heb 1:1—13:21) and personal note (Heb 13:22-25) are intended as a substitute for his presence until he can come in person (Heb 13:19, 23).

We have already noted that the assembly was in crisis. Their numbers had been depleted (Heb 10:25), and those who remained were subject to a loss of confidence in their convictions. Their former sense of identity as the new covenant people of God had been undermined, and in the writer's analysis they are no longer listening to the voice of God (Heb 2:1, 3; 3:7—4:14; 5:11; 12:25). Their formerly bold commitment in the face of public abuse, imprisonment and loss of property (Heb 10:32-34) has given way to discouragement (Heb 5:11; 6:12; 12:12-13) and a weariness of sustaining their Christian confession in the face of hostility (Heb 12:3-4).

The writer is alarmed at the group's attraction to traditions that he regarded as inconsistent with the word of God proclaimed by their former leaders (Heb 13:7-9). This may account for the tension between the community and their current leaders (Heb 13:1, 17-18), and it may also explain their apparent isolation and lack of accountability to the larger network of house churches (Heb 13:24). These factors would have exposed them to the corrosive impact of their sociopolitical and religious environment.

We should probably understand Hebrews to be addressing the concerns of second-generation Christians. The root of the problem may have been the delay of the Parousia* (Heb 10:25, 35-39), social ostracism and impending persecution (Heb 12:4; 13:13-14) or a general waning of enthusiasm and erosion of confidence (Heb 3:14; 10:35). A significant symptom was the faltering of hope (Heb 3:6; 6:11, 18-20; 10:23-25; 11:1), and the writer sensed the grave danger of apostasy* among some members, which he defined as turning away from the living God (Heb 3:12) and subjecting Jesus Christ to public contempt (Heb 6:4-6; 10:26-31). Once the sacred covenant bond between God and his people was violated, they would be excluded from covenant fellowship. Weaker members might reject the grace* of God and forfeit participation in the new covenant through personal carelessness (Heb 3:12-13; 4:1, 11; 6:4-8, 11; 10:26-31; 12:15-17, 25-29). These factors might well account for the urgent tone and pastoral strategies adopted by the writer.

3.2. Date of Composition: General Considerations. In assigning a date for the composition of Hebrews, we must first allow for the fact that both the writer and his audience had come to faith through the preaching of those who had heard Jesus (Heb 2:3-4) and had subsequently served as leaders during the formative period of the community (Heb 13:7). Further, we learn that the present members had been believers for an extended time (Heb 5:12). If we allow that at least three or four decades have elapsed since the beginning of the Christian movement, the earliest date we can assign for the composition of Hebrews would be around A.D. 60.

In seeking to establish an upper limit for a date of composition we need to consider the use of Hebrews in *1 Clement* (see *1 Clem.* 17.1 for the use of Heb 11:37; *1 Clem.* 36.2-6 for direct literary dependence on Heb 1:3-5, 7; *1 Clem.* 36.3 for the quotation of Ps 104:4 [103 LXX] in the precise wording of Heb 1:7 [in variation from the LXX]). Internal evidence and external attestation indicate that *1 Clement* was composed some time between 80 and 140 (for issues of dating, *see* Clement of Rome). Thus no firm inference concerning the date for the composition of Hebrews may be drawn from its use by Clement of Rome.

Some scholars have set an upper limit at 70, the year in which the Jerusalem temple* was destroyed by Titus. This conclusion is based on the writer's referring to cultic activity in the present tense (e.g., Heb 7:27-28; 8:3-5; 9:7-8, 25; 10:1-3, 8; 13:10-11) and the presumption that cultic activity was being carried out in Jerusalem. But the writer shows no interest in the Jerusalem temple or in contemporary sacrificial praxis. In Hebrews 9:1-10, for example, the focus is on the tabernacle* in the wilderness rather than the temple. Since the sanctuary is considered in relation to the old and new covenants and the contrast between the two, the writer refers to the tabernacle (and its association with the old Sinai covenant) rather than to the temple (see Heb 8:5). The use of the present tense evokes a sense of timelessness rather than indicating a continuing temple cult in Jerusalem. (Such use of a "timeless" present tense to describe the temple and its sacrifices after the temple had been destroyed may be observed in Josephus *Ant.* 4.8.17-23 §§224-57; *1 Clem.* 41.2; *Barn.* 7—8; *Diogn.* 3.) It has no bearing on the dating of Hebrews.

3.3. The Edict of Claudius. The most explicit reference to a specific event in the audience's past occurs in Hebrews 10:32-34. This description of the suffering endured is congruent with the hardships borne by the Jewish Christians who were expelled from Rome by the emperor Claudius in A.D. 49. Among them were the Jewish Christian leaders Aquila and Priscilla, who arrived in Corinth about 49 or 50 "because Claudius had commanded all the Jews to leave Rome" (Acts 18:2). This edict of expulsion is known from Suetonius, who in his *Lives of the Caesars* (A.D. 120) comments on Claudius's official actions toward certain foreign groups in Rome: *Iudaeos impulsore Chresto adsidue tumultuantes Roma expulit* (Suetonius *Claudius* 25.4). This may be translated in either of two ways: "He expelled from Rome the Jews constantly making disturbances at the instigation of Chrestus," or "Since the Jews constantly made disturbances at the instigation of Chrestus, he expelled them from Rome." Suetonius's comment can be interpreted to mean that either Claudius expelled only those responsible for the disturbances among the Jews, or the entire Jewish community in Rome was affected by the edict because they had been implicated in frequent rioting. The first translation is preferred because in Rome the Jewish community was divided into a number of district synagogues. In all probability the edict of expulsion was directed to the members of one or two specific synagogues, who would have been compelled to leave the city until there was a guarantee of no further social disturbances.

Although *Chrestus* was a common name among Roman slaves,* signifying "good" or "useful," it was not a recognized Jewish name. The garbled reference to "Chrestus" is almost certainly evidence of the presence of Christians within the Jewish community of Rome. The confusion between *Chrestus* and *Christus* ("the Messiah") is understandable, since in antiquity the distinction in spelling and pronunciation was negligible. There is every reason to believe that the source of the disruptions was the Jewish Christian preaching* of a crucified Jesus as Messiah. We can well imagine members of the Jewish community being thrown into violent debate, and this attracting the unfavorable attention of the imperial authorities. Claudius issued a decree of expulsion affecting those most directly involved (i.e., those Jewish Christians labeled under the name of *Chrestus*). Insult, public abuse and the loss of property were normal under the conditions of a decree of expulsion. If this reading of the evidence is correct, some of the recipients of Hebrews were Jewish Christians who had shared banishment from Rome with Aquila and Priscilla.

The date of the Claudian edict is contested, but the year 49 is plausible. It was in the period 47-52 that Claudius engaged in a campaign to restore the old Roman rites (*see* Religions, Greco-Roman) and to check the spread of foreign cults. Independent corroboration of this date is provided by the Gallio inscription from Delphi, which has made it possible to determine when Paul entered Corinth and made the acquaintance of Aquila and Priscilla, who had arrived in Corinth from Rome "only recently" (Acts 18:1-2). We conclude that the experience referred to in Hebrews 10:32-34 took place in 49.

Hebrews was written at a later time in which a new crisis had emerged, posing its own threat to the welfare of the members of the house church. The fear of death (Heb 2:15), loss of heart (Heb 12:3) and the fact that the community had not yet contended to the point of bloodshed (Heb 12:4; cf. Heb 11:35—12:3) suggest a situation more serious than that under Claudius. This suggests the persecution and martyrdom endured by Roman Christians under Nero following the devastating fire of 64 (Tacitus *Annals* 15.42-44). Christians then experienced the loss of life, not simply property. Hebrews appears to have been composed for members of a house church that had not yet borne the brunt of Nero's repressive measures, or less probably, for Jewish Christians who returned to Rome after that terrifying event. This suggests a tentative date of composition in the interval between the great fire of Rome (64) and Nero's suicide in June 68. Incidental features of the text, such as the imminent expectation of the Parousia (Heb 10:25, 36-39) or the notice of Timothy's release from prison (Heb 13:23), are consistent with this relatively early dating of Hebrews.

4. Integrity.

Few scholars have doubted the integrity of Hebrews 1—12, but questions have been raised concerning the authenticity of Hebrews 13 (for discussion, see Filson). The reasons are several: the chapter appears to begin abruptly and is marked by a sharp change in tone and theme; it appears to lack the writer's normal care to link a new section to the preceding unit of exhortation (Heb 12:14-29); the form of the chapter, marked by catechetical precepts characteristic of the paraenesis of Paul or Peter (e.g., 1 Thess 5:12-22; Rom 12:9-21; 13:8-10; 1 Pet 3:8-12), is without parallel in Hebrews 1—12; and its contents distinguish this section from the rest of the Hebrews.

Nevertheless Hebrews 13 exhibits the characteristic vocabulary and significant concepts, the appeal to the Pentateuch and Psalms and the elements of structure that are found in Hebrews 1—12. This constitutes a strong, cumulative argument for the authenticity of Hebrews 13.

A number of literary devices form a literary signature that identifies the author of Hebrews 13 as the author of Hebrews 1—12: the use of chiastic structure (Heb 13:2, 4, 10, 14, and 10-16); paronomasia, or play on words (Heb 13:2, 18, 20, 22); unusual word order designed to arouse attention (Heb 13:8, 11, 20); elegant style (Heb 13:17); linguistic rhythm (Heb 13:3); assonance (Heb 13:4, 5, 9, 13, 14, 16); alliterative arrangement of lines (Heb 13:5, 19); the use of syntax to display emphasis (Heb 13:3, 4, 5, 9, 11, 15, 18, 20) and the use of classical idioms (Heb 13:2, 5, 15, 17).

Hebrews 13 not only was composed by the same writer as Hebrews 1—12 but also was designed to accompany the preceding discourse. Its essential message can scarcely be separated from the primary concerns and conceptual themes expressed in Hebrews 1—12. The connection of Hebrews 13:1-21 to the preceding section (Heb 12:14-29) is established through Hebrews 12:28, where the community is called to serve God through thanksgiving. This concept of worship* is an expansive one, and the varied aspects of life (Heb 13:1-21) are to be regarded as an expression of devoted service* to God.

5. Genre.

The canonical ordering of Hebrews among the letters of the NT predisposes one to regard this document as a letter. This understanding of Hebrews can be traced back as early as the beginning of the third century and the Chester Beatty Papyrus (P^{46}), where Hebrews is positioned after Romans and before 1 Corinthians and is identified by the superscription "To the Hebrews" (cf. the uncials B A C H I K P, where it appears after 2 Thessalonians and before 1 Timothy).

Hebrews does not possess the form of an

ancient letter (*see* Letters). It lacks the conventional prescript of a letter and has none of the characteristic features of ordinary letters from this period. The writer offers no opening prayer for grace and peace,* no expression of thanksgiving or blessing.* Its beginning with a stately periodic sentence acclaiming the transcendent dignity of the Son of God through whom God spoke his final word (Heb 1:1-4) is more characteristic of rhetorical discourse that compels attention and engages a reader or auditor immediately. Hebrews begins like a sermon.

5.1. The Homily or Sermon Form. The writer confirms the sermonic genre when he describes the discourse as a "word of exhortation" (Heb 13:22), an idiomatic expression for a sermon in Hellenistic-Jewish and early Christian circles, where the public reading of Scripture was followed by preaching (cf. Acts 13:15 with Acts 13:16-41). Hebrews may be classified as a paraenetic homily in the Hellenistic-Jewish synagogue tradition (see Thyen). As such it is the oldest complete early Christian sermon that has been preserved. It possesses the eloquence of a discourse but the form of a homily. Like the paraenetic homilies of its period, Hebrews consists of strong encouragement and stern warning.

5.2. Defining the Genre. Recent research has identified a common form of Hellenistic-Jewish and early Christian oral sermon. The synagogue hortatory homily, or "word of exhortation," found in Acts 13:16-41 follows a threefold pattern: authoritative *exempla* (i.e., evidence in the form of biblical quotations, examples from the past or present, or reasoned exposition set out to commend the points that follow); a conclusion inferred from the preceding examples, indicating their relevance for the audience; a final exhortation. This threefold pattern can be found in many early Christian writings (Hebrews; *1 Clement;* other speeches in Acts; 1 Cor 10:1-14; 2 Cor 6:14—7:1; 1 Peter* and 2 Peter,* the letters of Ignatius; *Barnabas*) and in Jewish sources from the Hellenistic period (see Lane, lxxii).

This oral form was flexible and could be developed in a variety of ways. It could stand alone, as in Acts 13:16-41, or it could be extended in a cyclical fashion as the pattern is repeated in a longer sermon (e.g., Heb 1:5—4:16; 8:1—12:28; *1 Clem.* 4.1-13; 37.2—40.1; Ign. *Eph.* 3.1—4.2; 5.1-36; 7.2—10.1). Hebrews appears to follow a modified form of the latter pattern, creating in the process a complex sermonic text.

The study of Hebrews in light of Greco-Roman rhetoric, as outlined in the handbooks of Aristotle, Quintilian and Cicero, reveals the manner in which Hebrews addressed its hearers with the intent to persuade (cf. Aristotle *Rhetoric* 1.2.1355B). Hebrews exhibits highly nuanced and sophisticated forms of proof. In its various hortatory cycles, in which complementary ideas are augmented with multiple arguments, the writer engages in what the rhetorical handbooks call amplification or refinement.

Even the lengthy interruption in the "word of exhortation" of Hebrews 5:1—10:18, where the writer turns from the established hortatory pattern to present an extended exposition, finds explanation in the rhetorical setting. The writer aims not only to exhort his audience but also to stimulate and fortify them in their present convictions on the basis of an exposition of the surpassing, unrepeatable priestly sacrifice of Jesus for the sins of the many.

An alternative approach takes note of the formal pattern that serves as a structuring device in important sections of Hebrews (Heb 3:1—4:16; 8:1—10:18; 12:1-13). The pattern consists of formal introduction (e.g., Heb 3:1-6; 8:1-6; 12:1-3), scriptural citation (e.g., Heb 3:7-11; 8:7-13; 12:4-6), exposition or thematic elaboration (e.g., Heb 3:12—4:13; Heb 9:1—10:18; Heb 12:7-11) and application (e.g., Heb 4:14-16; 10:19-21; 12:12-13). This pattern has left its partial imprint in other portions of Hebrews as well (e.g., Heb 7:1-28). This genre of "word of exhortation" (Heb 13:22; Acts 13:15), or "paraclesis" (i.e., "exhortation"), emerged in the hellenistic synagogue, where it served to actualize traditional Scripture for a Jewish community in a nontraditional environment. The writer of Hebrews adapted this form in order to confirm the values and commitments of a group of Christians who were experiencing social ostracism and alienation in their environment.

5.3. The Impact of the Sermonic Discourse. The writer of Hebrews skillfully projected the impression that he was present with the gathered audience, delivering the sermon. Until the postscript (Heb 13:22-25), he studiously avoids any reference to writing or reading, which would tend to emphasize his geographical distance from the audience. Instead the accent is on speaking and listening, and he directly identifies himself with the audience and establishes a sense of presence (Heb 2:5; 5:11; 6:9; 8:1; 9:5; 11:32).

As a gifted preacher, the writer skillfully employs alliteration, oratorical imperatives, euphonic phrases, unusual word order and literary devices, all calibrated for rhetorical effectiveness. The alternation between exposition and exhortation provides an effective vehicle for oral impact. As the discourse was read aloud to the gathered assembly, Hebrews would have communicated its point as much aurally as logically.

Interpreters should be aware of the difference between oral preaching and written discourse. The dynamic relationship between speaker and audience is distinct in each case. The writer expressly declares in Hebrews 13:22 that his "word of exhortation" has been reduced to writing. As such, it is available for study to a modern reader, taking on a life of its own independent of the audience for whom it was written. But it is clear that this was not the writer's intention. It is also clear that the writer would have preferred to have spoken directly with the men and women he addressed (Heb 13:19, 23). In the realm of oral speech, the speaker and the auditors are bound together in a dynamic relationship within a world of sound. Although forced by geographical distance and a sense of urgency to reduce his homily to writing, the writer of Hebrews never loses sight of the power of the spoken word.

5.4. Rhetorical Analysis. In Hebrews the voice of the writer is the voice of the speaker. It was essential to provide verbal clues to enable the audience to discern where one unit of the discourse ended and another began. These verbal clues were also necessary for the reader, because in ancient documents there was no indication where parts of a composition began or ended. Thus the organization of the argument was revealed by devices such as repetition, anaphora, *inclusio, responsio,* parallelism, catchwords (or "hook words") and the like. By attending to these clues, the one reading the discourse to the assembled group could give the discourse a coherent delivery. Hebrews was crafted not for the eye but for the ear, and its forceful, artistic prose provided the vehicle for the argument.

It is attractive to view Hebrews as a deliberative discourse since it consists of advising and dissuading (cf. Quintilian *Inst. Orat.* 3.8.6). Hebrews includes a rhetorical *prooemium* (prologue, Heb 1:1-4), *narratio* (necessary background information, Heb 1:5—2:18) with the *propositio* (a lucid thematic statement, or the statement that is to be proved, Heb 2:17-18), *argumentatio* with *probatio* and *refutatio* (argumentation with the presentation of proof and refutation, Heb 3:1—12:29), *peroratio* (peroration, Heb 13:1-21) and *postscriptum* (postscript, Heb 13:22-25) that identifies the discourse in Hebrews 1:1—13:21 as an exhortation or urgent appeal (*see* Rhetoric).

It is difficult, however, to classify Hebrews as a specific type of ancient rhetoric. Deliberative rhetoric attempts to persuade an audience to make a choice on the basis of some future benefit or to dissuade them from inappropriate action. This type of rhetoric agrees with the earnest pastoral character of much of Hebrews. Epideictic rhetoric, however, is concerned with reinforcing beliefs accepted by the audience. The tone is more instructive, seeking to buttress a set of convictions already embraced. This also is a feature of Hebrews and may be observed in the exhortation not to cast aside the confidence and hope once firmly held, for the One who had promised is faithful (e.g., Heb 3:6, 14; 10:23, 35-39; 11:11).

The state of research is such that no one has yet produced a structural analysis of the homily that conforms strictly to the type of rhetoric discussed in the ancient Greco-Roman handbooks. We must conclude that Hebrews resists being cast into any single mold of classical rhetoric. Although rhetorical devices are clearly discernible, an identifiable rhetorical structure is less evident. The writer of Hebrews (like Paul and Philo) was not bound by rhetorical conventions. He freely adapted rhetorical conventions to suit his purposes.

5.5 Discourse Analysis. As a written communication, Hebrews lends itself to discourse, or text-linguistic, analysis. As a technique of biblical criticism, discourse analysis is in its infancy. Discourse analysis is concerned with semantic cohesion, the relationships within a unit of discourse and the identification of unit boundaries within a discourse. Its primary goal is an understanding of the individual paragraphs that constitute the building blocks of a discourse. This is based on the premise that the paragraph, rather than individual semantic units like words, phrases or sentences, provides the key to understanding the total (or main) discourse. A writer organizes sentences to form larger semantic units (i.e., paragraphs) that are assigned a variety of semantic functions in the development of the discourse.

The fundamental assumption of discourse analysis is that written texts originate in a writer's conceptualization of a theme. This theme is given expression by linguistic choices (diction, grammar, style), which lend meaning and structure to paragraph units. In order to comprehend the writer's development of his theme, it is necessary to examine the text on the lexical, syntactic and rhetorical levels. Discourse analysis attempts to understand how a writer linguistically marked his paragraphs and embedded discourses (i.e., those identifiable, distinct units of discourse that have a beginning and an end) in the process of developing the main discourse. (For further discussion, *see* Structuralism and Discourse Analysis.)

One analysis of Hebrews has identified a discourse structure that may be broadly outlined as follows:

Thematic introduction (Heb 1:1-4)
Point 1 (embedded discourse 1, Heb 1:5—4:13)
Point 2 (embedded discourse 2, Heb 4:14—10:18)
Peak (embedded discourse 3, Heb 10:19—13:19)
Conclusion (Heb 13:20-21)
Finis (Heb 13:22-25)

According to this analysis, Hebrews comprises three major embedded discourses bracketed by an introduction and a conclusion. The formal closing at the end of the homily is unrelated semantically to the thematic development of the discourse (for further details, see Lane, lxxx-lxxxiv; Vanhoye).

It must be emphasized that discourse analysis represents a purely linguistic approach that takes into account such factors as literary devices, shifts in genre, the semantic cohesion of individual sections, the functional role of subsections and the development of the discourse. It is not concerned with social or historical factors that may have affected the surface structure of the discourse. One of its major contributions to understanding Hebrews lies in its identification of techniques that not only effect

a transition but also give cohesion to a unit of discourse.

6. Literary Structural Devices.

The literary structure of Hebrews is complex and elusive. The range of proposals concerning its literary structure attests to the artistic and literary complexity of this discourse. Nevertheless the quest for a literary structure is legitimate and assumes that there were literary and rhetorical conventions for the orderly arrangement of a discourse and that in reducing the discourse to writing verbal clues would need to be provided to assist the auditors in following the argument (see Lane, lxxxiv-xcviii).

The writer of Hebrews has used a number of literary devices to indicate the beginning and ending of unified sections. These verbal clues to the development of Hebrews may be enumerated as follows:

(1) Announcement of subject. The writer announces the primary theme just prior to the introduction of the unit in which the theme is developed. For example, in Hebrews 2:17 Jesus is designated a "merciful and faithful high priest in the service of God." These primary themes are developed in inverse order. In Hebrews 3:1—5:10 the writer directs attention to Jesus as "faithful" (Heb 3:1-4:13) and then to Jesus as "merciful" (Heb 4:14—5:10).

(2) Transitional hook words. Hook words were a rhetorical device developed in antiquity to tie together two or more blocks of material. The introduction of a key word at the end of one section and its repetition at the beginning of the next served to mark formally the transition between the two units (e.g., "the angels" in Heb 1:4/5 joins the sections Heb 1:1-4/5-14).

(3) Change of genre. The writer alternates between exposition and exhortation throughout the discourse.

(4) Characteristic terms. The concentration of key vocabulary or of cognate terms within a unit of discourse frequently serves to articulate and develop a primary theme. For example, the term *angels* is found eleven times in Hebrews 1:5—2:16 and only twice after that. This density of usage serves to build cohesion in a block of material.

(5) *Inclusio.* Bracketing a unit of discourse by the repetition of a striking expression or key word at the beginning and close of a section provides an objective means of determining the beginning and end of a unit of discourse. For

example, the repetition of the verb "to see" and the noun "unbelief" in Hebrews 3:12 and 19 marks Hebrews 3:12-19 as a discrete literary unit of commentary on the biblical text found in Hebrews 3:7-11.

7. Purpose and Plan.

The purpose and plan of Hebrews is integrally related to the literary structure of the document. The key issue is the distinctive role assigned by the writer to the expository and hortatory sections of the homily. How is the writer's essential purpose served by the blocks of exposition or of exhortation throughout the discourse? What is the intended relationship between the indicative and the imperative, between thesis and paraenesis, within the total work?

There are sound reasons for arguing that in Hebrews paraenesis takes precedence over thesis in expressing the writer's purpose. Argumentation serves exhortation. Hebrews may be designated a pastorally oriented sermon whose goal is given expression in the paraenetic sections of the discourse. When the writer characterized his entire discourse as paraenesis or *paraclesis* (Heb 13:22, "my word of exhortation" *[paraklēsis]*), he was identifying his work as an earnest, passionate and personal appeal. The writer's biblical and theological exposition is therefore subordinate to his paraenetic purpose. Hebrews was composed to arouse, urge, encourage and exhort the audience to maintain their Christian confession and to dissuade them from a course of action the writer regarded as catastrophic. The writer calls them to fidelity and obedience and seeks to prepare them for suffering.

The primary function of the exposition is thematic development. The primary function of the exhortation is to motivate the community to appropriate action. Exhortation confronts, with implications for obedience and disobedience. Exposition instructs, showing why obedience will be amply rewarded. In Hebrews, exposition provides an essential foundation for the exhortation and ultimately serves a hortatory purpose. The expository units of the discourse do not stand on their own but furnish the presupposition for the paraenesis. At the same time, the persuasive force of the exhortation is derived from the convincing thematic development in the expository sections of the sermon. The basis for the exhortation in Hebrews 2:1-4, for example, is provided in the demonstration of the superior dignity of God's Son in Hebrews 1:5-14.

As we have argued, the purpose of Hebrews is to strengthen, encourage and exhort the weary members of a house church to respond courageously to the prospect of renewed suffering in view of the gifts and resources God has lavished upon them. The plan of the homily complements its practical purpose. The finality of God's revelation in his Son is set forth in moving language (Heb 1:1-4). The transcendent dignity of the Son is superior both to the angels (Heb 1:5-14) and to Moses (Heb 3:1-6). Within this setting the writer warns his auditors against indifference to the gospel message they have heard (Heb 2:1-4) or blatant unbelief (Heb 3:7—4:13). The unique priesthood of Jesus is introduced in Hebrews 2:17—3:1 and Hebrews 4:14—5:10, and it is treated at length in Hebrews 7:1—10:18. Three contrasts are developed that demonstrate the superior dignity of Jesus as priest and sacrifice: the temporal, ephemeral character of the Aaronic priesthood is overshadowed by the eternal ministry of the priest like Melchizedek* (Heb 5:1-10; 7:1-28); the priestly ministry in the tabernacle of the old covenant is superseded by the priestly ministry of Jesus in the heavenly sanctuary of the new covenant (Heb 8:1—9:28); the inadequacy of the sacrifices under the law* is contrasted with the efficacy and finality of Jesus' sacrifice (Heb 10:1-18).

The thematic development of Jesus' priesthood and unique sacrifice is foundational to the paraenetic warnings concerning the peril of immaturity and apostasy, which can be avoided only through faith, endurance and hope (Heb 5:11—6:20; 10:19-39). The audience is exhorted to steadfast endurance and the exercise of eschatological* faith that acts in light of the certainty of the future (Heb 11:1—12:3). The heroes and heroines of the past, whose faith was attested by God (Heb 11:1-40), are paraded before the audience. This appeal is then crowned by the supreme example of faith, Jesus himself (Heb 12:1-3). In the pastoral and theological climax to the sermon (Heb 12:14-29), the congregation is warned of the peril of refusing God's gracious word. A concluding exhortation summons them to a lifestyle of worship and unqualified identification with the confessing community (Heb 13:1-25).

Any analysis of the plan of Hebrews must reflect an intensive listening to the detail of the text. The analysis in figure 2 attempts to distinguish between thesis and paraenesis and to indicate the primacy of paraenesis in the discourse by italicizing the five warning passages that expose the danger to which the community was vulnerable (Heb 2:1-4; 3:7—19; 5:11—6:12; 10:19-39; 12:14-29). The passages listed in the right-hand column point out the extent to which Hebrews has been organized around paraenesis.

8. Structural Function of Old Testament Texts.
Every chapter in Hebrews is marked by explicit or implicit references to the OT text (for a full discussion, *see* Old Testament in Hebrews; Thomas). The writer's use of Scripture expresses his firm belief in the continuity between God's speaking and action under the old and new covenants which has urgent ramifications for Israel and for the church. A detailed knowledge of the OT is indispensable for following what the writer of Hebrews was endeavoring to say, for he assumes on the part of his audience a deep familiarity with the detail of the biblical text.

The argument of Hebrews is focused upon a succession of OT themes and figures so as to draw out both the continuity and the discontinuity between the period prior to the coming of Christ and the time of fulfillment in Christ. In the course of Hebrews a number of OT texts gain particular prominence. The rhetorical use of these OT texts defines the arrangement and the argument of Hebrews as a whole.

The writer appears to have arranged his argument as a series of six scriptural explications, each of which is framed by exhortation. He introduces a key biblical text, clarifies its eschatological significance and draws out the paraenetic implications for the community. This rhetorical strategy accounts for the arrangement of the entire discourse from Hebrews 2:5 to Hebrews 13:19. The argument is directed to the eschatological appeal for unqualified faithfulness in light of the fact that Christ's high-priestly ministry* has now secured the promised "good things" (Heb 9:11). Once this is recognized, the structural organization is clearly perceived. It is evident that the para-

enetic passages are grouped fairly uniformly in proximity to the six primary scriptural quotations (see figure 1).

Section	OT Text	Placement	Paraenesis
Introduction			
1:1—2:4	Catena		2:1-4
First Point:	"You Crowned Him"		
2:5-18	Ps 8	2:6-8	
Second Point:	"Today"		
3:1—4:13	Ps 95	3:7-11	3:1-2, 12-14 4:1, 11
Third Point:	"A Priest Forever"		
4:14—7:28	Ps 110	5:6	4:14-16 5:11—6:12
Fourth Point:	"A New Covenant"		
8:1—10:31	Jer 31	8:8-12	10:19-29
Fifth Point:	"By Faith"		
10:32—12:2	Hab 2	10:37-38	10:32-36 12:1-2
Sixth Point:	"Do Not Lose Heart"		
12:3—13:19	Prov 3	12:5-6	12:3-29 13:1-19
Closing			
13:20-21			

Fig. 1. Six Primary OT Texts

This analysis demonstrates the consistency of the paraenesis in Hebrews 10:19—13:19 with the earlier sections of the discourse. It displays the same rhetorical arrangement and permits the argument of the homily to proceed directly to its crowning paraenetic conclusion.

An appreciation of the thematic development, of the form of certain segments and of the transitions between sections often depends on an understanding of the function of OT texts in defining the arrangement and argument in Hebrews.

The manner in which the writer makes use of the OT shows that he stands in the mainstream of Judaism* and early Jewish Christianity.* The distinctiveness of his interpretation of Scripture was determined by his Christian theology of the interrelationship of history, eschatology and revelation. But the principles that guided his approach to the OT text and the forms of exposition he adopted were drawn from synagogue preaching. It is safe to assume that his audience was thoroughly familiar with the approaches to the scriptural text that char-

	Thesis	*Paraenesis*
1:1—2:18	**I. The Revelation of God Through His Son**	
1:1-4	A. God Has Spoken His Ultimate Word in His Son	
1:5-14	B. The Transcendent Dignity of the Son	
2:1-4		*C. The First Warning:* The Peril of Ignoring the Word Delivered by the Son
2:5-9	D. The Humiliation and Glory of the Son	
2:10-18	E. The Solidarity of the Son with the Human Family	
3:1—5:10	**II. The High Priestly Character of the Son**	
3:1-6		A. Consider That Jesus Was Faithful to God Who Appointed Him
3:7-19		B. *The Second Warning:* The Peril of Refusing to Believe God's Word
4:1-14		C. Strive to Enter God's Rest, the Sabbath Celebration for the People of God
4:15—5:10	D. A High Priest Worthy of Our Faith Because He Is the Son of God Who Is Compassionate	
5:11—10:39	**III. The Highly-Priestly Office of the Son**	
5:11—6:12		A. *The Third Warning:* The Peril of Spiritual Immaturity
6:13-20	B. A Basis for the Confidence and Steadfastness	
7:1-10	C. Melchizedek, the Royal Priest	
7:11-28	D. Jesus, Eternal Priest like Melchizedek	
8:1-13	E. Sanctuary and Covenant	
9:1-10	F. The Necessity for New Cultic Action	
9:11-28	G. Decisive Purgation through the Blood of Christ	
10:1-18	H. The Ultimate Character of Christ's Single, Personal Sacrifice for Sins	
10:19-39		I. *The Fourth Warning:* The Peril of Disloyalty to Christ
11:1—12:13	**IV. Loyalty to God Through Persevering Faith**	
11:1-40	A. The Triumphs of Perseverance in Faith	
11:1-7	1. In the Antediluvian Era	
11:8-22	2. In the Patriarchal Era	
11:23-31	3. In the Mosaic Era	
11:32-40	4. In the Subsequent Era	
12:1-13		B. Display the Necessary Endurance
12:14—13:25	**V. Orientation for Life as Christians in a Hostile World**	
12:14-29		A. *The Final Warning:* The Peril of Refusing God's Gracious Word
13:1-25		B. Serve God Acceptably Within the Confessing Community

Fig. 2.   Analysis of Hebrews: The Primacy of Paraensis

acterize this homily, for they also were conversant with the liturgy and preaching that were the mainstay of Hellenistic synagogues of the Diaspora.

Hebrews is a reminder that the OT remains a valid and significant witness to God's redemptive word and deed. Christians must appreciate this witness in the light of God's decisive act of speaking through the Son (Heb 1:1-2). The words of the OT are invoked not for their significance in the past but for their significance in the present. For the writer of Hebrews, Scripture in its entirety remains a revelation of God's unalterable plan of redemption for the human family.

9. Canonical Recognition.

Hebrews asserted an intrinsic authority in the early church, both in the West and in the East. But there was reluctance to acknowledge it as integral to the church's rule of faith and practice. In the West we find early evidence for the impact of Hebrews on the life of the Christian community in Rome through *1 Clement*. As we have earlier noted, *1 Clement* reflects a detailed literary acquaintance with Hebrews, and the manner in which he made use of Hebrews indicates that he recognized its authority (*1 Clem.* 9.3-4 [cf. Heb 11:5-7]; 12.1-3 [cf. Heb 11:31]; 17.1 [cf. Heb 11:37]; 19.2 [cf. Heb 12:1]; 21.9 [cf. Heb 4:12]; 27.2 [cf. Heb 6:18]; 36.1-6 [cf. Heb 1:3-13; 2:17-18; 4:15-16]; 43.1 [cf. Heb 3:2-5]).

The *Shepherd of Hermas*, an apocalyptic* prophecy* written in Rome between 120 and 140, appears to have known Hebrews. *Hermas* reflects questions raised in the Roman church concerning repentance* and the possibility of "second" repentance. The writer of Hebrews is the only teacher in the period prior to *Hermas* who is known to have expressed precisely the eschatological singularity of baptismal* repentance and of forgiveness.* Since Hebrews was circulating within the Roman Christian community, the writer may have been the teacher from whom *Hermas* received the instruction concerning the singularity of repentance. *Hermas* developed its prophetic message concerning a second repentance in formal recognition of the teaching of Hebrews but in substantial contrast to Hebrews (*Herm. Vis.* 2.2.4-5). (Other passages in *Hermas* that appear to reflect an acquaintance with Hebrews are *Visions* 2.2.7 [cf. Heb 11:33]; *Visions* 2.3.2 [cf. Heb 3:13]; *Visions* 3.7.2 [cf. Heb 3:13]; *Visions* 4.2.4; *Similitudes* 9.13.7 [cf. Heb 11:33]; *Similitudes* 9.22 [cf. Heb 10:19-20].)

Justin Martyr clearly knew Hebrews (Justin *Apol. I* 12.9 [cf. Heb 3:1]; *Dial. Tryph.* 13.1 [cf. Heb 9:13-14]; 19.3 [cf. Heb 11:5]; 19.4 [cf. Heb 5:6; 6:20; 7:1-2]; 46.3; 56.1 [cf. Heb 3:5]; 67.9 [cf. Heb 12:21]; 96.1 [cf. Heb 7:17, 24]; 113.5 [cf. Heb 5:6, 10]; 121.2 [cf. Heb 4:12-13]). Hebrews was known and used by Irenaeus (Eusebius *Hist. Eccl.* 5.26.3), by Gaius of Rome (c. 200, Eusebius *Hist. Eccl.* 6.20.2) and by Hippolytus (*Refut.* 6.30.9), all of whom recognized that it was not Pauline in origin.

The absence of Hebrews from Marcion's* *Apostolicon* (Tertullian *Marc.* 5) is sufficiently explained by its strong reliance upon the OT and upon Jewish thought forms. The Muratorian canon, which appears to date from the last quarter of the second century and provides a list of the documents received as authoritative by the church in Rome, makes no mention of Hebrews. In the West, Hebrews was seldom quoted in the third century and in the first half of the fourth century.

Some church leaders in the West questioned the authority of Hebrews. Confusion over the distinction between authorship and authority was widespread (*see* Canon). By the end of the second century and the beginning of the third, Roman opinion had crystallized in excluding Hebrews from the Pauline letter canon. The voice of Hebrews was muted for the church in the West. Even when its authority was formally recognized in the fourth century and Hebrews was admitted to the canon* of sacred Scripture, there is little evidence that it exercised any considerable influence upon the thought, life and liturgy of the church in the West.

In the East the early Alexandrian fathers and the Eastern church in general appear to have recognized the intrinsic authority of Hebrews and attributed it to Paul. It is probable that in the East the superscription "To the Hebrews" was first added to manuscripts. Hebrews was known to Pantaenus (c. 180) and to Clement of Alexandria (c. 200) (Eusebius *Hist. Eccl.* 6.14.1-4). Pantaenus, Clement of Alexandria and Origen (Eusebius *Hist. Eccl.* 6.14.1-4; 6.25.11-14) acknowledge the presence of Hebrews among a collection of Paul's letters and sense the necessity of justifying that association. The arguments advanced by Clement and Origen to defend the legitimacy of this arrangement are a witness to recognition of the intrinsic authority of Hebrews in the East by the end of the second century.

Late in the fourth century, under the influence of Western fathers who had spent time in the East, an agreement was reached between East and West that Hebrews was a letter of Paul's (see Hilary of Poitiers *Trin.* 4.11). Jerome was aware of the diversity of opinion regarding Hebrews. Although he displayed caution in his citations of Hebrews, he had no reservations concerning its intrinsic authority and its right to be included in the NT (Jerome *Vir.* 5; *Ep.* 53.8; 129.3). Augustine recognized its authority and listed Hebrews among the letters of Paul (Augustine *Doctr. Christ.* 2.8; *Civ. D.* 16.22).

10. Concluding Observations.
The authority of a text is ultimately determined by the "performance" (i.e., its power to influence and effect change in the readers) of the text. Hebrews was preserved and transmitted because Christian leaders continued to use it, and positive results followed. The concern of the early church was with praxis, with piety, with an experienced, vital faith, with spiritual usefulness, and Hebrews demanded that its voice be heard.

The authority asserted by Hebrews early in the life of the church is a reminder that this document is more than a sensitive pastoral response relevant only to a specific occasion in the past. Rather a specific occasion was a catalyst for creative and prayerful theologizing. More than that, it was a response to revelation. It conveys a word from God addressed to the church in response to the often harsh realities of Christian discipleship in a troubled world. Within the NT canon Hebrews is an essential witness to the decisive eschatological character of God's redemptive action through Jesus Christ and to the urgency of unwavering commitment to him.

Its canonical status both reflects and confers normative status. The particular text was universalized, endowed with a life of its own so that it may address a variety of situations not identical with the situation that called forth the text. The authority of Hebrews to function as a rule of faith was recognized when Hebrews was used by the believing community for teaching, correcting, equipping and leading the community into the reality of the holiness that is indispensable to the enjoyment of the vision of God (Heb 12:14).

Hebrews has acquired a reputation for being formidable and remote from the world in which we live. Ironically Hebrews is a call for ultimate certainty and ultimate commitment. It concerns itself with the issue of certainty by confronting ultimate questions about life and death with ultimate realities. Its presentation of the way in which God responds to the human family as the God who speaks, creates, covenants, pledges, calls and commits himself is intended to breathe new life into men and women who experience a failure of nerve because they live in an insecure, anxiety-provoking society. Hebrews is a scriptural gift to be appreciated especially when God's people find themselves prone to discouragement or distraction from any cause. It is a gift the church sorely needs.

See also ABRAHAM; ANCESTORS; ANGELS, HEAVENLY BEINGS, ANGEL CHRISTOLOGY; CHRISTOLOGY; COVENANT, NEW COVENANT; DEATH OF CHRIST; JERUSALEM, ZION, HOLY CITY; JEWISH CHRISTIANITY; MELCHIZEDEK; MOSES; OLD TESTAMENT IN HEBREWS; PRIEST, HIGH PRIEST; PROMISE; REPENTANCE, SECOND REPENTANCE; RHETORIC, RHETORICAL CRITICISM; ROME, ROMAN CHRISTIANITY; SACRIFICE, OFFERINGS, GIFTS; TABERNACLE, SANCTUARY; WORSHIP AND LITURGY.

BIBLIOGRAPHY. **Commentaries:** H. W. Attridge, *A Commentary on the Epistle to the Hebrews* (Herm; Philadelphia: Fortress, 1989); S. Bénétreau, *L'épître aux Hébreux* (2 vols.; CEB 10; Vaux-sur-Seine: ÉDIFAC, 1989, 1990); H. Braun, *An die Hebräer* (HNT; Tübingen: J. C. B. Mohr, 1984); F. F. Bruce, *The Epistle to the Hebrews* (rev. ed.; NICNT; Grand Rapids: Eerdmans, 1990); G. W. Buchanan, *To the Hebrews* (AB; Garden City, NY: Doubleday, 1972); P. Ellingworth, *Commentary on Hebrews: A Commentary on the Greek Text* (NIGTC; Grand Rapids: Eerdmans, 1993); H. Feld, *Der Hebräerbrief* (BF; Darmstadt: Wissenschaftliche Buchgesellschaft, 1985); E. Grässer, *An die Hebräer* (2 vols.; EKK; Zürich: Benzinger, 1990, 1993); D. A. Hagner, *Hebrews* (NIBC; Peabody, MA: Hendrickson, 1990); H. Hegermann, *Der Brief an die Hebräer* (THKNT; Berlin: Evangelische Verlagsanstalt, 1988); P. E. Hughes, *A Commentary on the Epistle to the Hebrews* (Grand Rapids: Eerdmans, 1977); S. J. Kistemaker, *Exposition of the Epistle to the Hebrews* (NTCom; Grand Rapids: Baker, 1984); W. L. Lane, *Hebrews* (2 vols.; WBC; Dallas: Word, 1991); O. Michel, *Der Brief an die Hebräer* (MeyerK; 13th ed.; Göttingen: Vandenhoeck & Ruprecht, 1975);

J. Moffatt, *A Critical and Exegetical Commentary on the Epistle to the Hebrews* (ICC; Edinburgh: T & T Clark, 1924); V. C. Pfitzner, *Hebrews* (ANTC; Nashville: Abingdon, 1997); E. Riggenbach, *Der Brief an die Hebräer* (Wuppertal: Brockhaus, 1987); C. Spicq, *L'Épître aux Hébreux: Traduction, notes critique, commentaire* (SB; Paris: Gabalda, 1977); A. Strobel, *Der Brief an die Hebräer* (NTD; Göttingen: Vandenhoeck & Ruprecht, 1975); H. F. Weiss, *Der Brief an die Hebräer* (MeyerK; Göttingen: Vandenhoeck & Ruprecht, 1991). **Studies:** K. Backhaus, *Der Neue Bund und das Werden der Kirche: Die Diatheke-Deutung des Hebräerbrief im Rahmen der frühchristlichen Theologiegeschichte* (NTAbh 29; Münster: Aschendorff, 1996); A. Cody, *Heavenly Sanctuary and Liturgy in the Epistle to the Hebrews: The Achievement of Salvation in the Epistle's Perspectives* (St. Meinrad, IN: Grail, 1960); M. R. D'Angelo, *Moses in the Letter to the Hebrews* (SBLDS 42; Missoula, MT: Scholars Press, 1979); D. A. DeSilva, *Despising Shame: Honor Discourse and Community Maintenance in the Epistle to the Hebrews* (SBLDS 152; Atlanta: Scholars Press, 1995); J. Dunnill, *Covenant and Sacrifice in the Letter to the Hebrews* (SNTSMS 75; Cambridge: Cambridge University Press, 1992); L. Dussaut, *Synopse structurelle de l'Épître aux Hébreux: Approche d'analyse structurelle* (Paris: Desclé, 1981); F. V. Filson, *"Yesterday": A Study of Hebrews in the Light of Chapter 13* (SBT 2/4; London: SCM, 1967); E. Grässer, *Der Glaube im Hebräerbrief* (Marburg: Elwert, 1965); idem, "Der Hebräerbrief 1938-1963," *TRu* 30 (1964) 138-236; G. H. Guthrie, *The Structure of Hebrews: A Text Linguistic Analysis* (NovTSup 73; Leiden: E. J. Brill, 1994); D. M. Hay, *Glory at the Right Hand: Psalm 110 in Early Christianity* (SBLMS 18; Nashville: Abingdon, 1973); G. Hughes, *Hebrews and Hermeneutics: The Epistle to the Hebrews as a New Testament Example of Biblical Interpretation* (SNTSMS 36; Cambridge: Cambridge University Press, 1979); L. D. Hurst, *The Epistle to the Hebrews: Its Background of Thought* (SNTSMS 65; Cambridge: Cambridge University Press, 1990); M. E. Isaacs, *Sacred Space: An Approach to the Theology of the Epistle to the Hebrews* (JSNTSup 73; Sheffield: JSOT, 1992); E. Käsemann, *The Wandering People of God* (Minneapolis: Augsburg, 1984); W. L. Lane, "Hebrews as Pastoral Response" in *The Newell Lectures* (Anderson, IN: Warner, 1996) 3:91-201; S. Lehne, *The New Covenant in Hebrews* (JSNTSup 44; Sheffield: JSOT, 1990); D. F. Leschert, *Hermeneutical Foundations of Hebrews: A Study in the Validity of the Epistle's Interpretation of Some Core Citations from the Psalms* (Lewiston, NY: Edwin Mellen Press, 1994); B. Lindars, *The Theology of the Letter to the Hebrews* (NTT; Cambridge: Cambridge University Press, 1991); W. R. G. Loader, *Sohn und Hoherpriester: Eine traditionsgeschichtliche Untersuchung zur Christologie des Hebräerbriefes* (WMANT 53; Neukirchen/Vluyn: Neukirchener Verlag, 1981); J. C. McCullough, "Hebrews in Recent Scholarship," *IBS* 16 (1994) 66-86, 108-20; G. Mora, *La Carta a los Hebreos como Escrito Pastoral* (Barcelona: Herder, 1974); L. L. Neeley, "A Discourse Analysis of Hebrews," *Occasional Papers in Translation and Textlinguistics* 3.4 (1987) 1-146; D. G. Peterson, *Hebrews and Perfection: An Examination of the Concept of Perfection in the "Epistle to the Hebrews"* (SNTSMS 47; Cambridge: Cambridge University Press, 1982); D. J. Pursiful, *The Cultic Motif in the Spirituality of the Book of Hebrews* (Lewiston, NY: Edwin Mellen Press, 1993); M. Rissi, *Die Theologie des Hebräerbiefs: Ihre Verankerung in der Situation des Verfassers und seiner Leser* (WUNT 14; Tübingen: Mohr-Siebeck, 1987); J. M. Scholer, *Proleptic Priests: Priesthood in the Epistle to the Hebrews* (JSNTSup 49; Sheffield: JSOT, 1991); J. Swetnam, *Jesus and Isaac: A Study of the Epistle to the Hebrews in the Light of the Aqedah* (AnBib 94; Rome: Biblical Institute Press, 1981); K. J. Thomas, "The Old Testament Citations in Hebrews," *NTS* 11 (1964-65) 303-25; J. W. Thompson, *The Beginnings of Christian Philosophy: The Epistle to the Hebrews* (CBQMS 13; Washington, D.C.: The Catholic Biblical Association of America, 1981); H. Thyen, *Der Stil der jüdisch-hellenistischen Homilie* (FRLANT 47; Göttingen: Vandenhoeck & Ruprecht, 1955); A. Trotter, *Interpreting the Book of Hebrews* (Grand Rapids: Baker, 1997); W. G. Übelacker, *Der Hebräerbrief als Appel: Untersuchungen zu exordium, narratio und postscriptum (Hebr 1—2 und 13:22-25)* (CBNTS 21; Stockholm: Almqvist & Wiksell, 1989); A. Vanhoye, *Structure and Message of the Epistle to the Hebrews* (Rome: Pontificio Istituto Biblico, 1989); idem, *La structure littéraire de l'Épître aux Hébreux* (StudNeot 1; 2d ed.; Paris and Bruges: Descléer de Brouwer, 1976); R. Williamson, *Philo and the Epistle to the Hebrews* (ALGHJ 4; Leiden: E. J. Brill, 1970); H. Zimmermann, *Das Bekenntnis der Hoffnung: Tradition und Redeaktion im Hebräerbrief* (BBB 47; Cologne and Bonn: Hanstein, 1977). W. L. Lane

HELL, ABYSS, ETERNAL PUNISHMENT

A belief in divine punishment* after death was widespread in Jewish and Greco-Roman thought. In our literature one finds the specific expectation of everlasting torment by the one righteous God,* directed against all who are outside of Christ.* The canon* of Scripture and the apostolic fathers* refrained from the elaborate descriptions of hell that are found in other later literature.

1. The Canonical Material
2. Postapostolic Literature
3. Is Punishment Everlasting?

1. The Canonical Material.

1.1. Acts. The implication in Acts 1:25 is that when Judas Iscariot went to his "own place," it was to hell, although *ho idios topos* may be heaven or hell in other contexts (Ign. *Magn.* 5.1; Pol. *Phil.* 9.2). But compared with Luke's Gospel, Acts* hardly mentions hell or eternal punishment.

1.2. Hebrews. The author of Hebrews* pronounces destruction on those who fall away from Christ (Heb 10:39). These apostates* will perish like the Israelites under Moses,* but their end is no mere physical death. Rather, a fire will consume the enemies of God (Heb 10:26-27; cf. Heb 12:9). Those who hear the word but are "unfruitful ground" (Heb 6:7-8) will be cursed and burned, an image that the author apparently understands as fiery eschatological* judgment.* None of these passages, with their cursing, perishing and burning, are easily made to refer to the fire of correction during this life (as in *Herm. Sim.* 6—7) or to the testing fire of 1 Corinthians 3:13-15 (Ellingworth, 535).

1.3. James. God has the power to "save and destroy" (Jas 4:12). In James 5:3 the author (*see* James) may be speaking of the fire of hell, and he certainly does in James 3:6: "the tongue is a fire . . . and it is set ablaze by hell *(geenna)*."

1.4. 1 Peter. What is meant by the intriguing reference to Christ preaching to the "spirits in prison" in 1 Peter 3:19 (*see* 1 Peter)? If it is linked with 1 Peter 4:6 and Ephesians 4:9-10, it could mean that between his death and resurrection,* Christ "descended into hell." This doctrine was firmly established by the second century, mentioned for example by Justin Martyr and Irenaeus as well as the apocryphal* *Gospel of Nicodemus* (Goppelt, 260-63).

The trend of late has been to see a chrono-

logical sequence in 1 Peter 3:18-22. This proclamation occurred after Christ's death (*see* Death of Christ) and resurrection and before he was enthroned at God's right hand (*see* Exaltation). Perhaps this was a part of his ascension,* in which he announced to the dead or to the angels* his victory over death and demons (Michaels, 194-222).

1.5. Jude and 2 Peter. Both Jude* and 2 Peter* agreed with the tradition that evil angels have been imprisoned since their primeval rebellion. They have "sinned" (2 Pet 2:5) or left their positions of heavenly authority* (Jude 6), but there is no explicit reference to whether their sin was consorting with human women, as in the Jewish tradition (e.g., *1 Enoch* 12, based on Gen 6). In 2 Peter 2:5 the verb *tartaroō* means to "confine to Tartarus," which in Greek and Jewish literature referred to the deep abyss to which angels were consigned. They are bound by chains, a feature that turns up often in Greek, Jewish and Christian writings (see esp. *1 Enoch* 10:5). Both 2 Peter 2:17 and Jude 13 connect their fate to the destiny of false teachers. For the errorists too are the chains of darkness reserved, since they have fallen away from the true faith.* Jude 23 alludes to Zechariah 3:2 when it speaks of snatching the dupes of false teaching from the "fire," that is, arresting their slide into eschatological judgment.

The end of the wicked is "destruction" in 2 Peter 2:1, 3; 3:16 *(apōleia)* and 2 Peter 1:12 *(phthora)*. 2 Peter and Jude, again following tradition, use the destruction of Sodom as an example of fiery judgment (Jude 7; 2 Pet 2:6-10; cf. Mt 10:15; *1 Clem.* 11.1-2). Along the same lines, God will rescue the righteous from the fire as he did Lot. He will destroy both heaven* and earth with fire (2 Pet 3:7, 12).

1.6. Revelation.

1.6.1. Abyss, Hades. In the literature under consideration "abyss" *(abyssos)* has reference to the infernal regions only in Revelation (*see* Revelation, Book of). Elsewhere it denotes the deep places of the seas. Despite its etymology, this abyss is not a "bottomless pit" (Rev 9:1 KJV) but an enclosed subterranean chamber. The phrase "the shaft *[phrear]* of the abyss" in Revelation 9:1 may mean that the abyss itself is a shaft or more likely that its entrance is a shaft (see Rev 9:2; 11:7; 17:8). It is critical to the book's plot that the abyss may be shut up from the outside. Once secured, it may be locked with a key and sealed

(Rev 20:1-3) so that it serves as a prison (*phylakē*, Rev 20:7; cf. Lk 8:31; 1 Pet 3:19). In Revelation 9:1-2 an angel from heaven is given the key to the abyss, from which he allows the "locusts" to escape in a billow of smoke. In the Greek version of *1 Enoch* 20:2, the good angel Uriel is placed over Tartarus, but in Revelation the king of the abyss is an angel named Abaddon or Apollyon, "the Destroyer." Possibly a different angel is put in charge of the "fire" in Revelation 14:18, but his relationship to the abyss is not made clear. We are also told indirectly that the first beast* comes up from the abyss (Rev 11:7; 17:8).

The abyss plays its major role in Revelation 20:1-3. Satan* is chained and thrown into the abyss, and his underworldly cell is locked and sealed for a thousand years.

Where "abyss" appears in the apostolic fathers (*1 Clem.; Diogn.* *), it takes its other meaning, that is, "the watery deep" (based on the Heb *t^ehôm*, "the deep").

1.6.2. Death and Hades. In Revelation there may be an implicit connection between the abyss and Hades or hell (as in Ps 71:20; Rom 10:7; and the first-century *Apoc. Zeph.* 6:15). Just as heaven holds the key to the abyss, Jesus possesses the keys to death and Hades or hell (Rev 1:18; see also Rev 6:8).

1.6.3. The Lake of Fire. The final abode of wicked angels and human beings is "outside" the new Jerusalem* (Rev 21:27; 22:14-15), or more specifically in the "lake of fire." A lake of fire or burning sulfur is not uncommon in apocalyptic* literature, and it is equivalent to "gehenna" in the NT.

The destruction of Babylon,* after the fashion of Sodom's fall, is a foreshadowing of the eternal fire (Rev 18:9, 18; 19:3). The beast and the false prophet* are the first to be cast in (Rev 19:20), followed by the devil (Rev 20:10), death and Hades (Rev 20:14) and the wicked, where they undergo the "second death" (Rev 20:15; 21:8).

2. Postapostolic Literature.
Christ is the savior from future punishment. Even further, with language similar to that of John's Gospel, *2 Clement* 2.7 asserts that before Christ came, the Christians were perishing already.

Didache 16 refers only to the resurrection of the righteous and makes no reference to the resurrection or judgment of the wicked (*see*

Didache). Curiously, some scholars have offered this silence as proof that its author(s) took an "annihilationist" view, that damnation leads to nonexistence forever.

There is clearer information in other literature. When the *Epistle of Barnabas** spoke of the Two Ways, the way of the devil is the "way of eternal death with punishment" (*Barn.* 20.1). Clement of Rome* is more detailed. The destruction of Sodom presaged eternal fire for the wicked, salvation* for the righteous and destruction on the "double-minded," who like Lot's wife look back to the world (*1 Clem.* 11.1-2).

Ignatius* foresaw hell for those who threatened the united catholic church.* Twice he updated the warnings against the immoral in 1 Corinthians 6:9-10; in his new version, corrupting teachers with their followers will not enter the kingdom of God (*see* Kingdom of God) but will go into the "unquenchable fire" (Ign. *Eph.* 16.1-2; Ign. *Phld.* 3.3). As in Hebrews, an eternity in hell is within the realm of possibility as a warning for people who are professedly Christians. The author of *2 Clement* foresees the same reversal (*2 Clem.* 6.7-9; 7.6; 10.5).

The literature of this period originated from a church under persecution,* and the prospect of eternal torture was offered as a counterpoint to the pains of earthly suffering.* The Jews of the Second Temple period had already grasped that truth (cf. 4 Macc 9:7-9), and it was taught by the Lord* himself (Mt 10:28; cf. *2 Clem.* 5.4). In that vein the author of *Diognetus* 10.7 promised his hearers that at their conversion, "you will recognize that which is true life in heaven, then you will scorn that which is here thought to be death, then you will fear that which is truly death." Theory comes to life in the *Martyrdom of Polycarp*, as Polycarp* was forced to weigh the everlasting fire of God's judgment against a dreadful but fleeting martyrdom* at the stake (*Mart. Pol.* 11.2). As for all the martyrs of Smyrna, "to them the fire of the inhuman torturers was cold, for they had set before their eyes an escape from the fire that is eternal and is never quenched" (*Mart. Pol.* 2.3).

The scant references to hell's destruction in the *Shepherd of Hermas** are reserved for those who defect from Christ (*Herm. Vis.* 3.7.2; *Herm. Sim.* 6.2.4; cf. *Herm. Sim.* 9.31.2). These will face "double punishment," perishing forever (*Herm.*

Sim. 9.18.2; *apothanountai eis ton aiōna).*

At the close of this period Justin Martyr made the fullest use of the fires of hell for apologetic purposes. He argued before the Roman government that if Christians believe that wickedness leads to hell, then they are highly motivated to live as good citizens (Justin *Apol. I* 12; 17). Plato and other thinkers, claimed Justin, borrowed their ideas about hell from the OT (Justin *Apol. I* 20; 44; 54; cf. Justin *Cohor. Graec.* 27). The existence of hell implies that human responsibility, not fate, controls our destiny (Justin *Apol. I* 43). In his *Dialogue with Trypho* Justin kept citing Isaiah 66:24 and Matthew 8:11-12 in tandem to show that some Jews will be sent to hell and some Gentiles* will enter the kingdom of God; everything hinges on one's response to Christ.

3. Is Punishment Everlasting?

If the extant literature is any indication, then an overwhelming majority within the ancient church were persuaded that damnation leads to everlasting, conscious suffering. The main historical alternatives are annihilationism, the view that the wicked eventually are consumed by the fire and forfeit their existence, or Origen's "curative" approach, in which the wicked are eventually purged and reconciled to God (Bernstein, 308; Kelly, 483-85).

3.1. Lexical Background. It has been argued that the key adjective *aiōnios* does not mean "everlasting" when it defines hell's torments but rather "lasting a long period of time." This interpretation rests partly on a few scattered passages in which *aiōnios* could be read that way and partly on its etymological relationship to *aiōn* ("ages"). This leads to the precarious logic that *aiōnios* must therefore mean "for many ages" rather than forever.

A search of early Christian literature reveals that, apart from a few places where it means "from eternity past" (e.g., 2 Tim 1:9; never in the apostolic fathers), *aiōnios* transparently takes the meaning of "everlasting" (e.g., Heb 5:9; 1 Pet 5:10; 2 Pet 1:11). The expectation of eternal punishment (*2 Clem.* 5.4-5) frequently provides the counterpart to "eternal life," which no one would argue is merely long-lasting. The real issue is whether God's punishment is consciously experienced by the wicked for eternity or whether it is everlasting in its permanence but not in its infliction of torment.

3.2. Canonical Material. Jude 7 contains the threat of "eternal fire" *(pyros aiōniou)* for the apostates. This was the "eternal fire" that destroyed Sodom, which fire was thought to burn perpetually. It is not said whether the wicked feel its pain forever.

In Revelation the devil, beast and false prophet "will be tormented day and night, forever and ever" (Rev 20:10). Although there is no explicit matching statement for wicked humanity, it is the natural reading of "the smoke of their torment arises forever and ever" (Rev 14:11, based on Is 34:10; cf. Rev 19:3).

While the author of Revelation joins the rest of the canonical writers in calling the fate of the wicked "death," death in that case is defined not as extinction but as existence in the inferno (Rev 20:14).

3.3. Later Developments. The postapostolic literature abounds in stereotyped language about everlasting punishment (e.g., *2 Clem.* 6.7; *Mart. Pol.* 11.2; Ign. *Eph.* 16.2; *Barn.* 20.1; also Justin Martyr *Apol. I* 8; 12; 17; 19; 45; Justin *Apol. II* 1; 2; Justin *Dial. Tryph.* 45; 117; 120; 130; Justin *Fragm.* 3; 4). Hermas referred to eternal destruction in *Hermas Similitude* 6.2.4 *(apōleian . . . aiōnion),* a fate that he repeatedly contrasted with life in the kingdom of God.

Another common motif, the "unquenchable fire," is borrowed from Isaiah 66:24 by way of Mark 9:48 (see also Sir 7:17; Jdt 16:17). Gehenna is the place "where their worm never dies, and their fire is never quenched" (*2 Clem.* 17.5; Ign. *Eph.* 16.2; *Mart. Pol.* 2.3).

A singular exception to this model turns up in *Diognetus* 10.7 in a reference to "the everlasting fire that shall punish to the end *(mechri telous)* those who are given over to it," perhaps a prediction of the eventual annihilation of the wicked. The ambiguity lies in the fact that in actual usage "unto the end" did not necessarily imply a conclusion or termination (cf. Heb 3:14) and likely meant "forever" (see the similar wording in 1 Thess 2:16; *Herm. Sim.* 8.8.5).

In the writings of Justin Martyr "eternal fire" was certainly intended to intimate everlasting suffering. Justin could not content himself with merely repeating the traditional formulations, since his books were designed to explain concepts such as the resurrection to a Greek audience. Christ himself will assign the wicked to hell once their souls are reunited with their bodies (Justin *Apol. I* 8), and, immortal, they have an eternal consciousness of pain (Justin *Apol. I* 52). Their torment will be everlasting *(aiōnios)*, not a mere thousand years, as Plato had taught (Justin *Apol. I* 8). When Justin predicted that wicked angels and humans will "cease to exist" in *Apology II* 7, he was speaking of ceasing from the earth, in the tradition of 2 Peter 3:3-13.

See also DAY OF THE LORD; ESCHATOLOGY; JUDGMENT; LIFE AND DEATH; MORTALITY AND IMMORTALITY.

BIBLIOGRAPHY. A. E. Bernstein, *The Formation of Hell: Death and Retribution in the Ancient and Early Christian Worlds* (Ithaca: Cornell University Press, 1993); J. W. Cooper, *Body, Soul and Life Everlasting: Biblical Anthropology and the Monism-Dualism Debate* (Grand Rapids: Eerdmans, 1989); P. Ellingworth, *Epistle to the Hebrews* (NIGTC; Grand Rapids: Eerdmans, 1993); L. Goppelt, *A Commentary on I Peter,* ed. F. Hahn (Grand Rapids: Eerdmans, 1993); J. Jeremias, "ἄβυσσος," *TDNT* 1:9-10; idem, "γέεννα," *TDNT* 1:657-658; J. N. D. Kelly, *Early Christian Doctrines* (rev. ed.; New York: Harper & Row, 1978); J. R. Michaels, *1 Peter* (WBC; Waco, TX: Word, 1988); H. Sasse, "αἰών, αἰώνιος," *TDNT* 1:197-209; W. R. Schoedel, *Ignatius of Antioch: A Commentary on the Letters of Ignatius of Antioch* (Herm; Philadelphia: Fortress, 1985). G. S. Shogren

HELLENISTIC CHRISTIANITY. *See* HELLENISTS, HELLENISTIC AND HELLENISTIC-JEWISH CHRISTIANITY.

HELLENISTIC-JEWISH CHRISTIANITY.
See HELLENISTS, HELLENISTIC AND HELLENISTIC-JEWISH CHRISTIANITY.

HELLENISTS, HELLENISTIC AND HELLENISTIC-JEWISH CHRISTIANITY

Acts 6:1-6 records the earliest known Christian controversy, a dispute between the Hebrews (those who spoke Aramaic) and the Hellenists (those who spoke Greek; *Hellēn,* "Greek") over the inequitable distribution of food to the Hellenist widows. According to Acts, the conflict was resolved by the appointment of a board of seven apparently Hellenist leaders charged with oversight of the church's* benevolent work. According to many biblical scholars, however, the controversy went much deeper and lasted much longer: Palestinian (Hebrew) and Dias-

pora* (Hellenist) Jews thought differently and so as Christians propagated divergent and competing forms of Christianity. Thus the essential distinction between Hebrews and Hellenists was theological, not linguistic, and their essential disagreement was a matter of religious perception, not charitable dispensation. In other words the Hebrews and Hellenists were the first Christian factions. Other scholars have challenged this approach, citing, for example, recent insights into the complex relationship between first-century Palestinian Judaism* and Hellenism (*see DPL,* Hellenism). It is ironic, according to this latter view, that the original dispute between the Hebrews and Hellenists, having been settled in a matter of days, has generated a controversy that remains unresolved after 150 years.

1. Background
2. Theoretical Questions
3. Exegetical Questions
4. Conclusion

1. Background.
Many influential nineteenth-century intellectuals regarded Hellenism and Judaism as diametrical opposites. For example, M. Arnold in "Hebraism and Hellenism" wrote that "between these two points of influence moves our world. . . . The uppermost idea with Hellenism is to see things as they really are; the uppermost idea with Hebraism is conduct and obedience" (Arnold, 165). Arnold sought the middle ground between what he regarded as two contrary but equally important positions. For many others the opposition between Judaism and Hellenism was absolute; choice, not compromise, was necessitated, and Judaism was decidedly the inferior partner in most such comparisons.

The contrasting of Judaism and Hellenism both owed much and offered much to a society largely contemptuous of the Jews. An example of the disparagement of Judaism may be found in nineteenth-century Gentile biblical scholarship, in which the religion of the Jews is derided as formalistic, idolatrous, superficial, stern and even perverse. Such characterizations were nowhere more commonplace than in Germany, where Luther himself earlier had extended if not established the precedent of Christian anti-Semitism.

In retrospect one may describe the task of many nineteenth-century (in particular German) NT scholars as the rescue of Christianity (in particular Pauline Christianity) from Judaism. The obvious strategy was to link Christianity to Hellenism and in so doing demonstrate Christianity's clear opposition to and superiority over Judaism. The obvious text on which to found such an argument was Acts 6:1.

1.1. F. C. Baur. Beginning in 1831 F. C. Baur advanced the theory that the early Jerusalem* church was divided into two theologically based parties corresponding to Luke's Hellenists and Hebrews. The conservative Hebrews "adhered as nearly as possible to the Jewish religion," whereas the liberal Hellenists came in a short time to recognize the clear "antagonism of Christianity to Judaism" (Baur 1873-75, 1:41-43).

According to Baur, Stephen,* the Hellenist leader, spoke out against the Mosaic law* and taught that the building of the temple* under Solomon had been contrary to the will of God,* who opposed "external, sensuous, ceremonial worship." "This inevitable rending asunder of Christianity from Judaism, whereby Judaism would be rendered negative as an absolute religion, and by which its final extinction was threatened, had been realized by Stephen; the high, liberal standpoint which he assumed, fostered in him the energetic zeal with which he laboured in the cause of Jesus" (Baur 1873-75, 1:48, 59).

A bloodthirsty mob lynched the radical Stephen, an incident that touched off a "great persecution" of the church in Jerusalem (*see* Persecution). According to Acts 8:1, all the believers were scattered, "except the apostles" (*see* Apostles). "This may justly surprise us," wrote Baur. What persecution is directed at followers but not leaders? "However, it cannot be doubted that they [the apostles] remained behind in Jerusalem. . . . But if they remained we cannot believe that they were the only ones who did so, but rather that the persecution first directed against the Hellenist Stephen was in fact carried on *against the Hellenistic part of the Church*" (Baur 1873-75, 1:39, emphasis added).

The consequences of this selective persecution of the Hellenist Christians were profound: "The two elements composing it, the Hellenistic and Hebraistic . . . now became outwardly separated from each other. At that time the Church at Jerusalem was purely Hebraistic; as such it adhered closely to its strictly Judaizing charac-

ter, and a strenuous opposition to the liberal Hellenistic Christianity was consequently developed" (Baur 1873-75, 1:40).

The Hellenists, having fled Jerusalem, founded the church of Antioch,* which soon became the second and only dynamic center of the Christian faith.* From the ranks of the Hellenists emerged Paul, whose great missionary work was obstructed and opposed by the Hebrew leaders Peter and James. Thus by mid-first century there appeared two separate but scarcely equal Christianities: the liberal-minded, universalistic, Hellenistic church and its moribund, legalistic and rigidly Jewish (= Hebrew) counterpart.

1.2. Baur's Influence. Baur was the first modern scholar to publish a comprehensive reconstruction of the history behind the earliest Christian texts. Moreover, Baur was one of the first commentators to take seriously disagreement within the primitive church. Baur's conclusions may be heavily disputed, but they cannot be and were not lightly dismissed.

Opponents, such as J. B. Lightfoot, focused their attack on two vital points: Baur's evaluation and use of sources (in particular his extreme skepticism toward Acts*) and his assertion of an open split between Paul and the Jerusalem apostles. Baur's views concerning the Hebrews and Hellenists were seldom challenged, being based on widely held assumptions about the relationship between Judaism and Hellenism. Lightfoot himself was convinced that the Hellenists would naturally "accept and interpret the new revelation in a less rigorous spirit than the Hebrew [Christian] zealot of Jerusalem" and that the Hebrews "regarded their Hellenist brethren with suspicion and distrust." Lightfoot is here indistinguishable from Baur: "a breach [with Judaism] was made, and the assailants as might be expected were Hellenists." Stephen "was the first . . . to sound the death-knell of the Mosaic ordinances and the temple worship, and to claim for the Gospel unfettered liberty and universal rights" (Lightfoot, 296-98).

Among those contemporaries who did attack Baur's interpretation of Acts 6:1—8:3 was L. Wolff, who rejected the notion that the "great persecution" was directed solely against the Hellenists. He also challenged Baur's reading of Stephen's speech in Acts 7: "Stephen's criticism is directed against the opinion that temple worship was in itself the complete fulfill-ment of the worship of God" (Wolff, 92-93, 96-97). Similarly M. Baumgarten wrote that Baur's Stephen is "an imaginary character" and that Baur's interpretation of Acts 7 "is a mere arbitrary conceit, which is opposed by the whole tenor of the discourse" (Baumgarten, 1:138, 158). Similar protests were penned a generation later by W. Soltau and W. Mundle, among oth-ers.

On this issue, however, Baur's opponents did not carry the day. Other, more influential schol-ars, including E. Zeller, F. Overbeck, H. J. Holtzmann and J. Wellhausen, assumed Baur's perspective. Gradually the core elements of Baur's proposal rose to the place of critical ortho-doxy. In contemporary NT commentaries, in-troductions, handbooks, theologies and histo-ries, in biblical annotations, dictionary articles and scholarly studies, we find these ideas consis-tently represented: the Hebrews and Hellenists were ideologically based parties, Stephen de-nounced temple worship and law observance, the Hellenists were selectively persecuted and the Hebrew church of Jerusalem and Hellenist church of Antioch were in constant tension and frequent conflict with one another. These opin-ions are repeated without attribution by teach-ers and writers across the theological spectrum at every level of academic sophistication. A few representative examples follow.

According to F. F. Bruce, "the Hellenists . . . were Jews who spoke Greek and whose way of life, in the eyes of stricter Palestinians, smacked too much of Greek customs." Stephen made "a vigorous attack on the Temple cultus," and at least some of Stephen's fellow Hellenists taught that "the coming of Jesus abrogated the Law," a position that would "inevitably cause tension between them and the more traditionalist 'He-brews.'" Bruce stated also that "the death of Stephen was the signal for a campaign of repres-sion by the authorities in Jerusalem against those who were of his way of thinking. Luke does not say explicitly that the Hellenists . . . were the principal targets of this campaign, but it emerges fairly clearly from his narrative that this was so" (Bruce 1972, 206, 208, 210, 214-15).

R. Bultmann made each of these same points in his seminal *Theology of the New Testament*. He also argued that the Seven were not deacons (contra Acts 6:2-3) but rather leaders of a Hel-lenistic party; as such "their office was by no means serving table, but . . . they were pro-claimers of the word" (Bultmann, 55-56). This observation is echoed by L. T. Johnson in his popular *The Writings of the New Testament: An Interpretation* (227).

J. C. Beker referred to "the Stephen group that founded the Antioch church" and " 'liber-alized' the Torah with respect to the validity of the temple and the cultic law" (Beker, 341-42). Similarly G. Bornkamm stated that the author of Acts concealed "a much more serious cleav-age" within the Jerusalem church. The Hel-lenists had come to "an understanding of the gospel altogether revolutionary in the eyes of the rest of the church." "Obviously, the non-Hel-lenistic part of the mother church was left un-molested" (Bornkamm, 14).

E. Haenchen provided an elegant restate-ment of Baur's interpretation of Acts 6:1—8:3 in *The Acts of the Apostles*. Equally prominent is the work of M. Hengel, whose analysis of early church history gives pride of place to the Hel-lenists, who "recognized above all" that "the protective attitude of Judaism over against its environment . . . most strongly expressed by the absolutizing place of the Torah" was "shattered in pieces" by the message of Jesus (Hengel 1974, 1:313-14).

If all academic questions were settled by vote, the clear winner in the precinct of Acts 6—8 would be Baur and his Hellenist party. All the same the choice would not be unanimous, and the incumbent's future would not be assured. Scholars are asking new and substantial ques-tions about the validity of Baur's interpretation.

2. Theoretical Questions.

Two key events have shaped NT interpretation during the past half century: the Holocaust, which has led many to an awareness of the role that anti-Semitism has played in the interpreta-tion of Christian Scripture; and the discovery of the Dead Sea Scrolls, which has alerted scholars to the diversity and complexity of first-century Palestinian Judaism. Let us consider the rele-vance of each of these points.

Horror at the ready use of the NT in support of Nazism—and shame at the silence of count-less Christians who witnessed the near annihila-tion of European Jewry—have motivated many recent scholars to take care to interpret the Bible from a point of view that is fair to Judaism. For example, commentators now recognize that much of the NT was composed in the nascent church's bitter conflict with Judaism; therefore, many of its harshest statements, such as John's sometimes vitriolic references to "the Jews," must be understood within their immediate argumentative context. A second consequence is the reinterpretation of some biblical passages whose exegesis had been prejudiced by anti-Jewish assumptions; much recent work on Romans 9—11 fits within this category. A third effect is the reclamation of passages that offer a favorable view of the Jews and Judaism, such as the depiction of Elizabeth and Zechariah in Luke 1:6.

These insights force the question, Is the standard view of the Hebrews and Hellenists founded on solid exegesis or simple prejudice? Was it really a case of good Hellenists versus bad Hebrews? Were the historical lines so conventionally and conveniently drawn?

The second point concerns the revolution in Judaic studies precipitated by the discovery of the Dead Sea Scrolls together with numerous lesser but complementary archaeological findings. In the past fifty years many pillar assumptions about the conservatism and homogeneity of Palestinian Judaism have fallen, notably the longstanding dichotomy between Judaism and Hellenism. To quote Hengel, "It is [now] certain that ancient Judaism was extremely pluralistic—even in Palestine itself—and in turn was influenced in many ways by its 'Hellenistic' environment" (Hengel 1983, xiv). M. Smith writes, "Greek thought, in one way or another, had affected the court and the commons, the Temple and the tavern, the school and the synagogue" (81). Palestine had been Hellenized for three centuries prior to Jesus; thus all of Palestinian Judaism was to an extent Hellenistic, as by extension was all of Christianity. Borders and minds were surprisingly open. Israel was not the hermit kingdom.

This means that one can no longer claim that because a Jew was from Palestine, he or she must have thought in certain predictable ways. This realization, like new wine bursting an old wineskin, has spattered the pages and scattered the ink of conventional wisdom. For example, prior to the discoveries at Qumran,* it was commonly believed that the Gospel of John was the most Hellenistic and therefore un-Palestinian of the canonical Gospels; however, in light of its many affinities with the Dead Sea Scrolls, John is now frequently regarded as the NT's most Palestinian Gospel.

The questions these facts raise about the interpretation of Acts 6:1—8:3 are obvious. If Judaism and Hellenism are not opposites, can the opposition of Hebrews and Hellenists be maintained? Would not the religious diversity of Palestinian Judaism be mirrored in Palestinian Jewish Christianity? Further, is it the case (as was supposed by W. Bousset, Bultmann and others) that many key Christian concepts could have developed only outside of Palestine?

I. H. Marshall has noted the problem: "If no hard and fast distinction can be made between Palestinian and Hellenistic Judaism, it is unlikely that one can press the distinction between Palestinian and Hellenistic Jewish Christianity." Therefore "we must conclude that the hypothesis of a theological distinction between Aramaic- and Greek-speaking sections of the Jewish church rests on inadequate grounds" (Marshall, 274).

3. Exegetical Questions.

Doubts concerning the adequacy of the Hebrew/Hellenist dichotomy have encouraged some scholars to take a second look at Acts 6:1—8:3 and related passages. What follows is a sampling of the questions they have raised about the traditional interpretation of these texts.

3.1. Acts 6:1-5. Does the author of Acts deliberately obscure a much deeper conflict between the Hebrews and Hellenists? One major component of the argument concerns the supposed domestication of the Seven: it is often claimed that these Hellenist leaders were assigned a minor role that is in conspicuous conflict with their (at least Stephen's and Philip's*) subsequent preaching* activity (Acts 6:8—8:40). This assumes the incompatibility of administrative and evangelistic* ministries. Acts does not preclude other forms of service* on the part of the Seven; it acknowledges that they had proven themselves already to be "full of the Spirit and wisdom" (*see* Holy Spirit; Wisdom). Moreover it was a common practice in Judaism to appoint boards of seven men to oversee important work (*see* Church Order).

More basic is a factor seldom included in the scholarly calculation: Acts 6:1-5 appears to be modeled in a fashion evident elsewhere in Luke-Acts on OT narrative (*see* Intertextuality), in this case the stories about the appointment of Moses'* assistants (Ex 18:13-27; Deut 1:9-18; Num 11). The account in Numbers describes even the "murmuring" of the people regarding the "daily distribution" of manna. The elders appointed to deal with the problem were filled with the Spirit, and two of them, Eldad and Medad (Num 11:26-30), were given prophetic* ministries—recalling the Spirit-endowed ministries of Stephen and Philip. The joining of the two forms of ministry is intentional, as are the echoes of the Exodus experience (Lk 9:31; Acts 2:22, etc.). The church succeeds when faced with challenges like those that threatened nascent Israel. (In similar fashion the earlier conflict over Ananias and Sapphira [Acts 5:1-11] harkens back to the paradigmatic story of Achan and his family, who "took some of the devoted things . . . acted deceitfully, and put them among their possessions" [Josh 7:11].)

3.2. Acts 6:11-14. Stephen is accused of teaching* that "Jesus of Nazareth will destroy this place [the temple] and will change the customs . . . [of] Moses" (Acts 6:14). Are these charges true? Many scholars argue that the "false witnesses" (Acts 6:13) were telling the truth*; Stephen was a radical critic of both law and temple. There are two basic problems with this view: (1) The actual charge concerns future, eschatological* destruction and change; this is a different belief from that usually credited to Stephen. (2) It would be obvious to the original readers of Luke-Acts that the temple charge at least was patently false; Jesus never threatened to destroy the temple himself (see Lk 13:34-35; 20:9-19; 21:6). The author's point throughout the narrative is that the Jews are guilty of disobedience (*see* Obedience), by which they themselves have brought about the destruction of their temple. Stephen's innocence is assumed.

3.3. Acts 7:2-53. Does Stephen dispense with the law and attack the building of the temple? The counter to the first of these points is simple: Moses and the law are treated almost glowingly in Stephen's speech; it is the Jews, who "received the law as ordained by angels," who "have not kept it" (Acts 7:53). The issue of temple criticism is much more complicated. It is certainly possible that Stephen made inflammatory statements about the temple, perhaps repeating Jesus' prophetic warning concerning its future destruction. The question is whether Stephen's teachings would have offended not only Jewish

authorities but also Hebrew (but not Hellenist) Christians. Did Stephen believe that temple worship was inherently wrong, that the building of the temple was an act of apostasy?*

At two principal places in the speech scholars claim to find radical criticism of the temple. The more important of these is in Acts 7:46-48:

> [David] found favor with God and asked that he might find a dwelling place for the house of Jacob.

> But it was Solomon who built a house for him.

> Yet the Most High does not dwell in things made with human hands.

Does the author intend to contrast "finding a dwelling place" and "building a house"? Scholars since Baur have claimed that, according to Stephen, David wanted only to locate a place in Jerusalem for the mobile tabernacle*; Solomon's mistake was to think he could confine God to a permanent locale, the temple.

Numerous challenges are raised to this interpretation. David clearly intended to build the temple; the reference to asking (Acts 7:46) almost certainly refers to 2 Samuel 7:1-2, in which David inquires of the prophet Nathan concerning his desire to construct a house* for God. Psalm 132, from which the phrase "find . . . a dwelling place for the house of Jacob" is borrowed, is a song of ascents celebrating the establishment of the Davidic monarchy and Jerusalem cult in toto. Reference to "building a house" (Acts 7:47) is found in a number of related verses in the Septuagint; in 1 Kings 5:3 it refers specifically to David's original wish. The categories *tent* and *house* are not treated elsewhere in Acts 7 in a way that would be consistent with Baur's reading: we are told of a bad tent ("the tent of Moloch") in Acts 7:43 and of a good house ("the house of Jacob") in Acts 7:46.

Almost always ignored is the fact that Acts 7:48, which summarizes Acts 7:46-47, omits the words *house, dwelling place* and *tent*. (Several translations wrongly insert the word *houses*, which does not appear in the Greek text.) The point is simple: God does not reside in human structures, whether tents or temples. This is a sentiment well known to Judaism (see Solomon's own statement in 1 Kings 8:27) and at most argues against any who would tend to localize the presence and worship of God in the Jerusalem temple. This theme would be of undoubted importance to the author of Acts, whose purpose is to chronicle the spread of the gospel* "to the ends of the earth" (Acts 1:16).

It is worth noting the string of charges that conclude the speech (Acts 7:51-53). The Jews are "stiff-necked" and "uncircumcised in heart" "and ears." They "are forever opposing the Holy Spirit"; having slain the prophets, they have now "betrayed" and "murdered" the righteous* One. The final accusation takes up the theme that dominated the central portion of the speech: the rejection of Moses and the law (see Acts 7:23-42). "You are the ones that received the law as ordained by angels, and yet you have not kept it" (Acts 7:53; *see* Angels). At its core the speech argues that present Jewish rejection of Jesus, the prophet like Moses (Acts 7:37; cf. 3:22; Deut 18:18) is well precedented, as are its tragic consequences. (The curious reference to Babylon* in Acts 7:43 [cf. "Damascus" in Amos 5:27] puts in parallel the first destruction of the Jerusalem temple in 587 B.C. and the second in A.D. 70.)

The second passage commonly cited in reference to Stephen's radical temple criticism is Acts 7:41-43. Many believe that there is an essential link between the wilderness story and the building of the temple. This is because the idolatrous Israelites are said in Acts 7:41 to have rejoiced "in the work of their hands," and Acts 7:48, which refers at least in part to the temple, makes the point that God does not dwell in "handmade" structures. Hence it is concluded that the building of the temple was an act continuous with the fashioning of the golden calf at Sinai. But what of the "tabernacle of testimony," which was also handmade? The shift from the terrible judgment* of Acts 7:42-43 to the construction of the tabernacle in Acts 7:44 is seamless. The point about the limitations of "handmade" shrines in Acts 7:48 is repeated in Paul's Areopagus speech in Acts 17:24, undoubtedly reflecting the author's own point of view.

Contrary to Baur, all evidence strongly suggests that the early church arrived at law (not to mention temple) criticism gradually and in response to specific circumstances, especially as occasioned by the Gentile mission* (e.g., as in Acts 11:19-20; Gal. 2:1-14; Acts 15).

3.4. Acts 8:1-3. Were the Hellenists the only Christians persecuted in Jerusalem? Absolutely not. In Acts 4:1-22 John and Peter are arrested and threatened; in Acts 5:17-41 the "apostles"

are apprehended, miraculously freed, rearrested and then beaten. Acts 12:1-11 tells us that Herod "laid violent hands upon . . . the church," killing James and arresting Peter. According to Josephus,* James, the brother of Jesus (*see* Relatives of Jesus) and by most accounts the leader of the Hebrews, was put to death at the instigation of the high priest Ananus the Younger (the brother-in-law of Caiaphas, the high priest who, according to Acts 7:1, sat in judgment of Stephen). Paul speaks in 1 Thessalonians 2:14-16 of the persecution of the churches in Judea. Certain passages in the Synoptic Gospels appear to presuppose a state of persecution; Matthew 10:23 locates this in Israel specifically. Clearly if persecution of the Hellenists means anything, then persecution of the Hebrews means something equally significant.

What are we to make of the notorious statement in Acts 8:1 that "all were scattered, except the apostles"? Probably the author wished to assure his readers that the captains of the church remained at the helm, which means in Jerusalem. It is no accident that Acts tells us nothing of the wider travels of Cephas, "the other apostles and the brothers of the Lord" (1 Cor. 9:5). It is in the author's design that the Twelve* (Acts 1:15-26) remain associated with the holy city, the capital of God's saving activity. (Concerning the unique importance of Jerusalem in Luke-Acts see Lk 1:38; 9:31, 51; 13:33; 21:24; 23:28 [statements found only in Luke].) Luke defends the continuity between Judaism and Christianity in part by highlighting the Jerusalem-centeredness of the Christian revelation.* As Paul says to King Agrippa, "This was not done in a corner" [Acts 26:26]).

3.5. Galatians 2:1-10 and Acts 15:1-35. Were the later Hebrew church of Jerusalem and the Hellenist church of Antioch in controversy with one another? We know of two meetings of representatives of these two congregations: the so-called Jerusalem council (Acts 15; Gal 2:1-10) and Antioch incident (Gal 2:11-14). In the first instance the leaders of the Jerusalem church (against the wishes of some) accepted the Antiochian practice of allowing uncircumcised Gentiles into the church. In the second case it appears that the Antiochian Christians (with the exception of Paul) accepted the ruling of the Jerusalem church that Jewish Christians as Jews ought to continue to obey the law. In both cases disagreement existed within each church;

between the two churches there was compromise and conciliation. The notion of an unbridgeable theological chasm separating Greek-speaking and Aramaic-speaking Christians is unsubstantiated.

4. Conclusion.

We have reviewed two very different models of early church history. According to the first, the primitive Christians were divided along cultural lines: old-style Jews and new-thinking Hellenists. Two different churches traveled on two different trajectories toward two different destinies. Unretouched, it is a black-and-white picture of starkly opposed alternatives. According to the second view, all of the earliest Christians were by heritage both Jewish and Hellenistic, and their methods of integrating these valuable but complex inheritances varied from individual to individual. Neither Judaism nor Hellenism was one thing; varieties of early Christian belief and expression (the fate of Israel* in Matthew and Romans; the Platonism of Hebrews and the Stoicism of 1 Thessalonians) were the inevitable products of so concentrated a mixture of ideas and allegiances. The result was complexity—and color.

See also ACTS OF THE APOSTLES; CHRISTIANITY AND JUDAISM: PARTINGS OF THE WAYS; LAW; PHILIP THE EVANGELIST; STEPHEN; TEMPLE.

BIBLIOGRAPHY. M. Arnold, *The Complete Prose Works of Matthew Arnold, 5: Culture and Anarchy with Friendship's Garland and Some Literary Essays* (Ann Arbor: University of Michigan, 1965); C. K. Barrett, "Acts and Christian Consensus" in *Context: Essays in Honor of Peder Borgen*, ed. W. Bockman and R. E. Kristiansen (Relieff 24; Trondheim: Tapir, 1987) 19-33; M. Baumgarten, *The Acts of the Apostles; or, The History of the Church in the Apostolic Age* (3 vols.; Edinburgh: T & T Clark, 1854); F. C. Baur, *History of the Church in the First Three Centuries* (London and Edinburgh: Williams & Norgate, 1878-79); idem, *Paul, the Apostle of Jesus Christ, His Life and Works, His Epistles and Teachings: A Contribution to a Critical History of Primitive Christianity* (2 vols.; London and Edinburgh: Williams & Norgate, 1873-75); J. C. Beker, *Paul the Apostle: The Triumph of God in Life and Thought* (Philadelphia: Fortress, 1980); J. Bihler, "Der Stephanusbericht (Apg 6,8-15 und 7,54-8,2)," *BZ* 3 (1959) 252-70; idem, *Der Stephanusgeschichte im Zusammenhang der Apostelgeschichte* (Munich: Max Hueber, 1963); G. Bornkamm, *Paul* (New York: Harper & Row, 1971); R. E. Brown, "Not Jewish Christianity and Gentile Christianity But Types of Jewish/Gentile Christianity," *CBQ* 45 (1983) 74-79; F. F. Bruce, *New Testament History* (Garden City, NY: Doubleday, 1972); idem, *Peter, Stephen, James and John: Studies in Early Non-Pauline Christianity* (Grand Rapids: Eerdmans, 1980); R. Bultmann, *Theology of the New Testament* (2 vols.; New York: Scribner's, 1951-55); J. D. G. Dunn, *Unity and Diversity in the New Testament: An Inquiry into the Character of Earliest Christianity* (Philadelphia: Westminster, 1977); W. W. Gasque, *A History of the Criticism of the Acts of the Apostles* (Peabody, MA: Hendrickson, 1989); E. Haenchen, *The Acts of the Apostles: A Commentary* (Philadelphia: Westminster, 1971); M. Hengel, *Between Jesus and Paul: Studies in the Earliest History of Christianity* (Philadelphia: Fortress, 1983); idem, *Judaism and Hellenism: Studies in Their Encounter in Palestine During the Early Hellenistic Period* (2 vols.; Philadelphia: Fortress, 1974); C. C. Hill, *Hellenists and Hebrews: Reappraising Division Within the Earliest Church* (Minneapolis: Fortress, 1992); L. T. Johnson, *The Writings of the New Testament: An Interpretation* (Philadelphia: Fortress, 1986); J. Kilgallen, *The Stephen Speech: A Literary and Redactional Study of Acts 7,2-53* (Rome: Biblical Institute, 1976); A. F. J. Klijn, "Stephen's Speech—Acts VII. 2-53," *NTS* 4 (1957) 25-31; E. Larsson, "Die Hellenisten und die Urgemeinde," *NTS* 33 (1987) 205-25; J. T. Lienhard, "Acts 6:1-6: A Redactional View," *CBQ* 37 (1975) 228-36; J. B. Lightfoot, *Saint Paul's Epistle to the Galatians: A Revised Text with Introduction, Notes and Dissertations* (10th ed.; London and New York: Macmillan, 1900); I. H. Marshall, "Palestinian and Hellenistic Christianity: Some Critical Comments," *NTS* 19 (1972-73) 271-87; H.-W. Neudorfer, *Der Stephanuskreis in der Forschungsgeschichte seit F. C. Baur* (Giessen-Basel: Brunnen, 1983); E. Richard, *Acts 6:1—8:4: The Author's Method of Composition* (SBLDS 41; Missoula, MT: Scholars Press, 1978); P. Richardson and D. Granskou, ed., *Anti-Judaism in Early Christianity, 1: Paul and the Gospels* (Waterloo, ON: Wilfrid Laurier University Press, 1986); M. Scharlemann, *Stephen: A Singular Saint* (Rome: Biblical Institute, 1968); M. Simon, *St. Stephen and the Hellenists* (London: Longmans, Green & Co., 1958); M. Smith, "Palestinian Judaism in the First Century" in *Israel: Its Role in Civilization*, ed. M. Davis (New York:

Seminary Israel Institute of the Jewish Theological Seminary of America, 1956); G. Stanton, "Stephen in Lucan Perspective" in *Studia Biblica, 1978, 3: Papers on Paul and Other New Testament Authors*, ed. E. A. Livingston (Sheffield: JSOT, 1980) 345-60; L. Wolff, "Der Bericht der Apostelgeschichte über Stephanus vertheidigt gegen die Angriffe Baur's," *ZLTK* 8 (1847) 86-97.   C. C. Hill

HERESY. *See* ADVERSARIES; APOSTASY; DOCETISM; GNOSIS, GNOSTICISM; MARCION.

HERMAS, SHEPHERD OF

The *Shepherd of Hermas* (or simply *Hermas*) is one of the more enigmatic documents to have survived from the sub-apostolic period. Relatively simple in style and widely popular in the second and third centuries, it is an important witness to the state of Christianity in Rome in the mid-second century. Expressing a Jewish Christian theological perspective by means of imagery, analogies and parallels drawn from Roman society and culture, the *Shepherd* reflects the efforts of its author(s) to deal with issues—for example, post-baptismal sin* and repentance*; the relationship between rich* and poor within the church—of concern to at least part of the Christian community in Rome.*
  1. Genre and Structure
  2. Contents
  3. Authorship and Date
  4. Concluding Observations
  5. Later Influence

1. Genre and Structure.
The external structure of five *Visions*, twelve *Mandates*, and ten *Similitudes* (or *Parables*) masks the fact that on the basis of its internal structure the document falls into two parts: *Visions* 1—4, and the *Shepherd* proper, comprising the *Mandates* and *Parables*, to which *Vision* 5 serves as an introduction.

The genre of *Visions* 1—4 is that of a Jewish Christian apocalypse.* A typical apocalypse (cf. Revelation) includes the following features: (1) a revelation from God, (2) usually in the form of a vision or dream, (3) often given through a mediator, (4) who provides an interpretation of the vision, (5) whose contents usually concern future events, especially the end times. *Visions* 1—4 neatly reflect this pattern, except for their contents: the focus is not on the end, but on the

possibility of repentance* because the end is not yet.

The *Mandates* reflect the form of a typical Jewish-Hellenistic homily. The closest parallels to the *Parables* of the *Shepherd* are found in the book of *1 Enoch*. These parables, in which typically the telling of the "parable" is followed by a request for and granting of an interpretation, and finally blessings and curses upon those who either do or do not heed it, are more like "allegorical similes" than the more familiar parables of the Synoptic Gospels.

There is some evidence to suggest that the two major sections, *Visions* 1—4 and *Vision* 5/*Parable* 10, were written and circulated separately. Two textual witnesses begin with *Vision* 5, and there are some discrepancies in the numbering of the *Parables* and internal inconsistencies which indicate that *Parable* 9 is a later addition. In all, it appears that two separate sections were later combined, at which time *Parable* 9 was added to unify and link them together, creating the *Shepherd* as it is known today. Whether these sections represent the work of two or three different contributors at different times (Giet), or the work of a single author, either written in stages over a period of time (Joly 1993, 529) or in a brief time (Maier, 58) continues to be debated.

2. Contents.
In *Vision* 1 Hermas sees a woman bathing and desires her, and then is confronted about his sin by an elderly woman, who represents the church. In *Vision* 2 he receives a revelation in the form of a book, and after fasting and prayer* is granted its interpretation: forgiveness* is possible for those who truly repent now and cleanse themselves of *dipsychia*, "doublemindedness." *Vision* 3 is of the church as a tower built on a foundation of apostles,* teachers, etc., with its diversity portrayed by the variety of stones used to build it. *Vision* 4, in which a huge monster appears, foreshadows tribulation.* The shepherd replaces the elderly woman as revelator in *Vision* 5, and proceeds to introduce the following twelve *Mandates* and ten *Parables*.

The *Mandates* consist of a series of commandments regarding ethical behavior, given by the shepherd and explicated by means of lists of virtues* and vices, with a smattering of dialogue between a patient shepherd and an unperceptive Hermas thrown in to advance matters. Key topics raised include faith, innocence, chastity, repentance, patience, truthfulness, cheerfulness and self-control, on the positive side, and evil desire, bad temper, doublemindedness and grief on the other.

The *Parables* (extended analogies or similes, utilizing cities, vineyards, trees, shepherds,* sticks, mountains, a tower and a garment) reflect similar concerns. *Parable* 8, for example, is a vision of a willow tree and various kinds of sticks (some green and budded, some half green and half dry, others dry and insect-riddled, etc.), each of which represents a certain type of believer (in the three examples, respectively, those who were persecuted for the law, those so engaged in business that they fail to associate with the saints, and apostates).

The book ends with a charge to Hermas to write down and communicate what he has seen, and to live in accordance with it.

3. Authorship and Date.

3.1. Authorship. The "Hermas" to whom the *Shepherd* is attributed is certainly not Paul the Apostle (a suggestion arising from Acts 14:12) or the Hermas mentioned in Romans 16:14 (Origen's suggestion). According to the Muratorian Canon, which may be the oldest (c. 180-200?) known list of NT and early Christian writings, Hermas was the brother of Pius, bishop of Rome (c. 140-154). Whether or not this is so, nothing else is known about the author(s); apparent autobiographical information is likely fictional.

3.2. Date. The date of the *Shepherd* is difficult to establish. Reference to it by Irenaeus (c. 175) establishes a date before which it must have been written, but on the other end dates as early as the 70s and 80s of the first decade have been proposed. The evidence of the Muratorian Canon (Hermas wrote the *Shepherd* in Rome while his brother Pius was bishop) must be used with caution, since it appears to reflect a subtle attempt to discredit the *Shepherd*. The internal evidence is inconsistent. Data in *Visions* 1—4, together with the reference in *Visions* 8.3 to "Clement,"* who may possibly be the Clement of Rome responsible for *1 Clement*, point to the end of the first century or the early part of the second, while the section comprising *Vision* 5/*Parable* 10 seems to come from a later time. Recognition of the composite nature of the *Shepherd* resolves many of the difficulties. *Visions* 1—4 likely represent the

earliest state of its formation, while the final editing, including the interpolation of *Parable* 9, may well have occurred about the time (mid-second century) suggested by the Muratorian Canon (*see* Canon).

4. Concluding Observations.

Throughout the book Hermas wrestles with whether repentance and forgiveness of post-baptismal sin are available. The answer, which seeks to balance God's justice and mercy* (cf. *4 Ezra*), is yes, once, but only for a limited while, so one must repent quickly before the opportunity passes. In sum, Hermas seeks to affirm God's mercy while attempting to maintain a strict moralism (Snyder 1992). A second major concern is the behavior of the rich, and their relationship to the poor within the church (Osiek); Hermas' solution (chap. 51 [= *Parable* 2]) stands in tension with the Sermon on the Mount. While scholarship has tended to dissociate the two concerns, sociological perspectives suggest they are intimately related (Maier).

The *Shepherd* offers a glimpse of a Christianity whose piety (much like that of the *Didache** and *Barnabas**) is centered on observing the divine commandments* and self-control. The distance from Romans (another document addressed to the Roman Christian community) in tone and perspective is considerable; its piety has much more in common with *1 Clement* (although its social location differs greatly [Jeffers, 120; Maier]). Christological* reflection is minimal (the Holy Spirit* or angels* carry out many christological functions). Although there is scarcely any direct use of the OT or early Christian documents, substantial parallels with Jewish wisdom traditions run throughout the document (Joly 1993). The use of Roman examples and categories is more than merely circumstantial (Reiling).

5. Later Influence.

The *Shepherd* was generally well received in the early church. Irenaeus, Clement of Alexandria and Origen (at least for a while) accepted it as Scripture, as apparently did Tertullian, although later, after he joined the rigorous sect of the Montanists, he referred to it as the "shepherd of the adulterers" for its "lax" approach to repentance. In the fourth century, Athanasius early on quoted it as canonical, and even after the Christology of the book proved to be congenial to his Arian opponents he continued to recommend it to new converts. His Alexandrian contemporary, Didymus the Blind, included it in his canon* of Scripture, and it stands at the end, following Revelation and Barnabas, of the important fourth-century biblical manuscript, Codex Sinaiticus.

See also APOSTOLIC FATHERS; REPENTANCE, SECOND REPENTANCE.

BIBLIOGRAPHY. **Text and Translation:** J. B. Lightfoot and J. R. Harmer, *The Apostolic Fathers: Greek Texts and English Translations of Their Writings*, ed. and rev. M. W. Holmes (2d ed.; Grand Rapids: Baker, 1992). **Commentaries and/or Editions:** M. Dibelius, *Der Hirt des Hermas* (Tübingen: J. C. B. Mohr, 1923); R. Joly, *Hermas le Pasteur* (Paris: Cerf, 1958; repr. with supplement, 1968); G. F. Snyder, *The Shepherd of Hermas* (AF 6; Camden, NJ: Nelson, 1968). **Studies:** L. W. Barnard, "The Shepherd of Hermas in Recent Study," *HeyJ* 9 (1968) 29-36; S. Giet, *Hermas et les Pasteurs: les trois auteurs du Pasteur d'Hermas* (Paris: Presses Universitaires de France, 1963); J. S. Jeffers, *Conflict at Rome: Social Order and Hierarchy in Early Christianity* (Minneapolis: Fortress, 1991); R. Joly, "Le milieu complexe du 'Pasteur d'Hermas'," *ANRW* 2.27.1 (1993) 524-51; H. O. Maier, *The Social Setting of the Ministry as Reflected in the Writings of Hermas, Clement and Ignatius* (Waterloo, Ont.: Wilfrid Laurier University Press, 1991); E. Massaux, *The Influence of the Gospel of Saint Matthew on Christian Literature before Saint Irenaeus*, 2: *The Later Christian Writings*, ed. A. J. Bellinzoni (NGS 5/2; Macon, GA: Mercer University Press, 1990); C. Osiek, *Rich and Poor in the Shepherd of Hermas: An Exegetical-Social Investigation* (Washington, D.C.: Catholic Biblical Association of America, 1983); L. Pernveden, *The Concept of the Church in the Shepherd of Hermas* (Lund: C. W. K. Gleerup, 1966); J. Reiling, *Hermas and Christian Prophecy: A Study of the Eleventh Mandate* (NovTSup 37; Leiden: E. J. Brill, 1973); G. F. Snyder, "Hermas' The Shepherd," *ABD* 3:148; W. Telfer, *The Forgiveness of Sins: An Essay in the History of Christian Doctrine and Practice* (Philadelphia: Muhlenberg, 1960).
M. W. Holmes

HERMENEUTICS

Some of the most difficult books in the Bible to interpret are found in the last part of the NT (e.g., Hebrews, Revelation), and scholars are just beginning to realize the value of the church fathers for understanding NT literature.

Among the difficulties is the peculiar use of the OT in Acts, Hebrews and Revelation. For these and other reasons the later NT literature provides fertile ground for exploring the value of recent techniques such as rhetorical theory, text-linguistics and intertextuality. This article will summarize the relevant hermeneutical issues and provide a general introduction to topics discussed more extensively in separate articles within this volume (*see DPL*, Hermeneutics/Interpreting Paul).

1. Recent Hermeneutical Developments
2. Hermeneutical Strategies
3. Hermeneutical Techniques
4. Hermeneutical Difficulties

1. Recent Hermeneutical Developments.
The postmodern attack on the classic hermeneutical quest for the author's intended meaning (maintained even in the Middle Ages with the Antiochian stress on the literal sense of the text) has intensified in recent years. Future generations will no doubt view twentieth-century hermeneutics as typified by the ascendance of the reader over the author in the production of meaning. For many scholars the author has no authority whatsoever over the texts he or she produces. Polyvalence, or multiple meanings, is becoming axiomatic in many circles of interpretation. This fits well with the pluralism and relativism that predominate in postmodern culture.

1.1. The Death of Modernism. Modernism per se began with the ascent of rationalism in the seventeenth century, epitomized by Descartes and his *cogito ergo sum* ("I think, therefore I am") and establishing the subject/object distinction as the heart of knowledge. At the same time knowledge was attained by empirical proof and was seen as certain in its results. Science replaced religion at the apex of the intellectual pyramid, and it was thought that a combination of reason and science could solve all problems. Optimistic humanism pervaded the social ethos, and it was believed that humankind was progressing upward on the path to a true paradise of modernistic life. In hermeneutics this produced the Schleiermachian objective hermeneutic, a method in which the subject (the interpreter) studies the object (the author's text) and derives a certain meaning that is deeper than even the author understood. This led to the grammatical-historical method and the historical-critical method, both of which were thought to produce assured results.

Several factors led to the demise of modernism on the historical as well as the scientific and hermeneutical levels. The Einsteinian revolution played havoc with the Newtonian closed-world nexus and the subject-object distinction (especially due to Heisenberg's "uncertainty principle"). Along with the Freudian emphasis on the power of the superego to subvert the objectivity of the subject, this revolution showed that knowledge is attained as much through the observer's perspective as through the data studied. Moreover, World War I and the century that followed destroyed the optimism of modernity. The last eighty years of the twentieth century have been characterized by a search for a new basis for meaning in the wake of modernism's demise.

1.2. The Hermeneutical Switch: Heidegger and Gadamer. M. Heidegger has often been called the most influential philosopher of the twentieth century. Heidegger's early thought was a primary influence on the theology of R. Bultmann, and Heidegger's later thought exercised influence on both the New Hermeneutic and H.-G. Gadamer. The early Heidegger of *Being and Time* (1927) developed the relationship of *Dasein* (the concrete, human "I") to its world in the quest for understanding. Preunderstanding informs Being and provides time-oriented content to this quest. Thus life itself is a hermeneutical process as one's *Dasein* addresses its existence and as understanding projects Being on the world. Meaning is the union of *Dasein* with existence, and the hermeneutical circle is the union of preunderstanding and interpretation; that is, the already understood unites with the object to be grasped. In his later works Heidegger developed the linguistic underpinning for his ontological approach to existentialism, relating the problem of language to the issue of Being. For him language is not a tool for imparting knowledge but an event that leads to the possibility of human existence. Language is grounded in being and not just in the thought life. It expresses Being by uniting both the subject and object into itself (see Thiselton 1980, 335-36).

Gadamer borrowed both Heidegger's ontology and the controlling metaphor of art or aesthetic appreciation. Although his major work is called *Truth and Method,* Gadamer opposes the methods of hermeneutics and the classical attempt to find the true meaning of the text. Perhaps more than anyone else, Gadamer was the hermeneutical precursor of postmodern interpretation. For him interpretation is not judging the meaning of the text but is to be found in the art or the act of reading. The community behind the reader and the prejudgments of readers are decisive as they enter the world of the text. Gadamer's most famous metaphor for this is the "fusion" of the "horizon" of the text with the "horizon" of the reader. This occurs not via foundational methods like grammar and semantics but via the reader's leap into the "stream of tradition," that is, the prejudices and understandings inherited from one's past and community. Thus Gadamer was opposing the myth of objective knowledge inherited from the Renaissance. Not only is the text cut off from its author, but also the reader is cut off from any purely rational interaction with the text. Instead there is a new relationship as both text and reader interrogate each other.

1.3. The Hermeneutical Centrality of the Reader: Poststructural Criticism. There are three schools within what is called the poststructural movement: poststructuralism, deconstruction and reader-response criticism. Building upon Heidegger and the French linguist F. de Saussure (1857-1913), structuralism was a short-lived movement that emphasized the text as an arbitrary system of signs that must be decoded. Saussure was the founder of modern linguistics and had developed the theory that language is a system of interdependent terms centering upon the interaction of *langue* (the language system) and *parole* (concrete acts of speech). The speaker chooses from the storehouse of linguistic conventions and puts arbitrary signs (individual terms) together into a meaning-context. Structuralists reworked this into a theory of "actantial" units to be decoded on the basis of binary opposites to get at the deep-structure message underlying the surface text.

However, there were serious philosophical problems in structuralism, and attention shifted quickly to poststructural considerations. With this came a serious attack on the Kantian subject-object distinction. Meaning was seen not in the object (text) but in the subject (reader). While Saussure considered the term to be an arbitrary sign that was given definition in the context of the sentence, poststructuralists saw the sentence also as an open-ended system of signs that compels the reader to complete its meaning. R. Barthes sums up this movement (Barthes, 74-81): The text is a production that continually develops and is open-ended by nature. It is without closure and has an infinite number of meaning-possibilities. It is intertextual by nature and contains within itself many different texts via its multiple meanings. The original author has no control over it and can come back only as a "guest" who is no longer necessary for interpretation. The author is "dead," and any return is only a projection of the reader's mind. Therefore the reader must complete its meaning and enter into the text, thereby producing a new text in the act of reading. The guiding metaphor is "play." The text becomes a playground on which readers may play whatever game they wish.

J. Derrida is the leading poststructuralist, and his deconstruction movement provides the greatest challenge yet to traditional hermeneutics. Derrida is trying to deconstruct, or decenter, Western philosophical reasoning inherited from Plato and Aristotle by blending Nietzsche with Heidegger to produce a metaphorical or rhetorical view of language. Communication is characterized by the "absence" of meaning, for when readers "interrogate" the text, they discover it is defined by "difference," which Derrida interprets two ways—the opposition between signifier and signified ("differ") causes an infinite number of sign-substitutions and endless play between the reader and the text ("defer"). Readers must deconstruct the text from any supposed connection with the author (who is no longer available) or previous interpretations of the text (which also cannot be truly understood) and reconstruct their own understanding of the text.

Reader-response theory is similar but centers on the reading strategy the reader employs. There are two schools of thought. Most biblical theorists follow the more moderate approach of W. Iser, who said that the text draws the reader into its narrative world and guides the process of coming to understanding by providing markers that work with the reader in producing meaning. The more radical approach of S. E. Fish states that the text itself exists only in the mind of the reader. As the text is read, the reading strategy drawn from the reading community determines the meaning of the text. The meaning is not discovered but created by the reader. There is no object, only a subject.

1.4. Hermeneutics and Social Context: Sociocritical Approaches. In line with the switch to the subject, this movement switches to the current cultural situation as the generating force in meaning. J. Habermas and K.-O. Apel propose a metacritical or "depth hermeneutic" that recognizes the worldview behind a text and its purpose to control or manipulate the reader into accepting its perspective. According to this view, one must go beneath the surface message to uncover the attempt to dominate the readers. Therefore interpretation must liberate itself from the ideology of the text and recreate the social world of the text into conformity with current needs.

Three recent movements are part of this school: liberation, feminist and black theologies. All seek to recreate biblical theology in light of the needs of the present community. For liberation and black theology, salvation* is freedom from economic and racial oppression. The Bible has been misused by the white, wealthy majority to oppress the poor and minorities, and the story of the exodus becomes the governing metaphor for the release of the oppressed from injustice. The primary need today is not spiritual but economic liberation, and this occurs when *theoria* (the meaning of the text) and *praxis* (the current needs of the community) are fused. God* is immanent (involved in the liberation of the oppressed) and not just transcendent (above this world), so practical action must replace theoretical speculation. Theology is redefined as action, and biblical parables about the lost sheep or the prodigal son are reinterpreted to center on the release of the oppressed poor rather than the search for the spiritually lost. The book of Revelation is a favorite text for this school of thought, centering as it does on the destruction of evil government.

Feminist hermeneutics takes a similar tack and critiques the patriarchal domination of women in the Bible, which has resulted in the male subjection and exploitation of women in society. A metacritical perspective must first unmask the pretense of objectivity in male-dominated biblical exegesis and both reiterate the femaleness of God and rediscover the centrality of women* in Christian religion. The basis of this reconstruction is women's experience of male domination, which provides the critical norm for biblical reflection (see Reuther). Moreover this reflection is praxis-oriented; that is, it must liberate the contemporary community from oppression.

1.5. The Counter Movement: Intentionalist Hermeneutics. While postmodern skepticism toward the intended meaning of the text has controlled many segments of higher criticism since the 1980s, there are some signs that its influence may be waning. A growing number of studies argue that such skepticism is unwarranted. N. T. Wright (50-69) argues that the solution is found in a critical-realist perspective in which the reader grapples with the text and attempts to ascertain what the author intended to say in the text. Two primary schools of thought espouse a similar realist approach.

The followers of E. D. Hirsch Jr. (W. C. Kaiser Jr., E. E. Johnson) argue for two elements in hermeneutics, the single intent of the author and multiple significances for the readers. There is only one true meaning of a text and that is the meaning the author intended to portray. However, that meaning can have more than one significance for readers in different situations. The task of readers is primarily to ascertain the original meaning and on that basis to see what impact that meaning has on their lives. P. D. Juhl agrees with an intentional approach but argues that one studies the author's text rather than the author's intention. Authors are still important, for they situate the text historically, but we know the author only to the extent that we know the text (Juhl, 12-15).

Others are more influenced by the language-game theory of the later L. Wittgenstein as filtered through the analytical philosophy of J. L. Austin and the speech-act theory of J. R. Searle. This is the view that language is first referential and then performative. The language-game theory of the later Wittgenstein developed the idea that communication depends upon the ever-changing linguistic context in which language operates. The context supplies rules whereby the utterance can be understood. Austin applied this to the performative function of texts in three aspects—the *locutionary* (cognitive, or propositional, message), *illocutionary* (what the text accomplishes—declaring, warning, etc.) and *perlocutionary* (what is effected or caused in the hearer or reader—persuading, changing, etc.). Searle has built on the illocutionary aspect and

developed a speech-act theory that blends the propositional or referential dimension of a text with its performative force. In other words, texts both assert truth and make demands of the reader, and in their contexts those different functions can be interpreted.

A. C. Thiselton (1992, 597-604) builds on this to develop his "action theory" of hermeneutics. He would see the locutionary and illocutionary functions as combining both meaning (proposition) and significance (demanding response) into a single act of communication. The author provides certain direction markers in the text that draw the reader into the extralinguistic world of the text and perform certain actions on the reader. A " 'believing' reading" allows the reader to participate in the text's effects and to discover its intended purpose. K. Vanhoozer (1995, 314-18) agrees that readers play a primary role in interpretation but argues that they must do so responsibly by seeking not just to "overstand" the text (ask only their own questions of it) but also to "understand" it (seek the meaning and sense of the text itself). The interpreter has an ethical responsibility to allow the communicative aim of the text to guide the reader to its intended meaning.

2. Hermeneutical Strategies.

2.1. Letter Forms. Of the nine Hellenistic letter forms (*see* Letters) adduced by S. K. Stowers (49-173) and D. E. Aune (162-69) (friendship; family; praise and blame; exhortation, or paraenesis; mediation, or recommendation; juridical, or forensic; private; official, or royal; and literary), several are reflected in the General Epistles. On the whole, however, it has been noted that even the personal letters (e.g., 3 Jn) are primarily literary and that rhetorical techniques dominate all of them. No single letter form suffices. Hebrews certainly fits into the paraenetic pattern and 3 John into the private letter form, but other types are mixed in as well (see below).

In general, all the letters follow Greco-Roman convention, such as the opening (sender to recipient followed by a greeting, a thanksgiving and prayer) and closing (greetings from friends, final exhortations and words of farewell). For the most part these conventions are followed, but Hebrews* and 1 John (*see* John, Letters of) have no opening, and James,* 2 Peter* and 1 John have no closing. Jude* closes without greetings or farewell, only with a doxology, and Revelation (*see* Revelation, Book of) with a benediction.

The General Epistles evidence a great variety in their letter forms. Hebrews is a paraenetic homily (Heb 13:22, "word of exhortation") containing several mini sermons (e.g., Heb 3—4, 5—7, 8—10) with rhetorical techniques centering upon warnings and encouragements to persevere. James does not easily fit any epistolary genre. It is primarily a moralistic letter that addresses several ethical* problems in a group of Hellenistic Jewish churches. 1 Peter* and 1 John might both be called pastoral letters, with 1 Peter a homily that tries to encourage churches of northern Galatia to persevere in times of persecution,* and 1 John a polemical tractate to encourage Christians to persevere in light of false teachers. 2 Peter and Jude are also polemical tractates. 2 Peter has often been called a testament or farewell address (2 Pet 1:13, 14 on his impending death) calling upon Christians to remain faithful to Christ* in light of false teachers. Jude contains an extensive midrash (Jude 5-19) with a strong prophetic emphasis on the judgment* awaiting the false teachers. 2 John and 3 John are personal pastoral letters addressing the treatment of church representatives (2 John of false teachers, 3 John of John's own representatives). The book of Revelation is the most complex of all. It contains many subgenres (epistle, prophecy, apocalyptic*) and does not fit any of the forms. The seven letters are virtually royal edicts with a paraenetic challenge to the churches, and the book as a whole is a prophetic-apocalyptic narrative designed to call the beleaguered Christians to a life of persevering faithfulness in the light of Roman persecution.

2.2. Rhetorical Approaches. Ancient rhetoric was developed by the Greeks (Aristotle and Quintilian) and utilized not only by them but by Jewish writers as well (*see* Rhetoric, Rhetorical Criticism). There were three primary types—judicial, or legal, argument, used to establish right and wrong; deliberative, or political/religious, used to persuade an audience of what is true or best; and epideictic, or praise/blame, used to argue for moral values. In most epistles one type will be primary with the others supporting it. There were six parts of ancient rhetoric: the *exordium,* or introduction; the *narratio,* or proposition; the *partitio,* or explanation of facts;

the *probatio,* or arguments presented in defense of the thesis; the *refutatio,* or refutation of opposing views; and the *peroratio,* or conclusion, providing final points to persuade the readers. The goal of the scholar (see Kennedy) is to study the rhetorical unit and the situation behind it and then to determine the type of argumentation employed, the arrangement and style by which it is presented and the effectiveness of the final product. The purpose is to understand the epistle better by studying the techniques the author used to address the ancient readers.

The epistle to the Hebrews* (see 2.1 above) is a paraenetic homily that places it under the general rubric of deliberative rhetoric, as the author tries to convince his Jewish Christian audience that Christianity is the true religion. Scholars have long noted that the key to the book is the juxtaposition of doctrinal and exhortatory sections, and in this sense the sixfold rhetorical division does not work easily. Therefore many interpreters (*see* Rhetoric) call this *synkrisis,* or comparison, comparing Christian with Jewish soteriological practices in order to call the readers back to Christ* as the only path to salvation.*

James* and 1 Peter* may well be epideictic rhetoric. James calls the readers to the moral values or ethics* of true Christianity. Attempts to outline it according to the six elements above have also proven difficult, and many different patterns have been suggested. Most likely it follows its own internal logic (the tendency recently is to see it as a unity rather than fragmented). 1 Peter attempts to call a persecuted church to persevere in the Christian values that characterized it in the past. As with James, it does not fall into any Greco-Roman literary pattern but centers on the twin themes of privilege (1 Pet 1:3-12; 2:4-10) and responsibility (1 Pet 1:13—2:3; 2:11—3:12), then applying these to the problem of persecution* (1 Pet 3:13—4:19), with a conclusion centering on the readers' responsibilities before Christ (1 Pet 5:1-14).

2 Peter* and Jude* are deliberative rhetoric attempting to persuade the readers of both the danger of the false teachers and the truths of the apostolic faith.* At the same time they utilize judicial rhetoric to prove the error of the heretics. The letters of John (*see* John, Letters of) combine deliberative rhetoric to challenge the false teachers and epideictic rhetoric to call

the readers to the true ethical precepts of the Christian walk. Revelation (*see* Revelation, Book of) cannot easily be classified since it is an apocalyptic* work, but it utilizes all three types: judicial rhetoric to address the false movements (e.g., the Nicolaitan heresy), deliberative rhetoric to call the readers to follow Christ at all costs and epideictic rhetoric to encourage the readers to worship* and persevere in Christ.

2.3. Historical and Social-Scientific Approaches. Ancient stories and texts originate in an historical context, and so it is important to ascertain the original social setting behind them (*see* Social Setting). There are two basic types of study. (1) Social description studies the facts and historical-cultural background behind the text, utilizing archaeological data to uncover details such as the type of homes people lived in as well as broad sociological patterns such as the patterns behind the house church* movement or Paul's tentmaking ministry.* (2) Sociological interpretation uses current sociological theory to explain what social forces led to the production of the text itself, such as the social codes as the product of Cynic influence or the early church as a millenarian movement. The problem with the latter is it is often reductionistic and a revisionist attempt to rewrite the history behind the ancient text on the basis of modern theories. The solution is to treat such study as heuristic and to allow the text rather than the theory to control the process. In this sense it is best to combine the methods of the historian and the sociologist and to let the data guide the results.

It is critical to center not just upon historical reconstruction but also upon biblical illumination, that is, to approach the text as a believer. This is the classic debate between the church and the academy, between a reasoned openness to the text and a historical-critical skepticism toward it. The solution is to amalgamate the two approaches, to search out what underlies the text but remain an obedient listener to its message. As historical documents, the biblical books must be studied critically; as divine revelation they must be obeyed implicitly. Moreover sociological analysis is an important aid to theological understanding when it is employed carefully. So long as one avoids the dangers of reductionism, revisionism, determinism, anachronism and overstatement (see Osborne, 141-44; Barton, 74-76) and allows exegetical

analysis to control the use of the social-scientific tools, social science is a valuable tool.

A couple of examples will help illuminate the value of this approach. First, the social implications of the Acts of the Apostles* are critical. Scholars have long noted the significant place social concern has in the two-volume work of Luke-Acts. In Luke there is a reversal of roles in which the rich will have nothing in the kingdom (*see* Kingdom of God) and the poor will have everything (Acts 6:20-26; 16:19-31; *see* Riches and Poverty). In Acts there is a strong theology of communal sharing at the core of the church (Acts 2:44-45; 4:32-35). In both the Jewish and Greco-Roman worlds the poor had a special place of privilege. In Rome the path to power lay in keeping the masses fed and happy, and politicians would spend fortunes financing the games to keep the masses happy and purchasing bread to keep them fed. In the Jewish world almsgiving was one of three primary acts of piety (with prayer and fasting). The early church built upon both to make the sharing of possessions a must for the mature Christian. The theology is this: when God blesses persons financially he is primarily giving them a ministry of helping and only secondarily a blessing* to enjoy.

One of the best known sociological works is J. H. Elliott's *Home for the Homeless,* a study of the situation behind 1 Peter.* Elliott focuses on the key terms "aliens and strangers" (1 Pet 1:1, 17; 2:11), arguing that they are sociological in nature and portray the "alienated" peoples of northeast Asia Minor who converted because they thought Christianity would provide a haven of rest for them. However, they became doubly oppressed and thereby depressed when their neighbors turned against them for becoming Christians. Peter writes to encourage them to embrace their "alien" status and join the "household of God" (1 Pet 4:17; *see* Household, Family). While Elliott does a service in tracing the rural, small-town life of that section of Asia Minor and the pressures that were exerted upon the original readers, he overstates the social nature of "aliens and strangers" and fails to understand its use as a religious metaphor for considering oneself separate from this world* (as in the black spiritual, "This world is not my home, I'm just a-passin' through"). Nevertheless, Elliott's study is helpful in placing 1 Peter in its first-century context.

2.4. Narrative Approaches. In the late 1970s and early 1980s, the weaknesses of form and redaction criticism, specifically the tendency to divide the narratives of the Bible into independent units (form) and to center only upon the differences between the Gospels (redaction), became apparent. Scholars realized that the biblical narratives were whole stories that contained plot, characterization, point of view and story time. Literary or narrative criticism had been developed by secular literary critics in their study of fiction, and their techniques were applied to the Bible (*see* Narrative Criticism). There are several premises: books like the Gospels, Acts and Revelation are to be considered as holistic pieces of literary art; they are to be treated as aesthetic works and studied in terms of literary artistry; the external or historical background behind the text is not the object of study, but the focus should instead be on the internal composition of the story itself.

The book of Revelation may be used as an example (for Acts as an example, *see* Narrative Criticism). Scholars have long recognized that Revelation (*see* Revelation, Book of) has a plot that centers on the conflict between God* and the forces of evil. The central theme is the sovereignty of God, with the correlative being the futility of Satan.* The first ten chapters juxtapose heavenly scenes (Rev 1, 4—5, 7) with earthly scenes (Rev. 2—3, 6, 8—9). The heavenly scenes are characterized by peace,* joy,* praise and worship.* The earthly scenes are characterized by chaos, persecution,* judgment* and sorrow. God alone is in control of the earthly and the heavenly. This theme is carried through in the central section (Rev 6—16) that details the seals,* trumpets* and bowls.* These series of seven judgments are seen not just as the wrath* of God upon the earth-dwellers but also as a final proof of his sovereignty (the first four trumpets and bowls are modeled after the Egyptian plagues) and a final opportunity for repentance* (see Rev 9:20-21; 14:6-7; 16:9, 11). It is clear throughout that the dragon has already been defeated by the slain Lamb* (Rev 5:6, 9, 12; 6:16; 12:11; 13:8).

The characterizations in the book are vivid. The dragon, the beast* and the false prophet* are clearly seen as a parody of the Trinity (Rev 13; 16:13), and everything Satan does is a "great imitation" of what God and Christ have already done, such as placing a mark on followers (Rev 13:16 = Rev 7:3), resurrection* from the "mortal wound" (Rev 13:3) and the "many crowns" (Rev 12:3/13:1 = Rev 19:12). Point of view is especially seen in the interludes between the seals, trumpets and bowls (Rev 7:1-17; 10:1—11:14; 12:1—14:20), which tend to typify the glory* of the heaven-dwellers and the battle between God and the forces of evil. The setting is in contrasting scenes of heaven* and earth, which demonstrates the choices that the churches have to make—will they follow the ways of God or the dictates of their world?

2.5. Text-Linguistics and Discourse Analysis. This is the latest hermeneutical development, coming to the fore in biblical studies within the last decade (*see* Structuralism and Discourse Analysis). It is also the most comprehensive school, moving from author to text to reader and combining sociolinguistics, anthropology, classical exegetical methods and reader-response theories. There are two primary types: the text-linguistics practiced by G. H. Guthrie, which utilizes semantic markers and grammatical and syntactical study of the surface text to analyze rhetorical development at the macro level of the text; and the discourse analysis practiced by S. E. Porter and J. B. Green, which studies the production of the textual strategy by the author and its effect upon the reader in the current reading situation. The one hermeneutical discipline missing is a consideration of historical background. The interest is not on what is behind the text but on what is in the text. The goal is to uncover not just the semantic interplay between words but also the process by which the text communicates to the reader (original reader and current reader).

When studying Hebrews,* one will first analyze the original linguistic situation that produced the book, including the first-century literary and rhetorical strategies employed. Second, it is necessary to ascertain the code or structure embedded in the book, utilizing a study of conjunctions, verb moods and tenses as they develop, and rhetorical strategies such as inclusion and meaning gaps to determine the major and minor breaks of the developing argument. Guthrie's analysis of Hebrews yields the following divisions: Hebrews 1:1-4 (introduction); Hebrews 1:5—4:13, 4:14—10:18, 10:19—13:19 (major sections); and Hebrews 13:20-25 (conclusion). At this stage there is also consideration of the multiple levels at which communication occurs, the relationship of the word to the sentence, of the sentence to the paragraph, and of the paragraph to the major section of the book.

Third, discourse analysis studies the effect upon the reader. The text is produced within one sociolinguistic situation but is read today within another sociolinguistic situation. This is where polyvalence occurs, for bridging the gap is difficult. The original readers understood the crisis behind the text (for Hebrews it is Jewish Christians tempted to return to Judaism* due to persecution*), but modern readers look at it from different vantage points, such as Arminian or Calvinist traditions. Discourse analysis analyzes the way the embedded discourse in Hebrews draws readers into the message of the text and guides them into participating in its narrative world.

2.6. Genre Approaches. Genre refers to a basic type of literature that provides hermeneutical guidelines so that the reader might understand its contents. It functions at the macro level (the book as a whole) and at the micro level (the subgenres utilized in the larger book). For instance, although Revelation is usually characterized as apocalyptic, it also utilizes epistolary (the seven letters of Rev 2—3), prophetic (the promises* and warnings) and poetic-liturgical (the hymns*) forms and material (*see* Liturgical Elements). J. L. Bailey notes three aspects: repeatable patterns that help the reader understand its message; a social setting that reveals a particular way of looking at reality; and rhetorical strategies that impact the reader in particular ways.

Genre is an indispensable aid to understanding Acts,* the General Epistles and Revelation (*see* Revelation, Book of). For instance, apocalyptic* has its own grammatical patterns (e.g., solecisms) and a unique set of syntactical devices (e.g., esoteric symbols, cyclical patterns and interludes). Knowing how these patterns operate can radically alter one's understanding of a text. The modern prophecy movement, for example, assumes that the apocalyptic symbols in the Bible were meant to be understood entirely in terms of current events and fails to understand how such symbols operated in their ancient context; namely, that they were drawn from a common store of such symbols in the Jewish and Greco-Roman worlds and made good sense to citizens of those cultures. It is

therefore a gross misinterpretation to identify the "eagle" as the United States and the "bear" as Russia. Likewise, to identify the symbol "666" as Hitler or Henry Kissinger or Ronald Wilson Reagan (whose three names each have six letters) falls far off the mark. The number refers to something or someone in the first century (perhaps to Nero Caesar, the letters of which name in Hebrew come close to 666).

2.7. Theology, Paraenesis and Ethics. The speech-act theory of Austin, Searle and Thistleton recognizes three types of utterances (see 1.5 above): locution (what the text means), illocution (what the text accomplishes) and perlocution (the effect the text causes in the reader). These three aspects correspond to the title of this section. Biblical theology is the message of the book; paraenesis the purpose of the book; and ethics the required response on the part of the reader. While there is no systematic theology in the Bible, all biblical books are inherently theological (*see* New Testament Theology). The key is to allow the developing embedded message of the text to emerge from the data. As one moves from one section to another, the theology is the thread that stitches the sections together. In 1 John (*see* John, Letters of) this would be the three "tests" that describe the true faith as opposed to the false teachers—an incarnational christology,* a binding love* between the members of the community and the necessity of righteous deeds. 1 Peter* contains some of the deepest teaching about God* (mentioned thirty-nine times in this epistle) in all the NT, about election* and a resultant holy living (*see* Holiness), about the church* as not belonging to this world,* and about a theology of suffering.*

Paraenesis describes the purpose of theology—to persuade the reader to live appropriately to the theological truths (*see* Teaching, Paraenesis). One mistake of theologians is to think of their discipline as primarily cognitive, as demanding logical or rational thought. While this is somewhat true, it is only part of the picture and not the more important part. The biblical authors intended their theology to be lived more than thought through. B. Fiore defines paraenesis as "discourse whose aim is to exhort or persuade the reader or auditor to do good." It refers to virtue* and vice lists, household codes* and general exhortations. The warning passages of Hebrews,* most of the wisdom sayings of James,* the ethical paragraphs (1 Pet 1:13—2:3) as well as household codes (1 Pet 2:11—3:12) of 1 Peter,* and the perseverance* passages of Revelation (see Revelation, Book of) are all examples of paraenesis.

Ethics refers to the action side of paraenesis (see Ethics). Theology informs, paraenesis persuades and ethics puts it into practice. As R. B. Hays argues, the NT cannot be understood apart from recognizing its moral dimension. The new life that Christ* made possible through his sacrificial death demands a new set of principles for living (see Death of Christ). This is true at the community level as well as at the individual level. The emphasis on community love in 1 John is a case in point. The theme begins with obedience* as the sign of the presence of God's love* (1 Jn 2:5) and proceeds to define this as "walking as Jesus did" (1 Jn 2:6). Finally this is applied to mutual love as the basis of "living in the light" of God (1 Jn 2:9-11; see Light). It is clear that no one can be in right relationship with God and "hate his or her brother and sister" (1 Jn 2:11).

3. Hermeneutical Techniques.
In recent years the study of the OT in the NT has centered more and more on the exegetical techniques employed by the NT authors. The OT is utilized in several ways in the NT. Often we find direct citations of OT passages; at other times allusions or echoes of passages can be detected; and at other times we have intertextual uses of OT stories (see Intertextuality in Early Christian Literature). Throughout the NT one fact is clear. The entire OT, not just the prophetic portions, is viewed as fulfilled in Jesus and the church* he established. What distinguishes the General Epistles and Revelation from the Gospels, Acts and Paul is the absence of apologetic quotations trying to prove Jesus is the Christ of prophecy.* Primarily these books use intertextual material in paraenetic fashion to call the readers to a life of Christian faithfulness and perseverance* in light of persecution* and pagan pressure to conform to the mores of the surrounding culture.

3.1. Exegetical Techniques in Acts. Most of the twenty quotations in Acts* can be found in the speeches, primarily Peter's (Acts 2:17-21, 25-28; 3:22-23, 25), Stephen's* (Acts 7:3, 5-7, 18, 27-28, 32-35, 37, 40, 42-43) and Paul's (Acts 13:22, 33-35, 41). The quotations are taken almost exclusively from the Septuagint (A text), primarily from the Psalms, Isaiah and the Minor Prophets (see Old Testament in Acts). Typology is central to the use of these passages, as Jesus, the church* and the mission* to the Gentiles* are all anchored in Israel's scriptural tradition. In his formula quotations Luke is quite specific, normally naming the OT author and often linking the text with God* (Acts 3:25; 7:2, 3, 5), the Holy Spirit* (Acts 4:25; 8:25) or the Lord* (Acts 13:47). As C. K. Barrett says (242), this shows Luke is writing "an account of a people, heir to Israel, told through the story of such men as Peter and Paul, and supplied with its meaning through their prophetic utterances, which were always in harmony with what the prophets of old had said."

Two subjects dominate the typological focus. As in Luke, Jesus is seen as the promised Messiah who must suffer (Is 53:7, 8 in Acts 8:32-33), die and be raised (Ps 16:8-11 in Acts 2:25-28, 13:35; Ps 118:22 in Acts 4:11; Is 55:3 in Acts 13:34; see Resurrection), and be exalted to the right hand of God (Ps 110:1 in Acts 2:34-35; see Exaltation). Also, the Gentile mission is steeped in scriptural fulfillment (Is 49:6 in Acts 13:47; Amos 9:11-12 in Acts 15:15-17), including God's turning from the Jews to the Gentiles (Is 6:9-10 in Acts 28:25-28) on the basis of Jewish unbelief (Ps 2:1-2 in Acts 4:25-26, applied to the Jewish people in Acts 4:27; as well as most of the quotations in Stephen's defense in Acts 7).

3.2. Exegetical Technique in Hebrews. Hebrews* may well be the most complex NT book in its use of the OT (see Old Testament in Hebrews). The presence of testimonia, or chain collections, the mixture of more than thirty direct quotations (Longenecker lists thirty-eight) with at least thirty allusions and several stories, and the absence of formula citations makes this a difficult subject to trace. Primarily it is God rather than the author who is the speaker (the predominant introduction to a quote is some form of "God says"—twenty-three times it is God, four times Christ and four times the Holy Spirit), so the emphasis at all times is on divine revelation rather than human mediation. The quotations are somewhat mixed, some from books exhibiting Septuagint text A and others from books exhibiting Septuagint text B.

There has been widespread disagreement over the hermeneutical technique used, with some interpreters arguing for a Philonic type (*see* Philo) of allegorical exegesis (e.g., Sowers, Spicq), but most recent studies (Hanson, Longenecker) have shown a much closer correspondence with Qumran* pesher, Jewish midrash and typology. Midrash is seen in several places (e.g., Ps 95:7-11 in Heb 3:7-19; Ps 39:7-9 in Heb 10:5-10), where a text is quoted and then explained. Chain citations dominate Hebrews 1—2, as the Son* is shown to be superior to the angels* by linking together passages on the superior relation of the Son and the inferior relation of the angels to God* the Father. Typology is demonstrated in the earthly tabernacle* as a "copy" or "shadow" of the heavenly sanctuary (Heb 8:5; 9:24).

Hebrews also has a unique purpose in the quotations, with two primary thrusts. The predominant issue is christology.* The writer demonstrates not so much that Jesus is the promised Messiah (as in the Gospels) but rather shows that he is superior to the Jewish cultus: first angels (Heb 1:5-14), then Moses* (Heb 3:1-6) and rest in the land* (Heb 4:8-11), then the priesthood* (Heb 5:1-10; 7:1-28), then the covenant* (Heb 8:1-11), sanctuary (Heb 9:1-10) and sacrifices* (Heb 10:1-18). In each area the fulfillment passages prove that Jesus alone is the path to salvation.* Linked to this is the use of texts for warning and example. In Hebrews 3:7-19 and Hebrews 4:7-13, Psalm 95:7-11 is used as a warning against testing God via a hardened heart, using Israel perishing in the wilderness as an example. The passage adduced in Hebrews 11 provide positive examples of triumph through persevering faith* and hope.* In Hebrews 12:5-11, Proverbs 3:11-12 exemplifies suffering* as loving discipline from the heavenly Father.

3.3. Exegetical Technique in James. James* contains only five direct quotes but numerous allusions, drawn primarily from the Pentateuch (in Jas 2:8-11) and Proverbs (which accounts for the centrality of wisdom* in James). So pervasive is the OT influence that it is common today to call James as a whole a midrash on OT themes (*see* Old Testament in the General Epistles). Its way of reasoning, its hermeneutical tradition and its themes are as Jewish as they are Christian. James quotes exclusively from the Septuagint, and there is no uniform citation formula. Three passages mention "Scripture" (Jas 2:8, 23; 4:6) and two have simply "he who said" (Jas 2:10, 11;

4:6). Scriptural "fulfillment" is emphasized in James 2:8, but as R. N. Longenecker says (199) this is *teleō*, not *plēroō*, and so points to literalistic midrash rather than pesher exegesis in James.

There are two major motifs in this book. First, the "whole law" is emphasized (Jas 2:8-11) in order to demonstrate the responsibility of the Jewish Christian reader to be impartial (*see* Law). Here James combines the Decalogue (Jas 2:11) with the "royal law" of love from Leviticus 19:15, 18. R. J. Bauckham (309) follows L. T. Johnson in noting the extent to which Leviticus 19:12-18 permeates the epistle. This leads to the second emphasis—a paraenesis that demands the believer conform to the ethical demands of God. Several "stories" are alluded to as examples of exemplary moral behavior (Abraham,* Sarah, Rahab, Elijah, Job, the prophets) and many OT echoes on issues such as wisdom, perseverance,* trials, the problem of the tongue, concern for the poor, misuse of riches (*see* Riches and Poverty) and the power of prayer.*

3.4. Exegetical Technique in 1 Peter. Like James, 1 Peter* is permeated with OT themes and allusions (*see* Old Testament in the General Epistles). There are nine direct quotes, all from the Septuagint, and many allusions, especially in the catenae collection in 1 Peter 2:4-10. There is great variety in the citation formulae, with the characteristic "it is written" occurring only in 1 Peter 1:16 and "in Scripture it says" in 1 Peter 2:6. There are simpler introductions elsewhere: *gar* (1 Pet 3:10), *dioti* and *hoti* (1 Pet 1:24; 5:5), *kai* (1 Pet 2:8; 4:18) and *hos* (1 Pet 2:22), and no introduction at all in 1 Peter 2:7.

Peter mingles his OT allusions with creeds* and catechetical teachings, so there is no standard introduction. The key to Peter's approach lies in 1 Peter 1:10-12, which tells us the "prophets" (including here the psalms) spoke of "the sufferings of the Messiah and the glories after these." As Bauckham points out (310), this has similarities to 1QpHab 7:1-8 and shows that 1 Peter's exegesis can be compared with the Qumran* pesharim. This style of "this is that" interpretation can also be found in 1 Peter 1:24-25 (applying Is 40:6-8 via "this is the word that was preached to you") and 1 Peter 2:4-10 (a pesher type stringing together the passages about the stone* of Ps 118:22 and Is 28:16; 8:14).

Peter's purpose is paraenetic and deeply

christological.* Christ* becomes the model for Christian suffering* in 1 Peter 1:11, 1 Peter 2:21-25 (utilizing Is 53:9) and 1 Peter 3:18-22 (cf. 1 Pet 4:13; 5:10), and one of the primary themes of the book is "suffering is the path to glory." Christians are called to realize (1) the transitory nature of life in contrast to the eternal nature of God's word (Is 40:6-8 in 1 Pet 1:24); (2) what it means to be the people of God (see Church as Israel), the "living stones" built up by God to be "chosen" and "honored" as the "spiritual house" (the stone testimonia in 1 Pet 2:4-10); (3) the necessity of a life of virtue* (Ps 34:12-14 in 1 Pet 3:10-12); (4) the value of suffering for Christ (Prov 11:31 in 1 Pet 4:18); and (5) the necessity of humility (Prov 3:34 in 1 Pet 5:5; see Pride).

3.5. Exegetical Technique in Revelation. While there are no formal citations in this work (see Revelation, Book of), it contains by far the most extensive list of allusions in the NT (see Old Testament in Revelation). H. B. Swete lists 278 allusions in the 404 verses of Revelation, and this does not count the numerous echoes permeating the book. All three major divisions of the OT are included, and Swete lists 46 references from Isaiah, 31 from Daniel, 29 from Ezekiel and 27 from the Psalms. Nowhere is there a verbatim quote from an OT passage, though at times John comes close, such as his conflation of Daniel 7:13 and Zechariah 12:10 in Revelation 1:7 or his apparent translation of the Hebrew of Psalm 2:9 in Revelation 2:27. There are two interpretive problems. (1) Normally references are strung together in catenae fashion, so that one must interpret each one in a series and then try to determine the cumulative effect. (2) John exhibits a creative use of the OT allusions, often altering details and seemingly ignoring the original context; the reader must be careful to note how the passages are applied and what they add to the context of Revelation.

On the whole Revelation utilizes midrash and typology. Yet there is a bewildering array of exegetical techniques within this broad pattern. G. K. Beale (323-32) notes several: (1) Literary prototypes, in which a particular OT pattern dominates the themes of a section, such as Daniel 3, 7 in Revelation 1, 4—5, 13, 17; (2) thematic use, such as the "abomination of desolation" or the divine warrior themes, which surface again and again in the book; (3) analogical

types, such as the "serpent of old" in Revelation 12:9, the judgment* motif, the four horsemen of Revelation 6:1-8, the plagues of the trumpets* and bowls* (= the Egyptian plagues), or Gog and Magog in Revelation 20:8; (4) universalization, as OT themes that belong to Israel* are applied to larger groups, such as "kingdom of priests" from Exodus 19:6 to the church* in Revelation 1:6 and Revelation 5:10, and "they will mourn" of Zechariah 12:10 to "all the tribes of the earth" in Revelation 1:7; (5) indirect fulfillment, in which nonprophetic passages such as historical events are applied, among them the tree of life (Rev 2:7; 22:7; Gen 2:9) or the wings of the eagle (Rev 12:14; Exod 19:4); (6) inverted use, as OT texts are used contrary to their original meaning, such as Revelation 3:9 (= Is 45:14; 49:23), in which the Gentiles* bowing down to the Jews is used of Jewish persecutors bowing down to believers.

3.6. Exegetical Technique in the Apostolic Fathers. Here the exegesis is of both the OT and NT. However, as the idea of canon* was just beginning, gegraptai ("it is written") is used only of OT quotes rather than of NT quotes (see Old Testament in the Apostolic Fathers). The NT books were well-known and treated as authoritative, especially the four Gospels and the Pauline letters, but they were not yet treated as Scripture. As with NT writers, literal midrash and typology were predominant, and the apostolic fathers* took a christocentric view of the OT, that is, the whole canon pointed forward and was fulfilled in Jesus.

The use of the OT varies widely among the Fathers. Perhaps the earliest work, 1 Clement, contains at least seventy quotations and nearly one hundred allusions from the OT but no formal quotations (though there are several allusions and references to the Pauline epistles, James,* 1 Peter* and Hebrews*) from the NT. Much of it is paraenetic, with Job and Proverbs among the most frequently cited. Clement (see Clement of Rome) characteristically used the heroes of the past (Enoch, Noah, Abraham,* Moses,* Rahab) as examples of proper conduct in the present. The Epistle of Barnabas* has an even more extensive OT presence (one hundred quotations, utilizing all three divisions), probably because it is a polemic against Judaism* and its ceremonial regulations. There is a heavy use of typology and a christological* emphasis. Christ not only fulfilled the OT but actually spoke through it.

In contrast, in the seven letters of Ignatius* there are only two formal quotations, though he writes against judaizing teachers in the church (as well as proto-Gnostics who denied the Incarnation). He argues that the prophets* and Judaism are subordinate to Christ, and so he uses a christological hermeneutic. The *Shepherd of Hermas** has no formal quotations but many allusions, most of them in liturgical* or catechetical contexts. *2 Clement* draws most of its OT quotations from NT parallels. In short, there is wide diversity in the use of the OT, probably due to the problems faced. Those fighting a judaizing or gnostic movement tend to see the OT as subordinate to the NT, while others view it (in ways similar to the General Epistles) in paraenetic fashion as anchoring the ethical* practice of Christians. A christocentric perspective dominates.

4. Hermeneutical Difficulties.

4.1. Interpretation of Acts. The critical issues in Acts of the Apostles* have been explored elsewhere in this volume, but several interpretive problems can be discussed. Two poles might be noted at the outset. Some modern Christian interpreters (especially those associated with the contemporary missionary movement) have tended to treat Acts as a strategy text that tells us how to conduct the church's* mission.* Yet this is counter to the hermeneutical dictum that historical books deal with contingent situations and the interpreter must keep that fact carefully in view. The theology of Acts, not the events, is programmatic. The second pole is to treat the book purely as a fictive narrative with virtually no theological thrust. This misses both its historical and its theological foci. The book is a narrative whole that traces a particular theological trajectory through the life of the early church.

Moreover, Acts is the second of a two-volume, integrated work and carries on themes prepared in the Gospel of Luke. The interpretation of any single part of this work must be done in terms of the place of the passage in the developing message of the two-volume work. One must consider structure (macro and micro), plot, setting and theological themes. L. T. Johnson (409-10) discusses some of the narrative devices (summaries, speeches, journeys, parallelism) and structures (geography, proph-ecy [literary, programmatic and speech-narrative types]) needed to understand the book. The best title for the book would be "The Acts of the Holy Spirit Through the Apostles," because the actant throughout is not Peter or Paul but God* through the Holy Spirit.* God decides, informs and guides the events throughout the book. Peter and Paul follow his dictates. Narrative criticism and biblical theology guide the exegesis of the Acts of the Apostles.

4.2. The Interpretation of Hebrews. There has been considerable debate regarding the possibility that the author of Hebrews* engaged in Alexandrian exegesis. Affinities with the platonic approach of Philo* in terms of such peculiarities as the law* as a "shadow" (Heb 8:5; 10:1) and of the heavenly tabernacle* (Heb 8:5; 9:23-24) have led many scholars to think this epistle stems from Alexandrian Judaism.* However, recent thought has demonstrated the lack of data for such an approach; Jewish parallels, particularly an eschatological* perspective, provide closer parallels (see especially Hurst). In similar fashion E. Käsemann and others have argued that the dualism of the book and the idea of a pilgrimage of the soul from the world* to the heavenly sphere shows that the author had a gnostic* background. Yet this too has problems, for the very myth Käsemann alludes to comes from a time later than Hebrews, and the parallels are not that close. Some interpreters (e.g., Buchanan, Hughes) see a pesher exegesis and Qumran* influence in this book. The Melchizedekian* high priesthood* of Hebrews 5:8-10 and Hebrews 7:1-28 has some affinities with Qumran, as does pesher exegesis in Hebrews 1:3-13 (similar to 4QFlor) and his use of Psalm 110:4 in Hebrews 5:6 and Hebrews 7:17, 21. While there undoubtedly are similarities, it is unlikely this is the provenance of the epistle, which is more Hellenistic Jewish than Essene in its thought (see Lane, cviii).

It is best to see a Jewish typology dominating the exegesis of the book and to note an eschatological* perspective that sees salvation* as a future entity demanding perseverance* in faith* and hope* in the midst of persecution.* As H. W. Attridge says (103), "the work is fundamentally the work of a Jewish-Christian rhetor, an individual who draws freely on a broad spectrum of legends, theological and philosophical patterns, scriptural interpretations, liturgical formulas, and oratorical commonplaces." More and more it is recognized that the warning passages (Heb 2:1-4; 3:7-19; 5:11—6:12; 10:19-39; 12:14-29) show the predominantly paraenetic purpose of the book. The peril and the solution in personal perseverance* and community undergirding (cf. Heb 12:12-17; 13:1-9) are keys to the book.

4.3. The Interpretation of Revelation. There is no biblical book whose interpretation depends more upon the perspective one brings to it than does the Apocalypse (*see* Revelation, Book of). Historically understanding has shifted among five hermeneutical approaches: (1) the historicist view that sees Revelation describing the entire period between the first and second coming of Christ* (*see* Parousia); (2) the preterist view that sees the book written to describe only the first-century situation of conflict between the church and the imperial cult (*see* Emperor; Roman Empire); (3) the sociological approach, which is a subset of the preterist but centers upon the social world behind the book (*see* Social Setting); (4) the idealist perspective, which sees the book as a set of timeless symbols addressing issues that Christians face at any time in history; and (5) the futurist approach, which understands the book to be describing the final eschatological* victory of God* over Satan* and the forces of evil.

Throughout Revelation's history of interpretation, it has been thought that one must choose a perspective, but it is being increasingly recognized (see Mounce, 39-45) that all the approaches have value for understanding the book. The Apocalypse addresses both present and future, it stems from a social world, and it contains symbols and emphases that speak to the church* in every age. The perspective shifts from one to another throughout the book, and often there is more than one emphasis in a given passage (e.g., the martyrdom* of the saints, combining the preterist, idealist and futurist into a single message).

The key to interpreting Revelation is in understanding how apocalyptic* functions and in interpreting the symbols accordingly:

Apocalyptic entails the revelatory communication of heavenly secrets by an otherworldly being to a seer who presents the visions in a narrative framework; the visions guide readers into a transcendent reality that takes precedence over the current situation and encourages readers to persevere in the midst of their trials. The visions reverse normal experience by making the heavenly mysteries the real world and depicting the present crisis as a temporary, illusory situation. This is achieved via God's transforming the world for the faithful. (Osborne, 222)

The symbols function within this environment. They are drawn from the ancient apocalyptic store of symbols and communicated well to the ancient reader. The modern reader needs to use background information (Jewish and Hellenistic) to unlock their meaning. One critical aspect is that the symbols function theologically and are not a description of exactly what will take place. The reader is to understand the text as a theological message, and what will really happen is not the intended message. In other words, an early-edition newspaper approach is hermeneutically indefensible. The message of the book is as open to careful students as that of any other biblical book, so long as they utilize the exegetical tools of structure, grammar, semantics and background information. The book is also narrative, and the tools of plot, characterization, point of view and setting are also critical.

See also CANON; INTERTEXTUALITY IN EARLY CHRISTIAN LITERATURE; LETTERS, LETTER FORMS; NARRATIVE CRITICISM; NEW TESTAMENT THEOLOGY; NONCANONICAL WRITINGS, CITATIONS OF; OLD TESTAMENT IN ACTS, HEBREWS, GENERAL EPISTLES, REVELATION, APOSTOLIC FATHERS; PREACHING FROM ACTS, GENERAL EPISTLES, REVELATION; PSEUDEPIGRAPHY; RHETORIC, RHETORICAL CRITICISM; SOCIAL SETTING OF EARLY NON-PAULINE CHRISTIANITY; STRUCTURALISM AND DISCOURSE ANALYSIS; TEXTUAL CRITICISM.

BIBLIOGRAPHY. K.-O. Apel, *Hermeneutik und Ideologiekritik* (Frankfort: Suhrkamp, 1971); H. W. Attridge, "Hebrews, Epistle to the," *ABD* 3:97-105; D. E. Aune, *The New Testament in Its Literary Environment* (LEC; Philadelphia: Westminster, 1987); J. L. Bailey, "Genre Analysis" in *Hearing the New Testament: Strategies for Interpretation,* ed. J. B. Green (Grand Rapids: Eerdmans, 1995) 197-221; C. K. Barrett, "Luke-Acts" in *It Is Written: Scripture Citing Scripture,* ed. D. A. Carson and H. G. M. Williamson (New York: Cambridge University Press, 1988) 231-44; R. Barthes, "From Work to Text" in *Textual Strategies: Perspectives in Poststructuralist Criticism,* ed. J. V. Harari (Ithaca, NY: Cornell University Press, 1979) 73-81; J. Barton, *Reading the Old Testament: Method in Biblical Study* (London: Darton, Longman & Todd, 1984); R. J. Bauckham, "James, 1 and 2 Peter, Jude" in *It Is Written: Scripture Citing Scripture*, ed. D. A. Carson and H. G. M. Williamson (New York: Cambridge University Press, 1988) 303-17; G. K. Beale, "Revelation" in *It Is Written: Scripture Citing Scripture*, ed. D. A. Carson, H. G. M. Williamson (New York: Cambridge University Press, 1988) 318-36; G. W. Buchanan, *To the Hebrews* (AB; Garden City, NY: Doubleday, 1972); J. Derrida, "Structure, Sign and Play in the Discourse of the Human Sciences" in *Writing and Difference*, ed. A. Bass (Chicago: University of Chicago Press, 1978) 79-153; J. H. Elliott, *A Home for the Homeless: A Sociological Exegesis of I Peter, Its Situation and Strategy* (Philadelphia: Fortress, 1981); B. Fiore, "Parenesis and Protreptic," *ABD* 5:162-65; S. E. Fish, *Is There a Text in This Class? The Authority of Interpretive Communities* (Cambridge, MA: Harvard University Press, 1980); H.-G. Gadamer, *Truth and Method* (2d ed.; New York: Crossroad, 1982); J. B. Green, "Discourse Analysis and New Testament Interpretation" in *Hearing the New Testament: Strategies for Interpretation*, ed. J. B. Green (Grand Rapids: Eerdmans, 1995) 175-96; G. H. Guthrie, *The Structure of Hebrews: A Text-Linguistic Analysis* (Leiden: E. J. Brill, 1994); J. Habermas, *Knowledge and Human Interests* (2d ed.; London: Heinemann, 1978); A. T. Hanson, "Christ in the Old Testament According to Hebrews," *SE* 2 (1964) 393-407; R. B. Hays, *The Moral Vision of the New Testament* (San Francisco: HarperCollins, 1996); E. D. Hirsch Jr., *Validity in Interpretation* (New Haven, CT: Yale University Press, 1967); P. E. Hughes, *A Commentary on the Epistle to the Hebrews* (Grand Rapids: Eerdmans, 1977); L. D. Hurst, *The Epistle to the Hebrews: Its Background of Thought* (SNTSMS 65; Cambridge: Cambridge University Press, 1990); W. Iser, *The Act of Reading: A Theory of Aesthetic Response* (Baltimore: Johns Hopkins University Press, 1978); E. E. Johnson, *Expository Hermeneutics: An Introduction* (Grand Rapids: Zondervan, 1990); L. T. Johnson, "Luke-Acts, Book of," *ABD* 4:403-20; idem, "The Use of Leviticus 19 in the Letter of James," *JBL* 101 (1982) 391-401; P. D. Juhl, *Interpretation: An Essay in the Philosophy of Literary Criticism* (Princeton, NJ: Princeton University Press, 1980); W. C. Kaiser, *Toward An Exegetical Theology: Biblical Principles for Teaching and Preaching* (Grand Rapids: Baker, 1981); E. Käsemann, *The Wandering People of God: An Investigation of the Letter to the Hebrews* (Minneapolis: Augsburg, 1984); G. A. Kennedy, *New Testament Interpretation Through Rhetorical Criticism* (Chapel Hill, NC: University of North Carolina Press, 1984); W. L. Lane, *Hebrews 1-8* (WBC; Dallas: Word, 1991); R. N. Longenecker, *Biblical Exegesis in the Apostolic Period* (Grand Rapids: Eerdmans, 1975); R. H. Mounce, *The Book of Revelation* (NICNT; Grand Rapids: Eerdmans, 1977); G. R. Osborne, *The Hermeneutical Spiral: A Comprehensive Introduction to Biblical Hermeneutics* (Downers Grove, IL: InterVarsity Press, 1991); S. E. Porter, "Discourse Analysis and New Testament Studies: An Introductory Survey" in *Discourse Analysis and Other Topics in Biblical Greek*, ed. S. E. Porter and D. A. Carson (Sheffield: Sheffield Academic Press, 1995) 14-35; R. R. Reuther, "Feminist Interpretation: A Method of Correlation" in *Feminist Interpretation of the Bible*, ed. L. M. Russell (New York: Blackwell, 1985) 111-24; P. Ricoeur, *The Rule of Metaphor* (Toronto: University of Toronto Press, 1977); J. R. Searle, *Expression and Meaning: Studies in the Theory of Speech Acts* (Cambridge: Cambridge University Press, 1979); C. Spicq, *L'Épître aux Hébreux* (2 vols.; Paris: Gabalda, 1952-53); S. K. Stowers, *Letter Writing in Greco-Roman Antiquity* (LEC; Philadelphia: Westminster, 1986); S. G. Sowers, *The Hermeneutics of Philo and Hebrews: A Comparison of the Interpretation of the Old Testament in Philo Judaeus and the Epistle to the Hebrews* (Richmond: John Knox, 1965); H. B. Swete, *Commentary on Revelation* (Grand Rapids: Kregel, n.d. [1911]); A. C. Thiselton, *New Horizons in Hermeneutics* (Grand Rapids: Zondervan, 1992); idem, *The Two Horizons: New Testament Hermeneutics and Philosophical Description* (Grand Rapids: Eerdmans, 1980); K. J. Vanhoozer, "The Reader in New Testament Interpretation" in *Hearing the New Testament*, ed. J. B. Green (Grand Rapids: Eerdmans, 1995) 301-28; idem, "The Semantics of Biblical Literature: Truth and Scripture's Diverse Literary Forms" in *Hermeneutics, Authority and Canon*, ed. D. A. Carson and J. D. Woodbridge (Grand Rapids: Zondervan, 1986) 53-104; D. F. Watson, *Invention, Arrangement and Style: Rhetorical Criticism of Jude and 2 Peter* (SBLDS 104; Atlanta: Scholars Press, 1988); N. T. Wright, *The New Testament and the People of God* (Minneapolis: Fortress, 1992).

G. R. Osborne

HIGH PRIEST. *See* PRIEST, HIGH PRIEST.

HOLINESS. *See* HOLY, HOLINESS.

HOLY, HOLINESS

"Pursue holiness," urges the writer to the Hebrews, for without holiness "no one will see the Lord" (Heb 12:14). The word *holy* and its cognates permeate the NT and find prominence in the postapostolic writings. Yet these words are not always readily understood, since the fundamental idea of the Greek words for holy or holiness and the Hebrew root word (*q-d-š*) that underlies them is embodied in such expressions as "different from," "distinct," "devoted to," "sacred," and the like. Moral and ethical* ideas derive from these words only insofar as people are devoted to or pledge themselves to a certain kind of god, in this instance to the God* of the OT and of the NT—the living and true God, the God who is sheer goodness, who is vitally concerned with the moral and ethical.

1. The Vocabulary of Holiness
2. The Old Testament Background
3. The Idea of the Holy in the New Testament and Apostolic Fathers

1. The Vocabulary of Holiness.

The words for "holy" and "holiness" used in the NT and the apostolic fathers belong to that cluster of words derived from an old Greek root, *hag-* : *hagiazō* (make holy, sanctify), *hagiasmos* (holiness, sanctification), *hagioprepēs* (holy, proper for one who is holy), *hagios* (holy, sacred), *hagiotēs* (holiness), along with words such as *hagneia* (purity), *hagnizō* (purify), *hagnismos* (purification), *hagnos* (pure, holy) and *hagnotēs* (purity, sincerity). Of this multiplicity of related words, however, *hagios* is the one used most frequently by all our authors.

Still other words, while from a different root, are related in meaning: *hosios* (holy), *hosiotēs* (holiness) and *hosiōs* (in a holy manner). These words are rarely used in early Christian writings, the latter two not at all in that part of the NT under consideration (but see *1 Clem.* 6.1; 21.7-8; 29.1; 32.4; 48.4; 60.2).

Hieros is still another Greek word denoting holiness—holiness or sacredness with no overtones of the ethical. It is used only infrequently in *1 Clement* (*see* Clement of Rome) and the *Shepherd of Hermas** (*1 Clem.* 25.5; 43.1; 45.2; 53.1; *Herm. Vis.* 1.10).

2. The Old Testament Background.

2.1. The Fundamental Character of God. The starting point for an understanding of these words in the NT and other early Christian writings is the OT. The OT writers reiterate that the Lord* God is holy (Lev 19:2; 21:8; Josh 24:19; Ps 22:3; Is 57:15, passim)—"holy" being the fundamental characteristic of God under which all other characteristics are subsumed—and that humans are sinful (Gen 18:20; 1 Kings 8:46; Ps 51:3; Eccles 7:20, passim).

As holy, God is transcendent above, different from, opposite to, Wholly Other (Otto, 6, 25), separate from sin and sinful people (Is 6:1-9; 55:8, 9; cf. Ex 19:20-24; Num 18:3; Heb 7:26). Sinful people, who have become so by their own choice against God (Gen 2:16, 17; 3:1-7; cf. Rom 5:12), are thereby alienated from God and powerless in that they are incapable of closing the chasm that exists between themselves and God, between the holy and the unholy (Is 50:1; 59:1, 2). God, the Holy, is also the "I am, the One who is" (Ex 3:14): God is Life. For people to be separated from God because of their sin is for them to be separated from Life. Those who were made for the purpose of living (cf. Gen 1:26) are faced with its opposite—death (Ezek 18:4).

2.2. The Actions of God. God, however, did what humans could not do. The holiness of God cannot be described merely as a state of being indicative of what God is, but also as purposeful, salvific action indicative of what God plans and carries out. The OT viewed God as transcendent in that he was distinct from sinful humans but not remote or indifferent to them (Snaith, 47). God took the initiative to make the unholy holy, to make the alien a friend, to reconcile sinners to himself (*see* Salvation).

An example of this is when God the holy One took the initiative to reveal himself to Israel* at Sinai and to call this people out from among other nations into a special personal relationship with himself through covenant,* law* and sacrifice* (Ex 20, 24:1-8; Lev 16). Thus, it was God who made Israel a priestly kingdom and a holy nation (Ex 19:6; Deut 7:6), a people that must preserve its distinctiveness by pursuing a way of life different from that practiced by other peoples (Deut 7:5-6; see Levine, 256), a people fit for the service of God and dedicated to do his will, a light to the nations around them (Is 49:6).

Because of God's special relation to parts of his creation* it was possible even for *things* to be called holy—holy only in the strict sense that they were different from the profane—wholly given over to divine purposes: the ground around a burning bush (Ex 3:5), Jerusalem* (Is 48:2), the temple* (Is 64:10), the Sabbath (Ex 16:23), priestly garments (Ex 31:10), and so on.

2.3. The Ethical Response to God. The OT meaning of "holy/holiness," however, is not exhausted with such ideas as "separate from," "dedicated to," "sacred" and the like, although these may have been the primary meanings of the words. There are also ethical and moral meanings attached to them. Again such meanings find their origin in the nature of God, for the nature of God is the determining factor that gives meaning to everything (2.1 above). Leviticus 19:1-18 clearly illustrates the moral side of God's holiness. Here it becomes clear that to be holy as God is holy is not simply to be pure* and righteous,* but to act toward others with purity and goodness, with truthfulness and honesty, with generosity, justice and love, particularly toward the poor and those who are in no position to help themselves (see esp. Lev 19:9-10, 14). Religion and ethics,* the sacred and moral, belong together in the OT; relationship to the Lord God of the OT demands an ethical/moral response. God's people must not only be like God but also act like God.

3. The Idea of the Holy in the New Testament and Apostolic Fathers.

The meaning of the words *holy* and *holiness,* although expanded in the literature under study, is squarely based on the writings of the OT. The primary meaning of holy as "separate from" is to be found in the actions of Paul and others who engaged in purification/sanctification rites *(hagnizō, hagnismos)* by which they ceremoniously separated themselves from the profane so as to be considered fit to enter the sacred precincts of the house of a holy God (Acts 21:24, 26; 24:18; cf. Num 6:5, 13-18; see Douglas, passim; also *Barn.* 8.1; 15.1, 3, 6-7). That narrow but fundamental meaning of "holy" is nevertheless inadequate to interpret all the texts that treat this concept.

3.1. The Holiness of God. In our early Christian writings "the holiness of God the Father is everywhere presumed . . . though seldom stated" (Procksch, 101). Nevertheless it *is* stated: God's name, the very essence of his person, is holy (*Did.* 10.2; *1 Clem.* 64). Making use of the vocabulary of Leviticus, especially the Holiness Code in Leviticus 19-26, Peter tells those to whom he writes that it is incumbent upon them to be holy as God is holy (*hagios,* 1 Pet 1:15-16; cf. Lev 19:2; see Selwyn).

The writer of Hebrews* explains the disciplinary action of God as his creative work in human lives so that they may share in his holiness (*hagiotēs,* Heb 12.10). Once again the trisagion (*see* Liturgical Elements) is sung to God (cf. Is 6:3), this time by the four living creatures of the Seer's vision*—*hagios, hagios, hagios* (holy, holy, holy). They acclaim that God is holy to the ultimate degree and as such is the Almighty, the *Pantokratōr,* the one who is, who was and who is to come, eternal and omnipotent, transcendent, Wholly Other (Rev 4:8; see also *1 Clem.* 34.6; 59.3). Those who were victorious over the beast sang, "Great and amazing are your deeds, Lord God the Almighty!. . . For you alone are holy" (*hosios [hagios]* Rev 15:3-4; *1 Clem.* 59.3), and the angel of the waters, "You are just, O Holy One" (*ho hosios,* Rev 16:5). The martyrs,* asking for vengeance upon those who slaughtered them for serving God, address God as "Sovereign Lord, holy and true *(ho hagios kai alēthinos),*" because they know that God, as holy, stands apart from and opposed to sin and evil and that he alone is able to administer justice and judge rightly (Rev 6:10).

God as holy is to be feared (cf. Ps 89:7; 99:3; 111:9); he is a consuming fire (Heb 12:29). He owns the right to judge and to take vengeance (cf. Deut 32:35). But in the NT and other early Christian writings God takes no delight in banishing sinners from him. He delights instead in making them holy, in creating a people fit for his presence, in bringing them close to himself and in giving them sacred work to do (cf. Is 6:1-8). As a consequence God sends his good news (*see* Gospel) out into the world so that sinful people may "turn from darkness to light and from the power of Satan to God, so that they may receive forgiveness of sins and a place among those who are sanctified *[hēgiasmenoi],*" i.e., among those who have been made holy and have been set apart to God (Acts 26:18; cf. 20:32). It is important to note here that the expression "those who are sanctified" is a passive participle (from *hagiazō*, make holy, consecrate, sanctify) that has been termed a "divine passive." That is, God is the agent of the action. He has taken the initiative not to destroy sinners but to make them holy (cf. *Herm. Vis.* 3.9.1).

It is God's will that sinful people be made holy (Heb 10:10). But it was costly for God to realize this wish. Under the old covenant sinners were made holy on the basis of animals being properly sacrificed year after year in their behalf (Lev 16)—tentatively made holy (cf. Rom 3:25; Heb 10:4). Under the new covenant sinners are made holy or sanctified (*hēgiasmenoi/hagiazomenous*) by a much more profound act—the conscious, deliberate choice of Jesus Christ,* God's Son, radically to obey his Father and offer his body in death as a single sacrifice for sins forever (Heb 10:5-10, 12, 14, 29; cf. Phil 2:8; *Diogn.* 9.2; *see* Death of Christ). The blood of Jesus (an expression that refers to the self-determined action of Jesus to die on behalf of sinful human beings) is that by which sinful persons are made holy. The explicit purpose of his suffering and death was that the unclean might become clean, that he might make unholy people holy (*hagiasē*, Heb 13:12; see also 9:13; *1 Clem.* 32.4; 59.3; *Barn.* 5.1).

In the writings under consideration, as in the OT, places and things as well as persons can be considered holy. Thus the temple is called "the holy place" (Acts 6:13; 21:28). The two tents of the tabernacle are referred to as "the holy place" (*hagia*, Heb 9:1) and "the Holy of Holies" (*hagia hagiōn*, Heb 9:3; see also 9:1, 12, 24, 25; 10:19; 13:11). The mountain on which Jesus was transfigured is designated as "the holy *[hagios]* mountain" (2 Pet 1:18; cf. *Barn.* 11.3). The Christian faith* is termed "the most holy *[hagiōtatē* faith" (Jude 20). Jerusalem is called "the holy *[hagian]* city" (Rev 11:2; 21:2, 10; 22:11, 19). Presbyters are holy (Ign. *Magn.* 3.1), the Eucharist is holy (*Did.* 9.5), the church* is holy (*Herm. Vis.* 1.1.6; *Mart. Pol.* presc.), prophets* are holy (Acts 3:21; 2 Pet 3:2), angels* are holy (Acts 10:22; cf. Jude 14; Rev 14:10; *1 Clem.* 39:7; *Herm. Sim.* 5.4.4; *Herm. Vis.* 5.5.3).

3.2. The Holiness of Jesus Christ. The NT describes Jesus as holy, a person set apart to God, anointed by him (Acts 4:27; *see* Anointing), dedicated to God and designated as his unique instrument to carry out his predestined plan in the world (Acts 4:28). But holy is also used of Jesus as it is used of God the Father.

The early church understood Psalm 16:10, said to be written by David and about David, to have had its fulfillment in the resurrected Jesus—"You will not . . . let your Holy *[hosion]* One experience corruption" (Acts 2:27; 13:35). Peter referred to Jesus as "the Holy *[ton hagion]* and Righteous One" (Acts 3:14), seemingly in the moral sense of innocent since he linked the word so closely with the anarthrous *dikaion* ("righteous"—*ton hagion kai dikaion;* cf. Lk 23:47 and see Conzelmann, 28). In a later sermon Peter speaks of Jesus as God's "holy *[hagion]* servant/son" (*pais*, Acts 4:27; 30).

But the NT and early Fathers say more than this about Jesus. He is the one who makes others holy (*ho hagiazōn*, Heb 2:11; 13:12), who consecrates them to God and his service that they might be admitted into his presence (cf. Procksch, 89-97). "Jesus is here [in Heb 2:11] exercising a divine function since, according to the OT, it is God who consecrates" (Montefiore, 62; cf. Ex 31:13; Lev 20:8; 21:15; 22:9, 16, 32; Ezek 20:12; 37:28; but see Attridge, 88 n. 107).

Borrowing the language of Isaiah 8:12-13 Peter calls upon Christians to "sanctify *[hagiasate]* Christ as Lord" (1 Pet 3:15). They are to acknowledge that he is holy (cf. Is 29:23; Ezek 20:41; Ecclus 36:4, Mt 6:9)—holy in the sense that God is holy—for as J. N. D. Kelly has remarked, this verse "has a bearing on 1 Peter's Christology. . . . [As] in ii,3 the title 'the Lord', which in the Hebrew original denotes God, is unhesitatingly attributed to Christ" (Kelly, 142; *see* Christology; 1 Peter).

"The Holy One," a frequent name of God in the OT (2 Kings 19:22; Ps 71:22; 78:41; Is 1:4, passim), appears also in 1 John 2:20 ("you have been anointed by the Holy One *[tou hagiou]*)." Although there is debate over whether this expression refers to God the Father or to Jesus Christ, in light of the context and especially in light of 2:27-28 it seems more likely that it is a title given to Jesus (see also *Diogn.* 9.2).

In his vision the Seer reads a letter addressed to the church at Philadelphia. It begins, "These are the words of the Holy One" (*ho hagios*, Rev 4:7). From the context of this letter (see Rev 2:18; 3:1) this Holy One is none other than the crucified, dead and risen Christ, the one who was and is and will forever be (Rev 1:17-18; cf. Rev 4:8; *Diogn.* 9.2). These writers want everyone to understand that Jesus is holy in the sense that God is holy—"holy *[hosios,* a word chosen to emphasize the moral dimension of holiness], blameless, undefiled, separated from sinners, and exalted above the heavens" (Heb 7:26). In naming him "the Holy One" they claim for him the title of deity.

3.3. The Holiness of God's People: Sanctification. In our writings Christians are God's holy people. These are sinful people who have responded with faith in and gratitude to God, who provided the means by which they might be reconciled to him, to be sanctified, to be made holy—action so radical that it required the death of his Son, Jesus Christ (Heb 10:5-10). All early Christian writings affirm this, but the letter to the Hebrews describes it most fully (Heb 2:11; 9:13; 10:10, 14, 29; 13:12; see also Acts 20:32; 26:18; Rev 22:11). Christians, therefore, but including grateful and believing Israel, have become the new Israel of God, "a chosen race, a royal priesthood, a holy nation" (1 Pet 2:9; cf. Ex 19:6; *see* Priest).

The most common term describing Christians is *hoi hagioi,* consistently translated "saints" (Acts 9:13, 32, 41; Heb 3:1; 6:10; 13:24; Rev 5:8; 8:3-4; 11:18; 13:7, 10; 14:12; 16:6; 18:20, 24; 19:8; 20:9; 22:21 [?]; *1 Clem.* 56.1; Ign. *Phld.* 5.2: *Did.* 4.2; 16.7, passim). "Saints" is perhaps not the most felicitous translation for this expression, since in popular usage it too often connotes people who rarely or never sin, when in fact this is not always the case (cf. Gal 2:11-14; Phil 1:14-16, passim). *Hagioi* (holy/saints) refers to persons who are holy because of God's gracious choice of them (Asting, 133-51). It primarily refers to persons who have a new ground of existence, who have been oriented away from the world and turned toward God, and not primarily to persons who are morally and ethically perfect.

Yet moral and ethical meanings do inhere in this word, for such meanings derive from the fact that Christians are persons who are set apart unto and dedicated to this God who has revealed himself in Jesus Christ, who is just, merciful, true, trustworthy, good, and so on (cf. 1 Jn 1:5). Therefore they are persons who have been turned toward God and toward doing his will. But doing the will of God does not come without conscious decision. Hence, the indicative of the verb—"we have been sanctified, made holy, made God's people" (*hēgiasmenoi esmen,* Heb 10:10)—is quickly followed by the imperative:

"As he [God] is holy, be holy *[genēthēte hagioi]* yourselves" (1 Pet 1:15). And again, "Cleanse your hands, you sinners, purify *[hagnisate]* your hearts, you double-minded" (Jas 4:8. The seriousness of this command is such that James* underscores it by addressing his Christian readers as "sinners" and "double-minded" people; see Martin, 153).

In Hebrews the perfect tense of the verb *hēgiasmenoi esmen* ("we have been sanctified, made holy," Heb 10:10) is followed by the present tense (*tous hagiazomenous,* "those who are being made holy," Heb 10:14 NIV). Thus, paradoxically, holiness is both an established fact for Christians and at the same time a process. Christians both are holy and are becoming holy. They are people who have been made holy, made God's special people by virtue of what God has done to them and for them in Christ (Heb 10:10). But they are also people who must allow the creative power of this redemptive act to work itself out in shaping their day-to-day behavior.

When Peter says, "Be holy as God is holy," he is not thinking of holiness in the abstract, for he goes on to say, "be holy in all your conduct" (1 Pet 1:15); you must be leading lives of holiness (2 Pet 3:11; cf. *1 Clem.* 48.5). Peter's "be holy in daily conduct" is not, however, holiness solely limited to that of sexual purity, as often is the case in the apostolic fathers (cf. *1 Clem.* 30.1; 38.2; *2 Clem.* 8.4, 6; *Herm. Man.* 4.1.1; Pol. *Phil.* 5.3), although it includes this. Peter's command is enlarged to embrace purity in the fullest sense of this word—utter goodness in every aspect of life (note how 1 Pet 1:15-16 recalls Lev 19:2-14, which defines the meaning of the word *hagios;* see also 1 Pet 1:22; 3:2; Jas 3:17-18; 1 Jn 3:3; *1 Clem.* 6.1; 21.7-8). Christians are holy and at the same time are people who are continually being shaped so as to share comfortably in God's holiness (*hagiotētos,* Heb 12:10; *1 Clem.* 56.16).

See also GOD; HOLY SPIRIT; PURITY AND IMPURITY.

BIBLIOGRAPHY. A. Asting, *Die Heiligkeit im Urchristentum* (FRLANT 46; Göttingen: Vandenhoeck & Ruprecht, 1930); H. W. Attridge, *The Epistle to the Hebrews* (Herm; Philadelphia: Fortress, 1989); D. Bloesch, "Salt and Light: Our Vocation to Holiness," *Touchstone: A Journal of Ecumenical Orthodoxy* 5 (1992) 25-28; R. Bultmann, *Theology of the New Testament* (2 vols.; New York: Scribners, 1951, 1955) 1:332-33; F. G. Carver, "The

Quest for the Holy: The Darkness of God," *WTJ* 23 (1988) 7-32; H. Conzelmann, *Acts of the Apostles* (Herm; Philadelphia: Fortress, 1987); M. Douglas, *In the Wilderness: The Doctrine of Defilement in the Book of Numbers* (Sheffield, JSOT, 1993); J. N. D. Kelly, *A Commentary on the Epistles of Peter and of Jude* (HNTC; New York: Harper & Row, 1969); B. A. Levine, "Biblical Concepts of Holiness" in *The JPS Torah Commentary, Leviticus* (Philadelphia: The Jewish Publication Society, 1989) 256-57; R. P. Martin, *James* (WBC; Dallas: Word, 1988); H. Montefiore, *The Epistle to the Hebrews* (HNTC; New York: Harper & Row, 1964); R. Otto, *The Idea of the Holy* (New York: Oxford University Press, 1946); O. Procksch and K. G. Kuhn, "ἅγιος κτλ," *TDNT* 1:88-115; E. G. Selwyn, *The First Epistle of St. Peter* (Grand Rapids: Baker, 1981 [1947]); N. H. Snaith, *The Distinctive Ideas of the Old Testament* (London: Epworth, 1944); N. Wolterstorff, "Liturgy, Justice, and Holiness," *Reformed Journal* 39 (1989) 12-20.

G. F. Hawthorne

HOLY CITY. *See* JERUSALEM, ZION, HOLY CITY.

HOLY SPIRIT

There is a sense in which the OT was the age of law* and prophecy,* a period when the Spirit of God came powerfully upon or into the lives of a variety of people—priests,* judges, kings, prophets* and the like—but only sporadically and for a brief time in order to accomplish certain specific tasks on God's behalf for God's people. With the coming of Jesus Christ, however, the eschatological* age dawned (see Heb 1:1-2), the age of the Spirit was inaugurated. Then not only did the Spirit come upon/into (Mk 1:10) Jesus at his baptism* and remain with him throughout his life (cf. Lk 4:1), but later and as a consequence of Jesus' death (*see* Death of Christ), resurrection* and exaltation,* the Spirit was "poured out," in the fulfillment of Joel's prophecy (Joel 3:1-5), upon all of Jesus' followers—irrespective of gender, age, race or social status—and upon them permanently (see Acts 2:4, 17-20, passim). The age of hope* had given way to the age of fulfillment, so that the gift of the Spirit is presently available to all who repent* and believe in the name of Jesus Christ. The promised gift of the Holy Spirit belongs now both to those who are near (Jews) and to those afar off (Gentiles*) (Acts 2:38).

1. Etymology
2. Terminology
3. The Holy Spirit in the Life of Jesus
4. The Holy Spirit and the Church
5. The Holy Spirit and the Inspiration of Scripture
6. The Holy Spirit and the Trinity

1. Etymology.

In all the writings under consideration the word translated "Spirit" (i.e., the Spirit of God, the Holy Spirit), is the Greek word *pneuma* (the equivalent of its Hebrew counterpart, *rûaḥ*) whose fundamental meaning is "air in motion." This word encompasses such ideas as wind, gale, storm or blast (see Ex 14:21; 15:8; Gen 1:2, where von Rad translates *rûaḥ 'elohim* [Spirit of God] as "Storm of God," von Rad, 49)—ideas of immense power,* force and uncontrollable strength; or ideas of peace, quietness and refreshment, for *pneuma* may also be used to describe something as gentle as a breeze (see Gen 3:8). Significantly, *pneuma* also means "breath," the breath of one's mouth or nostrils and by extension the breath of life—the stuff of existence for all living beings (see Gen 2:7; Ps 104:29-30).

It is this word that OT, NT and early Christian writers attach to God in an attempt to describe him, to tell in part who he is: God is *pneuma*, wind, and as such he is invisible, irresistible, unpredictable, uncontrollable power. He is *pneuma*, breath, and as such he imparts life and vitality into every living creature. He is *pneuma*, air in motion, and as such is movement and action, energy at work, everywhere and always present to create and re-create, to sustain, to order, to renew, to revive. This Spirit of God is God, the living God, who infuses new life into his people, filling them with strength, wisdom,* moral courage and power, heightening and enhancing their natural abilities, equipping them in an extraordinary fashion so as to take them beyond the borders of their own limitations, preparing them to carry out significant moral and ethical roles in the course of redemptive history (Hawthorne, 14-23).

2. Terminology.

The titles most frequently used for this "breath of God" in the OT and in the OT apocryphal and pseudepigraphal writings are "the Spirit," "the Spirit of God" and "the Spirit of the Lord." The name, "[the] Holy Spirit," occurs in only two places in the OT (Ps 51:11; Is 63:10-11) and somewhat more often in later writings (4 Ezra 14:22; *Asc. Is.* 5:14; cf. CD 2:11-13; 1QS 3:6-12). It becomes the standard term in rabbinical literature, meaning the Spirit of God as "an entity which stands outside [a person], and which comes to [that person] from God in special situations and under special circumstances" (Sjöberg, 6:381; for other, less frequently occurring titles see Is 11:1-2; Zech 12:10).

The NT and early Christian documents produce a plethora of titles by which attempts were made to catch in a net of words this elusive, universal, immediate, life-changing power that was daily being experienced by ordinary people. The Spirit of God, which many of Israel's* teachers taught had fallen silent or had ceased to be active in the world or was no longer needed now that the Hebrew Scriptures were complete (see Davies, 208-15; Scott, 47, 50; but cf. Aune, 103-47), was once again observed to be present and active. It is as though the world had suddenly awakened to the fact that the longed-for universal age of the Spirit had dawned (see Joel 2:28-29), that the hoped-for new era when God's people would continuously be infused with, inspired and motivated by the Spirit had at last arrived (Is 61). It is no wonder, then, that some of our literature abounds with references to the Spirit and that the titles now are far more varied than before.

As in the OT, especially in Ezekiel, "Spirit" or "the Spirit" are titles frequently used in the NT and the apostolic fathers* to designate the Holy Spirit (cf. Acts 6:3 with 6:5; 1 Pet 1:2; *1 Clem.* 42.4, passim). Surprising, however, is the fact that the familiar OT terms such as "the Spirit of God" and "the Spirit of the Lord" hardly occur in our literature. "The Spirit of God" appears in the NT only in 1 Peter 4:14 and 1 John 4:2 and in the early Fathers only in *Hermas, Mandates* 10.2.6; "the Spirit of the Lord" occcurs only in Acts 5:9; 8:39, *1 Clement* 21.2 and *The Epistle of Barnabas* 6.14 and 9.2.

Yet the excitement generated by the presence and power of the Spirit in the Christian community fostered an irresistible desire on its part to set forth in words the nature of this presence, to explain as clearly as possible the overwhelming significance of the Spirit, to try to make comprehensible the incomprehensible. This desire led to the creation of a variety of new terms to describe the person and work of the Spirit. Thus in addition to the aforemen-

tioned terms, the Spirit is called "the promise of the Father" (Acts 1:4; 2:33, 39; cf. Lk 24:49; Jn 14:16, 26; 15:26; Joel 2:28-29), "the Spirit of life" (Rev 11:11), "the Spirit of truth" (1 Jn 4:6; *Herm. Man.* 3.4), "the Spirit of grace" (Heb 10:29; *1 Clem.* 46.6), "the eternal Spirit" (Heb 9:14), "the blameless Spirit" (Ign. *Smyrn.* presc.), "the seven Spirits of God" (Rev 1:4; 3:1; 4:5; 5:6; see Bruce, 336), "the delicate *[trypheron]* Spirit" (*Herm. Man.* 5.2.6, indicating, no doubt, that the Holy Spirit is easily grieved by wickedness within the human heart), "the prophetic Spirit" and "the Spirit of prophecy" (*Herm. Man.* 11.9; Rev 19:10, calling attention to the Spirit as the inspirer of Scripture), "the Spirit of the Godhead (*theotētos; Herm. Man.* 11.10) and "the Divine (*theion*) Spirit" (*Herm. Man.* 11.7, 12, 21), terms that imply the deity of the Spirit, thereby moving the thinking of the church forward in its development of the doctrine of the Trinity.

Another new and important title given to the Holy Spirit, yet one that would be easily understood, is "the Anointing" (*to chrismon,* 1 Jn 2:20, 27): "You have an anointing from the Holy One and all of you have knowledge," an allusion to the Holy Spirit that Jesus poured out upon his followers like an anointing oil (Acts 2:32-33; cf. 1 Sam 16:17-18). This anointing* imparted to Christians a special gift of knowledge* about God* and about Christ and about their relation to God and Christ (see 1 Jn 3:24; 4:13).

The most common title for the Spirit is "[the] Holy Spirit" *(hagion pneuma, to hagion pneuma, to pneuma to hagion)*—rare in the OT but abundant in our literature. The reason for this radical alteration in terminology is not completely clear. Perhaps it is because now it is more fully understood that it is the Spirit who sets the people of faith* apart ("set apart" is the fundamental meaning of *hagion,* holy; *see* Holiness) from the profane world unto God and who consecrates them to God's service* (cf. 1 Pet 1:2). More likely, however, it is because the Spirit was being dramatically experienced as the power of God by which God was effecting changes in the lives of human beings on a very large scale, transforming them from sinners into a holy people as God himself is holy (1 Pet 1:15-16; cf. Lev 19), that is, effectively working out in them God's "personal will directed to a religious and moral end" (Baumgärtel, 365), making them ethically and morally good people (cf. Ezek 11:19; 18:31; 36:26; Acts 2:1-41; see

Herm. Man. 11.7-8; *see* Ethics).

Perhaps the titles for the Spirit that call for the greatest reflection are those that bring the Spirit and Jesus close together in a dialectical pattern of identity and distinction, arising no doubt from the fact that "Christ and the Spirit are so closely associated in the life of Christians that their names are interchangeable" (Hendry, 24): "the Spirit of Jesus" (Acts 16:7; see Stählin, 229-52), "the Spirit of Christ" (1 Pet 1:11), "the Spirit of Jesus Christ" (Ign. *Magn.* 1.2), "the unhesitating/unwavering *[adiakriton]* Spirit, who is Christ" (Ign. *Magn.* 15.1), "the Spirit is Christ" (*2 Clem.* 14.4) and "the Holy Spirit . . . is the Son of God" (*Herm. Sim.* 9.1.1). The preposition *of* in the expression "the Spirit of Jesus, of Christ, of Jesus Christ" need not necessarily lead one to identify the Spirit with Christ, since at base the function of the preposition is only to describe a close relationship existing between the two and may simply convey an idea similar to that of the Fourth Gospel, in which the Spirit of Christ is the Spirit who witnesses to Christ (cf. Jn 14:26; 15:26; 1 Cor 12:3). But the ambiguity of the expressions obviously led some of the Fathers to go beyond this and say that the one is the other and not to make a distinction between Christ and the Spirit (cf. Rom 8:9-10; 1 Cor 10:4; 2 Cor 3:18; see the confused and confusing passage in *Herm. Sim.* 5.6.5-7; also in the same vein, *2 Clem.* 9.5).

3. The Holy Spirit in the Life of Jesus.

The Gospel writers record decisive points in the life and ministry of Jesus, noting the presence of the Holy Spirit in each of these—his baptism, his temptation,* his preaching,* his exorcisms, and so on. Recording these events in this way, they make it clear that their intent was to describe the life of the Son of God become incarnate as that of a truly human person who was wholly guided and empowered by the Spirit (Hendry, 19). This theme is picked up in our literature and is clearly and succinctly summarized in Acts 2:22 and Acts 10:38. There it is stated that "Jesus the Nazarene was a man marked out by God with mighty works, wonders and signs which God did through him" (Acts 2:22), for "God had anointed him [made him Messiah] with the Holy Spirit and power"; as a consequence, "he always went about (*diēlthen,* see BDF 332.1) doing good *[euergetōn]* and healing *[iōmenos]* all who were overpowered by the

devil because God was with him" (Acts 10:38; see Robinson, 125; Swete 1976, 59). The whole of Jesus' ministry* is here regarded as "made up of a continuous series of acts of beneficence"— "God's decisive attack upon the (personally conceived) power of evil" (Barrett, 1:525)—performed by Jesus in the power of the Holy Spirit (cf. Is 61:1-2; 42:1; 11:1-3; see Hawthorne, 97-172).

It is of interest that in our texts only Ignatius* refers to the role that the Holy Spirit played at the birth of Jesus: "Our God, Jesus the Christ, was conceived by Mary . . . of *[ek]* the seed of David and of the Holy Spirit" (Ign. *Eph.* 18.2, an allusion to Rom 1:3).

The writer to the Hebrews* alone describes the presence and power of the Holy Spirit at the death of Jesus. He writes, "Christ, who through the eternal Spirit offered himself without blemish to God" (Heb 9:14). Behind these words "lies the portrayal of the Isaianic Servant of the Lord, who yields up his life to God as a guilt offering for many, bearing their sin and procuring their justification. When this servant is introduced for the first time, God says: 'I have put my Spirit upon him' (Is 42:1). It is in the power of the Divine Spirit, accordingly, that the Servant accomplishes every phase of his ministry, including the crowning phase in which he accepts death for the transgression of his people" (Bruce, 205; cf. the enigmatic words of *Barn.* 7.2-3).

In the literature we are considering there are repeated statements that God raised up Jesus and freed him of the pains, or pangs, of death (Acts 2:24, 32; 3:15, 26; 4:10; 5:30-31; 13:33-34; 17:31; 1 Pet 1:21; Ign. *Magn.* 9.3; [in one place Ignatius says that Jesus raised himself, Ign. *Smyrn.* 2]; Pol. *Phil.* 2.1-2). But how did God do this? By what power did God effect this mighty act of resurrection?

It is possible to infer that the power by which God did this was the power of the Holy Spirit, especially when one considers that the Holy Spirit of God was present in every significant event of Jesus' existence—at his birth, in his life and ministry, and at his death. This inference is strengthened by the implication of the somewhat enigmatic creedal* statement of 1 Peter 3:18, variously translated "He [Christ] was put to death in the flesh, but made alive *[zōopoiētheis]* in the spirit" (NRSV) or "He was put to death in the body but made alive by the Spirit"

(NIV). This statement has been taken by some to be an unmistakable reference to Jesus' resurrection by the Spirit. The parallels with the two other creedal statements involving flesh-spirit distinctions (i.e., Rom 1:3-4; 1 Tim 3:16) confirm the contention that "spirit" here refers to that sphere of Christ's existence "in which God's Holy Spirit was supremely and most conspicuously at work" (Dalton, 129-30). "Jesus was 'put to death' by human hands, not by God, but it was God who brought him to life by the power of the Spirit (cf. 4:6)" (Michaels, 204; cf. *Mart. Pol.* 14.2).

Further, the possibility that God raised Jesus by the power of his Spirit seems to be an increasingly reasonable supposition upon noting the words of Luke's introduction of his second treatise to Theophilus: "I wrote about all that Jesus began both to do and to teach until the day in which he was received up after he had given commandment [cf. Mt 28:19-20; Lk 24:45-49; Jn 20:21-23] through the Holy Spirit to the apostles he had chosen" (Acts 1:1-2; see Robinson, 125). This is to say, that during the forty-day period after his resurrection and before he was taken up to heaven Jesus continued to instruct his disciples, as he had done before, "by means of the Holy Spirit." Thus Jesus' entire time on earth, from his birth until his exaltation,* which includes his resurrection, is bracketed by references to the presence and power of the Holy Spirit effectively at work in every significant event of his life (see Hawthorne, 184-94).

4. The Holy Spirit and the Church.

4.1. The Initial Coming of the Holy Spirit. From the beginning of time the Spirit of God has been present and active in the world (Gen 1:2). Never has there been a period in human history when this has not been so—the Spirit creatively at work bringing order, relief and life in the midst of chaos, suffering* and death; the Spirit persistently and effectively reversing the process of destruction and decay; the Spirit in concrete ways acting "against the power of sin, despair, cynicism and death" (Welker, 340). If there was a time when the Spirit was thought to be absent, removed from the sphere of human affairs, no longer visibly evident (see Davies, 208-15; Scott, 47, 50), even then the Spirit was present and at work. There is, however, a difference in emphasis at different times with regard to the activity of the Spirit. The OT primarily focuses attention upon the presence and power of the Spirit in periods of national crisis and in the lives of select individuals. The NT, however, primarily focuses attention upon the presence and power of the Holy Spirit in the life of Jesus and then through him in the lives of all his followers.

After his resurrection Jesus told his disciples to wait in Jerusalem* until they should receive the promise of the Father, the promise of the Holy Spirit (Acts 1:4-5; 2:33). This waiting period ended on the day of Pentecost* (Acts 2:1), the fiftieth day after Passover (*hē pentēkostē [hēmera]* = the fiftieth [day]). Pentecost was the Jewish "feast of weeks" (Deut 16:9-12) or the "day of the first fruits" (Num 28:26), so called because it was when the first fruits of wheat harvest were offered to God (Ex 34:22; cf. Tob 2:1; Josephus *Ant.* 17.10.2 §254). Later Jewish writers viewed Pentecost as the commemoration of the giving of the law* by Moses* (Str-B 2:601). It is tempting to speculate about why this particular day was chosen to end the waiting period and mark the coming of the Holy Spirit—e.g., as Pentecost was thought to commemorate the gift of the Law that resulted in the old covenant* between God and his ancient people, so this same day was selected to celebrate the gift of the Spirit, based upon the life, death, resurrection and exaltation of Jesus that issued in a new covenant between God and his new or renewed people (see Schweizer, 411; *Jub.* 6:17-19; see also *Jub.* 1:1; 15:1; 44:4-5; Philo *Decal.* 33, 35; Philo *Spec. Leg.* 2.189). But such attempts have proved futile (see Lohse, 49-50; Barrett, 111). It appears that Luke was attempting only to state a fact, not make a theological statement.

Whatever may have been the significance of this particular day, Jesus' followers—no doubt the entire 120 (see Acts 1:15)—were together in one place. Then an unforgettable and decisive experience in the life of the church occurred—an event that was both audible and visible. Luke describes it as a sound like the rush of a violent wind and as the appearance of divided tongues of fire resting on each of the persons present (Acts 2:1-3). It is not possible adequately "to translate this experience into terms which convey the true significance to us" today (Bruce, 54), but certainly both wind and fire are familiar biblical terms that call to mind the presence and power of God, of the Spirit of God, creatively at work in the world (cf. Ezek

37:9-14; Ex 3:2-6). Thus it is not surprising to read immediately after this description of such an extraordinary happening that "all of them were filled with the Holy Spirit" (Acts 2:4), which Peter interprets both as the fulfillment of God's promise through the prophet Joel (Acts 2:17-21, quoting Joel 3:1-3) and as the direct result of the resurrected and exalted Christ lavishly bestowing on his church* the gift of the Holy Spirit which he had received from his Father (Acts 2:32-33).

Only in Acts 2—nowhere else in the NT or apostolic fathers—is this founding gift of the Holy Spirit described. Only here is the initial fulfillment of Jesus' promise to his followers that they would be infused with supernatural power detailed. Only here is the permanent coming of the Holy Spirit to live in the lives of the faithful, to indwell the community of believers, the church, made known. What then is one to make of the so-called additional comings of the Spirit described in Acts 8:16 and Acts 10:44 = 11:15? To be sure, the Greek verb that is used in these texts, *epipiptō* (lit. "to fall upon") is similar in meaning to other verbs—*eperchesthai* (Acts 1:8, "to come upon"), *pimplēnai* (Acts 2:4, "to fill"), or *baptizesthai en* (Acts 1:5, "to be baptized in")— used by Luke of that initial giving of the Holy Spirit.

Was there then more than one initial gift of the Spirit to the church? If the answer is no, perhaps the subsequent events recorded in Acts 8 and Acts 10 can be explained not so much as new comings but rather as necessary demonstrations that this same Spirit was no longer exclusively for believing Israel but was now present and available to all who believe. In other words, these so-called comings were concrete, visible proofs that Samaritans (Acts 8:16; *see* Samaria) and Gentiles (Acts 10:44 = 11:15)— people despised or looked down upon as outsiders by Israel—were now fully included among the recipients of God's gracious gift of the Spirit, proofs that the church, which from the beginning, though located only in Jerusalem, "is . . . a universal society in which universal communication is possible" (Barrett, 108). The Spirit once-for-all given at Pentecost to Jewish believers in Jerusalem is seen now to pervade every part of the believing community drawn from among all the nations of the world (Acts 1:8; 2:38-39; *Barn.* 1.3).

4.2. On Receiving the Holy Spirit. To discuss the initial coming of the Holy Spirit upon the faithful in Jerusalem at Pentecost is one thing. But when and how does the Spirit come upon or into each new believer subsequently? How does each new believer receive the Holy Spirit? Of the writings being studied in this volume only the book of Acts* gives an answer to this question, and its answer is unclear.

Certain texts seem to connect baptism so closely with the Holy Spirit (Acts 2:38; 19:1-7) that interpreters have come to understand that baptism is a necessary prerequisite for the coming of the Spirit into the life of the believer, a rite of the church by which the faithful receive the Spirit (e.g., Luther: "This doctrine is to remain sure and firm, that the Holy Spirit is given through the office of the church, that is through the preaching of the gospel and baptism," quoted by Lenski, 109; see more recently, Conzelmann, 22: "Baptism and receiving the Spirit belong together").

But if it is true that the gift of the Holy Spirit is contingent upon baptism, it is remarkable that there is such a varying relation in Acts of baptism to the coming of the Holy Spirit. In Acts 2:38 baptism precedes the gift of the Holy Spirit, from which it could be argued that baptism is a prerequisite for receiving the Spirit. But in Acts 8:16 baptism and the coming of the Spirit are not connected, and in Acts 8:36-39 the Ethiopian eunuch is baptized without any mention of the Holy Spirit coming upon him (see also Acts 9:17-19; 16:14-17, 31-33; 18:8; but note the variant reading to Acts 8:39). In Acts 10:44 the Spirit falls upon Cornelius* and his household* before their baptism takes place, whereas in Acts 18:24-26 baptism appears to be an unnecessary or at least an unmentioned element in the instruction given to Apollos. Finally, in Acts 19:5-6 it appears that the Holy Spirit is not so much conferred upon those who believe by baptism as it is by the laying on of the apostle's* hands (see Barrett, 154).

There is, then, in Acts no consistent tie to enable one to say unequivocally that the Spirit is received at baptism. Nor do the apostolic fathers make any such connection between baptism and the giving of the Spirit (*Barn.* 11.11 excepted, although the translation there of the key expression, *en tō pneumati,* is open to question: "in our spirit" [Swete 1912, 19], "in the Spirit" [Lake, Loeb trans.]).

If our texts will not permit one to argue with

complete confidence that water baptism (though important) is a prerequisite for the conferring of the Holy Spirit, it is possible to infer from them that whenever the Spirit "falls upon" or "fills" any person or group of persons it is because of their positive response to the divine person who encounters them in the gospel.* For example, even while Peter was proclaiming the gospel to the receptive Cornelius and his household the Holy Spirit "fell upon all who heard the word" (Acts 10:44), an event that brought to mind the word of the Lord: "John baptized with water, but you will be baptized with the Holy Spirit" (Acts 11:15-16). Thus the all-important baptism is the baptism with the Spirit, namely, the coming of the Holy Spirit upon or into the community or into the life of individuals. This baptism is predicated upon and coincident with faith in Jesus—in his person, life, death, resurrection and exaltation (cf. Acts 8:12, 14-17; 16:14-17, 31-33; 18:8, passim).

It seems clear from comparing Acts 1:5 with Acts 1:8 and Acts 2:4 that baptism with the Holy Spirit and being filled with the Holy Spirit are to be equated. Nothing is to be found in the book of Acts (and Acts is the principal source of information about the person and work of the Spirit in the literature under discussion) to indicate that the Holy Spirit once imparted was ever taken away from those to whom it was given—church or individual. In fact "Luke [in Acts] believes that the gift of the Spirit is constitutive of the Christian life (see [Acts] 19.1-6; there is something wrong with a disciple who has not received the Holy Spirit)" (Barrett, 115).

What then is meant when Acts says that at a later time Peter and the other believers "were filled" with the Holy Spirit (Acts 4:8, 31; 13:52; see also Acts 9:17 with 13:9)? Perhaps the answer to this question can be gained by comparing the Holy Spirit in the life of Jesus with that of the Spirit in the life of the church. Luke records that at Jesus' baptism the Holy Spirit descended upon him, filled him, was constantly leading (*hēgeto*) him during the forty days of his wilderness testing (Lk 3:21-22; 4:1-2) and was present with him throughout the remainder of his life (cf. Lk 4:14, 18), even at the cross (cf. Heb 9:4). Nevertheless, there are points noted by the Evangelists in the ministry of Jesus where it might be said that Jesus, "filled with the Spirit," healed, spoke, saw or rejoiced. That is, he who

was filled with the Spirit at all times was especially inspired by the Spirit at special moments during his ministry. For example, Luke records that on one such occasion "the power [= Spirit, see Acts 1:8; *Herm. Man.* 11.21] of the Lord was at hand for him to heal" (Lk 5:17). Again, when the woman with an incurable menstrual flow purposefully touched Jesus' clothes, he knew "that power [= Holy Spirit] had gone out from him" (Lk 8:46). Jesus' disciples returned to him with word of their success over the forces of evil. At that instant, it would appear, the Spirit gave him a flash of insight to see in their successes Satan's fall like a lightning bolt from heaven, for Luke goes on to say that "at that time Jesus, full of joy by the Holy Spirit," began to praise God (Lk 10:17-21).

So it is with Peter and all other Christians, initially and continuously filled with the Holy Spirit from conversion. When they are faced with especially difficult and challenging experiences they need from the Holy Spirit a special endowment of insight, inspiration, effective speech, power and emotional strength successfully to carry out their mission in life.

4.3. The Work of the Holy Spirit. It has already been noted that believers in Jesus who were filled with the Holy Spirit from the inception of the church (Acts 2:4) were also "filled with the Spirit" at certain important junctures in life (Acts 4:8). That is to say, they were especially empowered by the Spirit to go beyond the limits of their own innate human abilities so as to carry out a God-given mission in fulfillment of Jesus' words, "You will receive power [focused power, power to achieve some good end] when the Holy Spirit comes upon you" (Acts 1:8).

For example, it is the Holy Spirit who gives Peter, perceived as an "uneducated and ordinary" person, a special power of effective speech (Acts 4:8), so that even the learned elite are forced to recognize the unusualness of his eloquence (Acts 4:13). This power was not given solely to Peter in the history of the church, nor was it intended to be limited to him (Acts 6:10 with 6:5; cf. Lk 12:11-12; see Swete 1976, 84).

Further, it is the Holy Spirit that gives humble men and women, when faced with real threats to their life and welfare, supernormal courage to speak the word of the Lord with boldness and carry to completion the task they believed God wanted them to accomplish regardless of the consequences (Acts 4:31; 7:54-

56; 20:23; *Mart. Pol.* 14).

The Holy Spirit on occasion lifts certain people in an ecstatic, trancelike state above their confining human limitations and heightens their natural faculties, intellectual and spiritual, so that they are able to see and know things other people cannot see and know (Acts 7:55; 10:19; 20:23; Rev 1:10; 4:2; 17:3; 21:10; *Herm. Man.* 1.1.3; 2.1.1), to peer into the future and predict events yet to come (Acts 11:28; 21:12). Perhaps in a similar ecstatic manner, the Holy Spirit comes to the aid of God's people in prayer (Jude 20; cf. Rom 8:15-16, 26-37; Gal 4:6; Jn 4:23-24; Bauckham, 113; Dunn 1975, 245-46).

For whatever reason and in unspecified ways, the Spirit at times hinders people from doing what they intended to do or from going where they planned to go. The Spirit then turns them in quite different directions, giving them undreamed of work to accomplish (Acts 16:6).

The Spirit, living within believers, grants to them the possibility of a new understanding of existence, imparting to them right knowledge and instruction, so that they may come to realize that Jesus is the Christ (1 Jn 4:2, 6), know that God lives in them and they in God (1 Jn 3:24; 4:13) and recognize the difference between truth and error (1 Jn 2:20-21, 27; 4:6; see Bultmann, 80).

Still further, the Spirit is the silent, invisible one who sanctifies. The Spirit is the inner transformer of human lives, the one who acts through the preaching of the gospel to separate individuals from the world unto God (1 Pet 1:2; cf. 1:12; *Barn.* 6.14) so that they no longer indulge themselves in immoral behavior (Jude 18-19; Pol. *Phil.* 5.3) or engage their minds in attitudes hostile to God (Jas 4:4-5 and Martin's translation of 4:5: "The Spirit God made to dwell in us opposes envy," 149). The Shepherd of Hermas, however, seems not to realize the relation of the Spirit either to the life of God or to the human spirit and implies that a person must first be good in order for the Spirit to come and do a sanctifying work (*Herm. Sim.* 9.25.2; *Man.* 3.1.2; 5.1.2-3; 10.2.1, 5; 3.1-2).

Again, there are times when the Spirit constrains believers to achieve some worthwhile goal in life, as Paul felt himself constrained (*dedemenos*) by the Spirit to go to Jerusalem, while at the same time the Spirit warns them through other Christians or Christian prophets of impending disaster if they proceed as planned (Acts 20:22-23; 21:4, 12). Luke sees no contradiction in this, for to him it accords "with the common notion of prophecies and prodigies: they are fulfilled, but not to the exclusion of human decision. Paul 'must' go, but he freely affirms his destiny" (Conzelmann, 178).

It was the Holy Spirit who, in his own inexplicable way, appointed "overseers to shepherd the church of God" at Ephesus (Acts 20:28). Thus one should be careful not to make too sharp a distinction between the charismatic age of the Spirit and the ecclesiastical age, the age of the organized church, as though the latter automatically excluded from its midst the presence and power of the Spirit (see also *1 Clem.* 42.4; Ign. *Phld.* presc. 7.1-2).

The Spirit continues to be the Spirit of prophecy, i.e., the Spirit still inspires select men and women (see Acts 21:9), so that when they speak, they speak with power, so that they rank with the OT prophets in bringing to the people of God the word of God. Christian prophets resided in numbers in Syrian Antioch (Acts 13:1; cf. *Did.* 13.1); others were itinerant (Acts 11:28; 21:10; *Did.* 11). All were authoritative figures within the church, for the Spirit spoke through them. They were to be respected, even feared, certainly obeyed. Nevertheless, both they and their message could and should be put to the test (see *Did.* 11.7—12.11; *Herm. Man.* 1.7-17). This phenomenon of the Christian prophet survived, as far as our literature is concerned, at least into the fourth or fifth decade of the second century (Swete 1912, 25).

The postapostolic writers see in the presence and power of the Spirit the source and dynamic of peace and unity within the church—"A profound and rich peace was given to all; you had an insatiable desire to do good, because the Holy Spirit was poured out in abundance on you all" (*1 Clem.* 2.2; 46.6). Ignatius uses an extravagant metaphor to portray this unifying work of the Spirit: "You are the stones of the temple of the Father, made ready for the building of God our Father, carried up to the heights by the crane of Jesus Christ, that is the cross, and using as a rope the Holy Spirit" (Ign. *Eph.* 9.1). With this imagery he is saying that apart from the Spirit the cross* is a vast inert machine, with building stones around it unmoved. Only when the rope of the Holy Spirit is attached to it can it work to lift the individual stones, i.e., Christians, to fit them harmoniously into the place prepared for them.

The Holy Spirit, present and living within believers, is the companion (or author) of joy* even in the presence of the most adverse circumstances. For instance, Paul and Barnabas, persecuted and driven from city to city for preaching the gospel, nevertheless "were filled with joy and with the Holy Spirit" (Acts 13:52; see Swete 1976, 174; compare or contrast *Herm. Man.* 10.1.2; 10.2.1-6; 10.3.3).

The familiar NT triad of faith,* hope* and love* (1 Thess 1:3; 5:8; Gal 5:5-6; Col 1:4-5; Eph 4:2-5), words that "embrace the whole of Christian existence, as believers live out the life of the Spirit in the present age" (Fee, 212), appears in our literature only in The *Epistle of Barnabas* (*Barn.* 1.4; 11.8) and in Polycarp's *Letter to the Philippians* (Pol. *Phil.* 3.2-3).

When the church throughout Judea, Galatia and Samaria had endured fierce persecution* and had come through it into an era of peace* they found themselves living "in the comfort of the Holy Spirit" (NRSV; *paraklēsei tou hagiou pneumatos),* or as the NIV puts it, "encouraged by the Holy Spirit" (Acts 9:31)—a difficult word and phrase to translate. At times the noun *paraklēsis* can mean (prophetic) exhortation, as in Acts 13:15; at other times comfort, as is possible in Acts 15:31; at still other times, encouragement. "Followed here by the subjective genitive *tou hagiou pneumatos* it is not wrong to allow it to refer to whatever it is that the Holy Spirit does, and this will include both the (messianic) consolation . . . and the stirring up and enabling of Christians to live as they should (cf. 1.8)" (Barrett, 474; cf. *1 Clem.* 42.3).

4.4. How the Holy Spirit Works in the Church. It is clear from the literature that the Holy Spirit is God/Christ powerfully, mysteriously, sometimes quietly and unobtrusively at work in and through the church. But it is not always clear how this work is carried out.

Sometimes supernatural means are used, which defy further definition or explanation, as when Luke says that the Spirit of the Lord "snatched Philip away" and he later found himself in Azotus or when the Shepherd says that the Spirit "seized" him and took him away through a certain pathless district (*Herm. Vis.* 1.1.3; 2.1.1).

The chorus that is repeated seven times in the Apocalypse, "Let anyone who has an ear listen to what the Spirit is saying to the churches" (Rev 2:7, 11, 17, 28; 3:6, 13, 22), may find its explanation in the opening phrase of each letter addressed to the seven churches: "To the angel *[angelos]* of the church . . . write," for *angelos* may refer not to some supernatural being but to mortals, for it also means "messenger." These messengers may have been prophets—human beings especially prepared by God, people sensitive and open to receiving God's word—who wrote to each of these churches an authoritative word of the Lord, because the Holy Spirit inspired them to write. Thus each letter was in essence the Spirit speaking to the particular church addressed. The same might be said of Acts 13: 2—how did the Holy Spirit say to the church at Antioch, "Set apart for me Barnabas and Saul for the work to which I have called them"? Very likely the Spirit did so through the human voice of men or women—for there were prophets, people especially tuned to listening to the voice of the Spirit, in Antioch at that time (Acts 13:1). And when Luke goes on to say that Barnabas and Saul "were sent out by the Holy Spirit" (Acts 13:4), he meant for everyone to understand that the Spirit "sent them out" by means of the church.

That is to say, the Spirit infused God's people, who were praying and fasting, with the authority* necessary to commission these two men by the laying on of their hands (Acts 13:3). How was it that the Holy Spirit told Philip* to join the Ethiopian eunuch in his chariot? Perhaps he spoke to Philip in a human messenger *(angelos),* "the messenger of the Lord" who told him to leave Samaria and go south (Acts 8:29 with Acts 8:26).

Sometimes the Spirit acts in people's lives, communicates with and directs them through dreams, trances (Acts 10:9-20) or ecstatic experiences (Rev 1:10). At other times the Spirit concurs with and confirms the verbal witness of the church by external, visible miraculous signs and wonders (Acts 5:32 with Acts 2:32-39 and Lk 24:48-49; cf. Heb 2:4).

Sometimes the Spirit speaks through disappointing circumstances that cause people in whom he lives to take a different but better course of action than that originally planned (Acts 16:6-7).

Sometimes it is that still, small, inner voice of conviction (cf. *Barn.* 12.2)—perhaps it was in this way that the Spirit testified to Paul that in every city imprisonment and persecution were waiting for him (Acts 20:23). Whatever can be said of God, namely, that he "moves in mysterious ways his wonders to perform," can also be said of God's Spirit. But whenever the Spirit commands, he gives the power to carry out that command; wherever he directs, he gives the strength to traverse that course, however difficult.

5. The Holy Spirit and the Inspiration of the Scripture.

In the OT the formulas that the ancient prophets repeated over and over again as introductions to their prophecies were, "thus says the Lord" (Jer 9:23, passim), "the Lord has spoken" (Is 1:2, passim), "hear the word of the Lord" (Is 1:10, passim), "the word of the Lord came to me" (Ezek 33:1, passim), or the like. Such introductory formulas were intended to assure the audience that the message that came to them, whether spoken or written, did not originate with the prophet but with God. The word of the prophet was the word of the Lord and was to be received as such.

In the NT and the early fathers these older formulas for the most part have been replaced by the single formula, "the Holy Spirit said," or its like. The writers of our literature perceive the Holy Spirit as God's pervasive influence in the life of certain persons, inspiring them, validating their message by his power as words that are sacred, authoritative and final. Notice Peter's remarks to the 120 disciples after the resurrection and exaltation of Jesus: "Friends, the Scripture had to be fulfilled, which the Holy Spirit through David foretold" (Acts 1:16). These words of Peter give clear expression to the widespread belief of the early church about the OT as a whole—the Holy Spirit was its ultimate source; the Holy Spirit was speaking through persons, such as David, so that what was contained in the OT was the word of God, the word of the Spirit of God (see also Acts 4:25; 28:25; Heb 3:7; 9:8; 10:15; *1 Clem.* 13.1; 16.2; 22.1; 45.2; cf. 8.1; *Barn.* 9.2; 10.2, 9; 14.2). The remarks of the writer of 2 Peter 1:21-22 are apt at this point, even though the text is difficult to translate: "No prophecy of scripture is a matter of one's own interpretation, because no prophecy ever came by human will, but men and women moved by the Holy Spirit spoke from God" (NRSV, but see also the NIV). However one finally translates this verse, its message is clear: "The only point

which the author of 2 Peter is concerned to deny is that the prophets themselves were the originating source of their message. To counter this view he affirms that the Holy Spirit was the source of their prophecy, enabling them to speak as God's spokesmen" (Bauckham, 234; cf. Philo *Rer. Div. Her.* 259; Philo *Vit. Mos.* 1.281, 286).

The universal testimony of the earliest church concerning the OT is that it is the word of God, because those designated persons who spoke or wrote its message spoke or wrote by inspiration of the Holy Spirit and thus spoke or wrote for God. God spoke to his people through David, Isaiah, Jeremiah and others by the Holy Spirit (Acts 4:25). But what of the NT? Luke was aware that the Holy Spirit was still speaking in the apostolic period (Acts 13:2; 20:23), and the writer to the Hebrews refers to the Holy Spirit not only to say that the scriptural account of the tabernacle* and its priestly services was divinely inspired but also to say that the Holy Spirit was still speaking—in his day—and indicating that the way into the sanctuary could not be opened as long as the first tabernacle and its services still stood (Heb 9:8). Clement* seems more certain that the apostles* shared the same inspiration as the OT prophets. He wrote that they "having therefore received their commands, and being fully assured by the resurrection of our Lord Jesus Christ . . . went forth with the certainty that the Holy Spirit gives preaching the good news" (*1 Clem.* 42.3). Again, of Paul he writes, "With true inspiration (*ep' alētheias pneumatikōs*) he charged you concerning himself and Cephas and Apollos" (*1 Clem.* 47.3). From these few texts it is possible to infer that the Spirit was still speaking during the apostolic period, inspiring prepared persons to be God's voice in the world.

In contrast with the church's historic understanding of a closed canon* are the perplexing statements of Clement in which he appears to be claiming inspiration for himself. For example, he writes, "You will give us joy and gladness, if you are obedient to the things which we have written through the Holy Spirit" (*1 Clem.* 43.2). Ignatius,* too, claims to have the Spirit preaching and speaking through him, the Spirit who says, "Do nothing without the bishop" (Ign. *Phld.* 7.1-2). If indeed Clement and Ignatius viewed themselves as inspired prophets, on a par with the OT prophets, writing the words of God, there is not sufficient material in the writings under consideration to refute such claims. Such a refutation must be left to the later documents of the church, to the church universal, which apparently did not view them as inspired in the same way as the writers of the OT or those of the apostolic period were inspired.

6. The Holy Spirit and the Trinity.

The trinitarian formula that appears in Matthew 28:19, "baptize . . . in the name of the Father and of the Son and of the Holy Spirit," surprisingly appears neither in Acts nor in any other of the apostolic writings being considered. Nor does even a suggestive summary appear here such as that found in 2 Corinthians 13:14: "The grace of the Lord Jesus Christ, the love of God, and the communion of the Holy Spirit be with all of you." Seemingly none of our NT writers was concerned to construct a full-blown doctrine of the Trinity. Nevertheless, all the necessary ingredients to do so were present in our texts from the beginning, gathered up in the experience of Jewish Christians: "their inherited conception of God as 'Father,' their new faith in Christ as the 'Son,' . . . and their experience of the Spirit which [had] been given as the earnest and guarantee of the coming New Age" (Grant, 1015).

As time passed and Christian writers had more time to reflect, a gradual pulling together of these elements into a unified whole began to take shape, although there was still no developed doctrine of the Trinity. Nevertheless, several writers in the postapostolic period bring together the words "Father, Son and Holy Spirit" in a single sentence (*1 Clem.* 46.6; 58.2; Ign. *Magn.* 13.1). The earlier expression "baptize . . . in the name of the Father and of the Son and of the Holy Spirit" reemerges in the *Didache** (7.1, 3), the earliest noncanonical writing to give the trinitarian form of baptism (Swete 1976, 19). Polycarp's prayer at his martyrdom is the earliest instance of a doxology that glorifies the Spirit together with the Father and the Son: "I praise thee for all things, I bless thee, I glorify thee through the everlasting and heavenly high priest, Jesus Christ, thy beloved child, through whom be glory to thee with him and the Holy Spirit, both now and for the ages that are to come. Amen" (*Mart. Pol.* 14.3; cf. also 22.1). From this time on Christian thinkers had the materials that enabled them to theorize about the mystery of the nature of the Godhead and hammer out the doctrine of the Trinity.

See also CHRISTOLOGY; GOD; HOLY, HOLINESS; MIRACLES IN ACTS; NEW BIRTH; PENTECOST; POWER; SIGNS AND WONDERS; SPIRITS; TONGUES.

BIBLIOGRAPHY. H. W. Attridge, *The Epistle to the Hebrews* (Herm; Philadelphia: Fortress, 1989); D. E. Aune, *Prophecy in Early Christianity* (Grand Rapids: Eerdmans, 1983); C. K. Barrett, *The Acts of the Apostles* (ICC; Edinburgh: T & T Clark, 1994) vol. 1; R. J. Bauckham, *Jude, 2 Peter* (WBC; Waco, TX, 1983); F. Baumgärtel, "πνεῦμα κτλ (OT, Judaism)," *TDNT* 6:359-68; F. F. Bruce, *The Epistle to the Hebrews* (NICNT; Grand Rapids: Eerdmans, 1964); R. Bultmann, *The Johannine Epistles* (Philadelphia: Fortress, 1973); H. Conzelmann, *Acts of the Apostles* (Philadelphia: Fortress, 1987); W. J. Dalton, *Christ's Proclamation to the Spirits: A Study of 1 Peter 3:18—4:6* (AnBib 23; Rome: Pontifical Biblical Institute, 1965); W. D. Davies, *Paul and Rabbinic Judaism* (rev. ed.; Philadelphia: Fortress, 1980); J. D. G. Dunn, "Discernment of Spirits—A Neglected Gift" in *Witness to the Spirit: Essays on Revelation, Spirit, Redemption,* ed. W. Harrington (Dublin: Koinonia, 1979) 79-96; idem, *Jesus and the Spirit* (Philadelphia: Westminster, 1975); G. D. Fee, *God's Empowering Presence: The Holy Spirit in the Letters of Paul* (Peabody, MA: Hendrickson, 1994); F. C. Grant, "Trinity, the," *Dictionary of the Bible,* ed. J. Hastings (rev. ed.; New York: Scribners, 1963); M. Green, *I Believe in the Holy Spirit* (Grand Rapids: Eerdmans, 1975); G. F. Hawthorne, *The Presence and the Power: The Significance of the Holy Spirit in the Life of Jesus* (Dallas: Word, 1991); G. S. Hendry, *The Holy Spirit in Christian Theology* (rev. ed.; Philadelphia: Westminster, 1965); R. C. H. Lenski, *The Interpretation of the Acts of the Apostles* (Minneapolis: Augsburg, 1934); E. Lohse, "πεντηκοστή," *TDNT* 6:44-53; R. P. Martin, *James* (WBC; Waco, TX: Word, 1988); J. R. Michaels, *1 Peter* (WBC; Waco, TX: Word, 1988); R. H. Mounce, *The Book of Revelation* (NICNT; Grand Rapids: Eerdmans, 1977); G. von Rad, *Genesis* (rev. ed.; Philadelphia: Westminster, 1976); H. W. Robinson, *The Christian Experience of the Holy Spirit* (London: Nisbet, 1928); E. Schweizer, "πνεῦμα κτλ, (NT)," *TDNT* 6:396-453; E. F. Scott, *The Spirit in the New Testament* (London: Hodder & Stoughton, 1923); E. Sjöberg, "πνεῦμα κτλ (Palestinian Judaism)," *TDNT* 6:375-89; G. Stählin, "τὸ πνεῦμα Ἰησοῦ (Apostelgeschichte 16:7)" in *Christ and Spirit in the New Testament,* ed. B. Lindars and S. S. Smalley (Cambridge: Cambridge University Press, 1973) 229-52; H. B. Swete, *The Holy Spirit in the Ancient Church* (London: Macmillan, 1912); idem, *The Holy Spirit in the New Testament* (reprint ed.; Grand Rapids: Baker, 1976); M. M. B. Turner, "The Significance of Receiving the Spirit in Luke-Acts: A Survey of Modern Scholarship," *TJ* (1982) 131-42; idem, "The Spirit of Christ and Christology" in *Christ the Lord*, ed. H. H. Rowdon (Leicester: Inter-Varsity Press, 1982) 168-90; H. P. Van Dusen, *Spirit, Son and Father* (New York: Scribners, 1958); M. Welker, *God and Spirit* (Minneapolis: Fortress, 1994).   G. F. Hawthorne

HOMILY GENRE. *See* HEBREWS.

HOMOSEXUALITY. *See* SEXUALITY, SEXUAL ETHICS.

HOPE

In the later NT, hope is one of the defining marks of the believer. Despite the suffering that comes from living in a fallen world, the Christian is certain that God will one day complete what he has started in the lives of believers and in the whole cosmos.

1. Old Testament Background
2. Later New Testament
3. Apostolic Fathers

1. Old Testament Background.

In the OT, hope in God* is predicated on the mighty acts he has done for Israel.* God has acted on behalf of his people in the past, and thus the faithful can be certain that he will exercise his righteousness* on their behalf. That we do not see in the OT much in the way of hope for an afterlife sets the outstanding character of OT hope into bold relief. God can be counted on to act in the here and now. However, prophets* such as Isaiah (cf. Is 25:9; 42:4; 51:5) display a certainty that one day there will be a new order in which all the world* will recognize the sovereignty of God.

2. Later New Testament.

2.1. *The Object and Ground of Hope.* The meaning of "hope" and its cognates in the NT is radically different from that of the English word *hope*. Rather than expressing the desire for a particular outcome that is uncertain, hope in

the NT by definition is characterized by certainty. The object of hope in the later NT is variously described: it is seeing God himself (1 Jn 3:2), the resurrection* of the dead (Acts 23:6) and Christ,* who will bring his children* "to glory" (Heb 2:10; cf. Heb 12:23; *see* Glory). 1 Peter* encourages believers to endure unjust suffering*; Revelation (*see* Revelation, Book of) looks forward to the day God will put an end to such suffering. Although God's people may be persecuted, the Apocalypse encourages them to hope; it presents Christ as the supreme ruler of the universe who will one day be victorious and ensure victory for God's people (cf. Rev 2:21; 5:5; 6:2; 17:14). Revelation's vision of hope reaches its climax in Revelation 21:1—22:5, which describes in extravagant detail the new creation* and new Jerusalem* that await the faithful.

1 Peter instructs its audience that they must be ready to account for the hope that characterizes their lives as believers ("the hope that is in you" [plural]; 1 Pet 3:15). We do not have to decide if "in you" refers to individuals (Goppelt) or to the Christian community, for it is individual believers, all of whom have hope, that make up the community. They must be able to articulate the nature and content of their faith* to those who do not believe, that is, to those who persecute them because of their hope in Christ (cf. Kendall). The hope that believers enjoy is recognized by Peter to be a manifestation of God's grace.* It is by God's "great mercy"* that we believers have been born anew "into a living hope" (1 Pet 1:3). The description of hope as "living" is appropriate. Hope is not static; it is active, expressing itself in the hearts, minds and lives of Christians. It is not merely something to live by; it makes life as it should be possible (cf. Davids).

Hope looks with certainty toward the future God has promised his people, but at the same time it looks back to the Christ event. Throughout the NT the assurance* of future salvation* is grounded in the work of God in Christ, specifically in the resurrection of Christ. Because of this act, which has a decidedly future-looking character, believers are confident that God will finish what he has started (cf. 1 Pet 1:13). Regarding 1 Peter 1:13, L. Goppelt is correct when he notes that the believer does not hope for an atemporal, spiritualized utopia. He errs, however, in asserting that hope in 1 Peter 1:13

implies certain ethical* obligations. That is not made clear until the next verse (see 2.2 below).

2.2. Perseverance and Hope. The writers of the NT know that to hope is a decision that must be made continually. Thus the author of Hebrews* continually exhorts his readers to "hold fast" to the confession of hope "without wavering" (Heb 10:23). Hope is objective, referring to what believers hope for, but the basis for endurance* is hope of the reliability of God's promise* (cf. the discussion in Ellingworth). In Hebrews 3:6 the "hope" that is to be "held fast" looks forward to the day when Christians will enter into the "rest" promised to the people of God (cf. Heb 4:1). That believers should stand firm is predicated on God's character. It is impossible that God should prove false. If he was true to his promises to Abraham* (cf. Heb 6:15), and if he has been true to Christians, then he will continue to be so.

Persevering in hope also implies an ethical obligation. There is an "already" and "not yet" aspect to hope. The new birth* that Peter speaks of is to a living hope (1 Pet 1:3). If one has hope, then one must live up to one's hope and faith. This, J. Piper argues, is at the heart of 1 Peter's paraenesis. 1 Peter 1:13 is a call to hope fully, and in 1 Peter 1:14-15 the implications of that hope are spelled out. Those who hope in a future secured and given by Christ will not try to satisfy themselves with what the flesh* offers but will instead live in a manner that pleases the One who has graciously made a living hope available (cf. 1 Pet 1:14-15).

The possibility that believers can do so comes in an exhortation to slaves.* Slaves, Peter says, are to endure unjust suffering. And how is this possible? The answer comes in a verse that is not a mere digression (contrary to some scholars) but provides the theological underpinning for all of Peter's commands. Christ, he says, "bore our sins in his body on the tree so that we, having died to sin, might live for righteousness." Christ's death (*see* Death of Christ) makes possible to live up to our hope. In 1 John we see that hope functions similarly: the one who has "this hope" purifies himself as [God] is pure" (1 Jn 3:3). This hope, contrary to the view of R. E. Brown, here not only looks to the future ("we shall be like him") but also is experienced in the present ("we are God's children now").

2.3. Continuity and Discontinuity.

2.3.1. Continuity. The NT writers are heirs of the dynamic OT language of hope, expressing as they do an unwavering confidence that God will do as he has promised because of what he has done in the past. Thus in Acts* Paul assumes a continuity between the hope he, as a Christian, has in God and that of his Jewish ancestors* (Acts 24:25; 26:6-7; 28:20). In Acts 26:6 Paul says that he stands on trial for his hope in the promise made by God to Abraham. Paul describes his belief as being in continuity with the OT promise to Abraham. What Paul's hope has in common with the hope of the OT is its "anchorage in the past" (Moule).

2.3.2. Discontinuity. If, however, the character of NT hope is not substantially different from that of the OT, the divine action on which hope is grounded is new. In Acts we see that Paul's hope is based not only on the acts of God in the Hebrew Scriptures but also and ultimately in what God has done in Christ. The fulfillment of the promise given to Abraham is decidedly different from that which Paul's Jewish and non-Christian contemporaries believed it to be (cf. Minear's discussion). The author of Hebrews, working from the categories of type and antitype, says in Hebrews 7:19 that Christians have a "better hope." The OT realities were a shadow of what was to come, and since, for the writer of Hebrews, Christ is the fulfillment of the promise of the OT and the "anchor of the soul" (Heb 6:19), Christian hope is superior to any hope that is not based on Christ.

3. Apostolic Fathers.

Given the apostolic fathers'* dependence on the NT and the fundamental importance of hope therein, it is to be expected that they would refer to it frequently, and this is the case. *1 Clement* 59.3 reads, "[grant us] to hope on your name, the source of all creation." It would seem that it is God's name,* not that of Jesus Christ, to which the text refers. God is the object of hope. *1 Clement* also makes reference to one of fundamental facts of early Christian dogma. *1 Clement* 27.1 says "in this hope [the hope of the resurrection] let our souls be bound to him [God] who is faithful."

The certainty of Christian hope is used to encourage believers to remain steadfast in their faith in the face of persecution* (cf. *2 Clem.* 17.7). Hermas refers to the "hope of repentance," that is, the possibility of turning from one's morally bankrupt ways (*Herm. Sim.* 8.7.2;

8.10.2; *see* Repentance), which will lead to salvation.

Barnabas, writing from his post-A.D. 70 vantage point for a church that continues to define itself against the Judaism* from which it has now parted (*see* Christianity and Judaism), speaks of the superiority of Christian hope; Jews, he says, placed their hope in the temple*; this, however, "was vain" (*Barn.* 16.1-2). Hope, he says, is "put on the Name" (*Barn.* 16.8); it is only that way that people experience remission of sins and become part of the covenant* community (see also *Barn.* 6.3; 11.11). Faith and hope can become virtually synonymous: "Blessed are those who hoped on the cross and descended into the water" (*Barn.* 11.8).

Christian hope was also used to call for unity among the churches. *1 Clement* claims that "those who were the leaders of sedition and disagreement are bound to consider the common hope" (*1 Clem.* 51.1; see also *2 Clem.* 1.2; *see* Church Order). Since Christ is he who makes unity possible, the truth concerning him must be clung to. Ignatius* of Antioch* battles heresy by recalling the common hope of the things accomplished by Jesus Christ: his birth, passion and resurrection (Ign. *Magn.* 11.1; cf. Ign. *Trall.* 2.2; Ign. *Eph.* 1.2). For Ignatius "the gospel of the common hope" (Ign. *Phld.* 5.2) is to be preserved at all costs.

See also ASSURANCE; ENDURANCE, PERSEVERANCE; ESCHATOLOGY; FAITH, FAITHFULNESS; GLORY; LOVE; REDEMPTION; RESURRECTION; SALVATION; SUFFERING.

BIBLIOGRAPHY. J. C. Beker, *Suffering and Hope* (Grand Rapids: Eerdmans, 1994); R. E. Brown, *The Community of the Beloved Disciple* (New York: Paulist, 1979); P. H. Davids, *The First Epistle of Peter* (NICNT; Grand Rapids: Eerdmans, 1990); F. J. Denbeaux, "Biblical Hope," *Int* 5 (1951) 285-303; P. Ellingworth, *The Epistle to the Hebrews* (NIGTC; Grand Rapids: Eerdmans, 1993); L. Goppelt, *A Commentary on 1 Peter* (Grand Rapids: Eerdmans, 1993); E. Hoffman, "Hope," *NIDNTT* 2:238-46; D. W. Kendall, "1 Peter 1:3-9," *Int* 41 (1987) 66-71; P. S. Minear, *Christian Hope and the Second Coming* (Philadelphia: Westminster, 1954); C. F. D. Moule, *The Meaning of Hope* (Philadelphia: Fortress, 1963); J. Piper, "Hope as the Motivation of Love: 1 Peter 3:9-12," *NTS* 26 (1980) 212-31; K. H. Rengstorff and R. Bultmann, "ἐλπίς κτλ," *TDNT* 2:517-35; C. Spicq, "ἐλπίζω, ἐλπίς," *TLNT* 1:480-92; B. Studer, "Hope" in *Encyclopedia of the Early Church*, ed. A. Di Berardino (2 vols.; New York: Oxford University Press, 1992) 1:397-99.

B. Eastman

HOSPITALITY

The custom of hospitality was worldwide and highly regarded as a virtue in antiquity (Stählin, 17-20). It was rooted in a sense, given divine sanction, of the mutual obligation of all people to help one another, especially the stranger. Hence temples and altars were places of asylum, and the gods (such as Zeus Xenios, Zeus the patron of strangers) were believed to protect the oppressed foreigner or the abused host. Inns, hostels and other forms of shelter for travelers, often linked with temples and synagogues, also became important components of hospitality as an institution (Casson).

1. Definition
2. Background
3. The Later New Testament
4. The Postapostolic Period

1. Definition.
From the point of view of the anthropology of the cultures of the Mediterranean, hospitality (Gk *philoxenia;* Lat *hospitium*) is a social process by means of which the status of someone who is an outsider is changed from stranger to guest. The process has three stages: the evaluation and testing of the stranger to see whether incorporation as a guest is possible without undue threat to the purity lines of the group; the incorporation of the stranger as a guest under the patronage of a host and in accordance with a culture-specific code of hospitality imposing obligations upon both host and guest; the departure of the guest as a stranger now transformed into either a friend, if honor has been satisfied, or an enemy, if honor has been infringed (Malina, 181-87; Hobbs).

This conception of hospitality differs significantly from that of most Westerners today, for whom hospitality is personal and individualistic and has to do with entertaining relatives and friends with the prospect of the hospitality being reciprocated. In the first-century Mediterranean world, however, hospitality was a public duty toward strangers where the honor of the community was at stake and reciprocity was more likely to be communal rather than individual. Furthermore, whereas contemporary

Western hospitality has become secularized (so that a common synonym is "entertainment"), hospitality in antiquity was a sacred duty, not least because it opened up the possibility of revelatory encounter with strangers from another world. The story of the hospitality of Abraham* and Sarah to the "three men" by the oaks of Mamre (Gen 18; see also Gen 19) is a classic instance that became proverbial (cf. Heb 13:2; *1 Clem.* 10.7). Such strangers, precisely because they are outsiders and unknown, make hospitality a potential occasion for an epiphany. A classic instance from the NT is the revelation* of the risen Christ* to the two disciples during the meal at Emmaus (Luke 24:28-35).

2. Background.

2.1. Greco-Roman Background. For the Greeks and Romans hospitality was a mark of culture. Principal motivations were fear of the gods and human fellow-feeling *(philanthrōpia)* as well as the expectation of reciprocity. That hospitality was regarded as a basic aspect of civilized behavior is reflected in the recurrence of the motif in the Homeric sagas (Finley, 99-103). In this vein is the story of Paul's shipwreck at Malta (Acts 28:1-11). Hospitality is extended to the apparently ill-fated travelers both by the natives *(barbaroi)* of the island and by the Roman "first man," Publius; their hospitality is rewarded by manifestations of the divine mediated by the apostle*; and in turn the strangers-become-guests are sent on their way fully provisioned and bearing gifts.

2.2. Jewish Background. The practice of hospitality is fundamental in the Jewish tradition as well. Many biblical and Jewish texts give accounts of exemplary hospitality (usually associated with heroes and heroines like Abraham and Sarah, Lot, Rebekah, Rahab and Job), as well as of notorious inhospitality (the people of Sodom [Gen 19] and those of Gibeah [Judg 19]). Hospitality toward the stranger or the resident alien (Hebrew, *gēr)* is a duty that takes precedence over the obligation of neighborliness (Cohn, 49-57). In the Torah it is commanded no fewer than twenty-four times. It is an ideal rooted religiously both in an understanding of God* as one who "loves the sojourner, giving him food and clothing" (Deut 10:18) and in the story of the Israelites in Egypt: "you shall not wrong a stranger or oppress him, for you were strangers in the land of Egypt"

(Exod 22:21; cf. Lev 19:33-34; Deut 10:19). A powerful image in Jewish eschatology* is that of God as a bountiful host entertaining Israel* (Amos 9:13-15) and the nations (Is 25:6-8) at a great feast at the end of time.

2.3. Jesus. This latter point helps to explain Jesus' practice of hospitality and table fellowship (to which all the Gospels testify), for there can be little doubt that Jesus saw himself as God's eschatological envoy extending the divine invitation of heavenly hospitality to Israel and the nations (Koenig, 15-51). In contrast to other movements of his day (e.g., the Pharisees and the Qumran* covenanters), which were seeking to restrict table fellowship, Jesus seems to have become notorious for a practice of open hospitality that brought him the label "a glutton and a drunkard, a friend of tax collectors and sinners" (Mt 11:19; Lk 7:34).

Consistent with this are a number of other aspects of Jesus' teaching and action: the prominence of metaphors of meals and exuberant hospitality in the parables; the eschatological prayer* for bread that Jesus teaches his disciples; the positive reception Jesus gives to women,* children (*see* Sonship, Child, Children), the poor and the sick; the miraculous feeding of the multitudes; the alacrity with which Jesus accepts the hospitality of others and himself plays the host (not least at the Last Supper); the opposition he registers to fasting so long as he remains with his disciples; the teaching he gives on hospitality to itinerant preachers; and his teaching about God's hospitality in the kingdom of heaven: "Many will come from east and west to sit at table with Abraham, Isaac and Jacob in the kingdom of heaven" (Mt 8:11; Lk 13:28-29; *see* Kingdom of God).

2.4. Paul. But if Jesus' teaching and practice of hospitality is important for developments in early Christianity, so too is that of the apostle Paul (Koenig, 52-84; Theissen). A reading of Paul's letters shows us that Paul regarded hospitality as an important Christian virtue,* the practice of which builds up unity and helps meet practical needs. In his instructions, therefore, he exhorts his fellow believers to "contribute to the needs of the saints [and] practice hospitality" (Rom 12:13). As an itinerant apostle, Paul not only worked to support himself but also depended upon the hospitality of others (cf. 1 Cor 9:4-14; Acts 21:4, 7, 16-17); and the hardships he faced included the frequent absence of hospitality and even severe experiences of inhospitality from his enemies (1 Cor 4:11-13; 2 Cor 6:4-10; 11:21-33).

But hospitality, for Paul as for Jesus before him, is not just a practical issue. It is a fundamental expression of the gospel: a response to God's hospitality to humankind in providing Christ as the "paschal lamb*" (1 Cor 5:7) and an outworking of what it means to be members of the one "body of Christ," sharing Christ's eschatological table by eating bread, which is his body, and drinking wine, which is his blood (1 Cor 11:17-34). That is why Paul demanded a practice of hospitality that united the fellowship across lines both of social status and purity* and why he refused to compromise lest the gospel of unity in Christ be brought into disrepute (cf. Gal 2:11-14). It is also why he demanded the refusal of hospitality from those who ate and drank at the "table of demons," for this would have been to acknowledge the authority* of a host other than the risen Lord* (1 Cor 10:14-22). Instead of sharing hospitality in temple precincts, therefore, the primary locus of Christian hospitality was the meeting together of the believers in members' houses (oikoi). This explains the prominence Paul accords to various heads of households,* both men and women, who served as patrons of the fellowships* (ekklēsiai) meeting in their houses (cf. Rom 16). It also explains the prominence of instructions about godly household order in Paul's letters (cf. Col 3:18—4:1).

3. The Later New Testament.
Given the orientation of early Christianity toward universal mission,* as well as the self-understanding of the local churches as belonging together to one universal church,* it is not surprising that itinerancy was common and hospitality an essential aspect of Christian instruction and practice (Riddle). Outside the Gospels and main Pauline literature, specific references to hospitality come mainly in Acts, the Pastoral Epistles, Hebrews and the Johannine epistles, but the practice is presupposed and therefore implicit elsewhere also (e.g., Philem 22).

3.1. Acts. The narrative testimony of Acts* is illuminating. Here we find themes and motifs from the story of Jesus in Luke's first volume developed further in the stories of the apostles and the early church. Thus the motif of the journeys of Jesus as occasions for encounters with the divine is carried over into the missionary journeys of the apostles as the context for further experiences of the supernatural motif of "entertaining angels unawares." The conversion of households in response to Jesus' preaching and healing* is carried over into conversion by household in Acts; and among the converted householders who show hospitality are Cornelius,* Lydia and the Philippian jailer.

The exuberant table fellowship of Jesus is translated into the practice of the Jerusalem church, having "all things in common . . . [and] breaking bread in their homes . . . with glad and generous hearts" (Acts 2:44-47; cf. Acts 4:32-37). Jesus' hospitality to the socially marginalized is reflected in the care of the apostolic churches for the poor and the sick, whether men, women or children. The welcome Jesus gives to Gentiles becomes mission to all nations; and the formulation of new rules of table fellowship makes possible the integration of Gentile* converts with converts from Judaism* (Acts 15:1-29). The hospitality of women as well as men shown to Jesus in the Gospels is carried over into the patronage offered by both women and men to the apostles and the nascent church in Acts. The inhospitality of the leaders of the people (Jewish and Roman) to Jesus is reflected in the apostles' experiences of inhospitality among both Jews and Gentiles, culminating in the inhospitality of the Jews in Rome* toward Paul at the story's end (Acts 28:17-31).

There is no single explanation for this considerable interest in hospitality and related matters in Luke-Acts (cf. Esler, 71-109). First, the boundary-crossing hospitality expresses Luke's belief that with Pentecost* a new age of salvation* has dawned and a new people of God is being brought into being to share in the messianic banquet. Second, such hospitality as narrated has a moral thrust as well. It is a reminder (especially to the wealthy and influential?) that true conversion requires both detachment from household ties and material concerns generally and a generosity that overflows in acts of mercy* to the poor, the needy and the stranger. A third explanation may be of a more pragmatic kind. Luke may be wanting to encourage his readers to continue the practice of inclusive hospitality begun a generation earlier, as a way of contributing to the maintenance of church unity and Christian witness* in his own day. He may even want to encourage his readers not to neglect hospitality to itinerant missionaries.

3.2. Pastoral Epistles. In the Pastoral Epistles teaching about hospitality has a narrower focus, being related to the essential qualifications of overseers as officers in the local church (cf. 1 Tim 3:2; Tit 1:8). The Pastorals generally appear to reflect a stage in the development of early church organization in which the pre-dominantly charismatic ethos of Pauline church order* was becoming more formalized, perhaps due to the impact of structures that Jewish Christianity* inherited from the synagogue* or the Qumran community but also as a means of reinforcing the boundaries of the church against the threat of what were perceived as heretical doctrines and their proponents.

A striking feature of this process of routinization (to use M. Weber's term) is the dominance of the metaphor of the household, already pervasive in Paul's writings but now taken further (Verner). It is as if the model of orderly, hierarchical, gendered social relations provided by the household, a model fully recognized and acceptable in society, was seen as having the potential for protecting the church's life from dissolution within and maintaining its honor in relations with the world outside. Thus in 1 Timothy 3:15 the writer speaks of how believers are to behave in "the household *(oikos)* of God, which is the church *(ekklēsia)* of the living God, the pillar and bulwark of the truth"; and in Titus 1:7, the overseer *(episkopos)* is described as God's "steward" *(oikonomos)*, the one, that is, who manages the household on behalf of the master (in this case, God).

Given this conception of the church as God's household and of the overseer as God's household steward, it is not surprising that the overseer is to exhibit all the qualities of the good household head: "Now an overseer must be above reproach, the husband of one wife . . . hospitable *(philoxenos)*, an apt teacher. . . . He must manage his own household well, keeping his children submissive and respectful in every way; for if a man does not know how to manage his own household *(oikos)*, how can he care for God's church *(ekklēsia)*?" (1 Tim 3:2-5). In this context hospitality was important on two fronts. First, it was the means whereby the overseer welcomed traveling Christians, itinerant preachers and other strangers into the church

but in a way that made a process of testing possible, transformed the stranger into a guest and so avoided threats to church life and order. Second, it was the means whereby charitable activity within the fellowship of the church could be administered fairly, with due regard for the poor and for the maintenance of unity, so that the good name of the church could be upheld.

But hospitality is expected of "ordinary" (i.e., non-official) members of the church as well. Thus in the instructions about drawing up the list of the "real widows" (i.e., widows who have no household members of their own to support them and therefore need the support of the household of the church; cf. Young, 114-20, contra Thurston), the writer lays down certain criteria for eligibility: "she must be well attested for her good deeds, as one who has brought up children, shown hospitality *(xenodocheō)*, washed the feet of the saints, relieved the afflicted and devoted herself to doing good in every way" (1 Tim 5:9-10).

Several assumptions are noteworthy. First is that of reciprocity: the widow is to receive hospitality from the church household because, as a former householder, she has been hospitable herself. Second, hospitality occurs conventionally as a test of social and religious worth; and it is taken for granted that it involves washing the feet of traveling fellow believers (as a ritual of acceptance; cf. Lk 7:44; Jn 13:14) and helping people (the indigent, persecuted, imprisoned) in distress. Third, hospitality is not restricted to officials of the church, nor is it restricted to male members; rather it is an accepted moral virtue that is to characterize the behavior of believers as a whole. In context its appropriateness as a role for women is that it is a natural extension of their authority in the domestic sphere, a way of bringing the household into the church and the church into the household.

3.3. Hebrews. In a manner that reminds us of the ethical* injunctions (including the command to practice hospitality) with which Paul concludes his letter to the Romans (Rom 12), the writer of the epistle to the Hebrews* draws his letter to a conclusion with important practical recommendations for maintaining the life of faith,* prominent among which is the command "Do not neglect to show hospitality *(philoxenia)*" (Heb 13:2; cf. Rom 12:13). So for the author of Hebrews as for Paul, hospitality is a fundamental expression of Christian faith. For both it is also a fundamental outworking of love (*agapē* or *philadelphia*). Hence "Let brotherly love (*philadelphia*) continue. Do not neglect to show hospitality" (Heb 13:1-3: cf. Rom 12:9-13).

Worth noting also is the following. First, hospitality, according to Hebrews, is a virtue to be exercised first and foremost among fellow Christians. The RSV and NRSV misleadingly translate Hebrews 13:2 as a command to be hospitable "to strangers" (omitted by REB), if this is taken to imply unbelievers. As we might say, charity begins at home, and this is true of early Christianity as a whole (cf. 1 Pet 4:9, "Practice hospitality ungrudgingly to one another"). It is teaching especially relevant to the concerns of Hebrews, in which the author is trying to prevent apostasy* by recalling his readers to an active faith given expression in good works that strengthen the fellowship. But what of the motive, "for thereby some have entertained angels unawares" (Heb 13:2)? This is likely to be a reminder of the encounters of Abraham, Lot, Gideon, Manoah and Tobit with angelic* beings in contexts of hospitality. In Hebrews it fits well with the idea that believers are, like the ancestors,* "strangers (*xenoi*) and exiles (*parepidēmoi*) on the earth" (Heb 11:13), on a pilgrimage to heaven,* there to share with the angelic hosts in the divine worship* (cf. Heb 12:22-24). So hospitality is appropriate for a pilgrim people, especially if it entails the possibility of anticipations of that heavenly destination.

Heaven and earth remained firmly linked, however, in the command that follows: "Remember those who are in prison, as though in prison with them" (Heb 13:3; cf. Heb 10:32-34). Yet another aspect of early Christian hospitality comes to the surface: the practice of relieving the needs of fellow believers in prison by visiting them and providing their sustenance. This is not the only instance in the NT that juxtaposes the motif of "meeting angels unawares" and visiting fellow believers in prison. In the parable in Matthew 25:31-46, the heavenly king is revealed as present incognito with "the least of these my brethren" suffering imprisonment. There are also the two stories in Acts of imprisoned apostles being visited and miraculously released by "an angel of the Lord" (Acts 5:17-26; 12:1-19). Such evidence as this, together with the testimony of sources from the postapostolic period (see 4 below), shows that the instruction

in Hebrews marks an early stage in a significant, developing tradition of hospitality as solidarity with the oppressed.

3.4. Johannine Epistles. In the Johannine epistles (*see* John, Letters of) we encounter evidence of what becomes a recurring concern in the churches of the late first century and onward: how to discriminate between true and false prophets* or teachers who come as itinerants expecting hospitality but who may be the bearers of false doctrine or out for personal gain at the Christians' expense (cf. *Did.* 11—12). In 2 John the "elder" (*presbyteros*) writes to a "sister" church (the "elect lady") and recommends the strict refusal of hospitality to any itinerant who does not teach orthodox Johannine christology: "If anyone comes to you and does not bring this doctrine [of Christ], do not receive him into the house or give him any greeting; for he who greets him shares his wicked work" (2 Jn 10-11). This shows both how dependent Christian itinerant preachers were on the informal hospitality of those among whom they moved but also how vulnerable local churches were to the harmful influence of wandering schismatics.

3 John is even more revealing (Malherbe, 103-12). The elder writes a letter of recommendation on behalf of Demetrius to Gaius, who is presumably a household head and someone prominent in one of the local house churches. He commends Gaius for showing hospitality to itinerant believers (like Demetrius), even those who were "strangers" (*xenoi*). But he also complains bitterly of the behavior of Diotrephes, who has contested the elder's authority and expressed his rival claim by refusing hospitality to those who have come from the elder, even expelling from his own house church any members who break ranks and offer hospitality themselves. So, ironically, whereas in 2 John the refusal of hospitality is advocated, in 3 John it is a cause for complaint.

These texts contribute to our understanding of early Christian hospitality in a number of ways. They reinforce our impression of the importance of hospitality as an informal, household-based mechanism for sustaining itinerant mission and building unity among the churches. They show what hospitality involved: sending and receiving letters of recommendation testifying to the bona fides of the itinerants (3 Jn 9); "greeting" the strangers; receiving them into the household for a period (unspecified here); attending to the doctrine they brought; and sending them on their way provisioned for the next stage of their journey (2 Jn 10-11; 3 Jn 5-6). They show that hospitality was a practice that brought honor to the host and to the local church through the positive testimonials of the guests (3 Jn 6). They also show that hospitality (and its opposite) between churches could be a focus of tension in relation to evolving authority structures at both the local and translocal levels. In 3 John hospitality is obviously a barometer not only of relations between potential hosts and guests but also of relations between church leaders (Malina).

4. The Postapostolic Period.
Beyond the NT, the practice of Christian hospitality continues to be widely attested in both Christian and non-Christian sources. Even outsiders find it worthy of comment, if only for the purpose of ridicule.

4.1. A Non-Christian Source. The Roman satirist Lucian is a case in point. As he saw things, Christians were so hospitable that they could be taken advantage of by charlatans like the imprisoned Peregrinus (d. 165):

> From the crack of dawn on you could see grey-haired widows and orphan children hanging around the prison, and the bigwigs of the sect used to bribe the jailers so they could spend the night with him inside. Full-course dinners were brought to him, their holy scriptures read to him, and our excellent Peregrinus . . . was hailed as a latter-day Socrates. From as far away as Asia Minor, Christian communities sent committees, paying their expenses out of the common funds, to help him with advice and consolation. The efficiency the Christians show whenever matters of community interest like this happen is unbelievable; they literally spare nothing (Lucian *Peregr.* 12—13, in Greer, 119-20).

This remarkable testimony from a hostile witness shows that the Christians were renowned for their hospitality. It indicates that by the second century (if not earlier) hospitality was carried out in an organized fashion on a translocal basis drawing upon resources held in common (cf. Acts). It reinforces the impression from Paul and the Pastoral Epistles that Christians saw themselves as brothers and sisters together in a worldwide household. This makes it

unsurprising that the primary focus of their hospitality was on fellow believers, a particularity that impressed some outsiders and irked others (cf. Tacitus on the Christians' "hatred of mankind" in *Annals* 15.44). But Lucian clearly believes that Peregrinus was not worthy of hospitality because he was receiving it under false pretenses (since he was not a Christian). The question of how to distinguish true prophets from false seems to have been a perennial one.

4.2. Didache. The fact that hospitality was open to abuse and could even threaten church life (cf. 2 Jn; 3 Jn) meant that it continued to be a subject of reflection and instruction. The rules laid down in *Didache* 11—12 are significant in this regard. They show that a peripatetic ministry of teachers, apostles and prophets was taken for granted in the church of the late first century. Such travelers are to be received "as the Lord." But certain criteria are listed for testing the authenticity of incoming strangers: their teaching must be orthodox, their stay is to be strictly limited, they are to be sent on their way with (limited) provender but not money, and they are not to use their spiritual gifts for personal material gain (*Did.* 11). Similar rules apply to traveling Christians generally (*Did.* 12): they are not to be allowed to make a living off the name *Christian,* and they are not to "make traffic of Christ" (*christemporos*).

4.3. 1 Clement. Important also is the evidence of *1 Clement* (c. 96), a letter from the church at Rome to the Corinthian church (cf. Brown and Meier, 159-83). The fact that it was written to encourage harmony in a church plagued with dissension and insubordination toward the local elders (*presbyteroi*) now deposed (*1 Clem.* 3.2; cf. *1 Clem.* 46.5-9; 53.1-2; 57.1-2; *see* Church Order) goes a long way to explain why hospitality is a recurring motif. This is especially so if, as H. Chadwick suggests, the local divisions are being accentuated by the arrival from outside of fellow Christians expecting hospitality, receiving it from the elders who have been deposed and consequently being cold-shouldered by the rest of the church. What the visitors will have been aware of is not the hospitality of the church as a whole but its absence. This helps explain why, at the beginning of the letter, the writer reminds his addressees of the former, honorable practice of hospitality to which he wants to recall them: "For who has stayed with you without making proof of the virtue and steadfastness of your faith? . . . Who has not reported your character so magnificent in its hospitality *(philoxenia)*?" (*1 Clem.* 1.2).

In a recounting of the virtues of the biblical models Abraham, Lot and Rahab, hospitality is prominent once again, alongside faith and piety: "Because of his [Abraham's] faith and hospitality a son was given him in his old age" (*1 Clem.* 10.7); "For his hospitality and piety Lot was saved out of Sodom" (*1 Clem.* 11.1); "For her faith and hospitality Rahab the harlot was saved" (*1 Clem.* 12.1). Important from a theological point of view is the clear implication that salvation is social as well as individual: it comes not just through a certain kind of spiritual knowledge *(gnōsis)* but through a certain kind of hospitable practice as well.

4.4. Shepherd of Hermas. Finally we may cite the *Shepherd of Hermas,** written in Rome in the early second century. Among the list of good deeds whose reward* is salvation is the following: "To minister to widows, to look after orphans and the destitute, to redeem from distress the servants of God [and] to be hospitable *(philoxenos)*, for in hospitality may be found the practice of good" (*Herm. Man.* 8.10). The subject recurs in *Hermas Similitude* 9.27, where reference is made to "bishops and hospitable men *(episkopoi kai philoxenoi)* who at all times received the servants of God into their houses gladly and without hypocrisy; and the bishops ever ceaselessly sheltered the destitute and the widows by their ministration and ever behaved with holiness." The prominence of the *episkopos* in the exercise of hospitality (cf. 1 Tim 3:2) is evident.

The problem of itinerant false prophets who threatened local church life (cf. *Did.* 11-12) was probably one of the main reasons for the disappearance of a peripatetic ministry and the development in its place of the threefold ministry* of bishops, priests and deacons. Hospitality becomes more formalized, and the bishops become the agents of hospitality, assisted by the deacons (Greer, 125). Noteworthy also in *Hermas Similitude* 9.27 is a distinction between two types of hospitality: that toward visiting "servants of God," which strengthens the unity of the church ecumenically, and that toward the needy in the immediate vicinity, which strengthens the unity of the church locally. This conforms with the twofold conception of the church of which we know from Paul onward: the church in a particular place and the church universal.

See also HOUSEHOLD, FAMILY; SOCIAL SETTING OF EARLY NON-PAULINE CHRISTIANITY.

BIBLIOGRAPHY. R. E. Brown and J. P. Meier, *Antioch and Rome: New Testament Cradles of Catholic Christianity* (New York: Paulist, 1983); L. Casson, *Travel in the Ancient World* (London: George Allen & Unwin, 1974); H. Chadwick, "Justification by Faith and Hospitality," *SP* 4 (1961) 281-85; H. H. Cohn, *Human Rights in the Bible and Talmud* (Tel Aviv: MOD Books, 1989); P. F. Esler, *Community and Gospel in Luke-Acts: The Social and Political Motivations of Lukan Theology* (Cambridge: Cambridge University Press, 1987); M. I. Finley, *The World of Odysseus* (Harmondsworth, England: Penguin, 1979); R. A. Greer, *Broken Lights and Mended Lives: Theology and Common Life in the Early Church* (University Park, PA: Pennsylvania State University Press, 1986); T. R. Hobbs, "Man, Woman and Hospitality—2 Kings 4:8-36," *BTB* 23 (1993) 91-100; J. Koenig, *New Testament Hospitality: Partnership with Strangers as Promise and Mission* (Philadelphia: Fortress, 1985); A. J. Malherbe, *Social Aspects of Early Christianity* (2d ed.; Philadelphia: Fortress, 1983); B. J. Malina, "The Received View and What It Cannot Do: 3 John and Hospitality," *Semeia* 35 (1986) 171-94; W. A. Meeks, *The Origins of Christian Morality: The First Two Centuries* (New Haven, CT: Yale University Press, 1993); D. W. Riddle, "Early Christian Hospitality: A Factor in the Gospel Transmission," *JBL* 57 (1939) 141-54; G. Stählin, "ξένος," *TDNT* 5:1-36; G. Theissen, *The Social Setting of Pauline Christianity* (Edinburgh: T & T Clark, 1982); B. B. Thurston, *The Widows: A Women's Ministry in the Early Church* (Minneapolis: Fortress, 1989); D. C. Verner, *The Household of God: The Social World of the Pastoral Epistles* (Chico, CA: Scholars Press, 1983); F. Young, *The Theology of the Pastoral Letters* (NTT; Cambridge: Cambridge University Press, 1994).

S. C. Barton

HOUSE CHURCHES. *See* ARCHITECTURE, EARLY CHURCH.

HOUSE OF GOD. *See* HOUSE, SPIRITUAL HOUSE.

HOUSE, SPIRITUAL HOUSE

A house (Gk *oikos* and *oikia*) is a dwelling that is both a permanent shelter and a place where one's family is located. By extension of meaning, therefore, "house" can also mean "household" or "family" (for the sociological dimension of such "houses," *see* Households, Family) or an even larger social unit regarded as the descendants of a particular individual. A special use of "house" is in reference to the "house of God," which can refer either to God's symbolic dwelling place (the temple* or tabernacle*) or to the people of God's family.

1. Dwellings
2. Ancestral Families
3. The House of God
4. The People of God as the House of God

1. Dwellings.

The Septuagint uses the Greek words *oikos* and *oikia* almost exclusively for the Hebrew *bayit*, very rarely for *'ōhel* ("tent"), *liškâh* ("eating hall") or *hêkāl* ("temple"). *Bayit* in the OT most commonly refers to one's physical dwelling or place of residence, and similarly in NT and early Christian literature its most common use is in reference to a literal building where people reside (e.g., Acts 4:34, *1 Clem.* 12.6). For a physical description of dwellings in NT times see Dickie and Payne.

The author of Acts* locates many events of the early church's* development in the houses of particular individuals. It was in a house that the first believers were baptized by the Holy Spirit* (Acts 2:2), and the earliest church met in people's houses (Acts 2:46, 12:12). Saul (Paul*) raided these house meetings as a persecutor (Acts 8:3) and then later is healed in the house of Judas (Acts 9:11). Peter stayed in the house of Simon the tanner (Acts 10:6), upon whose roof he sees the vision* that encourages him to go to Cornelius.* Then, against Jewish practice, Peter enters the house of Cornelius, a Gentile* (Acts 10:25). This became a point of contention (Acts 11:3) from which it was established that, as Paul later put it, the old walls of separation between Gentile and Jew were coming down in Christ.* Paul stayed at the houses of many of his converts (Acts 16:15, 31; 17:7; 18:7). The book of Acts (see, e.g., Acts 16:40) makes it fairly clear that the early church's principal locus of operations was in the houses of individual Christians (for more on house churches, *see* Households, Family). The naming of so many particular houses (some by name, e.g., Acts 12:12) may also reflect the author's

intention to stress the historical reality of the events (*see* Architecture).

The only possible reference to a literal house in the General Epistles* is 2 John 10. The author urges the "elect lady" (either the church [note the plural verbs] or perhaps a prominent woman at whose house the church met) not to show hospitality* to heterodox teachers (literally, "do not receive them into the house") or even greet or speak to them. However, since churches met in people's houses, it is possible that this is also an injunction against receiving these people into the church (see 4 below). Thus this command would not forbid hospitality in general, even to heretics, but rather forbids receiving false teachers into the fellowship or allowing them to teach in the church.

In the OT, "house of" could be used metaphorically to mean a place or circumstance in which something is manifested (e.g., the "house of Lady Wisdom" in Prov 9). The Dead Sea community referred to itself as the true "house of the Torah," presumably because they regarded themselves as the only truly obedient people (CD 20:11-13). Early Christian literature occasionally makes such metaphorical use of "house." So, for example, an unregenerate heart is a "house of demons" in *Barnabas* 16.7, because it is where wickedness dwells.

2. Ancestral Families.

In the OT "house" was commonly used to refer to a sociological unit under a particular person's authority* (*see* Households, Family). Therefore, a greatly extended sociological unit such as a whole nation, if it regarded itself as a family, could be identified in terms of the common ancestor, understood as a kind of head of his descendants and their dependents. "House of Israel" means all those people who could claim a connectional identity with Israel's (Jacob's) descendants, and the "house of Judah" refers to the tribe that descended from Judah. Even smaller social units or families within tribes can be called houses, as with the house of Zadok.

"House" thus meaning "nation," "tribe" or "clan" occurs in our literature only as a rare carryover from OT usage. Acts twice uses the stock phrase "house of Israel," once in an OT citation by Stephen* (Acts 7:42) and once in Peter's first sermon at Pentecost* (Acts 2:36) where he solemnly tells the "house of Israel" that God has made Jesus whom they crucified to be both Lord and Christ. Hebrews 8:8 and 8:10 quote OT texts addressed to the "house of Israel" and the "house of Judah."

Instances of this use of "house" in the apostolic fathers occur in their reflections on OT material. Thus the phrase "house of Israel" occasionally is observed (e.g., 1 Clem. 8.2). Barnabas, who likes to see the symbolic meaning of everything, has Moses* prophesy that "in the last days the Son of God will cut off the house of Amalek by the roots" (Barn. 12.9), taking "the house of Amalek" as a metaphor for the unbelieving world. Just as Christians are spiritual descendants of Israel or Abraham* by faith, non-Christians are spiritually connected to Amalek by unbelief.

3. The House of God.

The OT speaks frequently of the "house of God" or "house of the Lord." This was generally applied to the temple or earlier to the tabernacle (e.g., Judg 18:31; 19:18), which was indeed some kind of physical accommodation. But the first use of the phrase "house of God" was in Jacob's naming of Bethel (which means "house of God" in Hebrew), which was not a domicile or building but simply a place where Jacob had experienced the presence of God. Later Israelites too were aware that the temple was not a literal abode of God, as Solomon testified when he dedicated the temple (1 Kings 8:27)—"the heavens, even the highest heaven, cannot contain you. How much less this temple I have built." The house of God was thus a symbol for the dwelling of God among his people, his spiritual presence in a special way.

Therefore the tabernacle or temple took on something of a metaphorical character in representing this presence of God. When the psalmist said, "Surely . . . I will dwell in the house of the Lord forever" (Ps 23), he was not referring to the physical tabernacle or temple but the fact that he would experience the presence of God always.

Since in the OT the "house of God" was the physical place that symbolized God's presence with his people, the temple is occasionally referred to as God's house. Stephen echoed the Chronicler's reference to Solomon's temple as "God's house" (Acts 7:46, 47, 49). But Stephen also refers to Isaiah's declaration that the temple cannot really be God's dwelling (Acts 7:48-

50, quoting Is 66:1-2). Stephen had been charged with "speaking against this holy place" (Acts 6:13), and thus his motive is to show that the physical building in Jerusalem* does not in any way guarantee God's presence and that the Jewish trust in the presence of the physical building is misplaced.

Though the dominant "house" motif in Hebrews 3 is the idea of the "people of God," the image of God's "house" as his dwelling place, or the place where God may be approached, is not absent. Hebrews 3 begins with an exhortation to consider Jesus, the apostle* and high priest* whom we confess. Hebrews* is clearly interested in Jesus' priestly service in the heavenly tabernacle, as is spelled out in Hebrews 8 and 9. Further, the readers of Hebrews would no doubt remember that Moses was in some sense the "builder" of the literal tabernacle in the wilderness. At least he is the one who took down the directions and then implemented them (see Heb 8:5). Thus there may be an implicit merging of the two ideas that the "house" of God, which is the people of God, is also the place where God is approached—echoing Paul's understanding of the people of God as being also the dwelling place of God (1 Cor 3:16; Eph 2:19-22). Thus when Hebrews 10:21 concludes that Jesus is also "great priest over the house of God," the author understands "house of God" both in terms of the tabernacle/temple imagery and in terms of the "people of God."

4. The People of God as the House of God.

In 2 Samuel 7:11 there is a hint of juxtaposing the two concepts of family and dwelling, for when David wishes to build a house for God (a temple) he is told that rather God will build a house for David (David's progeny). Since "house" was a common enough idiom for a social unit with familial connections who are under an individual's authority and share a common identity (see Household, Family), it was a small step to think of the "house of God" as the people of God.

In the intertestamental period the *Similitudes of Enoch* (probably dating to late second or early first century B.C.) speaks of God's house in spiritual terms and associates it with a messianic figure—"After this, the Righteous and Elect One will reveal the house of his congregation" (*1 Enoch* 53:6, trans. E. Isaac). There is some ambiguity here. Possibly this is a vague reference to a "hidden" temple like the hidden Jerusalem made manifest at the end of the world. Alternatively, "of his congregation" may simply be epexegetical (he will reveal the house, that is, his congregation). In any case the concept of house as family and house of God as temple is starting to merge into the idea found in the NT of the community as the house of God.

Apparently the Qumran* covenanters regarded the council of their community as a spiritual replacement for the temple (1QS 8:4-5: "When these [twelve men and three priests] are in Israel the Council of the Community shall be established in truth. It shall be a . . . house of Holiness for Israel"). The temple of Herod was apparently regarded as illegitimate, primarily because it was served by a priesthood* they regarded as illegitimate (because the priests were not Zadokite). The Temple Scroll suggests that the Qumran sectaries also expected the literal temple to be restored and the entire sacrificial system to be reestablished.

But the path was well-laid for the NT writers to think of the "house of God" as the people of God. As in Paul, who understood both the church as a whole (Eph 2:22) and the believer as an individual (1 Cor 3:16; 6:19) to be a dwelling place of God's Spirit, most references to "house of God" in our literature carry the meaning of "God's people," that is, the Christian community, although it is sometimes merged with the concept of "God's dwelling" as well.

Hebrews 3:2 refers to Numbers 12:7, which says that Moses, unlike ordinary prophets, is "faithful in all my house." Numbers may have simply meant that Moses was faithful in his words and actions in the Tent of Meeting and thus used the term *house* in a more or less literal fashion. But the author of Hebrews clearly saw a greater significance, understanding it to mean the "people of God," namely, Israel/church (*see* Church as Israel). Moses was faithful as a servant* in God's house (i.e., among God's people), in contrast to Jesus, who is a son over his house (i.e., over God's people; Heb 3:5-6). Further, Moses himself is part of the house, albeit an exalted one, whereas Jesus is the builder (Heb 3:3-4), which is an implicit statement of Christ's deity (Heb 3:4). Moses was chief minister among God's people, whereas Christ not only ministers but also has created the people of God by his redemptive acts.

Christians who persevere are "his house" (Heb 3:6), the house Christ built and in which Moses served. There are not two houses here, one for Moses (Israel) and one for Jesus (church), but a single house ("Israel" and "church" together). In fact, it is unlikely that Hebrews makes anything like our modern distinction between Israel and the church, since *ekklēsia* is the Greek word used for the congregation of Israel (Heb 2:12, quoting Ps 21:23 LXX [EVV Ps 22:22]). Both Moses and Jesus have to do with the one house of God; the difference lies in their respective positions and functions with regard to that house.

In 1 Peter,* particularly in 1 Peter 2:4-10, the two concepts of "house of God"—God's dwelling and God's family—are completely merged. The focus in this passage is on Jesus Christ, who is the chief cornerstone, which is the "guide" stone used in the foundation and building of a house (rather than the keystone of an arch). A catena of OT "stone" quotations is given in 1 Peter 2:6-8 to show how Christ is foundational to God's house, the church. But the underlying purpose is to show how believers are likened to and identified with Christ as God's elect.* Believers are also called "living stones" (1 Pet 2:5), which together with Christ "are being built up as a spiritual house for holy priesthood, to offer up spiritual sacrifices* acceptable to God through Jesus Christ" [author's trans.]. Thus when 1 Peter calls the believers a "spiritual house" it is not just saying they are a metaphorical house; they are the family of God constituted by and indwelt by God's Spirit (1 Pet 2:9-10).

In the OT the temple or tabernacle was the symbol of God's dwelling with his people, and the people are the family/house of God. Further, the Christian takeover of the OT concept that Israel is to mediate God's presence to the Gentile world at large makes the church as a whole a priesthood. Thus we have the combining of three OT images, the house of God as the temple, the house of God as God's family and the house of God as the priesthood. As was already mentioned, the Qumran community (which was probably a priestly sect) had already regarded its council as in some ways a temporary replacement for the temple. 1 Peter here uses a homiletical midrashic exegesis similar to the Qumran community's to present the church as the new temple community (Schutter). Thus they are both the house of God and also the maintainers (the "priesthood") of the house. Certainly it is surprising how many overlaps in OT citations there are between 1 Peter and the Dead Sea Scrolls. Even if 1 Peter is entirely independent of Qumranic influences, the thought-world is clearly parallel.

There are, however, certain clear differences. Most noticeable is that the "spiritual house" in 1 Peter is permanent rather than a stopgap until a proper temple can be reconstituted, as appears to have been the case with Qumran. The observation that the NT's exegesis is distinctly christological,* in contradistinction to exegesis in the Dead Sea Scrolls, obtains here as well, since this spiritual house has Christ as its determinative foundation. Peter's spiritual house exists only in connection with the chief cornerstone. Finally, the merging of the temple imagery with the idea of God's family as God's house gives a distinctly personal character to Peter's spiritual house.

With this as background it is possible to understand the enigmatic statement of 1 Peter 4:17 that "it is time for judgment to begin with the house of God," which appears to be saying that Christian suffering,* even for the sake of Christ, is a judgment* of God. This is probably an allusion to Ezekiel 9:6, where in Ezekiel's vision all God's people who were not marked as grieving over sin* were slaughtered, beginning with the elders at the temple. As the new spiritual "house of God," the church is subject to the winnowing trials that befell the literal temple and the people of Israel in the OT. The "house of God" must be purified (cf. Mal 3:3; 2 Chron 29:15-18) so that it is a suitable dwelling for God.

The merged image of God's house as his people and his dwelling found ready acceptance in the early church. *1 Clement* twice picks up on the quotation of Numbers 12 in Hebrews 3, understanding "God's house" in the same way to refer to God's people. *2 Clement* goes so far as to cite Jeremiah 7:11 ("my house has become a den of thieves") as applying to the church if it does not do the will of the Lord. *The Epistle of Barnabas* (16.6) follows Paul's lead in seeing Christians as God's temple. Gentile believers are now a house for God, though formerly they were a house for demons. In Hermas* the "house of God" is synonymous with the church. In a passage apparently based on 1 Peter 2, Hermas has a vision of a tower (the church) and

rejected stones, those who were formerly in the faith but were later deceived by the "women in black" (Unbelief, Self-indulgence, Disobedience, and Deceit). These rejected stones were cast out of the house of God, but they may reenter God's house as true stones if they repent (*Herm. Sim.* 13-14).

See also ARCHITECTURE, EARLY CHURCH; CHURCH; HOUSEHOLD, FAMILY; TABERNACLE, SANCTUARY; TEMPLE.

BIBLIOGRAPHY. A. C. Dickie and J. B. Payne, "House," *ISBE* 2:770-72; J. H. Elliott, *The Elect and the Holy: An Exegetical Examination of 1 Peter 2:4-10 and the Phrase* βασιλειον ἱερατευμα (Leiden: E. J. Brill, 1966); B. Gärtner, *The Temple and the Community in Qumran and the New Testament* (Cambridge: Cambridge University Press, 1965); J. Goetzmann, "House . . . ," *NIDNTT* 2:247-51; N. Hillyer, "Spiritual Milk . . . Spiritual House," *TynB* 20 (1969) 126; F. Manns, " 'La maison où réside l'Esprit'. 1 P 2,5 at son arrière-plan juif," *SBFLA* 34 (1984) 207-24; R. J. McKelvey, *The New Temple: The Church in the New Testament* (London: Oxford University Press, 1969); J. S. Marshall, " 'A Spiritual House and Holy Priesthood' (1 Peter ii, 5)," *ATR* 28 (1946) 227-28; O. Michel, "οἶκος κτλ," *TDNT* 5:119-31; P. Minear, "The House of Living Stones: A Study of 1 Peter 2:4-11," *ERev* 34 (1982) 238-48; W. Schutter, *Hermeneutic and Composition in 1 Peter* (Tübingen: J. C. B. Mohr, 1989). D. G. McCartney

HOUSEHOLD, FAMILY

The sociological unit in the Hellenistic world, as in the OT, was not the individual, the city or the state but the family or household. Early Christianity, including the NT itself, to a large degree addressed people not as separate individual entities but as connected to the household (*see DPL*, Households and Household Codes).

1. Households in the Ancient Mediterranean World
2. Evidence of Households in the New Testament
3. Households and the Social Structure of Early Christianity

1. Households in the Ancient Mediterranean World.

In the OT the term *house* is frequently used figuratively as a reference to one's family (e.g.,

Gen 7:1). A house or household included not only an immediate nuclear family but usually a somewhat extended family and those who were dependent on and connected to that family in some way, all under the authority* of the householder. Thus when Joshua promises that "I and my house will serve the Lord" (Josh 24:15), he means his family and other people living with his family under his authority will serve the Lord. Similarly, in Genesis (41:40; 45:8, etc.), as Acts 7:10 recounts, when Joseph was made governor over Egypt and over Pharaoh's household, it means he had stewardship both of the nation and of Pharaoh's family and attendants. (The NIV's "my palace" in Gen 41:40 probably misses the point.) These references also demonstrate that "house" did not include everyone under a person's authority but only those with some kind of familial or domestic attachment. Pharaoh's household (Gen 45) is distinguished from "all Egypt," which was also under his authority.

In the Hellenistic world the household was a social* unit with familial or domestic connections whose members lived in a particular house and were subject to the householder's authority. They shared a common identity as members of that unit. Its cohesiveness lay not only in its members' connection to the head of the house but also in various economic, psychological and religious factors. Prosperity (or want) came not to individuals in isolation but to their household (see *Herm. Sim.* 7.3). The very word *economy* comes from the Greek (*oikonomia*) for "house law," because financial and other administration pertained to the household, not the individual. Such administration was often the responsibility of the householder's wife. In our literature Clement of Rome* refers to women who have been taught "to manage the affairs of the household with dignity" (*1 Clem.* 1.3). Psychologically, a person's identity, from that of the householder to that of the slave,* resided in his or her connection to, responsibilities toward and function within a household. Ordinarily a household was held together by a common religion,* the family generally following the religious proclivities of the head of the household.

2. Evidence of Households in the New Testament.

It is therefore not surprising that the household, a social unit found both in the OT and in Hellenistic culture, is common in our literature. Since households were such strongly religiously-linked social units, they are often the target of evangelistic* effort. Several extended families whose heads believe the gospel* are said to be included in the salvation* that comes to that "house." Thus in Acts 10:2 Cornelius* "with all his household" feared God* and is later (Acts 11:14) told that Peter will bring a message "by which you will be saved, you and all your household." Similarly Lydia, a Thyatiran businesswoman in Philippi, is baptized "with her household" (Acts 16:15). This last reference demonstrates that a woman could be head of a household and was accepted as such in the church* (see also 1 Cor 1:11; Ign. *Pol.* 8.2; Rom 16 in Paul's tribute to women colleagues). The prison warden of Philippi and his whole household are saved and rejoice with him (Acts 16:31, 34), and in Acts 18:18 Crispus, the synagogue* ruler in Corinth, believed, along with his whole household. Clearly the author of Acts* regards the coming of the gospel as affecting whole families and household authority structures as well as individuals. The baptisms* of these entire households suggests an early Christian adoption of the OT covenantal* idea that included families and households, not just individuals, in the covenant and thus also the covenant signs (see Gen 17:23).

Likewise in the General Epistles* the family is a social unit to which salvation often comes. Hebrews 11:7 makes reference to Noah building an ark for the salvation of his "house." Although this was in the first instance a physical salvation rather than a spiritual one, Hebrews* is clearly applying it in a spiritual direction (see 1 Pet 3:20-21), since his emphasis is on Noah's faith. The rest of Hebrews 11 emphasizes how the OT family of God exercised faith.*

3. Households and the Social Structure of Early Christianity.

Since entire households of prominent people were converted, it is not surprising that the household remained the basis for early Christian meetings. In general the early Christians, having been expelled from the synagogues,* appear to have gathered in the homes of prominent converts for instruction and prayer* (Acts 12:12, 16:40; Rom 16). Several recent sociological studies on these house churches have argued that much of the social structure of early

Christianity stemmed from its being patterned after a household unit, with attendant responsibilities and claims to loyalty. In particular, as the household of God, the church was not a democratic institution but a patriarchal family consisting of people who are familially related to, dependent on, obedient to and loyal to the head of that house, Jesus Christ, and thus also to his subordinate officers (1 Pet 5:5; Heb 13:17).

Since the church as a whole, as well as in its manifestations in local houses, was regarded as a family, the mutual obligations of its members are thought of in terms of family responsibilities. Christians have an obligation to familial love (1 Pet 1:22; 2 Pet 1:7; 1 Jn 3:11; 4:7; etc.), and failure to show proper hospitality* in welcoming family members is grievous (3 Jn 10; *Did.* 12.1-5). The family must be protected against false teachers, to whom hospitality must not be given (2 Jn 10). 1 Peter 5:1-5 (see also 1 Jn 2:12-14) addresses the church as a household. Elders are to be shepherds, eager to serve but not lording it over their charges, themselves in service to the chief Shepherd (1 Pet 5:4). The "young men" are to be submissive and a model to all members, who are to be clothed with humility toward one another (1 Pet 5:5).

However, the early church's stress on believers as members of the household of faith did not obscure the significance of individual belief. The particular character of the household code* in 1 Peter* is partly the result of the fact that certain slaves* and women,* contrary to their household heads, have believed in Christ and are thus religiously at odds with their households. Much of the suffering* that 1 Peter envisages is due to the fact that, by adopting Christianity, individuals are disrupting one of the glues that held a household together. No doubt many non-Christian heads of households felt obligated for the sake of maintaining the household to discourage its members from departing from the accepted religion of the house, and this may at times have led to attempts at physical coercion. Thus slaves, specifically identified in 1 Peter 2:18 as *oiketai* or household slaves, could be beaten for their faith (1 Pet 2:20). Both slaves and wives (1 Pet 3:1-6) are put in the difficult position of being required to do all they can to maintain the stability of the household while at the same time holding fast to their religious convictions and commitments

to Christ. Suffering for so doing was commendable (1 Pet 2:20) because it brought glory to God (1 Pet 2:12; 4:16).

The fact that individuals may be saved in distinction from their household does not obviate the reality of their household connections. 1 Peter 3:1-2 even entertains the possibility of the household connectedness working in reverse of the usual pattern, suggesting that unbelieving heads of households might be won by the godly behavior of their believing wives.

The postapostolic period continued in this vein. Although the corporate idea of salvation continues, the necessity of personal belief and action is also stressed. Hermas* retains the corporate expectation when he exhorts people to "pray to God, and he will heal your transgressions, and those of your whole house and those of all the saints" (*Herm. Vis.* 1.1.9), but at the same time he struggles with the fact that his own family has not repented (*Herm. Vis.* 1.3.1-2), at least partly because Hermas did not care for the spiritual well-being of his house until rebuked (*Herm. Vis.* 2.3.1). Thus the early church to a large degree maintained the balance between corporate connectedness, even in respect to salvation, and individual responsibility.

See also HOSPITALITY; HOUSE, SPIRITUAL HOUSE; HOUSEHOLD CODES; SOCIAL SETTING OF EARLY NON-PAULINE CHRISTIANITY.

BIBLIOGRAPHY. R. Banks, *Paul's Idea of Community* (Grand Rapids: Eerdmans, 1980); E. A. Judge, *The Social Pattern of Christian Groups in the First Century* (London: Tyndale, 1960); A. J. Malherbe, *Social Aspects of Early Christianity* (Baton Rouge, LA: Louisiana State University, 1977); A. Strobel, "Der Begriff des 'Hauses' im griechischen und römischen Privatrecht," *ZNW* 56 (1965) 91-100; D. Tidball, *An Introduction to the Sociology of the New Testament* (Exeter: Paternoster, 1983).   D. G. McCartney

HOUSEHOLD CODES

NT writers adopted a number of conventional literary devices to aid them in the teaching of ethics.* One significant device of this sort is referred to by scholars as a household code. This term is a translation of the German term *Haustafel* ("house table"), which Martin Luther originally coined and which was taken up by scholars to describe the extended passages in the NT that address various members of a household.* A number of sections in the NT letters have been classified in this way (Col 3:18—4:1; Eph 5:22-33; 1 Tim 2:8-15; 5:1-2; 6:1-2; Tit 2:1—3:8; 1 Pet 2:13—3:7), and related teaching occurs in the writings of the late first- and second-century apostolic fathers.* The focus of the present article is on the non-Pauline NT and later usage of this form of instruction, but the lines of research have developed in such a way that some discussion of the Pauline usage must fall within our purview (*see DPL,* Households and Household Codes).

1. Definitions: The Parameters and Permutations of the Household Code
2. The Household Code Tradition in Recent Scholarship
3. Household and Church Codes in the Later New Testament and Apostolic Fathers
4. Conclusions

1. Definitions: The Parameters and Permutations of the Household Code.

1.1. The Form. The ideal household code is characterized by teaching addressed to the two members in a household relationship (wives and husbands; slaves* and masters; children and parents); use of an imperative verb expressing subordination (Gk *hypotassō)* or obedience* (Gk *hypakouō)*; grounds or motivation for the behavior enjoined; and reciprocal address. But close inspection of the various passages generally categorized as household codes reveals a number of differences that complicate the issues of the genesis and form of the NT device.

1.2. Variations Within the New Testament. The typical assumption is that the household codes of Colossians and Ephesians represent in some sense the basic form, with somewhat divergent later examples being understood as developments or expansions of an ideal form corresponding to developments in the church's sense of self-identity in relation to the world as the house church became the institutional church* (so esp. Herr).

Although this interpretation is open to question, it does seem clear from a comparison of the form and themes that the related passages belong to a common tradition(s) that in different settings and times proved to be capable of adaptation to new situations. Thus within the Pauline and Petrine writings we find passages that address believers specifically from the perspective of their place in the household (Eph; Col; cf. 1 Tim 6:1-2; 1 Pet 2:13—3:7). However,

other passages related in form and tone address believers according to their positions in the broader context of the Christian congregation. Injunctions may be divided along gender lines, whether generally or in the marriage relationship (1 Cor 11:3-16; 14:33-35; 1 Tim 2:8-15), and along generational lines (1 Tim 5:1-2); Titus 2:1-10 combines these perspectives. Elsewhere the church as a whole is instructed to acknowledge the secular authorities (Rom 13:1-7; Tit 3:1-2; 1 Pet 2:13-17; *see* Civil Authority). And several passages encourage the church similarly to submit to its leaders and/or exhort leaders to lead well (1 Cor 16:16; 1 Thess 5:12-13; Heb 13:17; 1 Tim 3:1-13; Tit 1:6-9; 1 Pet 5:1-5).

In view of both the similarity of form, content and tone in these passages and the variety of groups and concerns addressed, the adequacy of the term "household code" to describe the tradition as a whole has been questioned. D. Schroeder (1976, 1959) chose the more general term "station code," which identifies and links the passages on the basis of their common form and concern to teach believers how to behave in their various stations in life. Others (Balch, Weiser) prefer to think in terms of two subspecies of one tradition: the term "household code" applies to the form as it occurs in Colossians, Ephesians and 1 Peter,* but the term "church code," or "congregational code," more accurately describes the tradition's application or expansion in those passages that exceed the bounds of the household (e.g., 1 Tim 2:1—6:2; Tit 2:1—3:8).

Both of these approaches share the assumption that a basic form was altered or expanded as new situations warranted. The most recent work of H. von Lips suggests another explanation. He observed the relationship between the household code in 1 Peter and the code in Titus 2:1—3:7 and determined that these two examples share certain features that set them off from Colossians and Ephesians: the parent/child category is absent; instructions are addressed to slaves but not masters; subordination to the state, which Colossians and Ephesians do not mention, is enjoined; 1 Peter and Titus prefer the verb *subordinate* or *submit* (Gk *hypotassomai;* used throughout) to *obey* (Gk *hypakouō;* used in Col and Eph of slave and child) and the noun *despotai* of the masters (Col and Eph use *kyrioi);* and the codes in 1 Peter and Titus make extensive use of theological material to ground the instructions (Titus 2:11-14; 3:3-8; 1 Pet 2:21-24; 3:18-22). These points of contact, especially the addition of the instruction concerning the state, suggest the emergence of a new schema or a parallel tradition rather than one that has undergone transformation. Whether this explanation is an improvement remains to be seen. However, his attentiveness to the text and context, instead of primarily secular parallels, for clues about the meaning of the codes is noteworthy. This methodology has not always been followed.

2. The Household Code Tradition in Recent Scholarship.

Three crucial questions determine the direction that study of this teaching form has taken: Where did it come from? What circumstances in the Christian communities gave rise to its usage? What is the intention of the ethic it enjoins?

2.1. The Question of Source. For the most part scholars have concentrated on discovering the source of the code as it appears in the NT in the hope that this would provide the clue to its meaning. Initial investigations concluded that codes used in Stoicism had been modified only slightly for Christian use (Weidinger, Dibelius). Then some scholars noticed that the emphasis on subordination seemed closer to the teaching of Hellenistic Judaism* as seen, for instance, in Philo* (Schroeder 1959 and esp. Crouch). L. Goppelt (1973, 1993 [1978], 1982), building on the work of Schroeder, concluded that the NT household codes are genuinely Christian products; in some respects they compare with Stoic and Hellenistic Jewish relationship ethics but are more specifically the result of Christian reworking of Hellenistic ethics "on the basis of principles developed by Jesus and Paul" (Goppelt 1993 [1978], 173).

More recent scholarship emphasizes to a greater extent the influence of the Greco-Roman culture on the NT device (Lührmann, Thraede, Balch 1981, Müller, Lips). The structure of Aristotelian household ethics (addressing social relationships, reciprocality, placing one of the pair under the authority of the other) might explain the codes in Colossians and Ephesians. But the more likely immediate source of the NT tradition, which becomes more diverse in content, is to be found in the broader contemporary Hellenistic discussion of the theme "concerning the household" (Gk *peri oikonomou*), which developed from, but was not restricted to, Aristotle in terms of content and form.

For a number of reasons, looking to the contemporary culture for an understanding of the NT household codes is a useful approach. The absence of an identifable source for the form recommends caution and sensitivity (Hartman). It is clear that the NT writers were indeed influenced by their environment, and in this respect it is important to note how the early church utilized the Hellenistic "household" concept as its own sense of identity developed. This concept, rather than formal considerations alone, would seem to be the common denominator that links NT with secular social ethics. The ancient household* was regarded as the basic building block of society; its stability guaranteed the stability of the city-state, and so discussion of the relation of household members to the state authorities came naturally within the purview of a discussion of ethics related to the household. The teaching developed to safeguard the relationships and responsibilities in the household and respect for the state established some of the categories and suggested the method of instruction of the NT household code. But there is no question of an uncritical, wholesale adoption of secular ethics on the part of NT writers.

2.2. The Question of Causal Circumstances. Martin Dibelius and K. Weidinger answered this question on the basis of secularization in the early church. In their opinion the delay of Christ's* return and the pressing concern for survival in a hostile world led the church to find a way to make itself at home in society. The secular code, with some slight Christian modifications, encouraged the kind of behavior that would facilitate this transition. The codes were taken over so completely, however, that nothing about a particular church's situation might be learned from them. This view has been largely rejected, though it has still influenced the interpretation of later NT writings.

Other scholars maintain that the household code was applied to quiet the unrest caused in Christian communities by the enthusiastic enactment of the Pauline equality tradition preserved in Galatians 3:28 (Col 3:11; 1 Cor 12:13; Schroeder 1959; Crouch; Martin, 3:931-32). Goppelt argued similarly that the tradition called Christians undergoing stress because of the faith* to remain engaged in the social structure rather than emigrate out of it (Goppelt 1982).

E. Schüssler Fiorenza's feminist reconstruction combines the two preceding views, interpreting the household codes as evidence of the church's return to patriarchy. Early efforts to live according to the equality promised by Paul's gospel (Gal 3:28) led to some exuberant excesses and apparently drew criticism and hostility from secular critics. Rather than stand firm for the gospel and coequality of the sexes, church leaders in the name of Paul returned to the acceptable secular arrangement for the church in order to promote peace with the hostile world.

On the whole Schroeder, Crouch, Goppelt and Balch seem to be on the better track in their various ways. Balch (1981) especially pointed out that there is no sign of an emancipation movement in 1 Peter, much less one based on Galatians 3:28. What does seem evident in all cases is some sort of social instability in the church, whether brought on by errant theology or eschatology* (Col; 1 Tim; and perhaps linked to false teaching) or stressful conditions in society in which Christians were being alienated and persecuted (1 Pet; see Elliott). In either case the solution arrived at was for the Christian community to structure its social behavior in ways that reflected conformity rather than opposition to the outside world. The more fundamental question is the intention in encouraging such behavior.

2.3. The Question of Intention. Along with the search for the source has gone the search for the motive or intention of the ethic taught by the NT household code, and numerous suggestions have been made (accommodation to secular ethics, Weidinger, Dibelius and more recently Schüssler Fiorenza; quieting enthusiastic unrest, Crouch, Martin; preventing internal disintegration brought on by outside pressures, Elliott 1981; defense-apologetic, Balch; mission, Schroeder, Goppelt).

However, the variation in the form the tradition takes and in the circumstances it addresses in the NT, as well as the absence of a single secular prototype, suggest that any one of the proposed solutions may be too narrow. It can be said generally that the NT household and church codes are concerned with Christian behavior in typical life situations; as in the secular Hellenistic setting, so too in the church: household roles and the household context provided the typical forum for discussing social ethics. Once the household metaphor is taken over as an expression of congregational identity (Eph; 1 Tim; Tit; 1 Pet), the same pattern of teaching can be expanded and applied to address life within the relationships in the broader Christian community and life as a Christian in the world. Goppelt observed correctly that life lived at this level in the various social roles insured that Christians would be in daily contact with unbelievers with every opportunity to testify to the faith (Goppelt 1982, 2:170; 1993, 162-79).

Whether the household codes were specifically missionary in orientation in every NT application is another question. What can be said is that through them the NT writers reflect sensitivity to the expectations of society at large and seem to encourage Christians to live according to patterns that were widely accepted as respectable. But in view of the emphasis on justice and fairness and the extent to which the ethic is grounded in theology, none of the NT household codes reflect uncritical secularization. A creative middle ground was sought, and at least in some cases (Tit; 1 Pet) this would facilitate a "salt and light" Christian existence in the world. In other cases it might serve a different purpose or have in-house matters more in mind.

3. Household and Church Codes in the Later New Testament and Apostolic Fathers.

3.1. 1 Peter. As indicated, the circumstances of the recipients of a letter* containing a household code provide the more reliable clues to the intention of the teaching than anything inherent in the form itself. 1 Peter is somewhat distinct (as compared, for instance, with Titus) in that it addresses churches already experiencing or about to experience alienation and abuse in society. This dimension of Christian existence had apparently led some people in those churches to consider either a form of compromise to avoid this criticism and hostility or perhaps to pull out and attempt to live a Christian life beyond the range of pagan society.

Peter responds to these options by reinforcing rather than reducing the sense of tension felt by his readers with a theology that explained their experience of alienation. God's* election* to membership in his family set them in a paradoxical situation—nonmembers in a world in which they must continue to live (1 Pet 1:1-2). On the one hand Christians are "foreigners," those who reside without citizenship and without rights in a land that is not their own (1 Pet 1:1; 2:11). On the other hand they are the equivalent of resident aliens, a slightly different metaphor that implies the same sorts of limitations as "foreigners" but also implies the need to live on in that foreign country (1 Pet 1:17; 2:11). Since God's action in Christ for his people has determined their situation, they may rejoice; and however much the pressures of this life might seem to contradict it, the hope of salvation* to be realized in full only in the end is sure (1 Pet 1:3-7). This theology may explain how the predicament has come about and provide some assurance* about the future fulfillment of God's promises,* but there is little incentive in it for a continued commitment to living the arduous Christian life in a hostile world.

Another factor is mentioned to convince Christians to stay engaged in the social life of the world, whatever the perils: mission. At 1 Peter 2:11-12, Peter makes the turn from the theology of the Christian identity as aliens to appropriate Christian living. The main motive for living an exemplary life before pagans is the hope of their salvation (1 Pet 2:12; cf. 1 Pet 3:1, 15). If Christian living can lead to this, then the importance of continued engagement in social life can be seen. It is this point that the household code that immediately follows (1 Pet 2:13—3:7) seeks to explore. Engagement will mean living as far as possible in accordance with the patterns of social life, and the secular household ethos provides the essential categories.

1 Peter 2:13-17 calls for submission to the government authorities. This would include a general attitude of respect toward those in authority (cf. Tit 3:1; Rom 13:1-4), which would be demonstrated in the specific acts of paying taxes (cf. Rom 13:6-7) and offering prayers* in behalf of civil leaders (cf. 1 Tim 2:1-2; *1 Clem.* 61.1-3). The rationale is that the civil government has been ordained by God and that such behavior will disprove the false accusations of outsiders who have slandered Christian households as being disloyal to the city-state. Apparently this kind of accusation was a current problem; the implication from the letter is that

even exemplary behavior in this regard might not stop the abuse from unbelievers.

1 Peter 2:18-25 commands Christian slaves to submit to their masters. It is possible that it was more common in these churches for slaves to be Christians than masters, since masters are not addressed (cf. 1 Tim 6:1-2; Tit 2:9-10) and since the lengthy theological foundation establishes Christ's suffering* as the pattern for Christian slaves who must continue to suffer unjustly. The unique christological* grounding reveals the special circumstances of the churches to which Peter writes (cf. the confessional* material used to ground the behavior in Titus 2:11-14; 3:3-7). In any case, the church's calling to engagement in the world prohibited slaves from opting out of this social institution. To encourage anything else would be regarded by unbelievers as anarchy.

1 Peter 3:1-7 closes the household code with teaching addressed to wives and husbands (*see* Marriage). Wives are to be submissive to husbands, and the two possible scenarios of mixed and Christian marriages are envisaged. A Christian wife whose husband was an unbeliever might experience harsh treatment for insubordination because of her foreign religion (1 Pet 3:1-2). Exemplary behavior might also be linked to her faith and so win over the unbelieving mate to Christ. Outer adornment is the specific aspect of respectable conduct given to illustrate the teaching (cf. 1 Tim 2:9-10). Spiritual inner adornment is commended (a gentle and quiet spirit), and Sarah's demeanor provides a pattern. Christian husbands are to refuse to treat their wives harshly (1 Pet 3:7). They are fellow heirs of eternal life; failure to treat them with the respect they are due as human beings and fellow heirs will affect their relationship with God (cf. 1 Tim 2:8).

At this point in the letter the teaching addressed to the traditional household code categories comes to an end. There is no question of the wholesale adoption of a pagan ethical code. The conduct encouraged certainly corresponds to secular .ideals of respectability, but the grounds and intention of the teaching are thoroughly Christianized. What is unique about the code as it is applied in 1 Peter (in contrast to Col, Eph, 1 Tim, Tit) is the insistence on respectability and engagement by Christians in the social life of the world even when they have been marginalized by unbelieving society.

Church concerns continue in 1 Peter 3:8—5:11, with various themes being linked to the dominant one of suffering. In 1 Peter 5:1-5 Peter returns briefly to the traditional format, addressing the congregational categories of elders in authority* and younger believers who are to submit to that authority. The teaching to both parties is traditional (for leaders, cf. Acts 20:28; Rom 12:8; 1 Tim 3:1-13; Tit 1:6-9; for the younger, cf. 1 Cor 16:16; 1 Thess 5:12-13; Heb 13:17); the decision to expand the household code to address behavior within the broader congregational setting is in keeping with Peter's overarching concern for the church in the world; this "household" of God must maintain the lines of authority and order that will insure its acceptability in a society looking precisely for such things.

3.2. The Apostolic Fathers. Several passages in the group of late first- and second-century Christian writings known as the apostolic fathers assume the pattern observed in the NT household and church codes. Circumstances and concerns have changed. It is more likely that a less critical endorsement of the traditional patriarchal social order (such as Schüssler Fiorenza argues for the NT household codes) has now become evident in some cases.

3.2.1. 1 Clement. Clement's (*see* Clement of Rome) main concern as he addresses the Corinthian congregation is for unity and harmony (see esp. *1 Clem.* 20; 37—38; 46—48). One threat to church stability came from a group that had apparently challenged ecclesiastical authority (*1 Clem.* 21.5; 44.1, 4; 47.6). The two passages fashioned as household codes suggest that Clement urged a return to traditional family values as the key to harmony. Moreover, the authority of the male head of the house, central to Roman ethical thinking among the aristocracy, corresponded to Clement's views of ecclesiastical authority in the church.

Two passages in *1 Clement* take the form of household or church codes. *1 Clement* 1.3 addresses teaching meant for all to the head of the family according to a hierarchical organization: submission to leaders, honor to older men (elders?), instruction to younger men; women were to cherish their husbands and live in subjection. *1 Clement* 2.1 states the goal of this pattern: to live in humility* as characterized by a willingness to be in subjection (as the household ethic

dictates) rather than demanding subjection (cf. Eph 5:21).

1 Clement 21.6-8 serves the theme of harmony expounded in the hymn* of *1 Clement* 20. This time in the hortatory first person plural, the same basic order of instruction is followed: to honor leaders and elders (possibly church officers), to teach the younger, to guide women toward the good, to teach the children in the faith. Despite the first-person address, the absence of instructions to the husbands or fathers suggests the main addressee is the male leader of the household.

Differences between the NT household codes and those in *1 Clement* are evident and probably indicate changed circumstances and outlook. Instructions concerning children emphasize teaching rather than obedience to parents, perhaps because of the concern to safeguard the faith for succeeding generations. Slaves and masters are not addressed. In addition to addressing instuctions to the male head of the house, the emphasis on the behavior of wives (in terms of obedience, purity* and silence without reference to status in marriage or in Christ; cf. Eph 5:22-33; 1 Pet 3:1-7) reveals Clement's preference for the accepted order of things in his Roman setting. The household codes outline the divine pattern for unity and stability (*1 Clem.* 1.3; 20.11; 21.4). But the divine pattern, as Clement interprets it for household ethics, seems completely uncritical of Roman patriarchal assumptions (see Stambaugh and Balch, Bowe, Jeffers).

3.2.2. Ignatius and Polycarp. In the writings of Ignatius* and Polycarp* main concerns include false teachers (Ign. *Pol.* 3.1; Ign. *Eph.* 6.2; Ign. *Trall.* 6.1; Ign. *Magn.* 8.1; Ign. *Smyrn.* 6.2; Pol. *Phil.* 7), and the answer to their threat comes in maintaining unity in the church and ecclesiastical (episcopal) order (Ign. *Pol.* 1.2; 6.1; Pol. *Phil.* 5.3). To aid the church in achieving this unity Ignatius in his *Letter to Polycarp* 4.1—5.2 introduces a church code (somewhat closer in tone and content to the NT codes than *1 Clement*) that combines instructions concerning treatment of widows and slaves and reciprocal instructions to wives and husbands with instructions to Polycarp himself concerning ministry.* Although the immediate application of the code is to an internal matter, we should be aware of Ignatius's general positive attitude toward unbelievers and desire for their repentance* that underlie his instructions to live in harmony with the world (Ign. *Eph.* 10.1-3). Thus the pattern of life described in the household or church code might be applied to internal instability, but it is not without outward effect. Polycarp's *Letter to the Philippians* 4.2—6.1 instructs the church similarly, according to household groups and church-specific groups—wives, widows, deacons, young men, young women, elders—blending them much as Titus 2:1-10 does. Although he does not elaborate, the order of life Polycarp encourages is introduced as that which pleases the Lord* (Pol. *Phil.* 5.2; 6.1; 4.1).

3.2.3. The Didache and the Epistle of Barnabas. The *Didache** is partly (*Did.* 1.1—6.2) a catechetical work designed to prepare new believers for baptism* (*Did.* 7.1) and partly a text on church order* (*Did.* 6.3—16.8). The much different purpose of the *Epistle of Barnabas** is to demonstrate that Christians are the genuine children (*see* Son) of God. *Didache* 4.9-11 instructs parents to discipline their children, masters to treat their slaves reasonably and slaves to be subject to their masters. The reciprocity, the theme of submission and the motivation (the impartiality of God, who is over both master and slave) suggest a link with the tradition as used in Colossians and Ephesians. Probably the writer has incorporated material from the Pauline letters (the possibility that the writer had access to an earlier teaching source, which Colossians and Ephesians also knew, is explored by Munro). *Barnabas* 19.5, 7 uses the same material (the matter of source is unclear; there may have been a common source accessible to each writer) with slight alterations, reversing the order of instructions to slaves first, then masters. In each case the household code material has been incorporated into the collection of traditions used to explain the Two Ways teaching (of "life and death," *Did.* 1.1; of "light and darkness," *Barn.* 18.1). The household and community relationship ethics implied by these sections are not applied in any discernible way to immediate situations. The material is simply included as orthodox.

4. Conclusions.
The household codes of both the NT and the apostolic fathers reflect an awareness of the expectations of the Greco-Roman environment of the church. However, they also reveal some subtle differences in the way the church at different times and in different situations sought to interact with secular society. NT usage of the device demonstrates sensitivity to secular values and in critically adjusting certain features (emphasizing justice and fairness and providing a theological rationale) aimed to direct Christians to a constructive middle ground, avoiding either the simple return to patriarchy or emancipation. 1 Peter utilizes the household code with Christian engagement in the social life of the world in mind (cf. Tit 2—3), and it is significant that this engagement is necessitated by the church's identity and mission as aliens and foreigners who are God's elect.

In the writings of the apostolic fathers, household codes are used—without evidence of the critical reflection upon the church's responsibility in the world seen in 1 Peter—to preserve the status quo. The shape of the two codes in *1 Clement* suggests a preference for patriarchy on the Roman model; Schüssler Fiorenza's interpretation may fit this later situation. The *Didache* and *Epistle of Barnabas* have employed another recension of the household code but in any case offer its teaching as traditional without reflecting on its implications. Ignatius and Polycarp are more in touch with NT household codes but are mainly preoccupied with restoring church stability and unity. For this the codes provide a structure for respectable behavior in relationships that complement the writers' understanding of ecclesiastical authority. Although Ignatius's outlook on the church in the world may be an exception, the household codes in the late first- and second-century church seem to function less to keep the church on the cutting edge of eschatological tension with contemporary society and more to preserve a status quo.

See also HOUSE, SPIRITUAL HOUSE; HOUSEHOLDS, FAMILY; SLAVE, SLAVERY; SOCIAL SETTING OF EARLY NON-PAULINE CHRISTIANITY; WOMAN AND MAN.

BIBLIOGRAPHY. J.-P. Audet, *La Didachè: Instructions des Apôtres* (EB; Paris: Gabalda, 1958); D. L. Balch, "Household Codes," *ABD* (1992) 3:318-20; idem, *Let Wives Be Submissive: The Domestic Code in 1 Peter* (SBLMS 26; Chico, CA: Scholars Press, 1981); L. W. Barnard, *Studies in the Apostolic Fathers and Their Background* (Oxford: Blackwell, 1967); B. E. Bowe, *A Church in Crisis: Ecclesiology and Paraenesis in Clement of Rome* (HDR 23; Minneapolis: Fortress, 1988); J. E.

Crouch, *The Origin and Intention of the Colossian Haustafel* (FRLANT 109; Göttingen: Vandenhoeck & Ruprecht, 1972); M. Dibelius and H. Greeven, *An die Kolosser, Epheser an Philemon* (3d ed.; HNT 12; Tübingen: J. C. B. Mohr, 1953); J. H. Elliott, *A Home for the Homeless: A Sociological Exegesis of 1 Peter, Its Situation and Strategy* (Philadelphia: Fortress, 1981); L. Goppelt, *A Commentary on 1 Peter* (Grand Rapids: Eerdmans, 1993 [1978]); idem, "Jesus und die Haustafeltradition" in *Orientierung an Jesus*, ed. P. Hoffmann (Freiburg: Herder, 1973) 93-105; idem, *Theology of the New Testament* (2 vols.; Grand Rapids: Eerdmans, 1982) vol. 2; L. Hartman, "Some Unorthodox Thoughts on the 'Household-Code Form'" in *The Social World of Formative Christianity and Judaism*, ed. J. Neusner et al. (Philadelphia: Fortress, 1988) 219-34; T. Herr, *Naturrecht aus der kritischen Sicht des Neuen Testaments* (Munich, Paderborn and Vienna: Schöningh, 1976); J. S. Jeffers, *Conflict at Rome: Social Order and Hierarchy in Early Christianity* (Minneapolis: Fortress, 1991); J. B. Lightfoot and J. R. Harmer, eds. *The Apostolic Fathers: Greek Texts and English Translations of Their Writings* (2d ed.; ed. and rev. M. W. Holmes; Grand Rapids: Baker, 1992); H. von Lips, "Die Haustafel als 'Topos' im Rahmen der urchristlichen Paränese," *NTS* 40 (1994) 261-80; D. Lührmann, "Neutestamentliche Haustafeln und antike Ökonomie," *NTS* 27 (1980) 83-97; R. P. Martin, "Haustafeln," *NIDNTT* 3:928-32; W. Munro, *Authority in Paul and Peter: The Identification of a Pastoral Stratum in the Pauline Corpus and 1 Peter* (SNTSMS 45; Cambridge: Cambridge University Press, 1983); K. Müller, "Die Haustafel des Kolosserbriefes und das antike Frauenthema" in *Die Frau in Urchristentum*, ed. G. Dautzenberg, H. Merklein and K. Müller (QD 95; Freiburg, Basel and Vienna: Herder, 1983) 263-319; W. R. Schoedel, *Ignatius of Antioch: A Commentary on the Letters of Ignatius of Antioch* (Herm; Philadelphia: Fortress, 1985); W. Schrage, "Zur Ethik der NT Haustafeln," *NTS* 21 (1974) 1-22; D. Schroeder, "Die Haustafeln des neuen Testaments (ihre Herkunft und theologischer Sinn)" (unpublished dissertation; Hamburg: Mikrokopie, 1959); idem, "Lists, Ethical," *IDBSup* (1976) 546; E. Schüssler Fiorenza, *In Memory of Her: A Feminist Reconstruction of Christian Origins* (New York: Crossroad, 1984); J. E. Stambaugh and D. L. Balch, *The New Testament in Its Social Environment* (Philadelphia:

Fortress, 1986); G. Strecker, "Die neutestamentlichen Haustafeln" in *Neues Testament und Ethik: Festschrift für R. Schnackenburg*, ed. H. Merklein (Freiburg, Basel and Vienna: Herder, 1989) 349-75; K. Thraede, "Zum historischen Hintergrund der 'Haustafeln' des NT" in *Pietas, Festschrift für Bernhard Kötting*, ed. E. Dassmann et al. (Munich: JAC Ergänzungsband 8, 1980) 359-68; K. Weidinger, *Die Haustafeln: Ein Stück urchristlicher Paränese* (Leipzig: Hinrichs, 1928); A. Weiser, "Titus 2 als Gemeindeparänese" in *Neues Testament und Ethik: Festschrift für R. Schnackenburg*, ed. H. Merklein (Freiburg, Basel and Vienna: Herder, 1989) 397-414; K. Wengst, *Tradition und Theologie des Barnabasbriefes* (Berlin and New York: Walter de Gruyter, 1971).

P. H. Towner

HUMILITY. *See* PRIDE, HUMILITY.

HYMNS, SONGS

Singing hymns as spontaneous praise to deities in public assembly, with or without musical instruments, had been a common practice in Jewish and the pagan communities long before the NT era (Norden). When Christianity, with its Jewish and pagan converts and the presence of the Holy Spirit, came into existence, singing hymns to God* or Christ for his redemptive* grace* inevitably became a part of Christian public worship (MacDonald, 112-13; *see* Worship). Some of the Pauline communities, for example, were musically oriented (see 1 Cor 14:15, 26). Members were often encouraged to teach and admonish one another with psalms, hymns and spiritual songs (Eph 5:19; Col 3:16). No wonder one finds that incorporating christological* hymns for a didactic or epistolary purpose is a common literary practice within the Pauline corpus (e.g., Phil 2:6-11; Col 1:15-20; 1 Tim 3:16; see *DPL*, Hymns). Elsewhere in the NT and in the writings of the apostolic fathers,* the allusion to hymns or songs and the incorporation of hymnic fragments, although less frequent (except in Revelation; *see* Revelation, Book of), also provide windows to the hymns or songs used in other Christian communities during the first two centuries of the Christian era.

1. Acts
2. Hebrews
3. James

4. 1 Peter
5. Revelation
6. Post-Apostolic Writings
7. Conclusions

1. Acts.

Allusion to hymns or singing is expressed by two Greek words in Acts:* *aineō* (Acts 2:47; 3:8-9) and *hymneō* (Acts 16:25). The former, although it generally means "to praise" or "to extol" (Schlier, 177), is employed by the Septuagint to translate *hallel*, which in the Bible most commonly means "to praise [God] in song" (Stanley, 173). In Acts 2:46-47 Luke uses *aineō* to denote communal praises expressed by the early Christian converts during their daily assembly; in Acts 3:8-9 the same word is used to denote praises expressed by an individual in response to the healing* he has just experienced. If *aineō* includes musical expression, then in both of these cases the praises are mostly likely hymnic in form and are said to be directed to God. The content of these praise hymns is not recorded. However, in light of the communal prayer of praise *(deomai)* recorded in Acts 4:24-30 (which is possibly in musical or metrical form also; see Old, 27; Smith, 22), we see a blend of fragments quoted from the OT Psalms coupled with Christian motifs (Moule, 70). Through the apostolic preaching* and teaching,* their new recognition that Jesus is the Christ (see Acts 2:36; 8:5; 9:22; 17:3; 18:5; 28), their awaited Messiah (see Lk 24:26-27), is making a powerful impact in their lives. It is thus natural that their praises to God included a combination of the OT prophecies (esp. in the Psalms) and their new faith in Christ.

Luke's repeated reference to hymnic praises early in his book to Theophilus (just as in Luke 1-2, where four Jewish Christian canticles are recorded), while possibly reflecting actual incidences, may serve an apologetic purpose as well. Those events highlight the practice of hymnic praise as a key element in early Christian worship; both in form and content this practice resembles Jewish synagogue* worship in the Diaspora* (Hengel, 90). It is Luke's intention to provide a linkage between the Jewish and Christian communities. He wanted Theophilus (as well as others in Rome) to know that Christianity, like Judaism,* should be considered a *religio licita* (permitted religion), not a threat to the empire (Longenecker 1981, 218; *see* Roman Empire). The constant allusions to hymnic praise at the outset help to reinforce this message.

In Acts 16:25 the special reference to Paul's and Silas's corporate singing to God in the Philippian prison is expressed through the word *hymneō*, which commonly referred to praising God in songs. Philo uses *hymnos* regularly to describe the OT Psalms. In Ephesians 5:19 and Colossians 3:16 *hymnos* is mentioned with *psalmos* and *ōdē pneumatikē* to denote musical elements used in corporate worship for mutual edification. As some have suggested, Acts 16:25 perhaps reflects the writer's knowledge of a regular custom of night service (Acts 12:5, 12; 20:7-1; see Bradshaw, 39), but it is more likely that the writer wanted again to present a positive image of Christianity to his reader(s). Note the similarities between Acts 16:25 and Acts 4:21-31; namely, the *Sitz im Leben* (Christians being persecuted*), the reaction (they praised God) and the consequence (the earth was shaken). The writer repeatedly uses hymnic praise to stress that Christians are not a threat to the Roman Empire even when they face oppression. Rather, they are a people of praise, whether in Palestine (represented by Peter and John in Jerusalem, Acts 4:21-31) or in Hellenistic regions (represented by Paul and Silas in Philippi, Acts 16:25). So Luke uses the allusion to hymnic praise in Acts 4:23-31 and Acts 16:25 for an apologetic purpose: to show how Christians did not offer political resistance to Rome.

2. Hebrews.

The most obvious use of hymnic material is found in Hebrews 1:3, which on the basis of syntactical and stylistic criteria has been considered to be hymnic in form (e.g., Schille, 42; Deichgräber, 137-38; Sanders, 19-20; contra Ellingworth, 98). The introductory relative pronoun *hos*, followed by a present participle *ōn* in preference to main verbs, and the switch of person from God in Hebrews 1:1-2 to Christ his Son in Hebrews 1:3 also support the notion that this is possibly a piece of a preexisting hymn quoted by the writer (cf. Phil 2:6-11; Col 1:15-20; contra Frankowski) in this context.

The theme of this hymn is distinctly christological in addition to being ontological and soteriological: Christ is God in revelation,* sustainer of the creation,* savior of humanity, and the exalted one. These four brief phrases embody the four key roles of Christ. Perhaps the hymn was originally composed as a piece of liturgical confession and is being adopted by the writer of Hebrews* to highlight his or her message of Christ's supremacy to his or her readers, who are in danger of being misled by alien teachings (Heb 13:9) and falling away from their salvation* (Heb 2:1-3). Since it is hymnic material, its message would make a greater impact upon the readers (see Nida et al. on the contributions of poetic language to a text). And if Hebrews is a sermon, as some have suggested (Lane, lxxx), then the writer's inclusion of a piece of hymnic material with relevant content at the outset of his or her message is noteworthy (Black, 193).

The writer first shows the readers that the use of hymns is essential in corporate worship, just as they are reminded that they are to offer up sacrifice of praise *(aineseōs)* to God; that is, the fruit of lips that acknowledge his name (Heb 13:15). The saving act of Christ ushered in new forms of worship in which singing praises to God is considered a sacrifice* in lieu of animal sacrifices (cf. the prophecy of Hos 14:2). The writer also demonstrates that the content of a hymn sets the pattern for the message of the sermon. In the case of Hebrews, Christ's supremacy is the theme, and the hymn in Hebrews 1:3 effectively prepares the readers for the message to be delivered. This brief hymnic fragment is incorporated in the sermon at the outset to serve epistolary, didactic and even polemic purposes (cf. Col 1:15-20, which has similar purposes). Although the allusion to hymnic material is found only in Hebrews 1:3 and Hebrews 13:15 (in addition to Hebrews 2:12, where Christ is likened to a hymn singer leading his people's praises), the place of hymns in the Hebraic communities and the writer's use of hymn to serve his or her purposes are clearly shown.

3. James.

The letter of James* includes only one reference to singing: "Is anyone cheerful? Let him sing praises *[psalletō]*" (Jas 5:13). The allusion has been taken by many as merely an exhortation to remember God at all times. But considering the use of the word *psallō* (which appears almost sixty times in the LXX and generally indicates to praise by means of a harp or a song sung to God [e.g., Ps 33:2, 3; 98:4-5; 147:7;

149:3]) and the context (Jas 5:13-15), in which praying* and singing are mentioned together, we may conclude that the *Sitz im Leben* of this verse is communal worship (Martin 1988, 206). It is probable that, just as in other Christian communities (cf. 1 Cor 14:26), the members of the Jacobean congregation used to offer songs of praise and thanksgiving during corporate worship. But continual oppression by the wealthy (see Jas 5:1-6; cf. Jas 2:6, 15-16) has possibly depressed the exuberant spirit of these worshipers. James, by the use of the imperative *psalletō* ("let him sing a song [to God])," reminds as well as exhorts his readers to revert to what they used to do. Music (i.e., *psallō*, which is significant in the light of the paucity of possible references in the early Fathers) must be rehearsed in public worship if anyone is in good spirits despite distressing circumstances. This brief allusion to singing in the letter provides us insight into the place and practice of hymnic praise in the Jacobean congregation.

J. L. Wu

4. 1 Peter.

Five passages of 1 Peter* contain its essential christological testimony: 1 Peter 1:3-12, 18-21; 2:4-8, 21-25; and 3:18-22. Each of these texts contains traditional materials, whether from oral or literary sources. Four of the five passages (the exception is 1 Pet 2:4-8, a catena of three OT texts) have been identified by style and form as containing traditional liturgical deposits and, more specifically, hymnic fragments, which have been brilliantly woven into the text of 1 Peter.

4.1. Twentieth-Century Research. The identification of liturgical (creedal* or hymnic) passages in the text of the NT was begun in the early 1900s. Seeberg (1903) made note of the use of formula-like material in 1 Peter, and Norden (1913) listed some of the literary devices indicative of liturgical deposits in this epistle: *parallelismus membrorum* (the poetic technique of the Psalms in which lines are arranged in couplets or triplets), a pronominal beginning, descriptive participles and relative clauses. The studies that followed were concerned with detecting such preformed deposits on the basis of refined study of lexical and stylistic evidence (such as rhyming devices in the Greek, rare terms or dramatic language), including formal introductory phrases and the contextual dislocation produced by the insertion of such material into the prose style of narrative or epistle. Over the last century, form-critical study has identified a number of types of traditional material and formal sources (beyond the OT citations) found in 1 Peter, including topoi, ethical lists, kerygmatic and creedal* statements, hymns or hymn fragments, catechetical instructions, doxologies and eulogies, household* rules, testimonia and dominical sayings (Stauffer, Shimada and Martin have provided lists of the features of traditional materials, especially hymns in the NT).

The proposal that formal liturgical or hymnic materials are embedded in the text of 1 Peter has been advocated by a majority of scholars. B. Reicke (1946), R. Bultmann, J. Jeremias and H. Windisch all identified the following passages in 1 Peter as hymnic: 1 Peter 1:3-12, 18-21; 2:21-25; 3:18-22. (See also Best, Boismard, Cullmann, Dalton, Deichgräber, Goppelt, Hengel, Lohse, Martin, Sanders and Schutter.) Bultmann's study (12-14), the most speculative, went so far as to propose an original hymn that he reconstructed from three passages: 1 Peter 1:20; 2:21-24; 3:18-22. His proposal has been justifiably dismissed by such scholars as Jeremias and Lohse for his excessive freedom in alteration of the text and his faulty hypothesis of a Gnostic* redemption myth. But the enduring value of his analysis is that it provided the springboard for the modern discussion of the author's use of source materials, especially hymnic or creedal forms, in 1 Peter.

4.2. Hymnic Passages in 1 Peter.

4.2.1. 1 Peter 1:3-12. This christological pericope, composed of a single sentence, is a tightly woven declaration based upon at least six varieties of formal materials, including hymnic material. The *bᵉrākôt* ("blessed be") form that opens the pericope establishes the types of sources employed in the unit (1 Pet 1:3-12) and also the intent of 1 Peter; the passage is created from the language and forms of Christian worship for Christian worship. A hymnlike quality can be observed in 1 Peter 1:3-5 and probably even in the materials through 1 Peter 1:9. The christological pattern of sufferings* and glories,* explicitly stated in 1 Peter 1:11, creates the center of this exquisite literary poem which, in its final form, is best identified as a formal, didactic ascription.

4.2.2. 1 Peter 1:18-21. This pericope is a composite of formulary materials primarily determined by the Isaiah 53 tradition and deliberately reflecting the dynamic of the sufferings/glories pattern. The descending clauses, in two couplets (parallelism) and unusual liturgical language, preserve traces of the hymnic nature of the traditional sources.

4.2.3. 1 Peter 2:21-25. This passage stands out from its context by a different linguistic usage, terminology and style. Derived from Isaiah 53, this hymnic piece is based primarily on the feature of parallelism. The features that indicate the independence of this unit also give the unit the character of a traditional deposit (a preformed unit) and, more particularly, a hymn. The pericope includes the ethical* example of Christ as the archetypal righteous sufferer and the dominant theme of Christ's suffering as atonement.

4.2.4. 1 Peter 3:18-22. The fullest statement of the christology of the epistle lies in 1 Peter 3:18-22, five short verses that have been the focus of numerous articles and books. The passage is a self-contained unit of one sentence that fits into the context with coherence but is not defined by the context. 1 Peter 3:18-22 opens with a primitive creedal statement, moves into a hymn fragment that frames 1 Peter 3:18c-22 and expands in a sort of midrash (1 Pet 3:20-21) developed on Enoch/Noah traditions. The passage's theme of salvation and judgment* includes strong eschatological* overtones.

Whereas the pericope of 1 Peter 2:21-25 emphasized the obedience* of the Suffering Servant of Isaiah 53, the pericope at 1 Peter 3:18-22 moves immediately from the suffering of Christ to his vindication, exaltation* and triumphant rulership in the present, which assures the future. The progression of thought in 1 Peter 3:18-22 is produced by a long series of qualifying statements or dependent clauses, each one specifying the preceding statement. Then, 1 Peter 3:22 returns to the resurrection* inference of 1 Peter 3:18 in a resolution in which Christ has become the "Cosmocrat" and "judge of all history" (Martin 1978, 267).

Clear signs that creedal and hymnic material are present in 1 Peter 3:18, 22 include the preference for participles, the intentional antithesis with parallel clauses, the *men/de* construction and the assonance created by anaphora and epiphora. Also, the rhyming participles of 1 Peter 3:18b are both hapax legomena in the epistle. The features of antithetical parallelism are clearly related to the well-established hymn in 1 Timothy 3:16. The elevated language and content, which recall the basic facts of *Heilsgeschichte,* is a further indication of a poetic and hymnic character.

4.3. Suffering and Glory. The hymnic material of 1 Peter introduces the primary focus on the death and resurrection of Jesus Christ (*see* Death of Christ), which is presented as constituting a unity that reveals God's plan. The unity of death/resurrection is presented throughout 1 Peter in the scheme of "sufferings" and "glories" (1 Pet 1:11). Isaiah 53, referred to explicitly in 1 Peter 2:21-25, is the controlling source behind this scheme. Appearing sixteen times as a pattern in 1 Peter, this scheme declares that in God's plan righteous suffering is followed by vindication and exaltation, or "glories." The scheme, introduced in 1 Peter 1:10-12, is understood by the author(s) of 1 Peter to be the core of the prophets'* message and is the definitive statement of the hermeneutical* method of the document. The sufferings/glories pattern is derived from the humiliation/vindication theme of the Servant Songs of deutero-Isaiah (especially Is 53) and a closely related contrast of "rejected"/"chosen" (Ps 118 as quoted in 1 Pet 2:4-8). Preserved in the lyrical style and hymnic form of the traditional materials, the scheme has been used to address the dilemma of the righteous sufferer. In 1 Peter, Christ himself is presented as the model of righteous suffering and as the forerunner and archetype of one who has been "lifted up" (1 Pet 5:6) in vindication and exaltation.

The christology of the five major pericopae of 1 Peter, 1:3-12, 18-21; 2:4-8, 21-25; and 3:18-22, all of a poetic character, forms the conceptual unity of the document. It provides the foundation for the central motif of 1 Peter—righteous suffering and resulting glory. This christology controls the soteriological assurances and both reveals and responds to the sociological realities of the recipient community. These pericopae function as the rationale, the assurance, the requirement of the community of faith and as a theodicy that both assures vindication and justifies God's action or inaction. The genius of 1 Peter is expressed in a compositional strategy that directs extensive redaction of the christological and other formal materials. The hallmark of the composition of 1 Peter is the careful weaving of many types of source materials into a tapestry of reassurance that is developed through the use of eschatological perspectives along the lines of promise/fulfillment themes (now/then topoi and the pattern of sufferings/glories).   S. C. Pearson

5. Revelation.

The book of Revelation is richly embedded with liturgical elements (e.g., the *Ter Sanctus,* "Amen," "Hallelujah," doxology and benedictions; *see* Liturgical Elements) and hymnic materials (e.g., Rev 4:8, 9-11; 5:9-10, 12-14; 7:9-12; 11:15-18; 14:3; 15:3-4; 19:1-4, 6-8). These hymns are mainly praises directed to God (e.g., Rev 4:8, 11; 7:11-12; 11:15-17; 15:3-4; 19:1-4, 6-8) or to Christ (e.g., Rev 5:9-10; 14:3). Most of these hymns are placed in heavenly worship scenes (see Rev 4, 5, 7, 11, 15, 19); nevertheless, they are probably derived from songs sung in early Christian worship (Smith, 25-27). In particular, hymns that make constant allusion to OT motifs such as the *Ter Sanctus* ("three times holy") in Revelation 4:8 (cf. Is 6:3); the Song of Moses in Revelation 15:3-4 (cf. Ex 15:1-18); and the Hallelujah chorus in Revelation 19:6 (cf. the enthronement, Ps 96-99) are probably of Jewish Christian origin and betray the influence of the synagogue on Greek-speaking believers in the Diaspora (MacDonald, 112).

It must be noted that the writer's constant reference to hymns is not done arbitrarily. R. Deichgräber (45) observes that these hymns are evenly scattered in each of the vision* sections, so that each section has at least one hymn. He suggests, therefore, that hymns are used as a connecting thread to link the visions with one another. It is a literary style peculiar to the writer. But beyond the literary aspect, we should note that all these hymns are by nature songs of praises directed to God (as the Creator, Rev 4:11; the almighty Lord* who judges the world, Rev 11:17-18; the holy and righteous God, Rev 15:3-4; and the victorious King, Rev 19:1-6) and to Christ (as the Lamb* who was slain for the ransom of all nations, Rev 5:9-14; cf. Rev 14:3).

In view of the readers' predicament under imperial persecution, the writer's inclusion of these praise hymns into his vision narratives serves not only to present an exalted view of God and Christ in Christian worship but more specifically to provide a coherent message of comfort to the readers. God, who is the Creator of the universe, is still in sovereign control despite the hardships they are experiencing. He will triumph and execute judgment on evil powers. Christ, who is their Redeemer, has already made them a kingdom to God and will reign on earth eventually (Rev 5:10; see Thompson, 49-50; Carnegie, 254-56). The hymns in Revelation are skillfully interwoven into various visions to present messages of hope* and comfort to the readers according to their specific needs at that time. And poetic language usually contributes to a text a more effective impact to the readers (see Nida et al.). In the case of Revelation, the writer's use of hymnic materials, placed in a heavenly worship setting, uttered by large multitudes (namely the four living creatures, the twenty-four elders, the followers of the Lamb and/or a host of angelic beings), has indeed helped to convey his message more dynamically and to accomplish his goal even more effectively.

6. Post-Apostolic Writings.

6.1. Odes of Solomon. At least one Christian "hymnody" was composed in the post-apostolic era under consideration: the *Odes of Solomon,* dated in the mid or late second century. This work, generally acknowledged to be a product of a Syriac poet, contains songs of praise directed toward God and Christ with a sentimental tone. The wide variations in length and requirement for soloists or antiphonal choirs suggest that the *Odes of Solomon* may have served various functions, as anthem book, hymnal, psalter and even oratorio (Adey, 29). The author describes Christian worship as the sacrifice of praise offered by the righteous (*Odes* 8.1-2) and often speaks of the fruits presented to the Lord, which is the sacrifice of praise (echoing Heb 13:15). A close examination of the entire document reveals its incomplete (if sometimes faulty) presentations of christology and other doctrinal beliefs (e.g., the silence about sin and judgment; hence *Odes* is sometimes regarded as having a gnostic flavor). Yet its value of providing later Christians a window into the place of hymns and their thematic emphasis in early Christian communities is not to be overlooked (Old 1992, 68-75). According to the writer, songs of praise, when expressed with love, are essential in Christian worship:

My art and my service are in his hymns,

Because his love has nourished my heart,
And his fruits he poured unto my lips.
For my love is the Lord;
Hence I will sing unto him.
For I am strengthened by his praises,
And I have faith in him.
I will open my mouth,
And his spirit will speak through me
The glory of the Lord and his beauty. (*Odes* 16.2-5)

6.2. Ignatius. The earliest Father to mention hymns or songs in his writings is Ignatius,* the bishop of Antioch. On his journey to Rome before his martyrdom* (for dates, *see* Ignatius of Antioch), his letters to the Ephesians and Romans include several direct allusions to hymns of praise. In *Ephesians* 4 Ignatius exhorts the readers to live in unity so that Jesus Christ is sung and that they may sing to God the Father through Jesus Christ with one voice (*see* Worship). Here Ignatius stresses the importance of Christian unity. Hymnic praises to God or to Christ are meaningful only when they are sung by Christians who are united in heart and in voice. In *Ephesians* 13 the importance of hymnic praise in corporate worship is also made plain: "Take heed, then, often to come together to give thanks to God, and show forth his praise." In his letter to the Romans (Ign. *Rom.* 2) Ignatius beseeches his readers to sing praise to God upon his martyrdom, for he sees his death as the will of God and thus God is to be praised at its fulfillment. Ignatius's words to these churches reflect the place and functions of hymns in the Antiochean community under his supervision.

A more lengthy piece of Christ-hymn has also been attested in Ignatius, *Ephesians* 19, due to its elevated and poetic literary style, generally known as the "Song of the Star" (Martin 1997, 11). As a preface to the song three mysteries are being mentioned: the virginity of Mary;* her giving birth; and the death of the Lord. The song commences with the appearance of a star, which is depicted as above all stars and having the power to destroy the reign of all wicked astral powers. Ignatius's inclusion of this hymnic fragment in his letter is to be expected in the light of the popular worship of Fate and astral powers in the pagan world and the danger of false teachers intruding into the Ephesian community at that time (Ign. *Eph.* 16, 17). The necessity of reminding the readers about the essence of Christian faith* is urgent. Christ the incarnate one, as the supreme Star, is triumphant over all wicked astral powers that have kept many under bondage. This message, expressed in hymnic language, serves a polemic function in its context, just as in 1 Peter the hymns function also pastorally to refute the idea that alien powers are still triumphant.

6.3. Pliny. At about the same time as Ignatius, Pliny, the governor of Pontus and Bithynia, reports that some former Christians who have abandoned their faith are now worshiping the emperor's statue (*see* Emperor) and testifies to several key features of early Christian worship: on a fixed day they met before dawn to sing a hymn antiphonally to Christ as to a god (*carmenque Christo quasi deo dicere secum invicem;* Pliny *Ep.* 10.96). Although there is no mention of the content of the hymn, it is most likely a hymn of praise or thanksgiving, since it is directed to Christ on the day when his resurrection is commemorated (i.e., Sunday; cf. Justin Martyr *Apol. I* 67). And since it is mentioned before other matters (the making of an oath, the pledges and the meal), it indicates that Christians customarily begin their worship with hymns of praise sung antiphonally (i.e., in turn) by the congregation. Thus we see the prominent order of hymn singing in corporate worship (1 Cor 14:26) and the way they are sung (Eph 5:19) developed into the second century.

7. Conclusions.

The preceding survey provides a composite picture of the place, content and functions of hymns used in early Christian worship at different regions outside the Pauline communities. Hymn singing is an important element in Christian worship, being a spiritualized form of sacrifice replacing animal sacrifices of temple service (1 Pet 2:1-10; Heb 13:15). It is the opening element in a worship service (1 Pet 1:3-8; Pliny *Ep.* 10:96), and its ongoing practice is often encouraged and promoted whenever singing is neglected (Jas 5:13). The content of these hymns is mainly descriptive praise (in Westermann's term) directed toward God or Christ and blended with motifs derived from the OT (see Heb 1:3; Acts 4:24-26; Rev 4:8; 15:3-4; 19:6; later possible gnostic sources, *Odes of Solomon*). Devotional or self-reflecting hymns are not detected. Finally, hymns are commonly used or referred to by writers as an effective literary means to convey their messages to their readers whether for epistolary (Heb 1:3), exhortatory (Jas 5:13; Rev 4:11; 5:9-11, Ign. *Eph.* 4, 13) or polemic purposes (Acts 4:24-26; 16:25; 1 Pet 3:18-22; Ign. *Eph.* 19).   J. L. Wu

See also LITURGICAL ELEMENTS; 1 PETER; WORSHIP AND LITURGY.

BIBLIOGRAPHY. L. Adey, *Hymns and the Christian "Myth"* (Vancouver: University of British Columbia, 1986); D. E. Aune, "Excursus: Hymns in Revelation" in *Revelation* (WBC; Dallas: Word, 1997) 1:313-16; J. L. Bailey and L. D. Vander Broek, *Literary Forms in the New Testament* (Louisville: John Knox/Westminster, 1992); F. W. Beare, *The First Epistle of Peter* (Oxford: Blackwell, 1958); E. Best, *1 Peter* (NCB; Grand Rapids: Eerdmans, 1971); D. A. Black, "Heb. 1:1-4: a Study in Discourse Analysis," *WTJ* 49 (1987) 175-94; M.-E. Boismard, *Quatre Hymnes Baptismales dans la Première Epître de Pierre* (Paris: Cerf, 1961); P. Bradshaw, *Early Christian Worship: A Basic Introduction to Ideas and Practice* (Grand Rapids: Eerdmans, 1996); idem, *The Search for the Origins of Christian Worship* (New York: Oxford University Press, 1992); P. H. Davids, *The First Epistle of Peter* (NICNT; Grand Rapids: Eerdmans, 1990); R. Bultmann, "Bekenntnis- und Liedfragmente im 1 Petrusbrief," ConNT 11 (1947) 1-14; D. R. Carnegie, "Worthy Is the Lamb: The Hymns in Revelation" in *Christ the Lord: Studies in Christology,* ed. H. H. Rowdon (Leicester: Inter-Varsity, 1982) 243-56; D. A. Carson, ed., *Worship: Adoration and Action* (Grand Rapids: Baker, 1993); O. Cullmann, *Earliest Christian Confessions* (London: Lutterworth, 1949); W. J. Dalton, *Christ's Proclamation to the Spirits: A Study of 1 Peter 3:18-4:6* (Rome: Pontifical Biblical Institute, 1965, 1989); R. Deichgräber, *Gotteshymnus und Christushymnus in der frühen Christenheit* (Göttingen: Vandenhoeck & Ruprecht, 1967); G. Delling, "ὕμνος κτλ," *TDNT* 8:489-503; idem, *Worship in the New Testament* (London: Darton, Longman & Todd, 1962); P. Ellingworth, *Commentary on Hebrews* (NIGTC; Grand Rapids: Eerdmans, 1993); J. Frankowski, "Early Christian Hymns Recorded in the New Testament: A Reconsideration of the Question in the Light of Heb. 1:3," *BZ* 27 (1983) 183-94; W. H. Gloer, "Homologies and Hymns in the New Testament: Form, Content and Criteria for Identification," *PRS* 11 (1984) 115-32; L. Goppelt, "Der erste Petrusbrief," *Kritisch-exegetischer Kommentar über das Neuen Testament* (Göttingen: Vandenhoeck &

Ruprecht, 1987); D. Guthrie, "Aspects of Worship in the Book of Revelation" in *Worship, Theology and Ministry in the Early Church*, ed. M. J. Wilkins and T. Paige (Sheffield: JSOT, 1992) 70-83; M. Hengel, "Hymns and Christology" in *Between Jesus and Paul* (Philadelphia: Fortress, 1983) 78-96; J. Jeremias, "Zwischen Karfreitag und Osten," *ZNW* 42 (1949) 194-201; R. Karris, *A Symphony of New Testament Hymns* (Collegeville, MN: Liturgical Press, 1996); J. N. D. Kelly, *A Commentary on the Epistles of Peter and Jude* (Grand Rapids: Baker, 1969); W. L. Lane, *Hebrews* (WBC; 2 vols.; Dallas: Word, 1991); R. N. Longenecker, *The Acts of the Apostles* (EBC; Grand Rapids: Zondervan, 1981); E. Lohse, "Parenesis and Kerygma in 1 Peter" in *Perspectives on 1 Peter*, ed. C. Talbert (NABPRSS 9; Macon, GA: Mercer University Press, 1986) 37-59; R. P. Martin, *A Hymn of Christ* (Downers Grove, IL: InterVarsity Press, 1997) idem, "Hymns in the New Testament: An Evolving Pattern of Worship Responses," *Ex Auditu* 8 (1992) 33-34; idem, *James* (WBC; Waco, TX: Word, 1988); idem, *New Testament Foundations: A Guide for Christian Students* (2 vols.; Grand Rapids: Eerdmans, 1978) vol. 2; idem, "New Testament Hymns: Background and Development," *ExpT* 94 (1983) 132-36; idem, "Some Reflections on New Testament Hymns" in *Christ the Lord: Studies Presented to Donald Guthrie*, ed. H. H. Rowdon (Leicester: Inter-Varsity, 1982) 37-49; J. R. Michaels, *1 Peter* (WBC; Waco, TX: Word, 1988); P. S. Minear, "Singing and Suffering in Philippi" in *The Conversation Continues*, ed. R. Fortna and B. Gaventa (Nashville: Abingdon, 1990) 202-19; C. F. D. Moule, "The Influence of Liturgy on the Selection and Use of Christological Terms," *JTS* 10 (1959); C. M. Mountain, "The New Testament Christ-Hymn," *The Hymn* 44 (1993); idem, "The New Testament Epiphany-Hymn," *The Hymn* 45 (1994); L. Mowry, "Revelation 4-5 and Early Christian Liturgical Usage," *JBL* 71 (1952) 75-84; T. Mullins, "Ascription as a Literary Form," *NTS* 19 (1972-73) 194-205; E. Nida et al., *Style and Discourse* (New York: United Bible Societies, 1983); E. Norden, *Agnostos Theos: Untersuchungen zur Formengeschichte religiöser Rede* (Leipzig: Teubner, 1913); H. O. Old, "The Psalms of Praise in the Worship of the New Testament Church," *Int* 39 (1985) 20-33; idem, *Themes and Variations for a Christian Doxology* (Grand Rapids: Eerdmans, 1992); J. J. O'Rouke, "The Hymns of the Apocalypse," *CBQ* 30 (1968) 406-9; B. Reicke, *The Disobedient Spirits and Christian Baptism; A Study of 1 Peter 3:19 and Its Context* (Copenhagen: Munksgaard, 1946); idem, *The Epistles of James, Peter, and Jude* (AB; Garden City, NY: Doubleday, 1964); E. Richard, "The Functional Christology of 1 Peter" in *Perspectives on 1 Peter*, ed. C. Talbert (NABPRSS 9; Macon, GA: Mercer University Press, 1986) 121-39; J. T. Sanders, *The New Testament Christological Hymns* (SNTSMS 15; Cambridge: Cambridge University Press, 1971); G. Schille, *Frühchristliche Hymnen* (Berlin: Evangelische Verlagsanstalt, 1965); idem, "αἰνέω," *TDNT* 1:177; W. L. Schutter, *Hermeneutic and Composition in 1 Peter* (WUNT 2d series 30; Tübingen: J. C. B. Mohr, 1989); A. Seeberg, *Der Katechismus der Urchristenheit* (Leipzig: A. Deichert'sche Verlagsbuchhandlung Nachf. (Georg Bohme), 1903); E. G. Selwyn, *The First Epistle of St. Peter* (2d ed.; Grand Rapids: Baker, 1981); K. Shimada, "The Formulary Material in First Peter: A Study According to the Method of Traditionsgeschichte" (Ann Arbor, MI: Xerox University Microfilms, 1966); W. S. Smith, *Musical Aspects of the New Testament* (Amsterdam: Kok, 1962); D. M. Stanley, "Carmenque Christo Quasi Deo Dicere . . . ," *CBQ* 20 (1958) 173-91; G. Stanton, "Aspects of Early Christian and Jewish Worship: Pliny and the *kerygma Pertrou*" in *Worship, Theology and Ministry in the Early Church*, ed. M. J. Wilkins and T. Paige (Sheffield: Sheffield Academic Press, 1992) 84-98; E. Stauffer, *New Testament Theology* (New York: Macmillan, 1955); M. M. Thompson, "Worship in the Book of Revelation," *Ex Auditu* 8 (1992) 45-54; U. Vanni, "Liturgical Dialogue as a Literary Form in the Book of Revelation," *NTS* 37 (1991) 348-72; H. Windisch, *Die katholischen Briefe* (HNT; Tübingen: J. C. B. Mohr, 1951); K. Wengst, *Christologische Formeln und Lieder des Urchristentums* (Gütersloh: J. C. B. Mohr, 1972).

J. L. Wu and S. C. Pearson

I

IDOLATRY

Idolatry is the offering of sacrifice* to some deity other than the Creator, usually with a view to gaining temporal benefits (fertility, rain, health, good luck); by extension, a person dominated by anything in the created realm might be guilty of idolatry. Images of the god had little role in Greco-Roman cultic procedures, which used just an altar, but were defining symbols of the precinct.

1. Greco-Roman Images
2. The Jewish/Christian Outlook
3. Eating *Eidōlothyta* ("Things Sacrificed to Idols")
4. Gnosticism
5. Cult of the Emperor

1. Greco-Roman Images.

Gods were pervasive in Greco-Roman society. Birth, marriage, death, sickness and health, sowing and reaping, travel and business ventures, the customs of the home and the ideology of the empire (*see* Emperor; Roman Empire)—no aspect of life was without its divine charm secured by ritual. Scarcely a classical text lacks data for the historian of religion. One need only skim Pausanias's *Description of Greece* to get an impression of the plethora of visual reminders of the divine that greeted a tourist of the second century A.D. Industries in some places depended on trade in statuary (Acts 19:24-41), and temples suffered pillaging (Philo *Prou* 2.33-34; Rom 2:22). To escape the reach of images "you would have to exit the world" (1 Cor 5:10).

Local priests,* who opened a shrine in the morning and locked it at night, kept the statue within brightly painted and washed, rubbed it with oil, dressed its hair, decorated it with robes and garlands and carried it in parades once or twice a year. Suppliants who visited the shrine would gaze on the figure in admiration or pray* before it. Although it is hard to generalize across the multifarious cults of antiquity (*see* Religions), usually worshipers thought a deity existed on high, apart from its images in several cities, but was responsive to what people were doing with the images. Thus a statue was a concrete means of contact between the human and the divine. Devotees would call a god's statue an *agalma* (ornament) or a *theos* (god).

2. The Jewish/Christian Outlook.

The word *eidōlon* ("idol"), preferred by Jews and Christians, had the somewhat demeaning connotation "copy" or perhaps even "phantasm." To say "There is no idol [anywhere] in the world" (1 Cor 8:4) was to deny that images had any actual effect on the imagined realm of gods.

Early Christianity inherited its stance toward idols from Judaism.* The Second Commandment prohibited making a likeness and worshiping it (Ex 20:4-5). When the tempter (*see* Satan) urged Jesus to do obeisance, Jesus refused with indignation (Mt 4:10; cf. Lk 4:8). For a Christian to embrace idols is impossible: "don't be idolaters," "flee idolatry!" (1 Cor 10:7, 14; cf. 1 Jn 5:21; *Did.* 3.4). The Christian Eucharist and the feasts of the gods, God's temple* and idols, have nothing in common (1 Cor 10:21; 2 Cor 6:16). Idolatry brings excommunication (1 Cor 5:11); indeed it excludes one from God's kingdom* (1 Cor 6:9-10; 8:11; Gal 5:20-21; Rev 21:8; 22:15; *Did.* 5.1; *Barn.* 20.1).

Besides being unworthy of the one, spiritual Creator,* features of Greco-Roman idolatry that Jews and Christians found repulsive were the drinking bouts and sexual immorality in certain cults (*see* Purity). Notorious were the rites of Dionysus, the wine god whose cultic revelries used phallic symbols, and the Egyptian deities Isis, Osiris and Serapis, whose temples had a sordid reputation (Josephus *Ant.* 18.3.4 §§65-80; Ovid *Art of Love* 1.77-78; Juvenal *Sat.* 6.487-89, 526-41; 9.22-26). Literary, artistic and archeological remains attest the nexus at various times or places of idolatry and orgy. This explains the dictum of Rabbi Judah ("The Israelites knew that there was no reality to the idol and they only worshiped it in order to permit themselves public fornication"; *b. Sanh.* 63b), as well as collocations of the two things in NT texts (Rom 1:20-25; 1 Cor 5:11; 6:9; Gal 5:19-21; Eph 5:5; Col 3:5; 1 Pet 4:3).

A keynote of the Christian mission* to pagans was a call to turn "to God from idols" (1 Thess 1:9; cf. Acts 14:11-18; 17:16-31). Christians' rhetoric may have included ridicule: the gods have no divine nature (Gal 4:8-9); unlike God,* idols are or dwell in temples "made with hands" (Acts 7:41, 48; 17:24; 19:26); idols are useless (Acts 14:15), speechless (1 Cor 12:2) senseless and deaf (*Diogn.* 3.3) and nothing short of dead (implied by 1 Thess 1:9; *Did.* 6.3).

3. Eating *Eidōlothyta* ("Things Sacrificed to Idols").

3.1. Paul. Paul's Corinthian correspondence sets the scene for the issue of sacrificial food in the early church.* Some at Corinth in the early 50s refused to eat meat from animals, portions of which had been offered to pagan gods (1 Cor 8:7, 10-12). Others felt at liberty (*see* Freedom), by virtue of the impotence of idols, to party with unconverted friends in temples (1 Cor 8:10), where all would be served such meat (1 Cor 8:1, 4). Archaeology has uncovered dining rooms in or adjacent to sacred precincts that might be hired by adherents for private entertainment—only mansions could accommodate more than about nine persons at table. The church at Corinth wrote Paul for guidance (1 Cor 8:1; cf. 7:1).

His answer was threefold. (1) Love requires us voluntarily to suspend freedom at times, lest an imperfectly educated Christian be drawn to sin against conscience (1 Cor 8:1-3, 9-13; 9; 10:28-29a, 32-33). (2) Yet those with robust consciences have a valid point: idols do not spoil God's good gifts, which may be enjoyed without scruple, subject to the exception above (1 Cor 8:4-6, 8; 10:19, 23, 25-27, 29b-30). (3) Participation in an idolatrous festival, however, the purpose of which is to honor a pagan deity—by laying its statue on a couch at table, for example—is incompatible with the Christian Eucharist. There is this much reality to idols: they are tools of demons (1 Cor 10:1-22; cf. Rev 9:20).

3.2. Other Christian Leaders. Paul's answer is more nuanced than either the earlier decree of the Jerusalem council or John's later prophecy, both of which had other contexts. The apostolic letter (A.D. 49) was addressed to churches where Jews and Gentiles* formed mixed congregations (esp. Antioch*). It required Gentiles in such churches to avoid sacrificial meat altogether, so as not to offend Jewish-Christian sensitivities (Acts 15:20, 29; 21:25; *see* Jewish Christianity). Although Paul participated in the consultation (Acts 15:2, 12) and helped publicize its judgment* (Acts 16:4), he breathes not a word of it in 1 Corinthians, presumably because the abstainers at Corinth are former idolaters and not Jews, so other principles govern ethics.

According to John, those who eat what has been offered to idols face judgment (Rev 2:14, 20). This presupposes the sort of situation 1 Corinthians 10:1-22 warns against. About A.D. 95, Nicolaitans at Pergamum and Thyatira (maybe other places in western Asia Minor too) were openly practicing orgiastic rites. Blanket prohibition of eating meat offered to idols became characteristic of the catholic church in the second century (*Did.* 6.3; Justin *Dial. Tryph.* 34, 35; Irenaeus *Haer.* 1.6.3; 24.5; 28.2).

4. Gnosticism.

Gnostic* syncretism harbored idolatrous elements. According to one tradition the Samaritan Simon Magus, who claimed divinity (Acts 8:9-11), was honored by a statue in the river Tiber at Rome during the reign of Claudius (Justin Martyr *Apol. I* 26). Simon's followers down to the early fourth century allegedly prostrated themselves before images of him and of his consort, Helen, and worshiped them with incense, sacrifices and libations (Irenaeus *Haer.* 1.23.4; Eusebius *Hist. Eccl.* 2.13.6), and at least one other gnostic sect behaved similarly (Irenaeus *Haer.* 1.25.6), if patristic testimony may be trusted. A Jewish-Christian-pagan theosophy at Colossae seems to have served angels* (Col 2:18). If the schismatics who left the community that later read 1 John shared such practices, it would give point to the elder's parting shot: "Keep yourselves from idols" (1 Jn 5:21).

5. Cult of the Emperor.

One apocalyptic* expectation looked for antichrist* to set himself up as an object of worship* (2 Thess 2:4; Rev 13:4, 8, 12, 15; 14:9, 11; 16:2; 19:20; 20:4). John saw this partially fulfilled in the imperial cult (*see* Emperor), as enforced in proconsular Asia in the last decade of the first century, with its priests, counterfeit miracles, ventriloquistic use of statues and economic or capital punishment of Christians who would not offer incense or decorate their doors for civic processions (Rev 13:11-17).

See also Emperor, Emperor Cult; Food, Food Laws, Table Fellowship; Religions, Greco-Roman; Worship and Liturgy.

Bibliography. N. Bookidis, "The Sanctuary of Demeter and Kore in Corinth: Excavations 1970-72," *AJA* 77 (1973) 206-7; J. C. Brunt, "Rejected, Ignored, or Misunderstood? The Fate of Paul's Approach to the Problem of Food Offered to Idols in Early Christianity," *NTS* 31 (1985) 113-24; W. Burkert, *Greek Religion: Archaic and Classical* (Oxford: Blackwell, 1985); K. Donfried, "The Cults of Thessalonica and the Thessalonian Correspondence," *NTS* 31 (1985) 336-41; D. W. J. Gill, "Behind the Classical Facade: Local Religions of the Roman Empire" in *One God, One Lord in a World of Religious Pluralism*, ed. A. E. Clark and B. W. Winter (Cambridge: Tyndale House, 1991) 72-87; H.-J. Klauck, *Herrenmahl und hellenistischer Kult: eine religionsgeschichtliche Untersuchung zum ersten Korintherbrief* (NTAbh n.s. 15; Münster: Aschendorff, 1982); R. MacMullen, *Paganism in the Roman Empire* (New Haven, CT: Yale University Press, 1981); S. R. F. Price, *Rituals and Power: The Roman Imperial Cult in Asia Minor* (Cambridge: Cambridge University Press, 1984); S. J. Scherrer, "Signs and Wonders in the Imperial Cult: New Look at a Roman Religious Institution in the Light of Rev 13:13-15," *JBL* 103 (1984) 599-610; E. E. Urbach, "The Rabbinical Laws of Idolatry in the Second and Third Centuries in the Light of Archaeological and Historical Facts," *IEJ* 9 (1959) 149-65, 229-45; W. L. Willis, *Idol Meat in Corinth: The Pauline Argument in 1 Corinthians 8 and 10* (SBLDS 68; Chico, CA: Scholars Press, 1985).   P. A. Rainbow

IGNATIUS OF ANTIOCH

Ignatius, bishop of Antioch in Syria, was sent early in the second century as a prisoner to Rome* to be thrown to wild animals in the arena. While en route he wrote seven letters which offer a glimpse of post-apostolic Christi-

anity in Asia Minor and are virtually the only source of information about their remarkable author.

1. Authenticity
2. Date
3. Form and Style
4. Sources and Cultural Context
5. Setting and Occasion
6. Central Concerns

1. Authenticity.

The letters exist in three basic forms. The "long" recension is an expanded fourth-century version of the seven original letters to which six spurious letters have been added (some of these came to be associated with the "middle" recension as well); the "short" is a Syriac abridgment of the letters to the *Ephesians, Romans* and *Polycarp*; the "middle" (known to Eusebius) preserves the original form of the letters.

During the Renaissance and Reformation periods both the "long" and "middle" recensions became known in both Greek and Latin, although it was not until 1646 that the Greek text of the "middle" recension was published. This multiplexity of forms, together with the admixture of varying numbers of later spurious letters, created considerable confusion and debate about the authenticity of the letters. Progress in resolving the question was not helped by the fact that the discussion came to be heavily influenced by dogmatic concerns (generally Catholic vs. Protestant) extraneous to the issue.

A consensus favoring the "middle" recension eventually prevailed following the publication of Pearson's *Vindiciae Ignatianae* (1672), but the publication of the "short" recension in 1845 re-opened the question. Not until the independent work of T. Zahn (1873) and J. B. Lightfoot (1885) was general recognition of the authenticity of the seven letters comprising the "middle" recension attained, a situation which recent challenges (Joly; also Weijenborg, Rius-Camps) have not altered (Schoedel 1980, 1993, 345-46; Munier, 379-80).

2. Date.

There has long been a virtually unanimous consensus that Ignatius was martyred during the time of Trajan (A.D. 98-117). The Eusebian date of c. 107-8 is accepted by some, while many place it somewhere in the second half of Trajan's reign, c. 110-17. Attempts to fix the year more precisely have not been persuasive; if anything, the tendency is to enlarge the possible time frame in the direction of Hadrian's reign (A.D. 117-38; Schoedel 1993, 347-48; Munier, 380). The original collection of the letters was apparently compiled by Polycarp not long after Ignatius's death (cf. Pol. *Phil.* 13.2).

3. Form and Style.

Drawing on both Pauline and secular models of letters,* Ignatius utilizes them in distinctive ways (e.g., thanksgiving statements are notably absent), especially with respect to the greetings at the beginning and end and internal transitional devices (Schoedel 1985, 7). His dense, colorful (perhaps even florid) style reflects a popular type of rhetoric* known as "Asianism."

4. Sources and Cultural Context.

4.1. Old Testament. Ignatius makes little use of the OT, citing it only three times (Ign. *Eph.* 5.3; Ign. *Magn.* 12; Ign. *Trall.* 8.2). Allusions are no more numerous (cf. Ign. *Eph.* 15.1; Ign. *Magn.* 10.3; 13.1).

4.2. Early Christian Traditions and Literature. Ignatius is deeply indebted to early Christian tradition, which has pervasively shaped his vocabulary and thought. His heavy use of Pauline tradition (the way Paul responded to rejection likely offered a model for Ignatius) was shaped both by a more "mystical" tradition (represented also in the Gospel of John) and by a concern for order and discipline* (cf. Matthew).

Knowledge of only a limited range of written documents can be demonstrated conclusively. He probably worked with the Gospel of Matthew (e.g., Ign. *Smyrn.* 1.1; so Massaux, Köhler, contra Koester [all in Massaux, 118-21]); there is no evidence of Mark, and minimal (and not conclusive) evidence of Luke (Ign. *Smyrn.* 3.2). Use of John (cf. Ign. *Rom.* 7.2-3, Ign. *Phld.* 7.1) is unlikely (Paulsen 1978, 36-37). He has read 1 Corinthians and probably Ephesians. There are numerous echoes of other Pauline documents (his collection may have included 1 Corinthians, Ephesians, Romans, Galatians, Philippians, Colossians and 1 Thessalonians), but it is difficult to determine whether they reflect the use of traditional elements or literary dependence. The parallel between 1 John and *Letter to the Ephesians* 14.2 is notable, as are parallels between Ignatius and *1 Clement, 2 Clem-*

ent, and the *Shepherd of Hermas.* But the parallels are insufficient to demonstrate knowledge of written documents. In short, Ignatius may have known a wide range of early Christian literature, but the use of only a few can be demonstrated with any certainty.

4.3. Hellenistic Culture. The character of Ignatius's debt to Hellenistic culture is much debated. Gnostic* affinities have been alleged on the basis of mythological elements in such passages as Ignatius's *Letter to the Ephesians* 19 (Schlier; *see* Worship) or the themes of "oneness" and "silence" (Bartsch; cf. Paulsen 1978). But recent investigations have indicated that these elements are also found in the wider popular culture (Schoedel 1985, 15-17). Taken together with observations about the form and style of his letters (see 3 above), this suggests that Ignatius mirrors more the popular culture of his day than esoteric or gnostic influences.

5. Setting and Occasion.

The letters were written in extraordinarily stressful and difficult circumstances. After his arrest (it is not known why and in what circumstances he was arrested) in Syria,* which left the church in Antioch* leaderless and vulnerable, Ignatius was sent to Rome in the custody of ten soldiers (the "leopards" of Ign. *Rom.* 5.1) to be executed. As he traveled, he met with Christians in communities along the way, including Philadelphia. At Smyrna he was enthusiastically received by Polycarp, the local bishop, as well as delegations from Tralles, Magnesia and Ephesus (who had been informed in advance of Ignatius's route). Ignatius responded to this show of support (perhaps deliberately orchestrated; Schoedel 1985, 12) by sending a letter to each of the three churches, and he also sent one ahead to the church in Rome, alerting them to his impending arrival there and attempting to forestall any interference with his plans. At Troas, Ignatius's received the news that "peace" had been restored to the church at Antioch (cf. Ign. *Phld.* 10.1; Ign. *Smyrn.* 11.2; Ign. *Pol.* 7.1), about which he apparently had been quite worried, and he sent letters back to the two churches he had visited, Philadelphia and Smyrna, and to Polycarp. At Philippi, where he was warmly welcomed by the church (cf. Pol. *Phil.* 1.1), he disappeared from view; presumably he was taken on to Rome and thrown to the lions in the Coliseum. While it is not absolutely certain that he died a martyr's death (later accounts of his martyrdom* being historically worthless), there is no reason to think otherwise.

6. Central Concerns.
It appears that three concerns were uppermost in Ignatius's mind at this time: the struggle against false teachers within the churches, the unity and organization of the churches and his impending death.

6.1. False Teachers. To Ignatius, the false teachers within posed a greater threat than the pagan society without (*see* Adversaries). "Heresy" (cf. Ign. *Eph.* 6.2; Ign. *Trall.* 6.1), whether that of the "Judaizers" (*see* Jewish Christianity), whose teaching tended to diminish the importance and centrality of Christ,* or of the "Docetists,"* who tended to deny the reality of Jesus' humanity, threatened to split the church and thereby destroy the God-given unity which for Ignatius was one of the distinguishing marks of the true faith.* In response Ignatius strongly affirmed the divinity of Jesus and the reality of Christ's incarnation, suffering* and resurrection,* to such an extent that he grounded the meaning and reality of his own circumstances on the reality of what Jesus experienced (Ign. *Trall.* 10; Ign. *Smyrn.* 4.2).

6.2. Unity and Organization. In opposing the false teachers Ignatius also stressed the importance of the bishop in preserving the unity of the church (*see* Church Order; Early Catholicism). He does this on two levels. First, while Ignatius's ideal church may have a threefold ministry* that includes deacons and presbyters, it is the bishop who is most critical: where the bishop is, the church is, and no activity or service that takes place without either the bishop's presence or permission has any validity (Ign. *Smyrn.* 8.1-2; Ign. *Magn.* 7; Ign. *Trall.* 3.1). Thus those schismatics who gather separately cut themselves off from the true church (Ign. *Eph.* 5.3; Ign. *Smyrn.* 6.2). Second, the central role of the bishop organizationally has a theological rationale (in contrast to his near-contemporary Clement of Rome, who works with a concept of apostolic succession; *see* Worship): the bishop is in some sense God's representative to the congregation, and just as Christians are united with God spiritually in heaven, so it is their duty to be in communion or harmony with their bishop on earth (Ign. *Eph.* 6.1; Ign. *Magn.* 3; Ign. *Trall.*

2.2, 3.1; Ign. *Phld.* 2.1; Ign. *Smyrn.* 8.1). Conversely, one's attitude toward the bishop reflects one's attitude toward God, and thus one's behavior relative to the bishop becomes critically important.

The sociological implications of these first two concerns (community protection through definition of belief and legitimation of authority*) have been highlighted by Maier.

6.3. Impending Death and View of Martyrdom. Ignatius anticipates his impending death with a vivid, almost macabre, eagerness (Ign. *Rom.* 4.2; 5.3; 7.2). At least three elements shaped his complex attitude toward martyrdom* and contributed to the zeal with which he pursued it.

One factor is his sincere desire to imitate the suffering of Jesus and thereby become a true disciple; indeed, he goes so far as to claim that only since his arrest is he "beginning" to be a disciple (Ign. *Rom.* 5.3; 6.2). His positive attitude toward persecution finds parallels in both Paul and Matthew.

Some of his language, particularly in his *Letter to the Romans*, may reflect an understandable fear of failure (Ign. *Rom.* 7.2), an effort to bolster his courage so as not to fail in the course to which he had publicly committed himself. In addition, generally the only basis for releasing a Christian condemned to death was apostasy*; even if the Roman church had won his release for good reasons (something he feared they would attempt to do [Ign. *Rom.* 1.1—2.1; 4.1]), rumors that he had apostatized likely would have arisen, and he no doubt wished to avoid such a situation.

Finally there is the situation in Antioch, about which Ignatius is evidently quite worried. Schoedel notes (1) Ignatius's marked tendency towards self-effacement, and (2) that he relates to the churches to which he writes not on the basis of his status as bishop, but as a captive about to be martyred and persuasively suggests that the Antiochene church was on the verge of splitting (Schoedel 1985, 10-11, 13-14). If such a split were to occur it would mean that Ignatius was a failure as a bishop, because he would not have maintained the godly way of the congregation that had been entrusted to him. He may, therefore, have seen in his imminent martyrdom a means by which to reclaim the deteriorating situation in Antioch and/or to redeem his reputation as a bishop and a Christian.

See also ADVERSARIES; ANTIOCH; APOSTOLIC FA-

THERS; CHURCH ORDER, GOVERNMENT; MARTYR-
DOM; SYRIA, SYRIAN CHRISTIANITY.

BIBLIOGRAPHY. **Text and Translation:** J. B.
Lightfoot and J. R. Harmer, *The Apostolic Fathers:
Greek Texts and English Translations of Their Writ-
ings,* ed. and rev. M. W. Holmes (2d ed.; Grand
Rapids: Baker, 1992). **Commentaries and/or
Editions:** P.-Th. Camelot, *Ignace d'Antioche: Let-
tres. Lettres et Martyre de Polycarpe de Smyrne* (4th
ed.; SC 10; Paris: Cerf, 1969); R. M. Grant,
Ignatius of Antioch (ANF 4; Camden, NJ: Nelson,
1966); J. B. Lightfoot, *The Apostolic Fathers, Part
II: S. Ignatius. S. Polycarp* (2d ed.; 3 vols.; Lon-
don: Macmillan, 1889); H. Paulsen, *Die Briefe des
Ignatius von Antiochia und der Brief des Polykarp
von Smyrna* (Zweite, neubearbeitete Auflage der
Auslegung von Walter Bauer; Tübingen: J. C. B.
Mohr, 1985); W. R. Schoedel, *Ignatius of Antioch:
A Commentary on the Letters of Ignatius of Antioch*
(Herm; Philadelphia: Fortress, 1985). **Studies:**
C. P. H. Bammel, "Ignatian Problems," *JTS* 33
(1982) 62-97; H.-W. Bartsch, *Gnostisches Gut und
Gemeindetradition bei Ignatius von Antiochen*
(Gütersloh: Bertelsman, 1940); W. Bauer, *Ortho-
doxy and Heresy in Earliest Christianity,* ed. R. A.
Kraft and G. Krodel (Philadelphia: Fortress,
1971); H. von Campenhausen, *Ecclesiastical
Authority and Spiritual Power in the Church of the
First Three Centuries* (Stanford, CA: Stanford Uni-
versity Press, 1969); V. Corwin, *St. Ignatius and
Christianity in Antioch* (New Haven: Yale Univer-
sity Press, 1960); R. Joly, *Le dossier d'Ignace d'An-
tioche* (Brussels: Éditions de l'université de
Bruxelles, 1979); H. O. Maier, *The Social Setting
of the Ministry as Reflected in the Writings of Hermas,
Clement and Ignatius* (Waterloo, Ont.: Wilfrid
Laurier University Press, 1991); E. Massaux, *The
Influence of the Gospel of Saint Matthew on Christian
Literature before Saint Irenaeus, Book 1: The First
Ecclesiastical Writers,* ed. A. J. Bellinzoni (NGS
5/1; Macon, GA: Mercer University Press,
1990); C. Munier, "Où en est la question d'Ig-
nace d'Antioche? Bilan d'un siècle de recher-
ches 1870-1988," *ANRW* 2.27.1 (1993) 359-484;
H. Paulsen, *Studien zur Theologie des Ignatius von
Antiochien* (FKD 29; Göttingen: Vandenhoeck &
Ruprecht, 1978); J. Rius-Camps, *The Four
Authentic Letters of Ignatius, The Martyr* (Christianismos 2; Rome: Pontificium Institutum Orientalium Studiorum, 1979); H. Schlier,
*Religionsgeschichtliche Untersuchungen zu den Igna-
tiusbriefen* (BZNW 8; Giessen: Töpelmann,
1929); W. R. Schoedel, "Are the Letters of Ignatius of Antioch Authentic?" *RSR* 6 (1980) 196-
201; idem, "Polycarp of Smyrna and Ignatius of
Antioch," *ANRW* 2.27.1 (1993) 272-358; R. Weijenborg, *Les lettres d'Ignace d'Antioche* (Leiden: E.
J. Brill, 1969); T. Zahn, *Ignatius von Antiochien*
(Gotha: Perthes, 1873).   M. W. Holmes

ILLNESS. *See* HEALING, ILLNESS.

IMITATION

Many NT scholars are reluctant to accord imitation a prominent place in early Christian ethical* instruction, especially imitation of Christ*
or God.* However, recognizing the role this
pedagogical tool played in the Greco-Roman
environment justifies a reconsideration of this
important means of exhortation in the later
writings of the NT and other early Christian
literature.

  1. Imitation in Hellenistic Moral Instruction
  2. Imitation of Human Examples
  3. Imitation of Christ
  4. Imitation of God

1. Imitation in Hellenistic Moral Instruction.
The use of models for imitation was an important element of classical and Hellenistic moral
instruction. Examples served as demonstrations
of the appropriate manner of life. Calls for
imitation, both explicit and implicit, of personal example are among the most common
means of ethical exhortation across a wide variety of writings throughout the Hellenistic period (e.g., Socrates, Alexander the Great).
Additionally imitation of or assimilation to God
was central to Middle Platonism's understanding of the purpose of human existence.
Thus, as one might expect, imitation of God was
a crucial element in Philo's* ethics. Less philosophically inclined Judaism* also used example
as a motivation for proper behavior. The stories
of Eleazar and the seven sons who were tortured
and executed by Antiochus IV explicitly draws
on this motif (2 Macc 6:24—7:42; 4 Macc 5—
18). Likewise the *Testaments of the Twelve Patriarchs* regularly use this theme. Assuming the
effectiveness of personal example, Josephus*
(Josephus *Ant.* 1.11.3) asserts that Lot was hospitable (*see* Hospitality) to the angels* who destroyed Sodom because he had learned to
imitate the goodness of Abraham.* Since the
use of imitation was so widespread, its presence
in NT texts should be no surprise.

2. Imitation of Human Examples.

Late NT writings draw on many human examples. Hebrews* often utilizes this means of exhortation. Its readers are called to imitate those who through faithfulness "are inheriting the promises" (Heb 6:12). These inheritors include Abraham (Heb 6:13-15) and others among the faithful in Israel's* history, as the implicit invitation to imitate the faithful in Hebrews 11 shows. Citing both ancient and current examples was a common practice in contemporary hortatory writings. Readers are explicitly summoned to imitate their current leaders in Hebrews 13:7, and those "inheriting the promises" (Heb 6:12) may also include those who maintain proper beliefs (Heb 6:1-12) in the present ("inheriting" is in the present tense). Like Hebrews, James 5:10-11 cites figures from the past (the Hebrew prophets and Job) as examples to be imitated. The specific focus of this imitation is perseverance (see Endurance) in suffering.*

B. Fiore argues that the literary form of the Pastoral Epistles itself is a call for imitation. This form (see Letters), paralleled in the Socratic epistles, harks back to the group's founder and earliest associates as patterns for the readers' lives and teaching. 2 Timothy 1:13-14 explicitly gives Paul's teaching as the pattern for correct doctrine. 1 Timothy 1:11 implies the same ideal. 2 Timothy 3:10-17 gives both the teaching and life of Paul as examples for imitation, and in 2 Timothy 4:1-8, Timothy is exhorted to fulfill his ministry,* with Paul's acceptance of martyrdom* as his model. Titus 3:3-8 apparently gives both Paul and Titus as examples of the impact conversion is to have on Christians' lives. In Titus 2:6-8, Titus is told that he should be an example for other young men to follow. Finally, 2 Tim 1:5-6 gives members of Timothy's own family as examples to encourage him to perform his ministry vigorously. Using family members as models was also a common hortatory technique of this period.

Outside the canon,* *1 Clement* 17—19 exhorts its readers to be imitators of several OT characters (including Elijah, Ezekiel, Abraham, Job, Moses* and David). Clement (see Clement of Rome) uses their example to urge his readers to peace* and devotion to God, even asserting that their deeds, presumably through their examples, have "made us better" (*1 Clem.* 19.1-2).

As was common in Hellenistic moral exhortation, several late NT writings also provide examples to be avoided. Among others, Jude 5-7, 2 Peter 2:4, 6 and 1 John 3:12 all cite characters from the Bible whose conduct is to be avoided.

3. Imitation of Christ.

A call to imitate Christ presents difficulties for some modern interpreters. W. Michaelis narrowly circumscribes the idea by asserting that the primary meaning of imitation is obedience.* And W. Schrage delimits imitation by noting the unique soteriological significance of Jesus (e.g., Schrage, 273, 324-25). But ancient authors do not shy away from the idea of imitating Christ. 1 Peter 2:21 encourages slaves* to endure suffering at the hands of their masters by presenting Christ's sufferings as an example to imitate. Many interpreters see this verse as a foundation for all the following exhortations to wives, husbands and the whole Christian community as the household* of God. This aspect of Christ's example is especially appropriate for a church* enduring persecution. Similarly Timothy is exhorted to follow Christ's example by living up to his confession* of Christ (1 Tim 6:12-14). M. Reddish asserts that one of the central points of Revelation (see Revelation, Book of) is to present Jesus as the prototypical martyr whose example is to be imitated. This example of Jesus' endurance helps John prevent his readers from capitulating in persecution.

More broadly Ephesians 5:25 and 1 John 3:16-18 exhort their readers to imitate the love* of Christ: Ephesians exhorts husbands to imitate Christ in their love for their wives, and 1 John gives Christ's willingness to sacrifice himself as the model for relations within the Christian community (see John, Letters of).

Ignatius* reports that at Philadelphia his inspired preaching urged his hearers to become "imitators of Jesus Christ" (Ign. *Phld.* 7.2). In context this seems to be a general exhortation about how to conduct one's life, especially perhaps with regard to the unity of the church. More narrowly, Polycarp* (Pol. *Phil.* 8.2) urges his readers to imitate Jesus by enduring suffering. *1 Clement* 15—16 does not explicitly call for imitation of Christ, but the description of Christ as humble immediately preceding a list of those figures from the Bible whose humility* the readers are to imitate makes it clear that Christ is the foremost example. Clement encourages these readers to achieve unity by following these examples of humility.

Calls to imitate Christ in these writings usually have one of two foci: enduring suffering or living a life of love, especially (though not exclusively) in the context of the church, where such an attitude promotes unity.

4. Imitation of God.

The most problematic sort of imitation for modern interpreters is imitation of God (see, e.g., Lindars). But again late NT writings find God an appropriate model for imitation. Ephesians 5:1 straightforwardly calls its readers to be "imitators of God." In context the focus is on being loving, especially perhaps as that is manifested in forgiving fellow Christians. Christ serves as yet another model of love to emulate in Ephesians 5:2. Just as 1 Peter* supported specific ethical injunctions with the example of Christ, it also intimates that imitation of God is a foundation of Christian ethics more broadly by quoting Leviticus 11:44, "You be holy because I am holy" (1 Pet 1:16-17; *see* Holy). 3 John 11 gives the general exhortation to imitate the good and not the evil. This exhortation may involve imitation of God because the result of imitating the good is that one will be "of God."

Ignatius describes the Ephesians as "imitators of God" because they had sent him help while he was in prison (Ign. *Eph.* 1.1). Later he exhorts this same church to strive to be imitators of God by putting the good of the other above one's own good. The *Epistle to Diognetus** (10.3-6) asserts that by loving God and one's neighbor, believers become imitators of God. Anticipating some reaction, the author says one should not be amazed at this because it is possible for humans to be imitators of God if they so desire.

It is clear, then, that Christians of the first and second centuries found it appropriate to urge imitation not only of Christ but also of God. Imitation of God arises most often in contexts that exhort believers to live lives of love. This love is to be expressed in helping those in need or by putting the good of others, both within and outside the Christian community, before one's own good. Still, 1 Peter 1:16-17 and perhaps 3 John 11 make imitation of God a broad foundation for the conduct of the believer's life.

See also ETHICS; OBEDIENCE.

BIBLIOGRAPHY. H. D. Betz, *Nachfolge und Nachahmung Jesu Christi im Neuen Testament* (Tübingen: J. C. B. Mohr, 1967); J. H. Elliott, "Backward and Forward 'In His Steps': Following Jesus from Rome to Raymond and Beyond. The Tradition, Redaction and Reception of 1 Peter 2:18-25" in *Discipleship in the New Testament,* ed. F. F. Segovia (Philadelphia: Fortress, 1985) 184-204; idem, *A Home for the Homeless: A Sociological Exegesis of 1 Peter, Its Situation and Strategy* (Philadelphia: Fortress, 1981); B. Fiore, *The Function of Personal Example in the Socratic and Pastoral Epistles* (AnBib 105; Rome: Biblical Institute Press, 1986); L. E. Frizzell, "Education by Example: A Motif in Joseph and Maccabee Literature of the Second Temple Period" in *Of Scholars and Savants and their Texts; Studies in Philosophy and Religious Thought: Essays in Honor of Arthur Hyman,* ed. R. Link-Salinger (New York: Peter Lang, 1989); V. P. Furnish, *The Love Command in the New Testament* (Nashville: Abingdon, 1972); B. Gerhardsson, "Agape and Imitation of Christ" in *Jesus, the Gospels and the Church: Essays in Honor of William R. Farmer,* ed. E. P. Sanders (Macon, GA: Mercer University Press, 1987); B. Lindars, "Imitation of God and Imitation of Christ," *Theology* 76 (1973) 394-402; R. N. Longenecker, ed., *Patterns of Discipleship in the New Testament* (Grand Rapids: Eerdmans, 1996); A. J. Malherbe, *Moral Exhortation, A Greco-Roman Sourcebook* (LEC; Philadelphia: Westminster, 1986); W. Michaelis, "μιμέομαι κτλ," *TDNT* 4:659-74; H. P. Nasuti, "Identity, Identification and Imitation: The Narrative Hermeneutics of Biblical Law," *Journal of Law and Religion* 4 (1986) 9-23; M. Reddish, "Martyr Christology in the Apocalypse," *JSNT* 33 (1988) 85-95; R. Schnackenberg, *The Moral Teaching of the New Testament* (London: Burns & Oates, 1965); W. Schrage, *The Ethics of the New Testament* (Philadelphia: Fortress, 1988); R. A. Wild, " 'Be Imitators of God': Discipleship in the Letter to the Ephesians" in *Discipleship in the New Testament,* ed. F. F. Segovia (Philadelphia: Fortress, 1985) 127-43.　　　　　　　　J. L. Sumney

IMMORTALITY. *See* MORTALITY AND IMMORTALITY.

IMPERIAL CULT. *See* EMPEROR, EMPEROR CULT; RELIGIONS, GRECO-ROMAN.

IMPURITY. *See* PURITY AND IMPURITY.

INCARNATION. See CHRISTOLOGY; PREEXISTENCE.

INTERCESSION. See PRAYER.

INTERTEXTUALITY IN EARLY CHRISTIAN LITERATURE

This article focuses on the manner in which OT stories and narrative were a significant influence in shaping the literature of the later NT and early second-century writings. While OT quotations in many NT writings are apparent, numerous studies have argued for formative influence of the OT upon the NT also at the conceptual and structural level (*see DJG*, OT in the Gospels; see also studies by Evans and Sanders, Evans and Stegner, and Swartley, esp. 10-21 for history of scholarship on this topic). While these contributions focus on the canonical Gospels, similar evidence obtains for the Pauline writings (e.g., Hays). Both the OT and the stories of the Jesus tradition,* in oral and written Gospel* form, had significant influence also upon the writings considered in this volume. Occasionally the Pauline influence is prominent also.

    1. Types of Use
    2. Acts
    3. Hebrews
    4. James
    5. 1 Peter
    6. 2 Peter and Jude
    7. 1, 2 and 3 John
    8. Revelation
    9. Apostolic Fathers
    10. Concluding Comment

1. Types of Use.

Because of the varied nature of later NT literature, it is impossible to speak of one or even several patterns that characterize OT textual influence in these writings. To illustrate: the epistles of John (*see* John, Letters of) contain no OT quotations and utilize the OT only in recalling the Cain and Abel story for moral example, whereas Revelation* is saturated with OT allusions to Ezekiel, Daniel et al. (*see* Old Testament in Revelation). Similarly, two documents with unknown dates but likely from early- to mid-second century, the *Didache** and the *Epistle of Barnabas,** represent vastly different uses of and influences from the OT: the former has only several allusions to specific texts, while the latter

constructs a sustained argument effecting a mutation in foundational theology (*see* Old Testament in Apostolic Fathers).

As a whole, however, the later NT literature and the early patristic literature up to the mid-second century show seven ways in which earlier Scripture exerted influence: (1) quotations of earlier texts, often to claim fulfillment of prophecy;* (2) allusions, echoes or very brief quotations of older narrative to thus extend the older "truth-world" in a "just-as" pattern; (3) recital of Israel's* past or the story of Jesus to convince listeners of some truth; (4) citing persons or events for moral (or immoral) example; (5) typological argument to argue for fulfillment of hope;* (6) allegorical reflection on older texts to emphasize new theological realities; and (7) creative new use of older images, stock expressions and sequences of thought in a new ordering and composition. All these means of employing the older story contribute to intertextuality. Comment on the writings is oriented to these means by which older literature fashions younger narratives.

2. Acts.

In Acts* quotations abound, to effect chiefly a fulfillment pattern of type 1 above. Most remarkable theologically are the pouring out of the Spirit (*see* Holy Spirit) in the "last days" (Acts 2:17-21 par. Joel 2:28-32 [in LXX and MT 3:1-5]); raising up a prophet, Jesus, like Moses* (3:22-23 par. Deut 18:15-16, 19); the Messiah Jesus "led as a sheep to the slaughter" (Acts 8:32-33 par. Is 53:7-8); and the "raising of the fallen booth of David," so that the rest (the Gentiles*) can call on the name of the Lord* (Acts 15:16-18 par. Amos 9:11-12). The important texts of making God's* people a light to the nations (Acts 13:47 par. Is 49:6) and explaining the unbelief of God's own (Jewish) people (Acts 28:26-27 par. Is 6:9-10) are also fulfillment texts with some element of the "just-as" pattern of type 2. For the list of quotations and mode of citation, virtually all from the Septuagint, see J. A. Fitzmyer, who remarks that the Christian owning of the OT is largely due to Luke's legacy (Fitzmyer, 538; *see* Old Testament in Acts).

The extended kerygmatic* recital (type 3) of Israel's salvation* story—from Abraham* to Solomon in Acts 7 and from election* to David in Acts 13:16-23—is an important means of using earlier narrative to establish identity and call to decision. This recital is extended through the life, death (*see* Death of Christ) and resurrection* of Jesus in Acts 13:26-41 (cf. Acts 10:34-43) and includes a catena of OT quotations (Ps 2:7; Is 55:3; Ps 16:10 MT [15:10 LXX]; Hab 1:5). Paul's speech in front of the Areopagus is of type 2 with numerous allusions (1 Kings 8:27; Ps 50:12; Is 42:5; Deut 32:8; and the Adam story in Gen 3 in the phrase "from one ancestor" [Acts 13:26]; *see* Paul and Paulinisms). In the narrative as a whole, David as a royal person and the book of Isaiah figure prominently from the older story, providing promissory hope and warrant for Jesus as messianic fulfillment. David is of special significance since he connects prophecy with the messianic figure (Jervell, 84-85). The Elijah-Elisha stories are echoed in Acts 1:1-9 and Acts 8:9-40 and perhaps more broadly (see Brodie). The Moses story as prototype of God's revelation,* both in "raising up a prophet like unto Moses" (Acts 3:22) and the people's response of unbelief (esp. Acts 7), also plays a major role (see Soards).

3. Hebrews.

Even more than Acts, Hebrews* is laced with OT quotations, as well as numerous thought allusions to the older scriptural story (*see* Old Testament in Hebrews). Hebrews 1 contains eight such connections in a space of fourteen verses (Ps 110:1; 2:7; 2 Sam 7:14; Deut 32:43; Ps 104:4 MT [103:4 LXX]; 45:6-7; 102:25-27 MT [101:25-27 LXX]; 110:1 MT [109:1 LXX]). These uses combine a "just-as" with a fulfillment motif (see esp. Heb 2:6-9 par. Ps 8:4-6). The most notable fulfillment use is Hebrews 8:8-12, citing Jeremiah 31:31-34 to make the case that the new covenant replaces the Mosaic covenant (see Heb 8:13, "he [Jesus] has made the first one obsolete").

In addition to this extravagant use of OT texts to prove and provide warrant for arguments, Hebrews contains a sustained typological* argument to show the superiority of Jesus (type 5, above): first, to the OT prophets* (Heb 1:1-3), the angels* (Heb 1:5—2:18) and to Moses* (Heb 3:1-6); second, to the levitical priesthood* (Heb 4:14—7:28); and third, to sacrifices* as offered in Israel heretofore (Heb 8:1—10:39). Here the accent falls on fulfillment, so much so that the older pattern of piety is abolished (Heb 10:3-10).

One distinctive mark of the older story on Hebrews is the writer's use of the Melchizedek* narrative from Genesis 14, both in Hebrews 5 and 7. Here we have not a fulfillment typology, but an analogical typology wherein Jesus is likened to Melchizedek: to his mysterious origin and destiny and to his royal peace- and righteousness-making character. All these attributes are superior not only in quality, compared to the old levitical order, but in quantity—they are eternal, for Jesus is priest like Melchizedek forever (Heb 5:6; 7:17, 21; citing Ps 110:4 MT [109:4 LXX]).

The second distinctive imprint of the older story is the recital in Hebrews 11 with its litany of OT heroes of faith, including lesser well-known figures—Abel, Enoch, Isaac, Jacob, Joseph, Rahab, Barak, Samson, Jephthah, Samuel—as well as the famous ones— Noah, Abraham, Moses and David (*see* Ancestors). Abraham and Moses receive pride of space in the narration but all, including women, constitute the "great cloud of witnesses" that now functions to inspire faith in Jesus, the "pioneer and perfecter of faith" (Heb 12:2).

Third, the writer presents us with a metaphorical transformation of Zion in Hebrews 12:22, an extension of the "city that has foundations, whose architect and builder is God" (Heb 11:10; *see* Jerusalem, Zion). Here, the holy city and Zion imagery of Israel's Scripture, in Psalms and Isaiah especially, reaches a new level of meaning, loosed from its geospace and transmuted into a new transspace reality where its durability is unquestioned, for it "cannot be shaken" (Heb 11:28).

4. James.

James* has several quotations and numerous allusions to and variations on OT Scripture. Most notable are the citation of the command to "love your neighbor" in James 2:8 (Lev 19:18); citation of the commandments* not to commit adultery and not to kill in James 2:11 (Ex 20:14, 13 par. Deut 5:18, 17); "Abraham believed God . . . for righteousness" in James 2:23 (Gen 15:6); and "God resists the proud, but gives grace to the humble" in James 4:6 (Prov 3:34). The sense of Isaiah 40:6-7 is evident in James 1:10-11, as is Isaiah 5:9 in James 5:4. More distinctive is James's use (type 4) in which Abraham (Jas 2:21-24), Rahab (Jas 2:25), Job (Jas 5:11) and Elijah (Jas 5:17) are employed as moral examples of righteous action (*see* Righteousness), perseverance (*see* Endurance) and earnest prayer* respectively (but the reader needs to know these OT stories to make the points persuasive [Davids, 122]). This use of OT personages and the stories by which they are remembered signals a developing tendency in the literature of this later canonical portion (*see* Old Testament in General Epistles).

5. 1 Peter.

1 Peter* contains at least nineteen quotations, mostly in a "just-as" mode but with an added paraenetic punch: 1 Peter 1:16, an injunction to be holy (Lev 19:2); 1 Peter 3:6, that women* should behave toward husbands as Sarah obeyed Abraham, calling him lord (Gen 18:12); 1 Peter 3:10-12, keep your tongue from evil and seek peace* (Ps 34:12-16 MT [Ps 33:13-17 LXX]); 1 Peter 5:5, God resists the proud* but gives grace* to the humble (Prov 3:34 LXX); and the exhortation in 1 Peter 5:7 to cast all anxiety on God (Ps 55:22 MT [54:23 LXX]).

In a catena of quotations and massing up several sets of images, the author establishes a christological* and ecclesial foundation for the believers' identity that empowers ethical resistance (*see* Ethics) to the pressures of the larger society and sustains in the midst of suffering* (1 Pet 2:4-24). This series of images—a "living stone" (1 Pet 2:4); a stone* in Zion, a chief cornerstone, elect and precious (1 Pet 2:6) but rejected by the builders; and a stone that makes those who do not believe stumble (1 Pet 2:7-8)—build upon the joining of Isaiah 28:16; Isaiah 8:14 and Psalm 118:22 (Snodgrass, Oss). The images of elect race, royal priesthood,* and holy nation echo the stories of exodus and new exodus (Ex 19:5-6; 23:22; Is 43:20-21). The reality of a new people is clinched in 1 Peter 2:10 by dramatic flashback to Hosea 1:6, 9 and Hosea 2:1, 23, where God's faithless people are forgiven and reclaimed as a marriage partner. This creative use of Scripture testifies to deep intratextuality whereby the story of God's people's past infuses the identity-forming text for the readers of this epistle. Drawing on various OT texts (Ps. 33 LXX; Is 8; 53; Gen 18; Lev 19:2; 20:7, 26; Prov 3:34), he authorizes his instruction to shape moral conduct (Green).

But there is another important layer of story influence here. 1 Peter appeals directly to the example of Jesus (1 Pet 2:21-25). Without citing the passion narrative as such, Peter draws on the oral story of Jesus' suffering and death (1 Pet 2:21-24; cf. 1 Pet 4:1-6) and resurrection-exaltation victory (1 Pet 3:21c-22) to clinch his sustained paraenetic exhortations to nonresistance to evil (*see* Death of Christ; Exaltation; Resurrection). Referring to Noah (1 Pet 3:20) as a moral example also adds to the persuasion, showing God's provision to care for the faithful even while exercising divine wrath.* Hence the older and newer stories of God's people blend together as basis for ethical paraenesis.

6. 2 Peter and Jude.

While in these two brief epistles there are several quotations of OT Scripture (2 Pet 2:22 par. Prov 26:11; 3:8 par. Ps 90:4; 3:13 par. Is 65:17; Jude 9 par. Zech 3:2) and possibly one of a Gospel text (2 Pet par. Mt 17:5), as well as one from an extracanonical writing (Jude 14-15 par. *1 Enoch* 1:9; 5:4; 60:8), the more distinctive feature of these writings is an appeal to OT people or events that evoke episodes of divine salvation in the context of certain and devastating judgment* and provide either moral or immoral example (type 4).

While 2 Peter* accentuates the certainty of God's judgment upon perpetrators of destructive teaching and those who follow licentious ways (2 Pet 2), it also points to a moral example in two of the three citations: Noah saved from the devastating flood (Gen 6—8) and Lot saved from the destruction of Sodom and Gomorrah (Gen 19:12-29). Only in the first citation—God not sparing the rebellious angels (Gen 6:1-6)—no saving act occurs.

Jude* uses the same list (Jude 6-7) but does not mention those saved, rather only the terrible, pounding judgment. This is trumped by a second sequence of OT people who acted like "irrational animals" (Jude 10): Cain, a murderer; Balaam, erring for the sake of gain; and Korah, in rebellion. Unmitigated judgment is heaped upon all who behave similarly to these immoral and ungodly types. Here the OT story is used in a way opposite from that of Hebrews 11. Rather than portray the "hall of faith," Jude highlights the "hall of fate," of those who rebelled against God and fell under God's judgment. In these writings, stories of the past are used as warrant for harsh messages of judgment, especially upon apostasy* (*see* Old Testament in General Epistles).

7. 1, 2 and 3 John.

Of all the writings in this canonical grouping, 1, 2 and 3 John are least marked by influence of OT story. Here is mentioned only Cain as an immoral example—a murderer—while Abel is a model of righteousness (1 Jn 3:12). Whether one can deduce from this feature the nature of the audience to which these epistles are addressed—i.e., Gentiles*—is dubious. Important truths from the Jesus story punctuate these letters, however: the blood of Jesus, God's Son, cleanses us from sin* (1 Jn 1:7); Jesus Christ is our advocate with the Father and the expiation for our sins and for the sins of the whole world (1 Jn 2:1-2); and Jesus Christ has indeed come in the flesh—to deny this is antichrist* (1 Jn 4:2-3; 2 Jn 7). Here cardinal beliefs of the Jesus story, received either orally or through written Gospel, form the motivating goal of the exhortation: so the readers might believe correctly in Jesus as Son* of God and continue to know that they have eternal life (1 Jn 5:13; *see* Old Testament in General Epistles).

8. Revelation.

If the vote for common authorship in the Johannine corpus depends upon influence of the OT upon the narrative, then the Gospel and Revelation* are together and the epistles stem from another hand or group. Of the three, Revelation is by far the most thoroughly dependent upon the OT in its one-liner quotations (eleven listed by Bratcher), many stream-of-consciousness allusions, its symbolic codes, apocalyptic* genre and possibly even its structure (some have seen in it the reverse order of the exodus plagues as well as the days of creation* in Genesis). Lacking any direct appeal to OT Scripture, the narrative is replete with thunderous echoes of the OT, in collage fashion, so that it consummates the OT in its prophetic-apocalyptic essence (*see* Apocalyptic).

E. Schüssler Fiorenza suggests that the writer "adapts or borrows whole Old Testament sequences as patterns for his original compositions" (135). W. J. Harrington begins his commentary on short individual sections by printing six to nine OT texts, occasionally NT ones as well, to show the store of imagery from which the new composition arises (e.g., for Rev 12:1-4: Gen 3:14-16; Song 6:10; Is 66:7-8; Dan 7:7; 8:10 [164-65]). S. Moyise has shown John's extensive use of Daniel and Ezekiel but also

corrects misuses of the connections: G. Beale's virtually exclusive appeal to Daniel 7 for composition of Revelation 1:4-20 and Revelation 4—5 and M. Goulder's correlation of Revelation with the Ezekiel readings in the Jewish year (45-84) are notable. H. Ulfgard assesses various proposals that connect Revelation to the Feast of Tabernacles and concludes that not the feast itself, but what it eschatologically* represents provides an illuminating context for the grand vision of Revelation 7:9-17 (148-53).

The NT gospel story surely figures prominently also in understanding Revelation, both in its testimony to the suffering of the Messiah and in its promised exaltation of the Messiah. In this respect Revelation is the grand finale to both aspects of the Jesus story: the Lamb* that was slain (Rev 5:9-14) and the vindication of the Lamb through the triumph of God (Rev 19-22; *see* Old Testament in Revelation).

9. Apostolic Fathers.

Here are briefly considered *1 Clement,* the *Letters of Ignatius,* the *Didache,* the *Epistle of Barnabas,* and the *Shepherd of Hermas* (*see* Old Testament in Apostolic Fathers).

9.1. 1 Clement. An anonymous letter ascribed in ancient tradition to Clement,* the third bishop of Rome, and written likely at the end of the first century, *1 Clement* brims with OT personages, short citations, recitals of faithful people and their deeds, all within the purpose to emulate for moral action. All the first four types of OT uses noted above are present. Though Scripture is cited with a fulfillment motif, it is not for messianic proof but to authorize moral instruction (*1 Clem.* 3.1). Similarly, the heroes of faith, ancient and near contemporary (Peter and Paul), are cited to encourage faithfulness (*1 Clem.* 4—12). Rahab is given eight verses (*1 Clem.* 12.1-8) and later Judith and Esther are emulated for risking their lives for the faithful (*1 Clem.* 55.4-6).

Specific reference to Jesus Christ in his faithful life, unto death, is intertwined with citations from Isaiah 53 (*1 Clem.* 16). Elijah, Elisha, Ezekiel, Job, Moses and David are called forth, with brief key texts, to present models of godly response (*1 Clem.* 17—18). Later Isaac, Jacob, the priests and the Levites are listed, leading up to a christological reflection that in turn results in the call to "be energetic in doing 'every good deed' " (*1 Clem.* 31—33). Then, in language reminiscent of Hebrews 12:1-2, Jesus Christ is set forth to culminate these appeals (*1 Clem.* 36.1). Then follows a catena of OT quotations to magnify Christ (Pss 104:4; 2:7-8; 110:1). In a quite different manner from Revelation, *1 Clement* is formed by OT Scripture stories and appeals to the lives and teachings of Jesus Christ and the apostles.*

9.2. Letters of Ignatius. The *Letters of Ignatius,* written in the early second century by Ignatius* enroute to Rome for martyrdom and to churches that echo Revelation 2—3 and Paul's own mission, contain few references to the OT, but many to Gospel and Pauline texts. Paul is the real saint and martyr* (Ign. *Eph.* 12.2) and Ignatius's goal is to be worthy to die in union with the passion of Jesus Christ (Ign. *Magn.* 5). Ignatius takes refuge in the gospel as the flesh of Jesus, in the apostles as the presbytery of the church and in the prophets, who in anticipating Christ's coming were in unity with him. He warns against those preaching Judaism* but regards a circumcised person preaching Christ better than a Gentile* (Ign. *Phld.* 5—6.1). The clincher comes in a simulated argument between those claiming the documents and those claiming Christ as authority.* Ignatius's famous retort is, "To me Jesus Christ is the original documents" (Ign. *Phld.* 8.2). Ignatius's letters contain only occasionally the second type use of OT texts, with brief quotes to warrant his moral instruction (Ign. *Eph.* 5.3 par. Prov 3:34; Ign. *Magn.* 12d par. Prov 18:17 LXX; Ign. *Trall.* 8.2 par. Is 52:5). But his letters breathe Gospel and epistle language with frequent textual citations and this with type 3 use.

9.3. Didache. Likely written very early in the second century (likely before *Barnabas* and *Hermas*), this catechetical manual cites frequently from the Gospels (though rarely from John) but only occasionally from the Pauline epistles and the OT. The double love command, the Sermon on the Mount (with Luke's par.) including the Lord's Prayer (*Did.* 8.2), the Gospel Apocalypse (Mt 24) and the Great Commission (Mt. 28:19; *Did.* 7.3) shape the ethical exhortation. But the *Didache* often adds to these borrowed words some explicit instruction, as in the case of baptism.* The eucharistic words only slightly recall the NT texts, presenting a distinctive version of its own (*Did.* 9-10). The predominant type of use is 2, but the textual axis is mostly between the Gospel works of Jesus and the *Didache* writer(s).

9.4. Epistle of Barnabas. The *Epistle of Barnabas** demonstrates prominently the sixth use, as well as the third and fifth uses of numerous OT texts, laws* and stories. Many OT texts are cited briefly or at length and are interspersed with NT citations: in *Barnabas* 6 alone K. Lake lists twenty-two OT references and six from the NT. Barnabas cites the older story repeatedly to show it was intended spiritually for our (Christians') sake and was misunderstood by Jews in literally observing the laws and grasping the stories. Most famous are Barnabas's claim that the covenant* is not "both theirs and ours. It is ours" (*Barn.* 4.9; K. Lake trans.) and equating Abraham's 318 circumcised men (*Barn.* 8.8), via gemmatria play, with Jesus Christ and the cross* (of the 18, 10 = I; 8 = H and IH are the first two letters for Jesus in Greek and T (Tau), the cross, = 300).

The allegorical use of the OT, similar to that in Qumran* (Barnard), is not limited to christological* points but extends to moral instruction as well. The levitical food* prohibitions (Lev 11:13-16) mean that you shall not be like or associate with those people who manifest the traits of these animals (lazy, dirty swine or idle birds). In short, through spiritualized interpretation the whole OT is *for us* (including creation, sabbath, and temple in *Barn.* 15-16). The treatise concludes with ethical paraenesis on the "Two Ways," either borrowing from the *Didache* or a source common to both.

9.5. Shepherd of Hermas. Written in Rome sometime between A.D. 120 and 148 and in an apocalyptic genre that combines the visionary style of Ezekiel, overtones of Song of Solomon and Hosea in love and fidelity themes, and parables (some akin to Jesus'), this lengthy writing addresses itself primarily to the ethical challenge of maintaining a virtuous life and struggling against the insidious temptations of lust, wealth and anxieties that ruin simplicity of mind and heart (*see* Hermas, Shepherd of).

Echoes of Scripture, both Old and New, are sporadically frequent, but there is relatively little explicit use of biblical texts. The few exceptions include *Mandates* 4.4, which addresses whether one should remarry (1 Cor 7:38-40) after a spouse dies (*see* remarriage). In *Hermas* remarriage is not sin, but greater honor accrues to one who does not. The parable of the rock and the door (*Herm. Sim.* 9.12.3-8) employs imagery from John 3:5 and 14:6, with a prelude echoing Proverbs 8:17-20. The prominent biblical issue of how the rich stand before God (esp. Lk and Jas 4:13—5:6) is taken up numerous times (*Herm. Vis.* 3.6.5-7; 3.9.2-9; *Herm. Man.* 10.1.4-6) and genially resolved by the remarkable parable of the sterile elm and fruitful vine (*Herm. Sim.* 2). The rich man, poor in intercession and confession toward God because of his business, must lean upon (give to) the poor, who are rich in this regard, and the poor man must lean upon the rich (the elm), so the vine produces abundant fruit. In this way the rich are of service to God, and both together bear much fruit.

None of the seven patterns of employing Scripture neatly fit for *Hermas,* but elements of both 2 and 7 are clearly present in his creative use of biblical images and phrases, and through visionary genre these are used for the sake of exhorting unto holiness of life, to "glorify God's great and glorious name," which is a recurring phrase (*Herm. Vis.* 3.4.3; 4.1.3; et al. par. Ps 86:9, 12; 99:3). The Shepherd certainly echoes John 10 and is the visionary one who comes to remain with Hermas (*Herm. Sim.* 10.3) to assure him of his purity and life with God.

10. Concluding Comment.
Both the later NT canonical literature and these five early second-century writings exhibit a remarkable degree of intertextuality, utilizing various parts of the canon.* Moreover, the range of types of use is fully present in the canonical group and almost fully present in the early second-century group. The latter group lacks type 1 used as messianic fulfillment proofs, as in Acts and Hebrews. L. Goppelt (35) observes this point as well as other differences between *1 Clement* (representative of other second-century writings) and canonical Hebrews and 1 Peter: Hebrews and 1 Clement make use of the OT in exegetical argument, while 1 Peter uses it homiletically. In terms of content, the OT provides the writer of Hebrews with salvation-historical or typological correspondences, *1 Clement* with authoritative moral analogies and 1 Peter with wisdom* sayings and images. Its hermeneutical approach places 1 Peter, like Hebrews, in the middle of the "apostolic" witness, since it announces that the eschaton is present in the dialectic of the now-but-not-yet. This cannot be said for *1 Clement* or for the other documents of the apostolic fathers.

See also OLD TESTAMENT IN: ACTS, HEBREWS, GENERAL EPISTLES, REVELATION, APOSTOLIC FATHERS.

BIBLIOGRAPHY. L. W. Barnard, "The Epistle of Barnabas and the Dead Sea Scrolls: Some Observations," *SJT* 13 (1960) 45-59; R. G. Bratcher, ed., *Old Testament Quotations in the New Testament* (New York: United Bible Societies, 1967); T. L. Brodie, "Luke-Acts as an Imitation and Emulation of the Elijah-Elisha Narative" in *New Visions on Luke and Acts,* ed. E. Richard (Collegeville, MN: Liturgical Press, 1990) 78-85; G. B. Caird, *The Revelation of St John the Divine* (London: Adam & Charles Black, 1966); J. T. Carroll, "The Uses of Scripture in Acts," in *SBLSP* (1990) 512-28; P. H. Davids, "Tradition and Citation in the Epistle of James" in *Scripture, Tradition, and Interpretation,* ed. W. W. Gasque and W. S. LaSor (Grand Rapids: Eerdmans, 1978) 113-26; C. H. Dodd, *According to the Scriptures: The Substructure of New Testament Theology* (London: Nisbet, 1952); W. J. Dumbrell, *The End and the Beginning: Revelation 21-22 and the Old Testament* (Australia: Lancer, 1985); C. A. Evans and J. A. Sanders, *Luke and Scripture: The Function of Sacred Scripture in Luke-Acts* (Minneapolis: Augsburg Fortress, 1993); C. A. Evans and W. R. Stegner, eds., *The Gospels and the Scriptures of Israel* (JSNTSup 114; Sheffield: Academic Press, 1994); E. S. Fiorenza, *The Book of Revelation: Justice and Judgment* (Philadelphia: Fortress, 1985); J. A. Fitzmyer, "The Use of the Old Testament in Luke-Acts," in *SBLSP* (1992) 524-38; S. Freyne, "Reading Hebrews and Revelation Intertextually" in Intertextuality in *Biblical Writings* (Festschrift B. van Iersel) ed., S. Draisma (Kampen: J. H. Kok, 1989) 83-94; L. Goppelt, *A Commentary on 1 Peter* (Grand Rapids: Eerdmans, 1993); G. L. Green, "The Use of the Old Testament for Christian Ethics in 1 Peter," *TynB* 41 (1990) 276-89; W. J. Harrington, *Understanding the Apocalypse* (Washington, DC & Cleveland: Corpus, 1969); R. B. Hays, *Echoes of Scripture in the Letters of Paul* (New Haven, CT: Yale University Press, 1989); J. Jervell, "Die Mitte der Schrift: zum lukanische Verständnis des Alten Testaments," in *Einheit und Vielfalt Neutestamentlicher Theologie,* ed. U. Luz, and H. Weber (Festschrift E. Schweizer) (Göttingen: Vandenhoeck & Ruprecht, 1983); S. J. Kistemaker, *The Psalm Citations in the Epistle to the Hebrews* (Amsterdam: van Soest, 1961); S. Moyise, *The Old Testament in the Book of Revelation* (JSNTSup 115; Sheffield: Academic Press, 1995); A. P. O'Hagan, "Early Christian Exegesis Exemplified from the Epistle of Barnabas," *AusBR* 11 (1963) 33-40; C. Osiek, *Rich and Poor in the Shepherd of Hermas: An Exegetical-Social Investigation* (CBQMS 15; Washington, DC: The Catholic Biblical Association of America, 1983); D. A. Oss, "The Interpretation of the 'Stone' Passages by Peter and Paul: A Comparative Study," *JETS* 32 (1989) 181-200; F. Schröger, *Der Verfasser des Hebräerbriefes als Schriftausleger* (Regensburg, Germany: F. Pustet, 1968); K. R. Snodgrass, "I Peter II.1-10: Its Formation and Literary Affinities," *NTS* 24 (1977-78) 97-106; M. L. Soards, *The Speeches of Acts* (Louisville: Westminster/John Knox, 1994); W. M. Swartley, *Israel's Scripture Traditions and the Synoptic Gospels: Story Shaping Story* (Peabody, MA: Hendrickson, 1994); H. Ulfgard, *Feast and Future: Revelation 7:9-17 and the Feast of Tabernacles* (ConBNT 22; Lund: Almqvist & Wiksell, 1989).   W. M. Swartley

ISAAC. *See* ANCESTORS.

ISRAEL, TWELVE TRIBES

At its birth the Christian church had a lively sense of continuity with the historical Israel, as is clear from canonical books that relate to both the beginning of the NT period (the Gospels and the letters of Paul; *see DJG,* Israel; *DPL,* Israel) and its end (Revelation); this was replaced by a modified self-awareness as the church developed its own separate identity.

Biblical authors in the period in view do sometimes refer to some or all of the twelve tribes of Israel (Acts 26:7; Rev 21:12), but not frequently. They tend rather to use the name *Israel* both as a way to refer to historical, ethnic Israel and as a code word for a variety of related matters.

1. Shared Outlooks
2. Acts
3. Apostolic Fathers

1. Shared Outlooks.

1.1. The Historical Israel. Either "Israel" or "the people(s) of Israel" is used as a common shorthand for referring to all Jews (Acts 4:10, 27; 5:21; 9:15; 10:36) or as a way to refer to the central OT nation (Acts 13:17, 23-24; Rev 2:14; 21:12). These references are clear, even in the case of the passages in Revelation, in spite of the interpretive uncertainty frequently brought

about by symbolic imagery there.

1.2. The Church as the New Israel. It is more difficult to interpret Revelation 7:4-8, but G. R. Beasley-Murray (139-41) argues cogently that this passage, applied here to the church* as the new Israel, was originally written as a Jewish oracle and only later applied to the community of believers. If he is correct, then this passage is an example of the Christian view that the church is the new Israel.

That such a conception of the church was current in the late NT period and beyond can be amply demonstrated. James 1:1, which refers to "the twelve tribes of the dispersion," was surely addressed to ethnic Jews who were also practicing Christians and makes it plain, as R. P. Martin argues (Martin, 8-9), that the author thought of Jews who had become Christians as the true Israel. James* was not apparently written to a mixed group of Jews and Gentiles* but to Jews alone.

First Peter,* however, though it begins similarly (1 Pet 1:1), is written to churches that have a marked Gentile membership (see 1 Pet 4:3). To quote J. Ramsey Michaels, the author of this book "is addressing certain communities of Gentile Christians as if they were Jews" (Michaels, 6). In the language used to describe Petrine believers in 1 Peter 2:9-10, the Christians addressed are a "chosen race, royal priesthood, holy nation, God's own people" (cf. the OT passages behind these words in the Septuagint translation of Exod 19:6 and Is 57:15 and especially in the "not pitied/not my people" language of Hos 2:23 and context). These verses come at the end of a passage beginning at 1 Peter 1:13 and clearly delineate the believing community (see Elliott, esp. 38-48), Jew and Gentile alike, in terms that were originally applied to Israel in their OT contexts. God,* who chose the people of Israel to be his own people, through Christ* has now chosen Christian believers to be his own people as an extension of his salvation* to the race (Steuernagel, 13-14).

1.3. Jesus, God's Agent to Save and Restore Israel. The canonical books reflect an early Christian understanding of Jesus as the consummation of God's plan, as articulated by the prophets,* to redeem and restore Israel. This appears in our literature in Acts, both as an assumption underlying the thinking of the early disciples (Acts 1:6ff.) and as an idea expressed in addresses by Peter (Acts 3:18-21; 5:31) and

Paul (Acts 13:30-33; 26:6ff.; 28:20).

It is also a theme represented in Hebrews,* which views Jesus as the fulfillment of the promises* of salvation and restoration made to Israel by God and as the perfection of what was foreshadowed in that nation's institutions and history. Israel was the object of the conditional and passing Mosaic covenant,* whereas the church is in the line of the unconditional and permanent Davidic covenant (Beavis, 25-27). Hebrews portrays Jesus as the perfect representative of heaven,* making him superior to OT religion in every respect (Omanson, 25).

This contrast between the former, Israelite order and the new arrangement under Jesus is so pervasive in Hebrews that it is difficult to select some passages that demonstrate the point without neglecting others that equally deserve attention. But Hebrews 8:7-13 is exemplary of both the theme of the necessary supercession of the old covenant by the new and the citation of OT facts and passages (here Jer 31:31-34, the longest quotation of the OT anywhere in the NT). In the extended context of describing the new covenant and its high priest* Christ, the author writes of the obsolescence of the Israelite covenant and its replacement. As foretold by Jeremiah, the day had come for God in Christ to forge a new relationship with his people that does not partake of the provisional nature of the original one (Vanhoye, 182-83). Throughout its sustained argument Hebrews makes it clear, as here, that the new covenant will not be limited to the twelve tribes of Israel but will extend to the church that replaces them.

2. Acts.

The Gospels assign much of the blame for the crucifixion of Jesus to the Jews and their leaders (*see DJG*, Death of Jesus §6.1) who lived at that time. (In Christian history this has sometimes been taken to mean that all Jews of all subsequent times are guilty of Jesus' death; that is an erroneous deduction, but it lies beyond the scope of this article to address it.) Acts,* the second volume of Luke's bipartite work, portrays this understanding as carried on by the nascent church (on the authorship of Acts and its relationship to Luke see, e.g., Johnson, 197-210). God had predicted a Messiah who would do Israel good, but when that Messiah came in Jesus, the Jews (under the name of Israel) not only turned him away but made away with him.

This understanding of the state of affairs lies behind and is assumed in several places in Acts. But it is used variously, as a whip in the excoriating speech of Stephen* (Acts 7:2-53) and evangelistically in Peter's Pentecost* sermon (Acts 2:14-36; see esp. the climax in Acts 2:36 and the outcome).

3. Apostolic Fathers.

By the time of the writers referred to as the apostolic fathers,* the consciousness of the Christian body as being in direct succession to the historical nation Israel had receded somewhat into the background. That idea never completely dies in the church, and it comes to expression several times and in various places in subsequent Christian history. But it is directly and extensively expressed in the apostolic fathers in only one book, and even that book allegorizes the Jewishness of Israel away (cf. Bernard). There are isolated passages, such as the one in *1 Clement* 29 (*1 Clem.* 29.2-3), for example, that speaks of God's part in creating and electing historical, ethnic Israel. But it is the *Epistle of Barnabas* that stresses the theme of the Christian significance of the OT. This epistle urges Christians not to accept a Jewish reading of the Hebrew Scriptures but to understand their esoteric meaning, which speaks of the church. For the anonymous author of this epistle, there is not any literal significance to be assigned to commands of the Law.* Nevertheless, beyond a small handful of questionable words and phrases, neither these writings nor other Christian and fringe Christian writings to the middle of the second century make much at all of the literal Israel and its twelve tribes.

See also CHRISTIANITY AND JUDAISM: PARTINGS OF THE WAYS; CHURCH; CHURCH AS ISRAEL, PEOPLE OF GOD.

BIBLIOGRAPHY. C. K. Barrett, *A Critical and Exegetical Commentary on the Acts of the Apostles* (2 vols.; ICC; Edinburgh: T & T Clark, 1994); G. R. Beasley-Murray, *The Book of Revelation* (NCB; Grand Rapids: Eerdmans, 1983); M. A. Beavis, "The New Covenant and Judaism," *TBT* 22 (1984) 24-30; L. W. Bernard, "The Use of Testimonies in the Early Church and in the Epistle of Barnabas" in *Studies in the Apostolic Fathers and Their Background* (New York: Schocken, 1966) 109-35; J. H. Elliott, *The Elect and the Holy: An Exegetical Examination of 1 Peter 2:4-10 and the Phrase Basileion Hierateuma* (NovTSup 12;

Leiden: E. J. Brill, 1966); L. T. Johnson, *The Writings of the New Testament: An Interpretation* (Philadelphia: Fortress, 1986); W. L. Lane, *Hebrews* (2 vols.; WBC; Dallas: Word, 1991); R. P. Martin, *James* (WBC; Waco, TX: Word, 1988); J. R. Michaels, *1 Peter* (WBC; Waco, TX: Word, 1988); R. L. Omanson, "A Superior Covenant: Hebrews 8:1—10:18," *RevExp* 82 (1985) 361-73; V. R. Steuernagel, "An Exiled Community as a Missionary Community: A Study Based on 1 Peter 2:9, 10," *ERT* 10 (1986) 8-18; A. Vanhoye, *Old Testament Priests and the New Priest According to the New Testament* (Petersham, MS: St. Bede's Publications, 1986).   A. Casurella

J

JAMES, LETTER OF

The Letter of James is among the most neglected books of the NT canon. Many believers and their (especially Protestant) faith traditions still agree with Luther's negative verdict of its usefulness for Christian formation, pointing out its lack of reference to Christ and its apparent disagreement with Paul as good reasons for its marginal status within the church. During the modern period of biblical studies, some have even viewed the book's more practical bent as inherently inferior when compared to the theological profundity of Paul's correspondence. At the same time, others have come to depend upon the book's wise solutions to everyday situations, which insist that a fully biblical religion requires more than mere confessions of orthodox faith. In this sense James offers a complementary "check and balance" to the accents of the Pauline letters, helping to form a biblical witness that commends a firm trust in the saving work of the Lord Jesus (Pauline) and a practical wisdom patterned after his life (James).

1. The Author(s) of James
2. The Audience(s) of James
3. The Literature of James
4. A Canonical Approach to James
5. The Gospel According to James
6. The Argument of James

1. The Author(s) of James.

1.1. Candidates for Authorship. The identities of a book's author and his first audience are important considerations for any interpreter interested in a wide range of historical issues. For instance, it is difficult to locate a composition in its original world, to know something of what occasioned its writing and when and how it functioned among its first readers without good ideas of who wrote it and why.

The opening verse directly claims author-ship for "James, servant of God and of Jesus Christ" (Jas 1:1). Yet the author's identity remains a contested issue of modern scholarship. Two critical issues are at stake in this continuing discussion: who is this "James" referred to in the letter's address, and is he necessarily the author of the book? The evidence that may settle these issues is historical and lacking: we have no other writing from James by which to compare its literary style and subject matter; nor do we have a reliable contemporary of the author who confirms the author's identity.

Even if one agrees that the book's superscription identifies its "real" author, there are still several Christian leaders named James to choose from, including six mentioned in the NT. Some have even added an "unknown James" to this list (Moffatt), only by sheer conjecture. Among those named by Scripture are two apostles,* making them especially attractive candidates because of the close historical connection between canonicity (*see* Canon) and apostolicity, a point embraced for a time in the West, where some thought the book was written by the apostle James, son of Alphaeus (cf. Mk 3:18; Acts 1:13). Yet memory of his apostolic ministry outside of Scripture is lacking. In any case an apostolic credential does not seem required for the author: the book's address does not appeal to an apostolic office for personal authorization but rather to the more modest relationship to God and the Lord Jesus as their "servant." Origen and Jerome even held that no apostle could have written James, which disagrees so thoroughly with Pauline thought—a point followed by Luther centuries later.

Most scholars suppose the only viable candidate remains "James the Just," the brother of Jesus (*see* Relatives of Jesus), a verdict that has modest support from ancient tradition (see Eusebius *Hist. Eccl.* 2.23.4). While he was not one of the Twelve,* the biblical portrait of James commends him as a significant leader in earliest Jewish Christianity.* Jesus even singled him out following the resurrection* (1 Cor 15:7), apparently for an important ministry (see *Gos. Heb.* 7). It is not surprising, then, that Acts* introduces James as Peter's successor in Jerusalem* (Acts 12:17; Wall 1991, "Successors"), whose pastoral leadership over the Jerusalem church became increasingly strategic, first at the Jerusalem council (Acts 15:13-21) and then during his relations with Paul (Acts 21:17-26). Paul himself named James as the first of three "pillars" of the Jewish church (Gal 2:9), whose continuing observance of circumcision and laws* of ritual purity undermined the gospel* of his Gentile mission* in Antioch* (Gal 2:11-15).

In fact the robust memories of James the Just were preserved well into the second century by the Jewish church, who viewed him the model disciple (Martin, xli-lxi). Eusebius even cites Hegesippus, a second-century Jewish believer from Jerusalem, who describes in some detail the moral and religious superiority of James (Eusebius *Hist. Eccl.* 2.23.4). Indeed, a substantial body of apocryphal* (largely gnostic*) Christian writings, written in his name by pseudepigraphers during the second and third centuries (*1* and *2 Apoc. Jas.; Ap. Jas.; Protev.* (= *Book) Jas.;* also, *Gos. Heb., Epis. Pet.*), promote an exemplary, if not legendary, James whose vital piety and ascetic lifestyle corrected a church that had become too secular and middle-class for the taste of its more conservative Jewish and gnostic constituencies (Wall and Lemcio, 250-71). Almost certainly the canonizing church envisaged this James as the James of the biblical letter's address. Only his witness to Christ and abiding authority* within earliest Christianity, singular among possible candidates, justify the canonical status accorded this controversial composition. Thus W. G. Kümmel concludes, "Without doubt James claims to be written by [the brother of Jesus], and even if the letter is not authentic, it appeals to this famous James and the weight of his person as authority for its content" (Kümmel, 412).

1.2. Authorial Style and Subject Matter. Did "this famous James" write the book in his name? A majority of modern scholars think not and favor a postapostolic date and pseudonymity,* even though there are significant allusions to James already in *1 Clement* and *Hermas* at the end of the first century (Davids, 8-9). They suppose the composition's superior Koine Greek and literary artistry, as well as the author's substantial knowledge of current Hellenistic philosophy, lie beyond the ability and provenance of this working-class Jew from Galilee (Reicke, Laws). James may have even employed a trusted and well-educated amanuensis, or secretary, a common practice then, who knew Greek well and who transcribed James's pastoral exhortations into a more suitable idiom and literary form for a wider Greek-speaking audience (Mitton) while retaining their original Semitic "flavor" (cf. Mussner).

This compromise solution is hardly necessary. One need only appeal to the mounting evidence that demonstrates a fairly active social intercourse between Hellenistic and Palestinian cultures during the late Second Temple period. Religious Jews, especially in Galilee, may well have been anti-Hellenistic during the days immediately before and after the fall of Jerusalem in A.D. 70 (*see* Judaism); however, Jew and Greek intermingled, if a little uneasily. Thus Acts describes a Jerusalem congregation that included Greek-speaking Jews and a pastor (James) who cites the Greek translation (LXX) of Scripture when instructing them (Acts 15:17-18; cf. Jas 4:6). Sharply put, James grew up in a Hellenized Jewish culture where Greek was used and perhaps learned well enough to write this book.

Others contend that the epistolary writer could not be the brother of Jesus, whose biblical portrait values aspects of the Jewish law that finally disagree with the thrust of the letter (Kümmel). This objection too has little merit. A growing number of scholars think that the Jewish-Christian theological cast and pastoral intentions of the letter mirror those same commitments of the biblical James. For example, his concerns for religious purity* (Acts 21) and for the public performance of the biblical torah (Gal 2) are central concerns of this book (Jas 1:22-27; 2:8-26); and his commitment to the poor, which Paul mentions in Galatians 2:10, also reflects an important theme of the book (Jas 1:9-11; 2:1-7; 5:1-6). Even the conciliatory James of Acts 15 seems consistent with the spirit that undergirds this letter. Likewise the traditions used by Luke to narrate the speech of James to the Jerusalem council (Acts 15:13-21) and the subsequent letter to Antioch (Acts 15:23-29) reveal a remarkable similarity in both substance and vocabulary to the letter of James (Adamson, 18-20; Oesterley). Further, the many apocalyptic* images and themes found throughout James fashion a sociology of suffering* and vindication similar to that of the Jerusalem community James pastored, according to Acts and the social world of first-century messianic Judaism. Noteworthy also are the many allusions to targumic and midrashic materials found in James, which follow his speech in Acts where James settles a crucial intramural conflict by a midrash on the biblical book of Amos (Acts 15:17-21).

The agreement between this James and the subject matter of the letter is also secured by more implicit evidence. Many suppose that dates of compositions can be calculated by images and ideas of Jesus, so that a more full-bodied or developed christology* is contained in a later composition. By this reasoning the scant references to Jesus in James (Jas 1:1; 2:1), which does not include even an apparent allusion to his atoning death (*see* Death of Christ), is more easily explicable if James was written in the middle of the first century.

Finally, however, the most important consideration in this matter is whether the author is responding to controversial elements of Paul's teaching, including the relationship between faith* and works (*see* Faith and Works), and law and liberty (*see* Freedom). Since these combinations are found neither in Jewish sources nor in the earliest Christian traditions of the NT, some scholars assume the author is responding to ideas found in Paul's writings and only after their publication toward the end of the first century when they came into a wider circulation (Holtzmann, Dibelius, Laws, Aland). Since James was executed in 62 by the Sadducean high priest Ananus II, these same scholars further presume that James the Just could not have written the letter of James.

Yet many are reluctant to find in favor of the author's dependence upon the writings of Paul. Some find it impossible that any Christian reader of Paul's writings would criticize him so openly, especially at the close of the first century or beginning of the second when his writings already were being recognized as "Scripture" (2 Pet 3:15-16). Still others find the issue of literary dependency indeterminate (Mayor, Davids, Martin). Even if James and Paul mean the same thing by "faith and works" or by "law

and liberty," a view that remains contested among scholars, Paul could have as easily been responding to the kerygma* of Jerusalem Christianity (Spitta, Meyer), especially in his Romans and Galatians where numerous parallels are found. In support one may appeal to the well-known contention of G. Bornkamm that Paul wrote Romans as his "last will and testament" in order to recall and respond to the controversies generated by his missionary work, particularly among believers in Jerusalem (Donfried, 17-31). While the ideas and precise argument of James may not predate Paul's Gentile mission and his corpus of NT writings, their status in earliest Christianity may be more current and certain than is often supposed. In short there is no compelling reason to argue against the traditional position, which supposes a pre-Pauline date for this book and James the Just as its author (however, see 4. below).

1.3. Stages of Composition. Perhaps the persistent indeterminacy of this problem commends another solution that considers and integrates a wider field of available evidence. In this case J. Cantinat, more recently and cautiously followed by P. H. Davids, has suggested that the biblical form of James actually evolved in two discrete stages of composition (see Davids, 12-13). According to this hypothesis, James the Just is responsible for most of the book's raw material, delivered first as homilies and preserved by the Jewish Christian Diaspora (Jas 1:1; cf. Acts 8:4; 11:19). This may help explain the letter's "primitive" theological content.

These precious memories of James were then edited and written by another, probably (although not necessarily) after James's death, under the pressures of the educational mission of an expanding church.* The editor who actually wrote James may have done so without a religious agenda of his own: his intent was to compile and preserve the most enduring "sayings of James" for future readerships. If required at all, this conjecture may help explain the letter's articulation of Jacobean Christianity in the literary and intellectual idiom of Hellenistic culture.

Editors, however, are rarely this objective. Even editors who do not overlay a peculiar theological perspective on that of another still must select material from available traditions when composing a new work—a self-critical act of interpretation. Further, the reworking of old traditions is typically occasioned by the requirements of new readers. The letter's careful literary design and theological coherence seem to reflect this very sort of editorial decision-making: James is hardly the mere compilation of sayings, as some have suggested (see 3. below), or the exact copy of some former speech recalled. Indeed, if a two-stage composition is followed, one should probably assume that the editor had specific theological, sociological and literary intentions in mind, which are then reflected by the letter's final shape and subject matter.

For instance, the editor's arrangement of earlier traditions to combine Pauline catchwords (Jas 2:12-26) and to make strategic allusions to Jesus' ministry among the poor (Jas 2:1-5), along with the clever pairing of cited/alluded Scripture from Torah and wisdom* (Jas 1:19-27) and from the prophets* and wisdom (Jas 4:6-10; Jas 4:13—5:6), all intend to create a far richer context within which his audience could better hear and interpret the authoritative witness of James to the gospel. New audiences are addressed by a written composition unlike any sermon preached by James and in a fresh way that more effectively presents an inspired solution to their particular spiritual crisis. Even though the editor followed the core convictions of James the Just, his literary design accented certain theological convictions that were apropos for the new contingencies of his late first-century church, which occupied a very different geographical, linguistic and cultural turf than it did during the old days in Jerusalem. For these reasons the interpreter who decides in favor of the two-stage hypothesis of composition should consider the editor the "real" author of the Letter of James and the late first century its "true" date of composition.

2. The Audience(s) of James.

The letters of the NT are occasional literature, most often written to defend or nurture the tentative faith of immature audiences. While the author's advice only rarely takes a narrative form, every letter tells a story, however implicit, of an audience's struggle to confirm its faith. In the case of James, the story is plotted by the suffering of Jewish believers whose devotion to the Lord and to one another is tested by various kinds of conflicts, both spiritual and social.

2.1. Identity of the Audience. The precise identity of the first readers of James is indeterminate and opinion remains divided. Lacking specific details of the readers' identity, most exegetes are content to locate them in either of two places: post-Pauline Diaspora or in prewar (A.D. 66-70) Palestine-Syria.* All agree, however, that the proper place to begin this discussion is the letter's opening verse, which greets the audience as "the twelve tribes in the Diaspora." This enigmatic phrase, however finally understood, might then be employed to interpret subsequent references to the readership in the letter itself, resulting in a more detailed and focused picture.

If this opening phrase is taken at face value, the readers are probably Jewish believers ("twelve tribes") with an address in some Roman territory outside of Palestine ("in the Diaspora"), perhaps in Rome* (Laws), Alexandria* (Schneider) or even Syria (Davids) toward the end of Domitian's turbulent reign (Reicke). If, however, the phrase is taken metaphorically, the scope of possible meaning and setting is significantly widened. On this basis some have created complex settings of social and spiritual conflict, which are then confirmed by the images of hostility found throughout the book.

In fact a metaphorical reading of "the twelve tribes" certainly agrees with use of the phrase by other biblical writers. The biblical prophets, for instance, use the phrase (or "tribes of Israel") as a reference to a future, restored Israel* (Ezek 47:13, 22; Is 49:6; Zech 9:1). Paul contends that the "Israel of God" (Gal 6:16) is a spiritual rather than an ethnic people (cf. Rom 9—11; Gal 3—6) who belong to Christ (Rom 9:1-18) and are the true heirs of the biblical promise of salvation* (Gal 3:21-4:7; cf. Jas 2:5). In a similar way the audience of James consists of those whose primary identity appears religious and eschatological* rather than ethnic and national; that is, they form a spiritual people whose life is guided by God's word and whose destiny is the realization of God's promised blessing.*

The metaphorical use of "Diaspora"* is also attested in Jewish literature as a reference to believers, living in Palestine, but who are cut off from social and religious support systems (Overman; Maynard-Reid). In this case a reference to diasporic Jews need not place them in a geographical location but rather in a social world. Moreover, diasporic Jews were often driven from their homeland for political (e.g., criminals) and economic (e.g., unemployed workers or tax debtors) reasons; in this sense they were aliens both at home and abroad. Even in Palestine the "homeland" was typically in the hands of wealthy landowners (Jas 5:1) who controlled both the economic (Jas 5:4-6) and religious lives (Jas 2:2-7) of their poor workers, sometimes in venal and vicious ways (see 2.2 below).

In a similar way Scripture speaks of the Diaspora to accent this very kind of experience (cf. 1 Pet 1:1; Is 49:6) in which a people's present pain results from their separation from the plentiful land of divine blessing (whether land* of Israel or in heaven*). In a religious sense present suffering discloses one's status as "alien and stranger" but more significantly the absence of promised salvation that is still in the future. Indeed, this theological understanding of place adds another layer of meaning to "the twelve tribes," whose future inheritance of the kingdom's blessings ameliorates the trials and tribulations of their present exile.

The haunting ambivalence between the audience's present suffering in the Diaspora and its future restoration as the twelve tribes underscores the spiritual crisis that has occasioned the writing and reading of this composition. Its thesis neatly follows: Even though belonging to the redeemed and restored Israel, believers continue to face the hardships and heartaches of the Diaspora that test their devotion to God (Jas 1:2-3). Their possible spiritual failure carries this future consequence: the forfeiture of promised blessing (Jas 1:12-15); the passing of their spiritual testing, enabled by divine wisdom, ensures the community's future salvation (Jas 1:16-21). The community's joyful consideration of present suffering (Jas 1:2), then, has in mind the prospect of a future restoration, when all is made complete and perfect and when nothing is lacked (Jas 1:4).

2.2. Social and Spiritual Worlds of the Audience. References to the first readers of this letter, however vague and even opaque, supply several details about the nature of the conflict that may help us tell their unrecorded story. Clearly they are believers (Jas 1:2) who are members of a Jewish Christian synagogue* (Jas 2:1-2), who aspire to be "rich in faith" as heirs of the promised kingdom* (Jas 2:5) and at the same time pursue worldly pleasures that they lack (Jas 4:1-5). A measure of their current suffering is due to their poverty: they are a congregation of "humble" means (Jas 1:9-11; cf. 4:6-10), composed of members from the working-class poor (Jas 5:1-6) and from other social groups who are most neglected (Jas 1:27; cf. Acts 6:1-6), most oppressed (Jas 2:1-7; cf. Gal 2:9-10) and most poor (Jas 2:14-17).

Their enemies are the landed rich (Jas 5:1) and merchant middle class (Jas 4:13) who are members of a Jewish congregation attached to the local synagogue (Jas 2:2-4; cf. 1:9). However, their exploitation of the poor, their greed and maliciousness, which so fundamentally offend the moral essentials of their own biblical tradition (Jas 2:8-10), fortify the author's polemic against them: they are foolish to look in the "mirror" (= biblical law) and then turn away from it (Jas 1:22-24) without any further reflection of their own frailty (or their riches, Jas 5:1-3) under the eternal light of God's will (Jas 4:14-17) and the imminent coming of God's judgment* (Jas 5:4-6, 7-9). Indeed, they have become "outsiders" (Jas 2:6-7) to God's reign (Jas 2:5) who no longer belong to "the twelve tribes" and cannot look forward in joy* to their complete restoration. In demonstration of their outsider status they oppress the impoverished members of the Christian congregation (Jas 2:2), even using their political clout to exploit the working-class poor (Jas 5:1-6) and to demand favorable verdicts against them from the law court (Jas 2:6-7) and the synagogue court (Jas 2:3-4; Ward).

These outside pressures have created tensions inside the congregation that threaten its present unity and eschatological survival. The conflict that rages between believers is pluriform: some disregard their own poor in favor of the rich and powerful outsiders (Jas 1:22—2:26); abusive speech between rival teachers undermines their teaching* ministry and the congregation's spiritual formation (Jas 3:1-18); and hostilities between believers (Jas 4:1-2) and finally toward God (Jas 4:7-10) have their source in their frustration of not having the material goods they passionately desire (Jas 4:3-6).

Perhaps more troubling than this class conflict between rich and poor, which in turn threatens the solidarity of the congregation, is the spiritual or psychological conflict that threatens the believers' relationship with God. These same trials also occasion doubt about God's generosity (Jas 1:5-8) or even the self-destructive deception that God is to blame for the bad news of human life (Jas 1:13-16). Perhaps anxiety for personal safety prompts some believers to suppose that glib confessions of orthodox faith are sufficient for God's approval (Jas 1:22-27; 2:14-20), substituting them for a morally rigorous life that responds in mercy to the poor and powerless when they are exploited by the rich and influential (Jas 2:1-13; 2:21-26). An inward passion for lacking pleasure (Jas 4:1-2) gives one up to a consuming desire for things at the cost of relationships with God (Jas 4:6-12) and neighbor (Jas 4:3-5). Spiritual failure results from theological deception, when a faulty view of the word of God yields bad decisions and ultimately prevents participation in the new order (Jas 1:17-21; 2:12-13; 3:14-16; 4:11-12).

2.3. Social and Spiritual Tensions. To specify a locale in the first-century Roman world, whether Hellenistic or Palestinian, is extremely difficult to do with any precision. For this reason some continue to follow Dibelius's lead and contend that this form of literature (paraenesis) resists any reference to a particular historical contingency that may have occasioned the writing and first reading of this composition. One can speak perhaps of a moral culture that this literature helps to shape by its advice, which fixes the community's socioreligious borders within any hostile environment (Perdue, Elliot). Perhaps even the apocalyptic images found throughout this composition perform this same social role—images that anticipate a new cultural order that promises an alternative, more hospitable homeland for a poor and powerless people (Wall 1990).

Nevertheless, some continue to investigate James for a particular historical *Sitz im Leben* (life setting). The traditional position locates both the author and his audience in prewar Palestine; the details gathered from the letter fit this setting well (Davids, 28-34). Of course, no one who accepts a literal Diaspora would subscribe to this provenance. Further, while the images and metaphors of nature are brought to sharper focus against a Palestinian backdrop (Hadidian), S. S. Laws, for one, remains unconvinced by this evidence and counters by pointing to Greek literature for similar images, even as F. Mussner points to Scripture as the source of these images.

However, if the diasporic setting is viewed as a metaphor of spiritual or social dislocation, the references to class strife between rich and poor proffers a more convincing line of evidence for a Palestinian provenance (Maynard-Reid). In Palestine, as throughout the Roman world, rural land and wealth were concentrated in the hands of a few wealthy farmers (Jas 5:1). Middle-class merchants (Jas 4:13) could but dream of a future when they too could take their place among the landed gentry and share their life of luxury. Toward that end the merchants worked with the large landowners to control the agrarian marketplace, which only made the workers more dependent upon the landowner and the independent farmer's situation more difficult to endure.

Very little upward mobility was enjoyed between these classes, since Rome (*see* Roman Empire) maintained a stratified society as a means of managing the masses. While the continuing exploitation of the poor by the merchant-farmer coalition was not encouraged by Rome, for fear of a worker strike, it was tolerated in order to maintain the fragile prosperity of the region. Especially during times of famine (see Jas 5:17-18; Acts 11:27-30), the economic pressures of field hands and harvesters became more intense and their economic well-being more precarious as landowners tried to maximize their profits (Jas 4:4-6). The result is that some lacked even the basic requirements of a humane existence (see Jas 2:15-16). The great majority of the Palestinian population was thus confined to working-class ghettos, living a hand-to-mouth existence without any hope of an improved life. Such historical determinism either gave rise to social rage and the potential of peasant rebellion or to religious sentiment deeply rooted in a "piety of poverty" and apocalyptic hope.

In addition, Martin contends, James was written for a community of poor people and their religious leaders who were suffering under Sadducean rule. His argument recognizes Josephus's* historical record that James was executed in 62 by Ananus II, a Sadducean priest, at the height of tensions with the Jerusalem church; James might be read as another kind of record of that episode. His contention also makes considerable sense not only of the economic conflict mentioned in the letter (Jas 5:1-6; 2:6-7), since the landed aristocracy was essentially Sadducean if even religious, but also of the book's theological cast, since Sadducees also observed Torah (Jas 1:22-25; 2:8-13) and were deeply fearful of any apocalyptic-messianic movement—to which the readers of James belong (Jas 2:1; Martin, lxiv-lxv). However, unlike the Zealots, whose apocalypticism the Sadducees feared most of all, James takes his readers in a more spiritual and less violent direction, so that the struggles of the poor against the rich are then internalized as spiritual warfare with materialism (Jas 4:1-5).

2.4. Theological Tensions. Those who posit the audience within a Hellenistic culture tend to describe the audience's struggle in ideological rather than in sociological terms. The most interesting suggestion places the audience in a Roman (Laws, Deppe) or perhaps Corinthian (Syreeni) congregation, where the tensions are theological and between Jewish and Gentile believers. Common themes shared by the whole church, such as law and liberty, faith and works, perfection and wisdom, are now explored by James to distinguish more carefully between the two different Christian missions and their kerygmata (cf. Gal 2:7; Rom 16:3-4). For example, in Paul the "faith in and of Jesus Christ" is redemptive* (Rom 3:22; Gal 3:22) whenever confessed (Rom 10:9-10), whereas for James the "faith of Jesus Christ" asserts an ethical* principle (Jas 2:1)—do not favor the rich over the poor (Jas 2:2-11)—which is redemptive when practiced (Jas 2:12-13, 14-26).

The conflict between rich (= outsider) and poor (= insider) symbolizes the conflict between competing ideologies. The poor (= Jewish believers) are true heirs of the promised kingdom (Jas 2:5), while the salvation of the wealthy (= Gentile believers) is less certain, a view that seems to retain but reverse the sense of Paul's commentary on the same conflict (1 Cor 8-10; Rom 14). There are social and even economic results of this theological battle, which Paul notes. For example, his warning about settling intramural conflicts in civil court (1 Cor 6:1-6) is vaguely similar to James 2:6-7.

The intense tones of this conflict found in James 5:1-6 are not easily explained by this *Sitz im Leben.* Even if such a setting fails to explain the data, however, the thematic parallels between James and Paul and the dialogic manner by which they are related together may well provide the raw material for a more robust theological reflection (see 4 below).

2.5. A Way of Wisdom. T. B. Cargal has called

attention to the interplay between the book's opening address to those "in the Diaspora" and its concluding exhortation to those who "wander from the truth" (Jas 5:19-20). He proposes that the literary architecture of James is that of an inverted parallelism, with James 1:1 and James 5:19-20 providing the outside boundaries for the exhortations found within. In this sense the "Diaspora" is located wherever immature believers are found who have "scattered" from the truth; the exhortations are to encourage their repentance* and restoration in order to guide them back into the "homeland," which is the eschatological reign of God.

The ultimate importance of this address is not to identify the geographical location of first readers but rather to give shape to their theological location. Indeed, the audience of this book includes all those who find themselves pushed, pulled and moved away from the truth as Christian faith defines it. They are those who have been marginalized and alienated from the cultural order because of their piety and now question whether this testing of faith is worth their devotion to God. This book supplies a way of wisdom by which scattered believers are led back into the faith.

3. The Literature of James.

3.1. James as Exhortation. Most scholars accept with some qualification Dibelius's important form-critical conclusion that James is a paraenesis, a genre of ancient moral literature characterized by various collections of moral sayings and essays, loosely held together by common themes and linking catchwords but without literary rhyme, theological reason or specific social location. The dominant mood of paraenesis is imperative; the primary exhortation is to live a virtuous life. Readers are often reminded of moral truth that all should accept (e.g., Jas 1:19; 3:1-8; 4:3-4) and of heroic exemplars (e.g., Jesus, Abraham,* Rahab, Job, Elijah) whom all should imitate.

Even if one allows that James exhibits the conventions of paraenetic literature and has wide appeal, its final shape frames a carefully orchestrated witness to God that compels a faithful (and Christian) response to its claims. Since Dibelius, several have demonstrated that the composition develops along the lines of a specific rhetorical strategy (Wuellner, Cargel, Johnson, Watson) that argues for a specific theological point (Mussner, Hoppe). Johnson, who contends that James must be approached as an oral presentation, argues for a thematic and literary coherence that is organized by two competing worldviews between "friendship with the world" and "friendship with God" (1995, 13-15).

3.2. James as an Epistle. James may also be studied as epistolary literature (Francis; *see* Letters). Even though omitting many features of the Pauline (or Hellenistic) epistolary form, the structure of James is still vaguely parallel to other NT letters: it opens with an address (Jas 1:1) followed by a thesis statement (Jas 1:2-21) that both clarifies the letter's occasion and introduces the author's advice. It then sets forth various exhortations and oaths that promote Christian piety (Jas 5:7-8, 9-11, 12, 13-18), before the real purpose for writing is stated (Jas 5:19-20). Sandwiched between the opening thesis statements and concluding exhortations is the letter's main body (Jas 1:22—5:6), comprised of three extended essays on the wisdom of "quick to hear" (Jas 1:22—2:26), "slow to speak" (Jas 3:1-18) and "slow to anger" (Jas 4:1—5:6), which communicates more fully its pastoral message to an embattled readership.

Clearly the literary form of the main body of James differs in convention and substance when compared with the Pauline letters. However, its function is precisely the same: to provide the readers with a powerful interpretation of their present spiritual crisis and to offer them a practical solution that encourages their future salvation (see 4. below).

3.3. James as Wisdom Literature. The question of sources remains a thorny one: from whence comes this book's understanding of wisdom? In my view, wisdom is the orienting concern of this book by which all else is understood: after all, James refers to wisdom as the divine "word of truth," which is graciously provided to a faithful people to make sense of their trials and to guide them through those trials in order to insure their future destiny in the new creation (cf. Martin, lxxxii-lxxxiv). A strong case has been made that James shares in the moral world of the Greco-Roman world (Laws, Kee): the virtue of the community of the wise is aptly demonstrated during personal testing, when the actions of the wise result in personal and divine blessing (see Johnson 1995, 27-29). The well-known contrast between professions of trust

and an embodied faith may be less a response to Pauline teaching and more a reflection of the contrast between eloquent speech and moral action found among certain Hellenistic moralists such as Epictetus.

The characteristics of a virtuous life, concentrated by the catalog found in James 3:17 and complemented by the book's accent on a life of patience, perfection, consistency and self-control, are common themes among current moral philosophies (esp. Stoicism and Cynicism).

This article will seek to understand this same moral calculus and its various topoi under the light of Jewish wisdom literature. The theological subject matter of James is profoundly biblical, and the Greco-Roman literary patterns and moral topoi found in this composition are subsumed by the author's biblical vision. Morality, according to James, is concentrated by a believer's faith in God. It is not a virtue ethic, then, whose failure is vice and self-destruction. Rather it is a theological ethic, since the lack of wisdom threatens the believer's relations with God and imperils the prospect of future blessing in God's coming reign on earth. For this reason James fits much more comfortably in Scripture than in an anthology of Hellenistic moral philosophy.

Of course, these two sources, Hellenistic and biblical, are not dissimilar in either form or content and are found integrated in Jewish intertestamental writings such as Sirach and Wisdom of Solomon, which no doubt formed a part of the wisdom tradition this author inherited. There are frequent parallels to the writings of Philo.* James is a traditional wisdom, and its sensibilities are Jewish more than Greco-Roman. In passage after passage the crucial subtexts of this composition are not Greco-Roman but biblical—a perspective recently defended in L. T. Johnson's commentary on James (1995).

For this reason the interpreter seeks after the relationship between James and its principal subtexts in Scripture rather than in the writings of Greco-Roman moralists and philosophy: James offers one tradent's reading of biblical wisdom (Jas 1:19; see 6 below). The overarching interpretive strategy of James is sapiential in that nonwisdom and extrabiblical traditions are strained through the filter of Jewish wisdom. In this sense, then, the testing addressed by James is spiritual and not personal, and this "way of wisdom" promises eschatological blessing (Jas

1:12) for those who live and act under the light of the Lord's coming triumph (Jas 2:5; 5:7-9).

3.4. James as Midrash. James is midrashic literature. While several exegetes have discovered fragments of existing Jewish midrashim employed by James (e.g., Ward, Johnson), few go as far as M. Gertner, who claims that the whole of James is a midrash on Psalm 12. More modest is the suggestion of L. T. Johnson, who finds examples of a halakic midrash on Leviticus 19 throughout James that both anchors and warrants its moral vision (Johnson 1982).

Contemporary literary theory uses "midrash" as a metaphor of a literary text's reflexive interplay with another, earlier text. That is, a literary text is midrashic insofar as it interprets an earlier text as part of its own redaction and argumentation for a new audience and its particular situation. In this sense the primary indicator of biblical midrash is not a certain form of literature (e.g., halakic) that is produced by following certain rabbinical rules for commenting upon Scripture. Rather, the primary indicator is a text's intertextuality,* when the reader of a biblical text recognizes its citation, allusion or echo of another, earlier biblical text that then completes and commends its meaning. In my reading of the intertextuality of midrash, biblical texts echo other biblical texts as literary cues that point us to those stories or topoi, persons or places in order to construct a fuller biblical context within which the strong interpreter reflects upon the theological meaning of the passage under analysis.

With this understanding of midrash in mind, then, similar words and ideas found in different parts of Scripture are cited, alluded to and echoed in James and add a rich subtexture to its message—a message that is framed by a reflexive, mutually enriching conversation between James and these other biblical voices. Sometimes a meaningful contour is added to James by what is lacking from a biblical allusion. For example, the carefully worded reference to Rahab in James 2:25 presumes by what it omits that the reader knows the details of her story as told in Joshua 2. In this way James need not even mention Rahab's faith since her biblical story asserts that the works of her hospitality* are the real stuff of true religion. Thus I have come to read James as the literary product of an author whose "canon consciousness" (*see* Canon) first elevates the status of his Bible as the central symbol of his religious life and then routinely appeals to it, sometimes in subtle ways, to justify the moral authority of what he advises his readership to be and do.

The dynamic quality of an intertextual reading of James is envisaged even when the exegete narrows one's frame of reference to the *intra*textuality of the book of James itself. Following the lead of G. Lindbeck (see *The Nature of Doctrine: Religion and Theology in a Postliberal Age* [Philadelphia: Westminster, 1984]), the full meaning of James is discovered when a text is analyzed within (intra-) the literary and theological context of the composition, when the composition itself serves as the privileged medium of its own interpretation. In this sense the book of James is approached as an autonomous text that supplies its own special "grammar," which makes sense of its own "text-constituted world" (Lindbeck, 136). From this intratextual perspective, then, a fuller meaning of its most important catchwords can be discerned by their repetition in different locations of the argument (for example, follow the author's use of "perfect" [Jas 1:4, 17, 25; 2:22; 3:2; cf. 2:8; 5:11]). These words acquire new and enlarged meanings by their repeated use, while at the same time their prior uses alert the interpreter to possible meanings that may well be obscured by their new literary and linguistic context. This literary feature of James is especially important, since it provides a kind of literary coherence that otherwise has seemed lacking to some.

Both features of the literary art of James mentioned above are also important features of persuasive speech in the Greco-Roman literary culture (*see* Rhetoric), which also contributed to the shaping of this composition's main body (Watson). Clearly the repetition of key words and ideas in a composition was one such feature of ancient rhetorical writing and speaking. By repeating catchwords throughout a composition or speech, for example, an author like the writer of James could both organize and relate together different sections of a composition for his auditors. Especially important in this regard is the reflexive character of repetition, so that subsequent uses of a word or phrase would naturally expand and clarify how an auditor or a reader should understand an important thematic interest of the composition as a whole.

The use of prophetic exemplars in James also follows ancient rhetorical practice. In the case of James, references to familiar biblical personages (Abraham, Rahab, Job, Elijah) not only provided authoritative examples in support of the thesis—these were those who passed their spiritual tests. They provided role models for an eschatological community—these were those who received promised blessings from God. The use of these exemplars in James is more than rhetorical, since each calls attention to a biblical story that provides the primary subtext that in turn deepens the point James scores.

3.5. Literary Sources. The author's possible knowledge and use of NT traditions (specifically those found in the Synoptic Gospels and in the Pauline and Petrine letters*) remains debated. While there are significant linguistic and thematic parallels between James and the major letters of Paul (Syreeni) and 1 Peter* (Davids)—more numerous and certain than most scholars care to admit—the question of literary dependence remains indeterminate (see 1 above). The same can be said of the possible appropriation by James of Jesus sayings found in Q (Hartin 1991) and then in Luke (Davids) and especially Matthew (Shepherd). In fact the parallels between James and Matthew's Sermon on the Mount (par. Luke and Q) are remarkably close (Mayor, lxxxii-lxxxiv; Mussner, 47-52; Shepherd; cf. Hartin 1993; *see* Jesus Traditions). However, D. D. Deppe argues against a pre-Synoptic source by contending that the parallel sayings in James evince an even more primitive source and have in any case a different literary form and function than they do for Q and the Synoptic Evangelists. In any case B. Witherington correctly contends that James exhibits a more conventional, less prophetic theological conception than found on the lips of the Synoptic Jesus (Witherington, 236-47).

4. A Canonical Approach to James.
The canonical approach to biblical interpretation is interested in reading the whole of Scripture as the church's authoritative (or canonical) witness* to God and so formative and normative of the church's understanding of God (Wall 1995). The interpreter recognizes this theological role more clearly when reflecting upon Scripture within its biblical and ecclesiastical contexts rather than in terms of the conventions of its "original" historical or literary environ-

ments. While historical and literary reconstructions of the "original" James have had some value in determining the full meaning of a biblical text, to presume that critical historical investigation determines its normative meaning is mistaken. The principal property of the biblical text is neither historical nor literary but theological. For the exegete to locate this composition within its first-century milieu and to fix its meaning there is to mistake the true referent of the biblical witness who is God. If the interpreter's orienting concern toward Scripture is its authorized roles within the church, then all the various tasks and exegesis and interpretation will seek to understand a biblical writing as a resource for theological reflection and understanding.

Within its particular biblical *Sitz im Leben* the book of James supplies a distinctive and complementary witness to God, so that it functions neither as the single articulation of God's biblical word nor as an atonal voice that must be excluded from the chorus of voices that together harmonize on the word of God. In this sense Christian faith is distorted by not taking the distinctive witness of James seriously. The special significance of this book's particular witness to God is best understood in relationship to the witnesses of other biblical books and collections, precisely because each understands God in different, although complementary, ways and forms if finally by "mutual criticism" a more objective and discriminating faith.

Besides this overarching perspective on the study of Scripture, important guidance is provided the interpreter by the title that introduces a book within its discrete canonical collection; by the arrangement of canonical writings within the canon as a whole; by the final literary form of a composition that best articulates that variety of God's word; by the author's use of his Scripture as a decisive clue to how the canonical audience should read his book as Scripture; and by the history of its interpretation, whenever a biblical writing "becomes canonical" as faithful interpreters pick it up again and again to comfort the afflicted or afflict the comfortable.

4.1. Title. Titles are properties of the canonical process and as such are indicators of a theological tradition and a practical role that continues to exercise authority in forming the faith and witness of Scripture's current readerships. Even if one is not convinced that James should be read as a literary letter, the ancient church recognized its divine inspiration precisely when using it as a letter. Thus the inscription, *Iakbou Epistolē* ("the letter of James"), is added to this nonletter (or at least a literary letter different from those written by the Pauline school [*see* Pauline School]) to fit it into a wider collection of epistolary writings, all of which share a similar role in nurturing the faith of believers; that is, letters function as pastoral vehicles of instruction and exhortation, written for believers whose worship* of God is threatened by personal hardship or theological confusion. The canonical audience orients itself to James from this perspective to read it as Christian Scripture.

The importance of authorship statements in the address of a biblical letter is not exclusively historical; rather, names found in titles and greetings also locate compositions in particular theological traditions, each of which provides an authoritative witness to God's saving activity in Christ Jesus. This particular title locates the composition of James in a particular genre of literature to underscore its practical role in forming Christian faith; it also places the theological subject matter of James in a particular theological tradition—that belonging to James of Jerusalem, the brother of Jesus. In turn the name of James, found in both its biblical title and epistolary address, assigns this writing to the revelation tradition founded by James—that is, a conservative variety of Jewish Christianity.

4.2. Placement Within the Canon. The placement of the letters within the NT and then of James among them is suggestive of the role this book continues to perform as part of the biblical canon. James is placed within a second collection of NT letters. While the relation between the four NT Gospels has long been a topic of scholarly investigation, few have considered the relationship between the two collections of NT letters as significant: what possible relationship do the non-Pauline letters have with the Pauline in forming our theological understanding (the intended role of Scripture), and how might this consideration aid the interpreter in discerning the special role James might perform within the Christian Bible?

Especially within Protestantism, primary attention has been concentrated upon the Pauline collection to investigate not only the meaning of individual letters but also the rela-

tionship between them. Partial justification for this keen interest in Paul's witness to the gospel is claimed by the ordering of the letters, since the Pauline corpus comes first. Yet this very Pauline priority has also led to a reductionism in the study of the second, non-Pauline collection of letters. For example, James is typically viewed as envisaging either a Pauline faith, although in alternative wording, or an anti-Pauline faith. In either case the more complementary character of the intracanonical relationship between James and Paul is seriously distorted, as is their integral witness to God's gospel.

Accordingly one may suggest that a critical role performed by the second collection of (non-Pauline) letters is to enhance our understanding of the first (Pauline) by provision of an apparatus of checks and balances that prevents distortion of the full gospel (Wall 1992, 208-71). In light of the history of its interpretation, the interpreter is especially challenged to listen to James for a different voice from that heard when reading Paul. However, it is neither the voice of a ventriloquist nor the voice of an adversary but that of a colleague whose new perspective adds and even supplies a necessary balance to what has already been read and accepted from Paul (see 5 below).

4.3. The Canonical Audience. Even though their readerships constantly change, biblical letters allow for the continual adaptation of their practical message to every generation of believers. There is no guarantee that the current readers of James participate in any of the ancient worlds occupied by its first readers; nor should we expect to recover the full meaning of the words that James originally wrote. Precisely because James is canonical Scripture, readers must not interpret its meaning as belonging to a distant past. Not only does its central theme of spiritual testing seem pertinent, but readers often number themselves among the rich and powerful who disregard the powerless or among the powerless who require and are given God's support against the powerful. James sometimes exposes the foolishness of believers who substitute facile confession for an embodied devotion to God or use malicious words to gain an advantage over a rival—both important topics of James. The wise words of James may sound a prophetic tone, sharply critical of business as usual and often inviting our repentance or a pastoral tone for those in need of the gospel's assurance. The point is this: the book of James has found a place in Scripture not only because it provides us trustworthy contours of our understanding about God but also because it illumines our walk before God especially when considered an integral part of an inspired whole.

5. The Gospel According to James.

5.1. A Portrait of God. The old critical conclusion that James is not a theological writing has waned in recent years. At the very least, most scholars now acknowledge the importance of theological images and themes in communicating the message of this book. For instance, the portrait of God that James envisages is rather robust. God is Creator* who rules over all things (Jas 1:17) and who promises a new cosmic order (Jas 1:18) that is remade perfect and complete, lacking in nothing (Jas 1:4). In preparation for the coming triumph of the Creator, God gives only good gifts to the faith community (Jas 1:13-17), especially the gift of wisdom (Jas 1:5-6; 3:17), which is able to "save their souls" (Jas 1:21; 3:18). God also receives petitions for wisdom (Jas 1:5; 4:3) and healing* (Jas 5:13-18). God is faithful to the promise of salvation (Jas 2:5; 4:6-10) and will reverse the status of the faithful poor and powerless in the coming age (Jas 1:9-11; 2:1-5). Because God is Savior and Judge of all creation (Jas 2:12-13; 4:11-12, 13-17; 5:1-9), God is worshiped (Jas 3:9-10; 4:7-10) and God's law obeyed (Jas 1:22-27).

5.2. A Story of God's Salvation. Biblical scholarship has recently underscored the narrative aspect of Scripture's theological subject matter—in J. Sanders's tidy phrase, "God has a story too" (Sanders 1979). The functional importance of this line of inquiry is twofold. First, it supplies biblical theologians with a framework for building a comprehensive and coherent treatment of Scripture's theological subject matter. Second, foundational stories function to facilitate a more personal and immediate identification between the biblical narrative and its contemporary audience.

One fruitful effort in this regard is by R. Hays, who contends that Paul's theological vision is narrative in cast. According to Hays, Paul's core theological convictions comprise a sequence of six events, beginning with God's promise of blessing to Abraham* and concluding with the Lord's Second Coming. Between are those episodes that constitute the "Christ event," climaxed by Jesus's messianic death and resurrection* and their results in the faith community. While the Pauline accents are distinctive within the NT, the narrative theology of other contributors to the biblical canon, including James, follows a similar story line. Like Hays, E. E. Lemcio has isolated the basic ingredients of a "unifying kerygma" in every canonical unit (i.e., Gospels, Acts, Letters, Apocalypse) of the NT.

The fourfold Gospel frames and founds Scripture with a narrative substructure; that is, this story of Jesus becomes the interpreter's foundational presupposition in understanding the practical advice given and theological claims made by every subsequent book of the NT. From this perspective as well, James shares with other biblical writers a common story of God's salvation through Jesus Christ, which provides the structure and supplies the subject matter of a fully integrated biblical theology.

The story's inaugural event is (1) God's election of a people to save. James understands divine election in terms of social class: God chooses the poor as heirs of the promised kingdom (Jas 2:5). Their inheritance of the blessing first promised to the children of Abraham is not conditioned upon their national or ethnic identity but upon their devotion to God, whether they are "rich in faith" (cf. Jas 1:12; 2:5) as embodied by merciful deeds (Jas 2:8-26).

(2) God sends an agent of salvation into the world in order to free people from the results of their sin. According to James, God "gives" "the word of truth" to these pious poor in order to enable the passing of their spiritual tests (Jas 1:2-3) and to restore them as part of the coming order (Jas 1:4, 17-18). The subject matter of the divine word is proverbial wisdom (Jas 1:5), which demands that the community be "quick to hear, slow to speak and slow to anger" (Jas 1:19; see 6 below). This word of wisdom is capable of saving the community (Jas 1:21; 3:17-18) from all the foolishness (Jas 1:16) and filthiness (Jas 1:21) that bring forth death (Jas 1:14-15; 3:14-16; 5:19-20).

(3) God's word is disclosed in the messianic "faith of the Lord Jesus Christ" (Jas 2:1). Unlike Paul, who understands the faith of Jesus in terms of his messianic death and resurrection, James understands the faith of Jesus as exem-

plary of an observed wisdom ("the word of truth"). In particular Jesus' devotion to God is confirmed by his just treatment of the poor neighbor, which God demands according to the "royal" law (Jas 2:8; cf. 1:27).

(4) The divine word, already made known in Scripture's wisdom and exemplified by Jesus, illumines "the way" to divine blessing for any believer who asks God for it (Jas 1:5) and does not doubt its efficacy (Jas 1:6-8). Further, this same word has taken root within (Jas 1:21) and so marks out the boundaries of the elect community of the poor (Jas 1:27). Membership in this community, and with it the prospect of future blessing, is maintained by those who observe the word (Jas 1:22-25; cf. 4:13-17), who teach it without jealousy (Jas 3:1-18) and who resist those internal passions that undermine its performance (Jas 4:1-10; cf. 1:14-15).

(5) The current crisis that provokes spiritual testing is occasioned by every struggle of remaining faithful to God in an anti-God world (Jas 1:2-3; 3:13-16). In the present situation, when the community's suffering indicates a real "lack" of God's good intentions for creation, James contends that the word of proverbial wisdom empowers the passing of the spiritual test, so that the "first fruits" of a new creation might even now be demonstrated in the community's life together (Jas 1:18; 3:17-18). In this restricted sense, the witness of the wise community anticipates the coming age: the true and approved religion is an ethical people, whose witness to God is measured by the purity of its collective and personal life (Jas 1:27; 2:14-16). Thus it is finally the public works of wisdom, which demands the community's merciful treatment of its own poor (Jas 1:22—2:26), purity of speech among its word brokers (Jas 3:1-18) and a denial of materialistic affections among its aspiring middle class (Jas 4:1—5:6) that form the essential identity of an eschatological people.

(6) The community's hope is concentrated by the story's conclusion, the Lord's imminent Parousia* from heaven (5:7-9), which ushers into history the ultimate good and perfecting gift from above. At this climactic "any-moment" the eschatological community will be confirmed and vindicated: God will judge the foolish and bless the wise (Jas 2:13; 4:11-12; 5:4-6; 5:7-9; cf. Mt 7:24-27). James and Paul substantially agree on this final event. Both agree that

divine judgment and blessing are finally creational activities, which bring about the new order of things (Jas 1:4; 1:18; 3:18; 5:17-8). Both agree that the Lord's Parousia is imminent, so that the convictions of christological monotheism and the demands of public witness are made more urgently and embodied more readily. The time for repentance is short, because the time of judgment is at hand (Jas 5:7-9; 5:19-20).

6. The Argument of James.

6.1. Thematic Introduction (Jas 1:1-21). James is written to a community whose faith in God is threatened by a daily struggle with hardship (Jas 1:2-4). This "testing of faith" is provoked by a variety of external and historical circumstances or "trials." More importantly every test occasions a theological crisis, when the believer is more easily deceived or confused about who God is and how God acts (Jas 1:5-8). Within a crucible of theological reflection, largely internal and spiritual (Jas 1:13-15), a decision is called forth that ultimately measures the believer's "true" devotion to God, whether one is fit to participate in God's coming reign (Jas 1:12). To remain faithful to God in the present is the way to receive promised blessings from God in the future.

The community's decision for or against God is rooted in a sense of moral freedom. What form will this freedom take? On the one hand the wise believer loves God and trusts that God is a consistently loyal Father, who generously supplies the faith community with the "word of truth" that will guide the believer's pilgrimage on earth through the wilderness of trials and into the promised land of eternal life (Jas 1:16-18). The anticipated result of receiving this word, whose subject matter is proverbial wisdom (Jas 1:19-20), is an increased capacity to remain faithful to God during the testing of this age until the Lord comes in triumph over sin and death. The wise and faithful believer will enter into the coming age where all that is lacking is reversed and made perfect by the Creator, who alone completes humanity's material (Jas 1:9-11) and spiritual existence (Jas 1:21).

On the other hand the foolish Christian believes that God is disloyal to the promise of new life and actually is responsible for the community's hardships (Jas 1:13-16). The fool supposes that God is responsible for humanity's hardship and intends one's death; however, this deception results in refusing the merits of God's advice (cf. Jas 1:21). Such doubt gives birth to spiritual failure when facing present hardships, and the eschatological result of present spiritual failure is the forfeiture of the "crown of life" that is the blessing of all those who endure (Jas 1:12).

6.2. The Wisdom of "Quick to Hear" (Jas 1:22—2:26). In this first section of the main body of James, the wisdom of "quick hearing" is paired with biblical Torah: to "hear" is to "do the work" of Torah (Jas 1:22-25). More specifically the wisdom of "quick hearing" means to obey the levitical laws pertaining to the merciful treatment of the neighbor (Jas 1:26-27). This portion of the Torah is defined as the wise thing to do in order to address a situation in which the material needs of the poorest and most marginal members of the faith community are neglected. The occasion for this neglect is the favored treatment of rich and powerful outsiders in the legal proceedings of both the synagogue (Jas 2:2-4) and law courts (Jas 2:6-7). In this situation the biblical Torah demands jubilary justice in order to liberate the poor and powerless from their oppression (Jas 2:8-13).

The decision to favor these rich outsiders over poor insiders, even though perhaps a matter of short-term survival, fails the community's "test of faith" because God has in fact chosen the pious poor of the world to receive blessing (Jas 2:5). Further, favoritism of this sort envisages a compromise to the evils of the world order. Such is the nature of a theological failure that imperils the community's future salvation, which requires concrete works of mercy toward the poor (the social "diaspora"). Jesus was approved by God as "glorious Lord" (Jas 2:1) because he loved his poor and powerless neighbor according to the "royal law" (Jas 2:8). His example of divine mercy, which followed in the way of both ancestor Abraham (Jas 2:21-24) and prostitute Rahab (Jas 2:25), charts the way of wisdom for all which leads into eternal life.

The wise community is quick to hear and act upon what the Torah commands, knowing that it articulates God's will according to which all people will be either blessed or judged at the coming triumph of God's reign (Jas 2:12-13). If the Torah is centered on the command to love the neighbor, especially those who are like the "widow and orphan in distress," then it is foolish to favor the rich over the poor when the result

is eternal retribution. According to Torah, faith in God is embodied by works of mercy: true religion is an ethical religion, not confessional orthodoxy (Jas 2:14-26). To profess devotion to God without a complement of merciful works is foolish (Jas 2:20). Such religion is worthless for either heralding or entering the age to come (Jas 2:17, 26).

6.3. The Wisdom of "Slow to Speak" (Jas 3:1-18). James's essay on the proverbial wisdom of "slow speaking" is especially suited for the "wilderness" (Jas 3:11-12), when the spiritual journey is most unstable (Jas 3:3-6), when the guidance of "wise and understanding" teachers (Jas 3:13) is most critical, but also when harsh things are more easily said. The peril of speech is made even more pointed by the inherent difficulty of controlling what is said (Jas 3:7-8).

Every social crisis embodies a theological crisis as well; i.e., a crisis of faith in God as Creator (Jas 3:9-10). Slanderous speech, which curses the neighbor who should be loved (Jas 2:8), offends the good intentions of the Creator, who made people in God's image. The deeper logic of a creation theology is that God built certain patterns in the created order (Jas 3:11-12); in this sense profane speech will not yield spiritual results (Jas 3:15-16), whereas pure speech will (Jas 3:17-18).

That is, the result of speech that substitutes "earthly" wisdom (Jas 3:15) for "heavenly" wisdom (Jas 3:17) is "chaos" (Jas 3:16), which is opposite of the Creator's intentions for a restored creation (cf. Gen 1:2). Demonic speech destroys human relationships and prevents the sort of spiritual nurture that empowers the community's journey through present trials toward the future promise of a new order. The harvest of "pure and merciful" speech (Jas 3:17), which conforms to heavenly wisdom, is the blessing of peace for those "perfect" teachers (Jas 3:1-2) who practice it (Jas 3:18).

6.4. The Wisdom of "Slow to Anger" (Jas 4:1—5:6). James 4:1—5:6 interprets the meaning of the proverbial exhortation for believers to be "slow to anger." According to James, the source of the community's anger (Jas 4:1) is an inward passion for lacking material pleasures (Jas 4:2-3). The trial that imperils the community's participation in God's coming triumph stems from an inability to be content with one's humble conditions, coveting rather the material goods of others (Jas 4:4-5). This passion for things tests the community's dependence upon God, who resists the arrogant and exults those of humble means (Jas 4:6; cf. 2:5). The wise community humbles itself before God (Jas 4:7-10), who alone establishes the criterion for judge and salvation (Jas 4:11-12).

The foolish, however, continue to indulge in self-centered passion for material profit without consideration of God's will for human existence (Jas 4:13-17). Indeed, those who choose Mammon over God will also choose Mammon over people and treat their poor neighbor with inequity (Jas 5:4) and hostility (Jas 5:6). The misery of mistreated workers ironically foreshadows the misery of the rich in the last days, when they will lose their wealth (Jas 5:1-2) and lives (Jas 5:4) to an angry God.

6.5. Concluding Exhortations (Jas 5:7-20). James concludes as it opens, with a pair of integral statements. By recalling important catchwords and phrases from the opening statements, the author forms an *inclusio* with his thesis that frames the commentary on wisdom found in between. More than a retrospective on the way of wisdom according to James, this conclusion also supplies the principal motivation for following its advice: the coming of the Lord is near (Jas 5:7-9).

The concluding exhortations to endure the testing of faith, implicit throughout James, are made more urgent by the author's pointed assertions that the Parousia is imminent. The community is encouraged to exercise patience (Jas 5:7-8), like Job (Jas 5:10-12) rather than his complaining friends (Jas 5:9), and to be vigilant in prayers* for healing (Jas 5:13-16), like Elijah (Jas 5:17-18), in order to insure participation in the coming triumph of God's reign.

The final verses (Jas 5:19-20) form a commission that calls the readers to a special mission for those foolish believers who have been deceived by falsehood and have departed from the "word of truth" that defines the way of wisdom. Their spiritual healing will result in salvation rather than condemnation at the end of the age. To be the church is to be wise when tested in knowing that the present testing of faith determines the future entrance into the age to come.

See also FAITH AND WORKS; JEWISH CHRISTIANITY.

BIBLIOGRAPHY. **Commentaries:** J. B. Adamson, *The Epistle of James* (NICNT; Grand Rapids: Eerdmans, 1954); J. Cantinat, *Les épîtres de s. Jacques et de s. Jude* (SB; Paris: Gabalda, 1973); P. H. Davids, *Commentary on James* (NIGTC; Grand Rapids: Eerdmans, 1982); M. Dibelius, *James,* rev. H. Greeven (Herm; Philadelphia: Fortress, 1976); Z. C. Hodges, *The Epistle of James* (Irving, TX: Grace Evangelical Society, 1994); R. Hoppe, *Jakobusbrief* (SKKNT; Stuttgart: Katholisches Bibelwerk, 1989); F. Hort, *The Epistle of St. James* (London: Macmillan, 1909); L. T. Johnson, *The Letter of James* (AB; New York: Doubleday, 1995); S. S. Laws, *A Commentary on the Epistle of James* (HNTC; San Francisco: Harper & Row, 1980); R. P. Martin, *James* (WBC; Waco, TX: Word, 1988); J. Marty, *L'épître de Jacques* (Paris: Felix Alcan, 1935); J. B. Mayor, *The Epistle of St. James* (Grand Rapids: Zondervan, 1954); C. L. Mitton, *The Epistle of James* (Grand Rapids: Eerdmans, 1966); J. Moffatt, *The General Epistles* (MNTC; London: Hodder & Stoughton, 1928); D. Moo, *James* (TNTC; Grand Rapids: Eerdmans, 1987); F. Mussner, *Der Jakobusbrief* (HTKNT; Freiburg: Herder, 1967); W. E. Oesterley, *The General Epistle of James* (EGT; London: Hodder & Stoughton, 1910); P. Perkins, *First and Second Peter, James and Jude* (IntC; Louisville, KY: John Knox, 1995); B. Reicke, *The Epistles of James, Peter and Jude* (AB; Garden City, NY: Doubleday, 1964); J. H. Ropes, *The Epistle of St. James* (ICC; Edinburgh: T & T Clark, 1916); F. Spitta, *Der Brief des Jakobus untersucht* (Göttingen: Vandenhoeck & Ruprecht, 1896); G. M. Stulac, *James* (IVPNTC; Downers Grove, IL: InterVarsity Press, 1993); R. W. Wall, *The Community of the Wise: The Book of James* (NTC; Harrisburg, PA: Trinity Press, 1997). **Studies:** K. Aland, "Der Herrnbruder Jakobus und der Jakobusbrief," *TLZ* 69 (1944) 97-104; G. Bornkamm, "The Letter to the Romans as Paul's Last Will and Testament" in *The Romans Debate,* ed. K. Donfried (Minneapolis: Augsburg, 1977) 17-31; D. Boyarin, *Intertextuality and the Reading of Midrash* (Bloomington, IN: Indiana University Press, 1990); M. Brett, *Biblical Criticism in Crisis?* (Cambridge: Cambridge University Press, 1991); F. F. Bruce, *Peter, Stephen, James and John: Studies in Early Non-Pauline Christianity* (Grand Rapids: Eerdmans, 1979); T. B. Cargal, *Restoring the Diaspora. Discursive Structure and Purpose in the Epistle of James* (SBLDS 144; Atlanta: Scholars Press, 1993); A Chester and R. P. Martin, *The Theology of the Letters of James, Peter, and Jude* (NTT; Cambridge: Cambridge University Press, 1994); B. S. Childs, *The New Testament as Canon

(Philadelphia: Fortress, 1985); C. E. B. Cranfield, "The Message of James," *SJT* 18 (1965) 182-93, 338-45; D. D. Deppe, *The Sayings of Jesus in the Epistle of James* (Chelsea, MI: Bookcrafters, 1989); K. Donfried, ed., *The Romans Debate* (Minneapolis: Augsburg, 1977); J. H. Elliot, "The Epistle of James in Rhetorical and Social Scientific Perspective: Holiness-Wholeness and Patterns of Replication," *BTB* 23 (1993) 71-81; F. O. Francis, "The Form and Function of the Opening and Closing Paragraphs of James and I John," *ZNW* 61 (1970) 110-26; M. Gertner, "Midrashic Terms and Techniques in the New Testament: the Epistle of James, a Midrash on a Psalm," *SE* 3 (= TU 88 [1964]) 463; D. E. Gowan, "Wisdom and Endurance in James," *HBT* 15 (1993) 145-53; D. Hadidian, "Palestinian Pictures in the Epistles of James," *ExpT* 63 (1952) 227-28; P. J. Hartin, "Come now, you rich, weep and wail . . .' (James 5:1-6)," *JTSA* 84 (1993) 57-63; idem, "Call to Be Perfect Through Suffering (James 1:2-4)," unpublished paper presented to the Society of Biblical Literature (Philadelphia,1995); idem, *James and the Q Sayings of Jesus* (JSNTSup 47; Sheffield: JSOT, 1991); R. B. Hays, *The Faith of Jesus Christ* (SBLDS 56; Chico, CA: Scholars Press, 1983); M. Hengel, "Der Jakobusbrief als antipaulinische Polemik" in *Tradition and Interpretation in the New Testament*, ed. G. F. Hawthorne and O. Betz (Grand Rapids: Eerdmans, 1987) 248-78; idem, *Property and Riches in the Early Church* (London: SCM, 1974); H. J. Holtzmann, "Die Zeitlage des Jakobus- briefes," *ZWT* 25 (1882) 292-310; R. Hoppe, *Der theologische Hintergrund des Jakobusbriefes* (FB 28; Würzburg: Katholisches Bibelwerk, 1977); J. Jeremias, "Paul and James," *ExpT* 66 (1954-55) 368-71; L. T. Johnson, "Friendship with the World/Friendship with God: A Study of Discipleship in James" in *Discipleship in the New Testament,* ed. F. F. Segovia (Philadelphia: Fortress, 1985) 166-83; idem, "The Mirror of Remembrance (James 1:22-25)," *CBQ* 50 (1988) 632-45; idem, "The Social World of James" in *The Social World of the First Christians*, ed. L. M. White and O. L. Yarborough (Minneapolis: Fortress, 1995) 178-97; idem, "The Use of Leviticus 19 in the Letter of James," *JBL* 101 (1982) 391-401; W. G. Johnsson, "The Pilgrimage Motif in the Book of Hebrews," *JBL* 97 (1978) 239-51; H. C. Kee, *Who Are the People of God?* (New Haven, CT: Yale University Press, 1995); J. A. Kirk, "The Meaning of Wisdom in James," *NTS* 16 (1969) 24-38; G. Kittel, "Der Jakobusbrief und die apostolischen Vater," *ZNW* 43 (1950) 54-112; W. G. Kümmel, *Introduction to the New Testament* (rev. ed.; Nashville: Abingdon, 1975); E. E. Lemcio, "The Unifying Kerygma of the New Testament," *JSNT* 33 (1988) 3-17; J. G. Lodge, "James and Paul at Cross Purposes: James 2,22," *Bib* 62 (1981) 195-213; B. J. Malina, "Wealth and Poverty in the New Testament," *Int* 41 (1987) 354-67; P. U. Maynard-Reid, *Poverty and Wealth in James* (Maryknoll, NY: Orbis, 1987); A. Meyer, *Das Rätsel des Jakobusbriefes* (BZNW 10; Giessen: Töppelman, 1930); J. A. Overman, "The Diaspora in the Modern Study of Ancient Judaism" in *Diaspora Jews and Judaism*, ed. J. A. Overman and R. S. MacLennan (SFSHJ 41; Atlanta: Scholars Press, 1992) 63-78; T. C. Penner, *The Epistle of James and Eschatology* (JSNTSup 121; Sheffield: Sheffield Academic Press, 1996); L. Perdue, "Paraenesis and the Epistle of James," *ZNW* 72 (1981) 241-56; J. M. Reese, "The Exegete as Sage: Hearing the Message of James," *BTB* 12 (1982) 82-85; J. A. Sanders, *God Has a Story Too* (Philadelphia: Fortress, 1979); J. Schneider, *Die Briefe des Jakobus, Petrus, Judas und Johannes* (NTD 10; Göttingen: Vandenhoeck & Ruprecht, 1961); A. M. Shepherd, "The Epistle of James and the Gospel of Matthew," *JBL* 75 (1956) 40-51; K. Syreeni, "James and the Pauline Legacy," unpublished paper presented to the Society of Biblical Literature (Chicago, 1994); R. E. van Voorst, *The Ascents of James: History and Theology of a Jewish-Christian Community* (SBLDS 112; Atlanta: Scholars Press, 1989); R. W. Wall, *Colossians & Philemon* (IVPNTC; Downers Grove, IL: InterVarsity Press, 1993); idem, "James as Apocalyptic Paraenesis," *RQ* 32 (1990) 11-22; idem, "Reading the New Testament in Canonical Context" in *Hearing the New Testament: Strategies for Interpretation*, ed. J. B. Green (Grand Rapids: Eerdmans, 1995) 370-93; idem, *Revelation* (NIBC; Peabody, MA: Hendrickson, 1991); idem, "Successors to 'the Twelve' According to Acts 12:1-17," *CBQ* 53 (1991) 628-43; R. W. Wall and E. E. Lemcio, *The New Testament as Canon: A Reader in Canonical Criticism* (JSNTSup 76; Sheffield: JSOT, 1992); R. B. Ward, "The Works of Abraham: James 2:14-26," *HTR* 61 (1968) 283-90; idem, "Partiality in the Assembly: James 2:2-4;" *HTR* 62 (1969) 87-97; D. F. Watson,

"James 2 in Light of Greco-Roman Schemes of Argumentation," *NTS* 39 (1993) 94-121; idem, "The Rhetoric of James 3:1-12 and a Classical Pattern of Argumentation," *NovT* 35 (1993) 487-64; B. Witherington, *Jesus the Sage* (Minneapolis: Fortress, 1994); W. Wuellner, "Der Jakobusbrief im Licht der Rhetorik und Textpragmatik," *LB* 43 (1978) 5-65.

R. W. Wall.

JAMES THE JUST. *See* JAMES, LETTER OF.

JERUSALEM, ZION, HOLY CITY

Ever since the "stronghold of Zion" was seized by David (2 Sam 5:7; 1 Chron 11:5), Jewish attention has been focused upon one city, Jerusalem. Shortly after its capture Jerusalem became the political, economic, military, social and religious center for ancient Israel. The successful concentration of both earthly and heavenly power in Jerusalem insured that this city was destined to dominate Jewish geographical imagination forevermore. Not only was Jerusalem thought to be the "center," or "navel," of the whole earth (Ezek 5:5; 38:12; *1 Enoch* 26:1; *Jub.* 8:11, 19) but also ideal figurations of this holy city, this Zion, became stock symbols for Jewish worship and eschatology.* Jewish dreams of what ought to be and what would be were uniquely tied to this specific plot of land (Gowan). Jerusalem, or Zion, thus replaced Sinai as the mountain of Yahweh's presence (Levenson).

Given Jerusalem's importance for Jewish communal identity (Kee, 18-22), it is curious that imagery about Zion does not play a larger role within early Christian reflection. "Zion" *(Sion)* occurs only four times in the later writings of the NT and the apostolic fathers* (Heb 12:22; 1 Pet 2:6; Rev 14:1; *Barn.* 6.2), while the phrase "holy city" *(hagia polis)* appears only four times in the later writings of the NT (Rev 11:2, 21:2, 10; 22:19) and never in the apostolic fathers. References to "Jerusalem" *(Ierosolyma; Ierousalem)*, although more plentiful, are concentrated: fifty-nine occurrences in Acts; only five elsewhere (Heb 12:22; Rev 3:12; 21:2, 10; *1 Clem.* 41.2). Part of the explanation may be that Roman occupation and the destruction of Jerusalem held in check wholesale Christian appropriation of the tradition (see *Barn.* 16.4-5; Robinson). Further, Jesus, as the embodiment of God's presence, reshaped Jewish eschatology.

Since Christian hope was uniquely tied to a person and not to a place, the Zion tradition was reformatted in its application to Jesus (1 Pet 2:6; *Barn.* 6.2; cf. Is 28:16). Finally many of the royal themes associated with Zion were carried along without specific reference to the city; for example, language about kingdom, temple,* covenant* and priesthood.* The few places in which Christianity did explicitly use the Zion tradition in a substantive way thus merit close attention.

1. Old Testament Background
2. Jerusalem in the Geographical Theology of Acts
3. Zion in the Eschatological Warning of Hebrews
4. The Holy City in the Apocalyptic Vision of Revelation
5. Summary

1. Old Testament Background.

In the OT several motifs coalesce to form the idealized picture of Jerusalem, Zion or the holy city (Roberts, 329-44). The OT affirms that Yahweh specifically chose Jerusalem (Ps 78:68; 87:2; 102:16; 132:13) to be his special dwelling place (Ps 2:6; 9:11; 74:2; 87:2; 102:16). Jerusalem is thus considered to be a sacred place, a place of worship and celebration (2 Chron 5:2; Ps 99:2; 137:1-3; 146:10; 147:12). OT writers consistently glorify the city by describing it in epic proportions. Even though it is of modest size, Zion is depicted as a mountain of exceeding height (Ps 48:2; Is 2:2; Mic 4:1; cf. Ezek 40:2; Zech 14:10). All the heavenly host assemble at Zion (Is 14:13; Ps 48:1-2; 89:5, 12). From Zion flows a river that brings unparalleled fertility and abundance to the world (Ps 46:4; Ezek 47:1-12; Joel 3:18; cf. Is 51:3; Zech 1:17). Zion is also thought to be the site of a mighty theophany where Yahweh defeated, defeats or will defeat the evil powers of chaos (Is 14:32; 17:12-14; 18:1-6; 29:1-8; 31:4-9; Ezek 38—39; Joel 2:1; 3:21; Amos 1:2; Zech 12:1-9; 14:3, 12-15).

The OT also sees the city as playing a prominent role in Israel's and the world's future. After purification and cleansing (Is 4:4; 52:1), Jerusalem is the place where Israel will be regathered (Is 30:19; 46:13; 51:11; Jer 31:6); Jerusalem is the place where both Israel* and the nations with be judged (Is 10:12; Amos 6:1; Mic 3:12); from Jerusalem salvation* will pour to the ends of the earth (Ps 14:7; 50:2; 53:6; Is 37:32; 52:7; Joel 2:32; 3:16; Obad 1:17; Zeph 3:14); and to

Jerusalem all the nations will come to acknowledge Yahweh alone as king of the world (Ps 76:11-12; Is 2:2-4; Mic 4:2, 7; Is 18:7; Zech 14:16-19). The themes of election,* divine presence, worship,* prosperity, ingathering, conversion, transformation, judgment* and salvation are all closely associated with the tradition of Jerusalem, Zion and the holy city.

2. Jerusalem in the Geographical Theology of Acts.

Hans Conzelmann placed geography front and center in any discussion of the theology of Luke-Acts. While one may wish to quibble with some of Conzelmann's conclusions—for example, that Luke intentionally used geography to distance Jesus from John the Baptist (Conzelmann, 18-27; cf. Marshall, 145-47)—one cannot deny the programmatic role that geography in general and Jerusalem in particular played for the structure of this two-volume work. Jerusalem not only is the city of destiny for Jesus (Gospel of Luke) but also is the reference point for worldwide gospel expansion (Acts).

The first scene of Acts* takes place in Jerusalem (cf. Lk 1:5-23). The risen Jesus commands his disciples not to leave Jerusalem until "the promise" has been fulfilled (Acts 1:4). Jesus then recommissions his disciples (Acts 1:8; cf. Lk 24:47), and this commission provides the geographical plan for the entire work: "you shall be my witnesses beginning in Jerusalem [Acts 1—7], Judea and Samaria [Acts 8—12] and unto the ends of the earth [Acts 13—28]." If in the Gospel the story winds down to Jerusalem, then in the book of Acts the story spirals outward from Jerusalem.

Jerusalem continues to figure prominently in the narrative, even though the plot of Acts requires the movement away from the city. The entirety of Jerusalem becomes a collective and unwitting witness to the death of Christ,* his resurrection* and the coming of the Holy Spirit* (Acts 2:14; 4:16; 5:28). The disciples' ministry* and preaching* first enjoyed success in Jerusalem (Acts 5:16; 6:7). The critical events of Jesus' life that transpired in Jerusalem—his crucifixion, resurrection and appearances—became essential elements in the preaching of the disciples (Acts 10:39; 13:27, 31). The persecution of the church* at Jerusalem paradoxically led to the evangelization of Judea and Samaria* (Acts 8:1). The community of believers in Jeru-

salem provided supervision for the successive waves of expansion outside the city environs (Acts 8:14, 25; 11:2, 22, 27; 12:25; 15:2, 4; 16:4). And the Paul of Acts, like the Jesus of Luke's Gospel (Lk 9:51—19:27), makes a fateful, final journey to Jerusalem (Acts 19:31—21:17), replete with foreboding travel notices (Acts 20:16, 22; 21:4, 11, 12, 13, 15; cf. Lk 9:51, 53; 13:22; 17:11; 18:31; 19:11).

What drives this focus upon Jerusalem? Acts strategically places Jerusalem in the narrative horizon generated by the Zion tradition. The subtext for the programmatic commission of Acts 1:8 is Isaiah 49:6 (cf. Is 2:3 = Mic 4:2). The phrase "ends of the earth" specifically links these two texts and thereby places the commission in a larger narrative web of texts that spotlight God's universal saving intentions (e.g., Ps 2:8; 22:27; 72:8; 98:3; Is 45:22; 52:10). The disciples thus become intertextually positioned as the "light" that Yahweh or Jesus sends to "the nations" in order that "salvation might reach to the ends of the earth."

Pentecost* should also be read in light of the Zion tradition. "Devout persons from every nation under heaven" had gathered in Jerusalem, and it was to them, in their own language, that they heard the apostles* speaking. Peter appeals to Joel's prophecy about Zion (Joel 2:1, 15, 23) to explain this extraordinary event. God foretold that he would pour out his Spirit upon "all flesh" (Joel 2:28 = Acts 2:17). But, as Peter glosses his subtext, this blessing* is not limited to those who reside in Zion (Joel 2:32); this blessing is to be democratized upon "whoever calls upon the name of the Lord" (Acts 2:21). Peter's pesher of Joel 2 thus makes Jerusalem the nuclear center for world transformation.

Paul's missionary efforts, which dominate the latter half of Acts, are also narratively linked to the Zion tradition. The interpretation of Paul's conversion that God provides to Ananias identifies Paul as a (the) "chosen instrument" to carry Yahweh's name "before the nations" (Acts 9:15; cf. Acts 22:12-16; 26:16-18; Gal 1:16; Rom 1:5). Paul and Barnabas justify their Gentile* mission by explicitly citing Isaiah 49:6 (Acts 13:47). The citation clarifies Paul's "necessity" of preaching first to the Jews and, only after their rejection, of turning to the "nations" (Acts 13:46; 18:6; 28:26-28; cf. Rom 1:16-17). Such a procedure resonates with Isaiah's eschatological* vision: Zion's "servant" has a twofold mission: to restore Israel (Is 49:6) and to include the nations in this salvation (Is 49:6). Like Jesus (Lk 2:32) and the early disciples before him (Acts 1:8), Paul too is to be the "light to the nations."

Not only does Jerusalem provide the literary setting for the middle portion of Luke and Acts (Lk 20—Acts 7), but also the city is the theological epicenter for reaching the "ends of the earth" with the good news of Jesus (Kee, 192-207). Acts construes the events accomplished in Jerusalem—Jesus' death, resurrection, ascension*—as the topical sequence of a larger narrative, a narrative whose final sequence includes the conversion of the nations. Acts thus explains the ever outward spiral of expansion in terms of the Zion tradition: Jerusalem is the place where God begins to transform the world. The missionary exploits of Jesus' disciples, beginning in Jerusalem and stretching to the ends of the earth, represent nothing short of the world's "Zionization."

3. Zion in the Eschatological Warning of Hebrews.

The clearest and most expressive use of the Zion tradition occurs in Hebrews 12. In a tightly knit and internally cohesive unit, the author contrasts Sinai (Heb 12:18-21) with Zion (Heb 12:22-24). Specifically the author compares the terrifying aspects of Yahweh's theophany at Sinai with the festive joy of Zion under the new covenant. Prefaced by a hortatory appeal for perseverance (Heb 12:14-17), the descriptive analogy between Sinai and Zion forms the basis for the author's stern warning about the eschatological peril of falling away (Heb 12:25-29).

The dramatic differences between Sinai and Zion can be seen in the images the passage associates with the two locales:

You have not come to [Sinai]	But you have come to Mount Zion,
	to the city of the living God,
	to the heavenly Jerusalem
to what can be touched	to a myriad of angels in festal gathering
to a burning fire	to the congregation of the firstborn who are enrolled in heaven
to darkness	to God, a judge over all
to gloom	to the spirits of the just made perfect
to a whirlwind	to the mediator of the new covenant, Jesus
to the sound of a trumpet	to the sprinkled blood
to a voice of words	

The author compounds Zion imagery, to demonstrate the eschatological superiority of the new covenant revealed in and through Jesus. The juxtaposition of the phrases "the city of living God" and "the heavenly Jerusalem" with "Mount Zion" (Heb 12:22) identifies Zion as the "city whose builder and maker is God" (Heb 11:10), the city that God has "prepared" for the faithful (Heb 11:16) and the city believers earnestly "seek" in this life (Heb 14:13). Zion, the holy city and heavenly Jerusalem are also related to other royal geographical references in Hebrews; for example, to the "kingdom" (Heb 1:8; 11:33; 12:28), the "world to come" (Heb 2:5), "the throne" (Heb 4:14; 8:1), "the shrine behind the curtain" (Heb 6:19), "the sanctuary" (Heb 8:2, 5, 19), "homeland" (Heb 11:14) and the "better country" (Heb 11:16). Hebrews uses Zion imagery to define Jerusalem as the city of God's abiding presence and conversion as citizenship in God's cosmic and eschatological metropolis.

The atmosphere in Zion is festive, in direct contrast to Sinai. Joyful angelic praise (Heb 12:22) replaces the distressing images of fire, darkness, gloom, violent wind and unintelligible sounds (Heb 12:18). The festal gathering *(panyrgia)* recalls the unrestrained celebrations prefigured within the Zion tradition, while the presence of innumerable angelic hosts invokes the divine council who were thought to reside upon Zion.

The "congregation of the firstborn" *(ekklēsia prōtotokōn)* supplants the image of Israel huddled at the base of Sinai (Heb 12:23). That the earthly members of God's community share Zion's certain and sure election is emphasized by the inscription of their names in the heavenly city (cf. Ps 69:28; 139:16; Phil 4:3; Rev 3:5; 13:8; 17:8; 20:12, 15; 21:27). Zion's God is still "judge over all" (Heb 12:23); but the life that he makes possible in the heavenly city will entail full transformation. The "just" will undergo that final, eschatological metamorphosis into complete conformity with God's perfect character (Heb 12:23; cf. Ezek 36:24-32; Gowan, 73-81). The unapproachability, distance and mysteriousness of God under the old covenant are replaced by the full and unrestricted access of the new (Heb 12:24). This access is gained through the mediatory work of Jesus—specifically the offering of his sacrificial blood. This eschatological vision inaugurates the new covenant hope* of Jeremiah 31:31-34.

The author of Hebrews* uses the dramatic images of Sinai and Zion to demonstrate the eschatological superiority and greater responsibility of Christian identity. While affirming that the readers have already arrived (Heb 12:18) at the city gates of Zion (i.e., the "now" of salvation), the author also portrays the Christian life as a pilgrimage to the heavenly city (i.e., the "not yet" of salvation). Christians should persist in "drawing near" (Heb 4:16; 7:25; 10:1, 22; 11:6; 12:18, 22). Hebrews thus employs Zion imagery to draft a strong word to those who are experiencing spiritual fatigue in their journey.

4. The Holy City in the Apocalyptic Vision of Revelation.

"City" *(polis)* occurs twenty-six times in Revelation (*see* Revelation, Book of) and forms one of the book's key images. The plot of Revelation can be read as the tale of two cities—the new and heavenly Jerusalem and the corrupt and sinful Babylon.*

Revelation predicts that the "great" city of Babylon is destined to suffer a cataclysmic end (Rev 14:8). Revelation narrates this fate in the climatic judgment of the seventh cup (Rev 16:17—18:24), the final judgment before the apocalypse of Jesus and the new Jerusalem (Rev 19:1—22:5).

Babylon is singled out as the special object of God's wrath* (Rev 16:19). The city is metaphorically described as a woman (Rev 17:3; 17:18). Despite her regal appearance (Rev 17:4), the city is a harlot (Rev 17:1), the mother of all whores (Rev 17:5). Babylon is the dwelling place of demons, of all that is foul and hateful (Rev 18:2). Babylon has consciously persecuted those who side with God. She has become drunk with the blood of the saints and martyrs of Jesus (Rev 17:6): Her sins are heaped as high as heaven itself (Rev 18:4). This woman/city exercises an undue and tragic influence over all the cities of the earth (Rev 17:18). Revelation graphically demonstrates this connection: when Babylon was split into three parts, the cities of the nations fell (Rev 16:19). The nations have committed fornication with her and under her influence have grown rich with the wealth of her wantonness (Rev 18:3).

But God promises to punish her iniquities (Rev 18:5). He will repay double for all that she has done (Rev 18:6). Because she has usurped royal privilege (Rev 18:7), her plagues will come and they will come quickly—in a single day (Rev 18:8), even a single hour (Rev 18:10, 17, 19). The cities and kings of the earth will be amazed at the swiftness and completeness of her judgment (Rev 18:10). Babylon's destruction will collapse the world's domination system (Rev 18:11-20; see Wink, 319-24). God's judgment upon this great city will be complete: "she will be found no more" (Rev 18:21).

Like Babylon, Jerusalem also will undergo judgment because of her sinfulness; thus the renaming of Jerusalem "Sodom and Egypt" (Rev 11:8). Consequently the nations will "tread under foot" the holy city for forty-two months (Rev 11:2), and the city will be punished by a great earthquake (Rev 11:13). However, unlike Babylon, Jerusalem will also receive the protection of God. Just when the forces of evil are ready to destroy this great city, God will send "fire" to destroy them (Rev 20:6).

The final eradication of evil clears the way for the transformation of Jerusalem (Rev 21:2). The new Jerusalem is also likened to a woman, a faithful and chaste woman, adorned as a bride (Rev 21:2). This new city will enjoy the unmediated and full presence of God forevermore (Rev 21:3, 11). Sorrow, pain and suffering* will no longer plague the city, for all the former woes will have "passed away" (Rev 21:3-4).

Revelation draws freely upon the Zion tradition to describe the new Jerusalem. The city will be located upon a mountain of exceeding height (Rev 21:10) and of immense proportions—a great cube with its height, width and length measuring the same fifteen hundred miles (Rev 21:15-16). The four city walls, with three gates each, are made of jasper, while the city itself is constructed of gold. The foundations supporting the four walls are adorned with every kind of precious stones (Rev 21:18-21). This eschatological city needs no temple or sun or moon, for God's presence will be a beacon to all the nations (Rev 21:22-26). The river that flows from the city brings abundance and peace to the whole world (Rev 22:2). From this city God will reign forevermore (Rev 22:5).

The images of Babylon and Jerusalem provide comfort to a community suffering persecution* and wondering about its future. God will vanquish the great foe Babylon, the symbol of evil's cruel rule in this life, and will replace that city with the new Jerusalem, the symbol of transforming powers of God that will usher in the age of unparalleled blessing. The horrors and catastrophe of Babylon will be exceeded only by the greatness and shalom of the new Jerusalem.

5. Summary.
Christianity, like Judaism,* saw in Jerusalem, Zion and the holy city a rich array of possible evocations. Acts interprets Jerusalem's strategic role in worldwide expansion through the lens of the Zion tradition: the mission to include the nations in God's saving purposes inaugurates the hope of eschatological Zion. Hebrews translates the entirety of the Christian life into the language of Zion: conversion is arrival at the city gates, while discipleship is the progressive journey toward Zion. Revelation pits Babylon against Jerusalem to assure its readers of God's final victory: the new, heavenly Jerusalem embodies the greatness and certainty of complete world transformation.

See also CENTERS OF CHRISTIANITY; CHRISTIANITY AND JUDAISM: PARTINGS OF THE WAYS; ESCHATOLOGY; JEWISH CHRISTIANITY; TEMPLE.

BIBLIOGRAPHY. R. J. Bauckham, *The Climax of Prophecy: Studies on the Book of Revelation* (Edinburgh: T & T Clark, 1993); R. L. Cohn, *The Shape of Sacred Space* (AARSR 23; Chico, CA: Scholars Press, 1981); H. Conzelmann, *The Theology of St. Luke* (Philadelphia: Fortress, 1961); D. G. Gowan, *Eschatology in the Old Testament* (Philadelphia: Fortress, 1986); J. D. Levenson, *Sinai and Zion: An Entry into the Jewish Bible* (Minneapolis: Winston, 1985); H. C. Kee, *Who Are the People of God? Early Christian Models of Community* (New Haven, CT: Yale University Press, 1995); I. H. Marshall, *Luke: Historian and Theologian* (Grand Rapids: Zondervan, 1970); J. J. M. Roberts, "The Davidic Origins of the Zion Tradition," *JBL* 92 (1973) 329-44; J. A. T. Robinson, *Redating the New Testament* (Philadelphia: Westminster, 1976); W. Wink, *Engaging the Powers: Discernment and Resistance in a World of Domination* (Minneapolis: Fortress, 1992).

C. C. Newman

JESUS TRADITIONS
To what extent were traditions about the life and teaching of Jesus used in earliest Christianity? In what contexts were Jesus traditions used?

These questions continue to tease scholars. In the light of form criticism it is generally accepted that Jesus traditions circulated orally in early Christian communities for several decades before they were incorporated into the four Gospels. However, the evidence from Christian writings themselves for the use of Jesus traditions is difficult to assess.

There are few explicit quotations of Jesus traditions in writings that date from before the early decades of the second century. Many more possible allusions have been noted, but it is difficult to determine how many of them would have been understood by the first readers to be references to Jesus traditions. Some of the alleged allusions may result from the use of similar "biblical" phraseology in both the Jesus tradition and the allusion.

A decision on the extent of allusions to traditions of the life and teaching of Jesus is inevitably based partly on presuppositions. Scholars who insist that most early Christian writers took it for granted that their readers had an extensive knowledge of traditions about the teaching and actions of Jesus are naturally more willing to accept a considerable number of allusions. A very different view is taken by those who claim either that before about A.D. 150 interest in the earthly life of Jesus was less prominent in Christian preaching and teaching than we might suppose, or Jesus traditions did not circulate in all early Christian communities. Discussion of these questions has often focused on the Pauline epistles (*see DPL*, Jesus, Sayings of), but the equally important evidence of the later NT writings and second-century writings needs to be considered carefully.

An equally controversial issue arises in Christian writings from early in the second century onward. Are quotations or allusions to Jesus traditions taken from oral tradition or from written Gospels? Since Jesus traditions were known and used orally long after the Gospels were written, it is often difficult to decide whether an oral or a written Jesus tradition has been used.

1. Acts of the Apostles
2. Hebrews
3. James
4. 1 Peter
5. 2 Peter and Jude
6. The Johannine Epistles
7. Revelation

8. Apostolic Fathers
9. Other Early Christian Writings
   (Agrapha)
10. Jesus Traditions and the Fourfold Gospel
11. Conclusions

1. Acts of the Apostles.

There are few references to Jesus traditions in the speeches or sermons of Acts.* This is not surprising, given that Luke has already set out the story of Jesus at some length in his Gospel. Close examination of the speeches confirms that Luke is an economical writer who avoids unnecessary repetition: themes that are prominent in one speech are often treated cursorily or omitted in other speeches.

The speeches in the early chapters of Acts are set in Jerusalem,* where some knowledge of the life and teaching* of Jesus and in particular of the events that led to the crucifixion seems to be assumed. Once Luke's account of the post-Easter events moves beyond Jerusalem, however, it is necessary to include a sketch of the story of Jesus in Peter's evangelistic preaching* to Cornelius,* a Roman centurion (Acts 10:34-43).

Luke did not include such a sketch in Paul's lengthy speech in the synagogue* at Pisidian Antioch (Acts 13:16-41). Here there is more detailed reference to John the Baptist than there was in the previous speech (Acts 10) and a quotation of John's words concerning his relationship to Jesus (Acts 13:24-25). But the story moves directly from John the Baptist to the request of "the residents of Jerusalem and their leaders" to Pilate to have Jesus killed (Acts 13:27-28).

The citation of John the Baptist's words in Acts 13:24-25 does not correspond exactly to Luke 3:16: in Acts Luke may have abbreviated the words he included in his Gospel, or he may be quoting from a slightly different oral tradition.

The later speeches in Acts do not allude to, let alone cite, Jesus traditions. Paul's moving farewell speech to the Ephesian elders at Miletus, however, is an exception. It concludes with an explicit citation of a saying of Jesus that is not included in any of the Gospels: "It is more blessed to give than to receive" (Acts 20:35). Although quotations of the teaching of Jesus are rare in early Christian writings before Irenaeus, this verse confirms that extracanonical sayings of Jesus (often referred to as "agrapha," or "unwritten" sayings) were known. Unlike many of the agrapha found in later writings, this saying is usually accepted as a genuine saying of Jesus (see 9 below).

The quotation of these words of Jesus brings to a dramatic climax the final theme of Paul's speech at Miletus. In this way Luke shows his readers that Paul knows and obeys the teaching of Jesus and implies that they should follow Paul's example: Paul's last words to the Ephesian elders are not his own but the words of "the Lord Jesus." Luke makes this point so powerfully as the finale to this speech that there is no need to repeat it in the other speeches in Acts.

The context is significant. Paul quotes the words of Jesus as the climax of his insistence to the Ephesian elders that by his own hands he has supported himself and his companions. The use of a Jesus tradition in the context of community instruction in Acts 20:35 complements the use of Jesus traditions in an evangelistic context in Acts 10:36-43.

2. Hebrews.

In Hebrews* there are few references to events in the life of Jesus and probably no references to his teaching. Nonetheless the author's whole line of argument assumes broad familiarity with the story of Jesus.

The fullest reference to the earthly life of Jesus is in Hebrews 5:7-9 (NRSV):

> In the days of his flesh, Jesus offered up prayers and supplications, with loud cries and tears, to the one who was able to save him from death, and he was heard because of his reverent submission. Although he was a Son, he learned obedience through what he suffered; and having been made perfect, he became the source of eternal salvation for all who obey him.

Although this passage has often been related closely to the Gethsemane traditions in the Gospels, there is no significant verbal correspondence. However, nearly all the Greek words in this verse are found in several OT passages with a similar context of a prayer* uttered in deep anxiety; the closest parallels are in Psalm 116. Several scholars have suggested that Hebrews 5:7-9, like the partly similar Philippians 2:6-11, is based on an early Christian hymn.* While this view is plausible, it is worth noting that few of the stylistic features of the "hymn" in Philippians 2:6-11 (and other early Christian "hymns") are found here.

The context of Hebrews 5:7-9 assumes that the experiences of Jesus alluded to took place in connection with his passion (for some discussion see Cullmann, 95-98). While a variant Gethsemane tradition probably does lie behind these verses, they may refer in summary form to more than one period of earnest prayer shortly before the crucifixion.

Hebrews 13:12 refers to the suffering of Jesus "outside the city gate." This detail is not found in the Synoptic passion narratives, though it does seem to be presupposed in the Matthean and Lukan versions of the parable of the wicked husbandmen (Mt 21:39 par. Lk 20:15; cf. Mk 12:8). The closest parallel is in John 19:17-20, though verbal correspondence is minimal.

Two further references to the earthly life of Jesus need to be noted. In line with many NT passages, Hebrews 7:14 refers to the descent of Jesus from the tribe of Judah. Hebrews 4:15 states that Jesus, our high priest,* has been "tested in every respect as we are, yet is without sin." Since the previous chapter has compared Jesus and Moses* closely and has referred to the "testing" of Moses and those whom he led in the wilderness (Heb 3:1-19), it is possible that the general reference to the "testing" of Jesus in Hebrews 4:15 includes an allusion to his wilderness "testing" (Mk 1:13 and par.).

Knowledge and use of sayings of Jesus are even more difficult to trace. In two passages sayings of Jesus are quoted, but in both cases they are words of Scripture rather than sayings of the earthly Jesus. In Hebrews 2:12 we read: "For this reason he [i.e., Jesus] is not ashamed to call them brothers and sisters, saying, 'I will proclaim your name [i.e., the Father's name] to my brothers and sisters,'" a quotation of Psalm 22:22. Quotations of 2 Samuel 22:3 (or perhaps Is 12:2 or Is 8:17) and then Isaiah 2:13 follow. Although there is no indication of the point at which Jesus is considered to have spoken these words, they are not necessarily to be taken as words of the exalted Christ.* The author probably intends the citations of Scripture to be taken as comments made by Jesus at his incarnation.

This is certainly the case at Hebrews 10:5-6, where quotation and discussion of Psalm 40:6-8 is introduced as follows: "Consequently, when he [Christ] came into the world, he said. . . ."

Since Christ is the fulfillment of Scripture, then it is possible for the author of Hebrews to claim that at his coming into the world* Christ quoted verses from the psalm: his coming into the world is an act of submission to the will of God*; this is the sacrifice* God really desires.

In several paraenetic passages a saying of Jesus might have been used to clinch the argument, as at Acts 20:35, but for whatever reason this is not done. Hebrews 13:5 is a good example. In the opening clause readers are urged to keep their lives free from the love of money, but there is not so much as an allusion to Matthew 6:24 (par. Lk 16:13). The verse continues: "Be content with what you have," which might be taken as a summary of Matthew 6:31-34 (par. Lk 12:29-32), but there is no verbal reminiscence of this passage. Hebrews 13:5 ends with a quotation, "I will never leave you or forsake you." The introductory formula is unusual; it plausibly can be translated "For he [i.e., the Master] has said." However, in view of the immediate context and of the absence of sayings of the earthly Jesus elsewhere in Hebrews, the introductory phrase should almost certainly be translated (with the REB) "for God has said [in Scripture]" and the quotation taken as a reference to either Joshua 1:5 or a version of Deuteronomy 31:6, 8.

In spite of the paucity of references to Jesus traditions, the author of Hebrews is by no means uninterested in the earthly life of Jesus. Immediately after his highly rhetorical opening chapter, the author makes the first of his forceful exhortations: "Therefore we must pay greater attention to what we have heard" (Heb 2:1 NRSV). What has been heard is the message of salvation,* "declared at first through the Lord, and it was attested to us by those who heard him" (Heb 2:3 NRSV). While some interpreters insist that the exaltation* of Christ is in view as the moment when the message of salvation is first proclaimed, the immediate context refers to the incarnation rather than the exaltation of Christ (Heb 2:9-18). So Hebrews 2:3 is probably "a traditional summary of the spread of the gospel that started with a reference to Jesus" (Attridge, 67), a summary not unlike Acts 10:36-39, Peter's evangelistic proclamation to Cornelius.

In Hebrews 2:10 Jesus is referred to as the "pioneer" or "pathfinder" (see also Heb 12:2) who blazes a trail to glory* for his followers (see also Heb 6:20; 10:19-20). Because Jesus himself was tested by what he suffered, he is able to help those who are being tested (Heb 2:18; cf. Heb 4:15). At Hebrews 5:8 the Son* of God is said to have "learned obedience" through what he suffered (*see* Obedience). Since the obedient suffering* of the Son* is the path to exaltation and the pattern for his followers, the author has a deep-seated interest in the earthly life of Jesus.

It is difficult to assess the extent of the author's knowledge of the details of that life. It is significant that Hebrews 5:7, the most specific comment on the sufferings of Jesus, is couched in phrases from Psalm 116 rather than in echoes of Jesus traditions from the Gospels or their earlier sources.

3. James.
The letter of James* does not contain a single explicit citation of a saying of Jesus. Nonetheless as many as forty-five possible allusions to Jesus traditions have been noted. P. H. Davids has gone a step further and argued that at least one allusion lies at the heart of every major paragraph of the letter. While few scholars would be quite so bold, most accept that in at least a handful of passages the writer is indebted to oral Jesus traditions.

The clearest evidence of use of a Jesus tradition is at James 5:12 (NRSV): "Do not swear, either by heaven or by earth or by any other oath, but let your 'Yes' be yes and your 'No' be no, so that you may not fall under condemnation." A close relationship with Matthew 5:34-35, 37 is undeniable, for the verbal similarity of these two passages cannot be explained as independent use of the same OT, Jewish or Greek admonition. Although both Jewish and Greek ethical* teachers discouraged the use of oaths, Jesus seems to have been the first to prohibit their use. James 5:12 may well be closer to the original words of Jesus than is the fuller version in Matthew 5:34-35, 37; if so, Matthew 5:36 is probably an early expansion of the tradition, for there is no trace of these words in James.

Why does James fail to note that this striking and perhaps unique teaching comes from Jesus himself? Perhaps the writer and his readers were so well aware of this fact that ascription to Jesus was unnecessary. Or perhaps the writer was not aware of the origin of these words, for there is evidence elsewhere that Christian teachers wove sayings of Jesus into their ethical exhortation without indicating their origin.

James 2:8 also draws on Jesus tradition: "You are doing well if you really do fulfill the royal law according to the scripture, 'You shall love your neighbor as yourself.' " Here Leviticus 19:18 is quoted as Scripture, but James does not note that Jesus referred to this passage (Mk 12:31). Paul also quotes Leviticus 19:18 as the supreme command (Rom 13:9-10; Gal 5:14) but without referring to the authority* of Jesus for this conclusion. "It is probable that when James quotes Lev 19:18 as scripture he does so in the knowledge that this scripture has received the added authority of Jesus' use" (Laws, 110).

The following may be noted as further examples of allusions to Jesus traditions.

(1) "Ask God, . . . and it will be given to you" (Jas 1:5 recalls Mt 7:7 par. Lk 11:9). The same Q pericope seems to lie behind James 1:17 and perhaps James 4:2-3.

(2) James 2:5 is an extended paraphrase of Matthew 5:3, 5 (par. Lk 6:20): "Has not God chosen the poor in the world to be rich in faith and to be heirs of the kingdom that he has promised to those who love him?"

(3) James 3:12, "Can a fig tree . . . yield olives, or a grapevine figs?" may be based on Matthew 7:16 (par. Lk 6:44), though parallels in Stoic teaching may be closer.

(4) James 4:10, "Humble yourselves before the Lord, and he will exalt you," recalls Luke 14:11 and also Luke 18:14 and Matthew 23:12.

(5) The closing sentence of the letter, James 5:19-20, may be based on Matthew 18:15 (par. Lk 17:3), though there is little verbal correspondence.

How are these and many other alleged allusions to be assessed? If they are examined closely one by one, use of Jesus traditions is by no means certain. In some cases an equally plausible case can be made for partial dependence on OT, Jewish or Greek ethical teaching. However, once one accepts that Jesus traditions have been used at James 2:8 and at James 5:12, it becomes more likely that the writer has drawn on Jesus traditions elsewhere.

Some writers have attempted to show that in its use of Jesus traditions James depends directly on Q, on "M" or on Matthew's Gospel (see Hartin). The allusions are not confined to Q or to "M." While one cannot rule out dependence of James on Matthew's Gospel, few of Matthew's distinctive themes and turns of phrase are found in James; some of their shared vocabulary is common in other writings or is used rather differently by the two writers. In some respects James is closer in ethos to Luke than to Matthew.

The writer of James has drawn on his knowledge of a number of oral Jesus traditions in order to express his ethical concerns, but the extent of his indebtedness must remain an open question.

4. 1 Peter.

There are no explicit citations of sayings of Jesus in 1 Peter,* but more than thirty possible allusions to sayings of Jesus have been identified. Most scholars, however, accept no more than a handful of allusions to Jesus traditions.

Given that the author of this letter identifies himself in 1 Peter 1:1 as "Peter, apostle of Jesus Christ," the extent of allusions to sayings of Jesus has played a prominent part in discussion of the apostolic authorship of 1 Peter. Are there allusions to the sayings or events in the life of Jesus that could have come only from Peter himself? Or does the paucity of personal reminiscences tell against apostolic authorship?

In two detailed articles R. H. Gundry argued that 1 Peter was dictated by the apostle* Peter in Rome* and insisted that his dictation was peppered with frequent allusions to dominical sayings that were authentic and possessive of special interest to Peter. In a response to the first article, E. Best rejected most of the alleged allusions and concluded that contact between 1 Peter and Gospel traditions was confined primarily to two blocks, Luke 6:22-33 and Luke 12:32-45. Several more recent writers have assessed this debate and sided largely with Best, but they have added few fresh observations.

In the opening part of the great eulogy in 1 Peter 1:3-9 the writer includes himself along with the readers: "By God's great mercy he has given us a new birth" (*see* Mercy; New Birth). In 1 Peter 1:8, however, the writer switches to the second person plural: "Although you have not seen him, you love him; and even though you do not see him now, you believe in him." Is this an indication that although the readers have not seen the earthly Jesus, the writer (i.e., Peter) was an eyewitness? This seems unlikely. In the remainder of the letter* the second person plural is used frequently in passages in which the writer is not necessarily distinguishing himself from his readers.

When the writer refers to himself as a "wit-ness of the sufferings of Christ" (1 Pet 5:1), does he imply that he himself was an eyewitness to some of the events of the passion? Although this verse may be interpreted in this way, it should be noted that the phraseology of the references to the sufferings of Christ in 1 Peter 2:23-25 are taken from Isaiah 53, not from eyewitness testimony.

The following are some of the clearest examples of possible allusions in 1 Peter to Jesus traditions.

(1) The closing sentences of the Beatitudes (Mt 5:10-11 par. Lk 6:22) are alluded to in 1 Peter 3:14 and 1 Peter 4:14, even though these verses share only three Greek words.

(2) The whole of 1 Peter 2:12, a lengthy verse, is strikingly similar in content to Matthew 5:16 (which does not have a close parallel elsewhere in the Gospels), but they have only four Greek words in common.

(3) There are a number of similarities between 1 Peter 1:11 and Luke 24:26-27, but these verses have only one Greek word in common.

(4) 1 Peter 4:13 and Matthew 5:12 share two Greek verbs in the same order ("rejoice and be glad"), and this might be taken at first sight to indicate dependence. But the two contexts are very different, and the two verbs are hardly unusual.

Some interpreters argue that an allusion by the writer of 1 Peter to the content or a few words of Jesus traditions would have triggered in the minds of the readers recollection of larger blocks of traditions: the writer and the recipients of his letter were steeped deeply in traditions of the teaching of Jesus. This may have been the case, but if so, it would be difficult to understand why the writer frequently used his own turns of phrase and favorite terminology in passages that are similar in content to Jesus traditions.

We may be confident that 1 Peter drew on several clusters of Jesus traditions that were relevant to the points the writer wished to make. But it is impossible to be precise about the extent of the writer's knowledge and use of Jesus traditions. In several cases allusion to Jesus traditions is possible, but the influence of other early Christian catechetical traditions cannot be ruled out. However, the writer and perhaps his readers may have known many more sayings of Jesus that are not alluded to in this letter because they were not relevant to the themes being emphasized.

The writer knew oral Jesus traditions rather than written Gospels, but there is not enough evidence to decide whether or not he knew some form of Q. Since the clearest allusions are to Jesus traditions in Greek rather than Aramaic, it has often been claimed that they rule out Petrine authorship of this letter. This line of argument, however, is not compelling. We now know that Greek was spoken in some circles in first-century Galilee, and Greek may well have been used from time to time by Peter and Jesus, even though Aramaic was their native language.

5. 2 Peter and Jude.
2 Peter* includes an intriguing reference to the transfiguration in 2 Peter 1:16-18. The writer claims to have been an eyewitness of the majesty of Christ. "For he received honor and glory from God the Father when that voice was conveyed to him by the Majestic Glory, saying, 'This is my Son, my Beloved, with whom I am well pleased.' We ourselves heard this voice come from heaven while we were with him on the holy mountain" (2 Pet 1:17 NRSV).

Some scholars have claimed that the large number of differences from the transfiguration traditions in the Synoptic Gospels suggest that these verses are an account of a postresurrection appearance of Jesus (see Resurrection). But the words of the voice from heaven,* as well as the references to the visible majesty of Christ and to the presence of "Peter" and others on the mountain, confirm that this is a terse version of the transfiguration traditions. Although the phraseology of these verses is a little closer to Matthew than to the other Gospels, they almost certainly originated as an independent tradition that has been revised and perhaps abbreviated by the writer to fit its present context. If that is so, they provide important evidence for the continuing circulation of oral traditions of events in the life of Jesus as well as of his teaching. (For a full discussion see Bauckham, 205-12.)

There are three further references to Jesus traditions. At 2 Peter 1:14 "Peter" notes that he will die shortly, as indeed the Lord* Jesus Christ has told him clearly. This is usually taken to be a reference to the saying of Jesus recorded in John 21:18. While dependence on the final form of the Fourth Gospel is possible, there are no other indications in 2 Peter that the writer

and his readers knew this Gospel. 2 Peter 1:14 and John 21:18 are more likely to depend independently on a similar oral tradition concerning Peter's impending death.

At 2 Peter 2:20 there is close verbal agreement with the conclusion to the parable-like story of the returning unclean spirit (Mt 12:45 par. Lk 11:26). While the context suggests that the writer may know the whole story, this is unlikely in view of the fact that 2 Peter 2:22 quotes two proverbs rather than the Jesus tradition.

2 Peter 3:10, "the day of the Lord will come like a thief," is almost certainly related to the parable of the thief (Mt 24:43 par. Lk 12:39), for the image of a thief is found only in early Christian writings. Dependence on the version of this tradition in 1 Thessalonians 5:2 cannot be ruled out, for the verbal similarity is as close as it is to the Q tradition.

Several further phrases in 2 Peter may allude to Jesus traditions, but since there are similar phrases in OT or later Jewish writings, certainty is not possible.

The short letter of Jude* does not contain any clear allusions to Jesus traditions. Jude 17 urges readers to remember the predictions of the apostles of Christ; their words are quoted at a point where we may have expected a saying of Jesus. "They said to you, 'In the last time there will be scoffers, indulging their own ungodly desires.' " The next verse notes that these people are causing divisions. The theme of these two verses recalls Matthew 24:10-12 and related passages, so it might be argued that Jesus traditions are referred to here at second hand (i.e., via "the apostles"). But since there are no close verbal similarities, the link with Jesus traditions is at best tenuous.

6. The Johannine Epistles.
Although there are no traces of Synoptic Jesus traditions in the Johannine epistles (see John, Letters of), the relationship between John's Gospel and the Johannine epistles has long been a perplexing problem. Nearly every verse of 1 John contains a phrase or theme found in John's Gospel; there are also many links between 2 John and 3 John and the Gospel. There are so many differences, however, that common authorship is probably ruled out.

In the patristic period 1 John was often considered to have been written either to introduce the Gospel or to comment on its text. Variations on both these views are still advanced. R. E. Brown, for example, argues that 1 John is attempting to correct misinterpretation of the Gospel by the secessionists. On the basis of the impressively long list of parallels between 1 John and the Gospel (Brown, 757-59) and possible links between the structure of 1 John and the Gospel, Brown concludes that it is more likely that the author of 1 John knew some form of the written Gospel itself than merely the kind of tradition contained in it (Brown, 101, 86 n. 190). If this is so, 1 John would provide the earliest evidence for use of Jesus traditions in written rather than oral form.

Although Brown's views have been influential on recent scholarship, they have not won the day. For 1 John does not contain any proof of direct dependence either on Johannine Jesus traditions in oral form or on the written text of a version of John's Gospel itself. From time to time the rather unlikely view that the Johannine epistles were written before the Gospel has been defended.

In 1 John, as is the case in several other early Christian writings, there are a number of possible allusions to Jesus traditions. But careful consideration of the evidence suggests that it is unwise to draw bold conclusions about the ways Jesus traditions were used in Johannine circles.

7. Revelation.
Revelation (*see* Revelation, Book of) contains a handful of clear allusions to Jesus traditions. The following passages are among the most striking: Revelation 1:3, "blessed are those who hear and who keep what is written in it [the words of the prophecy]; for the time is near" (cf. Lk 11:28); Revelation 1:7, with its conflation of Daniel 7:13 and Zechariah 12:10, is closely related to Mt 24:30. In Revelation 3:3 (and cf. Rev 16:15) the Parousia* of Christ is likened to the coming of a thief, as in the Q tradition (Mt 24:42-23 par. Lk 12:39-40). A Q tradition (Mt 10:32 par. Lk 12:8) also lies behind Revelation 3:5: "I will confess your name before my Father and before his angels." Revelation 13:10, "if you kill with the sword, with the sword you must be killed," is dependent on the Jesus tradition in Matthew 26:52.

Most intriguing of all is the use in Revelation of the "hearing formula," "let anyone with ears to hear, listen," which is found in several strands of the Synoptic tradition (Mk 4:9 par. Mt 13:9 par. Lk 8:8; Mk 4:23; Mt 11:15; Mt 13:43; Lk 14:35). With the exception of Matthew 11:15 (which follows the statement that John the Baptist is the expected Elijah), these passages all conclude parables of Jesus. In Revelation, however, the similar hearing formula is used in a different context, at the end of all seven letters in Revelation 2—3 to churches in Asia Minor (Rev 2:7, 11, 17, 29; 3:6, 13, 22; cf. also Rev 13:9). In spite of the different contexts and the slightly different wording, in the Synoptic traditions and in Revelation the hearing formula is used to encourage careful attention to the preceding teaching; it is not a signal pointing to an esoteric meaning.

The relationship of Revelation to John's Gospel continues to baffle scholars. Most scholars accept that both writings, as well as the Johannine epistles, come from the same circles, though common authorship is unlikely. Although there is no clear evidence that Revelation depends on John's Gospel in its written form rather than on oral Johannine traditions, numerous passages echo its vocabulary and themes. For example, Revelation 21:6, "to the thirsty I will give water as a gift from the spring of the water of life," and Revelation 22:17, "let everyone who is thirsty come; let anyone who wishes take the water of life as a gift," are closely related to John 4:10 and John 7:37.

Revelation, probably written toward the end of the first century under Domitian, is thus the first early Christian writing that draws on both Synoptic and Johannine Jesus traditions. Decisive evidence of literary dependence is lacking, so whether the author knew oral traditions or written Gospels must be left as an open question. Nonetheless Revelation's evidence for the merging of two streams of Jesus traditions no later than about A.D. 95 is most important.

One further point needs to be noted. Although the author of Revelation has a deep knowledge of the OT Scriptures, he never quotes from them explicitly (*see* Old Testament in Revelation). This phenomenon should alert us to the possibility that early Christian writings may be deeply dependent on Jesus traditions even though they are not cited.

8. Apostolic Fathers.
Jesus traditions are used extensively in the writings of the apostolic fathers.* As is the case in

the canonical writings considered above, quotations are rare, and the extent of allusions is keenly debated. Unlike the canonical writings, however, the apostolic fathers provide some limited evidence of the use of *written* Gospels. As we shall see, opinions differ on the interpretation of individual passages.

8.1. The Didache. Several passages in this fascinating manual of early church instruction and discipline (*see* Didache) contain close parallels to sayings of Jesus included in the Synoptic Gospels.

In the opening six chapters traditional Jewish ethical teaching has been lightly christianized. Two ways are contrasted: the characteristics of the "way of life" are set out in *Didache* 1—4, and the sinful acts that are the "way of death" are listed in *Didache* 5; there is a short conclusion to the Two Ways traditions in *Didache* 6.

This lengthy section opens with a passage (*Did.* 1.2—2.1) that contains numerous parallels to traditions in Matthew and Luke. These verses include a negative form of the Golden Rule (cf. Mt 7:12 par. Lk 6:31) and a series of close parallels with Matthew 5:39-48 (par. Lk 6:27-36) and with Matthew 5:25-26. However, there is no indication in the text that Jesus traditions are being cited. Perhaps the first users of the *Didache* would have known this almost instinctively. It is then striking that in this section Jesus traditions are not singled out in any way and given a higher authority than is the traditional Jewish ethical teaching that follows this passage.

The *Didache's* version of the Lord's Prayer (*Did.* 8.1-2) is closely related to Matthew 6:9-13. The prayer is introduced in a similar way: "Do not pray as the hypocrites do, but as the Lord commanded in his Gospel, pray like this: Our Father in heaven, hallowed be your name." The *Didache* includes the earliest example of what came to be the traditional doxology: "For yours is the power and the glory for ever." The Lord's Prayer is followed by the instruction, "Pray like this three times a day." This regular Jewish practice (see Ps 55:17) is taken over for the first time in a Christian writing. But instead of Jewish prayers, the words of the Lord (Jesus) are to be used. In this way Christians are to differentiate themselves from Jews (*see* Worship).

In one key passage a saying of Jesus is quoted (probably from oral tradition) with an introductory formula: "The Lord has also spoken concerning this [i.e., participation in the Eucharist by unbaptized persons]: 'Do not give what is holy to dogs' " (*Did.* 9.5). In Matthew 7:6 an identical proverbial saying is enigmatic; here it is given a specific context.

The final chapter of the *Didache* opens with an exhortation, "Watch over your life: do not let your lamps go out, and do not let your loins be ungirded, but be ready, for you do not know when our Lord is coming" (*Did.* 16.1). Further numerous parallels to verses in Matthew 24 follow, at least some of which presuppose knowledge of Matthew's written Gospel rather than the sources on which the evangelist drew (see Tuckett, 200-214).

Four passages in the *Didache* refer to "the Gospel." In addition to *Didache* 8.2, cited above, these passages advise readers to "deal with the apostles and prophets in accordance with the decree of the Gospel" (*Did.* 11.3); "Reprove one another, not in anger but in peace, as you find in the Gospel. . . . Carry out all your prayers and acts of charity and actions just as you find in the Gospel of our Lord" (*Did.* 15.3-4). Although these passages may refer to an oral collection of the sayings of Jesus, Matthew's written Gospel is more probable, especially in the light of *Didache* 8.2, which reflects the Matthean context of the Lord's Prayer.

The date of the *Didache* cannot be settled easily, especially since it is clearly a composite document. While many traditions in the *Didache* have first-century roots and thus predate some NT writings, the final redaction seems to have taken place in the early decades of the second century. By this time Jesus traditions in both oral and written form were being used extensively in instruction of Christians.

8.2. 1 Clement. Although this lengthy letter (*see* Clement of Rome) has traditionally been dated to about A.D. 95, it may come from the early decades of the second century. Two passages use clusters of Jesus traditions; several others contain probable allusions. In *1 Clement* 13.1 seven maxims are introduced as follows: "Remember the words of the Lord Jesus, which he spoke as he taught gentleness and patience. For he said this:

> Show mercy that you may receive mercy;
> forgive that you may be forgiven.
> As you do, so shall it be done to you.
> As you give, so shall it be given to you.

As you judge, so shall you be judged.

As you show kindness, so shall kindness be
shown to you.

With the measure you use, it will be measured to you."

Five of the seven maxims are related, with varying degrees of closeness, to traditions in Matthew's or Luke's versions of the Sermon on the
Mount. Oral traditions seem to have been
reshaped for ready memorization.

The second passage opens with a similar
introductory formula, "Remember the words of
Jesus our Lord, for he said: 'Woe to that man! It
would have been good for him if he had not
been born, than that he should cause one of my
elect to sin. It would have been better for him
to have been tied to a millstone and cast into
the sea, than that he should turn aside one of
my elect' " (*1 Clem.* 46.7-8). Here there are links
with Mark 14:21 and Mark 9:42 and parallels,
but the verbal agreement is not extensive. Once
again oral rather than written Jesus traditions
seem to have been used.

8.3. Ignatius. In the seven letters of Ignatius*
there is only one explicit quotation of a saying
of Jesus: "after the resurrection, when Jesus
came to Peter and those with him, he said to
them: 'Take hold of me; handle me and see that
I am not a disembodied demon' " (Ign. *Smyrn.*
3.1-2). Although this saying recalls Luke 24:39,
it is probably taken from oral tradition rather
than Luke's Gospel, for these words are attributed by Jerome to the Gospel according to the
Hebrews and by Origen to the *Preaching of Peter.*

The letters include several allusions to sayings of Jesus, some probably from oral tradition,
some from a written Gospel. "The tree is known
by its fruit" (Ign. *Eph.* 14.2) is similar in wording
to Matthew 12:33. The proverbial character of
these words suggests oral tradition; there is no
indication in the context that a Jesus tradition
is being referred to. In *Trallians* 11.1 (and similarly in Ign. *Phld.* 3.1) the "opponents" of Ignatius are referred to as people who "are not of
the Father's planting." Here the allusion to a
redactional verse at Matthew 15:13 suggests dependence on Matthew's written Gospel. If so,
the context is altered: Matthew's attack on
Pharisees is adapted for use against docetists.*

In Ignatius's writings there are more references to the life of Jesus than occur in works of
other apostolic fathers. In *Ephesians* 17.1 the
reader is reminded that "the Lord received ointment upon his head," an allusion to Matthew
26:6-13. Several passages refer to the virgin birth
and Davidic descent of Jesus, his sufferings,
crucifixion under Pontius Pilate and resurrection (e.g., Ign. *Magn.* 11; Ign. *Trall.* 9.1-2; Ign.
Smyrn. 1.1-2; *see* Worship for a possible liturgical
setting). Although the full humanity of Jesus is
stressed, these passages move directly from the
birth of Jesus (and in the case of Ign. *Smyrn.* 1.1,
the baptism* of Jesus) to his passion.

Ignatius and his readers were probably acquainted with rather more of the teaching and
actions of Jesus than the references and allusions in the letters might suggest. This is
strongly suggested by the fact that in at least
some of Ignatius's references to the noun *gospel,*
he has a written Gospel (almost certainly Matthew) in mind. In *Philadelphians* 9.2 "the Gospel" includes the coming (Parousia), here
undoubtedly the life of Jesus Christ, as well as
his suffering and resurrection. This suggests
that a written rather than an oral proclamation
of the cross* and resurrection is being referred
to, but the latter interpretation is possible.

In the letter to the Smyrneans, however,
there is less room for doubt. The letter opens
(Ign. *Smyrn.* 1.1) with a creedal* summary of
christological* convictions that refers to the
baptism of Jesus by John, "in order that all
righteousness might be fulfilled by him." The
verbal agreement with Matthew 3:15, a verse
that bears the stamp of Matthew's redactional
hand, is sufficiently close to persuade most
scholars that Ignatius is here quoting Matthew's
Gospel.

In the same letter (Ign. *Smyrn.* 5.1) Ignatius
notes that neither the prophecies* nor the law*
of Moses nor "the gospel" has persuaded his
opponents. The juxtaposition of "the gospel"
with scriptural writings strongly suggests that, in
this letter at least, Ignatius is referring to a
writing, most probably Matthew's Gospel, which
he has quoted a few paragraphs earlier. A similar
juxtaposition of "the gospel" with scriptural
writings is found two paragraphs later (Ign.
Smyrn. 7.2). Here Ignatius urges his readers to
"pay attention to the prophets and especially to
'the Gospel' in which the passion has been
made clear to us and the resurrection has been
accomplished."

For Ignatius, as for the Didachist, Jesus traditions, whether oral or written, are "Gospel."

8.4. Polycarp. Two passages in Polycarp's*

letter to the Philippians are of special interest. At *Philippians* 2.3 the readers are exhorted to "remember what the Lord taught." Four Jesus traditions are then quoted:

Judge not, that you be not judged,
forgive and it shall be forgiven unto you,
be merciful that you may obtain mercy,
with the measure you use, it will be measured
to you again.

These sayings are closely related to four of the seven maxims quoted in *1 Clement* 13.1-2 (see 8.2 above) and the Q traditions in Matthew 7:1-2 (par. Lk 6:36-38). The order and the wording of the sayings are not fixed, so this passage is almost certainly drawn from oral tradition. A further Jesus tradition is attached with the word *and:* "Blessed are the poor and they who are persecuted for righteousness' sake, for theirs is the kingdom of God." This tradition is similar to Matthew 5:10, a redactional verse, so it seems to reflect Matthew's written Gospel. If that is so, then the juxtaposition of oral and written Jesus traditions in the one passage is striking.

At *Philippians* 7.2, a Jesus tradition, "the spirit is willing, but the flesh is weak," is introduced with the words "as the Lord said." Here it is difficult to decide whether oral or written tradition (Mk 14:38 par. Mt 26:41) has been used. This is also the case with the allusion to the Lord's Prayer at *Philippians* 6.1-2.

8.5. Barnabas. There are few references to Jesus traditions in the *Epistle of Barnabas.** Given this letter's concentration on the interpretation of OT passages, this is not surprising (*see* Old Testament in Apostolic Fathers). In *Barnabas* 4.14 a terse saying, "many are called but few chosen," is introduced by a phrase that points to use of a written document: "it is written." This may well be a reference to Matthew 22:14 in its written form, but since there is a similar proverbial saying in 4 Ezra 8:3, the question cannot be readily answered. In *Barnabas* 5.9 the writer states that Jesus "came not to call the righteous but sinners" (Mk 2:17 and parallels). There is no indication in the context that this is a Jesus tradition. Perhaps readers of *Barnabas* were so familiar with this saying that they would have recognized it immediately as a saying of Jesus. Or perhaps the writer knows many Jesus traditions and quotes one here instinctively, without any awareness that it is a saying of Jesus.

8.6. Shepherd of Hermas. In this lengthy writing (*see* Hermas, Shepherd of) there are a large number of possible allusions to Jesus traditions, but none of them is preceded by an introductory formula. Scholarly opinion is divided: some think that the writer is steeped in oral Jesus traditions, while others are convinced that he knew at least some of the Gospels that later became canonical. As in most of the writings under discussion, the allusions are all to sayings of Jesus.

8.7. 2 Clement. This sermon (whose relationship to *1 Clement* is unclear) probably dates from the middle of the second century, a little later than the writings discussed above. For several reasons its use of Jesus traditions is particularly interesting.

Immediately after citation and discussion of Isaiah 54:1 in *2 Clement* 2.1-3, a striking introductory formula precedes citation of a saying of Jesus: "And another Scripture says, 'I have not come to call the righteous, but sinners' " (cf. Mk 2:17 par. Mt 9:13). Here for the first time in an early Christian writing, a written Gospel or possibly a written collection of sayings of Jesus is quoted as Scripture and considered to have the same authority as Isaiah.

In *2 Clement* 8.5 an introductory formula introduces baffling Jesus traditions: "For the Lord says in the Gospel: 'If you did not guard something small, who will give you something great? For I say to you, the person who is faithful in a very little is faithful also in much.' " The latter part is in verbatim agreement with Luke 16:10, so perhaps this a rare early quotation of Luke's Gospel. While the first part of the quotation could be a free rendering of Luke 16:11-12, it may stem from a noncanonical source.

In three further passages, the formula "the Lord says" introduces Jesus traditions (*2 Clem.* 5.2-4; 6.1-2; 9.11). In each case there are close but not exact parallels in the Synoptic Gospels. The author could be quoting freely from memory from two or even all three Synoptic Gospels, he could be drawing on a harmonized written collection of Jesus traditions or an apocryphal* gospel, or he could be referring to oral traditions. The evidence does not allow us to settle the matter.

In *2 Clement* 13.4 a Jesus tradition very similar to Luke 6:32, 35 is introduced by "God says." Since *2 Clement* does not equate Jesus with God, the sense here seems to be, "God says in a [scriptural] Gospel," as in *2 Clement* 2.1-3 (see above).

In *2 Clement* 9.5-6 there seems to be clear dependence on John's Gospel: "If Christ the Lord who saved us was spirit at first but became flesh [cf. Jn 1:14] and so called us, so we shall receive the reward in the flesh. Let us then love one another [cf. Jn 13:34] so that we may all come to the kingdom of God." In this case there is no introductory formula, so at best we have here two allusions to John's Gospel. Nonetheless, this passage provides evidence that Johannine as well as Synoptic Jesus traditions were known and used in the same circles before the middle of the second century. As we shall see (10 below), this conclusion coheres with other evidence that suggests that the fourfold Gospel began to gain ground at this time.

8.8. Papias. About A.D. 110 Papias, bishop of Hierapolis in Asia Minor, wrote in five books his *Exposition of the Lord's Logia*. Perhaps as many as twenty fragments have survived. His comments on the origin and purpose of Matthew and Mark are intriguing and have been discussed repeatedly. More important for our purposes is Papias's attitude toward oral and written Jesus traditions.

In the preface to his work Papias commented as follows on his own careful search for "the commandments given by the Lord to the faith": "For I did not think that information from books would profit me as much as information from a living and abiding voice" (quoted by Eusebius *Hist. Eccl.* 3.39.3). Papias's preference for oral instruction by an authoritative teacher is clear. As we have seen, there is plenty of other evidence for the continuing importance of oral Jesus traditions well into the second century.

Papias, however, did not reject written Jesus traditions. The title of his work suggests that he himself collected and wrote down traditions of both the sayings and the deeds of Jesus: he uses the term *logia* to refer to the sayings and deeds of Jesus in Mark's Gospel. His comments on Matthew and Mark confirm that he was not opposed to written Jesus traditions.

The surviving fragments of Papias are terse and often difficult to interpret. Nonetheless they remind us of the complex relationship between oral and written Jesus traditions in the early decades of the second century.

9. Other Early Christian Writings (Agrapha).

In the preceding sections reference has frequently been made oral Jesus traditions that continued to circulate for some time among early Christian communities. In most cases these oral traditions are related to sayings found in the canonical Gospels. But some were either unknown to or ignored by the Evangelists; Acts 20:35 is a notable example.

The large number of sayings attributed to Jesus in early Christian writings, but not included in the four canonical Gospels, have been referred to as agrapha ("unwritten sayings") for more than two hundred years. Many of the agrapha are found in writings much later than the first- and second-century writings considered above. Do any of the agrapha in these later writings have strong claims to be authentic sayings of Jesus?

J. Jeremias assessed critically the references to sayings of Jesus outside the Gospels and concluded that in all probability eighteen such sayings were spoken by Jesus. The evidence has been reassessed recently by his former pupil and colleague O. Hofius, who concludes that only nine of the agrapha have strong claims to authenticity.

The nine sayings are as follows.

(1) In 1905 one damaged page of a tiny parchment book was discovered with writing on both sides. The forty-five lines of Greek text in microscopic script have still not received the attention they deserve. The tiny book was probably used as an amulet, a charm hung around the neck to ward off evil. The text includes an account of a discussion between Jesus and a pharisaic chief priest named Levi, who criticizes Jesus and his disciples for ignoring regulations for walking in the temple* court. Levi speaks to Jesus as follows:

> Who gave you leave to [trea]d this place of purification and to look upon [the]se holy utensils without having bathed yourself and even without your disciples having [wa]shed their f[eet]?

In his response Jesus echoes anti-pharisaic polemic found in Matthew 23 and concludes:

> But I and [my disciples], of whom you say that we have not im[mersed] ourselves, [have been im]mersed in the li[ving . . .] water which comes down from [. . . B]ut woe unto those who . . . (P.Oxy 840)

This passage is similar to discussions concerning purity* regulations in Mark 7, but it does not seem to be directly dependent on any of the NT Gospels. If in its original form it is an authentic tradition, it would provide further evidence that Jesus took a radical stance concerning purity regulations.

(2) In a sermon in Syriac we read: "As you are found, so you will be led away hence" (*Liber Graduum* 3.3.).

(3) Logion 8 of the *Gospel of Thomas:*

And Jesus said: A man is like a wise fisherman, who cast his net into the sea and drew it up from the sea full of small fish. Among them the wise fisherman found a good large fish. He threw down all the small into the sea. He chose the large fish without trouble. He who has ears to hear, let him hear.

(4) At the beginning of the third century, Clement of Alexandria quotes the following saying of Jesus: "Ask for great things, and God will add unto you the little things" (Clement of Alexandria *Strom.* 1.24.158).

(5) In the middle of the third century Origen quotes the following saying, which is also referred to by six other early Christian writers: "Be approved money changers."

(6) In Codex Bezae an additional short tradition is added to the text of Luke 6:4: "On the same day he [Jesus] saw someone working on the Sabbath and said to him, 'Man, if you know what you are doing, you are blessed; if you do not know, you are cursed and a transgressor of the law.' "

(7) *Gospel of Thomas* logion 82: "Whoever is near me, is near the fire; whoever is far from me, is far from the kingdom."

(8) Jerome (c. A.D. 400) claims that he found the following words in the *Gospel of the Hebrews* (now lost): "And never be joyful, save when you look upon your brother in love."

(9) A papyrus fragment (P.Oxy 1224), probably part of an apocryphal gospel, contains two sayings that are similar to Matthew 5:44 and Luke 9:50. A third saying that is not related to the canonical Gospels may be authentic: "[He that] stands far off [today] will tomorrow be [near you]."

Hofius notes that the first five of these nine sayings may be related in some way to the canonical Gospels, so perhaps only the last four have strong claims to be independent "new" sayings of Jesus. Hofius concludes, surely correctly, that the four NT Gospels contain nearly all that was known about the life and teaching of Jesus in the second half of the first century. A thorough search of all early Chris-

tian writings for possible references to words of Jesus confirms the value of the canonical Gospels and related oral traditions as evidence for the life and teaching of Jesus.

10. Jesus Traditions and the Fourfold Gospel.
From shortly after the middle of the second century, Justin Martyr's *Apology I* and his *Dialogue with Trypho* provide important evidence for the use of Jesus traditions. In *Apology I* 67 there is an explicit comment on the context in which Jesus traditions were used. In his well-known account of eucharistic worship, Justin refers to the reading of "the memoirs of the apostles or the writings of the prophets, as long as time allows." Here apostolic writings are being accorded a similar authority to the writings of the prophets, a Christian shorthand way of referring to the OT Scriptures. In the preceding chapter the reader is told explicitly that "the memoirs of the apostles" are "the Gospels" (*Apol. I* 66), the first Christian occurrence of the plural.

In addition to these two references to "the memoirs of the apostles" in *Apology I*, Justin uses the phrase thirteen times in one section of the *Dialogue* (Justin *Dial. Tryph.* 98—107), in which he seems to have incorporated his own earlier extended anti-gnostic exposition of Psalm 22 and in which he emphasizes the "writtenness" of "the memoirs of the apostles." At one point in this exposition Justin refers to Peter's memoirs; from the context this is a reference to Mark's Gospel (*Dial. Tryph.* 106.3). So in both the *Apology* and the *Dialogue* the "memoirs" are identified as written Gospels.

How many Gospels does Justin accept? In *Dialogue with Trypho* 103.8 he refers to "the memoirs composed by the apostles [of Jesus] and those who followed them." Although Justin never refers to the number of the Gospels he accepts, this passage implies that there were at least four. There is general agreement that Justin used Matthew and Luke regularly and that Mark's Gospel is referred to once (*Dial. Tryph.* 106.3). Justin's knowledge of the Fourth Gospel is much disputed, but *Apology I* 61.4 draws on John 3:3-5 and *Dialogue with Trypho* 88.7 shows knowledge of John 1:19-20. Justin's failure to refer to John's Gospel more frequently is puzzling, but it may be related to his strong interest in infancy narratives, in ethical teaching and in futurist eschatological* sayings, all in somewhat short supply in this Gospel. Since there is no clear evidence for Justin's knowledge of any Gospels other than the canonical four, we can be all but certain that he had in mind Matthew, Mark, Luke and John, no more, no less.

Justin uses the singular "Gospel" in only two passages, but in both cases he is referring to written Jesus traditions. Justin's opponent, Trypho, states that he has read with appreciation the commands of Jesus "in the so-called Gospel" (*Dial. Tryph.* 10.2) At *Dialogue with Trypho* 100.1 there is a similar usage: a citation of Matthew 11:27 is introduced with the words "it is written in the Gospel." These two references recall Irenaeus's much more frequent use of the phrase "in the Gospel" some thirty years later. For Justin, as for Irenaeus, the sayings of Jesus are of special importance: they are recorded "in the Gospel," "in the memoirs of the apostles."

It is not easy to account for the variations in wording from Matthew and Luke in Justin's citations of Jesus traditions. In some cases Jesus traditions from the Gospels have been harmonized; some of those harmonized traditions can be traced in his pupil Tatian's more thoroughgoing harmony of the Gospels. It is likely that for catechetical purposes (and possibly even to disarm critics) Justin himself gathered together topically harmonized clusters of sayings of Jesus from written Gospels, primarily Matthew and Luke. In this respect he partially anticipates Tatian. In his use of written Gospels alongside harmonized sayings of Jesus, his successor is Irenaeus.

Recent research suggests that Justin may well have possessed a four-Gospel codex in the library of his catechetical school in Rome. T. C. Skeat has shown that papyri fragments of Matthew (P^{64} + P^{67}) and of Luke (P^4) are from a late-second century codex that contained all four Gospels. G. N. Stanton (1997) has drawn attention to one of the codex's most striking features: its use of two columns to the page is rare in papyrus codices. This is the only example of a two-column Greek NT papyrus manuscript, though there are four examples in early fragments of OT papyri. The narrow columns, with only about fifteen letters in each column, would have assisted reading aloud in the context of worship. So the use of two columns in P^{64} + P^{67} + P^4 is almost certainly an indication of a high-class codex, a splendid "pulpit edition" of the four Gospels intended for liturgical use. This codex was an *édition de luxe* that was planned and executed meticulously. All these features indicate a handsome edition of the four Gospels, which would have been expensive to produce. This codex does not look like an experiment by a scribe working out ways to include four Gospels in one codex; it certainly had predecessors much earlier in the second century.

When Irenaeus set out the earliest defence of the church's fourfold Gospel in about A.D. 180, he almost certainly did so on the basis of his use of codices that contained all four Gospels. His main point is clear: there is one gospel in fourfold form, held together by one Spirit (Irenaeus *Adv. Haer.* 3.11.8). He frequently refers to "the Gospel," "the Gospel according to . . ." and only very rarely to "four Gospels." The gospel is primarily the faith* proclaimed and transmitted by the apostles and only secondarily the written record reported by such and such an Evangelist. The church has the one God-given gospel as recorded by two apostles and two of their immediate associates: the gospel has been given to the church in fourfold form.

Although Irenaeus often cites passages from the four Gospels accurately, he also regularly introduces sayings of Jesus with "the Lord said," "the Lord said in the Gospel" or "the Lord declared" without indicating from which particular Gospel the sayings are taken. At the end of the preface to book 3, for example, a version of Luke 10:18 is introduced with the words "the Lord declared." In this case the text is cited in abbreviated form. It is difficult to decide whether the variation occurs as the result of faulty memory, Irenaeus's knowledge of an otherwise unattested textual tradition, or his use of oral tradition. In the middle of his extended discussion of the opening chapters of Luke, Irenaeus refers to four verses from John 1 but without indicating that he has switched from Luke to John (Irenaeus *Adv. Haer.* 3.10.3). Matthew 12:18-21 is quoted as part of the discussion of the opening chapters of John's Gospel, but once again the reader is not told about the change of Gospels. Similar phenomena occur elsewhere. This is not surprising once we recognize that for Irenaeus "the Gospel" and in particular the words of Jesus have a higher authority than do the individual writings of the

Evangelists, even though the Gospels are referred to occasionally as "Scriptures."

Irenaeus is able to cite the written Gospels both carefully and carelessly, to weave together loosely passages from two or more Gospels and to introduce sayings with "the Lord said," some of which seem to be taken from the written Gospels, some from oral tradition. The fact that these various phenomena are found in a writer for whom the fourfold Gospel is fundamental stands as a warning sign for all students of Gospel traditions in the second century. Earlier Christian writers may also value the written Gospels highly even though they appeal directly either to the words of Jesus or to oral tradition, or even though they link topically sayings of Jesus taken from two or more Gospels. Irenaeus was not the only early Christian writer who cites "words of the Lord" and does not tell us whether he is quoting from written Gospels or from oral tradition.

11. Conclusions.

Although the use of Jesus traditions in early Christian writings raises a number of questions that must be left open, several conclusions can be drawn. The transition from the use of oral to written Jesus traditions is difficult to trace in detail, but the broad outline is clear. While it is possible that the Evangelists drew on written sources, in the very earliest post-Easter decades Jesus traditions were transmitted mainly in oral form. Even after the written Gospels began to circulate, oral traditions continued to be used, even as late as early in the third century. But by then the written fourfold Gospel was beginning to be accepted as primary, partly in the light of misuse of oral traditions by Montanists and Gnostics.*

Most of the examples of the use of Jesus traditions noted above are in the context of the catechetical instruction and exhortation of believers. This is not surprising since the writings referred to nearly all fall into that category. Some evidence suggests that Jesus traditions were also used in other contexts: Acts 10:36-43 indicates that the story of Jesus was an integral part of evangelism, and Justin's *Apology I* 67 confirms that readings from "the memoirs of the apostles" were part of eucharistic worship. Although the shape of some of the Jesus traditions included in the Gospels strongly suggests that they were used in apology and polemic, evidence for their use in these settings is scarce

from outside the Gospels. When Justin and his Jewish opponent, Trypho, enter into dialogue, they differ sharply in their interpretation of the OT Scriptures, but according to Justin, not in their interpretation of Jesus traditions: Trypho has read the sayings of Jesus "in the Gospel" and considers them to be "admirable and great" (*Dial. Tryph.* 10.2).

The quotations of Jesus traditions confirm their importance for Christians in the period under discussion. The even more numerous allusions are difficult to assess. In some cases the writers seem to assume that readers will be familiar with the traditions to which allusion is made. In many other cases it is impossible to determine whether the allusions are deliberate or merely casual use of familiar phraseology. It is important to note that even in the latter case the allusions confirm that the writer was steeped so deeply in Jesus traditions that use of its phraseology was almost instinctive.

From early in the second century we have evidence for the use of the term *gospel* for both oral and written Jesus traditions. It is likely that in this period the title "the Gospel according to . . ." began to be used for the four writings that came to be accepted as canonical. From early in the second century and probably from much earlier, traditions of the sayings of Jesus and of his story were considered to be an integral part of the gospel of Jesus Christ, the Son of God.

See also APOSTOLIC FATHERS; CHRISTOLOGY; MARK, SECRET GOSPEL OF; MATTHEAN COMMUNITY; NONCANONICAL WRITINGS, CITATIONS OF; PETER, GOSPEL OF; THOMAS, GOSPEL OF.

BIBLIOGRAPHY. H. W. Attridge, *A Commentary on the Epistle to the Hebrews* (Herm; Philadelphia: Fortress, 1989); A. J. Bellinzoni, *The Sayings of Jesus in the Writings of Justin Martyr* (Leiden: E. J. Brill, 1967); R. J. Bauckham, *Jude, 2 Peter* (WBC 50; Waco: Word, 1983); E. Best, "I Peter and the Gospel Tradition," *NTS* 16 (1970) 95-113; R. E. Brown, *The Epistles of John: Translated with Introduction, Notes, and Commentary* (Garden City, NY: Doubleday, 1982); O. Cullmann, *The Christology of the New Testament* (rev. ed.; Philadelphia: Westminster, 1963 [1959]); P. H. Davids, "James and Jesus" in *Gospel Perspectives* 5: *The Jesus Tradition Outside the Gospels,* ed. D. Wenham (Sheffield: JSOT, 1984) 63-84; K. P. Donfried, *The Setting of Second Clement in Early Christianity* (NovTSup 38; Leiden: E. J. Brill, 1974); A.-M. Enroth, "The Hearing Formula in the Book of Revelation,"

NTS 36 (1990) 598-608; R. H. Gundry, *"Verba Christi* in 1 Peter," *NTS* 13 (1966) 336-50; idem, "Further *Verba* on *Verba Christi* in First Peter," *Bib* 55 (1974) 211-32; D. A. Hagner, "The Sayings of Jesus in the Apostolic Fathers and Justin Martyr" in *Gospel Perspectives* 5: *The Jesus Tradition Outside the Gospels,* ed. D. Wenham (Sheffield: JSOT, 1984) 233-68; idem, *The Use of the Old and New Testaments in Clement of Rome* (NovTSup 34; Leiden: E. J. Brill, 1973); P. J. Hartin, *James and the Q Sayings of Jesus* (JSNTSup 47; Sheffield: Sheffield Academic Press, 1991); O. Hofius, "Unbekannte Jesusworte" in *Das Evangelium und die Evangelien,* ed. P. Stuhlmacher (WUNT 28; Tübingen: J. C. B. Mohr, 1983) 355-82; C. N. Jefford, *The Sayings of Jesus in the Teaching of the Apostles* (Leiden: E. J. Brill, 1989); J. Jeremias, *Unknown Sayings of Jesus* (rev. ed.; London: SCM, 1964); W. D. Köhler, *Die Rezeption des Matthäusevangeliums in der Zeit vor Irenäus* (WUNT 24; Tübingen: J. C. B. Mohr, 1987); H. Köster, *Synoptische Überlieferung bei den apostolischen Vätern* (TU 65; Berlin: Walter de Gruyter, 1957); S. S. Laws, *A Commentary on the Epistle of James* (HNTC; San Francisco: Harper & Row, 1980); E. Massaux, *The Influence of the Gospel of Saint Matthew on Christian Literature Before Saint Irenaeus,* ed. A. J. Bellinzoni (NGS 5/1, 5/2, 5/3; Macon, GA: Mercer University Press, 1990-93); J.-M. Sevrin, ed., *The New Testament in Early Christianity* (Louvain: Louvain University Press, 1989); T. C. Skeat, "The Oldest Manuscript of the Four Gospels?" *NTS* 43 (1997) 1-31; G. N. Stanton, "The Fourfold Gospel," *NTS* 43 (1997) 317-46; idem, *Jesus of Nazareth in New Testament Preaching* (SNTSMS 27; Cambridge: Cambridge University Press, 1974); idem, "Other Early Christian Writings: 'Didache,' Ignatius, 'Barnabas,' Justin Martyr" in *Early Christian Thought in its Jewish Context,* ed. J. Barclay and J. P. M. Sweet (Cambridge: Cambridge University Press, 1996) 174-90; W. D. Stroker, *Extracanonical Sayings of Jesus: Texts, Translations and Notes* (Atlanta: Scholars Press, 1988); C. M. Tuckett, "Synoptic Traditions in the Didache" in *The New Testament in Early Christianity,* ed. J.-M. Sevrin (Louvain: Louvain University Press, 1989) 197-230; D. Wenham, ed., *Gospel Perspectives* 5: *The Jesus Tradition Outside the Gospels* (Sheffield: JSOT, 1984).   G. N. Stanton

JEWISH CHRISTIANITY

The much discussed problem of defining Jewish Christianity is caused by the diversity of the phenomena to be explained and the difficulty of deciding what criteria to use in identifying it. One may, for example, focus on negative criteria, that is, on the lack of difference with Judaism (thus Baur, Hort). One may, on the other hand, establish certain positive criteria that are regarded as distinctive of Jewish Christianity. Daniélou found three such criteria, each representing a discrete group: a low christology* that denied the deity of Christ*; esteem for the Jerusalem* church ruled by the relatives* of Jesus; and an apocalyptic* orientation. One may focus on opposition to Paul and corresponding affirmation of the law* (*see DPL,* Opponents of Paul) R. E. Brown advocates speaking of four types of what he calls Jewish/Gentile Christianity, that is, Jewish Christianity and its Gentile* converts, depending on the degree of commitment to the observance of the law. In fact, as recent studies have emphasized, Jewish Christianity was anything but a single, unified phenomenon. We have to deal with something that extended over a period of three to four centuries, in locations throughout the Mediterranean world, phenomena further complicated by the mutual interpenetration of Judaism* and Hellenism, and the fact that Jewish Christianity expressed itself in a variety of both orthodox and heretical forms, known to us through widely different sources.

Broadly conceived, Jewish Christianity consists of those forms of Christian faith held by the Jewish Christians of the first few centuries. After that time Jewish believers in Christ were usually assimilated into the Gentile church, at least until the modern "Messianic Judaism" movement. Just as there were various manifestations of Judaism prior to A.D. 70, Jewish Christianity was itself also a varied phenomenon. We know orthodox varieties of Jewish Christianity directly from a number of NT writings and the apostolic fathers.* Even here, however, we find considerable diversity. Our knowledge of heterodox varieties of Jewish Christianity outside and later than the NT often comes to us more indirectly. Special caution is called for in considering the accounts of heterodox Jewish Christianity provided to us by the church fathers. The later sects known to us, for example, the Ebionites,* clearly reflect a departure theologically from the orthodoxy of the mainstream church on several key issues. This raises the question of the exact boundaries that mark out orthodoxy from heterodoxy.

1. Jewish Christianity in the New Testament
2. Jewish Christianity After the New Testament
3. Historical Observations
4. The Theology of Jewish Christianity
5. The Question of Orthodoxy and Heresy

1. Jewish Christianity in the New Testament.
It may fairly be said at the outset that there is no Christianity in the NT that is not Jewish. All of the writers of the NT, with the exception of Luke, were themselves Jews who had believed in Jesus Christ and the gospel.* Even Paul's Christianity, often categorized as reflecting "Gentile Christianity," remains deeply Jewish in character. Yet, for all the continuity between Paul's Christianity and that of, say, early Palestinian Judaism, there is a distinct difference. This can be admitted without accepting the so-called Tübingen hypothesis of F. C. Baur. Indeed, certain documents of the NT manifest a Christianity that is distinctly Jewish in a way that contrasts with Paul's. These represent an identifiably specific type of Christianity we call Jewish Christianity, and it is these that are the focus of this section.

1.1. Acts. We must begin with Acts,* not because it is written from the perspective of Jewish Christianity, but because it provides the only description we have of the beginnings of Christianity among the Jews of Palestine. And although Acts is written relatively late, we may for our purpose take its representation of matters as essentially accurate. Earliest Christianity—that described by the opening chapters of Acts—was exclusively Jewish. In Acts we first encounter a Gentile Christian, excluding the exception of the Ethiopian eunuch in Acts 8:27-39, in the story of the conversion of the Roman centurion, Cornelius,* to which Luke gives so much space (Acts 10:1—11:18). Even "the Hellenists"* of Acts 6 were not Greeks (the word used in Acts 6:1 is *Hellēnistai* rather than *Hellēnes,* which properly means "Greeks"). The argument in Acts 6 concerns Aramaic-speaking Jews and Greek-speaking Jews, that is, Jews who differed on the degree to which assimilation to Hellenism was to be tolerated.

What is remarkable about the earliest church is that it appears at first to be classifiable as a messianic sect within Judaism. The disciples are found frequently in the temple* (Acts 2:46; 5:21, 25, 42), going up at the hour of prayer,* presumably to pray (Acts 3:1, 3), and they are held in high regard by the people (Acts 2:47; 5:13). From this last point we may assume not only that they continued to observe the law, but that they continued in their Jewish practices and customs, including circumcision,* temple participation, Sabbath worship* and observance of food* laws. They were fully Jews, although to be sure they held the quite strange conviction that a recently crucified criminal had in fact risen from the dead and that he was the Messiah.

It was apparently Stephen,* a Hellenistic Jew, who first began to draw conclusions about the significance of Christ's death* for the practice of the Jewish church. He seems to have made the suggestion that the temple was of limited, or even outmoded, significance and that—undoubtedly leaning on some sayings of Jesus contained in the oral tradition—the law had now been significantly modified (Acts 6:13-14; although the witnesses against Stephen are "false" and distort the truth, what they say is not without basis). Stephen's radicalism ignited the first persecution* of the church, of Jews by Jews. It is unlikely that the more conservative, Aramaic-speaking Jewish Christians, including the apostles,* agreed with Stephen's radical analysis of the new situation. The ability of the twelve apostles to remain in Jerusalem (Acts 8:1) implies that the persecution was not directed against them, probably because they dissociated themselves from the views of the Hellenistic Christians.

While there is no need to put undue stress upon the differences between the Aramaic-speaking and Hellenistic Jews, that there were important differences between them seems clear. The attempt of C. C. Hill to overturn the common reconstruction just offered is hardly successful (*see* Hellenists). He correctly cautions against a polarizing in the fashion of Baur, pointing to the increasingly recognized influence of Hellenism even upon Palestinian Judaism, and the necessarily overlapping backgrounds of the two groups of Jewish Christians. But he minimizes the significance of Stephen,* arguing that there was no truth in the claims of the false witnesses, and that the critique of the law and temple began with Gentile Christianity. Acts, however, gives no evidence of this. To be sure, the Aramaic-speaking Jews are also persecuted in Acts, but apart from Peter* and John* in Acts 4 and Peter in Acts 5 (which the populace does not support: Acts 4:21; 5:26), this persecution occurs later when not even the conservative Jerusalem Christians can continue to be regarded as a sect within Judaism.

Evidence concerning the conservative attitude of the Aramaic-speaking Jerusalem Christians toward the law in particular is found much later in the book of Acts. In Acts 21:20 they are represented as saying to Paul: "You see, brother, that there are many thousands among the Jews who have believed and all of them are zealous for the law (zēlōtai tou nomou)." Because of Paul's reputation concerning the law, he is forced to make a symbolic gesture of fulfilling his vow (cf. Acts 18:18) together with several other Jewish Christians (Acts 21:23). Here too we have evidence of the continuing role of the temple in the lives of the conservative Jerusalem Christians.

Also to be mentioned is the presence of Judaizers at the Jerusalem council in Acts 15. These ultraconservative Jewish Christians, described as former Pharisees, were insisting on the need for Gentiles to be circumcised* and to keep the law in order to be Christians (Acts 15:5). Arguing with Paul and against the Judaizers, however, were both Peter and James. Thus the Judaizers cannot be taken to represent the typical Jewish Christianity of the Jerusalem church, who upheld the importance of the law for Jewish Christians but not for Gentile Christians (cf. Gal 2:12).

1.2. The Gospel of Matthew. Since this Gospel was written for Jewish Christians, it reflects concerns of the congregation or congregations of Jewish Christianity for which it was written (*see* Matthean Community). The Jewish character of the Gospel can be seen in such things as the stress on the fulfillment of the OT, especially in the fulfillment formula quotations, the omission of Mark's explanation of Jewish customs, and the use of rabbinic patterns of argument (e.g., Mt 19:3-9). Some sayings of Jesus unique to Matthew can only have been preserved by and have meaning for Jewish Christians (e.g., Mt 10:5-6; 15:24; 23:2). Of particular significance, however, is the stress on the fidelity of Jesus to the law (e.g., Mt 5:17-19) as it can be seen in Matthew's redaction of Mark 7 in Matthew 15 (note especially the omission of Mark's editorial comment "Thus he declared all foods

clean" [Mk 7:19 NRSV]). Also to be noted is the consistently strong call to "righteousness"* (*dikaiosynē* occurring in the Synoptic Gospels only in Matthew [except for the poetry of Lk 1:75], seven times). The insistence upon the permanence of the law and the emphasis on righteousness have been taken by some as a polemic against the Pauline gospel or at least against extreme Paulinists.

Other marks of a Jewish-Christian background to this Gospel can be seen in the narrative of the virgin birth, possibly written against Jewish claims of the illegitimacy of Jesus' birth, and in the resurrection* narrative, which addresses explicitly the Jewish claim that the missing body was stolen.

Matthew has always been somewhat of a puzzle to commentators because of several of its strong polarities. Thus, for example, for all the Jewish aspects of the Gospel that one might mention, there is at the same time a striking anti-Judaism (to be carefully distinguished from anti-Semitism) in Matthew. This can be seen in the distancing remarks "*their* synagogues" (Mt 4:23; 9:35; 10:17: 12:9: 13:54; cf. "*your* synagogues" [Mt 23:34]), "*their* scribes" (Mt 7:29), and in the striking reference to "the Jews" (Mt 28:15). More significant are the passages where Israel is in effect displaced by the church (Mt 8:11-12; 21:41, 43; 22:3, 8; cf. Mt 11:24; 13:10-15; 23:38; *see* Church as Israel). Worst of all, because it has been used to incite anti-Semitism, is the bitter statement in Matthew 27:25, "His blood be on us and on our children" (NRSV).

This strong anti-Judaism is precisely what one might expect among Jewish Christians who are in polemical debate with non-Christian Jews. This is an intramural polemic between Jews. Jewish Christians had to defend themselves against Jewish charges of disloyalty to the religion of Israel, abandonment of the law, and affiliation with an alien (if not pagan) religion whose membership was mainly Gentile. What can explain the polarities and distinctives of the Gospel is the life-setting of Jewish-Christian communities who exist between Jews who did not accept the new faith and a largely Gentile church. It is they above all who must be prepared to bring out of their treasure boxes "things both old and new" (Mt 13:52).

The Gospel of Matthew thus provides an interesting example of a Hellenistic Jewish Christianity that existed in the second half of the first century, very possibly as early as the late sixties, probably no later, however, than the mid-eighties. Torah righteousness is upheld in a distinctive way over against the Pauline view of the law, as articulated for the Gentile churches. It is not surprising to find Irenaeus reporting that many Jewish Christians accepted Matthew as the only authoritative Gospel (*Adv. Haer.* 1.26.2; 3.11.7).

1.3. Hebrews, James, Jude/2 Peter. If the tradition concerning the Petrine authorship of 1 Peter* may be relied upon, the letter may qualify for consideration as a product of Jewish Christianity. Although it is not without the marks of a Jewish perspective, however, 1 Peter appears to have been written to a Gentile readership, and its Christianity is not greatly different from that of Paul.

The epistle-homily we know under the title of Hebrews* was, by contrast, almost certainly addressed to Jewish Christians (cf. Heb 1:1; 2:16). The extent of the argument from the OT and its midrashic interpretation (*see* OT in Hebrews), the understanding of the cross through the detailed correspondences with the sacrificial ritual of the temple, the levitical priesthood* and the Mosaic covenant,* all point to the Jewish bedrock presupposed in this document. Hebrews is an exceptionally powerful statement about the final truthfulness of Christianity and the folly of returning to Judaism, perhaps a Judaism inclined to gnosticism.* What is remarkable about the Jewish Christianity of Hebrews is its very high christology, on the one hand, and its relative neglect of the subject of the law, on the other. Hebrews 13:9 (cf. Heb 9:10), however, does take a stand against the dietary laws—but perhaps only as abused within gnosticizing circles. The author and the readers were very probably Hellenistic Jewish Christians in Rome, probably in the late sixties of the first century.

James* represents one of the most distinctively Jewish Christian documents in the NT. Indeed, because it has no explicitly Christian doctrine and so few specifically Christian elements (Jas 1:1; 2:1; but, cf. Jas 1:18), many regard it as the slight reworking of an originally Jewish document. With its repeated imperatives, the letter emphasizes orthopraxy, stresses the importance of being doers, and not merely hearers, of the word, and lifts up the importance of social justice for the needy. In these and other

respects, James resembles the wisdom* tradition of Israel (cf. Jas 1:5; 3:13, 15, 17). The law, referred to uniquely as "the law of liberty" (Jas 1:25; 2:12) and "the royal law" (Jas 2:8), is also glorified (cf. Jas 4:11). And there is a famous polemic, if not against Paul, at least against extreme Paulinists (Jas 2:14-26). Consonant with the stress on the importance of the law is the reference to the position of James and the Jerusalem church in Acts 21:17-20.

The epistle of Jude* also reflects a Jewish-Christian background. The chief evidence for this is the reliance upon the apocalyptic* perspective, and specifically the quotation of, or allusion to, the non-canonical apocalyptic works *1 Enoch* and the *Testament of Moses* (*see* Non-Canonical Citations). The midrashic section of Jude 5-19 is decidedly Jewish. On the other hand, the law is not referred to at all, despite the obvious concern for orthopraxy. If the tradition concerning the authorship by Jude the brother of James and Jesus, is true, then the author's context might well reflect Palestinian Jewish Christianity. 2 Peter,* dependent upon Jude, is a testamentary document pertaining to Peter. It too reflects a high interest in Jewish apocalyptic, but now within the framework of a Hellenistic Jewish Christianity. While much of the imagery in the letter-testament is clearly Jewish, the language often reflects Hellenistic terminology.

1.4. The Johannine Literature. The tradition underlying the Fourth Gospel stems from Palestinian Jewish Christianity. Linguistically its idiom may be designated Semitic and at several points the author indicates his awareness of the rabbinic interpretation of the Bible (e.g., Jn 1:51; 5:17; 8:56). At the same time, however, the Gospel reveals considerable Hellenistic influence. As it stands, the Fourth Gospel is the product of a Christianity reflecting the Hellenistic Judaism of the Diaspora (Asia Minor). In this Gospel one again encounters an ambiguity with respect to the Jews (cf. Matthew). Jesus can say in response to the Samaritan woman: "We worship what we know, and salvation is from the Jews" (Jn 4:22). At the same time, some of the harshest words against the Jews in the whole of the NT are found here: "You are from your father the devil, and you choose to do your father's desires" (Jn 8:44). This reflects the bitter hostility between the Jewish Christians and the non-Christian Jews (cf. Jn 16:1-4). In the

Gospel of John there is a very high christology (directed in part against Jewish Christians with a low Christology?) together with a high view of the law (e.g., Jn 7:19, 49).

The three Johannine letters* appear to reflect similar characteristics and the same Hellenistic-Jewish-Christian milieu as the Gospel. All of the letters indicate a concern for righteousness, and 1 John reveals a high respect for the law (1 Jn 3:22; 5:2-3); sin is defined as "lawlessness" (*anomia*; 1 Jn 3:4).

1.5. The Apocalypse. The literary genre of the Book of Revelation* points in itself to its Jewish origin. Apocalyptic* is an essentially Jewish phenomenon and builds upon the precedent offered in the OT and in much of the literature between the testaments. The imagery of the book is repeatedly Jewish, reflecting the orientation of Jewish Christianity, from the reference to "a kingdom"* and "priests"* in Revelation 1:6 to "the holy city, the new Jerusalem" in Revelation 21:2. This Jewish Christianity too is in a hostile relationship to non-Christian Jews as can be seen especially from the reference to "those who say they are Jews and are not, but are a synagogue* of Satan" (Rev 2:9; 3:9). The Apocalypse is, of course, marked by a very high christology, one that makes much of Jewish imagery. The importance of the law is upheld (Rev 12:17; 14:12).

2. Jewish Christianity After the New Testament. Virtually from the beginning Jewish Christianity was diverse. Heterodox Jewish Christianity was also to be found from the beginning in, for example, the Judaizers against whom Paul fights in Galatians and Romans, and the gnosticizing Jewish Christians against whom he fights in Colossians. After the NT the diversity continues: orthodox forms continue, while heterodox forms of Jewish Christianity begin to harden in their opposition to the Gentile church.

2.1. Apostolic Fathers. Jewish Christianity is well represented in the apostolic fathers.* Both the *Didache** and *Barnabas** contain a description of the Christian life using the Jewish literary device of the "Two Ways" of life and of death. This may be a pre-Christian Jewish document used independently by the two writers. The *Didache* depends directly on the Gospel of Matthew and very probably reflects the same Jewish-Christian milieu. Orthopraxy is central and fasting is stressed, but on Wednesdays and Fridays,

in contrast to the Mondays and Thursdays on which the non-Christian Jews fast. The eucharistic prayers* of *Didache* 9—10 are based on originally Jewish patterns of prayer. The law remains important, and the document's christology employs Jewish images, particularly in its *pais* ("servant") christology (*Did.* 9.2, 3; 10.2, 3) and in the reference to Jesus as "the Holy Vine of David" (*Did.* 9.2; cf. 10.6).

Pseudo-Barnabas, which ends with the "Two Ways" tradition, is filled with OT quotations, many of which are interpreted allegorically. Jewish imagery is abundant together with a stress upon the importance of the law (*Barn.* 2.6 ["without a yoke of necessity"]; *Barn.* 4.11; 21.8; cf. 4.1). Barnabas is striking for the sharpness of its argument against the law as observed by the Jews in order to prevent "conversion to their law" (*Barn.* 3.6). Thus in turn, the author refutes the Jewish notion of the sacrifices,* the Sabbath, the food* laws and the temple. Most notable is the argument that the covenant belongs to the Christians and not to the Jews (*Barn.* 4.6-7).

The *Shepherd of Hermas,** also reflecting Hellenistic Jewish Christianity, is written in the form of a Jewish apocalypse similar to 2 Esdras. The central problem of *Hermas* is the possibility of repentance* after postbaptismal sin, and in the discussion of this subject the author reveals both extensive Jewish imagery and Hellenistic influence. The law is given high prominence in *Hermas Similitude* 8.3.1-8. Indeed, the second major section, *Mandates,* is given over entirely to an exposition of commandments for the penitent. Through the whole of the document the commandments receive the highest emphasis, with the refrain repeated again and again that the one who does the commandments will thereby live. A high christology is found in the exposition of the ninth *Similitude.*

1 Clement (*see* Clement) clearly comes from a Hellenistic Jewish Christianity in Rome. The letter-treatise is filled with OT quotations, examples from the history of Israel, and frequent Jewish imagery. The great prayer of *1 Clement* 59—61 employs much Jewish terminology. *1 Clement* contains a high christology (cf. *1 Clem.* 59.2; 64.1). The law, on the other hand, receives no emphasis (the word is not found in *1 Clement*). Indeed, the only place where the word "commandment"* (*entolē*) is found is in *1 Clement* 13.3, where it is used in connection with the sayings of Jesus.

The homily known as *2 Clement* (*see* Clement), not by the same author as *1 Clement*, again makes extensive use of Jewish language and reflects a Jewish-Christian perspective. A distance from Judaism is indicated by *2 Clement* 2.3. From the opening words of *2 Clement* 1.1, "we must think of Jesus Christ as of God," and sprinkled throughout the document is a very high christology. The importance of the commandments is insisted upon, but as interpreted by Jesus (cf. *2 Clem.* 4.5).

The seven authentic letters of Ignatius also contain language reflecting a Jewish Christianity. Here a more specific polemic against Judaism can be seen. Most striking is the statement in Ignatius *Magnesians* 8.1: "For if we are living until now according to Judaism, we confess that we have not received grace." This remark and the one following in Ignatius *Magnesians* 10.3: "It is monstrous to talk of Jesus Christ and to practice Judaism," are apparently addressed to Judaizers (so too Ign. *Phld.* 6.1; cf. 8.2). A high christology is present (Ign. *Eph.* 7.2; 18.2) and Jesus "the High Priest" can be described as "the door of the Father, through which enter Abraham and Isaac and Jacob and the Prophets and the Apostles and the Church" (Ign. *Phld.* 9.1). The law, however, is not emphasized.

2.2. Cerinthus. An early second-century Jewish Christian, influenced by incipient gnosticism, Cerinthus is known to us only indirectly through Irenaeus (*Adv. Haer.* 1.26.1; 3.11.1), Epiphanius (*Haer.* 28.4) and Hippolytus (*Omn. Haer. Ref.* 7.33). Cerinthus is significant because he represents the distinctives of Jewish Christianity as it begins to develop independently of the Gentile church. Thus one finds a strong emphasis on the law, especially circumcision and the Sabbath, and a low christology that describes Jesus as a man upon whom the Christ descended at the baptism and departed before the cross.

2.3. Justin Martyr. In his dialogue with Trypho the Jew, Justin reveals an awareness of Jewish believers in Christ. He allows their continuing obedience to the law, as long as they do not persuade Gentile Christians to join them in that obedience (*Dial.* 47). In the following chapter, Justin acknowledges that some Jews who confess Jesus as the Christ hold him to be only a man among men. Trypho later indicates that it would be acceptable to him if Christ had been

elected to be the Messiah because of his faithful obedience to the law (*Dial.* 67), a view held by some Jewish Christians of a later time.

2.4. The Pseudo-Clementines. In Syria at the beginning of the third century, a Jewish Christianity produced a corpus of literature, apparently using earlier materials to some extent, under the name of Clement (of Rome), known more specifically under the titles *Clementine Recognitions* and *Homilies*. This literature, although showing signs of gnostic influence, represents a classic form of Jewish Christianity somewhat similar to that of the *Gospel of Thomas*. James, "the Lord's brother," and Peter are exalted. Much disputed is the question of whether the Simon Magus debated by Peter is a cipher for Paul himself. A strong emphasis on the continuing importance of the law is present. Again the "Two Ways" idea is presented, described as "those of obedience and disobedience to the law" (*Hom.* 20.2). While Christ is the only Savior (*Recog.* 1.51) and is described as "the true Prophet" (*Recog.* 5.10; 10.51; *Hom.* 3.21), he is the Son of God but not God (*Hom.* 16.25).

2.5. Sects: Ebionites, Nazoreans, Elkesaites. The most conspicuous name applied by the church fathers to Jewish Christianity is Ebionism.* We know about the Ebionites mainly from the apologists of the late second and third century, although it may well be that what we have encountered in the Pseudo-Clementines represents Ebionite Christianity. In the Ebionites Jewish Christianity has hardened in its heterodoxy against the Gentile church. Irenaeus, in the earliest mention of them, indicates that they "use the Gospel according to Matthew only [cf. *Adv. Haer.* 3.11.7], and repudiate the Apostle Paul, maintaining that he was an apostate from the law," and that they "persevere in the observance of those customs which are enjoined in the law" (*Adv. Haer.* 1.26.2). As for Ebionite christology, Irenaeus reports that they do not accept "the union of God and man," but only that Jesus was a naturally born man (*Adv. Haer.* 5.1.3). According to Eusebius, the Ebionites viewed Christ as "a plain and ordinary man," and he adds that "they insisted on the complete observance of the law" (*Hist. Eccl.* 3.27). While some of the patristic writers trace the name of the sect back to an individual named Ebion, the name almost certainly is from the Hebrew *'ebyônîm*, meaning "the poor," and was probably indeed originally a reference to their actual poverty.

It is impossible to isolate distinctives of the Nazoreans (or Nazarenes; the spelling varies considerably), and the name refers probably to Jewish Christians indistinguishable from the Ebionites (*pace* Pritz, who distinguishes them from the Ebionites because of their orthodox christology). The fourth century Epiphanius used this name in his catalog of heresies (*Haer.* 29; cf. 18; cf. Jerome, *Ep.* 112.13).

A third sect, the Elkesaites, did not apparently differ much from the Ebionites. They took their name from Elkesai, who had produced a book containing the revelation he had received. They upheld the law strictly, a christology that spoke of Jesus as only a man, though a prophet, and they rejected totally the Pauline epistles. Most distinctive was their asceticism, which included vegetarianism. The Elkesaites are known to us from Origen (via Eusebius *Hist. Eccl.* 6.38; here the name is given the spelling Helkesaites), but primarily from Epiphanius (*Haer.* 19; 30.17; 53) and Hippolytus (*Philos.* 9.13-17; 10.29).

3. Historical Observations.

From the beginning, as we have seen, the only Christianity that existed was a Jewish Christianity. The church first spread from Jerusalem by means of Diaspora* Jews who had come to faith in Christ in the holy city. As they returned to their various communities in the Mediterranean world, they in effect founded Jewish-Christian communities. In this way the churches at Rome,* Antioch* of Syria, and Alexandria* in Egypt were founded. We have evidence of a thriving Jewish Christianity in these cities.

Paul's letter to the Romans indicates the existence in Rome, in the fifties, of the kind of tensions between Jewish and Gentile Christians that one might indeed expect (see esp. Rom 11:13-24; 15:7-13). This sort of problem undoubtedly existed in other places where there were sufficient numbers of Jewish and Gentile Christians. Eventually, it would appear, in many if not most places Jewish Christians eventually assimilated into the larger Gentile church. Where they did not, they usually began to polarize on certain issues in the process of establishing their identity against the larger church.

The events of the First Jewish Revolt of A.D. 66-70 were of course catastrophic for the Jerusalem church. According to a tradition increasingly challenged, but still to be regarded as trustworthy, the Palestinian Christians moved to Pella* in the Transjordan (perhaps believing that Jesus had directed them to do this; cf. Mk 13:14) around the year 67 (see Eusebius *Hist. Eccl.* 3.3.5). There some of them remained until perhaps the fourth century, apparently becoming more radical in their Jewishness, and eventually becoming known generally as Ebionites, or sometimes Nazoreans. Some, however, eventually returned to Jerusalem where they resumed leadership of the church. Although he probably overstates his case, Jervell's conception of the Jewish Christians as a "mighty minority" on through the first century into the second seems justified in light of the continuing strength of Jewish Christianity as it can be seen in the later NT writings and the apostolic fathers. It did not help the relation between Christians (whether Jewish or Gentile) and Jews when the former regarded the destruction of the temple as a vindicating expression of the judgment of God upon Judaism. Toward the end of the first century the polarization between Christian Jews and their non-Christian kinsfolk was aided by the expulsion of the Christian Jews from the synagogue through the deliberate alteration of the liturgical prayer called "the Eighteen Benedictions" (*Shemoneh Esreh*) to be directed against the "heretics" (*minîm*) and "Nazoreans" (*noṣrîm*), though this is debated.

To the credit of the Gentile church, it did not turn its back on its Jewish heritage (though this would happen later), nor did it in the late second century follow Marcion* in denying the Hebrew Scriptures their proper place in the Christian canon.* The church of the first four centuries knew the importance of its Jewish roots and the extent to which Christianity constituted the fulfillment of the OT (*see* Christianity and Judaism).

4. The Theology of Jewish Christianity.

Jewish Christianity was marked by diversity from the beginning. We see it already in the Aramaic-speaking and Hellenistic Jewish Christians of the early chapters of Acts, whose differences involved more than language, not to mention the Judaizers. As we move into later manifestations of Jewish Christianity, however, and particularly to increasingly heretical branches such as the Ebionites, more radical stances on key issues are often found.

4.1. The Law. Because of its central importance to Judaism, it is understandable that the law* becomes a crucial element within certain manifestations of Jewish Christianity. We have noted that already in the NT one encounters an amazing spectrum of opinion on the subject, from the Judaizers who insist on the law even for Gentile Christians, to the Jerusalem church under James, to Matthew's community, and to Paul and Hebrews. Commitment to the law in varying degrees may be said to characterize all of Jewish Christianity after the NT. Later Jewish Christianity, as represented by the Ebionites, solidified in its affirmation of the continuing validity of the commandments of the law (cf. Eusebius *Hist. Eccl.* 3.27) and its rejection of Paul's law-free gospel.

4.2. Anti-Paulinism. One can detect some tension between Jewish Christianity and Paul already in Acts 21:21. It seems probable, furthermore, that James 2:14-26 is directed against Paulinists—that is, those who took Paul's law-free gospel to an extreme. Since it was Paul who spoke out so clearly against the permanence of the law, it is to be expected that later Jewish Christianity would seek to separate itself from his teaching and authority. Irenaeus reports concerning the Ebionites that "they repudiate the Apostle Paul, maintaining that he was an apostate from the law" (*Adv. Haer.* 1.26.2; cf. Eusebius *Hist. Eccl.* 3.27). If, as some have argued, the Simon Magus of the Pseudo-Clementines represents Paul, then this body of literature would contain by far the most extensive polemic against Paul in the Jewish Christian literature we possess.

4.3. Christology. Certain strands of second-century Jewish Christianity apparently found a high christology* incompatible with the strict monotheism of the *shema*. The Johannine idea of Jesus as the Incarnation of God was rejected. Usually the virgin birth was denied and a type of adoptionism was accepted, wherein Jesus became designated Messiah because of his faithfulness to God (*Apost. Const.* 6.6; Irenaeus, *Adv. Haer.* 5.1.3). Eusebius goes so far as to say that the Ebionites (i.e., "the poor") received their name because "they had poor and mean opinions concerning Christ" (*Hist. Eccl.* 3.27). This is probably not the true explanation of the name, but it does point to the meager christol-

ogy of these Jewish Christians.

5. The Question of Orthodoxy and Heresy.
The Jewish Christianity of the early Jerusalem church was theologically primitive, yet not to be judged as unorthodox. As early as Stephen and the Hellenistic Jewish Christians there is growth in understanding of the theological significance of Jesus and his death. The later examples of Jewish christianity in the NT reflect a much more developed christology than that of the early Jerusalem church.

Yet from nearly the beginning there were also heterodox Jewish Christians, the so-called Judaizers (Gal 2:11-14; Phil 3:2; Acts 15:5). It seems probable that people of this persuasion concerning the law continued right through the first century. There were also undoubtedly Jewish Christians who remained relatively conservative in their christology, being unwilling to draw out the full implications concerning the person of Christ, for example his deity and his pre-existence.

As we move into the second century we begin more and more to encounter a Jewish Christianity of a decidedly heterodox kind. What is the reason for the increasing polarization between Jewish Christianity and the Gentile church, and the eventual demise of the former? With the passing of time, the Jewish Christians who did not integrate into the great church must have felt themselves under increasing pressure from both the church on the one hand, and the synagogue on the other. The pressure from the synagogue reinforced their own strong Jewish convictions and clearly had a great impact on them. The result was that despite their Christian leanings, they were unable to articulate a Christianity that was orthodox on the matters of law and christology. They found themselves in a quite impossible situation.

With much perceptivity Jerome said of them: "since they want to be both Jews and Christians, they are neither Jews nor Christians" (*Ep.* 112.13). Unlike the Jewish Christian scribes of Matthew's community, they were apparently unable to bring out of their storehouse things both old and new (Mt 13:52). For them the old was a hindrance to the new, and they were thus unable to arrive at that important balance wherein the newness of the gospel finds its proper place alongside the tradition of Israel of which it is the proper fulfillment.

See also CHRISTIANITY AND JUDAISM: PARTINGS OF THE WAYS; CHRISTOLOGY; CIRCUMCISION; EBIONITES; FOOD, FOOD LAWS, TABLE FELLOWSHIP; GOD; HOLY DAYS; JERUSALEM, ZION, HOLY CITY; LAND IN EARLY CHRISTIANITY; LAW; MATTHEAN COMMUNITY; SYNAGOGUES; TEMPLE; WORSHIP AND LITURGY.

BIBLIOGRAPHY. B. Bagatti, *The Church from the Circumcision* (Jerusalem: Franciscan, 1971); R. E. Brown, "Not Jewish Christianity and Gentile Christianity but Types of Jewish/Gentile Christianity," *CBQ* 45 (1983) 74-79; G. W. Buchanan, "Worship, Feasts and Ceremonies in the Early Jewish-Christian Church," *NTS* 26 (1980) 279-97; J. Daniélou, *The Theology of Jewish Christianity*, Vol. 1 of *The Development of Christian Doctrine Before Nicea* (London: Darton, Longman & Todd, 1964); J. A. Fitzmyer, "Jewish Christianity in Light of the Qumran Scrolls" in *Studies in Luke-Acts*, ed. L. E. Keck and J. L. Martyn (New York: Abingdon, 1966) 233-57; B. Gerhardsson et al., *Judéo-Christianisme*, Festschrift J. Daniélou [=*RSR* 60 (1972) 1-320)] (Paris: Recherches de Science Religieuse, 1972); C. C. Hill, *Hellenists and Hebrews* (Minneapolis: Fortress, 1992); G. Hoennicke, *Das Judenchristentum im ersten und zweiten Jahrhunderten* (Berlin: Trowitzsch, 1908); F. J. A. Hort, *Judaistic Christianity*, ed. J. O. F. Murray (reprint: Grand Rapids: Baker, 1980); J. Jervell, *The Unknown Paul* (Minneapolis: Augsburg, 1984); A. F. J. Klijn, "The Study of Jewish Christianity," *NTS* 20 (1974) 419-31; R. N. Longenecker, *The Christology of Early Jewish Christianity* (Naperville: Allenson, 1970); G. Lüdemann, *Opposition to Paul in Jewish Christianity* (Philadelphia: Fortress, 1989); F. Manns, *Bibliographie du Judéo-Christianisme* (Jerusalem: Franciscan, 1978); I. H. Marshall, "Palestinian and Hellenistic Christianity," *NTS* 19 (1972-73) 271-89; J. Munck, "Jewish-Christianity in Post-Apostolic Times," *NTS* 6 (1959-60) 103-16; R. Murray, "Defining Judaeo-Christianity," *HeyJ* 15 (1974) 303-10; R. A. Pritz, *Nazarene Jewish Christianity: From the End of the New Testament Period until Its Disappearance in the Fourth Century* (Leiden: E. J. Brill, 1988); S. K. Riegel, "Jewish Christianity: Definitions and Terminology," *NTS* 24 (1977-78) 410-15; H.-J. Schoeps, *Jewish Christianity: Factional Disputes in the Early Church* (Philadelphia: Fortress, 1969); A. F. Segal, "Jewish Christianity," in *Eusebius, Christianity and Judaism*, ed. H. W. Attridge and G. Hata (Detroit: Wayne State University Press, 1992) 326-51; G. Strecker, "On the Problem of Jewish Christianity," Appendix 1 in W. Bauer, *Orthodoxy and Heresy in Earliest Christianity*, ed. R. A. Kraft and G. Krodel (Philadelphia: Fortress, 1971) 241-85; idem, *Das Judenchristentum in den Pseudoclementinen* (Berlin: Akademie, 1958).

D. A. Hagner

JEWISH WARS. *See* CHRISTIANITY AND JUDAISM: PARTINGS OF THE WAYS.

JOHANNINE COMMUNITY/SCHOOL. *See* JOHN, LETTERS OF.

JOHN, LETTERS OF

Three of the NT's twenty-one letters are associated with John. Even though they do not bear John's name, an impressive church tradition and unmistakable thematic connections with the Fourth Gospel have suggested that they stem from John, the author of the Fourth Gospel.

Interest in the Johannine epistles has always been eclipsed by an untiring fascination with the Fourth Gospel. John's recasting of Jesus' life (compared with the Synoptic portrait), his theological probings into the essence of the Incarnation and his theological contributions (in christology,* pneumatology and eschatology*) have all drawn expected attention. The Johannine epistles, however, are an enigma. While 2 John and 3 John have the usual features of ancient letters,* 1 John bears no such marks: it is more like a tract or a broadside aimed at a particular problem sweeping the church.

In recent years, however, scholars have taken a second look at the letters as one more avenue into exploring the composition and social history of the Johannine community. As early as 1979, R. E. Brown's *The Community of the Beloved Disciple* brought to general audiences suggestions about the Johannine community that had been offered elsewhere by J. L. Martyn (1968), O. Cullmann (ET 1975), R. A. Culpepper (1975), and others (for bibliography see Brown 1982, 140-43). Today it is commonplace to speak of the Johannine school, or community, or circle, from which the teachings of John about Jesus were preserved and penned (the Gospel of John) and where John's correspondence was preserved (1 Jn, 2 Jn, 3 Jn). Just as the Fourth Gospel yields information about Jesus, it also betrays the consciousness of the community that shaped and cherished it. Just as the opening paragraph of 1 John and the Fourth Gospel mirror each other, so too the concerns of the letters fit into the compositional history of the Gospel.

Therefore in order for us to understand better the place of the letters of John, we would do well to reconstruct the social and theological history of the community as best we can from its surviving literature. There is considerable debate concerning the sequence of these four documents (Brown 1982, 14-35), but a consensus has emerged showing that they stem from the same community and, for many, they share the same author. Moreover, it is widely accepted that the problems addressed in the letters are reflected in the Fourth Gospel itself. A common compositional history argues that an early edition of the Fourth Gospel was followed by a theological crisis in the community. This crisis prompted a revision of the Gospel and the writing of 1 John. This explains, for instance, the parallels between the Gospel's prologue and that of 1 John, as well as parallels between 1 John and John 14-17, John's Farewell Discourse (Smalley 1984, xxix-xxx; see chart, Brown 1982, 757-59; Segovia). Finally, 2 John and 3 John were penned to address a subsequent local problem.

1. History of John's Church
2. Theological Struggle
3. John's Secondary Concerns
4. Authorship and Setting
5. Epistolary Structure

1. History of John's Church.

The Johannine literature does not provide us with chronological clues to reconstruct its life and setting. Nevertheless, we can confidently assume that these letters and the Gospel did not surface in a vacuum. It is not farfetched to assume that John himself—John the apostle, son of Zebedee, one of the Twelve*—was a pastor and an evangelist who built churches in the Mediterranean world and was a custodian of traditions about Jesus (see Jesus Tradition). If this is the case, then the literature that survives this community, the letters and the Gospel of John, provide important evidence of the character of these Christians. These documents tell us about the development of thought among John's followers: their passions, their wars, even their history.

1.1. John's Earliest Community. Early traditions indicate that John planted churches in Ephesus. Eusebius, the fourth-century historian, quotes Irenaeus (130-200), bishop of Lyons, who tells us that John was a leading ecclesiastical figure in Asia Minor (Eusebius *Hist. Eccl.* 3.23). He goes on to say that clergy from throughout the area would travel to Ephesus just to learn from John and hear his stories about Jesus. And how did Irenaeus know all this? Irenaeus says it was confirmed to him by Polycarp,* the bishop of Smyrna, who in his younger years was instructed by John (Irenaeus *Haer.* 2.22.5). Similarly Eusebius also preserves for us a letter by the bishop of Ephesus itself (Polycrates). In it the Ephesian bishop tells us that John who reclined near the Lord at the Last Supper (Jn 13:25) was buried in Ephesus. Today two tombs still exist near this ancient city, both claiming to be the burial place of John.

While the early church was well-known for its fanciful traditions about the apostles* (see the Syriac *History of John),* many scholars do not count this story of John among them. John was a leading pastor whose memory of Jesus and whose recollection of his teachings gave him unique stature in antiquity.

John's community of believers lived on the frontiers of Judaism.* His church was heterogeneous: Jews who had moved into the Greek world lived alongside Greeks who knew little of the OT. Their common bond was a firm allegiance to Jesus, their messiah, and John was their leader. And yet because John himself and his "Christian message" were rooted in Judaism, it was natural that this community would live in proximity to the synagogues* of his city. In fact it is here, in this relationship with the synagogue, that the Johannine community's "story" was forged.

1.2. The Fourth Gospel. The Gospel of John is a by-product of John's ministry. That is why it repeatedly anchors its message in John's "eyewitness" testimony (Jn 19:35; 20:24). Its text tells us about Jesus, to be sure, but the way its message is framed tells us about its author and his audience. This explains, for instance, why again and again the Gospel refers to "the Jews" (sixty-four times) as if they were the opponents of the church (neither Paul nor Luke writes with this same tone). Even though some have criticized the NT and especially the Fourth Gospel as anti-Semitic, such a view misrepresents the cultural and historical framework unique to these writings. In its earliest days John's congregation felt that it was under siege: external enemies particularly from the synagogue were in debate with them. This also explains the importance of John's lengthy story in John 9: the blind man's expulsion from the synagogue may have meant a lot to John's Jewish followers who themselves were being expelled.

At its earliest stages (before the writing of the epistles) this community was cultivating an outlook of division: the world outside the church was a place of darkness, persecution* and turmoil. In Jesus' prayer (Jn 17) there is not even a record of Jesus praying for the world: he simply prays for the survival and success of his followers. Stories that held deep meaning for the community ended up in the Johannine archive about Jesus: fights with Jewish leaders (see Jn 5, 8, 9 and 10), the continuing relevance of Jewish festivals like Passover (see Jn 6) and the ongoing importance of John the Baptist (see Jn 1:35-51; 3:22-36) to name a few. We know, for example, that Ephesus had a community of people who were followers of John the Baptist but not of Jesus (see Acts 19:1-7). Did these groups debate? Did a story like John 1:35-51 encourage many of them to join the followers of Jesus?

In these earliest days the Fourth Gospel may have been a loose collection of stories preached by John (see Stibbe). These were the formative years of the community when prized stories about Jesus were being preserved and polished, when a collection of John's best memories and personal accounts were being written down. To be sure, this was a Gospel to be proud of: it gave generous amounts of teaching* from Jesus, teaching that predicted the sort of persecution the church was having and yet promised an intimacy with Christ that made such suffering* immaterial. This was a Gospel that described the Holy Spirit* in detail—that talked about conversion using terms like "rebirth" and "drinking living water" and "eating the bread of life." This was a Gospel that encouraged those believers prone to mystical experiences of the faith.*

Indeed the Gospel of John was an empowering Gospel that shaped this Christian community so that it would expect dynamic spiritual experiences. Jesus and the Father were dwelling inside these spiritually reborn believers (Jn 14:23)! No other Gospel speaks like this. The Holy Spirit promised to provide them with incredible powers: power* to recall Jesus' very words (Jn 14:26), power to work miracles* greater than those of Jesus (Jn 14:12), power to have prayer answered (Jn 14:13-14) and power to confront a hostile world (Jn 16:7). They even had the power to forgive sin* (Jn 20:23). Above all the Spirit gave them the power of prophecy,* to continue speaking with Jesus' voice, revealing new things not recorded in Scripture (Jn 16:13).

John's Gospel suggests that John's community was a pneumatic community. This is not to say that the Johannine literature provides a detailed working-out of the spiritual gifts as, say, Paul does in 1 Corinthians 12-14. Rather, the Johannine literature evidences a community that was alert to the centrality of the Spirit and ready to experience the Spirit in its fullness. Johannine theology laid the context in which a pneumatic/charismatic Christianity would flourish.

1.3. Problems in the Community: The Letters. But we can only speculate that something serious happened at a later stage of the church's life. The once-unified congregation began to tear apart from within. Threats that were once external now were found within the ranks of the fellowship* itself. For John it must have been a crisis beyond belief. In 1 John 2:18 he even says that it is "the last hour" for the community.

Lengthy scholarly debate has centered on the identity of these dissenters. They were likely a select group of Johannine Christians who knew the Fourth Gospel well, claimed to be inspired by the Spirit and challenged John's understanding of Jesus Christ's personhood and work. And they were succeeding. The community was splitting, harsh words were being exchanged, and the vocabulary once reserved in the Fourth Gospel for those in "the world" now was being aimed at fellow Christians.

1 John supplies our primary evidence for this division. In its chapters we have evidence of severe social conflict: the painful departure of the group (1 Jn 2:19-26) and warnings about "deceivers" and "liars" who twist the truth of Christ (1 Jn 2:22; 2 Jn 7). There were also severe theological debates (1 Jn 5:5-8) that were being fought among teachers claiming to be filled with the inspiration of the Holy Spirit (1 Jn 2:20-21; 4:1-6). The letter's repeated emphasis on love* hints at the severity and desperation of the situation.

Brown believes that at this point the Fourth Gospel may have gone through a revision to correct some of these misunderstandings. The Gospel, for instance, gained its prologue (Jn 1:1-18), which emphasizes Jesus' full incarnation (Jn 1:14). These introductory verses have an uncanny resemblance to the opening verses of John's first letter (see 1 Jn 1:1-4). Some think that the event that inspired this "writing up" of the Gospel was John's death. John 21 implies that John has died even though his community thought that he would survive until Christ's second coming (see Jn 21:20-25). When John's disciples compiled their leader's story of Christ, they gave him a title of veneration that would make him famous: the Beloved Disciple (Jn 13:23; 19:26; 20:2; 21:7, 20).

Therefore we can say that in some respect John's letters are a response written in debate with those who may be misinterpreting the Fourth Gospel. For some scholars the epistles serve as a sort of commentary on the Gospel. Still other scholars would describe them as an "epilogue" to the Gospel designed to circulate with it so that erroneous interpretations would not be reached. S. S. Smalley prefers to describe 1 John as a paper that "sets out to expound Johannine teaching and ideas, now preserved in the tradition and theology of the Fourth Gospel, for the benefit of heterodox members of John's community who were also indebted to the teaching of the gospel but who were understanding it differently and, indeed, erroneously" (Smalley 1984, xxvii).

1.4. The Fate of the Johannine Church. But the Johannine church was not to survive the conflict. 2 John and 3 John give a glimpse of the sort of crises that must have gripped one congregation. The larger Johannine community divided, with strong leaders taking the fellowship into Gnosticism* and Docetism* while John's own disciples remained in communion with the other NT churches of Paul and the apostles. The earliest commentaries on John (e.g., Heracleon) were written by Gnostics, a fact that shows how the Fourth Gospel was embraced in these heretical circles. The *Odes of Solomon* (if they are gnostic) likewise bear marks of Johannine influence. Even the Nag Hammadi texts seem to describe a dualism that would fit the secessionists of John's church quite well. Concepts such as light and darkness, sinlessness, divine birth, the Spirit of Truth and God's seed all appear in Nag Hammadi.

Hippolytus (c. 170-c. 236)) describes how Johannine language was used by his gnostic opponents. This may explain why the orthodox church (the "Great Church" as some label it) embraced the Fourth Gospel reluctantly. In fact there is a surprising lack of interest in the Johannine writings among the leading second-century writers. The church's gnostic opponents were using the Fourth Gospel or a form of it. As many scholars believe, it was the epistles of John—1 John in particular—that redeemed the Fourth Gospel for the NT we possess today.

2. Theological Struggle.

The Johannine epistles everywhere betray the marks of struggle and conflict. 1 John 2:18 describes antichrists* in the world; 1 John 2:22 names them "liars" who are denying an orthodox christology. There is no doubt that the letters themselves were written in the midst of a severe and desperate theological debate.

2.1. John's Opponents. Who were these opponents whom John confronted? What were the issues that they debated? It is virtually impossible to name them specifically or label their "movement" (although some scholars attempt to do so). Some even believe that John is confronting two separate groups in the letters (Painter 1993; Smalley 1980). What we can do is outline their beliefs using the refutation that John has given us in his letters. But this is a difficult endeavor for a number of reasons. Writers rarely give a complete hearing to their opponents' views, and we have no first-hand information from John's adversaries.* None of their writings have survived. Moreover, sometimes John opposes things that may not be on the agenda of his opponents. For instance, in 1 John 4:18 he says there is no fear in love because perfect love casts out fear. John may be taking an opportunity to chastise his followers and not necessarily addressing anyone else.

2.2. Theological Issues. John returns to two major subjects repeatedly as he writes: christology and ethical* behavior. And it is likely that the two are intimately connected. The secessionists had embraced an aberrant form of christology that led them to make wrong judgments about Christian living.

2.2.1. Christology. The doctrine of Christ lived at the center of John's theological disputes. John says that his opponents hold the following beliefs: they deny the Son (1 Jn 2:23); they deny that Jesus Christ has come in the flesh (1 Jn 4:2; 2 Jn 7); they deny that Jesus is the Christ (1 Jn 2:22). These statements may be compared with affirmations in the epistles that buttress John's own christology. It is likely that these verses are connected to the opponents' christological error: Jesus is the Christ (1 Jn 5:1); Jesus Christ has come in the flesh (1 Jn 4:2); Jesus is the Son (1 Jn 2:23; 3:23; 5:11) or the Son of God (1 Jn 1:3, 7; 3:8, 23; 4:9, 10, 15); Jesus Christ came "by water and blood" (1 Jn 5:6).

From these statements a composite image begins to emerge. These are no doubt Christians who have begun to deviate from the traditionally received understanding of Jesus Christ. They affirm the idea of Christ but doubt if Christ became flesh and if the man Jesus was indeed the incarnation of God.

Today scholars have concluded that John's opponents embraced a "high christology" that elevated Christ's divinity at the expense of his humanity. The Hellenistic world commonly affirmed a cosmos populated by numerous deities. Elevating Christ into their company was easy given the tolerant, syncretistic outlook of the day. And yet this same Hellenistic world was predisposed to reject that such divinities would materially enter the world. Using a dualistic outlook, Christ was separated from the world, set apart with the divinities of heaven and there left to rule. One Christian variety of this view said that Christ may have "seemed" (Gk *dokein*, hence, Docetism) to appear in the flesh, but he did not. The notion that Christ would appear "in flesh" (Gk *sarx*) was ridiculous if not abhorrent. The strong emphases of John 1:14 and 1 John 1:1-3 are all salvos in John's theological struggle.

If the earthly life of Jesus Christ was now irrelevant, these people still claimed to have immediate access to God. In their view they had moved beyond the basic, elementary, orthodox teachings of Christianity and, inspired by the Spirit, could know God directly. I. H. Marshall describes them well: "They were like men kicking away the ladder on which they have climbed to the heights and leaving themselves without any visible means of support" (Marshall 21). The very gospel* that had given birth to their faith was being jettisoned. They are not abiding in the teaching of Christ but are going beyond it (2 Jn 8).

This tendency to divide the world along dualistic lines that separated reality into opposing forces (light/darkness, above/below, spirit/flesh, etc.) was quite common in the first century. Further, the notion of immediate revelation* through divine knowledge* (known as Gnosticism) was just coming to life. But the application of these principles to a Christian christology was something new.

2.2.2. Cerinthus. One of the first teachers to do so was Cerinthus. What we know about him is contained in the records of his opponents, particularly Irenaeus. In Irenaeus's *Adversus Haereses* (c. A.D. 180) we find an important story reported by Polycarp that bring Cerinthus and John together. Apparently John once was in the public baths at Ephesus and discovering Cerinthus there cried out, "Let us save ourselves; the bath house may fall down, for inside is Cerinthus, the enemy of the truth." Irenaeus goes on to say that John proclaimed his gospel in order to refute the errors of Cerinthus (Irenaeus *Haer.* 3.3.4; 3.11.1).

Cerinthus's theology is outlined for us by Irenaeus. Cerinthus may have been one of the first to carefully distinguish Jesus and Christ. He argued that Jesus was the earthly man of Nazareth well-known for his piety and wisdom.* Christ was a heavenly deity who descended on Jesus at his baptism* and departed before the crucifixion (*see* Death of Christ). Thus the man Jesus, not the Son of God, died on the cross.* Therefore when we read 1 John 2:22 ("Who is the liar but the one who denies that Jesus is the Christ.") many commentators wonder if it is just this sort of distinction that John has in mind (see also 1 Jn 5:1, 11, etc.). Someone is saying that Jesus the man is not the Christ.

In summary, for John's opponents the incarnate Jesus Christ was no longer occupying the central place in Christian faith. At best these secessionists had a nominal interest in the Jesus of history and tradition and instead were looking to inspired spiritual experiences that lifted them above the conventional views of John.

2.2.3. Ethics. John's letters also evidence a sustained critique of the moral disposition of certain persons. This is not like the usual exhortations we find in Paul's writings, in which believers are warned against catalogs of sins (1 Cor 6) or dispositions of the heart (Gal 5). In the Johannine context a theological rationale had formed making ethical behavior of no consequence for the Christian life. John mentions his opponents' views in a number of places:

☐ they boast that they are "free from sin" (1 Jn 1:8, 10)

☐ they boast that "they have fellowship" with God but walk in the darkness (1 Jn 1:6)

☐ they boast that they "know God" but nevertheless are disobedient (1 Jn 2:4)

☐ they boast that they "love God" but hate their brothers and sisters (1 Jn 4:20)

☐ they boast that they are "in the light" but hate their fellow Christians (1 Jn 2:9)

John also repeats a number of affirmations that shed some light on the nature of the secessionists' ethical position:

☐ to abide in God is to obey him—it is to walk as Jesus walked (1 Jn 2:6)

☐ to sin willfully shows that you have not known God (1 Jn 3:3-6; 5:18)

☐ whoever acts sinfully belongs to the devil (1 Jn 3:7-8, 9-10)

☐ we should love one another (1 Jn 3:11-12, 17-18)

☐ refusing to love your brother or sister means that you have not inherited eternal life (1 Jn 3:14-15)

☐ God is love—and to know him is to love (1 Jn 4:8-10)

While christology was the main battleground in the community, the tangible expression of these disagreements came in the form of open conflict and hostility. Faulty christology spilled into unethical conduct.

What does John mean when he says that these people are "not obedient"? There is no evidence that they were living immoral lives (*see* Purity). 1 John 2:15-16 is likely a general exhortation for the church not to be worldly. Instead, these people were not following the conventional authoritative teachings of the church. Since they denied the significance of Christ's incarnation, it stands to reason that they would deny the significance of his earthly teachings. Therefore they did not heed Jesus' words written in the Gospel. Likewise if they denied their own sinfulness, they would feel no need for Christ's atoning death on the cross. Theirs was a "deeper" religion, a mystical faith, fueled by nontraditional insights gleaned from the Spirit (1 Jn 2:20-23; 4:1). They refused to conform to traditional teachings, and as a result they refused to submit to the leadership that bore those teachings.

The secessionists were not simply indifferent to those who disagreed with them. They were intolerant. This explains the repeated times that John refers to "hating" fellow Christians. Conflict resulted from their superior spirituality. These people had become elitist in their view of themselves. And those who sought to exhort them who could not catalog similar experiences for themselves had no credibility.

We must not read John's words about "community love" as applying merely to John's opponents, however. Too often we have characterized these unorthodox Christians as difficult, haughty and unremitting in their attitudes toward the church. John is also exhorting his own followers to exhibit love because they are responding to the secessionists with equal hostility. And just because their theology is right by no means says that their angry attitudes are justified.

2.2.4. Incipient Gnosticism? This disposition to spiritualize the earthly career of Christ, giving it no great salvific importance, and to deny the spiritual importance of one's own physical, moral life had some currency in antiquity. Gnostic systems of religious thought were in intense debate with Christianity from about A.D. 150-300 (years after John's death) and yet the framework that would lead to these systems was already in place (*see* Gnosis, Gnosticism). This later literature speaks of a religion of enlightenment, of special knowledge, preserved only for the initiated. Believers were "reborn," creating a unique union with God that literally brought about a state of sinless perfection. "Sin" belongs to another nature, our material nature, which no longer matters in God's economy. Hence, enlightened spiritual experiences validated spirituality, while at the same time practical questions of moral conduct were deemed irrelevant.

Scholars who have compared the Johannine literature with second- and third-century gnostic writings find striking similarities of language and tone. For instance, when 1 John 3:9 talks about God's "seed" remaining in one born of God, this echoes the teaching of the Valentinian Gnostics who were great opponents to the orthodox church. In the nineteenth century this even led some to conclude that John was directly in debate with a fully developed gnostic religious system (and hence to be dated much later). But this is not necessary. The predisposition to divide the world along material and spiritual lines (dualism), to seek spiritual enlightenment (mysticism) and to deny personal moral responsibility were well-established by the end of the first century. Colossians and the Pastoral Epistles bear similar witness to Christians who have some christological deviation and who disregard the value of practical moral conduct.

3. John's Secondary Concerns.

A number of secondary themes are found throughout the epistles. In some sense these appear by accident because they are a part of the refutation the author is making against his opponents. In most cases these are intimately connected with the two primary subjects under debate in his church: christology and ethics.

3.1. The Holy Spirit. If study of the Fourth Gospel was central to this community's spiritual formation, it comes as no surprise that the Spirit would play a pivotal role in discipleship. No gospel places as much emphasis on the Spirit as John's Gospel (Burge). In fact the indwelling of Christ and the transformation of the believer are both framed in terms of Spirit-experience in this literature (Jn 14:23-24; 3:1-8). Even the Lord's Supper is defined as an assimilation of Christ in Spirit (Jn 6:52-63). This is why John's community had strong pneumatic or ecstatic tendencies. His followers were confident of their anointing,* and in his polemic against the secessionists he must take this pneumatic context into consideration.

In 1 John 4:13 John reassures his followers that possessing the Spirit is characteristic of those who "abide in God." Such abiding is not simply a matter of orthodox confession (1 Jn 4:15) or loving conduct (1 Jn 4:16), although these are important. Abiding in God is experiential: it is a personal experience with the Holy Spirit. Therefore John's opponents (the false teachers) must buttress their authority* with some pneumatic experience, some evidence that they have the Spirit too. This explains why in 1 John 4:1-3 the church is called to "test the spirits.*" These opponents are claiming to be prophets* (1 Jn 4:1 labels them false prophets), who under the inspiration of the Spirit are making striking new claims about Christ.

This is a pneumatic context. It is interesting to note what John does not say. He does not employ his apostolic authority as, say, Paul does in Galatians to refute the Judaizers there. He does not leverage pastoral authority as power anchored in a position. Instead he urges the church to test the spirits to see if they are affirming traditional beliefs about Jesus—thereby undercutting the authority of these prophets. His tactic therefore is characteristic of those struggling against rival leadership claims in a "charismatic" setting. One cannot deny the Spirit. One must teach discernment and urge believers to weigh claims made in the voice of the Spirit.

But John goes further. If these secessionists are claiming a superior spirituality, John reminds the church that each member has been equally anointed with the Spirit (1 Jn 2:20, 27). In other words, spiritual discernment is the task of every person. To be a Christian is to possess the Spirit, and no one may come along claiming exclusive spiritual insight. Thus 1 John 2:27 remarks, "As for you, the anointing you received from him remains in you, and you do not need to have anyone teach you." Christians must be well-grounded and confident in the authenticity of their own spiritual experience and not swayed by the seemingly more compelling experiences of others.

3.2. Discernment and Tradition. John reminds us that the church is the custodian of the truth. Foremost among John's concerns is the responsibility of the corporate community to discern false belief and practice, to distinguish between truth and error. While this theme is explicitly mentioned only in 1 John 4:1-6, nevertheless it is presumed throughout 1 John. The church must stand guard against any who would bring distortion or error (2 Jn 8).

But this presents a problem. How can we discern truth from falsehood? If a prophet urges something new under the authority of the Spirit how can it be weighed? In 1 Corinthians 14:29 Paul confronted a similar dilemma. His solution was to have the prophets weigh one another's words, thereby checking individual inspiration in a deliberative body. John nowhere uses that tactic, setting prophet against prophet. Instead he believes that the church is accountable to the historic revelation given in Jesus Christ and passed down through the apostles. Individual inspiration, therefore, must be weighed against truth revealed in Scripture and tradition.

Throughout 1 John the author affirms that what was "from the beginning" should be the anchor for what we believe now (1 Jn 1:1; 2:13,

14; 3:11). In fact "from the beginning" becomes a refrain as John urges his readers to recall what they first learned and measure all else by it. "Let what you heard from the beginning abide in you. If what you heard from the beginning abides in you, then you will abide in the Son and in the Father" (1 Jn 2:24 NRSV). He says that his commandments are not new, but "old commandment[s] that you have heard from the beginning" (1 Jn 2:7; 2 Jn 5).

John is not merely giving a stubborn defense of tradition, as if older is better. By "the beginning" he refers to the historic coming of Jesus Christ and the preservation of that revelation. What was revealed in the Incarnation must be the litmus test for all new theological insights. Thus in 1 John 1:1-3 John points to what he saw with eyes and touched with hands—the incarnate Christ. Historic christology must be the touchstone for all Christian belief. How do we know love? "God sent his son into the world" (1 Jn 4:9). Curiously his exhortation in 1 John 2:12-14 twice reminds the fathers—those who are older—to rekindle their acquaintance with the ancient teachings, things the younger generation may no longer treasure.

This theological anchor in historic christology is reminiscent of what we read in the Gospel of John. In his Farewell Discourse Jesus talks about the Spirit and the limits of what he will do. As Jesus' words cannot deviate from the Father's words (Jn 5:19), so too the Spirit will reiterate what Jesus himself has said in history (Jn 14:26). The Spirit "will not speak on his own, he will speak only what he hears" (Jn 16:13). In Christian faith Father, Son and Spirit provide a revelation that is self-consistent and harmonious. No later revelation contradicts what has gone before. John is affirming that Christian wisdom and truth, anchored in right christology, are cumulative and binding.

3.3. Love, Unity and Fellowship. The epistles of John as well as the Gospel of John place a high premium on the quality of Christian community. Jesus' command in John 13:34 and John 15:12, 17 made clear that love should be the hallmark of his followers. In John 17 Jesus prays for harmony and unity among his followers "so that they may be one" on the model of the oneness of the Father and the Son (Jn 17:20-23).

No doubt the schism in John's church has placed unity and love on the ecclesiastical agenda. He even makes love a command: Christians who love God must love their brother or sister in the church (1 Jn 4:21). This teaching John anchors "in the beginning" as well (1 Jn 3:11; 2 Jn 5), harking back no doubt to the Gospel. In 1 John 3:23 he almost sums up the Christian life giving two simple exhortations: belief in Jesus Christ and loving one another.

But John does not give an exhortation without offering some theological ground since there are indeed times when loving those who are unlovely seems impossible. God, he says, first loved us (1 Jn 4:19). Love, especially in difficult circumstances, cannot be fueled by human energy. Love originates from God when we apprehend the depth of his love for us (1 Jn 4:7a) and when we are born anew by his spirit (1 Jn 4:7b). For John intimate knowledge of God is the same as enjoying the intimate reciprocity of God's love: he loves us, we love him, and this love spills over to those near us. In harsher terms, not to love is evidence, severe evidence, that someone does not know God and has failed to experience him fully (1 Jn 4:8).

If we are uncertain about God's profound desire for us, we need only look to God's love shown to us in Christ. Christ is the material expression of God's tangible love, and so once again John is making a claim for the value of historic, incarnational christology to address issues of ethics. Because Christ laid down his life for us, so too we ought to do the same for one another (1 Jn 3:16). 1 John 4:10 says it succinctly: "This is love, not that we loved God, but that he loved us and sent his Son as an atoning sacrifice for our sins."

John describes living in God's love, knowing him and obeying his commands as "walking in the light." This is one more metaphor for normative Christian discipleship. Therefore in 1 John 1:7 he affirms that when people walk in the light together, when corporately they experience God's love, unity and fellowship result. Vibrant community is the natural outgrowth of people who genuinely live in God's presence. But the reverse is also true. When people exhibit hostility and division, when they "hate" (to use John's term), they prove that their lives are being lived "in the darkness" (1 Jn 2:9-11) or being lived "in death" (1 Jn 3:14). Such so-called Christians are "liars" and hypocrites (1 Jn 4:20). John spares no words for people who claim to know God but fail to exhibit genuine godliness.

There is an important nuance to John's

teaching. To anchor our love in God's affection might inspire passivity. That is, we wait for God's love to mature and change us, to shape us, before we apply any effort to our own growth. If we cannot feel God's love, John would have us exhibit love toward others as a way to step into God's presence. In 1 John 4:12 he talks about the limits of our experience of God: "No one has ever seen God; but if we love one another, God lives in us and his love is made complete in us." Loving the unlovely or the difficult to love is an avenue, a mystical avenue, to discover God in our midst.

A concrete example of how this love might be expressed is in simple acts of charity among God's people. 1 John 4:17 remarks: "How does God's love abide in anyone who has the world's goods and sees a brother or sister in need and yet refuses help? Little children, let us love, not in word or speech, but in truth and action" (NRSV). In 3 John 10 we are even given a negative example of someone named Diotrephes who is lacking in the practice of Christian charity and hospitality, according to the elder.

Are there limits to love? Of course, John says that we must not love the world (1 Jn 2:15)—not meaning the people of the world (Jn 3:16) or God's creation (Jn 17:24). This instead refers to everything that is hostile to God and inimical to the truth of the gospel. But in 2 John 10 we have an interesting problem. John urges his followers not to welcome (to receive into fellowship) anyone who intentionally professes false doctrine. Could John be referring to the secessionists who have divided the church? While participation with the unbelieving world is a necessary facet of Christian discipleship, if we are to have integrity there must be a limit to tolerance. There are lines of personal social intercourse and public participation that Christians must not cross.

4. Authorship and Setting.

4.1. Authorship. While Christian tradition has attributed these letters to John the apostle, the Johannine epistles are anonymous with the exception that 2 John and 3 John call their author "the elder" (2 Jn 1; 3 Jn 1). Locating his identity would of course solve the mystery. The title may simply refer to a man of high esteem in the community, although good evidence shows us that the apostles themselves were described as "elders" in antiquity (cf. 1 Pet 5:1).

The situation is sorely complicated by a ref-erence in Eusebius (*Hist. Eccl.* 3.39.4) to two Johns, one clearly the apostle and the other possibly an elder who lived later (some have speculated that he was a disciple of the apostle John). Could the elder in our epistles be this second John? Marshall, however, has shown that this does not necessarily have to be the case and that even if two persons named John lived in this period, the attribution of epistolary authorship to the later man is purely hypothetical (Marshall 42-48).

While 2 John and 3 John appear to come from the same pen, does 1 John originate with this author? Nowhere is he described as "the elder," who is so called in 2 John and 3 John. Careful comparisons of style and content show striking similarities among all three writings and suggest that common authorship is not at all unlikely (Brown 1982, 14-35, 755-59). A more compelling question is whether the same pen wrote the epistles and the Gospel of John. As early as the third century Dionysius the Great of Alexandria was making this claim based on similarities of content and style, and today the parallels between the Gospel and the letters is a commonplace in NT studies. This is particularly true of 1 John and the Gospel. In fact careful comparison of 1 John and the Gospel's Farewell Discourse (Jn 13—17) shows even more remarkable parallels. Parallels in style and content are comparable to those found in Luke and Acts or even Colossians and Ephesians. This has led the vast majority of scholars to affirm common authorship for 1 John and the Gospel. Those who disagree point to the absence of OT quotations in 1 John, stress on future eschatology, Jesus as paraclete (rather than the Spirit), 1 John's emphasis on Jesus' sacrificial death and the promotion of ecclesiastical authority. But for most these objections have not been decisive.

4.2. Date. Since the epistles have been closely associated with the Fourth Gospel, those who would place the Gospel in the late first century locate the epistles anywhere from A.D. 90-110. However, arguments for such a late date now must bear the weight of serious criticisms, and increasingly the Gospel has been given an earlier time frame closer to A.D. 70 or A.D. 80. Allowing time for the development of the heresy described in the epistles, a date between A.D. 70 and A.D. 90 would not be unreasonable.

4.3. Location. The traditional view that the

Johannine writings originated from Asia Minor is sound. The heresies addressed in the epistles (and perhaps the Gospel) are well-established in this area. Further, the Fourth Gospel is traditionally associated with Ephesus. We can also argue by inference. John 1:35-42; 3:22-4:3; and 10:41 suggest that the Johannine community was in a debate with followers of John the Baptist who had not affirmed the messiahship of Jesus. Acts 19:1-7 describes twelve such followers of the Baptist in Ephesus who find themselves at odds with the Christians in that city.

4.4. The Sequence of 1, 2 and 3 John. Since little supplemental information exists telling us about the circumstances of these letters, we cannot assume that they were written in the sequence in which they appear in our NT. Some scholars have rearranged the three letters in every conceivable configuration. Some have argued that 2 John precedes 1 John because the tone is quite different: in 2 John the false teachers are addressed mildly (2 Jn 7-9) while in 1 John the struggles are described more severely (1 Jn 2:19; 4:1-3). We can wonder then if the problems brought on by the secessionists are just beginning in 2 John (making it earlier) and only later come to blows in 1 John.

The differences in the epistles may be explained by geographical locale. That is, 1 John may be addressed to a community setting at the heart of the Johannine world, perhaps the very center where the secessionists had launched their campaign. This would explain the personal nature of the letter as well as its intensity. By contrast 2 John may be addressed to outlying house churches not fully embroiled in the controversy. Perhaps this is why 2 John is more formal and detached in the way it addresses its readers (see 2 Jn 1, 5, 13) and essentially is a warning about what is to come (2 Jn 8-11). Another possibility is that 2 John and 3 John were cover letters that were accompanied by the more substantial treatise 1 John. Some believe that this fits 3 John particularly well since it is addressed to "Gaius," and Demetrius, who is being commended to the church, may have been the letter's courier (3 Jn 12; cf. 3 Jn 8). But we cannot be confident about any of these theories.

It is no doubt best to view these letters as coming from the same approximate time period and addressing the same general crisis in the church. 1 John is the author's full broadside against his opponents. 2 John and 3 John are personal notes that either accompanied 1 John or were sent separately to another destination.

5. Epistolary Structure.
2 John and 3 John have all of the usual features of first-century letters: the author and recipient are identified at the beginning, a blessing or prayer follows ("Grace, mercy, and peace will be with us," 2 Jn 3; "I pray that all may go well with you," 3 Jn 2) and there is a concluding greeting (2 Jn 13; 3 Jn 15; cf. Gal 1:1; 1 Thess 1:1). The letters also contain personal references and allusions that suggest they are intended for a specific, personal situation. Some even suggest that 3 John is the best NT example of first-century epistolary format.

The same cannot be said, however, for 1 John. In fact of all twenty-one letters, 1 John is the least like a first-century letter. As B. F. Westcott wrote, there is "no address, no subscription, no name is contained in it of a person or place; no direct trace of the author, no indication of any special destination" (Westcott, xxix). No conclusion ends the document—1 John 5:21 even sounds as if the writer's thoughts have been cut off. Further, no personal comments suggest that the author is writing a personal letter. This is highly unusual when we consider the intensely personal character of the crisis in the church. It is all the more unusual if we believe that the same author penned 2 John and 3 John. If so, then he clearly knew epistolary form.

This absence of form has rightly led many to suggest that 1 John is not a personal letter at all but a general treatise aimed at wide distribution. Some prefer to call it a sermon or an address. Perhaps it is a pamphlet, a brochure or an encyclical. Some prefer to think of it as a tractate engaged in some sort of polemic, a kind of manifesto that addresses specific theological issues across a general front. This may explain why John mentions thirteen times that "he is writing" and that twenty-two times he uses the plural *you*.

The earliest patristic view understood that 1 John was a sort of introduction or explanation of the Fourth Gospel. It was not an exposition or a commentary but rather a correction, a clarification aimed at those who might distort its teachings. And in the end the Fourth Gospel would become more intelligible. This explains why John chooses an opening that deliberately imitates that of the Gospel and why in 1 John 5:13 his closing epilogue resembles John 20:31. Brown (1982, 116-29), who defends this view (following earlier scholars like Lightfoot) even finds a two-part structure to the epistle that imitates the two-part structure of the Fourth Gospel (cf. The Book of Signs, Jn 1—12; The Book of Glory, Jn 13—21).

5.1. The Structure of 1 John. Discovering a recognizable pattern or structure of thought in 1 John has proven impossible. Most scholars have sought to divide it into either two or three sections. Some commentators (Brooke, Dodd, Grayston, Houlden and Marshall) believe this is pointless and find instead either spirals of cyclical thought or a list of unconnected units. According to this view, John's units link up with each other only casually and are "governed by an association of ideas rather than by a logical plan" (Marshall, 26).

The most famous threefold division belongs to R. Law whose 1909 commentary argued that 1 John had three parts, each part offering three "tests of life:" righteousness, love and belief. The secessionists fail to acknowledge the importance of righteous behavior, do not love fellow Christians and deny belief in Jesus Christ, the Son of God. While such a theory's creativity is attractive it falls short in many places in the epistle, particularly in part three (1 Jn 4:7—5:13). Nevertheless a number of current scholars have defended such a three-unit theory: A. E. Brooke (1912), E. Malatesta (1973), P. R. Jones (1970), M. Thompson (1992) and R. Schnackenburg (1965). Those who find a threefold structure appealing generally look for thematic divisions at 1 John 2:27/28/29 and at 1 John 3:22/24, 4:6 or 4:12.

A twofold or bipartite division has traditionally been less popular but today is commanding renewed attention. The French scholar A. Feuillet defended this view in 1973 and most recently Brown (1982) and Smalley (1984) have become its champion in their commentaries. Two observations argue for this structure. First, John makes two declarations in the Gospel (Jn 1:5; 4:6) that Brown suggests are keys to John's master plan: "God is light" (Jn 1:5) and "God is love" (Jn 4:6). Second, the Gospel of John, which enjoys a bipartite form, may be the structural model for this second Johannine writing. Similarities between the two writings have often been observed. Each begins with parallel prologues, and the bodies of each writing move from doctrinal truths to practical applications for life.

Smalley would prefer to divide the epistle at 1 John 2:29 and 1 John 3:1, which would employ a division popularly used by those making a threefold division in the epistle. Brown's divisions shown here provide proportionally sized halves for the epistle and also find parallel introductory lines for 1 John 1:5 and 1 John 3:11, "This is the message we have heard."

A. Prologue, 1 John 1:1-4: The word of life which we have witnessed among us.

B. Part 1, 1 John 1:5—3:10: God is Light—and we should walk accordingly.

"This is the message we have heard from him and proclaim to you."

1 John 1:5-7: Thesis: walking in the light and walking in the darkness.

1 John 1:8—2:2: First Exhortation: Resist sinfulness.

1 John 2:3-11: Second Exhortation: Obey God's commands.

1 John 2:12-17: Third Exhortation: Defy the world and its allure.

1 John 2:18-27: Fourth Exhortation: Renounce those who distort the truth.

1 John 2:28—3:10: Fifth Exhortation: Live like God's children.

C. Part 2, 1 John 3:11—5:12: God is Love—and we should walk accordingly.

"This is the message you have heard from the beginning, that we should love one another."

1 John 3:11-24: Love one another in practical ways.

1 John 4:1-6: Beware of false prophets who would deceive you.

1 John 4:7-21: Love one another as God loves us in Christ.

1 John 5:1-4: Obey God and thereby conquer the world.

1 John 5:5-12: Never compromise your testimony.

D. Conclusion, 1 John 5:13-21: The boldness and confidence of those who walk in God's light and love.

5.2. The Structure of 2 and 3 John. Few have discovered a careful literary structure for these brief epistles. Like personal letters everywhere, they begin with a greeting and then develop one theme after another in a casual manner. Each letter is occasioned by the same concern: living the truth. This takes on two dimensions: it means loving those who abide in the family of

God, and it means chastising those who would dismantle that family. In each case John warns against community destroyers—a theme grounded in the concerns about division well-known throughout 1 John.

2 John

    2 John 1-3: Personal Greetings
    2 John 4-6: Loving the Family of God
    2 John 7-11: Protecting the Family of God
    2 John 12-13: Closing

3 John

    3 John 1-2: Personal Greetings
    3 John 3-8: Loving Christ's Emissaries
    3 John 9-12: Exhortations About Diotrephes
    3 John 13-14: Closing

See also ADVERSARIES; CHRISTOLOGY; DOCETISM.

BIBLIOGRAPHY. **Commentaries:** A. E. Brooke, *A Critical and Exegetical Commentary on the Johannine Epistles* (Edinburgh: T & T Clark, 1912); R. E. Brown, *The Epistles of John: Translated with Introduction, Notes, and Commentary* (AB; Garden City, NY: Doubleday, 1982); F. F. Bruce, *The Epistles of John: Introduction, Exposition, and Notes* (London: Pickering & Inglis; Old Tappan, NJ: Revell, 1970); R. Bultmann, *The Johannine Epistles: A Commentary on the Johannine Epistles* (Philadelphia: Fortress, 1973); G. M. Burge, *The Epistles of John* (Grand Rapids: Zondervan, 1996); C. H. Dodd, *The Johannine Epistles* (London: Hodder & Stoughton, 1946); K. Grayston, *The Johannine Epistles* (Grand Rapids: Eerdmans, 1984); J. L. Houlden, *A Commentary on the Johannine Epistles* (London: Adam & Charles Black; New York: Harper & Row, 1973); S. J. Kistemaker, *Exposition of the Epistle of James and the Epistles of John* (Grand Rapids: Baker, 1986); R. Law, *The Tests of Life: A Study in the First Epistle of St. John* (Edinburgh: T & T Clark, 1909); I. H. Marshall, *The Epistles of John* (NICNT; Grand Rapids: Eerdmans; London: Marshall, Morgan & Scott, 1978); R. Schnackenburg, *The Johannine Epistles: Introduction and Commentary* (New York: Crossroad, 1965/1992); S. S. Smalley, *1, 2, 3 John* (WBC; Waco, TX: Word, 1984); J. R. W. Stott, *The Letters of John: An Introduction and Commentary* (TNTC; 2d ed.; Grand Rapids: Eerdmans, 1988); M. M. Thompson, *1-3 John* (IVPNTC; Downers Grove, IL ; Leicester, UK: InterVarsity Press, 1992); B. F. Westcott, *The Epistles of St. John: The Greek Text with Notes* (4th ed.; Grand Rapids: Eerdmans 1966, [1883]). **Studies:** C. K. Barrett, *Essays on John* (London: SPCK, 1982); R. E. Brown, *The Community of the Beloved Disciple: The Life, Loves and Hates of an Individual Church in New Testament Times* (New York: Paulist; London: Geoffrey Chapman, 1979); idem, " 'Other Sheep Not of This Fold': The Johannine Perspective on Christian Diversity in the Late First Century," *JBL* 97 (1978) 5-22; idem, "The Relationship to the Fourth Gospel Shared by the Author of 1 John and by His Opponents" in *Text and Interpretation,* ed. E. Best and R. McL. Wilson (Cambridge: Cambridge University Press, 1979), 57-68; G. M. Burge, *The Anointed Community: The Holy Spirit in the Johannine Tradition* (Grand Rapids: Eerdmans, 1987); O. Cullmann, *The Johannine Circle* (London: SCM; Philadelphia: Westminster, 1975); R. A. Culpepper, *The Johannine School* (Missoula, MT: Scholars Press, 1975); A. Feuillet, "The Structure of First John: Comparison with the Fourth Gospel," *BTB* 3 (1973) 194-216; P. R. Jones, "A Structural Analysis of I John," *RevExp* 67 (1970) 433-44; J. M. Lieu, "The History and Background of 2 and 3 John," unpublished Ph.D. thesis, University of Birmingham, 1980); idem, *The Second and Third Epistles of John: History and Background* (Edinburgh: T & T Clark, 1986); idem, *The Theology of the Johannine Epistles* (NTT; Cambridge: Cambridge University Press, 1991); idem, "What Was from the Beginning: Scripture and Tradition in the Johannine Epistles," *NTS* 39 (1993); E. Malatesta, *The Epistles of St. John: Greek Text and English Translations Schematicallty Arranged* (Rome: Gregorian University, 1973); J. L. Martyn, *History and Theology in the Fourth Gospel* (Nashville: Abingdon, 1968); J. Painter, *The Quest for the Messiah: The History, Literature, and Theology of the Johannine Community* (Nashville: Abingdon, 1993); F. F. Segovia, "The Love and Hatred of Jesus and Johannine Sectarianism," *CBQ* 43 (1981) 258-72; S. S. Smalley, *John: Evangelist and Interpreter* (Exeter: Paternoster, 1978, 1983); idem, "What about 1 John?" in *Studia Biblica 1978,* 3: *Papers on Paul and Other New Testament Authors,* ed. E. A. Livingstone (JSNTSup 3; Sheffield: JSOT, 1980) 337-43; D. M. Smith, "Johannine Christianity: Some Reflections on Its Character and Delineation," *NTS* 21 (1974-75) 222-48; M. W. G. Stibbe, *John as Storyteller: Narrative Criticism and the Fourth Gospel* (SNTSMS 73; Cambridge: Cambridge University Press, 1992); J. C. Thomas, "The Order of the Composition of the Johannine Epistles," *NovT* 37 (1995) 68-75; U.C. von Walde, *The Johannine Commandments: 1 John and the*

Struggle for the Johannine Tradition (New York: Paulist, 1990); R. A. Whitacre, *Johannine Polemic: The Role of Tradition and Theology* (Chico, CA: Scholars Press, 1982).   G. M. Burge

JOSEPH THE PATRIARCH. *See* ANCESTORS.

JOSEPHUS

A politician and general during the Jewish war of A.D. 66-70, Josephus was the most significant Jewish historian* of the Roman period (*see* Roman Empire).

    1. Life of Josephus
    2. Historian and Apologist
    3. Josephus's Works
    4. Summary

1. Life of Josephus.

Born in the first year of Caligula (A.D. 37-38), Josephus was a priest* and claimed Hasmonean lineage. Never shy about his abilities, Josephus relates that he possessed a fine memory and great intellectual acuity. At twenty-six he was part of a delegation sent to Rome concerning several priests who had run afoul of Nero. He met and befriended Poppaea, the consort and then wife of Nero, and through her offices secured their release (Josephus *Life* 3 §16). Nero and his circle were known to favor eastern religions,* and Agrippa II issued coinage bearing the visage of Poppaea.

Upon returning to Judea, Josephus found seditious elements already at work and attempted to mollify them. Secretly hoping that Cestius, the governor of Syria, would be able to quell the rebellion in its infancy, he regarded the defeat of Cestius a terrible blow, as it encouraged the revolutionaries for whom Josephus had scant regard (Josephus *Life* 6 §24). Two years later Josephus was appointed general for Galilee. Captured soon after Vespasian arrived in A.D. 67 to direct Roman efforts against the revolutionaries, Josephus became a collaborator with the Romans, serving as an interpreter during the siege of Jerusalem.* In this Josephus was typical, as the Romans frequently preferred to entice conquered elites to act as their agents, granting in return positions of privilege. Josephus thereby earned the enmity of many Jews. After the war Josephus lived in Rome, where Vespasian granted him a pension and made him a Roman citizen (Josephus *Life* 76 §422-26).

2. Historian and Apologist.

Our richest source for information about Judea during the Second Temple period, the works of Josephus are often cited yet frequently judged "propaganda" and "distorted." Nevertheless, we owe him the courtesy of evaluation according to his apologetic aims and the literary standards then current.

Josephus was an apologist for his people and for himself. To appeal to Roman sensibilities he cited *hubris* to explain human behavior, noted parallels between the Pharisees and the Stoics, applied the four cardinal Hellenistic virtues to biblical figures and merged two schools of Hellenistic historiography: the sensationalism and rhetoric of the "pathetic" school (he added dramatic, romantic and even erotic elements to biblical stories) with the revived Herodotean tradition. He also was determined to appeal to fellow Jews who regarded him a traitor. For example, *The Jewish War*, sometimes judged a propaganda piece produced by a Roman minion, is actually the fruit of a striking thesis: a nonrepresentative minority Jewish faction corrupted Judaism* and caused the war (*J.W.* 2.17.10 §449-56; 4.3.6 §147-50), and by destroying Jerusalem the Romans acted as the agents of God.* This is consonant with Jewish views of history, respects Roman might and fortune and exonerates the Jewish people at large.

Josephus made use of a number of rhetorical conventions then standard (the child prodigy, lies that demonstrate wily resourcefulness), and while their presence may disturb us, to Josephus they no doubt appeared effective. That Josephus was capable of misrepresenting history pursuant to his apologetic or rhetorical needs is likewise seen in the discrepancies between *The Jewish War* and *Life*. While this renders our desire to achieve Rankean historicity (i.e., history "as it actually happened") difficult, Josephus remains in large measure a trustworthy guide.

Josephus provides crucial information on figures (Pilate, Herod, James), movements (the enormously complicated revolutionary/messianic terrain) and social conditions only alluded to elsewhere. His fondness for Daniel may be evidence of the popularity of apocalyptic* during this period. The relationship between Josephus and various NT documents (Luke-Acts,* Paul,* James*) constitute burgeoning fields of study, and recent work on the sociology of Palestine owes much to Josephus. Preserved by early Christians for the wealth of information he relates, Josephus was distorted by Origen and Eusebius to make the claim that the destruction of Jerusalem was God's punishment for the murder of Jesus. In Josephus the Jewish idea of God acting in history is combined with Greek historiographical styles. This is emblematic of a broader fusion of cultures and more narrowly points to the *Ecclesiastical History* of Eusebius and to the historiography of Christian Byzantium.

3. Josephus's Works.

In Rome Josephus produced four works that have survived.

3.1. The Jewish War. The earliest was *The Jewish War*, originally written in Aramaic. The stated purpose is to warn other nations against opposing Rome, but its pro-Roman apologetic is far more complex than this. Debate continues concerning its accuracy, but excavations at Masada by Yadin have in large measure affirmed its trustworthiness on that matter at least.

3.2. The Jewish Antiquities. The *Jewish Antiquities* is a survey of Jewish history from the biblical period through the Jewish war, occasioned by charges of Jewish hatred of humankind. In response Josephus highlights the antiquity of Judaism and the high moral character of its laws,* pictures Jewish leaders in terms reminiscent of Plato's philosopher-king and all but ignores the covenant.* Yet he notes the need for Jews to avoid assimilation with other cultures. Claiming to set out in "precise detail," "neither adding nor omitting anything," Josephus frequently alters the biblical material to suit his apologetic aims. The integrity of the claim can be preserved by arguing that Josephus used an early Aramaic Targum along with the Septuagint and the Masoretic Text, viewing each as authoritative. We are on more firm ground in noting that Josephus modeled his work on the *Roman Antiquities* of Dionysius of Halicarnassus, which had appeared a century before. Both comprise twenty books, and both make the rhetorical claim to historical accuracy. *The Jewish Antiquities* contains the famous *Testimonium Flavianum*, where Jesus is called the Messiah (*Ant.* 18.3.3 §63-64). Most scholars judge it a Christian interpolation.

3.3. Life of Josephus. Often called the first autobiography, the *Life of Josephus* is in large measure an apology for his career in Galilee, claiming that his actions followed the lead of his superiors in Jerusalem. A response to criticisms leveled at the account provided in *The Jewish War*, it differs in many respects from the longer work.

3.4. Against Apion. His last work, *Against Apion*, follows the model of the Greek apologists. It is an attack upon Greek anti-Jewish sentiment that had spread to Rome.

4. Summary.

Josephus is crucial to our understanding of the NT world. His work presents us with a complicated historical and apologetic landscape, causing many to express doubt concerning his reliability. Nevertheless, once apologetic aims are recognized, his value is unchallenged.

See also JUDAISM, POST-A.D. 70; PHILO.

BIBLIOGRAPHY. Z. Baras, "The *Testimonium Flavianum* and the Martyrdom of James" in *Josephus, Judaism and Christianity,* ed. L. Feldman and G. Hata (Detroit: Wayne State University Press, 1987) 338-48; G. Carras, "Paul, Josephus and Judaism: The Shared Judaism of Paul and Josephus," Unpublished D. Phil. thesis, Oxford, 1989); L. Feldman, "Josephus," *ABD* 3:981-98; L. Feldman and G. Hata, eds., *Josephus, Judaism and Christianity* (Detroit: Wayne State University Press, 1987); idem, *Josephus, the Bible and History* (Detroit: Wayne State University Press, 1989); S. Mason, *Flavius Josephus on the Pharisees* (Leiden: E. J. Brill, 1991); idem, *Josephus and the New Testament* (Peabody, MA: Hendrickson, 1992); T. Rajak, *Josephus* (Philadelphia: Fortress, 1984); H. Schreckenberg, "The Works of Josephus and the Early Christian Church" in *Josephus, Judaism and Christianity,* ed. L. Feldman and G. Hata (Detroit: Wayne State University Press, 1987) 315-24.   D. P. Nystrom

JOY

Joy is a major theme that runs throughout the writings of the OT, the NT and the literature of the early church fathers (*see* Apostolic Fathers). It is a word with great theological significance, because everywhere in these documents joy in the true sense, both individual and corporate, is rooted in an unshakable faith in God and originates in a realization that God has acted and is acting to save those who put their trust in him (Ps 16:11; Lk 1:46-47; Acts 2:26, 28; 5:41; 1 Pet 1:6; Rev 19:6, 7; *1 Clem.* 18.8; *Barn.* 10.11).

1. The Vocabulary of Joy
2. Joy in the Later New Testament
3. Joy in the Apostolic Fathers
4. Summary

1. The Vocabulary of Joy.

In the body of Christian literature under consideration there are numerous Greek words or clusters of words that give color to the idea of joy: *agalliasis/agalliaomai* ("exult," "be glad," "rejoice"), *asmenōs* ("gladly"), *gelaō/gelōs* ("laugh"/ "laughter"), *euphrainō/euphrosynē* ("gladden," "be glad," "take delight in," "joy," "cheerfulness"), *eudaimoneō* ("be happy," "fortunate"), *hēdeōs/hēdonē/hēdomai* ("gladly"/"pleasure," "have pleasure," "enjoyment," "cravings") *hilaros/hilarotēs* ("cheerful"/"cheerfulness," "glad"/"gladness," "merry," "graciousness"), *makarizō/makarios/makarismos* ("consider blessed," "happy," "fortunate," "a blessing"), *skirtaō* ("exult," "skip gaily about") and *chairō/chara* ("rejoice," "be glad"/"joy").

The very number of these words helps one to approach an understanding of the meaning of this elusive term. From the texts under study its meaning seems to range from an exuberant gaiety that expresses itself in frolic or exultant dance, to a happiness coming from a good mental outlook on life, to a feeling of well-being that is generated by confidence in the blessing of God, to a deep, quiet, settled joy that is more akin to peace* than it is to happiness.

2. Joy in the Later New Testament.

Some of these words or word groups are seldom used or used not at all by our NT writers. For example, the verb *to laugh* never appears and the noun *laughter* only once (Jas 4:9). These writers, familiar with and influenced by the OT, where laughter was most often used to convey ideas of scorn, doubt, derision or foolish thinking and behavior, not joy (cf. Gen 18:12; Prov 10:23 LXX; Eccles 7:6; Sir 21:20; 27:13), either avoided such words altogether or did as James did. He challenged certain of his Christian readers to change their "laughter to mourning" (Jas 4:9), not because he wanted to kill their joy but rather because he knew that their laughter was the foolish laughter of people who had turned from the ways of God and who needed to repent,* so that they might

discover true joy (see Martin, 154).

Other words such as *eudaimoneō, hilaros/ hilarotēs* and *skirtaō* also are absent from the vocabulary of these writers. Perhaps this was because some of these words may have been still too closely tied to their pagan roots (*eudaimoneō*), describing a happiness that was the result of a good genius (*daimōn*)—words not filtered by previous usage in the Septuagint—while others tended to emphasize a lighthearted gaiety that was not truly descriptive of a suffering* community that lived life under the cross.* *Hēdonē*, a word that writers in antiquity often made use of to convey both positive ideas of enjoyment and delight (Plato *Rep.* 9.583-85; Aristotle *Eth. Nic.* 7.14; Herodotus 4.139) and negative ideas of sensual pleasures that threaten to undermine the very meaning of life (Jaeger, 1:178-80), is a word that our writers use sparingly (three times) and only in the latter pejorative sense. They see *hēdonē* as contributing nothing to genuine joy, for it is sinful pleasure, evil passion, a selfish craving that works to destroy the self and the community (Jas 4:1, 3; 2 Pet 2:13; cf. 4 Macc 1:25-26; see Stählin, 2:917-18).

The words or word groups for joy that our NT writers make the most use of are *agalliaomai/agalliasis, euphrainomai/euphrosynē, makarizō/makarios* and *chairō/chara*.

The first of these, *agalliaomai/agalliasis,* is a word group that is found only in Jewish (especially in the Psalms) and Christian writings. It is strictly a religious term that always expresses the worshiper's* thankful exultation in God* and in his mercy.* It is a gladness that may be experienced in the present, e.g., through the contemplation of and the participation in what God has done through Christ* to redeem* human beings (Acts 2:46; 1 Pet 1:6, 8). It comes to full flower in the future when Christians will rejoice with rapturous joy as they stand with Christ in his glory* (1 Pet 4:13; Rev 19:6-7)—*agalliaomai* is a common eschatological* theme: "the jubilation of God's people in the attainment of his purpose" (Jude 24; Is 12:6; 25:9; 60:5; 61:10; Bauckham, 122). Yet time, present or future, is irrelevant to the meaning of this word, since such exultation is grounded in faith in God and in his unchangeableness (see Bultmann, 1:19-21, who nevertheless does emphasize the eschatological dimension).

Euphrainō/euphrosynē is a word group that appears rather infrequently in our NT writings.

It primarily identifies the inner, subjective feelings of merriment and good cheer describing a mood, a positive mental outlook on life; secondarily it refers to the outward expression of that cheer, such as banqueting, eating, drinking and making merry. It is the joy that a righteous* person (e.g., the Messiah) experiences, even in the face of death, because of his quiet confidence in the safekeeping of his person in the protective care of God (Acts 2:26, 28). These words also describe an inner mood that is a gift from God that can enable all people, if they will allow it, to recognize God's gracious providential care of them (Acts 14:17). It also expresses a joy that manifests itself in liturgical, jubilant celebration. Whenever it is so used in the NT, however, it always has a pejorative connotation (Acts 7:41; Rev 11:10).

Makarizō/makarios is a word group that finds its origin in a word first used of the gods and that denoted "the transcendent happiness of a life beyond care, labour and death" (Hauck, 4:362). Although it later became a weaker, more common everyday term, it seems never to have lost its meaning of well-being, fullness of life, bliss, settled joy in contrast to fleeting earthly happiness (Sir 11:28). In biblical writings it described those whose well-being had its basis in God and his will—knowing and doing it, trusting him, waiting for him, hoping in him and loving him (Mal 3:12; Ps 2:11; 33:8; Prov 16:20) irrespective of the situations in which these faithful might find themselves (Wis 5:15-23). In this same sense our NT writers often use this word group. Who is the person who experiences true well-being, bliss, settled joy *(makarios)*? Such is the person who holds up under testing and proves faithful (Jas 1:12); the person who both hears and does the will of God (Jas 1:25; Rev 1:3); the person who for the sake of God and Christ experiences suffering even when doing what is right (1 Pet 3:14; 4:14); the person who endures to the end (Jas 5:11; Rev 14:13). However one is to translate this word group, the translation "happy"/"count happy" is hardly the best, for "happy" suggests an emotional reaction based on circumstances, while in fact *makarios/makarizō* suggests rather a reaction to whatever life might bring based on the faithfulness of God (Martin, 193).

Chairō/chara, originally secular in usage, has become *the* word group for joy in the NT. Its frequent occurrences underscore the fact that joy is the hallmark of the Christian era—initiated at the birth of Jesus (Mt 2:10), accented at his death,* resurrection* and ascension* (Lk 24:52), persisting to the present even during periods when Christians are subjected to suffering (Jas 1:2; 1 Pet 1:6, 7).

At times joy may be an inner response to a life-changing event—conversion to Christ (Acts 8:39), hearing the gospel* for the first time (Acts 13:48); learning that the church* at Antioch* was manifesting the grace* of God (Acts 11:23); experiencing healing* acts of God (Acts 8:8); knowing Peter was released from prison (Acts 12:14); finding out about the conversion of Gentiles* (Acts 15:3), and so on.

At other times joy may be an inner response to the greatest of adversities—beaten and disgraced for the sake of Christ's name (Acts 5:41); having one's possessions plundered because of being a Christian (Heb 10:34); being painfully driven from city to city because of preaching the gospel (Acts 13:52); undergoing every kind of testing (Jas 1:2); sharing in the sufferings of Christ (1 Pet 4:13); enduring painful discipline* (Heb 12:11).

Sometimes joy was both a present and a not-yet experience—something future, anticipated, eschatological. For example, we may note these words: "Jesus, who for the sake of the joy that was set before him, endured the cross," where the joy, like the goal itself, lies in front of him yet to be attained (Heb 12: 2; Attridge, 357). Note also 1 Peter 4:13b, where the apostle links *chara* and *agalliaomai* in a kind of ascending parallelism from present gladness in experiencing suffering for Christ to an eschatological jubilation in the day when his glory will be revealed: "Rejoice insofar as you are sharing Christ's sufferings, so that you may also be glad *[charēte]* and shout for joy *[agalliōmenoi]* when his glory is revealed" (1 Pet 1:6, 8; see Michaels, 262; Marshall, 151; Selwyn, 222).

At times the NT writers cannot fully express precisely what they mean by joy with a single word, so they pile word on top of word to help them articulate what they have in mind: *euphrainomai/agalliaomai* (Acts 2:26); *chairō/agalliaomai* (1 Pet 4:13; Rev 19:7); *agalliaomai/chara* (1 Pet 1:8); *chairō/euphrainomai* (Rev 11:10), variously translated "glad"/"rejoiced," "be glad"/"shout for joy," "rejoice"/"exult," "rejoice with joy," "rejoice"/"celebrate." On occasion, almost as though they realized human beings are incapable of experiencing and adequately giving full expression to joy, they call upon the heavens and those who dwell there to join them in this (Rev 12:12; 18:20; cf. Ps 96:11, 12; *T. Levi.* 18.5). In our NT writings God is never made the subject of joy (but cf. *1 Clem.* 33.7).

3. Joy in the Apostolic Fathers.

Some of the words for joy omitted by the NT writers find a place, however, in the postapostolic writings.

The verb *gelaō* ("to laugh") appears only in the *Shepherd of Hermas** but with a positive connotation, where an old woman asks Hermas, "You who are patient and good-tempered, who are always laughing [*gelōn*], why are you . . . not merry?" (*Herm. Vis.* 1.2.3, 8).

Hilaros/hilarotēs ("cheerful," "glad," "merry," "joyful," "gladness") is still another word group found only and often in Hermas. The Shepherd says to Hermas: "Put on joyfulness [*hilarotēs*], which always has favor with God. . . . Every joyful man [*hilaros anēr*] does good deeds . . . and despises grief [*lypē*]. But the mournful man [*lyperos anēr*] always does wickedly . . . because he grieves the Holy Spirit which is given to man [*anthrōpō*] in joyfulness [*hilaron*]" (*Herm. Man.* 10.3.1, 2; *Herm. Sim.* 9.15.2; cf. *Herm. Vis.* 1.2.3; 1.4.3; 3.9.10; 3.10.5; *Herm. Man.* 5.2.3; 10.3.2; *Herm. Sim.* 6.1.6; 8.1.18; 9.9.7; 9.10.1). This word group seems to connote a lighthearted cheerfulness linked by this writer to the presence of the Holy Spirit* within the believer (cf. Gal 5:23), a cheerfulness that is the opposite of and incompatible with sorrow [*lypē*]. Perhaps it was for this reason that the other apostolic fathers avoided the use of these words: a hint and a silent reminder that true joy is not incompatible with sorrow and pain.

Eudaimoneō is found only in *Diognetus*: "For happiness [*eudaimonein*] consists not in domination over neighbors. . . . But whoever takes up the burden of his neighbor and works to help another" (*Diogn.* 10.5). This text, so used, demonstrates that a pagan word can be taken up, "baptized" and used to express a fundamental Christian idea.

Skirtaō, a word that in itself means "to leap, spring or skip about" as a sign of joy (cf. Lk. 1:41, 44), never appears in our NT writers and only twice in the early fathers—negatively in *Hermas* where the Angel of Luxury and Deceit shepherded skipping (*skirtaō*), joyful (*hilaros*) sheep that had given themselves to lusts of this world (*Herm. Sim.* 6.1.6; 2.3.4, 6) and positively in *Diognetus* where it is said that "the grace of the church exults" (*Diogn.* 11.6).

Those words and word groups used by our NT writers to connote joy also appear frequently in the writings of the fathers and with similar meanings.

Makarizō/makarios continues to give expression to that sense of supreme well-being that humans experience by participating in the forgiveness,* grace and salvation* of God even though they must endure suffering, pain and martyrdom (*1 Clem.* 50.6; *2 Clem.* 19.4; Pol. *Phil.* 2.3; *Mart. Pol.* 2.1-3).

Euphrainomai/euphrosynē still describes a joy born from knowing and trusting God who both provides and will provide; it refers to a joy both experienced and anticipated (*1 Clem.* 52.2; *2 Clem.* 19.4; *Barn.* 7.1; 10.11; 21.9; *Herm. Man.* 5.1.2). The apostolic fathers also carry on to a lesser degree the meanings of *chairō/chara* as they were used in the NT. For example, it is said of Christians that "when they do good they are buffeted as evildoers, when they are buffeted they rejoice as people who are receiving eternal life" (*Diogn.* 5.16); joy is experienced by leaders in the church upon seeing Christians living together in unity (*1 Clem.* 65.1); knowledge of God's love brings joy (*Diogn.* 10.3); obedience to Christian teachings given in the Holy Spirit gives joy and gladness to the teacher (*1 Clem.* 63.2); the blood of Jesus Christ is eternal and abiding joy to those within the church (Ign. *Phld.* presc.); Polycarp, when facing a cruel death, was nevertheless filled with courage and joy (*Mart. Pol.* 12.1). Polycarp's friends, although they had begged Polycarp to make his escape, remained to put his bones in a proper place where the Lord allowed them to come together in gladness and joy in order to remember him (*Mart. Pol.* 18.2).

Like the noun to which it is related (*hēdonē*, pleasure), the adverb *hēdeōs* ("with pleasure," "joyfully"), which is not used by our NT writers, sometimes expresses a negative idea: "What sort of luxuries are harmful? Every act which a person does with pleasure [*hēdeōs*]" (*Herm. Sim.* 6.5.5; *Herm. Man.* 2.2; cf. Ign. *Trall.* 6.2). But more often than not it describes an action done in a positive, gladsome, joyful spirit (*1 Clem.* 2.1; 31.3; *Herm. Sim.* 6.5.5; 8.10.3, 4; 9.14.6; 27.2). In using *hēdonē*, the apostolic fathers for the most part follow the example of our NT writers in giving it a negative connotation (Ign. *Trall.* 6.2; Ign. *Phld.* 2.2; Ign. *Rom.* 7.3; *Herm. Sim.* 6.5.7; 8.8.5; 9.4; *Diogn.* 6.5; contra *2 Clem.* 15.5).

While employing these same words for joy that are found in the NT writings under consideration, the apostolic fathers extend their usage. Not only do humans rejoice, but "the Word teaches the saints and rejoices *[euphrainomai]"* (*Diogn.* 12.9). God, too, rejoices: "The Lord adorned himself with good works" (by creating the world; Conzelmann, 9:371] and rejoiced (*chairō, 1 Clem.* 33.7; cf. *Herm. Vis.* 3.12.3). For some of these postapostolic writers, joy is a reward for keeping the commandments of God and going beyond them—doing anything good beyond what is required (*Herm. Sim.* 5.3.3). *Barnabas* addresses his readers as "children of gladness" (*euphrosynēs; Barn.* 7.1) and tells them of the three ordinances of the Lord, one of which is "love united with joy and gladness" (*agapē euphrosynēs kai agalliaseōs; Barn.* 1.6).

4. Summary.

Joy is a theme that pervades the earliest Christian writings. Words for joy are plentiful and seem easy enough to translate, but to understand precisely what these writers meant by them is much more difficult. There is something mysterious about this concept that is not always easy to grasp or express.

Perhaps one can say, on the basis of the texts examined, that for the vast majority of these early Christian writers true joy was not something that could be measured by external features, such as hilarity and exultant celebration —at least not on this side of the great eschatological banquet (Rev 19:7). In those places where such words for joy are used to describe a cultic dance or a dance of jubilation, they always are used in a pejorative sense (see Acts 7:41; Rev 11:10.) Further, these writers do not appear to equate joy with happiness, as happiness is commonly understood today (this in spite of the fact that *makarios* is translated as "happy" in numerous versions), nor can any of them be termed advocates of what might be called "holy laughter" or other such ecstatic, visible expressions of joy (see Jas 4:9).

Whatever joy is, it can be the result of an experience and awareness of beneficial things occurring either to oneself or to others, such as a vivid consciousness of the providential presence of God in life (Acts 2:28; *Barn.* 10.11), the coming of rain from heaven and a bountiful harvest (Acts 14:17), possessing and observing the commandments* of God (Jas 1:22-25; *Barn.* 1.8; 4:11; 10:11), hearing of the growth and stability of the church (Acts 11:23), knowing that the gospel is for Gentiles as well as for Jews (Acts 13:48), possessing an invitation to the eschatological wedding feast hosted by Christ (Rev 19:9), receiving the right to share in the first resurrection (Rev 20:6), and the like.

At the same time joy is not something that exists and thrives only when good things happen or when good news comes. Genuine joy cannot be extinguished or even dampened by the direst of circumstances or the worst kind of events. For example, the apostles, flogged and ordered by their religious leaders to desist from their mission in life, were nevertheless filled with joy because they were counted worthy to suffer disgrace for the sake of Christ's name (Acts 5:41). Christians living in the midst of fiery trials and themselves sharing in the sufferings of Christ rejoiced (1 Pet 4:13). People of faith accepted, even anticipated (*prosdexasthai*), the plundering of their possessions with joy (Heb 10:34). Furthermore, the possibility of life coming to a violent end could not keep Christians from walking forward to their own personal, painful death with courage and joy (*Mart. Pol.* 12.1).

What then is joy? One begins to suspect that for most of these Christian writers joy was more than a happy feeling, a pleasing mood or a sense of overflowing jubilation, although it might include these. Rather, by joy they seem to have been referring to something more profound, something more difficult to define yet real. Joy seems not to be laughter, gaiety, lightheartedness, and dance and song (at least in this present world) but something more akin to faith, more akin to a settled state of mind marked by peace. Joy is fundamentally an attitude toward life that views and accepts the world with equanimity, a confident way of looking at life that is rooted deep in faith, in a keen awareness of and trust in the sovereign God who has revealed himself in Jesus Christ and his death and resurrection. Joy thus was a perception of reality that generated hope* and endurance* in affliction and temptation or ease and prosperity. It enabled Christians to see beyond any particular event, judged good or bad, to God who stands above all events and ultimately has control over all events, which will be consummated at Christ's Parousia* (1 Pet). Joy included a readiness for martyrdom (*Mart. Pol.* 12.1), but equally it described an eagerness to go on living and serving even in the most difficult of circumstances (Hawthorne 1983, 17-18; 1987, 107-10).

See also ENDURANCE, PERSEVERANCE; ESCHATOLOGY; PEACE; SUFFERING; WORSHIP, LITURGY.

BIBLIOGRAPHY. H. W. Attridge, *Hebrews* (Herm; Philadelphia: Fortress, 1989); R. J. Bauckham, *Jude, 2 Peter* (WBC; Waco, TX: Word, 1983); E. Bey-reuther and G. Finkenrath, "Joy, Rejoice," *NIDNTT* 2:356-61; R. Bultmann, "ἀγαλλιάομαι κτλ," *TDNT* 1:19-21; idem, "εὐφραίνω κτλ, *TDNT* 2:772-75; H. Conzelmann, "χαίρω κτλ," *TDNT* 9:359-415; F. Hauck, "μακάριος κτλ," *TDNT* 4:362-70; G. F. Hawthorne, *Philippians* (WBC; Waco, TX: Word, 1983); idem, *Word Biblical Themes: Philippians* (Waco, TX: Word, 1987); W. Jaeger, *Paideia: The Ideals of Greek Culture Highet* (3 vols.; New York: Oxford University Press, 1939-44); I. H. Marshall, *1 Peter* (IVPNTC; Downers Grove, IL: InterVarsity Press, 1991); R. P. Martin, *James* (WBC; Waco, TX: Word, 1988); J. R. Michaels, *1 Peter* (WBC; Waco, TX: Word, 1988); W. G. Morrice, *Joy in the New Testament* (Grand Rapids: Eerdmans, 1985); J. Moltmann, *Theology and Joy* (London: SCM, 1971); E. G. Selwyn, *The First Epistle of Peter* (Grand Rapids: Baker, 1981); G. Stählin, "ἡδονή κτλ," *TDNT* 2:909-26.

G. F. Hawthorne

JUDAISM, POST-A.D. 70

Traditional Judaism began to take shape in the aftermath of the destruction of Jerusalem* and the temple* in A.D. 70. With the destruction of the temple and fading hopes of rebuilding it, Jewish faith* could no longer be centered around the temple and the priesthood.* At the time of the destruction of the temple there were many religious sects and doctrines, many of which were at variance with one another. In recent years J. Neusner has rightly criticized the tendency, still in evidence in the work of some scholars, to view Judaism of the first century as essentially unified or "normative." Judaism (or "Judaisms," as Neusner sometimes puts it) was quite diverse in faith and practice. It was only after A.D. 70 that Judaism began moving toward something approximat-

ing standardization. This process reached important stages with the production of the Mishnah and later the Talmud, which subsequently came to dominate Jewish religious understanding and practice.

1. Historical Factors
2. Literature
3. Rabbinical Schools, Authorities and Sects
4. Synagogue
5. Basic Tenets of Faith

1. Historical Factors.

The most important factors that changed the complexion of Judaism were the two major wars with Rome. The first war (A.D. 66–70) resulted in the destruction of Jerusalem and the temple. This destruction effectively brought the priesthood and the Jewish religious-political establishment to an end. The second war (A.D. 132-35) resulted in the destruction of the Jewish state and the banning of Jews from Jerusalem.

Both of these wars were to some extent driven by messianic hopes. To be sure, the first war was fueled by economic desperation on the part of many of Israel's marginalized, but according to Josephus* it was an "ambiguous oracle," more than anything else, that provoked his countrymen to rebellion (Josephus *J.W.* 6.5.4 §312-14; cf. 6.5.3 §289). This oracle, which foretold that "one from their country would become ruler of the world," was in all probability based on Numbers 24:17 ("a star shall come forth out of Jacob, and a scepter shall rise out of Israel"). This text is understood in an explicitly messianic sense in all four of the extant Pentateuch targums ("a king shall arise out of Jacob and be anointed the Messiah out of Israel"). Earlier traditions also provide evidence that the passage was understood in a messianic sense (*T. Jud.* 24:1-6; 1QM 11:4-9; CD 7:18-21; Philo *Praem. Poen.* 16 §95; Mt 2:2, 7, 9-10). Josephus, however, believed that the oracle was fulfilled in the accession of Vespasian.

The passage from Numbers seems to have played an important part in the second war as well. The leader of this rebellion, Simeon bar Kosiba, who in some of his letters calls himself "Prince of Israel" (cf. 5/6*H*evEp 1–15), was apparently dubbed bar Kokhba, that is, "Son of the Star" (Justin Martyr *Apol.* I 31.5-6; Eusebius *Hist. Eccl.* 4.6.1-4; *y. Ta'an.* 4.5). This triumphalistic messianism is probably what lies behind the Aramaic paraphrase found in *Targum Isaiah*

52:13—53:12. This targumic passage probably reflects messianic hopes as they were expressed in the period between the two Roman wars. These hopes were fixed on the advent of a conquering (not suffering) Messiah who would defeat Rome and liberate Israel: "He will build the sanctuary. . . . He will bring our exiles near. . . . He will take away the rule of the Gentiles from the land of Israel. . . . He will hand over the wicked to Gehenna. . . . They shall see the kingdom of their Messiah" (*Tg. Isa* 53:5, 8, 9, 10).

The Bar Kokhba defeat ended Israel's nationhood. The Jewish people were now almost entirely a dispersed people, a people of the Diaspora.* Jewish identity no longer was defined by support of the Jerusalem temple or life in the land of Israel. Jewish identity increasingly became Torah-centered. The context of Jewish worship and Torah study was the synagogue.* Although pluralism remained a reality, the rabbis, exerting greater influence, more precisely defined several teachings of Jewish faith and the liturgy of the synagogue. These definitions are preserved in the rabbinic writings.

2. Literature.

An extensive corpus of writings was produced after A.D. 70. These writings can be placed into three broad categories: legal or prescriptive; homiletical or speculative; and apocalyptic* and pseudepigraphal.

2.1. Legal. Rabbinic Judaism's foundational document is the Mishnah, a compendium of legal (or halakic, i.e., how one should "walk") opinions that was compiled and edited under the direction of Rabbi Judah ha-Nasi ("the Prince") in the early part of the third century. The Mishnah (lit. "repetition") is divided into six sedarim ("orders") treating major aspects of Jewish life under the authority* of Torah. The names of the sedarim are "Seeds," "Set Feasts," "Women," "Damages," "Holy Things" and "Cleannesses." Each seder contains several tractates, which treat various subtopics. The Mishnah seems to envision obedience to Torah mainly in terms of priestly holiness.*

Completed about one century after the Mishnah, the Tosefta (lit. "addition") supplements—as implied by its name—the contents of the Mishnah. In fact, the Tosefta cannot be understood apart from reading it alongside of the Mishnah. It too is divided into the six mishnaic sedarim, although the tractates are not always in the same order, nor are all of them represented.

The Talmud (lit. "learning") has taken form in two recensions, the Palestinian and Babylonian. The former may be dated to the fifth century, the latter to the sixth. The Talmud is made up of the Mishnah and the gemara (lit. "completion"), material that expands section by section upon portions of the Mishnah. In Hebrew the former is called *Talmud Yerushalmi* (Jerusalem Talmud). But this is a misnomer, for the Palestinian Talmud was not edited in Jerusalem. In Hebrew the latter is called *Talmud Babli*. The Talmud contains mostly legal discussion (as one would expect, given its dependence on and interaction with the Mishnah), but nearly one third of it is homiletical. It is in the Talmud, not the Mishnah and the Tosefta, that we find a rich assortment of messianic traditions and polemic directed against Jesus and Christians. Modern Judaism has its roots in the varieties of Judaism preserved and held in tension in the mishnaic-talmudic literature.

2.2. Homiletical. Much of the homiletical (or haggadic, i.e., story) material is found in the rabbinic Midrash (lit. "interpretation," or "commentary") and the Aramaic paraphrase of Scripture called the Targum (lit. "translation").

The early midrashim include *Mekilta* (lit. "measure," or "section"; commentary on Exodus), *Sipra* (lit. "the book"; commentary on Leviticus), and the two *Sipre* (lit. books; commentaries on Numbers and Deuteronomy). Later midrashim include *Midrash Rabbah* (lit. "the great commentary"; commentaries on the Pentateuch and the Five Scrolls), *Midrash Tehillim* (Psalms commentary), *Midrash Shemuel* (Samuel commentary), *Midrash Mishle* (Proverbs commentary). These last three are sometimes collectively referred to as *Midrash Shocher Tov* (from Prov 11:27: commentary of "the one who seeks good"). *Midrash Tanhuma* (commentary of [Rabbi] Tanhuma) is another important commentary.

The targums are interpretive Aramaic paraphrases that arose in the synagogue (see 4 below). There are three complete Pentateuch targums: *Onqelos,* the official targum and the one that is the most literal; *Pseudo-Jonathan,* the latest and most paraphrastic; and *Neofiti* (or Neophyti), the targum that may represent the oldest tradition. There are also several manuscripts of the so-called *Fragmentary Targum*. It is called this because it contains only selections of verses and passages. Finally, there are several fragments of the Pentateuch targums that have been recovered from the Cairo Genizah. There are also targums for all of the Prophets (the so-called *Targum Jonathan*). It has been argued that these targums contain many early (i.e., first-century) traditions. Finally, there are targums for most of the Writings (two targums, in the case of Esther).

The antiquity of the production of targums is attested at Qumran.* Among the fragments of caves 4 and 11 we have 4QtgLev (= Lev 16:12-15, 18-21), 4QtgJob (= Job 3:5; 4:16–5:4) and 11QtgJob (= major portions of Job 17–42). There are important differences between these targum fragments and the later, fully preserved targums. The discovery of them at Qumran demonstrates that targums were produced in the first century, but it does not prove that the style and traditions of the later targums can be assumed also to reach back to the first century. The later targums do contain traditions that reach back to the first century, but this has to be demonstrated on a case-by-case basis; it cannot be assumed.

Thanks largely to the numerous publications of Neusner, a lively and interesting debate has emerged that revolves around the related questions of the interpretation of rabbinic literature and of Jewish pluralism of late antiquity. Breaking with traditional modern Jewish interpretation, which tends to regard the contents of rabbinic literature as historically reliable and as offering a description of a unified Jewish faith, and applying several of the canons of Gospel criticism, Neusner has argued that each rabbinic document should be studied on its own terms. He finds that these documents reflect individual traits and distinctives and that very little of their contents can with confidence be assigned to the various named rabbinic authorities.

Nor is it legitimate, Neusner argues further, to infer from the rabbinic literature an ancient, monolithic Judaism. Rather, we should speak of "Judaisms." Although criticized for claiming too much with respect to a given document's overall perspective (often in the form of an argument from silence—what the document does not address we should assume that it is opposed to it) and sometimes for failing to engage in tradition

criticism that takes into account related materials found outside of the document in question, Neusner's work marks a major advance in the modern study of rabbinic Judaism. The older, largely uncritical, synthetic portraits of what "the rabbis" believed or what "Judaism" was like in the first century, portraits that included biographies of figures such as Hillel or Aqiba, should now be seen as obsolete.

2.3. Apocalyptic and Pseudepigraphal Literature. A great deal of apocalyptic (i.e., revelatory) and pseudepigraphal (i.e., pseudonymous) literature was produced in the aftermath of the destruction of Jerusalem in A.D. 70. In his English translation of the oldest and most important specimens of the pseudepigrapha, J. H. Charlesworth subdivides this literature into the following categories: apocalyptic literature; testaments; OT expansions; wisdom and philosophical literature; and prayers, psalms and odes. Among the most important writings in the first category are *1* and *2 Enoch*, *4 Ezra*, *2 Apocalypse of Baruch* and the *Apocalypse of Abraham*. In the second category the *Testaments of the Twelve Patriarchs*, the *Testament of Job* and the *Testament of Moses* are especially important. The *Epistle of Aristeas, Jubilees*, Pseudo-Philo's *Biblical Antiquities* and the *Lives of the Prophets* are among the most important pseudepigraphal writings of the third category (what is also sometimes called the "rewritten Bible"). In the fourth category, 3 and 4 Maccabees are especially important, while the *Psalms of Solomon* is arguably the most important specimen from the fifth category.

Common to all five of these categories of the pseudepigrapha is the role played by the OT. The OT provides names (of famous biblical characters), settings, themes, structures and language. At least two concerns stimulated the production of the pseudepigrapha: the perception of historical and theological problems or gaps in the OT and the need to update the message of the OT, so that it might speak more directly and effectively to later generations.

Pseudepigraphical writings attempted to update the OT and how it should be interpreted by clarifying points of law,* instructing in matters of piety and cultic practice, predicting Israel's history and predicting the timing and character of the eschaton* and day of judgment.* For these reasons it is true in a general sense to say that the pseudepigrapha bear an exegetical relationship to the OT.

In many of the pseudepigraphal writings there is a marked interest in theodicy and final judgment. Evidently many of the pseudepigraphal writers, in the aftermath of the devastating wars with Rome and the apparent dissolution of the locus of Jewish faith and practice, were seeking to validate faith in the God* of the OT Scriptures. Had God abandoned Israel? Was God just? What did the future hold? How should a believing Jew live? These are the principal questions that drive many of the pseudepigraphal writers. It might be added that the legal interpretation of the rabbis is also to some extent pseudepigraphic, in that it is understood as the "oral Torah," a detailed explication of the written Torah that ultimately derives from Moses* and is passed on by various famous rabbinic authorities (often fictitiously).

3. Rabbinical Schools, Authorities and Sects.

The rabbinic tradition makes reference to several pretannaitic sages, such as Shammai, Hillel, Admon, ben He He, Yose ben Yohanan, Yohanan ben Bag-Bag, Yohanan the High Priest, and Simeon the Just. Among the early sages also are the so-called holy men (e.g., Honi the Circle-Drawer and Hanina ben Dosa), who are remembered especially for their acts of piety and effectual prayers. One of the much-debated questions has to do with the relationship between the Pharisees and the rabbis. In the past it was often assumed that the rabbis were the heirs of the pharisaic tradition. Although it is true that many of the teachings and practices associated with the Pharisees appear to have been taken over by the rabbinic tradition, the exact nature of this continuity remains unclear.

The rabbis are divided into four basic classifications that correspond to four periods of time: the Tannaim, the Amoraim, the Saboraim and the Geonim. Each of these periods saw important works produced or compiled and edited.

3.1. The Tannaim. The tannaitic period extends roughly from A.D. 10 to 200, that is, from the establishment of the early academies, Bet Shammai (House of Shammai) and Bet Hillel (House of Hillel), to the compiling and editing of the Mishnah under Rabbi Judah ha-Nasi in the first decade or so of the third century. The teachers, or sages, of this period are called the Tannaim (lit. "teachers," from the Aramaic

word *t°nā*, which literally means "to repeat." This word is formulaic, occurring frequently in the literature.). It is in this period that teachers were given the more or less formal title *rabbi* (lit. "my master"). Some have argued that it was after Yabneh (c. A.D. 85) that this title became a mark of official ordination. The Gospels evidently attest its earlier, informal usage. The rabbis of this period produced what would become the Mishnah and the tannaitic midrashim *(Mekilta, Sipra Leviticus, Sipre Numbers* and *Sipre Deuteronomy).* The sayings of many of these rabbis (or at least many sayings attributed to them) are found in later collections and are referred to as *baraitot* (lit. "standing outside"; sing. *baraita).* Major Tannaim include Rabban Gamaliel, Rabban Gamaliel II, Eliezer ben Hyrcanus, Aqiba ben Joseph, Ishmael, Joshua, Judah ben Bathyra, Meir, and Yose the Galilean.

3.2. The Amoraim. The amoraic period extends roughly from A.D. 200 to 500. Rabbis of this period are called the Amoraim (lit. "expounders" or "spokesmen"). The achievement of the amoraic period was the production of the Tosefta and the gemara that, in combination with material from the Mishnah and the Tosefta, would make up the two versions of the Talmud. The oldest version of the Talmud (i.e., *Talmud Yerushalmi)* was completed toward the end of the amoraic period. The Amoraim also contributed to and edited many midrashic works. Major Amoraim include Hanina ben Hama, Joshua ben Levi, Rab, Simeon ben Lakish and Abbahu.

3.3. The Saboraim. The saboraic period extends roughly from A.D. 500 to 650. The relatively small number of rabbis of this period are called Saboraim (lit. "reasoners"). The Saboraim expanded and edited the Babylonian Talmud, their most important achievement, as well as some of the midrashim, and contributed to halakic debate. Major Saboraim include Sama ben Judah, Ahai ben Huna and Samuel ben Judah. 'Ena and Simuna were the last of these scholars.

3.4. The Geonim. The geonic period extends roughly from A.D. 650 to 1050. The major Babylonian rabbis of this period are called the Geonim (lit. "excellent ones"). "Gaon" was a title of honor reserved for the chief rabbis (sometimes in place of the title *Rosh Yeshiva;* lit. "head of the academy"). They edited several of the latest midrashic works and were students of the Talmud, often interacting with philosophy and secular academics. Perhaps best known is Saadia Gaon (Saadia ben Joseph, 892-942) who translated the Hebrew Bible into Arabic, complete with Arabic commentary. He also wrote a commentary on Ishmael's thirteen exegetical rules and a polemical work against the Karaites. Another famous Gaon was Natronai (eighth century) who, it is claimed, wrote out from memory a copy of the Talmud. With the death of Gaon Hai (1038) the geonic institutions went into decline.

4. Synagogue.

The roots of the synagogue* (from the Greek *synagōgē,* meaning "a gathering") are obscure but probably had their origin in the exilic period. In the Second Temple period the word referred both to the people who assembled for worship* and prayer* (hence, a synagogue may also be called a *proseuchē,* "a house of prayer") and to the building in which they gathered. Eventually the word comes to refer primarily to the building.

Many references to synagogues are found in the NT and in Josephus. Archaeological remains suggest that as distinctive buildings synagogues did not become commonplace until after the Bar Kokhba war. Only three first-century synagogues have been discovered (in Gamla, in Masada and within the Herodium). In the first century various buildings, public and private, served as synagogues. A first-century Greek inscription, however, does speak of the building of a synagogue: "Theodotus, son of Vettenos, the priest and *archisynagōgos,* son of an *archisynagōgos* and grandson of an *archisynagōgos,* who built the synagogue for purposes of reciting the Law and studying the commandments." There are NT references to *archisynagōgoi* (lit., "rulers of the synagogue"; Mk 5:22, 36-38; Lk 13:14; Acts 13:15; 18:8, 17).

In the aftermath of the destruction of the temple, the liturgy of the synagogue became increasingly fixed and formalized. Lectionaries developed. Older prayers and blessings were edited and new prayers and blessings were added. One of the best known prayers is the Qaddish (holy): "May His great name be glorified and made holy in the world which He created according to His will. May He establish His kingdom in your lifetime and during your days." This Aramaic prayer has often been compared with the Lord's Prayer. Another well known prayer is the Amidah (standing) or Shemoneh Esreh (eighteen). The twelfth benediction of this prayer was eventually supplemented in such a way as to discourage Christians from continuing with the synagogue: To the original line, "For apostates let there be no hope, and the kingdom of arrogance quickly uproot," has been added: "In a moment let the Nazorenes and the heretics be destroyed; let them be blotted from the Book of Life, and with the righteous not be inscribed" (for rabbinic discussion of this revision, see *b. Ber.* 28b-29a). The assurances in Revelation 21:27 that Christians' names are written in the book of life could very well be a response to the imprecations of this revised benediction.

The interpretive paraphrasing of Scripture into Aramaic, which resulted in the production of the targums, was another important activity of the synagogue. Although the targums contain traditions that date to the early Middle Ages, careful comparative work has isolated primitive traditions, sometimes reflecting ideas and events of the first century. Some of this early tradition has been useful in NT interpretation.

5. Basic Tenets of Faith.

According to Josephus, the Jewish people adhere to the Law of Moses and so live in "astonishing unity of mind *[homonoia]*" (Josephus *Ag. Ap.* 2.19 §179-81). He goes on to declare that Jews hold to a single concept and profession of God. The apologetic needs of his treatise have led Josephus to exaggerate, especially when he declares that among his people is "no difference in conduct of their lives." But there is much truth to his claim that the Jews, unlike the Gentiles,* hold to a common belief about God. But in most other matters touching faith and practice, Jewish religious views of the first century were quite diverse. Only in the rabbinic age did Jewish faith become more or less standardized.

5.1. God. Judaism's view of God* is squarely founded on the writings that make up the Hebrew Bible. The spiritual, transcendent and eternal character of God is affirmed. God is Creator and Sustainer. He is the final Judge. Absolute monotheism is affirmed. Jewish writings, especially rabbinic writings, vigorously oppose any idea that could be viewed as compromising monotheism. In some cases this means carefully qualifying statements in Scripture (e.g., Gen 1:26; 3:22), which Christians, Gnostics* and others at one time or another appealed to in support of the plurality of the Godhead (Segal 1977).

In post-70 Judaism, reverence for God's name exceeded the explicit requirements of written Torah. Whereas Exodus 20:7 (Deut 5:11) commands Israelites not to take the name of the Lord God in vain, Jewish piety would eventually require that the name of God normally not be uttered at all. The rabbinic writings reflect this reverence, as is seen in the formulaic and ubiquitous reference to God as "The Holy One, blessed be He."

5.2. Humankind. In contrast to Hellenistic dualism, in which the human being is understood as made up of an unworthy and flawed body and a worthy and good soul (the latter longing to escape from the former), Judaism understands the human being in monistic terms. There is a "soul" *(nepeš)*, to be sure, but it acts in concert with the physical being. Every aspect of the human being is potentially good, yet every aspect of the human being has been tainted by sin. In rabbinic writings the moral dimension of the human being is described in terms of the *yēṣer*, or "inclination," either to do good or to do evil (*m. Ber.* 9:5; *Gen. Rab.* 14.4 [on Gen 2:7]). Some rabbis believed that the evil *yēṣer* resides in all of the members, or organs, of the human being (compare Paul's comments in Rom 7:17-24, esp. 7:23).

One finds in Jewish writings a broad range of opinions with respect to the question of humanity's redemption.* There is a range of opinion even with respect to the fate of Israelites themselves. Certain Jewish groups, especially the Essenes and authors of some of the Dead Sea Scrolls, believed that persons outside of their community had little chance of salvation.* Jewish views with respect to Gentiles also varied greatly. Some believed that there is no hope for Gentiles; their corpses will feed the furnaces of hell.* Others believed that salvation was possible for righteous Gentiles if they obeyed the seven Noahic laws (based on Gen 9:3-4).

5.3. Written and Oral Torah. The most inspired and most authoritative writings of Judaism are the books of Moses, the Torah ("law" or, more literally, "instruction"). Because these books were written and so were public they could not remain the exclusive property of the Jewish people. Christians claimed the books for themselves as an important part of their heritage. The history of God's dealing with Israel and humanity in general had reached its climax in the coming of Jesus and his atoning death (*see* Death of Christ) on the cross. What the Jewish people were able to retain for themselves was the oral Torah, that is, the written traditions that elaborated and interpreted the written Torah. It was believed that the oral Torah also originated at Mount Sinai and so was invested with essentially the same authority as was the written Torah. For many Jewish teachers the oral Torah was Judaism's trump card. Christianity may well possess the written Torah, but only Judaism possessed the oral Torah and so was able to interpret the former fully and accurately.

5.4. Eschatology. One must be cautious when attempting to summarize Jewish eschatology. The literature generated in the first century following the destruction of Jerusalem and the temple is especially diverse. Apocalyptic and pseudepigraphal writings envision a variety of events and forms of judgment, both temporal and eternal, with or without a Messiah. Within the rabbinic corpus itself there is much diversity. Some authorities believe that the ten northern tribes will be regathered; others think not. Some rabbis apparently tried to predict when the Messiah would appear (e.g., "forty years after the destruction of the temple"); others expressed skepticism (e.g., "Aqiba, grass will sprout from your cheek bones and still Messiah will not have appeared"). Others speculated how long the messianic era would perdure (e.g., "four hundred years" or "one thousand years"). Later rabbinic speculation entertained a suffering Messiah, who was "son of Josephus" (or Ephraim), as opposed to the more traditional "son of David." This Messiah would suffer and die, paving the way for the triumph of the Messiah, son of David.

Even with all of the diversity, there emerged several common concepts in rabbinic Judaism. The hope for the "world to come"; the hope for the appearance of the Messiah, son of David; the anticipation of the day of judgment, with opinions varying as to the fate of the Gentiles; and the idea that Abraham* and other patriarchs guarded the gates that led either to heaven* or to hell (cf. Lk 16:22-25) are among the most commonly held eschatological beliefs.

See also CHRISTIANITY AND JUDAISM: PARTINGS OF THE WAYS; DIASPORA JUDAISM.

BIBLIOGRAPHY. I. Abrahams, *Studies in Pharisaism and the Gospels* (Cambridge: Cambridge University Press, 1917); G. Alon, *Jews, Judaism and the Classical World: Studies in Jewish History in the Times of the Second Temple and Talmud* (Jerusalem: Magnes, 1977); L. Baeck, *The Pharisees and Other Essays* (New York: Schocken, 1947); J. Bonsirven, *Palestinian Judaism in the Time of Jesus Christ* (New York: Holt, Rinehart & Winston, 1964); S. J. D. Cohen, *From the Maccabees to the Mishnah* (Philadelphia: Westminster, 1987); J. H. Charlesworth, ed., *The Old Testament Pseudepigrapha* (2 vols.; Garden City, NY: Doubleday, 1983, 1985); H. Conzelmann, *Gentiles, Jews, Christians: Polemics and Apologetics in the Greco-Roman Era* (Minneapolis: Fortress, 1992); W. D. Davies and L. Finkelstein, eds., *The Cambridge History of Judaism,* 1: *Introduction: The Persian Period* (Cambridge: Cambridge University Press, 1984); A. Eisenberg, *The Synagogue through the Ages* (New York: Bloch, 1974); C. A. Evans, "Mishna and Messiah 'in Context': Some Comments on Jacob Neusner's Proposals," *JBL* 112 (1993) 267-89; F. J. Foakes Jackson, *Josephus and the Jews* (London: SPCK, 1930); S. Freyne, *Galilee: From Alexander the Great to Hadrian* (Notre Dame, IN: University of Notre Dame Press, 1980); M. Goodman, *State and Society in Roman Galilee,* A.D. *132–212* (Oxford Centre for Postgraduate Hebrew Studies; Totowa, NJ: Rowman & Allanheld, 1983); L. L. Grabbe, *Judaism from Cyrus to Hadrian,* 2: *The Roman Period* (Minneapolis: Fortress, 1992); R. Hamerton-Kelly and R. Scroggs, eds., *Jews, Greeks and Christians: Religious Cultures in Late Antiquity* (SJLA 21; Leiden: E. J. Brill, 1976); M. Hengel, *The "Hellenization" of Judea in the First Century after Christ* (London: SCM; Philadelphia: Trinity Press International, 1989); H. Jagersma, *A History of Israel from Alexander the Great to Bar Kochba* (London: SCM, 1985); H. C. Kee, "The Transformation of the Synagogue after 70 C.E.: Its Import for Early Christianity," *NTS* 36 (1990) 1-24; P. Keresztes, "The Jews, the Christians, and Emperor Domitian," *VC* 27 (1973) 1-28; L. I. Levine, ed., *Ancient Synagogues Revealed* (Jerusalem: Israel Exploration Society, 1981); idem, ed., *The Galilee in Late Antiquity* (New York and Jerusalem: Jewish Theological Seminary of America, 1992); H. Maccoby, *Judaism in the First Century* (London: Sheldon, 1989); L. M. McDonald, "Anti-Judaism in the Early Church Fathers" in *Anti-Semitism and Early Christianity: Issues of Polemic and Faith,* ed. C. A. Evans and D. A. Hagner (Minneapolis: Fortress, 1993) 215-52; G. F. Moore, *Judaism in the First Century of the Christian Era: The Age of the Tannaim* (3 vols.; Cambridge: Harvard University, 1927-30); J. Neusner, *Early Rabbinic Judaism: Historical Studies in Religion, Literature and Art* (SJLA 13; Leiden: E. J. Brill, 1975); idem, "The Formation of Rabbinic Judaism: Yavneh (Jamnia) from A.D. 70–100," *ANRW* 2.19.2 (1979) 3-42; idem, *Formative Judaism: Religious, Historical, and Literary Studies* (2 vols.; BJS 37, 41; Atlanta: Scholars Press, 1982-83); idem, *Judaism: The Classical Statement. The Evidence of the Bavli* (Chicago: University of Chicago Press, 1986); idem, *Judaism: The Evidence of the Mishnah* (Chicago: University of Chicago Press, 1981); idem, *Judaism in Society: The Evidence of the Yerushalmi* (Chicago: University of Chicago Press, 1983); S. Safrai, ed., *The Jewish People in the First Century* (2 vols., CRINT 1.1-2; Assen: Van Gorcum; Philadelphia: Fortress, 1974-76); idem, ed., *The Literature of the Sages* (CRINT 2.3; Assen: Van Gorcum; Philadelphia: Fortress, 1987); S. Sandmel, *Judaism and Christian Beginnings* (New York: Oxford University Press, 1978); E. Schürer, *The History of the Jewish People in the Age of Jesus Christ (175 B.C.—A.D. 135),* rev. and ed. G. Vermes et al. (3 vols.; Edinburgh: T & T Clark, 1973-87); A. F. Segal, *Rebecca's Children: Judaism and Christianity in the Roman World* (Cambridge: Harvard University Press, 1986); idem, *Two Powers in Heaven: Early Rabbinic Reports about Christianity and Gnosticism* (SJLA 25; Leiden: E. J. Brill, 1977); P. Sigal, *The Emergence of Contemporary Judaism* (Pittsburgh, PA: Pickwick, 1980); E. M. Smallwood, *The Jews under Roman Rule: From Pompey to Diocletian: A Study in Political Relations* (SJLA 20; Leiden: E. J. Brill, 1981); G. Vermes, *Jesus and the World of Judaism* (London: SCM, 1983; Philadelphia: Fortress, 1984); I. M. Zeitlin, *Jesus and the Judaism of His Time* (Oxford: Blackwell, 1988).

C. A. Evans

JUDE

The letter of Jude is the last letter in what has become known as the "catholic," or "general letters," of the NT (i.e., James through Jude; Webb 1992). In this letter Jude warns his readers about false teachers and exhorts them to defend the faith. Rowston (1975) is correct in lamenting that Jude is "the most neglected book" in the NT. But careful study of it will richly repay the reader.

1. Literary Structure and Form
2. Character
3. Opponents
4. Authorship
5. Date
6. Recipients/Destination
7. Message

1. Literary Structure and Form.

Although Jude is one of the smallest letters of the NT, analysis of its structure reveals a carefully composed literary gem.

1. Epistolary Structure. While Jude has a letter opening (Jude 1-2) and a closing doxology (Jude 24-25), its epistolary character has been questioned (*see* Letters). For example, Fuller (160) considers Jude to be a tract, and the epistolary features to be "merely a conventional device." But such a claim cannot really be substantiated because it is these features which characterize the letter genre, and there are no formal means for distinguishing them as conventional devices or later interpolations (Bauckham 1988 *ANRW*, 3800). Furthermore, the body itself alludes to the epistolary character of the text (Jude 3); it also uses epistolary conventions (e.g., "I desire to remind you," Jude 5; cf. White).

As an epistle, Jude's epistolary structure may be outlined as follows:

Letter Opening (Jude 1-2)
    Opening Address (Jude 1)
    Salutation (Jude 2)
Letter Body (Jude 3-23)
    Body Opening (Jude 3-4)
    Body Middle (Jude 5-23)
Letter Closing (Jude 24-25)

Due to the brevity of the letter, there is no body closing. Neyrey (1993, 27) views Jude 17-23 as the body closing because of the use of a disclosure formula (cf. Watson, 67). However, the phrase "but you, beloved" (Jude 17, cf. Jude 20) with an imperative is not actually a disclosure formula. Rather, this use of direct address and a command indicates a major transition within the body middle itself (cf. White, 38). In this instance Jude 20-23 actually brings the body to a fitting climax by addressing the purpose of the letter itself: how to contend for the faith* (cf. Jude 3).

The body opening of a letter usually identifies the occasion for the letter and alludes to its purpose (White, 18-19). Thus the body opening of Jude indicates that the occasion for the letter is Jude's realization that false teachers have entered the church* (Jude 4), and the letter's dual purpose is to make his readers aware of them and their condemnation (Jude 4), as well as to exhort them to fight for the faith (Jude 3). As a body opening, Jude 3-4 lay the foundation for the discussion in the body middle (Jude 5-23). This relationship between the body opening and body middle produces a chiastic structure (cf. Bauckham 1983, 5-6):

A Appeal: need to contend for the faith (Jude 3)

   B Occasion for appeal: false teachers identified and condemned (Jude 4)

   B' Occasion for appeal: false teachers described and condemned (Jude 5-19)

A' Appeal: how to contend for the faith (Jude 20-23)

By concluding with a doxology, Jude does not follow the usual form for a letter closing. This form of the closing suggests that Jude envisions the letter being read to the Christian community gathered in worship,* and that he is addressing them with a sermon in letter form. This suggestion is confirmed by the midrashic style of the letter's body (see below), and thus, as Bauckham (1983, 1) suggests, Jude is an "epistolary sermon" (cf. McDonald, 60-61).

1.2. Rhetorical Structure. Within the past twenty years scholars have begun to analyze NT texts in light of Greco-Roman rhetorical* techniques and forms (cf. Kennedy; Mack). While originally an oral skill used in speeches, rhetoric was later used in written texts as well, particularly in those forms of literature which were meant to persuade. Rhetoric was taught to Greco-Roman students and included instruction in selecting the appropriate arguments (called "invention"), arranging the material into the most effective outline (called "arrangement"), and developing appropriate language for effective communication (called "style").

In a very helpful analysis, Watson (29-79) has applied rhetorical criticism to Jude's letter. All parts of a letter, including its opening and closing, may contribute to its rhetorical effectiveness. For example, while the identification of the readers in Jude 1 is necessary according to epistolary form, the description itself reassures the readers and contributes to their sense of goodwill toward the author. Thus a letter opening may contribute to the rhetorical function of an introduction (*exordium*) while at the same time conforming to the epistolary form.

Watson's analysis (29-79, esp. 77-78; cf. Neyrey 1993, 25-27) results in the following rhetorical outline of Jude, to which has been added brief definitions of the Latin terms.

1. Introduction (*exordium*; Jude 3)
(with Jude 1-2 as a quasi-*exordium*)
2. Narration (*narratio*; Jude 4)
3. Proofs (*probatio*; Jude 5-16
containing three proofs (Jude 5-10, 11-13, 14-16)
4. Conclusion (*peroratio*; Jude 17-23)
Recapitulation (*repetitio*; Jude 17-19)
Emotional Appeal (*adfectus*; Jude 20-23)
(with Jude 24-25 as a quasi-*peroratio*)

While this is an informative analysis, its weakness is the combination of Jude 17-19 and Jude 20-23 as the conclusion (*peroratio*). Jude 17-19 as a unit contains the same formal characteristics as the earlier three proofs (example/text, application to the opponents), and so it should be considered a fourth proof in the *probatio*. The unit of Jude 20-23 does not really qualify as an *adfectus*, or emotional appeal; it is, rather, completing the appeal stated in Jude 3 by giving instructions for how to contend for the faith. How to classify such paraenesis in NT letters is one of the questions still unanswered in the application of rhetorical analysis to biblical texts.

1.3. Midrash. Ellis (221-26; cf. Bauckham 1983, 4-5) first observed the midrashic style used in Jude 5-19, in which scriptural examples and quotations become "texts" which are then interpreted to apply to the situation facing Jude's readers. This midrashic pattern of "text" followed by interpretation is repeated four times in these verses. The first two "texts" are actually allusions to biblical stories (Jude 5-7, 11) which are then interpreted to apply to Jude's opponents (Jude 8-10, 12-13). The latter two are from authoritative (though not biblical) sources (Jude 14-15, 17-18) which are equally applied to the readers' situation (Jude 16, 19; cf. Bauckham 1990, 179-234).

This midrashic style may be compared profitably with the Qumran pesharim (scrolls interpreting biblical texts; from *pēšer*, "interpretation"; plural, *pᵉšārîm*), particularly the thematic pesharim that comment on diverse texts which have been brought together because they address a common theme (e.g., 4QFlor; 11QMelch; in contrast to continuous pesharim, e.g., 1QpHab). Both similarities and differences may be noted between Jude and these pesharim (cf. Bauckham 1983, 4-5; Bauckham later suggests avoiding the term midrash because of potential confusion with rabbinic midrashim; cf. Bauckham 1990, 180 n. 2).

2. Character.
Jude has frequently been viewed as characterized by the early catholicism* of the post-apostolic era (e.g., Schelkle 1963 *Spätapostolische*; Sidebottom, 77-78; Rowston 1971, 145-54; on date, see 5 below). As a category in which to understand the development of early Christianity, early catholicism has increasingly been called into question. But even if the characteristics of this category are granted for the sake of argument, Jude still should not be so characterized (e.g., Bauckham 1983, 8-9). The expectation of an imminent Parousia* has not faded (Jude 1, 14-15, 21, 24; cf. Webb 1996). Jude does not argue that the false teachers should submit to some form of ecclesiastical hierarchy; he does not even allude to such officials (*see* Church Order). There is no evidence of a developing Christian canon.* The evidence for this characterization is based on two things: (1) Jude 17 is interpreted to imply a post-apostolic date, but this is unnecessary (on date, see 5 below). (2) The reference to "the faith" in Jude 3 (cf. Jude 20) is interpreted as referring to a defined set of crystallized doctrines. But there is no need to view this phrase as anything more than a synonym for "the gospel." And even Paul, writing in the 40s and 50s, used "the faith" in this way (e.g., Gal 1:23; cf. Neyrey 1993, 55).

Rather than early-catholic, Jude is better understood as an apocalyptic* Jewish-Christian letter (e.g., Bauckham 1983, 8-11; Charles 1993, 42-64). This view is based on observing (1) the midrashic style of argumentation (see above), (2) the pervasive use of Jewish sources, especially apocalyptic ones (see 3.2 below), and (3) the prominence of an apocalyptic* worldview in the thought of the letter.

2.1. Literary Relationships. Packed within the twenty-five verses of this letter is an amazing number of literary allusions. Perceiving them aids the reader in appreciating Jude's literary richness.

2.2. Old Testament. While Jude does not actually quote any OT texts, a careful study reveals its extensive dependence on the OT, including its narratives (e.g., Israel's exodus and wilderness experience, Jude 5), theology (e.g., the people of God are "the called," Jude 1), and language ("feeding themselves," Jude 12, from Ezek 34:2; e.g., Rowston 1971, 37-48; Bauckham 1983; Charles 1990; Charles 1993, 91-127).

The author is evidently aware of Greek versions of the OT because he picks up some of its distinctive terminology (e.g., *gongystēs*, "grumbler", Jude 16; Symm. Prov 26:22; Is 29:24; cf. Bigg, 310-11). But his primary text appears to be the Hebrew because he alludes to OT passages in which the Hebrew text makes his point, but the Greek translation does not support it. For example, Jude 12 refers to "clouds without rain, carried away by winds," which probably alludes to the Hebrew version of Proverbs 25:14 ("clouds and wind, but there is no rain"). But Proverbs 25:14 LXX reads "winds and clouds and rain appear," and lacks the vivid image Jude is using (*see* Old Testament in General Epistles).

2.3. Jewish Traditions. While not quoting from the Hebrew canon, Jude is the only NT book to cite explicitly an extra-canonical Jewish source. This is clearly the case in Jude 14-15 which quotes *1 Enoch* 1:9 and probably also in Jude 9 which may quote the now lost ending of the *Testament of Moses* (Bauckham 1983, 65-76). For some later Christians this was a problem. Tertullian saw this as an argument for *1 Enoch's* authenticity (Tertullian *De Cult. fem.* 1.3), while Jerome on the other hand questioned Jude's canonicity (*Vir.* 4; cf. Bauckham 1990, 137-38). Given the other allusions to these and other Jewish apocalyptic texts in Jude (and in some other NT books), it is quite evident that these works were popular in the milieu in which this letter was composed and read. If this is the case, then Jude's quotations should not really be a problem to modern readers; it is similar to a minister in a sermon making a point by quoting a popular Christian writer who is a recognized authority on a subject (*see* Non-Canonical Writings, Citations).

Beyond these explicit quotations, Jude makes extensive allusions to *1 Enoch* and other Jewish writings and traditions of the Second-Temple period (Osburn 1977; Wolthuis; Charles 1991, "Jude's Use"; Charles 1993, 128-66). An appreciation of these allusions assists the reader in understanding what Jude is implying

in his dense and compact work. The use of these Jewish traditions often moves an OT story or reference beyond that which may be understood from the OT itself. For example, Jude 11 refers to Cain, Balaam and Korah. Jude has probably brought these three characters together in this woe oracle based on similarities between them, which they have in later Jewish tradition. In the case of each of these three men, Jewish tradition viewed them as leading people astray through false teaching (e.g., Cain, Josephus *Ant.* 1.2.1 §61; Balaam, Philo *Abr.* 114; Korah, *Pseudo-Philo* 16:1; cf. 16:5; Josephus *Ant.* 4.2.3 §21). That such points are made allusively rather than explicitly suggests that such Jewish traditions were a natural part of the milieu of Jude's readers.

2.4. 2 Peter. It is quite evident that some relationship exists between Jude 4-13, 16-18 and 2 Peter 2:1-18; 3:1-3. Until the nineteenth century the predominant view was that Jude used 2 Peter* as a source (e.g., Luther, 203; Bigg, 216-24), but more recently the predominant view has been reversed to 2 Peter having used Jude (e.g., Mayor 1978 [1907], i-xxv; cf. list in Bauckham 1990, 145), with very few holding the earlier view (e.g., Lenski, 241). A few have argued that both Jude and 2 Peter are dependent upon a common source (e.g., Reicke, 189-90; Green, 58-64), and common authorship by Jude has also been argued (e.g., Robinson, 192-95).

More recent work using redaction criticism (Fornberg, 33-59; Neyrey 1977, 119-67; Bauckham 1983) and rhetorical criticism (Watson 1988, 160-87) have strengthened the position that 2 Peter used Jude as a source, and this remains the most probable position. However, the lack of precise verbal links between 2 Peter and Jude renders the position of a common source a possibility.

2.5. Christian Traditions. It has frequently been asserted that Jude is indebted to Paul's thought and terminology (e.g., Bigg, 311-12; Sidebottom, 72-73), such as Jude's self description, "a servant of Jesus Christ" (Jude 1; cf. Rom 1:1), or use of the phrase "build yourselves up" (Jude 20; cf. 1 Thess 5:11; cf. the list of parallels in Rowston 1971, 60-61). The problem with this assertion is its assumption that parallels between Jude and Paul's letters are distinctively Pauline. But this assumption is questionable on two grounds. Paul himself makes use of common early Christian traditional materials, and many of the supposed examples of Jude's indebtedness to Paul may be better explained as traditional material common to early Christianity (Bauckham 1983, 8). Second, some of the common terminology may be better explained by the fact that Jude is addressing a situation similar to that which Paul sometimes faced (e.g., "worldly," Jude 19; cf. 1 Cor 2:14).

If Jude is not indebted to Paul in particular, it is more likely that he is indebted to early Christian tradition in general. This is the case not only with respect to his use of Christian terminology but also catechetical (Jude 20-21) and liturgical* material (Jude 24-25).

2.6. Other. A few suggestions have been made that Jude is dependent upon Greek literature for certain traditions (e.g., Glasson, 62-63; Oleson, Charles 1993, 162-63). The evidence substantiating this indebtedness is weak at best, and the imagery in Jude which is used to support this claim is better explained through links with Jewish apocalyptic literature (Osburn 1992, 302-303).

3. Opponents.

The opponents (*see* Adversaries) referred to in Jude have often been identified as Gnostics* and considered to be similar to or the same as the opponents in 2 Peter (e.g., Werdermann; Green, 42-46). Older scholars tended to identify the opponents with a specific gnostic group (cf. the list in Bauckham 1988 *ANRW*, 3809; Osburn 1992, 310), but more recently those holding to a gnostic identity have not made a specific identification, referring instead to some form of incipient Gnosticism (e.g., Sidebottom, 75-76; Kelly, 231; Fuchs and Reymond, 143). It is increasingly recognized that developed, second-century Gnosticism should not be read back into Jude, and the few defined features of Jude's opponents do not point in this direction. Other proposals for identifying Jude's opponents include political agitators in the employ of Rome (Reicke, 191-92), the Essenes (Daniel), deviant Hebraists who have rejected OT ethical codes (Ellis, 235) or "Pauline" antinomians (Sellin; cf. Bauckham 1993, 12). Werdermann argued that Jude probably does not describe a specific heresy. Wisse (142) concludes that Jude is not combating actual opponents at all because the letter is a general "eschatological tract" preparing Christians everywhere for the imminent Parousia. Desjardins, who blends Jude and 2 Peter,

suggests that the communities were eschatologically-minded and world-denying, whereas the opponents were becoming less radical because of the delay of the Parousia (*see* Eschatology). Winter (218-22), who translates Jude 23b as "hating the defiled garment of flesh," proposes that the author is encouraging sexual asceticism.

Many elements of Jude's language about the opponents must be understood as rhetoric rather than as description; nevertheless, certain elements do provide some sense of their character. The internal evidence of Jude itself indicates that the primary characteristic of the opponents is antinomianism; they reject the moral authority of Christ* (Jude 4) and the law* (Jude 8-10). As a consequence, they engage in immoral behavior, particularly sexual* immorality (Jude 6-8, 16, 18, 23). The authority* for these opponents is their own visionary* experiences (Jude 8). Jude's rhetorical statement that they are merely *psychikoi* (lit. "soulish;" i.e., functioning at a natural, human level) and were "devoid of the Spirit" (Jude 19) is probably countering their claim to prophetic* inspiration. These opponents did not arise within the community but rather entered in from the outside (Jude 4), have been accepted by the community (Jude 12) and were perhaps supported by them as well (Jude 16). The influence they were having on the community (Jude 11-13) and Jude's use of shepherding* imagery ("shepherding themselves," Jude 12) indicate that these opponents functioned as teachers. Their claim to prophetic inspiration supported their teaching role.

In light of these elements, Jude's opponents are most likely itinerant prophets whose charismatic experience led them to reject moral authority and to practice immorality. They also taught others to adopt these views and practices. There is no real indication of cosmic dualism underlying the thought of these false teachers, and so the evidence does not support the claim that these opponents are Gnostics. Other early Christian texts point to itinerant charismatic prophets being a problem for some churches (Mt 7:15; 24:11-12; 2 Pet 2:1; 1 Jn 4:1; 2 Jn 7-11; *Did.* 11—12; cf. Bauckham 1983, 11-13; Martin, 68-75), and it is against such that Jude is best understood to be writing.

4. Authorship.

Two related questions arise with respect to the

authorship of this letter. First, what is the identity of the "Jude" referred to in Jude 1? Second, is the name "Jude" used pseudepigraphally or not?

4.1. The Issue of Jude's Identity. In the NT the name "Jude" refers to at least eight different men (the Greek *Ioudas* is translated as "Judah," "Judas" or "Jude" depending on the person to whom reference is made). It is a common Jewish name held in honor because of its namesake, Judah, one of the twelve sons of Israel.

It is, of course, theoretically possible that this Jude is an otherwise unknown person and that the James referred to in Jude 1 is also unknown (e.g., Moffatt, 224-26). But it is very unusual to identify oneself as someone's brother, rather than using the name of one's father. As Bauckham (1983, 23) aptly observes, "The only theory which does explain it is that which identifies James as the James whom everyone knew." Equally, the phrase "brother of James" could be a later gloss (e.g., Barns, 393), but without manuscript evidence such a proposal begs the question.

Some older scholars identified the author as one of the twelve apostles, Judas of James (Lk 6:16; Jn 14:22; Acts 1:13; e.g., Calvin, 428), equating Jude the apostle with Jude the brother of Jesus. The weaknesses of this view are that (1) the expression "Judas of James" would naturally be understood as "Judas, son of James" rather than "Judas, brother of James"; (2) Jude does not identify himself as an apostle of Jesus Christ in Jude 1; and (3) the disciple, Judas of James, is better understood to be a different person than Jude, brother of Jesus, because Jesus' brothers were not disciples during his lifetime (*see* Relatives of Jesus).

A few scholars have identified Jude as the apostle Thomas who was known in the eastern Syriac* tradition as Judas Thomas or Didymus Judas Thomas (Koester, 247; Sidebottom, 69, 79; cf. *Gos. Thom.* title). The names Thomas and Didymus both mean "twin" in Syriac and Greek respectively, and thus in two works of this tradition the apostle Thomas was equated with the brother of Jesus named Jude, identified as his "twin," and so named Judas Thomas (cf. *Thom. Cont.* 138:1, 4, 7, 10, 19; *Acts Thom.* 10, 31, 39; cf. Jn 14:22 sy[s.(c)]). But this equation is probably a later confusion (Klijn 1970; Gunther 1980; Bauckham 1990, 32-36).

Another proposed identification is Judas called Barsabbas, who accompanied Paul, Barnabas and Silas to Antioch with the decision of the Jerusalem council (Acts 15:22, 27, 32; e.g., du Plessis; Ellis, 226-34). In this view the "James"* in Jude 1 is identified with the brother of Jesus, but the term "brother" in Jude 1 is interpreted not as a blood-brother but as a spiritual designation for those who were involved in ministry with the apostles in the Jerusalem* church (cf. Acts 11:1). Acts 15:22 describes Judas called Barsabbas as a leader among the "brothers" (Greek, *adelphoi*). This identification of Jude is possible, but its weakness is that, if this particular Jude's identity was clarified by also being called Barsabbas, he did not use it in his own letter.

Most scholars identify the author as the brother of Jesus (cf. Mt 13:55 par. Mk 6:3; Eusebius *Hist. Eccl.* 3.19.1—20.1; e.g., Bauckham 1983, 21-25) on the strength of the author's self-designation, "brother of James" (Jude 1). This Jude was not a disciple during Jesus' lifetime (Jn 7:5; cf. Mk 3:20-21), but, like his brother, James, he became a member of the early Christian movement after the resurrection of Jesus. The strength of this view is that it explains the evidence in Jude's letter in the simplest way. Its chief weakness is that Jude could have clarified who he was by identifying himself as "brother of Jesus Christ." It should be noted, however, that whereas the early church used the term "brother(s) of Jesus" (e.g., Mk 3:31; Acts 1:14; 1 Cor 9:5; Gal 1:19; *Gos. Thom.* 99; Eusebius, *Hist. Eccl.* 2.23.4; 3.19.1—3.20.1), it would appear that this expression was not used as a self-designation by these men (cf. Jas 1:1).

Of all these alternatives, the last two are the most plausible, with the identification of Jude as the brother of Jesus the more probable of the two.

4.2. The Issue of Pseudepigraphy. Ascertaining the probable identity of Jude does not address the second issue: whether or not this letter is pseudepigraphic.* Scholars are divided on this point, with an increasing number in recent years proposing that the letter is pseudepigraphic (cf. list in Bauckham 1990, 174 n. 261). There are two main arguments for the pseudepigraphic character of Jude's letter. First, the letter should be dated quite late (after the death of Jude, about which nothing is known) because

(1) Jude 17 is interpreted to refer to the apostolic age as being in the past, and (2) the letter is characterized by early catholicism opposing Gnosticism (e.g., Kelly, 233-34). But a careful reading of Jude 17 indicates that it is referring rather to the readers having heard the prediction by the apostles, probably at the time when this church was first established by these apostolic missionaries. In other words, Jude is bringing his readers back to their first instructions in the faith (cf. Jude 3, 5; with respect to Jude's letter not being characterized by early catholicism and the opponents not being Gnostics, see 2 above).

The second main argument for the pseudepigraphic character of Jude is the quality of the letter's use of language. It can be claimed that the letter's Greek is too good to have been written by a Palestinian Jewish peasant like Jude (e.g., Kelly, 233). But a couple of points call this argument into question: (1) While the letter is marked by a rich and varied vocabulary and it has quite clearly been carefully composed, the grammar itself is relatively unsophisticated. And much of this vocabulary echoes Jewish sources, so the language itself does not necessarily need to be entirely natural for this author. (2) In light of the increasing recognition of the bilingual character of Galilee,* and that, if written by Jude, it was written after many years experience in missionary activity, it is quite possible for someone like Jude to have used Greek competently (e.g., Bauckham 1983, 6-7, 14-16; Green, 48-52).

One objection to using Jude as a pseudonym is that he was too obscure a person for his name to be used in this way (e.g., Cranfield, 147-48; Green, 51-52). It may be noted, however, that, while Jude may be obscure to us, as one of "the brothers of the Lord" he would probably have been well known among Jewish Christians of the first century—the environment in which this letter arose (Cantinat, 286-87; Rowston 1975, 559-60). On the other hand, the fact that the letter uses the self-description "servant* of Jesus Christ" rather than "brother of Jesus Christ"—the description by which Jude would have been known in that environment—militates against the pseudepigraphic designation (Bauckham 1990, 176).

The evidence for the hypothesis of pseudepigraphy does not bear the weight placed upon it. The character and language of the letter is best explained as having come from the pen of Jude.

5. Date.

Scholarly opinion for the date of Jude varies widely, from the 50s and 60s (e.g., Ellis, 232-35; Bauckham 1983, 13; Green, 56), to the latter part of the first century (e.g., Schelkle 1980, 138; Fuchs and Reymond, 152); through the early second century (e.g., Leaney, 82; Sidebottom, 77) and even into the latter part of that century (e.g., Barns, 391-93; for a complete survey of dates, see Bauckham 1990, 168-69 n. 237; Fuchs and Reymond, 151 n. 1). The question of date is tied to a number of issues already discussed. If the letter is read as an early-catholic, post-apostolic document, then the later dates are more appropriate. But if, as discussed above, the letter is rather to be characterized by Jewish-Christian apocalypticism, then the door is open to considering an earlier date (though this characterization would not require an earlier date). The type of opponents (see 4 above) are not dissimilar to some that Paul faced in Corinth during the 50s.

If the letter is pseudepigraphic, then a later date is more appropriate; but if, as argued above, the letter was written by Jude, the brother of Jesus, then Jude's death provides a *terminus ad quem*. Unfortunately nothing is known about Jude's death, though Eusebius cites Hegesippus referring to grandsons of Jude who lived during the reign of Emperor Domitian (A.D. 81—96; Eusebius *Hist. Eccl.* 3.19.1—3.20.7). The citation begins, "Now there still survived of the family of the Lord grandsons of Judas, who was said to have been his brother according to the flesh" (*Hist. Eccl.* 3.20.1), which may imply that Jude himself was dead at this time. Since Jude was probably one of the youngest of the brothers (falling near the bottom of the list of names (Mk 6:3 par. Mt 13:55), he could have lived well into Domitian's reign, and an estimate of some date shortly before 90 for his death is reasonable (Mayor 1978 [1907], cxlviii). Paul alludes to the brothers of the Lord engaged in missionary* activity (1 Cor 9:5). If this includes Jude and is current with Paul's writing 1 Corinthians, then it would place Jude as engaged in ministry during the 50s. The tone of Jude's letter and Jude 3 in particular indicates that Jude is actively engaged in ministry, and this suggests a date earlier in his life rather than at its end.

If, as discussed above, Jude 17-18 does not support a post-apostolic date but is instead an allusion to the readers' initial reception of the gospel and the establishment of their church, then these verses imply that the readers are still the first-generation Christians who were part of the church's founding.

This meager evidence suggests a date for Jude's letter between the 50s and the 80s, with the earlier half of this spectrum being more probable.

6. Recipients/Destination.

Little real evidence exists to address the questions of the recipients and destination of this letter. Given the pervasive use of Jewish traditions it is plausible to suggest the readers are Jewish Christians* and Jude expects his readers to appreciate his allusions. But this evidence tells us more about the author than the recipients. On the other hand, problems with antinomianism as evidenced in this letter were more common among Gentiles* than Jews (but not unknown among Jews; cf. Bauckham 1983, 16). Yet this tells us more about the opponents who have come from outside than the recipients themselves. Given Jude's knowledge of his readers (Jude 3) it would appear that he is personally acquainted with them and pastorally concerned for them. If they are within the sphere of his pastoral ministry, then the weight of probability is that they are predominantly Jewish Christians, but their problems arose because the context in which they lived may have been dominated by Hellenistic values.

Destinations proposed for this letter include Palestine (e.g., Kelly, 234), Syria (e.g., Koester, 2.247), Egypt (e.g., Gunther 1984) or simply unknown (e.g., Fuchs and Reymond, 144). All destinations could meet the suggestion made above that the readers were Jewish Christians living in a Hellenistic environment. One indirect piece of evidence is that Jude was accepted as canonical in Alexandria* by the time of Clement,* but the Syriac* church did not accept it as canonical until the sixth century (Bauckham 1983, 16-17; See Canon).

7. Message.

In light of the preceding discussion (especially on literary structure and form), the message of the letter may now be more fully understood (cf.

Martin, 81-86).

Jude writes to address a specific situation facing his readers. He encourages them "to fight for the faith" (Jude 3) because false teachers "have infiltrated" them with a message and lifestyle, the implications of which Jude understands to be a perversion of God's grace and a denial of Christ's lordship (Jude 4). Jude's opponents, the false teachers, would not, of course, state matters in such blatant anti-Christian terms (if they had, they would probably not have been able to infiltrate this Christian community successfully). So before Jude can instruct them how to fight for the faith, he must convince his readers of the dangers of the opponents' teaching and lifestyle and of the certain divine judgment* awaiting them (Webb 1996).

Jude accomplishes this latter task by means of four sets of examples or texts which he applies to his opponents. Each of these sets have some point of commonality between them and the false teachers. Consequently, Jude can then point to the theme of judgment found in all four sets and conclude that divine judgment is the fate awaiting "these" (Greek, *houtoi,* Jude 7, 8, 10, 12, 14, 16, 19) false teachers. The first two sets are collections of examples from the past—OT narratives which were expanded in later Jewish traditions (see 3.2 above). In the first set the sins by and judgment of Israel in the wilderness, the disenfranchised angels,* and Sodom and Gomorrah (Jude 5-7) are then applied to Jude's opponents (Jude 8-10). Similarly in the second set the examples of Cain, Balaam, and Korah (Jude 11) are applied to the false teachers (Jude 12-14). The third and fourth sets are quotations from authoritative sources which are applied in similar fashion as the first two sets. In the third set a prophecy of divine judgment from *1 Enoch* 1:9 is quoted (Jude 14-15) and then applied (Jude 16), and in the fourth set a quotation from early Christian apostolic tradition is cited (Jude 17-18) and applied (Jude 19).

Having denounced the errors of the false teachers and announced their certain judgment, Jude returns to the purpose at hand in Jude 20-23, namely to instruct the readers how "to fight for the faith" (Jude 3). Their first concern must be to guard their own relationship with God (Jude 21; the verb "keep," *tēreō,* in Jude 21 is also used in Jude 1, 6 [2x], 13), which entails fulfilling certain responsibilities

(Jude 20) as well as maintaining an eschatologically oriented outlook (Jude 21). Their second concern is to assist those who have become tainted with this false teaching (Jude 22-23), while being careful not to be tainted with it themselves (Jude 23).

Jude's pastoral concern does not end with his advice in Jude 20-23 but concludes instead with a doxology (Jude 24-25) in which he returns to themes he alluded to in the letter's opening (Jude 1-2). As an expression of prayerful confidence, the doxology reassures the readers that God is able to preserve them not only through this situation but unto the Parousia, at which time they will be able to stand and rejoice in God's* presence.

See also ADVERSARIES; APOCALYPTIC, APOCALYPTICISM; EARLY CATHOLICISM; JEWISH CHRISTIANITY; NONCANONICAL WRITINGS, CITATIONS of; 2 PETER; RELATIVES OF JESUS.

BIBLIOGRAPHY. **Commentaries:** R. J. Bauckham, *Jude, 2 Peter* (WBC; Waco: Word, 1983); C. Bigg, *A Critical and Exegetical Commentary on the Epistles of St. Peter and St. Jude* (ICC 41; Edinburgh: T & T Clark, 1901); J. Calvin, *Commentaries on the Catholic Epistles* (Grand Rapids: Baker, 1979 [1551]); J. Cantinat, *Les épîtres de Saint Jacques et de Saint Jude* (SB; Paris: Gabalda, 1973); J. Chaine, *Les épîtres catholiques: La seconde épître de saint Pierre, les épîtres de saint Jean, l'épître de saint Jude* (2d ed.; EB; Paris: Gabalda, 1939); C. E. B. Cranfield, *I & II Peter and Jude* (TBC; London: SCM, 1960); E. Fuchs and P. Reymond, *La deuxième épître de saint Pierre: L'épître de saint Jude* (2d ed.; CNT 13b; Geneva: Labor et Fides, 1988); M. Green, *The Second Epistle General of Peter and the General Epistle of Jude* (2d ed.; TNTC; Grand Rapids: Eerdmans, 1987); D. E. Hiebert, *Second Peter and Jude: An Expositional Commentary* (Greenville, SC: Unusual Publications, 1989); N. Hillyer, *1 and 2 Peter, Jude* (NIBC; Peabody, MA: Hendrickson, 1992); J. N. D. Kelly, *A Commentary on the Epistles of Peter and of Jude* (BNTC; London: A. & C. Black, 1969); S. J. Kistemaker, *Exposition of the Epistles of Peter and of the Epistle of Jude* (Grand Rapids: Baker, 1987); A. R. C. Leaney, *The Letters of Peter and Jude* (CBC; Cambridge: Cambridge University Press, 1967); R. Leconte, *Les épîtres catholiques* (2d ed.; SBJ; Paris: Cerf, 1961); R. C. H. Lenski, *The Interpretation of 1 and 2 Epistles of Peter, the Three Epistles of John, and the Epistle of Jude* (Minneapolis: Augsburg, 1966); M. Luther, "Sermons on the Epistle of St. Jude" in *The Catholic Epistles*, ed. J. Pelikan and W. A. Hansen (*LW* 30; St Louis: Concordia, 1967 [1523]) 203-15; J. B. Mayor, *The Epistle of St. Jude and the Second Epistle of St. Peter* (Minneapolis: Klock & Klock, 1978 [1907]); J. Moffatt, *The General Epistles: James, Peter, and Judas* (MNTC; London: Hodder & Stoughton, 1928); J. H. Neyrey, *2 Peter, Jude* (AB; New York: Doubleday, 1993); H. Paulsen, *Der Zweite Petrusbrief und der Judasbrief* (MeyerK 12.2; Göttingen: Vandenhoeck & Ruprecht, 1992); P. Perkins, *First and Second Peter, James, and Jude. Interpretation* (Louisville: John Knox, 1995); B. Reicke, *The Epistles of James, Peter, and Jude* (AB; Garden City, NY: Doubleday, 1964); K. H. Schelkle, *Die Petrusbriefe, Der Judasbrief* (5th ed.; HTKNT 13.2; Freiburg: Herder, 1980); E. M. Sidebottom, *James, Jude, 2 Peter* (NCB; Grand Rapids: Eerdmans, 1967); H. Windisch, *Die katholischen Briefe* (3d ed. rev. H. Preisker; HNT 15; Tübingen: J. C. B. Mohr, 1951). **Studies:** T. Barns, "The Epistle of Jude: A Study in the Marcosian Heresy," *JTS* 6 (1905) 391-411; R. J. Bauckham, "James, 1 and 2 Peter, Jude" in *It is Written: Scripture Citing Scripture: Essays in Honour of Barnabas Lindars, SSF,* ed. D. A. Carson and H. G. M. Williamson (Cambridge: Cambridge University Press, 1988) 303-13; idem, "The Letter of Jude: An Account of Research," *ANRW* 2.25.5 (1988) 3791-826; idem, *Jude and the Relatives of Jesus in the Early Church* (Edinburgh: T & T Clark, 1990); idem, "Jude, Epistle of," *ABD* (1992) 3:1098-103; M. Black, "The Maranatha Invocation and Jude 14, 15 (1 Enoch 1:9)" in *Christ and Spirit in the New Testament: In Honour of Charles Francis Digby Moule,* ed. B. Lindars and S. S. Smalley (Cambridge: Cambridge University Press, 1973) 189-96; J. D. Charles, " 'Those' and 'These': The Use of the Old Testament in the Epistle of Jude," *JSNT 38* (1990) 109-24; idem, "Jude's Use of Pseudepigraphical Source Material as Part of a Literary Strategy," *NTS 37* (1991) 130-45; idem, "Literary Artifice in the Epistle of Jude," *ZNW* 82 (1991) 106-24; idem, *Literary Strategy in the Epistle of Jude* (London/Toronto: Associated University Presses, 1993); E. Cothenet, "La tradition selon Jude et 2 Pierre," *NTS* 35 (1989) 407-20; C. Daniel, "La mention des Esséniens dans la texte grec de l'Épître de S. Jude," *Mus* 81 (1968) 503-21; M. Desjardins, "The Portrayal of the Dissidents in 2 Peter and Jude: Does It Tell Us More about the 'Godly' than the 'Ungodly'?," *JSNT 30* (1987) 89-102; O.

J. du Plessis, "The Authorship of the Epistle of Jude" in *Biblical Essays 1966: Proceedings of the Ninth Meeting of 'Die Ou-Testamentiese Werkgemeenskap in Suid-Afrika,' and Proceedings of the Second Meeting of 'Die NuweTestamentiese Werkgemeenskam van Suid-Afrika'* (Potchefstroom, S. Africa: Potchefstroom Herald (Edms.) Beperk, 1966) 191-99; E. E. Ellis, "Prophecy and Hermeneutic in Jude" in *Prophecy and Hermeneutic in Early Christianity* (Grand Rapids: Eerdmans, 1978) 220-36; T. Fornberg, *An Early Church in a Pluralistic Society: A Study of 2 Peter* (ConB 9; Lund: Gleerup, 1977); J. Fossum, "Kyrios Jesus as the Angel of the Lord in Jude 5-7," *NTS* 33 (1987) 226-43; R. H. Fuller, *A Critical Introduction to the New Testament* (2d ed.; London: Duckworth, 1971); T. F. Glasson, *Greek Influence in Jewish Eschatology* (London: SPCK, 1961); J. J. Gunther, "The Meaning and Origin of the Name 'Judas Thomas,' " *Mus* 93 (1980) 113-48; idem, "The Alexandrian Epistle of Jude," *NTS* 30 (1984) 549-62; H. Harm, "Logic Line in Jude: The Search for Syllogisms in a Hortatory Text," *OPTAT* 3-4 (1987) 147-72; R. Heiligenthal, "Der Judasbrief: Aspekte der Forschung in den letzten Jahrzenten," *TRu* 51 (1986) 117-29; S. J. Joubert, "Language, Ideology and the Social Context of the Letter of Jude," *Neot* 24 (1990) 335-49; J. Kahmann, "The Second Letter of Peter and the Letter of Jude: Their Mutual Relationship" in *The New Testament in Early Christianity: La réception des écrits néotestamentaires dans le christianisme primitif*, ed. J.-M. Sevrin (BETL 86; Louvain: Leuven University Press, 1989) 105-21; G. A. Kennedy, *New Testament Interpretation through Rhetorical Criticism* (Chapel Hill: University of North Carolina Press, 1984); A. F. J. Klijn, "John xiv 22 and the Name Judas Thomas" in *Studies in John: Presented to Professor Dr. J. N. Sevenster on the Occasion of His Seventieth Birthday* (NovTSup 24; Leiden: E. J. Brill, 1970) 88-96; idem, "Jude 5 to 7" in *The New Testament Age: Essays in Honor of Bo Reicke*, ed. W. C. Weinrich (Macon: Mercer University Press, 1984) 1.237-44; H. Koester, *Introduction to the New Testament, 2: History and Literature of Early Christianity* (FF; Philadelphia: Fortress, 1982); M. A. Kruger, "ΤΟΥΤΟΙΣ in Jude 7," *Neot* 27 (1993) 119-32; S. Kubo, "Jude 22-3: Two-Division Form or Three?" in *New Testament Textual Criticism: Its Significance for Exegesis: Essays in Honor of Bruce M. Metzger*, ed. E. J. Epp and G. D. Fee (Oxford: Oxford University Press, 1981) 239-53; J. I. H. McDonald, *Kerygma and Didache: The Articulation and Structure of the Earliest Christian Message* (SNTSMS 37; Cambridge: Cambridge University Press, 1980); B. L. Mack, *Rhetoric and the New Testament* (GBS: NT; Minneapolis: Fortress, 1990); R. P. Martin, "The Theology of Jude, 1 Peter, and 2 Peter" in *The Theology of the Letters of James, Peter, and Jude*, ed. A. Chester and R. P. Martin, (NTT; Cambridge: Cambridge University Press, 1994) 63-163; J. B. Mayor, "The Epistle of St Jude and the Marcosian Heresy," *JTS* 6 (1905) 569-77; J. H. Neyrey, "The Form and Background of the Polemic in 2 Peter" (Yale University: unpublished Ph.D. dissertation, 1977); J. P. Oleson, "An Echo of Hesiod's *Theogony* vv. 190-2 in Jude 13," *NTS* 25 (1978-79) 492-503; C. D. Osburn, "The Christological Use of 1 Enoch 1:9 in Jude 14, 15," *NTS* 23 (1977) 334-41; idem, "Discourse Analysis and Jewish Apocalyptic in the Epistle of Jude" in *Linguistics and New Testament Interpretation: Essays on Discourse Analysis*, ed. D. A. Black, K. Barnwell and S. Levinsohn (Nashville: Broadman, 1992) 287-319; B. A. Pearson, "James, 1-2 Peter, Jude" in *The New Testament and its Modern Interpreters*, ed. E. Epp and G. MacRae (Philadelphia: Fortress Press, 1989) 371-406; J. A. T. Robinson, *Redating the New Testament* (Philadelphia: Westminster, 1976); D. J. Rowston, "The Setting of the Letter of Jude," (Southern Baptist Theological Seminary: unpublished Ph.D. dissertation, 1971); idem, "The Most Neglected Book in the New Testament," *NTS* 21 (1975) 554-63; K. H. Schelkle, "Der Judasbrief bie den Kirchenvätern" in *Abraham unser Vater; Juden und Christen im Gespräch über die Bibel: Festschrift für O. Michel*, ed. O. Betz, M. Hengel, and P. Schmidt (AGJU 5; Leiden: E. J. Brill, 1963) 405-16; idem, "Spätapostolische Briefe als frühkatholisches Zeugnis" in *Neutestamentliche Aufstäze: Festschrift für Josef Schmid zum 70. Geburtstag*, ed. J. Blinzler, O. Kuss and F. Muner (Regensburg: Pustet, 1963) 225-32; G. Sellin, "Die Häretiker des Judasbriefes," *ZNW* 77 (1986) 206-25; M. L. Soards, "1 Peter, 2 Peter, and Jude as Evidence for a Petrine School," *ANRW* 2.25.5 (1988) 3827-49; D. F. Watson, *Invention, Arrangement, and Style: Rhetorical Criticism of Jude and 2 Peter* (SBLDS 104; Atlanta: Scholars Press, 1988); R. L. Webb, "Epistles, Catholic," *ABD* (1992) 2:569-70; idem, "The Eschatology of the Epistle of Jude and its Rhetorical and Social Functions," *BBR* 6 (1996) 139-51; H. Werdermann, *Die Irrle-*

hrer des Judas- und 2. Petrusbriefes (BFCT 17.6; Gütersloh: C. Bertelsmann, 1913); J. L. White, *The Form and Function of the Body of the Greek Letter: A Study of the Letter-Body in the Non-Literary Papyri and in Paul the Apostle* (SBLDS 2; Missoula: Scholars Press, 1972); S. C. Winter, "Jude 22-23: A Note on the Text and Translation," *HTR* 87 (1994) 215-22; F. Wisse, "The Epistle of Jude in the History of Heresiology" in *Essays on the Nag Hammadi Texts in Honour of Alexander Böhlig*, ed. M. Krause (NHS 3; Leiden: Brill, 1972) 133-43; T. R. Wolthuis, "Jude and Jewish Traditions," *CTJ* 22 (1987) 21-41. R. L. Webb

JUDGMENT

The NT expectation of a final judgment is derived from biblical tradition and therefore is based on God's right as Creator to execute justice in the earth. The "day of the Lord," in which righteous judgment will take place, is not a matter of calculation but of patient hope, faith and obedience. The coming day of judgment is integral to the gospel, and to the comfort, warning and call to perseverance which proceeds from it. Christ himself shall judge each one according to his or her deeds. The eternal destiny of each person shall be determined in this judgment.

1. The Background of the New Testament Understanding
2. The Day of Judgment in Acts, the Non-Pauline Letters and Revelation
3. The Context and Function of the Theme of Judgment in the Earliest Church
4. The Early Christian Conception of Judgment

1. The Background of the New Testament Understanding.

Early Christian belief in a final divine judgment represents a development of biblical faith* in the one God* of Israel,* the judge and ruler of all the earth (e.g., Gen 18:25). The Psalms celebrate Yahweh as the righteous king who punishes the wicked and intervenes on behalf of the downtrodden (e.g., Ps 72:1-4). He has the sovereign right to determine justice and execute judgment (e.g., Ps 96—99). The prophets announce that divine visitation will bring punishment not only to the nations that oppose God but first and foremost to the disobedient within Israel (e.g., Is 1:1-31). The covenant renders Israel, the object of divine favor, more and not

less liable to judgment (e.g., Amos 3:2). Wisdom literature anticipates that deeds, whether good or evil, will receive recompense (Prov, passim). Ultimately the hope grew for a revelation of divine glory* at the end of human history, including a judgment at which all human beings would be brought to account (e.g., Dan 12:2-3; *1 Enoch* 1:1-9; 4 Ezra 7:70-74).

This understanding of final judgment characterized the message of Jesus. The Gospels record numerous instances in which Jesus warned of future punishment and—subject to the paradox of grace*—promised reward* for the faithful (e.g., Mt 19:27—20:16). His proclamation of coming judgment represented not a new teaching but a reassertion of the biblical tradition. Before him, John the Baptist had announced that the impending wrath* of God demanded repentance* from all and insisted, like the classical prophets, that membership in the covenant nation was insufficient for deliverance from judgment (Mt 3:7-10). In continuity with John, Jesus issued a call to repentance* in anticipation of the coming judgment with his announcement of the kingdom (Mk 1:15; 9:42-48; Mt 11:20-24; *see DJG*, Kingdom of God).

The authors of the NT writings and other early Christian literature likewise shared the conviction of many of their Jewish contemporaries that a final divine judgment was coming upon the world. Continuity with the biblical tradition, in which God the Creator and his claim upon his creatures is central, sets the NT understanding of final judgment apart from Egyptian and Greco-Roman conceptions of the afterlife (see in this regard *m. 'Abot* 4:22). Particularly in the latter, the torments of the wicked are of primary interest, a tradition to which Dante's *Inferno* was an heir. Some early extrabiblical writings from the first through fifth centuries, both Jewish and Christian, show such influence (although they are not simple developments of Greek ideas; see Himmelfarb) and stand at a distance from the NT materials (e.g., *Apoc. Zeph., Apoc. Peter, Apoc. Paul;* with time attention shifted from future to postmortem punishment [Bauckham]). In contrast even the NT Apocalypse of John (Revelation), which vividly depicts the outpouring of wrath, focuses not on the experience of perdition but on the wickedness of humanity and on the certainty and justice of divine judgment.

2. The Day of Judgment in Acts, the Non-Pauline Letters and Revelation.

In the Hebrew Scriptures the predominant expression for the time at which God visits judgment on the earth is "the day of the Lord."* The NT writers take up this term, give nuance to the basic phrase with varying forms and use it to signify the final judgment at the end of the present age (e.g., "the Day," Heb 10:25; "the day of visitation," 1 Pet 2:12; "the day of the Lord," 2 Pet 3:10; "the day of judgment," 1 Jn 4:17; "the great day," Jude 6; "the great day of wrath," Rev 6:16-17).

There is little basis in the NT for the thesis that a crisis resulted from the so-called delay of the Parousia,* i.e., the supposed disappointment of the first generation of believers who are thought to have believed that Christ's coming (Parousia) would certainly occur within their lifetime (see inter alia Moore). In 2 Peter,* where the delay of the day of the Lord is treated explicitly as a theological problem, the challenge to Christian faith arises not from a failure of Christ* to appear immediately but from a teaching that denied biblical faith more broadly considered (2 Pet 3:1-10). "Scoffers" have used the apparent continuity of the world from the time of the ancestors to advance what seems to have been a monistic, materialist view of the world (*see* Creation, Cosmology). Such philosophy, the author declares, ignores the biblical witness to creation *ex nihilo*, the patriarchal deluge and the divine word that has determined a fiery end to the present order (2 Pet 3:5-7).

The tenor of the NT anticipation of the day of the Lord reflects that of numerous passages in the Hebrew Scriptures, particularly the Psalms, in which the faith of the righteous* is proved in their patiently waiting in hope* for God to act on their behalf (e.g., Ps 25; 27; 31; 37—39). The NT writings are distinct in their sense of imminence, but for them the nearness of the Parousia is not subject to calculation. As with their biblical precedents, it is rather a matter of faith and obedience.* Christ has appeared, in whom God's saving purposes have culminated (e.g., Acts 10:43; 1 Pet 1:20). With him the last days have arrived (e.g., Acts 2:17; Heb 1:2; Jas 5:3). Judgment now impends since no saving event will intervene before the end (e.g., Heb 10:26-27; 1 Pet 4:5, 6). The "day" will come unexpectedly upon the unbelieving and disobedient (e.g., 2 Pet 3:10; Rev 3:3; 16:15).

Those who belong to Christ are to be prepared by their faith and upright behavior (e.g., Heb 10:35-39; 1 Pet 4:7; 1 Jn 2:28-29).

3. The Context and Function of the Theme of Judgment in the Earliest Church.

The expectation of a final judgment not only motivated the apostolic mission* and witness* of the earliest church but is basic to all instruction, exhortation and comfort in the NT. The NT authors invariably address threats to the life and faith of Christians that bear the potential of bringing condemnation on them. Often such threats prompt the composition and sending of the letters, as is the case with Hebrews,* 2 Peter* and Jude,* 1 John* and Revelation.* It is crucial to remember that the proclamation of the gospel* included a call to repentance coupled with the warning of coming judgment (e.g., Acts 2:38-40; 3:19; 10:42; 11:18; 17:30-31; 26:19-20; cf. Rom 2:4; Rev 9:20-21; 16:9) and that new converts were instructed on the final judgment (Heb 6:1-2; cf. Acts 24:24-25). Frequently the prospect of facing divine judgment is joined to specific admonitions (e.g., Heb 6:10-12; 13:4; Jas 1:12; 2:12-13; 5:9). Christian leaders and teachers are singled out as being especially accountable to God (Heb 13:17; Jas 3:1; cf. 1 Pet 5:1-4). Strikingly, three NT letters conclude with encouragement to restore the disobedient in view of their perilous state (Jas 5:19-20; 1 Jn 5:14-17; Jude 22-23; see also 1 Pet 4:8).

It is equally clear, however, that the expectation of a final judgment alone does not adequately describe the NT writings. They bear as their central message the conviction that God through Christ has provided forgiveness* and salvation* at the final judgment (e.g., Acts 20:32; Heb 7:23-28; Jas 1:18; 1 Jn 4:17-21). Between these two beliefs there exists an inescapable tension (see 4 below). Here it is important to note that the NT writers regarded the judgment to come not merely as a basis for warning but as an offer of hope, comfort and encouragement. The author of Hebrews, for example, reminds his readers that God is not unjust. He will not forget the labor and love* of believers (Heb 6:10). James* assures his audience that those who endure trial will receive the crown of life that God has promised to those who love him (Jas 1:12; cf. Rev 2:10). The hope of divine deliverance underlies the Apocalypse of John (e.g., Rev 6:9-11; 7:13-17; 11:16-19; 19:1-4).

Of fundamental significance for Christian theology and ethics* is the broadly attested stance of the NT writers that judgment and retribution belong to God alone and that believers consequently are not to take vengeance themselves or to condemn one another (Mt 7:1; Rom 12:19-21; 14:10-12; Jas 2:4, 12-13; 5:9; cf. 1 Cor 5:1-13: church discipline* is not thereby excluded). To assume such authority* is to trespass upon the divine role itself, an act of hubris that even the angels* of God do not dare (Jas 4:11-12; 2 Pet 2:11; Jude 9). Following the pattern of Christ, Christians are to entrust their rights to "the one who judges righteously" (1 Pet 2:21-23, 4:19; Jas 5:7-11; Rev 6:9-11).

4. The Early Christian Conception of Judgment.
A prominent and distinctive aspect of NT and early Christian teaching is the prospect that Christ himself will judge all humanity at his Parousia.* The formulaic description of Christ as the "one who is to judge the living and the dead" provides an indication of the centrality of this belief to early Christian thought (Acts 10:42; 2 Tim 4:1; 1 Pet 4:5; *Barn.* 7.2; Pol. *Phil.* 2.1). Judgment hinges upon one's response to Jesus (Acts 13:40-41; 13:46; 18:6). Disobedience to the word that God has spoken in his Son brings a more severe punishment than rejection of Moses* (Heb 4:12-13; 6:7-8; 10:26-31; 12:25). The book of Revelation stresses that it is supremely right that Jesus, who suffered innocently and thereby secured salvation, should be the agent of divine judgment (e.g., Rev 1:4-7; 5:9-10). Jesus' resurrection* and ascension* signify God's vindication of his messianic claims and place him in a role that otherwise was reserved for God alone (Acts 10:42; 17:30-31; see the christologically significant *2 Clem.* 1.1). To some extent parallels may be found within some circles of early Judaism* in which the Messiah was expected to act as judge, yet in these instances no historical figure is in view (*1 Enoch* 62:1-16; 4 Ezra 13:1-58).

No less prominent is the theme of individual judgment according to works* (Heb 9:27-28; Rev 1:7; 2:7; 2:23). Each one will be called to give an account for his or her deeds (Heb 4:13; 13:17; 1 Pet 4:5-6). The NT authors are careful to apply the prospect of judgment to Christians themselves. As the judge of all, God will render his verdict impartially. Believers, although they name God as "Father," must not presume upon

grace (1 Pet 1:17-19; Heb 10:30; cf. Jas 2:9). Frequently the authors bring reminders that punishment will be meted out to those who practice immorality, greed and similar vices (Heb 13:4; *see* Purity).

NT exhortations are frequently based upon final recompense for obedience and hardly make sense apart from this prospect. Moreover, the NT writers regularly depict final punishment as corresponding to deeds done in this life, underscoring the manifest justice of the final divine verdict (*lex talionis*, Jas 2:13; 5:1-3; Jude 6; cf. Rev 2:10; 3:10). Measure-for-measure retribution is not unique to the biblical writings and appears with particular prominence in early Jewish and Christian "tours of hell." Yet since the biblical materials lack detailed descriptions of torment, they give greater prominence to the divine verdict, implicitly emphasizing the justice of God. The "tours of hell" instead portray a correspondence between deeds and gruesome destinies, suggesting an inherent connection between deed and outcome (cf. Himmelfarb).

The NT describes reward* as intrinsically related to God and Christ, the object of hope and trust. Those who love Christ and consequently serve him now will be rewarded by seeing him in his glory. Moreover, such reward always paradoxically issues in glory to Christ, who has worked the believer's salvation. Nevertheless the NT writers do not regard retribution as mere divine confirmation of human decision. Punishment and reward are actively imposed by God from without upon the human being (contra Travis; see, e.g., Heb 10:26-31; Jas 5:1; 2 Pet 2:6).

If the cross* has worked a right standing with God for the believer, how is it that the believer must yet face judgment? Between this prospect and the proclamation of forgiveness in Christ stands an irreducible paradox. Yet to a certain extent lines of convergence can be traced. In the first place, as we have noted, the NT writers anticipate that Christ himself will judge humanity. Faith in him is a moral act, the fundamental obedience that God requires of human beings (e.g., Heb 3:12-19; 1 Pet 1:3-9; 1 Jn 2:22-25). Furthermore, the NT writings display a deep confidence in the power of God to effect salvation for those who have received the forgiveness offered in Christ (e.g., Acts 20:32; Jas 1:9; 2 Pet 2:9; Jude 24). That is not to say that all uncertainty is removed from the visible community of Christians; otherwise the warnings of judgment would hardly make sense. The church on earth yet remains under testing. Nevertheless, where saving realities are present they manifest themselves in persevering faith and obedience, which secure the believer in the final judgment (e.g., Heb 10:39; 1 Jn 2:29-3:3; Rev 1:9).

Paul's understanding of the gospel therefore does not stand at odds with the rest of the NT. While there are distinctions which cannot be ignored, there is no final contradiction between Paul and James. James speaks of a final justification by faith with works (*not* by faith and works; Jas 2:22-24) and therefore thinks of works which proceed from faith. When Paul affirms that a person is justified by faith and not by "works of the law," he rejects the saving value of deeds of obedience apart from faith, which are always incomplete and proceed from the self-seeking heart of the fallen human being. Any claim to righteousness is thereby ruled out, and the whole of justification is located in the atoning work of the cross, which is grasped by faith alone. Paul thereby in no way diminishes James's demand for deeds of obedience. In fact he too expects a judgment according to deeds (2 Cor 5:10). James speaks of the justification at the final judgment (Jas 2:14-26), while Paul speaks of a final justification worked already by the cross (e.g., Rom 3:21-26). The two loci stand in tension but not in contradiction. There is evidence in James's letter that he would embrace Paul's interpretation of the cross. He views the gospel as the source of life, one the basis of *unconditioned* divine mercy (Jas 1:18; 2:12-13). Both Paul and James share the expectation that acceptance of the gospel will issue in new obedience (Jas 1:21, "the word [i.e., gospel] implanted, which has the power to save"; Rom 6:19).

An immediate postmortem judgment, which is implicit in the parable of the rich man and Lazarus (Lk 16:19-31; but cf. Acts 10:42), is likewise suggested in a few NT passages such as the vision* of the righteous martyrs (Rev 6:9-11; cf. Jas 3:6) and occasionally in both Jewish and Christian sources (e.g., 4 Ezra 7:78-80; cf. 7:104-5; *1 Clem.* 20.5; *2 Clem.* 19.4). This expectation does not eliminate the judgment of the last day, upon which the focus is set.

Understandably, judgment imagery similar to some of that employed in the NT may be found in the Greco-Roman world, including Egypt. Sometimes borrowing is evident (e.g., the imprisonment of angels in Tartarus, 2 Pet 2:4), but similarities do not necessarily constitute parallels or influence (contra Griffiths). The NT writers generally appeal more directly to biblical tradition, as do early Jewish writings. Probably the image of the opening of books in which deeds have been recorded derives from Daniel (Dan 7:10; e.g., Rev 20:12; *Jub.* 30:22; *1 Enoch* 98:8; 2 Bar 24:1; *m. 'Abot* 2.1). The juxtaposed "book (of life)," which paradoxically contains the names of the elect,* appears here as well (Dan 12:1; cf. Ps 69:28; Phil 4:3; Rev 3:5; 20:12; 20:15; cf. *Jub.* 30:23). Divine judgments in the past serve as patterns for what is yet to come, especially the deliverance of the righteous and the destruction of the wicked. The salvation of Noah through the flood prefigured baptism,* by which believers lay claim to forgiveness (cf., *1 Enoch* 54). Here baptism itself entails a self-judgment in anticipation of the eschaton* (1 Pet 3:20-22; cf. 2 Pet 2:5; Heb 11:7). The destruction of Sodom and Gomorrah by fire serves as an example of what is coming on the ungodly (2 Pet 2:6; Jude 7; cf. Lk 17:29; Rev 14:9-11), just as the divine rescue of Lot prefigures the rescue of the righteous (2 Pet 2:7; cf. Lk 17:28-32).

In some passages of the NT the punishment of unbelievers is described as enduring eternally. There has been some recent debate over this matter, naturally involving the interpretation of various occurrences of the Greek word *aiōn*, which may signify "eon" or "forever," and the corresponding adjective, *aiōnios*. Nevertheless, it is sufficiently clear that the adjective is regularly used in the sense of everlasting (see Sasse; Heb 5:9; 6:2; 9:12; 9:14; 9:15; 13:20; 2 Pet 1:11). Various references in which the noun is employed envision an everlasting punishment (Rev 14:9-12; 19:1-3; 20:10-15). Moreover, the anticipation of everlasting punishment is attested outside the NT (e.g., *1 Enoch* 91:12-16; *Pss. Sol.* 3:11-12). Explicit teaching of eternal punishment appears only occasionally in the NT, probably because it was an uncontested part of elementary Christian instruction (Heb 6:1-2). There is no indication that the NT writers derived the belief that punishment would be eternal from the presupposition that the soul is naturally immortal. They rather regard it as an expression of the justice of God (e.g., Rev 19:1-4).

See also APOCALYPTIC; DAY OF THE LORD; ESCHATOLOGY; HELL, ABYSS, ETERNAL PUNISHMENT; REWARDS; UNIVERSALISM; WRATH, DESTRUCTION.

BIBLIOGRAPHY. R. J. Bauckham, "Early Jewish Visions of Hell," *JTS* 41 (1990) 355-85; A. E. Bernstein, *The Formation of Hell: Death and Retribution in the Ancient and Early Christian Worlds* (Ithaca, NY: Cornell University Press, 1993); S. G. F. Brandon, *The Judgment of the Dead: An Historical and Comparative Study of the Idea of Post-Mortem Judgment in the Major Religions* (London: Weidenfeld & Nicolson, 1967); D. Cohn-Sherbok, "Rabbinic Judaism and the Doctrine of Hell" in *Rabbinic Perspectives on the New Testament* (SBEC 28; Lewiston, NY: Edwin Mellen, 1990) 1-18; J. G. Griffiths, *The Divine Verdict: A Study of Divine Judgment in the Ancient Religions* (Studies in the History of Religions 52; Leiden: E. J. Brill, 1991); M. Himmelfarb, *Tours of Hell: An Apocalyptic Form in Jewish and Christian Literature* (Philadelphia: University of Pennsylvania, 1983); A. L. Moore, *The Parousia in the New Testament* (NovTSupp 13; Leiden: E. J. Brill, 1966); L. Morris, *The Biblical Doctrine of Judgment* (Grand Rapids: Eerdmans, 1960); C. F. D. Moule, "The Judgment Theme in the Sacraments" in *The Background of the New Testament and Its Eschatology,* ed. W. D. Davies and D. Daube (Cambridge: Cambridge University Press, 1956) 464-81; idem, "Punishment and Retribution" in *Essays in New Testament Interpretation* (Cambridge: Cambridge University Press, 1982) 235-49; H. Sasse, "αἰών, αἰώνιος," *TDNT* 1:197-209; P. Toon, *Heaven and Hell: A Biblical and Theological Overview* (Nashville: Thomas Nelson, 1986); S. H. Travis, *Christ and the Judgment of God: Divine Retribution in the New Testament* (Grand Rapids: Zondervan, 1987); G. Vermes, F. Millar and M. Black, "The Last Judgment" in *The History of the Jewish People in the Age of Jesus Christ (175 B.C.—A.D. 135)* (2 vols.; Edinburgh: T & T Clark, 1979) 2:544-47. M. A. Seifrid

JUSTIFICATION. *See* RIGHTEOUSNESS.

K

KERYGMA AND DIDACHE

The nature of the early Christian preaching of the gospel has been a central issue in mid-twentieth-century NT scholarship. In particular debate has focused on the question and content of the kerygma. Related to the Greek verb *kēryssō*, which means "to herald," "kerygma" refers to either the matter that is heralded or the act of heralding itself. The gospel about Christ stood at the center of the preaching, but the issue turns on the main emphasis that was given to the theme. The verbal usages generally always have an object, a content for the preaching, whether it is Christ Jesus (2 Cor 1:19; 4:5) or the "crucified Christ" (1 Cor 1:23), the "Word" (2 Tim. 4:2) or the "word of faith" (Rom 10:8), the Messiah (Acts 8:5) or "Jesus as Son of God" (Acts 9:20), or "the kingdom of God" (Acts 20:25; 28:31).

Sometimes the content of the preaching is something other than the gospel about Christ. It can be John the Baptist's message of repentance (Acts 10:37), the law* of Moses* (Acts 15:21) or even the judaizing message that circumcision* is necessary for salvation (Gal 5:11). Of fundamental importance has been the question whether there ever existed a type of preaching that had no passion story, as in the so-called Q tradition, a corpus of Jesus' teaching found in Luke and Matthew, or whether the apocryphal* and Gnostic* gospels like *The Gospel of Thomas** should be appealed to as evidence of Christian communities that cherished the person of Jesus as a sage delivering wise oracles (the *logoi sophōn*) but with no mission to redeem from sins by his death and resurrection.

1. Early Reconstructions of the Kerygma
2. Multiple Kerygmas
3. The Didactic Element in the Kerygma

1. Early Reconstructions of the Kerygma.

Historically M. Dibelius believed that most of the gospel tradition was passed on in the preaching of the apostles* as recorded in Acts.* He proposed that the early Christian preaching is found partially preserved in the speeches of Acts and contains three main elements: the basic kerygma of salvation* in Christ,* scriptural proofs and an exhortation to repentance* (Dibelius, 17). C. H. Dodd also maintained that the kerygma had this content. Like Dibelius, he believed that the kerygma, or gospel message of the early church, could be reconstructed from the speeches in Acts. His reconstruction included six main elements (Dodd, 21-23). First, the kerygma proclaimed that the age of fulfillment of the OT prophecies* about the Messiah had come. Second, this was seen to have come through the ministry,* death and resurrection* of Christ (*see* Death of Christ). Third, as a result of his resurrection, Christ has been exalted* to the right hand of God. Fourth, the presence of the Holy Spirit* in the church* is the guarantee of Christ's living presence. Fifth, the return of Christ will bring the messianic age to its consummation. Sixth, the listeners were exhorted to repent of their sins, be baptized* and enter the community of Christ, receiving the gift of the Spirit.

Dodd insisted that this kerygma of the church was totally distinct from its didache, which was its ethical* teaching and was taught subsequent to the believer's response to the basic kerygmatic or gospel message (Dodd, 7). Further, Dodd argued, the basic points of the kerygma provided the outline for the Gospel of Mark, and this Markan kerygmatic outline was later expanded with didache (Jesus' teachings) by Matthew and Luke.

Initially Dodd's work met with acceptance of his basic thesis of a recoverable early Christian message. Recent investigation into the nature of early Christianity, however, is apt to conclude that patterns of diversity corresponding to geographical location, cultural ethos and theological challenges were in evidence (see Dunn), thus making the idea of a monolithic kerygma less likely (see Worship). Thus Dodd's thesis has been challenged at some points and refined at others. In particular, his kerygmatic outline has been shown to be too rigid (Evans, Nineham) and limited, and his elimination of didache from kerygma has been challenged (Worley).

2. Multiple Kerygmas.

On a broader front Dodd's reconstruction of the kerygma is open to challenge. The speeches in Acts do not support the basic six points of Dodd's outline. His synopsis of the kerygma is assembled only by piecing it together from the various speeches, primarily from three (Peter's speeches in Acts 2; 3; 10). In fact the emphasis on Jesus' ministry is found mainly in Peter's speech at Cornelius's* home (Acts 10:37-39), though there are data in Peter's speech at Pentecost* (Acts 2), and yet this is the main foundation for his argument that the kerygma provided the outline for Mark's Gospel.

Dodd claimed that his reconstructed kerygma was that only of the Jerusalem* church. This was a wise restriction, for the extensive OT proofs found in it would have been more appropriate for the immediate audience. Does Acts depict other kerygmas more pertinent to Gentiles*? The speeches at Lystra (Acts 14:15-17) and on the Areopagus at Athens (Acts 17:22-31) seem to provide a basic kergymatic message for Gentiles, a kerygma that is not based on OT proofs and that begins with a basic monotheistic appeal. Perhaps the best summary of this Gentile kerygma appears in 1 Thessalonians 1:9-10 (see Kemmler, Munck). It consists of four main points, and it is striking to note how closely these correspond with the emphases of the speech on the Areopagus: turning from idols to God (cf. Acts 17:29), serving the one living and true God (cf. Acts 17:23-27), waiting for his Son* from heaven,* whom he raised from the dead (cf. Acts 17:31), and being delivered by Jesus from the wrath* to come (cf. the emphasis on judgment* in Acts 17:31). As with all gospel appeals, there must also have been a call for the Gentiles to repent (as in Acts 17:30).

Noting the problems in Dodd's treatment, a number of scholars have suggested different reconstructions but with no consensus among themselves (e.g., Reicke, 139; Mounce, 77). Perhaps the most promising avenues for future research on the kerygma are the recent attempts to recover the kerygma on the basis of the NT creedal, hymnic and confessional passages (Sloan, 573), with the basic work in E. Stauffer, O. Cullmann and V. H. Neufeld (see Creeds; Hymns). The most significant of these creedal statements is in 1 Corinthians 15:1-8, where Paul rehearses his debt to an earlier credo that he both inherited from his predecessors (in Antioch* or Jerusalem?) and in turn passed on to the Corinthians. All the marks of a confessional formulary are present (e.g., verbs of traditioning, recitative use of "that," an appeal to OT testimonies).

Yet the important items are the way the death of Christ for sins and the resurrection in fulfillment of the divine purpose form a central part of God's *Heilsplan* for human salvation (1 Cor 15:1, 2). This piece of evidence, obviously pre-Pauline and preformed before its use in Paul's letter points back to the earliest kerygma that centered in the cross* and resurrection. There is no substantial evidence to indicate any Christian community in which these saving events were not central, just as the Lord's Supper* meal (1 Cor 11:17-34) focused on the sacrificial* death of Christ and was integral to Christian community from the beginning.

The witness of early "hymns to Christ" (see Hengel) tells a similar story in the pre-Pauline period and was continued in the later NT books that draw on these liturgical elements (see Liturgical Elements; Worship). The centrality of Christ's cross and victory is seen in documents as diverse as 1 Peter* (1 Pet 2:21-24; 3:18-22), 1 Timothy (1 Tim 3:16) and Revelation (Rev 5:9-14; see Revelation, Book of), with these texts all credibly regarded as hymnic praise formulas in celebration of cosmic redemption in turn centered on the cross and triumph of Christ the Lord* of the universe.

3. The Didactic Element in the Kerygma.

Dodd was wrong in his sharp distinction between kerygma and didache. The lexical evidence of the NT is sufficient witness against such a dichotomy. Regularly the terms *teaching* and *preaching* are used together or are regarded as interchangeable (Paul's ministry in Acts is so regarded). Nonetheless, we should mark the distinct emphasis that belongs to each word group, as kerygmatic preaching is aimed at converting outsiders and didactic preaching serves to build up the congregations. The words tend to be used together in the later Christian writings. Hermas, for example, speaks of "teachers of the son of God who preached" (*Herm. Sim.* 9.16.5).

So it is natural that the kerygmatic terminology is used with a didactic content, as when Paul speaks of the content of his message (1 Cor 15:1-8). The word *preaching* continued to be used with a didactic application in the later Christian writings. Ignatius,* for example, reminded the Philadelphians of the Spirit's "preaching," which had for its content loving unity and keeping one's body untainted (Ign. *Phld.* 7.2).

More common, however, is the use of teaching terminology in what is clearly an evangelistic, missionary context, a context in which preaching would be called for. This is the dominant use in Acts, both for the verb *didaskō* ("to teach") and for the noun *didachē* ("teaching"). "Teaching" and "evangelizing" are used together (Acts 5:42; 15:35). Teaching in Acts includes an evangelistic endeavor, preaching to non-Christians, whether they are Jews (Acts 4:2, 18; 5:21, 28) or Gentiles (Acts 13:12; 17:19; 18:11).

Early Christian preaching almost certainly contained a didactic element. The exact nature of the teaching emphasis would differ from context to context. For example, among the Jews, teaching from the OT prophecies would be an essential element in the preaching of Christ as Messiah (Lk 24:44-47; Acts 17:2-3, 11-12). For Gentiles, turning from idolatry* and the immorality of pagan lifestyles would be a basic part of the appeal to place one's faith in the only true God.

A major area for contemporary investigation is the study of the various types of early Christian teachings. These have left their mark on the literature in a variety of forms. The Pastoral Letters hold up the "deposit" *(parathēkē)* as important for the pastor to maintain and teach (1 Tim 4:11-16; 6:20) and cite confessional materials that seem to have a setting in baptismal and/or martyr contexts (2 Tim 2:11-13). There are the more lengthy doctrinal statements seen in Hebrews,* as the readers are encouraged to be teachers (Heb 5:11-14), as a warning against being led astray (Heb 13:9), or the use of catechetical form of elementary Christian in-

struction known as household codes,* or station codes, represented in the Pastorals and 1 Peter. Sometimes entire letters (e.g., Jude, *2 Clement*) or substantial portions of epistolary correspondence are given over to exhortation based on didactic preaching (1 John) and conform to rhetorical* patterns of deliberative persuasion (Hebrews, 2 Peter; see Watson).

The *Didache** (or Teaching of the Twelve Apostles) gives us some idea of the various categories of teaching in the early church of the late first or early second century. Of its sixteen chapters the first six deal with ethical instruction (paraenesis). *Didache* 7—15 deal with church practice and consist of teaching in proper practice (catechesis) and tradition (paradosis). *Didache* 16 deals with eschatology* and belongs to a more prophetic type of teaching. The hymnic and creedal portions of the NT, as we have observed, provide a further area for research into the development of Christian theology from the early didache of the church.

It is highly unlikely that preaching and teaching were ever entirely separated in early Christianity. Kerygma and didache belong together. To set one over against the other would be a loss for the church and an abandonment of the NT pattern (see Glen, Smart).

See also CREEDS, CONFESSIONAL FORMS; EVANGELISM IN THE EARLY CHURCH; GOSPEL; NEW TESTAMENT THEOLOGY; TEACHING, PARAENESIS.

BIBLIOGRAPHY. O. Cullmann, "The Tradition" in *The Early Church*, ed. A. J. B. Higgins (Philadelphia: Westminster, 1956) 55-99; M. Dibelius, *From Tradition to Gospel* (New York: Scribners, 1965); C. H. Dodd, *The Apostolic Preaching and Its Development* (London: Hodder & Stoughton, 1936); J. D. G. Dunn, *Unity and Diversity in the New Testament* (2d ed.; Philadelphia: Trinity Press International, 1990); C. F. Evans, "The Kerygma," *JTS* (n.s.) 7 (1956) 25-41; G. Friedrich, "κῆρυξ κτλ," *TDNT* 3:683-719; T. F. Glasson, "The Kerygma: Is Our Version Correct?" *Hibbert Journal* 51 (1953) 129-32; J. S. Glen, *The Recovery of the Teaching Ministry* (Philadelphia: Westminster, 1960); M. Hengel, *Studies in Early Christology* (Edinburgh: T & T Clark, 1995); D. W. Kemmler, *Faith and Human Reason: A Study of Paul's Method of Preaching as Illustrated by 1-2 Thessalonians and Acts 17:2-4* (NovTSup 40; Leiden: E. J. Brill, 1975); J. I. H. McDonald, *Kerygma and Didache* (SNTSMS 37; Cambridge: Cambridge University Press, 1980); R. H. Mounce, *The Essential Nature of New Testa-*

ment Preaching (Grand Rapids: Eerdmans, 1960); J. Munck, "1 Thessalonians 1:9-10 and the Missionary Preaching of Paul," NTS 9 (1962-63) 95-110; D. E. Nineham, "Eyewitness Testimony and the Gospel Tradition," JTS (n.s.) 9.1 (1958) 13-25; 9.2 (1958) 243-52; 11.2 (1960) 253-64; B. Reicke, "A Synopsis of Early Christian Preaching" in The Root of the Vine, ed. A. Fridrichsen et al. (London: Dacre, 1953) 128-60; K. H. Rengstorf, "διδάσκω κτλ," TDNT 2:135-65; R. B. Sloan, "Canonical Theology of the New Testament" in Foundations for Biblical Interpretation, ed. D. H. Dockery et al. (Nashville: Broadman & Holman, 1994) 565-94; J. D. Smart, The Teaching Ministry of the Church (Philadelphia: Westminster, 1954); K. Stendahl, "Kerygma und Kerygmatisch: Von Zweideutigen Ausdruechen der Predigt der Urkirche—und Unserer," TLZ 12 (1952) 715-20; J. J. Vincent, "Didactic Kerygma in the Synoptic Gospels," SJT 10 (1957) 262-73; D. F. Watson, Invention, Arrangement and Style: Rhetorical Criticism of Jude and 2 Peter (SBLDS 104; Atlanta: Scholars Press, 1988); R. C. Worley, Preaching and Teaching in the Earliest Church (Philadelphia: Westminster, 1967).

J. B. Polhill

KINGDOM OF GOD

Most of the writings under discussion show that the kingdom of God continued to be a vital theme in the preaching of the church. They maintain several characteristics of Jesus' conception of the kingdom of God, although sometimes they express them in new ways in adjustment to their new salvation-historical and missionary situations.

1. Acts
2. Hebrews
3. General Epistles
4. Revelation
5. Apostolic Fathers
6. Gospel of Thomas

1. Acts.

1.1. The Kingdom of God as the Central Theme of Acts. In the introduction to the book of Acts,* the second volume of his two-volume work, Luke summarizes the teaching* that the risen Jesus imparted to his apostles* during the forty days before his ascension* as having been about "the kingdom of God" (Acts 1:3). Luke concludes the volume with Paul's preaching* of the "kingdom of God" and "about the Lord Jesus

Christ" in the heart of the Roman Empire* (Acts 28:31; see also Acts 28:23). With this *inclusio,* linking the beginning of the book's message with its ending, Luke appears to indicate that his central theme in the second volume is the kingdom of God in continuation with that in his first volume, the Gospel of Luke. This is confirmed by his summaries of the messages of Philip* and Paul in terms of the kingdom of God in the main body of Acts (Acts 8:12; 19:8; 20:25; see also Acts 14:22; 17:7).

Yet Luke's combination of "the kingdom of God" with "the name of Jesus Christ" and with "the Lord Jesus Christ" as the gospel of Philip (Acts 8:12) and of Paul (Acts 28:23, 31) suggests a shift: in the Gospel of Luke the gospel of Jesus was about "the kingdom of God," but in Acts the gospel of the apostles includes the Lord* Jesus Christ along with the kingdom of God. In his summaries of the apostolic preaching, Luke has as the object of the verb *euangelizomai* not only the kingdom of God (Acts 8:12) but also the Lord Jesus Christ (Acts 5:42; 8:35; 10:36; 11:20; 17:18; cf. Acts 15:35). Using the verb *keryssō* to summarize the apostolic preaching, he likewise specifies as the object of the verb Jesus the Christ* or the Son of God (Acts 8:5; 9:20; 19:13; see also Acts 17:3, 7; *see* Son of God) as well as the kingdom of God (Acts 20:25; 28:31). These phenomena, especially those in the various summaries of Philip's gospel (Acts 8:5, 12, 35), suggest that the preaching of the kingdom of God was in effect the preaching of Christ Jesus. As is well known, Jesus' gospel of the kingdom of God in the Synoptic Gospels is generally replaced with the apostolic gospel of Christ in the rest of the NT, and the preacher Jesus in the former becomes the preached Christ in the latter. In Acts Luke also reflects this general change and in his own way shows how and why this has taken place.

1.2. The Future Kingdom of God. The final coming of the kingdom of God is expected to be an event in the future, but we are not to be anxious to know its "times or dates the Father has set in his authority" (Acts 1:6-7). It will be the "times of refreshing" or the "times of restoration of all things," and it will take place with the second coming of Christ (*see* Parousia) when all Israel* repent (Acts 3:19-21). So the kingdom of God represents the consummation of salvation,* and we must maintain faith* and bear sufferings* patiently "to enter the kingdom of God" (Acts 14:22).

1.3. The Lord Jesus Christ, the Present Regent and Savior. However, Luke is more concerned with the reign of God* in the present. God's reign takes place in the present through the exalted Christ and the Holy Spirit.* In his earthly existence Jesus was the agent through whom God did miracles, wonders and signs (*see* Signs and Wonders) or displayed his saving reign (Acts 2:22-23). God has raised this Jesus from the dead and exalted him to his right hand to be his viceroy in fulfillment of the promise of Psalm 110:1 (Acts 2:32-35; 5:31). So "God has made this Jesus . . . both Lord and Christ" (Acts 2:36). In Acts the title *Lord (Kyrios)* is applied to Jesus as well as to God, with the implication that Jesus Christ now exercises God's lordship on his behalf. This is the reason the apostolic preaching of the kingdom of God regularly involves preaching Jesus' messianic kingship or lordship or occasionally is replaced by the latter.

In the OT it is Yahweh as the *Kyrios* who forgives the sins of his people and saves them, but now it is Jesus the *Kyrios* who exercises this divine prerogative. In the OT it was by calling on the name* of Yahweh the Lord that one was saved (e.g., Joel 3:5 cited in Acts 2:21), but now this Lord is none other than Jesus Christ, so it is through the name of "Jesus Christ who is Lord of all" (Acts 10:36), "the judge of the living and the dead" (Acts 10:42), that forgiveness* of sins or salvation is obtained (Acts 10:43; see also Acts 3:16; 4:12, 30; 16:18; 22:16).

The exalted Lord Jesus Christ's exercise of divine kingship or lordship is manifested in his direction of the church's* mission.* As the Son of Man or the Lord standing at the right hand of God, he receives the spirit of his martyr Stephen* (Acts 7:56, 59). He arrests Saul/Paul near Damascus and calls him to be his apostle to the Gentiles* (Acts 9:1-19; 22:3-16; 26:9-18), assures Paul of his protection (Acts 18:9), redirects his mission (Acts 22:17-21) and leads him to Rome* (Acts 23:11). The Lord Jesus Christ opens Lydia's heart to appropriate Paul's gospel (Acts 16:14-15), makes Christian mission in Antioch* successful and leads a great number of people to turn to himself by faith (Acts 11:21). In his exercise of divine lordship, Jesus Christ uses the agency and power of the Holy Spirit and the ministry* of his apostles.

1.4. Through the Agency and Power of the Spirit. God's exaltation of Jesus at his right hand involved not only mandating him with his lordship but also giving him his Holy Spirit and making him the dispenser of the divine Spirit: "Exalted to the right hand of God, [the Lord Jesus Christ] has received from the Father the promised Holy Spirit and has poured [the Spirit] out" (Acts 2:33). So, if through his exaltation God the Father made Jesus his vicegerent to exercise his kingship or lordship on his behalf, at Pentecost* the Lord Jesus Christ poured out the Holy Spirit to be his agent and execute his kingship or lordship on his behalf. While the Lord Jesus Christ remains at the right hand of God in heaven* until his second coming for "the restoration of all things" or the consummation of the kingdom of God (Acts 3:19-21), on earth the Holy Spirit exercises his lordship on his behalf. Thus there is a trinitarian structure in the present manifestation of the kingdom of God: God the Father reigns through his Son* (Acts 9:20) Jesus Christ, who in turn reigns through the Holy Spirit. Hence the direction of the church and the mighty saving acts that are ascribed to the Lord Jesus Christ are also ascribed to the Spirit. They are the Lord Jesus Christ's exercise of God's reign through the agency of the Holy Spirit. Therefore they may be ascribed to the Spirit as well as to the Lord Jesus Christ.

So the Lord Jesus Christ's direction of the church is through the agency and power of the Spirit. Before his ascension he gave instructions to his apostles through the Holy Spirit (Acts 1:2). But after his ascension the apostles received the Holy Spirit given by the Lord Jesus Christ, and the Holy Spirit empowered and directed their mission (Acts 1:5, 8; 2:33). While there are references to the Lord Jesus Christ's directing and empowering the apostles' mission, there are parallel references to the Spirit's directing and empowering the apostles' mission: Acts 8:29; 10:19; 11:12, 28; 13:2, 4; 15:28; 16:6, 7; 19:21; 20:22, 23; 21:4, 11. That the two kinds of statements refer to the same reality is suggested in Acts 16:6-7: the Holy Spirit who directed Paul to leave Asia for Macedonia is explicitly identified as "the Spirit of *Jesus*." Paul concludes from this experience "that *God* had called [him] to preach the gospel" to the Macedonians (Acts 16:10). Thus Acts 16:6-10 implies the trinitarian structure of divine lordship exercised in regard to the church's mission.

During his earthly existence Jesus actualized

God's saving reign through his exorcism and healing* ministry that he wrought through the power of the Holy Spirit (Lk 11:20 par. Mt 12:28; Acts 2:22; 10:38). Now, as the exalted Lord, he has poured out the Holy Spirit to his church (Acts 2:33). Those who believe in him and are baptized in his name are given the Spirit (Acts 2:38; 9:17-18; 10:43-44; 11:16-17; 19:5-6; *see* Baptism) and thus are made to enjoy the blessings* of the eschatological* power of God in the sphere of Jesus Christ's lordship.

Further, the exalted Lord Jesus' dispensing the Holy Spirit to his apostles had the purpose of empowering them (Acts 1:8) to preach the gospel effectively and to perform many exorcisms and healing miracles* as demonstrations of the eschatological salvation. Such "signs and wonders" are often said to have been performed by the apostles "in the name of Jesus Christ" (Acts 3:6, 16; 4:30; 8:6-12; 16:16-18; cf. Acts 19:13-20) or are attributed directly to God (Acts 15:12; 19:11-12) or to the Lord (Jesus?) (Acts 14:3). However, not only from Acts 1:8 and Acts 2:33 but also from Acts 4:29-31, Acts 6:8 and Acts 8:5-19 the clear implication is that the apostles performed the healing miracles through the power of the Holy Spirit given by the Lord Jesus Christ. So the Holy Spirit is the agent who actualizes the Lord Jesus Christ's saving reign, which is in reality God's saving reign. We are to respond affirmatively to the rhetorical question of J. D. G. Dunn: "If the Kingdom's presence in Jesus was determined by the coming of the Spirit upon Jesus at Jordan, then may we, indeed must we not say that the Kingdom became present in the disciples by the coming of the Spirit at Pentecost in the same way?" (Dunn, 40).

1.5. The Lord Jesus and His Apostles. Along with the Holy Spirit, the church, especially the twelve apostles, is also the agent that actualizes the kingdom of God or Christ in the present, or to be more precise, the church led and empowered by the Holy Spirit fulfills this role. In his Farewell Discourse, the earthly Jesus promised to vest by way of a covenant* *(diatithemai)* the kingdom to the Twelve,* just as the Father had vested it by way of a covenant *(dietheto)* to him, so that they might participate in Christ's kingdom and become rulers and judges over Israel (Lk 22:29-30). Through his death, which was the sacrifice* for establishing the new covenant (Lk 22:20), Jesus fulfilled this promise* and created a new people of God with the Twelve as

the nucleus, in typological correspondence to Israel with the twelve tribes. Thus by way of a covenant he constituted a new people of God, a new people under God's kingship. Then the risen Christ taught them about the kingdom of God (Acts 1:3), empowered them with the Holy Spirit and commissioned them to bear witness* to the kingdom of God or Christ (Acts 1:8; 2:1-36).

The twelve apostles, represented by Peter, and others like Stephen, Philip, Paul and Barnabas go to Judea, Samaria* and the Gentile world as far as Rome, proclaiming the kingdom of God or the lordship of Christ and demonstrating the salvation of the kingdom ("signs and wonders" of exorcism and healing) through the power of the Holy Spirit. Those who respond to their gospel by repentance* and faith are incorporated into the sphere under the lordship of Jesus Christ (i.e., the kingdom of God) by being baptized in the name of the Lord Jesus Christ, and they receive the blessings of the kingdom, the forgiveness of their sins and the eschatological power of the Holy Spirit (Acts 2:38; 19:5-6; 22:16). Thus through the mission of the church the kingdom of God or Christ is extended.

1.6. The Messiah, the Kingdom of David or Israel, and the Twelve. Along with the title *Kyrios,* the "Christ" (= Messiah) is used to designate Jesus as the regent in the kingdom of God: God has exalted the crucified Jesus to his right hand and made him both Lord and Christ (Acts 2:33, 38). This exaltation* as the Messiah means Jesus' enthronement on the throne of David in fulfillment of God's promise to David (Acts 2:30; 13:23, 32-39; cf. 2 Sam 7:12-14). As such it represents the restoration of "David's fallen tent" (Acts 15:16), and "the remnant" of the Jews who "seek the Lord" and "all the Gentiles who bear [Christ's] name" are the eschatological people of God, the restored kingdom of David or Israel, over which Jesus the Davidic Messiah reigns (Acts 15:17). The twelve apostles are set as his representatives so that they may rule and judge them in his name (Lk 22:30). However, this restored kingdom of David, or Israel, is not to be thought of in terms of a Jewish nationalistic political system, as it was in some of the contemporary Jewish parties (Acts 1:6), but rather in terms of a community of the Jews and the Gentiles who call on the name of the Lord (i.e., submit to the kingship of Jesus the

Messiah, who represents the kingship of Yahweh [Acts 2:21]).

1.7. Conclusion. In Acts Luke records the salvation history of God's exaltation of Jesus at his right hand to execute his lordship and kingship, of the Lord Jesus Christ's execution of God's kingship or lordship through the Holy Spirit and his church and of the Jewish and Gentile believers being brought into the kingdom of God or Christ for salvation. Luke concentrates on the present manifestation of the kingdom but views it as a process toward the consummation, "the restoration of all things," at the Parousia of Christ.

2. Hebrews.

2.1. The Kingdom of God. In Hebrews* there is only one explicit reference to the kingdom of God: "Since we are receiving an unshakable kingdom, let us be thankful and so worship God acceptably with reverence and awe" (Heb 12:28). Here "kingdom" does not seem to refer to God's kingly reign, and the verse does not seem to have in view either our submitting to it or our sharing in it.

Throughout the epistle there is little teaching about God's kingly rule. Rather, "kingdom" seems to be used as a synonym for "the city of God" (Heb 11:10, 16; 12:22), "the city that is to come" (Heb 13:14), "Mount Zion" or "the heavenly Jerusalem"* (Heb 12:22) and the "fatherland" (Heb 11:14). Like these terms, "kingdom" seems to denote the place where God reigns and the believers are to obtain the blissful rest *(katapausis,* Heb 3:11, 18; 4:1, 3, 5, 10-11; *sabbatismos,* Heb 4:9), the consummation of their salvation.

To be sure, God's heavenly "throne" is referred to (Heb 4:16; 8:1; 12:2). In the formulation "the throne of the Majesty" *(megalōsynēs)* in heaven (Heb 8:1) there may be a connotation of divine power or sovereignty, and from the contrast between the cross* Jesus endured and the divine throne Jesus eventually obtained (Heb 12:2) we may discern a similar connotation of the divine throne. However, in both cases the connotation cannot be said to be strong. In Hebrews 8:1 as well as in Hebrews 4:16 the cultic meaning of the divine throne is much more prominent than is its political meaning.

2.2. Jesus Christ Exalted to the Right Hand of God's Throne. A similar phenomenon takes place with reference to Jesus Christ. It belongs to the central theme of Hebrews that Jesus

Christ was exalted to sit at the right hand of God or his throne in fulfillment of Psalm 110:1 (Heb 1:3, 13; 8:1; 10:12; 12:2). Besides the fact that in several books of the NT Psalm 110:1 functions prominently to substantiate the lordship or kingship that the exalted Jesus Christ has come to exercise on God's behalf, several factors in Hebrews point to a political connotation of the theme. (1) It is accompanied by references to God's appointment of Jesus as his Son, his "heir of all things" in fulfillment of Psalm 2:7-8 (Heb 1:2, 5; 5:5; 7:28) and 2 Samuel 7:14 (Heb 1:5), which were interpreted as prophecies* for the messianic king in Judaism* and in the early church. (2) Psalm 45:6-7 and Psalm 8:4-6 are applied to Christ respectively in Hebrews 1:8-9 and Hebrews 2:6-8 to emphasize his exaltation to universal kingship or lordship. Note especially the language of the former:

> Your throne, O God, will last for ever and ever, and righteousness will be the scepter of your kingdom.
>
> You have loved righteousness and hated wickedness; therefore God, your God, has set you above your companions by anointing you with the oil of joy.

(3) Christ is said to be "faithful as a son over God's house," in contrast to Moses,* who was faithful as a servant (Heb 3:5-6). (4) The name *Melchizedek** is interpreted in terms of "king of Salem [or peace]" and "king of righteousness" (Heb 7:1-3), in whose order Christ is supposed to have been appointed the high priest (Heb 5:6; 7:13-28). These factors clearly indicate that in Hebrews there is an understanding of Jesus Christ as the messianic king who exercises divine kingship on God's behalf. Here may be involved something more than a simple reflection of the primitive church's common kerygma. The statement in Hebrews 2:3-4 appears to reflect Jesus' ministry of kingdom preaching and healing (e.g., Mt 12:28 par. Lk 11:20), and further it is possible that the presentation of the consummation of salvation in terms of the sabbath rest in this epistle (Heb 4:9) reflects Jesus' ministry of healing on the sabbath as a proleptic actualization of the sabbath perfection or the restored creation* in the kingdom of God.

However, it can hardly be said that the theme of Jesus' messianic kingship is expounded in the epistle. As little is said about the reign of the exalted Lord Jesus Christ over his people or the world* as is said about God's reign. Since his exaltation to the right hand of God, Christ waits for his enemies to be made his footstool (Heb 10:13; cf. Ps 110:1). Beyond affirming his exaltation to universal kingship, this is all that is said about the exalted Christ's current political activity. Instead the exaltation of Christ to the right hand of God is expounded almost exclusively in terms of his ministry as the high priest (cf. Davies, 388-89), just as God's throne in the heavenly sanctuary is almost exclusively interpreted in its cultic significance. Having entered the holy of holies once for all by his own blood, obtaining eternal redemption* for us (Heb 9:12) and mediating the new covenant (Heb 8:6-13; 9:15-22), Christ now serves in the heavenly sanctuary as the high priest, interceding for us (Heb 2:17-18; 4:14-16; 7:25; 8:1-2; 9:24; 10:19-22).

2.3. Based on the Jesus Tradition? Hebrews's exposition of God's throne in the heavenly sanctuary and of Christ's exaltation to the right hand of it chiefly in terms of their cultic significance, while retaining their political significance in the background, is based on the common conception of the temple* both as the sanctuary where God is worshiped and as the palace from which God reigns (cf. Hengel and Schwemer). Jesus also combined the concept of the kingdom of God and the temple: he sometimes pictured the former in terms of the latter (cf. Aalen) and concluded his kingdom preaching with a sign-act for God's impending destruction of the Jerusalem temple and for his building a new temple (Mk 11:15 par.; Mk 14:58 par.).

Even if *cheiropoiētos* ("made with hands") or *acheiropoiētos* ("not made with hands") in Mark 14:58 should be inauthentic, the appearance of the vocabulary in Acts 7:48 and Hebrews 9:11, 24 as well as Mark 14:58 suggests that it was part of a common early church tradition to express with the vocabulary a contrast between the Jerusalem temple and the new cult made possible by Jesus Christ. Then it appears that the idea of Christ's entering "the greater and more perfect tabernacle that is not made with hands" (Heb 9:11), the heavenly reality of which the Jerusalem temple or its predecessor (the wilderness tabernacle*) "made with hands" was only a copy and a shadow (Heb 8:2, 5; 9:24), reflects this common tradition.

Since Hebrews shows some awareness of the Jesus tradition* (e.g., Heb 2:3-4; 5:7-8; 13:12), it is possible that beyond the common tradition the author was aware of Jesus' negative attitude to the Jerusalem temple and his claim to build a new temple as part of his kingdom preaching. Thus the genius of the author may lie in his systematic exposition of the cultic element at least secondarily present in Jesus' kingdom preaching (cf. Gaston, 65-243) in the light of Psalm 110:1, 4. If so, his gospel is also based ultimately on Jesus' gospel of the kingdom of God.

2.4. Already But Not Yet. The believers are to receive "an unshakable kingdom" (Heb 12:28), that is, "the heavenly Jerusalem," "the city of God." In the "kingdom," "city" (e.g., Heb 11:10) or sanctuary (Heb 6:19-20) of God there is to be the sabbath rest (Heb 4:9) and the festival that God's people celebrate with myriads of angels.* They are at present on pilgrimage toward it, and they must press forward by faith and with perseverance, following Jesus Christ, "the pioneer and perfecter of our faith" (Heb 12:2; *see* Endurance). Yet by appropriating Christ's atonement and new covenant, in a real sense they "have [already] come to Mount Zion, to the city of the living God, the heavenly Jerusalem" to celebrate the sabbath in the festal gathering of angels and saints (Heb 12:22-23). Besides the tension between the "already" and the "not yet," a tension that is characteristic of NT eschatology as a whole, we may observe that this imagery is not far from Jesus' favorite picture of a feast for the kingdom of God and from his actualization of the salvation of the kingdom of God through his healing ministry on the sabbath.

3. General Epistles.
In the rest of the General Epistles, the term "the kingdom [of God]" appears only in James 2:5 and 2 Peter 1:11; related concepts are found in 1 Peter 2:4-10.

In 2 Peter 1:11 the readers are exhorted to cultivate Christian virtues* so that they may be "provided with an entrance into the eternal kingdom of our Lord and Savior Jesus Christ." It is possible that in 1 Peter 2 the ideas of the church as the "spiritual house"* or the temple founded on the cornerstone or a foundation stone* (1 Pet 2:4-8) and as "a chosen race, a royal house, a priesthood, a holy nation, a people for God's possession" (1 Pet 2:9; Exod 19:6) reflect what Jesus aimed at in his kingdom preaching and temple saying: to create a new, eschatological people of God or to build a new "temple."

Reminding the readers that God has chosen the poor "to be rich in faith and to inherit the kingdom he promised to those who love him" (Jas 2:5), James* urges them to keep "the royal law" *(nomos basilikos)*, "Love your neighbor as yourself" (Jas 2:8). He also warns them with a contrasting picture of the rich: they are those who exploit others and slander the name of God (Jas 2:6-7). Here Jesus' language is clearly echoed in the idioms "the poor" (Lk 4:18; Mt 5:3 par. Lk 6:20) and "to inherit the kingdom" (e.g., Mt 5:5; 25:34).

Jesus' teaching is also clearly reflected: Jesus gave as the law of the kingdom the double command of love*: love your God with your whole being and your neighbor as yourself (Mt 22:34-40 par.) and concretized it (e.g., in the Sermon on the Mount or Plain [Mt 5—7 par. Lk 6:20-49]). The rich violate this law of the kingdom, or "the royal law": instead of loving God, they slander the name of God and love rather the idol Mammon (cf. Mt 6:24 par. Lk 16:13) and so inevitably exploit their neighbors. In consequence they are excluded from the kingdom of God. In contrast "the poor" are rich in faith: they rely on God and love him, and so they love their neighbors too. Thus they prove themselves to be people of the kingdom of God, and they are to "inherit the kingdom" when it comes in its consummation. The contrast between the poor and the rich echoes closely the Beatitudes in the Lukan form (Lk 6:20-26). The poor will inherit the kingdom, it is implied, when the Lord comes as the judge, and so they are to wait patiently, as "the Lord's Parousia is at hand" (Jas 5:7-9).

4. Revelation.

"The kingdom of God" is the theme of Revelation, and so to study it is to survey the whole content of the book (*see* Revelation, Book of).

4.1. The Kingdom of God in Heaven. God, as "the Alpha and the Omega" and "the First and the Last," is the Creator and goal of all things and, as the *pantokrator* ("all-sovereign" or "almighty"), is the sovereign Lord of the whole universe. He is "the One who sits on the throne" in heaven, and from there he directs the course of history. This fact is dramatically presented to the seer John in a vision* described in Revelation 4.

In the vision John sees God sitting on the heavenly throne and receiving the worship* of the "four living creatures" and the "twenty-four elders." In the heavenly throne room, the prototype of the holy of holies in the earthly temple, the four living creatures, appearing respectively like a lion, an ox, a human being and an eagle, as representatives of all creatures worship God on the throne. In their hymn* the holiness* of the eternal and sovereign God is highlighted. God the Creator and Ruler of the whole universe is properly hallowed (Rev 4:8). The "twenty-four elders," the angelic beings who make up the heavenly council and rule the heavenly sphere on God's behalf, also worship God, acknowledging the sovereign will and power of the Creator (Rev 4:11). So John sees that in heaven God's name is hallowed, he reigns, and his will is done (cf. Mt 6:9-10).

4.2. The Kingdom of Satan. However, on earth Satan* (the dragon or serpent), the primeval adversary* of God and the supernatural source of all evils, reigns, misleading all the nations with falsehood to worship him instead of the true God (Rev 12). John sees this reign of Satan taking a concrete form in the tyrannical and exploitative Roman Empire: the Roman imperial power incorporated in the emperor* is the beast* or sea monster that rules the world on behalf of the dragon (Rev 13; 17). The dragon, the beast and the second beast or land monster that persuades nations to worship the beast are a parody of the triune God, the Father, the Son and the Holy Spirit. The satanic trinity forces the nations to submit to the imperial cult by deceiving them with the wine of the harlot of Babylon* (i.e., the ideology of *pax romana*, Rev 17), as well as by overwhelming them with the apparently invincible power of the Roman Empire (Rev 13).

Thus on earth the Roman emperor masquerades as god, and so the name of the true God is not hallowed, his reign is usurped, and his will is not done.

4.3. The Kingdom of God on Earth: The Christ Event (Already).

God, "who is and who was," "is to come" to earth in order to establish his rightful kingship, destroying the satanic forces. This is the main message of Revelation. John is sure of this because he saw in a vision the heavenly reality of God's triumph through Jesus Christ, which is to be unfolded on earth (Rev 5). In a real sense

God has already come and triumphed in Jesus Christ. As the one who bears his names ("the First and the Last," "the Alpha and the Omega" and "the Beginning and the End") and shares his throne, Christ is the agent of God who establishes God's kingship on earth. He is the one who turns "the kingdom of the world" into "the kingdom of our Lord and his Christ" (Rev 11:15). Christ is completely identified with God, so that God's future coming for salvation and judgment* is none other than Christ's (Rev 22:12, 20).

This Christ has already come and conquered the satanic forces and is now enthroned in heaven (Rev 3:21). For Christ's conflict with the satanic forces and his redemption of humankind, John uses two metaphors: the messianic war and the exodus. Jesus is the Messiah, "the Lion of the tribe of Judah, the root of David" (Rev 5:5; 22:16) and has overcome the rebellious nations (cf. Ps 2:8-9) with a sharp two-edged sword issuing from his mouth (cf. Is 49:2; Rev 1:16; 2:12, 16; 19:11, 15, 21). Jesus is the Passover Lamb* (Rev 5:6, 9-11) who by his blood has ransomed a people from all the nations of the world and "made them a kingdom and priests to serve God" (Rev 5:9-10; cf. Exod 19:5-6).

Jesus Christ has conquered the satanic forces by bearing a faithful witness to God and then by his death (see Death of Christ). Jesus Christ was "the faithful and true witness" to God even unto his death (Rev 3:14; cf. Rev 1:5; 12:17; 19:10). This must refer to Jesus' proclamation of the kingdom of God during his earthly life. But the decisive victory was by his death. This is made clear in the vision of Revelation 5 (Bauckham): in Revelation 5:5 it is declared that Jesus as the Davidic Messiah has triumphed, but in the subsequent verses this triumphant Messiah appears as a Lamb slaughtered, standing in the center of the divine throne and receiving the worship of the four living creatures and the twenty-four elders. Then a myriad of angels and eventually all creatures in the universe are seen joining in their worship and praising him for his triumph won through his sacrificial death. In Revelation 12:5-12 Christ's decisive victory over Satan through his death is depicted in two vivid pictures: Christ is enthroned in heaven while Satan is driven out of heaven and cast down to the earth.

This is in complete agreement with Jesus or the Gospels: Jesus Christ has triumphed over the satanic forces through his preaching of the kingdom of God and his sacrificial death on the cross. Again in full agreement with Jesus' own teaching or the testimonies of the Gospels, the result of Jesus' victory over the satanic forces is the creation of the people of God, a people he has ransomed from the kingdom of Satan and made "a kingdom and priests to serve God" (Rev 5:10). They are the people over whom God reigns as King, or they are the kingdom of God that has already come into being. In this way Jesus Christ has already brought about the kingdom of God.

Thus Jesus has fulfilled the OT or Jewish expectation of the Davidic Messiah. However, again in agreement with Jesus or the Gospels, John also reinterprets messiahship: Jesus' messianic victory was a victory over the evil forces of Satan (Rev 12:7-9) rather than the Gentile nations as such; the means of his victory was his witness to truth or to the true God and his sacrificial death rather than military conquest; and the people gathered into the kingdom of God to share in God's reign was not the Jewish nation but a new people of God who would hold faithfully to "the testimony of Jesus" or faithfully adhere to the kingdom of God that Jesus proclaimed (Rev 12:17; 17:6; 19:10).

By describing the vision of God enthroned in heaven and of Jesus Christ as the Lamb slain to establish his kingdom on earth (Rev 4—5), John presents an image of God who rules in self-giving love and righteousness* over against the satanic forces, who rule by self-assertion and oppression. Because God reigns in love, his kingship means salvation for humankind, and the message of his coming to establish his kingship is the gospel. Thus the message of John is the same as the gospel of Jesus, the Evangelists and Paul.

4.4. The Kingdom of God in or Through the Church (Now). The church or the people of God ransomed from the kingdom of Satan through Christ's sacrificial death is the kingdom of God present on earth (Rev 1:6; 5:10). The Christians make Christ's triumph over the satanic forces effective on earth. In parallel to the work of Christ, this role of the church is pictured in terms of the messianic war. The dragon, which has been conquered at Christ's death and cast down from heaven, now tyrannizes the world through the sea beast and the land beast. With

Satan's authority and at his behest, the emperors and the local rulers of the Roman Empire make war against the church (Rev 12:13—13:18). The church is the army of the Messiah (numbering 144,000) drawn from the twelve tribes of Israel (Rev 7:4-8; i.e., 12 x 12 x 1,000—all symbolic ciphers). The risen Christ, the victorious Lamb, is present with his church (Rev 1:13; 2:1) and leads it as his army (Rev 14:1, 4; 17:14) into the battle against the satanic trinity, empowering the church with the Holy Spirit, which is his power operating in the world (Rev 3:1; 5:6).

Again in parallel to the work of Christ, the church's holy war against the satanic forces is cast in terms not of a military conquest but a witness to the kingship of God or Christ and Jesus' sacrificial death (Rev 11:1-13; 12:11). The Christians are an army, but an army of the Lamb slain (Rev 14:1-5). As such they participate in the Lamb's victory over the satanic forces through their martyrdom,* which is their participation in the Lamb's sacrificial death (Rev 7:14). Their holy war consists in continuing the "testimony of Jesus" to the kingship of the true God (Rev 12:17; 19:10) and resisting the idolatry* of the false god, the beast.

The persecution of the beast (the Roman imperial power) is fierce, and the deception of the harlot of Babylon (the ideology of *pax romana)* is seductive. Yet the church is empowered by the Spirit of prophecy (Rev 11:3-6; 19:10), and its faithful witness to the kingship of the true God and the Lamb unto death among all the nations brings about the conversion of the nations from idolatry to the worship of the true God (Rev 11:13; 15:2-4). Thus God's kingship is made effective over the nations at present through the church's witness.

4.5. The Consummation of the Kingdom at the Parousia of Christ (Future). However, there remain those who neither heed God's warning judgments (the two series of judgments: Rev 6:1-17; 8:1, 3-5; 8:2, 6-11; 11:14-19) nor accept the church's witness. They continue to be under the rule of the satanic trinity so long as the latter exist, blaspheming against God and coercing and deluding nations into their worship. The saints continue to suffer under their tyranny, and even the souls of those who have already been martyred must wait for the consummation of their salvation and the judgment of the wicked (Rev 6:9-11).

The consummation of salvation and judgment is to take place with the Parousia of Christ. Christ will come as "King of kings and Lord of lords" (Rev 17:14; 19:16) and finish off the holy war against the satanic forces. There will be the final judgment (Rev 15:1, 5—16:21), in which Babylon, the satanic regime, will fall (Rev 16:16—18:24), the rulers of the world allied with it will be destroyed (Rev 19:17-21) and the wicked will be condemned (Rev 14:17-20; 17:12-14; 19:15). The satanic trinity of the dragon, the beast and the false prophet themselves will be destroyed (Rev 19:19—20:10). But the saints will be harvested into Christ's kingdom (Rev 14:15-16).

John depicts the destruction of the dragon, Satan, in two stages and accordingly the consummation of the salvation of the saints also in two stages. The dragon is first to be captured and locked in the abyss* for a thousand years, and during that period only the martyrs are to be resurrected to participate in Christ's reign. Then Satan is to be released to muster Gog and Magog (from Ezek) for the final battle against God's people, only to be cast into the lake of fire forever. Together with Satan, death and hades are to be destroyed. This results in the general resurrection* and the last judgment of all the dead (Rev 20:1-10). It is disputed whether this picture of the millennial kingdom of Christ should be interpreted in such a way as to be identified with any objective period in the eschaton (e.g., premillennialism and postmillennialism), beyond making the theological point that unlike the paradise of the *Urzeit,* the universe restored under God's kingship at the *Endzeit* is no longer vulnerable to Satan (Bauckham).

Then John depicts the consummation of the kingdom of God in terms of a new creation, "a new heaven and a new earth" and "the Holy City, the new Jerusalem, coming down out of heaven from God" (Rev 21:1—22:5). The new creation is more than just a restoration of the original creation. In it there will be "no longer any sea" (Rev 21:1), whereas in the first creation the "sea," the primeval source of evil (cf. Rev 13:1), remained as the potential threat to the cosmos (Gen 1:2; 7:11).

Filled with God's presence, the new creation will be the city of God, the new Jerusalem, and also the temple where God and the Lamb will be enthroned. There God will dwell with his people, and those who "conquer" by faith in Christ will be his people and will dwell with God. There will be no more death but only the fullness of life, as the "river of the water of life" will flow from the throne of God and the Lamb and the fruits of "the tree of life" will be available. There will be no more darkness (*see* Light), but the glory* of God and the Lamb will enlighten the whole city. There will be no more satanic deception and impurity (Rev 21:27), but God's Word and his truth* will prevail (Rev 19:11, 13). God's people as his children will inherit all these blessings and participate in God's reign, and the nations will come with their treasures to worship God and walk by his light, in fulfillment of the prophecies of the OT prophets and Jesus. So will the kingdom of God be consummated and God's intent in his creation and covenant be fulfilled.

4.6. Conclusion. Revelation presents a faithful interpretation of Jesus' gospel of the kingdom of God in the light of Christ's death, resurrection and exaltation and a creative contextualization of it to the latter half of the first century in which the Roman Empire appeared as the incarnation of the satanic kingdom.

5. Apostolic Fathers.
According to H. M. Herrick, in the apostolic fathers* there are fifty-two references to the kingdom, of which ten are quotations from the NT; the full phrase "kingdom of God" occurs twenty-seven times. These references maintain several features of Jesus' and his apostles' preachings as well as beginning to enunciate some new features.

5.1. The Coming Kingdom of God. The main emphasis is put on the eschatological or futuristic nature of the kingdom of God. Having been commissioned by the risen Lord Jesus Christ, "the apostles went forth in the assurance of the Holy Spirit and preached the gospel that the kingdom of God was about to come" (*1 Clem.* 42.3). In contrast to the mean and brief life in this world, "the promise of Christ, namely, the rest of the coming kingdom and of eternal life, is great and wonderful" (*2 Clem.* 5.5). We must "await anytime the kingdom of God in love and righteousness, since we know not the day of God's appearing" (*2 Clem.* 12.1). With regard to the kingdom of God that is coming, the NT language of entering into the kingdom of God (e.g., *2 Clem.* 9.6) and inheriting the kingdom

of God (e.g., Ign. *Eph.* 16.1; Ign. *Phld.* 3.3; Pol. *Phil.* 5.3) is also used.

We cannot enter into the kingdom of God by ourselves but only "by God's ability" (*Diogn.* 9.1). God loved humankind and sent his only Son to them, and he promised them the kingdom in heaven and will give it to them (*Diogn.* 10.2). The Son of God is "the rock and the gate" of the kingdom of God; the entrance into the kingdom is only through him or by receiving his name (*Herm. Sim.* 9.12-15). Yet in order to enter or inherit the kingdom we must live a life of love and righteousness (*2 Clem.* 6.9; 9.6; 11.7; 12.1; *Barn.* 21.1) and avoid sins (Pol. *Phil.* 5.3).

5.2. The Kingdom of Christ Future and Present. Sometimes the coming kingdom of God is identified as the kingdom of Christ: the righteous dead "shall be manifested at the visitation of the kingdom of Christ" (*1 Clem.* 50.3). The Lord Jesus will come to redeem the believers and condemn the unbelievers, who will regret bitterly seeing Christ having the sovereignty over the world (*2 Clem.* 17.4-7). Those who desire to attain to his kingdom must receive him through suffering (*Barn.* 7.11).

Yet the kingdom of Christ is already a present reality. "The kingdom of Jesus is on the cross," and "in his kingdom there shall be evil days, in which we shall be saved" (*Barn.* 8.5-6). These sentences seem to express the tension of "already but not yet." It is implied that we have been redeemed out of the kingdom of Satan and transferred into the kingdom of Christ when we are exhorted not to slumber over our sins, lest "the prince of evil should gain power over us [again] and thrust us out of the kingdom of the Lord" (*Barn.* 4.13; cf. Ign. *Eph.* 19.3). So Christ is the king who reigns forever (*Mart. Pol.* 9.3; 17.3; 21.2). Further, *Martyrdom of Polycarp* 22.1, 4 may indicate the beginning of the doctrine of the kingdom of Christ as the present reality in heaven into which the believers enter at death.

5.3. The Kingdom and the Church. In *Didache* 9.4 and *Didache* 10.5-6 there are prayers* for the Lord to gather the church from the four corners of the earth into his kingdom. So the kingdom of God is distinguished from the church. However, in the *Shepherd of Hermas* we begin to see a close association of the church and the kingdom, which is achieved apparently with the help of the conceptions of the temple in Jesus, Paul (1 Cor 3) and 1 Peter 2:4-8: Christ is the rock upon which is built "the building of the tower" (i.e., the church; *Herm. Vis.* 3.3; *Herm. Sim.* 9.13) or "the house of God" (*Herm. Sim.* 9.14). Christians are stones for the building (*Herm. Vis.* 2.4). They enter into the building through its gate, which is Christ, and entrance into it is entrance into the kingdom of God (*Herm. Sim.* 9).

5.4. The Millennial Kingdom. Papias is said to have thought of Christ's millennial kingdom to be set up on earth after the resurrection (Eusebius *Hist. Eccl.* 3.39; Jerome *Vir.* 18).

6. Gospel of Thomas.
There are twenty-two references to the kingdom of God or heaven in this Gnostic* apocryphon. Some of them have parallels in the canonical Synoptics: logion 20 (mustard seed); 22 (entrance as children); 46 (one in the kingdom is superior to John the Baptist); 97 (leaven); 99 (those who do the will of God are Jesus' brothers and mother and will enter the kingdom of God); 107 (a shepherd* seeking one lost sheep); see also 113. The others are quite disparate, but all the kingdom sayings in the *Gospel of Thomas* tend to emphasize the wisdom* motif, minimize the apocalyptic* motif and understand the kingdom in terms of the community of Thomas.

See also CREATION, COSMOLOGY; ESCHATOLOGY; EXALTATION, ENTHRONEMENT; GLORY; GOD; HEAVEN, NEW HEAVEN; LAND IN EARLY CHRISTIANITY; LORD; MILLENNIUM; PAROUSIA.

BIBLIOGRAPHY. S. Aalen, " 'Reign' and 'House' in the Gospels," *NTS* 8 (1961-62) 215-40; R. J. Bauckham, *The Climax of Prophecy: Studies on the Book of Revelation* (Edinburgh: T & T Clark, 1992); G. R. Beasley-Murray, *The Book of Revelation* (Grand Rapids: Eerdmans, 1983); F. F. Bruce, *The Acts of the Apostles* (Grand Rapids: Eerdmans, 1990); P. H. Davids, *Commentary on James* (NIGTC; Grand Rapids: Eerdmans, 1982); J. H. Davies, "The Heavenly Work of Christ in Hebrews," *StEv* 4 (1968) 384-89; J. D. G. Dunn, "Spirit and Kingdom," *ExpT* 82 (1970-71) 36-40; P. Ellingworth, *Commentary on Hebrews* (NIGTC; Grand Rapids: Eerdmans, 1993); E. Ferguson, "The Kingdom of God in Early Patristic Literature" in *The Kingdom of God in 20th-Century Interpretation,* ed. W. Willis (Peabody, MA: Hendrickson, 1987) 191-208; L. Gaston, *No Stone on Another* (Leiden: E. J. Brill, 1970); M. Hengel and A. M. Schwemer, eds., *Königsherrschaft*

Gottes und himmlischer Kult (Tübingen: J. C. B. Mohr, 1991); H. M. Herrick, *The Kingdom of God in the Writings of the Fathers* (Chicago: University of Chicago Press, 1903); K. King, "Kingdom in the Gospel of Thomas" in *Foundations and Facets Forum* 3 (1987) 48-97; H. Koester and T. O. Lambdin, "The Gospel of Thomas" in *The Nag Hammadi Library in English,* ed. J. M. Robinson (San Francisco: Harper, 1988) 124-138; W. L. Lane, *Hebrews* (2 vols.; WBC; Dallas: Word, 1991); J. B. Lightfoot and J. R. Harmer, *The Apostolic Fathers: Greek Texts and English Translations of Their Writings,* ed. and rev. Michael W. Holmes (2d ed.; Grand Rapids: Baker, 1992); I. H. Marshall, *Luke: Historian and Theologian* (Exeter: Paternoster, 1970); K. Wengst, *Schriften des Urchristentums 2: Didache (Apostellehre), Barnabasbrief, Zweiter Klemensbrief, Schrift an Diognet* (Darmstadt: Wissenschaft Buchgesellschaft, 1984). S. Kim

KNOWLEDGE
Knowledge, according to the OT and NT, is attained through a personal relationship between the subject and the object to be known, rather than the Greek idea of theoretical pursuit through observation.

1. Terminology
2. Knowledge in the Old Testament
3. Knowledge in the Later New Testament
4. Knowledge in the Apostolic Fathers
5. Knowledge and Ethics

1. Terminology.
The OT uses the verb *yāḏaʿ* ("to know") and its various cognate forms to express knowledge through experience or learning. The predominant words in the NT include *ginōskō,* ("to know," "to understand," 222 times) and *gnōsis* ("knowledge," 29 times). Other forms that appear include the compounds *epignōsis* and *epiginōskō,* as well as *gnōstos* ("the knowable," "that which is known"). Another word, *oida* (318 times, primarily by John), is used synonymously with *ginōskō* (see Seesemann).

2. Knowledge in the Old Testament.
The meaning and use of *yāḏaʿ* implies a type of knowledge that is personal, experiential, emotional and relational. Thus it is not so much propositional knowledge about something based upon scientific or intellectual comprehension but knowledge discovered through a

personal relationship between the subject and object. Spouses, for example, "know" each other through the sexual intimacy they experience (Gen 4:1, 17, 25; 1 Sam 1:19; cf. Mt 1:25 where *ginōskō* is used for marital relations).

Israel's* knowledge of God* comes from a covenantal* relationship in which God reveals himself through certain historical events (Lev 23:43; Deut 4:32-39, 11:2-7; Ps 9:10; Is 1:2-3, 41:20; Hos 2:19-23), and from which he expects obedience. "Israel's lack of knowledge," notes O. Piper, "is not theoretical ignorance, but rather failure to practice the filial relationship in which they stand with God" (3:43).

3. Knowledge in the Later New Testament.

3.1. General Observations. For the Greeks knowledge is rational, theoretical and speculative. They were more concerned with the essence of things than a relationship between subject and object that carried certain moral obligations. In the mystery religions* *gnōsis* is used as a technical term for secret and esoteric knowledge obtained through visions* and special illumination. The Gnostics* also believed that *gnōsis* was the key to their salvation.* Much of what Paul and John write about knowledge is a corrective to gnosticizing ideas that were threatening the church* in the first century.

The NT continues the OT understanding of knowledge as a relationship (for a detailed analysis and supporting Scripture of the various uses of *ginōskō* see articles in BAGD, *EDNT* and *NIDNTT*). John explains that believers know the Father through the Son (Jn 1:14; 14:7-10; 17:7-8, 25-26; cf. Mt 11:25-27) and continues to describe the importance of the covenantal bond between Jesus and his disciples with the metaphor of sheep and shepherd (Jn 10:14-15). For Paul knowledge of God comes to those who hear the gospel* and are possessed by the Spirit of God (Rom 1:14-17; 10:17; 1 Cor 2:11-14; 8; Eph 3:4-5; Col 1:6; 1 Thess 4:9; *see* Holy Spirit).

3.2. Knowledge in John. Much of the Johannine literature is written to counteract the teachings of Gnosticism and Docetism* (the verb *ginōskō* appears 87 times; *oida,* 127 times). The absence of the noun, *gnōsis,* may be a deliberate attempt on John's part to extricate the term from the Gnostics and replace it with other metaphors for knowing.

John will not tolerate any gnostic concepts that deny the reality of the Incarnation (1 Jn 1:1-4). He sees Jesus as the one whom God sent into the world to reveal the Father (Jn 1:1-14; 14:7-10; 17:7-8, 25-26). One comes to know God through the earthy ministry of Jesus and the signs* *(sēmeion)* that he performs. In distinction from the Gnostics, "John uses *ginōskō* in a theological sense parallel to 'believe' or 'love God' or 'see God,' thereby giving the Gnostics' term an OT and Christian sense" (Schmithals, 1:250). In other words, those who do not believe, see or love* God cannot claim to know God.

3.3. Knowledge in Other New Testament Letters and Revelation. The problem that Paul had with some form of incipient Gnosticism in Corinth became more acute after his death (esp. 1 Cor 1:18—2:16; for further discussion on Paul, *see* DPL, Gnosticism). In the Pastorals, for example, the readers are warned to avoid "profane myths and old wives' tales" (1 Tim 4:7) and "the profane chatter and contradictions of what is falsely called knowledge *[gnōsis]"* (1 Tim 6:20). In order to avoid any confusion between Gnostic and Christian knowledge, it appears the author deliberately changes words, using *epignōsis* instead of *gnōsis* to talk about true knowledge, that is, "knowledge of the truth" (1 Tim 2:4; 2 Tim 2:25, 3:7; Tit 1:1).

The same word is used in Hebrews 10:26 and several places in 2 Peter that emphasize knowledge of God and/or the Lord Jesus Christ* (2 Pet 1:2, 3, 8; 2:20). In Colossians *epignōsis* is used in passages that deliberately distinguish knowledge of God from human knowledge and traditions (Col 1:9, 10; 2:2; 3:10). This appears to confirm W. Hackenberg's observation that although *epignōsis* is used in a general and nontheological way, in a number of places it specifies Christian truth (doctrine) and conduct—"an almost technical sense for the call to the Christian faith" (Hackenberg, 24-25; but note 2 Pet 3:18: "knowledge *[gnōsis]* of our Lord and Savior Jesus Christ"). In 2 Peter 3:3 it clearly refers to understanding the character of the last days (*see* Eschaton). It is probably knowledge of God and his will as expressed in the paraenetic tradition that is referred to in the virtue* list in 2 Peter 1:5-6.

A final ethical* use of knowledge is the instruction to husbands in 1 Peter 3:7 to live with their wives "according to knowledge" (NRSV: "show consideration for your wives"). This is probably a recognition of their "weak" social status and physical strength in comparison with their husbands and of their equality with their husbands as "fellow heirs of the gift of life." Failure in this area, for example, by taking advantage of their wives' vulnerability, will hinder the husbands' prayers.*

Revelation 2:4 has what is probably an ironic use of "knowledge." The knowledge that "Jezebel" probably presented as deep prophetic insight into divine truth is referred to by John as knowledge of the "deep things of Satan," which may or may not have had gnosticizing elements.

4. Knowledge in the Apostolic Fathers.

Both *gnōsis* and *epignōsis* appear in the early fathers in a general, nonreligious sense as knowing someone or something (*Barn.* 2.3; 9.8; *Diogn.* 12.2; 12.4; *1 Clem.* 41.4; 48.5; *Barn.* 13.7; Ign. *Rom.* 10.2). Far more frequent and important, however, are the number of times the Fathers use these terms while addressing moral and religious concerns. Clement* (*1 Clem.* 1.2; 36.2; 59.2; *2 Clem.* 3.1), Barnabas* (6.9; 11.4; 21.5), Ignatius* (Ign. *Eph.* 17.2), Justin (Justin *Dial. Tryph.* 14.1) and Tatian (Tatian *Or. Graec.* 42.1), for example, speak about the knowledge of God* and Jesus (see also *Herm. Sim.* 9.18.1; *Diogn.* 10.1; *Did.* 9.3; 10.2). In other cases there are specific references to "the truth"*—i.e., true doctrine (*Barn.* 18.1; Tatian *Or. Graec.* 13.1; Justin *Apol.* II 2.2; Justin *Dial. Tryph.* 27.4; 39.5; 69.1; Ign. *Phld.* 1.2).

5. Knowledge and Ethics.

The preceding discussion revealed a consistent relationship between knowledge and ethics. To know something is to act upon that knowledge. In the OT those who know God and are known by him through a covenant relationship are summoned to obedience.* In Paul, those who know God through Christ continue in the faith* (2 Cor 4:6; Gal 4:9), serve God (Phil 1:9; 1 Thess 1:9), live by the Spirit and value love as the highest gift (1 Cor). True knowledge for John also expresses itself in action. To know God is to abide in him, obey the truth, keep his commandments* and love their family members (e.g., Jn 15; 1 Jn 2:3-5, 29; 3:16, 19, 24; 4:7-21; *Barn.* 5.4; 19.1). A similar focus is observable in later documents and some of the Fathers (Col 1:9-10; 3:10; 2 Pet 1:8; 2:20-21; *Barn.* 5.4; 19.1; *2 Clem.* 3.1).

See also GNOSIS, GNOSTICISM; REVEAL, REVELATION; TRUTH; WISDOM.

BIBLIOGRAPHY. J. Bergman and G. Botterwick, "עדי" *TDOT* 5:448-81; R. Bultmann, "γινώσκω," *TDNT* 4:689-719; E. E. Ellis, "Wisdom and Knowledge in 1 Corinthians," *TynB* 25 (1974) 82-98; W. Hackenberg, "ἐπιγνώσκω" "ἐπίγνωσις," *EDNT* 2:24-25; O. Piper, "Knowledge," *IDB* 3:42-48; K. Rudolph, *Gnosis* (San Francisco: Harper, 1983); W. Schmithals, "γινώσκω," *EDNT* 1:248-51; idem, *Gnosticism in Corinth* (Nashville: Abingdon, 1971); idem, *Paul and the Gnostics* (Nashville: Abingdon, 1972); E. Schmitz, "Knowledge," *NIDNTT* 2:393-406; H. Seesemann, "οἶδα," *TDNT* 5:116-19.

A. G. Patzia

KOINONIA. *See* FELLOWSHIP.

L

LAMB

Jesus appears as God's lamb at significant points in early Christian texts. This article surveys the uses in Revelation (*see* Revelation, Book of), Acts* and 1 Peter,* giving special attention to Revelation (which calls Jesus the Lamb* more than twenty-five times, making "lamb" one of the book's primary christological* titles).

1. The Lamb in Johannine Texts
2. 1 Peter 1:19
3. Acts 8:32
4. Conclusion

1. The Lamb in Johannine Texts.

1.1. The Lamb in the Fourth Gospel. Because many scholars concede that the Fourth Gospel and Revelation issued from the same community, discussions concerning the term *lamb* in one Johannine document may be relevant to the other. Scholars have proposed various backgrounds for the Johannine lamb (sometimes separate ones for Jn 1:29 and Rev 5:6): apocalyptic* lambs, the lamb of Isaiah 53:7, and Passover and sacrificial* lambs. Dodd (230-38) and Barrett (218) compare John's lamb to the eschatological* horned lambs of the messianic era in *1 Enoch* 89-90 (Morris, 146, sees this as relevant for Revelation but not for the Fourth Gospel).

But *1 Enoch's* apocalyptic lambs bear no specific function more relevant to Jesus than most of *1 Enoch's* other numerous symbols; indeed, some other Jewish texts speak of horned lambs without eschatological significance (e.g., paschal lambs in *t. Pesaḥ* 6.7). The image of a lamb conveyed more general nuances in literature widely read in this period (Wis 19:9; cf. Lk 10:3). The earliest supposedly non-Christian use of "lamb" for the Messiah himself is a Christian interpolation in *Testament of Joseph* 19:8, so one cannot appeal to a messianic lamb to support the theory of an eschatological lamb.

Many find in John 1:29 the language of Isaiah's Suffering Servant (e.g., Taylor, 138-39; Schnackenburg, 1:300). As common as this image became in early Christianity, however, more dominant lamb imagery overshadows the isolated mention of the Servant as a lamb in Isaiah 53:7 (e.g., *1 Clem.* 16.7). The Fourth Gospel portrays Jesus' death in terms of the Passover lamb (Jn 18:28; 19:36) and reports John the Baptist proclaiming Jesus as a lamb (Jn 1:29) in the context of a new exodus and a new redemption* (Jn 1:23) expected by Judaism* (regardless of how John the Baptist may have meant it; Barrett, 218). The primary background of the Johannine lamb must be that of the sacrificial Passover lamb, whatever other elements may also appear (e.g., Schnackenburg, 1:299-300). (Early Judaism apparently attached the nuances of sacrifice to Passover; cf. Josephus *Ant.* 2.312.)

1.2. The Paschal Lamb in Revelation. The image of the paschal lamb that fits the Fourth Gospel also seems to fit Revelation and the reference in 1 Peter (Rev. 5:6; 7:14; 1 Pet 1:19; cf. 1 Cor 5:7; Minear, 102-3). In Revelation 5, the "lamb having been slaughtered" is the Passover lamb (with possible additional allusions to Isaiah 53:7; Taylor, 36; Hillyer) whose blood delivers God's people from the coming plagues (Rev 7:3). But this passage also portrays the lamb in union with the martyrs,* for Revelation 6:9 identifies the martyrs as sacrifices:* they appear beneath the altar, where the blood of sacrifices was poured (Beasley-Murray, 135; Ladd 1978, 39). (This interpretation seems secure; 4 Macc 9:24 also portrays martyrs as sacrifices, and early Christian texts often used similar imagery: Phil 2:17; 2 Tim 4:6; Ign. *Eph.* 8.1; *Mart. Pol.* 14.2; cf. Ign. *Rom.* 4.1.)

Commentators often find in the seven horns a symbol of strength and power* borrowed from apocalyptic texts (Ford, 86; Beasley-Murray, 125); this being the case, the most significant feature of the text is that the power appears in weakness. The great lion (Rev 5:5) turns out to be a slain lamb (Rev 5:6). That the lamb's eyes derive from God's eyes in Zechariah 4:10 also underscores Revelation's divine christology (see Bruce, 335). Legal documents typically had seven seals: seven witnesses imprinted their signet rings in hot wax to seal the seven threads surrounding the document, thus ensuring that no one tampered with it until it was opened under official circumstances. Some commentators have suggested that a specific legal document, namely, a will, is in view here (Ladd 1974, 623). In this case the book may be the inheritance in the Lamb's book of life, the validity of its contents attested by the judgments* of the seven seals (see Scrolls). Significantly, however, wills could not be opened until the death of the one who made the will (so Heb 9:16). Thus only when the sacrificed Lamb took the throne could the book begin to be opened.

2. 1 Peter 1:19.

Commentators have suggested that the redemptive blood is the counterpart to the sacrifice at Jewish proselytes' conversion (Reicke, 85), an interpretation that makes sense if Peter's audience represent Gentile* converts who rejected their former idolatry.* Because texts addressing conversion primarily stress circumcision and baptism,* however, so narrow an allusion might have been obscure to ancient hearers (especially Gentiles). That the allusion is to Passover is far more likely (e.g., Selwyn, 146), especially given probable contextual allusions like "girding one's mind up" (1 Pet 1:13; see Ex 12:11; Kelly, 65; Reicke, 83; contrast Best, 84).

3. Acts 8:32.

Some think the emphasis of this quotation from Isaiah 53 is waiting on God* while suffering persecution,* rather than Jesus' vicarious death (e.g., Decock; see Death of Christ). But Luke often assumes his readers' knowledge of the rest of a text (e.g., Lk 4:18-19) as Jewish teachers generally did (e.g., y. Qidd. 4:1, §2), and the widespread use of Isaiah 53 in early Christianity suggests that the citation would recall the whole passage to many hearers' memories.

4. Conclusion.

The primary background for the image of Jesus as a lamb in early Christianity was the Passover lamb, combined with allusions to sacrificial lambs; the secondary background was probably the image of the Suffering Servant as a lamb in Isaiah 53:7, a passage to which early Christians devoted much attention. In the person of Jesus early Christians found both paschal lamb and Suffering Servant; hence, they often may have failed to draw a significant distinction between the two roles.

See also CHRISTOLOGY; REVELATION, BOOK OF; SHEPHERD, FLOCK.

BIBLIOGRAPHY. C. K. Barrett, "The Lamb of God," *NTS* 1 (1955) 210-18; G. R. Beasley-Murray, *The Book of Revelation* (NCB; Greenwood, SC: Attic, 1974); E. Best, *1 Peter* (NCB; Greenwood, SC: Attic, 1971); F. F. Bruce, "The Spirit in the Apocalypse" in *Christ and Spirit in the New Testament: Studies in Honour of C. F. D. Moule*, ed. B. Lindars and S. S. Smalley (Cambridge: Cambridge University Press, 1973) 333-44; P. B. Decock, "The Understanding of Isaiah 53:7-8 in Acts 8:32-33," *Neot* 14 (1981) 111-33; C. H. Dodd, *The Interpretation of the Fourth Gospel* (Cambridge: Cambridge University Press, 1965); J. M. Ford, *Revelation* (AB; Garden City, NY: Doubleday, 1975); N. Hillyer, " 'The Lamb' in the Apocalypse," *EvQ* 39 no. 4 (1967) 228-36; J. N. D. Kelly, *A Commentary on the Epistles of Peter and Jude* (Grand Rapids: Baker, 1981); G. E. Ladd, *The Last Things* (Grand Rapids: Eerdmans, 1978); idem, *A Theology of the New Testament* (Grand Rapids: Eerdmans, 1974); P. S. Minear, *Images of the Church in the New Testament* (Philadelphia: Westminster, 1960); L. Morris, *The Gospel According to John: The English Text with Introduction, Exposition and Notes* (NICNT; Grand Rapids: Eerdmans, 1971); B. Reicke, *The Epistles of James, Peter, and Jude* (AB; Garden City, NY: Doubleday, 1964); R. Schnackenburg, *The Gospel According to St. John,* (3 vols.; New York: Herder & Herder, 1968) vol. 1; E. G. Selwyn, *The First Epistle of St. Peter: The Greek Text with Introduction, Notes and Essays* (2d ed.; New York: Macmillan, 1947); V. Taylor, *The Atonement in New Testament Teaching* (London: Epworth, 1945). C. S. Keener

LAND IN EARLY CHRISTIANITY

The land of Israel belonged to Judaism's understanding of itself. Early Christianity's identity, however, was not closely tied to the land, and the NT focuses not on the holiness* of a place but the holiness of a person, Jesus Christ; in

Christian literature christology* displaces territorial theology. The land, nonetheless, retained significance (if sometimes perhaps only symbolic) for Christian eschatology.*

1. Jewish Background
2. Earliest Christianity
3. Acts of the Apostles
4. Revelation
5. Conclusion

1. Jewish Background.

The importance of and veneration for the land appear from a number of legends about Palestine: it was protected during Noah's flood and remained dry (Pseudo-Philo *Bib. Ant.* 7.4; *b. Zebaḥ.* 113a); it lies at the center of the earth (*Jub.* 8:19; *Sib. Or.* 5:250); it is holier than any other land (*m. Kelim* 1:6-9); to leave it for a foreign country is to lose the merits of the fathers (*b. B. Bat.* 91a); in the great tribulation at the end of time those within its borders will be spared affliction (*2 Apoc. Bar.* 29:2; 40:2; 71:1; cf. Joel 2:32); at the resurrection of the dead the just outside the land will roll through underground tunnels until they emerge from a cleft Mount of Olives, in the middle of—to use a term found already in Zechariah 2:12—"the holy land" (*b. Ketub.* 111a [which also records the opinion that those who die outside the land will not rise from the dead]; *Tg.* Cant 8.5; *Gen. Rab.* 96:5). This glorification of the land is especially strong in the rabbinic sources. *b. Berakot.* 15a asserts that God gave Israel three precious gifts: "the Torah, the land of Israel, the world to come."

1.1. The Old Testament. In Genesis 15:18-21 God promises the land of Israel to Abraham's* descendants (cf. Gen 17:8). This promise is central to the Hexateuch, whose major events revolve around the land: the Hebrew ancestors enter the land; famine later moves them to leave the land and enter Egypt, where their descendants become enslaved—until Moses* intervenes to free them and lead them back to the promised land; when Moses dies without having achieved his goal, Joshua becomes his successor and leads the conquest of Canaan. Israel's foundational narrative then is largely about the land, which is given to Abraham's offspring by divine authority—it belongs to God (Lev 25:23; Josh 22:19)—and for the obtaining of which God works many miracles.

1.2. The Land in Eschatology. In the OT proph-

ets there are not only predictions of doom against the land (as in Jer 6:8; 25:38; Joel 2:3) but also many prophecies of its restoration (Is 2:2-4; Amos 9:11-15; etc.). In later times such prophecies were read as properly eschatological: a regathered Israel will forever live in a renewed land. As *Psalms of Solomon* 17:28 puts it, in the latter days God will distribute the tribes of Israel "upon the land according to their tribes." This belief was widespread.

2. Earliest Christianity.

2.1. The Jesus Tradition. There is surprisingly little about the land in the sayings attributed to Jesus. Matthew 5:5 does refer to inheriting the land (*gēn;* cf. Ps 36:11 LXX), and Matthew 8:11 par. Luke 13:29 may presuppose that Jerusalem or Palestine is the goal of the eschatological pilgrimage of either Gentiles* (so most interpreters) or (more likely) diaspora Jews. But Matthew 19:28 speaks of a "new world" (*palingenesia*) in which the Twelve will rule over the twelve tribes; and while this could refer to a literal messianic kingdom centered in Israel, it more probably refers to a new or renewed earth. This raises the possibility that for Jesus, as already for some Jews, restoration to the land had become a symbol of some transhistorical reality (cf. *m. Sanh.* 10:1 and *b. Sanh.* 110b, where inheriting the land is equated with life in the world to come). In any case the paucity of material shows that Jesus neither offered details on future cosmological states nor spoke much about the land.

2.2. The Primitive Community. It is plausible that some of Jesus' Galilean followers remained in Jerusalem*—the quintessence of the land—in part because they thought it would be the center of eschatological events; that is, they hoped that the Messiah would return to the Mount of Olives and establish in the capital an earthly kingdom. According to Acts 1:6, some wondered whether Jesus might not "restore the kingdom to Israel" in the near future; and Acts 1:11 has been taken to mean that when Jesus returns from heaven for his Second Coming he will descend to the Mount of Olives.

3. Acts of the Apostles.

In Luke-Acts, which retells the story of God's promise of the land to Abraham (Acts 7:2-8), a mystique surrounds the land and its capital. Jesus' story begins and ends in the holy city (Lk

1—2; 24); the church has its birth there (Acts 1—9); and even the apostle to the Gentiles feels bound to return to Israel (Acts 20—23). There is also, however, simultaneously a demoting of Jerusalem (and so necessarily the land): the capital rejects Jesus and the prophets (Acts 7:52). Especially noteworthy is Stephen's* speech in Acts 7. It implicitly rejects the sort of territorial theology later found in rabbinic sources such as *Mekilta* on Exodus 12:1, where divine revelation given outside Israel is a stumbling block. According to Stephen, God revealed himself to Abraham not in Israel but in Mesopotamia (Acts 7:2); Joseph received divine assistance when he was outside the land (Acts 7:9-10); Israel's deliverer, Moses, was raised in a foreign court, spent years in Midian, and stood on "holy ground" outside Israel (Acts 7:20-43); the exile to Babylon was God's will (Acts 7:43); and the Jerusalem temple does not contain God, whose throne is heaven, whose footstool is earth (Acts 7:44-50). There appears to be in all this an emphasis upon God's extra-territorial activity—an emphasis consistent with a book which tells of God's Spirit falling upon people regardless of their location or ethnic identity. Still, Acts contains very little explicit teaching, positive or negative, on the land of Israel. As in the Gospels, the land is a vital presence whose significance is assumed rather than discussed; and it is overshadowed by other things.

4. Revelation.

The Apocalypse not only seems to assume that certain eschatological events will take place in the land of Israel (Rev 11:1-13; 14:1), it also may teach a millennial kingdom (*see* Millennium): Jesus will return and reign for a thousand years (Rev 20:1-10). But if so, nothing is said about the territorial aspects of that kingdom. (Contrast Justin Martyr *Dial. Tryph.* 80: the saints will live a thousand years in Jerusalem.) We do not, for instance, read that it is to be centered in Jerusalem or located in Palestine (cf. Papias in Irenaeus *Adv. haer.* 5.33.3; there too the dramatic fertility of the earth during the messianic kingdom is not localized). Perhaps the location of events in Palestine is assumed by the text, but there is certainly no plain statement to that effect. Once more, then, we see that despite the influence of Jewish eschatological expectation there is no focus upon the land as such. This is characteristic of early Christianity in general.

5. Conclusion.

There is a dearth of explicit reflection upon the Jewish doctrine of the land in Acts and other early Christian writings. The silence is surprising given the large amount of reflection on the other central symbols of Jewish theology— the one God who acts in history, the Torah, the people of God. Whatever be the explanation for this—lack of interest on the part of the Jesus tradition, a similar lack of concern among Gentiles, religious experience outside the land, the spiritualization of territory (already attested in Jewish sources: Philo and *T. Job* 33:5-7)—the theological point is clear: holy space is where Jesus Christ is (Ign. *Smyrn.* 8.2); and because as risen Lord he is free to move where he wills, there can be no sacred as opposed to profane territory, no genuine "holy land." Christ's ubiquity as a spiritual presence universalizes the notion of holy space and so inescapably relativizes the sanctity and significance of the land promised to Abraham's descendants.

See also ABRAHAM; CHRISTIANITY AND JUDAISM; CREATION, COSMOLOGY; ESCHATOLOGY; MILLENNIUM.

BIBLIOGRAPHY. W. Brueggemann, *The Land* (Philadelphia: Fortress, 1977); W. D. Davies, *The Gospel and the Land: Early Christianity and Jewish Territorial Doctrine* (Berkeley: University of California, 1974); idem, *The Territorial Dimension of Judaism* (Minneapolis: Fortress, 1991).

D. C. Allison Jr.

LAST DAYS. *See* ESCHATOLOGY.

LAW

The relationship between Christians and the Mosaic Torah was one of the most disputed and complex issues in the early church.* The law* comes to the forefront in the Pauline writings (*see* DPL, Law) and receives considerable attention in the Synoptics and the Gospel of John (*see* DJG, Law). In the literature under consideration in this volume, the Mosaic law is not as prominent. For instance, the Mosaic law is not the subject of discussion in Revelation (*see* Revelation, Book of), 1 and 2 Peter,* Jude* and 3 John (*see* John, Letters of). In 2 John 4-6 it is treated in a glancing way when the author commends keeping the commandments,* but the relationship of commandments to the Mosaic law here is disputed. More promising, although frustratingly brief and ambiguous, are texts relating to the law in James* and 1 John. The law crops up in Acts* on a number of occasions and is prominent in the letter to the Hebrews.*

1. James
2. 1 John
3. Hebrews
4. Acts of the Apostles
5. Apostolic Fathers

1. James.

James describes the law as "the perfect law of liberty" (Jas 1:25), "the royal law" (Jas 2:8) and "the law of liberty" (Jas 2:12). To what does the word *law (nomos)* refer here? Scholars have often remarked that James hails from conservative Jewish Christian circles (*see* Jewish Christianity), and thus one might think that the entire OT law is intended. For instance, the early Christian sect called the Ebionites* demanded the observance of circumcision.* But it is doubtful that the reference is to whole OT law, for James nowhere commands believers to keep any part of the ceremonial law. For instance, he never says anything about circumcision, food laws* and sabbath. And his letter would be a fitting place to address these matters, for he probably corrects a false understanding of Paul's view of justification. So too the letter would be an appropriate place to counter the Pauline teaching on circumcision. His silence on this issue is likely to be an indication that he agreed with Paul that circumcision was unnecessary. Indeed, Acts 15:13-21 and Galatians 2:1-10 confirm that James did not believe circumcision should be required of Gentile* converts. We may conclude then that James 2:10, "For whoever keeps the whole law, but stumbles in one matter, has become guilty of all," does not require adherence to the ceremonial law.

If *nomos* does not refer to the ceremonial law, to what does James refer? James 2:8-12 is the central text for answering this question. The "royal law" is in accord with the OT command to love one's neighbor as oneself (Lev 19:18). It seems, therefore, that the "royal law" is from the OT. James 2:11 substantiates this interpretation, for there the law is explained in terms of the prohibitions against murder and adultery (Ex 20:13-14; Deut 5:17-18). The "law" in James, therefore, seems to refer to the moral norms of the OT law, and love* is the apex and heart of the law's requirement.

It is also instructive to note that James estab-

lishes a connection between "law" *(nomos)* and "word" *(logos)* in James 1:21-25. The readers are commanded to "receive the implanted word which is able to save your souls" (Jas 1:21) and to be "doers of the word" and not just hearers of it (Jas 1:22-23). In James 1:25 the doing of the word is explained in other terms, i.e., abiding "in the perfect law of liberty." We conclude that doing the "word" and keeping the "law" are synonymous for James. The idea that the word is "implanted" and "saves" most likely reflects Jeremiah 31:31-34, a passage in which Jeremiah promises that the law will be written on the heart and that people will be enabled to keep God's commands when the new covenant* is fulfilled. This is probably why James says the law is one of "liberty" (Jas 1:25; 2:12), for the implanting of the law indicates God has provided the strength to keep the law and that doing the word is a freeing and liberating experience, not a burden.

The reference to the "word" and the "law" in this text must also be explained in terms of the gospel* of Jesus Christ, for it is this gospel which saves. Many scholars have rightly argued that the letter to James depends on the teaching* of Jesus, especially the Sermon on the Mount (the *Didache** also witnesses to the tradition shared by Matthew and James, *Did.* 1.2-5). The "law of liberty" and "the royal law," therefore, cannot be separated from the message of the gospel and the teaching of Jesus. The moral norms of the OT law and the call to love are realized to their fullest extent in the teaching of Jesus of Nazareth and reflected in the teaching of James. It seems fair to conclude that the OT law is interpreted by James in the light of the Christ event, and it would even be fitting to say that the "law of Christ" is the authoritative standard for believers and that this law contains the moral norms of the OT law.

2. 1 John.

John often emphasizes that believers should keep God's commandments (1 Jn 2:3, 4, 7, 8; 3:22, 23, 24; 4:21; 5:2-3; 2 Jn 4, 5, 6). The content of the commandments is not specified in detail, except the command to love one another and to believe in Jesus as Messiah (1 Jn 3:22-24; 4:21; 5:2; 2 Jn 4-6). The love commandment is presumably what John has in mind when he refers to the "old" command that is "new" in him (1 Jn 2:7-11). Jesus' call to love one another as he has loved the disciples (Jn 13:34-35) is likely the "old" command. John probably calls it old to emphasize that the message he imparts does not deviate from the truth they have always known (cf. 1 Jn 2:18-27). But love has now become a reality because of the coming of Jesus Christ, who has begun to dispel the darkness of the old age by introducing the light of the new age. John seems to be saying that the ability to love one another is a gift of the new age inaugurated by Jesus.

R. E. Brown has remarked that there is a close connection between "word" *(logos)* and "commandment" *(entolē)* in Johannine writings. This is borne out by 1 John 2:3-6, where knowing God is described in terms of keeping "his commandments" (1 Jn 2:3-4) and also as "keeping his word" (1 Jn 2:5; cf. 2:7). The "commandments" and the "word" probably hearken back to the "ten words" (Ex 34:28) Moses inscribed upon the stone tablets. Thereby John suggests that those who believe Jesus is the Christ and love their brothers and sisters fulfill the OT law, which is itself summed up in the Ten Commandments. John does not envision keeping the commandments in one's own strength. Those who do so "have been born of God" (1 Jn 5:1), signifying that his seed provides the power.* And "the victory which overcomes the world is our faith" (1 Jn 5:4), indicating that our trust in God's power is the foundation of our obedience.*

3. Hebrews.

The letter to the Hebrews contains an elegant argument for the supersession of the Mosaic law, in particular the obsolescence of the Aaronic priesthood* and the OT sacrifices.* The author's thesis is that Jesus is the Melchizedekean priest predicted in the OT (Ps 110:4). The fact that a new priesthood was anticipated demonstrates that the Aaronic priesthood was not intended to be permanent (Heb 7:11). And if a new priest has arisen, a new law must be enacted, "for when the priesthood is changed, of necessity there is a change of law also" (Heb 7:12).

The inferiority of the old priesthood is impressed upon the reader with a series of stunning contrasts: Aaronic priests served without an oath while Jesus received an oath (Heb 7:21-22); there were many priests in the old order because death prevented them from continuing

to serve as priests, but Jesus abides as a priest forever since he always lives to make effective intercession for his people (Heb 7:23-25); Aaronic priests had to offer sacrifices for their own sins* as fallible and flawed human beings, whereas the sinless Son offered up one effective sacrifice for the sins of all human beings (Heb 7:26-28). Aaronic priests stand daily since their work of atoning for sins is never finished (Heb 10:11), but the Son sits triumphantly at the right hand of God since his one sacrifice was definitive and effective (Heb 10:12-14). Similarly the sacrifice of Jesus is infinitely superior to the sacrifices offered under the old covenant. Animal sacrifices have to be repeated since they do not cleanse the conscience* from sin (Heb 10:1-2, 11), but Christ through one sacrifice has cleansed the conscience from sin forever (Heb 9:25-28; 10:12-14). Animals are brute victims whose blood is spilled, but they have no conception of the significance of their sacrifice (Heb 10:3-4); the Son as a human being offered himself voluntarily for the salvation* of others (Heb 10:5-10).

When the author refers to the "weakness and uselessness" of the "former commandment" (Heb 7:18) and claims that "the law made nothing perfect," he is reflecting on its inability to effect forgiveness of sins and to bring believers into God's* presence. This is evident in Hebrews 7:19, for the work of Christ on the cross* was effective because through it "we draw near to God." It is here that the author finds fault with the old covenant; it could not accomplish forgiveness* of sins (Heb 8:7-13; 10:16-18). The very promise that a new covenant would commence signals that the old is inadequate and doomed to obsolescence.

The author of Hebrews does not deny the historical validity of the old covenant, nor does he allegorize the laws of the OT so that they are robbed of their literal meaning, nor does he dismiss OT practices as absurd and irrational (see the discussion in 5 below by way of contrast). He has a sense of salvation history that is remarkably lacking in the *Epistle of Barnabas** and the *Epistle to Diognetus.** The OT priesthood, sacrifices and covenant are inferior to the new covenant according to Hebrews, but they played a positive role in redemptive history. The priests, sacrifices and tabernacle* (Heb 8:1—9:28) functioned as types or patterns of the work of Christ. The content of OT revelation* is not denigrated as in *Barnabas* but is ascribed a particular place in the history of salvation. OT sacrifices and priests played a proper role in their era, pointing to the fulfillment that would be enacted when the true priest and sacrifice arrived. Now that the fulfillment of the old covenant has arrived returning to the old way deserves judgment, but the old way was instituted by God himself as a prelude and pointer to the salvation to come. For instance, the entrance into the land under Joshua anticipates the heavenly rest available for God's people (Heb 3:7—4:13). Similarly, resting on the sabbath anticipates the eschatological* sabbath rest (Heb 4:3-11).

4. Acts of the Apostles.
The Lukan view of the law may be discerned from both Luke's Gospel and Acts, but here we shall confine ourselves to Acts (see *DJG*, Law, for a discussion of the Gospel of Luke). The Lukan theology of the law is a matter of debate. For instance, J. Jervell thinks that Luke's view is the most conservative in the NT, while S. G. Wilson argues that Luke is ambiguous on the question. One can understand why Luke would be designated as conservative, for the church in Acts seems to abide by the Torah. They worship* in the temple (Acts 3:1-10), the charge that Stephen violates the law is false (Acts 6:11-14), and Stephen says the law contains "living words" (Acts 7:38; cf. Acts 7:53). Paul is portrayed as a law-abiding Jew: he accepts the apostolic decree (Acts 15:22-29), circumcises Timothy (Acts 16:3), takes a Nazirite vow (Acts 21:21-26; cf. 18:18) and insists that he has never transgressed the law (Acts 24:14-16; 25:8; 28:17).

C. L. Blomberg and M. A. Seifrid (see also Turner) have convincingly argued that the most satisfying perspective from which to understand Luke's theology of the law is salvation history. The OT prophecies are fulfilled in the ministry, death and resurrection of Jesus (Acts 2:16-36; 3:11-26; 4:11; 8:32-35; 13:16-41; 15:13-21; 24:13-14; 26:22-23, 27; see Death of Christ). The Mosaic law was provisional but has been displaced now that the fulfillment of the law has come, Jesus the Messiah. Thus Paul proclaims in Acts 13:38-39 that forgiveness and justification are now available through Jesus Christ and that the law of Moses did not provide forgiveness or justification. Similarly in Acts 15:10-11 Peter argues that the law was a yoke that the Jews

could not bear. J. Nolland has rightly argued that the intention of the verse is not to say that the Mosaic law is an oppressive burden. Instead the purpose is to say that no one could keep the law. Thus Peter concludes in Acts 15:11 that salvation is through the grace of the Lord Jesus Christ rather than through the Mosaic law.

The salvation-historical dimension of the law is also apparent in Acts 10:1—11:18 and Acts 15:1-29. In the former text Peter is enjoined in a vision* to eat unclean foods. Peter is puzzled as to why he is commanded to violate the OT law that specifically prohibits consuming the foods that were represented in the vision (Lev 11:1-45; Deut 14:3-21), but the rationale for the vision dawns upon him as the story unfolds. Immediately after this ecstatic experience he was summoned to the house of Cornelius.* As Gentiles Cornelius and his friends were considered to be "unclean," and thus Jews could eat with them only if purity laws were observed. While Peter was explaining the gospel of Jesus Christ, God poured out his Spirit (see Holy Spirit) upon Cornelius and his friends to indicate that Gentiles could be part of the people of God without the imposition of the Mosaic law.

The relationship of Jews and Gentiles in the church came to a head in the apostolic council of Acts 15. The successful missionary tour of Paul and Barnabas (Acts 13—14) led to an influx of Gentiles into the church. Some Jewish Christians from the pharisaic wing of the church were concerned that the OT law and the distinctive place of the Jews were being abandoned since Gentiles were streaming into the church without being circumcised. They argued that circumcision was necessary for salvation (Acts 15:1, 5). A meeting of the church was called in Jerusalem* to discuss this matter, and it was determined that Gentiles could be members of the church without being circumcised. The gift of the Holy Spirit to Cornelius and his friends played a decisive role in the debate (Acts 15:7-11), for if God gave the Spirit apart from circumcision, then it must not be required for entrance into the church. James argued that the OT Sriptures themselves anticipated the inclusion of Gentiles apart from the imposition of the law (Acts 15:13-21). Both Acts 10:1—11:18 and Acts 15:1-29 demonstrate that Luke should hardly be characterized as the most conservative writer in the NT with reference to the law, for the OT law required circumcision and the observance of food laws. Luke sees these as passé now that the fulfillment of the OT law has arrived and the promise to Abraham* that all nations should be blessed is becoming a reality.

The addition of the four requirements of the apostolic decree (see *DPL,* Jerusalem §4.2.3), namely, abstention from immorality *(porneia; see* Purity), blood, food contaminated by idols, and that which was strangled, seems puzzling. Has Luke introduced other requirements of the law after circumcision has been dismissed as necessary? The complexity of the apostolic decree warrants more discussion than is possible here, but these four requirements were probably retained as a means of facilitating fellowship* between Jews and Gentiles. The church emphatically rejected the notion that Gentiles must observe the law (i.e., circumcision) in order to obtain salvation, but they were not opposed to the temporary observance of parts of the law as a way of preserving fellowship between Jews and Gentiles. Jewish sensibilities received some consideration at the apostolic council, while the idea that circumcision should be required for salvation was rejected.

It is probable that not all Jewish Christians concurred with or abided by the decision of the council (*see* Jewish Christianity). This seems confirmed by second-century evidence, for the Jewish Christian sect called the Ebionites* (lit. "the poor") demanded the observance of the OT law and circumcision. Most of our information about the Ebionites derives from the early church fathers, but the sources are fragmentary and thus our understanding of Ebionism is partial and cannot be harmonized into a coherent unity. They rejected Paul's view of the law. Most Ebionites denied the Virgin Birth and all seem to have rejected the preexistence* of Christ. Scholars debate whether the Pseudo-Clementines derive from the Ebionites, especially the *Kerygmata Petrou* (Sermons of Peter). Certainty eludes us since the literary history and composition of the Clementine literature are complex. One interesting feature is that the Pauline view of the law is fiercely rejected by Peter in this literature. The Pseudo-Clementines may also reflect in places the views of the sect called the Elkesaites, for the latter required circumcision and sabbath observance, although they rejected OT sacrifices. Some scholars have suggested that the Ebionites are derived from the Elkesaites, but again this is hypothetical and cannot

be established. The relationship of the Ebionites to the *Gospel of the Nazoraeans* has also been intensely studied, but unfortunately no firm conclusions may be drawn.

The law-abiding Paul of Acts has stimulated much discussion. Many scholars contend that the circumcision of Timothy by Paul (Acts 16:3) and his taking of a Nazirite vow (Acts 21:21-26) are historically incredible and betray Lukan theology rather than Pauline history. Several things should be said briefly in response to this. Lukan history and theology need not and should not be pitted against each other. Modern scholarship rightly stresses that Luke is a theologian, but theology and history are not mutually exclusive. Nor are the Pauline accommodations to the law in Acts foreign to the spirit of the Pauline letters. 1 Corinthians 9:19-23 indicates that Paul adopted a flexible stance on the law in order to advance his mission. Paul invariably resisted the imposition of the law on Gentiles for salvation, but he was not averse to some observance of the law by Gentiles to accommodate Jewish culture. The narrative of Acts 15—16 underscores this very point: circumcision is not required to be part of the people of God, yet Paul accedes to the circumcision of Timothy (Acts 16:3) in order to advance his mission.

5. Apostolic Fathers.

The writer of the *Epistle of Barnabas* moves in the direction of Marcion,* although he does not dispense with the OT as Marcion did. He not only argues that the "new law" of Jesus Christ is in force (*Barn.* 2.6) but also strenuously argues against submission to the Mosaic law (*Barn.* 3.6) by suggesting that the Mosaic covenant was flawed from the outset. He declares that God did not even command the sacrifices enjoined in the OT (*Barn.* 2.4-10). Food laws, circumcision, the sabbath and the temple* are stripped of their literal meaning even in the OT and are understood to refer to spiritual realities: the food laws are understood to refer to moral commands, circumcision is spiritual and anticipates the cross of Christ, the sabbath anticipates the eschatological rest that is celebrated in advance on the Lord's day, and the church is the Lord's true temple (*Barn.* 9.1—10.12; 15.1—16.10). The writer of Barnabas apparently expected the Jews to understand that the OT law from its inception pointed to Christ and rebuked them for observing the law literally. Indeed, the covenant with the Jews was abolished from the time that Moses broke the tablets (*Barn.* 4.6-8; 14.1-4). The author also suggests (*Barn.* 9.4) that physical circumcision was instituted at the behest of an evil angel,* criticizes the Jews because they understood the food laws literally (*Barn.* 10.9) and contends that the temple was never a special place for God's residence (*Barn.* 16.1).

Another instructive comparison is with the *Epistle to Diognetus.* The author rejects circumcision, fasting, sabbath, food laws and the observance of days because these things are ridiculous and irrational (*Diogn.* 4.1-6). OT sacrifices are virtually equivalent to idolatrous offerings since they imply God needed our offerings (*Diogn.* 3.1-5; *see* Idolatry).

Interestingly Ignatius* in *The Letter to the Magnesians* 9.1 says Christians should observe the Lord's day (called the eighth day in memory of the resurrection*) rather than the sabbath. No sustained explanation for this exhortation is supplied, but elsewhere Ignatius categorically rejects Judaism* because it is not according to grace* and it deters one from centering on Christ (Ign. *Phld.* 6.1; Ign. *Magn.* 8.1; 10.2-3). Ignatius's critique of Judaism is frustratingly brief, and further details are lacking to supplement the picture. His fundamental objection appears to be that devotion to Judaism detracts from Jesus Christ. We have already noted that the new law of Jesus Christ is authoritative for Barnabas (*Barn.* 2.6). The *Shepherd of Hermas** does not provide a treatise on the law, but he does define God's law as the gospel of his Son that is proclaimed throughout the world (*Herm. Sim.* 69.2).

See also CHRISTIANITY AND JUDAISM: PARTINGS OF THE WAYS; CIRCUMCISION; COMMANDMENTS; FOOD, FOOD LAWS, TABLE FELLOWSHIP; JEWISH CHRISTIANITY; OLD TESTAMENT.

BIBLIOGRAPHY. H. Attridge, *The Epistle to the Hebrews* (Herm; Philadelphia: Fortress, 1989); C. L. Blomberg, "The Law in Luke-Acts," *JSNT* 22 (1984) 53-80; R. E. Brown, *The Epistles of John* (AB; Garden City, NY: Doubleday, 1982); P. H. Davids, *The Epistle of James* (NIGTC; Grand Rapids: Eerdmans, 1982); H. Frankemölle, "Gesetz im Jakobusbrief. Zur Tradition, kontextuellen Verwendung und Rezeption eines belaseten Begriffes" in *Das Gesetz im Neuen Testament,* ed. K. Kertelge (QD 108; Freiburg: Herder, 1986) 175-221; C. J. Hemer, *The Book of Acts in the Setting of Hellenistic History* (WUNT 49; Tübingen: J. C. B. Mohr, 1988); M. Hengel, "Der Jakobusbrief als antipaulinische Polemik" in *Tradition and Interpretation in the New Testament: Essays in Honor of E. E. Ellis,* ed. G. F. Hawthorne and O. Betz (Grand Rapids: Eerdmans, 1987) 248-65; J. Jervell, *Luke and the People of God: A New Look at Luke-Acts* (Minneapolis: Augsburg, 1972); L. T. Johnson, "The Use of Leviticus 19 in the Letter of James," *JBL* 101 (1982) 391-401; M. Klinghardt, *Gesetz und Volk Gottes* (WUNT 32; Tübingen: J. C. B. Mohr, 1988); R. P. Martin, *James* (WBC; Waco, TX: Word, 1988); D. J. Moo, *The Letter of James* (TNTC; Grand Rapids: Eerdmans, 1985); J. Nolland, "A Fresh Look at Acts 15:10," *NTS* 27 (1980) 105-15; K. Salo, *Luke's Treatment of the Law: A Redaction-Critical Investigation* (DHL 57; Helsinki: Annales Academiae Scientiarum Fennicae, 1991); O. F. J. Seitz, "James and the Law," *SE* 2 (1964) 472-86; M. A. Seifrid, "Jesus and the Law in Acts," *JSNT* 30 (1987) 39-57; M. M. B. Turner, "The Sabbath, Sunday and the Law in Luke/Acts" in *From Sabbath to Lord's Day: A Biblical, Historical and Theological Investigation,* ed. D. A. Carson (Grand Rapids: Zondervan, 1982) 100-157; S. G. Wilson, *Luke and the Law* (SNTSMS 50; Cambridge: Cambridge University Press, 1983).

T. R. Schreiner

LAWLESSNESS. *See* OBEDIENCE AND LAWLESSNESS.

LETTER OF PETER TO PHILIP. *See* APOCRYPHAL AND PSEUDEPIGRAPHAL WRITINGS.

LETTER, LETTER FORM

The early church relied upon the letter because of the necessity of communicating important matters of the gospel and the Christian community over long distances. There were several factors peculiar to the early church that influenced how these letters were written. Among many others, these factors included the understanding of relationships among Christians in terms of family ties, the unique authority of apostles and their successors, the desire persuasively to present the gospel and its consequences for practical living and the influence of liturgical language. Early Christian letter writers, whose works are found both within and without the NT, adapted the epistolary and rhetorical forms of the Greco-Roman world to create sophisticated, literary creations.

1. Classification of Early Christian Letters
2. The Form of Early Christian Letters
3. The Letter Form of Hebrews, the General Epistles and Revelation
4. The Letter Form of the Works of the Apostolic Fathers

1. Classification of Early Christian Letters.

Earlier in the twentieth century Adolf Deissmann made the questionable distinction between nonliterary or documentary letters (situational, private) and literary epistles (for posterity, public, rhetorically sophisticated), a distinction that persists. He classified the letters of the NT as documentary, but rhetorical analysis of NT letters has demonstrated that they fall between his categories, being situational yet possessing rhetorical sophistication.

Ancient letters are of various types, depending on the contexts from which they arose and the purposes they served. The relationships of friendship, family and client-patron generated the bulk of ancient letters. Ancient epistolary handbooks classify letters into their many types, including friendship, family, praise and blame, and exhortation and advice. These are ideal types that can be elaborated and mixed with other types.

Ancient letters contemporary with those of the NT were influenced by rhetorical conventions. These letters can be classified according to the three species of rhetoric*: judicial (accusation and defense), deliberative (persuasion and dissuasion) and epideictic (praise and blame). For example, accusing and apologetic letters are judicial, letters of advice and exhortation are deliberative, and letters of recommendation and praise are epideictic.

The more early Christian letters are compared with literary letters rather than with documentary letters (as has been the case in the past) the more their rhetorical sophistication is noted. Early Christian letters exhibit patterns of argumentation and arrangement as well as many stylistic features of Greco-Roman rhetorical convention used in literary letters. Rhetorical analysis has been helpful in determining the structure of the elusive body of the letter, which was least bound by letter conventions.

Early Christian letters generally are a mix of the ideal types of letters and rhetorical classifications and often are not adequately classified with any one letter type or rhetorical species. Hebrews* and the General Epistles are usually classified as letters of exhortation and advice, but they show characteristics of other letter types as well. They have been classified in part or whole according to all three species of rhetoric. Determination of letter and rhetorical classification are interdependent, since letters were influenced by rhetorical conventions at various points.

2. The Form of Early Christian Letters.

Christian letters followed the conventions of Greek letters with some modifications attributable to Christian experience. Greek letters, especially the opening and closing, are governed by convention. They begin with the letter opening, or prescript, composed of this formula: sender (*superscriptio*) to recipient (*adscriptio*), greetings (*salutatio*). Christian letters typically expand the prescript by describing the sender and recipient in relation to God (e.g., "apostle," "chosen by God"). The Greek letter greeting uses a verb of greeting (*chairō*) and a wish for the recipient's health (*hygianō*), but in Christian letters these become "grace" (*charis*) and "peace" (*eirēnē*) respectively, often presented in the form of a benediction ("may grace and peace be yours").

The Greek letter greeting is usually followed by the sender's wish for the health of the recipient (*hygianō*), an expression of joy* at the receipt of the letter from the recipients (*chairō*), a thanksgiving for good health and deliverance from disaster (*eucharisteō*, "to rejoice"), a report of a prayer* for the addressees (*proskynēma*) and/or a mention that the sender remembers the recipients (*mneia*). In Christian letters these are often subsumed into the thanksgiving or a benediction, which introduces the key topics of the letter.

The body of Greek and Christian letters has three parts: the body-opening, body-middle and body-closing. The body-opening establishes the common ground between the sender and recipient by alluding to shared information or by disclosing new information. It provides the principal occasion or purpose of the letter that prompts the sender to write and introduces the main points the letter will develop. The purpose of the letter can be expressed in one of three ways: (1) a full disclosure formula giving the sender's wish or command that the recipients know something ("I want you to know that"), consisting of a verb of disclosure *(thelō, boulomai)* and a verb of knowing *(ginōskō)*, (2) a motivation for writing *(graphō)* or (3) a petition that the audience take some course of action, composed of a verb of petition *(parakaleō, erōtaō* and the reason for the petition.

The body-middle both develops the subject(s) introduced in the body-opening and introduces new material. It often begins with a disclosure formula that conveys that the sender desires or commands that the recipients know something. The body-closing accentuates and reiterates the principal motivation for writing and establishes bridges to further communication. It often begins with the imperative form of the disclosure formula using the verb *ginōskō* ("to know") followed by responsibility statements urging the recipients to be attentive to the content of the letter and to respond as desired. It may notify the recipients of the sender's intention to visit, which is motivated by a desire to talk face to face rather than to use pen and ink. It may also contain recommendation of a third party who will deliver the letter.

The letter closing or postscript maintains contact between sender and recipient and enhances their friendship. This is accomplished by using greetings *(aspazomai)*, a health wish and/or words of farewell. In Christian letters a doxology or benediction (*see* Liturgical Elements) can replace the last two.

3. The Letter Form of Hebrews, the General Epistles and Revelation.

The degree to which the books of Hebrews, the General Epistles and Revelation (*see* Revelation, Book of) conform to the conventions of the Greek and early Christian letter forms varies according to purpose and associated genres.

3.1. Hebrews. Hebrews has been identified as a Jewish-Hellenistic and early Christian homily or sermon influenced by classical rhetoric. More recently it has been classified as a written speech of encomium. It does not conform to the letter form; it does not even possess a formal letter prescript. It does have a postscript incorporating a benediction (Heb 13:20-21), a formal petition functioning as a responsibility statement *(parakaleō,* Heb 13:22), an announcement of the sender's plan to visit (Heb 13:23), greetings from the sender and secondary greetings from those with him *(aspazomai,*

Heb 13:24) and a second benediction (Heb 13:25). The appeal to obey the exhortation given (Heb 13:22) indicates that seeking such obedience* was the main reason for writing.

3.2. James. James* is protreptic literature in letter form. It tries to persuade the recipients to live a particular life of virtue.* It begins with a prescript that includes sender, recipients and greeting (*chairō,* Jas 1:1). The prescript indicates that James is a circular letter meant to be distributed to numerous churches ("twelve tribes of the Dispersion"). James does not exhibit a clear body-opening, middle or closing, nor does it have a postscript. However, James 1:2-27 acts like a body-opening in introducing topics that are developed in James 2:1—5:12, and James 5:13-20 acts like a body-closing in recapitulating some of those same topics. Also included in its letter form are diatribal elements (dialogue and question and answer in pursuit of truth*), paraenesis (moral instruction) and three examples of a complete elaboration of an argument according to Greco-Roman rhetoric (Jas 2:1-13; 2:14-26; 3:1-12).

3.3. 1 Peter. 1 Peter* conforms only partially to the ancient letter form. It begins with a prescript (1 Pet 1:1-2) containing a reference to the sender (Peter) and the recipients (exiles of the Diaspora*), each with a theological description (1 Pet 1:1-2), and a greeting in the form of a benediction (1 Pet 1:2). The prescript is followed by a benediction substituting for the health wish or thanksgiving (1 Pet 1:3-9). The body of the letter (1 Pet 1:13—5:12) is not easily divided into body-opening, middle and closing. The body-opening begins with a petition in the form of a command to "set all your hope on the grace that Jesus Christ will bring you when he is revealed" (1 Pet 1:13). An imperatival petition often begins the body-opening. It gives the sender's main reason for writing which the body of the letter will elaborate. The body-closing contains a motivation-for-writing formula and a responsibility statement which echoes the petition which begins the body-opening: "Stand fast in it [the true grace of God]" (1 Pet 5:12). The postscript (1 Pet 5:13-14) is comprised of greetings from a third party and the sender *(aspazomai;* 1 Pet 5:13-14) and a benediction (1 Pet 5:14).

First Peter has been identified as a diaspora letter modeled on those in the OT sent from Jews in Jerusalem* to those in exile (cf. 1 Pet

1:1), but the diaspora letter is not a specific genre. 1 Peter is better identified as a circular letter sent to several congregations. Among other traditional materials, it incorporates a household code* that describes the role of members of the household* in relation to one another (1 Pet 2:18—3:7). Although it has been surmised that a catechism or a baptismal* liturgy underlies the body of the letter, these features can be attributed to shared early Christian tradition.

3.4. 2 Peter. In a Jewish or Christian farewell speech or testament a dying community leader announces his death and exhorts the community to be faithful to its traditions after his death. The sender of 2 Peter* creates the unusual combination of a testament in letter form. This allows the sender in the postapostolic era to portray the apostle Peter as communicating over time to the recipients.

2 Peter begins with the typical prescript referring to sender and recipients and a benediction (2 Pet 1:1-2). The letter prescript is followed by elements borrowed from the testament genre: the rehearsal of the traditions central to the community (2 Pet 1:3-11) and an announcement of Peter's death (2 Pet 1:12-15). This announcement functions as the body-opening of the letter (2 Pet 1:12-15). Reminding the recipients of the traditional teachings works like a full disclosure formula ("I wish you to know that") and a motivation for writing. The body-middle of 2 Peter (2 Pet 1:16—3:13) develops the motif of the coming of false teachers, so common to a testament, by refuting their main doctrines (*see* Adversaries). The body-closing (2 Pet 3:14-18) is indicated by the vocative *beloved* and a responsibility statement (2 Pet 3:14). A doxology serves as the postscript (2 Pet 3:18).

3.5. 1 John. 1 John (*see* John, Letters of) does not exhibit the typical letter opening conventions needed to classify a document as a letter. The opening (1 Jn 1:1-4) is modeled on the prologue of the Fourth Gospel (Jn 1:1-18) and introduces topics to be developed in the remainder of the work. The closing of 1 John 5:13-21 reiterates main topics but does not contain letter closing conventions. The reason for writing (1 Jn 1:4, 5:13) is the only true letter convention to be noted.

3.6. 2 John. In contrast to 1 John, 2 John conforms to letter conventions. It begins with a prescript (2 Jn 1-3) referring to the sender (the

elder) and the recipients (the elect lady), accompanied by theological description of the latter (2 Jn 1-2). A benediction replaces the greeting (2 Jn 3). Although it is not formally a thanksgiving, 2 John 4 functions as one as it rejoices in the recipient's welfare. The body-opening (2 Jn 4-5) begins with an expression of joy (*echarēn lian*), alludes to subject matter shared by both parties so as to provide a common basis for matters of the letter body (the commandment*) and presents a petition. The petition is standard: 2 John 4 providing the background ("walking in the truth") and 2 John 5 providing the petition itself (*erōtaō*, "Let us love one another"; i.e., to continue to walk in the truth).

The body-middle (2 Jn 6-11) develops the concerns presented in the body-opening and introduces other concerns of equal importance. It is indicated by the presence of responsibility statements (2 Jn 8, 10) and the concluding short paraenetic section common to Christian letters (2 Jn 11). The body-closing (2 Jn 12) reiterates and accentuates what has been said. It presents the motivation for writing ("much to write"), forms a bridge to further communication and notifies the recipients of the sender's coming visit to discuss further issues. The letter closing sends traditional greetings from a third party (*aspazomai*, 2 Jn 13).

3.7. 3 John. 3 John also follows letter conventions. The prescript refers to sender (the elder) and recipient (Gaius) but lacks the typical greeting (3 Jn 1). Although 3 John 2 contains a conventional health wish (*hygianō*) within a report of a prayer for the recipients, both of which are typical of the prescript, the initial vocative, *beloved*, of 3 John 2 marks the transition to the body-opening (3 Jn 2-6). The body-opening contains an expression of joy over the welfare of the recipient (*echarēn lian*, 3 Jn 3-4) and a petition that expresses its purpose (3 Jn 5-6). The petition contains the petition proper ("you will do well," *kalōs poiēseis*, 3 Jn 6) and its background, beginning with the formula "you do faithfully" (*piston poiēseis*, 3 Jn 5-6), a variation of "you will do well" (*kalōs poiēseis*). The body-middle (3 Jn 7-12) contains responsibility statements (3 Jn 8, 11) and a recommendation of a third party carrying the letter (Demetrius, 3 Jn 12). The body-closing (3 Jn 13-14) presents a reference to writing and notifies the recipients of the sender's upcoming visit, techniques that enable the body-closing to form a bridge to further communication. The postscript consists of a benediction and greetings from the sender and a third party (*aspazomai*, 3 Jn 15).

3.8. Jude. It has been suggested that Jude* is a homily in letter form or that it incorporates a midrash in Jude 5-19. At least it can be said that elements of these genres have been incorporated into a rhetorically complex letter that tries to prove that the opponents are the ungodly of whom the prophets spoke. Jude begins with a prescript containing reference to sender (Jude) and recipients, described in their relationship to God (Jude 1), and a benediction (Jude 2). The letter body (Jude 3-23) is divided into the body-opening (Jude 3-4), body-middle (Jude 5-16) and body-closing (Jude 17-23), all beginning with the transitional vocative *beloved*. The body-opening (Jude 3-4) begins with a reference to "the salvation we share," providing the common ground for the letter. It supplies the occasion for the letter as a petition (*parakaleō*, Jude 3) and its background (Jude 4). The body-middle (Jude 5-16) provides further background for the petition, beginning with a full disclosure formula that employs the idea of wishing (*boulomai*) the recipients know (*oida*) something. The body-closing (Jude 17-23) begins with the imperative form of the disclosure formula ("remember," *mnēsethēte*) and contains many responsibility statements in the form of exhortation. The postscript is a doxology (Jude 24-25).

3.9. Revelation. Revelation can be classified as several genres, including letter, prophecy and apocalyptic.* It exhibits few features of the Greek letter tradition. After a brief prologue (Rev 1:1-3) there is a letter opening referring to sender (John) and recipients (seven churches of Asia) (Rev 1:4), a benediction (Rev 1:4-5) and a doxology (Rev 1:6). After an epilogue (Rev 22:6-20) the letter closes with a benediction (Rev 22:21). The remainder of the book is dominated by the forms of the prophetic and apocalyptic genre.

Mention must be made of the letters to the seven churches in Revelation 2—3. These seven letters each have some forms of ancient letters, including reference to recipients (one of seven churches) and sender (Christ) in the prescript and a reference to knowing (*oida*), which often begins the body-opening. However, David Aune's careful analysis shows that the seven

letters are to be classified as ancient royal or imperial edicts or proclamations, with the mode used being the paraenetic salvation*-judgment* oracles of early Christian prophecy.

4. The Letter Form of the Works of the Apostolic Fathers.

Several works of the apostolic fathers* are genuine letters, one takes on the guise of a letter, and some are not letters at all. Works that are not letters include *2 Clement*, a homily or sermon calling itself an appeal (*enteuxis*, *2 Clem.* 19.1); the *Didache,** a manual of church instruction; the *Shepherd of Hermas*, a Christian apocalypse (*see* Hermas, Shepherd of); and the *Epistle to Diognetus*, which in spite of its title is an apology for Christianity. Although it is a polemical tractate, the *Epistle of Barnabas* (*see* Barnabas, Epistle of) takes on the guise of a letter. The genuine letters of the apostolic fathers are *1 Clement*, the seven letters of Ignatius,* the *Epistle of Polycarp to the Philippians* and the *Martyrdom of Polycarp* (*see* Polycarp). They are modeled after the letters of Paul (cf. Ign. *Trall.* inscr.) and use other facets of Hellenistic epistolography.

4.1. The Epistle of Barnabas. The letter opening refers to the recipients as "sons and daughters" but does not refer to the sender. A greeting (*chairete*) and a wish for peace (*eirēnē*, *Barn.* 1.1) are followed by an expression of joy concerning the audience (*Barn.* 1.2-3). The body-opening gives the motivation for writing as perfecting the knowledge* of the recipients (cf. the disclosure formula; *Barn.* 1.5) followed by the main points to be addressed (*Barn.* 1.6-8). The body-closing is composed of exhortation (*Barn.* 21.1-9), a command to remember the sender (*mnēmoneuō*), a reference to writing, a responsibility statement and a benediction (*Barn.* 21.7-9).

4.2. 1 Clement. *1 Clement* begins with a prescript referring to sender and recipients and their relationship to God and the modified greeting "grace and peace" (*charis kai eirēnē*) in the form of a benediction. The body begins with an introduction of the occasion of the letter, a schism caused by youth illegitimately taking authority from elders (*1 Clem.* 1—3; *see* Church Order), followed by an exposition of the nature of the Christian life (*1 Clem.* 4—39) and proposed solutions for the schism (*1 Clem.* 40—61). The letter ends with a summary of the letter's contents (*1 Clem.* 62), a recommendation of the letter bearers and responsibility statements (*1 Clem.* 63), a benediction and doxology (*1 Clem.* 64) and a request that the messengers be sent back speedily, as well as a final blessing and doxology (*1 Clem.* 65).

4.3. The Seven Letters of Ignatius. The seven letters of Ignatius warn of false teachers, uphold the organization of the church (especially the office of bishop) and acknowledge Ignatius's impending death. Like Paul, Ignatius Christianizes the standard opening and closing letter formulae, but he does so in a non-Pauline way. The letters typically begin with a prescript referring to sender and recipient and their relationship to God and an initial greeting (*aspazomai* and/or *pleista chairein,* "abundant greeting"). The first chapter usually praises the spiritual life of the recipients in a fashion akin to a joy expression. There are appeals (*parakaleō*) throughout the body of the letters (e.g., Ign. *Trall.* 6.1). The letters usually conclude with a call to remember certain churches and Ignatius in prayer* (*mnēmoneuō*), final greetings from Ignatius and third parties (*aspazontai*) and a farewell (*hrōnnymi*).

4.4. The Epistle of Polycarp to the Philippians. the *Epistle of Polycarp to the Philippians* begins with a letter prescript, referring to sender and recipients and their relationship to God, and the benediction "mercy and peace . . . be multiplied" (*eleos hymin kai eirēnē . . . plēthyntheiē*). This is followed by an extended expression of joy concerning the spiritual well-being of the Philippians (Pol. *Phil.* 1). The body of the letter contains the reason for writing (Pol. *Phil.* 3.1-3) and closes with a benediction and an exhortation (Pol. *Phil.* 12.1-3) and a recommendation of the letter carrier (Pol. *Phil.* 13.1—14.1). A farewell comprises the letter closing (Pol. *Phil.* 14.1).

4.5. The Martyrdom of Polycarp. The *Martyrdom of Polycarp* is a letter sent from the church of Smyrna to the church of Philomelium. The letter opening refers to sender and recipient without theological description followed by the benediction "mercy, peace and love . . . be multiplied." The body of the letter opens with the reason for writing—to inform the recipients about the martyrdom of Polycarp (*Mart. Pol.* 1.1)—and closes with an exhortation to send the letter to others, a doxology and greetings from the church (*Mart. Pol.* 20.1-2), followed by a date and doxology (*Mart. Pol.* 21.1).

See also HERMENEUTICS; LITURGICAL ELEMENTS; PSEUDEPIGRAPHY; RHETORIC, RHETORICAL CRITICISM.

BIBLIOGRAPHY. C. Andresen, "Zum Formular frühchristlicher Gemeindebriefe," *ZNW* 56 (1965) 233-59; D. E. Aune, "The Form and Function of the Proclamations to the Seven Churches (Revelation 2-3)," *NTS* 36 (1990) 182-204; K. Berger, "Apostelbrief und apostolische Rede/Zum Formular frühchristlicher Briefe," *ZNW* 65 (1974) 190-231; R. E. Brown, "Appendix V: General Observations on Epistolary Format" in *The Epistles of John* (AB; Garden City, NY: Doubleday, 1982) 788-95 (deals with 2 and 3 John; see 86-92 on 1 John); J. D. Charles, *Literary Strategy in the Epistle of Jude* (Scranton: University of Scranton Press, 1993) 20-64; A. Deissmann, *Bible Studies* (Edinburgh: T & T Clark, 1901) 3-59; idem, *Light from the Ancient East,* (New York: Doran, 1927) 146-251; W. G. Doty, *Letters in Primitive Christianity* (Philadelphia: Fortress, 1973); J. A. du Rand, "Structure and Message of 2 John," *Neot* 13 (1979) 101-20; idem, "The Structure of 3 John," *Neot* 13 (1979) 121-31; F. O. Francis, "The Form and Function of the Opening and Closing Paragraphs of James and 1 John," *ZNW* 61 (1970) 110-26; R. W. Funk, "The Form and Structure of II and III John," *JBL* 86 (1967) 424-30; J. Lieu, *The Second and Third Epistles of John: History and Background,* ed. J. Riches (SNTW; Edinburgh: T & T Clark, 1986) 37-51; T. W. Martin, *Metaphor and Composition in 1 Peter* (SBLDS 131; Atlanta: Scholars Press, 1992) 41-79; E. Peterson, "Das Praescriptum des 1. Clemens-Briefes" in *Pro Regno Pro Sanctuario* (Nijkerk: G.F. Callenbach, 1950) 351-57; X. Roiron, "Les plus anciens prologues épistolaires chrétiens," *RSR* (1913) 382-96; F. Schnider and W. Stenger, *Studien zum neutestamentlichen Briefformular* (NTTS 11; Leiden: E. J. Brill, 1987); H. J. Sieben, "Die Ignatianen als Briefe: Einige formkritische Bermerkungen," *VC* 32 (1978) 1-18; S. K. Stowers, *Letter Writing in Greco-Roman Antiquity* (LEC 5; Philadelphia: Westminster, 1986); L. Thurén, *The Rhetorical Strategy of 1 Peter: With Special Regard to Ambiguous Expressions* (Åbo: Åbo Academy Press, 1990) 84-88; D. F. Watson, *Invention, Arrangement, and Style: Rhetorical Criticism of Jude and 2 Peter* (SBLDS 104; Atlanta: Scholars Press, 1988) passim; idem, "A Rhetorical Analysis of 2 John According to Greco-Roman Convention," *NTS* 35 (1989) 104-30; idem, "A Rhetorical Analysis of 3 John: A

Study in Epistolary Rhetoric," *CBQ* 51 (1989) 479-501; J. L. White, "Ancient Greek Letters" in *Greco-Roman Literature and the New Testament,* ed. D. E. Aune (SBLSBS 21; Atlanta: Scholars Press, 1988) 85-105; idem, *The Body of the Greek Letter* (SBLDS 2; Missoula, MT: Scholars Press, 1972); idem, *Light from Ancient Letters* (Philadelphia: Fortress, 1986); idem, "New Testament Epistolary Literature in the Framework of Ancient Epistolography," *ANRW* 2.25.2 (1984) 1730-56; idem, "Saint Paul and the Apostolic Letter Tradition," *CBQ* 45 (1983) 433-44.

D. F. Watson

LIBERTY. *See* FREEDOM, LIBERTY.

LIFE AND DEATH

God* is the "living God" (Heb 3:12) and the Creator, and thus he has the power to give life. Human beings live or die at God's sufferance, and they may be divided into "the living and dead" (Acts 10:42; 1 Pet 4:5; *2 Clem.* 1.1; *Barn.* 7.2).

1. Background
2. Acts
3. Hebrews and General Epistles
4. Revelation
5. Later Developments

1. Background.

1.1. Terminology. The words for life are mainly cognates of *zōē,* while death is expressed by *nekros* or *thanatos* and their cognates. Also *psychē* at times means "living person" or "life" (1 Pet 3:20; 1 Jn 3:16). *Bios* means "life" in the apostolic fathers*; its cognate verb *bioō* ("to live") occurs in the scope of our canonical literature only in 1 Peter 4:2.

1.2. Concepts. The world of the early church offered a variety of opinions on the nature of life and death. The Epicureans thought that human existence begins at birth and ends at death, while the Platonists thought of life as the soul's temporary sojourn in a mortal body.

Christians countered that God gives life to human beings, and life consists of body and soul. Death came only as a consequence of sin. While human existence is possible out of the body, God's plan for humanity is the rolling back and defeat of death in resurrection.*

2. Acts.

The church testified to the Gentiles* that the one true God lives and that other deities do not (Acts 14:15). Paul adapted a remark by the Stoic poet Aratus (*Phaen.* 5), claiming that in the one true God "we live and move and exist" (Acts 17:28).

Central to the apostolic kerygma are the death and resurrection of Christ* (Acts 2:23-24, etc.; *see* Death of Christ). The resurrected Jesus is the "originator" or "prince" of life (Acts 3:15). Through the apostles* he even restored life to Tabitha and to Eutyches (Acts 9:40-41; 20:10).

People may forfeit their lives because of flagrant sin (Acts 1:16-18; 5:5, 10; 12:23). In Acts,* however, many more people presumably die or risk death for the sake of their faith* than for any other cause (Acts 5:33; 7:57—8:1; 9:1). Still the Christian experience is properly labeled "life" (Acts 5:20).

3. Hebrews and General Epistles.

3.1. Hebrews. Despite his own revulsion at what was to come (Heb 5:7), Jesus died to free humanity from the numbing terror of death (Heb 2:15) and to destroy the devil (*see* Satan), who held the power of death (Heb 2:14). The new covenant* could not be activated until the death of the testator (Heb 9:16-17). God raised Jesus and made him the living high priest* for all time (Heb 7:3, 16, 20, 23-25).

Christians likewise must persist even to the point of death (Heb 11:13). They will be resurrected, but in the meantime their spirits will go to be with Christ in heaven* (Heb 12:22).

3.2. James. Death is the result of sin, not nature (Jas 1:15; 5:20). It will cut short all human plans (Jas 1:11; 4:14-15), but those who persevere with God will receive the "crown of life" (Jas 1:12; cf. 1 Pet 5:4; Rev 2:10; *Mart. Pol.* 17.1; 19.2; *2 Clem.* 20.2).

If a person professes faith and does not display it with loving actions, that faith is "dead," just like a body without a spirit (Jas 2:17, 26; cf. 2 Pet 1:14; *Diogn.* 6.3, 8). James's* interest here is illustration, not explaining the afterlife (Martin, 98).

3.3. 1 Peter. God gives "life" or a "living hope" (1 Pet 1:3; 1:23; 3:7, based on the resurrection of Jesus, 1 Pet 1:21), and the Christians have rejected the old way of life (1 Pet 1:18; 4:2-4). They have died to sin already in order to live to righteousness* (1 Pet 2:24; cf. Michaels, 148-49).

In 1 Peter 4:6 it is said that the gospel was

preached "even to the dead" (Michaels, 235-41; Reicke). Perhaps these are the spiritually dead, but it is more natural that they are literally dead, as in 1 Peter 4:5. In that case 1 Peter* may teach to Jesus' descent into the realm of the dead; more likely its reference is to people who were alive when they heard the gospel and are "now dead" (NIV).

3.4. 2 Peter and Jude. If 1 Peter is about hope in the midst of trial, 2 Peter* and Jude* are about gloom for those apostates* who flourish in this age. Jude 12 calls them the "twice dead," perhaps an allusion to the "second death" of Gehenna (Bauckham, 88). And true Christians must remember that they are equipped to live godly lives in the world (2 Pet 1:3-4).

3.5. Johannine Epistles. Life and death are presented as parallel courses: "We know that we have crossed over from death into life, because we love one another. The one who loves not remains in death" (1 Jn 3:14; Strecker, 202-8; *see* John, Letters of). Just as Jesus laid down his life for us, so "we should lay down our lives for one another" (1 Jn 3:16). The grasping after satisfaction and glory consisting in mere possessions is the sin of the "pride of life." Rejecting that worldly value, the Christian will live forever (1 Jn 2:15-17).

1 John 5:16-17 mentions a class of sins that lead to death. What constitutes so grievous a sin is not delineated. "Death" may be physical demise (as in 1 Cor 11:30; perhaps Jas 5:20) or damnation (as in Jude 22-23; see Smalley, 297-301).

4. Revelation.

History is driven by the predetermined triumph of Jesus (Rev 1:5) over the beast* who mimics his death and resurrection in order to deceive the world (Rev 13:3). The book (*see* Revelation, Book of) answers two troubling questions: If Christians are rejected by the world, is their God really in control? And how should Christians react to a government that usurps divine prerogatives? The Christian must decide between acquiescence to the "mark of the beast" and "overcoming" through martyrdom* (Rev 2:10-11; Boring, 21-23). The first resurrection is the hope of all faithful martyrs (Rev 20:4, 6).

Meanwhile, the inhabitants of the earth will be plagued by the pale horse of death and hades (Rev 6:8). Although the slaughter is great, the survivors will envy the dead (Rev 9:6). Still death

is not the end for the enemies of God. They will rise in the second resurrection to judgment* (Rev 20:12-13). With all humanity resurrected, death and Hades will also be thrown into the lake of fire (Rev 20:14).

Revelation uses several traditional symbols for life, notably the water of life and the tree of life (Rev 22:1-2) and the book of life (Rev 20:12; cf. Dan 12:1; *Jub.* 30.22). The "second death" is also known from the Jewish targums and is the counterpart to entering the life to come (Abrahams, 41-49). Philo* likewise speaks of the "undying death" to which God subjects the wicked after they pass through physical death (Philo *Praem. Poen.* 69-70).

5. Later Developments.

Postapostolic Christians esteemed the Jewish tradition of the Two Ways, so we read: "There are two ways: one of life and another of death, and there is a great difference between the two ways" (*Did.* 1.1; cf. *Barn.* 18—20; *Herm. Sim.* 8.6-11). In *Hermas Similitude* 9.16.3-5 baptism* is the passing over from life to death.

Christ is the true life of the Christian (*2 Clem.* 20.5; Ign. *Eph.* 7.2; Ign. *Magn.* 9.2; *Diogn.* 9.6). He has secured the "abolition of death" (Ign. *Eph.* 19.3). Ignatius* was particularly concerned that the Docetists* were denying the true humanity of Christ and thereby his death and resurrection (Ign. *Trall.* 9—10; Ign. *Magn.* 11.1; Ign. *Smyrn.* 2-7).

The times being what they were, Christians wrote about the proper response to death threats. The faithful should rejoice as if they are being made alive (Ign. *Rom.* 6.1-3; *Diogn.* 5.12, 16). *Diognetus* 10.7 even went as far as remarking that physical death is not really death; eternal death is the menace (*Diogn.* 1). All true Christians should be prepared to die after the example of Christ (Ign. *Magn.* 5.1-2). Although Polycarp* had spent eighty-six years serving Christ (*Mart. Pol.* 9.3), he willingly gave up his life to find immortality in heaven (*Mart. Pol.* 17.1; 19.2; cf. *2 Clem.* 19.4). After the veneration of martyrs became a feature of Christian worship, the date of their death was observed as their "birthday" into heavenly life (the earliest reference is *Mart. Pol.* 18.2).

2 Clement, which speaks often of "life" and "eternal life," underscored the finality of death: "Thus let us too, while we are in the world, repent with our whole heart of the things that we do in the flesh, so that we may be saved by the Lord, while we have opportunity for repentance. For after we depart from the world, we can no longer make confession nor any longer repent" (*2 Clem.* 8.2-3; cf. Heb 9:27; *see* Repentance).

The early Christians generally agreed that the soul is conscious after death, either in torment or in heavenly bliss. It does not transmigrate to another body (Justin Martyr *Apol. I* 18). The orthodox view ran counter to that of the Gnostics,* who adopted the docetic christology* that had earlier rankled Ignatius. For them death was not a consequence of sin but the result of the creator god's attempt to fuse immortal spirit with mortal flesh. Death was the undoing of that awkward combination, freeing the Gnostic initiate to ascend back to the spirit world. The church understood that this idea rejected not only God's work of creation* but also any gospel based on the death and resurrection of the Logos.*

See also ESCHATOLOGY; HELL, ABYSS, ETERNAL PUNISHMENT; MARTYRDOM; MORTALITY AND IMMORTALITY; RESURRECTION.

BIBLIOGRAPHY. I. Abrahams, *Studies in Pharisaism and the Gospels* (LBS; 2d series; Cambridge: Cambridge University Press, 1924); R. J. Bauckham, *Jude, 2 Peter* (WBC; Waco, TX: Word, 1983); M. E. Boring, *Revelation* (IntC; Louisville, KY: John Knox, 1989); R. P. Martin, *James* (WBC; Waco, TX: Word, 1988); J. R. Michaels, *1 Peter* (WBC; Waco, TX: Word, 1988); B. Reicke, *The Disobedient Spirits and Christian Baptism* (Copenhagen: Munksgaard, 1946); W. R. Schoedel, *Ignatius of Antioch: A Commentary on the Letters of Ignatius of Antioch* (Herm; Philadelphia: Fortress, 1985); S. S. Smalley, *1, 2, 3 John* (WBC; Waco, TX: Word, 1984); G. Strecker, *The Johannine Letters* (Herm; Minneapolis: Fortress, 1996). G. S. Shogren

LIGHT AND DARKNESS

In Jewish thought "light" (Heb *'ôr;* Gk *phōs*) is not merely a philosophical term or a poetical term but rather it "becomes a fundamental religious reality" (Spicq, 3:474-75). In the beginning God* created light (Gen 1:3), and it was deemed "good" (Gen 1:4). Light provides understanding (Ps 119:130) and engenders life (Ps 36:9). "Darkness" (Heb *ḥōšek;* Gk *skotia*), comprised of chaos (Gen 1:2) and evil, is the antithesis of God's light (Is 5:20); but merely to

juxtapose light and darkness, as if they represent a cosmic dualism, is misleading: darkness is subservient to God, its Creator (Is 45:7). The OT understanding of light and darkness informs the understanding and gives content to the same in the NT and apostolic fathers* (see esp. Achtemeier, 439). Others scholars find significant parallels to the NT (esp. the Johannine) concept of light and darkness in the *Corpus Hermeticum,* the Mandean Literature and the Dead Sea Scrolls.

1. Imagery of Light and Darkness
2. Light as Epiphany
3. Related Words: "Day" and "Night"
4. Summary

1. Imagery of Light and Darkness.
The third account of Paul's conversion in Acts* (Acts 26:12-18) relates a typically Jewish understanding of light and darkness, and it is this same figurative dichotomy created between light and darkness (i.e., "good" and "evil") that runs through the General Epistles and into the apostolic fathers. In Acts 26:18 the conjunction *kai* ("and"), when it is epexegetically understood (when it is translated "that is" or "namely"; see BDF, §442.9), equates darkness with the power of Satan* and light with God (Marshall, 396-97; cf. Col 1:12-13).

1.1. Light and Darkness and the Moral Spheres of Good and Evil. Most often in the NT, light and darkness illustrate the moral sphere of good and evil (cf. Lk 11:34-35; Jn 8:12; 12:35, 46); thus in the Johannine epistles (*see* John, Letters of), those who "walk in darkness" speak lies concerning their fellowship* with God,* whereas those who "walk in light" are cleansed from their sins by the blood of Jesus (1 Jn 1:6-7). Those who "hate their brother or sister" are still "in darkness" (1 Jn 2:9), but those who "love their brother or sister abide in the light" (1 Jn 2:10; see Neufeld, 84-86). Morality counts because God is "light, and in him is no darkness whatsoever" (1 Jn 1:5; cf. 1 Tim 6:15-16; *Diogn.* 9.6; Justin *Apol. I* 6). Thus the author of 1 John "is not interested in any metaphysical implications of the idea that God is light, but in its ethical implications" (Dodd, 19). In the *Epistle of Barnabas* this moral sphere is represented by the Two Ways, one of light and one of darkness. "The way of light" (*Barn.* 18.1—19.12; or "the way of righteousness," *Barn.* 5.4) consists of commands, both positive and negative, whereas "the way of darkness" (*Barn.* 18.1; or "the way of the Black One," *Barn.* 20.1-2), consists essentially of one long vice list (cf. *Did.* 5; *see* Virtues).

1.2. Light and the Saints. In the book of Hebrews* and the writings of Ignatius* of Antioch* and Justin Martyr, saints are those who have been "enlightened" or "illumined" (Heb 6:4; 10:32; Ign. *Rom.* presc.; Justin *Dial. Tryph.* 122; cf. Justin *Dial. Tryph.* 7). This enlightenment arguably refers to the catechumenate's moment of baptism* (see esp. Spicq, 3:487, 491, who cites Justin *Apol. I* 61: "and this washing is called illumination," as well as the v.l. in *Acts Thom.* 25: *ebaptisen/ephōtisen;* cf. Conzelmann, 9:355-58). In 1 Peter,* as well as in the thought of Clement of Rome (*see* Clement of Rome), Christians have been "called out of darkness into God's glorious light" (1 Pet 2:9; *1 Clem.* 59.2; cf. *Barn.* 14.5-7) and have light "graciously given" to them (*2 Clem.* 1.4; cf. Ps 118:27). Again, in Ignatius, saints are "children of light" (Ign. *Phld.* 2.1; cf. Jas 1:17); yet in some sense they still await the "pure light" (Ign. *Rom.* 6.2).

1.3. Darkness and the Sinners. We may note Luke's contrast between Paul and the false prophet, Bar-Jesus (Acts 13:6-12). The latter was blinded not by a light from heaven* but in judgment* was covered by a "mist and darkness" and, unlike Paul, had to search for someone to lead him about by the hand (Acts 13:11; cf. Deut 28:29; 1 Jn 2:11). In *2 Clement* darkness and mist is not a punishment for individuals but a preexistent condition in all of humankind (*2 Clem.* 1.6; cf. Mt 23:16, 24; Lk 6:39; *1 Clem.* 36.2; *Barn.* 8.7; Justin *Resurrec.* 4). Still, it should be noted, even believers can be darkened in their understanding (*2 Clem.* 19.2; quoting Eph 4:18). On a broader scale, in Revelation 16:10 darkness is a judgment on the kingdom of the beast* (see also Rev 8:12; 9:2; 18:23; cf. Exod 10:22; Is 8:19-22; Amos 5:18, 20; Zeph 1:15). Ultimately, eternal darkness has been reserved for the wicked (2 Pet 2:17; Jude 13; see Bauckham, 90-91; cf. Mt 8:12; 22:13; 25:30).

1.4. "Proclaiming Light" and "Publishing Darkness." In what appears to be an odd metaphor and one unique to the NT (but see Aeschylus *Pers.* 300), Paul states that Christ,* specifically in his resurrection,* "proclaims light" to Jews and Gentiles* (Acts 26:23). Perhaps a similar point is made in 2 Timothy 1:10: "Christ Jesus did away with death, bringing immortal life to light via the gospel" (cf. 1 Tim 6:16). In both

passages "light" is bound up with resurrection. Likewise Clement of Rome metaphorically links "day" and "night" to resurrection (*1 Clem.* 24.3). In one instance in the General Epistles, not wholly unrelated to the metaphor in Acts 26:23, the prophetic word is likened to "a lamp shining in a dark place" (2 Pet 1:19; cf. Ps 119:105). In the writings of Justin Martyr, Jews do not proclaim light; rather they relish each opportunity to "publish dark and unjust things against the . . . righteous Light sent by God" (Justin *Dial. Tryph.* 17).

2. Light as Epiphany.

Six of the ten occurrences of the word *light* in Acts refer to the intense light that arrested and blinded Paul on the road to Damascus (Acts 9:3; 22:6, 9, 11; 26:13, 18; cf. Mt 17:2). That Luke narrates the events surrounding Paul's conversion in such significant detail and then retells them twice more through Paul, once for the crowds in Jerusalem* (Acts 22:1-21) and once for Agrippa (Acts 26:2-23), demonstrates their significance for his story (see further Haenchen, 327-29). Paul, blinded by the epiphanic light, would later see his ministry* in terms of bringing light to the Gentiles (Acts 13:47; quoting Is 49:6; cf. *Barn.* 14.8) and thereby "opening blind eyes" (Is 42:7; see esp. Acts 26:18; cf. *Barn.* 14.7).

3. Related Words: "Day" and "Night."

The related words *day (hēmera)* and *night (nyx)* should be discussed. In the literature considered here, the word *day* serves little purpose more than as a chronological indicator of time (Heb 11:30; *Did.* 11.5; passim; in contrast see 1 Thess 5:5). Still, several times "day" is coupled with "night" for the sake of intensification and/or symmetry (Acts 9:24; 20:31; Rev 4:8; 7:15; *1 Clem.* 2.4; Ign. *Rom.* 5.1; *Did.* 4.1; *Mart. Pol.* 5.1; Justin *Dial. Tryph.* 1; cf. Lk 2:37; 18:7). On one occasion, however, "day" is used to illustrate the absolute depravity of humankind, who typically prefer darkness to light because their works are wicked (Jn 3:19) but in some cases become so "insatiable for sin" (2 Pet 2:14 RSV) that "they count it a pleasure to revel in the daytime" (2 Pet 2:13 RSV).

The word *night* not only functions as a chronological indicator of time but also serves a purpose in the following two kinds of scenes. (1) Dramatic escapes by Christians occur at night (Acts 5:19; 9:23-25; 12:6-11; 17:10; 23:23-31; cf. Mt 2:14; but see *Mart. Pol.* 5.1), as do (2) heavenly visions* (Acts 16:9; 18:9; 23:11; 27:23; *Herm. Vis.* 2.4.1; 3.1.2; 10.7; cf. Lk 2:8); but note the emphasis laid on Cornelius's* and Peter's respective daytime visions (Acts 10:3, 9, 30).

While even now "darkness continues to pass away and the true light already shines" (1 Jn 2:8), in Revelation (*see* Revelation, Book of) "night" is finally abolished forever in the heavenly city (Rev 21:25; 22:5; cf. Zech 14:7). Doubtless this is due to night's associations with darkness and evil (Jn 3:19), but more importantly it is abolished because the "glory of God" will be the city's light and the Lamb* its lamp (Rev 21:23; *see* Glory).

4. Summary.
Light in Acts is normally to be understood literally, regardless of whether it is epiphanic or utilitarian. In the General Epistles and the apostolic fathers it should normally be understood figuratively. Light serves the positive function of dispelling the darkness of the mind and heart. Further, it is emblematic of both godliness and truth. Darkness should normally be understood figuratively; it represents all that is evil and morally corrupt; note also, however, even the literal use of "darkness" (as in Acts 13:11; cf. Jn 6:17) is often not without symbolic import and drama.

See also APOCALYPTIC, APOCALYPTICISM; ESCHATOLOGY; GLORY; GNOSIS, GNOSTICISM; QUMRAN.

BIBLIOGRAPHY. E. R. Achtemeier, "Jesus Christ, the Light of the World: The Biblical Understanding of Light and Darkness," *Int* 17 (1963) 439-49; R. J. Bauckham, *Jude, 2 Peter* (WBC; Dallas: Word, 1983); R. Bultmann, "Zur Geschichte der Lichtsymbolik im Altertum," *Exegetica* (1967) 323-55; H. Conzelmann, "σκότος κτλ," *TDNT* 7:423-45; idem, "φῶς κτλ," *TDNT* 9:310-58; G. Delling, "νύξ," *TDNT* 4:1123-26; C. H. Dodd, *Johannine Epistles* (MNTC; New York: Harper & Row, 1946); W. Hackenberg, "σκότος," *EDNT* 3:255-56; E. Haenchen, *Acts* (Philadelphia: Westminster, 1971); I. H. Marshall, *Acts* (TNTC; Grand Rapids: Eerdmans, 1980); P. G. Müller, "νύξ," *EDNT* 2:481-83; D. Neufeld, *Reconceiving Texts as Speech Acts: An Analysis of 1 John* (Leiden: E. J. Brill, 1994); H. Ritt, "φῶς," *EDNT* 3:447-48; C. Spicq, "φῶς κτλ," *TLNT* 3:470-91; M. Winter, "φωτίζω," *EDNT* 3:449-50.   S. A. Hunt

LITURGICAL ELEMENTS

The notion that "the New Testament was, in a sense, a liturgical book" (Cabaniss 1989, 44-45) is a growing trend among NT interpreters. This suggestion is based on the observations that the letters or books of the NT were first read during public worship* (1 Thess 5:27; Col 4:16) and that liturgical elements are richly embedded in these writings. Some scholars have even proposed that certain NT letters are essentially liturgical documents written for religious rites such as the baptismal* service or the Eucharist (Cabaniss 1989, 44). Frequent allusions to liturgical elements, however, may not imply that being "a liturgical book" was the original intent for their composition (Bradshaw, 30-37). Especially when one recalls how the presence of the Holy Spirit* had enacted a new dimension in Christian worship (cf. 1 Cor 14:26; van Unnik 1959, 294), it is unconvincing to conclude that Christian worship had already developed fixed liturgical forms with fixed sequences in the early decades when the NT letters were written (Delling, 76; Cullmann, 27, 32; Williams, 451).

In fact most of these documents or letters were responses to various needs within scattered Christian communities (e.g., 1 Pet, Jude and Heb). A close examination of the Pauline corpus shows that although liturgical elements (e.g., creedal confessions, benedictions, doxologies, hymnic fragments and prayer acclamations such as "amen," "Abba," "maranatha") appear in many letters, they are not always uniform in expression or placed in locations in line with the order of worship. Rather, liturgical elements are often tailored to highlight relevant contents and placed in strategic contexts to clarify or underscore the writer's messages to his readers (*see* DPL, Liturgical Elements). In this study of the liturgical elements found in the later canonical writings and in the writings of the early apostolic fathers we further explore what types of liturgical elements are alluded to most often, whether they are uniform in expression and why are they mentioned in their contexts.

1. Liturgical Elements in the Later
    Canonical Writings
2. Liturgical Elements in the Apostolic Fathers
3. Conclusions

**1. Liturgical Elements in the Later
Canonical Writings.**
As in the Pauline corpus, liturgical elements

such as benedictions, doxologies, hymnic fragments (*see* Hymns), creedal* confessions and some acclamations such as amen, *Ter Sanctus*, hallelujah and maranatha are incorporated in Acts,* Hebrews,* the General Epistles and the Apocalypse (*see* Revelation, Book of) by different writers in their addresses to different groups of readers at scattered locations.

1.1. Benedictions. The inclusion of benedictions in a letter to express the writer's wish-prayers for the readers may have been derived from Jewish worship, in which benediction was a common practice. In the Pauline corpus each letter commenced and ended with a benediction. In the group of writings we are considering, however, there are some distinctive features: not every letter includes a benediction (e.g., Jas and 1 Jn) and, except for 1 Peter,* each letter includes only one benediction, either at the beginning (1 Pet 1:2; 2 Pet 1:2; 2 Jn 3; Jude 2; Rev 1:4) or at the end (Heb 13:20-21, 25; 1 Pet 5:14; 3 Jn 15; Rev 22:21). Even though benediction is frequently included in a letter, it is not a necessary element. The Johannine epistles provide strong evidence: there is no benediction in 1 John, one introductory benediction in 2 John and only a brief closing benediction in 3 John (*see* John, Letters of). Here the same writer does not follow a stereotyped format in his letters.

Benedictions are essentially wishes of grace* and/or peace*: "Grace be with you [all]" (Heb 13:25; Rev 22:21) or "Peace be with [or to] you" (1 Pet 5:14; 3 Jn 15). In some letters benedictions are elaborated with additional features such as mercy* (2 Jn 3) or love* (Jude 2) or with a closing "Amen" (Heb 13:25; Rev 22:21). In Hebrews 13:20-21 and Revelation 1:4, both letters include lengthy introductions about God,* the source of the benefaction, with epithets that coincide with the major motifs of the letters (Lane, 560). The Pauline formula "The grace of the Lord Jesus Christ be with you" and the so-called *Dominus Vobiscum* ("The Lord be with you"; see Lk 1:28; van Unnik 1959), are not shared by these writings. Thus we see the contents of benedictions are also subject to modification by each writer according to personal choice or the needs of the recipients (Delling, 76).

1.2. Doxologies. Out of gratitude for God's redeeming grace, early Christians were constantly offering praise (see Acts 2:46; 4:24). Just as in the Pauline letters, two doxological formulae are found in this group of writings. One is expressed by the formula "Blessed [be] God" (also known as the *Berakhah*, or Eulogy; 1 Pet 1:3; cf. 2 Cor 1:3; Eph 1:3), which is a common expression in OT worship and also resembles the *Shemoneh Esreh*, the Eighteen Benedictions used in the synagogue.* The other is expressed by the phrase "to him be glory [and dominion] for ever and ever," which is less formal in structure but more commonly used (e.g., Heb 13:21b; 1 Pet 4:11; 5:11; 2 Pet 3:18; Jude 24-25; Rev 1:6; 5:13; 7:12). The former type often occurs at the beginning of a letter and the latter at the end of a letter or a section (e.g., 1 Pet 4:11), sometimes with a liturgical "amen" attached to it. But exceptions are also found in the Apocalypse, where doxological expressions are placed in various contexts to maximize the tone of worship. Some follow the common formula "to God be glory for ever and ever" (Rev 1:6; 5:13; 7:12), and some begin with the expression *axios ei/estin* ("worthy art thou"/"is he"; Rev 4:11; 5:9, 11).

Although most of the doxologies in this group of writings follow the formulaic expressions, they may also be modified with motifs that bring out meanings relevant to the readers (Lane, 565). For example, the doxology in Jude* has been considered as one of the most fulsome doxologies in the NT (Martin, 66). It contains a declarative praise for God's specific deeds ("to keep you from falling and to present you without blemish," Jude 24) and a descriptive praise for who God is ("the only God, our Savior," Jude 25; in Westermann's definitions, 31), and it is expressed with motifs evidently tailored to meet the subjective needs of the readers whose faith* was endangered by the false teachings* of the intruders (Martin, 80-81). Many doxologies in the Apocalypse are also more elaborate in content (cf. Rev 4:11; 5:12, 13). Some of them are directed to Christ (Rev 5:9, 12, 13) with similar wordings as those directed to God (cf. Rev 4:11; 7:12). The purpose is to emphasize his deity, thereby comforting the suffering* readers during the imperial persecution.* Doxologies are not confined to a limited range of thought or stereotyped expression (Delling, 65; cf. Piper, 17).

1.3. Creedal Confessions. Creed, in its modern sense as an article of the Christian faith, is not discernible in the NT (*see* DPL, Creed). Yet fragments of creedal confessions are traceable. Among this group of writings, Acts provides us with a window on one of the earliest forms of creedal confessions in the Christian communities, namely, "Jesus is the Lord [and/or Christ]" (Acts 2:36; 8:35-38 [the Western text]; 10:36; 16:31; cf. Rom 10:9; Phil 2:11, where *homologeō,* "confess," is directly connected with the formulaic expression). This is possibly a baptismal confession, for it is consistently connected with baptism in various geographical locations: Jerusalem,* Samaria,* Caesarea and Philippi. And since the document is written partly with a polemic objective, it is probably the writer's intention to show his recipients (Theophilus and eventually the Romans) that Christian communities as outlined in Acts 1:8 are founded on the same faith, "Jesus is the Lord/Christ." They are not political rebels against the Roman government (*see* Hymns, for similar usage of hymnic materials in Acts; *see* Civil Authority; Roman Empire). The creedal confessions found in 1 John such as "Jesus is the Christ" (1 Jn 2:22), "Jesus Christ is come in the flesh" (1 Jn 4:2) and "Jesus Christ is the Son of God" (1 Jn 4:15; cf. Heb 4:14), however, are mentioned as criteria for discerning one's faith and are most likely introduced for apologetic purposes.

In Hebrews the writer refers to the *homologia* three times (Heb 3:1; 4:14; 10:23; also the verb form in Heb 11:13; 13:15) and exhorts his readers to hold fast to it. This repeated allusion has been generally acknowledged (e.g., Bornkamm; Michel; and more recently Lane, with some modifications; contra Delling, 79-80) as evidence for the existence of certain fixed forms of creedal confession in the latter part of the first century (see 1 Tim 3:16; 4:6; 6:20; 2 Tim 1:13, 14; 2:11-13; 4:3; Tit 1:9, 13; Jude 3; "the faith," "the deposit" and "sound teaching/doctrine" all clearly support this notion). In the case of Hebrews, Christ's sonship* (Heb 4:14) and high priesthood* (Heb 3:1) are the key confessions acknowledged by the members of the community. The reason for exhortation is also directly related to the urgent needs of the readers. Being Jewish converts in the Diaspora,* the readers have been attracted by a form of heretical and gnosticizing* Judaism* and are at the stage of returning to their former beliefs. Thus the writer's allusions to the *homologia* that spells out the supremacy of Christ are intended to serve as powerful reminders to the readers of

the belief they once confessed (Lane, 103-4). They should "hold fast" to it and not fall back (Heb 10:39). Creedal confessions in early Christian communities are all christocentric* and are designed for the presentation, identification and defense of this new faith.

1.4. Prayer Acclamations. The most familiar prayer acclamation found in this group of writings is "āmēn," a transliteration of the Hebrew word *'amen,* meaning "firmness, certainty." This word is frequently used in the OT and the intertestamental period as a vocal expression signifying a person's agreement to or endorsement of or affirmation of another person's words or prayers (e.g., 1 Chron 16:36; Neh 8:6; Ps 41:13; Tob 8:8; 1 Esdr 9:47). In the Jewish synagogue, "amen" became a liturgical term attached to various forms of prayer. When early Christians began their worship they readily adopted this usage. Evidences are found in the General Epistles, where "amen" is consistently added to the end of doxologies (Heb 13:21; 1 Pet 4:11; 5:11; 2 Pet 3:18; Jude 25) and benediction (Heb 12:25). This is not done perfunctorily by the writers. By adding an "amen" at the end of doxologies, the readers are given an opportunity to make the message of praise their own (Delling, 64) as well as to unite with one another through their simultaneous utterance of this liturgical acclamation. The unified "amen" is a means for promoting the corporate spirit of worship (MacDonald, 109).

In the Apocalypse, however, "amen" has richer connotations besides being added to the end of various doxologies (Rev 1:6; 7:12b) and the final benediction (Rev 22:21). It is seen as an expression of affirmation of another person's prayer* (Rev 5:14; 19:4) or serves as an emphatic yes (Rev 1:7; 7:12a; 22:20). But a more significant use of "amen" is found in Revelation 3:14. There it is identified as a christological title, and the meaning of "amen" is clearly spelled out in the following phrase, "the faithful and true witness" (RSV), serving as a double emphasis of Christ's faithfulness. It must be noted that the choice of epithets for Christ in this context, just as in Revelation 2:1, 8, 12, 18; 3:1, 7, is directly related to the specific needs of the church. In the case of the Laodicean church (Rev 3:15), believers have failed to follow the One who was faithful in carrying out God's promise of salvation* and made it possible for them to utter the "amen" together in corporate worship. Here we see another example of using "amen" as a christological title to convey the writer's message to his readers (cf. Paul's similar use of "amen" in 2 Cor 1:20 for underlining his argument; *see DPL*, Liturgical Elements, §5.1). The use of "amen" may be more than just a formal consent or endorsement.

There are two other liturgical acclamations in the Apocalypse: *Ter Sanctus* (the "Thrice Holy," Rev 4:8) and "hallelujah" (Rev 19:1, 3, 4, 6). Both acclamations are also found in the OT (Is 6:3; Pss 104-06, 111-13, 115-17, 135, 146-50, the so-called Alleluia Psalms) and are not alluded to in other parts of the NT.

The origin of *Ter Sanctus* is a song of praise sung by celestial beings, the seraphim, in the presence of God (Is 6:1-3; there, probably the triune God or Yahweh, in contrast to Brock's view, which suggests that *Ter Sanctus* is directed to Christ), proclaiming his holiness* and his sovereignty, which eventually led Isaiah to an awareness of his own unworthiness (Brock, 32). Although this acclamation is not found elsewhere in the NT, its presence in Revelation 4:8 indicates its continual usage in Jewish worship (possibly as a liturgical element used in the Jewish synagogue; see Spinks, 46-54, 194, cf. van Unnik 1951, 213). It was adopted by Jewish Christians* in the Diaspora to be cited on occasions such as the Eucharist (Brock, 31-32; van Unnik, 205; contra Moule, 64). Notably the *Ter Sanctus* is the first song of praise that commences the heavenly worship in the book of Revelation.

Since Revelation 4:8 is the only place in the NT where *Ter Sanctus* is mentioned, the writer's purpose must not be overlooked. As in Isaiah 6:3, *Ter Sanctus* is also sung by celestial beings, the four living creatures, in the presence of God (Rev 4:6-8). The similarities between these two passages strongly suggest that the writer's intention is to stress the holiness of God. The writer uses this acclamation to highlight God's holiness as the foundation of universal worship. The acclamation is followed by the description of God as one "who was, who is and who is to come" (Rev 4:8)—a theme repeated throughout the book (Rev 1:4, 8, 14, 17, 18; 2:8). God's eternal character implies his sovereign control in human history. This twofold message of God's holiness and sovereignty, laid out side by side through the acclamation *Ter Sanctus* in a worship setting, helps to remind as well as comfort

the suffering readers who were undergoing persecution.

The other acclamation, "hallelujah," is a Greek transliteration from the Hebrew word *haľlûâh*, meaning "praise [ye] the Lord." In the OT it is found frequently in the Psalter (e.g., Ps 104—6, 111—13, 115—17, 135, 146—50). The plural imperative form of the verb indicates that the term was a directive to the worshiping congregation in the temple* and was meant to evoke a response. In the course of time it became an independent exclamation of joy,* so that the Greek-speaking Jews simply transliterated it (see LXX) instead of translating it (Cabaniss 1970, 116). Although it is not found in other NT writings, its presence in Revelation 19 testifies to its continual usage in the Jewish communities and its adoption by Jewish Christians in the Diaspora as a joyful chant. Since "hallelujah" is mentioned only here, the writer's intention is also evident. In Revelation 19 "hallelujah" is placed at the last song of praise, shared by both celestial and human beings in exuberant response to God's sovereign judgment* upon the evil (Rev 19:1, 3, 4) and his final victory (Rev 19:6). Just as the Hebrew Psalter closes with God's chosen people singing "hallelujah" (Ps 150 ends with this word), the Apocalypse also closes with the "hallelujah chorus," inviting the readers to join. The book closes on a high note. While reminding his readers to focus on God's power and sovereignty, the writer skillfully incorporates the familiar acclamation *hallelujah* to achieve his goal more effectively.

The frequent references to liturgical language in Revelation do not make it a liturgical book, as some have overstated (e.g., Shepherd, Cabaniss, Piper, Vanni). Prayer acclamations (*Ter Sanctus* and hallelujah) are selected and incorporated in strategic locations to bring out a cohesive picture of victory and hope* for the comfort and encouragement of the readers as they are reminded of God's holiness and sovereignty. Their presence in the book goes far beyond serving merely liturgical purposes.

2. Liturgical Elements in the Apostolic Fathers.
Around the turn of the first century of the Christian era, liturgical elements were still a common literary element in letters.* For example, benedictions were found either at the beginning of a letter (*1 Clem.* 1; Pol. *Phil.*; Ign.

Trall.; Ign. *Rom.)* or at the close of a letter (*1 Clem.* 58, 59; *Barn.* 21; Ign. *Eph.* 21; Ign. *Pol.;* Ign. *Smyrn.* 12). The expression of benediction as a wish-prayer for readers, however, is very flexible in wording (esp. in Ignatius's* letters) and in length (e.g., *1 Clem.* 58). Doxology is a more fixed expression (mostly following the popular formula "to God be glory for ever and ever, amen"; *Diogn.* 12; *1 Clem.* 20, 32, 38; [except in Ign. *Eph.* 1, where the formula "blessed be God" is employed]) and less restricted in location (e.g., *1 Clem.;* doxologies are found throughout the letter: 20, 32, 38, 43, 45, 50, 58 and 59). Therefore, while fixed formats provide guidelines for expression, flexibility in wordings and usages is always allowed and accepted.

Besides benediction and doxology, prayer acclamations such as "amen," *Ter Sanctus,* "hosanna" and "maranatha" are also attested in some of the early fathers' writings, indicating a continual usage of these acclamations in the later and postapostolic era. The acclamation *amen* is always attached to the end of a doxology (*1 Clem.* 20, 32, 38, 58, 59) or a letter (see Ign. *Eph.;* Ign. *Pol.;* also Ignatius's letters to St. John and the Virgin Mary) as a symbol of confirmation of the blessing uttered. In *Didache* 10.6 and Justin Martyr's *Apology I* 65, "amen" is explicitly an acclamation of consent to the leader's prayer at the eucharist. In other words, the liturgical usage of "amen" is quite fixed by the end of the first century. The second acclamation, *Ter Sanctus,* is found in *1 Clement* 34 and is considered a loose quotation of Isaiah 6:3 (van Unnik 1951, 247), warning the readers against laziness and calling them to follow the example of angels* in submitting to God's will. The emphasis there evidently is not directly related to God's holiness as in Revelation 4:8. Nevertheless, its allusion may reflect its regular usage in early church worship (van Unnik 1951, 248).

A more significant use of prayer acclamations is found in *Didache** 10.6:

Let grace come and let this world pass away
Hosanna to the God of David
If any man is holy, let him come
If any be not, let him repent
Maranatha
Amen

The *Sitz im Leben* of this paragraph is generally acknowledged to be the Eucharist (Audet, Jungmann, Cabaniss). It was recited antiphonally by the leaders and the congregation. Appar-

ently these three words were already familiar liturgical acclamations employed in early church worship; thus no translation is deemed necessary. "Hosanna" derives from two Hebrew elements: *hôsha* 'and *nā* ', meaning "save, please" and thus signifying a cry for help (Ps 118:25). In the NT this word is only found in the Gospels in the context of the triumphal entry (Mt 21:9; Mk 11:9, 10; Jn 12:13). Although the original meaning of this word may have been familiar to the Jewish people in the Christian era, it seems more likely that this acclamation had developed into an expression of exuberant joy (Hart, Hawthorne, Brown, contra Werner, Pope), as indicated by the occasion and the manner in which this cry was expressed (also see Luke's use of *doxa* in place of "hosanna" in Lk 19:38). In *Didache* 10.6 the utterance of "hosanna" in connection with God as the God of David (similar to the expression directed to Jesus at his triumphal entry) also supports the idea that it was understood by Jews and Gentiles* in the Christian era to be an expression of joy rather than a call for help or deliverance.

"Maranatha" is a Greek transliteration of an Aramaic word, *marana' ta* ', probably denoting an imperative cry ("Our Lord, come!") rather than a statement ("Our Lord has come"; *see DPL,* Liturgical Elements, §5.3). It is most likely the earliest Christian prayer (Cullmann, 13) and originated among Jewish Christians in Palestine or Syria* as a plea for the fulfillment of Christ's eschatological Parousia* (cf. Rev 22:20) as well as for his immediate presence at the Lord's table. This prayer is quickly and widely adopted by Gentile Christians in the Diaspora (1 Cor 16:22) as a part of the eucharistic liturgy. In *Didache* 10.6 "maranatha" is placed at the end of the antiphonal recitation followed by the close of the eucharistic meal. It represents the congregation's climactic hope. And by adding the liturgical "amen" to it, the congregation is provided an opportunity to adopt the prayer to themselves. Thus the order of arrangement of these three words in *Didache* 10.6 reflects the beliefs and practices of early Christians in their worship.

3. Conclusions.

The above study provides us some clearer understandings of the forms and functions of liturgical elements in later canonical writings and the writings of early apostolic fathers.

The presence of some liturgical elements in various NT writings and the allusion to prayer acclamations such as "amen," "hallelujah," *Ter Sanctus* and "hosanna" without translation or explanation testifies to the existence of certain fixed expressions and worship formats (e.g., to commence a letter with introductory benediction and/or doxology and to close with benediction and/or doxology) that had already been adopted by scattered Christian communities in their corporate worship.

The inclusion of these liturgical elements, however, is selective according to the genre of the letters and/or the themes of the writers. The absence of "Abba" in this group of writings does not mean that "Abba" is not used or known outside the Pauline communities (Delling, 71). Similarly the inclusion of *Ter Sanctus* and "hallelujah" in the Apocalypse (Rev 4:8; 19:1, 3, 6) does not imply that these are elements unique to the Johannine circles.

In the light of diverse motifs or themes that were often added to the somewhat fixed formulas, it is also clear that liturgical elements were still in the stage of development. Doxologies and benedictions, while generally following similar formats, are occasionally tailored to motifs in order to meet the specific needs of the readers or to coincide with the overall message of the writers (see Jude 24-25 versus 2 Pet 3:18; Heb 13:20-21 versus 1 Pet 1:2). In this respect there is a solidarity between Paul and other NT writers in their use of liturgical elements.

Liturgical language is still employed by early apostolic fathers in their writings as a literary style and occasionally for didactic or polemic purpose. Nevertheless, the forms and usages are comparatively fixed despite the fact that varieties are still attested.

NT writers' use of liturgical elements witnesses to a blend of form and freedom in early church worship as well as literary works. Freedom* must operate within the accepted framework to ensure orderliness, whereas formality must also allow flexibility of expression to guarantee meaningful practice—this is the essence of NT worship.

See also BAPTISM; HYMNS, SONGS; LORD'S SUPPER, LOVE FEAST; WORSHIP AND LITURGY.

BIBLIOGRAPHY. J.-P. Audet, *La Didaché: Instructions des Apôtres* (Paris: Gabalda, 1958); G. Bornkamm, "Das Bekenntnis im Hebräerbrief," *TBl* 21 (1942) 56-66; P. F. Bradshaw, *The Search for the Origins of Christian Worship* (New York: Oxford University Press, 1992); S. P. Brock, "The Thrice-holy Hymn in the Liturgy," *Sobornost* 7 (1985) 24-34; R. E. Brown, *The Gospel of John* (AB; Garden City, NY: Doubleday, 1970); A. Cabaniss, "Alleluia: A Word and Its Effect" in *Liturgy and Literature* (Tuscaloosa, AL: University of Alabama Press, 1970) 114-21; idem, "A Note on the Liturgy of the Apocalypse," *Int* 7 (1953) 78-85; idem, *Pattern in Early Christian Worship* (Macon, GA: Mercer University Press, 1989); J. D. Charles, *Literary Strategy in the Epistle of Jude* (London: Associated University Presses, 1993); A. Chester and R. P. Martin, *The Theology of the Letters of James, Peter, and Jude* (NTT; Cambridge: Cambridge University Press, 1994); O. Cullmann, *Early Christian Worship* (London: SCM, 1953); G. Delling, *Worship in the New Testament* (Philadelphia: Westminster, 1962); P. Fiedler, "Neues Testament und Liturgie," *Archiv für Liturgiewissenschaft* 25 (1983) 207-32; H. Hart, "Hosanna in the Highest," *SJT* 45 (1992) 283-301; G. F. Hawthorne, "Hosanna," *ISBE* 2:761; J. A. Jungmann, *The Mass* (Collegeville, MN: Liturgical Press, 1976); W. Lane, *Hebrews* (WBC; Dallas: Word, 1991); H. Lietzmann, *Mass and Lord's Supper: A Study in the History of the Liturgy* (Leiden: E. J. Brill, 1979); A. MacDonald, *Christian Worship in the Primitive Church* (Edinburgh: T & T Clark, 1934); O. Michel, "*f*," *TDNT* 5:199-220; C. F. D. Moule, *Worship in the New Testament* (London: Lutterworth, 1961); O. A. Piper, "The Apocalypse of John and the Liturgy of the Ancient Church," *CH* 20 (1951) 10-22; M. H. Pope, "Hosanna: What It Really Means," *Bible Review* (1988) 16-25; J. M. Ross, "Amen," *ExpT* 102 (1991) 166-71; B. D. Spinks, *The Sanctus in the Eucharistic Prayer* (Cambridge: Cambridge University Press, 1991); S. Schulz, "Maranatha und Kyrios Jesus," *ZNW* 53 (1962) 138; D. E. Smith and N. H. Tauffig, *Many Tables: The Eucharist in New Testament and Liturgy Today* (London: SCM, 1990); K. Trudinger, "Amen, Rev. 3:14 . . . ," *NovT* 14 (1972) 277-79; W. C. van Unnik, "1 Clement and the 'Sanctus,' " *VC* 5 (1951): 204-48; idem, "Dominus Vobiscum: The Background of A Liturgical Formula" in *New Testament Essays: Studies in Memory of Thomas Walter Manson*, ed. A. J. B. Higgins (Manchester: Manchester University Press, 1959) 270-305; U. Vanni, "Liturgical Dialogue as a Literary Form in the Book of Revelation," *NTS* 37 (1991) 348-72; G. Wainwright, "The Praise of God in the Theological Reflection of the Church," *Int* 39 (1985) 34-45; N. Walker, "The Origin of the 'Thrice-holy'," *NTS* 5 (1958-59) 132-33; E. Werner, "'Hosanna' in the Gospels," *JBL* 65 (1946) 97-122; C. Westermann, *Praise and Lament in the Psalms* (Atlanta: John Knox, 1981); R. B. Williams, "Liturgy and the New Testament," *Worship* 42 (1968) 450-65.   J. L. Wu

LITURGY. *See* WORSHIP AND LITURGY.

LOGOS CHRISTOLOGY

Logos christology* is the use by a Christian writer of the popular Hellenistic religio-philosophical term *logos* ("word") as a title or predicate of Christ to express Christ's preincarnate existence; his role as the mediator and sustainer of creation*; the universality of his revelatory activity; or his personal distinction from and subordination to God* while sharing God's essence. The term "Logos christology" became common in NT scholarship in the middle of the twentieth century, when a spate of studies appeared on NT titles of Christ. Among these, Logos is most closely related to certain wisdom* motifs in Alexandrian* Judaism* (Wis; *see* Philo*). Within the NT the high-water mark of Logos christology is John 1:1, 14. (On Logos in the wider environment and in the Fourth Gospel, *see DJG,* Logos.) The present article covers echoes of Logos christology in other NT writings and sketches its development in early Christianity to the time of Justin.

1. Later New Testament Documents
2. Ignatius and Preaching of Peter
3. Early Apologists
4. Jewish Mysticism and Gnosticism

1. Later New Testament Documents.

1.1. Hebrews. A current debate about whether Hebrews* presents a Logos christology is epitomized by R. Williamson's recent abandonment of the overly cautious line he took in his dissertation (1970). A weighty christological passage at Hebrews 1:3 draws upon language used formerly at Alexandria to describe Wisdom: God's Son is the "shining" (*apaugasma*) of God's glory and the "representation" (*charaktēr*) of his substance, even as Wisdom is the "shining" of eternal light and the "representation" (*eikōn*) of its goodness (Wis 7:26). The Christian author may well have read the Jewish work. Besides sharing a rare term (*apaugasma*) and

synonyms, both texts say the transcendent divine essence is known to humanity by some agency. In Hebrews the Son is the agent of God's final revelation* (Heb 1:1-2) and the medium of God's creative act (Heb 1:2; cf. Heb 1:10-12), which in turn implies the Son's pretemporal existence (cf. Heb 7:3; 13:8). The Son is also honored as "God" (Heb 1:8, quoting Ps 45:6). So Hebrews 1:3 ranks with John 1:1, 14; 1 Corinthians 8:6; and Colossians 2:9 in preparing for binitarian developments of the early patristic era. Elsewhere in Hebrews, some of Philo's characteristic titles for the Logos are applied to Christ: e.g., "firstborn" (*prōtogonos,* Philo *Conf. Ling.* 146; cf. *prōtotokos,* Heb 1:6) or "high priest" (Philo *Gig.* 52; cf. Heb 7:26). What prevents our concluding that Hebrews has a full-blown Logos doctrine is the lack of the word *logos* itself.

Recently a few scholars have tried to revive the traditional exegesis of Hebrews 4:12-13 in terms of the personal Logos. More likely, however, the word of God described in Hebrews 4:12 is the "living" and "discerning" address of God (Heb 4:13) through the recorded words of Psalm 95:7-11 (cf. Heb 3:7-11) as pressed home by this author (Heb 3:7—4:11). In the last phrase in Hebrews 4:13 *logos* is well translated "an account" (NRSV).

1.2. 1 John. In 1 John (*see* John, Letters of) the Logos occurs but once (1 Jn 1:1). Like the opening of the prologue to the Fourth Gospel ("In the beginning"), this passage affirms the Word's existence "from the [absolute] beginning." "Word of life" denotes the Logos as the source of life (cf. Jn 1:4, 12-13). His presence revealed an eternal life that has its natural abode with the Father (1 Jn 1:2; cf. Jn 1:1-2), identified as God's Son, Jesus Christ (1 Jn 1:3; cf. Jn 1:14-17). All the elements of a classical doctrine of the Incarnation of the Logos are here. The new touch is an emphasis on the apostolic circle's direct experience of the Logos: "what we heard, saw [thrice—1 Jn 1:1, 2, 3], beheld and handled." Their report must be limited to "what" they learned "concerning" (*peri*) the Word's unfathomable reality. The claim remains that this privileged group encountered the Logos in the realm of sense, making a dualism of matter and spirit unacceptable. Probably the paragraph opposes a contemporary Cerinthian-Gnostic* teaching that the Christ was a pure spirit-being who descended on Jesus only from baptism* (1 Jn 5:6; cf. Irenaeus

Haer. 1.7.2; 1.26.1; 3.3.4; 3.11.1).

An interpolation at 1 John 5:7 (the *Comma Johanneum*) applies the term *logos* to the second member of the Trinity, but it is first documented in the fourth-century *Liber apologeticus* 4.

1.3. Revelation. An apocalyptic* description of Christ names him "the Word of God" (Rev 19:13), perhaps because the judgment* he executes fulfills God's promises (cf. Rev 19:11, 13 with Rev 21:5; 22:6). Since the passage does not treat of his personal relation to God or of his cosmological functions, its contribution to Logos christology proper is peripheral.

2. Ignatius and Preaching of Peter.

2.1. Ignatius (c. A.D. 110; Syria). Elaborate theories have sometimes been built upon Ignatius's* simple statement, "There is one God, who revealed himself through Jesus Christ his son, who is his Word coming forth from silence" (Ign. *Magn.* 8.2). This sentence paraphrases John 1:18; need it mean more than that Christ expresses what can be known of the divine mystery? We might compare phrases elsewhere in Ignatius that call Christ "the will (*gnōmē*) of the Father" (Ign. *Eph.* 3.2) or "the mouth without falsehood, by which the Father speaks truly" (Ign. *Rom.* 8.2). Ignatius adds little to the biblical Logos christology.

2.2. The Preaching of Peter (c. A.D. 80-140; Egypt). A phrase, the exact wording of which is now lost, in the *Preaching of Peter,* no longer extant, denoted Christ as both Torah and Logos (Clement of Alexandria *Strom.* 1.29.182; 2.15.68; Clement of Alexandria *Ecl. Proph.* 58). If the phrase comes from Isaiah 2:3, it presents Christ as the eschatological* revelation of God for all nations. Some rabbis speculated that the Torah existed before the world and was God's instrument for creation: "God consulted the Torah and created the world" (*Gen. Rab.* 1). A profound Logos christology may be hidden here, but with such scant data we cannot be sure.

3. Early Apologists.

3.1. The Epistle to Diognetus (c. A.D. 130-50). The most signal evidence for Logos christology in this anonymous work has often been overlooked. The invisible God "himself, from heaven, set among humans the truth and the holy and incomprehensible Word," by sending not a servant* or an angel* or a ruler but "the workman (*technitēs*) and demiurge (*dēmiourgos*) of the universe himself, by whom he created the sky." As a king sends a son, so God sent him as king: "he sent him as God" (*Diogn.* 7.2, 4). Here the Logos is distinct from God but is also God's Son and representative, superior to the celestial retinue; his cosmological functions, as well as the universality of the revelation he brings from God, are clear. This exposition, addressed to a high-ranking aristocrat (*Diogn.* 1), couches it in terms of the Platonic demiurge known to popular philosophies of the day and so marks a concerted attempt to persuade the educated elite.

The Logos also made possible God's recent act of revelation (*Diogn.* 11.2-8; 12.9). The Word who appeared and was rejected by the Jews "was from the beginning," at once new and old (*Diogn.* 11.3-4). He is "the eternal one", God's Son, who continues to unfold grace* in the church* (*Diogn.* 11.5) through those he chooses (*Diogn.* 11.7).

3.2. Justin Martyr (mid-second century). Justin, a philosopher converted to Christianity, deepened and refined the church's Logos christology. Salient are his points that the Logos disclosed fragments of truth through Greek and barbarian philosophers (Justin *Apol. I* 5; 46; Justin *Apol. II* 10; 13); that it was the actual subject of the OT theophanies (Justin *Dial. Tryph.* 56-60; 126-27); and that it constituted a "second god," distinct from God in number but not in essence, sharing God's essence without diminishing it (Justin *Dial. Tryph.* 55-56; 61-62; 127-28). Some suppose Justin to be the first witness* to a liturgical tradition that invoked the descent of the Logos upon the eucharistic elements (Srawley, 32-34). Many have expounded Justin's important contribution (see Barnard; Kelly; Price).

4. Jewish Mysticism and Gnosticism.

The subject of Logos christology is potentially vast, for historians of religion find no empirical boundary between first- and second-century ideas that came to be recognized as orthodox and others later ruled out as heretical, whether by rabbinic academies or by ecclesiastical councils. Taking up the scriptural figure of the angel of the Lord (e.g., Ex 23:20-21; Josh 5:13-15), named Michael in late texts (Dan 10:13, 21; 12:1; 1QM 9.15-16; 17:6-7), Jewish authors at Alexandria identified him with the Logos (Wis

18:15-16) and made the Logos the principal archangel (Philo *Conf. Ling.* 146; *Migr. Abr.* 174; *Rer. Div. Her.* 205-6).

For several centuries Jewish Christianity* used the concept of the Logos-archangel to describe Christ, meaning not that he was a created being but that he was sent by God. This tradition may inform the book of Revelation (cf. Dan 10:6 with Rev 1:12-16; Wis 18:15-16 with Rev 19:11-13; *see* Revelation, Book of). Its exegetical conclusions underlie Justin's dialogue with Trypho, where Justin lists "Word" and "Angel" as OT titles of Christ (Justin *Dial. Tryph.* 126-28). The christology of *Shepherd of Hermas** is angelomorphic (cf. *Herm. Sim.* 8.1.2; 8.3.3; 9.6.1-6; 9.7.1-2), putting Christ in charge of six archangels (*Herm. Sim.* 9.12.7-8). Various Gnostic* sects speculated further on seven archons who created the universe (e.g., Irenaeus *Haer.* 1.30.4-5); some placed the Logos in an aboriginal Ogdoad (Irenaeus *Haer.* 1.1.1; 1.8.5; 1.15.3). Related Jewish mystical revelations about God's principal angel, whether known as Yaoel ("Yahweh-El": *Apoc. Abr.* 10:3, 8; *3 Enoch* 48D:1(1)) or as Metatron, the "lesser Yahweh" (*b. Sanh.* 38b; *3 Enoch* 12:5; 48C:7; 48D:1(90)), also provided matter for the gnostic science of God's chariot-throne (*Orig. World* 105.1-12; *Hyp. Arch.* 95.27-29). The best approach to the whole knotty field is through specialized monographs (Daniélou; Segal; Fossum; Hurtado).

See also CHRISTOLOGY; PREEXISTENCE; WISDOM.

BIBLIOGRAPHY. L. W. Barnard, *Justin Martyr: His Life and Thought* (Cambridge: Cambridge University Press, 1967) 85-100; J. Daniélou, *The Theology of Jewish Christianity: A History of Early Christian Doctrine Before the Council of Nicaea* 1 (London: Darton, Longman & Todd, 1964) 117-46; J. D. G. Dunn, *Christology in the Making: A New Testament Inquiry into the Origins of the Doctrine of the Incarnation* (London: SCM, 1980) 213-50; J. E. Fossum, *The Name of God and the Angel of the Lord: Samaritan and Jewish Concepts of Intermediation and the Origin of Gnosticism* (WUNT 36; Tübingen: Mohr-Siebeck, 1985); R. Holte, "Logos Spermatikos: Christianity and Ancient Philosophy According to St. Justin's Apologies," *ST* 12 (1958) 109-68; L. W. Hurtado, *One God, One Lord: Early Christian Devotion and Ancient Jewish Monotheism* (Philadelphia: Fortress, 1988); J. N. D. Kelly, *Early Christian Doctrines* (5th ed.; London: Adam & Charles Black,

1977) 90-101; R. M. Price, "'Hellenization' and Logos Doctrine in Justin Martyr," *VC* 42 (1988) 18-23; W. Rodorf, "Christus als Logos und Nomos: Das Kerygma Petrou in seinem Verhältnis zu Justin" in *Kerygma und Logos: Beiträge zu den geistesgeschichtlichen Beziehungen zwischen Antike und Christentum,* ed. A. M. Ritter (Göttingen: Vandenhoeck & Ruprecht, 1979) 424-34; A. F. Segal, *Two Powers in Heaven: Early Rabbinic Reports About Christianity and Gnosticism* (SJLA 25; Leiden: E. J. Brill, 1977) 182-233; W. Schneemelcher, ed., "The Kerygma Petri," in *New Testament Apocrypha,* ed. W. Schneemelcher (2d ed.; 2 vols.; Louisville, KY: Westminster/John Knox, 1990-92) 2:34-41; W. R. Schoedel, *Ignatius of Antioch: A Commentary on the Letters of Ignatius of Antioch,* ed. H. Koester (Herm; Philadelphia: Fortress, 1985); J. H. Srawley, *The Early History of the Liturgy* (2d ed.; Cambridge: Cambridge University Press, 1947); J. Swetnam, "Jesus as *Logos* in Hebrews 4, 12-13," *Bib* 62 (1981) 214-24; M. Theobald, *Die Fleischwerdung des Logos: Studien zum Verhältnis des Johannesprologs zum Corpus des Evangeliums und zu 1 Joh* (NTAbh n.s. 20; Münster: Aschendorff, 1988); R. Williamson, "The Incarnation of the Logos in Hebrews," *ExpT* 95 (1983) 4-8.   P. A. Rainbow

LORD

Any survey of the NT literature, particularly Paul's letters,* will show the importance of the term *kyrios* for the early church* (*see DPL*, Lord). The faith* of the early church involved confessing that Jesus is the risen and exalted* *kyrios* (1 Cor 9:1; 12:3; Rom 10:9; Phil 2:9-11). That this confession* was largely based on what was true about Jesus after his death (*see* Death of Christ) is shown by the fact that the term *kyrios,* when it is found in the dialogue portions of the Gospels as a mode of address to Jesus, almost without exception means "master" or "respected sir," not "divine being" (but cf. Mk 12:35-37 and Witherington 1990).

Kyrios, like its Aramaic equivalent *marē,* normally conveyed the idea of a human being who was superior to or over another human being or group of people. *Kyrios* tells us something about a person's position in relationship to other things or persons. This is shown by the fact that in social contexts *kyrios* is often paired with the term *doulos,* "slave" or "servant." The former is lord of and lord over the latter. It is not surprising that early Christians appropriated this terminology to speak of the risen Jesus; it was commonly used in the Greco-Roman world to refer to exalted beings, including gods and demigods (cf. 1 Cor 8:5), and early Christians felt that their relationship to the risen Jesus was like that of the relationship of a *doulos* to a *kyrios* (cf. Rom 1:1 to 2 Pet 1:1). With this background we are prepared to consider the use of the term *kyrios* outside the Gospels and the Pauline literature.

The term *kyrios* is used in a variety of ways outside of the Gospels and the Pauline portions of the NT. In some cases it seems to have a simple functional connotation, indicating a role that Jesus or God plays, but in other contexts it seems also to imply something about who Jesus is, namely, one who can be placed on the Creator side of the Creator/creature distinction. This sort of distinction, however, has its limitations. A review of the relevant passages shows how *kyrios* can be used almost interchangeably of God and Jesus by early Christians. We will review the data beginning with the book of Acts,* then turning to Hebrews,* James* and Jude,* the Petrine epistles (*see* 1 Peter; 2 Peter), the Johannine letters (*see* John, Letters of) and the Apocalypse (*see* Revelation, Book of), concluding with a sampling of the use of *kyrios* in the early Christian literature outside the canon.*

1. The Acts of the Apostles
2. Hebrews
3. James and Jude
4 1 Peter and 2 Peter
5. The Johannine Epistles and the Apocalypse
6. The Apostolic Fathers
7. Summary

1. The Acts of the Apostles.
The term *kyrios* appears 104 times in Acts, with at least eighteen of these occurrences referring to God, forty-seven referring to Jesus, four referring to secular masters, owners or rulers, and the remainder referring to either Jesus or God, though in these instances it is not clear who is meant (cf. Kee, 19). Luke is familiar with the use of the term, even with the article, to refer to a secular ruler (Acts 25:26, of Nero) or to an owner or a master of a slave* (Acts 16:16, 19), but his interest lies elsewhere.

We can be certain that *kyrios* refers to Jesus in some texts because the term is combined either with the name* *Jesus* (Acts 1:21; 4:33; 8:16; 15:11; 16:31; 19:5, 13, 17; 20:24, 35; 21:13) or with the combined referent *Jesus Christ* (Acts 11:17; 15:26; 28:31). In other cases the context makes evident that Jesus is meant (e.g., Acts 9:5, 10, 11). In some instances, primarily in quotations of the OT that have the combination of *kyrios* with *theos*, it is evident that God and not Jesus is meant (Acts 2:39; 3:22; *see* Old Testament in Acts). Some of the confusion could be resolved if we could know that Luke does not draw on the concept of the preexistent* Son of God,* but texts like Acts 2:25 may suggest he knows of such an idea.

The remarkable quotation from Psalm 110:1 in Acts 2:34, in which both God and Jesus are referred to as *kyrios*, shows how flexible Luke was prepared to be in his use of the term. It would be wrong, however, to conclude from such a text that Luke saw Jesus as merely the believers' Lord, for in Acts 10:36 he is called the Lord of all (*pantōn kyrios*). It was not merely the use of the term *kyrios* of Jesus that caused the parting of the ways between Christianity and early Judaism (*see* Christianity and Judaism; Judaism). Christians also wished to appropriate the term and the OT texts in which *kyrios* had the more exalted sense of divine Lord (referring to Yahweh) and to apply those texts and their attendant concepts to Jesus (cf. Dunn 1991).

In general when an OT phrase or concept such as the "Day of the Lord" (Acts 2:20; *see* Day of the Lord), "the angel of the Lord" (Acts 5:19; 12:11, 23), "the fear of the Lord" (Acts 9:31) or "the hand of the Lord" (Acts 13:11) appears in the text it is likely that "Lord" means "God" in such texts. The phrase "the Word of the Lord," especially if one takes it as an objective genitive (the Word about the Lord), appears to refer to Jesus (Acts 8:25; 13:44, 49; 15:35, 36; 19:20), as is likely the case with the phrase "the way of the Lord" (Acts 18:25). Further, the phrase "the name of the Lord" (Acts 9:28) likely refers to Jesus, especially in view of the clearer texts such as Acts 19:5, 13 and 17.

One of the keys to understanding Luke's use of *kyrios* in Acts is to recognize the narrative framework, which includes a historical component, in which he views all christological* matters (on theology in a narrative framework see Witherington, *Narrative* 1994). The references to *kyrios* in Acts must be compared and contrasted to the material in Luke's Gospel, but what Luke says about Jesus depends on what point in the trajectory of his career Luke is discussing. One must ask whether Luke is referring to Jesus during his historical ministry* or to what Luke's believes to be true about Jesus after the resurrection* and ascension.*

For example, it is widely recognized that Luke uses the term *kyrios* in the narrative framework and in the editorial comments in his Gospel in a way the other Synoptic writers do not, while at the same time no character in the Gospel narrative calls Jesus *kyrios* unless it is under inspiration (Lk 1:43, 76), involves an angel* (Lk 2:11) or involves Jesus obliquely alluding to himself (Lk 19:31, 34; cf. Fitzmyer 1981). However, as soon as the narrative gets beyond Easter various human beings can and do use *kyrios* of Jesus (cf. Lk 24:34; Acts 10:36-38; Moule). This may be explained in part as an example of Luke's desire to avoid historical anachronisms, but it also shows that he does not wish to violate the internal logic of the narrative and so have characters get ahead of what they ought to be saying at a particular juncture in the story.

The assertion that Luke is adoptionist in his christological thinking is based on texts like Acts 2:36—"God has made this Jesus whom you crucified both *kyrios* and Christ." The problem with this conclusion is that here, as elsewhere in Acts, Luke uses his christological language in a way that suits his narrative. From Luke's point of view Jesus did not in any full sense assume the roles of Lord* and Messiah over all until after the resurrection and ascension. It was not that Jesus became someone different from who he was before but that he entered a new stage in his career or assumed new roles after the ascension (cf. Dunn 1980). Only as an exalted one could Jesus take on the tasks of Lord over all and universal Messiah.

Luke's basic interest is in the story of Jesus from his birth until he assumes and begins to exercise the role of Lord from heaven,* though a text like Acts 2:25 may imply that Luke knew of the concept of the preexistent Lord (cf. Acts 2:24 and Craddock). It is the narrative about Jesus and its progress that affects how the terminology is used, not a concern to settle a later debate about functional over against ontological christology. Furthermore, nice distinctions between being and doing would probably have seemed inappropriate to Luke. The Lord Jesus

is able to do what he does because he is who he is. The roles he assumes are roles that are appropriate in Luke's mind for the exalted Jesus to assume. Jesus' lordship is viewed not as a mere honorary title but as a description of his status and activity since at least the resurrection.

The term *kyrios* is the most frequently used christological title in all of Luke-Acts, used almost twice as frequently as the term *Christ.* * Of 717 occurrences of *kyrios* in the NT the vast majority are to be found either in Luke-Acts (210) or in the Pauline letters (275) (Bietenhard, 2:513). This emphasis in Luke-Acts comports with Luke's basic stress on God's sovereignty over and in history as it is expressed in the form of God's plan of salvation* for the world that comes to fruition through Jesus (cf. Squires). Jesus is the one who expresses and in a sense executes this salvation plan both by his acts in space and time and also by his acts as the exalted Lord sending the Holy Spirit* to work on earth in his behalf and place. It becomes clear that the basic connotation for Luke of the term *kyrios* is one who exercises dominion over the world and in particular over human lives and events.

It is important not to underestimate the significance of the transfer of the term *kyrios* from Yahweh to Christ at various points in Acts. As J. A. Fitzmyer says, "In using kurios of both Yahweh and Jesus in his writings Luke continues the sense of the title already being used in the early Christian community, which in some sense regarded Jesus as on a level with Yahweh" (Fitzmyer 1981, 203).

Acts indicates, as the Pauline epistles also suggest, that the basic confession of the early church was that Jesus is the risen Lord (cf. Acts 10:46; 11:16; 16:31; 20:21). It is Jesus the risen and exalted Lord whom people are called upon to turn to and believe in (Acts 5:14; 9:35; 11:17). This risen Lord confronts Saul on Damascus road (Acts 9:10-17; 18:9), and to him believers must remain faithful (Acts 20:19). It is the Lord Jesus with whom the original disciples traveled (Acts 1:21), whose teaching* Paul can quote (Acts 20:35) and who commissions people for ministry (Acts 20:24). In these texts the name *Jesus* seems to be appended to *kyrios* to make clear the identity of this Lord. The continuity of the Lord's identity before and after Easter makes it possible for Luke to refer to Jesus' earthly activity and teaching using the term *kyrios,* even though he knows that Jesus does not fully or truly assume the roles of exalted Lord until after Easter.

In other texts where the Lord God and not Jesus is meant by *kyrios* (Acts 2:39; 3:19, 22; 4:26; 7:31; 10:4, 33), these references are found either in the first few chapters of Acts or on the lips of Jews or apparent proselytes to Judaism. The further one gets into Acts and the more Christians speak for themselves, it is almost always Jesus who is referred to as the Lord. After the crucial apostolic council and decree (Acts 15), there is only one text in which *kyrios* seems clearly to refer to God and not Jesus: in the apologetic speech of Paul before the Areopagus (Acts 17:24). That is, in almost half of Acts, where Luke himself may have drawn on his own knowledge and travel accounts beginning in Acts 16, references to God as *kyrios* are strikingly lacking.

In some passages one could debate whether Jesus or God is the referent. For example, in Acts 2:47 "the Lord" is probably God (cf. Acts 2:34), but in a text like Acts 21:14 *kyrios* could refer to either Jesus or God (cf. Acts 21:13). In Acts 12:11, 17 (cf. Acts 12:5) the "Lord" seems to refer to God, as is more clearly the case in Acts 12:23. But in Acts 7:60, Acts 13:2 and Acts 16:14-15 it appears that Jesus who is prayed to, worshiped and believed in (cf. Kee, 20). This sort of ambiguity does not trouble Luke because in his view the terminology is equally appropriate when used of either God or Jesus, not least because he viewed Jesus as a proper object of worship* and petitionary prayer.*

2. Hebrews.
Of the sixteen references to *kyrios* in Hebrews only three refer to Jesus (Heb 2:3; 7:14; 13:20); the remainder refer to God. Of these thirteen references to God all but one (Heb 8:2) are found in quotations or paraphrases of several OT texts that are important to the writer's argument: Psalm 102:26 cited in Hebrews 1:10; Psalm 110:4 cited in Hebrews 7:21; Jeremiah 31:31-34 cited in Hebrews 8:8-11 and Jeremiah 31:33 cited in Hebrews 10:16; Proverbs 3:11-12 cited in Hebrews 12:5-6; and Psalm 118:6 cited in Hebrews 13:6. That the author does not see an allusion to Jesus as Lord in any OT texts is surprising, since the prologue (Heb 1:1-4) speaks of a role the preexistent Son of God played in the acts of creation* (cf. Wither-

ington, *Sage* 1994; *see* Old Testament in Hebrews). This may in part be explained by the fact that the author does not indulge in midrashic contemporizing of the OT so much as he uses it for typology (cf. G. Hughes).

The author of Hebrews feels free to refer to the earthly Jesus who announced salvation to his first followers as "Lord" (Heb 2:3), and even more tellingly he speaks of Jesus' ancestry as the ancestry of "our Lord." The closing benediction in Hebrews 13:20 refers to God bringing back from the dead "our Lord Jesus." Nothing here suggests an adoptionist christology, but equally clearly there is no stress on Christ's cosmic roles as Lord of the universe. The author rather focuses on the fact that Jesus is "our Lord," and wherever "Lord" refers to Jesus in Hebrews the subject is his historical roles and experiences (e.g., birth, proclamation, death and resurrection). One reason the author feels free to use the term *kyrios* of Jesus during his earthly ministry may be that he sees him as a perfect human being, without sin, and thus above all other mortals (cf. Hoekema).

3. James and Jude.
The usage of *kyrios* in James is easier to analyze than in some NT books. In thirteen instances *kyrios* is used, and in all but four it seems certain that the reference is to God, not Jesus. The references to the Lord Jesus Christ in James 1:1 and James 2:1 provide almost the only clear evidence that this homiletical document is a Christian one, if one did not recognize the echoes of the Sermon on the Mount in various portions of James (see Witherington, *Sage* 1994). In the context of a Christian document James 5:7-8 is also likely a reference to Christ's Second Coming (*see* Parousia). As for the other ten instances of *kyrios,* none reflect any theological meanings, insights or nuances that are specifically Christian in character or that could not be found in general in early Jewish sapiential literature. Thus it is God the Lord to whom one prays (Jas 1:5-7; 5:4—the "Lord Sabaoth" or "almighty") and whom one worships (Jas 3:9). The odd phrase "the Lord and Father" in James 3:9 is surely a reference to one person in view of the single article. It is to God the Lord that one submits or humbles oneself (cf. Jas 4:7 and Jas 4:10) and whose will determines the length of one's life (Jas 4:15).

The prophets spoke in the name of the Lord

God (Jas 5:10), and it was the Lord who finally had compassion on Job (Jas 5:11). The final references to "Lord" (Jas 5:14-15) are ambiguous. Is it in the name of the Lord Jesus that one is to anoint* the sick and to expect the Lord to raise them up (*see* Healing), or is this also a reference to the Lord God who responds to prayers and various forms of petition, as was seen in James 1:5-7 and James 5:4? The latter seems likely. The term *Lord* in James then normally refers to the One who is and has always been sovereign over all the universe and has always been the object of prayer. The references to Jesus as Lord at James 1:1, James 2:1 and probably James 5:7-8 all refer to roles he assumed or will assume after the resurrection, hence the apt qualifier at James 2:1 ("our glorious Lord Jesus"). This way of putting the matter may refer to Jesus as risen in glory* or Jesus as exalted to God's right hand or both. The writer of this document seems to reflect the earliest period of Christian thinking about Jesus, including the early fervency and hope* for his imminent return.

The preceding makes for a striking contrast in terms of emphasis with the use of *kyrios* in another early Jewish Christian document—Jude. Here, with the probable exception of the reference to the Lord God in Jude 9, five other references to *kyrios* in this book apply to Jesus. It is textually uncertain as to whether "Lord" or "Jesus" should be read in Jude 5, but "Jesus" or perhaps "Joshua" is the better attested reference (cf. Metzger, 726). In Jude 4 Jesus is called "our sovereign *[despotēn]* and Lord." His Second Coming with the holy ones (angels?) is referred to in Jude 14, and he is three times called "our Lord Jesus Christ" (Jude 17, 21, 25). He is the one who not only is coming but also will bring the gift of eternal life to the believers (Jude 21). Jude 25 suggests that he is the one through whom one relates to and petitions the only God. Finally the Lord's apostles or sent ones are referred to in Jude 17, the sole reference where "Lord" may be predicated of Jesus during his earthly ministry (cf. Bauckham).

4. 1 Peter and 2 Peter.

Of the eight references to *kyrios* in 1 Peter, one is an example of the mundane use of the term to refer to a human master (what Sarah called Abraham*—1 Pet 3:6), and most of the remaining examples involve an allusion to or quotation of an OT text (*see* Old Testament in the General Epistles). For example, Psalm 34 is alluded to several times. At 1 Peter 2:3, Psalm 34:8 is quoted; and at 1 Peter 3:12, Psalm 34:15-16 is cited, accounting for two further examples of *kyrios*. While in the latter citation it seems clear that the Lord God is meant, at 1 Peter 2:3 the reference could be to Christ, whom the audience has now experienced and found good. More clearly 1 Peter 3:15 is an appeal to acknowledge Christ as the holy Lord, a text that may include a possible allusion to Isaiah 8:13. If so, this provides us with another example in which OT texts are used homiletically to affirm what is true about Jesus (cf. Davies).

In 1 Peter 1:25 *kyrios* seems a clear reference to God, in view of the parallel "word of God" in 1 Peter 1:23. Again an OT text, Isaiah 40:6-8, is being quoted. In the initial thanksgiving at 1 Peter 1:3 we find a clear distinction between God who is Father and "our Lord Jesus Christ." The text says that the one praised is both the God and Father of Jesus. What is less evident in 1 Peter is any connection of the *kyrios* references to a subtext of the story about the various stages in Jesus' career (*see* Intertextuality), though hints in this direction can probably be seen in 1 Peter 1:20 (preexistence) and 1 Peter 3:18-22 (suffering* and atonement). When Christ is the subject, however, the focus is on what Christ now is and should be confessed to be. When God is the subject, *kyrios* is usually introduced because the author is citing the OT. Nevertheless the writer is apparently not shy about using the OT to describe the exalted qualities of Christ as heavenly Lord—he is both holy and good and as such is to be acknowledged and experienced (Krafft).

Of the fourteen references to *kyrios* in 2 Peter, none clearly quote an OT text, but 2 Peter 2:9 and 2 Peter 2:11 are part of a recitation of the stories of God's judgments* by flood and fire (Gen 6—8; 18—19), and in this context it is not surprising that *kyrios* refers to the Lord God. It appears too that when the author reflected on the day of the Lord, he thought of it in terms of the *yôm Yahweh* ("Day of the LORD") spoken of in the OT, and thus it is likely that *kyrios* in 2 Peter 3:8, 9, 10 and 15 refers to God (cf. 2 Pet 3:12 and Witherington 1992 on the *yôm Yahweh*).

All the other references in this letter refer to Christ, as is made evident by the coupling of *kyrios* with either "Jesus" (2 Pet 1:2), "Jesus

671

Christ" (2 Pet 1:8, 11, 14, 16; 3:18) or *sōtēr* (2 Pet 3:2). This writer has a penchant for coupling the term *kyrios* with the term *savior* (2 Pet 1:11; 2:20; 3:2, 18). In neither of the Petrine letters is there any major focus on the cosmic dimensions of Christ's lordship (but cf. 1 Pet 3:21-22). Rather, as the qualifier *our* shows, the focus is on Christ's rule and dominion over the Christian community and individual Christian life (esp. 2 Pet, but see also 1 Pet 1:3). 2 Peter does not reflect the ambiguity we have seen in some of the other NT documents in the use of *kyrios*. In each instance it is clear when Christ is and is not meant. This author does not show the subtlety of use of the OT to speak about lordship that the author of 1 Peter does.

5. The Johannine Epistles and the Apocalypse.
In view of the use of *kyrios* in the Fourth Gospel and the Apocalypse and considering the high christology one finds in 1 John, it comes as a surprise that there are no references to either God or Christ as *kyrios* in the Johannine epistles nor any more mundane uses of the term. Accordingly we must turn our attention to the Apocalypse.

There are twenty-one uses of *kyrios* in the Revelation; in this book, which is a pastiche of OT allusions and images with few direct quotations (*see* Old Testament in Revelation), the use of *kyrios*, particularly in the first half of the book, is like that found in the OT (cf. Black). Besides Revelation 7:14, where the vocative *kyrie* is little more than a term of respect meaning something like "sir," all the references prior to Revelation 11:8 seem clearly to refer to God and not to Jesus as Lord. John likes to use the phrase "the Lord God" (*kyrios ho theos*; Rev 1:8; 4:8; 11:17; 15:3; 16:7; 18:8; 19:6; 21:22; 22:5-6), and especially in a text like Revelation 21:22, where the term is used to distinguish God from the Lamb,* it becomes clear that this phrase does not refer to Jesus, with only one possible exception (see below). This phrase comes up particularly in contexts in which prayer or praise is being offered up to God, and it is sometimes combined with the term *pantokratōr* ("almighty"; Rev 15:3; 19:6; 21:22) to indicate the magnitude of God's sovereignty.

The first clear reference to Jesus as *kyrios* comes at Revelation 11:8, and this is made clear in two ways: by reference to the crucifixion and by the modifier *their* attached to "Lord." It is

unclear with a text like Revelation 14:13 whether dying in the Lord refers to dying for Jesus, but in view of Revelation 14:12 this seems likely. Twice Jesus is acclaimed as King of kings and Lord of lords (Rev 17:14; 19:16) in a context where Christ's eschatological* role of subduing the opposition at the end of history is stressed. He is not merely sovereign over the church but also will exercise his sovereignty over the nations of the world on behalf of the faithful. The more familiar early Christian usage "Lord Jesus" (see above) occurs twice at the end of the document, where Christ's Second Coming and a benediction in Christ's name is invoked (Rev 22:20-21; *see* Liturgical Elements).

One of the most debatable issues in this book is whether at its beginning it is God or Jesus who is called the Lord and the Alpha and Omega (Rev 1:8), especially since the terminology comes up again in Revelation 21:6 and Revelation 22:7, and in the lattermost example it seems rather certain the reference is to the returning Lord Jesus (*see* Christology). However, everywhere else the phrase "the Lord God," especially when qualified by the term *Almighty*, does not refer to Jesus; most scholars think this is also likely the case in Revelation 1:8. Revelation 1:17 may suggest the opposite conclusion, however (cf. Rowland). The point of mentioning this ambiguity is that John, especially in a doxological context, is willing to predicate of Jesus what he predicates of the Lord God, because he sees them as on the same level, being divine and proper objects of worship unlike the angels (cf. Rev 19:10). Jesus, like God's Spirit, is part of John's vision* of what the Godhead is, without at the same time denying the oneness of God. In such circumstances it is understandable that some of the references to *kyrios* in this book could refer to either the Lord Jesus or the Lord God.

6. The Apostolic Fathers.
The use of *kyrios* in the early Christian noncanonical literature, besides reflecting the Christian tendency to use the term of both the Lord God and the Lord Jesus, also reveals some new trends to which we will pay particular attention as we survey the data from the *Epistle of Barnabas*,* the letters of Clement of Rome* to the Corinthians, the epistle of Polycarp to the Philippians, the *Didache*,* the *Shepherd of Hermas*,* and the letters of Ignatius* of Antioch.

6.1. The Epistle of Barnabas. One of the more Jewish and eschatological of the early Christian noncanonical books is the *Epistle of Barnabas.* At *Barnabas* 15.4 we find the speculation that the Lord will make an end of human history in six thousand years, since Genesis 2:2 talks about God finishing his work in six days and since one day is as a thousand years for the Lord. Also, the "day of the Lord" is said to last one thousand years (*see* Day of the Lord). As in the other places in this work where the OT is the basis of the discussion (*see* Old Testament in the Apostolic Fathers), "Lord" seems to mean God, not Jesus.

This is the case at *Barnabas* 2.6, where a quote from Isaiah 1:1-13 is introduced with "says the Lord" (so also at *Barn.* 4.8, introducing Ex 32:16; *Barn.* 6.14, introducing Ezek 11:19; 36:26; *Barn.* 9.1, which uses Jer 4:4), or at *Barnabas* 2.10, where Psalm 51:19 is quoted about "sacrifice for the Lord." The same phenomenon can be seen at *Barnabas* 3.1, which uses Isaiah 58:4-5; *Barnabas* 3.3, which borrows from Isaiah 58:6-10; or *Barnabas* 4.7, where Exodus 34:28 is quoted about the finger and covenant* of the Lord. One may also note the use of Isaiah 1:2 and Isaiah 1:10 at *Barnabas* 9.3 or the use of Jeremiah 9:25-26 at *Barnabas* 9.5. The reference to the commandments* of the Lord after the citation of the Mosaic law* (Lev 11:3; Deut 14:6) suggests that "Lord" means "God" in this text. And the reference to the Lord foretelling the cross* and the baptism* at *Barnabas* 11.1 is likely also a reference to God, not Jesus.

The phrase "Lord God" (*kyrios ho theos*) is found in a quote of Isaiah 45:2-3 at *Barnabas* 11.4, and immediately thereafter we hear of the fear of the Lord (*Barn.* 11.5). The conglomerate citations (Ex 24:18; 31:18; 32:7-19; Deut 9:12-17) in *Barnabas* 14.1-5 all involve reference to the Lord God. The quote of Isaiah 42:6-7 ("I the Lord thy God") at *Barnabas* 14.7-8 is followed by the juxtaposition *kyrios . . . theos* (*Barn* 14.8). This Lord speaks in Scripture (cf. *Barn.* 16.2), gives the OT commandments (*Barn.* 19.2) and is the one whose name must not be taken in vain (*Barn.* 19.5, quoting Deut 5:11). He is the Lord from eternity to eternity (*Barn.* 18.2). Yet it may be we should distinguish him from "the Lord of glory" referred to in the closing benediction (*Barn.* 21.9). Other ambiguous references could refer to Christ or God, such as the mention of the kingdom* of the Lord at *Barnabas* 4.13 (cf. *Barn.* 1.1, 4, 6).

Yet the term *Lord* can also be used of Jesus, even during the course of his earthly ministry. Thus at *Barnabas* 5.1 we hear of the Lord delivering his flesh* up to corruption, or at *Barnabas* 7.2 we hear of the Son of God who was the Lord and suffered to make us alive. Yet at *Barnabas* 7.3 "the Lord" seems to refer to Yahweh as the one who commanded what is recorded in Leviticus 23:29. Again at *Barnabas* 2.6 the phrase "Lord Jesus Christ" (who gives the new law) is used for the only time in this document.

Perhaps the most important clue about the use of *kyrios* comes at *Barnabas* 12.10, where the familiar citation of Psalm 110:1 ("the Lord speaking to my Lord") is used. The author makes clear that the "my Lord" is Christ, while "the Lord" is God. Since this verse was widely used in early Christianity and perhaps even by Jesus himself (see Witherington 1990, 189-91), it may be that this verse and its influence guided early Christians in distinguishing between God as Lord and Jesus as Lord, namely, that the use of the possessive with *kyrios* would signal Christ, while the phrase "the Lord" would normally refer to the Father unless further contextual data were added to clarify the meaning. In tone, use of the OT and christological character, *Barnabas* seems most like Jude and as such likely reflects the first- or at latest early-second-century milieu of Jewish Christianity (*see* Jewish Christianity).

6.2. The Letters of Clement. The first letter of Clement to the Corinthians is in some respects the noncanonical letter most like the canonical Pauline ones, with various allusions to Paul's Corinthian correspondence and possibly also to Hebrews (cf. Goodspeed). We might expect from this that there would be a similar christological use of the term *Lord* in both contexts. For instance, at *1 Clement* 12.7 we hear about the blood of the Lord and at *1 Clement* 21.6 about the blood of the Lord Jesus Christ. Even more clearly we find the quotation that Paul uses several times about boasting in the Lord (cf. *1 Clem.* 13.1 with 1 Cor 1:31; 2 Cor 10:17). We also find the mention of the Lord Jesus Christ, who is the first fruits from the dead (*1 Clem.* 24.1; 42.3; cf. 1 Cor 15:20). The Lord Jesus Christ is said to be the elect* or chosen one at *1 Clement* 64.1 (cf. 1 Cor 1:2), and he concludes at *1 Clement* 65.2 with the Pauline benediction "the grace of our Lord Jesus Christ." It is the Lord Jesus Christ who now lives as God lives (in heaven), according to *1 Clement* 58.2. Finally we are told that the apostles knew that later there would be strife over the title of bishop through our Lord Jesus Christ.

It is also true that when Clement uses the OT in this letter, "Lord" seems to refer only to the Lord God. Thus the reference to Isaiah 1:16-20 at *1 Clement* 8.4 is followed with the familiar "says the Lord." In the discourse on Isaiah 53:1-12 at *1 Clement* 16 "Lord" means God not only in the quotation of the text but also after it when Clement refers to the fact that "the Lord delivered him [i.e., Christ] up for our sins." The quotation of Proverbs 20:27 about "the Spirit of the Lord" is of a similar nature, as is the reference to the fear of the Lord at *1 Clement* 22.1, where Psalm 34:11-17 is alluded to. One may also note the conglomerate citation of texts from Deuteronomy and Numbers at *1 Clement* 29.2-3, where the subject is the portion of the Lord. The Genesis creation* story is cited as proof that the Lord God adorned the divine self with good works, and the believer is urged to do likewise at *1 Clement* 33.4-8. Exodus 31 and Exodus 32 are used to speak of the pardoning of sins* by the Lord God (*1 Clem.* 53.4), and Job 5:17-26 is used to stress the Lord's chastening and reproving of his people (*1 Clem.* 56.3-6).

The use of the OT in 1 Clement shows that this author stands in some contact with the earliest Jewish Christian reflections on Jesus (see 1, 2 above) and writes before the overly christological reading of the OT has become dominant (cf. Hanson and Hagner).

2 Clement deserves a separate treatment, not least because it was not likely written by Clement but is a later document. This document, unlike *1 Clement*, is full of allusions to sayings of Jesus rather than those of Paul and also has some OT quotes or allusions in which "Lord" means "God." For examples of the former phenomenon we may examine *2 Clement* 4.1-2, where Matthew 7:21 is quoted and the author refers to the fact that lip service to the Lord will not save a person. At *2 Clement* 6.1 the phrase "the Lord says" introduces a quote of Matthew 6:24/Luke 16:13, and at *2 Clement* 8.5 it prefaces a partial quote from Luke 16:10-12. This text is said to be part of the commandments of the Lord (*2 Clem.* 8.4). At *2 Clement* 9.11 the phrase "the Lord said" prefaces a paraphrase of Mark 3:35 and its parallels. A saying, sometimes attributed to the apocryphal* *Gospel of the Egyptians*, is attributed

to the Lord (Jesus) at *2 Clement* 4.5: "If you are gathered together into my bosom and do not do my commandments, I will cast you out." There seems to be a partial quotation from 1 Corinthians 2:9 at *2 Clement* 14.5 speaking about "what the Lord has prepared" for his elect. The preceding suggests that by the time the author of *2 Clement* was writing, the Gospels and Paul's writings were being treated as sacred texts, equally useful as the OT to be used in saying something authoritative about God and "the Lord Jesus."

The author of *2 Clement* seems to go further than the other authors we have surveyed in saying that Christ the Lord "saved us, though he was originally spirit, became flesh and so called us" (*2 Clem.* 9.5). In other words he speaks of a preexistent Lord (cf. Craddock).

OT quotations are not frequent in this document, but where we find them and the term *kyrios* it seems to refer to God *simpliciter*. For example, the quote of Isaiah 52:5 is introduced by "For the Lord says"; Isaiah 66:24 is quoted at *2 Clement* 17:4, and in both instances "Lord" refers to God. The reference to the will of the Lord in the first part of *2 Clement* 14.1 is followed by the quote of Jeremiah 7:11 and seems to refer to God, since in the first part of *2 Clement* 14.1 the phrase "the will of the Father" is found.

6.3. The Letter of Polycarp to the Philippians. Polycarp's *Letter to the Philippians* is a brief work in which we find various explicitly Christian uses of the term *kyrios*. Thus we find the phrase "the Lord Jesus Christ" repeatedly (Pol. *Phil.* 1.1-2; 2.1; 12.2; 14.1). There appear to be no examples in this letter where "Lord" does not mean Jesus. Lord and God are clearly distinguished in the interesting image of standing before the eyes of the Lord and of God (Pol. *Phil.* 6.2). At the same time the author speaks of "our Lord and God Jesus Christ" (Pol. *Phil.* 12.2, in the Latin portion of the manuscript). This phrase is followed immediately by the comment that God raised this Lord and God from the dead (see also Pol. *Phil.* 2.1, which speaks about the raising of the Lord).

Various references are less explicitly christological. Thus we hear about what the Lord taught, with a quote of Matthew 7:1-2 (Pol. *Phil.* 2.3; see 6.2 above on *2 Clement*), about walking in the commandment of the Lord at 4:1 (Pol. *Phil.* 4.1; see 6.5 below) or about the oracles of the Lord (Pol. *Phil.* 7.1; *see* Jesus Traditions). We hear about the truth of the Lord who was servant of all, a clear reference to his earthly ministry (Pol. *Phil.* 5.2), and Polycarp speaks about "those who had known the Lord," by which he means those who had known the historical Jesus (Pol. *Phil.* 11.3; cf. Pol. *Phil.* 13.2). As we shall see with the letters of Ignatius, this letter also focuses on Christ as Lord and makes no distinction between the Jesus of history and the risen Lord, using the latter terminology even of the earthly Jesus. While the Lord Jesus may be called God in this document, God the Father is not called the Lord.

6.4. The Didache. The *Didache* uses as its most consistent term for Jesus Christ *kyrios,* beginning in the prescript with a reference to the Lord that unmistakably refers to Christ (the "Lord's teaching to the heathen by the twelve apostles"). At *Didache* 8.2 we have a clear reference to Christ as Lord who commanded his disciples to pray the Lord's Prayer. A saying of Jesus is quoted at *Didache* 9.5 (cf. Mt 7:6) as a saying of the Lord, and this is immediately preceded by a reference to baptism in the Lord's name. There is a good deal of discussion in this work about honoring and receiving those who come and speak in the name of the Lord as if it were the Lord who had come in person (*Did.* 4.1; 11.2, 4; 12.1), for they bring the knowledge* of the Lord. The Jewish concept of agency ("a man's agent [*šāliaḥ/apostolos*] is as himself"; cf. Hurtado 1988) seems evident in such cases. The test of whether a prophet speaks in the name of Christ is whether "he has the behavior of the Lord" *(tous tropous kyriou, Did.* 11.8). Probably the reference to bearing the yoke of the Lord is an allusion to Jesus' yoke (Mt 11:29-30). Even clearer is the reference to the gospel* of the Lord at *Didache* 15.4 or the Lord coming on the clouds at *Didache* 16.8 (cf. *Did.* 16.1).

There are also various uses of *kyrios* referring to God, especially when an OT passage is cited or alluded to (*Did.* 4.12-13, quoting Deut 4:2; *Did.* 14.3, alluding to Mal 1:11, 14). In general when the Gospel material is quoted or alluded to, "Lord" means Jesus, while when the OT is used God is meant. Like James, the *Didache* arises out of a Jewish Christian milieu that is in close contact with the Matthean form of Jesus' sayings (cf. Witherington, *Sage* 1994; *see* Matthean Community; Worship).

At *Didache* 14.1 we have the redundant expression "on the Lord's day of the Lord" *(kyriakēn de kyriou),* which suggests that by the time this document was written the phrase "Lord's day"* was conventional. The idea of a Lord's day is found in Revelation 1:10, but there it is not specified as a day of Christian worship or identified as being the first day of the week. There is, however, a contrast between the Lord's day and the Jewish sabbath in Ignatius's writings (Ign. *Magn.* 9.1), where it is said that Christians no longer live for the sabbath (on Ignatius see 6.6 below). We may conclude from these various hints that a Lord's day was set apart and special for various early Christians (Rom 14:5-6), but there was probably not a uniform practice in this matter in early Christianity.

One may also point out the use of *marana tha* in *Didache* 10.6, in a context similar to what one finds in 1 Corinthians 16:22. In both cases the Aramaic phrase is not translated and occurs just before the close of a section of the document. In both cases the phrase probably should be seen as a prayer formula, especially in view of the similarity to Revelation 22:20, and should be translated as "Come, Lord" (*marana tha* rather than *maran atha,* which would probably be translated "the Lord [has] come"; cf. Witherington 1995).

The author of the *Didache* uses the term *kyrios* in some of the same diverse ways we find in the canonical texts. He shows no hesitancy to refer to the earthly Jesus as already the Lord, who gave various teachings and did various things. There is no hint of adoptionism in this work.

6.5. The Shepherd of Hermas. In the lengthy Jewish Christian work commonly called the *Shepherd of Hermas* the term *kyrios* appears dozens of times, and almost without any possible exception the term refers to God, not to Jesus. The author prefers to use the term "the Son" to refer to Jesus and uses the term "the Lord" in its OT manner, including the use of such familiar OT phrases or concepts as "the fear of the Lord" (*Herm. Man.* 7.1; 10.1.6, paralleling "the fear of God"), "knowing the Lord" (*Herm. Vis.* 3.3.1), the angel of the Lord (*Herm. Sim.* 8.1.2; 8.2.1), "the commandment(s) of the Lord" (*Herm. Vis.* 3.5.3; 3.8.2; *Herm. Sim.* 5.2.4; 8.3.8; 8.7.6), "sinning against the Lord" (*Herm. Vis.* 1.3.4; 3.1.5-6), blaspheming the Lord (*Herm. Vis.* 2.2.2; *Herm. Sim.* 6.2.4), serving the Lord (*Herm. Man.* 5.1.3; *Herm. Sim.* 7.6; 9.27.3; in

Herm. Sim. 1.7; 4.5 appropriately using *douleuontes tō kyriō)* and praying to or petitioning of the Lord (cf. *Herm. Vis.* 1.1.3; 2.2.1; 3.1.2; 3.9.6; 3.10.6; *Herm. Sim.* 5.3.7; 5.4.3).

The vocative *kyrie* is used repeatedly in direct address to God and others with no particular nuances about the divinity of the one addressed (cf. *Herm. Sim.* 3.1; 4.1; 5.1; 6.5.5; 7.1 and passim). *Kyrios* also appears to refer to a human ruler of a country (*Herm. Sim.* 1.1.4).

Some debate could be offered as to whether Christ might be alluded to in the references to suffering in the name of the Lord (*Herm. Vis.* 3.5.2; cf. *Herm. Sim.* 8.1.1), but the author does not make clear that such is the case. A christological reference is more probable when the author speaks of those who had the name of the Lord called over them (presumably at baptism; *Herm. Sim.* 8.6.4, apparently a quote of Jas 2:7; see also *Herm. Sim.* 9.26.6). The use of *kyrios* with the possessive *their* may suggest that Jesus is meant (*Herm. Vis.* 3.6.5), but the author does not say so explicitly. It seems clear that some later Christian scribes felt frustrated with lack of clear reference to Christ, for there are places in some manuscripts where the possessive *our* is added to "Lord" in a way that suggests a christological reference (*Herm. Vis.* 3.9.10 and the textual variants). Whenever the OT is quoted or alluded to with a reference to "the Lord," a theological rather than christological reference seems clear (*Herm. Vis.* 3.11.3, quoting Ps 55:22; *Herm. Vis.* 4.2.4, where "God" parallels "Lord"; *Herm. Man.* 4.2.2, using a phrase similar to that found in Judg 2:11; 3:12; *Herm. Man.* 9.6 cf. with Prov 3:5).

A reference to the indwelling Lord (*Herm. Man.* 3.1.1) seems to be further identified as the spirit (*pneuma*) that dwells within "this flesh." The one who has the Lord in his heart is contrasted with the one who has the Lord only on his lips (*Herm. Man.* 12.4.3-5). One finds the phrase "put on the faith of the Lord" (*endysai tēn pistin tou kyriou, Herm. Sim.* 6.1.2; also at *Herm. Sim. 6.3.6),* which may mean faith in the Lord but could equally well mean the faith that the Lord had and modeled for believers to follow (cf. Witherington, *Narrative* 1994). In either case, but especially if we are dealing with a subjective genitive, we likely have a christological reference. A christological reference seems even more probable in *Similtudes* 5.4.3, in which we hear about the "sayings of the Lord" (*ta*

rhēmata tou kyriou; also at *Herm. Sim.* 9.11.8).

Toward the end of the work, in the section of parables, christological references to the Son* become more prevalent, and we also find the remarkable reference to "the glorious man and Lord of all the tower" (i.e., the church; *Herm. Sim.* 9.7.1). The first two major sections of the document have little if any christology, but this is not the case as the third section of the book draws to a close. Yet at places in this third division of the work a clear distinction is made between "the Lord" and the Son, the former referring to the Father. For example, the Son is the only gate or entrance to the Lord (*Herm. Sim.* 9.11.6); we also we find the phrase "those who believe on the Lord through his Son" (*Herm. Sim.* 9.13.5). Even as late as *Similitudes* 9.19.1 we find "Lord" paralleling and alluding to God, not Christ. *Similitudes* 9.23.4 says, "God and our Lord who [singular] rules over all . . . bears no malice"; "God" and "Lord" refer to one person, and the verb that follows is also in the singular (*mnesikakei*).

All these permutations and combinations bear witness to a Jewish person who has become a Christian, and while he is familiar with the language of the Hebrew Scriptures, he has made some adjustments in his language to include God's Son, who on some occasions he alludes to as the Lord. This document may reflect the sort of ethos that existed among Jewish Christians in Rome.* It was so highly valued that various Christian writers in the second and third centuries regarded it as Scripture (cf. Duffy, 437.)

6.6 The Letters of Ignatius. The letters of Ignatius of Antioch display a plethora of uses of *kyrios,* and some uses are of special interest as they show how ideas developed after the canonical period.

In these letters *kyrios* seems always to refer to Christ. The phrase "the Lord Jesus Christ" is frequently coupled with "God the Father" in initial greetings (Ign. *Pol.;* Ign. *Phld.;* also at Phil 1:2) or closing remarks as the one who rewards the faithful (Ign. *Smyrn.* 11.2), or it is used when Ignatius speaks of the cross (Ign. *Smyrn.* 1.1). This comports with his other references to the flesh of the Lord (Ign. *Trall.* 8.1) or the passion of the Lord (Ign. *Phld.* presc.). He can even use the phrase the "flesh of the Lord Jesus Christ" to refer to what one is united with in partaking of the Eucharist *(Ign. Phil.* 4.1). This phrase is also used when he refers to the coming of the Savior "our Lord Jesus Christ" (Ign. *Phld.* 9.2).

Ignatius is influenced by Paul's letters, and so he speaks about being imitators of the Lord (cf. Ign. *Eph.* 3.2 with 1 Cor 11:1 and Trakatellis). He also closes a letter using a Pauline phrase, *en kyriō* (Ign. *Pol.* 8.3). It is the Lord about whom Ignatius gives testimony (Ign. *Trall.* 10.1), and he stresses that bishops should be regarded as the Lord himself (Ign. *Eph.* 6.1). The Lord is the one who forgives those who repent (Ign. *Phld.* 8.1; *see* Forgiveness; Repentance), who receives believers (Ign. *Smyrn.* 11.1) and who knows the secrets of the heart (Ign. *Eph.* 15.3). It is the Lord Jesus who came and acted upon the earth (Ign. *Smyrn.* 4.2). As D. Trakatellis stresses, Ignatius did not invent the idea of applying God language to Jesus, but he, more than any other figure in the literature surveyed, reflects the theology of the church that was to become orthodoxy through the councils of Nicea and Chalcedon. In particular he reflects the idea of the Incarnation and the full lordship of Christ even before his earthly ministry.

In insistence and emphasis, though not in substance, Ignatius breaks new christological ground. "What Ignatius did was to interpret the Johannine and Pauline christological traditions or formulas in a way that could serve the immediate and pressing needs of the church. . . . One of the results of his interpretation is his fascinating God language" (Trakatellis, 430). It is probable that the influence of Docetists* on some of Ignatius's flock pressured him in this direction.

6.7. Justin Martyr. Of the material that has been generally accepted as coming from the hand of Justin Martyr (*Apology I, Apology II* and the *Dialogue with Trypho*) only a little needs to be said. When Justin quotes the OT, *kyrios* tends to refer to God the Father rather than Christ (cf. Justin *Apol. I* 37 with *Dial. Tryph.* 27), but there are exceptions: he appears to quote some form of Psalm 96, referring to "the Lord has reigned from the tree," or he quotes Lamentations 4:20 (LXX) as speaking of "the breath before our face is the Lord Christ." On the basis of texts like Psalm 110:1, Justin argues that David calls Jesus both "Christ and God" (Justin *Dial. Tryph.* 126). In a striking manner Justin speaks of the Lord who rained fire from heaven and the other Lord who descended to behold the cry of Sodom, thus following the tradition of the christological interpretation of the OT (Justin *Dial. Tryph.* 129).

Justin regularly uses the phrase "God the Father and Lord of all" (e.g., Justin *Apol. I* 36, 44; *Dial. Tryph.* 7), but he can speak of "the Lord or his Father" immediately after speaking of "God the Lord and Father" (Justin *Apol. I* 36). Again Justin says, "I will mention to you other words also spoken by the blessed David, from which you will perceive that the Lord is called the Christ . . . and that the Lord, the Father of all, has brought him again from the earth setting him at his own right hand until He makes his enemies his footstool . . . from the time that our Lord Jesus Christ ascended to heaven" (Justin *Dial. Tryph.* 32). This and other texts show that Justin, like other early Christian writers, stresses that Christ is especially "our Lord" (cf. Justin *Dial. Tryph.* 133). It becomes clear that for Justin the term *kyrios* is not used simply to refer to what has become true of Christ since the resurrection. Because of the christological interpretation of the OT, Christ is seen to be referred to as Lord not only in Jewish prophecy about the future but also in the narratives. The Son at various points is the Lord who is involved in events that transpired long before the Incarnation. The clarity and frequency of these sorts of references show a development beyond what we find in the NT, but it is in a direction already seen or hinted at in the canon.

7. Summary.

In all these documents we have seen both certain repeated patterns and a considerable variety in the use of the term *kyrios*. It is noticeable that only some of the canonical texts (e.g., Acts) seem to reflect an attempt to use the term *kyrios* in a way that reflects the narrative subtext about Jesus' earthly and heavenly career.

It is also noticeable that the more a document is influenced by the OT and Jewish ideas, the more the term *kyrios,* if it stands alone, is likely to refer to the Lord God, not the Lord Jesus. Yet this is only a trend, not a universal pattern. This lack of clear and universal patterns suggests it is well not to exaggerate the image of Jewish Christian communities developing their own theologies apart from Gentile* Christians and their communities. Rather, one must think in terms of cross-fertilization; all early Jewish Christians were at least somewhat Hellenized, though a particular author will normally reflect his primary background and influences most of the time.

All this material suggests that Jewish ways of thinking about Jesus and God persisted well into the second century and that the high christology one finds in Ignatius of Antioch had precedents in earlier Christian documents that came to be seen as canonical, particularly the Pauline and Johannine ones. The old, neat dichotomies between early and primitive Jewish christologies versus later, higher and more Hellenistic christologies are too simplistic when one studies the material carefully, especially in view of the enormous importance of sapiential ways of thinking about Jesus from the beginnings of early Christianity (cf. Witherington, *Sage* 1994).

See also CHRIST; CHRISTOLOGY; DOCETISM; LAMB; LITURGICAL ELEMENTS; LOGOS CHRISTOLOGY; LORD'S DAY; PREEXISTENCE; SHEPHERD, FLOCK; SON OF GOD; STONE, CORNERSTONE; WISDOM.

BIBLIOGRAPHY. R. J. Bauckham, *Jude, 2 Peter* (WBC; Waco, TX: Word, 1983); H. Bietenhard, "Lord," *NIDNTT* 2:510-20; M. Black, "The Christological Use of the Old Testament in the New Testament," *NTS* 18 (1971-72) 1-14; F. B. Craddock, *The Preexistence of Christ in the New Testament* (Nashville: Abingdon, 1968); O. Cullmann, *The Christology of the New Testament* (Philadelphia: Westminster, 1959); P. E. Davies, "Primitive Christology in 1 Peter" in *Festschrift to Honor F. W. Gingrich,* ed. E. H. Barth and R. E. Cocraft (Leiden: E. J. Brill, 1972) 115-22; S. H. Duffy, "The Early Church Fathers and the Great Councils: The Emergence of Classical Christianity" in *Jesus One and Many: The Christological Concept of New Testament Authors,* ed. E. Richard (Wilmington, DE: Michael Glazier, 1988) 435-86; J. D. G. Dunn, *Christology in the Making* (Philadelphia: Westminster, 1980); idem, *The Partings of the Ways Between Christianity and Judaism and Their Significance for the Character of Christianity* (Philadelphia: Trinity Press International, 1991); J. A. Fitzmyer, *The Gospel According to Luke 1-9* (Garden City, NY: Doubleday, 1981) 143-270; idem, "The Semitic Background of the New Testament Kyrios-Title" in *A Wandering Aramean: Collected Aramaic Essays* (Missoula, MT: Scholars Press, 1979) 115-42; W. Foerster, "κύριος κτλ," *TDNT* 3:1039-98; E. J. Goodspeed, "First Clement Called Forth by Hebrews," *JBL* 30 (1911) 157-60; D. A. Hagner, *The Jewish Reclamation of Jesus: An Analysis and Critique of the Modern Jewish Study of Jesus* (Grand Rapids: Zondervan, 1984); A. T. Hanson, *Jesus Christ in the Old Testament* (London: SPCK, 1965); M. Hengel, *Between Jesus and Paul* (Philadelphia: Fortress, 1983); idem, "Christological Titles in Early Christianity" in *The Messiah: Developments in Earliest Judaism and Christianity,* ed. J. H. Charlesworth (Minneapolis: Fortress, 1992) 425-48; A. A. Hoekema, "The Perfection of Christ in Hebrews," *CTJ* 9 (1974) 31-37; G. Hughes, *Hebrews and Hermeneutics: The Epistle to the Hebrews as a New Testament Example of Biblical Interpretation* (SNTSMS 36; Cambridge: Cambridge University Press, 1979); P. E. Hughes, "The Christology of Hebrews," *SWJT* 28 (1985) 19-27; L. W. Hurtado, *One God, One Lord* (Philadelphia: Fortress, 1988); D. L. Jones, "The Title *kyrios* in Luke-Acts" in *SBLSP* (1974) 2:85-101; H. C. Kee, *Good News to the Ends of the Earth: The Theology of Acts* (Philadelphia: Trinity Press International, 1990); H. Krafft, "Christologie und Eschatologie im 1. Petrusbrief," *EvT* 10 (1950-51) 120-26; R. N. Longenecker, *The Christology of Early Jewish Christianity* (SBT 2d series 17; Naperville, IL: Allenson, 1970); B. M. Metzger, *A Textual Commentary on the Greek New Testament* (New York: United Bible Societies, 1971); C. F. D. Moule, "The Christology of Acts" in *Studies in Luke-Acts,* ed. L. E. Keck and J. L. Martyn (Nashville: Abingdon, 1966) 159-85; R. C. Nevius, "*Kyrios* and *Iēsous* in St. Luke," *ATR* 48 (1966) 75-77; C. Rowland, "The Vision of Christ in Rev. 1.13ff. The Debt of an Early Christology to an Aspect of Jewish Angelology," *JTS* 31 (1980) 1-11; J. T. Squires, *The Plan of God in Luke-Acts* (Cambridge: Cambridge University Press, 1993); D. Trakatellis, "God Language in Ignatius of Antioch" in *The Future of Early Christianity: Essays in Honor of Helmut Koester,* ed. B. Pearson et al. (Minneapolis: Fortress, 1991) 422-30; B. Witherington III, *The Christology of Jesus* (Minneapolis: Fortress, 1990); idem, *Conflict and Community in Corinth: A Socio-Rhetorical Commentary on 1 and 2 Corinthians* (Grand Rapids: Eerdmans, 1995); idem, ed., *History, Literature and Society in the Book of Acts* (Cambridge: Cambridge University Press, 1996); idem, *Jesus, Paul and the End of the World* (Downers Grove, IL: InterVarsity Press, 1992); idem, *Jesus the Sage: The Pilgrimage of Wisdom* (Minneapolis: Fortress, 1994); idem, *Paul's Narrative Thought World: The Tapestry of Tragedy and Triumph* (Louisville, KY: Westminster/John Knox, 1994).

B. Witherington III

LORD'S DAY

Lord's day observance in weekly commemoration of Jesus' resurrection* on "the first day of the week" began at an early point in the apostolic age and in the post-apostolic age involved transfer of Mosaic law* to new covenant* structures and norms.

1. Introduction
2. Linguistic Considerations
3. Historical Considerations
4. Theological Considerations

1. Introduction.

Discussion of the Lord's day treats the development leading to second-century and later Sunday worship* in relation to the Jewish sabbath. Was there a transfer during the apostolic age wherein a creation ordinance, involving the principle of one day in seven, was shifted along with the fourth "word" of the Decalogue to the Lord's day (e.g., Beckwith and Stott; Murray)? Or did a shift from sabbath to Sunday begin only in the second century in the context of increasing anti-Judaism in the church* and in direct contravention of the practice and teaching of the Lord* and his apostles,* who had upheld sabbath observance (Bacchiocchi; Strand)? Or did Lord's day observance arise during the apostolic age alongside sabbath observance and essentially independently from it, while the Mosaic sabbath was seen to find its fulfillment in the work of Christ* broadly conceived (Carson)? The discussion thus involves the interrelationship of both historical and theological issues. Recent study has tended to highlight the sparsity and ambiguity of the earlier historical evidence, and this article will devote most of its space to that side of the question, followed by a briefer treatment of related theological issues.

2. Linguistic Considerations.

The adjective kyriakos first appears in Greek literature in 1 Corinthians 11:20 and elsewhere in the NT only in Revelation 1:10. Nor is it used in non-Christian Jewish literature. In secular Greek, where the word begins to appear A.D. 68, after but independent of Paul's usage, it almost always refers to the emperor* and has the sense of "belonging to the emperor" or "imperial."

Among second-century Christian writers the phrase kyriakē hēmera or kyriakē alone means "the Lord's day" in the following passages: Didache 14.1; Ignatius Magnesians 9.1; Gospel of Peter 35, 50; Dionysius of Corinth (Eusebius Hist. Eccl. 4.23.11 [PG 20.388C]); Epistula Apostolorum 18 (Coptic); Acts of Peter (Actus Vercellenses 29-30); Acts of Paul; Melito of Sardis (Eusebius Hist. Eccl. 4.26.2 [PG 20.389A]); Irenaeus Fragment 7 (PG 7.1233); and Valentinian (Clement of Alexandria Excerpts from Theodotus 63 [PG 9.689B]). In Clement of Alexandria the phrase kyriakē hēmera occurs twice: Stromateis 5.14 (PG 9.161A) and 7.12 (PG 9.504C). In addition kyriakos is used several times in other connections. For further linguistic considerations see LSJ 1013; MM 364; BAGD 458; PGL 785-86; Louw-Nida, 1:139; Bietenhard, 518; Fitzmyer, 331; Foerster; Spicq; Stott NIDNTT 3:411-12.

Examination of usage leads to the conclusion that "in meaning the word kyriakos is simply synonymous with (tou) kyriou in all cases where (tou) kyriou is used adjectivally with a noun, with the exception of the objective genitive" (Bauckham, 224); kyriakos and (tou) kyriou seem to be interchangeable. The sparse usage of the adjective in the NT (twice) corresponds to contemporary usage in general and is probably not due to any special meaning. The expression "Lord's day" was not likely in use when 1 Corinthians and Acts* were written, so that its absence in those works does not count as evidence against any custom. The use of the adjective kyriakos in this particular expression does become relatively common, however, probably due to the fact that hēmera (tou) kyriou was already a technical expression for the eschatological* Day of the Lord (see Day of the Lord). There is also no linguistic support for the thesis (Rordorf 1968) that the use of the same adjective in 1 Corinthians 11:20 and Revelation 1:10 indicates that the Lord's day grew out of the Lord's Supper.* The terminological correlation could have been noted already in the first century, but the thesis that the name of the day grew out of the name of the meal is unproven (Bauckham, 226-27, 233-36).

3. Historical Considerations.

It will be taken for granted that many Christians would have kept sabbath throughout the apostolic period and beyond (e.g., Bacchiocchi, 132-64); Jesus himself had done so, and Easter was observed annually in connection with the Passover (Jeremias, 900-904). The question is not whether Christianity created a rival "feast" but whether there is any evidence for a practice, within the apostolic period, of meeting to "break bread" on the first day of each week due to the fact that the Messiah's resurrection had occurred on that day.

3.1. 1 Corinthians 16:2. At a fairly early date Paul directs the Corinthians to provide for his collection campaign by following a rule that he had also established for the churches in Galatia, that is, to lay up an amount of money weekly, specifically on "the first day of the week" (1 Cor 16:2). The traditional approach to the passage has been to assume that the last detail has no rationale unless Paul is assuming that this day was already a special occasion for the church. The chief objection to this interpretation has been that Paul directs the Corinthians to lay up funds privately. No regular gathering or common coffer (cf. Acts 4:34—5:2) in connection with an assembly is mentioned, let alone commanded.

This point can nonetheless be made to prove too much if it is made to suggest that the church did not meet on that day. The fact remains that Paul specifies "the first day of the week" and takes for granted that the choice of this particular day would have made sense to the Corinthians (as it also had to the churches in Galatia). Did Paul pick that day at random, simply wanting to encourage regular giving? Possibly. Did he select it due to budgetary principles? Perhaps, though the argument is at best conjecture and possibly special pleading (nor is there evidence that the first day was pay day). If we have not excluded on dogmatic grounds the possibility of a regular assembly on the day in question, then some such custom remains the most likely explanation.

First, it should not be overlooked that the phrase "the first day of the week" occurs in the NT outside of 1 Corinthians 16:2 and Acts 20:7 only in the resurrection narratives (Mk 16:2; Mt 28:1; Lk 24:1; Jn 20:1,19; in the LXX only the title to Ps 23 [24]) and that in spite of the passion prediction concerning the "third day." Given that the planetary week was in general use at the time (Bacchiocchi, 238-51), it is reasonable to expect that Paul's casual usage of the Jewish name of the day with a predominantly Gentile audience has behind it some further explanation. We may assume what is probable (1 Cor 11:23-26; 15:1-8, though Paul alludes to the "third day"), namely, that this church has in some fashion been exposed to the narrative

traditions that would later with one voice identify the day of the resurrection and appearances as the "first day of the week" (and John does so emphatically; see 3.4 below). We may also note the usage (and nonusage) of the expression in the literary remains of apostolic Christianity and observe the contextual proximity of 1 Corinthians 16:1-4 to the discussion of the resurrection in the previous chapter (although no thematic link is demanded). In view of the absence of any other explanation for the selection of this day, it is no matter of eisegesis to find hints of "resurrection day" in Paul's use of the expression in 1 Corinthians 16:2.

Second, Paul invested this collection with far-reaching theological significance (e.g., Rom 15:27). Such a *diakonia tēs leitourgias* (ministry of service; 2 Cor 9:12; cf. Rom 15:27) and a gathering for celebration of the Eucharist would presumably be mutually augmentative and fittingly joined on the day of the resurrection, even if they did not transpire at the same time on that day. Even if the church met other days as well it remains suggestive that Paul singled out this day for the purposes of personal participation (weekly) in a profoundly spiritual act. It therefore seems better to conclude that Christians did customarily meet on the "first day of the week" and to infer that there is a good reason for the private nature of the collection than to assume that the private nature of the collection excludes any meeting. Even so, at best the text only assumes a custom of meeting on the first day, and the directions regarding the collection would seem to highlight that day's observance; there is no imperative stated or assumed.

3.2. Luke 24:1. In his account of the resurrection Luke records the appearance of Jesus to two disciples on the way to Emmaus (Lk 24:13-35), noting that this took place on the same day as the resurrection (Lk 24:13), that is, "on the first day of the week" (Lk 24:1). Upon arriving at the village, Luke reports, Jesus took bread, blessed and broke it, and gave it to them (Lk 24:30). The wording is quite similar to that of Luke 22:19, and we may with some confidence take this as an allusion to the Last Supper. Whether we have here an account of the founding of first-day observance cannot be demonstrated. Yet from the standpoint of Luke's Gospel we have a celebration of the Lord's Supper on the day of the resurrection (the two are not unrelated), specifically, "on the first day of the week." No custom is indicated, nor is there any basis for finding here details of eucharistic liturgy. But the memory of Lord's Supper observance on that particular "first day of the week" is fixed in tradition.

3.3. Acts 20:7. This text contains a remarkable convergence of three suggestive ideas: the expression "the first day of the week"; a "gathering" for the purpose of "breaking bread"; a story revolving around a resurrection. In view of the fact that the Jewish expression "the first day of the week" is used by the Gentile author and that it is used only in Luke 24:1 and Acts 20:7 (concerning a Gentile* church), both times associated with the breaking of bread, there might be yet more justification for sensing here an allusion to Jesus' resurrection in the use of this expression. This is all the more likely in view of a key motif of the story for which Paul's discourse and the burning lamps are stage props: the "resurrection" of the sleepy lad. The expression "to break bread" is not a typical Jewish expression for a meal (versus "to eat bread") but is more likely a peculiar way of referring to the Lord's Supper, in this case probably combined with an actual meal. This likelihood is increased by the combination of "to break bread" with "gathering" (cf. 1 Cor 11:20, 24; *Did.* 14.1; Ign. *Eph.* 20.2). We have to do, then, with a formal gathering of the church on the first day of the week, the stated purpose of which is to celebrate the Lord's Supper rather than to say farewell to Paul.

Though it is no longer clear whether the evening in question would have fallen on Saturday (after sabbath, by Jewish reckoning) or Sunday (by Roman reckoning), the issue is immaterial since practice may have varied; from Luke's point of view the meeting took place on "the first day of the week." A journey on Sunday would have given no offense since it was not a Christian sabbath, but a Roman reckoning is more likely (see Acts 3:1; further Turner, 129-30), and the delay of the meal until early Monday morning in spite of the stated purpose (Acts 20:7) is a merely circumstantial delay.

All of this does not establish that there was a weekly pattern of holding a special meeting on Sunday. In favor of such a custom it can be noted that as Luke phrases it the gathering is not for the purpose of giving Paul an opportunity to speak but for the purpose of "breaking bread."

Though the timing of the meeting could have been occasioned by Paul's imminent departure, Luke does not say that. Rather, he mentions that Paul was going to be leaving the next day by way of explaining the discourse, especially its length (its content is of no interest). It is also improbable that Luke mentions which day of the week it was merely by way of indicating chronology, as in that case he leaves too many gaps. Without any other satisfactory explanation either for mentioning that it was the first day of the week (beyond the resurrection of the lad, which is itself suggestive of a particular regard for that day) or for stating what the purpose of the gathering was, we are left with the likelihood that the clause ("we gathered together to break bread") is the natural accompaniment to the prepositional phrase ("on the first day of the week"); in other words there is an assumed and close relationship between them. The suggestion is strong that this type of gathering was customary on that particular day.

Again there is no imperative, nor does this look like this is intended to be a normative model. We cannot say how representative this account is of what was practiced at the time by other churches in other areas. It does indicate, however, the existence of a custom in Troas and presumably among Luke's intended readers (*see* Worship).

3.4. John 20:1, 19. Twice John underlines the day of the week on which Christ arose and appeared ("the first day of the week"; Jn 20:1, 19). John 20:19, in which Jesus appears to his gathered disciples, is especially emphatic insofar as the phrase "the first day of the week" follows a demonstrative pronoun pointing back to John 20:1. Is it merely coincidental that the next appearance of Jesus in the midst of his gathered disciples is exactly one week later (Jn 20:26), that is, on the first day of the week? This must be phrased as a question, for the matter is left unclear, but the suggestion is very strong. We need only suppose that "the first day of the week" had already come to carry a special meaning in the gatherings of the John's churches to appreciate how this passage would have resonated with them.

3.5. Revelation 1:10. The cause of our uncertainty in this passage, as it will be in the early postapostolic period, is that the writers take for granted that the readers know what the referent is while the form of the statement requires only the idea of a specified day. A day does not, however, need to be twenty-four hours long, and it can be specified in different ways: by calendar (weekly, monthly, etc.) or some other established reference point (e.g., an expected event). The adjective in Revelation 1:10 narrows the options, but only to a point. The three primary alternatives (leaving aside the sabbath) are the eschatological Day of the Lord, Easter, and the weekly meeting on the first day of the week, or Sunday.

The difficulty that any argument runs into is that the relevant passages from the first through the early second century must be treated as mutually corroborative precisely because of their ambiguity. The thesis that Revelation 1:10 refers to Easter gains its force from arguing that the NT evidence we have already surveyed does not indicate the existence of first-day observance prior to Revelation 1:10 and that the early- second-century evidence (esp. *Did.* 14.1 and Ign. *Magn.* 9.1) refers to an annual observance. On the contrary, we have shown it is likely that weekly observance was already a custom before Revelation (*see* Revelation, Book of) was written. The general argument that Easter observance preceded and precipitated Sunday observance is problematic, and *Didache** and Ignatius* probably also refer not to Easter but to Sunday (Bauckham, 227-31). This means that only a short while before Ignatius makes mention of weekly observance under the name "Lord's day" and in the same geographical area (the province of Asia), John uses the same expression in Revelation 1:10.

Might not John's reference be to the Day of the Lord? G. W. H. Lampe cites one instance in which the adjective refers to the "last day" (Origen *Comm. Joh.* 10.35), but it may not be an equivalent expression for "the Day of the Lord" (Stott 1965, 71) and is in any event the exception that proves the rule. There are many ways of referring to the Day of the Lord, and Revelation 1:10 may be one more. But given that the semantic content of the phrase would be the same, whether it is formed with the adjective or the genitive, there is no apparent reason for John to depart from the standard form. This manner of expression would become all the more confusing if the same form of words had already come into use in Asia as a name for the first day, as *Didache* and Ignatius might indicate. It is also to be observed that the content of

Revelation is not concerned exclusively with the Day of the Lord (Rev 1:1—3:22; Rev 21—22), and the standpoint of the vision* does not appear to be consistently from that "day." Thus neither the word or phrase nor the context of Revelation would indicate to the reader that the Day of the Lord is in view.

There may be no exegesis without presuppositions, but a prima facie reading of Revelation 1:9-10 suggests that we are being told the historical where and when of John's vision regarding the seven churches. Patmos does not appear to be a metaphor for an eschatological reality, and we do not expect the Lord's day to be mentioned in that connection either. Given the considerations already raised against the other alternatives, particularly in view of the probable preexistence of first-day observance (possibly even under the name of "Lord's day"), a reference to the first day of the week is most likely.

Why did the day come to be called the "Lord's day"? The thesis that the name of the day stemmed from the name of the Eucharist (Rordorf 1968) is possible but unproven. The suggestion that the name was chosen in conscious contrast to the use of *sebastē* as a name for the monthly "emperor's day" and that the regular (weekly) observance of the day was due to the same (Deissmann, 357-61; Charles, 1:22-23) is plausible but essentially conjectural. That the adjective was chosen because the alternative phrasing (genitive of the noun, *kyrios*) was already a technical expression when used with "day" is likely but leaves unexplained why this day should be characterized as "the Lord's." A general allusion to the decisive victory won by the Lord of lords on the first day of the week with a view to its eschatological and final achievement is most probable in the context of Revelation and is suggestive as a setting for the reception of the vision. Outside of that context there are any number of possible connotations.

3.6. Postapostolic Literature.

3.6.1. Didache 14.1. The *Didache* is notoriously difficult to date, not least because it seems to have grown over time, and *Didache* 14.1-3 appears to some scholars to be an intrusion into the flow of community instructions. Most, however, are probably inclined to date some form of the document around or just before the turn of the century and to locate it in Syria or Syro-Palestine. The expression used in *Didache* 14.1 is difficult: *kata kyriakēn de kyriou* (according to the Lord's [?] of the Lord). It has been taken as equivalent to the Jewish "Sabbath of the Lord" (Clemens, 708), as the Lord's teaching, as Easter and as the Lord's day (i.e., Sunday). Elsewhere when the noun is implied it is "day," and this is how the *Apostolic Constitutions* (7.30.1; c. 380) interprets *Didache*. There are serious problems with the argument for an Easter allusion (Bauckham, 230-31), and the context does not indicate that these are anything other than ordinary meetings centering in the breaking of bread. "Lord's day" is the likely alternative of choice. There is no hint of sabbath theology here.

3.6.2. Ignatius Magnesians *9.1 (c. 100-110).* The expression used (following the Latin text with most: *mēketi sabbatizontes alla kata kyriakēn zōntes;* "no longer sabbatizing but living according to the Lord's [day]") is again opaque, and it is not clear whether it is a comment on OT prophets* or Jewish Christians (Schoedel, 123, favors the latter; *see* Jewish Christianity). The concern is with ways of life *(kata)* so that it is not possible to be sure, but an allusion to weekly Lord's day observance gets the nod over annual observance in view of the parallel with what is probably centered in weekly sabbath observance (Bauckham, 228-29). This would be confirmed if it could be shown that the choice of the verb (*aneteilen;* "arose"), more often associated with the rising of the sun than with the resurrection, was a play on the name *Sunday*. The text may oppose and so give evidence of Gentile sabbath observance, but it is also possible that the sabbath is introduced simply to make a point. It is also possible that Ignatius knew and was partially dependent on *Didache* 14.1 (Jefford). If so this would confirm not only an earlier date for *Didache* 14.1 but also that the two passages have the same idea in mind. It should be noted that observance of the day is connected to the resurrection. Again there is no trace of transfer theology, and in this case sabbath observance seems to be universally excluded.

As for the remaining usages of *kyriakos* noted above, *Gospel of Peter* 35 and 50 (Syria; mid-second century) cannot be definitely construed as allusions to Sunday observance, and the title to Melito* of Sardis's work provides little information, but the other instances are clearer in their reference to Sunday. To these can be added Pliny's letter to Trajan (c. 112; Bithynia in Asia Minor), which refers to meetings of Christians on an appointed day *(stato die)* in both morning and evening (Pliny *Ep.* 10.96). Pliny gives no reference point by which we can fix the "appointed day" (it need not have been the same day each week), but taken together with the other evidence of regular meetings in that geographical area it is reasonable to suppose that the reference is to Sunday. Certainly *Barnabas* 15.9 (c. 130-35, possibly earlier; provenance uncertain) uses the phrase "eighth day" to refer to Sunday. His comment grounds the significance of the day in the resurrection and seems to assume that the day's observance is a longstanding custom. Like Ignatius, *Barnabas* desires to exclude sabbath observance entirely, yet without transferring the sabbath to Sunday. Finally Justin Martyr (c. 100-165) not only makes definite mention of Sunday but also provides details of the day's activities (*Apol. I* 67; *see* Worship).

3.7. Conclusions and Further Observations. The evidence for or against a weekly commemoration of the resurrection in the apostolic age is ambiguous, especially when each passage is examined in isolation. Yet one hypothesis does fit comfortably over all the data and for that reason is to be favored. From a very early point, at least some believers recognized the "first day of the week" as a special day for the celebration of the Eucharist. The resurrection of Messiah, the Son* of God, does not happen often and would itself be sufficient cause for the establishment of a novel, Jewish custom. In a Jewish setting a weekly rhythm is natural, all the more so among believers who may not have anticipated a long delay before their Lord's return.

We cannot say that within the apostolic period this practice was universally recognized or that it was uniform with respect to how the day was reckoned, by Jewish or Roman calculation. It did not necessarily exclude gatherings on other days of the week and it existed peacefully alongside sabbath observance for many Christians (see the analogous practice of Acts 2:46). There is no indication in the NT evidence that the day displaced or rivaled the sabbath, that it was a day of rest, that it had anything to do with the Fourth Commandment or that it involved any sort of transfer theology. If the NT evidence for it gives any explanation for the fact of the day's observance and of its significance, it is in the resurrection.

By the turn of the first century it can be taken

for granted not only that the weekly observance of Jesus' resurrection is customary but even that it can be referred to intelligibly in shorthand fashion (adjective only) as the Lord's (day). The early postapostolic literature also confirms that the absence of evidence for a transfer theology in the NT is not accidental. There is not only a lack of evidence for connecting the Lord's day to the OT sabbath command, but also there is evidence against it (e.g., in the fact that the Lord's day was not a day of rest; see below). The tendency visible in Ignatius and *Barnabas* to oppose the Jewish and Christian days has been put in its proper perspective when viewed as a facet of the "partings of the ways" of Judaism and Christianity (Bacchiocchi; *see* Christianity and Judaism), but it must be stressed that there is no evidence for an anti-Judaism motive behind Lord's day observance in the NT itself, and it would be a serious mistake to read that type of opposition into the apostolic period. In any event the Fathers' polemic leaves no room for the thesis that they construed Sunday as the Christian sabbath.

As to how the day was observed, we have nothing solid to go on in the NT beyond the rather sure point that the celebration of the Eucharist was central. Acts 20:7-36, with its evening meeting, is no sure guide to what was universally customary (nor is it clear whether in that case it was the evening following sabbath or Sunday evening), and the resurrection narratives do not clearly point to an evening meeting. During the second century, however, the picture gains detail. The *Didache* alludes to a (public?) rite of confession preceding the Eucharist. Pliny's letter indicates that in his area (c. 112) believers met before dawn, probably on Sunday, to sing a hymn and take an oath and then come together again in the evening for a meal. Following Trajan's edict outlawing dinners of unlicensed clubs the evening meeting was eliminated. Justin Martyr's account (*Apol. I* 65-67) supplies further details of the service, including (in this order) reading of Scripture, instruction and exhortation, rising for prayer* (versus remaining seated as on other days; cf. Tertullian *De Orat.* 23; canon 20 of the Council of Nicea), celebration of the Eucharist and a collection for the needy. Tertullian (c. 160-225) is the first on record to suggest that business be deferred so as to enhance worship (*De Orat.* 23), but otherwise Sunday was a work day, and ces-

sation from other activities on that day was not widespread until about the third century (Cyprian *Ep.* 64.4). Even then there is no connection with the fourth Commandment (on the Fourth Commandment and the sabbath rest in postapostolic Christianity see Bauckham, 252-87), and the point is to clear more time for worship. Only with Constantine's edict in 321 does Sunday, the "venerable day of the sun," becomes an official day of rest (at least partially). Ambrose (*Ps.* 47) and Chrysostom (*Gen. Hom.* 10.7) firmly attached the rest of Sunday to the Fourth commandment (versus the imperial edict), and following the fourth century there is a steady move toward identifying the sabbath with Sunday.

The different names of the day—first day of the week; Lord's day; eighth day (e.g., *Barn.* 15.8-9; Justin Martyr *Dial. Tryph.* 41.4; 138.1; Origen *Selec. Ps.* 118.164 [*PG* 12.1624] Ambrose *Exp. Ev. Luc.* 5.49 [*PL* 15.1735]; *Abr.* 2.11 [*PL* 14.494]); Sunday—are briefly discussed by Rordorf (1982).

4. Theological Considerations.
Thorough treatment of this matter is beyond the scope of this summary article. A few words are in order, however, if only as an indication of a necessary part of the discussion of our topic.

In three passages Paul makes specific comments that transfer Mosaic sabbath observance from the realm of law to that of *adiaphora* ("matters of indifference") that positively oppose the legal imposition of the sabbath on believers of any ethnic background and that by extension also oppose investing Lord's day observance with normative force. The meaning of these passages is debated, and they must be discussed in the broader context of the law-gospel discussion, but we will only mention them. The upshot of Galatians 4:8-11 in its context is that sabbath observance is not to be imposed on any believer in the name of the Mosaic law, nor is it to be taken up on legal grounds as a promise of anything beyond that which already belongs to believers in Christ. To violate this rule is in Paul's argument to make Christ's death purposeless (Gal 2:21). Romans 14:5-6 gives passing notice to the sabbath issue but makes evident that observance of days, sabbath and Lord's day included, is now a matter of conscience* rather than law. Nor is it possible to reconcile a one-in-seven principle with Romans 14:5-6, at least when it is grounded in law. Legal imposition of sabbath observance as a condition of spirituality is likewise assumed to be inappropriate in Colossians 2:16, for the sabbath was properly a shadow of the eschatological reality that is Christ (cf. Dunn, 171-87, 23-35).

None of these comments proscribes observance of days, and such observance can be a manifestation of either "weak" or "strong" faith. Yet it is not possible against that background to find any grounds for treating the Mosaic sabbath as a continuing legal requirement for Christians. Taken together with the historical evidence, it is difficult to find any basis for transferring the legal force and theological content of the sabbath to the Lord's day. There is certainly no positive evidence for such a transfer or even for a new holy day as such. At the same time these comments of Paul comport with both the historical decline of the sabbath and the initially low profile of Lord's day observance.

Does the NT indicate, then, that the sabbath, of so much theological import in the OT, was only a cul-de-sac? That, robbed of its covenantal-legal force, it was destined merely to come to a close, having been effectively replaced by something unrelated to it? To the contrary, the NT indicates that the sabbath followed its own channel and found its goal in Christ's redemptive work. Here is where John 5:17 should be discussed (cf. also Jn 7:23), as also Colossians 2:16, to which we have already referred, and Matthew 11:28—12:14. It is less evident that controversy over sabbath observance gave any impetus to that treatment of the topic in Hebrews 3:7—4:11 (Laansma), yet there at least we are pointed to the ultimate goal of the creation sabbath (here an exclusively future *Heilsgut*) and are thus reminded that the sabbath was by no means a cul-de-sac.

It is true to the NT to say that the Mosaic sabbath as a legal and weekly matter was a temporary symbol of a more fundamental and comprehensive salvation, epitomized by and grounded in God's own creation sabbath, and brought to fulfillment (in already-not yet fashion) in Christ's redemptive work. Believers are indeed to "keep sabbath," no longer by observance of a day of the week but now by the upholding of that to which it pointed: the gospel of the cross.* Along independent lines the Lord's day emerges as a nonmandatory but increasingly revered custom by which the cen-

tral import of the cross is commemorated and its final realization anticipated. It thus augments that which was ordained, the Lord's Supper.

The label used in Revelation 1:10 suggests an underlying, profound regard for what that day of the week symbolically represented and what it would presently come to represent. That in itself, to the extent that it was appreciated, would fill that day with significance and lift it above the others in the hearts of many believers. Yet that this label suggested that the day as such had been claimed by the Lord for religious observance is probably outside of Revelation's horizons.

See also LORD; LORD'S SUPPER, LOVE FEAST; RESURRECTION; WORSHIP AND LITURGY.

BIBLIOGRAPHY. S. Bacchiocchi, *From Sabbath to Sunday* (Rome: The Pontifical Gregorian University Press, 1977); R. J. Bauckham, "The Lord's Day" in *From Sabbath to Lord's Day,* ed. D. A. Carson (Grand Rapids: Zondervan, 1982) 221-50; idem, "Sabbath and Sunday in the Postapostolic Church" in *From Sabbath to Lord's Day,* ed. D. A. Carson (Grand Rapids: Zondervan, 1982) 251-98; R. T. Beckwith and W. Stott, *This Is the Day* (London: Marshall, Morgan & Scott, 1978); H. Bietenhard, "Lord, Master," *NIDNTT,* 2:508-20; D. A. Carson, ed., *From Sabbath to Lord's Day* (Grand Rapids: Zondervan, 1982); R. H. Charles, *Revelation of St. John* (2 vols.; ICC; Edinburgh: T & T Clark, 1920); J. S. Clemens, "Lord's Day" in *Dictionary of the Apostolic Church,* ed. J. Hastings (2 vols.; Edinburgh: T & T Clark, 1915) 1:707-10; A. Deissmann, *Light from the Ancient East* (Grand Rapids: Baker, 1965, repr.); J. D. G. Dunn, *The Epistles to the Colossians and to Philemon* (NIGTC; Grand Rapids: Eerdmans, 1996); T. C. Eskenazi et al., eds., *The Sabbath in Jewish and Christian Traditions* (New York: Crossroad, 1991); J. A. Fitzmyer, "κύριος, κυριακός," *EDNT* 2:331; W. Foerster, "κυριακός," *TDNT* 3:1095-96; C. N. Jefford, "Did Ignatius of Antioch Know the *Didache?*" in *The* Didache *in Context,* ed. C. N. Jefford (NovTSup 77; Leiden: E. J. Brill, 1995), 330-51; J. Jeremias, "πάσχα," *TDNT* 5:896-904; P. K. Jewett, *The Lord's Day* (Grand Rapids: Eerdmans, 1971); J. Laansma, " 'I Will Give You Rest': The Background and Significance of the Rest Motif in the New Testament with Special Reference to Mt 11 and Heb 3—4" (Ph.D. dissertation, University of Aberdeen, 1995; Tübingen: J. C. B. Mohr, forthcoming);

J. Murray, "Romans 14:5 and the Weekly Sabbath" in *Epistle to the Romans* (NICNT; Grand Rapids: Eerdmans, 1959, 1965) 257-59; W. Rordorf, *Sabbat und Sonntag in der Alten Kirche* (Zürich: Theologischer Verlag, 1972) [texts of primary sources]; idem, *Sunday* (London: SCM, 1968); idem, "Sunday: The Fullness of Christian Liturgical Time," *StudLit* 14 (1982) 90-96; W. R. Schoedel, *Ignatius of Antioch* (Herm; Philadelphia: Fortress, 1985); C. Spicq, "κυριακός" in *Theological Lexicon of the New Testament* (3 vols.; Peabody, MA: Hendrickson, 1994) 2:338-40; W. Stott, "A Note on the Word ΚΥΡΙΑΚΗ in Rev. 1:10," *NTS* 12 (1965) 70-75; idem, "Sabbath, Lord's Day," *NIDNTT* 3:405-15; K. A. Strand, ed., *The Sabbath in Scripture and History* (Washington, DC: Review and Herald Publishing Association, 1982); M. M. B. Turner, "The Sabbath, Sunday and the Law in Luke-Acts" in *From Sabbath to Lord's Day,* ed. D. A. Carson (Grand Rapids: Zondervan, 1982) 99-157.

J. C. Laansma

LORD'S SUPPER, LOVE FEAST

The term Lord's Supper, *kyriakon deipnon*, occurs in the NT only at 1 Corinthians 11:20 (*see DPL*, Lord's Supper). When the Corinthian Christians gather "as a church [*en ekklēsia*]" (1 Cor 11:18), their assembly includes a meal to which belong the eating of that bread and the drinking of that cup which "proclaim the Lord's death until he comes" (1 Cor 11:26). It is not clear whether that bread and that cup framed the full meal, bread at the beginning and cup at the end (as would be the case if the Corinthian practice took the same pattern as the apostle Paul's account of Jesus' Last Supper, 1 Cor 11:23-25); or whether that bread and that cup both rather came together after people had otherwise eaten and drunk. It is certain that by their abusive behavior—"each goes ahead with his own meal, and one is hungry and another drunk" (1 Cor 11:21)—the Corinthians are, in the judgment of the apostle Paul and apparently of God also (1 Cor 11:27-34), denaturing "the Lord's Supper." Scholars generally agree that conduct such as that found at Corinth was the likely reason for an eventual separation between the *agapē*, or love-feast (a designation full of irony in such circumstances), and the sacrament (to speak anachronistically for the apostolic period). In treating the NT and the early postapostolic writings, it will be necessary to speak of the *agapē* and the Eucharist together; as the second century progresses, a clearer distinction emerges between the love-feast and the Holy Communion.

The Synoptic Gospels and Paul all report the institution by Jesus, at the Last Supper, of a rite with bread and wine as his own memorial (Mt 26:26-29; Mk 14:22-25; Lk 22:17-20, 29-30; 1 Cor 11:23-26; *see DJG*, Last Supper). The Acts of the Apostles mentions the meals at which the memorial actions probably took place in the primitive Church. A few other echoes of the ritual meal are found elsewhere in the later NT writings. The most important evidence for developments in the second century is provided by the *Didache*,* the letters of Ignatius* of Antioch, and the *Apologies* of Justin Martyr and of Tertullian.

1. The Breaking of Bread in Acts
2. The Non-Pauline Epistles and Revelation
3. The Early Postapostolic Period
4. *Agape* and Eucharist Distinguished
5. Conclusion

1. The Breaking of Bread in Acts.

By noun or by verb Luke speaks five times in Acts* of "the breaking of bread": Acts 2:42 and 46, as part of a description of the life of the Jerusalem* church directly after the outpouring of the Spirit* at Pentecost*; Acts 20:7 and 11, in the narrative of Paul's visit to the assembly at Troas; Acts 27:35, in telling how Paul encouraged the ship's company to take food when in danger of shipwreck. The matter of "tables" in Acts 6:1-6 is also relevant.

In Jewish practice, bread was broken when God was blessed at the start of a meal. In primitive Christianity, the breaking of bread bore the special imprint it had acquired from its significant usage by Jesus. In the Gospel of Luke (in whose light Acts has particularly to be read), Jesus broke the loaves when he fed the five thousand (Lk 9:16); the Savior broke the bread when he gave it to his disciples at the Last Supper, saying, "This is my body which is given for you. Do this in remembrance of me" (Lk 22:19); and the risen Lord broke the bread at Emmaus (Lk 24:30) and was known to his two companions "in the breaking of the bread" (Lk 24:35). Around those highly significant occasions cluster then all the multiple words and deeds of Jesus involving food and drink that also give weight and texture to the observance which the church of Acts called by metonymy "the breaking of bread."

Jesus had pictured God's coming reign as a feast: "People will come from east and west, and from north and south, and sit at table in the kingdom of God" (Lk 13:29). Apart from the messianic act of already feeding the multitudes in anticipation of the kingdom, Jesus had been notorious also for eating and drinking with publicans and sinners (Lk 7:34; 15:1-2; *see DJG*, Table Fellowship); he thereby invited them to repentance (Lk 5:30-32), for the mere eating and drinking in his presence was no guarantee of salvation (Lk 13:22-30). At the Last Supper he spoke of himself as being among his disciples "as one who serves" (Lk 22:27), yet he was also able to promise them a place at his table in the kingdom which his Father had given him (Lk 22:28-30). After his resurrection, his appearance at Emmaus was not the only one in which he shared in a meal with his followers: he ate with the others in Jerusalem (Lk 24:36-43), and in Acts Luke gives Peter the summary statement that "God raised Jesus on the third day and made him manifest . . . to us who were chosen by God as witnesses, who ate and drank with him after he rose from the dead" (Acts 10:40-41). (Acts 1:4 implies the same, if *synalizomenos* is to be associated with *hals*, salt, and then understood as a reference to the risen Jesus' *eating with* the apostles, as in fact the Latin, Syriac and Coptic versions translate.) These, then, are the associations which accompany the meal assemblies perpetuated by the primitive church after the Lord's exaltation.

1.1. Acts 2:41-46. According to Acts 2:41-42, those who at Pentecost repented and were baptized were added to the company of those who "devoted themselves to the apostles' teaching and fellowship* [*koinōnia*], to the breaking of bread and the prayers." It is hard to determine the precise relationship among the elements in this foursome, chiefly because of the difficulty in specifying the meaning of the somewhat elastic word *koinōnia*. It has been suggested that the four items constitute a service, in liturgical sequence, of preaching, *agapē*, Eucharist and prayers* (*see* Worship). Another suggestion is that *koinōnia* designates a collection (of money or goods), so that "the breaking of bread" might then stand for either an *agapē* or the Eucharist or both. In any case, the context indicates that the believers *shared* several things together: not only apostolic instruction, the "breaking of

bread" and prayers, but also attendance at the temple (Acts 2:46) and the distribution of material goods as need arose (Acts 2:44-45). Thus the breaking of bread is associated with a common faith, the common worship of God and a common life of mutual service; the "breaking" is for the purpose of "sharing," as Léon-Dufour insists (*le partage du pain*), and so brings to expression the unity of the community in Christ. The breaking of bread took place in the homes of believers and in conjunction with a meal of which they partook "with glad and generous hearts" (Acts 2:46; cf. du Toit).

The joy* which characterized these meals has led some scholars (notably Lietzmann) to postulate an original "Jerusalem-type" Lord's Supper in distinction from a Pauline type, where the apostle, perhaps in dependence on Hellenistic memorial meals, would have shifted the theme to the Lord's death. While different emphases may have marked the Christian meal at different times and in different places, it is unwise and unnecessary to exaggerate the difference between Jerusalem and Paul in this matter. According to Luke, the Jerusalem church was well aware that the redemption* in which it rejoiced had been bought at the price of the Lord's crucifixion (Acts 2:23), while Paul himself may, in his reminder that the Supper proclaimed the Lord's *death** until he *comes*, have been correcting an overenthusiastic Corinthian supposition that the divine kingdom was already here. The joy (*agalliasis*) that marked the meals of the Jerusalem church was experienced by the Philippian jailer (*ēgalliasato*, Acts 16:34), who "set a table" (*parethēken trapezan*) for Paul and Silas after his baptism.

1.2. Acts 6:1-6. "Tables" had been an issue between the Greek-speakers ("Hellenists"*) and the Aramaic-speakers ("Hebrews") in the Christian community at Jerusalem (Acts 6:1-6). The primitive church inherited a Jewish tradition of provision for the poor and needy at festive meals, which would be extended to all the needy sisters and brothers in their regular gatherings (Reicke 1948). The Hellenists complained that their widows were not treated fairly in the distribution of food. The daily dole had apparently taken place under the general oversight, though not detailed supervision, of the apostles ("It is not right that we should give up preaching the word of God to serve tables"). The apostles proposed that seven other men be elected to the duty. Seven people with Greek names were chosen, and the apostles prayed and laid their hands upon them. Traditionally this event has been seen as the origin of the diaconate as an order of ministry. The apostles could now devote themselves "to prayer and to the ministry of the word." Some have regretted the divergence between a preaching and a diaconal ministry.* It is in any case sad that, as would be the case at Corinth, the sharing of food should be a divisive issue among Christians. Table-fellowship—this time explicitly as a matter of theological principle between Jewish and Gentile Christians—would emerge as a question again in Acts 10—11, where the episode concerning the apostle Peter* and the centurion Cornelius* would be settled by the recognition that "to the Gentiles also God has granted repentance unto life" (Acts 11:18).

1.3. Acts 20:7-12. The next occurrence of "the breaking of bread" in the narrative of Acts falls during the apostle Paul's visit to Troas (Acts 20:7-12). The Christians "gathered together to break bread" on "the first day of the week." The assembly took place (the verb *synagō* is used) during the evening and night.

Whether it was the evening and night of our Saturday/Sunday or of our Sunday/Monday is uncertain. If Luke is using the Roman system of reckoning, which begins the day in the morning, then the meeting started on Sunday evening. If he is using the Jewish liturgical reckoning, however, the assembly would have started on the evening of Saturday, the beginning of "the first day of the week." It has been suggested that the Christian Sunday originated as a prolongation of the Jewish Sabbath: Christians kept the Sabbath by attending Jewish worship and then, because the Sabbath no longer sufficed since it has been fulfilled by Jesus, they assembled in houses for specifically Christian worship as soon as the Sabbath was over (Riesenfeld; *see* Lord's Day). If such a Jewish-Christian influence affected the church at Troas, then the assembly of Acts 20:7-12 would have taken place on Saturday/Sunday. On the other hand, *Sunday* evening may have imposed itself on the earliest church, as the time for the main weekly assembly, on account of the memory of the meals which the risen Lord had shared with his disciples on the first Easter Sunday.

In any case, we find that Paul "prolonged his speech until midnight"; and only then, after incidentally reviving the hapless Eutychus, did the apostle "break bread and eat." This pattern of preaching and meal—recalling the risen Lord's exposition of the Scriptures to the two on the road to Emmaus and his being made known to them in the breaking of the bread (Lk 24:27-35)—may already show a regular practice of "word and table" in the main weekly assembly of the Christians.

1.4. Acts 27:33-38. The most intriguing case of "breaking bread" in Acts occurs during the story of Paul's shipwreck. Acts 27:33-38 reads:

As day was about to dawn, Paul urged them all to take some food, saying 'Today is the fourteenth day that you have continued in suspense and without food, having taken nothing. Therefore I urge you to take some food; it will give you strength [literally: "this will be for your salvation"], since not a hair is to perish from the head of any of you.' And when he had said this, he took bread, and giving thanks to God in the presence of all he broke it and began to eat. Then they all were encouraged and ate some food themselves. (We were in all two hundred and seventy-six persons in the ship.) And when they had eaten enough, they lightened the ship, throwing out the wheat into the sea.

Strikingly, Paul's actions with the bread mirror those of Jesus at the Last Supper and presage what modern scholarship has called "the 'four-action' shape of the eucharist" (G. Dix): the apostle "took bread" (the "offertory"), he gave thanks (the "eucharistic prayer"), he broke the bread (the "fraction"), he ate (the "communion"). Because Paul was in this way presiding over a meal shared by a whole boatload of presumably heathen sailors and passengers (for there is no indication of two separate meals, one for Paul, Aristarchus and "the travel-diarist," and another for the heathen), it is usually said that this cannot have been a Eucharist but was rather a case simply of Paul observing the Jewish custom of grace before food.

One modern exegete has tried to do more justice to the "eucharistic" tone of Acts 27:35: B. Reicke argued that Acts 27:33-38 is a further stylized account of an incident upon which Paul himself had already put a quasi-eucharistic stamp at the time of its happening; Paul had let the people on board participate in "a prefiguration of the Christian Eucharist as a potential preparation for later discipleship," and the author of Acts, understanding the episode in the same way, had used the story of what happened on the voyage to open up also the prospect of the work that Paul would do in the wider context of the mission when he reached Rome (cf. Acts 28:28-30). It may be wondered whether even this interpretation goes far enough. Those on board a ship running on the rocks (Acts 27:29) were confronted by "the last things": it was a matter of life and death, both physically and, for the heathen, spiritually. The possibility should not be excluded that when the apostle proposed they should all take food, telling them "This will be the saving of you" (Acts 27:34) and having already announced to them that their destiny was in the hands of his God whose will it was that there should be no loss of life among them (Acts 27:21-26), he then celebrated for them the very meal which is life to all who will choose life. Certainly this episode provides the clearest instance of what J. Wanke sees as a eucharistic motif characteristic of Lukan meal stories: the Lord is present to protect and preserve his people.

2. The Non-Pauline Epistles and Revelation.

2.1. Jude 12. This verse may represent the only use in the NT of *agapē* in the sense of love-feast (the regular meaning of *agapē* is simply "love"). (In the closely related passage of 2 Peter 2, the manuscripts are divided in verse 13 between *agapais* ("love-feasts") and *apatais* ("pleasures," "dissipations"); and I. H. Marshall suggests that the former reading may result from a later scribe's ironing out of a deliberate pun.) In any case, the fiery epistle of Jude* declares that the Christian assembly has been infiltrated by "ungodly persons who pervert the grace of our God into licentiousness and deny our only Master and Lord, Jesus Christ." They are said to be "blemishes on your love-feasts, as they boldly carouse together, looking after themselves."

2.2. Hebrews. It has been argued that "there is little or no evidence in Hebrews* of involvement, on the part of the author or of the community of Christians to which the epistle was addressed, in eucharistic faith and practice" and indeed suggested that, for the writer, "the sacrifice of Christ was of a kind that rendered obsolete every form of cultus that placed a material means of sacramental communion between God and the worshiper" (Williamson).

Other exegetes see the Letter to the Hebrews as shot through with allusions to the Eucharist. It is certain that Hebrews contains language that the later Christian tradition has associated with the Eucharist.

Two verses are of particular interest: "Through [Jesus Christ] let us continually offer up a sacrifice* of praise to God, that is, the fruit of lips that acknowledge his name. Do not neglect to do good and to share what you have, for such sacrifices are pleasing to God" (Heb 13:15-16). The "sacrifice of praise (and thanksgiving)" became a designation for the Eucharist; and John Chrysostom, in expounding the gospel story of the healed leper, commented that we offer thanks to God not because God has need of anything but in order to bring us closer to God (*Hom. Mt. 25*, Migne, *PG* 57.331). In the Hebrews passage the sacrifice is not limited to verbal confession of God's name but includes also sharing (*koinōnia*) and good works.

More generally, the Letter to the Hebrews has been considered important in the Christian liturgical tradition for its description of Christ's continuing intercession after his entrance from Calvary into the Holy of Holies: the Eucharist is traditionally seen to represent in ritual mode the high-priestly work of Christ before the face of the Father. Moreover, Hebrews' references to "the blood of the covenant*" resonate with the cup-word at the Eucharist, and in particular Hebrews 13:20 finds an echo in the words of consecration at the Roman Mass: "This is the cup of my blood, the *blood of the* new and *everlasting covenant.*"

2.3. 1 Peter 2:3. The phrase from Psalm 34:8 echoed in 1 Peter 2:3 about "tasting the goodness of the Lord" has been used as a communion verse in traditional liturgies of the Eucharist. In the Petrine context it comes close to the notion of Christians as "a spiritual house," "a holy priesthood, to offer spiritual sacrifices acceptable to God through Jesus Christ" (1 Pet 2:5).

2.4. Revelation. At the beginning of Revelation,* the seer says that he "was in the Spirit on the Lord's day" (Rev 1:10). Modern scholarship has suggested that the Apocalypse reflects the church's worship in which John found inspiration, either the Sunday assembly of the congregation or the annual Easter liturgy (depending on the sense of "Lord's Day"). In traditional Christian rites for the Lord's Supper, participants have been summoned by the *Sursum Corda* ("Lift up your hearts") to join in the heavenly worship and add their voices to the angelic company in singing the *Sanctus:* "Holy, holy, holy, Lord God Almighty" (Rev 4:8; *see* Liturgical Elements). Besides the praise of God, life in the city of God includes the messianic feast, "the marriage supper of the Lamb." In the Roman Catholic Mass, the invitation to communion borrows from Revelation 19:9: "This is the Lamb of God. . . . Happy are those who are called to his supper." The Jesus of the Apocalypse extends the invitation: "Behold I stand at the door and knock; if any one hears my voice and opens the door, I will come in to him and eat with him, and he with me" (Rev 3:20).

3. The Early Postapostolic Period.

3.1. Didache. The earliest nonscriptural material related to Lord's Supper and love-feast probably comes from the *Didache,** or "Teaching of the Twelve Apostles," which may belong around the turn of the first century (although scholarly dating of this text, rediscovered in 1875, varies between A.D. 60 and 200). Opinion is divided concerning the Jewish-style table prayers given in chapters 9 and 10, as to whether they belong to an *agapē* or to the Eucharist (*see* Worship). The text reads as follows:

About the thanksgiving, give thanks thus. First about the cup: "We give thanks to you, our Father, for the holy vine of your child (*pais*) David, which you made known to us through your child (*pais*) Jesus; glory to you for evermore." And about the broken bread: "We give thanks to you, for the life and knowledge which you made known to us through your child Jesus; glory to you for evermore. As this broken bread was scattered over the mountains, and when brought together became one, so let your church be brought together from the ends of the earth into your kingdom; for yours are the glory and the power through Jesus Christ for evermore." But let no one eat or drink of your thanksgiving but those who have been baptized in the name of the Lord. For about this also the Lord has said, "Do not give what is holy to the dogs."

And after you have had your fill, give thanks thus: "We give thanks to you, holy Father, for your holy name which you have enshrined in our hearts, and for the knowl-

edge and faith and immortality which you have made known to us through your child Jesus; glory to you for evermore. You, almighty Master, created all things for the sake of your name, and gave food and drink to human beings for their enjoyment, that they might give you thanks; but to us you have granted spiritual food and drink and eternal life through your child Jesus. Above all we give you thanks because you are mighty; glory to you for evermore. May grace come, and may this world pass away. Hosanna to the God of David." If any is holy, let him come; if any is not, let him repent. Maranatha. Amen.

Although the introductory word is about "the thanksgiving" (*eucharistia*), it is likely that the first two prayers, over the cup and over the bread, belong to an *agapē* (the order of cup before bread is perhaps to be found at the communal meal in the later church order reconstituted by modern scholarship and identified with *The Apostolic Tradition* of Hippolytus, although the text is very confused around chapter 25/26; cf. also perhaps 1 Cor 10:16-17). All food over which thanks have been said is sanctified (cf. 1 Tim 4:4-5), and so the application of the Lord's word from Matthew 7:6 ("Do not give what is holy to the dogs") does not necessarily imply a sacramental Eucharist. The rubric "after you have had your fill" implies that a meal has occurred before the next prayer. However, that prayer itself has a more "redemptive" cast than the previous ones, bringing it closer to the themes of the Eucharist proper; and the fourth-century compiler of *Apostolic Constitutions* VII was easily able to make it unmistakably sacramental in his adaptation of the text (and in fact obviously understood all the prayers in the *Didache* in a sacramental sense).

Whatever may be the case with chapters 9 and 10 of the *Didache*, scholars are agreed that chapter 14 refers to what would be called "the Eucharist." The text reads:

On the Lord's day of the Lord, come together, break bread and give thanks, having first confessed your transgressions, that your sacrifice may be pure. But let none who has a quarrel with his companion join with you until they have been reconciled, that your sacrifice may not be defiled. For this is that which was spoken by the Lord, "In every place, and at every time, offer me a pure sacrifice; for I am a great king, says the Lord, and my name is wonderful among the nations."

The timing is for Sunday (although some have wanted to make the rather strange turn of phrase refer only to Easter). The requirement for prior confession of sin may derive from Leviticus 5:5-6, while the requirement for reconciliation within the fellowship certainly comes from the saying of Jesus recorded at Matthew 5:23-24 (a text frequently evoked later in connection with the Eucharist, e.g. by Irenaeus *Haer.* 4.18.1, and by Cyril of Jerusalem *Myst. Cat.* 5.3). The application of Malachi 1:11 concerning the "pure sacrifice" will be repeated in Justin (*Dial. Tryph.* 41; cf. 117) and Irenaeus (*Haer.* 4.17.5), and it will become a commonplace that the Eucharist is to be offered "always and everywhere" (*semper et ubique*).

3.2. Pliny's Letter. From the early years of the second century comes both external and internal evidence, of a fragmentary kind, concerning the ritual meal practice of the Christians in Asia Minor. The imperial official Pliny reports to the emperor Trajan on his investigations into the group (Pliny *Ep.* 10.96).

On a fixed day [presumably Sunday], [the Christians were] accustomed to meet before dawn, and to recite a hymn antiphonally to Christ, as to a god, and to bind themselves by an oath [*sacramentum*]. . . . After the conclusion of this ceremony it was their custom to depart and meet again to take food; but it was ordinary and harmless food; and they had ceased this practice after my edict in which, in accordance with your orders, I had forbidden secret societies.

Some have seen in the early morning meeting a garbled reference to the Eucharist, while the later gathering would have been for an *agapē*. The suspicion that Christians engaged in cannibalism recurred throughout antiquity, doubtless provoked by reference to communion in the body and blood of the Lord.

3.3. Ignatius of Antioch. The letters of Ignatius,* bishop of Antioch (martyred about A.D. 110), contain several references to *agapē* and Eucharist. A passage in the *Letter to the Smyrnaeans* suggests that the Eucharist was held in conjunction with an *agapē*.

Let that be regarded as a valid Eucharist which is under the bishop or someone appointed by him. Where the bishop is present, there let the congregation gather, just as where Jesus Christ is, there is the catholic church. Without the bishop it is not lawful either to baptize or to hold a love-feast. (Ign. *Smyrn.* 8.1-2)

The writer's main concern here, in any case, is for the unity of the congregation, which is grounded christologically, sacramentally and ministerially:

Take care to observe a single Eucharist, for there is one flesh of our Lord Jesus Christ and one cup to unite us with his blood, and one altar, as there is one bishop with the presbytery and the deacons, my fellow servants, in order that what you do, you do according to God. (Ign. *Phld.* 4.1)

The sacramental reality corresponds to the reality of the Incarnation:

[The Docetists] abstain from the Eucharist and prayer because they do not confess that the Eucharist is the flesh of our Savior Jesus Christ which suffered for our sins and which the Father in his goodness raised. (Ign. *Smyrn.* 7.1)

Ignatius speaks of "breaking the one bread," which is "a medicine of immortality, and an antidote against dying, but rather that one may live in Jesus Christ for ever" (Ign. *Eph.* 20.2).

4. *Agapē* and Eucharist Distinguished.

4.1. Justin Martyr. By the middle of the second century Justin Martyr describes the church in Rome as holding a regular Sunday service of word and table, where the reading and exposition of the Scriptures are followed by prayers and the Eucharist of the Lord's body and blood. The description in chapter 67 of Justin's *First Apology* runs as follows:

And on the day called Sunday an assembly is held in one place of all who live in town or country, and the memoirs of the apostles or the writings of the prophets are read as time allows. Then, when the reader has finished, the president in a discourse admonishes and exhorts us to imitate these good things. Then we all stand up together and send up prayers; and as we said before, when we have finished praying, bread and wine and water are brought up, and the president likewise sends up prayers and thanksgivings to the best of his ability, and the people assent, saying the Amen; and the elements over which thanks have been given are distributed, and everyone partakes; and they are sent through the deacons to those who are not present.

And the wealthy who so desire give what they wish, as each chooses; and what is collected is deposited with the president. He helps orphans and widows, and those who through sickness or any other cause are in need, and those in prison, and strangers sojourning among us; in a word, he takes care of all those who are in need.

And we all assemble together on Sunday, because it is the first day, on which God transformed darkness and matter, and made the world; and Jesus Christ our Savior rose from the dead on that day; for they crucified him the day before Saturday; and the day after Saturday, which is Sunday, he appeared to his apostles and disciples, and taught them these things which we have presented to you also for your consideration. (Justin *Apol. I* 67)

Several points are noteworthy, some of them capable of supplementation from other passages in Justin, particularly his description of the Eucharist celebrated after baptisms* (*Apology I* 65):

(1) Sunday is the chosen day of the liturgical assembly as a commemoration and celebration of creation and of Christ's resurrection,* the day marked by the risen Lord's appearances to his followers.

(2) The service includes reading from what became the NT ("the memoirs [*apomnēmoneumata*] of the apostles") as well as the OT ("the writings of the prophets"), and these Scriptures are expounded in a homily by the presider.

(3) The presider is not further identified; but if the practice follows that stipulated by Ignatius, it will be the bishop or someone appointed by him.

(4) Bread and wine are the food and drink, the wine probably being mixed with water (the word *krama*, "mixture," is used in *Apol. I* 65).

(5) The presider improvises the eucharistic prayer ("to the best of his ability"), though probably according to certain guidelines. He "sends up praise and glory to the Father of all in the name of the Son and of the Holy Spirit" (*Apol. I* 65). The people's assent ("Amen") is significant enough to be mentioned in both chapters.

(6) Only the baptized may participate in the Eucharist: "We call this food 'thanksgiving'; and no one may partake of it unless he is convinced of the truth of our teaching, and has been cleansed with the washing for forgiveness of sins and regeneration, and lives as Christ handed down" (*Apol. I* 66). But it is important that Christians enjoy their privilege: "Everyone partakes, and [the bread and wine] are sent through deacons to those who are not present" (presumably the sick and the imprisoned are in mind).

(7) The reason for the restriction of communion to baptized believers and the purpose of their participation are spelled out in *Apology I* 66:

For we do not receive these things as common bread or common drink; but just as our Savior Jesus Christ, being incarnate through the word of God, took flesh and blood for our salvation, so too we have been taught that the food over which thanks have been given by a word of prayer which is from him, (the food) from which our flesh and blood are fed by transformation, is both the flesh and blood of that incarnate Jesus. For the apostles in the records composed by them which are called Gospels, have handed down thus what was commended of them: that Jesus took bread, gave thanks, and said, 'Do this for the remembrance of me; this is my body'; and likewise he took the cup, gave thanks, and said, 'This is my blood'; and gave to them alone.

(8) The material care for the needy recalls the situation in Acts 2:42-47. No *agapē* is mentioned by Justin; but later writers envisage that for some time the church continued a practice they saw as apostolic: "When the assembly [*synaxis*] was over, after the communion of the mysteries, they all went to a common banquet [*euōchia*], the rich bringing their provisions with them, and the poor and destitute being invited by them, and all feasting in common. But afterwards this custom also became corrupt" (John Chrysostom *Homily 27 on 1 Corinthians*; Migne, *PG* 61.223-24).

4.2. Tertullian. In the late second century, Tertullian gives some account of the purposes for which Christians assemble ("The scriptures are read, psalms are sung, sermons are given, prayers are offered"; *De Anim.* 9); and to prayers, Scriptures and exhortations he adds, in the *Apologeticus*, the making of modest and voluntary contributions to the needy (*Apol.* 39.5-6). The fuller description contained in this latter writing includes also, by name, a love-feast:

> Our supper (*coena*) explains itself by its name, which is the Greek word for love [i.e., *agapē*]. Whatever it costs, our outlay in the name of piety is gain, for it is the needy that we benefit by that banquet [*refrigerio isto*]. . . . We taste first of prayer to God before we recline to food; we eat only what suffices hunger, and drink only what befits such as are chaste. We satisfy appetite as those who remember that even during the night they have to worship God. We converse as those who know that they are in the hearing of their Lord. After water for washing the hands, and the lights have been brought in, everyone is called forward to sing praises to God, either from the Holy Scriptures or of his own composing. And this is a proof of the measure of the drinking. As we began, so the feast is concluded with prayer. We depart not like a pack of ruffians, nor in gangs of vagabonds, nor to break out into licentiousness, but with as much regard for our modesty and chastity as if we had been taking in a moral lesson rather than a supper. (Tertullian *Apol.* 39.16-19)

Here there is nothing specifically "eucharistic," but in other writings Tertullian makes reference to what can only be the sacramental Eucharist: for example, "the sacrament of the Eucharist [*eucharistiae sacramentum*]" (*De Cor.* 3; *Marc.* 4.34); "the sacrament of the bread and the cup [*panis et calicis sacramentum*]" (*Marc.* 5.8); "the body of the Lord [*corpus domini*]" (*De Idol.* 7; *De Orat.* 19). There is no clear indication as to how this Eucharist was liturgically or ritually related to the assemblies in which the Scriptures, psalms, prayers, collection and *agapē* took place. His terms *convivium dominicum* (in *Ad Ux.* 2.4) and *coena Dei* (in *De Spect.* 13) could apply either to an *agapē* or to the Eucharist or to both.

5. Conclusion.

In the anonymous *Epistle to Diognetus*, dating perhaps from the middle of the second century, the author's description of the life of the Christians states: "They spread a common board [*trapezan koinēn paratithentai*], though not a common bed [reading *koitēn*]" (*Diogn.* 5.7). Pictorial testimony to the importance of the common meal is borne by the frequency of table scenes in the mural paintings of the Christian catacombs, where loaves and fishes are also a recurrent motif. It is impossible to know whether the reference is to *agapē* or to Eucharist. In NT times the behavior of the participants at the meals varies from the idyllic to the problematic to the reprehensible. In the second and third centuries, apologists defend the community against accusations of debauchery and cannibalism by explaining the charitable nature of the love-feast and the sacramental character of the memorial of the Lord under bread and wine. By the late fourth century we find Augustine and other African bishops and synods prohibiting the *agapē* on account of revelry (e.g., Augustine *Ep.* 22, to Aurelius; Migne, *PL* 33.90-92). At the same time, under the imperial establishment of Christianity, there sets in the decline from that regular participation in eucharistic communion which had been, according to Ignatius of Antioch and Justin Martyr, a hallmark of membership in the church.

See also BAPTISM, BAPTISMAL RITES; DEATH OF CHRIST; FOOD, FOOD LAWS, TABLE FELLOWSHIP; LITURGICAL ELEMENTS; LORD'S DAY; SACRIFICE, OFFERINGS, GIFTS; WORSHIP AND LITURGY.

BIBLIOGRAPHY. A. Bouley, *From Freedom to Formula: The Evolution of the Eucharistic Prayer from Oral Improvisation to Written Texts* (Washington, DC: The Catholic University of America, 1981); O. Cullmann, "The Meaning of the Lord's Supper in Primitive Christianity" in *Essays on the Lord's Supper*, ed. O. Cullmann and F. J. Leenhardt, (ESW 1; Richmond, Virginia: John Knox, 1958); G. Dix, *The Shape of the Liturgy* (London: Dacre Press/A. & C. Black, 1945); A. B. du Toit, *Der Aspekt der Freude im urchristlichen Abendmahl* (Winterthur: Keller, 1965); P. F. Esler, *Community and Gospel in Luke-Acts* (SNTSMS 57; Cambridge: Cambridge University Press, 1987); J. L. Espinel Marcos, *La Eucaristia del Nuevo Testamento* (Salamanca: San Esteban, 1980); A. J. B. Higgins, *The Lord's Supper in the New Testament* (SBT 6; London: SCM, 1952); R. C. D. Jasper and G. J. Cuming, *Prayers of the Eucharist: Early and Reformed* (3d ed.; New York: Pueblo, 1987); J. Jeremias, *The Eucharistic Words of Jesus* (New York: Scribner's, 1966); A. A. Just, *The Ongoing Feast: Table Fellowship and Eschatology at Emmaus* (Collegeville, MN.: Liturgical Press, 1993); J. F. Keating, *The Agapé and the Eucharist in the Early Church* (London: Methuen, 1901); H.-J. Klauck, *Herrenmahl und hellenistischer Kult* (Münster:

Aschendorff, 1982); J. Kodell, *The Eucharist in the New Testament* (Wilmington, DE: Michael Glazier, 1988); X. Léon-Dufour, *Sharing the Eucharistic Bread: The Witness of the New Testament* (Mahwah, NJ: Paulist, 1987); H. Lietzmann, *Mass and Lord's Supper* (Leiden: E. J. Brill, 1953, 1979); I. H. Marshall, *Last Supper and Lord's Supper* (Grand Rapids: Eerdmans, 1981); P. H. Menoud, "Les Actes des apôtres et l'eucharistie" in *Jésus-Christ et la foi* (Neuchâtel: Delachaux & Niestlé, 1975) 63-76; B. Reicke, *Diakonie, Festfreude und Zelos in Verbindung mit der altchristlichen Agapenfeier* (Uppsala: Lundequistska Bokhandeln, 1948); idem, "Die Mahlzeit mit Paulus auf den Wellen des Mittelmeeres Act. 27, 33-38," *TZ* 4 (1948) 401-10; J. Reumann, *The Supper of the Lord: The New Testament, Ecumenical Dialogues, and Faith and Order on Eucharist* (Philadelphia: Fortress, 1985); H. Riesenfeld, "Sabbat et jour du Seigneur" in *New Testament Essays*, ed. A. J. B. Higgins (Manchester: Manchester University Press, 1959) 210-17; W. Rordorf et al., *The Eucharist of the Early Christians* (New York: Pueblo, 1978); M. H. Shepherd, *The Pascal Liturgy and the Apocalypse* (ESW 6; Richmond, Virginia: John Knox, 1960); G. Wainwright, *Eucharist and Eschatology* (London: Epworth, 1971; New York: Oxford University Press, 1981); J. Wanke, *Beobachtungen zum Eucharistieverständnis des Lukas auf Grund der lukanischen Mahlberichte* (ETS 8; Leipzig: St. Benno-Verlag, 1973); L. Wehr, *Arznei der Unsterblichkeit: Die Eucharistie bei Ignatius von Antiochien und im Johannesevangelium* (NTAbh n.s. 18; Münster: Aschendorff, 1987); R. Williamson, "The Eucharist and the Epistle to the Hebrews," *NTS* 21 (1975) 300-12.

G. Wainwright

LOT. *See* ANCESTORS.

LOVE

"This is love: not that we loved God, but that he loved us and sent his Son as an atoning sacrifice for our sins" (1 Jn 4:10). These words point to the revolutionary new understanding of love the Christians brought into the world. They learned from the love of God for the unworthy and they came to love not because they found people worthy to be loved but because they had become loving people. They loved now not because of the attractiveness they discerned in other people but because they themselves had become loving people. The love of God in Christ had transformed them; they had been reborn into a life in which they had become loving people. They loved God, they loved one another and they loved people outside their fellowship.

1. The Love of God
2. Love for God
3. Love of Fellow Believers
4. Love for Non-Christians
5. Love in the Postapostolic Church

1. The Love of God.

The love God* has for his people is the primary truth.* It is this love that undergirds all Scripture: were it not that God loves the people he has made, there would have been no revelation* to record. And especially it is due to the love of the heavenly Father that he sent his Son* into the world* to bring salvation* to repentant sinners. That love of God for the people he has made is fundamental. Sometimes the love of Christ* is referred to (Rev 1:5), sometimes that of God (Heb 12:6). Either way the priority of the divine love is insisted upon (1 Jn 4:19).

The writer to the Hebrews* includes a series of quotations from the OT that he applies to "the Son" (Heb 1:6, 8-13). Mostly these are concerned with the greatness of the Son, but one of them concerns love, namely, "you loved righteousness and hated lawlessness" (Heb 1:9, the quotation is from Ps 45:7; [*see* Old Testament in Hebrews]). The love for what is right runs through the whole of Scripture, and it is one of the important things about God. Here we find that the Son, who shares the divine nature of the Father, shares also the Father's love of what is right.

The Seer tells his readers that Jesus "loves us and has loosed us from our sins in his blood and made us a kingdom, priests to his God and Father" (Rev 1:5-6). "Loves" is in the present tense: the writer is pointing to a love that never ceases, while "loosed" in the aorist refers to an action based on that love but occurring at a point in time. It indicates that Jesus has set us free from the bondage of sins, and the reference to "his blood" makes it clear that John is referring to Jesus' saving death (*see* Death of Christ). He is drawing attention to that great offering made in love when Jesus died on the cross* and to its effects in dealing comprehensively with all the sins of all who come to him. Here we have the thought, emphasized by Paul, that salvation proceeds from the love of God so strikingly shown on the cross (most clearly in 1 Jn 4:7-12). Throughout the NT this important truth undergirds the whole Christian way.

"Keep yourselves in God's love" writes Jude* (Jude 21), bringing out the importance of the love of the heavenly Father and also the dreadful truth that in some way believers can minimize its effect. "Without obedience to God's will, fellowship with God can be forfeited" (Bauckham, 114). Believers are reminded that the love of God demands a response.

Another part of the Christian life comes before us when the writer to the Hebrews quotes Proverbs 3:11-12: "For whom the Lord loves he chastens, and he scourges every son whom he receives" (Heb 12:5-6). W. Bauer's lexicon gives the meaning of the verb *(paideuō)* in this passage (translated "chastens") as "discipline with punishment." There is the thought of chastisement, and the writer is reminding his readers that the Christian way is not all roses and joy. Even the best of Christians sometimes do things that ought not to be done or fail to do things that ought to be done. Hebrews is telling us that some of the pain we feel as we go through life is in fact divine discipline, helping us become better people. It is to be welcomed accordingly, and we are to heed the lessons God is teaching us.

The same passage from Proverbs (Prov 3:11-12) is behind the rebuke to the church* of Laodicea (Rev 3:19), where the message from God includes the words, "As many as I love I rebuke and discipline." In this most unsatisfactory of the seven churches, one in which there is nothing to praise and much to condemn, there is this message of love and a reminder of the divine purpose in the suffering* that would come upon the little group. R. H. Charles comments, "It is a touching and unexpected manifestation of love to those who deserve it least among the Seven Churches" (Charles, 1:99). And it is of continuing importance that believers are to discern the loving hand of God in the chastisements that are part of life as well as in their happy days.

The love of Christ is seen in the message to another of the seven churches, the church in Philadelphia, one of the two out of the seven that receive no blame. This church had evidently suffered at the hand of some Jews whom John calls "the synagogue of Satan," but they are assured that these persecutors will in due course come to give honor to the church and will know that Christ has loved those believers (Rev 3:9).

2. Love for God.

Love for God is equally important. It is everywhere assumed in the NT, though it does not often come to expression. One such passage, however, is that in which James* assures his readers of the blessing* that comes to the person who "endures temptation" (Jas 1:12). Such a person, being approved, "will receive the crown of life that he [God] promised to those who love him." James does not spell out what "the crown of life" means (cf. Rev 2:10), but clearly it points to a royal blessing, the life of the age to come. Temptation* is part of life as we know it, and James is making it clear to his readers that God expects that those who love him will resist temptation and do what is right. When this happens, James assures us, the believer will not lack divine recognition. For those who love him, there is a promise* of God. And nothing could be more reliable than such a promise.

It is in this spirit that Peter can write of Christ, "whom not having seen, you love," and he goes on to speak of the blessings that come to those who love in this way. Though they do not see Christ, they believe and rejoice with unspeakable joy* that is full of glory*; they receive the salvation of their souls (1 Pet 1:8-9). Another significant passage is that in which James refers to the poor people in this world whom God has chosen and who are "rich in faith." They are thus the possessors of spiritual riches that contrast with their temporal poverty (Jas 2:5). And that is not all. James goes on to speak of these poor people as "heirs of the kingdom that God promised to those who love him." Our love for God is important now as we make our way through this world's problems, and it means incredible spiritual riches in the life to come. James does not wish those who are poor in this world to be depressed at their experience of financial stringency. Riches in faith* now and the promises of the kingdom (*see* Kingdom of God) to come mean that such poor people are not to be despised.

Thus both Peter and James speak of love for God, one for God the Father and the other for God the Son. Both assure the reader of the wonderful blessing that is the inevitable consequence of such love.

3. Love of Fellow Believers.

Again and again the writers of the later NT books insist that the saving work of Christ means that believers must live in love to one another. This was a virtue widely insisted on in antiquity, but the Christians seem to have had a special interest in it. There are many exhortations to familial love in the NT, and we must understand this not of love toward the human race in general but of love for those who have entered the fellowship* of the church, those who have been remade by the saving work of Christ. It is true that the early Christians were to take a benevolent interest in people at large, but "brotherly love" (Heb 13:1 NRSV, "let mutual love continue") meant for them love in a special sense for fellow believers.

Thus Peter exhorts his readers: "Above everything keep your love for one another at full strength" (1 Pet 4:8; J. N. D. Kelly's trans.); believers are to work at making their love for others in the household* of faith stronger day by day. They are not to think that brotherly love automatically goes on and on. While in many respects it is self-sustaining, it must also be supported by the exercise of the will. Believers must not take it for granted that they will continue in love for other believers. It is the case that some of those with whom we share membership in the household of faith are difficult people. So Peter is saying that we must take it as a high priority ("above all") to keep our love for others in the church at full strength, even for people who do not naturally appeal to us. Those who have been saved by Christ must not live selfishly. Christian love must not be seen as an option for those who like that sort of thing. It is an imperative laid on all those who have experienced the salvation of Christ brought about at Calvary.

Peter goes on in this passage to point out that "love covers a multitude of sins" (1 Pet 4:8; a quotation from Prov 10:12, "love covers all wrongs"). Some exegetes hold that this refers to the sins of the coverer, but it seems much more likely that it is the sins of other people that are in mind. Peter is surely saying that believers must not dwell on other people's sins but "cover" them. Love "is ready to forgive again and again. It finds a way to shelter the wrongdoer from exposure and condemnation. This is how God has treated us. This, therefore, is how we ought to treat one another" (Stibbs, 154).

Peter comes back to the importance of familial love when he lists some desirable qualities in believers, beginning with "be all of you of one mind, sympathetic, loving the brothers, compassionate" (1 Pet 3:8). The exhortation to be of one mind seems to reflect the situation of the early church where the many foes outside made it imperative that there be unity within the fold. And it is natural in such circumstances for the exhortation to include sympathy and genuine love for one another. Such bonds meant that the house church would not easily be split asunder.

The writer to the Hebrews evidently was satisfied with the way his readers were behaving, but love is so important that he could say, "Let brotherly love continue" (Heb 13:1). It cannot be taken for granted, but believers must work at it. J. Calvin comments on this verse, "We can only be Christians if we are brethren." James gives an example when he exhorts his readers as "my beloved brothers and sisters" (Jas 2:5 NRSV).

With so many exhortations to love in the literature of the early church, there must have been the temptation for people who linked themselves to the church without being really committed people to pretend to be more loving than they were. So Peter can look for "genuine mutual love" and proceed, "love one another deeply from the heart" (1 Pet 1:22 NRSV). Such an exhortation seems to indicate that there were some whose profession of love was insincere.

But such insincerity was unavailing, for God knows the love his people show to one another and the service they render (Heb 6:10). The writer to the Hebrews can argue that believers are to spur one another on to love and to good works (Heb 10:24). When people come to believe in Jesus and to become members of the church they are to love all the other members. Life in the Christian community is meant, among other things, to introduce new believers to a community of love, a community in which the members strive to build one another up and to do this in love; believers help one another in love.

And love is so much part of community life in the early Christian church that Jude can begin his letter by addressing its members as people "beloved in God the father," after which he goes on to a prayer* that mercy,* peace* "and love" be multiplied among them (Jude 1-2). Peter similarly can urge believers to greet one another with "a kiss of love" (1 Pet 5:14). The first thing Christians do when they meet is give evidence of their love.

In the social setting of the early church it was of first importance that the members of the church should stand by one another. There are quite a few exhortations to them to love one another. It was not enough for them to refrain from in-fighting: in a hostile world it mattered that believers saw one another as brothers and sisters and acted accordingly. It is clear that some people who fell far short of the Christian ideal found their way into church membership and that this presented problems that come to the surface from time to time in the NT. The causes of disunity may have been trivial, but the writers of the later NT books saw it as most important that such disunity be overcome. Believers were brothers and sisters in Christ, and it mattered immensely that they behave as family in Christ.

It is not surprising accordingly that the NT contains exhortations to believers to behave toward one another with love. Thus we read of certain converts who had "purified their souls in obedience to the truth" with the result that they now had "genuine mutual love." They are exhorted to "love one another deeply from the heart" (1 Pet 1:22 NRSV). The writer agrees that these converts had come to love their new family when they became Christians. But he does not want there to be any doubt as to the importance of going on in the faith and of continuing to live in love toward their brothers and sisters. It was love that held the church together. There was no law compelling people to belong to it. Its members could leave at any time.

But if they remained as church members it was of the utmost importance that they loved other church members. This does not mean that they were to pretend that others in the church were faultless. They were not to love them because they were perfect, for they were not perfect. They were to love them because the salvation they themselves had received in Christ made them loving people. They were to love other church members not because they had many excellent qualities (though doubtless some of them did). They were to love them because they themselves were now loving people. Love makes allowances. Love tries to help. Love looks at the good people do in preference to dwelling on their defects. "Love for the broth-ers" was of the utmost importance in the life of the early church.

Later in his letter* Peter comes back to the theme. "Honor all people," he writes, "love the brotherhood, fear God, honor the king" (1 Pet 2:17). It is interesting that when the writer is exhorting his readers to give honor to people at large, to fear God and to honor the ruler he should think it suitable to tell them to love the brotherhood of believers. Religion is not one department of life, tucked away from all other things we do. Loving the Christian family is of the first importance for those who seek to live out their lives as the servants of God in a troubled and all too often evil world.

Jude has a warning against false teachers who were "rocks in your love feasts" (Jude 12; see commentaries for translation). This glimpse of the early church at worship* shows that the Holy Communion was called a "love feast," a name that is found in Ignatius, Clement of Alexandria and others. It is perhaps worth reflecting that this is not a name for the service that would spontaneously occur to modern Christians. It may be that later generations have lost something that the early believers valued.

The expression shows us that the communion service was a full repast and not a token meal as commonly in modern times. And, however we understand the word translated as "rocks," it was a meal that gave some opportunity to false teachers to disrupt the life of the church in some way instead of preserving the unity the service suggests.

4. Love for Non-Christians.

Christians are required to love other Christians, but they are also required to live lives of love where non-Christians are concerned. Perhaps the clearest indication of this is 2 Peter's* injunction that his readers should "add to piety love of the brothers, and to love of the brothers, love" (2 Pet 1:7). The point is that believers are bound to one another with the special tie that they have all been saved through Christ's atoning death. But Peter is clear that they should not reason that their attitude to nonbelievers does not matter. They are to be loving people, and their attitude to those who do not believe is to be one of love.

Similarly James can tell his readers to obey "the royal law, according to the Scripture, 'you shall love your neighbor as yourself'" (Jas 2:8).

There is a problem in the words to the church in Ephesus, "you have forsaken your first love" (Rev 2:4), where "love" might mean love for Christ (GNB) or "love for one another" (Moffatt) or even love for people in general. Perhaps all three are included. There is a similar problem with the love of the church in Thyatira, where John says simply, "I know your works and love and faith" (Rev 2:19). What is clear in such passages is that believers are expected to be loving people.

Sometimes people love what is wrong, and we find the permanent consequence of this in a passage in Revelation. After speaking of the blessedness of those who go into "the city," John writes, "Outside are the dogs and the magicians and the fornicators and the murderers and the idolaters and everyone who loves and practices falsehood" (Rev 22:15). The linking of loving and lying points to an unreliable way of life. It is clear that lying is more than the telling of a little fib, which modern people sometimes see as of no great consequence. As in Revelation 21:8, lying comes last with emphasis.

Some passages do not fit into our classification, for they do not refer to love for people. This is the case with 1 Peter 3:10, where the writer quotes from Psalm 34:12-16: "For he who wills to love life and to see good days" (in LXX "love" refers to seeing the good days, rather than to life). It is unusual to find a reference to loving life rather than to loving people, but it directs attention to an important part of the service* of God. There are people who are depressed by the burdens of life, and this must have been a temptation to first-century Christians, harassed as they were by officialdom and without redress for the mistreatment they might expect and sometimes experienced. Peter is quoting Scripture to point them to the truth that life is a good gift from God and it is to be loved as such. To live in the service of the God who loves with the love we see on Calvary is to live a life we may well love to live. Our wills are to be set on this love.

In 2 Peter we have a reference to another kind of love, one with which we are not unfamiliar, namely, the love of money. The writer is making a reference to Balaam the son of Beor who, he tells us, "loved the wages of unrighteousness" (2 Pet 2:15). His fate is a reminder to Peter's readers that they are called to a very different kind of love.

The last book of the Bible has some memorable passages about the contest God's people have with evil, and in one of them we read of Michael and his angels doing battle with Satan* and his angels.* Victory went to the forces of good and it is said of the martyrs, "they did not love their life unto death" (Rev 12:11). They gave their all in the struggle against evil, and that is their commendation.

5. Love in the Postapostolic Church.

Christians have always found it difficult to live up to all that is taught them in the NT, and this goes for the early church as well as for the later periods. We do not have a complete picture of life in the early church, but the writings that survive show that the NT teaching on love was held to be of great importance. And, when we consider what we know of life in general at that time, it was put into practice to a remarkable extent.

In the letter known as *1 Clement,* after the opening greeting in the first sentence, the readers are addressed as "beloved" (an address that recurs in other parts of the letter), and the writer speaks of the church in Corinth as "worthy of all people's love" (*1 Clem.* 1.1). He says that God wills "to give to all his beloved repentance" (*1 Clem.* 8.5), so that it is the love of God that brings the church into existence.

Clement (*see* Clement of Rome) can speak of the church of Corinth as striving "on behalf of all the brothers and sisters" (*adelphotētos,* *1 Clem.* 2.4); it is significant that he sees believers everywhere as brothers and sisters. Clement looks for the strong to care for the weak and for the rich to help the poor, duties that are part of the outworking of love (*1 Clem.* 38.2). The loving person is to carry out the commandments* of Christ (*1 Clem.* 99.1), so that obedience* is necessary for the believer as well as love. It is in love that all God's elect* were perfected, and without love nothing pleases God (*1 Clem.* 49.5). And Clement reminds his readers that it was in love that Christ "gave his blood" for us (*1 Clem.* 49.6). He sees love as "great and marvelous" and urges his readers to "pray and ask" for it. He further says that it is to be found only where God gives it (*1 Clem.* 50.1-2); it is not to be seen as a human achievement. He selects Moses,* Judith and Esther as examples of people who showed great love (*1 Clem.* 53.4-5; 55:4-6).

The writer of *2 Clement* does not have as many

references to love as does the author of *1 Clement,* but he clearly sees love as a most important part of living out the Christian faith. He cites the words in Matthew 7:21 that not all those who say "Lord, Lord" are saved and goes on, "So then, brothers, let us confess him in works, in loving each other" (*2 Clem.* 4.1-3). We are to "await God's kingdom in love and righteousness" (*2 Clem.* 12.1). If Christians do not love other people, and specifically other believers, outsiders "laugh us to scorn" with the result that "the name is blasphemed" (*2 Clem.* 13.4). Anyone who "speaks and hears" should "speak and hear with faith and love" (*2 Clem.* 15.2). The writer quotes from 1 Peter 4:8, "love covers a multitude of sins," and he sees this as surpassing almsgiving, fasting and prayer (*2 Clem.* 16.4).

Ignatius* comes before us as a bishop of the church, sentenced to death by the authorities and on his way to Rome* to be thrown to wild beasts. He writes a number of letters, mostly to churches, and consistently urges people to do nothing to hinder his martyrdom.* He is perhaps more fanatical than loving, but he has some wonderful things to say about love. Even this fiery spirit was touched by the love of God and saw love as the most important part of Christian service. He commends bishop Onesimus of Ephesus as "a man of inexpressible love" and urges the Ephesians to return that love (Ign. *Eph.* 1.3). Faith and love are "the beginning of life and its end" (Ign. *Eph.* 14.1). He speaks of love "which is the blood of Jesus Christ" (Ign. *Trall.* 8.1). He can give directions to the Trallians introduced with "yet not I but the love of Jesus Christ" (Ign. *Trall.* 6.1). He was sure of what Christ would say in love in the situation in which the Trallians found themselves.

Ignatius was convinced of the love of the Roman Christians. He speaks of them as "preeminent in love" (Ign. *Rom.* presc.). He also says, "I fear your love, lest it do me wrong" (Ign. *Rom.* 1.2). He was keen on being martyred, and he evidently was afraid that the Roman Christians would somehow influence the authorities to spare his life. He could say, "If you are silent about me, I am a word of God, but if you love my flesh, then I shall be only a voice." He looks for the Roman church to be "a chorus in love" while he is offered on the altar (Ign. *Rom.* 2.1-2).

Ignatius tells the Philadelphians that the Spirit was saying to him, among other things,

"love unity" (Ign. *Phld.* 7.2). The bishop later says that "where there is division and anger God does not dwell" (Ign. *Phld.* 8.1). He also remarks that all things are good "if you believe in love" (Ign. *Phld.* 9.2).

There is a letter of Polycarp* to the Philippians in which it is said that "he who has love is distant from all sin" (Pol. *Phil.* 3.3). Wives are exhorted to remain in the faith and "in love and purity, loving their own husbands in all truth and loving all people equally" (Pol. *Phil.* 4.2). The letter calls for love of the brotherhood (Pol. *Phil.* 10.1). There is a call to prayer for those who persecute them (Pol. *Phil.* 12.3). The letter carries repeated warnings against love of money (Pol. *Phil.* 4.3; 5.2; 6.1), so evidently this form of love was prevalent. There is an account of the martyrdom of this good man from which we learn that "it belongs to true and steadfast love not only to wish to be saved oneself but all the brothers and sisters also" (Pol. *Phil.* 1.2).

The *Didache** explains the way of life: "The way of life is this: First you shall love the God who made you; secondly, your neighbor as yourself. And whatsoever you do not wish to be done to you, do not do to another" (*Did.* 1.2).

Throughout the literature that comes down to us from the early church, it is clear that there was emphasis on the importance of believers showing love in such ways as helping the poor (a practice insisted upon even when there is no specific mention of love). There are also rebukes for the hypocritical, which show both that it was expected that those who had this world's goods would show their love for their fellows by helping the less fortunate and also that all too often this was outward show that lacked genuine love (1 Jn 3:11-17; 4:20; cf. Jam 2:1-16). But the impression that is left is that the early church on the whole took seriously the fact that its members had been saved by the love of God and that this demanded that those members live in love to one another.

See also ETHICS; FAITH, FAITHFULNESS; GRACE; HOPE; MERCY.

BIBLIOGRAPHY. R. J. Bauckham, *2 Peter, Jude* (WBC; Waco, TX: Word, 1983); R. H. Charles, *The Revelation of St. John* (2 vols.; ICC; Edinburgh: T & T Clark, 1920); A. Chester and R. P. Martin, *The Theology of the Letters of James, Peter and Jude* (NTT; Cambridge: Cambridge University Press, 1994); M. C. D'Arcy, *The Mind and Heart of Love* (2d ed.; London: Faber & Faber, 1954); R. H.

Fuller, ed., *Essays on the Love Command* (Philadelphia: Fortress, 1978); V. P. Furnish, *The Love Command in the New Testament* (Nashville: Abingdon, 1972); L. E. Keck, "On the Ethos of Early Christians," *JAAR* 42 (1974) 435-52; J. N. D. Kelly, *A Commentary on the Epistles of Peter and Jude* (HNTC; New York: Harper & Row, 1969); L. L. Morris, *Testaments of Love: A Study of Love in the Bible* (Grand Rapids: Eerdmans, 1981); J. Moffatt, *Love in the New Testament* (London: Hodder & Stoughton, 1929); A. Nygren, *Agape and Eros* (Philadelphia: Westminster, 1953); J. Piper, *"Love Your Enemies": Jesus' Love Command in the Synoptic Gospels and the Early Christian Paraenesis* (SNTSMS 38; Cambridge: Cambridge University Press, 1979); C. Spicq, *Agape in the New Testament (3 vols.; London: Herder, 1963-66); idem, Agapé: Prolégomènes à une étude de théologie néotestamentaire* (Leiden: E. J. Brill, 1955); A. M. Stibbs (with A. F. Walls), *1 Peter* (TNTC; London: Tyndale, 1959); O. Wischmeyer, *Der höchste Weg: Das 13 Kapitl des 1. Korintherbriefes* (Gütersloh: Gütersloher Verlaghaus, 1981).

L. L. Morris

LOVE FEAST. *See* LORD'S SUPPER, LOVE FEAST.

LUKE-ACTS. *See* ACTS OF THE APOSTLES.

LUST. *See* MARRIAGE, DIVORCE AND ADULTERY.

M

MAGIC AND ASTROLOGY

In the ancient world magic was a method of harnessing supernatural power to gain protection from evil spirits or to obtain what one desired (*see DPL*, Magic). The practice of astrology was based on a belief that there is an inextricable link between the movements of the sun, moon and stars and what happens to people in the courses of their lives. Popular astrology conceived of the heavenly bodies as governed by spirits, gods or angels.* Thus astrology and magic became linked as people attempted to use incantations and rituals to thwart the astral spirits and alter their fate. An understanding of the presuppositions and beliefs of magic and astrology are essential to appreciating the worldview of the mass of people—both Gentile* and Jew—in the Roman world. This awareness is, in turn, helpful to students of the NT in understanding what kind of shifts in worldview were necessary for people in becoming Christians.

1. Nature and Characteristics
2. Magic and the Demonic in Acts
3. Magic and the Apocalypse
4. Anti-Magic Polemic in the Apostolic Fathers
5. Astrology and Early Christianity
6. Magic and Astrology in the Rise of Gnosis

1. Nature and Characteristics.

Magic presupposed the existence of thousands of spirits—good and evil—involved in the affairs of day-to-day life. These spirits were thought of as gods and goddesses (e.g., Apollo and Artemis), divine mediators (e.g., Hermes, *angeloi, paredroi*), spirits of the untimely dead (*biaiothanatoi*), astral spirits, underworld spirits or various kinds of chthonic, or terrestrial spirits (*see* Religions). The practice of magic also assumed a system of inner connections between physical objects in the universe. An action performed on one object was thought to have a corresponding impact on another(the principle of sympathy and antipathy).

Those who engaged in the ancient art of magic sought to solicit the help of various gods and spirits or to utilize the system of correspondences throughout the universe. This was achieved through various acts of ritual power.* Through many literary texts and especially now through the numerous recently discovered papyrus texts (see Betz), lead curse tablets (see Gager), amulets and various other magical paraphernalia, we have a good idea of how much of this procedure was carried out.

Magical conjurations typically consisted of three parts: an incantation, a ritual and a command. The naming of various spirits and gods was the key part of the incantation (e.g., "I entrust this binding-charm to you gods of the underworld: Pluto and Kore-Persephone, Ereschigal, Adonis also called Barbaritha, Hermes Katachthonios-Thoth . . . I conjure all daimones in this place to assist this daimon Antinoos" [*New Documents*, no. 8, lines 1-3]). Often various kinds of power rituals, sometimes involving the principle of sympathy and antipathy, accompanied the incantation. For example, one magical formula for attaining great success in business calls for the performance of the following rite:

Take beeswax . . . and fashion a man having his right hand in the position of begging and having in his left a bag and a staff. Let there be around the staff a coiled snake, and let him be dressed in a girdle and standing on a sphere that has a coiled snake, like Isis. . . . Fashion him during the new moon and consecrate it in a celebrating mood, and read aloud the spell over his members. (*PGM* IV.2379-91)

Finally, after invoking the deities or spirits and performing the requisite rights, the person could make his demands of the attendant spirit. Many of the papyrus texts and most of the amulets are calls for protection (apotropaic magic for "warding off" harmful spirits), deliverance or help. People also frequently used magic simply to get something they wanted—victory in a race, a sexual liaison, influence over another person or healing. The darkest dimensions of magic are the various maledictions, or curses. Most prominent among these are the lead curse tablets (*defixiones*) in which a "fix," or "binding," is placed on another person by the spirits conjured (see Gager).

Although magic in the Roman world was an identifiable phenomenon with objective characteristics and with specialists who identified themselves as magicians, the terms *magic* and *magician* could also be used as pejorative labels for deviant religious behavior in the context of a cult. Early Christians, however, tended to interpret magic in terms of its source of power, Satan and his demons. Thus in its own self-understanding, Christianity could not be a type of magic because it relied on the power* of God* and the Lord* Jesus Christ.*

Like magic, astrological beliefs and practices permeated the Mediterranean world. Because of the belief in an inextricable link between the position and movements of the stars over time and the events of a person's life, *mathematikoi* or *Chaldaei* (astrologers) could cast a horoscope and predict certain outcomes in the life of an individual. While Stoics resigned themselves to destiny, many thought that the horrors of a foul fate could be altered. Since it was widely believed that deities and spirits animated the heavenly bodies, fate could be altered through ritual acts of power that would compel the spirit to a different course of action. Thus magic and astrology became intertwined in popular belief.

In our literature, "magic" figures prominently in Acts and Revelation, but it is not at all in the foreground in James, Hebrews, 1 and 2 Peter, 1—3 John and Jude. Nevertheless, keeping in mind the fact that many of the readers of these letters were people who had been involved in the magical arts and astrology to some degree prior to their conversions may help to understand some of the theological accents in these works. In the apostolic fathers, however, there is a strong anti-magic and anti-astrology polemic that characterizes many passages.

2. Magic and the Demonic in Acts.

The book of Acts* narrates three dramatic and important accounts involving the practice of magic. In each of these, magic is cast in a bad light and is seen as the tool of Satan to keep people from the gospel of Christ and a true dependence upon him.

As the gospel* spread from Jerusalem* to Samaria* through Philip's* preaching, a wonder worker named Simon became enamored with the means by which the Spirit of God came upon people after the Apostles laid their hands upon them (Acts 8:9-25). The text explicitly says that Simon practiced magic (*mageuōn*) in the city (Acts 8:9) and that he had amassed a significant following because people were amazed with his magic (*mageia*, Acts 8:11). They had in fact hailed him as "the Great Power" (Acts 8:10). In spite of Simon's ostensive conversion ("he believed and was baptized"), Peter rebuked him in the severest of terms because Simon sought power rather than Jesus Christ. In fact, Peter discerned bitterness in his heart and an abiding bondage (*syndesmon*) to sin (Acts 8:23).

The theme of conflict with magic and the demonic surfaces once again in Luke's narration of Paul's confrontation with Elymas, or Bar Jesus, on the island of Cyprus (Lk 13:4-12). Elymas is twice termed a "magician" (*magos*) by Luke. What makes the account even more intriguing is that he is a *Jewish* magician. Many Jews in antiquity were deeply involved in the magical arts, exorcising demons, making protective amulets, and creating various magical spells (see Alexander). Luke saw Elymas as a satanically inspired opponent of the gospel of Jesus Christ, hindering the proconsul of the island from positively responding to the truth. God's power proved greater than the diabolic power of Elymas (*see* Signs and Wonders). The hand of the Lord was against this "son of the devil," and he was struck blind. The proconsul then heard the teaching about the Lord and believed. S. Garrett aptly notes, "Paul's victory over Satan's servant demonstrates again the reliability of Jesus' promise that Christians will have authority to trample on 'snakes and scorpions,' and over all the power of the Enemy" (Garrett, 86).

The final account explicitly mentioning magic is the story of the burning of the magical papyri in Ephesus (Acts 19:8-20). Magical practices flourished at Ephesus, thus giving it the reputation of being something of a center for magic (see Arnold, 14-20). The catalyst for this mass renunciation of occultic practices was the quickly spreading news of the foiled attempt of Sceva and his sons to cast demons out of a man. The Jewish exorcists had attempted to use the name of Jesus in their incantational repertoire of names—without success. In fact, they were physically assaulted and hurt in the encounter. As a result of this, fear gripped people living in the city, even those in the new Christian community. The surprising twist in the story is that *many Christians* became convicted of their continued involvement in magical practices, openly renounced it and burned their scrolls (Acts 19:18-19). There was a strong temptation for Christians to continue wearing amulets, consulting magicians and using incantations and formulas. Not all Christians in the Mediterranean world, however, renounced their occult practices. Many individuals syncretized their Christianity with magic (*see* Syncretism). This is well illustrated in the published corpus of Christian magical texts (see Meyer and Smith).

3. Magic and the Apocalypse.

The Apocalypse contains some very strong and explicit polemic against magic (*see* Revelation, Book of). The harshest appears in Revelation 21:8 where sorcerers (*pharmakoi*) are doomed to the lake of fire and the second death.* Similarly, magicians (*pharmakoi*) are consigned to a place outside the new heavenly city (Rev 22:15). The reason for this is partly explained in Revelation 18:23 where the personified Babylon* is upbraided for leading all the nations astray by her magical spells (*pharmakeiai*). Practicing magic is placed on the same level as worshiping demons, stealing, committing murder and engaging in sexual immorality (Rev 9:21).

In denouncing magic the Apocalypse consistently uses *pharmakeia* and its cognates (cf. Paul's use of *pharmakeia* as a deed of the flesh in Gal 5:19). Although the term *pharmakos* could be used in referring to poison and drugs, it was also widely used as a way of generally speaking of magic and did not necessarily entail the use of potions or drugs in the magic ritual. Thus *pharmakeia* and *mageia* could be used interchangeably.

The practice of magic in Rome is well-attested in the literature (e.g., *Sib. Or.* 5.165) and by the discovery of numerous curse tablets (Gager). As in the book of Acts, the indictment of the magical arts in the Apocalypse is that it is a tool of Satan* to lead people away from a true knowledge* of God (cf. Rev 18:23).

D. Aune has demonstrated that the author of the Apocalypse actually incorporates certain images from the conceptual world of magic (Aune 1987). He points in particular to the expressions "I have the keys to Death and Hades" (Rev 1:18), "I am coming quickly" (e.g., Rev 22:20) and "I am the Alpha and the Omega" (e.g., Rev 1:8). After noting the uniqueness of these expressions in early Christian literature, Aune illustrates each with striking parallels from the language of magical revelation. Aune then argues that the Apocalypse presents Jesus as a counter to many of the assumptions of Greco-Roman revelatory magic. In effect, the language represents "an extensive and creative anti-magical polemic the purpose of which is to nullify the revelatory claims of the pagan competitors of Christian prophets" (Aune 1987, 494).

4. Anti-Magic Polemic in the Apostolic Fathers.

The early patristic literature leaves no option to new Christians other than giving up and renouncing their magical arts, including astrology. The *Didache* unequivocally asserts, "my child, do not be an auger (*oionoskopos*), since it leads to idolatry. Do not be an enchanter (*epaoidos*) or an astrologer (*mathematikos*) or a magician (*perikathairōn*), or even desire to see them, for all these things breed idolatry" (*Did.* 3.4; cf. also *Did.* 2.2). The practice of magic is listed with idolatry and other evils as part of the way of death (*Did.* 5.1).

Second-century orthodox Christians saw magic as a constituent part of "the ancient kingdom"—the domain of Satan which Christ had come to destroy (Ign. *Eph.* 19.3). The *Epistle of Barnabas* speaks of sorcery and magic (*pharmakeia* and *mageia*) as part of the way of "the Black One" (Satan) that destroys people's souls and leads to punishment and eternal death (*Barn.* 20.1). *Diognetus* also speaks of "the illusion and deceit of the magicians" (*Diogn.* 8.4). Again, the real reason for the rejection of the popular amulets, incantations and spells has to do with the source for the power. It is connected with Satan and his evil demons, not with God and his redemptive and relational purposes through the Lord Jesus Christ. As an antidote to the spiritually fatal effects of magic, Ignatius prescribes the Eucharist, which he characterizes as *Pharmakon athanasias*, "medecine of immortality (Ign. *Eph.* 20.2). This accompanies the confession of Jesus as Son of Man and Son of God, fellowship with the people of God and submission to the leadership of the church.

In contrast, some scholars have seen *Hermas** as influenced by a magical worldview evidenced by the terms and concepts from ancient magic found in his revelatory visions. This borrowing was primarily formal, however, and the worldview assumptions in *Hermas* stand at a significant distance from the magical practices of ancient Rome. Furthermore, *Hermas* makes a number of unfavorable comments about magic and sorcery (*Herm. Vis.* 3.9.7; *Herm. Man.* 11.2).

5. Astrology and Early Christianity.

With the exception of *Didache* 3.4, there is no overt anti-astrology polemic in our literature. One can certainly assume, however, that astrology was frowned upon by leaders in the church. As the early church appropriated much of the OT tradition regarding idolatry, it would also have taken over the negative perspective on astrology. The Torah expressly prohibited Israel from worshiping the stars (Deut 4:19). One may also assume that the anti-magic polemic of Acts, the Apocalypse and the apostolic fathers includes an anti-astrology stance.

Nevertheless, astral imagery holds a prominent place in the book of Revelation.* Jesus is introduced as holding "seven stars" in his right hand (Rev 1:16). These stars are subsequently identified as angels associated with the seven churches (Rev 1:20). In fact, Jesus is termed "the bright Morning Star" at the end of the book (Rev 22:16). In a more negative vein, stars/angels are involved in the outpouring of wrath.* A star called "Wormwood" turns all of the waters bitter (Rev 8:10-12) and another star is given the key to the Abyss (Rev 9:1). Many interpreters have seen the third of the stars swept out of the sky by the tail of the dragon as an allusion to the fall of Satan and his angels* (Rev 12:4; cf. 12:7). The astral imagery, here and elsewhere, would have communicated powerfully to people who came into the church steeped in a background of astrological practices. One message that comes out strongly is Jesus' supremacy and sovereignty over all the stars.

Astrology and astral phenomena are quite rare in the apostolic fathers. In *Clement** the stars are represented as purely physical objects that circle unerringly in their courses at the direction of God (*1 Clem.* 20.3). Yet in Ignatius the personified sun, moon and stars join in a chorus around the star of Bethlehem at the birth of Christ (Ign. *Eph.* 19.2; *see* Worship). This imagery, as in Revelation, points to the superiority of the Son.*

6. Magic and Astrology in the Rise of Gnosis.

Magic and astrology ultimately fed into the grand amalgam of teachings commonly called Gnosticism.* Individual Gnostic teachers incorporated magical incantations, rituals of power, and astrological beliefs and symbols into their various systems of thought. Magical passwords and seals, for instance, are given in the two books of Jeu to assist the individual Gnostic in the treacherous heavenly ascent through the demonically controlled planetary spheres after death (see Rudolph, 172-75). Thus the phenomena of magic and astrology—so popular with the masses—found a companion in Gnosticism, but continued to be opposed by the mainstream church.

See also GNOSIS, GNOSTICISM; MIRACLES IN ACTS; POWER; RELIGIONS, GRECO-ROMAN; SATAN, DEVIL; SIGNS AND WONDERS; SPIRITS.

BIBLIOGRAPHY. P. S. Alexander, "Incantations and Books of Magic" in *The History of the Jewish People in the Age of Jesus Christ*, rev. and ed. G. Vermes, F. Millar and M. Goodman (3 vols.; Edinburgh: T & T Clark, 1986) 3.1.342-79; C. E. Arnold, *Ephesians: Power and Magic* (SNTSMS 63; Cambridge: University Press, 1989; Grand Rapids: Baker, 1992 repr.); D. Aune, "The Apocalypse of John and Graeco-Roman Revelatory Magic," *NTS* 33 (1987) 481-501; idem, "Magic in Early Christianity," *ANRW* 2.23.2 (1980) 1507-57; idem, "Magic," *ISBE* 3.213-19; H. D. Betz, ed. *The Greek Magical Papyri in Translation*, 1: *Text* (Chicago: University of Chicago Press, 1986); idem, "Magic and Mystery in the Greek Magical Papyri" in *Hellenismus und Urchristentum. Gesammelte Aufsätze I* (Tübingen: J. C. B. Mohr, 1990) 209-29; F. Cumont, *Astrology and Religion Among the Greeks and Romans* (New York & London: G. P. Putnam's, 1912); idem, *The Oriental Religions in Roman Paganism* (New York/London: Dover, 1956 [1911]); C. A. Faraone and D. Obbink, eds., *Magika Hiera: Ancient Greek Magic and Religion* (New York: Oxford University Press, 1991); E. Ferguson, *Backgrounds of Early Christianity* (2d. ed.; Grand Rapids: Eerdmans, 1993); J. G. Gager, *Curse*

Tablets and Binding Spells from the Ancient World (New York: Oxford University Press, 1992); S. R. Garrett, *The Demise of the Devil: Magic and the Demonic in Luke's Writings* (Minneapolis: Fortress, 1989); E. R. Goodenough, *Jewish Symbols in the Greco-Roman Period, 2: The Archaeological Evidence from the Diaspora* (BS 37; New York: Bollingen Foundation, 1953); H. G. Gundel, *Weltbild und Astrologie in den griechischen Zauberpapyri* (MBPAR 53; München: Beck, 1968); W. Gundel, *Dekane und Dekansternbilder: Ein Beitrag zur Geschichte der Sternbilder der Kultervölker* (2d ed.; Darmstadt: Wissenschaftliche Buchgesellschaft, 1969); T. Hopfner, *Griechisch-Ägyptischer Offenbarungszauber* (SPP 21; Amsterdam: Adolf M. Hakkert, 1974 [= Leipzig: Haessel, 1921]); G. H. R. Horsley, *New Documents Illustrating Early Christianity. A Review of Greek Inscriptions and Papyri Published in 1976* (North Ryde: Macquarie University, 1981); G. Luck, *Arcana Mundi* (Baltimore: Johns Hopkins, 1985); R. Merkelbach and M. Totti, *Abraxas. Ausgewählte Papyri Religiösen und Magischen Inhalts* (3 Vols.; ARWAW: Sonderreihe, Papyrological Coloniensia 17.1, 17.2, 17.3; Opladen: Estdeutscher Verlag, 1990, 1991, 1992); M. W. Meyer and P. Mirecki, *Ancient Magic and Ritual Power* (RGRW 129; Leiden: E. J. Brill, 1995); M. W. Meyer and R. Smith, *Ancient Christian Magic: Coptic Texts of Ritual Power* (San Francisco: Harper, 1994); A. Segal, "Hellenistic Magic: Some Questions of Definition" in *The Other Judaisms of Late Antiquity* (BJS 127; Atlanta: Scholar's Press, 1987) 79-108; E. M. Yamauchi, "Magic in the Biblical World," *TB* 34 (1983) 169-200.   C. E. Arnold

MAN. *See* WOMAN AND MAN.

MANDATES OF HERMAS. *See* HERMAS, SHEPHERD OF.

MARANATHA. *See* LITURGICAL ELEMENTS.

MARCION

Marcion (c. 80-c. 155) was the most influential heretical Christian of the second century. He rejected Judaism* and the OT and with them the God* of the OT. Preaching a gospel of love, Marcion focused on what he implied was a second, higher and better God of the NT. He established the earliest closed canon* and the first independent Christian organization to rival successfully the mainstream church.

1. Career
2. Teaching and Works
3. Marcionism
4. Marcion and the New Testament
5. Legacy

1. Career.

Marcion was a native of Sinope, a Hellenistic city in the province of Pontus in Asia Minor and a center of commerce on the shore of the Black Sea. Marcion was a wealthy ship owner whose father, we are told, was a bishop. He was supposedly excommunicated for "seducing a virgin." This is no doubt a false report, since it hardly fits with our knowledge of Marcion's character and is found in only one source. It may be a garbled memory of his leading astray some local Christians with false teaching (cf. 2 Cor 11:2-4). Marcion appears to have moved to other ports in Asia Minor, scattering his gospel everywhere. There is some evidence that he taught in Ephesus and was rejected there. It is possible that Polycarp's epistle to the Philippians (c. 125) was written against Marcionite teachings and indicates some of the early spreading of his ideas.

Like most thinkers who wished to influence the empire, Marcion made his way to Rome and gave the church a handsome gift of 200,000 sesterces (*see* Roman Empire). In Rome he came under the influence of Cerdo, a Christian philosopher from Syria.* In 144 (the one firm date we have for his life) Marcion was excommunicated by the council of presbyters in Rome, and his money was returned to him. Marcion then organized his own church, which grew rapidly. He solidified his teachings, created an abbreviated and closed canon of Scripture and stayed in Rome until his death sometime after 150.

2. Teaching and Works.

In the second century there were no written standards by which heresy was identified and no fixed list of canonical books for the NT. Only the universal rejection of Marcion by the orthodox and his mutilation of Christian documents identify him as a heretic. Marcion himself no doubt sincerely believed that he was restoring the true gospel* of Jesus from the corrupting influence of Judaizers and pseudoapostles (*see* Apostle).

2.1. Theology. Scholars continue to debate the central concern of Marcion, the key points of departure that lead to his aberrant theology, his short canon of Scripture and his establishment of a separate church organization. This debate is greatly complicated by the lack of Marcionite documents. As with most heretics, we know of Marcion only through the writings of his Christian opponents. We are fortunate, however, to have Tertullian's five books against Marcion, from which (along with other patristic sources) we can reconstruct his ideas and writings.

The key to understanding Marcion's thought is his anti-Judaism. From this center we can explain the rest of his work (contra Hoffmann, 226-34). It is important to remember that Marcion had philosophical and religious problems with Judaism but was not anti-Semitic in the modern sense. No doubt the anti-Judiac character of Marcion's thought derives from the general conflict between synagogue* and church following the bloody suppression of Jewish revolt in Palestine (A.D. 66-70 and 116-17). We know there was a large Jewish population in Pontus. It is suggestive of conflict between Jews and Christians in Pontus that Aquila (not the NT Aquila) was likewise a native of Sinope. Aquila was a re-convert to Judaism from Christianity who produced a literal Greek translation of the OT to replace the Septuagint, which the church used. The motive for this translation is clearly polemical and anti-Christian. If Marcion's father was a bishop, his family may have been involved in this conflict.

Marcion accepted a literal interpretation of the OT, rejecting the widespread use of typology and allegory among Christians. He distinguished, however, between the inferior Creator God (or Demiurge) of the OT and the God of the NT. The OT God gave the law* and was just but also incompetent. He was responsible for the creation of matter and for allowing Adam and Eve to fall into sin.* A second and superior God, the "unknown" God (cf. Acts 17:23) who is alien to this world, is the true author of salvation* and Father of Jesus Christ. This God was unknown prior to the ministry of Christ and is a God of light and love, the true savior of humanity. Only the NT God is worthy of worship* and adoration. The God of the Jews Marcion rejected. This dualism also provided a simple answer to the problem of evil, which no doubt added to the popularity of Marcionism.

Because of this theological dualism and rejection of matter, early writers like Irenaeus identified Marcion as a Gnostic.* While Marcion was no doubt influenced by Gnosticism, he differed from it in too many ways to be called a Gnostic. A more probable influence upon Marcion was the dualism and world-denying asceticism of several popular Hellenistic religions and philosophies, such as Cynic philosophy and Mithraism, in his native Pontus (see Religions). This suggests that Marcion developed his anti-Judaism in a thorough and consistent manner, using the intellectual tools that he found at hand. On this basis he was able to affirm the savior Jesus while relegating the God, the future Messiah (not Jesus) and the Bible of the Jews to second-class status. Marcion was consistent in his rejection of the material world* and the flesh.* Christ did not assume a physical body, and his work consisted of announcing the forgiveness* of the God of love and goodness. To join the Marcionites one renounced sex and could not be married (see Marriage). One also avoided wine and meat but was allowed fish. After death only the soul is raised to eternal life (see Resurrection).

2.2. Writings. Some scholars (Harnack, Hoffmann) have understood Marcion to be an extremist follower of Paul, merely a biblical theologian. This interpretation ignores the influence of anti-Judaism, dualism and asceticism on his thought. Such an interpretation is a good antidote to the traditional hypothesis but founders on the fact that the letters of Paul do not of themselves lead to Marcionism and in fact have elements in them that contradict it. Marcion himself knew better than modern critics how true this is, since he had to cut out the offending elements in Paul's letters. But there can be no doubt of Marcion's attachment to the apostle to the Gentiles. Paul alone among the apostles and evangelists understood the true gospel, the others being deluded by Jewish influence.

Marcion's canon included only an edited version of Luke and ten letters of Paul (excluding the Pastorals). The OT was completely rejected as an inferior Bible. To be consistent, Marcion removed from Paul's writings all quotations from the OT and most positive references to the Jews (e.g., the word *first* in Rom 1:16). To be fair to him, Marcion based this mutilation of NT documents on the theory that judaizing false apostles had corrupted the works of Paul and the gospel stories of Jesus. Careful work, therefore, was needed to restore the true, uncorrupted text. The edited version of Paul he called the *Apostolicon.*

Marcion's Gospel, the first part of his canon, was an edited version of Luke "restored" according to the same method. No doubt the tradition associating Luke with Paul was one reason Marcion preferred this Gospel to the others. Portions of Luke that did not fit the "true" (Marcionite) gospel were removed from the text, being interpolations by the false (Jewish) apostles. Marcion removed such elements as the Jewish genealogy of Jesus and the infancy narratives. Some have suggested that Marcion had a shorter text, a kind of proto-Luke, to work from. The evidence for this is necessarily scant, since Marcion's Gospel does not exist. It seems unlikely, however, given the late date of Marcion's work, relative to Luke-Acts. Furthermore, Marcion was willing to cut out offending portions even from the letters of his beloved Paul. How much more was he willing to edit the work of a mere follower, such as Luke? Marcion also wrote the *Antitheses,* which sets forth the contradictions between the teachings of Jesus and Paul and the OT. This functioned as a "key to the Scriptures" in the Marcionite churches and established Marcion as the first radical NT critic in church history.

3. Marcionism.

Marcion broke away from the catholic churches and established his own organization. This was successful and soon spread throughout the empire, "to every nation" wrote Justin Martyr, c. 150 (Justin *Apol. I* 26). Tertullian devoted his longest work to a refutation of Marcion. Numerous other orthodox writers in the Middle East, Africa and Europe felt compelled to condemn his work. These developments demonstrate the strength of the Marcionite church. Besides its own doctrine and canon of Scripture, the Marcionite church had its own bishops, presbyters, catechumenate and liturgy. Marcionite churches could be found in cities throughout the Roman Empire and in fact were so similar to the mainstream church that orthodox pastors warned new converts not to enter a Marcionite church by mistake. The oldest inscription (A.D. 318-19) we have from any Christian house of worship is Marcionite: "Place of worship [*synagōgē*] of the Lord and Savior

Jesus Christ of the Marcionites in the village of Lebabon" (Harnack 1924, 342). This indicates that Marcionites used the name of their founder to identify themselves and their buildings. Like other Christians, Marcionites faced martyrdom* at the hands of their Roman leaders, until the age of Constantine. The Marcionite church was absorbed, for the most part, into Manichaeism by the end of the second century but survived in the East (especially Syria) until the middle of the fifth century.

The popularity of Marcionism can be explained by many factors. Not least among them is the widespread anti-Judaism among Christians and pagans alike (Gager 1983). The dualism and asceticism of the Marcionites must have fit well into the popular mindset of late antiquity. His simple solution to the problem of evil, to the multiplicity of gospels and to the difficulty of an Incarnation must likewise have been attractive.

4. Marcion and the New Testament.

Some scholars (Bauer, Knox, Hoffmann) have argued that anti-Marcionite sentiments may lie behind some portions of the NT itself. In particular they find anti-Marcionite elements in Luke-Acts and the Pastoral Letters (1 and 2 Tim; Tit). This is most unlikely, given the probable dates for Marcion's Bible and for the NT documents (*see DJG,* Luke, Gospel of and *DPL,* Pastoral Letters). Even if Marcion was teaching heresy in the East prior to 144, there is no evidence of his Bible until Irenaeus (c. 190). There was no reason to publish his *Gospel* and *Apostolicon* until he had founded a new church after his expulsion from the Roman one.

Even leaving aside the issue of dating, the hypothesis collapses on careful consideration of the evidence. The heresy that prompted the writing of the Pastorals is best understood as a kind of Jewish proto-Gnosticism. All the evidence for anti-Marcionism can be explained with this far more likely theory. In addition the proto-Gnostic theory fits the fact that these false teachers devoted themselves to endless myths and genealogies (1 Tim 1:4) and wished to be teachers of the law (1 Tim 1:7)—such cannot have been Marcionite. Even the word *antitheseis* (contradictions, 1 Tim 6:20) need not point to Marcion. The word is a common one in Hellenistic rhetoric, which both 1 Timothy and Marcion used independently (cf. Esther 3:16; Job

32:3 LXX). The notion that Luke-Acts was written in part against Marcion (Knox, Hoffmann) is even more unlikely. The minimal evidence for such a bias can easily be explained by internal conflicts in the first-century church, a theory that fits much better with the date and purpose of Acts.*

4.1 Marcion and the Canon of the New Testament. Marcion's influence on the canon of the NT, as opposed to the NT itself, is beyond doubt. While the early church would have eventually created a list of authorized books in any case, the work of Marcion gave a sharp impetus to the creation of a catholic canon. He was the first to create a closed list of books, and the larger church was bound to respond with its own list. Even the shape of our NT (Gospels and Epistles) is due to Marcion's two-part canon. In terms of the Pauline corpus, Marcion gives us a ten-letter list without Hebrews or the Pastorals. The earliest papyrus of the Pauline letters (P^{46}) also does not include the Pastorals (but does include Hebrews). This may indicate an early, shorter Pauline corpus. It is certainly striking that brief, ancient prologues to Paul's letters seem to have been written in Marcionite circles in Rome. These prologues eventually made their way into many manuscripts of the Vulgate. At the same time, short prologues to the four Gospels in early Latin manuscripts seem to be anti-Marcionite. Marcion thus made a definite impact upon the canonical process, and this may be his most enduring legacy.

4.2 Marcion and the Text of the New Testament. Marcion's editorial cuts have also influenced the textual history of NT manuscripts (Blackman, 128-71). For example, some manuscripts of Romans 1:16 omit the word "first." But the extent of Marcion's influence upon the textual tradition in Paul and Luke is slight. Since Marcion's Gospel has to be reconstructed, we owe citations from his text to other sources. For many of the nontheological changes Marcion made, it is difficult to tell whether the alteration is due to Marcion himself or to a variant textual tradition that Marcion (or his critic) is quoting. For example, at 1 Corinthians 6:20 Marcion's text, along with many Latin texts, reads "Glorify and bear God in your body" (rather than "therefore, glorify God in your body.") It appears that this is a common variant (mis)reading rather than one that Marcion introduced into the textual traditions of the NT.

5. Legacy.
Marcion's canon and separate church forced the mainstream of Christianity to clarify its own NT canon. He also helped the mainstream church affirm its relationship to Judaism and the OT. Marcionism led early Christian thinkers to recognize the OT roots of their religion and the Jewish element in any true Christian faith. These were valuable lessons for Christianity. Given the unfortunate anti-Semitic tradition in Christian history, one can only wish they had been better learned.

See also CANON.

BIBLIOGRAPHY. D. Balas, "Marcion Revisited" in *Texts and Testaments,* ed. W. E. March (San Antonio, TX: Trinity University Press, 1980) 95-108; W. Bauer, *Orthodoxy and Heresy in Earliest Christianity* (ET; Philadelphia: Fortress, 1971); E. C. Blackman, *Marcion and His Influence* (London: SPCK, 1948); J. J. Clabeaux, *A Lost Edition of the Letters of Paul* (CBQMS 21; Washington, DC: Catholic Biblical Association, 1989); H. J. W. Drijvers, "Marcionism in Syria," *SecCent* 6 (1987-88) 152-72; J. G. Gager, "Marcion and Philosophy," *VC* 26 (1972) 53-59; idem, *The Origins of Anti-Semitism* (New York: Oxford University Press, 1983); A. von Harnack, *Marcion: Das Evangelium vom fremden Gott* (TU 45; 2d ed.; Leipzig: J. C. Hinrichs, 1924), partial ET, *Marcion: The Gospel of the Alien God* (Durham, NC: Labyrinth, 1990); R. J. Hoffmann, *Marcion: On the Restitution of Christianity* (AARAS 46; Chico, CA: Scholars Press, 1984); J. Knox, *Marcion and the New Testament* (Chicago: University of Chicago Press, 1942); G. May, "Marcion in Contemporary Views," *SecCent* 6 (1987-88) 129-51; B. M. Metzger, *The Canon of the New Testament* (New York: Oxford University Press, 1987); R. S. Wilson, *Marcion: A Study of a Second-Century Heretic* (London: Clarke, 1933).   A. G. Padgett

MARK, SECRET GOSPEL OF

The *Secret Gospel of Mark* is a title given to a version of Mark's Gospel mentioned and briefly cited in a fragment of a Letter "to Theodore," attributed to "the most holy Clement, the author of the *Stromateis*" (*Theod.* 1.1; i.e., Clement of Alexandria [c. 150-215]). Since its discovery, the *Secret Gospel of Mark* has remained of interest especially among scholars who have sought source material beyond the limits of the canonical Gospels for a reconstruction of the life and teaching of the historical Jesus (e.g.,

Smith 1978; cf. Crossan 1991) or the history of the Gospel traditions (e.g., Koester).

1. Text and Context
2. The Question of Authenticity
3. *Secret Gospel of Mark* and Canonical Mark
4. Conclusion

1. Text and Context.

The only extant manuscript of the *Letter to Theodore*, discovered in 1958 by Morton Smith (published in Smith 1973, reprinted in Stählin and Treu) at the Orthodox monastery at Mar Saba, southwest of Jerusalem, is a fragmentary copy. This copy was written on the last page (both sides) and the inside back cover of a volume of Isaac Voss's edition of the letters of Ignatius,* published in 1646, in what Smith and nine other scholars, relying on Smith's photographs, have judged to be an eighteenth-century hand (for the full text of the *Letter to Theodore* in translation, see Bruce, Cameron, Smith 1973, 1982; for the fragments of the *Secret Gospel of Mark* see also Merkel 1991 and Elliott). Since all scholarly judgments on the authenticity of the *Letter to Theodore*, and thus the value of the brief citation from the *Secret Gospel* that it contains, have been dependent to date on Smith's uncorroborated published photographs and report of his discovery (but cf. Talley), they must remain tentative (cf. Quesnell).

The *Letter to Theodore* is a warning against the teaching of the Carpocratians, an Alexandrian Gnostic* sect known for its libertine practices of "carnal and bodily sins" (*Theod.* 1.4; cf. Chadwick, Daniélou, Rudolf, Hultgren and Haggmark; *Letter to Theodore* draws allusively on polemical phrases from Prov 26:5; Eccl 2:14; Mt 5:13 par. Lk 14:34; Mt 25:29 par. Lk 19:26; Lk 1:78 [?]; 2 Cor 3:17; 1 Thess 5:5; Tit 1:15; Jude 13; Rev 2:24).

In particular the *Letter to Theodore* accuses the Carpocratians of misinterpreting and falsifying "the divinely inspired Gospel according to Mark" (*Theod.* 1.11-12), which is known in Alexandria* in two editions. According to the *Letter to Theodore*, Mark composed the first edition of his Gospel during Peter's stay in Rome for use in the instruction of catechumens. After Peter's death, the *Letter to Theodore* relates, Mark came to Alexandria, where he composed a "more spiritual Gospel" (*Theod.* 1.21-22), expanding his first edition with additional acts and sayings of Jesus from his memoirs and those of Peter

(but excluding the "hierophantic teaching of the Lord" [*Theod.* 1.23-24]) to produce a "secret Gospel" (*Theod.* 2.6, 12; hence the title *Secret Gospel of Mark*) for use by those who were being perfected in knowledge through initiation into the "great mysteries" (*Theod.* 2.2).

The *Letter to Theodore* alleges, however, that Carpocrates deceitfully obtained a copy of the "most carefully guarded" (*Theod.* 2.1) *Secret Gospel* and polluted it with "shameless lies" (*Theod.* 2.8-9), making it the basis of his "blasphemous and carnal opinion" (*Theod.* 2.7). Carpocrates had so corrupted the *Secret Gospel* that the *Letter to Theodore* advises Theodore, when confronted by Carpocratian teaching, to deny "with an oath" that it is by Mark (*Theod.* 2.12).

To aid in the refutation of Carpocratian falsifications, the *Letter to Theodore* cites about eighteen lines of Greek text from the *Secret Gospel*. The first citation of about fifteen lines (*Theod.* 2.23—3.11) is identified as being located between Mark 10:32-34 and Mark 10:35. This citation relates an account of Jesus' raising of a rich "young man" in Bethany whose sister has prostrated herself before Jesus (an apparent variant of the Johannine story of the raising of Lazarus [John 11]). The account concludes with Jesus staying in the young man's house and after six days teaching him "the mystery of the kingdom of God" during a nocturnal session in which the young man is clothed with "a linen robe thrown over his naked body." The second citation of about three lines (*Theod.* 3.14-16) is located after Mark 10:46 and recounts Jesus' failure to receive "the sister of the young man whom Jesus loved and his mother and Salome." A further alleged citation, the cryptic phrase "naked to naked" (*Theod.* 3.13), is regarded by the *Letter to Theodore* to be spurious.

2. The Question of Authenticity.

Smith has copiously and vigorously argued for the authenticity of the *Letter to Theodore*, dating it between 175 and 200. He notes that letters of Clement, though no longer extant, are cited in the *Sacra Parallela*, attributed to John of Damascus (c. 675-749), who spent some time at Mar Saba, and it is possible that the fragment of the *Letter to Theodore* found at Mar Saba may have been preserved from the destruction of a fire in the eighteenth century documented by the monastery's historian.

With the aid of detailed indices in the critical

edition of Clement's works by O. Stählin, Smith demonstrates the similarities between the *Letter to Theodore* and the extant works of Clement with reference to vocabulary, style, use of Scripture (including a preference for the Western textual tradition) and classical writers, and theological and ethical perspective. Parallels with the works of Clement that specially favor the authenticity of the *Letter to Theodore* are knowledge of Mark's relationship with Peter (cited by Eusebius *Hist. Eccl.* 2.15.1-2; 6.14.5-7 [see also Mullins]) and Mark's founding of churches in Alexandria on the basis of his Gospel (perhaps implied by Eusebius *Hist. Eccl.* 2.16.1; 2.24 [see also Pearson; denied by Bauer]); the polemic against the libertinism of the Carpocratians (Clement *Strom.* 3; cf. Irenaeus *Haer.* 1.25.1-6; 1.28.2); and the promotion of a higher knowledge for those seeking perfection beyond catechetical instruction (Clement *Strom.* 5.10), which may be based on an oral tradition from the risen Lord* (Clement *Excerpta* 66; cf. Eusebius *Hist. Eccl.* 2.1.4-5). Smith also finds a possible corroboration for the Carpocratian use of Mark in Irenaeus's reference to unnamed heretics "who separate Jesus from Christ, alleging that Christ remained impassible, but that it was Jesus who suffered, preferring the Gospel by Mark" (Irenaeus *Haer.* 3.11.7; cf. Irenaeus *Haer.* 1.25.5).

Smith's case for the authenticity of the *Letter to Theodore*, though accepted by many scholars, is diminished by some discrepancies from the known writings of Clement. Eusebius reports that Clement regarded the Gospel of John as the "spiritual Gospel" (Eusebius *Hist. Eccl.* 6.14.7), and although Clement cites the apocryphal* *Gospel of the Egyptians* (Clement *Strom.* 3.6.45; 3.9.63, 64, 66; 3.13.92-93) in his major polemic against the Carpocratians (Clement *Strom.* 3), he traces the source of their libertinism to their interpretation of Matthew 5:42 (par. Luke 6:30; Clement *Strom.* 3.4.27; 3.6.54) and another unidentified apocryphal writing (Clement *Strom.* 3.4.29), with no mention of the *Secret Gospel.*

Likewise no reference to the *Secret Gospel* is made in Clement's lengthy homily on the rich man in Mark 10:17-31 (*Quis Div.*), which presumably would have been enhanced by the story of a rich man who became a disciple of Jesus (the fragment of the *Secret Gospel* in *Theod.* 2.23—3.10, placed after Mark 10:34). Further-

more, the *Letter to Theodore*'s advocacy of deception regarding the existence of the *Secret Gospel* because of Carpocratian corruption and misuse (*Theod.* 2.11-19) seems contrary to Clement's teaching regarding truthfulness and the taking of oaths (Clement *Strom.* 7.8-9 [pace Smith]) and may betray a forger's "seal of authenticity" (C. E. Murgia in Wuellner; cf. Musurillo).

The *Letter to Theodore*'s argumentative strategy also appears inauthentic, "since for Clement true gnosis is not attained by acquaintance with hidden documents but by faith and love as learned through interpretation of public apostolic writings," and his polemic against the Carpocratians is argued elsewhere "on ethical grounds" (Osborn, 224; cf. Clement *Strom.* 3.4.39; 3.5.42; 3.18.109-10; cf. Clement *Quis Div.* 5, 11, 17, 27-30, 36-37).

Finally, although the Carpocratians were notoriously sexually promiscuous (Clement *Strom.* 3.2.5, 10; cf. Irenaeus *Haer.* 1.28.2), there is no clear evidence that this involved homosexual relations (with the exception of stereotyped lists of vices [Clement *Strom.* 3.4.36; 3.18.109]), as Smith infers from the phrase "naked to naked" in *Letter to Theodore* 3.13 (cf. Grant; the texts adduced by Smith to interpret this phrase as implying a homosexual union also can be disputed [Plato *Symp.* 175c-e; Plutarch *Iside* 17, *Mor.* 357d; *Iside* 19, *Mor.* 358e; Aelian *De Nat. Anim.* 16.28; Philostratus *Vit. Ap.* 6.16 (cf. Clement *Strom.* 3.7.60); Hippolytus *Apos. Trad.* 21.5, 11; Clement *Excerpta* 66]).

3. *Secret Gospel of Mark* and Canonical Mark.
Smith has developed a complex hypothesis defending the antiquity of the *Secret Gospel*, arguing, with some divergence from the testimony of the *Letter to Theodore*, that the *Secret Gospel*, although it was compiled after the canonical Gospel of Mark in an imitation of Mark's Greek style, preserves an Aramaic source that antedates canonical Mark and thus provides a window to the historical Jesus. As evidence for this hypothesis, Smith adduces the form of the miracle story in the *Secret Gospel* (*Theod.* 2.23—3.6), which appears more primitive than the story in John 11 and exhibits some Semitisms (additional form-critical arguments are offered by R. H. Fuller in Wuellner); the similarity between the geographical outlines of Mark 6:32—16:8 and John 6:1—20:2 when the material from the *Secret Gospel* is added to Mark; a liturgy for Easter

baptism* that can be discerned in Mark 10:13-45 with the addition of the *Secret Gospel* (see also Richardson); the apparent dependence of Matthew and the Western textual tradition on the *Secret Gospel*; and the resolution of an aporia in Mark 10:46, explained as the result of later censorship of the *Secret Gospel* material cited in *Letter to Theodore* 3.14-16, and the enigma of Mark 14:51-52, interpreted in light of the *Secret Gospel* as another nocturnal baptism (see also Scroggs and Groff). (Similarly Koester, Crossan, Schenke, Meyer, and Munro, with various arguments, find canonical Mark to be an abridgment of the *Secret Gospel*. Cf. also Levin's analysis of the value of the *Secret Gospel* for interpreting canonical Mark.)

Ranging widely through the nooks and crannies of early Jewish, pagan and Christian literature and armed with an unrelenting hermeneutic of suspicion, Smith ferrets out evidence of a secret but pervasive libertine mysticism in the ancient world. From this background Smith interprets the *Secret Gospel* as proof that the historical Jesus was part of this libertine movement and engaged in magical practices possibly involving homosexual acts (a thesis defended further in *Jesus the Magician*).

Smith's hypothesis, and others like it, concerning the priority of the *Secret Gospel* in relation to canonical Mark, is even less compelling than his case for the authenticity of the *Letter to Theodore*. The *Secret Gospel* is "too much like Mark," according to E. Best (204), using criteria for determining Markan style developed by E. J. Pryke, and is much more easily explained as a secondary "pastiche of phrases from Mark" (Bruce, 306), demonstrably dependent on the stories of Nicodemus and Lazarus in John (John 3; 11; cf. Brown) and the "young man" stories in the Synoptic Gospels (Mt 19:20, 22; Mk 14:51; 16:5; Lk 7:14; cf. Neirynck).

The phraseology of the *Secret Gospel* betrays the harmonizing tendency of a hand familiar with all the canonical Gospels (see the tabular surveys in Brown, Merkel, Wink), perhaps through Tatian's Diatessaron, which frequently follows the Western textual tradition (cf. D. Schmidt in Wuellner). The secondary character of the *Secret Gospel* is also confirmed by the way it spoils a carefully constructed Markan climax to Jesus' deliberate journey "on the way" from Caesarea Philippi to Jerusalem (Mk 8:27—10:52) by introducing a superfluous visit to Bethany, acclamation of Jesus as "Son of David" and return to the other side of the Jordan (*Theod.* 2.23—3.11) before blind Bartimaeus hails Jesus as the "Son of David" and follows him "on the way . . . drawing near to Jerusalem, to Bethphage and Bethany" (Mk 10:52—11:1), where he will be exalted as the Davidic king (Mk 11:9-10). As a pastiche or cento, the *Secret Gospel* bears a strong resemblance to other apocryphal Gospels from the second century (e.g., *Gospel of the Ebionites* [cited in Epiphanius *Haer* 30.13.2-3], Papyrus Egerton 2; cf. Brown, Merkel, Neirynck).

4. Conclusion.

It is difficult to assess the historical value of documents as problematic as the *Letter to Theodore* and *Secret Gospel*. If the *Letter to Theodore* is authentic, it confirms Clement's belief in a higher knowledge for Christians who were being perfected and reveals another apocryphal Gospel, the *Secret Gospel*, used by his church (cf. Clement's use of *Preaching of Peter* [Clement *Strom.* 2.15.68; 6.5.39; etc.], *Apocalypse of Peter* [cited in Eusebius *Hist. Eccl.* 6.14.1], *Gospel of the Hebrews* [Clement *Strom.* 2.9.45; 5.14.96] and *Gospel of the Egyptians* [Clement *Strom.* 3.6.45; 3.9.63; 3.13.99]; cf. Bruce). It also shows that the *Secret Gospel* was another source of contention in the debate with the Carpocratians. It can be doubted, however, that the portion of the *Secret Gospel* cited in the *Letter to Theodore* was the basis of a baptismal rite in Clement's church since there is no explicit reference to baptism (cf. Merkel; Best 1986 "Mark 10:13-16"), and the rich young man with "a linen robe thrown over his naked body" may be demonstrating his renunciation of wealth (cf. Mk 10:21; 15:46), an ideal of poverty that Clement later rejects (cf. *Quis Div* 11; so Gundry). Because the *Secret Gospel* is likely a secondary apocryphal work, it probably offers no value for source and tradition criticism of the Gospel of Mark (cf. Neirynck, Gundry; against Koester, Crossan, Schenke, Meyer) or for insight into the life and teaching of the historical Jesus (cf. Merkel against Smith), including the role of women among his followers (against Munro).

See also APOCRYPHAL AND PSEUDEPIGRAPHICAL WRITINGS; PETER, GOSPEL OF; THOMAS, GOSPEL OF.

BIBLIOGRAPHY. W. Bauer, *Orthodoxy and Heresy in Earliest Christianity* (Philadelphia: Fortress,

1971); E. Best, "Mark 10:13-16: The Child as Model Recipient" in *Disciples and Discipleship* (Edinburgh: T & T Clark, 1986) 80-97; idem, "Uncanonical Mark" in *Disciples and Discipleship* (Edinburgh: T & T Clark, 1986) 197-205; R. E. Brown, "The Relation of 'The Secret Gospel of Mark' to the Fourth Gospel," *CBQ* 36 (1974) 466-85; F. F. Bruce, "The 'Secret' Gospel of Mark" in *The Canon of Scripture* (Downers Grove, IL: InterVarsity Press, 1988 [1974]) 298-315; R. Cameron, *The Other Gospels* (Philadelphia: Westminster, 1982); H. Chadwick, "Clement of Alexandria: General Introduction" in *Alexandrian Christianity*, ed. J. E. L. Oulton and H. Chadwick (Philadelphia: Westminster, 1954) 15-39; J. D. Crossan, *Four Other Gospels* (Sonoma, CA: Polebridge, 1992 [1985]); idem, *The Historical Jesus* (San Francisco: Harper San Francisco, 1991); idem, "Thoughts on Two Extracanonical Gospels," *Semeia* 49 (1990) 155-68; J. Daniélou, *The Theology of Jewish Christianity* (Philadelphia: Westminster, 1964); J. K. Elliott, *The Apocryphal New Testament* (Oxford: Clarendon, 1993); R. M. Grant, "Morton Smith's Two Books," *ATR* 56 (1974) 58-64; R. H. Gundry, "Excursus on the Secret Gospel of Mark" in *Mark* (Grand Rapids: Eerdmans, 1993) 603-23; A. J. Hultgren and S. J. Haggmark, eds., *The Earliest Christian Heretics* (Minneapolis: Fortress, 1996); H. Koester, *Ancient Christian Gospels* (Philadelphia: Trinity Press International, 1990); idem, "History and Development of Mark's Gospel: From Mark to Secret Mark and 'Canonical' Mark" in *Colloquy on New Testament Studies*, ed. B. C. Corley (Macon, GA: Mercer University Press, 1983) 35-58; S. Levin, "The Early History of Christianity in the Light of the 'Secret Gospel' of Mark," *ANRW* 2.25.6 (1988) 4270-92; H. Merkel, "Appendix: The 'Secret Gospel' of Mark" in *New Testament Apocrypha*, ed. W. Schneemelcher (2 vols.; rev. ed.; Louisville, KY: Westminster/John Knox, 1991) 1:106-9; idem, "Auf den Spuren des Urmarkus? Ein neuer Fund und seine Beurteilung," *ZTK* 71 (1974) 123-44; M. W. Meyer, "The Youth in the Secret Gospel of Mark," *Semeia* 49 (1990) 129-53; T. Y. Mullins, "Papias and Clement and Mark's Two Gospels," *VC* 30 (1976) 189-92; W. Munro, "Women Disciples: Light from Secret Mark," *JFSR* 8 (1992) 47-64; H. Musurillo, "Morton Smith's Secret Gospel," *Thought* 48 (1973) 327-31; F. Neirynck, "The Apocryphal Gospels and the Gospel of Mark" in *The New Testament in Early Christianity* (BETL 86; Louvain: Leuven University/Peeters, 1989) 125-75; E. Osborn, "Clement of Alexandria: A Review of Research, 1958-82," *SecCent* 3 (1983) 219-44; B. A. Pearson, "Earliest Christianity in Egypt: Some Observations" in *The Roots of Egyptian Christianity*, ed. B. A. Pearson and J. E. Goehring (Philadelphia: Fortress, 1986) 137-45; Q. Quesnell, "The Mar Saba Clementine: A Question of Evidence," *CBQ* 37 (1975) 48-67; C. C. Richardson, "Review of *Clement of Alexandria and a Secret Gospel of Mark* and *The Secret Gospel*, by Morton Smith," *TS* 35 (1974) 571-77; K. Rudolf, *Gnosis* (San Francisco: Harper & Row, 1983); H.-M. Schenke, "The Mystery of the Gospel of Mark," *SecCent* 4 (1984) 65-82; R. Scroggs and K. I. Groff, "Baptism in Mark: Dying and Rising with Christ," *JBL* 92 (1973) 531-48; M. Smith, *Clement of Alexandria and a Secret Gospel of Mark* (Cambridge, MA: Harvard University Press, 1973); idem, "Clement of Alexandria and Secret Mark: The Score at the End of the First Decade," *HTR* 75 (1982) 449-61; idem, *Jesus the Magician* (San Francisco: Harper & Row, 1978); idem, *The Secret Gospel* (Clearlake, CA: Dawn Horse, 1982 [1973]); O. Stählin and U. Treu, eds., *Clemens Alexandrinus* (2d ed.; GCS; Berlin: Akademie-Verlag, 1980) vol. 4.1; T. J. Talley, "Liturgical Time in the Ancient Church: The State of Research," *StudLit* 14 (1982) 34-51; W. Wink, "Jesus as Magician," *USQR* 30 (1974) 3-14; W. Wuellner, ed., *Protocol of the Eighteenth Colloquy, 7 December 1975, The Center for Hermeneutical Studies in Hellenistic and Modern Culture* (Berkeley, CA: The Center for Hermeneutical Studies in Hellenistic and Modern Culture, 1976).

L. A. Losie

MARRIAGE, DIVORCE AND ADULTERY

This article addresses the development of early Christian conceptions of marriage, divorce and adultery in post-Pauline Gentile Christianity. (For questions of roles in marriage relationships *see* Woman and Man.) The focus is primarily the sanctity and inviolability of the marriage union as expressed negatively in early Christian sanctions against divorce and marital unfaithfulness (*see* DJG, Divorce; DPL, Marriage and Divorce, Adultery and Incest).

1. Marriage and Divorce
2. Lust and Adultery
3. Conclusion

1. Marriage and Divorce.

1.1. Marriage and Divorce in Jesus' Teachings.
Although scholars disagree widely about the precise implications of Jesus' teachings on divorce, these teachings clearly impacted the later church.* Divorce was common in the Roman world (Carcopino, 95-100), Roman law dissolved a marriage at the request of either partner (Cary and Haarhoff, 144), and Jewish law* dissolved a marriage at the request of the man (Harrell, 64). Although the School of Shammai accepted only unfaithfulness as valid grounds for divorce—a standard charge in the dissolution of marriages—they nevertheless accepted as valid divorces for other reasons (see Keener 1991, 39-40.)

Jesus introduced a stricter ethic based not on the biblical law of divorce (Deut 24:1-4) but on the biblical principle of marriage (Gen 2:24)—that is, he opposed divorce because the permanence of marital harmony is God's* ideal. By implication he also opposed disharmony in marriage. Although scholars differ on the precise background and use of Jesus' divorce saying in the earliest church (for one redactional study see Collins), it seems most likely that Jesus offered a general prohibition of divorce in a graphic, hyperbolic saying that portrayed all divorce as invalid and remarriage as adulterous (Mk 10:11; Lk 16:18). Given the context of Jesus' Jewish teaching style, Matthew and Paul are undoubtedly correct to allow exceptions for the innocent party whose marriage is broken against his or her will (for infidelity and abandonment, respectively—Mt 5:32; 19:9; 1 Cor 7:15; see Stein; Keener 1991). That Paul never needs to address the dissolution of second or third marriages in his congregations in a divorce-ridden society also indicates that the earliest Christians regarded repentance* as a sufficient response to past errors, without regarding the divorcing partner as still literally married to the first spouse. In the context of rising sexual asceticism and strict legal applications of Jesus' teachings in the increasingly Gentile second-century church, however, Jesus' Jewish teachings were pressed to produce a harsher ethic than Jesus seems to have intended, one that restricted the victim as well as the perpetrator of a unilateral dissolution rather than simply upheld the sanctity of marriage.

1.2. Marriage and Celibacy in Ignatius. The
second century witnessed a gradually increasing tendency toward sexual asceticism, reflecting not merely earlier Jewish chastity but a broader climate of growing asceticism in late antiquity (cf., e.g., Wimbush on antecedents; on the second- and third-century church, e.g., Brown). One might detect some hints of the tendency as early as Ignatius's* mention of "the virgins who are called widows" (Ign. Smyrn. 13.1), whether this refers to widows who had pledged not to remarry (cf. 1 Tim 5:11-12) or to virgins who had chosen to maintain their singleness as in a particular ideal of widowhood from the Republic (see Keener 1991, 92-94). As early as 1 Timothy 4:3 and possibly 1 Corinthians 7:1, some schismatics within the church counseled abstention from marriage; by the time of Ignatius such celibacy appears as a noble calling, but Ignatius warns that one who boasts in this calling is "lost" (Ign. Pol. 5.2). Both celibates and couples seeking marriage needed to seek counsel from the bishop, the latter lest they marry for reasons of lust rather than for the Lord (Ign. Pol. 5.2). This may suggest the somewhat popular philosophical view that one should avoid lust even in marriage (e.g., Muson. Ruf. Sexual Indulgence Frag. 12).

1.3. Marriage and Divorce in Hermas. The
mild hints of sexual asceticism in the church world Ignatius knew increased in subsequent decades, however. Among early Christian writings the Shepherd of Hermas* may have been especially responsible for popularizing the tendency in the mainstream churches; unfortunately, if any ancient document is genuinely amenable to Freudian interpretation, it is the Shepherd of Hermas. Whereas biblical visions* and dreams typically involved angels,* departed (or sometimes living human) spirits frequently appeared in extrabiblical dreams (e.g., Plutarch Mul. Vir., Mor. 252F; Chariton Chaer. 2.9.6; Apuleius Met. 8.8; 9.31; cf. 'Abot R. Nat. 40A; 46, §§128-29B; y. Hag. 2:2, §5; y. Sanh. 6.6, §2; Pesiq. Rab Kah. 11:23). The initial visions of Hermas involve women, and though they may symbolize the church (Herm. Vis. 2.8.1) his visions also include rebuke for the unexpressed lust of a woman whose slave he was and whom he had seen undressed (Herm. Vis. 1.1.1-2). Although he claimed to love her only as a sister and to think nothing impure (Herm. Vis. 1.1.1-2), her image appeared to condemn him for desiring her subconsciously (Herm. Vis. 1.1.7-8) and to

warn him to repent lest he perish (*Herm. Vis.* 1.1.9). If one asks why Hermas had to repress such a sin,* one should keep in mind that he felt that this meant his salvation* was in danger (*Herm. Vis.* 1.2.1); such fear could naturally lead either to denial of sin or to the introspective conscience* of traditional Western theology.

But another visionary woman allows Hermas to project his guilt against those with whom he was already frustrated; as it turns out God was angry at Hermas not because he once lusted (as the first woman had indicated, *Herm. Vis.* 1.1.9) but because he had not made his family follow his Christian convictions (*Herm. Vis.* 1.3.1; *Herm. Sim.* 7.66.1-3). One may suspect that Hermas hoped these visions would scare his children (cf. *Herm. Vis.* 2.6.2) and wife (*Herm. Vis.* 2.6.3) into obedience*; as a Roman *paterfamilias* he was responsible for the behavior of his family (Keener 1991, 98), and as the head of the house he had to suffer for their misdeeds first (*Herm. Sim.* 7.66.3; *see* Household, Family).

Hermas indicates a deeper sexual asceticism than had prevailed previously. He threatens to become celibate if his wife does not stop her ungodly speech (*Herm. Vis.* 2.6.3). Although widowers or widows who remarried did not sin (cf. 1 Cor 7:27-28, where the parallel use of "freed" must apply also to those divorced), Hermas indicates a definite preference for remaining single after widowhood (*Herm. Man.* 4.32.1-2). This preference for people remaining single after the death of a spouse gained prominence in the church, picking up some streams of popular culture but reacting against the earlier ideals of the Augustan era (see Keener 1991, 68-72). Caring for widows remained part of the church's obligation (*Herm. Man.* 8.38.10).

His "shepherd," apparently a combination of the Jewish guardian angel and the Roman *genius*, instructs him that the man who learns that his wife is in adultery must divorce her; should the man remarry, however, he himself commits adultery (*Herm. Man.* 4.29.7). This statement represents the first recorded instance in history where remarriage was considered adulterous in the case of a valid divorce (all those citations thoroughly collected in Heth and Wenham that clearly prohibit remarriage—others may be intended as generally as Jesus' original prohibition—follow Hermas and hence cannot confirm earlier Christian views). Although this statement misinterprets the likely sense of Jesus'

teaching in its Palestinian context, this view became the prevailing one in the increasing climate of sexual asceticism (despite Hermas's somewhat defective christology,* e.g., *Herm Sim.* 5.58.2; 9.78.1; perhaps 9.89.2). But one should note the shepherd's reason for this instruction: the husband is to remain single so that if the wife repents, he may take her back (*Herm. Man.* 4.29.10). Yet if he takes her back and she sins after her repentance, the shepherd's reason would no longer be valid, for the shepherd allows her only one repentance (*Herm. Man.* 4.29.8). (The doctrine of only one permissible repentance—cf. e.g., *Herm. Man.* 4.31.2; *Herm. Sim.* 9.96—would aid church discipline but could compound problems for the church in following centuries, when some Roman officials waited for deathbed baptisms to avoid the danger of postbaptismal sin—e.g., Chadwick, 127.) Hermas was likewise strict on the necessity of penance (e.g., *Herm. Man.* 4.30.2); even wholehearted repentance was not adequate for the forgiveness* of sins until the person had suffered sufficiently (*Herm. Sim.* 7.66.4).

1.4. Marriage in Second-Century Christian Values. Especially in its earliest and mildest forms, early Christian opposition to divorce stemmed from the high honor early Christians bestowed on marriage and family relations. Because marriage makes one flesh, jealousy between spouses is harmful in a marriage (*1 Clem.* 6.3; *1 Clem.* 3—6 focuses largely on jealousy over church offices; *1 Clem.* 43—44). Husbands should love their wives as Christ loves the church (Ign. *Pol.* 5.1; cf. Eph 5:25). Because marriage was in part an economic contract, the church felt a special need to care for unmarried, hence economically deprived, older women. (Younger women could easily enough find husbands, given the relative shortage of women compared to men in Greek and Roman society—1 Tim 5:14; Gardner, 82; on probable female infanticide, see Lewis, 54-55.) Ignatius felt that bishops were to look after the widows in their congregations (Ign. *Pol.* 4.1).

2. Lust and Adultery.

2.1. Lust and Adultery in Antiquity. Whereas most Greek society rarely objected to sexual desire if it were not acted out toward other men's wives (Diogenes Laertius *Vit.* 6.2.4.6; *Clit.* 1.4-6; *Ach. Tat.*; *Grk. Anth.* 5.267), some Greek and more Jewish teachers did object to it (e.g.,

Epictetus *Disc.* 2.18.15-18; Sir 9:8; *1 Enoch* 67:8; *b. Nid.* 13b; *b. Šabb.* 64ab). Jesus actively condemned it as adultery of the heart, using the Septuagint's language from the Tenth Commandment about coveting one's neighbor's wife (Mt 5:28; Ex 20:17). Mediterranean societies universally condemned adultery, however; a wife was viewed as her husband's sexual property and hence any other man's use of that property was viewed as wife-stealing (*Pseud.-Phoc.* 3; *Sib. Or.* 1.178; 3.38). Under various circumstances this offense could be punished by banishment or worse (Seneca *Ben.* 6.32.1; Quintilian *Inst. Orat.* 7.1.7; Richlin, 228); law mandated that a husband who learned of his wife's affair divorce her immediately (Gardner, 89; Safrai, 762) or risk himself being prosecuted for the offense of *lenocinium*—pimping (Gardner, 131-32; Richlin, 227).

2.2. Marriage and Adultery in Hebrews 13:4. Whether Hebrews 13 was appended later or is, as we think, an original part of the letter-essay as a whole, it provides a list of moral exhortations in typical Greek paraenetic style. The exhortation in Hebrews 13:4 reflects especially Jewish marriage values. Sanctity of the "bed" was a common expression for sexual fidelity in marriage (Wis 3:13, 16; cf. Juvenal *Sat.* 4.21; Moffatt, 227) and could also depict fidelity in advance (*Jos. and As.* 2:9, 16; 15:14); other ancient writers also acknowledged that extramarital sex defiled it (Lane, 516). Here both sexual immorality (*see* Purity) in general and adultery in particular invite God's judgment (see also 1 Cor 6:9; 1 Thess 4:6) and are dishonorable (see also 1 Thess 4:4).

2.3. Lust and Adultery in 2 Peter. Early Christians understood that lust frequently characterized false teachers. Many of their contemporaries mistrusted the motives of traveling charlatans, who found it easier to convert women than men to their followings (Lucian *Alex.* 6; Liefeld, 239; cf. Juvenal *Sat.* 1.38-39; 6.540-50; *Pesiq. Rab Kah.* 24:15); the Christians, too, suspected the sexual activity of false teachers who particularly or nearly exclusively sought women converts (cf. 2 Tim 3:6; Irenaeus *Haer.* 1.13). Like clergy who abuse positions of influence to molest members of their congregations, false teachers had "eyes full of adultery" (2 Pet 2:14; cf. 1QS 1.6-7; CD 2.16), seeking to exploit others sexually (for the expression, see Bauckham, 266; for "ensnare" as deceptively exploit-

ing the naive, see Kelly, 342).

These teachers' secret desires reflect their enslavement to their corrupt fleshly passions (2 Pet 2:10), and they interpret believers' daylight love feasts as an occasion for sexually immoral revelry (2 Pet 2:13; for night as the time for revelry, see, e.g., Rom 13:12-13; Horace *Sat.* 1.3.17-18; Seneca *Ep. Lucil.* 47.7; Juvenal *Sat.* 8.9-12); such behavior was typically viewed as pagan (1 Pet. 4:3; Josephus *Ag. Ap.* 2.195; *Pesiq. R.* 52:1; *Gen. Rab.* 39:8; *Lev. Rab.* 5:3). Peter borrows a common philosophic description of those who follow their passions as beasts (2 Pet 2:12; 4 Macc. 12:13; Epictetus *Disc.* 1.3.7, 9; 2.9.3; 4.1.127; 5.21; Plutarch *Bride* 7; *Mor.* 139B; *Praec. Ger. Reipub.* 5, *Mor.* 802E; *Reply to Colotes* 2; *Mor.* 1108D; Marcus Aurelius *Med.* 3.16; 4.28; *Diogn.* 28; in a legal text, Gardner, 36).

Peter's language and image of "greed" (2 Pet 2:14-15) may apply to sexual covetousness or to literal financial covetousness, as with Balaam (2 Pet 2:3; Num 22:17; *Bib. Ant.* 18:13), or may link the two, as in other ancient texts (see Moffatt, 228). This sexual sin is conjoined with their rejection of proper authorities, including angelic ones (2 Pet 2:10-12; cf. *1 Enoch* 46:7 but perhaps especially Gen 19:5, 12-14). Thus Peter compares them with Balaam (2 Pet 2:15), who urged harlotry. While respecting his prophetic (e.g., Josephus *Ant.* 4.104; Philo *Vit. Mos.* 1.264-65; *Sipre Deut.* 343.6.1; 357.18.1-2) or philosophic (*Gen. Rab.* 65:20; *Pesiq. Rab Kah.* 15:5) skill, Jewish tradition regularly condemned Balaam as foolish (e.g., Philo *Cher.* 32; *Qoh. Rab.* 2:15, §2) and evil (e.g., Philo *Vit. Mos.* 1; *b. 'Abod. Zar.* 4a). Balaam had led Israel into sexual immorality and hence divine judgment (Num 25:1-3; 31:15-17; Rev 2:14; see Philo *Vit. Mos.* 1.300-301) but also paid for his sin with his life (Num 31:8). Jewish tradition naturally extended his punishment to damnation (e.g., *m. 'Abot* 5:19; *y. Sanh.* 10:2, §8), as these false teachers would also be damned (2 Pet 2:4-9, 19-22); a tradition of uncertain date even declares that Balaam ignored the impending day of judgment (*Pesiq. R.* 41:3).

Peter indicates that Balaam's donkey was wiser than Balaam (2 Pet 2:16; cf. Philo *Vit. Mos.* 1.272; *Gen. Rab.* 93:10), again implying the bestial character of these slaves of passion (2 Pet 2:12). The sensuality and fleshly desires of these who have barely escaped (2 Pet 2:18) contrast starkly with those who partake of the divine nature, who have escaped the corruption that is in the world by desire (2 Pet 1:4; cf. 1:9; 2:20; 3:3; cf. Bauckham, 180-82; unlike Jews many Greeks associated "corruption" with physicality—see, e.g., Plutarch *Iside* 78, *Mor.* 382F). These false teachers acted thus because, in keeping with their Hellenized perspective, they neglected or rejected a future day of judgment* (2 Pet 3:3-14; cf. 2:1, 3-6, 9, 12-13; we accept the third chapter as an integral part of the letter—cf., e.g., Kelly, 352-53).

2.4. Lust and Sexual Immorality in Jude. 2 Peter draws heavily on Jude* for its materials. Although some commentators may go too far in regarding Jude's opponents as full-blown Gnostics,* it seems likely that he was combating a sort of antinomian heresy and that the false teachers were exploiting this heresy of false grace* as an excuse for sexual immorality (Jude 4). Thus Jude condemns the behavior of the fallen angels who wanted to have intercourse with women (Jude 6, following a common Jewish reading of Gen 6:1-4 in his day—e.g., see documentation in Keener 1992, 40, 61-63). He likewise provides as an example Sodom and Gomorrah; the men who wanted to rape Lot's guests again provide an example of sexual perversion (either because they sought intercourse with angels or because they sought it with those they thought were men—see Bauckham, 54, for the former). The false teachers followed evil passions (Jude 16, 18); the people of the Spirit* could resist this behavior by Spirit-inspired prayer* and perseverance* (Jude 20-21; cf. Jude 24).

2.5. Spiritual Adultery in James and Revelation. The OT often speaks of spiritual adultery, especially in the context of Israel's* unfaithfulness to God (e.g., Lev 17:7; Is 1:21; Jer 3:1-14), but occasionally other people's also (Is 26:16-18; Nahum 3:4). James* addresses an audience experiencing economic oppression, some of whom are tempted to favor the growing resistance against Rome (see Martin). He warns his audience that God's wisdom* is gentle and peaceful* in contrast to the selfish and striving wisdom of the world* and the devil (Jas 3:13-18). Those who seek violent solutions to their situation, while claiming to follow God (Jas 4:1-2), pursue their own desires rather than God's will (Jas 4:3) and hence are spiritual "adulteresses" (Jas 4:4). James undoubtedly alludes to the common image of Israel's harlotry here (Davids, 160), not to a narrower allusion like

Proverbs 30:20 (pace Schmitt). James offers a solution to this adultery: instead of trying to follow both God's values and those of the world, they should submit to God and resist the devil (Jas 4:7-10), seeking peace with their neighbors (cf. Jas 4:11-12).

Scholars are divided as to whether the condemnation of immorality in Revelation 2:14, 20-23 refers to literal or spiritual prostitution. Balaam (Rev 2:14) led Israel to literal immorality and idol food; Revelation 9:20 may refer to literal immorality. Yet especially if Jezebel may be linked with influence from a Thyatiran Sibyl (for divergent views see Hemer, 119; Ramsay, 337-38) and/or more likely strategic compromises with the imperial cult (for imperial cult meals, e.g., *CIL* 3:550; *see* Emperor), spiritual immorality is more likely (Caird, 39, 44; cf. 2 Kings 9:22, where Jezebel's immorality is probably figurative). The figurative use of the term continued in contemporary usage (4Q169 Frags. 3-4, 2:7; perhaps Wis 14:12), and probably the prostitute Jezebel provides a prototype for the vision of the great spiritual prostitute Babylon* (Rev 17—18).

2.6. Lust and Adultery in Early Second-Century Christian Writers. Lust was dangerous because it could lead to fornication or adultery (*Did.* 3.3); according to the thought-world of Hermas, where sexual dangers abounded on every side, the mere thought of another woman was a mortal sin, and the best protection was to focus one's mind on one's own wife (*Herm. Man.* 4.29.1-2). Adultery was damnable but often appears in vice lists as one damnable sin among many—e.g., deceit, theft and slander (*1 Clem.* 35.8, quoting Ps 50:18-20); deceit and love for money (*2 Clem.* 6.4); drunkenness, luxury and slander (*Herm. Man.* 8.38.3), or drunkenness, slander and lying (*Herm. Sim.* 6.65.5). According to Hermas, a man who finds his wife in adultery must divorce her or he becomes a participant in her adultery (*Herm. Man.* 4.29.5-6); in this, Hermas echoes the charge in Roman law: a man who failed to divorce his adulterous wife would be charged with *lenocinium* ("pimping," 2.1 above). Christian writers could employ the phrase "corrupting households" (normally a depiction of adultery) as a metaphor for distorting the faith with false teaching (Ign. *Eph.* 16.1).

3. Conclusion.
Following the lead of Jesus and biblical Juda-

ism, early Christians restricted all expressions of sexuality to marriage. To some extent, however, especially on remarriage and later on first marriages for clergy, later Christians began to adopt the values of sexual asceticism that began to flourish in some circles in late antiquity.

See also SEXUALITY, SEXUAL ETHICS; WOMAN AND MAN; WOMEN IN THE EARLY CHURCH.

BIBLIOGRAPHY. R. J. Bauckham, *Jude, 2 Peter* (WBC; Waco, TX: Word, 1983); P. Brown, *The Body and Society: Men, Women and Sexual Renunciation in Early Christianity* (New York: Columbia University Press, 1988); G. B. Caird, *A Commentary on the Revelation of Saint John the Divine* (San Francisco: Harper & Row, 1966); J. Carcopino, *Daily Life in Ancient Rome: The People and the City at the Height of the Empire,* ed. H. T. Rowell, (New Haven, CT: Yale University Press, 1940); M. Cary and T. J. Haarhoff, *Life and Thought in the Greek and Roman World* (4th ed.; London: Methuen, 1946); H. Chadwick, *The Early Church* (Baltimore: Penguin, 1967); E. A. Clark, *Women in the Early Church* (MFC 13; Wilmington, DE: Michael Glazier, 1983); R. F. Collins, *Divorce in the New Testament* (Collegeville, MN: Liturgical Press, 1992); P. Davids, *The Epistle of James* (NIGTC; Grand Rapids: Eerdmans, 1982); J. F. Gardner, *Women in Roman Law & Society* (Bloomington, IN: Indiana University, 1986); P. E. Harrell, *Divorce and Remarriage in the Early Church: A History of Divorce & Remarriage in the Ante-Nicene Church* (Austin, TX: Sweet, 1967); C. J. Hemer, *The Letters to the Seven Churches of Asia in Their Local Setting* (JSNTSup 11; Sheffield: University of Sheffield, 1986); W. A. Heth and G. J. Wenham, *Jesus and Divorce: The Problem with the Evangelical Consensus* (Nashville: Thomas Nelson, 1984); C. S. Keener, *And Marries Another: Divorce and Remarriage in the Teaching of the New Testament* (Peabody, MA: Hendrickson, 1991); idem, *Paul, Women & Wives* (Peabody, MA: Hendrickson, 1992); J. N. D. Kelly, *A Commentary on the Epistles of Peter and Jude* (Grand Rapids: Baker, 1981 [1969]; W. L. Lane, *Hebrews* (WBC; 2 vols.; Dallas: Word, 1991); N. Lewis, *Life in Egypt Under Roman Rule* (Oxford: Clarendon, 1983); W. L. Liefeld, "The Wandering Preacher As a Social Figure in the Roman Empire" (unpublished Ph.D. Dissertation, Columbia University, 1967); R. P. Martin, *James* (WBC; Waco, TX: Word, 1988); J. Moffatt, *A Critical and Exegetical Commentary on the Epistle to the Hebrews* (ICC; Edinburgh: T & T Clark, 1924); W. M. Ramsay, *The Letters to the Seven Churches of Asia* (London: Hodder & Stoughton, 1904; Grand Rapids: Baker, 1979); A. Richlin, "Approaches to the Sources on Adultery at Rome," *Women's Studies* 8 (1981) 225-50; S. Safrai, "Home and Family" in *The Jewish People in the First Century: Historical Geography, Political History, Social, Cultural and Religious Life and Institutions,* ed. S. Safrai and M. Stern with D. Flusser and W. C. van Unnik (2 vols.; Assen: Van Gorcum, 1974; Philadelphia: Fortress, 1976) 728-92; J. J. Schmitt, "You Adulteresses! The Image in James 4:4," *NovT* 28 (1986) 327-37; V. L. Wimbush, "Renunciation towards Social Engineering, An Apologia for the Study of Asceticism in Greco-Roman Antiquity," *Occasional Papers of the Institute for Antiquity and Christianity* 8 (Claremont, CA: Claremont Graduate School, 1986). C. S. Keener

MARTYRDOM

In the NT the Greek term *martys* ("martyr") means "witness" in a legal sense, often having to do with testimony related to Jesus Christ,* and may include the opposite concept of false witness. Of the thirty-four NT uses of *martys,* twenty-one are found in Acts, the non-Pauline epistles and Revelation; eighteen of the twenty-one references occur in Acts, which documents Christians' efforts to fulfill the Great Commission and the Apocalypse. Such uses frequently include the idea of faithful witness* for Jesus, even in the face of intense suffering* or death.

The latter nuance is most evident in the biblical text in Revelation, where the concept of faithful witness connects with the climactic phase of the Great Commission (see 4 below). However, martyrdom as death becomes the common understanding only in the writings of some of the apostolic fathers, notably Ignatius. For those Fathers, martyrdom became an active choice in completing the Christian witness.

1. Judaism and Hellenism
2. Acts of the Apostles
3. Non-Pauline Letters
4. Book of Revelation
5. Postapostolic Period

1. Judaism and Hellenism.

Both Jewish and Greco-Roman ideas about martyrdom likely influenced the understanding of the NT writers and the apostolic fathers. The familiarity of the NT writers with the OT, which is apparent through its extensive and striking usage in Hebrews (*see* Old Testament in Hebrews), James,* 1 Peter, 2 Peter,* Jude* and Revelation, strongly implies such an influence.

Jewish law* required two or more witnesses to verify accusations (Deut 17:6-7; 19:15), a principle often appealed to in the NT (Mt 18:16; Heb 10:28). In the OT both reliable witnesses (Ruth 4:9-11; Is 8:2) and false witnesses (Ex 23:1; Prov 6:19) are common.

In Daniel 7—12 there is developed a concept of the suffering of God's "holy ones," some even unto death, before their sharing in the future kingdom (*see* Kingdom of God). In Daniel 7:18, 22, for example, these sufferers are called "the saints [LXX *hagioi*] of the Highest One," apocalyptic* terminology that seems to inform the concept of witness in the book of Revelation (see 4 below). Perhaps partly due to the influence of the book of Daniel, some Jewish intertestamental writers (see 1-2 Macc) reflect a fairly developed concept of martyrdom (Tabor).

Alongside the examples of witnesses in the OT are the accounts of faithful ones among the people of God* who died, starting with Abel (Gen 4:8). This point was underscored by Jesus (Mt 23:35), Stephen (Acts 7:52) and the writer of Hebrews (Heb 11:35, 37). There is also an emphasis in the NT on the death of the OT prophets,* those who proclaimed and witnessed to the Word of God (Mt 23:35; Acts 7:52).

There also existed a contemporary Greco-Roman understanding of martyrdom (see Seeley). In some strands of the Roman thought, martyrdom was considered to be a particularly noble way to die (Tabor). This may be observed in writers such as Seneca, Epictetus and Plutarch (see Seeley, 113-41).

2. Acts of the Apostles.

From the beginning of the book of Acts,* the thirteen uses of *martys* occur primarily in the context of the Christian mission.* *Martys* is conceived as a solemn legal witness regarding Jesus, a witness that focused on his resurrection* and also emphasized his unjust but voluntary death (Acts 1:22; 2:32; 3:15; 5:32; 10:39-41). This witness provided the kind of legally recognized testimony needed to substantiate the preaching* of the gospel (Gk *euangelizō;* Acts 13:31-32), which began in Jerusalem* and continued to the remotest part of the earth (Acts 1:8).

When the apostle Paul recounts his conversion on the Damascus road and its aftermath (Acts 9:1-19), he refers to his apostolic* calling as being a "witness" to all people (Acts 22:15). That included both the Jews and the Gentiles* (Acts 26:16), though his primary emphasis would be on the witness to the Gentiles (Acts 22:21). Paul's witness made available to this diverse audience spiritual enlightenment, release from the power of Satan* and forgiveness* of sins to those who responded by faith* in Jesus (Acts 26:16-18).

There also were false witnesses in the infant church* (Acts 6:13). They played a decisive role in the first recorded death by martyrdom in the church, that of Stephen* (Acts 7), even as false witnesses had strategically testified against Jesus (Mt 26:60). Jesus had spoken of the stoning of those sent by God to Jerusalem and her leaders (i.e., as witnesses; Mt 23:37), and Stephen died (Acts 7:57-60) as a faithful witness (Acts 22:20). Paul was able to provide an eyewitness (Acts 7:58; 8:1) account of Stephen's death as a "martyr" (Acts 22:20, NIV).

Though the term *martyr* is not found in the context, the death of James the apostle (Acts 12:1-2), the brother of John, at the hands of King Herod Agrippa I is another example of martyrdom. Soon thereafter Peter also was arrested but was miraculously released and perhaps spared from martyrdom (Acts 12:3-11). Paul almost died a martyr's death in Lystra (Acts 14:19-20) while he was preaching the gospel (Gk *euangelizō;* Acts 14:15).

3. Non-Pauline Letters.

In the non-Pauline letters* there are only two uses of *martys* in Hebrews (Heb 10:28; 12:1) and one in 1 Peter (1 Pet 5:1). Hebrews 10:28 refers to the necessity of "two or three witnesses" for a just death sentence under the law of Moses.* The other instance refers to witness related to the past, with suffering as the backdrop. In 1 Peter 5:1 *martys* applies to suffering but distinctively so: "the sufferings of Christ."

Up to the time that Hebrews* was written, no one in the community had suffered death as witness for their faith (Heb 10:32-39), though there had been suffering and persecution* (Heb 10:32-34). But the possibility of a martyr's death continued to exist (Heb 12:4).

The mention in Hebrews 11 of those who died in faith, such as Abel (Heb 11:4) and the unnamed believers performing the faithful acts described in Hebrews 11:35, 37, prepares for the usage of *martyr* in Hebrews 12:1. The "great cloud of witnesses" (Heb 12:1 NIV) includes a substantial number of martyrs (Heb 11:4, 35, 37). Their persevering witness serves to motivate the recipients of the epistle to focus on Jesus, even if witness and endurance* mean bloodshed and martyrdom (Heb 12:1-4).

The lone use of *martyr* in 1 Peter 5:1 may seem to provide little evidence that Peter's idea of witness might include death. It initially appears that Peter merely describes himself as a legally valid eyewitness to Jesus' suffering, perhaps at the hands of the authorities, at the time of his denial of Christ (Mt 26:58, 69-75). Yet 1 Peter* presents an extensive theology of suffering, and each of the extended passages dealing with suffering (1 Pet 2:19-24, 3:14-18, 4:12-13) also refers to the sufferings of Jesus. Those sufferings include Christ's death (i.e., martyrdom) on the cross* (1 Pet 2:24; 3:18; *see* Death of Christ).

In 1 Peter 5:8-9 the devil is portrayed as a "roaring lion" who causes suffering in the lives of God's people (*see* Satan). 1 Peter 5:10 then provides the readers assurance* that their experience of suffering in the spiritual warfare will last only "a little while" before God brings them to the point of spiritual completeness. Though this is not stated explicitly, it is possible to infer that martyrdom completes this process. Scripture (2 Pet 1:14-15) and extrabiblical tradition combine to testify that Peter himself suffered and died as a martyr (*1 Clem.* 5; see Cullmann).

4. Book of Revelation.

The five uses of *martys* in the Apocalypse are spread through the book (*see* Revelation, Book of). One reference appears in the introductory portion (Rev 1:5), two in the letters to the churches in Asia Minor (Rev 2:13; 3:14) and two in the visions* that form the body of the Apocalypse (Rev 11:3; 17:6). Two of the five uses refer to Jesus as the ultimate or foundational faithful "witness" (Rev 1:5; 3:14). The other three describe those who die as witnesses for the faith (Rev 2:13; 11:3; 17:6), either in the setting in which the Apocalypse was written (Rev 2:13) or in the apocalyptic setting its visions portray (Rev 11:3; 17:6).

In several works R. J. Bauckham has examined how the Apocalypse utilizes numerous OT passages and intertestamental ideas in reflect-

ing the conversion of the nations, although Bauckham has not adequately linked this latter, overarching theme, which he views as taking place in the apocalyptic setting in Revelation, to the worldwide preaching of the "gospel of the kingdom" just before "the end" *(to telos)* comes (Mt 24:14). Both conversion and fulfillment take place in the context of persecution and death (Mt 24:9).

Revelation's portrayal of the proclamation of "the eternal gospel" *(euangelion aiōnion)* to "every nation *(pan ethnos)*, tribe, language and people" (Rev 14:6) does parallel the Matthean wording. Further, the reference to "all the nations" *(pasin tois ethnesin)* as the target audience in Matthew 24:14, as well as in the Matthean and Lukan versions of the Great Commission (Mt 28:19; Lk 24:47), and the closing mention of "the end of the age" *(heōs tēs synteleias tou aiōnos)* in Matthew 28:20 seem to establish that the conversion of the nations (see esp. Rev 7:9, "all nations" *[pantos ethnous]*), in the midst of great suffering and martyrdom, echoes the Synoptics as much as prior Jewish thought and expectation.

Further, in Revelation apocalyptic terminology resembles that of the book of Daniel (see 1 above). It is likely that the suffering of the saints, depicted in the visions in Daniel 7—12, is a scriptural basis for the "prayers of the saints" (Rev 5:8; 8:2-4), the temporary conquest of the saints by the beast* (Rev 13:5-7), the need for patient endurance* by the saints (Rev 13:10) and the shedding of the blood of the martyred saints (Rev 16:6; 17:6).

Foundational in this apocalyptic drama is the loud cry from the heavenly altar of "those who had been slain because of the word of God and the testimony *(martyrian)* they had maintained" (Rev 6:9 NIV). Their impassioned prayer demands, "How long, Sovereign Lord, holy and true, until you judge the inhabitants of the earth and avenge our blood?" (Rev 6:10 NIV). The answer seems to sum up the remaining scenes in Revelation: "they were told to wait a little longer, until the full number of their fellow servants and brothers who were to be killed as they had been was completed" (Rev 6:11 NIV). Echoes of this prayer and its divine answer, chillingly describing a "full number" *(plērōthōsin)* of future martyrs, reverberate through the Apocalypse to the Parousia* (Rev 18:20, 24; 19:1-2).

Unlike the single passage in 1 Peter 5, the

Apocalypse develops another aspect of martyrdom: its satanic origin. The intense though limited persecution of the contemporary churches at Smyrna and Pergamum (Rev 2:10, 13) is attributed directly to Satan. There had already been a death for the faith in Pergamum, that of Antipas, "my faithful witness" (Rev 2:13 NIV; *ho martys mou ho pistos mou*), wording that echoes the initial description of Jesus in Revelation 1:5 *(ho martys ho pistos)* and the closely parallel description in Revelation 3:14. Other martyrdoms may follow soon after the writing of the letter to Smyrna (Rev 2:10).

In the apocalyptic visions, the death of the two witnesses *(dysin martysin,* Rev 11:3) at the hand of the beast (Rev 11:7) is empowered by Satan (Rev 13:1-2). The deaths of many faithful martyrs also are attributed to the fury of the devil (Rev 12:11-12), though the counterpoint is made clear. Such deaths are victories in God's plan, even as was the shedding of the "blood of the Lamb" (Rev 12:11; *see* Lamb). That victory celebration is vividly described in Revelation 15:2.

Since the unbelieving world* follows and worships the beast (Rev 13:2-4), they worship and follow the great dragon (Rev 13:4), who is Satan (Rev 12:9), in opposing God and in rejoicing over the demise of God's faithful witnesses (Rev 11:9-10). The beast's evil consort, the pseudo-queenly Babylon* the Great, drunk with the blood of the martyrs (Rev 17:6), is ultimately exposed as "a home for demons and a haunt for every evil spirit" (Rev 18:2 NIV).

It should not be assumed, however, that all who are faithful witnesses for "the word of God and the testimony of Jesus" die as a result. John, the writer, was alive in spite of persecution that saw him exiled to the island of Patmos (Rev 1:9). Only a relatively few believers in Revelation 2—3 would die (Rev 2:10, 13). Even the "great multitude" standing before the heavenly throne in Revelation 7:9, 14 are not all or necessarily martyrs. The comment about making their robes "white in the blood of the Lamb" may refer not to martyrdom but to Christ's redemptive death.

While there is a special beatitude for those who persevere and die in the Lord* (Rev 14:12-13), especially for those who take a fatal stand against the beast (Rev 20:4), they are not the only witnesses who are divinely blessed.* Other than the descriptions in Revelation 12:11 and Revelation 15:2, all the promises* for overcoming (Rev 2—3; 21:7), which includes faithful witness (Rev 2:10-11), are offered to all believers, as is the promised destiny of those purchased with Christ's blood: to be a kingdom and God's priests* who will also reign (Rev 5:9-10).

5. Postapostolic Period.

With increased persecution came increased martyrdom. Tertullian is credited with saying: "The blood of the martyrs is indeed the seed of the church. Dying we conquer." Thus he held that the witness of the church was furthered decisively by the martyrdom of the faithful. But the popular perception of thousands of early Christians being fed to the beasts in the arena is a distortion. In W. H. C. Frend's estimation, the total number of early Christian martyrs should probably be measured in "hundreds, not thousands" (Frend, 413).

The apostolic fathers* wrote during a time of transition. They look back on the developing NT usage of *martys* as well as provide insight on the perspectives of early centuries of church history. The most striking attitude toward martyrdom is found in the voices of those who fully embraced it. The strongest expression is found in Ignatius,* who regarded martyrdom as the highest expression of discipleship to Jesus Christ (Ign. *Rom.* 4.2), a true act of following in his passion (Ign. *Rom.* 6.3). Ignatius wrote his letters as he was transported under Roman escort from Antioch to Rome* (probably during the first two decades of the second century; *see* Ignatius). His letter to the Romans reflects his eagerness to suffer and die (Ign. *Rom.* 7.2), and his determination that the Roman Christians not interfere with the process (Ign. *Rom.* 2; 4.1). Martyrdom offered the opportunity for the highest form of spiritual attainment (Ign. *Rom.* 4), for it was the pathway to God (Ign. *Rom.* 7.2). As Ignatius memorably phrased it:

> Allow me to be eaten by the beasts, through whom I can attain to God. I am God's wheat, and I am ground by the teeth of wild beasts that I may be found to be pure bread of Christ. (Ign. *Rom.* 4.1)

Or again he writes, "I long for the beasts that are prepared for me. And I pray that they may be found prompt for me" (Ign. *Rom.* 5.2). This attitude of Ignatius toward martyrdom was not the norm, but it does point out that for some the rewards of martyrdom far outweighed its costs (see Stark, 163-89). It was not driven by an irrationalism or masochism, as some modern interpreters have supposed.

The earliest example of martyrological literature is *The Martyrdom of Polycarp,* a letter written from the church at Smyrna to the church at Philomelium shortly after Polycarp's death in c. 155-160. The aged Polycarp, bishop of Smyrna, does not seek martyrdom but, refusing to take an oath to Caesar, he accepts his execution with steadfast courage and saintliness: "For eighty-six years I have been his servant, and he has done me no wrong. How can I blaspheme my king who saved me?" (*Mart. Pol.* 9.3). The honor of martyrdom is maintained (*Mart. Pol.* 2.1-2), but those who "give themselves up" willingly are not commended (*Mart. Pol.* 4.1). Those who die the martyr's death are imitators of the Lord (*Mart. Pol.* 1.2; 19.1) and partakers of Christ (*Mart. Pol.* 6.2). As he faces the flames, Polycarp prays that he might be "a rich and acceptable sacrifice" (*Mart. Pol.* 14.2). After his death his fellow Christians collect Polycarp's burnt bones and preserve them as precious artifacts, with the intention of celebrating "the birthday of his martyrdom" (*Mart. Pol.* 18.3).

Several accounts from beyond our time period are worth mentioning. Eusebius quotes in his *Ecclesiastical History* a *Letter of the Churches of Lyons and Vienne* (*Hist. Eccl.* 5.1.3-63), which gives an account of the persecution of the church at Lyons in c. 177 or 178. The letter presents a moving account the sufferings and deaths of the martyrs and employs the motif of Christ suffering in the martyrs, and the martyrs as athletes engaged in a contest, with the victors receiving the crown of immortality (*Hist. Eccl.* 5.1.23, 36, 42). The *Passion of Perpetua and Felicitas* is the account of the martyrdom in 202 at Carthage of a young woman, Perpetua, and her slave Felicitas, and three catechumens, Saturus, Saturninus and Revocatus. The document is particularly valuable for its preservation of Perpetua's prison diary, which occupies eight of the twenty-one chapters. Another category of martyrological literature is the "acts of the martyrs" (*acta,* or *gesta martyrum*), which purport to contain official court proceedings. Acts of first-century martyrs are *The Acts of Justin and His Companions* (Justin Martyr, martyred c. 165 in Rome) and *The Acts of the Martyrs of Scilli in Africa* (martyred c. 180 in North Africa). Tertullian's

To the Martyrs (*Ad Martyras,* c. 200) is addressed as an encouragement to fellow Christians held in prison and awaiting their inevitable martyrdom.

See also ENDURANCE, PERSEVERANCE; PERSECUTION; SUFFERING; WITNESS.

BIBLIOGRAPHY. R. J. Bauckham, *The Climax of Prophecy: Studies on the Book of Revelation* (Edinburgh: T & T Clark, 1992); idem, "The Martyrdom of Enoch and Elijah: Jewish or Christian?" *JBL* 95 (1976) 447-58; idem, *The Theology of the Book of Revelation* (NTT; Cambridge: Cambridge University Press, 1993); H. von Campenhausen, *Die Idee des Martyriums in der alten Kirche* (2d ed.; Göttingen: Vandenhoeck & Ruprecht, 1964); A. Y. Collins, "Persecution and Vengeance in the Book of Revelation" in *Apocalypticism in the Mediterranean World and the Near East,* ed. D. Hellholm (Tübingen: J. C. B. Mohr, 1983) 729-49; O. Cullmann, *Peter: Disciple, Apostle, Martyr* (Philadelphia: Westminster, 1953); B. Dehandschutter, "The Meaning of Witness in the Apocalypse" in *L'Apocalypse johannique et l'Apocalyptique dans le Nouveau Testament,* ed. J. Lambrecht (Louvain: Louvain University Press, 1980) 283-88; S. de Dietrich, " 'You are My Witnesses'—A Study of the Church's Witness," *Int* 8 (1954) 273-79; G. Dragas, "Martyrdom and Orthodoxy in the New Testament Era," *Greek Orthodox Theological Review* 30 (1985) 287-96; A. Droge and J. Tabor, *A Noble Death: Suicide and Martyrdom Among Ancient Jews, Christians, Greeks, and Romans* (San Francisco: Harper & Row, 1989); W. H. C. Frend, *Martyrdom and Persecution in the Early Church* (Grand Rapids: Baker, 1981); A. B. Luter Jr., "End Times and Mission," *Evangelical Dictionary of World Missions,* ed. S. Moreau (Grand Rapids: Baker, forthcoming); idem, "Great Commission," *ABD* 2:1090-91; M. G. Reddish, "Martyr Christology in the Apocalypse," *JSNT* 33 (1988) 85-95; W. R. Schoedel, *Ignatius of Antioch* (Herm; Philadelphia: Fortress, 1985); D. Seeley, *The Noble Death: Greco-Roman Martyrology and Paul's Concept of Salvation* (JSNTSup 28; Sheffield: JSOT, 1990); R. Stark, *The Rise of Christianity* (Princeton, NJ: Princeton University Press, 1996); H. Strathman, "μάρτυς κτλ," *TDNT* 4:474-514; J. P. M. Sweet, "Maintaining the Testimony of Jesus: The Suffering of Christians in the Revelation of John" in *Suffering and Martyrdom in the New Testament,* ed. W. Horbury and B. McNeil (Cambridge: Cambridge University Press, 1981) 101-17; R. Tabor, "Martyr, Martyrdom,"

ABD 4:574-79; C. H. Talbert, *The Apocalypse: A Reading of the Revelation of John* (Louisville, KY: Westminster/John Knox, 1994); A. A. Trites, "Μάρτυς" and Martyrdom in the Apocalypse: A Semantic Study," *NovT* 15 (1973) 72-80; idem, *The New Testament Concept of Witness* (SNTSMS 31; Cambridge: Cambridge University Press, 1977); A. A. Trites and L. Coenen, "Witness," *NIDNTT* 3:1038-51; M. J. Wilkins, *Following the Master: Discipleship in the Footsteps of Jesus* (Grand Rapids: Zondervan, 1992); H. B. Workman, *Persecution in the Early Church* (Oxford: Oxford University Press, 1980 [1906]).

A. B. Luter Jr.

MARTYRDOM OF POLYCARP. *See* POLYCARP OF SMYRNA.

MARY

Apart from the four Gospels, the NT documents provide scanty information concerning the life or role of Mary in the early Christian era. There is no reference to her in the General Epistles, and even in Paul's several references to Christ's birth or biological origin (Gal 4:4; Rom 1:3; 9:5), Mary's name is consistently withheld. Why is the person who was once closely related to Jesus thus ignored by early Christian writers? What is her role after the ascension of Jesus? How is she understood by Christian leaders before the end of the second century?

1. Biographical Data
2. Literary Analysis
3. Theological Development
4. Conclusion

1. Biographical Data.

John, the last composed or compiled canonical Gospel at the turn of the century, reveals that Mary was committed by Jesus to the care of his beloved disciple at the foot of the cross (Jn 19:26-27; Beasley-Murray, 350). Apparently this disciple had a place or a family of his own in Jerusalem (*eis ta idia,* Jn 19:27), and Mary went to reside with him at that time (Tenney, 182-83). After the ascension* of Jesus she was listed among the first group of disciples who gathered to pray (Acts 1:14) and probably experienced the coming of the Holy Spirit* at Pentecost* (Acts 2:1-4). Beyond this point no canonical record or writing of the early apostolic fathers* refers to the events of her later years.

According to church tradition it is possible that Mary also went to Ephesus with John when he migrated there in the 60s (see Eusebius *Hist. Eccl.* 3.1, 23, 28, 31; 5.20; Irenaeus *Haer.* 3.1). A record of Jesus' word of commission from the cross to Mary and the beloved disciple (Jn 19:26-27) seems to suggest that the writer was explaining to the Christians at Ephesus about Mary's residence there. The apocryphal* *Protevangelium of James,* a product of the second century, provides a detailed description of Mary's life: her parents, family background (*Protev. Jas.* 1.1—5.1), birth and childhood (*Protev. Jas.* 5.2—8.1), betrothal to Joseph (*Protev. Jas.* 8.2—10.2) and her conception and delivery of Jesus (*Protev. Jas.* 11—20). The entire record aims at exalting Mary as a pure and perfect figure whose conception was miraculous and whose marriage* to Joseph was without physical contact. Although this document was soon widely accepted by the Eastern church (Gaventa, 122) and became a foundational document for the full development of Mariology in the fourth century, its historical value has always been questioned on the basis of its second-century origin. Besides, its information on Mary has never been confirmed in any previous writings. Other apocryphal literature, such as the *Gospel of Thomas* and the *Gospel of the Nazareans,* also provide glimpses of Mary's character and activities; these too represent a gnostic* variation on the canonical records.

2. Literary Analysis.

Besides the queries about who Mary was and in what manner she was being portrayed in the canonical accounts, it is important to explore the reason(s) why Mary's place is recorded as such in the NT. From the literary perspective the Gospel writers are believed to have selected and tailored their sources according to the purpose of their presentations and need of their audiences. Thus Mary's role as it appears in Jesus' birth narratives is not identical in Matthew's and Luke's accounts (see Gaventa, Brown 1993), and the seemingly harsh portrayal of Mary in Mark's Gospel (Mk 3:21, 31-33) has also to be explained as a critique of the holy family as representing Jewish Christianity* (Jelly, 33-37, Trocmé, 132-37).

In the Fourth Gospel Mary is mentioned twice, in the beginning (Jn 2:1-11, the feast of Cana) and at the end (Jn 19:25-27, the foot of the cross) of Jesus' public ministry. The writer's intention in these two instances is meant to underscore the humanity of Jesus, "whose earthly father and mother and brothers and geographical origin are known" (Gaventa, 80, 95-97; see Relatives of Jesus). But perhaps it is more likely that the inclusion and arrangement of these two events found only in John are meant to provide a powerful witness to Jesus' role as the Son of God* (Jn 20:31). Mary, like many other figures recorded in the Fourth Gospel, is called to provide eyewitness testimony. Despite her unique relationship to Jesus (see Jn 2:1, 3, 5, 12; 19:25-26, where the writer does not hesitate to introduce her repeatedly as the mother of Jesus), Jesus is not her son but the Son of God. The two addresses of "woman" (*gynai*, Jn 2:4; 19:26) by Jesus to Mary strongly support this.

The brief reference to Mary as one who gathered and prayed with other disciples in Acts 1:14 is to reinforce the notion that Mary is an obedient disciple of Jesus—an image repeatedly portrayed by the same writer in his Gospel (cf. Lk 1:38; 2:19, 51).

The silence about Mary in Paul's letters and the General Epistles is noteworthy, since the later documents view Christ's person from the postresurrection perspective. In the Gospels Jesus' earthly life was the focus, and his birth and family background are natural means of introducing him. The other NT writings, however, are characteristically christocentric and soteriocentric. Jesus' biological origin was soon superseded by his divine origin and redemptive work after the dawn of the church age (cf. 2 Cor 5:16).

Ignatius* (c. A.D. 112) also alluded to Mary (Ign. *Trall.* 9; 10; Ign. *Eph.* 18.1) and her virginity (Ign. *Eph.* 19.1; Ign. *Smyrn.* 1) in his letters. He stressed the reality of Mary's childbearing and that Jesus was by God's design to be carried in Mary's womb, all for the purpose of arguing against the docetic teachings of his day (Kelly, 492). The mention of Mary serves to support his assertion of Jesus' true humanity.

3. Theological Development.
The Synoptic Gospels provide glimpses of Mary's biographical information. Some scholars have suggested that the records of Mary in John are more theologically oriented. Jesus' word from the cross to Mary and the beloved disciple (Jn 19:25-27) is an evidence that Mary

was commissioned as the mother of all disciples, or Christians, by Jesus. Although this view has generally been adopted by the Roman Catholic church (Jelly, 67; Brown 1978, 215-16), the issue remains disputed among NT interpreters. This estimate would cover the use of Revelation 12 to refer to Mary as "the woman clothed with the sun" (see Prigent).

A more certain theological emphasis of Mary is seen in Ignatius's letters, in which Mary is consistently described as a virgin (Ign. *Eph.* 18.1; 19.1; Ign. *Trall.* 9; 10; Ign. *Smyrn.* 1). Evidently Mary's virginity in the birth of Christ, though hidden from the prince of this world (in the Song of the Star, Ign. *Eph.* 19.1), was a familiar concept among Christians at that time, since Ignatius can allude to it without additional explanation. By the middle of the second century Justin Martyr (*Dial. Tryph.* 100.5) first made an explicit comparison between Mary and Eve,

> For Eve, who was a virgin and undefiled, having conceived the word of the serpent, brought forth disobedience and death. But the virgin Mary received faith and joy, when the angel Gabriel announced the good tidings to her . . . , by whom God destroys both the serpent and those angels and men that became like it.

This identification of Mary the virgin who gives birth to the Redeemer as "the second Eve," just as Christ is "the second Adam" (Rom 5:12-17; 1 Cor 15:22), was adopted and further developed by Irenaeus (c. A.D. 185) in the West (Lyons) and Tertullian (c. A.D. 200) in the East (Alexandria*). Irenaeus applied the principle *recircumlatio* to Christ and Adam as well as to Mary and Eve (Irenaeus *Haer.* 3.22.3-4; 5.19.1). With him Mariology became accepted (Jelly, 71).

4. Conclusion.
After Jesus' ascension Mary evidently was recognized as one of the disciples of the risen Lord* (Acts 1:14; Bauckham, 52). Early Christians, awaiting for Christ's imminent Parousia,* devoted their energies to proclaiming Christ and his cross* (cf. 1 Cor 1:17-18; 2:2). Mary's life, like Jesus' earthly life, was no longer a matter of concern in primitive Christianity, both in Jewish and Gentile* circles. Her natural family relationship with Jesus was replaced by the eschatological* family relationship (Brown 1978). Thus, despite her unique role in the early life of Christ, Mary is essentially acknowledged as

one of God's instruments (like the apostles*) in carrying out his plan of salvation.* It is in this light that she was remembered by early Christians. The identification of Mary as an exalted figure in the church belongs to a later development.

See also RELATIVES OF JESUS; WOMEN IN THE EARLY CHURCH.

BIBLIOGRAPHY. R. J. Bauckham, *Jude and the Relatives of Jesus* (Edinburgh: T & T Clark, 1990); G. R. Beasley-Murray, *John* (WBC; Waco, TX: Word, 1987); D. D. C. Braine, "The Place of the Virgin Mary in Dogmatics," *STJ* 37 (1984) 145-62; G. W. Bromiley, "Mary the Mother of Jesus," *ISBE* 3:269-73; G. J. Brooke, ed., *Women in the Biblical Tradition* (Lewiston, NY: Edwin Mellen, 1992); R. E. Brown, *The Birth of the Messiah* (rev. ed.; Garden City, NY: Doubleday, 1993); R. E. Brown et al., eds., *Mary in the New Testament* (Philadelphia: Fortress, 1978); B. R. Gaventa, *Mary, Glimpses of the Mother of Jesus* (Columbia, SC: University of South Carolina Press, 1995); F. M. Jelly, *Madonna: Mary in the Catholic Tradition* (Huntington, IN: Our Sunday Visitor, 1986); J. N. D. Kelly, *Early Christian Doctrines* (5th ed.; New York: Harper & Row, 1978); J. McHugh, *The Mother of Jesus in the New Testament* (Garden City, NY: Doubleday, 1975); H. A. Oberman, *The Virgin Mary in Evangelical Perspective* (Philadelphia: Fortress, 1971); P. Prigent, *Apocalypse 12: Histoire de l'exégèse* (Tübingen: J. C. B. Mohr, 1959); R. Russell, "The Blessed Virgin Mary in the Bible" in *Mary's Place in Christian Dialogue*, ed. A. Stacpoole (Wilton, CT: Morehouse-Barlow, 1983) 45-50; M. C. Tenney, *The Gospel of John* (EBC; Grand Rapids: Zondervan, 1981); E. Trocmé, *The Formation of the Gospel According to Mark* (Philadelphia: Westminster, 1975); M. Warner, *Alone of All Her Sex: The Myth and the Cult of the Virgin Mary* (rev. ed.; London: Picador, 1990).   J. L. Wu

MATTHEAN COMMUNITY

Inferring from the Gospel of Matthew that the community for which this Evangelist wrote is reflected in the pages of the First Gospel, scholars today have attempted to reconstruct the church life and social conditions in which Matthew was written (*see DJG*, Matthew, Gospel of). Not infrequently scholars contend that various bits of information in the First Gospel are a "transparency" of the Matthean community and show little connection with the life of Jesus (Luz). Others are more cautious in their judgments and contend that inferences about a community are limited more or less to major trends and themes (e.g., Hagner). In general, however, most specialists would agree that some things can be known, by way of inference and confirmation from other evidence, about the community for which the First Gospel was intended. Furthermore, a fundamental issue for appreciating this debate and the evidence of Matthew is the complex relationship of Matthew's kind of Christianity to the evolving, diversifying world of Judaism, with its wide range of toleration and differences. This development was highly complex and chaotic; it was further exacerbated by the complex and changing place Judaism had within the Roman legal world (Dunn, Goodman).

1. Scholarship
2. Methodology
3. Suggestions for Reconstructing a Matthean Community

1. Scholarship.

There are two broad trends in studies regarding Matthew's community: some argue that Matthew's community was within Judaism* *(intra muros)* while others argue that Matthew's community was outside of Judaism *(extra muros)*. (For an early survey of scholarship, see Stanton 1984, 1910-21.) Within each of these trends there are significant differences. Alongside this issue of the relationship of Matthew's community to Judaism there is also the placement of Matthew's community within the broader, developing Christian movement (Dunn, Stanton 1984, 1908-10; *see* Christianity and Judaism). A consensus seems to have emerged that Matthew is not opposing Pauline Christianity (Davies, 316-66) or opposing any specific set of antinomians (Strecker). In addition the majority would argue that Matthew's community is Jewish and is seeking to bring together its historical covenant with Abraham,* Moses and David with its newly discovered faith* and obedience* to Jesus the Messiah, along with the stresses this new faith generates (e.g., Hagner 1993, Overman, Saldarini).

The debate today concerns the relationship of Matthew's supposed community to its parent religion, Judaism. On the one end of the spectrum are those who contend that Matthew's community sees itself as true Israel,* even part of Judaism, even if there are tensions created by the community's faith in Jesus as the Messiah (Saldarini, Dunn, Kilpatrick). For this view Matthew's community defines itself over against the Gentile* world and over against nonmessianic Judaism but does not identify itself as a new religion. It is the true Israel, the remnant of the end times, that has found God's promises fulfilled in Jesus Messiah. Its mission* is still to the Jews (Mt 10:5-6; 15:24), it pays the Jewish tax (Mt 17:24-27), and its acerbic attacks against the Pharisees (e.g., Mt 23) reflect actual debates between the true Israel and the others within Judaism over the Law* (Hummel; Dunn, 98-102, 151-56), the rightful leaders (the apostles* or the Pharisees; see Mt 9:35—11:1; 21:43; 23:1-3) and who ought to be in "their synagogues" (e.g., Mt 4:23). W. D. Davies went so far as to specify that Matthew, especially Matthew 5—7, was a response to the contemporary events of the reorganization of Judaism at Jamnia. (Scholars have become much more cautious about inferences about Jamnia due to the paucity of evidence; see Hagner 1993, lxviii-lxix.) The opponents of Matthew's community and its leaders were the Pharisees. They may well have seen this particular brand of Judaism as sectarian or even heretical (if such a term can be appropriately used for this period in light of the diversity of Judaism), but such a categorization is a natural reaction to an upstart movement of this sort (Saldarini; Dunn, 156).

Basing their arguments on the Gentile emphasis (Mt 1:1-17; 2:1-12; 4:12-16; 8:5-13; 15:21-28; 28:16-20), the use of the phrase "their synagogues" (Mt 4:23) and the heated debate with the Pharisees (e.g., Mt 23), a number of scholars now argue that Matthew's community was already separated from Judaism and is to be understood as the church,* a new religion of faith in Jesus, and some have proposed that the author of the First Gospel was a Gentile (Strecker, Trilling). Arguing from the basis of a careful delineation of how Matthew depicts salvation history, R. Walker argues that the time of Israel is in a distant past and that Matthew's present is one concerned with the Gentile mission. The work of G. Strecker on salvation history and of W. Trilling on Matthew 21:43 support the same view: Matthew's community is no longer a part of Judaism; this community is largely Gentile and sees the debate with Judaism as a chapter in its history. J. P. Meier contends

that the First Gospel was written by a Gentile and that it mirrors the historical evolution of the church of Syrian Antioch*.

Somewhere between these two trends, other scholars have argued that the Matthean community has made the break with Judaism but has made this move reluctantly because it still defines itself within Judaism and over against nonmessianic Judaism (Stanton 1984, 1992; Hagner). They are, in effect, in "no man's land" (Hagner, lxx). As proposed by Hagner, Matthew's community is a reflection of several polar-opposite spectrums, but this is seen most clearly in the tension between universalism (Mt 2:1-12; 4:12-16; 8:5-13; 21:43; 28:16-20) and particularism (Mt 1:21; 10:5-6, 23; 15:24). This Gospel contains references to "their synagogues" (Mt 10:17) and to the privilege of Jews (Mt 5:17-48; 6:1-18; 13:16-17; 19:28). "In short, Jews are naturally put on the defensive by their non-Christian Jewish community, and probably more so if they have insisted on preservation of their Jewishness and have resisted assimilation, thus making at least the implicit claim of being the true Israel" (Hagner 1993, lxix). The First Gospel, then, is a reflection of this difficult position: a combination of the desire to anchor one's faith in the traditions of Israel (particularism; true Israel) and, because of the new faith in Jesus Messiah, the desire to anchor one's hope* for the future in a totally inclusive people of God (universalism; new Israel). This is why Matthew adds "so both are preserved" to the parable of new and old wine (Mt 9:17).

2. Methodology.

The discussion above is loaded with methodological issues. It must be asked how modern scholars can discern what the "community" of Matthew was like. Questions must be raised about how much can be known and whether it is even reasonable to talk about the profile of this community. It must be admitted that too often scholars have speculated far too much and have drawn heavy inferences from scanty informtation. When scholars propose a full-scale profile of Matthew's community, to the point of knowing what titles their leaders preferred, what kind of catechism they preferred and the demographic makeup of that community, we must exercise caution. Some scholars "know too much," meaning they know much more than the data permit. The assumption of a "transparency," or of Matthew's text being a window onto his community, is at times gratuitous and without support (Kingsbury 1991, 259-63).

It is reasonable to argue, however, that a document such as the First Gospel will in some measure reflect its community's concerns and its author's general orientations that correspond to the reality of that community. At times the text is transparent (Luz, Segal) and a fairly clean window onto Matthew's community. Few scholars would counter this methodological point: the First Gospel spoke to the community to which it was addressed because it addressed concerns of that community. And if it did speak to that community's concerns, we ought to be able to infer some things about that community. No one would imagine that this Gospel is simply a theoretical "life" of Jesus that has no relationship to the community to whom it was given.

But how do we reconstruct this community? Several suggestions are worthy of following up with a patient investigation of the evidence of Matthew. First, the redactional emphases of Matthew will be the most natural place to begin for a reconstruction of the Matthean community. Two points immediately emerge: Matthew's penchant for contrasting "their synagogues" (Mt 4:23; 9:35; 10:17; 12:9; 13:54), "their scribes" (Mt 7:29) and "your synagogues" (Mt 23:34); and Matthew's unrelenting attack on Pharisees and, in a broader sense, the leaders of Israel (Mt 23). These two traits, and there are other such emphases, illustrate the kind of evidence that ought to be used to reconstruct a profile of Matthew's community (Overman).

Second, the evidence so discovered ought to be discussed in the context of the Judaism that emerged alongside early Christian development. Thus the emphasis Matthew gives to the Pharisees probably also reflects contemporary Judaism. This is where J. A. Overman's work advances beyond that of the majority of scholars on Matthew (see also Stanton 1992, Saldarini, Segal).

Third, the contours that begin to take shape in light of these kind of procedures need to be set within the context of the development of early Christianity. A reconstruction of Matthew's community, in other words, ought to bear resemblance to some kind of known Christianity in the first century, whether we date Matthew early or late. This is the advantage of the approach taken by J. P. Meier in seeking to

locate Matthew's redactional interests, along with the tradition-critical historical development of the Gospel itself, into the development of the church at Syrian Antioch (see Meier and Brown). Here Meier places Matthew's theological and social interests in a believable construction of early Christianity. Even if one does not go the whole way with Meier, one has to admire the sweep of his argument and its contextually sensitive nature. The same can be said of J. D. G. Dunn's reconstruction of the "partings of the ways": Matthew's theology and concerns, especially as they touch on the law and the temple,* are placed into a broader, believable portrait of the growing separation of Christianity and Judaism (*see* Christianity and Judaism).

Fourth, informed judgments can be gleaned at times from sociological theories and models. If one can assume that humans of the first century behave similarly to humans of modern cultures, then one can infer general behavioral and cultural patterns (esp. White; Overman, who borrows heavily from the sociology of knowledge theory of Berger and Luckmann). Overman, for instance, argues fairly persuasively that Matthew's Gospel fits the pattern of sectarian argument and legitimation characteristic of formative Judaism in the post-A.D. 70 period.

Fifth, J. D. Kingsbury has proposed what amounts to a "narrative approach" to constructing the Matthean community. He tries to construct what he calls the "intended readers" or the "implied reader." This approach infers from the text of Matthew a correspondence to the actual readers (the community), and this approach allows Kingsbury to avoid the logically difficult issues of the redactional approach mentioned above. At the same time he carefully seeks to construct a historically believable community. He infers that Matthew's community was set in Antioch of Syria, late in the first century, and Greek was its language. It was urban rather than rural; it had neighbors who were both Jewish and Gentile. The atmosphere was characterized by conflict, both from without and within. The community had already made its break with Judaism and defined itself in terms of a fellowship* under the leadership of the exalted Son of God, with the important corollary that hierarchy was to be avoided. While this approach is reasonable, it fails to distinguish the various levels of Matthew and how those various levels relate to the communities they addressed. It is hard to believe that all of Matthew reflects Matthew's community.

Sixth, cautions need to be raised at every juncture. No matter how solid a redactional conclusion might seem, it is nonetheless rooted in a theory about the source relations of Matthew to previous traditions, and that theory is not certain. No matter how close an observation about Matthew's community might be to contemporary Judaism or Christianity, that observation is still an inference drawn and not a certain piece of evidence. No matter how confident we might be about our conclusions, we are still faced with the fact that the words of Matthew purport to be words from Jesus (and not about Matthew's community). Thus we are forced to admit that we are sometimes arguing that words in the mouth of Jesus are being suggested to be words that are more reflective of Matthew's community than of Jesus. These decisions, while they may be defensible at some general methodological level, are always open to dispute and difference of opinion.

It has, for instance, been argued over and over that Matthew 22:7 reflects a post-A.D. 70 *vaticinium ex eventu*. Therefore, it is inferred, Matthew's Gospel was written after A.D. 70 and probably not by the apostle Matthew, and therefore the parable reflects the time of Matthew's community. This is all reasonable historical speculation. But, as others have argued, it was a topos of ancient Jewish literature to describe destructions of big cities in terms of burning. Therefore this piece of evidence does not necessarily mean Matthew's Gospel was written after A.D. 70, and it could have been written by the apostle, and it could reflect a much earlier setting, even one during the time of Jesus. Nearly every argument advanced in this debate suffers from this kind of reasoning and counterarguments.

Finally, one ought not deny the impress of the author, and one ought to recognize that what was important to an author may not have been as important to a community and may not have any relationship to that community. Maybe, one might argue, the author of the First Gospel had had a decisively bad experience with pharisaic Judaism and the author alone was responsible for this heated polemic. While this argument may not be provable, it is not beyond the scope of our reasoning, and it is a factor that

ought to be considered by anyone speculating on the nature of Matthew's community. An author's stamp on a book, unless that author is merely a representative of that community (which is exceedingly difficult to prove for NT books), may be distinct from the community's stamp and its concerns. Maybe, then, it was only Matthew who had conflict with the Pharisees over the law.

3. Suggestions for Reconstructing a Matthean Community.

Though cautions are in order, it is not beyond our capacities to infer some things for a profile of Matthew's community. What is presented here is in part a consensus of current Matthean scholarship (see Kingsbury 1991, 264-65).

3.1. Date, Provenance and Authorship of Matthew. In spite of traditional scholarship's insistence that Matthew the apostle wrote the First Gospel, the case has not been proven. It probably will never be proven because the evidence for this kind of argument is unavailable (McKnight 1992, 528). If our knowledge of the author is far from certain, the date is even more uncertain. While some have argued that Matthew 22:7 clearly proves that the First Gospel was not given its final shape until after the destruction of Jerusalem,* others have argued convincingly that this piece of evidence is best explained as a Jewish topos. Thus the evidence is unclear. And even if a considerable number of scholars today think Matthew originated in Syrian Antioch, numbers are not definitive proof: the data for this conclusion are not unambiguous, and a number of other scholars are arguing for other provenances (Kingsbury 1991, 264). Because the Gospel was written in Greek, however, it seems fair to argue that Matthew was not written in the land of Israel; rather, it was composed where the vast majority of his readers would have been at home in Greek. The redactional interest of Matthew in cities may indicate Matthew's community was at home in an urban environment (Kingsbury 1988, 152-53).

3.2. A Jewish Community. If there is any consensus about Matthew's community it is that it was mostly Jewish. This best explains the interest in OT fulfillment, in the Pharisees and in the Jewish flavor of the Gospel (Dunn, Stanton 1992, Hagner, Overman, Kingsbury). But this Jewish community is probably in the Diaspora,* since the language of communication is Greek. It is possible that a Greek-speaking community in the land of Israel is the home of this Gospel, (*see* Galilean Christianity), even a Greek-speaking synagogue* in Jerusalem, but these are much less likely than a Diaspora home.

3.3. The Community as the True Israel. The constant appeal to the OT, as well as passages like Matthew 1:21 and 19:28, clearly evince a case for Matthew's community seeing itself as the true people of God who are in direct continuity with Israel's biblical heritage (McKnight 1993, Hagner, Stanton). The persistent haggling with the Pharisees demonstrates that Matthew's community was defining itself in the context of such a debate. Whether or not the community of Matthew was perceived as Jewish or whether they were accepted as "members" of a local synagogue is unclear from the side of the opponents, but "sectarian" would seem to apply (see Saldarini, Overman). However, it seems clear to most scholars that Matthew's community thought they were true and even new Israel (Stanton).

3.4. Conflict with the Pharisees. Matthew's answers were not, however, acceptable to the pharisaic leadership. Matthew contends that the apostles of Jesus are the true leaders of Israel (Mt 9:35—11:1; see McKnight 1986) and have in fact replaced the Pharisees (Mt 21:43). He further contends that the destruction of Jerusalem took place as God's judgment* on the Pharisees for leading the people astray (McKnight 1993). Thus one of Matthew's major themes is that the followers of Jesus must abandon the leadership of the Pharisees (Mt 15:13-14; 23:1-7). We cannot know much about the leadership of Matthew: whether Matthew 23:8-12 implies the absence of hierarchy is less clear than his desire not to see them fighting for power*. It is probably the case that there were some prophets* (Mt 7:15-27; 10:41; 23:34), but it less clear that there was a group of "righteous ones" who were teachers (Mt 10:41). The leaders of this community seem to be, somewhat indirectly, the apostles. It is precisely here that we probably see history rather than transparency: the leaders of Matthew's community are not as visible through some title as they might be had the author used other titles.

This debate with Pharisaism was undoubtedly over the place of Jesus and over the proper interpretation of the law of Moses. Thus the early chapters of Matthew seek to show that Jesus is the fulfillment of OT patterns and promises*: whatever happened to Israel has happened to Jesus (Mt 4:1-11). Jesus is in every sense Jewish, but he is also more than his Jewish patterns (e.g., Mt 12:1-8). Further, it is to Jesus that the community of Matthew looks for the proper interpretation of the Law (Mt 5:17-48). Jesus is not against the Law or the Prophets: he fulfills the Law and the Prophets by bringing them to their fullest expression in both his person and teaching* (Mt 5:17-20). It seems reasonable to think that the debates preserved in the First Gospel are the debates Matthew's community had with Pharisaism: thus they fought over at least the issues of the sabbath (Mt 12:1-8), of table purity (Mt 9:9-13; *see* Food Laws) and of taxation (Mt 17:24-27).

3.5. The Community's Meeting Place. Whatever we make of the acerbic nature of Matthew's polemic with the Pharisees (Mt 23), the use of the expression "their synagogues" seems to suggest that Matthew's community was no longer meeting in the synagogue. This, however, does not mean that the community was *extra muros,* since this separation would be only a physical one. The real issue is religious, and Matthew's Gospel does not indicate that the followers of Jesus are a different religion. They may be the church (Mt 16:18; 18:17), but "church" here probably means only a newly defined group that fulfills the OT concept of remnant. Thus the best model is seeing Matthew's community meeting across the street from the synagogue (separated) but contending that they are the rightful members of that synagogue from which they have been expelled *(intra muros).* They did not leave; they were forced out. But in being forced out, they continued to think of themselves as Jews, as true Jews, as the fulfilled Judaism, the Judaism that brought into reality the dreams of their prophets.

See also GALILEAN CHRISTIANITY; JEWISH CHRISTIANITY.

BIBLIOGRAPHY. D. L. Balch, ed., *Social History of the Matthean Community: Cross-Disciplinary Approaches* (Minneapolis: Fortress, 1991); W. D. Davies, *The Setting of the Sermon on the Mount* (Cambridge: Cambridge University Press, 1966); J. D. G. Dunn, *The Partings of the Ways: Between Christianity and Judaism and their Significance for the Character of Christianity* (Philadelphia: Trinity Press International, 1991);

M. Goodman, "Nerva, the fiscus Judaicus and Jewish Identity," *JRS* 79 (1989) 40-44; D. A. Hagner, *Matthew 1-13* (WBC; Dallas: Word, 1993), lxv-lxxi; idem, "The *Sitz im Leben* of the Gospel of Matthew," in SBLSP (1985) 243-69; R. Hummel, *Die Auseinandersetzung zwischen Kirche und Judentum im Matthäusevangelium* (BET 33; Munich: Christian Kaiser, 1963); G. D. Kilpatrick, *The Origins of the Gospel According to St. Matthew* (Oxford: Clarendon, 1946), esp. 101-23, 124-34; J. D. Kingsbury, "Conclusion: Analysis of a Conversation" in *Social History*, ed. Balch, 259-69; idem, *Matthew as Story* (2d ed.; Philadelphia: Fortress, 1988) 147-60; U. Luz, "The Disciples in the Gospel According to Matthew" in *The Interpretation of Matthew*, ed. G. N. Stanton (IRT 3; Philadelphia: Fortress, 1983) 98-128; S. McKnight, "A Loyal Critic: Matthew's Polemic with Judaism in Theological Perspective" in *The New Testament and Anti-Semitism*, ed. C. A. Evans and D. A. Hagner (Minneapolis: Fortress, 1993) 55-79; idem, "New Shepherds for Israel: A Historical and Critical Study of Matthew 9:35-11:1" (unpublished Ph.D. dissertation, University of Nottingham, 1986); J. P. Meier, "Matthew, Gospel of," *ABD* 4:622-41; J. P. Meier and R. E. Brown, *Antioch and Rome: NT Cradles of Catholic Christianity* (New York: Paulist, 1983); J. A. Overman, *Matthew's Gospel and Formative Judaism: The Social World of the Matthean Community* (Minneapolis: Fortress, 1990); A. J. Saldarini, *Matthew's Christian-Jewish Community* (CSHJ; Chicago: University of Chicago Press, 1994); A. F. Segal, "Matthew's Jewish Voice" in *Social History*, ed. Balch, 3-37; G. N. Stanton, *A Gospel for a New People: Studies in Matthew* (Edinburgh: T & T Clark, 1992); idem, "The Origin and Purpose of Matthew's Gospel: Matthean Scholarship from 1945 to 1980," *ANRW* 2.25.3 (1984) 1889-1951; G. Strecker, *Der Weg der Gerechtigkeit* (FRLANT 82; 3d ed.; Göttingen: Vandenhoeck & Ruprecht, 1971); W. Trilling, *Das wahre Israel: Studien zur Theologie des Matthäus Evangeliums* (SANT 10; 3d ed.; Munich: Kösel Verlag, 1964); R. Walker, *Die Heilsgeschichte im ersten Evangelium* (FRLANT 91; Göttingen: Vandenhoeck & Ruprecht, 1967); L. M. White, "Crisis Management and Boundary Maintenance: The Social Location of the Matthean Community" in *Social History*, ed. Balch, 211-47.   S. McKnight

MELCHIZEDEK

Melchizedek is an enigmatic figure who appears only briefly in Genesis and is thereafter named only once in the OT. But he became the subject of much speculation in Judaism, as the Dead Sea Scrolls in particular prove; and Hebrews pays considerable attention to him in developing its distinctive christology.

1. The Old Testament
2. The Dead Sea Scrolls
3. *2 Enoch*
4. Hebrews

1. The Old Testament.

1.1. Genesis. In Genesis 14:17-20, after Abraham* defeats Chedorlaomer, the patriarch is met by the king of Sodom and (heretofore unmentioned) Melchizedek, king of Salem (= Jerusalem; cf. Ps 76:2). The latter, "a priest of God Most High," brings out bread and wine and utters a blessing, after which Abraham gives Melchizedek "a tenth of everything"—or vice versa: the Hebrew simply reads, "and he gave him." Melchizedek then disappears from the narrative as suddenly as he appeared.

1.2. Psalm 110. Melchizedek is named only one other time in the OT, in Ps 110:4. Here, in what appears to be a royal psalm of coronation, the Davidic king in Jerusalem is said to be "a priest for ever after the order of Melchizedek." In other words, because Melchizedek was a king and priest in Jerusalem, the Jewish king, who also has priestly functions, can be likened to Melchizedek. The Psalm came to read as properly messianic (as in the NT and the targum).

2. The Dead Sea Scrolls.

Although 1QapGen 22:14-17 retells the story of Melchizedek without elaboration, in 11QMelchizedek (a fragmentary eschatological midrash from the first century A.D. or B.C.) Melchizedek ceases to be an earthly figure. He rather becomes an angel* called "the heavenly one" (*'lōhîm*, cf. Ps 82:1), and he is a central figure in the eschatological drama. At the end of days he proclaims release to the captives (11QMelch. 2:6; cf. Lev 15:10), exacts "the vengeance of the judgements of God" (11QMelch 2:13) and delivers the sons of light from Belial (11QMelch 2:13).

Although the text is fragmentary, Melchizedek seems also to be named in 4QNAmram[b] frag. 3:2: "[My] three names [are Michael, Prince of Light, and Melchizedek]." The speaker is the "watcher" who rules over all the light and "all that is of God," including the saints. His opponent is Belial, the prince of darkness, whose other name is Melchireša'. If the text cited is correctly restored, then Melchizedek is here identified with the archangel Michael as in the *Zohar* and other medieval Jewish sources. (According to Jerome *Ep.* 73.2, already Origen and Didymus thought Melchizedek to be an angel.) The identification is consistent with the significant resemblances between the two: they are both angelic beings and priests (for Michael see, e.g., *'Abot R. Nat.* 34; *b. Ḥag.* 12b; *b. Zebah.* 62a) who protect Israel (cf. Dan 10:13, 21; *1 En.* 20:5), play eschatological roles (cf. Dan 12:1-3), head angelic forces (cf. 1QM 17:7), war against demonic foes (cf. Rev 12:7-9) and defeat Belial (cf. 1QM 17:5-8). Moreover, if in 1QM 17:5-8 the eschatological war establishes the reign of Michael, in 11QMelch Melchizedek reigns in the latter days.

It is also likely that Melchizedek is referred to in 4Q401 11 3 and 4Q401 22 3, both fragments of 4QShirot 'Olat Ha-Shabbat. The former refers to "[Melchi]zedek, priest in the assemb[ly]." The line alludes to Psalm 82:1, which in 11QMelch 2:10 is applied to Melchizedek. We likely have here the identification of Melchizedek (= Michael) with the highest archangel in charge of the heavenly priesthood. As in 11QMelchizedek, he is elevated over the angelic court.

The sources of Melchizedek's exaltation are unclear. One guesses that the enigmatic appearance in Genesis of a priest without a genealogy (cf. Heb 7:3) stimulated reflection; so too the circumstance that Abraham, the ancestor of the Levites, offered him a tithe: this might suggest the superiority of Melchizedek's priestly order over that of the Levites (cf. Heb 7:4-10). But Psalm 110:4 especially must have provoked thought. At least it is plain that some eventually came to understand "priest of the Most High" to mean that Melchizedek serves in the heavenly temple. It is also probable that "priest forever" was taken to imply Melchizedek's immortality, and so his being something other than a man. And once he was thought of as a heavenly figure, his status as king (Gen 14:18) could further lead to speculation about an eschatological role.

3. 2 Enoch.

The Dead Sea Scrolls are not the only evidence that Melchizedek was the subject of speculation in early Judaism. The Jewish prayers preserved in *Apostolic Constitutions* 7.39.3; 8.5.3; and 8.12.23 name Melchizedek alongside OT worthies such as Abraham, David and Job. Plainly these prayers presuppose traditions beyond those in Genesis; and the sometime rabbinic animosity toward Melchizedek is likewise telling (cf. *b. Ned.* 32b and the probable excision of the Melchizedek story from *Jub.* 13:25). Also revealing are the closing chapters of *2 Enoch*; these relate the story of Melchizedek's birth. Sothonim, the wife of Nir, grandson of Methuselah and brother of Noah, is found to be pregnant in her old age. (This is not a virginal conception.) She has not slept with her husband, who therefore shuns her—until it is revealed to him that her conception has a supernatural cause. When the time for birth comes, Sothonim dies; but the baby emerges from her dead body fully clothed—with "the badge of priesthood on his chest"—and fully developed physically. He even speaks and blesses the Lord. Later he is carried away by an angel to paradise so that he will not be destroyed by Noah's flood.

Although *2 Enoch* 68—73 appears to be an integral part of the original work, unfortunately the date and place of the writing as a whole are unknown: we may or may not be dealing with pre-Christian tradition. There is seemingly in any case no other trace of the strange story in old Jewish or Christian literature, so it would be hazardous to base much upon it.

4. Hebrews.

Unless the Gnostic* book named "Melchizedek" be dated to the first half of the second century, before Justin Martyr (*Dial. Tryph.* 33; 118) the only Christian work of our period to name Melchizedek is Hebrews.* The book several times refers to Jesus as "a priest forever after the order of Melchizedek" (Heb 5:6, 10; 6:20; 7:17). And Hebrews 7 is largely an exposition of this line from Ps 110:4, which is taken to establish the existence of a non-Aaronic priesthood in contrast to a mortal levitical priesthood.

Melchizedek is the king of righteousness* and king of peace* and a priest* without beginning or end. In all this he resembles Jesus, his antitype. With such resemblance established, three main arguments follow, designed to show the superiority of Jesus' priesthood, gained by the power of an indestructible life (Heb 7:6), to that of Aaron. Melchizedek's lack of genealogy (this suggests immortality), his reception of tithes (the inferior pays tithes to the superior) and his blessing of Abraham (the inferior is blessed by the superior) all prove Melchizedek to be greater than the Levites, the descendants of Abraham; and because Jesus belongs not to the Levitical priesthood but to the order of Melchizedek (cf. Psalm 110), he too must be superior to the Levites.

Although Hebrews 7:1-2 simply summarizes Genesis 14:17-20, the argument is informed by postbiblical tradition. The translation of Melchizedek's name by "king of righteousness" (Heb 7:2; cf. Josephus *Ant.* 1.10.2 §180 and the targums on Gen 14:18), his status as "king of peace" (Heb 7:2; cf. Philo *Leg. All.* 3.79) and his reception of tithes from Abraham (rather than vice versa: Heb 7:4; cf. 1QapGen 22:17; Josephus *Ant.* 1.10.2 §181) reflect extrabiblical tradition. It may also be that, even if Hebrews 7:2-3 does not (as has been thought) borrow from a non-Christian source, the words depend upon pre-Christian tradition about Melchizedek. "Without father or mother or genealogy" might in fact refer to Melchizedek's status as a heavenly being (cf. the Dead Sea Scrolls). So too his continuing as a priest "forever." The view (still held by Horton) that Hebrews derives Melchizedek's eternal priesthood from Psalm 110:4 and the failure of Genesis to narrate the priest's death (according to the principle that what is not in the Torah is not in the world) is now problematic. We have pre-Christian sources in which Melchizedek is an angelic being without beginning or end of days, and this raises the strong possibility that the argument in Hebrews presupposes the identification of Melchizedek with a heavenly high priest (so Kobelski). There is to be sure no evidence of direct dependence upon the Qumran materials. But the Scrolls and Hebrews both appear to be heirs to related Jewish speculation about the enigmatic Melchizedek.

See also ANGELS, HEAVENLY BEINGS, ANGEL CHRISTOLOGY; HEBREWS; PRIEST, HIGH PRIEST; QUMRAN.

BIBLIOGRAPHY. J. A. Fitzmyer, "Further Light on Melchizedek from Qumran Cave 11"; " 'Now this Melchizedek . . .' (Heb 7:1)" in *Essays on the Semitic Background of the New Testament* (SBLSBS 5; Missoula: Scholars Press, 1974) 187-204; 221-43; F. L. Horton, Jr., *The Melchizedek Tradition* (SNTSMS 30; Cambridge: University Press, 1976); M. de Jonge and A. S. van der Woude, "11QMelchizedek and the New Testament," *NTS* 12 (1966) 301-26; P. J. Kobelski, *Melchizedek and Melchireša'* (CBQMS 10; Washington, DC: Catholic Biblical Association, 1981); J. T. Milik, "*Milkî-ṣedeq* et *Milkî-rešd* dans les ancients écrits juifs et chrétiens," *JJS* 23 (1972) 95-144; A. S. van der Woude, "Melchizedek als himmlische Erlösergestalt in den neugefundenen eschatologischen Midraschim aus Qumran-Höhle XI," *OTS* 14 (1965) 354-73.   D. C. Allison Jr

MELITO OF SARDIS

Melito was bishop of Sardis, a prominent city of Asia Minor, during the second half of the second century A.D. He was a theologian, an eloquent preacher and a prolific writer (Eusebius *Hist. Eccl.* 4.26.1-3), yet only fragments of his works have been preserved.

1. The Paschal Homily
2. Rhetorical Context
3. Christology

1. The Paschal Homily.

An incomplete manuscript of Melito's Paschal Homily *(Peri Pascha),* the oldest Christian Easter sermon, came to light in 1940 (Bonner). In 1960 another manuscript of this sermon, one that was almost complete and in excellent condition, was discovered and published (Testuz). Since then additional fragments of *Peri Pascha* have surfaced, written in Coptic, Georgian, Latin, Syriac and Greek. Consequently all lacunae have been filled, and the homily has been reconstructed (Blank, Hall, Hawthorne, Perler).

This sermon of Melito may have been part of the ancient Easter service of the Asian church, a service that likely began with a vigil that included a homily, a baptismal* service, a love* feast and the celebration of the Eucharist that took place in the early hours of Easter morning (cf. *Ep. Apos.* 15). It is reasonable to believe that sermons in the Easter vigil were based on the OT Passover text. As the Jews annually recounted the events of the exodus and pondered the significance of the lamb* and the redemption* it effected, so Christian pastors also read from Exodus and preached about a redemption greater than the redemption from Egypt and about the true Passover lamb, Jesus Christ.

Melito's homily begins, "The Scripture about the Hebrew Exodus has been read . . . but I will clearly set forth the significance of the words of this Scripture" (*Peri Pascha* 1, 11). Later he writes, "For this one [Jesus Christ], who was led away as a lamb, and who was sacrificed as a sheep, by himself delivered us from servitude to the world as from the land of Egypt, and released us from bondage to the devil as from the hand of Pharaoh, and sealed our souls by his own spirit, and the members of our bodies by his own blood" (*Peri Pascha* 68).

2. Rhetorical Context.

When Christianity came to Asia Minor it came to that part of the Roman Empire where education was widespread and intellectual culture was well developed. Education and culture were dominated by grammarians and rhetoricians; rhetorical schools flourished, each with its own distinctive style. This style was shaped by those who appreciated an oratory rich in metaphor, figures of speech, poetic elements and staccato-like rhythms.

Not until the second century and later did the popular rhetoric of the day begin to influence Christian preaching,* and even then it was slow in taking hold. The oldest Christian sermon in postapostolic literature, the second letter of Clement of Rome* (c. A.D. 120-170), displays simplicity in its composition.

For years scholars considered that Hippolytus (d. A.D. 235) was the first Christian preacher to introduce secular rhetoric into the church. The discovery of Melito's Paschal Homily, however, makes it clear that Hippolytus was not the first Christian writer or preacher who attempted to put the Christian message in a form that would be appreciated and welcomed by its hearers. By examining the features of Melito's homily it becomes clear that Melito was influenced by his environment and in harmony with his culture. He was also familiar with the Bible, the form of Jewish Passover Haggadah, and philosophy and oratory. *Peri Pascha* may have been the first serious attempt to employ contemporary communication techniques as a tool for spreading the gospel* (see Hawthorne 1969, 36, 37, 188-255).

The homily shows Melito to have possessed a large vocabulary that he employed to stir the emotions of his hearers or readers. His grammar was nearly flawless; his short, rhythmic sentences were intended to create a sense of urgency; his use of figures of speech was designed to hold an audience. In addition he shows a flair for typological exegesis.

3. Christology.

Scholars have scrutinized the homily in an attempt to determine Melito's motivation for writing, concluding that his motivation was multifaceted (Norris). Yet Melito appears to have focused all his education, training and oratorical ability upon one clearly defined goal: exalting Jesus Christ, the central person in the universe and in Melito's own life and thought (*see* Christology; Exaltation).

The centrality of Jesus lay in the fact that he was more than a human being. Melito was among the first of the church fathers (*see* Apostolic Fathers) clearly to articulate the doctrine that Jesus shared two natures. He wrote, "For the one [i.e. Jesus Christ] who was born as Son, and led to slaughter as a lamb, and sacrificed as a sheep, and buried as a man, rose up from the dead as God, since he is by nature both God and man" (*Peri Pascha* 8). He alludes further to this dual nature by saying:

When the Lord had clothed himself with humanity,
And had suffered for the sake of the sufferer,
And had been bound for the sake of the imprisoned,
And had been judged for the sake of the condemned,
And buried for the sake of the one who was buried,
He rose up from the dead, and cried aloud with this voice:
Who is he who contends with me?
Let him stand in opposition to me.
I set the condemned man free.
I gave the dead life.
I raised up the one who had been entombed.
Who is my opponent?
I, he says, am the one who destroyed death,
And triumphed over the enemy,
And trampled Hades under foot,
And bound the strong one,
And carried off mankind to the heights of heaven.
I, he says, am the Christ.
(*Peri Pascha* 100-102)

The salvation* of the human race, which sin* made necessary and which Jesus Christ had achieved, inspired Melito to attribute to the resurrected* and triumphant Christ this dramatic cry:

Come to me all families of the earth!
You who have been defiled with sins.
Come and receive forgiveness for your sins.
I am your forgiveness.
I am your ransom.
I am your light.
I am your savior. I am your resurrection. . . .
I am the one who leads you up to the heights of heaven.
I am the one who will show you the eternal Father. (*Peri Pascha* 103)

Clearly Melito believed in Christ as the Person of cosmic significance, the Savior of the world, and he crafted this sermon to proclaim Christ's worth and work. *Peri Pascha* has the power to arrest even the attention of a modern audience and make savingly clear to those who hear it the essence of the gospel.

See also APOSTOLIC FATHERS; HYMNS; WORSHIP AND LITURGY.

BIBLIOGRAPHY. J. Blank, *Meliton von Sardes, Vom Passa* (Freiburg: Lambertus Verlag, 1963); C. Bonner, *Melito of Sardis: The Homily on the Passion and Some Fragments of Ezekiel* (Studies and Documents 12; Philadelphia: University of Pennsylvania, 1940); S. G. Hall, *Melito of Sardis, On Pascha and Fragments: Texts and Translations* (Oxford: Clarendon, 1979); G. F. Hawthorne, "Melito of Sardis: His Rhetoric and Theology" (unpublished Ph.D. dissertation, University of Chicago, 1969); idem, "A New English Translation of Melito's Paschal Homily" in *Current Issues in Biblical and Patristic Interpretation,* ed. G. F. Hawthorne (Grand Rapids: Eerdmans, 1975) 147-75; B. Lohse, *Die Passa-Homilie des Bischofs Meliton von Sardes* (Textus Minores 24; Leiden: E. J. Brill, 1958); F. W. Norris, "Melito's Motivation," *ATR* 68 (1986) 16-24; O. Perler, *Méliton de Sardes, Sur la Pâque et Fragments* (Paris: Editions du Cerf, 1966); J. S. Sibinga, "Melito of Sardis, the Artist and His Text," *VC* 24 (1970) 81-104; M. Testuz, *Papyrus Bodmer XIII: Méliton de Sardes Homélie sur la Pâque* (Geneva: Bibliotheca Bodmeriana, 1960).   G. F. Hawthorne

MERCY

The early Christian understanding of mercy has its roots in the Old Testament, but it is also shaped by the teaching and example of Jesus (*see DJG,* Mercy). In the later NT and apostolic fathers, as in Jesus and Paul (*see DPL,* Mercy), the primary accent is on God's* mercy toward sinners, from which human mercy toward others is derived.

1. Background of Meaning.
2. Hebrews
3. James
4. 1 Peter, 2 John, Jude
5. Apostolic Fathers

1. Background of Meaning.
In the NT and apostolic fathers, *eleos,* the Greek word frequently translated into English as "mercy," is primarily used in the sense of compassion, pity, sympathy or clemency (BAGD, 250; Esser, 594). The word occurs mainly in the context of ethical exhortation. In addition, since ethics is related to relationships, *eleos* appears especially where person-to-person relationships are involved, whether it is God having compassion or pity on a person, or individuals having compassion toward one another (Mt 9:13; 12:7). The background of this NT use of *eleos* seems to lie primarily in the OT idea of *ḥesed* (*eleos* is frequently used for *ḥesed* in the LXX), which, depending on its context, can be translated as "mercy," "kindness," "faithfulness" or "steadfast love" (see Sakenfeld; *see DJG,* Mercy §1).

The OT idea of *ḥesed* (Bultmann, 479) is to be understood in the context of a covenantal agreement between two parties, a greater with a lesser party, usually God and Israel. Given the likelihood of covenantal default, the stronger party, showing *ḥesed,* provides resources to the weaker party for the sake of preserving the covenant. Fidelity to the covenantal partner becomes more important than the debt itself. Thus the Hebrew notion of divine, covenant *ḥesed* very likely stands behind this canonical and apostolic idea of *eleos,* "mercy." This OT tradition shows how *ḥesed/eleos* acts as a balance to divine judgment,* as that which restrains the wrath of God. It also acts as grace.* It can mean unmerited forgiveness.* Sometimes it appears as deliverance. It is always related to God's unsolicited love and nurturing care of Israel. For example, in Psalm 136:1 God's mercy delivers, it reaches down to the poor, it is compassionate grace, and it elicits thanksgiving from those who are blessed. In short, the canonical and apostolic roots of *eleos* are primarily found in the OT, but we should not rule out or ignore the understanding of mercy in Greek and Roman thought.

In its classical Greek background, *eleos* could carry the sense of an emotion and its related action aroused by observing the affliction of another (Bultmann, 477; cf. *Mart. Pol.* 2.2). But the idea of a god or goddess being merciful, or showing clemency (Lat. *clementia*), though not unheard of, was not developed in any notable manner in popular pagan theology or by the philosophers (see Harris for evidence). "The most common picture was of gods who were more to be feared than loved, more malevolent than beneficent. . . . The gods must be propitiated, won over, persuaded to be more kindly, and the fear of them which lay behind many rituals accorded ill with ideas of divine mercy" (Harris, 102-3). While an emperor might display mercy, or clemency, this was not because he had received divine mercy but because he, like the gods, was in the position to dispense his beneficence, and clemency would solidify and perpetuate his power among those who received it (see Harris, 98-99, on Seneca *De Clem.*). As E. A. Judge writes of classical antiquity, "the cry of the undeserving for mercy remained unanswered, whether it arose from guilt in the inner man, or from the evil of society at large" (Judge, 107).

2. Hebrews.

Although the term *eleos* occurs only once in Hebrews,* where the author speaks of the community receiving mercy (Heb 4:16), within the context of the letter's discourse various facets of this divine and priestly* mercy are suggested. In the immediate context mercy is closely linked with grace.* It issues from the "throne of grace," and both mercy and grace are set in parallel formation as gifts received "in the time of need." In the broader context of Hebrews, mercy appears as that divine ability to forgive and to set aside wrath.* In this context mercy is also an ethical incentive to hold fast the faith* (Heb 4:14). Mercy is made available by a heavenly high priest (Heb 9:11), who being taken from among humans (Heb 4:15—5:1), is able to sympathize (*sympathēsai*) with their weaknesses and be merciful to them (Heb 4:15).

The pastoral problem of apostasy* is addressed by ethical exhortation in Hebrews. The author makes it clear that choosing Christ, as opposed to returning to the old religion, was a pivotal decision. Rejecting Christ would incur judgment "without mercy" (*chōris oiktirmōn*, Heb 10:28, where *oiktirmos* carries a sense very close to *eleos*), pity or reprieve, as under the Mosaic covenant. The threat of mercy withheld could be seen as both a deterrent to apostasy and a threat of actual judgment.

In Hebrews the continuity between the OT and the NT ideas of mercy is apparent. The new way of life flows out of the same God who showed his mercy to Israel.

3. James.

For James* Christian faith goes beyond "saying" (Jas 2:18) that one has faith: Faith is made perfect by (1) works of mercy (Jas 2:15); (2) justice to the poor (Jas 2:6; 5:1-6); and (3) the systematic dismantling of economic (Jas 2:2), cultural (Jas 2:3) and even racial prejudice (Jas 2:6, 8, 9). As James uses it, *eleos* has an OT prophetic ring. In contrast with Paul's interpretation of Abraham* in Galatians 3 and Romans 4, James views Abraham as the father of works, not "faith only" (Jas 2:21-26). It is in this context of practical Christianity that *eleos* appears four times in James. Once in James we find the negative form, *aneleos*, "without mercy" (Jas 2:13, its only occurrence in the NT, but cf. Heb 10:13).

Ethical exhortation frames the context of the use of *eleos* in James. James 2:6 and 13 show that judgment, the absence of mercy, awaits those who despise the poor. Mercy must be a characteristic of the Christian life, and in order to receive mercy, one must demonstrate mercy to others. The Lord's own exhortation, "Do not judge, so that you may not be judged" (Mt 7:1; Lk 6:36-38, NRSV), finds its echo in James 2:13: "For judgment will be without mercy to anyone who has shown no mercy; mercy triumphs over judgment" (NRSV). As a characteristic of the Christian life, mercy comes from above as wisdom* (Jas 3:17) from God. This special wisdom is a life of faith, full of works of human mercy: (1) caring for the fatherless (Jas 1:27); (2) helping the widow (Jas 1:27); (3) respecting the poor (Jas 2:1-8); (4) feeding the hungry and clothing the naked (Jas 2:1-16). In this practical, ethical context, mercy is seen as compassion for others.

4. 1 Peter, 2 John, Jude.

In 1 Peter the idea of mercy comes into immediate ethical focus. The mercy referred to in 1 Peter 1:3 is no ordinary mercy. This is "great mercy" from God, especially related to resurrection* power (1 Pet 1:3), for a holy* life (1 Pet 1:15), for self-control (1 Pet 1:13), for imitating* Christ (1 Pet 2:21). This "great mercy" (a phrase used only here in the entire NT) is the ethical basis for the Christian life. Thus the idea of "great mercy" is here to be understood in terms of empowerment for righteousness,* and in this sense it may be seen as grace. It is a great and encouraging mercy to Christians scattered throughout the eastern Mediterranean world who perhaps face some form of proportionally "great" persecution.*

The verb *eleaō* appears twice in 1 Peter 2:10: "once you had not received mercy, but now you have received mercy" (NRSV; based on Hosea 1:6, 9; 2:1, 23). The divine mercy which in 1 Peter 1:3 has given birth to a new humanity now calls this humanity to a new way of life (1 Pet 2:9). Rather than being the object of wrath, this new humanity, because of mercy, is now "a chosen generation, a royal priesthood, a holy nation, a people of [God's] own" (1 Pet 2:9). The ethical context of mercy calls this new people to "good works," since mercy is the basis for obedience.* The imperative is based on the indicative: what believers must do is based on what God has already done (cf. Rom 12:1; Betz).

In 2 John 3 and Jude 2 we find *eleos* used in a customary Christian epistolary greeting. In Jude 21 the readers are urged to "look forward to the mercy *[eleos]* of our Lord Jesus Christ that leads to eternal life" (NRSV). It is notable that Jesus, rather than God, is said to be the dispenser of mercy. The verb *eleaō* appears in Jude 22 and 23, though the textual evidence is problematic for both verses, with some texts reading *elegchete* ("convince") instead of *eleeite* ("have mercy"). Nevertheless, a good case can be made for *eleaō* being the original reading (see commentaries). Those who await the mercy of the Lord Jesus Christ are to have mercy on those who are wavering or are even engulfed in the flames of destruction.

5. Apostolic Fathers.

For Clement* *eleos* can mean something like divine favor. It is almost as if an errant slave is on his knees entreating or begging for a king's forgiveness, when suddenly the great monarch turns with open arms toward the slave. Such is the face of mercy in *1 Clement* 9.1: "Let us be obedient, then, to that sovereign and glorious will. Let us entreat his mercy and goodness, casting ourselves upon his compassion" (cf. *1 Clem.* 22.8, citing Ps 32:10, where *eleos* = *ḥesed; Hermas Vis.* 3.9.8). For Barnabas,* however, the new dispensation transcends the old (*see* Old Testament in Apostolic Fathers). The OT promise* that God would reward* with mercy Israel's keeping of the Sabbath (*Barn.* 15.2; cf. Jer 17:24-25) is transcended in Christ. True Sabbath keeping will only be possible when "all things have been made new by the Lord" (*Barn.* 15.7).

Mercy has an ethical thrust in *1 Clement* when the Corinthians are reminded that obedient faith renounces arrogance and embraces humility and mercy toward others. Echoes of the Lord's own words on mercy (Mt 5:7; 7:1) and forgiveness are heard in Clement and Polycarp's exhortations: "Be merciful . . . that you may obtain mercy" (*1 Clem.* 13.2; Pol. *Phil.* 2.3). In other words, humility and obedience in human relations are required in order to receive forgiveness and mercy from God. Ethical exhortation also forms the context as both the *Didache* and *Barnabas,* in charting the doctrine of the "Two Ways," include being "unmerciful toward the poor" among their lists of vices (*Did.* 5.2; *Barn.* 20.2; *see* Virtues and Vices). By way of contrast, *Didache* 3.8 mentions being "merciful" (*eleēmōn*) in a list of virtues (echoing Mt 5:7).

Clement can point to a story of humility rewarded by divine mercy in the humble king David whom God anointed with eternal mercy (*en eleei aiōniō echrisa auton, 1 Clem.* 18.1). David obtained the divine favor of the King of the Universe. And instead of becoming arrogant about his status as favored, David himself begged God for mercy: "Have mercy upon me *[Eleēson me],* O God, according to your great mercy *[kata to mega eleos sou]*" (Ps 51:1). Elsewhere Clement entreats God in prayer for mercy on behalf of the lowly (*1 Clem.* 59.4).

Mercy is used in *1 Clement* 28.1 in a manner consistent with the canonical literature: believers should "leave off foul desires of evil deeds" that they may be "sheltered by his mercy from the judgments to come." Mercy restrains God's wrath. Repentance from sin in the shadow of divine wrath is again the background for mercy in *1 Clement* 48.1.

In a twist on the theme of mercy, a stream of

early Christian tradition sees divine chastening and even martyrdom* as occasions of severe mercy. The righteous person who is reproved is corrected in mercy (*1 Clem.* 56.4-5). In this view of mercy Clement follows the apostolic tradition reflected in a passage such as Hebrews 12:6: "Do not lose heart when he rebukes you, because the Lord disciplines those he loves." As discipline is divine love in Hebrews, so martyrdom is an affirmation of divine mercy in Ignatius's *Letter to the Romans,* for it is the means by which Ignatius attains to God (Ign. *Rom.* 9.2; cf. 8.3). In a powerfully moving phrase, Ignatius reflects this understanding of martyrdom's mercy: "I am God's wheat, ground up by the teeth of wild beasts, so that I might be the pure bread of Christ" (Ign. *Rom.* 4.1). Ironically, however, in writing to the Ephesians Ignatius contrasts his own state of danger and condemnation with that of his readers who have "obtained mercy" in their physical safety and freedom (Ign. *Eph.* 12.1).

Finally, mercy occurs in the apostolic fathers in introductory letter greetings (e.g., Ign. *Rom.*; Ign. *Phld.*; Pol. *Phil.*) or conclusion (Ign. *Smyrn.* 12.1). In these contexts, as in the canonical epistles, mercy is part of a formulaic wish for God's blessings.*

In conclusion the canonical and apostolic literature complement each other in their uses of mercy. In both bodies of literature the term largely appears in ethical contexts as divine encouragement to ethical action and as discouraging disobedience. It also refers to the grace of martyrdom as mercy from God. But whether it is compassion from God or person-to-person pity, mercy has its roots in the OT idea of the infinite love of God for a helpless and needy covenantal partner.

See also FORGIVENESS; GRACE; LOVE; VIRTUES AND VICES.

BIBLIOGRAPHY. F. I. Andersen, "Yahweh, the Kind and Sensitive God" in *God Who Is Rich in Mercy,* ed. P. T. O'Brien and D. G. Peterson (Sydney: Lancer, 1986) 41-48; H. D. Betz, "The Foundations of Christian Ethics According to Romans 12:1-2" in *Witness and Existence,* ed. P. E. Devenish and G. L. Goodwin (Chicago: University of Chicago Press, 1989) 55-72; R. Bultmann, "ἔλεος κτλ," *TDNT* 2:477-87; idem, *Theology of the New Testament* (2 vols.; New York: Scribner's, 1951, 1955); H.-H. Esser, "Mercy, Compassion," *NIDNTT* 2:593-601; B. F. Harris, "The Idea of Mercy and Its Graeco-Roman Context" in *God Who Is Rich in Mercy,* ed. P. T. O'Brien and D. G. Peterson (Sydney: Lancer, 1986) 89-105; E. A. Judge, "The Quest for Mercy in Late Antiquity" in *God Who Is Rich in Mercy,* ed. P. T. O'Brien and D. G. Peterson (Sydney: Lancer, 1986) 107-21; G. W. H. Lampe, *A Patristic Greek Lexicon* (Oxford: Oxford University Press, 1976); K. D. Sakenfeld, "Love (OT)," *ABD* 4:375-81; idem, *The Meaning of Hesed in the Hebrew Bible: A New Inquiry* (HSM 17; Missoula, MT: Scholars Press, 1978); N. H. Snaith, *The Distinctive Ideas of the Old Testament* (London: Epworth, 1944); F. Staudinger, "ἔλεος κτλ," *EDNT* 1:429-31.   I. Canales

MESSIAH. *See* CHRIST; CHRISTOLOGY; KINGDOM OF GOD.

MIDRASH. *See* JUDAISM, POST-A.D. 70.

MILK, SOLID FOOD

The contrasting designations "milk" and "solid food" are metaphorical expressions used to describe spiritual nourishment. They naturally indicate accompanying stages of spiritual growth in Christians who have experienced a spiritual new birth.*

1. Terminology
2. Background
3. Necessity of Milk
4. From Milk to Solid Food
5. Milk and Solid Food in the Apostolic Fathers

1. Terminology.

The term *milk* occurs forty-eight times in the Bible, but the NT term for milk, *gala,* occurs five times (1 Cor 3:2; 9:7; Heb 5:12, 13; 1 Pet 2:2). Only in 1 Corinthians 9:7 is *gala* used of literal milk. The other four times it is used metaphorically. The term occurs only in the *Epistle of Barnabas** in the apostolic fathers,* four times citing the OT expression for the promised land as "the land flowing with milk and honey" (*Barn.* 6.8, 10, 13, 17), which becomes the basis for discussing milk as a metaphor for Christian spiritual nourishment (*Barn.* 6.17).

Two primary terms, *brōma (brōsis)* and *trophē,* are used to designate "food" in the NT. *Brōma* occurs fifteen times, three of which are metaphorical uses (Jn 4:34; 1 Cor 3:2; 10:3—"spiritually typical" might be a better designation for the latter), while *trophē* occurs sixteen times, two of which are metaphorical (Heb 5:12, 14). The adjective *stereos* ("firm, solid") occurs four times in the NT (2 Tim 2:19; Heb 5:12, 14; 1 Pet 5:9). Two of those four are linked with *trophē* to give us the metaphorical expression "solid food" *(hē sterea trophē)*, which contrasts with "milk" *(gala,* Heb 5:12, 14).

These terms for food are also used by the apostolic fathers: *brōma* occurs only three times but is used both literally (Ign. *Trall.* 2.3; *Barn.* 10.9-10) and metaphorically *(Barn.* 10.9), while *trophē* occurs twelve times, ten times referring to literal food (*1 Clem.* 20.4; Ign. *Rom.* 7.3; *Did.* 10.3; 13.1-2; *Barn.* 10.4, 11; *Herm. Vis.* 3.9.3; *Diogn.* 9.6) and twice referring to metaphorical food (Ign. *Trall.* 6.1; *Did.* 10.3).

2. Background.
While the metaphors "milk" and "solid food" are found abundantly in the Greek ethical* tradition (e.g., the Stoics), the pedagogical emphasis appears to draw more upon an OT usage (contra Williamson). "Food" and "drink" are important metaphors in both the OT and NT. Isaiah rebukes those who spend their money on what cannot satisfy. The wine and milk and bread of which he speaks will delight one's soul; hence, "seek the Lord while he may be found" (Is 55:1-6). The godly thirst for God* (Ps 42:2; 63:1; 143:6) and thirst after wisdom (Sir 51:24-25).

Jesus' allusion to himself as the bread of life (Jn 6) draws upon one of the chief metaphorical uses of food in Scripture. Israel ate manna in the wilderness, to which Paul refers as "spiritual food" *(pneumatikon brōma,* 1 Cor 10:3; cf. Deut 8:3; Mt 4:4 par. Lk 4:4), quite likely a typological reference to the Lord's Supper* (Fee, 446-47). Jesus gave his body and blood as the necessary sacrifice* so that those who eat his flesh and drink his blood would have eternal life* and never want again (Jn 6:25-59).

Jesus also said, "My food is to do the will of him who sent me and to complete his work" (Jn 4:34). Jesus is not disparaging material food but rather is emphasizing that even as literal food sustains and satisfies one's physical mission in life, so the greatest sustenance and satisfaction of the spiritual life is to carry out God's will and work in this world.

3. Necessity of Milk.
Peter introduced the concept of spiritual new birth with the compound verb *anagennan* ("to

give new birth," "to be born anew"; (1 Pet 1:3, 23). He continues that theme with the metaphor "newborn babies" *(artigennēta brephē)* in 1 Peter 2:2 and expands the metaphor by emphasizing that "pure, spiritual milk" is a necessary nourishment for the spiritually newborn baby. A primary characteristic of a healthy new baby is its yearning for its mother's milk. Peter draws not on the smallness or innocence of the baby but on this strong and instinctive longing. Continuous nourishment from "spiritual milk" causes the newborn to grow up in its spiritual salvation* (1 Pet 2:2). Here "milk" is not set in opposition to "food" but is itself the necessary nourishment for Christians. "Pure, spiritual milk" becomes a symbol of imperishable life and divine mercy* in contrast to the perishable evil desires in which the readers had lived in ignorance (1 Pet 1:14). All Christians are to have a longing for spiritual nourishment similar to the longing of a baby for its mother's milk. The medium by which this milk is received is the proclaimed message of the gospel (1 Pet 1:25), but the milk "itself is more appropriately interpreted as the sustaining life of God given in mercy to his children" (Michaels, 88-89).

4. From Milk to Solid Food.
The author of Hebrews* has a slightly different approach to the issue of metaphorical "milk" from that of Peter. The author has expected better things of his readers than they display. They should have made more progress in the Christian life than they have. The author is disturbed by their immaturity. Enough time has transpired in their spiritual lives that by now they should qualify to be teachers. Instead they need instruction.

Milk is necessary and adequate for infants. No baby is criticized for taking milk. But when a baby grows into an adult it is absurd to envision it still feeding only on milk. Milk is insufficient for the needs of an adult. With a twist of irony, the author rebukes these believers for such an absurdity: they have had enough time in the faith to be adults feeding on solid food; instead they are still feeding on milk.

Here "milk" refers to "the basic elements of the oracles of God," which any newborn Christian is able to understand (Heb 5:12; 1 Cor 3:2). It takes no advanced spiritual skill to acquire this nourishment. Possibly a preliminary and insufficient teaching based upon the OT is meant (Lane, 140), or the entire Jewish system. In the light of the similar phrase "the basic word about Christ" (Heb 6:1), however, it more likely refers generally to the basics of Christianity, especially the fulfillment in Jesus Christ of all that God has spoken (Hughes, 190). Changing the metaphors, the author suggests that spiritual milk is necessary when the "foundation" of the Christian life is laid, the "foundation of repentance from dead works and faith toward God" (Heb 6:1; *see* Repentance), which is in apposition to the accompanying items of catechetical instruction concerning cleansing rites, laying on of hands, the resurrection* of the dead and eternal judgment.* This foundational teaching or milk develops a distinctively Christian perspective in the beginning stages of the Christian life (Heb 6:1-2).

The author is not demeaning milk. Rather, milk is insufficient for those who should be mature. The readers should have progressed to the point in their growth where they desire solid food. This is similar to the way in which Paul told the Corinthian Christians that they still could not be treated as "spiritual persons" ready for "solid food" since they still acted like "carnal" or "fleshly persons" (1 Cor 3:1-3). Solid food (*brōma*) in the Corinthian context is the hidden wisdom* of God, which is imparted by the Spirit to those who possess the mind of Christ (cf. 1 Cor 2:6-7; 12-16). Solid food (*hē sterea trophē*) in Hebrews points to the priesthood* of Christ, which is likened to the priesthood of Melchizedek* (cf. Heb 5:4-10 with the connective in Heb 5:11) and the instruction of the high-priestly office of Christ that will be provided in Hebrews 7:1—10:18 (Bruce, 108-9; Lane, 138-39). The mature person is acquainted, experienced or skilled with the "word of righteousness" (Heb 5:13), which is linked with training to distinguish between good and evil (Heb 5:14), an ethical or moral maturity.

The teaching of elementary Christian truth is described as "milk." Milk is the first teaching given to newborn Christians who had been converted through the missionary message (cf. 1 Cor 3:2). This milk was appropriate for newborn Christians (1 Pet 2:1-2). Newborn Christians are not ready for solid spiritual food, because they would not be able to handle its acquisition (chewing) or its digestion. However, there comes a point in the natural maturing process when the Christian needs solid spiritual food for full health. This solid food is advanced teaching on Christ and his sacrificial death, the full teaching of the wisdom of God and exercise of ethical discernment (Heb 5:12—6:3).

5. Milk and Solid Food in the Apostolic Fathers.
The metaphorical use of "milk" and "solid food" is similar yet somewhat different in the apostolic fathers. In the *Epistle of Barnabas* we find a use of "milk" similar to that in 1 Peter 2. The author draws upon the OT expression "land of milk and honey" to make metaphorical reference to the wisdom and understanding of the secrets of Jesus Christ, which are now the nourishment of those newly created in Christ (*Barn.* 6.8-17).

In an interesting variation Ignatius writes to the Trallians, who are mere babes, that he does not want to give them nourishment that might choke them, since they are not ready for advanced spiritual teaching (Ign. *Trall.* 5.1-2). Hence he admonishes them to take only "Christian food" (*christianē trophē*), as opposed to "every strange plant, which is heresy" (Ign. *Trall.* 6.1-2). "Food" is used to indicate nourishment for spiritual babes.

In an important passage on the practice of the Eucharist in the early church,* the author of the *Didache** gives thanks for the "spiritual food and drink" (*pneumatikēn trophēn kai poton*) that God has given for spiritual nourishment (*Did.* 10.3). This is similar to Paul's expression in 1 Corinthians 10:3 (*pneumatikon brōma*; cf. 1 Cor 10:16-18).

See also TEACHING, PARAENESIS.

BIBLIOGRAPHY. W. Bauder and H. Dropatschek, "Hunger, Thirst, Food," *NIDNTT* 2:264-73; J. Behm, "βρῶμα, βρῶσις," *TDNT* 1:642-45; F. F. Bruce, *The Epistle to the Hebrews* (NICNT; Grand Rapids: Eerdmans, 1964); G. D. Fee, *The First Epistle to the Corinthians* (NICNT; Grand Rapids: Eerdmans, 1987); P. E. Hughes, *A Commentary on the Epistle to the Hebrews* (Grand Rapids: Eerdmans, 1977); W. L. Lane, *Hebrews 1—8* (WBC; Dallas: Word, 1991); J. P. Lewis, "Food," *ZPEB* 2:581-87; J. R. Michaels, *1 Peter* (WBC; Waco, TX: Word, 1988); H. Schlier, "γάλα," *TDNT* 1:645-47; R. Williamson, *Philo and the Epistle to the Hebrews* (ALGHJ 4; Leiden: E. J. Brill, 1970). M. J. Wilkins

MILLENNIUM

Millennium refers to a thousand-year period expected by some Christian and Jewish eschatological texts as the coming, intermediate phase before the full reestablishment of God's kingdom. In the NT it is explicitly mentioned only in Revelation 20, but it may be referred to in the earlier text of 1 Corinthians 15:23-28 and the later text of 2 Peter 3:8. The millennium functions as a reward* for the servants of God* who remain faithful amid persecution,* "those who are steadfast to the end," in the words of a refrain of Revelation. Furthermore, the millennium in Revelation establishes a double contrast: between the evil one's impotence and Christ's authority* and between the evil one's destiny and the reward awaiting the saints. Interpretation of the millennium is crucial for eschatology*; the elusiveness of consensus on the meaning of the millennium is reflected in the diverse eschatological conceptions that abound.

1. Millennium in the New Testament
2. Millennium in Jewish Apocalyptic and Early Patristic Thought
3. Contemporary Interpretations of the Millennium

1. Millennium in the New Testament.

1.1. Revelation 20. Revelation 20 contains the only explicit references in the NT to a temporary, thousand-year *(chilia etē)* reign of Christ.* Revelation 20:4-6 is one of the most difficult passages in the book *(see* Revelation, Book of), but it is clear that the function of the millennium is to reward the servants of God who remain faithful through the trials of their faith.*

There are several things to note about the millennial period as it is described in Revelation 20. First, the devil is "bound" and "thrown into the pit," which is then sealed to keep him from further "deceiving the nations" during this interval (Rev 20:2-3). Second, Christ reigns throughout this era, attested by the silence and absence of the evil one's activity. Though Paul does not mention the thousand-year period, some scholars infer from 1 Corinthians 15:23-28 that he too believes in an intermediate period in which Christ "must reign until he has put all his enemies under his feet" (1 Cor 15:25).

A third thing to note about the thousand years of Revelation is that those who were martyred for their confession of Jesus reign with him during this time (Rev 20:4, 6; *see* Martyrdom). The text identifies those who reign with

Christ as martyrs, but some interpreters take this as synonymous with "all Christians" (e.g., Sweet). This in turn affects our understanding of who are "the rest of the dead" (Rev 20:5). Are they non-Christians? Or should we take the more straightforward reading that "the rest of the dead" are nonmartyrs, both Christian and non-Christian?

A fourth observation is that there is no mention of the relationship of this millennium to the time of the Second Coming of Christ *(see* Parousia). Does Christ return before or after the millennium? This question is not explicitly answered by Revelation 20.

A fifth thing to note is that the thousand years does not signify the permanent establishment of Christ's kingdom but is portrayed as a temporary government, an interregnum before the end. After this thousand-year hiatus, the devil will "be let out for a little while" (Rev 20:3, 7; cf. Rev 12:12), Christians who were not martyred for their faith will be resurrected (Rev 20:5) and ultimately the dead will be judged (Rev 20:12) and death destroyed (Rev 20:14). After that comes the eternal kingdom of God: "Then I saw a new heaven and new earth" (Rev 21:1; *see* Heaven; Judgment; Kingdom of God; Satan).

1.2. 2 Peter 3:8. In 2 Peter 3:8 there may be an implicit reference to a millennial kingdom: "But do not ignore this one fact, beloved, that with the Lord one day is like a thousand years, and a thousand years are like one day." The context suggests that 2 Peter* reflects an eschatology like that of Revelation, since here we find the readers facing doubts about Christ's second coming because they do not perceive any changes in the fabric of history (2 Pet 3:4). The author reminds them of the unpredictability of the Day of the Lord,* which comes like a bandit (2 Pet 3:10). As in Revelation, what follows is a "new heavens and a new earth, where justice dwells" (2 Pet 3:13).

Even so it appears that 2 Peter 3:8 is more likely an echo of Psalm 90:4 than of Revelation's eschatology. The emphasis in 2 Peter 3 is not on a human perception or symbol of the length of Christ's intermediate reign (as in Rev 20) but on how the vast human time line appears so brief to God. In the words of the psalmist, "For a thousand years in your sight are like yesterday when it is past, or like a watch in the night" (Ps 90:4 NRSV).

2. Millennium in Jewish Apocalyptic and Early Patristic Thought.

2.1. Millennium in Jewish Apocalyptic. Revelation 20 draws on traditional eschatological themes but construes them in a unique way. The Jewish apocalypses of this period are diverse both in themes and in literary forms (cf. *1 Enoch* 91:12-17; 4 Ezra 7:26-30; 12:31-34; *2 Apoc. Bar.* 29—30; *see* Apocalyptic). Revelation is distinctive yet indebted to its Jewish background for literary forms, theological ideas, symbolic images and the way it interprets OT texts. The relationship of Revelation to these other apocalypses is not one of literary dependence but rather a reliance on a common tradition that takes different forms in the different sources they utilize. Revelation is as similar to and different from Jewish apocalypses as they are from each other, and the differences are pronounced when we factor in the Christian orientation of Revelation. That is, the reign of the martyrs with Christ during the thousand years resembles nothing else in Jewish apocalyptic (Gourgues). John's Revelation stands distinct because of its particularity as a pastoral word to the Christian churches of Asia Minor near the end of the first Christian century (Bauckham 1993).

Similar elements of the millennial expectation of Revelation are evident in a Jewish Christian contemporaneous work. The *Ascension of Isaiah* is a Palestinian Christian addition to the Jewish *Martyrdom of Isaiah*. There the expectation of a resurgence like that of the antichrist* before the end is described. Beliar, "a king of iniquity, a murderer of his mother," will domineer and deceive just before the end of the evil age (*Asc. Isa.* 4.1-13). Then God tosses Beliar and his servants into gehenna, "and he will give rest to the pious whom he finds in the body in this world" (*Asc. Isa.* 4.15). The offer of rest turns out to be a significant characteristic of the millennial period. As in Revelation 20, the promise of the millennium is the offer of reprieve from persecution.

2.2. Resistance to and Acceptance of the Millennium in Early Patristic Thought. Papias is the first patristic thinker to espouse belief in the millennium (Irenaeus *Haer.* 5.33.4; Eusebius *Hist. Eccl.* 3.39). He explicitly taught that the thousand years is not to be taken in an allegorical sense. His witness is crucial, since he claimed to be a "hearer" of John.

Millennial teaching was not universally ac-cepted in the early church. Justin Martyr had to address the Greco-Roman audience that held that there is no resurrection* but rather an immediate ascent of the soul to heaven. Justin made it a matter of orthodox belief that there will be a millennium and a resurrection body, and he detailed the scene of the millennium as the restored Jerusalem* prophesied of old (Justin *Dial. Tryph.* 80—81). He concedes that not all Christians are of this mind, but he exhorts that "right-minded Christians" agree with him. Origen (c. 185-254) was the first orthodox patristic writer to attempt to discredit a millennial interpretation of Revelation 20:4-6.

From the *Epistle of Barnabas*★ onward, including almost all of the early church fathers, the millennial expectation was of a thousand-year period of rest within the framework of a universal week of seven thousand years. History was broken down into seven thousand-year periods paralleling the seven days of the creation story. The final period of time, the millennium, was to be a period of rest like the seventh day of creation when "God finished the work that he had done, and he rested on the seventh day" (Gen 2:2). Naturally 2 Peter 3:8 and Revelation 20 were read as a part of this dispensationalist understanding of history (e.g., *Barn.* 15.3-9). According to *Barnabas*, the millennial sabbath is followed by the "eighth day" of the new creation* (*Barn.* 15.8; cf. Irenaeus *Haer.* 5.32-39).

3. Contemporary Interpretations of the Millennium.

3.1. History of Interpretation. Since the literalism of the early church period there have been three main phases in interpreting the millennium. (1) The allegorical or spiritual interpretation of the thousand-year reign was adopted by the most influential exegetes from the fourth to the eighteenth centuries. (2) In the last century the majority view suggests that the author is not overly concerned with creating a fully consistent eschatological scheme. When there are apparent inconsistencies these are attributed to the disparate traditional eschatological materials the author has drawn together in his apocalyptic mosaic (e.g., Court). (3) A recent trend in interpretation is to disregard chronological concerns in favor of discerning the theological freight of the text. This approach suggests that Revelation uses a traditional picture of the future messianic age in order to communicate an essentially theological message and therefore not one about time (e.g., Mealy).

3.2 Premillennial, Postmillennial and Amillennial Interpretations. Current interpretations tend to fall into one of three groups, premillennialist, postmillennialist and amillennialist. Those who take Revelation's mention of one thousand years as an actual period that stretches over one thousand rotations of the earth around the sun are usually premillennialists. The label refers to their belief about when the return of Christ (1 Thess 4:17) will happen in relation to the millennial rule of Christ. Premillennialists believe Christ's return mentioned in 1 Thessalonians 4 happens before the millennial kingdom.

Some postmillennialists also believe in a literal, thousand-year reign of Christ, which is then followed by the Second Coming of Christ. Other postmillennialists believe that the one thousand years stand for the current effectiveness of the gospel in the present age, after which Christ returns. Neither premillennialism nor postmillennialism is explicitly supported by Revelation 20, since it makes no mention of the return of Christ.

Amillennialists do not believe "one thousand years" refers to a literal time frame. It is a symbol for the whole period of time between Jesus' first and second comings. This interpretation was first championed by Augustine of Hippo. Augustine read Revelation through a Pauline lens. Colossians 3:1 and Ephesians 2:6 declare that we already are "raised with Christ" and "enthroned with Christ in heavenly places," and this must mean that the reign of saints with Christ (Rev 20:4-6) must describe the present reign of Christians (Augustine *Civ. D.* 20.6-20). The difficulty of this line of interpretation is that it must overlook the current experience of evil in the world, which the author of Revelation conveys is due to the evil one's awareness of the shortage of time left to covort and corrupt (Rev 12:12). A variation on this view is to take the millennium to represent not the entire church age but only the periods of reprieve from persecution.

3.3. Concluding Comments. The search for a cosmic calendar that plots out the future days and weeks according to the book of Revelation is misguided. The book's message is not in its details but in its impact on a beleaguered church. Those Christians needed to hear what Revelation had to offer, that suffering* is temporary but a necessary experience of those who profess Christ in a corrupt age; that Christ and the church ultimately prevail over this present evil; that believers should hold on to faith even through suffering; and that God's justice and peace* will ultimately prevail, even if it is not yet evident to us. This is the message of Revelation to the church militant in every age: the church, like Christ, will soon be triumphant. Patience and faithfulness are required, but we will soon join "all the saints, who from their labors rest."

See also APOCALYPTIC, APOCALYPTICISM; CREATION, COSMOLOGY; ESCHATOLOGY; KINGDOM OF GOD; REVELATION, BOOK OF.

BIBLIOGRAPHY. R. J. Bauckham, *The Climax of Prophecy: Studies on the Book of Revelation* (Edinburgh: T & T Clark, 1993); idem, *Jude, 2 Peter* (WBC; Waco, TX: Word, 1983); H. Bietenhard, "The Millennial Hope in the Early Church," *SJT* 6 (1953) 12-30; R. G. Clouse, ed., *The Meaning of the Millennium: Four Views* (Downers Grove, IL: InterVarsity Press, 1977); J. M. Court, *Myth and History in the Book of Revelation* (London: SPCK, 1979); M. Gourgues, "The Thousand-Year Reign (Rev 20:1-6): Terrestrial or Celestial?" *CBQ* 47 (1985) 676-81; J. M. Ford, "Millennium," *ABD* 4:832-34; J. W. Mealy, *After the Thousand Years: Resurrection and Judgment in Revelation 20* (JSNTSup 70; Sheffield: JSOT, 1992); R. H. Mounce, *The Book of Revelation* (NICNT; Grand Rapids: Eerdmans, 1977); J. P. M. Sweet, *Revelation* (WPC; Philadelphia: Westminster, 1979).

B. J. Dodd

MIND. *See* PSYCHOLOGY.

MINISTRY

The ministry and leadership of the church* is variously depicted in the literature covered by this dictionary. The roles of the Twelve, Paul and his colleagues, other apostles,* prophets,* bishops, elders, teachers and deacons, as well as the empowering of the Holy Spirit,* are all mentioned. At one end of the spectrum there is an emphasis upon the work of the Spirit in all believers, and at the other submission to the bishop and elders is stressed. Throughout the literature leadership of some kind in the Christian community is assumed.

1. The Acts of the Apostles
2. Hebrews to Revelation
3. Apostolic Fathers

1. The Acts of the Apostles.

1.1. Fundamentals: Jesus and the Spirit.

In Acts* Jesus begins to fulfill what John the Baptist prophesied about him, i.e., that he would baptize* his people with the Spirit (Acts 1:4-5; 2:1-4, cf. Lk 3:16). By virtue of his resurrection* Jesus entered a new relationship with the Spirit. He who was anointed* with the Spirit at his baptism to become the end-time prophet, liberator and Messiah now became the one who baptizes his people with the Spirit. Jesus' new relationship with the Spirit forms a bridge between his ministry as the historical Jesus and the ministry that he continues as the exalted Christ through the church (Acts 1:1; see Exaltation). It is no surprise, then, that Acts presents the ministry of the early church as something initiated and empowered by the Holy Spirit (Acts 1:8; 2:4; 4:8, 31; 5:32; 6:3, 10; 7:55; 8:15, 18, 29, 39; 9:17, 31; 10:19, 44-47; 11:12, 15, 16, 24, 28; 13:2, 4, 9, 52; 15:8, 28; 16:6, 7; 19:6, 21; 20:22, 23, 28; 21:4, 11).

1.2. The Apostles.

The designation *apostles* is applied to two groups only in Acts: the Twelve and Paul and Barnabas. The Twelve, reconstituted by the selection of Matthias after the suicide of Judas, included men who had accompanied Jesus from the time of John's baptism to the time when Jesus was taken up (Acts 1:21-22). The Twelve constitute a second bridge between the ministry of the historical Jesus and that of the early church.

Jesus said the Twelve would sit on twelve thrones judging the tribes of Israel* (Lk 22:30), so they stand as a sign of God's* continued purposes for Israel. They also played an important role in legitimizing the expansion of the church among Samaritans (see Samaria) and Gentiles* (Acts 8:14-17; 11:1-18; 15:1-35). Their actual ministry involved preaching* and bearing witness* to the resurrection of Christ (Acts 1:22; 4:33), teaching* (Acts 2:42) and prayer* (Acts 6:2-4). Their preaching was often accompanied by signs and wonders* (Acts 2:43; 5:12) and was directed mainly but not exclusively to Jews.

Because all the references to apostles in Acts except Acts 14:4, 14 refer to the Twelve, some scholars argue that the term *apostle* applied to Paul and Barnabas in these texts means something else (e.g., missionaries rather than apostles), or reflects the tradition Luke was using at this point and therefore not his own view of apostleship, or is a later gloss. However, the account of the ministry of Paul and his colleagues in Acts replicates in many ways that of the Twelve, especially that of Peter: their ministry also involved preaching the gospel* (Acts 9:15; 19:8-10; 22:14-15; 26:15-18) and teaching and encouraging new Christian communities (Acts 14:21-22; 18:11; 20:25-26). It too was accompanied by signs and wonders (Acts 13:8-12; 14:3, 8-9; 16:16-18; 19:11-12; 20:7-12). While Paul and his companions had not accompanied Jesus from his baptism to the ascension and so could not be regarded as apostles in exactly the same way as the Twelve were, nevertheless it is apparent that their apostolic ministry was very much the same. The one real difference was that the ministry of Paul and his colleagues was directed mainly but not exclusively to Gentiles. The pattern of Paul's itinerant ministry was to preach first in Jewish synagogues,* where he could speak to Jews, proselytes and God-fearers, and afterward to the wider Gentile community (Acts 13:46-48; 18:5-8; 19:8-10). The ministry of apostles, whether of members of the Twelve or of Paul and his colleagues, was marked by the involvement of the exalted Christ through the Spirit (Acts 1:1, 5, 8; 2:4; 4:8; 5:32; 8:14-17; 9:17; 10:19, 44-48; 11:12-17, 24; 13:1-4; 16:6-7; 19:6; 20:22-23).

1.3. The Seven.

Because of the rapid growth of the early Jerusalem* church and problems that arose in it, the Twelve were unable to cope with the daily distribution to the needy as well as their own ministry of the word of God and prayer. It was to resolve this problem that the Twelve gathered all the disciples together and asked them to choose seven men, full of the Holy Spirit and wisdom, to take over responsibility for the daily distribution (Acts 6:1-6). This incident probably provided the model for the later institution of the office of deacon. However, the word *deacon (diakonos)* is not used in Acts 6. The work of the Seven is described as a "ministry" *(diakonia)*, as is the work of the Twelve (Acts 6:1, 4). However, it is the function rather than any office that is depicted here. The task the Seven were appointed to carry out (Acts 6:1-3) appears to have been taken over by the elders shortly afterward (Acts 11:27-30).

In later chapters of Acts the activities of two members of the Seven are highlighted. Stephen* and Philip* carry out a powerful preaching ministry that is accompanied by miraculous signs (Acts 6:8-10; 8:4-8). Stephen's ministry brought him into opposition with members of the Synagogue of the Freedmen, and this led to his arraignment before the Sanhedrin and subsequent martyrdom* (Acts 6:8-12, 54-60). Philip's ministry resulted in a turning to Christ on the part of many Samaritans and the conversion of the Ethiopian eunuch (Acts 8:4-13, 26-39). This shows that, while the Seven might have been made responsible (temporarily) for the daily distribution to the needy, their ministry, as people filled with the Holy Spirit, was not limited to that.

1.4. Ordinary Believers. While members of the Seven and the Twelve were responsible for the initial evangelization* of Samaritans (Acts 8) and Gentiles (Acts 10) respectively, it was ordinary believers, scattered by persecution,* who carried the gospel far and wide. They spoke to Gentiles as well as Jews, and because God's hand was with them, they were responsible for a remarkable turning to Christ among Gentiles (Acts 8:4; 11:19-21).

1.5. Elders. In the earliest days the Twelve took the lead in the Jerusalem church, but it was not long before they were joined by a group called "the elders." It was to the elders that Paul and Barnabas brought aid from the church in Antioch* (Acts 11:27-30). It was to the apostles and elders in Jerusalem that they were sent to discuss the demands for circumcision being placed upon Gentile converts in Antioch, and it was in the name of the apostles and elders that the decision about this matter was communicated to the Gentile churches (Acts 15:2, 4, 6, 22-23; 16:4). It was the elders, together with James, the brother of the Lord (*see* Relatives of Jesus), whom Paul and his company greeted when they returned to Jerusalem at the end of the third missionary journey, and it was they who urged Paul to take specific action to neutralize rumors that he was teaching the Jews of the Diaspora* to turn away from the law* of Moses (Acts 21:18-26). From all this it appears that the Jerusalem elders were a group distinct from the Twelve and did not include James. There is no information in Acts concerning their selection and appointment or what qualifications they had to have. Their function, as far as we can tell, was to work alongside the Twelve and then James in the leadership of the church. This involved receiving (and distributing) aid and handling controversial issues as they arose. Paul and Barnabas appointed elders for the churches they founded (Acts 14:23). Some hints about their appointment and responsibilities are found in Paul's address to the Ephesian elders. The elders, or at least some of them, were made overseers *(episkopoi)* of the flock (see Phil 1:1) by the Holy Spirit and were responsible for guarding it against those who sought to lead people astray. They were to shepherd the church of God, bought with his own blood (Acts 20:28-31).

1.6. Women in Ministry. There are a number of references to the ministry of women in Acts. The women, including Mary the mother of Jesus, joined in constant prayer along with the men when all the disciples met in the upper room (Acts 1:13-14). Peter, quoting from the prophet Joel, explained the phenomena of the day of Pentecost* in terms of the pouring out of the Spirit on all people, both men and women, so that both would prophesy (Acts 2:17-18). Dorcas's ministry of doing good and helping the poor was praised, and it moved the apostle Peter to pray for her restoration to life (Acts 9:36-44). Mary, the mother of John Mark, hosted the gathering of the Jerusalem church (Acts 12:12). Priscilla and her husband, Aquila, provided hospitality* for Paul in Corinth (Acts 18:1-3), accompanied him on his journey to Ephesus (Acts 18:18-19) and provided hospitality for Apollos and instructed him in the way of God (Acts 18:26). The four unmarried daughters of Philip the Evangelist prophesied (Acts 21:8-9).

1.7. Prophets. Acts mentions the ministry of various Christian prophets. There were prophets who came down from Jerusalem to Antioch, including one named Agabus who predicted a severe famine during the reign of Claudius (Acts 11:27-28). Later Agabus predicted Paul's arrest in Jerusalem (Acts 21:10-11). In Antioch there were prophets and teachers, and it was to these that the Holy Spirit gave directions to set apart Barnabas and Paul for their missionary work (Acts 13:1-3). Judas and Silas, who were part of the delegation from Jerusalem that conveyed the Jerusalem decrees to the Gentile churches, are described as prophets who exhorted and strengthened the disciples (Acts 15:30-32), and the four unmarried daughters of Philip the Evangelist used to prophesy (Acts 21:8-9). The ministry of the prophets in Acts included prediction, receiving specific directions, exhortation and encouragement.

2. Hebrews to Revelation.

2.1. Hebrews and James. Hebrews* exhorts its readers to respect their leaders who spoke the word of God to them, whose lives provided an example to be followed and who kept watch over them as those who must give an account of their ministry (Heb 13:7, 17). James* speaks of the heavy responsibility of teachers; they will be judged more strictly (Jas 3:1). He also refers to the role of elders in praying for and anointing the sick (Jas 5:15).

2.2. 1 and 2 Peter and Jude. In 1 Peter* believers are depicted as stones* that are built into a spiritual temple,* to function as a holy priesthood* offering spiritual sacrifices* and declaring the praises of God who called them out of darkness into his glorious light* (1 Pet 2:4-10; see Glory). All believers are urged to use whatever gifts they have, whether gifts of speaking or of serving (1 Pet 4:10-11; see Service). Elders are urged to carry out the role of shepherds, caring for God's flock, not in a domineering way, but providing an example of godly living (1 Pet 5:1-4). In 2 Peter and Jude,* the readers are reminded of what the apostles of Christ commanded (2 Pet 3:2) and foretold (Jude 17) and in particular of the teaching of Paul found in his letters (2 Pet 3:15-16).

2.3. 1, 2 and 3 John and Revelation. The letters of John (see John, Letters of) reflect a situation in which itinerant preachers, both orthodox and heretical, had gone out and were moving around the (Johannine) churches (1 Jn 2:18-19, 26; 3:7; 2 Jn 7; 3 Jn 5-10). The orthodox itinerants are described as those who went out "for the sake of the Name" and therefore deserved to receive hospitality (3 Jn 7-8). The elder who in 2 John and 3 John exhorts his readers to provide hospitality to the orthodox and withhold it from the heretical expects his readers to heed his exhortation, though it was rejected by one Diotrephes who wanted preeminence (3 Jn 9-10). The author of 1 John acknowledges that his readers need no one (especially not the false teachers) to instruct them, because they have an anointing from God (1 Jn 2:20-21, 26-27). Nevertheless he provides them with quite explicit teaching about assessing the claims of false teachers. The book of Revelation (see Revelation, Book of) speaks of the twelve apostles of the Lamb as the twelve foundations of the wall of the new Jerusalem (Rev 21:14).

3. Apostolic Fathers.

3.1. Clement. This letter is addressed to a church that had, on account of one or two persons, dismissed from office its presbyters (1 Clem. 47.6). Clement* wrote to urge the church, which previously had a reputation of obedience* to its rulers (1 Clem. 1.3), to respect those who ruled over them (1 Clem. 21.6). In the process he asserts that the apostles' practice of appointing bishops and deacons from among their first converts was in accordance with the Scriptures (1 Clem. 42.4-5; cf. Is 60:17). And because the apostles had foreknowledge of the strife that would arise concerning the episcopate, they added the codicil that, if those appointed by them died, other approved men should succeed to their ministry (1 Clem. 44.1-2). Clement insists that it is no small sin* to remove from the episcopate those appointed by the apostles or those appointed by other eminent men with the consent of the whole church (1 Clem. 44.3-4).

Applying all this to the situation in Corinth, Clement stresses that it is shameful that the Corinthians are being disloyal to their presbyters (1 Clem. 47.6) and urges those who instigated the sedition to repent* and submit themselves to the presbyters (1 Clem. 54.1-2; 57.1). From all this it emerges that, as far as Clement was concerned, the apostles had inaugurated the ministry of bishops and deacons by appointing people to this task and had provided for its continuance following the death of those whom they appointed. Clement appears to use the terms bishop and presbyter synonymously. Perhaps the reason for this is, as H. O. Maier suggests, that some of the elders of a larger presbyteral body acted as bishops in the Roman church (see Rome).

3.2. The Didache. In the Didache* the readers are urged to honor those who teach them the Word of God as they would the Lord himself, because when they teach about the Lord's nature, the Lord is present (Did. 4.1). The readers are instructed to allow prophets to hold eucharists (or give thanks) as they will (Did. 10.7) and to receive itinerant apostles as the Lord* (Did. 11.1-3). Normally they are not to test prophets when they are speaking "in a spirit" (Did. 11.7). However, sometimes this will be necessary. Prophets who order a meal "in a spirit" to eat of it themselves are false prophets, as are those who do not practice what they teach

(*Did.* 11.9-10). Apostles or prophets who want hospitality for more than two days or ask for money may be regarded as false (*Did.* 11.3-6, 12). Yet instructions are given to support genuine prophets and teachers who take up residence. They are to be given the first fruits of the readers' produce (*Did.* 13.1-7). The *Didache* makes no mention of the apostles appointing bishops and deacons; rather, the readers are told to appoint for themselves worthy men as bishops and deacons. Once appointed they are not to be despised, because they minister to the people the ministry of prophets and teachers (*Did.* 15.1-2). The *Didache* reflects a situation similar to that reflected in 1, 2 and 3 John when it speaks of itinerant preachers and teachers, both orthodox and heterodox, who were moving about among the churches.

3.3. The Epistles of Ignatius. In his letters* Ignatius* is at pains to bring the Christians of Asia under the authority of their leaders. His letters include many clear references to the three orders of ministry: bishops, presbyters and deacons. Some of each are mentioned by name (Ign. *Eph.* 1.3; 2.1; Ign. *Magn.* 2.1; 15.1; Ign. *Trall.* 1.1; Ign. *Phld.* 11.1; Ign. *Smyrn.* 10.1). The bishop appears as the leader of the Christian community in a given city (Ign. *Magn.* 15.1; Ign. *Trall.* int.; 1.1; Ign. *Phld.* presc.; 1.1). Believers are exhorted to live in harmony with their bishops and presbyters (Ign. *Eph.* 4.1; Ign. *Magn.* 6.1-2; 7.1), who provide an example for them to follow (Ign. *Eph.* 1.3; Ign. *Magn.* 6.2). Believers must, with their bishop, come to the unity of the church (Ign. *Phld.* 3.1; 8.1). They are to be subject to the bishop as to God and to the presbyters as to the apostles, for the bishop presides in the place of God and the presbyters in the place of the council of the apostles (Ign. *Eph.* 2.2; 6.1; 20.3; Ign. *Magn.* 2.1; 3.1; 6.1-2; 13.2; Ign. *Trall.* 2.1-2; 3.1; 13.2; Ign. *Phld.* 7.1; Ign. *Smyrn.* 8.1; Ign. *Pol.* 6.1). Believers are to remain loyal to the bishop and "do nothing" without him and the presbyters and deacons (Ign. *Magn.* 7.1; Ign. *Trall.* 7.1-2; Ign. *Phld.* 7.2; Ign. *Smyrn.* 9.1).

When a bishop is youthful people should not take advantage of that but submit to him, yet not to him but to the Father of Jesus Christ who is the bishop of all (Ign. *Magn.* 3.1). Those who honor the bishop are honored by God (Ign. *Smyrn.* 9.1). The prayer of the bishop and the whole church (in the eucharist) is powerful (Ign. *Eph.* 5.2). In each church there was one bishop with the presbytery and the deacons (Ign. *Phld.* 4.1). Deacons must be in every way pleasing to all, for they are not only ministers of food and drink but servants of the church of God (Ign. *Trall.* 2.3). They are entrusted with the service of Jesus Christ (Ign. *Magn.* 6.1), and they must be respected as Jesus Christ (Ign. *Trall.* 3.1) and as the command of God (Ign. *Smyrn.* 8.1). Deacons could be sent as ambassadors from one church to another (Ign. *Phld.* 10.1).

3.4. Polycarp. Polycarp* wrote the Philippians a letter of exhortation in which he urged the deacons to be blameless in their conduct (Pol. *Phil.* 5.2) and believers to be subject to the presbyters and deacons as to God and Christ (Pol. *Phil.* 5.3). Presbyters were exhorted to be compassionate to all, restoring those who wander and caring for the weak, in particular widows and orphans (Pol. *Phil.* 6.1).

3.6. The Shepherd of Hermas. This document, commonly understood to be primarily concerned with postbaptismal sin and repentance, has in recent times been seen to be concerned more with the preservation of the purity* of the Christian community. This it seeks to do by inculcating proper attitudes toward the use of wealth (Maier). Corrupt deacons who receive goods to assist widows and orphans and devour them themselves are given warnings (*Herm. Sim.* 9.26.2). Contrasted are bishops who ceaselessly shelter the destitute and receive the servants of God into their houses gladly (*Herm. Sim.* 9.27.2).

The *Shepherd of Hermas** contains numerous other references to Christian leaders. Hermas saw in a vision a building with square white stones representing apostles, bishops, teachers and deacons, all of whom agreed among themselves and some of whom had died (*Herm. Vis.* 3.5.1). In the ninth similitude forty stones represent the prophets and teachers of the preaching of the Son of God (*Herm. Sim.* 9.15.4) and apostles and teachers who, having preached the name of the Son of God, fell asleep and then preached to those who had fallen asleep before them (*Herm. Sim.* 9.16.5; cf. *Herm. Sim.* 9.25.2). The eleventh mandate reflects a time when the charismatic ministry of genuine prophets was highly regarded. The Shepherd instructs Hermas how to distinguish between genuine and false prophets: genuine prophets are godly in behavior and give no answers to those who ask but speak only when God wishes them to speak: when they are filled with the Holy Spirit. False prophets are shameless and talkative, live in luxury and prophesy only if paid to do so, something genuine prophets do not do. When genuine prophets enter assemblies of righteous men who make intercession, they are filled with the Holy Spirit and speak to the congregations as the Lord wills. But when false prophets enter such assemblies and intercession is made, they become dumb and have nothing to say *(Herm. Man.* 11.7-15).

See also APOSTLE, APOSTLESHIP; AUTHORITY; CHURCH ORDER, GOVERNMENT; MISSION, EARLY NON-PAULINE; PASTORAL THEOLOGY; PROPHECY, PROPHETS, FALSE PROPHETS; SERVANT, SERVICE; TEACHING, PARAENESIS; WOMEN IN THE EARLY CHURCH.

BIBLIOGRAPHY. D. L. Bartlett, *Ministry in the New Testament* (Minneapolis: Fortress, 1993); H. von Campenhausen, *Ecclesiastical Authority and Spiritual Power in the Church of the First Three Centuries* (London: A. & C. Black, 1969); J. N. Collins, *Diakonia: Reinterpreting the Ancient Sources* (New York and Oxford: Oxford University Press, 1990); E. E. Ellis, "The Role of the Christian Prophet in Acts" in *Apostolic History and the Gospel: Biblical and Historical Essays,* ed. W. W. Gasque and R. P. Martin (Exeter: Paternoster, 1970) 55-67; K. Giles, *Patterns of Ministry Among the First Christians* (Melbourne: Collins Dove, 1989); A. T. Hanson, *The Pioneer Ministry* (London: SCM, 1961); A. E. Harvey, "Elders," *JTS* 25 (1974) 318-32; A. Lemaire, "From Services to Ministries: *Diakonia* in the First Two Centuries," *Concilium* 10 (1972) 35-49; idem, "The Ministries in the New Testament: Recent Research," *BTB* 3 (1973) 133-66; idem, *Ministry in the Church* (London: SPCK, 1977); J. B. Lightfoot, "The Christian Ministry" in *Saint Paul's Epistle to the Philippians* (London: MacMillan, 1898) 181-269; H. O. Maier, *The Social Setting of the Ministry as Reflected in the Writings of Hermas, Clement and Ignatius* (Waterloo, ON: Wilfrid Laurier University, 1991); R. P. Martin, *The Family and the Fellowship: New Testament Images of the Church* (Grand Rapids: Eerdmans, 1979); E. Schillebeeckx, *Ministry: A Case for Change* (London: SCM, 1981); W. Schmithals, *The Office of Apostle in the Early Church* (London: SPCK, 1971); E. Schweizer, *Church Order in the New Testament* (London: SCM, 1961); C. Trevett, "The Much-maligned Ignatius," *ExpT* 93 (1981) 299-302.

C. G. Kruse

MIRACLES IN ACTS

Miracles, or divine interventions in the observed order of human events, are part of most biblical narratives. Acts* contains twenty to twenty-five miracle stories, the latter figure including five summary statements referring to the working of multiple miracles. These stories serve to point to divine activity and to authenticate the teaching and mission of the divinely authorized agent. While the healing miracles are in continuity with the miracles of Jesus in the Gospel, they reflect an independent tradition; there are also a number of miracles unique to Acts, such as miraculous releases from prison, transportation and especially judgment.*

1. Miracle Story Evidence
2. Critical Assessment of the Miracle Stories
3. Paul as a Miracle Worker
4. Judgment Miracles
5. Function of Miracle Stories

1. Miracle Story Evidence.
The miracles in Acts continue the miracle narratives in Luke. However, along with the similarities there are significant differences. Healing miracles are more prominent in Luke, while protection or deliverance miracles are more prominent in Acts. Yet both works have miracles in each of the categories described below (see 1.2-4 below), which makes Luke-Acts different from the other Gospels (i.e., none of the others have judgment miracles, except the cursing of the fig tree, while John is the only other Gospel with clear miracles of deliverance or protection).

When we examine the miracles in Acts we will divide them into four groups, combining exorcism and raising of the dead with healing miracles (Neirynck, 170-71, uses seven groups; Hardon, 303-5, uses five groups). To this we could add a fifth type of miracle, that of the ascension* (Acts 1:9-11; so also Hardon), which is presented as a significant event of salvation history and is thus in a class apart from the other miracles.

1.1. Miracles of Inspiration. The most prominent miracle of inspiration is Pentecost* (Acts 2:1-13), although one could group with this other references to glossolalia or prophecy* (Acts 10; 19) as well as references to Peter, Paul or others laying hands on people and the Holy

Spirit* coming upon them (which appears to include some experiential component) and to guidance by visions,* angels* or God's* Spirit. Many writers would not count any of these experiences among the miracles in Acts in that no physical phenomena are involved (e.g., Gen, 4, 6), while others would count Pentecost since it involved observable phenomena but not the miracles of guidance (e.g., Praeder, 108). Yet surely these distinctions are modern, not those of the author of Acts. For him all of these events are part of his evidence that God through his Spirit was directing and empowering the mission of the church* (Stronstad, 49-74).

1.2. Miracles of Healing. The healing miracles (including the summary statements) are common enough that they can be best presented in a table:

Reference	Miracle	Agent	Result
Acts 2:43	Summary	Apostles	evangelization (in context)
Acts 3:1-10	Lame man healed	Peter (and John)	evangelization
Acts 5:12-16	Summary	Apostles/ Peter	evangelization/high regard
Acts 6:8	Summary	Stephen	hostility
Acts 8:4-8	Summary	Philip	evangelization
Acts 9:10-19/ Acts 22:12-16	Blind receives sight	Ananias	evangelization
Acts 9:32-35	Paralytic healed	Peter	evangelization
Acts 9:36-43	Dead woman raised	Peter	evangelization
Acts 14:3	Summary	Paul and Barnabas	evangelization/division
Acts 14:8-18	Lame man healed	Paul	high regard
Acts 15:12	Summary	Paul and Barnabas	context of evangelistic report
Acts 16:16-24	Spirit exorcised	Paul	hostile attack
Acts 19:11-12	Summary	Paul	evangelization/high regard
Acts 20:7-12	Dead man raised	Paul	comfort
Acts 28:7-10	Man with fever healed	Paul	high regard

What one notes is that these miracles, dealing with diseases stemming from both spiritual and nonspiritual causes, concern a variety of anatomical regions (although not as wide a variety as in Luke, possibly indicating real if

limited results of redemption*; Pilch), and these miracles are normally connected to an evangelistic result or at least a rise in the status of the miracle workers (Praeder, 113-14).

1.3. Miracles of Protection or Deliverance. Each of the miracles of protection or deliverance in some way extricates a person from danger or difficulty, allowing him to get on with the work of evangelization. While many scholars do not count Paul's deliverance from the shipwreck as a miracle, Acts announces it as divine deliverance (Acts 27:23-24), and so it appears miraculous from Luke's perspective. Furthermore, the survival of Paul from stoning could also be grouped with healing miracles (similar to the raising of Eutychus); what it shares with the protection or deliverance miracles is the absence of a named agent.

Reference	Miracle	Subject	Result
Acts 5:17-21 (26)	release from prison	Apostles	preaching
Acts 8:39	man transported	Philip	preaching
Acts 12:1-19	release from prison	Peter	fear ?
Acts 14:19-20	Paul survives stoning	Paul	continues mission
Acts 16:16-24	release from prison	Paul and Silas	evangelization
Acts 27:13-44	deliverance from shipwreck	Paul	effect on sailors
Acts 28:1-6	deliverance from snakebite	Paul	high regard

1.4. Miracles of Judgment. The miracles of judgment are the most unusual miracles in Acts. These appear to be the opposite of the salvation or healing miracles. There is some question as to whether to include among these miracles Paul's being blinded on the Damascus Road (see 4 below).

Reference	Miracle	Agent	Result
Acts 5:1-11	Couple dies	Peter	fear
Acts 9:1-9/ Acts 22:6-11	Paul blinded?	Jesus	conversion/call
Acts 12:19-24	Herod dies	Angel of the Lord	Word of God increases
Acts 13:6-12	Bar-Jesus blinded	Paul	evangelization

2. Critical Assessment of the Miracle Stories.

The modern criticism of the miracle stories in Acts began with the *Tendenzkritik* of the past century pointing out that in Acts, Peter and Paul work similar miracles. This led to F. C. Baur's assertion that Luke had deliberately modeled Paul on Peter to equate the two. In a related development B. Bauer, building on the work of others, argued that miracle stories about Jesus were the original out of which both Peter's and Paul's miracles were built. The significance of this issue of the Jesus-Peter-Paul parallelism became a much discussed topic in further critical works.

A second approach to the miracles, developing in the nineteenth century, was that of source criticism. Scholars such as E. Zeller and A. von Harnack viewed the miracles not as Luke's creation but as stemming from his sources. Usually the sources included a Petrine source for Peter's miracles (often viewed as legendary) and the "we" source for Paul's (sometimes viewed as historical). Without the controls found in Synoptic source criticism, no firm conclusions have resulted from this research.

With the coming of the twentieth century, Martin Dibelius and Rudolf Bultmann pioneered the form-critical approach to the miracles in Acts, classifying them similarly to the Gospel pericopae (Conzelmann, 25; see DJG, Form Criticism). However, more recent criticism (J. Roloff and S. H. Kanda) has pointed to the differences between the miracles in Acts and the miracles of Jesus, particularly in the use of prayer* and the divine name,* and thus views them as similar to Jewish miracles (Neirynck, 172-202). The most recent research has focused on the function of miracles in the Lukan redaction (see 5 below).

The present critical consensus is that the miracles in Acts are rarely if ever directly built upon the miracles in Luke's Gospel (although this does not deny influence) but instead stem from independent tradition available to Luke (Praeder, 120; Schreiber, 140-43; Conzelmann, 25, 76, 164). There are in fact few verbal or structural parallels with Gospel miracles other than the essential terms needed to describe a given type of healing.* The historical validity of the underlying tradition is variously evaluated, as is the degree to which Luke may have embellished it for theological reasons. What is clear is that the miracle summaries are Lukan, although they too may indicate his knowledge of a tradition of miracle working by Peter, Paul, Stephen* and others.

3. Paul as a Miracle Worker.

The critical discussion of the miracle stories in Acts pointed out as a major issue the portrait of Paul. There is no question that Paul in Acts is said to work miracles. Five miracle narratives (including one judgment miracle) and three summary statements present Paul as a charismatic wonderworker. Does not this picture of Paul stand at odds with Paul's self-presentation as "weak"? Could it be that this picture of Paul is a deliberate attempt to parallel Paul to Peter? Or is Paul being presented as a theios anēr (divine man)?

Five observations have been made about this issue. First, given that there was no unified "divine man" ideal in the ancient world, the use of the term theios anēr is itself problematic. Furthermore, the evidence usually cited points to persons who were viewed as having power in themselves and thus as revealing their own status through their wonders. Paul's miracles are normally connected to his message, and this message is about someone other than he, that is, Jesus or God, who is said to be the real power working the wonder (Adams, 247-52).

Second, while Paul is undoubtedly a miracle worker in Acts, his miracles are spread thinly over his ministry. Two are at the beginning of his first missionary journey (including the judgment miracle), one in the second missionary journey and one in the third. The final miracle is an incidental event after the final shipwreck. One can hardly say that the miracle stories are a major part of the picture of Paul. Only the miracle summaries give that impression.

Third, there is no reference to the miracles in the speeches of Paul, which is not true of the speeches of Peter (miracles form the basis for at least three of them). Thus miracles function differently in relation to Paul than they do in relation to Peter. With Peter they initiate evangelism* and are a theme of his preaching while with Paul they only accompany evangelism.

Fourth, Paul's letters also refer to Paul as a miracle worker. Twice he uses the vocabulary of the Lukan summaries and notes that "signs and wonders"* were worked through him, which he identifies as the "signs of an apostle" (2 Cor 12:12; Rom 15:19). Elsewhere he makes passing reference to miracles having accompanied his ministry (1 Cor 2:4; 1 Thess 1:5; Gal 3:1-4). Therefore the Lukan summaries do not differ significantly from Paul's self-presentation of the presence of the role of the miraculous in his ministry.

Fifth, Acts does have a suffering Paul. He is chased from Damascus and Jerusalem* (the former of which incidents he viewed as showing "weakness," 2 Cor 11:30-33). Later he was forced out of the various cities of his first missionary journey, being stoned in one of them. Much the same could be said for his second missionary journey. His third journey ends with Paul imprisoned for two years. On his way to Rome* he experiences a storm at sea and a shipwreck. Acts ends with Paul still a prisoner. What becomes clear in Acts is that while there are miracles of deliverance, the miracles are not about Paul. They are about the gospel. Nothing stops Paul (or Peter) from presenting the gospel, flight and rejection serving to continue its spread. And even when the doors of the prison are shaken open, the main result is evangelization, for it is by political means rather than the miracle that Paul eventually leaves the prison. Luke's triumph is a triumph of God, not of Paul.

Given that the Pauline letters* are occasional letters and thus do not discuss the whole of Paul's theology and given the preceding data, it is arguable that Paul's self-presentation is compatible with Luke's perspective on the triumph of the gospel through Paul (so Jervell, Praeder).

4. Judgment Miracles.

Acts reports at least three and possibly five judgment miracles. The deaths of Ananias and Sapphira, the death of Herod and the blinding of Bar-Jesus clearly fall in this category. There is debate as to whether the blinding of Paul is an act of judgment. Some interpreters view this as a judgment on Paul, while others view it as a natural result of the encounter with a divine epiphany. If it is judgment, we have a fourth judgment miracle; if it is not then we have a healing after an "accident." The fifth possible judgment miracle is the storm at sea culminating in the shipwreck, which Luke presents as the result of not heeding Paul's advice (Acts 27:9-10, 21-26); however, in this case divine intervention is indicated only as the cause of deliverance, not as the cause of the storm.

Judgment miracles are not unique to Acts, since one, the muting of Zechariah, is included in Luke (Lk 1:19-22, 62-65). However, this is the only judgment miracle in the Gospels (other than the cursing of the fig tree, which concerns an object rather than a person). Thus we can conclude that judgment miracles are part of Lukan theology, continuing OT precedents. For instance, F. F. Bruce (102) has noted that the judgment of Ananias and Sapphira functions similarly to the judgment on Achan in Joshua in that the community is warned against ignoring the presence of God in their midst. In all of the judgment stories someone is ignoring or opposing the activity of God. The results may be temporary (Zechariah, Paul, Bar-Jesus) or permanent (Ananias and Sapphira, Herod), but in each case God intervenes to stop the opposition and demonstrate his presence.

The function of judgment miracles, therefore, is similar to the function of healing miracles. Each of them results in either fear (i.e., awe in the face of God's action) or evangelization (conversion of Paul, spread of the Word, conversion of Sergius Paulus). Thus God is attributed a higher status (fear) or more people submit to him. His presence and his teaching have been authenticated, even though the process was a negative one (Gen). They also prefigure the final judgment, which Acts warns about on more than one occasion (Acts 2:40; 10:42; 17:30-31).

A function of one of the judgment miracles (Acts 13:6-12) is to differentiate miracle from magic.* It is clear that historically magic was a polemic term that identified the person or activity so designated as socially or religiously unacceptable (Garrett 1989, 11-17, 31-32). Ethnographically, however, magic indicates the attempt to manipulate the world through the use of divine powers.* This manipulation may take place through the use of a term of power or an incantation or other means at the disposal of the magician (Adams, 241-44).

Both of these types of definitions reveal aspects of Luke's methodology. Elymas Bar-Jesus and Simon Magus are both pictured as magicians, thus individuals with a source of power other than God in Jesus. Both meet their match in Paul and Peter, with a shaming of the alternative powers through a judgment miracle (the blinding of Elymas) and a miracle of inspiration (the giving of the Holy Spirit through Peter) respectively. This contest with magic is carried out most fully by Paul in Acts 19, where he exhibits "extraordinary" power, while Jewish exorcists get only shame in trying to usurp that power. The result is that the Ephesian believers forsake magic (burning their books; Fiorenza, 8-16; Conzelmann, 163). This contrast with magic is a subtheme of the contrast between the God and pagan deities found in several places in Acts (e.g., Acts 14; 17; 19).

In that all of the miracles are referred to God's power rather than to power resident in the miracle worker and in that technique goes almost unmentioned (other than in the references to Paul's "handkerchiefs," Tobin, 278); there is also a deliberate, unannounced contrast between magic and miracle (although clear to anyone involved in magic). Miracle is not about technique or influencing God but about God's sovereign activity in spreading the gospel. Thus when Simon Magus wants to purchase Peter's "secret" he is rebuked, for his magical mindset is inimical to what Peter is about.

The contrast with magic is most clearly seen in the miracles of protection or deliverance, for none of them are brought about by the person they benefit. The various apostles* appear surprised upon being released from prison. And when Paul is stoned or bitten by a snake we do not learn of anything that he does to heal himself. In the shipwreck incident, far from being in control, he appears to need encouragement himself. When combined with the fact that Stephen and James are not delivered, these miracles reveal a power of God that is not under the control of God's agents but that sometimes works through those agents.

5. Function of Miracle Stories.

We have already mentioned the function of the miracle stories in Acts as part of the Christian apologetic that contrasted the divine miracles of Jesus and the apostles with the magic of the Jewish and Hellenistic worlds (Fiorenza). Beyond this function, the miracles also serve as indicators of divine intervention in the world. There are two types of direct statements concerning divine intervention in Acts: statements concerning God's intervention in creation,* Israel's* history, the life of Jesus and (more rarely) the eschatological* future, all of which have miraculous aspects but are outside the narrative context, and statements concerning God's intervention in the narrative, both in terms of miracles of inspiration and in terms of signs and wonders (Mowery). In other words, it is through the miraculous, including the advent

of the Spirit (which is often said to be the force behind the miracles), that God becomes the most important actor in Acts. Peter and Paul are visible on the stage but only as agents for God, Jesus or the Spirit.

This is Luke's reason why the gospel advances as it does. The various messengers are sent out by the Holy Spirit and directed by the Spirit as they are under way. When the gospel encounters obstacles, God overcomes them so that it is not stopped. This is the message behind the judgment miracles: someone has opposed God, and God will not be stopped. In these miracles God may act without a human agent (as in the case of Herod) or speak through a human agent (as in the case of Ananias and Sapphira, where divine revelation of the deceit comes through Peter), yet whatever the means God is more to the fore than in the healing miracles. This is also the message behind the nondeliverance of Stephen (indeed, his vision—that is, divine intervention—triggers his death) and James and the deliverance of the apostles Peter and Paul on other occasions. Stephen dies, and the gospel spreads as the church scatters. Paul is sent on mission, and chasing him out of town only spreads the gospel further. Even stoning the messenger cannot stop the progress of the gospel. Put him in prison and the power of God converts the jailer. A storm at sea only serves to move him further toward Rome, for it was God who said that Paul would go to Rome. While the church does pray for Peter (we are not told if it was for his deliverance), in none of these cases are we told that a miracle is requested. God appears to decide whether to spread the gospel through a martyrdom* or a miracle. Thus again the most important actor in Acts is God (Barrett, 277).

Related to God's central role is the function of miracles to authenticate the gospel message. According to Acts, Jesus was attested by signs and wonders (Acts 2:22), so it is no surprise when the apostles ask God to stretch out his hand to attest to their message through signs and wonders "through the name of your holy servant Jesus" (Acts 4:30). As the charts demonstrate (see 1.2-4 above), the various miraculous events are connected to evangelization either through a rise in the status of the messenger or through direct evangelistic effect. Peter's first miracle (and the one reported in the most detail) is accomplished not by Peter's skill (magic) but through faith in Jesus, for God has chosen to glorify Jesus (Acts 3:13,16; 4:10). The miracle is the evidence that the message about the resurrected Jesus is true. Without the message, the miracle is at best an equivocal communication. In Acts 14 a miracle is misinterpreted (even though "faith to be healed" was present), and it is only with difficulty that the apostles can communicate enough of the truth to prevent pagan sacrifice.* The miracle then is God's authentication of the message and the messenger.

Another function of the miracles stories in Acts is to advance the Lukan theology of salvation.* In Acts 3:1-10 the healing of the lame man parallels the offer of salvation in the following two speeches. Thus at the time of prayer the lame man outside the temple* is healed ("saved"; the verb *sōzō* is used) through the power of Jesus mediated through the apostles. The man then enters and leaps about in the temple illustrating the fulfillment of salvation-historical hope (cf. Is 35:6). Along with the formerly lame man, the offer of salvation comes through the apostles to the people in the temple, presenting to them the fulfillment of salvation history in Jesus (Hamm, without endorsing everything he sees in the text). This serves as a grid through which to read the other miracles in Acts as limited outward demonstrations of eschatological salvation.

Finally, miracles serve to tie NT and OT salvation history together. We have already mentioned that the story of Ananias and Sapphira reminds one of the story of Achan in Joshua. That parallel (judgment among the people of God as they are taking a new promised land* [the whole world]) shows the salvation-historical continuity Luke demonstrates other ways. In the healing of the two mobility-challenged men, the salvation-historical hope of Isaiah 35:4 comes to the fore. Thus the OT and its hope is mirrored in the Lukan context. Salvation history is also seen in the parallels with Jesus. As Jesus drove out demons, so the disciples in Acts continue his conflict with Satan,* driving out demons. As Jesus healed, so the disciples healed. They advance the new eon begun in Jesus. Yet they do not act exactly like Jesus, for Luke is conscious of his uniqueness. Jesus acted sovereignly, while the disciples act in his name or through the power of the Spirit he promised. In other words their miracles point back to the Lord (and at times to the promise of his eschatological return), for it is Jesus who is and remains the real miracle worker even in Acts.

See also ACTS OF THE APOSTLES; HEALING, ILLNESS; SIGNS AND WONDERS.

BIBLIOGRAPHY. M. M. Adams, "The Role of Miracles in the Structure of Luke-Acts" in *Hermes and Athena: Biblical Exegesis and Philosophical Theology*, ed. E. Stump and T. P. Flint (Notre Dame, IN: University of Notre Dame, 1993) 235-72; C. K. Barrett, *A Critical and Exegetical Commentary on the Acts of the Apostles* (ICC; Edinburgh: T & T Clark, 1994); F. F. Bruce, *The Book of Acts* (NICNT; Grand Rapids: Eerdmans, 1988); H. Conzemann, *Acts of the Apostles* (Herm; Philadelphia: Fortress, 1987); J. C. Fenton, "The Order of the Miracles Performed by Peter and Paul in Acts," *ExpT* 77 (1966) 381-83; E. Schüssler Fiorenza, "Miracles, Mission and Apologetics: An Introduction" in *Aspects of Religious Propaganda in Judaism and Early Christianity*, ed. E. S. Fiorenza (Notre Dame, IN: University of Notre Dame, 1976) 1-25; J. M. Ford, "The Social and Political Implications of the Miraculous in Acts" in *Faces of Renewal: Studies in Honor of Stanley M. Horton Presented on his Seventieth Birthday*, ed. P. Elbert (Peabody, MA: Hendrickson, 1988) 137-60; S. R. Garrett, *The Demise of the Devil: Magic and the Demonic in Luke's Writings* (Minneapolis: Fortress, 1989); idem, "Light on a Dark Subject and Vice Versa: Magic and Magicians in the New Testament" in *Religion, Science and Magic: In Concert and in Conflict*, ed. J. Neusner (Oxford: Oxford University Press, 1992 [1989]) 142-65; R. M. Gen, "The Phenomena of Miracles and Divine Infliction in Luke-Acts: Their Theological Significance," *Pneuma* 11 (1989) 3-19; D. Hamm, "Acts 3:1-10: The Healing of the Temple Beggar as Lukan Theology," *Bib* 67.3 (1986) 305-19; J. A. Hardon, "Miracle Narratives in the Acts of the Apostles," *CBQ* 16 (1954) 303-18; P. W. van der Horst, "Peter's Shadow," *NTS* 23 (1977) 204-12; J. Jervell, "The Signs of an Apostle: Paul's Miracles" in *The Unknown Paul: Essays on Luke-Acts and Early Christian History* (Minneapolis: Augsburg, 1984) 77-95; R. L. Mowery, "Direct Statements Concerning God's Activity in Acts" in *SBLSP* 29 (1990) 196-211; F. Neirynck, "The Miracle Stories in the Acts of the Apostles: An Introduction" in *Les Actes des Apôtres*, ed. J. Kremer (Gembloux: J. Duculot, 1979) 169-213; L. O'Reilly, *Word and Sign in the Acts of the Apostles:*

A *Study in Lukan Theology* (*Analecta Gregoriana* 243.82; Rome: Editrice Pontificia Universita Gregoriana, 1987); J. J. Pilch, "Sickness and Healing in Luke-Acts" in *The Social World of Luke-Acts,* ed. J. H. Neyrey (Peabody, MA: Hendrickson, 1991) 181-209; S. M. Praeder, "Miracle Worker and Missionary: Paul in the Acts of the Apostles" in *SBLSP* 22 (1983) 107-29; R. Reitzenstein, *Hellenistische Wundererzählungen* (3d ed.; Stuttgart: B. G. Teubner, 1974); S. Schreiber, *Paulus als Wundertäter* (BZNW 79; Berlin: Walter de Gruyter, 1996); R. Stronstad, *The Charismatic Theology of St. Luke* (Peabody, MA: Hendrickson, 1984); T. H. Tobin, "Miracles, Magic and Modernity: Comments on the Paper of Marilyn McCord Adams" in *Hermes and Athena: Biblical Exegesis and Philosophical Theology,* ed. E. Stump and T. P. Flint (Notre Dame, IN: University of Notre Dame, 1993) 275-81; M. Turner, "The Spirit and the Power of Jesus' Miracles in the Lukan Conception," *NovT* 33 (1991) 124-52.   P. H. Davids

MISHNAH. *See* JUDAISM, POST-A.D. 70.

MISSION, EARLY NON-PAULINE

On the morning of Pentecost in the year A.D. 30, seven weeks after Jesus' death and resurrection, we read of 120 followers of Jesus constituting the first community of believers (Acts 1:15). There also may have been sympathizers meeting in small communities in Galilee (cf. perhaps 1 Cor 15:6). We do not know the number of Christians in the Roman Empire at the time the "evangelists" wrote the canonical Gospels and John wrote Revelation. Pliny the Younger, governor of Bithynia-Pontus (c. A.D. 110), complains to Trajan about the aggressive expansion of the repulsive "superstition" to which the crucifixion had given rise as people of every age and social standing were affected by it, even in villages and the countryside (Pliny *Ep.* 10.96.8-10; cf. Hengel 1983, 48). How was it possible that religious convictions inseparably linked with the Jewish faith came to be accepted by increasing numbers of non-Jews? (*See DJG,* Gentiles; *DPL,* Mission.)

1. The Early Christian Mission and Jesus
2. Vision, Strategy and Methods
3. Mission in Acts
4. Mission in the Letter to the Hebrews
5. Mission in the General Epistles
6. Mission in the Revelation

7. Mission in the Early Noncanonical Writings

1. The Early Christian Mission and Jesus.
The early Christian mission cannot be understood without the person, the ministry, the death (*see* Death of Christ) and resurrection,* and the commission of Jesus. If the early Christians had not believed Jesus to be the Messiah, they would have had no reason whatsoever to talk about Jesus' death and resurrection as the event by which evil was once for all defeated, or to believe that the fate of their Galilean teacher should be of significance for pagans.

1.1. The Call to Be Fishers of People. The apostles* (Lk 6:14-16; Acts 1:13) had been called by Jesus to be "fishers of people" (Mk 1:17 par. Mt 4:19; cf. Lk 5:10), that is, to participate in his mission of rescuing the lost by devoting their entire energies ("leaving their nets") to get people to repent and recognize the presence of God's* reign. The aspects of the verbs in Mark 1:17 and its parallels imply a promise and prediction: the vocation of the Servant of Yahweh to be the light of the world, realized in his redemptive suffering* (Is 40—55), would come true in his own ministry, climaxing in his death on the cross (Mk 8:31-18 par. Mt 16:21-27 par. Lk 9:22-26), and then in the ministry of his followers, who would regroup after his vindication (Wright, 610). The Twelve, symbolizing the reconstitution of the people of God (redefined in terms of allegiance to Jesus rather than to the old national symbols of Israel), were called and prepared by Jesus for their future missionary task (*see DJG,* Gentiles).

1.2. The Mission to Jews. The observation of Jesus' own ministry of proclamation and healing* among his Jewish contemporaries prepared his followers for an initial itinerant ministry in Galilee with the injunction to work among the "lost sheep of the house of Israel" (Mt 10:6), as well as for the later commission (Acts 1:8) to a worldwide mission starting in Jerusalem* (Acts 2—7) and continuing in Judea and Samaria* (Acts 8—9). The praxis of the apostle Paul demonstrates that even the most prominent missionary to the Gentiles* went first to the Jews and then to the non-Jews (cf. Rom 1:16; Acts 9:15) on account of the special applicability of God's promise* to his chosen people. The first Christian missionaries were Jews, the first churches* were Jewish Christian communities (Jerusalem, Damascus, Antioch*). Most if not all the churches that were established in Asia Minor, Greece and Italy started with Jews being converted to faith* in Jesus. As the followers of Jesus accomplished the task of proclaiming the Good News, they could not exclude their fellow Jews.

1.3. The Mission to Gentiles. The early Christian mission to non-Jews was not an innovation introduced by Paul from Tarsus (thus Hengel 1979, 93-98; 1995, 36). The "Gentile factor" has its roots in the teaching and ministry of Jesus (*see DJG*, Gentiles §2; Schnabel). Jesus' proclamation of the fulfillment of time and the appearance of God's kingdom (Mk 1:14-15; Mt 4:17; *see* Kingdom of God), an announcement that belongs to Jesus' commission to the disciples as well (Mt 10:7 par. Lk 10:9), was bound to encompass the world on the basis of promises and expectations such as Isaiah 2:2-5 (= Mic 4:1-5), Isaiah 49:1-6 and Zechariah 8:20-23. Thus he challenged the true Israel to be light of the world and salt of the earth (Mt 5:13-16).

In his praxis Jesus ministered occasionally to Gentiles who sought him out (Mk 5:1-20; 7:24-30; Mt 8:5-13; Jn 12:20-22; cf. Jn 4:1-42). He announced that Gentiles would share in the blessings* of the kingdom (Mt 8:11-12 par. Lk 13:28-29) and that the consummation would not occur until the gospel of the kingdom had been preached in the entire *oikoumenē* ("inhabited world") to "all nations" (Mt 24:14), thereby predicting the necessity of worldwide evangelism* (Mk 13:10). After his victory on the cross and his vindication in the resurrection, he commanded the eleven disciples to go to the "end of the earth" (Acts 1:8) and make disciples of all nations (Mt 28:19; cf. the commission to Paul, Acts 9:15; 26:15-18).

The following observations confirm the view that the apostolic Gentile mission has its roots in Jesus' word and praxis. (1) If Jesus foresaw his rejection at the hands of the Jewish leaders ensconced in the temple,* it is not impossible to assume that he replaced the OT expectation of the nations streaming to the temple with a mission that would actively take the messianic salvation* to the nations. (2) If Jesus expected to die and then be raised from the dead, it would be natural for him to leave his messianic mission to his disciples. (3) Jesus' teaching suggests both that God's rule has taken effect among his disciples and that it has not yet taken full effect in the world at large, thus implying a period of worldwide evangelism. (4) There was no debate in the early church over the Gentile mission as such, only a discussion about the status of the converted Gentiles and their relations to the converted Jews, and there was no discussion whether they should wait for the nations to stream to Jerusalem at the consummation.

As the followers of Jesus proclaim the Good News, they cannot limit themselves to Israel; as the eschatological* messianic salvation has dawned, the nations worldwide are now invited into the kingdom of God.

1.4. Reaching Both Villages and Cities. References to Jesus' geographical movement in Mark 6:6 (*periēgen . . . kyklō*), 9, 35 and Luke 4:43 might be taken to indicate that he planned his travels in an organized manner. As the early church engaged in mission it would have been challenged by the example of Jesus to reach all people of a region whether they lived in cities, in villages or in small hamlets.

1.5. Reaching All Kinds of People. As Jesus proclaimed his message to the simple and the sophisticated, to powerless Galileans and to influential leaders of the Jerusalem establishment, to people with bad reputations and to the pious, comparing the arriving kingdom of God with a dragnet in which fish "of all kinds" get caught (Mt 13:47), the early Christian missionaries who had practiced "following Jesus" were confronted with the task of reaching everybody prepared to listen to them, irrespective of traditional, social or religious barriers.

2. Vision, Strategy and Methods.
As Jesus' announcement of the arrival of God's kingdom was accompanied by a redefinition of what the kingdom meant, with the symbols of Israel's identity either missing (circumcision, sabbath, food) or transformed (nation, land, Torah, Temple; Wright 1996, 369-442, 467-72), the traditional vision of nations coming to Jerusalem (Is 2:2-5 par. Mic 4:1-5; Zech 8:20-23) was replaced by the reality of Christian missionaries going to the nations. The anticipated movement from the periphery to the center is redirected to a mission from the center (Jerusalem, where Jesus had died and was raised from the dead) toward the periphery (the ends of the earth). An essentially stationary model of communication—God reveals himself on Zion, Gentiles are attracted to Israel and become

proselytes, nations flock to Jerusalem—is transformed into a fundamentally mobile pattern of communication: Christians carry their convictions from Jerusalem to Damascus and Antioch, to Athens and Corinth, to Ephesus and Rome.*

The basic missionary strategy was to win as many people as possible for Christ* before his expected return and to do this "in the whole world" (*en panti tō kosmō,* Col 1:6).

2.1. Reaching All Nations. If the Twelve were indeed commanded by the risen Lord* to reach all nations (*panta ta ethnē,* Mt 28:19) even unto the "end of the earth" (*heōs eschatou tēs gēs,* Acts 1:8) with the good news of God's salvific revelation* in Jesus the Messiah and invite them to become his followers, and if they took this commission seriously, the question arises as to how they might have perceived their task.

The apostles could have thought of the "nations" (*ethnē*) of the world, including Israel (cf. LXX), in terms of "all the nations" in distinction from the nation Israel (cf. *Pss. Sol.* 9:9) or in terms of the individual "Gentiles" or non-Jews (cf. *4 Bar.* 6:19). A messianic mission to "all the nations" would remind the apostles, in terms of geography and ethnography, of the table of nations in Genesis 10 and its continuing significance as the "Jewish" description of the world (cf. Scott 1994, 492-522; Scott 1995, 5-56). That their geographical horizon was not limited to the Roman Empire* is demonstrated by the evidence in Acts* that mentions regions independent of Rome: Parthia (Acts 2:9) in the east and Ethiopia (Acts 8:27) in the south. As regards a feasible policy to fulfill the Great Commission, the apostles would have thought in terms of specific nations or "tribes" or, from a political perspective, in terms of Roman provinces (cf. Rom 16:4 with Gal 1:2; 1 Cor 16:19; 2 Cor 8:1; Gal 1:22).

An exclusively biblical-Jewish outlook might interpret the phrase "end of the earth" in terms of the extent of the Jewish Diaspora (cf. Acts 2:9-11), whereas a wider perspective would extend the geographical horizons to the furthest points on the edge of the inhabited world: the Indians in the east (or even the Seres, the "silk people" further east, as the *Periplous Maris Erythraei* of the first century A.D. reflects existing commercial contacts with China?), the Scythians in the north, the Germani at the Atlantic in the west (or Britannia, known to the Mediterranean world from at least the third

century B.C. and annexed by Claudius in A.D. 43?) and the Ethiopians in the south (Homer *Odys.* 1.23 calls the "distant Ethiopians" "people at the edge [of the earth]"; cf. Herodotus 3.25.114). The singular *eschatos (tēs gēs)* in Acts 1:8 should not be understood in terms of a single goal of the disciples' mission (pace Ellis, who thinks of Spain); it affirms that there is no spatial limit to their mission.

It appears that the early Christians had the broader perspective: for the Scythians see Colossians 3:11 (Michel, 7:449-50, seems to assume a converted Scythian in the Colossian church); for Spain see Romans 15:24, 28; for Ethiopia see Acts 8:27-39. India is not mentioned in the NT (but is referred to in Esther 1:1 [LXX] passim; 1 Macc 6:38). Would such a perspective mean that the apostles planned to travel to all territories known at that time? Considering the audacious courage of at least some of the apostles, this possibility should not be discarded. Intriguing are the later traditions that speak of missions to India, Scythia and Ethiopia (see 2.8 below).

J. M. Scott has advanced the thesis that according to the evidence in Acts and in Paul's letters the early Christians had a missionary policy based on the table of nations. The apostles seem to have decided on territorial jurisdictions in their respective missions drawn along the lines of the sons of Noah (which Luke supposedly adopts in the literary structure of Acts): Peter was responsible for the mission to "Shem" (Acts 2:1—8:25), Philip* is involved in the mission to "Ham" (Acts 8:26-40), Paul is responsible for the mission to "Japheth" (Acts 9:1—28:31; Scott 1994, 522-44; 1995, 135-80). This proposal seems convincing from a tradition-historical point of view, and it illuminates various aspects of Paul's travels, although it is impossible to verify whether Paul consulted the table of nations tradition when making tactical decisions. His responsiveness to divine guidance seems to point to a high degree of flexibility, and Scott's view that an infringement of Peter and the "men of James" on Japhetite territory (Gal 2:11-14) caused Paul's strong reaction is doubtful. The dispute was not about territorial jurisdiction but about proper relations between converted pagans and messianic Jews.

R. Riesner suggested a different OT background for Paul's mission strategy. As Paul regarded himself part of the eschatological missionary enterprise to the nations portrayed in Isaiah, it is perhaps no coincidence that the movement in Isaiah 66:19, beginning in Tarshish (Tarsus) and turning in a northwest semicircle to Javan (Greece) and the "distant islands," corresponds to Romans 15:19 and thus to Paul's mission, explaining at the same time why Paul evidently did not plan a mission in the provinces between Rome and Spain, especially Gaul (Riesner, 216-25). A problem with this view is the fact that Isaiah 66:19 does not mention the two geographical limits of Paul's mission (Rom 15:19) and that Put is more naturally linked with Libya than with Cilicia.

2.2. The Feasibility of the Missionary Commission. As the early Christians believed that the eschatological age had arrived with the ministry of Jesus Christ and that the consummation may arrive soon, praying for the Parousia* of the Lord (1 Cor 16:22; Rev 22:20), one might conclude that the early missionaries would not have been interested in strategy and planning. However, the eschatological factor must not be seen as the most important motivation of the early Christian movement. Paul's extended periods of missionary work at Corinth and Ephesus, his repeated visits to the churches in south Galatia, Macedonia and Achaia, and the dispatch of coworkers and letters demonstrate that the early Christian mission was not attempting to preach to a maximum number of people over brief spells of evangelism in as many areas as possible. Rather, they evidently saw from the beginning the need of consolidating their missionary efforts notwithstanding their eschatological convictions.

However, the belief that Christ may return soon must have shaped their view of the feasibility of their task of proclaiming the gospel to all nations. They would not have thought in terms of presenting the Good News to every individual in all regions of the earth. Paul said that he had "fulfilled the message of good news" between Jerusalem and Illyricum (Rom 15:19) and thus had to go to Spain in order to be able to do pioneer missionary work. He seems to have been satisfied that he had completed all the preaching of the gospel that must have happened before the Parousia (Mk 13:10) when he had preached to a representative number of people in a given province (or Japhetite nation).

2.3. Human Planning and Divine Guidance. Is it conceivable that the Twelve had left the practical realization of the missionary task entrusted to them by the risen Lord to more or less accidental developments? This is the impression that Luke's depiction of the earliest Christian mission in Acts seems to convey. (1) The first missionary sermon, preached by Peter on the day of Pentecost,* seems to be a spontaneous statement (Acts 2:12-14, 37-38) explaining to a bewildered crowd the significance of the outpouring of the Spirit of God. (2) The apostles appear to have stayed in Jerusalem after Pentecost (Acts 8:1), as there is no hint at missionary travels of the Twelve. (3) The first journeys Luke mentions are the flight of some Christians of the Jerusalem church to Judea and Samaria after the martyrdom* of Stephen,* and Luke specifically points out that the apostles were spared this initial persecution (Acts 8:1). (4) The first major expansion of the Jerusalem church into Samaria is related, as regards initiative and quantitative success, to one of the leaders of the Hellenist house churches rather than to an apostle, and it appears as a spontaneous event in the midst of a persecution* rather than as a planned undertaking. Hence some scholars regard the leaders of the Jerusalem church as a conservative body that was never responsible for new ventures.

Several observations indicate, however, that this is not the whole picture. The apostles were clearly aware of their responsibility for an active missionary outreach, even to the Gentiles. (1) We must not forget that Luke portrays in a highly selective manner the ministry of only one of the Twelve, that of Peter. Otherwise he mentions only John, always in connection with Peter (he prays in Acts 3:1, looks at a crippled man in Acts 3:4, is arrested in Acts 4:3, defends himself before the Sanhedrin in Acts 4:19, ministers with Peter in Samaria in Acts 8:14-25) and his brother James (who is executed in Acts 12:2). If Luke has given a limited picture of Paul's mission, without however misrepresenting him (Marshall, 91-98), it should come as no surprise that his sketch of the mission of the Twelve is fragmentary.

(2) This is all the more remarkable since Luke begins his treatise on the history of the early Christians and their expansion from Jerusalem to "the end of the earth" after having narrated Jesus' renewed instructions about his disciples' vocation and Jesus' departure (Acts

1:1-12; *see* Ascension) with a list of the eleven remaining disciples (Acts 1:13) and a comparatively long section on the replacement of Judas as the twelfth apostle (Acts 1:15-26).

(3) When Luke reports that the Jerusalem apostles had enormous courage and were prepared to challenge with great boldness a political institution that may call for their execution, refusing to stop their public proclamation and their private teaching of Jesus Christ (Acts 4:18-20; 5:28-29), this seems to speak against the view that they were timid leaders unwilling to initiate new ventures. This is supported by the content of the long prayer of the Jerusalem church after the release of Peter and John, who had been arrested. Even in view of "raging nations" they ask for strength and boldness to carry on their task of preaching* God's word (Acts 4:29). Further, if Paul was prepared (without "Christian" preparation) to respond quickly to the divine call to evangelize the Gentiles by traveling to the nearby territory of the Nabatean Arabs (Gal 1:17; 2 Cor 11:32-33; *see DPL*, Paul in Acts and Letters, §2.5), it is not unreasonable to expect that the apostles were not only willing to face martyrdom (as Jesus had predicted they would) but also responsive to the commission of missionary outreach (as Jesus had predicted, exemplified and commanded).

(4) The Sanhedrin was concerned that the messianic movement linked with Jesus of Nazareth would spread to new territories (Acts 4:17; Barrett), thus witnessing to the dynamic vitality and drive toward expansion of the Jerusalem church and its leaders. The Sanhedrin became increasingly apprehensive as the apostles had "filled Jerusalem" with their teaching* (Acts 5:28), underscoring the impressive impact of their preaching.

(5) The fact that the Twelve are at first permanently based in Jerusalem reflects Luke's Jerusalem-centered perspective, which is congruent not only with the Jewish conceptions of world geography (Scott 1994, 492-522) but also with the prophecies of exiled Jews returning to Jerusalem from all four points of the compass and Gentile nations coming from all directions to Jerusalem as well (Is 2:2-3; 11:12; 43:5-6; 49:12; 60:3-16; Zech 8:20-23; Tob 13:11-13). In this context it would be natural for the leaders of the first Christian community, which saw itself as the messianic temple, to locate the foundation of the new temple in Jerusalem rather than

in Galilee* and to see themselves as responsible for the oversight of the active missionary movement.

(6) As the prophecies regarding the nations describe not only a movement to Jerusalem but also a prior movement of the word of the Lord out from Jerusalem (Is 2:3), it is possible that in the earliest period of the Jerusalem church the expectation was that through the proclamation of the gospel in Jerusalem (cf. Is 40:9) its sound would reach to the ends of the earth, through the constant stream of pilgrims to Jerusalem and back into the countries where they lived. "In that case, Luke provides us, in his portrayal of the first preaching of the gospel in Jerusalem to a crowd drawn from all nations under heaven (Acts 2:5-11), with a programmatic account of the earliest mission strategy of the Jerusalem church" (Bauckham 1995, 426).

(7) The narrative in Acts indicates that the Jerusalem apostles acted in accordance with their call to missionary outreach. They send Peter and John to Samaria when they hear of converts there (Acts 8:14; there is no hint that the apostles might have found the news from Samaria to be surprising; Dunn). They liaise with Paul and hear not only of his conversion but also of his work as a missionary in Damascus (Acts 9:27). Peter appears to be involved in a missionary journey through all the cities and villages of Judea, Galilee and Samaria (Acts 9:32 with 9:31; 8:25; a link offered by Barrett as a possibility, regarding it unlikely that *dia pantōn* anticipates "the saints") and the coastal areas (Acts 9:35). Peter also plays a pioneering role in the first breakthrough to the Gentiles in Caesarea (Acts 10:1—11:18). The Jerusalem church feels responsible for the missionary outreach to Gentiles in Antioch (Acts 11:19-24); all the early coworkers in Paul's mission to the Gentiles came from Jerusalem: Barnabas, John Mark and Silas.

(8) R. J. Bauckham has argued convincingly that up to Acts 11:1 the apostles (the "Twelve"; cf. Acts 1:13, 25-26) were the leaders of the Jerusalem church, Peter being the preeminent figure, and they remained so even after the persecution following the martyrdom of Stephen caused the permanent dispersion of many prominent members of the Jerusalem church (Acts 8:1, which does not say that the apostles escaped persecution). This period comes to a close after about twelve years as a

result of the persecution under Herod Agrippa I (A.D. 41-44) that led to the martyrdom of one of the Twelve, James the brother of John (A.D. 41/42) and to the imprisonment and eventual escape of Peter (Acts 12:1-17).

Evidently this persecution put an end to the leadership of the apostles in Jerusalem. When Barnabas and Paul deliver the famine relief, they are sent by the church in Antioch to the "elders" of the Jerusalem church (Acts 11:30), who appear as the group that replaced the Twelve as leaders in Jerusalem, with James the brother of Jesus being the new preeminent figure (Acts 12:17; 15:13-21; 21:18; *see* Relatives of Jesus). Peter's leading role in Jerusalem and in the outreach from Jerusalem with the breakthrough to the Gentiles passes to James (Acts 12:17) in Jerusalem and to Paul (Acts 13:2) in the outreach to the Gentiles (Bauckham 1995, 427-41).

If it is correct that in Acts 12 Luke's narrative "has reached the point where leadership at the center in Jerusalem can no longer be combined with personal leadership in the missionary movement out from the center" (Bauckham 1995, 436), we may conclude that the necessity to leave Jerusalem did not lead to Peter's retirement; his role may have become even more important as a traveling missionary (cf. 1 Cor 9:5) among both Jews and Gentiles (see 2.8 below). This scenario coincides with later patristic evidence in which the disciples are said to have stayed in Jerusalem for twelve years before moving out into the world. See Apollonius (in Eusebius *Hist. Eccl.* 5.18.14); *Acts of Peter* 5; *Kerygma Petrou* 3 (Clement of Alexandria *Strom.* 6.5.43, regarded as historical by Harnack; but cf. Bauer in Hennecke and Schneemelcher, 2:45).

(9) Paul's statement of missionary policy in Romans 15:20, which includes the principle "not to build on another's foundation," does not establish him as the only pioneer missionary to Gentiles (so evidently most commentaries) but indicates that others were actively involved in the mission to the Gentiles. This is also implied by 1 Corinthians 9:5 and 1 Corinthians 15:10 (*see DPL*, Paul in Acts and Letters §3.2). Even the judaizers wanted to win Gentiles (Gal 6:13).

Apart from strategic planning of missionary outreach the often spontaneous guidance by the Lord or the Holy Spirit* or by supernatural factors were an important factor. Consider Philip's mission to an Ethiopian official (Acts 8:26), Peter's mission in Caesarea (Acts 10), the mission of Christians from Jerusalem in Phoenicia, Cyprus and Antioch (Acts 11:19) or Paul's mission to south Galatia (Gal 4:13: "because of an illness") and to Europe (Acts 16:6-10). Circumstances also determined the planning of missionary travels (cf. Paul's plans to visit Rome, Rom 1:10-11, 13).

2.4. Geographical Expansion. Within forty years the Christian missionaries had planted churches in the Roman provinces of Syria-Cilicia, Cyprus, Galatia, Asia, Mysia, Macedonia, Achaia, Cappadocia and Pontus-Bithynia; in Italy and in Rome; in Dalmatia; on Crete; perhaps in Illyricum; perhaps in Egypt (apart from the record in Acts see Gal 1:1, 21; 1 Thess 1:7; Rom 15:19; Tit 1:5; 2 Tim 4:10; 1 Pet 1:1; Rev 1:11; for Egypt see Acts 18:24-25).

An important factor of the early Christian mission was the planting of churches in the main urban centers of the Roman Empire. After the rapid quantitative growth of the church in Jerusalem (Acts 2:41; 4:4; cf. Acts 21:20), churches were planted in Damascus (by A.D. 31/32), Caesarea (A.D. 31-33), Antioch (A.D. 35?), Rome (before A.D. 49), Corinth (A.D. 50), Alexandria* (before A.D. 52? cf. Acts 18:24-25) and Ephesus (A.D. 52). The history of the church in Colosse indicates that churches in large centers such as Ephesus served as bases for regional outreach through other missionaries (cf. Col 1:7; 4:12). Local and regional expansion is the result of the preaching in the congregational services (1 Cor 14:23-25; cf. 1 Cor. 11:26; Rom 10:9), of individual Christians responding to questions about the faith (1 Pet 3:15; cf. Lk 12:11) and of the proclamation ministry of evangelists (*euangelistēs*, Acts 21:8; cf. Acts 8:14-17, where the term is used for the missionary Philip; 2 Tim 4:5 for the church leader Timothy; Eph 4:11 for members of local churches engaged in mission; cf. 1 Thess 1:8; Phil 1:14).

Some Christian communities were established by Christians who traveled for other than missionary purposes. The church in Rome may have been established by Roman Jews who were converted during their pilgrimage to Jerusalem around Pentecost in A.D. 30, by Jewish Christian traders such as Aquila from Pontus (Lampe, 3-4) or by Jewish Christian associates of Stephen whose ancestors were Roman *liberti* (cf. Acts 6:9) and who returned to their Roman relatives when they were persecuted in Jerusalem (Lampe, 53). Similar assumptions may explain the foundation of the churches in the north Anatolian provinces of Pontus-Bithynia and Cappadocia (1 Pet 1:1; Michaels, 9, refers to Paul's refusal to enter Bithynia in Acts 16:7 and the possible links with Paul's policy of not doing missionary work where others had already been pioneers).

Apart from the churches in the urban centers, which have already been mentioned, there were churches in as many as fifty other towns: Samaria—villages (Acts 9:25); coastal plain—Azotus (Acts 8:40), Lydda (Acts 9:32), Sharon (Acts 9:35), Joppa (Acts 9:36), Ptolemais (Acts 21:7); Syria—Tyre (Acts 21:3-4), Sidon (Acts 27:3), Pella* in the Decapolis (Eusebius *Hist. Eccl.* 3.5.3, referring to A.D. 66/67), possibly in towns in Arabia (Nabatea, Gal 1:18) and presumably in towns in Syria-Cilicia (Acts 15:23, 41; Gal 1:21-23), presumably Tarsus (Acts 9:30; 11:25); Cyprus—Salamis and Paphos (Acts 13:5, 6; 15:39, cf. Acts 11:19); Pamphylia—Perge (Acts 14:25); Pisidia—Antioch (Acts 13:14-52), Iconium (Acts 14:1-7), Lystra (14:8-19), Derbe (14:20-21); Phrygia—Laodicea (Acts 2:1), Hierapolis (Acts 4:13), Smyrna, Pergamum, Sardis and Philadelphia (Rev 1:11); Lydia—Thyatira (Rev 1:11); Asia—Colosse (Col 1:2); Mysia—Troas (Acts 20:5-12; 2 Cor 2:12); Cappadocia—several towns (1 Pet 1:1); Pontus/Bithynia—presumably Amisus (1 Pet 1:1; Pliny *Ep.* 10.96); Macedonia—Philippi (Acts 16:12-40; Phil 1:1), Thessalonica (Acts 17:1-4; 1 Thess 1:1), Berea (Acts 17:10-12); Epirus—Nicopolis (Tit 3:12); Achaia—perhaps Athens (Acts 17:32-34; cf. Eusebius *Hist. Eccl.* 3.4.10), Cenchreae (Acts 18:18; Rom 16:1).

Other churches existed in Italy—Puteoli (Acts 28:13-14); Dalmatia (south Illyria, 2 Tim 4:10)—perhaps Scodra or Salonae; possibly in Spain (cf. Rom 15:24, 28; *1 Clem.* 5.5-7; Muratorian fragment lines 38-39); and possibly even in Gaul (in 2 Tim 4:10 "Galatian" may refer to Gaul; cf. the usage of Polybius; the v.l. in ℵ C and others that read *Gallian,* "to Gaul," perhaps intends to dissipate the terminological confusion; cf. Spicq, 811-13, who wants to think of Lugdunum [Lyons], Vienna [Vienne] and Massilia [Marseille]).

According to later sources there were further churches by A.D. 180 in as many as sixty other towns in Syria: several towns near Antioch; Edessa; Parthia: Zabdiene, Adiabene; Cappadocia; Caesarea, Melitene; Isauria; Laranda; Pisidia: Philomelium; Mysia: Patium; Bithynia: Nicomedia; Asia: Magnesia, Tralles, towns near Smyrna and other towns; Phrygia: Apamea, Cumane, Eumanea, Hieropolis, Otrus, Pepuza, Synnada, Tymion; Galatia: Ancyra, Sinope; Pontus: Amastris; Thrace: Anchialus, Deultum; Thessaly: Lacedaemon, Larissa; Crete: Cnossus, Gortyn; Cephallene: Same; Egypt: several towns; Sicily: Syracuse; Italy: Neapolis; Gallia: Lugdunum, Vienne and among the Celts; Germania: in several places; Spain: in several towns; Africa: Carthage; Numidia: Madaura, Scilium (Harnack 1924, 626-28; cf. Harnack 1908, 2:94-96).

As regards the postapostolic expansion of the church, we have no information of the beginnings of the church in Egypt. We do not know where Apollos (Acts 18:24-25) was converted; the Western addition to Acts 18:25 (D) says that Apollos had been instructed "in his own country," implying that the gospel had reached Alexandria around A.D. 50, which some scholars accept as historical fact, whether the addition is based upon personal knowledge or on inference (Metzger, 413). According to Eusebius (Eusebius *Hist. Eccl.* 2.16), it was John Mark who preached the gospel "which he had written down" in Egypt and was the first to plant churches in Alexandria. When the rebellion of the Jews from the Cyrenaica to Egypt was ruthlessly quelled in A.D. 116, thousands of Jews were massacred; if the Jewish Christian churches ceased to exist as a result, this may explain the silence of the sources (Hengel 1979).

The early Christians evidently were not too interested in precise figures of quantitative growth. The only figures from the NT period are given by Luke as rounded figures (*hōs[ei]*), and only for the growth of the Jerusalem church, which numbers "about three thousand" (Acts 2:41), then five thousand (Acts 4:4; *myriades,* "thousands," in Acts 21:20 is more general and seems to include at least all Jewish Christians in Palestine). These figures can be shown to be reliable (Reinhardt). In view of the fact that Luke, in writing Acts, used biblical language and models and surely knew the historical books of the OT where not only approximate but often precise numbers are given (particularly in connection with the exodus and the return from the exile, although the tradition of exile and return is not prominent in Luke-Acts), it is astonishing that he does not give more precise figures, repeated censuses of members of individual churches and sum totals of the number of churches and/or the number of Christians. Paul never mentions statistics with regard to the churches he has founded or he writes to.

We have only one statistic about the numbers of Christians before Constantine: 154 ministers of varying rank (including 46 presbyters and 7 deacons) and "more than 1,500 widows and poor people" who are said to be supported by the Christians in Rome in 251 (Eusebius *Hist. Eccl.* 6.43.11-12). How these figures can be used to arrive at a total figure (between ten thousand and thirty thousand Christians?) remains precarious (cf. Lampe, 116).

2.5. Means of Communication. Language is the basic constituent of communication, and thus we notice that the NT and the early Christian documents contain hints of various local languages being spoken besides Greek. On the day of Pentecost, Diaspora Jews (*see* Diaspora Judaism) from Parthia, Media, Elam, Mesopotamia, Cappadocia, Pontus, Asia, Phrygia, Pamphylia, Egypt, Libya, Rome, Judea, Crete and Arabia (Nabatea) hear the apostles speak the great deeds of God in their own languages (*idios dialektos,* Acts 2:11). The people of Malta are designated *barbaroi* (Acts 28:2, 4), a term that denotes that they had retained their Phoenician dialect and did not speak Greek well. The inhabitants of Lystra spoke Lycaonian (Acts 14:11), corresponding to the fact that there is evidence from inscriptions that most of the ethnic Phrygians, Paphlagonians, Pisidians, Lycaonians and Celts (Galatians in Asia Minor, Gauls) had maintained their own languages; however, they presumably knew enough Greek to understand what the Christian missionaries said to them.

In Philippi and in Corinth the official language seems to have been Latin, but Greek was also used. The dividing line between Latin or Greek being used as official language was the border between Macedonia/Thrace and Dalmatia/Moesia (apart from colonies as languages enclaves). With regard to Thomas's alleged mission in India, *Acts of Thomas* 1.8 states that the Indians "did not understand what he said" since he spoke in Hebrew. As the first

Christian missionaries were bilingual Jews, speaking Hebrew and/or Aramaic and Greek, the translation of important news was a normal practice.

There is no evidence from the NT period that the earliest Christian missionaries used any languages other than Hebrew/Aramaic and Greek. Since the Gospels are attested about A.D. 180 in Latin and Syriac, Christian teaching in these languages must have been older; there is no evidence that other translations of the Bible were promoted by church leaders. This need not indicate a lack of missionary interest. Anyone who could read or write was likely to know Greek or Latin; many of the spoken dialects (e.g., in Asia Minor) lacked any literary history and often any alphabet; and in and around the towns there is evidence of an easy bilingualism. When Irenaeus of Lyons refers (c. A.D. 180) to his "exertions" in barbarian dialect (Irenaeus *Haer.* presc. 1.3), this should probably be seen not as a reference to the use of Celtic or Latin but as a literary disclaimer. But we do not know what missionaries and preachers in small townships in Pontus, Persia, Egypt or Africa may have tried. We should not rule out exceptional Christian missionaries like Ulfilas, whose Cappadocian parents had been taken captive by the Goths and who invented a Gothic alphabet in the 350s and taught the Goths the Scripture in their own language (Lane Fox, 284-87).

The fulfillment of Jesus' mission charge required travel. Overland journeys could be undertaken by camels, donkeys, mules, horses or wheeled conveyances—or by foot, the means of transport of the early Christians missionaries, covering twenty to thirty kilometers per day. On the highways and byways of the empire, traffic was heavy, as "the people of the Roman empire traveled more extensively and more easily than had anyone before them—or would again until the nineteenth century" (Meeks, 17). The missionaries would have encountered imperial officials, judges, soldiers on the march, municipal magistrates, traders, letter carriers, pilgrims, tourists, poets, actors, doctors, artisans, conjurers, transients and philosophers. The wayside inns where ordinary travelers would put up were run-down and unclean facilities; the NT encouragements to hospitality* (Rom 12:13; 1 Tim 3:2; Tit 1:8; 3:13; Heb 13:2; 1 Pet 4:9; cf. *Did.* 11—13; *1 Clem.* 10—12) and the recognition of those with whom traveling missionaries stayed (3 Jn 5-8; cf. Acts 16:15, 34; 21:7-8, 17; 28:14) have to be understood in the context of the churches' involvement in spreading the gospel. The dangers involved in land and sea travel are mentioned in 2 Corinthians 11:26-27.

The means for the dissemination of news that could potentially be used by the early church were speeches, conversations, messengers carrying letters, graffiti and the "grapevine" (Reck, 106-51). For internal communication the churches used messengers and letters. For missionary purposes only public speeches and personal conversations were viable and reliable options; persuasion, in the sense of changing convictions of others, happens primarily through personal relationships; and the other means of mass communication were either unreliable or, in the case of the government communication network (postal service, gazette, edicts), not accessible. Personal contacts in the street were possible only on the horizontal level; contacts in the house allow vertical relationships of a personal nature. Thus the early churches meeting in houses—mixed communities of everyday life, of work, trade and business—had definite advantages for communicating the gospel as widely as possible (cf. 1 Cor 14:22-25; see Households).

The early Christian missionaries, on entering a new town, arrived as strangers. Thus they could either stay at inns and attempt to reach people in the marketplace and in the streets; or, and more naturally, they could find immigrants and temporary residents from their own country or ethnos and practitioners of their own trade who tended to gather in the same areas of the town (Meeks, 29). This is precisely what Acts reports concerning the mission of Paul: being a Jew he first contacted other Jews and started to preach to them; being a tentmaker he got in contact with such workshops, presumably using them as another locus of his preaching ministry (see DPL, Tentmaking).

For conversions to happen the missionaries must have been seen by the later converts to possess high initial credibility. This included (1) their competence, that is, their knowledge of their message about God's revelation in Jesus' person and work (as witnesses of Jesus' resurrection or as disciples of the apostles, having spiritual authority), as well as their ability to perform miracles* (with regard to the second century see Eusebius Hist. Eccl. 3.37.3); (2) their charac-

ter (i.e., their trustworthiness); and (3) their composure, that is, their exemplary and courageous behavior in stressful situations (Acts 20:18-21; 1 Thess 2:1-12; 1 Pet 5:1; 2 Pet 1:12-21; 3:2; 1 Jn 1:1-3; Jude 3, 17).

2.6. Challenges for Missionary Outreach. A first challenge for international missionary outreach—which tried to convince people to change their religious convictions, to alter patterns of behavior in everyday life and to switch loyalty from family, city or country to a new community—was the lack of relevant models. There was neither an organized active mission of Jews to Gentiles (McKnight) nor much evidence of any organized or conscious missionary outreach of pagan cults (see Religions, Greco-Roman). There is no sign of any pagan god whose cult required active evangelism; not even the emperor* cult tried to change anyone's religion (MacMullen 1981, 97-105). The expansion of oriental cults was evidently not the result of successful recruitment of new converts but a function of mobility: the relocation of families from the east (MacMullen 1981, 116-17). The military conquests of Alexander the Great or the expansion of Greek culture or of Roman administration were hardly patterns that "fishers of men" could emulate.

The "herald" (kēryx) of secular society was not regarded as a generally suitable model either, presumably since it designated subordinate officials and was associated with institutions, although the designation was useful in underlining the effective act of proclamation (cf. 1 Tim 2:7; 2 Tim 1:11). The contact between the Jewish Diaspora communities and the religious center in Jerusalem by šᵉlûḥîm ("messengers," i.e., Gk apostoloi) may be regarded as a personal and relational model for global communication (Reck, 157) but could hardly serve as a model for the universal Christian mission that wanted to reach Jews and Gentiles and that aimed at more than maintaining existing contacts as it focused on winning "people of different faiths" for Christ.

A second challenge to easy communication of the gospel was the dissimilarity of basic beliefs and values, with the vitality of pagan faiths continuously introducing and adapting new forms and rites of worship (MacMullen 1981, 106; cf. Acts 14:11-15; 17:19-23) and with the gospel message that spoke about a Jewish Messiah who died on the cross and was raised from the dead being deeply incompatible with traditional Jewish and pagan conceptions of God and of salvation (cf. 1 Cor 1—2). In this context Acts relates the direction and the success of the early Christian mission to the power of the Holy Spirit (Acts 4:8, 31; 5:32; 6:5; 7:55; 8:29, 39; 10:10-20, 47; 13:4, 9; cf. 1 Thess 1:4-6; 1 Cor 2:5).

A third challenge to the early Christian mission was social and cultural barriers. The first cultural barrier was between Jewish Christians (see Jewish Christianity) and Jews, occasioned by the different views on the land and the temple, on sacrifices* and on salvation, on circumcision,* and on food. The early missionaries, even Paul the apostle to the Gentiles (cf. Acts 16:3; 18:18; 21:20-26), sought to care for some Jewish susceptibilities.

A second cultural barrier was that between Jewish Christians and Gentiles, with many Jews' basic inclination toward segregation (cf. *Ep. Arist.* 139.142), and with potential hostility of pagans against Jews (cf. Cicero *Pro Flacco* 28.67). The former was solved, at least on a theological level, rather early in connection with Peter's encounter with a Roman military commander, Cornelius* (Acts 10:1—11:18), in which the leader of the apostles learns that he must not regard anybody as unclean (Acts 10:28). The latter was addressed by admonishing the Christians to be good citizens and live in accordance with cultural conventions (1 Cor 10:32-33; Col 4:5; 1 Tim 3:7; 1 Thess 4:12; 1 Pet 2:12-14), not to give legitimate cause for action by the Roman state (cf. Acts 16:35-39; 18:12-17; 19:21-41; 21—28), not to try to impose Christian behavior on pagans (1 Pet 4:15), not to retaliate, to pray, and to be willing to suffer. Paul preaches to "Jews and Greeks" (i.e., to the entire population of the Hellenistic cities; Acts 11:19-20; 14:1; 18:4; 19:17; cf. Rom 1:16; 10:12).

A third cultural barrier existed between educated Jewish or Gentile Christians in the towns and cities and the non-Hellenized barbarians and between poor Christian missionaries and the well-to-do (among them houseowners as patrons and/or potential hosts of churches). Awareness of such social distinctions is reflected in Romans 1:14. A similar barrier, for potential converts from the upper class or even the urban artisans, constituted the presence of poor freedmen and dispossessed slaves.

There also was always potential conflict between missionaries subject to the jurisdiction of hostile Jewish authorities or as noncitizen residents *(metoikoi)* subject to local magistrates. The Christian missionaries are portrayed as being unimpressed by threats and willing to go to prison (cf. Acts 4:1-31; 5:17-42). When the option existed, they defended themselves on legal grounds (cf. Acts 18:12-17; 2—26); when the situation became too explosive they evacuated the city (cf. Acts 17:5-10; 20:1).

A fourth challenge to missionary outreach may have been psychological barriers, such as the high self-esteem of officials of synagogues* and towns; skepticism with respect to the central place of the resurrection of Jesus and of his death on the cross in Christian evangelistic preaching; apprehension of pagans concerning to the prospect of joining a new Jewish-related sect; apparent similarities between the practices of wandering philosophers (sometimes regarded as charlatans) and the Christian missionaries (cf. 1 Thess 2:1-12?). Many scholars have tried to explain the appeal of Christianity in psychosocial terms, implying that potential converts feel some kind of conflict in their present social state, including a sense of anxiety (F. Cumont), and gravitate naturally toward a message of appeasement. Since we must reckon with a vast variety of economic and personal situations and since this model hardly explains the conversion of people of higher social standing, this approach does not answer all questions concerning the motives for conversions (cf. White, 123).

Fifth, for a pagan to switch allegiance to the worship of one God while denying the existence of all the other gods would incur the charge of atheism, which (as in the case of the Jews) might lead to vilification and slander or (as happened in the second century) to outright persecution involving charges of treason or disloyalty, since the Christian faith could not claim to be an old and venerable religion and could not point to a protracted period of official patronage as could the Jewish faith. The fact that the Christians met in house churches could be interpreted as secret gatherings where, it was alleged, mysterious and immoral things happened (Lane Fox, 419-34).

Sixth, there were structural and organizational issues such as finance, with the option of being supported by an existing church that sends gifts (cf. Phil 4:10-18) or by manual work of the missionaries who thus support themselves (cf. 1 Thess 2:9; 2 Thess 3:8; 1 Cor 4:12; Acts 18:3; 20:33-34); headquarters, with great flexibility (e.g., Paul's move from Damascus to Tarsus, from Antioch to Corinth and to Ephesus and the expected move to Rome in order to establish a base for a planned mission to Spain); the lack or scarcity of social networks capable of providing patronage and benefaction that would ensure social acceptance in the community, which seems to have been a major factor in the expansion of oriental cults (although Corinth may have been an exception in this regard); coworkers (cf. *DPL*, Coworkers, Paul and His) and their availability; the need to evangelize as quickly as possible on account of the expected Parousia and to see others as firmly as possible established in a committed Christian position (cf. Jas 5:19-20; 2 Pet 3:17).

Seventh, there were potential personal obstacles: family members who came along on missionary journeys (1 Cor 9:5) and their needs; cramped urban living conditions, with an average population density in cities approaching two hundred per acre (corresponding to conditions in industrial slums in Western cities); the hardships and dangers of travel; and the demands of contacts with a formidable variety of people.

2.7. Words and Deeds. In accordance with Jesus' own example and his previous injunction to preach and to heal (Mt 10:7-8), to teach and to make new disciples among the pagans (Mt 28:19-20), as witnesses of the crucified and risen Jesus (Acts 1:3, 8) the early Christian missionaries are portrayed as preaching the gospel, occasionally healing people and helping the Christians to form caring communities characterized by selfless love.*

The message that the apostles preached concentrated on the atoning death of Jesus the Messiah who was raised from the dead and who, as living Lord, commands both Jews and pagans to repent—the Jews over the misunderstanding that occasioned Jesus' death, the pagans of their idolatry*—and to commit themselves to God's new and conclusive revelation as the exclusive source of salvation that the prophets* looked forward to (cf. 1 Cor 15:3-5; 2 Cor 5:21; Rom 4:25; Acts 2:36; 5:30-31; 10:34-43; 13:25-41; 17:30).

According to the evidence in Acts, the missionary preaching of the apostles interacted with the religious views of the audiences (in Acts 14:8-20 with popular superstition, in Acts 17:16-34 with the natural theology of the Stoics and Epicureans), resisting accommodation to popular piety in spite of Roman imperial religious policy. When Paul discusses the appropriate Christian interaction with the religious pluralism of contemporary society (1 Cor 8—10), both in public and in private situations, he aims to help the church to find a response that would not only help to fulfill its social obligations to society but also enhance its evangelistic task (cf. Winter).

The "deed" accompanying the "word" of the missionaries (cf. Rom 15:18) would include their irreproachable conduct, miraculous events such as healings, loving concern and personal involvement with individual people for their spiritual welfare and steadfast endurance* amid suffering (cf. 1 Thess 2:1-12; 2 Cor 12:12; Acts 20:18-21, 31).

The message of the Christian missionaries and the life of the Christian communities caused the separation of church and synagogue (*see* Christianity and Judaism). The cause was not principally the Gentile mission of Paul (cf. Martin) but the public preaching about Jesus and the missionary success of the Jerusalem church, leading to opposition and hostile actions by the Sanhedrin (Acts 4:1-21; 5:12-33; 6:8-15; 7:54-60; 8:1-3) and by Herod Antipas (Acts 12:1-4) that culminated in the killing of Stephen and James and a large-scale persecution. Whether there was an official excommunication of the Christians from the synagogue or not, the record of Acts shows its reality, or confirms, if the evidence of the Gospels regarding vehement opposition to Jesus is included, that Jewish antagonism against the followers of Jesus existed from the beginning and quickly included institutional consequences (cf. Acts 6:1, the need to care for widows).

2.8. The Missionaries. Terms used for missionaries include *apostolos* ("apostle"), first of all the Twelve as witnesses* of all that Jesus did in Judea and in Jerusalem, including his death and resurrection (Acts 1:21-22; 10:39-41); then Paul as the "last" of the apostles (1 Cor 15:8; cf. 1 Cor 1:1; Acts 14:4, 14); finally other commissioned missionaries (1 Cor 9:5; 12:28; 2 Cor 11:13; Eph 4:11) such as Barnabas (Acts 14:4, 14) and the husband-and-wife ministry teams of Aquila and Prisca (Rom 16:3), and Andronicus and Junia (Rom 16:7).

Martys ("witness") designates those who were personally present when Jesus ministered and when he had been raised from the dead, who interpret the person and work of Jesus and who stand up for the gospel message (Acts 1:8, 22; 2:32; thirteen times in Acts).

Halieus anthrōpōn ("fisher of people"), used only by Jesus in the initial calling of his disciples (Mk 1:17; Mt 4:19; cf. Lk 5:10), defines the missionary commission as "catching" human beings, that is, getting them to repent, leading them to faith in the good news of the kingdom and joining the new community. The context implies the call to a full-time itinerant life of ministry.

Euangelistēs ("evangelist," a person who announces good news), is used for Philip in Caesarea (Acts 21:8), who was a missionary in Samaria (Acts 8:4-40); for Timothy in Ephesus (2 Tim 4:5), designating part of the work of a church leader; and for ministers of the church "between" the itinerant apostles and the stationary pastors (Eph 4:11).

Hypēretēs ("servant") is used by Luke for the disciples as eyewitnesses (Lk 1:2) and for Paul as divinely called missionary (Acts 26:16; cf. 1 Cor 4:1); the term emphasizes the centrality of the gospel message and implies both the authority* of God's revealing Word, which is the person and work of Jesus, and the unreserved nature of their dedication to Jesus' cause.

Kēryx ("preacher," a "herald" or "proclaimer" of new or important information) is used for Paul (1 Tim 2:7; 2 Tim 1:11).

Synergos ("fellow worker") is used for missionaries generally as they participate in God's work (1 Cor 3:9; 1 Thess 3:2), specifically for the members of a missionary team who shared in the ministry of evangelization, such as Prisca and Aquila, Urbanus, Timothy, Titus, Epaphroditus or Clement (Rom 16:3, 9, 21; 1 Thess 3:2; 2 Cor 8:23; Phil 2:25; 4:3).

Ergatēs ("worker"), characterizing the activity of the ministry as one of labor, is used for Timothy (2 Tim 2:15; in a negative setting 2 Cor 11:13; Phil 3:2).

Koinōnos ("partner"), used for Titus as Paul's associate in mission (2 Cor 8:23), describes personal relationship, with a nuance of confidence and joy in service (Ollrogg, 77).

The NT refers to the activity of at least thirty-two (not counting the ten of the Twelve mentioned only in lists) and possibly forty-two

missionaries, by far the largest group of Christian ministers for whom personal names are given in the NT period. Of the Twelve, only the ministry of Peter and of John is referred to. Peter was primarily involved in the mission to the Jewish people (Gal 2:9; cf. Acts 2—12); he joins the missionary outreach to the Samaritans (Acts 8:14-25) and is instrumental in inaugurating the mission to the Gentiles (Acts 10:1—11:18). We do not know why he came to Syrian Antioch (Gal 2:11) and how long he stayed; the tradition of the third century that Peter was the first bishop of Antioch (Eusebius *Hist. Eccl.* 3.22.36; Origen *Homily on Luke* 6.100) is historically suspect in view of Acts 11:19-26 and Ignatius's* letters.

The tradition that Peter left Jerusalem after twelve years (i.e., in A.D. 41/42) and went to Rome (*Acts of Peter* 5.22) to become the original missionary who founded the church in the capital of the empire and was its first bishop, implying that the "other place" (Acts 12:17) to which Peter went after leaving Jerusalem was Rome (Eusebius *Hist. Eccl.* 2.14.6; 2.17.1; 15.2; *Chronicon* 261F [ed. Helm 179]; Jerome *Vir.* 5.8) is held by some to be reliable (Thiede, 153-56), while others regard this claim as erroneous (Brown and Meier, 98.102-3) or remain undecided (Riesner, 106). Peter may have been involved in missionary work among both Jews and Gentiles (cf. the evidence of 1 Peter*) in the territories in Asia Minor north and west of the Taurus Mountains (1 Pet 1:1) sometime after he left Jerusalem (Acts 12:17) until his martyrdom in Rome around A.D. 64 (Davids 1990, 8).

The only other member of the circle of the Twelve mentioned as a missionary in the NT is John, who appears besides Peter as commissioned with outreach to the Jewish people (Gal 2:9); in Acts 8:14-25 he appears with Peter as evangelizing among the Samaritans.

Paul as the "last" of the apostles (1 Cor 15:8), commissioned primarily to outreach among the Gentiles (Gal 2:9; Acts 9:15; 26:17-18) but determined to reach "the Jews first" (Acts 13:14; 14:1; 17:1-2; 18:1-4, 19; 19:18), evangelized in Nabatea (Arabia), Syria-Cilicia, Cyprus, south Galatia, Asia, Mysia, Macedonia, Achaia, in Rome, probably in Crete (Tit 1:5) and also possibly in Spain.

James, the brother of Jesus and leader of the Jerusalem church, appears beside Peter and John as charged with the mission to the Jewish people (Gal 2:9). If he is the author of the epistle of James,* he seems to appear as exercising ecclesial authority over Jewish Christians outside of Palestine, probably in Syria* and Asia Minor (Davids 1982, 64). His authority over the mission to Diaspora Jews is referred to in *Gospel of Thomas* 12 (the saying probably dates from James's lifetime and reflects the outlook of the early Jewish Christian mission to east Syria; cf. Bauckham 1995, 451).

Some scholars posit a mission to the Gentiles—independent of Paul's mission—by ultraconservative Jewish Christians from Jerusalem who insisted on full observance of the Torah, including circumcision (Martyn; Dunn 1993, 10-12). This inference is based on Paul's insistence on the independence of his own apostolic commissioning (Gal 1:1, 11-24); this does not prove, however, that the opponents of Paul in Galatia (and Greece?; cf. 2 Cor 11—12; Phil 3) could claim the authorization of leaders of the Jerusalem church such as James and were thus part of an official mission from Jerusalem. There is no evidence for such an ultraconservative Jewish Christian mission to Gentiles independent of Paul's letters or outside the churches established by him. The fact that such people traveled to Galatia and perhaps other areas in order to correct, improve and "complete" Paul's gospel does not make them missionaries; it is best to call them "teachers" (Martyn), and many interpreters find it reasonable to argue that they were the "false brothers" of Jerusalem who "belonged to the party of the Pharisees" and were not supported by the Jerusalem apostles (Acts 15:5; *see DPL,* Opponents of Paul §3), though they may have claimed the support of the mother church (2 Cor 10—13).

Stephen, a converted Diaspora Jew living in Jerusalem and one of the Seven (Acts 6:5), is portrayed as a spokesman for God (Acts 6:8) whose preaching in Jerusalem provoked vehement opposition as it replaced the continuity of God's revelation in Israel centering in the temple with his revelation in Jesus (Acts 7). His friends and followers opened up the next phase in the early Christian mission (Acts 8:1-4). Philip, the second of the Seven (Acts 6:5), emerges in this context as missionary in Samaria (Acts 8:5-13), as evangelist to an Ethiopian (Acts 8:26-39) and as evangelist in "all the cities" between Azotus/Ashdod and Caesarea, the official capital of Judea and the official seat

of the procurator, where he eventually had his base (Acts 11:19; 21:8).

Barnabas (Joseph), a Cypriot Jew (Acts 4:36) living in Jerusalem, becomes involved in the mission to Syrian Antioch (Acts 11:22-26), is a partner of Paul in the mission to Cyprus and south Galatia (Acts 13—14) and then concentrates on Cyprus (Acts 15:39). If Acts 13:1 may be linked with Acts 11:20, we have further names of leaders of the early Jewish Christian mission to Syria, particularly Antioch: Simeon called Niger (no inference about his race seems possible; cf. Barrett, 603), Lucius of Cyrene, and Manaen, who had court connections with Herod Antipas.

Timothy, son of a Jewish mother living in Lystra and a convert of Paul (1 Cor 4:17), was drafted as a missionary worker into Paul's team (Acts 16:1). He participated in Paul's Gentile mission to Macedonia and Achaia (Acts 17—18), with special responsibilities for Thessalonica (1 Thess 3:1-6), and to Ephesus (cf. Acts 19:22), with special responsibilities for Corinth (1 Cor 16:10-11) and later for Ephesus (1 Tim 1:3).

Silas (Silvanus), a leading member of the Jerusalem church (Acts 15:22) and perhaps a Roman citizen like Paul (Acts 16:37-38), belonged to Paul's missionary team when it worked in Macedonia and Achaia (Acts 15:40; 16:19; 17:4, 10; 2 Cor 1:19), with special responsibilities in Berea (Acts 17:15). Luke, a physician (Col 4:14) originating probably from Antioch (Eusebius *Hist. Eccl.* 3.4.6), was one of Paul's "coworkers" (Philem 24). According to long-established tradition he was the companion of Paul in his mission to Macedonia, possibly with particular responsibilities in Philippi between A.D. 50 and 57 (cf. the "we" passages in Acts).

Prisca (Priscilla) and Aquila, a Jewish Christian couple from Rome, who later resided in Corinth and in Ephesus before returning to Rome, were business people who provided Paul with the opportunity to earn money. They worked as a husband- and-wife-team in Ephesus and provided the meeting point for a house church in Rome (Rom 16:4).

Titus, a Greek Christian, perhaps a convert of Paul (Tit 1:4) who (presumably) remained uncircumcised (Gal 2:3), was Paul's partner and fellow worker (2 Cor 8:23). He undertook assignments in Corinth (2 Cor 7:6-7, 13-15; 8:6) and presumably accompanied Paul to Crete, where he became responsible for further missionary work (Tit 1:5). He may have been involved in a mission to Dalmatia (2 Tim 4:10) and is reported to have returned to Crete (Eusebius *Hist. Eccl.* 3.4.5). Another close associate was Tychicus, of the province of Asia (Acts 20:4), whom Paul calls "a faithful servant and fellow slave in the Lord" (Col 4:7); we see him on missions to Colosse, Ephesus and Crete (Col 4:7-9; Eph 6:21; 2 Tim 4:12; Tit 3:12).

Other fellow workers mentioned by Paul are John Mark (Philem 24), a member of the Jerusalem church (Acts 12:12, 25; 13:13) and a companion of Paul during the mission to Cyprus, where he continued to work with Barnabas (Acts 13; 15:37-39), later becoming a member of Paul's most intimate circle (cf. Col 4:10-11; 2 Tim 4:11) and an associate of Peter (1 Pet 5:13; cf. Eusebius *Hist. Eccl.* 3.39.15).

Apollos of Alexandria (Acts 18:24) served in Achaia (Acts 18:27), particularly in Corinth (1 Cor 3:5-6, 9), later perhaps in Ephesus (1 Cor 16:12) and on Crete (Tit 3:13). Epaphroditus of Philippi, presumably a Gentile convert, labored at Paul's side when the latter was in prison (Phil 2:25-30). Euodia and Syntyche, two women who were highly valued coworkers, had energetically participated in Paul's mission, perhaps in Philippi (Phil 4:3); Clement, presumably a Philippian Christian, was another coworker (Phil 4:3). Aristarchus, presumably of Thessalonica (Acts 19:29; 20:4; 27:2), belonged to the group that accompanied Paul on his final journey to Jerusalem and thence to Rome (Col 4:10-11; Philem 24). Epaphras of Colosse, presumably converted during Paul's mission to Ephesus (Acts 19:8-10), led the mission to the Lycus valley and evangelized in Colosse, Laodicea and Hierapolis (Col 1:7; 4:12; Philem 23).

Jesus Justus was a coworker of Jewish birth (Col 4:11); and Demas, a coworker of Gentile birth (Col 4:14; Philem 24), later deserted Paul (2 Tim 4:10). Perhaps the (released?) slave Onesimus (Philem 13) was a "helper in the work of mission" (Ollrogg, 104). Philemon may have founded the church at Laodicea, Philip and his daughters (Acts 21:8) the church at Hierapolis (cf. Papias, in Eusebius *Hist. Eccl.* 3.39.9).

We hear further of the husband-and-wife ministry team of Andronicus and Junia, Jewish Christians presumably of the Hellenistic circle in Jerusalem who were "apostles" (Rom 16:7;

i.e., traveling missionaries); of Urbanus, a Christian worker known to Paul (Rom 16:9); of Crescens, who went to Galatia or perhaps to Gaul (2 Tim 4:10). Perhaps other Christians mentioned by Paul could be seen as coworkers: Tertius, who helped Paul write the letter to the Romans (Rom 16:22); Erastus of Corinth (Rom 16:23); Quartus (Rom 16:23); Phoebe in Cenchreae (Rom 16:1); Mary, who "worked hard" among the Christians of Rome (Rom 16:6); Tryphena and Tryphosa (twin sisters?), who are "workers in the Lord" (Rom 16:12); Persis, who "labored much in the Lord" (Rom 16:12); perhaps also Onesiphorus (2 Tim 1:16-18; 4:19); and Zenas the lawyer (Tit 3:13).

In early patristic sources we are given further evidence for early Christian missionaries. The apostle Thomas is said to have become missionary in India; the apocryphal *Acts of Thomas* describe his ministry to the Indian king Gundophar, who ruled A.D. 20-40 at Taxila in the Punjab, which belonged to the Indo-Parthian empire (Eusebius *Hist. Eccl.* 3.1.1 [Origen?] and *Pseud.-Clem. Recog.* 9.29 link the apostle Thomas with Parthia), and the oral tradition of the church in south India speaks of a ministry of Thomas in Kerala. Some scholars credit this twofold tradition as being derived from a historical core and assume that Thomas was a missionary in the Punjab before traveling to south India (Farquhar), while others regard the tradition as legendary and deriving from the mission of the Syrian church in the Parthian empire in north India about 200 (Dihle). Proof for Christians in India dates to the third century.

As Indian products were readily available in Palestinian markets (Lott, *ABD* 3:410) and since the routes for merchant shipping between Egypt, Arabia and south India were well established since the first century B.C. (cf. *Periplous Maris Erythraei*, written A.D. 40-70 on the basis of oral tradition), it is not unlikely that the apostle Thomas might have traveled to India. He displays in John's Gospel a strange but understandable mixture of pessimism and impulsiveness and appears in John 11:16 as a leading disciple who seems courageously prepared to follow Jesus into death (Collins, *ABD* 6:528-27). According to another tradition, the apostle Bartholomew was involved in a mission to India as well (Eusebius *Hist. Eccl.* 5.10.3; Gelasius), as was Pantaenus of Alexandria (c. A.D. 190; Eusebius *Hist. Eccl.* 5.10.2-3; Lane Fox,

278, regards this tradition as largely true).

The apostle Andrew is said to have led a mission to Scythia (Eusebius *Hist. Eccl.* 3.1.1; cf. *Acts of Andrew and Matthias* of the sixth century). The apostle Matthew went to Ethiopia (cf. Rufinus *Hist. Eccl.* 1.9-10), where the converted official of Acts 8:26-39, according to Irenaeus (Irenaeus *Adu Haer* 3.12.8), had already been active as a missionary proclaiming "the message which he had believed." Thaddeus, one of the seventy disciples of Jesus, evangelized in Edessa in the empire of Abgar V Ukhama (A.D. 9-46) east of the Euphrates, commissioned by the apostle Thomas (Eusebius *Hist. Eccl.* 1.13.4, 11). Another source mentions Addai as the pioneer missionary to Edessa and to Adiabene in Mesopotamia (*1 Apoc. Jas.* 36.15-24; cf. the later *Doctrina Addai, Chronicle of Arbela; see* Syria, Syrian Christianity). Mark is said to have been the first missionary to Alexandria (Eusebius *Hist. Eccl.* 2.16; see 2.6 above).

While the historical value of the apocryphal acts of various apostles (*see* Apocryphal and Pseudepigraphal Writings)—a genre that became established after the third quarter of the second century—is generally regarded as negligible, apart from some of the earlier ones, it is difficult to assess the reliability of other early Christian traditions. Although details of some of the accounts are obviously fictitious, one should often reckon with a historical core; however, in most cases it is impossible to attain certainty. Thus A. Harnack (1924, 679-70) and L. W. Barnard accept the historicity of Addai and the beginnings of Christianity in Edessa in the first century, while others (cf. Lane Fox, 279-80) regard the relevant traditions as legends of the third century while accepting the presence of Christians in Edessa in the second century.

3. Mission in Acts.

The life and faith of the Christians and the churches portrayed in Acts are characterized by missionary witness from beginning to end (Acts 1:8; 28:30-31).

3.1. A Theology of Mission. A survey of the relevant vocabulary shows that "mission" (*apostolē, [ex]apostellō, [ek]pempō*) refers in Acts primarily to the work of God in sending Jesus the Messiah to the Jews and to the Gentiles through the word of his witnesses and that "witness" (*martys, martyreō, martyria, martyrion*) refers to

the activity of the twelve apostles and Paul (Bolt).

The following elements are relevant to a theology of mission of Acts:

(1) The missionary outreach of the church is directed by God at crucial stages (by the Spirit: Acts 8:29, 39; 10:19; 13:2; 15:28; 16:6; by angels*: Acts 8:26; by the Lord himself: Acts 18:9; 23:11); the apostolic mission is carried out by God himself (Acts 15:4).

(2) According to God's will (Acts 10:1—11:18) and Jesus' commission (Acts 1:8; 9:15) the preaching of the gospel moves from Jewish and Samaritan audiences to pagan Gentiles.

(3) The story of the early Christian mission is a story of geographical expansion from Jerusalem and Judea to Samaria and the coastal plain, to Antioch in Syria, to Asia Minor and to Greece and finally to Rome.

(4) The mission of the church is Israel's mission to the nations and therefore an essential aspect of Israel's restoration (Acts 1:6-8; 2:39; 3:17-26; 15:14-18; 26:22-23; 28:23).

(5) Jesus' status means that he can impart forgiveness,* rescue from God's judgment,* the gift of the Spirit and salvation (cf. Acts 2:38; 10:43; 17:31; 22:16).

(6) The Twelve, who had witnessed the main events in the life of Jesus, particularly his death and resurrection, are the primary witnesses to the fact that God has fulfilled his earlier promises.

(7) The personal experience of the living power of Jesus Christ entitles other Christians to be regarded as witnesses as well.

(8) The proclamation of the Word is a decisive factor in the passing on of the message of salvation; the witness of the apostles and other missionaries, delivered in the form of speeches that were intended as a medium of persuasion, includes elements of reasoned argument.

(9) In the encounters with Jews the decisive point is whether Jesus is the Messiah whose life and death correspond with the plan of God and whose status as *kyrios* ("Lord") accords him an authoritative position similar to that of God.

(10) In the encounters with pagans the proclamation centers on biblical conceptions of God, who demands repentance* and has designated Jesus as Lord and future judge.

(11) Jesus' position enables the apostles to do the same kind of mighty works as Jesus had done.

(12) The success of the mission is dependent on and enabled by the Holy Spirit (Acts 4:8, 31), as the crucial factor in conversion is the gift of the Spirit (Acts 2:38; 8:14-17; 9:17; 10:44-48; 11:15-18); the missionaries are inspired to speak with an effectiveness that often transcends their native ability (Acts 4:13).

(13) In the conversion of individual people several factors come together (cf. Acts 10:1—11:18): God's initiative, human instruments of God's purpose, points of contact with the religious and ethical disposition of the hearers, the reception of salvation as gracious gift.

(14) The church needs to be open for new challenges and new developments (Acts 6:1-7; 10:1—11:18).

(15) The Christian mission involves progress despite opposition: missionaries are threatened by the Sanhedrin in Jerusalem, they are brought before magistrates of Greek or Roman cities; some are killed, others are maltreated, some escape by a miracle; despite the opposition, the word of God continues its triumphal progress (cf. Marshall, 56-76; Dunn 1996, xix-xx).

3.2. The Vision of Acts 1:8 and Paul. The vision of Acts 1:8 is a worldwide mission of the apostles. What Luke then narrates is the Judean and Samaritan mission of the Jerusalem apostles (Acts 1—12) and Paul's mission from Jerusalem to Rome (Acts 13—28). As Rome is not "the ends of the earth," Luke does not report the fulfillment of Acts 1:8 but rather the most significant events leading to this goal (Hengel 1995, 35-36). This may help explain why the area depicted by the list in Acts 2:9-11 stops short of the traditional "ends of the earth" in each direction: India, Scythia, Spain and Ethiopia. As Luke had assumed a Roman view of the world in his Gospel, presenting Augustus as the ruler of the whole *oikoumenē* (Lk 2:1), he presents in the Jewish, Jerusalem-centered geographical perspective (at the beginning of Acts) how the good news of Jesus was carried from Jerusalem toward the ends of the earth. Luke presents Paul's mission as representative of the entire worldwide mission of the church: it took him to only the northwest part of the world as defined by the Jewish Diaspora, with the ends of the earth lying beyond the extent of the Diaspora. But Luke knows that there are other stories besides Paul's: when the converted eunuch continued his journey to Ethiopia (presumably to Meroe, the capital of Ethiopia/Nubia) he was "on his way" (Acts 8:39) to one of the "ends of the earth" (Bauckham 1995, 422).

3.3. Missionary Speeches and Mission Reports. The attempt to extract from the missionary speeches in Acts (Acts 2:14-39; 3:12-26; 4:9-12; 5:30-32; 10:34-43; 13:16-38; 14:15-17; 17:22-31) a common standard pattern (Wilckens, 81-91, who also analyzes 1 Thess 1:9-10 and Heb 6:1-2) has been criticized on account of basic differences between the various passages (Holtz, 55).

Luke regularly includes reports that missionaries give to churches (Acts 14:27; 15:3, 12; 21:19; cf. Acts 11:5-17; 12:17).

4. Mission in the Letter to the Hebrews.

Without showing evidence of an interest in the Gentile mission, the author's theology has been seen as grounded in the theology of the early Hellenist Christians of Jerusalem, represented by Stephen and Philip, which fostered world mission whose biblical support was a reinterpretation of Israel's redemptive history (Manson, 25-46; cf. Lane, cxlvi-cl).

4.1. Preaching as the Work of God. The Christians to whom this letter was addressed had come to faith in response to the preaching of people who had heard Jesus teach (Heb 2:3; *see* Hebrews). The witness of these preachers had been made effective through visible signs that confirmed that God continued to speak and act through the missionaries (Heb 2:4; cf. Lane, 1:39-40). The reminder of elementary instruction in Hebrews 6:1-2 should probably not be interpreted in terms of missionary preaching or in terms of a rule for accepting new believers into the church; it is more generally a reflection of catechesis in a Jewish Christian environment.

4.2. The Preaching of the Missionaries. The reference to the "leaders" (*hēgoumenoi*) in Hebrews 13:7 may refer to the founders of the local Christian community the writer addresses; that is, to the missionaries whose preaching of the word of God and its effects in leading people to faith in Jesus Christ made them leaders (Lane). Their daily behavior was such that they remained faithful to the end and is therefore a model for the faith of the community. In the context of Hebrews 13:7, the statement in Hebrews 13:8 asserts that although the missionaries and preachers change, the preaching must remain the same. In the context of Hebrews 13:9, the acclamation of Hebrews 13:8 implies that to the extent that Jesus Christ was presented authoritatively in the preaching of the missionary leaders, they continue to have authority in the local Christian community, even after their deaths (Lane, 528-29).

5. Mission in the General Epistles.

The General Epistles do not discourse on the task of mission; several references to the commission of spreading the gospel indicate, however, that the active participation in mission was regarded as a matter of course.

5.1. James. The letter of James* does not contain evidence for missionary concern or activity (Davids 1982, 18). The comment on the believer who "turns back a sinner from the error of his way" (Jas 5:20) relates to members of the church who have deliberately forsaken the "way of truth." When a fellow believer turns a brother or a sister back from the error of wrong behavior, the "wandering" Christian is saved from destruction and freed of his or her sins through repentance. However, the notion of a concern for missionary involvement among pagan sinners must be regarded as a logical extension of the passage.

5.2. Jude. The athletic metaphor of the "fight for the faith" (Jude 3) does not suggest primarily the negative task of opposing the false teachers but refers, as in Paul, to the offensive contest of promoting the advance and victory of the gospel (*see* Jude). Resisting the influence of the false teachers and their denial of the moral implications of the gospel is part of the struggle for the gospel. The people who are to be "snatched from the fire" (Jude 22) are not unbelievers who should be introduced to faith in Jesus Christ but church members who indulged in sinful behavior and were thus in imminent danger of judgment at the Parousia (Jude 14-15).

5.3. The Letters of Peter. At the end of the opening thanksgiving (1 Pet 1:3-12) Peter describes the present as the culmination of salvation history (1 Pet 1:10-12): the salvation that the prophets spoke about belongs to the Christians living in Asia Minor scattered as homeless among the Gentiles (1 Pet 1:1), presently suffering affliction (1 Pet 1:6). They received God's "saving grace" (1 Pet 1:10) as a result of the preaching of missionaries who announced the good news (1 Pet 1:12: *hoi euangelisamenoi*). These "evangelizers" remain anonymous. According to Peter, their "success" is the work of

God himself: the missionary proclamation of the gospel is accompanied by the power of "the Holy Spirit sent from heaven." Thus the evangelistic mission of the church, carried out in the present where God finally fulfills the promises given to the prophets and where the righteous* suffer the affliction of the messianic end time, is seen as the decisive world-historical and eschatological process by which the promised and long-hidden salvation is being revealed and imparted (*see* 1 Peter).

Although Peter is hardly positive about the culture and its lifestyle that the Christians face (cf. 1 Pet 1:14; 2:25; 4:3-4), he does not advocate withdrawal, as this is impossible and "because he shares the early church's sense of evangelistic mission" (Davids 1990, 21). One of the purposes of the privileged position of the Christian community as the chosen and holy people of God (1 Pet 2:9) is to "announce the praiseworthy deeds of him who called you out of darkness into his marvelous light" (1 Pet 2:9; *see* Light). This has been interpreted as defining the outer-directed priestly* ministry of the church in terms of proclaiming to the world the mighty acts of God; this interpretation too narrowly highlights a single title in the list. The interpretation that concludes from the use of *exangellō* in the Septuagint that 1 Peter 2:9 refers to proclamation directed to God in worship* rather than to missionary preaching (cf. Michaels, 110) is dubious on semantic grounds. There seems to be no reason why one should view the interpretation in terms of worship and in terms of missionary preaching as alternatives, particularly in view of 1 Peter 1:10-12 and 1 Peter 3:1, 15.

In 1 Peter 3:1 Peter speaks to Christian women of the hope that their unbelieving husbands "who are disobedient to the word" (i.e., who did not respond to the preaching of the gospel by faith) might be "won" (*kerdainō*) by their devoted and commendable lifestyle (*anastrophē*) "without word" (*aneu logou*). Where preaching did not lead to conversions, an exemplary lifestyle might save unbelieving spouses (*see* Household Codes; Marriage; Woman and Man). More generally, as believers live among unbelievers and as pagan acquaintances might inquire after the reasons for their Christian faith and for their changed behavior (cf. 1 Pet 3:13), they are called upon to "always be ready" to give an "accounting" (*apologia*) to anyone who questions them (1 Pet 3:15).

The twofold effort of maintaining the Christian identity (of the church corporately and of one's life personally) in the context of pagan society without discarding social responsibilities (1 Pet 2:13—3:12) and of missionary outreach to non-Christians (1 Pet 3:15) had both positive results in that one could expect that people would be converted (cf. 1 Pet 3:1) and negative effects in that nonconformity might lead to self-isolation, rejection and even persecution (cf. 1 Pet 4:1-4). If *allotriepiskopos* in 1 Peter 4:15 is understood in the sense of "busybody in other people's affairs," Peter seeks to calm Christians who, in their zeal for the gospel, behave in culturally unacceptable forms as guardians of morality (cf. Michaels, 267). Although this interpretation fits the early Christian missionary situation (cf. the polemic against Christians in the second and third centuries by Celsus and Pophyry), it does not seem to fit the context in 1 Peter 4:14-16: Peter's exhortation would amount to dissuading the believers from missionary efforts, which is not possible in view of 1 Peter 1:12; 3:15. The assumption that he warns of importunate, overzealous practices of missionary involvement on account of which Christians became a nuisance is too harmless: consistent Christian mission will always bring disturbance and irritation into families and communities of people, and the term *allotriepiskopos* in 1 Peter 4:15 should more plausibly be interpreted in a criminal sense, perhaps as "embezzlement" as the vice typical of traders and brokers.

In 2 Peter 1:16 the charge of the false teachers is refuted that the teaching about the Parousia of Jesus Christ is a "myth," a fairy story fabricated with an unworthy motive. Peter stresses that the common apostolic teaching about the Parousia is based on eyewitness testimony and implies that the missionary preaching that led to the establishment of the churches addressed included the expectation of the Parousia (*see* 2 Peter).

5.4. The Letters of John. Harnack visualized a large-scale mission led by John the presbyter who, based in Ephesus, worked in the Pauline churches of Asia Minor, sent out traveling missionaries and maintained oversight over the churches by itinerant emissaries, an oversight which some churches sought to throw off (Harnack 1908, 1:81-82; *see* John, Letters of). This

view is not usually held today. According to another reconstruction, the presbyter tells the Christians who are faithful to him to refuse hospitality to secessionist missionaries by not even talking to them (2 Jn 10-11). Diotrephes, the host of a house church, took this policy further and refused hospitality to all missionaries in order to save the church from contamination (3 Jn 9-10); as a result the presbyter requests Gaius to offer hospitality to traveling Johannine missionaries (3 Jn 5-8), which is the main concern of 3 John.

Whatever the situation of the Christian communities to which the epistles of John belong and their relationship to other churches in Asia Minor was, the missionaries of whom 3 John 5-8 gives evidence (the "brothers" in 3 Jn 5 are clearly missionaries, as is shown by the urgency of the demand) are characterized in the following ways.

(1) They have "gone out" *(exerchesthai)*, that is, they have left their homes in order to embark on missionary travels (cf. Acts 14:20; 15:40). (2) They travel "for the sake of *[hyper]* the Name"; that is, they went out in the service of Christ and also to make him known, proclaiming the divine name given to Jesus (proclaiming Jesus as God's presence in the flesh; *see* Name). (3) They have been "accepting nothing from the pagans" *(ethnikoi,* "unbelievers"); they carry out their missionary work without either expecting or begging for support, presumably in order to avoid being confused with itinerant Cynic philosophers. (4) The church is "bound to support" such men, as they are "brothers." Such support *(hypolambanein,* 3 Jn 7) includes a hospitable welcome, protection and the provision of practical help and supplies that would enable them to journey to the next stop *(propempein,* 3 Jn 6). (5) Christians who thus support missionaries prove themselves to be "coworkers *(synergoi)* in the cause of the truth"; that is, they have a share in the ministry of the missionaries who proclaim the truth,* the reality of God as it has been revealed in the gospel.

6. Mission in the Revelation.

6.1. A Vision for the World. The last book of the NT canon* begins and ends with the theme of "witness" (Rev 1:2, 5; 22:20), and it most frequently refers to the whole world ("the inhabitants of the earth," ten times), indicating the universal worship of the beast,* or to "[all] the nations" (fifteen times); seven times we find the phrase "every tribe and language and people and nation" (Rev 5:9; 7:9; 10:11; 11:9; 13:7; 14:6; 17:16). One of the main themes of Revelation is that of witness (Bauckham 1993 *Theology*, 72-73). Jesus is "the faithful and true witness" (Rev 3:14; cf. Rev 1:5), referring to the verbal witness to the truth of God (cf. Rev 1:2, 9; 6:9; 20:4), as are his followers (Rev 2:13; 17:6) who hold "the witness of Jesus" (Rev 12:17; 19:10), which is their own witness (Rev 6:9; 12:11), the witness "to the true God and his righteousness, which exposes the falsehood of idolatry and the evil of those who worship the beast." In the judicial contest that is carried out in the courtroom of the world in order to decide who is the true God, Jesus and his followers bear witness to the truth.

6.2. Encouraging Faithful Witness. In the oracle to the church in Philadelphia, which received unqualified commendation from Christ who holds the "key of David" (Rev 3:7), Christ assures the believers that he has set before them an "open door which nobody is able to shut" (Rev 3:8). Unless this statement refers to free entrance into the messianic kingdom (after having been excommunicated from the local synagogue, Rev 3:9), it may mean that Christ opens up a good opportunity for missionary activity (cf. 1 Cor 16:9) even though the church has "little power" and has to endure conflict, perhaps referring to the strategic location at the juncture of trade routes leading to Mysia, Lydia and Phrygia. The two interpretations are not mutually exclusive (Hemer 1989, 162-63).

6.3. The Missionary Nature of the Church. Unless the vision of the measuring of the temple and of the two witnesses (Rev 11:1-13) is a prediction of a return of Moses and Elijah seeking to restore the nation of Israel to its land, it is best interpreted as a parable that depicts in dramatic language the nature of the church's witness: the two witnesses symbolize the church (cf. Rev 11:14 with Rev 1:12, 20), the eschatological temple of Ezekiel 40—48 (cf. the presence of worshipers in Rev 11:1), in its role of witness (two *martyres*) to the nations to which it is called even in the midst of persecution and martyrdom.

Bauckham links the content of the scroll* of Revelation 5:1-9 that is unsealed in Revelation 10:1-10 with the missionary witness and death of faithful Christians depicted in Revelation 11:1-13, pointing to John's central prophetic

concern about the coming of God's kingdom on earth. The sacrificial death of the Lamb* and the ministry of his followers, who have been redeemed "from all the nations" (Rev 5:9) to bear prophetic witness "to all the nations" (cf. Rev 11:3-13), are God's strategy for winning all the peoples of the world (cf. Rev 14:14-16; 15:3-4) from the dominion of the beast to his own kingdom (Bauckham 1993 *Theology*, 84-108; cf. Bauckham 1993 *Climax*, 238-337). This interpretation in terms of a universalistic missionary vision must be balanced by pointing out that John does not predict the degree of success that the witness of the faithful Christians will have; that John not only depicts the eschatological fulfillment of the history of God's covenant* people redeemed from all the nations in the full inclusion of all the nations but also pictures the unrepentant in their persistent adherence to the beast so that they will be condemned in final judgment; that John does not predict the salvation of each and every human being: unrepentant sinners have no place in the new Jerusalem (Rev 21:8, 27; 22:15; cf. Bauckham 1993 *Theology*, 103, 139).

7. Mission in the Early Noncanonical Writings.
Noncanonical and patristic texts of the second century (*see* Apostolic Fathers) still reflect awareness of the worldwide missionary program of the church that we see in the Gospels (Mk 13:10; 14:9; 16:15; Mt 28:19; Lk 24, 47) and in Acts (Acts 1:8); for Rome around 150 see generally Justin Martyr (Justin *Apol. I* 6.2; 10.5; 12.11; 14.3; 16.3-4; 18.2; 23.2).

7.1. Mission as Ongoing Perspective. In *Barnabas* 16.10 we find an echo of the apostolic conviction that God himself speaks in the preaching of missionaries. The *Kerygma Petrou* (c. 90-140) incorporated assumed discourses of Peter with the proclamation of the one God, repudiation of polytheism and Jewish worship and exposition of the death and resurrection of Jesus. The text is not to be regarded as simply apologetic but as accentuating certain elements in early Christian missionary preaching (Schneemelcher in Hennecke and Schneemelcher, 2:97). In recounting the "Martyrdom of Christians in Vienna and Lugdunum" (cf. Eusebius *Hist. Eccl.* 5.1.3-63; 5.2.2-7; the events took place in 177/178) we hear of a certain Alexander, a doctor from Phrygia, who was known for his love for God and his *parrēsia tou logou* ("boldness in preaching," described as an apostolic gift) and who had traveled throughout Gaul (Eusebius *Hist. Eccl.* 5.1.49), evidently preaching the gospel.

The apocryphal acts of individual apostles contain descriptions of the missionary work of the apostles in different regions and the effects of their preaching, but the particular apostle and the description of his character is usually given such prominence "that we can no longer describe them in terms of missionary history, conceived as the history of the Word of God and its publication throughout the world" (Schneemelcher in Hennecke and Schneemelcher, 2:173). Thus the miracle stories, which often describe fantastic and bizarre effects, are included not to describe the mission of the church as the work of God but rather to glorify the apostles as miracle workers, with the consequence that the apocryphal acts are more entertaining than edificatory.

The *Acts of Andrew* (c. 150-190) mention a journey of the apostle from Pontus to Achaia via Amasea, Sinope, Nicea, Nicomedia, Byzantium, across Thracia to Perinthus, to Philippi and Thessalonica in Macedonia, and finally to Patrae in Achaia (cf. Hornschuh in Hennecke and Schneemelcher, 2:397-98). In *Acts of John* 33—36 (c. 150-180, possibly of written in Egypt) we are given a missionary speech of John in Ephesus: the pagans are addressed as depraved people as in a catalog of vices; they are called upon to change their ways in order to escape eternal doom; the "mercy and goodness" of Jesus Christ are briefly mentioned (*Acts of John* 33.8-9).

7.2. Lack of Missionary Strategy? However, the evidence of the apocryphal gospels, the apocryphal acts of individual apostles and other patristic texts (evidence that has not been newly assessed on a large scale since Harnack, but see Lane Fox) indicates that the church(es) of the second and third centuries did not seem to have had an operative program of world mission.

N. Brox (194-215) gives four reasons. First was the conviction that world mission was the task of the twelve apostles given by the risen Christ (Mt 28:16-20; Acts 1:8), linked with the implication that they fulfilled this task, dividing up the world. *Acts of Thomas* 1 begins with a list of the twelve apostles who were "all in Jerusalem" and then "divided the regions of the world, that each one of us might go to the region which fell to his lot, and to the nation to which the

Lord sent him." *Hermas Similitudes* 9.17.1-2 refers to the twelve nations *(ethnē)* that inhabit the earth and among whom the apostles exclusively preached "the Son of God" (cf. *Herm. Sim.* 9.25.2). Syriac *Didascalia* 43.12-17 states the universality of Jesus' missionary commission: "Jesus Christ sent out us, the twelve, to teach the (chosen) people and the Gentile peoples" (Eusebius *Hist. Eccl.* 3.1; cf. Maiburg). Thus Irenaeus describes the church as having spread over the entire world to the ends of the earth—as the work of the apostles (Irenaeus *Haer.* 1.10.1-2; 3.11.8; 5.20.1; cf. Tertullian *Adv. Jud.* 7.3—6.9; Origen *Peri Arch.* 4.1.2-5). Rather than reflecting on the permanent task of world mission, the postapostolic teachers reflected on the success of the worldwide mission of the apostles.

Second was the certainty that conversion of people is the sovereign work of God. A third reason was the conviction that as a result of the mission of the apostles the gospel is presently offered everywhere; that is, the missionary commission of the Lord has been fulfilled in the geographically universal distribution of Christians. Therefore, the fact that not all people are Christians does not necessitate geographical expansion (i.e., mission) but refers to the coming Parousia and God's judgment of the world (cf. later Augustine *Ep.* 199.48).

A fourth reason was the attitude that the primary task of the churches was their appearance before the world, that is, their holiness.* There are only eight instances of prayer* for "mission" or for the conversion of people in pre-Constantine literature: *1 Clement* 59.4; Ignatius *Ephesians* 10.1; Aristides *Apology* 17.3; Justin Martyr *Dialogue with Trypho* 35.8; 108.3; Syriac *Didascalia* 2.56; Cyprian *De Dominica Oratione* 17; *Apostolic Constitutions* 8.10.16-17. Tertullian's prayer for the delay of the Parousia (Tertullian *Apol.* 30.7; 39.2) may be motivated by a missionary interest.

Even though the postapostolic church retained a missionary vision with universal claims (cf. *Herm. Sim.* 8.3.2; Justin *Dial. Tryph.* 53.5), it seems that there were no professional missionaries, no missionary schools or a systematic missionary strategy until the fifth century (Frohnes and Knorr, 3-67). In the post-NT period up to the age of Constantine we have unambiguous reports about only two active Christian missionaries: the Alexandrian Pantaenus, who went to India about 110 (Eusebius *Hist. Eccl.* 5.10) and the heretical Mani (216-276) from southern Mesopotamia, the founder of Manichaeism (Lane Fox, 282, 561-62); another missionary of the second century was perhaps Addai in Edessa (see 2.8 above) and, later, Gregory the Wonderworker around Neocaesarea in Pontus (third century). The lack of great missionary personalities is sometimes explained by the loss of Jerusalem as the center of the church after A.D. 70: apparently neither Antioch, Corinth, Ephesus nor Rome took up the apostolic task of sending missionaries to foreign lands.

7.3. Missionary Methods. When Pliny deplores the fact that the abominable "superstition" of the Christians has reached people of every age and social standing and has spread even to the villages and the countryside (Pliny *Ep.* 10.96.8-10) this testifies that the numbers of Christians and of churches had increased considerably during the second century. One should not explain the astonishing growth of the churches only by referring to Harnack's dictum that the "church exerted a missionary influence in virtue of her very existence" (Harnack 1908, 2:511). The geographical expansion of the church cannot thus be accounted for.

Eusebius writes that disciples of the apostles "whose hearts had been ravished by the divine Word" gave up their possessions and "set out on long journeys, doing the work of evangelists, eagerly striving to preach Christ to those who had never heard the word of faith," appointing others as pastors of the newly found churches while they themselves proceeded "to other countries and other peoples." He says that it is not possible to mention by name all the men who served as pastors or evangelists in the generation that followed the apostles (Eusebius *Hist. Eccl.* 3.37.1-4). With respect to the second century he asserts that "there were still many evangelists of the Word eager to use their inspired zeal after the example of the apostles for the increase and building up of the divine Word" (Eusebius *Hist. Eccl.* 5.10.2; cf. Origen *Cont. Cels.* 3.9).

Even though the names of the early Christian missionaries are lost, it appears that the gospel was spread by traveling Christians (cf. *Did.* 11—13, referring to wandering preachers, apostles and prophets whom the churches are to support), by the exemplary behavior of Christian traders (cf. Justin *Apol. I* 16.4), by Christians being scattered as a result of persecution (initi-

ated by hostile pagans or by fellow Christians who would not tolerate differing beliefs) or as captives of wars, and mainly through conversations with neighbors in apartment houses (Justin *Apol. I* 6.4; Justin *Apol. II* 1.2) and with family members in private houses (cf. Justin *Apol. II* 1.2). Many conversions are due to the witness and testimony of Christian women to husbands and slaves,* particularly in the higher strata of society (Grech, 92); Christian slaves witness to women and children (thus Celsus; cf. Origen *Cont. Cels.* 3.55). Some of the teachers, such as Justin Martyr and others, were missionaries in the sense that pagans entered their schools and listened to their teaching. Conversions in church services were presumably rare, since the originally unrestricted admission was increasingly limited to baptized* Christians and approved catechumens due to the danger of denunciation (cf. Lampe, 81-82; MacMullen 1984, 111; Lane Fox, 280-81).

Marcion's* activities, which reached all Roman provinces after he had left Rome in 144 (cf. Justin *Apol. I* 26; 58), are usually not interpreted in terms of missionary outreach (the two hundred thousand sesterces that the church of Rome gave him back would go a long way toward financing the extensive travels).

7.4. Explaining the Spread of Christianity. Several factors that a former generation of scholarship saw as having facilitated the spread of Christianity are either rejected or seen in a more nuanced manner today (cf. Praet):

(1) The critique of polytheism by Platonist and Stoic philosophers, for this never had any practical consequences for participation in pagan cults.

(2) The disintegration of the Greek city states *(poleis)* discrediting the gods, an explanation that focuses too much on Greece.

(3) Religious syncretism with its tolerance and its occasional dissolution of several gods into a single one; syncretism did not lead to monotheism.

(4) The Hellenistic ruler cult implying the possibility of a god-man, a parallel that does not encourage or explain faith in a crucified Messiah.

(5) Pagan religiosity saw a steady decline climaxing in the third century; this crisis theory has been abandoned or heavily modified, as it does not fit either chronologically or geographically and is selective in its appeal to the extant

data, and there is much evidence for the confident spirit of paganism.

(6) Status inconsistency among independent women, wealthy Jews in pagan cities, well-to-do freedmen stigmatized by their origin, embracing "substitute careers" as Christian converts (cf. Meeks, 191); an explanation that does not fit the facts or reckon with the complex way in which people view their own status (cf. Lane Fox, 319-22).

(7) The material and moral insecurity, leading to anxiety and a yearning for salvation in the second and especially third centuries; the evidence for optimism and firm belief in the pagans gods more than neutralizes the anxieties of some intellectuals of the time (Lane Fox, 65-66).

(8) The Christian exclusiveness, refusing all compromises and explicit forms of syncretism, as attractive features; however, pagans did not complain about the numerous options, and polytheism also had its advantages (Lane Fox, 575).

(9) The anonymity and loneliness of life in the cities made the Christian communities with their sense of belonging attractive; this sociopsychological explanation, although not entirely without value, seems to be in tune with more modern feelings: apart from Rome and Alexandria, the Mediterranean towns were small and remained connected with the countryside, and their populations consisted of identifiable social groups that maintained the traditional social controls.

The three most popular explanations for the success of the early Christian mission before Constantine are (1) miracles and exorcisms (for MacMullen the most important, if not the only, reason for conversion to Christianity during this time; cf. MacMullen 1981, 49-112; MacMullen 1984, 17-42); however, pagan gods were also believed to produce miracles, or differing explanations for miracles could be offered, and excitement about miracles wrought by Christians does not necessarily lead to acceptance of Christian exclusivism (cf. Lane Fox, 329-30). (2) The courage of the martyrs, impressing spectators with the evident inspiration of a powerful God and the value of a faith worth dying for (cf. Justin *Apol. II* 12; Tertullian *Apol.* 50.13-15); however, pagans like Epictetus offered less flattering explanations for Christian martyrdoms, and inquiry by spectators would not by necessity lead to acceptance of the Christian faith. (3) The ideal and practice of Christian love and charity impressed many (cf. Tertullian *Apol.* 39.7 and the statement by the emperor Julian reported by Eusebius *Hist. Eccl.* 9.8.11-14); however, pagan heartlessness could be exaggerated, and Christian intolerance and even hatred directed against fellow Christians who had different persuasions did not go unnoticed.

Occasionally other factors are mentioned: (4) The Christian view of life after death, with the offer of resurrection and eternal bliss; however, the idea of bodily resurrection remained unacceptable to many pagans (cf. Origen *Cont. Cels.* 5.14), and the message about a second coming of Jesus initiating the end of the world was not easy to believe either. (5) The historical nature of the Christian faith, including the unique personality of its founder, contrast with elaborate mythologies of numerous pagan gods; however, pagans countered by asking why the Christian savior came so late, leaving generations of people without salvation, and what he accomplished for his faithful other than persecution (thus Celsus; cf. Origen *Cont. Cels.* 4.7; 8.69). (6) The Christian inclusiveness, transcending national and ethnic ties, social and financial barriers, geographical boundaries, being open to both men and women; however, depending on one's personal situation such advantages might be disadvantages, and there is no evidence of pagans deciding for the Christian faith on the basis of an evaluation of these features.

Whether the Christian faith needed the conversion of Constantine in 312 (or slightly earlier) and the ensuing political support to become a world religion, having been a minority religion before then (MacMullen, Lane Fox, Praet), or whether the decisive period was the third century with a rapid numerical expansion and a growing respectability (W. H. C. Frend, P. Brown), is still disputed by historians. As none of the factors mentioned (7.4) and no combination of factors sufficiently explains the astonishing spread of Christianity, it may be more than Christian bias if we see the growth of the church as the work of divine providence.

See also ACTS OF THE APOSTLES; CENTERS OF CHRISTIANITY; EVANGELISM IN THE EARLY CHURCH; GENTILES; PENTECOST; SOCIAL SETTING OF EARLY NON-PAULINE CHRISTIANITY.

BIBLIOGRAPHY. L. W. Barnard, "The Origins

and Emergence of the Church in Edessa During the First Two Centuries," *VC* 22 (1968) 161-75; C. K. Barrett, *The Acts of the Apostles* (ICC; Edinburgh: T & T Clark, 1994); R. J. Bauckham, *The Climax of Prophecy: Studies on the Book of Revelation* (Edinburgh: T & T Clark, 1993); idem, *The Theology of the Book of Revelation* (NTT; Cambridge: Cambridge University Press, 1993); idem, "James and the Jerusalem Church" in *The Book of Acts in Its Palestinian Setting*, ed. R. J. Bauckham (BAFCS; Grand Rapids: Eerdmans, 1995) 415-80; P. G. Bolt, "Mission and Witness" in *The Book of Acts in Its Theological Setting*, ed. I. H. Marshall and D. Peterson (BAFCS; Grand Rapids: Eerdmans, 1997); R. E. Brown and J. P. Meier, *Antioch and Rome: New Testament Cradles of Catholic Christianity* (New York: Paulist, 1983); N. Brox, "Zur christlichen Mission in der Spätantike" in *Mission im Neuen Testament*, ed. K. Kertelge (QD 93; Freiburg: Herder, 1982) 190-237; R. F. Collins, "Thomas," *ABD* 6:528-29; P. H. Davids, *The Epistle of James* (NIGTC; Grand Rapids: Eerdmans, 1982); idem, *The First Epistle of Peter* (NICNT; Grand Rapids: Eerdmans, 1990); A. Dihle, "Neues zur Thomas-Tradition," *JAC* 6 (1963) 54-70; J. D. G. Dunn, *The Acts of the Apostles* (London: Epworth, 1996); idem, *The Theology of Paul's Letter to the Galatians* (NTT; Cambridge: Cambridge University Press, 1993); E. E. Ellis, "'The End of the Earth' (Acts 1:8)," *BBR* 1 (1991) 123-32; J. N. Farquhar, "The Apostle Thomas in North/South India," *BJRL* 10 (1926) 80-111; ibid., 11 (1927) 20-50; H. Frohnes and U. W. Knorr, eds., *Kirchengeschichte als Missionsgeschichte*, 1: *Die Alte Kirche* (Munich: Kaiser, 1974); P. Grech, "The Daily Life of Second Century Christians," *MTh* 41 (1990) 87-96; F. Hahn, *Mission in the New Testament* (London: SCM, 1981); A. von Harnack, *Die Mission und Ausbreitung des Christentums in den ersten drei Jahrhunderten* (4th ed.; Leipzig: Hinrichs, 1924); idem, *The Mission and Expansion of Christianity in the First Three Centuries* (2d ed.; 2 vols.; New York: Putnam, 1908); M. Hengel, *Acts and the History of Earliest Christianity* (Philadelphia: Fortress, 1979); idem, *Between Jesus and Paul: Studies in the Earliest History of Christianity* (Philadelphia: Fortress, 1983); idem, "The Geography of Palestine in Acts" in *The Book of Acts in Its Palestinian Setting*, ed. R. J. Bauckham (BAFCS; Grand Rapids: Eerdmans, 1995) 27-78; E. Hennecke and W. Schneemelcher, *New Testament Apocrypha* (2 vols.; Philadelphia: Westminster, 1963, 1965); C. J. Hemer, *The Book of Acts in the Setting of Hellenistic History*, ed. C. Gempf (WUNT 49; Tübingen: J. C. B. Mohr, 1989 [1986]; T. Holtz, *Der erste Brief an die Thessalonicher* (EKK; Neukirchen-Vluyn: Neukirchener Verlag, 1986); P. Lampe, *Die stadtrömischen Christen in den ersten beiden Jahrhunderten: Untersuchungen zur Sozialgeschichte* (WUNT 2.18; 2d ed.; Tübingen: J. C. B. Mohr, 1989); W. L. Lane, *Hebrews* (2 vols.; WBC; Dallas: Word, 1991); R. Lane Fox, *Pagans and Christians in the Mediterranean World from the Second Century A.D. to the Conversion of Constantine* (2d ed.; London: Penguin, 1988); J. K. Lott, "India," *ABD* 3:410; S. McKnight, *A Light Among the Gentiles: Jewish Missionary Activity in the Second Temple Period* (Minneapolis: Fortress, 1991); R. MacMullen, *Christianizing the Roman Empire (A.D. 100-400)* (New Haven, CT: Yale University Press, 1984); idem, *Paganism in the Roman Empire* (New Haven, CT: Yale University Press, 1981); U. Maiburg, "Und bis an die Grenzen der Erde . . . Die Ausbreitung des Christentums in den Länderlisten und deren Verwendung in Antike und Christentum," *JAC* 26 (1983) 38-53; W. Manson, *The Epistle to the Hebrews: A Historical and Theological Reconsideration* (London: Hodder & Stoughton, 1951); I. H. Marshall, *The Acts of the Apostles* (NTG; Sheffield: JSOT, 1992); V. Martin, *A House Divided: The Parting of the Ways Between Synagogue and Church* (New York: Paulist, 1995); J. L. Martyn, "A Law-Observant Mission to Gentiles: The Background of Galatians," *SJT* 38 (1985) 307-24; W. A. Meeks, *The First Urban Christian: The Social World of the Apostle Paul* (New Haven, CT: Yale University Press, 1983); B. M. Metzger, *A Textual Commentary on the Greek New Testament* (2d ed.; Stuttgart: Deutsche Bibelgesellschaft, 1994); J. R. Michaels, *1 Peter* (WBC; Waco, TX: Word, 1988); O. Michel, "Σκύθης," *TDNT* 7:449-50; J. Murphy-O'Connor, *Paul: A Critical Life* (Oxford: Clarendon, 1996); W.-H. Ollrogg, *Paulus und seine Mitarbeiter* (WMANT 50; Neukirchen-Vluyn: Neukirchener Verlag, 1979); D. Praet, "Explaining the Christianization of the Roman Empire: Older Theories and Recent Developments," *Sacris Erudiri* 33 (1992-93) 5-11; R. Reck, *Kommunikation und Gemeindeaufbau: Eine Studie zu Entstehung, Leben und Wachstum paulinischer Gemeinden in den Kommunikationsstrukturen der Antike* (SBS 22; Stuttgart: Katholisches Bibelwerk, 1991); W. Reinhardt, "The Population Size of Jerusalem and the Numerical Growth of the Jerusalem Church" in *The Book of Acts in Its Palestinian Setting*, ed. R. J. Bauckham (BAFCS 4; Grand Rapids: Eerdmans, 1995) 237-65; R. Riesner, *Die Frühzeit des Apostels Paulus: Studien zur Chronologie, Missionsstrategie und Theologie* (WUNT 71; Tübingen: J. C. B. Mohr, 1994); E. J. Schnabel, "Jesus and the Beginnings of the Mission to the Gentiles" in *Jesus of Nazareth: Lord and Christ*, ed. J. B. Green and M. Turner (Grand Rapids: Eerdmans, 1994) 37-58; J. M. Scott, "Luke's Geographical Horizon" in *The Book of Acts in Its Greco-Roman Setting*, ed. D. W. J. Gill and C. Gempf (BAFCS 2; Grand Rapids: Eerdmans, 1994) 483-544; idem, *Paul and the Nations* (WUNT 84; Tübingen: J. C. B. Mohr, 1995); C. Spicq, *Les Épîtres pastorales* (4th ed.; Paris: Gabalda, 1969); C. P. Thiede, *Simon Peter: From Galilee to Rome* (Exeter: Paternoster, 1986); L. M. White, "Adolf Harnack and the 'Expansion' of Early Christianity: A Reappraisal of Social History," *SecCent* 5 (1985-86) 97-127; U. Wilckens, *Die Missionsreden der Apostelgeschichte: Form- und traditionsgeschichtliche Untersuchungen* (WMANT 5; 3d ed.; Neukirchen-Vluyn: Neukir-chener Verlag, 1974); B. W. Winter, "In Public and in Private: Early Christian Interactions with Religious Pluralism" in *One God, One Lord in a World of Religious Pluralism*, ed. B. W. Winter and A. D. Clarke (Cambridge: Tyndale House, 1991) 112-34; N. T. Wright, *Jesus and the Victory of God* (Minneapolis: Fortress, 1996).   E. J. Schnabel

MONARCHICAL BISHOP. *See* CHURCH ORDER, GOVERNMENT.

MONOTHEISM. *See* CHRISTIANITY AND JUDAISM: PARTINGS OF THE WAYS; GOD.

MONTANISM. *See* PROPHECY, PROPHETS, FALSE PROPHETS.

MORALITY. *See* ETHICS.

MORTALITY AND IMMORTALITY

Human beings are mortal, that is, subject to bodily death. God* is immortal (Rev 4:8-10; 10:6), but he bestows immortality as a grace.

   1. Background
   2. Acts
   3. Hebrews and General Epistles
   4. Revelation
   5. Postapostolic Developments

1. Background.

1.1. Vocabulary. The distinctive vocabulary is rare in our canonical material but regular in the apostolic fathers.* *Aphtharsia* ("immortality") and its cognates *phthartos* and *aphthartos* ("mortal," "immortal") appear there. Words from another etymology, *athanatos* and *athanasia* ("immortal" and "immortality") and *thnētos* ("mortal"), appear in the Fathers; the last is used also in 1 Peter.* Human beings are designated "mortals" in *1 Clement* 39.2 and the *Epistle to Diognetus* 9.2.

1.2. Concepts. The church's growing interest in immortality is understandable, given its expansion into Hellenistic territory. In the pagan mind the gods were held to be immortal (see Acts 28:6), but there the certainty ended. For Epicureans such as Lucretius (*On the Nature of Things*) death was the end of human existence. Others believed that the soul would be reincarnated or would exist eternally apart from a body. The Platonists taught that the soul was preexistent and immortal, its connection with a body only temporary. That shaped the thinking of some Hellenistic Jews (Wis 2:23; 8:19-20; Philo *Sacr.* 5-7). But in Second Temple Judaism* it was more conventional to suppose that the soul was conscious after death and would be reunited with the body at the resurrection* (e.g., *1 Enoch* 51; *4 Ezra* 8:53). According to contemporary witnesses, the Pharisees believed in resurrection, while their opponents, the Sadducees, denied any survival after death (Josephus *J. W.* 2.8.14 §165; Acts 23:6-8). The Essenes meanwhile taught either the soul's natural immortality (*Jub.* 23:30-31; Josephus *J. W.* 2.8.11 §154-55; perhaps 1QH 6:34) or immortality as the result of resurrection (Hippolytus *Refut.* 9.22).

Christians tried to steer a course amid the competing views. They were uncomfortable at first with calling the soul immortal by nature. Nevertheless they affirmed the soul's survival of death and above all the resurrection hope. In addition there was the predictable tension between the reception of immortality in the age to come and the realization of some of its spiritual benefits in this life.

2. Acts.

As Stephen* died, he cried out "Lord Jesus, receive my spirit!" (Acts 7:59, recalling Lk 23:46). Left unstated is the implication that Stephen would go to be consciously present with Christ* (who rises to greet him, a unique description) after death, in the manner of Luke 23:43 (cf. Lk 16:22-26).

The resurrection of Christ was of course central to the apostolic kerygma. They took Psalm 16:8-11 as a proof-text in Acts 2:25-32: God "would not allow your holy one to see corruption," but Jesus had to be that holy one. He, not David, rose with immortal body, no longer to see the corruption of mortal existence (cf. Acts 13:34-37). It was this aspect of the gospel that so riled the Sadducees (Acts 4:2; 23:6) and amused the Athenian Epicureans and Stoics (Acts 17:32), all of whom scoffed at the suggestion of personal immortality.

3. Hebrews and General Epistles.
The author of Hebrews urges believers to cling to Christ because they have approached the heavenly city, in which are "the spirits of righteous ones made perfect" (Heb 12:23), an allusion to Christians who have died and gone to heaven* (see Ellingworth, 680-81). Unique to Hebrews* is the argument for Christ's superior priesthood* based on his immortality. The Aaronic priests kept dying and needed replacements. Jesus is not only human, but also he lives forever (Heb 7:23-25) to make perpetual intercession for his church.* In Christ people are set free from death's terrors.

For James mortality cannot be given a naturalistic explanation. Rather, it results from the flowering of sin (Jas 1:15). Those who persevere will receive the crown of life (Jas 1:12). 1 Peter draws a contrast between the perishable things of earth, such as gold and silver, and the imperishable gospel that leads to new life* (1 Pet 1:3, 8-19; 1:23; cf. Did. 4.8). According to a difficult passage, the gospel was preached to the dead (1 Pet 4:6), an event that according to one reading implies conscious existence after death (see Michaels, 235-41). In Jude we read that it is Jesus who brings the Christians to eternal life (Jude 21), apparently in the future. In 2 Peter 1:4, 11 it is unclear whether the faithful participate in the divine nature and enter the eternal kingdom of Christ upon death or at the resurrection, although possibly Peter will enter it when he "departs" (2 Pet 1:14-15). Some interpreters have read 2 Peter 1:4 as either a Hellenization of the Christian hope or more likely a recasting of the traditional message in Hellenistic terms (Bauckham, 183-84).

As in the Gospel of John, in 1 John eternal life is the possession of the Christians alone (1 Jn 2:25; 3:14; 5:11-13, 20). Still there is a reservation of immortality until the future (1 Jn 3:2), since only at Christ's appearance will Christians be fully "like him."

4. Revelation.
Jesus has brought about resurrection life by his own victory over death (Rev 1:5, 18; 2:8). In the kingdom his people will partake in resurrection existence and will be able to drink from the water of life (Rev 22:1-2) and eat from the tree of life (Rev 2:7; 22:2).

The reader is invited to escape the second death that is the lake of fire (Rev 2:11; 20:6, 14; 21:8). The most natural reading of Revelation is that people in the lake of fire will experience conscious torment forever (Rev 14:11) after they have been resurrected (Rev 20:13; cf. Dan 12:2), although the beast* and the false prophet* will be cast "alive" into the fire (Rev 19:20).

There is also some indication that human souls are conscious between death and resurrection. In Revelation 6:9-11 martyred Christians are able to speak and ask questions and can wear robes. The "great multitude" of Revelation 7:9-17 seems likewise to comprise deceased saints.

5. Postapostolic Developments.
The issue that pressed upon the church was how to proclaim the gospel to an audience that denied an afterlife or held that immortality was theirs by natural endowment. Their usual formulation was that only God the Creator is immortal in himself (Aristides *Apol.* 7, Syriac recension). Human beings are mortal (*1 Clem.* 39.2), but they may find immortality as a supernatural grace in Christ (*1 Clem.* 35.1-2; 36.2; *2 Clem.* 6—7; 14.5; *Herm. Sim.* 9.23.4), a gift that will reveal itself in resurrection existence but in a lesser manner in conscious fellowship* with Christ between death and the Parousia.* When modern readers pick up these writings, they must remember that those Christians could deny the soul's immortality in one breath but in the next talk of going to be with Christ at death (compare *1 Clem.* 39.2 with *1 Clem.* 5.4, 7).

There were exceptions. The *Epistle to Diognetus* * resembles James 2:26 in a superficial way, but it seems to have been influenced, albeit unevenly, by Hellenistic thought: "the soul dwells in the body, nevertheless it is not of the body. . . . The immortal soul dwells in a mortal vessel" (*Diogn.* 6.3, 8; parallels with Wisdom of Solomon are evident). But even this author returned to traditional categories in *Diognetus* 9.2-6.

Ignatius* emphasized that Christ had to take on mortality in order to bring the church to immortality (Ign. *Eph.* 7.2; 20.1; Ign. *Phld.* 9.2; Ign. *Pol.* 3.2). It is no wonder, said Ignatius, that the Docetists* refrained from the Eucharist (Ign. *Smyrn.* 6.2), since without a real incarnation there can be no "bread of life." In a memorable turn of phrase communion became for Ignatius the "medicine of immortality" (*see* Lord's Supper; Worship). It was an antidote not, apparently, due to its inherent powers but because it placed the communicant within the catholic church (cf. Ign. *Eph.* 20.1; Ign. *Rom.* 7.3; and the comments by Schoedel, 97-99). The eucharistic prayer in *Didache* 10.2 may indicate a traditional association between communion and immortality: "We thank you . . . for the knowledge and faith and immortality that you have made known to us through your child Jesus."

Hermas suspected that Platonist notions might lead to Christians to think they could defile the flesh with impunity (*Herm. Sim.* 5.7.3). Similarly the preacher of *2 Clement* 14.5 predicted that a person may expect life and immortality in the next life but only if the Holy Spirit* is manifestly joined with the flesh in this life. In *2 Clement* 9.1-2, likewise: "And let none of you say, 'This flesh is not judged nor will it rise.' Realize this: in what you were saved? In what did you receive your sight, if not in fleshly existence?"

The *Martyrdom of Polycarp* took a new direction: immediately upon death the bishop of Smyrna was to receive the crown of immortality (*ton tēs aptharsias stephanon, Mart. Pol.* 17.1; 19.2; cf. the "prize" of immortality in Heb 2:9; Jas 1:12; *2 Clem.* 6—7; Ign. *Pol.* 2.3). That is the same impression given by Ignatius's embracing of the martyrs' sufferings*: "The pangs of birth are upon me! Share my understanding, brothers. Do not hinder me from living! Do not wish my death!" (Ign. *Rom.* 6.1-2). Polycarp* also stated his hope that he would go immediately to heaven to be with the apostles* and martyrs* and that he would that day be granted a portion in the resurrection of both soul and body (*Mart. Pol.*

14.2; cf. 4 Ezra 7.96-98), an event that earlier he had linked with Christ's return (Pol. *Phil.* 2.2).

The Hellenized Jewish-Christian *Odes of Solomon* (early second century?) are similar to the Johannine viewpoint of eternal life as a present possession, but now immortality appears without reference to the future resurrection (*Odes Sol.* 10.2; 15.10).

In the second century the Gnostics* took a view of the soul that echoed Platonism. For them a human being is composed of a preexisting spirit or spark (*Gos. Thom.* 4; cf. the late second-century Gnostic *Treatise on Resurrection*) that was put into a mortal body by a dull-witted creator god. It will be freed from the body upon death, and should it possess the "gnosis" or knowledge* of its true nature, it will return to its home in the spiritual realm.

Whether responding to Hellenism or Judaism or Gnosticism, most Christians trod a careful path, denying (Origen being a later exception) the soul's preexistence and affirming that the soul is conscious after death but insisting that immortality be connected with bodily resurrection at Christ's return. These themes would receive full expression in the writings of Justin Martyr in the mid-second century (see Justin Martyr *Resurrec.* 10; *Dial. Tryph.* 69; 117; 130).

See also ESCHATOLOGY; HELL, ABYSS, ETERNAL PUNISHMENT; JUDGMENT; MARTYRDOM; RESURRECTION.

BIBLIOGRAPHY. R. J. Bauckham, *Jude, 2 Peter* (WBC; Waco, TX: Word, 1983); J. W. Cooper, *Body, Soul and Life Everlasting: Biblical Anthropology and the Monism-Dualism Debate* (Grand Rapids: Eerdmans, 1989); P. Ellingworth, *The Epistle to the Hebrews* (NIGTC; Grand Rapids: Eerdmans, 1993); M. J. Harris, *From Grave to Glory: Resurrection in the New Testament* (Grand Rapids: Zondervan, 1990); J. R. Michaels, *1 Peter* (WBC; Waco, TX: Word, 1988); G. J. Riley, *Resurrection Reconsidered: Thomas and John in Controversy* (Minneapolis: Fortress, 1995); E. Rohde, *Psyche: The Cult of Souls and Belief in Immortality Among the Greeks* (London: Routledge & Kegan Paul, 1925); W. R. Schoedel, *Ignatius of Antioch: A Commentary on the Letters of Ignatius of Antioch* (Herm; Philadelphia: Fortress, 1985).

G. S. Shogren

MOSES

Moses, Judaism's most important and imposing figure, plays a prominent role in early Christian literature. The prominence is inevitable, for Christians claimed to be the authentic heirs of Israel's* history, and in first-century Judaism that meant they had to show themselves to be the rightful children of Moses.

1. The Life of Moses
2. The Death of Moses
3. The Return of Moses
4. Moses as Prophet
5. Moses as Type of Christ
6. Moses as Lawgiver
7. Moses as Moral Model
8. The Generation of Moses
9. Jesus as Greater than Moses

1. The Life of Moses.

1.1. Acts. Stephen's* speech in Acts 7 contains an overview of the life of Moses. The primary purpose is to show that, although God worked through Moses to save Israel, the people "did not understand" (Acts 7:25), they "refused" to accept Moses as ruler and judge (Acts 7:35), and they disobeyed the "living oracles" received by him and instead offered sacrifice to an idol of their own making (Acts 7:39-41)—wherefore God judged them (Acts 7:42-43). The implicit lesson is that in the story of Jesus history is repeating itself (see 8.1 below).

Although most of Luke's biographical facts can be found in the OT, postbiblical traditions are also followed. For it is not the OT but extrabiblical sources which tell us that Moses was instructed in all the wisdom of the Egyptians (Acts 7:22; cf. Philo *Vit. Mos.* 1.21-24), that he decided to "visit" his people (Acts 7:23; cf. Philo *Vit. Mos.* 1.40-44), and that he was forty years old when he went into exile (Acts 7:23; cf. *Sipre Deut.* §357).

1.2. Hebrews. Hebrews 11:23-28, part of a catalogue of figures of faith,* briefly recounts the life of Moses. Four incidents are mentioned—his birth, his decision to join Israel rather than be called the son of Pharaoh's daughter, his leaving Egypt (probably a reference to Ex 2:15, not the exodus), and his keeping of the Passover and sprinkling with blood. Several elements go beyond Exodus. One is the assertion that Moses willingly chose to share ill-treatment with his own people rather than a royal life. The same thought appears in Philo (*Vit. Mos.* 1.149) and Josephus (*Ant.* 4.3.2 §42). Also extra biblical is the association of Moses' flight from Egypt with faith (if the reference is

to Ex 2:15). For in Exodus Moses flees in fear (cf. Acts 7:29). But in postbiblical sources this is toned down and his motives are made more noble (e.g., Philo *Leg. All.* 3.14). Finally, the statement that Moses considered "opprobrium" (*oneidismon*; cf. Ps 68; 88:51-52 LXX) suffered "for the Christ" greater wealth than the treasures of Egypt is plainly Christian interpretation. It is often explained in terms of the solidarity (in Christ) of the people of God throughout history. But a literal interpretation—Moses the visionary foresaw the sufferings of Jesus Christ—is equally possible (cf. Lk 24:26-27, 44); for the visionary powers of Moses are, in Jewish sources at least, almost unbounded (cf. *Jub.* 1:1-4; 4 Ezra 4:5; *Sipre Deut* §357; *Tg. Ps.-Jn.* on Deut 34:1; Philo *Vit. Mos.*).

2. The Death of Moses.

According to Deuteronomy 34:6 (MT) Moses died in the land of Moab, and no one knows the place of his burial "until this day." The text—which Josephus and others took to be autobiographical and therefore prophetic—also says that "he buried him" (so MT; the LXX, like the Samaritan Pentateuch, has "they buried him"). This was commonly taken to mean that God himself buried the lawgiver (*Bib. Ant.* 19:16; *m. Soṭa* 1:9; *b. Soṭa* 14a; *Memar Marqah* 2:12). But there also developed the tradition that Moses never died (*b. Soṭa* 13b; *Sipre Deut.* §357; this may be implicit in Josephus *Ant.* 4.8.48 §326).

2.1. Jude. Jude 8-10, in discussing the topic of slander, cites the example of the archangel Michael: when he buried Moses—Moses' physical death is assumed—there was a debate with the devil in which Michael did not presume to condemn him for slander but simply said, "May the Lord rebuke you!" This obviously is not a retelling of the OT's story of Moses' burial, Deuteronomy 34:1-6. But, as noted, Deuteronomy 34:6 was commonly taken to mean that God buried Moses; and this in turn developed into the tradition that the deed was done by Michael, God's instrument, or perhaps by several angels* (so Philo *Vit. Mos.* 2.291; cf. the LXX and the Samaritan Pentateuch?). There also developed the notion (based in part upon Zech 3:1-5) that when Michael went for Moses' body, the devil—Michael's traditional antagonist (cf. Rev 12:7)—met him and demanded, on the ground that Moses had sinned, that he be allowed to dispose of the body (he wanted to give it to Israel as an idolatrous object of worship).

While Jude only alludes to this story, it appears in fuller form in later sources. These include the *Palaea Historica* (a collection of Byzantine legends), the *Slavonic Life of Moses* and Severus of Antioch. These sources in turn seem to have drawn upon the lost ending of the ancient *Assumption of Moses*. The correlation between Jude 9 and that document is confirmed by patristic sources (the earliest being Clement of Alexandria, *Frag. in Ep. Jude*).

3. The Return of Moses.

Many have identified Moses with one of the two witnesses of Revelation 11:1-13. The two eschatological figures resemble Moses and Elijah respectively, for they are able to call down fire from heaven (cf. 2 Kings 1:10-16: Elijah prays and God sends fire from heaven), shut the sky so that no rain falls (cf. 1 Kings 17:1: Elijah successfully prays that there be no rain), turn the waters into blood (cf. Ex 7:14-24: at Moses' command the Nile turns to blood) and smite the earth with every plague (cf. Ex 7—13: Moses smites Egypt with ten plagues).

These parallels make the common identification with Moses and Elijah more likely than other proposals—identification with Enoch and Elijah (the dominant patristic tradition) or Peter and Paul (J. Munck). If so, we should detect the influence not only of Malachi 4:5 ("I will send you Elijah the prophet before the great and terrible day of the Lord comes") but also of the Jewish expectation of the eschatological return of Moses himself—an expectation attested in *Lives of the Prophets: Jeremiah* 14; *Fragmentary Targum* on Ex 12:42; and *Deuteronomy Rabbah* 3:17, but not otherwise in the earliest Christian writings.

4. Moses as Prophet.

While moderns do not always think of Moses as a prophet, it was otherwise with the ancients. In the Pentateuch Moses has the Spirit of God (Num 11:17), receives a divine calling (Ex 2—3) and speaks God's word, and he is explicitly called a prophet in Deuteronomy 18:15, 18; 34:10; Hosea 12:13; Sirach 46:1; and Wisdom 11:1. In fact, Deuteronomy 34:10 makes Moses the greatest of Israel's prophets: "and there has not arisen a prophet since in Israel like Moses, whom the Lord knew face to face." That Moses continued to be regarded as a prophet appears

from numerous sources (cf. *T. Mos.* 1:5; *Asc. Isa.* 3:18; *m. Soṭa* 1:9; etc.). Particularly impressive for those who assumed Moses' authorship of the Pentateuch was his ability to narrate his own death and burial (cf. Philo *Vit. Mos.* 2.291).

4.1. Acts. Early Christians also thought of Moses as a prophet (cf. *1 Clem.* 43:6), and in Acts the conviction comes to clear expression twice. Acts 3:22-23 and 7:37 cite Deuteronomy 18:15(18) and proclaim fulfillment of the oracle in Jesus: "Moses said, 'The Lord God will raise up for you a prophet from your brethren as he raised me up. You shall listen to him in whatever he tells you.'" This text, which also probably lies behind the "listen to him" of Mark 9:7 par., was, as 4QTestimonia suggests, the source of lively speculation in the first two Christian centuries. Several "messianic" figures attempted to perform wonders reminiscent of Moses because an eschatological Mosaic prophet was expected (see, e.g., Josephus *Ant.* 20.5.1 §§97-99; *J.W.* 2.13.5 §§261-63).

4.2. Epistle of Barnabas. The appellation "prophet" is used of Moses three times (*Barn.* 6:8; 12:8; 14:2). Moreover, in *Barnabas* 12 several deeds of Moses are interpreted as prophetic of Jesus. When Moses stretched forth his hands to gain victory in battle (Ex 17:8-13) he became a type of the suffering Christ on the cross (cf. Justin, *Dial. Tryph.* 97; 111; 112; *Sib. Or.* 8:251-4). When Moses set a bronze serpent upon a pole so that those who looked upon it might live (Num 21:9), he prefigured the intercession of Jesus (cf. Jn 3:14). And when Moses commissioned Joshua (= Jesus) that all the people might hearken (*akousē*) to him alone, the revelation of the Father in Jesus was intimated. This last, which cites Numbers 13:16-17, also appears to allude to Deuteronomy 18:15, 18 (cf. Acts 3:22; 7:37) and, if so, offers the same interpretation found later in Clement of Alexandria's *Paedagogus* 1.70: Moses "said, 'God will raise up for you a prophet from among your brethren like me,' meaning Joshua, son of Nun, but implying Jesus, the Son of God."

5. Moses as Type of Christ.

Many Jewish and Christian sources offer Moses typologies (see Allison). In the Hexateuch Joshua is a new Moses. In Judges it is Gideon. In Kings Elijah is like the lawgiver. In 4 Ezra events from the life of Moses are moved to the life of

Ezra. In Matthew Jesus is a new Moses. In Eusebius Constantine is Moses' antitype. And in Gregory of Nyssa Basil the Great lives a life which constantly reminds one of items in Exodus. Moses was a well-used type because he was so many different things—saint, preeminent prophet, ideal king, suffering servant, paradigmatic deliverer, giver of the law.* Further, comparison with Moses served to exalt a man: to be like Moses was the highest praise one could give or receive.

5.1. Acts. Both Acts 3 and 7, when read in the light of the rest of Luke-Acts, offer a Moses typology: Jesus is like the lawgiver. Both "visited" Israel (Acts 7:23; Lk 7:16; cf. Lk 1:68). Both gained "wisdom" (Acts 7:22; Lk 2:40, 52). Both were "sent" by God (Acts 7:34-35; Lk 10:16). Both did "signs and wonders"* (Acts 7:36; Lk 2:22; 4:30). Both were "denied" by their own people (Acts 3:13-14; 7:35). Moses was the "redeemer" (Acts 7:35) while Jesus came to "redeem"* Israel (Lk 24:21). Moses was *archōn* and *dikastēs* (Acts 7:27, 35) while Jesus was *dikaios* and *archēgos* (Acts 3:14, 15). And whereas Moses was "mighty in his words and deeds" (Acts 7:22), Jesus was "mighty in deed and word before God" (Lk 24:19).

The Moses typology of Acts has two main functions. The first is to characterize Jesus as the prophet like Moses. According to Deuteronomy 18:15-18, which is cited in both Acts 3 and 7, Moses foretold that God would raise up for Israel a prophet like himself. Early Christians saw this prophecy as fulfilled in Jesus and so naturally found Mosaic features in Jesus. Thus the quotation of Deuteronomy 18:15-18 supports the Moses typology and the Moses typology supports the quotation. Secondly, the parallelism between Jesus and Moses extends beyond them as individuals to encompass their unfaithful generations and so becomes a warning to Israel and an explanation for the unbelief of so many: just as Moses found opposition within Israel, so too Jesus (see 8.1 below).

5.2. Hebrews. Hebrews 3:2 likens Jesus to Moses: the lawgiver was "faithful to him who appointed him, just as Moses was also faithful in God's house." The text, however, goes on not to compare the two figures but to contrast them (see 9.1 below). Yet in Hebrews 9:15-22 a second likening of Jesus to Moses appears. Here the surpassing self-sacrifice of Jesus is compared with the sprinkling of blood told of in Exodus

24:6-8. Moreover, the formulation of Hebrews 9:20 ("This is the blood of the covenant which . . .") shows assimilation to the tradition of the Lord's Supper (cf. Mk 14:22, 24; 1 Cor 11:24-5). The implication is that Jesus' mediation of a new covenant* at the Last Supper is comparable with Moses' mediation of the first covenant: the last redeemer is as the first.

5.3. Revelation. Moses is mentioned only one time in the Apocalypse, in Revelation 15:3. Here reference is made to "the song of Moses," sung by victorious martyrs in heaven. This harks back to Exodus 15 and is part of a larger exodus typology. Revelation refers to the sacrifice of the Lamb* (Rev 13:8, etc.) and to the twelve tribes (Rev 7:4-8); there are trumpets* (Rev 8:7) and thunders and lightnings (Rev 8:5)—the signs of Sinai (Ex 19:16); and the plagues of Egypt recur—hail falls (Rev 8:7), the sea is turned into blood (Rev 8:8; 16:3), darkness descends (Rev 8:12; 16:10), locusts swarm (Rev 9:3). Clearly Revelation depicts the eschatological redemption as analogous to the redemption from Egypt.

6. Moses as Lawgiver.

For Judaism Moses was above all the lawgiver (Jn 1:17); and occasionally in early Christianity Jesus becomes a second lawgiver (cf. Matthew's Moses typology). But because Christianity came to reject so much of the Mosaic legislation as obsolete, Christians generally did not esteem Moses primarily as lawgiver. It is natural then that the giving of the law receives only brief notice in the review of Moses' career in Acts 7 and that Hebrews 11:23-28 can pass over it altogether (contrast the review in Sir 45:1-5). Where the topic does receive some treatment, in *Barnabas*, the author argues that Judaism has totally misunderstood the Mosaic law, which was intended from the beginning to be symbolic; and further that Moses threw the two tables from his hands because the people were not worthy. For *Barnabas* Moses ceases to be the lawgiver of Israel and becomes instead the mystical prophet of Jesus.

7. Moses as Moral Model.

Already the Pentateuch praises Moses as most meek among all on the face of the earth (Num 12:3). This acclaim of Moses' virtue only grew as time passed, and in writers such as Philo (cf. *Vit. Mos.* 1.66; 2.9-10) and Josephus (cf. *Ant.*

4.7.49 §§328-29) Moses becomes the moral model *par excellence* (cf. 4 Macc 2:17). Hebrews 11:23-28 reflects this tradition, which later found a permanent home in the monastic tradition, where Moses became both saint and ascetic (cf. already Clement of Alexandria *Strom.* 3.7.57).

7.1. Hebrews. The primary function of Hebrews 11:23-28 is to present Moses as an exemplar of faith. "By faith Moses/he," a phrase which appears four times altogether, introduces concrete illustrations of faith in action. Moses chose to share ill-treatment rather than "to enjoy [as the son of Pharaoh's daughter] the fleeting pleasures of sin." He determined to suffer abuse for the Christ rather than enjoy the treasures of Egypt, for he looked forward to another reward. And in leaving Egypt "he endured as seeing him who is invisible." All this recalls the martyr* tradition of Jewish Hellenism, for which "choice" (*haireō*), "fleeting" (*proskairon*), "pleasure" (*apolausis*) and "endure" (*kartereō*) were key words (D'Angelo). Further, the description of Moses' trials strongly recalls Hebrews 10:32-39, where the former afflictions of the addressees are recounted. In this way Moses becomes a model of Christian discipleship.

7.2. 1 Clement. This epistle nowhere likens Jesus to Moses, and there is no Moses christology.* Rather Moses appears solely as a moral model. In *1 Clement* 17 (which cites Num 12:7) he is an example of humility. (Moses' meekness or humility was proverbial: Num 12:3; Sir 45:4; Philo *Vit. Mos.* 1.26; *b. Ned.* 38a; etc.) In *1 Clement* 43—44 he is the faithful servant in God's house* (cf. again Num 12:7) who serves as a model for Christian leaders. And in *1 Clement* 53—54 Moses is an exemplar of compassion and love* (cf. *Apoc. Sed.* 1:18).

8. The Generation of Moses.

In the OT the generation in the wilderness is called "faithless," "evil," "sinful," "perverse" and "crooked" (e.g., Deut 1:35; 32:5, 20). In the rabbis this particular generation came to be seen, along with the generation of the flood, as especially corrupt (cf. *m. Sanh.* 10:3; *Mek.* on Ex 15:1). Given this, and the polemic against "this generation" in the Jesus tradition (Mt 12:39; 16:4; etc.), it was natural for early Christians to liken their generation to that of Moses.

8.1. Acts. The review of Moses' life in Acts 7:20-44 (see 1.1 above) is almost as much about Moses' contemporaries as Moses himself. They did not understand his killing of the Egyptian (Acts 7:23-25). Two of them, instead of listening to Moses' council for reconciliation, rebuked him and caused him to leave Egypt (Acts 7:26-29). Upon his return Israel refused to obey him, thrust him aside, turned back to Egypt, made a golden calf, worshipped idols and did not keep the law (Acts 7:39-43, 53). This negative salvation-history is part of a speech which ends with Stephen's rebuke: "You stiff-necked people . . . you always resist the Holy Spirit" (Acts 7:51). Here Moses' generation serves as a type for the generation of Jesus and Christian missionaries and so helps make more explicable the rejection of the gospel.

8.2. Hebrews. The comparison and contrast between Jesus and Moses in Hebrews 3:1-6 is immediately followed by an exhortation based on the sad fate of the wilderness generation. Psalm 95:7-11 is quoted to illustrate what happened to those who "left Egypt under the leadership of Moses," namely, their bodies fell in the wilderness and they did not enter into rest, that is, the promised land. Hebrews here warns that the situation that once obtained with those who followed Moses can likewise obtain with those who now follow Jesus: they too can, through disobedience, miss the promise given them (cf. Heb 4:1-13). Here then the theme of the faithless generation is no longer applied to Jews who have rejected Jesus (as in Acts) but to Christians (who in the author's eyes were running the risk of losing their salvation).

8.3. Epistle of Barnabas. In *Barnabas* 4 and 14, Moses is the wise lawgiver and servant who, after meeting God "face to face on Mount Sinai" (cf. Ex 33:11; Deut 34:9-12), broke the tablets of the law because Israel had turned to idols. Israel was unworthy to receive the law (which she wrongly understood literally) and the covenant. The church, however, has so far proven worthy. But her favor is not irrevocable: she must remain on guard (*Barn.* 4.9-14). As in Hebrews, the generation of the wilderness is not a type of unbelieving Jews but a warning to Christian believers.

9. Jesus as Greater than Moses.

In early Christianity the parallelism between Jesus and Moses did not, of itself, communicate the subordination of the latter to the former, and the traditions in Acts 3 and 7, the typology in Luke-Acts, the proclamation of the Pseudo-Clementines, and many of the incidental comparisons found in patristic literature betray little or no anxiety about Jesus' status over against Moses. But it is otherwise in John (see esp. Jn 1:17-18 and 6:32-33); so too in Hebrews.

9.1. Hebrews. Hebrews 3:1-6 exalts Jesus above Moses. The former has been counted worthy of much more glory* than the latter; and whereas Moses was faithful in all God's house as a servant (cf. *1 Clem.* 17.5; 43.1), Christ was faithful over God's house as a Son.* Whatever the precise meaning of these remarks (see D'Angelo), they gain force against the exaltation of Moses in Judaism. The *Epistle of Aristeas* affirms that Moses understood "all things" (*Ep. Arist.* 139). Philo more than once calls him "god" (*theos;* see, e.g., *Vit. Mos.* 1.158). Artapanus (in Eusebius *Praep. Ev.* 9.27.6) says he was worthy of "godlike honor." Ezekiel the Tragedian has a scene in which Moses sits on God's throne (Eusebius *Praep. Ev.* 9.29.4-6). Ezekiel also tells us that Moses counted the stars and saw all "things present, past, and future." *Deuteronomy Rabbah* 11.4 refers to Moses as half man, half divine. Given such traditions as these, one understands why it might have been necessary to make explicit Jesus' superiority over Moses. Those traditions also help us appreciate how significant the exaltation of Jesus over Moses could be. It is striking that Hebrews argues for Jesus' superiority over Moses the man *after* already proving Jesus' superiority over the angels.* The implication seems to be that one could be greater than the angels and still not greater than Moses (cf. the judgment of R. Jose in *Sipre* on Num 12:7).

See also CHRISTOLOGY; COVENANT AND NEW COVENANT; HEBREWS; LAW; OLD TESTAMENT.

BIBLIOGRAPHY. D. C. Allison, Jr., *The New Moses: A Matthean Typology* (Minneapolis: Fortress, 1994); M. R. D'Angelo, *Moses in the Letter to the Hebrews* (SBLDS 42; Missoula: Society of Biblical Literature, 1979); *Moïse: L'Homme de L'Alliance* (Paris: Desclée, 1955); R. F. Zehnle, *Peter's Pentecost Discourse* (SBLMS 15; Nashville: Abingdon, 1971).   D. C. Allison Jr.

MYSTERY

G. Bornkamm begins his article on *mystērion* by noting that the etymology of the word itself is "a mystery" (803). Some authors suggest that the term originated from the Greek *myein,* meaning

"to close the mouth or lips," thus indicating that something is to be kept silent or secret. This may account for its use as a technical term of initiation (*mye*) into the mystery religions* that were popular in the ancient world from the seventh century B.C. to the fourth century A.D. (see Wis 12:5; 14:23; 3 Macc 2:30). Those initiated into the mysteries were required to keep the nature of their initiation rites secret. As a result we know very little about the content and process of initiation (*see DPL,* Religions, Greco-Roman, §4.4). Other uses of the word *mystērion* need to be determined from the context in which it appears.

1. Background
2. The New Testament
3. The Postapostolic Fathers

1. Background.

1.1. Greek. The concept of *mystērion/ta mystēria* appears in noncultic settings as well. In ancient philosophy it retains the idea of an initiation of individuals who advance through stages of philosophical inquiry and who eventually are able to comprehend the ultimate realities of truth*. One can therefore speak of "the initiatory rites of philosophy" (see Harvey's analysis, 322-23, of several philosophers, including Philo,* where mystery terminology is used as a metaphor for initiation into philosophical knowledge).

1.2. Semitic. The Greek idea of *mystērion* mystrion as something hidden, obscure or secret is expressed by the Hebrew word *sôd* and the Aramaic word *rāz.* Several occurrences of *sôd* in the OT simply convey the idea of human secrets (Ps 64:2; Prov 11:13; 20:19; 25:9); some prophets* specify a heavenly council to which they had access and from which God's* secrets were revealed (Jer 23:18; 23:22; Amos 3:7). In no case, however, is *sôd* translated as *mystērion* in the Septuagint, although it does occur several times in the Qumran* literature.

The word *rāz,* thought to be a Persian loan word, first appears in the Aramaic of Daniel where it is translated as "mystery" or "mysteries" (Dan 2:18, 19, 27, 28, 29, 30, 47; 4:9). Including Daniel, *rāz* occurs twenty-one times in the Septuagint as *mystērion* (see Tob 12:7; Jdt 2:2; Sir 22:22; 27:16; Wis 2:22; 6:22; 14:15). All of these occurrences refer to eschatological* and cosmic mysteries that once were hidden but now have been revealed by God to the apocalyptic* seer. The Qumran literature refers to the revelation* of divine mysteries about God, creation,* providence and evil (e.g., 1QM 3:9; 14:14; 1QS 3:15, 21-23; 4:18; 9:18; 1QH 1:9; 4:27; 9:23; 1QpHab 2:1-3; 7:4, 8, 13-14).

2. The New Testament.

2.1. The Revelation to John. In Revelation 1:20; 17:5, 7 (*see* Revelation, Book of) "mystery" connotes secret and symbolic meaning in the form of "the seven stars," the name *Babylon** and a "woman" who is known only to God and/or the seer. Revelation 10:7, however, has no symbolic meaning but refers to the fact that the entire "mystery of God" has been made known to the prophets and will publicly be revealed after the seventh angel* blows his trumpet.* This idea is comparable to the Synoptics, where *mystērion* (Mk 4:11) and *ta mystēria* (Mt 13:11; Lk 8:10) refer to God's rule ("the secrets of the kingdom of God") made known through the person and teaching* of Jesus.

2.2. Pauline Literature.

2.2.1. Origin. Most of the references to *mystērion* in the NT occur in the literature attributed to Paul. Attempts by the history of religion school *(Religionsgeschichtliche Schule)* to explain the origin and use of *mystērion* mystrion from the Greek mystery cults have not been convincing even though we recognize that these cults were contemporaneous with Christianity during the first four centuries of the Christian era. Similarities between the two can be explained by their common religious, social and cultural contexts.

2.2.2. Mystery as a Disclosure of God's Saving Activity. The largest number of references to mystery in Paul deal directly with the salvation* of the Gentiles* and his apostolic* role as a revealer of this mystery. This hidden wisdom* of God is now being revealed through the proclamation of the gospel* (see Rom 16:25) and stands in sharp contrast to the wisdom *(gnōsis)* cherished by the Corinthians (1 Cor 2:1, 2, 7 [cf. 2:10]; 4:1; for further discussion *see DPL,* Mystery).

The two references in 1 Timothy appear as fixed formulae in the context of warnings against false teachings in the Christian community. The "mystery of faith" (1 Tim 3:9) is that which is believed as truth, while "the mystery of our religion" (1 Tim 3:16) includes those elements of the faith* mentioned in this brief

confessional or hymn* (*see* Liturgical Elements).

2.2.3. Colossians and Ephesians. Both of these epistles contain the early Pauline idea of mystery as something revealed that formerly was hidden (see Rom 16:25; 1 Cor 2:7). In Colossians this revelation is to "the saints" (Col 1:26-7; 2:2). In Ephesians, although the mystery is revealed to the church* (Eph 1:9) and God's holy apostles and prophets (Eph 3:5), the main focus is on the revelation given to Paul (esp. Eph 3:3, 4, 7, 8).

There is considerable development and clarification of *mystērion* mystrion in these two epistles, and their general dating as either late in Paul's career or as post-Pauline pseudepigrapha* makes their discussion pertinent in a review of the later apostolic and postapostolic period. Colossians, in response to the false teaching in the church that apparently relegated Christ to a minor role, deliberately emphasizes that the mystery that was hidden "throughout the ages and generations" (Col 1:26) and "is now revealed to all the saints" (Col 1:27) is Christ himself (Col 1:27; 2:2; 4:3). Thus the Colossians need not seek beyond Christ because he is "first place in everything" (Col 1:18) and in him are hidden "all the treasures of wisdom and knowledge" (Col 2:3).

Ephesians likewise equates mystery and gospel (Eph 6:19) but goes farther than Paul and Colossians by defining it as God's ultimate plan of reconstituting the entire cosmos (*see* Creation; World) under Christ's rule (Eph 1:9-10; 3:9-10). In Ephesians 3:1-11, the longest treatment of mystery in the NT, Paul clarifies the *mystērion* mystrion as the good news of salvation to the Gentiles, including their incorporation into the body of Christ, the church (specifically Eph 3:3-5, 9). This focus on ecclesiology is unique to Ephesians and is taken up again in Ephesians 5:32, which refers to the intimate—hence mysterious—union between Christ and the church (see further Lincoln, 380-81).

3. The Apostolic Fathers.

There are a significant number of references to mystery terminology in the early church fathers. Justin Martyr (Justin *Apol. I* 66.4; Justin *Dial. Tryph.* 70.1), Tertullian (Tertullian *De Praesc.* 40) and Clement of Alexandria (Clement *Protr.* 12.120), for example, view the mystery religions, particularly Mithraism, as demonic imitations of Christianity. Others refer to such salvific events as Christ's Incarnation,* suffering,* death (see Death of Christ) and resurrection* as "mysteries" of the Christian faith (Justin *Dial. Tryph.* 40.1; 44.2: 74.3; 134.5; 138.2; Ign. *Eph.* 19.1; Ign. *Magn.* 9:1-2; *Diogn.* 4.6; 7.1; 8.10-11; 10.7; 11.2, 5).

The meaning of *mystērion* in *The Teaching of the Twelve Apostles* (an early secondcentury document commonly called the *Didache**) at *Didache* 11.11 is difficult to determine. The Greek phrase *poiōn eis mystērion kosmikon ekklēsias* could be translated as "symbolizing the mystery of the church," "enacting a worldly mystery," "symbolizing the church in an earthly manner," "[a prophet] who in his action has in view the earthly mystery of the church" or "though he [a prophet] enact a worldly mystery of the church." The meaning, however, in this document is uncertain and may refer to some type of prophetic symbolism.

This verse falls within the context (*Did.* 11-13) that gives some criteria whereby the Christian community may or may not judge whether certain prophets and teachers are true or false. It appears that some early Christian prophets entered into sexual or marriage* relationships similar to that of the prophet Hosea and Gomer and that this was meant to symbolize, in some "mysterious" earthly way, the heavenly union between Christ and his church (see Eph 5:25-33; for further discussion see Lincoln, 362).

According to this passage such marriages by early Christian prophets are not subject to the judgment* of the community. Certain Gnostic* teachers may have participated in such marriages as well ("the mystery of conjunction," Irenaeus *Haer.* 1.6.4.).

The Greek word *mystērion* usually was translated in Latin as *sacramentum* and by the fourth century A.D. became a fixed term for baptism* and the Lord's Supper*—two sacraments of the church.

See also APOCALYPTIC, APOCALYPTICISM; KNOWLEDGE; REVEAL, REVELATION; VISIONS, ECSTATIC EXPERIENCE

BIBLIOGRAPHY. G. W. Barker, "Mystery," *ISBE* 3:451-55; M. Bockmuehl, *Revelation and Mystery in Ancient Judaism and Pauline Christianity* (Tübingen: J. C. B. Mohr, 1990); G. Bornkamm, "μυστήριον," *TDNT* 4:802-27; R. E. Brown, *The Semitic Background of the Term "Mystery" in the New Testament* (Philadelphia: Fortress, 1968); C. C. Caragounis, *The Ephesian Mysterion* (Lund: Gleerup, 1977); J. Coppens, " 'Mystery' in the Theology of Saint Paul and Its Parallels at Qumran" in *Paul and Qumran*, ed. J. Murphy-O'Connor (Chicago: Priory Press, 1968) 132-58; G. Finkenrath, "Mystery," *NIDNTT* 2:501-6; A. E. Harvey, "The Use of Mystery Language in the Bible," *JTS* n.s. 31 (1980) 320-36; H. Krämer, "μυστήριον," *EDNT* 2:446-49; A. T. Lincoln, *Ephesians* (WBC; Dallas: Word, 1990).

A. G. Patzia

MYSTERY RELIGIONS. *See* RELIGIONS, GRECO-ROMAN.

N

NAG HAMMADI TEXTS. *See* GNOSIS, GNOSTICISM.

NAME

Of 331 NT uses of the noun *name (onoma)*, 112 occur in the later NT (60 of these in Acts alone). The verb form *(onomazō)* occurs 10 times in the NT and only once in the later NT (Acts 19:13).

1. Name and Persons
2. Name and Christ
3. Name in the Apostolic Fathers

1. Name and Persons.

In the NT, when "name" is used of persons it is used in the sense of "reputation." Thus in Revelation 3:5 the angel* (or "messenger") of the church in Sardis says that they "have a reputation" for being spiritually alive (lit., they "have a name" that they live), although in fact they are not spiritually alive. Individuals are to be greeted "by name" (3 John 15). In three places "name" is used as a synonym for "person" (as in Acts 1:15— the group consisted of about 120 persons [see also Rev 3:4; 11:3]).

2. Name and Christ.

In our literature "name," when it is used in connection with Christ,* is theologically significant.

2.1. Names of Christ. The belief, widespread in the ancient world, that to know a person's or a deity's name is to know something fundamental about him or her, helps one to understand the significance of some occurrences of the term *name.* In Hebrews 1:4 the ascended Christ is said to have "become as much superior to angels as the name he has obtained is more excellent than theirs." To say that Christ has a superior name is to say that he is superior to all others, but what is the specific name to which the author of Hebrews* refers? The immediate context points towards its being "Son" (Heb 1:5, "You are my Son, today I have begotten you"), a term that refers not only to Christ's relationship to God* but also to his role as God's chosen Messiah.

In Revelation 19:11-16 we see a typical NT phenomenon: what the OT applies to God, the NT unabashedly applies to Christ. Christ, appearing in apocalyptic* glory,* is called "faithful and true" (cf. Ps 96:13), and Revelation 19:13 calls him "The Word of God" (cf. Gen 1:3, 7, 9). "Faithful and true" words that echo the OT, recall how God acts with respect to his people and all humanity. As the God of the OT was faithful and true, so also is Christ to the new people of God. The latter term is reminiscent of Genesis, where God speaks and worlds spring into being. Here Christ, the Word of God, will create a world* in which his church* will live in the grandeur of his triumph over evil.

There are also clear echoes of Deuteronomy 10:17 (a text that emphasizes God's sovereignty by calling him "God of gods and Lord of lords") in Revelation 19:16, where the warrior Christ is seen to be worthy of the titles "King of kings and Lord of lords" (cf. Rev 17:14).

2.2. Belief in Christ's Name. 1 John 3:23 insists that it is God's will for all to "believe in the name of his Son, Jesus Christ," and in 1 John 5:13 he refers to those who "believe in *(eis)* the name of the son of God" (*see* Son of God; Sonship). In both places this belief involves more than mere mental assent to what has been said about or by Christ. It means fidelity to Christ, and it is to enter into a relationship with him signified in baptism* (according to Acts 2:38; 8:16; 10:48; 19:5; 22:16) and characterized by a certain lifestyle.

2.3. Suffering for the Name. According to 1 Peter 4:14-16, those who have the honor of bearing the name of Christ can expect to suffer for it, which means they will be rejected by society at large (*see* Persecution). This is not a condition that is to be considered unusual but is rather to be expected. Those who suffer for the name of Christ should consider it a privilege. In Revelation 2:3 the risen Christ praises the endurance* of the Ephesian believers, saying that they have borne suffering "for my name's sake." To do a thing for "the sake of the name" is to do it for the sake of the nameholder. Thus "holding fast" to a name (Rev 2:13) is a way of saying that someone is being true to the nameholder. In Revelation 2:13 the Lord* commends the Christians in Pergamum for holding fast to "my name," which is to say that they have been faithful to him. Revelation, with its view of a future in which God finally defeats the enemies of the church, encourages the persecuted with the promise* that those who suffer for Christ will be rewarded (*see* Revelation, Book of).

2.4. Forgiveness for Christ's Sake. In 1 John 2:12 and Revelation 2:3 we encounter *onoma* as the object of the preposition *dia*. The prepositional phrase, meaning "for the sake of his [Christ's] name," is causative; thus in 1 John 2:12 believers are said to be forgiven not because of their response to the message (though that is presupposed) but rather "for his name's sake." Forgiveness* therefore is predicated primarily on what Christ has done (cf. 1 John 1:7), although a human response is necessary.

2.5. Invocation of Christ's Name. Acts* uses the OT expression of "calling upon the name of the Lord" but applies it to Christ (Acts 2:21; 9:14, 21; 22:16). In Acts, by calling upon the name of Jesus one becomes a believer and then belongs to God himself. In the act of calling upon God, a person gives up the right to control his or her life and acknowledges that Christ is Lord.

In Acts 4:12 we read that there is no other name given by which humanity might be saved. For Luke (and Peter) salvation* is summed up in the name *Jesus* (see also Acts 3:6; 8:12). In Acts 10:43 we read that it is "through [Christ's] name" that forgiveness of sins is obtained. Because of such claims for the name, the religious authorities are said to have forbidden the apostles* to preach "in this name." However, the fledgling church believed that Christ was God's agent of salvation and thus they had to preach salvation in his name. It should be noted, however, that from the perspective of Acts, invoking Christ's name does not mean that one is automatically saved; faith* is also required.

James 2:7 indicates that to mistreat a person over whom the name of Christ has been invoked is to mistreat Christ. The verb translated "invoke" (*epikaleō*) refers to the act of calling the name of one over another to indicate that the former owns the latter (cf. in the LXX Deut 28:10; Is 43:7; Jer 14:9). Thus James 2:7 claims that the rich who treat less fortunate believers badly "blaspheme" the "good name" that was invoked (probably in baptism) over these poor. To mistreat the poor is mistreat those who belong to God, a serious sin indeed.

In James 5:14 the author encourages the sick to call for the elders to pray, "anointing him with oil in the name of the Lord." The elders are to act in the name of the Lord, and in doing so they call upon God's power. It is important to note that James is not speaking about magic*— to invoke God's name is not to use a formula in order to manipulate supernatural forces. Rather, invoking "the name of the Lord" implies a relationship with him. It means that one can ask God to heal (*see* Anointing; Healing), and it is his power that will heal the person, not the act itself. To do something "in the name of the Lord" is to do something according to his will, and as such it represents a bending of the human will, not the divine. It is this that is misunderstood by the unbelievers who attempt to use the name of Jesus to cast out evil spirits (Acts 19:13-16).

3. Name in the Apostolic Fathers.

Despite the belief that a name reveals something fundamental about its owner, Justin Martyr makes the claim that although people are baptized in the name the Father, Son and Spirit, no name can express God's true nature (Justin *Apol. I* 61.11). Names may reveal something about God, but for the most part he is unknowable. In the apostolic fathers* we also see that the practice of invoking God's name in baptism continues, although Athanasius does not believe that one can merely repeat divine names and thereby count oneself as a Christian. They are not magic; one must live a Christian life and believe rightly or baptism avails nothing (Athanasius *Ar.* 2.43). As Hermas says, no one can enter the kingdom of God unless he takes the name of God's Son (*Herm. Sim.* 9.12.4). For Hermas that means that one must have faith in God's Son who is, as Hermas puts, the gate into the kingdom (*see* Kingdom of God). Finally it is worth noting that in a world populated with demons and spirits, Christ's name was believed to protect those who believe against evil, since "even the demons fear the power of his name" (Justin *Dial. Tryph.* 30.3). This for Justin was proof of the superiority of the Christian faith.

See also AUTHORITY; BAPTISM, BAPTISMAL RITES; CHRISTOLOGY; MAGIC AND ASTROLOGY.

BIBLIOGRAPHY. C. K. Barrett, *The Acts of the Apostles* (2 vols; ICC; Edinburgh: T & T Clark, 1994-); H. Bietenhard, "Name," *NIDNTT* 2:648-55; idem, "ὄνομα κτλ," *TDNT* 5:242-83; P. H. Davids, *The Epistle of James* (NIGTC; Grand Rapids: Eerdmans, 1982); idem, *The First Epistle of Peter* (NICNT; Grand Rapids: Eerdmans, 1990); P. Ellingworth, *The Epistle to the Hebrews* (NIGTC; Grand Rapids: Eerdmans, 1993); L. Hartmann, "ὄνομα," *EDNT* 2:519-22; R. H. Mounce, *The Book of Revelation* (NICNT; Grand Rapids: Eerdmans, 1977); S. S. Smalley, *1, 2, 3 John* (WBC; Waco, TX: Word, 1984). B. Eastman

NARRATIVE CRITICISM

Narrative critics analyze the complex ways in which stories are told in biblical books written in narrative form. Their hybrid method concentrates on the plot, points of view, character development, dialogue, settings, repetitions, gaps in the story line, uses of irony and the effects on readers of these and other literary features that distinguish a particular biblical text from a letter,* treatise, speech or collection of unrelated stories. During the 1970s scholars of the Bible created this new method by drawing on various analytical methods that had been developed recently by literary critics in their study of modern novels, short stories and films (see Booth, Chatman), referred to collectively as "narratology" (see Bal). These biblical scholars developed their own narrative criticism as a tool for analyzing the final, canonical forms of biblical narratives as coherent, integrated wholes rather than as composites of various sources. Scholars of various perspectives have been persuaded of the value of this approach, making narrative criticism the most widely employed variety of the new literary criticism now used in investigations of biblical narrative texts (see Spencer).

1. The Development of This Method
2. The Applications of This Method

1. The Development of This Method.

1.1. Origins. Biblical scholars invented the phrase "narrative criticism" to parallel the estab-

lished designations of text, source, form, redaction and composition criticism (see Rhoads and Michie). This new approach to understanding biblical texts was rooted in composition criticism, which under the influence of general literary theories about narrative ("narratology") developed into a hybrid method in which at least three such theories for analyzing the final form of the text have been integrated: as communication between an author and reader through a set of intermediate voices (see the chart in 2.1 below); as the presentation of an autonomous story world whose basic elements are characters, plot and settings; and as the combination of rhetorical techniques (*see* Rhetoric) that the author chose in order to transmit the story in just the way it is.

This newly synthesized method was nurtured by members of the Markan Seminar of the Society of Biblical Literature, who were eager to explore the ways in which this approach might break through the limits set by historical criticism. The initial focus on Mark's Gospel, made widely known by D. Rhoads and D. Michie, was followed in the 1980s by major narrative studies of Matthew by J. D. Kingsbury, of John by R. A. Culpepper and of Luke-Acts by R. C. Tannehill, each of whom drew on general literary theories in his own way.

In the 1990s narrative critics of Acts* have continued to treat Luke and Acts as one extended narrative; the method has been further refined in book-length treatments by R. L. Brawley, D. B. Gowler, J. A. Darr and W. S. Kurz (see Powell, 308-24 for an extensive bibliography on Luke-Acts to date). In contrast, work on the remaining canonical narrative, the Revelation to John (*see* Revelation, Book of), seems just to have begun; and narrative analyses of such second-century narratives as the *Shepherd of Hermas,* * the *Martyrdom of Polycarp* (*see* Polycarp) and the apocryphal* Acts will surely appear soon.

1.2. Assumptions. While those scholars who practice narrative criticism have demonstrated various ways of applying this method, they share at least three basic assumptions:

Biblical narrative texts are to be analyzed as internally interactive unities in their finished, canonical forms, not as composites of various sources.

Biblical narratives are to be read with the goal of grasping and entering the story world created by the text and not first of all for reconstructing their historical context or their relation to reality outside of the world presented in the text.

Biblical narratives display significant literary artistry that can be appreciated by close attention to the way the narrator tells these stories: that is, to how characters are presented; to how the plot is developed (including creation and resolution of conflicts); to foreshadowing; to gaps in the story line; to repetition of words, scenes, themes and literary patterns; to points of view; to temporal, spatial and social settings; to relative duration of focus on each scene; to uses of implicit commentary (such as irony, misunderstandings and symbolism); and to other rhetorical strategies for persuading readers to enter the world and agree with the story created by the narrator.

1.3. Relation to Previous Methods. Narrative critics are convinced that a biblical book in narrative form should be analyzed on its own terms before it is studied as evidence of something else outside of the text. This approach seems to be a logical development of the methods used by redaction and composition criticism. Philosophically, however, narrative criticism is based on theories about communication applied to the text as an end in itself rather than on any methods of historical analysis in which texts are treated as means to the end of reconstructing the events and the traditioning process that resulted in the finished text.

Yet in contrast to the narratologists' chief interest in analyzing texts to develop theories about narrative, narrative critics draw on literary theories in various ways to exegete their texts. And while composition critics sought the primary meaning of the biblical text in the text's theological or ideational content, which is separate in principle from the narrative form, narrative critics seek the primary meaning in the details of the text's structure: what the text says, its story, may not be separated from the way it is said, its discourse or rhetoric (see Moore, 41-45). By no means does this approach entail a rejection of theological interest as such; rather it introduces a distinct shift in focus that holds significant theological promise (see Osborne, 153-73 and Powell, 85-105).

The functional difference between the methods of historical criticism and narrative criticism is aptly compared to that between a window and a painting. Historical criticism seeks to look *through* the text in order to see the events, circumstances and motivations that led to the production of the text. Literary criticism, including narrative criticism, looks *at* the text in order to discern there the inner workings of the story world presented by the text. In other words, while historical criticism focuses on the degree to which a narrative refers to the real world (its referential function), narrative criticism deals directly with the contributions the various literary features of the text make to the telling of the story itself (its poetic function). Narrative critics do not deny the values of referential inquiry, but they leave this work to others and concentrate on the text as literature, with the goal of describing what and how the author communicates to the narrative's readers.

2. The Applications of This Method.

2.1. The Communication Model. Many narrative critics operate explicitly with adaptations of the narrative communication model proposed by S. Chatman (6, 151). As the diagram seeks to clarify, the real (historical, flesh and blood) author communicates with the real reader (the one reading the text today) through the creation of an implied author (see Booth, 70-76) who advances the story by speaking through a narrator, who may or may not be the voice of one of the characters. The narratee is the person or persons directly addressed by the narrator. And the implied reader is the real reader's image of the original reader who is presupposed by or produced by the text.

Since the real author stands outside the text as such, the only author available to the real reader is the implied author, a complex image of the real author as a selecting and structuring intelligence that is gradually inferred by the real reader while reading. The real author's creation of this textual persona, as in Luke 1:1-4, is the profound rhetorical move that begins the communication. And with the famous "we" narrator of Acts (who first appears in Acts 16:10-17 and then in Acts 20:5-15; 21:1-18; 27:1—28:16) and the narrator of the Revelation to John, the respective authors have created narrators who participate as characters in their stories.

Much more frequently in biblical texts it is impossible to distinguish between the implied author and the narrator as the invisible speaker, whose voice may be most obvious in editorial comments. This is especially the case if the real reader regards the narrator as fully reliable. Early in Acts, for example, the narrator appears frequently to inform the reader about the wonderful success of the Holy Spirit's* work through the church* despite the opposition endured from without and the problems faced from within (see Acts 2:43-47; 6:7; 9:31; 12:24); and the implied reader does not doubt the truth of these claims. A reliable narrator's authoritative voice expresses the point of view (ideology) that the implied author seeks, in the face of possible opposition, to establish as the implied reader's own norm for evaluating both what happens in the story and the veracity of the characters (see Powell, 23-25). Alert real readers are thus influenced to perceive the error in Simon Magus's judgment (Acts 8:18) that Peter controlled the giving of the power of the Holy Spirit (see Tannehill 1990, 106).

The text does not give today's real readers access to the original readers of the biblical narratives, but the text does bid real readers to read from the standpoint of the text's implied readers; that is, to identify with the issues they faced and the relevance of the text's message to their situation. The narratee is the literary figure to whom the author explicitly directs the text, such as Theophilus in Luke 1:3 and Acts 1:1. In most biblical narratives the implied reader and the narratee are functionally indistinguishable, which is the case for the relation between Theophilus, the narratee, and the Christians Luke wanted to influence, the implied readers. For the narrator clearly addresses summaries and explanations to both (see Kurz, 9-16).

The goal of narrative criticism is to enable a real reader to read the text from the perspective of the implied reader. This aim requires a real reader to obtain such knowledge as the text assumes was known by the implied reader and to "forget" everything that the text does not assume such a reader would know. To be sure, the goal of reading as if one were in the shoes of the hypothetical implied reader may be fully unattainable, but narrative critics are persuaded that this aim sets important criteria for interpretation. "With regard to any proposed reading, the question may be asked, Is there anything *in the text* that indicates the reader is expected to respond in this way?" (Powell, 21).

2.2. The Narrative Analysis of the Text.

2.2.1. Plotting, Gaps and Repetitions. Narrative critics seek to explicate the characteristics of narrative that distinguish it from a recorded series of discrete incidents. The primary feature that they analyze is the text's plot, a interrelated succession of actions ordered to present a beginning, a middle and an end. An author has a large range of freedom regarding where to begin (compare the openings of Mark and Luke) as well as how to end (compare the endings of Matthew and Luke). And for the middle an author can choose, for example, to follow one or another character, to include or omit events (compare the middle sections of Mark and Luke), to flash back (note Luke's placement of Jesus' genealogy), to foreshadow (note how Simeon's prophecies* in Luke 2:29-35 anticipate the main plot turn of Acts) or to proceed in chronological order (see Kurz, 17-36). The choice of the ending may be the most critical expression of an author's freedom, for the end sheds much light on the entire narrative since it appears to be the goal toward which the plot has been moving. Thus the ending of Acts has generated enormous controversy.

In Acts the author's process of selecting and structuring has resulted in emphasizing some events (e.g., Saul/Paul's call/conversion) while deemphasizing or omitting others (such as Peter's activities after Acts 12:17-19), thus leaving gaps to be filled by the reader's imagination. Whether an author has intended an omission to trigger such reflection can be debated (see Sternberg, 235-37), but the gaps in the plot line of Luke and Acts have generated discussion at least from the time of John Chrysostom. Perhaps the most striking and problematic gaps occur at the end of each text. Mikeal C. Parsons has used narrative criticism to illuminate the ways in which the end of Luke and the beginning of Acts both overlap and conflict with each other. And the open-ended character of Acts provokes the reader both to wonder about what happened to Paul after "two whole years" under house arrest and to remain uncertain about the implied author's anticipation regarding further reception of "this salvation of God" by Jews (see

Tannehill 1990, 347-48). Yet as the result of artful plotting, the reader's attention is drawn away from Paul's fate to the concluding emphasis on his "proclaiming the rule of God and teaching about the Lord Jesus Christ with great boldness and without restriction" (Acts 28:31).

While historical critics have usually regarded both gaps in the plot line and repetitions as evidence for an author's use of multiple sources, narrative critics observe that these features appear frequently in narratives and that they can be effective literary devices for communicating the author's message. M. Sternberg (365-440) detects five forms of repetition and variation that may be employed singly or in combination: change of order, substitution, grammatical transformation, addition or expansion and ellipsis or truncation. A narrator may use these strategies to communicate emphasis, contrast, climax, correspondence or irony. Such repetition is common to classical literature as well as to folklore and is one of the most ancient methods of conveying information.

Perhaps the most striking example of repetition in early Christian documents is the thrice-told story of Saul/Paul's conversion/call in Acts 9, 22 and 26 (see Witherup 1992). The reader first hears the story from the authoritative, third-person point of view of the narrator. Saul the aggressive persecutor is reduced to blind helplessness and must be led by the hand for three days before the divine restoration of his sight, mediated by a certain Ananias. The truth of the story is then confirmed by two subsequent tellings that are presented from a subjective, first-person point of view with variations that highlight additional aspects and implications. In Acts 22 Paul uses insider language (Aramaic) to tell an expanded version of the story of his dramatic conversion in the form of a defense to a Judean audience in Jerusalem.* In this apologia the reader learns more about Saul's zeal as a Judean and his own responsibility as a former persecutor of those he has joined, that Paul was more aggressive than portrayed in Acts 9 in his questioning the source of his visions* and that he received his call to witness to Gentiles* directly from the risen Jesus in a vision in the Jerusalem temple* (Acts 22:17-21), rather than earlier in Damascus.

The context of the third recounting, with Paul now speaking Greek, is a hearing before civil authorities in Caesarea (*see* Civil Authority). In this version of Paul's apologia, Luke displays the rhetorical features of a classical defense speech, by which the reader should be persuaded not only that Paul was not helpless but also that he had become an orator of some stature. In Acts 26 the narrator continues the trend begun in Acts 22 to intensify the descriptions both of Saul's activities as a persecutor (who ironically is now being persecuted by those who are like his former self) and of his experience of the light in the vision. And in a further expansion the risen Lord* expounds at length on his sending Paul to the Gentiles. There is also truncation of the narrative: Paul's blindness, his having been led into Damascus, and Ananias are not mentioned. The narrative bypasses these events and substitutes Paul's summary: "I was not disobedient to the heavenly vision" (Acts 26:19-20).

Such modified repetitions have helped lead narrative critics to two important conclusions. First, the reader should pay close attention to how the placement of any element in a developing narrative affects that material's function. Expectations created or implied early in a narrative may be reversed later. Thus it is not appropriate to derive a biblical writer's view of a particular subject by collecting and summarizing relevant internal references without regard to their functions in the whole narrative. Second, the reader is led to build an image of the central characters as relevant information is revealed in an unfolding narrative.

2.2.2. Characterization. "Characterization refers to the process by which characters are formulated, depicted, and developed," and a character is defined as any figure or group presented in a literary work (Darr, 173). As Darr points out, "Some of the most vivid, enduring, and effectual characters in all of Western literature appear in Luke-Acts." Until the rise of narrative criticism, however, scholars' awareness of just how these characters are employed by the narrator to advance the story line has been quite limited.

Darr has summarized the questions that narrative critics should use in uncovering the author's techniques of characterization as follows: "What roles do characters play and how are such roles recognized by the reader?" "What devices give a personage depth and individuality?" "Are figures illustrative (typed/symbolic) or more realistic?" "What contemporary literary stereotypes and social conventions are evoked?" "How is distance (the level of identification between reader and character) controlled?" (11). Darr emphasizes that readers build their images of characters in a narrative in response to the author's presentations of figures within "a web of interrelationships that develops among all of the figures in the story world. . . . Characters are delineated in terms of each other, just as we are defined by our relationships in real life" (41). It follows then that God also must be regarded as such a character whose image in the reader's mind is built up as divine intervention is presented (see Brawley).

2.2.3. Setting. Chatman observes that authors provide social, historical, geographical and temporal settings for their stories. The implied author of Luke and Acts presents more details than does any other NT author about the historical, physical and institutional settings of the activities of Jesus and his early followers. The function of this detail is often not simply to provide interesting local color but to emphasize significant aspects of the implied author's message. For example, the beginnings and endings of Luke and Acts present contrasting physical settings and economic systems for the activity of the people of God. The Gospel opens with Zechariah, Simeon, Anna and then the young Jesus in the temple in Jerusalem; the narrator closes this book by describing the postresurrection disciples as "continually in the temple blessing God." Acts emphatically changes the setting by opening with the disciples waiting for the power of the Holy Spirit in an "upstairs room" of a household; it closes with Paul teaching boldly and without hindrance in a household setting. Along the way the narrator provides many clues that God intends for the household* and its economy of mutual sharing to replace the temple and its unjust economy of exploitive redistribution (see Elliott).

2.2.4. Implicit Commentary. An author's narrative techniques may include expressions of irony, misunderstanding and symbolism to guide the implied reader into an advanced understanding of the narrator's point of view. With these rhetorical devices the implied author encourages the rejection of certain interpretations as well as the exploration of alternative ones. In symbolic communication the reader recognizes that something means more than it

initially seems to mean; the narrative critic seeks to uncover the "more" that would have been sensed by the implied reader. And awareness of the use of irony leads to the conclusion that the true interpretation must be contrary to the apparent meaning. In Acts, for example, the reader becomes aware of a major, extended irony: those who attempt to oppose God and repress evangelization unwittingly facilitate the actualization of God's will and the spreading of the "word of the Lord" (see Kurz, 144-47).

The misunderstanding motif that the implied author used effectively in the Gospel of Luke (e.g., Lk 4:22/4:34; 22:36-38) appears early in Acts (Acts 1:6-7). When the disciples ask the risen Jesus whether he is now going to restore the kingdom of Israel, the readers of the Gospel have superior insight that the narrator already conveyed to them in Luke's passion narrative. Following many other uses of this motif in Acts, the narrator returns to it emphatically in Acts 28:26-28, now taken to its ultimate: spiritual blindness. Suddenly the narrator presents Paul gravely citing the famous passage from Isaiah 6:9-10 ("you shall indeed hear but not understand") to leaders of the Judeans living in Rome.* In light of the narrator's report in the same context of a mixed response from Roman Jews to Paul's message (Acts 28:24), whether the implied author intended to convey a tragic sense of the final rejection of the gospel by the Jews (with implicit encouragement of the implied reader to reject non-Christian Jews) remains one of the most vexing questions in Lukan scholarship (see Tannehill 1990, 344-57).

See also ACTS OF THE APOSTLES; HERMENEUTICS; RHETORIC, RHETORICAL CRITICISM; STRUCTURALISM AND DISCOURSE ANALYSIS.

BIBLIOGRAPHY. M. Bal, *Narratology* (Toronto: University of Toronto Press, 1985); W. Booth, *The Rhetoric of Fiction* (2d ed.; Chicago: University of Chicago Press, 1983); R. L. Brawley, *Centering on God: Method and Message in Luke-Acts* (Louisville, KY: Westminster/John Knox, 1990); S. Chatman, *Story and Discourse: Narrative Structure in Fiction and Film* (Ithaca, NY: Cornell University Press, 1978); J. A. Darr, *On Character Building: The Reader and the Rhetoric of Characterization in Luke-Acts* (Louisville, KY: Westminster/John Knox, 1992); J. H. Elliott, "Temple versus Household in Luke-Acts: A Contrast in Social Institutions" in *The Social World of Luke-*

Acts: Models for Interpretation, ed. J. H. Neyrey (Peabody, MA: Hendrickson, 1991) 211-40; D. B. Gowler, *Host, Guest, Enemy and Friend: Portraits of the Pharisees in Luke and Acts* (ESEC 2; New York: Peter Lang, 1991); W. S. Kurz, *Reading Luke-Acts: Dynamics of Biblical Narrative* (Louisville, KY: Westminster/John Knox, 1993); D. L. Matson, *Household Conversion Narratives in Acts: Pattern and Interpretation* (JSNTSS 123; Sheffield: Sheffield Academic Press, 1996); S. D. Moore, *Literary Criticism and the Gospels: The Theoretical Challenge* (New Haven, CT: Yale University Press, 1989); G. R. Osborne, *The Hermeneutical Spiral* (Downers Grove, IL: InterVarsity Press, 1991) 153-73; M. C. Parsons, *The Departure of Jesus in Luke-Acts: The Ascension Narratives in Content* (JSNTSS 21; Sheffield: JSOT, 1987); M. A. Powell, *What Is Narrative Criticism?* (Minneapolis: Fortress, 1990); M. A. Powell, C. G. Gray and M. C. Curtis, eds., *The Bible and Modern Literary Criticism: A Critical Assessment and Annotated Bibliography* (New York: Greenwood, 1992); D. Rhoads and D. Michie, *Mark as Story: An Introduction to the Narrative of a Gospel* (Philadelphia: Fortress, 1982); F. S. Spencer, "Acts and Modern Literary Approaches" in *The Book of Acts in Its Ancient Literary Setting,* ed. B. W. Winter and A. D. Clarke (BAFCS 1; Grand Rapids: Eerdmans, 1993) 381-414; M. Sternberg, *The Poetics of Biblical Narrative: Ideological Literature and the Drama of Reading* (Bloomington, IN: Indiana University Press, 1988); R. C. Tannehill, *The Narrative Unity of Luke-Acts* (2 vols.; Minneapolis: Fortress, 1986, 1990); R. Witherup, "Cornelius Over and Over and Over Again: 'Functional Redundancy' in the Acts of the Apostles," *JSNT* 49 (1993) 44-66; idem, 'Functional Redundancy in the Acts of the Apostles: A Case Study," *JSNT* 48 (1992) 67-86.

S. S. Bartchy

NATIONS. *See* GENTILES, GENTILE MISSION; MISSION, EARLY NON-PAULINE.

NAZOREANS. *See* JEWISH CHRISTIANITY.

NEW BIRTH

The NT witnesses to a radical change in the life of those who have placed their faith* in Jesus Christ. Among the many terms that mark the initiation of a changed relationship with God* (e.g., justification, redemption,* reconciliation), "new birth" especially points to a change in the life of the believer that initiates a process of growth and development into a new person in Christ.*

1. Terminology
2. Background
3. James: Born to Be Firstfruits
4. Petrine Epistles: Born by Resurrection and the Word
5. Johannine Epistles: Born with Characteristics of a New Family
6. Apostolic Fathers: New Birth and the Church

1. Terminology.
A variety of terms lie behind the NT concept of new birth. The term *palingenesia* ("regeneration") is found only in Matthew 19:28 and Titus 3:5. The former refers to the end-time renewal of all things, while the latter is linked with *anakainōsis* ("renewal") to refer to the initiation of new life* in the believer. The production of new life in the believer is expressed by *ktizein* ("to create"; Eph 2:10), resulting in a *kainē ktisis,* a "new creation" (2 Cor 5:17; Gal 6:15), or a *kainos anthrōpos,* a "new person" (Eph 4:24). The related term *anakainoun* ("to renew") and its cognates occur most frequently in the Pauline letters (Rom 12:2; 2 Cor 4:16; Eph 4:23; Col 3:10; Tit 3:5; cf. Heb 6:6).

The concept of new birth is expressed especially in the later NT by the verb *gennaō* ("to give birth," "to be born"; e.g., 1 Jn 2:29; 3:9; 4:7; 5:1, 4, 18; cf. Jn 1:13; 3:3-8) and the compound verb *anagennaō* ("to give new birth," "to be born anew"). The latter occurs in the NT only in 1 Peter 1:3, 23 and not at all in the Septuagint (except as a variant in Sir prol. 28). Other terms and expressions round out the concept of new birth, including *apokueō* ("to bring forth, give birth to," only in James 1:15, 18 in the NT) and *ek tou theou estin:* the one doing good "is from God" (3 Jn 11).

2. Background.
The older history of religions school sought to find the derivation of the notion "new birth" in the mystery religions of the Hellenistic world, where initiates passed from death into life by being brought into a mysterious intimacy with the deity (e.g., Bultmann, 45-46; *see* Greco-Roman Religions). But in the light of the scarcity of early "new birth" terminology such as *anagennaō* in the mystery religions, recent scholarship

has sought an origin of the concept elsewhere (Büchsel, 673-75; Nash, 174-79).

A more likely origin has been found in the OT and Judaism. While the Jews did not describe themselves or others as possessing new life, they hoped for a new life for the world and themselves. This hope was expressed especially in the prophecies of a new covenant, whereby God would give Israel a new heart and put a new spirit in them and restore to them new life* (cf. Ezek 11:19-20; 36:25-27; 37:1-14; Jer 31:31-34). Jesus' words of institution at the Last Supper indicate that the covenant is initiated through his blood (Mk 14:22-25), and Peter's proclamation after the resurrection* and Pentecost* indicates that the pouring out of the Holy Spirit* upon all believers is the fulfillment at least in part of the OT expectations (Acts 2:16-41; 3:17-26). New life is now the possession of Christians as a present reality because of the new birth (cf. Toon, 55-61).

3. James: Born to Be Firstfruits.
We gain an important understanding of new birth in the context of James's* apologetic for God's innocence with regard to temptation.* James denies that God is the author of temptation, because God acts constructively. The result of yielding to temptation moves from evil desire to sin, and full-grown sin gives birth (apokyei) to death. But God's purpose is different. "He chose to give us birth (apekyēsen) by the word of truth, so that we would become a kind of firstfruits of all he created" (Jas 1:18). This "birth" could be the birth of humanity in the creation (Gen 1:26-27; 2:7), the birth of Israel, God's chosen people (Deut 32:18), or the birth of Christians. The last appears to be the most likely interpretation. Those who have been chosen by God for salvation* in Christ are the firstfruits of a redeemed creation* (cf. 2 Thess 2:13; Rev 14:4; Rom 8:19-23). James appeals to the spiritual new birth of Christians as an illustration of the good things that God gives. God accomplishes this new, spiritual birth through the "word of truth," a reference to the divine action upon the life of the believer. Christians therefore stand as the first installment ("firstfruits") in the universal redemptive plan of God (Moo, 76-77; Johnson, 197-98).

4. Petrine Epistles: Born by Resurrection and the Word.
Peter (see 1 Peter; 2 Peter) alone among NT authors uses the compound verb anagennaō ("to give new birth," "to be born anew"; 1 Pet 1:3, 23). The event denoted by the term is neither a natural nor a magical process, nor is it something that a person can take up and dispose of at will. Peter tells his readers that they have been born anew into a living hope through the resurrection of Jesus Christ (1 Pet 1:3). God has made believers his children (see Son) by raising Jesus from the dead; resurrection means life and makes life possible (cf. Jn 11:25; Michaels, 19). And that life points to the future, because the goal of regeneration is "a living hope." "Birth, while wonderful, does not exist for itself but rather to start a child on its way to maturity and adult life" (Davids, 52).

Peter returns to the new birth motif in 1 Peter 1:23 to say that it is effected by the creative agency of imperishable seed, through the living and enduring word of God (1 Pet 1:23). The term for seed, spora, occurs only here in the NT (the more common word for seed, sperma, is also used in conjunction with the new birth in 1 Jn 3:9). Both spora and sperma can be used either of producing plants or of biological procreation. The former is suggested when Peter metaphorically equates humanity and grass (1 Pet 1:24), but the latter is suggested by the metaphor "newborn babies" (artigennēta brephē) in 1 Peter 2:2. The new birth is effected by the seed of the word of God (cf. Jesus' parable, Lk 8:11; Mk 4:14), which will never perish (1 Pet 1:24). Peter draws not on the smallness or innocence of a baby but on its strong and instinctive longing for mother's milk. Continuous nourishment from "spiritual milk" causes the newborn to grow up in its salvation (1 Pet 2:2).

Through the preaching of the gospel (1 Pet 1:25) of Jesus, the divine seed has sprouted in believers' souls by the power of the Spirit and has produced Jesus' resurrection life in newborn babies who will grow by feeding on pure, spiritual milk.*

5. Johannine Epistles: Born with Characteristics of a New Family.
The Johannine idiom gennēthēnai ek theou ("to be born of God") is a description of the origin of the believer (1 Jn 2:29; 3:9; 4:7; 5:1, 4, 7, 18; cf. 3 Jn 11; Jn 1:13; 3:3-21) whose true existence begins and ends in God through Jesus Christ, and the idiom is used as a description of Jesus himself (1 Jn 5:18; cf. Heb 1:5; 5:5). John uses

the idiom to point to characteristics of the new life that have resulted from being born of God (*see* John, Letters of).

5.1. New Life and Righteousness (1 Jn 2:29). John declares that everyone who does what is right has been born of God (1 Jn 2:29). The metaphor indicates that Christians have received new life from God by a creative act comparable with physical birth. Righteous conduct is not a condition for obtaining rebirth but rather is both a consequence and an evidence that a person has truly been born of God. This kind of righteousness* was displayed by Jesus and is therefore truly possible only for those who have been born of God. Righteousness is a family characteristic shared by the Father and the Son and the children of God. The new life given to those born of God is both transforming and enabling: it makes the believer righteous and enables the believer to live life rightly.

5.2. New Life, Sin and the Seed of God (1 Jn 3:9; 5:18). John continues the thought of 1 John 2:29—the person born of God does what is right—by making the same point negatively: a person who is born of God does not sin. The divine birth explains the Christian's moral character. The Christian does not continue in sin because God's seed (*sperma*, the more common word for seed than *spora* in 1 Pet 1:23) remains in him or her. The Christian shares something of the nature of God (cf. 2 Pet 1:4) through the new birth, which ultimately will result in the believer being conformed to the image of Christ (Rom 8:29; 2 Cor 3:18). This is a principle of life in which the word of God operates in the heart of the believer by the inward power of the Spirit and the indwelling presence of Christ (cf. Eph 3:14-19) to produce a godly life. This new life is characteristic of God's own life and will enable the believer to resist sin and live a godly life (cf. Smalley, 171-75).

John expands this thought in 1 John 5 by drawing on a parallel between the believer and Jesus: "We know that those who are born of God do not sin, but the one who was born of God protects them, and the evil one does not touch them" (1 Jn 5:18). The expression "the one who was born of God" is most probably a reference to Jesus Christ (Marshall, 252; Smalley, 303), not the believer (Brown, 620-22). This corresponds to Jesus' divine sonship, which the author of Hebrews* unfolds when citing the messianic prophecy of Psalm 2:7, a text that likewise describes Jesus as born of God (Heb 1:5; 5:5; cf. Acts 13:33). This divine begetting of the believer and the Son joins them in participating in divine life. Once again we see that the new birth for believers results in a family trait. The children of God now are protected from the evil one by the Son of God.* Children of the devil (*see* Satan) naturally sin (Jn 8:38-47; cf. 1 Jn 5:19), but children of God now are kept from sin by their own new life and also by the protection of the Son of God (cf. Jn 17:12).

5.3. New Life and Love (1 Jn 4:7; 5:1). John begins an extended discussion of love* as the third family characteristic of the new life that results from being born of God by stating, "Beloved, let us love one another, because love is from God; everyone who loves is born of God and knows God" (1 Jn 4:7; cf. 1 Jn 5:1-12). As believers receive God's love they experience a transformation of heart by which they are now able and impelled to love each other with God's love. This was the emphasis of Jesus' new command to the disciples at the Last Supper (Jn 13:34-35).

Not only do regenerate persons have a new heart that will love, but also they have an endless supply of love from God by which the new heart can continually pour forth love (esp. 1 Jn 4:12-16, 19-21). If people do not love, they show that they do not know God. God's love brought life, and it is his love that guarantees that believers will love one another.

5.4. New Life and Faith (1 Jn 5:1, 4). John continues the emphasis upon love in 1 John 5 but additionally gives a final family characteristic of new life: victorious faith. "Everyone who believes that Jesus is the Christ has been born of God . . . for everything born of God conquers the world. And this is the victory that conquers the world, our faith" (1 Jn 5:1, 4). In 1 John 5:1 we can see that the continuing exercise of faith (*pisteuōn*, present tense) is the result of having been born of God (*gegēsanta*, perfect tense). This kind of faith takes God at his word by delighting in the will of God and thereby conquering the presence and power of Satan in the world. Whoever is born of God has the kind of faith that also triumphs over the trials and troubles that arise whenever one seeks to do what is right in a sinful world (Toon, 35).

6. Apostolic Fathers: New Birth and the Church. While the terminology of new birth is scarce in the apostolic fathers,* we do find the concept developing from the NT teachings.

6.1. Inward Transformation. The apostolic fathers continue to emphasize the inward change that occurs in the new birth. Ignatius* of Antioch describes the transformation as moving from death to life, and the new life is like bearing inwardly "the stamp of God the Father in love through Jesus Christ" (Ign. *Magn.* 5.2). This irreversible stamp of God's ownership also produces the power of Christ's life within one's experience. Ignatius elsewhere refers to fellow believers as "God-bearers, temple-bearers, Christ-bearers, bearers of holy things" (Ign. *Eph.* 9.2), emphasizing the separation of the Christian community from the profane world through the indwelling of individual believers (Schoedel, 67).

The *Epistle of Barnabas** likewise speaks of inward transformation, so that believers "became new, created again from the beginning; therefore God truly dwells in us" (*Barn.* 16.8; cf. 6.11). He goes on to emphasize that the indwelling God speaks through the believer to witness to unbelievers (*Barn.* 16.9-10).

6.2. Baptism and the New Birth. Most of the discussion by the apostolic fathers of the new birth is in the context of the rite of baptism.* It was beginning to be taken for granted that Jesus' expression "born of water and Spirit" (Jn 3:5) and Paul's reference to "the washing of regeneration and renewing by the Holy Spirit" (Tit 3:5) refer to the outward act of baptism and the inward act of regeneration. While this connection arguably does not imply that baptism produces regeneration (Downing, 112), without the caution Peter inserts in 1 Peter 3:21 it may have set the direction for such a doctrine in the later fathers.

The *Epistle of Barnabas* contends that the cross* and baptism are vitally connected, so that "while we descend into the water laden with sins and dirt, we rise up bearing fruit in our heart and with fear and hope in Jesus in our spirits" (*Barn.* 11.11). In the *Shepherd of Hermas**we find the declaration concerning believers that it was necessary "for them to come up through water in order to be made alive, for otherwise they could not enter the kingdom of God" (*Herm. Sim.* 9.16.2; cf. *Herm. Man.* 4.3.1). The water is the seal by which deadness is laid aside and through which believers come up alive (*Herm. Sim.* 9.16.4; 9.31.1, 4). *2 Clement* likewise speaks

of the seal of baptism as the confidence that believers will enter into the kingdom of God (*2 Clem.* 6.9; 7:6; *see* Clement of Rome). However, the author of *1 Clement* is careful to declare that believers are justified not by piety or works but through faith in God who justifies (*1 Clem.* 32.4).

6.3. New Birth and Community. In an intriguing passage the author of *1 Clement* apparently harks back to Peter's discussion of Noah and says, "Noah . . . proclaimed a regeneration (*palingenesia*) to the world, and through him the Master saved the living creatures that entered into the ark in harmony" (*1 Clem.* 9.4). The analogy suggests that spiritual rebirth can take place only within the community of the church. While this was taken too far in later centuries, it presents a NT understanding of the new birth taking place within the corporate life of the community of faith (Downing, 105-6).

See also BAPTISM, BAPTISMAL RITES; FORGIVENESS; HOLY SPIRIT; LIFE AND DEATH; RESURRECTION.

BIBLIOGRAPHY. R. E. Brown, *The Epistles of John: Translated with Introduction, Notes, and Commentary* (Garden City, NY: Doubleday, 1982); F. Büchsel, "γεννάω κτλ," *TDNT* 1:665-75; R. Bultmann, *The Johannine Epistles* (Philadelphia: Fortress, 1973); P. H. Davids, *The First Epistle of Peter* (NICNT; Grand Rapids: Eerdmans, 1990); V. K. Downing, "The Doctrine of Regeneration in the Second Century," *Evangelical Review of Theology* 14.2 (April-June 1990) 99-112; L. T. Johnson, *The Letter of James: A New Translation with Introduction and Commentary* (AB; Garden City, NY: Doubleday, 1995); I. H. Marshall, *The Epistles of John* (NICNT; Grand Rapids: Eerdmans, 1978); R. P. Martin, *James* (WBC; Dallas: Word, 1988); J. R. Michaels, *1 Peter* (WBC; Waco, TX: Word, 1988); D. J. Moo, *The Letter of James: An Introduction and Commentary* (TNTC; Grand Rapids: Eerdmans, 1985); R. Nash, *The Gospel and the Greeks* (Dallas: Word, 1992); F. Porsch, "ἀναγεννάω," *EDNT* 1:76-77; A. Ringwald, "γεννάω," *NIDNTT* 1:176-180; W. R. Schoedel, *Ignatius of Antioch* (Herm; Philadelphia: Fortress, 1985): S. S. Smalley, *1, 2, 3 John* (WBC; Waco, TX: Word, 1984); P. Toon, *Born Again: A Biblical and Theological Study of Regeneration* (Grand Rapids: Baker, 1987).

M. J. Wilkins

NEW COVENANT. *See* COVENANT, NEW COVENANT.

NEW HEAVENS. *See* HEAVEN, NEW HEAVENS.

NEW TESTAMENT THEOLOGY

If theology is discourse about God, then there has been NT theology, i.e., discourse about God that is based on the NT documents, as long as those documents have existed. But so expansive an approach proves unhelpful: no serious reflection on the NT throughout the entire history of the church could be excluded. NT theology is best thought of as a subset of biblical theology and restricted to movements that adopt that label.

1. Biblical Theology and New Testament Theology
2. Historical Criticism and New Testament Theology
3. Some Responses to the Historicist Impulse
4. Recent Visions of the Nature of New Testament Theology
5. Roman Catholic Contributions
6. New Testament Theology: 1985-95
7. Other Influences That Shape New Testament Theology
8. Controlling or Defining Elements of New Testament Theology
9. Focal Issues

1. Biblical Theology and New Testament Theology.

The first known use of "biblical theology" was by W. J. Christmann in 1607, in the title of his book (no longer extant) *Teutsche biblische Theologie.* It was a compilation of *dicta probantia,* prooftexts drawn from the Bible to support Protestant systematic theology. This usage enjoyed long life: a century and a half later, G. T. Zachariae published his four-volume *Biblische Theologie oder Untersuchung des biblischen Grundes der vornehmsten theologischen Lehren* (1771-75). This was an exegetically rigorous and detailed version of the same approach, prepared within the framework of traditional views of inspiration well established from the time of the magisterial Reformation yet reflecting very little consciousness of historical development within the canon.*

A rather different usage is found in P. J. Spener and the Pietists he influenced. In his *Pia Desideria* (1675) Spener distinguished *theologia biblica* (i.e., his own theology) from *theologia scholastica,* the prevailing Protestant orthodoxy that had returned to the Aristotelianism Luther had rejected. Thus "biblical theology" took on an aura of protest, of being "more biblical" than the prevailing dogmatics.

In the second half of the eighteenth century, under the impact of English Deism and the German *Aufklärung,* a handful of biblical theologians protested against the prevailing dogmatics, not in favor of Pietism but in favor of rationalism. The aim of several of these works was to extract from the Bible timeless truths in accord with reason, truths that were still largely, if sometimes uneasily, acceptable to the confessional stance of the ecclesiastical establishment. The most influential by far was J. P. Gabler, whose inaugural lecture at the University of Altdorf captured the rising mood and precipitated the next step: "An Oration on the Proper Distinction Between Biblical and Dogmatic Theology and the Specific Objectives of Each" (Gabler 1787). Gabler charged that dogmatic theology is too far removed from Scripture, constantly changing, perpetually disputed. Biblical theology, by which Gabler seems to mean a largely inductive study of the biblical text, has much more likelihood of gaining widespread agreement among learned, godly and cautious theologians. The fruit of such study may then serve as the basis on which dogmatic theology may be constructed. Thus Gabler's primary appeal was not that the Bible must first be read historically or that the documents be set out in historical sequence (though a little of this is implicit in what he said) but that biblical theologians may properly go about their task without being directly bound by doctrinal aims—an epoch-making suggestion at the time and one that has earned him the sobriquet "father of biblical theology."

The first part of Gabler's proposal, the rupturing of the link between biblical study and confessional application, was soon widely adopted, but the second part, that the results of such biblical theology should then be deployed in the construction of dogmatics, was largely ignored. Moreover, the more that scholars worked at a merely descriptive level, with decreasing concern or responsibility to synthesize and prescribe what is normative, the more the diversities in the biblical material achieved prominence. Encouraged to think through the biblical text inductively without reference to confessional constraints, G. L. Bauer produced not a biblical theology but an OT theology (1796), followed by a two-volume NT theology (1800-1802). Biblical theologies (i.e., of the entire Christian canon) continued to be written for the next century and beyond, the most influential being that of J. C. K. von Hofmann (1886), whose contribution to A. Schlatter's thought was significant. Moreover, some biblical theologians accepted the mandate to produce distinctive OT and NT theologies while still trying to spell out what bearing their work had for dogmatics (e.g., de Wette, 1813—although his push toward the unified was a synthesis of faith and aesthetics, or faith and feeling, attempting to isolate the timeless and the general while the particular data of the NT could be peeled away as the particular phenomena of one phase or other of the history of religions). But the drift of biblical theology was toward the increasingly atomistic, cut off from any obligation to traditional dogmatics.

2. Historical Criticism and New Testament Theology.

The long-standing ferment over the historical worth of the Bible, traceable in no small measure to Spinoza and Richard Simon generations earlier, erupted in the 1830s and the 1840s in D. F. Strauss's *Das Leben Jesu* (1835; ET 1972) and in the impact of F. C. Baur's historical reconstruction of how the Pauline epistles, the book of Acts* and the Gospels came to be written. The influence of the Tübingen School was far wider than the law/grace, Peter/Paul dichotomies at the heart of their historical criticism. The posthumous publication of Baur's NT theology (1864) marked the beginning of a passionate commitment by many biblical theologians to a developmental view of critically reconstructed history. Moreover, Baur's fairly radical naturalism meant that the NT documents could not properly be thought of as revelatory in any sense, still less theologically binding. They merely provided information about the first century.

Although few who followed him during the next half-century indulged in his degree of skepticism, Baur's insistence on the primacy of developmental history in the interpretation of NT documents shaped the leaders in the field— not only the best of the liberal biblical theologians (e.g., Holtzmann 1897, 1911) but the best of the conservative ones as well (e.g., Weiss

1868, 1903; ET, 2 vols., 1882-83). The focus on smaller and smaller parts of the Bible and the turn-of-the-century interest in a naturalism-inclined history of religions prompted many to doubt that one could meaningfully speak of NT theology: one must speak rather of NT theologies. And since the discipline of NT theology was disappearing into the wasteland of naturalistic histories of early Christianity, what need was there for the discipline? Hence the cheeky title of W. Wrede's work, written at least in part as a critique of Holtzmann: *Über Aufgabe und Methode der sogenannten neutestamentliche Theologie* (1897; lit. *Concerning the Task and Method of So-Called New Testament Theology*). Wrede argued that to treat each book of the NT separately was absurd, since each book provided too little information to enable an interpreter to reconstruct the entire "theology" of its author. The only responsible way forward was to construct "the history of early Christian religion and theology." Any unified NT theology, let alone biblical theology, is a chimera. This emphasis on the developmental-historical and on the descriptive remains a driving influence on not a few works dubbed NT theology today.

3. Some Responses to the Historicist Impulse.

The liberal track from these developments tended to produce works that were inherently unstable. Reconstructions of the historical Jesus, for instance, produced a Jesus who was acceptable to the current climate. Further historical work overthrew the construction. Three related but quite different developments responded to the growing crisis in the discipline.

The first was the impact of K. Barth. His commentary on Romans (1919, 1921) reflected a theological approach to the text that had been progressively eroded in the name of history. In part Barth was building on the outstanding conservative historical scholarship of T. Zahn, J. B. Lightfoot, and others. Thus in his 1922 debate with R. Bultmann, Barth was unwilling to allow a place for *Sachkritik*, a criticism of the content of the biblical texts on the basis of what is perceived to be the gospel* the text intends to articulate (Morgan). Barth had persuaded Bultmann to abandon classic religious liberalism; he could not persuade him to abandon the formation he had received in historical criticism of a skeptical variety (a background that Barth himself sometimes held on to in tension with his own theology of the Word). Thus Barth diminished the importance of historical research for the understanding of the Bible, underscoring instead the importance of theological interpretation. For many this was an oasis in a parched land; for others this was escapism that could not long be sustained unless the underlying historical and hermeneutical questions were firmly addressed, not summarily dismissed.

The second was the tack taken by Bultmann. Attentive to Barth's insistence that merely historical description is arid but not to his call to abandon classic liberal historical criticism, Bultmann, in a series of articles and books and finally in his *Theology of the NT* (1948-53; ET 1952-55), developed a new path. The naturalism and historical approaches of Wrede dominate the work at one level, but instead of eschewing theological formulation or dogmatic synthesis, Bultmann "demythologizes" what he thinks "modern man" can no longer believe and seeks to isolate the real, unchanging nature of the gospel in terms that can still be believed. At one level his historical reconstructions are heavily indebted to the turn-of-the-century history of religions school, worked out on a Procrustean bed of source criticism now largely abandoned and on an assumption that early and well-developed Gnosticism* shaped many features of nascent Christianity—a reconstruction that finds fewer and fewer adherents because evidence for well-formed pre-Christian Gnosticism is distinctly lacking.

At another level, in his effort to make the text speak today Bultmann abandons the historicism of Wrede. His hermeneutical program enables him to find, especially in Paul and John, a kernel of kerygma* that is remarkably akin to Heideggerian existentialism. Along the way revelation,* God,* faith* and much else become redefined. Bultmann advocates using the ancient vocabulary because lay people who belong to the old ways will hear the words and be comforted by the repetition of the ancient mythologies, while the cognoscenti will understand them in an existentialist framework. More importantly this theological content is cast in such a way that it is independent of the historical reconstructions, so that changing historical fashions cannot by themselves challenge his theological construction.

Despite the enormous influence wielded by Bultmann's work, however, very few hold it up as a suitable model today. Scholars with a historical bent find little merit in reading late nineteenth- and early twentieth-century existentialism into the first century. Scholars with a higher view of revelation insist that history and faith cannot properly be driven into disjunctive camps. Many complain how profoundly unfaithful to the NT documents is the resulting theological synthesis: faith whose object is not tied to historical revelation; a Jesus about whom little can be said except for a raw *Dass,* a thatness of his existence; a resurrection* whose significance lies not in its reality but in the psychological faith of the community, and so forth.

The third development was the rise of the biblical theology movement. Influenced in part by Barth and in part by Hofmann's work in the nineteenth century, hungry to be theologically and pastorally relevant in a world rent by two world wars, the Great Depression and the cold war, exponents of the movement developed various emphases in Britain and the continent during the 1930s, 1940s and 1950s and in America during the 1940s and 1950s. Perhaps the movement's most influential theologian was O. Cullmann, whose insistence on salvation history *(Heilsgeschichte)* attempted not only to bring together two components that had been flying apart in the disputes over biblical theology at the turn of the century but who wrote in a style calculated to be edifying. His insistence that salvation history is the theme that unites both Testaments has not gained wide acceptance even though only a few would deny that he has rightly emphasized one important unifying theme. In the English-speaking world A. Richardson's more popular writings, culminating in his own NT theology (1958), exerted wide influence. But the biblical theology movement had many facets. R. Morgan (*ABD* 6:479) includes within its scope G. Kittel's *Theological Dictionary of the New Testament* (1933-74; ET 1964-74), which was, after all, dedicated to Schlatter.

But the biblical theology movement as such could not last. In the hands of some of its exponents, the locus of revelation was in God's mighty acts, but the connection these acts enjoyed with the biblical text was less than clear. In the hands of others, entire theological structures were being made to depend on word studies of doubtful linguistic probity (a criticism leveled by J. Barr). *Heilsgeschichte* underwent several semantic metamorphoses. Hesitations about the movement climaxed in B. Childs's critique (1970).

4. Recent Visions of the Nature of New Testament Theology.

The contemporary scene is flooded with diversity as to what is understood by NT theology, though most kinds betray threads drawn from one strand or another of the twisted historical skein briefly untangled here. It may be helpful to classify some of the NT theologies of the past hundred years, especially those of the last half-century.

One strand follows a pattern of generally conservative historical judgments, a commitment to describe the theological content of the NT books and an assumption that such content is of authoritative (*see* Authority) and religious significance. In succession to the substantive work of Weiss and Schlatter is the shorter but robust NT theology of Zahn (1928), who conceived of NT theology not as a scientific system or ordered religion, in the history of religions model, but as a presentation of the theology of the Bible in its historical development. Zahn begins with John the Baptist as the one who opens the final epoch of redemptive history; only occasionally does he make connections with the OT.

Along somewhat similar lines in the English-speaking world is G. B. Stevens (1901, 1906), most of whose historical judgments are conservative (e.g., he places Acts, James,* 1 Peter,* Jude* and 2 Peter in the section on "The Primitive Apostolic Preaching," before the section on Paul) but whose theology is sometimes cast in the artificial optimism of turn-of-the-century pious liberalism. R. E. Knudsen's subtitle (1964), *A Basis for Christian Faith,* displays his theological interest, but his structure of thought owes more to systematics than to inductive description of the NT corpora.

More recently the more substantial works of G. E. Ladd (1974, 1993), D. Guthrie (1981) and, at a slightly more popular level, L. Morris (1986) more faithfully honor the tradition from Hofmann and Weiss. Ladd and Morris interpret the NT corpus by corpus, working inductively from the text and generally following a developmental approach whose structure is built on generally conservative historical judgments. On some themes Ladd draws important links to the OT (e.g., kingdom*); neither Ladd nor Morris attempts to integrate his findings into a synthetic NT theology, let alone a "whole-Bible" biblical theology (cf. Oeming). Guthrie's massive volume addresses the demand for synthesis by choosing themes and tracing them through the various NT corpora. By and large the themes are dictated by the material; occasionally they have been dictated by the categories of systematic theology. The gain achieved by placing side by side treatments of how the various NT corpora treat selected themes (e.g., Son of Man) is somewhat mitigated by the loss in clearly seeing how the individual corpora are put together, how they tie together their own themes. In any case there is no attempt at integration of biblical or NT thought.

Although Hofmann's emphasis on what is now called salvation history helped shape both Cullmann and Ladd, his influence is felt in slightly different ways in E. Stauffer (1941; ET 1955) and especially in L. Goppelt's posthumous work (2 vols., 1975-76; ET 1981-82). Stauffer does not follow the chronological order of the NT books but opts for a christocentric theology of history (his approach to salvation history), running from Judaism* to post-NT times. At one level he follows Wrede in denying the need of a canon but not for the same reason: Stauffer holds that a canon is unnecessary for the writing of NT theology since it is the christocentric theology of history that runs in a straight line from "the old biblical tradition" (Stauffer 51) to the subapostolic fathers (*see* Apostolic Fathers).

By contrast Goppelt, in his far more rigorous work, builds on Hofmann but wants to distance himself from any association of salvation history with universal history. In Goppelt's hands salvation history is more narrowly tied to the notions of promise* and fulfillment and must not be abstracted from regular history. Moreover, however important the theme is to him, he tries to avoid elevating it to exclusive importance and accepts many standard historical-critical conclusions. He eschews mere description, arguing that modern human beings must be brought into "critical dialogue" with the NT writers. His first volume explores the theological meaning of Jesus' activity. NT theology is grounded in the reporting of the earthly ministry of Jesus. If we do not have direct access to this historical Jesus, we do have access to Jesus as he showed himself to his followers, and study of this Jesus is as necessary as the study of the post-Easter developments (reserved for the second volume).

Certain works are so individualistic that they cannot easily be identified with a particular stream of the heritage of NT theologies. One thinks in particular of M. Albertz, who studied under both Zahn and A. von Harnack and who follows neither. The first two of his four volumes (1946-57) recast NT introduction along form-critical lines, and the next two unfold the NT's message. Against Bultmann he argues that it is improper to demythologize the NT writings since these documents contain no myths (but he distorts what Bultmann means by "myth"); against Baur he argues that naturalist ("philosophical") historical approaches fail to treat the NT on its own terms; against Weiss, von Harnack, Bultmann, Stauffer and others, he argues that NT theology is far too entrenched in a modern worldview and must return to the NT itself. His attempt to unfold the NT message he ties to the formula found in 2 Corinthians 13:13. But as G. Hasel (1978, 69) comments, it is far from clear how Albertz "can hold on to form criticism which is also influenced by the *Zeitgeist* and disclaim the validity of other branches of research which also reflect the *Zeitgeist.*"

H. Conzelmann (1968, 1987; ET 1969) is the only student of Bultmann to write an entire NT theology, and in many ways his work is indebted to his master. But his work eclipses Bultmann at several points. Whereas for Bultmann the historical Jesus was a presupposition for NT theology rather than a part of NT theology, for Conzelmann the historical Jesus is not a necessary presupposition. The basic problem of NT theology, according to Conzelmann, is why the church maintained "the identity of the Exalted One with Jesus of Nazareth after the resurrection appearances" (xviii). Even Bultmann's *Dass* disappears. (By contrast many other post-Bultmannians embarked on the so-called new quest for the historical Jesus [e.g., E. Käsemann, as early as 1954].) In line with his own commitment to redaction-critical study, Conzelmann supplements Bultmann with a section on the Synoptic kerygma. Further, taking up a suggestion from H. Schlier, who thinks of theology as the interpretation of early creedal formulations, Conzelmann seeks to trace out the trajectories that lead back to the earliest Christian creeds.* But once he has reconstructed them to

his satisfaction, he regards them as no more than the objectification of early Christian self-understanding. As a true disciple of Bultmann, for him (and especially for H. Braun, ET 1965) theology is finally nothing more than anthropology. Even his fellow post-Bultmannians have roundly criticized him for the speculative nature of his creedal reconstructions.

Also reacting against Bultmann but in the center of the stream of discussion stand several NT theologies that survey the content of the NT corpora and adopt historical stances that are more or less conservative but are invariably more conservative than that of Bultmann and Conzelmann. These offer useful exegeses and theological insights but break little new methodological ground. Most of them offer descriptive sections to each of the various NT corpora. Included here are W. G. Kümmel (1969), J. Jeremias (1971), E. Lohse (1974) and J. Gnilka (1989). Kümmel's first chapter reconstructs the proclamation of Jesus, and his fourth section compares and contrasts Jesus and Paul, noting not only their commonalities and differences but also their different salvation-historical situations. Thus he is far removed from Bultmann, Braun and Conzelmann. Only Jeremias's first volume, on the proclamation of Jesus, appeared in print. He felt it was possible to reconstruct with a fair degree of certainty what Jesus had taught. But because so much of his historical work is based on a fairly doctrinaire form of redaction criticism, he has been criticized from many parts of the theological spectrum, even while those who are convinced that Christian theology must be grounded in responsible history are grateful for the antidote he provides against Bultmann.

At a somewhat more popular level Lohse similarly incorporates the proclamation of Jesus into NT theology. Lohse's "postulate of non-derivability" (*Unableitbarkeitsthese*, 21)—i.e., his confident affirmation that some sayings attributed to Jesus must be accepted as authentic because they could not reasonably have been derived from the early church—makes this stance possible and places him in the mainstream of his time. In any case the debate has moved on: the more liberal scholars discover little that they cannot assign to the creativity of the church, while the more conservative find odd any criterion that confuses the eccentric with the historical. (In what other field of historical research would the most influential sayings of an extraordinarily influential individual be denied authenticity on the ground that because they were believed and repeated by the individual's followers they could not have been authentic?) The rest of Lohse's work follows roughly the chronological development of the NT, with a closing chapter devoted to its unity. This unity rests, Lohse asserts, on the fact that although the various NT corpora develop a variety of theological syntheses, all of these syntheses are based on the same kerygma of the crucified and risen Christ.

In the English-speaking world a handful of works plot roughly the same course. The volume by M. Burrows (1946) selects themes drawn from the categories of systematic theology and tracks them across the NT corpora. F. C. Grant's large volume (1950) disavows that it is a NT theology, but it is indistinguishable from some strands of the discipline. Grant strongly emphasizes the importance of historical anchoring (he is not far from Wrede in this regard and far removed from Bultmann) and emphasizes the differences he detects among the various "theolog*ies*" of the NT, which as a whole is not more than "a theology in process" (Grant, 60). The rest of the book treats an array of "doctrines" (e.g., doctrine of God, doctrine of man, doctrine of Christ, doctrine of miracles*), considering each in turn as it appears in the NT but refusing to trace any chronological development. By contrast F. Stagg (1962) seeks to highlight the unity within the diversity, as does the influential work of S. Neill (1974) and the more popular work of A. M. Hunter (1957). The contributions of C. C. Ryrie (1959) and C. R. Lehman (1974) are aimed at a popular readership. They primarily serve their respective theological constituencies without significantly engaging with the broader discipline.

5. Roman Catholic Contributions.
Roman Catholic scholars have come late to the discipline. Despite the popular, confessional works of A. Lemonnyer (1928; ET 1930) and O. Küss (1936), it has been the years since the publication of *Divino Afflante* (1943) that have increasingly displayed among Catholics the diversity of approaches that characterizes Protestant scholars.

M. Meinertz (1950) works inductively with the separate NT writings but attempts no assess-

ment of their chronological or historical development. J. Bonsirven (1951) is much the same, but a gentle piety pervades his work as he sees his task as providing a responsible basis for Christian dogmatics. His historical judgments are almost always conservative: for example, he reconstructs the life of Jesus from the Synoptics and John. The later NT writings he denotes as "Works of Christian Maturity," thereby refusing to tarnish them with the pejorative adjective *late*, much loved by scholars whose NT theology is a historical discipline but little else.

R. Schnackenburg (1962) deals first with the kerygma and theology of the primitive church, reconstructs the teaching* of Jesus according to the Synoptics, summarizes the contributions of the individual Synoptists and follows with treatments of Paul, John and the rest of the NT writings. What is distinctive about his work is the space at the end that Schnackenburg devotes to some central topics that recur thematically in the sequence. The four-volume work by K. H. Schelkle (1968-76; ET 1971-78) is structured on traditional dogmatic categories: creation,* world-time-history (vol. 1); revelation,* redemption* and salvation* (vol. 2); ethos (vol. 3); completion (vol. 4/1); disciple, congregation and church* (vol. 4/2). But within each category Schelkle traces, in continuous dialogue with dogmatics, the diachronic development of the movement from the OT through Judaism to the NT.

The contribution of Goppelt has already been described. W. Thüsing (1981) identifies the unity of the NT in two kinds of criteria: the structures of the life and works and teaching of Jesus, as Thüsing reconstructs them, and the structures of christology* and soteriology in the post-Easter period. Gnilka adopts the now traditional form of NT theology that treats the various authors or corpora of the NT separately, with the caveat that James and 2 Thessalonians are treated in excurses. Gnilka begins with the seven Pauline epistles whose authenticity is least disputed, glancing back at the same time to the generation before Paul. He then moves on to the Gospels, pausing to consider Q and his reconstruction of a primitive passion narrative. John is treated with the Johannine Epistles (*see* John, Letters of). Gnilka goes on to the so-called deutero-Paulines, the rest of the letters and the Apocalypse (*see* Revelation, Book of). In each case he organizes his material by focusing on humanity, salvation, community and the sacraments (though he admits other themes as they crop up). His concluding chapter probes for unity and concludes that, whatever the extraordinary diversity, salvation is always through Jesus Christ, and the response of faith is always mandated. As with Lohse, what holds this together is the kerygma of the death and resurrection of Jesus (*see* Death of Christ).

6. New Testament Theology: 1985-95.

If one focuses on the most recent NT theologies, those published in the approximate decade of 1985-95, despite the fact that H. Räisänen (1990) has pronounced that the discipline is fundamentally impossible, the diversity of approaches is staggering.

Although much of his writing focuses on the OT side of biblical theology, H. Gese, who represents one wing of the so-called new Tübingen school, has left a plethora of studies that have a bearing on NT theology. (For English readers he is most easily approached through his 1981 volume.) Gese argues that in the time of Jesus and of the writers of the NT there was still no closed OT canon (a thesis increasingly questioned), and therefore biblical theology must be understood to deal with the process of tradition viewed as a whole—not with earlier and later forms or canonical forms but with the entire process.

Somewhat similarly P. Stuhlmacher, using the law* as a sample topic appropriate to this notion of biblical theology, traces developing and quite differing concepts of law through both Testaments (Stuhlmacher 1986). But his more recent work is nuanced and complex. After an extensive introduction to the aims and structure of the discipline, the first volume of his NT theology begins with the rise and distinctiveness of NT proclamation: first the preaching of Jesus, followed by a much shorter section on the preaching of the primitive church (i.e., the period between the resurrection and Paul) and concluded by a section on the preaching of Paul. The subtitle of this volume is critical: *The Foundation: From Jesus to Paul.* Here is neither massive historical skepticism nor a Bultmannian trench between theology and history.

In the second edition of his book on NT hermeneutics (1986) one detects a rapprochement between Stuhlmacher and G. Maier

(Stuhlmacher 1986, 33-34), whom he no longer places in the fundamentalist camp because of the latter's commitment to take the text and history seriously, even if his judgments are sometimes more conservative than those of Stuhlmacher and his criticism of the historical-critical method more scathing (Maier, who had earlier proclaimed the "end of the historical-critical method," prefers "historical-biblical method"). Among the luminaries of German scholarship, however, Stuhlmacher, O. Hofius, M. Hengel and one or two others stand alone in the seriousness with which they treat the historical dimensions of the NT text.

H. Hübner has completed his three-volume NT theology (1990-95). The first raises questions about the extent and nature of the canon, evaluates canon criticism and explores what is meant by covenant* and revelation. The chapters devoted to the NT expression of revelation treat Romans 1:16-17 and Romans 3:21 (the self-revealing righteousness of God), the parables of Jesus, the focus on Jesus as the revealer of God in the Fourth Gospel and the Parousia* as the revelation still to come, concluding with some reflections from systematic theology on these chapters. This sets up Hübner for a chapter on the one God and both Testaments and an epilogue on Jewish and NT methods of exegesis. The second volume treats Pauline theology, both the theology of the "undisputed" Paulines and of "Pauline theology" as it works itself out in other NT epistles, including James and 1 and 2 Peter. The final volume considers Hebrews,* the four Gospels and the Apocalypse. It concludes with a lengthy section on the "interval" *(Zeit-Raum)* of grace* that harks back to the "being and time" categories of the existentialist theology of the first half of this century. Despite valiant efforts to identify points of continuity between the Testaments, the last chapter lays much more stress on discontinuity: the NT takeover *(in novo receptum)* of the Old demands this assessment.

The brief work by E. Schweizer (1989) is of mixed genre, simultaneously a NT introduction and a NT theology. The former component offers common critical judgments with sovereign disregard for alternative views. The NT theology component restricts itself to the NT canon. There is no separate treatment of the historical Jesus. Schweizer emphasizes diversity, with a typical scheme for the development of eschatology,* christology,* ecclesiology (*see* Church) and the like: the diversity is in the canon, not in history. The brevity of the book ensures there is no reflection on the aims or methods of NT theology.

The contribution of W. Schmithals (1994) is in some respects not a NT theology but an independent reconstruction of early Christianity into which the NT is squeezed. Schmithals asks why the traditions* about the historical Jesus should ever have been attached to the post-Easter kerygma and its related confessions. He argues that such passages as 1 Corinthians 15:20-28 suggest a link between the theme of the kingdom of God in the teaching of Jesus and Paul's theology. From this base Schmithals develops a fundamental polarity (methodologically akin to Baur's reductionism a century and a half earlier) between Antioch* theology and Damascus theology. Antioch theology was apocalyptic,* focused on the righteousness* of God and on salvation and had gnostic overtones. The theology of Damascus, where Paul was converted and molded, had by that time abandoned distinctions between Jews and Gentiles,* enjoyed a christology that affirmed preexistence* and Incarnation, taught a radical view of sin* and espoused a realized eschatology. From this polarity Schmithals proceeds to trace a number of subjects through the NT and into the apostolic fathers.

K. Berger's large, recent volume (1994) similarly traces the history of NT thought, but the picture is quite different. His book develops the metaphor of a tree: NT thought is like a large tree with roots in Jerusalem,* but the primary branching takes place in Antioch. The first Christians were charismatic, nurtured by the OT, and saw themselves as the new Israel.* Those more influenced by Hellenism moved to Antioch. The Jerusalem group shaped the early Roman church and the epistle of James. The more influential streams flowing from Antioch became the Pauline and the Johannine branches. A secondary node in the large Antioch branch generates the Gospels, including Mark, Q and John (in Berger's thought John antedates Matthew and Luke). All this material is laid out before Berger begins his systematic examination of the NT books. These are then studied to see how they fit into this grid, and Berger believes he can detect how the various branches repeatedly cross and influence one another. Berger traces his pattern beyond the NT into the second century. Although all of this generates many novel ways of looking at things, sometimes the speculation is palpable. More importantly for our purposes, there is no significant attempt to seek out what is unifying in NT thought or to wrestle with questions of revelation, theological normativity or canon.

Quite different is the posthumously published work of G. B. Caird (1994). Caird candidly assesses and criticizes previous approaches to NT theology—what he calls the dogmatic approach, the chronological approach, the kerygmatic approach and the author-by-author approach—and proffers another, the conference-table approach. "The presupposition of our study is simply stated: to write a New Testament theology is to preside at a conference of faith and order. Around the table sit the authors of the New Testament, and it is the presider's task to engage them in a colloquium about theological matters which they themselves have placed on the agenda" (Caird, 18). Caird sets forth his answers to possible objections, e.g., How many conferees are around the table? What is the presider's role? What about the troubling fact that the conferees are all dead? The latter leads into an important discussion on how and to what extent things from the past may be known.

Caird then works through various central concepts (e.g., predestination, sin,* ethics,* eschatology,* christology*), which are "discussed" by the participants (including Caird, the presider), the discussion moving on to a presentation of the theology of Jesus himself. The epilogue on dialogue, meaning and authority offers a brief, trenchant critique of both postmodernist readings of the NT and their antithesis in the denial of all development but mere reliance on original intention. In the latter case, he writes, "the infallibility of Scripture becomes a cypher for the infallibility of the interpreter" (Caird, 424). As for the postmodernist option of endlessly polyvalent meanings, these are "Gadarene precipitations into the Dark Ages. . . . Language is in essence a medium of communication. If the hearer takes words in a sense not intended by the speaker, that is not an enlargement of meaning but a breakdown of communication. This claim applies to all uses of language, but it is especially apposite where a claim of revelation is involved" (Caird, 423).

The creativity, exegetical sanity and fresh writing of much of Caird's work makes this volume one of the most useful and suggestive in the field of NT theology. But methodologically his approach is closer to Guthrie (whom he dismisses) than he thinks, though frequently with slightly less conservative results: much of Caird's book, talk of the conference-table approach aside, is an exploration of selected themes as they are developed by the various writers of the NT canon. There is only sporadic reflection on how these themes relate to the OT. Moreover, for all its strengths Caird's approach proves less able than some other approaches to provide a portrait of the overall structure of thought of a major NT writer (e.g., Paul), precisely because of the vertical trenches that are cutting across the corpora.

7. Other Influences That Shape New Testament Theology.

Eight further influences can be seen to be shaping what is meant in some circles by NT theology.

1. Some scholars have not yet produced anything like a NT theology but have in their writings given a lot of thought to certain dimensions of it. One thinks, for example, of some of the work of J. D. G. Dunn, who argues that the fundamental christological unity in the NT is the conviction that the predeath Jesus is to be identified with the postresurrection Christ. Whereas this is decidedly more conservative than, say, Conzelmann, the thesis is surprisingly minimalistic. Other instances of embryonic NT theology include th work of N. T. Wright (1991, 1992) and of R. B. Hays (1989).

2. Countless volumes have been written on the theology of particular NT books or corpora or on major themes within them. Such treatments are to NT theology what NT theology is to biblical theology.

3. A smaller but nevertheless substantial number of books and essays explore a chosen theme across the NT or across the entire Christian canon and refer to themselves respectively as NT theology or as biblical theology (e.g., Moberly).

4. The rise of canon criticism in its two dominant forms cannot be excluded from the discussion. By this expression J. A. Sanders (1972, 1987, 1995) refers to the canonical process begun at the first recitation of oral tradition and continuing beyond closure to our own (and future) adaptations and interpretations developed in living communities. Sanders does not mean to devalue the authority of what was originally said or written, so far as it can be reconstructed, but to elevate the later appropriations. By contrast, for Childs (1992), who disavows the expression "canon criticism" (though it is frequently applied to his work), the final form of the text and thus the closure of the canon is critical: the challenge is to understand the texts as they have been handed down in final form by the church. Childs never abandons historical criticism and rarely steps outside the bounds of "mainstream" critical judgments, but their hermeneutical and theological value is relatively small.

At the risk of simplistic judgments, one can say that it is not clear how Sanders can avoid sliding into an open-ended form of postmodernism, despite his mild interest in the original utterance; this at a time in which a number of biblical theologians are displaying a rising interest in discovering some form of enduring or authoritative theological message in Scripture (Hasel 1994). Conversely, despite his many useful suggestions as to how the Bible can be read as one canonical book, it is not clear how Childs's leap of faith to accept the church's canonical judgments, divorced from Childs's historical-critical judgments, will prove more epistemologically enduring than Barth's theology of the Word. Theologically Childs reaches conclusions that are very close to those of, say, Stuhlmacher. But the latter arrives at his destination by means of historical-critical judgments that leave his thought world a unified whole, while the former reaches them by consciously refusing to make much of a tie between his theology and his history.

5. More broadly the rising pressures from postmodernism are generating readings of biblical text that are distanced from what the texts originally meant. The most rigorous postmodernists deny that the notion of what a text "originally meant" is coherent. Inevitably these new "biblical theologies" or NT theologies use the text to support some current agenda. Some forms (certainly not all) of liberation theology fall into this camp, as do some forms of feminist reading (on the latter see Fiorenza 1994). There is now a plethora of literature that celebrates whatever is novel in a reading, a literature

that roundly denounces the very possibility of any "right" reading of a text.

6. Overlapping other developments (e.g., postmodern readings, Childs's form of canon criticism) but differentiable from them is the rising interest in narrative theology and related literary-critical readings of the NT and of the Bible. The results are extraordinarily variable. Although some scholars see these new tools as nothing more than an extension of the historical-critical method, itself the offspring of the Enlightenment, increasingly these tools are viewed rightly as the product of Romanticism, itself often in conflict with an Enlightenment view of the world. The results may often be seen as a branch of aesthetics: plot, implied author, characterization and the like are carefully laid out with no concern for historical claims in the text or with how the absence of such concerns may itself decisively shape one's understanding of the text (e.g., the choice of the nineteenth-century novel as a model to unpack the Fourth Gospel: Culpepper). Such works abound in insight at the level of details but substantially distort the whole.

7. Similarly, because meanings in language are inevitably tied to a social system, the current interest in the social structure or the social history that is presupposed in biblical books is sometimes useful in understanding the texts themselves. In the hands of some scholars, sociological analysis of past bodies is undertaken with a sovereign disregard for other branches of history and exegesis, usually with the aim of gaining biblical warrant for present fads in behavior. On the positive side one thinks (to choose a few at random) of the contributions to our understanding of the text of the NT and thus of NT theology by W. Meeks (1983), C. Hemer (1989) and M. Hengel (1991), whose work is less interested in imposing modern sociological categories on the NT documents than on delineating the social history behind those documents.

8. Especially in Britain and sometimes in Germany, "theology" can function as a generic term describing the study of anything to do with Christianity. In that framework NT theology may refer to collections of studies on the NT that have only accidental connection with NT theology in any sense that deals with the entire NT, any corpus within it or any theme running through it. For example, see the titles of books

by I. H. Marshall (1990), J. Blank (1992) and W. Thüsing (1995).

8. Controlling or Defining Elements of New Testament Theology.
The controlling elements have been alluded to and occasionally evaluated in the historical recital, but they demand separate reflection.

Morgan's analysis of NT theology (*ABD* 6:473-83) turns on the interplay of three elements: the biblicist, the historical and the hermeneutical; Corley's (1994) on three lines: the purely historical, the existential and the salvation-historical. Others proffer somewhat different categories (e.g., Ladd, *ISBE* 1:498-509; Via, 369-88). Whatever the breakdown, none of the elements or lines or categories can be evaluated in isolation. One's conception of the discipline of NT theology and of its present state turns on what one makes of the peculiar interplay of the defining categories.

8.1. Theology. NT theology is above all theology: i.e., it is discourse about God. For Christians this means it is discourse about the God and Father of our Lord Jesus Christ, about his character, nature, self-disclosure; about his acts of creation, providence and redemption; about his people, their origin, circumstances, salvation, destination. It is thus not to be reduced to the history of the Jews or the early history of Christians. NT theology is theology, not religion. It follows that the track worked out from Baur is profoundly mistaken not in this or that peculiar historical judgment but in its increasing collapse of the discipline into nothing but history.

But the interplay of theology with other elements must not be overlooked. Because this theology is our discourse about God (however much it is based on his self-disclosure), hermeneutical considerations must not be forgotten. To overlook them is not to escape them; it is to foster the illusion, characteristic of a great deal of modernity, that the latest opinion is the truly objective and culture-transcending one. Because this theology is grounded in God's revelation in history and because God's self-revelation in history "has often caught up elements from the relgous [sic] milieu and incorporated them in *Heilsgeschichte*" (Ladd, *ISBE* 1:505), theology's relationship with history is exceedingly complex. It is not always antagonistic, nor is the experience of the people of God set antithetically to all others in every respect. Israel was not the only group that practiced circumcision, the church did not invent elders out of whole cloth and "house-tables" of duties were well known in the pagan world before Christianized forms were incorporated into the NT (*see* Household Codes; Household, Family). Thus theology cannot be abstracted from historical questions.

8.2. Supernaturalism and Revelation. In Morgan's view (*ABD* 6:474) the biblicist element in NT theology "is the tendency (more or less extreme) to attach greater weight to these writings than would be rational for non-Christians. It is necessary because Scripture is indispensable for knowing God in Jesus Christ, and that is central to Christianity. . . . But actually identifying Scripture with revelation is irrational biblicism."

Morgan is correct to insist that the biblicist element is necessary to NT theology. But if by this he means no more than that apart from the NT documents we have few other early sources regarding Jesus and the early church and that these are the earliest witnesses,* such that if Christianity is to survive at all we are necessarily forced to draw on them, he has conceded too little. The God of the Bible not only acts providentially in history but sometimes chooses to reveal himself openly in history, thus perpetually threatening all merely naturalistic readings of history. More importantly he is a talking God, and the very witnesses to which Morgan points insist that not only has this God talked with human beings in concrete historical situations in the past but that he has not left himself without verbal witness, choosing to use the words of mortals to convey something of himself. To fail to see that this is a recurring presupposition of the biblical writers is to assign too great a veto power to non-Christian perspectives.

It is true that an emphasis on supernaturalism without careful consideration of the other dimensions of Scripture can treat the Bible as a magic book and produce NT theology that is bizarre. It is true that focusing on revelation without perceiving that God has commonly disclosed himself in the "accidents" of history with all their "secondary causalities" may end up denying providence, hunting for a mysterious God-of-the-gaps. It is true that espousing revelatory authority without grasping that God's self-disclosure has commonly been through means,

progressive in nature, and as often through institutions (temple*), rites (sacrificial system; *see* Sacrifice) and dynasties (the Davidic) as through words is to tumble into reductionism. It is true that the words of Scripture perform many functions in addition to conveying truth*: they bear witness to Christ, evoke worship,* call to repentance* and so forth, and these various speech-acts must not be overlooked. But it is never a responsible solution to meet one reductionism by another.

8.3. Canon. NT theology properly presupposes a NT canon. Many in the name of historical objectivity refuse any distinction between the canonical and the noncanonical (e.g., Wrede), and others (e.g., Morgan, *ABD* 6:481) argue that the notion of canon has no place in historical research and no place in demarcating books that are different in kind from other books (e.g., possessing some revelatory quality). For Morgan the notion of canon can be preserved only to mark out books that enjoy, for whatever historical reasons, a "special use" among Christians.

It is warranted to insist that the NT books are not different in every way from other books written about the same time. But to recognize a canon of books based purely on historical accident means that the discipline of NT theology improperly looks for any unity: at best it can describe the individual contributions of this accidental canon inductively and historically (where "historically" presupposes naturalism). But if the canonical books are bound up with the self-revealing God and are identified not with the totality of that revelation but as one crucial component of it, then the concern of many NT theologians not only to identify differences among the NT books but to work out what holds them together becomes a possible, even a praiseworthy, task. Because of the historical elements in NT theology, it is appropriate to make connections between the NT and the apostolic fathers. But that is not itself NT theology. R. B. Sloan (1994) is partly right to point out that a theological core helped to precipitate the books that came to make up what we call the NT canon and that this core can in large part be inferred by exegesis and historical analysis from those books themselves. But that reconstructed core must not be thought of as canon (a canon to which we have no agreed or direct access): that would be to confuse the means by which canonical distinctions were made with the canon itself.

The point to underline is that the note of authority that most biblical theologians want to recover, namely, the connection between NT theology and the NT documents, has to be found in the text itself. It cannot be found behind the text, in realities to which the text points or in parts of the text. It cannot be found in the theology that apparently precipitates the text, in the lowest common denominator of the assembled NT texts or in the communities to which the text bears witness.

In much the same way a tighter connection between text and reality is necessary to make epistemologically viable Childs's approach to canonical (including NT) theology. To some extent the later works of Childs depend on H. Frei (1974), who argues that the triumph of rationalism in the historical-critical method during the eighteenth and nineteenth centuries abandoned reading the narratives of the Bible as narratives. These rationalists, discounting the supernatural, tried incessantly to make the meaning of the text turn on what happened (as the critics reconstructed it), which was then read back into the text in circular fashion and found there. Reacting against this, conservatives stressed the historicity of the biblical accounts, thus making meaning depend on the history while failing to return to a narrative conception of meaning.

To some extent this analysis is astute. But what it fails to address directly is the relationship between ostensibly historical narrative and the historicity of the ostensible events. If while insisting on the primacy of a narrative conception of meaning one perpetually fails to address that question, one is inviting a faith based on a story line, regardless of the relationship (if any) between that story line and extratextual reality. Neither Judaism nor Christianity is Buddhism: we are not invited to an atemporal system of thought whose authority turns on the credibility and aesthetics of an abstract philosophical system. We are instead invited to the personal-transcendent Creator-God who deigns to address his rebellious imagebearers in "the scandal of [historical] particularity." "Were the biblical narratives written or read as fiction, then God would turn from the lord of history into a creature of the imagination with the most disastrous results. ... Hence the Bible's determination to sanctify

and compel literal belief in the past" (Sternberg, 32). One way of reading Childs is to see that the leap of faith that Frei seem to be advocating at the level of individual narratives, Childs seems ready to take at the level of the entire canon.

If the notion of the NT canon briefly articulated here is extended to the entire canon, then by similar reasoning one is driven to the importance of trying to discover "a whole Bible theology" *(eine gesamtbiblische Theologie)*. At issue is not simply whether the OT provides the most important matrix out of which to understand the NT but whether there is a continuous story line around which the canonical books are clustered and to which each book makes its own contribution. Granted the degree of specialization and the bias of naturalistic biblical scholarship against such a move, the task is daunting. Some envisage intensive cooperation between OT and NT specialists (e.g., Ebeling, 96); others anticipate that a specialist in one area might branch out into the canonical framework (as Childs 1992 and Seebass 1982 have done). But even those who do not feel confident to undertake the writing of canonically framed biblical theology may discipline themselves to careful exegesis that never loses sight of the canonical horizon. "A biblical-theology-orientated exegesis is the only way, in the field of Old Testament and New Testament studies, that a first step can be taken, and a first thrust ventured. Thus, we will not only ask for a 'theology of the Old Testament' or a 'Pauline theology,' but also, in these limited areas, keep the wider context constantly in sight" (Harrington, 373).

8.4. History. However much we eschew all reduction of NT theology to the study of the history of religions, a proper emphasis on history is essential to NT theology. "Biblical Theology is that branch of exegetical theology which deals with the process of the self-revelation of God deposited in the Bible" (Vos 1948, 5); or again, "Biblical Theology ... is nothing else than the exhibition of the organic process of supernatural revelation in its historic continuity and multiformity" (Vos 1980, 15). The critical expressions are progress, process, and historical continuity and multiformity. Several factors need examination, in each case tied to other elements in this list.

First, one must insist that the historical narratives refer to objective (i.e., extratextual) reality. "If there is anything that distinguishes Christianity from all other religions and philosophies it is this: Christianity in the first instance is neither a set of doctrines nor a way of life, but a gospel; and *a gospel means news about historical events, attested by reliable witnesses, and having at its centre a historical person*" (Caird, 422, emphasis his). Adequately formulated NT theology will not permit a retreat to the study of texts as if they were naked art forms and nothing else.

Second, although the God of the Bible commonly works in the context of history that could reductionistically be explained in naturalistic terms, he sometimes enters this order with deeds and words that cannot possibly be explained in such terms. They may be explained away or discounted or relegated to the category of faith on the dubious ground that they are outside the historian's domain. But such a view of history is imprisoned by naturalistic presuppositions. We have returned to supernaturalism and revelation by another route. At no point in the discipline of NT theology are these issues more important than in assessing the place of Jesus the Christ (cf. Hasel 1978, 133-35). The resurrection of Jesus, for instance, cannot be historical according to the canons of a form of historical criticism committed to naturalism; it is difficult to see why historical criticism that is not committed to naturalism yet that is interested in determining what actually took place in the space/time continuum should not come out with a positive assessment (cf. Ladd, *ISBE* 1:507).

Third, although for the Christian salvation history is thus part of real history (i.e., it did take place), no one should think this represents all of what took place or that it is unbiased or uncommitted. We thus encroach on questions of hermeneutics and postmodernism (see 8.7 below).

Fourth, precisely because God's self-disclosure has taken place over time, NT theology, as part of the larger discipline of biblical theology, is committed to understanding the constitutive documents within that temporal framework. In this respect NT theology differs widely in emphasis from systematic theology, which tends to ask atemporal questions of the biblical texts, thereby eliciting atemporal answers.

8.5. Literature. However anchored in history, the NT documents, like the documents of the entire biblical canon, are cast in an extraordinary array of literary genres that demand both historical knowledge and literary sensitivity on the part of the interpreter. There are several entailments, which again lap onto the domains of other elements in this list.

First, NT theology is committed to inductive study of the texts. The texts are not first and foremost a quarry for abstract doctrines or the source of answers to questions they are at best only marginally interested in addressing but are texts that demand study on their own terms (cf. Schlier, 1-25; Harrington, 363-64). Thus at its best biblical theology has the potential for reforming dogmatics.

Second, NT theology will not on this ground treat the texts as literary forms to be studied on their own terms but, precisely because they are the sorts of texts they are, perceive the extratextual realities to which they point. This is powerfully elucidated by R. J. Bauckham in a review (*BI* 2 [1994] 246-50) of Childs (1992). In his laudable insistence on the theological integrity of the texts and in his focus on the historical reconstruction of the development of the text, Childs "seems to treat as insignificant for biblical theology any relationship of the theological witness of the texts to the concrete historical circumstances in which that witness originated" (Bauckham, 249). There is no attempt to illuminate Paul's thought by trying to understand what it was like to live in first-century Corinth, for instance. Real depth in a text is not found by most readers in a knowledge of the text's prehistory, any more than a reader will perceive Hamlet to be shallow until he or she knows about Shakespeare's sources, successive drafts and the ostensible contributions of later editors. Thus a careful reading of Gospels and Epistles will not endorse either a literary isolationism or a retreat to the most sterile forms of historical criticism. Depth will be found in a rich appreciation of their historical rootedness, their profound truth, their astonishing interconnections and their powerful vitality.

Third, such inductive and historical study cannot be set over against canonical considerations. "The work of New Testament theology is still not complete when the theology of the individual books or groups of writings is presented. The task is done only when we have succeeded in showing the unity of the different 'theologies'; and this underlying theological unity must be brought out as explicitly as possible" (Harrington, 365; see 9 below). Given the occasional nature and literary quality of so many of the biblical writings, there is plenty of scope for cautious integration and synthesis instead of the penchant for finding closed and mutually conflicting systems of thought in each of the various NT documents.

8.6. Existential Bite. Ideally NT theology will have existential bite, a profoundly religious dimension (a point emphasized by Terrien, though regrettably at the expense of other factors). Gabler's success in abstracting biblical theology from dogmatic theology fostered an unhealthy independence: biblical theology is soon also abstracted from reverence, from commitment, from faith. In the name of objectivity that was in fact too often infected by naturalism, anything corresponding to doxological study in NT theology was viewed with suspicion.

Given the spiritual vibrancy and fervor of the early witnesses, it would have been unthinkable for them to have pleaded their cause with dispassionate neutrality. So it is equally unthinkable that modern Christians would engage in NT theology with aloof detachment. This is what Schlatter (1905) dismissed as "atheistic method," writing elsewhere, "As soon as the historian sets aside or brackets the question of faith, he is making his concern with the New Testament and his presentation of it into a radical and total polemic against it" (in Morgan 1973, 152; see also the comments of Ladd, *ISBE* 1:509).

8.7. Hermeneutics and Postmodernism. If, from Gabler on, classic modernism was too confident of its ability to produce timeless and culture-transcending biblical theology, postmodernism is too confident of its ability to say nothing that is true beyond what the individual or interpretive community perceives to be true. Postmodernism has released us from the hubris of a pretended omniscience only to introduce us to the no less dogmatic hubris of epistemologically determined relativism. Thus in his analysis of NT theology Via (380-81) follows L. Montrose's chiasm as a proper poststructuralist orientation to history: historical study is reciprocally concerned with the historicity of texts and the textuality of history (Montrose, 20). The historicity of texts insists that all texts "are embedded in a specific social and cultural setting"; the textuality of history means that "we have no access to

a lived, material past that is unmediated by textual traces and that these traces are subject to further textualization (figuration), when the historian uses them in constructing a narrative." Although Via affirms "the possibility of some degree of knowledge about the real past" (Via, 384), in fact historical knowledge "is knowledge acquired by making interpretive meaning" and "history is about the creation of meaning" (Via, 384).

Via's views are now commonplace among many NT scholars. The element of truth in such postmodern epistemology is that no finite and fallen mortal perceives anything from the vantage of omniscience. All of our knowledge is in certain respects an approximation. But the antithesis that is then often assumed—either one enjoys absolute knowledge or all our knowing is utterly relative—is unnecessary. Various models suggest that one can enjoy true knowledge without absolute knowledge (e.g., the fusion of horizons; the hermeneutical spiral; the asymptotic approach: see Carson 1995b; *see* Hermeneutics). Although no interpreter can entirely escape his or her own culture and heritage and flee into another that is removed by millennia and distanced by language barriers, by patient distanciation and careful reading and rereading it is possible to have authentic contact with another mind through what that mind has written. Most texts are not as autonomous as many postmoderns assume, and the meaning of texts does not reside primarily in the interpreter. Poststructuralists do not like reviewers to misread their books: apparently they are prepared to invest their own texts with authorial intent. Why cannot they accord the same courtesy to Paul or for that matter to God, if he is a God who discloses himself through verbal revelation?

Reflections on postmodernism thus take us back to both questions regarding the nature of history and the issues of supernaturalism and revelation, for epistemological questions take on a different hue if there is an omniscient "God who speaks" and has chosen to disclose some things. Granted our finiteness and fallenness, God himself cannot disclose everything to us. But it is difficult to see why he cannot disclose true things even if he cannot exhaustively disclose all their relationships.

The bearing of these reflections on the writing of NT theology is obvious. The leading intellectual movements of the day often foster the illusion that NT theology as a discipline that moves toward canonical synthesis is impossible and certainly disreputable. Those who configure the elements of NT theology and of biblical theology in a different way, lightly sketched here, must get on with the task.

9. Focal Issues.

To accept the configuration of NT theology just articulated does not mean that all the issues have been resolved. Among the most important challenges are three.

First, many of the fundamental questions pertaining to how NT theology should be constructed remain. The most pressing of these is how simultaneously to expound the unity of NT theology (and of the larger canon of which it is a part) while doing justice to the manifest diversity; or, to put it the other way, how simultaneously to trace the diversity and peculiar emphases and historical developments inherent in the various NT (and biblical) books while doing justice to their unifying thrusts. Methodologically it may be necessary to do something of both (Dunn 1977) or to invoke a creative device (Caird). But the tension will continue.

In addition to such large-scale strategic questions there are countless procedural issues. Those who write NT theology should ideally become intimately acquainted with the text of the NT, develop a profound grasp of the historical (including social and cultural) frameworks in which the NT books were written, maintain and sharpen the horizon provided by the entire canon, foster literary skills that permit varied genres to speak for themselves, spot literary devices and correctly interpret them, learn to fire imagination and creativity in a disciplined way and acknowledge and seek to accommodate and correct their own cultural and theological biases. All of these elements must be maintained in appropriate balance, nurtured by love for God and fear of God and growing hunger to serve his people.

Second, the issue of the unity and the diversity of the NT documents is not only a matter of presentation but of substance (cf. Hasel 1978, 140-70). The quest for the center of NT theology has three challenges (see DPL, Center). (1) What does "center" mean, and how might it be discovered? Does it refer to the most common theme, determined by statistical count, or to the controlling theme or to the fundamental theological presuppositions of the NT writers, so far as they may be discerned? Precisely how does one determine what a "controlling theme" is? Is pursuit of the "center" legitimate in literature that all sides admit is largely occasional? (2) How does one avoid mere generalities? One might say that the center of NT theology is Jesus Christ, but although at one level that is saying everything at another level it is saying almost nothing. Or one might say (with Dunn) that the fundamental tenet of NT christology is the belief that the predeath Jesus is to be identified with the postresurrection Jesus—but this too is anemic. (3) How shall one avoid the tendency to elevate one book or corpus of the NT and domesticate the rest, putting them on a leash held by the themes of the one, usually the book or corpus on which the biblical theologian has invested most scholarly energy?

There are no comprehensive answers. But we shall not go far astray if we adopt some such prescriptions as the following.

1. The pursuit of the center is chimerical. NT theology is so interwoven that one can move from any one topic to any other topic. We will make better progress by pursuing clusters of broadly common themes, which may not be common to all NT books. For example, we might examine how the temple functions and develops in the OT and, in terms of NT theology, observe how it is variously treated by the Synoptists (both Jesus' observance of temple ritual and his cleansing of the temple), note such features as the rending of the veil at the time of Jesus' death (Mt 27:51), study the peculiar Johannine emphases (including Jesus' self-identification with the temple destroyed—Jn 2), chart the tensions and changing role of the temple in Luke-Acts as the church increasingly becomes defined by Christ and not by any of the traditional Judaisms, examine the varied metaphorical uses of temple in Paul's writings, study the complex links between various aspects of temple ritual and Christ's work according to the epistle to the Hebrews and plot the development of the temple theme in the Apocalypse, which ultimately celebrates the absence of any temple in the new Jerusalem, because the Lord God and the Lamb* are its temple (Rev 21—22). In this last step there is no further need for mediation as the people of God are ushered into the unshielded glory* of the consummat-

ing new heaven and new earth. Out of such material it is possible simultaneously to treat the contributions to this theme made by individual books, entirely within the framework of thought provided by those books, and to reflect on the significance of the pattern that develops to so glorious a consummation. This sort of endeavor can be undertaken with scores of themes.

2. Clearly it is essential to treat each theme or passage within the framework of each book or corpus before treating it as part of the larger NT horizon. The comprehensiveness of such work will go a long way toward warding off falling victim to an arbitrary canon within the canon.

3. In particular it is imperative that relatively light themes in a particular book or corpus be teased out first within the context of the major themes of that book or corpus. For example, studies on discipleship in Mark that fail to work out how that theme plugs into Mark's story line that takes Jesus to the cross* and beyond will prove fundamentally flawed. Not infrequently the points of connection from corpus to corpus must be delineated through these major themes. Thus although it seems wise to avoid committing oneself to one disputable center, inevitably the texts themselves will force a hierarchializing of unifying themes.

4. It is essential to avoid the dogmatic antitheses that have afflicted so much of the discipline, antitheses that spot distinctive treatments while dismissing both complementarity and sweeping development.

5. Careful literary and historical examination of certain biblical themes may foster renewed ability to see that the shape of the theme in a particular corpus (e.g., temple and related matters in Hebrews) is tightly tied to the social, ecclesiastical and theological situation the writer is addressing. Such examination therefore encourages insight not only into the way that separate NT treatments may be complementary but also into the way that such themes should properly function pastorally.

6. Time invested in the history of interpretation will not only enlarge the horizons of the interpreter but also tend to foster appropriate distanciation and thus a degree of proper objectivity in exegesis and creation of NT theology.

Third, the most difficult question by far is the relation of the NT to the OT and in particular the use of the OT in the NT. The most recent collection of essays on biblical theology (Pedersen) reflects how strongly most biblical theologians struggle to avoid saying that the NT interpretation of the OT is the only correct one. The reasons vary from interpreter to interpreter but are reducible to three: (1) some think the NT interpretation of the Old so implausible that it should not be given such status; (2) others are so committed to the canons of postmodernism that any claimed hegemony in the field of interpretation must be dismissed with an anathema; (3) others, moved not least by the Holocaust, refuse to be a party to what some label "cultural genocide" even while they recognize that the writers of the NT themselves betray little doubt about the rightness of their reading of the OT.

Those are the large issues that help to determine the outcome when the countless little issues weigh in: what constitutes a quotation and what an allusion; the text form of quotations; the form and function of introductory formulae; the appropriation techniques deployed by the NT writers and their relationship to Jewish middoth; the hermeneutical axioms that govern many NT citations of the OT; the many forms of typology; how various NT uses of the OT fit into larger questions regarding the relations between the covenants*; ethical uses of antecedent Scripture; the place of Torah in Matthew or Paul; the meaning of "fulfillment" language; the symbol-laden, imagination-firing associational uses common in the Apocalypse; the assumption of various societal givens (e.g., God/family/society); and much more of the same. Such considerations are the stuff of studies on the use of the OT in the NT, and clearly no responsible NT theology, insofar as it sees itself part of a broader biblical theology, can proceed very far without taking them into account.

See also CANON; CHRISTOLOGY; CHURCH; COVENANT, NEW COVENANT; DEATH OF CHRIST; ESCHATOLOGY; ETHICS; GOD; HERMENEUTICS; HOLY SPIRIT; KINGDOM OF GOD; OLD TESTAMENT; PASTORAL THEOLOGY; REVEAL, REVELATION.

BIBLIOGRAPHY. **Articles from Standard Reference Works:** J. Barr, "Biblical Theology," *IDBSup* 104-11; M. Dibelius, "Biblische Theologie und biblische Religionsgeschichte," *RGG*[2] 1:1091-94; G. E. Ladd, "Biblical Theology, History of," *ISBE* 1:498-509; O. Merk, *TRE* 6:455-77; R. Morgan, "Theology (NT)," *ABD* 6:473-83; H. G. Reventlow, "Theology (Biblical), History of," *ABD* 6:483-505; H. Riesenfeld, "Biblische Theologie und biblische Religionsgeschichte," *RGG*[3] 1:1261-61; K. Stendahl, "Biblical Theology, Contemporary," *IDB* 1:418-32; A. Vögtle, "New Testament Theology," *SM* 4:216-20. **Works Treating the Methods and Problems of NT Theology:** H. R. Balz, *Methodische Probleme der neutestamentlichen Christologie* (Neukirchen: Neukirchener Verlag, 1967); K. Berger, *Exegese und Philosophie* (Stuttgart: Katholisches Bibelwerk, 1986); idem, *Hermeneutik des Neuen Testaments* (Gütersloh: Gütersloher Verlagshaus Gerd Mohn, 1988); H. Boers, *What Is New Testament Theology? The Rise of Criticism and the Problem of a Theology of the New Testament* (Philadelphia: Fortress, 1979); H. Braun, "The Problematics of a New Testament Theology," *JTC* 1 (1965) 169-83; idem, "The Sense of New Testament Christology," *JTC* 5 (1968) 89-127; G. Bray, *Biblical Interpretation: Past & Present* (Downers Grove, IL: InterVarsity Press, 1996); R. Bultmann, "The Problem of a Theological Exegesis of the New Testament" in *The Beginnings of Dialectical Theology*, ed. J. M. Robinson (Richmond, VA: John Knox, 1968) 47-72; D. A. Carson, "Current Issues in Biblical Theology: A New Testament Perspective," *BBR* 5 (1995) 17-41; idem, *The Gagging of God: Christianity Confronts Pluralism* (Grand Rapids: Zondervan, 1995); B. Childs, *Biblical Theology in Crisis* (Philadelphia: Fortress, 1970); B. Corley, "Biblical Theology of the New Testament" in *Foundations for Biblical Interpretation*, ed. D. Dockery, K. A. Mathews and R. B. Sloan (Nashville: Broadman and Holman, 1994) 545-64; R. A. Culpepper, *Anatomy of the Fourth Gospel* (Philadelphia: Fortress, 1983); G. Ebeling, "The Meaning of 'Biblical Theology'," *JTS* 6 (1955) 210-25; idem, *Word and Faith* (Philadelphia: Fortress, 1963); E. S. Fiorenza, *In Memory of Her* (London: SCM, 1983); H. Frei, *The Eclipse of Biblical Narrative: A Study in Eighteenth and Nineteenth Century Hermeneutics* (New Haven, CT: Yale University Press, 1974); E. Fuchs, *Studies of the Historical Jesus* (London: SCM, 1964); K. Haacker et al., *Biblische Theologie heute* (Neukirchen-Vluyn: Neukirchener Verlag, 1977); W. J. Harrington, *The Path of Biblical Theology* (Dublin: Gill and Macmillan, 1973); G. F. Hasel, "The Nature of Biblical Theology: Recent Trends and Issues," *AUSS* 32 (1994) 203-15; idem, *New Testament Theology: Basic Issues in the Current Debate* (Grand Rapids:

Eerdmans, 1978); C. J. Hemer, *The Book of Acts in the Setting of Hellenistic History*, ed., C. H. Gempf (Tübingen: J. C. B. Mohr [Paul Siebeck], 1989); M. Hengel, *The Pre-Christian Paul* (Philadelphia: Trinity, 1991); E. Käsemann, ed., *Das Neuen Testament als Kanon* (Göttingen: Vandenhoeck & Ruprecht, 1970); idem, "Das Problem des historischen Jesus," *ZTK* 51 (1954) 125-53; H.-J. Kraus, *Die biblische Theologie: Ihre Geschichte und Problematik* (Neukirchen-Vluyn: Neukirchener Verlag, 1970); E. E. Lemcio, "The Unifying Kerygma of the New Testament," *JSNT* 33 (1988) 3-17; idem, "The Unifying Kerygma of the New Testament," *JSNT* 38 (1990) 3-11; G. Maier, *Biblische Hermeneutik* (Wuppertal: R. Brockhaus, 1990); W. A. Meeks, *The First Urban Christians: The Social World of the Apostle Paul* (New Haven: Yale University Press, 1983); O. Merk, *Biblische Theologie des Neuen Testaments in ihrer Anfangszeit* (Marburg: N. G. Elwert, 1972); J. Moltmann, "Zur neutestamentlichen Theologie," *EvT* 51 (1991) 307-95; L. Montrose, "Professing the Renaissance: The Poetics and Politics of Culture" in *The New Historicism*, ed. H. A. Veeser (New York: Routledge, 1989) 15-36; R. Morgan, "The Historical Jesus and the Theology of the New Testament" in *The Glory of Christ in the New Testament*, ed. L. D. Hurst and N. T. Wright (Oxford: Clarendon, 1987) 187-206; idem, *The Nature of New Testament Theology* (London: SCM, 1973); C. F. D. Moule, *The Birth of the New Testament* (3d ed.; New York: Harper & Row, 1982); M. Oeming, *Gesamtbiblische Theologie der Gegenwart* (2d ed.; Stuttgart: Kohlhammer, 1987); J. Pelikan, ed., *Twentieth Century Theology in the Making*, 1: *Themes of Biblical Theology* (New York: Harper & Row, 1970); P. Pokorný, "The Problem of Biblical Theology," *Horizons* 15 (1993) 83-94; H. Räisänen, *Beyond New Testament Theology* (London: SCM, 1990); H. G. Reventlow, *Problems of Biblical Theology in the Twentieth Century* (London: SCM, 1986); J. A. Sanders, "Scripture as Canon for Postmodern Times," *BTB* 25 (1995) 56-63; A. Schlatter, "Atheistische Methoden in der Theologie" [1905], in *Zur Theologie des Neuen Testaments und zur Dogmatik, Kleine Schriften*, ed. U. Luck (Munich: Christian Kaiser, 1969) 134-50; H. Schlier, *The Relevance of the New Testament* (New York: Herder & Herder, 1968); R. Schnackenburg, *New Testament Theology Today* (London: SCM, 1963); C. H. H. Scobie, "The Challenge of Biblical Theology," *TynB* 42 (1991) 3-30; idem,

"The Structure of Biblical Theology," *TynB* 42 (1991) 163-94; R. B. Sloan, "Canonical Theology of the New Testament" in *Foundations for Biblical Interpretation*, ed. D. Dockery, K. A. Mathews and R. B. Sloan (Nashville: Broadman and Holman, 1994) 565-95; J. Smart, *The Past, Present, and Future of Biblical Theology* (Philadelphia: Westminster, 1979); M. Sternberg, *The Poetics of Biblical Narrative: Ideological Literature and the Drama of Reading* (Bloomington, IN: Indiana University Press, 1985); D. F. Strauss, *The Life of Jesus Critically Examined*, (Philadelphia: Fortress, 1972 [1835]); G. Strecker, ed., *Das Problem der Theologie des Neuen Testaments* (Darmstadt: Wissenschaftliche Buchgesellschaft, 1975); D. O. Via, "New Testament Theology: Historical Event, Literary Text, and the Locus of Revelation," *PRS* 19 (1992) 369-88; G. Vos, "The Idea of Biblical Theology as a Science and as a Theological Discipline" in *Redemptive History and Biblical Interpretation: The Shorter Writings of Geerhardus Vos*, ed. R. E. Gaffin (Phillipsburg, NJ: Presbyterian & Reformed, 1980) 3-24. **Works on NT Theology (with Some Biblical Theology):** M. Albertz, *Botschaft des Neuen Testaments* (Zollikon/Zürich: Evangelischer Verlag, 1946-57); J. Barr, *The Semantics of Biblical Language* (Oxford: Oxford University Press, 1961); F. C. Baur, *Vorlesungen ber Neutestamentlichen Theologie* (Leipzig: Fues's Verlag [L. W. Reisland], 1864); G. L. Bauer, *Biblische Theologie des Neuen Testaments* (2 vols.; Leipzig: Weygand, 1800-1802); idem, *Theologie des Alten Testaments* (Leipzig: Weygand, 1796); K. Berger, *Theologiegeschichte des Urchristentums* (Tübingen: Francke, 1994); J. Blank, *Studien zur biblischen Theologie* (Stuttgart: Katholisches Bibelwerk, 1992); J. Bonsirven, *Theology of the New Testament* (London: Burns and Oates, 1963 [1951]); R. Bultmann, *Theology of the New Testament* (2 vols.; London: SCM, 1952-55 [1948-53]); M. Burrows, *An Outline of Biblical Theology* (Philadelphia: Westminster, 1946); G. B. Caird, *New Testament Theology*, ed. L. D. Hurst (Oxford: Clarendon, 1994); B. S. Childs, *Biblical Theology of the Old and New Testaments: Theological Reflection on the Christian Bible* (Minneapolis: Fortress, 1992); H. Conzelmann, *An Outline of the Theology of the New Testament* (London: SCM, 1969 [1968, 1987]); O. Cullmann, *Salvation in History* (New York: Harper & Row, 1967); J. D. G. Dunn, *Christology in the Making* (Philadelphia: Westminster, 1980); idem, *Unity and Diversity in the New Testament* (Philadelphia: Westminster, 1977); E. S. Fiorenza, *Jesus, Miriam's Child, Sophia's Prophet: Critical Issues in Feminist Christology* (New York: Continuum, 1994); D. P. Fuller, *The Unity of the Bible: Unfolding God's Plan for Humanity* (Grand Rapids: Zondervan, 1992); J. P. Gabler, "Oratio de iusto discrimine theologiae biblicae et dogmaticae regundisque recte utriusque finibus" in *Kleinere theologische Schriften*, ed. T. A. Gabler and J. G. Gabler (2 vols.; Ulm: Verlag des Stettinischen Buchhandlung, 1831) 2:179-98 [available in English in J. Sandys-Wunsch and L. Eldredge, "J. P. Gabler and the Distinction Between Biblical and Dogmatic Theology: Translation, Commentary and Discussion of His Originality," *SJT* 33 (1980) 133-58]; H. Gese, *Essays on Biblical Theology* (Minneapolis: Augsburg, 1981); J. Gnilka, *Neutestamentliche Theologie: Ein Überblick* (Würzburg: Echter Verlag, 1989); idem, *Theologie des Neuen Testaments* (Freiburg: Herder, 1994); L. Goppelt, *Theology of the New Testament* (2 vols.; Grand Rapids: Eerdmans, 1981-82 [1975-76]); F. C. Grant, *An Introduction to New Testament Thought* (New York: Abingdon, 1950); D. Guthrie, *New Testament Theology* (Downers Grove, IL: InterVarsity Press, 1981); J. C. K. von Hofmann, *Biblische Theologie des Neuen Testaments* (Nördlingen: Beck, 1886); H. J. Holtzmann, *Lehrbuch der neutestamentlichen Theologie* (Tübingen: J. C. B. Mohr [Paul Siebeck], 1897, 1911); H. Hübner, *Biblische Theologie des Neuen Testaments* (Göttingen: Vandenhoeck & Ruprecht, 1990-95); A. M. Hunter, *Introducing New Testament Theology* (London: SCM, 1957); J. Jeremias, *New Testament Theology: The Proclamation of Jesus* (New York: Scribner's, 1971 [1971]); R. E. Knudsen, *Theology in the New Testament: A Basis for Christian Faith* (Valley Forge, PA: Judson, 1964); W. G. Kümmel, *The Theology of the New Testament According to Its Major Witnesses* (London: SCM, 1974 [1969]); O. Küss, *Die Theologie des Neuen Testaments: Eine Einführung* (Regensburg: Pustet, 1936); G. E. Ladd, *A Theology of the New Testament* (Grand Rapids: Eerdmans, 1974 [rev. ed. 1993]); C. R. Lehman, *Biblical Theology, 2: New Testament* (Scottdale, PA: Herald, 1974); A. Lemonnyer, *La Théologie du Nouveau Testament* (Paris: Bloud & Gay, 1928; ET 1930); E. Lohse, *Grundriss der neutestamentlichen Theologie* (Stuttgart: Kohlhammer, 1974); I. H. Marshall, *Jesus the Savior: Studies in New Testament Theology* (Downers Grove, IL: InterVarsity Press, 1990); M. Meinertz, *Theologie* *des Neuen Testaments* (2 vols.; Bonn: P. Hanstein, 1950); R. W. L. Moberly, *From Eden to Golgotha: Essays in Biblical Theology* (Atlanta: Scholars Press, 1992); L. Morris, *New Testament Theology* (Grand Rapids: Zondervan, 1986); S. Neill, *Jesus Through Many Eyes: Introduction to the Theology of the New Testament* (Philadelphia: Fortress, 1974); S. Pedersen, ed., *New Directions in Biblical Theology* (Leiden: E. J. Brill, 1994); A. Richardson, *An Introduction to the Theology of the New Testament* (London: SCM, 1958); C. C. Ryrie, *Biblical Theology of the New Testament* (Chicago: Moody, 1959); J. A. Sanders, *From Sacred Story to Sacred Text* (Minneapolis: Fortress, 1987); idem, *Torah and Canon* (Philadelphia: Fortress, 1972); K. H. Schelkle, *Theology of the New Testament* (4 vols.; Collegeville, MN: Liturgical Press, 1971-78 [1968-76]); A. Schlatter, *Die Theologie des Neuen Testaments* (2 vols.; Stuttgart: Verlag der Vereinsbuchhandlung, 1909, 1910 [ET of the first volume of the 2d ed., 1923, forthcoming from Baker]); W. Schmithals, *Theologiegeschichte des Urchristentums* (Stuttgart: Kohlhammer, 1994); R. Schnackenburg, *The Moral Teaching of the New Testament* (London: Burns and Oates, 1965 [1954, 1962]); E. Schweizer, *Theologische Einleitung in das Neuen Testament* (Göttingen: Vandenhoeck & Ruprecht, 1989 [ET 1991]); H. Seebass, *Der Gott der ganzen Bibel: Biblische Theologie zur Orientierung im Glauben* (Freiburg: Herder, 1982); F. Stagg, *New Testament Theology* (Nashville: Broadman, 1962); E. Stauffer, *New Testament Theology* (London: SCM, 1955 [1941]); G. B. Stevens, *The Theology of the New Testament* (Edinburgh: T & T Clark, 1901, 1906); P. Stuhlmacher, *Biblische Theologie des Neuen Testaments. 1: Grundlegung: Von Jesus zu Paulus* (Göttingen: Vandenhoeck & Ruprecht, 1992); idem, "The Law as a Topic of Biblical Theology," in *Reconciliation, Law and Righteousness* (Philadelphia: Fortress, 1986) 110-33; idem, *Vom Verstehen des Neuen Testaments* (2d ed.; Göttingen: Vandenhoeck & Ruprecht, 1986); S. Terrien, *The Elusive Presence: The Heart of Biblical Theology* (San Francisco: Harper & Row, 1978); W. Thüsing, *Die neutestamentlichen Theologien und Jesus Christus, Band 1: Kriterien auf Grund der Rückfrage nach Jesus und des Glaubens an seine Auferweckung* (Düsseldorf: Patmos, 1981); idem, *Studien zur neutestamentlichen Theologie* (Tübingen: J. C. B. Mohr [Paul Siebeck], 1995); G. Vos, *Biblical Theology: Old and New Testaments* (Grand Rapids: Eerdmans, 1948); B. Weiss, *Biblical Theology of the New Testament* (2 vols.; Edinburgh: T & T Clark, 1882-83 [1868, 1903]); W. M. L. de Wette, *Lehrbuch der christlichen Dogmatik in ihrer historischen Entwicklung dargestellt. Erster Teil. Die biblische Dogmatik, enthaltend Biblische Dogmatik Alten und Neuen Testaments. Oder kritischer Darstellung der Religionslehre des Hebraismus, des Judenthums, und Urchristentums* (3d ed.; Berlin: G. Reimer, 1831 [1st ed. 1813]); W. Wrede, *Über Aufgabe und Methode der sogenannte neutestamentliche Theologie* (Göttingen: Vandenhoeck & Ruprecht, 1897) [trans. into English by R. Morgan as "The Task and Methods of 'New Testament Theology'" in *The Nature of New Testament Theology* (London: SCM, 1973) 68-116]; N. T. Wright, *The Climax of the Covenant: Christ and the Law in Pauline Theology* (Edinburgh: T & T Clark, 1991); idem, *The New Testament and the People of God* (London: SPCK, 1992); G. T. Zachariae, *Biblische Theologie, oder Untersuchung des biblischen Grundes der dolfvornehmsten theologischen Lehren* (5 vols.; Tübingen: Frank & Schramm, 1771-86); T. Zahn, *Grundriss der neutestamentlichen Theologie* (Leipzig: A. Deichertische Verlagsbuchhandlung, 1928).

D. A. Carson

NOAH. *See* ANCESTORS.

NONCANONICAL WRITINGS, CITATIONS IN THE GENERAL EPISTLES

The General Epistles—James,* 1 Peter* and Jude* in particular—reflect a conspicuous debt to Jewish exegetical tradition. In their use of both the Hebrew Scriptures and noncanonical tradition material, they mirror a Jewish religiocultural matrix by which their message as well as mode of literary expression are shaped.

The arguments set forth in James, 1 Peter and Jude, for example, betray the hand of a skilled haggadist, exercised in the application of Jewish midrash for didactic purposes, not unlike what one finds in rabbinic literature. Jude and 2 Peter contain instances of prophetic typology that are applied to the Christian community for the purpose of condemning the apostate and exhorting the faithful. James unfolds as a collection of loosely knit paraenetic sayings cast in the form of a diatribe. Both Jude and 2 Peter offer a targumic assessment of OT characters while simultaneously making use of pagan proverbs or legends that underscore the reality of divine truth.* In Jude and 1 Peter we encounter christologized allusions to apocalyptic* writings of sectarian Judaism.* And 1 John in its theological dualism shows conceptual resemblance to the literature of Qumran.*

The significance of noncanonical sources for biblical exegesis lies in their ability to clarify theological concepts, inform us of Jewish religious history, elucidate Jewish attitudes toward the Scriptures and illuminate the first-century Jewish-Christian context of which the General Epistles are a part.

1. Jewish Hermeneutical Tendencies and the General Epistles
2. Jewish Exegetical Practice in the General Epistles

1. Jewish Hermeneutical Tendencies and the General Epistles.

The General Epistles present the reader with a remarkably clear window through which to observe the scope and variety of first-century Jewish-Christian hermeneutics. To observe exegetical method is to gain understanding into the religiocultural milieu from whence it derives. While biblical scholarship in the main has categorized first-century Jewish hermeneutical practice according to three broad types—literalist (found in rabbinic literature), allegorical (as practiced by Philo*) and midrashic (as practiced both by mainstream and sectarian Judaism)—it is the latter, haggadic midrash, that is of primary interest in our consideration of the General Epistles.

The volumes by H. L. Strack and P. Billerbeck have long been the primary source for observing parallels between rabbinic literature and the NT. While midrash (from the Hebrew verb *dāraš* "to search out," "to seek") has historically and generically designated rabbinic commentary on the OT Scriptures, it is also understood in the sense of a procedure or hermeneutical activity. Accordingly, midrashic interpretations of the Bible have as their goal the contemporary application of the Scriptures for later generations. Jewish midrash can either be halakic (i.e., prescriptive) or haggadic (i.e., moralistic and historical) in its teaching emphasis. The latter category occurs with relative frequency in the General Epistles, where in the form of moral typology it serves to interpret or reinterpret the Scriptures according to present pastoral need.

2. Jewish Exegetical Practice in the General Epistles.

2.1. James. NT scholarship has largely held James to be an expression of Palestinian Jewish-Christian thought, in spite of evidences of Hellenistic rhetorical influence in the document and its use of the Septuagint in citing the OT. James draws from a wide assortment of Jewish tradition material—the OT legal corpus (Ex 20; Lev 19; Deut 5), Jesus' sayings and wisdom literature (Prov, Sir, Wis).

Among the General Epistles and aside from Jude, James cites OT characters most frequently. Following the letter's greeting, Abraham* and Rahab (Jas 2), Job, the prophets* and Elijah (Jas 5) are cited as models of validating faith* and patience in the face of adversity. What sets these figures apart, however, is the manner in which the author employs them. As paradigms they frequently emit a greater correspondence to current Jewish notions of righteousness* than to the OT narratives themselves. While the meaning, derived from the letter's broader thematic flow, is clear, the exegetical process is not always readily apparent to the reader.

James 1:12-15 is illustrative, containing striking parallels from Jewish wisdom tradition—notably the wisdom of Sirach (second century B.C.). In Sirach 15:11-20 the writer argues that in the context of testing God* does not cause sin*; rather, sin proceeds from human desire. God is depicted as omniscient, wise, all-powerful; he watches those who fear him. Humans, by contrast, will face temptation; indeed, testing is inevitable. The faithful are exhorted in Sirach to prepare their souls for testing (Sir 2:1), in much the same way that James admonishes his audience (Jas 1:2, 12). Yet one can choose to obey and resist sin. Observing the law* and keeping the commandments* while one endures trial are praised in Sirach.

James 1:22-25 also suggests reliance on extracanonical tradition material. The "mirror of remembrance" as a teaching device appears to have achieved fairly wide currency both in Jewish and Hellenistic circles. For both Plutarch and Epictetus (late first century) self-examination was understood to be the moral equivalent of gazing into a mirror. In *The Education of Children* Plutarch applies the mirror imagery in the context of moral education. Significantly this includes control of the tongue (cf. Jas 1:26; 3:1-12) and control of one's anger (cf. Jas 1:19-20). Wisdom literature also incorporates this theme. The mirror is a "reflection of eternal light, a spotless mirror of divine working" (Wis

7:26). Such wisdom* cannot be produced, however; it is granted by God (Wis 8:19-21; cf. Jas 1:17; 3:13). Moreover, those who live by this wisdom are "friends of God" (Wis 7:27; cf. Jas 4:4).

Contemporary midrashic parallels are particularly helpful in probing James 2:14-26. While James 2:21-23 shows notable similarity to Genesis 22 and 15:6, less obvious is the connection between *pistis* and *erga,* a connection the author seems to presuppose. In rabbinic literature (e.g., *m. Soṭa* 5:5; *m. 'Abot* 5:19; 6:10) Job and Abraham are paradigms for the "God-fearing" and "God-loving" individual. Other Jewish sources confirm this portrait of Abraham. In Philo, for example, the idea of Abraham's love* for God is developed more extensively (*T. Abr.* 10, 32, 167). In *Testament of Abraham* [A] 17:7 the patriarch is noted both for his righteous deeds and for the greatness of his love toward God. In 1 Maccabees 2:52 Abraham is found faithful in trial. Contemporary Jews viewed Abraham as righteous based on his works (*Jub.* 17:16; 18:11, 16), the culmination of which was his willingness to offer Isaac (4 Macc 16:20; *Jub.* 17:17; 19:8; *m. Ta'an.* 2:4,5; *m. 'Abot* 5:6; *see* Faith and Works).

It is noteworthy that allusion to Rahab immediately follows James's use of Abraham as a model. In Jewish lore both Abraham and Rahab are paradigms of hospitality* (e.g., *T. Abr.* [A] 17:7; *Gen. Rab.* 49:4; 56:5; *t. Soṭa* 10a-b); both express genuine faith through deeds. While the idea of faith being validated by works is implicit in the OT, in later Jewish tradition this attestation is magnified (e.g., *Midr. Ruth* 2:126). James's argument is that true faith will evidence itself.

James 5:17-18, an allusion to the prophet Elijah, finds a close parallel in the pseudepigraphic 4 Ezra 7:39 (109) and *Lives of the Prophets* 21:5. The context of 4 Ezra is especially illuminating. The writer lists Israel's mighty who had prayed with authority*—Abraham for Sodom, Moses* for the fathers in the wilderness, Joshua for Israel in the days of Achan, David for the plague, Solomon in the sanctuary and Elijah for rain. The lesson is stated flatly: "If therefore the righteous have prayed for the ungodly now, when corruption has increased and unrighteousness has multiplied, why will it not be so then as well?" (4 Ezra 7:45 [115]). In contrast to contemporary Jewish notions of Elijah, which

tended to stress the supernatural (e.g., *m. Soṭa* 9:15; *m. Šeqal.* 2:5; cf. Mal 4:5-6; Mt 17:3-4; Mk 9:4, 5; Lk 9:30; Jn 1:21), James attempts to humanize the prophet. His method of doing so is to depict him as an intercessor, a role that accords both with biblical and extrabiblical tradition (see also *y. Sanh.* 10; *b. Sanh.* 113; *m. Ta'an.* 2:4).

Paraenetic sayings on patience in trial both open (Jas 1:2-18) and conclude (Jas 5:7-12) the epistle, thus forming something of an inclusio. As a model of patience in suffering* James cites the prophets and Job (Jas 5:10-11). The OT depicts Job foremost as upright before the Lord; his patience is less clear. In extracanonical Jewish tradition, however, the patience of Job is explicit and well-developed, achieving proverbial status (e.g., *T. Job* 4:5-6; 27:3-10; 39:11-13; *m. 'Ed.* 2:10). Whether written or oral this tradition is apparently familiar to James's readers.

Other traces of Jewish tradition material in the letter appear in James 1:1 (reference to those "serving" God in the "diaspora," as in 2 Macc 1:27); James 1:3-4 (emphasizing the virtue of endurance, e.g., 4 Macc 1:11); James 1:5 (God granting wisdom liberally and not upbraiding as a fool upbraids, Sir 18:18; 20:15; 41:22); James 1:12 (a crown of glory* promised to those who persevere, *2 Apoc. Bar.* 15:8; *Apoc. Elijah* 1:8); James 1:8 (the double-minded person over against the perfect, undivided heart, as in Sir 2:12-14; *T. Benj.* 6:5; *Tg. Neof.* Gen 22:14; *Tg. Neof.* Ex 19:8); James 1:19 (the admonition to be quick to hear, slow to speak and slow to become angry, Sir 5:13 and *m. 'Abot* 5:12); James 2:1-7 (rabbinic texts such as *Deut. Rab.* 5:6 and *b. Šebu.* 31a making reference to the dichotomy between rich and poor in judicial proceedings); James 2:10 (contradicting the law* in small or in great measure, e.g., 4 Macc 5:20); James 3:2, 6, 10 (the person not sinning with the mouth as blessed, Sir 5:13 and 14:1); James 3:13-17 (the true wisdom, as described in Sir 19:18-22); James 3:13—4:10 (paraenesis on envy, strife and murder that resembles allusions to "the envious eye" in 1 Macc 8:16 and Tob 4:4, 16, and envy and murder in *T. Sim.* 2:6-14); James 4:4-6 (a probable midrash on Noah, illustrated in Sir 15:11-20); James 5:10 (the prophets being persecuted, e.g., in *T. Levi* 16:2 and *Asc. Isa.* 1—5); James 5:16 (confession of sin and pardon in Jewish liturgy, resembling texts such as *m. Sanh.*

6:2 and *Tg. Ps.-J.* Ex 33:7).

2.2. 1 Peter. In our consideration of the literary strategy at work in 1 Peter, it becomes self-evident that a significant part of this strategy entails the author's lavish use of OT material. Less apparent, however, is the extent to which noncanonical tradition-material is utilized. Several examples of the use of tradition material deserve comment.

One trace of noncanonical allusion occurs in 1 Peter 1:12, where the author observes parenthetically that the angels* yearn to look into the things of salvation* brought from heaven* through Christ. No explanation of or direct parallel to this phenomenon is to be found in the OT. A Jewish apocalyptic reference to angelic activity and a targumic expansion on Jacob's ladder, however, are suggestive. In the text of *1 Enoch* 9:1, the angels are said to observe carefully from the heavens the events on earth. The verb that describes the angels' activity, *parakyptein*, is the same verb used in 1 Peter 1:12. In *Targum Neofiti* Genesis 28:12 one finds a description of the angels ascending and descending in order to observe Jacob. According to the text they "earnestly desired" to see this righteous man. It is possible that in his allusion to the angelic aspect of divine mystery* Peter is making use of imagery and language associated with a midrashic tradition.

One instance of the use of tradition material in 1 Peter to which much literature is devoted is 1 Peter 2:4-17, a midrash employing a christologized metaphor of a stone.* 1 Peter 2:4-10 would appear to combine OT references with contemporary Jewish notions of God's people. While a clear link to the metaphor in Isaiah 28:16 and Psalm 118:22 is evident, its reinterpretation as it is applied to the community bears some resemblance to Qumran exegesis. In 1QS 8:7 the community is depicted as a stone. In the same context it is also described as a holy house* (1QS 8:5; see also 1QS 5:5-6; 1QH 6:25-26). The reinterpretation, moreover, is reminiscent of Isaiah 44:28, which correlates Israel's return with the building of the temple.* Whereas in the OT the stone is the king, in later Jewish tradition it is the actual people of God. Christologization of the image in 1 Peter is in keeping with this theological development.

After employing the metaphor of the stone, the writer summarizes in 1 Peter 2:9 by combining several images that are reminiscent of both OT paschal narratives as well as Qumran terminology. A priesthood,* a holy nation, the chosen of God and the dualism of darkness and light* find parallels in both canonical and noncanonical Jewish texts. (On light and darkness see 1 John.)

The readers are subsequently admonished to behavior that is honorable in the sight of surrounding pagan culture (1 Pet 2:11-12). The result is that though they may be maligned as "evildoers," others will "see your honorable deeds and glorify God on the day of visitation." The linkage of glorifying God and commendation through good deeds occurs with relative frequency in Jewish tradition. As evidenced by 1QH 6:8-12, the covenanters of Qumran understand the effects of holiness* as leading to the revelation* of God's mighty acts and the Gentiles seeing God's glory (see also 1QH 10:17-21). The link between good works, honor and glorifying God (cf. Mt 5:16) is also found in the pseudepigraphal *Testaments of the Twelve Patriarchs* (second century B.C.): "If you achieve good, my children, men and angels will bless you, and God will be glorified through you among the Gentiles" (*T. Naph.* 8:4).

1 Peter 3:6, part of a Petrine paraenesis on Christian ethics* in a secular world, would appear to be a reference to Genesis 18. However, in the OT narrative Sarah's obedience* to Abraham is not the principal theme. The text of 1 Peter reads: "Thus Sarah obeyed Abraham and called him lord." While this accent is absent from Genesis, it appears with great frequency in the *Testament of Abraham* (first century). In this pseudepigraphal work Sarah's submissiveness is a virtual subtheme, illustrated by the abundant use of the title "my lord Abraham" (e.g., *T. Abr.* [A] 5:12; 6:2, 5, 8; 15:4). Peter is less concerned to recount the Genesis narrative than he is intent on identifying a point of correspondence between Sarah and Christian women.* From an exegetical standpoint, more important than citing the OT is the establishment of a moral paradigm for the sake of Christian ethics.

In one of the more enigmatic texts of the NT, 1 Peter 3:18-20, the writer in a rather cryptic way expands his discussion of suffering and baptism.* Christ also suffered, his readers are reminded; thereby a point of identification is made. Yet this suffering and subsequent rising entailed more than meets the eye. Part of this great redemptive act included "proclamation to the spirits in prison who in former times did not obey."

The preaching to the spirits is best explained in light of the prepositional phrase *en phylakē* (in prison). In the genre of apocalyptic literature, prison is not the location of human souls but of punishment, as evidenced by the language of the NT Apocalypse (e.g., Rev 18:2; 20:7; *see* Revelation, Book of). In Jewish apocalyptic literature "imprisoned spirits" figure quite prominently. *1 Enoch* is exemplary and casts helpful light on the cryptic allusion found in 1 Peter. Christ's descent is not unlike that depicted in Enoch's commission to go and preach to the fallen angels (*1 Enoch* 12). Given the attention to fallen angels in first-century apocalyptic, Peter may well be portraying Christ as the end-time Enoch who proclaims judgment* on the fallen spirits, having disarmed the principalities and powers and triumphed over them (cf. Col 2:15). In 1 Peter 3 angelic typology serves an important pastoral function. The readers pass from Christ's sufferings to Christ's triumph with the reminder that just as the fallen angels are reserved for judgment, those who persecute Christians and refuse to believe also "will give account to him who will judge the living and the dead" (1 Pet 4:4).

A final cluster of exhortations, relating to oversight of the flock of God (1 Pet 5:1-11), finds a parallel in the Qumran literature. In the community's *Manual of Discipline* leaders are warned not to be domineering ("The sons of Aaron should only rule in justice and with appropriate authority") and to avoid reaching decisions independently that refract detrimentally on others (1QS 9:7). Peter's admonition is strikingly similar: the elders are to shepherd God's flock not out of compulsion but willingly before God. Moreover, they are not to lord it over the flock but serve as *typoi* or examples (1 Pet 5:2-3). In so doing they will receive a crown of great glory that will never fade (5:4; cf. *2 Apoc. Bar.* 15:8).

2.3. Jude and 2 Peter. The epistle of Jude may be assumed to mirror a distinctly Jewish-Christian audience. The abundant use of triplets, apocalyptic imagery and midrashic typology that borrows heavily from Jewish tradition material are together indicative of a markedly Jewish-Christian social matrix. 2 Peter, by contrast, strongly suggests an audience that finds itself in a pagan Gentile* environment. The writer, ac-

cordingly, appropriates the language of philosophical mysticism, a catalog of Stoic virtues, a reference to Tartarus, two common secular proverbs and flood-fire typology directed against moral relativists.

Lists of historical paradigms depicting hardheartedness appear in intertestamental literature with relative frequency. Among the most commonly cited in these lists are apostate Israel, Sodomites, the fallen angels, Assyria, the giants, the generation of the flood, Korah and the Canaanites. Such lists are employed as a teaching device in the Apocrypha, in the pseudepigrapha and in rabbinic literature (e.g., 3 Macc 3:7; Sir 16:5-15; *1 Enoch* 1—36, *T. Naph.* 2:8—4:3; *Jub.* 20:2-7; CD 2.14—3.12; *m. Sanh.* 10:3). Both Jude and 2 Peter enlist the use of paradigms for typological purposes.

In order to magnify the irrationality of his opponents, Jude casts the apostates as polar opposites of Michael the archangel, who though possessing greater authority remains within his bounds. The tradition according to which the conflict between Michael and the devil reputedly derives, the *Assumption of Moses,* is apocryphal in origin, perhaps circulating in oral form during the first century and having numerous parallels in Qumran literature. The *Assumption,* which admits of no apparent connection to Deuteronomy 34 but incorporates imagery from Zechariah 3, is known to us through several subapostolic sources, initially through Origen (*De Princ.* 3.2.1).

Jude's description of the judgment of the ungodly includes a near-verbatim citation of *1 Enoch* 1:9, a pseudepigraphal expansion of theophanic statements that occur with frequency throughout the OT, most notably Deuteronomy 33. In Jude, as in *1 Enoch,* theophany and judgment merge in response to the apostate. The fate of the wicked is certain. Further borrowing of Jewish apocalyptic imagery appears in the same contextual flow—Jude 12-13 (cf. *1 Enoch* 67:5-7; 80:2-8)—where Jude's opponents are cast as "wandering stars."

Because Jude's citation of *1 Enoch* is direct and because he states that Enoch "prophesied," commentators assume that Jude regarded Enochic literature as authoritative and on the level of the Hebrew Scriptures. However, if Jude's literary strategy may have called for exploiting a work that was highly esteemed not so much by himself as by his audience, it is plausible that in this case Enoch can be said to "prophesy" in much the same way as a Cretan poet is said to be a "prophet" by the apostle Paul (Tit 1:12). Thus Jude's citation of *1 Enoch* may derive less from his personal elevation of Enochic literature than from that of his readers.

Lacking the distinctly Palestinian flavor that is manifest in Jude, 2 Peter incorporates extrabiblical tradition material with a pagan social context in view. To the list of characteristic Stoic virtues such as moral excellence, knowledge,* endurance and self-control are added the Christian virtues of faith, brotherly love and agape (2 Pet 1:5-7). The present situation, in which the writer seeks to counter a faith weak in ethical fiber, calls for a rhetorical response that is immediately perceptible. Furthermore, the general structure of 2 Peter, with its use of paraenesis (2 Pet 1), moral typology (2 Pet 2) and caricature of the moral skeptic (2 Pet 3), suggests a pervasively pagan social location in which unrestricted human autonomy stands in denial of moral accountability.

The profile of apostasy* in 2 Peter 2 shows the greatest degree of literary relationship to Jude. Whereas the historical paradigms in the latter underscore irrevocable judgment, in the former they highlight both certain judgment on evildoers as well as deliverance of a righteous remnant. That the situation behind 2 Peter calls for a unique response is shown by the presence of Noah and Lot as midrashic types of God's merciful deliverance (*see* Mercy). Contrary to the emphasis of most commentaries, Lot is not a "model of righteous suffering." He is "righteous" not by personal example but by comparison; Lot illustrates the mercy of God. In Wisdom 10:4-10, significantly, Lot appears alongside Noah, Abraham, Jacob and Joseph as a "virtuous" man.

Taken together the paradigms in 2 Peter are reminiscent of one notable OT character—Balaam, "who loved the wages of evil" (2 Pet 2:15). Balaam is notorious in standardized Jewish tradition. Allusions to this OT character are evidence of a Jewish mindset fascinated with the prophet who led Israel into idolatry* (Philo *Vit. Mos.* 1.295-99; Josephus *Ant.* 4.6.6; cf. Num 31:16) and thus had no place in the life to come (*m. Sanh.* 10:2-4). In rabbinic literature Balaam is the antithesis of Abraham (e.g., *m. 'Abot* 5:19). Curiously absent from 2 Peter are Cain and Korah as paradigms (cf. *t. Soṭa* 4:9, where Cain,

Balaam and Korah appear together in a list), the former serving as "type and teacher" of ungodliness in Jewish tradition (Philo *Poster. C.* 38), the latter being arguably the most arresting case of insubordination in the OT in that he opposed Moses, the man who talked with God. With Balaam as their spiritual mentor, the apostate are vividly depicted by means of a double metaphor—a dog returning to its vomit and a pig returning to the mud from whence it was washed. While the metaphor of the dog finds a parallel in the book of Proverbs (Prov 26:11), the metaphor of the pig finds its analogue in the Egyptian Story of Ahiqar: "My son, you were to me like a pig which had been in a hot bath. . . . And when it was out and saw a filthy pool went down and wallowed in it" (*APOT* 2:772).

2.4. 1 John. The form of expression in 1 John, both in style and substance, is strikingly similar to that of Qumran literature. Principal among the parallels to be noted is a theological dualism—e.g., sons or children (*see* Sonship, Children) of light and truth versus sons or children of darkness, deceit and the devil (*see* Satan); spirits* of truth and light versus spirits of deceit and darkness; angels of truth versus angels of darkness (1 Jn 3:10, 13, 24, 25; 4:5, 6, 17; 3:18-21, 24; 5:10; cf. 1QS 1:9, 10; 2:2, 5).

Several thematic links are also to be detected: angels, spirits and the devil (1 Jn 3:8-10; 4:1-6; cf. 1QS 3:13-14, 20-22; 5:20-21, 24; 9:14); love, community and *koinōnia* (1 Jn 1:3-7; 2:9-11; 3:10; 4:7-12; cf. 1QS 1:1, 12, 16; 2:22; 3:12; 5:1; 8:1, 5); knowledge (in 1 Jn, *oida* is used eleven times and *ginōskō* fourteen times; cf. 1QS 4:26; 1QH 12:11; 13:18, 19; 14:12, 13, 25; 16:2-7); cleansing from and confession of sin and lies (1 Jn 1:6-10; 2:13; cf. 1QS 1:23-26; 4:20-22; 11:9-10; 1QH 1:21-26; 3:23-25; 17:18-19); and hatred of the world (1 Jn 3:13; cf. 1QH 2:12-17, 23-25; 3:6-8; 4:7-27; 5:1-32).

From this comparison 1 John is not to be regarded as a theological development of Qumran theology, despite the many similarities. Rather, the parallels are useful insofar as they help elucidate the first-century Palestinian and Jewish mindset. We are once more reminded that the writers of the NT did not express themselves in a cultural vacuum but were in conversation with contemporary religious ideas and language.

See also JAMES; JUDE; OLD TESTAMENT IN GENERAL EPISTLES; 1 PETER.

BIBLIOGRAPHY. R. Bauckham, "James, 1 and 2 Peter, Jude" in *It Is Written: Scripture Citing Scripture. Essays in Honour of B. Lindars,* ed. D. A. Carson and H. G. M. Williamson (Cambridge: Cambridge University Press, 1988) 303-17; R. Beckwith, *The Old Testament Canon of the New Testament Church and Its Background in Early Judaism* (Grand Rapids: Eerdmans, 1985); J. D. Charles, *Literary Strategy in the Epistle of Jude* (Scranton, PA: University of Scranton; London and Toronto: Associated University Presses, 1993); idem, "The Use of Tradition-Material in the Epistle of Jude," *BBR* 4 (1994) 1-14; J. H. Charlesworth, *The Old Testament Pseudepigrapha and the New Testament* (Cambridge: Cambridge University Press, 1985); A. Chester and R. P. Martin, *The Theology of the Letters of James, Peter and Jude* (NTT; Cambridge: Cambridge University Press, 1994); P. Davids, "Tradition and Citation in the Epistle of James" in *Scripture, Tradition and Interpretation,* ed. W. W. Gasque and W. S. LaSor (Grand Rapids: Eerdmans, 1978) 113-26; E. E. Ellis, *Prophecy and Hermeneutic in Early Christianity* (WUNT 18; Tübingen: J. C. B. Mohr, 1978); C. A. Evans, *Noncanonical Writings and New Testament Interpretation* (Peabody, MA: Hendrickson, 1992); J. T. Forestell, *Targumic Traditions and the New Testament: An Annotated Bibliography with a New Testament Index* (SBLAS 4; Chico, CA: Scholars Press, 1979); M. Gertner, "Midrashim in the New Testament," *JSS* 7 (1962) 267-92; T. A. Hoffman, "1 John and the Qumran Scrolls," *BTB* 8 (1978) 117-25; R. N. Longenecker, *Biblical Exegesis in the Apostolic Period* (Grand Rapids: Eerdmans, 1975); M. McNamara, *Targum and Testament: Aramaic Paraphrases of the Hebrew Bible: A Light on the New Testament* (Grand Rapids: Eerdmans, 1982); J. H. Neyrey, "The Form and Background of the Polemic in 2 Peter," *JBL* 99 (1980) 407-31; W. L. Schutter, *Hermeneutic and Composition in 1 Peter* (Tübingen: J. C. B. Mohr, 1989); H. L. Strack and P. Billerbeck, *Kommentar zum Neuen Testament aus Talmud und Midrasch* (4 vols.; Munich: Beck, 1922-28). J. D. Charles

O

OBEDIENCE AND LAWLESSNESS

The particular words *obedience (hypakoē)* and *lawlessness (anomia)* do not occur much in the General Epistles and Revelation (*see* Revelation, Book of). In fact the noun *obedience* is found only in 1 Peter* (1 Pet 1:2, 14, 22), and the verb is restricted to Hebrews 5:9; 11:8 and 1 Peter 3:6. The word *lawlessness* and its cognates appears only in Hebrews 1:9; 10:17; 2 Peter 2:8 and 1 John 3:4. From this evidence we could easily come to the mistaken conclusion that the concepts of obedience and lawlessness are of little significance in our literature. Drawing such an inference highlights the danger of relying upon word studies to establish the theology of biblical writers, for a careful examination of the contents of the General Epistles and Revelation reveals that the concepts of obedience and lawlessness are central to the thinking of virtually every piece of literature in this corpus. Since the necessity of obedience is woven so consistently throughout the literature, we can only touch upon the theme in a cursory way here.

1. Hebrews
2. James
3. 1 Peter
4. 2 Peter and Jude
5. 1 John
6. Revelation
7. Apostolic Fathers

1. Hebrews.

The letter to the Hebrews* is best characterized as an epistolary exhortation (Heb 13:22) in which the author warns his readers against forsaking the new covenant* established through Jesus Christ by returning to the Jewish cult. The letter is punctuated by exhortations (Heb 2:1-4; 3:7—4:11; 5:11—6:8; 10:26-39; 12:25-29) that warn the readers against the danger of apostasy.* Warnings permeate the letter because of the specific situation that called forth the letter:

the readers were apparently tempted to tone down the distinctiveness of their Christian faith* and to compromise with Judaism*. S. McKnight has rightly argued that these warnings are addressed to the Christian community and that the punishment threatened for apostasy is eternal destruction, although his conclusion that genuine believers may forsake and abandon their salvation* is more controversial (see Grudem for a different view).

The cruciality of obedience, therefore, can scarcely be exaggerated. One of the consistent themes in the warning texts is that if God punished sin* under the Sinai covenant, then the punishment will be even stricter in the covenant inaugurated by Jesus Christ. The theological argumentation contained in Hebrews—in which the superiority of the new covenant over the old is featured—is designed to motivate the believers to continue in obedience. The obedience to which the readers are summoned should not be severed from faith, for Hebrews 10:35—12:3 demonstrates that obedience is rooted in faith. For instance, Abraham's* obedience in leaving his homeland stems from his faith. Faith for the author of Hebrews is in God's promises* and includes the conviction that God rewards "those who seek him" (Heb 11:6). Thus Abraham left his homeland because God promised him a better city and country (Heb 11:10, 13-16). Moses* suffered the indignity of identifying himself with the people of God* because of the promised reward (Heb 11:23-26), and even Jesus obeyed the call to suffer* on the cross* "for the joy set before him" (Heb 12:2).

2. James.

Even though James* does not contain the words *obedience* and *lawlessness,* there is no doubt that his paramount concern is that his readers live out their faith in a concrete and practical manner. Apparently the churches addressed were becoming complacent in their Christian faith, perhaps because they wanted to curry favor with the rich and were experiencing economic hardship in the Christian community (see Jas 1:9-11; 2:1-13; 4:13—5:6). James emphasizes that genuine Christian faith is inseparable from obedience (see Faith and Works). To demonstrate this in detail would require a survey of virtually the entire letter. In any case a sampling of themes reveals that his primary concern is ethical*: enduring trials (Jas 1:2-18); avoiding partiality, which is a sin tantamount to transgression of the law* (Jas 2:1-13, esp. Jas 2:9); proper use of the tongue (Jas 3:1-12); the danger of riches (Jas 1:9-11; 2:2-7; 4:13-17; 5:1-6). The purpose of James could be summarized in his terms, for he emphasizes that people must "do the word" and not just hear it (Jas 1:22-25). Wisdom,* according to James, does not pertain to intellectual ability but is manifested in righteous behavior (Jas 3:13-18). So too, as James says in his most famous passage, faith cannot be separated from works* (Jas 2:14-26). Those who claim to have faith but are lacking in works are deceived. Genuine faith inevitably displays itself in a transformed life. If works are not present, then the only prospect is judgment.* Here James and the author of Hebrews concur on the cruciality of obedience.

3. 1 Peter.

1 Peter* is addressed to churches encountering suffering.* The suffering was probably not a sustained and empire-wide persecution* directed from Rome (see Roman Empire) but sporadic persecution in the provinces. Peter appears to use the term *obedience* in reference to conversion. Obedience is the result (*eis*) of the sanctifying work of the Spirit* and the electing and foreknowing work of God the Father (1 Pet 1:1-2; see Election). Believers are characterized as "obedient children" (1 Pet 1:14; see Sonship, Children), and this obedience is traced back to the initial reception of the truth* (1 Pet 1:22). Nonetheless, Peter summons his readers to a holy lifestyle throughout the letter (see Holiness). His particular concern is that the readers manifest righteousness* in the midst of suffering, and thus he appeals to the example of Christ (1 Pet 2:21-25; 3:18-22). The imperative of obedience is also grounded in the promise of the heavenly inheritance that awaits them (1 Pet 1:3-9). The certainty of this inheritance should motivate the churches to endure the persecutions arising in the social order, which was hostile to the Christian faith (1 Pet 4:4, 12-19).

4. 2 Peter and Jude.

Both 2 Peter and Jude* were written to counteract adversaries* influencing the church. A comparison of Jude and 2 Peter 2 reveals that the issues facing the two writers were remarkably similar but not identical. In both cases the opponents are severely criticized for their licentious and morally loose behavior (see Purity), and such behavior indicates that they will face future judgment (2 Pet 2:20-22; Jude 14-15). Discussion has often centered on whether the opponents were Gnostics,* but the description of the false teachers is too vague to draw any firm conclusion about their identity. The adversaries in 2 Peter can be distinguished from those in Jude in that the former denied the Parousia* (2 Pet 3:3-7).

The readers in both letters are warned about the danger of presuming on God's grace,* for he judged angels* who overreached their appointed station, the world* at the time of Noah, Israel* after saving them from Egypt, and Sodom and Gomorrah (Jude 5-7; 2 Pet 2:4-9). Apostasy warrants eternal judgment, and believers will face the same if they adopt the morally loose lifestyle of the false teachers. Thus Jude commands his readers to "keep themselves in the love of God" (Jude 21), and this cannot be a reality without obedience. 2 Peter summons his readers to practice Christian virtues* (2 Pet 1:5-11), teaching them that this is necessary in order to enter into the kingdom* of Jesus Christ. His coming should motivate believers to holiness and godliness (2 Pet 3:11-18). The absolute necessity of human obedience for eternal reward does not nullify God's grace, for Jude says that it is God "who is able to keep you from stumbling" (Jude 24), which means that he keeps believers from apostasy. Nonetheless, this does not rule out the need for believers to obey, for the word of promise* cannot be used to nullify the threat of judgment.

5. 1 John.

1 John also underscores the importance of obedience in response to the threat of proto-Gnostics who were indifferent to moral issues (1 Jn 1:8) and adopted a docetic* christology* (1 Jn 2:22; 4:3; cf. 2 Jn 7). Those who genuinely know

God keep his commandments* and live the same way Jesus did (1 Jn 2:3-6; 5:2-3). John specifically defines sin as lawlessness in 1 John 3:4, and he goes on to argue that those who are born of God do not practice sin (see 1 Jn 3:4-10; 5:18). This does not mean that believers are sinless (1 Jn 1:6-10) The purpose of Christ's coming was to do away with sin (1 Jn 2:1; 3:5), and sin is no longer the dominating force in the life of the believer since the old age of darkness is passing away and the true light* is now shining (1 Jn 2:8).

6. Revelation.

The book of Revelation contains a theme similar to that of the other writings we have examined, even if the social and theological setting is different. Revelation is likely addressed to churches that were tempted to compromise in order to escape persecution. The persecution involved loss of life for some believers (Rev. 2:13; 17:6: 18:24; 19:2; cf. Rev 16:6; 20:4), although it is doubtful that the persecution was prosecuted and enforced with equal rigor in every part of the empire. Nonetheless it was quite intense, since it threatened believers with loss of life* and imprisonment (cf. Rev 1:9; 2:10). John insists that only those who overcome will obtain the promised reward (Rev 2:7, 11, 17, 26; 3:5, 12, 21). An analysis of these texts indicates that the reward promised refers to eternal life, for those who overcome are promised a tree of life and victory over the second death. Revelation 20:14 demonstrates that the second death is synonymous with the lake of fire, and thus John teaches that obtaining the heavenly inheritance is conditioned upon overcoming. This theme coheres with the purpose of Revelation as a whole, for the readers are called upon to endure even though "Babylon" is implacably opposed to their faith. Those who capitulate will face God's wrath* and torment, but those who endure will enjoy the triumph realized when the new heavens (*see* Heaven) and new earth become a reality (Rev 14:10-12; 21:1—22:5).

7. Apostolic Fathers.

One of the most remarkable passages about the "lawless" is in the *Epistle to Diognetus*.* The lawless and ungodly are declared to be justified in the Son of God, and the author speaks of the "sweet exchange" (*Diogn.* 9.4-5) whereby sinners are justified through the Son. The text is extraordinary because the apostolic fathers typically emphasize that obedience is necessary for eternal life. The "Two Ways" section in both the *Didache** and the *Epistle of Barnabas** stress that obedience is the path of life (*Did.* 1.1—6.2; *Barn.* 18.1—21.1). So too, the *Shepherd of Hermas** says that the lawless will not be saved (*Herm. Vis.* 14.1; 73.6; cf. *Herm. Sim.* 96.1). The author of *1 Clement* offers forgiveness for the lawless if they repent (*1 Clem.* 8.3; 35.4-9; 60.1; cf. *Barn.* 14.5; *see* Clement of Rome). The Shepherd also held out hope for the repentant, although he is famous for his teaching that such repentance* is available only once after baptism.* The *Didache*, in dependence on the apocalyptic* discourse in the Gospels (Mk 13 par.), predicts that lawlessness will increase immediately before the coming of the Lord (*Did.* 16.4; *see* Second Coming).

See also APOSTASY; COMMANDMENTS; DISCIPLINE; ENDURANCE, PERSEVERANCE; FAITH AND WORKS; FORGIVENESS; JUDGMENT; LAW; REWARDS; SIN, WICKEDNESS.

BIBLIOGRAPHY. R. J. Bauckham, *Jude, 2 Peter* (WBC; Waco, TX: Word, 1983); R. E. Brown, *The Epistles of John* (AB; Garden City, NY: Doubleday, 1982); P. H. Davids, *The Epistle of James* (NIGTC; Grand Rapids: Eerdmans, 1982); W. Grudem, "Perseverance of the Saints: A Case Study from Hebrews 6:4-6 and the Other Warning Passages in Hebrews" in *The Grace of God, The Bondage of the Will.* 1: *Biblical and Practical Perspectives on Calvinism*, ed. T. R. Schreiner and B. A. Ware (Grand Rapids: Baker, 1995) 133-82; P. E. Hughes, *A Commentary on the Epistle to the Hebrews*(Grand Rapids: Eerdmans, 1977); S. McKnight, "The Warning Passages in Hebrews," *TJ* 13 (1992) 21-59; R. P. Martin, *James* (WBC; Waco, TX: Word, 1988); D. J. Moo, *The Letter of James* (TNTC; Grand Rapids: Eerdmans, 1985); R. H. Mounce, *The Book of Revelation* (NICNT; Grand Rapids: Eerdmans, 1977).

T. R. Schreiner

ODES OF SOLOMAN. *See* APOCRYPHAL AND PSEUDEPIGRAPHAL WRITINGS; HYMNS, SONGS; SYRIA, SYRIAN CHRISTIANITY.

OFFERINGS. See SACRIFICE, OFFERINGS, GIFTS.

OLD TESTAMENT IN ACTS

Use of the OT in the NT is one of the most debated aspects of NT study outside of the Gospels. When we refer to the OT, we use the term anachronistically. In the time of Jesus what we know as the OT often was simply called "the Scripture." The term described the venerated writings of Israel. There is much agreement on the nature of the OT text appearing in Acts,* on the forms some passages reflect and even on the topics that such citations address. However, there is much debate about the Lukan hermeneutics. This article examines the text of the citations, the topics covered, the forms of OT use and the nature of Luke's hermeneutic.

1. The Text of Old Testament Citations in Acts
2. The Topics of Old Testament Use
3. The Forms of Old Testament Use
4. The Type of Hermeneutics

1. The Text of Old Testament Citations in Acts.
There is considerable consensus that in most cases Luke has used an OT text much like the manuscript A text of the Septuagint. This consensus ranges from studies done early in the twentieth century (Clarke) to those done much later (Holtz). T. Holtz's detailed study saw Luke as so consistent in using a Septuagint text that any significant deviation was automatically evidence for the use of traditional material. Such a source is clearest in the Twelve Prophets and in Isaiah. The only place where one is less certain is with regard to the Pentateuch, while the use of the Psalms exhibit a greater degree of variation than do other books.

2. The Topics of Old Testament Use.
C. K. Barrett has argued that three topics dominate OT discussion: preaching* (Acts 2:17-21, 25-28, 34-35; 3:22-23, 25; 7:3, 5-7, 18, 27-28, 32-35, 37, 40, 42-43; 8:32-33; 13:22, 33-35, 41), prayer* (Acts 4:25-26) and direction for the church's* life (Acts 1:16, 20; 13:47; 15:16-18; 23:5; 28:26-27). These are good general categories, but more detail is possible (Evans).

In fact most texts are christological,* emphasizing Jesus as the fulfillment of messianic and Davidic hope* or highlighting how he fulfills promises* associated with the end-time activity of God* or a righteous sufferer (see Righteousness; Suffering Servant). The Psalter, Isaiah, Joel and Amos are keys to this portrait (Ps 2:7 in Acts 13:33; Ps 16:10 in Acts 2:25-28, 13:35; Ps 110:1 in Acts 2:34-35; Ps 118:22 in Acts 4:11; Ps 132:11 in Acts 2:30; Is 53:7-8 in Acts 8:32-33; Is

55:3 in Acts 13:34; Amos 9:11-12 in Acts 15:15-17; Joel 2:28-32 in Acts 2:17-21). In addition Acts 3:18-21 highlights the general promises of Scripture in indicating that, as Israel's Messiah, all that Jesus did not fulfill in his first coming, he will realize in his return.

Drawing on themes already raised in Luke 1:76-79; 2:30-32; 3:3-6; and 4:18-20, Luke uses the image of light* to declare that the church's message is to go out to all nations (Is 49:6 in Acts 13:47; see Gentiles). In this text (Acts 13:47) Paul and Barnabas use the servant imagery to refer to their own ministry* rather than that of Jesus, as does Luke's Gospel, though undoubtedly this use of the imagery connects their ministry to him.

Other texts serve to explain how Israelite unbelief should not be a surprise but reflects a divine pattern of either Israel's or humanity's response to God (Ps 2:1-2 in Acts 4:25-26; Is 6:9-10 in Acts 28:25-28; the various allusions in Acts 7, where the theme is stated in Acts 7:51-53). According to Stephen* (Acts 7), Israel's misunderstanding of the role of the tabernacle* or temple* reflects such a pattern.

Some texts warn of the danger of unbelief and urge response to the gospel* as a result (Deut 18:19 in Acts 3:23; Lev 23:29 in Acts 3:23; Hab 1:5 in Acts 13:41). It is a dangerous thing to scoff at God's work. Judgment* and separation from God loom for those who do not accept the gospel.

A few texts indicate how those who hear the speeches should not respond (Amos 5:25-27 in Acts 7:42-43; Is 66:1-2 in Acts 7:49-50). The point is to learn from history and not make the same error. Israel is the predominant audience for such points. The use of Isaiah 6 in Acts 28:25-28 seems to fit here also.

Peter's appeal to Scripture serves as a guide to the replacement of an enemy from within, namely, Judas (Acts 1:19-20 citing Ps 69:26 and 109:8, possibly also an allusion to Ps 41:10). A lack of surprise at opposition emerges when one reflects on Psalm 2:1-2, as the prayer of Acts 4:25-26 indicates. To be opposed is to stand in God's will. One need only be bold. This latter text shows that some passages can perform two functions at one, since this text also is used to explain opposition. James's advice to leave the Gentiles alone when it comes to circumcision is fueled by his appeal to Amos 9:11-12 as evidence that God would include the Gentiles when the authority* of the Davidic house was restored. The use of Exodus 22:7 appears to argue for the showing of respect to those Jewish leaders who persecute* believers.

The Scripture is put to a wide array of use in Acts, though most uses concentrate on describing who Jesus is and the reactions to him among various groups. Our survey has concentrated on citations. Luke loves to cite the OT in summary as well, speaking of what the OT or what the prophets* since Samuel have taught (e.g., Acts 3:24; 26:22). Such general appeals and allusions usually accompany texts making christological points (Acts 10:42-43; 17:30-31).

3. The Forms of Old Testament Use.

Two speeches are singled out here for treatment. Acts 13:16-41 is seen as the early Christian equivalent to the synagogue* *proem* homily (Bowker, Bruce). The *proem* is a type of bridge text that linked together the Torah reading and the reading from the Prophets during the synagogue service. This third text served to expound the theme raised by the two other passages and make their point clear. 1 Samuel 13:14, cited in its targumic form, is seen as the bridge text for connecting Deuteronomy 4:25-46 and 2 Samuel 7:6-16 in Acts 13. This speech then is an exposition of Israel's history in light of God's promise to David and its initial fulfillment in Jesus, though we are less than certain what the base texts were.

A second form is sometimes mentioned in association with Acts 15 and James's remarks. Some appeal here to the *yelamedenu* ("let the [rabbi] teach") speech form, in which a teacher tackles a practical problem scripturally and comes to a conclusion. In Acts 15 the problem concerns what to do about the Gentiles. James reasons his way to not requiring circumcision of them though his appeal to Amos 9:11-15. The possible evidence of remnants of these forms may well suggest the age and ancient quality of the traditions they represent.

In addition one should note the use of link words to bind the argument of passages together. This happens frequently throughout Luke-Acts, but three speeches give significant use of the technique. The first, Acts 2:16-40, has several such links between texts or between texts and exposition. The term "pour out" appears in Acts 2:17 and Acts 2:33. The title *Lord* appears in Acts 2:21 and Acts 2:36. The term *Hades* links

Acts 2:27 with Acts 2:31. The concept of being seated or set on a throne ties together Acts 2:30 and Acts 2:34, linking an allusion to Psalm 132:11 to Psalm 110:1. The concept of "at the right hand" links Acts 2:33 and Acts 2:34. The combination of links argues that the initial fulfillment of the promise of the Spirit's (*see* Holy Spirit) distribution is evidence of Jesus' ascension to authority in fulfillment of ancient promises made to David. Acts 13, the second speech, has similar links, as the concept of "holy things" (Is 55:3) and "holy one" (Ps 16:10) unite Acts 13:34-35 to make a similar point about Jesus fulfilling Davidic hope. The third example is Acts 15, in which "Gentiles" ties together Acts 15:17 and Acts 15:19. Again the realization of Davidic hope is in view, since the nations are included as a result of rebuilding the Davidic dwelling. These texts evidence basic Jewish technique in expounding the Scripture. The promises of old are fulfilled in Christ.

4. The Type of Hermeneutics.

There are two major schools of thought about the hermeneutics of Luke. Some have argued that Luke took his view of events and used the language of Scripture as a hermeneutical tool to explain current events without appeal to straight-line promise and fulfillment (Rese, Soards). Some have argued in addition that Luke told his story, framing it in language where Scripture is imitated (Brodie). This latter variant argues that Luke rewrote and retold the OT story through the event associated with Jesus.

Others have argued that Luke used Scripture as one of the major means of explaining how the plan of God works and in doing so appealed to fulfillment through prophecy* and the historic pattern (or typology) of God's activity (Schubert, Bock; Evans and Sanders speak of "prophetic critique" in many of Luke's uses of the text). This approach recognizes that Luke's use of the text is often reflective, so that the events frequently triggered the awareness of fulfillment. It also argues that the texts used were already being used in Judaism* as texts that expected fulfillment with the arrival of promised salvation.* The events surrounding Jesus are told in the language and idiom of Scripture, but it is the story of Jesus, not that of the OT, that is being told in these terms. The repetition serves to reveal the presence of the pattern of God's activity, which itself points to fulfillment. This latter approach is more satis-factory in understanding Luke's appeal to Scripture, especially as he seeks to validate Christianity's claim to be God's way in the face of debate over the nature of the OT hope.

A key issue in this debate is whether typology, being a comparative category, is seen as a pro-phetic category. C. H. Talbert has argued that it is not a prophetic category. But the question is a complicated one. Are comparisons made be-cause after the fact one matches event to Scrip-ture and so the exercise is fundamentally retrospective? Or do texts have an interpreta-tion in Judaism that creates an expectation of certain kinds of events that come with fulfill-ment, so that when the event comes it is associ-ated with the hope of the text? Many of the texts Luke uses fall into this latter category (e.g., Deut 18; Joel 2, Is 61; Ps 2, 110, 118, 132). This would seem to indicate that such texts were read in the first century as describing a prophetic fulfillment. Other texts, where the Christian reading appears to be unique, also seem to parallel such Jewish expectations, though it does seem likely that events became a catalyst to their recognition (Is 53, though the idea of a representative death did exist in Judaism [Wis 2—5]). Other texts appeal to the repetitions of certain patterns of activity in history (Amos 5; Is 66). They prove nothing either way.

Luke's juxtaposition of the plan of God with Scripture is an appeal to design and expectation that one should appreciate upon reflection on the events. Prophecy to be prophetic need not always be anticipatory, since sometimes God reveals himself through the saving event itself which causes one to see better how his plan holds together. Thus the prospective-retrospec-tive test for defining a prophetic presence is not a good one. It is better to see how Luke frames his texts by how he appeals to God's activity being defined as present and anticipated through what God had previously said. Proph-ecy or pattern fulfillment need not be a straight-line interpretive approach to be present. If we listen to him carefully, we will see the design in what God planned to do and did in Jesus.

See also ACTS OF THE APOSTLES; INTERTEXTU-ALITY IN EARLY CHRISTIAN LITERATURE.

BIBLIOGRAPHY. C. K. Barrett, "Luke/Acts" in *It Is Written: Scripture Citing Scripture: Essays in Honour of Barnabas Lindars*, ed. D. A. Carson and H. G. M. Williamson (Cambridge: Cam-bridge University Press, 1988) 231-44; D. L. Bock, "Framing the Account: Alleviating Confu-sion in the Lukan Portrait of Jesus" in *SBLSP* (1994) 612-26; idem, *Proclamation from Prophecy and Pattern: Lukan Old Testament Christology* (JSNTS 12; Sheffield: Sheffield Academic Press, 1987); J. Bowker, "Speeches in Acts: A Study in Proem and Yelammedenu Form," *NTS* 14 (1967-68) 96-111; T. L. Brodie, *Luke the Literary Interpreter: Luke-Acts as a Systematic Rewriting and Updating of the Elisha-Elijah Narrative* (Rome: Pontifical University of St. Thomas Aquinas, 1987); F. F. Bruce, "Paul's Use of the Old Testa-ment in Acts" in *Tradition and Interpretation in the New Testament: Essays in Honor of E. E. Ellis*, ed. G. F. Hawthorne with O. Betz (Grand Rapids; Eerdmans, 1987) 71-79; W. K. L. Clarke, "The Use of the Septuagint in Acts" in *The Beginnings of Christianity*, 1: *The Acts of the Apostles*, ed. F. J. F. Jackson and K. Lake (5 vols.; Grand Rapids: Baker, 1979 [1922]) 2:66-105; C. A. Evans and J. A. Sanders, *Luke and Scripture* (Minneapolis: Fortress, 1993); T. Holtz, *Untersuchungen über die alttestamentlichen Zitate bei Lukas* (TU 104; Berlin: Akademie Verlag, 1968); M. Rese, *Alttestamen-tliche Motive in der Christologie des Lukas* (SNT 1; Gerd Mohn: Gütersloher Verlagshaus, 1969); P. Schubert, "The Structure and Significance of Luke 24" in *Neutestamentliche Studien für Rudolf Bultmann zu seinem siebzigsten Geburtstag am 20. August 1954*, ed. W. Eltester (BZNW 21; Berlin: Alfred Töpelmann, 1954); M. Soards, *The Speeches of Acts: Their Contents, Context and Con-cerns* (Louisville, KY: Westminster/John Knox, 1994); C. H. Talbert, "Promise and Fulfillment in Lukan Theology" in *Luke-Acts: New Perspectives from the Society of Biblical Literature*, ed. C. H. Talbert (New York: Crossroad, 1984).

D. L. Bock

OLD TESTAMENT IN APOSTOLIC FATHERS

Apostolic fathers is an artificial category, both historically and literarily, for the noncanonical but orthodox Christian writings nearest in time to the NT. Although diverse in purpose, geo-graphical location and type of literature, they exhibit a substantial agreement about the OT as the Word of God,* inspired by God's Spirit (*see* Holy Spirit) and constituting the Scriptures of the church. In common with other early Christian literature but unlike Jewish literature, they make greater use of the Prophets (especially Isaiah) and the Writings (especially the Psalms) than the Law. The two writings that make the most extensive use of the OT, *1 Clement* and *Barnabas,* permit conclusions to be drawn about the authority* of the OT and its interpretation.

1. *Didache*
2. *Barnabas*
3. *1 Clement*
4. *2 Clement*
5. The *Shepherd of Hermas*
6. Polycarp
7. Ignatius
8. Alternatives and Relationships

1. *Didache*.
The manual of church life and order known as the *Didache** ("The Teaching of the Lord Through the Twelve Apostles to the Nations") is saturated with the Jewish environment, from the moral instruction of the "Two Ways" at the beginning of the work to the apocalyptic* picture in the last chapter. The language of the OT, especially the Wisdom Literature, is readily used as part of that Jewish context but with little explicit quotation.

1.1. Quotations. The *Didache* contains three formula quotations, introduced by "It was [or, has been] spoken" rather than "written." Two of these are from the prophets*—Malachi 1:11, 14 cited as "spoken by the Lord" (*Did.* 14.3) and Zechariah 14:5 (*Did.* 16.7)—and one is from an unknown source (*Did.* 1.6, "Let your alms sweat in your hands until you know to whom you give"—cf. Sir 12:1; 7:22). The "Two Ways" (*Did.* 1.2) begins with a quotation of the two commandments* to love* God (Deut 6:5) and to love your neighbor (Lev 19:18) as refracted through Jesus' teaching.* The language of the two ways of life* and death itself is taken from the OT (Jer 21:8; cf. Deut 30:15-20). The content of the "Two Ways" (*Did.* 2-5) is an expansion of the Ten Commandments (Ex 20; Deut 5).

1.2. Phrases and Allusions. The *Didache* draws on imagery from Judaism*—"yoke of the Lord" (*Did.* 6.2); "holy vine of David your servant" (*Did.* 9.2)—and refers to institutions and practices in Judaism—fasting (*Did.* 8); first fruits (*Did.* 13); sacrifices* (*Did.* 14.1); priests* (*Did.* 13.3). In addition phrases from the OT are often picked up: "the snare of death" (Prov 14:27; 21:6 in *Did.* 2.4); "fearing [my] words" (Is 66:2; *Did.* 3.8); "judge righteously" (Deut 1:16,

17; Prov 31:9; *Did.* 4.3); "neither adding to nor taking away" (Deut 4:2; 12:32 [13:1 LXX]; *Did.* 4.13); "loving vanity" (Ps 4:3; *Did.* 5.2); and "pursuing a reward" (Is 1:23; *Did.* 5.2). Such phrases may have been in common use so that a specific biblical allusion was not in mind. Where the same phrase is in the OT and the NT we cannot determine the immediate source, especially since these are in Matthew, with which the *Didache* has closest affinities: "for the meek shall inherit the earth" (Ps 37:11 [36:11 LXX]; Mt 5:5; *Did.* 3.7); "four winds" (Zech 2:6 [2:10 LXX]; Mt 24:31; *Did.* 10.5); "who comes in the name of the Lord" (Ps 118:26 [117:26 LXX]; Mt 21:9; *Did.* 12.1).

Several phrases come from the wisdom books of the Apocrypha*: "love . . . your Creator" (Sir 7:30; *Did.* 1.2); "Do not be one who extends his hands to receive but closes his fist to give" (paraphrased—Sir 4:31; *Did.* 4.5); "do not turn away from the needy" (Sir 4:5; *Did.* 4.8); "murderers of children" (Wis 12:5; *Did.* 5.2). Where a phrase is frequent in Jewish and Christian sources, as "He created all things" (Wis 1:14; Sir 18:1; 24:8; cf. Rev 4:11; *Did.* 10.3), it may have been a common expression (especially in worship*) that was not drawn immediately from a written source.

From these quotations and allusions it is impossible to determine the limits of the Didachist's canon, for he not only appropriates but also lives in the whole world of the Jewish heritage, and in this work he was not concerned to make an explicit differentiation between canonical and noncanonical.

2. *Barnabas*.
2.1. Relation to Judaism. The *Epistle of Barnabas,** like the *Didache*, contains the teaching of the "Two Ways," but instead of the biblical language of "the way of life and way of death" (Jer 21:8) the author speaks of "the ways of light and darkness" (*Barn.* 18.1, as at Qumran*—1QS 3.18-25; 1QM). Both documents breathe the atmosphere of Judaism, but *Barnabas*, unlike the *Didache*, has a strong sense of a break with Judaism. *Barnabas* represents an extreme form of the claim that only Christians correctly understand the OT (*Barn.* 8.7; 10.12). In *Barnabas's* community Jews and Christians struggled over who were the people of God: Whose was the covenant* and to whom did the Scriptures belong? *Barnabas's* argument is that

the Jews had misunderstood the Scriptures from the start.

Claiming a special insight into the meaning of Scripture (*Barn.* 1.4-8; 5.3), the author takes the position otherwise unknown in early Christianity that God did not intend the literal observance of the law,* charging that the Jews had fashioned their own religious observances contrary to the will of God. His is perhaps the strongest assertion in this literature that the OT is a Christian book. He discusses the principal institutions and religious practices of Judaism: God does not need sacrifices (*Barn.* 2), and the true atonement is the death of Christ (*Barn.* 7—8; *see* Death of Christ); the acceptable fast is good deeds (*Barn.* 3); circumcision is of the heart and the hearing (*Barn.* 9); the food laws* prohibit association with immoral persons (*Barn.* 10; *see* Purity); the true washing is baptism* (*Barn.* 11); there is only one covenant, given to Christians and not to Jews (*Barn.* 13-14); the sabbath is really the eschatological* rest (hence, Christians keep the "eighth day," *Barn.* 15); the true temple* is the heart and the believing community (*Barn.* 16). All is buttressed with scriptural quotations.

2.2. Quotations. The argument of *Barnabas* has to do with the OT. There are approximately 100 explicit quotations of Scripture. The most frequently quoted books are Isaiah (about one-fourth), the Pentateuch (especially Genesis) and Psalms. These were also favorite books in the NT and other Christian literature. "Scripture says" introduces quotations from the three parts of the Hebrew Bible: Law (*Barn.* 4.7; Ex 34:28; 31:18), Prophets (*Barn.* 4.11; Is 5:21) and Writings (*Barn.* 5.4; Prov 1:7). Two quotations are from outside the Hebrew canon: "Another prophet says," introducing 4 Ezra 4:33; 5:5 (*Barn.* 12.1) and "Scripture says," referring to *1 Enoch* 89:56, 66, 67 (*Barn.* 16.5). The use of Sirach 4:31 (*Barn.* 19.9) may be due to its earlier presence in the "Two Ways." Two other quotations are unknown (*Barn.* 6.13, introduced by "The Lord says," and *Barn.* 7.8, perhaps a commentary on Lev 16:21-22). An example of a quotation in an expanded, interpreted form comes from Exodus 20:8, "Sanctify the sabbath of the Lord with pure hands and a pure heart" (*Barn.* 15.1, 6).

In the introductory formulas the author prefers verbs of speaking over writing (so for other authors in this literature) and prefers the pre-

sent tense, emphasizing that the word is addressing people in the present.

Although the formula quotations show respect for the OT as the Word of God, there are arbitrary uses of the Scriptures. Some are intentional changes in the wording of texts. In *Barnabas* 5.12 Zechariah 13:6-7 is quoted, "When they smite their shepherd, then the sheep of the flock will perish," stressing the responsibility of the Jews ("their") for Christ's death and making the verse say that the Jews themselves will be destroyed. In *Barnabas* 11.2 Jeremiah 2:12-13 is quoted as "this people" rather than "my people" to avoid saying that Israel* was God's people. In *Barnabas* 13.4-6 Genesis 48:14-15 is quoted so as to have Jacob bless only Ephraim, the younger son, and not Ephraim and Manasseh. *Barnabas* furthermore ignores certain facts, as the giving of a second set of the tablets of stone and so a renewing of the covenant with Israel (Ex 34:1-10; *Barn.* 4.6-8).

2.3. Authority and Interpretation. Scripture for the author of *Barnabas* is clearly authoritative, giving both revelation* (e.g., *Barn.* 1.7; 2.4; 3.6; 5.3; 7.1) and commands (e.g., *Barn.* 6.1; 7.3, 6; 8.1; 9.5; 10.2; 12.6; 14.6; 21.1). God speaks through Scripture (*Barn.* 1.7; 2.4, 9). The divine origin is indicated by the frequency with which the speaker is said to be the Lord* (*Barn.* 4.8; 6.16; 9.1 [twice]; 14.3; 16.2) or God (*Barn.* 5.5, 12), but sometimes the human author is specified—Moses* (e.g., *Barn.* 10.1), David (e.g., *Barn.* 10.10), Isaiah (*Barn.* 12.11) or Daniel (*Barn.* 4.5). All of Scripture is seen as prophetic* (*Barn.* 6.4, 6, 7, 8, 13; 12.10; 13.4). The Holy Spirit is the Spirit who prophesies (*Barn.* 9.2). Scripture speaks of Christ: "The prophets who received grace from him prophesied of him" (*Barn.* 5.6) "because all things are in him and for him" (*Barn.* 12.7). Moreover, Christ himself speaks in Scripture: The "Lord" in *Barnabas* 6.16 and *Barnabas* 7.2-3 is Christ.

In some texts *Barnabas* finds his prophetic message in the literal meaning of the text (*Barn.* 2—3; 4.7-8; 6.18). The author sometimes follows the usual Christian reading of the OT prophecies about Christ and his sufferings* (*Barn.* 5.1—6.7). Perhaps most characteristic of *Barnabas* is his typological* reading of the OT story: *typos* ("type") is a favorite word (*Barn.* 7.3, 7, 10, 11; 8.1-2; 12.2; 12.5-6; 12.10; 13.5). Although he understands the events to have occurred, they had no historical significance except as prophetic types; the history happened in order to be a prophecy. Instances of allegory in the strict sense are not as numerous as usually assumed. Most often noted are the interpretations of the forbidden foods as types of persons whom one is to avoid (*Barn.* 10) and of the 318 servants of Abraham as referring to Christ and him crucified (*Barn.* 9). Unlike most allegorical interpretations, for *Barnabas* there were not multiple meanings in the text, not an obvious plus a deeper meaning; for him there was only one meaning, the spiritual sense. More than claiming that the ordinances of Israel had been abrogated (*Barn.* 2.6; 9.4; 16.2), *Barnabas* presents the spiritualizing interpretation as the real, intended meaning of the text from the beginning (*Barn.* 2.7-8; 9.4; 16.6). Moses "legislated well," but he did so "spiritually," "as the Lord intended" (*Barn.* 10.2, 9, 12).

The context of discussion with the Jews is made evident in the way Barnabas distributes the texts between the "two peoples" (see *Barn.* 13.2): "For what has been written . . . relates in part to Israel and in part to us" (*Barn.* 5.2). The literal or negative words are those addressed "to them," the Jews (*Barn.* 2.7; 3.1; 5.2; 6.8; 9.5; 10.2; 12.7); the positive, spiritual words are addressed "to us," the Christians (*Barn.* 2.4; 2.10; 3.3; 5.2; 6.13; 9.1-3). *Barnabas* distances himself from "their law" (3.6) but claims the covenant for Christians (*Barn.* 4.6-7). Instead of a new covenant he speaks of a "new people" (*Barn.* 5.7; 7.5).

3. 1 Clement.

3.1. Quotations and Allusions.

OT quotations or allusions pervade the letter of the church at Rome* to the church at Corinth known as *1 Clement* (*see* Clement of Rome). The approximately seventy direct quotations constitute about one-fourth of this long epistle, making it second only to Barnabas among the apostolic fathers in the frequency of quotation from the OT. Allusions and examples drawn from the OT and Apocrypha would increase this percentage considerably. For instance, the prayer* in *1 Clement* 59—61 may be described as a pastiche of phrases from the Septuagint. Some of the quotations are lengthy. Psalms, Isaiah, Job, Genesis and Proverbs, in this order, are the most frequently cited. The heavy use of Job and Proverbs is unusual in comparison with the NT and

Christian literature generally in the early period. Nearly all the quotations have introductory phrases; these include "It is written" and various forms of "It says."

Although some of the quotations vary widely from the Septuagint, thirty-nine are essentially verbatim and nine moderately variant. *1 Clement* four times quotes documents we do not know: *1 Clement* 8.3 (following a quotation from Ezek 33:11, so this may be a paraphrase of Ezek 33:11-27, an interpolated version or an Ezekiel Apocryphon); *1 Clement* 17.6 (ascribed to Moses); *1 Clement* 23.3-4 (also found in *2 Clem.* 11.2-4, which has an additional sentence); *1 Clement* 46.2.

No conflict with Judaism is in evidence in *1 Clement*. Sometimes the author derives doctrinal lessons from the OT: for example, *1 Clement* 26 supports the resurrection by a catena of references (Ps 27:7; 3:6; 22:4 LXX; Job 19:26) given an overly literal interpretation in the fashion of some rabbinic interpretations. The regulations of the OT priesthood serve as a model for the Christian ministry* (*1 Clem.* 41). The author primarily uses the OT for moral and practical purposes.

3.2. Arrangement of Materials.

For each of the attitudes or qualities that the author of *1 Clement* considers the Corinthians to need, he cites biblical passages and gives examples. Although the examples include Gentiles* (*1 Clem.* 55) and Christian figures (*1 Clem.* 5—6), the great majority come from the OT. In the treatment of the topics in *1 Clement* we can likely observe the method of preaching* and teaching that Clement employed in church.

1 Clement 4 cites seven instances in their biblical order where jealousy enters the story—Cain and Abel; Jacob and Esau; Joseph and his brothers; Moses, Aaron and Miriam; Dathan and Abiram; David and Saul (*1 Clem.* 4)—followed by seven statements of what jealousy had caused, citing both pagan and Christian examples (*1 Clem.* 5—6). The treatment of repentance* (*1 Clem.* 7—8) cites two examples of OT preachers of repentance, Noah and Jonah (*1 Clem.* 7.6-7), and quotes two texts, a paraphrase of Ezekiel 33:11-27 and Ezekiel 18:32 (or an Ezekiel Apocryphon) joined with Isaiah 1:16-20 (*1 Clem.* 8.3-4). *1 Clement* 9—12 brings together obedience,* faith* and hospitality* as interrelated qualities. Seven examples are given: Enoch (*1 Clem.* 9.3), Noah (*1 Clem.* 9.4), Abraham* three times (*1 Clem.* 10.1; 10.2; 10.7), Lot (*1 Clem.* 11.1-2) and Rahab (*1 Clem.* 12.1-7).

Humility is taught in *1 Clement* 13—15 by a combination of OT texts (Jer 9:23-24; Is 66:2; Prov 2:21-22 [cf. Ps 36:9, 38]; Ps 36:35-37; Is 29:13; Ps 61:5; 77:36-37; 30:19; 11:4-6 LXX) with sayings of Jesus (*1 Clem.* 13.2) and in *1 Clement* 16—18 by the examples of Christ (Is 53 quoted in entirety as an indication of Christ's humility), three prophets (Elijah, Elisha and Ezekiel) and four others (Abraham, Job, Moses and David). The pattern followed is to state why the hero may be regarded as approved by God and then to cite passages that give evidence of his humility: Abraham (Is 41:8 contrasted with Gen 18:27), Job (Job 1:1 contrasted with Job 14:4-5), Moses (Num 12:7 contrasted with Ex 3:11; 4:10 and an unknown source); David (1 Sam 13:14; Ps 88:21 contrasted with Ps 50:3-19 LXX). Scriptures on confession of sin* and praying for forgiveness* are brought together in *1 Clement* 52—53 (Ps 68:31-33; 49:14-15; 50:19 LXX; Ex 32:7-10, 31-32; Deut 9:12-14).

3.3. Doctrine of Scripture. Of the apostolic fathers *1 Clement* offers the fullest doctrine of Scripture. The sacred and authoritative character of the OT books is affirmed both by introductory formulas ("The Holy Spirit says," *1 Clem.* 13.1, quoting Jer 9:23-24; *1 Clem.* 16.2, quoting Is 53:1-12) and by descriptions ("the holy word," *1 Clem.* 13.3, introducing Is 66:2, and *1 Clem.* 56.3, introducing Ps 117:18 LXX; and "sacred Scriptures . . . and oracles of God," *1 Clem.* 53.1). A particularly strong statement occurs in *1 Clement* 45.2-3: "You searched deeply into the sacred Scriptures, which are true and given by the Holy Spirit. You know that nothing unjust or counterfeit is written in them."

Christ is of supreme importance for Clement (*1 Clem.* 13.1-2). The OT speaks of Christ (e.g., Is 53 in *1 Clem.* 16.2; cf. *1 Clem.* 17.1 of other prophets and the passages quoted in *1 Clem.* 36); and Christ himself speaks in the OT, especially the Psalms (*1 Clem.* 16.15-16, quoting Ps 21:7-9; and *1 Clem.* 22.1, "He himself through the Holy Spirit exhorted us," followed by Ps 33:12-18 and 31:10 LXX). His words are quoted alongside the words of the OT as something to be remembered (*1 Clem.* 13.2; 46.7-8).

1 Clement, in warning against opposition to the righteous, appeals in sequence to "the sacred Scriptures" (the OT, *1 Clem.* 45.2), "the words of Jesus our Lord" (*1 Clem.* 46.7) and "the

epistle of the blessed Paul the apostle" (*1 Clem.* 47.1). The order may not be important, but it corresponds to the triad of prophets, Lord and apostles* frequently found in works of the early writers. Clement makes a twofold summary of the OT when he refers to what "Moses signified in the sacred books, whom the other prophets followed, testifying to the laws laid down by him" (*1 Clem.* 43.1). He seems to refer to the third division of the Hebrew Scriptures (the Writings) when he identifies Psalm 138:7-10 (LXX) as found in the "Writing" (*1 Clem.* 28.2-3). Clement's references include some of the Apocrypha: Judith (the person, given as an example along with Esther, *1 Clem.* 55.4-6) and Wisdom of Solomon (*1 Clem.* 3.4; 27.5 citing Wis 2:24; 12:12 respectively without introductory formula).

1 Clement offers some interpretations that can be classified as allegorical and typological. As instances of the former, one may refer to the interpretation of the scarlet cord of Rahab (Josh 2:18) as a prophecy of redemption* through the blood of Christ (*1 Clem.* 12.7) and the interpretation of the "gate" through which the righteous enter (Ps 117:19-20) as Christ (*1 Clem.* 48.2-4). These interpretations are part of the early church's general christological* reading of the OT. As instances of typology* may be cited the parallels to the situation in the church at Corinth drawn from Deuteronomy 32:15 (*1 Clem.* 3.1); Isaiah 3:3-4 (*1 Clem.* 3.5); and Numbers 17 (*1 Clem.* 43). These latter agree with Clement's predominantly paraenetic use of the OT for moral and ecclesiological lessons.

Clement can make a direct application of the OT to the church because for him Israel merges into the church* (*see* Church as Israel) The contrast of his situation and his use of the OT with *Barnabas* may be seen in the different ways they treated the incident in which Moses broke the tablets of the Ten Commandments (Ex 32:7-19; Deut 9:12-17). *1 Clement* 53 refers to the incident in order to prepare for the appeal to the troublemakers at Corinth to depart for the good of the congregation by recalling Moses' willingness to be killed himself in order that the people may be spared. *Barnabas* 4.6-8 sees in the incident the breaking of the covenant between God and Israel so that the covenant of Jesus might be given to Christians.

4. 2 Clement.

The sermon known as *2 Clement* shows less explicit indebtedness to Christianity's Jewish roots in general and the OT in particular. There are several quotations from the OT, but the striking thing is that nearly all of these are also found in the NT.

4.1. Quotations from the Old Testament also in the New Testament.
The formula quotations in *2 Clement* are introduced "[He (or, it)] says [or, said]," but several citations have no introductory formula. The following list notes the use of the same passage in the NT or other early Christian literature: *2 Clement* 2.1 = Isaiah 54:1 (Gal 4:27); *2 Clement* 3.4 = Deuteronomy 6:5 (Mk 12:30 par.); *2 Clement* 3.5 quotes Isaiah 29:13 by name (but closer to Mt 15:8 and Mk 7:6 and identical to *1 Clem.* 15.2); *2 Clement* 7.6 and *2 Clement* 17.5 = Isaiah 66:24 (Mk 9:48, but *2 Clem.* quotes more than Mk does); *2 Clement* 8.2 uses the example of the potter, as does Jeremiah 18:4-6 (Rom 9:19-21); *2 Clement* 13.2 = Isaiah 52:5, including the latter's introductory words, "The Lord says" (close to Ign. *Trall.* 8.2; since the quotation is combined in *2 Clem.* with an unknown quotation, the author has received the quotation from a source other than Isaiah); *2 Clement* 14.1 quotes Jeremiah 7:11 as "Scripture" (Mt 21:13); *2 Clement* 14.2 quotes Genesis 1:27 as "Scripture" (Mk 10:6; the preceding reference in *2 Clem.* to Eph 1:22 makes it possible that Eph 5:31 has pointed the author to the Genesis account). The frequent use *2 Clement* makes of gospel* tradition* adds support to the possibility that the author may have received much of his knowledge of the OT by way of Christian materials.

4.2. Other Quotations.
2 Clement, however, does have citations from the OT that do not have a parallel use in the NT: *2 Clement* 15.3 = Isaiah 58:9, introduced "God says"; *2 Clement* 16.3 = Malachi 4:1 (Mal 3:19 LXX); *2 Clement* 17.4-5 = Isaiah 66:18 (cf. Dan 3:7) and Isaiah 66:24. The phrase in *2 Clement* 17.4, "each according to his works," is in Psalm 61:13 and Proverbs 24:12; *2 Clement* 10.2 is a possible allusion to Psalm 33:15 but is not close, and *2 Clement* 19.3 may allude to Hosea 10:12. *2 Clement* 6.9 may show a familiarity with 4 Ezra 7:102-6, and *2 Clement* 16.4 alludes to Tobit 12:8-9. Some quotations are problematic: *2 Clement* 4.5 is a quotation of unknown origin (it contains a phrase from Is 40:11), but it may derive from a Christian source; *2 Clement* 6.8 quotes Ezekiel 14:14, 20 as Scripture but in a different order and with changed wording, suggesting indirect appropriation or a summary reference; *2 Clement* 11.2 quotes an unidentified "prophetic word" that is also cited but not as extensively in *1 Clement* 23.3-4 (this could be from a Christian prophet; if it is not from a Christian source, a Christian source may have pointed to the passage).

The author of *2 Clement* often cites as authority "the Lord," referring to the teachings of Jesus (*2 Clem.* 3.2; 4.2; 5.2; 6.1; 8.5; 9.11; 12.2). The phrase in *2 Clement* 14.2, "the books and the apostles," refers to two other sources of authoritative teaching, the Jewish Scriptures and the Christian apostles. This phrase anticipates the two-part Christian canon.* For the most part the author is dependent on Christian material, which included OT quotations; but *2 Clement's* own independent use of the OT may have been limited.

5. The *Shepherd of Hermas*.

This work is ascribed to Hermas (*see* Shepherd of Hermas) and in spite of theories of composite authorship may be accepted as the work of one person, perhaps written over a period of two or three decades. The work—containing *Visions, Commandments* (or *Mandates*) and *Parables* (or *Similitudes*)—is an apocalypse in literary form, although it lacks the usual content of apocalyptic literature.

The only quotation by Hermas attributed to its source is to a lost work: "'The Lord is near to those who turn to him,' as it is written in Eldad and Modat, who prophesied to the people in the wilderness" (*Herm. Vis.* 2.3.4 = 7.4 [references will give both the old and the new form of division of the text]). A rare quotation introduced by a formula cites Ecclesiastes 12:13 as "he says" (*Herm. Man.* 7.1 = 37.1). Many phrases, however, are drawn ultimately from the OT: A recent edition cites forty-five. Some occur more than once: "glorify his name" (Ps 85:9, 12 LXX; Is 24:15; 66:5; *Herm. Vis.* 2.1.1 = 5.2; 3.4.3 = 12.3; 4.1.3 = 22.3; *Herm. Sim.* 9.18.5 = 95.5); "cast your cares on the Lord" (Ps 54:23 LXX; 1 Pet 5:7; *Herm. Vis.* 3.11.3 = 19.3; 4.2.4 = 23.4; 4.2.5 = 23.5); "work righteousness" (Ps 14:2 LXX; Acts 10:35; Heb 11:33; *Herm. Vis.* 2.2.7 = 6.7; 2.3.3 = 7.3; *Herm. Man.* 12.3.1 = 46.1; 12.6.2 = 49.2; *Herm. Sim.* 9.13.7 = 90.7).

These and many other phrases sound formulaic and may have come to Hermas through use in liturgy*: "God who dwells in heaven" (Ps 2:4; 122:1 LXX; *Herm. Vis.* 1.1.6 = 1.6); "God of powers" (common in Ps—e.g., 58:6; 79:5; 83:9 LXX; *Herm. Vis.* 1.3.4 = 3.4); "the great King" (Ps 46:3 LXX; *Herm. Vis.* 3.9.8 = 17.8); "trusting in the Lord" (Ps 2:12 and often; *Herm. Man.* 9.6 = 39.6); "fear of the Lord" (Ps 110:10 LXX; Prov 1:7, etc.; *Herm. Man.* 10.6 = 40.6); "sacrifice acceptable to God" (Is 56:7; cf. Sir 35:6; Phil 4:18; *Herm. Sim.* 5.3.8 = 56.8); "righteous Judge" (Ps 7:12 LXX; *Herm. Sim.* 6.3.6 = 63.6); "pure heart" (Ps 50:12 LXX; *Herm. Sim.* 6.3.6 = 63.6).

Some of the ideas that may go back to the OT were proverbial: "tried by fire" (Job 23:10; Prov 17:3; Sir 2:5; 1 Pet 1:7; *Herm. Vis.* 4.3.4 = 24.4); "each according to his deeds" (Ps 61:13 LXX; 2 Cor 5:10; *Herm. Sim.* 6.3.6 = 63.6); "fruit of righteousness" (Prov 3:9; 11:30; frequent in the NT; *Herm. Sim.* 9.19.2 = 96.2).

Understandably, in terms of Hermas's theme, many of his biblical phrases relate to repentance and forgiveness: "he shall heal your sins" (Deut 30:3; cf. Jer 3:22; *Herm. Vis.* 1.1.9 = 1.9); "he has done wickedly before the Lord" (Judg 2:11 and frequently; *Herm. Man.* 4.2.2 = 30.2); "turn to the Lord with your whole heart" (Jer 24:7; Joel 2:12; *Herm. Man.* 6.1.5 = 35.5; 9.2 = 39.2; 12.6.2 = 49.2); "remembering his commandments" (Ps 102:18 LXX; *Herm. Sim.* 1.7 = 50.7).

Even this incomplete listing from Hermas illustrates the extent to which the language of the OT became a part of common Christian speech.

6. Polycarp.

The bishop of Smyrna, Polycarp,* wrote to the church at Philippi a letter that is saturated with the language of the letters of Paul, Peter and John. Making the maximum allowance for Polycarp's dependence on the OT still results in only meager use. Such infrequency would not be surprising in a relatively short letter; it becomes noteworthy when compared with the heavy adoption of language from the NT.

If something is to be made of Polycarp's allusions to the OT, they fit the pattern of other early Christian writings in being mainly dependent on the Prophets, Psalms and Wisdom Literature. Occasional OT phrases are picked up: "serve God with fear" (Ps 2:11; Pol. *Phil.* 2.1 and

6.3; cf. Heb 12:28); "all breath" (Ps 150:6; Pol. *Phil.* 2.1); "his blood is required" (Gen 42:22; Pol. *Phil.* 2.1); "iniquitous things" (Job 27:6; Pol. *Phil.* 5.3); "before God and men" (Prov 3:4; Pol. *Phil.* 6.1); "swift judgment" (Wis 6:5; Pol. *Phil.* 6.1); "do not know the judgment of the Lord" (Jer 5:4; Pol. *Phil.* 11.2); "be angry and do not sin" (Ps 4:5; Pol. *Phil.* 12.1; Eph 4:26). The clearest and fullest use of a passage from the old Scriptures by Polycarp is Tobit 4:10 and Tobit 12:9 in the discussion of almsgiving in *Philippians* 10.2.

The employment of the same brief phrase does not necessarily indicate direct use. Isaiah 52:5 ("name blasphemed"), for instance (Pol. *Phil.* 10.2-3), seemingly had become something of a commonplace (see on *2 Clem.* 13.2 in 4.1 above).

Significant for Polycarp's perspective is the application of Psalm 2:11 ("serve him with fear and all reverence") to Christ and the further expansion, "As he himself commanded, and also the apostles who preached the gospel to us, and the prophets who foretold the coming of our Lord" (Pol. *Phil.* 6.3). This kind of statement is common in the second century of Christians' threefold source of authority: the Lord, the prophets and the apostles. This three-part "canon" centers in the Lord who also spoke through the apostles and prophets. In Polycarp's letter to the Philippians the Jewish heritage and the OT virtually disappear into the Christian message.

7. Ignatius.

Ignatius,* bishop of Antioch,* while a prisoner on his way to martyrdom* in Rome, wrote letters to six churches and one individual (Polycarp). Although he had assistance in the preparation of his correspondence, the circumstances were not conducive to bookish correspondence, so we should not expect careful quotation by Ignatius. His letters are full of NT allusions and parallels, but there are few to the OT.

7.1. Quotations and Allusions to the OT. Ignatius has two quotations introduced "It is written," both to Proverbs (Prov 3:34; Jas 4:6; 1 Pet 5:15; Ign. *Eph.* 5.3; Prov 18:17, Ign. *Magn.* 12.1) and both likely proverbial apart their written source. The clearest allusions to the OT were similarly common tags: "He spoke and it came to be," introduced by reference to the "one Teacher" (Ps 32:9; 148:5 LXX; Jdt 16:4, all with reference to God's creation, Ign. *Eph.* 15.1); "my name is blasphemed" (Is 52:5; cf. Pol. *Phil.* 10.2; Ign. *Trall.* 8.2); "loose every bond" (Is 58:6; Ign. *Phld.* 8.1); "set up an ensign" (Is 5:6; Ign. *Smyrn.* 1.2). "Living water" (Ign. *Rom.* 7.2) more likely comes from John (Jn 4:10; 7:38); at least there is no compelling reason to think Ignatius took this phrase from Zechariah 14:8. Some language of the OT came into the church from its early days and was used in worship and teaching without direct reference to the OT; that could be the case with these quotations and allusions.

7.2. The Prophets. Ignatius conducts a strong polemic against judaizing teachers in the church (Ign. *Phld.* 6) and against Docetists* with a christology that denied the reality of Christ's human flesh,* "whom neither the prophecies nor the law of Moses and not even so far the gospel did persuade" (Ign. *Smyrn.* 5.1). Against these teachers Ignatius claimed the prophets as servants* of Christ and as belonging to the Christians. To live according to Judaism is to confess that one has not received grace,* "For the most divine prophets lived according to Jesus Christ" (Ign. *Magn.* 8.2), and "Even the prophets" were his "disciples in the Spirit" (Ign. *Magn.* 9.2). "We love [or, let us love] the prophets because they announced the gospel, hoped in him, and waited for him, in whom they also having believed in him were saved, being united with Jesus Christ" (Ign. *Phld.* 5.2). Although Ignatius refers to the prophets as persons, he knew them because of their writings and so treats them as a group.

7.3. Authority. As these passages about the prophets indicate, the prophets derived their authority from Christ, and their message was subordinated to him. Ignatius felt that it was "improper" (or "absurd") "to speak of Jesus Christ and to practice Judaism, for Christianity did not base its faith on Judaism but Judaism on Christianity" (Ign. *Magn.* 10.3). Thus he strongly affirms the superiority of the new dispensation over the old. "The priests are noble, but the High Priest [Christ] is better." Christ is the door to the Father for the ancestors,* prophets, apostles and the church: "The gospel has a certain preeminence. . . . The beloved prophets pointed to Christ, but the gospel is the completion of immortality" (Ign. *Phld.* 9.1-2). Hence Ignatius exhorts "to give heed to the prophets and especially to the gospel" (Ign. *Smyrn.* 7.2). "In order to prosper in whatever

you do [Ps 1:3], give diligence to be confirmed in the ordinances of the Lord and the apostles" (Ign. *Magn.* 13.1).

These passages indicate that for Ignatius, as for Polycarp, the authority is the Lord Jesus Christ, and his message may be found in the prophets when interpreted with reference to him but especially in the gospel preached by the apostles (see Ign. *Phld.* 5.1-2 on the apostles and prophets as preaching the gospel of Christ—another indication of the triad of the Lord, prophets and apostles). Another passage may further indicate Ignatius's subordination of the OT to Christ: "For I heard some say, 'If I do not find [it] in the archives, I do not believe [it to be] in the gospel.' And when I said, 'It is written,' they answered me, 'that is just the question.' But for me the archives are Jesus Christ, the inviolable archives are his cross and death and his resurrection and faith through him" (Ign. *Phld.* 8.2, trans. Schoedel). "Archives" would be the OT, and the debate between Ignatius and his opponents concerned whether certain Christian teachings were in the OT. Ignatius appeals to Christ as superior authority. The translation of "archives" as OT may not be certain, but it fits the perspective of Ignatius that the OT has its meaning and value in relation to Christ.

8. Alternatives and Relationships.

The common conviction that the OT is the church's book allowed for a variety of ways in which it might be used. Jewish Christians* continued to live in the atmosphere of the OT, although making various modifications in its institutions and ordinances, an approach reflected in the *Didache*, whoever the author might have been. Gentile Christians might largely leave it in the background (*2 Clem., Herm.*) or subordinate it to the teachings of Christ (Polycarp). Others took the OT seriously but came to terms with it in differing ways. *Barnabas,* in comparison to other early Christian writings, has a singular viewpoint on the OT, but his spiritualizing interpretation may be seen as anticipating the Alexandrian* allegorization that found Christian teaching under the letter of the old law, especially in matters of the spiritual life. *1 Clement* anticipates the Western church's appropriation of the OT as a guidebook whose instructions could be transferred from the OT institutions to their NT equivalents, especially in the moral and organizational life of the church. Ignatius appears to anticipate the view of Justin Martyr and Irenaeus that the OT was valid for a time but has now been superseded by the revelation through Christ.

See also BARNABAS, EPISTLE OF; CLEMENT OF ROME; DIDACHE; HERMAS, SHEPHERD OF; IGNATIUS; POLYCARP.

BIBLIOGRAPHY. J. D. M. Derrett, "Scripture and Norms in the Apostolic Fathers," *ANRW* 2.27.1 (1993) 649-99; K. P. Donfried, *The Setting of Second Clement in Early Christianity* (Leiden: E. J. Brill, 1974) 49-97; E. Ferguson, "Christian Use of the Old Testament" in *The World and Literature of the Old Testament*, ed. J. T. Willis (Austin: Sweet, 1979) 346-57; E. Flesseman-van Leer, *Tradition and Scripture in the Early Church* (Assen: van Gorcum, 1954); R. M. Grant, *The Apostolic Fathers: A Translation and Commentary*, 1: *An Introduction* (New York: Thomas Nelson, 1964) 35-86; D. A. Hagner, *The Use of the Old and New Testaments in Clement of Rome* (Leiden: E. J. Brill, 1973) 21-132; R. Hvalvik, *The Struggle for Scripture and Covenant: The Purpose of the* Epistle of Barnabas *and Jewish-Christian Competition in the Second Century* (Tübingen: J. C. B. Mohr, 1995) 109-44, 349-57; J. Reed, "The Hebrew Epic and the *Didache*" in *The Didache in Context: Essays on Its Text, History, and Transmission*, ed. C. N. Jefford (Leiden: E. J. Brill, 1995) 213-25; W. R. Schoedel, "Ignatius and the Archives," *HTR* 71 (1978) 97-106.

E. Ferguson

OLD TESTAMENT IN GENERAL EPISTLES

Rich in their appropriation of characters, events and imagery associated with Israel's history, the General Epistles reflect a conspicuous debt to the OT and to contemporary Jewish exegesis of the OT. The literary tendency of the General Epistles is to display their relationship to the OT through indirect allusions rather than direct citations (*see* Intertextuality). This is frequently found in the context of moral and hortatory instruction.

More so than the Pauline epistles (*see DPL*, Old Testament in Paul), many of which are formulated in explicitly theological or doctrinal terms, the General Epistles mirror the practical dimensions of moral tensions arising from the church's contact with surrounding culture. And unlike the Gospel narratives (*see DPL*, Old Testament in the Gospels), whose apologetic aim is to demonstrate that Jesus Christ fulfills the Law,

the Prophets and the Writings, the General Epistles are paraenetic, alluding to the OT for the sake of ethical illustration. Where a Palestinian Jewish Christian substratum is evident, these epistles exhibit a stronger indebtedness to OT and Jewish tradition. By comparison, where a more Gentile social environment is suggested, the literary strategy of the writer calls for more numerous touch points with pagan culture.

Recent scholarship, stimulated by interest in Christian origins, Jewish apocalyptic* and the Dead Sea Scrolls (*see* Qumran), has devoted itself to the question of the NT writers' exegetical technique. Creative and penetrating interpretations can thus be seen to arise from the awareness that the writers of the NT are in conversation with Jewish contemporaries. Elucidating the extent to which the language and thought-world of both the OT and contemporary Judaism* pervade the General Epistles is the aim of the discussion that follows.

1. Literary Strategy and Exegetical Technique in the General Epistles
2. The Role of Typology in the General Epistles
3. The Old Testament in the General Epistles

1. Literary Strategy and Exegetical Technique in the General Epistles.

An investigation of NT dependence on the OT is no cut-and-dried matter. Intertextual* relationships are complex and often defy neat categorization. Even determining whether we are dealing with a quotation or an allusion is at times problematic. Moreover, the citation or allusion may be unidentified. Thus proof of literary borrowing can be elusive. The main lines of recent research have followed the question of exegetical method, particularly in tracing current Jewish exegetical practice in Pauline literature, Acts* and the Gospels (e.g., in the use of formula quotations, collections of OT texts [*testimonia*] and the role of the LXX in citation).

More recent attempts (e.g., Ellis and Bauckham) have been made to uncover the midrashic structure of passages in the General Epistles. Midrashic or paraphrastic use of the OT is typically applied to current events, with a scriptural allusion serving as a means of illustration or reapplication. Certain phenomena in the General Epistles are best understood in light of contemporary midrashic techniques and not merely the OT passage from which the tradition derives. A comparison of extrabiblical Jewish writings that are roughly contemporary to the NT documents offers material parallels.

NT writers refer to the OT in a diversity of ways and for a variety of reasons. For the purposes of the present discussion, several general categories of usage may be assigned.

The OT may be cited in a direct, literal-historical fashion, an illustration of which is James 2:11, a citation from the Decalogue. In this context the author reminds his readers of the Mosaic covenant's* ethical* imperatives that are still binding in the Jewish-Christian community. The historical connection is essential to this category of OT allusion. A similar instance may be found in 1 Peter 1:16, a reaffirmation of a Pentateuchal exhortation to holy conduct. In this sense the OT is not superseded by Christian revelation; it is presupposed as an abiding foundation. What was ethically prescribed by Yahweh is literally and fully binding.

Another category of appropriating the OT is typological. This genus of usage is primarily illustrative, without any necessary historical or organic correspondence. The General Epistles abound with such examples that become a part of the writer's pastoral theology and form the basis for a Christian ethical or paraenetic tradition.

A typological exegetical approach grows out of the conviction that contained within Israel's history are all the principal forms of divine activity that point to the ultimate purposes of God.* The theological center of this is the life, death and resurrection* of Jesus Christ (*see* Death of Christ). Beyond christological* or theological typology, however, lies moral typology. OT characters and events project themselves in ways that allow them to serve as paradigms in the Christian paraenetic tradition. The abundance of this category makes the General Epistles a rich and distinct contribution to the NT canon.

Much of the illustrative material in James, for example, consists of moral exhortation to endure as the people of God. With no direct or discernible OT passages in support, Abraham, Rahab, the prophets, Job and Elijah are cited as exemplars. (Extrabiblical Jewish traditions frequently fill in the gap in explaining the context of those particular references.) In 1 Peter, Sarah is the model wife, submissive to her husband's authority (1 Pet 3:6), while Noah is a paradigm of divine patience (1 Pet 3:20). In Jude and 2 Peter, the fallen angels, Sodom and Gomorrah, and Balaam function in the context of evocative warnings to the readers. Noah and Lot illustrate in 2 Peter the need for perseverance amid pagan surroundings, while unbelieving Israel, Cain, Korah and Michael the archangel are added to the catalog of paradigms in Jude. Most if not all of these are meaningful as they find reinterpretation and reapplication in extrabiblical Jewish literature (*see* Noncanonical Writings). The use of these paradigms in the General Epistles frequently has more in common with contemporary exegetical practice than they have with any OT passages to which they might be traced.

The moral and spiritual health of the community surfaces as a primary theme in the General Epistles. Admonitions to good works (James), patient endurance* (1 Peter), faithfulness (Jude), virtuous living (2 Peter) and undivided commitments (1 John) are the didactic trajectory of these epistles.

In addition to citations and allusions to OT material, the stylistic influence of the Hebrew Scriptures on Christian literary composition is extensive. Terms, phrases, literary forms and conventions all are reflected in the writings of the NT, even when the modern reader or the apostolic writer may not be consciously aware of their presence. This is particularly true of the General Epistles. James's use of the Septuagint in citing the OT, for example, may reflect both his immersion in the OT and his ability to adapt himself to Hellenistic cultural influences. The metaphor of the stone (1 Peter) intertwines OT imagery with more contemporary Jewish exegesis in the letter's commentary on the people of God. Furthermore, as "exiles of the Diaspora," Peter's audience struggles with the challenges of persecution* for the name* of Christ. And because the readers are exiles in the world,* continuity is established between the OT and Christian community. Jude and 2 Peter are written in a style and vocabulary that bespeak both an OT prophet as well as a literary master. The fiery imagination normally associated with prophetic judgment speeches in the OT engages the reader. Waterless clouds driven by the winds, fruitless trees, waves of the sea, wandering stars, slaves of corruption—the apostates are thus branded and stand under the irrevocable threat of divine judgment.* This judgment accords with a day of reckoning prophesied by the prophetic messengers of old, even when subtle linguistic nuances on the part of the writer suggest slightly different literary strategies at work in each epistle.

Of the General Epistles, only 2 John and 3 John fail to show strong evidence of dependency on the OT.

2. The Role of Typology in the General Epistles.
Given the illustrative use of the OT in the General Epistles and the fact that these letters* have not received the attention accorded other NT books, we may appeal to two test cases for viewing the paraenetic use of typology.

2.1. 1 Peter. The first case involves a use of double typology in 1 Peter.* Throughout the epistle the readers are admonished that suffering* is a normative experience in the Christian journey. The literary strategy calls for marshaling evidence to support the thesis that patient endurance of suffering has a precedent and suffering is not an end in itself. To illustrate, Christ suffered on our behalf in order to bring us to God (1 Pet 3:18). However, while Christ suffered and was put to death, he also was made alive by the Spirit of God. Injected parenthetically into the writer's exhortation is a cryptic but rhetorically decisive pronouncement. Christ is portrayed as an end-time Enoch who was commissioned by God to preach to "the spirits in prison" (i.e., the enemies of God in the unseen world who became subject to Christ's conquest [1 Pet 3:19]). These enemies—"angels, authorities and powers"—are in the plan of God "subjected to" Christ the Lord, who reigns "at the right hand of God" (1 Pet 3:22). This awareness is critical for the readers, since they are presently suffering because of Christ's name. Yet their enemies, like the fallen angels, are subject to the same effects of Christ's work that brought his enemies under his feet. Suffering brought about unqualified victory.

Sandwiched within this literary context is a second use of typology. In this connection the writer employs a type from an earlier epoch in history to illustrate that "baptism now saves you" (1 Pet 3:21). Just as Noah and his family endured much persecution and abuse for their faithfulness in an unbelieving generation, so the Christian community is to be cognizant that perseverance leads to God's salvation.* In this way baptism* separates the church from the world. The generation of the first-century Christians is compared to the generation of Noah, both of which move to their appointed end. Just as few from the whole human race were rescued, so relatively few are to be saved from the current generation. The typology, however, relates the flood not to final judgment but to baptism. The water is symbolic: it serves as "the antitype which now saves you through baptism" (*ho kai hymas antitypon nyn sōzei baptisma,* 1 Pet 3:21; *see* Hymns). Baptism now saves, much as deliverance from slavery* lies in the past (1 Pet 1:18).

2.2. Jude. Literary strategy in Jude* calls for a rhetorically sophisticated use of triplets to illustrate the fate of the ungodly. After citing unbelieving Israel (Jude 5), the disenfranchised angels (Jude 6), and Sodom and Gomorrah (Jude 7) as types of apostasy* upon whom divine judgment fell, Jude introduces a second triplet of OT paradigms (Jude 11). These are objects of a woe cry or prophetic denunciation. Having blasphemed and rejected authority (Jude 8), the opponents, in contrast to Michael (Jude 9), have brought themselves under divine curse.

The text of Genesis 4 describes Cain bringing the "fruits" of the earth as an offering to the Lord (Gen 4:3), while his brother Abel is said to have brought the "firstborn" from his flock (Gen 4:4). The Lord subsequently looked with favor upon Abel but not Cain (Gen 4:5). To the Jewish mind Cain represents the epitome of wickedness. He is the first man in the Hebrew Scriptures to defy God and despise another person; hence he is prototypical, the "type and teacher" (Philo*) of ungodliness. Although there exists in the OT collectively a mixed review of Balaam, son of Beor, he is portrayed in the main as a negative memorial, having hired himself out to curse Israel. Greedy and self-serving, Balaam led Israel into idolatry* and immorality at Baal-Peor (Num 31:16). As a type Balaam "loved the wages of wickedness" (cf. 2 Pet 2:15). The third of this triad, Korah, is arguably the most arresting illustration of insubordination in all the OT. It is he who challenged the authority of Moses,* the man who talked with God. Moreover, siding with him were 250 among Israel's leaders (Num 16:17, 35). Korah's rebellion (*antilogia*) is symbolic of strife and contention. In its effect Korah's fate is commensurate with his deed.

For Jude's purposes this trio foreshadows the fate of those who blaspheme and demonstrate irreverence in the face of spiritual authority.* At first they depart, but ultimately they perish. With the cry of condemnation and the threat of divine vengeance hanging over their heads, Jude's opponents await the execution of certain judgment (see also 3.3 below).

3. The Use of the Old Testament in the General Epistles.

The extent to which the General Epistles exhibit a Semitic cast and literary relationship to the OT can be demonstrated by noting examples of the writers' exegesis. Although similarities in their use of the OT are evident, notable differences can be detected as well.

3.1. James. James's* discussion of the law* requires citing the OT (*mē moicheusēs . . . mē phoneusēs,* "do not commit adultery . . . do not murder," Jas 2:11) for two principal reasons—underscoring the unity of the law as well as one's final moral accountability to the lawgiver. Neglecting or breaking any part of the law is tantamount to disregarding the whole law. Why, in James's treatment of the law, does he quote central commandments?* His preceding discussion of partiality provides a clue (love* of one's neighbor), while the exhortations to good works that immediately follow intensify the emphasis on moral accountability for one's actions. Social conditions existing among James's audience may be such that the temptation to envy, hatred and murder are real. In sum, James is contending that the ethical foundations of Mosaic law are in no way set aside; rather they retain their full force in the life of the Christian community.

One feature of Jewish midrashic practice is alternating summary allusions to scriptural texts and related commentary (Longenecker, 36-37). James 2:23 appears to fit this pattern. Abraham,* as a moral paradigm, serves to illustrate a different point for James than he does for Paul (cf. Rom 4:3). In Pauline teaching belief in and of itself deserves God's commendation. For James faith validating itself through works is meritorious (*see* Faith and Works). Thus in the writer's mind the fulfillment of Scripture by Abraham ("Abram believed the Lord, and he credited it to him as righteousness," Gen 15:6) is the patriarch's works that lead ultimately to the binding of Isaac. This understanding,

though it is not in opposition to the OT narrative, nevertheless shares with contemporary Judaism an interpretive shift. In addition, Abraham as the "friend of God," an idea that finds striking parallels in the Jewish apocrypha, can be deduced from 2 Chronicles 20:7 and Isaiah 41:8.

The rhetorical question framed in James 4:5-6 ("Or do you suppose that it is for nought that the Scripture says, 'God yearns jealously for the spirit that he has made to dwell in us'?") is reminiscent of Moses' response to Joshua in Numbers 11:29: "Are you jealous for my sake? I wish that all the Lord's people were prophets and that the Lord would put his Spirit on them!" The emphasis in Numbers is the manifestation of the Spirit's power; in James there is something of an interpretive shift. In a more generic sense, jealousy connotes friendship with God over against friendship with the world. A second midrashic citation of the OT follows, deriving from Proverbs 3:34: "The Lord resists the proud but gives grace to the humble." Mindful of the reality of judgment for sins not purged, the writer expresses with different words what was stressed earlier: mercy triumphs over judgment in the act of human repentance* and embrace of God's mercy* (cf. Jas 2:13; 5:1-8).

The words *kai kalypsei plēthos hamartiōn* ("will cover a multitude of sins") in James 5:20 are more a reminiscence than a citation of the OT (cf. Prov 10:12). Moreover, James has altered the subject of "to cover," while the sense in which the phrase is used is not immediately transparent. The context in which it occurs has to do with regulations in the congregation (e.g., Jas 2:1; 3:1; 4:11; much of Jas 5). Sins covered is meant to be the counterpoint to sins provoked—for example, those manifest through the tongue, hatred or partiality. In the author's line of reasoning, the restoration of the neighbor, an act that "covers sins," is the pastoral calling of the church and hence a vital service that it should render.

In addition there are numerous scattered resemblances or reminiscences to the OT in James. Among these are the language of humility and exaltation (Jas 1:9; cf. Job 5:11, 12; Prov 29:23); the imagery of the sun and heat in relation to riches (Jas 1:10-11; cf. Job 14:2; 24:24-25; 27:21; Ps 37:2, 14; 73:12; 78:18-20; 113:7-8; Is 40:6-7; Ezek 21:31); the language of testing (Jas 1:12; cf. Job 5:17); the sphere of riches (Jas

2:6; 5:1-2, 5; cf. Job 14:20-21; 20:22; 24:4-12); the language of sin and lust (Jas 1:5; cf. Ps 7:15); the world of the tongue (Jas 1:26; 3:5-6,8; cf. Ps 39:1; 82:14-15; 139:4; 141:3); speaking and listening (Jas 1:19; cf. Prov 11:12; 29:20); anger (Jas 1:19; cf. Prov 14:29; 16:32; 29:22); tomorrow's uncertainty (Jas 4:13-15; cf. Prov 27:1); partiality (Jas 2:9; cf. Prov 28:21); dishonoring the poor (Jas 2:6; cf. Prov 14:21); the association of a crown with endurance (Jas 1:12; cf. Zech 6:14); orphans and widows (Jas 1:27; cf. Is 1:17; Mal 3:5); the relationship of poverty of the world and faith (Jas 2:5; cf. Is 29:19); the triumph of mercy (Jas 2:13; cf. Mic 6:8; Jer 9:23); Abraham as the friend of God (Jas 2:23; cf. 2 Chron 20:7; Is 41:8); drawing near to God (Jas 4:5; cf. Zech 1:3); and the call to mourn (Jas 4:9; cf. Amos 8:10).

3.2. 1 Peter. 1 Peter 1:16, a citation of Leviticus 11:44 ("You shall be holy, for I am holy"), expresses the essence of Israel's identity as a nation and continued to have the same literal force in the early church (cf. Mt 5:48). Holiness* is required because it was commanded in the law of Moses. The ethical foundation for the Christian life is nothing less than that of the OT. The significance of the law transcends theonomic Israel.

The relationship of 1 Peter 1:24-25 to the OT (Is 40:6-8) is also evident. The citation "All flesh is like grass . . . the grass withers, the flower fades, but the word of the Lord endures forever" indicates that the writer is quoting from the Septuagint rather than the Hebrew text. The context of Isaiah 40 is the enduring purposes of God—the sure word of the Lord in the midst of changing and at times calamitous events in Israel's history. In 1 Peter the accent is similar. The author wishes to assert the efficacy of the word of God in contrast to all that changes and perishes.

A catena of OT citations and allusions accompanies the depiction of the people of God in 1 Peter 2. This includes references to Exodus 19:6; Isaiah 8:14, Isaiah 28:16 and Isaiah 43:20-21; Psalm 118:22; Hosea 1:9-10 and Hosea 2:23. The initial quotation about the cornerstone, with minor alterations, derives from Isaiah 28:16. Additional citations from Psalm 118:22 and Isaiah 8:14 incorporate the metaphor of the stone while midrashically supporting the broader theme of persecution and rejection. The stumbling and rejection are due to an unwillingness, not an inability, to believe. The rejected stone as the capstone (Ps 118:22) is applied by Jesus to himself (Mt 21:42; Mk 12:10; Lk 20:17; *see* Stone, Cornerstone). Furthermore, all three of the citations in 1 Peter 2:6-8 are found elsewhere in the NT (Mt 21:42; Acts 4:11; Rom 9:33), while the christological application of the metaphor occurs also in Pauline literature (1 Cor 3:11; Eph 2:20). The reference at this point to "Zion" (1 Pet 2:6) is fitting, given that the writer has just described the temple* as made of "living stones." Its multiple use in the NT, including its Petrine application, indicates that the metaphor was fairly widespread in first-century Jewish exegesis.

The concept of the believing community as a building, although having noteworthy parallels in Qumran* literature, also has numerous traces in the OT: the "house"* of Israel (Ex 16:31; Lev 10:6; Num 20:29; Ruth 4:11; 2 Sam 1:12; 12:8; 16:3; Ps 98:3; 115:12; 135:19; Is 5:7; 46:3; Jer 2:26; 5:15; 9:26; Ezek 2:5; 3:1; cf. Mt 10:6) and the Lord's "house" (Num 12:7). The prophets utilize the imagery of a building or a house in denouncing Israel and Judah during times of corporate apostasy.

The notion of Israel as a nation of priests,* suggested in Exodus and Isaiah, is carried over and applied to spiritual Israel as well. All of Israel's history constitutes a loud proclamation that its people are "chosen" (cf. Exod 19:6; Deut 7:6; 14:2; 25:18; Is 43:20-21; Mal 3:17). In 1 Peter 2:5 we encounter not a citation but rather imagery called forth by an amalgam of OT allusions. Although the precise form of the OT reference is not reproduced in 1 Peter 2:4-10, the substance is. The final OT allusion in this exhortation to be the people of God derives from Hosea. In one sense the saints are the fulfillment of the prophetic promise.

In connection with the metaphor of priesthood, the idea of "spiritual sacrifices," prominent in Qumran, also surfaces in the OT: in Psalm 50:13, 14, 23, Psalm 51:17 and Psalm 141:2; Isaiah 1:11-17; Hosea 6:6; and Micah 6:6-8.

Turning to the broader theme of suffering (1 Pet 2:18-25), Peter quotes (1 Pet 2:22) from Isaiah 53:9: "He committed no sin, neither was there found any deceit in his mouth." In the Suffering Servant of Isaiah the writer finds a type of the suffering Christ, the "lamb without spot or blemish" (1 Pet 1:19; cf. Is 53:7): "Christ also suffered for you, leaving you an example [hypogrammos], so that you follow in his steps." The metaphor of the righteous sufferer is extended in 1 Peter 2:24, borrowing further from Isaiah 53:4, 11-12. In targumic fashion the writer supports allusion to one text with another to underscore the fact that suffering is redemptive in nature. In 1 Peter, Christ's example functions as an ethical paradigm; it is meant to yield an increase in righteous living (see Righteousness).

Extending the theme of suffering, in 1 Peter 3:10-12 the writer cites Psalm 34:13-17, reproducing the text of the Septuagint with the exception of a stylistic alteration: he changes the imperatives from second to third person. This quotation is meant to support the preceding admonition concerning well-doing (1 Pet 3:8-9). Material such as is cited almost verbatim from Psalm 34 was probably catechetical for the early Christian community. The admonition, moreover, is reminiscent of the Jewish-Christian wisdom* tradition that laces much of the epistle of James. Divine blessing* ultimately prevails upon those who control their speech and who do good.

Unlike the OT allusions in 1 Peter 2:22 and 1 Peter 3:10-12, 1 Peter 3:14 reflects little correspondence to Isaiah 8:12-13, from which it borrows. "Do not fear what they fear, and do not be afraid" in the mouth of the prophet is directed toward the people of Israel as they wilt before the threat of Assyria and its minions. In the prophet's eye the Lord Almighty is the one whom Israel should dread. The context in 1 Peter relates to the saints who are suffering for good. In Isaiah the oracle is delivered in the midst of prophetic rebuke; in 1 Peter the words are intended to convey blessing and encouragement for those being persecuted. What both passages have in common is the exhortation not to lean on human resources. The object of trust in Isaiah is the Lord Almighty; in 1 Peter it is Christ the Lord. Reverencing Christ the Lord has an apologetic thrust. It prepares the individual to "be ready at all times to give an answer [apologia] to anyone who inquires as to the reason for the hope within you" (1 Pet 3:15).

The final OT allusion in the epistle occurs in 1 Peter 4:8. Whereas in James 5:20 similar words constitute a reminiscence, here we have a citation ("Love covers a multitude of sins"). Peter has in mind the community of Christians, who are to be "good stewards of the manifold grace of God, serving one another." Love covers everything, that is, sins and wrongs in the community (see the parallel in 1 Cor 13). The proverbial statement rings forever true.

In sum, 1 Peter is replete with prophetic interpretation and paraenetic application, even when, as R. J. Bauckham (309) notes, the two are not always distinct from one another.

3.3. 2 Peter and Jude. Although OT allusions in 2 Peter* are not as numerous as they are in James, 1 Peter or Jude, they are noteworthy. Particularly important is the use of typology. The flood is frequently represented by Jewish literature as a prototype of eschatological judgment. Hence in 2 Peter, Noah and Lot become types of faithful Christians who are to expect deliverance. Noah's generation is prototypical of a faithless generation in Jesus' teaching as well (Mt 24:37-39; Lk 17:26-28). In Luke's Gospel, Noah's and Lot's generations appear side by side. Both are united by a common thread: life proceeding as normal in spite of pending judgment. While Noah is a herald of righteousness* in Jewish tradition, Lot is by no means a righteous model in the OT. Lot's "righteousness" (thrice he is depicted as dikaios, "righteous," in 2 Pet 2:4-10) is developed more in Jewish intertestamental literature, although it can be indirectly attributed to Abraham's pleading with God (Gen 18:16-33).

The double proverb in 2 Peter 2:22 consists of one part OT and one part extrabiblical tradition (the Egyptian Story of Ahiqar). The OT source is Proverbs 26:11: "As a dog returns to its vomit, so a fool repeats his folly." Although only the first clause is quoted, the readers are familiar with the saying and will appreciate its appropriateness to the situation. More important than citing from Jewish tradition material per se, in 2 Peter is the use of sources in general that will resonate with the audience. The epistle mirrors a pagan social environment; thus, in contrast to Jude, Jewish sources would be less effective in the development of a literary strategy.

While not a single explicit citation from the OT is found in Jude, the brief epistle is nevertheless replete with examples of prophetic typology. No fewer than nine subjects—unbelieving Israel, the fallen angels, Sodom and Gomorrah, Michael the archangel, Moses, Cain, Balaam, Korah and Enoch—are employed by the writer in a polemic against ungodly antitypes who through stealth have infiltrated the community. These ungodly persons are the focus of Jude's invective.

Several OT motifs are prominent in Jude, among them the antithesis of the ungodly and the faithful, theophany and judgment, and divine foreknowledge or divine preservation. Two sets of triplets (Jude 5-7 and Jude 11) illustrate the fundamental antithesis between the faithful and faithless. The ungodly, furthermore, are described as the antithesis to Michael the archangel, who though he possessed divine authority still deferred to the Lord of Hosts (Jude 8-9). Members of the second triad of faithless are united by means of a woe cry. Each is signified by a formula—"the way of Cain," "the error of Balaam," "the rebellion of Korah"—which would give the appearance of a standardization of type that had emerged in Jewish circles. A significant part of the Genesis account is given to Cain, whose murder of his brother qualifies him as the archetype of disobedience (Gen 4:10-12, 15-16). In Balaam we encounter an individual who is seduced by riches, who counseled Balak to corrupt Israel through defilement, and whose greed assisted Israel's enemies, prompting the intervention of an angel (Num 22—25). And in Korah we find a notable example of defying authority; his fate was commensurate with his rebellion (Num 16). These three might be seen as depicting Jude's opponents in three levels of ascending gravity, from initial departure to final ruin (see also 2.2 above).

One of the most central of themes in the OT is that of Yahweh's coming, frequently depicted in the form of fire, flood or storm. Often, though not exclusively, theophany in the OT occurs in the context of judgment and destruction. The prediction employed in Jude 14-15 (*1 Enoch* 1:9) appears to derive from the theophany recorded in Deuteronomy 33. The text of Jude 14-15, a christological reshaping of the theophany tradition, and *1 Enoch* 1:9 bear striking resemblance to the general pattern of theophany statements throughout the OT (e.g., Deut 33:2; Judg 5:4; Ps 18:9; 46:8-9; 68:17; 76:9; 96:13; Is 19:1; 31:4, 27; 40:10; 66:15; Jer 25:31; Dan 7:10; Amos 1:2; Joel 3:2; Mic 1:3; Hab 3:3; Zeph 1:7-9, 12; Hag 2:22; Zech 3:8; 9:14; Mal 3:3-5). A common link between Jude, *1 Enoch* and the OT is the catchword *ungodly (asebeia/asebeis/asebeō)*.

Jude's hermeneutic facilitates two goals: he is faithful to the OT tradition of theophany statements, and in *1 Enoch* he exploits a literary work of sectarian Judaism* with which his readers were more than likely acquainted (Charles 1993, 153-62). The statement in *1 Enoch,* rooted in antecedents from the OT, rings prophetically true concerning Jude's adversaries.* In Jude theophany and judgment merge to counter the distortions of the ungodly.

A feature common to the OT and Jewish intertestamental literature is the notion of names recorded in heavenly books (e.g., Exod 32:32-33; Ps 40:4; 56:8; 69:29; 139:16; Is 4:3; Jer 22:30; Dan 7:10; 12:1; Mal 3:16; *1 Enoch* 81:1-2; 89:62; 90:14, 17, 20, 22; 104:7; 108:3, 7; *2 Apoc. Bar.* 24:1; cf. Rev 3:5; 5:1, 7-8; 10:8-11; 20:12). These heavenly books reflect a religious self-understanding fundamental to Hebrew thought: the divine purpose, though hidden from human view, is predetermined and revealed in history. The scroll* of Revelation 5, for example, is a view of that history from the divine standpoint. The heavenly books point to the divine foreknowledge by which "the chosen" of Israel were called to be Yahweh's own possession and instrument in the earth (see esp. Ps 139:16; Jer 1:5).

The reference in Jude 4 to the ungodly as "those whose judgment was written down long ago" conforms to this apocalyptic convention of heavenly books and resembles the juridical pronouncements found in Jeremiah 22:30 and Malachi 3:16, which carry specifically penal ramifications. Moreover, this designation is contrasted with Jude's description of the faithful, who are depicted as "chosen" *(klētoi)* and "preserved" *(tetērēmenois)* in the letter's introduction. At the same time, just as God has "reserved" *(tērein)* for the great day of judgment the angels who deserted their heavenly position (Jude 6), "blackest darkness" has been "reserved" for the ungodly (Jude 13). Casting his opponents as godless antitypes for whom judgment, long since prescribed, has already been established, Jude views judgment as fulfilled in the ungodly of the present.

Three paradigms underscore the certainty of this judgment: unbelieving (apostate) Israel, the fallen angels and Sodom and Gomorrah (Jude 5-7). Each of the three exhibits for the readers an unnatural brand of rebellion. Israel, God's chosen, had been redeemed "once for all" *(hapax),* yet tragically was later *(deuteron)* destroyed because of unbelief. Although material from Numbers 11, 14, 25 and 32 is most explicit in describing Israel's unbelief, the whole of the OT corpus is a constant calling to remember Israel's unrepeatable deliverance from Egypt. The present as well calls for a prophetic reminder.

The angels, despite their created exaltedness, chose to desert their heavenly dwelling. Although Jewish angelology is far more systematic and imaginative following the exile, several precedents for angel typology suggest themselves in the OT: Isaiah 14:5-23, a taunt against "the king of Babylon"; Isaiah 24:21-22, a symbolic representation of Yahweh's judgment; and Ezekiel 28:1-19, a prophetic funeral dirge against the "king of Tyre." With the angels these figures share a common fate: each is stripped of an exalted rank. While the idea of "imprisoned spirits" is unrefined in the OT and pronounced in Jewish apocalyptic, Jude appears to combine typological treatment of the OT with conventional notions of angelology. Apocalyptic mythology frequently exhibits a conspicuous pattern: war erupts in heaven (depicted in astral terms), followed by a spilling over of this rebellion to earth, resulting in ultimate vindication and punishment by the king of heaven.

Sodom and Gomorrah, the third part of this prophetic triplet, consistently stand out in the OT as a model of finality in judgment (e.g., Deut 29:23; 32:32; Is 1:9-10; 3:9; Jer 23:14; 49:18; 50:40; Ezek 16:46-59; Amos 4:11). Having given themselves over to unnatural sexual expression, the cities of the plain serve as an abiding example (*prokeintai deigma*) of divine punishment. Jude's burden is to remind his audience that moral agency is the defining human characteristic.

3.4. 1 John. Although it is generally conceded that direct influence of the OT, with the exception of 1 John 3:12, is absent from the Johannine epistles (*see* John, Letters of), it should be noted that the substructure underlying the writer's polemic in 1 John reveals more about his opponents' confession than it does about their social location. Parallels between Johannine and Essene literature (*see* Noncanonical Writings) suggest that 1 John initially circulated in a Jewish Christian orbit and thus is firmly rooted in a Jewish Christian milieu (Longenecker, 193).

See also INTERTEXTUALITY IN EARLY CHRISTIAN LITERATURE; JAMES; JOHN, LETTERS OF; JUDE; NONCANONICAL WRITINGS, CITATIONS IN THE GENERAL EPISTLES; OLD TESTAMENT IN HEBREWS; 1 PETER; 2 PETER.

BIBLIOGRAPHY. R. J. Bauckham, "James, 1 and 2 Peter, Jude" in *It Is Written: Scripture Citing Scripture: Essays in Honour of B. Lindars*, ed. D. A. Carson and H. G. M. Williamson (Cambridge: Cambridge University Press, 1988) 303-17; E. Boehl, *Die Alttestamentliche Zitaten im Neuen Testament* (Wien: W. Braumueller, 1878); J. D. Charles, *Literary Strategy in the Epistle to Jude* (Scranton: University of Scranton Press, 1993); idem, "'Those and These': The Use of the Old Testament in the Epistle of Jude," *JSNT* 38 (1990) 109-24; P. H. Davids, "Tradition and Citation in the Epistle of James" in *Scripture, Tradition and Interpretation*, ed. W. W. Gasque and W. S. LaSor (Grand Rapids: Eerdmans, 1978) 113-26; W. D. Davies, "Reflections about the Use of the Old Testament in the New in Its Historical Context," *JQR* 74 (1983) 105-36; E. E. Ellis, *The Old Testament in Early Christianity* (Tübingen: J. C. B. Mohr, 1991); idem, *Prophecy and Hermeneutic in Early Christianity* (WUNT 18; Tübingen: J. C. B. Mohr, 1978); J. A. Fitzmyer, "The Use of Explicit Old Testament Quotations in Qumran Literature and in the New Testament," *NTS* 7 (1960-61) 297-333; M. Gertner, "Midrashim in the New Testament," *JSS* 7 (1962) 267-92; L. Goppelt, *TYPOS: The Typological Interpretation of the Old Testament in the New* (Grand Rapids: Eerdmans, 1982); G. L. Green, "The Use of the Old Testament for Christian Ethics in 1 Peter," *TynB* 41-42 (1990) 277-89; A. T. Hanson, *Living Utterances of God: The New Testament Exegesis of the Old* (London: Darton, Longman & Todd, 1983); R. N. Longenecker, *Biblical Exegesis in the Apostolic Period* (Grand Rapids: Eerdmans, 1975); M. P. Miller, "Targum, Midrash and the Use of the Old Testament in the New Testament," *JSJ* 2 (1970) 29-82; D. M. Smith, "The Use of the Old Testament in the New" in *The Use of the Old Testament in the New and Other Essays*, ed. J. M. Efird (Durham, NC: Duke University Press, 1972) 3-65; K. R. Snodgrass, "The Use of the Old Testament in the New" in *New Testament Criticism and Interpretation*, ed. D. A. Black and D. S. Dockery (Grand Rapids: Zondervan, 1991) 409-34; R. W. Wall, "James as Apocalyptic Paraenesis," *RestQ* 32 (1990) 11-22.

J. D. Charles

OLD TESTAMENT IN HEBREWS

Of all the NT literature no document cites the

OT text more extensively than Hebrews.* By implicit and explicit references the author weaves a tapestry presupposing and proposing points of continuity and contrast between the old and new covenant eras. The author's art in using the OT follows patterns discerned in early Judaism* and that shed light on the book's structure, theology and methods of argumentation.

1. Phenomena
2. Text Type
3. Employment of the Old Testament
4. Theological Implications
5. Conclusions

1. Phenomena.

The exact enumeration of OT references in Hebrews frustrates even the most careful analyst on account of the author's mix of direct quotations, allusions to specific passages, uses of biblical phraseology and general references to OT historical events and persons. However, there are roughly thirty-six quotations, thirty-five allusions, eighteen cases where OT material is summarized and fourteen where an OT name* or topic is referred to without reference to a specific context. In his discourse the author depends most heavily on the Pentateuch and the Psalms, deriving his comments concerning redemptive history mostly from the former and his christology* from the latter.

Hebrews never mentions an OT author and never introduces a quotation with Paul's favorite introductory formula *gegraptai* ("it is written"). Rather, forms of *legein* ("to say") are employed most often, especially the present participle *legōn* ("saying"). Quotations of the OT are almost always framed as falling from the lips of God;* twenty-three of the thirty-six quotations in Hebrews have God as the speaker. Four passages are attributed to Christ and four others to the Holy Spirit.* In addition Moses* speaks concerning a command of God (Heb 9:20) and expresses terror at God's revelation* (Heb 12:21). Although the quotations in these passages have a human speaker, the context is still that of divine revelation. Finally, the unusual introductory formula at Hebrews 2:6 ("but somewhere one has testified saying") was likely a rhetorical device employed to add effectiveness to the discourse and to keep the focus on God as the primary speaker.

2. Text Type.

One of the primary issues surrounding the use of the OT in Hebrews concerns the author's text. The assumption among NT scholars is that a Greek rather than a Hebrew text was used. In recent years attention has shifted to the question of which set of manuscripts the author accessed. The format for the current debate was initiated in the last century by F. Bleek. In *Der Brief an die Hebräer* Bleek argued against Pauline authorship of Hebrews, partly on the basis that Paul used a text similar to Codex Vaticanus when quoting a Greek text. According to Bleek, Hebrews gives evidence of its author's partiality to a text similar to Codex Alexandrinus. However, scholars such as P. Katz have questioned Bleek's observations, and discussions in this century have dealt with how the author's text relates to one or both of these major codices. J. C. McCullough has emphasized the need to focus research on recensions of the Greek text on a book-by-book basis rather than on one or two extant manuscripts. McCullough concluded that for several books of the OT, such as Jeremiah and Psalms, the recension from which the text quoted is taken is fairly clear, whereas a great deal of uncertainty surrounds other OT books. It seems the author of Hebrews used and reproduced faithfully the local text of various OT books available to him.

3. Employment of the Old Testament.

In the past the exegetical methodology of Hebrews has been most often associated with the allegorical exegesis of Philo.* This argument was made by such commentators as J. Moffatt and C. Spicq. A number of scholars, however, have noted the sharp differences between Hebrews and Philo, placing Hebrews in the mainstream of Jewish and primitive Christian thought and methodology (e.g., Caird, Hurst, Williamson).

3.1. General Forms.

3.1.1. Midrash. Although the ambiguous term *midrash* may refer to a genre of literature produced by rabbis of the tannaitic and amoraic periods, most recent work on the OT in the NT has focused on midrash as an expositional activity in which the NT author cites and then explains an OT text on the basis of Jewish-rabbinic hermeneutical* principles. E. E. Ellis distinguishes between this type of exposition, which he designates "explicit midrash" and "implicit midrash," by which the author integrates interpretive elements into the OT quotation (Ellis 1978, 152-57). The author of Hebrews employs the latter sparingly. His quotation of Haggai 2:6 at Hebrews 12:26 offers a possible example. The LXX text reads *eti hapax egō seisō ton ouranon kai tēn gēn* ("yet once more I will shake heaven and earth"). However, Hebrews 12:26 offers *eti hapax egō seisō ou monon tēn gēn alla kai ton ouranon* ("yet once more I will shake not only the earth but also heaven"). The author reverses the references to heaven* and earth and includes the phrases "not only" and "but also" to bring out the significance of the text for his discussion.

Much more prevalent is the author's use of explicit midrash. For example, he quotes Psalm 39:7-9 (LXX) at Hebrews 10:5-7 and in Hebrews 10:8-10 presents an explanation of the OT text built around the words *tote* ("then") and *thelēma* ("will"). Based on the psalmist's use of *tote* the author explains that there is a temporal relationship between the first part of the passage, having to do with God's lack of desire concerning sacrifices,* and the second part concerning what does afford God pleasure. He interprets *tote* to mean that the old order has been set aside prior to establishing the new order.

Another example of explicit midrash comprises the content of Hebrews 7:1-10. In this passage the author summarizes Genesis 14:17-20 and then examines various aspects of the OT text. He discusses Melchizedek's* name (Heb 7:2), his lack of genealogy and the lack of information concerning his birth and death (Heb 7:3), and his greatness in comparison to the levitical priesthood* (Heb 7:4-10). J. A. Fitzmyer has observed that this exposition resembles that found in *Genesis Rabbah* 43:6.

3.1.2. Chain Quotations. The rabbis and the interpreters of Qumran* at times used *Stichworte* ("catch words") to chain together a number of OT texts. The chain quotations, or *ḥaraz* ("to string"), were used to support a topic under discussion by virtue of the quantity of scriptural quotations brought to bear. In Hebrews 1:5-12 the author presents three pairs of passages supporting the Son's* superiority to the angels.* The first pair (Ps 2:7; 2 Sam 7:14) concerns the Son's superiority by virtue* of his unique relationship to the Father (Heb 1:5); the second (Deut 32:43/Ps 96:7 LXX; Ps 103:4 LXX), the angels' inferior position (Heb 1:6-7); and the third (Ps 44:7-8 LXX; Ps 101:26-28 LXX), the

Son's eternal reign (Heb 1:8-12). Each of the three pairs is joined by a *Stichwort* (see 3.2.6 below): *hyios* (Heb 1:5), *angelos* (Heb 1:6-7) and forms of the pronoun *su* (Heb 1:8-12). This chain's climax comes with the quote of Psalm 109:1 (LXX) at Hebrews 1:13. The effect of the *ḥaraz* is to impress the unqualified superiority of the Son upon the hearers in order to set up the a fortiori exhortation of Hebrews 2:1-4 (see 3.2.7 below).

3.1.3. Example Lists. Another use the author of Hebrews makes of the OT is in line with rhetorical practices of the ancient world. The formulation of example lists *(exempla)* to prove or illustrate an author's exhortation finds expression in a number of literary traditions (e.g., 4 Ezra, Cicero's *De Orat.*, Philo, the CD of Qumran and 1 Macc). Although these lists are diverse in expression, their common function is exhortation. By presenting the examples cited as representative of a much larger body of evidence, the author challenges his hearers to action (Cosby). In Hebrews 11 the author uses this technique, listing biblical heroes in chronological order. These heroes are presented as people of *pistis* ("faith"), a term used anaphorically to drive home the author's point. The list impresses upon the audience the effectiveness of living by faith* and their responsibility to live faithfully in the face of great difficulties.

3.2. Principles Used in Interpretation.

3.2.1. Dispelling Confusion. It was common practice among the rabbis to clear up a verse open to theological misunderstanding (Cohn-Sherbok). In Hebrews 2:8-9 the author offers comment on Psalm 8:5-7 (LXX). After asserting the comprehensive nature of all things being made subject to the Son of Man, he clarifies with the statement "but now we do not yet see all things as subjected to him." The clarifying statement shows the author's concern to alleviate any confusion this passage might cause for his hearers, who are struggling with forces obviously not submitted to God's rule. He asserts that the reality perceived by the hearers does not contradict the OT text and that all has indeed been subjected to Christ's rule.

3.2.2. Reinforcement. Reinforcement is a technique by which a rabbi adds support to an exhortation by quoting a biblical phrase, often using "for" as part of the introductory formula. In Hebrews 10:19-39 the author exhorts the readers to persevere in their confession of faith (*see* Creeds), concluding with a conflated quotation from Isaiah 26:20 and Habakkuk 2:3-4: "For in a very short time the coming one will arrive." Similarly the exhortation to financial contentment in Hebrews 13:5-6 finds reinforcement in a scriptural reference: "I will never desert or forsake you" (Deut 31:6, 8).

3.2.3. Implications. Another common rabbinic procedure involved drawing out the implications of a text. At Hebrews 8:7-12 the new covenant* is introduced through Jeremiah 38:31-34 ([LXX] = Jer 31:31-34). After the extensive quote—the longest OT quotation in the NT—the author presents the implication of the text, focusing on the word *kainēn*. Hebrews 8:13 contains the inference, tersely expressed with *en tō legein kainēn pepalaiōken tēn prōtēn* ("By saying 'new' he has declared the first obsolete").

3.2.4. Literal Sense. This principle refers to a teacher seizing upon and emphasizing a word's meaning with great precision, and it is used extensively in Hebrews. The idea is to focus the hearer's attention on a specific aspect of the text's proclamation in order to support the speaker's case. The author utilizes this principle to advantage at Hebrews 4:7-8 where, concentrating on the term *sēmeron* ("today"), he argues that the word refers to a day of rest other than the one offered to the wilderness wanderers.

3.2.5. Typology. When interpreting Hebrews one must make a distinction between the way the author uses the words *typos* and *antitypos* and his practice of typology. The noun *typos* finds expression in this letter only at Hebrews 8:5 and based on the context should be translated "pattern" or "model." *Antitypos,* used in Hebrews 9:24, means "copy" or "counterpart," referring to the earthly holy place over against the heavenly. Although some have associated Philo's use of the *typos* word group with that of Hebrews, the two utilize these terms quite differently. In Philo's interpretation of Exodus 25:40 (Philo *Vit. Mos.* 2.76; Philo *Som.* 1.206) *archetypos* designates the original pattern as conceived in the mind of God, *typos* the copy of the *archetypos* as impressed on the mind of Moses and *mimēma* the completed structure. For our author the heavenly tabernacle* was a structure built by God, not merely an ideal blueprint (Heb 9:11). This concept represents apocalyptic* symbolism rather than Philonic idealism. Jewish apocalyptic traditions held belief in a heavenly city containing a heavenly place of worship.*

The author's practice of typology, in the sense of identifying preordained connections between events, persons or institutions in the span of salvation history, finds considerable expression in his section on the superior heavenly offering of the heavenly high priest* (Heb 8:3—10:18). For example, the writer describes regulations for old covenant tabernacle worship (Heb 9:1-7), stressing that only the high priest could enter the holy of holies once a year. The author then explains this as indicating the need for Christ's superior, high-priestly ministry* (Heb 9:8-10), which would open the way for all God's people to enter the true holy of holies. The OT pattern serves as a type for the new covenant ministry of Christ.

3.2.6. Verbal Analogy. Of the seven hermeneutical principles traditionally attributed to Hillel (*t. Sanh.* 7.11; *'Abot R. Nat.* [A] §37), two play key roles in Hebrews' appropriation of the OT. The first, *Gezērâšāwâ,* suggests that verbal analogy between two passages warrants the consideration of both passages in an interpretation of each. The author of Hebrews uses this principle to pair one OT text with another at numerous places in the development of the discourse. Examples include Hebrews 4:3-5 and Hebrews 5:5-6. "Rest" constitutes a main topic of Hebrews 3:7—4:11, the author following the quotation of Psalm 94:7-11 (LXX) with a treatment of the OT wilderness wanderers who through disobedience (*see* Obedience) failed to enter God's rest (Heb 3:12-19). After a transitional statement in Hebrews 4:1-2, he continues with a discussion of the promised rest for those who are obedient, introducing Genesis 2:2 for consideration: *kai katepausen ho theos en tēn hēmera tē hebdomē apo pantōn tōn ergōn autou* ("and God rested on the seventh day from all his works"). The cognates *rest* and *rested* provide the connection between the two passages and demonstrate that the "rest" addressed in the psalm is sabbath rest, a rest that involves the cessation of one's own work.

The verbal analogy between two passages may even be based on the common use of a pronoun, as is the case with the pairing of Psalm 2:7 and Psalm 109:4 (LXX) in Hebrews 5:5-6. These two OT texts, among the most important texts in the discourse's development, meet by virtue of the pronoun *su* ("you"). *Gezērâšāwwâ* is employed to effect a transition from a discussion focused on Jesus as Son to a discussion focused on Jesus as high priest. These passages proclaim Christ's two eternal, exalted positions, each specified in an oath of God: "You are my Son"; "You are a high priest."

3.2.7. Argument from Lesser to Greater. Qal *waḥômēr*, also referred to as a fortiori argumentation, states that what applies in a less important situation applies in a more important situation, often with greater implications. For example, the logic of Hebrews 10:28-29 is as follows: those who rejected the law* of Moses in the OT were severely punished; those who reject the Son, rejecting the superior covenant and insulting the Spirit of grace,* deserve an even greater punishment. Other examples of *qal waḥômēr*, are found at Hebrews 2:2-3; 9:13-14; 12:9; 12:25.

For a complete listing of OT references in Hebrews, see figure 1.

4. Theological Implications.

Having considered the author's methods of employing the OT, we turn to his theological presuppositions and motives. We first examine the presuppositions that seem evident from the ways in which he uses the OT and then analyze the theological content grounded in the author's uses of the OT.

4.1. Presuppositions Evident in the Author's Use of the OT. First, with the rabbis of his day, the author of Hebrews utilizes methods presupposing God's inspiration of the exact words and phrases of the OT text. In Hebrews, as in other Jewish-Hellenistic synagogue* homilies of the day, one notices a propensity to cite Scripture as falling from the lips of God (Thyen 1955, 69-74). Also, principles such as the literal sense and argument from lesser to greater (see 3.2.4 and 3.2.7 above) depend on exact meanings in the OT text. The presupposition seems to be that God has built those exact meanings into the text for specific didactic and hortatory purposes. Second, and following from the first point, the words of the OT, as the words of God, are authoritative* both in the sense of reflecting truth and possessing the right to command adherence.

4.2. Explicit Theological Teachings Grounded in the OT.

4.2.1. God as Communicator. "God as communicator" also finds explicit expression as a key aspect to the book's overarching message. The first words of the discourse proclaim "God, hav-

ing spoken formerly in many and various ways to the fathers by the prophets, at the inception of these last days he spoke to us by a Son." The people of God should listen to the voice of God through the OT Scriptures and the NT kerygma* (Heb 2:1-4; 3:7-19; Ps 94:8-11 LXX) and should do so on the basis of God's promises* (e.g., Heb 8:8-12; Jer 38:31-34 LXX), warnings (e.g., Heb 3:11; 4:3; Ps 94:11 LXX) and proclamations concerning the Son (e.g., Heb 5:5-6; Ps 2:7; 109:4 LXX). Hebrews addresses an audience in danger of turning away from the Christian faith and returning to Judaism (Bruce, 8-9; Lindars, 4-15). The purpose of the book, therefore, is to exhort the readers to endure in their quest for the promised, new covenant reward in obedience to the word of God and on the basis of their relationship with God's superior Son. God's proclamations concerning the Son are developed in four steps and comprise the expositional sections of the book.

4.2.2. The Son's Superiority to the Angels. Hebrews 1:5-14 argues for the superiority of the Son in relation to the angels (see 3.1.2 above). Each of the three main movements of this passage presents the Son as superior on the basis of a pair of OT texts. Psalm 2:7 and 2 Samuel 7:14 support the unique father-son relationship Jesus enjoys with God (Heb 1:5). The first is a declaration to the Son ("You are my son") and the second a declaration about the Son ("I shall be a father to him and he shall be a son to me"). The second pair (Heb 1:6-7), a conflation of Psalm 96:7 (LXX) and Deuteronomy 32:43 (LXX) presented in tandem with Psalm 103:4 (LXX), proclaim the inferior position of the angels, and the third (Heb 1:8-12), Psalm 44:6-7 (LXX) and Psalm 101:25-27 (LXX), proclaim the eternal reign of the Son. In the second pair the Son's preexistence* and his right to worship by the angels finds expression. In the third, the Son is called "God" *(ho theos),* is said to have an eternal reign and is said to have been the agent of creation.*

The passage ends with the quote of Psalm 109:1 (LXX) on the exaltation* of the Son to the right hand of God. The theological message of Hebrews 1:5-14 is that the Son of God has a unique and supreme status in the universe.

4.2.3. The Incarnation. The superior, heavenly Son became incarnate* to render the devil *(see* Satan) powerless, to become a high priest and to bring the sons of earth to glory.* Use of Psalm 8:5-7, a text that includes references to

Figure 1: Chart of Old Testament References in Hebrews

Hebrews	Old Testament	Quote	Allusion	Summary	Name/Topic
1:3d	Ps 110:1		*		
1:5a	Ps 2:7	*			
1:5b	2 Sam 7:14	*			
1:6	Ps 96:7 (LXX) = Ps 97:7/Deut 32:43	*			
1:7	Ps 103:4 (LXX) = Ps 104:4	*			
1:8-9	Ps 44:6-7 (LXX) = Ps 45:6-7	*			
1:1-12	Ps 101:26-28 (LXX) = Ps 102:25-27	*			
1:13	Ps 109:1 (LXX) = Ps 110:1	*			
2:6-8	Ps 8:5-7 (LXX) = Ps 8:4-6	*			
2:9-10	Ps 8:5-7 (LXX) = Ps 8:4-6		*		
2:12	Ps 21:23 (LXX) = Ps 22:22	*			
2:13a	Is 8:17	*			
2:13b	Is 8:18	*			
2:16	Is 41:8-9		*		
2:17	(high priest)			*	
3:1	(high priest)				*
3:2	Num 12:7		*		
3:7-11	Ps 94:7-11 (LXX) = Ps 95:7-11	*			
3:13	Ps 94:7-8 (LXX) = Ps 95:7-8	*			
3:15	Ps 94:7-8 (LXX) = Ps 95:7-8	*			
3:16-19	(wanderings)			*	
3:18	Ps 94:11 (LXX) = Ps 95:11		*		
4:1	Ps 94:11 (LXX) = Ps 95:11		*		
4:3, 5	Ps 94:11 (LXX) = Ps 95:11	*			
4:4	Gen 2:2	*			
4:7	Ps 94:7-8 (LXX) = Ps 95:7-8	*			

4:10	Ps 94:11 (LXX) = Ps 95:11 + Gen 2:2			*		
4:14-15	(high priest)					*
5:1-4	(high priest)					*
5:4	(Aaron)					*
5:5	Ps 2:7	*				
5:6	Ps 109:4 (LXX) = Ps 110:4	*				
5:7-9	Ps 114, 115 (LXX) = Ps 116			*[1]		
5:10	Ps 109:4 (LXX) = Ps 110:4			*		
6:8	Gen 3:17-18			*		
6:13-15	Gen 22: 16-17			*		
6:14	Gen 22:16-17	*				
6:19	Lev 16:12			*		
6:20	Ps 109:4 (LXX) = Ps 110:4			*		
7:1-2	Gen 14:17-20				*	
7:4	Gen 14:20			*		
7:5	(Levi, Abraham)					*
7:5-11	(Levi, priests)				*	
7:14	(Judah, Moses)					*
7:19	(Law)					*
7:21	Ps 109:4 (LXX) = Ps 110:4	*				
7:22	(covenant)					*
7:24	Ps 109:4 (LXX) = Ps 110:4			*		
7:26-28	(Law)					*
7:28	Ps 2:7			*		
8:1	Ps 109:1 (LXX) = Ps 110:1			*		
8:5	Ex 25:40	*				
8:6	Jer 38:31-34 (LXX) = Jer 31:31-34			*		
8:8-12	Jer 38:31-34 (LXX) = Jer 31:31-34	*				
8:13	Jer 38:31-34 (LXX) = Jer 31:31-34			*		

---

[1]See A. Strobel, "De Psalmengrundlage der Gethsemane-Parallele hbr. 5, 7ff.," *ZNW* 45 (1954) 252-66.

9:1-7	(ministry of priests			*	
9:12-14	(sacrifice)				*
9:15	Jer 38:31 (LXX) = Jer 31:31		*		
9:18-19	Ex 24:6-8			*	
9:20	Ex 24:8	*			
9:21-22	Ex 24:6-8			*	
9:28	Is 53:12		*		
10:1	(Law)				*
10:5-7	Ps 39:7-9 (LXX) = Ps 40:6-8	*			
10:8-9	Ps 39:7-9 (LXX) = Ps 40:6-8	*			
10:10	Ps 39:9 (LXX) = Ps 40:8		*		
10:12-13	Ps 109: (LXX) = Ps 110:1		*		
10:16-17	Jer 38:33-34 (LXX) = Jer 31:33-34	*			
10:27	Is 26:11 (Zeph 1:18)		*		
10:28	Deut 17:6		*		
10:30a	Deut 32:35	*			
10:30b	Deut 32:36	*			
10:37-38	Is 26:20-21 + Hab 2:3-4	*			
11:3	Ps 33:6, 9; Gen 1		*		
11:4	Gen 4			*	
11:5	Gen 5:24		*		
11:7	Gen 6:13-22			*	
11:8-12	Gen 12-17		*		
11:12	Gen 22:17		*		
11:17	Gen 22:1-10			*	
11:18	Gen 21:12	*			
11:20	Gen 27:27-29			*	
11:21	Gen 47:31		*		
11:22	Gen 50		*		
11:23-26	Ex 2			*	

11:30-31	Josh 6		*		
11:32	(various heroes)				*
12:2	Ps 109:1 (LXX) = Ps 110:1		*		
12:5-6	Prov 3:11-12	*			
12:12-13	Is 35:3/Prov 4:26 Job 4:3-4		*		
12:15	Deut 29:18		*		
12:16-17	Gen 25-27			*	
12:18-21	Ex 19			*	
12:20	Ex 19:12-13		*		
12:21	Deut 9:19	*			
12:24	Jer 38:31-34 (LXX) = Jer 31:31-34; Gen 4:10			*	
12:26	Hag 2:6	*			
13:5	Deut 31:6, 8	*			
13:6	Ps 117:6 (LXX) = Ps 118:6	*			
13:11	Lev 16:27		*		

both exaltation and incarnation, effects the transition from the exalted position of Hebrews 1:5-14 to the earthly ministry of Hebrews 2:10-18. The OT texts employed in Hebrews 2:12-13, Psalm 21:23 (LXX) and Isaiah 8:17-18, have to do with the Lord's brotherly relationship with God's people and presence among God's people. The sons are called "brothers" and "children," and the Son is in their midst. This solidarity with family members, with whom he shares flesh and blood, was a necessary prerequisite for the Son's death and appointment as high priest.

4.2.4. Appointment as High Priest. The high-priestly christology of Hebrews appears nowhere else in the NT. Hebrews 5:1-7:28, strategically interrupted by the hortatory material of Hebrews 5:11-6:20, addresses the appointment of the Son as high priest. The focal OT text providing the basis for this section is Psalm 109:4 (LXX), the author also offering a midrashic treatment of Genesis 14:17-20 (Heb 7:1-10). These two OT passages alone mention the enigmatic Melchizedek. Based on these texts the author reasons that the Melchizedekean priesthood of Jesus is superior to the Aaronic priesthood of the older covenant (Heb 7:11-28). The appointment stems from Christ's imperishable nature (Heb 7:16) rather than tribal descent. His indestructibility and God's pronouncement of his position with an oath ("You are a priest forever") assure the permanence of his priesthood, offering believers a superior basis of hope.*

4.2.5. The Superior Offering. This superior high priest has offered a superior new covenant offering (Heb 8:3-10:18). Hebrews sets forth Jeremiah 31:31-34 as proof that the new covenant has superseded the old (Heb 8:7-13). The new covenant offering is greater than the old covenant offerings on three bases (Heb 9:1-18). First, the new covenant offering was made in the true, heavenly tabernacle (Heb 9:11) rather than the earthly copy. Second, Christ's offering consisted of his own blood rather than the blood of animals (Heb 9:12-14). Third, his offering, rather than having to be repeated year after year, was made once for all time (Heb 10:1-18). Since his superior offering perfects new covenant believers permanently, God no longer remembers their sins* (Heb 10:14-18) and they receive a superior basis for endurance* in the Christian way.

4.2.6. Promise and Punishment. Eschatologically,* the wandering people of God are traveling toward the heavenly kingdom and city. In addition to their relationship to Jesus, they have the promise of rest (Heb 4:1-11; Gen 2:2; Ps 94:7-11 LXX), the example of the OT faithful (Heb 11) and the knowledge* that true children face discipline* from the heavenly Father (Heb 12:4-13; Prov 3:11-12) to sustain them. At the same time the OT warns that punishment awaits those who prove faithless (e.g., Heb 3:7-19; Ps 94:7-11 LXX; Heb 10:30; Deut 32:35-36). The harsh warnings of the hortatory sections of Hebrews have the OT wilderness episodes as their backdrop. The important motif of falling must be understood in light of those faithless ones who incurred God's wrath* through their unbelief.

5. Conclusions.

It is clear that the author of Hebrews drew from a wide range of homiletical and hermeneutical techniques common to his milieu. Rather than employing these in a fantastic and reckless appropriation of the OT, his discourse evinces careful study, reflection and craftsmanship. The importance of understanding his methodology and therefore his logic can hardly be overemphasized. Furthermore, and most importantly, the author uses the OT as one vitally important basis for his theology. The theological tapestry he weaves, although grounded in the early Christian kerygma, cannot be understood apart from a comprehension of his uses of the OT text.

See also ANCESTORS; INTERTEXTUALITY IN EARLY CHRISTIAN LITERATURE; MELCHIZEDEK; MOSES; PRIEST, HIGH PRIEST; PROMISE; SACRIFICE, OFFERINGS, GIFTS; TABERNACLE, SANCTUARY.

BIBLIOGRAPHY. M. Barth, "The Old Testament in Hebrews" in *Issues in New Testament Interpretation,* ed. W. Klassen and G. F. Snyder (New York: Harper & Row, 1962) 65-78; F. Bleek, *Der Brief an die Hebräer* (Berlin: Ferdinand Dümmler, 1828); F. F. Bruce, *The Epistle to the Hebrews* (NICNT; rev. ed.; Grand Rapids: Eerd- mans, 1990); G. B. Caird, "The Exegetical Method of the Epistle to the Hebrews," *CJT* 5 (1959) 44-51; R. E. Clements, "The Use of the Old Testament in Hebrews," *SWJT* 28 (1985) 36-45; H. Cobrink, "Some Thoughts on the Old Testament Citations in the Epistle to the Hebrews," *Neot* 5 (1971) 22-36; D. Cohn-Sherbok, "Paul and Rabbinic Exegesis," *SJT* 35 (1982) 117-32; M. Cosby, "The Rhetorical Composition of Hebrews 11," *JBL* 107 (1988) 257-73; E. E. Ellis, *Paul's Use of the Old Testament* (Grand Rapids: Baker, 1981); idem, *Prophecy and Hermeneutic in Early Christianity: New Testament Essays* (Grand Rapids: Eerdmans, 1978); J. A. Fitzmyer, " 'Now This Melchizedek' (Heb 7:1)," *CBQ* 25 (1963) 305-21; G. Howard, "Hebrews and the Old Testament Quotations," *NovT* 10 (1968) 208-16; G. Hughes, *Hebrews and Hermeneutics: The Epistle to the Hebrews as a New Testament Example of Biblical Interpretation* (Cambridge: Cambridge University Press, 1979); L. D. Hurst, *The Epistle to the Hebrews: Its Background of Thought* (SNTSMS 65; Cambridge: Cambridge University Press, 1990); P. Katz, "The Quotations from Deuteronomy in Hebrews," *ZNW* 49 (1958) 213-23; S. J. Kistemaker, *The Psalm Citations in the Epistle to the Hebrews* (Amsterdam: van Soest, 1961); B. Lindars, *The Theology of the Letter to the Hebrews* (NTT; Cambridge: Cambridge University Press, 1991); R. N. Longenecker, *Biblical Exegesis in the Apostolic Period* (Grand Rapids: Eerdmans, 1975); J. C. McCullough, "The Old Testament Quotations in Hebrews," *NTS* 26 (1979-1980) 363-79; J. Moffatt, *A Critical and Exegetical Commentary on the Epistle to the Hebrews* (New York: Charles Scribner's Sons, 1924); K. J. Thomas, "The Old Testament Citations in Hebrews," *NTS* 11 (1965) H. Thyen, *Der Stil des jüdisch-hellenistischen Homilie* (Göttingen: Vandenhoeck & Ruprecht, 1955); J. Van der Ploeg, "L' exégèse de l'Ancien Testament dans l'Épître aux Hébreux," *RB* 54 (1947) 187-228; M. Wilcox, "On Investigating the Use of the Old Testament in the New Testament" in *Text and Interpretation: Studies in the New Testament Presented to Matthew Black,* ed. E. Best and R. Wilson (Cambridge: Cambridge University Press, 1979) 231-44; R. Williamson, *Philo and the Epistle to the Hebrews* (Leiden: E. J. Brill, 1970).

G. H. Guthrie

OLD TESTAMENT IN REVELATION

No book of the NT is more thoroughly saturated

with the thought and language of ancient Scripture than the book of Revelation (*see* Revelation, Book of). Yet, in contrast to much of the NT, Revelation never mentions the Scriptures *(hai graphai)* and never cites as Scripture *(graphē)* any individual passage from either the Hebrew Bible, now known to Christians as the OT, or the Greek Bible, known as the Septuagint. Nor does John, the writer of Revelation, ever appeal to the authority* of Scripture with the phrase "it is written" *(gegraptai)* or state that something happened "to fulfill" *(hina . . . plērōthē)* some prophecy written in the Bible.

1. Writing and Books in the Revelation of John
2. Characters and Authors
3. The Hebrew Bible as Prophecy
4. Biblical Language in the Revelation

1. Writing and Books in the Revelation of John.

A great deal of writing goes on in the book of Revelation itself. John is repeatedly told to "write" *(grapson;* an imperative) what he sees (Rev 1:11, 19; 2:1, 8, 12, 18; 3:1, 7, 14; 14:13; 19; 21:5; cf. 10:4). When he looks at his own finished work he speaks of "the things written" in it *(ta gegrammena,* Rev 1:3; 22:18, 19). Names especially are often "written": a new name* on a white stone* for Christian believers (Rev 2:17); the name of God or God's city written on the believers themselves (Rev 3:12); the names of the Lamb* and of the Father on their foreheads (Rev 14:1); a name of mystery* on the forehead of Babylon* the prostitute (Rev 17:5); an unknown name written on the rider on the white horse (Rev 19:12); and the name "King of kings and Lord of lords" on his clothing and armor (Rev 19:16).

Books or scrolls* are said to be "written," with the implication that the writing was done before the book of Revelation itself was written. John sees in heaven* "a scroll *[biblion]* written on the inside and on the back, sealed with seven seals" (Rev 5:1, NRSV; *see* Seals). At the last judgment* "books *(biblia)* were opened," and "another book *[biblion]* was opened, which is the book of life. And the dead were judged by what was written *[ek tōn gegrammenōn]* in the books, by what they had done. . . . And if any one's name was not found written in the book of life, he was thrown into the lake of fire" (Rev 20:12, 14, RSV). Earlier visions* mention the beast* "whose name is not written" (Rev 13:8) and "the

dwellers on the earth whose names are not written" (Rev 17:8) in this book of life. In one of the prophecies* to the seven churches* the victorious Christian is promised that "I will not blot his name out of the book *[biblos]* of life" (Rev 3:5).

Few interpreters will argue that either the "book of life" or the other "books" opened at the judgment represent the Hebrew Bible. The "book of life" is a list of all who are chosen for salvation* (cf. Ex 32:32-33), while the other books are divine records of deeds done by every person on earth (cf. Dan 7:10; *1 Enoch* 90:20; *4 Ezra* 6:20; *2 Bar* 24:1). The writer of Revelation knows of many "books" written before his own, yet he is strangely silent about the one Christians would come to call the OT.

2. Characters and Authors.

Unlike many Jewish apocalyptic* works, the book of Revelation does not claim to be written by an OT character or author such as Enoch, Ezra or Baruch. Other than Moses,* the only characters from the Hebrew Bible who are mentioned are the twelve patriarchs listed in Revelation 7:5-8 (see also Judah in Rev 5:5), David (in the phrase "the root of David," Rev 5:5; 22:16), and Balaam, Balak and Jezebel as examples of false prophecy (Rev 2:14, 20). The only biblical author named is "Moses, the servant of God" (Rev 15:3), and he is mentioned not as a writer of Scripture but as the one who led Israel* across the Red Sea, even as Christian believers cross the "sea of glass mixed with fire" in John's immediate context (Rev 15:2). The term "servant of God" (*see* Servant) identifies Moses as a prophet,* the only one of God's "servants the prophets" (Rev 10:7) who is designated by name—possibly because John viewed him as the first prophet and a standard by which all prophecy was measured (see Deut 18:15-18). Moses' "song" (Rev 15:3-4) has no direct links to the "song of Moses" found in Exodus 15:1-18 but is jointly the song of Moses and of the Lamb (Rev 15:3). Possibly it is the same as the "new song" that only the 144,000 on Mount Zion could learn (Rev 14:3; *see* Jerusalem, Zion).

If Moses is the only named biblical prophet (other than false prophets) in the Revelation, John himself is the only named Christian "servant" or "prophet" (Rev 1:1, 9-10; 22:8-9). This fact may help to illumine John's use of the OT. John as a prophet seems to have viewed all

Scripture as prophecy. His role is not that of a scribe interpreting a written text but of a prophet incorporating the spoken words of ancient prophecies into new prophecies for a new time. To John, the truth* he presents is not derivative from those ancient prophets he knows but never identifies by name—Daniel, Ezekiel, Isaiah, Jeremiah, Zechariah. Rather, it comes from the same wellspring of divine inspiration on which they drew. His visions and auditions, no less than theirs, are revelations* from God.

Some scholars, while granting this in theory, still use the OT as a framework within which the book of Revelation must be interpreted. For example, the system commonly known as dispensationalism adds together two of the time periods designated in the Revelation as "42 months" (Rev 11:2, 13:5) or "1,260 days" (Rev 11:3, 12:6) to make a total of seven years, which are then understood to be the "seventieth week" of Daniel 9:27. In a different vein, G. K. Beale suggests that when John mentions "what will [or must] take place after this" (e.g., Rev 1:19; 4:1) he refers to what was future from Daniel's standpoint (Dan 2:45), not necessarily his own. A better approach is to recognize that in the book of Revelation the language and thought of the OT are not only preserved and reaffirmed but transformed. The lasting contribution of A. Farrer (even though many of his examples are questionable) is the insight that in the Revelation biblical images are reborn and given not just life but new life.

3. The Hebrew Bible as Prophecy.

To introduce a modern analogy from the world of computers, John uses the OT not as hard copy but as soft copy. Because he himself is a writing prophet who goes so far as to insist that nothing be added to or subtracted from what he has written (Rev 22:18-19), John understands that the hard copy—the written text of the Bible—exists, and he has no desire to change it. What is written in Daniel is written. What Ezekiel has written, he has written. John is more interested in the soft copy, the revelation as it came orally from God to the prophets. These ancient oracles inform and shape his own work in his own time. To be sure, John knows them from written texts, whether texts he has read or texts he has heard read in Christian congregations. Such written prophecies, when

read aloud, become oral once again and in that sense soft copy. They take on new life in John's visions as part of the language by which he speaks to situations not imagined at the time the prophecies were given. This phenomenon, known to students of literature as intertextuality,* is nowhere better illustrated in the NT than in the Revelation. John is not so much rewriting ancient texts as creating from them (he would say transmitting) something new. John anticipated that his prophecies too would have a continuing life, both written (Rev 22:18-19) and oral (Rev 1:3) in Christian communities, and that they would not replace but stand alongside the Jewish Scriptures. This is what happened.

4. Biblical Language in the Revelation.

How do John's visions make use of the OT, and what parts of it do they use? Only a small sampling is possible.

4.1. Genesis. From the early chapters of Genesis John draws the image of the "tree of life" (Gen 2:9; 3:22, 24) with the promise* that victorious Christians will gain access to that long-guarded treasure (Rev 2:7; 22:2, 14, 19). The "ancient serpent" in the Garden of Eden (Gen 3:1-5) becomes "the great dragon," also known as "the Devil and Satan, the deceiver of the whole world" (Rev 12:9; *see* Satan). While the curse on the serpent in Genesis 3:14 is ignored in the book of Revelation, the curse's continuation in Genesis 3:15 is taken seriously indeed.

The conflict between the woman and her offspring and the serpent-dragon and his "offspring" becomes the controlling image of Revelation 12 and 13, where the dragon tries unsuccessfully to destroy first the woman's child as soon as he is born (Rev 12:4-5), then the woman herself (Rev 12:13-16) and finally "the rest of her offspring—those who obey God's commandments and hold to the testimony of Jesus" (Rev 12:17, NIV; *see* Commandments). The dragon carries out the last of these evil intentions by summoning from the sea a beast who looks like him, with "ten horns and seven heads" (Rev 13:1; cf. 12:3), giving the beast his own "power and his throne and great authority" (Rev 13:2, NRSV). Significantly one of the beast's heads "seemed to have received a death-blow, but its mortal wound had been healed" (Rev 13:3, NRSV; cf. Rev 13:12, 14). The beast bears the scars of the conflict prophesied in Genesis 3:15. If Revelation 12 describes the first stage of the prophecy, "enmity between you and the woman," Revelation 13 describes the second, "enmity between your offspring and hers."

4.2. Daniel. At the same time the beast is painted in colors taken from Daniel's dream in Babylon (Dan 7:1-8). Daniel saw four beasts, one like a lion, one like a bear, one like a leopard and the fourth "different from all the beasts that preceded it, and it had ten horns" (Dan 7:7, NRSV). John sees just one beast, with ten horns and seven heads, "and on its horns were ten diadems, and on its heads were blasphemous names. And the beast that I saw was like a leopard, its feet were like a bear's, and its mouth was like a lion's mouth" (Rev 13:1-2, NRSV). It is as if John sees Daniel's four beasts rolled into one. The beast's seven heads are the only conspicuous detail of the vision not rooted in Daniel's dream. Moreover, the grotesque appearance of the beast in Revelation 13 has already shaped to some extent the transformation of the serpent of Genesis in Revelation 12 into a dragon "with seven heads and ten horns" (Rev 12:3).

The use of Daniel in the book of Revelation is evident in John's first vision (Rev 1:12-20). John, on the island of Patmos, sees an angelic figure recognizably similar to one Daniel saw on the bank of the Tigris River: "I looked up and saw a man clothed in linen, with a belt of gold from Uphaz around his waist. His body was like beryl, his face like lightning, his eyes like flaming torches, his arms and legs like the gleam of burnished bronze, and the sound of his words like the roar of a multitude" (Dan 10:5-6, NRSV; cf. Rev 1:13-15). John, like Daniel, falls to the ground but is touched by the figure he sees and told, "Do not fear" (Dan 10:9, 10, 12; cf. Rev 1:17).

Instead of simply "a man," John's angel* is identified as one "like a son of man" (Rev 1:13, NIV), a phrase echoing such passages as Daniel 10:18 ("one in human form," NRSV) and in different settings Daniel 7:13 ("one like a human being") and Ezekiel's vision of the throne of God* with "something that seemed like a human form" above it (Ezek 1:26). That Daniel 7 at least is in John's mind alongside Daniel 10 is clear from other details of his description of the figure he saw: "His head and his hair were white as white wool, white as snow" (Rev 1:14). These comparisons come neither from Daniel's description of the man by the Tigris in Daniel

10 nor from his reference to the "one like a human being" in Daniel 7:13 but from his description of the "Ancient One" into whose presence the "one like a human being" came, whose "clothing was white as snow, and the hair of his head like pure wool" (Dan 7:9, NRSV). Daniel's "Ancient One," his "one like a human being" and his man by the Tigris River all merge into one in John's remarkable opening vision.

John's figure finally identifies himself as the risen Jesus, not by name but with the words "I am the first and the last, and the living one. I was dead, and see, I am alive forever and ever; and I have the keys of Death and Hades" (Rev 1:17-18, NRSV). The point, however, is not to assert that Daniel repeatedly saw Jesus in his visions. Revelation is not interpreting Daniel in the sense in which Jewish or Christian scribes customarily interpreted ancient written texts. Nor is its use of the OT like that of John's Gospel, where Isaiah is quoted with the notice that the prophet saw Jesus' glory* and wrote about him (Jn 12:42), nor like that of Paul, who claimed that the Israelites in the desert "drank from the spiritual rock that followed them, and the rock was Christ" (1 Cor 10:4, NRSV). Instead Revelation borrows Daniel's language to articulate visions that Daniel never saw. There is no interest in Daniel as a book of the Bible or in the intentions of its author, for John is preoccupied with his own visions and consequently with his own authorial intentions.

4.3. Ezekiel. The same is true of the book of Ezekiel. When John first looks into heaven (Rev 4 and 5) he echoes Ezekiel more than Daniel. What he sees there resembles in part what Ezekiel saw centuries before—the throne of God, a rainbow, an expanse of shining crystal and four living creatures around the throne, each with four wings and the four faces of a human being, a lion, an ox and an eagle. In John's vision each living creature has one of the four faces, the expanse of crystal has become a sea of glass, and other details (such as twenty-four elders on twenty-four thrones) have been added, yet John's heaven is still recognizably Ezekiel's. Later, when John receives his call to "prophesy again about many peoples and nations and languages and kings," his experience of taking a scroll, eating it and finding it sweet in his mouth but bitter in his stomach (Rev 10:8-11) virtually reenacts the prophetic call of Ezekiel (Ezek 2:8-3:3).

4.4. Narrative as Prophecy. John's visions do not distinguish biblical prophecy from narrative, and his choice of narratives is not limited to the early chapters of Genesis. Narrative too is prophecy to him. In telling the story of two witnesses who will confront an ungodly world in Jerusalem (Rev 11:1-13), he draws freely and simultaneously on Zechariah's prophecy of two olive trees and a lampstand representing "the two anointed ones who stand by the Lord of the whole earth" (Zech 4:11-14, NRSV) and on well-known biblical stories about Elijah withholding rain from the land (1 Kings 17:1) and Moses turning the waters of Egypt to blood (Ex 7:17-19; see Rev 11:4-6). If Jewish thought customarily summed up the Hebrew Bible as "the law and the prophets" (see e.g. Mt 5:17) without regard for other genres such as poetry, history or wisdom, the book of Revelation largely ignores the category of law and views the whole Bible under the single rubric of prophecy.

4.5. A New World and a New Covenant. John's concluding visions of "a new heaven and a new earth" (Rev 21:1) and of "the holy city, the new Jerusalem, coming down out of heaven from God, prepared as a bride adorned for her husband" (Rev 21:2; see also 21:9—22:5) blend visions from the books of Ezekiel and Isaiah. The new heaven and new earth echo Isaiah 65:17 and 66:22, while a number of details in John's description of the holy city correspond to Ezekiel's blueprint for a restored temple* (Ezek 40—48)—but with one conspicuous and decisive exception: John "saw no temple in the city, for its temple is the Lord God the Almighty and the Lamb" (Rev 21:22). The key to Revelation's use of the Hebrew Bible is perhaps John's vision of consummation in the new heaven and new earth (Rev 21:3), where "a loud voice from the throne" confirms certain biblical promises made in connection with God's covenant* with Israel, above all Leviticus 26:11-12 ("I will place my dwelling in your midst. . . . And I will walk among you, and will be your God, and you shall be my people") and Ezekiel 37:27 ("My dwelling place shall be with them; and I will be their God, and they shall be my people"). Again, however, there is a decisive difference. What John hears from God is a promise not to "people" but to "peoples." The promise to Israel has been broadened to embrace "a great multitude that no one could count, from every nation, from all tribes and peoples and languages, standing be-fore the throne and before the Lamb" (Rev 7:9).

The use of the Bible in the book of Revelation is quite different from its use in Paul's letters, but one passage in Paul (not altogether typical and often said to be non-Pauline) closely parallels John's way of using the Bible, in particular John's vision of the new covenant in Revelation 21:1-8. The only difference is that what John assigns to the future, Paul places in the present: "For we are the temple of the living God; as God said, 'I will live in them and walk among them, and I will be their God, and they shall be my people. Therefore come out from them, and be separated from them, says the Lord, and touch nothing unclean; then I will welcome you, and I will be your father, and you shall be my sons and daughters, says the Lord Almighty'" (2 Cor 6:16-18, NRSV). Without specific citation Paul combines Leviticus 26:11-12 and Ezekiel 37:17 in much the same fashion as John does in Revelation 21:3, and Paul applies the promise of 2 Samuel 7:14 to faithful Christians just as John does in Revelation 21:7. The parallels suggest that John's method of drawing freely on OT language was not unique in early Christianity but surfaced from time to time wherever emphasis was placed on the conviction that the same Spirit (*see* Holy Spirit) who had inspired the biblical prophets was speaking again through Jesus Christ and his servants.

See also APOCALYPTIC, APOCALYPTICISM; BABYLON; BEASTS, DRAGON, SEA, CONFLICT MOTIF; ESCHATOLOGY; INTERTEXTUALITY; REVELATION, BOOK OF.

BIBLIOGRAPHY. G. K. Beale, *The Use of Daniel in Jewish Apocalyptic Literature and in the Revelation of St. John* (Lanham, MD: University Press of America, 1984); J. Cambier, "Les images de l'Ancien Testament dans l'Apocalypse," *NRT* 77 (1955) 113-23; R. H. Charles, *A Critical and Exegetical Commentary on the Revelation of St. John* (2 vols.; Edinburgh: T & T Clark, 1920); A. Farrer, *A Rebirth of Images: The Making of St. John's Apocalypse* (Boston: Beacon, 1963); J. Fekkes III, *Isaiah and Prophetic Traditions in the Book of Revelation* (Sheffield: Sheffield Academic Press, 1994); A. Feuillet, *The Apocalypse* (Staten Island, NY: Alba House, 1965) 77-80; F. Jenkins, *The Old Testament in the Book of Revelation* (Grand Rapids: Eerdmans, 1976); E. Lohse, "Die alttestamentliche Sprache des Sehers Johannes," *ZNW* 52 (1961) 122-26; F. D. Mazzaferri, *The Genre of the Book of Revelation from a Source-critical*

Perspective (Berlin and New York: Walter de-Gruyter, 1989); J. R. Michaels, *Interpreting the Book of Revelation* (Grand Rapids: Baker, 1992) 107-27; S. Moyise, *The Old Testament in the Book of Revelation* (JSNTSup 115; Sheffield: Sheffield Academic Press, 1995); J. Paulien, "Elusive Allusions: The Problematic Use of the Old Testament in Revelation," *BibRes* 33 (1988) 37-53; M. Rist, "The Use of the Old Testament by the Author of Revelation," *Iliff Review* 17 (1960) 3-10; J. P. Ruiz, *Ezekiel in the Apocalypse* (New York: Peter Lang, 1989); H. B. Swete, *The Apocalypse of St. John* (Grand Rapids: Eerdmans, n.d.) cxl-clviii; P. Trudinger, "Some Observations Concerning the Text of the Old Testament in the Book of Revelation," *JTS* 17 (1966) 82-88; J. T. Willis, "The Old Testament and the Book of Revelation" in *Johannine Studies,* ed. J. Priest (Malibu, CA: Pepperdine University, 1989).

J. R. Michaels

OPPONENTS. *See* ADVERSARIES.

ORACLES. *See* RELIGIONS, GRECO-ROMAN.

P

PARABLES OF HERMAS. *See* HERMAS, SHEPHERD OF.

PARAENESIS. *See* TEACHING, PARAENESIS.

PAROUSIA

Parousia is a quasi-technical term usually used with reference to the future coming of Jesus Christ* in glory* at the end of the world as the consummation of the saving actions of God* and as the culmination of the eschatological process. More popularly (and much less precisely) the term is often equated with the Second Coming of Jesus Christ on the clouds of glory, based mainly on passages which occur in the Gospels (such as Mt 24:3, 27, 37, 39) and in the Pauline epistles (such as 1 Cor 15:23; 1 Thess 2:19; 3:13; 4:15; 5:23; 2 Thess 2:1, 8-9; *see DJG* and *DPL*, Eschatology). The Parousia is important in that it serves as an intersection of Christian understandings of christology,* eschatology* and soteriology: as the supreme moment of revelation of Jesus Christ as Lord* for all the created order to see, as the culmination of God's eternal purposes as they are worked out in human affairs and as the time at which the world is judged and believers are granted resurrection* existence and are ultimately united with their Lord.

At the same time, perhaps no other single idea has engendered so much theological debate over the centuries as has the Parousia, given that it has challenged Christians to think afresh about the meaning and significance of eschatological hope.* Insofar as the so-called "delay of the Parousia" (discussed below) has prompted discussion about Jesus' own expectations as well as raise questions about the extent of his human nature (did he know the time of the final Parousia or was he just mistaken?), it has remained an important item on the christological agenda of many modern theologians.

Insofar as the Pauline letters, and indeed most of the rest of the NT documents, contain references to the Parousia within them, questions about the reliance of these materials upon Jesus' own ideas about the Parousia arise. Similar questions are prompted about the nature and extent to which specifically Christian eschatological ideas are to be seen as natural developments of Jewish literature in its prophetic, wisdom and apocalyptic traditions.

All of this is to say that the Parousia stands as an important theological crossroads at which many strands of NT theology* and hermeneutical debate come together. To engage in a discussion of the Parousia of Jesus Christ, seemingly at any point, is to enter an exegetical minefield; yet to refuse to engage in such a discussion is to run the risk of overlooking a central feature of NT teaching, one which may in fact go a long way toward clarifying many other critical issues of Christian faith and belief. We will concentrate our discussion on the NT materials addressed within the confines of this volume, but we will necessarily spill over in our analysis into the Gospels, the Pauline letters and other early Christian writings. This is unavoidable given the complex interconnection between them all on such a matter as foundational as the Parousia of Jesus Christ.

1. The Background of the Idea of the Parousia within Jewish Thought
2. The Parousia of Jesus Christ in Acts, Epistles and the Book of Revelation
3. The Delay of the Parousia

1. The Background of the Idea of the Parousia within Jewish Thought.

The concept of the Parousia of Jesus Christ is best viewed as a development of the generalized hope for the future which is found throughout the OT, particularly within the prophetic literature. It is to be seen as intimately related to

God's promises to his people that a better future awaited them, a time when injustices would be righted, the world order transformed and divine values made to hold sway in human lives. Within the NT these ideas are particularly associated with expectations of the coming of the kingdom* of God and are given explicit christological content.

There is much to suggest that the idea of an imminent arrival of the kingdom of God was a foundational idea within the thought and teaching of Jesus of Nazareth. Yet insofar as his own messianic self-understanding led him to see his life and ministry as the means of bringing the kingdom of God to earth, it can be said to be realized in the present. It is therefore reasonable to infer that the idea of the Parousia, as it is expressed in the various writings of the NT, is an extension of Jesus' own thought, although understandably it shows signs of Christian expansion and development (see Ladd 1975 on this point). The Pauline letters are especially significant in this regard, inasmuch as they stand as the earliest extant Christian writings. We see within Paul's letters how the apostle reinterpreted the Jewish idea of the Day of the Lord (as contained in such passages as Amos 5:18; Is 2:6-22 and Zech 14:3-5) and reshaped it christologically.

We can also detect the same process of reinterpretation going on in a variety of subsequent Christian writings, especially with regard to Zechariah 14:3-5; the same OT theophany is explicitly cited in *Didache* 16:7 and is applied to the Parousia of Jesus Christ. Many other Jewish documents of the first and second century A.D. also help to provide an understanding of the idea of the Parousia, notably *Jubilees*, *1 Enoch* 37—71, *4 Ezra* and *2 Baruch* (although Glasson 1945, 1953 and 1971 strongly disagrees). In short, Christian declarations about the coming Parousia of Jesus Christ arise out of Jewish eschatological thought about the coming of the kingdom of God. At the same time it appears to be rooted more in theophanic descriptions than in messianic belief, although it is difficult to draw hard and fast distinctions between these two focal points, so intertwined are they within Christian writings, apparently from the very beginning.

Such a consideration helps explain how frequently it happens that confusion reigns in the NT writings when it comes to identifying who it is that comes (God or Christ?) in judgment at the final consummation (see the discussion of the various NT documents below). Nevertheless, there is an additional linguistic consideration to keep in mind as well, since the term *parousia* was used in the larger Hellenistic world at the time that many of the NT writings were being produced.

1.1. Terminological Considerations. It is often noted that the meaning of *parousia* in Hellenistic Greek is used to denote the "presence" or "arrival" of someone (the Latin equivalent is *adventus*). Both *parousia* and *adventus* are thus used with reference to the arrival of a Roman emperor in a province, such as the visit of the emperor Hadrian as proclaimed on Roman imperial coinage (as Kreitzer 1988 argues). The key thing to be observed here is how the term is used non-eschatologically. It is also interesting to note in this regard that Josephus uses the term *parousia* in a non-eschatological sense to describe the epiphany of God at Sinai and in the temple,* as well as the revealing of his presence to the Roman legate Petronius during the tension-filled incident when the Emperor* Caligula wished to have his image placed in the temple at Jerusalem (Josephus *Ant.* 3.5.2 §80; 3.8.5 §203; 18.8.6 §284). At the same time it is important to remember that the expectation of a future deliverer was widespread within the first-century world and that it was often linked to imperial aspirations. We find clear evidence that some writers entertained the suggestion that the future world leader would rule from Judea. A classic example of this is Josephus's prophecy about the Roman Emperor Vespasian being hailed as the Messiah (Josephus *J.W.* 6.6.4 §§312-313 ; cf. Tacitus *Hist.* 5.13 and Suetonius *Vespasian* 4).

We are so accustomed to using the term Parousia exclusively with reference to Jesus Christ, effectively taking it to be shorthand term for "Christian eschatology," that it sometimes comes as a surprise to find that outside of Matthew and the Pauline letters the term *parousia* occurs only six times in the whole of the NT (Jas 5:7, 8; 2 Pet 1:16; 3:4, 12; 1 Jn 2:28). However, a wide number of related terms and expressions are used outside the Gospels and the Pauline corpus to express the idea of an eschatological fulfillment wherein Jesus Christ is presented as the one who comes to bring God's kingdom to its completion. In this connection, forms of the verb *phaneroō* appear fourteen times (Heb 9:8, 26; 1 Pet 1:20; 5:4; 1 Jn 1:2 (twice); 2:19, 28; 3:2, 5, 8; 4:8; Rev 3:18; 15:4); and forms of the verb *erchomai* occur numerous times in (seemingly) eschatological contexts (including Acts 1:11; 3:20; Rev 1:7; 2:5, 16; 3:11, 20; 22:7, 12, 20). Meanwhile, the noun *apokalypsis* is used three times in 1 Peter 1:7, 13 and 4:13 to speak of the "revelation"* of Jesus Christ in a context which clearly implies his Parousia at the final judgment, and a verbal form of the same word appears in 1 Peter 5:1. Similarly, in Acts 2:20 the writer quotes the LXX of Joel 3:4 using the noun *epiphanēs* within Peter's sermon at Pentecost.

Several equivalent expressions for the future day of eschatological judgment* are contained in the NT. For example, in Hebrews 10:25 the phrase "the day" is found; in Jude 6 mention is made of "the great day"; and in Revelation 6:17 and 16:14 the complementary phrases "the great day of wrath" and "the great day of God Almighty" appear (*see* Day of the Lord). It is not always clear within these passages whether the writer(s) has the (so-called) first coming or the Second Coming (or Advent) of Jesus Christ in mind, or even (as in Jude 6 and Rev 6:17; 16:14) whether they are speaking more generally of the great eschatological Day of the Lord and have not yet recast what was originally an OT theological concept into a specifically NT christological form. It needs to be remembered that it is not until the writings of Justin Martyr (c. A.D. 110) that a formal distinction is made between the first and second comings of Christ (they are distinguished in his *Apol. I* 52.3; cf. *Dial. Tryph.* 14.4; 118.2), although Hebrews 9:28 is very close to making such a distinction (for further lexicographical details see Oepke, McArthur, Brown, Radl).

1.2. Conceptual Considerations. Different ways of conceptualizing the Parousia of Jesus Christ are to be found within the NT, most arising directly out of the matrix of Jewish eschatology. These are indicative of the astonishing range of theological truth associated with the concept and they witness to its importance as a focal point of Christian belief. They also serve as gathering points for theological interpretation by NT scholars who seek to explore the multifaceted concept we describe as the Parousia. Thus, the Parousia has been understood as an act of vindication, a time of visitation, a decisive moment of judgment, a time of deliverance and the climactic event of consummation. The boundaries of these ideas are difficult to define. At times one dimension, one facet of belief in the Parousia may be focussed upon more than another, but collectively they constitute the multi-dimensional nature of Christian proclamation about the Parousia, the advent of Jesus Christ.

2. The Parousia of Jesus Christ in Acts, Epistles and the Book of Revelation.

References or allusions to the Parousia of Jesus Christ are to be found in nearly all of the NT documents under consideration, the only clear exception being 3 John. However, since 1 John does contain an explicit reference to the Parousia (in 1 Jn 2:28), we can safely say that the idea of the final eschatological act of God in the return of Jesus Christ is one of the few theological ideas to enjoy unanimous support in all strata of the NT.

2.1. The Book of Acts. The interpretation of the eschatology of Acts* is closely tied up with the interpretation of the Gospel of Luke. It is quite impossible to separate the ideas contained within the two documents, and they are best viewed as complementing one another at several key points in matters of eschatology, including the presentation of the Parousia of Jesus Christ (contra Wilson, who argues for a subtle, but important, difference between the eschatology of Lk and that of Acts on this point). Inevitably decisions about the place that eschatology has within the thought of the writer of Luke-Acts become intertwined with suggestions as to the purpose the author had in mind when writing his two-volume work.

Following the lead (if not agreeing with the conclusion) of H. Conzelmann, most scholars accept that in Luke-Acts eschatological hope has been deferred in some way and the belief in the imminent arrival of the Parousia is in some measure downplayed. This adjustment is most notable in the Lukan reworking of Jesus' discourse contained in Mark 13, in the reworking of some of the parables of Jesus (as evidenced in such verses as Lk 18:1; 19:11) and in the ascension* story (Lk 24:50-51; Acts 1:6-11) which prompts a new understanding of the fulfillment of history. Indeed, the very existence of Acts itself may be taken to indicate this shift of eschatological emphasis. As J. D. G. Dunn puts it: "the very act of writing a history of earliest Christianity (rather than an apocalypse) was an admission that the earliest Parousia hope was mistaken and that the Parousia hope itself had faded" (Dunn, 348).

Conzelmann is well known for arguing that the motivation for the composition of Luke-Acts was disappointment over the non-fulfillment of the Parousia. Many important German interpreters of Acts have followed Conzelmann on this point (notably Grässer, Haenchen and Lüdemann, with English-speaking interpreters generally less enthusiastic, the important work of Esler being a notable exception). However, caution needs to be exercised here, and has been in more recent investigation. In the words of W. W. Gasque: "One conclusion that unites nearly all recent study of Lk-Acts is that Conzelmann's classic formulation of the purpose of the Lukan writings, put forward in *The Theology of St. Luke*, was incorrect. Lk-Acts was certainly not written to deal with the problem of the delay of the parousia" (Gasque, 346). Something of a scholarly consensus has been reached to the effect that Luke-Acts contains many passages which maintain a firm belief in the possibility of an imminent Parousia (contra Conzelmann), while containing at the same time many passages which present it as coming sometime in the indefinite future (Hiers 1973-74 and Wilson offer interpretations along these lines).

So central has the question of the delay of the Parousia been for studies of Luke-Acts (in light of Conzelmann's work) that it is worth considering briefly some of these scholarly investigations, complex and novel though they tend to be. Some interpreters of Luke-Acts have ruthlessly followed the logic of the de-eschatologizing process which is said to be going on in Luke-Acts and identified the resurrection of Jesus with the arrival of the kingdom of God, thus rendering the future Parousia secondary, if not superfluous. Several passages are cited as supporting such an interpretation, including Luke 23:42 and Acts 1:3 which speak of resurrection and the arrival of the kingdom of God together. Others (such as Flender and Franklin) have come to similar conclusions about the ascension as the central eschatological event in the theology of Luke-Acts, an approach which relegates the future Parousia to a position of serving as mere confirmation for the ascension and, conversely,

takes the ascension to be an anticipation of the Parousia (see Parsons for a full discussion).

The vision of Stephen* contained in Acts 7:54-60 has also attracted some discussion about it as implying the Parousia of the Son of Man. The fact that the Son of Man is described as "standing" (*estōta*), in contrast to the description of him as sitting (*kathēmenos*) in Luke 22:69, is sometimes taken to mean that he stands in order to come at the Parousia. Since the context of the pericope is concerned with the martyrdom* of Stephen, this has led to interpretations of the passage as a personal Parousia which Stephen experiences when he is stoned to death (H. P. Owen and C. K. Barrett [1964] both offer interpretations along these lines). Similarly, the stress placed on the Jewish-Gentile mission within Luke-Acts is sometimes said to be related to the author's handling of the theological problems raised by the delay of the Parousia. Thus in Acts 1:6 the disciples question the risen Lord about the timing of the arrival of the kingdom of God only to find Jesus reply by exhorting them against date-fixing (Acts 1:7), promising them the gift of the Holy Spirit* (Acts 1:8a) and commissioning them with the mission to the Gentiles (Acts 1:8b). The incident is then rounded off by the ascension story which concludes with an assurance of his Parousia in the future (Acts 1:11). Other key passages in Acts also associate the fulfillment of the church's mission with the Parousia, including Acts 3:19-21 where Peter addresses the Jews in Solomon's portico and calls them to repentance so as to hasten the sending of the appointed Christ Jesus; and Acts 10:42 where Jesus Christ is described by Peter (in his speech following the Cornelius* episode) as the judge of the living and the dead who is ordained by God.

The connection between the Parousia and the future judgment that it brings is found in several other places in Acts. Included are: Acts 2:20 where the Day of the Lord is described in the words of a prophecy of Joel 2:31 as "the great and manifest day"; Acts 3:19-21 where it is portrayed as the fulfillment of OT prophecy and the provocative phrase "until the time of the restoration of all things" is used; Acts 17:31 where mention is made of the day on which Christ will judge the world as God's divinely appointed judge; and Acts 24:25 where mention is made of Paul's talking to the Roman procurator Felix and his Jewish wife Drusilla about the future judgment (*tou krimatos tou mellontos*). It may well be that the open-ended references to future salvation* (such as Acts 2:21, 40; 4:12; 11:14; 13:26; 15:1, 11; 16:17, 30-31) and to hope (such as Acts 2:26; 23:6; 24:15; 26:6-7; 28:20) also have the Parousia as a backdrop in that it is the time of both deliverance and assurance.* The curious linking of persecution* and entry into the kingdom of God contained in Acts 14:22 is taken by some to reflect traditional ideas about persecution of the faithful as a sign of the end times (as it is in 1 Pet). If the Parousia is taken to be the moment of vindication for the persecuted, then a connection can be set up between it and the "entry into the kingdom of God."

One final observation is worth noting in that it is intimately connected with interpretations offered of the Parousia in Acts, particularly those which suggest (partly on an interpretation of key passages in Acts) that the idea of the Parousia was not part of Jesus' own thought and teaching. We have noted (see 1.2 above) that one common conceptualization of the Parousia is to view it as an act of vindication. J. A. T. Robinson (1957), for example, pursued this line of thought, suggesting that early on in Christian thinking the Parousia was taken to be the vindication of Jesus Christ to God, and that this was accomplished in his resurrection* from the dead. A crucial point here is that there is no temporal lag between the resurrection of Jesus Christ and his vindication as Lord at the Parousia; in fact, Jesus' resurrection is seen as the event which serves as his vindication. Thus Robinson argues that the two (resurrection and Parousia) are twin aspects of a single event, and he points to Acts 2:36 as evidence for this association of Parousia with Jesus' resurrection/vindication (Acts 17:31 might also be called into service on this point since it declares that the resurrection of Jesus from the dead serves as a guarantee [*pistis*] for the Parousia).

Even so, Robinson continues (1956), there is a stage of theological thinking which is prior to this, a stage reflected in Acts 3:18-21. This is a passage that is generally accepted as expressing expectation of the Parousia of Jesus Christ following the conversion of the Jews. However, Robinson argued, highly contentiously, that the passage merely proclaims that Jesus is the Messiah-elect and that the messianic age is yet to be inaugurated. The net result of this line of argu-

mentation is that the future Parousia, far from being the eschatological culmination of God's purposes in the glorious appearance of Jesus Christ, is taken to be the time at which Jesus will be confirmed as the Messiah (cf. Rom 1:3-4, a passage which figures prominently in debates about adoptionism). As a result, Robinson describes Acts 3:18-21 as "the most primitive christology of all," while decrying the tendency for interpreters of Acts to read traditional Parousia beliefs into it (F. F. Bruce 1988, 60, counters by describing the passage as arguably containing "the most primitive eschatology of all"; C. K. Barrett 1985 offers additional discussion). In that Acts 3:18-21 does not explicitly speak of Jesus as the Messiah by virtue of his resurrection (in contrast to Acts 2:36) it paves the way, so Robinson concluded, for the eventual development of a belief in the Second Coming of Jesus Christ at the end of time.

There has been much critical reaction to Robinson's theory and his interpretation of the Parousia passages in Acts has been largely rejected (his handling of Acts 10:42 seems almost sleight-of-hand!). Nevertheless, it has engendered much discussion about the place of the Parousia in Christian belief and his views are a reflection of the thinking of many today.

2.2. Hebrews. Few would dispute the essentially pastoral nature of Hebrews.* The fact that the anonymous author is addressing real concerns within the congregation he writes to is clear, as is the fact that he sets all of his "word of exhortation" (*logos parakleseos*, Heb 13:22) against a backdrop of traditional Jewish eschatological expectations, an approach which distinguishes him from the platonic ideas of Philo of Alexandria with whom he is often compared. The frequent use of the term "salvation (*soteria*) is a good indication of this; generally it is used in contexts which are eschatological in tone and associate the salvation hoped for with the Parousia of Jesus Christ as the time it is either granted or finds its fulfillment (Heb 1:14; 2:3, 10; 5:9; 6:9). Nowhere is this made more explicit than in Hebrews 9:26-28 where the future Parousia of Jesus Christ (verse 28) is set over against the reference in verse 26 to his appearance as a human being who dies a sacrificial death* "once for all at the end of the age." Clearly the writer thought Christians to be living in "the last days" (Heb 1:2) with the "powers of the age to come" (Heb 6:6) impinging upon them.

Not only does the key word "salvation" (*sōtēria*) appear in Hebrews 9:28, but so too does the curious description of Christ's future "appearance" for a second time (the verb *ophthēsetai* is here used of him, a verb which is often used with eschatological overtones). Nowhere else in the NT is the future Parousia described in terms of the *second* appearance of Jesus Christ. So unusual is this expression that it has led to an interesting suggestion (as argued by Bruce 1964 and Lane 1985) that the cultic imagery of the high priest entering the temple* to make sacrifice* on behalf of the people on the Day of Atonement is ultimately responsible for the description of the *re-appearance* of Jesus Christ the High Priest (*see* Priest). Just as the people of Israel* waited for the Jewish high priest to return after he had offered sacrifice, so too do the people of the new covenant* now wait eagerly for Christ's return following his sacrifice offered once and for all (Sir 50:5-10 is an important comparative text for this idea).

The other key text which makes explicit reference to the future coming of Christ is Hebrews 10:35-37. Here allusion is made in Hebrews 10:37 to an expectation of the imminent coming of the Messiah by means of a midrashic reworking of Habakkuk 2:3-4 (*see* Old Testament in Hebrews). The effect is reminiscent of the description of Jesus as "the coming one" (*ho erchomenos*) in the Gospels (Mt 11:3; Luke 7:19-20; Jn 6:14; 11:27) and Isaiah 26:20 (see Lewis for an interesting interpretation of the passage). The explicitness of the language used in Hebrews 10:37 is probably an indication that the delay of the Parousia was one of the pastoral problems in the church to which the anonymous writer addresses his exhortation (as Attridge argues).

In general the future Parousia of Christ is described throughout Hebrews in terms of its being a time of judgment, as in Hebrews 10:25 where the readers are warned to act accordingly as they "watch for the approaching day," a phrase which is sometimes seen as predictive of the fall of Jerusalem and is often invoked as an argument for the pre-A.D. 70 dating of Hebrews. Beyond this key passage the judgment theme is a prominent one throughout Hebrews, finding explicit reference in a number of places, many of which speak of God as the judge (Heb 2:2; 4:1, 12-13; 6:2, 4-8; 9:27; 10:27, 30-31; 12:5-11,

18-19, 23, 25, 29; 13:4, 17). Given the frequency of this theme, the suggestion of G. Buchanan that the original letter (Heb 1:1—12:29) ended with the citation of Deuteronomy 4:24 ("The Lord your God is a devouring fire") and that the concluding chapter 13 is thus to be viewed as an appendix, is not as far-fetched as it might first appear. However, his argument that Hebrews 1:1—12:29 is a midrashic homily based upon Psalm 110 does not seem to provide a sufficient base for the eschatological element so determinative in the letter.

B. Lindars, in contrast, offers an interpretation which makes Hebrews 13 the key to understanding the letter as a whole, including its eschatological teaching. As a means of emphasizing the terrible nature of the future judgment the author cites several passages from the OT about the giving of the law* on Mount Sinai (drawn from Ex 19—20 and Deut 4—5). His point is that the future Parousia of Jesus Christ will be an even greater cataclysm than was the giving of the Mosaic law. The prominence of the idea of future judgment, whether exacted by God or Jesus his Messianic agent, is hardly surprising given the author's basic intentions of warning his audience against the dangers of apostatizing from their Christian faith. Interestingly, some recent interpretations of Hebrews have linked this move toward apostasy* specifically with the idea of the Parousia of Christ. Thus Lindars suggests a crisis arose within the church about postbaptismal sin which was causing a drift toward apostasy. As Lindars remarks: "They simply assumed that they would remain in a state of grace until the parousia" (Lindars, 13). Not all would agree with such an assessment of the root problem being addressed by the author, but it certainly demonstrates how the idea of the Parousia figures prominently in recent interpretations of Hebrews.

The novel idea of a "Sabbath rest" in Hebrews 4:9 (*sabbatismos*, a hapax in the NT; but see *Barn.* 15.1-5) is also to be seen as a demonstration of the eschatological context of the epistle as a whole (the related term *katapausis* appears eight times in Heb 3:11, 18; 4:1, 3, 5, 10, 11; the corresponding verb *katapauō* is used three times in Heb 4:4, 8, 10). This is closely related to the way in which the Christian life is described as a journey of faith throughout Hebrews. In Hebrews 11:13 the believers on such a journey are specifically noted to be "pilgrims" (*parepidēmoi;* Käsemann 1984, whose assumption about Gnosticism as generating the idea must be questioned; cf. R. McL. Wilson; Johnsson provides a thorough discussion of the theme using a phenomenological model).

Such a travel motif becomes all the more related to an eschatological mindset when we recall that Jesus is described in Hebrews 12:2 as the "Pioneer and Perfector" of faith,* the one who not only begins but brings to completion the journey of faith. It is difficult not to see the future Parousia of Jesus Christ as the time when his role as "Perfector" is played out, a suggestion which also helps to make sense of the curious declaration made in Hebrews 4:9 about Joshua not giving "rest" to the people of God. It seems certain that the author is playing with the name "Joshua" (*Iēsous*), seeing the OT character as a prefiguration of the Lord Jesus Christ.

The frequent use of forms of the verb *teleioō* (9 times), together with the abstract nouns "maturity" (*teleiotēs*) in Hebrews 6:1 and "perfection" (*teleiotēs*) in Hebrews 7:11, are also related to this journey motif. Taken together they indicate the ultimate goal, the Parousia of Christ, to which everything, including Christian discipleship as well as the world order, is moving (see Hübner, Carlston, Peterson). This future perspective also finds expression in Hebrews 12:18-24 and 13:14 where it is connected with the coming heavenly Jerusalem* (Barrett 1956 offers a solid discussion of both the journey motif and the heavenly city motif as integral parts of the author's eschatological mindset; MacRae develops the heavenly temple motif further, although the distinction he makes between the Alexandrian imagery of the author and the apocalyptic imagery of the recipients of the epistle seems forced upon the text).

In summary, most commentators agree that eschatology has a central, if not overtly expressed, place within the thought of Hebrews. The controlling idea of Christianity as a new covenant* is based upon the eschatological understanding of the author, who saw Jesus, particularly through his atoning death, as the fulfillment of the promises made by God to his people of old. To the author of Hebrews, therefore, Christians are seen to be delicately poised between an inaugurated eschatology and a futuristic one which focussed on the Parousia of Jesus Christ as the moment of hope and judgment. As W. Manson puts it: "He sees all things in the light of the crisis brought about by the announcement of the Eternal World in Jesus and the swift approach of the end of the present order, including the Last Judgment." (Manson, 9, who argues on the basis of the story of Stephen in Acts 7 that there is a close connection between Heb and the early Christianity of Jerusalem, especially with the drive toward world-wide mission). The ability to combine both spatial and temporal models of reality (the horizontal and the vertical) so as to form his eschatological message and to do so while employing the cultic and sacrificial imagery drawn from Judaism stands as the distinctive contribution of Hebrews within the NT.

2.3. James. This epistle (*see* James) has been called "the most consistently ethical document in the New Testament." (Laws, 27). It should not be surprising, therefore, that the eschatological materials are closely intertwined with its ethical* sections; effectively eschatological punishment and reward are used to reinforce the author's demands for righteous living. Some commentators (such as Reicke) have interpreted the ethical demands made by the author as arising out of a setting of real persecution. Others (such as Laws) have taken the tribulations* to reflect the everyday struggles of an individual and downplay a setting of real persecution. In either case, the application of traditional eschatological forms, including the sober warning of a future Parousia of Jesus Christ, is made by the author of the epistle.

There are a number of passages in James which reflect a traditional eschatological viewpoint concerning the certainty of future judgment. Thus we see in James 1:12 a powerful declaration that the faithful follower of Christ who has endured a time of trial will receive a crown of life in the future judgment (cf. Rev 2:10 and 1 Pet 5:4); whereas James 2:12-13 promises a future judgment according to the law of freedom*; and James 4:11-12 where judging one's brother is condemned in view of the fact that God judges us all. It is not unreasonable to assume that the future Parousia of Jesus Christ is the time at which God's judgment is enacted. Judgment is to be seen as a key eschatological motif for the author of James and is thus closely connected to his understanding of the Parousia of Christ. Similarly, another eschatological image is found in James 1:18, where Christians are described as "firstfruits of his

[God's] creation." If the eschatological use of *aparchē* in Paul's letters (as in Rom 8:23; 1 Cor 15:20, 23; cf. Rev 14:4) is anything to go by, it suggests that the idea of the Parousia underlies the author's thought here by virtue of its association with the present possession of the Spirit and the future resurrection of the body.

However, the most sustained section of James which deals with eschatological matters is James 5:1-11, an exhortative section which blends a severe pronouncement of future judgment and a comforting word of assurance about God's mercy* together with a double-barreled declaration about the Parousia of the Lord (Jas 5:7-8; Feuillet's attempt to interpret the passage as the historical coming of Jesus to the nation Israel culminating in the debacle of A.D. 70 must be regarded as unconvincing). The passage contains several interesting references to the judgment, including James 5:9 where Christians are told to stop complaining about each other since the Judge stands ready at the door (as in Rev 3:20?); and James 5:12 where the prohibition against oath-taking is asserted lest believers fall under God's judgment.

Of these passages, James 5:9 provides the most opportunity for interpretative debate in that it raises questions about who is understood to be the judge. Most commentators (including Laws, Davids, Martin and Moo) interpret Jesus Christ as the judge, usually on the basis of the parallelism between James 5:9 and the preceding verse. Yet despite the clear reference to the future Parousia of Christ in James 5:7-8, the urgency and frenetic concern which often characterizes other discussions of the theme is missing here; it is simply asserted with a calm assurance which is encapsulated in the call for patience among the "brethren" (*makrothymēsate oun adelphoi*). As R. P. Martin says: "The postponement of the Parousia is not the problem vexing James's readers, nor the question of why the end does not come soon" (Martin, 188).

There is some debate about whether *kyrios* in James 5:7-8 means God or Christ (as Laws rightly notes). There is something to be said for it being God, especially since the verses immediately preceding (Jas 5:4-5) speak of a "day of slaughter" and seem to use traditional Day of the Lord battle imagery drawn from Jewish prophetic and apocalyptic literature (such as Is 34:2; Ezek 21:15; Jer 12:3; 25:34 and *1 Enoch* 94:8-9; contra Blackman who takes the "day of slaughter" to be

an image of feasting following victory). Likewise, the three references to *kyrios* following (in Jas 5:10-11) are also best taken as having God in mind, although some have interpreted the allusion in James 5:10 to refer to the Parousia of Jesus Christ on the strength of the unusual phrase "the end" in the verse (see Gordon). This leaves James 5:7-8 as one of the few places in the epistle where something explicitly Christian is said, making it (together with the two mentions of *Iēsous* in Jas 1:1 and 2:1) a key focal point in debates about whether James is a Christian or a Jewish document.

2.4. 1 Peter. Of all of the epistles in the NT 1 Peter* demonstrates most clearly an atmosphere of persecution and oppression (whether this is to be regarded as actual or potential is a matter of considerable scholarly debate). Given the frequent reference to the trials and tribulations that are faced by the church, it is perhaps understandable that the Parousia of Jesus Christ has such a high profile within the letter in that it concentrated on a time of future hope and certainty in the midst of a time of despair and uncertainty. As E. G. Selwyn remarks (1956, 394): "there is no book in the New Testament where the eschatology is more closely integrated with the teaching of the document as a whole" (Davids 1990, 17, concurs: "apocalyptic eschatology colors the whole of the epistle").

The term *parousia* does not appear in the epistle, although *apokalypsis* is used as a virtual equivalent three times (Selwyn argues that the use of *apokalypsis* reflects Petrine authorship of the letter, based upon the use of the term in the Gospel materials; Michaels 1988 suggests a comparison between 1 Peter and Jewish apocalypses, such as *2 Baruch* and *4 Ezra*, on the basis of questions of genre raised by the use of the term). Nevertheless, allusions and veiled references to the Parousia are scattered throughout the epistle, although most simply give tacit expression to traditional eschatological expectations rather than adding anything startlingly new or taking the idea in a different direction. Indeed, the one wholly distinctive passage in the epistle, the story of Christ preaching to the spirits of Noah in prison (1 Pet 3:19-20), does not appear to contain any explicit link to the author's hope in the Parousia (although Michaels 1966-67 offers an eschatological interpretation based on 1 Pet 3:17 which introduces the passage).

The epistle opens with a hymn* of praise and thanksgiving (1 Pet 1:3-12), followed by an exhortation to holy living (1 Pet 1:13-25) which contains a cluster of images and terms calling to mind the future Parousia of Jesus Christ. The term *apokalypsis* appears twice in these verses (1 Pet 1:7, 13), offering consolation to a persecuted congregation based upon the assurance of his appearing. The Christians are said to have an "imperishable inheritance" (1 Pet 1:4), which is "kept in heaven"; is "guarded through faith" (1 Pet 1:5); and is "to be revealed in the last time" (1 Pet 1:5). In 1 Peter 1:13 they are exhorted to set their hope "completely" (*teleiōs*) on the coming revelation of Jesus Christ, an exhortation which grounds the development of Christian maturity firmly in eschatological expectation and demonstrates yet again how central the idea of "completion" (whether it be moral or historical) is to the notion of the future Parousia. In 1 Peter 1:23 the Christians are said to be born "not of perishable but imperishable," an image Paul uses in 1 Corinthians 15:42 with reference to the resurrection of Jesus and applies to his description of what happens to the believers at Christ's Parousia.

The unusual phrase "the day of visitation" (*en hēmera episkopēs*) occurs in 1 Peter 2:12, an expression probably taken from Isaiah 10:3 and used here as part of the author's exhortation to his readers to live as befits their status as aliens and exiles in the world until the coming of the Parousia (a similar phrase also occurs regularly in the Qumran materials, such as in 1QS 3:18: "the time of his visitation"). In 1 Peter 3:9 mention is made of inheriting a blessing* (presumably given at the Parousia) and in 1 Peter 3:15 the readers are called to the apologetic task and "to account for the hope" that is within them, a hope that (presumably) finds its fulfillment in the Parousia of Jesus Christ.

In 1 Peter 4:5 the lawless are said to have to face Christ "who is ready to judge the living and the dead"; and in 1 Peter 4:7 it is declared in no uncertain terms that "the end of all things is at hand" (*pantōn de to telos ēngiken*, note the use of the perfect; cf. Mk 1:15; Jas 5:8) with a corresponding list of ethical demands following in 1 Peter 4:7-11. Similarly, 1 Peter 1:9 asserts that the result of the believers' faith is that they obtain the "salvation of their souls." Meanwhile, in 1 Peter 4:13 we have the third explicit reference to the *apokalypsis* of Christ contained in

1 Peter; the declaration here is given to console the Christians in light of the persecution they were undergoing. The imagery of this verse is somewhat obscure and many commentators turn to the apocalyptic idea of "the messianic woes" (as a prelude to the arrival of the Messiah) in explanation (Best is a good example). This is followed by another passage (1 Pet 4:17-19) in which God exercises judgment in the church.* This stands as a prefiguration of what he will do to the world at the end of time when Christ comes (Selwyn 1956, 397, suggests that with the exception of 1 Pet 4:5 it is the Father rather than Christ who is thought of as the judge throughout the epistle). The verb "to make manifest" (*phaneroō*), which appeared already in 1 Peter 1:20 as an expression of the incarnation, is used again in 1 Peter 5:4, this time as an expression of the Parousia. Here it occurs in conjunction with a rather unusual title for Jesus (found only here in the NT), describing him as "the Great Shepherd*" (*ho archipoimēn*, cf. Heb 13:20).

As further evidence of the prominence of eschatological concerns in 1 Peter we note that the key word "glory"* (*doxa*), often associated with the idea of the Parousia, appears ten times in the epistle; the corresponding verb (*doxazō*) occurs four times. Most of these occurrences appear in contexts which refer to, or at least imply, the future Parousia of Christ (including 1 Pet 1:7, 11, 21 (?); 2:12; 4:11, 13; 5:1, 4, 10). 1 Peter uses the word "salvation"* (*sōtēria*) four times (1 Pet 1:5, 9, 10; 2:2), again as another key expression of his hope in the Parousia of Christ. The single instance of the verb "exalt" (*hypsoō*) in 1 Pet 5:6 is perhaps related to this expression of hope, particularly as it appears to speak about a time of future exaltation,* although here it is again interesting to note that God, not Christ, is the active agent. The idea of Christian life as an earthly pilgrimage toward a heavenly destination, which finds the Parousia as the time of fulfillment, is sometimes argued to underlie the letter (see the discussion of Heb above). The references to such terms as *paroikos* ("stranger") and *parepidēmos* ("stranger") might be taken to support such an eschatological interpretation, although sociological studies of the epistle (like that of Elliott) offer another way of interpreting these.

Some debate about the tense of the verb "rejoice" (*see* Joy) in 1 Peter 1:8 (*agalliate/ agalliasthe;* Is it present or future?) has arisen, a matter which is tangentially related to the question of the Parousia in 1 Peter. If the present tense variant is adopted then the delicate balance between the present experience of the believers and their future hope, so characteristic of the epistle as a whole, is maintained (see Davids 1990 and Michaels 1988 for differing views on this particular point).

2.5. 2 Peter. The interpretation of the eschatological teaching of 2 Peter* is intimately tied up with questions about its authorship, intended audience and date. Decisions about who wrote the document, to whom and when tend to govern how the eschatological teaching contained within the epistle is interpreted. The fact that Paul's letters are mentioned (in 1 Pet 3:15-16); that allusions appear to both 1 Peter and the epistle of Jude (in 2 Pet 2:1-18; 3:1-3); and that the first explicit citation of 2 Peter occurs in the work of Origen (c. A.D. 215-51) have all been used to date the epistle. For many, the operating assumption that 2 Peter is a pseudonymous* work of the second century (c. 150), employing the form of a dying saint's last testament and probably directed to the church in Rome,* offers the best way to proceed. However, the matter is still a subject of some debate, and a wide range of dates has been proposed (M. Green suggests a date in the 60s; R. Bauckham [1983] a date of 80-90; B. Reicke a date of 90; J. N. D. Kelly a date of 100-110; J. H. Elliott [1992] a date in the first quarter of the second century; and C. E. B. Cranfield a date in the first half of the second century).

There are several passages in 2 Peter which might be described as expressing a generalized eschatological hope and which thus have the Parousia as a backdrop. It is clear that matters relating to the future are central to the author's thought and form the basis of his reply to his doubting opponents who perhaps are motivated by an over-realized eschatological perspective (although Bauckham [1983] has reservations about this). Explicit reference to "the power and the coming of our Lord Jesus Christ" is made in 2 Peter 1:16; a number of supportive echoes of this essentially eschatological belief are also to be noted. For example, in 2 Peter 1:14 the author makes reference to his future resurrection by means of the curious phrase "the putting off of my bodily-tent" (perhaps as a deliberate echo of 2 Cor 5:1-4?). This, the author of 2 Peter asserts, is something which

will take place in the near future and was revealed to him by the Lord Jesus Christ.

References to a time in the future when the believer will be provided "an entrance into the kingdom" (2 Pet 1:11); to the future "dawning of the day" and "the appearance of the morning star" (2 Pet 1:19; cf. Rev 2:28); to "the destruction" (2 Pet 2:3); to "the day of judgment" (2 Pet 2:9); and to "destruction" (2 Pet 2:12) might all legitimately be seen as expressive of the eschatological framework of the author's thought in which the Parousia of the Lord holds central place. It appears that even the curious reference to the transfiguration of Jesus Christ contained in 2 Peter 1:17-18 is to be viewed as a prefigurement of the glory of the Lord Jesus Christ, which is to be revealed in the Parousia. It is a matter of some speculation, however, why the author chooses the transfiguration rather than the resurrection of Jesus Christ for this (perhaps the gospel tradition that Peter was an eye-witness at the transfiguration is central here).

It is 2 Peter 3 which has occupied the major share of exegetical discussion since the chapter contains the most explicit treatment of the delay of the Parousia in the NT (see below). Based on his interpretation of this chapter, E. Käsemann (1964) described the epistle as "an apologia for primitive Christian eschatology," arguing that the Petrine community to whom the letter was written was disturbed and embarrassed by the nonappearance of Christ. In Käsemann's estimation any interpretation of the epistle as a whole must proceed giving due weight to this fact (it is worth noting that Käsemann effectively defines apocalyptic as belief in the imminent Parousia of Christ). Primitive Christian hope in the imminent Parousia of Christ has given way to skepticism and downright derision by certain segments of the community. It is to this that the author of 2 Peter 3 (so Käsemann argues) responds.

Yet, ironically (Käsemann concludes), the apologia which the author of 2 Peter puts forward is rather inadequate to the task, misunderstanding the very nature of the eschatological message as it does and thus reflecting the retrograde step toward "early Catholicism"* (*Frühkatholizismus*) which the church took. The author of 2 Peter appeals to traditional apocalyptic eschatology, the idea of the coming of the Lord at the Parousia, but betrays via his unconvincing use of Psalm 90:4 that he himself has given up on any belief in Christ's imminent return. In fact Käsemann goes so far as to suggest that the apologia is in effect "the demonstration of a logical absurdity" (Käsemann, 194) as far as the delay of the Parousia is concerned (a remark which causes Bauckham 1983 to summarize Käsemann's interpretation as a "full-scale theological attack on 2 Pet").

Such an interpretation of 2 Peter 3 has been contested in various quarters, not least because of its assumption that the challenge to traditional eschatological beliefs is being generated by Christian sectarians who are Gnostic* in orientation (Käsemann assumes that there is an inherent conflict between Gnosticism and primitive Christian eschatological belief, which saw fulfillment as a future, as opposed to a present, matter). Influential though Käsemann's interpretation has been, and there have been important variations of it (such as that offered by Talbert, which focuses on the identification of the heresy being confronted as the key to the eschatology of the epistle, and Fornberg, which places the epistle within a concrete situation, namely a thoroughly Hellenized society), it is now recognized to be an anachronistic interpretation which is badly in need of correction (both Moore and Bauckham 1983 offer solid critiques of Käsemann's interpretation).

It is important to remember that the crucial verse which mentions the nonappearance of the Parousia (2 Pet 3:4) is in fact a citation of the mocking words of his opponents (see Adversaries) by the author of the epistle, which elicits his rebuking quote of Psalm 90:4 ("With the Lord one day is as a thousand years, and a thousand years as one day") in 2 Peter 3:8. This verse, incidentally, is cited by M. Green as evidence for the Petrine authorship of the letter in that it does not go on to express an explicit chiliasm (see Millennium) so common of most second-century works (such as Barn. 15.4 and Justin Martyr Dial. Tryph. 81.3-4) which cite the OT passage. The author Peter then moves on in 2 Peter 3:9 to interpret the OT verse as demonstrating God's forbearance by providing additional time for people to repent, as well as warning in 2 Peter 3:10 against precise calculations of the exact time of the Parousia of the Lord by means of the stock image of a thief coming in the night at an unknown hour (see Mt 24:43 and 1 Thess 5:2). The passage also

makes reference in 2 Peter 3:12 to "the day of God," effectively reinforcing the OT prophetic tradition which underlies the hope in the Parousia (Sidebottom stresses the way in which the Parousia is generally presented as theophany rather than christophany within the letter). It is clear that there is a close connection between the Parousia and the judgment theme which appears frequently within the letter. Illustrations of how God judged the world in the past, notably through the flood in the days of Noah (2 Pet 3:5-7), are given as a warning of the judgment which is to come at the Parousia of Christ.

Interestingly, the author of 2 Peter offers some novel ideas about the cosmic implications of this Parousia of Jesus Christ in 2 Pet 3:10-13, closely associating the Parousia with the final conflagration of creation (the nearest OT equivalent is Zeph 3:8, although many Stoic parallels are in evidence). He says that the "heavens and the earth are reserved for fire" (2 Pet 3:7; see Heaven, New Heaven); that the "elements will be dissolved with fire" (2 Pet 3:10, 12), and that "a new heaven and earth will issue forth in which righteousness dwells" (2 Pet 3:13).

J. H. Neyrey (1993) attempts to follow through literary approaches of interpretation, giving attention to the rhetorical argument being pursued within the epistle as a whole. At the same time Neyrey combines this insight with a number of social-science models designed to help facilitate understanding of the letter in that they sensitize us to the fact that the cultural perspective of the author of 2 Peter is so vastly different from our own. What is important to note for our purposes is the way that Neyrey identifies the debate about the Parousia as central to this formal structure of the letter. He outlines a highly formalized series of challenges and replies about some aspect of divine truth (notably eschatological matters associated with the Parousia and judgment) which are addressed by the author. A five-part division of the body of the letter results, which emphasizes its nature as a document juxtaposing polemic and apology (2 Pet 1:16-18; 1:19-21; 2:1-3, 4-10a; 3:1-3, 4-7; 3:8-9, 10-13).

While we may feel that the outline structure Neyrey imposes on the epistle is not without its problems, his interpretation does give proper stress to the centrality of the Parousia as one of the central matters being debated. The proposal is imaginative and has much to offer, including some interesting suggestions about a possible connection between the opponents being addressed in the letter and the Epicurean philosophical school which wrestled with the problems of theodicy and the delay of divine judgment. We find, so Neyrey argues (1980), precisely these issues being debated within 2 Peter (an argument supported by the association of both 2 Pet 2:11 and 3:9a with 3:4 in terms of reconstructing the opponents' views).

It seems clear that the writer used the Parousia-judgment motif as a means to exhort his audience, notably the sectarians he is seeking to correct, to right ethical behavior and dutiful Christian service (2 Pet 3:11-12). The delay between the resurrection of Jesus Christ and his Parousia is thus to be viewed as a period of God's grace, offering time for the church to enjoy both eager expectation and to discharge its responsibilities. In 2 Peter 3:12 this is characterized by the expression "waiting and hastening the Parousia." The author of the letter concludes his exhortation to the church with another unusual, if indirect, reference to the Parousia of Jesus Christ when he says, "To him be the glory both now and to the day of eternity" (2 Pet 3:18).

2.6. Jude. Like its literary counterpart 2 Peter, the epistle of Jude* contains a number of passages which speak of or allude to the future Parousia of Jesus Christ and the judgment that his appearing brings, including Jude 4, 6, 9, 13. Evocative imagery is used by the author to communicate this idea of future judgment, including "fire" (Jude 22), "gloomy darkness" (Jude 13) and analogy from the three OT figures (Cain, Balaam and Korah) upon whom divine judgment is pronounced in Jude 5-7 (note "the eternal fire" in verse 7). On a more positive note, the letter is addressed (Jude 1) to "those called and kept" by Jesus Christ (cf. 1 Pet 1:4 where a similar expression is also used with reference to the believers at the Parousia); in Jude 21 it exhorts its readers to "wait for the mercy of our Lord Jesus Christ unto eternal life" (Bauckham 1983 takes the verb to be an imperative); and in Jude 24-25 the author also speaks of a future time of glory and joy accomplished through the saving act of God in Christ. Again it seems likely that Christ's future Parousia is in mind within all of these passages.

Moreover, the most important of the references in Jude to the Parousia occurs in Jude 14-16 where the author cites from the pseudepigraphal *1 Enoch* 1:9, creatively reworking an OT image of theophany to serve his own particular purposes (*see* Non-Canonical Writings). It appears that he does this in order to proclaim the assurance of Christ's judgment upon the godless opponents who have invaded the church and are causing problems for it (we see hints of their disruptive influence in Jude 4 and 19). This is so despite the fact that the reference to *kyrios* in Jude 14 is probably a christological refinement of the passage from *1 Enoch* 1:9, which speaks more vaguely of "he" (meaning God). The result is that the passage is better viewed as a christophany rather than a theophany (see Osburn and VanderKam for a discussion of this). Further debate about Jude 14 focuses on the aorist tense of *ēlthen* (a change from the Greek versions of *1 Enoch* which have the present tense verb *erchetai*). Most commentators take this to reflect a Semitic prophetic perfect, expressing what is meant to be a future event as if it has already happened. The openness to Jewish pseudepigraphal literature in Jude is also evidenced by the allusion to legends surrounding the dispute between Michael and the devil over the body of Moses in Jude 8-9, probably based on *Testament of Moses* (see Bauckham 1983, 65-76, for a detailed study of this). Again the Lord's "rebuke" (at the end of Jude 9) could be associated with the judgment that comes at Christ's Parousia.

In any event, the epistle of Jude does not deal with the problem of the delay of the Parousia as explicitly as does 2 Peter, although his opponents seem to have adopted an overrealized eschatology which led them to deny the Lord Jesus Christ (Jude 4) in that they denied the need for a future resurrection and judgment at the Parousia (similar to the situation we see recorded in 2 Tim 2:17-18). If such an interpretation of the opponents' "denial of the Lord Jesus Christ" is allowed, we can infer a similarity of circumstance between Jude and 2 Peter wherein proponents of these ideas are challenged and rebuked by the respective authors of the letters. The fact that within the two epistles the same word is used to describe the opponents (the noun "scoffers" *[empaiktai]* which appears only in these two places within the NT) lends weight to this suggestion (Rowston and

Cavallin both discuss the possibility of a relationship between the opponents being addressed within the two epistles). However, the word may appear in 2 Peter 3:3 simply because it is borrowed from Jude, and it is by no means certain that the situation addressed in 2 Peter is also at the root of the problems tackled in Jude. Debates about an early dating of Jude may have some bearing on the question of the Parousia hope that is contained within it (Ellis suggests a date between 55-65; Robinson 1976 a date of 61-62), although a later date has also been proposed.

2.7. *The Johannine Epistles*. The most important text in the Johannine epistles (*see* John, Letters of) which makes mention of the Parousia of Jesus Christ is 1 John 2:28. Remarkably, this is the only instance in the Johannine letters where the term *parousia* is used, a fact which has led some commentators (such as Bultmann 1973) to assign the verse to a later editor (Schnackenburg 1992 is more cautious on this point, although he too sees the problems posed by the expression; Marshall 1978, 166, is more dismissive of Bultmann's theory of a later redactor, describing it as "unnecessary and unconvincing"). The verse concludes a short section (1 Jn 2:18-29) which demonstrates the eschatological mindset of the author. The declaration "it is the last hour" occurs twice in 1 Jn 2:18, and it clearly is meant to indicate the author's belief that his readers were living at the point of the consummation of the age and argues that this is confirmed by severe tensions within the community (the appearance of antichrists*!) which has led to some members breaking fellowship and leaving (1 Jn 2:19).

The declaration made in 1 John 2:28 is somewhat unusual in that no explicit mention is made of Jesus Christ himself—the key verb *phanerōthē* ("revealed") is left indefinite, as is the *autou* ("his") which qualifies the word *parousia*. The obscurity of 1 John 2:28—3:2, with its fluctuation of focus between Jesus and God, is noted by J. Lieu, who remarks that the lack of precision in the author's thought means that "we cannot speak with any confidence of Jesus' eschatological role in 1 John" (Lieu, 73). Nevertheless, there is little serious doubt that the Parousia of Jesus Christ is in mind within the passage, especially since the verse begins with a reference to "remaining in him"; the verb *menein* ("to remain") is used seven times in 1 John

2:18-29 and ultimately links back to "Jesus Christ the righteous" in 1 John 2:1.

The writer's injection of the imminent future Parousia in 1 John 2:28 is sometimes taken as a response to the disputes within the Johannine community which have become overbalanced in favor of a realized eschatology (both Houlden and Brown offer discussion on this, as does Grayston, although he suggests that the writer of 1 Jn means the past resurrection of Jesus Christ and not a future coming when he uses the term *parousia* here). In any event, the verse prompts a call for Christian faithfulness and steadfastness, so that shame can be avoided when Christ comes and boldness (*parrēsia*) be seen to characterize the believer's life (Smalley thinks that the author is making a deliberate play on the words *parousia* and *parrēsia* in the verse).

However, the hope of the Parousia is not restricted to the single reference to the term in 1 John. Several other passages also hint at the importance of the future revelation of Jesus Christ for the writer. For example, 1 John 3:2-3 appears to make veiled allusion to the future appearance of Jesus Christ and the fact that when he appears the faithful believers shall be like him. However, there is some debate about the meaning of these verses, especially since the subject of the instances of the verb "to reveal" is not clear (both Schnackenburg 1992 and Brown 1982 take it to be an impersonal subject and not an explicit reference to the Parousia of Christ). Meanwhile, in 1 John 4:17 the "day of judgment" is mentioned, again with the hope that the believer may be able to meet it with confidence (the term *parrēsia* is here again used; cf. 1 Jn 3:21; 5:14). On the strength of these passages it is sometimes argued (as for example by Dodd 1946) that 1 John represents a departure from the realized eschatology of the Gospel of John and a return to a more futuristic eschatology which characterized the early church. Needless to say, much depends on the assumptions one has about the eschatology contained in John's Gospel in making such a claim.

The reference to "receiving the full reward" in 2 John 8 could be taken to imply the future Parousia, in that it is at the Parousia at the end of time that such a reward* would be granted to the faithful. Beyond this possible allusion, however, there are no further clear references to the Parousia in either 2 John or 3 John.

2.8. The Revelation to John. Most of the difficulties which arise generally in the interpretation of NT eschatology come into sharp focus within the book of Revelation.* Nowhere is this better illustrated than when we come to consider the question of the timing of the Parousia as it is expressed within this work, a question which is inevitably related to a consideration about the historical situation being addressed within the document (is a dating during the reign of the emperor Domitian [A.D. 81-96] to be assumed or not?).

The idea of the imminent Parousia of the Messiah is woven through the very fabric of the Revelation to John like a golden thread, giving consistency to the eschatological pattern contained within it. Although the term *parousia* itself is not found in Revelation, it seems clear that the idea of the imminent Parousia is what is meant in Revelation 1:1 when, in the opening paragraph of his work, the author describes his *apokalypsis* as a revelation of "the things that are soon to take place." He follows this up by pronouncing a blessing on the readers in Revelation 1:3, concluding with the declaration that "the time is near." At the same time, the phrase "the time is near" is repeated in Revelation 22:10, with the declaration "I am coming soon" repeated three times in Revelation 22:7, 12, 20. Thus it could be argued that the expectation of an imminent Parousia of the Messiah effectively provides a literary framework for the composition as a whole.

Beyond this eschatological framing, there are many passages which also seem to allude to or speak of the imminent Parousia of Jesus Christ, including Revelation 1:7 where a pair of OT passages (from Dan 7:13 and Zech 12:10) are used to express the idea (see Scott for a discussion of this verse); Revelation 1:19 where John is commissioned to write down the contents of his vision, which is described as a revelation of "what is and what is to take place" (see Beale's study of this crucial verse); Revelation 4:1 where a similar declaration is made as part of the introductory vision given to John: "I will show you what must take place after this"; Revelation 12:12 where the devil is said to know that "his time is short"; and Revelation 22:6 where God is again said to send his angels to reveal "the things that are soon to take place." The threefold declaration of the divine being as "He who is, and was, and is to come" (Rev 1:4, 8; 4:18) is

also significant (although note the deletion of *ho erchomenos* in Rev 1:17 and 16:5). A comparable description is applied to Satan* and his personification in Revelation 17:8, 10.

Likewise, the threefold reference to Jesus Christ coming soon (in Rev 22:7, 12, 20) has parallels in the so-called Seven Letters to the Seven Churches (Rev 2—3), namely in Revelation 2:16 where Jesus Christ threatens to come to the church of Pergamum and war with them; in Revelation 2:25 where Christ exhorts the church at Thyatira to hold fast to what they have until he comes, at which time he will give the faithful "the morning star" (cf. 2 Pet 1:19); in Revelation 3:3 where the traditional image of Christ coming like an unexpected thief is invoked to the church at Sardis (cf. Rev 16:15 where the same image is used; it is a common image within eschatological literature and is also found in Mt 24:43 and 1 Thess 5:2); and in Revelation 3:11 where Christ promises to arrive soon in order to vindicate the faithful of the church at Philadelphia. Similarly, the "coming" of Christ to judge the churches of Ephesus and Smyrna in Asia Minor (the verb *erchomai* is used in both Rev 2:5 and 2:16) is also worth noting, although it is by no means certain that the final Parousia of Christ at the end of time is in view here. It may well be that a spiritualized coming of the Lord in judgment within the life of the churches concerned is in mind.

In any event, future tense verbs abound throughout Revelation 2—3, and each of the so-called Seven Letters to the Seven Churches contains a declaration of what will happen to them in the future when the Lord comes to them. The element might properly be considered a highly-structured pattern which unites the seven letters in terms of form (see Hemer). In short, there are a number of passages within Revelation which reflect the idea of an imminent Parousia.

At the same time there are one or two places within the body of the Apocalypse where the Parousia of Jesus Christ is presented as if it has already been realized, especially as the future judgment of God becomes the focal point within the imagery of the vision. Thus in Revelation 6:16-17 we have the declaration that the great day of the wrath* of the Lamb* has already arrived upon the world as part of the destruction wrought by the opening of the sixth seal (*see* Scrolls, Seals); in Revelation 14:7 it is said that the hour of judgment has come as part of the extended description following the sounding of the seventh trumpet*; in Revelation 14:15 the time for reaping the harvest is said to have arrived; and in Revelation 18:10 the hour of judgment upon the city of Babylon is said to have fallen. In all these instances the aorist verb *ēlthen* ("has come") is used. The same point might be raised in connection with Revelation 15:4 where it is said that the judgments of God have been revealed (the aorist passive verb *ephanerōthēsan* is used here); in Revelation 16:17 where the seventh angel pours out his bowl of judgment upon the earth, accompanied by a solemn declaration from heaven, "It is done!"; and in Revelation 19:2 where God is said to have "judged the great harlot."

Given these frequent references to the judgment as something in the past, it is understandable how it might be argued (as by Hanson) that the judgment which comes to Babylon* (Rome!), particularly as expressed through the "wine of wrath imagery," refers to the processes of history and not only to the final eschatological act. As Hanson puts the key point: "This is not to say that the wrath has no reference to the end of history; but it never refers purely to that end. It is always a process; sometimes a process viewed as culminating in the End" (Hanson, 165).

Given the frequent references to the idea of the imminence of the Parousia which are juxtaposed with those passages that speak about judgment as if it is a past event, what are we to make of the idea of the delay of the Parousia in Revelation? Is there any evidence within this work that the Parousia of Jesus Christ is an event which is to take place far off in the distant future, following a period of delay? When Revelation is viewed as a whole there is certainly room for precisely just such an interpretation. Indeed, it could also be argued that Revelation 6—11, which trace the movement from the victorious cross of Jesus Christ to his final Parousia in glory by means of a series of images (the seven seals and the seven trumpets), are concerned precisely with this question. These chapters appear to presume something of a delay before the final consummation in the revelation of Jesus Christ. Indeed, it is precisely this which gives rise to the anguished cry by the martyrs in Revelation 6:10 as the fifth seal is opened: "O Sovereign Lord, holy and true, how long before

thou wilt avenge our blood on those who dwell upon the earth?" In short, it appears that the idea of a delay of the Parousia was also an integral part of the apocalyptic vision presented by the writer of Revelation. The theme appears explicitly, or is at least lurking behind the scenes, in many of the key passages of the work (as Bauckham 1980 correctly notes).

This motif of delay adds to the complexity of the picture of judgment as it is contained in Revelation, heightening our awareness of the delicately balanced handling of judgment as something which is past, present and future. Thus it is also important to remember those passages which speak of the judgment as something which is yet to be awaited. A key text for this is Revelation 17:14 which, in describing the war of the powers of evil against the Lamb of God (*arnion* is used some twenty-eight times in Rev with reference to Jesus Christ), concludes with a resounding note of future victory: "the Lamb will conquer them." In short, we need to remember that the past, the present and the future are not rigidly separated in the thought of the Seer, and that he freely moves from one to the other with ease. As Thompson helpfully puts the crucial point: "past, present, and future are not separated by fixed, absolute boundaries." On the contrary, he says, there are "soft boundaries in time" (Thompson, 84).

The declaration in Revelation 22:20, "Come, Lord Jesus!" has been the subject of considerable scholarly debate in view of the fact that it appears to be a translation of the Aramaic *marana tha*, an expression found only in the NT in 1 Corinthians 16:22 (cf. *Did.* 1.6 where it is used as a prayer in connection with the Lord's Supper). The basic question is whether in 1 Corinthians 16:22 the word is to be taken as a perfect ("Our Lord has come!") or an imperative ("Our Lord, come!"). Although both translations of the Aramaic are linguistically possible, the latter is to be preferred if for no other reason than the vocative parallel contained in Revelation 22:20. (Moule and Black offer interesting interpretations of the expression).

There are two specialized items of interpretation which need to be mentioned in connection with the idea of the Parousia in Revelation. Each has generated a considerable amount of scholarly debate. It is to these that we now turn.

2.8.1. The Divine Warrior of Revelation 19:11-16. One of the fullest mythological descriptions of the future Parousia is contained in Revelation 19:11-16, a passage which builds creatively upon the ancient Jewish mythic language surrounding the Divine Warrior and reinterprets it so as to express christological belief. A key issue here is whether the essentially Jewish idea of a Divine Warrior is ultimately incompatible with the Christian idea of the Parousia of Jesus Christ in judgment. Most commentators feel that the two ideas are not to be so rigidly juxtaposed (among others, A. Y. Collins and Ford 1975 and 1984 usefully discuss the background to the Divine Warrior motif, although Ford's suggestion, partly based on her consideration of the motif, that a disciple of John the Baptist is the author of Rev 12—22 must be judged as suspect).

As we noted above, Revelation contains perhaps the most detailed treatment of the judgment theme in the NT, interweaving complex images of judgment (past, present and future) within the apocalyptic vision related by the Seer. The use of the Divine Warrior motif might be seen as an extension of this judgment theme which is so central to the book of Revelation as a whole. Yet its intimate connection to other images of judgment, notably the "wrath of the Lamb" motif (Rev 6:16) and the "wine-press" motif (as in Rev 14:19-20; a common OT image found in Joel 3:13 and Is 63:1-6), is not to be overlooked. This is particularly so when it is recognized that the appearance of the Divine Warrior is presented as a vindication of the sacrificial slaughter of the Lamb (Jesus Christ!) which took place on the cross of Calvary and has been prefigured earlier within the book in the crucial vision of the worthy Lamb who was slain in Revelation 5:6-14 (Hanson discusses this point at length, arguing that it is this christological feature which defines Revelation as a distinctively Christian work).

Thus, there is an overlapping of images of divine judgment occurring here, which is hammered home most powerfully by the reference in Revelation 19:13 to the Divine Warrior as having his robe "dipped in blood." This is a profound image which effectively integrates all three motifs (Divine Warrior, wine-press, slaughter of the Lamb) and points to the death of Jesus Christ as the place where God's judgment is firmly and decisively anchored in world history, although the effects of that death transcend the boundaries of time. Thus the Lamb can be described in Revelation 13:8 as having

been slain "before the foundation of the world."

2.8.2. The Millennium of Revelation 20:1-4. The book of Revelation has been described as "the playground of the eccentrics." Nowhere is this more evident in the variety of ways in which the idea of the final Parousia of Jesus Christ has been interpreted, particularly in connection with its relationship to the millennium* described in Revelation 20:1-4. There are a number of curious, not to say down-right bizarre, interpretations which may be noted in passing. It would take too much space to discuss these at length, but given the centrality of the millennial kingdom within discussions of Revelation in particular and within Christian apocalyptic literature in general it seems appropriate that we mention briefly some of these interpretations as well as some of the critical reactions to them.

Some interpretations of the millennium approach it from the standpoint of the contents of the book of Revelation as a whole. For example, R. H. Charles takes Revelation 13—20 to teach that the Parousia of Jesus Christ is applicable only for those who have been martyred in the great tribulation* (for it is only they who will be raised at the Parousia). This has been described as "the universal martyrdom of the church." However, this interpretation is plagued with difficulties, not least the fact that it runs against the presentation of the Parousia contained in Revelation 1—3, where the hope of the Parousia is presented as something for all of the church (not just those who have suffered martyrdom) to await eagerly (as Marshall 1964 rightly notes in his critique of Charles). However, more generally it is true to say that the main battleground of interpretative debate is to be found in Revelation 20 itself.

Debates about the interpretation of Revelation 20:1-10 are among the most heated, particularly in some conservative circles where one particular line or another is made an axiom of Christian belief. Does the passage teach a literal one-thousand-year reign of Christ on earth, or is it to be taken as a symbolic or metaphorical reference to God's kingdom? It is striking that the word translated "millennium" (*chilioi*) occurs some six times in Revelation 20:2-7, and probably should be associated with the idea of a cosmic week based on the statement contained in Psalm 90:4 (see Brown "Number" for a discussion of this.) How do time and eternity come together within the Seer's apocalyptic vision?

And most importantly for our consideration, where does the Parousia or, as it is popularly described when speaking about Revelation 20, "the rapture," fit into the author's scheme of things? In fact, the appropriateness of the term *rapture* to describe the future Parousia of Christ has been the subject of considerable theological interest (Ladd 1956 offers a study of this question). Does the Parousia inaugurate the messianic kingdom, come during it or conclude it? Are we to interpret the passage as espousing a pretribulation rapture, or is it expressing a posttribulation rapture, or perhaps even a midtribulation rapture? Or are we much nearer the truth when we adopt the position of amillennialism when interpreting the book, effectively refusing to be drawn on the question of how the Parousia and the millennium fit together by refusing to see the millennium in literal, chronological terms? Should we see the judgment following the millennium described in Revelation 20:7-10 as merely a doublet for the judgment enacted at the Parousia of Christ which is portrayed in Revelation 19:11-21 (as Schnackenburg 1963 suggests)?

These matters of millennial interpretation have long been contentious within the history of the church, even from its earliest days (as Bietenhard argues). It is possible to find early Christian writers arguing for a literal millennium based upon the passage (a classic example being *Barn.* 15.3-9); at the same time it is also possible to find other Christian writers vehemently opposing such a literalism (a classic example being Augustine *Civ. D.* 20.6-7). Indeed, within this century volume after volume, article after article, sermon after sermon, have been put forward to debate this matter of millennialism, often with an aggressiveness of spirit not in keeping with Christian demands of tolerance and charity. In fact, a wide variety of positions have been credibly argued by competent scholars and most good commentaries of recent years will provide some discussion of the issue (such as those by Beasley-Murray, Lane, Caird, Ladd, Wilcox, Morris, Goldsworthy, Walvoord, Summers and Rowland). Beyond that, several useful volumes and articles offering an in-depth comparison of the various millennial perspectives are well worth considering (including Barr, Clouse and Osborne).

3. The Delay of the Parousia.

We now discuss briefly the so-called "delay of the Parousia" (a translation of the German word *Parusieverzögerung* first launched onto the agenda of NT studies by A. Schweitzer in *The Quest for the Historical Jesus* [1906]). The "delay of the Parousia" has been a subject of considerable debate since it inevitably invites discussion on a number of fronts, not least the development of Christian understandings about the purposes of God in history, the connection with Jewish eschatological hopes and the nature of the church. A wide variety of approaches to the subject are in evidence, as NT scholars attempt to unravel this veritable "Gordian knot" of NT theology.

Some have attempted to solve the problem of the "delay of the Parousia" by seeing it against the backdrop of the gradual diminishment of eschatology in apocalyptic belief which occured as the church moved from an essentially Jewish provenance into the wider Hellenistic world. Thus Schweitzer saw the Parousia as an element of Jewish apocalyptic thought which is eventually jettisoned by the church in light of its nonfulfillment. Others, such as C.H. Dodd (1936) and J. A. T. Robinson (1957), have attempted to explain it in terms of the church's inability to reckon with Jesus' proclamation of the completely realized nature of the kingdom of God. In this instance the church is viewed as responsible for the refocusing on or indeed the creation of the idea of the Parousia by failing to grasp with the import of Jesus' life and teaching. Others, notably Rudolf Bultmann (1953) and his followers, have attempted to demythologize the meaning of the Parousia in favor of an existentialist encounter with the risen Lord, thereby loosing the bonds that the Parousia has with future history. This has led others, such as O. Cullmann (1951), to reassert the future Parousia as the culminating event in salvation-history. Each of these solutions has its own strengths and weaknesses, although each represents, in some way or another, a response or a reaction to the program of consistent eschatology proposed by Weiss and Schweitzer (their suggestion was that Jesus' message was consistently, or thoroughly, eschatological in nature and that everything taught and believed was conditioned by this perspective). Each is, in the evocative phrase of R. H. Hiers (1966, 171), who is echoing A. Schweitzer, part of "the struggle against eschatology."

More recently there has been a considerable

move to re-assess the idea of the "delay of the Parousia" altogether. It is by no means clear that the delay of the Parousia ever evoked quite the crisis of faith among the early Christians that it is sometimes assumed to have done. Even the proof text often appealed to by those who want to argue for the position, namely 2 Peter 3:1-13, is taken by many NT scholars (such as E. Käsemann) to be rather the exception than the rule when it comes to establishing what was normative Christian eschatological belief. In fact, explicit formulation of the delay of the Parousia as a theological question is found only in 2 Peter 3:4 within the whole of the NT; elsewhere it is an inference at best.

Indeed, many NT interpreters would dispute that the delay of the Parousia necessitated the kind of theological accommodation it is often assumed to have required, effectively rendering the extremes of interpretation outlined above somewhat irrelevant. It may well be that early Christians were able to believe in the imminent arrival of the Lord Jesus at the Parousia while recognizing fully the difficulties posed by the lapse of time between the death, burial and resurrection of Christ, and his future coming at the end of time in order to fulfill God's redemptive purposes. As D. Aune puts it: "The very paucity of references to a supposed delay of the eschaton is indicative of the fact that the delay of the Parousia was largely a nonproblem within early Christianity" (Aune, 103).

In this regard, the theological problems raised by the delay of the Parousia, which the Christians were wrestling with, are precisely the same sorts of problems that other Jewish authors were wrestling with in their works (notably the authors of *2 Apoc. Bar.* and *4 Ezra*). In short, many of the theological problems associated with eschatological delay are endemic to the literature of apocalypticism as a whole (as Bauckham 1980 argues). Indeed, the idea of a delay of God's eschatological judgment surfaces in some of the OT prophetic literature, as Ezekiel 12:21-25 and Habakkuk 2:2-5 serve to indicate. In other words, there are good grounds for suggesting that imminence and delay are held in creative tension by many Jewish and Christian writers of the NT period, and any credible interpretation of the idea of the Parousia of Jesus Christ can only be offered when this crucial fact is kept in mind. Passages in the NT which stress the imminence of the Parousia of Jesus Christ may be much more concerned with *theological* relationship between the present reality and future hope than they are with the *chronological* relationship between them (contra Cullmann).

Once this crucial point is recognized, the "problem of the delay of the parousia" diminishes greatly in importance (see Smalley; Travis). As C. C. Rowland states in his summary of the issue: "Within the apocalyptic framework adopted by the early Christians there lies the resource to cope with the delay in the fulfillment of the promise" (Rowland 1985, 293). That resource, which is absolutely central to the early Christians as they sought to hold together the reality of what has already happened in Christ and their faith in what is yet to be accomplished, is the confident assurance that they share in the heavenly life of the risen Lord (see Col 3:1-4 for the classic Pauline expression of this).

See also APOCALYPTIC, APOCALYPTICISM; ASCENSION; DAY OF THE LORD; ESCHATOLOGY; JUDGMENT; MILLENNIUM; RESURRECTION.

BIBLIOGRAPHY. H. W. Attridge, *The Epistle to the Hebrews* (Herm; Philadelphia: Fortress, 1989); D. E. Aune, "The Significance of the Delay of the Parousia for Early Christianity" in *Current Issues in Biblical and Patristic Interpretation: Studies in Honor of Merrill C. Tenney*, ed. G. F. Hawthorne (Grand Rapids: Eerdmans, 1975) 87-109; J. Barr, *Fundamentalism* (Philadelphia: Westminster, 1978); C. K. Barrett, "The Eschatology of the Epistle to the Hebrews" in *The Background of the New Testament and Its Eschatology: Festschrift for C.H. Dodd*, ed. W. D. Davies and D. Daube, (Cambridge: Cambridge University Press, 1956) 363-93; idem, "Stephen and the Son of Man" in *Apophoreta: Festschrift für Ernst Haenchen*, ed. W. Eltester and F. H. Kettley (BZNW 30; Berlin: Töpelmann, 1964) 32-38; idem, "Faith and Eschatology in Acts 3" in *Glaube und Eschatologie: Festschrift für W.G Kümmel*, ed. E. Grässer and O. Merk (Tübingen: J. C. B. Mohr [Paul Siebeck], 1985) 1-17; R. J. Bauckham, "The Delay of the Parousia," *TynB* 31 (1980) 3-36; idem, *Jude, 2 Peter* (WBC; Waco, TX: Word, 1983); G. K. Beale, "The Interpretative Problem of Rev. 1:19," *NovT* 34 (1992) 360-87; G. R. Beasley-Murray, *The Book of Revelation* (NCB; rev. ed.; Grand Rapids: Eerdmans, 1978); idem with H. H. Hobbs and R. F. Robbins, *Revelation: Three Viewpoints* (Nashville: Broadman, 1977); E. Best, *1 Peter* (NCB; Grand Rapids: Eerdmans, 1977); H. Bietenhard, "The Millennial Hope in the Early Church," *SJT* 6 (1953) 12-30; M. Black, "The Maranatha Invocation and Jude 14, 15 (I Enoch I.9)" in *Christ and Spirit in the New Testament: in honour of Charles Digby Moule*, ed. B. Lindars and S. S. Smalley (Cambridge: Cambridge University Press, 1973) 189-96; E. C. Blackman, *The Epistle of James* (TBC; Naperville, IL: Allenson, 1957); C. Brown, "Number," *NIDNTT* 2.683-704; idem, "Present, Day, Maranatha, Parousia," *NIDNTT* 2.886-935; R. E. Brown, *The Community of the Beloved Disciple* (New York: Paulist, 1979); idem, *The Epistles of John* (AB; New York: Garden City, 1982); F. F. Bruce, *The Epistle to the Hebrews* (NICNT; Grand Rapids: Eerdmans, 1964); idem, "Eschatology in Acts" in *Eschatology and the New Testament: Essays in Honor of George Raymond Beasley-Murray*, ed. W. H. Gloer (Peabody, MA: Hendrickson, 1988) 51-63; G. W. Buchanan, *To the Hebrews* (AB; New York: Doubleday, 1972); R. Bultmann, "History and Myth" in *Kerygma and Myth* 1, ed. H.-W. Bartsch (London: SPCK, 1953) 1-44; idem, *The Johannine Epistles* (Herm; Philadelphia: Fortress, 1973); G. B. Caird, *The Revelation of St. John the Divine* (HNTC; New York: Harper & Row, 1966); C. Carlston, "The Vocabulary of Perfection in Philo and Hebrews" in *Unity and Diversity in New Testament Theology: Essays in Honor of George E. Ladd*, ed. R. A. Guelich (Grand Rapids, MI, 1978) 133-60; R. G. Clouse, ed., *The Meaning of the Millennium: Four Views* (Downers Grove, IL: InterVarsity, 1980); H. C. C. Cavallin, "The False Teachers of 2 PT as Pseudo-Prophets," *NovT* 31 (1979) 263-70; R. H. Charles, *The Revelation of St. John* (2 vols.; ICC; Edinburgh: T & T Clark, 1920); A. Y. Collins, *The Combat Myth in the Book of Revelation* (Missoula, MT: Scholars Press, 1976); H. Conzelmann, *The Theology of St. Luke* (New York: Harper, 1960); idem, *Acts of the Apostles* (Herm; Philadelphia: Fortress, 1987); C. E. B. Cranfield, *I & II Peter and Jude* (TBC; London: SCM, 1960); O. Cullmann, *Christ and Time* (Philadelphia: Westminster, 1951); P. H. Davids, *The Epistle of James* (NIGTC; Grand Rapids: Eerdmans, 1982); idem, *The First Epistle of Peter* (NICNT; Grand Rapids: Eerdmans, 1990); C. H. Dodd, *The Apostolic Preaching and Its Developments* (London: Hodder & Stoughton, 1936); idem, *The Johannine Epistles* (MNTC; London: Hodder & Stoughton, 1946); J. D. G. Dunn, *Unity and Diversity in the New Testament* (Philadelphia: Westminster, 1977) 344-51; J. H. Elliott, *A Home for the Homeless* (London: SCM, 1982); idem, "Peter, Second Epistle to," *ABD* 5.282-87; E. E. Ellis, *Prophecy and Hermeneutic in Early Christianity* (Grand Rapids, MI: Eerdmans, 1978) 221-36; P. Esler, *Community and Gospel in Luke-Acts* (SNTSMS 57; Cambridge: Cambridge University Press, 1987); A. Feuillet, "Le sens du mot *Parousia* dans l'Evangile Matthieu—Comparaison entre Matth. 24 et Jac. 5, 1-11" in *The Background of the New Testament and Its Eschatology: Festschrift for C. H. Dodd*, ed. W. D. Davies and D. Daube (Cambridge: Cambridge University Press, 1956) 261-80; H. Flender, *St. Luke: Historian and Theologian* (Philadelphia: Fortress, 1967); J. M. Ford, *Revelation* (AB; Garden City, NY: Doubleday, 1975); idem, "Tribulation and Peace: The Fate of Shalom in Jewish Apocalyptic," *HBT* 6 (1984) 1-26; T. Fornberg, *An Early Church in a Pluralistic Society: A Study of 2 Peter* (CB 9; Lund: Gleerup, 1977); E. Franklin, "The Ascension and the Eschatology of Luke-Acts," *SJT* 23 (1970) 191-200; W. W. Gasque, *A History of the Interpretation of the Acts of the Apostles* (Peabody, MA: Hendrickson, 1989); T. F. Glasson, *The Second Advent* (London: Epworth, 1945); idem, *His Appearing and His Kingdom* (London: Epworth, 1953); idem, "The Second Advent—25 Years Later," *ExpT* 82 (1971) 307-9; G. Goldsworthy, *The Gospel in Revelation* (Exeter: Paternoster, 1984); R. P. Gordon, "KAI TO TELOS KURIOU EIDETE (JAS. V.11)," *JTS* 26 (1975) 91-95; K. Grayston, *The Johannine Epistles* (NCB; Grand Rapids: Eerdmans, 1984); M. Green, *2 Peter and Jude* (TNTC; Leicester: Inter-Varsity; Grand Rapids: Eerdmans, 1968); E. Haenchen, *The Acts of the Apostles* (Oxford: Basil Blackwell, 1971); A. T. Hanson, *The Wrath of the Lamb* (London: SPCK, 1957); C. J. Hemer, *The Letters to the Seven Churches of Asia in Their Local Setting* (JSNTSup 11; Sheffield: Sheffield Academic, 1986); R. H. Hiers, "Eschatology and Methodology," *JBL* 85 (1966) 170-84; "The Problem of the Delay of the Parousia in Luke-Acts," *NTS* 20 (1973-74) 145-55; J. L. Houlden, *A Commentary on the Johannine Epistles* (HNTC; New York: Harper & Row, 1973); H. Hübner, "τέλειος," "τελειόω," "τελέω," "τέλος" *EDNT* 3.342-48; W. G. Johnsson, "The Pilgrimage Motif in the Book of Hebrews," *JBL* 97 (1978) 239-51; E. Käsemann, "An Apologia for Primitive Christian Eschatology" in *Essays on New Testament Themes* (London: SCM, 1964) 169-95; idem, *The*

Wandering People of God (Minneapolis: Augsburg, 1984); J. N. D. Kelly, *A Commentary on the Epistles of Peter and of Jude* (HNTC; New York: Harper & Row, 1969); L. J. Kreitzer, "Hadrian and the Nero Redivivus Myth," *ZNW* 79 (1988) 92-115; G. E. Ladd, *The Blessed Hope* (Grand Rapids: Eerdmans, 1956); idem, *A Commentary on the Revelation of John* (Grand Rapids, Eerdmans, 1972); idem, "Apocalyptic and New Testament Theology" in *Reconciliation and Hope: New Testament Essays on Atonement and Eschatology Presented to L. L. Morris on his 60th Birthday*, ed. R. Banks, (Grand Rapids: Eerdmans, 1975) 285-96; W. Lane, *Call to Commitment: Responding to the Message of Hebrews* (Nashville: Thomas Nelson, 1985); S. Laws, *The Epistle of James* (HNTC; New York: Harper & Row, 1980); T. W. Lewis, "'. . . And if He Shrinks Back' (Heb. X. 38b)," *NTS* 22 (1976) 88-94; J. Lieu, *The Theology of the Johannine Epistles* (NTT; Cambridge: Cambridge University Press, 1991); B. Lindars, *The Theology of the Letter to the Hebrews* (NTT; Cambridge: Cambridge University Press, 1991); G. Lüdemann, *Early Christianity According to the Traditions in Acts: A Commentary* (Minneapolis: Fortress, 1989); G. W. MacRae, "Heavenly Temple and Eschatology in the Letter to the Hebrews," *Semeia* 12 (1978) 179-99; W. Manson, *The Epistle to the Hebrews* (London: Hodder & Stoughton, 1951); I. H. Marshall, "Martyrdom and the Parousia in the Revelation of John," *SE* 4 (1964) 333-39; idem, *The Epistles of John* (NICNT; Grand Rapids: Eerdmans, 1978); R. P. Martin, *James* (WBC; Waco, TX: Word, 1988); H. K. McArthur, "Parousia," *IDB* 3.658-61; J. R. Michaels, "Eschatology in 1 Peter III.17," *NTS* 13 (1966-67) 394-401; idem, *1 Peter* (WBC; Waco, TX: Word, 1988); D. J. Moo, *The Letter of James* (TNTC; Leicester: Inter-Varsity, 1985); A. L. Moore, *The Parousia in the New Testament* (NovTSup 13; Leiden: E. J. Brill, 1966); L. Morris, *The Revelation of St. John* (TNTC; Leicester: Inter-Varsity, 1969); C. F. D. Moule, "A Reconsideration of the Context of Maranatha," *NTS* 6 (1959-60) 307-10; R. H. Mounce, *The Book of Revelation* (NICNT; Grand Rapids: Eerdmans, 1977); J. H. Neyrey, "The Form and Background of the Polemic in 2 Peter," *JBL* 99 (1980) 407-31; idem, *2 Peter, Jude* (AB; New York: Doubleday, 1993); A. Oepke, "παρουσία," *TDNT* 5.858-71; G. R. Osborne, "The 'Rapture' Question," *Themelios* 2 (1977) 77-80; C. D. Osburn, "The Christological Use of 1 Enoch I.9 in Jude 14-15," *NTS* 23 (1977) 334-41; H. P. Owen, "Stephen's Vision in Acts VII.55-56," *NTS* 1 (1954-55) 224-26; M. C. Parsons, *The Departure of Jesus in Luke-Acts* (JSNTSup 21; Sheffield: Sheffield Academic, 1987); D. Peterson, *Hebrews and Perfection* (SNTSMS 47; Cambridge: Cambridge University Press, 1982); W. Radl, "παρουσία," *EDNT* 3.43-44; B. Reicke, *The Epistles of James, Peter, and Jude* (AB 37; New York: Doubleday, 1964); J. A. T. Robinson, "The Most Primitive Christology of All?," *JTS* 7 (1956) 177-89; idem, *Jesus and His Coming: The Emergence of a Doctrine* (New York: Abingdon, 1958); idem, *Redating the New Testament* (Philadelphia: Westminster, 1976); C. C. Rowland, *Christian Origins* (SPCK: London, 1985); idem, *Revelation* (EC; London: Epworth, 1993); idem, "Parousia," *ABD* 5.166-70; D. J. Rowston, "The Most Neglected Book in the New Testament," *NTS* 21 (1974-75) 554-63; R. Schnackenburg, *God's Rule and Kingdom* (Edinburgh: Nelson, 1963); idem, *The Johannine Epistles* (Tunbridge Wells: Burns & Oates, 1992); R. B. Y. Scott, "Behold, He Cometh With Clouds," *NTS* 5 (1959-60) 127-32; E. G. Selwyn, *The First Epistle of Peter* (London: Macmillan, 1947); idem, "Eschatology in 1 Peter" in *The Background of the New Testament and Its Eschatology: Festschrift for C. H. Dodd*, ed. W. D. Davies and D. Daube (Cambridge: Cambridge University Press, 1956) 394-401; E. M. Sidebottom, *James, Jude, 2 Peter* (NCB; Grand Rapids: Eerdmans, 1971); S. Smalley, "The Delay of the Parousia," *JBL* 83 (1964) 41-54; idem, *1, 2, 3 John* (WBC; Waco, TX: Word, 1984); R. Summers, *Worthy is the Lamb* (Nashville: Broadman, 1951); J. Tabor (with P. Arnold), "The David Koresh Manuscript: Exposition of the Seven Seals" (Houston, TX: Reunion Institute, 1994); C. H. Talbert, "II Peter and the Delay of the Parousia," *VC* 20 (1966) 137-45; L. Thompson, *The Book of Revelation: Apocalypse and Empire* (Oxford: Oxford University Press, 1990); S. Travis, *I Believe in the Second Coming of Jesus* (Grand Rapids: Eerdmans, 1982); J. VanderKam, "The Theophany of Enoch I 3b-7, 9," *VT* 23 (1973) 129-50; J. F. Walvoord, *The Revelation of Jesus Christ* (Chicago: Moody, 1966); M. Wilcox, *The Message of Revelation* (BST; Downers Grove, IL: InterVarsity, 1975); R. McL. Wilson, *Hebrews* (NCB; Basingstoke: Marshall, Morgan & Scott, 1987); S. G. Wilson, *The Gentiles and the Gentile Mission in Luke-Acts* (SNTSMS 23; Cambridge: Cambridge University Press, 1973). L. J. Kreitzer

PASCHAL HOMILY. *See* MELITO OF SARDIS.

PASCHAL LAMB. *See* LAMB.

PASTORAL THEOLOGY

Pastoral theology in the most general sense is the application of Christian truth* to pastoral situations. Therefore pastoral theology is both a contemporary pursuit as well as a historical phenomenon. The latter is the primary focus of this article, as the authors of our literature reveal the pastoral concerns that lie behind their purposes for writing.

1. Definitions
2. Backgrounds
3. Pastoral Emphases

1. Definitions.

1.1. Pastoral Theology as a Contemporary Pursuit. T. C. Oden defines pastoral theology as "that branch of Christian theology that deals with the office and functions of the pastor" (Oden, x). It is theology because it treats the consequences of God's* self-disclosure in history and concerns itself with theological meaning of life events. It is pastoral because it concerns itself with the appropriate methods by which Christian pastors should function in the practice of ministry,* including roles, tasks and duties. Therefore as a contemporary pursuit pastoral theology is a theology of the practice of ministry, including the church disciplines of pastoral care and counseling, preaching, liturgy, religious education, mission, evangelism and social ministries (Oden, x; Malony, 631; Tidball 1995, 42).

Four representative traditions in pastoral theology—Roman Catholic, Lutheran, Anglican and Reformed—reveal special emphases. With its emphasis upon sin as the problem of life and penance and acts of satisfaction as the solution, the traditional Roman Catholic teaching sees that the goal of pastoral theology is to nurture souls and prepare them for heaven* through spiritual discipline. The Lutheran tradition became more concerned with the problem of faithlessness, including the concerns of pride,* self-righteousness, lack of trust and anxiety, so that the approach of pastoral theology is to induce feelings of despair and repentance,* followed by encouragement to have faith.* The Anglican tradition sees sin as disorder, inward, interpersonal and social, so the

pastoral role is to restore order by embodying the grace* of God that allows the possibility of Christian growth. With their emphasis upon predestination, Reformed Christians need concrete assurance* of their foreordination to salvation,* so much of pastoral theology focuses on the procedures to determine the true state of their souls and to achieve evidence of their security (see Malony, 631; Cooke, 1-24).

1.2. Pastoral Theology in Early Christian Literature. Pastoral theology is the subject of exegesis and is at least in part the source for contemporary pursuits. From an exegetical perspective, pastoral theology surfaces through three primary levels of inquiry. These three levels of exegetical analysis are combined to provide the broadest perspective of pastoral theology as "the application of Christian truth to pastoral situations" (Tidball 1986, 17).

First, the authors of the biblical texts and the apostolic authors (*see* Apostolic Fathers) had pastoral intentions as they wrote to their respective audiences. Pastoral theology is revealed in the text as the exegete determines an author's purpose for writing to a particular audience. For example, the "elder" in 2 John displays a pastoral concern for the elect lady and her children, encouraging them to continue to walk in truth and love (2 Jn 4-6), while at the same time—like a good shepherd—warning them of the false teachers who want to deceive them (2 Jn 7-11; *see* John, Letters of).

Second, a biblical theology of "shepherding" surfaces from these texts that can be systematically organized as pastoral theology to provide pastoral help for general readers and also provide a resource for those engaged in pastoral ministry. When Paul declares that the goal of pastoral ministry is to proclaim Christ, "admonishing and teaching everyone in all wisdom, so that we may present everyone perfect in Christ" (Col 1:28), this task can be clarified throughout the NT by other texts that echo that goal and specify aspects of it (e.g., 1 Pet 1—2). For example, Peter focuses his readers' attention on the process of growth in this life (1 Pet 1:3-9), calls them to obedient living (1 Pet 1:13-25; *see* Obedience) and admonishes them to follow the example of Jesus (1 Pet 2:21-24), all with a pastoral goal in mind: "for you were going astray like sheep, but now you have returned to the shepherd and overseer of your souls" (1 Pet 2:25).

Third, specific texts give instruction in the pastoral office or describe the pastoral role within the early church.* These texts can be organized into a pastoral theology that provides a statement of pastoral responsibilities. Caregiving is a distinctive of NT faith, both of individual believers toward one another and for those engaged in the pastoral office. Paul admonishes the Galatian readers to "bear one another's burdens, and in this way you will fulfill the law of Christ" (Gal 6:2), which is supplemented by the statement of the author of Hebrews*: "Let us consider how to stimulate one another to love and good deeds, not neglecting the meeting together, as is the habit of some, but encouraging one another" (Heb 10:24-25). When Paul emphasized the gifted person who would be "pastor-teacher" of the church (Eph 4:12), he furthers the shepherding motif that he had admonished the Ephesian elders to assume as their role among the flock or church (Acts 20:25-31). This theme is expanded upon when compared with Peter's instructions to the sheep and undershepherds among his readers (1 Pet 5:1-5; cf. Jn 21:15-19) and the various other terms that lay out the variety of pastoral roles (e.g., bishop, elder; cf. Ign. *Magn.* 6:1-2; Ign. *Trall.* 3.1; Ign. *Phld.* 5.1).

Our focus in this article is upon pastoral theology as an exegetical concern, although we recognize that this exercise is intended to inform the contemporary pursuit as well.

2. Backgrounds.

2.1. Gospels. The Gospels traditionally have been seen as historical and theological documents, but recent approaches (e.g., redaction criticism) have demonstrated an awareness of their pastoral dimensions. In the attempt to provide a historically credible document, Luke provides pastoral help to Theophilus (either individually or representing the community), who appears to have doubts and uncertainties about the faith (Lk 1:1-4; cf. Marshall, 21-52). The author of the Fourth Gospel wished to present various signs* Jesus performed in his historical ministry in such a way that they would convince his readers that Jesus was the Christ,* the Son of God,* and that they would have life* through this belief (Jn 20:31). This is pastoral concern, whether of mission or of edification and comfort (cf. Carson, 87-95; 660-63).

Therefore the Gospels provide different pastoral perspectives. The first is the pastoral emphasis of Jesus. One of the striking metaphors Jesus used to define his relationship to his followers was as the shepherd* of the sheep (Jn 10:1-18; 21:15-19), terminology that was followed explicitly by the early church to designate those who had responsibility for caring for the church (e.g., 1 Pet 5:1-5). Jesus in his shepherding role becomes the pivotal analogy of pastoral care as he calls, protects, leads, feeds and even lays down his life for his sheep (Oden, 51-53). The author of Hebrews refers to Jesus as the great Shepherd of the sheep (Heb 13:20; cf. Mt 26:31), a metaphor we will see Peter allude to as well (cf. 1 Pet 2:25). The second is the pastoral emphasis of the Evangelists. When seen as pastoral pamphlets, the Gospel records become models of pastoral care for communities of faith. Through the stories of Jesus and his interaction with his followers and even opponents, the Evangelists instruct, admonish, comfort, warn and edify their readers. Third, we begin to gain insight to the pastoral functioning of the communities, an insight that will be fleshed out in the Epistles. Since new disciples are to be taught to obey all that Jesus had commanded (Mt 28:19-20), the Gospels become in part manuals of discipleship by which the pastoral teaching role in the church can be facilitated (cf. Wilkins, 172-239).

2.2. Paul. Paul testifies that pastoral concerns loomed large in his apostolic ministry: "there is daily pressure upon me of concern for all the churches" (2 Cor 11:28; *see DPL*, Pastor, Paul as). Paul's pastoral ministry was rooted in the character and meaning of the gospel message he carried and is seen in the three major facets of his ministry: his proclamation of the gospel, his establishing of congregations and his nurture of them (cf. Furnish).

The letters* of Paul are explicit in their pastoral thrust. The needs of the recipients are usually addressed directly, and the letters contain immediate instruction and exhortation to meet the doctrinal, corporate and personal needs and problems of believers. Paul's pastoral approach is normally didactic, relating the experience of his readers to the doctrines of the faith. Even though he may not be the present leader of the local church to which he writes (e.g., Philemon) and never uses the term *pastor* of himself, Paul brings a translocal authority to the text that is intended to influence the church to remember that, since they are in Christ, they are responsible to heed Paul's pastoral guidance. He appeals to his readers to heed him as their spiritual father and to heed also his spiritual offspring who share his pastoral role among them (e.g., Timothy in 1 Cor 4:14-17; cf. Petersen, 287-302; *see DPL*, Pastor, Paul as)

3. Pastoral Emphases.

The book of Acts,* the General Epistles, the Revelation (*see* Revelation, Book of) and the writings of the apostolic fathers are varied in their approach but nonetheless are pastoral in their intent, designed to apply Christian truth to specific conditions and needs.

3.1. Acts: Purpose and Spiritual Power. As was the case with his Gospel, so the author of Acts had a pastoral intention in composing his document. R. P. Martin (1978, 53-67) demonstrates that this is revealed first in the emphasis upon the power of the Holy Spirit* through God-ordained messengers in the universal spread of the church, which compels the readers to accept that this movement truly is "of God" (Acts 5:39). Second, the author confirms to Theophilus that the Christian church is not politically dangerous: It is innocent of the charges leveled against it, as was its Lord* (Acts 5:39). This should encourage him to continue (or begin) to identify with the movement. Third, the author challenges the readers, now a multiracial church that has come out of Judaism,* to recognize that it continues to have links that cannot be severed with God's program of the ages because of its place in salvation history. Ernst Haenchen, who goes too far with his suggestions of the writer's freedom from historical reporting, nonetheless points rightly to the writer's pastoral intent of impressing upon the reader unforgettably the truth of the power of God in his unfolding narrative (Haenchen, 103-10). Such a narrative is sure to offer to the church the confidence to accept that the life of the Christian community on this earth is now relatively fixed and settled and that its future shares the same task of the apostles,* to offer the gospel message to a waiting world (Martin 1978, 56-63).

3.2. Hebrews: Defection and Real Confession. W. L. Lane concludes that the book of Hebrews is "a pastorally oriented sermon." The author, concerned that his readers are in danger of forsaking Christianity and lapsing back into Judaism, possibly to avoid persecution,* engages in a careful exposition of the superiority of the new covenant* to the old. But biblical and theological exposition ultimately serve the paraenetic purpose. The book was written to arouse, urge, encourage and exhort those addressed to maintain their Christian confession. The writer wants to dissuade the readers from a course of action that would be catastrophic (Lane, c).

Throughout the document the author encourages the readers to reexamine the basis of their faith by looking closely at Jesus (Heb 2:9; 3:1; 12:2-3). On the one hand they must recognize that in every possible way Jesus Christ is superior to all, whether angels* (Heb 1:5—2:18), Moses* (Heb 3:1-19), Joshua (Heb 4:1-13), the high priest* (Heb 4:14—5:10) or Melchizedek* (Heb 7:1-28). Jesus Christ is superior to the revelation* that came through the law,* especially as the law was applied through the levitical priesthood. Although the law was God's revelation and the argument of Hebrews is founded on the OT, the new revelation in Christ has superseded the old. Jesus provides a better way from humans to God (Heb 8:1—10:18). But on the other hand the author recognizes that in addition to intellectual needs, the readers have pressing situational needs. As a tried and tested people, they must look to Jesus who was fully human (Heb 2:14) and who can sympathize with their temptations (Heb 4:15), their sufferings* (Heb 5:7-9) and their perseverance (*see* Endurance), even if it must be to death (Heb 2:14; 13:12).

The author applies pastoral care to his readers. Intermittent exhortations (Heb 2:1; 3:12; 4:11, 14; 5:11-12; 6:1; 10:35-36; 12:1, 12, 25; 13:9, 22) call the readers to apply what they know about Jesus to make a firm intellectual stand in their faith. The author also uses direct warnings (Heb 2:2-3; 6:1-8; 10:26-31; 12:25) about the direction their spiritual lives seem to be taking to call them to recognize the consequences of traversing that path. Even while the author speaks directly of judgment,* a note of encouragement quickly follows (Heb 6:6-10; 10:32-35) that apprises the readers that they can recover from their present dilemma, because the history of God's people is filled with examples of others who have faced similar difficulties (Heb 6:13-15; 11:1—12:1; 13:7). But these truths must now be applied by the readers. They must take them to heart as the only means of withstanding the influence of the false teachers (Heb 13:9) so that they can carry out the will of God through Jesus Christ (Heb 13:20-21; cf. Tidball 1986, 124-30).

3.3. James: Economics and True Faith. While the precise location of writing, destination and dating of James* remain problematic, the pastoral nature of the letter is widely acknowledged. D. J. Moo states, "First and most prominent is the strong tone of pastoral exhortation. . . . James issues his commands, for the most part, in a tone of tender pastoral concern" (Moo, 36; see also Chester, 15). The author writes to urge his readers to make necessary changes in their lives and in their relationships with one another within the community. Writing to a community (or communities) that apparently is well versed in fundamental Christian teaching, the author has at least two overriding pastoral concerns (see Martin 1988, lxvii-lxix; Davids, 34).

First is the author's regard and sympathy for the poor and disadvantaged (Jas 1:9-11; 1:26-27; 2:1-13; 4:13—5:6). The author offers both comfort to those suffering under economic trials and denunciation to those who are taking advantage of them. He draws on the rich OT background of God's regard for the poor and downtrodden by reminding his readers that the wealth of this world does not always indicate those whom God has chosen to enjoy the eschatological* riches of the kingdom (Jas 2:5; *see* Kingdom of God). He declares that the essence of true religion is evidenced by social and economic concern for those in need (Jas 1:26-27). Rich merchants (Jas 4:13-17) and landowners (Jas 5:1-6) are condemned both because of their arrogant attitude that forgets God and because of their exploitation of the poor in general and their poor workers. The poor must not fawn on the rich by showing them favoritism (Jas 2:1-7), because the rich who have not humbled themselves will wither under the scorching of God's judgment (Jas 1:9-11).

The second pastoral concern is vitally connected to the first. The poor and oppressed must not allow their circumstances to destroy the unity of the church, nor must they succumb to the temptation to take the path of social revolution as the means of rectifying their plight. They must be single-minded in relying upon the wisdom* of God (Jas 1:2-7) or else anger and envy (Jas 1:19-27) will turn both inward to cause quarreling (Jas 4:1-3, 11-12) and outward to attempt to rectify their plight by aligning themselves with worldly powers (Jas 4:4-10; cf. Jas 3:13-18; 5:7-11).

The poor and oppressed are called to act upon the truths of the faith. They must rely on the wisdom of God, not their own. They must patiently wait for the Lord's coming judgment, not taking judgment into their own hands. They must show by their actions that they have true faith in God, not in themselves or the world.

3.4. 1 Peter: Persecution and Living Hope. The primary distinctive of 1 Peter's* pastoral theology is found in the author's caregiving to those who are suffering persecution. The persecution comes from local rather than imperial sources. The readers appear to be relatively new Christians (cf. 1 Pet 1:22-23; 2:2-3; 3:21) who are a minority social group within the local pagan environment. The genre of 1 Peter can be classified at least in part as paraenesis, since the author does not attempt to convince the readers of new ethical rules. Rather he assumes that they already know and accept the rules. The author's main task is to enhance their right attitudes and make them more steadfast in their convictions, which in turn will lead to right action (cf. Thurén, 226).

Three of the readers' critical needs become the focal points for author's pastoral caregiving. First, since the readers were at odds with society around them, they were feeling persecution from local authorities and community pressures (1 Pet 1:6; 3:13-14; 4:4, 12-16; 5:9-10). The author suggests that the readers' attractive conduct is the best apologetic to hostile neighbors and authorities (1 Pet 2:12, 16-17; 3:16; 4:12-16). Second, since the readers have only recently been converted to Christianity, their social status has been thrown into question; they are now an alienated social group that needs to understand their identity (1 Pet 2:10; 4:4). The author boldly declares that they now belong to the people of God that stretches back to Abraham* and Sarah (1 Pet 3:5-6) and forward to the complete household* of faith one day to be realized (1 Pet 2;4-10; 4:17-19). Third, these new believers apparently were struggling with age-old questions: Why do good people suffer? Why does God allow suffering to occur? Where is God in the middle of suffering? (1 Pet 1:6; 2:19; 4:12). The author offers classic pastoral help through his theodicy: God's plan is at work in and through human pain, misery and affliction, and at the end of history this plan will be fully known (1 Pet 1:5-9; 4:7; 5:10). Therefore the Christian life is centered in a living hope in the God whose purposes are known in Christ (1 Pet 1:3, 21; 3:5, 15; 4:11; see Martin 1994, 89-90, 123).

A second distinctive of pastoral theology in 1 Peter is the discussion of the pastoral leaders (1 Pet 5:1-5). The group of elders (1 Pet 5:1) are told to "shepherd the flock of God" among them (1 Pet 5:2) until the appearing of the chief Shepherd (1 Pet 5:4; cf. Jn 10:1-18; Mt 26:31). The verb *shepherd (poimainō;* cf. Jn 21:16; Acts 20:28) points to a pastoring or shepherding role for the elders. They have a unique responsibility to care for the household of God. They must guide and shepherd their charges willingly and without complaint, not for financial gain or ego satisfaction. Their lives are to an example for the rest of the assembly (1 Pet 5:3). The mention of the younger men (1 Pet 5:5) indicates either a second, junior branch of church leadership or more likely a call to the rest of the assembly to recognize the designated authority* of the elders. But all, whether or not elders, are to act in humility toward one another (1 Pet 5:5; cf. Michaels, 288-91).

3.5. 2 Peter and Jude: Guard and Grow. 2 Peter* and Jude* take the approach of apocalyptic,* which can be effective in providing a strong dose of pastoral medicine. Serious inroads and threats against the church were being made by false teaching, so 2 Peter and Jude mount polemics against it (2 Pet 2:1-20; Jude 4-19). The authors take seriously their responsibility to guard their readers from false teaching but also to help them grow in their faith until the coming of the Lord. The pastoral concerns of these two letters are devoted to three issues. First, the false teaching and its adherents are not unlike the godless, false teachers that have plagued the human race in general and the people of Israel* in particular throughout history. Second, by twisting the truth these false teachers fall prey to their own wicked teaching and plunge into moral perversion and degradation (but see Bauckham for the view that the moral perversion is the false teaching). Third, the judgment that will accompany the coming of the Day of Lord* (2 Pet 3:1-13; Jude 14-15) will vindicate the long-suffering of God and the maintenance

of his promises* (2 Pet 3:8-9).

It was the authors' responsibility to remind the readers of the truth (1 Pet 1:12; 3:1-2, 14-17; Jude 3, 5, 17), so that they could identify the false teachers. But just as importantly the truth will encourage the readers in their personal and corporate growth (2 Pet 3:18; Jude 20), it will remind them to keep pure until the coming of the Lord (2 Pet 3:11-12, 14-17; Jude 21), and it will equip them to rescue others who are under the influence of the false teachers and teaching (2 Pet 3:17-18; Jude 22-23).

3.6. Johannine Epistles: Truth and Love. The cardinal tenet of pastoral theology in the Johannine epistles, following that of the Fourth Gospel, is found in the interrelatedness of christology* and ethics*: knowing the truth about Jesus' identity will be evidenced in love* within the community of faith. The Johannine community behind the three epistles seems to be composed of two groups of believers. One group was made up of Jewish Christians, whose background in Judaism would have made it difficult to accept the full messiahship of Jesus. Another group was made up of Hellenistic Christians, whose background in pagan religions (*see* Greco-Roman Religions) with dualistic systems of salvation would have made it difficult to accept the full humanity of Jesus.

John writes with an eye toward both of these groups as he strikes a christological balance. Both groups had begun to discern the real identity of Jesus, but in neither group was the estimate adequate. In fact, from the time of the writing of the Fourth Gospel to the epistles, fringe members of both groups were moving toward heretical polar positions (for details see Brown). Friction was increasingly evident as the groups took their theological stances. John's task was to move them closer to christological truth while at the same time emphasizing that Jesus' love for his disciples (Jn 13:34-35) is recapitulated in their love for one another (1 Jn 4:7-12). Secession from the community had begun (1 Jn 2:18-19). Ethical implications on both sides emerged. An emphasis on law marked the Jewish Christian sector (1 Jn 2:7-8), and an indifference to right conduct, including love, marked the Hellenistic Christian sector (1 Jn 3:10-11). By the time of 2 and 3 John the theological and ethical divisions had widened. Further secessions occur (2 Jn 7), and an organizational threat to the unity of the community was embodied in persons like Diotrephes (3 Jn 9-10).

John writes as one who has a solid base of relationship with his readers. While he writes to correct error, he especially writes to instruct and encourage the faithful. They are his "dear children" (1 Jn 2:1, 12-13, 18; 3 Jn 4) and "dear friends" (1 Jn 2:7; 3:2, 21; 3 Jn 1, 2, 5), and he intends to build on this solid pastoral relationship. He continually reminds them of what they already know (1 Jn 2:7-8, 21-22; 2 Jn 5). He calls them to lay claim to that truth, which will then enable them to love each other, which in turn will bring them into healthy moral and ethical relationships with one another. The epistles emphasize certainty and assurance in the light of the uncertainty and confusion surrounding the readers. There is a clear statement of truth in these epistles, and the readers must cling to it to avoid being swayed by the errors of the day and to enable them to love one another truly (see Smalley, esp. xxiii-xxxii; Smith, 222-26).

3.7. The Revelation: Eschatology and Perseverance. Early in the twentieth century H. B. Swete caught the essence of the book of Revelation: "In form it is an epistle, containing an apocalyptic prophecy; in spirit and inner purpose, it is a pastoral" (Swete, *The Apocalypse of St. John*, xc). The opening verse declares the eschatological purpose: "The revelation of Jesus Christ, which God gave him to show his servants what must soon take place" (Rev 1:1). Through the revelation God shows that even as humankind and the satanic forces in the last days will attempt to establish the antikingdom on the earth, God will finally bring judgment upon the earth for its wickedness, he will finally fulfill his promise of restoration to the people of God, and he will finally establish his kingdom on the earth.

The author also has a profound pastoral purpose. The book is designed to encourage the readers to persevere in the middle of their suffering and testing. When the temptation comes to forsake the Lord while being persecuted, one must recognize that God will ultimately be victorious. When the temptation comes to choose the wicked ways of the world because it is more convenient and comfortable to do so, one must recognize that the ways of the world will finally be judged, and the one who remains faithful to God will finally be rewarded. The author encourages authentic Christian living by explaining suffering and martyrdom* in the light of the way in which Jesus' death brought victory over evil.

3.8. Apostolic Fathers: Institutionalism and Clergy. D. J. Tidball identifies four factors that stand out when considering the development of pastoral theology in the writings of the apostolic fathers. First, the church was subject to the natural processes of institutionalization. Second, the increasing need to define and defend orthodox belief began to result in divisions within the church. Third, the leaders of the church were products of their culture and intellectual environment and often unconsciously shaped the ministry to conform to it. Fourth, the church begins this period as a persecuted minority, but there are signs of the change to come, when Christianity will be the recognized religion of the empire and the baptizer of its culture (Tidball 1986, 147).

Nearly all of the apostolic fathers say something about pastoral ministry. While itinerant teachers and prophets* continue to be valuable as they traverse the landscape, the *Didache* lays down precautionary guidelines for their reception: for example, if they stay longer than three days, they are suspect of being a false prophet (*Did.* 11.5; 12.1-5); they were to be dismissed as charlatans if they asked for money for themselves (*Did.* 11.6) or asked for food while "in a spirit" (*Did.* 11.9); and their behavior is the proof of the validity of their prophecy (*Did.* 11.8). But it is clear that local leaders were assuming greater significance than the itinerants (*Did.* 15; Tidball 1986, 148).

The most significant issue for pastoral theology is in the development of the pastoral office (cf. Volz, 19-26; Tidball 1986, 148-49). We find an increasing division between clergy and laity in the apostolic fathers (*1 Clem.* 42—47), especially in Ignatius's* writings (cf. Schoedel, 10-27). A threefold ministry of bishops, priests and deacons is in existence. Ignatius writes, "Similarly let everyone respect the deacons as Jesus Christ, just as they should respect the bishop, who is a model of the Father, and the presbyters as God's council and as the band of the apostles. Without these no group can be called a church" (Ign. *Trall.* 3.1). These offices now are the essence of the church. Ignatius time and again exhorts his readers to obey the bishops, because power was conferred on them by God (Ign. *Magn.* 3.1) and they were to be followed like sheep (Ign. *Phld.* 2.1). Obeying them was like obeying the voice of God (Ign. *Phld.* 7.1;Ign. *Smyrn.* 8), for all those who belong to God and Jesus Christ are with the bishop (Ign. *Phld.* 3.2; Ign. *Eph.* 4.1; see Wilkins 1992 "Interplay of Ministry").

The hierarchical mentality was surely motivated by the desire to protect the flock, but it was not universal. Polycarp* likewise encourages obedience to the clergy and deacons, but he does not mention the office of bishop. Instead he emphasizes the qualities desired of the clergy: they are sympathetic and compassionate for humanity; they turn back those going astray; they visit the sick, widows, orphans and the poor; they aim for what is honorable in the sight of God and people; they avoid anger, partiality and unjust judgment; they are free from love of money; they do not believe things spoken against others; they are not harsh in judgment; and they are included in the debt of sin (Pol. *Phil.* 6.1).

See also APOSTASY; ASSURANCE; CHURCH; CHURCH ORDER, GOVERNMENT; DISCIPLINE; ENDURANCE, PERSEVERANCE; HOUSEHOLD CODES; HOUSEHOLD, FAMILY; MARRIAGE, DIVORCE, ADULTERY; MILK, SOLID FOOD; MINISTRY; REPENTANCE, SECOND REPENTANCE; SERVANT, SERVICE; SEXUALITY, SEXUAL ETHICS; SHEPHERD, FLOCK; SOCIAL SETTING OF EARLY NON-PAULINE CHRISTIANITY; TEACHING, PARAENESIS; WOMEN IN THE EARLY CHURCH; WORSHIP AND LITURGY.

BIBLIOGRAPHY. D. J. Atkinson, "Pastoral Theology" in *The Blackwell Encyclopedia of Modern Christian Thought,* ed. A. E. McGrath (Oxford: Blackwell, 1993) 426-28; R. J. Bauckham, *Jude, 2 Peter* (WBC; Waco, TX: Word, 1983); R. E. Brown, *The Community of the Beloved Disciple* (New York: Paulist, 1979); J. T. Burtchaell, *From Synagogue to Church: Public Services and Offices in the Earliest Christian Communities* (Cambridge: Cambridge University Press, 1992); D. A. Carson, *The Gospel According to John* (Grand Rapids: Eerdmans, 1991); A. Chester, "The Theology of James" in A. Chester and R. P. Martin, *The Theology of the Letters of James, Peter and Jude* (NTT; Cambridge: Cambridge University Press, 1994); B. Cooke, *Ministry to Word and Sacraments: History and Theology* (Philadelphia: Fortress, 1976); P. H. Davids, *The Epistle of James: A Commentary on the Greek Text* (NIGTC; Grand Rapids: Eerdmans, 1982); idem, *The First Epistle of Peter* (NICNT; Grand Rapids: Eerdmans, 1990); V. P. Furnish, "Theology and Ministry in the Pauline Letters" in *A Biblical Basis for Ministry,* ed. E. E. Shelp and R. Sunderland (Philadelphia: Westminster, 1981) 101-44; E. Haenchen, *The Acts of the Apostles: A Commentary* (14th ed.; Philadelphia: Westminster, 1971); C. G. Kruse, *New Testament Models for Ministry: Jesus and Paul* (Nashville: Thomas Nelson, 1985); W. L. Lane, *Hebrews* (2 vols.; WBC 47; Dallas: Word, 1991); H. N. Malony, "Pastoral Theology" in *New Twentieth Century Encyclopedia of Religious Knowledge,* ed. J.D. Douglas (2d ed.; Grand Rapids: Baker, 1991) 631-32; I. H. Marshall, *Luke: Historian and Theologian* (3d ed.; Exeter: Paternoster, 1988); R. P. Martin, *James* (WBC; Dallas: Word, 1988); idem, *New Testament Foundations: A Guide for Christian Students,* 2: *The Acts, the Letters, the Apocalypse* (Grand Rapids: Eerdmans, 1978); idem, "The Theology of Jude, 1 Peter and 2 Peter" in A. Chester and R. P. Martin, *The Theology of the Letters of James, Peter and Jude* (NTT; Cambridge: Cambridge University Press, 1994); D. J. Moo, *The Letter of James: An Introduction and Commentary* (TNTC; Grand Rapids: Eerdmans, 1985); T. C. Oden, *Pastoral Theology: Essentials of Ministry* (San Francisco: Harper & Row, 1983); N. R. Petersen, *Rediscovering Paul: Philemon and the Sociology of Paul's Narrative World* (Philadelphia: Fortress, 1985); W. R. Schoedel, *Ignatius of Antioch* (Herm; Philadelphia: Fortress, 1985); S. S. Smalley, *1, 2, 3 John* (WBC; Waco, TX: Word, 1984); D. M. Smith, "Theology and Ministry in John" in *A Biblical Basis for Ministry,* ed. E. E. Shelp and R. Sunderland (Philadelphia: Westminster, 1981) 186-228; L. Thurén, *Argument and Theology in 1 Peter: The Origins of Christian Paraenesis* (JSNTSup 114; Sheffield: Sheffield Academic Press, 1995); D. J. Tidball, "Practical and Pastoral Theology" in *New Dictionary of Christian Ethics and Pastoral Theology,* ed. D. J. Atkinson et al. (Downers Grove, IL: InterVarsity Press, 1995) 42-48; idem, *Skillfull Shepherds: An Introduction to Pastoral Theology* (Grand Rapids: Zondervan, 1986); C. A. Volz, *Pastoral Life and Practice in the Early Church* (Minneapolis: Augsburg, 1990); M. J. Wilkins, *Following the Master: A Biblical Theology of Discipleship* (Grand Rapids: Zondervan, 1992); idem, "The Interplay of Ministry, Martyrdom and Discipleship in Ignatius of Antioch" in *Worship, Theology and Ministry in the Early Church,* ed. M. J. Wilkins and T. Paige (JSNTS 87; Sheffield: Academic Press, 1992) 294-315.   M. J. Wilkins

PAUL AND PAULINISMS IN ACTS

The role of Paul (Saul) in Acts can be summarized as follows. We are introduced to Saul, the persecutor of the earliest followers of Jesus, in Acts 7:58. In Acts 9 we read of the conversion of Saul the persecutor into Paul the Christian missionary. Paul drops from view until Acts 13, when he and Barnabas are commissioned by the believers in Antioch* to go and spread the gospel. This is usually referred to as Paul's first missionary journey. While he plays a surprisingly limited role in the council of Jerusalem, from Acts 15:20 onward Paul is the central character of the narrative.

Paul's second missionary journey begins at Acts 15:36. It is here that Paul and Barnabas part company, Paul taking Silas and eventually Timothy along with him. The highlight of this second journey is the founding of the church in Corinth, where Paul remains "for a considerable time" (Acts 18:18). Paul's third and final journey begins hard on the heels of the second. The narrative of this journey is focused on Ephesus (Acts 19). This journey reaches its climax with Paul's arrival and eventual arrest in Jerusalem (Acts 21).

The rest of the narrative explains how Paul the prisoner eventually reaches Rome, having appealed his case to Caesar (Acts 25:11). The narrative of Paul's arrest and travel to Rome takes up more space in Acts than do the narratives of his missionary activities. We do not learn of Paul's death (except by inference in Acts 20:29). Rather, the narrative ends with his arrival in Rome. Throughout these chapters Paul is cast as a charismatic visionary, a preacher, a healer and a worker of miracles.*

An extensive body of scholarly literature compares the Paul of Acts with the Paul of the epistles. The vast majority of such comparative work aims to make historical judgments about the nature of earliest Christianity, about the biographical and chronological details of the life of the historical Paul and about the historical author of Acts and that person's relationship to Paul. (*See DPL,* Chronology of Paul; Intineraries, Travel Plans, Journeys, Apostolic Parousia; Paul in Acts and Letters.) This article will focus primarily on the narrative of Acts and the picture of Paul that emerges in it. When comparisons between Acts and the epistles are made, it is to help clarify the picture presented in Acts rather than to establish a picture of the

"real" Paul (see Fowl for a discussion of the "real" Paul). This discussion will begin with an examination of the way Paul characterizes himself in Acts. The picture of Paul that emerges from that examination will then be situated within the broader scope of Acts as a whole.

1. Paul's Characterizations of Himself
2. Paul's Place Within the Scope of Acts

1. Paul's Characterizations of Himself.

Paul gives two kinds of accounts of himself in Acts,* both of which are central to an understanding of Paul in Acts as a whole. First, we have Paul's farewell address to the Ephesian elders in Acts 20:18-35, an account rendered before friends. Second, there are three occasions on which Paul has to defend himself before hostile or potentially hostile audiences (Acts 22; 24; 26).

In all of the speeches in which Paul gives an account of his life and ministry,* there is always some reflection on his conversion. In Acts Paul's encounter with the resurrected Christ* on the road to Damascus (Acts 9:1-19) and the accounts of this which Paul later gives in Acts (Acts 22; 24; 26) play a much more explicit and important role than they do in the epistles (see Gaventa, chap. 2). Acts 9 narrates the events of Paul's miraculous encounter with Christ. This passage does several important things for our understanding of Paul in Acts. It establishes Paul as an apostle* who has seen the resurrected Christ and has been given a special task (Acts 9:15). In addition we learn of the sufferings* that are to characterize Paul's ministry (Acts 9:16). As important as Acts 9 is, we come to a fuller understanding of Paul's character as he reflects on his conversion in the accounts he gives of himself in the later chapters of Acts (see Witherup).

1.1. Paul's Farewell Address to the Ephesian Elders (Acts 20:17-35). This account of Paul's life and ministry is given to fellow believers. This account has the most in common with the accounts Paul gives of himself in the epistles (cf. Gal. 1:11—2:21; Phil. 3:2-16). Paul is known to his audience. He is not introducing or defending himself before strangers. Paul's speech is occasioned by the fact that he is soon to be permanently separated from the Ephesians.

In addition to saying good-bye and to foreshadowing his impending imprisonment, Paul wishes to leave the Ephesians with an account of his ministry that will be a guide and a re-source to them in the future (see Tannehill, 2:253). Paul reminds the Ephesians of his per-sistence and boldness in proclaiming the gospel to them. As the plot of Acts has unfolded, the progress of the gospel has been unremitting, spreading out from Jerusalem* and soon to reach Rome.* As opposition has become more violent, the message and the messengers have grown more resilient. According to Paul, noth-ing can thwart the plan of God.* It is this plan that Paul boldly proclaimed to the Ephesians (Acts 20:27) and in which Paul willingly partici-pates. Paul notes the tribulations he has en-countered and that more await him (Acts 20:22). Nevertheless he intends with the Holy Spirit's* help to finish the course of his ministry (Acts 20:24).

As Paul sees it, his sufferings are roadblocks that threaten to derail his pursuit of the course of his ministry. This perspective is consistent with that of Acts more generally. Paul, like Peter, Stephen* and others, has been made a witness* to the work of God, and God has providentially overseen the success of that testimony by means of visions,* auditions, miraculous escapes and the aid of various sympathizers. Paul's sufferings provide both tests for his ministry and occasions for the providential work of God.

Rather than focus on the content of this message, Paul emphasizes his way of life among the Ephesians. He notes that he was not a finan-cial burden on them (Acts 20:33). Since he did not preach good news to them for a living, his preaching had no ulterior motives (cf. 1 Thess 2:1-12). Paul's support of himself allowed re-sources to be given to those in need (Acts 20:35). As the Ephesians prepare for a future without him, Paul characterizes his own minis-try among them as a standard against which they can measure both their own ministry of service* and the faithfulness of future teachers.

1.2. Paul's Accounts of Himself Before Various Authorities (Acts 22; 24; 26). The other occasions on which Paul gives an account of himself are all situations in which he defends himself before authorities (see Neyrey; *see* Civil Authority). Al-though there are obvious differences among these passages, they do not warrant individual treatments of each of these chapters. The Ro-man authorities are the ones who ultimately sit in judgment, but Paul's accusers are Jews. Paul's characterization of himself is framed by Jewish accusations, particularly in Acts 22 and Acts 26. As a result Paul goes to great lengths to charac-terize himself as a faithful and loyal Jew (Acts 22:3-5; 26:4-11). Even when Paul characterizes himself before Felix he asserts that he "worships the God of our ancestors, believing in the things written in the law, the prophets and the writ-ings" (Acts 24:14). He aims "to keep a clear conscience before God" (Acts 24:16). One fur-ther way in which Paul characterizes his faithful-ness is to note that he was a persecutor of Christians (Acts 22:4-21; 26:9-18). Paul portrays this aspect of his life in a matter-of-fact way. He does not express remorse. Rather it marks his diligent adherence to the truth of God as he then saw it (this seems to parallel the way Paul discusses this aspect of his life in Phil 3:6 and Gal 2:13, but cf. 1 Cor 15:9).

In these defensive contexts Paul's charac-terization of himself seems to have a dual rhe-torical* aim. On the one hand he wishes to make it clear that he was and is still a faithful Jew. He has broken neither Roman nor Jewish law.* Hence the charges brought against him are baseless. On the other hand he wants to convince his audience that the only way to ac-count for his transformation from persecutor to witness is by assenting to his claims about the resurrected Christ (Tannehill, 2:279). This point is not lost on King Agrippa, and Paul implies that this is his ultimate aim (Acts 26:28-29).

It is here, in these three speeches rather than in Acts 9, that we begin to get an insight into how we are to view Paul's conversion. Paul por-trays himself as a faithful defender of the truth of God, devoted to the law and the prophets* and more committed to Jewish ways than are most of his contemporaries. This commitment and devotion are channeled in a new direction when he encounters the resurrected Christ. Paul characterizes himself as one who initially found his direction and coherence by partici-pating in a story of conquest that moved in a seemingly irresistible path from Jerusalem to-ward Damascus. Paul's participation in this story ceases when he encounters the resur-rected Christ.

Prior to his conversion Paul characterizes himself as an independent though faithful agent. He controls his own actions. From the time he encounters the resurrected Christ on the road to Damascus, Paul presents himself as someone who is called and acted upon (see also the similar perspective in Paul's self-characterization in Phil 3:12-16). As soon as Ananias restores Paul's sight we find out that God has set aside things for Paul to do (Acts 22:10). Rather than be a defender of the truth, he is to become a witness to it (Acts 22:14-15, 18; 26:16, 22).

As Paul tells it, he has been incorporated into God's story, a story that he now sees as having a basis in the history of the people of Israel,* which has its climax in the death and resurrection* of Jesus and that is leading to the incorporation of the Gentiles* into the people of God (Acts 22:15, 21; 26:22-23; *see* Church as Israel; Death of Christ). Paul sees himself as having a significant role to play in this divine drama. By characterizing himself as he does in these chapters, however, Paul makes it clear that this is not a role he could have anticipated, nor is it a role he could have chosen himself. He had to be acted upon by God. Even then his opportunities to be a witness are the result of divine aid (Acts 26:22).

2. Paul's Place Within the Scope of Acts.
While an examination of Paul's accounts of himself is crucial to an understanding of Paul in Acts, it is hardly sufficient. It is important to remember several things about these accounts. First, Acts or even the second half of Acts is not primarily about Paul. Rather, Paul is a chief character in the story of the spread of the gospel from Jerusalem to Rome (see Witherup's point, 85, that in Acts characterization is in the service of plot). Acts ends not with Paul's death but with the gospel's arrival in Rome. Although Paul is a crucial character, his importance derives from his role in the spread of the gospel.

With this in mind, it is also important to remember that these accounts are not Paul's autobiography. They are not written by Paul; these are Luke's accounts. There seems to be little reason to question the historicity of the overall scope of events related in these chapters, but we should not assume, for example, that Luke was producing the transcripts from Paul's various trials. The accounts Paul gives of himself in Acts are not given for their own sake, to chronicle the life and adventures of an interesting person. Rather, Luke characterizes Paul as he does to serve the larger aims of Acts. Hence noting what Paul says about himself will not be sufficient. In the case of Acts there is a larger

story being told, the story of God's action in the maintenance and spread of the gospel. How one tells that story shapes and is shaped by the ways in which Paul's account of himself fits into that larger story about God. Questions about how Luke tells this larger story will be important for understanding the picture of Paul that emerges in Acts. It is also useful to notice how the picture of Paul in Acts fits into patterns and themes that are already developed in Luke's Gospel.

2.1. Paul as Luke's Ideal Disciple. If one compares the picture of Paul in Acts with that in Luke's Gospel, Paul can be seen as an example of the ideal disciple, presenting a sharp contrast, for example, with those pictures of failed discipleship narrated in Luke 9:57-62. As Jesus begins his journey to Jerusalem and the cross* (Lk 9:51), we are presented with three characters who for various reasons fail to join the journey. This prompts Jesus to say, "No one who puts a hand to the plow and looks back is fit for the kingdom of God" (Lk 9:62). Alternatively, having been called by the resurrected Christ, Paul joins in what is to become his own cruciform journey, never looking back. Paul, as a Pharisee (Acts 22:3; 23:6; 26:5) who follows Jesus, stands as an antitype to the pharisaic opposition Jesus encounters in Luke (see Lk 11:37-54).

2.2. Paul as Witness and Example of Restored Israel. More generally, Paul stands as an example of the reformed and reconstituted people of Israel. As Luke presents it, the reformation and ingathering of the people of God is one of the crucial aims of Jesus' mission. This mission continues in Acts. The picture of Paul fits into this emphasis on the eschatological* reconstitution of Israel (*see DPL*, Restoration of Israel). As Paul understands it, God's activity in the life, death and resurrection of Jesus is intimately connected to the story of God's ongoing dealings with Israel. This means that Paul views his conversion as a homecoming. That is, he does not see his conversion to be at odds with his Judaism.* This is seen in Paul's customary missionary practice of going to the synagogue* first. Only in the face of rejection there does he turn to the Gentiles.

Paul even sees the preaching of the gospel to the Gentiles as one of God's ultimate ends in restoring Israel. In his extensive engagement with the Jews of Pisidian Antioch Paul cites

Isaiah 49:6 (LXX: "I have appointed you as a light for the Gentiles that you may be for salvation to the ends of the earth") to just this effect (Acts 13:47). The claim that God's restoration of Israel is at least in part to "bring salvation to the Gentiles" surprises and divides the Jews in Paul's audience. For an attentive reader of Luke-Acts, however, this should come as no surprise. The citation from Isaiah 49:6 echoes the prophecy of Simeon that Jesus would become a "light to enlighten the Gentiles" as well as a glory to Israel (Lk 2:29-32). John the Baptist, also citing Isaiah, indicates that with the advent of Jesus "all flesh shall see God's salvation" (Lk 3:6). According to the resurrected Christ, the Scriptures themselves note that repentance* and forgiveness* of sins in Jesus' name* are to be proclaimed to "all nations" (Lk 24:44-47). In addition there is the commission of the resurrected Christ to be witnesses "to the ends of the earth" (Acts 1:8). Preceding Paul's arrival in Antioch of Pisidia, Peter had encountered Cornelius* (Acts 10), and we read about the recognition that "God has given even the Gentiles the repentance that leads to life" (Acts 11:18).

2.3. Paul and the Gentiles in Acts. Paul's primary concern with Gentiles is with their place in God's restored people, Israel. In addition, although we learn that Paul is a Roman citizen and this fact ultimately brings him to Rome, Paul in Acts never reflects on issues of his own citizenship and its relationship to the gospel (cf. Rom 13). As J. Lentz (24) notes, however, the combination of Pharisee of Pharisees and Roman citizen in a single individual is astonishing (it is less clear that Paul is "proud" of his Roman citizenship [Lentz, 6]).

Gentile opposition to Paul is typically generated by those who profit materially from pagan worship (Acts 16:16-24; 19:21-41). This fits in with the more general Lukan theme that pursuit of riches is a substantial threat to one's abilities to respond well to the gospel. This sort of opposition results in a disturbance of civic peace (Acts 19:40-41) in Ephesus and the charge against Paul and Silas that they are disturbers of the peace in Philippi (Acts 16:20).

Acts 17:16-35 is Paul's most sustained address to the pagan world* on its own terms. This is Paul's speech before the Athenians at the Areopagus, where Paul "discusses" (*dielegetō*) the gospel as a "philosopher." Paul does not argue

from Scripture. Instead he quotes a pagan poet, calling the Athenians to learn of the gods they already revere as creator. He uses this longing to know the Creator of all things as a way to call the Athenians away from ignorance and idolatry* (Acts 17:24-30). The resurrection proves to be a major stumbling block for the Athenians (Acts 17:34; cf. 1 Cor 1:20-25). Paul does not enjoy a great deal of success in Athens, but he does come across as a philosopher, and Christianity is seen as cultured learning rather than superstition (see Pervo, 61-62).

2.4. Paul, Suffering and the Gospel. The picture of Paul that emerges in Acts presents an account of the suffering and opposition Paul faced that differs somewhat from what we find in the epistles. In this respect P. Vielhauer rightly notes that the issue of the cross provides the sharpest contrast between Luke's picture of Paul and that found in the epistles (see Vielhauer, 45-49). I am unconvinced that one can extrapolate from this to make larger claims about differences between Lukan and Pauline theologies as Vielhauer does. This larger question goes beyond the confines of this article; however, it will be useful to summarize the differences between Acts and the epistles on these matters as a way of enabling further debate about these issues.

Acts generally, and the Paul of Acts in particular, has an unfailing confidence in God's providence. Paul's imprisonment, persecutions,* arrest, beatings and shipwreck are seen as hurdles placed by Satan* in the way of the gospel. These hurdles are all overcome. For example, Paul is forewarned of the rejection he will face in Jerusalem (Acts 20:23; 21:11). When this happens, it does not raise questions about Paul's message and mission. Instead the Lord informs Paul (and us) that this is all part of the divine plan to move the gospel to Rome (Acts 23:11). Paul's appeal to the emperor,* which initially saves him from a plot by the Jews, keeps him in prison when he should be set free. Even this is not seen as a problem. It provides both opportunity for authorities to proclaim Paul's innocence (Acts 26:31-32) and the mechanism to get Paul on his way to Rome.

Without question, Paul in Acts has an unshakable confidence in God's providential care. This is true of the epistles as well. Nevertheless, because of the aims of the narrative of Acts and his place in that narrative, Paul does not have to address seriously those who would see the opposition and persecution Paul faces as signs of the unworthiness of Paul and his message. Luke's narrative of God's providential oversight of the Christian mission not only gives direction and coherence to the narrative's paradigmatic missionary but also provides a particular perspective from which Paul can characterize his own tribulations. In contrast to Philippians, Galatians and especially the Corinthian correspondence, in Acts Paul does not have to address questions about his status or his message based on the fact that he suffers persecution and opposition. The Maltese quickly judge him to be a malefactor when he is bitten by a viper. Within the space of a verse, however, they are convinced he is a god when he shows no ill effects from the snakebite (Acts 28:5-6).

In the epistles, too, Paul is convinced that he and his gospel will ultimately be vindicated by God. His own sufferings, however, appear to raise questions both about the importance of the cross for Christian living and about Paul's status as an apostle. These questions are most directly addressed in Philippians and the Corinthian correspondence. It is clear that Paul recognizes his suffering and humiliations as real and significant, but these things are to be transformed finally. In these texts the cross provides Paul with an ironic perspective. From this ironic perspective past achievement can be seen as rubbish; present weakness becomes an opportunity for God's power; current judgments about status and wisdom* are overturned by the "foolishness of God." The Paul of the epistles struggles (often against fellow believers) with the scandal of the cross and its moral and theological significance to a much greater degree than in the picture of the apostle found in Acts.

In Acts it is clear the Paul is an example of cruciform living, but in Acts this does not seem to raise the problems that such a life raises in the epistles. This further reminds us that Acts is not primarily a story about Paul but a story about the gospel in which Paul is a central character.

See also ACTS OF THE APOSTLES; MISSION, EARLY NON-PAULINE; PAULINE LEGACY AND SCHOOL.

BIBLIOGRAPHY. R. Brawley, "Paul in Acts: Aspects of Structure and Characterization" *SBLSP* (1988) 96-103; J. T. Carroll, "Literary and Social Dimensions of Luke's Apology for Paul" *SBLSP* (1988) 106-18; S. Fowl, "Who's Characterizing Whom and the Difference This Makes: Locating and Centering Paul" *SBLSP* (1993) 537-53; B. R. Gaventa, *From Darkness to Light: Aspects of Conversion in the New Testament* (Philadelphia: Fortress, 1986); J. Jervell, "Paul in the Acts of the Apostles: Tradition, History and Theology" in *The Unknown Paul: Essays on Luke-Acts and Early Christian History* (Minneapolis: Augsburg, 1984) 68-76; L. T. Johnson, *The Acts of the Apostles* (SacP; Collegeville, MN: Liturgical Press, 1992); J. Lentz, *Luke's Portrait of Paul* (SNTSMS 77; Cambridge: Cambridge University Press, 1993); D. Moessner, "Paul in Acts: Preacher of Eschatological Repentance," *NTS* 34 (1988) 96-104; J. Neyrey, "The Forensic Defense Speech and Paul's Trial Speeches in Acts 22—26" in *Luke-Acts: New Perspectives from the Society of Biblical Literature Seminar,* ed. C. H. Talbert (New York: Crossroad, 1984); R. I. Pervo, *Luke's Story of Paul* (Minneapolis: Augsburg Fortress, 1990); *SBL Seminar Papers* (Atlanta: Scholars Press, 1983, 1988, 1993), essays on Paul and Acts; R. Tannehill, *The Narrative Unity of Luke-Acts* (2 vols.; Minneapolis: Augsburg Fortress, 1990); P. Vielhauer, "The Paulinisms of Acts" in *Studies in Luke-Acts,* ed. L. E. Keck and J. L. Martyn (Nashville: Abingdon, 1966) 33-50; R. Witherup, "Functional Redundancy in the Acts of the Apostles," *JSNT* 48 (1992) 67-86.

S. E. Fowl

PAULINE LEGACY AND SCHOOL

Paul was the most significant Christian theologian of all time. His writings have been an indispensable starting point for creeds* and confessions more or less from the first. Most of the greatest restatements of Christian theology have understood themselves as a reworking or an elaboration of Paul's theology, and all theologians have found it necessary to justify their enterprise by reference to Paul in some degree. In that sense all who take the NT seriously as a theological book share in Paul's legacy. In a more precise sense we would have to make special mention of Irenaeus and Augustine from the early centuries, Luther and Calvin from the Reformation period and Baur and Barth from the nineteenth and twentieth centuries.

Within the first two generations of Paul's death, however, we can recognize two groups of early Christian writers who deserve to be called Paul's heirs in a fuller sense—one group in which the legacy is clear and boldly attested, the other in which the legacy is more a matter of influence, still direct but less obvious.

1. The Immediate Heirs
2. The Wider Circle of Pauline Influence
3. The Legacy of Paul

1. The Immediate Heirs.

If we ask who were the immediate heirs of Paul, those who could be said to belong to a Pauline school, the focus narrows properly and appropriately to the question of the post- or deutero-Pauline epistles, that is, letters written in his name but today generally regarded as written after his death by a disciple (*see* Pseudepigraphy). The majority of scholars regard the Pastoral Epistles as the clearest example, with Ephesians not far behind. There is much greater dispute over 2 Thessalonians and Colossians. I regard both as Pauline, but since the latter is so closely related to Ephesians and thus also gives a clear indication as to how we should understand the transition from Pauline to post-Pauline, it shall be included here too.

1.1. Colossians. Colossians may be said to stand at the transition point from Pauline to post-Pauline. The most detailed stylistic analysis (W. Bujard) demonstrates that it was composed by someone other than Paul. At the same time the detail of the final section (Col 4:7-17), including the overlap with Philemon, and the final autograph of Colossians 4:18 strongly indicate the personal involvement of Paul himself. The most obvious solution is that Timothy, named as joint author (Col 1:1), composed the letter on their behalf and that Paul was able to give his approval of the sentiments and to add a final confirmatory signature before the letter was dispatched. Even if we cannot be sure whether this hypothesis is correct, the detailed specification of Paul's colleagues (Timothy, Tychicus, Onesimus, Aristarchus, etc.), and the typical Pauline concern for a church founded within his mission, albeit not by him, is evidence enough that the letter stems immediately from a circle of Paul's closest associates. (For arguments in favor of Pauline authorship, *see DPL*, Colossians.)

If it is Pauline, Colossians is already being shaped by the concerns that became more prominent in the post-Pauline period; if it is post-Pauline, Colossians is the clearest echo of and reflection on Paul's own concerns. The point can be best illustrated by three aspects characteristic of Paul's theological and pastoral emphases.

On the new movement's relationship with Israel* and Israel's inheritance, Colossians is as Pauline as Galatians. Here is the same insistence on Gentiles* fully sharing in that inheritance ("saints," Col 1:2, 12; 3:12; Gal 3:6-29), the same pointing to the cross* and experience of grace (Col 2:6-15; Gal 3:1-5), the same warning against circumcision (implied), festivals and food laws (Col 2:11, 16, 21; Gal 2:4-5, 11-16; 4:10), the same talk of "the elemental forces" (Col 2:8, 20; Gal 4:3, 9) and the same assertion that distinctions between Jew and Gentile have lost their force (Col 3:11; Gal 3:28). The characterization of "uncircumcision" as a state of deadness (Col 2:13) and the warning against "sexual sin, impurity, evil desire and the covetousness which is idolatry" (Col 3:5) are characteristically Jewish (*see* Idolatry; Purity). At the same time the mystery motif, introduced in Romans 11:25-26, has shifted slightly from the thought of God's eschatological* purpose to unite Jew and Gentile to the thought of "Christ in you, the hope of glory" (Col 1:26-27; 2:2; 4:3). And there is no real polemic against the law as such (the term *nomos* is absent from the letter), as distinct from particular regulations (Col 2:14-17, 20-23).

The central concern of Colossians to highlight the full sufficiency of Christ* as redeemer, reconciler and victor over the powers (particularly Col 1:14, 20-22; 2:15) naturally shapes the emphases of the letter. Most interesting is how the so-called Christ hymn (Col 1:15-20) goes well beyond anything earlier in Paul (1 Cor 1:24, 30; 8:6) in lauding Christ in terms of divine Wisdom. Still more striking is the way the ecclesiology is linked into this Wisdom christology* in what appears to be a continuum—cosmos, body (of Christ), church (Col 1:18; 2:10). This ties in with a significant variation of the earlier Pauline body imagery (1 Cor 12; Rom 12:4-8)—Christ as the head of the body (Col 1:18; 2:19). At the same time the body imagery is stretched the other way by the unusual emphasis on the fleshly nature of Christ's crucified body (Col 1:22; 2:11), highlighting the christological claim of Colossians 2:9 still more starkly (*see DPL*, Head, Christ as).

It is not quite correct to say, as many scholars have, that Colossians's eschatology is wholly realized (note particularly Col 3:2-4), but it is true that more weight seems to be attributed to the "already" stage in the process of salvation (Col 1:13; 2:12; 3:1; cf. Rom 6:4-5; 8:11). At the same time the characteristic balance of Pauline ethics, between indicative and imperative, is maintained with fresh vigor (Col 3:5-12). But we also note the first appearance of what was to become a recurrent feature in second- and third-generation Christianity, the list of "household rules" (*Haustafeln;* Col 3:18—4:1; Eph 5:22—6:9; 1 Pet 2:18—3:7; cf. 1 Tim 2:8-15; 6:1-2; Tit 2:1-10; *Did.* 4.9-11; *Barn.* 19.5-7; *1 Clem.* 21.6-9; Ign. *Pol.* 4.1—5.2; Pol. *Phil.* 4.2-3). In each case the inference is probably sound that the *Haustafel* expresses a realization that the Christian community must settle to a pattern of responsible living within the structures of society as it was traditionally ordered (*see* Household Codes).

In the continuity of Pauline theology, Colossians thus stands at a crucial transition point. Colossians indicates how the Pauline legacy would be stewarded in the generation following Paul's death and may be said to provide the canonical validation for subsequent Pauline school works to be designated as Pauline and properly attributed to Paul himself.

1.2. Ephesians. Ephesians looks like a conscious attempt by a disciple of Paul to preserve the heritage of Paul in a form that was of general rather than specific use, that was easy to incorporate within congregational worship and that maintained the earlier Pauline emphases regarded as of greatest continuing value. (For arguments in favor of Pauline authorship, *see DPL,* Ephesians.) This would explain its general character: not directed to a particular church—the words "in Ephesus" (Eph 1:1) are not present in the earliest and best manuscripts; not addressed to particular issues; and lacking Paul's normal list of greetings.

It would also explain the richly resonant style, the first three chapters almost taking the form of a lengthy thanksgiving prayer, full of what might be called "liturgical redundancies" (Eph 1:17-19; 2:13-18; 3:14-19), and the elaboration of the body imagery in Ephesians 4:7-16, of the marriage imagery in Ephesians 5:21-33 and of the warfare imagery in Ephesians 6:10-17, all serving to nurture a Pauline congregation's devotion and dedication more effectively than Paul's more typically epigrammatic exhor-

tation. The number of passages in which Ephesians seems to have drawn on Colossians (e.g., Eph 1:15-17/Col 1:3-4, 9-10; Eph 2:5/Col 2:13; Eph 4:16/Col 2:19; Eph 5:19-20/Col 3:16; Eph 6:21-22/Col 4:7) gives particular point to the suggestion that Colossians provided the precedent for further post-Pauline attempts to preserve the Pauline legacy for continuing use. Again the case can be illustrated in three ways.

First, the typically Pauline emphasis on the Jewish character of the faith proclaimed is enhanced. The recipients are described as "saints" or "holy" more often than in any other Pauline letter (ten times), and their share in the promised "inheritance" is a reiterated assertion (Eph 1:14, 18; 5:5). The unique and impressive blessing (Eph 1:3-14) and the following prayer (particularly Eph 1:17-19) use characteristic Jewish language throughout. And there are regular citations of and allusions to Jewish scriptures and apocrypha* throughout Ephesians 4—6 (explicitly Eph 4:8-10, 25-26; 5:31; 6:2-3).

Most notable is Ephesians 2:11-22, which serves as a clearer statement of Paul's vision of Jew and Gentile integrated within eschatological Israel than anything Paul wrote earlier, not least with its Jewish sense of Gentile lack ("alienated from the commonwealth of Israel and strangers to the covenants of promise, having no hope and without God in the world") now made good by the reconciling death of Christ* ("no longer strangers and aliens but . . . fellow citizens with the saints and members of the household of God"). Equally striking is the elaboration of the mystery motif. The language is drawn most directly from Colossians (Eph 3:3-5, 9/Col 1:26-27; Eph 6:19/Col 4:3), but the emphasis reflects the earlier Pauline concern (Gentiles as fellow heirs, Eph 3:6, 8) more closely than does Colossians. These were evidently still living concerns or at least represent an attempt to harvest the full benefit of this central emphasis in Paul's ministry and theology (cf. Rom 9—11). The echo of the earlier Pauline polemic against works (of the law) and boasting (Eph 2:8-9), however, is little more than that—an echo (contrast Gal 2:15—3:14; Rom 3:20—4:6; 9:11, 32). And the *Shema,* so creatively reworked in 1 Corinthians 8:6, seems to have been absorbed into a more ecclesiastically structured confession (Eph 4:4-6).

Second, in an odd way the christology, so powerful in Colossians, seems to have been somewhat diminished in emphasis as the vision of the church becomes more glorious. The church, characteristically the local church (in house, city or region) in the earlier Paulines is now for the first time understood consistently as the universal church (*see DPL,* Church). The cosmic christology of Colossians 1:17-19 has been developed into the striking, not to say astonishing, cosmic ecclesiology of Ephesians 1:22-23 ("the church that is his body, the fullness of him who fills all in all"). Christ's ascension* had as a primary purpose the giving of gifts to the church, and the measure of the resulting maturity of the church is "the full stature of Christ" (Eph 4:7-13). The first part of the Colossians's *Haustafel* has been transformed by the glorification of the church as bride of Christ (Eph 5:23-27). Analogously the eschatology is more consistently realized: "salvation" is an accomplished act (Eph 2:5, 8; 6:17); they are already raised and seated with Christ "in the heavenly places" (Eph 2:6); and there is no reference to Christ's coming again (contrast Eph 4:15; 5:27).

Third but not least in significance is the way in which the writer seems to be looking back to an apostolic age and to Paul as the archetypal apostle.* "The apostles" belong to the church's foundation, with the implication that the superstructure built thereon is well advanced (Eph 2:20), and they are designated as specially "holy" (Eph 3:5). The self-reference to Paul in Ephesians 3:1-13 at first looks to be strong evidence of Pauline authorship. But as the paragraph proceeds, the measure of boasting goes well beyond what Paul had previously claimed for his own role and sounds more and more like a eulogy penned by an admirer (cf. 1 Tim 1:15-16). Even with Ephesians 3:1 and Ephesians 4:1, the addition of the definite article turns the humble self-designation of Philemon 1 and 9 ("a prisoner of Christ Jesus") into something more like a title ("the prisoner of Christ Jesus," "the prisoner in the Lord").

All in all Ephesians can fairly be called the high point of Paulinism, as having harvested much of the most distinctive of the earlier Paul and having done so in such a memorable and inspirational way.

1.3. The Pastorals. With the Pastorals the question is provoked as to whether the Pauline legacy is beginning to be stretched too far and too thin. (For arguments in favor of Pauline authorship, *see DPL,* Pastoral Letters.) It is not that the traditional Pauline emphases and concerns are lost to sight. It is rather that the typical balance of emphasis that Paul achieved and sustained is in danger of being lost and of being replaced by one that Paul himself may not have recognized. The claim of the author is that what he writes does indeed stand within the tradition that Paul inaugurated. The verdict of the churches in accepting the Pastorals as Pauline is to accept and affirm that same claim. And since many of those involved stood a good deal closer to Paul in time and probably in personal knowledge, it ill behooves those writing nineteen centuries later to think we know Paul better than they did. Nevertheless a close comparison between the Pastorals and the undisputed Pauline letters does raise the question as to whether the Pauline legacy is beginning to be decisively eroded. And we are not surprised that the Pastorals had no successors (the drop in quality as we move into the subapostolic age is often noted), the Pastorals themselves having already begun to draw near to the boundaries of what could justifiably claim the epithet *Pauline.*

If we follow a similar sequence of analysis as in the last two cases, we should note first how remote the Jew/Gentile issue, still so prominent in Ephesians, seems to be. Paul's ministry to the Gentiles is recalled (1 Tim 2:7; 2 Tim 4:17) but with none of the fiery passion so characteristic of the earlier Paul. The mystery, so prominent in Colossians and Ephesians, has become something more formalized: "the mystery of faith," "the mystery of our religion" (1 Tim 3:9, 16; *see DPL,* Mystery). The positive value attributed to the law in 1 Timothy 1:7-9 echoes earlier assertions (Rom 2:12-16; 7:12-13; 13:3-4), but without the more characteristically negative thrust of so much of Paul's earlier teaching (echoes in 1 Tim 4:3-5 and Tit 3:9) the earlier balance is lacking. So too the talk of grace and works in 2 Timothy 1:9 and Titus 3:5 seems even more dispassionate and formulaic than even Ephesians 2:8-9, with the consistent commendation of "good works" (twelve times) underlining how much the perspective has shifted.

The developments in Pauline christology seem also to have shifted gear and to be moving in a direction different from the cosmic christology of Colossians and Ephesians. A stronger concern to reassert a clear monotheism seems evident (1 Tim 1:17; 2:5; 6:15-16); God is consistently described as "Savior" (1 Tim 1:1; 2:3; 4:10; Tit 1:3; 2:10, 13; 3:4). In correlation the christology is more in terms of Jesus as mediator' with God (1 Tim 2:5) and as sharing in God's role as Savior (2 Tim 1:10; Tit 2:13; 3:6). Most striking is the designation of Christ as "the glory of our great God and Savior" (Tit 2:13), which reads more like a variation of the earlier Wisdom christology, with Christ designated as the visible manifestation of the transcendent God (see DPL, Christology).

Equally noteworthy is the way in which faith in this Christ has become something more established and fixed: "the faith" (eleven times); "the teaching," "sound teaching" or "good teaching" (eleven times). "The faithful sayings" represent a similar sense of consolidation of tradition, not least in terms of the faith to be believed regarding Jesus (1 Tim 1:15; 2 Tim 2:11; Tit 3:5-8). It is not that such emphases are foreign to the earlier Paul. It is rather that the sense of a faith being freshly forged, of a dynamic tension between older traditional understandings and fresh revelation is lacking. A primary concern of the churches of Paul is now to gird themselves for the safe transmission of the tradition that began with Paul (2 Tim 1:12-14; 2:2).

The greatest development in the Pauline heritage of the Pastorals comes in the ecclesiology. The charismatic interplay of gifts and ministries so vividly portrayed in Paul's metaphor of the body of Christ in Romans 12:4-8 and 1 Corinthians 12, and still influential in the reworking of Ephesians 4, seems to have been left behind—understandable as that would be in a second-generation situation. "Elders" are in evidence for the first and only time in the Pauline corpus (1 Tim 5:1-2, 17, 19; Tit 1:5). "Overseers" (1 Tim 3:1-7; Tit 1:7-9) and "deacons" (1 Tim 3:8-13) now appear as established offices (1 Tim 3:1). "Charism" is spoken of as though it denoted an engracing of more limited scope (1 Tim 4:14; 2 Tim 1:6). Timothy and Titus begin to assume something of the role of a monarchical bishop with supreme responsibility (1 Tim 1:3; 4:6, 11; 5:1-16, 19-22). Again parallels can be drawn with particular features of Paul's earlier letters, but again the point is that the overall balance, which included the responsibility of Paul's churches to test and admonish and encourage, seems to have been lost, and the attempt to achieve a structured and ordered charismatic community has already largely given way to a straightforward hierarchical structure (see Church Order, Government).

2. The Wider Circle of Pauline Influence.

The second circle of Pauline influence includes several other writings within the NT itself.

2.1. Hebrews. An obvious candidate is Hebrews,* still attributed to Paul in the King James Version. And certainly there is a considerable overlap of concern between them, particularly in their perception of the importance of Christianity's relationship with its Jewish heritage and the terms in which they each conceive of that relationship. At each point, however, the weight of emphasis is significantly different, so that the question is whether the influence is specifically Pauline or a feature of early Christianity in general.

For example, the theme of the new covenant* is central to Hebrews in a way that is somewhat paralleled in 2 Corinthians 3; but the use of the covenant motif in Romans and Galatians, the fullest treatments of the relationship between Christianity and pre-Christian Judaism,* is quite different (Rom 9—11; Gal 3—4). The law* is a major theme in common; but Paul's concern is with circumcision* and other works of the law; the concern of Hebrews is almost exclusively with the temple cult (Heb 7—10). The most Hebrews-like feature in the Paulines at this point is Colossians 2:18/Hebrews 10:1. Faith* is another prominent Pauline word in Hebrews; but the great roll call of faith in Hebrews 11 starts from a somewhat different definition of faith (Heb 11:1) from Paul's in Romans 4. The overlap of Wisdom christology in Hebrews 1:3-4 is primarily with Colossians 1:15-20. And the high-priestly christology that dominates Hebrews has a foothold in Paul only at Romans 8:34.

2.2. 1 Peter and James. Of the other NT letters 1 Peter* can properly be called Pauline, at least on a number of key points. The christology of the suffering servant (1 Pet 2:24) is an explicit exposition of what is usually only alluded to by Paul (particularly Rom 4:25; 2 Cor 5:21). The conduct encouraged in 1 Peter 3:16 has several echoes of Pauline paraenesis, as the commentaries indicate. Most striking is the theology of charisms in 1 Peter 4:10-11, the only passage outside the Paulines to use the term *charisma* (cf. particularly Rom 12:3-8; 1 Cor 12:8-10). But the idea of sharing Christ's sufferings* (1 Pet 4:13) is also distinctively Paul's (e.g., Rom 8:17; 2 Cor 1:5; Phil 3:10).

The implication that the Petrine school was influenced by the Pauline school is confirmed by 2 Peter 3:15-16. Evidently Paul's letters were well known in Petrine circles, and the "things in them hard to understand" were being all too influential for the writer of 2 Peter.*

Somewhat similar is the obvious allusion to Paul's teaching on faith and works (particularly Rom 3:28—4:22; *see* Faith and Works) in James 2:18-24. The influence of Paul's formulation seems to have been similarly "twisted" and so misapplied, in the view of James.*

2.3. Mark. It is even plausible to regard the Gospel of Mark as falling within the circle of direct influence from Paul (*see DJG*, Mark). The argument is that Paul both introduced the term *gospel* (the noun itself) into Christian vocabulary and fixed its meaning as focused on the death and resurrection of Christ (particularly 1 Cor 15:1-5; Gal 1:6-7; 3:1). It was evidently Mark who introduced the same term into the Gospel tradition, and his own use of it in Mark 1:1 effectively fixed the form of a Gospel as a "passion narrative with an extended introduction" (Kähler). The possibility that Mark wrote his Gospel to correct a misplaced emphasis on Jesus as miracle worker (particularly Mk 8) may also reflect a challenge to the gospel similar to that which drew forth Paul's most striking exposition of the power of Christ as strength in weakness (2 Cor 12:1-10; 13:4).

2.4. Acts of the Apostles. The most plausible candidate for the title of disciple of Paul outside the Pauline corpus, however, is the author of Acts* (Luke). At the least he was obviously a great admirer of Paul (*see* Paul in Acts). More than half of his book has Paul as the principal hero. Paul's missionary work particularly in the Aegean basin is the decisive expansion of Christianity into the Gentile world. And the final quarter of Acts is chiefly occupied with an elaborate defense of Paul against any charge of apostasy* from his ancestral faith. At these points Acts properly echoes and defends Pauline concerns. The case would be all the stronger if the minority view that Luke also wrote the Pastorals could be sustained. But the parallels suggest more the extent of Paul's influence than a common hand.

Despite his admiration for Paul, Luke seems to have been equally concerned to display the coherence and connectedness of Paul's mission with the Christianity that first emerged in Jerusalem.* In so doing, however, he underplays the points that Paul himself emphasized (Paul's apostleship, his confrontations in Antioch* and Galatia, the collection) and plays up points that run counter to Paul's own claims (his repeated visits to Jerusalem, his part in disseminating the apostolic decree and his concern to observe the law). Luke, we may say, was a disciple or an admirer of Paul trying to integrate the Pauline legacy within a missionary church, where Spirit and good order went hand in hand, where the apostolic decree was the basis for mixed congregations and where elders provided a common form of church government (*see* Worship).

2.5. 1 Clement. Beyond the NT itself we would have to make special mention of *1 Clement,** written from Rome to Corinth in the second half of the 90s. Clement obviously admired Paul greatly (*1 Clem.* 5.6-7). He certainly knew several of Paul's letters (cf. particularly *1 Clem.* 35.5-6 with Rom 1:29-32) and evidently modeled his own on 1 Corinthians (*1 Clem.* 47; cf. also *1 Clem.* 24 with 1 Cor 15; *1 Clem.* 37.5—38.2 with 1 Cor 12; *1 Clem.* 49—50 with 1 Cor 13; and *1 Clem.* 42.4 with 1 Cor 16:15). The most interesting Paulinism is the reference to "justification by faith" in *1 Clement* 32.4. But equally striking is the way he treats Abraham* as a model of obedience* (*1 Clem.* 9—10) and links faith with "hospitality"* (*1 Clem.* 10.7) in a manner closer to James than to Paul (*1 Clem.* 30.3; 31.2-3). It would be widely agreed that the echoes of Paul's distinctive theology lack the cutting edge of Paul's own perception and formulation.

2.6. Ignatius. The only other person with a real claim to belong to the wider circle of Pauline influence is Ignatius,* who wrote his sequence of letters while being taken prisoner through* Asia Minor on the way to martyrdom* in Rome sometime in the 110s. Like Clement, he admired Paul greatly (Ign. *Eph.* 12.2; Ign. *Rom.* 4.3). Like Clement, he knew 1 Corinthians (Ign. *Eph.* 16.1; 18.1; Ign. *Rom.* 5.1; 9.2). And *Ephesians* 12.2 also makes it clear that he knew that Paul had written several letters. The evidence of specific influence, however, is often hard to evaluate. For example, while the "in Christ" phrase of *Ephesians* 8.2 is no doubt derived from Paul, the echo of Romans 1:3-4 (Ign. *Eph.* 18.2; 20.2; Ign. *Rom.* 7.3) may equally be explained as knowledge of common creedal material.

The substantive parallels are enhanced by the fact that both could evaluate their suffering positively, precisely because they understood it as a sharing in Christ's sufferings—"imitating the passion of my God" (Ign. *Rom.* 6.3)—and the similar opposition they waged against judaizing movements within the churches addressed (Ign. *Magn.* 8—10; Ign. *Phld.* 6.1). In the first case, however, Ignatius's eagerness for martyrdom strikes many readers as somewhat unhealthy, and in the latter the antithesis is between "Judaism" and "Christianity" with a sharpness that Paul would probably have regretted. And while Ignatius's strong advocacy of episcopacy can be seen as an extension of the line of development through the Pastorals, his abandonment of Paul's clear distinction (1 Cor 15:44-50) between a spiritual (resurrection) body and the body of flesh (Ign. *Smyrn.* 3.1) contributed, ironically, to early Christianity's loss of the sense of the present body as a positive feature of createdness.

4. The Legacy of Paul.
It is the measure of the greatness of an innovative or inspirational figure that he gathers disciples and generates imitators. Rarely do such disciples and imitators rise to the heights of the master, though Ephesians could be said to do so in this case. What is important for us at this distance is (1) to recognize the character of the original inspiration, its theological insights and pastoral concerns, and not allow the shifting emphases of the Pauline school or the circles of diminishing influence to blur or dull the impact of that original inspiration; (2) to observe how the content and emphases of Paulinism changed in character in the succeeding generation but were still acknowledged as Pauline and legitimate bearers of his name; and (3), if we cherish the legacy of Paul, to engage in the equivalent reworking of that legacy in relation to the changing circumstances, needs and challenges of our own day as Augustine and Luther and Barth did in their day. Only so will the legacy of Paul be preserved in its full value.

See also NEW TESTAMENT THEOLOGY; PAUL AND PAULINISMS IN ACTS.

BIBLIOGRAPHY. C. K. Barrett, *Paul: An Intro- duction to His Thought* (Louisville, KY: Westminster/John Knox, 1994) chaps. 4—5; J. C. Beker, *Heirs of Paul: Paul's Legacy in the New Testament and in the Church Today* (Minneapolis: Fortress, 1991); W. Bujard, *Stilanalytische Untersuchungen zum Kolosserbrief* (SUNT 11; Göttingen: Vandenhoeck & Ruprecht, 1973); H. Conzelmann, "Die Schule des Paulus" in *Theologia Crucis-Signum Crucis*, ed. C. Andresen and G. Klein (Tübingen: J. C. B. Mohr, 1979) 85-96; E. Dassmann, *Der Stachel im Fleisch: Paulus in der frühchristlichen Literatur bis Irenäus* (Münster: Aschendorff, 1979); J. D. G. Dunn, "The Deutero-Pauline Letters" in *Early Christian Thought in Its Jewish Context*, ed. J. Barclay and J. Sweet (Cambridge: Cambridge University Press, 1996) 130-44; G. S. Holland, *The Tradition That You Received from Us: 2 Thessalonians in the Pauline Tradition* (Tübingen: J. C. B. Mohr, 1988); K. Kertelge, *Paulus in den neutestamentlichen Spätschriften* (QD 89; Freiburg: Herder, 1981); A. T. Lincoln and A. J. M. Wedderburn, *The Theology of the Later Pauline Letters* (NTT; Cambridge: Cambridge University Press, 1993); A. Lindemann, *Paulus im ältesten Christentum: Das Bild des Apostels und die Rezeption der paulinischen Theologie in der frühchristlichen Literatur bis Marcion* (Tübingen: J. C. B. Mohr, 1979); D. R. MacDonald, *The Legend and the Apostle: The Battle for Paul in Story and Canon* (Philadelphia: Westminster, 1983); M. Y. MacDonald, *The Pauline Churches: A Sociohistorical Study of Institutionalization in the Pauline and Deutero-Pauline Writings* (SNTSMS 60; Cambridge: Cambridge University Press, 1988); I. H. Marshall, "Prospects for the Pastoral Epistles" in *Doing Theology for the People of God: Studies in Honor of J. I. Packer*, ed. D. Lewis and A. McGrath (Downers Grove, IL: InterVarsity Press, 1996) 137-55; H. Räisänen, " 'Righteousness by Works': An Early Catholic Doctrine? Thoughts on 1 Clement" in *Jesus, Paul and Torah: Collected Essays* (JSNTSup 43; Sheffield: JSOT, 1992) 203-24; F. Young, *The Theology of the Pastoral Letters* (NTT; Cambridge: Cambridge University Press, 1994).
J. D. G. Dunn

PEACE

The idea of peace (*eirēnē*), primarily in the objective sense of a state of affairs or a type of relationship, is widely employed in early Christian literature as an important component of the salvation* accomplished by Jesus Christ and therefore as a basic characteristic of Christian existence and behavior (*see DJG*, Peace; *DPL*, Peace, Reconciliation). NT usage draws heavily on the OT (see esp. *šālôm*), both through direct exegesis and as the OT (Hebrew and/or Greek) was mediated to the individual writers through Jewish and antecedent Christian thought. (For the concept of peace in the Hebrew OT, *see DJG*, Peace, and note also Durham. On the Hebrew OT but also on the Septuagint, other Jewish literature and secular Greek and Latin literature, with further details regarding terminology, see Foerster and von Rad; Healey and Klassen; Yoder and Swartley.)

Ideas of *eirēnē* stemming from Greco-Roman traditions (usually summarized as "the absence of war") can also be detected. Yet attempts to separate and tag Hebrew and Greek ideas, although they sometimes provide useful references points, can lead to artificially precise distinctions, especially in a milieu where Judaism and Hellenism are not distinct categories. In terms of the Christian literature before us, it must be said that the idea of peace was in the public domain and therefore conforms in each case to the particular historical and theological contexts of the separate writings. Of interest is not merely how the words are defined in each case but how the idea is employed and developed in the given context as well as its place in Christian traditions.

Only Jude* will be omitted from the following treatment of the General Epistles. "Peace" appears verbally only in the letter's greeting (Jude 2), where it is joined with mercy* and love.* Though the absence of peace is evident in the lives of the itinerant teachers or prophets (e.g., Jude 12-13) and is notably absent in the wake of their activities (Jude 19), Jude shows no interest in promoting peace as such. His desire is rather to rouse the church to "contend for the faith."

1. Acts
2. Hebrews
3. James
4. 1-2 Peter
5. 1-3 John
6. Revelation
7. Postapostolic Writings
8. Conclusions

1. Acts.

In Acts 10:36 (*see* Acts), probably an allusion to Isaiah 52:7, *eirēnē* is a summary of the message

God had preached through Jesus to the people of Israel* (cf. Acts 3:19-20, which employs the related idea of "refreshment"; see Laansma, 274-75) and that has already spread through Judea. It conveys the comprehensive "salvation" (cf. Lk 1:79; 2:14) attending reconciliation (cf. *DPL*, Peace, Reconciliation) between God and Israel; in the context of Peter's inaugural sermon to the Gentiles* ("He is Lord of all!"), it signifies reconciliation between God and humankind and thus between Jews and Gentiles. The action of Moses* in Acts 7:26 ("reconcile in peace") might be noted in this connection if this detail is included as a parallel to Jesus.

Luke notes that the "church throughout all Judea and Galilee and Samaria enjoyed peace, being built up" (Acts 9:31). The image is of a church both relatively free from internal strife and external persecution* and positively thriving (see also, e.g., Acts 2:43-47). Then, in the context of the council's decision on the status of the Gentiles, we read of Judas and Silas, itinerant prophets* whom the church at Antioch* "sent off in peace [probably in a formal setting] . . . to those who had sent them [believers in Jerusalem]" (Acts 15:33 NRSV; cf. 3 Jn 5-8; Jas 2:15-16; Acts 20:7-12; Acts 20:36-38), thus marking harmony between the churches.

The expression probably used on that occasion is used also by the converted Philippian jailer when he releases Paul from prison: "Go in peace" (Acts 16:36). This Jewish expression on the lips of a Gentile converted only a few hours earlier serves to underline the genuineness of the man's conversion, while setting the stage for Paul's attempt to secure peace for the converts he leaves behind.

In two instances the term *eirēnē* is used in a political setting, both of which ring hollow. In Acts 12:20 the people of Tyre and Sidon seek peace (reconciliation) with Herod because they are economically dependent on Judea. The lawyer Tertullus begins his case against Paul by declaring to Felix, "We have through you attained much peace" (Acts 24:2). The statement is mere flattery and exaggeration, since Felix's tenure of office was far from peaceful, but it sets the stage for the case against Paul as a rabble-rouser. It is possible then that Luke views the peace that is brought through the Messiah-king's birth (Lk 2) and proclamation (Acts 10) and that is spreading geographically and ethnically (Acts 9:31; cf. Acts 10:36-37; 15:33) as the true counterpart to the *Pax Romana* (Hasler, 395-96).

2. Hebrews.

Each usage of the term *eirēnē* (*eirēnikos*, used once) in Hebrews* bears the stamp of the old link of peace and righteousness* (e.g., Is 9:7; 11:1-10; 32:17; Ps 72:7 [LXX 71:7]; Ps 85:10 [LXX 84:11]; Rom 5:1; see 3 and 4 below), whether verbally (Heb 7:2; 12:11; 12:14 [*hagiasmon*, "holiness," in the last]) or conceptually (Heb 11:31; 13:20-21).

The nonscriptural detail that Rahab received the spies "with peace" (Heb 11:31) probably indicates that she is a model of the hospitality* enjoined in Hebrews 13:2. In James 2:25 Rahab's faith* is noted for its hospitality (*hypodexamenē*) to the spies (James's term is *angelous;* a short route to the idea of Heb 13:2?) in a list that may be dependent on the same tradition as *1 Clement* 12, where she is also noted for her "hospitality" (*philoxenia;* cf. Heb 13:2). This sort of hospitality was an essential complement to the itinerant nature of much early ministry* (cf. Acts 15:33; Jude in the introduction above; 5 below [2 Jn and 3 Jn]; Mt 25:35; *Did.* 11; often elsewhere); in Hebrews it is a specific application of Hebrews 12:14.

Also similar to James* is the way in which the "peaceful fruit of righteousness" caps an ethical* section drawing on wisdom* (Heb 12:4-11; cf. Jas 3:18; *eirēnikos* occurs in the NT only here and in Jas 3:17). The latter expression is a compact way of saying that the harvest of God's parental discipline consists in peace (broadly conceived as *šālôm*) and righteousness, which are gifts of the eschatological* salvation (e.g., Is 32:17) and are linked to the enjoyment of God's presence. The exhortation to "pursue peace with [not: in company with] all" (Heb 12:14) draws on the language of Psalm 34:14 [LXX 33:15] (see 4 below [1 Pet]) and probably refers to internal affairs of the church. There is no apparent problem with strife among community members, but willing participation in the disciplinary process that leads to full peace (Heb 12:4-11) is flagging (e.g., Heb 10:24-39; 13:3, 13). The exhortation of Hebrews 12:14 is probably included in that broad sense, that is, "pursue the things that lead to salvation and well-being with all" (Heb 12:12-13). This idea is then developed in general (Heb 12:15-29; cf. Heb 10:32-34) and particular (Heb 13:1-19)

ways. It is noteworthy that peace is here linked with the cultic notion of sanctification. "Communal 'peace,' in the broadest sense, is rooted in, and is the fullest expression of, the holiness of the community gathered around Christ's 'altar'" (Attridge, 367).

It is against the background of Hebrews 12:11, 14 that the benediction (Heb 13:20-21, "God of peace") is to be understood in the first instance, although the language is traditional (1 Thess 5:23; Rom 15:33) and probably cannot be contextually restricted (cf. "covenant of peace"; Num 25:12; Is 54:10; Ezek 34:25). The expression "king of peace" (Heb 7:2) is likewise semantically ambiguous (subjective or descriptive genitive?) and of uncertain thematic importance. "King of peace" is one element in a dense midrash, and the etymology of Melchizedek's* name was apparently well known (Philo *Leg. All.* 3.79; Josephus *Ant.* 1.10.2 §180). It is possible that the combination of "king of righteousness" and "king of peace" was meant to highlight Jesus' messiahship (cf. e.g., Is 9:7), but this is not developed. Nor is this "peace" obviously related to the *katapausis* theme of Hebrews 3:7—4:11 (but see, e.g., 1 Chron 22:6-10; Is 32:17; Sir 47:13, 16), as the latter passage focuses primarily on the image of a sabbath celebration in God's resting place (on the motif of rest see Laansma). It is difficult to know, therefore, either what the author meant by "king of peace" or how integral this idea is to his "word of exhortation," unless it is in anticipation of the ethical applications in Hebrews 12.

3. James.

The shock value of James's illustration (Jas 2:15-16; cf. 1 Jn 3:17) may be partially lost on a society foreign to oriental norms of hospitality, but in his own context the profound incongruity of such an empty pronouncement in the face of such need would have registered even with many pagans. "Go in peace" was a common Jewish farewell (for parallels, see Judg 18:6; 1 Sam 1:17; Jdt 8:35; *Jub.* 18:16; Mk 5:34; Acts 16:36), and that it here carries the broader sense of *šālôm* is evident from the additional comments: "keep warm and eat your fill" (NRSV). The utterance was misguided but probably sincere. The illustration is suited to the context (Jas 2:1-13) and is probably chosen because peacemaking, thus defined as the active promotion of *šālôm*, epitomizes James's ethic (Jas 3:18; see also Guelich, 106-7, on Mt 5:9). The point is not merely that deficient faith would make such a hollow pronouncement but that "saving" faith would express precisely that sentiment and follow through with appropriate action.

Wisdom's gentle peacemaking (Jas 3:13-18) is in contrast to the wisdom that brings disorder (*akatastasia*), but it also consists positively in impartial acts of mercy (Jas 1:27; cf. Jas 2:1-13) and good fruits, and the "fruit of righteousness is sown in peace by those who make peace" (probably an attached proverb). The close association of righteousness and peace in the OT (see 2 above) can be felt here, possibly with a sense of eschatological fulfillment (Jas 1:16-18; Jas 5:3, 7-9). In the light of the broad idea of *šālôm* in James 2:16, the meaning is not merely that harmony is the soil in which righteousness flourishes, as true as that is (Jas 1:20), but that righteousness and *šālôm* (*eirēnē*) are materially related and necessarily joined. The way to peace is then portrayed in James 4:1-12 and elsewhere in the letter.

4. 1-2 Peter.
The greetings and closings of 1 Peter (1 Pet 1:2; 1 Pet 5:14), although formulaic (*see* Letters; 1 Peter; 2 Peter), convey not only the pastoral desire that these people would possess in the fullest measure the source (grace*) and content (peace) of the divine blessings* in the midst of a hostile world but also the assumption that these blessings of *šālôm*, along with the other privileges of Israel (1 Pet 2:9-10), have now been assigned restrictively to those who are "in Christ."

Wives are to adorn themselves for God's eyes first (1 Pet 3:4; cf. Mt 6:4, 6, 18), resulting in a display of beauty that emanates from a "meek and quiet spirit" on behalf of their unbelieving husbands. This is to shape, rather than to exclude, bodily adornment and is social rather than private, having to do with how wives relate to their potentially hostile husbands both actively and passively. As the centerpiece of Peter's counsel on submission, for which Sarah is an example, 1 Peter 3:4 involves the wives' domestic application of the general injunction borrowed from Psalm 34:13-17: "seek peace and pursue it" (*zētēsatō eirēnēn kai diōxatō autēn*, 1 Pet 3:11).

The latter expression is unique in the OT

with the possible exception of Jeremiah 29:7 (LXX 36:7: *zētēsatō eirēnēn kai diōxatō autēn*, Ezek 7:25 has a different sense), and its wording can be detected in several NT texts (see also Rom 14:19; Heb 12:14; possibly 2 Tim 2:22), indicating that Psalm 34:14 was popular in apostolic Christianity. The expression in its present context suggests an indefatigable promotion of peace in all dealings with unbelievers, and, as in Hebrews and James, the idea includes "doing good" and "righteousness." Numerous comments in the epistle give shape to the sentiment, drawing prominently on the example of Christ.* It may also be, as B. Winter has suggested (Winter, 22-23 and passim), that the idea of Jeremiah 29 underlies it, namely, that the believers are literally to seek the welfare (*šālôm*) of the city (Jer 29:7) in which they live as resident aliens through civically recognized acts of public beneficence so that "the Gentiles . . . though they malign you as evildoers . . . may see your honorable deeds and glorify God when he comes to judge" (1 Pet 2:12 NRSV).

The greeting of 2 Peter 1:2 specifies that it is in the sphere of "the knowledge of God and of Jesus our Lord" that believers will receive the full measure of grace and peace. This idea is carried through to the end of the letter where, in view of the inevitability and nature of the coming judgment,* the readers are to "strive to be found [in the eschatological judgment] by him without spot or blemish, in peace" (2 Pet 3:14), which is accomplished positively by growing "in the grace and knowledge of our Lord and Savior Jesus Christ" (2 Pet 3:18). The peace in view is not merely harmony as opposed to dissension, nor is this an inner feeling. The idea may be one of peace with God (a state of reconciliation) at the time of judgment, but it probably also includes the life (*šālôm*) after which they are to strive (2 Pet 1:3-11) and which stands in contrast to the existence of the false teachers (2 Pet 2).

5. 1-3 John.
The idea of peace is not expressed verbally in 1 John (*see* John, Letters of) and it receives formulaic expression in 2 John 3 (cf. 1 Tim 1:2; 2 Tim 1:2) and 3 John 15. 2 John 3 substitutes an affirmation for a prayer* in its greeting and groups together grace, mercy, and peace (*eirēnē*) as gifts from God for those who walk in

the realm of the gospel's truth and love. 3 John closes (3 Jn 15) with the simple benediction pronounced by the elder on Gaius: "Peace to you" *(eirēnē soi)*. The same epistle confirms that the full OT sense of *šālôm* is intended: "I pray that all may go well with you and that you may be in good health *[hygiainein]*, just as it is well with your soul" (3 Jn 2 NRSV). This prayer is then developed in terms of life consistent with the gospel's truth (3 Jn 3-4) and love (3 Jn 5-8), making evident that peace consists of fellowship* with God and with one another and by extension that peace from God is mediated through human fellowship (cf. 3 Jn 2, 5-8 with 1 Jn 3:17; Jas 2:16). In this case the elder is concerned that *šālôm* (Judg 19:20) should be extended to the itinerant preachers and that they should be sent out in proper fashion (see 1 above [Acts 15:33]), although they are strangers to Gaius (cf. Heb 13:2), in contrast to Diotrephes' practice.

1 John does not allude verbally to peace but everywhere develops the associated ideas of walking in truth and love as well as fellowship with God and one another. That the idea of peace is everywhere present in 1 John can also be seen, for example, in the references to "confidence" *(parrēsia;* 1 Jn 2:28; 1 Jn 3:21; 1 Jn 4:17; 1 Jn 5:14) available to believers and related comments: being "unashamed" (1 Jn 2:28); "reassure our hearts before him" (1 Jn 3:19; cf. Jn 14:27); and "casts out fear" (1 Jn 4:18; cf., with differences, Jn 14:27; Jn 16:33).

6. Revelation.

War and peace are of thematic significance in Revelation *(see* Revelation, Book of). The Apocalypse speaks to a church suffering persecution at the hands of Rome, within the sphere of the militarily imposed *Pax Romana,* but also to one subject to the insidious, corrupting and powerfully alluring religious and economic influence of the beckoning "harlot." Drawing on the OT as well as Jewish traditions of martyrdom* and holy war, the book offers its vision of the holy war to be waged against this power (Bauckham).

God himself removes both human peace (Rev 6:4; probably with an eye on the *Pax Romana)* and war and establishes his own lasting and perfect peace through the Lamb's* death and eschatological warfare (Rev 5:5-6; 19:11—20:15). The role of believers on the earth is secondary but significant: to resist assimilation to Rome's corruption; to have a faithful testimony (completed by martyrdom); to engage in works of faith, love, service and patient endurance;* and to keep the commandments* of God. They conquer after the pattern of the slaughtered Lamb: "by the blood of the Lamb and by the word of their testimony, for they did not cling to life even in the face of death" (Rev 12:11). Though martyrs are present with the Lamb in the battle preceding the thousand-year earthly reign (Rev 19:14-15; cf. Rev 17:14; Rev 2:27), they play no specified role in the fight (Rev 19:21). Before that time, in the heavenly regions they cry out for vengeance but are told to rest, to wait quietly until their number has been completed (Rev 6:11).

Again it is said in one of the seven beatitudes, " 'Blessed are the dead who die in the Lord from now on.' 'Yes,' says the Spirit, 'they shall rest from their labors, for their works follow them'" (Rev 14:13). Meanwhile the book's greeting pronounces "grace and peace" on those still alive on the earth (Rev 1:4-5). The tailoring of this greeting to the book's contents suggests that peace takes the form of a confident assurance gained from the transcendent and eschatological perspective of the prophecy but also consists in the salvific victory already achieved on behalf of the living (Rev 1:5-6; cf. Jn 16:33), while it anticipates the universal victory and ensuing peace of the book's final three chapters. The peace of God is not established through human force, whether military or political, nor is it brought in through social transformation. Yet the saints' martyrdom is construed as active participation in the holy war—as conquering—and their righteousness presumably leaves its mark.

7. Postapostolic Writings.

Most of the documents included in groupings of the early apostolic fathers* contain scattered references to peace or concord by name *(eirēnē, homonoia* and cognates; see also *hēsychia, diallagē, apallagē, epikatallagē* and cognates), with the highest concentration in *1 Clement,* Ignatius* and the *Shepherd of Hermas.* *The following examples are largely restricted to passages using the preceding terms, although passages exhorting to peace and concord in other ways could be multiplied. In particular the idea is embedded in the Two Ways doctrine and is stressed in connection with the Eucharist. Peace in the sense of rest is characteristic of gnostic thought (for the idea of rest in the non-gnostic literature of this period see Laansma, 118-33; *see* Gnosis).

7.1. The Two Ways. Both the *Didache** and the *Epistle of Barnabas** contain extended Christian versions of the Two Ways doctrine, and among their several points of similarity are the command "you shall not desire a schism but shall reconcile *[eirēneuseis]* those who strive" (*Did.* 4.3; cf. *Barn.* 19.12; on the idea of reconciliation see *DPL*, Peace, Reconciliation) and the virtues of "meekness" and "quietness" (*Did.* 3.7-8; *Barn.* 19.4). In the NT the latter pair occurs in 1 Peter 3:4 (see 4 above [1 Pet]). This pair occurs frequently in *Hermas* as well (*Herm. Man.* 5.2.3; 5.2.6; 6.2.3; 11.8; with the last compare Jas 3:17-18), which is usually considered to reflect Two Ways thinking (esp. *Herm. Man.* 6.2.3 above).

7.2. Instructions on the Eucharist. According to *Didache* 14.2 it was necessary for those quarreling to be reconciled *(diallagōsin)* before participating in the Eucharist, or else the sacrifice would be defiled. Ignatius exhorts the Ephesian believers to come together more frequently "to give thanks" (probably a reference to the Eucharist), but he assumes rather than commands that the meeting will be imbued with *homonoia* ("concord") and *eirēnē* ("peace"). The reason for the frequency of the meetings is that by their concord Satan's* mischief is brought to nothing, and by peace every war in heaven and on earth is destroyed (Ign. *Eph.* 13.1-2; cf. Ign. *Eph.* 5.2). Redemption* is thereby advanced.

7.3. 1 Clement. The occasion for *1 Clement* is dissension *(stasis)* within the Corinthian community involving a few younger men who have unseated the older bishops. This dissension Clement* of Rome attributes chiefly to jealousy and envy (*zēlos kai pēteonos*—specifics are unclear) so that the entire, wide-ranging letter is summed up as an "entreaty for peace and concord" *(tēn enteuxin . . . peri eirēnēs kai homonoias, 1 Clem. 63.2)*, beginning with the reestablishing of good order: the exile of the pretenders and the restoration of the deposed bishops (*see* Church Order). The usage of relevant terminology (esp. *eirēnē, homonoia*) is therefore extensive, and the epistle abounds with illustrations of and arguments for concord drawn from the OT, Jesus' teachings, the apostles* and nature.

Yet the expression "peace and concord" was a standard way of referring to the well-being of the Roman Empire* from the first century B.C. on, and this is the basic source of Clement's thought. His letter conforms closely to a specific type of deliberative discourse, an "appeal for concord," of which there are several extant examples; their authors, "generally philosophers or rhetoricians, seek to calm the outbreak of faction, within cities or between cities, by dissuading from strife *(stasis)* and exhorting to concord *(homonoia)*" (Welborn, 1058). In general, Clement's, or the Roman church's, response is favorably disposed toward the Roman *imperium* and seems to follow the approach of the Roman senate and emperor in dealing with strife within the empire, possibly indicating an early and presumptuous (if well-intentioned) move toward that church's primacy. Compared to the NT, the center of Clement's idea of peace seems to have shifted from soteriology and christology* to ecclesiology, drawing on pagan models.

7.4. Ignatius. The political background of *homonoia* is less pronounced in Ignatius. His characteristic concern that bishops be regarded as the Lord* himself (*Eph.* 6.1) is reflected in a repeated appeal for *homonoia* on behalf of the bishops (Ign. *Eph.* 4.1; Ign. *Magn.* 6.1-2; Ign. *Trall.* 12.2; Ign. *Phld.* presc.). In one of these (Ign. *Eph.* 4) he works the idea up into the memorable image of harmonious *(symphōnos)* love and concord in which Jesus Christ is sung in the key of God. He also appeals to several churches to send a delegation to Antioch in Syria, Ignatius's own church, to congratulate the church there for having restored to itself peace (*eirēnē;* Ign. *Phld.* 10.1; Ign. *Smyrn.* 11.2; Ign. *Pol.* 7.1). He does not elaborate on the situation behind that request, but it may have involved an earlier attack on his own authority* as bishop that had been properly dealt with after his departure.

7.5. The Shepherd of Hermas. Hermas's emphasis on quietness as an ethical quality has already been noted. Several times 1 Thessalonians 5:13 (cf. Mk 9:50) is alluded to in slogan fashion (*Herm. Vis.* 3.6.3; 3.9.2; 3.9.10; 3.12.3; *Herm. Sim.* 8.7.2): "be at peace among yourselves" (*eirēneuete en heautois*). The idea is associated with the sharing of material goods (*Herm. Vis.* 3.9.2), with mutual correction (*Herm. Vis.* 3.9.10; cf. *Did.* 15.3; 4.3; 14.2; *Barn.* 19.2) and with the promise of further visions* (*Herm. Vis.* 3.12.3). Evil speech in particular is cited as detrimental to communal peace; those refraining from such speech will have well-being at all times with all (*Herm. Man.* 2.3; *Herm. Sim.* 8.7.2). *Homonoia* is included in a list of the best things in life (*Herm. Man.* 8.9), bringing a blessing. When it is possessed along with other virtues* and the name of the Son of God,* it brings entrance into the kingdom of heaven* (*Herm. Sim.* 9.15.2; in *2 Clem.* 10.2 peace is the eschatological reward* for righteousness).

7.6. Gnosticism. The idea of rest is characteristic of gnostic thought, where the term *anapausis* ("rest") is a synonym of *eirēnē* (Helderman, 47-84) and is expressed in terms of most of the major features of the system(s) (see Helderman; Williams; Laansma, 134-39, 142-46; these syntheses utilize several gnostic writings, many of which are later than A.D. 150). Thus rest is the original state of the Pleroma and the original home of the Gnostic. Since the "fall," existence for the Gnostics is characterized by "unrest" and turbulence (cf. *Gos. Truth* 28.29—30.4). The divine Logos comes to reveal to the Pneumatics their original resting place, and the fruit of the gnosis he bestows is rest (*Gos. Truth* 22.9, 12). "Rest" is also descriptive of the unity *(homonoia)* of the Pneumatics with each other (*Gos. Phil.* 72.22-23; 79.3-13). Upon death the light particle is freed from the material body and returns to the repose of the Father. At the end of history, when all of the estranged particles of light have been restored to the Pleroma, the original condition of absolute rest and silence will return (*Gos. Truth* 41.3—43.3; *Gos. Mary* 17.4-7). The concept is deeply indebted throughout to Platonic traditions of the stability of the transcendent and of the mind that contemplates it in contrast to the instability, movement and flux of the material creation (Williams). (For further developments following A.D. 150 see Hamman; Yoder and Swartley, 189-91; Dinkler, 466-93; Huber et al., 618-46.)

8. Conclusion.
The following generalizations seem to constitute a fair representation of the idea as indicated by the specific terms used within the literature we have surveyed. Within the apostolic period "peace" is spoken of in christological and soteriological terms, as the eschatological gift of reconciliation in Christ from the God of peace and as an appropriate behavioral reflection of the new covenant* relationship between believers and God and each other. There are significant implications for the relationship of believers to the society in which they live (e.g., 1 Pet 3), though there is no social or political agenda separate from the advancement of the gospel. Among the Fathers, where the idea is utilized most prominently in connection with developing notions of the church as an institution, the communal aspect in an ecclesial setting is the most outstanding development. Clement in particular relies heavily on the model of the Roman state and its promotion of concord. In Gnosticism the idea of peace is expressed most characteristically in the frequent references to "rest." The latter concept is drawn from Greek metaphysical ideas of transcendent stability in contrast to the instability and flux of the material world. In this sense it is characteristic of all the major elements in the gnostic system(s) and is one of its most important soteriological concepts.

Certain features seem to link the various NT usages of the idea, beyond the common reliance on the OT and Jewish concept of *šālôm.* For example, Psalm 34 underlies both Hebrews 12 and 1 Peter 3. Its use elsewhere in the NT suggests that it had a fixed place in early paraenesis. Hebrews and James both place the fruit of righteousness and peace at the climax of an exhortation drawing on wisdom, and the reference to Rahab in Hebrews may reflect early Christian lists of OT examples also used by James and Clement of Rome. But there are also differences in emphasis. For example, Luke may be quietly positing the peace of the gospel as an alternative to the *Pax Romana,* while the author of Revelation rejects the latter in favor of an eschatological peace issuing from the Lamb's final victory. Not long after Revelation is written, Clement of Rome draws on the Roman state as a positive model of concord for the church. Other differences arise due to the differing theological emphases of the letters and writers.

See also DEATH OF CHRIST; FELLOWSHIP; REDEMPTION; RIGHTEOUSNESS.

BIBLIOGRAPHY. H. Attridge, *Hebrews* (Herm; Philadelphia: Fortress, 1989); R. J. Bauckham, *The Climax of Prophecy* (Edinburgh: T & T Clark, 1993); E. Dinkler, "Friede," *RAC* 8:434-505; J. I. Durham, "שלומ and the Presence of God" in *Proclamation and Presence: Old Testament Essays in Honour of Gwynne Henton Davies,* ed. J. I. Durham and J. R. Porter (London: SCM, 1970) 272-93; W. Foerster and G. von Rad, "εἰρήνη κτλ," *TDNT* 2:400-420; R. A. Guelich, *The Sermon on the Mount* (Waco, TX: Word, 1982); A. Hamman, "Peace" in *Encyclopedia of the Early Church*, ed. A. Di Berardino (New York: Oxford University Press, 1992), 664-65; V. Hasler, "εἰρήνη," *EDNT* 1:394-97; J. P. Healey and W. Klassen, "Peace," *ABD* 5:206-12; J. Helderman, *Die Anapausis im Evangelium Veritatis* (NHS 18; Leiden: E. J. Brill, 1984); W. Huber et al., "Frieden," *TRE* 11:599-646; J. Laansma, " 'I Will Give You Rest.' The Background and Significance of the Rest Motif in the New Testament with Special Reference to Mt 11 and Heb 3—4" (Ph.D. dissertation, University of Aberdeen, 1995; Tübingen: J. C. B. Mohr, forthcoming); C. Spicq, "εἰρηνεύω" in *Theological Lexicon of the New Testament* (3 vols.; Peabody, MA: Hendrickson, 1994) 1:424-38; L. L. Welborn, "Clement, First Epistle of," *ABD* 1:1055-60; K. Wengst, *Pax Romana and the Peace of Jesus Christ* (Philadelphia: Fortress, 1987); M. A. Williams, *The Immovable Race: A Gnostic Designation and the Theme of Stability in Late Antiquity*, ed. F. Wisse (NHS 29; Leiden: E. J. Brill, 1985); B. Winter, *Seek the Welfare of the City* (FCCGRW, Grand Rapids: Eerdmans, 1994); P. B. Yoder and W. M. Swartley, eds., *The Meaning of Peace* (Louisville, KY: Westminster/John Knox, 1992).   J. C. Laansma

PELLA, FLIGHT TO

Early Christian sources speak of a group of Jewish Christians fleeing from Jerusalem prior to or during the Jewish war of A.D. 67-70 and settling in the Perean city of Pella. One of the cities of the Decapolis, Pella was located at the base of the foothills in the northern Jordan Valley, about two miles east of the Jordan River and eighteen miles south of the Sea of Galilee. Despite critical issues that have been raised, the historical probability of this event seems well grounded.

1. The Pella Tradition
2. Critical Issues
3. Conclusions

1. The Pella Tradition.

Eusebius provides the earliest account of this tradition in *Ecclesiastical History* 3.5.3. He tells us that "the people of the church of Jerusalem, in accordance with a certain oracle given by revelation," were instructed to depart from Jerusalem* before the war "and dwell in one of the cities of Perea which they called Pella." This was so that when the Christian believers had deserted the capital and all of Judea, "the judgment of God might at last overtake them [the Jews] for all their crimes against the Christ and his apostles" (cf. 1 Thess 2:14-16). What was the source for Eusebius's tradition? We cannot be certain. It may have been from Hegesippus or from Aristo of Pella (see Lüdemann 1980, 165-66), a Christian apologist of the mid-second century.

Epiphanius, writing in A.D. 377 in his *Panarion* ("medicine chest"), mentions the flight to Pella in his discussions of the Nazoreans (Epiphanius *Pan.* 29.7.7-8) and of the Ebionites (Epiphanius *Pan.* 30.2.7). These two Jewish-Christian sects, according to Epiphanius, had roots in Pella. In 392, writing in his *Treatise on Weights and Measures* 15 (a biblical reference work), Epiphanius describes the small "church of God" existing in Jerusalem when Hadrian and his Jewish interpreter, Aquila, visited the ruined city in 129. He speaks of how the "disciples of the disciples of the apostles" had returned to Jerusalem from Pella and briefly recounts their original flight to Pella. When Jerusalem was "about to be seized by the Romans," the disciples were "forewarned by an angel to depart from the city." They settled in Pella "of the Decapolis," "across the Jordan." "But after Jerusalem was destroyed, they returned."

In the Syriac version of the Pseudo-Clementine *Recognitions* 1.37, 39, we find an indirect testimony to what appears to be the Pella tradition (for the text, see Koester, 98-101). Christian believers "would be led to a secure place of the land that they might survive and be preserved from the war" (*Recog.* 1.37.2), and "they would be saved from the war which was about to come for the destruction of those who were not persuaded" (*Recog.* 1.39.3). This text may reflect a second-century tradition that circulated among Christian communities in Transjordan, where the allusion to "a secure place of the land" would have been understood as a reference to Pella (Koester, 101-2).

In Luke 21:20-22 we find Jesus warning his disciples, "When you see Jerusalem surrounded by armies, then know that its desolation has come near. Then those in Judea must flee to the mountains, and those inside the city must leave it" (NRSV). Here Luke differs from Mark 13:14, where the "abomination of desolation set up where it ought not to be" serves as the warning for those in Judea to flee to the mountains.

Does Luke's version of this saying reflect a knowledge of the Pella tradition? While "the mountains" might be understood as alluding to the mountains east of the Jordan, including the region of Pella, there is no compelling reason to understand it in this manner. Since the warning is directed toward "those in Judea," the mountains of Judea are more likely in view (see Marshall, 772).

If Luke is writing post-A.D. 70, it is not clear that he is shaping these words in light of the Pella tradition. Is this saying of Jesus, or a version of it, perhaps the oracle of which Eusebius speaks? In other words, has an oracle that was received during 67-70 been placed on the lips of Jesus or shaped an already existing saying of Jesus? This possibility cannot be ruled out, but the evidence does not demand the conclusion, and the fact that Eusebius does not point out the correlation with Jesus' warning is notable. On the whole, the Lukan version of Jesus' warning of the coming destruction of Jerusalem, though giving the verisimilitude of specificity informed by hindsight, is no more specific than what one might generally expect of the siege of a city in the ancient world. In fact, some details are at variance with the account we have from Josephus* (see *DJG*, "Destruction of Jerusalem" §3). It remains questionable that Luke provides an additional testimony to the Pella tradition.

2. Critical Issues.

Do we have two testimonies to Pella in Eusebius and Epiphanius, or only one? In other words, was Epiphanius dependent on Eusebius's account? While G. Lüdemann concludes that Epiphanius was dependent on Eusebius (Lüdemann 1980, 164-65), C. Koester has examined the vocabulary of both accounts and effectively shown that Epiphanius was not dependent on Eusebius's account, though the "main elements . . . are essentially the same" (Koester, 94-95). There is good reason to conclude that in Eusebius and Epiphanius we have two explicit and independent accounts of the flight to Pella, and to these may be added another independent though indirect testimony in the Pseudo-Clementine *Recognitions*.

Granted that Christians did reside in Pella

after the war, was their origin in Jerusalem, as the Pella tradition claims, or was the story of the flight from Jerusalem a tradition that emerged in the interest of claiming an apostolic lineage for Transjordanian Jewish Christianity? Lüdemann has argued that the latter was the case. According to Lüdemann, when Epiphanius speaks of the postwar church in Jerusalem as consisting of returnees from Pella, he is combining his knowledge of the (actually unhistorical) Pella tradition with his knowledge of a postwar Christian community in Jerusalem. In placing the postwar heirs of the apostles* in Jerusalem, he is counteracting the claim of apostolic lineage made by Jewish Christian heretics in Pella. In Epiphanius's mind, the true descendants of the Jerusalem apostles returned to Jerusalem after the war. But Koester has pointed out that if the Pella tradition emerged out of this interest, Epiphanius, who locates the origin of the "Nazorean heresy" in the region of Pella (Epiphanius *Pan.* 19.7.7-8), would surely have taken opportunity in his *Panarion* to refute any claim they made to apostolic descent. But he does not. And there is no indication of a tradition that the refugees included apostles. Instead Epiphanius calls the refugees "disciples" (Epiphanius *Pan.* 29.7.8), and in *Weights and Measures* he explicitly refers to them as "disciples of the apostles" (*Weights* 15).

A more probable motivation behind the tradition may be found near the surface of the texts: to recount historical events that testified to the divine favor shown to the Jewish Christian community as they were warned through supernatural revelation* (Eusebius *Hist. Eccl.* 3.5.3; Epiphanius *Weights* 15) to flee from Jerusalem and thus escape the divine judgment,* which would befall non-Christian Jews remaining in Jerusalem.

There seems to be no substantial reason for doubting the historical authenticity of the account that Jewish Christian refugees from Jerusalem did settle in Pella. Their flight probably took place "before the war," as Eusebius asserts, and prior to the siege of Jerusalem, as Epiphanius maintains (Epiphanius *Pan.* 29.7.8). The Jewish Christians who settled in Pella gradually took on distinctive beliefs that Epiphanius would later identify as the "Nazorean heresy" (*nazōraious hairesis, Pan.* 29.7.8; see Jewish Christianity). And Epiphanius traces the origin of the Ebionites* to Pella, where

"Ebion's pretense began" (Epiphanius *Pan.* 30.2.7).

If these Jewish Christians did flee Jerusalem, when would they have done so? Eusebius's report that they did so "before the war" allows more possibilities than does Epiphanius's account, that they did not flee until "the city was about to be conquered." From Josephus we learn that the first outbreak of fighting took place in the summer of 66 (Josephus *J. W.* 2.15.4 §284), while Vespasian's campaign was begun in 67. Josephus also recounts how many Jews fled the city immediately after the Jewish victory over the Twelfth Legion in November of 66 (Josephus *J. W.* 2.20.1 §556). Jewish Christians might well have been among these refugees (for objections, see Brandon, 168-78). Although Brandon appeals to Josephus (Josephus *J. W.* 4.413-39) for evidence of Vespasian's carrying out a punitive campaign in the vicinity of Pella in 68, Pella is not mentioned by Josephus in that account, and there is no reason to believe that a Hellenistic and pro-Roman city such as Pella would have been the target of punishment any more than was Gadara, which was spared (see Sowers, 307-10, for a rebuttal of Brandon). Its political safety may have been an attractive reason for Jewish Christians to seek refuge in Pella, perhaps under the sponsorship of Gentile* Christians (so Sowers, 310 n. 14).

3. Conclusions.

It is plausible that prior to the siege of the city, Jewish Christians fled Jerusalem for Pella while there was still opportunity. Their presence in the city until a relatively late hour is what we might expect of Jewish Christians, for Jerusalem held for them a significant role in history and theology. Their departure as described in the Pella tradition, however, indicates a self-identity that was distinct from Jewish nationalism and zealotry. Eusebius is offering his own interpretation in saying that the coming defeat under the Romans was the judgment of God upon unbelieving Jews, but given the historic destruction of Jerusalem under the Babylonians, the interpretation would seem naturally to have followed for the refugees themselves. For Jewish Christians the event must have represented a defining moment in distinguishing themselves from "mainstream" Judaism.*

Epiphanius's report (Epiphanius *Weights* 15) that some of these Jewish Christians returned to Jerusalem after 70 is not difficult to believe. It fits with the Eusebian picture of a Christian community in Jerusalem after the war, "the whole church consisting of believing Hebrews," and his recounting of a succession of fifteen "bishops in Jerusalem" until the siege of Hadrian in 135 (Eusebius *Hist. Eccl.* 4.5). There is no reason to assume that all of those who fled to Pella returned to Jerusalem after the war, and the evidence from Epiphanius and elsewhere (see Van Elderen) of a continuing Jewish Christian presence in Transjordan suggests that some of the original refugees remained in Pella and its environs.

See also EBIONITES; GALILEAN CHRISTIANITY; JEWISH CHRISTIANITY.

BIBLIOGRAPHY. S. G. F. Brandon, *The Fall of Jerusalem and the Christian Church* (2d ed.; London: SPCK, 1957); B. C. Gray, "The Movements of the Jerusalem Church During the First Jewish War," *JEH* 24 (1973) 1-7; J. J. Gunther, "The Fate of the Jerusalem Church: The Flight to Pella," *TZ* 29 (1973) 81-94; C. Koester, "The Origin and Significance of the Flight to Pella Tradition," *CBQ* 51 (1989) 90-106; G. Lüdemann, "The Successors of Pre-70 Jerusalem Christianity: A Critical Evaluation of the Pella Tradition" in *Jewish and Christian Self-Definition*, vol. 1, ed. E. P. Sanders (Philadelphia: Fortress, 1980) 161-73 and as "Appendix: The Successors of Earliest Christianity: An Analysis of the Pella Tradition" in *Opposition to Paul in Jewish Christianity* (Minneapolis: Fortress, 1989) 200-13; I. H. Marshall, *Commentary on Luke* (NIGTC; Grand Rapids: Eerdmans, 1978); S. S. Sowers, "The Circumstances and Recollection of the Pella Flight," *TZ* 26 (1970) 315-20; B. Van Elderen, "Early Christianity in Transjordan," *TynB* 45.1 (1994) 97-117.   D. G. Reid

PENTECOST

Acts 2:1-42 contains Luke's dramatic story of the giving of the Spirit (*see* Holy Spirit) to Jesus' followers at the Jewish feast of Pentecost (*see* Judaism). This distinct event, occurring fifty days after the resurrection,* is depicted as the miracle* that began the period of the church* and energized its mission.* Extraordinary audible and visible phenomena accompany a filling with the Holy Spirit that enables each person to speak in other languages. Crowds of Jerusalem residents, who represent every nation, gather and recognize in their native language praise* of God's* mighty works. Others mock at this scene and believe the disciples are drunk. Peter, as representative of the Twelve, replies to the accusation in a discourse that explains what has occurred and its relation to Scripture and God's activity in Jesus of Nazareth. He concludes by calling on his audience to repent* and be baptized.* About three thousand people respond positively and become part of a new community.

1. The Role of Pentecost in the Narrative of Luke-Acts
2. Historical Issues
3. The Theological Significance of Pentecost

1. The Role of Pentecost in the Narrative of Luke-Acts.

1.1. Narrative Linkage. The account about Pentecost is linked with the open-endedness of the closure of Luke's first volume, which foretells the disciples' witness,* involving a proclamation to all nations, beginning from Jerusalem* (Lk 24:47-48), and its unfulfilled promise*: "And see, I am sending upon you what my Father promised; so stay here in the city until you have been clothed with power from on high" (Lk 24:49; *see* Power). This link between the two parts of Luke's narrative is reinforced when the latter saying is substantially repeated in Acts 1:4-5.

In Luke's second volume, Acts,* Pentecost constitutes a decisive part of the commissioning element of the plot, which leads through conflict to a resolution that has features of both closure and open-endedness. Insight into the commissioning and a partial outline of the plot are provided in Acts 1:8: "But you will receive power when the Holy Spirit has come upon you; and you will be my witnesses in Jerusalem, in all Judea and Samaria, and to the ends of the earth" (*see* Samaria). Pentecost enables Jesus' followers to begin carrying out this commission.

1.2. Narrative Shaping. Pentecost as part of the promise-fulfillment schema not only joins Luke's two volumes but also helps to shape the overall narrative, because Pentecost also fulfills John the Baptist's promise that "he will baptize you with the Holy Spirit and with fire" (Lk 3:16). The eschatological* judgment* and purification by the wind and fire of the Spirit begin in the experience at Pentecost. The fulfillment of the promise that launches the story line of Acts has parallels in the Gospel's plot with the commissioning element at the baptism of Jesus, which launches his ministry* (Lk 3:21, 22). While Jesus is at prayer,* the Holy Spirit descends on him, accompanied by visible and audible phenomena. Shortly thereafter Jesus, filled with the power of the Spirit, gives a discourse that is programmatic for the rest of the Gospel's narrative (Lk 4:16-30). In Acts this pattern is repeated with the praying disciples (Acts 1:14) as the recipients of the Spirit and Peter providing the programmatic speech (Acts 2:14-42).

The theophanic elements and the miracle in which the Spirit produces not just ecstatic utterances (Acts 10:46; 19:6) but other languages make the manifestation of the Spirit at Pentecost unique in the narrative (see also 2.4 below). Despite the unrepeatable character of Pentecost as inaugurating a decisive new stage in God's saving purposes, there are references back to Pentecost or mini-Pentecosts at key points in the narrative's depiction of the church's expansion—in Samaria, with Cornelius,* at the Jerusalem council and in Paul's work at Ephesus (Acts 8:14-17; 10:44-48; 11:15-17; 15:7-9; 19:1-7).

1.3. Characterization of the Spirit. While Jesus' followers are the human protagonists in the plot of Acts, the narrator shows that the primary character at Pentecost is a divine character, the Spirit. The disciples are at first passive recipients; the action is that of the divine Spirit (Acts 2:1-4). The sound that fills the house comes from heaven* (i.e., from God; Acts 2:2) and the event is depicted in terms of a theophany. In Jewish literature wind and fire accompany divine manifestations. Wind is mentioned in 2 Samuel 22:11, 16; Job 37:9, 10; 38:1; Ezekiel 13:13. Fire is a common feature in theophanies and an integral element in the theophany at Sinai (Ex 19:18). The account in Exodus does not mention wind at Sinai, but other versions of the event do (Josephus *Ant.* 3.80). Philo mentions the noise created by God's *pneuma,* breath or wind (Philo *Decal.* 33) and has the voice of God visible as flames and becoming articulate speech in the language familiar to the audience (Philo *Decal.* 46). The interpretation of the event in Peter's discourse also emphasizes that the Spirit is God's Spirit (Acts 2:27, 28) and that what Christ pours out he has first received from the Father (Acts 2:33).

From now on the divine Spirit will be a

significant character with a prominent and determinative role in the narrative. The Spirit will give courage to the Jerusalem community under persecution* (Acts 4:31) and to Stephen* in the face of martyrdom* (Acts 7:55) and will be responsible for extraordinary acts of power* (e.g., Acts 13:9). The Spirit will guide new departures and crucial stages in the church's mission, such as singling out Barnabas and Saul (Acts 13:2), inspiring the apostolic decree (Acts 15:28), directing the second journey of Paul (Acts 16:6, 7), leading Paul to go to Jerusalem (Acts 19:21) and making known to him what would befall him there (Acts 20:22, 23; 21:4, 11). At the end of the narrative Paul in Rome attributes to the Holy Spirit the passage from Isaiah that justifies his decision to turn from the Jews to the Gentiles* (Acts 28:25-28).

1.4. Intertextuality. Pentecost as the fulfillment of promise provides continuity between Luke's narrative and an earlier text, the Jewish Scriptures (see Intertextuality; Old Testament in Acts). This is most clearly seen in the use of the citation from Joel 3:1-5 (LXX) in Peter's discourse (Acts 2:17-21). Through the introductory *pesher* formula—this which has happened is that which was spoken of in Scripture—Pentecost is interpreted as the fulfillment of the promise that in the end times God will pour out his Spirit on all flesh.* The continuity motif is strengthened as Peter points out that the Christ who has poured out the Spirit (Acts 2:33) is the fulfillment of Psalm 16 and Psalm 110 and more generally of God's plan in Scripture (Acts 2:23).

2. Historical Issues.
Views on the historicity of the account range from acceptance of the substantial historicity of all its elements (Marshall) to skepticism about any historical tradition underlying most of them (Zehnle). Of the historical issues that have been raised, five major ones should be mentioned.

2.1. Diverse Views of Christian Origins. Questions are raised by the absence of any other NT reference to an event so extraordinary and so significant for the church's existence. Paul appears to see Christ's resurrection, exaltation* and his becoming life-giving Spirit as a single complex. John's equivalent to Pentecost occurs on the same day as the resurrection and is for a small group of disciples (Jn 20:22). It does not follow that because John may be considered to have a tendency to bring out the unity of salva-

tion* events, Luke's presentation is to be preferred historically. Luke can be shown to have an equal tendency to separate salvation history into distinct though related episodes. Elsewhere in the NT, such as in Paul's view of the commissioning of an apostle* or in the Great Commission (Mt 28:18-20), resurrection appearances are the presupposition for mission. Luke's schema of separating the resurrection appearances from Pentecost entails that in his narrative the Pentecostal experience of the Spirit rather than resurrection appearances is the indispensable presupposition for mission.

2.2. Place. Another well-known tendency of Luke is to give Jerusalem a central role in the structure of his narrative. In contrast to the other Gospels, the disciples are told not to leave Jerusalem between the resurrection and Pentecost (Lk 24:49; Acts 1:4), and Luke omits Mark 14:28 and alters Mark 16:7 (cf. Lk 24:6), thereby suppressing the tradition of resurrection appearances in Galilee. For this reason some have held that it is likely there were independent origins of churches with accompanying experiences of the Spirit in places such as Galilee and Damascus (Acts 9:19) and that Luke has again suppressed these in order to retain a neater schema with Jerusalem at the center. Two arguments suggest otherwise. The chief leaders of the earliest Jerusalem church were Galileans— James, Peter and John, as Paul attests independently. This makes it unlikely that Galilee* played any major role as the place of the church's origins, and in view of current eschatological expectations and their convictions about Christ's imminent Parousia,* it would make sense if there had been an early move of disciples from Galilee back to Jerusalem, where the events of the end were expected to unfold. It is also clear that Paul, particularly in Galatians, knows of only one place that could lay claim to be the center of the early Christian movement or the mother church, and that is Jerusalem.

2.3. Time. If, as Mark and Matthew indicate, the first resurrection appearances took place in Galilee, then, although this runs counter to Jesus' command in Luke's narrative, it might still be said that Pentecost would provide the obvious time to return to Jerusalem. But the issue of dating is tied up with Luke's depiction of a period of forty days of resurrection appearances with an ascension* as a separate event bringing the period to a close, and a number of reasons suggest that the dating may be part of Luke's reshaping of his traditions. Both Luke's Gospel and John's have the ascension on the day of the resurrection. A comparison of Acts' forty-day schema with the sequence of resurrection appearances, including an appearance to more than five hundred at one time (1 Cor 15), also suggests that the Acts schema is a narrative construct. Luke has separated what others regarded as one saving event. He has distinguished the resurrection from a physical exaltation by confining appearances to a symbolic period of forty days between the two events and has separated the bestowal of the Spirit from both by having it at the next appropriate date, the fiftieth day. Given Luke's interest in the notion of a renewed Israel,* Pentecost was a particularly appropriate date because of the associations of this festival with the renewal of the covenant* (see 3.3 below).

2.4. The Miracle of Language. In terms of the narrative itself there appears to be no particular need for a language miracle (see also 1.2 above). The audience of Jews would have understood either Aramaic or Greek. Elsewhere in Acts and in 1 Corinthians the Spirit produces glossolalia, ecstatic speech that ordinarily does not involve foreign languages. The comment of some within the narrative about the disciples' drunkenness (Acts 2:13) makes sense as a reaction to ecstatic speech (see also 1 Cor 14:23) but not as a response to hearing foreign languages. Some scholars have therefore proposed that originally the disciples spoke glossolalia but that some hearers recognized phrases as their native language. But if Luke or an earlier stage of the tradition could reinterpret a hearing miracle as a language miracle, they could equally well have reinterpreted glossolalia as languages in an attempt to show the special and universal features of the first experience of the Spirit (*see* Tongues).

2.5. Peter's Speech. As with other speeches in Acts, there are questions about the relation between tradition, if any, and redaction. In this case prior traditions, such as the christological* use of Psalm 110 and other OT texts, the primitive kerygma* and the invitation to repentance and faith,* may well have been incorporated, but the style is similar to that of other speeches in Acts and reflects Luke's hand. Its form is similar to that of a synagogue* homily, quoting a text at the beginning, weaving other texts into

the address and finishing with an allusion to the original text. Some of its points appear to depend on the Septuagint text. Would Peter have quoted this to his Jewish audience?

2.6. Conclusions. Given that NT narratives consist of a mixture of historical tradition and theological shaping whose final form is authoritative* for the church, we cannot be certain of some aspects of this narrative's historicity. These include the dating at Pentecost and the miracle of languages. Luke, however, is likely to have known of traditions of an initial powerful experience of the Spirit by the first followers of Jesus in Jerusalem that involved visionary elements and glossolalia, of Peter's early leadership and of early Christian preaching about Jesus that involved use of OT proof-texts. These constitute the materials he has reworked and reinterpreted for his narrative presentation.

3. The Theological Significance of Pentecost.

Aspects of the theological significance of Pentecost, such as the outpouring of the Spirit as fulfillment of promise, the divine nature of the Spirit, prayer and the reception of the Spirit and the Spirit's role in the church's expansion, have already emerged from a consideration of narrative features of this episode. Four further theological themes will be highlighted.

3.1. Pentecost and Christ. Just as the Spirit poured out at Pentecost is the Spirit of God, so that same Spirit does not operate in isolation from Christ but is the Spirit of Christ. The Spirit who descended on Jesus and filled him with power for his mission to bring good news to the poor and release to captives is the Spirit with whom he will baptize others (Lk 3:16; 24:49). In the narrative the Pentecostal experience depends on Christ's ascension as its presupposition, and Peter's speech makes clear that because of Christ's exaltation he has received the Spirit from the Father in such a way that he can now bestow the Spirit on others (Acts 2:33, 34).

3.2. Pentecost and the Filling of the Spirit. With the exception of Ephesians 5:18 the notion of being filled with the Spirit is a distinctively Lukan one. It can be employed for the initial and permanent endowment of a person who is to serve God, such as John the Baptist (Lk 1:5) or Paul (Acts 9:17). It is especially used when a person is inspired by the Spirit to make a prophetic statement or preach (e.g., Lk 1:41, 67;

Acts 4:8, 31; 13:9). In Luke's terminology the filling with the Spirit at Pentecost is synonymous with the baptizing, the gift or the outpouring of the Spirit. It may well be that "filling" is the term chosen for the Pentecost experience because of the association with inspired utterances, both those of all the disciples and that of Peter. It is significant also that in Peter's speech "and they shall prophesy" is added to the citation from Joel after "I will pour out my Spirit" (Acts 2:18). For the disciples Pentecost involved a filling of the Spirit that was both an equipping for inspired speech and an initiation into a new eschatological epoch ("in these last days" is another addition to the Joel prophecy in Acts 2:17).

3.3. Pentecost and the People of God. Pentecost produced not simply Spirit-filled individuals but a new community. The three thousand who were baptized "devoted themselves to the apostles'. . . fellowship" and "were together and had all things in common" (Acts 2:42, 44). The outpouring of the Spirit was appropriate at Pentecost because for many Jews this festival was a celebration not simply of the offering of the first fruits of the wheat harvest but of the renewal of the covenant made by God with Israel, particularly the covenant at Sinai (*see* Church as Israel). This significance of the festival existed from the middle of the second century B.C. (cf. *Jub.* 1:5; 6:11, 17; 15:1-24; 1QS 1:7—2:19). The narrative depicts Pentecost as the end-time renewal of the people of God, "the whole house of Israel" (Acts 2:36, 39), and the Spirit is therefore also the fulfillment of covenant promise (cf. Acts 3:25).

3.4. Pentecost and Mission. Pentecost is not only the inauguration of the renewed Israel with the Twelve as its foundation and the Jerusalem church as its representative. It also foreshadows the universality of the mission of this renewed people of God. The Jerusalem residents who appear on the scene turn out to be representatives "from every nation under heaven" (Acts 2:5-11). The citation from Joel speaks of "all flesh" and "whoever calls on the name of the Lord" (Acts 2:17, 21). Although Gentiles are not mentioned in their own right but appear only as proselytes to Judaism* (Acts 2:11), Pentecost launches the church's mission, which will take it to the ends of the earth (Acts 1:8).

The outpouring of the Spirit produces the energizing power for witness (Lk 24:48, 49; Acts 1:8). This witness of proclamation and mission is not something believers can carry out unaccompanied. The initial filling and the continuing impetus and empowering of the Spirit are its indispensable prerequisites. The account indicates that not only preaching* but also signs and wonders* will be part of the witness as a consequence of the Spirit's empowerment. The citation from Joel is revised to read of "portents in the heavens above and signs on the earth below" that will accompany the outpouring of the Spirit (Acts 2:19); Peter's speech emphasizes that Jesus himself was "a man attested to you by God with deeds of power, wonders and signs" (Acts 2:22); and as a result of their Pentecost experience such deeds are replicated in the mission of his followers, as "many wonders and signs were being done by the apostles" (Acts 2:43).

See also ACTS OF THE APOSTLES; HOLY SPIRIT; SIGNS AND WONDERS; TONGUES.

BIBLIOGRAPHY. C. K. Barrett, *Acts 1-14* (ICC; Edinburgh: T & T Clark, 1994); J. D. G. Dunn, *Baptism in the Holy Spirit* (London: SCM, 1970); idem, "Baptism in the Spirit: A Response to Pentecostal Scholarship on Luke-Acts," *JPT* 3 (1993) 3-27; idem, *Jesus and the Spirit* (Philadelphia: Westminster, 1975); J. A. Fitzmyer, "The Ascension of Christ and Pentecost," *TS* 45 (1984) 409-40; L. T. Johnson, *The Acts of the Apostles* (Collegeville, MN: Liturgical Press, 1992); A. T. Lincoln, "Theology and History in the Interpretation of Luke's Pentecost," *ExpT* 96 (1985) 204-9; G. Lüdemann, *Early Christianity According to the Traditions in Acts* (London: SCM, 1989); I. H. Marshall, "The Significance of Pentecost," *SJT* 30 (1977) 347-69; R. P. Menzies, *The Development of Early Christian Pneumatology with Special Reference to Luke-Acts* (Sheffield: JSOT, 1991); M. C. Parsons, *The Departure of Jesus in Luke-Acts* (Sheffield: JSOT, 1987); J. B. Shelton, *Mighty in Word and Deed: The Role of the Holy Spirit in Luke-Acts* (Peabody, MA: Hendrickson, 1991); R. B. Sloan, "'Signs and Wonders': A Rhetorical Clue to the Pentecost Discourse," *EvQ* 63 (1991) 225-40; R. Stronstadt, *The Charismatic Theology of St. Luke* (Peabody, MA: Hendrickson, 1984); R. C. Tannehill, *The Narrative Unity of Luke-Acts* (2 vols.; Minneapolis: Fortress, 1990) vol. 2; A. J. M. Wedderburn, "Traditions and Redaction in Acts 2:1-13," *JSNT* 55 (1994) 27-54; R. F. Zehnle, *Peter's Pentecost Discourse: Tradition and Lukan Reinterpretation in Peter's Speeches of Acts 2 and 3* (New York: Abingdon, 1971). A. T. Lincoln

PERSECUTION

The NT and church history in general highlight various episodes of persecution against the followers of Jesus and typically treat them as defining moments in the life of the church. For the purposes of this article, persecution is the violation of anyone's property or physical person because of the victim's identification with a religious group.

1. Overview of Persecution Against Christians
2. Reasons for Persecution
3. Christian Attitudes to Persecution
4. Theological Significance of Persecution

1. Overview of Persecution Against Christians.

In order to understand the significance of persecution in the NT and its place in the first two centuries A.D., a literary survey of the NT and a chronological survey are presented below. Such surveys as follow are clearly incomplete. The NT and other early Christian works never had as their purpose to provide a complete catalog of persecutions. These surveys focus on the significant instances of persecution preserved in the literary evidence; it is certain that many of our ancestors in the faith experienced persecutions concerning which we have no record.

1.1. Literary Survey of the New Testament. With the exception of 2 Peter,* Jude* and the Johannine epistles (*see* John, Letters of), the NT books under consideration in this volume provide a variety of descriptions of persecution and responses to it by the Christians.

1.1.1. Acts. Acts* is an account that is focused on Peter's early ministry* and on Paul's part in the spread of Christianity from Jerusalem* to Rome.* As such it does not provide an exhaustive account of the persecutions occurring in the time period it covers (c. 30-62). It is also clear from his Gospel and Acts that Luke is pro-Roman in political orientation. Given these caveats, the testimony of Acts is worth consideration.

Acts describes persecution by the Jews who were against the message of Jesus' followers, persecution that included commands for silence about Jesus (Acts 4:18; 5:40); beatings (Acts 5:40; 18:17; 21:30-32); imprisonment (Acts 5:18); stoning (Acts 7:58-60); and legal prosecution (Acts 18:12-16; 24:2-9). Of special interest is the repeated account of the persecutions that Saul brought against believers: arresting and imprisoning them (Acts 9:2; 22:4-5; 26:10) and approving of their executions (Acts 8:1; 26:10). In a dramatic reversal, this same Saul becomes the target of Jewish plots after his conversion (Acts 9:23-24; 20:19; 23:12-14) and appears as the central victim of persecution in the last half of the book.

There are also accounts of persecutions brought against believers by Jews in complicity with Gentiles: stonings (Acts 14:5 [attempted]; 14:19) and unspecified persecution (Acts 13:50; 17:5-9, 13).

We also have a description of Agrippa I (called King Herod by Acts and Eusebius) executing James the apostle* and imprisoning Peter (Acts 12:2-4; Eusebius *Hist. Eccl.* 2.9). Eusebius's account adds the detail (from Clement of Alexandria *Hypotyposes* 7) that the bailiff who escorted James to trial professed his faith after hearing James's court testimony and was executed with James.

Gentiles* who persecute believers include the mantic slave girl's owners, who bring Paul and Silas to be beaten and imprisoned (Acts 16:22-23). If we take Suetonius's *impulsore Chresto* ("by the instigation of Chrestus") as descriptive of Christ* as the point of contention among tumultuous Jews (with Lampe), then Claudius's expulsion of Jews in 49 might be considered an instance of persecution against Jews and Jewish Christians in Rome (Acts 18:2; Suetonius *Claudius* 25.4; Dio Cassius *Hist.* 60.6.6; Orosius *Pag.* 7.6.15), though Claudius may have been motivated by concern for the Jews' safety, as his policies in Alexandria* and Judea show (Eusebius *Hist. Eccl.* 2.19). This was one of two expulsions of Jews under the Julio-Claudians (the other in 19 by Tiberius), both of which seem to be attempts to quiet unrest rather than persecutions of Jews for religious reasons. There is also a description of a disturbance in Ephesus against "the Way" (Acts 19:23-41). Paul's final imprisonment in Acts is portrayed as a Roman action against him (Acts 28:16-17, 30), though Paul blames it on the Jews (Acts 28:17-19).

1.1.2. Hebrews. The author of Hebrews* knows that the letter's* first readers had experienced significant though not continued persecution, including confiscation of property (Heb 10:32-34). Hebrews 12:4 might indicate that the readers had not yet been put to death for their faith.

1.1.3. James. The text of James* does not single out persecution as a challenge for Christian experience, though the trials mentioned in James 1:2 may include persecution. James the Just, as Eusebius calls the author, was martyred at the temple* in Jerusalem for his testimony to Jesus. Eusebius identifies the persecutors as "scribes and Pharisees" who threw James off the top of a wall around the temple, stoned him and then allowed one of their number to club his head (Eusebius *Hist. Eccl.* 2.23.8-18; cf. Epiphanius *Haer.* 78.14). Epiphanius connects this martyrdom* to the beginning of Vespasian's siege, thus dating James's death to 66, since this would have been the last time that Jews from around the Mediterranean would be able to gather for a Passover (Meyer and Bauer). Josephus, however, dates James's death to about 62, since he links it to the beginning of Albinus's tenure as procurator (Josephus *Ant.* 20.9.1 §§200-201). This is the preferred date for James's death, since Josephus is writing in the same century and the passage bears no evidence of emendation by Christian scribes (cf. Josephus *Ant.* 18.3.3 §§63-64).

1.1.4. 1 Peter. Of the two Petrine letters, 1 Peter* is clearly written at a time when Christians have experienced persecution. The command in 1 Peter 4:12 not to think it strange that "the fiery trial" has occurred among the readers is strong evidence that this letter, written from Rome (= Babylon,* 1 Pet 5:13), dates from around the time of Nero's persecution of Christians after the fire in Rome (64).

Tacitus (Tacitus *Ann.* 15.38-44) describes the fire and how Nero shifted the blame for the fire from himself to the Christians and then began to persecute them. Tacitus is not at all sympathetic to Christianity, calling it a *superstitio* and including Christians among the dregs of the Roman Empire.* His record of Nero's persecution of them is therefore reliable, since he has no intention of making the Christians look good. Tacitus tells us that Nero had some Christians dipped in oil and then set afire to serve as lights in his gardens at night. Thus "the fiery trial" of 1 Peter 4:12 could refer both to the persecution that arose because of the fire and one mode of persecution that Nero used. The translations that offer words outside of the semantic field of "burning" or "fire" for the noun *pyrōsis* miss the historical allusion here, as well as the link with "the trial by fire" of 1 Peter 1:7,

and the intertextual, eschatological connection made between this fire and a fire God will use to judge the earth and vindicate his people (2 Pet 3:7, 12; *Did.* 16.5). The fact that 1 Peter deals so much with persecution (1 Pet 1:6-7; 3:13—4:19) and mentions obedience* to the government (1 Pet 2:13-17) makes the connection between this letter and the fire of 64 most probable. Since 2 Peter* is more concerned with false teaching than with persecution, it does not have the emphasis on faithfulness in persecution that 1 Peter does.

1.1.5. Revelation. The book of Revelation (*see* Revelation, Book of) contains many references to persecution, since persecution forms the occasion for this book's composition. As the Apocalypse begins, the author is depicted as being in exile for his Christian message (Rev 1:9). In his letters to the seven churches, reference is made to affliction (Rev 2:9-10) and martyrdom* (Rev 2:10, 13).

The second and third visions* in the book also include references to martyrdom (Rev 6:9-11; 16:6; 17:6; 18:24; 19:2). The woman who is drunk with the blood of the saints is clearly identified as Rome in Revelation 17:9. The descriptions at least of this woman therefore refer to the execution of Christians by Roman authorities; we cannot say whether the mention of martyrdom made to the churches of Smyrna and Pergamum was carried out by local residents (note "those called Jews" in Rev 2:9) or Roman authorities. The problem of persecution drives this Apocalypse (*see* Apocalyptic) and forms the occasion for John's visions that climax in Christ's ultimate vindication of the elect* (Rev 19:11-21), God's judgment* of all according to their works (Rev 2:23; 18:6; 20:12-13; 22:12) and the final rest of the redeemed in a restored creation* (Rev 21:1—22:15). Revelation is primarily a theodicy of persecution, not a definitive time line of the future or a sure guide to persecutions that were taking place. W. H. C. Frend links the high prices (Rev 6:6) and boycotts (Rev 13:16-17) to the famine that occurred in 92-93 in Asia Minor. This is possible, but it is equally possible that the author imagined how the persecution related to the imperial cult might progress.

1.2. Chronological Survey. This survey begins with Domitian, the first emperor* after Nero known for persecuting Christians (see 1.1.1 for a rough chronological outline through Nero's persecution). The survey ends with Marcus Aurelius, emperor in 161-80.

1.2.1. Domitian's Persecution. According to Melito* of Sardis (in Eusebius *Hist. Eccl.* 4.26.9) and Tertullian (*Apol.* 5.4), Domitian was the second emperor who persecuted Christians. We have little certain evidence of what Domitian did; Tertullian tells us that he did not persecute the Christians for long and that he recalled those whom he had exiled. Among those may have been Domitilla, Domitian's niece, whom he exiled to Pontia (Eusebius *Hist. Eccl.* 3.18.4; Eusebius's identification of Domitilla as Flavius Clemens's niece is probably mistaken).

Also noteworthy is Dio Cassius's description of Domitian's persecution of those who were practicing Jewish ways. They were charged with atheism; some were deprived of property, while others were executed (Dio Cassius 67.14.1-3). Given Judaism's* status as a legal religion, his reference to the charge of atheism makes one wonder whether his source had confused Jewish ways with Christianity.

Dio's description at least confirms Domitian's reputation as a persecutor. Suetonius describes how "Lord God" became Domitian's standard title in correspondence and conversation, how images of this emperor in Rome had to be of a certain weight of gold or silver and how various architectural embellishments proliferated as means of encouraging worship of Domitian (Suetonius *Domitian* 13). Because of this strong push toward deification within his lifetime and the record that he did persecute Christians, Domitian remains the best candidate for being identified as the second beast* of Revelation, whose image was supposed to be worshiped (Rev 13:15; note also Suetonius's remark that his troops referred to him as "God" immediately after his assassination [Suetonius *Domitian* 23]).

Although there is not agreement on his number (Rev 13:18), it is likely that 666 refers to Nero, who then would be identified as the first beast (Rev 13:1-8), since this is the numerical value of "Neron Caesar" when it is spelled in Hebrew letters. This would then make sense of the statement that the second beast had the authority of the first beast (Rev 13:12), since both these emperors are known to have persecuted Christians. Domitian's number would thus identify him as another Nero. E. Stauffer has suggested that the number derives from an abbreviated form of Domitian's titular name, spelled in Greek. No claim to certainty on these apocalyptic codes can be made, but Revelation 17:7-9 clearly associates the beast with Rome; thus the best interpretations of the beasts depicted in Revelation equate the beasts with Roman emperors. Evidence for early Christian understanding of them in this way may be found in the letter concerning the martyrs of Lyons, where the crowd is stirred up by the "wild beast," perhaps a reference to the emperor or the governor of Gaul, though Kirsopp Lake takes this beast to be the devil (in Eusebius *Hist. Eccl.* 5.1.57; 5.2.6).

1.2.2. Policy of Trajan and Hadrian. With the younger Pliny's correspondence with Trajan, we have valuable evidence for how Christians were perceived and treated by the authorities in the province of Bithynia in 112-13. If those who were indicted as Christians persisted in admitting this several times before Pliny, the emperor's legate with praetorian power (*legatus Augusti pro praetore*) there, he executed them, though he would send Roman citizens who were guilty of being Christians on to Rome (Pliny *Ep.* 10.96.3-4). The emperor affirmed Pliny's policy, cautioning him only not to seek out Christians and to acquit any who chose to deny being a Christian and proved such denial by worshiping "our gods" (Pliny *Ep.* 10.97). More important for a general understanding of persecution, however, is the second sentence of this imperial letter, which states that no universal policy can be enacted for dealing with Christians. This makes explicit what is obvious for the first two centuries: there was no single, official policy on Christians; Roman authorities responded to them differently in various times and places of the Principate.

Hadrian's rescript to the proconsul of Asia, Minucius Fundanus, about 124 or 125, also illustrates this nuanced treatment of Christians. He gives the proconsul freedom to punish Christians who can conclusively be identified as such, with punishments in proportion to the laws they have violated. He also rules that false informers are to be prosecuted with stiffer penalties.

1.2.3. Persecution Under the Antonines. The martyrdom of Justin and his colleagues occurred under the urban prefect Rusticus, but it was this man's emperor, Marcus Aurelius, who has achieved greater notoriety for persecuting Christians. It is clear that Marcus knew of Christians and approved of their execution. But it has never been shown conclusively that Marcus enacted laws explicitly against Christians or initiated persecution against them as Nero and Domitian did. Indeed, a decree of the joint emperors during 166-68 to offer sacrifices* to the gods so that the empire could survive a plague and invasions by German tribes may have led to mob reactions against Christians in certain locations.

Rescripts to Asia (not necessarily originating with the emperor; perhaps from the proconsul) apparently made it easier for people to inform on Christians (Melito, in Eusebius *Hist. Eccl.* 4.26.5), and this time period is known more for outbreaks of persecution throughout the empire: in 166-67 Christians were sought out in Smyrna, where Polycarp* met his death *(Mart. Pol.);* some scholars would date this as early as 156-57, based on information about the presiding consul, L. Statius Quadratus. Dionysius of Corinth mentions a martyrdom and persecution in Athens that occurred perhaps around 170 (Eusebius *Hist. Eccl.* 4.23.2).

Eusebius (*Hist. Eccl.* 5.1.3-3.3) includes much from a letter by Christians in Gaul about the persecution in the Rhône Valley in Lyons during Marcus Aurelius's reign, in 177. Here we have a record of a persecution that began by local antipathy toward the Christians, many of whom were Asian in ethnic extraction, at the time of a festival in Gaul. The literary evidence indicates a significant persecution, since it records how all of the most devout Christians of Lyons and Vienne were arrested. Even non-Christian servants of these believers were arrested. The Christians were tortured in order to get them to recant. Some of the Roman citizens among the accused were jailed while the governor awaited word from Rome. The emperor's word was that those who recanted should be released, while noncitizens who continued to identify themselves as Christians should be exposed to the animals in front of the festival crowd. Roman citizens who remained firm in their identification as Christians were beheaded. Eusebius preserves the record that those who had experienced some of this persecution did not want to be called "martyrs" but stated that Christ was the true martyr (Eusebius *Hist. Eccl.* 5.2.2-3). This illustrates the fluidity in the use of the term *martyr,* which did not become a technical term for one who had died for

religious belief until the middle of the third century.

1.2.4. Conclusion. While the available evidence makes us wonder whether persecution was as pervasive within Christendom as 2 Timothy 3:12 hints at (cf. 1 Pet 5:9), this overview shows that there were significant though not constant outbreaks of persecution within the first 150 years of the church's existence.

2. Reasons for Persecution.
The reasons for persecution do not always seem clear from the early Christian literature available to us. For example, in most of Acts, it is the believers' commitment to Jesus as Messiah that brings persecution from the Jews (e.g., Acts 5:40). Yet in Acts 16:20-21 the charge brought against Paul and Silas in the Roman colony of Philippi is that they are Jews who teach things unlawful for Romans. The theological significance that persecution carried for the early Christian writers (see section 4 below) obscures our understanding of the historical reasons behind some of the persecution accounts. For the most part, however, the NT presents persecution as arising from identifying with Jesus (Rev 1:9; 12:17; 19:10) or from rivalry with the Jews (see references in 1.1.1 above), presumably over the Christians' claim to inherit the promises* made to Israel (e.g., Acts 13:32-41).

2.1. Reasons for Official Persecution by Rome.
In the Roman sources available to us, the reasons for persecution seem similar to the reasons the Romans persecuted the followers of Bacchus in 186 B.C., the Jews in A.D. 19 or the astrologers (*see* Magic), who were occasionally expelled from the city of Rome in the first century A.D. In the instances of persecution against these groups as well as against Christians, what prompted the Roman authorities to take hostile action was not an ideological problem with the religious practice but rather a threat to the Romans' ideas of a properly ordered society.

Though they were particularistic in different ways, both Judaism and Christianity were regarded by some Romans as antisocial (Philostratus *Vit. Ap.* 5.33; Tacitus *Ann.* 15.44). The practice of Christians to meet in private, behind closed doors, also seemed suspicious to Roman sensibilities. This was because some *collegia,* Roman social clubs, had been looked on as extremely disorderly (e.g., Bacchanales; see *CIL*

1.196; *ILS* 18; Livy 39.8-18) or politically dangerous, as Augustus's law from around A.D. 7, requiring either senatorial or imperial approval
for any club to exist (*ILS* 4966), shows. Emperors could shut down these *collegia* at any time
(Pliny *Ep.* 10.34). Pliny was aware of this and
shows the Roman suspicion of unauthorized
collegium when he describes for Trajan how
Christians used to meet in his province (Pliny
Ep. 10.96.7). Pliny's request of imperial permission for a group of firemen to be formed for the
safety of Nicomedia was rejected by Trajan, on
the grounds that all groups of people inevitably
become political (Pliny *Ep.* 10.34). This illustrates well for us the Roman preoccupation with
order and the imperial suspicion of anything
that might upset such order.

Besides the Christians' suspicious practice of
gathering for worship,* the social leveling that
occurs in some early Christian literature (e.g.
Gal. 3:28) perhaps was a threat to the highly
stratified Roman conception of an ordered society (Dio Cassius *Hist.* 52.19.1-4). This possibility supports R. Scroggs's claim that the
egalitarian nature of the early church was one
of the factors that makes it identifiable as a
sectarian movement (Scroggs, 25, 39-40).
Rome's official acceptance of Christianity in the
fourth century is due not only to the ground-
swell of Christians in the empire but also to a
fundamental change in Roman society, which
made lower-status groups such as the Christian
house churches more acceptable than they had
been in preceding centuries. This change included the growing acceptance of provincials
with lower status into the senatorial order
(Gager, 107-8). Before this time the composition of Christian house churches would have
naturally sparked Roman disdain.

One might object to the alignment at the
beginning of this section of the persecution of
Christians alongside the Roman persecution of
the Jews, citing the identity of Judaism as a legal
religion *(religio licita)*, a recognition that Christianity did not receive until 313. But Rome
continued to persecute followers of Judaism in
the first and second centuries (e.g., Vespasian's
destruction of the Jewish temple in Leontopolis
[Josephus *J.W.* 7.10.2 §§420-2]) for the same
reasons that it persecuted Christians: in order
to reestablish a sense of Roman boundaries and
order in places within the empire where such
order appeared in question. This similarity in

the reasons for Roman persecution of various
religions accounts for the association that is
made between practicing Jews and followers of
Isis in accounts of the expulsion of 19 (Philo
Leg. Gai. 159-61; Josephus *Ant.* 18.3.4-5 §§65-84;
Suetonius *Tiberius* 36.1; Tacitus *Ann.* 2.35.4-5;
Dio Cassius *Epit.* 57.18.5A). It may also account
for Suetonius's reference to Chrestus (Christ?)
when he wrote of Claudius's expulsion of the
Jews from Rome (Suetonius *Claudius* 25).

Any attempt at explaining Roman persecution of Christians, therefore, must include an
account of Roman action toward other foreign
religions, beginning at least with the Bacchanalia incident of 186 B.C. (Livy *Hist.* 39.8-18). Rome
sought to rid itself of any threat to its understanding of law and order; it did not persecute
Christians because of a religious antipathy toward Christianity. As G. E. M. de Ste. Croix has
shown, persecutions by Roman authorities were
not directly about what Christians believed or
confessed but were carried out because the
Christians refused to sacrifice to the gods. This
refusal was a violation of the Roman sense of
order.

*2.2. Reasons for Popular Movements Against
Christians.* The reasons the masses opposed
Christians were not always as spiritual as a believer might wish. Christians typically were
thought to be countercultural. Suspicions of
such counterculturalism and the resultant antipathy might operate along ethnic lines.
Claudius's expulsion of Jews, if it was because of
arguments over Chrestus (Christ), may have
been partially motivated by anti-Semitism directed toward the Jewish Christians in Rome.
Similarly Tacitus's description of the "depraved
superstition" known as Christianity makes clear
its origins in Judea (Tacitus *Ann.* 15.44).

Justin's first apology, written about 150 in
Rome, indicates that there were charges against
Christians (Justin *Apol. I* 3) that included accepting the name *Christian* (Justin *Apol. I* 4),
atheism (Justin *Apol. I* 5—6) and evil deeds
(Justin *Apol. I* 7). His martyrdom (c 165) with
that other believers, including the imperial
slave Euelpistus, is narrated in the *Acts of Justin*.
Here it is clear that they are executed because
they freely admit to being Christians and refuse
to offer sacrifices to the gods (*Acts Just.* Rec. A,
B, C 3-5). Atheism (*Mart. Pol.* 3; 9; Justin *Apol. I*
5—6), cannibalism (Justin *Dial. Tryph.* 10.1)
and incest (Athenagoras *Leg.* 3.1) seem to have

remained within the popular caricature of Christianity. In addition there is evidence that Christians were blamed for earthquakes (c. 152) and the plague (c. 165) in Asia Minor, much as Christians were blamed for the decline of the Roman Empire in Augustine's time (Augustine *Civ. D.* 1.1-36). These are probably some of the reasons behind Tacitus's enigmatic remark that Christians were arrested in Nero's persecution because of the Christians' hatred of the human race (Tacitus *Ann.* 15.44).

It is also probable that Christians were caricatured in some circles as a rebellious people. Origen preserves the charge that Christianity is a group that arose out of rebellion against Jews (Origen *Cont. Cels.* 5.33). Marcus Aurelius depicts Christians as those who abandon the fatherland (Marcus Aurelius *Med.* 3.16; also included in this passage are charges of atheism and doing things behind closed doors). This stereotype of rebellion was associated with the way Christianity arose, its followers worshiping someone crucified by the Romans. The charge of insubordination may explain why NT authors take pains to tell Christians to follow the government (Rom 13:1-7; 1 Tim 2:1-4; 1 Pet 2:13-17; *see* Civil Authority) and why Justin wants to say that Christians keep the law (Justin *Apol. I* 12).

3. Christian Attitudes to Persecution.

Both the NT and extracanonical early Christian literature provide ample testimony that Christians reacted in a variety of ways to persecution.

3.1. Eagerness to Be Persecuted. The most well known example of this wish to experience persecution is Ignatius* of Antioch.* His eagerness to experience martyrdom is amply sprinkled throughout his letters (Ign. *Eph.* 1.2; 8.1; 11.2; 18.1; Ign. *Trall.* 4.2; 10; Ign. *Rom.* 1.2; 2.2; 3.2; 4.1-3; 5.2-3; 6.1-3; 7.2; 8.3). Inherent in this attitude is the motivation that persecution is a way to reach God or Jesus (see 4.2.3 below). But this attitude was not universally held throughout Christendom.

3.2. Avoidance of Persecution. An equally attested attitude was one that would seek to avoid persecution. Such avoidance was carried out in different ways that gave evidence of different attitudes toward it.

3.2.1. Flight from Persecution. The dominical command to flee (Mt 24:16; Mk 13:14; Lk 21:21) endorses the natural human response to the violence of persecution. At the same time such flight is based on the stubborn refusal to surrender and change one's religious identity to avoid the persecution. We see flight from persecution in the example of the early believers (Acts 8:1) and in the experiences of Paul (Acts 9:23-25; 23:12-35), Polycarp* (*Mart. Pol.* 5.1; 6.1), Cyprian (Cyprian *Ep.* 2; Cyprian *Laps.* 10) and Lactantius (Lactantius *Div. Inst.* 4.18.1-2; Athanasius *Fug.*). It is also worth noting that the deserts of Egypt swelled with monks in the years of the great persecution (303-13).

3.2.2. Apostasy. Another well attested response was to say the words and perform the sacrifices necessary to avoid persecution. In Pliny's letter to Trajan we read of those who recanted their Christian confession in front of Pliny and of others who said that they had abandoned their identity as Christians three to twenty years previously (Pliny *Ep.* 96.6). Because some renounce their faith during persecution, the church's response to such lapsed who later seek restoration is a recurring point of contention throughout church history (Jn 21:15-19; Rev 20:4-5; Cyprian *Laps.*; Augustine *Ep.* 93). Some Gnostics,* because of a docetic* or otherwise nuanced christology* and the view of the passion that this entails, as well as their independence from what came to be orthodox church authority,* did not value martyrdom as did other believers and may have outwardly recanted to avoid persecution (Heracleon, according to Clement of Alexandria *Strom.* 4.71-72).

3.3. Orthodox Attitudes to Persecution. It is an established tradition within the Christianity that became identified as orthodox that those who intentionally sought martyrdom would not be recognized as martyrs (Clement of Alexandria *Strom.* 4.17.1; *Mart. Pol.* 1.4; Council of Elvira canon 60). The *Martyrdom of Polycarp* is carefully written to show that Polycarp did not seek his martyrdom. Those who were persecuted were certainly honored, as any perusal of the martyrologies will show. But if one engineers persecution upon oneself, one has annulled its value. What is valuable is to suffer for doing good (1 Pet 3:13-17).

4. Theological Significance of Persecution.

Already in the NT we see a complex of theological issues embedded in the persecution texts. Persecution itself is not simply a historical phenomenon; it is also a theologoumenon in its own right.

4.1. The Origin of Persecution. The descriptions of persecution in the NT and early Christian literature demonstrate tensions in defining the identity of the forces behind persecution of Christians.

4.1.1. The Divine/Diabolical Tension. In Revelation 6:9-11 we have a strong affirmation that God allows persecution and sets limits on its extent, an idea already affirmed in Job 1:12 and Job 2:6. As in the book of Job, however, Revelation identifies the immediate powers involved in persecution as diabolical (Rev 2:10; 13:2, 4, 11; 16:13), with its references to the dragon clearly identified as Satan* in the description of the millennium (Rev 20:2). Origen makes the point that martyrs' souls destroy the power of demons, as if the very act of martyrdom carries spiritual significance. Since the demons have learned this point, he says, Christians will not be persecuted until the time the demons forget it (Origen *Cont. Cels.* 8.44). This statement is predicated on the causal connection between the diabolical and persecution, a similar link to that in Revelation 13 (see also Eusebius *Hist. Eccl.* 5.1.16; Origen *Pass. Perp. Fel.* 20.1).

4.1.2. The Divine/Human Tension. The NT also seems to balance its descriptions of persecution as arising from divine or human agency. The exchange between Pilate and Jesus concerning Pilate's authority to persecute Jesus illustrates this well (Jn 19:10-11). Peter's description of responsible parties in the death of Jesus also illustrates this. He refers to Jewish leaders ("you") and Roman soldiers ("godless men"), but these agents are all subsumed under God's predetermined will (Acts 2:23).

4.1.3. Depictions of Jewish Persecutors and Anti-Semitism. Within the human side of persecution the NT identifies a significant amount of persecution from the Jews. The Gospels seem cognizant of such persecution (Mt 10:17; 23:34; 24:17 par. Mk 13:9; Lk 21:12; Jn 9:34; 16:2). Acts also contains such descriptions (see 1.1.1. above), and Paul does not hesitate to identify some of his persecutors as Jewish (Rom 15:31; 2 Cor 11:24; Phil 3:2; 1 Thess 2:14-16). Revelation 2:9 and Revelation 3:9 do identify some persecution as arising from Jews, though they are not the main agent of persecution in Revelation.

Such descriptions inevitably give rise to a consideration of the alleged anti-Semitism in the NT. A full consideration of the evidence demands that we note that many of the NT writers consider themselves still within the Judaisms present in first-century Judea and the Diaspora (Mt 5:17-20; 19:28 [= Lk 18:30]; 23:1-3; Acts 23:6; 2 Cor 11:22; Gal 6:16; Heb 7; Jas 1:1; 1 Pet 1:1; 2:9; Rev 7:4-8; 21:12; *see* Diaspora Judaism). They continue to look at being Jewish as though it has inherent value (Mt 13:52; Rom 3:1-2; 9:3-5; 11:26-29; Rev 5:5; 14:1-5; 22:16). In Acts 2:23 the crucifixion is God's plan in which Jews and Romans participated; in 1 Corinthians 2:8 "the rulers of this age," if they are political agents rather than spiritual powers who crucified Jesus, were ignorant. The sins of the elect put Jesus on the cross, not any specific group's malevolence (1 Cor 15:3; Gal 3:10-14). However anti-Semitic later Christian authors appear on the issue of persecution (e.g., *Barn.* 5.11; *Mart. Pol.* 12.2; 17.2), the charge of anti-Semitism based on NT persecution texts betrays an anachronistic reading of an intra-Jewish struggle for legitimacy.

4.2. The Spiritual Value of Persecution. Though persecution is never identified as a sacrament, it is clear in the NT that Christians valued persecution (Acts 5:41). This valuation arose from Judaism and was articulated by Christians in terms of following Jesus' example, drawing closer to God or Jesus and gaining rewards.*

4.2.1. The Origin of the High Appraisal of Persecution. Frend's thesis that early Christians valued persecution and respected its victims because of Jewish attitudes toward persecution is essentially correct. It is clear that the writers of the NT and later Christian authors have adopted a Jewish theology of persecution (Rom 8:36; Heb 11:35-38; Origen *Exhort. Mart.* 22—27). But they do not emphasize dying for Torah as in descriptions of Jewish martyrs (2 Macc 7:9, 11; 4 Ezra 7:89); they rather add the idea of following Christ through persecutions. At least one link was explicitly made between Christian persecution and a Hellenistic respect for martyrdom, but this is not the norm (*Acts Apoll.* 39—41, citing Plato *Rep.* 2.5.361E and the example of Socrates).

4.2.2. A Means of Following Jesus. The Gospels include the idea that Jesus' followers will imitate him in experiencing persecution (Mt 10:24 par. Lk 6:40; Jn 13:16; 15:20). This idea is also espoused throughout the NT (Phil 3:10; Heb 12:2-3; 1 Pet 2:21-25; Rev 1:9).

4.2.3. A Means of Approaching the Divine. Persecution is also linked to drawing near to God or Jesus (Rom 8:17; Phil 3:10-11; Ign. *Rom.* 5.3; 7.2; Ign. *Smyrn.* 4.2). Sometimes persecution is causally linked to becoming pure (1 Pet 4:1; Origen *Exhort. Mart.* 30) or accomplishing something that is spiritually necessary, thus allowing one to approach the divine (Col 1:24; Ign. *Rom.* 3.2-3; *Mart. Pol.* 2; *Apoc. Pet.* 74.4-16; Tertullian *Apol.* 50). Intimate knowledge of Jesus' own sufferings qualifies one for authority in the church (Jn 19:34-35; Gal 6:17; 1 Pet 5:1).

4.2.4. A Means of Gaining Rewards. The dominical saying on rewards for persecution (Mt 5:11-12 par. Lk 6:22-23) fuels the idea of otherworldly rewards for persecution. Revelation describes such rewards for those who endure persecution, especially martyrs (Rev 2:10; 6:11; 7:13-14; 11:18; 22:12). This idea would inspire Christians through the centuries.

4.3. The Necessity of Persecution. There is one strand in the persecution material that treats it as a necessary component of any believer's life. Perhaps arising from an absolute reading of such texts as Luke 6:26 and 2 Timothy 3:12, this has led Christians to expect and in some cases orchestrate their own persecutions. Early Christian tradition did not universally hold this view, however, as the ample evidence of flight from persecution attests (see 3.2.1 above).

While persecution therefore is not a requirement for every believer, the NT and early Christian literature attribute to persecution such results as church growth (Acts 8:1-4; Eusebius *Hist. Eccl.* 5.1.48-49) and spiritual gain (Phil 1:21; Rev 14:13; Origen *Exhort. Mart.* 14).

See also ADVERSARIES; APOSTASY; BABYLON; BEASTS, DRAGON, SEA, CONFLICT MOTIF; EMPEROR, EMPEROR CULT; ENDURANCE, PERSEVERANCE; MARTYRDOM; SUFFERING.

BIBLIOGRAPHY. T. D. Barnes, "Legislation Against the Christians," *JRS* 58 (1968) 32-50; W. H. C. Frend, *Martyrdom and Persecution in the Early Church* (New York: New York University Press, 1967); idem, "Persecutions," *Encyclopedia of the Early Church*, ed. A. Di Berardino (2 vols.; New York: Oxford University Press, 1992); J. G. Gager, *Kingdom and Community: The Social World of Early Christianity* (Englewood Cliffs, NJ: Prentice-Hall, 1975); P. Keresztes, "Marcus Aurelius a Persecutor?" *HTR* 61 (1968) 321-41; P. Lampe,

Die stadtrömischen Christen in den ersten beiden Jahrdunderten (WUNT 2.13; 2d ed.; Tübingen: J. C. B. Mohr, 1989); A. Meyer and W. Bauer, "The Relatives of Jesus" in *New Testament Apocrypha,* ed. E. Hennecke, W. Schneemelcher and R. McL. Wilson (Philadelphia: Westminster, 1963) 418-32; O. Nicholson, "Flight from Persecution as Imitation of Christ," *JTS* 40 (1989) 48-65; N. M. P. Nilsson, "Bacchanalia," *OCD,* 2d ed.; E. Pagels, "Gnostic and Orthodox Views of Christ's Passion: Paradigms for the Christian's Response to Persecution?" in *The Rediscovery of Gnosticism,* ed. B. Layton (Leiden: E. J. Brill, 1980) 262-83; L. V. Rutgers, "Roman Policy Towards the Jews," *Classical Antiquity* 13 (1994) 56-74; R. Scroggs, "The Earliest Christian Communities as Sectarian Movement" in *The Text and the Times* (Minneapolis: Fortress, 1993) 20-45; A. N. Sherwin-White, *Roman Society and Roman Law in the New Testament* (New York: Oxford University Press, 1963); M. Slusser, "Martyrium 3.1 NT/Alte Kirche," *TRE;* E. Stauffer, "666," *ConNT* 11 (1947) 237-41; G. E. M. de Ste. Croix, "Why Were the Early Christians Persecuted?" in *Studies in Ancient Society,* ed. M. I. Finley (London: Routledge & Kegan Paul, 1974) 210-49; G. H. Stevenson, "Clubs, Roman," *OCD,* 2d ed.

M. Reasoner

PERSEVERANCE. *See* ENDURANCE, PERSEVERANCE.

1 PETER

The Gospels consistently present the apostle* Peter as leader and spokesperson among Jesus' disciples, a role he continues to play in the beginnings of the Christian movement as described in the first half of the book of Acts.* It is not surprising, therefore, that two NT letters* bear his name. The first of these (traditionally called "first" because the other, shorter letter explicitly calls itself the "second," 2 Pet 3:1) is a remarkably concise and powerful summary of Christian belief and practice.

1. Author and Readers
2. Integrity and Literary Structure
3. Historical and Social Situation
4. Theological Contributions to the Canon

1. Author and Readers.
First Peter follows closely the literary format of the letters of Paul, identifying both author and readers in the first two verses of the letter and

following the identification with a "grace and peace" formula. It differs from Paul's letters (except for Galatians and Ephesians) in being addressed not to one specific local congregation but to a circle of congregations spread over a considerable geographical area (in this respect compare Revelation [see Revelation, Book of], esp. Rev 1:4-6, 10-11).

1.1. Peter as Implied Author. Just as Paul in five of his letters is "Paul, apostle of Jesus Christ," so this author identifies himself as "Peter, apostle of Jesus Christ" (1 Pet 1:1). Whoever the real author may be, he is writing as the apostle Peter. In the context of the NT canon* it appears that Peter is here exercising the judicial authority* Jesus gave him (according to Mt 16:19) to bind and loose or is carrying out the command of Jesus (according to Jn 21:15-17) to feed or shepherd* the Christian flock.

Little is made explicitly of this claim of apostolic authority in the rest of the letter. Only three times does the author write in the first person singular. In the first of these instances (1 Pet 2:11) he says "I appeal" *(parakalōn);* in the second, "I appeal to any elders among you," referring to himself not as an apostle but as a "fellow elder and witness to the sufferings of Christ and a sharer as well in the glory to be revealed" (1 Pet 5:1; see Glory; Witness). On the surface this is a more modest claim, but its apparent purpose is to establish collegiality and common ground with the readers, precisely as a great authority figure might do. We might compare Peter to John the prophet* describing himself to his readers as "your brother and sharer in the tribulation and kingdom and patient endurance in Jesus" (Rev 1:9; see Endurance; Kingdom of God) or even to the angel* who, addressing John, claimed to be a "fellow servant with you and your brothers" (Rev 19:10; 22:9; see Servant). Such language presupposes a certain status and sense of personal authority on the part of the speaker, and this kind of authority is evident throughout 1 Peter.

In his third use of "I," Peter concludes, "I have written these few lines through Silvanus (whom I consider a faithful brother) to appeal *[parakalōn]* and give testimony that this is true grace from God" (1 Pet 5:12; see Grace). Then he sends greetings from "the sister [congregation] in Babylon, chosen along with you, and Mark, my son" (1 Pet 5:13). The effect is to locate Peter geographically in "Babylon"*

(probably a metaphorical name for Rome, as in Revelation) and to link him with two of Paul's companions, Silvanus (1 Thess 1:1; 2 Thess 1:1; 2 Cor 1:19) and Mark (Philem 24; Col 4:14; 2 Tim 4:11).

Because of his adoption of the Pauline letter form and his references to Paul's companions, some have inferred that the author of 1 Peter wants to present Peter as a friend or an associate of Paul (compare the explicit reference to "our beloved brother Paul" in 2 Peter 3:15). This tendency to make the implied author a Paulinist is a matter of indifference in itself, though the idea is hardly verifiable. But when it leads interpreters to measure the letter by the standards of Paul's writings it fails to do justice to 1 Peter, for then that letter is found to be either lacking the great Pauline themes of justification by faith* and life* in the Spirit (see Holy Spirit) or (somewhat inconsistently) as exhibiting a derivative brand of Paulinism. Instead 1 Peter should be read on its own terms as a significant independent witness* to Christian faith and life.

Not only where he specifically refers to himself but also throughout the letter this author wears his identity as "Peter, apostle of Jesus Christ" rather lightly. Jesus called Simon Peter a "rock" (Mt 16:18), but in 1 Peter the "living Stone" is Jesus Christ himself (1 Pet 2:4; see Stone). Jesus also said to Peter, "You are a scandal to me" (Mt 16:23), but in 1 Peter it is Jesus Christ who is "a stone of stumbling and a rock of scandal" (1 Pet 2:8)—not to the people of God* but to unbelievers. The irony is unmistakable. Jesus designated Peter as shepherd to his flock (Jn 21:15-17), but again the author of 1 Peter assigns this role to Jesus himself, "the Shepherd and Guardian of your souls" (1 Pet 2:25). "Shepherd the flock of God that is in your care," he tells the elders (1 Pet 5:2), but he gives no particular significance to his own role as shepherd. Instead he and the elders together wait for Christ to be revealed, for Christ is the "chief shepherd" (1 Pet 5:4) to whom all sheep and all shepherds are accountable.

The implied author's claim to be "witness to the sufferings of Christ and a sharer as well in the glory to be revealed" (1 Pet 5:1) should not be understood as emphasizing Peter's eyewitness role in relation to either Jesus' life or his death (see Death of Christ) on the cross* (e.g., as in 2 Pet 1:16-18). Strictly speaking Peter was not an eyewitness to Jesus' sufferings because, with other disciples, he deserted Jesus in Gethsemane and was not present at the crucifixion. Moreover, this author is stressing that which he has in common with the "elders" to whom he is writing, not that which he can claim and they cannot. He is saying that like them (and like the prophets of old, 1 Pet 1:11) he bears his witness or testimony to the gospel* of Jesus' suffering* and vindication as he waits for the future glory to be revealed.

1.2. Peter as Real Author. Early church tradition, where it mentions this letter at all, is unanimous in identifying Peter as its real author. Papias of Hierapolis, writing in the mid-second century from within the general area to which the letter is addressed, accepts the letter's claim to come from Peter, to be written from "Babylon" (which Papias understood as Rome) and to convey greetings from Mark, whom Peter called his "son" (1 Pet 5:13; see Eusebius *Hist. Eccl.* 2.15.2). Irenaeus too, who lived first in Asia Minor and then in Gaul, cited 1 Peter late in the second century as Peter's work (Irenaeus *Haer.* 4.9.2; 4.16.5; 5.7.2). The same is true of Tertullian in Roman North Africa (*Scorp.* 12) and Clement of Alexandria in Egypt (e.g., Clement *Paed.* 1.6; Clement *Strom.* 3.12). Origen, also from Alexandria, expressed in one breath acceptance of 1 Peter and doubt about 2 Peter: "Peter, on whom Hades shall not prevail, has left one acknowledged epistle, and, it may be, a second one, for it is doubted" (Eusebius *Hist. Eccl.* 6.25.8; this claims to be from a portion of Origen's commentary on John that is not extant).

Modern scholars, unlike the ancient church, do not universally accept this letter's claim to come from Peter's hand. Peter is indeed the implied author, but is he the real author? Some who hold that 1 Peter is pseudonymous (i.e., that a later author adopted Peter's name as a literary device) argue that the style is far too elegant for Simon Peter, the Galilean fisherman. In Acts 4:13, just after Peter had quoted Psalm 118:22 (the same text he quotes in 1 Pet 2:7), he and his companion, John, are described as "uneducated and ordinary men" (NRSV). Yet 1 Peter contains some of the finest Greek in the NT. Others, pointing to traditions about Peter's martyrdom* c. A.D. 64 in the persecution* under Nero, contend that 1 Peter cannot have been written before that date.

The latter argument is precarious because no one knows when or how Peter died. The testimony of 2 Peter (2 Pet 1:12-15) is that he had ample time to prepare and plan for his departure and is consistent with the notion that he died a natural death. This testimony carries weight even if Peter did not write 2 Peter, for it reflects early Christian belief about Peter's death. The same is true of the reference to his death in John's Gospel (Jn 21:18-19), which is more like a riddle about youth and old age than a prediction of martyrdom. Only later traditions make Peter into a martyr (e.g., Origen, Tertullian, Eusebius and above all *Acts of Peter* 30-41; *1 Clement* 5.4, written from Rome near the end of the first century, is far from clear on the subject).

As to the letter's style, a number of scholars (Selwyn, Kelly, Davids, Marshall) have attributed its actual composition to Silvanus ("through Silvanus," 1 Pet 5:12), but the expression is more likely a commendation of Silvanus as the bearer of the letter—as in the letters of Ignatius to the Philadelphians (Ign. *Phld.* 11.2), Smyrneans (Ign. *Smyr.* 12.1), Romans (Ign. *Rom.* 10.1) and Polycarp (Ign. *Pol.* 8.1) and of Polycarp to the Philippians (Pol. *Phil.* 14.1). Although this hypothesis has become popular among some scholars as a defense of Petrine authorship, its effect is to make Silvanus and not Peter the real author of the letter, just as Mark and not Peter was identified as author of the Gospel of Mark (*see DJG*, "Mark, Gospel of" §1.2). At least one defender of this hypothesis allows the possibility that Peter "may have never even seen" the letter, "having given only the briefest of instructions" to Silvanus (Davids, 7).

The notion that Peter had help in the composition of this letter does not stand or fall with the theory about Silvanus. If 1 Peter is, as it appears to be, an encyclical on behalf of the church at Rome* ("Babylon") to a wide circle of churches on the frontiers of the Roman Empire* in five provinces of Asia Minor ("Pontus, Galatia, Cappadocia, Asia and Bithynia," 1 Pet 1:2), then the author would likely have had scribal help with vocabulary and style, and his helpers would likely have remained anonymous. The burden of proof is still on those who reject the letter's claim to come from Peter the apostle.

1.3. The Implied Readers. 1 Peter shows little or no knowledge of the circumstances of its readers because they are spread over a huge and distant geographical area, and all we can know about the readers is the way in which the author visualizes them. Like the readers of Paul's letters, these implied readers are Gentiles* who have come to believe in Jesus. They are no longer slaves* to "the impulses that once drove [them] in [their] ignorance" (1 Pet 1:14) but are "redeemed from the empty way of life that was [their] heritage" (1 Pet 1:18). They have given up their former "acts of immorality and lust, drunken orgies, feasts, revelries and lawless acts of idolatry" (1 Pet 4:3; *see* Idolatry; Law; Purity). Through Jesus Christ they have come to faith and hope* in the one true God, the God of Israel* (1 Pet 1:21). Christian salvation* is theirs, but they lack a past and a sense of identity. The letter confers on them a Jewish past and a quasi-Jewish identity by claiming that certain titles of privilege once given to Israel are now theirs as well. They are "a chosen race, the king's priesthood, a holy nation, a people destined for vindication" (1 Pet 2:9a; cf. Ex 19:6; Is 43:20-21; *see* Priest).

Just as in ancient Israel, such privileges carry corresponding responsibilities. Like the Jews, these Gentile Christians are a *diaspora,** a chosen people scattered and living as strangers in a hostile world* (1 Pet 1:1). Their task is to "be holy in all [their] conduct" (*anastrophē,* 1 Pet 1:15) and in this way to "sound the praises of him who called [them] out of darkness to his marvelous light" (1 Pet 2:9b; *see* Light). The society they live in is hostile, but Roman magistrates are fair (1 Pet 2:13-17; *see* Civil Authority). Their responsibility is to "show respect for everyone and love for the brotherhood, reverence toward God and respect for the emperor" (1 Pet 2:17; *see* Emperor). This will not keep them from being accused of wrongdoing (1 Pet 2:12; 3:15-16; 4:15-16), but the hope is that when they are, their accusers will either be "put to shame" (1 Pet 3:16) or will, "from observing your good works, glorify God on the day of visitation" (1 Pet 2:12).

The readers' life situation is not a local or specific one but rests on the author's generalization about the situation of Christians in Roman society at the time the letter was written. In the author's mind his readers represent all Christian believers everywhere. For this reason the classification of 1 Peter as one of the catholic or general letters is an appropriate one.

2. Integrity and Literary Structure.
2.1. Integrity. Efforts to call into question the

literary integrity of 1 Peter have been largely rejected in recent years. Arguments that part of the letter (1 Pet 1:3—4:11) was originally a baptismal* sermon for new converts or even a full baptismal liturgy (*see* Liturgical Elements; Worship), common in an earlier generation (e.g., Windisch, Preisker, Cross), are seldom made today. Nor has C. F. D. Moule's suggestion of a break between 1 Peter 4:11 and 1 Peter 4:12 found much recent support. Moule argued that persecution, a rather remote possibility in 1 Peter 1:3—4:11, becomes an urgent matter in 1 Peter 4:12—5:11. Either the author received sudden news of a wave of persecution or deliberately planned two letters, one for congregations faced with social pressures but not outright persecution (1 Pet 1:1—4:11; 5:12-14) and a shorter, more urgent one for congregations already suffering the "fiery trial" (1 Pet 1:1—2:10; 4:12—5:14). All such theories are speculative and without support in ancient manuscripts.

2.2. Literary Structure. There is a discernible break in structure between 1 Peter 4:11 and 12, even though it does not call the letter's integrity into question. The break is marked by the direct address "Beloved" (NRSV) or "Dear friends" (NIV; *agapētoi*) in 1 Peter 4:12. The same personal address marks a similar break at 1 Peter 2:11. The two appeals divide the letter into three main parts (followed by a postscript): 1 Peter 1:1—2:10; 1 Peter 2:11—4:11; 1 Peter 4:12—5:11.

The first part centers on the implied readers' identity as people of God, based on their spiritual rebirth (1 Pet 1:3, 22-23; 2:2-3) and consequent hope of salvation (1 Pet 1:5, 9-10; 2:3). Peter announces their identity programmatically in 1 Peter 1:1-2 and confirms it in 1 Peter 2:9-10, framing the whole section. Within this framework he interweaves a recital of what God has done and will do (1 Pet 1:3-12, 18-21, 2:4-8) with a reminder of their responsibility to live in hope as a holy* people (1 Pet 1:13-16), in reverent fear* of the God who saved them at infinite cost (1 Pet 1:17-19), with love* for each other and a desire for God (1 Pet 1:22; 2:1-3).

The second section is an appeal to the implied readers (1 Pet 2:11) focusing on their responsibility to show reverence toward God, love for one another and honor and respect for everyone, starting with the emperor (1 Pet 2:13-

17). Peter urges peace* and respect specifically toward those who denounce their Christian faith and accuse them of wrongdoing (1 Pet 2:12; 3:16). He envisions social conflict in the setting of the Roman household,* among Christian slaves owned by non-Christian masters (1 Pet 2:18-25) and Christian wives married to unbelieving husbands (1 Pet 3:1-6; *see* Marriage). His so-called household duty codes (unlike those in Col 3:18—4:1; Eph 5:21—6:9; *see* Household Codes) are oriented more to relationships of Christians with unbelievers (even in the same household) than with one another and stand at the heart of the letter's ethical* demands. Christians are called to do good in the face of slander and threats (1 Pet 3:8-9), just as Christ did (1 Pet 2:22-23), with full assurance that God will vindicate them (1 Pet 3:16-17; 4:5-6) as he vindicated Christ in the resurrection* and victorious journey to heaven* (3:18-22). Peter then accents the responsibility of Christians toward God and one another by urging mutual love, ministry* and hospitality* within the believing community and concludes with a doxology (1 Pet 4:7-11).

The third section reiterates the themes of the second, with particular attention to congregations ruled by the older members, or "elders." The address in 1 Peter 4:12 ("dear friends") anticipates 1 Peter 5:1, "To any elders among you I appeal" (cf. 1 Pet 2:11, "Dear friends, I appeal"). Peter's intent is to develop further the admonitions he began in 1 Peter 4:7-11 by spelling out more fully the mutual responsibilities of older and younger members of the congregations (at least those congregations that operated with such a distinction). But he digresses (1 Pet 4:12-19) in order to highlight again and with greater urgency the themes of the previous section in light of his stated conviction that "the end of all things is near" (1 Pet 4:7). Peter sees a "fiery ordeal" (1 Pet 4:12) breaking out and divine judgment* beginning "from the house of God" (1 Pet 4:17). With Ezekiel he interprets this to mean that the judgment begins "from the elders" among the people (cf. Ezek 9:6). Therefore he starts with elders and their responsibilities (1 Pet 5:1-4) and moves on to the younger persons and thus to everyone in the congregations (1 Pet 5:5) in relation to the coming crisis (1 Pet 5:6-9). Again he concludes with a doxology (1 Pet 5:10-11).

Rhetorically 1 Peter is best described as an appeal, or persuasive discourse (*see* Rhetoric). In his postscript (1 Pet 5:12-14) Peter seems to describe the letter as a combination of appeal and testimony (*parakalōn kai epimartyrōn,* 1 Pet 5:12), but the two terms are not to be separated. Peter's "testimony" here is not so much the announcement of salvation that underlies his appeal (e.g., in 1 Pet 1:3-12) as the conclusion to the appeal itself. Specifically it is Peter's solemn assurance that the letter he has just written is "true grace from God" (1 Pet 5:12). The letter is his own demonstration of the principle that Christians should use their respective spiritual gifts in ministry to one another, "faithfully administering God's grace in its various forms" (1 Pet 4:10, NIV).

3. Historical and Social Situation.

For the past two hundred years biblical scholarship has tried to determine the precise historical situation out of which or to which individual books of the Bible were written. For the past twenty years or so, equal or greater attention has been given to the social situation or social world of biblical writings.

The difference between the two enterprises, at the simplest level, is that historical investigation deals with what is unique, datable and historically and geographically fixed about the life setting *(Sitz im Leben)* of these ancient works, while social scientific theory looks at factors that are not unique but closely paralleled in other times, places and different—sometimes very different—cultures. In the past social scientific study was done under the broad canopy of historical study but the recent trend has been to separate the two, especially when historical investigation by itself proved inconclusive. In the case of 1 Peter the two disciplines are interrelated but not quite interchangeable.

3.1. Historical Setting. It has become commonplace to define the life setting of 1 Peter as one of suffering or persecution. This has tended to locate the letter historically in a time of known persecution* in the Roman Empire, either under Nero (c. A.D. 64) on the assumption that Peter is the real author (Selwyn) or under Trajan in the early second century on the assumption that the letter is pseudonymous (Beare). A third option, that it was written in Domitian's time (between A.D. 81 and 96) is less common, possibly because the evidence for persecution during that period is weak. But does the letter presuppose a situation of outright persecution? Peter's attitude toward the Roman Empire seems similar to Paul's: "Defer to every human creature for the sake of the Lord, whether to the emperor as sovereign or to magistrates as those sent by him to punish wrongdoers and commend those who do good deeds" (1 Pet 2:13). If anything he is clearer and more explicit than Paul, who spoke vaguely of "governing authorities" or "those authorities that exist" (Rom 13:1, NRSV). It is difficult to imagine either Paul or Peter writing such words in a time of systematic persecution of Christians.

Yet Peter does refer to "various trials" or ordeals, of faith being "tested by fire" (1 Pet 1:6-7), even of "the fiery ordeal that is taking place among you to test you" (1 Pet 4:12, NRSV). At least some of his rhetoric is the rhetoric of persecution and martyrdom. Christ is the supreme example for Christians precisely as a vindicated martyr, the One who was "put to death in the flesh but made alive in the Spirit" (1 Pet. 3:18; cf. 2:21-24; 4:1-2).

Undeniably Peter saw himself and his readers in danger but not from the emperor or provincial governors, whose legitimate task it was "to punish those who do wrong and to praise those who do right" (1 Pet 2:14, NRSV). The threat he saw was from fellow citizens in Rome (and, Peter assumes, in the provinces) who did not share the implied readers' Christian faith and who consequently rejected their distinctive worship* and lifestyle. Peter urges, therefore, "that by doing right you should silence the ignorance of the foolish" (1 Pet 2:15, NRSV). The persecution in view is the kind carried out not with fire or sword but with words—words of ridicule, slander and sometimes formal accusations of crimes against society (see 1 Pet 2:12; 3:13-17; 4:14-16).

Such persecution is difficult to locate either chronologically or geographically. It could fit almost any time and place in the Mediterranean world in the late first or early second century. The uncomfortable fact is that we know little or nothing of the historical setting of 1 Peter. It is possible that when Peter says the "time for judgment to begin from the house of God" has come (1 Pet 4:17), he has in mind the destruction* of Jerusalem* and the Jewish temple* in A.D. 70 by the Romans ("Babylon," 1 Pet 5:13) and sees this event as heralding danger for all who worship the God of Israel, Christians as well as Jews.

But there is no proof of this. Without clearer points of reference we cannot use contemporary history to illumine the text of 1 Peter.

3.2. Social Setting. Since the 1970s studies of 1 Peter (e.g., Goppelt, Elliott and Balch) have centered more on its social than its historical setting. Whatever its precise historical context, the letter speaks to a situation in which the implied readers are visualized as outsiders in the Roman Empire. Peter writes from a Christian community in "Babylon" (1 Pet 5:13), in Jewish tradition the place of exile and alienation, to Christians who are similarly in exile, a "diaspora" (1 Pet 1:1) scattered as strangers throughout the Roman provinces. For author and implied readers alike, dramatic differences separate their values from those of the societies in which they live.

The works of J. H. Elliott and D. Balch uncovered a tension in 1 Peter between "acculturation" (i.e., conforming where possible to dominant values) and "boundary maintenance" (i.e., the preservation of Christian distinctives in a hostile society). As one observer put it, the letter has two goals at once: "(1) the social cohesion of the Christian groups, and (2) the social adaptation of the Christian groups to their cultural setting. Without the first, Christian identity would have been lost. Without the second, Christians would have had no social acceptability, which is also necessary for survival and outreach" (Talbert, 148).

Christians did have some values in common with the culture of the Mediterranean world, notably the contrasting social realities of honor and shame. Virtually all recent studies of the social world of the NT deal in some way with honor and shame, and in no book of the NT is the contrast highlighted more than in 1 Peter. Both to those addressed in the letter and to their enemies in Roman society, honor was a desirable goal, perhaps the supreme goal in life, while shame was something to be avoided at almost any cost. The radical difference between Christians and their contemporaries lay in what constituted honor and what constituted shame.

Honor to the Romans involved the praise* and esteem of fellow citizens, usually with some kind of public recognition of their good deeds either within the household or on behalf of the larger community. Individual deeds of honor brought honor to the family, the state, the emperor and the gods. Shame was the result of antisocial behavior that tended to undermine or discredit these same institutions and consequently to disgrace in the eyes of the community those guilty of such behavior.

According to 1 Peter, honor and shame are determined not by public opinion, the emperor or the Roman gods but solely by the God of Israel, who is Father of those who believe in Jesus and the universal Judge to whom all are accountable (1 Pet 1:17; 4:5). Not their acts of public service but their loyalty to God and faithful endurance of "various trials" are what Christians will exchange for "praise, glory and honor" at the future "revelation of Jesus Christ" (1 Pet 1:6-7; *see* Revelation). Jesus was slain as God's "faultless and flawless lamb," but God "raised him from the dead and gave him glory" (1 Pet 1:19, 21; *see* Lamb). Drawing on biblical language (Is 28:16), Peter compares Jesus to "a choice and precious stone, a cornerstone in Zion" and announces that "the person who believes in him will never be put to shame" (1 Pet 2:6). This honor (of never being put to shame) belongs to Christians (1 Pet 2:7), while to unbelievers Christ becomes "a stone for stumbling and a rock to trip over"—a fate to which they were "appointed" (1 Pet 2:8). The dualism of such texts is absolute: Christians are destined for honor and non-Christians for eternal shame.

Yet Peter's values also overlap those of the wider society, for he is willing at times to measure honor and shame by a person's responsibilities to family, the wider community and the state, as well as to God and fellow believers: "Honor everyone," he writes, "love the brotherhood, fear God, honor the emperor" (1 Pet 2:17).

Peter urges his readers to answer the slanderous words of their detractors with kind words and good conduct, "so that in a case [*en hō*] where they accuse you of doing wrong they may, from observing your good works, glorify God on the day of visitation" (1 Pet 2:12). His goal is not to undermine the social world in which his readers live but to win it over—or at least to win converts from it who will honor the Christian God and receive in return the honor that only God can give. Peter knows this will not always happen. He writes at times as if he suspects it may never happen. But regardless of the outcome, Christians must "always be ready to answer anyone who demands from you an accounting of the hope that is yours . . . out of humility and reverence, with a good conscience, so that in a case [*en hō*] where you are accused, those who denounce your good conduct in Christ may be put to shame" (1 Pet 3:15-16).

These imagined cases, or occasions when Christians are charged with wrongdoing or antisocial behavior, are for Peter the decisive tests of honor or shame respectively, whether for the accused Christians themselves or their accusers. "Let none of you suffer as a murderer or a thief," he concludes, "or any kind of criminal, or even as a busybody. But if you suffer for being a Christian, do not be ashamed, but glorify God in such a case" (1 Pet 4:15-16, where the text followed by the KJV is to be preferred). To be accused of criminal acts, as Christians occasionally were, or to be slandered as "busybodies" (self-appointed guardians of public morality), as they often were (and still are), is no reason for shame, according to Peter. Shame is appropriate only when such charges are true.

Honor in 1 Peter is the reward* not of suffering as a virtue in itself but of suffering for doing good. Peter is not encouraging either paranoia or masochism. Make sure, he says, that when you are denounced or accused it is not because you are guilty of wrongdoing or antisocial behavior but solely because of your Christian faith. The Roman ideal of honor and good citizenship is transcended and relativized but not negated. Christians are a counterculture in Roman society, sharing the commitments of other Romans and provincials to the household and the state as long as these commitments do not entail worship of the Roman gods (*see* Religions).

At the time of writing, the author is confident of his readers' conduct. While martyrdom is not out of the question (1 Pet 4:6; 5:8-9), neither is it a major theme of the letter. "Babylon" is still the place of exile, not the throne of Satan* or the antichrist,* as in the Book of Revelation. The stark dualism of 1 Peter is qualified by the realities of life in what we would call a pluralistic society. For Western Christians at the close of the twentieth century, this brief tract written within a culture not yet Christian becomes a relevant textbook on Christian living in a culture no longer Christian.

4. Theological Contributions to the Canon.
1 Peter's place in the NT canon has been a

humble one, given Peter's prominence as the rock on which the church would be built (Mt 16:18-19) and the shepherd whose responsibility it was to feed Christ's sheep (Jn 21:15-17). This could be because of the letter's brevity, or because Peter has only two NT letters bearing his name while Paul has twelve, or because 1 Peter has long been yoked with 2 Peter, whose authenticity was disputed from the start. Or perhaps the author's self-deprecating attitude toward his own identity as "Peter" (see 1.1 above) had a lasting influence on how his letter was read. For whatever reason, when Christians spoke of "the apostle" (especially in connection with the canon) in the early centuries, they almost always meant Paul, not Peter.

Yet 1 Peter strikes a more even balance than Paul between the teaching* and example of Jesus on the one hand and his death and resurrection on the other. More than any other NT letter, 1 Peter completes or extends the testimony of the four Gospels, especially Mark. It does so in three respects: first, it gives the reader a sense of living in a world where Jesus is no longer or not yet visible; second, it accents Christian discipleship as a journey in Jesus' footsteps to the cross and beyond the cross to heaven; finally, the victory over "unclean spirits" (see Spirits) that began in Jesus' ministry continues in 1 Peter in his resurrection and ascension,* assuring his disciples of vindication against their oppressors when he becomes visible once again.

4.1. The Hidden Christ. The "living hope" of Christians (1 Pet 1:3) is not the "coming" (parousia)* of Jesus, but rather his revelation or apocalypse* (apokalypsis; see 1 Pet 1:7, 13). When he is revealed "salvation" (1 Pet 1:5, 9) and "glory" (1 Pet 4:13) will be revealed as well. Jesus appeared or was made visible in the world once and will be again (phanerōthentos, 1 Pet 1:20, 5:4).

These are clearly apocalyptic themes in that they deal with a decisive apocalypse or revelation. Yet 1 Peter is not an apocalyptic letter like the book of Revelation. It never calls itself an apocalypse, as the Revelation does (Rev 1:1), nor does it claim that Peter, like Paul (Gal 1:12), received a direct revelation from Jesus Christ (contrast 2 Pet 1:16-18). The decisive revelation or apocalypse is future. The only other revelation mentioned was a sort of nonrevelation to the ancient prophets, telling them that their prophecies of Christ were not for themselves or their own time but for a distant future that to Peter and his readers is present (1 Pet 1:10-12). 1 Peter is not so much an apocalytic as a preapocalyptic letter. Christians cannot see Jesus now (1 Pet 1:8), but they stand on the threshold of a great apocalypse in which they will see him in all his glory and joyfully embrace the salvation he holds in store for them.

4.2. Discipleship as a Journey. One might conclude from this that the revelation of Jesus Christ and of full salvation is something for which Christians simply wait. Peter's reference to "an indestructible, incorruptible and unfading inheritance reserved in heaven for you" (1 Pet 1:4) is open to such an interpretation. But this is not the case. Salvation is not something that comes to us but something standing at "the end" of an active life of faithfulness (1 Pet 1:9) and toward which we "grow" (1 Pet 2:2). Jesus is viewed not as one who comes to us but as one toward whom we are coming (1 Pet 2:4), first in conversion and then in a lifelong process of being "built into a spiritual house for holy priesthood" (1 Pet 2:5; see House). Peter's favorite metaphor for this process is that of the journey, or "following in Jesus' footsteps" (1 Pet 2:21).

This is the metaphor of the Gospel writers, above all Mark (see Mk 1:16-20; 8:34), and presumably of Jesus himself. Paul preferred for the most part the nonmetaphorical notion of faith, or believing. Although it can be plausibly argued that Paul himself understood faith as the equivalent of following Jesus' example of faithfulness, it remained for 1 Peter to bring together Paul's notion of faith and the command of Jesus in the Gospels to follow him as disciples. Whatever "faith" means in Paul, in 1 Peter it includes faithfulness (see 1 Pet 1:5, 7, 9), and faithfulness means following Jesus on a journey to the cross—and beyond (1 Pet 2:21-25).

Already in Mark there is a hint that the journey extends beyond the cross. If it were only a journey to the cross it would be a failure, for the disciples deserted Jesus at his arrest (Mk 14:50). Yet when Jesus predicted their desertion (Mk 14:27), he added, "But after I am raised up, I will go before you [that is, lead you as a shepherd] into Galilee" (Mk 14:28). Ironically it was Peter who protested, "Even though all become deserters, I will not" (Mk 14:29), and it is Peter who seems to allude to the incident: "For you were going astray like sheep, but you have turned now to the Shepherd and Guardian of your souls" (1 Pet 2:25).

The situation of the implied readers corresponds to that of Peter and the original disciples. The journey of Jesus in 1 Peter reaches beyond the cross, beyond Galilee, to heaven itself. As the next chapter makes clear, Jesus not only was "put to death in the flesh" and "made alive in the Spirit" (1 Pet 3:18) but also has "gone to heaven, with angels and authorities and powers in submission to him" (1 Pet 3:22). Consequently the journey of Christian disciples is a journey to heaven as well, like the Christian pilgrimage in the letter to the Hebrews* (e.g., Heb 11:10, 16; 12:22; 13:14) or the journey of Christian in John Bunyan's *The Pilgrim's Progress*. The goal of Jesus' faithful followers is nothing less than God's "marvelous light" (1 Pet 2:9) or "eternal glory" (1 Pet 5:10).

1 Peter is not alone in the NT in accenting the truth that a believer's "whole life" (*anastrophē;* see 1 Pet 1:15, 17; 2:12; 3:1-2, 16) is a journey to heaven in the footsteps of Jesus. Yet its testimony stands as a serious caution against three popular misconceptions: that salvation is merely something that happened to Christian believers in the past, that their only responsibility now is to wait passively for the Second Coming and that "going to heaven" is something that begins when they die.

4.3. Victory over Evil Spirits. At one other point 1 Peter extends the Markan testimony to Jesus beyond Jesus' ministry on earth and into the time and circumstances of its implied readers. Mark's Gospel pays special attention to incidents in which Jesus drove "unclean spirits" out of those who were demon-possessed (see Mk 1:23-28, 32-34; 3:11-12; 5:1-20; 7:24-30; 9:14-29). Although several of these stories are repeated in Matthew and Luke, exorcism has no place among the gifts and ministries mentioned by Paul in his letters and plays only a minor role in narratives of the early Christian mission* (see Acts 16:16-18, 19:11-16).

Only 1 Peter develops the theme of victory over evil spirits in connection with Jesus' resurrection and ascension (1 Pet 3:18-22). On his way to heaven Jesus "made proclamation" to the spirits, described here as "disobedient spirits" and viewed as offspring of an unnatural union between women and evil angels (Gen 6:1-6; see

1 Enoch 15:8-10 and the discussions of Dalton and Michaels 1988). In doing so he gained victory over these spirits on behalf of his followers. The implication drawn in 1 Peter is not that those who have passed (like Noah) through water, the saving water of baptism (1 Pet 3:20), now have the power to perform exorcisms but that they have nothing to fear from human oppressors in Roman society who (like the spirits) are "disobedient" to God (see 1 Pet 2:8; 3:1; 4:17; *see* Obedience). Peter's triumphant message is that Jesus Christ reigns from heaven over all "angels and authorities and powers" (1 Pet 3:22).

4.4. Conclusion. These and other features of 1 Peter not only justify its inclusion in the NT canon but also suggest that its importance within the canon has been underrated. Despite its association with 2 Peter by virtue of common attribution of authorship, all it has in common with 2 Peter is a strong emphasis on the coming judgment of God. Its more significant function in the NT is as a link or a bridge between the Gospels and the letters of Paul.

First Peter itself seems to signal such a function with its terse references at the end to Paul's companion Silvanus and to "Mark, my son" (1 Pet 5:12-13). Mark was for centuries a neglected Gospel, and if we begin to think of 1 Peter as a sort of companion piece to Mark (in keeping with Papias's tradition about Mark as the inscribing of Peter's memoirs; Eusebius *Hist. Eccl.* 3.39.15), it is perhaps not surprising that this short letter has been neglected as well. The abundance of recent studies may indicate that this "exegetical step-child" (Elliott's term) within the canon is on its way to the rehabilitation it deserves.

See also Household Codes; Old Testament in General Epistles; 2 Peter.

Bibliography. **Commentaries:** P. J. Achtemeier, *1 Peter* (Herm; Minneapolis: Fortress, 1996); F. W. Beare, *The First Epistle of Peter* (3d ed.; Oxford: Blackwell, 1970); E. Best, *1 Peter* (NCB; Grand Rapids: Eerdmans, 1971); N. Brox, *Der erste Petrusbrief* (2d ed.; EKK; Zurich: Benziger, 1986); P. H. Davids, *The First Epistle of Peter* (NICNT; Grand Rapids: Eerdmans, 1990); L. Goppelt, *A Commentary on 1 Peter,* ed. F. Hahn (Grand Rapids: Eerdmans, 1993); F. J. A. Hort, *The First Epistle of St. Peter 1:1-2:17* (London: Macmillan, 1898); J. N. D. Kelly, *A Commentary on the Epistles of Peter and Jude* (HNTC; Harper

& Row, 1969); I. H. Marshall, *1 Peter* (IVPNTC; Downers Grove, IL: InterVarsity Press, 1991); J. R. Michaels, *1 Peter* (WBC; Waco, TX: Word, 1988); B. Reicke, *The Epistles of James, Peter and Jude* (AB; Garden City, NY: Doubleday, 1964); E. G. Selwyn, *The First Epistle of Peter* (2d ed.; London: Macmillan, 1947); D. Senior, *1 and 2 Peter* (NT Message 20; Wilmington, DE: Michael Glazier, 1980); H. Windisch and H. Preisker, *Die katholischen Briefe* (HNT; 3d ed.; Tübingen: J. C. B. Mohr, 1951). **Studies:** D. Balch, *Let Wives Be Submissive: The Domestic Code in 1 Peter* (SBLMS 26; Chico, CA: Scholars Press, 1981); A. Chester and R. P. Martin, *The Theology of the Letters of James, Peter and Jude* (Cambridge: Cambridge University Press, 1994); F. L. Cross, *1 Peter: A Paschal Liturgy* (London: Mowbray, 1954); W. J. Dalton, *Christ's Proclamation to the Spirits: A Study of 1 Peter 3:18-4:6* (2d ed.; Rome: Pontifical Biblical Institute, 1989); J. H. Elliott, *1 Peter: Estrangement and Community* (Chicago: Franciscan Herald, 1979); idem, *A Home for the Homeless: A Sociological Exegesis of 1 Peter, Its Situation and Strategy* (Philadelphia: Fortress, 1981); T. W. Martin, *Metaphor and Composition in 1 Peter* (SBLDS 131; Atlanta: Scholars Press, 1992); J. R. Michaels, *Word Biblical Themes: 1 Peter* (Dallas: Word, 1989); C. F. D. Moule, "The Nature and Purpose of 1 Peter," *NTS* 3 (1956-57) 1-11; W. L. Schutter, *Hermeneutic and Composition in 1 Peter* (WUNT; Tübingen: Mohr/Siebeck, 1989); C. H. Talbert, ed., *Perspectives on First Peter* (NABPRSS; Macon, GA: Mercer University Press, 1986); W. C. van Unnik, "The Teaching of Good Works in 1 Peter," *NTS* 1 (1954-55) 92-110; B. W. Winter, *Seek the Welfare of the City: Christians as Benefactors and Citizens* (Grand Rapids: Eerdmans, 1994). J. R. Michaels

2 PETER

Second Peter presents itself as a testament or farewell discourse of the apostle* Peter, written in the form of a letter* shortly before his death (2 Pet 1:14). Its object is to remind the readers of Peter's teaching* and to defend this teaching against objections raised by false teachers who were casting doubt on the Christian expectation of the Parousia* and advocating ethical* libertinism.

1. Literary Structure and Genre
2. Attribution to Peter and Date
3. Opponents and Response
4. Theological Character

1. Literary Structure and Genre.

The structure of 2 Peter can be analyzed as follows

(A = apologetic; E = exhortation/denunciation; L = letter; T = testament):

(L^1) Address and Greeting (2 Pet 1:1-2)

(T^1) Theme: A Summary of Peter's Message (2 Pet 1:3-11)

(T^2) Occasion: Peter's Testament (2 Pet 1:12-16)

(A^1) First Apologetic Section (2 Pet 1:16-21)
Two replies to Objection 1: that the apostles based their preaching of the Parousia on human-made myths (2 Pet 1:16-19)
Reply to Objection 2: that OT prophecies were the products of human minds (2 Pet 1:20-21)

(T^3) Peter's Prediction of False Teachers (2 Pet 2:1-3a)

(A^2) Second Apologetic Section (2 Pet 2:3b-10a)
Reply to Objection 3: that divine judgment never happens (2 Pet 2:3b-10a)

(E^1) Denunciation of the False Teachers (2 Pet 2:10b-22)

(T^4) Peter's Prediction of Scoffers (2 Pet 3:1-4) (including Objection 4: 2 Pet 3:4)

(A^3) Third Apologetic Section (2 Pet 3:5-10)
Two replies to Objection 4: that the expectation of the Parousia is disproved by its delay (2 Pet 3:5-10)

(E^2) Exhortation to Holy Living (2 Pet 3:11-16)

(L^2) Conclusion (2 Pet 3:17-18)

Second Peter is clearly a letter, since it has a formal letter opening (2 Pet 1:1-2), and the conclusion (2 Pet 3:17-18), while not specifically epistolary in character, can function as a letter closing. Moreover, 2 Peter seems to be addressed to those churches or some of those churches to which 1 Peter* had been addressed (2 Pet 3:1). As well as being a letter, 2 Peter belongs to the literary genre of testament, well known in the Jewish literature of the period (e.g., *T. Mos.; 1 Enoch* 91-104; *2 Bar* 57-86; *4 Ezra* 14:28-36). In such testaments an OT figure, such as Moses* or Ezra, knowing that his death is approaching, gives a final message to his people, which typically includes ethical exhortation and prophetic revelations of the future. In 2 Peter four passages (marked T^1-T^4 in the analysis above [2 Pet 1:3-11, 12-16; 2:1-3a; 3:1-4]) particularly resemble the Jewish testament literature and clearly identify the work as Peter's testament. In 2 Peter 1:12-15, a passage full of conventional testament language, Peter describes the occasion for writing as his awareness of approaching death and his desire to provide for his teaching to be remembered after his death. The teaching is summarized in 2 Peter 1:3-11, which is a miniature homily, following a pattern used in farewell speeches. It plays a key role in the book as a definitive summary of Peter's ethical and religious instruction. There are also two passages of prophecy* (2 Pet 2:1-3a; 3:1-4) in which Peter foresees that after his death his message will be challenged by false teachers.

The rest of 2 Peter is structured around the four passages that belong to the testament genre. It includes three apologetic sections (marked A^1-A^3 [2 Pet 1:16-21; 2:3b-10a; 3:5-10]) whose aim is to answer the objections the false teachers raise against Peter's teaching. There are four such objections, only the last of which is explicitly stated as such (2 Pet 3:4). In the other three cases the objection is implied in the author's denial of it (2 Pet 1:16a, 20; 2:3b). These apologetic sections give 2 Peter its polemical character as not simply a testamentary statement of Peter's message but also a defense of it against objections. Two passages (marked E^1, E^2 [2 Pet 2:10b-22; 3:11-16]) contrast the libertine behavior of the false teachers, denounced in 2 Peter 2:10b-22, with the holy* living expected of the readers if they are faithful to Peter's teaching (2 Pet 3:11-16).

2. Attribution to Peter and Date.

The problem of the authorship of 2 Peter arises in part out of the form and structure. In the Jewish literature of this period, testaments were pseudepigraphal.* They were attributed to OT figures long dead and were probably understood as exercises in historical imagination, putting into the mouth of these figures the kind of thing they might have been expected to say in farewell speeches. This establishes an initial presumption that 2 Peter is likewise a work written in Peter's name by someone else after his death, though it remains possible that the testament genre could have been used by Peter to write his own, real testament.

But it should be noted how the predictive character of the testament genre is used in 2 Peter. Nothing in the letter reflects the situation in which Peter is said to be writing; the work is addressed to a situation after Peter's death. Peter's two predictions of false teachers (2 Pet 2:1-3a; 3:1-4) function as pegs on which is hung the apologetic debate with these false teachers about the validity of Peter's message.

Moreover, whereas the testamentary passages speak of the false teachers in the future tense, predicting their rise after Peter's death (2 Pet 2:1-3a; 3:1-4; cf. 3:17), the apologetic sections and the denunciation of the false teachers refer to them in the present tense (2 Pet 2:3b-22; 3:5-10, 16b). It is hardly possible to read 2 Peter without supposing the false teachers to be contemporaries of the author with whom he is already in debate. The alternation of predictive and present-tense references to them (most obvious in 2 Pet 3:1-10, 16b-17) is therefore best understood as a deliberate stylistic device by which the author conveys that these apostolic prophecies are now being fulfilled. In other words, Petrine authorship is a fiction that the real author does not feel obliged to maintain throughout his work. In that case it must be a transparent fiction, a literary convention that the author expected his readers to recognize as such. (That the author inadvertently slips into the present tense, forgetting that he is meant to be referring the false teachers from Peter's perspective in the past, is not plausible, because 2 Peter is a carefully composed work, and the alternation of future-tense and present-tense references to the false teachers follows a structural pattern.)

These considerations of literary genre are probably the most important elements in the scholarly consensus that 2 Peter is pseudepigraphal, from which only a few recent discussions of the work still dissent. The most cogent additional reasons for denying Peter's authorship are the Hellenistic religious language and ideas and the evidence for dating the work after Peter's death in the mid-60s (see below). While the use of Hellenistic religious language and ideas by a Palestinian Jew should no longer be regarded as incredible, nevertheless the use of Hellenistic religious terminology is a particularly striking feature of 2 Peter and is more easily attributed to a Christian of Diaspora* Jewish or Gentile origin. However, since Peter could have employed a collaborator in writing the letter, this argument cannot be decisive. The dating of the work is probably more significant for the question of authenticity.

It has been common to regard 2 Peter as the latest of the NT writings, to be dated well into the second century, even as late as 150. But there is no good reason to postulate such a late date. The clearest evidence of a postapostolic date is 2 Peter 3:4, which indicates, in the context of raising the problem of the delay of the Parousia, that the first Christian generation (here called "the fathers") has died. The probability is that the letter was written when this had only recently become true, c. A.D. 80-90. This was the time when those who had expected the Parousia during the lifetime of the generation of the apostles would face the problem of the nonfulfillment of that expectation. There is no evidence that this particular issue continued to be felt as a problem in the second century (though John 21 may hint at the problem).

The literary relationship between 2 Peter and Jude* is another consideration that could be relevant to the date of 2 Peter. There are such close resemblances (especially between Jude 4-13, 16-18 and 2 Pet 2:1-18; 3:1-3) that some kind of literary relationship seems certain. Some scholars have held that Jude is dependent on 2 Peter or that both depend on a common source, but most conclude that 2 Peter has used Jude as a source. However, this requires a late date for 2 Peter only if Jude is dated late.

If 2 Peter was written not by Peter but after Peter's death, why did the real author present the work as Peter's testament? Probably because his intention was to defend the apostolic message in the period after the death of the apostles (2 Pet 3:4) against teachers who held that in important respects the teaching of the apostles was discredited. Whereas they were claiming to correct the apostles' teaching, the author of 2 Peter regards it as normative for the postapostolic church. By writing in Peter's name he claims no authority* of his own except as a faithful mediator of the apostolic message, which he defends against attacks. The form of the letter as an apostolic testament is therefore closely connected with its apologetic purpose as a vindication of the normative authority of the apostolic teaching. That the author chose to write Peter's testament is probably best explained if he was a leader in the Roman church (*see* Rome), which had counted Peter as the most prestigious of its leaders in the previous generation.

3. Opponents and Response.

The false teachers whom the letter opposes have usually been identified as Gnostics,* but this identification, as recent scholarship has recognized, is insecure. The only features of their teaching that are clear from the author's refutation of it are eschatological* skepticism and moral libertinism. The Parousia had been expected during the lifetime of the apostles, but the first generation of Christians had passed away and in the opponents' view this proved the primitive Christian eschatological hope* to have been mistaken (2 Pet 3:4, 9a). There would be no eschatological judgment* (2 Pet 2:3b), no divine intervention to eliminate evil and to establish a world* of righteousness.* This attitude seems to have been based on a rationalistic denial of divine intervention in history (2 Pet 3:4b), as well as on the nonfulfillment of the Parousia prophecy. But it also related to the ethical libertinism of the opponents. They claimed to be emancipating people from the fear* of divine judgment and therefore from conventional Christian morality (2 Pet 2:19a). Evidently they felt free to indulge in sexual immorality (*see* Purity) and sensual excesses generally (2 Pet 2:2, 10a, 13-14, 18).

This teaching involved a critique of the traditional teaching inherited from the apostles. The opponents claimed that the apostles had invented the idea of the Parousia (2 Pet 1:16a) and denied the inspiration of the eschatological prophecies of the OT (2 Pet 1:20-21a). Either they appealed to Pauline teaching about freedom* in support of their libertine views or they considered that Paul's expectation of the imminent Parousia discredited his teaching. The claim that they distort what Paul wrote (2 Pet 3:16b) could be taken in either of these senses.

There is no basis in 2 Peter itself for supposing that these teachings had a gnostic basis. There is no indication, for example, of the dualism that is a defining characteristic of gnostic thought. The views of the opponents are more plausibly understood as reflecting popular pagan attitudes and deploying pagan skeptical arguments (such as were used by the Epicureans) about eschatology and revelation.* The opponents probably aimed to disencumber Christianity of elements that seemed to them an embarrassment in their pagan cultural context: its cosmic eschatology, alien to most Hellenistic thinking and especially embarrassing after the apparent failure of the Parousia hope, and its ethical rigorism, which contrasted with more permissive attitudes in the cultural context.

In response to this challenge, the author of 2 Peter mounts a defense of the apostolic expectation of judgment and salvation* at the Parousia and of the motivation for righteous living this provides. His definitive summary of Peter's teaching (2 Pet 1:3-11) stresses the need for moral effort if eschatological salvation is to be assured. This positive statement is then backed up by apologetic arguments in the rest of the letter.

The author argues that the apostles' preaching of the Parousia was soundly based on their witnessing of the transfiguration of Jesus, when God* appointed Jesus to be the eschatological judge and ruler (2 Pet 1:16-18), and on the divinely inspired prophecies of the OT (2 Pet 1:19-21). OT examples prove that divine judgment does happen and prefigure the eschatological judgment (2 Pet 2:3b-10a). As God decreed the destruction (see Wrath) of the ancient world in the flood, so he has decreed the destruction of the present world in the fire of his eschatological judgment (2 Pet 3:5-7, 10). The problem of the delay of the Parousia is met by traditional arguments drawn from Jewish tradition: that the delay is long only by human standards, not in the perspective of God's eternity,* and should be seen as God's gracious withholding of judgment so that sinners may repent (2 Pet 3:8-9; see Repentance; Sin). Such arguments enable the author, at a time when the hope of the Parousia had become problematic, not to let it fade by postponing it indefinitely but vigorously to reassert the traditional Christian hope and its relevance. Throughout 2 Peter the author is concerned that the hope for the vindication and establishment of God's righteousness in the future (2 Pet 2:9; 3:7, 13) necessarily motivates the attempt to realize that righteousness in Christian lives (2 Pet 3:11, 14).

4. Theological Character.

The distinctive theological character of 2 Peter is found in its remarkable combination of Hellenistic religious language and Jewish eschatological ideas and imagery. On the one hand, for example, the author summarizes Peter's teaching in a passage that in its religious and ethical terminology is perhaps the most typically Hellenistic in the whole NT (2 Pet 1:3-11). This can be seen both in the ethical terms drawn from Hellenistic moral philosophy (2 Pet 1:5-7; see Virtues and Vices) and in the promise* of escaping corruption and sharing divine nature (2 Pet 1:4). Such Hellenistic terminology is carefully situated in a context that gives it Christian meaning (e.g., the list of virtues* in 2 Peter 1:5-7 is given Christian definition by its first and last items: faith* and love*) but seems nevertheless a striking and deliberate attempt to make contact with the Hellenistic religious environment. On the other hand, 2 Peter accurately and effectively reproduces the concepts and imagery of Jewish cosmic eschatology, especially in 2 Peter 3:3-13, which may be drawing directly on a Jewish apocalypse.*

This combination of two different theological styles can be explained by the author's intention of both interpreting and defending the apostolic message in a postapostolic period and a pagan cultural context. When he states the Christian message positively (2 Pet 1:3-11) he does so in terms that make contact with the ideals and aspirations of contemporary pagan culture. He is engaged in the task of translating the gospel* into terms intelligible in a new cultural environment. But this is a delicate task that requires care lest the real Christian content of the gospel be lost. In the author's view that was happening in his opponents' version of Christianity. In their attempt to adapt Christianity to Hellenistic culture they were compromising essential features of the apostolic message, advocating mere pagan skepticism about eschatology and mere acquiescence in moral permissiveness.

In order to defend the gospel against this excessive Hellenization, therefore, the author resorts to sources (including the letter of Jude) and ideas close to the eschatological outlook of early Jewish Christianity (see Jewish Christianity). He sees that if Hellenized Christianity is not to become paganized Christianity, cosmic eschatology—the hope for the triumph of God's righteousness in the whole of his creation*— has to be reasserted, along with the ethical motivation it provides. 2 Peter thus maintains a careful balance between a degree of Hellenization of the gospel message and a protest, in the name of cosmic eschatology, against an extreme Hellenization that would dissolve the real Christian substance of its message. It is a valuable witness to the church's difficult transition from a Jewish (albeit Hellenized) context to a predominantly non-Jewish Hellenistic environment and from the apostolic to the postapostolic age.

This understanding of the theological character of 2 Peter, it may be claimed, does better justice to its content than the tendency of older scholarship to assign it to the category of early catholicism,* a classification that has usually been at the same time a way of denigrating the book as a lapse from the theological standards of earlier (usually meaning Pauline) Christianity. This classification of 2 Peter requires attributing to it features of so-called early catholicism that cannot be found in the text—such as ecclesiological institutionalization and the crystallization of the faith into rigid formulae. It also fails to explain or to appreciate 2 Peter's deliberate and creative combination of Jewish eschatology and Hellenistic religious terminology.

See also ADVERSARIES; EARLY CATHOLICISM; JUDE; PAROUSIA; 1 PETER; PSEUDEPIGRAPHY.

BIBLIOGRAPHY. R. J. Bauckham, *Jude, 2 Peter* (WBC; Waco, TX: Word, 1983); idem, "2 Peter: An Account of Research," *ANRW* II.25.5 (1988) 3713-52; A. Chester and R. P. Martin, *The Theology of the Letters of James, Peter and Jude* (Cambridge: Cambridge University Press, 1994); T. Fornberg, *An Early Church in a Pluralistic Society* (ConNT; Lund: Gleerup, 1977); E. Fuchs and P. Reymond, *La Deuxième Epître de Saint Pierre; L'Epître de Saint Jude* (CNT; Paris: Delachaux & Niestlé, 1980); A. E. Harvey, "The Testament of Simeon Peter," in *A Tribute to Geza Vermes: Essays on Jewish and Christian Literature and History,* ed. P. R. Davies and R. T. White (JSOTSup 100; Sheffield: JSOT, 1990) 339-54; E. Käsemann, "An Apologia for Primitive Christian Eschatology," in *Essays on New Testament Themes* (London: SCM, 1964) 169-95; J. B. Mayor, *The Epistle of St. Jude and the Second Epistle of St. Peter* (London: Macmillan, 1907); D. G. Meade, *Pseudonymity and Canon* (WUNT; Tübingen: J. C. B. Mohr [Siebeck], 1986); J. H. Neyrey, *2 Peter, Jude* (AB; Garden City, NY: Doubleday, 1993); A. Vögtle, *Der Judasbrief; Der 2. Petrusbrief* (EKK; Solothurn: Benziger Verlag, 1994); D. F. Watson, *Invention, Arrangement and Style: Rhetorical Criticism of Jude and 2 Peter* (SBLDS 104; Atlanta: Scholars Press, 1988); A. Wolters, "'Partners of the Deity': A Covenantal Reading of 2 Peter 1:4," *CTJ* 25 (1990) 28-44.
R. J. Bauckham

PETER, GOSPEL OF

The *Gospel of Peter* is an apocryphal Christian writing from the mid-second century bearing the name of Peter, extant only as a fragmentary account of the trial, death, burial, resurrection* and appearances of Jesus (*see DJG,* Gospels [Apocryphal]).

1. Discovery and Identification
2. Narrative Perspective
3. The Question of Sources

1. Discovery and Identification.

Eusebius notes that Bishop Serapion of Antioch,* who flourished from c. 190, developed a concern regarding a *Gospel of Peter* because it had been used by some at the church in Rhossus to support docetic* ideas (*see* Canon). Brief mention is also made of a *Gospel of Peter* by Origen (Origen *Comm. Mt.* 10.17). No such book was known, however, until the end of the nineteenth century. In 1886-87 a French archaeological team excavating in a cemetery in Akhmîm (Egypt) found a small codex including a fragment of a work that begins in mid-sentence with an account of the trial of Jesus and ends in mid-sentence with Simon Peter and others at the sea where, presumably, it would be recorded that the risen Lord* appeared to them. Because of the spacing and ornamentation preceding and following the text, it appears that the scribe had access only to this excerpt.

Initial examination noted that Simon Peter speaks in the first person (*Gos. Pet.* 14.60; cf. 7.26) and drew attention to alleged docetic features, leading to the identification of this text with Serapion's *Gospel of Peter.* The Akhmîm fragment has been dated as early as the fifth century or as late as the ninth. Two small papyrus fragments from Oxyrhynchus (POxy 2949) provide a second witness to the manuscript tradition of the *Gospel of Peter* (*Gos. Pet.* 2.3-5), and these were written c. 200 (On the relation of these two witnesses see Treat.) A further papyrus (POxy 4009), also dated to the second or third century, may bear witness to a postresurrection scene similar to that in John 21, possibly witnessed in the *Gospel of Peter* following the point at which the Akhmîm fragment breaks off (Lührmann).

The Greek text is available (e.g., in Neirynck, 171-75; for photographs see von Gebhardt, I-X) and in recent English translation (e.g., in Brown, 2:1318-21).

2. Narrative Perspective.

Although one may observe points of contact between the extant material from the *Gospel of Peter* and what is said of earlier, now lost portions of the narrative (Brown, 2:1317-18 n. 4), it is impossible to reconstruct its story line and theological tendencies before the trial of Jesus. Certain themes are brought into the foreground by the extant text, however.

First, one finds a strong anti-Jewish sentiment. According to the *Gospel of Peter*, the Jews bear sole responsibility for the crucifixion of Jesus. The account begins with the Jews and Herod, their king, refusing to wash their hands, presumably after Pilate had done so (Mt 27:24); later Pilate proclaims, "I am clean of the blood of the Son of God," blaming the Jews for the execution of this just man (*Gos. Pet.* 11.46). It was Herod who handed "the Lord" over to death (*Gos. Pet.* 1.2). When Joseph, "friend of Pilate and the Lord" (*Gos. Pet.* 2.3; and not a faithful Jew, as in the canonical Gospels), requests the body of Jesus, Pilate must gain permission from Herod (*Gos. Pet.* 2.4-5). The Jews, the elders and the priests* mock and crucify Jesus (*Gos. Pet.* 3.6—7.25); following his death they recognize their wrongdoing and mourn because of the judgment* that would now befall them—namely, the fall of Jerusalem (*Gos. Pet.* 7.25). Even if the Jewish people are rehabilitated somewhat in their responses to the portents following the crucifixion (*Gos. Pet.* 7.25-26), the negative portrayal of the Jewish leaders, who fear the people more than God (*Gos. Pet.* 11.48), is relentless.

Is the *Gospel of Peter* docetic? That it can be read in this way is clear from Serapion's response (see 1 above). Certainly there are phrases that would be attractive to gnostic* Christians, including the narrator's statement upon Jesus' crucifixion, "He was silent, as if having no pain" (*Gos. Pet.* 4.10); in addition, the description of the moment of his death (*Gos. Pet.* 5.19) is susceptible to the interpretation that the divine element of Jesus left him prior to his suffering* and death.* Of course, canonical materials, including the Gospel of John and certain Pauline epistles, also were used by gnostic Christians.

The *Gospel of Peter* evidences a relatively high christology.* This is perhaps most recognizable when Jesus' body, taken from the cross and placed on the ground, causes an earthquake (*Gos. Pet.* 6.21), and when the body of the risen Lord stretches from the earth to the heavens, taller even than the angels* supporting him (*Gos. Pet.* 10.40). In addition Jesus is never referred to by personal name but usually by "Lord" or "Son of God"*; even "the Jews, elders and priests" recognize him as righteous* (*Gos. Pet.* 7.25), and those who guard his tomb, both soldiers and Jews, acknowledge him as God's Son (*Gos. Pet.* 10.38; 11.45; cf. 3.6-9).

Finally, not least in contrast with the canonical Gospels, the *Gospel of Peter* presents a fail-safe apologetic for the resurrection of the Lord (*Gos. Pet.* 8.31—11.49). Pilate provides a centurion and soldiers who together with the Jewish elders close off the tomb and seal it with seven seals, and they all stay through the night in order to safeguard the tomb. Moreover, they all witness the Lord's exit from the tomb in the company of two angels (unlike the canonical Gospels, which never describe the emergence from the tomb).

3. The Question of Sources.

From the beginning of scholarly study of the *Gospel of Peter*, opinions divided over the relationship between this apocryphal* writing and the canonical Gospels. J. A. Robinson has been joined by others, both in the decades following his publication of the text in 1892 and more recently, in holding that the *Gospel of Peter* depended on the NT Gospels (e.g., Brown, Green, Mara, Neirynck, Vaganay). A. von Harnack, however, insisted that the *Gospel of Peter* bore witness to a tradition independent of the canonical Gospels, and this view has found subsequent support and restatement (e.g., Crossan, Denker, Koester). A century after those first studies of the problem, the source-critical initiative appears in many circles to lie with the views of H. Koester, who argues that the *Gospel of Peter* was a very early form of the passion and resurrection accounts, or J. D. Crossan, who insists that the *Gospel of Peter* contains within it a very early, precanonical account (the "Cross Gospel").

This view is problematic for two reasons. First, the modern reaffirmation of the independence of the *Gospel of Peter* is assumed or asserted more than argued by its proponents; in particular Crossan's work suffers from his failure to provide any detailed analysis of the text of the apocryphal Gospel that would lead to the conclusion of its early and independent origins (see Brown, Green, Kirk). Second, the views of both Crossan and Koester depend on an unsupported theory—in Koester's words, "The details and individual scenes of the narrative do not rest on historical memory, but were developed on the basis of allegorical interpretation of Scripture" (Koester, 224). Evidence for this sort of allegorical interpretation, leading to the creation of narrative in the absence of historical data either in earliest Christianity or in contemporary Judaism,* has not been presented by Koester or Crossan, however, and counterevidence is easy to find (e.g., the measured comments in Marcus; also Green). Greater attention at the level of presuppositions and precision of argument is thus needed, but the way forward in this debate is undoubtedly in the more nuanced exploration of the role of oral tradition in the formation of the *Gospel of Peter* (Schaeffer).

When was the *Gospel of Peter* written? It had to have been written before the end of the second century, since it was by then a source of controversy in Rhossus. A further judgment on this question is dependent upon one's views on the relationship between this writing and the canonical Gospels. Those who believe that the *Gospel of Peter* evidences a precanonical passion narrative may date it into the mid-first century. As seems more likely, however, the *Gospel of Peter* borrows from and builds on the canonical Gospels and so must be dated after 100, probably in the first half of the second century.

See also APOCRYPHAL AND PSEUDEPIGRAPH AL WRITINGS; MARK, SECRET GOSPEL OF; THOMAS, GOSPEL OF.

BIBLIOGRAPHY. R. E. Brown, *The Death of the Messiah—From Gethsemane to the Grave: A Commentary on the Passion Narratives* (2 vols.; ABRL; Garden City, NY: Doubleday, 1994) 2:1317-49; idem, "The *Gospel of Peter* and Canonical Gospel Priority," *NTS* 33 (1987) 321-43; J. D. Crossan, *The Cross That Spoke: The Origins of the Passion Narrative* (San Francisco: Harper & Row, 1988); J. Denker, *Die theologiegeschichtliche Stellung des Petrusevangeliums: Ein Beitrag zur Frühgeschichte des Doketismus* (EH 23: Theologie 36; Frankfurt: Peter Lang, 1975); O. von Gebhardt, *Das Evangelium und die Apokalypse des Petrus* (Leipzig: J. C. Hinrichs, 1893); J. B. Green, "The *Gospel of Peter:* Source for a Precanonical Passion Narrative?" *ZNW* 78 (1987) 293-301; A. von Harnack, *Bruchstücke des Evangeliums und der Apokalypse des Petrus* (2d ed.; TU; Leipzig: J. C. Hinrichs, 1893); A. Kirk, "Examining Priorities: Another Look at the *Gospel of Peter's* Relationship to the New Testament Gospels," *NTS* 40 (1994) 572-95; H. Koester, *Ancient Christian Gospels: Their History and Development* (London: SCM; Philadelphia: Trinity Press International, 1990) esp. 216-40; D. Lührmann, "Ein Neues Fragment des Petrusevangeliums" in *The Synoptic Gospels: Source Criticism and the New Literary Criticism*, ed. C. Focant (BETL 110; Louvain: Louvain University, 1993) 579-81; J. W. McCant, "The Gospel of Peter: Docetism Reconsidered," *NTS* 30 (1984) 258-73; M. G. Mara, *Évangile de Pierre: Introduction, Texte Critique, Traduction, Commentaire et Index* (SC; Paris: Cerf, 1973); J. Marcus, "The Old Testament and the Death of Jesus: The Role of Scripture in the Gospel Passion Narratives" in *The Death of Jesus in Early Christianity*, ed. J. T. Carroll and J. B. Green (Peabody, MA: Hendrickson, 1995) 205-33; F. Neirynck, "The Apocryphal Gospels and the Gospel of Mark" in *The New Testament in Early Christianity*, ed. J.-M. Servin (BETL 86; Louvain: Louvain University, 1989) 123-75; J. A. Robinson and M. R. James, *The Gospel According to Peter and the Revelation of Peter: Two Lectures on the Newly Discovered Fragments Together with the Greek Texts* (London: C. J. Clay, 1892) 83-88; S. E. Schaeffer, "The Gospel of Peter, the Canonical Gospels and Oral Tradition" (unpublished Ph.D. dissertation, Union Theological Seminary, 1991); J. C. Treat, "The Two Manuscript Witnesses to the Gospel of Peter," *SBLSP* (1990) 391-99; L. Vaganay, *L'Évangile de Pierre* (2d ed.; EB; Paris: Librairie Lecoffre, 1930). J. B. Green

PHILIP THE EVANGELIST

The description—"the evangelist, one of the Seven"—in Acts 21:8 distinguishes this Philip from his apostolic namesake (Lk 6:14; Acts 1:13) and recalls his roles as pioneering proclaimer of the Christian gospel* (Acts 8; *see* Evangelism) and partner in charitable ministry* (Acts 6:1-6). Other traditions about Philip must be compared with the primary portrait provided in the canonical Acts.*

  1. Philip in Acts
  2. Philip in Other Early Christian Traditions

1. Philip in Acts.

1.1. Table Servant in Jerusalem.

Philip first appears, after Stephen,* in a list of seven servants (*see* Service) chosen to oversee the Jerusalem* church's daily dole of food, especially to poor Hellenist widows (Acts 6:1-3, 5). With established reputations as wise, Spirit-filled persons (Acts 6:3; *see* Holy Spirit), Philip and his associates seem to have been community leaders prior to this new assignment. Moreover, any supposed inconsistency between Philip's social duty and subsequent evangelistic activity vanishes in light of the Lukan emphasis on "serving tables" and "serving the word" as complementary diaconal *(diakoneō)* ministries (Acts 6:2, 4; cf. Lk 9:1-6, 10-17; 12:37-42; 17:7-10; 22:14-27).

1.2. Evangelist to the Samaritans.

A campaign of persecution* against the Jerusalem church, beginning with the stoning of Stephen, drives Philip to Samaria,* where he performs miracles* of healing* and exorcism and proclaims the good news of Jesus Christ (Acts 8:5-8, 12). This mission* marks the gospel's first advance beyond Jerusalem, following the plan outlined in Acts 1:8. Apart from geographical expansion, Philip's outreach also crosses socioreligious boundaries dividing Samaritans and Jews, as evidenced earlier in the Lukan narrative in the Samaritan villagers' refusal to host the Jerusalem-bound Jesus, as well as James and John's hotheaded retort (Lk 9:51-56).

The character and strength of Philip's Samaritan mission is particularly demonstrated in his overwhelming of Simon Magus (*see* Magic), who had previously dazzled the crowds with his grandiose claims and wondrous displays. In contrast to Simon's soliciting devotion to himself as "the Great Power *[dynamis megalē]* of God," Philip promotes commitment to "the kingdom of God and the name of Jesus Christ" (Acts 8:9-12; *see* Kingdom of God). And whatever the greatness of Simon's feats, Philip's "great powers" *(dynameis megalas)* are notably superior, prompting even Simon's amazement and apparent conversion (Acts 8:13). This discomfiture of a popular magician-sorcerer characterizes Philip as a Moses*-style prophet* (Ex 7:22; 8:7, 18-19; Deut 18:9-18) and matches Paul's work at the beginning of his three main missionary journeys (Acts 13:6-12; 16:1-18; 19:11-20).

Subsequent events involving Peter and John's conveyance of the Spirit to the Samaritan believers (*see* Pentecost) and exposure of Simon's greedy insincerity (Acts 8:14-24) raise possible questions about Philip's discernment. Such concerns are offset, however, by the Lukan emphasis on the Spirit as God's sovereignly bestowed gift—irrespective of human channels (Lk 11:13; Acts 2:38; 8:20; 10:44-48; 11:15-17)—and frank acknowledgment of other fraudulent disciples, including Jesus' own apostle,* Judas (Lk 22:3-6; Acts 1:16-20; cf. Lk 8:14; Acts 5:1-11).

1.3. Evangelist to the Ethiopian Eunuch.

Philip also spreads the gospel along Israel's Mediterranean coast from the Gaza region to Caesarea (Acts 8:26, 40). The most memorable encounter is with a eunuch returning home to Ethiopia from Jerusalem. Starting with the text of Isaiah 53:7-8, which the eunuch had been reading, Philip expounds the good news about Jesus (Acts 8:32-35). The eunuch responds with a request for baptism,* which Philip promptly fulfills just before the Spirit whisks him away (Acts 8:36-39).

Once again Philip proves to be a boundary-breaking pioneer. Geographically, he extends the gospel not only to the Judean coastal plain but also toward the eunuch's Ethiopian homeland, situated at "the ends of the earth" in Greco-Roman thought (Homer *Odys.* 1.22-24; Strabo *Geog.* 17.2.1; cf. Acts 1:8; Ps 68:31). Ethnically, Philip evangelizes a black African, Jewish-sympathizing Gentile* ("God-fearer"). Socially, Philip's witness spans two poles. On the one hand he advises an elite government official *(dynastēs)*, the queen's treasurer (Acts 8:27). On the other hand, however, he reaches out to a castrated male *(eunouchos)*, who, despite his interest in Judaism,* would have been regarded according to traditional law* as impure and disgraceful, forever cut off from the covenant* community (Lev 21:18-20; Deut 23:1; Josephus *Ant.* 4.8.40 §290-91; Philo *Spec. Leg.* 1.324-25). Within this scenario Philip's identification of Jesus with the shorn and scorned figure of Isaiah 53 becomes especially relevant.

Philip's interaction with an inquiring foreign official, culminating in the latter's baptism, recalls Elisha's dealings with Naaman (2 Kings 5:1-15; cf. Lk 4:27) and previews Peter's breakthrough to Cornelius* (Acts 10:1-48). Interesting links have also been noted between the revelatory ministries of Philip and Jesus to confused travelers on the roads to Gaza and Emmaus respectively (cf. Lk 24:13-35).

1.4. Resident Host in Caesarea. Philip ultimately settles in Caesarea with his four unmarried daughters, known for their prophetic vocation. For several days Philip hosts Paul and his companions (the "we" group) on their way to Jerusalem (Acts 21:8-14).

Philip's domestic-residential service in Caesarea both parallels his table waiting in Jerusalem and balances his evangelistic-itinerant mission in Judea and Samaria. Moreover, his gracious hosting of Paul (*see* Hospitality) constitutes a remarkable conciliatory gesture to this former instigator of persecution surrounding Philip's earlier ministry (Acts 8:1-3; 9:1-2). In sum, Philip emerges as a key agent of unity in Acts, bringing together different forms of service* and different types of people.

2. Philip in Other Early Christian Traditions.

2.1. Johannine. In four passages, unparalleled in the Synoptic tradition, the Fourth Gospel refers to a disciple of Jesus named Philip from Bethsaida in Galilee (Jn 1:43-48; 6:5-7; 12:20-22; 14:8-9). Although this Philip is not identified as one of the twelve apostles and does bring Nathanael and some Greek seekers into contact with Jesus, any tie-in with Philip the evangelist in Acts remains speculative. Presumed connections between the anonymous "other" laborers in the Samaritan mission field in John 4:38 and Philip in Acts 8 are also tenuous.

2.2. Patristic. Eusebius reports the claims of the second-century Ephesian bishop, Polycrates, and the Montanist leader, Proclus, that the luminous apostle Philip and his unmarried, prophetic daughters were laid to rest in Asia Minor. Eusebius clearly associates this Philip with Acts 21:8-9, thus blurring the distinction between apostle and evangelist (Eusebius *Hist. Eccl.* 3.31.2-5; 5.24.2). He also mentions that Philip's daughters recounted a wondrous resurrection* story (involving their father?) to Papias of Hierapolis and cites the opinion of Clement of Alexandria that Philip eventually gave his daughters in marriage (Eusebius *Hist. Eccl.* 3.39.9; 3.30.1; Clement of Alexandria *Strom.* 3.52.5).

2.3. Gnostic. In various gnostic* traditions Philip becomes one of the main channels of special revelation* among Jesus' disciples (*Gos. Phil.* 73.8; *Soph. Jes. Chr.* 92.4; 95.19; *Pistis Sophia*). In *The Letter of Peter to Philip* (late second or early third century) Peter urges his estranged "brother" Philip to rejoin the apostolic fold (*Ep. Pet. Phil.* 132.10—133.19), signaling perhaps some conflict among gnostic circles involving these two figures. Although this tractate makes no explicit reference to the material about Philip in Acts, numerous allusions to Acts 1—12 may suggest that the letter's addressee again represents an amalgam of Philip the evangelist and Philip the apostle.

See also ACTS OF THE APOSTLES; HELLENISTS; SAMARIA; STEPHEN.

BIBLIOGRAPHY. C. K. Barrett, "Light on the Holy Spirit from Simon Magus (Acts 8,4-25)" in *Les Actes des Apôtres: Traditions, rédaction, théologie,* ed. J. Kremer (BETL 48; Paris-Gembloux: Duculot; Louvain: Louvain University, 1979) 281-95; F. Bovon, "Les Actes de Philippe," *ANRW* 2.25.6 (1988) 4431-527; T. L. Brodie, "Towards Unraveling the Rhetorical Sources in Acts: 2 Kgs 5 as One Component of Acts 8,9-40," *Bib* 67 (1986) 41-67; S. R. Garrett, *The Demise of the Devil: Magic and the Demonic in Luke's Writings* (Minneapolis: Fortress, 1989); A. M. Johnson Jr., "Philip the Evangelist and the Gospel of John," *AbrN* 16 (1975-76) 49-72; C. H. Lindijer, "Two Creative Encounters in the Work of Luke: Luke xxiv 13-35 and Acts viii 26-40" in *Miscellanea Neotestamentica,* ed. T. Baarda, A. F. J. Klijn and W. C. van Unnik (NovTSup 48; Leiden: E. J. Brill, 1978) 77-85; C. J. Martin, "A Chamberlain's Journey and the Challenge of Interpretation for Liberation," *Semeia* 47 (1989) 105-35; M. W. Meyer, *The Letter of Peter to Philip: Text, Translation and Commentary* (SBLDS 53; Chico, CA: Scholars Press, 1981); D. M. Parrott, "Gnostic and Orthodox Disciples in the Second and Third Centuries" in *Nag Hammadi, Gnosticism and Early Christianity,* ed. C. W. Hedrick and R. Hodgson Jr. (Peabody, MA: Hendrickson, 1986) 193-219; F. S. Spencer, "The Ethiopian Eunuch and His Bible: A Social-Science Analysis," *BTB* 22 (1992) 155-65; idem, *The Portrait of Philip in Acts: A Study of Roles and Relations* (JSNTSup 67; Sheffield: JSOT, 1992).

F. S. Spencer

PHILO

Philo Judaeus, also known as Philo Alexandrinus, lived in Egypt from about 20 B.C. to A.D.

50. He is never mentioned in the NT and in his writings never directly address Christianity or any of the leaders of the early Christian church. Yet Philo's extant works provide a window on the first-century world shared by Christianity.

1. The Man
2. The Writings of Philo
3. Philo and the New Testament
4. Summary

1. The Man.

Philo was a member of one of the most prominent Jewish families in Alexandria.* His brother, Alexander, was a political ally of Herod Agrippa (Josephus *Ant.* 18.6.3, §159). Alexander's son Marcus was wed to Agrippa's daughter Bernice (cf. Acts 25:13, 23; 26:30). Another of Philo's nephews, Tiberius Julius Alexander, served as procurator of the province of Judea in A.D. 46-48 (Josephus *Ant.* 20.5.2 §100-104; Acts 11:28; 12:20-23). Despite these connections with Palestine, Philo mentions only one visit to Jerusalem (Philo *Prov.* 2.64).

Philo's writings reveal a creative, educated man struggling to synthesize the two most prominent elements of his personal existence: Greek wisdom and the Jewish religious tradition (*see* Judaism). The early Christian church struggled to work a similar synthesis as it proclaimed the message of the Messiah in a Hellenized Gentile world. As a result, the Christian church found Philo's writings helpful, and his works survived primarily in the church.

2. The Writings of Philo.

Two of Philo's writings have survived as complete documents only in Armenian: *Questions and Answers on Genesis* (*Quaestiones et Solutiones in Genesin*) and *Questions and Answers on Exodus* (*Quaestiones et Solutiones in Exodum*). These occupy the final two volumes of the twelve-volume Loeb collection. Organizing Philo's other works into helpful subdivisions has proven difficult. Scholars typically find from three to six major divisions but confess that the content of the documents in these divisions frequently overlaps.

2.1. Historical Works. Two of Philo's most notable historical documents are *Flaccus* (*In Flaccum*) and *On the Embassy to Gaius* (*De Legatione ad Gaium*). Flaccus, the prefect of Egypt, was responsible for the Jewish pogrom of A.D. 38. The Jews sought to counter the pogrom by sending Philo as the leader of an embassy to the emperor,* Gaius Caligula. Eventually Flaccus was recalled to Rome, exiled and executed. Philo used the account to make the theological point that evil will ultimately reap divine punishment. Another historical work, *On the Contemplative Life* (*De Vita Contemplativa*), focuses on a religious order, the Therapeutae, which Philo compared briefly to the Essenes. The Essenes are also mentioned in *That Every Good Man Is Free* (*Quod Omnis Probus Liber sit*), which reflects Stoic wisdom by drawing a sharp distinction between the spiritual nature of virtue* and the physical origin of vices.

2.2. Philosophical Works. This grouping of writings (occupying the first five Loeb volumes following *On the Creation of the World* [*De Opificio Mundi*]) could easily be labeled Philo's allegorical digressions. This series of treatises follows the order of Genesis 1-17, 27, 37. Philo began each treatise with a biblical citation but allegorized the text and moved rapidly to a rambling discussion of spiritual-philosophical matters in general.

2.3. Exegetical Works. Philo's exegetical works begin with *On the Creation of the World* (*De Opificio Mundi*) which strives to demonstrate the harmony between natural law and divine law. A series of treatises on key figures (*On Abraham* [*De Abrahamo*], *On Joseph* [*De Iosepho*] and *On the Life of Moses* [*De Vita Mosis*]) provide living examples of the goodness of the law. These in turn lead the reader to Philo's treatises *On the Decalogue* (*De Decalogo*) and *On the Special Laws* (*De Specialibus Legibus*).

3. Philo and the New Testament.

Much has been written regarding Philo and the NT texts. Scholarly attention has focused primarily on three areas: Hebrews,* some sections of the Gospel of John and some portions of the writings of Paul. Each of these demonstrates varying degrees of affinity with the writings of Philo.

3.1. Hebrews. The author of Hebrews reveals an impressive knowledge of the Jewish Scriptures, an unmistakable commitment to the supremacy of the Christian gospel* and a greater similarity to Philo than any other NT writer. The book delivers its lesson based on the Greek text of the OT and reflects training in the art of Greek rhetoric. This combining of Hebrew revelation* and Greek wisdom* gives Hebrews a Philonic flavor.

Philo and Hebrews both show a preference for the Pentateuch. Both give considerable attention to Moses* (cf. Heb 3:1-6 and Philo *Vit. Mos.*), the priesthood* and the Jewish cult (cf. Heb 4:14—5:10; 7:23-28 and Philo *Spec. Leg.*). Both treat OT persons and events as symbols of deeper realities and both distinguish between an immature knowledge of the revelation versus a true deeper understanding.

In spite of these commonalities, significant differences also exist. For the author of Hebrews it was Christ and the work of Christ that defined all wisdom (Heb 1:1-4). Thus he interpreted the Septuagint via typology and finds Christ there. Philo interpreted the Septuagint via allegory and found there the foundation for all wisdom, especially Greek wisdom. In line with Greek wisdom, Philo's dualism is ontological. Matter and spirit are opposed, God* is transcendent, and ascending to the enlightened level of true spiritual being is humanity's goal. The dualism of Hebrews is eschatological. Material existence is not essentially evil and God is directly involved with it. The two worlds discernible in Hebrews (the heavenly and the earthly) are tightly tied to one another as the present age flows into the age to come (Heb 9:23-28). Such deep discontinuities between the thought of Hebrews and that of Philo outweigh their superficial similarities and should prevent us from labeling Hebrews as Philonic.

3.2. John. The Gospel of John also exhibits several parallels with the writings of Philo. Dualism is evident in John and is predominantly an ontological dualism. For both authors true spiritual enlightenment or true life is attained through the knowledge of the one true God. For both the knowledge of God derives from the Jewish Scriptures. Both John and Philo also struggled to communicate the knowledge of this one true God to the broader Hellenized world. This attempt is perhaps best seen in the use by both authors of Logos terminology (Jn 1:1-18; Philo *Som.* 1.75; Philo *Migr. Abr.* 102). Yet at this point the most basic difference between Philo's writings and John can be seen.

In general in Hellenistic philosophy the Logos (the "word") is an impersonal force. It is the reason or logic that unified and made sense of the world. The wise and enlightened person sought to understand and cooperate with the Logos (*see* Logos Christology). Both Philo and John made use of the Hellenistic Logos concept by linking it to the biblical concept of the "Word" of God. For Philo the Word reveals God and wise persons allow that Word to inform and shape their lives. In its prologue, however, John takes an additional crucial step by proclaiming that the Word became flesh* and identifying that Word as Jesus Christ (Jn 1:14-17).

Philo used personification to discuss the Logos (Philo *Conf. Ling.* 146), but his Hellenistic worldview would never allow its actual incarnation (Philo *Conf. Ling.* 147). By contrast the incarnation of the Logos made sense for John. His understanding of the world was dominated by his knowledge of the divine in the man Jesus. Through Jesus true life is secured and God is revealed. Jesus serves as the bridge between humanity's darkness and divine light.* The Logos was for John what it could never be for Philo.

3.3. Paul. Numerous parallels in terminology exist also between Paul's and Philo's writings. Both revered the Jewish Scriptures and cited or alluded to the Septuagint frequently. Both worked primarily in the Diaspora* communicating the revelation of the Jewish God to Hellenized audiences. Both wrote of humanity as a complex of body, soul and spirit (or in Philo "mind") and as persons capable of living dominated by the flesh or guided by the spirit (Philo *Gig.* 36-37; 1 Thess 5:23).

However, the distance between Paul's gospel and Philo's philosophy is great. As in John, Paul's Logos was the Christ, Jesus. For Philo it was a timeless, noncorporeal reality. So for Paul the separation between the transcendent God and humanity had been bridged in a way that was impossible for Philo. Likewise the hope* of the Parousia* and of a physical resurrection* in Paul (1 Cor 15:3-57) bring together the world of the divine and the human in a way that Philo's dualism could not countenance.

Philo and Paul both respect and comment on the law as the wisdom of God. Philo integrated the law and Hellenistic wisdom by means of allegorical interpretation. The law, properly understood, was for Philo a guide that humanity should and can obey and that if obeyed would lead to an enlightened, spiritual existence (Philo *Migr. Abr.* 89-93). Paul laments that humanity is incapable of keeping the law. Salvation* is accomplished through faith* in Christ completely apart from obedience* to the Law. Thus Paul's writings are centered on a dilemma (humanity's inescapable captivity to sin* and death, Rom 3:9-20) and a solution to that dilemma (deliverance by grace* through faith in Christ, Rom 3:21-26) that Philo's writings do not reflect.

4. Summary.
John, Hebrews, Paul and Philo clearly shared common vocabulary and engaged in dialogue with the same Hellenized world. As a result our knowledge of that world is greatly enhanced through a familiarity with Philo's writings. It is unlikely, however, that any of the biblical authors were directly influenced by a knowledge of Philo's works.

See also HEBREWS; JOSEPHUS; LOGOS CHRISTOLOGY.

BIBLIOGRAPHY. P. Borgen, *Philo, John and Paul* (Atlanta: Scholars Press, 1987); G. Meyer, *Index Philoneus* (New York: Walter de Gruyter, 1974); R. Radice and D. T. Runia, *Philo of Alexandria: An Annotated Bibliography 1937-86* (Leiden: E. J. Brill, 1988); D. T. Runia, *Philo in Early Christian Literature* (Minneapolis: Fortress, 1993); idem et al., *The Studia Philonica Annual* (BJS; Atlanta: Scholars Press, 1989—); S. Sandmel, *Philo of Alexandria* (New York: Oxford University Press, 1979); R. Williamson, *Jews in the Hellenistic World: Philo* (Cambridge: Cambridge University Press, 1989); idem, *Philo and the Epistle to the Hebrews* (Leiden: E. J. Brill, 1970).   D. M. Martin

POLEMIC, JEWISH-CHRISTIAN. *See* CHRISTIANITY AND JUDAISM: PARTINGS OF THE WAYS.

POLYCARP OF SMYRNA
Bishop of Smyrna, Polycarp (c. A.D. 69/70—c. 155-160) was an important Christian leader in Asia Minor in the first half of the second century, the author of a letter to the church in Philippi and the subject of the earliest extant Christian martyrdom.

1. Polycarp of Smyrna
2. The Letter of Polycarp to the Philippians
3. The Martyrdom of Polycarp

1. Polycarp of Smyrna.
Already bishop of Smyrna when his friend and mentor Ignatius* of Antioch addressed a letter of encouragement and advice to him (c. 110 or later), Polycarp died a martyr's death (see 3.5 below) several decades later at age 86 (c. 155-

160), having served as bishop for at least forty and possibly sixty or more years. His one surviving letter reveals a direct and unpretentious style and a sensitive pastoral manner, while in the *Martyrdom* he is described as the "teacher of all Asia" (*Mart. Pol.* 12.2). His life and ministry spanned the time between the end of the apostolic era and the emergence of catholic Christianity (*see* Early Catholicism), and he was deeply involved in the central issues and challenges of this critical era: the growing threat of persecution* by the state; the emerging gnostic* movement (he is particularly known for his opposition to one of the movement's most charismatic and theologically innovative teachers, Marcion,* whom he reportedly encountered, perhaps while in Rome* [Irenaeus *Adv. Haer.* 3.3.4; Eusebius *Hist. Eccl.* 4.14.7]); the development of the monepiscopal form of ecclesiastical organization (*see* Church Order, Government); and the formation of the canon* of the NT.

Both Irenaeus (who as a child met Polycarp) and Eusebius considered him to be a significant link in the chain of orthodox apostolic tradition. (Their claim that he had known John the apostle among others [Irenaeus *Adv. Haer.* 3.3.4; Eusebius *Hist. Eccl.* 4.14] is unverifiable and perhaps confused). Irenaeus also associates him with Papias (Irenaeus *Adv. Haer.* 5.33.4) and Florinus (before he became a heretic; Eusebius *Hist. Eccl.* 5.20.4-8) and reports (probably correctly) that he traveled to Rome to discuss the Quartodeciman controversy (a dispute over the date for celebrating Easter) with Anicetus, bishop of Rome (Irenaeus *Adv. Haer.* 3.3.4; Eusebius *Hist. Eccl.* 5.24; 4.14). Conservative and traditional, Polycarp exercised influence far beyond Asia as he sought to protect and maintain the orthodox faith.

2. The Letter of Polycarp to the Philippians.
Only a single document by Polycarp survives (Campenhausen's attempt to show that Polycarp was also the author of the Pastoral Epistles has met with very little acceptance). Written in response to a letter from the church in Philippi (cf. Pol. *Phil.* 3.1, 13.1), it seeks to define and reinforce community boundaries (Maier) while responding to their request for a discussion of "righteousness"* (Pol. *Phil.* 3.1) and dealing with the problem of Valens, an avaricious presbyter (Pol. *Phil.* 11.1-4).

2.1. Integrity and Date of the Letter. Determination of the date of Polycarp's letter is dependent upon the question of its integrity, because it has been suggested that the document as we now know it preserves not one but two letters.

The references to Ignatius in *Philippians* 1.1 and 9.1 (which imply that Ignatius is already dead) and *Philippians* 13.2 (where Polycarp asks for information about his fate) are usually understood to indicate that while sufficient time has passed since Ignatius's final departure for Rome for Polycarp to assume that Ignatius has by now been martyred, he has not yet received a confirmatory report. Thus the letter is customarily dated within a few weeks (or at most a few months) of the time of Ignatius's death (c. 110 or later).

Harrison has argued that Polycarp's "letter" is actually two letters: a brief one, comprising chapters 13—14, that was written shortly after Ignatius left Philippi, and a longer one (chapters 1—12) written some decades later, about 135-137 (the basis for this date being alleged anti-Marcionite elements in the letter, such as Pol. *Phil.* 7.1). While initial reaction to Harrison's thesis was enthusiastic, subsequent investigations have pointed out (1) the absence of any distinctively Marcionite aspects of the teaching refuted in the letter and (2) that the remembrances of Ignatius and his companions in *Philippians* 1.1 and 9.1 are far too fresh and vivid to allow for the passage of two or three decades since the event being remembered. Recent discussions, whether rejecting (Schoedel 1967, Paulsen, Dehandschutter 1989) or accepting (Barnard 1966) the possibility of division into two letters (a division which a formal epistolary analysis permits but does not require), insist on a date very close to the time of Ignatius's death.

Theories of interpolation (e.g., Joly) arise out of Polycarp's testimony to Ignatius (cf. Schoedel 1987, Dehandschutter 1989), and thus more properly belong to a discussion of the authenticity of the Ignatian letters (a collection which Polycarp apparently initiated [Pol. *Phil.* 13.2]).

2.2. Genre. Polycarp's letter is a complex hortatory letter that (1) combines elements of at least three common letter* types (paraenesis, advice and admonition), and (2) employs in portions of the letter a sermonic or homiletic style of discourse, the "word of exhortation." While its structure owes more to the "word of exhortation" model than to either Hellenistic

epistolary conventions or rhetorical* theory, awareness of the latter two is evident throughout the letter.

2.3. Contents. The following topical outline of the body of the letter offers an overview of the document's contents.

I. Righteousness (2.1—10.3)
  A. Righteousness defined (2.1-3)
  B. Occasion for letter: a request about righteousness (3.1-2)
  C. Faith/Hope/Love: the essence of righteousness (3.3)
  D. Table of duties: the living out of righteousness (4.1—6.2)
    1. "Weapons of righteousness" combat a love of money (4.1)
    2. Men (4.1)
    3. Wives (4.2)
    4. Children (4.2)
    5. Widows (4.3)
    6. Whole community (5.1)
    7. Deacons (5.2)
    8. Younger men (5.3)
    9. Younger women (5.3)
    10. Presbyters (6.1)
    11. Forgiveness: the duty of all (6.2)
  E. Follow the Lord, not false brothers (6.3)
  F. Rejection of heretics who reject Christ 7.1-2)
  G. Christ the guarantee of our righteousness (8.1-2)
  H. The martyrs as examples of righteousness (9.1-2)
  I. Exhortation to godly living (i.e., righteousness) (10.1-3)
II. The matter of Valens (11.1-4)
  A. Comments about Valens (11.1-2)
  B. Commendation of the community (11.3)
  C. Concern for Valens (11.4a)
  D. Instructions to the community (11.4b)

2.4. Central Concerns. The central interpretive question is the relationship (or lack thereof) between the two main issues and the pervasive exhortation. The shortcomings of purely theological readings (which stressed the antiheretical aspects at the expense of other elements) have been indicated by sociological* analyses (Maier), which give due weight to the exhortation but are unable adequately to account for the historical particularities of the situation. Recent investigations stressing the thematic unity of the letter have differed regarding its precise delineation (Meinhold,

Schoedel 1967, Steinmetz).

Analyses of the historical context (e.g., the antiheretical elements likely reflect the situation in Smyrna, not Philippi, and Marcion is nowhere in view) and of the epistolary, rhetorical and sociological aspects of the letter converge to suggest that Polycarp's key goal was to maintain and protect the integrity of the community in terms of both its beliefs and behaviors. It was Polycarp's conviction that wrong behaviors were prima facie evidence of wrong beliefs, and wrong beliefs axiomatically produced wrong behaviors. Further, wrong beliefs and/or behaviors are characteristic of outsiders, not insiders; consequently Valens's behavior represents a major threat to the stability and self-understanding of the Philippian community.

This understanding makes sense of the way Polycarp stresses so strongly the behavioral aspects of what is usually viewed as a purely "theological" concept, righteousness. For him, orthopraxy is the other side of the coin of orthodoxy; if the community is behaving properly, it is also likely believing properly. Here may be the explanation of the vigor with which he reinforces the community's sense of norms and standards throughout the letter.

2.5. Written Sources. The letter reveals a deep indebtedness to the Scriptures (in the form of the Septuagint; *see* Old Testament in Apostolic Fathers) and early Christian writings. It is "fairly certain" that the letter "reflects more or less direct contact" with the following writings: Psalms, Proverbs, Isaiah, Jeremiah, Ezekiel, Tobit; Matthew, Luke, Acts, Romans, 1—2 Corinthians, Galatians, Ephesians, Philippians, 1—2 Timothy, 1 John, 1 Peter and 1 Clement* (Schoedel 1967); Polycarp seems to be particularly familiar with the last two. The way he uses these documents is noteworthy: (1) while apparently none of the NT books are cited as "Scripture" (the reference to Ephesians in Pol. *Phil.* 12.1 is a possible exception), (2) the manner in which he refers to them clearly shows that he considered them to be authoritative.

3. The Martyrdom of Polycarp.

3.1. Genre and Content. The letter from the church at Smyrna to the church at Philomelium known as the *Martyrdom of Polycarp* is the oldest written account of a Christian martyrdom* outside the NT. A genuine letter which integrates narrative and paraenetic elements (Buschmann), it became the model for what would become a very popular genre of literature, the martyrdom. Apparently written by eye-witnesses (*Mart. Pol.* 15.1) not long after the event (*Mart. Pol.* 18.1), it records, in sometimes gruesome detail, the death of Polycarp at age 86. An introduction (*Mart. Pol.* 1) precedes a brief account of the martyrs who preceded Polycarp (*Mart. Pol.* 2-3) and of Quintus who, after volunteering, turned coward and sacrificed to the emperor (*Mart. Pol.* 4). The bulk of the account describes Polycarp's pursuit and arrest (*Mart. Pol.* 5—8), trial in the stadium before the proconsul (*Mart. Pol.* 9—12), death (*Mart. Pol.* 13—17) and final disposition (*Mart. Pol.* 18). A conclusion (*Mart. Pol.* 19—20) and several appendices (*Mart. Pol.* 21—22) complete the narrative.

3.2. Context. The account illuminates a growing challenge confronting the church around the middle of the second century. Because of its belief in one God,* the church found itself engaged in a struggle with the Roman state which permitted no compromise and from which eventually only one of the two parties would emerge victorious. The *Martyrdom* sets out quite clearly both the issue at stake—Lord* Christ* vs. Lord Caesar (*Mart. Pol.* 10.1)—and the state's (as well as the general population's) view of Christians as disloyal atheists (*Mart. Pol.* 9.2) who threatened the well-being of the Empire (*see* Roman Empire).

3.3. Central Themes. The narrative is clearly intended to set forth "a martyrdom in accord with the gospel" (*Mart. Pol.* 1.1) as a corrective of erroneous conceptions. The portrait of the havoc caused by Quintus (who volunteered himself and forced others to go forward, and then turned coward) and the community's response (no praise for volunteers) demonstrate an awareness of the dangers of enthusiasm to the well-being and stability of the community. Further, *Martyrdom of Polycarp* 17.3 may reflect an attempt to circumscribe an incipient tendency to overvalue the role and significance of martyrs (Saxer).

Polycarp's behavior is presented as exemplary in every respect. The concept of "imitation" (Ger. *Nachahmung*), which could lead to a focus on the martyr, is subordinated to "following after" (Ger. *Nachfolge*), which emphasizes more the concept of obedience and faithfulness to God, to whose will Polycarp conforms

(Schoedel 1967; Dehandschutter 1982, 1993, 514; Buschmann places greater weight on imitation). This view is reinforced by Polycarp's prayers*; instead of seeking personal glory, Polycarp takes advantage of his circumstances to pray for God's people (*Mart. Pol.* 7.2—8.1). In short, the narrative displays a balanced response that seeks both to preserve the stability of the group and also to meet the challenge of external threats (Schoedel 1992, 394).

3.4. Integrity. Chapters 21—22 and certain incidental details (e.g., the dove in *Mart. Pol.* 16.1) may be (and the notes by Gaius, Socrates and Pionius certainly are) later additions to the text. Moreover, there are differences between Eusebius's citations and the text preserved by the manuscript tradition. These circumstances have led to suggestions that the main narrative itself has been interpolated; in particular, that the story has been expanded in light of the Gospels by a later interpolator in order to make more obvious the parallels between the sufferings of Jesus and Polycarp (Campenhausen, Conzelmann). But the value of the differences between the manuscripts and Eusebius is questionable, especially as Eusebius himself may be responsible for some of them. Moreover, the *imitatio Christi* motif is no indicator of lateness, since it occurs as early as Paul's writings. Consequently in recent studies Campenhausen's thesis has been modified (Schoedel 1967) or rejected (Barnard 1970, Saxer, Dehandschutter 1993). Ronchey's thesis that it is a mid-third-century forgery is even less compelling.

3.5. The Date of Polycarp's Martyrdom. The information in *Martyrdom of Polycarp* 21 mentions the month and day (February 22, or perhaps 23), but not the year of Polycarp's death. According to Eusebius he died in 167, but the reliability of his information is questionable. Evidence regarding the proconsulship of Statius Quadratus suggests a date around 156; this squares well with the report that not long before his arrest Polycarp visited Bishop Anicetus of Rome, who became bishop there not earlier than 154 (Barnard 1970) Dehandschutter 1993). In view of the various difficulties, including a possible leap year, greater precision than c. 155 to 160 may be unwarranted (Schoedel 1967, 1993). If the information provided by *Martyrdom of Polycarp* 21 is discounted as a later addition (note the last sentence of *Mart. Pol.* 20), the Eusebian date becomes possible

(Frend, Brind'Amour). A date as late as 177 (Grégoire and Orgels) is unlikely.

See also APOSTOLIC FATHERS; IGNATIUS; MARTYRDOM.

BIBLIOGRAPHY. **Text and Translation:** J. B. Lightfoot and J. R. Harmer, *The Apostolic Fathers: Greek Texts and English Translations of Their Writings*, ed. and rev. Michael W. Holmes (2d ed.; Grand Rapids: Baker, 1992). **Commentaries and/or Editions:** P.-Th. Camelot, *Ignace d'Antioche: Lettres. Lettres et Martyre de Polycarpe de Smyrne* (4th ed.; SC 10; Paris: Cerf, 1969); J. B. Lightfoot, *The Apostolic Fathers, Part II: S. Ignatius. S. Polycarp* (2d ed.; 3 vols.; London: Macmillan, 1889); H. Paulsen, *Die Briefe des Ignatius von Antiochia und der Brief des Polykarp von Smyrna* (Zweite, neubearbeitete Auflage der Auslegung von Walter Bauer; Tübingen: J. C. B. Mohr, 1985); W. R. Schoedel, *Polycarp, Martyrdom of Polycarp, Fragments of Papias* (AF 5; Camden, NJ: Nelson, 1967). **Studies:** L. W. Barnard, "The Problem of St. Polycarp's Epistle to the Philippians" in *Studies in the Apostolic Fathers and their Background* (New York: Schocken, 1966) 31-39; idem, "In Defence of Pseudo-Pionius' Account of Saint Polycarp's Martyrdom" in *Kyriakon: Festschrift Johannes Quasten*, ed. P. Granfield and J. A. Jungmann (2 vols.; Münster: Aschendorff, 1970) 1.192-204; G. A. Bisbee, *Pre-Decian Acts of Martyrs and Commentarii* (HDR 22; Philadelphia: Fortress, 1988); A. Bovon-Thurneysen, "Ethik und Eschatologie im Philipperbrief des Polycarp von Smyrna," *TZ* 29 (1973) 241-56; P. Brind'Amour, "La date du martyre de saint Polycarpe (le 23 février 167)," *AnBoll* 98 (1980) 456-62; G. Buschmann, *Martyrium Polycarpi— Eine formkritische Studie: Ein Beitrag zur Frage nach der Entstehung der Gattung Märtyrerakte* (*BZNW* 70; Berlin/New York: de Gruyter, 1994); H. von Campenhausen, "Polykarp von Smyrna und die Pastoralbriefe" in *Aus der Frühzeit des Christentums* (Tübingen: J. C. B. Mohr, 1963) 197-252; idem, "Bearbeitungen und Interpolationen des Polykarpmartyriums" in *Aus der Frühzeit des Christentums* (Tübingen: J. C. B. Mohr, 1963) 253-301; H. Conzelmann, "Bermerkungen zum Martyrium Polykarps" *Nachrichten der Akademie der Wissenschaften zu Göttingen: Philologisch-historische Klasse* 1978.2 (Göttingen: Vandenhoeck & Ruprecht, 1978) 41-58; B. Dehandschutter, "The Martyrium Polycarpi: a Century of Research," *ANRW* 2.27.1 (1993) 485-522; idem, "Le Martyre de Polycarpe et le développement de la conception du martyre au deuxième siècle" in *Studia Patristica XVII*, ed. E. A. Livingstone (3 vols.; Oxford: Oxford University Press, 1982) 2.659-68; idem, "Polycarp's Epistle to the Philippians: An Early Example of 'Reception' " in *The New Testament in Early Christianity*, ed. J.-M. Sevrin (BETL 86; Leuven: Leuven University Press and Peeters, 1989) 275-91; W. H. C. Frend, *Martyrdom and Persecution in the Early Church: A Study of a Conflict from the Maccabees to Donatus* (Oxford: Blackwell, 1965); H. Grégoire and P. Orgels, "La véritable date du martyre de S. Polycarpe (23. 2. 177) et le 'Corpus Polycarpianum'," *AnBoll* 69 (1951) 1-38; P. N. Harrison, *Polycarp's Two Epistles to the Philippians* (Cambridge: Cambridge University Press, 1936); R. Joly, *Le dossier d'Ignace d'Antioche* (Brussels: Éditions de l'université de Bruxelles, 1979); H. O. Maier, "Purity and Danger in Polycarp's Epistle to the Philippians: The Sin of Valens in Social Perspective," *JECS* 1 (1993) 229-47; E. Massaux, *The Influence of the Gospel of Saint Matthew on Christian Literature before Saint Irenaeus, Book 2: The Later Christian Writings*, ed. A. J. Bellinzoni (NGS 5/2; Macon, GA: Mercer University Press, 1990); P. Meinhold, "Polykarpos," *RE* 21.2.1662-93; S. Ronchey, *Indagine sul Martirio di San Policarpo: Critica Storica e fortuna agiografica di un caso giudiziario in Asia Minore* (Rome: Istituto Storico Italiano per il Medio Evo, 1990); V. Saxer, "L'authenticité du Martyre de Polycarpe. Bilan de 25 ans de critique" in *Mélanges de l'Ecole française de Rome. Antiquité* 94 (1982) 979-1001; W. R. Schoedel, "Polycarp, Epistle of," *ABD* (1992) 5:390-92; idem, "Polycarp, Martyrdom of," *ABD* (1992) 5:392-95; idem, "Polycarp of Smyrna and Ignatius of Antioch," *ANRW* 2.27.1 (1993) 272-358; idem, "Polycarp's Witness to Ignatius of Antioch," *VC* 41 (1987) 1-10; P. Steinmetz, "Polykarp von Smyrna über die Gerechtigkeit," *Hermes* 100 (1972) 63-75. M. W. Holmes

POSTMODERNISM. *See* HERMENEUTICS.

POSTSTRUCTURALISM. *See* HERMENEUTICS.

POVERTY. *See* RICHES AND POVERTY.

POWER

The concept of power in early Christianity is intimately linked to a knowledge* of the one true God.* He is represented as powerfully at work in history creating a people for himself, redeeming them through the work of the Lord* Jesus Christ* on the cross, defeating death* by raising Jesus from the grave, and empowering them to lead holy lives and fulfill the mission he has given them.

1. Terminology and Expressions of Power
2. The Almighty God
3. The Power of the Lord Jesus Christ
4. Power to Live a Godly Life
5. Power to Proclaim the Gospel
6. Power to Do Signs and Wonders
7. Power over Demons
8. Power in Suffering

1. Terminology and Expressions of Power.

The most common term for power in this literature is *dynamis,* although some authors (e.g., Hermas) use *ischys* and its cognates just as frequently. Both terms refer to the inherent or derived ability to perform an action. A third term, *kratos,* was used in the same sense, but occurs most commonly in doxologies. The right to exercise power is expressed by the word *exousia,* "authority." The verbs *dynamoō* and *endynamoō* were regularly used to convey the notion of divine empowerment of individuals. Hermas, however, prefers *ischyropoieō,* "to make powerful"—a term that never occurs in the NT. The common verb *dynamai* appears most frequently as a simple modal ("I can"), but in certain contexts the notion of ability or power may be emphasized.

The concept of power is expressed through numerous other terms and ideas. Whenever God* acts, the concept of power is present because of God's limitless ability to accomplish whatever he intends. Similarly the Holy Spirit* represents God's empowering presence in the lives of his people. Words such as grace* and glory* are further expressions of the power of God.

The early Christian view of supernatural power is deeply rooted in the OT concept of relationship to the one true almighty God, who redeems a people for himself, fights for them and superintends the course of history. This stands in contrast to some of the prevailing notions of power in the Greco-Roman world. A. D. Nock described popular belief in the Roman Empire as "directed to divine power rather than to divine personalities" (Nock, 35). Certainly we find this to be true of Simon Magus— "the Great

Power"—who valued access to new supernatural abilities far more than forgiveness* of sin and a relationship to Christ (Acts 8:19). The *Epistle of Barnabas* 20.1 warns that among the many vices on the evil path is the exaltation of power.

The concept of power in our literature is also distinct from the popular notion of supernatural power as an impersonal substance. The power of God is not stored in names, amulets, precious stones or metals, or certain combinations of vowels. Neither is the power of God mediated through incantations or formulas. The background for the early Christian conception of divine power is a knowledge of the personal God and a submission to his will. God's self-revelation to his people is decisive: "I am the Lord . . . I will redeem you with an outstretched arm and with mighty acts of judgment. I will take you as my own people, and I will be your God" (Ex 6:6-7).

2. The Almighty God.

The one God* is unequalled in power and sovereignty. He is therefore acclaimed *pantokratōr,* "all powerful." The epithet appears nine times in the Apocalypse (e.g., Rev 4:8; 11:17; 15:3), seven times in *1 Clement* (e.g., *1 Clem.* 2.3; 8.5; 32.4) and elsewhere in the apostolic fathers* (*Herm. Vis.* 3.3.5; Pol. *Phil.* prologue; *Did.* 10.3). He is "marvelous in strength and majesty" (*1 Clem.* 60.1).

Numerous doxologies acknowledge and proclaim his power throughout our literature. 1 Peter 4:11 exclaims, "to him be the glory and the power *[kratos]* for ever and ever" (see also 1 Pet 5:11; Rev 4:11; 5:13; 7:12; 19:1; *1 Clem.* 64.1; 65.2; *Mart. Pol.* 20.2; *Did.* 9.4; 10.5).

This one God is worthy of praise because he is the Creator and the one who sits on the heavenly throne (Rev 4:11; cf. also *1 Clem.* 33.3;). The heavenly temple* is filled with his glory and his power *(dynamis)* (Rev 15:8). As Creator of all the angelic* forces he is "Lord of Hosts," or "Lord of the Powers" *(kyrios tōn dynameēn, Herm. Vis.* 1.3.4)—a title deeply rooted in the OT (e.g., 2 Sam 6:2; Ps 89:8 [LXX 88:9]). He has power over the sun, moon, stars and all of creation.* Angels serve him and worship* him. He is the one who manifests his power in providing salvation* (Rev 7:12), conquering and judging evil, and completely realizing all of his plans for a reign of peace* (Rev 11:17; 12:10; 19:1).

The Lord God has no rival. The doxology at the end of Jude* ascribes glory, majesty, power *(kratos)* and authority* *(exousia)* to the *only* God (Jude 25). Yet God has his enemies. There are supernaturally powerful forces that oppose God and his purposes (*see* Satan). Any description of the power of God needs to be understood against the power of this opposing sphere. John understood the entire world as under the grip of the power of the evil one (1 Jn 5:19). It is against these forces of darkness that God fights, rescuing a people for himself (Acts 26:18) and working to bring about the demise of their evil purposes, most notably the power of death (Heb 2:14). Satan's* power is limited. There is nothing in our literature that even hints of a thoroughgoing cosmic dualism. According to the Apocalypse, one of God's angels can even bring about the fall of the devil in heavenly warfare (Rev 12:7-9). Satan "was not strong enough *(ouk ischysen)*" to withstand Michael and his angels (Rev 12:8).

3. The Power of the Lord Jesus Christ.

The Lord Jesus Christ, the Son* of God, shares in the awesome power of the Father. The prologue to Hebrews* describes the Son as "the radiance of the glory of God" as well as the agent and sustainer of creation (Heb 1:1-3).

In his account of Peter's Pentecost* message, Luke portrays Jesus as performing works of power *(dynameis),* signs* and wonders in his earthly ministry (Acts 2:22). Luke later observes that "God anointed Jesus of Nazareth with the Holy Spirit and power *[dynamis]*" which made it possible for Jesus to heal* those under the oppression of the devil (Acts 10:38).

The writer to the Hebrews makes it clear that one of the primary purposes of Jesus' incarnation and death* was to nullify the power of the devil and thereby free those held in bondage by this evil tyrant (Heb 2:14). The writer claims that the devil had "the power *[kratos]* of death." W. L. Lane rightly comments, "the devil did not possess control over death inherently but gained his power when he seduced humankind to rebel against God" (Lane, 61). The death of Jesus effectively dealt with this problem because "he made atonement for the sins of the people" (Heb 2:17). Death itself was not able to keep its hold on Christ, because the one God manifested his almighty power in raising Jesus from the grave (Acts 2:24; *see* Resurrection). The

Apocalypse can therefore portray death as ultimately having no authority over the people of God (Rev 20:6). Those who have "washed their robes" by appropriating the blood of Christ for the forgiveness* of sins have the right (exousia) to the tree of life (Rev 22:14).

The people of God properly respond to the Messiah by giving him doxological praise alongside the Father: "to him who loves us and has freed us from our sins by his blood, and has made us to be a kingdom and priests to serve his God and Father—to him be glory and power for ever and ever!" (Rev 1:6; cf. also Rev 5:12, 13; 12:10). Thus in a development that demarcated early Christianity from the synagogue,* believers worship* Christ and ascribe to him the glory once reserved only for the Father (see Hurtado; see Christology).

4. Power To Live a Godly Life.
The coming of Christ inaugurated the beginning of a new era. According to the writer of Hebrews, people can now experience the power of the age to come (Heb 6:5). God imparts divine power to his people so they can overcome the evil one, proclaim the message of the gospel, and faithfully endure until the end.

Peter reminds his readers of the unchanging purpose of God that his people become holy and pure (1 Pet 1:15-16). God empowers believers to this end: "His divine power [theia dynamis] has given us everything we need for life and godliness" (2 Pet 1:3). Believers are therefore called to "escape the corruption in the world caused by evil desires" (2 Pet 1:4) and to acquire the ethical virtues* consistent with their calling as Christians. In his eloquent doxology, Jude* assures his readers that God exercises his power on behalf of believers to keep them from falling (Jude 24-25). John has seen Christians appropriate this power in his community and find victory over the evil one in his attempts to inspire sin* and apostasy* (1 Jn 2:14).

It is essential that the people of God exercise faith* in their Lord to obtain the strength they need for life and service. Peter stresses the role of faith* in experiencing God's protecting and keeping power (1 Pet 1:5). The writer to the Hebrews strongly emphasizes the importance of faith in God for accomplishing what he calls his people to do. Those who look to God in faith are strengthened in their weakness (edynamōthēsan apo astheneias, Heb 11:34).

The Mandates of the Shepherd of Hermas have much to say about drawing on God's strengthening power for getting rid of sinful tendencies and acquiring virtue. In Mandates 5.2, for example, Hermas stresses the need to deal with an angry temper. He sees it as a dangerous vice that opens the believer up to the influence of evil spirits. Hermas suggests that those who are filled with faith can overcome it "because the power of the Lord is with them [hē dynamis tou theou met' autōn estin]" (Herm. Man. 5.2.1). For Hermas, since faith is powerful (ischyra), believers should "trust God that you will receive all the requests you make" (Herm. Man. 9.7; cf. also Herm. Man. 9.10; 11.4). One needs to guard against doubt (dipsychia) because it is from the devil (Herm. Man. 9.9). In drawing on the power of God, Hermas also emphasizes the need to repent* from sin (Herm. Vis. 3.5.5.), fear* the Lord (Herm. Man. 7.4: "the fear of the Lord is powerful"), and trust in the Holy Spirit* (Herm. Man. 11.21: "the divine Spirit that comes from above is powerful").

Of utmost importance for Ignatius was the maintenance of doctrinal purity among the churches. He asserts that the power (dynamis) of Jesus is what has enabled believers at Ephesus to remain in agreement with the apostles (Ign. Eph. 11.2). He also calls believers to persevere to the end "by the power of faith [en dynamei pisteōs]" in pursuing love and eliminating sinful practices (Ign. Eph. 14.2). One of the keys for receiving the power of God, according to Ignatius, is united prayer (Ign. Eph. 5.2).

5. Power to Proclaim the Gospel.
Luke records that before Jesus ascended* to heaven, he promised his disciples that they would receive power (dynamis) when the Holy Spirit* came upon them, and they would become his witnesses throughout the world (Acts 1:8). The book of Acts* thus becomes the story of the powerful spread of the gospel of the Lord Jesus Christ throughout the Mediterranean region. The apostles testified to the resurrection* of the Lord Jesus "with great power [dynamei megalē]" (Acts 4:33) and "the word of the Lord grew mightily and prevailed" (Acts 19:20). Luke depicts, for example, how Apollos powerfully (eutonōs) refuted unbelieving Jews by showing that Jesus is the Messiah (Acts 18:28). Immediately after his conversion, "Saul grew more and more powerful [enedynamouto] and baffled un-

believing Jews in Damascus by proving that Jesus is the Messiah" (Acts 9:22). James declares the life changing impact of this gospel when he urges his readers to "receive the implanted word which has the power *[ton dynamenon]* to save your souls" (Jas 1:21). W. Grundmann thus aptly comments, "the Gospel is saving power" (Grundmann, *TDNT* 2.310).

6. Power to Do Signs and Wonders.

God bestowed his power on the apostles and other leaders in the early Christian movement to perform various kinds of miraculous deeds (*see* Signs and Wonders; Miracles). Luke presents Stephen as full of grace and power (*plērēs charitos kai dynameōs*) to do signs and wonders (Acts 6:8). Philip,* likewise, did many astonishing works of power (*dynameis,* Acts 8:13) as also did Paul in Ephesus and throughout his ministry (see esp. Acts 19:11). The writer to the Hebrews teaches his readers that these signs and wonders were God's means of vouching for the message of salvation* that these servants were proclaiming (Heb 2:4).

7. Power Over Demons.

The exorcisms recounted by Luke in Acts graphically demonstrate the power and authority bestowed on the church by Christ to defeat the powers of darkness in carrying out the mission* (Acts 16:16-18; 19:11). John commends the young men in his community for their strength and for overcoming the evil one (1 Jn 2:14). Ignatius exclaims that the powers of Satan* are overthrown by faith (Ign. *Eph.* 13.1). Likewise, Hermas tries to reassure his readers that Christians have power to conquer the works of the devil (*Herm. Man.* 12.6.2, 4). He says that, "those who are full in the faith resist him mightily *[ischyrōs],* and he leaves them alone, because he finds no place *[topos]* where he can gain entrance" (*Herm. Man.* 12.5.4; cf. Eph 4:27).

8. Power in Suffering.

The empowering presence of God does not guarantee a life devoid of suffering* and struggle but enables believers to endure to the end. This is particularly clear in 1 Peter—a letter written to people facing localized outbreaks of persecution and suffering in Asia Minor. Peter assures his readers of God's protective power in spite of the inevitable suffering and trials they would face (1 Pet 1:5-6). God's power would help them in their quest toward holiness.* He promises that "the God of all grace . . . after you have suffered a little while, will himself restore you and make you strong *[sthenōsei],* firm, and steadfast" (1 Pet 5:10).

Journeying toward his martyrdom,* Ignatius urges the Roman Christians to pray that God would strengthen him to be faithful as a true Christian (Ign. *Rom.* 3.2). When he writes to the church of Smyrna, he is exultant over Christ's strengthening power: "Only let it be in the name of Jesus Christ, that I may suffer together with him! I endure everything because he himself, who is perfect man, empowers me *[me endynamountos]*" (Ign. *Smyrn.* 4.2).

See also AUTHORITY; GLORY; GOD; HOLY SPIRIT; MAGIC AND ASTROLOGY; MIRACLES IN ACTS; RESURRECTION; SIGNS AND WONDERS; SPIRITS; SUFFERING.

BIBLIOGRAPHY. C. E. Arnold, "Power, New Testament Concept Of," *ABD* 5.444-46; O. Betz, "Might, Authority, Throne," *NIDNTT* 2:601-16; G. Friedrich, "δύναμαι," "δύναμις," *EDNT* 1:355-58; W. Grundmann, *Der Begriff der Kraft in der Neutestamentilichen Gedankenwelt* (Stuttgart: Kohlhammer, 1932); idem, "δύναμαι κτλ," *TDNT* 2.284-317; L. Hurtado, *One God, One Lord* (Philadelphia: Fortress, 1988); W. L. Lane, *Hebrews* (WBC 47; 2 vols.; Dallas: Word, 1991); A. D. Nock, "Studies in the Graeco-Roman Beliefs of the Empire" in *Arthur Darby Nock: Essays on Religion and the Ancient World,* ed. Z. Stewart (Oxford: Clarendon, 1972) 32-48 (= *JHS* 48 [1928] 84-101); C. H. Powell, *The Biblical Concept of Power* (London: Epworth, 1963).

C. E. Arnold

PRAYER

Prayer played a central role in the activities of the early church.* From the records in Acts* of the earliest Christian community in Jerusalem* (Acts 1:14, 24; 2:42; 3:1; 4:31) to the records of the apostolic fathers* in the Mediterranean world at the beginning of the second century (e.g., Ign. *Eph.* 1.2; Ign. *Magn.* 7.1; Ign. *Smyrn.* 7.1), prayer was a central activity and unifying feature of the Christian community.

    1. Categories of Prayer
    2. Types of Praying

1. Categories of Prayer.

The richness of prayer in the life of the early church is indicated by the diversity of expressions used to record practice, form and teaching of it. Various categories have been proposed to isolate aspects of prayer. While it is commonly understood primarily as some form of request, prayer overlaps in NT usage with other Christian activities. We isolate here four broad, overlapping categories: petition, worship, thanksgiving and conversation.

1.1. Prayers of Petition. We find in early Christian usage a variety of terms for making petition to God.* The most general term for prayer is *proseuchomai,* which in ancient Greek was a technical term for invoking a deity. In the early church *proseuchomai* (Acts 1:24; *proseuchē,* Acts 2:42; *euchomai,* Jas 5:16; *euchē,* Jas 5:15) covers every aspect of invocation, including request, entreaty, vow or consecration.

Another term, *aiteō* (1 Jn 5:14; *aitēma,* 1 Jn 5:15), meaning "ask, petition, demand," has both a secular use, as when the Jewish crowds asked or demanded to have Barabbas released instead of Jesus (Acts 3:14), and a religious use, as when obedient believers can receive from God whatever they ask (1 Jn 3:22).

Deomai (Acts 4:31; *deēsis,* 1 Pet 3:12), "ask, seek," denotes the powerful prayer of the righteous person (Jas 5:16). *Hiketēria,* found only once in the NT, means "supplication" (Heb 5:7). *Entygchanō* (Heb 7:25; *hyperentygchanō,* Rom 8:26; *enteuxis,* 1 Tim 2:1; 5:5), used infrequently in the NT (only in Heb 7:25; Rom. 8:26 1 Tim 2:1; 5:5; see *1 Clem.* 56.1), carries a meaning of "intercession" (Heb 7:25).

Epikaleō occurs frequently in contexts of calling on God or his name in prayer, as in Peter's famous declaration, "And it shall be that everyone who calls (*epikaleō*) on the name of the Lord shall be saved" (Acts 2:21).

Petitions made to God are of two broad types: petitions for the one asking and petitions for others (Hultgren, 27-33).

1.1.1. Petitions for the Petitioner. Men and women of faith* regularly petition God for themselves. One can petition the Lord* for salvation* from sin (Acts 2:21; 22:16; *epikaleō*), as Ananias told Saul in Damascus: "Get up, be baptized and wash your sins away, calling on his name" (Acts 22:16; *epikaleō*). The person who is suffering is to pray (Jas 5:13; *proseuchomai*). If one lacks wisdom or is in want, that person is to ask God (*aiteō;* Jas 1:5-6; 4:2; 1 Jn 3:22; see also *Herm. Man.* 9.7.8). A person who has committed wickedness is to pray in repentance* for his or her forgiveness* (Acts 8:22; *deomai*). Jesus of-

fered up prayers (*deomai*) and supplications (*hiketērias*) with loud cries and tears to the one who was able to save him from death (Heb 5:17).

1.1.2. Petitions for Others. Even more frequently men and women pray for others. This is often rendered as "intercession," as when the writer to the Hebrews* declares that Jesus "always lives to make intercession for them" (Heb 7:25; *entynchanō*). A person who has performed wickedness can ask for another to pray for his or her forgiveness (Acts 8:24; *deomai*), and the church must intercede (*entnchōmen*) for those who have fallen into transgression (*1 Clem.* 56.1).

Fellow believers can offer significant help for each other. As they confess their sins to one another they are to pray for one another (Jas 5:16; *euchomai*). The elders are to pray for the healing of those who are sick (Jas 5:14; *proseuchomai*), even as Peter effectively prayed for Tabitha's healing and Paul prayed for Publius's father (Acts 9:40; 28:8; *proseuchomai*). The apostles* and the early church prayed (*proseuchomai*) for workers (Acts 6:6), converts (Acts 8:15) and missionaries who were being sent off (Acts 13:3; see also Ign. *Eph.* 21.2; Ign. *Magn.* 14.1; *entynchanō,* 1 *Clem.* 56.1; Pol. *Phil.* 4.3; *1 Clem.* 59.2 combines *aiteō, deēsis, hikesia*). The author of Hebrews can ask for prayer from his readers (Heb 13:18), while he or she can offer a wish-prayer for the readers, expressing a desire that God take action on their behalf (Heb 13:20-21). The prayer of a righteous person accomplishes much for others of the assembly (Jas 5:16; *deomai*), in the same way that Elijah's prayer for rain resulted in earth's bounty (Jas 5:17; *proseuchomai*).

1.2. Prayers of Worship. Prayer is consistently linked with worship, whether it is the spontaneous outburst of the individual believer or the developed liturgical response of the community of faith. The earliest gathering of the Christian community involved devotion to the apostles' teaching, fellowship,* breaking of bread and prayers (Acts 2:42; *proseuchomai*). The worship and prayers of the church combined to mark them as filled with the Holy Spirit* and bold to proclaim the word of God (Acts 4:23-31). In the heavenly scene when the elders fell down to worship the Lamb,* the sacrifice* of the golden bowls* of incense were the prayers of the saints (Rev 5:8; *proseuchomai*).

A number of activities relate prayer to worship, such as reverence (*proskyneō,* Rev 4:10), glorify (*doxazō,* Rev 15:14), praise (*aineō,* Heb 13:15) and singing hymns* (Acts 16:25, *hymneō;* cf. *exomologeō, 1 Clem.* 61.3; *Barn.* 6.16; *proseuchomai,* Ign. *Magn.* 7.1). The Jewish *berakah* ("benediction") style of prayer occurs rarely in the NT—only three times in our material (1 Pet 1:3; Ign. *Eph.* 1.3; *Barn.* 6.10). The structure of the *berakah* suggests a liturgical setting, since the "blessing" formula is followed not by petitions but by praise (Bradshaw, 30-31). Another liturgical type of prayer inherited from Judaism* was *anamnēsis,* a "recollection" of God's mighty works, which proceeded directly from recollection to petition or intercession without any introductory formula (see Acts 4:24-30; Bradshaw, 33-34).

1.3. Prayers of Thanksgiving. Closely related to the praise of God in worship is thanksgiving (*eucharisteō*), but thanksgiving especially entails remembering God's answers to prayers as well as remembering what God has done for the individual believer and the believing community (Acts 28:15; Rev 11:17; *2 Clem.* 18.1; *Herm. Sim.* 2.5; 9.14.3). So important is thanksgiving that P. Miller subsumes all prayer under two categories, prayers for help and prayers of thanksgiving, whether in the OT generally, in the Eighteen Benedictions of Judaism or in the prayers of the NT (Miller, 305). Like Hellenistic Judaism, Christians frequently used the *hodayah* ("thanksgiving") pattern of prayer, which characteristically began with the phrase "I/we thank you," using variations of *eucharisteō* (Rev 11:17-18) and *homologeō* (Heb 13:15; Bradshaw, 31-33).

Giving thanks to God at the breaking of bread is a recollection that God is Creator and Provider. Even as Jesus blessed God (Lk 9:16; 24:30; *eulogeō;* not a bestowal of blessing on the bread, Turner, 60 n. 7) and gave thanks (Lk 22:[17], 19; *eucharisteō*) to God in typically Jewish fashion, so the early church gave thanks at the breaking of bread (even at crisis times) as a testimonial of God's protection and provision (see Acts 27:35). Thanksgiving took such a prominent place in the celebration of the Lord's Supper* that the verb *eucharisteō* ("give thanks") provided the name *Eucharist* for the church's thankful acknowledgment of the redemptive work of Christ (cf. *Did.* 9—10). Prayer that is offered without a corresponding thankfulness is ingratitude.

1.4. Prayers of Conversation. Prayer of a general sort can be seen as a dignified conversation and personal communion with God. Indeed, Oscar Cullmann declares that "the essence of all prayer is that it is a conversation with God as the partner" (Cullmann, 17). While formal prayer in the OT is often tied to a particular occasion, in the later OT (e.g., Dan 6:10-12), in Judaism at the time of the NT and in the further development in NT teaching and practice, we find prayer as "a *spiritual discipline,* that is, as an ongoing and regular part of the relationship with God" (Miller, 312).

The intimacy that the disciples enjoyed with Jesus during his earthly ministry* could now be maintained through prayer. They devoted themselves to prayer not only to petition his help, not only to worship, but also to maintain the personal nature of their unique master-disciple relationship (Wilkins, 276-78). One can enter into living, personal contact with Jesus, talking with him just as one did when he was on earth (cf. Acts 9:10-16; 2 Cor 12:8-9). Even at a specified time of prayer Peter did not recite a standardized prayer; he held a conversation with his risen Lord (Acts 10:9-16). The early church experienced the presence of the risen Lord to the degree that Stephen,* in his dying moments, speaks to the Lord Jesus (Acts 7:59; Polycarp also in *Mart. Pol.* 15.1). The intimacy of prayer is revealed as believers confess Jesus' name and their sins to God (Heb 13:15; 1 Jn 1:9; 2:23; *homologeō*). Those who suffer injustice can cry out to the listening Lord (Jas 5:4; *krazō* and *boē*), even as those martyred can cry out to the Lord to avenge them (Rev 6:10; *krazō*). Jesus used "knocking" as a metaphor of the prayers of his followers (Mt 7:7-8; Lk 13:25), and in John's vision* the risen Lord Jesus "knocks" so that the church would hear and open themselves to the intimacy of his fellowship (Rev 3:20; *krouō*).

2. Types of Praying.

2.1. Acts: Prayer in a New Age. The prayer life of the early church as recorded in Acts was influenced by two primary features: its roots in Judaism and its relationship to Jesus.

2.1.1. Influence from Judaism. The early church was thoroughly Jewish, which meant that its prayer life was governed by the common practices of Jewish prayer, informal and formal, private and public, individual and corporate.

While continuing the ancient practice of personal, spontaneous prayers (note that Cornelius* as a God-fearer both kept traditional times of prayer as well as prayed "continuously," Acts 10:2-4), Jews of the late Second Temple period gathered for increasingly fixed, communal prayer (Charlesworth, 265-66). In Diaspora Judaism* Jews were characterized by their commitment to times of communal prayer (see Acts 16:13, 16). The synagogue* and temple* were places Jews gathered to pray. We find that the early church was a distinct entity gathered for prayer (Acts 1:13-14; 2:42), while at the same time they carried out the traditional times of prayer individually (Acts 10:9) and at least at the beginning attended the temple at the prescribed hour of prayer (Acts 3:1; cf. Acts 2:42, 46, "the prayers"). The apostle Paul regularly went to the synagogue upon arriving at a new location on his missionary journeys (Acts 13:5, 14; 14:1; 16:13; 17:1-2, 10, 17; 18:4, 19: 19:8).

2.1.2. Influence from Jesus. The prayer life of the early church was also influenced by its relationship to Jesus. In the first place Jesus' personal practice of prayer set an example for the early church. Jesus derided public, ostentatious prayers and called his followers to personal prayer with the Father (Mt 6:5-8), thereby enhancing private prayer and leading to silent prayer as a discipline (cf. van der Horst, 16-18). Jesus prayed at special times of crisis and need, but prayer was also the "daily inspiration of His life" (Martin 1974, 28-29).

Second, Jesus' practice of prayer reflected his relationship to Judaism. All four Evangelists concur that Jesus frequently attended synagogue services on the sabbath, and his cleansing of the temple was based upon his desire that it should be a "house of prayer" (Mk 11:17). These activities established continuity with Judaism but also set the stage for the breach between the church and Judaism (*see* Christianity and Judaism). "The originality of Christian worship is not that it rejects Jewish worship but that it reforms and develops that worship, in accordance with Jesus' teaching and in recognition of his saving work" (Beckwith, 65).

Third, therefore, "the prayers the church offers are now *Christocentric*" (Turner, 73-74). What Israel had identified as divine prerogatives the church now attributes to Jesus: he is the one Lord on whose name (in Joel's terms) people are now to call for salvation (Joel 2:17-39); he

speaks to Saul in conviction (Acts 9:4-6) and Peter in direction (Acts 10:13-16); prayer is offered to him by Stephen (Acts 7:59) and Ananias (Acts 9:10-16). Soon after the ascension* of Jesus, the nascent church gathered to pray (Acts 1:14). They prayed for the Lord to show them which of the two who qualified—Joseph Barsabbas and Matthias—should take Judas's place (Acts 1:15-26). This scene marks a central aspect of the new form of discipleship: although their Lord is no longer with them personally, they can still ask him and the Father for help in times of need through prayer.

Fourth, the age of fulfillment that was announced by John the Baptist and Jesus (Mt 3:2; 4:17) was now experienced in the outpouring of the Spirit (Acts 2:14-41). The earliest gathering of the Christian community involved devotion to the apostles' teaching, fellowship, breaking of bread and the prayers (Acts 2:42). The primitive church, already both within and outside Israel, now offered prayers in "Easter joy" (Alsup, 34) and in the power of the Holy Spirit.

2.2. Hebrews: Jesus the High-Priestly Intercessor. The substantive contribution of Hebrews to the NT view of prayer is the portrayal of Jesus, the Son of God, as high priest (Cullmann, 115). Jesus is the champion of his people both through what he accomplished in his earthly ministry and in what he is doing now (Lane, cxl-cxliii). He wrestled with spiritual forces in his earthly life, overcoming all temptation* to sin. Therefore he can sympathize with our weaknesses, and we can with confidence *(parrēsia)* draw near to the throne of grace (Heb 4:14-16). His prayers and supplications in the most difficult of his circumstances acknowledge the intimate, Father-Son relationship that led him to obey the Father's will for his life, even though it meant suffering* (Heb 5:7).

Jesus offered the perfect sacrifice in his death and now sits enthroned in the heavenly sanctuary. He applies the benefits of his finished work to those who draw near to God through him (Heb 10:11-23; Peterson, 104), giving NT believers confidence, which is the basis of the certainty that prayer will be heard (see 1 Jn 5:14-15). His high-priestly ministry of intercession (Heb 7:25) includes eschatological* salvation (Heb 1:14; 5:9; 9:28) but also reflects the current experience of the community. Because of his sustained interest in the welfare of his people, his support is available to those who turn to him at each critical moment (Lane, 189-90).

2.3. James: Prayer of Faith. If we understand "testing of faith" (Jas 1:2-3) to be a central concern for James* (Davids, 57), then we should expect to find this theme in his discussion of prayer. This is the case in the three primary passages on prayer (Jas 1:5-8; 4:1-4; 5:13-18), all of which are critical of the community's practice.

2.3.1. Faith Without Doubt (Jas 1:5-8). James offers a general principle when he reminds his readers that God gives good gifts, namely, "wisdom," to those who ask him (Jas 1:5, 17). But prayer must be of the right sort: one must ask in faith, without doubting (Jas 1:6). This seems to reflect Jesus' teaching on prayer (cf. Mt 7:7-12; 21:21-22) and understands faith as a whole-hearted commitment of oneself to God. The person who doubts wavers in commitment to God; he or she is a "double-minded" person (Jas 1:8), doubting God's ability or willingness to give the wisdom* that God has said he would give to those who ask. The right sort of prayer turns the person away from other, competing allegiances, especially one's own human resources and devices, and places full confidence in God to bring about deliverance from life's trials (Martin 1988, 21).

2.3.2. Faith Without Wrong Motives (Jas 4:1-3). In a community torn by wars and fightings caused by internal "passions," James gives another general principle on prayer: "you do not have because you do not ask" (Jas 4:2). But further, his readers ask with wrong motives: "to spend it on your passions" (*hēdonai*, the same term as in Jas 4:1). Instead of asking God for solutions that will advance one's own desires, the right sort of prayer seeks God's solutions—God's kingdom* and righteousness*—within the community, even if his solution goes contrary to our own desires. "God is no magic charm which must help if the proper words are uttered" (Davids, 159). God's solution to the problem is within reach if one will only ask and receive.

2.3.3. Faith Without Sin (Jas 5:13-18). In a major passage on prayer, a final general principle of prayer echoes the first: as one must "ask in faith" (Jas 1:6), so one must offer a "prayer of faith" (Jas 5:15). One must pray with single-minded devotion to God, a genuine trust in God

and his promises.* All of the circumstances of life offer opportunities for different kinds of prayer. If one suffers, direct communion with God in prayer brings an empathetic companion in God (Jas 5:13). If one is cheerful, one can offer a prayer of praise to God (Jas 5:13). If one is weak, especially with illness, calling for the intercession of church leaders brings healing* and forgiveness of sins (Jas 5:14-15). Although anointing* with oil can indicate medicinal care, it more likely is a symbolic action, possibly indicating that the sick person has been set aside for special attention, favor or use by God (Moo, 180-81; Martin 1988, 208-9). If one has committed sins, confession to one another and prayer for one another brings spiritual and physical healing within the community of faith (Jas 5:16).

Prayer is a powerful activity of faith (the participle *energoumenē* is most likely in the middle voice; see Martin 1988, 211-12; Moo, 187) for the person who in purity* of life has confessed sin and is available as a righteous channel through whom God can bring healing (Jas 5:16). The OT prophet* Elijah is used by James as an example ("of like nature with ourselves," RSV) for the church of the intense prayer (*proseuchē prosēuxato*) of faith that accomplished the impossible (Jas 5:17-18).

But the prayer of faith is not to be equated with magical manipulation of the divine. James has boundless confidence in the promise of answered prayer, but not all prayer is answered in the way the person requests. James has already indicated that some prayer is not answered in the way requested because the person prays with wrong motives (Jas 4:1-3). Jesus also instructed his disciples to pray with unlimited expectation (Mk 11:22-24; cf. Jn 16:23); however, his own prayers and supplications (Heb 5:7) ultimately were not answered according to his own request but rather were subject to the Father's will (Mk 14:36), a theme we see echoed for all believers by John (cf. 1 Jn 5:14-15). "All prayer is bounded by the providence and sovereign favor of God, who knows believers' truest needs and may not grant their natural requests in just the way they would choose" (Martin 1988, 215-16).

2.4. Petrine Epistles: Unhindered Prayer. The importance of prayer in 1 Peter* and 2 Peter* is indicated by the wide range of prayer material. It includes opening and closing wish-prayers (1 Pet 1:2; 5:14; 2 Pet 1:2), brief doxologies (1 Pet 4:11; 5:11; 2 Pet 3:18), the longer praise form related to the Jewish *berakah* style of liturgical prayer in which praise (1 Pet 1:3-4) merges into exhortation (1 Pet 1:5-12), and specific exhortations to prayer, including invocation of (1 Pet 1:17), entrusting themselves to (1 Pet 4:19) and casting their anxieties upon (1 Pet 5:7) God, who cares for them while they encounter various difficulties (1 Pet 4:17).

Of special interest in 1 Peter are passing references to conditions that can either enhance or hinder prayer (1 Pet 3:7, 12; 4:7). Within a discussion of godly marital relationships (1 Pet 3:1-7) Peter motivates husbands to live considerately with their wives by warning, "so that nothing may hinder your prayers" (1 Pet 3:7). "Your *(hymōn)* prayers" may point only to the prayers of the husband (Reicke, 103) or to the common prayers of husbands and wives (Michaels, 171), but either way in the background resides the principle that a genuine relationship with God depends on right relationships with other people (cf. Mt 5:23-24; 1 Cor 11:1-34; Jas 4:1-4; Peterson, 114). The hindrance may result from lack of attention on the part of those praying, from lack of cooperation in the prayer effort by the marital partners or from divine judgment* for disobedience. The last may be more likely in view when we see the warning in the light of Peter's quotation from Psalm 34:15-16: God's ears are open to the prayers of the righteous, but his face is against evildoers (1 Pet 3:12). Personal righteousness, especially practiced in all relationships between "coheirs" (1 Pet 3:7), enhances the effectiveness of prayers to God.

A final passing reference to prayer is found in Peter's exhortation to prepare for the end of all things through mental alertness in "attending to prayers" (1 Pet 4:7) within the loving fellowship of the community of faith (1 Pet 4:8-11). Alert, clear-headed prayer keeps the community from being distracted during spiritual warfare and the trials associated with the end of the age (Michaels, 246).

2.5. Johannine Epistles: Confidence in Prayer. Some general forms of prayer appear in 1, 2 and 3 John *(see* John, Letters of), such as an assurance* of blessing* to the readers (2 Jn 3), a petition for the good health and well-being of body and soul (3 Jn 2) and a wish-prayer in the form of a blessing (3 Jn 14). But the chief contribution lies in the confidence believers have that results from prayer. The prayer of confession brings confidence that one's sins are forgiven and confidence to walk in fellowship with God and his people (1 Jn 1:5-10). This confidence is secured because Jesus Christ the righteous is our advocate or intercessor *(paraklētos)* with the Father (1 Jn 2:2; cf. *entynchanō* in Heb 7:25).

One may have confidence before God that we will receive what we ask when we have a clear conscience* and we are obedient to God (1 Jn 3:21-22). Similar to the image in John 15:7, the thought here is of a person whose life is lived in conformity to Christ's. A Christlike person has confidence in prayer because he or she is intent upon carrying out the will of God the Father, a theme that surfaces explicitly in 1 John 5:14-17. The true child of God is confident that God cares enough to hear and that this caring God does not simply hear prayers of his children but also gives to them whatever they ask. The key to this assurance is the will of God. A true child of God seeks to carry out the will of God in prayer for self and for others, even for those who sin (1 Jn 5:16-17). Jesus instructed his disciples to pray that the Father's will be accomplished (Mt 6:10), and he submitted his own destiny to his Father's will (Mt 26:39, 42). Prayer then becomes not a self-gratifying pursuit but a means by which his children become more effective at seeking first the kingdom of God and establishing his will in their own lives and in the lives of those around them.

2.6. Jude: Prayer in the Spirit. Jude offers a wish-prayer for his readers in the salutation (Jude 2), renders a magnificent doxological prayer to God our Savior in the conclusion (Jude 24-25) and exhorts the readers to "pray in the Holy Spirit" (Jude 20). While this last expression may indicate charismatic prayer, glossolalia, in which the words are given by the Spirit (Dunn, 245-46; Bauckham, 113), the connection with the preceding exhortation to "build yourselves up in your most holy faith" suggests that prayer in the power and under the guidance of the Holy Spirit brings the strength necessary to confront the false teachers who do not have the Spirit (Jude 18-19; cf. Eph 6:18; see Miller, 318-21).

2.7. Revelation: Worship in Prayer. The prayers of the Revelation *(see* Revelation, Book of) are many and varied, but generally they bear marks of worship in its manifold splendor. Apart from the cry of prayer ("Come, Lord Jesus," Rev 22:20), it does not contain petitionary prayer (Cullmann, 116). As John addresses the recipients of the book, he launches into a doxology to Christ that merges with a staccato exclamation concerning the coming of Christ (Rev 1:4-7). A benediction reminiscent of Paul (e.g., Col 4:18; 5:28) concludes the book (Rev 22:21).

As is the case with its other pictures of worship, the book of Revelation sets dramatic scenes of prayerful thanksgiving in worship. From the four living creatures gathered around the throne (Rev 4:9), to the angels* standing around the throne and the Lamb (Rev 7:12), to the twenty-four elders sitting on their thrones before God, thanksgiving is given to Lord God Almighty, "for you have taken your great power and begun to reign" (Rev 11:17).

Three special features in Revelation expand our understanding of NT prayer. The first special feature are hymns of praise and gratitude to Christ, the Lamb who was slain (e.g., Rev 5:9-10, 12, 13; 7:10, 12; 11:15, 17-18; 15:3-4; 19:1-8), which will become a standard feature of later Christian worship in prayer.

The second is the emphasis upon "hearing." The risen Lord "knocks" so that the church might open the door to fellowship with him (see 1.4 above). Genuine prayer is not monologue but dialogue in which the person praying is often silent in order to listen to Jesus' word and command. At the end of the seven letters the churches are admonished, "He who has an ear, let him hear what the Spirit says to the churches" (Rev 2—3). As in the OT, prayer is something personal and specific, a genuine conversation with God or Jesus Christ or the Spirit of God (Schönweiss, 867).

The third special feature is the eschatological character of prayer that anticipates the end of the book and the end of the age: "Amen. Come, Lord Jesus!" (Rev 22:20; Cullmann, 117-18). These fervent words, part of the liturgy of the early church (cf. *Did.* 10.6), are a prayer of invocation. The equivalent of the transliterated Aramaic formula *marana tha* (1 Cor 16:22), it is the oldest Christian prayer of which we have record, showing how those who had invoked the name of their covenant God as "Lord" in the synagogue worship "now came to apply the same divine title to Jesus the Messiah" (Martin 1974, 32-33; see also Mundle, Brown; *see* Worship; Liturgical Elements).

2.8. Apostolic Fathers: Developing a Life of Prayer. The wide diversity of prayer terms found in the NT continues in the writings of the apostolic fathers (Maschke, 103-11). We find also three important developments in the apostolic fathers: prayer as discipline, the use of the Lord's Prayer and prayer for civil authorities.*

2.8.1. Prayer as Discipline. While the apostolic fathers emphasize that prayer is to be a continuous activity for all Christians (Ign. *Pol.* 1.3), as Paul had admonished his readers (1 Thess 5:17), they reflect an increasing movement toward prayer occurring in a pattern of spiritual discipline. The *Didache** admonishes the church that fasts are not to be held on Monday and Thursday, as do the hypocrites (i.e., Jews), but rather on Wednesdays and Fridays. Further, they were to pray three times daily (*Did.* 8.1-3). These prayers were likely intended to be said for the church as a whole, but they set a pattern that later was to include a private, personal discipline of prayer (Volz, 37-40; cf. Hippolytus *Apos. Trad.* 36.2). Polycarp,* harking back to the account of Jesus in Gethsemane, combines the admonition "giving attention to the prayers" with an admonition to fasting (Pol. *Phil.* 7.2), likewise reflecting a pattern of spiritual discipline.

2.8.2. The Use of the Lord's Prayer. The *Didache,* in the same context in which fasting and thrice-daily prayers are admonished, directs the church not to pray as the hypocrites "but as the Lord commanded in his Gospel" (*Did.* 8.2). Then the so-called Lord's Prayer is quoted with the added doxology. Whether we understand the author to intend that the Lord's Prayer itself was the prayer to be prayed or whether it was to be used as an example of the kind of prayer to be prayed three times daily, we can see that the Lord's Prayer had become an integral part of Christian worship by this time (cf. Bradshaw, 26-28; Volz, 40-44).

2.8.3. Prayer for Civil Authorities. 1 Clement includes a lengthy prayer that continues a tradition in the NT to pray for civil authorities (e.g., 1 Tim 2:1-2). But the prayer's length and repeated positive assessment of rulers and governors goes beyond anything found in the NT. While some scholars see the prayer as a theological apology for the *Pax Romana* and others suggest that it reflects an attempt to build a

947

bridge from the emerging church to larger Roman society (Jeffers, 198), it probably applies the enigmatic saying of Jesus to "render to Caesar the things that are Caesar's and to God the things that are God's" (Mk 12:21; see Bowe, 93).

See also BLESSING; FELLOWSHIP; GOD; LITURGICAL ELEMENTS; WORSHIP AND LITURGY.

BIBLIOGRAPHY. J. Alsup, "Prayer, Consciousness and the Early Church: A Look at Acts 2:41-47 for Today," *Austin Seminary Bulletin* 101 (1985) 31-37; R. J. Bauckham, *Jude, 2 Peter* (WBC; Waco, TX: Word, 1983); R. T. Beckwith, "The Daily and Weekly Worship of the Primitive Church in Relation to Its Jewish Antecedents," *EvQ* 66 (1984) 65-80; B. E. Bowe, "Prayer Rendered for Caesar? *1 Clement* 59.3—61.3" in *The Lord's Prayer and Other Prayer Texts from the Greco-Roman Era,* ed. J. H. Charlesworth with M. Harding and M. Kiley (Valley Forge, PA: Trinity Press International, 1994) 85-99; P. F. Bradshaw, *Daily Prayer in the Early Church: A Study of the Origin and Early Development of the Divine Office* (New York: Oxford University Press, 1982); J. H. Charlesworth, "A Prolegomenon to a New Study of the Jewish Background of the Hymns and Prayers in the New Testament," *JJS* 33 (1982) 265-85; O. Cullmann, *Prayer in the New Testament* (OBT; Minneapolis: Fortress, 1995); P. H. Davids, *The Epistle of James: A Commentary on the Greek Text* (NIGTC; Grand Rapids: Eerdmans, 1982); J. D. G. Dunn, *Jesus and the Spirit* (Philadelphia: Westminster, 1975); A. J. Hultgren, "Expectations of Prayer in the New Testament" in *A Primer on Prayer,* ed. P. R. Sponheim (Philadelphia: Fortress, 1988); J. S. Jeffers, *Conflict at Rome: Social Order and Hierarchy in Early Christianity* (Minneapolis: Fortress, 1991); W. L. Lane, *Hebrews 1—8* (WBC; Dallas: Word, 1991); R. P. Martin, *James* (WBC; Dallas: Word, 1988); idem, *Worship in the Early Church* (1964; rev. ed.; Grand Rapids: Eerdmans, 1974); T. Maschke, "Prayer in the Apostolic Fathers," *SecCent* 9 (1992) 103-18; J. R. Michaels, *1 Peter* (WBC; Waco, TX: Word, 1988); P. Miller, *They Cried to the Lord: The Form and Theology of Biblical Prayer* (Minneapolis: Fortress, 1994); D. J. Moo, *The Letter of James: An Introduction and Commentary* (TNTC; Grand Rapids: Eerdmans, 1985); W. Mundle and C. Brown, *"maranatha," NIDNTT* 2:895-98; D. G. Peterson, "Prayer in the General Epistles" in *Teach Us to Pray: Prayer in the Bible and the World,* ed. D. A. Carson (Grand Rapids: Baker, 1990) 102-18; B. Reicke, *The Epistles of James, Peter and Jude* (AB; 2d ed.; Garden City, NY: Doubleday, 1964); H. Schönweiss, C. Brown and G. T. D. Angel, "Prayer, Ask, Kneel, Beg, Worship, Knock," *NIDNTT* 2:855-86; M. M. B. Turner, "Prayer in the Gospels and Acts" in *Teach Us to Pray: Prayer in the Bible and the World,* ed. D. A. Carson (Grand Rapids: Baker, 1990) 58-83; P. W. van der Horst, "Silent Prayer in Antiquity," *Numen* 41 (1994) 1-25; C. A. Volz, "Prayer in the Early Church" in *A Primer on Prayer,* ed. P. R. Sponheim (Philadelphia: Fortress, 1988) 36-47; M. J. Wilkins, *Following the Master: A Biblical Theology of Discipleship* (Grand Rapids: Zondervan, 1992).
M. J. Wilkins

PRAYER ACCLAMATIONS. *See* LITURGICAL ELEMENTS; PRAYER.

PREACHING, APOSTOLIC. *See* KERYGMA AND DIDACHE.

PREACHING FROM ACTS, HEBREWS, GENERAL EPISTLES AND REVELATION

Preachers committed to proclaiming faithfully the whole counsel of God* must not limit themselves to the riches of the Gospels and the epistles of Paul but must also attend to the rest of the NT, not only despite but also because of the challenges and perplexities confronting interpreters of these diverse materials. Some of these challenges are the same for preaching texts chosen from any part of the Bible: discerning the original cultural setting and the concerns the biblical writer intended to address; understanding how the grammatical constructions and formal literary characteristics of the passage bear on interpretation; hearing the word God would speak through this ancient text to God's people in a particular setting in today's world; shaping a sermon that effectively and engagingly presents the claim of the passage upon the modern hearer. Other challenges, however, present themselves with particular force in one or more of the books under consideration, such as how to read apocalyptic* symbolism or how to hear the one voice of the Spirit (*see* Holy Spirit) in statements that appear theologically discrepant.

1. General Considerations
2. Cultural Considerations
3. Theological Considerations
4. Formal Considerations

5. Issues Related to Particular Books
6. Shaping the Sermon

1. General Considerations.

The preacher may regard the diversity of style and viewpoint found in Acts,* the General Epistles and Revelation (*see* Revelation, Book of) not as a thorny problem to fight one's way through or a series of peaks and valleys begging to be made level but rather as an encouraging, intriguing manifestation of the Lord's preservation of the individuality of his messengers and suggestive of the particularity of the Lord's concern for his people. An analogous maintenance of one's own faithful individuality and a particularity of concern for one's own people will rightly be reflected in the words spoken from the pulpit. While God's eternal truth is not internally contradictory, preachers should not treat aspects of that truth as if they were disembodied and independent of their context, as Job's friends heard to their sorrow when their utterances—many of them fully orthodox—were rejected by God (Job 42:7). A fitting word for the energetically self-justifying (some of Paul's hearers?) may be a dangerous word for those slothfully certain of their safety (some of James's hearers?).

Furthermore, preachers may be instructed by the extent to which biblical writers freely assumed the prevailing understandings of their own culture not only in terms of common knowledge (as presumably of the meaning of many of the symbols in Revelation) but also and more problematically in terms of some incorporation of what may be seen as noncanonical materials and worldview (in particular the use Jude* apparently made of *Enoch).* Granting the need for discernment and caution, preachers may yet believe from the model of Scripture itself that they ought not to be so elitist as to scorn or ignore popular culture if they wish to be heard and understood. However, sensitivity to the realities of diversity and of biblical engagement with the culture of the writers' own day should also inoculate preachers against falsely universalizing the particular: points of great doctrinal and practical consequence ought not to be made to rest upon isolated statements not elsewhere attested in Scripture, nor should ideas taken from very different contexts (e.g., Thess and Rev) be asked to march hand in hand.

2. Cultural Considerations.

2.1. The Culture of the Writer and of the Original Recipients. What the text meant (what the writer intended to communicate and expected the reader or hearer to understand) sets limits for what the text may be legitimately taken by contemporary readers to mean. Therefore it is incumbent upon preachers to do that research in commentaries and their introductions, Bible dictionaries and Bible encyclopedias that will enable them not only to clarify obscurities, like what the archangel Michael's dispute over the body of Moses* (Jude 9) might have been about, but also to understand such matters as what might be tempting John's contemporaries to deny that Christ has come in the flesh* (1 Jn 4:2) or what it was like to be a first-century beggar in Jerusalem (Acts 3). The point is not to find material for a speculative psychologizing of the text but rather to discipline a too-direct identification of an earlier situation with a superficially similar one of today (see Best on the difference between situation and the much deeper issue of culture: similar situations may have different weights and meanings in different cultures). Need for outside resources becomes more evident when one recognizes that the biblical writers did not have to state directly what was the common knowledge of those for whom they wrote, whether cultural specifics or details related to problems of particular churches*—knowledge that we by no means automatically share (Ericson, 249).

2.2. The Culture of the Preacher. Regarding their own cultures, preachers have two sometimes conflicting responsibilities: to be keen participant-observers of their cultures, so as to know the images, symbols and examples that will help them communicate clearly, effectively and movingly; and to seek that measure of critical distance that will allow them to be attuned to at least some of the underlying values and unexamined, unarticulated assumptions that govern the culture's understanding of Scripture (and everything else), so that the Bible does not become captive to the culture. The Bible must be preached in culturally specific ways, but no culture rightly escapes God's judgment,* as if its ways can be identified with God's ways.

2.3. The Problem of Cultural Relativism. Because communication can take place only by utilizing the forms, symbols and options available or at least conceivable in a given culture, it sometimes becomes difficult to discern what belongs to the essential message of Scripture and what is a function of the circumstances in which a passage was written. Common sense easily betrays us here, for it is precisely the "common sense" of a particular culture (see Fee and Stuart, 61-77). By the late twentieth century (though not earlier) most preachers might agree that the word to slaves* in 1 Peter* (1 Pet 2:18-25) is a means of granting human dignity to those scarcely considered persons rather than a word to slave owners sanctioning their keeping slaves. But that a similar interpretation should be given to the immediately following words to wives (1 Pet 3:1-6) would be less generally accepted.

There is no infallible path through this thicket, except by a trust in the Holy Spirit to continue to guide the church as a whole into a better understanding of God's will. Meanwhile, if only one cultural option or institution appears to have been open or viable when a text was written, the likelihood that a scriptural expression of that option is culturally relative increases. When a biblical writer goes against the commonly accepted norm, the likelihood that the writer is making known a truth of cross-cultural importance increases. When biblical writers take different positions on an issue (e.g., two attitudes to the Roman government [see Civil Authority] in Revelation 13 versus Romans 13), the likelihood that their words reflect situational differences and that the principles they articulate should be applied in ways sensitive to situational differences increases. Responsible preachers will ponder questions of these kinds. They will then seek ways of handling them that are faithful to their central theological understandings of the Lord's provision in Christ for fallen humanity and that tend to shape Christlike behavior in the hearers. Interpretations of ambiguous matters that compromise the core of the gospel or that tend to generate self-serving, immoral, bigoted or hateful attitudes or behaviors are always suspect.

2.4. Crossing the Cultural Gap. Neither "bridging" nor "leaping" metaphors for crossing the cultural gap are satisfactory, the first because it suggests too wooden and mechanical a process, the second because it might seem to sanction flights of fancy. A legitimate homiletical crossing involves first the faithful exegetical work that leads to as deep an understanding of the text and its original setting as possible and then the pastorally sensitive, imaginative approach that not only discerns directly comparable situations in contemporary life but also risks seeking those parallels and analogies that capture the inner dynamic and intended impact of the scriptural text. The preliminary reestablishing of the strangeness and alien quality of the biblical world may help the preacher to be fresh and relevant, for one needs a certain amount of distance in order to hear a text afresh, to be freshly confronted by it and to ask of it those questions that may, by the grace* of the Holy Spirit, help its truth to come alive for modern hearers.

3. Theological Considerations.

Although some preachers seek to avoid theology on the grounds that doctrinal systems distort particular texts in the interests of their own internal coherence, these preachers will either utilize an unacknowledged grid of their own to make sense of diverse materials, read so selectively or undiscerningly that they miss many important questions, or allow such intellectual chaos to reign that this week's sermon from James* flatly contradicts last week's from Paul. The better preachers comprehend how their own traditions treat the range of major theological loci and also particular problems, the better they will be able to maintain balance in their preaching, avoid undoing next week what they accomplished this week and also see where particular texts challenge their tradition's understanding. A broad theological awareness becomes especially significant when one must consider the diverse perspectives of Acts, the General Epistles and Revelation.

3.1. Doctrinal Diversity. Acts, the General Epistles and Revelation have been especially fruitful sources of denominational differences (not to mention a seedbed for sects that may find their justification in isolated and perhaps hard-to-interpret texts). Preachers from Pentecostal or primitivist groups turn often to Acts; those from holiness groups concerned about backsliding will emphasize warnings in Hebrews* about apostasy* more than Paul's teaching on perseverance (see Endurance); millenarian groups rely heavily on Revelation and may mute Jesus' affirmation that no one knows the time of the end; preachers in the liberation theology camp may find the perspective on the state in Acts 4 and 5 and Revelation 13 pertinent to the current scene, while those with conservative political commitments may turn instead to Romans 13 and 1 Peter 2:13-17. It behooves preachers both to be faithful to their own convictions and to be candid that other Christians may have legitimate biblical grounds for a different viewpoint. Charity to those who differ will serve the church better than pulpit bombast (Liefield, 147).

3.2. Unity Without Homogeneity. Those who acknowledge the superintendence of the Holy Spirit in the writing and transmission of Scripture will grant a fundamental unity to the Bible (despite some anomalies they may not be able conscientiously to sort out) and believe that the whole of it serves God's purpose for our salvation, but they need not draw the false corollary that therefore every writer is saying the same thing or that a theologically loaded word has the same sense no matter which writer uses it. "Faith" *(pistis)*, for instance, does not have the full Pauline sense of heartfelt trust when used by James (who employs the word more in the sense of orthodox opinion) or the writer of Hebrews (who is thinking more of faithfulness, of persevering while holding on to God's promises*). Preachers alert to such variations in usage will spare themselves many theological conundrums. Or, to take a different example, suppose one grants that James, John and Paul were all concerned about right action but that (to oversimplify) James spoke of it directly while John started from love* and Paul from faith.* One may then grant the importance and note the hazards of each style. The direct approach can foster works-righteousness (*see* Faith and Works) and moralism; the love route, too little regard for the shape love must have truly to be loving; the faith route, quietism. Preachers sensitive to the whole counsel of God will avoid false alternatives and seek not to err on any of the available sides.

3.3. Holding on to the Center. Whatever they take up in a sermon, preachers should not let a particular problem or the intricacies of a particular text obscure their fundamental duty to preach the gospel—good news of what God has done, is doing and will do in Christ for us sinners. That does not mean that every sermon will mention directly the cross* and resurrection,* but it does mean that preachers will not forget them and the necessity for them as they construct their sermons. Keeping a firm grip on the theological center will help preachers to avoid majoring in the minors or designing sermons that offer primarily moralisms, good advice, mental hygiene, pop psychology, social or political commentary or the preacher's present view of life. The focus on God must not be swallowed up in discussion of what we are or ought to be doing. At the same time biblical truth is never truth meant only for intellectual apprehension and having no practical consequences: the sermon that remains at the level of abstract discussion of the dimensions of the new Jerusalem (Rev 21) has failed as seriously as the one that lets the transcendent slip from view in a practical discussion of the wrong use of the tongue (Jas 3).

4. Formal Considerations.

4.1. Genre. The books considered here fall into three main genres, with some books showing aspects of more than one: history (regarded as an expression of salvation history), epistles and apocalyptic.

4.1.1. History. Acts is the continuation of a narrative that Luke plainly says is intended as a careful account of events (Lk 1:1-4), a historical narrative. Truthfulness about what occurred and disinterested objectivity are not, however, the same thing. Luke's account is marked by his theological concern to perceive and vividly set down real events that showed what God was doing in history; his purpose was not to present a series of uninterpreted, coldly objective facts. (Hellenistic history generally did not conform to our ideas of critical historiography, and all history is of necessity selective and interpretive.) Therefore the preacher does well to ask why Luke has placed a speech in a particular location or why he has chosen to include certain events and not others, remembering that the speeches, letters and sermons in Acts are almost certainly Lukan compositions in their present form, probably combining research and memory with materials that would be seen as suitable to the occasion, and that the events narrated are selected to make a point. Given the large number of miracles* in Acts and the Hellenistic skepticism regarding the miraculous, it is notable that Luke emphasizes "many convincing proofs" for the resurrection: whatever freedom current literary standards gave him, he obviously wished to emphasize the factual grounding of his account (Acts 1:3; Aune, 125, 135).

4.1.2. Epistles. James, 1 and 2 Peter (*see* 2 Peter), 1, 2 and 3 John (*see* John, Letters of) and Jude constitute what have been called the catholic or General Epistles. A few scholars would add Hebrews to the list. These books, although they are identified as letters, vary in their adherence to traditional letter form and tend to show signs both of conscious literary effort and of being directed to a more general audience than the letters of Paul. They manifest a kind of church consciousness: even when they mention specific people, they do so because of the danger these people pose to the church at large (Doty, 67). Despite the intent of the authors to address the whole church, the modern preacher must recall that the documents come from the early days of the church and assume specific and diverse circumstances by no means identical with our own. Thus they may not directly address certain present-day questions the preacher brings to them but need to be understood first within their own context.

Because of the literary conventions governing Hellenistic letters,* elaborated by Paul (*see DPL,* Letters, Letter Forms), the preacher needs to distinguish those components dictated by convention from those expressive of the writer's particular purpose: in our culture, for instance, the salutation *dear* does not imply affection between the correspondents. Additions to, omissions from and alterations of traditional forms may give significant clues to the writer's attitude and purpose. 2 and 3 John largely exemplify the common Greek letter tradition, as do the letters in Acts (Acts 15:23b-29; 23:26-30), whereas 1 John has no formal elements of a letter. The opening letters in Revelation are the creation of the writer, but Revelation as a whole may, especially given the closing benediction (*see* Liturgical Elements), be seen as a letter to the churches (Tate, 130).

That these books are presented as epistles should not obscure characteristics of other literary forms that may be significant to how they are to be interpreted and preached. Hebrews, 1 Peter and 1 John all have sermonic qualities. James resembles a moral tract with similarities to wisdom literature. 2 Peter has characteristics of a last testament, while Jude is a single-purpose polemic tractate (Ericson, 245).

4.1.3. Apocalyptic. The only NT apocalypse is the Revelation of John (which also manifests prophetic* and epistolary characteristics), but Hebrews 1 and 2, 2 Peter 2 and 3 and Jude, as well as the Gospels and Pauline epistles, have apocalyptic aspects. Apocalyptic works, common in certain Jewish circles between about 200 B.C. to A.D. 200, were literary creations. They were not generally intended to give a precise chronology of future events but were designed to help their recipients think and act in terms of a transcendent perspective, since God would shortly intervene and do away with the present order (only a few apocalypses lack this latter, eschatological,* component). They offer revelatory* visions* characterized by imaginative, symbolic language; conflicts between supernatural forces; reference to extreme suffering* and final judgment; and a view of history that does not expect development but rather the final inbreaking of God.

Preachers do well to honor the intent of the biblical apocalypse to encourage godly behavior and give hope* and power* to persevere in the face of affliction rather than to derive from it eschatological schemas and timetables. They should also pay careful attention to the symbolism and how it is used, getting help from responsible commentators in discerning OT allusions as well as images that were common to the nonbiblical apocalyptic, mythology or culture of the day. However, the meaning of many symbols comprehensible at the time may be lost to us. Such gaps ought not to be filled by flights of speculation, nor should details of symbolic presentations be allegorized. Above all preachers should recognize that they are being less, not more, faithful to the text if they interpret literally what was initially intended to be taken symbolically.

4.2. Literary Structures and Rhetorical Devices. The alert preacher will be sensitive to the inclusion in the biblical text of traditional materials, perhaps adapted for the occasion, and also to the use of rhetorical devices that give emphasis to particular ideas. Vice and virtue* lists and household codes* were common in Greek writing. When used in the literature we are considering (e.g., Rev 9:20-21; 2 Pet 1:5-8; 2:13—3:7) they may in many respects be quite stereotyped, not necessarily addressing specific problems in the community and apparently intended to show that Christianity was not subversive of the social order (Doty, 57; Aune, 196). Liturgical materials, including hymns* and hymn fragments, creedal statements (*see* Creeds) and doxologies, may give a sense of the tone as well as the content of early worship* (e.g., Rev 4:8-11; 1 Pet 3:18-22; Jude 24-25). Diatribes, as in James 2:1—3:12 and 4:13—5:6, are marked by a dialogical character, and the preacher should be alert for imaginary opponents, hypothetical objections and false conclusions that provide a foil for the writer (Aune, 200). Techniques such as repetition of words and ideas, chiasm (an a b b′ a′ pattern, as in Heb 1:5-8), parallelism and antithesis all provide ways of giving weight to main ideas.

5. Issues Related to Particular Books.

5.1. Acts. Luke, the only Evangelist who adds a second book to his narrative, clearly wishes to affirm the historical continuation (see also 4.1.1 above) of the whole biblical drama in the time of the church (note his use of OT prophecy; *see* Old Testament in Acts). By his way of detailing the proclamation of Jesus, the maintenance of an apostolic* group that will guard the tradition* and the rejection of deviants like Simon Magus (*see* Magic), he does present a kind of normative Christianity (Gasque, 120; Aune, 137-38). Thus the preacher may be tempted to frame merely historical sermons or sermons that present some narrated detail of early church life as prescriptive for all time—temptations to be avoided (see Fee 1991, 83-104). The preacher will rightly observe, however, the overriding faithfulness of God in fulfilling his promises, the importance of the church (over against its cultured despisers) and striking evidences of mutual care (e.g., Acts 4:34; 6:1-3; 11:27-30) as well as attend to diverse examples of church life and individual conversion.

Acts shows the spread of the church from Jewish sect (*see* Christianity and Judaism) to worldwide movement, breaking down barriers between people by the power of the word of God and the activity of the Holy Spirit, which will not be thwarted. Triumphalists should be chastened, though, by the striking alternation of successes with suffering on the part of the disciples and scoffing on the part of the unconvinced: the trials are not to be ignored in proclamation of the triumphs. Those moved by the inclusive reach of the gospel should take equal note of its conditions (Acts 4:12; 10:35-36; 13:46) and the demands for repentance* and change of life. Those with an unnuanced view

of the proper relationship of Christians and secular or religious authorities should observe both how often the disciples are at odds with them and the fact that Paul is willing to make use of his status as a Roman citizen to gain protection (e.g., Acts 16:35-40; 25:10-12).

5.2. Hebrews. The writer of the letter to the Hebrews seeks to steady wavering Christians in their faith by presenting the surpassing excellence of Christ, an excellence that makes turning away to any other or for any reason absurd as well as fatal. The author uses a sermonic style, and the preacher may note both the attention given to rhetorical effect and the way exhortation frequently interrupts complex arguments. The preacher may also observe strong contrasts of realm (heavenly versus earthly) and time (ways of the past made obsolete by Christ; the present marked by the finality and sufficiency of Christ's work on our behalf; the promised perfection of the future to be pursued with hope and faith, following the One who has gone before us). The writer's high christology* is combined with an equally strong emphasis on the full humanity of Jesus, which makes him a fit help for us. The preacher will need to pay special attention to the writer's use of the OT, since most of the argument of the epistle turns on key OT passages (*see* Old Testament in Hebrews). Recognition that the writer usually quotes the Septuagint rather than the Hebrew text and that he or she uses extensive typology and interprets christocentrically will help resolve some difficulties, as will familiarity with Jewish midrashic styles of commentary on texts (Hagner 1981, 217-33).

5.3. James. James writes with the practical purpose of calling people to live the Christian life, taking up topics with sometimes little discernible order (though he may return to topics, so preachers should be alert to what has gone before and what follows). Preachers may note resonances with the wisdom tradition (*see* Old Testament in the General Epistles) and in particular with the Gospel of Matthew. Though christological teaching is scant, one must keep in mind the grace to which response is necessary and the point that the Christian duty to fulfill the royal law* (Jas 2:8) rests precisely on its author being king of the universe (Ladd, 638).

5.4. 1 Peter. Peter writes with sermonic tone to a church on the fringes of society and threatened by persecution*—a difference of setting that preachers in secure, mainstream contexts should keep in mind. His stress on God's providence in unmerited suffering surely applies to all Christians, yet Christians in positions of power may have different responsibilities in this regard, especially as regards others who suffer, than do the powerless. One may note that his strong emphasis on future hope is put in the service of discipline* in the present and is not a means of escape from present duties (e.g., 1 Pet 1:13-17).

5.5. 2 Peter. 2 Peter addresses the problem of false teachers—about which some in the contemporary church may be insufficiently concerned—in the context of the power and truth of the gospel (2 Pet 1) and the certainty, despite delay, of the end (2 Pet 3). Preachers need to pay special attention to specialized vocabulary, background ideas and allusions to noncanonical literature.

5.6. 1 John. 1 John maintains a warmly pastoral tone while addressing the effects of the teaching of errorists who deny the Incarnation. The preacher might reflect on various ways in which false doctrine leads to failures in living and hence on the importance of right knowledge of Christ. John's ethical* and theological terminology will also repay exploration. The preacher should be forewarned that John's line of thought is by no means so straightforward as it may at first appear: particular attention to coherent sermonic structure will likely be needed.

5.7. 2 and 3 John. 2 and 3 John provide brief case studies of particular situations in churches facing challenges from without and within. These are true letters, so the preacher should be careful not to overinterpret the merely formal elements.

5.8. Jude. Jude makes clear his purpose that his readers hold on to and contend for their faith in the face of false teachers (Jude 3), an ongoing need in a pluralistic society. The letter is closely related to 2 Peter but has a particularly harsh and urgent tone, suggestive of imminent crisis; preachers addressing less immediately critical situations should be careful of their own sermonic tone when preaching from Jude.

5.9. Revelation. Revelation affirms that the omnipotent God, the nature of whose power is defined by the slain and risen Lamb,* is Lord of history, despite what historical evils and suffering might suggest to the contrary—an affirma-tion desperately needed by those who have been sobered by the Holocaust and other overwhelming historical evils. It also depicts the church and individual Christians in unequivocal opposition to the corporate forces of evil, as manifested in the state and in social and economic structures. This latter emphasis may give grounds for preachers to raise questions about too-easy accommodation to seemingly all-determining corporate forces even in times of cultural tranquility, where the power of Caesar is transmuted into the power of money: late-twentieth-century cases in which tranquility has erupted into overt or covert conflict reveal a contemporary church that has often been unable to separate its calling from its temporal self-interest. But Revelation makes clear that death itself is far from the worst thing that can happen to believers (contrast Rev 14:13 with Rev 9:6).

Preachers do well to preach from the whole of Revelation, not least to help inoculate hearers against popular literalist misinterpretations of the book (see also 4.1.3. above). They also do well to observe the prominence of worship and praise in the midst of suffering and to read large portions of the book aloud so as to begin to sense the evocative power of the language and imagery. A sermon that reflects this evocative power will be in harmony with Revelation's purpose not only to convince people that it is right to worship God instead of the beast but also to persuade them to stake their lives on it (Fiorenza, 134).

6. Shaping the Sermon.

6.1. Choosing a Text. Pastoral discernment must be employed at the level of choice of an appropriate passage of Scripture as well as at the level of illustration and application: not every biblical truth is fitting for every situation. The text should be a coherent unit of thought, usually at least a paragraph. The preacher may avoid a text so long that it raises too many diverse issues, but he or she may not responsibly avoid considering how the context bears on the proper interpretation of the passage selected. Occasional efforts to bring home the central idea of a short letter will be fruitful for preacher and congregation alike.

6.2. Clarifying Theme and Purpose. The preacher should be able to state the theme of the sermon (what it is about) and the purpose of the sermon (what the preacher intends the sermon to accomplish) each in a clear, focused, simple sentence; this theme and purpose should govern the whole development of the sermon. While they may not be identical with the biblical writer's own theme and purpose in a given passage, they must be in fundamental harmony with it. The preacher should beware of purposes that do not go beyond the cognitive (e.g., that hearers understand something without its implications for life being addressed) or those that are merely moralistic (telling hearers to do or be good without grounding the imperative in the enabling acts of God on our behalf).

6.3. Sermon Structure. The text itself should suggest not only the theme of the sermon but also the way the theme will be developed. Keeping the sermon close to the text will help the sermon not only to be faithful to what the text is saying but also to do what the text is doing. Within those guidelines, openness to using a variety of forms will aid in keeping preaching fresh and perhaps suggest approaches especially effective for bringing out the force of a particular text. Introduction and conclusion, as points of special prominence, need extra attention so that the lead-in is accurate and engaging and the culmination brings the main idea home.

6.4. Connecting with Hearers. Preachers who bore themselves will almost certainly bore their hearers. Preachers need to wrestle with their text until it speaks compellingly to them. Having done faithful exegetical work, they should avoid proclaiming historical background or exegetical detail for its own sake but rather include only what moves the sermon forward. The background work is not lost; it provides grounding for a faithful but also imaginative discernment of contemporary connections by which the gospel and its implications come alive in a new setting.

See also HERMENEUTICS; LETTERS, LETTER FORMS.

BIBLIOGRAPHY. R. J. Allen, *Contemporary Biblical Interpretation for Preaching* (Valley Forge, PA: Judson, 1984); D. E. Aune, *The New Testament in Its Literary Environment* (Philadelphia: Westminster, 1987); E. Best, *From Text to Sermon: Responsible Use of the New Testament in Preaching* (2d ed.; Edinburgh: T & T Clark, 1988); M. E. Boring, "The Theology of Revelation: 'The Lord Our God the Almighty Reigns,'" *Int* 40 (1986) 257-

69; J. W. Cox, ed., *Biblical Preaching: An Expositor's Treasury* (Philadelphia: Westminster, 1983); F. B. Craddock, "Preaching the Book of Revelation," *Int* 40 (1986) 270-82; W. G. Doty, *Letters in Primitive Christianity* (Philadelphia: Fortress, 1973); N. R. Ericson, "Interpreting the Petrine Literature" in *The Literature and Meaning of Scripture*, ed. M. A. Inch and C. H. Bullock (Grand Rapids: Baker, 1981) 243-66; G. D. Fee, *Gospel and Spirit: Issues in New Testament Hermeneutics* (Peabody, MA: Hendrickson, 1991); idem, *New Testament Exegesis: A Handbook for Students and Pastors* (Philadelphia: Westminster, 1983); G. D. Fee and D. Stuart, *How to Read the Bible for All Its Worth: A Guide to Understanding the Bible* (2d ed.; Grand Rapids: Zondervan, 1993); E. S. Fiorenza, "The Followers of the Lamb: Visionary Rhetoric and Social-Political Situation," *Semeia* 36 (1986) 123-46; W. W. Gasque, "A Fruitful Field: Recent Study of the Acts of the Apostles," *Int* 42 (1988) 117-31; S. Greidanus, *The Modern Preacher and the Ancient Text: Interpreting and Preaching Biblical Literature* (Grand Rapids: Eerdmans, 1988); D. A. Hagner, "Biblical Theology and Preaching," *ExpT* 96 (1985) 137-41; idem, "Interpreting the Epistle to the Hebrews" in *The Literature and Meaning of Scripture*, ed. M. A. Inch and C. H. Bullock (Grand Rapids: Baker, 1981) 217-42; S. J. Kistemaker, "The Theological Message of James," *JETS* 29 (1986) 55-61; G. E. Ladd, *A Theology of the New Testament*, ed. D. A. Hagner (rev. ed.; Grand Rapids: Eerdmans, 1993); W. L. Liefeld, *New Testament Exposition: From Text to Sermon* (Grand Rapids: Zondervan, 1984); R. P. Martin, "Approaches to New Testament Exegesis" in *New Testament Interpretation: Essays on Principles and Methods,* ed. I. H. Marshall (Grand Rapids: Eerdmans, 1977) 220-51; W. R. Tate, *Biblical Interpretation: An Integrated Approach* (Peabody, MA: Hendrickson, 1991); W. H. Willimon, " 'Eyewitnesses and Ministers of the Word': Preaching in Acts," *Int* 42 (1988) 158-70.

M. Shuster

PREACHING OF PETER. *See* APOCRYPHAL AND PSEUDEPIGRAPHAL WRITINGS.

PREEXISTENCE

In NT studies preexistence refers to the notion that a person or a thing exists in heaven* prior to its entrance into history. This idea is not unique to early Christianity; it is also present in various forms in Plato, some eastern philosophies and Jewish theology, particularly the apocalyptic* and wisdom* traditions during the Second Temple period (*see* Judaism). The preexistent state may be described as ideal (existence in the mind or plan of God*) or actual (existence alongside and distinct from God; Hamerton-Kelly, 1-13). Although the term *preexistence* does not occur in the NT, the notion is expressed in descriptions of the person and work of Christ as well as other entities.

1. The Origin of the Concept
2. New Testament Writings
3. Post-New Testament Writings
4. Conclusion

1. The Origin of the Concept.

1.1. Hellenism. Scholars debate the background out of which the concept of preexistence emerged. Some locate the origin of a preexistence christology* in the Hellenistic church, a community allegedly far removed from the practices and beliefs of monotheistic Judaism. R. H. Fuller (93-97, 203-32) posits a distinction between the Palestinian Jewish, Hellenistic Jewish and Hellenistic Gentile* church (*see* Hellenists). During the Gentile mission,* he maintains, preachers translated the kerygma* of the Palestinian church into Hellenistic categories and thought-forms in order to reach Greeks and Romans with the gospel.* This conscious and unconscious assimilation resulted in theological formulations not present in the earliest Jewish congregations.

According to this approach, the most likely analogue to christological preexistence would have been the gnostic* redeemer myth. In this story a heavenly figure descended into the material world to effect redemption* and ascended back to the heavenly realm. The parallels between christological preexistence and the preexistence of the redeemer, it is assumed, are obvious. Other scholars (Hengel, 33-41) disagree and consider the gnostic redeemer myth to be the construct of scholarly imagination rather than an accurate reading of the data. There is no evidence to suggest that such a myth existed early enough to influence NT writings. Moreover, most scholars today reject hard divisions between Palestinian Jewish and Gentile congregations, since it is apparent Hellenistic culture had made inroads in Palestine centuries before the beginnings of Christianity. Consequently, because Second-Temple Judaism provides an adequate conceptual base, the view is that the background for a preexistence christology is found in Judaism.

1.2. Second-Temple Judaism. Preexistence requires prior existence somewhere; that somewhere is understood generally as heaven. OT writers, particularly exilic and postexilic authors, envisaged a heavenly, transcendent world that ran concurrent with the earthly realm. From time to time the heavenly would break through to the faithful in visions* and revelations.* During the crisis of exile, for example, Ezekiel experiences the heavenly realm in his vision of the throne-chariot by the Chebar River and glimpses at the manlike figure identified as the "glory of the Lord" (Ezek 1:1-26; *see* Glory). Another national crisis precipitates Isaiah's vision of the Lord* who appears high and lifted up, accompanied by ministering seraphim (Is 6:1-12). In a related way the priestly* tradition found significance in Israel's* covenant* story at Mt. Sinai. In it God reveals to Moses* a heavenly tabernacle* and orders him to construct the earthly model and its furnishings according to its heavenly prototype (Ex 25:9, 40; 26:30; 27:8; Num 8:4).

These images become important for the Jewish apocalyptic and mystical traditions. Echoing the story of the tabernacle, 2 Baruch 4:1-7 promises the eschatological* revelation of the heavenly temple and paradise that God created but took away when Adam sinned. On Mt. Sinai God showed Moses the heavenly temple that was to serve as a pattern for the earthly tabernacle and its furnishings. Among the Dead Sea Scrolls (*see* Qumran) the Angelic Liturgy (4Q400-407) portrays the heavenly worship* of angels* as exemplary to the community and assumes a celestial sanctuary as well as the throne-chariot of God's glory. *1 Enoch* 46—48 describes a heavenly Messiah called the Righteous One, the Chosen One and the Son of Man. He is a preexistent, heavenly being described in majestic symbols of power.* He appears at the end of the age to reward* the righteous and punish the evil. In the same way 4 Ezra 7:26-30 portrays the end of the age and declares that God's eschatological promises, including the city, the land* and his Son,* the Messiah, will be revealed.

1.3. Wisdom. While the priestly, apocalyptic and mystical traditions in Judaism provided a cosmology suitable for the expression of preexistence, most scholars today point to the wisdom tradition as the matrix of preexistence christology. Therein Lady Wisdom is personified. Proverbs 8:22-31 describes the divine origin of Wisdom; she was created before the earth and present with God as a "master worker" (Prov 8:30, NRSV). Similarly Wisdom 7:22-25 portrays her *(sophia)* as the "fashioner of all things" and "a pure emanation of the glory of the Almighty" (Wis 7:25, NRSV). In Sirach 24:1-29 God commands Wisdom to dwell with Israel and identifies her with the book of the Law* of Moses (cf. Bar 3:9-4:4).

Interpreters disagree over the significance of such reflection. J. D. G. Dunn (168-76) and L. W. Hurtado (42-50), for example, conclude that Wisdom is not a hypostasis or intermediary figure independent of YHWH. Wisdom language, they say, emerged as a vehicle to express the immanence and redemptive activity of the one, transcendent God. J. E. Fossum (345-46) argues that these texts demonstrate the belief in Judaism that entities such as divine Wisdom existed independently of God. The crux of the disagreement lies in the nature of Jewish monotheism and how the language of personification should be understood.

As Jews, the earliest Christians inherit the cosmology and reflection on Wisdom's role in the creation,* redemption and governance of the world. Preexistence christology then emerges first as wisdom christology. What devout Jews said of Sophia, devout Jewish Christians said of Christ. The early Christians' experience of Jesus both before and after Easter led them to envisage Jesus as the embodiment of divine Wisdom. Given this category, they were able to apply to Jesus the language and the ideas associated formerly with Wisdom. This transference appears to occur in some of the earliest NT documents (1 Cor 8:6; Col 1:15-20) and continues into the latest (e.g., Jn 1:1-18).

2. New Testament Writings.

2.1. Hebrews.
Scholars generally agree that this anonymous letter (*see* Hebrews) represents the setting and doctrine of second-generation Christianity (as Heb 2:1-5 may suggest). Preexistence language is present and less ambiguous than in earlier writings (e.g., those of Paul). Many interpreters assume that, in addition to a Jewish background, a modified Platonic cosmology undergirds the worldview of the author of Hebrews. This dualistic perspective envisaged a heavenly world of ideas and forms that preceded and corresponded to the earthly world of shadows and copies (Plato *Tim.* 51-52; Plato *Rep.* 7.1-3; 9.592b; Plato *Soph.* 246-47; see also Philo *Leg. All.* 3.100-103).

Hebrews begins with clear affirmations of Christ's preexistence in what may be a preformed hymn* about the Son, a key christological title throughout the book. First, God created the universe through his Son, and the Son sustains the world by his powerful, enabling word (Heb 1:2-3; cf. Jn 1:1-3; Col 1:15-16). The same idea is expressed when the author quotes Psalm 102:25-27 and applies it christologically to the role of the Lord *(kyrios)*, who made heaven and earth (Heb 1:10). As God's agent of creation, the Son exists before his earthly manifestation as the man Jesus and takes on functions attributed to Wisdom in Hellenistic Judaism.

Second, the Son is "the reflection *[apaugasma]* of God's glory" (Heb 1:3). Though this statement by itself does not require a claim for preexistence, inasmuch as it draws upon notions of creation and Wisdom, the claim appears to be implied. No literary dependence can be proven, yet the christological affirmation in Hebrews 1:3 may conflate two statements made about Wisdom in the Wisdom of Solomon. Wisdom is "a reflection *[apaugasma]* of eternal light" and "a pure emanation of the glory of the Almighty" (Wis 7:24-25, NRSV). Philo* uses the same Greek word to speak of the Logos* in relation to the most high God (Philo *Op. Mund.* 146; Philo *Plant.* 50). Philo's Logos doctrine appears closely associated with the christological reflection in Hebrews 1:1-3 (e.g., Philo *Plant.* 18; Philo *Som.* 1.241; Philo *Cher.* 127; Philo *Vit. Mos.* 1.155).

Third, the author quotes Psalm 45:7-8 as God's address to the Son: "Your throne, O God, is forever and ever, and the righteous scepter is the scepter of your kingdom" (Heb 1:8). The application of "God" *(theos)* to the Son is rare but not without parallel (cf. Jn 1:1; 20:28); it is nevertheless more significant since it is contained in a scriptural quotation. The phrase "forever and ever" may imply the eternality of the Son's rule and carries the preexistence of Christ beyond a precreational context (Harris, 205-27).

The preexistence of Christ in Hebrews becomes all the more potent when contrasted with his humanity. Employing Psalm 8:4-6 (LXX), the writer depicts Jesus as one who "for a little while was made lower than the angels" (Heb 2:7-9). Moreover, he refers to Jesus' high-priestly duties "in the days of his flesh" (Heb 5:7; *see* Flesh), the Son's obedience* learned through suffering* (Heb 5:8) and his ability to sympathize with every human weakness since he was subject to every human temptation but did not sin* (Heb 4:14-15). Hebrews stresses Jesus' humanity and his earthly pilgrimage while contextualizing this state between the time of his preexistent work and his exaltation* (Heb 1:3). What results is a descent-ascent christology typical of other presentations of Christ in the NT (cf. Phil 2:6-11; 2 Cor 8:9). In a similar vein the author utilizes incarnational language to describe Christ's thoughts as he came into the world to accomplish God's will and entered a body that God prepared for him (Heb 10:5-7; cf. 1:6). Therefore it is evident that Hebrews presents God's Son as preexistent, the agent of creation and incarnate in the man Jesus.

Other entities in Hebrews are characterized in the language of preexistence. Hebrews 11:3, for example, states the creation was prepared by the word of God so that the visible world was made from things that are invisible. Some interpreters understand this as *creatio ex nihilo*. Others consider it an expression of Platonic cosmology whereby the invisible things precede and correspond to the visible world. Perhaps more explicit is the description of the sanctuaries in Hebrews 8:1-7. In the heavens the great high priest sits at God's right hand and ministers in the one, true sanctuary and tabernacle of the Lord, a tabernacle that no mortal has erected. In contrast, priests on earth sacrifice* daily in another sanctuary that is "a copy and shadow of the heavenly" (Heb 8:5). The author grounds his argument in the Sinai narrative and alludes to God's command to Moses to make the tabernacle according to the pattern shown him on the mountain (Ex 25:40; cf. 25:9; 26:30; 27:8). For the author the heavenly, eternal sanctuary existed prior to the earthly and constituted the pattern by which the latter was made.

2.2. 1 Peter and Jude. Traditions associated with Peter (*see* 1 Peter) and Jude* also speak of Christ in language linked to preexistence. In what may be part of an early hymn the author writes that Christ was "predestined before the foundation of the world, made manifest at the end of the times for you" (1 Pet 1:20). While the first clause could be interpreted that the Messiah is God's eternal plan for saving the world (ideal preexistence), the second clause containing the word *phanerōthentos* ("made manifest") rules this out. The verb *phanerousthai* ("to be manifested") implies the revelation of something concealed. The idea appears to be that Christ existed with God, not merely in the plan or mind of God. Formerly, however, Christ was kept in heaven awaiting the eschatological day of redemption (cf. 1 Pet. 1:3-5). A similar thought is reflected earlier in 1 Peter 1:11, which claims the "Spirit of Christ" spoke through the OT prophets about salvation* in general and the sufferings of the Messiah in particular. For the "Spirit of Christ" to communicate to and through the prophets means that Christ must have existed prior to the man Jesus. Herein his preexistent reality is described as "spirit" (*pneuma*), a concept suggested elsewhere in the NT (2 Cor 3:17-18; 1 Tim 3:16; Heb 9:14) and taken up later in a developed "Spirit Christology" (Kelly, 142-45).

A reference to the preexistence of Christ in Jude is less certain. Jude 5 states that the Lord (*kyrios*) saved Israel from Egyptian bondage and also destroyed the unbelieving element of Israel sometime later. The original reading of this text is uncertain. Two manuscripts, Codex Alexandrinus and Codex Vaticanus, which are generally considered reliable witnesses,* contain the name *Jesus* instead of the title *Lord*. This would be the more difficult reading and if original would indicate that Jesus existed during the period of OT history and was God's agent in leading the captives out of bondage. But if "Jesus" is not original the author may still have intended a reference to the "Lord Jesus" since *kyrios* is most often a christological title in the NT, and elsewhere in Jude *kyrios* is used almost exclusively in reference to Christ (Jude 4, 14, 17, 21, 25). If the writer intended to refer to God the Father and not the Lord Jesus, there is no allusion to the preexistent Christ in this book. Nevertheless, the manuscripts containing the name *Jesus* instead of "Lord" evince the tendency of copyists and theologians to read the preexistent Christ into OT history at an early date (cf. Justin Martyr *Dial. Tryph.* 120.3).

2.3. The Johannine Epistles. Close linguistic and conceptual ties exist between the prologue of the Fourth Gospel (Jn 1:1-18) and the beginning of 1 John (1 Jn 1:1-4; *see* John, Letters of).

The author of the epistle purposes to witness to the "Word of Life" *(tou logou tēs zōēs)* and describes it as present with the Father "from the beginning." This phrase may refer to creation, a reading suggested by 1 John 2:13-14 and 1 John 3:8, or the moment when true faith* came to the believing community, a reading made possible by 1 John 2:7, 24 and 1 John 3:11. The ambiguity may be deliberate since the birth of the Christian community may be described as a new creation in which "the darkness is passing away and the true light already is shining" (1 Jn 2:7-8; cf. 2 Cor 5:17; *see* Light). The parallel with the Gospel's prologue renders creation a likely motif. The writer affirms that the "Word of Life" has been manifested to "us" (the apostolic community) and is confirmed by the testimony that "we have heard," "we have seen" and "our hands handled" it. The language certainly speaks of preexistence but stops short of speaking unambiguously of Christ. What preexists and is manifested is called the "Word of Life" and "eternal life." Clarity begins to dawn in 1 John 1:3 when the proclamation and reception of the "Word of Life" promises to engender "fellowship with the Father and His Son, Jesus Christ" (*see* Fellowship). By linking the Father and the Son in this way, the author apparently connects the Son with the "Word of Life" and envisages the preexistence of Christ.

1 John 4:2 and 2 John 7 describe the confession (*see* Creeds) of genuine believers as those who confess that "Jesus Christ has come in the flesh." The phrase "in the flesh" is similar to the incarnational language of John 1:14 and assumes existence prior to "fleshly" existence, although the manner of existence is left undefined. Most interpreters agree the discourse combats an incipient Gnosticism that denied the Incarnation and emphasized the divinity of Christ to the exclusion of his humanity. Those who deny the Incarnation are not "from God" and carry the "spirit of the antichrist" (*see* Antichrist). Evidently the author or authors of 1 and 2 John insist on a real, lasting union between the preexistent Son of God and the flesh in Jesus.

2.4. Revelation. As the only thoroughgoing apocalyptic book in the NT, Revelation's (*see* Revelation, Book of) images and symbols move about on two dimensions, time and space. The temporal duality juxtaposes "things which are" with "things which are going to happen," while a corresponding spatial duality contrasts heaven and earth. As a result the apocalyptic notion of preexistence suggests things exist in heaven that will be revealed in the last days. John experiences visions of "things which are" in heaven with the promise they are also "things which are about to happen" for the benefit of believers suffering persecution* in Asia Minor (Rev 1:19). He sees events (e.g., the worship of all God's people, Rev 4:1-11; the final battle, Rev 19:11-21; the last judgment,* Rev 20:11-15) as well as entities (e.g., the tree of life, Rev 2:7; the throne of God, Rev 4:1-5; the new Jerusalem,* Rev 21:1-2). These events and entities exist in heaven, as the visions suggest, and will occur or be revealed at the proper time. How they exist or when they come to be is never stated. The vision nevertheless guarantees the future deliverance of God's suffering people.

Besides these preexistent entities and events, Revelation also portrays the preexistent Christ. In the initial vision John sees one like a Son of Man whom he represents in images used to describe the Ancient of Days in Daniel 7:9-14. He discovers that this one is none other than the crucified and risen Jesus. The merging of this Son of Man with the Ancient of Days modifies the story in Daniel 7 and appears to identify Jesus with God. The basis for this revisionary reading is the resurrection,* which exalts the crucified one and makes him worthy of the worship accorded God (Rev 4:1—5:14). Such a claim clearly assumes the preexistence of Christ. This interpretation is made sure by the words of the Son of Man, who says, "I am the first and the last" (Rev 1:17; cf. 2:8). The claim to be "first" implies pretemporal existence.

The same expression is found at the end of the prophecy; this time, however, it is merged with other expressions implying preexistence: "I am the Alpha and the Omega, the first and the last, the beginning and the end" (Rev 22:13). The claim to be "the Alpha and the Omega" echoes the beginning of the prophecy (Rev 1:8) and the vision of the throne (Rev 21:6) in which the same formula expresses God's existence. By associating protology and eschatology so closely, the author envisions the dissolution of the present age and the arrival of the new creation that results in a new heaven and earth. The authority* Christ has to consummate the age is based ultimately upon his pretemporal activity as "the Alpha."

The Son of Man instructs John to write seven letters* to seven churches in Asia Minor. The letter addressed to the church in Laodicea comes from "the Amen, the faithful and true witness, the beginning of God's creation" (Rev 3:14). To be "the beginning of God's creation" may mean either the first created being or the origin or source of creation. It is likely that the latter is intended, given the use of similar language in other NT writings with creational mediation as the driving motif (cf. Jn 1:1-3; Col 1:15-16; Heb 1:2). Yet even if the writer intends the former, the first created being exists prior to the creation of other entities and before his historical manifestation as the man Jesus (Rev 1:18).

3. Post-New Testament Writings.

At the end of the apostolic age not all strains of Christianity profess the preexistence of Christ. The Ebionites,* for example, consider Jesus the Messiah but know nothing of the deity of Christ, his Virgin Birth or any notion of his personal preexistence.

The prevailing orthodoxy as expressed in the apostolic fathers* assumes the preexistence of Christ. Clement* of Rome writes that Christ spoke through the Spirit in the Psalms (*1 Clem.* 22.1). The author of the *Epistle to Barnabas** declares that the Lord Jesus was present at creation and affirms that God addressed the statement "Let us make humanity in our image" (Gen 1:26) to him (*Barn.* 5.5; 6.12). Ignatius* states that the Son was "born and unborn, God in man" (Ign. *Eph.* 7.2), "God manifest in human form" (Ign. *Eph.* 19.3). According to R. E. Brown, Ignatius may be the first Christian theologian to link clearly the Virgin Birth with the Incarnation (Ign. *Smyrn.* 1.1), an association not made in the NT (Brown, 134). The author of *2 Clement* understands that Christ was first Spirit and then became flesh to call humanity to salvation (*2 Clem.* 9.5). The *Shepherd of Hermas** appears to evidence a spirit christology as well. It describes the Holy Spirit* as "preexistent" *(proon)*, the agent of creation and made to dwell in human flesh (*Herm. Sim.* 5.6.5). As a reward for admirable service* to the Spirit, God chose this flesh to be a "companion" with the Spirit and so identified the Son with the Spirit (*Herm. Sim.* 9.1.1). At the same time *Hermas* can say the Son of God is older than creation, the Father's "counselor" *(symboulon)* in fashioning

the world (*Herm. Sim.* 9.12.1-3).

In his defense of Christianity Justin Martyr develops a logos christology. Beginning with the Logos idea current in Stoicism and later Jewish thought, he presents the divine "Word" *(logos)* as God's agent of creation and revealer of truth* to humanity. Accordingly he narrates the OT and claims the Jewish ancestors and Moses experienced the Logos, God's offspring (Justin *Dial. Tryph.* 62.4), in a variety of forms. Called "angel," "God" and "Lord," the Logos is distinct from "the Maker of all things" numerically but not in will (Justin *Dial. Tryph.* 56.1-10). In Jesus Christ, the Logos took shape and became human (Justin *Apol. I* 5.4; Justin *Apol. II* 10.1). As a result Justin concludes that the OT theophanic appearances of the angel of YHWH were manifestations of the preexistent Christ (e.g., Justin *Dial. Tryph.* 56.1-10; 58.3; 59.1).

2 Clement envisions also the preexistence of the church. It states the first church, the spiritual church, was created before the sun and moon. The church, which is the body of Christ (cf. Eph 1:20-23), was Christ's companion from the beginning. Just as Jesus was manifest in the last days, so the preexistent church was manifest in him (*2 Clem.* 14.1-3).

4. Conclusion.

The presence of a preexistence christology in several books under a variety of forms suggests this doctrine held wide currency in Christian communities during the first and second centuries. Through the apocalyptic and wisdom traditions, Second Temple Judaism provided the cosmology and images to facilitate the attribution of preexistence to Christ and to see heavenly entities before they become earthly realities. The way NT and early patristic writers approached the subject insinuates it is known already in the churches. Since they do not give systematic treatment to the doctrine, important considerations are left undefined: the nature of preexistent entities and the point when they came to be.

Foundational to the doctrine of the preexistence of Christ is the belief that the crucified Jesus had been resurrected and exalted to the right hand of God. Scholars think most christological development proceeds from the resurrection. Early Christians' belief in and experience of the resurrected Christ served as the catalyst of many christological formulations, including preexistence. This perspective prompted them to apply to Jesus language and functions originally attributed to God the Father and Wisdom. In addition it led to revisionary readings of the OT that place the preexistent Christ in key moments of creative and redemptive history.

See also CHRISTOLOGY; GOD; LOGOS CHRISTOLOGY; LORD.

BIBLIOGRAPHY. R. E. Brown, *An Introduction to New Testament Christology* (New York: Paulist, 1994); D. B. Capes, *Old Testament Yahweh Texts in Paul's Christology* (WUNT 47; Tübingen: J. C. B. Mohr, 1992); F. B. Craddock, *The Preexistence of Christ in the New Testament* (Nashville: Abingdon, 1968); O. Cullmann, *The Christology of the New Testament* (Philadelphia: Westminster, 1959); J. D. G. Dunn, *Christology in the Making: A New Testament Inquiry into the Origins of the Doctrine of the Incarnation* (Philadelphia: Westminster, 1980); J. E. Fossum, *The Name of God and the Angel of the Lord: The Origins of the Idea of Intermediation in Gnosticism* (WUNT 36; Tübingen: J. C. B. Mohr, 1985); R. H. Fuller, *The Foundations of New Testament Christology* (New York: Charles Scribner's Sons, 1965); J. Habermann, *Präexistenzaussagen im Neuen Testament* (EH series 23, vol. 362; Frankfurt: Peter Lang, 1990); R. G. Hamerton-Kelly, *Preexistence, Wisdom and the Son of Man: A Study of the Idea of Preexistence in the New Testament* (Cambridge: Cambridge University Press, 1973); M. J. Harris, *Jesus As God: The New Testament Use of* Theos *in Reference to Jesus* (Grand Rapids: Baker, 1992); M. Hengel, *The Son of God: The Origin of Christology and the History of Jewish-Hellenistic Religion* (Philadelphia: Fortress, 1976); L. W. Hurtado, *One God, One Lord: Early Christian Devotion and Ancient Jewish Monotheism* (Philadelphia: Fortress, 1988); R. Jewett, ed., *Christology and Exegesis: New Approaches* (Semeia 30; Decatur, GA: Scholars Press, 1985); M. de Jonge, *Christology in Context: The Earliest Christian Response to Jesus* (Philadelphia: Westminster, 1988); J. N. D. Kelly, *Early Christian Doctrines* (rev. ed.; San Francisco: Harper & Row, 1978); I. H. Marshall, *Jesus the Savior: Studies in New Testament Theology* (Downer's Grove, IL: InterVarsity Press, 1990); idem, *The Origins of New Testament Christology* (Leicester: Inter-Varsity Press, 1976); H. Merklein, "Zur Entstehung der urchristliche Aussage vom präexistenten Sohn Gottes" in *Zur Geschichte des Urchristentums,* ed. Gerhard Dautzenberg et al. (QD 87; Freiburg: Herder, 1979); J. T. Sanders, *The New Testament Christological Hymns: Their Historical Religious Background* (SNTSMS 15; Cambridge: Cambridge University Press, 1971). D. B. Capes

PRESBYTERS. *See* CHURCH ORDER, GOVERNMENT.

PRIDE AND HUMILITY

In the NT a number of colorful words express the idea of pride. *Alazoneia* is the loud boasting of someone who has no basis for bragging. Closely related is *kenodoxia* ("empty conceit, vainglory"). Paul's favorite term for boasting, *kauchēma,* is found only once in later NT texts, where, however, it has a good connotation, "pride in hope" (Heb 3:6). *Tolmēros,* which is not found in later NT literature, means "audacious," and *hybris* is "pride" or "injury." *Hybris* is the main Greek word for the Promethian pride that resists the will of the gods and must be punished. It is rarely used with that meaning in the NT but more commonly with the idea of "insult" (Heb. 10:29) or "injury" (Acts 16:12, 22-24; 27:10, 21). The more common NT word for arrogant pride is *hyperēphania* or the adjective *hyperēphanos,* the latter of which occurs in several places (e.g., Jas 4:6; 1 Pet 5:5; *1 Clem.* 16.2; 30.2; 59.3; Ign. *Eph.* 5.3). *Hypsoō* means "to exalt," and when it is used reflexively it can mean "self-exaltation." *Physioō* ("to blow up"), common in Paul's writings, with the same twist—to be puffed up with one's sense of self-importance—is not represented in the later NT but appears in Ignatius* (Ign. *Trall.* 4.1; Ign. *Smyrn.* 6.1).

The range of words for humility—mainly *prajtēs* ("meekness") and *tapeinophrosynē* ("lowliness," "humility")—is more limited. *Prajtēs,* meaning the gentle self-control that takes all of life in stride, was a favorite word with the Stoics. In the NT it refers more to one's relationship to God.* "Lowliness" was not considered a virtue by the Greeks but was viewed as weakness. Sometimes this negative meaning appears in the NT, as when Paul's opponents at Corinth remarked about the "weakness" of his personal demeanor (2 Cor 10:1) and when he referred to the artificial acts of self-abasement of the Colossian false teachers (Col 2:18, 23). The joining of humiliation with fasting is found in the *Shepherd of Hermas* (*Herm. Man.* 4.2.2; *Herm. Sim.* 5.3.7) and in Barnabas (*Barn.* 3.5, based on Is 58:10). Several times it refers to "humiliation" through persecution* in Acts* (Acts 20:19) or physical deprivation (Phil 4:12). The more usual NT meaning is "humility" in one's relationships, whether to God or to other persons (e.g., 1 Pet 5:8; Jas 4:6, utilizing the Gospel tradition of Mt 11:29; 23:12, and frequently in *1 Clement*, e.g., *1 Clem.* 62.2; cf. *1 Clem.* 56.1; 58.2).

1. Humility in One's Relationship to God
2. Humility in One's Relationships with Others

1. Humility in One's Relationship to God.

The OT view of Israel's* relationship to God provides the background for the NT understanding of humility. God is Creator, and the creature should humbly submit to the Creator's will. Over against God, all human pride is sin and rebellion (Is 2:6-22; Ezek 16:49-50; Amos 6:8). God will not tolerate the haughty (Ps 101:5). The arrogant nation will not escape God's punishment (Is 10:12-19; Jer 50:29-32; Obad 1—4; neither will the arrogant person (2 Chron 26:16; Dan 5:20). God protects the humble (Is 61:1), however, and heeds the contrite spirit (Is 66:2). He defends the physically poor (Ex 23:6, 11; Deut 15:4, 7, 11). The "poor" are often virtually synonymous with the righteous*; they will experience God's mercy* (Zeph 2:3;,3:12-13). In Second-Temple Jewish literature the suffering righteous are those whom God exalts (Wis, Sir) in a pattern that the rabbis were to elaborate (see Kleinknecht).

The NT follows the same line: the proper religious attitude is submission to God, a teaching reflected in James 4:6-7 and 1 Peter 5:5. The congregants in James* are to have this spirit, which befits those who receive meekly God's word (Jas 1:21; 3:13), and in 1 Peter* leaders are to be examples to the people.

On the other side stands the arrogant, self-confident attitude that does not recognize any dependence on God or humbly submit to his will. It is the error of the merchants in James 4:16, who made all their plans but in their arrogant self-sufficiency left God out of the picture. It is a common trap for the rich, ensnared by the lust of the eyes and the pride of life (1 Jn 2:16; cf. 1 Tim 6:17). Later Christian writers often pointed to the danger of self-pride, born from the delusion of riches (*Herm. Sim.* 8.9.1). Not restricted to the rich, the peril is present as well for would-be teachers, to anyone who falls

into the sin of presumption (*Herm. Sim.* 9.22.1-3; cf. Jas 3:1-12). Humanity owes all to the Creator; there is no room for his creatures to boast (*1 Clem.* 38.3-4).

Running throughout the NT teaching on humility is the theme of eschatological* reversal that goes back to the teaching of Jesus and beyond him to Jewish martyrology: "Whoever exalts themselves shall be brought down, and whoever brings themselves down shall be exalted" (Mt 23:12; Lk 14:11; 18:14). It is the OT theme of God overthrowing humanity's injustices, exalting the lowly and abasing the proud. It is the song of the coming messianic age that Mary* sings (Lk 1:51-53). It is echoed in James 1:9-10 and reechoed in James 4:6 and 1 Peter 5:5-6. The latter two are strikingly similar and may reflect a common teaching in the early church. Both quote Proverbs 3:34, which shares the same sentiment as Jesus' saying, which in turn is based on the rabbinic teaching of "my humiliation is my exaltation" (see Kleinknecht, Schweizer): God opposes the proud and shows favor to the lowly. Later Christian writers were also familiar with the proverb (*1 Clem.* 30.2; cf. Sir. 3:17-18).

Not only did Jesus teach reversal of the world's norms but also he embodied it in his own ministry.* He was "meek and lowly of heart" and bade his disciples to be the same (Mt 11:29). He entered Jerusalem* as its meek King in fulfillment of Zechariah 9:9 (Mt 21:5) and set an example of servanthood* by washing his disciples' feet (John 13:14-15; cf. 1 Tim 5:10). Above all he was obedient to God's will, even to the death of the cross* (Phil 2:5-11; *see* Death of Christ).

Later Christian writers appeal to Christ's* humility as an example to imitate (Heb 12:2-3; 1 Pet 2:18-24; and Rev 14:4, where "following the lamb" is a key idiom; see Bauckham, 66-108; *see* Imitation; Lamb). This is particularly true of *1 Clement*, where humility is held up as the essence of Christian living (*1 Clem.* 13, 14), and Christ's sufferings* are portrayed as the supreme example of humility (*1 Clem.* 2.1). Clement quotes all of Isaiah 53:1-12 and Psalm 22:6-8 to depict the humiliation of Christ (*1 Clem.* 16.16) and concludes with the question, If Christ was so humble in spirit what else could his followers be? (*1 Clem.* 16.17). Not content to end there, Clement launches into a long roll call of "pioneers in humility," a list that includes

Abraham,* Job and Moses* (*1 Clem.* 17), David (*1 Clem.* 18), Jacob (*1 Clem.* 31.4), and Esther (*1 Clem.* 55.6-7).

2. Humility in One's Relationships with Others.

There are frequent references to pride and humility in the ethical* sections of the NT, especially in the virtue* and vice lists. In Mark 7:22 Jesus lists blasphemy and arrogance together as vices that come from within people and defile them. A similar linkage of self-willfulness and blasphemy occurs in 2 Peter 2:10. 2 Timothy 3:2 links boastfulness with love of money and self-love. Titus 1:7 lists arrogance as a quality that should not be found in a bishop. Later Christian literature continues to list pride among the deadly sins. Hermas, for example, lists five pride words in his vice catalog (*Herm. Man.* 8.3-5; cf. *Didache* and *Barnabas* with their common Two Ways moral teaching).

"Humility" often appears in lists of virtues. Sometimes the word is "meek" (*praÿs,* Mt 5:5; 1 Pet 3:4); sometimes it is "lowliness" (*tapeinophrosynē;* the adjective is found in 1 Pet 3:8). Meekness is necessary when sharing the faith* in adverse circumstances (1 Pet 3:15). People cannot claim meekness for themselves; it must be seen in them by others (*1 Clem.* 38.2).

Another traditional form of ethical teaching came into Christianity through Judaism*: that of the Two Ways. A section in the Qumran* *Rule of the Community* is devoted to the "two spirits" in humans, the spirit of truth and the spirit of error (1QS 3.13—4.26). Hermas employs the same device, sometimes speaking of "two angels" (*Herm. Man.* 6.2.2), sometimes of "two spirits" (*Herm. Man.* 11.8). The *Epistle of Barnabas** and the *Didache** both draw on a common source of Two Ways and are closely parallel in their treatment of pride (*Barn.* 19.6; *Did.* 3.9). In all these the evil way or spirit is characterized by arrogance, the righteous way or spirit by humility.

From Paul's emphasis on humility as a key to church unity, it was a small step for later writers to insist on humility for maintaining authority* in the congregation. This is true for 1 Peter and the Pastorals as well as for Ignatius, who condemned as being arrogant those who opposed the bishops (Ign. *Eph.* 5.3; *see* Church Order and Government). *1 Clement* dwells on the virtues of humility, viewing meekness as a means of overcoming the Corinthians' opposition to their leaders (*1 Clem.* 48.6). It is better to be a humble member of Christ's flock than to be rich and famous but not share its spirit (*1 Clem.* 57.2).

See also ETHICS; MERCY; REPENTANCE, SECOND REPENTANCE; SIN, WICKEDNESS; SUFFERING; VIRTUES AND VICES.

BIBLIOGRAPHY. R. J. Bauckham, *The Theology of the Book of Revelation* (NTT; Cambridge: Cambridge University Press, 1993); E. Best, *1 Peter* (NCB; Grand Rapids: Eerdmans, 1977); E. J. Cook, "Meekness," *IDB* 3:334-35; P. H. Davids, *The Epistle of James* (NIGTC; Grand Rapids: Eerdmans, 1982); B. S. Easton, "New Testament Ethical Lists," *JBL* 51 (1932) 1-12; W. Grundmann, "ταπεινός κτλ," *TDNT* 8:1-26; F. Hauck and S. Schultz, "πραΰς, πραΰτης," *TDNT* 6:645-51; K. T. Kleinknecht, *Der leidende Gerechtfertige* (WUNT 2.13; Tübingen: J. C. B. Mohr, 1984); L. H. Marshall, *The Challenge of New Testament Ethics* (London: Macmillan, 1946); W. A. Meeks, *The Moral World of the First Christians* (LEC 6; Philadelphia: Westminster, 1986); G. E. Mendenhall, "Humility," *IDB* 2:659-660; R. Schnackenburg, *The Moral Teaching of The New Testament* (New York: Herder & Herder, 1965); E. Schweizer, *Lordship and Discipleship* (London: SCM, 1960); M. J. Suggs, "The Christian Two Ways Tradition: Its Antiquity, Form and Function" in *Studies in New Testament and Early-Christian Literature,* ed. D. E. Aune (Leiden: E. J. Brill, 1972).   J. B. Polhill

PRIEST, HIGH PRIEST

In the later NT writings the word *priest (hiereus)* occurs three times in Acts, fourteen times in Hebrews and three times in Revelation. In Acts* it is used in a straightforward way during Luke's historical account, twice to refer to the Jerusalem priests (Acts 4:1; 6:7) and once to refer to a pagan priest of Jupiter (Acts 14:13). Revelation (*see* Revelation, Book of) uses it collectively to refer to the Christian church* ("kings and priests," Rev 1:6; 5:10; "priests," Rev 20:6). In Hebrews the old Israelite priesthood forms the framework for the author's depiction of Christ.

The term "high priest" (*archiereus*) follows the same pattern, being used in the historical sense twenty-two times in Acts for the leader(s) of the temple complex in Jerusalem, while in Hebrews it is used seventeen times either for Christ or for the OT figures who foreshadowed his work in the heavenly tent.

The word *priest* is never used in the NT for

an individual Christian, and priestly language is used only once to explain a specifically ministerial role, when Paul, in a violent metaphor, speaks of his "priestly administration (*hierourgounta*) of the gospel of God that the sacrificial offering of the Gentiles may be acceptable, sanctified in the Holy Spirit" (Rom 15:16). In 1 Peter 2:9-10 the term is broadened to include the role of the people of God, who are designated in language drawn from Exodus 19 as the "new people" or God's choice, exercising the priestly ministry of praise.

1. Hebrews
2. Post-Apostolic Writers
3. Conclusion

1. Hebrews.

Hebrews* has been justly called the epistle of priesthood. Nowhere else in the NT is Christ's* work set forth against the background of the OT priesthood. He is our great high priest (Heb 4:14) who is able to "sympathize with our weaknesses" and who was "tempted in every point as we are" (Heb 4:15). But in setting forth Christ as a priest the author does not limit himself to the common Jewish stereotypes of a Jerusalem* priest. The epistle understands the sacrifice* of Christ in language taken from the levitical ritual but in no other way connects it with levitical sacrifices.

In setting forth the priesthood of Christ the author points his readers' attention away from Aaron, who embodies what might be called an exclusive priesthood (to which only a select few were admitted) to another OT figure, Melchizedek.* For this author the OT is a book of anticipation, and as such the priesthood of Christ is anticipated by Aaron only as "sketch" and "shadow" (Heb 8:5; 10:1), whereas in Melchizedek is seen the "likeness" of Christ (Heb 7:15). These two words, "shadow" and "likeness," are not used casually by the author; they point to two competing models of ministry.* The OT priesthood is "but a shadow of the good things to come instead of the true form of these realities" (Heb 10:1). Aaron had the trappings of priesthood, but he lacked the ability to enable worshipers to draw near to God.* The sacrifices appeared to solve the problem of human misery, but they did not have the power to purify the conscience* from dead works. It is different with Melchizedek, of whom the author declares, "resembling the Son of God he continues a

priest forever" (Heb 7:3).

1.1. The Role of Melchizedek. Many modern interpreters have attempted to discover the true identity of Melchizedek in Hebrews, he who is "without father, without mother, without genealogy" (Heb 7:3), but most of their efforts have been unnecessary. For the author tells his readers plainly what Melchizedek's significance is. His priesthood is no shadow but participates in the reality of the priesthood of Christ. It was a genuine anticipation. For in Jesus "another priest arises in the likeness (*homoiotēs*) of Melchizedek, who has become a priest not according to a legal requirement concerning bodily descent but by the power of an indestructible life" (Heb 7:15). In other words, Melchizedek embodies a priesthood that is based not upon heredity or outward appointment but on the inner spiritual resources of a person's character. Through Melchizedek, Abraham* was enabled to draw near to God; even though he did not have any of the outward requirements of priesthood (e.g., correct parents or genealogy), nonetheless he acted as priest to Abraham.

The author's handling of Melchizedek requires careful and detailed examination. His interest in Psalm 110, one of the most popular testimonies used by the NT writers (cf. Mk 12:36; Acts 2:33-34; Rom 8:34; Eph 1:20; 1 Pet 3:22), leads him to ask after the identity of the mysterious personage of Hebrews 7:4. It would then be natural to go back to Genesis 14 for the answer. Part of the problem of modern interpreters who have grappled with the author's use of Melchizedek is the frugality of his explanations. He never explains, for instance, how for him Melchizedek became a priest or of what his "greatness" (Heb 7:4) consisted. Confining himself to the biblical account, he mentions only signs of that greatness—the blessing* of Abraham and the reception of tithes (Heb 7:1-2). Yet the most logical inference would be that for this author both Melchizedek's priesthood and his greatness resided in the quality of life he lived. This must remain the central point of comparison between the two figures—the possession of an ability to stand on the "godward" side of the human race (to borrow A. Nairne's phrase), an ability found not in any external system of law* but in the eternal will of God, a will that may be performed by those who know what that will is (Heb 10:5-18).

The so-called hymn* of Hebrews 7:3 continues to vex commentators and remains the main stumbling block to construing Melchizedek in purely human, historical terms. How is he "without father, without mother, without genealogy"? To this question there continue to be two frequent answers.

(1) The author intends a literal understanding of *apatōr, amētōr, agenealogētos*. Thus Melchizedek is seen as a supernatural, heavenly being. In defense of this view it must be admitted that *apatōr* and *amētōr* are used in pagan texts for the miraculous birth of deities or demigods. Its fatal objection in the context of Hebrews may be stated simply: if Melchizedek was not understood by the author to be a human being, his extensive arguments for the authority of Melchizedek over Abraham and Levi are unnecessary.

(2) The author intends a typological significance of these words that rests upon the rabbinical principle of quod non in Thora, *non in mundo* ("what is not in the Torah does not exist in the world"). Into this class fall those commentators who understand the author to be combating a view (such as is found in Qumran*) of Melchizedek as a supernatural, heavenly being similar to the archangel Michael. Thus through the use of typology the author is said to provide his counterargument; namely, that Melchizedek, far from being a supernatural being, anticipates only symbolically (in the remarks and silences of Scripture) the actual attributes of the eternal Son.*

But this view also has stumbling blocks. If Hebrews 5—7 constitutes the author's answer to a too-exalted view of Melchizedek, why then is nothing negative said about him? The other figures from the old covenant* are all treated in negative fashion: angels* (Heb 1—2) lack the exalted titles; Moses* is a servant* in God's house,* not Son (Heb 3—4); Aaron and the system he represents were never really able to remove sin (Heb 8—10). Nothing negative, however, is recorded against Melchizedek. In Hebrews, Melchizedek and Christ are not, as are Aaron and Christ, related as shadow to substance. It is not that Jesus has something really that Melchizedek has merely symbolically. The author's use of *homoiotēs* (Heb 7:15) strongly implies that what is said about the one must be construed in the same way as applying to the other.

The difficulty lies in finding the author's

point of comparison between Melchizedek and Christ. It is useful to recall B. F. Westcott's (7) description of Christ's appointment as Son in Hebrews: it is an eternal appointment that has inceptive fulfillments in time but with no particular time at which it begins. Similarly the priesthood of Melchizedek and Christ is founded upon an eternal decree, and the force of their indestructible lives puts that decree into operation. Since their appointment is grounded in the eternal will of God and not in any set of outward human ordinances, there is no "beginning of days" to their priesthood; and since both live beyond death, there can be no end to their lives. (The author's reasoning comes very close to that of Mark 12:26-27: because God is the father of Abraham, Isaac and Jacob, he is the God of the living, not of the dead.) Insofar as the figure of Psalm 110:4 is "like" the priest Melchizedek, it is "witnessed" that Melchizedek "lives." And if he lives, his priesthood must therefore be perpetual. In other words, a comparison of Hebrews 7:3, 8 with Hebrews 7:24 suggests that the same thing is being said about both Melchizedek and Christ.

For this writer Melchizedek and Christ are priests "continually" (*eis to diēnekes*, Heb 7:3; *eis ton aiōna*, Heb 7:24). F. L. Horton and D. M. Hay have correctly perceived that the burden of Hebrews 7:13-28 is the question of priesthood rather than that of any divine qualities. This then puts the expositor into a position to understand the author's distinctive use of Melchizedek. The question he is asking is, What is the basis of the respective OT priesthoods? Since Aaron's was founded on an external system of rules and regulations, his days as priest were numbered: they commenced with the initiatory rite (when the Levite reached a certain age—thirty) and were terminated by death. Melchizedek's days as priest had no such temporally conditioned beginning, insofar as they were rooted in the eternal will of God. It is important to recognize that the phrases "no beginning of days" and "no end of life" are not strictly parallel. One looks backward, drawing the readers' attention to a superior priesthood within God's predestining purposes; the other looks forward, impelling the readers to consider the afterlife. While "no end of life" includes the idea of perpetual priesthood, it widens in scope to include the resurrection* life* itself.

That the known terms *apatōr* and *amētōr* are combined with *agenealogētos,* a word apparently coined by the author, suggests strongly that he employs the first two terms in an unusual sense. He is qualifying the two familiar terms with the third, as if to say, "and by that I mean . . . " *Agenealogētos* thus indicates not biology but the absence of any genealogical credentials for priesthood. Remaining doubts as to this point are removed by Hebrews 7:13-14: there the author admits that Jesus did come from the tribe of Judah. What is true of Jesus—that he had a human genealogy—for this writer cannot have been untrue of Melchizedek.

The term *taxis* in the Septuagint of Psalm 110:4 has also resulted in considerable misunderstanding. The common translation, "order," implies "succession," but this is not the author's idea. It is much better translated "character" (see Heb 7:15, whereas *tēn homoiotēta* is a clear paraphrase of the *kata* of Ps 110:4). The author's argument in Hebrews 5:6, Hebrews 6:20, and so forth, may therefore be paraphrased, "You are a priest forever, according to the character of Melchizedek" (or, "just as Melchizedek is"). Melchizedek has a character dependent upon not any external ordinance but the prior, eternal will of God, and as such his priesthood is of the same substance as that of Christ.

1.2. The Role of Aaron and the Levitical Priests. The correspondences between Christ and the Aaronic priesthood are, as we have seen, drawn differently from those of Melchizedek. Aaron's priesthood relates to Christ's as shadow to substance (Heb 8:5; 10:1). Positive correspondences are clearly drawn, but the ancient rituals are a "sketch and shadow" (*hypodeigma kai skia*, Heb 8:5 NRSV) of the heavenly things and Christ's ministry in them. The author is interested in the levitical service in which the priest is chosen from among men and appointed by God (Heb 5:1; 8:3) to serve in the earthly sanctuary (*see* Tabernacle), and he is particularly interested in the ritual of the Day of Atonement, wherein the animal was killed and its blood brought into the holy of holies by the high priest (Heb 9:7) so that the people might have access to God (Heb 4:16; 7:18-28; 10:1, 19, 22).

In a similar but superior way Jesus has entered the "greater and more perfect tent made without hands" (Heb 9:11) and into "the holy place, not through the blood of goats and calves but through his own blood, thus securing an eternal redemption" (Heb 9:12). Despite what is often said, the author is not saying anything platonic in these passages, as if countering the heavenly to the earthly as ideal versus material. He is working with a biblical, horizontal promise-fulfillment scheme, maintaining that, once the superiority of Christ's priesthood is recognized, the OT ritual has much to offer as a picture book (or sketchbook) of Christ's priestly work. It makes the real thing recognizable when it comes. The old covenant priesthood was valuable in its day in that it pointed the way forward to Christ's priesthood (cf. Paul's similar point in Gal 3:23-26; there the law* is our "tutor" to lead us to faith*).

2. Post-Apostolic Writers.
Among the apostolic fathers* the idea of Christ as priest or high priest is found in Ignatius* ("Priests are a fine thing, but better still is the high priest who was entrusted with the holy of holies"; Ign. *Phld.* 9.1); *1 Clement* 91.3 ("through the high priest and guardian of our souls") and *1 Clement* 36.1 ("the high priest of our offerings, the protector and helper of our weakness"); and the *Martyrdom of Polycarp* 14.3 ("through the eternal and heavenly high priest, Jesus"). For Justin Martyr the twelve apostles* are "the bells on the garment of the high priest." Clement of Alexandria and Origen refer to Jesus as "great" high priest (Clement of Alexandria *Strom.* 6.153-54; Origen *Comm. Joh.* 6.53, 275), while Origen adds the terms *true (alēthinos)* and *perfect (teleios)* to the term *archiereus* (Origen *Hom. in Jos.* 26.3; *Comm. Joh.* 28.1, 6). Other phrases such as "*logos* high priest" and "*Christ priest*" are found in Justin, Clement of Alexandria and Origen (cf. the references in Schrenk). In these various instances the Fathers are clearly developing the metaphorical language of the author of Hebrews in ways consistent with but less imaginative than his usage.

The apostolic fathers also refer to humans as priests. Both Justin (Justin *Apol. I* 2) and Ignatius (Ign. *Eph.* 5.9) refer to the whole people of God (*see* Church as Israel) as a "royal priesthood," following 1 Peter.* *Didache* 13.3 cites the prophets* as high priests, indicating the respect due to them. And Ignatius frequently refers to the bishop as priest or high priest (e.g., Ign. *Eph.*; Ign. *Magn.* 3.11, 19; Ign. *Phld.* 4.11; Ign. *Smyrn.* 9.17).

3. Conclusion.
The author of Hebrews bases much of his understanding of Jesus as priest on one OT passage, Psalm 110. Since this text was composed at a time when the temple* ritual was in the hands of the levitical priests who traced their ancestry to Aaron, the question is raised, Why should the psalmist imagine a day when God would inaugurate a new priestly order? The answer is that for the author the present order was unsatisfactory. He then takes his readers on a relatively modern exegesis of Genesis 14, not to provide a fantastic allegory like that of Philo* of Alexandria but to ask the question, What did the words "priest forever after the order of Melchizedek" mean to the psalmist who wrote them? For him Psalm 110 is a claim by the psalmist that a new priesthood was needed to intercede between God and his creatures, and he found that in the figure of the priest-king Melchizedek of Genesis 14, who is like Jesus in that his priesthood is based on character and rooted in the eternal will of God rather than in any outward human ordinances.

Aaron's role in the levitical ritual is then seen (Heb 8—10) as a helpful sketching, ahead of time, of Christ's work in the heavenly sanctuary, but Aaron's priesthood relates to that of Christ as shadow to reality rather than partaking of the substance of Christ's work. The readers of Hebrews, failing to see this, are in danger of lapsing back into the than benefiting from the full substance of Christ's sacrificial ministry on their behalf.

See also MELCHIZEDEK; TABERNACLE, SANCTUARY; TEMPLE.

BIBLIOGRAPHY. H. W. Attridge, *The Epistle to the Hebrews* (Herm; Philadelphia: Fortress, 1989); J. Baer, "Priest," *NIDNTT* 3:32-44; F. F. Bruce, *The Epistle to the Hebrews* (NICNT; Grand Rapids: Eerdmans, 1964); G. B. Caird, "The Exegetical Method of the Epistle to the Hebrews," *CJT* 5 (1959) 44-61; idem, *New Testament Theology,* completed and ed. L. D. Hurst (Oxford: Clarendon, 1994); P. Ellingworth, *The Epistle to the Hebrews* (NIGTC; Grand Rapids: Eerdmans, 1993); D. A. Hagner, *Hebrews* (San Francisco: Harper, 1983); D. M. Hay, *Glory at the Right Hand: Psalm 110 in Early Christianity* (Nashville: Abingdon, 1973); F. L. Horton, *The Melchizedek Tradition* (SNTSMS 30; Cambridge: Cambridge University Press, 1976); L. D. Hurst, *The Epistle to the Hebrews: Its Background of Thought* (SNTSMS 65; Cambridge: Cambridge University Press, 1990); M. Isaacs, *Sacred Space: An Approach to the Theology of the Epistle to the Hebrews* (JSNTSup 73; Sheffield: JSOT, 1992); D. Juel, *Messianic Exegesis: Christological Interpretation of the Old Testament in Early Christianity* (Philadelphia: Fortress, 1988); S. J. Kistemaker, *The Psalm Citations in the Epistle to the Hebrews* (Amsterdam: van Soest, 1961); G. E. Ladd, *A Theology of the New Testament,* ed. D. A. Hagner (Grand Rapids: Eerdmans, 1993); W. L. Lane, *Hebrews* (2 vols; WBC; Dallas: Word, 1991); B. Lindars, *The Theology of the Letter to the Hebrews* (NTT; Cambridge: Cambridge University Press, 1991); O. Michel, "Μελχισέδεκ," *TDNT* 4:568-71; A. Nairne, *The Epistle of Priesthood* (Edinburgh: T & T Clark, 1913); D. Peterson, *Hebrews and Perfection: An Examination of the Concept of Perfection in the Epistle to the Hebrews* (SNTSMS 47; Cambridge: Cambridge University Press, 1982); G. Schrenk, "ἱερός κτλ," *TDNT* 3:221-83; B. F. Westcott, *The Epistle to the Hebrews* (London: Macmillan, 1989 [1892]); R. Williamson, *Philo and the Epistle to the Hebrews* (Leiden: E. J. Brill, 1970).   L. D. Hurst

PRISCILLA. *See* WOMEN IN THE EARLY CHURCH.

PROMISE

In Christian literature God's activity spans the time frames of past, present and future. The concept of promise weds the three into a composite picture of God's involvement in the concerns of his people. In the NT and the apostolic fathers,* promise refers to both the pledge made by God* and the substantive fulfillment of that pledge in relation to his covenant* people, centering especially in God's gift of salvation* through Jesus Christ, who inaugurates salvation in the present age and will consummate it at the Parousia.*

1. The Concept as Expressed in the New Testament
2. The Concept Outside the New Testament
3. Promise in Acts, Hebrews, General Epistles and Revelation
4. Promise in the Apostolic Fathers
5. Conclusions

1. The Concept as Expressed in the New Testament.
Although authors of the NT utilize the words *hosios* (Acts 13:34) and *pistis* (1 Tim 5:2) to communicate the idea of promise, *epangelia* and

its cognates are the primary conveyors of the concept. The term *epangelia* occurs fifty-two times and has wide distribution especially in Acts,* portions of Pauline literature and Hebrews.* Usage is noticeably absent from the Gospels with the exception of Luke 24:49, where Jesus speaks of the promised Holy Spirit.* The verbal form *epangellomai* enjoys a similar distribution but is employed only fifteen times. *Proepangellomai*, "to promise beforehand," and *epangelma* each are used only twice in the NT.

2. The Concept Outside the New Testament.

No single term conveys the idea of promise in the OT, the authors using a variety of common words such as *dbr* ("to speak") and *'amar* ("to say") to express the idea of God's pledge. God's declaration of his intentions for his people nevertheless plays a central role in the OT. God's promises to his covenant people are grounded especially in the foundation stories of the nation (Weinfeld, 353) and particularly in the promises to Abraham* concerning the land,* the greatness and vastness of his descendants and the nation's role in blessing* all the peoples of the earth (Gen 15:1-6; 17:3-8; 22:15-18).

In the Septuagint the translators use the term *epangelia* most often to communicate the promise one person makes to another, especially in political contexts (e.g., 1 Esdr 1:7; Esther 4:7; 1 Macc 10:15). God's covenant promise is in view only at 2 Maccabees 2:17-18 and 3 Maccabees 2:10, where the verbal form is used. These two passages are especially significant since they address God's attention to and salvation of his people, notions related to uses made of the *epangelia* word group in the NT.

In the broader Greco-Roman world the term *epangelia* could convey the idea of a command, summons, notification, offer, promise, profession or undertaking. As in the Septuagint, the most common usage is in military and diplomatic contexts. In these contexts a commander or an official might make a promise communicating self-resolve, exhortation to the promisee, deception or encouragement. Furthermore, a speaker might point to past promises, made by himself or another, as reminders, exemplary illustrations, exhortations to purity* and endurance,* thanksgivings, appeals or criticisms (Worley, 18-67).

3. Promise in Acts, Hebrews, General Epistles and Revelation.

Almost half the uses of *epangelia* in the NT are found in Acts and Hebrews, their authors employing the word twenty-two times. The term also finds expression at 2 Peter 3:4, 2 Peter 3:9 and 1 John 2:25. Nine of the fifteen occurrences of *epangellomai* in the NT are found in Acts, Hebrews, James,* 2 Peter* and 1 John (*see* John, Letters of). 2 Peter 1:4 and 2 Peter 3:13 contain the only two uses of *epangelma* in NT literature. When these uses of *epangelia* and its cognates are surveyed three distinct categories may be delineated: a person's promise to another person; promise as a component of Israel's* foundation stories; and promise and eschatological* salvation.

Acts 23:12-22 records a plot against Paul's life and the report concerning that plot made by Paul's nephew to the Roman commander in Jerusalem. In the boy's report he says that the Jews await the commander's promise *(epangelia)* granting their request for another interrogation of Paul. Of the NT occurrences this one fits the most common secular uses of the day. 2 Peter 2:19 also records the promise made on the person-to-person level. In this text false teachers offer the empty promise of freedom* to the immature.

The promises made to Abraham form not only the foundation of Israel's history but also the foundation of the NT theology of promise. Especially in Acts and Hebrews Abraham is presented as the paradigmatic receptor of God's promises. God called Abraham out of Mesopotamia and promised him descendants and a new land (Acts 7:5, 17). As the promisee, Abraham exercised faith* in response to the promise and thus received God's favor. Remaining faithful to God, although he did not receive the fulfillment of the promise in his lifetime, he offers an example to those promised the new covenant (Heb 6:13-15; 7:6; 11:8-19).

The great theological focal point for the NT teaching on promise lies in a soteriological framework. God's promises through the ages are summed up in the person of Christ and the salvation he brings. This salvation has been inaugurated in his new covenant community and will be consummated at the end of the age.

Most uses of the promise motif in Acts relate to aspects of salvation as inaugurated in God's people in the present age. The Holy Spirit about whom Jesus spoke to his disciples (Acts 1:4), that Spirit he received from the Father (Acts 2:33) and poured out on the new community, is the promised gift received at the inauguration of salvation (Acts 2:38-38). The coming of Jesus, a Savior who would provide forgiveness* of sins* and justification, was promised to the ancestors* (Acts 13:23, 32). God's fulfillment of that promise appears dramatically in the resurrection* of Jesus from the dead (Acts 13:33-39; 26:6-8).

Some scholars have seen this promise-fulfillment motif as a theological center for Acts, guaranteeing continuity with OT Israel and instilling hope* in the persecuted Christian community (Karris; *see* Persecution). The motif is better seen as one important component in the complex of Luke's theology (Talbert, 91). Although Acts seems to emphasize the inauguration of eschatological salvation, the close ties to resurrection from the dead and the day of the Lord (Acts 2:20) also anticipate the consummation of that salvation at the end of the age (Kaiser, 116-22).

The exact delineation of now-and-not-yet tensions in Hebrews is notoriously difficult and displayed in the author's uses of *epangelia* and *epangellomai*. The promises found in the new covenant certainly relate to the establishment of a relationship with God and forgiveness of sins (Heb 8:6-12; Jer 31:31-34; Heb 9:15). In Hebrews 4:1 the promise of rest as presented concerns hearing the gospel* with faith, but the author's audience needs perseverance to receive what has been promised (Heb 4:11; 6:12; 10:23, 36). As a future component in the author's message, the promised inheritance plays an important role in the dichotomy of decision facing the hearers. The word of God to them is either a word of punishment (e.g., Heb 2:1-4; 3:7-11) or a word of promise. If they do not heed the warnings they will fall back through unbelief; but if they endure by receiving the author's encouragement and the positive examples of the OT faithful, they will inherit the fulfillment of the promises. This hope ultimately resides in the faithfulness of God as the new-covenant promise maker (Heb 6:17; 10:23) (Rose, 188-89). He has brought new-covenant salvation to his people on the basis of his promises and will consummate that salvation at the end of the age, at which time he has promised to shake heaven* and earth (Heb 12:26).

The scope of God's promises also becomes apparent in the General Epistles. At 2 Peter 1:4 and 1 John 2:25 God's promises concern the quality of life experienced by believers. However, the full realization of God's promises will be obtained at the promised coming of Christ (2 Pet 3:4; 3:9). Believers will receive the crown of life (Jas 1:12) and a kingdom* (Jas 2:5) and will experience the new heaven and earth (2 Pet 3:13).

4. Promise in the Apostolic Fathers.
When one considers the concept of promise as utilized in the so-called apostolic fathers, there appears both continuity with and some slight divergence from Acts, Hebrews and the General Epistles. Forms of the noun *epangelia* and its verbal cognate *epangellomai* occur thirty-three times in the apostolic fathers, nineteen of these being nouns and fourteen appearing as verbs or participles. In general the uses may be categorized as in our treatment of the NT literature.

For example, one finds a person's promise to another person in the *Shepherd of Hermas** (*Herm. Vis.* 3.2.3; *Herm. Sim.* 5.2.7). In the former Hermas begs a heavenly messenger, the "Lady," to show him the vision* she had promised him. In the latter passage (*Herm. Sim.* 5.2.7) the master in the parable promises freedom to his faithful slave.* The master makes good his promise and eventually makes the servant (*see* Servant) joint heir with his son. One also finds an interesting reference (*Herm. Man.* 9.10) in which faith is personified and said to promise and perfect all things.

Promise also occurs in the apostolic fathers with reference to the foundation stories. In *1 Clement* 10.2 the author speaks of the faithfulness and obedience* of Abraham, who inherited the promises of God. This passage plays part in an example list (*1 Clem.* 9-12) similar to that found in Hebrews 11:1-40. *1 Clement* 32.2 notes the promise "your seed shall be as the stars of heaven," a promise fulfilled by God's blessings on the patriarch's kingly descendants.

As in the NT, the apostolic fathers are most interested in promise as related to the character of God. God may give a specific promise (*2 Clem.* 15.4; *Herm. Vis.* 3.1.2; Ign. *Trall.* 11.2) or may be referred to as one who is faithful to his promises in general (*1 Clem.* 27.1; *Herm. Vis.* 2.2.6; 5.7; *Herm. Sim.* 1.7). However, unlike the NT, the apostolic fathers are far more focused on God's promises as they relate to future reward* than the promise of salvation's inauguration, possible references to the latter occurring only in the *Epistle of Barnabas* * 5.7, 6.17 and 16.9. For those who persevere in waiting and are faithful, Christ leads them to rest in the coming kingdom (*Barn.* 15.7; *2 Clem.* 5.5; *Diogn.* 10.2), and the evil pleasures of this life cannot compare with the joys* and rewards of that promised life to come (*1 Clem.* 35.4; *2 Clem.* 10.3-4; 11.6). In *1 Clement* 26.1 the author speaks of the promised resurrection, having used the dying and rising phoenix as an illustration. Those who have suffered for the Name* have greater glory* than the rest of believers but share in the same gifts and promises (*Herm. Vis.* 3.2.1).

5. Conclusions.

It is important to note that the promise motif in Acts, Hebrews and the General Epistles finds expression most often in the context of preaching.* In Acts the preachers Peter, Stephen* and Paul use the motif in their sermons (Acts 2:33-39; 7:17; 13:23-32; 26:6). The author of Hebrews, an excellent example of early Christian homiletics, makes ready use of *epangelia* in the hortatory sections of the work. Just as promises were used to motivate hearers in military and diplomatic contexts of the ancient world, NT preachers appropriate *epangelia* and cognates to help their hearers draw the connection between the faithfulness of God and the hearers' faith response to God's promises. The apostolic fathers continue this message, focusing on the eschatological hope of future, promised rewards.

See also ABRAHAM; ESCHATOLOGY; HEBREWS; HOPE.

BIBLIOGRAPHY. F. F. Bruce, ed., *Promise and Fulfillment: Essays Presented to Professor S. H. Hooke* (Edinburgh: T & T Clark, 1963); J. A. Fitzmyer, "The Use of the Old Testament in Luke-Acts" in *SBLSP* (1992), 524-38; E. Hoffmann, "Promise," *NIDNTT* 3:68-74; W. C. Kaiser Jr., "The Promise of God and the Outpouring of the Holy Spirit" in *The Living and Active Word of God: Studies in Honor of Samuel J. Schultz,* ed. M. A. Inch and R. Youngblood (Winona Lake, IN: Eisenbrauns, 1983), 109-22; R. Karris, *What Are They Saying About Luke-Acts?* (New York: Paulist, 1979); P. S. Minear, "Promise," *IDB* 3:893-96; C. Rose, "Verheissung und Erfühllung: Zum Verständnis von ἐπαγγελία im Hebräerbrief," *BZ* 33 (1989)

178-91; A. Sand, "ἐπαγγελία κτλ," *EDNT* 2:13-16; C. H. Talbert, "Promise and Fulfillment in Lukan Theology" in *Luke-Acts,* ed. C. H. Talbert (New York: Crossroad, 1984) 91-103; M. Weinfeld, "The Promise to the Patriarchs and Its Realization: An Analysis of Foundation Stories" in *Society and Economy in the Eastern Mediterranean (c. 1500-1000 B.C.),* ed. M. Heltzer and E. Lipiski (Louvain: Uitgeverij Peeters, 1988) 353-69; D. R. Worley, "God's Faithfulness to Promise: The Hortatory Use of Commissive Language in Hebrews," (Unpublished Ph.D. dissertation, Yale University, 1981).   G. H. Guthrie

PROPHECY, PROPHETS, FALSE PROPHETS

The Gospels depict John the Baptist and Jesus as prophets and make Jesus the one who bestows the Holy Spirit* on his disciples. For Paul the universal gift of the Holy Spirit means among other things that the Christian community is a body in which there are many members, each with his or her own ministry.* These ministries exercised by the grace* *(charisma)* given by God are numerous and varied, and none is more important than that of prophecy (1 Cor 14:1-5). Luke, the author of the book of Acts,* and John, the author of the book of Revelation (*see* Revelation, Book of), also highlight the ministry of prophecy, but each in his own way says something distinctive on this matter. In the second century, prophets and prophecy continue to be known, although a diminution in prophetic ministry can be seen.

1. Acts
2. General Epistles
3. Revelation
4. Postapostolic Age

1. Acts.

The importance of prophecy for Luke is immediately brought to the reader's attention by the prominent use of the extended quotation from the OT prophet Joel in Acts 2:17-21 (*see* Old Testament in Acts). This text assumes that when the Spirit is universally given to God's* people they will all prophesy (Acts 2:17-18). Luke understands that this prediction was fulfilled when the Holy Spirit was given on the day of Pentecost,* thereby inaugurating "the last days" (Acts 2:17). A new age of prophecy had dawned. All agree that Luke is especially interested in prophecy, but who should be considered a prophet in Acts and how we are supposed to understand this ministry are debated questions. In broad terms two schools of thought about early Christian prophecy bear upon the interpretation of the data in Acts. One limits early Christian prophecy to episodic, oracular utterances that are spoken on the basis of supernaturally given revelation* via dreams, visions* and angelic* visitors (e.g., Aune, Dautzenberg). The other holds that early Christian prophecy was not a narrowly defined phenomenon and could take many forms, the oracular utterance given by direct divine intervention being but one form (e.g., Ellis, Hill, Dunn). It would seem that the Lukan writings support the latter position. Luke defines Jesus (see DJG, Luke, Gospel of §3.2) and all the leading figures in Acts in prophetic terms and allows that all forms of authoritative proclamation may be thought of as prophecy.

1.1. The Prophetic Spirit in Acts. In Lukan theology a disciple is someone who knows the blessing of sins forgiven (see Forgiveness) and the experience of the divine presence. In the Gospel narrative the disciple encounters the divine presence in the company of Jesus; in Acts the divine presence is known in the gift of the Holy Spirit whom Luke can call "the Spirit of Jesus" (Acts 16:7). When Luke speaks of the gift of the Spirit he insists that it is given to "all" who respond to the proclamation of the gospel* (Acts 2:4, 17; 4:31; 10:44), but he does not inseparably link believing in Christ, water baptism* and the reception of the Holy Spirit. The three can be conjoined (Acts 2:38), but sometimes believing and baptism go together and the reception of the Spirit follows (Acts 8:12-15), and sometimes believing comes first and the reception of the Spirit and baptism follow (Acts 9:17-18). Luke implies that all three are part of the normal Christian life, but in telling his story he does not let doctrine determine the order.

The Spirit as the divine presence with the believer enables prophecy (Acts 2:17-18; 19:6). But while the Spirit makes it possible for all to prophesy Luke insists that prophecy tended to manifest itself preeminently through certain "leading men" (Acts 15:22) who thus became known as "prophets," as well as a few leading women* (Acts 21:9).

1.2. The Prophets in Acts. Luke suggests that prophecy was pervasive in the early church and that a number of people in each Christian community came to be recognized as prophets. He mentions one group of prophets who belong to the church in Jerusalem,* among whom he names Agabus (Acts 11:27-28; 21:10), Judas and Silas (Acts 15:22-32). Another group is found at Antioch,* of whom he names Barnabas, Symeon, Lucius, Manaen and Paul (Acts 13:1). The four daughters of Philip* resident in Caesarea are usually taken as another group since Luke makes it clear by the use of the present tense (prophēteuousai) that they prophesied regularly (Acts 21:9). Although these prophets are associated with particular Christian communities, some of them at least on occasion traveled. In two instances Agabus is found outside Jerusalem, once in Antioch (Acts 11:27-28) and once in Caesarea (Acts 21:10). After the Jerusalem council (Acts 15) the assembled leaders send the prophets Judas and Silas to Antioch with Paul and Barnabas to pass on the decree, given in letter form (Acts 15:22-32). Luke then speaks of them exercising their prophetic ministry by encouraging and strengthening the church (Acts 15:32).

It seems that Luke deliberately draws Christian leaders as prophets. This is often indicated by speaking of such people as "full" (plērēs) of the Holy Spirit (Acts 6:3, 5, 8; 7:55; 11:24)—a continuous state. Barnabas, for example, is one of those so designated (Acts 11:24), but in introducing him in Acts 4:36 Luke says he was given this name presumably to indicate his characteristic ministry. Previously he had been known as Joseph the Levite from Cyprus. Barnabas is a Semitic name that Luke takes to mean "son of exhortation or encouragement" (hyios paraklēsis). Hebrew or Aramaic parallels and other uses of the word paraklēsis in Acts and the NT suggest that Luke is introducing Barnabas as "a son of prophecy" (i.e., a prophet; Ellis, Hill, Brock). In Acts 13:1 Barnabas (see DPL, Barnabas) is called a prophet.

Paul likewise is drawn as a prophet (see DPL, Prophet, Paul as). At the conclusion of the first account of his encounter with the risen Christ Paul is filled with the Holy Spirit (Acts 9:17). Luke gives this story three times (Acts 9:1-19; 22:4-16; 26:9-19), and while it is usually called Paul's conversion, the OT parallels suggest Paul's life-changing experience should also be understood as his commissioning as a prophet to the nations (cf. Is 49:6; Jer 1:5-7; see DPL, Conversion and Call, §3.3).

Peter, the leader of the twelve apostles,* is never explicitly called a prophet, but when Luke says Peter preached "filled with the Holy Spirit" (Acts 4:8; cf. 2:4, 14) he is indicating that the apostle spoke under divine initiative: as a prophet.

Stephen* is also depicted as a prophet. He is permanently "full of the Holy Spirit" (Acts 6:4; 7:55). His long sermon not only appeals frequently to the OT prophets but also reads like one of their speeches. He denounces Israel's* leaders for their hardness of heart and vain confidence in the temple.* This leads to his death, which Luke understood is the fate of the prophet (Lk 6:23; 11:48-50; 13:34).

Philip, another of the Seven, is also said to be "full of the Spirit." Admittedly Luke once calls him "the evangelist" (Acts 21:8), probably to distinguish him from one of the Twelve* with that name, but otherwise he too is depicted in prophetic terms. An angel of the Lord sends him on his mission (Acts 8:26), the Holy Spirit directs him to approach the Ethiopian eunuch (Acts 8:29), and when Philip had baptized him, "the Spirit" snatched Philip away. The imagery of the Spirit transporting a person is reminiscent of what happened to certain OT prophets (see 1 Kings 18:12; 2 Kings 2:9-16; Ezek 3:12, 14).

1.3. Prophetic Speech. D. E. Aune (262-68) limits the examples of early Christian prophetic speech in Acts to two predictive oracles by Agabus (Acts 11:28; 21:11) and three oracles of assurance given to Paul (Acts 18:9-10; 23:11; 27:23-24). In Acts 11:28 Agabus predicts through the Spirit that a severe famine will soon come and in Acts 21:11 that Paul will be arrested and handed over to the Gentiles* if he goes to Jerusalem. The second of these narratives is particularly important, first, because it provides the only example in the NT of a prophecy with the introductory formula "the Holy Spirit says." This is to be taken as the Christian counterpart of the OT messenger formula "thus says the Lord." Second, only here is there to be seen an instance of a Christian prophet performing a symbolic action that he then interprets by a prophetic word. The three assurance oracles are given by dream or vision to Paul. The first two are recounted by Luke, and the third is retold by Paul in a speech to the crew and passengers in the storm-tossed ship. The revealer in the first two is the Lord (Jesus) and in

the third an angel of God.

But if Luke has a broader definition of prophecy than Aune allows, then many more examples of prophetic speech may be found in Acts (see in particular Turner 1992, 38). These include (1) prophecies grounded on specific revelation that at some later time are passed on to one or more persons—an example of this is when Peter tells those assembled in the home of Cornelius* of his vision (Acts 10:30-33); (2) prophecies that come from immediate inspiration such as when the Holy Spirit directed the church at Antioch to "set apart for me Barnabas and Saul" (see also Acts 13:9; 21:11; cf. Lk 1:41, 67); (3) words of exhortation and encouragement spoken by prophets to assembled believers (Acts 14:22; 15:32, 41; 18:23); (4) expository sermons in which the interpretation and the application are given by the Holy Spirit (Acts 4:8-12; 7:2-53; 13:16-41); (5) praise addressed to God in a language not known to the speaker (Acts 2:4, 11; 10:46; 19:6; in this view tongues* is a special form of prophecy.) Examples can be multiplied, but Luke does not give enough information to enable exact classification of all his allusions to prophetic speech. The fact that Luke can speak of certain people as "prophets and teachers" (Acts 13:1) also suggests that for him prophecy was not narrowly defined.

1.4. The Source of the Prophetic Message. The differing forms of prophecy imply differing means of charismatic revelation. The quotation from Joel highlights the importance of visions and dreams (Acts 2:17) in imparting revelation that provides the content for specific prophecies. Except for the book of Revelation no other writing in the NT says more about visions, supernatural voices and dreams than Acts (see Acts 8:26; 9:10; 10:3, 17, 19; 11:5, 7; 16:9; 18:9; etc.). But Luke seems to allow that prophetic inspiration can come in less specific ways as well. Sometimes prophetic speech erupts as the Holy Spirit comes upon a person in an episodic way (Acts 4:18-31; 13:9). At other times, such as with the ministry of exhortation and charismatically inspired expository preaching,* the mind of the speaker seems to be more active. In these examples, Luke suggests, the Spirit imparts divine wisdom* and boldness of speech (Acts 4:13, 29, 31; 9:29; etc.) rather than specific content. In Luke's account of Stephen's ministry he notes not only that Stephen is full of the Spirit but also that he is full of wisdom (Acts 6:3, 5, 10). If

Stephen's sermon illustrates such inspiration, then prophetic speech, at least as far as Luke is concerned, is not always grounded in supernaturally disclosed revelation. Prophecy may also be a form of Spirit-guided preaching that builds on perceived insights into how Scripture once given now speaks to the present, particularly in relation to the Christ event.

1.5. False Prophecy. There are no warnings about or examples of false Christian prophets or prophecy in Acts, but Luke recounts one story about "a false Jewish prophet" (Acts 13:6) and one about a slave* girl, presumably a pagan, "who had a spirit of divination which brought her owners much gain by soothsaying" (Acts 16:16). These narratives are a reminder that prophecy of one form or another was a common feature of first-century Mediterranean life. In Paul's final address to the Ephesian elders (Acts 20:17-35) he says, "I know that after my departure savage wolves will come in among you, not sparing the flock. Some even from your own group will come distorting the truth" (Acts 20:29-30). The introductory "I know" suggests that this is a prophecy (cf. Rev 2:2, 9, 13, 19; 3:1, 8, 15), but the "savage wolves" are not identified as prophets. The task of the elders is to guard the flock (*see* Shepherd) against such persons (Acts 20:28), some of whom may be false prophets.

2. General Epistles.

2.1. The Johannine Epistles. John's Gospel and the epistles of John (*see* John, Letters of) reflect an abiding awareness of the dynamic presence of the Holy Spirit, and in the latter case this is explicitly associated with prophetic activity. In 1 John 2:20, 26-27 the author claims that the anointing* (*chrisma*) of the Holy Spirit gives personal knowledge* of the truth* that will protect believers from those "who would deceive." In 1 John 4:1-3 these deceivers are identified as false prophets. The readers are told "to test the spirits to see whether they are from God; for many false prophets have gone out into the world." This comment suggests that prophecy was well known and usually accepted as from God. The author does not question the prophetic ministry as such but insists that it must be judged by its content: a true prophecy will acknowledge that Jesus Christ has come in the flesh* (1 Jn 4:2-3). Prophecies that do not make this confession (*see* Creeds) come from

the antichrist* (1 Jn 4:3).

2.2. 2 Peter and Jude. Both 2 Peter* and Jude* are polemical documents written to counter the influence of false teachers in the churches addressed. Most modern commentators hold that 2 Peter is dependent on Jude, but from this it should not be concluded that the same group or error is combated in both epistles.

In Jude the author's adversaries* are drawn as itinerant, antinomian prophets. They reject all moral authority* (Jude 4, 8-10), arguing that those who possess the Spirit (Jude 19) are the judge of their own actions (cf. Jude 9). These people clearly claim to be Christians, for they take part in the Eucharist (Jude 12). Jude's categorical reply is that they are in fact "devoid of the [Holy] Spirit" (Jude 19). In Jude 18 an apostolic prophecy is quoted that foretold these very problems.

The major error combated in 2 Peter is "eschatological scepticism" (Bauckham). The false teachers were undermining belief in the return of Christ and of future judgment* (2 Pet 2:3, 4, 9). One argument the author uses in reply is an appeal to "the [OT] prophetic writings" (2 Pet 1:19; *see* Old Testament in General Epistles). Such prophecies, he insists, did not come "by human impulse but as men [and women] moved by the Holy Spirit spoke from God" (2 Pet 1:21). In this affirmation, albeit in reference to OT prophecy, a broad definition of prophecy is given. Prophecy is proclamation inspired by the Holy Spirit which expresses the mind of God. The author then warns against false teachers who he sees as the counterpart of the false prophets under the old covenant* (2 Pet 2:1). On the basis of the parallel made the question follows, Is he speaking of false prophets who give false teaching or of false teachers as such? The latter is a distinct possibility, as prophets and teachers can be equated (Acts 13:1), prophets can be said to teach (Rev 2:20; cf. 1 Cor 14:31), and Jude seems to be combating false prophetic teachers.

3. Revelation.

Prophets and prophecy play an important part in the book of Revelation. Although the book is often taken as a classic example of early Christian apocalyptic* literature, it is important to note that the author intended it to be taken as a prophecy (Rev 1:3; 22:7, 10, 18, 19). Revelation reflects the influence of the Jewish apocalyptic tradition but shows many differences, the most significant for this discussion being that the author, John, writes in his own name and bases his authority on the fact that he has been called and addressed directly by the risen Christ. The identity of this John is not given, but he was probably a Palestinian Jewish Christian because Hebrew or Aramaic seems to have been his native tongue.

3.1. Church Order. The church order reflected in the book of Revelation is undeveloped, with little fixed structure. The whole church is described as "kings and priests" (Rev 1:6; 5:10; *see* Priests); all are God's servants (Rev 2:20; 7:3; 19:2; 22:3), and all can be named saints (Rev 5:8; 8:3, 4; 13:7). When the Spirit speaks to the churches (Rev 2 and 3) he addresses the whole community. The only group standing apart somewhat are "the prophets" (Rev 10:7; 11:18; 16:6; 18:20, 24; 22:6, 9). But even here the idea that all members of the church were at least potentially able to prophesy (cf. Acts 2:17-18; 1 Cor 14:1, 5) appears to be maintained. This we can take to be the meaning of the somewhat enigmatic statement, "for the testimony of Jesus is the spirit of prophecy" (Rev 19:10). "The testimony of Jesus" is the testimony to Jesus that elsewhere in Revelation is said to be borne by all Christians (Rev 1:9; 6:9; 11:7; 12:11), and "the spirit of prophecy" is a Jewish expression for prophecy itself.

3.2. Eschatological Prophecy. John describes his work as "the revelation of Jesus Christ" (Rev 1:1), and he says the revelation came to him while he was "in the Spirit" (Rev 1:10; cf. 1:3; 4:2; 21:10). As the phrase is repeated, we presume this was an intermittent state. Some of the book is in the first person as if Christ himself is speaking, notably in the letters to the seven churches, but most of the book is a record of seven sets of visions that John apparently received and then put in writing. The prophecies are in part predictive. They are given "to show to his servants what soon must take place" (Rev 1:1). We find the same expression again in Revelation 22:6 and a similar one in Revelation 2:16; 3:11; 22:7, 12, 20. Some have supposed that the book therefore maps out human history until Christ returns. But we would agree with D. Hill (86), who says that John's "interest in the prophetic portrayal of eschatological events which are regarded as rapidly approaching is really in their significance for John's own time. He offers no

review of past history; he is not concerned with predicting events in the near or distant future, but addresses a church presently involved in a situation of stress and oppression." Thus, in the letters to the seven churches, the Lord through John offers words of exhortation, consolation and a warning of impending judgment to the recipients. The welfare of the church is the vital issue in this period of great testing. Trials facing the churches, John maintains, show that the end of all things is close at hand.

3.3. The Prophetic Use of the Old Testament. The profound dependence on the Jewish Scriptures evident in this piece of prophetic writing is also to be noted (*see* Old Testament in Revelation). The book is saturated with words and phrases drawn from the OT, which is not quoted in a deductive fashion but rather is read typologically so that the creation,* exodus, covenant, Jerusalem and temple motifs are transposed and become eschatological* realities. In this way a living unity is established between the revelation under the old covenant and the new. This method of appropriating the OT may be taken as a classic example of prophetic exegesis. The ultimate meaning of the OT text is given by revelation to the prophet.

3.4. Examples of Prophetic Speech. Aune makes it his special concern to isolate and analyze originally independent prophetic utterances that have been incorporated into the text of Revelation. He maintains that the seven letters to the churches (Rev 2-3) represent a typical form of prophetic speech. In each case the letters begin "thus says" *(tade legei);* the prophecy is said to come from the risen Christ (identified by one or more picturesque titles); the actual prophecy is introduced by the revelatory indicator "I know" *(oida);* and then a stereotyped message follows. Other examples in Revelation are where God or Christ is quoted in the first person singular (e.g., Rev 1:7-8, 17-20; 16:15; 21:5-8; 22:7, 12-14, 18-20) and where oracular speech is evident (e.g., Rev 13:9-10; 14:6-11; 18:21-24; 19:9; 21:3-4, 5-8).

4. Postapostolic Age.

In the second century the prominence and importance of prophets and prophecy declined. The ministry of the prophet was still known, but the impression is given that it was not always encouraged because local bishops often assumed the prophetic ministry themselves and false prophecy had become a growing problem.

4.1. 1 Clement, the Didache, Ignatius and Hermas. The occasion for the writing of *1 Clement* (c. A.D. 96) was a schism at Corinth (*see* Clement of Rome), caused by a revolt of young men who set themselves against the elders of the church. As these young men claimed special revelations (*1 Clem.* 48.5) and are said to have had powers of persuasive speech (*1 Clem.* 21.5; 57.2), we may take it that they were claiming prophetic gifts.

In the *Didache** (c. A.D. 100) prophets are frequently mentioned and held in great esteem (*Did.* 10.7-8; 11.3-12; 13.1-4), but the bishops and deacons are seen as the successors to the prophets (*Did.* 15.1-2).

Ignatius,* the bishop of Antioch in the early years of the second century, assumes the title *God-inspired* (Ign. *Magn.* 1.1), which is a claim to be a prophet. Writing to the Philadelphians, he refers to one of his prophecies by saying, "When I was among you, I cried aloud . . . with the voice of God, 'Give heed to the bishop and the presbytery and the deacons.'" These words, he adds, were given to him by the "Spirit" (Ign. *Phld.* 7.1-2). In his letter to the Ephesian church he speaks of revelations granted to him (Ign. *Eph.* 2.20), and in another letter he urges Polycarp,* the bishop of Smyrna, to seek heavenly revelations (Ign. *Pol.* 2.2). In the mid-second-century work the *Martyrdom of Polycarp,* the bishop is called a "prophetic" man (*Mart. Pol.* 16.2).

The charisma of prophecy is also associated with Melito,* the bishop of Sardis. Polycrates describes him as "one who lived entirely in the Holy Spirit" (Eusebius *Hist. Eccl.* 5.24). Melito's homily *On the Passover,* apparently written in A.D. 167-68, contains a long section in which the Lord speaks through Melito in the first person of prophetic speech. In these examples the bishop has assumed the prophetic ministry and it would seem silenced others.

The *Shepherd of Hermas** (c. A.D. 140) takes it for granted that prophets and prophecy will be prominent in the church. Hermas does not claim for himself the title *prophet,* but he clearly functions as a prophet. He insists that true prophecy takes place when "the prophetic spirit rests on a man and fills him, and being filled with the Holy Spirit, he speaks to the congregation as the Lord wills" (*Herm. Man.* 11.9).

4.2. Justin and Irenaeus. Justin Martyr, in his *Dialogue with Trypho* (A.D. 160), several times speaks of Christian prophecy. He says that in contrast to Judaism* the church still has those who have the spirit of prophecy (Justin *Dial. Tryph.* 39.1). Later he says even more explicitly, "The prophetic gifts remain with us even to the present time" (Justin *Dial. Tryph.* 82.1). They are evident "among us" as gifts given to both "women and men" (Justin *Dial. Tryph.* 88.1).

Similarly Irenaeus, in about A.D. 190, insists that the *charismata* are still evident in the Christian church. He writes that some "have foreknowledge of things to come: they see visions and utter prophetic expressions" (Irenaeus *Haer.* 2.32.4). In the same treatise he adds that the heretics reject both "the gospel and the prophetic Spirit. . . . They set aside the gift of prophecy. . . . They cannot admit the apostle Paul either. For, in his epistle to the Corinthians he speaks expressly of prophetic gifts, and recognizes men and women prophesying in church" (Irenaeus *Haer.* 3.11.9). But in our churches, he adds, "we do hear many brethren . . . who possess prophetic gifts" (Irenaeus *Haer.* 5.6.1).

4.3. Montanism. One deviation that significantly escaped the lash of Irenaeus in his monumental work *Against Heresies* was Montanism. This was a late-second-century apocalyptic movement that began in Phrygia when Montanus, and later Maximilla and Prisca, began to prophesy about the end of the world and other matters. The movement soon gained a wide following.

But while Irenaeus did not denounce this movement, many other church leaders did. They did not deny prophecy as such but denied that the Montanists were true prophets. It was claimed that they had introduced into the church pagan ecstatic prophecy (see Eusebius *Hist. Eccl.* 5.16.6-9). All the major features of early Montanism, however, can be paralleled in the apostolic writings. Aune argues that Montanism is better seen as a "renewal movement" within the church (the Montanists called themselves "the new prophecy"). Eusebius says that one of their opponents drew up a "catalog" of authentic Christian prophets insisting that "the apostle grants that the prophetic gift shall be in all the church until the final coming" (Eusebius *Hist. Eccl.* 5.17.4). Unfortunately Eusebius mentions only two names from this list of Christian prophets, Amnia and Quadratus, apparently because these two were widely known.

Condemnation of the Montanists was by no means universal. "The Confessors of Lyons," for instance, sent a letter by Irenaeus to Rome* admonishing Pope Eleutherius and the church of Asia not to quench the Spirit by condemning the Montanists. The next pope, Victor, almost gave official acknowledgment to the prophetic gifts of Montanus, Prisca and Maximilla and was persuaded only at the last moment not to do so. Most significant of all is the fact that Tertullian (A.D. 160-220), the brilliant exponent of trinitarian theology, joined the movement and became its apologist.

4.4. False Prophecy. In the postapostolic age the issue of false prophecy comes to the fore. In the *Didache* the true prophet can be recognized because he exhibits "the behavior of the Lord." He does not order meals or ask for money "in the Spirit" but "teaches the truth" (*Did.* 11.8-12). *Mandate* 11 in the epistle of Hermas deals almost entirely with the problem of false prophecy. Again the behavior of the prophet is the key issue. The true prophet is "meek, gentle, lowly-minded, refrains from all wickedness and evil desire of the world, and makes himself poorer than all men" (*Herm. Man.* 11.8). The true prophet also does not give oracular answers to questions put to him, especially in private. The authentic prophetic ministry is a congregational one that arises as the community is in prayer (*Herm. Man.* 11.9).

4.5. The Demise of Prophecy. But while the prophetic ministry was known throughout the second century, it was not as evident or as widespread as it was in the Pauline churches while the apostle was alive or as Luke suggests. The earliest hint that prophecy was to come under threat is seen in the Pastoral Epistles (*see DPL,* Pastoral Letters), the latest epistles ascribed to Paul. Here the ministry of the prophecy is subordinated to more ordered leadership. In the *Didache* the suggestion is that the bishops and deacons are to take the place of the prophets (*Did.* 15.1). The way this happened in regard to bishops is illustrated in the writings of Ignatius, and other examples are seen in the case of Polycarp and Melito. Later in the century Justin and Irenaeus know of prophets and prophecy but speak about prophecy only to argue that this characteristic ministry of the apostolic age is still to be seen in orthodox churches. After the activity associated with Montanism prophecy is only rarely mentioned.

Some scholars following A. von Harnack argue that the growing importance of the canonical Scriptures silenced the prophets as it was thought no new revelation was needed. But both Irenaeus and Eusebius appeal to Scripture in support of the ministry of prophecy. Other scholars hold that the growing problem of false prophecy rang the death knell for prophecy, but this was not a new problem. The most important factor seems to have been the growing importance of the ordered ministry, especially that of the bishop (*see* Church Order). Human organizations have a tendency to move from the more spontaneous to the more ordered. As this happened in the life of the church an uneasy tension between recognized office bearers, especially the bishop as the leader of the local church, and charismatic prophets developed. The more the church became institutionalized, the less free expression of charismatic gifts, and prophecy in particular, was encouraged. This trend progressed throughout the second century of Christian history. Gradually the prophets were silenced as the bishops assumed their ministry and usurped their place. The fundamental issue raised by Montanism was whether or not the church should be led by prophets. The verdict was a resounding no. In the face of this threat to its institutional life, the church closed ranks. The Montanists and prophecy itself were pushed to one side. Thus Montanism represents the last flare-up of prophecy in the early church and its virtual demise. Eventually Montanism, and by implication prophecy itself, was condemned in about A.D. 200 by Asian synods.

See also ADVERSARIES; ESCHATOLOGY; HOLY SPIRIT; REVEAL, REVELATION; VISIONS; WORSHIP AND LITURGY.

BIBLIOGRAPHY. J. L. Ash, "The Decline of Ecstatic Prophecy," *TS* 37 (1976) 227-52; D. E. Aune, *Prophecy in Early Christianity* (Grand Rapids: Eerdmans, 1983); R. J. Bauckham, *Jude, 2 Peter* (WBC; Waco, TX: Word, 1983); idem, *The Theology of the Book of Revelation* (NTT; Cambridge: Cambridge University Press, 1993); idem, *The Climax of Prophecy* (Edinburgh: T & T Clark, 1993); S. P. Brock, "Barnabas: Hyios Parakleseos," *JTS* 25 (1974) 93-98; G. Dautzenburg, *Urchristliche Prophetie* (Stuttgart: Kohlhammer, 1975); J. D. G. Dunn, *Jesus and the Spirit* (London: SCM, 1975); E. E. Ellis, *Prophecy and Hermeneutic in Early Christianity* (Grand Rapids:

Eerdmans, 1978); K. N. Giles, *Patterns of Ministry Among the First Christians* (Melbourne: Collins-Dove, 1989); idem, *What on Earth is the Church?* (Downers Grove, IL: InterVarsity Press, 1995); T. W. Gillespie, *The First Theologians: A Study in Early Christian Prophecy* (Grand Rapids: Eerdmans, 1994); D. Hill, *New Testament Prophecy* (Basingstoke: Marshall, Morgan & Scott, 1979); R. P. Menzies, *The Development of Early Christian Pneumatology* (Sheffield: JSOT, 1991); J. Reiling, *Hermas and Christian Prophecy: A Study of the Eleventh Mandate* (NovTSup 37; Leiden: E. J. Brill, 1973); M. Turner, *The Holy Spirit and Spiritual Gifts: Then and Now* (Carlisle: Paternoster, 1996); idem, *Power from on High* (JPTSup 9; Sheffield: Sheffield Academic Press, 1996); idem, "The Spirit of Prophecy and the Power of Authoritative Preaching in Luke-Acts: A Question of Origins," *NTS* 38 (1992) 66-88.

PROPHETS. *See* PROPHECY, PROPHETS, FALSE PROPHETS.

PROSELYTISM, JEWISH. *See* GENTILES, GENTILE MISSION.

PROVIDENCE. *See* GOD.

PSEUDEPIGRAPHAL WRITINGS, CHRISTIAN NONCANONICAL. *See* APOCRYPHAL AND PSEUDEPIGRAPHAL WRITINGS.

PSEUDEPIGRAPHAL WRITINGS, JEWISH. *See* JUDAISM, POST-A.D. 70.

PSEUDEPIGRAPHY

The issue of pseudepigraphy has a bearing on the NT because several of the writings included in the NT have commonly been regarded as pseudepigraphal or pseudonymous. The terms denote literary works falsely *(pseud-)* attributed *(epigraphos* = "superscription") or falsely named *(onoma* = "name"), although only the former goes back to antiquity (attested as early as the second century B.C. in an inscription from Priene). In both cases what is in view are writings that explicitly claim to have been written by a certain person but that by common consent were written by someone else.

It is on the issue of falseness that the significance of pseudepigraphy within the NT hangs. The issue should not be confused with that of anonymity. Many NT writings are anonymous (the Synoptic Gospels, for example), but that fact raises no point of principle about such writings being included in the NT. Nor should pseudepigrapha be confused with apocrypha. Both terms were used in the early church regarding those books that today are almost universally known as the OT Pseudepigrapha (the books of Enoch, the testamentary literature attributed to the patriarchs), but in this case "apocryphal" has the sense of suitable for private reading, as opposed to the public reading of recognized apostolic and hence canonical works (*Synopsis sacrae scripturae* 75, attributed to Athanasius).

By putting the emphasis on false attribution, however, the term *pseudepigraphy* implies a negative value judgment as to a document's integrity and acceptability. This is clear from its earliest attested use in Christian circles, where Serapion (second century A.D.) applies it to the *Gospel of Peter:* "the writings that falsely bear their names [Peter and the other apostles] we reject . . . knowing that such were not handed down to us" (Eusebius *Hist. Eccl.* 6.12.3). It is this judgment of falseness, of an intent to deceive and mislead, particularly by passing off as apostolic what should not be so regarded, that makes the issue of pseudepigraphy in the NT so sensitive. J. I. Packer put the point tersely: "Pseudonymity and canonicity are mutually exclusive" (Packer, 184; similarly Ellis; cf. Marshall).

In the light of the negative judgment implicit in the term itself, the claimed presence of pseudepigraphy in the NT would seem to pose a moral and theological problem for the notion of an authoritative canon* of Scripture. The uncomfortable fact is, however, that a large consensus of NT scholarship maintains that certain NT writings, particularly Ephesians, the Pastorals and 2 Peter, are pseudepigraphic, the first two attributed to Paul, the last attributed to Peter. How then to handle the seeming contradiction within the very phrase "NT pseudepigraphy"?

1. Attempts to Ease the Problem of New Testament Pseudepigraphy
2. Pseudepigraphy as Living Tradition
3. Pseudepigraphy in the New Testament
4. Conclusion

1. Attempts to Ease the Problem of New Testament Pseudepigraphy.
In the modern period there have been various

attempts to hold together the conflicting ideas of pseudepigraphy within the canon.

1.1. Intellectual Ownership in the Ancient World. An early attempt was to argue that writers in antiquity did not share the modern idea of copyright. If writings had no author ownership as such and were in effect common property, then use of another's name need not be understood as an attempt to deceive by claiming the named person's authority for the writing. The strength of this argument is that there is a difference between modern copyright mentality and the lack of inhibition among ancient writers in the way they freely incorporated material written by others within their own works. Nevertheless, W. Speyer has shown that the sense of intellectual ownership was already well developed in Greek culture long before the first century B.C. And though the Israelite literary tradition was characterized by anonymity, the influence of Greek culture brought the concept into Judaism in the Hellenistic era. This is evident, for example, in the ready acknowledgment that the writer of 2 Maccabees makes to the five volumes of Jason of Cyrene (2 Macc 2.23) and in the sensitivities regarding false attribution in 2 Thessalonians 2:2 and Revelation 22:18.

1.2. An Accepted Literary Device? A second suggestion is that pseudepigraphy was widely recognized as an acceptable literary device in the ancient world. This argument works well with documents that first appeared centuries after the claimed author had died. As B. M. Metzger observes, the Neo-Pythagoreans attributed their writings to Pythagoras himself, even though he had lived many centuries earlier; according to Iamblichus (c. A.D. 300), it was an honorable act to publish one's treatises in the name of so venerable a teacher (Metzger, 7). It is hard to believe that such a convention was not recognized, at least by most thoughtful readers, in the case of the Enoch corpus, the *Testaments of the Twelve Patriarchs* or the *Apocalypse of Adam,* all written probably between second century B.C. and second century A.D.

Similar in the Christian period are the sixth-century works claiming Dionysius (or Denys) the Areopagite (cf. Acts 17:34) as their author but clearly drawing on Neo-Platonic philosophy. But does the argument work so well in the case of Ephesians, appearing within a decade or two of Paul's death? There is a major difference between a writer adopting the pseudonym of an ancient or symbolic figure from an earlier epoch, particularly one not hitherto known as an author, and someone purporting to continue a particular literary tradition within a few years of its author's demise. The former may count as an acceptable device that was not seriously intended to deceive. The issue of deception is more delicate in the latter, and there is enough evidence that the ancients were alive to the issue (Metzger, 12-16).

1.3. Mystical or Spiritual Identification. A more popular view has been that pseudepigraphy was acceptable when it embodied the writer's claim to some sort of mystical or spiritual identity with the one whose name was used. This is certainly possible to conceive within cultures where inspired individuals could assume the persona of the one in whose name they spoke or acted as the mouthpiece for the divine being who inspired or possessed them. The OT prophets so spoke, and in the second century A.D. Celsus claimed that there were many such (Origen *Cont. Cels.* 7.9).

K. Aland in particular saw a solution here to the problem of pseudepigraphy in the first century and a half of Christianity: the attribution of authorship in effect to the Holy Spirit* by the Spirit-inspired author threw "a bridge across the generations"; the Spirit being the real author, the identity of the human author did not matter. But in so arguing he ignores the widespread recognition in earliest Christianity of the danger of false prophecy* (e.g., 1 Cor 12:3; 1 Jn 4:1-3; *Herm. Man.* 11). The argument does have greater plausibility when it is applied to writings that themselves purport to describe visions* and heavenly journeys on the part of the author; hence, presumably, its appeal to D. S. Russell in his treatment of apocalyptic* writings (similarly Speyer's category of "echte religiöse Pseudepigraphie"). But even there the sense of a mystical or an ecstatic identification of actual author with his pseudonym is lacking in the writing itself. And whether the argument works at all with a letter* genre must be regarded as highly questionable.

1.4. Revered Antiquity and the Noble Falsehood. Among more recent studies N. Brox draws attention to three features in particular that at least help us understand the why of the phenomenon of pseudepigraphy. One is the characteristic love of antiquity that is such a feature of the epoch. So, for example, since what was ancient called for respect, it was evidently important for the Jewish apologist Aristobulus (second century B.C.) to argue that famous Greek thinkers like Pythagoras and Plato had been imitators of Moses. Pseudepigraphy then was a way of expressing the value of the past and of enabling readers to participate in it.

Another relevant point is the similarly widespread idea of the noble falsehood, the idea that falsehood in support of a noble cause like religion was acceptable and did not attract the stigma of deceit. Brox notes that the Fathers too seem to have accepted the principle of what we might call the white lie, the good objective legitimating the questionable means.

The third feature is the related principle, again evident in the Fathers, that the content of the writing was deemed more important than its authorship. An illustration would be Serapion's evaluation of the *Gospel of Peter,* where Serapion goes on to note "that the most part [of the *Gospel*] was in accordance with the true teaching of the Savior but that some things were added." However, valuable as these observations are in catching something of the relevant attitudes of the times, it is questionable how much they contribute to the specific issue of NT pseudepigraphy.

1.5. Authoritative Tradition. The most promising contribution to the discussion of NT pseudepigraphy in recent years has been the thesis of D. G. Meade. He argues that the most obvious context within which to examine the issue of NT pseudepigraphy is not Greco-Roman literary genres and practices (as still Donelson, 14-15), and not simply particular Jewish apocrypha and pseudepigrapha, but the process in Jewish religious writing whereby tradition has accrued to a prominent historical figure and particularly the process whereby an original oral or literary deposit has been expanded by the attribution of further material to the originating figure. He instances Isaiah, the Solomonic corpus and the Daniel and Enoch traditions. In each case he finds that "attribution is primarily a claim to authoritative tradition, not a statement of literary origins" (Meade, 102).

When he turns to the NT Meade observes similar features in the letters usually regarded as pseudepigraphal, "a consistent relationship between the development of the Petrine and Pauline traditions and the literary forms which they take" (Meade, 192-93). In other words the relation of Ephesians and the Pastorals to the undisputed Paulines could be regarded as equivalent to the relation of Second and Third Isaiah to First Isaiah. In each case the motivation was to "make present, contemporize" *(Vergegenwärtigung)* or renewedly actualize the authoritative Petrine and Pauline traditions for the following generation.

Of all the approaches to the issue of NT pseudepigraphy, Meade's seems to have the greatest potential to explain the conundrum of pseudepigraphy within the canon; that is, how it could be that the earliest Christians may have accepted documents claiming as author someone who was already dead.

2. Pseudepigraphy as Living Tradition.
It is important to recognize the degree to which the elaboration of original tradition (attributed to a particular figure) in the NT mirrors the same process in the OT. The point can be illustrated by reference to the three traditional divisions of the OT before we turn to the NT.

2.1. The Torah/Pentateuch. Few scholars today would wish to dispute the consensus that the canonical Pentateuch is the result of a lengthy tradition process, including the later emergence of Deuteronomy and the postexilic editorial work of Ezra in establishing that canonical form—a process, it should be noted, stretching over several centuries.

Several features are to be noted. First, the process had a clear and authoritative starting point: Moses. However much or little of the Torah goes back to Moses himself, the tradition is unanimous in attributing its character and authority to Moses. Second, Moses did not leave a rigid tradition, fixed and closed, but a living tradition, one that was expanded and elaborated as circumstances changed and new insights emerged. This process was obviously not regarded as illegitimate or deceitful. On the contrary it was understood as a restatement of the tradition stemming from Moses; it was still the law of Moses. Only an elaboration that was in the spirit of the earlier and in recognizable continuity with it would have succeeded in this. And the community accepted the result as "the book of the law of Moses," the account of Nehemiah 8—9 presumably representing the climax of that process. Third, there was a point of transition when the process of *Vergegenwärtigung* changed in character, from an elaboration within the tradition itself to an interpretation of the tradition now more or less fixed. The tradition having become established in canonical form (though textual variations retain a certain fluidity) the role of the targumist and halakist takes over. The vitality of the tradition is maintained, not least in the claim of Mishnah *Aboth* 1:1 of an unbroken tradition of Torah from Moses, through Joshua, the elders and the prophets to the men of the great synagogue.* But any suggestion of pseudepigraphal elaboration has long been superseded.

2.1. The Prophets. If we take the example of Isaiah, the scholarly consensus is that while much of Isaiah 1—39 can be referred to the eighth-century Isaiah of Jerusalem, Isaiah 40—55 come from an unknown hand during the exilic period and Isaiah 56—66 are probably a collection of multiauthored oracles from a still later period. Variations on the basic consensus still have to reckon with a tradition that, on the most plausible reading of the text(s), spans several generations, in which case we see the same three features present.

First is an authoritative starting point for the tradition. Isaiah of Jerusalem was evidently a prophet who made a huge impact and whose prophecies were treasured as living resources within the circle that most revered his memory.

Second, there is a clear continuity and fundamental identity of religious perspective between the first two Isaiahs. That is to say, Second Isaiah consciously stood within the living tradition that stemmed from Isaiah of Jerusalem and can be seen quite properly as a creative reinterpretor of the earlier oracles.

Third, with Third Isaiah the earlier tradition seems to have become more fixed: the material is full of near or complete citations from the two earlier stages; and the reworking of the tradition begins to assume more the character of a midrashic exposition of these texts. It would appear then that the process of pseudographical elaboration within such a tradition can last only so long as there is an appropriation and reworking of the tradition that can legitimately claim to reexpress the mind of the tradition's originator and be recognized and accepted as doing so.

2.3. The Writings. Here we might instance the Psalms. The attribution of the book of Psalms to David is an attribution of genre rather than necessarily of each of the 150 psalms. Nevertheless the point once again is that David was regarded as the founder and originator of the canonical psalms, and the addition of subsequent psalms is a vivid illustration of the vitality of the tradition of psalm writing and singing that he inaugurated and authorized. The vitality of that tradition is well illustrated by the presence of further psalms naming David as their author among the Qumran* scrolls (Charlesworth, 2:609-24). In this case the function of the psalms as part of regular worship must have helped maintain the vitality of the tradition, raising the question as to whether canonical closure was ever an issue. Perhaps we should best compare the sense of living tradition in Orthodox liturgy that is such a distinctive character of the Orthodox churches.

More apposite here is probably the Solomonic corpus. There was evidently an early memory of Solomon's wisdom (1 Kings 4:29-34) that can be said to legitimate the attribution of the proverbial tradition (Prov 1:1) to him as, once again, the authoritative starting point of the tradition. The tradition was so powerful that it attracted also Qoheleth (Ecclesiastes) to his name (Eccles 1:1, 12; 12:8-14). In this case the process consisted not of a reworking of older traditions from within but in the attribution of a separate book to Solomon. And in this case the attribution proved to be successful in its claim to stand within the tradition of Solomon, at least to the extent that Qoheleth made it (just!) into the Hebrew canon. At the same time, however, although the name of Solomon continued to gather fresh works around it (Wisdom of Solomon, *Psalms of Solomon, Odes of Solomon*) there was never any question of their acceptance into the canon. By then the connection and continuity with Solomon was too remote for the attribution to be regarded as anything other than a literary fiction honoring the memory of Solomon as a sage and composer of psalms and odes but not constituting a claim to stand within Solomon's authoritative tradition.

The Jewish background to the issue of NT pseudepigraphy thus reveals a consistent pattern of living tradition with the same three features: a revered figure in the past to whom a particular character of authoritative tradition could properly be attributed; an elaboration of that tradition from within or at least in a manner whose continuity with and contemporizing of the original tradition was widely acknowledged; and a recognition that the vitality of the tradition could not be maintained in that way when the connection and continuity with the authoritative originator became too distant, tenuous or artificial.

3. Pseudepigraphy in the New Testament.

In the light of the preceding discussion it becomes possible to recognize an element of pseudepigraphy within the NT without any implication of deceit or fraud and without triggering the antithesis between pseudepigraphy and canonicity.

3.1. The Gospels. There is a striking parallel between the Gospels and the Pentateuch. The parallel is not in quantity but in the quality of the traditioning process. There need be little doubt that the great bulk of the Synoptic tradition goes back to Jesus (sayings) and his immediate circle (narratives). Even so, however, there is a measure of organization and interpretation incorporated into the Synoptic tradition that shows clearly enough that it was a living tradition, used and reflected on and elaborated within the churches that cherished these memories of Jesus, that fed on them as spiritual food and that found in them inspiration for their own living in often adverse conditions. As C. F. D. Moule has demonstrated, this is one of the lasting fruits of form criticism. In contrast the longer ending of Mark (Mk 16:9-20) represents a later elaboration of the tradition that went just beyond general acceptance.

Pursuing the parallel between the Gospels and the Pentateuch, we may further say that John's Gospel is somewhat equivalent to Deuteronomy—a distinctive unit within the whole but with sufficient continuity and overlap with the Synoptics for it to be recognized as a legitimate restatement of the original or earlier tradition. In John's case the degree of elaboration of the Jesus tradition brought it close to the boundary of what was and was not counted acceptable. It was Irenaeus's advocacy of John as part of the fourfold Gospel witness, despite its attractiveness to the Gnostic* sects, that made its place within the emerging orthodox canon secure. Others, like the *Gospel of Peter** and the *Gospel of Thomas,** were judged to have transgressed the boundary of acceptable *Vergegenwärtigung.*

The issue, it should be noted, was not settled simply on the question of attribution of authorship. It was the character of the tradition so attributed, whether it stood in sufficiently close continuity with and as an acceptable elaboration within the living tradition that was decisive. If so, the later attribution to John, however elaborated the tradition, was acceptable; if not, the attribution to Peter or Thomas was insufficient to secure its widespread acceptance. In an important sense, therefore, the issue of pseudepigraphy was secondary. Of course, the issue of the authorship of John's Gospel is a question for another volume than this (*see DJG,* John, Gospel of). I touch on it only to make the point that a parallel needs to be recognized between John's elaboration of the Jesus tradition and the Pastorals' elaboration of the Paul tradition. Those who recognize John as an authentic reexpression of the Jesus tradition arguably need feel no qualms in recognizing the Pastorals as acceptable Pauline pseudepigraphy.

3.2. Colossians and Ephesians. In the light of the tradition process illustrated, these two letters are the best place to start a discussion of the issue of Pauline pseudepigraphy. By broad consent Colossians stands close to the border that marks off Pauline from post-Pauline authorship: either very late in his life or very early after his death. And as agreed by a larger majority, Ephesians shows marked dependency on Colossians. In other words Colossians probably represents such a development of Pauline thought as to illustrate and even document the way in which Pauline merged into post-Pauline, itself an expression of the continuity and vitality of the Pauline tradition.

This last observation gains in plausibility when we recall a number of features in Colossians. First, as W. Bujard in particular has demonstrated, the style of Colossians is so different from that of the earlier Paulines as to make it very difficult to maintain that Paul himself composed the letter. Second, the theological and paraenetic content is also significantly different in content and character. In both cases, whether we use the term *Pauline* or *post-Pauline*, we have to speak of development, of a "late Paul" if not of someone writing in Paul's name. The close overlap with Philemon, the detailed personal requests made in Colossians 4:7-17 and the concluding autograph (Col 4:18) make it hard to doubt that Paul himself stood behind the letter in some personal capacity. The best solution is probably that the letter was composed by Timothy (named as coauthor in Col 1:1) but approved by Paul with the addition of his own name at the end. If so, then indeed we can speak of Colossians as the bridge between Pauline and post-Pauline. More to the point, the line between personal authorship and pseudepigraphy begins to become blurred and the evidence of continuity and proper claim to represent the named author's views becomes crucial in validating the means used. (See Pauline Legacy and School §1.1; for arguments in favor of Pauline authorship *see DPL,* Colossians.)

In the case of Ephesians the arguments for post-Pauline authorship are more compelling. (1) The style is quite distinct from anything else in the Pauline corpus, marked for example by long sentences, repetition and piling up of adjectives, phrases and clauses such as we find in Ephesians 1:17-19, 2:13-18 and 3:14-19. (2) At point after point, particularly in Ephesians 4—6, the phraseology of Colossians reappears in Ephesians (e.g., Col 3:12/Eph 4:2; Col 2:19/Eph 4:16; Col 3:5-6/Eph 5:5-6; Col 3:18-19/Eph 5:22, 25; Col 3:22—4:1/Eph 6:5-9; Col 4:7/Eph 6:21-22), indicating probably that the less personal and more general Ephesians has used Colossians as a kind of model. (3) The perspective seems to be more that of a second generation looking back to a past foundation period (cf. Eph 2:20; 3:5). (4) And the theological perspective seems to have shifted beyond that even of Colossians (e.g., Eph 1:22-23; 2:5-8). Here, in other words, the developments in the Pauline tradition are such that a defense of Pauline authorship in effect dissolves the distinction between "late Paul" and "disciple of Paul." The explanation that makes best sense of the evidence is that Ephesians was written by an associate or a disciple of Paul who stood within the tradition begun by Paul and was recognized to do so, was seen to represent the Pauline tradition after Paul's death and was able to reexpress it in significant measure in his own terms but in Paul's name and without deceit. (See further Pauline Legacy and School §1.2; for arguments in favor of Pauline authorship *see DPL,* Ephesians.)

3.3. Pastoral Epistles. If the debate on the Pauline authorship of Colossians and Ephesians is more evenly balanced, there is a much clearer majority opinion in favor of the post-Pauline

authorship of the Pastorals. The language is more characteristic of a later generation (e.g., "epiphany," "godliness"), and stylistic features are again markedly different. The opposition confronted in the Pastorals seems to reflect developments that led to the gnostic systems of the second century (e.g., 1 Tim 1:4; 6:20; *see* Adversaries). The structure envisaged for the churches in view seems to demonstrate the sort of institutionalizing tendencies (overseers, deacons and elders) that are characteristic of the second and third generations of charismatic movements (*see* Early Catholicism). And the earlier, more vital understanding of "faith" seems to have crystallized into more set forms of "the faith" ("sound teaching," "faithful sayings"). It is not appropriate to debate the significance of these features in detail, and it must suffice to indicate the typical features that have led most scholars to the conclusion of post-Pauline authorship (*see* Pauline Legacy and School §1.3).

The significance for the present discussion is that documents so markedly different from the earlier Paulines could still claim Pauline authorship and the claim not be regarded as illegitimate. It can be and is still argued conversely by an important minority that the letters' own claim to have been written by Paul outweighs the above evidence (*see DPL,* Pastoral Letters). But the earlier discussion shows how equally plausible it is that associates or disciples of Paul could legitimately write in the name of Paul, as a claim to represent Paul's counsel in the face of later challenges, and that the literary device could be accepted without demur because the writings were recognized as standing in a direct line of continuity with those of Paul himself (note 2 Tim 2:2)—possibly aided by the incorporation of brief notes (particularly 2 Tim 4:9-15) from Paul's final imprisonment. Though no one need have been in any doubt as to their post-Pauline authorship, what mattered was their Pauline character. In Meade's terms, their attribution to Paul was primarily "a claim to authoritative tradition, not a statement of literary origins." The living Pauline tradition, despite already solidifying into "sound teaching," was still sufficiently fluid and developing from within.

In contrast, the line of continuity was presumably not sufficiently sustained in the case of *1 Clement,* or Clement was a sufficiently independent figure of authority in his own right for it to be necessary to present its exhortation under Paul's name. Subsequently the *Acts of Paul* (including *3 Corinthians*) never gained much credibility, and the *Epistle to the Laodiceans* was too obviously a clumsy pastiche, though it was widely disseminated in the West.

3.4. 1 and 2 Peter. It is unnecessary to repeat the various arguments about authorship in this case. The particular problem with 1 Peter is that we have no undisputed Petrine tradition with which to compare it. Meade, however, has drawn renewed attention to repeated echoes of Jesus' teaching (in the Gospel tradition) and to a number of parallels between 1 Peter and the sermons attributed to Peter in Acts (Meade, 173-74). These may not be enough to sustain a hypothesis of Petrine authorship as such; though, given that our knowledge of Peter is always allusive and at best second-hand, what would count as sufficient evidence? Such cross-references and allusions may, however, be sufficient to sustain the conclusion that 1 Peter was accepted as Petrine because it was recognized to embody Petrine traditions, to stand directly in a line of tradition and emphasis that began with Peter himself. The value of this conclusion once again would be that 1 Peter's canonical status and authority therefore need not depend on a verdict as to whether Peter himself was actually responsible for the letter. The judgment of those who first received and cherished this letter as authentically Petrine would be sufficient to authenticate it, and the claim expressed in its opening word ("Peter . . . to the exiles") can be seen still today as properly inviting that judgment and not contradicting it. (For arguments in favor of Petrine authorship, *see* 1 Peter.)

Whatever the precise status of 1 Peter, 2 Peter* can be said to stand within and indeed as the most striking example of the accepted tradition of canonical pseudepigraphy. It was written to meet the danger of false interpretation of older revelation (2 Pet 1:20; 3:15-16). It did so by appealing back to the already acknowledged Petrine tradition (2 Pet 1:16-18; 3:1). In particular it presents itself as Peter's last testament and by implication as the means by which Peter's teaching could be recalled after his death (2 Pet 1:12-15). All this speaks strongly of the tradition of legitimate pseudepigraphy already outlined. Here is the appeal to authoritative tradition and the claim to a continuity with that tradition that maintains its authentic voice. This claim almost failed in the subsequent evaluation of the letter; presumably it was written so much later than Peter that its claim to continuity and still to speak with Peter's voice had become more open to question. Its close relationship with Jude (Jude 4-13, 16-18/2 Pet 2:1-18; 3:1-3) cannot have helped (why was it not designated 2 Jude?). But in the event the greater pull of Petrine authority succeeded—it was deemed to be genuinely Petrine and part of the Christian canon—whereas the verdict went the other way in the case of the *Gospel of Peter.*

3.5. 2 Thessalonians, James and Jude. We need say little more about the other claimed pseudepigrapha in the NT: 2 Thessalonians, James and Jude. In the first case the issue is more disputed; but if 2 Thessalonians should be regarded as post-Pauline, it may introduce one new element into the discussion. This is the suggestion that the warning against a letter falsely claiming to be by Paul (2 Thess 2:1-2) refers to 1 Thessalonians itself—the pseudepigrapher attacking the authoritative originator of the tradition. But the suggestion runs counter to the character of the pseudepigraphic traditioning process outlined; its warning was surprisingly ineffective if both letters were accepted as authoritatively Pauline; and that very acceptance indicates clearly enough that the allusion in 2 Thessalonians 2:1-2 was understood from the first as to some letter other than 1 Thessalonians. (For arguments in favor of Pauline authorship *see* DPL, Thessalonians.)

In the case of James* and Jude,* "brother of James," the parallel of 1 Peter covers the ground sufficiently for present purposes. The fact is that we know so little of the style and teaching of these brothers of Jesus that the letters themselves constitute the major testimony to an authentic Jacobean and Jude traditions. In such circumstances both attest the same principle of a characteristic tradition acknowledged and cherished as deriving from an authoritative member of Christianity's founding generation. Whether the letters should be attributed to James and Jude themselves or to collaborators or reworkers of teachings stemming from them is of secondary concern. In James and Jude in particular (as with 1 Peter) the distinction between genuine and pseudepigraphic is more or less meaningless.

4. Conclusion.

There is, then, what might be called a biblical practice of continuing and developing a literary tradition, begun by an authoritative figure in the past, after his death. That second phase could be and in various well-documented cases evidently was recognized as sharing in the authority of the tradition's originator and accepted as also authoritative under his name. In each case the traditioning process that bore the author's name was also recognized to be of limited duration, after which the tradition had become too fixed or claims to write in the authoritative name were no longer widely accepted.

If pseudepigraphy continues to be the appropriate name for what was composed within the second phase of that process, then we have little choice other than to regard it as legitimate and to distinguish what we might call canonical pseudepigraphy from other kinds. It also follows that in such cases the charge of deceit and falsehood leveled against these writings becomes inappropriate; what we have rather is a legitimate speaking in and use of the great teacher's name, recognized as such by the churches that first used the letters in question. In this case also the choice between pseudepigraphy and canonicity need not be pressed to an either-or. Perhaps the most appropriate analogy is therefore the paintings that come from the studio of a great master, where the brushstrokes may not have been made by the master himself, but the character and quality and inspiration of the work can properly be said to be his, even when the work was conceived and executed after his death.

See also PAULINE LEGACY AND SCHOOL; 2 PETER.

BIBLIOGRAPHY. K. Aland, "The Problem of Anonymity and Pseudonymity in Christian Literature of the First Two Centuries" in *The Authorship and Integrity of the New Testament* (SPCK Theological Collections 4; London: SPCK, 1965) 1-13; N. Brox, *Falsche Verfasserangaben: Zur Erklärung der frühchristlichen Pseudepigraphie* (SB 79; Stuttgart: KBW, 1975); idem, ed., *Pseudepigraphie in der heidnischen und jüdisch-christlichen Antike* (Darmstadt: Wissenschaftliche Buchgesellschaft, 1977); J. H. Charlesworth, *The Old Testament Pseudepigrapha* (2 vols.; Garden City, NY: Doubleday, 1983, 1985); L. R. Donelson, *Pseudepigraphy and Ethical Argument in the Pastoral Epistles* (Tübingen: J. C. B. Mohr, 1986); J. D. G. Dunn, *The Living Word* (London: SCM, 1987) chap. 4; E. E. Ellis, "Pseudonymity and Canonicity of NT Documents" in *Worship, Theology and Ministry in the Early Church: Essays in Honor of R. P. Martin*, ed. M. J. Wilkins and T. Paige (JSNTSup 87; Sheffield: JSOT, 1992) 212-24; K. von Fritz, ed., *Pseudepigrapha I* (Vandoeuvres-Geneve: Fondation Hardt, 1972); D. Guthrie, "The Development of the Idea of Canonical Pseudepigrapha in New Testament Criticism" in *The Authorship and Integrity of the New Testament* (SPCK Theological Collections 4; London: SPCK, 1965) 14-39; I. H. Marshall, "Prospects for the Pastoral Epistles" in *Doing Theology for the People of God: Studies in Honor of J. I. Packer*, ed. D. Lewis and A. McGrath (Downers Grove, IL: InterVarsity Press, 1996) 137-55; D. G. Meade, *Pseudonymity and Canon* (WUNT 39; Tübingen: J. C. B. Mohr, 1986); B. M. Metzger, "Literary Forgeries and Canonical Pseudepigrapha," *JBL* 91 (1972) 3-24; C. F. D. Moule, *The Birth of the New Testament* (3d ed.; San Francisco: Harper & Row, 1982); J. I. Packer, *"Fundamentalism" and the Word of God* (London: Inter-Varsity Fellowship; Grand Rapids: Eerdmans, 1958); S. E. Porter, "Pauline Authorship and the Pastoral Epistles: Implications for Canon," *BBR* 5 (1995) 105-23; idem, "Pauline Authorship and the Pastoral Epistles: A Response to R. W. Wall's Response," *BBR* 6 (1996) 133-38; M. Rist, "Pseudepigraphy and the Early Christians" in *Studies in New Testament and Early Christian Literature*, ed. D. E. Aune (Leiden: E. J. Brill, 1972) 75-91; D. S. Russell, *The Method and Message of Jewish Apocalyptic* (London: SCM, 1964); W. Speyer, *Die literarische Fälschung im Altertum* (Munich: Beck, 1971); R. W. Wall, "Pauline Authorship and the Pastoral Epistles: A Response to S. E. Porter," *BBR* 5 (1995) 125-28.   J. D. G. Dunn

PSEUDO-CLEMENTINES. See APOCRYPHAL AND PSEUDEPIGRAPHAL WRITINGS; CLEMENT OF ROME; JEWISH CHRISTIANITY.

PSYCHOLOGY

By *psychology* we mean the terms used for the parts of the human person and their mutual relationship, whether the author implies by them a Hellenistic dualism or a higher and lower part of the human being or a functional holism or holistic dualism characteristic of Paul, in which the person is viewed as essentially a psychosomatic unity (*see DPL,* Psychology). The following discussion will survey the use of various psychological terms, testing in particular whether the writers' use of these expressions implies an acceptance of the functional holism or holistic dualism characteristic of Paul.

1. The New Testament
2. After the New Testament

1. The New Testament.

1.1. Use of Old Testament Terms. Many instances of psychological terms occur in OT quotations or allusions, suggesting that the authors took over a Hebraic understanding of humanity as fundamentally holistic. See, for example, the use of "hearts" from Psalm 95 in Hebrews 3:8, 10, 15; 4:7; and "all flesh is like grass" (Is 40:6) in 1 Peter 1:24.

1.2. Aspects of Human Persons. Significant features of the use of the main terms may be summarized as follows.

"Body" *(sōma)* sometimes denotes the physical body of either humans or animals (Heb 13:3, 11; Jas 2:16). Elsewhere it is used by synecdoche to represent the whole person with its physical aspect particularly in view. In Hebrews 10:5-10 the sacrifice* of Jesus' body means not merely his physical suffering* but also his total self-offering expressed in his suffering on the cross.* Other passages that appear to divide the person into distinct parts do so only to stress different aspects of a unified person. For example, James* says that the body without the spirit is dead (Jas 2:26) in order to insist that the two belong together. Or the body may be contrasted with the heart or conscience* to distinguish between inward and outward aspects of a person (Heb 10:22; cf. *sarx,* "flesh," in 1 Pet 3:21).

"Flesh"*(sarx)* can denote a complex range of meanings similar to that found in Paul. In James 5:3 it means human flesh literally. Sometimes it denotes the earthly, physical life of human beings (1 Pet 4:2) or specifically of Jesus (Heb 2:14; 5:7; 1 Jn 4:2; 2 Jn 7). Or it expresses the sinfulness of humanity out of harmony with God's will, as in the phrase "desire of the flesh" *(epithymia sarkos,* 1 Jn 2:16; cf. 1 Pet 2:11; 2 Pet 2:18). In Jude 8 it probably refers specifically to sexual sin. But even here there is no suggestion that the physical body is inherently sinful or inferior to other parts of a person.

"Soul" *(psychē)* refers to physical life in Reve-

lation 12:11. More commonly it denotes the center of personality, the inner person in its capacity to direct one's life and to relate to God* (Heb 6:19; 1 Pet 1:21; 2 Pet 2:8; Rev 18:14). It is therefore the object of salvation* (Jas 1:21; 5:20; 1 Pet 1:9; cf. Heb 10:39; 13:17). But again this is an aspect, not a part, of personality. *Psychē* clearly represents the whole person in 1 Peter 3:20, 1 Peter 4:19 and 2 Peter 2:14. In Revelation 18:13 both *sōma* and *psychē* refer to slaves* as whole persons (cf. Ezek 27:13). A distinct usage is the description of the dead martyrs as *psychai* in Revelation 6:9-11 and Revelation 20:4. Though they await resurrection* they are not less than whole persons, as is indicated by the masculine pronoun in Revelation 20:4.

"Heart" *(kardia)* is the seat of human will and desire. It is the source of emotions and passions (Jas 3:14), understanding and reflection (Heb 4:12), and hence the whole inner being in contrast with the external aspect (Heb 10:22; 1 Pet 3:4; 1 Jn 3:19-21). Its desires may be in tune with God's will (Heb 8:10; 1 Pet 1:22; 3:15) or in conflict with it (Heb 3:12; Jas 1:26; 2 Pet 2:14). It naturally stands for the whole self in James 1:26 and James 5:5.

"Mind" *(nous, dianoia)* is the faculty of thought and understanding and the attitudes that it produces (Heb 8:10; 10:16; 1 Pet 1:13; 2 Pet 3:1). Since the mind of the Christian is open to God, both Greek words may represent God-given insight (1 Jn 5:20; Rev 13:18; 17:9).

"Spirit" *(pneuma)* is used much more frequently to refer to the Holy Spirit* (and occasionally to angels,* evil spirits or the breath of life) than to the inner life of human beings. But in 1 Peter 3:3-4 we see "heart" and "spirit" contrasted with outward appearance. The *pneuma* as the self in its capacity to relate to God is implied in Hebrews 12:9, where the unique description of God as "father of [our] spirits" is contrasted with "our fathers of the flesh" (i.e., our earthly ancestors).

The statement in Hebrews 4:12 that God's word "penetrates even to divide soul and spirit" has sometimes been taken to imply a dualism (or a trichotomy of spirit, soul and body). But probably the author does not intend to be precisely analytical. He wants to express vividly how God's word probes the inner recesses of human personality (Bruce, 113). In Hebrews 12:23 the plural *pneumata* denotes dead saints, a usage similar to that of "souls" in Revelation 6:9-11 and Revelation 20:4.

1.3. The Inner Conflict and the Person Made Whole. These writers give ample evidence of the distance that people may travel from the will of God and of the external temptations* and inner forces that may drive them there. They know too that believers in their own strength are weak and subject to temptation (Heb 4:15-16). Christians may become "double-minded" *(dipsychoi)*, with their passions *(epithymiai)* at war within them (Jas 1:8; 4:8; 4:1). But their hearts may be purified (Jas 4:8). They may learn to live not for evil human desires *(anthrōpōn epithymiai)* but for God's will (1 Pet 4:2). This vision of the human personality reintegrated around a new center and oriented toward God is expressed particularly in 1 Peter 1:14-15 (cf. 1 Pet 1:22-23; 2:9-12).

1.4. Some Hellenistic Traits? The issue arises as to whether there are not some Hellenistic traits in our literature; namely, passages in which the human is divided into body and spirit/soul in such a way that the spiritual is viewed as higher in contrast with the lower, physical part of the person. Two passages will be discussed here. E. Schweizer has called 1 Peter 2:11 "the most strongly hellenized *psychē* passage in the New Testament" (Schweizer, 653). The conflict between the soul and the desires *(epithymiai)* of the flesh* recalls Plato's division of the soul into three, of which the lowest part was the *epithymētikon,* the seat of desires, which must be controlled by the highest part, the rational. This is the only NT passages in which *sarx* clearly stands in opposition to *psychē*, suggesting that the soul is a higher part of the person than is the flesh. The idea is different from Paul's description of the conflict between *sarx* and *pneuma,* since in Galatians 5:18-23 it is God's Spirit that fights against the flesh. Yet the dualistic thrust of the statement in 1 Peter* can be exaggerated. The thought is not very different from that of Romans 7:23, where Paul acknowledges the reality of conflict within a person. And *psychē* here may be interpreted not as the immaterial or superior part of a human being but as "life" in the sense of Mark 8:35-37 (Michaels, 116-17).

In 1 Peter 3:18 and 1 Peter 4:6 the author contrasts *sarx* and *pneuma* in a way that may suggest that he is influenced by the Hellenistic idea of two spheres or levels, of which *pneuma* represents the higher sphere and *sarx* the lower. In both instances *sarx* refers to the death of the body, not to sinful human nature. According to 1 Peter 3:18, "his death took place in the sphere of 'the flesh', the earthly, temporal existence; his resurrection took place in the sphere of 'the spirit', the eternal, the indestructible, the heavenly. This does not imply any rejection of the thought of a bodily resurrection, but rather that the body in which He is 'made alive' is itself 'spiritual' " (Beare, 143; on the interpretation of this problematic passage see especially Dalton). In Pauline literature we find parallels in Romans 1:3-4 and especially 1 Timothy 3:16—both, like 1 Peter 3:18-21, generally agreed to derive from earlier Christian tradition. Although the idea of two spheres is present in all three passages, there is no suggestion that spirit and flesh are two distinct parts of the person. Death and resurrection happened to the whole Christ* (1 Pet 3:18) and to the whole persons referred to in 1 Peter 4:6.

1.5. Conclusion. Though we have seen limited evidence of Hellenistic forms of thought, the evidence gathered shows that these authors affirm a fundamentally Hebraic understanding of humanity that may be described as holistic dualism. In a variety of expressions they speak of persons in their various aspects but always think of the person as a unified whole. Even where Hellenistic influence may be detected, there is no reference to the immortal soul as the guarantee of eternal life,* no clear suggestion that the soul is superior to other aspects of humanity or that sin resides in one part of the person.

2. After the New Testament.

2.1. The Biblical Tradition Continued. There is clear continuity between biblical perspectives and literature of the early second century. Psychological terms appear frequently in quotations from the OT and less frequently from the NT. For OT examples see *1 Clement* 2.8; 8.4; 15.2-4; 16.11-3; 18.10-12, 17; 52.4; *Barnabas* 6.7; 9.1-5; 10.12; for NT examples see *1 Clement* 36.2; *2 Clement* 19.2; Ignatius *Polycarp* 1.3; Polycarp *Philippians* 4.3; 7.2; 8.1.

As the seat of desire the heart may be focused on evil thoughts (*Herm. Vis.* 3.6.3) or on God (*Herm. Man.* 9.2; 12.5.2; *2 Clem.* 11.1); it is a shrine of God (*Barn.* 6.15; 16.7). The spirit is the inner person (*Herm. Vis.* 3.11.2) or the whole person (*2 Clem.* 20.4). The meaning of "soul" is frequently very similar. It is the inner being (*2 Clem.* 13.1) or the whole person

(*1 Clem.* 64.1; Ign. *Phil.* 1.2; *Barn.* 3.5; 17.1) and therefore the object of salvation (*Barn.* 19.10).

The apostolic fathers* continued the range of meanings for *sarx* that are found in the NT, including the physical body (on which see below). As in Paul, to act "according to the flesh" (*kata sarka*) can mean to operate on a merely earthly level without reference to God (Ign. *Magn.* 6.2; Ign. *Rom.* 8.3). It rarely means "sinful nature," though Ignatius* has this sense in mind when he stresses the impossibility of being fleshly (*sarkikos*) and spiritual (*pneumatikos*) at the same time (Ign. *Eph.* 8.2). In *1 Clement* 38.2 it denotes sexual sin (in contrast to *enkrateia*, sexual restraint). These examples perhaps indicate a tendency to equate sinful desires with bodily indulgence. But in *Barnabas* 10.9 "desire of the flesh" (*epithymia tēs sarkos*) refers to an inability to understand Scripture on a spiritual (allegorical) level. *Diognetus* 5 provides an interesting example of a thoroughly Pauline use of the phrases "in the flesh" and "according to the flesh" (*en sarki . . . kata sarka*), referring respectively to neutral living in the world and living in a sinful way.

Some significant passages, by combining terms such as "spirit," "soul," "body" and "flesh," show concern to express the relationship between various aspects of human personality. Ignatius refers to acting and being "in flesh and spirit" (Ign. *Magn.* 13.1-2; Ign. *Trall.* 12.1; Ign. *Pol.* 1.2; 5.1). Perhaps *Polycarp* 2.2 ("You consist of flesh and spirit, that you may deal tenderly with the things which appear visibly") shows that Polycarp* understands the relationship of spirit to flesh in terms of the inner and outward aspects of personality. Though the spirit is perhaps more important than the flesh in that it operates on a deeper level, Ignatius is not negative about the body (cf. Ign. *Phil.* 7.1; *1 Clem.* 64.1; *2 Clem.* 12.3-4). The *Shepherd of Hermas, Similitudes* 5.7.1-4 says that spirit and flesh must both be kept pure because one cannot be defiled without also defiling the other. In *Diognetus* 6, however, there is a stronger insistence that "the immortal soul inhabits a mortal tent" and directs the body; paradoxically, "the flesh hates the soul," but "the soul loves the flesh."

This essentially positive view of the body is related to a specific understanding of the person of Jesus. Christ himself in his incarnation, death (*see* Death of Christ) and resurrection was "both spiritual and fleshly" (Ign. *Eph.* 7.2; Ign.

Smyrn. 3.2; 12.2). His fleshly or bodily nature was essential for the salvation of ours, and that salvation includes resurrection of the flesh (*1 Clem.* 49.6; *2 Clem.* 9.5). There is here the idea of two spheres or levels (see 1.4 above). Christ came from the spiritual sphere to the earthly sphere to unite the two. He did not come to rescue humanity from the flesh but in the flesh. Hence there will be a "resurrection of the flesh" (*sarkos anastasis*, not a NT phrase, appears in Justin Martyr *Dial. Tryph.* 80.5; cf. *Ep. Apos.* 21).

2.2. The Gnostic Strand. In contrast with the orthodox concern to hold together the different aspects of humanity, gnostic* texts display an evident dualism. Although *Gospel of Thomas* affirms Jesus' appearance in the flesh, it stresses the subsidiary role of the body and even asserts that the division of the two is desirable (*Gos. Thom.* 28—29, 112). In the *Treatise on Resurrection* the flesh is viewed negatively, as the temporary, earthly mode of existence for both the Savior and the elect.* It is abandoned at death, to be replaced by a new transformed flesh (*Treat. Res.* 47.6-8; *see* Resurrection). Rheginos is warned in this epistle against living "according to the flesh" (*Treat. Res.* 49.9-16). Though the language echoes that of Paul, the author apparently identifies the physical flesh with the seat of sin and thus advocates an ascetic ethic. The mind or soul, however, survives death (*Treat. Res.* 46.21-4; 47.38—48.2). By an act of faith, therefore, it must direct its thought away from the body and toward the truth. Bodily resurrection becomes irrelevant.

2.3. Conclusion. After the NT Christians continued to grapple with the task of interpreting a biblical understanding of the person in a predominantly Hellenistic culture. In the orthodox strand there is a recognizable continuity with the NT's holistic dualism; in the gnostic strand there is a much sharper dualism, which upholds the significance of the soul or mind at the expense of the essentially bodily nature of human personality.

See also CONSCIENCE; FLESH; SIN, WICKEDNESS.

BIBLIOGRAPHY. F. W. Beare, *The First Epistle of Peter* (Oxford: Blackwell, 1947); F. F. Bruce, *The Epistle to the Hebrews* (rev. ed.; NICNT; Grand Rapids: Eerdmans, 1990); W. J. Dalton, *Christ's Proclamation to the Spirits: A Study of 1 Peter 3:18—4:6* (Rome: Pontifical Biblical Institute, 1965); A. A. Hoekema, *Created in God's Image* (Grand Rapids: Eerdmans, 1986); W. G. Kümmel, *Man in the New Testament* (Philadelphia: Westminster, 1963); J. R. Michaels, *1 Peter* (WBC; Waco, TX: Word, 1988); M. L. Peel, *The Epistle to Rheginos: A Valentinian Letter on the Resurrection* (London: SCM, 1969); E. Schweizer et al., "ψυχή, κτλ," *TDNT* 9:608-66. **S. H. Travis**

PUNISHMENT. *See* HELL, ABYSS, ETERNAL PUNISHMENT.

PURITY AND IMPURITY

Purity is best understood as the condition which God* demands of his people for contact with him. In the case of Israel, specific foods, objects and physical characteristics are demanded for any approach of the divine. Even then, priests* mediate in the final acts of sacrifice,* because greater purity is required the closer one comes to God's holiness.*

Two sorts of impurity threatened Israel: impurity by contagion and impurity by holiness. Impurity by contagion results from contact with anything which should not exist. A corpse or a monstrous beast (e.g., Dan 7:3-8), for example, are not a part of the created order intended by God, and must not be brought near God. But it is equally dangerous to approach what belongs to God alone: blood, for example, threatens Israel's existence because it is too holy to be eaten, containing the very "life" *(nep̄eš)* of an animal as given by God, and not because it is essentially impure.

Both forms of impurity can be mortal, unless they are prevented or dealt with once they emerge. Nadab and Abihu offer an unwarranted sacrifice, and they are consumed by fire (Lev 10:1-3). But God also "broke out" against Uzzah, because he had touched the ark in order to steady it during transport (2 Sam 6:6-10). Such stories show that Israel's existence was balanced on a knife's edge according to this overall concept of purity. On the one side were the basic impurities which God categorically would not tolerate. On the other side was the holiness which destroyed even what was pure by simple contact. Defining what is pure was held to be Israel's charter for existence. Earlier inhabitants of the land had been expelled because they did not attend to the purity required by God (see Lev 18:24-30). That belief clearly marks the systemic importance of the observation of the clean and the unclean within Israel.

Issues related to the overall definition of purity were prominent within Jesus' discussions and disputes with his contemporaries. His stance in regard to those questions was so coherent as to amount to a program. As the cultural milieu of Jesus' movement changed after the resurrection, the principal circles of the primitive church (represented by Peter,* James* and Paul) developed distinctive understandings of purity. Tensions among those positions were resolved in the equation of purity with virtue. That resolution is one of the most important theological achievements of the NT.

1. Strategies of Purity Within Early Judaism
2. Jesus' Program of Purity
3. The Conflicting Strategies of Peter, James and Paul
4. The Resolution of Purity and Virtue in Hellenistic Christianity

1. Strategies of Purity Within Early Judaism.
That purity is required of Israel is axiomatic within the Hebrew Bible, but distinct strategies of defining, achieving and maintaining purity were developed. The best known and most comprehensive strategy is the priestly scheme represented in the book of Leviticus, and most discussions understandably begin at that point (*see DJG*, Clean and Unclean). But that picture is to be supplemented by the alternative strategies of other circles within Israel. Ezekiel, Leviticus and Deuteronomy provide patterns of understanding which were classic within the understanding of Israel and formative for several groups within Judaism during the time the NT emerged.

In Ezekiel 40—48 a vision establishes the purity by which Israel gains access to the holy, the powerful source of its inheritance. Only Zadokite priests are to serve God in his sanctuary (Ezek 44:15-16). Foreigners are to be excluded, as "foreskinned in heart and foreskinned in flesh" (Ezek 44:9). Levites are relegated to an ancillary function, owing to their previous involvement in idolatry (Ezek 44:10-14): service in the funeral cult of dead kings (Ezek 43:6-9). The Zadokite priests, in turn, are carefully regulated in respect of their clothing (Ezek 44:17-18), coiffeur (Ezek 44:20), temperance (Ezek 44:21) and marriages (Ezek 44:22). The priests are to leave their clothing in sacred chambers and put on other clothing before they meet the people in the outer court, "lest they make the people holy with their garments" (Ezek 44:19).

Purity and sanctity are complementary and yet distinct. What is pure is accessible to the holy and for that very reason must be protected from the holy.

The priests are also charged with teaching the people the difference between the holy and the profane and with making known the difference between the defiled and the clean (Ezek 44:23). Both basic impurity and any outbreak of holiness are dangers which must be guarded against. Priestly concerns within the logic of cleanness are developed further in Leviticus. Certain things, such as blood and the parts of beasts which are to be offered, are unclean because they belong to the divine alone (e.g., Lev 7:22-27; 17:10-14). But other things, impure beasts and carcasses, are not fit for consumption, whether human (Israelite) or divine (Lev 7:19-21; 17:15-16). But whether viewed from the perspective of impurity or of holiness, the thread of the argument is the same: the laws of cleanness are Israel's means of maintaining a solidarity of sacrifice with God, apart from which the land* may not be retained. Indeed, the claim is here explicitly made that the former inhabitants of the land failed to keep the rules of purity and for that reason were expelled, so that Israel might suffer the same fate (Lev 18:24-30). The land, in Leviticus, is not for Israel; Israel is for the service of God in his land. The conditionality of Israel's presence is cognate with the fierce emphasis on cutting off what is unclean (cf., e.g., Lev 7:19-21, 22-27), and separating from the Gentiles (cf., e.g., Lev 18:3; 20:23).

Holiness is a curiously ambivalent force. It is what gives Israel the land, but also what destroys anything that is not compatible with it. The priests are to be the instruments of Israel's compatibility with the holy, and for that reason they are both oddly privileged and fiercely punished. They partake of holy sacrifices, and are held to a higher order of sanctity than the generality of Israel (Lev 21:6, 8, 14, 15, 22, 23). When Nadab and Abihu, sons of Aaron, offer incense in a foreign manner, they are consumed in fire, and God announces without remorse, "I will be sanctified among those who are near me, and I will be glorified before all the people" (Lev 10:1-3). Death then becomes the sanction for breaking the specific requirements of priesthood (cf. Lev 10:6-11; 16:1-2). God's desire is to consume a part of what is pure, but he will

extirpate the impure, and his destruction of what he does not want is more comprehensive than his consumption of what he sets aside for himself. The priests are to keep those laws of purity which they teach and more, because they are the guardians of Israel's cleanness, the peoples' tenuous compatibility with the holy (Lev 10:10, 11).

The notion that there are three feasts which all male Israelites are to keep is paradigmatic within the Torah (cf. Ex 23:14-17; Lev 23; Num 28, 29), but Deuteronomy 16 is especially plain in its requirement. In Deuteronomy the emphasis is not on what is offered to God, as in Leviticus and Numbers, nor on appearing before him, as in Exodus, but on the fact that a pilgrimage is necessary (*see* Temple). From the perspective of Moses, of course, Jerusalem itself is not at issue, but readers or hearers can only identify that city with the single "place" (*hāmāqôm*) where God is to be worshiped (Deut 12:5-14). Because the ambit of activity in Deuteronomy extends far from Jerusalem (to which pilgrimage is necessary), the slaughter and consumption of animals outside of Jerusalem, explicitly as non-sacrificial, is permitted, provided the blood is poured out and the beast concerned is not owed as a sacrifice (Deut 12:15-28).

The assumption of Leviticus is quite different; the priestly focus of its scheme imagines all meat being offered in sacrifice prior to consumption (see Lev 17:1-9). Just as Deuteronomy replaces that impracticable requirement with a concept of a secular meal, so it widens the definition of the meat that may be eaten. The gazelle and the hart are specifically authorized for eating in Deuteronomy 12:22, although they are not mentioned in Leviticus 11. Deuteronomy establishes a conception of purity which functions as related but not identical to the category of what may be sacrificed. Yet Ezekiel, Leviticus and Deuteronomy all represent the covenantal regulation of sacrifice and make the temple in Jerusalem the sole focus of that regulation.

Sacrifice includes certain pragmatics, things offered in the appropriate place by certain people. The pragmatic offering is associated with specific emotions and is justified by articulated ideologies. Ezekiel defines a particular space and its priests by visionary means; the pragmatics of Leviticus are the animals offered by specified procedures; Deuteronomy motivates Israel to join in sacrifice on festive occasions. Ezekiel looks forward to security, Leviticus to separation from Gentiles, Deuteronomy to the joy of households. What justifies the particular sacrifices of each book? The memory of idolatry in Ezekiel; the picture of those expelled from the land in Leviticus; the anticipation of prosperity in Deuteronomy.

The Hebrew Bible attests, then, that the single covenant with Israel was consistent with varying emphases and practices within the conception of purity. Variation in that regard was also characteristic of well known Judaic groups in the first century (*see DJG*, Judaism, 400-404). Priests, Essenes and Pharisees evolved characteristic concerns of purity. The parable of the Good Samaritan presents a priest and Levite avoiding a man left for dead on the side of the road; their fear of contamination from an unclean corpse overcame their compassion (Lk 10:31-32). Similar attitudes may be the source of Josephus's complaint that the Sadducees generally are boorish and suspicious (*J.W.* 2.8.14 §166). Josephus also describes the Essenes' peculiar habits in regard to purity: among other things, he specifies the avoidance of oil, the practice of ablution and changing clothes prior to ritual meals, and the treatment of the eating hall "as if it were a holy temple" (*J.W.* 2.8.3-5 §§123-131). The Pharisees also used changing clothes as a marker of purity: an associate was not to accept the hospitality of a person of the land and could only receive a person of the land as a guest if a fresh clothing was provided for the guest (see *m. Dem.* 2:3).

2. Jesus' Program of Purity.

Jesus' circle was centered in Galilee and was characterized by fellowship at meals involving various people with different practices of purity (see Mt 11:18-19 par. Lk 7:33-35). That description applies to the period of Jesus' own activity and also to the period after his death when Peter appears to lead the movement. In either phase, the circle of Jesus needed to cope with the social issue of possible defilement as one member of Israel (with one set of practices) met another member of Israel (with a different set of practices).

One of the best attested of Jesus' sayings is his assertion that defilement is a matter of what comes from within, not from without (Mk 7:14-15). The point of this saying (and those to which it may be compared, Mt 15:10-11 and Lk 11:40-41) is that there is a link between integrity and cleanness: that Israelites are properly understood as pure and that what extends from a person, what he is and does and has, manifests that purity. Paul was to write some twenty-five years later (and for his own purposes), "Do you not know that your body is a temple of the Holy Spirit within you, which you have from God?" (1 Cor 6:19). Paul may be alluding to a particular saying of Jesus (cf. Jn 2:21) or to what he takes to be a theme of Jesus; in either case, he refers his readers to what he assumes to be elementary knowledge of the gospel.

That Jesus and especially Paul (who associated himself with the Pharisees, cf. Phil 3:5) speak from such a perspective is not unusual. It is said that Hillel took a similar point of view and expressed it in a more heterodox manner. He defended an Israelite's right to bathe in Roman installations on the grounds that if Gentiles deem it an honor to wash the idols of their gods, Israelites should similarly deem it an honor (indeed, a duty) to wash their bodies, the image of God (Lev. *Rab.* 34.3). In other words, bathing does not make one pure but celebrates the fact of purity; in their quite different ways, Hillel and Paul demonstrate that representatives of the Pharisaic movement conceived of purity as a condition which all Israelites could be assumed to enjoy, and out of which they should act. Fundamentally, Jesus' concern appears similarly to have been with cleanness as a matter of production rather than of consumption.

Jesus' interest in the definition of purity is also evident in the Synoptic story of what is known as Jesus' cleansing of a leper (Mt 8:2-4; Mk 1:40-44; Lk 5:12-14). In the story, a leper approaches Jesus and for no stated reason asserts that Jesus is able to cleanse him. Jesus assents, touching the man and pronouncing him clean and ordering him (a) to show himself to a priest and (b) to offer the sacrifice prescribed by Moses for cleansing. The terms of reference of the actions described are explicitly given within the book of Leviticus (chaps. 13 and 14). The assumption of Leviticus 13 and 14, and therefore of the story in the Synoptics, is that "leprosy," which might more literally be rendered "outbreak" (*ṣāra'at*), comes and goes and that its presence and absence can be detected. In Leviticus 13, when the issue is "outbreak" in humans (as distinct from cloth and houses), it is clear that the great concern and the cause of uncleanness is broken flesh (Lev 13:15). The suspicion of "outbreak" arises when there is a change in the pigmentation of the skin and accompanying hair, but a total change signals a return to cleanness (Lev 13:12, 13), since the fundamental concern is broken flesh (and therefore blood), to which no human correctly has access. Accordingly, sufferers are banned (Lev 13:45, 46).

In the event one is declared clean by a priest, two quite distinct offerings are enjoined in Leviticus 14. The first is a local sacrifice and may take place wherever there is flowing water. The priest kills a bird in a earthen vessel over the water and dips a living bird in its blood, having beforehand attached cedar, scarlet and hyssop to it. He then sprinkles the sufferer from "outbreak" with the living bird and releases it (Lev 14:1-8). Purification follows (cf. Lev 14:9), after which the sufferer needs to offer two male lambs, a ewe, cereal and oil; together they constitute a sacrifice for guilt, a sacrifice for sin, a burnt sacrifice and a cereal sacrifice, all with the sufferer particularly in view (Lev 14:10-20). Exceptional provisions are made for instances of poverty (Lev 14:21-32), but the requirement of ownership remains onerous.

Within the setting envisaged in Leviticus, the story concerning Jesus therefore refers to a specific moment. The sufferer from "outbreak" attributes to Jesus the ability to adjudicate the status of his skin, and Jesus accepts the responsibility of telling him he may proceed directly to the sacrificial moment which is to occur after cleanness has been declared. Although Jesus is not portrayed as taking over any sacrificial function, he is explicitly assigned—within the terms of reference the story itself establishes—the authority to pronounce on matters of purity. Pharisees were similarly involved, as an entire tractate of the Mishnah (*Nega'im*) attests. Jesus and his circle appear to have been keenly concerned with purity as such, in a manner similar to the Pharisees (although purity was generally a focus of discussion and controversy within early Judaism). Jesus' stance is perhaps more similar to the Pharisees' than to the sectarians' of Qumran (who separated from ordinary worship in the temple) or the priests' (who perpetuated that worship), but the formal categorization of Jesus as a Pharisee is not warranted.

The essential assumption in Jesus' cleansing of the man with "outbreak" is that purity is not merely a function of diagnosis by observation. The integrity of the skin proceeds from the integrity which animates the skin. Others concerned with purity might tell priests how to declare on the basis of their observations, advise concerning the removal of suspicious growths or counsel when the priest could best be visited (so the tractate *Nega'im*); Jesus appears in the story to hold that the determinative factor is the man's approach in the expectation of purity and his own agreement to purification by contact with the man. The link between purity and righteousness is implicit within the sacrificial systems of the Hebrew Bible, and Psalms brings to open expression the systemic association of righteousness and purity (cf. Ps 18:20 [MT 18:21]; Ps 24:3-6; 26:4-7; 51:2, 6, 7, 10 [MT 51:4, 8, 9, 12]; Ps 119:9).

Jesus' perspective in regard to purity is reflected within a passage which is also common to the Synoptics, but which is particularly articulated in the source of Jesus' teaching commonly called Q. (Q is principally attested in Matthew and Luke, but parts of the source are also reflected in Mark. *See DJG*, Q.) In the commission to his twelve followers (and, in Luke, seventy followers) to preach and heal, Jesus specifically commands them to remain in whatever house they are received within a given village, until they depart (Mt 10:11-14; Mk 6:10; Lk 9:4; 10:5-7). That commandment by itself is a notable development compared with a Pharisaic construction of purity because it presupposes that what the disciples eat, within any house which might receive them, is clean. Jesus' itinerancy and that of his disciples, treated in much recent literature as if it were an obviously Greco-Roman practice, was a profound statement of the general purity of food in Israel. The sayings source underscores that statement by having the disciples pronounce their peace upon the house in question (Mt 10:12, 13; Lk 10:5, 6), and Luke's Jesus particularly insists that the disciples should eat what is set before them in whatever town they might enter (Lk 10:7, 8 see also *Gos. Thom.* 1:14). The pronouncement of peace and the injunction not to go from house to house within a given community (cf. Lk 10:7) but to stay put until the visit is over had obvious utility within the missionary* concerns of the movement after the resurrection. (The message of the resurrection proved to be more divisive than Jesus' own preaching. The temptation to try to find especially sympathetic households prior to settling into a mission must have been great.) But the particular focus upon purity, all but obscured in Q within missionary directives, appears to have belonged to Jesus.

A last peculiarity of the commission in Q, which has long seemed incomprehensible, finds its sense according to our analysis. Although Mark's Jesus has the disciples without bread, bag, money or a change of clothes, he does permit them a staff and sandals (Mk 6:8, 9). In the mishnaic-like source of Jesus' instruction ("Q"), however, just those obviously necessary items are singled out for exclusion (cf. Mt 10:9, 10; Lk 9:3; 10:4). The traditional attempt to explain differences within the lists as the result of missionary practices within the early church is reasonable superficially, but that attempt only diverts attention from the obvious fact that the commission makes extremely poor sense as a missionary instrument. Why tell people not to take what on any journey they, practically speaking, might need? But if we understand the commission to treat every village they might enter as clean, as purely Israel as the temple itself, the perplexing imperatives of the commission makes eminent sense. The disciples are to enter villages exactly as pilgrims were to enter the temple within Pharisaic teaching: without the sandals, the staffs and the purses (cf. *m. Ber.* 9:5; *b. Yebam.* 6b) which would normally accompany a journey. Q makes Jesus' commission into a missionary discourse; within his ministry, it was designed to be an enacted parable of Israel's purity.

Whether in the triply attested material of the Synoptics (a probable reflection of Petrine tradition) or in the doubly attested mishnaic source known as Q, a circle of concern associated with Jesus is held to see purity as proceeding from Israel. Once one is identified with Israel, it is not that which is without which defiles, but those things which come from oneself. Separation from that which is outside one does not therefore assure purity, and non-Jews in the mixed environment of Galilee* pose no particular danger to Israel. The circle of Jesus frames its rhetoric for its specific, social circumstance of Israel in the midst of the nations. Defilement here is a matter of failing to recognize the others of Israel, refusing to produce

from within and to contact on that basis the pure Israel which those others represent.

3. The Conflicting Strategies of Peter, James and Paul.

Peter shared with Jesus the hope of a climactic disclosure of divine power, signaled in the willingness of nations to worship* on Mount Zion (*see* Jerusalem, Zion). That hope is certainly attested within sources extant by the first century. Chief among them, from the point of view of its influence upon the NT, is the book of Zechariah.

Zechariah provided the point of departure for Jesus' inclusive program of purity and forgiveness as the occasions of the kingdom. Jesus is said to have mentioned the prophet by name (see Mt 23:34-36; Lk 11:49-51). The book programmatically concerns the establishment of restored worship in the Temple, especially at the feast of Sukkoth (Zech 14:16-19). "All the nations" are to go up to Jerusalem annually for worship (Zech 14:16), and the transformation of which that worship is part involves the provision of "living waters" from the city (Zech 14:8, cf. Jn 4:10, 14). That image is related to an earlier "fountain opened for the house of David and the inhabitants of Jerusalem in view of sin and uncleanness" (Zech 13:1). Here we see the association of forgiveness and purity which is a feature of Jesus' program, as well as the notion of an immediate release, without any mention of a preliminary act of sacrifice, from what keeps Israel from God. God himself is held to arrange the purity he requires, so that the sacrifice he desires might take place. Zechariah features the commissioning of a priest (Zech 3, see Mt 16:18, 19), an oracle against swearing (Zech 5:3, 4, see Mt 5:33-37), a vision of a king humbly riding an ass (Zech 9:9, see Mt 21:1-9; Mk 11:1-10; Lk 19:28-40; Jn 12:12-19), the prophetic receipt of thirty shekels of silver in witness against the owners of sheep (Zech 11:4-17, see Mt 26:14-16; 27:3-10; cf. Mk 14:10, 11; Lk 22:3-6).

It is obvious that the connections between Jesus' ministry and Zechariah do not amount to a common agenda, and Matthew clearly reflects a tendency to increase the fit between the two. But the similarities are suggestive of Jesus' appropriation of Zechariah's prophecy of eschatological purity, as a final, more fundamental connection would indicate. The climactic vision of Zechariah insists that every vessel in Jerusalem will belong to Yahweh and become a fit vessel for sacrifice. As part of that insistence, the text asserts that no trader will be allowed in the temple (Zech 14:20, 21). In the light of Zechariah, Jesus' occupation of the temple appears an enactment of prophetic purity in the face of a commercial innovation, a vigorous insistence that God would prepare his own people and vessels for eschatological worship (*see* Temple).

Peter perpetuated that vision by means of his fidelity both to breaking bread at home with the disciples and in worship within the temple. At the same time, Acts portrays Peter's activity much further afield (*see* Temple). The reason for this connection between Peter's residence in Jerusalem and his activity in Syria and beyond is provided by the vision which he relates as the warrant for his visit to the house of Cornelius,* the Roman centurion (Acts 10:1-48). Peter is praying on a roof top in Joppa around noon. His vision occurs while he is hungry and concerns a linen lowering from heaven, filled with four-footed animals, reptiles and birds. A voice says, "Arise, Peter, slaughter and eat," and he refuses (in words reminiscent of Ezek 4:14). But a voice again says, "What God has cleansed, you will not defile" (see Acts 10:9-16).

In the course of a dispute with those who argued that circumcision* was a requirement of adherence to the movement, Peter defends his baptisms* in the house of Cornelius on the basis of his vision (Acts 11:1-18). He cites his activity among non-Jews at a later point, in the context of what has come to be called the Apostolic Council (Acts 15:7-11). Throughout, the position of Peter appears to have been consistent: God may make and has made eschatological exceptions to the usual practice of purity. Those exceptions include the acceptance of uncircumcised men in baptism and fellowship with them.

The policy of accepting non-Jews, who were baptized but not circumcised, was perhaps the most important decision which the primitive church made. It is presented as formalized in the book of Acts in a single session (Acts 15:1-35), but the reference to the dispute earlier (Acts 11:1-3) shows that the policy was framed over a number of years. Moreover, what appears as a single meeting in Acts 15 addresses two distinct issues. The first issue was whether non-Jews might be baptized without being circumcised (Acts 15:1-12). The second issue was whether such baptized Gentiles could be embraced in a single fellowship with Jews who had been baptized (Acts 15:13-29).

In his letter to Galatians, Paul reflects the discussion and dispute over the two issues as a vitally concerned participant (Gal 2:1-10). Paul records the agreement of the "pillars" of the church in Jerusalem that there should be an apostolate to the uncircumcised (represented by Paul) as well as to the circumcised (represented by Peter). (Of course, other apostolates—such as James's and his emissaries [Gal 2:12; cf. 2 Cor 10—13]—also concentrated on the circumcised; Paul's point is that Peter was especially concerned with the circumcised outside of Jerusalem and even beyond territorial Israel.) Those pillars include James, Jesus' brother, Peter himself and John. Paul goes on to describe the contention which emerged in Antioch,* a dispute which split the church for decades, but the remarkable agreement on a central point should not be overlooked: James, Peter and Paul agreed that there was a place for non-Jews within the movement.

Those who disagreed with them, the adherents to the Abrahamic requirement of circumcision (see Gen 17:10-14), were not silenced and maintained their position (see Acts 11:2-3; 15:1; Gal 5:2-12). Ebionite* Christianity, however, appears to have been the only wing of the church in the second century in which their stance prevailed (see Irenaeus *Haer.* 1.26.2; *see* Jewish Christianity). However much the position of the circumcisers could claim the warrant of Scripture, the vision of Peter represents the dominant tendency toward an acceptance of non-Jews.

The inevitable question emerged: did the acceptance of non-Jews imply their full fellowship with Jewish believers? In their response to that question, Peter, James and Paul went their separate ways. Paul reports favorably on the practice in Antioch before emissaries from James came, when meals could be conducted with common fellowship among Jewish and non-Jewish followers of Jesus (see Gal 2:12). According to Paul, the arrival of those emissaries caused Peter to separate from non-Jews, and even Barnabas acceded to the separation (Gal 2:12-13). The tendency of Hellenistic communities of Christians to mix their Jewish and non-Jewish constituencies and therefore to relax or ignore issues of purity in foods* is here documented by Paul (c. A.D. 53).

When Acts gives an account of the Jacobean policy toward Gentiles,* James appears much more sympathetic but nonetheless rigorous. The occasion of his statement of policy is said to be the suggestion that one must be circumcised in order to be saved (Acts 15:1), a suggestion which is associated with a form of Christian Pharisaism (Acts 15:5). Peter is said to side with Paul, with the argument that Gentiles who receive the Holy Spirit should not have the burdens laid on them "which neither our fathers nor we were able to bear" (Acts 15:10, within verses 7-11). Peter sounds remarkably Pauline at this juncture: Paul uses a similar line of argument *against* Peter in Galatians 2:14-21, and Peter, according to Acts 15:11, sums up by averring that both Jews and Gentiles are to be saved "through the grace of the Lord Jesus" (cf. Eph 2:5). Whatever the precise relationship between Acts 15 and Galatians 2 (*see DPL*, Galatians; Jerusalem), it is apparent that the Lukan portrayal of Peter has been framed in the interests of an accommodation with a Pauline perspective. James in Acts agrees that Gentiles who turn to God are not be encumbered (Acts 15:19), and yet he insists they be instructed by letter to abstain "from the pollutions of idols and from fornication and from what is strangled and from blood" (Acts 15:20).

The grounds given for the Jacobean policy are that the law* of Moses is commonly acknowledged (Acts 15:21); the implication is that to disregard such elemental considerations of purity as James specifies would be to dishonor Moses.* Judas Barsabbas and Silas are then dispatched with Paul and Barnabas to deliver the letter in Antioch along with their personal testimony (Acts 15:22-29), and they are said particularly to continue their instruction as prophets (Acts 15:32, 33). They refer to the regulations of purity as necessities (Acts 15:28), and no amount of Lukan gloss can conceal that what they insist upon is a serious reversal of Paul's position (see 1 Cor 8). The dispatch of Judas and Silas implicitly undermines the standing of Paul and Barnabas, and James's policy amounts to a constraint upon the behavior of Gentiles who joined the movement. The constraints are sometimes compared to the so-called Noachic commandments of *b. Sanhedrin* 56a-b, which are held to be binding on non-Jews.

While Paul held that there was a new "Israel* of God" (Gal 6:16), defined by having faith in Jesus just as Abraham had faith in God (Gal 3:6-9), Peter conceived of the acceptance of non-Jews in baptism more as a gracious inclusion than the "new creation" of which Paul spoke (Gal 6:15). Once non-Jews had been accepted in baptism, Peter might sometimes have fellowship* with them and sometimes not. As an apostle,* such contact might be necessary; as a faithful Jew, it was not natural. Within Paul's perspective, that was hypocrisy; within Peter's perspective, it was a consistent consequence of proceeding by the revelation of whom and what God accepts (and when) rather than a predetermined policy. James, while accepting the baptism of non-Jews, nonetheless maintained that a policy of their separation from Jews should be followed, unless they observed enough of the commonly acknowledged rules of purity to honor in practice the status of the Torah as the revelation to Moses, warranted in Scripture.

4. The Resolution of Purity and Virtue in Hellenistic Christianity.

The logical extension of Paul's conception was that all things are pure to the pure, precisely the formulation of Titus 1:15. But Paul's actual practice turned out to be otherwise. He indeed departs from the policy of James in 1 Corinthians 8, by accepting that food offered to idols* might be eaten, on the grounds that idols represent entirely fictional gods (1 Cor 8:4-6). But he also warns against eating such food if some who believe in such gods are confirmed in their idolatry, "and their conscience, being weak, is defiled" (1 Cor 8:7-13, esp. v. 7). The defilement here is internal and moral rather than pragmatic, but it is nonetheless dangerous; Paul declares that he would prefer not eat meat at all rather than cause a brother to sin (1 Cor 8:13; see the restatement of the principle in Rom 14:13-23). By means of his own characteristic argument, Paul approximates to what the rabbis would come to teach concerning the danger of idolatrous feasts (see *b. 'Abod. Zar.* 8a, instruction in the name of R. Ishmael). Paul in this aspect reflects a more general tendency in Hellenistic* Christianity. In his letters and in letters attributed to him there is an express connection between named vices (which are catalogued) and "impurity" (Rom 1:24; Gal 5:19; Eph 4:19;

5:3; Col 3:5). Early Christianity saw a shift in the understanding of the medium of impurity: no longer foods, but moral intentions, conveyed the danger of defilement. And those intentions are as specifically identified in the NT as impure foods are discussed in rabbinic literature, because the danger in both cases was understood to be an impurity which made a real and dangerous separation from God.

The cataloguing of sins and their classification with impurity is scarcely a Christian invention. It is represented, for example, in Wisdom 14:22-31. But the genre is mastered to brilliant effect in Romans 1:24-32; Galatians 5:19-21; Ephesians 5:3-5; Colossians 3:5-6, and is taken up in the period after the NT (see *Did.* 5; *Herm. Man.* 8). What is striking in each case is not only the equation of impurity and sin, but a clear indication that impurity as such remains a fundamental category: sexual* contact, a concern from at least the time of Leviticus 18, survives the declining significance of alimentary purity, even within Paul's thought. There is no question, therefore, of purity simply being abstracted into the realm of intention. Rather, intentionality of practice as well as observation of the integrity of one's body are together held to define an ambit of purity. On such an understanding, one's body was indeed a temple of the Holy Spirit (see 1 Cor 6:18-20; see 1 Cor 3:16-17), and a rigorous attitude toward marriage is completely coherent with the emphasis that a new purity is required by God for the inheritance of his kingdom* (see Mt 5:27-28, 31-32; 19:3-12; Mk 10:2-12; Lk 16:18; 1 Cor 7:10-16).

The success of the gospel of Jesus within the Hellenistic environment of primitive Christianity was in no small measure a function of its ability to frame a rational, practical but stringent system of purity. The marketplace is declared pure in itself, provided it does not encourage the defilement of idolatry, and the requirements of James are largely forgotten. But moral, and especially sexual, requirements make it clear that purity has not been abandoned as a regulatory system, despite the efforts of Paul in regard to alimentary purity.

The success of the resolution of virtue* and purity within primitive Christianity was sealed by the attribution to Jesus of the identification between the two. The attribution appears in Mark (and the Matthean parallel) just after Jesus' own teaching about what truly defiles (Mk 7:15). First by means of comment in response to a question (Mk 7:17-19) and then by means of comment and catalogue (Mk 7:20-23) the rhetoric attributes the shift in the medium of impurity to Jesus himself. The rhetoric is the product of an interpretative community, a circle sufficiently influential to cast what it had been taught concerning Jesus' principle into the terms of reference of the Hellenistic mission. The circle is concerned with issues of fellowship at meals but is unwilling to dismiss purity as a divine category, as Pauline rhetoric could do (Rom 14:14). The circle responsible for Mark 7:20-23, on the other hand, insists upon the danger of impurity but sees the contagion in moral terms. Such an attitude is closer to that of the lists of vices which Paul repeats than it is to the innovative aspects of his argument and rhetoric.

The identification of the authority behind the circle is obviously a matter of inference, but—among the possibilities given by Paul in Galatians 2—the most plausible suggestion is that it represents the apostolate of Barnabas. Barnabas is described by Paul as being less engaged with purity than either James or Peter but also as having been taken up in their "hypocrisy" (Gal 2:11-13). In effect, once Jesus enters the house in Mark 7:17, a new social setting is addressed, and the point of his teaching, as commented upon and expanded by means of a catalogue, is that vices rather than foods are sources of impurity. The categories of the pure and the impure are maintained, but they are worked out on the basis of moral rather than alimentary materials.

The dramatic shift in rhetoric and meaning within the Barnaban circle could not have succeeded by means of the comment (Mk 7:17-19) and the catalogue (Mk 7:20-23) alone. After all, they were by way of appendix to the principal matter of the emerging text, which still concerned corban (Mk 7:6-13) and the direction of impurity (Mk 7:14-15). In order to recast the whole of the tradition as an assertion of a new medium of impurity, defined on Jesus' authority, a rhetorical method needed to be found which would point all of the arguments in the same direction which the latest developments indicated.

The solution was a synthetic device of enormous power: narrative context. The arguments generally—with their varying rhetorics and different topics—are presented in the context of a single dispute. Pharisees and scribes observe that Jesus' disciples do not wash their hands before meals; they object, and Jesus goes on to reply by means of the material already described (Mk 7:1-2, 5). The new context, of course, has nothing precisely to do with the arguments which are then attributed to Jesus. Corban, the direction of defilement and the comparative danger of foods and vices are all interesting matters more or less related by a common interest in what true purity is, but none of those arguments actually answers the Pharisaic/scribal objection to not washing prior to a meal. The narrative context proceeds on the assurance that the readership already understands that all Pharisaic/scribal practices are to be grouped together and accorded the same sort of weight one would attribute to washing one's hands.

The power of the rhetoric is demonstrated by the fact that Jesus never actually answers the question which is posed to him. The response needs to be filled in by the hearer or reader who has been catechized to the point that it seems evident that there is a new, inner purity of moral intention which supersedes the practices of Judaism. The Gospels, as well as the more obviously Hellenistic documents of the NT, attest the resolution of virtue and purity which was a vital part of the genius of Christianity.

See also FOOD, FOOD LAWS, TABLE FELLOWSHIP; GENTILES, GENTILE MISSION; HOLY, HOLINESS; SACRIFICE, OFFERINGS, GIFTS; SEXUALITY, SEXUAL ETHICS; SIN, WICKEDNESS; TEMPLE; VIRTUES AND VICES.

BIBLIOGRAPHY. R. P. Booth, *Jesus and the Laws of Purity: Tradition and Legal History in Mark 7* (JSNTS 13; Sheffield: JSOT, 1986); A. Büchler, *Studies in Sin and Atonement* (New York: Ktav, 1967); R. Caillois, *L'homme et le sacré: Edition augmentée de trois appendices sur le sexe, le jeu, la guerre dans leurs rapport avec le sacré* (Paris: Gallimard, 1989); D. R. Catchpole, "Paul, James and the Apostolic Decree," *NTS* 23 (1977) 428-44; B. Chilton, *A Feast of Meanings: Eucharistic Theologies from Jesus through Johannine Circles* (NovT-Sup 72; Leiden: E. J. Brill, 1994); M. Detienne and J.-P. Vernant (with J.-L. Durand, S. Georgoudi, F. Hartog and J. Svenbro), *The Cuisine of Sacrifice Among the Greeks* (Chicago: University of Chicago Press, 1989); M. Hengel, "Jakobus der Herrenbruder—der erste 'Papst'?" in *Glaube und Eschatologie: Festschrift für Werner Georg Kümmel zum 80. Geburstag*, ed. E. Grässer and O. Merk (Tübingen: J. C. B. Mohr, 1985) 71-104; J. D. Levenson, *Theology of the Program of Restoration of Ezekiel 40-48* (HSMS 10; Atlanta: Scholars Press, 1986); J. Milgrom, *Studies in Cultic Theology and Terminology* (SJLA 36; Leiden: E. J. Brill, 1983); E. P. Sanders, *Jewish Law from Jesus to the Mishnah: Five Studies* (Philadelphia: Trinity Press International, 1990); J. Z. Smith, *To Take Place: Toward Theory in Ritual* (Chicago: University of Chicago Press, 1987); D. P. Wright, *The Disposal of Impurity. Elimination Rites in the Bible and in Hittite and Mesopotamian Literature* (SBLDS 101; Atlanta: Scholars Press, 1987). B. Chilton

Q

QUMRAN

The chance discovery in 1947 of the ancient manuscripts known as the Dead Sea Scrolls in many ways marked a new chapter in biblical study. Found at Wadi Qumran on the northwest shore of the Dead Sea, the writings were secreted in caves (most likely by a monastic Jewish sect, possibly the Essenes) about the time of Christ. From the eleven caves at Qumran came a total of approximately eight hundred documents, many of them fragmentary. Written in Hebrew, Greek and Aramaic, the material consists of a variety of literary genres: biblical texts (all books of the OT in whole or more frequently in fragments, except for Esther), commentaries (targums), hymns,* benedictions, psalms, prayers, a monastic rule (the Manual of Discipline, or Community Rule), a War Scroll (predicting a final, apocalyptic battle between the forces of good and evil) and a Temple Scroll. The last, describing an idealized Jewish temple* and its people, is thought by some to predate the Jewish sect that produced the rest of the documents (for a survey of the entire range of material, *see DJG*, Dead Sea Scrolls).

A number of the NT writings, particularly John, Acts, Revelation and Hebrews, not to mention the historical figure of John the Baptist, have been seen in a new perspective owing either to possible influence from Qumran or to light that the Qumran documents may shed upon ideas and practices reflected in the NT writings. Scholars, however, have not been able to achieve a consensus on how much influence or overlap should be seen, and the discussion will continue in the foreseeable future.

1. Qumran, Acts and Revelation
2. Qumran and Hebrews
3. Conclusion

1. Qumran, Acts and Revelation.

1.1. Qumran and Acts. Some scholars have detected similarities between the communal life of the Qumran sect and the life of the early church as it is reflected in the Acts* of the Apostles. This is seen primarily in two ways. (1) The emphasis on the Holy Spirit* and baptism* at Qumran (e.g., 1QS 4:6, 21) is said to be reminiscent of Acts 2:38: "Repent, and let each of you be baptized in the name of Jesus Christ for remission of your sins, and you will receive the gift of the Holy Spirit" (cf. Johnson, 10-11). For the Qumran sect the water rituals were frequent and continuous, whereas for the early church baptism was a once-and-for-all, unrepeatable act of identification with Christ.* (2) Some scholars have seen a parallel between the communal sharing of Acts 2:44-45 and 1QS 1.12 and 1QS 6.16-20 (see Capper). The attempt to trace a direct relationship has been generally less appealing than the explanation that the sharing of the early church grew out of Jesus' instructions to his followers as recorded in such texts as Matthew 5—7, 18 and 25.

1.2. Qumran and Revelation. Occasionally parallels are drawn between the apocalyptic* dualism of the Qumran War Scroll and that of Revelation (*see* Revelation, Book of). The Qumran community looked forward to the final, great battle between the sanctified people of God ("the Sons of Light"), led by the warrior angels* Melchizedek and Michael, and the forces of evil ("the Sons of Darkness"). Revelation similarly sees history reaching its climax in the final battle of Armageddon (Rev 16:16). There is, however, a major difference. "In the Qumran War Scroll, the final battle takes place here on earth; in Revelation, the final battle takes place in Heaven, and only the backlash of that battle is felt on earth" (LaSor, 198-99). In all probability the similarities between the two literatures result form a common indebtedness to OT apocalyptic such as is found in Isaiah 24—27, Daniel 7—9 and Zechariah 12—14.

2. Qumran and Hebrews.

In 1958 Y. Yadin advanced the thesis that before their conversion to Christianity, the recipients of Hebrews* had been members of the Qumran sect (the Essenes) who came into the church "carrying with them some of their previous beliefs" (Yadin, 38). According to Yadin, the primary similarities between the scrolls and Hebrews are as follows. The sect had an overly exalted view of angels, which the author of Hebrews combats in Hebrews 1—2. Further, the sect expected not one but two messiahs, a priestly* and a lay figure, which is countered by the argument in Hebrews that Jesus combines both offices in one person. Hebrews 1:1, which places the revelation* brought by Jesus over against that of the prophets,* "is obviously directed against the belief . . . that in the eschatological era a prophet should appear—a prophet who is not to be identified with the Messiah himself" (Yadin, 53). For Yadin this figure is the Mosaic prophet of Deuteronomy 18:15-16, which accounts for much of the concentration on Moses* in Hebrews. The frequency of quotations in Hebrews from the Pentateuch is a direct answer to the sect's focus on its wilderness calling.

Thirteen years later H. Kosmala went beyond Yadin by claiming that the readers of Hebrews were members of the Qumran sect who had not yet converted to Christianity but were in process of being instructed as part of a Christian mission to the Essenes (Kosmala, x). Central to the theologies of both groups, claimed Kosmala, was the prophecy of Malachi, in which Elijah is identified with the high priest of the last days (Kosmala, 76-81). In order to mount his thesis, Kosmala had to eliminate such passages as Hebrews 5:11-14 and Hebrews 6:6 as later interpolations (Kosmala, 17-30).

The Qumran hypothesis for Hebrews still exercises some popularity in NT studies, but it has been experiencing a gradual drop-off of interest. This was largely the result of the simultaneous judgments of F. F. Bruce (1963) and J. Coppens, both of whom felt the similarities to be largely illusory. Interest was regenerated, however, with the publication in 1965 of the Melchizedek fragment from Qumran cave 11 and the possible light it might shed on Hebrews 5—7.

The main points in the debate may be summarized briefly under the following headings (for a much fuller treatment, see Hurst, 45-65).

2.1. The Role of Angels. Yadin urged strongly that at Qumran angels are regarded as God's sons* and dominate eschatology.* Michael, the Prince of Light, assists the saints and has absolute authority.* Thus, Yadin claimed, the readers of Hebrews were angel worshipers. This, however, is highly unlikely. The author's concern with angels in Hebrews 1—2 is not part of a polemic against angel worship but is an attempt to prove the superiority of the new covenant* to the old. He connects angels with the Torah (Heb 2:2), and this serves to link the angels of Psalm 8 (cf. Heb 2:5-18) with those of Hebrews 1. If Jesus mediates a superior covenant, he must be superior to all those covenant mediators with whom the readers are familiar (angels, Heb 1—2; Moses, Heb 3—4; Aaron, Heb 5—7). It is therefore highly unlikely that Qumran can be seen as the background of one of the central themes of Hebrews 1—2.

2.2. Messianic Conceptions. For Yadin the epistle depicts Christ as priest because "this subject is forced upon the author . . . his readers' conceptions regarding the Aaronic priestly Messiah make it impossible for them to accept Jesus' unique authority" (Yadin, 44). The readers of Hebrews are said to have held the notion, reflected in CD and 1QS, that a messiah of the levitical line was expected who would dominate the Davidic Messiah and who would reinstate the levitical sacrifices* in the new age. Thus it was difficult for the readers to accept the supremacy of Jesus, who was not of the levitical line.

There are two points, however, at which this theory falls to the ground. First, there never was a heterodox, two-messiah doctrine at Qumran. The messianism of Qumran was identical to that of the OT, which spoke of two "anointed ones" (not "Messiahs" with a capital "M")—an anointed king and an anointed priest—who would accompany him (Zech 4:14; cf. Hurst, 47-48). Second, the presentation of the high priesthood of Jesus in Hebrews is sharply at variance with such a preconception. The lack of an emphasis on Jesus' Davidic lineage would be odd if the author were striving to establish a union of the so-called levitical and Davidic messiahs into one person. Psalm 110, rather than any alien notions of priesthood, forms the impetus for his speculations.

2.3. The Prophet Like Moses. Both Hebrews

and the Qumran documents emphasize the role of prophets. For Yadin Jesus' superiority to "the prophets" in Hebrews 1:1-2 corrects a Qumranian belief, reflected in 1QS 9:11 ("until the coming of a prophet and the messiahs from Aaron and Israel") and 4QTestimonia (the quotation of Deut 18:18-19) of a prophet like Moses who would accompany the messiahs and found the new covenant. But this, again, is unlikely. Hebrews has comparatively little to say about the prophets as a group or any individual prophet in particular, and there is virtually no evidence that the Mosaic "prophet" of 1QS 9:11 is in view in Hebrews. There Moses is not Moses redivivus but rather falls into the category of traditional biblical typology. Deuteronomy 18, furthermore, is never used in Hebrews, nor is Moses anything other than a figure of the past who points forward to the "better things" of Christ.

2.4. Melchizedek. When he first launched his case Yadin could not claim that the author's arguments regarding Melchizedek* had any parallel at Qumran because until then not a trace of him had been found. Then A. S. van der Woude published his version of the fragmentary text from cave 11, 11QMelch, in which Melchizedek is connected to the eschatological deliverance of the righteous* and the annihilation of the wicked. Claims for Hebrews began appearing immediately, notwithstanding the fact that the problems of interpreting the Melchizedek of Hebrews against 11QMelch are multiple. The text of 11QMelch is so mutilated as to make certainty about its meaning impossible. Further, scholars cannot agree whether in 11QMelch Melchizedek is a supernatural figure or a contemporary human figure of great prominence. In Hebrews the author interprets him as the historical figure of Genesis 14 (*see* Priest, High Priest). The ideas connected with Melchizedek in 11QMelch have nothing to do with Psalm 110 or Genesis 14, the two texts crucial to Hebrews 7; the picture of him at Qumran, while employing OT language, has little to do with the OT. The superiority of Melchizedek over Aaron in Hebrews is never the result of any angelic status of the former; it is seen in the fact that Abraham* paid him tithes and that he blessed Abraham. What is remarkable about the two treatments of the same figure is that they have nothing in common.

2.5. The Use of the Old Testament. Since the Qumran sect and the author of Hebrews both use the OT extensively (*see* Old Testament in Hebrews), this has frequently been seen as an area of agreement. S. J. Kistemaker and F. C. Fensham, for instance, claim to find an affinity in text form and interpretation. According to Kistemaker, "nearly every chapter of Hebrews reveals the peculiar feature of the *midrash pesher*" (Kistemaker, 74). Here comparison is often made with the Habakkuk Commentary (1QpHab) and 4QFlorilegium (4QFlor), which use various devices—textual variations, conflations, plays upon words and an application of Scripture to the present. It is unlikely once again, however, that any overlap between the two literatures can be traced. The use of Habakkuk 2:3-4 in 1QpHab and Hebrews 10:37-38, for instance, is totally different (see Hurst, 64-65), while G. B. Caird has shown convincingly that the *midrash pesher* label does not fit Hebrews: its author is an exegete who asks after the original meaning of his texts in a way similar to the method of modern interpreters. Thus in a comparison of the use of the OT in Hebrews and Qumran, nothing has been found that requires or even suggests a Qumran background for the former.

3. Conclusion.
Points of contact have been traced between the Qumran writings and Acts, Revelation and Hebrews, with the bulk of the comparisons centering on Hebrews. The enthusiasm that was initially attached to these alleged parallels has dissipated somewhat with time. In many cases the overlaps are apparent rather than real, and in the case of Hebrews a certain distortion of its argument, not to mention that of the evidence of Qumran, has been required to sustain the argument. Most of the points of comparison are probably due to a common background—the influence of the OT. It is improbable that any situation other than that of the pastoral problem of the readers, discouragement in the face of persecution,* called forth the response of the epistle.

See also JOSEPHUS; JUDAISM, POST-A.D. 70; PHILO.

BIBLIOGRAPHY. H. W. Attridge, *The Epistle to the Hebrews* (Herm; Philadelphia: Fortress, 1989); M. Black, *The Scrolls and Christian Origins* (Chico, CA: Scholars Press, 1961); H. Braun, *Qumran und das Neue Testament* (2 vols; Tübingen: J. C. B. Mohr, 1966); R. E. Brown, "The

Messianism of Qumran," *CBQ* 19 (1957) 53-82; F. F. Bruce, *The Epistle to the Hebrews* (Grand Rapids: Eerdmans, 1954); idem, " 'To the Hebrews' or 'To the Essenes,' " *NTS* 9 (1963) 217-32; G. B. Caird, "The Exegetical Method of the Epistle to the Hebrews" *CJT* 5 (1959) 44-61; B. Capper, "The Palestinian Cultural Context of Earliest Christian Community of Goods" in *The Book of Acts in Its Palestinian Setting,* ed. R. J. Bauckham (BAFCS 4; Grand Rapids: Eerdmans, 1995) 323-56; J. Carmignac, "Le document de Qumran sur Melkisékeq," *RevQ* 7 (1970) 348-78; J. J. Collins, "Dead Sea Scrolls," *ABD* 2:85-101; J. Coppens, Les Affinités qumrániennes de l'épître aux Hébreux," *Nouvelle revue théologique* 84 (1962) 128-41, 257-82; F. M. Cross, *The Ancient Library of Qumran and Modern Biblical Studies* (rev. ed.; New York: Doubleday, 1961); J. Daniélou, *The Dead Sea Scrolls and Primitive Christianity* (New York: Mentor Omega, 1962); P. Ellingworth, *The Epistle to the Hebrews* (NIGTC; Grand Rapids: Eerdmans, 1993); F. C. Fensham, "Hebrews and Qumran," *Neot* 5 (1971) 9-21; J. A. Fitzmyer, *Essays on the Semitic Background of the New Testament* (London: Chapman, 1971); E. F. Harrison, *Interpreting Acts* (Grand Rapids: Zondervan, 1986); D. M. Hay, *Glory at the Right Hand: Psalm 110 in Early Christianity* (Nashville: Abingdon, 1973); F. L. Horton, *The Melchizedek Tradition* (SNTSMS 30; Cambridge: Cambridge University Press, 1976); L. D. Hurst, *The Epistle to the Hebrews: Its Background of Thought* (SNTSMS 65; Cambridge: Cambridge University Press, 1990); S. J. Kistemaker, *The Psalm Citations in the Epistle to the Hebrews* (Amsterdam: van Soest, 1961); H. Kosmala, *Hebräer-Essener-Christen* (Leiden: E. J. Brill, 1971); W. L. Lane, *Hebrews* (2 vols.; WBC; Dallas: Word, 1991); W. S. LaSor, *The Dead Sea Scrolls and the New Testament* (Grand Rapids: Eerdmans, 1972); R. N. Longenecker, *Biblical Exegesis in the Apostolic Period* (Grand Rapids: Eerdmans, 1975); idem, *The Christology of Early Jewish Christianity* (London: SCM, 1970); S. Johnson, "The Dead Sea Manual of Discipline and the Jerusalem Church of Acts" in *The Scrolls and the New Testament,* ed. K. Stendahl (Westport, CT: Greenwood, 1957) 129-42; J. C. Vanderkam, *The Dead Sea Scrolls Today* (Grand Rapids: Eerdmans, 1994); A. S. van der Woude, "Melchizedek als himmlische Erlösergestalt in den neugefundenen eschatologischen Midraschim aus Qumran Höhle XI," *Oudtestamentliche Studiën* 14 (1965) 354-73; Y. Yadin, "The Dead Sea Scrolls and the Epistle to the Hebrews," *ScrHier* 4 (1958) 36-53.

L. D. Hurst

QUOTATIONS OF OLD TESTAMENT.
See OLD TESTAMENT.

R

RABBINICAL SCHOOLS. *See* JUDAISM, POST-A.D. 70.

RAHAB. *See* ANCESTORS.

READER-RESPONSE CRITICISM. *See* HERMENEUTICS.

REDEMPTION

The word group and motif of redemption are employed outside the Gospels and the Pauline corpus (*see DJG*, Ransom Saying; *DPL*, Redemption) to explain the significance of the work of Jesus in delivering believers from captivity to sin* and its consequences.

1. Background
2. The Gospels and Paul
3. The Rest of the New Testament
4. The Common Teaching
5. The Doctrine in the Early Second Century

1. Background.

A typical act of redemption in the OT is the buying back of somebody or something that has passed into another person's possession. If a member of a family fell into debt and was enslaved by his creditor, it was the duty of another member to secure his release if possible by making the appropriate payment. If family property fell into somebody else's hands, a member of the family would attempt to buy it back.

In the same way God's action in delivering the people of Israel from their bondage in Egypt was spoken of as an act of redemption in which he acted as their next of kin and did what was needed to set them free (Ex 6:6-8; *see* Freedom). Later the return of the people from exile in Babylon to live again in their own land was identified as an act of God and understood, by analogy with the deliverance from Egypt, as an act of redemption (Is 48:20). The language of payment was used metaphorically of God's action (Is 43:3-7; but see Is 52:3), but there is no thought of God paying anybody to set his people free. Yet the thought is not confined to that of deliverance. Rather, when he acts in sovereign power to liberate them, it costs him something to do so.

Alongside this concept of national redemption there stands the belief in God as the deliverer of sinful individuals who trust in him from dire situations, including the threat of death (Job 33; Ps 49).

In NT times the idea of redemption was commonplace in the Greco-Roman world with reference to the freeing of slaves.* Slaves were not necessarily bound for their lifetime; various possibilities of manumission existed, normally by a monetary payment to the owner. For example, slaves could pay money out of the small wages that they received into a temple.* When sufficient funds had accumulated, the money could be used to purchase freedom. However, since slaves were not legal persons in their own right, able to enter into and make legal contracts, a fictitious arrangement was created whereby the god worshiped at the temple bought a slave from an earthly master; the slave was freed in respect of earthly masters but was technically the property of the god who had bought him or her. A. Deissmann claimed that this practice forms the background to the metaphor of redemption used in the NT. It would be a vivid way of bringing home to freed slaves in the congregation the nature of what happened to them when they became Christians.

However, there are weighty arguments against this explanation. First, E. Pax has noted that in the secular world the chief actor is the slave's master, and the god is scarcely ever mentioned. But in the Christian use of the picture the old master of believers is not mentioned and all the stress lies on Christ as the new master.

Second, the slave was not wholly free from the old master; the slave still had an obligation to serve the master but as a freed person. Third, the aim of Greeks was to belong to themselves. Fourth, there were no personal relationships between the slave and the master or the god. And fifth, the vocabulary used in the secular and Christian usages is different. These points are sufficient to show that Paul's usage is not derived from Greek sacral manumission, although it shows parallels to it.

Pax himself looks to Jewish slavery for the background. In the OT, Hebrew slaves, who were normally enslaved because of debt, served for a maximum of seven years and then had to be set free; they could, however, be redeemed for payment at an earlier point. (They might also be unwilling to leave their master at the end of the seven-year period and could become permanent slaves of the master whom they loved.) After the OT period we find examples of slaves being adopted by masters as their children.* Further, the stress is on the person who frees the slave rather than on the master who lets him go. This practice of redeeming slaves was the basis for the OT picture of divine redemption in which the Israelites were set free from Pharaoh to become the servants (see Servant) of Yahweh (e.g., Deut 7:8).

2. The Gospels and Paul.

In the NT redemption is a general term for the end-time act and resulting state of deliverance promised by God and awaited by his people, who were conscious that they were still oppressed politically by their enemies and morally by their own sinfulness (Lk 2:38; cf. 1:68). The latter emphasis is in mind when Jesus states that as Son of Man he gives himself as a ransom for many (Mk 10:45; par. Mt 20:28). In the Pauline writings two related ideas appear. The first is that of redemption in the strict sense: people are released from some kind of bondage or slavery. They are delivered from being under the law* and the curse that it inflicts on those who are under it but do not keep its requirements (Gal 3:13; 4:5). In a second type of imagery slaves are bought from their previous master in order to belong to a new master whom they are under obligation to serve (1 Cor 6:20; 7:23). The church is a people purchased by God with the blood of "his own" (Acts 20:28), presumably Christ.

3. The Rest of the New Testament.

3.1. The Book of Revelation. In Revelation 1:5 (see Revelation, Book of) Jesus is described as the one who loved us and loosed us from our sins by his blood, making us into a kingdom* and priests.* The language is of deliverance from sin and its effects, and the motivation for the action lies in the love* of Christ. Behind the language lies Psalm 130:8, where God redeems Israel from all its iniquities. When the motif is repeated (Rev 5:9), the thought of deliverance from sin is replaced by that of believers having been purchased for God by the blood of the Lamb.* Similarly, believers present in heaven* are those who were bought from the earth as first fruits for God and the Lamb (Rev 14:3-5). The means of redemption from sin or purchase for God is the blood of Jesus, i.e., his sacrificial death (see Death of Christ). Thus the concept is understood not in terms of the payment of a monetary price but of the offering of a sacrifice.* When believers are said to have been bought, the question is, Out of what? or From whom? The question is not answered directly, but the implication is that they are set free from their sins or alien powers by the sacrifice of Jesus. The recurrence of the verb in 1 Corinthians 6:20; 7:23; 2 Peter 2:1 shows that traditional language is being used.

3.2. 1 Peter. 1 Peter 1:18 (see 1 Peter) describes believers as those who have been ransomed from their pointless way of life* with the precious blood of Christ, who is likened to a spotless and unblemished lamb. Here the deliverance is not so much from a master as from a way of life that was godless, sinful and leading nowhere. The concept of sacrifice is linked with that of redemption. The comparison with a monetary payment suggests that a parallel is being drawn with the state of slavery, from which people could be released by a ransom. But in the case of sinners a sacrifice is involved. Their way of life stands under condemnation from God, and only by a sacrifice can the condemnation be cancelled. The cancellation of the condemnation carries with it release from the captivity to the futile way of life.

3.3. Hebrews. In Hebrews 11:35 (see Hebrews) the word is used of people, doubtless the Maccabean martyrs* and others, who refused to accept deliverance for themselves when they were being tortured to death, in order that they might attain a better resurrection. This usage is nonreligious and refers to release from torture and imprisonment at the price of apostasy.*

In Hebrews 9:11-14 Christ obtained eternal redemption by entering into the heavenly tabernacle* with his own blood. The result is explained in that he offered himself as a sacrifice to God and so was able to purify the consciences* of believers from dead works to serve the living God. In Hebrews 9:15 it becomes clear that Jesus died in order to secure redemption from the transgressions committed in the time of the first covenant.* Thus once again redemption is linked to the remission of sins and is tantamount to forgiveness.*

4. The Common Teaching.
A motif in NT theology is like an object that is being tossed around just beneath the surface of a turbulent sea; whenever it emerges from the waves it is seen from a slightly different angle, and therefore different parts of it are observed, but it is one and the same object that keeps appearing. By combining the observations it is possible to form a fair idea of the total shape and appearance. From the various references to redemption we can see that there was a general understanding of the motif that surfaces and shows different facets. The controlling background lies in the OT. The basic idea of deliverance at great cost persists. The agent is always Christ, the motive is the love of God for humankind, and the thought leads to praise. Human beings are enslaved by a futile, sinful way of life that leads ultimately to death, as God's judgment* upon sin. The deliverance is from the rather than from a specific captor, and it is effected by the death of Jesus understood as a sacrifice. The sacrifice, which is both provided by God and offered to him, is the means of cancelling the effect of sin. At the same time it acts as a price that is paid to set people free from their , and the result is that they are bought by God to be his people to serve him. The language of purchase is retained, not because a purchaser is in view but in order to express the tremendous cost to God without which deliverance would not have been possible.

5. The Doctrine in the Early Second Century.
In the immediate post-NT writings there are some hints of salvation* by human effort: "If you have anything passing through your hands, you shall give a ransom for your sins" (*Did.* 4.6; *see*

Didache). The way of light* includes not only "saving souls by your word" but also "you shall work with your hands for a ransom for your sins" (*Barn.* 19.10; *see* Epistle of Barnabas). When *2 Clement* 17.4 (*see* Clement of Rome) refers to "the day of his appearing when he shall come and redeem us, each according to his works," it confuses judgment by works (*see* Faith and Works) with redemption by grace.*

Elsewhere the thought is more in line with canonical writings. In *1 Clement* 12.7 the scarlet thread hung out of the window by Rahab "shows beforehand that through the blood of the Lord there shall be redemption for all them that believe and hope on God." *Barnabas* 14.5-8 speaks of the "Lord Jesus who was prepared beforehand for this purpose, that appearing in person he might redeem out of darkness our hearts which had already been paid over to death" (cf. *Barn.* 19.2). The statement is backed up with prophecies* from Isaiah 42:6-7 and Isaiah 49:6-7 in which the Lord,* who sends his servant, is himself "the Lord who ransomed you, even God" (see also Justin Martyr *Dial. Tryph.* 86).

But the brightest star in the collection is the *Epistle to Diognetus*:
When our iniquity had been fully accomplished, and it had been made perfectly manifest that punishment and death were expected as its recompense, and the season came which God had ordained . . . he hated us not, nor rejected us, nor bore us malice, but was long-suffering and patient, and in pity for us took upon himself our sins, and himself parted with his own Son as a ransom for us, the holy for the lawless, the guileless for the evil, the just for the unjust, the incorruptible for the corruptible, the immortal for the moral. For what else but his righteousness would have covered our sins? In whom was it possible for us lawless and ungodly people to have been justified, save only in the Son of God? O the sweet exchange, O the inscrutable creation, O the unexpected benefits; that the iniquity of many should be concealed in One Righteous man, and the righteousness of One should justify many that are iniquitous! (*Diogn.* 9.2-5, Lightfoot/Harmer trans.).

See also SALVATION; SLAVE, SLAVERY.

BIBLIOGRAPHY. F. Büchsel, "λύω κτλ," *TDNT* 4:328-56; W. Haubeck, *Loskauf durch Christus:*

Herkunft, Gestalt und Bedeutung des paulinischen Loskaufmotivs (Giessen/Basel: Brunnen, 1985); D. Hill, *Greek Words and Hebrew Meanings* (Cambridge: Cambridge University Press, 1967) chap. 3; B. Janowski, "Auslösung des verwirkten Lebens. Zur Geschichte und Struktur der biblischen Lösegeldvorstellung," *ZTK* 79 (1982) 25-59; I. H. Marshall, "The Development of the Concept of Redemption in the New Testament" in *Reconciliation and Hope,* ed. R. Banks (Exeter: Paternoster, 1974) 153-69; L. Morris, *The Apostolic Preaching of the Cross* (3d ed.; London: Tyndale, 1965) chap. 1; E. Pax, "Der Loskauf. Zur Geschichte eines neutestamentlichen Begriffes," *Antonianum* 37 (1962) 239-78; J. Schneider and C. Brown, "Redemption, etc.," *NIDNTT* 3:177-223; J. Unterman and G. S. Shogren, "Redemption," *ABD* 5:649-57; B. B. Warfield, *The Person and Work of Christ* (Philadelphia: Presbyterian and Reformed, 1950) 325-48, 429-75.   I. H. Marshall

REIGN OF GOD. *See* KINGDOM OF GOD.

RELATIVES OF JESUS

Various relatives of Jesus are the subject both of historical traditions and of legendary imagination in early Christian literature. Historical traditions attest the important role they played in the leadership of the early Christian movement. Legendary developments focus especially on Jesus' mother.

1. The Known Relatives of Jesus
2. The Brothers and Sisters of Jesus
3. The Relatives as Early Christian Leaders
4. Mary and Joseph

1. The Known Relatives of Jesus.

From the NT and other reliable early sources, especially the second-century writer Hegesippus, who preserves Palestinian Jewish Christian traditions, the following relatives from the generation of Jesus' parents onward are known:

Jesus' mother Mary* and adoptive father Joseph.

Joseph's brother Clopas (Hegesippus, quoted in Eusebius *Hist. Eccl.* 3.11; 3.32.6; 4.22.4). "Mary of Clopas" (Jn 19:25) is probably his wife. He may well be the same person as Cleopas (Lk 24:18). Clopas is a Semitic name and Cleopas is a Greek name; Jews of this period frequently used both a Semitic name and a Greek name that sounded similar.

Elizabeth, the mother of John the Baptist, was a relative of Jesus' mother, Mary, according to Luke 1:36 (the precise relationship is not specified).

Jesus' four brothers: James, Joses (or Joseph; Joses is an abbreviated form), Judas (or Jude, an English variant of the name that is sometimes used for this brother of Jesus) and Simon (Mt 13:55; Mk 6:3).

Jesus' sisters (at least two: Mt 13:56; Mk 6:3). Later sources, perhaps correctly, name them Mary and Salome (*Protev. James* 19.3—20.4; *Gos. Phil.* 59.6-11; Epiphanius *Haer.* 78.8.1; 78.9.6).

Simeon (Simon) son of Clopas (Hegesippus, quoted in Eusebius *Hist. Eccl.* 3.11; 3.32.6; 4.22.4).

Zoker and James, two grandsons of Jesus' brother Jude (Hegesippus, quoted in Eusebius *Hist. Eccl.* 3.19.1-3.20.7; 3.32.5-6; and in Paris MS 1555A; Bodleian MS Barocc. 142).

Abris, Abraham and his son James, three descendants of the family of Jesus. They are named in medieval chronicles, which may preserve early sources, as bishops of Ctesiphon-Seleucia in central Mesopotamia in the second century.

Conon of Magydos, martyred in 250-51, was probably a descendant of the family of Jesus (*Martyrdom of Conon* 4.2).

2. The Brothers and Sisters of Jesus.

Since the terms *brother* and *sister* could be used of relatives other than full blood siblings, the precise relationship of these persons to Jesus has been debated. The issue has been closely connected with the traditional belief in the perpetual virginity of Mary, which can be found already in early second-century Christian literature. The three major views have come to be known by the names of their fourth-century proponents: Helvidius, Epiphanius and Jerome. The Helvidian view, which most modern exegetes hold, is that the brothers and sisters were children of Joseph and Mary, born after Jesus. The Epiphanian view, which is the traditional view in the Eastern Orthodox churches, is that they were children of Joseph by a marriage prior to his marriage to Mary (and therefore Jesus' adoptive siblings). The Hieronymian view, which through Jerome's influence became the traditional Roman Catholic view, is that they were first cousins of Jesus (usually considered children of Clopas). The last view depends largely on identifying Jesus' brothers with other persons of the same names (Mt 10:3; 27:56; Mk 3:18; 15:40, 47; 16:1; Lk 6:15-16; 24:10; Hegesippus, quoted in Eusebius *Hist. Eccl.* 4.22.4) but is rendered improbable by the fact that the brothers of Jesus are invariably called "the brothers of the Lord" in early Christian literature. If they were cousins of Jesus we should expect them to be occasionally so described, as Hegesippus describes Simeon son of Clopas (Eusebius *Hist. Eccl.* 4.22.4).

It is much more difficult to decide between the Helvidian and the Epiphanian views. Nothing in the NT provides decisive evidence either way, while the only works from an early period that are unambiguous about the relationship take the Epiphanian view. These are the *Protevangelium of James,* the *Gospel of Peter* (*see* Peter, Gospel of) and the *Infancy Gospel of Thomas,* probably all from second-century Syria. In the *Protevangelium of James* the perpetual virginity of Mary is also implied, and so a belief that it was inappropriate for the mother of Jesus also to bear other children may have produced the Epiphanian view of Jesus' brothers and sisters. Alternatively it may be that these prominent early Christian leaders were known from tradition to be children of Joseph but not of Mary and that belief in the perpetual virginity of Mary was possible only for this reason.

The apostle Thomas, known in east Syrian Christian tradition as Judas Thomas, is considered in some east Syrian Christian literature to be the twin brother of Jesus (*Acts of Thomas* 11; 31; 39; *Book of Thomas* 138.4, 7, 19), presumably identified with Jesus' brother Jude. The tradition stems from the fact that the name *Thomas* means "twin" (Jn 21:2) and probably at first indicated a relationship of spiritual rather than physical twinship with Jesus.

3. The Relatives as Early Christian Leaders.

There is good evidence that a considerable number of members of the family of Jesus, from the earliest period of the church down to the early second century, were prominent leaders in the Jewish Christian movement in Palestine and perhaps also were missionaries outside Palestine (*see* Jewish Christianity). Jesus' brother James,* whose importance as a Christian leader of the first generation is equaled only by that of Peter and Paul, quickly became prominent in the leadership of the Jerusalem* church* and

then its unique head until his martyrdom in 62. Since the Jerusalem church was the mother church of all the churches and by many early Christians accorded a central authority* over the whole Christian movement, James played a key role throughout the Christian movement. In the letter of James he writes from this position of central authority in Jerusalem to Jewish Christians throughout the Diaspora.* Many references to him (e.g., *Gos. Thom.* 12) and works associated with him in early Christian literature outside the NT also attest the remarkable impact he made.

After James's death (whether immediately or after 70 is unclear) his cousin Simeon son of Clopas succeeded him as leader of the Jerusalem church. Simeon occupied this position for at least forty years, until he was put to death by the Roman authorities on a charge of political subversion, since he belonged to a Davidic family (either between 99 and 103 or between 108 and 117; Hegesippus, quoted in Eusebius *Hist. Eccl.* 3.11; 3.32.6; 4.22.4). It is possible but not certain that the third leader of the Jerusalem church, named in the Jerusalem bishops' lists as either Justus or Judas, was also a relative of Jesus.

While James occupied the position of central authority in Jerusalem, the other three brothers of Jesus and perhaps also his sisters were traveling missionaries. Paul's reference to them in this role (1 Cor 9:5) is revealing, since it shows that they, along with Peter, were the obvious examples for Paul to cite, even when writing to Corinth, of people well known as traveling missionaries, whose right to the support due to apostles* was unquestionable. The letter of Jude* can be understood in relation to the implication of 1 Corinthians 9:5 that Jude the brother of Jesus was a very well-known Christian leader.

Paul's reference correlates with the later testimony of Julius Africanus, who lived at Emmaus in the early third century and derived his information from a Palestinian Jewish Christian source. He says that the relatives of Jesus, who were known as the *desposynoi,* "from the Jewish villages of Nazareth and Kokhaba traveled around the rest of the land" (quoted in Eusebius *Hist. Eccl.* 1.7.14). The term *desposynoi,* meaning "those who belong to the Master [or Sovereign: *despotēs*]," is not known from any other source and must be the term by which members of the family of Jesus were known in those Palestinian Jewish Christian circles in which they were revered leaders. It demonstrates that not only "the brothers of the Lord" but also a wider circle of relatives (including, for example, Clopas and his wife, Mary) played a prominent leadership role. Kokhaba is a village close to Nazareth. Evidently the traditional Galilean homes of Jesus' relatives remained the base from which they traveled and exercised leadership elsewhere in Jewish Palestine.

Among those who were prominent in the leadership of the Christian movement at the end of the first century were the two grandsons of Jude. This at least must be a reliable inference from the somewhat legendary account that Hegesippus gives about them. He says that, like Simeon son of Clopas, they came under suspicion, since they were descendants of David, and were brought before the emperor Domitian himself. As evidence that they were not politically dangerous, they pointed out that they were merely hard-working peasant farmers, farming only 39 plethra of land (quoted in Eusebius *Hist. Eccl.* 3.19.1—3.20.7; 3.32.5-6). The precise figure suggests an accurate knowledge of the size of the family's small holding in Nazareth, which had passed down to Zoker and James and would have been well known to Palestinian Jewish Christians.

4. Mary and Joseph.

From the second century onward Christian literary and legendary imagination gave much attention to Jesus' family background and especially to his mother, Mary. From the early second century onward, not only Joseph but also Mary was considered a descendant of David (Ign. *Eph.* 18.2; Ign. *Trall.* 9.1; Ign. *Smyrn.* 1.1; *Asc. Isa.* 11.2; Justin *Dial. Tryph.* 45.4; 100.3; *Protev. Jas.* 10.1). The mid-second-century *Protevangelium of James* tells of the birth of Mary to her parents Joachim and Anna, her childhood spent in the temple,* her marriage to Joseph, already an aged widower with children who takes her into his house as her guardian, and the birth of Jesus in a miraculous manner, leaving Mary's virginity unimpaired. The work seems designed especially to celebrate the role of Mary as pure virgin and instrument of God's salvation.* The miraculous birth of Jesus also appears in Ignatius* (Ign. *Eph.* 19.1), the *Ascension of Isaiah* (*Asc. Isa.* 11.2-14) and the *Odes of Solomon* (*Odes Sol.* 19).

Later birth and infancy gospels follow the model provided by the *Protevangelium of James,* but only the Coptic *History of Joseph the Carpenter* (probably fourth or fifth century) focuses on Joseph, featuring especially an account of his death narrated by Jesus. Of Mary's life after the ministry of Jesus the NT gives only a very early glimpse in Acts 1:14. According to later tradition, reflected in the *Assumption* literature (fourth century onward), she stayed in Jerusalem, where this literature describes her death and burial and the assumption of her body to heaven. That she moved to Ephesus with the apostle John (cf. John 19:27) and died there is an alternative later tradition with no support in the earlier Christian traditions associated with Ephesus.

See also JAMES; JEWISH CHRISTIANITY; JUDE; MARY.

BIBLIOGRAPHY. R. J. Bauckham, "The Brothers and Sisters of Jesus: An Epiphanian Response to John P. Meier," *CBQ* 56 (1994) 686-700; idem, *Jude and the Relatives of Jesus in the Early Church* (Edinburgh: T & T Clark, 1990); idem, "Mary of Clopas (John 19:25)" in *Women in the Biblical Tradition,* ed. G. J. Brooke (Lewiston, NY: Edwin Mellen, 1992) 231-55; W. A. Bienert, "The Relatives of Jesus" in *New Testament Apocrypha,* ed., W. Schneemelcher and R. McL. Wilson, (2 vols.; rev. ed.; Louisville: Westminster/John Knox, 1991) 1: 470-91.

R. J. Bauckham

RELIGIONS, GRECO-ROMAN

The traditional religions of Greece and those of Rome underwent significant changes in the Hellenistic and Roman imperial periods. Nevertheless it would be a mistake to minimize the influence of the traditional religion and traditional religious attitudes in NT times. Against the background of the old cults and their practices, certain expressions of the religious spirit attained new prominence or new manifestations in the period of the rise of Christianity: the imperial cult (*see* Emperor), the mysteries, oracles and healing,* magic,* demons, astrology and fate (*see DPL,* Religions).

1. Ancient Greek and Roman Religion
2. Characteristics of Religion in the Hellenistic-Roman Age
3. Civic Cult
4. Imperial Cult
5. Mysteries

6. Other Features

7. Concluding Observation

1. Ancient Greek and Roman Religion.

The difference between the traditional religion of Greece and that of Rome is typified by the fact that Greek religion derived from the myths in the epics of Homer and Roman religion was ascribed to the institutions of the lawgiver Numa. The Greeks dealt with their deities as they would with larger-than-life human beings, whereas Roman religion had a definite legal cast. The Greek deities were anthropomorphic, displaying human passions, portrayed as human beings and taking an interest in and interfering in human affairs but differing from humans by being ageless and deathless, not limited by space and being above ordinary morality (*see* Purity). Sacrifices did not require a professional priesthood and were governed by the bargaining spirit that "I give gifts to the gods and ask that they may do things for me" (see Plato *Euthyphro* 14C-E). Roman deities were less personalized powers *(numina)* that had specific and limited functions. Human relations with the divine were of a more contractual nature so that ceremonies had to be exactly followed, and many religious observances were performed for the people by the professional experts (*pontifices* and *augures*). The domestic cult in both Greece and Rome continued with great consistency. Meals began with a sacrifice of food and ended with a libation.

2. Characteristics of Religion in the Hellenistic-Roman Age.

The modern distinction between religion and the state did not operate. Since idolatrous practices permeated all aspects of life (politics, the military, the theater, athletics, business), Jews and Christians were at a severe social and economic disadvantage.

Syncretism was encouraged by the transplanting of Greek gods to foreign lands and the immigration of foreign gods into the Greek and Roman worlds, resulting in the identification of deities and borrowing of ideas.

Polytheism was tolerant, or nonexclusive; the exclusivism of Judaism* and Christianity was highly offensive to the pagan mentality. There was an inclination toward monotheism, but even where a supreme god was acknowledged, the old gods were kept as subordinate powers.

The increased individualism of the Hellenistic age put more emphasis on chosen relationships at the expense of inherited relationships, but the chosen relationships continued to express the corporate or social side of religion.

Piety (Lat *pietas;* Gk *eusebeia*) had to do primarily with external rites rather than inner attitudes. The pious person was the one who performed the required duties properly.

Morality was not derived primarily from the religious cult. The literary tradition provided examples of what was and was not done, and philosophers assumed the role of teachers of popular morality. Some of the cults began to include moral regulations along with rules for ritual purity.

By the first century, psychological needs included a feeling of helplessness before fate, uncertainty about the hereafter, curiosity about the supernatural and a sense of the instability of human affairs.

3. Civic Cult.

Contrary to what is often said, the traditional civic cults remained vibrant in the early centuries of the Christian era. The decline of local autonomy in Hellenistic and imperial times seemingly led to an awakening of loyalty and pride in the civic cult. As the political importance of the Greek cities diminished, their glory became associated with their temples and gods. The patriotism of the leading classes found expression in commissioning the writing of local histories, the study of old customs and myths, the building of new temples, instituting festivals and setting up commemorative or celebratory inscriptions. The civic cults were nurtured by primary and secondary education, where Homer was the basic textbook. Thus the educational curriculum transmitted the traditional myths and with them the traditional values of Greek culture.

The civic authorities determined the selection of cult personnel, requirements for ritual purity, distribution of items brought for sacrifice, order of march in processions, and other such externals of cultic affairs, and these regulations were often inscribed on stone monuments. The essential requirement of a religious sanctuary was an altar for sacrifice. Grain or bread, vegetables, olive oil and wine were more common sacrifices than meat, but the latter was the principal sacrifice at the periodic (often annual) state-sponsored festivals, the main time the poorer people had meat in their diet. Roman sacrifices were accompanied by the burning of incense and the playing of a pipe *(tibia)*, with the priest wearing a veil over the head. The altar was outside the temple, which was the house of the deity, not an assembly hall for worshipers (*see* Worship). The deity's presence was symbolized by the cult statue, the central point of focus in the temple. The periodic festivals, in addition to the public procession and sacrifices, often included games and contests. The principal occasion of private sacrifice was the votive offering, the gift brought to the deity in fulfillment of a vow, a central act of personal piety and religious life.

Two narratives in Acts* illustrate important features of local civic cults. In the episode at Lystra (Acts 14:11-13), which may have its background in the story recorded by Ovid (Ovid *Met.* 8.620-724), note may be taken of the following items: the anthropomorphic nature of the gods, who appear in human form; the giving of Greek names (Zeus, the chief god, and Hermes, the messenger of the gods) to native deities; the priest assigned to a deity; the identification of the cult as "Zeus-Outside-the City" (NRSV footnote), where the sanctuary was located; and the intention to sacrifice bulls (the most expensive sacrifice and so an indication of the perceived importance of the occasion) that are garlanded, a common decoration of the sacrificial animal.

In one of the episodes at Ephesus (Acts 19:23-41) other features related to civic cults stand out: once more the giving of a Greek name to a local deity (Artemis of the Ephesians is not the classical Greek goddess of the hunt but an Asia Minor mother goddess; although the fertility feature is not specifically attested for Artemis of the Ephesians, the analogy with other Anatolian mother goddesses suggests fecundity of nature but not sexual immorality); the alliance of the most important local deity with the civic magistrates (Acts 19:35, 38-39), provincial authorities (Acts 19:31, 38) and economic activity (Acts 19:24-27); the making of images of the deity for sale as souvenirs or as votive offerings (Acts 19:24); the use of acclamations (Acts 19:34); the designation of Ephesus as "temple keeper" *(neōkoros)* of Artemis (Acts 19:35); and a divine origin attributed to the image or symbol of the deity (Acts 19:35).

4. Imperial Cult.

Under the empire the principal local civic cult was often joined to the imperial cult. Giving divine honors to the rulers was the climax of civic cult in the Greco-Roman world, only now the city (Rome) was the world and the city was personified in the royal family. Precedents for the ruler cult were provided by the Near-Eastern view of kings as divine by reason of office and by the Greek cult of heroes, notable human beings who by reason of their achievements were elevated to the status of divinities. Alexander the Great and his successors received divine honors, and the Roman emperors succeeded to these honors in the Greek East and ultimately received them in the Latin West as well. Such was the great power exercised by the rulers and such was the gratitude for the peace and prosperity brought by the emperor that only the honors shown to the gods seemed an adequate expression of homage. The social elite, who benefited the most from Roman rule, were especially active in promoting the ruler cult, and generally the impetus came from the provinces, but certain rulers like Caligula and Domitian insisted on receiving divine honors.

The external forms taken by the imperial cult included the dedication of altars and temples, erection of statues to the person in the appearance of a deity, commemorative inscriptions, sacrifices in the ruler's honor, instituting new festivals or renaming old ones and ascribing divine titles. Although miracle* stories were often associated with the birth of the ruler, there seems to have been no expectation that the ruler would act supernaturally. Prayers* and votive offerings to the ruler were rare or nonexistent. The imperial cult was an acknowledgment of what seemed almost supernatural power and an act of gratitude for benefactions (*see* Blessing) received or an anticipation of them. It was an expression of the status of the ruler, of loyalty to him or her and of the unity of the subjects. Thus its importance was more political and social than religious.

The story of Herod Agrippa I (Acts 12:20-23) illustrates the hyperbole of court flattery to a king from those who expected benefits from him (cf. the fuller account in Josephus *Ant.* 19.8.2 §343-352). The Asiarchs mentioned in Acts 19:31 were members of the provincial council of Asia, who without necessarily being personally involved, oversaw the imperial cult as part of their duties. The book of Revelation (*see* Revelation, Book of) shows the greatest antagonism of any NT writing toward Rome and its embodiment in the imperial cult. The religious aspect of the beast* who will be overthrown by the Lord* stands out (Rev 13:1, 4-8, 11-15; 19:20). Astral imagery, associated not only with the gods of paganism but also on the coins of Domitian with the imperial family, is subordinated to Christ, who holds in his hands "the seven stars" (Rev 1:16), which are really the "angels of the seven churches" (Rev 1:20; *see* Angel), and who is the true world conqueror (Rev 3:21). Revelation from its beginning counters the imperial ideology by asserting that Christ is "ruler of the kings of the earth" (Rev 1:5) and that he has made his people "to be a kingdom" (Rev 1:6, 9; *see* Kingdom of God). It gives great emphasis throughout to the royal rule of God (Rev 11:15, 17; 12:10; 15:3; 19:6), to Christ as "Lord of lords and King of kings" (Rev 17:14; 19:16) and to the rule of the saints (Rev 5:10; 20:4, 6; 22:5).

5. Mysteries.

The mysteries, secret cults in which the uninitiated could not participate, were a feature of classical Greek religion. One of the oldest and the most influential was the Eleusinian mysteries celebrated in honor of Demeter. They were a local mystery, in that a person had to go to Eleusis, near Athens, to receive the initiation. A site mentioned in the NT where local mysteries were celebrated is Samothrace (Acts 16:11), where were worshiped the "Mother of the gods" and the Cabiri, the latter in Roman times confused with the Dioscuri, Castor and Pollux, who were protective deities of sailors (Acts 28:11). Also known in classical times were the mysteries of Dionysus, which were not confined to one locality.

Several Eastern cults, when their devotees became part of the Greek world, copied the Greek practice of mystery initiations. Especially widespread were the Egyptian deities Isis and Osiris (the latter largely replaced by Sarapis in the Greek world). Two second-century sources attest their popularity: the philosophical interpretation of the cult myth by Plutarch (Plutarch *Iside* 12-21, *Mor.* 355D-359) and the circumstantial account of the initiation (without divulging its secrets) by Apuleius (*Met.* 11), who also describes other features of the religion.

Numerous archaeological remains attest the spread of the mysteries of Mithras, especially in the second and third centuries after Christ. Although worshiping the Persian god Mithras, Roman Mithraism seems not to have been derived from Persian religion. Mithras was associated with astrological phenomena and was worshiped as having control over celestial forces. There were seven grades of initiation, from the rank of "raven" to that of "father." That Mithraism initiated only men and that it placed an emphasis on loyalty perhaps account for its popularity with soldiers and government officials.

The mysteries flourished around the beginning of the Christian era, especially in the second century, because they conveyed an assurance of higher status, a sense of a closer relationship with the deity and the hope of blessedness in the hereafter. They have in common with Christianity a concern with salvation,* but their salvation was from fate and the terrors of the afterlife, not from sin.* The "dying and rising" of the deities in the mysteries, where it occurs, relates to the cycle of nature and was no true resurrection.* The NT terminology of mystery has to do with the divine plan, previously hidden but now revealed. The Christian initiation was not secret. Where washings occur in the mysteries, this was part of the purification preliminary to the initiation, not the initiation itself as in Christian baptism.* The mysteries were rather expensive and were for the few deemed already worthy, whereas Christianity invited everyone (as the pagan critic Celsus pointed out—according to Origen *Cont. Cels.* 3.59).

6. Other Features.

6.1. Oracles and Healing. The sanctuary of Apollo at Delphi had been the principal site for receiving divine communications in classical times, but it was in decline at the beginning of the Christian era, a fact for which Plutarch sought explanations (*On the Obsolescence of Oracles, Mor.* 409E-438E). Its influence was partially inherited by daughter sanctuaries at Claros and Didyma in Asia Minor and Daphne near Antioch* in Syria. By the beginning of the Christian era the oracles were no longer determinative of political and religious developments, but they continued to be consulted by cities on formal sacred affairs and by individuals on affairs of personal life. Delphi was also known by the name Pytho, from Python, the female serpent representing the earth goddess who was killed by Apollo, and his priestess through whom the oracles were given was known as Pythia; hence "Pythian spirit" was used for the power* to utter oracular messages such as the fortunetelling by the slave* girl in Acts 16:16 (*see* Prophecy).

Dreams (*see* Visions) were considered another important source of divine communication, a belief shared by pagans and Jews and a frequent medium of providential guidance in the book of Acts (Acts 10:10-16; 16:9-10; 23:11; 27:23-24).

Many of the healing sanctuaries were properly shrines for oracles. The most important healing deity in the Greco-Roman world was the hero Asclepius, son of Apollo. In addition to his important sanctuary at Epidaurus, he had healing sites at Cos, Corinth, Athens and Rome. Rivaling Epidaurus was the sanctuary of Asclepius at Pergamum (Rev 2:12-17; see Hemer), celebrated by the second-century orator Aelius Aristides in his *Sacred Tales*. The satirist Lucian of Samosata, also second century, tells the story of *Alexander the False Prophet*, who created his own healing and oracular sanctuary in Asia Minor and duped many people, in a narrative that reveals the religious mentality of the age as well as the author's rationalist criticism. The sanctuaries of Asclepius often worked in cooperation with the medical profession to effect healing, but there were also told miracle stories of the most extraordinary kind. The expectation that divine power works miracles of healing is evident in many passages in Acts (Acts 3:1-10; 8:4-7; 9:32-41; 14:8-11; 28:8-9), but these accounts are more sober than the propaganda stories for Asclepius and are related to the saving work of Jesus as carried out by his messengers.

6.2. Magic. Religion and magic* were considered distinct, but they are not easily distinguished in the ancient world. In spite of laws against its practice, magic was widespread. As a somewhat artificial modern construct, the word *magic* as applied to ancient religion is used for efforts to compel supernatural forces by means of certain material objects and verbal formulas. Curse tablets sought to bring punishment on an enemy, and amulets were used to ward off potential attacks by evil forces. An extensive magical literature is preserved on papyri, often containing, it seems, the recipe books of practicing magicians (see Acts 19:19).

The term *magic* was derived from the name of a Persian priestly tribe and was used by the Greeks to refer to strange rites and formulas and then as a semitechnical term for the activity of those considered magicians. The use in Acts 8:9-11 illustrates the association of magic with the supposed control of supernatural power. The title *magos* is used for Bar-Jesus (or Elymas), also called a "false prophet," in Acts 13:6, 8. The Jews were widely regarded in the Greco-Roman world as possessing magical power. This association is evident also in the story in Acts 19:11-20, appropriately occurring in Ephesus, a city known as a center of magical activity (see Arnold). The story illustrates the use of formulas of constraint in magic and the common belief that knowledge of the name* of a supernatural power gave one control over that power (Acts 19:13), but it also exemplifies the different significance "the name of the Lord Jesus" had for Christians (Acts 19:15).

6.3. Demons and Superstition. By Hellenistic times the word *daimōn* had come to be used for intermediate divine beings that might be either good or bad. Plato's student Xenocrates had classified the kinds of demons; another Platonist, Plutarch, gives considerable information on demonology at the end of the first Christian century. The tendency by philosophers to blame the intermediate beings for bad things and for the less acceptable features of pagan religion prepared for the Jewish and Christian appropriation of *daimonion* for evil spiritual beings (Jas 2:19; 3:15; Rev 9:20; 16:14; 18:2).

The term *deisidaimonia* ("fear of the demons") became the common Greek term for "superstition" (see Plutarch *On Superstition, Mor.* 164E-171F). The word could have a neutral sense, even as *daimoniōn* ("divinities") does in Acts 17:18. Whether it is used in a neutral or a negative sense in Acts 17:22 depends on whether Paul is making a factual observation about the religiosity of the Athenians or is identifying with the philosophical criticism of Greek popular religion.

6.4. Astrology and Fate. Astronomy and astrology were not distinct in the ancient world (*see* Magic and Astrology). The belief that the movements of the heavenly bodies in absolute regularity control earthly events up to the smallest detail was developed by Greeks in Egypt in the Hellenistic age and began to be popularized under the early Roman Empire. The emperor Tiberius became so absorbed in astrology (Suetonius *Tiberius* 69) that he neglected the practice of religion, but few went that far. The religious aspect of astrology came from the identification of the planets with the traditional deities of Greece and Rome, but the planets themselves did not receive cultic devotion. The learned astronomy gave a new worldview that distinguished the sublunary world and the seven planets, characterized by change and corruption, from the supralunary world of the fixed stars, characterized by unchangability and perfection. Astrology became a principal support for the idea of absolute fate. Although some people gladly embraced this view, the popular religions were those that offered deliverance from fate—the mysteries of Isis and Mithras as well as Christianity (*see DPL*, Worship, §2.1).

7. Concluding Observation.

A snake was associated with many of the Greco-Roman deities. Among the forms that Zeus took, particularly in the household* cult, was that of a snake. A snake was portrayed on the shield of Athena, the patron goddess of Athens, and a snake was associated with Apollo at Delphi. The snake entwined around a staff was the symbol of Asclepius, and, from confusion of that with the twin snakes on the herald's staff of Hermes, this symbol has continued in use by the medical profession. The protective spirit of the Greek household, the Agathos Daimon, was depicted as a snake, and a snake represented the genius, or life principle, of the family on Roman household altars. Considering the biblical associations of the snake with Satan* (Rev 20:2), there is little wonder that Jews and Christians saw pagan religion as inspired by the devil.

See also GNOSIS, GNOSTICISM; IDOLATRY; MAGIC AND ASTROLOGY; ROMAN EMPIRE, CHRISTIANS AND THE.

BIBLIOGRAPHY. C. E. Arnold, *Ephesians: Power and Magic* (SNTSMS 63; Cambridge: Cambridge University Press, 1989); E. Ferguson, *Backgrounds of Early Christianity* (2d ed.; Grand Rapids: Eerdmans, 1993) 137-298; J. Ferguson, *The Religions of the Roman Empire* (Aspects of Greek and Roman Life; Ithaca, NY: Cornell University Press, 1970); A. J. Festugière, *Le Monde Gréco-Romain au temps de notre-Seigneur*, 2: *Le Milieu Spirituel* (Bibliothèque Catholique des Sciences Religieuses 7.2; Paris: Blond & Gay, 1935); D. Fishwick, *The Imperial Cult in the Latin West* (2 vols. in 4 pts.; Leiden: E. J. Brill, 1987-92); D. W. J. Gill and B. W. Winter, "Acts and Roman Religion" in *The Book of Acts in Its Greco-Roman Setting*, ed. D. W. J. Gill and C. Gempf (BAFCS 2; Grand Rapids: Eerdmans, 1994) 79-103; F. C. Grant, ed., *Ancient Roman Religion* (The Library of Religion; New York: Liberal Arts Press, 1957); idem, *Hellenistic Religions: The Age of Syncretism* (The Library of Religion; New York: Liberal Arts Press, 1953); C. J. Hemer, *The Letters to the Seven Churches of Asia in their Local Setting* (JSNTSup 11; Sheffield: JSOT, 1986); H. C. Kee, *Medicine, Miracle and Magic in New Testament Times* (Cambridge: Cambridge University Press, 1986); R. MacMullen, *Paganism in the Roman Empire* (New Haven, CT: Yale University Press, 1981); M. W. Meyer, *The Ancient Mysteries: A Sourcebook* (San Francisco: Harper, 1987); M. P. Nilsson, *Geschichte der griechischen Religion*, 2: *Die hellenistische und römische Zeit* (Handbuch der Altertumswissenschaft; Munich: C. H. Beck, 1950); A. D. Nock, *Conversion: The Old and the New in Religion from Alexander the Great to Augustine of Hippo* (Oxford: Clarendon, 1933); idem, *Essays on Religion and the Ancient World*, ed. Z. Stewart (2 vols.; Oxford: Clarendon, 1972); S. R. F. Price, *Ritual and Power: The Roman Imperial Cult in Asia Minor* (Cambridge: Cambridge University Press, 1984); J. Z. Smith, *Drudgery Divine: On the Comparison of Early Christianities and the Religions of Late Antiquity* (Chicago: University of Chicago Press, 1990); D. Ulansey, *The Origins of the Mithraic Mysteries* (Oxford: Oxford University Press, 1989); A. J. M. Wedderburn, *Baptism and Resurrection: Studies in Pauline Theology Against Its Greco-Roman Background* (Tübingen: J. C. B. Mohr, 1987).

E. Ferguson

REPENTANCE, SECOND REPENTANCE

Repentance is the divinely appointed means of repairing the relationship between God and humankind. It is God's gift, allowing the wayward the opportunity to repudiate sin and turn again to please God and honor God with one's life. It is a gift not to be taken for granted, nor is God's favor to be presumed upon. Repentance permits a person to return to God and seize upon a regenerate life, but provides no license for entering lightly into sin and apostasy.

1. Jewish and Greco-Roman Background
2. Acts
3. Hebrews
4. General Epistles
5. Revelation
6. Other Early Christian Literature

1. Jewish and Greco-Roman Background.

1.1. Old Testament and Hellenistic Judaism. The idea of repentance in Judaism* arose within the context of the covenant* between God* and Israel.* The people individually and collectively transgressed the law* and stood in need of reconciliation with God and restoration to favor. This was sought through inward contrition, accompanied by outward signs of regret such as confession, lamentation, wearing sackcloth and offering sacrifices* (Joel 2:12-13; Hos 14:2-5; Ezek 14:6; Pr Man 7-14). The OT speaks of repentance as a "turning" (Heb *šûb*) away from sin* and rebellion and "returning" to God, covenant loyalty and obedience.* R. D. Witherup correctly observes that the summons to repent is often an internal call to Israel, not an invitation to the nations (though some exceptions exist, such as Jonah's ministry). The OT and related texts speak of God's favorable acceptance of the penitent, a conviction dramatically expressed in the Prayer of Manasseh. Texts such as Jeremiah 31:31-34 provide a crucial link between this notion of repentance under the Mosaic covenant and the NT call to repent in response to God's promise* of the new, eschatological* covenant. Qumran* also links repentance with joining the covenant of the true Israel.

1.2. Greco-Roman Literature. While *metanoia* carries the general sense of a "change of mind," sometimes accompanied by a certain feeling of regret for having held to a former opinion, J. N. Bailey has convincingly shown (versus Behm) that it often achieves the full sense of conversion in the usage of certain philosophical schools. Some Stoics disparaged repentance, for one ought to approach all things with circumspection so as not to have any regrets (Epictetus *Ench.* 34; Marcus Aurelius *Med.* 8.2); others, however, viewed repentance favorably as an opportunity to change for the better, to put away vice and error in favor of virtue* and wisdom* (Dio Chrysostom *Or.* 12.44). Repentance is often occasioned by a philosopher's oration, which stings the conscience* and motivates re-

form (Plutarch *Adulat., Mor.* 56A). This has special significance for the call to repentance often attached to the speeches of Acts.*

2. Acts.

Repentance figures prominently in Acts, particularly as the desired response to the speeches of Peter and Paul. In the earlier sermons Peter calls the Jewish people and rulers to repent of the specific sin of rejecting and murdering the chosen Messiah, Jesus (Acts 2:36-39; 3:17-21; 5:29-32; cf. Tannehill) and to turn to a vital trust in him. Jews in the Diaspora* are not implicated: the benefits of Jesus' death and exaltation* are proclaimed to them as "release" from the sins committed under the Mosaic covenant (Acts 13:27-39). Gentiles* are called to repent of their former ignorance concerning the one God (despite God's self-revelation in creation,* Acts 17:26-27; cf. Rom 1) and their worship* of idols (*see* Idolatry), since the true knowledge* of God is now made available to them in the Christian mission* (Acts 14:15; 17:24-31; cf. 1 Thess 1:9-10). Bailey rightly observes that for both Jew and Gentile repentance in Acts means commitment to ethical* behavior (Acts 26:20) as well as assimilation to the new people God is forming (Acts 2:38-42), symbolized through baptism.* The result for both groups, now made one people, is "life"* (Acts 11:18) and "forgiveness of sins" (Acts 5:19; *see* Forgiveness) so that the new people of God may receive the promised blessings* of the "times of refreshing" (Acts 3:19).

3. Hebrews.

Believers enter the community of the saved in part through "repentance from dead works" (Heb 6:1). Turning away from dead works or sin, in the sense of directing one's life toward attaining the temporary goods of this world* (cf. Heb 11:25), is linked with "faith towards God" (Heb 6:1), a complete reorientation of loyalty, commitment and service.* This repentance is made possible and effective through God's favor, won by the unique sacrifice of Jesus, who provides the benefaction of "remission of sins" (Heb 10:18) and thus a cleansed conscience that enables one to stand before God as favored child (*see* Son) rather than condemned offender (Heb 4:14-16). The battle against sin is lifelong and may result in the loss of life (Heb 12:4), property and status (cf. Heb 10:32-34).

Since these penalties are exacted of the believer by the society, sin appears to entail much more than recognized vices. It includes adopting society's goals, values and ideals where these conflict with God's. Jesus' continued intercession assumes that believers will sin after baptism and thus continue to need his mediation (Heb 7:25).

Hebrews* raises the special problem of a "second repentance." For those who turn away from God (Heb 6:6; cf. 3:12) and renounce their allegiance to the divine patron, thus dishonoring God and showing contempt for Jesus' costly mediation of God's favor (Heb 6:6; 10:29), the author threatens the impossibility of a second repentance. Just as Christ's sacrifice is unrepeatable, so coming to faith* is unrepeatable (Heb 10:18-19: his mediation, however, continues for believers who sin without reorienting their hearts toward the world). The theological concern for "eternal security" and "final perseverance of the saints" (*see* Endurance) often obscures the first-century context of these warnings (cf. Sailer), which is the set of expectations attached to patron-client relationships (see deSilva). As with the wilderness generation (Heb 3:7-4:11; cf. Num 14:1-35) and Esau (Heb 12:16-17), distrust in God to provide greater gifts than the world offers and disloyalty to the divine patron amount to the cardinal sin of ingratitude, from which one could not expect a return to favor, or grace* (cf. Dio Chrysostom *Or.* 31.65: "those who insult their benefactors will by nobody be esteemed to deserve a favor"). When assessing the theological weight of such statements, it is important to consider their rhetorical purpose. Hebrews addresses believers, whom it seeks to confirm in loyalty and endurance at any cost. The author thus urges them to consider the irreplaceable value of the favor in which they stand and not to do anything that might jeopardize it. We should not assume that this author would say the same words to those who had left the fellowship* and sought to return with penitent hearts (so Carlston and Solari). Nevertheless it is clear that this author would urge us not to take grace for granted but rather to consider it the pearl of greatest price, not to be sacrificed for anything.

4. General Epistles.

First John (*see* John, Letters of) offers a particular challenge when speaking of sin and repentance. 1 John 3:4-10 leaves one with the impression that there is no place for sin in the life of the believer. 1 John 1:8—2:2, however, makes clear provision for dealing with postbaptismal sin, while 1 John 2:1 and 3:3 amount to injunctions against sin and exhortations toward purification. J. Painter offers a plausible solution: 1 John 3:4-10 answers not the question, Can believers sin? but rather, What shows one to be a true believer? Against his opponents, John stresses that it is not the mere possession of God's "seed" but rather the imitation of God's character, seeking holiness and purity (1 Jn 3:2-3). Praise of an ideal (cf. Marshall) effectively exhorts the hearers to strive for that ideal, thus making 1 John 3:4-10 another exhortation to put away sin. The hearer is stirred up by the desire to show himself or herself God's true child and so returns to the battle against sin with greater drive. Repentance is therefore an essential part of the ongoing life of believers when they fall into sin and must seek the means provided by God for cleansing and renewal in life and fellowship (1 Jn 1:8—2:2).

Both 1 Peter* and James* emphasize the call to leave behind all manner of sin and pursue holiness,* the call which began with conversion ("returning to the shepherd and guardian of your souls," 1 Pet 2:25; *see* Shepherd). For both the initial experience of repentance and conversion leads to a lifelong process of overcoming sin and progressing toward the holiness of God (1 Pet 1:14-16; Jas 4:8). James envisions a community in which confession of sin and mutual prayer* for forgiveness of sins is a regular occurrence, always with the promise of healing* and restoration (Jas 5:16, 20). 2 Peter also emphasizes the ethical fruit that repentance must bear in order to be genuine and effective (2 Pet 1:5-9). Defection from the true gospel* is a most serious offense, placing one in a worse position than the unbelievers (2 Pet 2:20-22; cf. Heb 6:4-8; 10:26-31). While 2 Peter* does not, like Hebrews, indicate that such people as the false teachers he opposes are beyond repentance, he suggests that such people will become hardened, so as not to repent and thus be kept "under punishment until the day of judgment" (2 Pet 2:9; *see* Judgment). This age, however, is an age for repentance, and God in God's mercy* has delayed the end in order to extend this opportunity for all to return (as God's patience is often linked, as R. J. Bauckham notes, with the opportunity for sinners to repent [cf. Jon 4:2]). Believers are thus urged not to presume upon God's patience as well as God's mercy by continuing in sin and taking repentance for granted.

5. Revelation.

Revelation (*see* Revelation, Book of) begins as a call to the churches, urging them to repent from lack of love,* doctrinal impurity, accommodation with the religious demands of the unbelieving society and imperfect commitment (Rev 2:5, 16, 21, 22; 3:3, 19). The call to repent is a continuing sign of Christ's love and desire to save (Rev 3:19) and has a continuing place in the life of the church.* There is a stark contrast between the expectation that the churches will respond in repentance during the period of preparation and the depiction of a recalcitrant world refusing God glory once the tribulation begins (Rev 9:20-21; 16:9, 11), despite repeated appeals from God's messengers (Rev 11:3; 14:6-7). They display a hardness of heart reminiscent of Pharaoh, which accords well with Revelation's borrowings from Exodus.

Repentance includes a call to Gentiles to turn away from "worshiping demons and idols" and from all manner of sinful behaviors (Rev 9:20-21; 16:11) and to turn toward the one God who created all things and whose Messiah redeemed a people for God through his blood (Rev 4:11; 5:9). It is synonymous with the call to "fear God and give God honor" (Rev 14:6-7; cf. 11:13)—thus an acknowledgment of God's legitimate claim on our lives and a repudiation of the illegitimate claims made by society's gods and rulers. John calls the churches to remain firm in their repentance, making firm their commitment to this one God and God's people. He reinforces this not by denying apostates (*see* Apostasy) a chance to repent but by depicting the hardness of heart that falls upon the partners of the beast* and dragon, assuring their dismal destiny (Rev 22:4).

6. Other Early Christian Literature.

6.1. Clement. The shed blood of Jesus "won the gift of repentance for the entire world" (*1 Clem.* 7). Repentance is thus a gift from God but one that God is most eager to give. Following the OT, this repentance involves both a renunciation of former sins as well as a commitment to a life of holiness, justice and charity (*1 Clem.*

8). Clement* allows a place for repentance in the life of the believing community, urging the Corinthians not to harden their hearts but rather to repent of their rebellion against their justly installed presbyters (*1 Clem.* 19, 44, 51) with tears, humility and submission to their discipline.* The homily attributed to Clement also speaks of repentance as a characteristic of the believer, who is continually being molded and reshaped by the Potter. Repentance is accessible as long as the believer remains in the world, just as the clay may be remolded up to the time it is put in the kiln (*2 Clem.* 8).

6.2. Ignatius, Polycarp and Didache. Ignatius,* like Clement, allows repentance for postconversion sin. He exhorts those who have broken with the bishop: "as many as repent, let them come into the unity of the church" (Ign. *Phld.* 3.2; 8.1; Ign. *Smyrn.* 4.1). The *Didache** presents repentance as a normal part of church worship: in order that prayers may be unhindered and the "sacrifice" pure, any believers who have sinned are to repent, confessing their transgressions (*Did.* 4.14; 10.6; 14.1; cf. *Barn.* 19.12). In *Martyrdom of Polycarp* the proconsul urges Polycarp* to repent of his Christian convictions on pain of death. Polycarp answers that Christians may not repent of the "better" in order to turn to the "worse," for they have already exchanged baseness for righteousness* (*Mart. Pol.* 11.1). The believer's initial repentance thus involves both the repudiation of sin and the beginning of a life of virtue, along which road the believer must continue to move forward, even in the face of death.

6.3. The Shepherd of Hermas. Repentance dominates *Hermas*—the shepherd is none other than the angel of repentance. The book begins by addressing Hermas's need and the need of his children for repentance (*Herm. Vis.* 1.2-3) but quickly moves on to call all believers who have sinned to hasten to repent (*Herm. Sim.* 8.11). By repentance the "Gentiles" may join the church, represented as a tower being built in a vast plain; it is also the means by which believers who have fallen again into sin may be restored to their place in the church. L. Pernveden helpfully distinguishes between the church as a historical institution and the church as the eternal assembly of the purified that receives the promise of God. Sinners may be found in the midst of the former, but only those who repent shall attain to the latter.

Hermas lends urgency to repentance by stressing the proximity of the end of the age, when the tower shall be completed and the unrepentant shut out forever (*Herm. Vis.* 3.5; *Herm. Sim.* 10.4). He lends seriousness to repentance by proclaiming that there is only one repentance for the believer (*Herm. Man.* 4.1). Believers may be forgiven and restored, but they must repent speedily and not fall away again; novitiates must not fall away at all (Behm). Repentance is always the gift of God (*Herm. Sim.* 8.6), who desires that "all who were called through his Son should be saved" (*Herm. Sim.* 8.11; cf. 1 Tim 2:4). It is an understanding that a certain action is wrong and blameworthy, combined with a commitment to walk thereafter in the right way (*Herm. Man.* 4.2). For repentance to be shown to be pure and genuine, and thus to result in remission of sin, it must bear the fruit of obedience to the commands of God (*Herm. Man.* 2; *Herm. Sim.* 9.33), given in a sort of shorthand in the *Mandates*. As in 1 and 2 Peter, repentance for sins is inseparable from the positive counterpart of commitment to righteousness (*Herm. Sim.* 6.1). The one repentance must be kept undefiled: the Christian life is a preservation of one's withdrawal from the control of sin and Satan* and one's submission to the works and commands of God (*Herm. Man.* 12.3).

As P. Henne observes, it is noteworthy that despite the severity of Hermas's doctrine of repentance, no sin excludes a person from coming to repentance save that of apostasy (thus continuing the tradition of Hebrews). This sin involved blaspheming the name* of God, showing Hermas's affinity with early Jewish notions of the gravity of *hillûl ha-šēm,* "profaning the Name" (cf. *Herm. Vis.* 3.7; *Herm. Sim.* 9.19). These have utterly abandoned themselves to the lusts of the world, by which they have brought dishonor to God's name (*Herm. Sim.* 6.2; cf. Rom 2:24). *Hermas* allows those who formerly denied Jesus to repent but allows no chance for repentance for those who, after his proclamation, deny the Lord* (*Herm. Vis.* 2.2), suggesting that Hermas's situation is one of high tension between church and society. His rhetoric promotes fidelity at any cost, as did the rhetoric of Hebrews. It is better for a person to remain an unbeliever than to come to the knowledge of God only to fall away again (*Herm. Sim.* 9.17.5—18.2; cf. 2 Pet 2:20-22).

Hermas combines a sharpened eschatological consciousness with a keen sense of God's mercy, for the building of the tower is halted to allow for an opportunity to repent (*Herm. Sim.* 9.14; 10.4). God's mercy, however, is a precious gift, not to be trampled (*Herm. Man.* 9.32) or taken for granted. Such a view provides powerful motivation for the believer to seize the opportunity and to pursue a regenerate life, so as not to have received God's mercy in vain.

See also ASSURANCE; ENDURANCE, PERSEVERANCE; FAITH, FAITHFULNESS; FORGIVENESS; HEBREWS; HERMAS, SHEPHERD OF; SIN, WICKEDNESS.

BIBLIOGRAPHY. J. N. Bailey, *Repentance in Luke-Acts* (unpublished Ph.D. dissertation, University of Notre Dame, 1993); R. J. Bauckham, *Jude, 2 Peter* (WBC; Waco, TX: Word, 1983); J. Behm and E. Würthwein, "μετανοέω, μετάνοια," *TDNT* 4:975-1008; C. E. Carlston, "Eschatology and Repentance in the Epistle to the Hebrews," *JBL* 78 (1959) 296-302; D. A. deSilva, "Exchanging Favor for Wrath: Apostasy in Hebrews and Patron-Client Relations," *JBL* 115 (1996) 91-116; B. R. Gaventa, *From Darkness to Light: Aspects of Conversion in the New Testament* (Philadelphia: Fortress, 1986); J. Goetzmann, "μετάνοια," *NIDNTT* 1:357-59; P. Henne, O.P., *L'Unité du Pasteur d'Hermas* (CRB 31; Paris: Gabalda, 1992); J. C. McCullough, "The Impossibility of a Second Repentance in Hebrews," *BibTh* 20 (1974) 1-7; I. H. Marshall, *The Epistles of John* (NICNT; Grand Rapids: Eerdmans, 1978); J. Painter, "The 'Opponents' in 1 John," *NTS* 32 (1986) 48-71; L. Pernveden, *The Concept of the Church in the Shepherd of Hermas* (STL 27; Lund: Gleerup, 1966); W. S. Sailer, "Hebrews Six: An Irony or a Continuing Embarrassment?" *EvJ* 3 (1985) 79-88; J. K. Solari, *The Problem of Metanoia in the Epistle to the Hebrews* (unpublished Ph.D. dissertation, Catholic University of America, 1970); R. C. Tannehill, "The Functions of Peter's Mission Speeches in the Narrative of Acts," *NTS* 37 (1991) 400-14; R. D. Witherup, *Conversion in the New Testament* (ZS:NT; Collegeville, MN: Liturgical Press, 1994).   D. A. deSilva

REST. *See* PEACE.

RESURRECTION

The resurrection of Jesus Christ from the dead is referred to explicitly in three of the NT documents considered here. It is difficult to imagine that the remaining documents could have been written without an underlying conviction that Jesus was risen and accessible to Christian believers. In the second century the resurrection of Jesus and of believers continued to be a significant theme in Christian writings. Divergent interpretations of it marked the emerging divide between orthodox and gnostic streams in the church.

1. Hebrews, 1 Peter, Revelation
2. After the New Testament
3. Conclusion

1. Hebrews, 1 Peter, Revelation.

1.1. Terminology of Resurrection. Like the English verbs *raise* and *rise,* the verbs used in the NT do not refer exclusively to the raising of people from among the dead (see, e.g., Heb 7:11, 15; Jas 5:15). The only occurrence in these documents of *egeirō* with reference to the resurrection of Jesus is 1 Peter 1:21. *Anastasis* refers to Jesus' resurrection in 1 Peter 1:3; 3:21; to a general future resurrection in Hebrews 6:2; 11:35; and to what John calls "the first resurrection" in Revelation 20:5-6. The verb *zaō* ("live") describes Jesus' resurrection in Revelation 1:18 and Revelation 2:8 and "the first resurrection" in Revelation 20:4-5. *Zōopoieō* ("make alive") denotes Jesus' resurrection in 1 Peter 3:18. Finally, *anagō* is used of God "bringing back" Jesus from the dead in Hebrews 13:20.

1.2. Hebrews: Resurrection and Exaltation. For the writer of Hebrews* "resurrection of the dead" is part of basic Christian instruction (Heb 6:2). The linking of resurrection with "eternal judgment" suggests that he envisages a future universal resurrection, of the righteous* to eternal life* and of the wicked to condemnation (cf. Dan 12:2; Jn 5:28-29; Acts 24:15). Later he sees restoration to physical life (*egeirein,* Heb 11:19; *anastasis,* Heb 11:35) as a picture of the future resurrection of the faithful to eternal life.

Jesus' resurrection is mentioned explicitly only once, in the prayer* of Hebrews 13:20-21. Elsewhere the focus is on his exaltation* to the right hand of God.* The writer's distinctive emphasis on Jesus' exaltation rather than on resurrection is a natural consequence of his concentration on Christ's* work as high priest* foreshadowed in the ritual of the Day of Atonement. Just as the high priest of the OT entered the holy of holies with the blood of the sacrificial victim, so the crucified Jesus appeared at God's right hand in the heavenly sanctuary (Heb 9:11-

12; *see* Tabernacle). In this pattern stressing Jesus' exaltation to heaven* there is no separate place for his resurrection. It is presupposed (cf. the linking of these two themes in Rom 8:34; Eph 1:20; Col 3:1; 1 Pet 3:22). Christ's exaltation to God's right hand presupposes his resurrection from the dead; his resurrection was the way to exaltation.

Theologically, Jesus' resurrection-exaltation is linked with other key themes in Hebrews. It demonstrated God's acceptance of his atoning sacrifice* (Heb 10:12; 13:20-21). It confirmed his divine sonship (Heb 1:3-5, 13; *see* Son), his high priesthood (Heb 5:5-10; 8:1) and his status as the last Adam (Heb 1:13—2:9, combining Ps 110:1 with Ps 8:4-6; see Dunn, 108-13).

The connection between Jesus' past resurrection and believers' future resurrection is hinted at in Hebrews's unique description of Jesus as "forerunner" (*prodromos,* Heb 6:20). Meanwhile he "is permanently alive to plead their cause" (Heb 7:25). The knowledge that he went via the cross* to God's right hand inspires them to remain faithful, confident that they will share his destiny.

The question of the timing of future resurrection is raised by the reference to "the spirits of the righteous made perfect" (Heb 12:23). This is commonly taken to mean dead believers (cf. *1 Enoch* 22:9), waiting in an intermediate state to receive resurrection bodies at Christ's second coming (*see* Parousia). However, Hebrews 12:22-24 seems to portray the ultimate encounter with God in the heavenly Jerusalem* rather than in a preliminary or an intermediate state. Hence the "spirits" are probably the righteous in their ultimate state, in their "spiritual bodies" (1 Cor 15:44). If this is so, the text does not address the question whether there is an interim, disembodied state between death and the Parousia (see further Peterson, 163-67).

1.3. 1 Peter: Hope of Vindication. The resurrection of Jesus is the foundation of hope* for the author of 1 Peter* and for his readers in churches facing persecution* (1 Pet 1:3, 21; 3:15). The key passage is 1 Peter 3:18-22, which is widely regarded as drawing on primitive liturgical traditions (*see* Hymns; Liturgical Elements), especially in 1 Peter 3:19-21 (see Michaels, 197-99).

Christ was "put to death in the flesh but made alive in the spirit" (1 Pet 3:18). The contrast between flesh* and spirit has sometimes been taken to imply a dualism within Christ's human nature or a contrast between his divine and human natures. These terms, however, denote not two parts of Christ but two spheres of existence. His earthly life ended in death, but that was succeeded by his risen life in what Paul calls his "spiritual body" (1 Cor 15:42-44; note the similar contrast between flesh and spirit in Rom 1:3-4; 1 Tim 3:16; and discussion in Dalton, 124-34; Michaels, 204-5).

1 Peter 3:21-22 leads the readers' thought from Jesus' resurrection to his exaltation to God's right hand (cf. 1 Pet 1:21; Eph 1:20-22). So whatever the meaning of the intervening passage about his preaching to the spirits in prison, the focus is on his vindication by God and his lordship over all things.

For Peter's readers, God's vindication of Jesus gives them solid hope that he will also vindicate them. Through Jesus' resurrection God has given to believers new birth, a secure inheritance to be revealed at the last time (1 Pet 1:3-4), conveyed through baptism* (1 Pet 3:21). Because God has called them in Christ to eternal glory* they may stand firm in suffering* (1 Pet 5:10).

The author maintains the typically Pauline tension between salvation* already experienced and salvation yet to be received in its fullness (e.g., in 1 Pet 1:3-9). The link between baptism and resurrection in 1 Peter 3:21 echoes the language of Romans 6:1-14. But because he addresses Christians in the context of persecution, Peter uses the theme of resurrection with more focus on the future than does Paul in Romans. Although Jesus' resurrection means that believers enter into new life now, it inspires a greater hope that God will in the future bring them through suffering to glory.

1.4. Revelation: "I Was Dead and Am Alive For Ever." The threat of persecution and the promise* of vindication shape John's message also in Revelation (*see* Revelation, Book of). The death of believers for their witness* *(martyria)* to Christ has already occurred, and for others it will occur (Rev 2:10, 13; 6:9-11; 12:11; 17:6; 20:4).

The book is introduced with a vision* of the risen Christ, "the first and the last and the living one" (Rev 1:18; cf. Rev 2:8). Since "the first and the last" is a title of God in Isaiah 44:6 and Isaiah 48:12 (cf. Rev 1:8; 21:6), the resurrection points to Christ's participation in the eternal being of God and his rule over creation* (Bauckham 1993 *Theology*, 54-58).

More specific references to resurrection indicate the centrality of this theme in John's thought. Jesus is introduced as "the firstborn from the dead and the ruler of the kings of the earth" (Rev 1:5). This phrase combines the idea that Christ pioneered for others the way to resurrection (cf. Col 1:18; "firstfruits" in 1 Cor 15:20) with the language of Psalm 89:27, where the Davidic king is described as "my firstborn, the highest of the kings of the earth." By virtue of his resurrection Jesus is already establishing God's rule over earthly powers* (cf. Rev 5:3-5).

The risen Lord has begun to fulfill the hope of establishing God's rule over the earth, so that ultimately God will through him make all things new (Rev 21:5). In the new heaven and new earth God will live with his resurrected people (Rev 21:3-4). John nowhere speaks of resurrection bodies, but the imagery of Revelation 21—22 would hardly fit with the notion that God's people are permanently disembodied spirits (see Charles, 1:81-83, 176, 184-88, 210, 213-14; 2:127-28, for the argument that in Revelation white robes represent resurrection bodies). He does not speculate about the separation or reassembly of bodies and spirits or souls but speaks simply of the death and resurrection of persons (Bauckham 1993 *Climax*, 62-70). John's hope, like the Jewish hope out of which it sprang, is not merely for the resurrection of individuals but also for resurrection of God's people in fellowship* with each other in a renewed world.

Two related passages require special attention. According to Revelation 6:9-11, those who have been killed because of their faithful witness are told that they will be vindicated against their persecutors when the full number of martyrs is complete. Like some Jewish apocalyptic* texts, this passage refers to dead saints awaiting resurrection as "souls" (*psychai;* cf. *1 Enoch* 22:3; *2 Bar.* 21:23). The text provides some support for the concept of an intermediate state, though the fact that the "souls" are described as wearing robes shows that they are not purely spiritual entities. Probably John's concern is not to teach about an intermediate state but to speak of the eschatological* delay during which the church must continue its witness (Bauckham 1993 *Climax*, 55-56).

The promise of Revelation 6:9-11 finds its fulfillment in the millennium (Rev 20:4-6). The souls of the martyrs "came to life *(ezēsan)* and ruled with Christ for a thousand years." John comments that those who take part in this "first resurrection" *(anastasis)* are protected from "the second death" (eternal, spiritual death, cf. Rev 20:14). In contrast with them, "the rest of the dead did not come to life until the thousand years were completed." (For the view that in Revelation 6:9-11 and Revelation 20:4-6 John is concerned exclusively with Christian martyrs see Beasley-Murray, 293-94. For the view that a wider group of believers is implied see Harris, 178-79, 228; Mealy, 110-15.)

After the thousand years there is a scene of universal judgment,* for which all the dead are gathered before God's throne (Rev 20:11-15). This must be the "second resurrection" implied by the earlier reference to the "first resurrection" (Rev 20:5). But it may be significant that John refrains from calling their standing before God for judgment a resurrection. Perhaps, like Paul, he prefers to reserve resurrection language for the raising of people to eternal life with Christ.

1.5. Other New Testament Literature. In the shorter letters* resurrection language hardly occurs, though there are occasional promises of "eternal life" (Jude 21), "a new heaven and a new earth" (2 Pet 3:13), entry into "the eternal kingdom" (2 Pet 1:11) or into "the presence of his glory" (Jude 24). In James,* Jesus Christ is "our glorious Lord" (Jas 2:1) who promises "the crown of life" to those who remain faithful under testing (Jas 1:12).

Though 1 John (*see* John, Letters of) retains the Fourth Gospel's stress on eternal life as a present possession (1 Jn 3:15; 5:11-12), there is also an important future perspective. "We know that when he appears we shall be like him, for we shall see him as he is" (1 Jn 3:2). There are uncertainties of interpretation. For example, is "he" God or Christ? Shall we be "like him" in character, or in form or appearance? Though most commentators take John to refer to transformation of character at the Parousia, it is likely that his focus is on the prospect of having resurrection bodies like that of Christ (cf. Phil 3:21; Col 3:4).

1.6. Conclusions on New Testament Literature. Most of this literature expresses, like Paul, the central importance for Christian faith* of the resurrection of Jesus and the expectation of the resurrection of believers. But there is no sustained reflection on the nature of resurrection

such as we find in 1—2 Corinthians.

Like Paul, these writers see Jesus' resurrection as the prototype of the resurrection of believers. They focus on resurrection as God's vindication of those who suffer for Christ's sake. They make no sharp distinction between Christ's resurrection and his exaltation. They offer only limited material on the timing of the resurrection of believers or the nature of an intermediate state. While there is implicit affirmation of the idea that all the dead will be raised for final judgment, no writer explicitly speaks of a resurrection for judgment. Evidently, like Paul, they prefer to reserve the term *resurrection* for God's raising of Jesus and of believers to eternal life in his presence.

2. After the New Testament.

On his journey toward martyrdom* in Rome* Ignatius* wrote of Jesus "who was truly raised from the dead . . . , just as his Father will raise up in Christ Jesus us who believe in him, without whom we have no true life" (Ign. *Trall.* 9.2). He thus affirms the traditional Christian belief in Jesus' resurrection and the future resurrection of believers. But the emphatic "truly" (used four times in the passage) indicates that the affirmation is being made in the context of criticism by docetists.* In the period A.D. 95-150 attitudes to the resurrection became an important indicator of the rift between orthodox and gnostic Christians.

2.1. The Apostolic Fathers and the Development of Orthodoxy. NT themes are easily recognizable in the works of most of the apostolic fathers,* but there are signs of development in response to controversy. Jesus' resurrection is celebrated in quasi-creedal statements (Ign. *Magn.* 11.1; *see* Creeds). The God who raised Jesus will also raise those who do his will (Pol. *Phil.* 2.2; 9.2; 12.2). The idea that Jesus' resurrection is a prototype of believers' resurrection, so typical of Paul, is combined with a more moralistic emphasis on future resurrection as a reward for the righteous and as compensation for present suffering (cf. *1 Clem.* 26.1; *2 Clem.* 19.3-4; *Barn.* 21.1; Ign. *Pol.* 7.1).

In defense against Docetism it is insisted that Jesus rose "in the flesh" or "in flesh and spirit" (Ign. *Smyrn.* 3.1-3; 12.2) and that for Christians too "this flesh" will be raised (*2 Clem.* 9.1-5). Ignatius warns that docetists will find themselves without bodily reality, just as they imagine

Christ to have been (Ign. *Smyrn.* 2.1). And although these writers sometimes seem, like Paul, to reserve resurrection language for believers only (Ign. *Trall.* 9.2; *Did.* 16.6), some speak explicitly of the resurrection in flesh, or in the body, of all people for judgment (*Barn.* 5.6-7; cf. later *Ep. Apos.* 26; Justin Martyr *Apol. I* 19—20).

There are two apologetic concerns apart from the argument against Docetism. First, orthodox Christians saw belief in resurrection of the flesh as a deterrent against asceticism and libertinism. Since the flesh will rise for judgment it is necessary to treat it responsibly in this life (*2 Clem.* 9; Aristides *Apol.* 15—16; cf. the stress in *Apoc. Peter* 4—12 on the reassembly of body, soul and spirit for judgment, followed by eternal physical torment for the wicked). Belief in immortality of the soul without resurrection of the body, or in the mere dissolution of persons at death, is an inadequate bulwark against immorality (Justin *Apol. I* 18; Justin *Dial. Tryph.* 80; *see* Purity). Second, the emphasis on the futurity of resurrection and judgment counterbalances an overrealized eschatology such as that already found among the false teachers criticized in 2 Timothy 1:18 (cf. Polycarp *Phil.* 7.1; and see Donfried, 103-7, 141-45 on this motivation in *1-2 Clem.*).

A more general apologetic motive is evident in *1 Clement* 24—26 (*see* Clement of Rome), where the future resurrection of humanity is argued from the sequence of the seasons, grains of seed, the story of the phoenix, scriptural prophecy and God's omnipotence and providence. Justin develops similar arguments, concluding that "we will receive again our own bodies, though they be dead and cast into the earth, for we maintain that with God nothing is impossible" (Justin *Apol. I* 18). The use of analogy is designed not only to counter specific heresy but also to make the case for Christian orthodoxy in a pagan world that accepts only the immortality of the soul.

2.2. The Development of Gnosticism. The preceding discussion shows that orthodox Christians were in conflict with others whose approach to resurrection was different. There were not two clear-cut schools of thought, and some documents do not fit neatly into one category or another. For example, the *Gospel of Peter*, which was probably used by the orthodox Justin and Melito of Sardis,* gives a vivid portrayal of the rising of Jesus from the tomb which

seems intended to exclude a resurrection of the flesh (*Gos. Pet.* 9—10). This description is echoed in the *Ascension of Isaiah* 3.16-17, which elsewhere says that the righteous will ascend "from the body" to receive garments representing angelic glory (*Ascension of Isaiah* 4.16-17; 8.14-15, 26; 9.2, 9-11, 26; 11.40).

In the documents that show gnostic* traits three features highlight the contrast with orthodoxy. First, a number of documents take the form of revelation discourses in which the risen Lord addresses disciples (e.g., *Ap. John, Soph. Jes. Chr.;* see Perkins 1980, 37-58). This genre is used to further the claim to reveal the hidden teaching* of Christ. It is probably this alleged distortion and creation of sayings of Jesus that Polycarp* has in mind when he denounces those who "pervert the sayings of the Lord for their own desires" (Pol. *Phil.* 7.1).

Second, they affirm that resurrection has already been experienced by Christians, sometimes with an appeal to texts such as Ephesians 2:5-6 or Colossians 3:1-4. In *Gospel of Thomas* 51 Jesus' disciples ask when the repose of the dead and the new world* will come, and Jesus replies: "What you expect has come, but you do not know it." The *Treatise on Resurrection* makes a similar affirmation (*Treat. Res.* 43.35—44.2) and appeals to Rheginos: "Do not live in conformity with this flesh . . . but flee from the state of dispersion and bondage, and then you already have resurrection" (*Treat. Res.* 49.9-16).

Third, they reject resurrection of the body or the flesh in favor of a more spiritual understanding. *Gospel of Thomas* 71 may be a polemic against belief in Jesus' bodily resurrection: "Jesus said: 'I shall destroy [this] house and no one will be able to build it.' " In the gnostic revelation discourses the risen Lord appears not in bodily form but as a luminous presence (e.g., *Soph. Jes. Chr.* 91.10-13).

Though its basic thought patterns are undoubtedly gnostic, the *Treatise on Resurrection* does not reject the involvement of flesh in resurrection. A highly paradoxical passage seems to mean that physical flesh is not resurrected, but resurrection involves a transformed flesh: "You received flesh when you entered the world. Why will you not receive flesh when you ascend to the aeon? That which is better than the flesh is for it the cause of life" (*Treat. Res.* 47.5-10; see Donfried, 138-41). If it is "transformed flesh" of which the writer speaks, perhaps his thought is closer to Paul's idea of a transformed "spiritual body" than the orthodox insistence on the resurrection of the flesh of the present physical body. But, like other Gnostics, he lacks any sense of future corporate resurrection at the Parousia. The NT vision of the resurrection of all God's people at Christ's coming has been reinterpreted as resurrection as a present spiritual experience and a return at death to the heavenly world.

3. Conclusion.
After the NT, Christian thought about resurrection developed along two distinct trajectories. The orthodox trajectory saw Jesus' resurrection as the climax of his life, teaching and death, affirmed the literal resurrection of his flesh and looked forward to a future resurrection of the physical flesh of believers at the Parousia. The gnostic trajectory reinterpreted and created sayings of Jesus to convey hidden teaching, affirmed that resurrection is fundamentally already past in the true believer's experience and played down or rejected the bodily nature of resurrection. Both strands distort the fine balance in Paul's thought about resurrection, between the already and the not yet, and between continuity and discontinuity of the person between this life and the next.

See also ASCENSION; CHRISTOLOGY; CREATION, COSMOLOGY; ESCHATOLOGY; EXALTATION, ENTHRONEMENT; GLORY; HEAVEN, NEW HEAVEN.

BIBLIOGRAPHY. R. J. Bauckham, *The Climax of Prophecy: Studies on the Book of Revelation* (Edinburgh: T & T Clark, 1993); idem, *The Theology of the Book of Revelation* (NTT; Cambridge: Cambridge University Press, 1993); G. R. Beasley-Murray, *The Book of Revelation* (NCB; London: Marshall, Morgan & Scott, 1974); R. H. Charles, *A Critical and Exegetical Commentary on the Revelation of St. John* (2 vols.; ICC; Edinburgh: T & T Clark, 1920); B. E. Daley, *The Hope of the Early Church: A Handbook of Patristic Eschatology* (Cambridge: Cambridge University Press, 1991); W. J. Dalton, *Christ's Proclamation to the Spirits: A Study of 1 Peter 3:18—4:6* (Rome: Pontifical Biblical Institute, 1965); K. P. Donfried, *The Setting of Second Clement in Early Christianity* (NovTSup; Leiden: E. J. Brill, 1974); J. D. G. Dunn, *Christology in the Making* (London: SCM, 1980); M. J. Harris, *Raised Immortal: The Relation Between Resurrection and Immortality in New Testament Teaching* (Grand Rapids: Eerdmans, 1983); D. M. Hay, *Glory at the Right Hand: Psalm 110 in Early Christianity* (Nashville: Abingdon, 1973); J. W. Mealy, *After the Thousand Years: Resurrection and Judgment in Revelation 20* (Sheffield: Sheffield Academic Press, 1992); J. R. Michaels, 1 Peter (WBC; Waco, TX: Word, 1988); M. L. Peel, *The Epistle to Rheginos: A Valentinian Letter on the Resurrection* (London: SCM, 1969); P. Perkins, *The Gnostic Dialogue: The Early Church and the Crisis of Gnosticism* (New York: Paulist, 1980); idem, *Resurrection: New Testament Witness and Contemporary Reflection* (New York: Doubleday, 1984); D. Peterson, *Hebrews and Perfection* (SNTSMS 47; Cambridge: Cambridge University Press, 1982); J. M. Robinson, "Jesus: From Easter to Valentinus (or to the Apostles' Creed)," *JBL* 101 (1982) 5-37. S. H. Travis

REVEAL, REVELATION

Revelation signifies the unveiling or disclosure of that which is hidden or secret. In the NT it refers usually to the disclosure of divine things, which cannot be known apart from a divine act of revelation often attributed to the Spirit of God (*see* Holy Spirit).

1. Terminology
2. The Gospels and Paul
3. The Rest of the New Testament
4. Post-Apostolic Writers

1. Terminology.

1.1. The Terms Used. In the NT the idea of revelation is presented in two ways: by descriptions or associations of the making known of the divine counsel that transcend the meaning of single words and especially by the specific use of a number of terms that signify revelation. The focus on the later literature of the NT (Acts,* Hebrews,* the General Epistles and Revelation [*see* Revelation, Book of]) makes concentration on specific terms inevitable, though descriptions or associations will be also kept in view. Not all of these terms had religious significance in pre-NT times.

Apokalyptō since Herodotus has both the sense of "to uncover" (e.g., the head, Plutarch *Crassus* 6, cf. Herodotus 1.119; the breast, Plato *Protag.* 352a) as well as the secular sense of "to reveal" (e.g., rhetoric, Plato *Protag.* 352a; *Gorg.* 455d; 460a; one's mind, Plutarch *Alex.* 55; Diod. Sic. 17, 62. The religious sense of "to reveal" occurs first in the Septuagint; *apokalypsis* occurs in a nonreligious sense four times in the Septuagint (1 Kings and Sir) as well as in Philodemus *Vit.* 38 (first century B.C.) of the uncovering of the head and in its religious sense first in the NT.

Gnōrizō, "to make known," since Aeschylus and Sophocles does not occur in a religious sense before the Septuagint.

Dēloō, "to declare" or "to make manifest or clear," since Aeschylus and Sophocles occurs in the sense of "to reveal" (through dreams, Aeschylus *Pers.* 519, as well as of divine revelation, Sophocles *Oed. Tyr.* 77).

Epiphainō, "to show" or in the middle "to show oneself," since Herodotus (1.24) has also the religious sense of revelation by visions* or dreams (Herodotus 2.91; 3.27) and especially of the revelation of a deity (e.g., of Artemis, *Syll. Inscr. Graec.* 557.5 (third century B.C.).

Phaneroō since Herodotus has the secular sense of "to make or to be made known" (Dion. Hal. 10.37); the passive, "become famous" (Herodotus 6.122), occurs once in the Septuagint (in a defective text with unclear meaning, Jer 40:6). Its religious sense is witnessed first in the NT.

1.2. Definition of the Terms Used. In the NT *apokalyptō* (LXX: mainly for pi'el of *gālah:* "to unveil," "to uncover," "to disclose," "to reveal") implies the unveiling or uncovering of something objectively existing but unknown (e.g., a *mystērion*, Rom 16:25; Eph 3:3-5) or something that is hidden from sight (e.g., Mt 10:26; Lk 2:35; Jn 12:38; Rom 1:17-18), especially something that necessitates divine (i.e., the Holy Spirit's) activity for its disclosure (1 Cor 2:10-16).

Gnōrizō, (LXX: mostly for hiph'il/haph'el of *yada'*), or "make known" (e.g., Lk 2:15-20; Jn 15:15; 1 Cor 12:3; 15:1; Gal 1:11), is used especially of something unknowable by natural means but communicated by divine initiative (e.g., a *mystērion*, Eph 1:9).

Dēloō, (LXX: mainly for hiph'il of *yada'*), meaning "to make clear" or "to show," especially implies explanation or interpretation (1 Cor 1:11; Col 1:8). Occasionally it also indicates something verging on revelation (Heb 9:8; 2 Pet 1:14).

Epiphainō (LXX: mainly for hiph'il of *'ōr*) means "to let light come upon," "to let appear" or "to show" (Lk 1:79). The middle, "to appear" or "to show oneself" (*epiphaneia*, "appearance,"

esp. of the self-revelation of a divinity; e.g., 2 Thess 2:8; 2 Tim 1:10), emphasizes the outcome of the process of revelation (Tit 2:11: 3:4).

Phaneroō (LXX: only Jer 40 (33):6 for pi'el of *gālah)* means "to make visible," obvious, manifest, open, clear or known (e.g., Mk 4:22; Jn 3:21). The idea is that what once was invisible, unclear, in the dark has now become evident and can be apprehended. This may be in reference to the introduction of Jesus to Israel* (Jn 1:31); to the revelation of Jesus' glory* (Jn 2:11); to God's works (Jn 9:3), his name* (Jn 17:6) or his righteousness* (Rom 3:21); to the *mystērion* kept silent since ages past (Rom 16:25); or to the Christian life that is hidden in God (2 Cor 3:3; 4:10-12; Col 3:4; see also Warfield, 97-99; Bultmann *TDNT* 1:718; 2:61-62; Bultmann and Lührmann, 9:1-10).

However, once these terms have come to be used of the disclosure of God or of his counsel or of some of its details, it is practically impossible to distinguish neatly among them. Except for *epiphaneia* all the terms occur in our literature, though not all of them in the technical sense of revelation.

2. The Gospels and Paul.
In the Gospels and Paul the idea of revelation is the great presupposition and basis of the teaching of Jesus, encompassing not only his various acts making up his complex proclamation of the kingdom of God in word and deed (Mt 11:25-27 par. Lk 10:21-22 *[apokalyptō];* Jn 15:15 *[gnōrizō];* Jn 17:6 *[phaneroō]*) but also and especially his person (Mt 16:16-17; Lk 17:30 *[apokalyptō];* Jn 1:31; 2:11 *[phaneroō]*), who thus brings the revelation of God (cf. Jn 17:26) to its hitherto most complete expression (Jn 14:9).

In the Pauline corpus revelation is of central significance: the revelation of God's person as well as the whole complex of his salvific counsel. In Romans the two loci of God's revelation are heaven and the gospel. From heaven is revealed his wrath* and his righteous judgment (Rom 1:18—2:6), while in the gospel is revealed his righteousness (in the sense of salvific justifying grace, representing the whole Christ event; e.g., Rom 1:16-17; 3:21-26). The Pauline understanding of the revelation occurrence implies two conditions: revelation occurs when it is both given objectively by God and apprehended subjectively by people (Caragounis 1990, 23). These two conditions find an illustration in the contrast between Ephesians 1:9; 3:3, 5 *(apoka-lyptō)*, which refers to God's revelation of his *mystērion* to the apostles,* and Colossians 1:24-28; 4:4 *(phaneroō* = Eph 6:19, *gnōrizō)*, which refers to the apostles' revelation, the proclamation of it to the church* (Caragounis 1977, 102, esp. n. 24), thus enabling the church to apprehend the revelation.

3. The Rest of the New Testament.

In our literature the terms occur sparingly and without the rich variation found in the Pauline texts. Of the five books—Hebrews, 1 Peter,* 2 Peter,* 1 John (*see* John, Letters of) and Revelation—in which the idea of revelation figures through one or more of these terms, 1 Peter and 1 John are the most important. In these the idea of revelation is expressed chiefly by *apokalyptō* or *apokalypsis* and *phaneroō* respectively.

3.1. Acts. The book of Acts does not fully develop the concept of revelation with reference to God's eternal counsel. However, Acts abounds with echoes or hints of revelations, appearances or visions* by means of the Holy Spirit* or an angel.* These intimations of the divine will concern the Spirit's manifestations in the church of the end time through the fulfillment of the prophecy* from Joel (Acts 2:16-36); God's fulfillment of his old plan through the Christ event (Acts 3:13-26); the revelation of the risen Christ to Paul (Acts 9:3-7; 22:6-9; 26:13-16); the church's mission* strategy (Acts 13:1-2), as well as the guidance of the church or its leaders in the progress of the gospel (e.g., Philip* and the eunuch, Acts 8:26-29; Peter and Cornelius,* Acts 10:3-22); Agabus's prophecies about the famine (Acts 11:28) and Paul (Acts 21:11); the Spirit's guiding Paul to bypass certain parts of Asia Minor in order to reach Macedonia (Acts 16:6-10); the encouragement given to Paul in Corinth (Acts 18:9-10); the witness* of the Spirit to Paul that "prison and hardships are facing [him]" (Acts 20:23); and the salvation* of Paul's companions in the shipwreck, where *epiphainō* is used (Acts 27:20-24). Acts 14:17 and Acts 17:26-31, though not developing a natural theology (see Gärtner, esp. 73-83, 144-69; Caragounis 1990, 23-26 and the literature), imply an elementary witness to God's constant care of his creation.*

3.2. Hebrews. This letter develops no concept of revelation in the strict sense. However, the idea of revelation is implicit in God's communi-

cation of his will through the prophets and in particular through the Son* (Heb 1:1-2). The recipients' faith* and new life* in Christ, spoken of as an enlightenment (Heb 6:4), presuppose a revelation of some sort. The earthly counterparts of heavenly realities (Heb 9:23-26), as well as the law's* being a shadow of future reality (Heb 10:1-4), cannot be understood apart from the concept of revelation.

In addition, Hebrews uses the terms *dēloō* and *phaneroō* in the sense of "to indicate" and "to appear" or "to disclose." Thus at Hebrews 9:8 the entrance of the high priest into the holy of holies, once a year and never without blood, was the way that the Holy Spirit had chosen to indicate *(dēlountos)* that the way into the Most Holy Place had not yet been disclosed *(pephanerōsthai)* as long as the first tabernacle* was still standing. At Hebrews 9:26 *pephanerōtai* is used of Jesus' earthly appearance to offer himself as a sacrifice,* while at Hebrews 12:27 *dēloi* introduces an explanation of an OT phrase.

3.3. 1 Peter. Unlike the Pauline corpus, where these terms occur particularly about the revelation of God's purposes, a revelation that has already been effected through Christ and cover a wide spectrum of ideas, in 1 Peter the revelation is wholly eschatological,* or future, and relates primarily to the final salvation with one exception (1 Pet 1:20). In 1 Peter 1:5 those "born again" (*see* New Birth) are said to be watched over by God's power* through faith for the eschatological, definitive salvation, which is about to be revealed *(apokalyphthēnai)* in the last time. Thus, although salvation is understood also as a present event, it is above all an eschatological reality. It will come in its full force with the eschatological *apokalypsis* of Jesus Christ (1 Pet 1:7, 13), where again the multifaceted revelation of Christ as depicted in the Gospels and Paul is limited to the vindication of those saved and their entrance into their inheritance.

This same salvation had engaged the OT prophets intensely *(exēraunēsan, exezētēsan,* 1 Pet 1:10), who searched for the intended times indicated by the Spirit of Christ *(edēlou to en autois pneuma Christou).* To them was revealed *(apekalyphthē)* both the fact of Christ's salvific sufferings* and coming glory* as well as the time when these were to take place (1 Pet 1:11-12). This last passage goes counter to the so-called *Revelationsschema* as found in certain but not all Pauline texts (Bockmuehl 1990, 208-10), according to which the revelation through Christ was withheld from God's people of old. At 1 Peter 1:20 we approach the earlier *Revelationsschema* when it is said that Christ was chosen before the creation of the world but was revealed *(phanerōthentos)* at the end of time, referring again to his first advent. This ambivalence is found also in the Pauline corpus.

It appears that for this author the eschatological revelation of Christ in glory (1 Pet 4:12-14; 5:1) is set in sharp contrast to his protological coming in lowliness and his sufferings. In this connection it is worth noting that the protological appearance of Christ for the purpose of suffering, which is placed "in these last times," is expressed by *phanerōthentos* (1 Pet 1:20). This contrast has undoubtedly a paraenetic pastoral function assisting the recipients of this letter, whose perseverance (*see* Endurance) in the faith was put to hard test on account of persecution.* This is exemplified by the paraenesis to the presbyters to shepherd* the flock of God faithfully and thus be in a position to receive the unfading crown of glory at the appearing *(phanerōthentos)* of the chief Shepherd (1 Pet 5:4).

3.4. 2 Peter. This letter uses only *gnōrizō* and *dēloō*, once each. *Gnōrizō* occurs at 2 Peter 1:16, an ambiguous passage that refers to either the first or the Second Coming of Christ. The first alternative is supported by the context, which has the present Christian life in view, eschatology and the Second Coming not being taken up until 2 Peter 3:4. In addition *gnōrizō* in the NT is always used of making known past events, especially the kerygma* and the *mystērion* (it would thus correspond to Eph 6:19, *gnōrizō*, and Col 1:24-28; 4:4, *phaneroō*, never future, eschatological events. The other alternative, accepted by most commentators, has in its favor the fact that in the NT *parousia* is always used of the Second Coming, as at 2 Peter 3:4 (the delay of the Parousia,* Bauckham 1980, 19-28) — though 2 Peter 1:16 need not be interpreted in the light of 2 Peter 3:4, since the context in the latter passage is eschatological (it is used of the first coming by Ignatius,* Justin, and others). In this case the reference to the transfiguration may have paradigmatic significance, giving a hint of what the Second Coming will be like. The combination of *dynamis* and *parousia*, even if it is taken as a hendiadys (i.e., "his coming in power"), makes good sense of both comings of Christ. However this may be, the verb refers to the author's making known the power and coming of Christ through proclamation, not to any revelatory event.

At 2 Peter 1:14 the author's approaching death is said to have been made clear (*edēlōsen*) to him by Christ himself, but no further indication is given as to when or how this took place (see Bauckham 1983, 199-201). Almost certainly it does not imply a revelation in the strict sense.

3.5. 1 John. This letter contains only *phaneroō* and that no fewer than nine times. This word occurs another nine times in the Fourth Gospel, making it a well-nigh Johannine term (in the Pauline corpus it occurs twenty-two times). All but one of its nine occurrences refer to revelation, which relates both to the first and the second advent. 1 John, unlike Paul, is not concerned with the revelation of God's counsel but concretizes divine revelation in the Incarnation of the Logos (*see* Logos Christology) and the Second Coming. Revelation consists not in the disclosure of abstract truth* or even of the things that God has in store for his chosen ones but in the one act of God whereby his person, attributes and salvific intentions for humankind were made manifest through the manifestation of his Son.

Thus at the outset of his letter the author, emphasizing the reality of the Incarnation, states as an incontrovertible fact (here the polemic against heretical deniers of the Incarnation is obvious) that life was manifested (1 Jn 1:2). Though life here may not be quite equivalent to Jesus as the Logos, this life is said to have been with the Father (*pros ton patera;* cf. Jn 1:1, where a similar grammatical expression is used of the Logos), and the manifestation is connected with the earthly life of Jesus (e.g., *heōrakamen, epsēlaphēsan,* "we have seen," "they have handled," 1 Jn 1:1). This manifestation of the Son of God is related to two salvation-historical activities coming under the purview of the Incarnation: to take away our sins (1 Jn 3:5) and to destroy the works of the devil (1 Jn 3:8; *see* Satan). These concrete acts of God, leading to eternal life for humankind, are the best proof that the Incarnation and the earthly life of Jesus as well as his death make up the supreme manifestation of God's love* (1 Jn 4:9). God is revealed concretely through his acts.

The concreteness that revelation has for John, exemplified in the manifestation of Jesus in his first coming, leads him to speak in identical terms about Jesus' Second Coming. The recipients of this letter are exhorted to abide in him, so that when he appears *(phanerōthē)* at his Second Coming they may have confidence and not be ashamed at his Parousia (1 Jn 2:28). In the same vein, in describing the love of God that has raised them to the status of being his children, the author says that the character of their future existence has not yet been disclosed *(oupō ephanerōthē)*. However, his revelation *(ean phanerōthē)* at his Parousia will imply for them their total conformity to him (1 Jn 3:2).

At 1 John 2:19 the term *phanerōthōsin* occurs once in a nontechnical sense of the exposure of the real character of the heretics, who by leaving the community proved that they had never really belonged to it.

3.6. Revelation. In Revelation 1:1 the titular *apokalypsis* has assumed the technical sense of denoting a literary genre (having given its name to the apocalyptic* movement as well as its literature), though it also covers the contents of that book. In this book the heavenly curtain is lifted up and a vision of what is in store for the near future is shown to the servants (*see* Servant) of God (*ha dei genesthai en tachei,* "the things that must shortly take place"). "In this eschatological orientation and the related visionary apparatus the last book of the NT shows great affinity to the Jewish apocalyptic to which it has given its name. But it is closer to genuine prophecy and has more of the content of biblical revelation" (Oepke, 3:589). At Revelation 3:18 *phaneroō* is used in the nonreligious sense of the appearance (of nakedness), but at Revelation 15:4 it seems to have the sense of the disclosure of God's "sentence of condemnation" (BAGD).

It may be conceded that in the NT "the word-group is just in the process of attaining a firm religious content" and that the idea of revelation is influenced by Jewish apocalypticism (Holtz, 1:132). But that the idea of uncovering what has been there previously is retreating before an understanding according to which revelation unfolds as God acts in history seems to be only partly true. Even in Revelation 13:8 the Lamb,* which figures conspicuously in half of the chapters of this book, is described as slain from the creation of the world.

4. Postapostolic Writers.

In the early Christian writings the concept of revelation is put forward mainly by means of the terms referred to. Of these *apokalyptō* or *apokalypsis* occurs in *1 Clement* (once, in a quotation; *see* Clement of Rome), Ignatius (once), the *Martyrdom of Polycarp* (twice), the *Epistle to Diognetus* (twice) and the *Shepherd of Hermas** (thirty-three times). *Gnōrizō* occurs in the *Didache** (three times), the *Epistle of Barnabas** (twice), *Diognetus* (once) and *Hermas* (eleven times). *Phaneroō* or *phaneron* occurs in *1 Clement* (three times), *2 Clement* (four times), Ignatius (seven times), *Martyrdom of Polycarp* (three times), *Barnabas* (seventeen times), *Diognetus* (six times) and *Hermas* (eight times). All three terms are quite frequent in the later Pseudo-Clementine writings.

The conspicuous fact about these writings is that the idea of revelation of God's counsel or of Jesus' person has lost its NT content and has been reduced chiefly to visionary and apocalyptic experiences. Characteristically these terms do not refer to the counsel of God or to the Second Coming of Christ. The picture is, however, more varied than A. Oepke implies (3:591). Thus Ignatius speaks of God manifesting himself through Christ (Ign. *Magn.* 8.3; see also Ign. *Eph.* 19.3). *Diognetus* states that no man has ever seen God; he himself has manifested himself *(heauton epedeixen, Diogn.* 8.5), or Christ manifested himself as Son of God (*Barn.* 5.9), or the Logos manifested himself to the disciples (*Diogn.* 11.2), or God has revealed *(ephanerōsen)* the truth through his Son (*2 Clem.* 20.5), his goodness for our salvation (*Diogn.* 9.2) or what he has prepared from the beginning (*Diogn.* 8.11; 11.8).

One unusual example with cosmological interest is *1 Clement* 60.1. While the first coming of Christ is hinted at as a revelation in the flesh (*2 Clem.* 14.3; *Barn.* 6.7; 14.5; Ign. *Eph.* 19.2; *Herm. Sim.* 9.12.3), the nearest we come to his Second Coming is when Barnabas says, "For the Lord has made known *[egnōrisen]* to us through the prophets things past and things present and has given us the firstfruits of the taste of things future" (*Barn.* 1.7; see also *Barn.* 5.3) and *1 Clement* refers to the "visitation of Christ's kingdom" (*1 Clem.* 50.3).

For the rest, and this means the great majority of instances, revelation is used of visionary experiences and their interpretation (almost all of the examples from *Hermas* [more than fifty]), of personal directions (e.g., Ign. *Eph.* 20.2; Ign. *Rom.* 8.2; Ign. *Pol.* 2.2; *Mart. Pol.* 12.3; 14.2; 22.3) or the disclosure of various matters (e.g., *Barn.* 7.1, 3; 8.7; 11.1; 16.5; *Diogn.* 11.5). Even though Oepke's apposite conclusion with regard to Hermas—"Even the word 'apocalyptic' would be a little too exalted for these well-meaning but tepid outpourings of a limited soul" (3:591)—would not apply to the rest of these writings, all of these works have distanced themselves considerably from the NT center of gravity with regard to the concept of revelation.

The *Didache* uses *gnōrizō* three times in connection with the eucharistic prayer for God's making known "the Holy Vine of David, Thy Child," "life and knowledge" (or knowledge of life) and for "thy Holy Name . . . for the knowledge and faith and immortality which thou didst make known to us through thy child" (*Did.* 9.1—10.2).

See also APOCALYPTIC, APOCALYPTICISM; ESCHATOLOGY; GLORY; GNOSIS, GNOSTICISM; KNOWLEDGE; MYSTERY.

BIBLIOGRAPHY. R. J. Bauckham, "The Delay of the Parousia," *TynB* 31 (1980) 3-36; idem, *Jude, 2 Peter* (WBC; Dallas: Word, 1983); idem, *The Theology of the Book of Revelation* (NTT; Cambridge: Cambridge University Press, 1993); M. N. A. Bockmuehl, *Revelation and Mystery in Ancient Judaism and Pauline Christianity* (WUNT 2/38; Tübingen: J. C. B. Mohr, 1990); idem, "Das Verb *phaneroō* im Neuen Testament," *BZ* 32 (1988) 87-99; R. Bultmann, "The Concept of Revelation in the New Testament" in *Existence and Faith* (New York: Meridian, 1960) 58-91; idem, "δηλόω," *TDNT* 2:61-62; idem, "γινώσκω κτλ," *TDNT* 1:689-719; R. Bultmann and D. Lührmann, "φαίνω κτλ," *TDNT* 9:1-10; C. C. Caragounis, *The Ephesian Mysterion: Meaning and Content* (ConBNT 8; Lund: Gleerup, 1977); idem, "L'Universalisme moderne: Perspectives bibliques sur la révélation de Dieu," *Hokhma* 45 (1990) 17-45; B. Gärtner, *The Areopagus Speech and Natural Revelation* (ASNU 21; Uppsala and Lund: Gleerup, 1955); T. Holtz, "ἀποκαλύπτω," *EDNT* 1:130-32; A. Lindemann, *Die Aufhebung der Zeit: Geschichtsverständnis und Eschatologie im Epheserbrief* (Gütersloh: Gütersloher Verlagshaus Mohn, 1975); D. Lührmann, *Das Offenbarungsverständnis bei Paulus und in paulinischen Gemeinden* (WMANT 16; Neukirchen-Vluyn: Neukirchener Verlag, 1965); A. Oepke,

"καλύπτω κτλ," *TDNT* 3:556-92; B. B. Warfield, "The Biblical Idea of Revelation" in *The Inspiration and Authority of the Bible* (Philadelphia: Presbyterian and Reformed, 1948; repr. 1970); U. Wilckens, "Das Offensbarungsverständnis in der Geschichte des Urchristentums" in *Offenbarung als Geschichte,* ed. W. Pannenberg (Göttingen: Vandenhoeck & Ruprecht, 1961) 42-90.

C. C. Caragounis

REVELATION. *See* REVEAL, REVELATION.

REVELATION, BOOK OF

The Book of Revelation is acknowledged to be a closed book by the majority of modern readers. This is largely due to the unfamiliarity of the prophetic books in the OT, the almost total ignorance of Jewish apocalyptic writings and the historical setting of the book which determines its content. In this article we shall endeavor to clarify these features and so enable the message of the last book of the Bible to be grasped.

1. Genre
2. Date
3. Historical Situation
4. Content and Structure
5. Authorship
6. The Expectation of Antichrist
7. The Purpose of the Revelation
8. The Significance of the Revelation for Today
9. The Revelation in the Earliest Post-New Testament Writings

1. Genre.

1.1. Apocalypse. The book of Revelation is the only work of its kind in the NT, but there were many like it in the ancient world, written especially by Jews but later also by Christians. These were called apocalypses, which is a Greek term from the verb *apokalyptō,* meaning "to uncover," "to reveal" or "to disclose" what is hidden. The characteristic motive of such works was to keep alive the flame of faith in difficult times and to maintain hope in the coming of the Day of the Lord (*see* Day of the Lord) and of the kingdom of God (*see* Kingdom of God). Accordingly the apocalyptic* movement is commonly viewed as the child of prophecy.* Jewish apocalypses, however, were not entirely concerned with the eschatological* hope of their people, for they frequently contain descriptions of the heavens* and the earth and their inhabitants, including angelic* and demonic powers. Nevertheless it is the eschatology of the apocalyptic writings that is most commonly in mind when one speaks of apocalyptic literature.

The most notable example of apocalypse in the OT is the book of Daniel, which became the model for subsequent apocalyptic writings. Other prophetic works, however, contain features that are related to apocalyptic thought and mode of expression. Ezekiel, for example, is sometimes called "the father of apocalyptic." Many passages in Isaiah 40—55 anticipate the apocalyptic style and content, along with Isaiah 25—27 and Zechariah 9—14. All these and other passages from the OT prophets contain representations of the intervention of God* for the salvation* of his people.

The book of Revelation opens with the words, "The Revelation *(apokalypsis)* of Jesus Christ that God gave him." We cannot be certain as to whether John intended to describe his work as an apocalypse. Was he implying that this revelation,* given by God to Jesus (Rev 1:1-2), provided the definitive declaration of that which other writings of this kind sought to give? The nature of that which follows may be thought to justify it. If this admission is acknowledged, it would be of utmost importance in interpreting the language and symbolism of the book. Much of the teaching of Jesus is conveyed in parables; the book of Revelation employs parabolic pictures for setting forth its representation of the past, present and future of history. An understanding of the use of such parables in related literature is invaluable for their interpretation in John's apocalypse. The pictorial language of Jewish apocalypses is itself rooted in the OT, and in turn the authors of the OT used imagery familiar to the nations of the Middle East. John the prophet was evidently acquainted with all that background, for it is recognized by virtually all scholars that his work reflects a mind soaked in the OT, and his language is dominated by it. A knowledge of this background is a prerequisite for a right understanding of his book.

1.2. Prophecy. The second sentence of the Revelation reads, "Happy is the one who reads [to others] and they who listen to the words of the prophecy and keep the things that are written in it." It is evident that John is aware that he was commissioned by the Lord to write this prophecy and that he is numbered among the prophets of God. As such he will have realized that he stands in the succession of the prophets of the new covenant.* More than once this is mentioned in his book. The epilogue relates how John fell at the feet of the angel who had showed him the visions* he had seen in order to worship him, but this he was forbidden to do: "You must not do that! I am a fellow servant with you and your brothers the prophets, and those who keep the words of this book. Worship God" (Rev 22:8-9). In Revelation 19:10 the angel tells John, "I am a fellow servant with you and your brothers who hold the testimony of Jesus . . . for the testimony of Jesus is the Spirit of prophecy." That appears to mean that the Holy Spirit* who inspires prophecy enables prophets to bear witness to the revelation that Jesus brought and brings. It accords with the description of the content of the Revelation in its first sentence, where it is stated to be "witness to the word of God and the testimony of Jesus" (Rev 1:2). In light of these statements, indeed of the content of the entire book, we are to recognize that the Revelation is the work of the Spirit, who from Pentecost* on has enabled Christians to bear prophetic witness to "the word of God and the witness of Jesus." That witness includes God's word concerning his will for humankind in the present and in the future.

It is evident, accordingly, that John's work is not to be viewed either as an apocalypse or as a prophecy, as though those terms were mutually exclusive; rather one should acknowledge that it has the features of both; that is, his work is to be defined as an apocalyptic prophecy and/or a prophetic apocalypse.

1.3. Letter. After the first paragraph John greets his readers in the conventional manner of one writing a letter* (Rev 1:4-5). Correspondingly he concludes the prophecy with a benediction such as is normal in the NT epistles (Rev 22:21). Moreover John was commanded to write what he was about to see and to send the work to seven churches* in the Roman province of Asia (Rev 1:11). All these churches have a short letter addressed to them. The latter always includes the exhortation, "Let anyone who has an ear listen to what the Spirit is saying to the churches" (e.g., Rev 2:11).

It is clear that the seven letters were intended for the benefit of all the seven churches addressed. Significantly the cities in which the seven churches were located were centers of civic administration and of postal distribution in their areas. It was therefore possible for copies of the whole prophecy to be dispatched to churches in other cities of the province. NT letters were clearly intended to be read to gathered congregations; the same applies to the entire book of Revelation, as is clear from the beatitude in Revelation 1:3 and from the epilogue in Revelation 22:6-21. If then the book of Revelation was a letter to the churches of Roman Asia, it is manifest that it was addressed to their situations.

In this respect Revelation stands in contrast to the opening paragraph of *1 Enoch,* which states that what the prophet saw was "not for this generation, but for a remote one which is to come." The situations and needs of the churches to which John wrote were as truly in John's mind as the situations and needs of the churches to which Paul and other Christian leaders wrote. The recognition of this fact has important consequences for the interpretation of the whole work. The prophet was bidden to write to the churches of Roman Asia in view of events that were developing in their time and to prepare them for their future. Just as the rest of the letters in the NT require the circumstances of the churches to which they were addressed to be known for understanding their content, so it is with the book of Revelation. Failure to grasp this fact has led innumerable readers to misinterpret the book by identifying the figures and events described in it with persons and events of their own times. Such misunderstanding is corrected by every effort to perceive the situation addressed in the book and its message for those living in it and for all subsequent generations.

1.4. Liturgy. Not a few books in the NT reflect liturgical elements in them (*see* Liturgical Elements), especially prayers* and hymns* and confessions of faith (*see* Creeds). One thinks of Ephesians 1 and the prayer of Ephesians 3:14-21; the christological* hymn in Philippians 2:6-11 and that in Colossians 1:15-20; the short snatch of a hymn in Ephesians 5:14 (all thought by some scholars to have been composed for the celebration of baptism*) and the various "faithful sayings" of the Pastoral Epistles. The book of Revelation has more such songs scattered through its pages than does any other writing in the NT. Their substance and contexts led M. H. Shepherd to suggest that the early paschal lit-

urgy of the churches formed the model for the Revelation. This interpretation has not found acceptance by most scholars, but the presence of liturgical forms in so many sections of the book is important; their combination with other liturgical forms should be acknowledged.

1.5. Drama. In the Greek tradition, worship* and drama are closely linked. The presence of the many hymns in the book of Revelation has encouraged some interpreters to see in the book a drama of the end time. J. G. Bowman observed that the book is made up of seven acts and seven scenes. The hymns have a similar function to the choruses in Greek drama: they throw light on the visions of the book. This E. Schüssler Fiorenza acknowledges: "They [the hymns of Revelation] function in the same way as the chorus in Greek drama, preparing and commenting upon the dramatic movements of the plot"; but she asserts that the Revelation is not a drama (Schüssler Fiorenza, 166), and with this most concur while readily admitting that the book is a remarkably dramatic work.

2. Date.

Two chief possibilities as to the time of writing the Revelation have been and still are maintained by scholars, namely, either in the turbulent period shortly after the death of Nero (A.D. 68-69) or toward the end of Domitian's reign, about A.D. 95.

The former view is held on the basis of the likelihood that John had endured the fearful persecution* of Christians by Nero and also because there is no clear reference in the book to the destruction of Jerusalem* in A.D. 70. If Revelation 11:1-2 is interpreted literally, it can indicate that Jerusalem had been under prolonged attack and that the altar and outer court of the temple* either had been seized or could not be kept from the Roman forces, whereas the sanctuary itself continued to be preserved by God.

In the latter chapters of the book Rome is called "Babylon" (see Rev 14:8; 16:19; 17:5; 18:2, 10, 21). The most probable reason for giving the name *Babylon* to Rome was that as Nebuchadnezzar, king of Babylon, had destroyed Jerusalem in 586 B.C. so Rome had done in recent times. The dirge over Babylon* in Revelation 18 views the current tyrant city as another Babylon. The apocalypses 4 Ezra and *2 Baruch* were written at the end of the first century of the Christian era and also gave the name of Babylon to Rome for the same reason.

In Revelation 13:3 (cf. Rev 13:14) it is stated that one of the heads of the "beast,"* the antichrist,* had received a deadly wound, but he lived again and was empowered by Satan* to rule the empire (cf. Rev 17:8). This appears to refer to the contemporary belief that the wounded "head" was Nero and that he had not been killed, whether by himself or another, but had escaped and would return to rule the empire (see Roman Empire). Revelation 17 has a developed form of this notion and represents the belief that the Beast Nero had risen from the dead and would come with a confederate army from the East and destroy "Babylon the Great." This expectation would require a later date than the death of Nero.

The majority opinion as to the date of Revelation is that of Irenaeus, who wrote concerning the book, "That was seen no very long time since, but almost in our own day, toward the end of Domitian's reign" (Irenaeus *Haer.* 5.30.3). Eusebius cited this judgment with approval (Eusebius *Hist. Eccl.* 3.18-20; 5.8.6). This assessment of the date of Revelation suits other evidence of the character and contents of the book, above all the delineation of the antichrist as another Nero.

The explanation in Revelation 17:9-11 as to the meaning of the seven heads of the beast has been investigated with a view to determining the date of the Revelation, but in vain. Two meanings are given in the text, the one identifying the seven heads with the seven hills of Rome, the other representing seven emperors. Both explanations are secondary, since they are applications to a contemporary situation of an ancient myth or saga of the seven-headed monster of the deep who opposed the powers of heaven. The list of emperors up to Domitian is Julius Caesar, Augustus, Tiberius, Gaius, Claudius, Nero, Galba, Otho, Vitellius, Vespasian, Titus, Domitian—twelve in all. Of these John states that five have fallen, one is (the sixth), one is to come (for a short time only), the eighth is one of the seven and will be the antichrist. Starting from Julius Caesar, John would be writing in Nero's reign, but the difficulties discussed remain. The simplest solution is to assume that the "five" that have "fallen" represent the majority, the sixth is the reigning emperor, Domitian; the seventh will reign for a short time and the antichrist will follow.

3. Historical Situation.

3.1. The Imperial Cult in Roman Asia. It is imperative to bear in mind that the churches for which Revelation was written were situated in the province of Roman Asia and that the emperor* cult (i.e., the worship of the emperor) was enthusiastically adopted in that area, possibly more than elsewhere in the Roman Empire. L. L. Thompson pointed out that the imperial cult had its high point in the reign of Augustus: "Language praising him is lofty and is similar to that offered to the gods" (Thompson, 159). All the cities of the seven churches had the worship of the emperor in their midst. In many cities annual festivals were held, especially on the emperor's birthday, and such festivals were supported by people from all walks of life. Thompson, however, urges that the importance of the worship of the emperor for the early Christians should not be exaggerated. In his view the greater issue revolved around Christians' relation to adherents of traditional religious cults rather than their relation to the cult of the emperor, for sacrifices were made in connection with them also (see Religions, Greco-Roman).

Domitian, in whose reign the Revelation is believed to have been written, has had the reputation of being a monster, who carried to an extreme the imperial cult. He is said to have erected an immense number of statues of himself, demanded that he be addressed as "our Lord and God" (*dominus et deus*) and embarked on a vicious persecution of the churches. Thompson has investigated the truth of these claims and come to the conclusion that they are false. The portrait of Domitian was drawn a few years after his death by a circle of writers around Pliny the Younger, which included Tacitus, Dio Chrysostom and Suetonius. After Domitian's assassination Nerva became emperor, but his reign lasted only two years (A.D. 96-98). He was succeeded by Trajan, who recognized his need of writers and orators who could promote his ideas. He found them in Pliny and his friends. They pursued a common policy of exalting Trajan by contrasting him with Domitian. Pliny, for example, wrote of the pleasure of being appointed consul during September, a month of triple rejoicing "which saw the removal of the worst of emperors [Domitian], the accession of the best [Nerva] and the birth of one even better than the best" (i.e., Trajan; see Pliny *Panegyr.* 92.4).

On this procedure Thompson comments: "Propagandists for a new age have to sharpen both edges of their two-edged sword; both the ideal present and the evil past have to be exaggerated" (Thompson, 115). Contrary to the claim that Domitian demanded to be addressed as "our Lord and God," Statius reports that when Domitian was acclaimed as *Dominus* at one of his Saturnalia he forbade those who did so to address him in this manner (Statius *Silvae* 1.6, 81-84). There are no references to Domitian as *dominus et deus* on any inscriptions, coins or medallions from the Domitianic era. Certainly there were people who referred to Domitian as *dominus et deus,* but Thompson urged that one must reckon with popular opportunism among those seeking benefits from the emperor (Thompson, 105-6).

If Thompson has made a strong case for clearing Domitian's name as a monster obsessed with his inherited divinity, with others he has underestimated the threat of the emperor cult to the churches and instead has imputed to John the prophet an obsession with Jewish apocalyptic. While recognizing that apocalyptic writings have frequently been due to crises precipitated by persecution, Thompson denies that such action of governing authorities in Roman Asia existed in John's day. He cites the concept of "perceived crisis" put forward by J. J. Collins: that is, the apocalyptist sees in the situation in which he lives a crisis that is nonexistent but is "perceived" through interpreting his situation from the viewpoint of apocalyptic beliefs (Collins, 2-8). Far from being an objective analysis of society at that time, Thompson affirms, "First century Roman life was . . . one of the most integrated, peaceful, meaningful periods of history for most of those who lived in the empire. This confusion of a particular social location with society as a whole is not uncommon in the study of early Christianity" (Thompson, 237 n. 10).

When one bears in mind that Roman society was dependent on sixty million slaves,* many whose life of slavery was largely due to conquest of their countries by Rome's armies, the compulsion of many male slaves to become gladiators for the entertainment of crowds in the amphitheaters and female slaves to become prostitutes, such a statement is beyond compre-

hension. John the prophet refers to these in his doom-song over the fall of Babylon as he concludes his list of the trades of the city with the words, "cattle and sheep, horses and chariots and bodies and souls of men" (Rev 18:13). He was no small-minded man, limited to an isolated congregation in a restricted area. He exercised an influential ministry over a group of churches in what was probably the most Christianized area of the Roman Empire in the late first century A.D. He was in a position to know what happens when emperors take measures against subjects whose conscience* forbids them to acknowledge his divinity; for example, the action of Antiochus Epiphanes to compel the Jews to forsake their own religion and adopt that of the rest of his domain, including sacrificing to himself as the representative of Zeus; Caligula's attempt to set his own statue in the temple of Jerusalem and the panic caused by that among the Jews of Jerusalem; and the appalling cruelty of Nero in his persecution of Christians in Rome during John's own lifetime.

Certainly John knew the teaching of the book of Daniel and its attitude to rulers who claimed to be not only divine but above the gods. Not that he interpreted the reigning emperor as holding that notion of himself, but it is evident that he saw in the enthusiastic pursuit of the emperor cult a preparation for the emergence of an antichrist who would not only declare war on the church but, astonishingly, destroy the empire itself (see Rev 17:12-17).

3.2. Persecution. Earlier beliefs that Domitian had already begun a severe persecution of the church are not borne out by the Revelation itself. References such as Revelation 2:10 and Revelation 2:13 indicate a present hostility toward Christians but speak of a future increase of such opposition. Nevertheless, the fact that John had been removed to Patmos is evidence that the governing authorities in Roman Asia were taking action against the Christian church. John had been banished to Patmos because of his powerful ministry* of the word of God and witness* of Jesus and therefore was viewed by the authorities as a dangerous leader of the Christian sect. His perception of the nature of the imperial cult accordingly was conditioned by his experience, not his prejudice.

4. Content and Structure.

4.1. Introduction (Rev 1). The opening chapter forms an introduction to the book, with a prologue (Rev 1:1-8) and a vision of the risen Christ* given to the prophet John (Rev 1:9-20). The former makes known the origin and nature of the book, pronounces the first of seven beatitudes in the work on its readers and hearers, gives a greeting from the triune God, a doxology to Christ and two prophetic sayings stating the theme of the book. The vision that follows contains a commission to John to write what he sees to seven churches in Roman Asia. The description of the risen Lord echoes that of the Ancient of Days in Daniel 7:9 and the powerful angel in Daniel 10:5-62.

4.2. Letters to Seven Churches (Rev 2—3). A series of seven letters to the churches named in Revelation 1:11 is given in Revelation 2—3. They are very brief, reminding us of the eight short oracles of Amos 1—2. The letters have an identical structure: an introductory statement from the risen Christ, drawn from the opening vision and usually pertinent to the contents of the letter; praise for the good qualities of the church and/or criticism of its faults; a promise* to the victor relating to the blessings* to be bestowed in the kingdom of Christ; and an exhortation to listen to what the spirit is saying to the churches.

4.3. Vision of the Heavenly Throne Room (Rev 4—5). As the vision of Christ in Revelation 1 leads into the seven letters, so the vision of heaven in Revelation 4—5 leads into the main body of the Revelation. It initiates the process of events leading to the unveiling of the final kingdom of God (Rev 6—19) and at the same time determines the symbolism of the first series of messianic judgments* (Rev 6:1—8:5).

4.4. Seals, Trumpets and Bowls (Rev 6—16). At this point we have to make a decision on how to interpret the relation of the three series of judgments that dominate the major part of the Revelation (Rev 6:1—19:10), portrayed under the symbolism of the opening of seven seals* of the document in God's hands (Rev 6:1—8:5), the sounding of the seven trumpets* (Rev 8:6—11:19) and the outpouring of seven bowls* of wrath (Rev 15—16). These three series of judgments in Revelation have been interpreted as following in chronological sequence (see, e.g., Charles, 1:xxiii; Farrer 1964, 9-23; Court, 74-75; Rowland, 416).

There is, however, one major feature of the three series of judgments that makes this inter-

pretation difficult to accept: each of the three series concludes with a description of the Day of the Lord, which leads to a revelation of the final kingdom of God. The first series of judgments is closely paralleled with features of the eschatological discourse of Mark 13, although ostensibly it employs the imagery of four riders on horses, adapted from Zechariah 1 and 6. The fifth seal reveals the cry of martyrs beneath the throne of God, "How long?" but the sixth seal brings the judgments to a climax as it tells of a great earthquake, the sun becoming black as sackcloth, the moon as blood, the stars falling to earth, the sky vanishing like a rolled up scroll, and every island and mountain removing from its place. The kings and the mighty call on the rocks of the mountains to fall on them and hide them from the face of God and the wrath* of the Lamb,* "for the great day of their wrath has come, and who is able to stand?" The passage is made up of citations from OT prophetic descriptions of the Day of the Lord (e.g., Is 13:10, 13; 34:4; Zeph 1:14-15), the meaning of which is not the destruction of the universe but a pictorial representation of the terror of the universe when the God of heaven steps forth to judge the world (cf. the last judgment scene, Rev 20:11).

In Revelation 6:12-20 the end of the rebellion of humankind in history has been reached, and with the opening of the seventh seal in Revelation 8:1-5 the prayers of the martyrs beneath the throne of God and of the saints on earth are answered, and the accompaniments of the coming of Christ in his kingdom take place (with Rev 8:5 cf. Rev 11:19; 16:17-18).

The judgments of the seven trumpets are described in a similar fashion as those at the opening of the seven seals: the judgments of the first four trumpets are adaptations of those on Egypt at the exodus; they are followed by the announcement of three woes to come on earth, but the third woe is withheld until later, and instead a song of triumph that celebrates the consummation of the kingdom of God is sung in Revelation 11:15-18:

"The kingdom of the world has become
  the kingdom of our Lord and of his Christ,
 and he will reign for ever and ever."
The twenty-four elders then fall on their faces and worship God:
"We give you thanks, Lord God Almighty,
 who is and who was,

for you have taken your great power
and begun your reign."

Observe that whereas the elders in Revelation 4:8 sing to him "who was, and who is, and who is to come," they now sing of him "who was, and who is," for God has come, and his reign of ultimate salvation in the fulfilled kingdom of God has begun.

The same goal has evidently been reached on the completion of the outpouring of the seven bowls of wrath. A voice from the temple and the throne proclaims "It is done" (Rev 16:17; cf. Rev 21:6, where the cry signifies that the completion of God's purpose in creation has arrived). It would appear that with the end of each series of messianic judgments, the end of history that precedes the triumph of the kingdom of God has also arrived. A corollary of this element of parallelism is that the period of divine judgments is not elongated into an interminable series of punishments but is a comparatively short period of intensified judgments executed by the Lord of history.

It is, however, important to note that John has linked the three series by a technique that has been variously described as "overlapping or interweaving" (Bauckham 1994, 8-9), "interlocking" (A. Y. Collins 1976, 16-18), "intercalation" (Schüssler Fiorenza, 172-73). Between the silence in heaven and the offering of prayers to God for the kingdom's coming the seven angels who are to sound the trumpets are introduced (Rev 8:1-5). After the sounding of the seventh trumpet the opening of the temple of God in heaven is mentioned, and thereby the ark of the covenant is seen (Rev 11:19). Similarly Revelation 15:5-6 tells of the opening of the temple of the tent of witness in heaven out of which proceed the angels with the seven last plagues, so bridging the extensive gap of Revelation 12-14 (Bauckham 1994, 8-9). By this method of repetition and development John builds up to the advent of Christ in an awe-inspiring climax.

4.5. Interludes: Glimpses of the Church and Its Conflicts (Rev 7; 10:1—11:13; 12—14). Between the three descriptions of the messianic judgments are set episodes that throw light on what happens to the church during the period of tribulation* and also the nature of its task.

In Revelation 7, between the opening of the sixth and seventh seals, occur two visions, the first of which recounts the sealing of God's people for protection in the time of trial (cf.

Ezek 9:1-11), the second giving a proleptic description of their joy* in the final kingdom of God. Likewise between the sixth and seventh trumpets a more extensive interlude takes place in which John is confirmed in his prophetic ministry (Rev 10), and an oracle reveals the church's vocation to carry out a powerful prophetic witness expected of Elijah and Moses* in the last days (Rev 11:1-13). Revelation 12—14 provide the longest interruption in the judgment visions; these chapters set the opposition between the emperor worship and the church in the context of the age-long conflict between the powers of darkness (*see* Light) and the God of heaven.

4.6. The City of Antichrist and the City of God (Rev 17:1—22:5). One would have expected that after completing the description of the messianic judgments John would portray at once the coming of the Christ and his kingdom. Instead he reveals the doom of the antichristian empire as it falls prey to its own forces of destruction (Rev 17—18) and the praise of God's people and heaven's hosts over it (Rev 19:1-10). Then John is free to describe the coming of Jesus to defeat the enemies of God by his all-powerful word (Rev 19:11—21:3), the kingdom of Christ in the world (Rev 20:4-6), the last vain attempt of Satan to overthrow that kingdom (Rev 20:7-10), the last judgment of the human race (Rev 20:11-15), the new heaven and earth (Rev 21:1-8) and the city of God, the new Jerusalem (Rev 21:9—22:5).

It is important to observe that, strictly speaking, the story of salvation, the new exodus, ends at Revelation 21:8 with its depiction of the new creation.* The description of the city of God, the bride of the Lamb, is given in a deliberate contrast to the antichristian city described in Revelation 17. The book of Revelation reaches its climax as the story of the harlot and the bride. It is in truth a tale of two cities!

4.7. Epilogue (Rev 22:6-21). The concluding paragraphs of the Revelation sum up and press home on the conscience of the readers and hearers the practical lessons of the book. It primarily emphasizes the authenticity of the book as a true revelation from God and the nearness of the fulfillment of its message.

5. Authorship.

The author makes himself known in the first sentence of the Revelation as "his [God's] slave,

John." The use of that term *slave* jolts the modern reader, as it did the translators of the King James (Authorized) Version, for although the term frequently appears in the original languages of both Testaments, it occurs once only in the KJV OT (Jer 2:14) and once in the KJV NT (Rev 18:13). Paul began his letter to the Romans, "Paul, a slave of Christ Jesus, called to be an apostle." John wrote in the same way, but whereas he often refers to himself in his book, he never speaks of himself as an apostle* (contrast 1 Cor 1:1; 2 Cor 1:1; Gal 1:1; Eph 1:1; Col 1:1).

From the latter part of the second century it was assumed that the Fourth Gospel, the letters of John (*see* John, Letters of) and the book of Revelation were all written by John the son of Zebedee. Nevertheless, from early times it was recognized that there are difficulties in that assumption, notably with respect to the differences between the Revelation and the Gospel. The issues were clearly stated by Dionysius, bishop of Alexandria in the third century. He had been disturbed by the spread of millennial teaching in his diocese and wished to discourage it. He therefore sought to establish first that the Revelation is not to be interpreted literally and then to demonstrate that the book could not have been written by John the apostle. He adduced three reasons for the latter position.

First, the author did not claim to be the Beloved Disciple, or brother of James, or an eyewitness and hearer of the Lord, as John the Evangelist did; many Christians had the name John, and there were two Christian leaders of that name in Roman Asia and two tombs in Ephesus that were acclaimed to be the tomb of John.

Second, there are many contacts of thought between the Gospel and letters of John, but the Revelation is utterly different from both: "It scarcely, so to speak, has a syllable in common with them."

Third, the style of the Gospel and letters is different from that of the Revelation; the former are written in excellent Greek, but the latter is often ungrammatical and uses barbarous idioms.

While Dionysius has been applauded for his insight in the critical evaluation of the Revelation, the issues are much more complicated than he realized. That he was right on the last point there is no doubt: John does break rules of Greek grammar frequently but not always through lack of knowledge; it has been said that for every solecism in Revelation there is an example of correct linguistic usage (note, e.g., John's refusal to decline the divine name after a preposition in Rev 1:4, immediately followed by the correct use in relation to the seven spirits before God's throne). It is now generally recognized that behind the Revelation is the mind of a Semitic author, one whose native language is Hebrew or Aramaic, but how that relates to the style and language of the book is uncertain.

R. H. Charles held that John thought in Hebrew and wrote in Greek (Charles, 1:cxliii). H. H. Rowley maintained that John's first language was Aramaic and that he thought in Aramaic as he wrote in Greek (a view he communicated in a letter to this author). C. C. Torrey affirmed that John wrote his book in Aramaic and someone else translated it into Greek very literally out of reverence for the master (Torrey, 158). If Torrey's view were adopted, it would complicate discussion on the linguistic differences between the language and style of the Gospel and the Revelation. Ironically, however, C. F. Burney wrote a book entitled *The Aramaic Origin of the Fourth Gospel* (Oxford: Oxford University Press, 1922) to demonstrate that the Gospel of John was written in Aramaic and later translated into Greek! It will be appreciated that recent scholars are wary of accepting that whole books of the NT were originally written in Aramaic and translated into Greek. In this case the argument has reached stalemate.

Dionysius's statement that Revelation has scarcely a syllable in common with the Gospel and letters of John is an exaggeration. Part of the problem of determining the relation between the Gospel and the Revelation is precisely their differences and likenesses. Both works alone, for example, use the term *logos* (the "Word") of Christ, both see in the Lamb of God a coalescence of the concept of the apocalyptic Warrior Lamb and the Passover Lamb (see Beasley-Murray 1978, 124-26; and 1986, 24-25, 354-55). Moreover the terms for witness, life, death, thirst, hunger and conquer in a spiritual or moral sense occur so frequently in the Gospel and the Revelation as to suggest a positive relationship in the area of soteriology between the two works.

Yet these two books almost uniquely express

the minds and personalities of two authors. Their works were composed with utmost care and in a peculiarly intricate manner. It is increasingly agreed that the Fourth Gospel contains material that not only has been thought over carefully but also has been preached a great deal through the years, and it displays a first-hand knowledge of rabbinic thought and Greek philosophical theology. The Revelation comes from a mind imbued with the OT but also reflects a first-hand knowledge of apocalyptic literature, so that John finds it natural to express himself in this mode of writing.

How then are we to account for the relationships between the two works? Their authors must have been well acquainted. Of late the postulate of a school of John has been put forward to explain the origin of the Johannine writings, which is a highly plausible hypothesis (see esp. Culpepper). There is, however, a further feature about this problem: it never occurred to Dionysius that the son of Zebedee may have been John the prophet and not the author of the Gospel.

H. B. Swete, in his discussion on the authorship of Revelation, was impressed with the kinship between the character of John the apostle as he appears in the Synoptic Gospels and what one would expect of John the prophet. He and his brother James were named by Jesus "Boanerges," that is, "Sons of Thunder" (Mk 3:17); John forbade one who was not a member of the apostolic group to cast out demons in the name of Jesus; he wanted to call down fire from heaven on Samaritans who would not give Jesus and his disciples hospitality* (Lk 9:52-55); he was a witness of the transfiguration of Jesus and of his resurrection.* Swete therefore was inclined to view John the apostle as the author of the Revelation and to divorce the problem from that of the authorship of the Fourth Gospel, but he wished to keep an open mind on the issue (Swete, clxxx-clxxxv).

M. Kiddle, forty years later, adopted a similar attitude and stated, "The authorship of the Revelation may prove to be the one mystery of the book which will never be revealed in this world" (Kiddle, xxxvi). W. G. Kümmel, yet another generation after Kiddle, wrote, "We know nothing more about the author of the Apocalypse other than that he was a Jewish Christian prophet by the name of John" (Kümmel, 331). Do we need to know more? In no other book of

the Bible is the identity of the author of so little importance, for it is not, as earlier editions of the Bible had it, "The Revelation of St. John the Divine," but the revelation of Jesus Christ to his servant John. The question of authorship is settled not by the name of the person who received the Revelation and wrote it down but by the nature of the work, which in the providence of God completes the canon* of the Scriptures as its crown.

6. The Expectation of Antichrist.

We have already observed the connection between the emperor cult and the anticipation of the appearance of an antichrist who shall rule not only the empire but also the world. This expectation dominates Revelation 12—14 and Revelation 16—17, passages in which the apocalyptic style reaches its height in the Revelation. The imagery of a woman clothed with the sun, with the moon beneath her feet and twelve stars above her head, and a dragon in the sky that throws a third of the stars down to earth clearly reflects ancient sources. These were known not only to writers of the OT but also to all the nations of the Middle East and were utilized in many ways. Common to all of them was the concept of a monster of the sea who fought the gods of heaven and sought to overthrow them. The imagery is clear in such a passage as Isaiah 27:1: "The Lord with his cruel and great sword will punish Leviathan the fleeing serpent, Leviathan the twisting serpent, and he will kill the dragon that is in the sea." The vision of the world empires in Daniel 7 that are symbolized by beasts that emerge from the sea, culminating in a fearful adversary of God and man, is an application of that same imagery to a contemporary tyrant who not only oppressed God's people but also sought world domination.

This symbolism was applied frequently in the OT as a cartoon for oppressive rulers, all of whom were doomed to be overcome by Israel's God, the Lord of heaven and earth. That cartoon was applied by the prophet John to the awaited antichrist emperor. It must be emphasized, however, that John did not look upon the reigning emperor as the antichrist; rather he viewed the emperor cult as preparing the way for an antichrist who would exploit it to the full, in a comparable manner as Paul in 2 Thessalonians 2:7 spoke of "the mystery of lawlessness" as already at work in the world. More precisely,

John applied the dragon symbol to Satan (Rev 12), to the antichrist (Rev 13) and to the city and empire over which he ruled (Rev 17).

But John goes further in that he conjoins the antichrist concept with the contemporary expectation of the return of Nero to Rome. This is seen first in his description of the antichrist as smitten by a deadly wound and coming to life after it (Rev 13:3), secondly by Revelation 13:18: "Let anyone with understanding calculate the number of the beast, for it is the number of a person. Its number is 666." The possibility of representing a name by a number lies in the fact that Hebrew and Greek did not have separate signs for numbers but used instead letters of the alphabet, so that "a" = 1, "b" = 2, "c" = 3, and so on. On this basis any name could be calculated by adding up the values of its letters. A. Deissmann, for example, cites a graffito on a wall in Pompeii reading, "I love her whose name is 545" (Deissmann, 275).

Through the centuries many names that add up to 666 have been suggested as the answer to the puzzle set by John, but in recent years a large measure of agreement has arisen that the name John had in mind is Nero Caesar in Hebrew. If one asks how Greek-speaking congregations could have known that, the answer is that it almost certainly arose among Hebrew- and Aramaic-speaking Jews; they had no reason to love Nero (the Roman-Jewish war began in his reign), and it would have become common knowledge among the churches, just as *Abba* and *Maranatha* became known among them all. Confirmation of this is found in an alternative reading of Revelation 13:18 in some manuscripts; that is, 616, which is the Hebrew number of the Latin form of Nero. By contrast it was early known among Christians that the name Jesus in Greek totals 888, which represents an advance upon perfection (777), as the antichrist shows a consistent falling below it. That indicates that the antichrist of Satan falls as far short of being the deliverer of humanity as the Christ of God exceeds all the hopes of humanity for a redeemer.

As to the historic Nero, Suetonius reported that when Nero learned that the Roman senate had proclaimed him a public enemy and troops were on their way to capture him, he committed suicide by slitting his throat and was buried in the tomb of his family (Suetonius *Nero* 49-50). This lack of a public burial for Nero led to widespread doubt that he really had died and contributed to the supposition that he had fled to the East. No fewer than three claimants to be Nero rose in subsequent years, one in the year following his death (A.D. 69), the second in A.D. 80 and the third in A.D. 88-89; this last one almost convinced the king of Parthia that he was Nero and nearly led to an invasion of the Roman Empire. Whereas earlier it was often supposed that Nero was still alive, a generation later it was thought that he had risen from the dead and would return to take vengeance on Rome. That is so expressed in the third, fourth and fifth books of the *Sibylline Oracles*.

John made use of this widespread expectation. In Revelation 13:3 he wrote that one of the beast's seven heads "was as it were slaughtered to death," a peculiar way of stating it, "and its deadly wound was healed." This is a reminiscence of Revelation 5:6, where the Lamb is described as "standing as it were slaughtered." The Christ of Satan is plainly a parody of the Christ of God, in this as in all other respects (see Rissi 1966, 66). The adaptation of the Nero anticipation to the coming antichrist appears again in Revelation 17:7-18 but with a different emphasis, in that the beast represents both the empire and the antichrist. On the one hand the beast on which the woman sits "was, and is not, and is to ascend from the abyss and go off to destruction" (Rev 17:8) and on the other hand it is said, "The beast who was and is not is the eighth [head], and is of the seven, and he goes off to destruction."

In light of Revelation 13 the eighth king is plainly Nero, in whom the nature and the destiny of the antichristian empire were embodied. Both share in the likeness of the dragon (Satan), both oppose the Lord in his people, both belong to the "abyss" (*see* Hell, Abyss) and both are doomed to suffer the fate of those who make war on the Lamb (Rev 16:14). But one major difference is apparent in the representations of the antichrist in Revelation 13 and Revelation 17: in the former the empire receives a boost from the antichrist, so that all in the world, apart from those whose names are written in the Lamb's book of life, receive the mark of the beast and worship him (Rev 13:8, 16-18). In Revelation 17 the fears of many are fulfilled, and the Christ of Satan persuades the kings of the East to join him in attacking "Babylon the Great," and the city is destroyed and burned with fire (Rev 17:15-17). Such is the outcome of the emperor cult. The beast and his allies remain in the hand of the God they defy, and by the impulse of the devil they fulfill the words of God (Rev 17:16-17; on this see Bauckham 1994, 329-417).

One point must be clarified concerning John's use of the so-called Nero myth. There is no question that John looked for Nero literally to return from the dead to fulfill the role of the antichrist. He utilized the current expectation to portray the works of the antichrist as those of *another* Nero, and that for a good reason: Nero was the first Roman emperor to persecute the Christian church, and he did so with such bestial cruelty as to provide a pattern for the beast of Satan to follow in his war with the Lamb (Rev 11:7-10; 13:7; 17:12-14). By his presentation of antichrist as another Nero, John has made it clear that the cult of the emperor is a projection of what will take place when the seeds of its beginning reach their full harvest. It could not be otherwise. The emperor cult, as R. J. Bauckham observed, was a deification of power (Bauckham 1994, 451-52). History, not least in the twentieth century, shows that such deification is capable of reappearing with appalling results. Humankind ignores that to its peril.

7. The Purpose of the Revelation.

E. F. Scott described the Revelation as "a trumpet call to faith" (174). For the Christians of John's generation, especially in Roman Asia, the exaltation of Rome and the popularity of the emperor cult made the living of the Christian life difficult and the future dismaying, in light of the pressure to join the majority in the celebration of Caesar's divinity and the readiness of informers to report to the authorities their refusal to do so. Yet to yield to such pressure entailed the denial of the Christian faith in its entirety, which was unthinkable. John therefore wrote at the behest of the risen Lord to strengthen the faith and courage of believers, to nerve them for battle with antichristian forces in the world and to help them to bear witness to the one true Lord and Savior.

The whole book of Revelation is rooted in its portrayal of God Almighty as the Lord of history and his redemptive activity in Christ. So surely as Jesus has accomplished the first and most important stage in the redemption* of humanity, so he will complete his appointed task of bringing to victory the kingdom of God and thereby the total emancipation of humanity from the powers of evil. The followers of the Lamb cannot expect to avoid sharing his sufferings;* hence the call early in the letters to the churches: "Be faithful until death, and I will give you the crown of life" (Rev 2:10). And that will be to participate in life eternal in the company of God and the redeemed in the eternal city of God.

8. The Significance of the Revelation for Today.

The book of Revelation has been an inspiration for the church through the ages, above all when it has known the fierce opposition of ruling authorities (*see* Civil Authority). From time to time, however, it has been criticized as a sub-Christian book. R. Bultmann, to cite one example, considered that it presents "a weakly Christianized Judaism" (Bultmann 1955, 2:175). Bultmann's criticism reflects his rejection of all apocalyptic, yet he is aware that the NT presents the atonement as involving both the love* and judgment of God. This is seen especially in John 12:31-32 but also in John 3:16-21; on the latter Bultmann made the striking comment, "There would be no judgment at all were it not for the event of God's Love" (Bultmann 1971, 154).

A. Y. Collins cites D. H. Lawrence as asserting that the book vents the anger, hatred and envy of the weaker against the strong, against civilization and even against nature (cited by A. Y. Collins 1984, 169). Lawrence's evaluation of the Revelation is typical of his outlook on life, but it is disturbing that Christian exegetes should adopt such a view. Collins considers that John sought to overcome the tension between reality and faith, what is and what ought to be. Faith* includes that God is ruler of all, Jesus is King of kings and Lord of all and that in the messianic kingdom all Christians will rule with him. The reality is the power of Rome and the powerlessness of Christians, their fear of denunciation before Roman authorities, their recollection of Nero's persecution, the destruction of Jerusalem and the banishment of John. This led to aggressive feelings of envy of the wealthy, frustration about the emperor cult and desire for vengeance for the violent acts of the empire. But these violent images were transferred to God and Christ in the Revelation; hence Jesus will make war with the sword of his mouth against followers of Balaam, Nicolaitans and Jezebel ("fellow Christians"!) as well as the generals and rich and strong (Rev 6:15-17) and the armies that follow antichrist (Rev 19:21; see A. Y. Collins 1984, 156-57).

Much more is written in this vein, which requires more space to answer than is possible here. A few points, however, need to be made. If it be a question of realism, John the prophet has it. The followers of Balaam, the Nicolaitans and Jezebel are not broadminded Christians but those affected by the antinomianism of emerging Gnostics,* and their influence had to be opposed. The hostility to the emperor cult is inevitable in any generation, and use of the cartoons derived from the ancient Middle East religions is justified. Regarding the violence in applying the latter, it is essential to recall the tradition of hyperbole used by the OT prophets. An outstanding example is seen in Zephaniah's language. In Zephaniah 1:2-6 the judgments of God are described in terms that involve the destruction of all living creatures on the Day of the Lord. That language is repeated in Zephaniah 3:8.

"In the fire of my passion all the earth shall be consumed."

This is immediately followed by Zephaniah 3:9:
"At that time I will change the speech
     of the peoples
     to a pure speech,
   that all of them may call on the name
     of the Lord
     and serve him with one accord."

Such contradiction of utterance cannot be taken literally, but the judgment and salvation of the Jews and Gentiles* is seriously meant, as the rest of the book makes plain. The like holds good in the Revelation, as Revelation 11:10 and Revelation 15:3-4, the survival of earth's inhabitants in the millennium, Revelation 20:4-6, and the kings of the earth bringing their gifts into the new Jerusalem (Rev 21:24-27) indicate. The picture of the city of God in Revelation 21:9—22:5 goes far beyond abating alleged anger and envy of Christians; its ultimate motive is to reveal the fulfillment of God's purpose for his creation in a redeemed humanity in fellowship* with himself. In declaring this revelation the prophet John was truly led by the spirit (Rev 19:10). The church today will do well to give heed to the appeal that appears in every one of the letters to the seven churches: "Let anyone who has an ear

listen to what the spirit is saying to the churches."

9. The Revelation in the Earliest Post-New Testament Writings.

A number of the apostolic fathers* indicate the influence of the book of Revelation in their works, though not all do so. Didache,* 1 Clement (see Clement of Rome), the letters of Ignatius* and the letter of Polycarp* to the Philippians show little or no reflection of the Revelation and are more concerned with the life of the church, its order (see Church Order) and worship. The conclusion of the Didache (Did. 16) has an "apocalyptic postscript," but it clearly echoes the eschatological discourse of the Gospels (Mark 13 par.) rather than the Revelation. The Epistle of Barnabas* adopts the interpretation of creation in six days as a figure of the cosmic week of history: the latter lasts for six thousand years and is followed by the sabbath rest of the kingdom of God (Barn. 15). This could well be one of the traditions that contributed to John's picture of the millennium. It is also found in 2 Enoch 33, a book possibly of the same period as the Revelation.

The Visions of the Shepherd of Hermas* are also in the apocalyptic tradition. They concern the life of the church and are therefore close to the Revelation. The like may be said of the Similitudes of Hermas, especially in the prominence given to angels, who are represented as responsible for creation, and a good and an evil angel are set over people (Herm. Man. 6.2.1; Herm. Vis. 3.4.1).

Papias above all was enthusiastic about the millennium.* His famous statement relating to the extraordinary fruitfulness of the earth in that time is attributed to "the Lord" as made known by "presbyters who saw John." Vineyards will have "ten thousand vines, and each vine ten thousand branches, and each branch ten thousand shoots, and on every shoot will be ten thousand clusters, and in every cluster ten thousand grapes, and every grape when pressed will yield twenty-five measures of wine." Such growth will apply to wheat grains, fruit trees, seeds and herbs, and animals who eat them will be peaceable to each other and to man (reported by Irenaeus Haer. 5.33.3-4). A related but less extravagant statement is found in 1 Enoch 10:19.

L. Gry suggested that Papias's concept of the millennium was gained from the followers of Aristion and the elder John. It is evident that Papias's ideas were widespread in the church of his time and led to the endeavor of Dionysius to diminish the influence of the Revelation. Nevertheless, the millennial interpretation of Revelation 20 was firmly held by Justin Martyr, Irenaeus, Hippolytus and Victorinus. Origen, however, was "the vehement opponent of millenarianism" (Beckwith, 323). Tyconius in his commentary followed in Origen's steps, and Augustine buried chiliasm by his doctrine of the millennium as the age of the church. Needless to say, the doctrine of the earthly kingdom of Christ has been resurrected in later centuries and espoused by many interpreters.

See also Antichrist; Apocalyptic, Apocalypticism; Babylon; Beasts, Dragon, Sea, Conflict Motif; Bowls; Christology; Eschatology; Heaven, New Heaven; Jerusalem, Zion, Holy City; Judgment; Lamb; Liturgical Elements; Martyrdom; Millennium; Old Testament in Revelation; Parousia; Persecution; Prophecy, Prophets, False Prophets; Scrolls, Seals; Trumpets; Visions, Ecstatic Experience; Worship and Liturgy; Wrath, Destruction.

Bibliography. **Commentaries:** D. E. Aune, *Revelation* (WBC; Dallas: Word, 1997); G. R. Beasley-Murray, *The Book of Revelation* (rev. ed.; NCB; Grand Rapids: Eerdmans, 1978); I. T. Beckwith, *The Apocalypse of John* (New York: Macmillan, 1919); M. E. Boring, *Revelation* (IntC; Louisville, KY: John Knox, 1989); G. B. Caird, *The Revelation of St. John the Divine* (HNTC; New York: Harper & Row, 1966); R. H. Charles, *A Critical and Exegetical Commentary on the Revelation of St. John* (2 vols.; ICC; Edinburgh: T & T Clark, 1920); J. M. Ford, *Revelation* (AB; New York: Doubleday, 1975); W. J. Harrington, *Revelation* (SacP 16; Collegeville, MN: Liturgical Press, 1993); M. Kiddle, *The Revelation of St. John* (MNTC; New York: Harper, 1940); G. E. Ladd, *A Commentary on the Revelation of John* (Grand Rapids: Eerdmans, 1972); H. Lilje, *The Last Book of the Bible* (Philadelphia: Muhlenberg, 1957); E. Lohmeyer, *Die Offenbarung des Johannes* (2d ed.; HNT; Tübingen: J. C. B. Mohr, 1953); E. Lohse, *Die Offenbarung des Johannes* (NTD; Göttingen: Vandenhoeck & Ruprecht, 1960); L. Morris, *The Revelation of St. John* (2d ed.; TNTC; Leicester: Inter-Varsity Press, 1987); R. H. Mounce, *The Book of Revelation* (Grand Rapids: Eerdmans, 1977); A. Schlatter, *Die Briefe und Offenbarung des Johannes* (Stuttgart: Calver Verlag, 1938); E. F. Scott, *The Book of Revelation* (London: SCM, 1939); J. P. M. Sweet, *Revelation* (Philadelphia: Westminster, 1979); H. B. Swete, *Commentary on the Book of Revelation* (3d ed.; London: Macmillan, 1909). **Studies:** D. E. Aune, "The Apocalypse of John and the Problem of Genre," *Semeia* 36 (1986) 65-96; R. J. Bauckham, *The Climax of Prophecy* (Edinburgh: T & T Clark, 1994); idem, *The Theology of the Book of Revelation* (NTT; Cambridge: Cambridge University Press, 1993); G. R. Beasley-Murray, *John* (WBC; Dallas: Word, 1986); J. G. Bowman, "The Revelation of John: Its Dramatic Structure and Message," *Int* 9 (1955) 436-53; R. Bultmann, *Gospel of John* (Oxford: Blackwell, 1971); idem, *Theology of the New Testament* (New York: Scribners, 1951, 1955); A. Y. Collins, *The Apocalypse* (Wilmington, DE: Michael Glazier, 1979); idem, *The Combat Myth in the Book of Revelation* (HDR 9; Missoula, MT: Scholars Press, 1976); idem, *Crisis and Catharsis: The Power of the Apocalypse* (Philadelphia: Westminster, 1984); J. J. Collins, *The Apocalyptic Imagination* (New York: Crossroad, 1984); J. Comblin, *Le Christ dans l'Apocalypse* (Paris: Desclée, 1976); J. M. Court, *Myth and History in the Book of Revelation* (Atlanta: John Knox, 1979); A. Culpepper, *The Johannine School: An Evaluation of the Johannine School Hypothesis Based on an Investigation of the Nature of Ancient Schools* (SBLDS 26; Missoula, MT: Scholars Press, 1975); A. Deissmann, *Light from the Ancient East* (Grand Rapids: Baker, 1978 [repr.]); A. M. Farrer, *A Rebirth of Images* (Westminster: Dacre, 1949); A. Feuillet, *The Apocalypse* (Staten Island, NY: Alba House, 1965); L. Gry, "Henoch X,19 et les belles promesses de Papias," *RB* 53 (1946) 197-206; P. D. Hanson, *The Dawn of Apocalyptic* (Philadelphia: Fortress, 1979); C. J. Hemer, *The Letters to the Seven Churches of Asia in Their Local Setting* (Sheffield: JSOT, 1986); T. Holtz, *Die Christologie der Apokalypse des Johannes* (TU 85; Berlin: Akademie Verlag, 1962); W. G. Kümmel, *Introduction to the New Testament* (Nashville: Abingdon, 1975); F. D. Mazzaferri, *The Genre of the Book of Revelation from a Source-Critical Perspective* (BZNW 54; Berlin and New York: Walter de Gruyter, 1989); M. Rissi, *The Future of the World: An Exegetical Study of Revelation 19:11—22:15* (SBT 2d ser.; London: SCM, 1972); idem, *Time and History* (Richmond, VA: John Knox, 1966); C. C. Rowland, *The Open Heaven* (New York: Crossroad, 1982); E. Schüssler Fiorenza, *The Book of Revelation: Justice and Judgment* (Philadelphia: Fortress, 1985); M. H. Shepherd, *The Pas-*

chal Liturgy and the Apocalypse (Richmond, VA: John Knox, 1960); L. L. Thompson, *The Book of Revelation: Apocalypse and Empire* (Oxford: Oxford University Press, 1990); C. C. Torrey, *Documents of the Primitive Church* (New York and London: Harper, 1941).

G. R. Beasley-Murray

REVERENCE. *See* FEAR.

REWARDS

A reward may be defined as a benefit promised or given in response to fulfilling a specified requirement. Spiritual blessings* as well as material ones may be included, for while biblical writers seldom use the specific term for blessings such as fellowship* with God,* they are "an aspect of the New Testament concept of reward, and a fundamental one" (Reicke). Such rewards therefore have great power* to motivate biblically mandated actions, positively through the hope* of enjoying them and negatively through the threat of their loss. Thus both Jesus and Paul offer rewards to encourage needed changes in the lifestyles of their hearers (e.g., Mt 10:42; Lk 6:35; 1 Cor 3:12-15; 9:24-27; Col 3:22-24). Material benefits are limited to this age (Lk 18:29-30). Spiritual blessings, however, are both present and future, though their enjoyment in the age to come will be greater (1 Jn 3:2; 1 Cor 13:12-13). This same understanding of rewards is carried on in the remainder of the NT and with some modification into the writings of the apostolic fathers.* Like the teachings* of Jesus and Paul, here the prospect of rewards is used to motivate the readers to turn from sinful (*see* Sin) ways and to live holy (*see* Holy, Holiness) lives. (For a response to the objections that such an appeal to self-interest might raise *see DPL,* Rewards.) In the apostolic fathers, however, a new note is sounded with the teaching that rewards can be earned or merited.

1. The General Epistles
2. Revelation
3. The Apostolic Fathers

1. The General Epistles.

1.1. Hebrews. Hebrews 10:35-36 (*see* Hebrews) provides the key to the author's understanding of rewards: "Do not throw away your trust in God, which has a great reward. For you need to persevere so that you keep on doing the will of God and thus receive what is promised."

The rewards enjoyed by the readers therefore consist of all that God has promised to do for those who persevere in trusting him (Heb 11:6; *see* Endurance). And while the full realization of these promises* awaits the age to come, to "share in Christ" (Heb 3:14) in this age is a great reward.

Though initially bold in enduring persecution* (Heb 10:32-34), in the face of a renewed threat the readers appear to be leaning toward a reversion to Judaism,* a protected religion in the empire (*see* Roman Empire). But this means a rejection of Christ, who is vastly superior to and has now superseded the OT cult. For them to turn their backs on Christ would be to call down the most dire consequences (Heb 10:28-31).

Thus powerful incentives are given to persuade the readers to continue cleaving to Christ even in the face of persecution. Though there is some mention of material gain—sons and land* (Heb 11:8, 11-12)—the emphasis is on the unsurpassed benefits of salvation*: deliverance from the fear* of death, forgiveness* of sins, having a faithful helper in times of temptation* (Heb 2:15-18); having God always with them so that they have no need to fear (Heb 13:5-6); complete equipping to do God's will (Heb 13:20-21). With Jesus as their model in perseverance they are to keep their eyes on him (Heb 12:2), who was able to endure even the terrible suffering* of the cross* because of the joys* that awaited him. The wonders of God's promises should therefore similarly strengthen the readers if they are called to further suffering. They should also be strongly motivated by stern warnings of the fearful consequences of failure to trust Christ: unless the readers' downward slide is arrested, they are in danger of forfeiting the blessings of salvation (Heb 2:2-3); only if they hold fast to their courage are they members of God's household* (Heb 3:6); only if they hold their first confidence firm unto the end will they share in Christ (Heb 3:14; also 4:1; 6:4-6, 11; 12:14, 25).

At the outset such threats might seem to remove any assurance* of being able to persevere unto the end. But because the threats are directed against unbelief, they serve as one of God's means to keep believers trusting in him (Heb 4:1-2). Being forced to consider the fearful alternative to persevering in faith* serves as an incentive to fight diligently against unbelief and thus to be assured of enjoying the blessings of God both in this life* and the next.

1.2. James. A specific reward borrowed from the Greek world is the "crown of life" (Jas 1:12; *see* James). As a wreath, or crown, of leaves was awarded to winners of the athletic contests, so God will award his crown of eternal life to those who have persevered in trusting and loving him in the face of trials. Allusion is also made to present blessings that faith in God brings: wisdom* (Jas 1:5; 3:17), forgiveness of sins (Jas 4:8-10; 5:15); victory over the devil (Jas 4:7; *see* Satan); friendship with God (Jas 1:18; 4:8).

Unlike Hebrews, where persecution was in view, here the test that must be steadfastly withstood is "all kinds" of trials and temptations (Jas 1:2). The author's goal therefore is to encourage his readers to persevere in faith so that they become mature and complete in God's sight, not deficient in any way (Jas 1:4).

To be genuine, faith must express itself in actions, and James, therefore, admonishes his readers to comply with many commands. He reinforces them with both reminders of the great advantages of commitment to the messianic faith and warnings of what failure to act in line with that faith will mean. Among the advantages of steadfastly trusting and obeying God is the inheritance of the riches* of his kingdom* and his blessing on all the readers' activities (Jas 2:5; 1:25). Material as well as spiritual bounties are in view, for God is the giver of every good gift. Warnings also abound against actions that betray a lack of trust: do not just listen to God's commands; do them, for this shows you are trusting him to guide you (Jas 1:22). Do not neglect the care of widows and orphans, for unless your faith in God's provision of your needs is sufficient to cause you to care for the needs of others, it is dead (Jas 1:27; 2:14-26). Do not presume to plan your life on your own; only God knows the future (Jas 4:13-15). Do not grumble and complain, for this shows you do not believe that your present lot is God's wise and gracious way of looking out for you (Jas 5:9). Along with these admonitions come assurances that God's wisdom and grace* is always available to those who humbly trust him, so that they, like Abraham,* will be called God's friends (Jas 2:22-24).

1.3. 1 Peter. The writer describes these benefits glowingly: a living hope and an imperishable inheritance (1 Pet 1:3-4); inexpressible and glorious joy (1 Pet 1:8). His readers are a chosen people, a royal priesthood,* God's precious possession (1 Pet 2:4-5, 9-10) whose sins have been forgiven through Christ's death on the cross (1 Pet 2:24). Tangible recognition is also in view in the promise that steadfast faith will receive praise, glory and honor at the revelation* of Jesus Christ (1 Pet 1:7). Visible too is the "crown of glory" promised to shepherds* (i.e., pastoral leaders) who faithfully care for their sheep (1 Pet 5:4).

The writer's concern is to stiffen his readers' resolve to stand firm in adversity by continuing to trust that God will soon bring great blessing (1 Pet 5:9-10). Though their painful trials are attributed to their being Christians (1 Pet 4:12-14, 16), these are less likely an officially sanctioned persecution than the sufferings that being different from the world inevitably involves.

The marvelous blessings promised are powerful incentives to the holy living enjoined by the writer. But perhaps even more effective is his warning to "live your lives in fear" (*phobos,* 1 Pet 1:17) so that the readers will not fail to set their hope fully on Christ and live solely to glorify God (1 Pet 1:13; 2:12). They are warned too that every deed will be judged by God, whose "face is against those who do evil" (1 Pet 1:17; 3:12). As further encouragement they are assured that the faith they must fight to maintain is of the greatest value in God's sight (1 Pet 1:7).

1.4. Conclusion. Thus God's rewards offer the strongest of incentives to persevere in faith, both by the promise of enjoying them and the threat of forfeiting them. Those who believe him take seriously the threats of what a failure to trust will mean—not only the loss of the blessings of salvation in this life but also in the next the fearful prospect of falling into the hands of the God who justly and severely punishes every unforgiven sin (Heb 2:2-3; 10:31), especially apostasy,* which at least hypothetically was the readers' chief peril (see Heb 6:9). These threats reinforce the motivating power inherent in the promised rewards. Allusion is made to material benefits as well as tangible recognition, but the emphasis is on spiritual blessings such as the forgiveness, fellowship and imperishable inheritance that are promised to those whose faith is steadfast. Though this faith must result in appropriate actions (Jas 2:14-26), these are never works in which the readers could boast (see Faith and Works), for what motivates them is the firm belief that God will keep his promises and will honor their faith with his blessings. Thus because they so greatly desire to enjoy these benefits (e.g., Heb 11:8-10; 24-27), they are to bend every effort to make their calling and election* sure (2 Pet 1:4-11) by firmly resisting Satan's efforts to destroy their faith (1 Pet 5:8-9). This faith is not in their own abilities to persevere but in the "God of all grace," who promises to keep them from succumbing to unbelief in this life and to bring them without fault into the next, there to enjoy to the full his rewards (Jude 24).

2. Revelation.
With one exception—being kept in the hour of trial (Rev 3:10)— the rewards proffered are all heaven-oriented and astonishing in their richness: the right to eat of the tree of life and of hidden manna (Rev 2:7, 17); being given the crown of life, a new name* and the morning star (Rev 2:10, 17, 28); being acknowledged by God and seeing his face (Rev 3:5); the right to sit with Jesus on his throne (Rev 3:21); the end of all tears and pain (Rev 21:3). Tangible recognition is also in view, for the deeds of the dead are said to follow them (Rev 14:13), and Jesus declares that each will receive according to his or her works (Rev 2:33). But whatever form this may take, it is clear that such recognition is given only that it may in some way reflect and honor the power and glory of God.

As a prediction of events leading to the establishment of the new heavens* and earth, Revelation (see Revelation, Book of) speaks in ultimate terms. The condition for the enjoyment of the blessings is "overcoming" present hindrances to faith (Rev 2:7, 17, 26; 3:5, 12, 21). This includes refusing either to allow one's initial, fervent love for Jesus to waver for any length of time or to condone false teaching and immorality (see Purity). And because eternity is at stake, the punishments that await those who fail to persevere are likewise eternal: being forced to drink the wine of God's fury as they suffer forever in the lake of fire (Rev 14:9-12; 20:15; 21:8).

Here the motivating power both of rewards and punishments is seen at its highest. Only two eternal futures lie before humankind: to be forever with the Lord, enjoying the unimaginable delights of life with him, or being tormented in the lake of fire. With issues of such great consequence in view the incentive to persevere in faith, though it entails great suffering and even martyrdom,* could scarcely be stronger.

As the culmination of NT teaching the ultimate nature of God's rewards and his punishments stand as awesome means to motivate believers to the firmness in faith essential for the enjoyment of his blessings.

3. The Apostolic Fathers.
The fullest treatment of rewards is found in 1 Clement and 2 Clement, where the writer(s) (see Clement of Rome) make explicit the NT's implicit equating of spiritual blessings with rewards: an inheritance of glory and honor, being confessed by Christ and the joys of eternal life (1 Clem. 45.7; 2 Clem. 3.2-3; 8.4). This understanding of rewards is found throughout the apostolic fathers, as is the condition for receiving them: perseverance in suffering and a holy, righteous life (1 Clem. 5.2-7; 2 Clem. 5.6; Pol. Phil. 5.2; Herm. Vis. 5.7). What awaits the disobedient (see Obedience) is seen both as torture in unquenchable fire (2 Clem. 17.7) and a double punishment that culminates in eternal death (Herm. Sim. 9.18.2).

As in the NT, rewards play a crucial role in motivating righteous living. But a new note appears in the teaching that believers can earn blessings from God, both by their repentance* and by turning others to him (2 Clem. 9.7-8; 15.1-2). Similarly Ignatius,* in response to the Smyrneans' love for him and loyalty to the bishop, assures them that "God is your reward," not misthos but amoibē, implying "repayment or return" (Ign. Smyrn. 9.2). Drawing on a Roman custom in the military, he writes to Polycarp,* "Let your works be your deposits that you may receive the back-pay due you" (Ign. Pol. 6.2). The Didache* and the Epistle of Barnabas* warn against reluctant giving, because "thou shalt know who is the good Paymaster of the reward" (Did. 4.7; Barn. 19.11). And of the martyrs it is said that by a single hour of despising worldly tortures they purchased eternal life (Mart. Pol. 2.3). A belief that rewards can be earned or merited leads to the teaching that even greater benefits result from works of supererogation, or going beyond what is commanded (Herm. Sim. 5.2.1—3.3).

In the apostolic fathers rewards appear in a new light. Though still understood primarily as spiritual blessings, they are also seen as benefits that are earned. And this opens the door to the self-sufficiency so firmly denounced by the NT.

See also BLESSING; ESCHATOLOGY; GLORY; HOPE; JUDGMENT; MARTYRDOM; SUFFERING.

BIBLIOGRAPHY. C. Boettger and B. Siede, "Recompense," in *NIDNTT* 3:134-144; R. Bultmann, "ἐλπίς κτλ," *TDNT* 2:517-33; R. M. Fuller, "A Pauline Understanding of Rewards" (unpublished Ph.D. dissertation, Fuller Theological Seminary, 1990); W. Grundmann, "στέφανος κτλ," *TDNT* 7:615-36; H. Kraft, "στέφανος κτλ," *EDNT* 3:273-74; C. S. Lewis, *The Weight of Glory* (New York: Macmillan, 1949); W. Pesch, "μισθός," *EDNT* 2:432-33; J. Piper, *Desiring God* (Portland: Multnomah, 1986); H. Preisker, "μισθός κτλ," *TDNT* 4:695-728; B. Reicke, "The New Testament Conception of Reward" in *Aux sources de la tradition chrétienne* (Neuchâtel: Delachaux & Niestlé, 1950), 195-206; W. Telfer, *The Forgiveness of Sins* (London: SCM, 1959); T. F. Torrance, *The Doctrine of Grace in the Apostolic Fathers* (Grand Rapids: Eerdmans, 1959).

R. M. Fuller

RHETORIC, RHETORICAL CRITICISM

The rhetorical criticism of the General Epistles and apostolic fathers* is still in its infancy. Most works have appeared only during the 1980s and 1990s. Current practitioners are using a variety of methodologies based on Greco-Roman rhetoric, modern rhetoric or both. Much is being discovered about the argumentation, arrangement and style of these books. Our understanding of the interplay of their rhetorical and historical contexts, authors, audiences and purposes is increasing.

Although rhetorical criticism of the General Epistles and apostolic fathers has begun, it will take time for synthesis of the rhetorical studies of each work to emerge. This is especially true of the works of the apostolic fathers, which have undergone little rhetorical analysis. Thus the major rhetorical analyses of each work can be discussed, but no definitive rhetorical analysis can be offered. However, these books are involved in the emerging discussion of the distinctives of Christian, Jewish and Greco-Roman rhetoric, as well as social-scientific study of the NT.

1. The Practice of Rhetorical Criticism
2. Rhetorical Criticism of Hebrews, the General Epistles and Revelation
3. Rhetorical Criticism of the Apostolic Fathers

1. The Practice of Rhetorical Criticism.
Rhetorical criticism of the NT and apostolic fathers has used the Greco-Roman rhetorical conventions and more modern rhetoric and related literary criticism. The former has the advantage of placing these works in their oral and written culture, while the latter helps these texts to function in addressing modern audiences and their concerns.

1.1. Using Greco-Roman Rhetoric. Rhetorical analysis of the General Epistles and apostolic fathers has often concentrated on the use of Greco-Roman rhetoric, with the methodology of George Kennedy being prominent. Kennedy proposed the following five-step methodology: determine the rhetorical unit; define the rhetorical situation; determine the rhetorical problem or stasis and the species of rhetoric; analyze invention, arrangement and style; and evaluate the rhetorical effectiveness. To understand this methodology and its current application, a brief overview of Greco-Roman rhetoric is necessary.

There are three main species of rhetoric: judicial, deliberative and epideictic. Their use is determined by the audience and the context. Judicial rhetoric is concerned with accusation and defense, usually in a legal setting. It stresses what is just or unjust. Deliberative rhetoric is advice giving, persuasion and dissuasion, usually in the political arena. It emphasizes what is advantageous or harmful. Epideictic rhetoric praises and blames, and concerns itself with what is honorable or the dishonorable with a view to increasing or decreasing assent to values. In a NT book one species of rhetoric typically predominates while the other two are supportive.

The stasis is the basis of the conflict addressed. There are three stases: fact, definition and quality. The stasis of fact involves whether something was done or whether it was done by the person accused. The stasis of definition admits the facts but denies that they have been defined correctly. The stasis of quality admits the facts but denies any wrong was committed. It also inquires into the nature of something, a function it frequently has in the NT.

Invention, arrangement and style are employed to compose the speech or document. Invention is the creation of convincing proofs. These can be either created or found by the rhetor. Those proofs not found by the rhetor include previous judgments or documents, which in the NT are usually eyewitness testimony and quotations of the OT. Those proofs created by the rhetor are ethos, pathos and logos. Ethos is the moral character of the rhetor, which is demonstrated in the discourse. Pathos is the arousal of the audience's emotion for the position of the rhetor and against the position of any opponent. Logos is reason from induction and deduction, proof from example and argument respectively. Examples used in the NT are often drawn from the OT, Jewish tradition and nature. Rather than the formal syllogism, arguments used in the NT often take the form of an enthymeme, a proposition with one supporting reason. Argumentation makes use of topics, some common to many types of argumentation (e.g., possible-impossible). In addition detailed schemes for elaborating themes and complete arguments are used in proof.

Arrangement is the persuasive ordering of the discourse. It requires an *exordium,* an introduction that strives to make the audience attentive, well-disposed and receptive to the message. This was often followed by a *narratio,* a narration of pertinent facts, and a *partitio,* an enumeration of the propositions to be discussed. The body of the discourse, the *probatio* (sometimes called *argumentatio* or *confirmatio),* follows and presents the argumentation. It both proves the rhetor's case *(confirmatio)* and disproves the case of any opposition *(refutatio,* sometimes called *confutatio).* It concludes with a *peroratio,* a recapitulation of the main points and an appeal to the audience's emotion in order to facilitate a desired response.

Style is presenting a discourse in language appropriate and expedient to the subject, audience and situation addressed and promoting the desired persuasive effect. Prominent in the discussion of style were figures of speech and thought. Important for the NT are repetition, hyperbole, paronomasia, metaphor, antithesis, irony and personification.

Greco-Roman rhetorical conventions had been incorporated in part into Jewish rhetorical practice by the Christian era. Within Hellenistic culture rhetoric was central to secondary education. Even if a NT writer had not been formally educated, rhetorical practice was everywhere and its forms would have been familiar. Much of Jewish and Greco-Roman rhetorical practice was shaped by the needs oral culture. Most people were illiterate and could only hear the message, and the forms devised to facilitate that hearing were well recognized (e.g., repetition and parallelism).

1.2. Using Modern Rhetoric. Many forms of modern rhetoric are used for rhetorical analysis. These include the new rhetoric of C. Perelman and L. Olbrechts-Tyteca (ancient rhetoric reconceptualized), Continental theories of literary rhetoric and American rhetoric within social-science hermeneutics. Modern rhetoric is also used in combination with other related methodologies, including literary criticism, reader-response criticism and discourse analysis. The position is that Greco-Roman rhetoric, while it is historically anchored in the NT era, does not address all theoretical, practical or philosophical questions posed by speech.

2. Rhetorical Criticism of Hebrews, the General Epistles and Revelation.

2.1. Hebrews. Greco-Roman and Jewish rhetorical features in Hebrews* are so prevalent that David E. Aune can state, "The author obviously enjoyed the benefits of a Hellenistic rhetorical education through the tertiary level" (212). For example, the comparative argument from the lesser to the greater *(argumentum e minori ad maius/qal wahomer,* "light and heavy") is common in Hebrews. There are many studies of particular rhetorical features such as antithesis and chiasm in Hebrews. Notable is M. R. Cosby's study that shows how the example list in Hebrews 11:3-40 provides the readers with famous examples illustrating the enduring faith* encouraged in Hebrews 10:19-39 and defined in Hebrews 11:1-2.

In spite of obvious rhetorical features, the genre, the overall rhetorical strategy and the social matrix of the Hebrews are elusive. Regarding genre, Hebrews calls itself a "word of exhortation" *(logos paraklēseōs,* Heb 13:22), a designation also used of Paul's sermon in Acts 13:15. L. Wills argues that Hebrews is a sermon or homily that in both individual units and larger cycles exhibits a threefold pattern of Hellenistic-Jewish and early Christian sermonic material: the presentation of biblical examples and authoritative exposition of theological points; a conclusion based on the examples, which indicates their significance to those addressed; and exhortation based on the conclusion (e.g., Heb 3:1—4:16; 8:1—10:25). In response C. C. Black states that the features noted by Wills are to be placed in the Greco-Roman rhetorical tradition. Many of these we will now explore.

Barnabas Lindars classifies Hebrews as deliberative rhetoric. It seeks to persuade a Jewish-Christian* audience, driven by a guilty conscience* due to sin, to return to the apostolic faith after it turned to Judaism* for purification. W. Übelacker agrees that Hebrews is deliberative rhetoric. It seeks to persuade the audience to accept Jesus' sacrifice* as sufficient to provide access to God.* He outlines Hebrews as *exordium* (Heb 1:1-4), *narratio* (Heb 1:5—2:18, with 2:17-18 as the *propositio), argumentatio* with *probatio* and *refutatio* (Heb 3:1—12:29), *peroratio* (Heb 13:1-21) and *postscriptum* (Heb 13:22-25). His work builds upon that of K. Nissilä, who analyzed the passages pertaining to the high priesthood* and devised a similar outline, also classifying Hebrews as deliberative rhetoric. However, the following developments make it more difficult to argue that Hebrews conforms to the standard Greco-Roman arrangement of a speech.

C. F. Evans explores the recurrent and dominant role in Hebrews of synkrisis, or comparison. This rhetorical form compares representatives of a type in order to determine the superiority of one over the other. It is a means of praise or blame by comparison and usually makes the comparison with people using the topics of family, natural endowments, upbringing and education, achievements and death. Through comparison, Hebrews shows Christ to be superior to angels,* the levitical priesthood and human worthies of salvation history. Synkrisis helps explain the christology* of Hebrews, in which the types of Christ are demoted or depreciated by comparison with Christ, the divine hero.

Also noting synkrisis in Hebrews, T. H. Olbricht classifies Hebrews as both epideictic and deliberative rhetoric and proposes that the book is modeled on the funeral orations of classical Greece and the early church fathers. Central to such orations was comparison of the deceased with illustrious personages of the past in order to prove the superior status of the deceased. In Hebrews the comparison of Christ with worthies of salvation history serves to amplify the argument as a whole. In each case the christological comparison is followed by exhortation to spiritual renewal based on the christology.

While rejecting the comparison with the funeral oration, T. W. Seid builds on Olbricht's observations on synkrisis. Rejecting the typical identification of Hebrews as a midrash or homily, Seid classifies Hebrews as a written speech of encomium belonging to the genre of synkrisis. The synkrisis alternates with exhortation (paraenesis) based on the synkrisis (as in Plutarch's *Parallel Lives)* for the purpose of moral exhortation. Such exhortation is found in encomia in the Greek protreptic tradition. The synkrisis/paraenesis alternation gives structure to the book: comparison of Son and angels (Heb 1:1-14) and paraenesis (Heb 2:1-18), comparison of Moses* and Christ (Heb 3:1-6) and paraenesis (Heb 3:7—4:16), comparison of Aaron and Christ (Heb 5:1-10) and paraenesis (Heb 5:11—6:20), comparison of Melchizedek* and Christ and the levitical priesthood (Heb 7:1-25) and paraenesis (Heb 7:26—8:3), comparison of the first covenant* and the new covenant (Heb 8:4—10:18) and paraenesis (Heb 10:19—12:29), and epistolary appendix (Heb 13:1-25). This alternation shows the superiority of Christ over the elements of the first covenant. It encourages the audience to progress in moral conduct by remaining faithful to the greater revelation* in Jesus Christ and emulating the models of its scripture. It also warns the audience of the greater judgment* to befall those unfaithful to the greater revelation.

2.2. James. Commentators have long noted the seemingly chaotic nature of James,* often attributing it to its paraenetic content. Usually paraenesis is viewed as unstructured exhortation strung like pearls. However, paraenesis can be an integral part of a rhetorically sophisticated text. Consensus is emerging that James is a thematic and rhetorical unity, even though there is disagreement on how to describe this unity.

W. H. Wuellner outlines James as epistolary prescript (Jas 1:1), *exordium* (Jas 1:2-4), *narratio* (Jas 1:5-11), *propositio* (Jas 1:12), *argumentatio* (Jas 1:13—5:6) in five units and *peroratio* (Jas 5:7-20). Modifying the work of Wuellner, E. Baasland classifies James as a protreptic, wisdom* speech in letter* form. He gives the outline of *exordium* (Jas 1:2-18), *transitus* (Jas 1:16-18), *propositio* (Jas 1:19-27), *confirmatio* (Jas 2:1—3:12), *confutatio* (Jas 3:13—5:6) and *peroratio* (Jas 5:7-20). The figures of style used in James are numerous and serve to clarify and amplify the argumentation.

Also building upon the work of Wuellner, J. H. Elliott uses rhetorical and social-scientific study to affirm the thematic cohesion of James. He outlines James as an introduction (Jas 1:1-12) composed of epistolary address and salutation (Jas 1:1-2), statement of the main theme concerning completeness and wholeness and its implied opposite of division and fragmentation (Jas 1:3-4), and related contrasts (Jas 1:5-12). The body of the argument (Jas 1:13—5:12) consists of exhortation in seven subsections contrasting negative indictments of division with positive recommendations for integrity and wholeness. James concludes with material echoing the introduction (Jas 5:13-20). Central is encouragement to reestablish the distinctive Christian ethos over against society at large. This is done by choosing heavenly versus earthly wisdom (Jas 3:13-18) and observing distinctions of purity* versus pollution (Jas 1:26-27). This choice ultimately leads to wholeness and holiness* rather than division and the devilish on the correlated personal, social and cosmic levels.

L. Thurén claims that James is epideictic rhetoric, reinforcing values the audience already holds. He analyzes the rhetoric of the entire letter according to Greco-Roman categories. The *exordium* (Jas 1:1-18) introduces the two central themes of perseverance* in trials in the practical areas of wisdom/speech and money/action. The *propositio* (Jas 1:19-27) is to accept the word and live by it. The *argumentatio* (Jas 2:1—5:6) develops the two themes of the *exordium* in three parts: James 2:1-26 on action and money, James 3:1—4:12 on speech and wisdom, and James 4:13—5:6 supplying a climax dealing with both themes focused on the rich man. The *peroratio* (Jas 5:7-20) consists of *recapitulatio*, or reiteration of the theme of perseverance in speech (Jas 5:7-11), and *conquestio*, or final exhortation (Jas 5:12-20). Thurén explains the obscurity of the surface level of the letter as the use of *insinuatio* or subtlety in rhetorical approach to avoid being too obvious to a rhetorically sophisticated audience. How-

ever, it is more likely that James does not conform to Greco-Roman standards in its overall arrangement.

D. F. Watson demonstrates that the central portion of James is deliberative rhetoric aimed at advising the audience to take certain courses of action and dissuade it from others. It contains three sections that use the Greco-Roman pattern of elaboration for themes and the complete argument. In these sections James advises his audience that partiality is inconsistent with faith (Jas 2:1-13), faith without works does not profit (Jas 2:14-26; *see* Faith and Works), and not many should become teachers (Jas 3:1-12). The pattern used to elaborate each of these propositions into complete arguments is *propositio* (proposition), *ratio* (reason for the proposition), *confirmatio* (proof of the reason by comparison, example and amplification), *exornatio* (embellishment of the argument) and *conplexio* (conclusion drawing the argument together). Paraenetic materials and diatribal features are incorporated into this pattern of argumentation.

2.3. 1 Peter. 1 Peter* is addressed to churches in Asia Minor undergoing local persecution.* Thurén classifies 1 Peter as epideictic rhetoric intended to reinforce the audience's adherence to values it already holds. He uses ancient and modern rhetoric to determine the function of ambiguous expressions in 1 Peter, such as whether the participles are indicative (encouraging) or imperative (exhorting). This ambiguity allows the author to address simultaneously two different groups in the audience and their individual response to suffering*: those passively assimilating to the world* to avoid suffering* and those actively avenging injustice and incurring more suffering. To the first group the author directs a critique of unacceptable portions of pagan culture to help them avoid undue assimilation. To the second group he upholds acceptable portions of pagan culture to help increase such assimilation. Ambiguous expressions allow each group to hear the letter differently according to its predisposition. Thurén outlines the letter as *exordium* (1 Pet 1:1-12); *argumentatio* aimed mainly at the passive audience (1 Pet 1:13—2:10), the active audience (1 Pet 2:11—3:12) and both audiences (1 Pet 3:13—5:7); and *peroratio* (1 Pet 5:8-14).

J. W. Thompson identifies 1 Peter as a sermon and analyzes it according to Greco-Roman rhetoric. As indicated in the conclusion (1 Pet 5:12), the letter is meant to exhort (*parakaleō*) and testify (*epimartyreō*). It is hortatory literature with a deliberative purpose of encouraging the audience to a certain course of action; that is, maintaining hope* and good works in spite of suffering (1 Pet 2:13-15, 20; 3:6, 17). Although it does not conform to the typical elements of rhetorical arrangement, 1 Peter 1:3-9 functions like an *exordium,* 1 Peter 1:10-12 like a *narratio,* 1 Peter 1:13—5:5 like a *probatio* and 1 Peter 5:6-11 like a *peroratio.* The subsections of the *probatio* are patterned as exhortation followed by justification for the prescribed conduct based on Scripture and the tradition of the community.

T. Martin discovered three distinctive clusters of metaphors in 1 Peter that describe the status of the audience and define three main sections: the elect* household* of God (1 Pet 1:14—2:10), the concept of aliens in this world (1 Pet 2:11—3:12) and sufferers in the Diaspora* (1 Pet 3:13—5:11). The Diaspora is the controlling metaphor that provides the thematic motif of 1 Peter. All the metaphors contribute to the author's objective of demonstrating conduct appropriate for the Christian eschatological* journey and dissuading the audience from defecting from the faith. In comparison P. J. Achtemeier sees "the Christian community as the new people of God constituted by the Christ who suffered and rose" as the controlling metaphor of 1 Peter. The author contrasts the audience's past in Greco-Roman social and religious life with their present life as the new people of God (*see* Church as Israel) and the suffering of their present with the greater glory* of the future. The argumentation and exhortation are based on the assurance that as long as the audience remains faithful, as the present transformed the past, so the future will transform the present and its suffering.

2.4. 2 Peter. 2 Peter* was probably written about A.D. 80-90 from Rome* to churches in Asia Minor in a time of eschatological crisis caused by the delay of the Parousia* of Christ. It seeks to counter the infiltration of these churches by false teachers whose solution to the crisis was denial of the Parousia (2 Pet 1:16-21; 3:1-4, 8-13) and the judgment expected to accompany it (2 Pet 2:3-10; 3:1-7), with immoral behavior resulting (2 Pet 2:10-22). Watson proposes that 2 Peter is mainly deliberative rhetoric intended

to advise the churches to adhere to the promises* of Christ and the apostolic tradition and to dissuade them from accepting the teaching of the false teachers (*see* Adversaries). However, judicial rhetoric is used to refute the teachings of the false teachers and affirm the Parousia and judgment as eschatological realities (2 Pet 1:16—2:10; 3:1-13). Also, epideictic rhetoric is used to denounce the character of the false teachers (2 Pet 2:10-22). The stasis or basis of the argument is one of quality: determining the truth* of the apostolic doctrines of the Parousia and its judgment. The arrangement of the letter is epistolary prescript (2 Pet 1:1-2); *exordium* (2 Pet 1:3-15) upholding apostolic doctrine; *probatio* (2 Pet 1:16—3:13) refuting the doctrinal challenges of the false teachers and confirming apostolic doctrine; and *peroratio* (2 Pet 3:12—16) summing up key points and eliciting emotion. The style is complex and plays an important role in amplifying the refutation and denunciation. The letter gives us a glimpse into early Roman Christian apologetics and rhetorical approach to false teaching.

2.5. Jude. Jude* was probably written in A.D. 50s from Jerusalem* to Jewish Christian churches in Palestine. It addresses the problem of the infiltration by itinerant prophets* or teachers who denied the authority* of the law* of Moses and Christ and were sexually immoral (Jude 4, 6-8, 10, 16). Watson contends that Jude uses deliberative rhetoric to advise the churches to contend for the apostolic faith (Jude 3) and to dissuade them from following the teaching and practice of the false teachers. Jude works through a variety of proofs from example (Jude 5-10) and prophecy (Jude 11-13, 14-16, 17-19) to demonstrate that the false teachers are those prophesied as coming in the last days and that they will be judged for their sexual immorality and their rejection of authority. In order to destroy the authority of these teachers, Jude also uses epideictic rhetoric to denounce them as comparable to notorious sinners of the past and the subject of prophecies of judgment (Jude 4-13). The stasis or basis of the argumentation is quality, showing that the words and deeds of the false teachers are ungodly and subject to judgment.

Watson arranges Jude as epistolary prescript (Jude 1-2), *exordium* (Jude 3) using a petition giving the main reason for writing as contending for the apostolic faith, *narratio* (Jude 4) providing the need to contend for the faith as the infiltration of false teachers who are the ungodly of prophecy, *probatio* (Jude 5-16) proving that the false teachers are the ungodly of prophecy, *peroratio* (Jude 17-23) summing up key points and instructing the churches on how to respond to the crisis, and epistolary postscript as a doxology (Jude 24-25; *see* Liturgical Forms). Style plays an important role in proving the false teachers are ungodly, especially strong metaphors and triads. The letter gives us a glimpse into early Jewish Christian polemic and rhetorical approach to opponents.

S. J. Joubert, while apparently unaware of the work of Watson, reaches many of the same conclusions. He stresses the positive/negative presentation strategy of the letter: the positive presentation *(laudatio)* of the congregation as faithful to apostolic tradition and the negative presentation *(vituperatio)* of the opponents as intruders rejected by God. This presentation gives the faithful the opportunity to live within the image of themselves projected by the text and reject the opponents and their teachings. J. D. Charles adopts Watson's outline while discussing literary strategies in general. E. R. Wendland analyzes the discourse structure of Jude to find that the entire letter is an extended structural and thematic chiasm or introversion.

2.6. The Johannine Epistles. The Johannine Epistles (*see* John, Letters of) address a schism within the Johannine community caused by secessionists who were espousing a corrupt christology and becoming morally indifferent. They denied that Jesus was the Christ, the Son of God, come in the flesh* and come by water and blood (1 Jn 2:22-23; 3:23; 4:2-3; 5:1, 5-6; 2 Jn 7). Minimizing the earthly ministry* of Jesus, they also minimized the moral walk that he modeled. They had formed their own community in opposition to those addressed by these epistles (1 Jn 2:18-19, 2 Jn 7).

Watson proposes that the author uses epideictic rhetoric to try to increase the adherence of the faithful to the traditional christology and ethics* of the Johannine community. The author upholds pursuing these as the honorable and beneficial course of action. The stasis or basis of 1 John is quality, for the author claims what is the best course of action and inquires into the nature of both the traditional and the aberrant christology and ethics. The *exordium* (1 Jn 1:1-4) affirms that the discourse is authorita-tive because its content derives from eyewitnesses of the revelation of the word of life. The *probatio* (1 Jn 1:5—5:12) upholds the teachings of the Johannine community and refutes those of the secessionists. As is typical of epideictic rhetoric, it abounds in propositions advanced as certain, antitheses, enthymemes and exhortation. Amplification of topics is a major part of the inventional strategy. The *peroratio* (1 Jn 5:13-21) enumerates points made and proposes policies to be pursued in light of them.

F. Vouga proposes that 1 John is deliberative rhetoric and has the following outline: epistolary prescript (1 Jn 1:1-4); *exordium (captatio benevolentiae)* (1 Jn 1:5—2:17), which gives the content of the revelation announced in the prescript; *narratio* (1 Jn 2:18-27) explaining the implications of the schism; *propositio* (1 Jn 2:28-29) concerning abiding in Christ; *probatio* (1 Jn 3:1-24) confirming the convictions of the *exordium* and interpreting the situation to show that the letter is justified; *exhortatio* (1 John 4:1-21) exhorting the churches to preserve the unity of the community; *peroratio* urging the maintenance of unity (1 Jn 5:1-12); and epistolary conclusion (1 Jn 5:13) and epistolary postscript (1 Jn 5:14-21). However, 1 John is not deliberative rhetoric because the churches addressed are faithful and do not need to be persuaded to a course of action.

The Presbyter wrote 2 John to further address the problem of secessionists, perhaps between A.D. 90-110. Watson proposes that he uses deliberative rhetoric to advise that the most beneficial course of action: to love* one another (2 Jn 5) and maintain the teachings of the community so as not to lose eternal life and fellowship* with the Father and the Son (2 Jn 8-9). To do otherwise is to share in the wicked deeds of the secessionists (2 Jn 11) and become antichrist* (2 Jn 7). The stasis of the argument is quality, for it is concerned with whether the christology of the secessionists is appropriate for the Christian life. The letter is arranged rhetorically as epistolary prescript (2 Jn. 1-3); *exordium* (2 Jn 4) giving the main topic as walking in the truth; *narratio* (2 Jn 5) petitioning the churches to adhere to the love commandment,* which embodies the proper understanding of christology and ethics; *probatio* (2 Jn 6-11) using exhortation and amplification to persuade the churches to adhere to the love commandment and not to extend the secessionists hospitality* or give them a hearing; *peroratio* (2 Jn 12) amplifying the importance of the message; and epistolary postscript (2 Jn 13).

The Presbyter wrote 3 John because a leader, Diotrephes, refused to receive missionaries and has ordered the members of his church to do the same (3 Jn 9-10). This refusal may be due to prideful rebellion (*see* Obedience; Pride) or an attempt to prevent the spread of secessionist influence. The Presbyter urges a Christian named Gaius to continue extending hospitality (3 Jn 3-8, 11-12). Watson proposes that 3 John is best classified as epideictic rhetoric of praise and blame. It commends Gaius for his hospitality and encourages him to continue to demonstrate it and accuses Diotrephes of refusal to extend hospitality and rebuffing the authority of the Presbyter. The stasis is quality, for it concerns the nature and necessity of hospitality. The letter is composed of an epistolary prescript (3 Jn 1); *exordium* (3 Jn 2-4) praising Gaius for walking in the truth; *narratio* (3 Jn 5-6) praising Gaius for hospitality and petitioning him to continue extending it; *probatio* (3 Jn 7-12) demonstrating the need for hospitality, amplifying Gaius's hospitality and denouncing the lack of the same by Diotrephes; *peroratio* (3 Jn 13-14) emphasizing the importance of the message; and epistolary postscript (3 Jn 15).

H.-J. Klauck qualifies the work of Vouga and Watson on the Johannine Epistles, arguing for the structural priority of the epistolary form. He questions the assumption that rhetorical invention and arrangement are found in the detail proposed for these letters.

2.7. Revelation. Reid shows that apocalyptic* literature relies upon contrasting metaphors, particularly the animalistic metaphors (e.g., Jesus as Lamb,* Satan* as serpent) and the light* and darkness metaphors (good and evil). Such literature is persuasive with people who are deeply dissatisfied with their present and whose future is uncertain. It explains their present distress as part of God's plan and reassures them that they are God's instruments in working out that plan, which is near to fulfillment. In its argumentation apocalyptic identifies a specific object of hatred and arouses fear while also giving the oppressed divine authority and purpose in working in God's service.*

S. D. O'Leary views the rhetoric of Revelation (*see* Revelation, Book of) as epochal discourse in which the systematic and symbolic division of historical time accords weight to events in history and mediates the relationship of past, present and future. Using dramatistic theory he proposes that the argument of Revelation is dramatic because it is placed within the cosmic drama depicted by the myth and symbolic universe it creates. Within the plot, the fate of the wicked is a tragic movement downward while the fate of the faithful is a comic movement upward. This drama helps the community deal with the apparent contradiction of salvation* and suffering and ultimately with death itself.

J. T. Kirby classifies Revelation as deliberative rhetoric. It is prophecy intended to persuade the seven churches to take a certain course of action in light of future events (Rev 1:1, 3) for its own advantage (Rev 22:11-12). Revelation 1:1-8 acts like a proem, while the vision* of Revelation 1:9-20 establishes the ethos of John as a prophet and elicits pathos (awe) from the churches. Each of the seven letters of Revelation 2-3 falls into four parts roughly corresponding to the proem, narration, proposition and epilogue. In the proem Jesus identifies himself and establishes his ethos for the pronouncements that follow. The narration is tailored to the nature of the individual churches addressed and forms the basis of the pronouncements and warnings of the proposition. Metaphor and paradox are the stylistic hallmarks of the narration and proposition. The epilogue is a promise promoting pathos in terms appealing to Christians undergoing persecution.

E. Schüssler Fiorenza proposes that Revelation is at once deliberative (call for decision), judicial (indictments and warnings) and epideictic (liturgical and hymnic) rhetoric. Regarding style, it uses sacred language and images from Jewish and Greco-Roman tradition to create the narrative symbolic universe in which the audience is to participate. Socioeconomic language and political-mythological imagery predominate because political and social issues predominate in the audience addressed. Regarding arrangement, the composition of Revelation is dramatic. It is unified by the appearance of key symbols and images throughout (e.g., Babylon*), preannouncements and cross-references, contrasts and numerical patterns. Interludes in which eschatological promises are clarified show the audience that the future gives meaning to their present and vice versa. Intercalation, the ABA' pattern (material sandwiched between two similar episodes or symbols), organizes smaller units and larger portions. Overall there is movement from promise to fulfillment.

Schüssler Fiorenza also describes how invention in Revelation functions. As a poetic work with symbolic language and images, Revelation evokes rather than defines meanings. It creates or organizes imaginative experience. The structure and strategy of Revelation and its function within a particular historical-rhetorical situation help the symbols and images make sense within a symbolic universe that invites participation. The rhetoric channels audience perceptions and emotions in an attempt to persuade it to change attitudes and motivations. Revelation seeks to fit a rhetorical situation—to clarify audience allegiances in a time of emperor* worship, social and economic ostracism, and even death. The audience is struggling with the seeming contradiction of participating in Christ's kingship and power* yet being persecuted by an empire challenging Christ as Lord.* It is struggling also with the temptation* of adaptation and acquiescence to political powers. Revelation encourages the audience to align itself with the heavenly world of God and to dissociate itself with the idolatry of the emperor cult backed by Satan. Using Jewish symbolic language it creates an alternative symbolic universe that gives meaning to the suffering of the community and individual death. It gives the audience a dramatic-cathartic journey that moves the audience to control its fear and sustain its vision.

3. Rhetorical Criticism of the Apostolic Fathers. Little study has been made of the rhetoric of the apostolic fathers. Further study of these works will yield important information about Christian rhetorical practice at the close of the first century and the beginning of the second century A.D., especially in its relationship to the rhetoric of the NT, Judaism and the Greco-Roman world. Among other things such study will reveal early Christian argumentative schemes and apologetic strategies. This in turn will reveal community values and assumptions that support such argumentation and ultimately our study of early Christianity in general.

3.1. 1 Clement. 1 *Clement* was written by Clement of Rome* to the church of Corinth around the turn of the first century A.D. The letter describes itself as one of counsel (*symboulē, 1 Clem.* 58.2), indicating that its rhetoric is deliberative. Using exhortation and warning, it is intended to persuade the Corinthians about what is beneficial and honorable and to dissuade them from what is harmful and dishonorable. The letter also describes itself as an appeal to peace* and concord or harmony (*enteuxis . . . peri eirēnēs kai homonoias, 1 Clem.* 63.2), a type of deliberative rhetoric necessitated by the uprising of younger men who have removed several presbyters from office and caused division in the church (*1 Clem.* 3; 44; 46.5-9; 47.5-7; *see* Church Order).

3.2. 2 Clement. Baasland argues that *2 Clement* is a sermon. It is deliberative speech designed not to win outsiders but to strengthen the self-understanding of insiders (having the force of protreptic). It begins with an *exordium* (*2 Clem.* 1.1-2), providing the theme "Christ as God who suffered for our salvation" as the grounding for the exhortation to follow. The *propositio* (*2 Clem.* 1.3-5) poses questions that are answered in the body of the sermon: What service will we render to God in return? and What fruit is worthy to render? The body of the sermon (*2 Clem.* 1.6-18.2) answers these questions but not by using logical argumentation intended to elicit a judgment. Rather, the topics of gift/reward* and gift in turn/service in return, which are introduced in the *exordium* and *propositio*, are developed throughout the body, most particularly in *2 Clement* 3.3; 9.5-11; 11.5-7; 15.1-2; and 19.1. The sermon concludes with a *peroratio*, summarizing this development (*2 Clem.* 19.1—20.5).

3.3. The Letters of Ignatius of Antioch. Ignatius,* bishop of Antioch,* wrote his seven letters approximately A.D. 100-118 to churches in Asia Minor and Rome while he was on his journey from Syria to Rome to face martyrdom.* These letters exhibit short cola (often in parallelism), rhythmic prose and such rhetorical figures as anaphora, homoeoteleuton, antithesis, metaphor, paronomasia and hyperbole (*see* Worship). This vigorous style has been attributed to the emotion of their epistolary situation. However, O. Perler more accurately identifies the style as Asian rhetoric common to Antioch of Syria and Asia Minor in the first and second centuries A.D. Asian rhetoric was a popular, exaggerated form of rhetoric that emphasized pathos (arousing emotion; *see* Melito of Sardis).

H. Riesenfeld adds that the sophistication in the subtleties of Asian rhetoric imply that Ignatius had a formal rhetorical education. He shows that the images and metaphors Ignatius uses are drawn from the Hellenistic rhetorical practice, such as a sailor waiting for fair wind or taking a storm-tossed vessel to the shelter of a harbor (Ign. *Pol.* 2.3).

D. L. Sullivan claims that the letters of Ignatius are epideictic rhetoric. They are intended to construct a social structure and maintain and increase the communities' adherence to its values. Ignatius helps the communities distinguish orthodoxy from the emerging heresies of judaizing and Docetism.* He does this using proofs from ethos, logos and pathos to create alter ego ideologies (images of what the community is not or what those outside the community are) and ego ideologies (images of what the community is). Alter ego ideology is created by forming negative images of the heterodox (ethos), exposing the falsity of their teaching (logos) and fostering a negative attitude toward them (pathos). However, the positive creation of ego ideology to foster community identity is the emphasis. Ignatius portrays the church as a dwelling place and a city and the leadership as hierarchial (Christ, bishop, clergy, laity) and worthy of imitation (ethos); describes the truth using semicreedal* passages and strong assertions of truth (logos); and enjoins the church to embrace certain attitudes and emotions (pathos).

3.4. Epistle to Diognetus. C. S. Wansink observes that the *Epistle to Diognetus** is protreptic; that is, literature aimed at extolling the truth and virtue of a certain philosophy or school of thought as opposed to others in order to convince the uninitiated to embrace it. This obscure work with an unknown past is probably an exercise of a young Christian convert in catechetical school. It focuses on the use of protreptic, subordinating theology to the rhetorical forms. The rhetoric is highly stylized and comes from rhetorical training. Of note is the use of well-balanced sentence structure, antithesis, paronomasia, alliteration, chiasm and repetition.

3.5. Other Apostolic Fathers. The epistle of Polycarp* to the Philippians (second century A.D.) is comprised of a series of exhortations often supported by citation of the NT. The *Didache**is a manual of church instruction, per-

haps from the second century A.D. Both works exhibit Christian rhetoric that relies more on the ethos or authority of the author and citation of Scripture and church tradition than on example or logical argumentation. Neither their argumentation nor arrangement reflects Greco-Roman conventions typical of the speech.

The *Martrydom of Polycarp* was written from the church of Smyrna to the church of Philomelium about A.D. 155. A narrative of the martyrdom of Polycarp in terms of the passion of Christ, the letter upholds Polycarp and ultimately Christ for imitation* (*Mart. Pol.* 1.1-2; 17.3; 19.1; 22.1). The weaving of allusions to the passion of Christ into the narrative is a rhetorically sophisticated use of comparison and exemplification. The *Epistle of Barnabas* (*see* Barnabas, Epistle of) presents what the author feels is the correct understanding of the OT. It argues logically throughout with many enthymemes, a proposition with supporting reason. The reason is often a quotation of the OT. Rhetorical questions amplify the significance of individual points of an argument as well as move the argumentation along. The *Shepherd of Hermas* (*see* Hermas, Shepherd of) is not arranged according to Greco-Roman rhetorical convention but does exhibit some important rhetorical features. In all three main divisions (the *Visions,* *Mandates* and *Similitudes)*development depends upon Hermas and various interlocutors using rhetorical questions to develop the revelation or teaching. The *Mandates* are commandments that are carefully developed in much the same way as an ancient thesis or proposition, using examples and contraries. The *Similitudes* or parables use diverse imagery drawn from such things as comparison of two cities, trees, vineyards, shepherds,* mountains and a tower.

See also HERMENEUTICS; LETTERS, LETTER FORMS; NARRATIVE CRITICISM; STRUCTURALISM, DISCOURSE ANALYSIS.

BIBLIOGRAPHY. P. J. Achtemeier, "Newborn Babes and Living Stones: Literal and Figurative in 1 Peter" in *To Touch the Text: Biblical and Related Studies in Honor of Joseph A. Fitzmyer, S.J.,* ed. M. P. Horgan and P. J. Kobelski (New York: Crossroad, 1989) 207-36; D. E. Aune, *The New Testament in Its Literary Environment* (LEC 8; Philadelphia: Westminster, 1987); E. Baasland, "Der 2.Klemensbrief und frühchristliche Rhetorik: 'Die erste christliche Predigt' im Lichte der neueren Forschung," *ANRW* 2.27.1 (1993) 78-157; idem, "Literarische Form, Thematik und geschichtliche Einordnung des Jakobusbriefes," *ANRW* 2.25.5 (1988) 3646-84; C. C. Black, "The Rhetorical Form of the Hellenistic Jewish and Early Christian Sermon: A Response to Lawrence Wills," *HTR* 81 (1988) 1-18; J. D. Charles, *Literary Strategy in the Epistle of Jude* (Scranton, PA: University of Scranton Press, 1993); M. R. Cosby, *The Rhetorical Composition and Function of Hebrews 11: In Light of Example Lists in Antiquity* (Macon, GA: Mercer University Press, 1988); idem, "The Rhetorical Composition of Hebrews 11," *JBL* 107 (1988) 257-73; J. H. Elliott, "The Epistle of James in Rhetorical and Social Scientific Perspective: Holiness-Wholeness and Patterns of Replication," *BTB* 23 (1993) 71-81; C. F. Evans, "The Theology of Rhetoric: The Epistle to the Hebrews" (Friends of Dr. Williams's Library, Lecture 42; London: Dr. Williams's Trust, 1988); S. J. Joubert, "Persuasion in the Letter of Jude," *JSNT* 58 (1995) 75-87; G. A. Kennedy, *New Testament Interpretation Through Rhetorical Criticism* (Chapel Hill, NC: University of North Carolina, 1984); J. T. Kirby, "The Rhetorical Situations of Revelation 1-3," *NTS* 34 (1988) 197-207; H.-J. Klauck, "Zur rhetorischen Analyse der Johannesbriefe," *ZNW* 81 (1990) 205-24; I. Lana, "La cristianizzazione di alcuni termini retorici nella *Lettera ai Corinti* di Clemente" in *Forma Futuri: Studi in Onore del Cardinale Michele Pellegrino* (Turin: Bottega d'Erasmo, 1975) 110-18; B. Lindars, "The Rhetorical Structure of Hebrews," *NTS* 35 (1989) 382-406; T. Martin, *Metaphor and Composition in 1 Peter* (SBLDS 131; Atlanta: Scholars Press, 1992); K. Nissilä, *Das Hohepriestermotiv im Hebräerbrief: Eine exegetische Untersuchung* (SFEG 33; Helsinki: Oy Liiton Kirjapaino, 1979); T. H. Olbricht, "Hebrews as Amplification" in *Rhetoric and the New Testament: Essays from the 1992 Heidelberg Conference*, ed. S. E. Porter and T. H. Olbricht (JSNTSup 90; Sheffield: Sheffield Academic Press, 1993) 375-87; S. D. O'Leary, "A Dramatistic Theory of Apocalyptic Rhetoric," *Quarterly Journal of Speech* 79 (1993) 385-426; C. Perelman and L. Olbrechts-Tyteca, *The New Rhetoric: A Treatise on Argumentation* (Notre Dame, IN: University of Notre Dame Press, 1969); O. Perler, "Das vierte Makkabaeerbuch, Ignatius von Antiochien und die aeltesten Martyrerberichte," *Rivista di Archeologia Cristiana* 25 (1949) 47-72; R. F. Reid,

"Apocalypticism and Typology: Rhetorical Dimensions of a Symbolic Reality," *QJS* 69 (1983) 229-48; H. Riesenfeld, "Reflections on the Style and the Theology of St. Ignatius of Antioch," *SP* 4 (= *TU 79*), ed. F. Cross (Berlin: Akademie, 1961) 312-22; E. Schüssler Fiorenza, *Revelation: Vision of a Just Word* (Minneapolis: Fortress, 1991), esp. 20-37, 117-39; idem, "Visionary Rhetoric and Social-Political Situation" in *The Book of Revelation: Justice and Judgment* (Philadelphia: Fortress, 1985) 181-203; T. W. Seid, "The Rhetorical Form of the Melchizedek/Christ Comparison in Hebrews 7" (unpublished Ph.D. dissertation, Brown University, 1996); D. L. Sullivan, "Establishing Orthodoxy: The Letters of Ignatius of Antioch as Epideictic Rhetoric," *JCR* 15 (1992) 71-86; J. W. Thompson, "The Rhetoric of 1 Peter," *RQ* 36 (1994) 237-50; L. Thurén, *The Rhetorical Strategy of 1 Peter: With Special Regard to Ambiguous Expressions* (Åbo: Åbo Academy Press, 1990); idem, "Risky Rhetoric in James?" *NovT* 37 (1995) 262-84; W. Übelacker, *Der Hebräerbrief als Appell: I. Untersuchungen zu exordium, narratio, und postscriptum (Hebr 1-2 und 13,22-25)* (ConBNT 21; Stockholm: Almqvist & Wiksell, 1989); F. Vouga, "La réception de la théologie johannique dans les épîtres" in *La Communauté Johannique et son histoire: La trajectoire de l'évangile de Jean aux deux premiers siècles*, ed. J.-D. Kaestli, J.-M. Poffet and J. Zumstein (Le Monde de la Bible; Geneva: Labor et Fides, 1990) 283-302; C. S. Wansink, "*Epistola ad Diognetum*: A School Exercise in the Use of Protreptic" in *Church Divinity 1986*, ed. J. Morgan (Church Divinity Monograph Series; Bristol, IN: Wyndham Hall Press, 1986) 97-109; D. F. Watson, "Amplification Techniques in 1 John: The Interaction of Rhetorical Style and Invention," *JSNT* 51 (1993) 99-123; idem, "An Epideictic Strategy for Increasing Adherence to Community Values: 1 John 1:1-2:27," *Proceedings: Eastern Great Lakes and Midwest Biblical Societies* 11 (1991) 144-52; idem, *Invention, Arrangement and Style: Rhetorical Criticism of Jude and 2 Peter* (SBLDS 104; Atlanta: Scholars Press, 1988); idem, "James 2 in Light of Greco-Roman Schemes of Argumentation," *NTS* 39 (1993) 94-121; idem, "The Rhetoric of James 3:1-12 and a Classical Pattern of Argumentation," *NovT* 35 (1993) 48-64; idem, "A Rhetorical Analysis of 2 John According to Greco-Roman Convention," *NTS* 35 (1989) 104-30; idem, "A Rhetorical Analysis of 3 John: A Study in Epistolary Rhetoric," *CBQ* 51 (1989)

479-501; L. L. Welborn, "Clement, First Epistle of," *ABD* 1:1055-60; E. R. Wendland, "A Comparative Study of 'Rhetorical Criticism,' Ancient and Modern—With Special Reference to the Larger Structure and Function of the Epistle of Jude," *Neot* 28 (1994) 193-228; L. Wills, "The Form of the Sermon in Hellenistic Judaism and Early Christianity," *HTR* 77 (1984) 277-99; W. H. Wuellner, "Der Jakobusbrief im Licht der Rhetorik und Textpragmatik," *LB* 43 (1978) 5-66.   D. F. Watson

RICHES AND POVERTY

The abundance or lack of material possessions was not a dominant concern for Christians of the late first and early second centuries. There is little apocalypticism,* and most paraenetic statements are continuous with Jewish piety rather than the radical statements of the Gospels. More distinctively Christian developments include a stress on hospitality* and an exchange of prayers* on the part of the poor for the beneficence of rich believers.

1. New Testament Writings
2. Early Noncanonical Literature

1. New Testament Writings.

1.1. Acts. Two key summary passages, Acts 2:43-45 and Acts 4:32-37, focus on the unity of believers in the first Jerusalem* church.* With respect to material possessions the passages contain two distinct features: that property was held in common (Acts 2:44; 4:32) and that possessions were sold to prevent anyone from being needy (Acts 2:45; 4:35). These features appear to represent a departure from the radical renunciation demanded of disciples in the Gospel (e.g., Lk 5:11; 14:33; 18:22), but it may be a way to meet that demand (cf. Lk 8:3; 12:33; 16:9; 19:8). Material giving in Acts* may assume what is stressed in the Gospels—that is, the need of the disciple to express complete dependence on God*—but the focus is on the need of community members. This is consistent with the praise given to other characters who give charitably to the needy (Acts 9:36; 10:2, 4; cf. Acts 6:1-6) and the condemnation of those who would put money above the needs of others (Acts 5:1-11; 8:14-24). It is also consistent with the Hellenistic ideal of friendship or unity of mind, often expressed in terms of common possessions, but here the practice is driven by the Spirit (*see* Holy Spirit) rather than by friendship.

Some scholars have suggested that community of possessions is not mentioned in early Christian writings after Acts 4 because it failed as a social experiment or because it was a temporary measure to help itinerant pilgrims who left when it became apparent that the eschaton was delayed (*see* Parousia). But a more likely implication of silence following such a glowing description of early church communal life is that believers failed to sustain their initial level of obedience.*

1.2. Hebrews, General Epistles and Revelation. The Pastoral Epistles and Hebrews* reflect what we might term middle-class values. These letters* share an interest in contentment with one's current economic status (1 Tim 6:6-10; Heb 13:5b) and condemn love* of money (1 Tim 6:10; 2 Tim 3:2; Heb 13:5a; cf. Tit 1:7) without condemning those who possess much. The recommendation to the rich is "to do good, to be rich in good works, generous, and ready to share" (1 Tim 6:17-18, NRSV). All believers are enjoined to practice hospitality (1 Tim 5:10; Heb 13:2, 16).

The letters of Peter (*see* 1 Peter; 2 Peter) and John (*see* John, Letters of) contain little relevant material. Peter warns against mercenary motives in ministry* (1 Pet 5:2; 2 Pet 2:14-15) and John recommends generosity toward needy believers (1 Jn 3:17); both command hospitality (1 Pet 4:9; 3 Jn 5-8).

James* and Revelation (*see* Revelation, Book of) evince more of the critical attitude toward the rich and praise for the poor that are characteristic of the Gospels, but this does not mean that the audience is from the lowest stratum of society. Diatribes against the rich in James 5:1-6 appear to be directed toward non-Christian oppressors, but other passages (Jas 1:10-11; 2:1-7; 4:13-15) imply the presence of affluent believers. Moreover, both rich and poor are described as "they" in relation to the recipients of the letter (Jas 2:1-7). James tells poor believers to boast that they will soon be "lifted up" and rich believers to boast that they will soon be "brought low" (Jas 1:9-11). The boasting is in the transitoriness of their wealth as compared to the permanence of the coming kingdom,* but James does not allow humility to remain at the level of attitude. "Doers of the word" (Jas 1:22) must care for the needy (Jas 1:27) and renounce worldly pleasures (Jas 4:3-10).

In Revelation Jesus commands the church of

Laodicea to turn from its boast that "I am rich" to "buy from me gold refined by fire" (Rev 3:17-18, NRSV), a possible allusion to Gospel passages (Mt 13:44-45; Lk 16:9) in which "buying" is a metaphor for renunciation of possessions. Elsewhere in Revelation earthly riches are associated with the powers of evil, and Revelation 18 offers a lengthy woe against Babylon,* who "glorified herself and lived luxuriously" (Rev 18:7, NRSV). Although the depiction of commercial enterprise is to some extent a metaphor for spiritual rebellion, the recommendation for believers is plain: "Come out of her, my people, so that you do not take part in her sins" (Rev 18:4, NRSV).

Revelation closes with a contrasting description of a heavenly kingdom made of gold, crystal and jewels (Rev 21:1-22:6; *see* Heaven). This too is metaphorical, a representation in prophetic* language of a community perfectly ordered by God. But in its almost ironic depiction of unimaginable material riches as the reward for those who renounced the same on earth, it partakes of a tradition going back at least to Job and continuous with Matthew 5:3-5, 2 Corinthians 8:13-15 and Revelation 2:9: "I know your affliction and your poverty, even though you are rich" (NRSV).

2. Early Noncanonical Literature.

Writings from the late first to mid-second centuries are dominated by defense of the gospel* against paganism or heresy and exhibit a relative lack of interest in either the rich or the poor. What references are made generally lack force or originality. Modern curiosity about the early Christian social situation is frustrated by the paucity of evidence and the inability to be certain about the import of the evidence. Does an author criticize the rich because he wants to partake in a prophetic or paraenetic tradition? to encourage an audience of (mostly) poor people? to exhort an audience of (partly) rich people? Does the author know his audience well, or is he simply concerned about the needy or the danger of wealth? Is his concern typical of Christian leaders at that time or in that region? Since it is impossible to answer such questions on the basis of literary evidence alone and since there is little other evidence, we do best to defer reconstructions of the social situation and consider instead the intrinsic meaning of the texts.

2.1. Themes Continuous with Jewish and New Testament Ethics. Late Second Temple Jewish writings share with early Christian writings an interest in almsgiving, which was at that time not a matter of giving loose change to beggars but a significant economic sacrifice* in the interest of others. There is ample evidence that both Jews and Christians regarded the practice as so significant that it had an atonement function. While this function may be evident in Gospel passages (e.g., Mt 6:19-21; Lk 16:9; 19:8), it is more explicit in Jewish and noncanonical early Christian writings. Polycarp* quotes Tobit 4:10, "almsgiving delivers from death" (Pol. *Phil.* 10.2; cf. *Did.* 1.5). *2 Clement* 16.4 asserts that "almsgiving is good as repentance for sin." *The Shepherd of Hermas* enjoins believers, "instead of lands, buy afflicted souls . . . and you will be saved" (*Herm. Sim.* 1.8-11; cf. 10.4.1-3).

In other respects late first- and early second-century writers have much in common with OT prophetic writers and NT authors, but no particular theme dominates. God makes both rich and poor (*1 Clem.* 59.3). One should be content (*2 Clem.* 20.1-4) and not love money (e.g., *2 Clem.* 4.3; Ign. *Rom.* 7.2-3; *Barn.* 19.6; Pol. *Phil.* 2.2) or indulge in luxury (*2 Clem.* 6.1-6; *Herm. Man.* 8.3; *Herm. Sim.* 6.2-5; 9.20, 31).

2.2. Hospitality. The alternative to avarice or luxury is generosity, especially hospitality*— and that especially to Christian workers. This is a common theme in the literature. Clement of Rome* begins his letter to the Corinthians by praising their "character so magnificent in its hospitality" and for their "giving more gladly than receiving" (*1 Clem.* 1.2; 2.1; 10.7; 12.1; 35.5). Numerous other passages exhort believers to practice hospitality or generosity to needy believers (*Did.* 13.4, 7; *Barn.* 19.6-11; 20.1-2; *Herm. Man.* 2.4; 8.10; *Herm. Sim.* 8.10.3; 9.27.2; *Diogn.* 5.13).

2.3. Exchange Between Rich and Poor. The most interesting development in attitudes toward rich and poor appears to have emerged from the tension between the presumed piety of the poor (Lk 6:20; Jas 1:9) and the presumed difficulty of the rich to enter heaven (Mt 19:24; Lk 6:24). How is it "possible for God" (Mt 19:26) to receive the rich? From the late first century on, we come across the idea that the poor, who had spiritual power, could pray for the salvation* of the rich if the rich, who had economic power, would keep the poor from becoming destitute.

The arrangement may have its roots in passages like Acts 4:42, but the early Christian expressions of it do not explicitly rely on any biblical text. Clement writes, "Let the strong care for the weak and let the weak reverence the strong. Let the rich man bestow help on the poor and let the poor give thanks to God, that he gave him one to supply his needs" (*1 Clem.* 38.2). Similarly *Hermas* enjoins, "Let therefore they who have overabundance seek out those who are hungry. . . . See to it then . . . that the destitute may not groan, and their groans go up to the Lord, and you with your goods be shut outside the door of the tower" (*Herm. Vis.* 3.9.5-6). *Hermas Similitude* 2.5-10 is the fullest statement:

> The rich man has much wealth, but he is poor as touching the Lord, being busied about his riches. . . . But . . . the poor is rich in intercession and confession, and his intercession has great power with God. . . . The poor man, being helped by the rich, makes intercession to God. . . . Therefore the two together complete the work, for the poor works in the intercession in which he is rich . . . and the rich man likewise provides the poor, without hesitating, with the wealth which he received from the Lord.

This solution to a practical problem is nothing if not creative, and it survives in less explicit form alongside more modern attempts to resolve the same tension presented by the biblical material.

See also HERMAS, SHEPHERD OF; HOSPITALITY; JAMES; SOCIAL SETTING OF EARLY NON-PAULINE CHRISTIANITY.

BIBLIOGRAPHY. L. W. Countryman, *The Rich Christian in the Church of the Early Empire: Contradictions and Accommodations* (Lewiston, NY: Edwin Mellen, 1980); R. Garrison, *Redemptive Almsgiving in Early Christianity* (Sheffield: JSOT, 1993); J. Gonzalez, *Faith and Wealth: A History of Early Christian Ideas on the Origin, Significance and Use of Money* (San Francisco: Harper & Row, 1990); M. Hengel, *Property and Riches in the Early Church* (Philadelphia: Fortress, 1974); L. T. Johnson, *Sharing Possessions: Mandate and Symbol of Faith* (Philadelphia: Fortress, 1981); P. U. Maynard-Reid, *Poverty and Wealth in James* (Maryknoll, NY: Orbis, 1987); C. Osiek, *Rich and Poor in the Shepherd of Hermas: An Exegetical-Social Investigation* (Washington, D.C.: Catholic Biblical Association of America, 1983).

T. E. Schmidt

RIGHTEOUS ONE. *See* RIGHTEOUSNESS.

RIGHTEOUSNESS

In the biblical tradition the noun *righteousness* and the adjective *righteous* normally denote the character, behavior and status appropriate to the covenant* relationship God* formed with the world through Israel.* God demonstrates righteousness through faithfulness to his promises,* while humanity expresses righteousness in and through loyal obedience.* "To justify" denotes the activity of "putting right" (in the case of God) and "being put right" (in the case of humans). This "being put right" can be ethical* (i.e., "to be transformed"), forensic (i.e., "to be declared right") or relational (i.e., "to be reconciled").

Despite a long and cherished history in Christian theology (see McGrath), the varied theological nuances of righteousness language within the Bible have sometimes been overlooked. Part of the problem is that English employs two word families ("righteousness"/"righteous" and "justify"/"justification") to translate only one family of words in Greek—the noun *dikaiosynē*, the adjective *dikaios* and the verb *dikaioō*. Because the word *justification* has obtained prominence as a legal term in English, there is a strong temptation to read juridical connotations into any occurrence of a *dik-* stem word in Greek. The forensic interpretation of the Protestant slogan "justification by faith alone" has further blinded readers to the diverse and often ethical uses of righteousness language. Moreover, the supposed anthropological orientation of righteousness in Paul has unfairly truncated the meaning of justification: as the antidote to a guilty conscience,* it primarily relates to the resolution of an individual's existential crisis (Stendahl). However, the kaleidoscopic contextual meanings and the variegated theological uses of the noun *dikaiosynē*, the adjective *dikaios* and the verb *dikaioō* mean that righteousness or justification cannot be reduced to a single theological concept. Righteousness justification language is one of the many ways that early Christians sought to convey the meaning and significance of God's saving deeds wrought in Jesus.

Thus it is not surprising to find that in the later NT documents and the apostolic fathers* language about righteousness or justification falls into four, broad domains of usage: a theological domain (to speak of God), a christological* domain (to define the person and work of Jesus), a soteriological domain (to describe the means and consequences of salvation*) and an ethical domain (to depict the character and behavior associated with spiritual transformation). Informing and guiding the use of language about righteousness or justification in each of these domains is an eschatological* perspective common to early Christianity.

1. The Righteousness of God
2. Jesus, the Righteous One
3. Justification by Faith as a New Pattern of Religion
4. Righteousness and Ethics
5. Righteousness and Eschatology
6. Summary

1. The Righteousness of God.
Given the supposed foundational character of "righteousness of God" (*dikaiosynē theou*) as God's saving activity in Paul's thinking (Rom 1:17; 3:5, 22; 10:3; 1 Cor 1:30; 2 Cor 5:21; cf. Phil 3:9; see Käsemann, Stuhlmacher), it is remarkable that the phrase so rarely appears in post-Pauline Christianity. Outside of Paul the phrase occurs only twice (Mt 6:33; Jas 1:20; on 2 Pet 1:1 see 2 below).

James* states that the "anger of man does not work the righteousness of God" (Jas 1:20). There are three ways to understand the phrase *dikaiosynēn theou*. (1) Human anger does not produce (*ergazetai*) the proper moral disposition or behavior (*dikaiosynēn*) within humans (see discussion in Davids, 93). (2) Human anger does not achieve (*ergazetai*) the level of perfection that God demands (*dikaiosynēn*), especially that demand to be revealed at the last judgment* (Ziesler 133, 135). Or, preferably, (3) human anger does not bring into being (*ergazetai*) the state of affairs that God desires (*dikaiosynēn*). By tying together the moral, forensic and eschatological senses, this last reading conceptually links the "righteousness of God" here with the "kingdom of God"* in the teaching of Jesus (Martin, 48). This reading also reveals that James is not reacting against Paul's notion of *dikaiosynē theou* (cf. Dibelius, 111). James stands much closer to Matthew, where righteousness is indicative of God's kingdom (Mt 6:33; cf. Przybylski, 89-92).

While Clement's quotation of Psalm 50:16 (LXX) does delimit the meaning of righteous-ness as "salvation" (*1 Clem.* 18.15: "My tongue will rejoice in your righteousness"), it is hard to see that Clement (*see* Clement of Rome) quoted the psalm specifically for this sense of *dikaiosynē*. The closest we come to Paul's rich and highly charged notion of *dikaiosynē theou* is in 1 John. The author claims that "If we confess our sins, he [God] is faithful and just [*pistos estin kai dikaios*] and will forgive our sins and cleanse us from all unrighteousness" (1 Jn 1:9). The paralleling of *dikaios* with *pistos* points to God's activity of forgiving sins and echoes his long-standing commitment to honor repentance* and sacrifice* (e.g., Ex 34:6-7). God's faithfulness thus becomes synonymous with his righteousness (Schnackenburg, 83).

The other uses of righteousness with reference to God are all clearly forensic (*see* God). Paul in his Areopagus speech (Acts 17:31) declares that God has a fixed day in which he will "judge the world in righteousness" (*krinein . . . en dikaiosynē*). This quotation of Psalm 95:13 (LXX) positions God in a traditional role as judge. 1 Peter (1 Pet 2:23) depicts Jesus as trusting the one (i.e., God) "who judges justly" (*tō krinonti dikaiōs*). Three times in Revelation (Rev 16:5, 7; 19:2; cf. Rev 15:3) is it said of God that his judgments are "just" (*dikaios*). *1 Clement* too affirms that God is righteous in his judgments (*1 Clem.* 27.1; 60.1). The *Shepherd of Hermas** (*Herm. Sim.* 6.3.6) even calls God a "righteous judge" (*dikaios kritēs*). Finally Polycarp* (Pol. *Phil.* 5.2), within a general admonition to "live in a manner that is worthy of his commandment," singles out the deacons for special attention. They "must be blameless before his righteousness" (*katenōpion autou tēs dikaiosynēs*). God is a righteous judge who demands purity.

2. Jesus, the Righteous One.
Righteousness language is also applied to Jesus. In fact various traditions entitle Jesus the "Righteous One" (*ho dikaios*). In their speeches Peter, Stephen* and Paul all name Jesus the "Righteous One" (*ho dikaios*). Peter (Acts 3:14) charges his Jewish listeners with having denied "the Holy and Righteous One" (*ton hagion kai dikaion*). Stephen (Acts 7:52; cf. Heb 10:37-38) understands the prophets* as preaching about the "coming of the Righteous One" (*tēs eleuseōs tou dikaiou*). Ananias (Acts 22:14) interprets Paul's christophany as an apocalyptic appearance of

the "Righteous One" *(ton dikaion)*.

Jesus' priestly* role as an advocate with the Father earns him the title "Jesus Christ, the Righteous" *(Iēsoun Christon dikaion)*, a confession common within the Johannine community (1 Jn 2:1, 29; 3:7). 1 Peter* and the *Epistle to Diognetus* also name Jesus the "Righteous One" *(dikaios)* in early confessions* of faith* (1 Pet 3:18; *Diogn.* 9.2). Hebrews* applies Psalm 45:7 to Jesus to show that God's Son* "loved righteousness and hated lawlessness" (Heb 1:9). *1 Clement* interprets the life of Jesus according to the Servant of Isaiah when he designates Jesus as the "Just One *[dikaion]* who is a good servant to many" (*1 Clem.* 16.12; cf. Is 53:11 [LXX]). Polycarp likewise appeals to Isaiah 53: he identifies Jesus as "the guarantee of our righteousness *[arrabōni tēs dikaiosynēs hēmōn]*, the one who bore our sins in his own body upon the tree" (Pol. *Phil.* 8.1; Is 53:3-5 [LXX]; cf. 1 Pet 2:24). *Diognetus* invokes more Adamic imagery when describing Jesus as that "one righteous man *[dikaiō heni]* who justifies many sinners" (*Diogn.* 9.5; cf. Rom 5:15).

The special endowment of a figure with one of God's attributes (e.g., wisdom,* holiness* or glory*) or the outright personification of an attribute were important ways Jews portrayed divine meditation (Hurtado, 41-50). In Second Temple Judaism* God's attribute of righteousness was often personified or given as a special endowment to some heavenly figure (e.g., *1 Enoch* 38:2; 53:6; 1QM 1:8; 17:8; 1QMyst 5-6; 1QIsa^a 51:5; 11QPsa^a 26:11; see Baumgarten, 219-39). Entitling Jesus the "Righteous One" positions him as God's chief agent.

As the "Righteous One" Jesus manifests what P. G. Davis calls the "triple pattern" of divine mediation. Jesus' substitutionary death (1 Pet 3:18; *1 Clem.* 16.12; Pol. *Phil.* 8.1; *Diogn.* 9.2-3; cf. Jas 5:5; *Barn.* 6.7) represents the legacy pattern, emphasizing the soteriological consequences of his past mediatorial deeds. Jesus' continuing role as an advocate with God the Father (1 Jn 2:1) reveals an interventionistic pattern, emphasizing the efficacy of his present mediatorial deeds. And the revelation of Jesus as a righteous judge at the Parousia* (Rev 19:11; cf. Acts 7:52) displays the consummation pattern, emphasizing the forensic character of his future mediatorial deeds. Thus while the title "Righteous One" closes the gap between God and Jesus (i.e., Jesus is marked as a special agent of God

because he embodies one of God's attributes), the mediatorial deeds ascribed to Jesus as the "Righteous One" also represent a significant innovation: the concentration of the triple pattern of mediation in Jesus—a rarity in Judaism (Davis, 502)—highlights his unique status. The title "Righteous One" may well have been one of the earliest ways that Christians expressed their belief in the divinity of Jesus (Longenecker, 47).

One reading of 2 Peter's opening address supports such a view. There the author affirms that the readers have obtained a "faith in the righteousness of God and Christ" *(pistin en dikaiosynē tou theou hēmōn kai sōtēros Iēsou Christou,* 2 Pet 1:1; cf. 2 Thess 1:12; Tit 2:13). Since it is best to understand both *theou* and *sōtēros* as appellations of Jesus (Brown, 184; Cullmann, 314), this text refers to Jesus as God (not to Jesus and God). The resulting translation would be "faith in the righteousness of our God and Savior, Jesus." 2 Peter* then seems to endorse a belief in the righteousness (= divinity or divine status) of Jesus (cf. Harris, 237). Like the attributes glory and wisdom, righteousness not only associates Jesus with God as his chief vizier but also helps demarcate Jesus as God (the embodiment of God's divine presence).

3. Justification by Faith as a New Pattern of Religion.

E. P. Sanders helpfully outlines the way in which Palestinian Judaism worked. He describes a five-fold soteriological pattern: Jews believed (1) that they were elected* by grace*; (2) that God gave the commandments* as a gift; (3) that obedience to the commandments brings blessing* while disobedience brings cursing; (4) that repentance and atonement for sin (5) will yield God's forgiveness.* Sanders terms this pattern of religion "covenantal nomism." Within this pattern of religion, righteousness was seen as a way of maintaining the covenant relationship and never as a means of obtaining or earning a relationship with God (Sanders, 205, 544).

This makes Paul's theology of justification distinctive. For Paul, in direct contrast to Judaism, both "righteousness" and "faith" were used as entry terms: justification by faith was the means of obtaining a right relationship with God. Furthermore, Paul insisted that a person initially justified by faith remains so through faith (Gal 3:1-3; Col 2:6-7; see Gundry). Paul, for all of his indebtedness to Judaism, conceptualized a completely new pattern of religion. The clarity and force of Paul's soteriological innovations make an examination of statements about justification in other Christian writers all the more intriguing.

3.1. Acts. Acts* twice depicts Paul as preaching about righteousness or justification. In his Areopagus speech (Acts 13:38-39) Paul declares that through Jesus God forgives sins and that belief in Jesus "justifies" (*dikaiountai*) when the law* was unable to do so (*ouk . . . dikaiōthēnai*). Justification here describes the movement from being unsaved to being saved and consequently fits closely to the pattern of religion envisioned by Paul (see esp. Rom 8:2-4). In his defense before Felix, Paul again preaches about "faith in Christ Jesus" (Acts 24:24). This "faith in Christ" is further defined as "righteousness [*dikaiosynēs*], self-control and judgment" (Acts 24:25; cf. *Barn.* 1.6). As Acts styles it, Paul's christocentric preaching consisted in a message about salvation (righteousness), ethics (self-control) and eschatological judgment (but see Reumann, 141). "Righteousness" here again describes "entrance" into salvation.

3.2. Hebrews. The use of righteousness language in two short comments about Abel and Noah in Hebrews allows a glimpse of that author's soteriological pattern. "By faith" Abel offered a better sacrifice and thereby "received approval as righteous" (*emartyrēthē einai dikaios*), in that God accepted his gift (Heb 11:4; cf. 1 Jn 3:12). Noah became an "heir of righteousness that comes by faith" (*tēs kata pistin dikaiosynēs egeneto klēronomos*) when he constructed the ark (Heb 11:7; cf. 2 Pet 2:5). Although it does not employ the formula "justified by faith," Hebrews, in its retrofitting of these two OT stories, represents a perspective that coheres with Paul's (Lane, 2:340; cf. Bacon, 14). Abel and Noah exemplify the faith praised at Hebrews 11:1 and Hebrews 10:37-38 (quoting Hab 2:4; Bruce, 71-72) and illustrate that faith serves as the only legitimate ground for righteousness.

3.3. James. Ever since Luther, James 2:14-26 has long plagued interpreters with its apparent contradictions with Paul at the point of justification. However, a close reading of James's rhetoric reveals that this passage complements rather than contradicts Paul.

James's opponents contend that faith and works (*see* Faith and Works) can legitimately be separated from each other (Jas 2:18; see Martin, 82-84). James responds by arguing for the interdependence of faith and works (Jas 2:18). Through an ironic appeal to the "faith" of demonic powers, James shows that "faith" is a necessary but insufficient basis for enjoying salvation (Jas 2:19). "Faith apart from works is barren" (Jas 2:20). James finds proof for this in the figure of Abraham* (Jas 2:21-22). In the offering of his son Isaac (Gen 22:1-14) Abraham "was justified" (*edikaiōthē*). Faith "was active" (*synērgei*) in Abraham's works, and works "completed" (*eteleiōthē*) his faith. Genesis 15:6—"Abraham believed God, and it was reckoned to him as righteousness [*dikaiosynēn*]"—was fulfilled (*eplērōthē*) in Genesis 22 (Jas 2:23). Thus for everyone, and not for Abraham alone, the presence of justifying faith is demonstrated by works (Jas 2:24). To this, James provides a second example, that of Rahab, whose faith was also completed in her works (Jas 2:25). James finally reiterates his point that faith apart from works is "dead" (Jas 2:26)

James is obviously seeking to correct something in early Christianity that he saw as a error (Reumann, 150). Specifically James is responding to opponents who had either misunderstood Paul or improperly radicalized Paul's teaching of "justification by faith alone" (Davids 51, 130-31). Because of his opponents' misuse of the words, "faith" and "justify" take on different meanings for James than they do for Paul. Faith in James refers to intellectual assent, whereas for Paul faith means the commitment of one's life, which includes a change in one's behavior. Thus what Paul means by faith (as in Gal 5:6) is functionally equivalent to James's faith-as-demonstrated-by-works formula. For James the verb *justify* (Jas 2:21, 24, 25) bears a demonstrative meaning, whereas *dikaioō* in Paul should be read most often as forensic declaration.

What James and Paul do agree upon is that "faith" and "justify" are entry terms (Sloan, 8-9), that complete and utter commitment to God is the means of justification and that good works should follow initial justification.

3.4. 1 John. 1 John (*see* John, Letters of) makes nearly the same point as James: righteous deeds are evidence of salvation. (This lends credence to the theory that [Paul's?] teaching on justification by faith alone had been greatly misunderstood; see 2 Pet 3:16.) The author explicitly ties the practice of righteousness *(ho poiōn tēn dikaiosynēn)* with conversion (1 Jn 2:29; 3:7, 10). Good works become the mark of conversion. While not specifically connecting righteousness or justification with faith, 1 John does ground the practice of righteousness with christology. "He who does right is righteous, as he [Jesus] is righteous" (1 Jn 3:7). Laying claim to righteousness involves a christoformic pattern of living.

3.5. **1 Clement.** Although some scholars have defended him as a "Paulinist" (e.g., Buchanan, 84), most see Clement as corrupting Paul's doctrine of justification (e.g., Wrede, 84-86; Torrance, 44-55) or as hopelessly inconsistent on the matter (e.g., Lightfoot, 1.1:397-98). Two things can and should be said about Clement's theology of justification.

It is clear that Clement embraced "justification by faith" as the way to obtain salvation (contra Räisänen). Abraham "attained righteousness and truth through faith" (*1 Clem.* 31.2), and all who experience salvation in Christ are "justified" *(dikaioumetha)* "through faith" *(dia tēs pisteōs)* and not through "wisdom," "piety" or "works" (*1 Clem.* 32.4; see also *2 Clem.* 6.9). In fact faith is the means by which God has "justified" *(edikaiōsen)* everyone from the beginning of time (*1 Clem.* 32.4). Thus Clement, like Paul, sees initial, forensic justification as occurring through faith.

It is also clear that Clement understood good works as the means to maintain salvation. Clement exhorts (*1 Clem.* 30.3) his readers to "clothe" themselves in unity, "being justified by works and not words *(ergois dikaioumenoi kai mē logois)."* Here Clement addresses the issue of how those who have already experienced salvation are expected to maintain it. The disunity within the congregation, according to Clement, is a great soteriological threat; Clement advises the Corinthians to remain saved through their practice of works, specifically hospitality* (Chadwick; *1 Clem.* 3.4; 12.1; 13.1; 17.3; 22.6-7; 30.7; 33.7; 35.1; 50.5).

Clement thus evinces a twofold soteriological pattern (Newman, 113-35); like other Christian writers (especially Paul), Clement sees that one is initially justified by faith and that (in distinction from Paul) one remains justified by works.

3.6. **Epistle to Diognetus.** When *Diognetus* questions "In whom was it possible for us, the lawless and ungodly, to be justified, except in the Son of God alone?" (*Diogn.* 9.4) and then details the unexpected way in which Jesus "should justify many sinners" (*Diogn.* 9.5), it is hard to determine if the two uses of *dikaioō* should be construed ethically ("make righteous") or forensically ("declare righteous"). While the context argues for the former (note the opposition of righteousness to wickedness in *Diogn.* 9.1; Ziesler, 215), the clear substitutionary flavor of *Diognetus* 9.3-5 argues for the latter. In either case *Diognetus* embraces a pattern of religion that emphasizes entrance into salvation though justification by faith.

4. Righteousness and Ethics.

In the later documents of the NT the noun *dikaiosynē* and the adjective *dikaios* always have an "ethical content" (Ziesler, 141). This ethical content can be expressed in many ways. Righteousness language can refer to the character of a human (2 Pet 2:8; Rev 22:11); behavior (Acts 10:35; 1 Pet 2:24; 3:13-14; 1 Jn 3:12); a person's status, which is grounded in behavior (Acts 10:22; 1 Pet 4:18; 2 Pet 2:7-8; Jas 5:16); or to the process of moral transformation (Heb 12:11; Jas 3:18; 2 Pet 2:21).

A near identical situation holds in the apostolic fathers; the noun and the adjectives always have an ethical connotation (Ziesler, 214). Again this ethical connotation can include the character of a human (e.g., *2 Clem.* 13.1; Ign. *Eph.* 1.1; *Mart. Pol.* 11.1; *Herm. Vis.* 3.9.1; *Herm. Man.* 1.2; 12.2.4), behavior (e.g., *1 Clem.* 9.3; 33.8; 42.8; *2 Clem.* 6.9; 19.3; Ign. *Smyrn.* 1.1; Pol. *Phil.* 2.3; 3.3; *Herm. Vis.* 3.3.3; *Diogn.* 10.8), a person's status grounded in behavior (e.g., *1 Clem.* 33.7; *2 Clem.* 2.4; 20.3-4; Ign. *Magn.* 12.1; *Mart. Poly.* 14.1; *Did.* 3.9; *Barn.* 5.9; 10.11; 17.1; *Herm. Vis.* 1.1.8) or the process of transformation (e.g., *2 Clem.* 5.7; 18.2; *Did.* 5.2; 11.1; *Barn.* 1.7; 15.4; *Herm. Man.* 5-6 passim). The verb *dikaioō* in all but four occurrences bears a forensic meaning, "acquit" (Ziesler, 214); in the four exceptions the verb refers to the process of "making righteous" (*Barn.* 15.7; *Herm. Vis.* 3.9.1; *Herm. Man.* 5.1.7; 5.7.1).

5. Righteousness and Eschatology.

The soteriological and ethical uses temporally anchor righteousness or justification language to the writers' past or present. However, early Christianity also employed righteousness language to describe what the future was to be like. The new heavens* and new earth will be a place in which righteousness dwells (2 Pet 3:13). The righteous person should look forward to the age to come (*Barn.* 10.11), despite the prospect of a righteous judgment (Acts 17:31; Rev 19:11). The future will entail a resurrection* of both the just and unjust (Acts 24:15). The future will be a time of final salvation for the righteous (1 Pet 4:18), a time in which final transformation (Heb 12:23) and reversal will occur (Ign. *Rom.* 5.1; Ign. *Phld.* 8.2; *Diogn.* 5.14). Because the future kingdom is immanent, there is an ethical urgency for the righteous to practice righteousness (Rev 22:11). To live this life as though one were already justified is a significant error (*Barn.* 4.10). Even those who have already experienced salvation should take care "for the time for the righteous to repent is at hand" (*Herm. Vis.* 2.2.5).

6. Summary.

Teaching about righteousness or justification formed part of early Christian catechesis. Along with hope* and love,* righteousness was, according to Barnabas (*Barn.* 1.6), one of the "three basic doctrines of the Lord" (*tria dogmata kyriou*). Christians were to be skilled in the "word of righteousness" (Heb 5:13; Pol. *Phil.* 3.1). This instruction emphasized God's righteousness (his faithfulness and his righteous character), Jesus as the Righteous One (his unique status and past, present and future deeds), the proper place of faith and works in salvation, and a hope for a future in which righteousness will rule. Early Christianity's use of the language of righteousness or justification is as diverse as it is evocative.

See also ABRAHAM; COVENANT, NEW COVENANT; DEATH OF CHRIST; ESCHATOLOGY; FAITH AND WORKS; FORGIVENESS; GOD; JUDGMENT; LAW; OBEDIENCE, LAWLESSNESS.

BIBLIOGRAPHY. B. W. Bacon, "The Doctrine of Faith in Hebrews, James and Clement of Rome," *JBL* 19 (1900) 12-21; J. M. Baumgarten, "The Heavenly Tribunal and the Personification of *Sedeq* in Jewish Apocalyptic," *ANRW* 2.19.1 (1979) 219-39; R. E. Brown, *An Introduction to New Testament Christology* (New York: Paulist, 1994); F. F. Bruce, "Justification by Faith in the Non-Pauline Writings of the New Testament," *EvQ* 34 (1952) 66-77; J. Buchanan, *The Doctrine of Justification* (Edinburgh: T & T Clark, 1867); H. Chadwick, "Justification by Faith and Hospitality," *TU* 79 (1961) 281-85; O. Cullmann, *The Christology of the New Testament* (Philadelphia: Westminster, 1959); P. H. Davids, *The Epistle of James* (NIGTC; Grand Rapids: Eerdmans, 1982); P. G. Davis, "Divine Agents, Mediators and New Testament Christology," *JTS* 45 (1994) 479-503; M. Dibelius and H. Greeven, *James* (Herm; Philadelphia: Fortress, 1976); R. H. Gundry, "Grace, Works and Staying Saved in Paul," *Bib* 66 (1985) 1-38; M. J. Harris, *Jesus as God: The New Testament Use of* Theos *in Reference to Jesus* (Grand Rapids: Baker, 1992); L. Hurtado, *One God, One Lord: Early Christian Devotion and Ancient Jewish Monotheism* (Philadelphia: Fortress, 1988); E. Käsemann, " 'The Righteousness of God' in Paul" in *New Testament Questions of Today* (Philadelphia: Fortress, 1969) 168-82; W. L. Lane, *Hebrews* (2 vols.; WBC; Dallas: Word, 1992); J. B. Lightfoot, *The Apostolic Fathers,* part 1: *Clement of Rome* (2 vols.; London: Macmillan, 1890); R. N. Longenecker, *The Christology of Early Jewish Christianity* (London: SCM, 1970); A. E. McGrath, *Iustitia Dei: A History of the Christian Doctrine of Justification* (2 vols.; Cambridge: Cambridge University Press, 1986); R. P. Martin, *James* (WBC; Waco, TX: Word, 1988); C. C. Newman, "Righteousness/Justification Language in 1 Clement: A Linguistic and Theological Enquiry" (unpublished M.Th. thesis, University of Aberdeen, 1985); B. Przybylski, *Righteousness in Matthew and the World of His Thought* (SNTSMS 41; Cambridge: Cambridge University Press, 1980); H. Räisänen, "Righteousness by Works: An Early Catholic Doctrine? Thoughts on 1 Clement" in *Jesus, Paul and Torah: Collected Essays* (JSNTSup 43; Sheffield: JSOT, 1992) chap. 8; J. Reumann, *Righteousness in the New Testament* (Philadelphia: Fortress, 1983); E. P. Sanders, *Paul and Palestinian Judaism* (Philadelphia: Fortress, 1977); R. Schnackenburg, *The Johannine Epistles* (New York: Crossroad, 1992); R. B. Sloan, "The Christology of James," *CTR* 1 (1986) 3-29; K. Stendahl, "The Apostle Paul and the Introspective Conscience of the West" in *Paul Among Jews and Gentiles* (Philadelphia: Fortress, 1976) 78-96; P. Stuhlmacher, *Gerechtigkeit Gottes bei Paulus* (2d ed; FRLANT 82; Göttingen: Vandenhoeck & Ruprecht, 1966); T. F. Torrance, *The Doctrine of Grace in the Apostolic Fathers* (London: Oliver and Boyd, 1948); W. Wrede, *Untersuchungen zum ersten Klemensbriefe* (Göttingen: Vandenhoeck & Ruprecht, 1891); J. A.

Ziesler, *The Meaning of Righteousness in Paul: A Linguistic and Theological Enquiry* (SNTSMS 20; Cambridge: Cambridge University Press, 1971).

C. C. Newman

ROMAN ADMINISTRATION. *See* ROMAN EMPIRE, CHRISTIANS AND THE.

ROMAN CHRISTIANITY. *See* ROME AND ROMAN CHRISTIANITY.

ROMAN EMPIRE, CHRISTIANS AND THE

The expression "Roman Empire" most frequently calls to mind the extensive territory under Roman rule during the period from Augustus's victory at Actium in 31 B.C. until the fifth century A.D. It may also be helpfully considered in terms of the network of political, military, economic and judicial arrangements by which Rome exercised dominion over much of the ancient world.

1. The Geographic Extent of the Empire
2. Imperial Administration
3. Travel and Commerce
4. Empire and Christianity

1. The Geographic Extent of the Empire.

Rome was founded, according to tradition, in 753 B.C. Its power increased initially under the direction of kings until 509 B.C., when it was reconstituted as a republic headed by consular magistrates elected annually by the Senate. Through a two-century period of internal conflict and warfare with the league of Latin cities, Rome emerged in 275 B.C. in effective control of much of Italy. It next annexed, through war and the failure of treaty negotiations, Sicily (241 B.C.), Sardinia (233 B.C.), Corsica (231 B.C.), the two Spains (197 B.C.) and Africa and Achaia (146 B.C.). The territories of Asia (133 B.C.) and Bithynia and Cyrene (74 B.C.) came into Rome's hands as bequests from foreign monarchs.

During the instability of social turmoil and civil war and as a result of the adventurism of powerful Roman generals, Crete (68 B.C.), Syria (63 B.C.), Cyprus (58 B.C.) and a reorganized Gaul fell within the Roman orbit. The forty-five years of Augustus's reign and the efforts of the Julio-Claudian emperors who followed added a dozen more provinces, notably Egypt (31 B.C.), Galatia (25 B.C.) and Judea (A.D. 6). The grave crisis of the year of the four emperors (A.D. 69)

ushered in nearly a century of consolidating gains, suppressing rebellious provinces and repulsing invading foreigners at the periphery of the empire.

2. Imperial Administration.

2.1. The Roman Interest. It would be incorrect to assume that the geographic extent of the empire represented a conscious centuries-long strategy to Romanize the entire Mediterranean world. Rome's involvement was essentially pragmatic, and its objectives were limited. The principal interest was a peace that ensured Roman prosperity. Threats to the integrity, sovereignty or material prosperity of Rome or to buffer states with whom alliances had been made called for decisive response. Ongoing instability resulted in Rome's ongoing presence. The security advantages of a relationship with such an honorable and zealous partner as Rome were clear.

Roman administration was less intrusive in the affairs of its subject peoples than is oftentimes thought. Taxation was generally structured by Rome, but collections were farmed out to successful bidders among the élite of the local communities. Where local laws and structures of governance were generally serviceable to the objective of peace for prosperity, they were permitted with a minimum of intrusion. Intervention usually occurred only where the Roman interest was threatened.

2.2. Governors. Provincial government was in the hands of senatorial and imperial nominees. Their duties included managing finances, hearing cases and employing the military forces in their charge for security and peacekeeping operations. They were granted the "power of the sword" (*ius gladii;* cf. Dio Cassius *Hist.* 52.22; 53.13.6-7; 53.14.5; Rom 13:4), a nontransferable jurisdiction to punish with death provincials and Roman citizens. Such powers held great potential for abuse, as did the fact that only in the year following their return to Rome could governors be prosecuted by aggrieved provincials for maladministration.

Proconsular provinces were governed by former praetors or consuls appointed by lot by the Roman senate. Appointments were generally for a year but could be renewed. These provinces had generally been pacified and so required smaller military forces to ensure the peace. Sergius Paulus at Cyprus (Acts 13:7),

Gallio at Achaia (Acts 18:12) and the unnamed individual(s) identified by the Ephesian town clerk (Acts 19:38) are NT examples of proconsuls.

The governance of strategic and/or unpacified territories had been voted to the emperor Augustus early in his reign; hence their designation as imperial provinces. He appointed ex-praetors and consuls from the Senate as imperial legates (*legati Augusti pro praetore*) in some. Quirinius served in this capacity in Syria-Cilicia (Lk 2:1-2; cf. Acts 5:37). Other provinces, like Judea, were governed by equestrian nominees called prefects or procurators whose terms could be considerably extended. The procurators Felix (Acts 23:24—24:27; Josephus *Life* 3 §13; Josephus *Ant.* 20.7.1—20.8.9 §137-82; Josephus *J.W.* 2.12.8—2.13.7 §247-70; Tacitus *Ann.* 12.54; Tacitus *Hist.* 5.9) and Porcius Festus (Acts 24:27—26:32; Josephus *Ant.* 20.8.9—20.9.1 §182-200; Josephus *J.W.* 2.14.1 §271-72) dealt with the politically charged case of Paul in the last years of the sixth decade A.D. Felix's venality and his and Festus's pliability in the hands of irate provincial élites show both the character of these men and the considerable pressures they faced.

2.3. Army. Following the heavily militarized period leading up to the battle of Actium, the victorious Augustus consolidated the Roman army. Despite its reduced size, it was still the chief means of enforcing peace in the provinces and at the periphery of the empire. It was comprised of legionary and auxiliary forces. A legion, of which there were twenty-five at Augustus's death, consisted in a force of between 4,000 and 6,000 men who were divided into ten cohorts of six centuries each (a century having a nominal strength of 100 men). The maniple, consisting of two centuries, was the basic fighting unit. A division (*ala*) of 120 or more cavalry was also attached to the legion. Men were enlisted in the legions from the Roman citizen population and after a twenty-year (earlier, sixteen-year) term of service were discharged with a lump-sum cash payment and a land grant somewhere in the empire.

The auxiliary forces, whether *alae* or *cohortes,* were comprised of freeborn noncitizen soldiers levied from the local tribes and cities of imperial provinces on the frontier. Often they had specialized skills (e.g., the two hundred *dexiolaboi* of Acts 23:23?). They received proportionately less pay and a more extended term of service than did their legionary counterparts; auxiliary soldiers received Roman citizenship as part of their discharge.

Four regular legions were in Syria by A.D. 23, and several more were added from Nero's reign to the time of the Jewish rebellion. There is also evidence for the presence of significant numbers of auxiliary troops there during the first and second centuries A.D. In Judea auxiliaries were the dominant military force. Five cohorts were stationed in the Judean capital, Caesarea, and one in Jerusalem. Briefly in the hands of King Herod Agrippa I until his death (A.D. 44; Acts 12:23; Josephus *Ant.* 19.8.2 §343-50), these troops eventually reverted to the charge of a procuratorial appointee.

We meet soldiers of several ranks in the pages of Acts.* Peter's first Gentile* converts are a God-fearer named Cornelius,* a centurion of the Italian Cohort, and his household* (Acts 10:1-2). His forebears were among the ten thousand slaves granted freedom by P. Cornelius Sulla in 82 B.C. He had risen to the command of a nominal force of one hundred men. The Italian Cohort, which would have been first called up in Italy, may well be the *cohors II Italica civium Romanorum,* which was in Syria in A.D. 69, though there is no record of its being in Judea before A.D. 41. The presence of Cornelius's extended household in Caesarea may suggest that he was retired.

If Herod's forces were structured on Roman lines, as seems likely, the four squads of four soldiers who guarded Peter (Acts 12:4-10, 18-19) represent either two units of "bunkmates" (*contubernales;* the *contubernium* was the basic army unit; cf. Vegetius *Epit. Rei Milit.* 2.8, 13; 3.8) or eight pairs of "privates" from every barracks unit in one of the centuries stationed in Jerusalem. If the soldiers were executed on account of Peter's escape instead of being punished in some other way (cf. *Code Just.* 9.4.4; *Dig. Just.* 48.3.12, 14), this would represent the nominal decimation of an entire century, no doubt shattering military morale and further explaining the great hostility of the troops toward the Jewish Herod (cf. Josephus *Ant.* 19.9.1-2 §356-65).

Paul was taken into custody by a tribune in Jerusalem (Acts 21:31—23:30). The tribune was the highest-ranking officer in Jerusalem, commissioned to lead a double cohort, as the title *chiliarchos* suggests. He must have worked his way through the ranks of the auxiliary forces in Syria, purchasing his Roman citizenship, as he indicates, and probably his equestrian status and military tribunate as well. The name Claudius Lysias (Acts 23:26; 24:22) and the "great cost" of his citizenship (Acts 22:28) make it likely that he was a Greek and had received the franchise early in the emperor Claudius's reign (cf. Dio Cassius *Hist.* 60.17.5-6).

The fact of increasing hostility and tension between Jews and non-Jewish provincials and auxiliary forces throughout this period in Judea (cf. Josephus passim) ought not to be forgotten when gauging what custodial relations must have been like for the Jewish Paul in the Fortress Antonia at Jerusalem (Acts 22:23-29; 23:16-22) and in Herod's *praetorium* at Caesarea (Acts 23:35; 24:23, 27; 26:29). They would have been far from pleasant despite the indications in the text of formal benevolence.

Julius, a centurion of the Augustan Cohort, was charged with heading up a military detail to take Paul and other prisoners to Rome (Acts 27:1). He would hardly have used the name Julius unless he possessed citizenship. Claudius had capitally punished individuals who illegitimately used the Roman *nomen gentile* (Suetonius *Claudius* 25.3). The designation *Augusta* for an auxiliary unit is more likely to be official than honorific. There is record of a *cohors I Augusta* levied from the Syrian population and found in Syria during the time of Quirinius (A.D. 6; *ILS* 1.2683) and a prefect "of the Augustan cohort" stationed in Batanaea east of Galilee some time during the reign of Herod Agrippa II (*OGIS* 421).

The Western text, if it can be accounted a reliable record at this point, indicates that on arriving in Rome Paul was handed over to the *stratopedarchēs* (Acts 28:16). We may doubt that this person should be identified with the prefect of the urban cohorts or for that matter the *princeps peregrinorum,* who had charge of a force responsible for the imperial grain supply and security. The urban prefect was concerned with local police matters; the *princeps* and his staff and force were of centurial rank (note the assignment to a regular soldier at Acts 28:16), too small and mobile and probably too late in time to guard Paul. We should rather understand the designation to indicate, if not the prefect of the praetorian forces located near the Viminal Gate, then more probably one of his subordinates.

For Ignatius* of Antioch (c. A.D. 108) the military constitute a great trouble. He writes to the Roman* church that his Syrian military escort of ten soldiers (likened to leopards) treats him with unremitting animosity. They respond to Christian kindnesses with increased harshness (Ign. *Rom.* 5.1).

3. Travel and Commerce.

3.1. Pax Romana. One of the legacies of Augustus's efforts to ensure security for prosperity was a two-century period of unprecedented peace, the *pax Romana* (cf. Philo *Leg.* 47; Plutarch *Fort. Rom., Mor.* 317B, C). Extending the Roman road network and clearing the seaways of pirates not only aided better official communications but also opened up the empire to increased commercial and private traffic (Pliny *Nat. Hist.* 14.1.2). This aided immensely the spread of the gospel (Acts 1:8).

3.2. Land and Sea Travel. Mention is made in Acts of a wheeled conveyance that could cover twenty-five to thirty miles a day (Acts 8:28-29, 38); travel by horse (Acts 23:23-24, 33) might double that distance. The most common means of travel, however, was by foot. The average distance of about twenty miles per day is confirmed by the journeying of Peter and Cornelius's servants between Caesarea and Joppa (Acts 10:23-24, 30). Even Paul's official Damascus mission appears to have been by foot (Acts 9:7-8). Greater distances in a day's time might be achieved, as during the forced march from Jerusalem to Antipatris (Acts 23:23-35). What Paul was prepared to brave in his various travels (2 Cor 11:26-27) suggests that he pushed the seasonal limits for travel as a professional merchant would, rather than being a fair-weather traveler.

Christians also frequently traveled by ship (Acts 13:4, 13; 14:26; 16:11; 17:15; 18:18, 22; 20:6, 13-17; 21:1-6; 27:2—28:13). Maritime transport, for all the safety that the Roman peace afforded, was still a risky business, and this Paul knew by experience (2 Cor 11:25-26; cf. Josephus *Life* 3 §14-16; Lucian of Samosata *Tox.* 19). Weather and sea conditions could be quite changeable, and there were generally agreed good and bad times for travel (cf. Vegetius *Epit. Rei Milit.* 4.39; Pliny *Nat. Hist.* 2.47-48.122-130; Tacitus *Hist.* 4.81). Rich imperial inducements for merchants to risk the season to supply grain for Rome, however, were difficult to resist (Suetonius *Claudius* 18-19; cf. Dio Cassius *Hist.* 60.11; Pliny *Nat. Hist.* 2.47.125). It is not surprising to find the centurion Julius requisitioning passage for himself, Paul and the rest of his prisoner detail on two Alexandrian free merchant grain carriers in the off season (Acts 27:6; 28:11). Ignatius's guards would have made similar arrangements (Ign. *Rom.* 5.1; Pol. *Phil.* 8.1).

3.4. Hospitality. Travelers had to make stops along the way. If they could not avail themselves of private lodging, prevail upon friends or requisition the facilities of the public post *(cursus publicus)* by virtue of their office, they might have to put up in a boarding house or wayside inn. Such rented accommodation was generally of poor quality (e.g., Petronius *Sat.* 94-99; *Acts of John* 60). It is not difficult, therefore, to understand the pattern of hospitality* found throughout Acts, epistolary encouragements to assistance (1 Pet 4:9; Heb 13:2) and epistolary recognitions of those who helped Christians on their way (e.g., Ignatius, passim).

4. Empire and Christianity.

4.1. The Roman Attitude to Christianity. The Roman stance toward Christianity underwent some change over time. In the earliest period Christianity, as a faction within Judaism,* was a matter of mild Roman interest (Acts 24:22, 24-25). Jewish religious objections to Christianity appear not to have provoked a Roman inclination judicially to intervene (Acts 18:15-16; 22:30; 23:29; 25:19-20, 25; 28:18); Roman religious objections, however, did (Acts 16:20-21). Manifest disturbances of the Roman peace (Acts 18:2-3; 21:30-40; cf. Suetonius *Claudius* 25.4) and formal accusations to that effect by Jewish ruling élites or their Roman proxies (Acts 17:6-7; 24:5-9, 12) received immediate official attention. Prosecutions during this time were localized, isolated and privately entered rather than being undertaken by the Roman state.

Before the great fire of A.D. 64 in Rome and Nero's persecution,* it appears that Christians had come to be detested in their own right. Tacitus notes with some irony that Christians, whom he indicates deserved exemplary punishment because of their *superstitio* and its "degraded and shameful practices," began to evoke Roman pity because they were unjustly accused by Nero of incendiarism and punished viciously (Tacitus *Ann.* 15.44; cf. Suetonius *Nero* 16.2).

The fact that believers became the objects of imperial delation was a significant downward turn in Roman and Christian relations. State prosecutions on the charge of simply being a Christian would be initiated later (cf. Pliny *Ep.* 10.95-96; *Acts of the Christian Martyrs,* passim).

4.2. The Christian Attitude to the Empire. The Christian attitude to imperial authority and governance was enlightened yet restrained in the early period. Paul saw a belated advantage (owing to his Christian Jewish commitments) in intimating his Roman citizenship to the appropriate authorities (Acts 16:37-38; 22:22-29; 23:27). He initially affirmed at Caesarea the equity of Roman provincial governance (Acts 24:10) but ultimately preferred to entrust himself to an imperial legal decision by appealing to Caesar (Acts 25:10-12, 25; 26:32; 28:19).

Peter acknowledged that believers were suffering in the imperial capital ("Babylon"; 1 Pet 5:13) and in the provinces at the hands of hostile communities and officials. He advised exemplary behavior and political quietism (1 Pet 2:13-15; 4:19). Suffering* as a Christian was the will of God (1 Pet 3:17; 4:13, 19) and was to be patiently endured because it inaugurated the apocalyptic* judgment* of the world and would end in joy* (1 Pet 4:1, 7, 17; 5:6-10; *see* Endurance). While the devil (*see* Satan) is identified as the ultimate enemy (1 Pet 5:8-9), a clear connection is not made with him to anti-Christian communities or Roman authorities (*see* Civil Authority). Christians are called to submit to the "king" (= emperor) and to the governors sent to punish malefactors and commend those who do right (1 Pet 2:13-14, 17; cf. Rom 13:1-7).

Hebrews,* which may well have been written to Rome, indicates past and present Christian sufferings at the hands of government officials (Heb 10:32-34). The recipients are challenged to see in this God's discipline, to persevere in their faith, to help fellow sufferers and to wait upon God's apocalyptic sweeping aside of the old order in favor of the new (Heb 10:32—12:29). Here too the writer does not, as it were, pass judgment upon government authority.

Revelation, to the contrary, in a later decade expresses an apocalyptic picture of anti-Christian government and its ultimate end (*see* Revelation, Book of). There is no reason to doubt that John, exiled on Patmos by the provincial authority (Rev 1:9), has Roman emperors* particularly in view when he speaks of "beasts"* with horns, heads and crowns who rule over the earth's inhabitants, utter blasphemy against God, martyr Christians and demand worship (Rev 13; 17; *see* Martyrdom). The references suggest the ruler cult in which deificatory honors were voted by the Senate to deceased emperors. Some emperors, however, not content to be known as "sons of the gods," ambitiously pressed for divinization in their lifetimes—with disastrous effects. Christians are challenged by John to endure patiently and in faith (Rev 14:12) until the beast is divinely judged (Rev 19:19-20).

Clement (*1 Clem.* 60.4—61.2), Ignatius (passim) and Polycarp* (Pol. *Phil.* 12.3) seem to follow the earlier apostolic attitude of a prayerful and cooperative rather than stridently negative attitude toward the Roman authority.

See also CHRONOLOGY; EMPEROR, EMPEROR CULT; MARTYRDOM; PERSECUTION; ROME AND RO-MAN CHRISTIANITY.

BIBLIOGRAPHY. S. Benko and J. J. O'Rourke, *The Catacombs and the Colosseum: The Roman Empire as the Setting of Primitive Christianity* (Valley Forge, PA: Judson, 1971); T. R. S. Broughton, "The Roman Army" in *The Beginnings of Christianity,* ed. F. J. Foakes Jackson and K. Lake (5 vols.; Grand Rapids: Baker, 1979 [1932]) 5:427-45; P. A. Brunt, "Charges of Provincial Maladministration Under the Early Principate," *Historia* 10 (1961) 189-227; L. Casson, *Ships and Seamanship in the Ancient World* (Princeton, NJ: Princeton University Press, 1971); idem, *Travel in the Ancient World* (London: George Allen & Unwin, 1974); P. Garnsey, "The Criminal Jurisdiction of Governors," *JRS* 58 (1966) 51-59; idem, *Social Status and Legal Privilege in the Roman Empire* (Oxford: Clarendon, 1970); P. Garnsey and R. Saller, *The Roman Empire: Economy, Society and Culture* (Berkeley: University of California Press, 1987); R. M. Grant, "Roman Empire," *IDB* 4:103-9; B. Levick, *The Government of the Roman Empire: A Sourcebook* (London and Sydney: Croom Helm, 1985); H. Musurillo, ed., *The Acts of the Christian Martyrs* (Oxford: Clarendon, 1972); B. M. Rapske, *Paul in Roman Custody* (BAFCS 3; Grand Rapids: Eerdmans, 1994); A. N. Sherwin-White, *Roman Society and Roman Law in the New Testament* (Sarum Lectures 1961-62; Oxford: Clarendon, 1963); J. Wacher, *The Roman Empire* (London and Melbourne: J. M. Dent & Sons, 1987); G. Webster, *The Roman Imperial Army of the First and Second Centuries A.D.* (3d ed.; London: A & C Black, 1985); C. Wells, *The Roman Empire* (2d ed.; London: Fontana/Harper Collins, 1992).   B. M. Rapske

ROME AND ROMAN CHRISTIANITY

Rome of the first and early second centuries A.D., as principal city of Italy and administrative seat of so much of the ancient world, is synonymous with both the empire and the civilization it spawned. The focus of this article, however, is drawn somewhat more narrowly upon the city itself as well as Christianity's early establishment in and relations with it.

1. The City of Rome
2. Roman Christianity

1. The City of Rome.

1.1. Situation. According to legend, the city of Rome was founded by Romulus in 753 B.C. Cicero wrote: "It seems to me that Romulus must at the very beginning have had a divine intimation that the city would one day be the seat and hearthstone of a mighty empire; for scarcely could a city placed upon any other site in Italy have more easily maintained our present widespread dominion" (Cicero *De Repub.* 2.5.10). The movement from republic to empire and the corresponding increase in the sphere of Rome's governance only confirmed this assessment. The city was ideally located at a crossroads of several major land routes, the bridgehead of the river Tiber, connected with the sea and at the geographic heart of the Mediterranean.

About 15 miles inland from the mouth of the river Tiber, Rome spread on the east over the seven hills (the central Palatine encircled by the Capitoline, Aventine, Caelian, Esquiline, Viminal and Quirinal), northeast from the seven hills over the floodplain known as the Campus Martius and over the Transtiberim in the area west of the river. The Tiber gave Rome an access to the Mediterranean Sea that was of immense importance to its commercial development. The strategic weaknesses in security implicit in such easy maritime access, however, were significantly counterbalanced by the seven hills, which acted as a natural fortress, and by the 13.2 miles of walls that circumscribed them.

1.2. Population. Rome was both populous and cosmopolitan. During the later republican period, Italians displaced and destitute because of war migrated to Rome as a place of refuge and opportunity. Prisoners of war were the human fuel of its ancient economy and a means whereby the wealthy might demonstrate their place in the élite hierarchy. The population may have quintupled during this time.

After the turbulence of the shift to imperial administration came a period of relative stability and growth that had profound effects upon the capital city. The increasing inflow of resources through taxation and commerce furnished Rome with the means to feed, maintain, build, entertain and significantly enrich itself. Foreign merchants, entrepreneurs and fortune seekers were drawn to this concentration of wealth. As the most significant administrative and juridical seat of the Mediterranean, Rome was also a place of great influence and opportunity for those who sought social and political advancement. A city so awash in wealth and greatness also drew educators and tourists and with them all, invariably, new cultural and religious practices and philosophical ideas.

The population was comprised of the few and the many: At the tip of the pyramid was the emperor and his household. Next was a group of some six hundred aristocratic citizen families who met the minimum property requirement of one million sesterces and from whose ranks magistracies, places in the Senate and consular posts were filled. The larger equestrian order was comprised of freeborn and highborn citizens possessing a minimum of four hundred thousand sesterces who might better their standing in the social hierarchy through serving in a number of salaried military, procuratorial and Roman civic posts. This was the fractional community of Rome.

The great mass of the city's population consisted of lowborn citizens, freedmen, foreigners and slaves. The poor vastly outnumbered the rich; men outnumbered women; and there were fewer children than adults. Average life expectancy is generally agreed to have been about twenty-five years.

Rome probably had a first-century A.D. population of about one million inhabitants. This figure is based upon a combination of indicators: the average dietetic value of grain, records of the amount of grain sent annually to Rome, records of the number of adult male citizens who qualified for the official public grain distribution (5 *modii* monthly, year round) and calculations of what proportion of the total

population the grain distribution recipients would have represented.

1.3. Accommodation. The capital city was a cripplingly expensive place to live. If Julius Caesar's maximum remittances to soldiers were an attempt at general parity, they suggest that accommodation in the city was about four times more expensive than anywhere else in Italy (Suetonius *Julius Caesar* 38.2; cf. Martial *Epigr.* 3.38.5; 12.32.2-3; Juvenal *Sat.* 3.164-66, 223-25; 9.63-64; 10.18). Only the very wealthy and privileged few could afford to own or rent a spacious private house *(domus)*. These were generally situated on the ridges or slopes of the seven hills where ventilation, drainage and view were best. They were designed for comfort and as a means of displaying wealth and social position.

The rest of Rome's million inhabitants lived in the valleys between the hills and in the areas close to the river Tiber, in a room or rooms in one of the many thousands of multistory tenement buildings *(insulae)*. A typical structure might be three to five stories high, having a central courtyard and shop dwellings at street level and apartments above.

The need to house a large population and investors' prospects for speculating in the rental market often frustrated sound architectural principles and imperial legislation for safety. Structures were frequently built cheaply, as high as legally permissible and with a mix of rent levels and degree of tenant crowding that generated the highest profits. In consequence, fires and building collapses were all too common (cf. Strabo *Geog.* 5.3.7; Seneca *Ben.* 6.15.7; Seneca *De Ira* 3.35.5; Juvenal *Sat.* 3.190-98; Aulus Gellius *Noc. Att.* 15.1.2-3).

Height was inversely proportional to rental cost and therefore reflected the renter's status and means. Ground- and first-floor units could only be afforded by the better-off, and leases were generally long-term and end-paid. The less easily accessible and more dangerous upper floors and rooftop garrets housed much poorer renters; lease arrangements for them were less favorable (cf. Martial *Epigr.* 1.117.7; Juvenal Sat. 3.198-208, 232-35).

Those who could not afford even a rooftop garret might seek accommodation in a boarding house or an inn. These were often disreputable places peopled by individuals of dubious morals (cf. Petronius *Sat.* 94—97). The most destitute—and Rome would have had many—

slept in shanties against walls, in stairwells, cellars, vaults and tombs or wherever they might find a relatively safe place.

1.4. Administration. It was evident in the latter years of the republic that existing administrative institutions were incapable of dealing efficiently with a city of such size and population density. Augustus, in consequence, created a new administrative order. Rome was divided into fourteen *regiones,* each of which was in the charge of a praetor, tribune or aedile chosen by lot (cf. Suetonius *Augustus* 30; Dio Cassius *Hist.* 55.8). These *regiones* were further divided into 265 neighborhood wards *(vici),* and each ward was under the care of four district superintendents (Pliny *Nat. Hist.* 3.66-67).

Specific administrative and policing responsibilities in the capital were assigned to various individuals. The urban prefect, a senatorial appointee, was charged with general oversight of the city, including siting new statues, repair work to public buildings and peacekeeping. He presided over his own court. Under him were three cohorts (the *cohortes urbanae)* charged with keeping law and order in the city. The praetorian prefect, drawn from the equestrian ranks, had oversight of a military force of nine cohorts (the *cohortes praetoriae),* of which no more than three were to be situated in the city at a time. These were the emperor's personal bodyguards who, outside of duties during wartime, discharged ceremonial functions and could also assist in quelling civil disturbances. They were eventually housed by Tiberius in barracks at the Viminal gate.

Because of the continuing fire risk to the capital, Augustus instituted a seven-cohort corps (the *cohortes vigilum)* under the direction of an equestrian prefect. Their duties were night patrol or peacekeeping and firefighting. Each cohort was quartered in and had charge of two *regiones* of the city.

Mention should also be made of the two detachments of soldiers in Rome whose principal tasks were the supervision of navigation on the river Tiber and patrol of the military harbors. They were stationed at the *castra Misenatium.*

The water supply of the capital was also a matter of official interest. The construction and care of aqueducts fell to *curatores aquarum.* Near the end of the first century A.D., 9 aqueducts fed 591 open water basins throughout the city (Frontinus 2.78; cf. Strabo *Geog.* 5.3.8; Pliny *Nat. Hist.* 36.123). A. Scobie calculates that these furnished 992,000 cubic meters of fresh water daily for Rome's consumption and bathing needs. Aediles supervised the building and maintenance of the extensive sewer network of the city. Few dwellings, however, were directly connected to it. The resulting refuse disposal and sanitation methods (cf. Martial *Epigr.* 10.5.11-12; Juvenal *Sat.* 3.269-77; *Dig. Just.* 43.10.1.5) probably contributed significantly to the low average life expectancy.

Except for wagons used during official religious events, wheeled traffic was banned during daylight hours. While this reduced congestion and fatalities when the populace was up and about the streets, the resultant nighttime traffic led to great disturbance and sleeplessness (Juvenal *Sat.* 3.232-39, 254-61).

1.5. Food. It was a challenge to feed the vast population of Rome. The Roman diet consisted of such produce as olives and olive oil, wine, honey, onions, radishes, turnips and other tubers, green vegetables, fruits, fish and poultry and, for those who could afford it, pork, mutton and beef. Condiments included salt, pepper and a briny fish sauce called *garum.* The staple of the Roman diet, however, was grain.

The regular supply of grain to the capital was an absolute priority for the imperial administration, requiring importation from various points, notably Africa and Egypt. A large segment of the citizen population was dependent upon the monthly distribution of grain *(frumentum publicum).* The numbers of those entitled to subsidized or free grain fluctuated over time from 150,000 to 320,000 through the later republican to early imperial period. Scarcity of grain and inflated prices at Rome had resulted in civil disorder in Rome (cf. Seneca *Brev. Vit.* 18.5; Dio Cassius *Hist.* 55.26.2-3; 60.11; Tacitus *Ann.* 2.87; 6.13; 12.43; Suetonius *Claudius* 18—19). As such, the grain supply was a matter of considerable political importance to the emperors. Responsibility for supervising the supply from the provinces to Rome's grain market fell to an imperial appointee of equestrian rank called the *praefectus annonae.*

2. Roman Christianity.

2.1. Early Developments. No clear indication can be found of the first appearance of Christianity in Rome. Earliest exposure of Latin speakers to the gospel seems to have occurred at Pentecost* in Jerusalem* (Acts 2:5, 10-11, 14). Whether these were residents or pilgrims, Luke's information suggests the probable line of interchange along which Christianity made its way to the imperial capital in the fourth decade A.D. (cf. Tacitus *Ann.* 15.44.2). Christian proselytism in Rome appears to have been vigorous in the fifth decade. The Claudian expulsion edict of A.D. 49 (Suetonius *Claudius* 25.4) caught the tentmaking missionaries Aquila and Priscilla in its wake (Acts 18:2-3, 18-28). Whether the unrest had to do with Christianity is somewhat uncertain (Suetonius uses the phrase *impulsore Chresto;* Luke is silent). By the late sixth decade Paul could acknowledge the Roman church's long existence (Rom 15:23-24; cf. Acts 19:21), renowned faith (Rom 1:8) and evangelistic zeal (Rom 16:3-16).

2.2. Paul. Paul arrived in Rome as a prisoner missionary at the beginning of the seventh decade A.D. (Acts 28:14). Like Ignatius* on the way to Rome and Peregrinus in Palestine at a later time, Paul received the official and public support of the church's leadership in Rome (namely, the "brothers," Acts 28:15). His motivation in early calling the leaders of the Jews together to speak with them was strategically wise. The Jewish community, dating back to before 139 B.C., might have numbered as many as fifty thousand in the city. They were a significant, if not generally loved, presence with vital connections to official Judaism* in Jerusalem (Acts 28:21). Though probably not centrally organized, they could exert considerable power through public demonstration, and they had influence in high places (cf. Josephus *Life* 3 §16; Josephus *J.W.* 2.6.1 §80; 2.7.1 §105 [Josephus *Ant.* 17.11.1 §300; 17.12.1 §330-31]; Josephus *Ant.* 20.8.11 §195; Tacitus *Ann.* 16.6). Non-Christian Jews and Christians in Rome appear not to have interacted at that time if Acts 28:22 is any indication.

Because he was a prisoner under restraint and not likely to have been permitted to ply his trade, Paul's rented accommodation was probably a third-floor or higher room in a tenement rather than a spacious house or lower-level apartment (Acts 28:16, 23, 30). The increasingly larger numbers of those who came to hear him (Acts 28:17, 23, 30) imply the availability of a gathering place (perhaps an apartment court-yard?). Paul's ministry in these circumstances,

far from being frustrated or fruitless, was effective (Acts 28:24-25, 30-31; cf. Phil 1:12-15). Luke's description of Paul's engaging in a free, house church type of ministry (Acts 28:30-31; cf. Acts 1:13; 9:37; 20:8; *Mart. Justin* Rec. A & B 3.3 on the use of upper rooms) is positive, forward reaching and powerful by ancient Christian reckoning. The custodial arrangements suggest both official tolerance and a favorable Roman assessment of Paul's prospects for release at the end of the two full years.

Being a Roman citizen, of legal age and formally domiciled in the city, Paul may have been able to defray some of the high living costs by sharing in the monthly grain distribution. That he was a prisoner would have been immaterial to his legal entitlement (cf. Seneca *Ben.* 4.28.2).

2.3. 1 Peter, Hebrews and Revelation. 1 Peter 5:13 appears to make the connection between the apostle* Peter, the "elect lady" (referring to the church) and Babylon,* the image of the conquering world power that, most scholars agree, refers to Rome. Ignatius asserts that Peter "commanded" the Roman church (Ign. *Rom.* 4.3); Clement (*see* Clement of Rome) indicates that he was martyred there (*1 Clem.* 5—6). Peter and the Roman believers can well identify with the trouble and hostility being experienced by the letter's recipients (1 Pet 4:17; 5:9). Peter instructs them to exemplary living in the face of community slander and submission rather than militancy toward the secular authority (1 Pet 2:13-17; *see* Civil Authority). The challenge to good domestic relations and hospitality* (1 Pet 2:18—3:7; 4:9, 17) intimates the Roman pattern of using homes as meeting places. Church leadership is in the hands of "elders" (1 Pet 5:1-5). We may doubt that Peter visited Rome as early as the fourth decade (see Acts 12:17 for the cryptic reference to "another place"). The date of the letter is probably the eve of the Neronian persecution* of A.D. 64 (Tacitus *Ann.* 15.44; Suetonius *Nero* 16; *see* 1 Peter).

There is reason, beyond the rather ambiguous greeting from the "Italians" (Heb 13:24), to believe that the book of Hebrews* may have been written to the Roman church. The earliest attestations to Hebrews come from *1 Clement* and *Shepherd of Hermas,** which both are connected with Rome. The writer's concern is that Roman believers not reject Jesus in order to return to something like Judaism. He recalls to them their steadfastness in earlier sufferings* of public ridicule and persecution, imprisonment and the confiscation of their property (Heb 10:32-34) and encourages them to stand firm in faith and upright behavior and to maintain community cohesion (Heb 13). Again one sees a call to practice hospitality through the troubles. The reminder that they do not live in an "enduring city" (Heb 13:14) may serve warning against endearing themselves not only to Jerusalem and what it symbolizes but also to Rome as well.

While the image of Babylon in the Revelation (*see* Revelation, Book of) may not be exhausted by exclusive application to Rome, there is much about the imperial capital that well fits the apocalyptic* denunciation. Babylon is the "great city" (Rev 16:19; 18:10, 16, 19, 21) seated on "seven hills" (Rev 17:9) and "the waters" which are "peoples, multitudes, nations and languages" (Rev 17:1, 15). It is the political power which holds kings and nations in thrall (Rev 17:2, 18; 18:3, 9), the great parasite to which vast goods and wealth go (Rev 18 passim). Babylon is the prostitute; morally corrupt and a corruptor (Rev 14:8; 17:5; 18:2). It is the place where the blood of the apostles, prophets* and saints has been shed (Rev 17:6; 18:20, 24). John calls for believers to "come out of" or disassociate themselves from the city's sins (Rev 18:4). These indications and the exile of John (Rev 1:9) suggest a time of persecution somewhere in the final four decades of the first century A.D.

2.4. The Apostolic Fathers. 1 Clement, written from Rome about A.D. 96, refers to the church there as "sojourners" (*1 Clem.* presc.). This image of transience may spring in part from the "sudden and repeated" persecutions that have delayed the epistle's writing (*1 Clem.* 1.1). The apostles Peter and Paul are held up as past examples of endurance* to the point of martyrdom* "among us" (*1 Clem.* 6.1). The vigorous encouragements to hospitality and good order in homes (*1 Clem.* 1.2-3; 11.1; 12.1, 3) implies the continued use of house churches throughout the city.

Ignatius writes to the church at Rome shortly before his martyrdom (c. A.D. 108). He indicates the Roman church's primacy over other churches in Italy (Ign. *Rom.* presc.; 2.1) and reminds it of the directive ministry of the apostles Peter and Paul (Ign. *Rom.* 4.3). Ignatius's pleas that the Roman church not hinder his martyrdom (Ign. *Rom.* 1—2 et passim) may sug-

gest its ability successfully to influence the secular judicial power. It receives correspondence concerning the flow of Christian prisoners to the capital and is told to continue to help and encourage them (Ign. *Rom.* 10.2).

Shepherd of Hermas, written perhaps as early as the first or second decade of the second century A.D., indicates the Roman church's directive ministry to other churches: Clement, it is said, writes letters that are sent out in the name of the Roman presbyters and bishops (*Herm. Vis.* 2.4). The Roman church is led by elders, bishops, teachers and deacons (*Herm. Vis.* 2.4; 3.1, 5; *see* Church Order, Government) and has a ministry to and possibly of widows and orphans (*Herm. Vis.* 2.4; *Herm. Sim.* 9.28). Persecutions have caused certain wealthy believers to deny the faith (*Herm. Vis.* 3.2; 3.5-6; *Herm. Sim.* 1). True religion is expressed by, among other things, helping widows, orphans and the needy, ransoming believers from afflictions and being hospitable (*Herm. Man.* 8; cf. *Herm. Sim.* 1; 9.27).

See also BABYLON; CENTERS OF CHRISTIANITY; CLEMENT OF ROME; EMPEROR, EMPEROR CULT; HEBREWS; 1 PETER; REVELATION, BOOK OF; ROMAN EMPIRE, CHRISTIANS AND THE; SHEPHERD OF HERMAS.

BIBLIOGRAPHY. S. Benko and J. J. O'Rourke, *The Catacombs and the Colosseum: The Roman Empire as the Setting of Primitive Christianity* (Valley Forge, PA: Judson, 1971); R. E. Brown and J. P. Meier, *Antioch and Rome: New Testament Cradles of Catholic Christianity* (New York: Paulist, 1983); J. Carcopino, *Daily Life in Ancient Rome* (New Haven, CT: Yale University Press, 1940); A. D. Clarke, "Rome and Italy" in *The Book of Acts in Its Greco-Roman Setting*, ed. D. W. J. Gill and C. Gempf (BAFCS 2; Grand Rapids: Eerdmans, 1994) 456-78; B. W. Frier, *Landlords and Tenants in Imperial Rome* (Princeton, NJ: Princeton University Press, 1980); idem, "The Rental Market in Early Imperial Rome," *JRS* 67 (1977) 27-37; P. Garnsey and R. Saller, *The Roman Empire: Economy, Society and Culture* (Berkeley: University of California Press, 1987); A. G. McKay, *Houses, Villas and Palaces in the Roman World* (Aspects of Greek and Roman Life; Southampton: Thames & Hudson, 1975); R. Meiggs, *Roman Ostia* (2d ed.; Oxford: Clarendon, 1973); W. J. Oates, "The Population of Rome," *Classical Philology* 29 (1934) 101-16; J. R. Patterson, "The City of Rome: From Republic to Empire," *JRS* 82 (1992) 186-215; B. M. Rapske, *Paul in Roman*

Custody (BAFCS 3; Grand Rapids: Eerdmans, 1994); G. Rickman, *The Corn Supply of Ancient Rome* (Oxford: Clarendon, 1980); O. F. Robinson, *Ancient Rome: City Planning and Administration* (New York amd London: Routledge, 1992); A. Scobie, "Slums, Sanitation and Mortality in the Roman World," *Klio* 68 (1986) 399-433; J. E. Stambaugh, *The Ancient Roman City* (Ancient Society and History; Baltimore: Johns Hopkins University Press, 1988).

B. M. Rapske

RULE OF FAITH. *See* Creeds, Confessional Forms.

RULER OF THIS AGE. *See* Satan, Devil.

S

SABBATH. *See* LORD'S DAY.

SABORAIM. *See* JUDAISM, POST-A.D. 70.

SACRED SPACE. *See* LAND IN EARLY CHRISTIANITY.

SACRIFICE, OFFERINGS, GIFTS

In the world of the first century the offering of sacrifices was a common feature of the traditional religion of the Greeks and Romans (*see* Religions, Greco-Roman), as it was for adherents of Judaism,* even though Jewish ritual was differentiated from the former by its rejection of any kind of human sacrifice. This cultural background enabled the concept of Jesus' death as a sacrifice to be comprehended by Greeks and Romans without much difficulty. However, the early Christians' insistence that Jesus' death eliminated the need for any further animal sacrifices set them apart from both the pagan culture as well as the Jewish religion, which continued to offer animal sacrifices in Jerusalem until its destruction in A.D. 70.

1. Jesus' Death as Sacrifice
2. Christian Sacrifice

1. Jesus' Death as Sacrifice.

1.1. Acts. Jerusalem* with its temple* played an important role in the early chapters of Acts* as the locus of the fulfillment of God's* promises* to Israel.* To them God gave his law* as living oracles (Acts 7:38) with attendant instructions concerning sacrifices. However, Israel's worship of God was not always pure, for Israel's history was replete with either sacrifices offered to idols* (Acts 7:41) or sacrifices offered to God accompanied by a stubborn heart (Acts 7:42, 51). Nonetheless, Luke also indicates that, apart from Israel's disobedience, there was something deficient in this sacrificial system of Mosaic law: it was unable to free or justify the believer and thereby grant forgiveness* of sins, which the apostles* claimed was now possible through Jesus (Acts 13:38-39).

Although Luke's general treatment of salvation* is based upon the death and resurrection* of Jesus as a unified matrix of events (e.g., Acts 2:23-24; 3:15; 5:30-31; *see* Death of Christ), the significance of Jesus' death for procuring forgiveness of sins is not wholly absent (cf. Acts 20:28; and the citation of Is 53 in Acts 8:32-33). Moreover there is an underlying recognition that the death and resurrection of Jesus is in continuity with and fulfillment of the OT (cf. Acts 13:32; 24:14; 28:23). It may seem surprising, therefore, that Luke describes an occasion where Paul offers Nazarite sacrifices (Num 6:1-21) in the temple (accompanying his vow in Acts 21:23-26; cf. Acts 24:18), even though Christ's death has already secured forgiveness of sins by the shedding of his own blood (Acts 20:28). Paul was clearly indifferent to these Nazarite offerings (cf. 1 Cor 9:19-20), and there is no reason to infer that Luke's record of this incident suggests that Christ's sacrificial death required any further offering prescribed by the Mosaic law. The pressing need for Paul's involvement in these temple activities was not initiated by the apostle but suggested by the Jerusalem elders for the purpose of not offending the Jews. This was the reason for Paul's action, as was his decision to circumcise* Timothy (Acts 16:3). However, Paul's desire not to offend the Jews did not extend to his willingness to compromise the gospel (Acts 15:2-11), nor did it prevent him from turning to the Gentiles* in the face of Jewish opposition, in accordance with Isaiah's prophecy (Acts 28:25-28).

1.2. Hebrews. Like Paul, the author of Hebrews* recognizes the climactic finality of the death of Christ (see *DPL*, Sacrifice, Offering). The writer is at pains to emphasize that Jesus' death has made the first covenant,* with its sacrifices and offerings, obsolete (Heb 8:13). This has come about by way of fulfillment rather than merely by replacement.

The continuity between the old and the new is evident not only in the pattern of the tabernacle,* reflecting the heavenly original (Heb 8:5; cf. Acts 7:44), but also by the manner of Jesus' priestly sacrifice, which of necessity shares aspects with the levitical high priest's ritual (Heb 8:3; cf. Heb 13:11-12). Like the high priest,* Jesus is chosen rather than self-appointed (Heb 5:4-5); like the high priest, he offers gifts and sacrifices to God on behalf of men and women (Heb 5:1; 8:3); like the high priest, Jesus is able to sympathize with human frailty (Heb 2:17-18; 4:15; 5:2).

However, there are distinct differences. Jesus' high priesthood is not an earthly high priesthood but rather a heavenly one (Heb 5:6; 7:16-17); Aaron stands (Heb 10:11), whereas Jesus sits (Heb 10:12); unlike Aaron, Jesus takes office with an oath (Heb 7:21-22, 28); where the number of levitical high priests are multiple and each holds limited tenure (Heb 7:23-24), Jesus' priesthood is singular and forever; the high priests under the law make offering first for themselves and then for the people (Heb 5:3, 7:27; 9:7), yet Jesus, being sinless, has no need to offer sacrifice for his own sin. In summary, Jesus' high priesthood is of the order of Melchizedek,* the very existence of which presupposes the inadequacy of the Aaronic priesthood (Heb 6:20–7:28).

The reason for a careful description of Jesus' high priesthood, however, lies in the kind of offering that he makes. Unlike the Mosaic offerings of bulls and goats, it is the offering of himself, the offering of his body through his blood, that the writer to the Hebrews wishes to emphasize (Heb 9:12, 14, 26; 10:10). This sacrifice secures redemption,* which is an eternal redemption (Heb 9:12). Moreover, the efficacy of the old covenant sacrifices finds its explanation in the sacrifice of Christ. For under the typology of Mosaic sacrifices and offerings, the conscience* of the worshiper was not perfected. However, Christ's death is retrospective in efficacy. For whereas the blood of bulls and goats could never take away sins (Heb 10:4, 11), the sacrifice of Christ has guaranteed the forgiveness of sins committed under the old covenant, that is, the sins of the penitent living under the old covenant (Heb 9:15), as well as the sins of

the penitent living under the new covenant (Heb 10:19-22).

Previously forgiveness was declared to Israel through the work of the high priest (Lev 4:20, 26, 31, 35). Yet this forgiveness, while it was not illusory (contrary to Schenk), was promissory. For the efficacy of the ritual pronouncement of forgiveness lay not in the animal sacrifices of Mosaic legislation but in the future prospect of Jesus' sacrifice, of which the sacrifice of bulls and goats was but a copy, a shadow of the good things to come (Heb 8:5; cf. Rom 3:25-26).

The fullness of God's promise to save has arrived with the time of reformation (Heb 9:10), when Christ offered for all time a single sacrifice for sins (Heb 10:12; cf. Heb 1:3). In the light of this declaration of forgiveness, there is no longer any need of an offering for sin (Heb 10:18).

1.3. 1 Peter. Although Peter does not use the language of sacrifice and offering when describing Jesus' death, the concept is patently present (*see* 1 Peter). The ransom of believers by "the precious blood of Christ, like that of a lamb without blemish or defect" (1 Pet 1:19) is clearly cast in the sacrificial terms of the OT. Jesus bore our sins in his body on the tree (1 Pet 2:24), so that he might bring us close to God having died for sins once for all (1 Pet 3:18). This emphasis on the uniqueness of Christ's death, requiring no repetition, echoes the teaching found in the letter to the Hebrews.

1.4. 1 John. John (*see* John, Letters of), like Peter, does not explicitly use the language of sacrifice and offering, but he does speak of the removal of sin (1 Jn 3:5) and of Jesus' death as the propitiation for our sins (1 Jn 2:2; 4:10). The apostle is intent on teaching his readers that a remedy for sin is found in Jesus' death and that through that death we may be cleansed from all sin and find forgiveness. Moreover, while sin may still persist in the believer, the forgiveness flowing from Jesus' blood is constant, thus echoing the uniqueness and efficacy of Jesus' sacrifice.

1.4. Revelation. The technical language for offerings and sacrifice is not found in the Revelation to John (*see* Revelation, Book of); however, like some of the other later NT letters,* there is a focus upon the death of Christ that is unmistakably set within the sacrificial framework. The opening verses remind readers that they have been freed from their sins by the blood of Jesus (Rev 1:5). He is the lamb* that was slain (Rev 5:6,12; 13:8), and the blood of the lamb cleanses the saints (Rev 7:14) and makes them conquerors (Rev 12:11). The implicit finality and centrality of the lamb's sacrifice for the people of God (Rev 5:9) is highlighted by the absence of the temple in the new Jerusalem (Rev 21:22), since the final sacrifice has been made once and for all.

2. Christian Sacrifice.

2.1. Hebrews. The writer to the Hebrews, more than any other NT writer, stresses the finality and unrepeatable nature of Jesus' death as sacrifice and thus establishes the theological rationale for recognizing the obsolescence of offering any further animal sacrifices. However, like Paul, the writer to the Hebrews continues to employ the language of sacrifice when describing the Christian's response to the sacrifice of Christ. In this way the writer redefines the cultic categories, originally applying only to the temple and its sacrificial order, to the whole life of the Christian. This concept receives particular emphasis at the close of the letter, where the language of sacrifice and offering is now descriptive of lives of obedience* and praise* (Heb 13:15-16), a fulfillment of Psalm 40:6-8, which the author had previously cited in Hebrews 10:5.

In a similar vein to Paul's instruction to present one's body as a living sacrifice (Rom 12:1-2), Hebrews declares that the sacrifices pleasing to God are the fruit of lips that acknowledge his name and the display of good works that emanates from those sanctified under the new covenant. This is the acceptable worship* that Christians are to offer God with reverence and awe (Heb 12:28). This new covenant worship includes loving fellow Christians (Heb 13:1), showing hospitality* (Heb 13:2), remembering prisoners (Heb 13:3) and holding marriage* in honor (Heb 13:4). It is acceptable "worship" *(latreia)* that is offered by Christians, because it is offered in response to the one sufficient offering of the blood of Christ (Heb 9:14). This is aptly described as "the participation of believers in the worship of Jesus" (Peterson 1992, 238-46).

2.2. 1 Peter, James and Revelation. The concept of Christian sacrifice as a response to God's grace* in Christ* is also evident in Peter's first epistle. Christians are "like living stones being built into a spiritual house, to be a holy priesthood, to offer spiritual sacrifices acceptable to God through Jesus Christ" (1 Pet 2:5; *see* House; Stone). The nature of these spiritual sacrifices is not defined. However, the use of the word "spiritual" *(pneumatikos)* identifies them as those activities that are characteristic of new covenant believers, who have been sanctified by the Holy Spirit* (1 Pet 1:2). In contrast to the sacrifices regulated by the OT, which were only offered by the levitical priests, all believers are now a holy priesthood, and their whole lives, characteristic of children of obedience (1 Pet 1:14; *see* Son), are seen as a holy response to God.

In a similar vein James* describes the new covenant lifestyle as true "religion" *(thrēskeia)*. This term was originally replete with ritualistic content but now describes such practicalities as visiting orphans and widows (Jas 1:26-27). Although the book of Revelation describes the prayers* of the saints as an offering of incense rising up to God (Rev 5:8; 8:3,4), there is no explicit reference to Christian sacrifice apart from the tangential references to Christians as pillars in God's temple (Rev 3:12) and their worship day and night in the heavenly temple (Rev 7:15). On the last day this will be superseded by the new Jerusalem, which has no temple, though it is characterized by a worshiping, obedient people (Rev 21:22; 22:3-5).

2.3. Apostolic Fathers. In accordance with the later writers of the NT, the apostolic fathers* recognized Jesus' death as a fulfillment of OT sacrifices (note the elaborate detail of the description in *Barn.* 7.1-11; 8.1-7, which Behm, 190, calls a "rather crude spiritualising"). The fulfillment found in Christ has thereby abolished the need for ritual sacrifices in the Christian era (*Barn.* 2.6). The *Epistle to Diognetus,** when it compares the worship of Christians and Jews, suggests that the offering of ritual sacrifices to God is foolishness rather than reverence, because God has no need of such offerings (*Diogn.* 3.1-5; cf. *Barn.* 2.7-8). The sacrifice to be offered by Christians is that of praise (*1 Clem.* 35.12; 52.3); the sacrifice of a broken heart (*Barn.* 2.10; cf. *1 Clem.* 18.17; 52.4); the sacrifice of fasting (*Herm Sim.* 5.3). Nonetheless, Clement (*see* Clement of Rome) can also draw upon the stipulations for OT sacrifices to counter anti-institutional abuses in the church (cf. *1 Clem.* 41.2 and the comments of Daly 1978 *Origins*, 85-86).

Moreover, in the *Didache** is found the beginning of a trend, to be developed in later centuries, of associating the sacrificial language of the OT with the celebration of the Lord's Supper.* This text even describes the offering as a sacrifice (*Did.* 14.2; cf. Justin Martyr *Dial. Tryph.* 41) and cites Malachi 1:11 as the justification for this language. The reference to the "gifts" (*dōra*) of the bishop in *1 Clement* 44.4 may also allude to the Eucharist. Yet this development was a distinct break from the teaching of the apostles. While the authors of the NT guarded the uniqueness of the sacrifice of Christ, they were willing to use the language of sacrifice and offering when they described the ethical* obedience of Christians but never applied sacrificial language to a liturgical setting (Daly 1978 *Origins,* 82). Such a narrow focus was to play a major role in the development of the Christian priesthood and the sacrifice of the Roman Mass, but it always lacked the endorsement of the NT.

See also COVENANT, NEW COVENANT; CROSS, THEOLOGY OF THE; DEATH OF CHRIST; HEBREWS; LAMB; LORD'S SUPPER, LOVE FEAST; MARTYRDOM; PRIEST, HIGH PRIEST; TABERNACLE, SANCTUARY; WORSHIP AND LITURGY.

BIBLIOGRAPHY. R. T. Beckwith and M. J. Selman, eds., *Sacrifice in the Bible* (Grand Rapids: Baker, 1995); J. Behm, "θύω κτλ," *TDNT* 3:180-90; R. J. Daly, *Christian Sacrifice: The Judeo-Christian Background Before Origen* (Washington, DC: Catholic University of America, 1978); idem, *The Origins of the Christian Doctrine of Sacrifice* (Philadelphia: Fortress, 1978); D. Kidner, "Sacrifice, Metaphors and Meanings," *TynB* 33 (1982) 119-36; W. L. Lane, *Hebrews* (2 vols.; WBC; Dallas: Word, 1991); S. Lyonnet and L. Sabourin, *Sin, Redemption and Sacrifice: A Biblical and Patristic Study* (Rome: Biblical Institute Press, 1970); D. G. Peterson, *Engaging with God* (Leicester: Apollos, 1992); idem, *Hebrews and Perfection* (SNTSMS 47; Cambridge: Cambridge University Press, 1982); W. Schenk, "προσφέρω," *EDNT* 3:177-78; T. R. Schreiner, "Sacrifice and Offerings in the New Testament," *ISBE* 4:273-77; H. Thyen, "θυσία, θύω," *EDNT* 2:161-63; K. Weiss, "προσφέρω," *TDNT* 9:65-68; F. M. Young, *The Use of Sacrificial Ideas in Greek Christian Writers from the New Testament to John Chrysostom* (Cambridge, MA: Philadelphia Patristic Foundation, 1979). G. N. Davies

SALVATION

With the noun *salvation (sōtēria)* is directly associated the verb *save (sōzō)* and rather more obliquely the noun *savior (sōtēr)*. In both the Septuagint and secular Greek the first two are connected with the notion of physical deliverance (e.g., from peril, illness, death or). "Savior," however, issues from the vocabulary of the ruler cult of the Greco-Roman kingdoms of the NT era. According to the Priene inscription from Asia Minor, "Providence . . . has sent to us . . . a savior . . . who has put an end to war . . . Caesar [Augustus]" (Spicq, 3:353). Throughout the NT this word group lends itself metaphorically to the notion of eschatological* salvation.* The title *sōtēr* is applied to both God* and the Son* he sent into the world for its salvation (*see DPL,* Salvation).

1. Acts
2. Hebrews, the General Epistles and Revelation
3. Apostolic Fathers

1. Acts.

The underlying idea of physical deliverance from both illness and may be seen at several points (Acts 4:9; 14:9; 7:25).

The more prominent idea, however, is metaphorical as applied to eschatological salvation. This appears early in the narrative, on the day of Pentecost,* when, in light of the Holy Spirit's* coming, Peter quotes Joel 2:32 (LXX): "Whoever calls on the name of the Lord will be saved." The Spirit's arrival is evidence that the Lord,* uncorrupted by death, is risen and ascended* and that the gate to salvation, as heralded by the prophets,* is now open. Hence, "save yourselves," Peter exhorted his hearers; day by day the Lord added "those who were being saved" (Acts 2:40, 47). Peter makes clear that only in Jesus Christ of Nazareth, crucified but risen, is salvation to be found (Acts 4:12). He is the savior whom God has exalted to his right hand (Acts 5:31; *see* Exaltation). Against those who asserted that circumcision* was a prerequisite to salvation Peter declared that both Gentiles* and Jews will be saved "through the grace of the Lord Jesus Christ" (Acts 15:1, 11). The apostolic word is the announcement but also, as apprehended by the hearers, the means of salvation (Acts 11:14).

In the second part of Acts* Paul, speaking as a Jew to a synagogue* audience, stated that "to us has been sent the message of this salvation." This is the good news about a descendant of King David, Jesus, whom God has brought to Israel* as a "savior," whom, uncorrupted by the grave, God has raised up alive (Acts 13:26, 23, 30-41). But this message, rejected by those Jews, was also for the Gentiles. Indeed God had appointed Paul to be a "light for the Gentiles," to bring God's salvation to them (Acts 13:47). Paul's emphasis in his preaching on salvation may be seen in the Philippian soothsayer's parroting of the message, "These men . . . proclaim to you the way of salvation" (Acts 16:17). This is borne out by the jailer's question, "What must I do to be saved?" to which Paul replied, "Believe on the Lord Jesus Christ and you will be saved" (Acts 16:30, 31).

In short we learn from the ministries* of the apostles Peter and Paul in Acts that salvation is in fulfillment of OT prophecy (*see* Old Testament in Acts), has become a present but exclusive reality in the death for sins and the resurrection* from the dead of Jesus of Nazareth the descendant of David, and is apprehended by receiving the apostolic message.

2. Hebrews, the General Epistles and Revelation.
The language of salvation appears often in this literature, though with different nuances.

2.1. Hebrews. In the letter to the Hebrews* we find several references to physical salvation from death (Heb 5:7) and from the deluge (Heb 11:7). According to Hebrews, eschatological salvation belongs to the future (Heb 1:14), at the appearing of the Son of God (Heb 9:28; *see* Son of God). In Hebrews, faith is the active expectation of the salvation, a hope that unceasingly and against all odds presses forward toward it (Heb 11:1-40 passim). Such faith is exercised in obedience* to the good news, promising salvation (Heb 2:3; 4:1-6). This salvation is in the presence of the God who is holy,* whither the incarnate Son of God has already arrived in virtue of his faith and obedience. Thus he is the "file leader" *(archēgos)* of his people, the exemplar of perseverance and obedience, to be followed after in the path to God's salvation (Heb 12:2). Nonetheless access to this salvation is not by self-effort but "through" the One who is high priest* forever, after the order of Melchizedek* (Heb 7:25, 15-17). He is the "source" of eternal salvation to all who obey him

(Heb 5:9), having offered for all time a single sacrifice for sins (Heb 10:12).

2.2. James. In the letter of James* only the verb *save* is employed. It is the soul that is saved, and it is saved from death and from being "destroyed" (Jas 1:21; 4:12; 5:20). Thus salvation is eschatological. According to James, it is the Lawgiver and Judge, that is, God, who both "saves and destroys" (Jas 4:12). Nonetheless the Lord, that is, the Lord Jesus Christ who is to come (Jas 5:7), will "raise . . . up" those who offer the prayer* of faith,* a deliberate double meaning, pointing to both physical healing* and final resurrection (Jas 5:15). How is one saved, according to James? It is by a lively faith that is authenticated by works (*see* Faith and Works); an empty or hypocritical faith will not save (Jas 2:14).

2.3. 1 Peter, 2 Peter and Jude. The language of salvation is important in 1 Peter.* Such salvation is a present reality in Jesus Christ, who was predestined before the foundation of the world but who has been made manifest at the end of times (1 Pet 1:20), who "bore our sins on the tree" and who was raised from the dead as "a living hope [of salvation]" for those who believe in him (1 Pet 2:24; 1:3). This salvation, which will be "unveiled in the last time" (1 Pet 1:5), is entered into now through the preaching of the good news (1 Pet 1:12, 23). Baptism,* a response to the gospel, "saves," though not by its water but by the inner reality of a cleansed conscience* in relationship with the God who is holy, through the resurrection of Jesus from the dead (1 Pet 3:21). As not yet revealed, this salvation is the goal or end point of faith (1 Pet 1:9), a salvation for which the "newborn" is nourished by the "pure spiritual milk"* of the gospel (1 Pet 2:2).

There is an alternative to this eschatological salvation. It is the judgment* of the living and the dead by God, who is holy (1 Pet 4:5; 1:15), upon "the passions . . . of ignorance" (1 Pet 1:14; 4:2). Quoting Proverbs 11:31 (LXX), Peter asks, "If the righteous man is scarcely saved, where will the impious and sinner appear?" (1 Pet 4:18).

Only once in 2 Peter* does this language appear: "And count the forbearance of the Lord as salvation" (2 Pet 3:15). Here Peter is alluding to the salvation of which his "beloved brother Paul" wrote (in Rom 2:4?), "as he does in all his letters." Peter recognized the importance of salvation in the writings of the apostle Paul. In a context relating to the sudden, unheralded coming of the Day of the Lord* and its judgment, Peter is teaching that God's withholding of salvation is an expression of divine forbearance, providing space and opportunity for people to find salvation.

Second Peter, like the Pastorals, is marked by a number of references to "savior." Unlike the Pastorals, however, in which both God and the Lord Jesus Christ are called the, or our, savior, 2 Peter confines this title to Jesus Christ. This usage may have been a polemical rebuttal of the contemporary application of this title to the Roman emperors*; Jesus Christ is the true savior. This possibility is strengthened by Peter's bracketing with "savior" other imperial titles, "god" and "Lord" (2 Pet 1:1, 11; 2:20; 3:2, 18). Against pretentious and often evil rulers Jesus is God, Lord and Savior through whom we "escape the corruption that is in the world because of passion and become partakers of the divine nature" (2 Pet 1:4). This is salvation, which "is granted to us by way of God's precious and very great promises" (2 Pet 1:4)

Jude,* unlike 2 Peter, applies the title *savior* to "the only God our savior" (Jude 25). Thus "our common salvation" is to be attributed to God, who saved a people out of Egypt. The alternative to this salvation is a "punishment of eternal fire" in the "judgment of the great day" (Jude 5, 6, 7). Thus Jude warns, "Save some by snatching them out of the fire" (Jude 23).

2.4. Johannine Literature. The letters of John (*see* John, Letters of) have only one example from the word group: "the Father has sent the Son as the savior of the world" (1 Jn 4:14; cf. Jn 4:42). In a parallel passage John's meaning becomes clear: "God . . . sent his Son to be the expiation *(hilasmos)* of our sins" (1 Jn 4:10; cf. 1 Jn 2:2). The Son of God, Jesus Christ the righteous, is the savior because by his death he has propitiated the wrath* of God toward sins or has covered sins (cf. Rom 3:25). Access to this salvation is by means of the apostolic proclamation of the message of the incarnation and death of the Son of God (1 Jn 1:2-3; 2:1-2).

In the Revelation salvation belongs to God, who "sits on the throne" of history and whose "judgments are just and true" (Rev 7:10; 19:1). Sharing that throne with God is the Lamb* (Rev 7:10; 19:1), an indication of the divine sovereignty of the Lamb (cf. Rev 4:11; 5:1-5, 7, 13).

Although Revelation is interested in the unfolding of history leading to God's final, apocalyptic* conclusion (Rev 16—22), that history and its consummation are in light of the salvation that is a present reality. The present and the future, which are awesome in their evil, unfold out of the already completed salvation of God in the death and resurrection of the Lamb (Rev 5:7-13). "Now the salvation . . . of our God and the authority of his Christ have come" (Rev 12:10). Thus, despite appearances to the contrary, "the kingdom of the world has become the kingdom of our Lord and of his Christ" (Rev 11:15; cf. Rev 1:6; 2:8). Those who "follow the Lamb" in his faithful witness* and in purity* of life (Rev 14:3-5) already have this salvation, already have begun to reign with Christ, as a kingdom and priests to God (Rev 1:6; 20:4, 6) and will not be subject to the "second death" (Rev 2:11; 21:7).

In the General Epistles and the Revelation, for the most part salvation is eschatological in its realization, is a present reality in Jesus Christ, fulfills the expectations of the OT and is made available by the word of God. The letter of James is silent as to its present reality and the OT expectations.

3. Apostolic Fathers.
The "save"/"salvation" vocabulary appears to a limited degree in this literature (most commonly in *2 Clem.*). Although these writers are in close historical continuity with the NT, we now step into a different world (*see* Apostolic Fathers). If the concept of salvation is less, this is probably due to a rather more vague eschatology, both future and realized, than in the NT and unclear views of sin and redemption.*

In *1 Clement* the underlying secular notion of physical preservation occurs (e.g., in the reference to OT deliverances, *1 Clem.* 7.6-7). But it is not clear that "salvation" is related to the future general resurrection (*1 Clem.* 25—26) or that it is the eschatological alternative to eternal destruction. It does not appear that such salvation is one's certain possession now, based on the death and resurrection of Christ, as mediated by the gospel. Christ's blood was "poured out for our salvation," but this was to bring "the grace of repentance to all the world." It is this repentance and godly obedience, based on OT examples, that issues in "salvation" (*1 Clem.* 7.4-7; 9.1-4; 11.1; *see* Grace; Repentance).

By contrast *2 Clement* does appear to hold a view of salvation as a present possession (e.g., *2 Clem.* 1.4, 7; 2.7; 3.3; 9.2). *2 Clement,* however, lacks the sense of salvation as a "finished work" accessible to faith through the gospel. As with *1 Clement,* this author places great emphasis on the ongoing repentance and obedience of the "saved" person. "Keep . . . the seal of baptism undefiled, that we may obtain eternal life" (*2 Clem.* 8.6).

The letters of Ignatius,* unlike other literature in this period, make reference to the title *savior* as applied to Christ (e.g., Ign. *Eph.* 1.1; Ign. *Phld.* 9.2). Unlike the later NT writings, in which *sōtēr* is used of Christ polemically to establish an antithesis between him and the imperial rulers, this is not Ignatius's emphasis. The other language of salvation, however, is not prominent in Ignatius (cf. Ign. *Eph.* 18.1), though he does refer to "immortality" (e.g., Ign. *Eph.* 17.1) or the "abolition of death" (Ign. *Eph.* 19.3), the means to which is repentance, membership in the bishop-led church* (*see* Church Order) and participation in the sacraments, which are "the medicine of immortality" (Ign. *Eph.* 20.2; Ign. *Magn.* 6.2; *see* Worship).

In the *Epistle of Barnabas*° there is some reference to salvation (e.g., *Barn.* 1.3; 2.10; 14.8; 16.10; 17.1); however, the way to it is by "works," the keeping of the commandments* of God (*Barn.* 19.1-12). The vocabulary of salvation is infrequent in Polycarp,* the *Didache*° and the *Shepherd of Hermas.*° *Hermas* does make a connection between baptism and repentance and being saved, but there is no future certainty.

The future salvation brought into the present by the death and resurrection of Jesus Christ, in fulfillment of the prophets, as mediated by the word of the gospel—ideas that are so powerfully stated or implied across the later as well as the earlier NT writings—are muted or absent in the postapostolic literature. J. N. D. Kelly concluded that "while enumerating all sorts of benefits bestowed by Christ, the apostolic fathers nowhere co-ordinate their main ideas or attempt to sketch a rationale of salvation" (Kelly, 163).

See also ASSURANCE; BAPTISM, BAPTISMAL RITES; DEATH OF CHRIST; ESCHATOLOGY; FORGIVENESS; GRACE; NEW BIRTH; REDEMPTION; REPENTANCE, SECOND REPENTANCE; RIGHTEOUSNESS; SAVIOR.

BIBLIOGRAPHY. W. Foerster and G. Fohrer, "σώζω κτλ," *TDNT* 7:965-1003; E. M. B. Green, *The Meaning of Salvation* (London: Hodder, 1965); J. N. D. Kelly, *Early Christian Doctrines* (London: Black, 1980); A. McGrath, *Christian Theology: An Introduction* (Oxford: Blackwell, 1994); I. H. Marshall, *Luke: Historian and Theologian* (Exeter: Paternoster, 1970); D. G. Peterson, *Hebrews and Perfection* (SNTSMS 47; Cambridge: Cambridge University Press, 1982); W. Radl, "σώζω," *EDNT* 3:319-21; K. H. Schelkle, "σωτηρία," *EDNT* 3:327-29; C. Spicq, *Theological Lexicon of the New Testament* (3 vols.; Peabody, MA: Hendrickson, 1994) 3:344-57; B. H. Throckmorton, "Σώζειν σωτηρία in Luke-Acts," *SE* 6 (1973) 515-26. P. W. Barnett

SAMARIA

In the NT Samaria is mentioned only in the Gospels and Acts. We cannot be absolutely certain that the term when used in these documents refers to the province rather than a city by that name. Acts, however, makes it clear that this territory or city played a pivotal role in the expansion of early Christianity.

1. History
2. Samaria in Acts

1. History.

1.1. City of Samaria. Omri, king of the northern tribes of Israel, founded the city of Samaria in the latter part of the ninth century B.C. (1 Kings 16:24). From then on it served as the capital of the northern kingdom until the city's destruction by Sargon II of Assyria in 721 B.C. (2 Kings 17). The city of Samaria was then rebuilt as the administrative capital of the Assyrian province of Samaria.

Not much is known about Samaria until the time of the exiles' return from Babylon (*see DJG,* Samaritans §2.4). In Ezra 4 we find opposition (by those living in the cities of the province of Samaria) to the rebuilding of the temple* in Jerusalem.* Approximately 332 B.C. the capital city itself came under the control of Alexander the Great. However, he soon destroyed it in response to the burning to death of the prefect by the city's inhabitants. Alexander deported many of its inhabitants to Shechem and settled the city with Syro-Macedonians. It then became a non-Samaritan religious city, and Shechem became the Samaritan religious center.

John Hyrcanus captured Shechem in 128 B.C. and destroyed the city of Samaria between 111 and 107 B.C. Herod the Great rebuilt the latter in Hellenistic style and returned it to the glory it had in the Israelite period. He then changed the city's name to Sebaste (i.e., Augusta) in honor of the emperor,* Caesar Augustus.

In the beginning of the Jewish revolt against Rome, Samaria was one of the first cities to suffer. It was captured and sacked by the Jews in the first month of A.D. 66.

1.2. Territory of Samaria. In the centuries following the founding of the city by Omri, the name *Samaria* was used to designate the area or territory of the northern kingdom lying between Judea to the south and Galilee to the north as well as the city. When Herod the Great rebuilt the city and renamed it Sebaste, the term *Samaria* was used exclusively to identify the province. Thus it seems more than likely that when the term is used in the NT, in most instances the province is denoted (see Lk 17:11; Jn 4:4: Acts 1:8; 8:1; 9:31; 15:3; *see DJG*, Samaritans §4).

2. Samaria in Acts.

2.1. Jesus' Commission to Samaria. Acts 1:8 has been considered as a sort of table of contents for Acts* or the theme verse that provides an outline for the book. The geographical places mentioned are significant because Samaria is specifically mentioned. Although Judea and Samaria are attached without a repetition of the Greek article and preposition and thus appear to be a single compound, Luke has Jesus specifically authorizing a mission to Samaria (the only non-Jewish area or city identified). Jesus and Luke thus wish to highlight Samaria as an important place in the "history of salvation" (see Cullmann).

2.2. The Beginnings of the Church in Samaria. Acts 8 details the inception of the church* in Samaria. Persecution* and dispersion of the Jerusalem church (Acts 8:1) brought about the fulfillment of Acts 1:8. But the mission to Samaria was not an evangelistic outreach to Gentiles.* Samaritans were viewed not as Gentiles but as schismatics, heretics or half-breeds. They were regarded as a sort of *tertium quid*— neither Jew nor Gentile. Thus they stood as a halfway house between the Jewish and Gentile worlds leading to a transition to the Gentile mission.

O. Cullmann argued that the basis for this mission to Samaria was laid by Jesus in the event recorded in John 4. After her encounter with Jesus, the so-called Samaritan woman returned to the city and testified to Jesus. The result was that "many Samaritans from that city believed in him" (Jn 4:39). And it has also been suggested that the behind the speech of Stephen* in Acts 7 lies a Samaritan theology and that Stephen was either a Samaritan and not a Hellenist (Spiro) or that the Hellenists were markedly influenced by Samaritan theology (Scobie). But this understanding of Stephen and the Hellenists has been severely criticized (see, e.g., Hill).

2.2.1. Philip in Samaria. Philip's* venture in to Samaria was a significant break with Jewish tradition. From that point on the gospel began to know no geographic or ethnic bounds. In Samaria he preached, exorcised demons and performed physical healing* (Acts 8:5-8) He also confronted and converted the famous magician, Simon (Acts 8:9-13).

Where Philip did his preaching, signs* and miracles* is a source of debate. In the Greek text of Acts 8:5 the definite article is omitted in some manuscripts before the word *city*, while in others it is included. If the definite article is omitted, it would seem that the province of Samaria was meant (as it is in the rest of the NT). However, if we follow the earlier and better manuscripts and include the article, then we must decide whether the reference is to Shechem or Sebaste, or even Gitta, the traditional birthplace of Simon (Acts 8:8). Because the religious Samaritan's main center was Shechem and there is no trace of Hellenism in the narrative, it seems that Sebaste should be ruled out. Philip's mission therefore was in the main city of the indigenous Samaritans.

2.2.2. Peter and John in Samaria. When the apostles* in Jerusalem received the news of Philip's success in Samaria, they sent Peter and John to the province (Acts 8:14). The purpose of the visit was not to begin the church but to legitimize and endorse the new church and mission.* This was accomplished as they prayed for the new members and laid hands upon them to bestow the Holy Spirit* (Acts 8:14-17). They also enthusiastically participated in the evangelistic mission, preaching in many Samaritan villages as they returned home (Acts 8:25).

2.2.3. Simon Magus of Samaria. The most prominent person from Samaria in Christian literature is Simon, whose magical* activity was superseded by Philip (Acts 8:9-24). In postapostolic times Simon was depicted as the father of

Gnosticism.* Justin Martyr, himself a Samaritan, wrote that Simon was a native of Gitta with a large following not only in Samaria but also in Rome and was worshiped by many as the supreme deity (Justin *Apol. I* 26.3).

There is great uncertainty as to whether Justin's Simon is the same as the one mentioned in Acts. The fact that the earliest gnostic Simonian teachings lack a Judaic flavor suggests that their roots were not in early Samaritan Christianity. On the contrary, these second-century Gnostics seem to have co-opted the Lukan Simon in order to give their movement roots in the NT.

2.3. Post-Philip Mission. The Samaritans proved receptive to the gospel, as is evidenced not only in the result of Philip's mission but also in the fact that they are included in Luke's statement that the church throughout Judea, Galilee and Samaria was built up and increased in numbers (Acts 9:31).

The church in Samaria seemed to be more liberal than its counterpart in Jerusalem. Luke reported that as Paul passed through Phoenicia and Samaria the believers there rejoiced at the inclusion of Gentiles in the church (Acts 15:3).

After this we learn extraordinarily little about the church in Samaria. It is possible that the church there was devastated during and after the Jewish war under Vespasian. Samaria might be included in Eusebius's statement that just before the siege Christians left Jerusalem and the surrounding territories, and the whole land of Judea was left destitute of righteous persons (Eusebius *Hist. Eccl.* 3.5.3).

See also ACTS OF THE APOSTLES; HELLENISTS, HELLENISTIC AND HELLENISTIC-JEWISH CHRISTIANITY; PHILIP THE EVANGELIST.

BIBLIOGRAPHY. F. F. Bruce, *Commentary on the Book of Acts* (Grand Rapids: Eerdmans, 1979); A. D. Crown, *The Samaritans* (Tübingen: J. C. B. Mohr, 1989); O. Cullmann, "Samaria and the Origins of the Christian Mission" in *The Early Church* (London: SCM) 185-94; K. Haacker, "Samaritan, Samaria," *NIDNTT* 3:449-67; E. Haenchen, *The Acts of the Apostles* (Oxford: Blackwell, 1971); C. C. Hill, *Hellenists and Hebrews: Reappraising Division with the Earliest Church* (Minneapolis: Fortress, 1992); J. Jeremias, "Σαμάρεια κτλ," *TDNT* 8:88-94; J. B. Polhill, *Acts* (NAC; Nashville: Broadman, 1992); E. Richard, "Acts 7: An Investigation of the Samaritan Evidence," *CBQ* 39 (1977) 190-208; J. A. T. Robinson, "The

Others of John 4:38" in *Twelve New Testament Studies* (London: SCM, 1962) 61-66; C. H. H. Scobie, "The Origins and Development of Samaritan Christianity," *NTS* 20 (1972-73) 390-414; G. S. Sloyan, "The Samaritans in the New Testament," *Horizons* 10 (1983) 7-21; A. Spiro, "Stephen's Samaritan Background" in *The Acts of the Apostles,* J. Munck (AB; New York: Doubleday, 1967) 285-300; G. E. Wright, "Samaria," *BA* 22 (1959) 67-78.   P. U. Maynard-Reid

SANCTUARY. *See* TABERNACLE, SANCTUARY; TEMPLE.

SATAN, DEVIL

The documents of early Christianity consistently reflect a belief in a powerful, hostile, supernatural enemy of God* most commonly called "Satan" or "the Devil" (*See DJG,* Demon, Devil, Satan; *DPL,* Satan, Devil). This personal being maliciously works to thwart the redemptive purposes of God and to perpetrate evil throughout the world and among the people of God. His demise is certain, however, because of his defeat at the cross* of Jesus Christ. The consummation of the age will mark the end of his pernicious activities.

1. Names and Titles
2. The Nature and Authority of Satan
3. The Defeat of Satan at the Cross
4. Satan's Hostility Against the Church
5. Christian Means of Victory Over Satan
6. Final Overthrow and Judgment of Satan

1. Names and Titles.

1.1. Satan. Although *Satan* (*ho satanas*) is a common title for this evil being in Revelation (see Rev 2:9, 13, 24; 3:9; 12:9; 20:2, 7), it is less common elsewhere, only occurring in Acts 5:3 and 26:18 (see also, Ign. *Eph.* 1.13; Pol. *Phil.* 7.1; *Barn.* 18.1; Pap. *Frag.* 11), and not at all in Hebrews, James, 1 and 2 Peter, Jude or the Johannine letters. The term is a transliteration of the Hebrew *Šāṭān* (Job 1:6-8, 12; 2:1-7; Zech 3:1-2) and characterizes his role as one who brings accusation or slanders. In our literature it has become a proper name to designate this supernatural adversary.

1.2. Devil. Essentially interchangeable with the title *Satan* is the designation *devil* (*diabolos*). Although its original meaning also has to do with slander and accusation, it has simply become a common way of referring to Satan. The term is used widely throughout the NT (e.g., Acts 10:38; 13:10; Heb 2:14; Jas 4:7; 1 Pet 5:8; 1 Jn 3:8, 10; Jude 9; Rev 2:10; 12:9, 12; 20:2, 10) and the Apostolic Fathers (24 times in *Hermas*; *2 Clem.* 18.2; Ign. *Eph.* 10.3; Ign. *Trall.* 8.1; Ign. *Rom.* 5.3; Ign. *Smyrn.* 9.1; Pol. *Phil.* 7.1; Pap. *Frag.* 11).

1.3. The Evil One. The depraved character of Satan is unequivocally expressed in the title "the evil one" (*ho ponēros*), which appears frequently in 1 John (1 Jn 2:13, 14; 3:12; 5:18, 19) but rather infrequently in the apostolic fathers (Ign. *Eph.* 7.1; *Barn.* 2.10; 19.11; 20.2; *Did.* 8.2).

1.4. The Serpent. Satan is identified as "the serpent" (*ho ophis*) who tempted Eve in Revelation 12:9, 14, 15; 20:2 as well as in *Barnabas* 12.5, *Diognetus* 12.3, 6, 8, and Papias *Fragment* 11. His work of tempting is envisioned as ongoing.

1.5. The Dragon. In Revelation 12 and 13, Satan appears as "the great red dragon" (*drakōn*, Rev 12:3, 4, 7, 9, 13, 16, 17; 13:2, 4, 11; see also Rev. 16:13 and the quotation of Rev. in Pap. *Frag.* 11) who faces Michael in heavenly battle (*see* Beasts, Dragon).

1.6. The Ruler of this Age. The preferred designation for Satan in Ignatius is "the ruler of this age" (*ho archōn tou aiōnos toutou*, Ign. *Eph.* 1.17, 19; Ign. *Magn.* 1.2; Ign. *Trall.* 4.2; Ign. *Rom.* 6.3; Ign. *Phld.* 6.1; see also *Barn.* 4.13; 18.2). The inspiration for this usage comes from the Apostle Paul (see 1 Cor 2:6, 8).

1.7. Other Titles. There are a variety of other descriptive titles used for Satan in this literature: "the deceiver of the world" (*ho kosmoplanēs*, *Did.* 16.4), "the one who is in the world" (1 Jn 4:4), "the adversary" (*ho antidikos*, 1 Pet 5:8; *ho antikeimenos*, *1 Clem.* 51.1), "the accuser" (*ho katēgōr*, Rev 12:10), "the black one" (*ho melas*, *Barn.* 4.9; 20.1), "the lawless one" (*ho anomos*, *Barn.* 15.5) and "the worker" (*ho energoun*, *Barn.* 2.1).

2. The Nature and Authority of Satan.

The background of much of what is said in this literature about Satan is deeply rooted in the OT and Jewish thought (*see DPL*, Satan, Devil).

2.1. Nature. The various titles of Satan give poignant expression to his evil character. He is the personification of all that is evil and thereby stands in direct opposition to the righteous and loving God. John claims that from the very beginning of creation* he sinned and has worked to instigate and inspire sinful behavior among all people (1 Jn 3:8, 10). According to

John, evil behavior finds its paternity in Satan.

Satan is nowhere represented as an equal to God. There is not an absolute dualism as we find in certain strands of Persian religion which portrays a cosmic struggle between Ahriman and Ahura Mazda. Neither is there a two-god theology as we find in Gnosticism.*

Satan appears to be a major angelic figure: he is a heavenly being (Rev 12:10), he stands at the head of a host of evil angels* (*Barn.* 18.1; cf. Rev 16:13), he disputes with Michael (Jude 9), and ultimately he leads his angels in heavenly warfare against Michael and the hosts of God (Rev 12:7-10)

2.2. Authority. Satan's sphere of authority* and influence encompasses the whole of creation. John states this most emphatically when he declares, "we know that the whole world is under the control of the evil one" (1 Jn 5:19).

His malevolent exercise of power,* however, is limited only to the present evil age. This Jewish two-age understanding is a presupposition of all of these writings (*see* Apocalyptic; Eschatology). Ignatius speaks frequently of Satan as "the ruler of this age" and the *Epistle of Barnabas* describes him as "the ruler of the present era of lawlessness" (*Barn.* 18.2).

Deception is one of the primary means Satan uses to keep people from a knowledge* of the truth* and the revelation* of Jesus Christ. He deceives the entire world, leading people astray from the one true God (Rev 12:9). Satan is the animating power behind other religions* as well as magic* and sorcery. Therefore the temple of Zeus (or possibly the Asclepion) at Pergamum could be spoken of as "Satan's throne" (Rev 2:13), and the Jewish magician Elymas can be referred to as a "son of the devil" (Acts 13:10). The two beasts of Revelation 13 represent a satanically inspired intermingling of idolatry* and secular power through which the devil would "deceive the inhabitants of the world" (Rev 13:14). The early Christian apologetic document known as the *Epistle to Diognetus* refers to the devil only three times, each of which indicate his role as one who deceives (*Diogn.* 12.3, 6, 8).

Satan thus holds people in bondage (Acts 10:38; 26:18; 1 Jn 3:8, 10) from which they are unable to escape by their own ability or resources. The plight of humanity is extraordinarily grim since Satan holds the power of death (Heb 2:14)—a power he gained when he seduced humanity to rebel against God (Lane, 61).

3. The Defeat of Satan at the Cross.

The death* and resurrection* of Jesus Christ dealt an irrecoverable blow to Satan and his evil designs. The writer of Hebrews declares that "through his death" Christ destroyed (*katargēsē*) the one who holds the power of death, the devil (Heb 2:14). Satan was not in some way annihilated at the cross*; rather, it was through the once-for-all sacrifice of Jesus as an offering for sin that the compelling power of the evil one was thwarted (Heb 10:11-13). As a result, Christ brought the possibility of freedom* and release to all of those in and bondage (Heb 2:15).

In a similar way, John claims that the Son of God came "to destroy the works of the devil" (1 Jn 3:8). No longer is the entire world under the power of the evil one. Jesus has nullified Satan's power to enslave and thereby can gather people into a new community.

4. Satan's Hostility Against the Church.

In spite of his defeat at the cross, Satan continues to rage in powerful opposition to the people of God. Peter gives vivid expression to this in his portrayal of Satan as "the adversary" who prowls "like a roaring lion seeking someone to devour" (1 Pet 5:8). Most of our literature, in fact, is concerned precisely with recognizing and dealing with Satanic attack.

4.1. He Tempts. As John notes, from the very beginning Satan has sought to inspire people to sin* (1 Jn 3:8). Accordingly he put it in Cain's heart to murder Abel (1 Jn 3:12; cf. Jn 8:44). Luke credits Satan with influencing Ananaias and Sapphira to sin by saying, "Satan has filled your heart [*eplērōsen satanas tēn kardian sou*] to lie to the Holy Spirit" (Acts 5:3).

After attributing temptation* to the impact of the evil inclination within individuals (Jas 1:13-15), James draws a close connection between the evil impulse and the work of the devil. He observes that the tongue is set on fire by Gehenna (Jas 3:6; a way of referring to Satan as the ultimate source) and that the so-called wisdom of the opposition is not only "earthly and unspiritual" but "of the devil" (*daimoniōdēs*, Jas 3:15). Thus, "behind the evil impulse lies the devil" (Davids, 166).

In 2 Clement 18.2 we read of temptations as the "tools of the devil." Ignatius depicts sin and

vice as weeds planted by the devil (Ign. *Eph.* 10.3). When he writes to the Romans, he reflects on his own struggle with "the ruler of this age," who wants to "take me captive and corrupt my godly intentions" by inspiring him to desire the things of the world (Ign. *Rom.* 7.1).

Much of the *Shepherd of Hermas* discusses how to respond appropriately to Satan when he tempts believers to sin (e.g., *Herm. Man.* 4.4.6). Hermas remarks that "evil desire is a daughter of the devil" (*Herm. Man.* 12.2.2). In *Mandate* 5.1 he describes how an angry temper can be exploited by an evil spirit. He observes that "the devil lives in an angry temper" (*Herm. Man.* 5.1.3), and suggests that it severely restricts the work of the Holy Spirit.*

4.2. He Inspires False Teaching. Just as Satan worked to deceive humanity through idolatry, he continues his work of deception within the church by inspiring deviant teaching (*see* Adversaries). Thus the Johannine community is urged to "test the spirits to see whether they are from God" (1 Jn 4:1-4). Some who were once affiliated with the church are now teaching, among other things, that Christ did not come in the flesh. Some in the church at Thyatira, following the teaching of a prophetess, were learning "the deep things of Satan" (Rev 2:24). This probably refers to a syncretistic* teaching involving a combination of Christianity with the cultic worship of Apollo Tyrimnaeus in the context of the local pagan guild feasts (Hemer, 122-23).

The issue of unacceptable and dangerous teaching becomes a prominent topic in the postapostolic generations of Christianity. The sentiment that such teaching has demonic roots is emphatically asserted by these writers. Polycarp declared that the person who denies the apostolic traditions about Christ "is the first-born of Satan" (Pol. *Phil.* 7.1)! In his discussion about the inspiration of a false prophet, Hermas explains that "the devil fills him with his own spirit, to see if he will be able to break down any of the righteous" (*Herm. Man.* 11.3; cf. also 11.17). The *Epistle of Barnabas* urges vigilance "lest the evil one should cause some error to slip into our midst" (*Barn.* 2.10).

Ignatius, likewise, is deeply concerned about those who spread heresy (*hairesis*, Ign. *Trall.* 6.1). These are dangerous snares of the devil (Ign. *Trall.* 8.1). Part of the solution for Ignatius is the elevation of the role of the bishop (*epi-*

skopos) to function as a custodian of doctrinal purity for the church. Thus, he goes so far as to assert, "whoever does anything without the bishop's knowledge serves the devil" (Ign. *Smyrn.* 9.1; *see* Church Order)

4.3. He Creates Doubt and Fear. As "the Accuser," the evil one continuously brings indictments to God against believers (Rev 12:10). This can result in doubt and lack of assurance for the people of God. Hermas emphasizes Satan's work of inspiring doubt (*dipsychia*). He calls it "a daughter of the devil" and "an earthly spirit from the devil that has no power" (*Herm. Man.* 9.9, 11)

The image of Satan as "a roaring lion" (1 Pet 5:8) captures the fear he seeks to instill in people. Hermas was well aware of this stratagem of Satan and urged his readers not to fear the devil (*Herm. Man.* 12.4.7). He responds to a common worry many Christians felt about the inevitability of demonic oppression. They say, "the devil is hard and oppresses (*katadynasteuein*)" believers, but Hermas attempts to dispel this defeatist attitude: "He cannot oppress God's servants who hope in him with all their heart. The devil can wrestle with them, but he cannot throw and pin them. So, if you resist him, he will be defeated and flee from you in disgrace" (*Herm. Man.* 12.5.1-2).

4.4. He Incites Hatred of Christians. The church has faced violent opposition and persecution* since its inception. Peter perceived the devil as behind the suffering* which the believers in Asia Minor were experiencing when he wrote to them (1 Pet 5:8-9). The stringent opposition that Christians in Smyrna and Philadelphia faced at the hands of the local Jewish populace led to each of their synagogues being dubbed "the synagogue of Satan" (Rev 2:9; 3:9). The letter warns the church in Smyrna that "the devil will put some of you in prison to test you" (Rev 2:10). Satan is even seen as behind the martyrdom* of a Christian leader in Pergamum (Rev 2:13).

The seething violence of Satan toward the people of God is symbolically depicted in Revelation 12—13. The red dragon persecutes the woman (Rev 12:13) and wages war against her seed (Rev 12:17). The beast of the sea is animated by Satan and goes to make war with the saints (Rev 13:7).

Ignatius* saw his own suffering and eventual martyrdom as incited by Satan. He describes

"fire and cross and battles with wild beasts, mutilation, mangling, wrenching of bones, the hacking of limbs, the crushing of my whole body" as "cruel tortures of the devil" (Ign. *Rom.* 5.3). Yet at the same time he could say, "let these come upon me, only let me reach Jesus Christ!"

5. Christian Means of Victory Over Satan.
The basis for victory over Satan is the appropriation of his work on the cross (*see* Death of Christ). This is what makes it possible for people to turn "from darkness to light, and from the power of Satan to God" (Acts 26:18) where they experience forgiveness of sins and are incorporated into the people of God. As people in relationship to the almighty God, there is not only the possibility to resist Satan but a call to resist him (Jas 4:7; 1 Pet 5:8-9; *Barn.* 4.9). This potential for victory can be seen in the successful experience of the readers of 1 John: "I write to you, young men, because you are strong, and the word of God lives in you, and you have overcome the evil one" (1 Jn 2:13-14).

5.1. The Blood of Christ. Satan's ability to prevent or sever a relationship with God comes through his power to incite sin and transgression. The death of Christ on the cross has effectually dealt with this problem. Therefore in spite of Satan's ability to accuse, God's people overcome him "by the blood of the lamb" (Rev. 12:11; *see* Lamb). It is precisely the blood of Christ that redeems people from and bondage to sin and Satan (cf. Rev 5:9).

5.2. The Power of God. Successfully resisting Satan depends on drawing near to God, who in turn draws near to his people (Jas 4:8) and fights on their behalf. Peter assures his readers that "the God of all grace . . . will make you strong *[sthenōsei]*" (1 Pet 5:10) in resisting the adversary. In Revelation it is God who gives escape and protection to the woman by providing her the wings of an eagle (Rev 12:14; cf. Ex 19:4). Hermas counsels, "turn to the Lord with all your heart, . . . and you will have the power to conquer the devil's works" (*Herm. Man.* 12.6.2)

5.3. The Presence of Christ. The indwelling presence of Christ himself assists believers in their ongoing struggle with the evil one. John assured his readers in the face of demonically inspired false teaching that "the one who is in you is greater than the one who is in the world" (1 Jn 4:4). He also consoles them by affirming the protective power of Christ: "the one who was born of God [Christ] keeps him safe, and the evil one cannot harm him" (1 Jn 5:18).

5.4. Humility and Faith in Turning from Sin. Peter explicitly calls people to trust God and humble themselves in the midst of their struggle against Satan: "resist him, standing firm in the faith" (1 Pet 5:6-9). James provides much the same counsel, insisting on contrition for sin as a part of humility before God (Jas 4:7-10). In Revelation we read that faith* will be necessary for believers who face the hostilities of the beast* that comes from the sea (Rev 13:10). Hermas gives eloquent expression to the indispensability of faith when Christians are tested by the devil: "All those who are full in the faith resist him mightily, and he leaves them alone, because he finds no place where he can gain entrance" (*Herm. Man.* 12.5.4.). In a unique development of Christian doctrine, Hermas teaches the possibility of only one repentance after conversion (*Herm. Man.* 4.3.6; *see* Repentance, Second Repentance).

5.5. The Word of God. Echoing one of the lessons gained from the account of Jesus' temptation, John stresses the importance of "the word of God" dwelling in believers (1 Jn 2:14). He claims that the young men are strong and have overcome the evil one as a result of the word of God abiding in them.

5.6. Fellowship and Unity. Ignatius appeals to his Ephesian readers to strive for fellowship* and unity as a means of overcoming Satan. He notes, "for when you meet together frequently, the powers of Satan are overthrown and his destructiveness is nullified by the unanimity of your faith" (Ign. *Eph.* 13.1; cf. also *Barn.* 4.10).

5.7. Angelic Help. Hermas conceives of special angelic* help and strengthening for the struggle with the devil (*Herm. Man.* 12.6). He speaks of an "angel of repentance" who comes to strengthen people in the faith. The help does not come in response to someone calling on an angel but rather in response to repentance and turning to the Lord. Hermas says that the angel "will crush all the power of the devil," and he and the angel together "will rule over him [the devil] and prevail over all his works" (*Herm. Man.* 12.6.4).

6. Final Overthrow and Judgment of Satan.

The Apocalypse is dramatically clear that Satan's time of perpetrating incessant evil is limited, his doom is sure. The devil will finally be judged and punished for his deception and evil works (Rev 20:10; cf. also *Barn.* 21:3). In the words of the Apocalypse, the devil will be "thrown into the lake of burning sulphur" where he "will be tormented day and night for ever and ever."

What happens just prior to this time in the events leading up to the judgment* has been a matter of debate for centuries. The text of Revelation 20:2 speaks of a binding of Satan that lasts for a thousand years. Is the binding of the devil spoken of here something that has already taken place through the work of the Lord Jesus Christ and the thousand years a way of referring to the time between advents? Or is this binding of Satan something that is yet to be fulfilled, which will be followed by a thousand year reign of Christ on earth? Most supporters of the first view recognize the difficulty of seeing Satan as bound in some absolute sense by the cross/resurrection event. They contend that Satan is therefore bound only with respect to deceiving the nations (cf. Rev 20:3); that is, he is "unable to prevent the spread of the gospel throughout the Gentile world in the period between the advents" (Page, 219). Thus Satan may still be active, but he cannot thwart the evangelistic success of the church.

Although this is a difficult problem that requires a deeper treatment of many related issues to reach a conclusion (*see* Millennium), the text appears to point to a future binding of Satan. The language and imagery of the text is too strong to allow for this particular binding to have occurred in the work of Christ on the cross. The writer of the apocalypse uses a series of five aorist indicative verbs to express this total suppression of Satanic opposition: (1) the angel seizes Satan, presumably with the chain he carries, (2) binds him for a thousand years, (3) throws him into the Abyss (*see* Hell, Abyss), (4) locks the Abyss with the key he possesses, and (5) seals it over him. The seizing, binding, casting, locking and sealing imagery leaves little room for seeing Satan as active on earth, even in a partial sense.

See also ADVERSARIES; ANGELS, HEAVENLY BEINGS, ANGEL CHRISTOLOGY; ANTICHRIST; APOCALYPTIC, APOCALYPTICISM; BEASTS, DRAGON, SEA, CONFLICT MOTIF; DAY OF THE LORD; ESCHATOLOGY; HELL, ABYSS, ETERNAL PUNISHMENT; JUDGMENT; MAGIC AND ASTROLOGY; MILLENNIUM; PAROUSIA; SPIRITS.

BIBLIOGRAPHY. H. Bietenhard, "Satan,

Beelzebul, Devil, Exorcism," *NIDNTT* 3.468-72; P. Davids, *James* (NIGTC; Grand Rapids: Eerdmans, 1982); E. Ferguson, *Demonology of the Early Christian World* (SS 12; Lewiston: Mellen, 1984); S. R. Garrett, *The Demise of the Devil: Magic and the Demonic in Luke's Writings* (Minneapolis: Fortress, 1989); C. J. Hemer, *The Letters to the Seven Churches of Asia in Their Local Setting* (JSNTSup 11; Sheffield: JSOT Press, 1986); W. L. Lane, *Hebrews 1-8* (WBC 47a; Dallas: Word, 1991); T. L. Longman III and D. G. Reid, *God is a Warrior* (SOTBT; Grand Rapids: Zondervan, 1995); S. Page, *Powers of Evil: A Biblical Theology of Satan and His Forces* (Grand Rapids: Baker, 1995); K. van der Toorn, B. Becking, and P. van der Horst, *Dictionary of Deities and Demons in the Bible* (Leiden: E. J. Brill, 1995); C. E. Arnold

SAVIOR

The Greek term *sōtēr* ("savior, deliverer or preserver") is found twenty-four times in the NT, with twelve of those in the traditional Pauline literature (*see DPL*, Savior). There are two uses in Acts, five in 2 Peter, one in Jude and one in 1 John. Other than Titus (with six), 2 Peter contains more occurrences of *sōtēr* than does any other NT book.

In Acts, the General Epistles and Revelation, the description of God as *sōtēr* is seen only in Jude. Otherwise it is Jesus who is referred to as *sōtēr* in Acts, 2 Peter and 1 John, where he is also called the Savior of the "world" *(kosmos)*. The uses in Acts and 2 Peter likely imply deity for Jesus also.

    1. Judaism and Hellenism
    2. Acts
    3. 2 Peter and Jude
    4. 1 John
    5. Apostolic Fathers

1. Judaism and Hellenism.

In the OT, God* is the ultimate Savior, frequently in a military sense, though the spiritual aspect of salvation* is clearly present. It is unlikely to be a coincidence that in the Septuagint *sōtēr* so frequently renders the Hebrew *yᵉšûʿâh*, which is also the proper name Joshua, the Greek form of which is *Iēsous* (Jesus).

Greco-Roman thought reflects the idea of the gods as helpers and deliverers of humankind. Invocations of gods such as Asclepius or goddesses like Isis implore their assistance in delivering devotees from danger or promoting

physical health *(sōtēria* can mean either; see Wendland 1913). Certain human rulers were also called *sōtēr*, often indicating their desire to be attributed divine status and honor. Though it was not an official part of the titles of Roman rulers, it was common for certain Caesars to be referred to as "savior of the world" (Schneider and Brown, 217; *see* Emperor).

2. Acts.

Both inclusions of *sōtēr* in Acts* occur in Jewish contexts. In Acts 5:31 "Peter and the other apostles" (Acts 5:29) witness before the Jewish Sanhedrin. Their testimony is that God resurrected Jesus and exalted him to heaven* as "Prince *(archēgos)* and Savior," enabling Jesus to offer "repentance and forgiveness of sins to Israel" (Acts 5:31 NIV; *see* Exaltation; Resurrection; Repentance). The furious response of the members of the Sanhedrin at this point (Acts 5:34) indicates that the author believes they understood the apostles' words as an implicit claim of deity for Jesus, since the exalted Messiah is described as dispensing to Israel* forgiveness,* a prerogative belonging to God himself as Yahweh in the OT and rabbinic soteriology (cf. Mk 2:1-12 for similar ideas). Some scholars conclude, with R. J. Bauckham (169), that the "early Christians saw Jesus as the one who exercised the divine function of salvation."

In Acts 13:23 Paul (Acts 13:16) is addressing a Jewish synagogue* in Pisidian Antioch on the first missionary journey. His elaborate "message of salvation" *(sōtēria;* Acts 13:26; *see* Salvation) is that Jesus is the son of David, the promised messianic figure that the Jewish Scriptures and people had long anticipated (Acts 13:17-25). Paul argues that Jesus' death and resurrection were fulfilling God's plan as prophesied in the OT (Acts 13:27-37; *see* Death of Christ), then ties his climactic offer of forgiveness of sins to this presentation of Jesus (Acts 13:38-39). The negative reaction to Paul's claim that Jesus is the resurrected Messiah is delayed in this setting but again is significant (Acts 13:45, 48, 50).

Thus in Acts Jesus' status as *sōtēr* derives both from his messianic lineage and his death and resurrection. Though it is found only twice, the usage by both the apostles* in Jerusalem* (Acts 5) and Paul in a Diaspora* synagogue (Acts 13) strongly implies that the understanding that Jesus as Savior is a central part of the author's gospel message.

3. 2 Peter and Jude.

Three of the five uses of *sōtēr* in 2 Peter* occur in the exact phraseology "our Lord and Savior Jesus Christ" (*tou kyriou hēmōn kai sōtēros Iēsou Christou;* 2 Pet 1:11; 2:20; 3:18). A fourth inclusion is worded simply "our Lord and Savior" (2 Pet 3:2), though the mention of the apostles (2 Pet 3:2) and its proximity to 2 Peter 2:20 are likely to account for the abbreviated form.

The only varied wording is encountered in "our God and Savior Jesus Christ" (*tou theou hēmōn kai sōteros Iēsou Christou*) in 2 Peter 1:1. Since this is the initial usage in 2 Peter, though, this variation should be considered quite significant, especially since 2 Peter 1:2 immediately refers to "Jesus our Lord."

For the writer of 2 Peter, it is a basic understanding that Jesus the messianic (i.e., Christ) *sōtēr* is both God and Lord* (for these two titles in collocation, see Bauckham, 168-69). In the concluding benediction, the readers are instructed to "grow in the grace and knowledge of our Lord and Savior Jesus Christ" (2 Pet 3:18 NIV), which is sharply contrasted with being "carried away by the error of lawless men" (2 Pet 3:17 NIV), almost certainly the false teachers and their "destructive heresies" predicted in 2 Peter 2:1.

At the core of this false teaching is the denial of "the sovereign Lord" (*despotēn*) and his redemption* (2 Pet 2:1). The false teachers are later described as having turned their backs on the knowledge* of "our Lord and Savior Jesus Christ" (2 Pet 2:20). Therefore, 2 Peter's concluding benedictory admonition to grow in "the knowledge of our Lord and Savior Jesus Christ" (2 Pet 3:18) is seen to be crucial in combating the onslaught of heresy, though there is apparently no developed teaching on gnosticizing* "knowledge," against which the author inveighs (Bauckham, 338).

The single inclusion of *sōtēr* in Jude* is as "God our Savior" in the concluding doxology (Jude 24-25). Though this wording is found in proximity to "Jesus Christ our Lord" (Jude 25), the two are not directly connected, as might be expected because of the extensive parallels between Jude and 2 Peter. God is rarely called "savior" in early Christian literature (only in Lk 1:47 and six times in the Pastorals; cf. *1 Clem.* 59.3).

As a background to the usages in 2 Peter and Jude, we should remark that the phraseology "God our Savior" is common in the Pastorals (1 Tim 1:1; 2:3; 4:10; Tit 1:3; 2:10; 3:4), where Jesus is also affirmed as *sōtēr* (2 Tim 1:10; Tit 1:4; 2:13; 3:6) and apparently placed on par with God as divine Savior in Titus 2:13 (see Harris; Schneider and Brown, 220). Thus Jude 25 should not be viewed as contradictory to the emerging NT theological presentation of *sōtēr* but as in line with a complementary aspect of the overall understanding. Both applications of *sōtēr* to God and Jesus reach back to Jewish usage (in LXX "our savior" occurs in Ps 64:6; 78:9; 94:1; *Pss. Sol.* 8:33; 17:3).

4. 1 John.

The only use of *sōtēr* in 1 John (*see* John, Letters of) is in 1 John 4:14, where the "Savior of the world" (NIV) is also said to be the Son* of (God) the Father. The wording "Savior of the world" is virtually identical to that of John 4:42, where that description of Jesus ("this man") is on the lips of Samaritans (Smalley, 252).

Therefore 1 John's lone usage emphasizes the universal* offer of salvation made available by Jesus as *sōtēr*, as the centerpiece (1 Jn 4:10, 14) of God's initiating love* toward humanity (1 Jn 4:7-19). It is in properly responding to Jesus as Son of God (1 Jn 4:15) and Savior (1 Jn 4:14) that the believer (1 Jn 5:1) enters new spiritual life* (1 Jn 4:9) and receives God's love with which to love others (1 Jn 4:11-12, 19). The setting is evidently John's insistence that the Father and the Son are one in purpose and salvific design (Jn 10:30), which extends to embrace "all peoples" in its scope (Jn 11:52; 1 Jn 2:2; Smalley, 253). We should also include John's emphasis on Jesus' humanity as savior "come in the flesh."

The issue is often raised why the occurrence of "savior" is so limited in the NT and it is found mainly in the later (chronologically speaking) books. The Pauline references (Phil 3:20; Eph 5:23) are descriptive of Christ's work and should be regarded as adjectives, not as nouns. Only in the later letters* do we encounter the titular usage of *sōtēr*.

The most probable explanation lies in the way the title could easily have been misunderstood in public proclamation (akin to Son of God*), where it might well have evoked ideas of Hellenistic cult figures and Roman emperors who were hailed as "divine son" and "savior." Similarly when the church was reaching out to the Hellenistic world, the title came to signify that Christ was equally the answer to pagan longings for deliverance and hope. So *sōtēr* became part of the "religious vocabulary of [the] Hellenistic environment," where it was appropriate to "communicate the gospel meaningfully to Gentile converts" (Bauckham, 169) as an in-house christological* appellation rather than as a part of kerygmatic terminology. Additionally, at an earlier time there was the danger of tautology when the simple name *Jesus* (used frequently in Paul, e.g., 2 Cor 4) conveyed the thought of God the Savior (= Jeshua/Joshua).

5. Apostolic Fathers.

Whatever inhibitions restricted the usage in the NT writings, the term became much more frequent in early second-century Christian works (*2 Clem.* 20.5; Ign. *Eph.* 1.1; Ign. *Magn.* inscrip.; Ign. *Phld.* 9.2; Ign. *Smyrn.* 7.1; Pol. *Phil.* 19.2; *Diogn.* 9.6, *Gos. Pet.* 4:13; Quadratus in Eusebius *Hist. Eccl.* 4.3.2).

See also CHRISTOLOGY; SALVATION.

BIBLIOGRAPHY. R. J. Bauckham, *Jude, 2 Peter* (WBC; Waco, TX: Word, 1983); W. Bousset, *Kyrios Christos* (Nashville: Abingdon, 1970); O. Cullmann, *The Christology of the New Testament* (rev. ed.; Philadelphia: Westminster, 1963); W. Foerster and G. Fohrer, "σῴζω κτλ," *TDNT* 7:965-1024; R. H. Fuller, *The Titles of Jesus in Early Christology* (London: Lutterworth, 1969); E. M. B. Green, *The Meaning of Salvation* (London: Hodder & Stoughton, 1965); M. J. Harris, *Jesus as God: The Use of Theos in Reference to Jesus* (Grand Rapids: Baker, 1992); J. Schneider and C. Brown, "Redemption etc.," *NIDNTT* 3:216-23; S. S. Smalley, *1, 2, 3 John* (WBC; Waco, TX: Word, 1984); V. Taylor, *The Names of Jesus* (London: Macmillan, 1953); P. Wendland, "Hellenistic Ideas of Salvation in the Light of Anthropology," *AJT* 17 (1913) 345-51; idem, "Σωτήρ," *ZNW* 5 (1904) 335-53.

A. B. Luter Jr.

SCROLLS, SEALS

Revelation mentions the concept of a sealed book in connection with the following: the Apocalypse itself, the seven-sealed book shown to the Seer, the unsealed "little book" and the sealing of the words of the seven thunders. The concept of a sealed book is not found in the apostolic fathers.*

1. Revelation
2. The Words of the Seven Thunders
3. The Seven-Sealed Book
4. The Little Book

1. Revelation.

Revelation (*see* Revelation, Book of) uses the concept of a book that must remain sealed until the appointed time, as is found in apocalyptic* writings such as Daniel 12:1-4. In Revelation, however, the scroll in which the Seer is instructed to write what is shown to him (Rev 1:11) must not be sealed (Rev 22:10): because the prophecy* is about to be fulfilled, it must be published openly.

2. The Words of the Seven Thunders.

The exception to the Seer's commission to record what he sees is that he must "seal" (i.e., not write down) the utterances of the "seven thunders" (Rev 10:4).

3. The Seven-Sealed Book.

Revelation 5:2 depicts a seven-sealed scroll written on both sides, but no one is found qualified to open the seals* and reveal the scroll's contents, until "the Lion of the tribe of Judah," Christ,* is found worthy. The image is of a typical first-century document written on a scroll made of sheets of papyrus or (less often) parchment or leather sewn together. Letters,* legal documents and the Scriptures themselves were written on such scrolls. Wax seals were often affixed to a document to conceal its contents or (with the impression of the writer's or signatory's mark in the wax) to confirm its authenticity.

That a new vision* is seen as each seal is broken suggests that seals had been affixed to the scroll at seven different places as it was rolled up. Yet none of the contents of a real scroll with multiple seals would be visible until the last seal had been broken—and at that point the whole of its contents would be revealed. Perhaps we should not try to visualize the physical "reality" that the Seer saw but rather look beyond the image to its significance.

But what kind of document was this scroll? It could be "the Lamb's book of life" (Rev 13:8; 20:15; 21:27), but the seals suggest that it is a legal document, perhaps a testament, a document of divorce or a book of destiny and/or world history; yet they also recall Isaiah's lament that his vision concerning Jerusalem* and its fate has become like a sealed book to the people (Is 29:11-12). That it is written on both sides is reminiscent of the tablets of the Torah (cf. Ex 32:15) but also of the scroll whose contents Ezekiel was to proclaim to the rebellious Israelites (Ezek 9:3-6).

The first four visions (each depicting a rider on a horse of a different color—the four horsemen of the Apocalypse) are distinguished from the latter three. B. J. Malina argues that what the Seer actually saw and formed the basis of his visions (seen through the lens of the OT and other Jewish traditions) were comets, which the Greeks often envisaged as horses, with the constellations Leo, Virgo, Libra and Scorpio as the riders (Malina, 126).

Although the first four seal visions could have historical referents—such as the unrest in various parts of the Roman Empire,* the Jewish war and the severe famines of the first century— it is important to consider these visions as a whole against their OT background. There are clear parallels with Ezekiel 5—7, which warns the disobedient and idolatrous Israelites of judgments* similar to those depicted here. Ezekiel 4:16 warns that famine will overtake the inhabitants of Jerusalem (cf. Rev 6:5-6), while Ezekiel 14:21 threatens Jerusalem with the same punishments* as those in Revelation 6:8. Jeremiah too threatens the people and Jerusalem with punishments like those depicted in the seal visions (Jer 6:22-26; 14:11-12; 15:1-2; 16:4-5; 18:11-21; Jer 21:8-10; 38:2; 44:11-14). The same punishments are among the judgments to come upon Yahweh's covenant* people if they forsake him (Deut 32:23-35). Like these OT passages, the judgments in the Apocalypse are examples of "covenant judgment" on Israel in accordance with Leviticus 26 and Deuteronomy 28 (van der Waal 1971, 143).

The fifth seal vision parallels Jesus' words in Matthew 23:35, threatening Jerusalem with punishment because of its ill-treatment of the prophets.

The sixth seal vision could refer to the various earthquakes and solar eclipses that occurred during the first century. Yet language like this is found in such passages as Isaiah 2:10, 19, 21; Jeremiah 4:29; Hosea 10:8 (cf. Lk 23:30; cf. van der Waal 1971, 191; Vos, 113-16).

An interlude (Rev 7:1-17) between the opening of the sixth and seventh seals reflects Ezekiel's image of a man sent through Jerusalem marking the foreheads of those who grieve over the city's evils and who will escape the slaughter that will commence at the sanctuary itself and encompass the whole city (Ezek 9:4; cf. Sweet, 150).

The content of the seventh seal could be merely the brief "silence in heaven" (Rev 8:1); the silence, the introduction of the seven angels* with trumpets,* and the vision of the angel with the prayers* of the saints (Rev 8:1-5); the whole series of trumpet visions (Rev 8:1— 11:19); or even the whole of the rest of the book (Michaels, 56-57).

The striking resemblance between the whole series of seal visions and the Synoptic Apocalypse (Charles, 1:158), together with the use of so many OT texts referring to Jerusalem, suggests that the Seer has in mind either a calamity to come on Jerusalem or a worldwide judgment in which Jerusalem is especially afflicted.

4. The Little Book.
The Seer also sees an opened "little scroll" in the hand of a "strong angel" (Rev 10:2). This could be a separate scroll from the seven-sealed scroll seen earlier. It could also be the same scroll described differently; although strictly speaking *biblaridion* is a diminutive of *biblion*, the two words (together with *biblidion*) may be used interchangeably, as in *Hermas Vision* 2.1.3-4; 2.4.1-3. Moreover, Revelation 10:8 uses *biblion* of the scroll that is designated as *biblaridion* in Revelation 10:2; 10:9-10. Perhaps the diminutive is used to contrast the scroll with the "mighty angel" rather than with the scroll mentioned earlier (cf. Michaels, 60).

See also APOCALYPTIC, APOCALYPTICISM; REVELATION.

BIBLIOGRAPHY. R. J. Bauckham, *The Climax of Prophecy: Studies on the Book of Revelation* (Edinburgh: T & T Clark, 1993); A. J. Beagley, *The 'Sitz im Leben' of the Apocalypse with Particular Reference to the Role of the Enemies of the Church* (BZNW 50; Berlin: Walter de Gruyter, 1987); G. R. Beasley-Murray, *The Book of Revelation* (NCB; London: Oliphants, 1978); I. T. Beckwith, *The Apocalypse of John: Studies in Introduction with a Critical and Exegetical Commentary* (Grand Rapids: Baker, 1979 [1919]); G. B. Caird, *The Revelation of St. John the Divine* (HNTC; New York and Evanston: Harper & Row, 1966); P. Carrington, *The Meaning of the Revelation* (London: SPCK, 1931); R. H.

Charles, *A Critical and Exegetical Commentary on the Revelation of St. John* (2 vols.; ICC; Edinburgh: T & T Clark, 1920) vol. 1 ; J. M. Court, *Myth and History in the Book of Revelation* (London: SPCK, 1979); J. C. De Young, *Jerusalem in the New Testament: The Significance of the City in the History of Redemption and in Eschatology* (Kampen: Kok, 1960); G. Fitzer, "σφραγίς κτλ," *TDNT* 7:939-53; B. J. Malina, *On the Genre and Message of Revelation: Star Visions and Sky Journeys* (Peabody, MA: Hendrickson, 1995); J. R. Michaels, *Interpreting the Book of Revelation* (GNTE; Grand Rapids: Baker, 1992); R. H. Mounce, *The Book of Revelation* (NICNT; Grand Rapids: Eerdmans, 1977); G. Schrenk, "βίβλος, βιβλίον," *TDNT* 1:615-20; J. Sweet, *Revelation* (WPC; Philadelphia: Westminster, 1979); H. B. Swete, *The Apocalypse of St. John: The Greek Text with Introduction, Notes and Indices* (Grand Rapids: Eerdmans, 1968 repr.); C. van der Waal, *Openbaring van Jezus Christus 2: Inleiding en Vertaling* (Groningen: De Vuurbaak, 1971); idem, *Openbaring van Jezus Christus 2: Verklaring* (Oudkarspel: De Neverheid, 1981); L. A. Vos, *The Synoptic Traditions in the Apocalypse* (Kampen: Kok, 1965).

A. J. Beagley

SEA. *See* BEASTS, DRAGON, SEA, CONFLICT MOTIF.

SEALS. *See* SCROLLS, SEALS.

SECOND APOCALYPSE OF JAMES. *See* APOCRYPHAL AND PSEUDEPIGRAPHAL WRITINGS.

SECOND REPENTANCE. *See* REPENTANCE, SECOND REPENTANCE.

SECRET GOSPEL OF MARK. *See* MARK, SECRET GOSPEL OF.

SERMONIC GENRE. *See* HEBREWS.

SERVANT, SERVICE

Believers and their leaders are referred to as servants or slaves* of God* in the literature covered by this dictionary. In various places the work of the Twelve,* Paul and his colleagues, other apostles,* prophets,* bishops, presbyters, teachers, deacons and the compassionate acts of believers are referred to as service.

1. Acts
2. Hebrews, General Epistles and Revelation
3. Other Early Christian Writings

1. Acts.

Believers and their apostles are both referred to as servants (*douloi*, lit. "slaves"*) of God (Acts 2:18; 4:29; 16:17). In the Septuagint *doulos* is used not only for slaves of human masters but also for kings and prophets as servants of God. In Acts, the term probably reflects not only the servant/master relationship in which all believers stand with God but also their privileged position as God's servants.

The ministry* of the Twelve is described as service (*diakonia*). It was a *diakonia* of witness to the resurrection* of Jesus (Acts 5:42), which Judas was to have shared with them (Acts 1:15-17). But seeing that he forfeited his share in this ministry by betraying Jesus and subsequently committing suicide, another had to be chosen to take his place (Acts 1:21-26). The ministry of the Twelve is further described as a *diakonia* of the word and prayer* (Acts 6:2). The ministry of the word appears to have included the teaching* of believers (Acts 2:42) as well as public witness* to the resurrection. Paul's apostolic ministry of testifying to the gospel* of God's grace* among the Gentiles* is also depicted as *diakonia* (Acts 20:24).

The daily distribution of aid to needy people in the congregation, for which the Twelve would not take responsibility because it interfered with their ministry of the word and prayer, is also described as *diakonia* (Acts 6:1-2). Along similar lines the collection of material aid in the church* at Antioch* and its conveyance to the needy believers in Jerusalem* by Barnabas and Paul are both described as *diakonia* (Acts 11:29; 12:25), as is the assistance rendered to Paul by Timothy and Erastus (*tōn diakonountōn autō*, Acts 19:22).

2. Hebrews, General Epistles and Revelation.

In a number of these documents, particularly in Revelation (*see* Revelation, Book of), believers and their leaders are referred to or refer to themselves as servants or slaves (*douloi*) of God (Jas 1:1; 1 Pet 2:16; 2 Pet 1:1; Jude 1; Rev 1:1; 2:20; 7:3; 11:18; 19:2, 5; 22:3, 6). As in the case of Acts, the term *doulos* probably reflects not only the relationship in which believers stand with God but also their privileged position as God's servants.

The word *diakoneō* ("to serve"), used in relation to Christian ministry, is found in Hebrews 6:10, where the author assures his readers that

God will not forget the love* they have shown in serving his people. The best explanation of what such service involved is found in Hebrews 10:33-34, where the fact that readers stood with those in prison and joyfully accepted the confiscation of their property is reported. In 1 Peter 4:10-11 believers are urged to serve or minister to (diakoneō) one another as each has received a gift (charisma) to do so. These ministries are categorized as either speaking or serving (diakoneō). In Revelation 2:19 Christ assures the church of Thyatira that he knows about its works, love, faith,* service (diakonia) and forbearance. What the service involved is not made known.

3. Other Early Christian Writings.

The predominant designation for believers in the Shepherd of Hermas* is "servants of God" (douloi tou theou), an expression used more than forty times. Living as a believer is described as serving God (douleuein theō). Similar expressions are found scattered through the other literature under investigation (e.g., Ign. Rom. 4.3; 1 Clem. 60.2; 2 Clem. 6.1; Mart. Pol. 9.3; 20.1).

Beside the references to the service rendered by deacons in these documents (see Ministry) there are a number of references to the service rendered by other members of the Christian community and other Christian leaders. The Didache* says that care should be taken in the appointment of bishops and deacons because they minister (leitourgousi) the ministry or service (leitourgian) of prophets and teachers to the Christian community (Did. 15.1).

Clement* argues that the Master has fixed by his supreme will the places and persons who are to offer the oblations and that believers should not transgress the appointed rules of ministration or service (leitourgias) given by him (1 Clem. 40.1-4; 41.1). Clement asserts that the apostles, foreseeing the problems that would arise in the church, not only appointed their successors but also made provision for other approved men to succeed to the ministry or service (leitourgian) of these appointees (1 Clem. 44.2). Clement reprimanded the Corinthians who removed from their episcopate and ministry or service (leitourgias) those presbyters who ministered or served (leitourgēsantas) without blame (1 Clem. 44.3-6).

In the letters of Ignatius* also the service (diakonia) of Christian leaders receives some attention. Bishops are said to be entrusted with

a diakonia for the common good (Ign. Phld. 1.1). Deacons are entrusted with the diakonia of Christ (Ign. Magn. 6.1), and they are servants (diakonoi) not of food and drink only but are servants (hyperētai) of the church of God (Ign. Trall. 2.3). Deacons may also perform the diakonia of ambassadors from one church to another (Ign. Phld. 10.1-2).

The Shepherd of Hermas speaks of apostles, bishops, teachers and deacons serving (diakonēsantas) the elect (Herm. Vis. 3.5.1), but its main emphasis is upon the ministry of giving: the proper use of wealth (see Riches). In the second mandate Hermas is exhorted to give to all in need, because God wishes gifts to be made of his bounty. Such ministry or service (diakonia) is honorable before God (Herm. Man. 2.5-6). In the first similitude the purpose for attaining riches is that one might purchase afflicted souls and look after widows and orphans. It is in order that they may fulfill these ministries (diakonias) that the Master makes people rich (Herm. Sim. 1.8-9). In the second similitude the rich are said to need the poor as a vine needs an elm tree over which to grow so that it might produce abundant fruit (if it lies on the ground it produces little fruit and rotten). The wealthy who understand these things will be able to perform some good service (dynēsetai diakonēsai ti agathon); the good service being understood as providing for the poor (Herm. Sim. 2.1-10).

Corrupt deacons who serve amiss are given warnings (Herm. Sim. 9.26.2). These are guilty devouring the living of widows and orphans, making personal gain from the ministry (diakonias) they had received to administer (diakonēsai). Standing in contrast to these are the bishops who by their service (diakonia) ceaselessly shelter the destitute and receive the servants of God into their houses gladly (Herm. Sim. 9.27.2; see Hospitality).

See also CHURCH ORDER, GOVERNMENT; MINISTRY; SLAVE, SLAVERY.

BIBLIOGRAPHY. D. L. Bartlett, Ministry in the New Testament (Minneapolis: Fortress, 1993); H. W. Beyer, "διακονέω κτλ," TDNT 2:81-93; H. von Campenhausen, Ecclesiastical Authority and Spiritual Power in the Church of the First Three Centuries (London: A. & C. Black, 1969); J. N. Collins, Diakonia: Reinterpreting the Ancient Sources (New York and Oxford: Oxford University Press, 1990); K. H. Giles, Patterns of Ministry among the First Christians (Melbourne: Collins-

Dove, 1989); K. Hess, "Serve, Deacon, Worship," *NIDNTT* 3:544-53; A. Lemaire, "From Services to Ministries: *Diakonia* in the First Two Centuries," *Concilium* 10 (1972) 35-49; idem, "The Ministries in the New Testament: Recent Research," *BTB* 3 (1973) 133-66; idem, *Ministry in the Church* (London: SPCK, 1977); J. B. Lightfoot, "The Christian Ministry" in *Saint Paul's Epistle to the Philippians* (London: MacMillan, 1898) 181-269; H. O. Maier, *The Social Setting of the Ministry as Reflected in the Writings of Hermas, Clement and Ignatius* (Waterloo, ON: Wilfrid Laurier University Press, 1991). C. G. Kruse

SERVICE. *See* SERVANT, SERVICE.

SEVEN, THE. *See* MINISTRY.

SEXUAL ETHICS. *See* MARRIAGE, DIVORCE AND ADULTERY; SEXUALITY, SEXUAL ETHICS.

SEXUALITY, SEXUAL ETHICS
The guidance of the later NT and the early church fathers on sexual conduct was given against a backcloth of widespread sexual license in the Mediterranean world. They showed little or no interest in accommodation to prevalent mores. In general, they advocated rigorous marital and sexual discipline and evinced growing esteem for ascetic abstinence from sex.

    1. The Later New Testament Writings
    2. The Early Patristic Writings

1. The Later New Testament Writings.
The books of the NT other than the Gospels and the Pauline Epistles (*see DPL*, Sexuality, Sexual Ethics) confirm rather than add to the teachings on sexual issues given by the earlier books. Thus Hebrews* reminds its readers of the honorable estate of marriage* and the need to guard it against adultery and sexual irregularity in general (Heb 13:4; cf. Heb 12:16, which may echo post-OT tradition on Esau's sexual sins; Bruce, 366-67; *see* Purity). The seventh commandment against adultery is reiterated in James 2:11 (cf. metaphorical application in Jas 4:4; *see* James), and 1 Peter* beautifully commends holy and considerate marital relations (1 Pet 3:1-7). Revelation (*see* Revelation, Book of) employs the imagery used from the prophets to Paul of the church* as the bride, the wife of Christ* the Lamb* (Rev 19:7, 21:2, 9; cf. possibly 2 Jn 1, 5).

No particular context need be supposed for repeated warnings against licentiousness in sexual and other behaviors (cf. 1 Pet 4:3). The inclusion of abstinence from *porneia* among the three provisions of the so-called apostolic decree, which clarified the *modus vivendi* for Gentile* and Jewish Christians* to share congregational life together (Acts 15:20), illustrates the contrast felt to obtain between pagan Gentile and Jewish codes of sexual mores. Here the infant church's leaders agreed to build upon minimal Jewish standards of sexual ethics (i.e., the commands Jews believed were given to Noah), a fact significant in itself for present-day debates, in which it is often assumed that Christian sexual ethics should function on guidelines independent of the OT. From Jesus onward (cf. Mt 5:27-8, Mk 10:1-12) the ethical teachings of the new order witnessed the adaptation and adoption of OT standards.

The Revelation of John makes frequent use of the language of prostitution and fornication, sometimes literally (Rev 9:21) but more often figuratively of idolatry* and the excesses of debauched luxury (Rev 14:8, 17:1-5, 18:3, 19:2); clearly the sexual, religious and other moral dimensions are not neatly separable. In these later chapters pagan, Christian-persecuting (*see* Persecution) Rome* seems to embody these forces of evil, but the letters to the Asian churches in Revelation 2—3 reveal subtler internal threats. Local allusions probably explain the imagery of Revelation 3:4, 18, but the churches at Ephesus, Pergamum and Thyatira had been disturbed by the teachings of the Nicolaitans (Rev 2:6, 15, presumably named after some Nicolas), whose ranks included a prophetess (Rev 2:20; she may well have named herself Jezebel). They appealed to Jewish traditions about Balaam (Rev 2:14; cf. 2 Pet 2:15; Jude 11; Num 22-4) and propagated a religious and sexual libertinism (Rev 2:14, 20) with Jewish roots (especially if Rev 2:9 [Smyrna] and Rev 3:9 [Philadelphia] allude to the same movement). The Fathers from Irenaeus on incorporate the Nicolaitans into their inventories of gnosticizing heretics but apparently with no independent knowledge about them.

Finally, among the later NT writings, the interpretation of Jude 7 (cf. 2 Pet 2:6) is much contested: "Similarly Sodom and Gomorrah . . . , having indulged in sexual immorality in the same manner as these [i.e., the angels of Jude 6] and having pursued after different flesh, are set forth." The reference is clearly to Genesis 19:1-29, where the Sodomites sought sex with two male angelic visitors (*see* Angels). The issue focuses largely on the preciseness of the analogy with Jude 6, whose "angels" (i.e., "the sons of God" of Genesis 6:1-4) married human wives (Bauckham, 50-53). Does *heteras* ("different, strange") mean that the "flesh" the Sodomites sought was angelic (i.e., nonhuman rather than homosexual)? The tradition of Hellenistic Judaism,* insofar as it identified Sodom's sin as sexual, saw it as homosexual (more so than Bauckham, 54 allows) rather than as transspecies. *Testament of Naphtali* 3:4-5 correlates the sins of Genesis 19 and 6 as departures from the order of nature. But modern preoccupations may be dictating an unreal choice. Just as abuse of hospitality* in antiquity often involved sexual aggression rather than mere breach of etiquette, so the angelic dimension may be a submotif in the Sodomites' same-sex lust, given the charge of "defilement of the flesh" in Jude 8 (cf. Jude 23).

2. The Early Patristic Writings.

Against some of the Gnostics,* Irenaeus and others leveled charges of sexual license (Irenaeus *Haer.* 1.13.5-7, concerning the Marcosians), but restraint on sexuality was overwhelmingly the order of the day. "There is little in the writings of the church fathers that could bolster a modern argument for 'sexual liberation'" (Clark, 1054).

Almost without exception early church writers regarded divorce and remarriage as inconceivable, even when they allowed or even required separation in cases of adultery or sometimes unbelief. There are few issues on which the patristic testimony is so unanimous (see Crouzel).

On the issue of remarriage for widowed persons the trend is clear, but no obvious consensus prevails. The debate can be read in Tertullian. *To His Wife* 1 urges her not to remarry if he dies; book 2 relents, no doubt out of greater anxiety that she remarry to a pagan, and insists that she marry only a Christian; *Monogamy,* written in his later Montanist phase, excludes remarriage as little better than licensed fornication.

As the second century advanced, voices are heard suggesting that for Christian married couples intercourse has only procreation in view (Justin *Apol. I* 29; Athenagoras *Suppl.* 33). This position is unambiguous in Clement of Alexandria (long before Augustine, who is often blamed for it).

At the same time abortion and infanticide, including exposure of unwanted children, were condemned from the *Didache* 2.2 onward (*see Didache*). Both practices were often ranked along with killing, whether in homicide, warfare or capital punishment. The need to disown the abandonment of children (Justin *Apol. I* 27) starkly sketches the harsh backdrop to early Christian sexual and marital ethics.

The Fathers trod a middle path between unqualified denigration of sexual relations and denial of the superiority of total abstinence from them. The former was espoused by nearly all varieties of Gnosticism* and by Marcion,* as well as by extreme, rather than heretical, movements such as Montanism. Gnosticism proper was fired by a thoroughgoing flesh-spirit dualism that in effect regarded the material as evil. In Montanism renewed eschatological* urgency led to a ban on marriage, whereas in other fringe groups, such as those to which the apocryphal* acts of the apostles appealed, abandonment of sexual activity enjoyed a high profile as the ethic of the élite—and afforded Christian women a paradoxical liberation from being sex partner, wife and mother.

Yet while the Fathers vindicated the intrinsic goodness of the created order (*see* Creation) and of marriage and childbearing within it, there was no gainsaying the enormous attraction of the ascetic option within mainstream catholic Christianity. In the Syriac-speaking church even baptism* may have been open only to celibate people for a period in the early centuries. Tatian, the author of the Diatessaron, a harmony of the Gospels, came from eastern Syria and is portrayed as founder of the Encratites, who condemned matrimony and all sexual activity. But encratism (Gk *enkrateia,* "self-control") was more widely diffused than a single sect; it has been detected, for example, in the *Gospel of Thomas* from Nag Hammadi. And its influence is discernible in catholic writers such as Clement of Alexandria.

Individuals or groups (e.g., virgins and widows) committed to permanent continence are attested within congregations from the apostolic fathers* onward (*1 Clem.* 38.2; Ign. *Pol.*

5.2). Both widows and virgins appear in the Hippolytan *Apostolic Tradition* (c. 215) under the bishop's supervision. The "spiritual marriage" of ascetics of both sexes living together, perhaps already glimpsed in Hermas's symbolism (*see* Hermas, Shepherd of), is condemned for its abuses from the early third century.

The prevalence of asceticism cannot be traced to a single source or motivation. Selective use of the canonical Gospels and Paul, the Stoic ideal of *apatheia* ("passionlessness"), Platonic dualism, the influence of Essene and other Jewish communal practices and the widespread ascetic impulse in serious circles in the Greco-Roman world all contributed. From no later than the mid-second century, the *Protevangelium of James* propagated reverence for Mary's* perpetual virginity.

The import of the limited NT references to homosexuality (*see DPL*, Homosexuality) is left in no doubt from a patristic perspective. Although it was never made the subject of any extended treatment, male homosexual behavior is one of a trio of sexual sins (the others being adultery and fornication) found together from the *Didache* 2.2 onward. It is regularly regarded as contrary to the natural order and discerned in the offense of the Sodomites. Female homosexuality is similarly rejected, though rarely mentioned, as in antiquity in general. There is no evidence that the teaching mind of the early church viewed same-sex eroticism with other than disapprobation, but it was not singled out for special condemnation.

A society obsessed with freedom of sexual expression is badly disadvantaged in interpreting early Christian sexual ethics sympathetically. But Christian people called to holiness* in body and spirit in such a setting may well find them peculiarly challenging. Certainly they cannot be understood except against the backdrop of patterns of exploitation and license that sound familiar today. And they even remind us of easily forgotten notes of sexual self-denial in the NT itself.

See also ETHICS; MARRIAGE, DIVORCE, ADULTERY; WOMAN AND MAN.

BIBLIOGRAPHY. R. Bauckham, *Jude, 2 Peter* (WBC; Waco, TX: 1983); P. Brown, *The Body and Society: Men, Women and Sexual Renunciation in Early Christianity* (New York: Columbia University Press, 1988); F. F. Bruce, *The Epistle to the Hebrews* (NICNT; Grand Rapids: Eerdmans,

1964); V. Burrus, *Chastity as Autonomy: Women in the Stories of the Apocryphal Acts* (Lewiston, NY: Edwin Mellen, 1987); H. von Campenhausen, *Tradition and Life in the Church* (Philadelphia: Fortress, 1968); H. Chadwick, "Enkrateia," *RAC* 5 (1962) 343-65; E. A. Clark, "Sexuality," *Encyclopedia of Early Christianity*, ed. E. Ferguson (2 vols; 2d ed.; New York: Garland, 1997) 2:1053-54; H. Crouzel, *L'Eglise primitive face au divorce* (Paris: Beauchesne, 1971); M. Goguel, "Les Nicolaïtes," *RHR* 115 (1937) 5-36; R. B. Hays, *The Moral Vision of the New Testament* (San Francisco: HarperCollins, 1996); D. G. Hunter, ed., *Marriage in the Early Church* (SECT; Philadelphia: Fortress, 1992); T. E. Schmidt, *Straight and Narrow?: Compassion and Clarity in the Homosexuality Debate* (Downers Grove, IL: InterVarsity Press, 1995); D. F. Wright, "Early Christian Attitudes to Homosexuality," *SP* 18:2 (1989) 329-34; idem, "Homosexuality," *Encyclopedia of Early Christianity*, ed. E. Ferguson (2 vols.; 2d ed; New York: Garland, 1997) 1:542-43; idem, "Homosexuals or Prostitutes? The Meaning of *arsenokoitai* (1 Cor. 6:9, 1 Tim. 1:10)," *VC* 38 (1984) 125-53.

D. F. Wright

SHALOM. *See* PEACE.

SHEEP. *See* SHEPHERD, FLOCK.

SHEKINAH. *See* GLORY.

SHEPHERD, FLOCK

Shepherd and sheep imagery appear frequently in early Christian literature, reflecting the broader familiarity with the task of shepherding in ancient Mediterranean culture.

1. Background for the Image
2. Jesus as Shepherd in Early Christian Literature
3. Shepherds as Church Leaders
4. The Shepherd in the *Shepherd of Hermas*

1. Background for the Image.

1.1. Negative Background for the Shepherd Image. Whereas shepherding was a typical Israelite occupation through much of Israel's history (e.g., Gen 46:33—47:4; Bright, 81), the roles of shepherds had begun to change by the time of Jesus. Many scholars observe that Jewish people commonly despised shepherds (*b. Sanh.* 25; Jeremias 1972, 132-33; idem 1971, 110; idem 1975, 304; Talbert, 33; Bailey, 147; Tooley, 23).

Many Jewish people were employed as shepherds (e.g., *CPJ,* 1:15), and E. P. Sanders cautiously warns against reading the pharisaic prejudice against shepherds as indicative of all Judaism* (Sanders, 461-64). Nevertheless the pharisaic view probably reflects a wider view throughout the Roman Empire* that shepherds were of lower status than other peasants (MacMullen, 1-2, 15). Although members of particular trades presumably had more respect for their own professions than did the small number of aristocrats (cf. MacMullen, 120), aristocratic ideology toward pastoralists would have especially influenced the thinking of urban dwellers, who made up the majority of the readers of the documents under consideration.

1.2. Positive Background for the Shepherd Image. Yet Jewish people did not uniformly despise shepherds (Josephus *Ant.* 1.53), and they never imposed the prejudices of their own time onto the popular shepherds of the biblical record. The Hebrew Bible supplies various images of shepherds upon which early Christian writers could draw. Whereas the flock almost invariably represented God's people (e.g., Ps 74:1; 77:20; 78:52; 79:13; 80:1; 100:3; Is 49:9; 63:11; Jer 13:17; 31:10; Zech 9:16; 10:3)—Sirach 18:13 and Philo *De Agricultura* 50—53 are exceptions—writers felt free to assign the title *shepherd* slightly more diversely.

Shepherds long provided natural analogies for rulers or leaders (cf. Anacharsis *Ep.* 7; Artem- idorus *Oneir.* 2.12; Homer *Il.* 1.263). David, who first watched over his father's flock (1 Sam 16:15, 34-37; Ps 78:70-71), became a shepherd of Israel in his generation and the future (2 Sam 5:2; 1 Chron 11:2; Ps 78:70-72; Ezek 34:23; 37:24; in later literature cf. *Pss. Sol.* 17:40; *Gen. Rab.* 59:5). The psalmist calls Moses,* who had forty years' experience as a shepherd (Ex 3:1), a shepherd of Israel (Ps 77:20; Is 63:11; in later literature cf. *1 Enoch* 89:35; Pseudo-Philo 19.3; *Sipre* Deut. 305.3.1; *y. Sanh.* 10:1, §9; *Soṭa* 5:4, §1; *Pesiq. Rab Kah.* 2:8; *Ex. Rab.* 2:2; Marmorstein, 100-101).

This image naturally applied to the Davidic Messiah as well (Mic 5:2-4; cf. Jer 23:1-6; Longenecker, 48-49) and sometimes Jewish teachers (Derrett, 26-28). The leaders God assigned to care for his flock for him (prophets, priests, rulers and officials) were also "shepherds" (Num 27:17; 1 Kings 22:17; Jer 3:15; *Mek. Pisha* 1.162-63; CD 19.8-9); the righteous proph-

ets,* usually addressing wicked generations, especially apply the term ironically to Israel's leaders performing their work unjustly (Is 56:11; Jer 22:22; 23:1-4; 25:34-36; Zech 10:3; 11:5, 15-17; 13:4-7). When God portrays Israel as a scattered or lost flock, his shepherds are often to blame (Jer 10:21; 50:6-7; Ezek 34:1-10).

The primary biblical portrait of Israel's shepherd, however, applied to God himself, especially in the Bible (Ps 23:1-4; 28:9; 74:1-2; 77:20; 78:52; 79:13; 80:1; 100:3; Is 40:11; Jer 13:17; 31:10; Ezek 34:11-17; Mic 7:14; Zech 9:16; 10:3) but also in some later literature (Sir 18:13; *1 Enoch* 89:18; Philo *Agric.* 50—53; Pseudo-Philo 28.5; 30.5; *b. Ḥag.* 3; Pes. 118; *Ex. Rab.* 34:3; *Lam. Rab.* 1:17, §52; *Pesiq. R.* 3:2). He performed shepherdlike functions for his people, carrying the young (Ps 28:9; Is 40:11; 46:3-4) and leading his flock as in the first exodus (Ps 77:20; 78:52; 80:1; Is 40:11; 63:14; cf. Ex 13:21; 15:13; Deut 8:2; Ps 78:14; 106:9; 136:16; Neh 9:12; Is 48:21; Jer 2:6, 17; Hos 11:3-4; Amos 2:10). The image of God as shepherd was an image of leadership and protection moved by caring for and commitment to his people. Although it never became a predominant image, later Jewish teachers also recognized that God was a shepherd (*b. Ḥag.* 3; Pes. 118; *Ex. Rab.* 34:3; *Lam. Rab.* 1:17, §52; *Pesiq. R.* 3:2; cf. Philo *Agric.* 50) and Israel his flock (e.g., *1 Enoch* 89—90; *Ex. Rab.* 24:3; *Pesiq. R.* 9:2; 26:2).

2. Jesus as Shepherd in Early Christian Literature.

2.1. Jesus as Shepherd in Revelation and the Johannine Literature. Although early Christian literature may contain allusions to the David-shepherd tradition (in more literal translations cf. Jn 10:9 with 2 Sam 5:2; Ezek 46:10; but this was a common Semitism: Num 27:17; 1 Kings 3:7; Rev 3:12; *m. Mid.* 1:3), early Christians probably drew especially on the image of God* as the chief shepherd. Thus in John 9:39—10:18 Jesus defends the blind man (Jn 9) as one of his sheep, that is, part of the true Israel,* while excoriating the Pharisees (Jn 9) as "thieves and robbers" (Jn 10:8-10) comparable to the false shepherds of Jeremiah 23:1-2 and Ezekiel 34:1-10. He himself is no hireling but the ultimate shepherd who has come to save the lost sheep (Jn 10:11-16), fulfilling the role the Hebrew Bible assigns to God (Ezek 34:11-22; cf. Jer 23:6), as befits Johannine christology* (cf. Barrett, 163; Payne). Revelation, whose divine christology closely resembles that of John, undoubtedly intends the image in much the same way (Rev 7:17).

In Revelation (see Revelation, Book of), however, Jesus' roles as shepherd and lamb* appear closely connected (Rev 7:17), emphasizing that Jesus not only is the leader of the flock but also participated in the humanity and death that characterize the flock (for the image of a leading sheep see Beasley-Murray, 149). This accords with the OT image of sheep's vulnerability that early Christians applied to Jesus (Acts 8:32, from Is 53:7, the Suffering Servant) and his followers (Rom 8:36, from Ps 44:22). At the same time the text's verbal allusions to Isaiah 49:10 indicate that Jesus fills the role of God in this passage.

2.2. Hebrews 13:20. The christology of Hebrews* is often as explicit as that of John, and its closing blessing adduces the familiar Johannine image of shepherd of God's sheep. In this instance, however, Jesus and the salvation of the promised new exodus is compared with Moses and the salvation of the first exodus (cf. Heb 3:1-6), for the writer depends directly on the Septuagint of Isaiah 63:11-14. As God brought Israel and its shepherds up from the Red Sea (Is 63:11), he brought up the great shepherd from the dead (Heb 13:20; cf. similarly the midrash on Deut 30 in Rom 10:6-8).

2.3. 1 Peter 2:21-25. Although household codes* traditionally addressed only the *paterfamilias* (male head of the household), Peter addresses particularly the oppressed slaves* and wives in the Christian community. In contrast to Paul, who compared the role of the *paterfamilias* to Christ's authority* (Eph 5:23; 6:5), Peter compares the suffering* and submission of the slave and the wife to that of Christ (1 Pet 2:21-25; 3:1: "in the same way"). He cites Isaiah 53:9 to prove that Christ was punished unjustly, perhaps intending also to recall the context of the servant who is silent like a sheep (Is 53:7). He continues with implicit citations of Isaiah 53: Christ "bore our sins" (1 Pet 2:24 = Is 53:4), and believers' sins are "healed by his wounds" (1 Pet 2:24 = Is 53:5), because they had been "wandering like sheep" (1 Pet 2:25 = Is 53:6). Jesus' death (see Death of Christ), however, restored the wandering sheep to the Shepherd, which could mean the Father (cf. 1 Pet 4:19) but very probably refers to Jesus (1 Pet 5:4). Some scholars

believe that Peter here draws on a paschal homily that incorporated Isaiah 53 (Lindars, 82), but early Christians applied the passage to Jesus consistently with or without paschal associations (e.g., Acts 8:32-33; Pol. *Phil.* 8; probably Mk 10:45).

2.4. Other Christian Texts. The church* continues to be portrayed as Christ's flock in early Christian literature (*1 Clem.* 16.1), with Jesus as the shepherd and helmsman (*Mart. Pol.* 19.2). Jesus' followers are like lambs among wolves, and though the wolves may kill them, they should fear not those who can kill but the one who has authority to cast into hell* (*2 Clem.* 5.2-4; cf. Mt 10:16, 28). Ignatius* also speaks of wolves seeking to overcome the sheep (Ign. *Phil.* 2.1-2).

3. Shepherds as Church Leaders.

If most christological shepherd texts draw on biblical imagery associated with God, most shepherd texts applying to the church draw on biblical images of shepherds as human leaders of God's people.

3.1. 1 Peter 5:2-4. In some cases, such as 1 Peter 5, the two images are intertwined. When Peter first calls Jesus the "shepherd," he also calls him the "overseer" (1 Pet 2:25; cf. Acts 20:28; CD 13.7-9). Judaism frequently applied the title *overseer* to God (e.g., Wis 1:6; *Sib. Or.* 1.152; 2.177; Frag. 1.3. *T. Benj.* 4:3; 6:6; *4 Bar.* 7:35; cf. Wis 7:23; Theon *Progymn.* 11.194). But the Mediterranean world generally used it for broader leadership designations (e.g., 1 Macc 1:51; Plutarch *Numa* 9.5, Vit.; Epictetus *Disc.* 3.22.72; 1QS 6.12; CD 9.18-22; see Dibelius and Conzelmann, 54). Several texts in Ignatius (Ign. *Eph.* 1.3; Ign. *Magn.* 3.1; Ign. *Rom.* 9.1) imply Christ is a heavenly overseer. Both terms recur in Peter's exhortation to church leaders (elders, 1 Pet 5:1) in 1 Peter 5:2-3: they are to shepherd and oversee the flock, awaiting the appearance of the "chief shepherd" (1 Pet 5:4; for the term see Deissmann, 99-100). This text plainly alludes to the prophetic conception that leaders among God's people are undershepherds expected to answer in all respects to God, the ultimate shepherd of his people (Jer 23; Ezek 34; cf. Jn 10:10-16).

3.2. Shepherds as Pastors in General. Although overseers and elders (bishops and presbyters) are distinct as early as the early second century (Ign. *Trall.* 3), the local churches of the first century in Acts* (Acts 20:17, 28), 1 Peter* (1 Pet 5:1-2), the Pastoral Epistles (Tit 1:5-7) and apparently Philippians (Phil 1:1) still used them interchangeably. Because Acts (Acts 20:28) and 1 Peter (1 Pet 5:1-2) also employ "shepherd" ("pastor") interchangeably with "overseer" and "elder," we may assume that early Christians particularly employed "shepherds" for this local church office (Eph 4:11). Early second-century writers portrayed overseers as shepherds (Ign. *Phld.* 2.1) and recognized that if necessary God could function as shepherd in their place (Ign. *Rom.* 9.1; cf. Ezek 34:11). Ignatius believes that the flock should follow their shepherds (Ign. *Phld.* 2.1), although he claims less than apostolic authority for the bishops (Ign. *Rom.* 4.3; cf. *Mart. Pol.* 16.2; *see* Church Order, Government).

4. The Shepherd in the *Shepherd of Hermas*.

Hermas's use of "shepherd" is quite different from the earlier uses. In the *Shepherd of Hermas** the "shepherd" is a sort of guardian angel,* an "angel of repentance" (*Herm. Vis.* 5.3, 7; *Herm. Man.* 12.49.1; *Herm. Sim.* 2.1; 8.1.4; 8.2.5-8; 8.4.1; 8.6.1; 9.2.6; 9.5.7; 9.7.1; 9.10.1; 9.11.1; 9.23.5; 9.33.1; 10.1.1; 10.4.5). This angel seems to derive its character more from the Roman *genius* than from Jewish categories (just as the visionary experiences borrow from Jewish apocalyptic* but reflect Roman images like those of Virgil); the shepherd functions, however, as the angelic guide of apocalyptic literature (e.g., *Herm. Sim.* 8.2.5-3.1). Nevertheless the doctrine of deeds being ruled by either the good or the evil angel, also attested at Qumran,* informs *Hermas's* angelology (*Herm. Man.* 6.2). Hermas entitles even evil angels "shepherds" (*Herm. Sim.* 6.1.5—2.2; 6.3.2).

See also HERMAS, SHEPHERD OF; LAMB; MINISTRY; PASTORAL THEOLOGY.

BIBLIOGRAPHY. K. E. Bailey, *Poet and Peasant: A Literary Cultural Approach to the Parables in Luke* (Grand Rapids: Eerdmans, 1976); C. K. Barrett, "The Old Testament in the Fourth Gospel," *JTS* 48 (1947) 155-69; G. R. Beasley-Murray, *The Book of Revelation* (NCB; Greenwood, SC: Attic; London: Marshall, Morgan & Scott, 1974); J. Bright, *A History of Israel* (3d ed.; Philadelphia: Westminster, 1981); A. Deissmann, *Light from the Ancient East* (Grand Rapids: Baker, 1978 [repr.]); J. D. M. Derrett, "The Good Shepherd: St. John's Use of Jewish Halakah and Haggadah," *ST* 27 (1973) 25-50; M. Dibelius and H. Con-

zelmann, *The Pastoral Epistles: A Commentary on the Pastoral Epistles* (Philadelphia: Fortress, 1972); J. Jeremias, *Jerusalem in the Time of Jesus* (Philadelphia: Fortress, 1975); idem, *New Testament Theology* (New York: Scribner's, 1971); idem, *The Parables of Jesus* (2d rev. ed.; New York: Scribner's, 1972); B. Lindars, *New Testament Apologetic* (London: SCM, 1961); R. N. Longenecker, *The Christology of Early Jewish Christianity* (Grand Rapids: Baker, 1981 [1970]); R. MacMullen, *Roman Social Relations: 50 B.C. to A.D. 284* (New Haven, CT: Yale University Press, 1974); A. Marmorstein, *The Old Rabbinic Doctrine of God: The Names and Attributes of God* (New York: KTAV, 1968 [1927]); P. B. Payne, "Jesus' Implicit Claim to be Deity in His Parables," *TJ* 2 (1981) 3-23; E. P. Sanders, *Judaism: Practice and Belief, 63 B.C.E.—66 C.E.* (Philadelphia: Trinity Press International, 1992); C. H. Talbert, *Reading Luke: A Literary and Theological Commentary on the Third Gospel* (New York: Crossroad, 1982); W. Tooley, "The Shepherd and Sheep Image in the Teaching of Jesus," *NovT* 7 (1964) 15-25.

C. S. Keener

SHEPHERD OF HERMAS. *See* HERMAS, SHEPHERD OF.

SIBYLLINE ORACLES. *See* APOCRYPHAL AND PSEUDEPIGRAHAL WRITINGS.

SIGNS AND WONDERS

The word pair "signs and wonders" ("wonder," *teras,* was archaic by the NT period and is always paired with "sign") and in most cases "sign" (*sēmeion*) by itself refer in our literature to miracles* worked by humans or directly by divine agency. Generally these signs and wonders serve to attest a divine or pseudo-divine messenger, although by the time of the apostolic fathers the reference is either historical or eschatological.*

1. Background
2. Acts
3. Revelation
4. Post-New Testament Writers

1. Background.

In Greek literature the word pair "signs and wonders" occurs as early as the second century B.C. for a miracle produced by a miracle worker or a divinity (Polybius *Hist.* 3.112.18). In the Septuagint and Jewish literature the pair, which appears twenty-seven times, normally refers to the miracles worked by Moses* (Ex 3:20; 4:30; 7:3; Deut 4:34; 6:22; 7:19; Jer 32:20-21; see *DPL,* Signs, Wonders, Miracles). However, it can also refer to the signs that confirm a prophet's* call to others (Is 8:18) or attest to God's* sovereignty, usually including the attesting to the prophet as his spokesperson (Dan 4:3; 6:27).

2. Acts.
Acts* refers to signs thirteen times in Acts 2—15, often in the explicit word pair "signs and wonders." The use by Stephen* in Acts 7:36 for the signs of the exodus parallels the use in the Septuagint. However, when Acts 2:22 points to Jesus as one attested to by God through signs and wonders (which use is also found in Heb 2:4, where God witnesses to Jesus with signs and wonders), we receive an indication of the distinctive use of this term in Acts.

In the prophecy from Joel cited in Acts 2, signs and wonders are associated with the pouring out of God's Spirit (Acts 2:19), which the author stresses is the Spirit of prophecy. With this Spirit poured out on them, each of the most significant figures in Acts is attested to by signs and wonders as Jesus had been. In Acts 2:43 the apostles* in general receive this attestation, and in Acts 4:16, 22 it is Peter and John in particular. Later the collective group prays for evangelistic boldness (also associated with the pouring out of the Holy Spirit*) accompanied by signs and wonders from God (Acts 4:30). Acts 5:12 reports that this is exactly what happened. Furthermore, Stephen (Acts 6:8), Philip* (Acts 8:6, 13) and Paul and Barnabas (Acts 14:3; 15:12) all receive similar attestation as they proclaim the gospel among the Hellenists, Samaritans* and Gentiles* respectively. Thus in Acts (unlike Luke, where "sign" is associated with the deeds of Jesus only by unbelievers and "mighty deed," *dynamis,* is his term for Jesus' miracles) signs and wonders indicate those miraculous acts associated with the outpouring of the Spirit in "the last days" that God does to attest his messengers.

3. Revelation.
Revelation (*see* Revelation, Book of) refers to signs or signs and wonders seven times. Three passages (Rev 12:1, 3; 15:1) speak of signs in heaven* with no agent named, but four times Revelation refers to signs produced by an agent (Rev 13:13-14; 16:14; 19:20). In every case the

signs are the miracles of the "false prophet" of the beast* or the "demonic spirits" released by them. When Revelation speaks of judgment miracles produced through godly individuals, namely, the two prophetic witnesses* (Rev 11), they are not called signs. Instead these two are said to "have authority" to do this or that. While the "beast from the earth" or "false prophet" is also said to have authority* (i.e., that of the "beast from the sea"), thus we cannot conclude that "have authority" is the term for godly miracle workers and "signs and wonders" for ungodly ones, it is clear that Revelation avoids the use of "sign" or "signs and wonders" for godly miracles. (The three times "signs" is used without a named agent, it apparently stands for symbolic figures, and one of them is the devil.)

Could it be that in whatever form of the Johannine tradition with which Revelation had contact "sign" was appropriate only for the miracles of Jesus? That would explain the difference between Revelation and the Fourth Gospel. Or was it that some of the opponents mentioned in Revelation 2—3 (such as the prophetic "Jezebel") described the miracles they worked as signs (cf. 2 Cor 12:12)? Or does Revelation, with its stress on martyrdom,* wish to avoid giving Christians the impression that a miracle might deliver them and instead sees the conquering of evil coming mainly through faithfulness unto death? It is possible that all of these could play some role in Revelation's use of "signs and wonders."

4. Post-New Testament Writers.
If "signs and wonders" referred to the authentication of the godly miracle-working messenger in Acts and to that of the miracle-working evil messenger in Revelation, in the apostolic fathers it refers mostly to past events, especially those of the OT, returning almost full circle to the use of the phrase in the Septuagint.

The signs and wonders of the exodus and the wilderness wanderings are referred to in *1 Clement* 51.5; *Barnabas* 4.14, 5.8 and 12.5 (in the latter the sign is the bronze serpent, which points to Christ*). Three other signs referred to are Lot's wife (*1 Clem.* 11.2), Rahab's scarlet thread in Jericho (*1 Clem.* 12.7) and in pagan mythology the story of the phoenix (*1 Clem.* 25.1). Signs for these writers are generally events in the history of Israel that are then interpreted typologically.

The one exception to this use of "sign" is *Didache* 16.4, 6 where, in a passage drawing heavily on the tradition in Matthew 24, the terms are used eschatologically. There we learn that "in the last days" the "deceiver of the world" who impersonates Christ "shall do signs and wonders." Yet when all seems lost, "then shall appear the signs of truth," namely, "the sign spread out in heaven," the "sound of the trumpet" and "the resurrection of the dead." Here we revisit the use of "signs and wonders" in Revelation but with the optimistic teaching that, as in the exodus, God's signs are the true signs of the future.

See also ACTS OF THE APOSTLES; HEALING, ILLNESS; HOLY SPIRIT; MIRACLES IN ACTS; TONGUES.

BIBLIOGRAPHY. J. D. G. Dunn, *Jesus and the Spirit* (Philadelphia: Westminster, 1975); O. Hofius, "Miracle," *NIDNTT* 2:626-27, 629-35; H. C. Kee, *Medicine, Miracle and Magic in New Testament Times* (SNTSMS 55; Cambridge: Cambridge University Press, 1986); F. Neirynck, "The Miracle Stories in the Acts of the Apostles: An Introduction" in *Les Actes des Apôtres: Traditions, Rédaction, Théologie,* ed. J. Kremer (Gembloux: Duculot, 1979) 169-213; S. M. Praeder, "Miracle Worker and Missionary: Paul in the Acts of the Apostles," *SBLSP* (1983) 107-29; H. Rengstorf, "σημεῖον κτλ," *TDNT* 7:200-261; idem, "τέρας," *TDNT* 8:113-26; R. Stronstad, *The Charismatic Theology of St. Luke* (Peabody, MA: Hendrickson, 1984); M. Whitaker, "'Signs and Wonders': The Pagan Background," *SE* 5 (1968) 155-58; D. Williams, *Signs, Wonders and the Kingdom of God* (Ann Arbor, MI: Servant, 1989). P. H. Davids

SIMILITUDES OF HERMAS. *See* HERMAS, SHEPHERD OF.

SIMON MAGUS. *See* GNOSIS, GNOSTICISM.

SIN, WICKEDNESS

Sin and wickedness are concepts frequently mentioned in this body of NT writings and in the works of the apostolic fathers by means of a number of different Greek words. The major words used for sin and wickedness are *kakos* and *ponēros,* two general words for evil or bad behavior; *adikia,* a general word for evil or sin; *hamartia,* a more specific term for sin often involving the breaking of God's law; *asebeia,* a term for impiety; and *parabasis,* a specific word for sinful disobedience, and their cognates. Although in some contexts it is possible to distinguish clear meanings for these words, there is also a large amount of overlap, so much so that it is better to distinguish various senses of sin and wickedness rather than usage of individual lexical items.

Sin and wickedness are condemned as inappropriate and even law-breaking behavior in relation to one's fellow humans and God. Often sin and wickedness are contrasted with positive qualities, such as goodness and love. This dualism is in keeping with the hortatory moral and paraenetic nature of much of this writing. The results of sin and wickedness are the severing of human and divine relationships and consequent punishment, including final judgment and condemnation.

1. Sin and Human Behavior
2. Sin and Christ
3. Sin and Love of God
4. Sin and Final Judgment

1. Sin and Human Behavior.

One of the fundamental distinctions in this body of writings is the opposition of good and evil, usually in terms of acts or behavior. In the opposition, good is to be preferred and is a reflection of maturity, obedience* and seeking to do good things, while evil is to be shunned and is a reflection of immaturity, disobedience and the doing of wrong (e.g., Heb 5:14; Jas 2:9; 1 Pet 2:14; 3:8-12; cf. Ign. *Phld.* 2.2). In many contexts evil is directly equated with sin and wickedness, since it is behavior that contravenes God's* goodness and righteousness* (Heb 1:9; 3:12; 8:12; Jas 1:13; 4:17; 1 Pet 2:1, 16; 3:12; 3 Jn 11).

In these writings humans are often categorized by their sinful or evil behavior. Instruction is given not to be the kind of person who is found doing wicked or evil things (e.g., Acts 3:26; 8:23; Heb 12:1; Jas 2:4; 4:16; 2 Pet 2:13, 15; 3 Jn 11; Rev 2:2), who has an evil conscience* due to impurity (Heb 10:22; *see* Purity) or even who welcomes one who does evil into his house (2 Jn 11). In James* some sin is depicted not as outright disobedience to God's law* but as the result of desire that has been allowed to give birth to sin and then leads to death (Jas 1:15; 5:20). The classic example of this process may well be the evil that Cain did to his brother Abel (1 Jn 3:12). Because Cain belonged to the evil one (see also 1 Jn 2:13, 14; 5:18, 19), he did the evil deed of killing his brother, whose actions were righteous.

In Hebrews* as well as in James, a clear exposition of sin as disobedience to God's law is given. The book resonates with the language of the OT temple* and the cultus (e.g., purification, Heb 1:3; atonement, Heb 2:17; as well as the law as a shadow of that which was coming, Heb 10:2-4, 8). Analogies are drawn with the priesthood* performing its functions in relation to sin offerings (Heb 5:1, 3; 10:11; 13:11), in which the priest's role is now taken by Christ* (Heb 2:17). The author goes further and not only equates the priestly function with Christ but also depicts Christ himself as the singular sacrifice* itself (Heb 7:27; 9:28; cf. Rev 1:5) that removes any further need for sacrifice to remove sin (Heb 9:26). The result is forgiveness* of sins—their never being remembered (Heb 8:12; 10:18). Hebrews 9:15 well summarizes the discussion of sin in the book when it speaks of Christ as the mediator of a new covenant* with the reward of an eternal inheritance, since Christ died to free humans from their sins committed under the earlier covenant.

The apostolic fathers* have a view of sinful human behavior similar to that of the NT writings cited above. Four major emphases are worth noting. The first is that they draw upon examples from the OT in exhorting their readers to shun evil and do good. For example, the book of Job is frequently drawn upon (e.g., *1 Clem.* 17.3; 39.9; 56.8), and the psalms are invoked for their passionate call to depart from evil (e.g., *1 Clem.* 18.4; 22.3, 4, 6).

Second, the reality of sinful desires is recognized (e.g., *Did.* 2.6, where the Ten Commandments are adapted to a Gentile* audience; *Herm. Man.* 12.1.1, a highly controversial section in the Shepherd because of his apparent view of sin as eradicable; *Herm. Sim.* 9.25.2). Evil is often seen in contrast to that which is good. For example, in *Hermas Mandates* 8.2 there is exhortation to shun that which is evil and do what is good (see also *Herm. Man.* 7.4; 10.2.3, 4).

Third, conscience* is seen to play a role in determining what is evil. For example, *Didache* 4.14 exhorts the reader not to pray having an evil conscience (see also *Herm. Man.* 3.4).

Fourth, and perhaps most clearly, sexual sin looms large. It appears to be the single sin that solicits the greatest concern and merits specific and direct address at numerous places in the apostolic fathers (*Barn.* 4.12, 13), with explicit equation of sexual sin with wicked desire (see *Herm. Man.* 12.2.5; *Herm. Sim.* 5.3.6). The nature of the Shepherd* literature perhaps makes this inevitable, although the Shepherd itself perhaps reflects that in the early church sexual sin was seen to be particularly dangerous (e.g., *Herm. Vis.* 1.1.7, 8; 1.2.4; 3.7.3; 3.8.4; *Herm. Man.* 2.3; 4.1.1, 2; 8.3; 12.1.3; *Herm. Sim.* 5.1.5).

2. Sin and Christ.

In several passages in this body of writings, comments are made regarding the sinlessness of Jesus Christ, which stands in opposition to sinful human behavior. These passages have raised theological issues regarding the possibility of Christ's sinning—for example, whether he was perpetually sinless, whether he was ever able to sin, or whether he achieved sinlessness and was exalted in his attained sinless state.

In Hebrews 4:15 the author states that humans do not have a high priest who is incapable of sympathy with their weakness but have one who has been tempted in every way, just as humans are. Nevertheless he was without sin. It is this phrase, "without or apart from sin," that has caused the most difficulty. Sin in the context of Hebrews seems to revolve around Jesus' response to temptation* rather than some kind of inherent sinless nature or his kinship with fallen humanity. The assertion seems to be that Christ resisted temptation at every stage of his life, so that when he is offered without blemish before God (Heb 9:14), this reflects not a final or an achieved blamelessness but the perfection of one who had always resisted temptation.

There is the same sense in 1 Peter 2:22, when the author quotes Isaiah 53:9, stating that Christ committed no sin and no deceit was found in him (see also *1 Clem.* 16.10, which cites Is 53:9 in the midst of citing most of Is 53:1-12 in a similar way). This allows the author of 1 Peter to state in 1 Peter 3:18, the opening verse of the most important christological* section in the book, that Christ's death was that of a righteous person dying for the unjust concerning their sins (*see* Death of Christ). In language redolent of 1 Peter 3:18 as well as Paul, *Diognetus* 9.2 contrasts Christ and the wicked, with Christ depicted as the son* who was given as ransom, the blameless for the evil.

3. Sin and Love of God.

An assumption of this part of the biblical literature is that impiety and godlessness are forms of sinfulness and are to be rejected (Jude 4, 15, 18; 2 Pet 2:5, 6; 3:7). God is angry at sin, both in the past with disobedient angels* (2 Pet 2:4) and the Israelites (Heb 3:17) and with contemporary Christian behavior. This dynamic is well illustrated in 1 John, a letter concerned to explicate the ethical* mandate incumbent upon those who have seen and known Christ. The letter* exemplifies what it means to love God in terms of loving behavior toward others (see also 1 Pet 4:8).

Several passages in 1 John imply that sinlessness is achievable, while other passages recognize the factuality of human sinfulness. R. E. Brown lists seven possible solutions to the problems raised by these passages, although none is entirely convincing. For example, a standard distinction between the present and aorist tenses of the Greek verb, whereby although humans might continue the occasional one-time sin (aorist tense) they do not persist in sin (present tense), runs afoul of usage in the book. For example, 1 John 3:4, 6 and 8 use the present tense to describe actual sinful acts, and the perfect tense is used in 1 John 1:10 to make the opposite statement regarding sin.

A more plausible solution, and one not dependent upon the Greek tense forms, is that a balance is being struck in the letter between the ideal of one not sinning and thus being consistent with one's confession of Christ and the reality of persistent human sinfulness. The ethical ideal is tempered by moral reality, although without neglecting the provision for forgiveness. In the argument of the letter, the reality is stated before the ideal. In 1 John 1:8-10 the author states that if we say that we have no sin, we deceive ourselves. If we say that we do not sin, we make God a liar, and his word is not in us. The ideal is established in such passages as 1 John 3:6, where the author says that everyone who abides in Christ does not sin, and everyone who does sin has not seen him; and 1 John 5:18, where he states that everyone who is begotten from God does not sin. Sin is clearly seen here as a breaking of divine law (1 Jn 3:4). Although those abiding in Christ know the demand of loving behavior through obedience, they will inevitably fail. Nevertheless all is not lost. The solution of the dilemma is found in Christ. In

1 John 2:1, after stating that he is writing so that his audience may not sin, the author says that if they sin, they have an advocate with the Father, Jesus Christ the righteous. It is Christ who cleanses and forgives from all sin (1 Jn 1:7, 9; 2:12; 3:5), since he is the propitiatory sacrifice for sins (1 Jn 2:2; 4:10).

4. Sin and Final Judgment.

In a few passages in the NT writings and the apostolic fathers, there are explicit statements regarding the ultimate and final judgment* of sinners and the wicked. These passages impress the reader with the seriousness of sin and wickedness, in the light of God and his demand for righteous behavior. In the NT these passages often utilize apocalyptic* imagery in painting a picture of final judgment. For example, Hebrews 2:2-3 asks the rhetorical question that if the message of angels was that every violation of God's law and every act of disobedience received punishment, how can Christians expect to escape if they ignore the call of salvation? Similarly Hebrews 10:26 says that those who keep on sinning can expect God's judgment. Revelation 18:4-8 and following draw a contrast between those who share in Babylon's* sin and those who do not. Those who do can look forward only to trouble, including repayment for their sins in terms of ultimate death and fiery consumption meted out by a judging God.

Although this kind of apocalyptic language is fairly frequent in Revelation (see Revelation, Book of), one of the most concentrated passages with such imagery is 2 Peter 2:9-16. After discussing how God has not spared others in the OT, the author asserts that God certainly knows how to rescue the godly from their trials and to hold the unrighteous for their day of punishment. He then depicts such unrighteous people in a lengthy catalog of their vices, including blasphemy and other sins so wicked that not even the angels would dare do the same. But these people will be paid back for their sins. The author describes this in anticipation of the day of the Lord (see Day of the Lord), when the ungodly will be destroyed (2 Pet 3:7). A passage that uses similar imagery is *Diognetus* 10.7, which implores believers to choose heaven* over death and the everlasting fire that punishes for eternity.* Similar in perspective if not in language is *Didache* 5.1-2, which defines the "Way of Death" in terms of a catalog of sinful behavior (cf. *Barn.* 20.1, which mentions the devil; *see* Satan). This language is more typical of the apostolic fathers, who appear regularly to use death as a means of speaking of eternal punishment (cf. *Herm. Man.* 12.1.2, 3; 12.2.2, 4).

See also CONSCIENCE; FLESH; FORGIVENESS; JUDGMENT; OBEDIENCE; REDEMPTION; RIGHTEOUSNESS; VIRTUES AND VICES.

BIBLIOGRAPHY. R. E. Brown, *The Epistles of John* (AB; New York: Doubleday, 1982); A. Chester and R. P. Martin, *The Theology of the Letters of James, Peter and Jude* (NTT; Cambridge: Cambridge University Press, 1994); R. B. Edwards, *The Johannine Epistles* (NTG; Sheffield: Sheffield Academic Press, 1996); W. Günther, "Sin," *NIDNTT* 3:573-85; J. A. Kleist, *The Didache, Etc.* (ACW 6; Westminster, MD: Newman, 1948); J. Lawson, *A Theological and Historical Introduction to the Apostolic Fathers* (New York: Macmillan, 1961); J. Lieu, *The Theology of the Johannine Epistles* (NTT; Cambridge: Cambridge University Press, 1991); B. Lindars, *The Theology of the Letter to the Hebrews* (NTT; Cambridge: Cambridge University Press, 1991); D. Peterson, *Hebrews and Perfection* (SNTSMS 47; Cambridge: Cambridge University Press, 1982). S. E. Porter

SISTERS OF JESUS. *See* RELATIVES OF JESUS.

SLAVE, SLAVERY

In the hierarchical societies of the early Roman Empire,* the legal ownership of human beings who could be used as property (chattel slavery) had long been widespread and regarded as appropriate and moral. Polybius, the Greek historian of Rome's rise to power, noted that both slaves and cattle were essential to life (Polybius *Hist.* 4.38.4). As many as one-third of the population of the empire were enslaved, and an additional large percentage had been slaves earlier in their lives. Those laboring in rural slavery provided their owners' primary income, from which the owners drew to maintain a large number of domestic slaves who not only provided a wide range of personal services but also displayed their owners' economic status. The Christian movement developed in such a social and cultural context, with the result that many important passages in early Christian documents cannot be understood apart from keen awareness of those features that make Greco-Roman slavery unique.

    1. Modern Readers and Ancient Slavery: Avoiding Anachronism

    2. "Slaves of God" in the Biblical Tradition: Serving with Honor

    3. Terminology of Slavery or Enslavement in Early Christian Texts: Clarifying the Contexts

1. Modern Readers and Ancient Slavery: Avoiding Anachronism.

Throughout history a large number of societies have chosen not to kill their vanquished enemies but to force them to serve as slaves, subjecting them to a "social death," separated from blood kin, from homeland and from legal protections enjoyed by free persons (see Patterson). The Greeks and Romans, however, independently transformed such enslavement into something original, "namely, an institutionalized system of large-scale employment of slave labor in both the countryside and the cities" (Finley, 67). Scholars have identified these societies as two of only five in world history rooted in "slave economics," that is, as having developed an economy and high culture made possible by extensive use of involuntary labor (see Ste. Croix). The other three were created later in Brazil, the Caribbean and the southern United States of America. It is natural then to think that knowledge of New World slavery can provide the modern interpreter with insight into the social, economic and legal context of the early Christians. Yet such information has frequently created serious misunderstandings.

Modern readers must overcome their temptation to read into any ancient Jewish, Greek or Roman text their knowledge of modern slavery. The meanings of any familiar-sounding terms can be determined only by a close investigation of the particular social systems and cultural values the early Christian writers took for granted (see Malina). Among the distinctive and often surprising features of slavery as practiced around the Mediterranean in the early centuries of our era are these:

    1. An enslaved person generally could not be identified by appearance or clothing; racial or ethnic origins were not reliable indicators of social or legal status.

    2. The cultural and religious traditions of slaves were usually those of their owners and other free persons.

    3. Education of slaves was encouraged, enhancing their value; some slaves were better educated than their owners. Rome's cultural

leadership in the empire largely depended on educated, foreign-born slaves who had been taken there.

4. Partially as a result, many slaves functioned in highly responsible and sensitive positions such as workshop and household managers, accountants, tutors, personal secretaries, sea captains and physicians (see Martin, 1-49). An important minority of slaves had considerable influence and social power, even over freeborn persons of lesser status than the slaves' owners.

5. By no means were the enslaved regularly to be found at the bottom of the socioeconomic pyramid. Rather those free and impoverished persons who had to seek work each day without any certainty of employment occupied the lowest level. Some of them sold themselves into slavery in order to obtain job security, food, clothing and shelter.

6. Slaves could own property, including their own slaves. They could accumulate funds that they might use to purchase their own freedom.

7. Because slaves were owned by persons across the range of economic levels, they developed no consciousness of being a social class or of suffering a common plight (see Garnsey and Saller, 109-25). Thus no laws were needed to hinder public assembly of slaves.

8. In contrast to New World slavery, ancient owners did not regard their adult slaves paternalistically; they clearly distinguished the roles of parents and of owners and felt no need to justify the institution of slavery.

9. Persons not infrequently sold themselves to pay debts, to escape poverty, to climb socially or to obtain special governmental positions (see Dio Chrysostom 15.23).

10. A large number of domestic and urban slaves, perhaps the majority, could anticipate being set free (manumitted) by age thirty, becoming a freedman or a freedwoman (see Acts 6:9, "the synagogue of the freedmen"). At any moment innumerable ex-slaves throughout the empire were proof that slavery need not be a permanent condition (see Bradley 1987, 81-112). And even ancient Greek commentators expressed astonishment that slaves freed by Roman citizens usually became Roman citizens themselves at their manumission. Notable in Acts 23—25 is the Roman governor Marcus Antonius Felix, who had been a slave until Antonia, the emperor Claudius's mother, manumitted him.

Slavery then was a fundamental aspect of daily life in the early Roman Empire, and virtually no one questioned its morality. Roman jurists and philosophers, some of whom noted that holding human beings as slaves was *contra naturam,* seemed never to have doubted the practical necessity or moral appropriateness of this practice. Not even the Stoic-Cynic philosopher Epictetus, who was raised and educated in slavery, regarded release from legal slavery as a desirable goal in itself. For him, as for the Jewish philosopher Philo* of Alexandria,* a person's achieving *inner* freedom from domination by social conventions, life's circumstances and one's passions was far more important than any change in one's social-legal status.

2. "Slaves of God" in the Biblical Tradition: Serving with Honor.

Neither Greeks nor Romans used the phrase "slave of God" in self-description, for the lack of freedom* implied by such a metaphor would have been intolerable. Thus kneeling played no role in the ceremonies of Greek and Roman worship; such "slavish" behavior would have met with contempt and would have been a cause for shame (see Bartchy 1985, 121-25).

In sharp contrast, in the Hebrew tradition the Israelites are frequently identified as "slaves of Yahweh," emphasizing their exclusive loyalty to their new Lord* following his liberation of them from Egyptian chattel slavery at the exodus (Lev 25:55; see Ex 20:2). This is especially interesting, since in Palestine a peasant economy prevailed, with legal slavery (usually for debt) playing only a minor role. In the Hebrew Bible the phrase in the singular "slave of Yahweh" identifies persons who came to enjoy an especially honored relationship to Israel's God, such as Abraham,* Isaac, Jacob, Moses,* David and Job. Paul of Tarsus boldly claims this designation of honor for himself and Timothy (Phil 1:1), as do James* (Jas 1:1), Jude* and the author of 2 Peter* ("slave of Jesus Christ," Jude 1; 2 Pet 1:1). Once Paul even refers to freeborn, Greco-Roman Christians in general as "slaves of the Lord" (1 Cor 7:22). Early Christian writers freely extended this phrase to identify all Christians.

3. Terminology of Slavery or Enslavement in Early Christian Texts: Clarifying the Contexts.

3.1. Acts, Revelation and the Slaves of God.

Early in Acts* Peter quotes the prophecy* from Joel according to which God's Spirit will be poured out "even upon my slaves, both men and women," echoing Mary's* response to the angel* Gabriel in the words: "Here I am, the slave of the Lord" (Lk 1:38, 48). Luke uses the phrase again in the prayer* in Acts 4:29: "grant to your slaves to speak your word with all boldness." And in Acts 16:17 even a pagan diviner, herself a slave, identifies Paul, Silas and Timothy as "slaves of the Most High God." Paul's bold exorcism of her profitable "spirit of divination" infringed on the property rights of her owners, whose charges against Paul and Silas led to their flogging and imprisonment.

In the Revelation of Jesus to John (*see* Revelation, Book of), the author immediately identifies both himself and his intended readers as slaves of Jesus Christ.* While occasionally referring to "slave and free" in inclusive series (Rev 6:15; 13:16; 19:18), John uses slave terminology primarily to emphasize the exclusive loyalty of Moses, the ancient prophets and his readers to God (e.g., Rev 10:7; 11:18; 19:5; 22:6). Note also that in four of his letters* Ignatius* refers to himself as a "fellow slave" (*syndoulos*), especially of the "deacons" (*diakonoi*), perhaps because he has identified them as representatives of Christ (Ign. *Magn.* 6.1).

3.2. 1 Peter, the Treatment of Slaves and Christ's Suffering Example. After exhorting all Christians to "live as free people, yet without using your freedom as a pretext for evil; but live as slaves (*douloi*) of God" (1 Pet 2:16), the author of 1 Peter* turns to the vulnerable plight of those Christians in domestic slavery (*oiketai*) who were owned by pagans who perhaps treat them cruelly (1 Pet 2:18-23). The author urges them nevertheless to accept their owners' authority* (1 Pet 2:17).

How an enslaved person, especially a household slave, was treated day to day depended almost entirely on the character and disposition of the owner. Greco-Roman laws and customs gave slave owners much leeway to act cruelly or compassionately in response to slaves, who were conventionally expected to act with fawning deception. Slaves were vulnerable to corporal punishment, including whippings that reinforced both the owners' domination and the slaves' lack of honor and dignity. As Christians, such slaves are addressed here as moral agents who like Christ himself may also suffer even

though they are innocent of any wrongdoing (1 Pet 2:19-21; 3:14, 17; 4:1, 12-19; 5:10). Yet to endure abuse for doing what is right is honorable, not shameful. They, as Christians, are exhorted to refuse to return evil for evil, following Christ and sharing in his suffering* (see Elliott, 142-43, 205-8).

3.3. 1 Clement and Self-Sale into Slavery. Two former imperial slaves, Claudius Ephebus and Valerius Bito, were the delegates of Christians in Rome* to carry the letter now known as *1 Clement* to the house churches* in Corinth at the end of the first century. This letter had been written in hope of inspiring the troublemakers among the Christians in Corinth to repent. The author points to the exemplary behavior of "many of our own number who have had themselves imprisoned in order to ransom others. Many have sold themselves into slavery (*douleia*) and given the price to feed others" (*1 Clem.* 55.2). These heroic examples of self-sacrifice, subverting the system for the sake of the common good (contrast Seneca *Ep. Mor.* 47.7), may already have been well known to the Corinthians. C. Osiek observes that "the fact that the letter is written from the Roman church to the Corinthian church further indicates that the examples cannot be localized; they belong to a common tradition of early Christian hagiography" (Osiek 1981, 370). The "ransoming of others" through imprisonment probably refers to a Christian's self-substitution for a person imprisoned for debt.

3.4. Ignatius to Polycarp and the Manumission of Enslaved Christians. Ignatius of Antioch* is the first Christian writer after Paul (1 Cor 7:21) to comment on the manumission of Christian slaves. From his letter to Polycarp,* bishop of the Christians in Smyrna, it is clear that some slaves, presumably already members of some of the house churches, had come to expect that the price of their manumissions would be paid from the churches' common funds (Ign. *Pol.* 4.3). Ignatius took up this issue in a household code* dealing with care for widows and the behavior of slaves, wives, husbands and those practicing voluntary celibacy (see also Ign. *Smyrn.* 6.2).

First Ignatius exhorts Polycarp to lead in caring for every member of the house churches and especially by not acting arrogantly to enslaved Christians. In turn he urges these slaves not to permit the new honor in which they are held to lead to insolence. Rather they should honor God by giving "more devoted service, so that they may obtain from God a better freedom." Then Ignatius warns them against making themselves "slaves of selfish passion" by seeking to obtain funds from the common chest (to be used for the widows?) to purchase their manumission. Perhaps experiences in Antioch led Ignatius to oppose the assumption that becoming a Christian gave a slave a *right* to manumission paid from the common treasury. He may also have been wary of provoking public slander of the Christian community as a cause of social instability. J. A. Harrell argues that "Ignatius showed concern only for the abuses of corporate manumission, not private manumission," concluding correctly that neither Ignatius nor Paul expressed any opposition to the liberation of Christians in slavery (Harrell, 194).

3.5. The Didache and God's Impartial Judgment of Slaves and Owners. Only one passage in the *Didache** mentions slaves or slavery. In a long chain of admonitions to practice extraordinary forms of generosity, the author cautions slave owners: "Do not be harsh in giving orders to your male and female slaves" (*Did.* 4.10), for those in slavery "hope in the same God as you," and cruel treatment could lead them to "cease to honor the God over you both." Enslaved Christians then are exhorted to "obey [their] owners with reverence and respect, as if they represented God" (*Did.* 4.11). This God, however, gives no advantage to owner over slave: "when he comes to call us, he will not respect our station but will call those whom the Spirit has made ready."

These admonitions extend the tradition of the NT household codes (see Col 3:22-23; Eph 6:5-8) which sought to transform negative attitudes engendered by the Roman patriarchal system. Owners are urged to exchange casual cruelty for fairness and compassion and slaves to abandon servile deception in favor of honesty and hard work. Both owners and slaves should imitate God's impartiality, thus profoundly altering interpersonal relationships. Many aspects of the slaves' social death were effectively overcome in the Christian house church "families." But the slave system as such was not called in question. With improved relations between slaves and their owners, ironically the system worked better than ever before.

3.6. The Shepherd of Hermas and the Obligations of Formerly Enslaved Christians. The author of the *Shepherd of Hermas** employs terms of slavery or enslavement far more than does any early Christian author, referring to Christians in general as "slaves of God" at least thirty-five times. He claims to have been an ex-slave himself (*Herm. Vis,* 1.1), and he directed his writing about the uses of wealth and the dangers of social climbing "to a large and influential group of freedmen and women in the Christian community" (Osiek 1993, 134). Here, for the first time in Christian writing, prosperous Christians are exhorted "not to oppress poor debtors" (*Herm. Man.* 8.10); such oppression frequently led to imprisonment or enslavement for debt, which some of these Christian freedmen and freedwomen may have suffered themselves.

These former slaves had become the majority of small business people, tradesmen and craftsmen in Rome. *Hermas* challenged them to repent and use their wealth on behalf of the needy among the Christians, including "purchasing afflicted souls" (*Herm. Sim.* 1.8; see *Herm. Man.* 8.10), a phrase that may include the act of buying Christian slaves from pagan owners (Gülzow, 89, opposed by Osiek 1981, 372). In any case, later writings indicate that Christians became known for their efforts to rescue prisoners, captives and slaves (e.g., the *Apostolic Constitutions* 4.9.2; see Harrell, 178-82).

As the Christians moved into the second century, they continued to share with their pagan contemporaries the view that slavery was an integral part of civilization. But by referring to themselves as "slaves of God," in an extension of an honorable OT tradition, they risked deeply offending Greco-Roman sensibilities. In the awareness that "people are slaves to whatever masters them" (2 Pet 2:9), both slaves and their owners were exhorted as Christians to root their treatment of each other in their voluntary and exclusive enslavement to the holy master of them all.

See also FREEDOM, LIBERTY; HOUSEHOLD CODES; HOUSEHOLDS, FAMILY; ROMAN EMPIRE, CHRISTIANS AND THE; SOCIAL SETTING OF EARLY NON-PAULINE CHRISTIANITY.

BIBLIOGRAPHY. S. S. Bartchy, "MALLON CHRESAI," *First-Century Slavery and the Interpretation of 1 Corinthians 7:21* (Atlanta: Scholars Press, 1985); idem, "Greco-Roman Slavery,"

ABD 6:65-73 (Garden City, NY: Doubleday, 1992); K. R. Bradley, *Slavery and Society at Rome* (Cambridge: Cambridge University Press, 1994); idem, *Slaves and Masters in the Roman Empire: A Study in Social Control* (New York: Oxford University Press, 1987); J. H. Elliott, *A Home for the Homeless: A Sociological Exegesis of 1 Peter, Its Situation and Strategy* (Philadelphia: Fortress, 1981); M. I. Finley, *Ancient Slavery and Modern Ideology* (New York: Viking, 1980); P. Garnsey and R. Saller, *The Roman Empire: Economy, Society and Culture* (Los Angeles: University of California Press, 1987); H. Gülzow, *Christentum und Sklaverei in den ersten drei Jahrhunderten* (Bonn: Habelt Verlag, 1969); J. A. Harrell, *Manumission of Slaves in Early Christianity* (HUT 32; Tübingen: J. C. B. Mohr, 1995); K. Hopkins, *Conquerors and Slaves* (New York: Cambridge University Press, 1978); B. J. Malina, "Reading Theory Perspective: Reading Luke-Acts" in *The Social World of Luke-Acts: Models for Interpretation,* ed. J. Neyrey (Peabody, MA: Hendrickson, 1991); D. B. Martin, *Slavery as Salvation* (New Haven, CT: Yale University Press, 1990); C. Osiek, "The Ransom of Captives: Evolution of a Tradition," *HTR* 74 (1981) 365-86; idem, *Rich and Poor in the "Shepherd of Hermas"* (Washington, DC: Catholic Biblical Association of America, 1983); O. Patterson, *Slavery and Social Death: A Comparative Study* (Cambridge, MA: Harvard University Press, 1982); G. E. M. de Ste. Croix, *The Class Struggle in the Ancient Greek World: From the Archaic Age to the Arab Conquests* (Ithaca, NY: Cornell University Press, 1989); T. Wiedemann, *Greek and Roman Slavery* (Baltimore: Johns Hopkins University Press, 1981).   S. S. Bartchy

SOCIAL SETTING OF EARLY NON-PAULINE CHRISTIANITY

"Social setting" is an umbrella term for an aspect of the study of the historical context of (in this case) early Christianity. By studying its social setting we gain a deeper understanding of the relationship between the first Christians and the world in which they lived. This helps us to recognize that early Christian belief and practice did not take shape in a vacuum but rather in the daily struggle of individuals and groups to bear witness to the lordship of Christ in a Mediterranean culture that acknowledged "many gods and many lords" (1 Cor 8:5).

   1. Directions
   2. Method
   3. Later New Testament
   4. Postapostolic Period

1. Directions.

In an influential article J. Z. Smith sets out four directions that the study of the social setting of early Christianity can take.

A first direction is the description of the social facts to which the Christian texts refer often only in passing because those facts were well known to their first-century readers. Important sources of information that supplement the literary evidence are such nonliterary evidence as provided by archaeology, epigraphy and papyrology (cf. Horsley). Even basic facts such as the size of houses and therefore the likely number of people who would be able to gather for worship in a house church give significant insight into the ethos of early church life.

Then there is the creation of a genuine social history that integrates what is known about the social facts into an account of early Christianity as a religious, cultural and social movement within the geographic, social, economic and political framework of the Roman Empire.* Exemplary here is the work of R. MacMullen (1981, 1984) and, from an earlier generation, A. D. Nock.

The third direction addresses questions of social organization "in terms of both the social forces which led to the rise of Christianity and the social institutions of early Christianity" (Smith, 20). Examples of social forces behind the rise of Christianity include the kind of political, economic, ecological and cultural factors identified by G. Theissen in his studies of both the rural, Palestinian "Jesus movement" (1978) and the urban, Pauline house churches (1982). An early and influential study of the social institutions of the city-state *(politeia),* the household *(oikonomia)* and voluntary associations *(koinōnia)* presupposed in the NT and beyond is that of E. A. Judge.

A final direction of inquiry is one that draws its main inspiration from the sociology of knowledge and interprets early Christianity "as a social world, [that is,] as the creation of a world of meaning which provided a plausibility structure for those who chose to inhabit it" (Smith, 21). Attention focuses on describing the ethos of the Christian groups over against that of Qumran,* the synagogue,* the Cynics or the mystery cults (*see* Religions, Greco-Roman), what it felt like to convert and how the meaning of belonging was expressed through the particular language, rituals and symbols that the Christians developed (cf. Meeks 1983, 140-92).

2. Method.

In addition to understanding the various directions that the study of the social setting of early Christianity can take, it is important to be aware of ongoing debates over method. Two of these are particularly prominent in current discussion.

2.1. Social History or Social Science? One debate is whether study of the social setting of early Christianity is an exercise in social history using the standard tools and techniques of the contemporary historian or whether it is also an exercise requiring the models and methods of the social sciences. For those who favor the social-history approach, social-scientific method is rejected on various grounds: its models are anachronistic; the sources are not such as to make controlled social-scientific analysis possible; it fails to allow for incommensurability between the past and the present; its genealogy lies in a hermeneutic of suspicion that is hostile to theology and the supernatural; and it tends to reduce the meaning of particular historical realities to the level of their social function in relation to general underlying needs and forces.

For those who favor the social-scientific approach, the social-history approach is held to be seriously lacking. First, "the historian's conceptualization tends to be implicit, arbitrary and unsystematic, whereas the social scientist's is explicit and systematic" (G. Barraclough, in Malina 1986, 174); second, there is the historian's tendency "to evade so far as possible the theoretical issues, and also to deal for preference less with the underlying structure than with events and personalities" (G. Barraclough, in Malina 1986, 174). At first glance this looks like a difference between a theory-laden (social-scientific) approach and a theory-free (social-history) approach. In fact it is a difference between approaches that make explicit their theoretical foundation and those that leave them implicit. At issue are serious questions, perhaps not sufficiently acknowledged, that have to do with theology and the politics and ethics of interpretation (cf. Malina 1986; Holmberg, 145-57; Elliott 1993, 87-100). In this article

the insights of both the social-history and social-scientific approaches will be deployed depending on what is appropriate to the subject matter under discussion.

2.2. Social Setting and Canonical Scripture. The other important debate over method is how investigation of the social setting of early Christianity is to be related to reading the NT and other early Christian texts as Scripture and tradition of and for the church. For some scholars, study of social setting is part of that larger enterprise called historical criticism that drives a wedge between Scripture and the church (see Braaten and Jenson). It does so by treating the text as a source for historical reconstruction rather than spiritual illumination and by putting to the text (now referred to as the "documents") questions that are honed not by the Christian tradition and the life of faith but by the Enlightenment tradition of the academy. For others, study of the social setting, both of the world behind the text and of the world within the text, is not inimical to the scriptural approach. On the contrary, it is a way of attending with greater seriousness to the remarkable realities to which these historical texts bear witness (see Barton). It is a way of putting body and soul together again in biblical interpretation that Meeks (1986) calls a "hermeneutics of social embodiment" and of becoming better informed about what kinds of questions a text like this deserves.

Historically and hermeneutically speaking, the former position with its emphasis on church and tradition is more Catholic, while the latter position with its emphasis on the text in its original context is more Protestant. The former position is a helpful reminder that the work of students of the social setting of early Christianity is to some extent parasitic upon the church for the authority attaching to what they do. The latter position is a reminder that the authority of the early Christian writings as Scripture and tradition depends in part on ongoing, skilled attention to what these writings make known. Both positions have something important to offer the task of interpretation (cf. Levenson, 106-26).

3. Later New Testament.

It is not possible here to give a comprehensive account of what is involved in investigation of the social setting of the later NT and beyond.

We will proceed instead by selected case studies related to particular texts. The aim in each case will be to show the implications for interpretation of an understanding of issues of social setting.

3.1. Acts: Meals and Table Fellowship. The attention given to meals, table fellowship and table talk in Luke's two volumes is remarkable and all-pervasive (Moxnes). Clearly there is for Luke more to meals than the satisfying of physical hunger, although that is important in itself. What this extra dimension is becomes clearer in the light of the social and religious history of Israel* and the Jews, for whom food and meal practices were governed by the levitical purity rules (*see* Food, Food Laws) and marked them out as God's* elect* (Lev 11; Deut 14; cf. Dan 1:3-17; 2 Macc 7). But it also becomes clearer in the light of the broader, cross-cultural insights of social anthropology, according to which meals meet social needs as well as physical ones and have as much to do with the social body or the body politic as with the physical body (cf. Neyrey). This is because meals involve the consumption of food in a social context and are part of an elaborate system of communication within a particular culture. Food dealings generally are a barometer of social relations and a powerful mechanism for both creating sociability and, alternatively, for destroying it.

If we ask how meals communicate meanings, how they provide food for thought, as we might say, anthropologists like M. Douglas (1975) draw attention to the way whole societies or groups within a single society both constitute themselves and distinguish themselves from others by their meal practices. Significant factors tend to be the type of food consumed or abstained from (clean or unclean, cooked or raw, meat or vegetable); the time and frequency of eating and abstaining (or fasting); the time of and time taken for meal preparation (e.g., whether it is permitted on the sabbath or not); the quantity and quality of food consumed (e.g., the phenomenon of conspicuous consumption, in which what is vital is that the consumption is conspicuous); who is allowed or invited to eat with whom and who is excluded from table fellowship; the symbolic geography of the meal (including who sits where, the position of men in relation to women, whether the meal is in public or in private); the clothes worn by participants (formal or informal, colored or not);

and the sounds (if any) that are appropriate to accompany the meal (silence, table talk, prayers,* readings and hymns*).

Seen in the light both of the history of Israel and Judaism* and of the insights of social anthropology, meals and table fellowship in Luke-Acts take on a profound level of significance (cf. Esler, 71-109). First, by virtue of the inclusion of Gentiles* at table, they represent a challenge to the boundaries and self-understanding both of the Jewish ethnos and of the Jewish Christians* in Jerusalem* and elsewhere. The story of Peter and the Roman centurion Cornelius* is an obvious case in point (Acts 10—11). Second and related, meals and table fellowship constitute the starting mechanism of a new group, an eschatological* society based upon radically novel criteria of acceptability (cf. Lk 14:1-24) and therefore open to Jews and Gentiles, men and women, rich and poor. This helps to explain the repeated attention drawn to the first Christians' meal practice and the honor it attracted from outsiders: "And day by day, attending the temple together and breaking bread in their homes, they partook of food with glad and generous hearts, praising God and having favor with all the people" (Acts 2:46; cf. Acts 2:42; 4:32-35).

Third and conversely, it is not surprising that an important manifestation of problems in the Jerusalem church* was the breakdown in table fellowship represented by the neglect of provision for the widows of the Hellenists (Acts 6:1-6). If meals are a potential source of unity and honor, they are also a potential source of conflict and shame. Fourth, the offering of food serves as part of a larger pattern of social exchange based on reciprocity. This helps to explain the references in Acts* to the hospitality* offered to apostles* like Paul: after his own conversion, Paul receives food in the house of Judas in Damascus (Acts 9:19); the convert Lydia receives Paul and his companions into her house to stay (Acts 16:15); the Philippian jailer expresses his gratitude to Paul by feeding him in his own house (Acts 16:34); and in Troas, Paul's teaching all night long is punctuated by his receiving sustenance in the communal breaking of bread (Acts 20:11). Such hospitality makes it possible for beneficiaries of the apostle's ministry* to reciprocate and thereby play a part in the apostolic mission and the life of the church.

Finally, table fellowship in Acts has a mimetic quality. The breaking of the bread that takes place when the Christians gather together (cf. Acts 2:42, 46; 20:7, 11) is a solemn, but also joyful, reminder of the breaking of the bread by Jesus both at the Last Supper before the crucifixion (Lk 22:19) and at the house in Emmaus after the resurrection* (Lk 24:30, 35). Thus the meal is a symbolic act that communicates to participants the very heart of what unites them. Its repetition also is significant in social-scientific terms. In the day-to-day life of the church, it binds the believers not only to one another but also to the crucified and risen Lord* who is the true host, now ascended into heaven* (cf. Lk 22:30).

3.2. The Pastoral Epistles: Gendered Church Order.

As children of the Enlightenment who espouse democratic individualism and the equality of the sexes, many readers of the Bible in Western cultures find puzzling and offensive instructions on church life that presuppose neither democracy nor egalitarianism. A case in point is the gendered church order in the Pastoral Epistles: "I desire that in every place the men should pray, lifting holy hands without anger or quarrelling; also that women should adorn themselves modestly and sensibly in seemly apparel. . . . Let a woman learn in silence with all submissiveness. I permit no woman to teach or to have authority over men; she is to keep silent" (1 Tim 2:8-15). This instance is certainly not unique in the NT and beyond (cf. 1 Cor 11:2-16; 14:33-36), even if it is by no means the only side of the story (cf. Gal 3:27-28; Rom 16:1-16), as social historians and feminist theologians, among others, have pointed out (Meeks 1974; Fiorenza). Responsible interpretation of texts like these requires the exercise of Christian theological judgment within the life of the church. Understanding these texts in their original social setting is an important contribution to the wise exercise of such judgment. Here we can draw attention to just a few of the pertinent areas of consideration.

First, the genderization of church order* in the Pastorals should not come as a surprise. Christians were the heirs of traditions and practices in Israel and Judaism that took for granted a system of holiness* symbolically elaborated along lines of purity* that at certain points distinguished between men and women. In this complex symbolic system, the rationale for which remains largely unexplained and implicit, men and women were organized in ways that enabled them to symbolize the holy in complementary ways (Archer). This meant, for example, that in a system in which bodily wholeness symbolized the oneness of God and the holiness and set-apartness of the people of God, things that crossed or confused the boundaries of the physical body became potent symbols of the impurity or chaos that constantly threatened the holiness of the social body (Douglas 1966, 1973; Countryman).

Thus bodily emissions, especially menstrual blood in the case of women and seminal emissions in the case of men, were regarded as sources of contagious impurity that temporarily disqualified the impure person from participation in celebrations of God's holiness in the cult (cf. Lev 12; 15). Greater seriousness was attached to the impurity of women through menstruation, not (it may be argued) because of the lower status of women but because of the symbolic weight accorded to blood as the symbol of life, which is sacred (Lev 17:11, 14). Nevertheless the regularity of ritual impurity through menstruation (and, related to this, childbirth) did mean that men alone were able to function as priests of the cult. Even here, a single tribe, the Levites, was set apart for the purpose. This cult and this symbol system are part of Christianity's cultural inheritance and help to explain the gendered ordering of the church in the Pastorals and elsewhere.

A second, related social factor that throws light on church order in the Pastorals is that, in the Mediterranean world generally, social space was divided up and marked out in a number of ways, one of the most important of which was the differentiation of the public domain from the private along lines provided by the binary opposition of male and female. It is as if the physical bodies of men and women served as a kind of map not only of the moral ordering of the social body but of its spatial ordering as well. The male represents public space and what is associated with it: leadership in politics, philosophy, rhetoric,* litigation, business, warfare and the arena. The female represents the more circumscribed, private space of the household. This is where women have authority* that they are to exercise on behalf of the male household head in ways intended to protect his honor. This gendered ordering of social space is maintained by deep-rooted custom and convention and by the powerful social values of honor and shame. Eloquent expression of this gendered order comes from the Hellenized Jew Philo* of Alexandria*:

Marketplaces and council halls and law courts and gatherings and meetings where a large number of people are assembled and open-air life with full scope for discussion and action—all these are suitable to men both in war and peace. The women are best suited to the indoor life that never strays from the house, within which the middle door is taken by the maidens as their boundary and the outer door by those who have reached full womanhood. Organized communities are of two sorts, the greater, which we call cities, and the smaller, which we call households. Both of these have their governors; the government of the greater is assigned to men under the name of statesmanship (*politeia*), that of the less, known as household management (*oikonomia*), to women (Philo *Spec. Leg.* 3.169-70).

In this light, the fact that the early Christians met together in houses (i.e., that a public or semipublic assembly took place regularly in a private place) makes it likely that conventional lines separating public and private spheres and related male and female authority became blurred. This blurring must have been accentuated also by claims by women as well as men to a new, charismatic authority that transcended legal and traditional household patterns; not to mention doctrines of an apocalyptic* or a gnostic* kind that encouraged celibacy and the reevaluation of the accepted social order (1 Tim 4:1-4; cf. *Acts of Paul and Thecla;* Kraemer). Thus it is not surprising that the Pastorals give such single-minded attention to the respective roles and authority of men and women and seek to put in place a gendered church order more in keeping with scriptural norms and wider cultural patterns (possibly including contemporary synagogue practice). This may reasonably be seen as an attempt both to protect the church against disintegration from powerful centrifugal forces and to maintain a credible witness to gospel truth in the society at large.

Interpreters may be right to see here the beginnings of the institutionalization and patriarchalization of the church and a decline from the discipleship of equals in the time of Jesus and his first followers (cf. Fiorenza, 288-94). But this may not be the fairest way to characterize either the Jesus movement (with its core of twelve male apostles) or what the Pastorals have in mind. For in their own social context, the issues dealt with are not primarily the politics of gender relations. They are to do much more with the disciplined ordering of the household* of God in the face of serious threats to its common life and public reputation.

3.3. 1 Peter: Household Order and Christian Benefactors. The central section of 1 Peter* contains remarkable and extensive instruction on the Christian's social obligations (1 Pet 2:11—3:17), making it one of the most significant non-Pauline texts to address the perennial theological question of the relationship between Christianity and culture. Particularly important are the metaphors *aliens (paroikoi)* and *exiles (parepidēmoi),* which are used to express the Christians' self-understanding (1 Pet 2:11; cf. 1 Pet 1:1, 17). Once we grasp what this designation implies, we have a key to interpreting the instructions about the Christian's social obligations. Are the instructions, in particular the so-called household code* (1 Pet 2:13—3:7), intended to separate the church from the surrounding culture? Or do they represent a compromise with society at large? Or should they be seen somewhat differently?

The first position is that taken by J. H. Elliott in one of the first works of sociological exegesis of the NT (1981). He argues that *paroikos* is as much a social as a religious category and that the addressees of the epistle were marginalized "resident aliens" *(paroikoi)* of Asia Minor who were attracted to Christianity because it offered, both socially and religiously, a home for the homeless. However, because their conversion increased the antagonism of the native residents toward them, they developed the ethos and identity of what we would call a conversionist sect in tension with the surrounding society. The strategy of the letter* is to confirm the believers in their social and religious separation from outsiders and to emphasize their incorporation into an alternative society, the household of God (1 Pet 4:17; cf. 1 Pet 2:5). The role of the household code and the wider instruction on social obligation is to accentuate the distance between believers and the world around them by increasing their self-understanding as the new eschatological people of God.

Not everyone has been persuaded by Elliott's proposal (cf. Winter, 11-23; Volf). While acknowledging the important point that "aliens and exiles" may have social as well as religious connotations, it appears rather one-sided to represent conversion and subsequent Christian instruction as the product of underlying social forces of marginalization when it appears more likely that the marginalization of the Christians is the result of their conversion and distinctive lifestyle. At the least the relation between social and religious factors is likely to be a complex one with lines of influence running in both directions. It may also be the case that Elliott's position is so predisposed toward accentuating the separatist, sectarian character of early Christianity that the relation between church and culture is polarized in a way that does not do justice to the more complex picture of the relation that 1 Peter implies. The act of distinguishing categories like "social" and "religious" (or "church" and "culture") that derive from our modern, secular way of seeing things may be a fundamental mistake. It predisposes us to define things from the beginning in terms of either the one or the other and to look for one-way causal relations that may be either simplistic or prone to ideological hostage-taking.

Different from Elliott's interpretation is that of D. Balch. On the basis of a comparison of the household code in 1 Peter with codes from the wider Hellenistic Jewish environment, Balch argues that the high degree of correspondence between the respective codes shows that, far from trying to distance themselves from society at large, the Christians in Asia Minor were being encouraged toward accommodation and greater integration. The motivation suggested is essentially apologetic. By accommodating to generally accepted social norms in relation to *politeia* and *oikonomia,* the Christians would counter the slander of outsiders who viewed them as a threat to civic order and household stability. In consequence the risk of discrimination or persecution* would be reduced.

Balch's comparative historical work is important for helping modern readers of the letter understand why the instructions on social ethics* tie together political obligation and household relations; why the household itself is given so much attention; and why the household code follows the pattern it does (with its overwhelm-

ing stress on the subordination of slave* to master and wife to husband). This makes sense in a historical and cultural context that viewed the stable household as the fundamental building block of society and that ordered itself according to class and gender in strictly hierarchical, patriarchal terms.

What is problematic, however, is the assumption that because the Christian household code is close to the Hellenistic Jewish code, the Christians must be losing their radical nerve and accommodating to the world around them. This implies that the Christians began as a minority group of outsiders and gradually accommodated to the majority by becoming insiders. But this kind of polarization obscures (in a way similar to Elliott's model of a conversionist sect) as much as it reveals. For, rather than involving a transfer from one society to another, it is far more likely that the effect of conversion was to bestow on converts membership of two societies simultaneously: earthly households and the household of God.

If so, 1 Peter may represent an attempt neither to bolster sectarian separation (Elliott) nor to encourage cultural accommodation (Balch) but to do something more subtle because the situation of the addressees is more complex (Volf). This something has to do with encouraging the Christians to realize more fully and in practice their own vocation as people who by God's mercy* "have been born anew to a living hope . . . [to be] a royal priesthood, a holy nation, God's own people" (1 Pet 1:3; 2:9). Sometimes this call to holiness is likely to involve rejection of the surrounding culture; at other times, acceptance and, even more, acts of public benefaction for the welfare of the city (Winter, 11-40). But the motivation for rejecting or accepting or serving as a public benefactor need not be those forces (sociological, political or others) that come solely from outside. To see things in this way reduces the profound theology and ethics of the letter to social pragmatics. It also distracts attention from the main point: the eschatological reality of God's holy people to which 1 Peter is both witness and summons (cf. 1 Pet 1:13-17).

4. Postapostolic Period.
Study of the social setting of early Christianity is not limited to the texts of the NT. Its range is much broader than that. This is partly because

the interests of the social historian tend not to be confined to the boundaries set by the canon* of Scripture; partly because study of what came later helps us to see the period of origins in a clearer perspective; and partly also because of the availability of a variety of source materials that cry out for investigation.

4.1. The Didache: *Morality and Greco-Roman Voluntary Associations.* One of the perennial questions of interest in the study of early Christianity is the question of conversion: what was involved in conversion, what motivated people to convert and what did people think they were converting to (cf. Nock)? The *Didache* is particularly interesting in this regard. It is a late first- or early second-century manual of Christian instruction intended for the preparation of catechumens for baptism.* Beginning with an extensive statement of moral rules (the so-called Two Ways; see also *Barn.* 18—20), it then proceeds to instruction on baptism, fasting and prayer, Eucharist, church order (apostles and prophets,* bishops and deacons), Sunday worship,* and warnings about the end time.

If we focus attention on the teaching about the Two Ways, which takes up the first half of the work as a whole, what is striking is the emphasis on moral rigor in conformity to traditions that, as the informed reader recognizes, are overwhelmingly biblical and evangelical. Addressed "to the pagans" *(tois ethnēsin)* as teaching of "the Lord" mediated through the apostles, this instruction marks out the "way of life" consonant with Christian profession (*Did.* 1—4) and the "way of death" to be shunned (*Did.* 5—6). But it is noteworthy how lacking this material is in Christian narrative setting and Christian doctrinal warrant. As W. A. Meeks (1987, 151) puts it: "At the lowest level, there is much here which a simple believer could take as simply rules for keeping in tune with the divine order of things, practices that the Greeks would call *eusebeia* and the Romans *religio*, but that a satirist might call 'superstition.' "

This observation is a useful reminder that the moral rigor that attracted pagans to Christianity and Judaism was not without parallel in Greco-Roman society beyond the church and synagogue. It needs to be recognized more widely that many pagans converted to Christianity because they found in the Christian groups moral standards that they recognized already as profoundly important for human welfare; and

many others scorned Christianity because they regarded the behavior of the Christians as reprehensible (e.g., Pliny *Ep.* 10.96: "I found nothing but a degenerate sort of cult carried to extravagant lengths."), a point about which a number of Christian writers from Paul on were particularly sensitive (cf. Wilken, 15-30).

A fine illustration of the high moral standards able to be found in Greco-Roman voluntary associations, for example, comes in the form of an inscription from a private cult group dedicated to a pantheon of gods in Philadelphia, Asia Minor, dated to the late second or early first centuries B.C. (text and translation in Barton and Horsley). This inscription sets out in considerable detail a moral code that those who enter cult meetings are to swear to uphold:

> When coming into this *oikos* let men and women, free people and slaves, swear by all the gods neither to know nor to make use wittingly of any deceit against a man or woman, neither poison harmful to men nor harmful spells. They are not themselves to make use of a love potion, abortifacient, contraceptive or any other thing fatal to children. . . . Apart from his own wife, a man is not to have sexual relations with another married woman, whether free or slave, nor with a boy, nor with a virgin girl; nor shall he recommend it to another. . . . A free woman is to be chaste and shall not know the bed of, nor have sexual intercourse with, another man except her own husband. . . . At the monthly and annual sacrifices may those men and women who have confidence in themselves touch this inscription on which the ordinances of the god have been written, in order that those who obey these ordinances and those who do not may be manifest.

Analogies with the early Christian groups are numerous and indicate the extent to which these groups must have appeared to outsiders as another form of club or voluntary society. The analogies include the open access given to "men and women, free people and slaves"; the regular meeting together for a religious purpose; the location of meetings in a privately owned house or shrine *(oikos);* the placing of moral responsibility on both men and women; a stringent sexual code; the respecting of marital and household ties; the protection of children (including the unborn); and the threat of divine sanction against oath-breakers. In relation to the Two Ways code in the *Didache,* especially noteworthy are the linguistic parallels to at least four of the forbidden practices: deceit *(dolos),* poison *(pharmakon),* destruction by abortion *(phthoros)* and murder *(phonos)* (cf. *Did.* 2.2). Comparable in meaning if not linguistically are the prohibitions against the enchanter, astrologer and magician,* the prohibition on infanticide and the command to "make no evil plan against your neighbor" (*Did.* 2.6).

These analogies are not fortuitous. They reflect the early Christians' indebtedness to the social patterns and moral consciousness of their times, Greco-Roman as well as biblical and Jewish. Thus we may assume that attraction to Christianity on the basis of its moral appeal had its parallels and precedents in attraction to cult groups like the one at Philadelphia. Such parallels and precedents allowed later apologists like Tertullian (c. 160-220) to use the language both of the voluntary religious association and of the philosophical school as a vehicle for persuading opponents that their fears about the Christian gatherings were groundless:

> We are an association *(corpus)* bound together by our religious profession, by the unity of our way of life *(disciplina)* and the bond of our common hope. . . . We meet together as an assembly and as a society. . . . We pray for the emperors. . . . We gather together to read our sacred writing. . . . After the gathering is over the Christians go out as though they had come from a "school of virtue" (Tertullian *Apol.* 39, in Wilken, 46).

In the light of such evidence, it is a mistake to attempt to explain conversion and baptism as simply a progression from darkness to light,* depravity to moral rigor, impiety to piety—however effective such an explanation might be from a rhetorical point of view. The reality of the social and religious setting was much more complex than this kind of polarization allows. The Philadelphian inscription is an important reminder that it was not only Jews and Christians who took morality and religion seriously.

4.2. Ignatius of Antioch and Judaism. If the previous example drew attention to aspects of the Greco-Roman social setting of early Christianity, this final case study looks at the continuing importance of Judaism for Christian practice and self-understanding into the second century. Good illustrations of this come in the letters written by Ignatius,* bishop of Antioch,* during his journey under arrest from Antioch to Rome,* where he was martyred* sometime toward the end of the reign of the emperor Trajan (98-117). However, relations between Christians and Jews are not Ignatius's principal concern. These become an issue primarily because they bear on something even more fundamental: the unity of the churches. As W. R. Schoedel puts it: "Ignatius' letters reflect the conviction that the success of his martyrdom depends on the establishment and maintenance of peace and concord in the churches. Thus he calls for obedience to bishops and avoidance of false teachers, and his views on these matters are uncompromising" (Schoedel, 12).

Of the seven letters, those to the Philadelphians and Magnesians are particularly relevant (Stanton, 176-81; translation in Schoedel). In the former Ignatius unambiguously identifies as one threat to unity those who are encouraging the Christians to follow Jewish practices: "But if anyone expounds Judaism to you do not listen to him; for it is better to hear Christianity from a man who is circumcised than Judaism from a man uncircumcised; both of them, if they do not speak of Jesus Christ, are to me tombstones and graves of the dead" (Ign. *Phld.* 6.1). This is striking evidence of the parting of the ways between church and synagogue in the early second century (*see* Christianity and Judaism), for Ignatius can speak of *Ioudaismos* and *Christianismos* as two separate religions (cf. Ign. *Magn.* 10.1-3, where the proper noun *Christianity* occurs for the first time in Christian literature).

Nevertheless, the possibilities of mutual influence and interaction remain strong, so much so that Christians are "not to listen" to people advocating the adoption of Jewish ways. Particularly repugnant for Ignatius is the phenomenon of Gentiles (the "uncircumcised") advocating Judaism, for it is acceptable to move from Judaism to Christianity, but quite unacceptable to move from Gentile Christianity to Judaism. The fact that Ignatius speaks so strongly on this to a church that he knows personally shows how real he felt the threat to be. This suggests in turn that Jewish laws and customs had an ongoing appeal to Christians of the second century and that this appeal was by no means limited to former members of the synagogue.

But it was not only the laws and customs of Judaism that exerted an influence: the Scriptures of the Jews were influential (and a source of division) also. Some of Ignatius's opponents appear reluctant to accept the teaching of Christ if it cannot be shown to be scriptural (Ign. *Phld.* 8.2). Ignatius's response is revealing, since it almost admits the point before appealing to a higher authority, reinterpreting "the charters" (i.e., the Scriptures) as Jesus Christ himself and his "cross and death and resurrection and faith through him."

Ignatius then brings his argument to a climax with a comparison between the old and new dispensations in order to convince potential dissenters of the superiority of the latter and of the divine and human unity to which it gives access: "The priests are also good; yet better the high priest entrusted with the holy of holies, who alone is entrusted with the secrets of God, since he is the door of the Father through which enter Abraham and Isaac and Jacob and the prophets and the apostles and the church—all these—into the unity of God" (Ign. *Phld.* 9.1-2). It is worth noting also that Ignatius passes in silence over Moses* and the law* in favor of the Hebrew ancestors* and prophets.* This is typical of his reinterpretation of the Jewish Scriptures and is a tendency found also in other contemporary Christian texts and writers, notably the *Epistle of Barnabas** and Justin Martyr (Stanton, 181-88). For the prophets in particular can be made to speak of Christ more easily than can the law, and in any case it is the law whose significance Ignatius wanted to play down because of its appeal to his Judaizing opponents.

The other letter of Ignatius that shows the prominence of Judaism in the social world of Christians in Asia Minor is the letter to the Magnesians, especially *Magnesians* 8—10. Once again the dominant concern is the unity of the church in the true faith* under the authority of the bishop, presbyters and deacons (Ign. *Magn.* 6—7). In single-minded pursuit of this unity, Ignatius's tendency is to polarize reality in terms of what brings life and what leads to death (e.g., Ign. *Magn.* 5; cf. Malina 1978, 82-95). Compromise is not an option. In particular compromise with Judaism and Judaizers is ruled out emphatically: "Set aside then the evil leaven, old and sour, and turn to the new leaven, which is Jesus Christ. Be salted with him to keep anyone among you from being spoiled, since you will be convicted by your odor. It is ridiculous to profess Jesus Christ and to Judaize; for Christianity did not believe in Judaism, but Judaism in Christianity, into which every tongue that has believed in God has been gathered together" (Ign. *Magn.* 10.2-3).

It is remarkable how far this uncompromising, polarized stance is from the position of Paul, who, in writing to the Corinthian church a generation or two earlier, can testify to having become "to the Jews as a Jew . . . to those under the law as one under the law" (1 Cor 9:20). For Ignatius the lines of continuity between Christianity and Judaism are weaker than they were for Paul; and the lines of discontinuity are greater. Whereas Paul distinguishes between grace* and the law, Ignatius distinguishes between grace and Judaism: "For if we continue to live until now according to Judaism *(kata Ioudaismon),* we confess that we have not received grace" (Ign. *Magn.* 8.1). In consequence the prophets are christianized in a radical way (Ign. *Magn.* 8.2; 9.2), and the way of life associated with sabbath observance is replaced by the way associated with the Lord's Day* (Ign. *Magn.* 9.1). It is plain, therefore, that for Ignatius Christianity is the negation of Judaism, and any reversion to it is anathema. This is the way he responds to the threat to church unity posed by Gentile Judaizers: not by what we would call interfaith dialogue but by strengthening the boundaries and sharpening the lines of demarcation. For Ignatius too much was at stake to allow compromise: the truth of the gospel of Christ crucified and risen, the unity of the churches under their respective bishops and the witness* of his own approaching martyrdom.*

See also ARCHITECTURE, EARLY CHURCH; CENTERS OF CHRISTIANITY; CHRISTIANITY AND JUDAISM: PARTINGS OF THE WAYS; CHURCH ORDER, GOVERNMENT; CIVIL AUTHORITY; EMPEROR, EMPEROR CULT; FOOD, FOOD LAWS, TABLE FELLOWSHIP; HOUSEHOLD CODES; HOUSEHOLDS, FAMILY; PERSECUTION; ROMAN EMPIRE, CHRISTIANS AND THE; SEXUALITY, SEXUAL ETHICS; SLAVE, SLAVERY; WOMAN AND MAN.

BIBLIOGRAPHY. L. Archer, "Bound by Blood: Circumcision and Menstrual Taboo in Post-Exilic Judaism" in *After Eve: Women, Theology and the Christian Tradition,* ed. J. M. Soskice (London: Marshall Pickering, 1990) 38-61; D. Balch, *Let Wives Be Submissive: The Domestic Code in 1 Peter* (Chico, CA: Scholars Press, 1981); S. C. Barton,

"Historical Criticism and Social-Scientific Perspectives in New Testament Study" in *Hearing the New Testament,* ed. J. B. Green (Grand Rapids: Eerdmans, 1995) 61-89; S. C. Barton and G. H. R. Horsley, "A Hellenistic Cult Group and the New Testament Churches," *JAC* 24 (1981) 7-41; C. E. Braaten and R. W. Jenson, eds., *Reclaiming the Bible for the Church* (Grand Rapids: Eerdmans, 1995); L. W. Countryman, *Dirt, Greed and Sex* (Philadelphia: Fortress, 1988); M. Douglas, "Deciphering a Meal" in *Implicit Meanings* (London: Routledge & Kegan Paul, 1975) 249-75; idem, *Natural Symbols* (2d ed.; London: Barrie & Jenkins, 1973); idem, *Purity and Danger* (London: Routledge & Kegan Paul, 1966); J. H. Elliott, *A Home for the Homeless: A Sociological Exegesis of I Peter, Its Situation and Strategy* (Philadelphia: Fortress, 1981); idem, *Social-Scientific Criticism and the New Testament* (Minneapolis: Augsburg Fortress, 1993); P. F. Esler, *Community and Gospel in Luke-Acts: The Social and Political Motivations of Lukan Theology* (SNTSMS 57; Cambridge: Cambridge University Press, 1987); E. Schüssler Fiorenza, *In Memory of Her* (New York: Crossroad, 1983); B. Holmberg, *Sociology and the New Testament* (Minneapolis: Augsburg Fortress, 1990); G. H. R. Horsley, *New Documents Illustrating Early Christianity* (5 vols.; Macquarie, Australia: The Ancient History Documentary Research Centre, Macquarie University, 1981-89); E. A. Judge, *The Social Pattern of Christian Groups in the First Century* (London: Tyndale Press, 1960); R. S. Kraemer, "The Conversion of Women to Ascetic Forms of Christianity," *Signs* 6 (1980) 298-307; J. D. Levenson, *The Hebrew Bible, the Old Testament and Historical Criticism* (Louisville, KY: Westminster/John Knox, 1993); R. MacMullen, *Christianizing the Roman Empire* (New Haven, CT: Yale University Press, 1984); idem, *Paganism in the Roman Empire* (New Haven, CT: Yale University Press, 1981); B. J. Malina, "The Received View and What It Cannot Do: III John and Hospitality," *Semeia* 35 (1986) 171-94; idem, "The Social World Implied in the Letters of the Christian Bishop-Martyr (Named Ignatius of Antioch)," *SBLSP* (1978) 2:71-119; W. A. Meeks, *The First Urban Christians* (New Haven, CT: Yale University Press, 1983); idem, "A Hermeneutics of Social Embodiment," *HTR* 79 (1986) 176-86; idem, "The Image of the Androgyne," *HR* 13 (1974) 165-208; idem, *The Moral World of the First Christians* (Philadelphia: Westminster, 1986); H. Moxnes, "Meals and the New Community in Luke," *SEÅ* 51-52 (1986-87) 158-67; J. H. Neyrey, "Ceremonies in Luke-Acts: The Case of Meals and Table Fellowship" in *The Social World of Luke-Acts,* ed. J. H. Neyrey (Peabody, MA: Hendrickson, 1991) 361-87; A. D. Nock, *Conversion* (Oxford: Clarendon, 1933); W. R. Schoedel, *Ignatius of Antioch* (Herm; Philadelphia: Fortress, 1985); J. Z. Smith, "The Social Description of Early Christianity," *RelSRev* 1 (1975) 19-25; G. N. Stanton, "Other Early Christian Writings: Didache, Ignatius, Barnabas, Justin Martyr" in *Early Christian Thought in Its Jewish Context,* ed. J. Barclay and J. Sweet (Cambridge: Cambridge University Press and 1996) 174-90; G. Theissen, *The Social Setting of Pauline Christianity* (Philadelphia: Fortress, 1982); idem, *The Sociology of Early Palestinian Christianity* (Philadelphia: Fortress, 1978) [published in U.K. as *The First Followers of Jesus: A Sociological Analysis of the Earliest Christians* (London: SCM, 1978)]; R. L. Wilken, *The Christians as the Romans Saw Them* (New Haven, CT: Yale University Press, 1984); B. W. Winter, *Seek the Welfare of the City* (Grand Rapids: Eerdmans, 1994); M. Volf, "Soft Difference: Theological Reflections on the Relation Between Church and Culture in 1 Peter," *Ex Auditu* 10 (1994) 15-30.　　　　　　S. C. Barton

SOLID FOOD. *See* Milk, Solid Food.

SON OF GOD

Application of the title "Son of God" to Jesus underwent considerable change in early Christianity. In the earliest Christian communities it was primarily a functional expression, taking an image from extant OT and Jewish thought and applying it in a generally imprecise way to articulate the meaning of the Christ event. In combination with insights drawn from other images (notably of the divine logos), "Son of God" was gradually invested with more metaphysical understandings until it eventually became the church's preferred christological title. Several phases of this development can be traced in the literature dealt with here, though by the end of the period there was still some way to go before the emergence of the mature Son of God christology* of the classic creeds.*

In the past this development engendered heated debate. The history of religions school highlighted the terminology of divine sonship as a leading example of the intrusion of alien categories in Christianity, and while there is still some peripheral argument about the possible influence of gnostic* categories, for example, most recent discussion has focused on theological concerns over whether the church* made an appropriate contextualization of its original faith in Jesus when it adopted the Son of God terminology. Was the notion of divine sonship alien to the teaching of Jesus and the beliefs of the first disciples, or did it make explicit in the context of Hellenistic culture what was already implicit in the Jewish culture within which the church originated?

1. Jewish Background
2. The Title and Its Development
3. Method

1. Jewish Background.
The generic term "son of God" had a wide currency in ancient culture. It could as easily be applied to the heroes of traditional Greek mythology (often referred to as sons of Zeus) as to Egyptian pharaohs or Roman emperors.*

Within Jewish culture the term was applied to Israel itself (Ex 4:22; Jer 31:9; Hos 11:1; Wis 9:7; 18:13; *Jub.* 1:24-25; *Pss. Sol.* 17:30), to leading individuals in the nation (Deut 14:1; Is 1:2; 43:6; Jer 3:22; 31:9; Hos 1:10; Wis 2:13-18; 5:5; 12:21; 16:10, 26; 18:4; Sir 4:10; 51:10; *Pss. Sol.* 13:8-9; 18:4; 2 Macc 7:34; Philo *Conf. Ling.* 145-47; Philo *Spec. Leg.* 1.318), to angels* and other heavenly beings (Gen 6:2-4; Deut 32:8; Job 1:6-12; 2:1-6; 38:7; Ps 29:1; 89:6; Dan 3:25; *1 Enoch* 13:8, 106:5), to the king (2 Sam 7:14; 1 Chron 17:13; 22:10, 28:6; Ps 2:7; 89:26-27; 4Q174; 4Q246; cf. Philo *Som.* 1.215; Philo *Conf. Ling.* 146), to the Messiah (2 Esdr 7:28; 13:32, 37, 52; 14:9 may be later Christian interpolations; 1QSa 2:11-12; 4QFlor 1:10-13; 4QPsDan A) and later to individual rabbis (*m. Taan.* 3:8; *b. Taan.* 24). It did not, however, denote a divine figure descending from heaven* as the bearer of salvation, except insofar as angels were messengers or agents of God or Philo's application of it to the divine logos could be so understood. On the contrary, when the status "son of God" was conferred on someone it was a recognition of a particular achievement. We therefore need to allow the literature itself to define the nature and scope of the term's meaning for early Christians.

2. The Title and Its Development.
2.1. General. Within the literature consid-

ered in this volume "Son of God" is absent from James* and the *Epistle of Polycarp*, while 1 Peter 1:3 and Jude 1 describe God as Jesus' Father (but without corresponding imagery of "son"; *see* 1 Peter; Jude). The *Martyrdom of Polycarp** has only a peripheral reference as part of a confessional formula (*Mart. Pol.* 17, with a similar statement in the Moscow manuscript of *Mart. Pol.* 22), and Revelation 2:18 is similar. The *Didache** likewise uses it as part of a formalized confession of faith (*Did.* 7.3), though *Didache* 16.4 testifies to continued currency of a more general understanding of the term not necessarily connected to Jesus.

2.2. Son of God as Functional Eschatological Image. Acts* uses "father" to describe God's* relationship with Jesus (Acts 1:4, 7), but "Son of God" is not among the many christological titles in the early chapters (unless Acts 8:37 is accepted as genuine, against the best manuscripts). It first appears in Paul's postbaptismal message (Acts 9:20) as a synonym for "Messiah" (Acts 9:22; cf. Acts 17:4; 18:5; 24:24). Acts 13:33, however, contains a typical eschatological* use of the term, in which Jesus' status as Son of God is conferred as a result of the resurrection,* in much the same way as are the titles *Lord** and *Messiah* (Acts 2:36). This usage is widespread throughout the earlier NT, usually associated (as here; see also 2 Pet 1:16-18) with a reference to Psalm 2:7, which celebrates the status of the king as God's adopted son.* There is an implied connection with belief in Jesus as Davidic king and Messiah, though understood in the functional sense that if Jesus was Messiah, then such imagery could appropriately be applied to him. There is no suggestion that Jesus was intrinsically related to God apart from his accomplishment as eschatological Messiah and not a hint of later notions such as preexistence.*

2.3. Son of God from Functional Savior to Incarnational Idea.
2.3.1. Hebrews. Hebrews* represents an important transition from early images of sonship to later metaphysical beliefs. Jesus as Son of God is a key theme and a basic confession of faith* (Heb 4:14). "Sonship" can be almost synonymous with the perfection and totality of salvation* (Heb 4:14—5:9; 6:6; 7:3, 28; 8—9), rooted in the assumption that Jesus achieved this status through suffering* and resurrection (Heb 5:8; 6:6; 10:29) and with the language of divine begetting (Ps 2) providing the frame of refer-

ence. However, other passages go well beyond this, identifying the Son as the agent of creation,* sharing God's own nature in language that is clearly related to philosophical categories applied elsewhere to the divine logos* (Heb 1:2-4). In Hebrews 3:2-6 Jesus is "appointed" (like Moses*), but as the Son he has a greater ontological (as distinct from functional) significance, a contrast that occurs again when Jesus' priesthood* is compared to that of Melchizedek.* While being "Son of God" is the typological fulfillment of Melchizedek's priesthood, this status also identifies Jesus with a preexisting ideal type, which explains why he is of greater significance than Melchizedek (Heb 5:6; 7:13, 15-17).

Little is known for certain about the background to Hebrews, but the author is clearly searching for relevant philosophical categories as a vehicle for Christian belief; hence the occurrence of a more obviously incarnational Son of God christology. At the same time Hebrews preserves the language of adoption while making no attempt to combine the two: they stand together in an unintegrated symbiosis. Jesus as Son is the heavenly (ideal world) archetype in comparison with which other (this world) claims are inadequate. As the church moved into a Hellenistic milieu with a Platonic worldview, it was natural for Jesus' eschatological significance to be described in these terms. For Hebrews, however, the starting point is the Platonic worldview, not reflection on the significance of Jesus per se. This fact explains why there is no concept of the personal preexistence of the Son who is Jesus but only the abstract theological idea of preexistence, which then demands explanation by reference to the more traditional category of sonship through adoption or achievement. Again, later concerns about ontological or metaphysical substance do not occur. In this sense Hebrews appears to represent a midpoint between the Christ event and its explanation in purely OT categories and the later development of a fully fledged, incarnational christology.

2.3.2. 1 Clement. *1 Clement* does not use the full term "Son of God," though like Hebrews it compares the Son with priests and angels (*1 Clem.* 36). Unlike Hebrews, it does not elaborate this in terms of preexistence but refers to Psalm 2 and the theme of divine begetting. The *Epistle of Barnabas** links preexistence more directly to

incarnation (*Barn.* 5.11) though still emphasizing Jesus' death and resurrection as key functional elements in his status as Son (*Barn.* 12.9; 15.5). But whereas Hebrews adopts the metaphysical language of sonship without personal reference to Jesus, *Barnabas* extrapolates the functional language of adoption from its personalized context in the story of Jesus' resurrection in such a way that the historical reality effectively becomes a theological abstraction (*Barn.* 6). *Barnabas* thereby takes the reformulation of the older understanding a stage nearer the point where it could be completely expressed in philosophical categories.

2.3.3. Johannine Literature. In the Johannine literature Son of God language is central. It defines the purpose of the Fourth Gospel (Jn 20:31) and is even more prominent in 1 John (it does not appear in 2-3 Jn, though 2 Jn 3, 9 use Father/Son imagery of Jesus and God; *see* John, Letters of). There is still a clear connection between Jesus' status as Son and his death and resurrection (1 Jn 1:7; 3:8; 4:10).

As in Hebrews, belief in Jesus as Son appears as the functional equivalent of a dependable salvation (1 Jn 5:18-21). But there is in addition a more cognitive, theological content to such belief, which serves to distinguish truth* from error (1 Jn 2:22-27; 3:23; 4:2, 9-12; 4:14-15; 5:5, 9-12). This entails metaphysical propositions, including belief that God and the Son are one and that the Son as a human being came from heaven. John's Jesus is Son of God not primarily because of his exaltation* or even as a by-product of the application of Platonic terminology to his functional importance but because he always had a personal existence with God that was of the same quality and purpose in this preexistence in heaven as it was during his lifetime on earth. This understanding probably emerged not from John's intrinsic concept of sonship but from a combination of that with the logos Christology that also features strongly in this literature. This association of preexistence with sonship goes further than does Hebrews, though 1 John still shows no interest in speculation about the precise ontological relationship between Jesus and God (yet the prologue, 1 Jn 1:1-4, comes near to that) and therefore never asks what oneness between Father and Son might mean.

2.3.4. The Epistle to Diognetus. The *Epistle to Diognetus** quotes from the Johannine literature in this connection with extensive considerations of the Son as preexistent agent of both creation and redemption* (*Diogn.* 8—11), though all these themes are expounded through the concept of the eternal logos rather than from an understanding of sonship itself. *Diognetus* 7 highlights the continued significance of the functional understanding of sonship related to OT themes of the king as son in his capacity as God's personal representative.

2.4. Toward Pragmatic Metaphysics.

2.4.1. Ignatius of Antioch. Ignatius* provides several examples of creedal statements incorporating Son of God terminology (Ign. *Eph.* 2; 4; 20; Ign. *Magn.* 1; 3). But the most significant passages are occasioned by his opposition to a docetic* christology not too different from that evidenced in 1 John (compare 1 Jn 4:21; 5:6 with Ign. *Magn.* 1.2; Ign. *Smyrn.* 1—3; 5.2). In counteracting, this Ignatius not only unhesitatingly uses Son of God terminology but also directly applies the epithet *God* to Jesus, in six instances quite explicitly (Ign. *Eph.* presc; Ign. *Eph.* 18.2; Ign. *Rom.* presc.; Ign. *Rom.* 3.3; Ign. *Smyrn.* 1.1; Ign. *Pol.* 8.9) and in others by implication (Ign. *Eph.* 1.1; 7.2; 15.3; 19.3).

Ignatius's primary focus, however, is not in relation to Christ's preexistence but in the opposite direction, in regard to the incarnation. His main concern was to affirm that Jesus was truly human while at the same time maintaining his divinity without raising later ontological questions as to how the two might be related. In this respect Ignatius goes little further than the same terminology used in the Fourth Gospel (Jn 20:28). At the same time he shows a clear awareness of some of the problems involved in relating the god of the philosophers (remote, nonmaterial, all-powerful) to the God incarnated in Jesus, even if he engages with them only tangentially as he discusses the relationship between the virginal conception of Jesus and Incarnation (Ign. *Eph.* 18.2) or by adopting Son of God language to distinguish Jesus' divinity from his human nature.

Ignatius's main concern was essentially practical and polemical. It is less important for him to explain the unity of Father and Son than it is to state it, in opposition to Docetism on the one hand and as the foundational principle of church unity on the other (Ign. *Eph.* 3.2; 5.1; Ign. *Magn.* 7.1-2; Ign. *Smyrn.* 3.3; 8.1; Ign. *Phld.* 7.2). In doing this he clearly builds on earlier

NT statements (compare, e.g., Ign. *Eph.* 7.2 with Jn 1; Ign. *Trall.* 9.1-2 with 1 Cor 15), though he extends them so as to address the needs of the churches in his day.

2.4.2. Shepherd of Hermas. In all this literature the *Shepherd of Hermas* reflects the most fully developed Son of God christology. There is only one passing reference to divine sonship in the *Visions* (*Herm. Vis.* 2.2), but *Similitude* 9 displays an increasingly close identification between different aspects of the Godhead, in which preexistence and incarnation are two sides of the one coin. Some scholars detect adoptionism in *Hermas Similitude* 5.2, 5-6 and in *Hermas Similitude* 8.3, 11. Consequently they dismiss *Similitude* 9 as a later interpolation, but that assumes a more integrated approach to christology than is necessary for this period. *Hermas Similitude* 9 shows a growing concern to define the functions of Father, Son and Spirit not in relation to the historical circumstances of Jesus of Nazareth but ontologically in relation to all that might be encompassed by the notion of God. So while the Son and the Father are the same in terms of being (including preexistence and involvement in creation), it is God who is surrounded by angelic majesty while the Son is the gate through which humanity can gain access to God. Likewise a distinction is made between thirty-five believers who are prophets* and ministers of God and another forty who are apostles* and teachers of the preaching of the Son of God (*Herm. Sim.* 9.15). There is still a long way to go from these statements to the more complex formulations embodied in the classic creeds, but *Hermas* foreshadows most of the raw materials from which the creeds were constructed.

3. Method.

A key consideration in all discussion of christology at this period is the need to avoid imposing later categories of thought. For example, by later standards the earliest understanding of Jesus as Son of God, based on Psalm 2, might well look like adoptionism, though in its context it was the opposite: not a denial of preexistent sonship but an affirmation of Jesus' actual status as Son. Similarly, preexistence never occurred to anyone until some denied it or the need emerged to justify Christian belief in philosophical categories. While earlier writers fail to affirm it, that does not mean they were denying it, and terms like kenoticism are inappropriately applied to them. During this period there was a gradual universalization of what were originally specific images as the articulation of theology moved from concern with the faith journeys of particular people to an effort to understand things in some absolute sense. As part of that process relational and functional statements about Jesus as Son of God were gradually displaced by metaphysical and ontological statements about the essence of God and Jesus as part of that.

See also CHRISTOLOGY; GOD; SONSHIP, CHILD, CHILDREN.

BIBLIOGRAPHY. O. Cullmann, *The Christology of the New Testament* (London: SCM, 1963); C. J. Davis, *The Name and Way of the Lord: Old Testament Themes, New Testament Christology* (JSNTSup 129; Sheffield: Sheffield Academic Press, 1996); J. D. G. Dunn, *Christology in the Making* (London: SCM, 1989); F. Hahn, *The Titles of Jesus in Christology* (London: Lutterworth, 1969); J. A. Grassi, "From Jesus of Nazareth to Christ, the Son of God," *Bible Today* 61 (1972) 826-34; M. Hengel, *The Son of God* (London: SCM, 1976); J. Hick, ed., *The Myth of God Incarnate* (London: SCM, 1977); P. E. Hughes, "The Christology of Hebrews," *SWJT* 28 (1985) 19-27; J. Knox, *The Humanity and Divinity of Christ* (Cambridge: Cambridge University Press, 1967); W. Kramer, *Christ, Lord, Son of God* (London: SCM, 1966); J. T. Lienhard, "The Christology of the Epistle to Diognetus," *VC* 24 (1970) 280-89; H. L. MacNeill, *The Christology of the Epistle to the Hebrews* (Chicago: University of Chicago Press, 1914); J. Macquarrie, *Jesus Christ in Modern Thought* (London: SCM, 1990); P. S. Minear, "The Idea of Incarnation in 1 John," *Int* 24 (1970) 291-302; E. Schweizer, "Variety and Unity in the New Testament proclamation of Jesus as the Son of God," *AusBR* 15 (1967) 1-12; D. Trakatellis, "God Language in Ignatius of Antioch," in *The Future of Early Christianity*, ed. B. A. Pearson (Minneapolis: Fortress, 1991) 422-32.

J. W. Drane

SONGS. *See* HYMNS, SONGS.

SONSHIP, CHILD, CHILDREN

The terminology of childhood features with remarkable infrequency in the NT (*see DJG*, Child, Children) and is not mentioned at all in most of the literature surveyed here. Where it

occurs the motif has three dominant usages.

1. Childhood as an Image of Growth
2. Childhood as a Theological Image
3. Children in the Christian Community

1. Childhood as an Image of Growth.

Modern understandings of childhood date from the Renaissance. For the Romans being a child was merely the necessary means to becoming adult (which was at an early age: girls might marry at twelve, boys typically at fourteen). Children were defined by reference to their function in the household* and so provided an appropriate image to apply to Christians, both in relation to God and to one another. As raw materials in process of formation, children were immature and undeveloped (cf. Plato *Leg.* 808D, E). Childhood could be synonymous with childishness, a fitting image for spiritual immaturity (Jas 1:6; Heb 5:13; 1 Pet 2:2-3).

Some scholars have seen the background for such terminology in the mystery religions (*see* Religions, Greco-Roman), with their notion of spiritual progression through various cultic rituals. Though some aspects of these texts can be understood in this context (e.g., the theme of milk* and solid food: Heb 5:12-14; 1 Pet 2:2; cf. *Barn.* 6.17), the notion of stages of faith was already present in some of the most distinctive teaching of Jesus, and ordinary family relationships provide a more plausible background here.

There is also a more positive use of the image. Christians could be addressed as "(little) children" (1 Jn 2:1, 12, 14, 18, 28; 3:7, 18; 4:4; 5:21; 2 Jn 1; 4; 13; 3 Jn 4; *Barn.* 7.1; 9.2; *Did.* 3.1; *1 Clem.* 22.1; *Herm. Vis.* 3.9.1), evoking teacher/pupil or parent/child relationships (cf. Sir 3:1; 4:1) and emphasizing the role of the child as a symbol of the future. The description suggests the focus for hope through whom the community's wider values would be perpetuated (cf. Rev 12:2). When it is used in this way the metaphor also heightens the significance of the message itself, in much the same way as a child's presence in the family underlined the importance of internalizing and living out the inherited tradition.

2. Childhood as a Theological Image.

The same image can also be applied as a theological metaphor of some substance to describe the Christian's relationship to God.* Here the focus is not on childhood but on the nature of Jesus as Son of God* and on believers as sharing in that. A major theme of 1 John is that because of Jesus' status as divine son *(hyios)*, Christians become "children of God" *(tekna)*. Paul used similar concepts (Gal 4:5; Rom 8:15, 23; Eph 1:5), though there are important differences. Paul applied the word *hyios* to describe the status of Christian believers as well as Jesus' own filial relationship to God *(see DPL*, Son of God). He also wrote of the "adoption" *(hyiothesia)* of Christians, just as Hebrews 2:10-12 depicts Jesus the Son as the firstborn in the eschatological* family of God, conferring the status of siblings on Christian believers *(see DPL*, Adoption, Sonship).

In 1 John, however (compare 1 Pet 1:3, 23), Christians are God's children by birth (cf. Heb 12:5-11). No doubt this reflects the more developed Johannine christology* as well as the particular circumstances addressed *(see* John, Letters of). Being children of God is not merely a metaphor for having a relationship with God (as it seems to be in Rev 21:7; *Herm. Sim.* 9.12; *Barn.* 6.11); it is a statement about the ontological nature of believers. The precise point at which they achieve this new birth* is never spelled out, though 1 John 5:6-8 may imply a baptismal context. 1 Peter 1:3, 23 use similar language about being born, though without explicitly including the imagery of childhood, and that certainly seems to be against the background of baptism.*

This concept leads to some unresolved tensions in 1 John. On the one hand children of God cannot sin, because God's nature is in them, and they are qualitatively different from "children of the devil" (1 Jn 3:8-10), for they belong to a place where sin is powerless (1 Jn 5:18). On the other hand the reality is that they do habitually sin (1 Jn 2:1; 5:16) and need constant encouragement to behave in accordance with their true nature. Though there is a hint of some eschatological tension, with Christians apparently awaiting the full outworking of the consequences of their being children of God (1 Jn 3:2), the ethical* questions raised by this perspective are not addressed directly (a contrast with Paul, whose imagery of a final adoption at the resurrection* ultimately leads to a more integrated theological outcome).

Other matters that gave rise to later debate are similarly left hanging in midair. For example, do people begin from a kind of neutral position and then choose to become children either of God or of the devil, or do they begin as children of the devil and remain so until they choose to become children of God? Nor is it obvious where we might helpfully locate any background to the Johannine use of this imagery. R. Bultmann's notion that there was some dualistic gnostic* influence here is hard to sustain in view of John's clear preference of an ethical dualism over against a material distinction (also found in Ign. *Phld.* 2.1). It is tempting to locate the origin of the imagery in those OT passages where sonship is a consequence of one's status within the covenant* people (e.g., Ex 4:22; Deut 32:5-6; Wis 12:19-20), but the dualistic contrast between children of God and children of the devil has no place there.

Qumran* might provide such a contrast (1QS 3:19—4:26), but unlike 1 John that is firmly within a covenantal context and provides no scope for the notion of divine begetting or new birth. The one thing that seems clear is that Jesus' relationship to God as Son is somehow to be shared with believers (1 Jn 2:24; 4:15; 5:20), though there is never complete identification since Jesus is the "only begotten" and "unique" son (1 Jn 4:9; cf. 1 Jn 3:1, 10), a distinction further underlined by the careful differentiation of *hyios* from *teknon*. One obvious place to look for further enlightenment would be Psalm 2:7, which was widely used in the early church* to explain Jesus' status as divine son. But unlike other writers, the author of 1 John makes no explicit reference to that passage, nor does he specifically say that Jesus' sonship is to be taken as a model for explaining the standing of disciples.

3. Children in the Christian Community.

The earliest Christian communities were based in the Roman household, and the place of children in the church was determined by their place in this wider social context. In this respect they were no different from women and men. Though there are few specific references to the role of children, Acts 2:39 gives theological legitimation to their inclusion in the church, while Acts 21:5 documents their presence and involvement. In general they were assumed to be part of the household of faith* (Ign. *Pol.* 8.2), sufficiently important that they could be singled out as a separate group (Ign. *Smyrn.* 13.1). The rejection of such common practices as abortion, sexual abuse and infanticide suggests they were valued in their own right (*Barn.* 19.5; 20.2; *Did.* 2:2; cf. *Did.* 5.2).

The most significant references to children are contained in the so-called *Haustafeln,* or household codes,* found in several places in the literature (1 Pet 2:18—3:7; *Did.* 4.9-11; *Barn.* 19.5-7; *1 Clem.* 21.6-9; Ign. *Pol.* 4.1—5.2; Pol. *Phil.* 4.2-3). These codes reflect concerns for the ordering and stability of society that were shared by Christians and non-Christians. They have often been perceived as the ultimate expressions of patriarchy and obviously originated in and reflect the concerns of a patriarchal culture (children are the responsibility of their fathers, as wives are the responsibility of their husbands). But the Christian codes reflect a more complex understanding than this. A purely patriarchal culture would have addressed only men, masters, fathers and husbands, whereas these lists (most of them quotations from or variations on Col 3:18—4:1) include instructions for children, slaves* and women,* suggesting they were accepted as equal members of the community. On this basis it has been argued that these codes were drawn up to affirm that Christian faith did not undermine family loyalties or social stability—and underlying this concern was a certain tension between the more open relationships of the church and what was culturally acceptable in the household in the wider culture.

Infant baptism had not yet developed within this period, though some passages imply that children had their own place within the regular catechetical programs of the church (*1 Clem.* 21.7; *Herm. Sim.* 7.6), albeit generally on the same terms as adult converts rather than in a context of a theology of childhood (e.g., *Herm. Vis.* 1.3.2). It would be some time before children, as children, found full acceptance in the life of the church, but already the seeds of radical change can be traced here, giving some hint of the direction in which theological reflection on personhood would later develop.

See also HOUSEHOLD CODES; HOUSEHOLD, FAMILY; MILK, SOLID FOOD; SON OF GOD.

BIBLIOGRAPHY. S. C. Barton, ed., *The Family in Theological Perspective* (Edinburgh: T & T Clark, 1996); J. Francis, " 'Like Newborn Babes'—The Image of the Child in 1 Peter 2:2-3," *Studia Biblica* 3 (1978) 111-17; C. J. A. Hickling, "John

and Hebrews: The Background of Hebrews 2:10-18," *NTS* 29 (1983) 112-16; J. M. Lieu, "Authority to Become Children of God," *NovT* 23 (1981) 210-28; B. Rawson, ed., *The Family in Ancient Rome* (Ithaca, NY: Cornell University Press, 1986); T. Wiedemann, *Adults and Children in the Roman Empire* (London: Routledge, 1989).

J. W. Drane

SOUL. *See* PSYCHOLOGY.

SPEAKING IN TONGUES. *See* TONGUES.

SPEECHES OF ACTS. *See* ACTS OF THE APOSTLES.

SPIRITS

The plural form "spirits" (Gk *pneumata*) is used in Acts and the General Epistles in ways mostly identical to its use in the Gospels and the Pauline literature. It may designate angels,* demonic spirits, human spirits, winds or the Holy Spirit.* All of these uses have their antecedents in OT and Second Temple Jewish literature. The designation *spirits (pneumata)* for evil supernatural beings is a usage not native to Greek, which favors *daimon* or *daimonion,* but has been imported from Jewish and Christian literature under the influence of the use of Hebrew *rûaḥ* (Paige, 198-220). "Spirit" (*rûaḥ* or *pneuma*) is increasingly used in later Jewish writing for angels or demons (usually in the plural) at Qumran* and in rabbinic and apocalyptic* literature (Sekki, chap. 5; Foerster, 13; Sjöberg, 375-76). Hence the reference to "evil spirits" and especially "unclean spirits" (Acts 5:1; 8:7; Rev 16:13, where the phrase is equated with "demonic spirits," *pneumata daimoniōn;* Rev 16:14; 18:2) clearly shows a Jewish Christian influence.

1. Acts
2. Hebrews
3. 1 Peter 3:19-20
4. 1 John
5. Revelation
6. Early Patristic Literature

1. Acts.
In Acts* we hear of the apostles,* in particular Peter, gaining such a reputation for healing* that people would bring those who were sick and afflicted with "unclean spirits" and lay them in the streets where they knew Peter would pass (Acts 5:15-16). Clearly this power over sickness

and supernatural evil echoes Jesus' healing ministry* (cf. Mk 6:56; Lk 6:17-18). Those who seek the apostle to exorcise these evil spirits are implicitly contrasted to Ananias, who also is said to be "filled" with Satan's* influence but yields to it and lies to the apostles (Acts 5:3-4). Ananias dies at God's* hand, while the demon-possessed seekers are healed.

In Acts 8:4-13 Philip* proclaims the gospel and performs "signs" (Acts 8:6, 13), including the exorcism of "unclean spirits" (Acts 8:7) and healings. His ministry echoes Peter's and Jesus' earlier ministries (cf. Mk 1:26; Lk 4:33). This power over evil spirits is a sign that God's presence is active in and with the proclamation of the gospel and that the kingdom of God has already begun to arrive (see Kingdom of God). The authentic, astounding power over the supernatural that Philip displays is contrasted with the pathetic chicanery of the self-proclaimed "Great Power," Simon (Acts 8:9-12).

In Acts 19 Paul is also shown as one who heals and exorcises evil spirits (Acts 19:11-12). As in Acts 8, authentic spiritual power is contrasted with the false. The sons of Sceva are Jewish exorcists who attempt to cash in on Paul's success, using "Jesus" as a magical name and throwing "Paul" in for good measure (Acts 19:13). But when they are confronted with the power of evil, they discover their magic formula is useless and are roughly assaulted by a demon-possessed man (Acts 19:16). The only security against such evil forces is repentance* and faith* in the Jesus who saves and delivers from the power of darkness (see Light). The magical* papyri confirm that pagans and Jews attempted to use the name* of Jesus, along with variations of the divine name YHWH and other Jewish terms (the ancestors' names, "sabaoth," e.g., *PGM* 4.3007-86, an exorcism spell that includes a reference to "the god of the Hebrews, Jesus").

It is thought by some scholars that the presentation of Paul as a miracle worker is the romantic fiction of a later age (see Jervell). Although Paul is reluctant to speak of any achievements in this regard, his own letters clearly state that the Spirit's "power" was at work in his evangelism (1 Thess 1:5; 1 Cor 2:4-5) and that "signs and wonders"* were performed through him (Rom 15:19; 2 Cor 12:12).

2. Hebrews.

In Hebrews* *pneumata* may stand for "winds" in a citation of Psalm 104:4 (Ps 103:4 LXX; Heb 1:7), for angels as "ministering spirits" (Heb 1:14) or for human "spirits of just people who have been made perfect" (Heb 12:23). Whose spirits these are is debated: whether they are of old covenant* or new covenant saints, and whether they include the living. It is probably best to take them as all the redeemed of all ages, who because of the new covenant can together participate in the ultimate worship* of God in heaven* (Heb 12:22-24; cf. Heb 11:40), either including the living (Dumbrell) or perhaps referring only to "the godly dead" of all ages, for this is the meaning of the expression "spirits of righteous persons" in Jewish apocalyptic literature (Lane, 2:470).

The significance of the title "Father of Spirits" (Heb 12:9) is also disputed. In the context the writer is comparing earthly fathers and the discipline of their children to God as Father (see Sonship), whose discipline may involve suffering.* Just as we give respect and obedience* to earthly parents, so all the more we owe this to God, who is worthy of it and who only has our good in mind, sharing his holiness* (Heb 12:10). P. E. Hughes suggested the title refers to God as "heavenly" Father, contrasted with "earthly" fathers. But even better is to take the term *spirits* as used at Hebrews 1:14 for angelic beings, in which case the term signifies God's majesty as ruler over the angelic armies of heaven, the supernatural world. This interpretation is supported by the parallel idea found in Numbers 16:22 (LXX) and Numbers 27:16 (LXX), where God is called "the God of spirits and of all flesh" (cf. 2 Macc 3:24). And M. Black has shown that the title "Father of spirits" in the Ethiopic translation of *1 Enoch* may be a paraphrase for the Hebrew title "the Lord of hosts," God as the commander of angelic armies. These texts reflect a traditional title known to early Christians and used in Hebrews.

3. 1 Peter 3:19-20.

There are three major questions here: Who are the "spirits" to whom Christ preached? What and where is the "prison"? And when did this happen? The context states that these spirits had "disobeyed" in the days of Noah (1 Pet 3:20), though it does not say that those were the days when Christ* preached (as if through Noah). The creedal statement of the preceding verse (1 Pet 3:18) sets the relative time for this "preaching": after Easter. Hence Jesus did not descend into hell* while in the grave. Neither does it make much sense in the context of Peter's exhortation to the church* if we interpret this of Jesus preaching to Noah's generation in hell. Furthermore, "spirits" in the Septuagint and apocryphal* literature usually refers to supernatural beings rather than human souls, especially when it is used without a qualifier such as "spirits of men" (Selwyn, 198-99; Kelly, 154).

This leaves the possibility that "spirits" refers to fallen angels, the "sons of God" of Genesis 6:1-4, which Jewish tradition held responsible for the wickedness that led to the flood (cf. Gen 6:5). These spirits who mated with humans were held to be a source of pagan idolatry* and continuing malevolent influence (Reicke, 109-11). J. R. Michaels prefers to connect these spirits to the "giants" (Gen 6:4) that Jewish tradition believed had become the evil spirits who trouble humanity and whom Jesus opposed during his ministry (Michaels, 207-8). But this requires a questionable interpretation of the word *prison* (Gk *phylakē*) as being the "sanctuary" of planet earth. There is a tradition in the apocryphal literature that the fallen angels were imprisoned by God (esp. in *1-2 Enoch;* cf. 2 Pet 2:4; Jude 6), and several times its location is above the earth, in some quarter of the heavens.

Further, the verb for "preaching" in 1 Peter 3:19 can also have the neutral sense of "proclaim." Therefore the reference may be to an event that occurred after or during Christ's ascent to the Father's throne, when Jesus "proclaimed" his victory to these who are the archetype of sin's rebelliousness and the source of paganism's evil orientation. If this is the case, then we do have an immediate link with Peter's exhortation to his readers to continue patiently living out their witness to Christ in the face of opposition. Peter says those who oppose the gospel have "disobeyed" (1 Pet 2:7-8; 3:1), following the pattern of the fallen angels (1 Pet 3:20). Just as Christ did not hesitate to proclaim his cosmic victory even to these archsinners, so Peter's readers may be emboldened to "give an answer to everyone who asks [them]" (1 Pet 3:15), and they may be consoled with the thought that those who now torment them and refuse to repent will share the fate of those "spirits in prison."

4. 1 John.
1 John 4:1-3 urges the readers to "test the spirits" and provides criteria by which this is to be done. The question is, Does "spirits" stand for the human spirits of prophets*; a multiplicity of spirit beings, good and evil; the one Spirit of God versus evil spirits; or spirit-inspired utterances?

The "because" (Gk *hoti*) of 1 John 4:1 shows the testing of spirits is necessary due to the activity of "false prophets" who have gone out "into the world." The false prophets are not activated by or informed by God's Spirit. They are the "antichrists" of 1 John 2:18-19 (cf. 2 Jn 7), the false prophets whom Jesus warned would arise (Mt 24:11). If they are listened to, they will lead God's people astray. Nowhere else in the NT does the term *spirits,* without qualification, refer to people; and the idea is common to all religious groups in the first century that supernatural beings may accompany, inspire and lead people (cf. the "Spirit of Truth" and "Spirit of falsehood" at Qumran, 1QS 4). So John refers in 1 John 4:1 to supernatural entities accompanying "prophets" and inspiring their messages. There is only one good Spirit for John, the Holy Spirit,* though many evil spirits may exist (Brown, 486, 491-92).

Some passages in 1 Corinthians could be read to suggest that for Paul the line between human and divine spirits could be blurred: so G. D. Fee understands that "my spirit" and "in spirit" in 1 Corinthians 14:14, 15 refer to both kinds of spirit simultaneously. Such an understanding might also be suggested for 1 John 4:1-3 by the references to the "confession" of "every spirit" (every human spirit of a prophet leaves telltale evidence of how it is inspired). But in light of 1 John 4:1, that the testing is whether the spirits are "from God" and considering that it would be odd to refer to the person of the prophets this way (their spirit being sent from God), it is better to understand the references to "every spirit" as vividly individualizing encounters with prophets. Though there is ultimately only one good spirit, the force of the expression (1 Jn 4:2-3) is, "every time you encounter a 'spirit' speaking through a prophet which agrees with the truth that Jesus Christ has come in the flesh, know that it is from God."

How does one test a "spirit"? Indirectly, by means of what effect it has on people's conception of Jesus and God (as here, 1 Jn 4:1-3) and by observing how it affects behavior (the test of love, 1 Jn 4:7-21). In the OT also an important test of a prophet was what he said about God (Deut 13:1-5; 18:15-22). There are false prophets or teachers who travel from one Christian community to another, living off their offerings and claiming to present a message from the Spirit (2 Jn 7-11). Perhaps for fear of committing the "blasphemy against the Holy Spirit," Christians were loath to publicly question or criticize a prophet. This attitude is illustrated in the *Didache:* "Do not put to the test, nor try to exercise judgment on any prophet speaking 'in Spirit,' 'for every sin will be forgiven, but this sin will not be forgiven.' But not everyone speaking 'in Spirit' is a prophet, unless that person has the behavior of the Lord. So you will know the false prophet and the true prophet by their lives." Even though the author of the *Didache** is aware that the "spirit" speaking through a prophet may not be the Holy Spirit, he cautions his readers not to challenge a prophet.

A similar reverence about enthusiastic spiritual manifestations in the Johannine community may have left them open to deception. In support of this the opening command of 1 John 4:1 could be translated "Stop putting your faith in every 'spirit' [that speaks through a prophet]!"—suggesting the community was already vulnerable to hypocritical swindlers.

5. Revelation.

In Revelation (*see* Revelation, Book of) the "seven spirits of God" make up four of the seven occurrences of *pneumata* (Rev 1:4; 3:1; 4:5; 5:6). Some scholars have suggested the phrase has reference to the famous seven archangels who serve God (Tob 12:15; *1 Enoch* 20:1-8; cf. Rev 8:2). Although "spirits" can stand for angels, the structure of Revelation 1:4 appears trinitarian: greetings from "him who is, and who was, and who is to come [God]," from "the seven spirits before his throne" and from Jesus Christ. In Revelation 3:1 the "seven spirits" are distinguished from angels (the "seven stars," cf. Rev 1:20).

In John's vision* of God's throne (Rev 4, echoing Isaiah's call, Is 6), the seven spirits are again pictured before God's throne, symbolized by seven lamps (Rev 4:5). The spirits are grouped with other manifestations of the theophany proper (lightning and thunder); signifi-

cantly the seven spirits are never said to join in the adoration of God by this court (Rev 4:8, 9-11).

In the final occurrence the seven spirits are pictured as members of the Lamb* of God, who shares God's awesome throne: "Then I saw a Lamb . . . standing in the center of the throne. . . . He had seven horns and seven eyes, which are the seven spirits of God sent out into all the earth" (Rev 5:6). All of these suggest that the "seven spirits" are another way of speaking of the Holy Spirit. The language and imagery are most likely influenced by Zechariah, who in one of his visions sees a gold lampstand with seven lights, representing "the eyes of the Lord, which range throughout the earth" (Zech 4:4, 10; cf. Rev 5:6). The number seven suggests completeness, "the Holy Spirit in his fullness of life and blessing" (Beasley-Murray, 56). Older interpreters (including patristic interpreters) looked to Isaiah 11:2-3, where the Septuagint lists seven descriptions of the spirit that will rest upon the promised future ruler, each beginning with "a spirit of . . ." Few modern interpreters hold this to be the source for Revelation. And the message that God will establish his people and his plans "not by might nor by power but by my Spirit" (Zech 4:6) fits Revelation's emphasis on God's sovereignty in history despite the appearance of powerful worldly opposition.

Two other references in Revelation are to evil spirits, called "unclean" and "demonic" (Rev 16:13, 14), who are sent out to deceive world rulers and draw them into a battle that will result in their destruction by God (cf. the deceiving spirit who draws Ahab to his last battle, 1 Kings 22:21-22).

"The God of the Spirits of the prophets" (Rev 22:6) is part of the conclusion to Revelation, which echoes themes of the introduction, bracketing the whole in a declaration of its divine origin and emphasizing that it contains true prophecy. Revelation's link of this Spirit that works in the prophets' "spirits" to God on the one hand and Jesus on the other ensures that the reader understands that the true prophetic working of the Spirit is the presence of Christ in the world and bears witness to him (cf. Rev 19:10, "the testimony of Jesus is the spirit of prophecy"). Fee has suggested that a similar expression in 1 Corinthians 14:32 may be understood as a reference to the prophets' human spirits (plural) as energized and informed by the Spirit (singular) who indwells them. A similar suggestion was already made by H. B. Swete: "the natural faculties of the prophets, raised and quickened by the Holy Spirit" (*The Apocalypse of St. John* [3d ed., Grand Rapids: Eerdmans, 1908], 303).

6. Early Patristic Literature.

The plural "spirits" (*pneumata*) does not occur in the *Didache*, *2 Clement*, Polycarp's* *Letter to the Philippians*, the *Martyrdom of Polycarp*, the *Epistle to Diognetus* or the letters of Ignatius.*

6.1. 1 Clement. *1 Clement* cites Hebrews 1:7 once (*1 Clem.* 36.3) and uses *pneumata* three more times, at which places it seems to refer to human spirits (souls) but may also include divine beings. *1 Clement* 59.3 speaks of God as "the creator and overseer (*episkopon*) of every spirit." This text and *1 Clement* 64.1 speak of God's role in relation to both "spirits" and "all flesh." Does Clement (*see* Clement of Rome) mean to speak of both sides of human nature (perishable and imperishable or spiritual and material), or does he present God's activity in its totality, over the supernatural world ("spirits") and the natural world ("all flesh")? On balance the contexts seem to indicate references to human beings. *1 Clement* 59.3 echoes Numbers 16:22 in its statement that the Lord* is "the finder of spirits and the God of all flesh" (some variants read, "benefactor of spirits"). He is the One in control of human fate, the One who raises the humble and brings down the proud. *1 Clement* 64.1 is a prayer* for the readers: "May God, who watches over all, is master of spirits and Lord of all flesh . . . give faith, fear, peace, endurance and patience, self-control, holiness and sobriety to every soul that has called upon his glorious and holy name."

6.2. Barnabas. For the writer of the *Epistle of Barnabas** the two plural uses of "spirits" occur in references to his readers, who have "blessed and glorious spirits" that cause the writer to rejoice (*Barn.* 1.2; cf. *Barn.* 1.5, where "such spirits" = "you").

6.3. Shepherd of Hermas. The *Shepherd of Hermas** has by far the most references to "spirits" among the works of the apostolic fathers* (seventeen times). Five of these refer to the human spirits (souls) of his readers, which have been or will be renewed by God (*Herm. Vis.* 3. 8.9; 3.12.3; 3.13.2; *Herm. Sim.* 8.6.3). And he tells his readers how to spot false prophets, warning

them not be gullible about self-proclaimed spiritual men: "For if you pack wine or oil into a pantry, and you put an empty jar in with them, and then you want to unpack the pantry, that jar that you put in empty you will find still empty. In the same way also, whenever the 'empty' prophets come to the spirits of just men, they are discovered to be just whatever sort of people they were when they came" (*Herm. Man.* 11.1.15).

Hermas refers to evil spirits (*pneumata*) six times, though some of these are references to things such as quick temper (*Herm. Man.* 5.2.4-5, 7) and sorrow (*Herm. Man.* 10.1.2), which are "earthly spirits" (*Herm. Man.* 11.1.19) contrasted with the influence of the Holy Spirit. They seem to be more than mere literary personifications and (like Paul's use of "sin" in Rom 7) are thought of as active forces opposed to God and in league with Satan (cf. *Herm. Man.* 11.1.15). He also has one vision explained as symbolizing the fate of Christians who have sinned so as to be cast out of God's church: "after they entered in together and became one body, some of them defiled themselves and were cast out from the family of the righteous. . . . Those who have come to know God and have seen his great works, and [yet] continue to do evil, they will be punished doubly and will die forever" (*Herm. Sim.* 9.17.5; 9.18.2). These are "stones"* taken from the "tower" that represents the church and are "handed over to evil spirits and thrown out from there" (*Herm. Sim.* 9.18.3).

The most idiosyncratic of *Hermas's* uses of *pneumata* occurs in relation to the Spirit of God. At several places he refers to "virgins" in his vision who "are holy spirits; and a person cannot be found to be in the kingdom of God in any other way except by them putting their clothes on him" (*Herm. Sim.* 9.13.2; cf. *Herm. Sim.* 9.13. 5, 7). These "clothes" that the believer receives may refer to the Spirit as marking those who are saved (as Eph. 1:13-14) or perhaps also to the godly virtues* that the Spirit engenders (see below on *Herm Sim.* 9.15.2). Further, "these virgins are powers of the Son of God" (*Herm. Sim.* 9.13.2). Hence the saving and sanctifying presence of the Holy Spirit is pictured as a plurality of Spirits (of God), as the presence of the Son and metaphorically as "virgins" who are also identified elsewhere as virtues (reminiscent of Paul's fruit of the Spirit, Gal. 5:22): faith, temperance, power, patience, simplicity (or generosity, *haplotēs*), guilelessness, holiness, cheerfulness, truth, understanding, agreement and love (*Herm. Sim.* 9.15.2). J. Quasten holds that *Hermas* has a binitarian theology: God the Father and God the Holy Spirit, who can also be known as the Son of God (Quasten, 100). *Hermas's* use of a plurality of spirits to represent the one Holy Spirit is reminiscent of Revelation, from which he may have gathered inspiration for his unique usage.

6.4. Justin Martyr. In his first and second apologies Justin never uses the term *pneumata* of good or evil spirits; for the latter he uses *daimonia*. Only in his *Dialogue with Trypho* (directed to a Jew) does he use *pneumata* of evil spirits, and this is the only way the term is used there. In four of his five uses of the word, Justin describes the "spirits" as being "deceitful" (or some translations, "spirits of error," *pneumata tēs planēs, Dial. Tryph.* 7; 30; 35; 39; 76). The association of these "spirits" with untruth and mental influence is echoed in his reference to "the unclean spirit [singular] of the devil," which shoots things into people's minds (Justin *Dial. Tryph.* 82).

6.5. Irenaeus. Irenaeus can speak of evil spirits, also known as "deceiving spirits" (Irenaeus *Haer.* 1.9.5; 1.16.3; 2.6.2). Valentinian Gnostics* teach that from grief came the "spirits of wickedness," along with the devil, Cosmocrator, and every wicked spiritual being (Irenaeus *Haer.* 1.5.4). The heretics can command spirits, which are actually sent forth by Satan (Irenaeus *Haer.* 1.13.4); and the antichrist* will deceive the world by means of "demons and apostate spirits" (Irenaeus *Haer.* 5.28.2). Christians exorcise evil spirits even in Irenaeus's day in the name of Jesus, and in doing this along with other miracles they show the power and truth resident in the true church (Ireneaus *Haer.* 2.32.4). At *Adversus Haereses* 4.6.7 he writes that even "apostate spirits and demons" testify to Jesus' deity, referring to Jesus' exorcisms (compare Irenaeus *Haer.* 4.6.6).

The Gnostic elite believe when they rid themselves of their bodies and (lower) souls, they will become "intelligent spirits" and companions of angels (Irenaeus *Haer.* 1.7.1-2; 2.29.1). Human "spirits" will be included with body and soul at the resurrection* of the righteous (Irenaeus *Haer.* 2.33.4); souls and spirits (human or other?) are part of God's creation*

and may exist as long as God so wills it (Irenaeus *Haer.* 2.34.3). "Spiritual people" are human saints, not "incorporeal spirits" (Irenaeus *Haer.* 5.8.2). Two instances are citations: Hebrews 1.7 (Ps 104:4) at *Adversus Haereses* 2.30.1, describing angels; and Revelation 5:6 at *Adversus Haereses* 4.20.11, the vision of the lamb with "seven horns and seven eyes, which are the seven spirits of God."

See also ANGELS, HEAVENLY BEINGS, ANGEL CHRISTOLOGY; CHRISTOLOGY; GOD; HOLY SPIRIT; IDOLATRY; RELIGIONS, GRECO-ROMAN; SATAN, DEVIL.

BIBLIOGRAPHY. R. J. Bauckham, "The Role of the Spirit in the Apocalypse," *EvQ* 52 (1980) 66-83; G. R. Beasley-Murray, *The Book of Revelation* (NCB; London: Oliphants, 1974); M. Black, "Two Unusual Nomina Dei in the Second Vision of Enoch" in *The New Testament Age: Essays in Honor of Bo Reicke*, ed. W. C. Weinrich (Macon, GA: Mercer University Press, 1984) 53-59; R. E. Brown, *The Epistles of John* (AB; Garden City, NY: Doubleday, 1982); F. F. Bruce, "The Spirit in the Apocalypse" in *Christ and Spirit in the New Testament*, ed. B. Lindars and S. S. Smalley (Cambridge: Cambridge University Press, 1973) 333-44; R. Bultmann, *The Johannine Epistles* (Herm; Philadelphia: Fortress, 1973 [1967]); A. Deasley, "The Holy Spirit in the Dead Sea Scrolls," *WTJ* 21 (1986) 45-73; W. J. Dumbrell, "Spirits of Just Men Made Perfect," *EvQ* 48 (1976) 154-59; W. Foerster, "δαίμων κτλ," *TDNT* 2:1-20; P. E. Hughes, *A Commentary on the Epistle to the Hebrews* (Grand Rapids: Eerdmans, 1977); J. Jervell, "The Signs of an Apostle" in *The Unknown Paul* (Minneapolis: Augsburg, 1984) chap. 5; J. N. D. Kelly, *The Epistles of Peter and of Jude* (BNTC; London: A. & C. Black, 1969); W. L. Lane, *Hebrews* (2 vols.; WBC; Dallas: Word, 1991); J. Lawson, *A Theological and Historical Introduction to the Apostolic Fathers* (New York: Macmillan, 1961); I. H. Marshall, *The Epistles of John* (NICNT; Grand Rapids: Eerdmans, 1978); J. R. Michaels, *1 Peter* (WBC; Waco, TX: Word, 1988); R. H. Mounce, *The Book of Revelation* (NICNT; Grand Rapids: Eerdmans, 1977); T. Paige, "Spirit at Corinth: The Corinthian Concept of Spirit and Paul's Response as Seen in 1 Corinthians" (unpublished Ph.D. dissertation, University of Sheffield, 1994); J. Quasten, *Patrology*, 1: *The Beginnings of Patristic Literature* (Westminster, MD: Christian Classics, 1986 [1950]); B. Reicke, *The Epistles of James, Peter and*

Jude (AB; Garden City, NY: Doubleday, 1964); A. E. Sekki, *The Meaning of* Ruaḥ *at Qumran* (SBLDS 110; Atlanta: Scholars Press, 1989); E. Sjöberg, "πνεῦμα κτλ: Palestinian Judaism," *TDNT* 6:375-89; S. Smalley, *1, 2, 3 John* (WBC; Waco, TX: Word, 1984).   T. Paige

SPIRITUAL HOUSE. *See* HOUSE, SPIRITUAL HOUSE.

STEPHEN

Stephen, member of the Seven, evangelist and the first known Christian martyr, makes his appearance in the NT solely in the Acts of the Apostles (Acts 6:1—8:3). The Jerusalem church,* acting at the direction of the Twelve, chose Stephen and six others to administer its charitable distribution of food in such a way that the widows among the Hellenistic Jewish Christians would be equitably served (Acts 6:1-6). Stephen also performed miracles* and preached the new faith* in one or more Hellenist synagogues* in Jerusalem* (Acts 6:8-10). This led to charges that he was guilty of blaspheming both Moses* and God* (Acts 6:10-11). Upon being arrested, he appeared before the Sanhedrin and delivered a speech that so infuriated his hearers that they stoned him to death (Acts 6:12—8:1). Saul of Tarsus, present at and consenting to this stoning, forthwith led a persecution* of the Jerusalem church, many of whose members were forced to flee the city (Acts 8:1-3).

    1. Stephen Within the Literary and Theological Context of Luke-Acts
    2. Tradition-Historical Issues Surrounding Stephen

1. Stephen Within the Literary and Theological Context of Luke-Acts.

In the story of Stephen, Luke is able to develop several themes that appear more widely in Luke-Acts. Most of these relate to the rejection of Jesus and his disciples by many of the Jews, particularly the authorities in Jerusalem. As Jesus faced rejection, he prophesied that his disciples would encounter the same hatred, with some having to suffer martyrdom* (Lk 9:23-24; 12:8-12; 21:12-19; Acts 7:54-60). Stephen is just such a martyr, who, as Jesus promised, was able to speak before his adversaries with a wisdom and a Spirit that they could not withstand (Lk 12:11-12; 21:12-15; Acts 6:10). Yet because he

acknowledged Jesus before others and lost his life for Jesus' sake, he saved his life and was acknowledged by the Son of Man (Lk 9:23-24; 12:8; 21:19; Acts 7:55-56).

The hostility of one or more Jerusalem synagogues and the Sanhedrin against Stephen typifies Jerusalem's unbelieving rejection of the prophets* up to and including Jesus, the prophet like Moses and the Messiah. Thus the obstinate disobedience of Stephen's adversaries underscores the guilt on account of which Jesus predicted that God would punish them by forsaking the city and its temple* to destruction, plundering and occupation by the Gentiles* (Lk 11:47-51; 13:33-35; 19:27-28, 42-44; 20:9-19; 21:5-6, 20-24; 23:28-31). In the first five chapters of Acts,* the apostles offer pardon and salvation* to all who incurred guilt on account of Jesus' death. But while many repent, the Sanhedrin only increases its opposition to the disciples. At first the Sanhedrin threatens Peter and John against any further preaching of Jesus (Acts 4:1-22). Next, all of the apostles are imprisoned and flogged (Acts 5:17-40). Finally this hostility climaxes with the stoning of Stephen and Saul's savage persecution (authorized by the high priest* [Acts 9:1]) that followed in its wake. Only following this decisive rejection does Luke's story turn away from Jerusalem toward various missions to regions beyond Judea.

Readers of Luke-Acts have long noticed that various details in the story of Stephen closely correlate him to Jesus and Paul, the dominant figures in these works. Stephen, like Jesus and Paul, is a Spirit-filled man whose empowerment is manifest in both speech and miracles (Lk 3:21-22; 4:1, 14-15, 18; Acts 6:3, 5, 8, 10, 51, 55; 9:17; 13:1, 4, 9-12; 14:3; 15:12). Stephen is especially at one with Jesus and Paul with respect to the opposition that they endured at the hands of Jewish unbelievers, particularly the authorities.

Stephen, like Jesus, was rejected in the synagogue, was arrested and brought before the Sanhedrin, faced trumped-up charges, appealed to the Son of Man at God's right hand, committed his spirit to the Lord,* prayed that his executioners would be forgiven and died as a martyr outside Jerusalem's walls (Lk 4:16-30; 22:54, 66; 23:1-5, 13-17, 34a [of uncertain textual status], 46; Acts 6:9-15; 7:55-60).

Like Paul, Stephen was a powerful speaker whose efforts to evangelize Hellenist Jews was repaid with persecution; he was arrested and brought before the Sanhedrin before whom he defended himself against the false charges of speaking against the law* and the temple; finally, due to the Sanhedrin's furious opposition, he suffered martyrdom (Acts 6:8-15; 7:54, 57-59; 9:28-29; 21:21, 24, 27-36; 22:22-23; 22:30—23:10; 23:12-15; 24:1-9, 11-21; 25:8; 28:17-19; Acts probably assumes Paul's martyrdom [Acts 20:22-24, 29, 37-38; 21:10-14; 23:11]).

Building on the work of O. Steck, D. Moessner has argued that these parallels exist because Luke views Jesus, Stephen, Paul and also Peter as Deuteronomistic rejected prophets. Thus "Israel's continued disobedience . . . is the linchpin of cohesion" (Moessner, 227) among these figures, despite Luke's conviction that Jesus is unique in salvation history.

Within Acts, Luke skillfully uses the narratives about Stephen to display the relationship between the earliest Jewish church, led by the Twelve, and later mission efforts and personalities. In his account of the choosing of the Seven (Acts 6:1-6), Luke continues his exclusive focus on the Jewish Jerusalem church. However, the mention of Stephen as one of the Seven (Acts 6:5) leads directly to an account of his evangelistic preaching, which in turn results in his stoning (Acts 6:8—7:60). At this point Luke introduces Saul (= Paul), who approvingly witnessed Stephen's death and thereupon led a persecution of the Jerusalem disciples so vicious that they, save the apostles, fled the city (Acts 7:58; 8:1-3).

This scattering of the disciples allows Luke to narrate momentous missionary developments, geographical and ethnic, that occupy almost all of the balance of Acts (see Acts 1:8). The flight of Philip* the Evangelist leads him to evangelize Samaritans* (Acts 8:4-25) and an Ethiopian treasurer, apparently a Jewish proselyte (Acts 8:26-40). These advances on the mission* to Judean Jews prepare for Peter's epoch-making evangelization of the household* of Cornelius,* an unqualified Gentile (Acts 10:1—11:18). The diaspora of the Jerusalem disciples also sets the stage for the importance of Paul and the church in Antioch* in Luke's story. It is on his way to Damascus to arrest dispersed disciples that Paul encounters the risen Jesus and thereby becomes the major witness of Jesus in the latter half of Acts (Acts 9:1-19). Stephen's death also leads to a Jewish

Christian mission to Gentiles in Antioch. Upon reaching the Syrian capital, scattered Jewish Christians originally from Cyprus and Cyrene exceeded the limits of their compatriots by evangelizing Gentiles (Acts 11:19-21). Subsequently this ethnically mixed church becomes the launching base for the three great Pauline mission trips.

Stephen's martyrdom leads to geographical and ethnic development of the Christian mission, but does Luke intend that we see in Stephen an instance of theological development? It is usually held that Stephen, perhaps since he was a Hellenist, plumbed the depth of the divine revelation* in Christ* and perceived that both the Mosaic law and the temple had been superseded. Stephen must have been critical of the law, since witnesses accused him of saying that Jesus would change the "customs" (ethē) delivered by Moses (Acts 6:14; cf. Acts 8:11, 14). Likewise he was charged with claiming that Jesus would destroy the temple (Acts 6:13-14). While this latter charge might not be entirely accurate, Stephen himself was allegedly critical of the temple (Acts 7:47-50). Against these considerations, however, one should note that Luke represents the charges against Stephen as false (Acts 6:13); Stephen refers to the law positively as "living oracles" (logia zōnta, Acts 7:38); Stephen accuses his hearers of refusing to keep the law "as ordained by angels" (Acts 7:53); the conjunction (de) introducing Acts 7:48 need not imply disapproval of the building of the temple; Acts 7:48-50 need not challenge the legitimacy of the temple but only its necessity; and Luke later takes pains to show that Paul too was charged with profaning the temple and sitting loose to the law but that these accusations were false (Acts 21:20-36; 22:30—23:5; 24:6, 10-21; 25:7-11; 28:17).

2. Tradition-Historical Issues Surrounding Stephen.

C. C. Hill has helpfully outlined a consensus of opinion surrounding the historicity, transmission and redaction of the Stephen traditions in Acts (Hill, esp. 5-16). This interpretation, rooted in the work of F. C. Baur and recently fortified in the main by M. Hengel, views the Hellenist (i.e., Greek-speaking) Jewish Christians, of which Stephen was a leader, as a group theologically distinct from the early Aramaic-speaking Christians, who continued their pre-

Christian devotion to the law and the temple. Stephen and other Hellenists, however, realized that temple worship and the law had become superfluous. Stephen's advocacy of such radical views brought him into violent conflict with a group of Jerusalem Jews who lynched him. This incident led to a persecution of the Hellenists. That the more conservative portion of the church was not targeted by the persecutors is deduced from Acts 8:1, which states that the apostles stayed in Jerusalem while other disciples were driven out.

It is widely agreed that at least some of Luke's Stephen narratives are attributable to a source or sources (emanating from the Antioch church, according to many, e.g., Harnack and Hengel), but many interpreters suspect that the appointment of the Seven to rectify problems in the charitable distribution to widows is an inaccurate explanation of a real distinction and tension between the Twelve and the Seven. It has also become popular to reject the historicity of Stephen's trial before the Sanhedrin and to regard Stephen's address as based upon something other than a reliable, remembered summary of his preaching. The source of the speech, for example, has been traced to a Samaritan tract (e.g., Scobie) or a Diaspora synagogue sermon (e.g., Haenchen); more recently there is a definite trend toward viewing it as Luke's own composition (Bihler, Richard, Kilgallen).

The identification of the extent and accuracy of the sources lying behind Luke's story of Stephen has proved to be notoriously difficult and controversial (Dupont). And yet apart from such information it is very difficult to assess the historicity of anything other than the barest outlines of the story. It is also difficult, however, to rule out with confidence disputed elements on historical grounds. Hill (24-28), for example, has recently argued that there is nothing inherently improbable in Luke's account of the Hebrew-Hellenist conflict and Stephen's role in its resolution. Furthermore, C. K. Barrett (1:321) has recently added his name to the list of those who believe that Stephen's trial before the Sanhedrin was already in a source employed by Luke. Finally, the general historical reliability of Stephen's speech still has its advocates (Bruce, Marshall), and even if Luke composed the speech or adapted a speech from a source other than Stephen, it is by no means impossible

that he did so on the basis of accurate knowledge concerning Stephen's theology and the accusations on account of which he was killed.

Apart from the question of sources, however, the consensual notion that Stephen and his fellow Hellenists held more radical views about the temple and the law than did their Aramaic-speaking fellow Christians rests on questionable arguments. Their tenuousness has been effectively demonstrated by Hill, who has explored in detail the considerations embedded in the last paragraph of the preceding section. Since Stephen's views and activity do not appear to represent an innovation in the Lukan outlook, it is precarious to look for it behind his presentation.

See also ACTS OF THE APOSTLES; HELLENISTS, HELLENISTIC AND HELLENISTIC-JEWISH CHRISTIANITY; MARTYRDOM; TEMPLE.

BIBLIOGRAPHY. C. K. Barrett, *A Critical and Exegetical Commentary on the Acts of the Apostles* (2 vols.; ICC; Edinburgh: T & T Clark, 1994-); J. Bihler, *Die Stephanusgeschichte im Zusammenhang der Apostelgeschichte* (MTS 1.16; Munich: M. Hueber, 1963); T. Brodie, "The Accusing and Stoning of Naboth (1 Kings 21:8-13) as One Component of the Stephen Text (Acts 6:9-14; Acts 7:58a)," *CBQ* 45 (1983) 417-32; F. F. Bruce, *Peter, Stephen, James and John* (Grand Rapids: Eerdmans, 1979); J. Dupont, *The Sources of Acts: The Present Position* (London: Darton, Longman & Todd, 1964); G. D. Fee, *God's Empowering Presence: The Holy Spirit in the Letters of Paul* (Peabody, MA: Hendrickson, 1994); E. Haenchen, *The Acts of the Apostles: A Commentary* (Philadelphia: Westminster, 1971); M. Hengel, "Between Jesus and Paul: The 'Hellenists,' the 'Seven' and Stephen (Acts 6:1-15; 7:54—8:3)" in *Between Jesus and Paul* (Philadelphia: Fortress, 1983) 1-29; C. C. Hill, *Hellenists and Hebrews: Reappraising Division within the Earliest Church* (Minneapolis: Fortress, 1992); J. Kilgallen, *The Stephen Speech: A Literary and Redactional Study of Acts 7:2-53* (AnBib 67; Rome: Pontifical Biblical Institute, 1976); E. Larsson, "Temple Criticism and the Jewish Heritage: Some Reflections on Acts 6—7," *NTS* 39 (1993) 379-95; D. Moessner, " 'The Christ Must Suffer': New Light on Jesus—Peter, Stephen, Paul Parallels in Luke-Acts," *NovT* 28 (1986) 220-56; H. Räisänen, *The Torah and Christ* (Suomen Eksegeettisen Seuran julkaisuja; Helsinki: Finnish Exegetical Society, 1986); E. Richard, *Acts 6:1—8:4: The Author's Method of Composition* (SBLDS

41; Missoula, MT: Scholar's Press, 1978); M. Scharlemann, *Stephen: A Singular Saint* (AnBib 34; Rome: Pontifical Biblical Institute, 1968); C. H. H. Scobie, "The Use of Source Material in the Speeches of Acts 3 and 7," *NTS* 25 (1979) 399-421; D. D. Sylva, "The Meaning and Function of Acts 7:56-60," *JBL* 106 (1987) 261-75.

B. L. Blackburn

STONE, CORNERSTONE

"Stone" and "cornerstone" represent several words and phrases in the original Greek. The idea and associations of stone are thoroughly exploited in the NT, owing to the fact that they lend themselves readily to various metaphorical usages to set forth such functions of Christ as his being a foundational stone or a cornerstone. From such a usage the meaning passes easily on to the believers' character of living stones built on him. This imagery is developed by the early Christian authors, especially Hermas, while in Revelation various kinds of precious stones adorn the foundations fo the heavenly Jerusalem.

1. Terminology
2. Usage in the Later New Testament
3. Usage in Early Christian Writers

1. Terminology.

Greek uses several words for stone: *petra* usually denotes "rock, bedrock, cliff" (often from Homer on) but has also, though less frequently, the sense of "stone" (for its many uses see Caragounis, "Petra"). It is normally distinguished from *petros,* a free-standing stone; however, *petros* sometimes is used interchangeably with *petra* for "rock" or "bedrock."

Lithos, which according to the database *TLG* occurs approximately ten thousand times times in Greek literature (including inscriptions and papyri), is the usual word for "stone" from Homer to post-Christian times. This is so less frequently in Byzantine and especially Modern Greek (often in the diminutive form *lithari[on]*), in which *petra* has been substituted, and its earlier meaning of "bedrock" is now expressed by *vrachos.* The variety of its uses include stones thrown by warriors (Homer *Il.* 5.308), stones for building (P Cair. Zen. 499.20), gravestones (Callimachus *Epigr.* 8.1; in the feminine), rostra (Aristophanes *Acharn.* 683), marble (Herodotus 3.57), an altar at Athens before which public servants took their oath (Demosthenes *Ag.*

Conon 1265), precious stones (Herodotus 2.44), hard-heartedness (Homer *Odys.* 23.103; metaphorically), as well as a stupid (Aristophanes *Nubes* 1202) or an insensitive person (Plato *Gorg.* 494).

The idea of "cornerstone" is expressed in two ways: by the adjective *akrogōniaios (akron* = "end," "extremity" + *gōnia* = "corner") with *lithos* (sometimes without *lithos*) and by the phrase *kephalē gōnias* ("head of the corner"). *Akrogōniaios* occurs first in Isaiah 28:16 (LXX), and its metaphorical significance is something that constitutes a solid or sure basis for deliverance. *Kephalē gōnias* occurs first in Psalm 118 (LXX Ps 117:22). Neither of these terms occurs in secular Greek literature.

2. Usage in the Later New Testament.

In our literature (Acts, the General Epistles and Revelation) the normal word for "stone" is *lithos.* This is the normal Septuagint translation of Hebrew *'eben. Petra* (which usually translates Heb. *sela'* and *ṣur* but never *'eben*) occurs only once in our literature with the sense of "stone" (1 Pet 2:8). In the entire NT *petros* occurs only as a proper name: that of the apostle Peter. *Akrogōniaios* occurs just once (1 Pet 2:6) in the quotation from Isaiah 28:16, being a neologism (Lust, Eynikel and Hauspie, s.v.).

2.1. Lithos. Our literature does not evince the rich variety of usage found in ancient authors or even in the NT as a whole. The word occurs only in Acts,* 1 Peter* and Revelation (*see* Revelation, Book of).

2.1.1. Acts. In his speech before the Jewish authorities in Acts 4:11 Peter quotes Psalm 118 (LXX Ps 117:22), "the stone *(lithos)* the builders rejected has become the capstone *(kephalē gōnias)."* Peter applies "the stone" as a building material in a metaphorical sense to Christ* and "the builders" to the authorities, who are thus declared guilty of having crucified the elect One of God.* In his Areopagus speech in Acts 17:29, Paul, in typical Jewish polemic against idolatry* (cf. Is 44:9-20), points out to the Athenians that the God whose offspring we all are *(tou gar kai genos esmen,* Acts 17:28, quoted from Aratus *Phaen.* 5 but probably echoing Cleanthes' *Hymn to Zeus* 4) cannot possibly be identified with "gold or silver or stone *(lithō),* an image made by man's design and skill." In a context such as this *lithos* is used of the statues of the Athenian gods made of stone or marble, which are thus contrasted to the God from whom human beings derive their existence (on Acts 17:29 see Gärtner, esp. 179-98, 219-28).

2.1.2. 1 Peter. A more varied usage of *lithos* is found in 1 Peter 2:4-8, where the word occurs five times. "Living stone . . . chosen and precious" *(lithon zōnta . . . eklekton kai entimon)* describes Christ who, though rejected by unbelievers, has been chosen by God (1 Pet 2:4). The imagery is one of building—a spiritual building—into which the recipients of this letter are drawn as living stones *(lithoi zōntes,* 1 Pet 2:5). The background to this is the quotation of Psalm 118 (LXX Ps 117:22), which is adumbrated in "rejected" *(apodedokimasmenon)* and is quoted in full in 1 Peter 2:7. The metaphorical use of "living stone" as applied to Christ passes on into the idea of the foundational stone.

Hence when the reasoning is being supported by the quotation from Isaiah 28:16 (1 Pet 2:6), the imagery of the "living stone" changes in accordance with the OT wording to that of "cornerstone" *(lithon akrogōniaion).* At this point the double function of this "stone" comes into view: for those who believe the stone is a "cornerstone" *(lithos akrogōnias,* 1 Pet 2:6), that is, a sure foundation upon which to build their existence; but for those who refuse to believe, the same stone turns out to be a "cornerstone" *(kephalēn gōnias,* 1 Pet 2:7) as well as, in the words of Isaiah 8:14, "a stone that causes men to stumble and a rock that makes them fall" (NIV; *lithos proskommatos kai petra skandalou,* 1 Pet 2:8). In this double function of the stone 1 Peter takes a different line from that of Paul (Rom 9:33), who embeds Isaiah 8:14, the saying on the stone of offense, within Isaiah 28:16, giving the combined quotation a mainly negative thrust though including an aspect of hope by quoting the last part of Isaiah 28:16. There is also a coincidence with the Greek idea expressed by *Lydia lithos* or *lithos basanou,* a "touchstone" or "testing stone" (on the above passage as a whole see Michaels, 94, 98-99).

2.1.3. Revelation. In Revelation the word *lithos* occurs eight times (once to describe a millstone and seven times to identify various types of precious stones) as well as in a variant reading at Revelation 15:6 (as a precious stone). At Revelation 4:3 the firelike appearance of the Almighty is described as one of "jasper and carnelian" *(lithō iaspidi kai sardiō),* obviously implying the red rather than the green type of jasper.

In Revelation 17—18 the great harlot, Babylon,* is attired with "gold, precious stones *(lithō timiō)* and pearls" (Rev 17:4; 18:16), while her destruction leaves the merchants of the earth without a buyer for their merchandise of "gold, silver, precious stones *(lithō timiō)* and pearls" (Rev 18:12). The sudden and violent destruction of this city is typified when an angel* throws into the sea "a stone large as a millstone" *(lithon hōs mylinon megan,* Rev 18:21; so correctly Luther's translation, Swedish translation, 1981; Modern Greek translation, 1989; against NEB, NIV following the AV: "like a great millstone").

At Revelation 21:11 the light *(phōstēr;* the same term in Gen 1:14, 16 is used of the sun and the moon, but here in view of Rev 21:23 it probably refers to the radiance emitted from the throne) of the heavenly Jerusalem is like "a most precious stone" *(lithō timiōtatō),* like "a jasper stone" *(lithō iaspidi),* clear as crystal, while at Revelation 21:19 the foundations of the heavenly Jerusalem are adorned with every kind of precious stone *(panti lithō timiō).* Revelation 21:19-20 mention twelve kinds of precious stones (jasper, sapphire [lapis lazuli], chalcedony, emerald, sardonyx, carnelian, chrysolite, beryl, topaz, chrysoprase, jacinth [turquoise], amethyst), one for each foundation. At Revelation 15:6, in spite of considerable manuscript support for *lithon,* the correct reading ought to be *linon* ("made of flux"; see, e.g., Charles, 2:38, to whose few classical examples of *linon* add those of the papyri).

2.2. Cornerstone. Three basic OT texts speak of a cornerstone. The first is Psalm 118, which refers to *'eben l'rōš pinnah* (LXX Ps 117:22, *lithon eis kephalēn gōnias),* "a stone for the head of a corner." Isaiah 28:16 reads *'eben pinnat* (LXX: *lithon akrogōniaion)* "a cornerstone"; and Jeremiah 51:26 reads *'eben l'pinnah* (LXX Jer 28:26, *lithon eis gōnian),* "a stone for a corner."

In all three cases the basic Hebrew word is *pinnah* ("corner"), showing that all three texts have the same meaning. The texts in Isaiah and Jeremiah clearly have foundational cornerstones in view. The referent of the passage from Psalms is uncertain, though it is understood as a foundational cornerstone by Matthew 21:42 and Luke 20:17 (Mk 12:10 is unclear). The function of such stones was to hold two walls together at their meeting point. This stone is spoken of in the singular not because there was only one such stone in every building but as representing its category and function.

Some scholars (e.g., Jeremias, *TDNT* 4:274-75) have tried to see in this stone "a keystone" or a "capstone" placed over the entrance or the porch of a building. This is done on the basis of Symmachus's (who uses *akrogōniaios*) and the Syriac ("head of the building") translations of Psalm 118:22, *Testament of Solomon* and a few authors such as Hippolytus and Tertullian. Such a stone would strictly apply to a pyramid. Besides, *Testament of Solomon* speaks of "a gigantic cornerstone" lying around, which Solomon decided *(eboulomēn)* to put into new use, that is, as a capstone. Moreover, the use of *akrogōniaios* in Psalm 118:22 by Symmachus shows only that this term had the same sense as *kephalē gōnias*. This is proved by the fact that both the MT *pinnat* "corner(stone)" and the "cornerstone" (LXX *akrogōniaios)* of Isaiah 28:16 are equivalents. Jeremias's theory of a capstone is thus difficult to maintain at least for the biblical texts.

2.2.1. Acts. The expression *kephalē gōnias* ("head of the corner" or "cornerstone") occurs once at Acts 4:11 in a citation from Psalm 118 (LXX Ps 117:22). Following the application of this term to Jesus in the Gospel tradition, Luke has Peter quote this text in his apology before the Jewish leaders in support of his claim that the one who was put to death by the Jewish nation (note Luke's addition of *hymas,* "you") ironically was the one chosen and destined by God to be their Savior. Since there is no building imagery in this context, this text is quoted solely for the contrast it provides between the despisedness and rejection of the earthly Jesus by the Jewish authorities and the exaltation of the resurrected Christ by God himself.

2.2.2. 1 Peter. Here too the expression *kephalē gōnias* occurs only once at 1 Peter 2:7 in the quotation of Psalm 118:22, which is embedded between the quotations of Isaiah 28:16 and Isaiah 8:14. The depiction of Christ as a living stone (i.e., a foundational stone) and of the recipients of the letter as living stones built on him to constitute a spiritual temple* calls forth three OT texts.

In the first text the stone is a "cornerstone" *(akrogōniaios;* its only other use in the NT is Eph 2:20), on whom people may put their trust without fear of being let down. The second quotation, from Psalms, addresses those who refuse to believe, for whom the same stone

becomes a *kephalē gōnias.* The question that arises is whether in this negative function the stone takes on a different character, for example, that of a keystone or capstone, the final stone of the building—in other words, its crown. Such an understanding would lend support to Jeremias's theory. That this is an unlikely interpretation is shown by the fact that the third quotation (Is 8:14), which is used in close conjunction with the psalm quotation, with both quotes making the same negative point (cf. *kai,* "and"), speaks of a "stumbling stone, a stone that makes them fall," that is, obviously a stone lying on the ground, not a capstone. Behind the "and" in the third quotation lies a Hebrew *waw-explicativum* ("and" in the sense of an elaboration of meaning). The text does not speak of two different stones or of one stone and one rock, one making people stumble and the other making them fall, but of one and the same stone: "a stone that causes people to stumble," that is, "a stone that makes them fall." Greek *lithos* and *petra* are here used synonymously and have the same referent (see Caragounis 1990, 14-16).

3. Usage in Early Christian Writers.

The combination of the texts found in Romans 9:33 and especially 1 Peter 2:4-8 probably implies that they had been brought together as christological proof-texts (i.e., *Testimonia)* and were so utilized even by other early Christian authors, such as Justin Martyr, who takes *lithos* (e.g., Justin *Dial. Tryph.* 34.2; 100.4; 114.2) and *lithos akrogōniaios* (Justin *Dial. Tryph.* 114.4; 126.1); as standing appellations of Christ.

Among the apostolic fathers* *lithos* occurs in the *Epistle of Barnabas** (4 times), the *Epistle to Diognetus** (twice), Ignatius* (once), *Martyrdom of Polycarp* (once) and the *Shepherd of Hermas** (85 times). *Akrogōniaios* and *kephalē gōnias* occur once each in *Barnabas* 6.2 and *Barnabas* 6.4 respectively. The *Epistle to Diognetus* ridicules the heathen idols as made of stone *(lithos)* and other materials (*Diogn.* 2.2), which like a stone *(lithos)* are insensitive of what humans do with them (*Diogn.* 2.9). In the *Martyrdom of Polycarp* the pious regard Polycarp's* bones, which they collect, as more precious than precious stones *(Mart. Pol.* 18.2). *Barnabas* 6.2, 4 applies stone *(lithos)* to Christ in connection with his citation of Isaiah 28:16 and Psalm 118:22, where he also uses, uniquely in the apostolic fathers, the terms *akrogōniaios* and *kephalē gōnias*.

The line initiated implicitly by Ephesians 2:20-22 and explicitly by 1 Peter 2:4-5, whereby the believers are said to constitute stones built upon Christ to form the new temple, is taken up once by Ignatius (Ign. *Eph.* 9.1).

This imagery is exploited by *Hermas* in his *Visions* 3 (17 times) and especially in his *Similitudes* 9 (66 times), in which the church, compared to a tower (*Herm. Sim.* 9.13.1), is built of various kinds of stones, some taken from the sea, others from the dry land. Upon the rock (*petra*), which signifies Christ, are built four rows of stones (*lithoi*) taken from the deep: the first two rows represent two generations of righteous, the third prophets* and servants and the fourth row apostles* and teachers (*Herm. Sim.* 9.4.3). Upon this foundation are built all other stones (*lithoi*) taken from various mountains and fields and representing various kinds of stones (*Herm. Sim.* 9.4.4): square, rounded, and so on. The building includes many unworthy elements, which are tested by the Lord* and rejected (*Herm. Sim.* 9.8.1-7). Many of these, however, after further work done on them are made fit to be reinserted into the building. Thus the parable not only shows that the visible church does not correspond entirely with the church approved by its Master but also adumbrates the later doctrine of purgatory, offering a second chance of salvation* for those who have expiated their sins: "they will fit another place much more inferior, and even this after they have been tormented and fulfilled the days of their sins" (*Herm. Vis.* 3.7.6).

See also CHRISTOLOGY; TEMPLE.

BIBLIOGRAPHY. C. C. Caragounis, *Peter and the Rock* (BZNW 58; Berlin: Walter de Gruyter, 1990); idem, "Petra," *Theologisches Begriffslexicon*, ed. K. Haacker and L. Coenen (2d ed.; Wuppertal: R. Brockhaus, forthcoming); R. H. Charles, *The Revelation of St. John* (2 vols.; ICC; Edinburgh: T & T Clark, 1920) 1975-76; B. E. Gärtner, *The Areopagus Speech and Natural Revelation* (ASNU 21; Uppsala: Gleerup, 1955); J. Jeremias, "λίθος," *TDNT* 4:268-80; idem, "γωνία," *TDNT* 1:791-93; H. G. Link, E. Tiedike and C. C. Caragounis, "Lithos," *Theologisches Begriffslexicon*, ed. K. Haacker and L. Coenen (2d ed.; Wuppertal: R. Brockhaus, forthcoming); J. Lust, E. Eynikel and K. Hauspie, eds., *A Greek-English Lexicon of the Septuagint* (2 vols.; Stuttgart: Deutsche Bibelgesellschaft, 1992, 1996) vol. 1; J.

R. Michaels, *1 Peter* (WBC; Waco, TX: Word, 1988); W. Mundle and C. C. Caragounis, *"Gōnia,"Theologisches Begriffslexicon*, ed. K. Haacker and L. Coenen (2d ed.; Wuppertal: R. Brockhaus, forthcoming). C. C. Caragounis

STRANGERS. *See* HOSPITALITY.

STRUCTURALISM AND DISCOURSE ANALYSIS

The field of NT studies is becoming increasingly interdisciplinary. As scholars bring the insights of other disciplines to bear on the interpretation of the NT, they are recognizing the inadequacies of the historical-critical method. Two disciplines recently brought to NT studies are structuralism and discourse analysis. Both are concerned with the final form of the NT texts and how the texts are constructed and read to generate meaning. They are valuable new tools which can supplement traditional methods of interpretation.

1. Structuralism
2. Discourse Analysis

1. Structuralism.
Structuralism is based on semiotic theories, which in turn are a development of structural linguistic theories. Structuralism deals with the implicit deep structures that generate a text rather than the surface structures of that text. It searches for the permanent and deep structures and categories that the mind uses to create order from its experience of the world. The method has been applied to virtually all disciplines in the sciences and humanities, especially literature, with narrative texts being the primary focus.

1.1. Origins. The work of the linguist Ferdinand de Saussure (1857-1913) is foundational to structuralism. Saussure argued that the meaning of a word is not found in its history (etymology), as was assumed at the time by linguists, but in its use in current language in relationship to other words. Language is a system of signs that are meaningful because of their interrelationships and their differences within structures. Linguistic systems with their structures and grammar are called *langue*. The langue constitutes the resources from which individual speech utterances or *parole* are drawn and derive their meaning. A piece of literature can also be considered a *langue* with its own conventions and system of meaning analogous to those of a language. These insights were incorporated by two groups of scholars developing semiotic theories. One group found in North America stresses the insight that language is a system of signs. The other group stresses that signs obtain meaning through their interrelations and differences.

M. W. Stibbe notes that Vladimir Propp (1928) was the first to apply structuralism to narrative (Russian fairy tales), discovering the typical structure with characters having a limited range of functions to perform in a wide-ranging possibility of manifestations. The anthropologist Claude Lévi-Strauss later applied Saussure's theories to myth. He discovered that myths are based on the permanent structure of oppositions and the desire to resolve these oppositions (e.g., immortal-mortal). Both Propp and Lévi-Strauss discovered the permanent structure through comparative analysis of and abstraction from the logical structure. A number of theories within structuralism have in turn generated a number of textual, exegetical strategies based upon them. Plot function (Propp) and resolution of oppositions (Lévi-Strauss) have been the focus of many studies of the NT. The following discusses structuralism in relation to written language and the NT.

1.2. Basic Assumptions. Structuralism assumes that a text is written in order to communicate or make sense to an audience. It presupposes that human communication, despite cultural differences, obeys similar rules throughout the centuries. Meaning does not reside in the text studied but is given to it by the cultural and intellectual systems in which it is found. A text has meaning if its features are recognized as different, and these features are interrelated in a structure. A word derives meaning from being recognized as being different from other words and from how it relates to words in its context and the language in general. Being recognized as different and in structure are also necessary for other text features such as sentences, paragraphs, plot, subplots and metaphors to have meaning. The focus of structuralism upon one or more of these features results in quite different analyses of the same text. A text has several dimensions that generate meaning, and the process of reading may produce several meanings. The context of the readers influences what meaning-producing dimensions of the text they

focus upon and what they find to be its meaning.

Structuralism is mainly a synchronic method, approaching the language at a given moment in time, rather than a diachronic method, which examines a language over time. It assumes that the meaning of language differs acording to focus: upon its own meaning system (synchronic connections) or upon it as part of a historical process (diachronic connections). It directs NT studies to move from diachronic word study to synchronic word study, which accounts for the use of a word in a particular text at a particular time.

D. Patte points out that historical-critical methodologies are concerned with what is new in a text, how material has been transformed. The approach is diachronic—the sources and traditions are traced through time to a text from a particular time. What is significant is viewed as what is different about the text in relationship to what went before. Structuralism assumes that what is significant in a text is how features of a communication are interrelated in a language system, with one another in a text, with other systems in the environment (religions, political, social) and how the text engages its readers and produces meaning.

1.3. Focus and Methodology. In biblical studies structuralism has been applied mainly to literary analysis as begun by the French structuralists, especially the literary critic Roland Barthes. It reveals the mechanisms by which biblical writers convey their message. It explains how meaning is created in the text and often finds new meaning not revealed by traditional exegesis. Special focus is upon the structure or arrangement of the text, elements such as formulas, repetition, comparison, contrast and chiasmus.

The role of structuralism in determining the faith convictions of a biblical author is particularly noteworthy. It isolates the author's system of convictions, as well as those he is using that belong to that of his audience, in order to convince them to adopt his own. Since the system of convictions derives from the text itself, structuralism moves beyond the limitations of the history of religions school, which determines the religion of biblical texts by comparison to religious texts of the period.

Patte has generated a six-step method for performing a structural exegesis of the NT that combines several of the individual textual approaches within structuralism. Step 1 is the delineation of the discourse unit within a larger discourse. Usually the final form of the discourse is selected, assuming the results of text, source and redaction criticisms. Unlike other criticisms, which examine the complete text through the characteristics of the smaller units, structuralism begins with elucidating the characteristics of the text overall. It is a working assumption that smaller units reflect the basic characteristics of the text as a whole. The whole text is structured with an inverted parallelism between the introduction and the conclusion. The introduction presents a theme as problematic in terms of the audience's old knowledge, and the conclusion presents the theme as resolved according to the audience's new knowledge. This new knowledge is derived from the transformation that the text has wrought on the audience's old knowledge in the process of argumentation. This inverted parallelism between the introduction and conclusion of the text is repeated within each subunit, thus serving to indicate subunit boundaries. To illustrate, John 3:1-21, the story of Nicodemus, is a unit as defined by inverted parallelism. It begins with Nicodemus coming to Jesus at night (John 3:1) and ends with Jesus calling people to the light* (John 3:21). It begins with Nicodemus affirming Jesus as a teacher* come from God* (John 3:2) and ends affirming that God sent Jesus into the world* (John 3:16, 17, 19).

Step 2 is identifying explicit oppositions of actions that express each author's system of convictions. Truths that authors believe are self-evident shape the way they view themselves and the purpose and meaning of their lives. Convictions are often stated by stipulations of what they do not mean—as explicit oppositions between what they want to say and what they do not want to say. Explicit oppositions of actions directly express the author's convictions and are expressed in the text by two verbs of doing; one action is positive and the other negative from the point of view of the discourse. For example, in John 3:2 the opposition of actions is of Jesus doing signs (positive action) and of others being unable to do signs (negative action).

Step 3 is identifying the qualifications through which the opposed subjects (the characters that perform the opposed actions) are contrasted. This clarifies the first series of convictions underscored by the oppositions. These convictions are identified by what qualifications

distinguish one person from all other persons, through negative comparisons (contrasts) and positive comparisons (correlations). In the opposition of actions in John 3:2, Jesus is able to perform signs because he is from God and God is with him, while others do not have these qualifications.

Step 4 is identifying the effects of opposed actions upon the receivers (the persons or things affected by the actions) and thus contrasting those opposed actions. This clarifies a second series of convictions underscored by the oppositions. It studies the contrasts between opposed receivers in each opposition of action and the correlations among either positive or negative receivers. In the case of John 3:2, receivers are not mentioned. This illustrates that not all steps will bear fruit for all oppositions of actions.

Step 5 is constructing the system of convictions of the author in the passage. It is using the convictions identified in steps 2-4 to demonstrate that the author's convictions are interrelated in categories posited by the theme, the inverted parallelism, and the oppositions of the passage and the work as a whole as discovered in step 1. These categories are about the divine, a mediator, religious leaders and believers, and their negative counterparts. All categories of convictions are organized according to a positive and negative hierarchies of values that are part of a shared pattern of the discourse unit and the discourse as a whole. This pattern reflects the author's way of perceiving human experience.

Step 6 is identifying the ways the author uses the theme of the discourse to communicate his or her pattern of convictions to the readers in order to have them accept this pattern as their own way of perceiving meaningful human experience. These convictions are usually expressed in terms of the readers' old views in order to facilitate their acceptance of them. This step is the typical starting point for historical-critical methods. This includes examination of metaphors and figurative language.

1.4. Strengths and Weaknesses of the Method. Structuralism is another methodology to add to the arsenal of the tools of biblical interpretation. It has helped us to see the role of oppositions in biblical narrative and the function of the elements of plot. Familiar texts can be seen from fresh vantage points. However, Stibbe points out five weaknesses of structuralism that need to be kept in mind when one uses the methodology in biblical studies. (1) It ignores the historical-critical method and its findings. It stresses the final form of the text to the exclusion of the historical and diachronic features of biblical narrative and the referential dimensions of the narrative. (2) The classifications used in structuralism are often arbitrary, especially when labeling binary oppositions and genre components. (3) The interpretative models employed are not as universal or as easily applied as is often claimed. (4) The characters and their relationships and other details of the narrative are often abstracted and obscured. (5) The anti-authorial stance of structuralism stands in opposition to the desire in biblical studies to discuss theological motivation and authorial intention.

1.5. Poststructuralism. There are new methodologies that can be labeled poststructuralism. These do not assume that the text contains a system of meaning that it seeks to impart but that the readers are themselves bringing meaning to the text from their own linguistic systems. Reading is a creative, interactive enterprise as the reader brings expectations and meaning to the text (cf. reader-response criticism).

2. Discourse Analysis.

Discourse analysis is the study and interpretation of spoken and written human communication. It is interested in the role of speaker or writer, oral communication or written text and the hearer or reader in the communicative process. It asks, How is language used? and How are discourses and texts produced and processed? It is a synthetic discipline within modern linguistics that seeks to unite many of the other disciplines of linguistics, such as semantics, pragmatics and sociolinguistics. In its quest to study and interpret language, discourse analysis is also interdisciplinary, seeking the aid of such other disciplines as reader-response criticism, anthropology, rhetoric,* semiotics, sociology and literary criticism. Once discourse analysis was confined to oral communication and text linguistics was confined to written communication, but the distinction is no longer made. Now both oral and written communication are discussed under the domain of discourse analysis.

2.1. Origins. Discourse analysis has emerged since the 1960s and 1970s and has only recently begun to be used as a methodology in NT studies. J. B. Green points out that the discipline is founded upon several shifts in hermeneutics. One is the shift away from the historical questions that lie behind the text to focus on the text itself as an act of communication. Historical questions are still asked (e.g., Are traditions used in the composition of the work?), but the focus is now on the function of the text (e.g., What is the function of the traditions being used in the text?). Another shift is the recognition that a discourse has multiple readings depending upon the readers and their reading situations. Although these readings are constrained by the discourse, they emerge in the interplay of the reader and the discourse. Finally, discourse is understood not just as something to be deciphered and understood but also, through embedded factors, as defining relationships and social positions (e.g., wealth, authority, solidarity) that motivate the audience to achieve certain aims.

There is as yet no single methodology or agreed-upon terminology in discourse analysis. Any discussion of discourse analysis will act more like a photograph of it at this stage in its development than as a definitive portrait of a mature discipline. The following explanation is such a photograph, and the discussion is oriented to written texts.

2.2. Basic Assumptions. Green highlights three main assumptions of discourse analysis. First, communication is social, transcending words and sentences. Communication is embedded in ongoing social interaction and cannot be interpreted apart from the context of that social interaction. Second, language is always embedded in culture and assumed common knowledge and experience. Cultural assumptions embedded in the text and those brought today to the text must be analyzed to understand communication. Third, human beings strive to make sense of their world. Discourse analysis assumes that communication is meant to be coherent and relevant and that readers try to make sense of the text. It seeks to understand how language is used to create a coherent communication.

2.3. Focus and Methodology. Discourse analysis moves beyond the traditional concern of linguistics with the sentence level. Rather it is concerned with the use of the smallest unit of language (morphemes), their use in constructing larger wholes (words, clauses, sentences, paragraphs, entire discourses) and the interrelationship of all the units; that is, with micro- and macrostructural analysis. Discourse analysis investigates the role of the writer in the production of discourse. How did the speaker or writer create the discourse? How did the original hearer or reader comprehend, process and respond to the discourse? Discourse analysis poses many challenges to the preoccupation of traditional NT studies with interpreting words to the neglect of the function of Greek in discourse.

S. E. Porter notes that in investigating language in use, discourse analysis combines the three main areas of linguistic analysis: semantics, syntax and pragmatics. Semantics pertains to the language forms conveying meaning (what the form means). Syntax entails the arrangement of language forms into meaningful units to form a cohesive piece of communication (how the forms create meaning together). Pragmatics is concerned with the meaning of language forms in linguistic contexts, between the discourse and shared, unarticulated presuppositions (what the speaker means when using the forms). Discourse must be analyzed in its social context to assess its social functions. This concern also ties the discipline with sociolinguistics, which investigates how language use fulfills social objectives.

Interrelated levels of reality influence the linguistic choices made in producing and comprehending discourse: *intertext* or *context of culture*, *discourse situation* or *context of situation* and *cotext*. *Intertext* or *context of culture* is the larger linguistic frame of reference on which a discourse consciously or unconsciously draws its meaning. It is where presuppositions and the reference of a discourse reside. This *context of culture* includes the standard *linguistic code* shared by a group of people, *variety of language* or dialects shared by various subgroups and *idolect* of a particular author. Readers bring assumptions and experiences drawn from the *context of culture* that allow the actualization of a text in the process of reading. When one analyzes the NT, knowledge of the oral, literary and rhetorical conventions of the first century is essential.

A second level is the *discourse situation* or *context of situation,* the sociohistorical realities in which a discourse is set. It is the moment of a communication act when the discourse was originally written and the time when it is read today. Thus discourse analysis is concerned with the multiple levels of communication and social interaction. This might include the communication occurring between characters within a discourse, the communication between the author and the audience receiving the discourse and the communication between the discourse and the modern audience. By reading a text the modern reader also generates meaning. Discourse analysis concerns how the use of language invites this participation, how meaning is generated in the reading and how the reader is shaped by the reading.

A third level is the *cotext* or the string of linguistic material in which a text is set (e.g., the relation of a sentence to a paragraph). It refers to previous discourse material written or read, which influences how material further along in the discourse is written or read. This includes giving prominence to some material *(staging)* that helps the reader comprehend what a discourse is about. For example, a formal opening introducing major themes to be developed in a discourse leads the reader to expect to find such themes in the process of reading.

2.4. Cohesion and Constituent Analysis. A key concern of discourse analysis is cohesion, the relationships within a unit of discourse and the identification of the boundaries and relationships between all these units within the discourse as a whole. G. H. Guthrie applies text linguistics (discourse analysis) to Hebrews* and gives one of the clearest discussions of the methodology. He is concerned with the author's selection of individual words, grammar and style to develop a theme into cola (grammatical structure with subject and predicate) and paragraphs. In order to understand the thematic development of Hebrews, Guthrie performs a lexical, syntactical and rhetorical analysis of the cola that make up the paragraphs. To understand the entire discourse he analyzes the relationship between the paragraphs that divide the discourse into smaller embedded discourses. These embedded discourses constitute the macrostructure of the discourse.

To isolate the paragraphs and embedded discourses, Guthrie investigates the signals that mark the beginnings and endings of units. Cohesion shifts (cohesion is a property of a text that gives it unity) and inclusion (the use of similar wording at the beginning and ending of a unit that acts like bookends to the intermediate material) mark these beginnings and endings. At the paragraph level cohesion is achieved by a variety of factors: genre (because a genre is established when literature consistently exhibits certain characteristics); topic or thematic development in a group of cola; connection or interdependence between cola, especially conjunctions; the consistent use of the same subject, verb tense, person or number; reference of the relation between an element of the text to something else in the text, especially pronominals (e.g., she, her, hers); lexical cohesion (the repetition of the same or similar lexical forms); and temporal and spatial indicators referring to the same time frame and location. Cohesion shifts and inclusion are also indications of cohesion in the larger embedded units of the macrostructure.

Once the units of a discourse are isolated, discourse analysis investigates the connection of these units as embedded discourse at the macrolevel. This interrelationship is indicated by inclusions comprising many discourse units, lexical and pronominal cohesion between units and transition devices such as hook words, reiterations and summaries. Once the macrolevel is delineated, the question remains as to why the units are arranged in their present position. On the macrolevel, discourse has an introduction, points that develop the argument, a peak or climax and a conclusion.

Investigating the macrostructure of Hebrews, L. L. Neely created the following outline of the constituent structure of Hebrews: thematic introduction (Heb 1:1-4), point 1 (embedded discourse 1, Heb 1:5—4:13), point 2 (embedded discourse 2, Heb 4:14—10:18), peak (embedded discourse 3, Heb 10:19—13:19), conclusion (Heb 13:20-21) and formalized closing (Heb 13:22-25). Guthrie has refined this outline with cohesion analysis and established the boundaries within the embedded discourse units and the transitions used to connect them into embedded units.

2.5. Schools of Discourse Analysis. Although it is difficult to categorize and although the works of major scholars overlap categories, Porter defines four models in the understanding and practice of discourse analysis in NT studies. The first is the North American school epitomized by the Summer Institute of Linguistics (SIL) at Dallas, which concentrates upon discourse analysis as related to biblical translation and the level of sentence grammar but has neglected work on the theory of discourse analysis in favor of textual analysis alone. The second is the English and Australian school, which stresses that language is a network of systems or groupings of choices that give it meaning. The third school is the continental European school, whose practice is wide-ranging and lacks a single model. It is particularly known by the model practiced in Scandinavian NT studies. This model focuses on the macrostructure of the text and tends to divide analysis into syntax, semantics and pragmatics. The fourth is the South African school, which has had a large influence on the theoretical and applicational levels. It is greatly influenced by the work of J. P. Louw, who concentrates on the level of the cola and their interconnections. However, there is no comprehensive theory underlying the work of this school.

See also HERMENEUTICS; NARRATIVE CRITICISM; RHETORIC, RHETORICAL CRITICISM.

BIBLIOGRAPHY. R. Barthes et al., eds., *Structural Analysis and Biblical Exegesis: Interpretational Essays* (PTMS 3; Pittsburgh: Pickwick, 1974); D. A. Black, ed., *Linguistics and New Testament Interpretation: Essays on Discourse Analysis* (Nashville: Broadman, 1992); G. Brown and G. Yule, *Discourse Analysis* (Cambridge: Cambridge University Press, 1983); P. Cotterell and M. Turner, *Linguistics and Biblical Interpretation* (Downers Grove, IL: InterVarsity Press, 1989); M. Coulthard, *An Introduction to Discourse Analysis* (2d ed.; London: Longman, 1985); J. B. Green, "Discourse Analysis and New Testament Interpretation" in *Hearing the New Testament: Strategies for Interpretation*, ed. J. B. Green (Grand Rapids: Eerdmans; Carlisle: Paternoster, 1995) 175-96; G. H. Guthrie, *The Structure of Hebrews: A Text-Linguistic Analysis* (NovTSup 73; Leiden: E. J. Brill, 1994); C. Lévi-Strauss, *Structural Anthropology* (New York: Basic, 1963); J. P. Louw, "Discourse Analysis and the Greek New Testament," *BT* 24 (1973) 101-18; L. L. Neely, "A Discourse Analysis of Hebrews," *OPTT* 3-4 (1987) 1-146; D. Nunan, *Introducing Discourse Analysis* (Harmondsworth, England: Penguin, 1993); D. Patte, "Structural Criticism" in *To Each Its Own Meaning: An Introduction to Biblical Criticisms and Their Application*, ed. S. L. McKenzie and S. R. Haynes (Louisville, KY: Westminster/John Knox, 1993) 153-70; idem, *Structural*

Exegesis for New Testament Critics (GBS; Minneapolis: Fortress, 1990); S. E. Porter, "Discourse Analysis and New Testament Studies: An Introductory Survey" in *Discourse Analysis and Other Topics in Biblical Greek,* ed. S. E. Porter and D. A. Carson (JSNTSup 113; Sheffield: Sheffield Academic Press, 1995) 14-35; V. Propp, *Morphology of the Folktale* (Austin: University of Texas Press, 1968); J. T. Reid, "Modern Linguistics and the New Testament: A Basic Guide to Theory, Terminology and Literature" in *Approaches to New Testament Study,* ed. S. E. Porter and D. Tombs (JSNTSup 120; Sheffield: Sheffield Academic Press, 1995) 222-65; F. de Saussure, *Course in General Linguistics* (New York: McGraw-Hill, 1966); M. W. Stibbe, "Structuralism" in *A Dictionary of Biblical Interpretation,* ed. R. J. Coggins and J. L. Houlden (London: SCM; Philadelphia: Trinity Press International, 1990) 650-55; M. S. Stubbs, *Discourse Analysis: The Sociolinguistic Analysis of Natural Language* (Language in Society 4; Chicago: University of Chicago; Oxford: Blackwell, 1983); T. A. van Dijk, ed., *Handbook of Discourse Analysis* (4 vols.; London: Academic Press, 1985).　　　　　　　D. F. Watson

SUFFERING

Certain NT books are more focused on the subject of suffering than are others. The authors of 1 Peter and Revelation are intensely interested in understanding and interacting with the problem of suffering in their communities. Since suffering is a central focus of these two works, their contribution will be developed at length. The theme of suffering plays an important but somewhat secondary role in Acts, Hebrews and James. In other works, such as 1, 2 and 3 John, 2 Peter and Jude, suffering is rarely mentioned. Beyond the NT, however, the early church fathers continued to theologize in the area of suffering, especially developing the theme with respect to martyrdom.

　　1. 1 Peter and Revelation
　　2. Acts, Hebrews and James
　　3. Early Church Fathers

1. 1 Peter and Revelation.

1.1. 1 Peter. The apostle* Peter probably wrote to the churches of Asia Minor in the early to mid-60s, during the reign of Nero (A.D. 54-68; *see* 1 Peter). Like the writer of Revelation, Peter uses the encrypted "Babylon" (i.e., Rome) as a backdrop to at least some of his concern (1 Pet

5:13; cf. Rev. 17:9-10). However, the suffering described in 1 Peter is not caused by official state persecution* or by any statewide program authorized by the Roman government. The reference to Babylon* is likely a way for the author to identify with the recipients in their struggles, rather than to define their situation.

Instead the plight of the Asian community is primarily social in nature. The Christians are referred to as "exiles of the dispersion" (*parepidēmoi diasporas,* 1 Pet 1:1), as "aliens" (*paroikoi,* 1 Pet 2:11) and "strangers" or "exiles" (*parepidēmoi,* 1 Pet 2:11). These Christians suffer the lot of outcasts and displaced persons in the very towns and cities where they lived and worked. As undesirable "resident aliens" they lacked the status and security that they used to enjoy. They had become the object of gossip, ridicule and social ostracism: "the hatred of the human race" (Tacitus *Ann.* 15.44.28). Their situation was one of homelessness and social disenfranchisement, instigated by those people the readers would encounter every day in their attempt to make a living. A dramatic change in their lifestyle—both withdrawing from immoral activities of their pagan past (1 Pet 2:11; 4:3-4) and a new quest for doing what was "right" and "good" (1 Pet 2:12, 14-15, 20; 4:14-15)—made them a vulnerable target for retaliation. 1 Peter does not describe a traumatic or climactic moment of acute suffering but the kind of suffering that wears people down because of its daily pressure (see Beker).

To these marginalized Christians Peter brings a message of hope that mirrors their sociological dilemma. He deals with their suffering as "aliens" or "homeless" (*paroikoi*) by finding them a new "home" (*oikos,* 1 Pet 2:5) in the covenant* community. To those now without a people, "strangers" (*parepidēmoi*), he grants a sense of belonging within the new "people" of God* (*laos,* 1 Pet 2:9-10; see Elliott). For readers sensing rejection, the new "house" or "home" is built upon the cornerstone of one who like themselves was "rejected by people but chosen by God." Along with this cornerstone, they too become the stones* out of which God is building a new temple* and people or house (1 Pet 2:4-10). The new community then adds a dimension of much-needed stability in the lives of these dispossessed people.

Within this new community christology* and slavery* are closely interwoven with suffering.

The Asian churches appear to have been composed of many individuals from a lower socio-economic status, since the household code* addresses primarily the underside of the social hierarchy and gives an unusual prominence to slaves (compared with other NT household codes). In this respect Christ's* role as Suffering Servant or slave (1 Pet 2:21-25, a portrait drawn from Isaiah's Suffering Servant) becomes the paradigm for all believers. The material about slavery along with Jesus' servantlike response to suffering (1 Pet 2:18-25) establishes a pattern for all believers within the community: exposure to harsh owners typifies the vulnerability of all to the hostilities of the "Gentiles"* (1 Pet 2:18; cf. 1 Pet 2:11-12; 3:13, 16; 4:4, 12, 16; 5:8-9); the possibility of slaves suffering though innocent is characteristic of the experience of all believers (1 Pet 2:19-20; cf. 1 Pet 1:6; 3:14, 17; 4:1, 13, 16, 19; 5:9-10); slaves as well as all Christians are instructed to suffer with clear consciences* (1 Pet 2:19; cf. 1 Pet 3:16, 21) and to do good (1 Pet 2:20; cf. 1 Pet 2:14-15; 3:6, 17; 4:19); both slaves and the congregation at large needed to "entrust themselves" to God (1 Pet 2:23; cf. 1 Pet 4:19); and both are "called" to act in the nonretaliatory manner like the christological Servant, who brought blessing* and healing* rather than exchanging insult for insult (1 Pet 2:21-22; cf. 1 Pet 3:9).

1 Peter adopts a bifocal strategy toward suffering. A future orientation and perspective motivates persistence in the face of suffering. Even if death should be the readers' fate (1 Pet 4:6), they have the assurance* of being "brought to God" along the path of Christ's vindication (1 Pet 3:18-22). Since justice and judgment* will ultimately fall upon the disobedient (1 Pet 1:7-8; 2:23; 4:17), the believers should entrust themselves to God and continue to do good (1 Pet 2:23; 4:19). Yet, as suggested above, the setting is one of social conflict in which only a few might encounter suffering as severe as death. Most of the readers would endure abuse from an everyday, common occurrence of social tension. As a result an other-worldly perspective (though clearly evident) is somewhat subdued and a present perspective has considerable room for development. There are hopeful possibilities in this immediate world. For instance, suffering offers the believer the opportunity for faith's refinement (1 Pet 1:6-7) as well as something of a missionary opportunity in the present. Suffering for "the name of Christ" (1 Pet 4:14) elicits paradoxical joy* and praise,* since one's faith is being refined in a manner that demonstrates its lasting quality (1 Pet 1:7-9; 4:16). Righteous suffering thus acts as a sign that the "Spirit of glory" rests upon believers (1 Pet 4:14) and they have found God's favor and blessing (1 Pet 2:20). Yet beyond these community borders, suffering functions redemptively in the lives of the outside, antagonistic society. A loving, nonretaliatory response to those inflicting the abuse (as well as the pursuit of what is good and commendable) should quiet, perplex, shame and possibly even bring about the salvation* of unbelievers (1 Pet 2:12, 15; 3:1-2, 9, 16; cf. 1 Pet 2:24-25; 3:18). Suffering then produces an internal and external witness* to the grace* of God in the present.

Since this present-redemptive feature to suffering is so strikingly different from what one finds in Revelation, it is worth highlighting some of the key texts. As the prologue to the entire household code, 1 Peter 2:11-12 significantly shapes the rest of the epistle. The way that the Asian community responded to social conflict was viewed as having a profound influence upon unbelievers: "As aliens and strangers . . . conduct your lives honorably among the Gentiles, so that, though they malign you as evildoers, they may see your good deeds and glorify God in the day of his visitation [eschatological appearing and judgment]." Although it is an interpretive crux, the expression "glorify God in the day of his visitation" should probably be understood as a conversion formula in view of its source connections to the Jesus tradition* with similar themes (cf. Mt 5:16) and its verbal tie to 1 Peter 3:2, where the unbelieving husband is won to the Lord through "seeing/intently watching" (*epopteusantes*) his wife's "lifestyle" (*anastrophēn*). Both terms appear in the prologue of 1 Peter 2:11-12. Along similar lines, the Christian's response to a hostile environment has the potential to "silence the ignorance of the foolish" (1 Pet 2:15), to "put them to shame" (1 Pet 3:16) and to create a certain "attractiveness" about Christianity (1 Pet 2:12; 3:8-9). It is likely that even the christological material was intended to be read within this "community mission" focus and not strictly from a soteriological perspective. As with Christ, the community's "stripes" and "wounds" in one sense also bring healing to the world around them (1 Pet 2:23-24; cf. 1 Pet 3:18).

1.2. Revelation. Although the date of Revelation is contested (*see* Revelation, Book of), the prophet* John may well have written his apocalypse* toward the end of Domitian's reign (81-96). The exact date and background are not essential for understanding his theology of suffering. Yet it is necessary to reach some kind of conclusion about the work in relationship to its political milieu. Certain recent studies have argued that the "dark images" of Nero and Domitian as portrayed by early writers such as Tacitus, Suetonius, Dio Chrysostom and Juvenal are entirely distorted (see Thompson) or that the political crisis in Revelation is more perceived than real (see Collins). L. L. Thompson, for example, goes so far as to suggest that John himself was on the island of Patmos by his own initiative as part of a missionary journey to evangelize the area, not because he had been banished there by political leaders. Such an understanding of John's opening words, "I was on the island of Patmos because of the word of God and the testimony of Jesus" (Rev 1:9), is rather dubious. A comparison of his rationale with the language of other texts places it in a negative context of persecution from external or political sources: the souls under the altar had been slain "because of the word of God and the testimony of Jesus" (Rev 6:9); the reigning saints of Revelation 20 had been beheaded "because of their testimony for Jesus and because of the word of God" (Rev 20:4). Most likely John was exiled for the same reason that these other Christians had lost their lives. The setting on Patmos creates an immediate affinity between John's life and the suffering circumstances of his audience.

While few NT scholars would lessen the political-religious conflict in Revelation to this extent, these studies have helped bring some balance to the portraits of terror that are frequently developed on a popular level. It is fair to say that Nero and Domitian have been somewhat caricatured by both the secular writers of their day and by Christians. The bloodbath portrayal of suffering in Revelation is a dramatic image and is more descriptive of collective, community pain felt from hostile actions taken toward certain individuals within the community. Also, it may have been escalated from historical reality as a way of fusing their present

situations with eschatological* expectations. Yet, as with the case of most apocalyptic literature, there seems to have been a significant and real threat (and on a political level in the case of Revelation) in order to account for this work and its images, even if the apocalyptic portrait goes beyond the historical reality.

Even with this guarded approach, the intensity and scope of the suffering in Revelation clearly transcends that of 1 Peter. The hostility in Revelation extends beyond the social plight of 1 Peter by taking on political and religious proportions. From the perspective of the Apocalypse, much of the persecution was due to a political movement to enforce the cult of emperor* worship. In Pergamum, the official center for emperor worship in Asia (comparable to Rome in the West; see Hemer), Antipas was put to death for not renouncing his faith (Rev 2:13). Other Christians appear to have been forced into economic hardship (Rev 2:9; cf. Rev 13:17), imprisoned (Rev 2:10) or slain for their faith (Rev 2:10; 6:9; 13:15; 18:24; 20:4; cf. Rev 2:10; 11:7-10) as a result of their refusal to participate in the emperor cults (cf. Rev 13:17; 14:9, 11; 15:2; 16:2; 19:20; 20:4). This political persecution was compounded by a growing antagonism from the Jewish population toward Christianity. Judaism* enjoyed a privileged status under Roman rule, so that Jews were sheltered from the demands for emperor worship. Christians were vulnerable to hostile Jews who found it an opportune time to shut the doors of the synagogue* on the followers of Christ (Rev 2:9; 3:9; cf. Rev 14:1-17).

The severity of persecution described in Revelation produces a markedly different theology of suffering. While 1 Peter responds to suffering in a bifocal manner, combining the hope of coming glory* with a hopefulness about present possibilities, Revelation's perspective is almost exclusively one-sided. John directs his readers to a unifocal and other-worldly hope found in the eschaton. His readers were to await the "soon" coming of the righteous* judge (Rev 19:11-16), the prospect of reigning with Jesus (Rev 20:4-6), the finality of God's judgment (Rev 19:11-15) and the rebirth of the old order into a "new heavens and earth" (Rev 21:1). Christians still act as witnesses for Jesus (Rev 1:2, 9; 6:9; 12:17; 19:10; 20:4). However, unlike 1 Peter, there is little optimism about the missionary outcome of their witness. The happy prospect of conversion resigns itself to the hardness and lack of repentance* of unbelievers (Rev 9:20-21; 16:9, 11; cf. Rev 11:10; 12:17). Antagonism has reach the point of open and antithetical conflict. Instead of blessing, curses fall upon the hostile society, and the reader enters into jubilant applause at the destruction of Babylon (Rev 18:1—19:8; cf. Rev 11:5).

Accordingly, the themes of cosmic transcendence and eschatological reversal dominate John's approach to suffering. The believer's individual suffering fuses with a much larger cosmic battle between Christ and Satan,* between good angels* and evil demons, between old-world Babylon and the new Zion (see Jerusalem). Christians are encouraged to endure* patiently the present crisis in view of a better world in the future, a world in which their fortunes will be different. For example, in the present Satan is enthroned and Christians are being thrown into prison (Rev 2:10, 13). Ultimately this picture will be reversed: one day Christians will reign with Christ and Satan will be imprisoned (Rev 20:1-6). Whether John envisioned this happening at the death of a believer or as a distinct eschatological reality (forging another epoch in salvation history) should not hinder contemporary readers from seeing the dramatic reversal in fortune. Similarly, while now the saints lament and cry out in anguish (Rev 6:10), in a future day God will "wipe away every tear," and "there will be no more death or mourning or crying or pain" (Rev 21:4; cf. Rev 7:15-17). Likewise the enduring wealth of eschatological Zion compared with the fall of opulent Babylon (Rev 17:4; 18:3, 7, 9-20; 21:11-21) would have clearly spoken to those readers who in their testimony for Jesus had lost property and wealth (Rev 2:10; cf. Rev 3:17).

Due to the book's apocalyptic framework, Christian suffering and martyrdom* in Revelation are typically spoken of as passive. Since the world is empty of redemptive possibilities, suffering becomes a passive form of victimization (see Beker). However, such a perspective has a growing number of challengers (see Boesak, Reddish). Suffering for the apocalyptists was passive only in the sense that hope for reforming this world had dwindled. It is probably more accurate to see suffering within Revelation as an act of open defiance against the social norms and political structures. Martyrdom was the supreme demonstration of rejecting the values of this present world and embracing those of the coming world and its new political structure. In that coming world a "slain lamb"* sits on the throne.

2. Acts, Hebrews and James.

2.1. Acts. The book of Acts* provides an invaluable glimpse into the experience of suffering of the early church.* The range of suffering experienced by Christians included being threatened (Acts 4:21, 29), conspired against (Acts 9:23, 29; 14:5), mocked and maligned (Acts 13:45; 17:32; 18:6), arrested and put in jail (Acts 4:3; 6:12; 8:3), placed in stocks or chains (Acts 16:24; 26:29; 28:20), brought before councils and courts (Acts 5:27; 22:30—23:10; 24:1; 25:23), falsely charged (Acts 25:7), flogged (Acts 5:40; 16:23; 22:19, 24), vilified by crowds (Acts 19:23-41; 21:27-36), forced to flee homes and relocate (Acts 8:1, 4; 11:19), displaced from synagogues (Acts 9:2; 22:19; 26:11; 18:7; cf. Acts 18:17), expelled from cities (Acts 13:50), stoned to death (Acts 7:54-60; 14:19; cf. Acts 26:10), and beheaded by the sword (Acts 12:1-2). Most of the persecution appears to have been motivated by jealousy from the Jewish community leaders and by a zeal to protect their religious traditions (Acts 13:45; 17:5; 22:3-5). At times the pagan cults were also threatened by the spread of Christianity and so responded with hostility (Acts 19:19, 23-27; cf. Acts 16:19). In contrast to these religious institutions, however, any threat to Roman political structures is minimized. Luke intentionally counters such an idea by presenting it as a "trumped-up" charge by the Jews (Acts 17:7; 25:8). Unlike Revelation, in Acts the relationship between Rome and Christians is a compatible one. Roman structures protect the preachers of the gospel from attack and facilitate their mission (Acts 17:1-9; 18:12-17; 19:23-41; 21:30-32; 23:12-35; cf. Acts 24—28; see Talbert 1983).

Luke portrays suffering as an integral part of Christian mission and particularly as a catalyst for the expansion of the gospel. In the book of Acts suffering repeatedly follows ministry* and mission.* In turn suffering provides a new opportunity for ministry. Through persecution the gospel spreads from Jerusalem to Samaria* (Acts 8:4-24): the scattering of Christians was a significant step forward in the mission of the early church. As I. H. Marshall aptly observes,

"One might say that it required persecution to make them [Christians] fulfill the implicit command in [Acts] 1:8" (Marshall, 152). In a similar way persecution and hardship causes the spread of the gospel to Rome* (Acts 20:17—28:31). Paul and his coworkers move on to other places as opposition arises (Acts 13:48-52; 14:5-6, 19-20; 16:25-40; 17:10, 13-15). This combination of suffering and mission exposes an underlying irony in Luke's theology. Far from dampening the spread of the gospel, persecution and suffering facilitated its geographical expansion.

Through suffering the church enters into the suffering mission of Jesus. For example, the language from Isaiah's texts about the Suffering Servant builds an affinity between the mission of Jesus and his followers (Acts 8:32-33; 26:23; cf. Acts 9:15-16; 13:47; 26:16-18; 28:28). In their suffering Christians extend the servant mission of Christ, especially in bringing the gospel to the Gentile world. The literary parallel between Luke and Acts also unites Jesus' suffering and Paul's suffering. Like Jesus, who "must" travel to Jerusalem and suffer (Lk 9:51; cf. Lk 13:22; 17:11; 18:31; 19:11), so too Paul "must" travel to Rome and suffer (Acts 20:22-23; 21:4, 12; 23:11; cf. Acts 25:12, 25; 26:32; 27:1, 24; 28:14, 16). The early church in effect completes the extended mission of Christ through its suffering. Its suffering is no more an accident than was Jesus' suffering. This affinity between Christ and his church's suffering is further illustrated in the response of Jesus to Saul on the Damascus road: "I am Jesus, whom you are persecuting" (Acts 9:4-5; cf. Acts 26:14-15). The ascended Lord* continues to suffer in and through his people's sufferings (a rather profound insight into the mysterious waters of suffering; see Bauckham, Moltmann).

2.2. Hebrews. If we accept the traditional view that this letter* addresses a movement from Judaism to Christianity, then the primary hardship on the Christians in Hebrews* is having to leave their cherished traditions and socioreligious roots. The role that suffering plays in trials and learning obedience* both for Christ and by implication for his people (Heb 2:18; 4:15; 5:8) should probably be read against this background of pain related to the departure from Judaism (e.g., the loss of participation in the religious festivals; Heb 9:10; 13:9-10). Beyond these central considerations, however, the external pressures appear to be a minimal component in the readers' crisis of faith. The writer does not place resistance to persecution at the center of his appeal (simple neglect by some and willful abandonment by others are only secondarily related to persecution). In earlier days the community had happily faced occasional insults, imprisonment and confiscation of property (Heb 11:32-34; cf. Heb 11:26, 35-38) and had helped each other through these difficult times (Heb 11:34; 13:3; cf. Heb 6:10). They are now encouraged to continue along this path. As Jesus endured the cross "for the joy set before him," the readers should likewise persevere in their present hardships, which have not reached the point of death (Heb 12:2-4), and function as loving discipline to ensure their legitimacy as God's children (Heb 12:5-12; *see* Sonship).

2.3. James. The epistle of James* adds yet another perspective to the suffering experienced by the early church. Along the lines of 1 Peter, suffering is related to social factors. However, in James the focus is further narrowed to socioeconomic injustice against the poor. Poverty-stricken readers were suffering from withheld wages (Jas 5:4), legal exploitation (Jas 2:6), social humiliation (Jas 2:1-4), hunger and the lack of adequate clothing (Jas 2:15). Unlike 1 Peter, the suffering in James is depicted more in economic than religious terms. It is possible that some of their suffering was due to religious conviction (Jas 2:7 is ambiguous). However, the struggle in James seems to be largely attributed to economic factors: a struggle between the poor as a class of people who were vulnerable to abuse by the wealthy. In order to show God's affinity with the poor, the author broadly depicts the wealthy class as "wicked oppressors" and the poor as "pious sufferers" (a poverty-piety equation rooted in Judaism; see Davids). Yet the church included some wealthy people (Jas 2:2, 16; 4:13; cf. the examples of wealthy Abraham* and Job), and obviously many poor lived outside the church community and would have been vulnerable to the same kind of abuse.

James responds to this economic injustice in two ways. Instilling a future hope, the community must wait patiently for the eschatological judge to bring justice and a reversal of fortunes (Jas 5:7-9; cf. Jas 1:9-11). However, he directs any present reformation toward the believing community. Within the church the poor are to be elevated in status and provided for in a tangible and generous manner as an expression of true religion (Jas 1:27; 2:14-26); the wealthy are not to be shown favoritism or held in higher esteem by the congregation (Jas 2:1-13). In sum, the hoped-for justice of the eschaton penetrates the community as a present reality.

3. Early Church Fathers.

In the early fathers a theology of suffering emerges with a marked emphasis on martyrdom.* One finds some discussion of social conflict as "strangers and aliens" along the lines of 1 Peter (*Herm. Sim.* 3.1.9-2.2) and even the suffering of humanity as part of a sin-cursed world (*Barn.* 6.9). However, an interest in martyrdom eclipses all other discussion about suffering. Early martyrs became the supreme standard and example of suffering for all Christians to follow even though their suffering may not be as severe (Pol. *Phil.* 9.1-2; *Mart. Pol.* 2.1; 3.1—5.2; 17.3; *1 Clem.* 6.2). Accordingly, various martyrs are named and spoken of as heroes within the Christian communities, both men (e.g., Ignatius,* Zosimus, Rufus, Polycarp,* Justin) and women (e.g., Danaids and Dirkai, mythic names in *1 Clem.* 6.1 that would cover a group of courageous women; see Hall). Aside from a status as role models, their place in the eschaton is significantly elevated. Martyrs are seated at the right hand of God, whereas other believers sit on the left (*Herm. Vis.* 3.1.9—3.2.2).

At its core, martyrdom was imitation and participation in the sufferings of Christ. Since Christ suffered for the martyr, the martyr is ready and glad to die for Christ. During the execution Christ comes and talks with the suffering believer (*Mart. Pol.* 2.2; 17.2). Through death the martyr enters into the sufferings of Christ in the most profound sense (Pol. *Phil.* 7.2; 9.2; *Mart. Pol.* 1.6-7; 6.2). On a number of occasions Ignatius argues that only death as a martyr would show him and others to be "true disciples" of Christ (Ign. *Eph.* 1.2; Ign. *Magn.* 9.1; Ign. *Rom.* 4.2; 5.1-2; 6.1-3; Ign. *Pol.* 7.1). As with Christ's death, the death of the martyr was an acceptable and pleasing sacrifice* to God (Ign. *Rom.* 2.2; *Mart. Pol.* 14.1-2). In view of the affinity between Christ's suffering and the martyr's plight, there was an added pragmatic need to establish the heretical nature of Docetism,* which taught that Christ's suffering was merely a semblance of reality (Ign. *Trall.* 10.1; Ign. *Smyrn.* 2.1).

The martyr lived out a "witness" toward the hostile realms. Whether burning at the stake or being torn apart by animals, the martyrs' deaths functioned as dramatic testimonies to their faith in Christ, which at times led some observers to convert (*Mart. Pol.* 1.2; 2.2; 7.3; Justin *Apol. II* 12). Far from being passive, martyrdom was viewed as a strong protest against the emperor and a statement of allegiance to the ascended and reigning Christ. In an act of civil disobedience, the Christian refused to denounce Christ and scoffed at Roman gods and political structures (*Mart. Pol.* 9.1—12.3; 21.1). As in Revelation, this earthly conflict entered into the larger cosmic battle between Christ and Satan (*Mart. Pol.* 19.2).

It is fitting to conclude our survey with Justin Martyr, since he departs from the typical approach to martyrdom found in the apostolic fathers.* Christian apologists, like Justin, spoke as philosophers about their quest for the supreme philosophy and of being persecuted for their pursuit of the truth (which they had come to realize in Christianity). As with Socrates of old, they were on trial as witnesses for the truth. Unlike Ignatius, Justin does not see martyrdom as a sacrifice, nor does he give special glory to the martyr as a hero of the faith. All Christians share in the witness to the truth*; the martyr expresses it more fully. Justin also abandons Ignatian mysticism about imitation* and union with Christ for more philosophical and rational categories that would be shared by his audience. A few words from his first apology capture the direction of his thought: "The lover of truth must, under all circumstances and even under threat of death, choose to say and do what is right, even when it may cost one their life" (Justin *Apol. I* 2.1).

See also DEATH OF CHRIST; ENDURANCE, PERSEVERANCE; HEALING, ILLNESS; MARTYRDOM; PERSECUTION.

BIBLIOGRAPHY. R. J. Bauckham, "'Only the Suffering God Can Help': Divine Passibility in Modern Theology," *Themelios* 3 (1984) 6-12; J. C. Beker, *Suffering and Hope: The Biblical Vision and the Human Predicament* (Grand Rapids: Eerdmans, 1994); A. A. Boesak, *Comfort and Protest: Reflections on the Apocalypse of John on Patmos* (Philadelphia: Westminster, 1987); A. Y. Collins, *Crisis and Catharsis: The Power of the Apocalypse* (Philadelphia: Westminster, 1984); P. H. Davids, *The Epistle of James* (NIGTC; Grand Rapids: Eerdmans, 1982); idem, "Sickness and Suffering in the New Testament" in *Wrestling with Dark Angels,* ed. C. P. Wagner and F. D. Pennoyer (Ventura, CA: Regal, 1990) 215-37; J. H. Elliott, *A Home for the Homeless: A Social-Scientific Criticism of 1 Peter, Its Situation and Strategy* (Minneapolis: Fortress, 1981); E. Schüssler Fiorenza, *The Book of Revelation: Justice and Judgment* (Philadelphia: Fortress, 1985); W. H. C. Frend, *Martyrdom and Persecution in the Early Church* (Oxford: Blackwell, 1965); L. Goppelt, *A Commentary on 1 Peter* (Grand Rapids: Eerdmans, 1993); S. G. Hall, "Women Among the Early Martyrs" in *Martyrs and Martyrologies,* ed. D. Wood (SCH 30; Oxford: Blackwell, 1993) 1-22; C. J. Hemer, *The Letters to the Seven Churches of Asia in Their Local Setting* (JSNTSup 11; Sheffield: Sheffield Academic Press, 1989); P. R. House, "Suffering and the Purpose of Acts," *JETS* 33 (1990) 317-30; I. H. Marshall, *The Acts of the Apostles* (Grand Rapids: Eerdmans, 1980); J. Moltmann, *The Crucified God: The Cross of Christ as the Foundation and Criticism of Christian Theology* (London: SCM, 1974); M. G. Reddish, *Apocalyptic Literature: A Reader* (Nashville: Abingdon, 1990); J. P. M. Sweet, "Maintaining the Testimony of Jesus: The Suffering of Christians in the Revelation of John" in *Suffering and Martyrdom in the New Testament,* ed. W. Horbury and B. McNeil (New York: Cambridge University Press, 1981) 101-17; C. H. Talbert, *Learning Through Suffering: The Educational Value of Suffering in the New Testament and in Its Milieu* (Collegeville, MN: Liturgical Press, 1991); idem, "Martyrdom in Luke-Acts and Lukan Social Ethic" in *Political Issues in Luke-Acts,* ed. R. Cassidy and P. Scharper (Maryknoll, NY: Orbis, 1983) 99-110; L. L. Thompson, *The Book of Revelation: Apocalypse and Empire* (New York: Oxford University Press, 1990). W. J. Webb

SYNAGOGUE

Recent research into the origin and development of the synagogue has confirmed its central importance for an understanding of the NT. Relationship to synagogues features as a major term of reference not only within the ministry of Jesus (*see DJG,* Synagogue) but also within the emergence of Christianity as a distinctive Judaic movement which finally separated from Judaism (*see* Christianity and Judaism).

1. The Functions of Synagogues
2. Jesus' Relation to Synagogues
3. Paul and the Hellenistic Synagogue
4. Rivalry Between Church and Synagogue

1. The Functions of Synagogues.

The earliest epigraphal references to synagogues come from Egypt (from the third century B.C.), where they were known generally as "places of prayer." But prayer was only one function of what might also be called a "house of learning" (Sir 51:23). Philo describes synagogues as "schools of prudence, courage, temperance, justice, piety, holiness and every virtue" (Philo *Vit. Mos.* 2.216), and he assumes that a reverent, communal reading of the Torah with exposition on the Sabbath is their principal purpose (Philo *Leg. Gai.* 156); In that the latter reference is to a longstanding custom in Rome, Philo attests the common knowledge that synagogues are a well known feature of Judaism, and hardly a local peculiarity of Egypt. It is a reasonable inference that Philo's own monumental exposition of the Torah was designed to complete the process of advanced education which synagogues sometimes occasioned.

The epigraphal remains of Jews in Egypt reflect their political situation. One slab of limestone refers to the synagogue as "in honor of King Ptolemy and of Queen Berenice," which permits a dating within the reign of Ptolemy III Euergetes (246-221 B.C.; Griffiths, 4-5). Evidently a degree of protection was claimed by such dedications (of which Griffiths gives further examples).

But to speculate from such evidence that the institution of the synagogue actually originated in Egypt is unwarranted. It has been claimed, for instance, that 1 Maccabees and 2 Maccabees contain "not a word" about the institution, so that evidence of synagogues in Palestine "is lacking before the first century B.C. and perhaps even until the first CE" (Grabbe, 21, 25). 1 Maccabees 3:46-54 in fact refers to a previous "place of prayer" in Mizpah, where the Israelites gathered after the desecration of the sanctuary. There they fast and do penance, read from the Torah and assemble what they can of the priestly vestments and the offerings, all the while seeking divine guidance. Mizpah, of course, is a place of sacrifice and assembly according to biblical precedent (Gen 31:44-54; Judg 20:1-3; 21:1-8; 1 Sam 7:5-16). But in 1 Maccabees it is presented as what Philo might have called a school of prudence and courage, a place where the Torah alone is guide, in terminology which corresponds well to the language of the epigraphal remains from Egypt.

What is evidenced in Egypt is an institution typical of the Judaism of the time, a gathering for accepting the guidance of the Torah with prayerful dedication. The generality of the synagogue is attested by the decree of Caesar Augustus that money for the temple tax might be stored in synagogues, and that confiscation should be regarded as sacrilege (Josephus, *Ant.* 16.6.2-3 §§162-66).

The range of purposes a synagogue might serve is attested by the inscription of Theodotus, which establishes that a synagogue was constructed in Jerusalem "for purposes of reciting the law and studying the commandments," as well as "to provide for the needs of itinerants from abroad" (*see DJG*, Synagogue, 783). The association with institutions such as the synagogues mentioned in Acts 6:9 is natural.

Unless synagogues needed to be public for some particular purpose (such as to claim political protection or to offer hospitality), they were for the most part "located in houses with the plan and facade of private homes" (Tsafrir, 79). Only from the third century in Palestine do typical patterns of construction for synagogues become widespread, and at the same time stunning artistic embellishments are widely represented. The Dura Europos synagogue in Dura, a Syrian town on the Euphrates, represents a similar development. The third-century building, the object of a famous excavation, was the result of successive adaptations of a private dwelling (Kraabel, 99). The magnificent paintings of Dura represent that same later phase, as does its prominent shrine for the Torah.

Synagogues built long after the destruction of the temple came to take on some of the aspects of the temple.* *Tosefta Megilla* 4(3):22, for example, insists that entrances for synagogues open only to the east, as in the temple. In the same vein, representations of the menorah, the lulav, the shofar and the incense shovel within synagogues reflect a consciousness of their quasi-cultic function (Dar and Mintzker, 163; Gal, 166-73).

Before the synagogue was felt to replace the temple, it had complemented it. The official function of receiving taxes for its upkeep is one example. Another is its function as a gathering of elders for the purpose of administering jus-

tice. When Paul refers to beatings in synagogues (Acts 22:19, see also 2 Cor 11:24), it corresponds to the judicial power that Mishnah also attributes to communal authorities (*m. Mak.* 3:1-14). A document from the Persian period in Babylonia (dated 511 B.C.) shows the attempt of a Jewish family to control the behavior of a daughter (Bickerman, 349-50); the emergence of the synagogue provided an occasion for such legal instruments. Although the implements of the temple were later associated decoratively with synagogues, the ark for the scrolls of the law is attested as early as Caesar's edict, as quoted by Josephus (*Ant.* 16.6.2 §164). The centrality of reading and interpreting the law is also conveyed in the scene of Nehemiah 8, which the rabbis of Talmud later associated with reciting the Scripture and giving its interpretation in Aramaic (*see DJG*, Targums; *b. Meg.* 3a; *b. Ned.* 37b).

The judicial function of the synagogue was not merely a punitive matter: Torah also provides for the support of the poor. Matthew 6:2 and *Tosefta Baba Batra* 8:4 in their differing ways agree that synagogues are places of charity (Safrai, 191-94). Within the first century, sites of synagogues are typically associated with *miqvaoth*, or ritual baths (Reich, 289-97), and that association is probable in the case of the synagogue in Arsinöē-Crocodilophilus (from 113 B.C.; Kasher, 217). A particular affinity between the synagogue and the adjudication of purity is therefore signaled by the archeological evidence.

The functions of the synagogue must be appreciated before the accumulating archeological data may be suitably assessed. It is a mistake of categories to expect Palestinian synagogues of the first century to be purpose-built structures, clearly labeled for the archeologist. As long as the Jerusalem temple stood, synagogues were usually no more than large rooms, typically in the midst of other smaller rooms (as in a private dwelling). Their purpose was the interpretation and application of the Torah, with the prayerful intent which the Torah presupposes. Some might criticize the ostentation of teachers and/or their prayer (see Mt 6:5; 23:6; Mk 12:39; Lk 11:43; 20:46), but the centrality of prayerful teaching is a matter of record. The diverse functions of the synagogue cannot be understood simply in terms of services of worship in churches today (so McKay), but most of what we call worship took place in that setting, no doubt with less organization (and decorum) than characterizes modern liturgies.

The synagogue at Migdal (Magdala) measures 8.16 m x 7.25 m; the one at Gamla measures 19.6 m x 15.1 m (Groh, 58-59). Both feature banked seats and columns arranged around a central area. They are designed for attentive listening. Beyond that, the use of such spaces for purposes of public meeting, the collection of alms, adjudication, higher learning, disputation, local administration and hospitality would vary from place to place, depending upon the needs, resources, and aspirations of the local community. Because local needs, resources and aspirations themselves can change before buildings can be altered, there is no reason to imagine all public functions took place in the same place in every community. The place of prayer in Philippi is said in Acts 16:13 to be beside a river. Local exigencies might demand outdoor meetings, as in the case of Judas Maccabeus at Mizpah. Only a simplistic obsession with monuments demands a marked, purpose-built structure for the claim to be made that those who revered the Torah read it regularly together and tried reverently to apply it.

2. Jesus' Relation to Synagogues.

The portrayal of Jesus' activity in the Gospels often corresponds to what may be known of synagogues within his period and place, although at times the presentation seems to reflect more the customs within Greek-speaking congregations in the Diaspora.* Luke 4:16-21 is the most vivid example of both aspects of the representation of Jesus (Chilton 1979, 123-77).

As the text reads, Jesus simply stands and recites a text and claims it has been fulfilled. General amazement is the result (Lk 4:22), and the congregation is startled even before Jesus announces the fulfillment of Scripture (Lk 4:20). What is missing from the text is an indication that Jesus has here provided a targum, a translation of the passage into Aramaic, because in the Hellenistic Diaspora the Scriptures were simply read in Greek, rather than read and then translated. It has often been observed that the citation from Isaiah 61:1-2a, the principal source Jesus cites here, omits the reference to divine vengeance in Isaiah 61:2b. That might have occasioned mild surprise, but scarcely astonishment. After all, the choice of where a passage of reading should end was largely left open during the first century. The key to an understanding of what Jesus says is that it is not a simple reading of Isaiah 61:1-2, but a conflation of that passage with Isaiah 58:6, which speaks of forgiving, that is, releasing, those who are oppressed. In the underlying tradition which informed the passage, Jesus stood in the synagogue and gave a new rendering of the book of Isaiah in Aramaic, targeted on the issue of forgiveness. That motivated his omission to speak of divine vengeance.

His assertion of the new activity of God is, it has been proposed, most accurately represented in the text of the Old Syriac Gospels:

> The Spirit of the Lord is upon you,
>> because of which he anointed you to
>>> preach to the poor,
> and he has sent me to preach to the captives forgiveness, and to the blind sight
>> —and I will strengthen the broken with forgiveness—
> and to preach the acceptable year of the Lord.

The reading reflects the linkage between Jesus personally and the distinctive issue of his new "reading": the issue of forgiveness. That linkage, the claim of an offer of forgiveness "fulfilled" by Jesus, causes astonishment in the synagogue.

In what follows in the text of Luke, astonishment turns inexplicably to scandal (Lk 4:22-30). The experience of preachers of Jesus in synagogues nearer Luke's time is reflected, as can be seen in the similarity of the pattern of presentation in Acts 13:13-52 concerning Paul and Barnabas at Pisidian Antioch. The sequel has Paul stoned by Jews in Lystra (Acts 14:19), so that the comparability with the presentation of Jesus in Nazareth becomes all the more plain.

Nonetheless, Jesus' activity in synagogues, including his sympathetic relations with leaders of synagogues such as Jairus, is amply attested (*see DJG*, Synagogue). The general pattern of teaching in synagogues (Mt 4:23; 9:35; 13:54; Mk 1:39; Lk 4:15; Jn 18:20) confirms the connection between Jesus and the targumic tradition (*see DJG*, Targums; Chilton 1984). There is no evidence to support the contention that lectionaries of readings were fixed within the first century, and that complements the NT's picture of the freedom which Jesus and his followers enjoyed to choose the texts which suited them. It is also striking that the question of healing is at issue in synagogues, in the idiom of disputes about keeping the Sabbath (Mt 12:9-14; Mk 3:1-6; Lk 6:6-11; 13:10-17; 14:1-6) and about purity* (Mk 1:21-28; Lk 4:31-37). Purity is also an implicit concern in approaching the supposed corpse of Jairus' daughter (Mt 9:18-19, 23-26; Mk 5:21-24, 35-43; Lk 8:40-42, 49-56). That issue is underlined within the tradition, as is shown by the inclusion of the story of the woman with a flow of blood (Mt 9:20-22; Mk 5:25-34; Lk 8:43-48). That Jairus would have lived adjacent to any meeting room now seems entirely plausible in light of archeological data.

Indeed, the synagogue may have featured more prominently in Jesus' ministry than appears at first sight. Peter and Andrew are depicted as residing adjacent to a synagogue in Capernaum (Mk 1:29; cf. Lk 4:38), and they may have been leaders there. Also at Capernaum, an appeal is made to Jesus to be sympathetic to a centurion on the grounds that he had built a synagogue (Lk 7:5); Jesus' high esteem of the institution is obviously presupposed (see also Jn 6:59). Likewise, Jesus himself is assumed to be an acceptable teacher in his own home town (Mt 13:54; Mk 6:2; Lk 4:16). Jesus' pronouncement that the "leper" who approached him was clean (Mt 8:1-4; Mk 1:40-45; Lk 5:12-16) may originally have been set in a synagogue, and that is the most appropriate setting for his teaching concerning defilement (Mk 7:15; Mt 15:10-11; see Purity). The "house" in which Jesus is placed at the time he declared the paralytic free of both sin and disease was possibly a synagogue (Mk 2:1-12; cf. Mt 9:1-8; Lk 5:17-26); that would explain the crowd and the degree of controversy involved.

3. Paul and the Hellenistic Synagogue.

Only at a later stage in the development of the Gospels was the synagogue assumed to be a place of persecution for disciples (Mt 10:17; 23:34; Mk 13:9; Lk 12:11; 21:12). That assumption reflects hard experience, as intimated, for example, in the allusion within the source called Q to failed missions in Chorazin and Bethsaida, and even in the formerly sympathetic Capernaum (Lk 10:13-15 par. Mt 11:20-24; see Catchpole, 171-76).

Acts* reflects something of the attempt after the resurrection, by some unsympathetic leaders of synagogues, to coordinate a denunciation of Jesus' followers with the help of the authorities of the temple (Acts 9:1-2; 22:19; 26:11; cf. 24:12). But the focus is so consistently upon Paul's reception in synagogues (together with Barnabas's, as Paul's companion) that it is a matter of supposition how other Christian leaders, such as Peter and James, were received in synagogues. Presumably their experience was as different from Paul's as their teaching was less radical, and James in fact cites the preaching of Moses* in synagogues as a reason for non-Jewish believers to maintain a rudimentary purity* (Acts 15:19-21). But Paul becomes the lens through which Acts views the institution of the synagogue.

Despite the radicalism of his message, Acts assumes that Paul is received into synagogues and that he is permitted to preach (Acts 13:13-43). The repeated opportunity permits Paul to reach non-Jewish hearers in the synagogues, which provokes jealousy among "the Jews" (Acts 13:44-52). That experience in Pisidian Antioch brings Paul and Barnabas to Iconium: some Jews and Greeks believe as a result of what they hear in a synagogue, but some people "sided with the Jews" (Acts 14:1-4). The threat of stoning (by both Gentiles and Jews) drives the apostles on to Lystra, where a similar pattern of experience results in the actual stoning of Paul because the people of Lystra are incited by antagonistic Jews from Antioch and Iconium (Acts 1:5-20).

Although much of the language of Acts suggests that there was a united Jewish front against Paul (and against Jesus before the time of Paul), the fact is that the synagogue remains Paul's customary point of entry into the communities he visits. Thessalonica (Acts 17:1-9), Beroea (Acts 17:10-14), Athens (17:16-17) all hear Paul first in their synagogues. The pattern of persecution from both religious and civic leaders is represented again, and the last example shows how dispute in the synagogue could spill over into the market place (Acts 17:18-34).

The link between the synagogue and wider civic debate was forged particularly by those known as "God fearers," those who acknowledged the God of Israel without accepting circumcision.* As a type of believer, they are represented by the centurion Cornelius* in Acts, who is converted by Peter (Acts 10:1-48). Paul is portrayed as even more effective in his ministry to them (Acts 13:16, 26). A similar group is referred to with the designation of those who "worship" God (see Acts 13:43, 50; 16:14; 17:4, 17; 18:7; the RSV often renders the usage with the adjective "devout").

But Paul's focus in Corinth continues to be the synagogue (Acts 18:1-4), and Crispus—ruler of the synagogue—is baptized with his household (Acts 18:5-11). The synagogue is Paul's introduction to Ephesus (Acts 18:19; 19:8), and it is also the place where Apollos preaches (Acts 18:26). Even the final chapter of Acts presents Paul in the company of local leaders of the Jews in Rome, gathered to hear him out, perhaps in their synagogue (Acts 28:17-22).

Paul's own letters do not use the term *synagogue*, because their concern is not with that institution. His interest is rather the definition and salvation of "Israel" (see Rom 9:6; 11:26; Gal 6:16), in which all who believe—Jew and Greek, slave and free, male and female (Gal 3:28)—are included (see Rom 4:1-25; Gal 3:6-7, 14, 27-29). The synagogue was therefore for Paul an occasion, not a limit, of operation. Even in his case, because the ultimate aim was to constitute Israel (however radically defined), the synagogue was a natural place to operate, no matter what the level of opposition to him (see 2 Cor 11:23-27). And in his case, as in the case of Christians leaders contemporaneous with him, it is difficult to imagine how the gospel could have been preached without the previous establishment of synagogues in the Mediterranean world and apart from their relative toleration of unconventional teachers.

4. Rivalry Between Church and Synagogue.

Although the letter of James* reflects a familiarity with the term *church* (*ekklēsia*) in order to refer to communities of believers (Jas 5:14), the term *synagogue* (*synagōgē*) also appears (Jas 2:2). The usage does not represent a formal claim to replace the most prominent institution of Judaism after A.D. 70, but the willingness to use the word itself is notable. It probably means no more than an assembly in context, but an assembly for the purpose of discerning and keeping the true, "royal law" (Jas 2:8) represents an implicit challenge to other congregations which claim to uphold the Torah.

James uses negative examples to insist by way of contrast that the poor should not be treated worse than the rich (Jas 2:1-7), that the whole of the law* is to be understood in the command-

ment* to love* (Jas 2:8-13), that faith* apart from actions is dead (Jas 2:14-26). The principal ethical interest of the letter closes with an explicit encouragement of prayer* (Jas 5:13-18), underlined—as the letter is generally—with scriptural example and allusion. The letter, in other words, is setting up the church as the true synagogue, a school of wisdom and action whose curriculum is the law correctly understood.

The irony is that the rivalry between church and synagogue was greatest when Christians most consciously adhered to their Judaic roots. The Revelation* of John sets up its vision as involving the divine court (Rev 1:12-16), the very throne of God (Rev 4:1-11); the terms of reference are principally drawn from Daniel and Ezekiel. But because this vision occurs on the "Lord's day"* (Rev 1:10), not during the Sabbath meeting in the synagogue, any opposing institution must be a "synagogue of Satan" (Rev 2:9; 3:9). That is the inevitable alternative to the discovery of the heavenly sanctuary under the guidance of Jesus as "one like a son of man" (Rev 1:13, alluding to Dan 7:13).

These developments in the Revelation presuppose the growing antipathy of leaders of the synagogue after A.D. 70, who were increasingly influenced by the Pharisees/rabbis. The period saw the development of the "blessing of the minim," a petition within the "Eighteen Benedictions" which cursed disloyal Jews such as the Christians (*see* Christianity and Judaism). Perhaps an even greater occasion of rivalry between churches and synagogues was the decision that certain of the rituals of the temple could be conducted in the synagogue. Such a decision was made by R. Yohanan ben Zakkai at Yavneh, when he permitted the shofar, the ram's horn, to be blown at the feast of the new year in the synagogue as it once had been in the temple (*m. Roš Haš.* 4:1-4). For those who saw Jesus as the true access to the sanctuary, any transfer of the temple's function to the synagogue necessitated the replacement of that institution; from that time, the attempt to replace the institutions of Judaism within Christianity became programmatic (*see* Temple).

See also ARCHITECTURE, EARLY CHURCH; CHRISTIANITY AND JUDAISM: PARTINGS OF THE WAYS; DIASPORA JUDAISM; JUDAISM; TEMPLE; WORSHIP AND LITURGY.

BIBLIOGRAPHY. E. J. Bickerman, "The Babylonian " in *The Cambridge History of Judaism*, ed. W.

D. Davies and L. Finkelstein (Cambridge: Cambridge University Press, 1984) 1.342-58; D. R. Catchpole, *The Quest for Q* (Edinburgh: T & T Clark, 1993); B. Chilton, *A Galilean Rabbi and His Bible: Jesus' Use of the Interpreted Scripture of His Time* (GNS 8; Wilmington: Glazier, 1984); idem, *God in Strength: Jesus' Announcement of the Kingdom* (SNTU 1; Freistadt: Plöchl, 1979), reprinted in *The Biblical Seminar* (Sheffield: JSOT, 1987); S. Dar and Y. Mintzker, "The Synagogue of Ḥorvat Sumaqa, 1983-1993" in *Ancient Synagogues: Historical Analysis and Archaeological Discovery*, ed. D. Urman and P. V. M. Flesher (SPB 47; Leiden: E. J. Brill, 1995) 157-64; A. Finkel, *The Pharisees and the Teacher of Nazareth* (AGSU 4; Leiden: E. J. Brill, 1964); P. V. M Flesher, "Palestinian Synagogues before 70 C.E.: A Review of the Evidence" in *Approaches to Ancient Judaism* 6, ed. J. Neusner and E. S. Frerichs (Atlanta: Scholars, 1989) 67-81, reprinted in *Ancient Synagogues*, ed. Urman and Flesher, 27-39; Z. Gal, "Ancient Synagogues in the Eastern Lower Galilee" in *Ancient Synagogues*, ed. Urman and Flesher, 166-73; L. L. Grabbe, "Synagogues in Pre-70 Palestine: A Re-assessment," *JTS* 39 (1998) 401-10, reprinted in *Ancient Synagogues*, ed. Urman and Flesher, 17-26; J. G. Griffiths, "Egypt and the Rise of the Synagogue," *JTS* 38 (1987) 1-15, reprinted in *Ancient Synagogues*, ed. Urman and Flesher, 3-16; D. E. Groh, "The Stratigraphic Chronology of the Galilean Synagogue from the Early Roman Period Through the Early Byzantine Period (ca. 420 C.E.)" in *Ancient Synagogues*, ed. Urman and Flesher, 51-69; A. Kasher, "Synagogues as 'Houses of Prayer' and 'Holy Places' in the Jewish Communities of Hellenistic and Roman Egypt" in *Ancient Synagogues*, ed. Urman and Flesher, 205-20; A. T. Kraabel, "The Diaspora Synagogue: Archaeological and Epigraphic Evidence since Sukenik," *ANRW* 2.19.1 (1979) 477-510, reprinted in *Ancient Synagogues*, ed. Urman and Flesher, 95-126; H. McKay, *Sabbath and Synagogue: The Question of Sabbath Worship in Ancient Israel* (RGRW 122; Leiden: E. J. Brill, 1994); L. Morris, *The New Testament and the Jewish Lectionaries* (London: Tyndale, 1964); idem, "The Saints and the Synagogue" in *Worship, Theology and Ministry in the Early Church*, ed. J. Wilkins and T. Paige (JSNTSup 87; Sheffield: Sheffield Academic Press, 1992); J. Neusner, *Development of a Legend: Studies on the Traditions concerning Yoḥanan ben Zakkai* (SPB 16; Leiden: E. J.

Brill, 1970); R. Reich, "The Synagogue and the Miqweh in Eretz-Israel in the Second-Temple, Mishnaic, and Talmudic Periods" in *Ancient Synagogues*, ed. Urman and Flesher, 289-97; Z. Safrai, "The Communal Functions of the Synagogue in the Land of Israel in the Rabbinic Period" in *Ancient Synagogues*, ed. Urman and Flesher, 181-204; Y. Tasfrir, "On the Source of the Architectural Design of the Ancient Synagogues in the Galilee: A New Appraisal" in *Ancient Synagogues*, ed. Urman and Flesher, 70-86; D. Urman and P. V. M. Flesher, *Ancient Synagogues: Historical Analysis and Archaeological Discovery* (SPB 47; Leiden: E. J. Brill, 1995).

B. Chilton

SYNCRETISM

The term *syncretism* is used by anthropologists and historians to refer to the blending of religious beliefs. This typically occurs when the social circumstances of one group bring them into contact with another. As the two groups interact, members of one group may begin to assimilate aspects of the religious beliefs of the other, resulting in a transformation of the traditional religion. For Christians throughout history, the notion of syncretism has had largely negative connotations and is sometimes associated with heresy. This is due to the fact that assimilation is often perceived as a departure from the purity of the original. Many modern-day missiologists thus distinguish syncretism from contextualization, with the latter understood as an appropriate expression of the gospel in culturally relevant forms.

1. Religious Syncretism in the Hellenistic and Roman World
2. Christianity as a Syncretistic Religion?
3. Syncretistic Trends in Early Christianity
4. Gnosticism and Christianity

1. Religious Syncretism in the Hellenistic and Roman World.

The political circumstances in the Mediterranean world from the time of Alexander the Great to the Roman imperial period resulted in an incredibly changed network of social and cultural contacts. Greeks made their way to the East, Persians came to the West, Egyptians did business in Asia Minor and Rome, Jewish communities were scattered throughout most of the important cities (*see* Diaspora Judaism) and Roman colonists were everywhere. This Hellenistic-era internationalism forced the various peoples to interact with other cultures and religious beliefs. As they did so, a variety of responses emerged, ranging from a reaffirmation of the pure form of the traditional religion to a borrowing and assimilation to the religions of the new environment (see Religions).

The syncretism of this era often extended to a complete identification of two deities with originally different mythologies, cults, rituals and functions (see Martin, 10-11). Thus the local fertility deity in Ephesus is identified as Artemis by early Greek settlers and as Diana by the Romans. In the second-century Isis aretalogy (ascription of praise) found in Egypt (P. Oxy. 1380), Isis is identified with nearly twenty other deities, including Aphrodite, Artemis, Astarte, Athena, Hera and Kore.

Judaism* struggled with syncretism throughout its history. The people of Israel often showed a tendency to assimilate Canaanite deities and religious beliefs. Thus there is frequent anti-idolatry polemic in the historical and prophetic writings of the OT. A king like Josiah is praised for demolishing the high places, cutting down the Asherah poles and removing cult objects associated with Baal from the Jerusalem temple (2 Kings 23).

There is ongoing scholarly debate as to the extent of Jewish syncretism in the Hellenistic and Roman periods. A writer like Philo* went a long way in absorbing the prevailing Greek philosophical views of the day (esp. Middle Platonism) and presenting Judaism in these terms to his pagan contemporaries. Yet he stops short of identifying Yahweh with Zeus or Sarapis. Neither does he attempt to transform Judaism by infusing it with rituals and beliefs from Egyptian or Greek religions. E. R. Goodenough's contention that Philo had assimilated many mystery-cult beliefs has been shown to be without support. Although Philo often uses the language of the mysteries, he does so more to present his own ancestral faith in language that would have been comprehensible to pagans. Furthermore, there is still no concrete evidence that Diaspora Jews had developed mystery cults based on and borrowing from the pagan mystery cults (see G. Lease).

Some scholars claim to have found evidence of Jewish syncretism in the cults of *Theos Hypsistos* and *Sabazios* in Asia Minor. We know very little about the worship of these two deities since they are only attested epigraphically. Based on this evidence, however, F. Cumont argued that the pagan use of *Hypsistos* ("most high god") was stimulated by the Jewish worship of Yahweh as *Hypsistos* in Asia Minor. He further suggested that a few pagan *thiasoi* (cult associations) had arisen independently of the synagogues devoted to the worship of the Most High and assimilated many Jewish religious concepts into a syncretistic fusion of pagan and Jewish ideas (see Cumont, 62-66, 162). Both Cumont and R. Reitzenstein contended that the Asia Minor cult of Sabazios represents the identification of the Jewish "Lord of Hosts" (LXX = *kyrios Sabaōth*) with a local Phrygian-Thracian deity (Sabazios) also identified with the Phrygian Jupiter and Dionysus (Cumont, 64; Reitzenstein, 123-25). Recent scholarship has called into question Cumont's interpretation that these two cults represent some sort of syncretism with Judaism. P. Trebilco and A. T. Kraabel contend that there is adequate reason to view both of these cults as purely pagan without postulating that they represent some sort of declension within Judaism or even Jewish influence on a pagan cult (see Trebilco, 127-44, and Kraabel, 450-51).

Nowhere is syncretism illustrated more clearly than in the magical and astrological beliefs of the era (see Magic and Astrology). In this realm power* takes precedence over personality. Commitment to one deity or fidelity to one cult gives way to rituals of power that work. Thus many gods and goddesses could be invoked at the same time by one person. Yahweh (or *Iao*) could be invoked in the same breath as Artemis and Hekate. Palestinian and diaspora Jews participated in this form of syncretism. Numerous Jewish magical amulets, spells and astrological documents attest to the prevalence of syncretistic Jewish magic (see Alexander).

2. Christianity as a Syncretistic Religion?

To what extent did the Hellenistic/Roman syncretism influence the development of early Christianity? H. Gunkel and other adherents of the History-of-Religions School argued that it was a major factor. Gunkel, in fact, concluded that, "Christianity is a syncretistic religion" (Gunkel, 95). He argued that the NT was strongly influenced by many foreign religions, but that these beliefs entered Christianity in the first instance through Judaism, which itself was very strongly syncretistic. R. Bultmann spoke of syncretism more often in connection with Hellenistic Christianity, which he sharply distinguished from Jewish Christianity. He noted, "on the whole, one could be tempted to term Hellenistic Christianity a syncretistic structure" (Bultmann, 1.164). For Bultmann the Jewish apocalyptic* kerygma of Jesus was combined with the gnostic* myth of redemption as Christianity spread to the Gentile world. Like Gunkel, however, he saw Hellenistic Judaism as "in the grip of syncretism" (Bultmann, 1.171) and therefore as the purveyor of these concepts to Christianity.

The subsequent course of scholarship has effectively dismantled many of the conclusions drawn by the History-of-Religions School. Various studies have demonstrated that there was not one coherent gnostic redeemer myth nor was there a common mystery-religion theology. We have already touched on the fact that Judaism was not the syncretistic religion that some scholars once thought that it was. Now most scholars are reluctant to assume that Gnosticism even existed during the genesis and early development of Christianity.

The majority of scholars are reaffirming the essential Jewishness of the early Christian movement. The background of various Christian rites, ideas and terms is being illustrated out of the OT and Judaism, in contrast to the previous generation that pointed to gnostic texts and the mystery religions. The background of the Christian practice of baptism,* for instance, is now seldom traced to the mystery initiation sacraments of Attis, Adonis or Osiris but to the OT initiation rite of circumcision* and the Jewish water purification rituals.

Gunkel, Bultmann and others clearly undervalued the formative influence of the OT and Judaism for early Christianity. Neither were they sufficiently open to the possibility that the NT writers could use religious language shared by adherents of other religions without adopting the full meaning of that language, as it was understood in other religious contexts. In other words, Christian writers could use the term *mystery** (e.g., Rev 10:7; Ign. *Magn.* 9.1; *Diogn.* 4.6) without implying that Christianity is a mystery religion like the cults of Cybele or Mithras. John could use the image of light* (1 Jn 1:5, 7; 2:8, 9, 10) without dependence on a gnostic light-darkness dualism. Both of these terms have long histories of usage in the OT that provide us with

the essential conceptual framework for understanding their NT usage. Yet at the same time they are terms that would communicate in a Gentile world, albeit now with a different set of connotations.

There is also evidence that the apostles and leaders in the early Christian movement made explicit and earnest attempts to resist the syncretistic impulses of the age. For example, when Paul preached in Lystra (Acts 14:8-20), he was faced with an opportunity to make a syncretistic innovation to the gospel. Luke records that after Paul healed a crippled man the people of the city mistook him for Hermes (the messenger of Zeus) and Barnabas for Zeus. Rather than allowing any form of identification with their gods (even the identification of "the living God" with Zeus), Paul takes the bold step of telling them to "turn from these worthless things" to the one God, the Creator (Acts 14:15). Earliest Christianity appears to have made stringent effort to resist the larger cultural trend toward the identification of deities and directed people to the God of Israel, who had now revealed himself in the Lord* Jesus Christ.

3. Syncretistic Trends in Early Christianity.

Nevertheless, there were clearly some syncretistic trends in the early Christian movement for which we can find evidence in the NT and the apostolic fathers. Invariably the NT writers portray the assimilationist tendencies as unacceptable. A few representative examples illustrate these trends.

3.1. Assimilation of Magic (Acts 8:9-25; 19:17-20). In Luke's portrayal of the Simon Magus episode (Acts 8:9-25), the reader is left with no uncertainty regarding the inappropriateness of understanding Christianity through the lenses of a magical worldview. The magician is severely upbraided for seeking power rather than forgiveness* of sin and a relationship of submission to the will of the risen Christ.

Many Christians did find it difficult to give up their magical practices and depend on Christ alone for protection and enablement. The great number who burned their magical texts in Ephesus were Christians, not pagans from the Gentile* population (Acts 19:17-20). The dramatic event involving the Jewish exorcist Sceva and his sons was the catalyst for these Ephesian Christians to reevaluate their involvements with magic. Again, Luke's narrative makes it clear that the most appropriate response for Christians converted from a background in the occultic arts is to renounce it completely and give their total allegiance to the Lord Jesus Christ. The fact that some Christians did not follow the example of this story and rid themselves of these practices is now well attested by a corpus of Coptic and Greek "Christian" magical texts found in Egypt (see Meyer and Smith).

3.2. Assimilation of Local Cult Practices (Rev 2:20-29). The church at Thyatira comes under strong rebuke in the Apocalypse for tolerating the teachings of a local prophetess whom the writer refers to as a "Jezebel" (Rev 2:20). She is said to deceive many of the believers in the church by leading them into sexual immorality and eating food sacrificed to idols. A brief look at the local religious milieu helps us to understand how this could have happened. The most popular deity of the city was Apollo Tyrimnaeus who was the patron god of the local trade guilds. C. J. Hemer has contended that the influential prophetess was probably urging an accommodation to the beliefs and practices of the local Apollo cult (Hemer, 118). Specifically she was arguing (perhaps appealing to prophetic inspiration) that Christians could maintain their membership in the guilds and participate in the temple feasts (where meat sacrificed to Apollo would be consumed and sexual liaisons in the name of the god would be made) without compromising their faith. This syncretistic accommodation to the local cult was deemed unacceptable. Hemer concludes that in the eyes of John, trade guild membership "necessarily involved contradiction of the Apostolic Decree and the needed repentance must necessarily involve repudiation of the guilds" (Hemer, 123).

3.3. Assimilation of Epicurean Rationalism (2 Peter). Recent study of 2 Peter* has shown that a strong tendency to assimilate an Epicurean set of beliefs into Christianity characterized the adversaries* (Neyrey; Bauckham, 154-57). This faction appears to have adopted a commonsense rationalistic view of the world after rejecting the traditional primitive Christian eschatological* expectation of a return (*see* Parousia) of Christ and judgment* (2 Pet 2:3; 3:4, 9). They also appeared to discount the power of the devil (*see* Satan) and his angels* (2 Pet 2:10). Their resultant "freedom" evi-

dently justified their participation in sexual* immorality, drunkenness and various other vices (2 Pet 2:2, 10, 13-14, 18). Neyrey suggested that these and other aspects of the beliefs of the opponents are more consistent with adopting an Epicurean point of view, as opposed to assuming that they represent a splinter group that have become Gnostics. The letter itself, however, reveals an early Christian resistance of assimilationist tendencies found in the churches.

3.4. Assimilation of Platonic Dualism (Johannine Letters). It has long been thought that the schismatics in the Johannine community were Gnostics of some sort. The trend in recent scholarship, however, has moved away from this facile identification since many crucial aspects of gnostic theology do not appear to be present in the teaching of the opponents. For instance, there is no polemic indicting the gnostic understandings of the demiurge as evil, the ascent of the soul after death or the preexistence of the souls of the *pneumatikoi*.

Many scholars have been content to look to the evidence of the text itself and identify the secessionists as having docetic* tendencies without appealing to developed Gnosticism for an explanation. R. E. Brown, for instance, describes the opponents in 1 John as docetists who arrived at their position through their idiosyncratic interpretation of the Gospel of John. After they were cut off from the Johannine community, they became even more "progressive" in their christology and ethics. This group, in the opinion of Brown, "offered a marvelous catalyst to docetic and gnostic strains of Christian thought" (Brown, 45-115, esp. 104).

Brown does not deal sufficiently with why one segment of the Johannine community would read the Gospel of John through a docetic lens. He isolates the Johannine community too much from the world in which it existed. At this juncture, one needs to factor into the discussion the increasing popularity of Platonic thought (viz. the rise of Middle Platonism). The example of Philo himself is sufficient to show the attraction of this philosophical system to some educated Jews in the diaspora. The platonic distinction between two levels of reality, in which the highest value is placed on the transcendent models (ideas) and little epistemological value is given to the level of sense perception, may have inclined some to interpret the gospel in a docetic direction. The end result is a syncretism of the gospel with platonic ideas that may have been mediated to the church through Hellenistic Judaism or directly through the pagan culture itself.

This trend toward docetism continues to be a problem well into the second century, not only in Asia Minor, but possibly also in Antioch* (Syria), if Ignatius* reveals anything of his own situation. Ignatius is aware of, and warns the church against, those who "do not confess that he [Jesus] was clothed in the flesh" (Ign. *Smyrn.* 5.2; cf. 4.2).

4. Gnosticism and Christianity.

Middle Platonic philosophy and a docetic view of Christ were indeed streams of thought that fed into the fully developed gnostic systems that we find reflected in the writings of Irenaeus, Hippolytus and others. Gnosticism represented the grandest form of syncretism in combining aspects of Judaism, Platonism, Greco-Roman and Egyptian religions (including mystery cults), magic, astrology and Persian thought into various systems of redemption (see Rudolph, 54-55).

See also ADVERSARIES; DIASPORA JUDAISM; DOCETISM; GNOSIS, GNOSTICISM; MAGIC AND ASTROLOGY; PHILO; RELIGIONS, GRECO-ROMAN.

BIBLIOGRAPHY. P. S. Alexander, "Incantations and Books of Magic" in *The History of the Jewish People in the Age of Jesus Christ*, rev. and ed. G. Vermes, F. Millar and M. Goodman (Edinburgh: T & T Clark, 1986) 3.1.342-79; C. E. Arnold, *The Colossian Syncretism: The Interface Between Christianity and Folk Belief at Colossae* (WUNT 2/77; Tübingen: J. C. B. Mohr, 1995); R. J. Bauckham, *Jude, 2 Peter* (WBC 50; Waco: Word, 1983); W. Bauer, *Orthodoxy and Heresy in Earliest Christianity*, ed. R. A. Kraft and G. Krodel (2d. ed.; Philadelphia: Fortress, 1971); R. E. Brown, *The Epistles of John* (AB 30; Garden City, NY, 1982); R. Bultmann, *Theology of the New Testament* (2 vols.; New York: Scribner's, 1951, 1955); C. Colpe, "Syncretism," ER 14.218-27; J. D. G. Dunn, *Unity and Diversity in the New Testament* (2d ed.; Valley Forge: Trinity Press International, 1990); E. Ferguson, *Backgrounds of Early Christianity* (2d ed.; Grand Rapids: Eerdmans, 1993); E. R. Goodenough, *By Light, Light: The Mystic Gospel of Hellenistic Judaism* (New Haven: Yale, 1935); H. Gunkel, *Zum religionsgeschichtlichen Verständnis des Neuen Testaments* (Göttingen, 1903); C. J. Hemer, *The Letters to the Seven Churches of Asia in their Local Settings* (JSNTSup 11; Sheffield: JSOT Press, 1986); A. T. Kraabel, "The Roman Diaspora: Six Questionable Assumptions," *JJS* 33 (1982) 445-64; G. Lease, "Jewish Mystery Cults Since Goodenough," *ANRW* 2.20.2 (1987) 858-80; L. Martin, *Hellenistic Religions* (New York: Oxford University Press, 1987); M. W. Meyer and R. Smith, *Ancient Christian Magic: Coptic Texts of Ritual Power* (San Francisco: Harper, 1994); J. H. Neyrey, "The Form and Background of the Polemic in 2 Peter," *JBL* 99 (1980) 407-31; H. Paulsen, "Synkretismus im Urchristentum und im Neuen Testament" in *Neu Glauben? Religionsvielfalt und neue religiöse Strömungen als Herausforderung an das Christentum*, ed. W. Grieve and R. Niemann (Gütersloh: Mohn, 1990) 34-44; R. Reitzenstein, *Hellenistic Mystery-Religions* (PTMS 15; Pittsburgh: Pickwick, 1978); K. Rudolph, *Gnosis: The Nature and History of Gnosticism* (San Francisco: Harper & Row, 1987); P. Trebilco, *Jewish Communities in Asia Minor* (SNTSMS 69; Cambridge: Cambridge University Press, 1991). C. E. Arnold

SYRIA, SYRIAN CHRISTIANITY

Syrian Christianity began in Syrian Antioch,* an important urban center of early Christianity, and spread into the greater Syrian-speaking world, with Edessa becoming another important Christian center. Although many questions remain to be answered regarding the origins and early history of Syrian church, the available evidence offers a valuable glimpse of an important sector of early Christianity.

    1. Ancient Syria
    2. The Arrival of Christianity in Syria
    3. Early Syrian Christianity
    4. Early Syriac Literature and Christian Life

1. Ancient Syria.

Syria, that most valued province of the eastern Roman Empire,* was bounded on the north by Cilicia, on the south by Galilee and Judea and on the east by the tiny kingdom of Osrhoene and the massive Persian (Parthian) Empire. The term *Syria* also refers to a West Asian Semitic culture and its ancient language, Syriac. The Syriac language developed in the regions around Edessa from the Mesopotamian tribal language of Aramaic, which in turn is a Syro-Arabian (Semitic) language. Syriac script was first found on inscriptions in the first century A.D. (around Edessa, present-day Urfa in southeast Turkey), and by the ninth century the language had virtually disappeared except in liturgical literature. There are three Syriac scripts: Estranghelo is the original uncial script from which the Serto (used by the Jacobites and Melkites) and Nestorian scripts developed.

The Syrian church, speaking mostly Greek, flourished from earliest times in Roman Syria, but in the Syriac language the gospel also spread from Edessa through Osrhoene, Adiabene, Armenia and Persia (modern-day Iraq and Iran). Before the end of the second century the church was well established in India. Syrian Christianity became very divided beginning in the fourth century because of the christological* controversies, persecutions* and imperial wars.

The main city of Roman Syria, Antioch,* was not only an important church center (Acts 11:26) but also a key military hub for Rome and an international trading center since it was the first city on the Old Silk Route through central Asia to Cathay (China). Flourishing trade created a cosmopolitan city with an especially large group of Jews. Jews had been encouraged by the Seleucids to settle in Antioch, and during the Maccabean wars other Jews fled from Judea to Antioch and further east to Edessa. Antioch, like the rest of Syria, was known for its schools: Jewish, pagan and then Christian. The intercultural mix made this third largest Roman city a strategic center for the church and for missionary activity (Acts 11:19-30; 13:1-3; 14:21-28; 15:22-35).

In the postapostolic age Antioch continued to be a theological and missionary center. Ignatius* (c. 35-c. 107) was either the second (after Peter) or third bishop (after Euodius) of Antioch, and though he was likely of pagan Syrian origin, his greatest influence was on the Western church through the letters he wrote on his way to martyrdom* in Rome.*

Christianity that was later called Syrian and characterized by its use of the Syriac, rather than the Greek language, flourished beyond the bounds of Antioch and the Syrian province of the Roman Empire. Edessa was a Syriac cultural center and the capital of the first Christian kingdom: Osrhoene. It was in the environs of Edessa and the eastern Persian city of Nisibis that Syrian Christianity developed its theological, monastic and missionary characteristics.

2. The Arrival of Christianity in Syria.

The early history of Syrian Christianity is clouded by myth and legend, yet it contains certain lines of historical development. Acts 2:9 records that Medes (from western Iraq), Parthians (Persians), Elamites (from Iran) and residents of Mesopotamia were present in Jerusalem* on the day of Pentecost* and witnessed the birth of the church. Although we have no record of these travelers returning to their homes and starting churches, we do know that by the end of the second century the church had spread to all of these areas, mostly along the Silk Route. Syrian Christianity of the first few centuries seems very Jewish in expression, but it shows no signs of the judaizing elements that Paul warned against in Galatians. We can say little with confidence about the heritage of Syrian Christianity, but later legends abound.

Legend has it that the apostle Thomas spread faith in Jesus to the East. Eusebius tells us that Thomas was designated to evangelize Parthia (Eusebius *Hist. Eccl.* 3.1), but Rufinus of Aquileia and Jerome (Jerome *Vita Apost.* 5) both say he was sent to Persia. Gregory of Nazianzus (Gregory *Oration* 33.11) held the traditional East Syrian view that Thomas was sent by Christ to India, where he planted churches and then was martyred (Gregory *Oration* 25). This story is told in the *Acts of Thomas* 1 (a third-century Syriac work) and was also accepted by the great Syrian saint Ephrem (c. 306-73; Ephrem *Hymns on Nisibis* 42), who explains that Thomas's body was later returned to Edessa. Thus traditions have Thomas going to south India, north India and Parthia, but all traditions have him going to Asia and dying in Asia. Indian Christians mark his place of martyrdom and his grave in Mylapore, south of Madras in southeast India. Nothing conclusive can be said about Thomas's mission to India, but it should be noted that Christianity in southern Tamil Nadu and Kerala first spread from the east, indicating that Christian missionaries or merchants arrived near Mylapore in the southeast and then, under persecution, spread westward.

3. Early Syrian Christianity.

As the Christian faith spread eastward from Jerusalem and Antioch, Edessa, capital of the client kingdom of Osrhoene, was the first major city to be reached. Eusebius (Eusebius *Hist. Eccl.* 1.13) records that Addai (Thaddeus) was sent by Thomas to the king of Osrhoene, Abgar V ("the Black"), to bring healing* from Jesus to the afflicted king. Eusebius claims to quote from an extant correspondence between Abgar and Jesus regarding the king's healing (Eusebius *Hist. Eccl.* 1.13.6-10). This story is also told in the *Doctrine of Addai* (late fourth or early fifth century), which also speaks of the later conversion of the entire city of Edessa. This story has historical elements (early Jewish converts, large national Christian movement, a king who converts to Christianity), yet it is not likely that Christianity became the national religion until the reign of Abgar VIII (177-212). Thus two Abgars may be confused in the *Doctrine of Addai.*

Although there are reports that Christianity moved to Edessa from the east rather than from the west, both geography and the strongest traditions suggest that the eastern city of Arbela (modern Erbil), the capital of Adiabene on the Tigris River, was evangelized after Edessa. Josephus (Josephus *Ant.* 20.21-5 §§17-53) reports that in about A.D. 36, King Ezad and Queen Helena both converted to Judaism.* This might have prepared the way for conversion to Christianity, but Christian tradition does not mention a Jewish king. According to Syrian tradition, it was either the successor of Addai, Aggai *(Doctrine of the Apostles),* Mari *(Acts of Mari)* or Addai himself *(Chronicle of Arbela)* who first planted the church in Arbela. Adiabene, located more deeply in Persian territory, claims no Jewish connection, and its church seems to have a Zoroastrian or pagan cultural heritage. Early persecutions from Zoroastrians must have been a common Christian concern, for there are numerous extant, though certainly embellished, martyr stories that tell of terrible persecutions.

4. Early Syriac Literature and Christian Life.
The early Syrian form of Christianity, found partially in the Roman Empire but mostly in the small kingdoms of Osrhoene and Adiabene and in Persia, developed a Christian Syriac literature at the turn of the second century that fully flowered from the fourth to the ninth centuries. The earliest Christian writings extant in the Syriac language are the Scriptures and the *Odes of Solomon.* The Syriac Bible, known as the Peshitta ("simple" or "plain" version), was prob-

ably the work of a number of translators in Edessa, translating at times very literally from the OT Hebrew text. NT portions were not fully translated from the Greek until the fifth century (Cureton and Siniatic manuscripts). Prior to the fifth century the Gospel account used was Tatian's Diatessaron (late second century), a single telling of the life of Jesus "through four" *(dia tessarōn)* Gospel accounts. Although there appears to be an Old Syriac version (c. 200) of Acts* and the Pauline epistles that was the basis of the Peshitta, this text is no longer extant. It must be noted that the development of the Syriac Scriptures was occurring almost simultaneously with the development of the Syriac language and script.

The *Odes of Solomon,* a corpus of forty-two Syriac and some Coptic Christian hymns,* seems to be the oldest extant Christian Syriac literature. The hymns have been dated as late as the early third century, but internal evidence (primitive Jewish Christianity,* a lack of NT quotations or images, inconsistent titles for church leaders) points to a very early stage when the Edessan church was developing in the midst of gnostic* movements and Jewish synagogues.* The hymns seem to have been written by a single author who claims direct inspiration for his oracles. They mention an incarnation (*Odes Sol.* 41.8-10) and a resurrection* (*Odes Sol.* 42.6) and have a strong missionary concern (*Odes Sol.* 12). The *Odes* read like OT psalms, with parallel lines in couplets (distichs), and are clearly meant for public reading or singing in worship.*

Syrian Christianity, although translating Greek Christian and philosophic works, developed a very different form of Christianity from that of the Roman Empire. Syrian Christianity spread first among Jewish trading communities and retained many Semitic characteristics. The Syrian literature, including exegesis, is more poetic than philosophic or dogmatic, often expressing ideas in hymns and parallel strophes. Images dominate over didactic or polemical discourse in the early literature. It is likely that the inferior position of Christians in Persian and Indian societies and the extensive persecutions produced the austere and at times ascetic life that is characteristic of the early Syrian church. From Syrian Christianity flowed both the extreme forms of asceticism (Stylites, Sons and Daughters of the Covenant) and the great

missionary zeal that had reached China by 635.
See also ANTIOCH; IGNATIUS OF ANTIOCH.

BIBLIOGRAPHY. A. Baumstark, *Geschichte der syrischen Literatur* (Bonn, 1922); S. P. Brock, *The Bible in the Syriac Tradition* (SEERI Correspondence Course on the Syrian Christian Heritage 1; Kottayam, 1989); idem, *Syriac Perspectives on Late Antiquity* (Collected Studies Series 119; London: Variorum Reprints, 1984); F. C. Burkitt, *Early Eastern Christianity* (London: John Murray, 1904); J. H. Charlesworth, *The Odes of Solomon: Syriac Texts Edited with Translation and Notes* (Oxford: Clarendon, 1973); J. M. Fiey, *Jalons pour une histoire de l'Eglise en Iraq* (Louvain: Secretariat du Corpus SCO, 1970); G. Howard, trans., *The Teaching of Addai* (Texts and Translations 16; Chico, CA: Scholars Press, 1981); A. F. J. Klijn, *The Acts of Thomas: Introduction, Text and Commentary* (Leiden: E. J. Brill, 1962); J. Labourt, *Le Christianisme dans l'Empire Perse sous le dynastie Sassanide* (Paris: Lecoffre, 1904); S. H. Moffett, *A History of Christianity in Asia*, 1: *Beginnings to 1500* (San Francisco: Harper, 1992); A. M. Mundadan, *History of Christianity in India*, 1: *From the Beginning Up to the Middle of the Sixteenth Century* (Bangalore: Church History Association of India, 1989); R. Murray, *Symbols of Church and Kingdom: A Study in Early Syriac Tradition* (Cambridge: Cambridge University Press, 1975); J. B. Segal, *Edessa, "The Blessed City"* (Oxford: Oxford University Press, 1970); A. Voobus, *Celibacy, A Requirement for Admission to Baptism in the Early Syrian Church* (CSCO 128, Subsidia 3; Stockholm; Secretariat du Corpus SCO, 1951); idem, *History of Asceticism in the Syrian Orient: A Contribution to the History of Culture in the Near East*, 1: *The Origin of Asceticism: Early Monasticism in Persia* (CSCO 184, Subsidia 14; Louvain: Secretariat du Corpus SCO, 1958); W. Wright, *A Short History of Syriac Literature* (Amsterdam: Philo Press, 1966 [1894]).   S. Sunquist

T

TABERNACLE, SANCTUARY

Paul applied the imagery and language of the temple* primarily to the people of God, defined in terms of their relationship to Christ (*see DPL*, Temple). This understanding is similarly expressed by Peter in his first letter and to an extent by John in the book of Revelation. However, John also recognizes that the dwelling of God in heaven is the locus of the true temple, and the believers' final incorporation into that temple is the consummation of God's purposes for his people. The writer to the Hebrews has a particular concern to establish the reality of the heavenly temple as the locus of Christ's redemptive activity, which has now superseded the earthly temple, being but a shadow of the true one in heaven. (For further background on the Jerusalem temple, which forms the basis of these writers' imagery, *see DJG*, Temple.)

1. Terminology
2. Acts
3. Hebrews
4. 1 Peter
5. Revelation
6. Apostolic Fathers

1. Terminology.

The Greek words for sanctuary (*naos*) and temple (*hieron*) are usually used to describe the inner sanctuary of the temple and the whole temple precincts respectively (Michel, 880-99); however, this is not an invariable distinction for all NT authors. In Acts, Luke uses *hieron* exclusively for the temple in Jerusalem* and *naos* when he refers to pagan temples (Acts 17:24; 19:24). When referring to the tabernacle of Moses,* he uses *skēnē* ("tent"; Acts 7:44; cf. Acts 15:16). In the book of Revelation, however, John uses *naos* exclusively for his description of the temple, whether earthly or heavenly. The writer to the Hebrews uses neither *hieron* nor *naos*. By contrast, this author uses *hagion* (or its

plural form, *hagia*) and *skēnē* when referring to either the earthly tabernacle or the heavenly sanctuary. The apostolic fathers, however, use *naos* exclusively when referring to the temple, whether literally or metaphorically.

2. Acts.

The opening chapters of the book of Acts* focus particular attention upon the temple in Jerusalem (Acts 2:46; 3:1—4:4; 5:20-32, 42; 6:13-14; 7:44-50), and toward the end of the book the temple again figures prominently in the record of Paul's arrest (Acts 21:15—23:35; 24:6-18; 25:8). However, unlike the Pauline letters, there is no attempt by Luke to regard the church* as the new temple or the replacement of the temple. On the contrary, as J. B. Chance argues, the temple appears as a mark of continuity between the people of God under the old and new covenants.*

It has been argued by A. Cole and others that Stephen's* speech (esp. Acts 7:44-50) has an intrinsic though not explicit reference to the new temple being the church. However, this view has been challenged by those who argue that Luke is not propounding a replacement theology of the temple, in terms of the Messiah or his people (McKelvey, 87; Chance, 39-40). The contrast expressed in Stephen's speech is not one of temple and Christ or temple and church; rather it is between a house made with hands and a house made without hands: a contrast between the earthly temple and the heavenly temple (the latter being the pattern for the former, Acts 7:44). Luke's interest in the physical temple in Jerusalem is not to be thought incompatible with a replacement theology in which that temple is replaced; it is merely that we should recognize Luke has omitted an explicit statement of this idea.

3. Hebrews.

The letter to the Hebrews* is well known for its

teaching concerning the heavenly temple. This is but one strand of many in the author's desire to establish the superiority of the new covenant to that of the old. Hebrews 8—10 are at the heart of the epistle, and here the writer expounds the relationship between the earthly tabernacle and its heavenly counterpart. As indicated (see 1 above), the usual words for temple and sanctuary are absent, the author preferring to use *skēnē* and *hagion* or *hagia*. The reason for this choice is most probably that the point of comparison for the writer is Moses' tabernacle rather than Solomon's temple, complementing the characterization of Jesus' superiority to Moses (Heb 3:3). Normally the author uses the two terms without any apparent difference in designation (Heb 13:11) and can even combine the two expressions in a hendiadys describing the one object (e.g., Heb 8:2; see Peterson, 130).

However, in Hebrews 9:11-12 the writer makes a distinction between the two terms, where the tent *(skēnē)* through which Jesus passed is distinguished from the holy place *(ta hagia)* that he entered (Peterson, 130; Lane, 237-38). However, it is likely that this distinction is made here only because it suits the author's purpose to distinguish between the front compartment and the rear compartment of the earthly tabernacle in order to draw a parallel between the first covenant and the second covenant. The spatial reference to the first (front) compartment is symbolized as a temporal reference, describing the Mosaic covenant with its attendant veil depicting, for the people, a barrier between them and the holy place. Yet now that Christ has entered through the *skēnē* and into the holy place, access to God's holy place has been permanently guaranteed.

For the writer to the Hebrews the sanctuary or holy place depicts the dwelling place and presence of God.* The Mosaic tabernacle is a copy of the true sanctuary in heaven* (Heb 8:5; cf. Heb 9:23) and therefore has pedagogic value for understanding the heavenly counterpart. However, the writer is not concerned to allegorize the various furnishings of the tabernacle, preferring instead to concentrate upon the broad sweep of redemptive history, which has been revealed by the Holy Spirit* (Heb 9:8). The heavenly sanctuary is not made with hands (Heb 9:11), unlike the earthly sanctuary (Heb 9:24); the heavenly sanctuary is not of this age

(Heb 9:11, "of this creation"), unlike the earthly tabernacle, which is symbolic for the present age (Heb 9:9). For with the accomplishment of Christ* a new age has dawned, access to God's presence has been established through his blood, and believers are invited to enter that sanctuary where Jesus now is (Heb 10:19-22). Yet there is an eschatological* tension here, in that believers "have [already] come to Mt. Zion, the city of the living God, the heavenly Jerusalem" (Heb 12:22). Entering the heavenly sanctuary, it would appear, has a present dimension to it as well as a future one, which provides a richer background for understanding Paul's concept of the people of God (*see* Church as Israel) being the temple of God in Christ.

4. 1 Peter.

The first letter of Peter (*see* 1 Peter) does not use the technical terminology for temple or sanctuary. However, the description of believers as living stones* being built into a spiritual house *(oikos)* to be a holy priesthood* offering spiritual sacrifices* is replete with temple imagery (1 Pet 2:4-10). Here the apostle* employs the language of the temple to describe Christians' relationship with Christ: they have come to him, the living stone (1 Pet 2:4). In the same way that the believers' inheritance is not in the land* of Israel but in heaven itself (1 Pet 1:3-5), it is not their relationship to the earthly temple that is of importance but their being joined to the eschatological temple that is being built in Christ. It is the temple of Christ's new community that is in view, and in this respect Peter's temple theology is an extension of Paul's understanding of the people of God as God's new temple, defined christologically.*

5. Revelation.

Unlike Hebrews, Revelation (*see* Revelation, Book of) uses the term *naos* (but neither *hieron* nor *hagion*) to describe the temple and *skēnē* to describe the tabernacle. The two words are virtually synonymous and always refer to the heavenly or eschatological reality (with the exception of Rev 11:1-2).

However, whereas Hebrews' use of temple imagery is primarily concerned with the redemptive historical accomplishment of Jesus' entrance into the holy of holies, Revelation has a focus upon the heavenly temple as the place of God's abode (Rev 15:8), the place from which the earth is governed and judgment* emanates (Rev 14:15, 17; 16:1, 17). Yet it is also the place of safety for the saints (Rev 3;12; 7:15). Where God is, there his temple is; from his throne issue both wrath* and mercy.* Although John does not show any interest in the earthly temple, his description of the heavenly temple containing the long-forgotten ark of the covenant (Rev 11:19) is clearly related to the sanctuary or temple of the OT. Yet there can be no physical temple in heaven. The saints themselves are pillars in God's temple (Rev 3:12). The reality of God dwelling with his people has arrived, and the need for copies of the original has passed. The city with its cubical dimensions (Rev 21:16-18) reflects the dimensions of the holy of holies, and John declares that there is no temple in the city, for the Lord God the Almighty and the Lamb* are its temple (Rev 21:22). In this final reference to the temple in the NT canon* the categories of temple are submerged in the vision* of God and the Lamb, in whose presence the saints experience the fulfillment of the promise* of God, to dwell with his people forever (Rev 22:1-5).

6. Apostolic Fathers.
Those postapostolic authors (*see* Apostolic Fathers) who make use of the temple imagery in their writings tend to follow the development of the Pauline corpus, where the focus is upon the Christian community or the individual Christian as the temple of the Holy Spirit. Thus Clement (*see* Clement of Rome) exhorts his readers to preserve the flesh as the temple (*naos*) of God (*2 Clem.* 9.3).

In the *Epistle of Barnabas** the author devotes a whole section of his letter to the temple. He castigates the Jews for having put their faith in a temple building instead of God himself. By faith, believers have received remission of sins, and "God truly dwells in us, in the habitation which we are" (*Barn.* 16.8). Since God dwells in us, we are "a spiritual temple being built in the Lord" (*Barn.* 16.10).

Likewise Ignatius* exhorts the Philadelphians: "Keep your flesh as the temple of God" (Ign. *Phld.* 7.2). To the Ephesians, borrowing the language of 1 Peter, he writes: "You are stones of the temple of the Father made ready for the building of God . . . you are then all fellow travelers and carry with you God and the temple and Christ" (Ign. *Eph.* 9.1-2).

All these examples reflect the consistent application of temple imagery to the earthly locus, where God dwells in and among his people. The heavenly locus, as it was developed by the authors of Hebrews and Revelation, does not explicitly appear in the writings of the first three centuries, even though such a conception would not have been at variance with their teaching. Their concern was to impress upon their readers the reality of God dwelling in them and that they were living temples of God. It was a much later development that saw the imagery of the sanctuary and the temple being used to describe church buildings, an association that was unknown to the apostolic church and the apostolic fathers.

See also COVENANT, NEW COVENANT; GLORY; HEBREWS; OLD TESTAMENT IN HEBREWS; PRIEST, HIGH PRIEST; SACRIFICE, OFFERINGS, GIFTS; TEMPLE; WORSHIP AND LITURGY.

BIBLIOGRAPHY. J. B. Chance, *Jerusalem, the Temple and the New Age in Luke-Acts* (Edinburgh: T & T Clark, 1988); E. P. Clowney, "The Final Temple" in *Studying the New Testament Today,* ed. J. H. Skilton (Nutley, NJ: Presbyterian & Reformed, 1974) 97-132; A. Cole, *The New Temple: A Study in the Origins of the Catechetical 'Form' of the Church in the New Testament* (London: Tyndale, 1950); Y. M.-J. Congar, *The Mystery of the Temple: The Manner of God's Presence to His Creatures from Genesis to the Apocalypse* (London: Burns & Oates, 1962); W. J. Dumbrell, *The End of the Beginning: Revelation 21—22 and the Old Testament* (Sydney: Lancer, 1985); W. L. Lane, *Hebrews* (2 vols.; WBC; Dallas: Word, 1991); R. J. McKelvey, *The New Temple: The Church in the New Testament* (Oxford: Oxford University Press, 1969); O. Michel, "ναός," *TDNT* 4:880-90; D. G. Peterson, *Hebrews and Perfection* (SNTSMS 47; Cambridge: Cambridge University Press, 1982); G. Schrenk, "τὸ ἱερόν," *TDNT* 3:230-48. G. N. Davies

TABLE FELLOWSHIP. *See* FOOD, FOOD LAWS, TABLE FELLOWSHIP; HOSPITALITY; SOCIAL SETTING OF EARLY NON-PAULINE CHRISTIANITY.

TALMUD. *See* JUDAISM, POST-A.D. 70.

TANNAIM. *See* JUDAISM, POST-A.D. 70.

TARGUM. *See* JUDAISM, POST-A.D. 70.

TEACHING, PARAENESIS
Paraenesis is a technical term for moral exhor-

tation and advice. While catechesis is the form of teaching that tends to emphasize basic instruction in the content of the faith, paraenesis is the instructional model in which ethical counsel and moral education were provided in a pattern of exhortation applied to practical problems or issues of living.

"Paraenesis" is a transliteration of the Greek noun *parainesis* ("advice"), a term that is abundant in secular Greek literature but absent from the NT. The verb *paraineō* ("advise," "exhort") occurs in the NT only at Acts 27:9, 22 in a nontechnical manner, where Paul "advises" the ship's officers not to sail the winter seas but then "exhorts" them to keep up their courage once they ignored his advice and set out to sea.

1. Background
2. Characteristics of Paraenesis
3. Paraenetic Forms

1. Background.
As an educational and literary form, paraenesis occurs throughout the ancient Mediterranean world. Since the major Hellenistic schools of philosophy (Stoics, Cynics, Epicureans) all emphasized ethics,* moral exhortation and advice, paraenesis is prominent in their writings. Seneca included consolation, warning, exhortation, scolding and praising as means of offering advice (Seneca *Ep. Mor.* 94.39).

The gulf from the fixed form of the Torah (and the later Prophets and Writings) to the situational needs of Israel's community contributed to the rise in the Jewish milieu of exegetical teaching traditions and paraenesis. The emergence of the paraenetic *topos* is bound up with the development of the wisdom tradition (e.g., Prov 10:1—22:16). The paraenetic Two Ways, as in Psalm 1, arises from the duality of Jewish ethical thinking (e.g., "the way of righteousness" and the "way of the wicked" and the "two inclinations" of the rabbinic tradition; cf. McDonald, 73-79).

2. Characteristics of Paraenesis.
Paraenesis is a complex subject that has recently become a focus of NT scholarship. While some scholars have attempted to draw distinct lines between forms of exhortation, such as *protrepsis* (exhortation to an agreed upon good), *paraklēsis* (exhortation of edification and encouragement) and *paraenesis*, recent scholarship has demonstrated that ancient usage was

more vague (cf. Gammie, passim; Stowers, 91-94). In the NT recognizable paraenetic material is intertwined with *paraklēsis* to form a broader "word of exhortation." For example, the author of Hebrews* concludes his epistle with *paraklēsis* (*parakaleō . . . paraklēseōs;* Heb 13:22), which is included within a larger section of paraenesis (Heb 13:1-21). This forms a model of apostolic paraenesis quite similar to paraenetic conclusions found in other NT letters,* especially Paul's (cf. Meeks, 79-82; Lane, 497-507). The expression "word of exhortation" in Hebrews 13:22 is strikingly similar to the invitation offered to Paul and Barnabas to speak "a word of exhortation" to the Jews gathered in the synagogue* at Antioch of Pisidia (Acts 13:15). This may have been a fixed Hellenistic-Jewish expression (cf. 1 Macc 10:24; 2 Macc 7:24; 15:11; cf. 1 Macc 12:9) that was then taken up and combined with paraenetic expression by the Christian community (cf. Wills, 278-85).

Several important characteristics are shared between the classical form of paraenesis found in Greek literature and that found in the NT. Paraenesis is traditional, reflecting conventional wisdom generally approved by society (Isocrates *Nicocles* 40-41; cf. Phil 4:8); applicable to many situations (Seneca *Ep. Mor.* 94.32-35; cf. Gal 5:13-14); related or adapted to the immediate setting (Seneca *Ep. Mor.* 64.6-10; cf. 1 Cor 7:10-11, 17); so familiar that it is often presented as a "reminder" (Seneca *Ep. Mor.* 13.15; 94.21-25; cf. 1 Thess 4:1-2); exemplified in exceptional people who are models of virtue for the audience (Seneca *Ep. Mor.* 6.5-6; 11.9-10; 95.72; cf. Acts 20:31-35; 2 Thess 3:7; Phil 3:17; 4:9); usually transmitted by persons who are socially and morally superior to those they address; used to commend or compliment the audience for what they are already doing (cf. 1 Thess 4:1, 10; 5:11; Ign. *Pol.* 1.2; Ign. *Eph.* 4.1; Ign. *Trall.* 2.2; see Aune, 191; Malherbe, 65-66, 125).

D. E. Aune states, "Paraenesis is really an indirect way of addressing a behavioral problem. Since the content of paraenesis is generally approved by society, it provides a basis of agreement in situations that are potentially divisive" (191). We must add that paraenesis does not simply have the goal of social control or changing behavior. It often confirms existing behavior (Stowers, 92) and intensifies and reinforces values, convictions and attitudes (Thurén, 17-18).

3. Paraenetic Forms.

Paraenesis sometimes refers to content, that is, traditional maxims or precepts of wisdom, especially moral wisdom.* It could also refer to the form or process of addressing words of encouragement or discouragement about behavior to persons (Stowers, 91).

Paraenesis as a hortatory style occurs in diverse forms. A distinctive feature of Pauline letters is the presence of a concluding section of paraenesis (e.g., Rom 12:1—15:13; Gal 5:1—6:10; 1 Thess 4:1—5:22). In other NT letters paraenesis is woven throughout the composition (e.g., James,* Hebrews, 1-2 Corinthians, Philippians). Among the paraenetic forms found in the later NT and the apostolic fathers* are *topos*, vice and virtue* lists, codes of household ethics (*see* Household Codes) and the Two Ways tradition.

3.1. Topos. One of the most common forms of paraenesis is *topos* (pl. *topoi*), a word whose connotation of location or place—including geographical, physiological, psychological or ethical—made it suitable to use in rhetoric* to denote a commonplace of subjects related to questions of justice or politics. In paraenesis *topos* denotes a particular topic of moral concern. On the one hand paraenetical exhortation as found in Xenophon could include a listing of *topoi* in his record of the teaching of Socrates as courage, wisdom, prudence, justice, madness, envy, leisure, kings and rulers (Socrates *Memorabilia* 3.9). On the other hand a minimal *topos* may consist of only a sentence or so devoted to one subject, including an imperatival or gnomic statement such as Isocrates' charge, "Fear the gods; honor your parents as you would wish your children to act toward you" (Isocrates *Dem.* 16; see McDonald, 70-71).

The authors of the later NT material and the apostolic fathers addressed similar paraenetic procedures to the particular situations that they confronted (e.g., 1 Pet 1:13-16; *1 Clem.* 38.1-4; cf. Bowe, 131-35). In addition they addressed paraenetical *topoi* to the institutional needs of the church and its ministry*; that is, paraenetical *topoi* were used by Christian writers to give guidance to Christians in areas of belief and conduct.

Topical figures in early church instruction were less frequent and less consciously rhetorical or literary than non-Christian counterparts. But when the extended simile and metaphor do occur they are integral to the purpose of the topic, such as in the simile in 1 Peter*: "Like newborn babes, long for the pure spiritual milk" (1 Pet 2:2; *see* Milk), or in the author's of Hebrews use of *parabolē* to denote Israel* being debarred from the inner sanctuary of the temple* as "symbolic for the present age" (Heb 9:9; cf. Heb 11:9), or the *Epistle of Barnabas's** use of the latter twice in relation to scriptural interpretation (*Barn.* 6.10, citing Ex 33:1-3; cf. McDonald, 94).

3.2. Virtue and Vice Lists. Virtue* and vice lists were common in antiquity as means of delineating desired and undesired behaviors and values. The content of these lists as they are found in the later NT often display traditional values that are common to Jews, Christians and pagans. In the literature of the later NT we find lists of vices (e.g., Jas 1:21; 1 Pet 2:1; 4:3) and lists of virtues (Heb 7:26; 1 Pet 2:1), while in the apostolic fathers the lists become more extensive (e.g., *1 Clem.* 13.1; 35.5; *Did.* 5; Pol. *Phil.* 2.2; 4.3; *Herm. Man.* 5.2; 6.2; 8.3-5; *Herm. Sim.* 6.5; 9.15).

3.3. Codes of Household Ethics. Household codes* of ethics (commonly referred to by the German *Haustafeln*, "house tablets") were widespread in the Greco-Roman world. These codes focused on three primary levels of reciprocal submission and obligations within the extended family: wives to husbands, slaves to masters, children to parents. Jewish forms of household codes are evident in the context of the *Shema* (Deut 6:4-9), in the Fourth Commandment and in the wisdom literature. The NT codes prominently include obligation to governmental authority (*see* Civil Authority). A code of household ethics is found in 1 Peter 2:11—3:12 (cf. 1 Tim 2:1-15; Tit 2:1-15; Eph 5:21—6:9; Col 3:19—4:1), in part occurring as an apologetic to show that Christianity was not culturally subversive (Balch, 81-109). Early Christianity apparently applied the household model to relationships within the church* itself, producing ecclesiastical station codes (e.g., *1 Clem.* 1.3; 21.6-9; Ign. *Pol.* 4.1—6.1; *Did.* 4.9-11; Pol. *Phil.* 4.1—6.3; Aune, 196; McDonald, 97-98, 190).

3.4. Two Ways Tradition. The Two Ways motif, drawing on two ways or paths as a metaphor for a life of vice or virtue, was frequently used in the Greco-Roman world. This metaphor was a staple of Jewish wisdom, eschatology* and apocalyptic* and is prominent in the teaching of Jesus and in early Christian paraenesis. We find the Two Ways motif in the paraenesis of James 4, the light* and dark contrasts in the epistles of John (*see* John, Letters of) and the eschatological contrasts in 2 Peter 2:1-2. The metaphor is introduced similarly in *Didache* 1—6 and *Barnabas* 18—21, leading to extensive Two Ways material. Ignatius* gives two ways of life* and death as ultimate alternatives, but no moral exhortation is included (cf. McKenna, 403-6; Bauckham, 238-43; van de Sandt, 40-41; Aune, 197).

See also COMMANDMENTS; ETHICS; HOUSEHOLD CODES; KERYGMA AND DIDACHE; MILK, SOLID FOOD; PASTORAL THEOLOGY; RHETORIC, RHETORICAL CRITICISM; VIRTUES AND VICES.

BIBLIOGRAPHY. D. E. Aune, *The New Testament in Its Literary Environment* (Philadelphia: Westminster, 1987); D. L. Balch, *Let Wives Be Submissive: The Domestic Code in 1 Peter* (SBLMS 26; Chico, CA: Scholars Press, 1981); R. J. Bauckham, *Jude, 2 Peter* (WBC; Waco, TX: Word, 1983); B. E. Bowe, *A Church in Crisis: Ecclesiology and Paraenesis in Clement of Rome* (HDR 23; Minneapolis: Fortress, 1993); J. G. Gammie, "Paraenetic Literature: Toward the Morphology of a Secondary Genre," *Semeia* 50 (1990) 41-77; D. Hill, " 'To Offer Spiritual Sacrifices. . . ' (1 Pet 2:5): Liturgical Formulations and Christian Paraenesis in 1 Peter," *JSNT* 16 (1982) 45-63; W. L. Lane, *Hebrews* (2 vols.; WBC 47; Dallas: Word, 1991); E. Lohse, "Parenesis and Kerygma in 1 Peter" in *Perspectives on First Peter,* ed. C. H. Talbert (NABPRSS 9; Macon, GA: Mercer University Press, 1986) 37-59; J. I. H. McDonald, *Kerygma and Didache: The Articulation and Structure of the Earliest Christian Message* (SNTSMS 37; Cambridge: Cambridge University Press, 1980); M. M. McKenna, " 'The Two Ways' in Jewish and Christian Writings of the Greco-Roman Period: A Study of the Form of Repentance Parenesis" (unpublished Ph.D. dissertation, University of Pennsylvania, 1981); A. J. Malherbe, *Moral Exhortation: A Greco-Roman Sourcebook* (Philadelphia: Westminster, 1986); W. A. Meeks, *The Origins of Christian Morality: The First Two Centuries* (New Haven, CT: Yale University Press, 1993); S. K. Stowers, *Letter Writing in Greco-Roman Antiquity* (Philadelphia: Westminster, 1986); L. Thurén, *Argument and Theology in 1 Peter: The Origins of Christian Paraenesis* (JSNTSup 114; Sheffield: Sheffield Academic Press, 1995); H. W. M. van de Sandt, "Didache 3.1-6: A Transformation of an Existing Jewish Hortatory Pattern," *JSJ* 23 (1992) 21-41; L. Wills, "The Form of the Sermon in Hellenistic Judaism and Early Christianity," *HTR* 77 (1984) 277-99.   M. J. Wilkins

TEACHINGS OF SILVANUS. *See* APOCRYPHAL AND PSEUDEPIGRAPHAL WRITINGS.

TEMPLE

The temple in Jerusalem* was of central importance within early Judaism. The primitive communities of Christians reflected in the NT are examples of Judaic movements, and they developed distinctive policies toward the cult and the temple. Those policies clearly reflect the theological processes which brought about the emergence of early Christianity as separable from Judaism at the close of the NT period (*see* Christianity and Judaism).

    1. The Operation of the Second Temple
    2. The Attitude of Jesus Toward the Temple and Its Cult
    3. The Cultic Piety of the Circle of Peter
    4. The Cultic Piety of the Circle of James
    5. The Assimilation of the Temple's Function by the Community
    6. The Theology of the Definitive Replacement of the Temple

1. The Operation of the Second Temple.
The temple was the place of God's* dwelling, where his "glory"* (or, as was said during the Rabbinic period, his "Presence" [*šᵉkinâ*]) abides. That understanding has been well established in research; the architecture of the temple in Jerusalem attests it (*see DJG*, Temple, §1). But the picture of the temple as a divine "house" is only helpful when it is borne in mind that the house was not only for God but for his people and his goods: the entire household was involved in sacrificial activity. Sacrifice* involved all Israel, and even those beyond the territorial limits of Israel.

Deuteronomy identifies Jerusalem as the single "place" (*hāmāqôm*) where God is to be worshiped (Deut 12:5-14). Sacrifices to the Lord elsewhere are specifically prohibited (Deut 12:13, 14), and the complete destruction of the "places" of all other gods is prescribed (Deut 12:2, 3). Provisions are made for the long journeys which centralization sometimes demanded: sacrifices of the tithe may be converted into money, which is then used to purchase food and drink to eat before the Lord (Deut 14:22-27). Contrary to the prescriptions of Leviticus, the slaughter and consumption of animals outside of Jerusalem, explicitly as non-sacrificial, is permitted, provided the blood is poured out and the beast concerned is not owed as a sacrifice (Deut 12:15-28; see Purity and Impurity).

The strict limitation of sacrifice to Jerusalem creates the imperative of the pilgrimage. Being in the "place" is naturally an occasion for joy (Deut 12:7, 12, 18). Sacrifice in Jerusalem is the celebration and at the same time a guarantee of prosperity. Disobedience, within the Deuteronomic scheme, can only result in Israel's destruction, its scattering in the manner of the Assyrian conquest (Deut 4:25-31). But keeping the commandments ensures that the Lord will give possession of the land to his people, thrust out their enemies, and provide physical and agricultural prosperity and freedom from disease (Deut 6:17-19; 7:1-16). The dynamic heart of the promise is that Israel is holy, a people for the possession of God (Deut 7:6): the central fact that God has acquired Israel is the sole cause of their redemption from Egypt and their future prosperity in just those aspects in which Egypt had been afflicted (Deut 7:7-16). Sacrificial "rejoicing" is a way both to celebrate and to secure that blessing of God which is Israel's prosperity.

The terms of reference established by sacrifice as an act of "rejoicing" in the single, sacred "place" from which God gives Israel prosperity are precisely observed in the calendar in Deuteronomy 16. The three feasts of Passover, Weeks and Sukkoth are carefully specified, and each—even Passover, originally a domestic meal (see Ex 12)—is made the occasion of pilgrimage. The feasts of pilgrimage are occasions on which both the map and the calendar of Israel are routinely redrawn. Three times a year, Israel is back in the desert, redeemed from Egypt, new in their freedom, living in booths. The land which has so desperately been sought and acquired disappears from view, in order to be received again as the gift of God to his own people, complete with the prosperity and health he alone can bestow. Variety in the understanding of the worship which God requires in the single temple is evident within the Hebrew Bible itself. But the Deuteronomic prescriptions give a good indication of the prevailing rationale of cultic practice, as it was based upon the Mosaic covenant. Pluralization in definitions of Judaism was more radical by the first century (see *DJG*, Judaism, §4; the discussion which follows supplements that description).

The Sadducees probably owe their name to Zadok (the priest of David's and Solomon's time), but their loyalty to the settlement in the temple, in which the Romans effectively chose high priests, made them appear to many to be upholders of privilege. Josephus describes attempts by prophetic pretenders and later Zealots to disentangle the operation of the temple from collaboration with Rome (see *J.W.* 2.13.3-6 §§254-65; 7.11.1-2 §§437-46; and, on the Zealots, *J.W.* 2.20.3 §§564-65; 4.4.1 §§224-25). Even among the priesthood, nationalism was a natural outgrowth of a desire for the cultic integrity of the temple (see *J.W.* 2.20.3-4 §§562-68).

The apocalyptic* perspective within early Judaism also resulted in critical attitudes toward the temple (cf. *DJG*, Judaism, §4.1; Dead Sea Scrolls, §1.2.1; Temple, §2). The book of Daniel (Dan 7—12) anticipates by visionary means an eschatological triumph, of which the principal agent is the archangel Michael (Dan 12:1-4); the temple's renewal is part of the scenario (Dan 12:11-12). Several of the documents found near Qumran represent an apocalyptic point of view and envisage that the sect of covenanters will direct the operation of the temple in the final days (see 1QM, 1QS, CD). More recently discovered materials (*Temple Scroll, New Jerusalem, Miqsat Ma'aseh Torah*) attest a directly practical interest in the conduct of sacrifice in Jerusalem. Josephus reports that one of the priestly nationalists involved as a general with him in the war against Rome was John the Essene (*J.W.* 2.20.4 §567; 3.2.1 §11; 3.2.2 §19), and he relates the repute of the Essenes for courage under Roman torture (*J.W.* 2.8.10 §§152-53). Indeed, the correspondence between Josephus's extensive description of the Essenes (*J.W.* 2.8.2-13 §§119-61) and the evidence which continues to emerge from Qumran is such as to make recent attempts to drive a wedge between the two seem even more apologetic than Josephus himself was.

The Pharisees, in their attempt to influence what the high priests did in the temple rather than to replace those institutions definitively, appear more conservative than the Essenes and nationalistic priestly families. Josephus reports that the Pharisees made known their displeasure at Alexander Jannaeus by inciting a crowd to pelt him with lemons (at hand for a festal procession) at the time he should have been offering sacrifice. His response to the claim that he was unfit to hold office was to have some six thousand people killed (*Ant.* 13.13.5 §§372-73). Josephus also relates, from a later period, the teaching of the rabbis (probably Pharisees) who were implicated in dismantling the eagle Herod had erected over a gate of the temple (*J.W.* 1.33.2-4 §648-55; *Ant.* 17.6.2-4 §§149-67). That gesture was less subversive of the established authority in the cult than what earlier Pharisees had done, but Herod correctly understood that it was a deliberate challenge to his authority, and he responded with summary executions.

Paradoxically the willingness of the Pharisees to consider the Hasmoneans and Herodians in their priestly function, in distinction from the Essenes, involved them not only in symbolic disputes but in vocal and bloody confrontations. Alexander Jannaeus is reported to have executed by crucifixion eight hundred opponents, either Pharisees or those with whom the Pharisees sympathized, and to have slaughtered their families; but his wife came to an accommodation with the Pharisees which guaranteed them considerable influence (*J.W.* 1.4.6—1.5.3 §96-114).

2. The Attitude of Jesus Toward the Temple and Its Cult.

The expulsion of traders in animals is the single point of consensus in the canonical Gospels concerning what Jesus did during his occupation of the temple. Indeed, it is the only specific point mentioned in Luke (Lk 19:45-48), which presents the sparsest account (cf. Mt 21:12-16; Mk 11:15-18; Jn 2:14-22). The expulsion of the traders is what is agreed in the Gospels (cf. *Gos. Thom.* 64) to have been the point of Jesus' action; the action was immediately directed at neither the Romans nor the high priests and had nothing whatever to do with destroying the fabric of the edifice itself. Once it is appreciated that Jesus' maneuver in the temple was in the nature of a claim upon territory in order to eject those performing an activity of which he evidently disapproved, it is more straightforward to characterize it as an "occupation," rather than a "demonstration"; the traditional "cleans-

ing" is obviously an apologetic designation. But the target of his activity makes good sense within the context of what we know of the activities of certain Pharisaic or early rabbinic teachers.

Hillel insisted that owners should lay their hands on their offerings prior to giving them over to priests for slaughter. Another rabbi was so struck by the rectitude of Hillel's position, he had some 3,000 animals brought to the temple, and gave them to those who were willing to lay hands on them in advance of sacrifice (*b. Beṣah* 20a, b; the passage is discussed further in *DJG*, Rabbinic Traditions and Writings, §4). The tradition concerning Hillel envisages the opposite movement from what is represented in the tradition concerning Jesus: animals are introduced rather than their traders expelled. But the purpose of the action by Hillel's supporter is to enforce a certain understanding of correct offering. Hillel's rule requires the participation of the offerer by virtue of his ownership of what is offered. Jesus' occupation may be understood—along lines similar to those involved in the provision of animals to support Hillel's position—as an attempt to insist that the offerer's actual ownership of what is offered is a vital aspect of sacrifice. Jesus wanted Israel to offer of its own, not to purchase sacrifices in the temple.

From a period slightly later than that of Jesus, Mishnah (*Ker.* 1:7) relates a story concerning Rabban Simeon b. Gamaliel, who crafted his teaching in order to bring down the price of offerings in the temple, which he considered to be exorbitant (see *DJG*, Rabbinic Traditions, §4.3). Hillel, Simeon and Jesus are all portrayed as interested in how animals are offered to the extent that they intervene in the court of the temple in order to influence the ordinary course of worship. Jesus can best be understood within the context of a particular dispute in which the Pharisees took part, a controversy over where action was to occur. In that the dispute was intimately involved with the issue of how animals were to be procured, it manifests a focus upon purity which is akin to that attributed to Hillel and Simeon.

The Gospels describe the southern side of the outer court as the place where Jesus expelled the traders. The exterior court was well suited for trade, since it was surrounded by porticos on the inside, following Herod's architectural preferences. But the assumption of rabbinic literature and Josephus is that the market for the sale of sacrificial beasts was not normally located in the temple at all, but in a place called Hanuth (meaning "market" in Aramaic) on the Mount of Olives, across the Kidron Valley. V. Eppstein has argued that rabbinic literature attests the innovation to which Jesus objected. It is recorded that, some forty years before the destruction of the temple, the principal council of Jerusalem was removed from the place in the temple called the Chamber of Hewn Stone to Hanuth (cf. *b. 'Abod. Zar.* 8b; *Šabb.* 15a; *Sanh.* 41a). Eppstein argues that Caiaphas both expelled the Sanhedrin and introduced the traders into the temple.

Caiaphas enjoyed a good relationship with Pilate, under whom he served for ten years, and on whose departure he was removed (Josephus *Ant.* 18.4.3 §90-95). Given that he enjoyed the support of the Romans, and that he was involved in disputes concerning the location of the council, the allegation of the Gospels that trade was permitted in the temple during his tenure seems plausible.

From the point of view of Pharisaism generally, trade in the southern side of the outer court would have been anathema. Purses were not permitted in the temple according to the Pharisees' teaching (*m. Ber.* 9:5). Sufficient money might be brought to put directly into the large containers for alms (cf. *m. Šeqal.* 6:1, 5; 7:1), to purchase seals redeemable for libations (cf. *m. Šeqal.* 5:4) and/or to exchange against Tyrian coinage in order to pay the annual half-shekel (cf. *m. Šeqal.* 1:3; 2:1), but the introduction of trade for animals into the temple rendered the ideal of not bringing into the temple more than would be consumed there impracticable. (References in Mt 21:12 and Mk 11:15 to people selling and buying animals within the court may even imply that serial transactions were involved.) Moreover, the installation of traders in the porticos would also have involved the removal of those teachers, Pharisaic and otherwise, who taught and observed in the temple itself (cf. *m. Sanh.* 11:2; *Pesaḥ* 26a).

From the point of view of the smooth conduct of sacrifice, of course, the innovation was sensible. One could know at the moment of purchase that one's sacrifice was acceptable and not run the risk of harm befalling the animal on its way to be slaughtered. It is therefore unnecessary to impute malicious motives to Caiaphas

in order to understand what was going on, although it may be assumed that additional profit for the temple was also involved. But when we look at the installation of the traders from the point of view of Hillelite Pharisaism, for example, Jesus' objection becomes understandable. Hillel had taught that one's sacrifice had to be shown to be one's own, by the imposition of hands; part of the necessary preparation was not just of people to the south and beasts to the north, but the connection between the two by appropriation. Caiaphas's innovation was sensible on the understanding that sacrifice was simply a matter of offering pure, unblemished animals. But it failed in Pharisaic terms and in the terms of Jesus, not only in its introduction of the necessity for commerce into the temple, but also in its breach of the link between worshiper and offering in the sacrificial action.

3. The Cultic Piety of the Circle of Peter.

One of the principal reasons that make it plain that Jesus himself was loyal to the temple, even as he attempted to insist upon a distinctive view of the purity God requires within it, is that the movement which continued in his name after the crucifixion was largely centered in the temple. The picture provided in Acts* is clear and consistent: under the leadership of Peter* and a group of Twelve, the followers of Jesus lived commonly, broke bread together regularly in their homes and participated in the cult in the manner of devoted, nonpriestly Israelites (see Acts 1:12-26; 2:46; 3:1-26; 4:1-37).

Within Jesus' practice, meals had been occasions on which eating together had been taken as a pledge of the festivity of the kingdom* of God (see Mt 8:11, 12; Lk 13:28, 29). Near the end of his life, Jesus had approved the communal wine and bread as more acceptable to God than regular sacrifice. With the words "this is my blood" and "this is my flesh" Jesus insisted that God approved a meal in his fellowship more than the conduct of worship* in the temple, where sacrificial arrangements had become too commercial (Mt 26:26, 28; Mk 14:22, 24; Lk 22:19-20; 1 Cor 11:24-25; Justin *Apol. I* 66.3).

The Petrine circle literally domesticated such meals, holding them at home and yet deliberately taking part in the worship of the temple (*see* Lord's Supper; Worship). At the same time, Peter's group accommodated the meal of fellowship to the general, ancient and widespread practice of blessing what was consumed at meals (see *m. Ber.* 6:5-8 and *b. Ber.* 41b—45a), beginning with bread (see *b. Ber.* 46a).

Acts also places Peter in Samaria* (Acts 8:14-25), Lydda (Acts 9:32-35), Joppa (Acts 9:36-43) and Caesarea (Acts 10:1-48; 12:19). Paul refers, as if as a matter of course, to Peter's presence personally in Antioch* (see Gal 2:11-14), and by the time of 1 Peter* he is pictured as writing from Rome with Silvanus (see 1 Pet 5:12-13) to churches in the northeast of Asia Minor (1 Pet 1:1, 2). If, then, Jerusalem* was a center for Peter in the way it was not for Jesus, it was certainly not a limit of his operations. Rather, the temple appears to have featured as the hub of a much wider network of contacts which linked Jews from abroad and even Gentiles* (see Acts 10:1-48; 11:1-18, 15:1-11 with Gal 2:1-14) in common recognition of a new, eschatological fellowship defined by the teaching of Jesus. The Petrine circle took part in worship within the temple, embracing it in a way Jesus had not, and yet at the same time viewed Jesus as the source of a teaching which envisaged the participation in worship of those far outside Jerusalem. Peter's activity, centered on but not limited to Jerusalem, was motivated by the eschatological* promise of Zion's place at the heart of the worshiping nations.

4. The Cultic Piety of the Circle of James.
Hegesippus—as cited by Eusebius (*Hist. Eccl.* 2.23.1-18)—characterizes James,* Jesus' brother, as the person to whom immediate control of the church in Jerusalem passed. James practiced a careful and idiosyncratic purity in the interests of worship in the temple. He abstained from wine and animal flesh, did not cut his hair or beard and forsook oil and bathing. If the report of Hegesippus is to be taken at face value, those special practices gave him access even to the sanctuary. Josephus reports he was killed in the temple c. 62 at the instigation of the high priest Ananus during the interregnum between the Roman governors Festus and Albinus (Josephus *Ant.* 20.9.1 §§197-203).

In addition to the sort of close association with the temple which could and did result in conflict with the authorities there, the circle of James is expressly claimed in Acts to have exerted authority as far away as Antioch, by means

of emissaries who spoke Greek (Acts 15:13-35). The particulars of the dispute (with both Pauline and Petrine understandings of purity) will not detain us here (*see* Purity and Impurity), but it is of immediate import that James alone determines the outcome of apostolic policy. James in Acts agrees that Gentiles who turn to God* are not be encumbered with needless regulations (Acts 15:19), and yet he insists they be instructed by letter to abstain "from the pollutions of idols, and from fornication, and from what is strangled, and from blood" (Acts 15:20).

The grounds given for the Jacobean policy are that the law* of Moses is commonly acknowledged (Acts 15:21); the implication is that to disregard such elemental considerations of purity as James specifies would be to dishonor Moses.* Judas Barsabbas and Silas are then dispatched with Paul and Barnabas to deliver the letter in Antioch along with their personal testimony (Acts 15:22-29) and are said particularly to continue their instruction as prophets* (Acts 15:32, 33). They refer to the regulations of purity as necessities (Acts 15:28), and no amount of Lukan gloss can conceal that what they insist upon is a serious challenge of Paul's position (compare 1 Cor 8, which is ignorant of the so-called decree).

James's devotion to the temple is also reflected in Acts 21. When Paul arrives in Jerusalem, James and the presbyters with him express concern at the rumor that Paul is telling Jews who live among the Gentiles not to circumcise* their sons. Their advice is for Paul to demonstrate his piety by purifying himself, paying the expenses of four men under a vow and entering the temple with them (Acts 21:17-26). The result is a disastrous misunderstanding. Paul is accused of introducing "Greeks" into the temple, a riot ensues and Paul himself is arrested (Acts 21:27-36). James is not mentioned again in Acts, but Hegesippus's notice would suggest his devotion to the temple did not wane.

Within the Gospels certain passages reflect the exceptional devotion of James's circle to the temple. The best example is Mark 7:6-13 (and, with an inverted structure, Mt 15:3-9); although the topic of the chapter overall is purity, the issue addressed in the passage itself is the sanctity of the temple (Mk 7:6-13). The issue is spelled out in terms of a dispute concerning *qôrbān*, the Aramaic term for a cultic gift (Mk 7:11).

The dispute reflects Jesus' own stance, that what is owed to one's parents cannot be sheltered by declaring it dedicated to the temple. The crucial point of such a gambit of sheltering is that one might continue to use the property after its dedication, while what was given to a person would be transferred forthwith. The basic complaint about the practice, especially as stated in the simple epigram of Mark 7:11-12, derives from Jesus. The complaint is characteristic of him; quite aside from his occupation of the temple, he criticized commercial arrangements there (see Mt 17:24-27; Mk 12:41-44; Lk 21:1-4).

The dominical epigram has here been enveloped in a much more elaborate argument. Mark 7:6-13 is a syllogism, developed by means of scriptural terms of reference. Isaiah's complaint (Is 29:13) frames the entire argument: the people claim to honor God, but their heart is as far from him as their vain worship, rooted in human commandments (Mk 7:6b-7). That statement is related in Mark 7:10-12 to the tradition of qôrbān, taken as an invalidation of the Mosaic prescription to honor parents. The simple and unavoidable conclusion is that the tradition violates the command of God (Mk 7:8-9, 13).

The argument as it stands insists upon the integrity of the temple and the strict regulation of conduct there; it attacks opponents for too little concern for the temple, not too much. At the same time the passage presents Jesus as maintaining a literal loyalty to the Scriptures (in their Septuagintal form), which the Pharisees did not. Those aspects of the presentation of Jesus' saying are arguably typical of the circle of James.

5. The Assimilation of the Temple's Function by the Community.

Jesus' conception at the end of his ministry was that his meals, his wine and bread, were more acceptable to God as "blood" and "flesh" than sacrifices in the temple were. In the circles of Peter and of James, as well as in other communities of primitive Christianity, a cultic understanding of the meal was preserved (and developed further). That practice led naturally to the claim that a church at worship* took the place of the temple.

The theme is evident in Pauline and deutero-Pauline passages such as 1 Corinthians 3:16-17; 6:19; 2 Corinthians 6:14-7:1; Ephesians 2:19-22 (see DPL, Temple). Comparable claims in the Dead Sea Scrolls (see, for example 1QS 9:5-6) demonstrate that the assimilation of cultic functions by a community need not imply that the temple is no longer the place of divinely mandated worship. The Essenes envisaged their place in the temple, as did James, Peter and Paul.

The assimilation of the functions of the temple, however, could develop into the expectation of its eschatological replacement. The Revelation of John represents that development clearly. The confident statement in the vision of the New Jerusalem in Revelation 21:22, "I saw no temple" in the city, probably reflects the awareness that the edifice had been destroyed as a result of the Roman siege of Jerusalem. But the theology of the passage is its real contribution, "for its temple is the Lord God the almighty and the lamb." Here a major theme of the Revelation that Jesus as the Lamb of God is the object of heavenly worship (see Rev 5 and Jn 1:29) finds its climax. In time to come, Jesus is to assume all the value of the temple itself.

The theme of the eschatological replacement of the temple is also voiced in the Gospels. The most obvious case is the interpreted compendium of Jesus sayings in Mark 13 (with Mt 24-25; Lk 21:5-36), a complex of material developing an apocalyptic scenario in which the most important elements are the destruction of the temple and Jesus' coming as the triumphant Son of Man of Daniel 7.

A less obvious instance of the theme of the eschatological replacement of the temple is the way in which Jesus' occupation of the temple is presented in Mark 11:15 and Matthew 21:12, but not in Luke 19:45. Instead of simply objecting on the ground of purity to trading in the temple, Jesus is made to attack those who were changing money for the annual tax of the half shekel. The fact of the matter is that every year money changing for that purpose went on publicly throughout Israel. The process commenced a full month before Passover, with a proclamation concerning the tax (m. Šeqal. 1:1), and exchanges were set up in the provinces ten days before they were set up in the temple (m. Šeqal. 1:3). Moreover, according to Josephus the tax was not even limited to those resident in the land of Israel (Josephus J.W. 7.6.6 §218; Ant. 18.9.1 §312), so that the procedure itself would not have been stopped by the sort of interruption the Gospels describe.

For reasons which have already been discussed, Jesus' occupation of the temple for the purpose of expelling vendors should be acknowledged as fully historical. The additional aspect of expelling the money-changers provided warrant at a later stage for the refusal of churches to participate in the collection of the half shekel (both in Jerusalem and abroad). John's picture (Jn 2:13-17), in which the smaller coins involved in the sale of animals were scattered, is historically plausible but also shows (in Jn 2:17-22) how the tradition developed toward the symbol of eschatological replacement, which Matthew and Mark present in narrative terms with the expulsion of the money-changers.

6. The Theology of the Definitive Replacement of the Temple.

The Epistle to the Hebrews* spells out how Jesus' replacement of the temple is not simply eschatological but already accomplished and definitive. Chapter nine of Hebrews begins with the "first" covenant's regulations for sacrifice,* involving the temple in Jerusalem. Specific mention is made of the menorah, the table and presented bread in the holy place, with the holy of holies empty but for the gold censer and the ark (Heb 9:2-5). The reference to the censer as being in the holy of holies fixes the point in time of which the author speaks: it can only be the day of atonement, when the high priest made his single visit to that sanctum, censer in hand (Lev 16).

That precise moment is only specified in order to be fixed, frozen forever. For Hebrews, what was a fleeting movement in the case of the high priest was an eternal truth in the case of Jesus. The movement of ordinary priests* in and out of the holy place, the "first tabernacle*" (Heb 9:6), while the high priest could only enter "the second tabernacle," the holy of holies (Heb 9:7), once a year, was designed by the spirit of God as a parable: the way into the holy of holies could not be revealed while the first temple, the first tabernacle and its service continued (Heb 9:8-10). That way could only be opened, after the temple was destroyed, by Christ,* who became high priest and passed through "the greater and more perfect tabernacle" of his body (Heb 9:11) by the power of his own blood (Heb 9:12) so that he could find eternal redemption in the sanctuary.

Signal motifs within the Gospels are developed in the Hebrews passage. The identification of Jesus' death* and the destruction of the temple, which the Gospels achieve in narrative terms, is assumed to be complete. (It is not even clear what exactly the author made of the interim between the two events.) Moreover, the passage takes it for granted that Jesus' body was a kind of "tabernacle," an instrument of sacrifice (Heb 9:11), apparently because the Gospels speak of his offering his body and his blood in the words of institution. (And John, of course, actually has Jesus refer to "the temple of his body," Jn 2:21.) "Body" and "blood" here are Jesus' self-immolating means to his purpose as high priest. In Hebrews the temple in Jerusalem has been replaced by a purely ideological construct. The true high priest has entered once for all (Heb 9:12) within the innermost recess of sanctity, so that no further sacrificial action is necessary or appropriate.

From the perspective of Hebrews there is only a short step to that of the *Epistle of Barnabas* (c. A.D. 130), where it is held that "the spiritual temple," God's word dwelling in the believer, takes the place of the temple of Jerusalem (*Barn.* 16.6-10). The physical temple was always a mistaken attempt to worship God; it was destined for destruction (*Barn.* 16.1-5). A proper, allegorical reading of such rites as the Day of Atonement (*Barn.* 7.3-11) and the red heifer (*Barn.* 8.1-7) testifies to the reality of Christ at the heart of Israel's Scripture; he is the truth behind the veil of the temple.

See also CHRISTIANITY AND JUDAISM: PARTINGS OF THE WAYS; EBIONITES; JERUSALEM, ZION, HOLY CITY; JEWISH CHRISTIANITY; JUDAISM, POST A.D. 70; LORD'S SUPPER, LOVE FEAST; PRIEST, HIGH PRIEST; SACRIFICE, OFFERINGS, GIFTS; SYNAGOGUE; TABERNACLE, SANCTUARY; WORSHIP AND LITURGY.

BIBLIOGRAPHY. G. A. Anderson, *Sacrifices and Offerings in Ancient Israel: Studies in their Social and Political Importance* (HSMS 41; Atlanta: Scholars Press, 1987); T. S. Beall, *Josephus' Description of the Essenes Illustrated by the Dead Sea Scrolls* (SNTSMS 58; Cambridge: Cambridge University Press, 1988); Th. A. Busink, *Der Tempel von Jerusalem von Salomo bis Herodes: Eine archäologisch-historische Studie unter Berücksichtigung des westsemitischen Tempelbaus*, 2 vols. (SFSMD 3; Leiden: E. J. Brill, 1970, 1980); B. Chilton, *The Temple of Jesus: His*

Sacrificial Program within a Cultural History of Sacrifice (University Park: Pennsylvania State University Press, 1992); idem, "[ὡς]" φραγέλλιον ἐκ σχοινίων [John 2:15]" in *Templum Amicitiae: Essays on the Second Temple Presented to Ernst Bammel*, ed. W. Horbury (JSNTS up 48; Sheffield: Sheffield Academic Press, 1991) 330-44; V. Eppstein, "The historicity of the Gospel account of the Cleansing of the Temple," *ZNW* 55 (1964) 42-58; J. Gnilka, "2 Cor 6:14-7:1 in the Light of the Qumran texts and the Testaments of the Twelve Patriarchs" in *Paul and Qumran. Studies in New Testament Exegesis*, ed. J. Murphy-O'Connor (London: Chapman, 1968) 48-86; M. Haran, *Temples and Temple-Service in Ancient Israel: An Inquiry into the Character of Cult Phenomena and the Historical Setting of the Priestly School* (London: Oxford University Press, 1978); J. Jeremias, *Jesus' Promise to the Nations* (Philadelphia: Fortress, 1982) 65-70; K. Lake, "The Apostolic Council of Jerusalem" in *The Acts of the Apostles*, ed. F. J. Foakes Jackson and K. Lake (Grand Rapids: Baker, 1979) 5.195-212; B. A. Levine, *In the Presence of the LORD: A Study of Cult and some Cultic Terms in Ancient Israel* (SJLA 5; Leiden: E. J. Brill, 1974); C. Roth, "The Cleansing of the Temple and Zechariah XIV 21," *NovT* 4 (1960) 174-81; W. R. Smith, *Lectures on the Religion of the Semites: Burnett Lectures* (London: Black, [1889] 1901); M. Weinfeld, *Deuteronomy and the Deuteronomic School* (Oxford: Clarendon, 1972); K. Wengst, *Tradition und Theologie des Barnabasbriefes* (AK 42; Berlin: de Gruyter, 1971); R. K. Yerkes, *Sacrifice in Greek and Roman Religions and Early Judaism: The Hale Lectures* (New York: Scribner's, 1952). **B. Chilton**

TEMPTATION

The NT assumes every Christian is destined to undergo temptation, even as Christ did. Temptation occurs when Satan uses life's circumstances to confront people with the opportunity to sin, to choose an action that goes against the character and will of God. Temptation focuses on causing Christians to fall away from faith in Christ.

1. New Testament Terminology
2. The General Epistles and Revelation
3. Evil Inclination
4. Early Church Fathers

1. New Testament Terminology.
The key Greek word that carries the concept of "tempt" in the NT is *peirazō*. This word describes the devil's approach to Jesus in the wilderness after his baptism* (Mt 4:1, 3; Mk 1:13; Lk 4:1, 3, 13) but also the predicaments the Pharisees and Sadducees set before Jesus, such as demanding a sign from heaven* (Mt 16:1; Mk 8:11; Lk 11:16), questioning him about divorce (Mt 19:3; Mk 10:2), handing him a coin (Mt 22:18; Mk 12:13), pressing him about which is the greatest commandment* (Mt 22:35) and casting an adulterous woman at his feet (Jn 8:6). Luke 22:28 uses this word to characterize his entire ministry.

Satan,* though not always named, is assumed to be the tempter or the agent wanting Christians to fail and sin (1 Cor 7:5; 1 Thess 3:5; Rev 3:1). However, Paul can characterize Jews as tempting him by their plots (Acts 20:19).

God* can be tempted in the sense that his character and will may be challenged, as when Ananias and Sapphira tempt the Holy Spirit* by lying to the church* (Acts 5:9) and when the church is said to tempt God by demanding Gentiles* be circumcised* before they can be Christians (Acts 15:10).

Peirazō most often is used in this pejorative sense. It can, however, convey the sense of a test or a trial in which success is likely. Thus before feeding the five thousand Jesus tests Philip* about acquiring bread (Jn 6:6). James 1:2 speaks of trials as beneficial to Christians. Paul encourages believers periodically to test themselves to determine if they are "in the faith" (2 Cor 13:5).

Used in this sense, *peirazō* overlaps in meaning with *dokimazō*, which means "test" in the sense of proving one's success or worthiness. Deacons must be proved (1 Tim 3:10). Spirits must be proved (1 Jn 4:1). Faith* must be proved genuine (1 Pet 1:7). After using *peirazō* initially in 2 Corinthians 13:5, Paul conveys his hope that believers will not fail their self-examination by using *dokimazō* five times in the next two verses. By definition James 1:12 asserts that one who "endures testing" *(peirazō)* is "proved" *(dokimazō)*.

2. The General Epistles and Revelation.
2.1. Temptation Expected and Welcomed. Because temptation in the form of testing provides opportunity for growth and maturity, James 1:2 emphasizes that it should be not only expected but also welcomed. This can happen "whenever" *(hotan)* it occurs, and it should be antici-

pated with "all joy." James 1:5 assumes that wisdom* from God is both attained and received during the course of succeeding against trial and temptation. According to James 1:12, opportunity to receive "the crown of life" necessarily depends not only on experiencing trials and temptations but also on overcoming them.

1 Peter 1:6-9 underlines the necessity of trials and temptations in believers' lives. They take place "so that your faith might demonstrate itself proved." Understanding that these experiences may be painful, 1 Peter 1:5 speaks of suffering.* Yet, precisely because of overcoming challenges to faith, 1 Peter 1:8 can anticipate "inexpressible and glorious joy" when Christ* is seen face to face and fullness of faith culminates in salvation* (*see* 1 Peter).

2.2. Identification with Christ. The temptation of Christians is connected to the temptation of Christ. 1 Peter 4:12-13 emphasizes that the Christians' anticipation of trial and temptation grows out of their identification with Christ. "Do not be surprised," this text says, "at the fiery ordeal to tempt you as a strange happening among you; rejoice, because you are sharing in the sufferings of Christ." Temptation desires to derail the divine mission first in Christ, then in Christians and the church. As Christians suffer rejection and persecution,* they demonstrate their oneness with him.

Certainly the cross* is the focus of Christ's suffering, as 1 Peter 2:23-24 elaborates. In this respect Christ's temptation to escape from the cross as pictured in the prayer* in Gethsemane (Mt 26:36-46; Lk 22:39-46) is the ultimate temptation of his human experience.

The wilderness temptations (Mt 4:1-11; Mk 1:12-13; Lk 4:1-13) provide a glimpse at this kind of unique temptation Christ experienced throughout his ministry in relation to his messianic mission. However, Hebrews 4:15 dwells not on the uniqueness of Christ's temptations but on their conformity with the temptations of all God's people: "He was tempted in every way we are." Christ does not escape any kind of suffering, whether common to humanity or unique to himself. He does not have special privileges. As M. Shuster (201) states, he experiences "the needs, limitations, and frailties of a human's body, mind, and circumstances."

Jesus' sinlessness despite the full range of temptations (Heb 4:15), according to Shuster, has to do with his ability to face suffering without giving in to the temptation to escape from it. Any faltering negates his mission. He stands as a model for Christians in precisely this way. As he did, so must Christians remain true to their purpose in God and not give in to the temptation to abandon it in the midst of suffering difficulties in life.

2.3. Power and Protection. Christ not only provides the spiritual strength to overcome temptation but also secures for Christians God's shielding hand from temptation that is greater than their level of maturity. Because Christ has experienced the temptations of life, as all humans do, yet never failed to obey God and do his will, he has much to teach about overcoming temptation. Christians are encouraged to call on Christ for help when temptation to sin becomes irresistible. Hebrews 2:18 assures the readers, "He is able to help those who are being tempted."

As high priest* Christ provides direct access to God, whose sovereignty allows him to monitor the level of temptations Christians undergo. Christians may confidently expect God "to help us in our time of need" (Heb 4:16). The Lord's* rescue of Lot, says 2 Peter 2:9, demonstrates that he "knows how to rescue the godly from temptation." Revelation 3:10 asserts that because of the church of Philadelphia's endurance,* Christ will prevent it from experiencing the temptation that will come upon the whole world. God's capability of shielding the godly from irresistible temptation is also assumed in the request in the Lord's Prayer ("Lead us not into temptation," Mt 6:13; Lk 11:4).

2.4. Varied Temptations. Circumstances that tempt people to sin vary widely and are rarely specified. Instead James 1:2 speaks of experiencing "many kinds of temptations," and 1 Peter 1:6 talks of suffering grief "in many kinds of temptations." Most translations correctly translate *peirasmos* as "trials" in these two places because they recognize that each passage has in mind external experiences and circumstances. Both passages use *peirasmos* because they have in mind any number of situations, including persecution, that can tempt a person to sin against God and perhaps fall from faith. Such situations will vary from one person to another and can only be gauged individually as spiritual challenges.

2.5. Sources of Temptation. Revelation 2:10 names the devil as the source of temptation.

Hebrews 11:17 uses *peirazō* when it refers to the time God "tempted" Abraham.* James 1:13-15 asserts vehemently that the responsibility for temptation lies with each individual's "evil desire." Can these positions be reconciled?

James 1:13 asserts: "When tempted, no one should say, 'God is tempting me.'" The passage demands that people take full responsibility for their participation in temptation. It also alerts people to the potential danger in compounding their resulting sin by blaming its irresistibility on God. The verse supplies two reasons for not blaming God. The second flatly denies the point by stating, "He tempts no one." The first reason varies in translation with the interpreter: "God cannot be solicited to evil" (Laws), "God is inexperienced in evil" (Martin), "God should not be tested by evil men" (Davids).

The interpretive problem revolves around the fact that the word *apeirastos* ("untempted") is not used anywhere else in the NT or the Septuagint and that the simplest translation, "God is untempted by evil," begs for a specialized sense more related to the point it is supposed to support. Although the parallel P. H. Davids draws with Deuteronomy 6:16 is interesting, it is not compelling because it places this first reason in disjunction with the second by focusing on the person being tempted rather than the character of God.

Regarding the other two interpretations, it goes without saying that God "cannot be solicited to" and is "inexperienced in" evil. Somewhere between these two interpretations most likely lies the point. Perhaps James means to assert that God and evil are separate or perhaps more pointedly that God is superior to or above evil. If God is so distant from evil as to be untouchable by its power, then surely he does not tempt anyone and is rightly affronted by any thought or utterance from one being tempted that suggests anything like it. Such a person is truly "doubleminded" or "unstable in all he does," as James 1:8 remarks.

James 1:14-15 go on to place the blame for temptation and the resulting sin squarely on each individual being "attracted" and subsequently caught by the enticing bait offered by his or her own "evil desire." In using the term "evil desire," James probably depends on rabbinic theology, which developed the concept of "evil impulse" as part of the makeup of every human being. Left unchecked, this evil impulse

leads people into sin (see 3 below). James proceeds to describe the process of sin in terms of conception and birth. The evil impulse penetrates the womb and fosters a child, who is publicly identified as sin, and this leads to conviction for adultery and the punishment* of death. The onus of sin lies with each individual, not on God or even on the devil, who is carefully ignored in all this.

Thus it is correct to translate *peirazomenos* (as in Heb 11:17) as "test," not "tempt." God allows temptation by the devil but is not associated with it himself. From his perspective it is testing, the opportunity to demonstrate endurance and hone maturity in believers. Although the devil is the external power involved in temptation, it is the internal source, the uncontrolled evil impulse, that provides the transition from temptation to sin.

2.6. Sin, Doublemindedness and Perfection. James 1:8 and James 4:8 introduce the vocabulary of doublemindedness *(dipsychos)* into the biblical picture of temptation and sin. In James 1:8 it is the chief characteristic of a person whose prayer God does not answer. Although some scholars (Wolverton) have tried to draw this term into the web of Jewish background discussions surrounding evil and good inclination *(yeṣer)* in spiritual battle over a person's sinful or wise actions, this is inappropriate. For James doublemindedness is not a neutral term describing someone on the borderline between temptation and sin. Rather doublemindedness describes a sinner who does not trust in God's loving care. In James 4:8 "doubleminded" is used as an alternative way of addressing "sinners" who need to repent. "Purify your hearts" indicates that the opposite of doublemindedness is singleminded devotion to God as in Deuteronomy 6:5 and as amplified in Jewish literature, including Sirach 1:28-29 and Sirach 2:12-14.

Both 1 Peter 4:1 and 1 John 3:6 apparently contemplate a Christian life free from sin. What do the authors mean by that, and does this mean a life free from temptation? Despite the wording of "ceases from sin" and "does not sin," the wider contexts of both books concern themselves with the reality of both temptation and sin in the lives of Christians. Although H. Swadling dismisses 1 John 3:6 as "polemical" (what his opponents advocated but he vehemently denies), V. K. Inman and especially S. Vitrano make a strong case for John's intending to separate the rebellious attitude of the worldly from the believer's orientation to sin. Regarding 1 Peter 4:1, I. Blazen's assessment (41) is similar when he says, "At rock-bottom, ceasing from sin has to do with the putting away of the old vices of pagan society." Ultimately the point of these passages is that a Christian never considers sin in his or her life acceptable. Sin is always at odds with the new sin-free life purchased with the blood of Christ.

So sin and its forerunner, temptation, remain real for the believer. Yet they should not be viewed as synonymous. Temptation is not sin. Recognition of temptation to sin is the essential spiritual function for ultimately choosing to follow God's way and not sin. Thus Jesus can be tempted and not sin. The truth of this is identifiable only because he was tempted.

3. Evil Inclination.

Most scholars consider the use of "evil desire" in James 1:14 the clearest example in the NT of *yēṣer* ("inclination") theology developed in Jewish extrabiblical literature. The starting point for this development, as F. C. Porter observed, is Genesis 6:5 and Genesis 8:21, both of which use *yēṣer* to grasp the tendency of humans to rebel against God, a state for which we are culpable. Later biblical texts, such as 1 Chronicles 28:9, 1 Chronicles 29:18 and Isaiah 26:3, use *yēṣer* not only assuming its innateness but also conceiving the possibility of a good *yēṣer*.

A key transition reference from the OT and James, as J. Marcus and others note, is Sirach 15:11-20. In this passage *yēṣer* becomes the buffer between humans' capacity for sin, which comes from being made in God's image, and humans' responsibility for sin, which comes from their own choice to follow their *yēṣer*. *Yēṣer* may be the vehicle for sin, but it is not sin itself. The domination of *yēṣer* can be diminished, according to Sirach 21:11, only by the observing the law.*

Considerable excitement stirred among scholars when *yēṣer* ideas were found in the Qumran* literature (Flusser, Kuhn, Murphy, Seitz, Malina). Numerous instances of the word occur in the primary sources. Most of these, as noted by Marcus, associate *yēṣer* with evil: a trait of the flesh (1QH 10:23), desire for wealth (1QH 10:22), lustful eyes (CD 2:16), something

to be circumcised (1QS 5:3-7) and the opposite of following God in all his ways (CD 2:14-15). Occasionally good or "steadfast" *yēṣer* is linked with concern for the poor, slowness in anger and wisdom (1QH 1:34-37) and standing up for faith in God (1QS 8:3). Marcus notes the startling similarities to concerns in James (Jas 1:5, 19; 2:1-7) at this point and in CD 3:2-3, where Abraham (Jas 2:23) is singled out as being a friend of God because "he kept the commandments of God and did not choose the will of his own spirit," presumably in the sense that he successfully resisted his evil *yēṣer*.

The direct association of "desire" (*epithymia*) and *yēṣer* ("evil inclination"), though noted in one Qumran passage (1QH 10:23) by D. Flusser (which he connects to Gal 5:16), becomes more evident in Philo.* Among other passages in Philo, Marcus mentions *De Specialibus Legibus* 4.15.85, in which Philo names desire as the originator of evil, and *De Decalogo* 28.150, in which Philo compares desire to the creeping sickness that spreads throughout the body.

Although Philo usually uses *diaboulion* ("deliberation") to translate *yēṣer* from Hebrew, the terms can overlap, as when *Testament of the Twelve Patriarchs* uses both *diaboulion* and *epithymia* ("desire") in conjunction with sexual sin (*T. Jud.* 11:1; 14:3).

Rabbinic literature further develops *yēṣer* ideas in its tendency to personify evil *yēṣer* and use it in place of the name of Satan (*b. Sukk.* 52; *b. B. Bat.* 16). Other passages (*b. Sabb.* 146; *b. Yebam.* 10:36) indicate that evil *yēṣer* came into humanity as a result of intercourse between Eve and the serpent. Yet in other references, as in Sirach, God himself creates evil *yēṣer* (*Gen. Rab.* 9:7; *b. Yoma* 69). The concept of two hearts is also associated with an evil and a good *yēṣer* (Midrash Tehillin, Ps 14:1, explaining 1 Chron 28:9; *b. Ber.* 9:5).

Despite the significance of *yēṣer* in Jewish literature for understanding James, it should be noted, as Marcus emphasizes, that although reference to evil *yēṣer* seems clear in James 1:14-15 and James 4:5, no specific reference to good *yēṣer* is present.

4. Early Church Fathers.

4.1. Continuity. In the early church fathers (*see* Apostolic Fathers) it is still assumed that not even Christians pursuing righteousness* escape temptation and that the "engines of the devil" are the source of temptation (*2 Clem.* 18.2). "Lead us not into temptation" remains a byword for seeking God's protection over and monitoring of temptation (*Did.* 8.2; Pol. *Phil.* 7.2). Yet testing continues to be viewed as a means of purification for the next age, even as fire purifies gold (*Herm. Vis.* 4.3.4).

Influence of good and evil *yēṣer* concepts may be observed particularly in *Hermas Mandates*, which can speak interchangeably of "two angels" (*Herm. Man.* 6—7), "two spirits" (*Herm. Man.* 5.2), "the desire of the devil" and "the desire of righeousness" (*Herm. Man.* 12), and of being filled with "the devil's spirit" and "the Divine Spirit" (*Herm. Man.* 11), as O. J. F. Seitz observes. It is less certain that *Barnabas* 18.1-2, when it refers to "two ways of doctrine," or *Didache* 1.1, when it speaks of "two ways, one of life and one of death," can be linked to Jewish *yēṣer* theology. In *2 Clement* 17.3 the power of desire continues to be a chief culprit in turning temptation into sin. Much as James tags evil desire (Jas 4:2-3) and doublemindedness (Jas 1:6-8) as impediments to successful prayer, so also *Hermas Mandate* 9.7 labels temptation as an interference.

4.2. Testing Prophets. In this postapostolic period concern for proving the genuineness of church leaders (*Did.* 12.1; 15.1, *1 Clem.* 42.4), especially prophets* (*Did.* 11.1, 7), increases dramatically. *Hermas Mandate* 11 provides lengthy commentary on how to "test the life" of those claiming to be prophets to determine if they truly have the "Divine Spirit." *1 Clement* 44.2 determines that after the apostles* fall asleep, other "proven men" should succeed them. A "proven spirit" is the mark of a mature believer in *Hermas Vision* 1.2.4.

4.3. God's Judgment and the Angel of the Lord. In *Hermas* testing by God takes a negative turn implying judgment and appears to have been turned over to the angel of the Lord. Those who escape the Shepherd's examination "I will try at the altar," says the angel of the Lord (*Herm. Sim.* 8.2.5). The tower (an image of the church) awaits completion until the Lord comes to test for the decayed stones, which he will remove (*Herm. Sim.* 9.5.2). In *Hermas Similitude* 7.1, Hermas is informed that his afflictions occur because "the glorious angel" intends to bring not Hermas but his household* to repentance.*

See also ENDURANCE, PERSEVERANCE; ESCHATOLOGY; FORGIVENESS; PASTORAL THEOLOGY; SATAN, DEVIL; SIN, WICKEDNESS; SUFFERING; TRIBU-LATION, MESSIANIC WOES; WATCHFULNESS.

BIBLIOGRAPHY. G. C. Berkouwer, "Perseverance and Temptation" in *Faith and Perseverance* (Grand Rapids: Eerdmans, 1958) 157-92; I. Blazen, "Suffering and Cessation from Sin According to 1 Peter 4:1," *AUSS* 21 (1983) 27-50; D. Bonhoeffer, *Temptation* (New York: Macmillan, 1955); R. B. Crotty, "The Literary Structure of the Letter of James," *AusBR* 40 (1992) 45-57; P. H. Davids, "The Meaning of ΑΠΕΙΡΑΣΤΟΣ in James 1:13," *NTS* 24 (1978) 386-92; idem, "Themes in the Epistle of James That Are Judaistic in Character" (unpublished Ph.D dissertation, University of Manchester, 1974); D. Flusser, "The Dead Sea Sect and Pre-Pauline Christianity" in *Aspects of the Dead Sea Scrolls*, ed. C. Rabin and Y. Yadin (Jerusalem: Magnes, 1958) 249-59; K. Grayston, "Satan and Job," *Scripture Bulletin* 23 (1993) 2-7; V. K. Inman, "Distinctive Johannine Vocabulary and the Interpretation of 1 John 3:9," *WTJ* 40 (1977) 136-44; K.-P. Kloppen, "The Interpretation of Jesus' Temptations (Mt 4:1-11; Mk 1:12-13; Lk 4:1-3) by the Early Church Fathers," *Patristic and Byzantine Review* 8 (1989) 41-43; K. G. Kuhn, "New Light on Temptation, Sin and Flesh in the New Testament" in *The Scrolls and the New Testament*, ed. K Stendahl (London: SCM, 1957) 94-113; S. Laws, *A Commentary on the Epistle of James* (BNTC; London: A. & C. Black, 1980); B. J. Malina, "Some Observations on the Origins of Sin in Judaism and St. Paul," *CBQ* 31 (1969) 18-34; J. Marcus, "The Evil Inclination in the Epistle of James," *CBQ* 44 (1982) 606-21; R. P. Martin, *James* (WBC; Waco, TX: Word, 1988); F. C. Porter, "The Yeçer Hara: A Study in the Jewish Doctrine of Sin" in *Biblical and Semitic Studies* (New York: Scribner's, 1901) 93-156; O. J. F. Seitz, "Antecedents and Signification of the Term ΔΙΨΥΧΟΣ," *JBL* 66 (1947) 211-19; idem, "Two Spirits in Man: An Essay in Biblical Exegesis," *NTS* 6 (1959) 82-95; M. Shuster, "The Temptation, Sinlessness and Sympathy of Jesus: Another Look at the Dilemma of Hebrews 4:15" in *Perspectives on Christology: Essays in Honor of Paul K. Jewett*, ed. M. Shuster and R. Muller (Grand Rapids: Zondervan, 1991) 211-30; H. Swadling, "Sin and Sinlessness in 1 John," *SJT* 35 (1982) 205-11; S. Vitrano, "The Doctrine of Sin in 1 John," *AUSS* 25 (1987) 123-31; W. Wolverton, "The Double-Minded Man in Light of the Essene Psychology," *ATR* 38 (1956) 166-75.   W. R. Baker

TER SANCTUS. See LITURGICAL ELEMENTS.

TESTAMENTARY LITERATURE. *See* 2 PE-
TER.

TEXTUAL CRITICISM

Textual criticism is the field of study whose
practitioners examine variant readings in various manuscripts in the effort to reconstruct the
original wording of a written text. This kind of
study is needed for texts whose autographs are
no longer extant, which is the case for most
ancient documents and all of the books of the
NT.

1. The Quest for the Original Text
2. Textual Criticism of Acts, Hebrews,
   General Epistles and Revelation

1. The Quest for the Original Text.

1.1. Earliest New Testament Copies. Because
not one original writing, or autograph, of any
NT book exists, we depend on copies for reconstructing the original text. According to most
scholars, the earliest copy of any NT book is a
papyrus manuscript designated P^{52}, dated
around 110-25, containing a few verses of John
(Jn 18:31-34, 37-38). This fragment, arguably
only thirty years removed from the autograph,
was part of one of the earliest copies of John's
Gospel.

Other scholars, however, believe there is an
even earlier manuscript, designated 7Q5, which
preserves two incomplete verses of Mark 6:52-
53. This fragment, found in a cave with all Greek
manuscripts, was first identified as Markan by
J. O'Callaghan and dated to about 65. But because of its smallness and because there is writing only on one side, this identification was
strongly contested. Yet in recent years scholars
did a complete computer search on 7Q5 and
concluded that this fragment does not fit anywhere in all of Greek literature except the Gospel of Mark. Subsequently its Markan identity
has been affirmed by several papyrologists.

Another very early manuscript is P^{46}, otherwise known as the Chester Beatty Papyrus II. It
contains Hebrews and all of Paul's epistles except the Pastorals, and it can be dated to the
early part of the second century. Other second-
century manuscripts are P^4, P^{64}, P^{67} (Matthew,
Luke), P^{32} (Titus), P^{66} (John), P^{75} (Luke, John),
P^{77} (Matthew), P^{87} (Philemon), P^{90} (John) and
P^{98} (Revelation).

1.2. Numbers of Copies. We possess many
other early copies of various parts of the NT;
several other papyrus manuscripts (about 40)
are dated in the third and fourth centuries. And
there are several other manuscripts of the NT,
which are called uncials (manuscripts written in
"biblical uncial" on vellum) and minuscules
(manuscripts written in cursive). At present we
have more than 6,000 manuscript copies of the
Greek NT or portions thereof. No other work
of Greek literature can boast such numbers.
Homer's *Iliad*, the greatest of all Greek classical
works, is extant in about 800 manuscripts; and
Euripides' tragedies exist in about 350 manuscripts. The numbers on all the other works of
Greek literature are far less.

Furthermore, it must be said that the span of
time between the original composition and the
next surviving manuscript is far less for the NT
than for any other work in Greek literature. The
lapse for most classical Greek works is about
eight hundred to a thousand years, whereas the
lapse for many books in the NT is around one
hundred years. Because of the abundant wealth
of manuscripts and because several of the
manuscripts are dated in the early centuries of
the church, NT textual scholars have a great
advantage over classical textual scholars. The
NT scholars have the resources to reconstruct
the original text of the NT with great accuracy,
and they have produced some excellent editions of the Greek NT.

1.3. Form of Texts. When speaking of the
original text, many scholars are referring to the
published text—that is, the text as it was in its
final edited form and as it was released for
circulation in the Christian community. For
some books of the NT, there is little difference
between the original composition and the published text. After the author wrote or dictated
his work, he or an associate made the final
editorial corrections and then released it for
distribution. As is the case for books published
in modern times, so in ancient times the original writing of the author is not always the same
as what is published—due to the editorial process. Nonetheless the author is credited with the
final edited text, and the published book is
attributed to the author and considered the
original published text.

Some scholars think it is impossible to recover the original text of the Greek NT because
they have not been able to reconstruct the early

history of textual transmission. Other scholars are less pessimistic but still quite guarded in affirming the possibility. And yet others are optimistic because we possess many early manuscripts of excellent quality and because we are quite certain that various sectors of Christianity, particularly Alexandria, maintained textual acumen to a large degree. Alexandrian manuscripts such as P^1, P^{23}, P^{39}, P^{65}, P^{75}, P^{91} and P^{98} must be very close replicas of the autographs.

The recovery of the text of the NT must be done on a book-by-book basis. The recovery pertains to individual books of the NT, not to the entire volume per se, because each book or group of books, such as the Pauline epistles, had its own unique history of textual transmission. The earliest extant copy of an entire NT text is the one preserved in Codex Sinaiticus (compiled about 375). (Codex Vaticanus lacks the Pastoral Epistles and Revelation.) Prior to the fourth century, the NT was circulated in its various parts: as a single book or a group of books, such as the four Gospels or the Pauline epistles. Manuscripts from the late first century to the third century have been found with individual books, such as Matthew (P^1), Mark (P^{88}), Luke (P^{69}), John (P^5, P^{22}, P^{52}, P^{66}), Acts (P^{91}), Revelation (P^{18}, P^{47}, P^{98}), or containing groups of books, such as the four Gospels with Acts (P^{45}), the Pauline epistles (P^{46}), the Petrine epistles and Jude (P^{72}). Each of the books of the NT has had its own textual history and has been preserved with varying degrees of accuracy. Nonetheless, all of the books were altered from the original state due to the process of manual copying decade after decade and century after century. And the text of each of the books has needed to be recovered.

1.4. Textual Transmission. By the end of the second century and into the third century many of the significant variant readings that we know today had entered into the textual stream. But the early period of textual transmission was not completely marred by textual infidelity and scribal liberty. Some scribes copied the text with exacting fidelity, due either to professional pride or perhaps to respect for a sacred text. The formalization of canonization did not ascribe this sacredness to the text. Canonization came about as the result of common, historical recognition of the sacredness of various NT books. Certain NT books, such as the four Gospels, Acts and Paul's epistles were considered

inspired literature from the onset. Certain scribes, therefore, copied them with reverential fidelity. Other scribes, however, felt free to make alterations in the text either in the interest of doctrine and harmonization or due to the influence of a competitive oral tradition (see Williams). The manuscripts produced in such a manner created a kind of popular text, that is, an uncontrolled text. This text type has usually been called the Western text, but some scholars argue that this is nothing more than a catch-all category for anything other than Alexandrian.

Most of the Alexandrian manuscripts are purer than other manuscripts because scribes from Alexandria or scribes familiar with Alexandrian scriptoral practices would generally take care in producing accurate copies. In the Hellenistic world there were many who had come to appreciate the scholarly practices of Alexandria.* Among the more noteworthy Alexandrian manuscripts are Codex Vaticanus (B) and Codex Sinaiticus (א). These are the two manuscripts that B. F. Westcott and F. J. A. Hort greatly esteemed, especially Codex Vaticanus, and these are the manuscripts that they believed most carefully preserved the original wording of the NT text. Based on this perspective, they developed a genealogical tree that traced back from Codices Vaticanus and Sinaiticus to the originals. According to their theory, Vaticanus is almost a perfectly transmitted text from the original. Westcott and Hort called this the "Neutral Text"—that is, a text void of textual corruption. Their theory was revolutionary, and their text was responsible for overthrowing the Textus Receptus.

1.5. Internal and External Criticism. Beginning in the middle of the twentieth century, however, textual critics became skeptical of recovering the original text through genealogical means. It was judged by several scholars that Westcott and Hort had made a subjective selection about the purity of Vaticanus and then used that to determine the impurity of other manuscripts. Thus Westcott and Hort's theory was no longer heartily endorsed. Left without a solid theory for making external judgments, textual critics turned more and more to internal evidence. They began to endorse the rule, or canon, that the reading that is most likely original is the one that best explains the variants. This canon is a development of J. A. Bengel's maxim *proclivi scriptoni praestat ardua* (the harder reading is to be preferred), a maxim he formulated in responding to his own question as to which variant reading is likely to have arisen out of the others. This canon for internal criticism involves several criteria, which one scholar or another has posited and/or implemented during the past three hundred years of NT textual criticism.

The internal criticism principle allows for the possibility that the reading selected for the text can be taken from any manuscript of any date. This produces subjective eclecticism. Modern textual scholars try to temper the subjectivism by employing a method called reasoned eclecticism. This approach employs a combination of internal and external criticism in the evaluation of the variant readings in light of the documentary evidence. This approach is aimed at producing a balanced view of the matter.

K. Aland favored a similar approach, calling it the local-genealogical method. According to this approach, the textual critic must make decisions on variant readings one by one. After carefully establishing the variety of readings offered in a passage and the possibilities of their interpretation, it must always then be determined afresh on the basis of external and internal criteria which of these readings is the original, from which the others may be regarded as derivative. This method assumes that for any given variation unit, any manuscript or manuscripts may have preserved the original text. Applying this method, however, can produce an uneven documentary presentation of the text. Furthermore, the danger of doing textual criticism on the local-genealogical basis is that the editors must decide what the authors most likely wrote on a phrase-by-phrase basis. This verges on claiming knowledge of the author's original intentions. But no one can do this with any degree of certainty. Those who say they can run the risk of falling prey to the intentional fallacy. Thus the recent trend in emphasizing internal criticism needs to be tempered by Hort's maxim, "knowledge of documents must precede all judgments on readings."

2. Textual Criticism of Acts, Hebrews, General Epistles and Revelation.

These books of the NT have had a textual and canonical history distinct and separate from those of the four Gospels and Paul's epistles (*see*

Canon). From as early as the second century, the four Gospels were being collected together into one volume, as were Paul's epistles (minus the Pastorals). But this was not so for the other NT books. In fact only a few other books were widely read in the Christian church—namely, 1 Peter and 1 John. The book of Acts was also well-known, but it was separated from its companion volume, Luke, when Luke was joined with the other four Gospels. And Hebrews was widely read in Christendom, especially in the East, where it was considered Pauline and therefore included in the Pauline corpus. All the other books had a difficult time making it into the NT canon: James, because of its apparent opposition to Pauline soteriology; 2 Peter, because of its dissimilarity to 1 Peter; 2 John, 3 John and Jude, because of their obscurity; and Revelation, because of its mystery.

By an act of providence the book of Acts and the General Epistles became companions. This is displayed in one manuscript, P^{74} (Papyrus Bodmer XVII), from the seventh century; it is a codex that contains only Acts and all the General Epistles. Incidentally, Westcott and Hort's *Greek New Testament* displays the same arrangement. Despite its late date, P^{74} is important because it presents an Alexandrian text and is an excellent witness for the book of Acts.

2.1. The Book of Acts. The book of Acts* existed in two distinct forms in the early church—the Alexandrian and the Western. The Alexandrian text is usually found in manuscripts such as P^{45}, P^{74} (א), A, B, C, 33. The other form has been called the D-text because this text is primarily represented by D (Codex Bezae of the fifth century). But this text was not created by the scribe who produced Codex Bezae, even though he may have added his own enhancements. The Western text or D-text of Acts existed as early as the late second century or early third century. We know this because a few third-century papyrus manuscripts display this text— namely, P^{29}, P^{38} and P^{48}. The Western text is also attested by the African Old Latin manuscripts, marginal readings in the Harclean Syriac translation and the writings of Cyprian and Augustine. The Western text, which is nearly one-tenth longer than the Alexandrian, is more colorful in circumstantial details.

Theories abound as to which form of the text is genuine or even if Luke wrote both. The major scholarly consensus is that the Alexandrian text is primary and the Western secondary. J. H. Ropes considered the Western text to be "a paraphrastic rewriting of the original," the "work of a single editor trying to improve the work on a large scale" (Ropes, ccxxii-xxiii). R. P. C. Hanson characterized this reviser as an interpolator who made large insertions into an Alexandrian-type text. Hanson hypothesized "that these interpolations were made in Rome between A.D. 120 and 150, at a time when the book of Acts was not yet regarded as sacrosanct and inspired"(Hanson, 224).

More often than not, the editors of Nestle-Aland text (27th ed.) and the United Bible Societies (4th ed.) considered the Alexandrian text, as the shorter text, to have preserved the original wording. In nearly every instance where the D-text stands alone against other witnesses, especially the Alexandrian, it is a case of the Western scribe functioning as a reviser who enhanced the text with redactional fillers. This reviser must have been a well-informed scholar who had a propensity for adding historical, biographical and geographical details. More than anything, he was intent on filling in gaps in the narrative by adding circumstantial details. Furthermore, he shaped the text to favor the Gentiles* over the Jews, to promote Paul's apostolic mission and to heighten the activity of the Holy Spirit* in the work of the apostles.*

2.2. Hebrews. In Egypt and the East the book of Hebrews* was considered part of the Pauline writings. So Hebrews was included in the Pauline corpus, according to P^{46}, the exemplar for B, as well as several other manuscripts. The copyist of another papyrus manuscript, P^{13}, used a manuscript very much like P^{46}, and the copyist of B used an exemplar very much like P^{46} and P^{13}. The original text of Hebrews has been largely preserved in P^{13}, P^{46} and B. Western manuscripts of Hebrews include Dp, Ep of the sixth century.

2.3. The General Epistles.

2.3.1. James. James* has been preserved in two third-century manuscripts: P^{23}, showing affinities with ℵ, and P^{20}, bearing resemblance to B. These manuscripts usually reflect the original wording of the text. The entire text of James is best preserved in the fifth-century manuscripts Codex Alexandrinus (A) and Codex Ephraem Rescriptus (C).

2.3.2. 1 and 2 Peter and Jude. Peter's first

epistle, accepted from the onset as authentic and apostolic, was quite well preserved in its early textual transmission (*see* 1 Peter). This textual fidelity is manifest in one late third-century manuscript, P^{72} (Papyrus Bodmer VII-VIII), and another fourth-century manuscript, P^{81}. P^{72} displays a text that resembles B and yet is closer to the original than B, while P^{81} has more affinity with (ℵ) than with B.

The original texts of 2 Peter* and Jude* were not as well preserved in the early period of textual transmission because these books were not readily acknowledged as apostolic, canonical texts by all the sectors of the early church. The manuscript evidence for these books is quite diverse, marked by independence. This is evident in the two papyri, P^{72} (especially for Jude) and P^{78}. All in all, Codex Alexandrinus (A) is the best witness for these epistles.

2.3.3. John's Epistles. Unlike John's Gospel, which was very popular throughout the early church, John's epistles (*see* John, Letters of) were far less known and read. A portion of 1 John exists in one third-century papyrus, P^9 (a product of careless copying) and a portion of 2 John exists in one fourth-century vellum manuscript, 0232 (which could have originally contained the Johannine corpus: Gospel, Epistles, Revelation). Out of all the manuscripts, 0232 bears the most resemblance to Codex Alexandrinus, which is the best witness to John's epistles.

2.4. The Book of Revelation. Although the early textual history of Revelation (*see* Revelation, Book of) is not as clear as we would like it to be, it is apparent that some scribes (generation after generation) treated the text carefully. According to J. Schmid, who produced a magnum opus on the text of Revelation, the best text was preserved in A and C. This text seems to have been antedated by two third-century manuscripts, P^{18} and P^{24}, and one second-century manuscript, P^{98}. The second best text is that found in ℵ, whose precursors are P^{47} and P^{85} (which accords almost completely with P^{47}). Two other trustworthy sources are a mass of manuscripts that follow Andreas of Caesarea's commentary on Revelation (marked as M^A) and a common group of other Koine manuscripts (marked as M^K).

See also CANON.

BIBLIOGRAPHY. K. Aland and B. Aland, *The Text of the New Testament* (Grand Rapids: Eerdmans, 1988); J. A. Bengel, *Gnomon Novi Testamenti,* ed. J. Steudel (3d ed.; Tübingen, 1855); P. W. Comfort, *The Quest for the Original Text of the New Testament* (Grand Rapids: Baker, 1992); P. W. Comfort and D. Barrett, *The Complete Text of the Earliest New Testament Manuscripts* (Grand Rapids: Baker, 1997); R. P. C. Hanson, "The Provenance of the Interpolator in the 'Western' Text of Acts and of Acts Itself," *NTS* 12 (1965) 211-30; M. Holmes, "New Testament Textual Criticism" in *Introducing New Testament Interpretation,* ed. S. McKnight (Grand Rapids: Baker, 1989) 53-74; Y.-K. Kim, "Paleographic Dating of P[46] to the Later First Century," *Bib* 69 (1988) 248-57; S. Kubo, "P[72] and the Codex Vaticanus," *Studies and Documents* 27 (Salt Lake City: University of Utah Press, 1965); B. M. Metzger, *The Text of the New Testament* (3d ed.; Oxford: Oxford University Press, 1992); J. O'Callaghan, "¿Papiros neotestamentarios en la cueva 7 de Qumran?" *Bib* 53 (1972) 91-100; J. H. Ropes, "The Acts of the Apostles" in *The Beginnings of Christianity,* ed. F. J. Foakes Jackson and K. Lake (London: Macmillan, 1926) vol. 3, pt. 1; J. Schmidt, *Studien zur Geschichte des griechischen Apokalypse-Textes* (3 vols.; Munich: Zink, 1955-56); C. S. C. Williams, *Alterations to the Text of the Synoptic Gospels and Acts* (Oxford: Clarendon, 1951). P. W. Comfort

THEOLOGY OF THE CROSS. *See* CROSS, THEOLOGY OF THE.

THOMAS, APOSTLE. *See* SYRIA, SYRIAN CHRISTIANITY.

THOMAS, GOSPEL OF

Since its publication in 1959 (see Guillaumont et al.) the Coptic *Gospel of Thomas* has been divided into 114 sayings, or logia. The title of this work is derived from a subscript at the conclusion, which reads *euangelion kata Thoman* ("the Gospel according to Thomas"), a phrase borrowed from the Greek Gospels. But *Thomas* is not a Gospel in the sense of narrative or biography; it is a "sayings" Gospel, as seen from the prologue's incipit: "These are the secret sayings that the living Jesus spoke." Many of these sayings are introduced with the words "Jesus said." On occasion a question or a request elicits a reply from Jesus. The incipit further claims that these sayings were recorded by "Didymos Judas Thomas," one of Jesus' disciples

and one whose standing among the disciples has been elevated (*Gos. Thom.* logia. §13). This pseudepigraphic* attribution suggests that *Thomas* was composed in eastern Syria, where legends about Thomas circulated. In recent years *Thomas* has figured prominently in discussion of the Gospels and the historical Jesus.

1. Manuscripts
2. Relation to the New Testament
3. Theology of *Thomas*

1. Manuscripts.

The *Gospel of Thomas* survives in Coptic as the second tractate in Codex II of the Nag Hammadi library (discovered in 1945) and survives partially in Greek in Oxyrhynchus Papyri 1, 654 and 655 (discovered at the end of the nineteenth century). POxy 654 contains the prologue to the *Gospel of Thomas,* logia §§1—7 and a portion of logion §30. POxy 1 contains *Gospel of Thomas* logia §§26—33. POxy 655 contains *Gospel of Thomas* logia §§24, 36—39 and 77. Although the point has been disputed, most scholars contend that *Thomas* was originally composed in Greek and that the Oxyrhynchus Papyri probably stand closer to the original form of the tradition than does the Coptic edition.

The Coptic text of *Thomas* is dated to the middle of the fourth century. The Oxyrhynchus papyri are much older, with POxy 1 dating to shortly after A.D. 200 and POxy 654 and POxy 655 dating to the middle of the third century. These three papyri appear to represent distinct copies of the writing, though what relation, if any, they may have to one another cannot be determined. The Coptic text itself suggests that other editions of Coptic *Thomas* were in circulation. Sometime near the end of the first quarter or first third of the third century, Hippolytus of Rome (Hippolytus *Haer.* 5.7.20) quotes a variant of logion §4 and explicitly identifies it as deriving from the *Gospel of Thomas.* All of this suggests that there were many editions, or recensions, of *Thomas* in the third and fourth centuries.

The date of the earliest editions of *Thomas* is hotly debated. This issue is tied closely to the question of this writing's relation to the NT. Those who have concluded that *Thomas* contains substantial amounts of material that is independent of the NT Gospels tend to argue for an early date, such as the last quarter of the first century (Cameron, Koester, et al.) or even as early as the middle of the first century (Crossan). Those who have concluded that *Thomas* contains little or no independent material tend to argue for a second-century origin (Blomberg, Evans 1994, Snodgrass).

2. Relation to the New Testament.

In recent years several scholars have argued that the *Gospel of Thomas* is a first-century composition, originally independent of the NT Gospels and only later influenced by them. This may be true, but numerous difficulties attend efforts to cull from this collection of logia material that can with confidence be judged primitive, independent of the canonical Gospels and even authentic. Quoting or alluding to more than half of the writings of the New Testament (Mt, Mk, Jn, Acts, Rom, 1—2 Cor, Gal, Eph, Col, 1 Thess, 1 Tim, Heb, 1 Jn, Rev; see Evans et al. 1993), *Thomas* could be little more than a collage of NT and apocryphal* materials that have been interpreted, often allegorically, in such a way as to advance second- and third-century Gnostic* ideas (see Blomberg, Brown, Dehandschutter, Fieger).

Moreover, the traditions contained in *Thomas* hardly reflect a setting that predates the writings of the NT, which is why J. D. Crossan and others attempt to extract an early version of *Thomas* from the Coptic and Greek texts that are extant. Assertions that a consensus is beginning to emerge in which *Thomas* is recognized as primitive and independent (see Davies) claim too much. Lately *Thomas* has enjoyed a great deal of publicity through the publications emanating from the Jesus Seminar. For example, *Thomas* is the fifth Gospel in the recently published *The Five Gospels* (see Funk and Hoover), a work that grades the authenticity of the sayings of Jesus with the colors red (= words of Jesus), pink (= approximation of something Jesus said), gray (= considerable doubt that Jesus said it) and black (= Jesus did not say it). In this work *Thomas* compares favorably with the canonical Gospels.

There are several indications that *Thomas* is secondary to the canonical Gospels. First, material identified as M (special Matthean material) and L (special Lukan material) is found in *Thomas* (cf. Evans 1994, 498). This is not easily explained on the basis of the independence of *Thomas*. Second, in places *Thomas's* readings agree with Matthean and Lukan redaction (cf.

Blomberg, Evans 1994, 499-502). This is so even in cases involving the Oxyrhynchus papyri. These observations should seriously undermine confidence in the antiquity and independence of *Thomas*. It is much more probable that *Thomas* is made up of materials derived from the canonical Gospels and extracanonical sources (though not necessarily directly) that in many cases have been edited to suit second- and third-century gnostic tastes. Although it is possible that *Thomas* may contain a few primitive sayings, it has little to offer Jesus research.

3. Theology of *Thomas*.

The *Gospel of Thomas* presents Jesus as a heavenly revealer, the embodiment of wisdom,* whose teachings, or "secret words," have an esoteric quality. This quality is underscored in the first two logia: " 'Whoever finds the interpretation of these words will not taste death.' Jesus said: 'Let him who seeks not cease seeking until he finds, and when he finds, he will be troubled, and when he has been troubled, he will marvel and he will reign over the All.' "

Although some scholars have insisted that the *Gospel of Thomas* is not Gnostic, most believe that it is. Several features suggest that this collection of the sayings of Jesus reflects a gnostic milieu. Interest in "the All" (log. §2; cf. log. §77) finds expression elsewhere in the writings of the Nag Hammadi library. The anticipation of becoming a "single one" (log. §4; cf. log. §11, §22, §106) probably reflects gnostic interpretation of Genesis 1—2 (cf. log. §85), in which humanity is divided into the two sexes. According to some strains of Gnosticism, man and woman will someday be reunited as an androgynous Human. The saying about being naked and unashamed (cf. log. §37) probably has to do with a return to a primordial state. The saying about coming from the light (log. §50) also has to do with gnostic cosmogony. The reference to the heaven that is above heaven* (log. §11) probably alludes to gnostic cosmology, in which an ultimate heaven is conceived. Criticism of the world as "drunk" (cf. log. §28) and in "poverty" (cf. log. §3, §29) is also a commonplace in gnostic writings. The quest for "rest" (cf. log. §50, §51, §60) is an important feature in gnostic eschatology.

See also GNOSIS, GNOSTICISM; JESUS TRADITIONS; MARK, SECRET GOSPEL OF; PETER, GOSPEL OF.

BIBLIOGRAPHY. C. L. Blomberg, "Tradition and Redaction in the Parables of the Gospel of Thomas" in *Gospel Perspectives* 5: *The Jesus Tradition Outside the Gospels,* ed. D. Wenham (Sheffield: JSOT, 1984) 177-205; R. E. Brown, "The Gospel of Thomas and St John's Gospel," *NTS* 9 (1962-63) 155-77; R. Cameron, *The Other Gospels: Noncanonical Gospel Texts* (Philadelphia: Westminster, 1982); J. H. Charlesworth and C. A. Evans, "Jesus in the Agrapha and Apocryphal Gospels" in *Studying the Historical Jesus: Evaluations of the State of Current Research,* ed. B. D. Chilton and C. A. Evans (NTTS 19; Leiden: E. J. Brill, 1994) 479-533; B. D. Chilton, "The Gospel According to Thomas as a Source of Jesus' Teaching" in *Gospel Perspectives* 5: *The Jesus Tradition Outside the Gospels,* ed. D. Wenham (Sheffield: JSOT, 1984) 155-75; J. D. Crossan, *Four Other Gospels* (Sonoma, CA: Polebridge, 1992) 3-38; S. Davies, *The Gospel of Thomas and Christian Wisdom* (New York: Seabury, 1983); B. Dehandschutter, "The Gospel of Thomas and the Synoptics: The Status Quaestionis" in *Studia Evangelica VII,* ed. E. A. Livingstone (TU 126; Berlin: Akademie, 1982) 157-60; idem, "L'évangile de Thomas comme collection de paroles de Jésus" in *Logia: Les Paroles de Jésus—The Sayings of Jesus,* ed. J. Delobel (BETL 59; Louvain: Peeters, 1982) 507-15; idem, "Recent Research on the Gospel of Thomas" in *The Four Gospels 1992,* ed. F. Van Segbroek et al. (BETL 100; Louvain: Peeters, 1992) 2257-62; C. A. Evans et al., eds., *Nag Hammadi Texts and the Bible: A Synopsis and Index* (NTTS 18; Leiden: E. J. Brill, 1993) 88-144; F. T. Fallon and R. Cameron, "The Gospel of Thomas: A Forschungsbericht and Analysis," *ANRW* 2.25.6 (1988) 4213-24; M. Fieger, *Das Thomasevangelium: Einleitung, Kommentar und Systematik* (NTAbh 22; Münster: Aschendorff, 1991); J. A. Fitzmyer, "The Oxyrhynchus *logoi* of Jesus and the Coptic Gospel According to Thomas" in *Essays on the Semitic Background of the New Testament* (SBLSBS 5; Missoula, MT: Scholars Press, 1974) 355-433; R. W. Funk and R. W. Hoover, eds., *The Five Gospels* (New York: Macmillan, 1993); B. Gärtner, *The Theology of the Gospel of Thomas* (London: Collins; New York: Harper & Row, 1961); A. Guillaumont et al., *The Gospel According to Thomas* (New York: Harper & Row, 1959); H. Koester, *Ancient Christian Gospels: Their History and Development* (London: SCM; Philadelphia: Trinity Press International, 1990) 75-128; idem, "Apocryphal and Canonical Gospels," *HTR* 73 (1980) 105-30; J. Ménard, *L'Évangile selon Thomas* (NHS 5; Leiden: E. J. Brill, 1975); R. J. Miller, ed., *The Complete Gospels* (Sonoma, CA: Polebridge, 1992) 301-22; S. J. Patterson, *The Gospel of Thomas and Jesus* (Sonoma, CA: Polebridge, 1993); idem, "The Gospel of Thomas and the Historical Jesus: Prospectus and Retrospectus" in *SBLSP* (1990) 614-36; J. M. Robinson, ed., *The Nag Hammadi Library in English* (rev. ed.; San Francisco: Harper & Row, 1988) 124-38; W. Schneemelcher, ed., *New Testament Apocrypha,* 1: *Gospels and Related Writings* (rev. ed.; Cambridge: James Clarke; Louisville, KY: Westminster/John Knox, 1991) 110-33; W. Schrage, *Das Verhältnis des Thomas-Evangeliums zur synoptischen Tradition und zu den koptischen Evangelienübersetzungen* (BZNW 29; Berlin: Töpelmann, 1964); K. R. Snodgrass, "The Gospel of Thomas: A Secondary Gospel," *SecCent* 7 (1989-90) 19-38; W. D. Stroker, *Extracanonical Sayings of Jesus* (SBLRBS 18; Atlanta: Scholars Press, 1989); R. McL. Wilson, *Studies in the Gospel of Thomas* (London: Mowbray, 1960).

C. A. Evans

TONGUES

The phenomenon of speaking in "unknown tongues," or glossolalia, has existed in many religious contexts, including the Old Testament (e.g., the prophesying of Saul in 1 Sam 10:5-6, 10) and various Mediterranean cults (*see* Religions, Greco-Roman). In the Christian context of our literature this phenomenon (i.e., making vocal sounds, under the influence of the Holy Spirit, that are unintelligible to at least some of those hearing), is mentioned by Paul (1 Cor 12, 14; *see DPL,* Tongues) and the author of Acts. This article will focus on tongues in Acts.

1. The Occurrence of Tongues in Acts
2. The Meaning of Tongues in Acts
3. Acts and the Rest of the New Testament
4. Acts and the Postapostolic Period

1. The Occurrence of Tongues in Acts.
The first reference to tongues occurs in Acts 2:4-13. When the Holy Spirit* comes at Pentecost,* he appears to those in the room as "divided tongues of fire" or "tongues of fire distributed among them" (Bruce), and they as a result began to speak in "other languages [tongues]" as the Spirit granted them ability. The text emphasizes that people from many nations each heard the praises of God* in their

own dialect (Acts 2:8) or language (i.e., tongue; Acts 2:11). Acts* then reports Peter explaining this phenomenon in terms of Joel's prophecy* (Joel 2:28-32).

The second reference appears in Acts 10:44-48, where the Holy Spirit interrupts Peter's address to the Gentile* Cornelius* and falls upon Cornelius and his associates. Peter recognizes the presence of the Spirit in their glossolalia and orders their baptism,* since they had received the Holy Spirit just as Peter and his fellow Jewish Christians had.

The final occurrence in Acts comes in Acts 19:1-7, where Paul finds a group of "disciples" who are ignorant of the Holy Spirit. The reason for this is that they know only John the Baptist's teaching and practice. After baptizing them in the name of Jesus, Paul lays hands on them, and the dozen disciples speak in tongues and prophesy.

There are other places in which Acts implies similar phenomena (e.g., Acts 8:17-19, where Simon observes some phenomenon) or refers to the explicit passages (e.g., Acts 11:15-17; 15:8), but none of them adds significantly to the three passages cited above.

2. The Meaning of Tongues in Acts.
When we examine the material in Acts, we can draw a number of conclusions.

First, Acts does not appear to differentiate clearly between tongues and prophecy. While the passage in Acts 19 mentions both spiritual gifts (to use the Pauline terminology), one wonders if this is not a type of emphasis. In Acts 2 the phenomenon is described as glossolalia, but in Peter's speech "this is that" refers to prophecy. In one place (Acts 2:18) "and they will prophesy" is added to Joel's prophecy to make his point clear. One might object that in Acts 2 the "tongues" are understandable as praise of God and thus prophetic, but Acts has already implied that because people from "every nation" were present presumably all languages were understood.

Second, Pentecost appears to reverse Babel. In Genesis 11:1, 6 it is underlined that humanity was monolingual; the confusion of language in Genesis 11:7 leads to the scattering of the nations (Gen 11:8-9). In Pentecost, people (both Jews and proselytes, thus former Gentiles) from all over the world* (the list in Acts 2:9-11 appears to parallel deliberately the geographic spread of the table of nations in Gen 10) are gathered in Jerusalem* and through the gift of tongues can all understand God's praise in their own language.

Third, glossolalia appears in Acts as an outward sign signaling the presence of the empowering Holy Spirit. If the point of Acts is that the mission* of the church was Spirit-driven rather than a human plan, then the function of glossolalia is to indicate that each phase of the mission is indeed the work of the Spirit. It is thus in Acts 2 a sign of the universal mission planned by the Spirit, then an indication of the initiative of the Spirit in the move to the Gentiles in Acts 10. The passage in Acts 19 probably demonstrates the universality of the presence of the Spirit in the church as a fringe group is integrated through the action of the Spirit. It is not the sole indicator of the presence of the Spirit, however, for such things as joy* (Acts 13:52; 16:34), the sharing of goods (Acts 4:32) and speaking the word with boldness (Acts 4:31) are also evidence of the Spirit cited in passages in which tongues are not mentioned.

3. Acts and the Rest of the New Testament.
The only other passage in the NT that refers to glossolalia is 1 Corinthians 12—14 (it does not appear in the shorter gifts lists in Rom 14, Eph 4 or 1 Pet 4). There Paul's concern is to dampen the Corinthian preference for tongues and to raise their appreciation of the more intelligible gift of prophecy. (Why this was not an issue for him elsewhere is unknown, just as it is unknown why Corinth in particular had a problem with the Lord's Supper.*) Neither the differentiation of the gifts nor the concern with intelligibility is a problem for Acts, possibly because in Acts the gifts are intelligible either by speakers of the various languages or as signs of the activity of God (ironically, in contrast to 1 Corinthians 14:22, tongues in Acts function as much a sign for believers as for unbelievers, especially in Acts 10).

4. Acts and the Postapostolic Period.
There are no references to glossolalia in the apostolic fathers, although there are twelve references to the tongue in terms of speech ethics* and one to the peoples of the languages of the world gathered in judgment.* Thus it appears that by the second century this phenomenon was subsumed under the term *prophecy* (i.e., the

lack of differentiation in Acts carried to its logical conclusion). This is clearly the case in Irenaeus (Irenaeus *Haer.* 3.12.15; 5.6.1; cf. Irenaeus *Haer.* 3.17.2; 2.32.4) and appears also to have been true of at least some Montanist "prophecy." M. T. Kelsey and A. Bittlinger therefore read *Martyrdom of Polycarp* 7.3 and the references to prophecy in Ignatius,* *Didache** and *Shepherd of Hermas** as including glossolalia. Whether their conclusion is accepted or not, what is clear is that speaking in tongues does not have a special significance in any of these works.

See also ACTS OF THE APOSTLES; HOLY SPIRIT; PENTECOST.

BIBLIOGRAPHY. A. Bittlinger, *Glossolalia: Wert und Problematik des Sprachenredens* (Schloss Craheim: Rolf Kühne Verlag, 1969); F. F. Bruce, *The Acts of the Apostles: The Greek Text with Introduction and Commentary* (Grand Rapids: Eerdmans, 1990); S. D. Currie, " 'Speaking in Tongues'; Early Evidence Outside the New Testament Bearing on 'Glossais Lalein,' " *Int* 19 (1965) 274-94; J. G. Davies, "Pentecost and Glossolalia," *JTS* n.s. 3 (1952) 228-31; J. D. G. Dunn, *Jesus and the Spirit* (Philadelphia: Westminster, 1975); J. M. Ford, "Towards a Theology of 'Speaking in Tongues,' " *TS* 32 (1971) 3-29; K. Haacker, "Das Pfingstwunder als exegetisches Problem" in *Verborum Veritas: Festschrift für Gustav Stählin,* ed. O. Böcher and K. Haacker (Wuppertal: Brockhaus, 1970) 125-32; H. Haarbeck, "Word," *NIDNTT* 3:1078-81; M. T. Kelsey, *Tongue Speaking: An Experiment in Spiritual Experience* (London: Hodder & Stoughton, 1964); G. J. Sirks, "The Cinderella of Theology: The Doctrine of the Holy Spirit," *HTR* 50 (1957) 77-89; R. Stronstad, *The Charismatic Theology of St. Luke* (Peabody, MA: Hendrickson, 1984).   P. H. Davids

TORAH. *See* LAW.

TRADITION. *See* JESUS TRADITIONS.

TRAVEL AND COMMERCE. *See* ROMAN EMPIRE, CHRISTIANS AND THE.

TRIBULATION, MESSIANIC WOES

In this portion of the NT and the apostolic fathers, tribulation is seen by these authors as something characterizing the Christian era, even if it intensifies nearer to the time of the return of Christ. The major word group regarding tribulation is *thlipsis* and its cognates, a word that is found in surprisingly few places in the NT or the apostolic fathers. Tribulation is one of the characteristics of what is sometimes called the messianic woes. The messianic woes were part of the Jewish eschatological framework in which it was thought that a certain number of tribulations and related signs needed to be experienced before the messianic age could be ushered in, a concept not well developed in the apostolic fathers. The relationship between tribulation and messianic woes indicates that the NT authors were probably heavily influenced by Jewish messianism such that they characterized both the first coming of Christ and their own age, culminating in the expected return of Christ, their Messiah, in such messianic terms.

1. Tribulation
2. Messianic Woes
3. Conclusion

1. Tribulation.
Reflecting apocalyptic language of the OT, especially Daniel, the book of Revelation (*see* Revelation, Book of) is the most extended depiction of tribulation in the NT, even though the word *thlipsis* is used only a few times. Although the reference in Revelation 7:14 to the great tribulation (cf. Mt 24:21) has caused unnecessary theological debate in terms of establishing the precise time and character of this tribulation in some futuristic eschatological* schemes, Revelation 6—19 clearly reflects a series of graphically depicted events of tribulation before the return of Christ* (Rev 19:11-21; *see* Parousia). This period is described in terms of the imagery of seven seals* (Rev 6:1—8:1), seven trumpets* (Rev 8:2—11:19) and seven bowls* (Rev 15:1—16:21), all containing various disastrous events culminating in judgment.* There have been numerous interpretations of how the seals, trumpets and bowls relate to each other, some interpreters seeing them consecutively and others with various degrees of overlap, some more and some less literally, but in any event in the end Babylon* is destroyed (Rev 17:1—18:24), making way for the return of Christ.

Although some persons have wanted to appropriate this book for their own theological purposes, interpretation in its original context indicates that it, like virtually all other biblical apocalyptic* passages, seems to reflect a time of imminent and impending if not already present persecution,* and hence persecution during the span of the Christian era. Although some writers have depicted this as a time when Christians are exempt from persecution, the evidence seems to indicate otherwise, with the tribulation being suffered by those by or for whom the books are written alongside others. This is certainly the case in Revelation. For example, in Revelation 1:9 the author, John, characterizes himself as a brother and companion in the tribulation or suffering,* kingdom and endurance* of his readers. In Revelation 2:9-10 the author speaks similarly to the church in Smyrna, recognizing their tribulation and poverty and instructing them that they can expect to have tribulation.

The same emphasis appears in other places in which tribulation is explicitly referred to in this literature (Heb 10:33; Jas 1:27; cf. Heb 11:37 regarding those in the OT). Even though the word for tribulation does not appear other than in James 1:27 in James,* A. Chester claims that such passages as James 1:2-4, 12-15 and James 5:7-12 also reflect tribulation. This is within the context of what the audience of the book is currently experiencing. This pattern is consistent with the rest of the NT. John 16:33 says that followers of Jesus can expect to have tribulation in this world,* and Acts 11:19 shows how the church* began to spread after persecution connected with the martyrdom* of Stephen.* Paul typifies his ministry* as one filled with tribulation (Acts 20:23) and admonishes Christians to whom he writes that tribulation is part of the endurance connected with faith* in Christ (Rom 5:3; 8:35; 12:12; 2 Cor 1:4, etc.).

The apostolic fathers* develop these concepts further in two important ways. The first is the recognition that the condition of the Christian is to have tribulation and suffer persecution. For example, in *1 Clement* 59.4, a passage that invokes a number of similar OT passages (*see* Old Testament in Apostolic Fathers), the author beseeches God* on behalf of all of those who have fallen into misfortune, including the overtly afflicted. In *Hermas Similitudes* 7.1-6, the shepherd* is told that his continued suffering of various forms of punishment is a means of inducing repentance* and purification for his sinful deeds. No other way is said to be effective.

2. Messianic Woes.

The messianic woes refers to the kinds of travails

to be experienced not only by the Messiah but by humankind in general in anticipation of the establishment of the messianic kingdom (*see* Kingdom of God). The travails include various kinds of turmoil and evil, including a general lack of humanity, earthquakes, famines, fire and various mysterious portents on earth and in the heavens. This was a fairly common idea in several strains of Jewish, especially apocalyptic, thought as well as some Greek thinking and is to be found specifically in Daniel (Dan 7; 9:20-27; 12:1-4), *1 Enoch* (*1 Enoch* 80:2-8; 99:4-9; 100), *Jubilees* (*Jub.* 23:11-25), 4 Ezra (4 Ezra 5:1-13; 6:17-28; 7:10-35), *Sybilline Oracles* (*Syb. Or.* 3.538-44, 633-51, 796-807; 5.512-31), *2 Apocalypse of Baruch* (*2 Apoc. Bar.* 25—27; 32:1; 70), *Testament of Moses* (*T. Mos.* 8; 10:1-10), the Qumran* literature (e.g., 1QH 3; 1QM 12; 19) and rabbinic literature (e.g., *m. Soṭa* 9:15; *b. Sanh.* 93; 98), among others.

The Suffering Servant passages in Isaiah, especially Isaiah 53:4-7, seem to have been instrumental in generating thought of a suffering Messiah. What characterizes those passages that introduce the Messiah is the expectation that the messiah, as a righteous person, was to be loaded down by God with cares, sorrows and even wounds and would suffer and possibly die. Whereas the vast mainstream of Jewish thought does not appear to have equated this death with an atoning death, on the basis of reflection upon Isaiah 53:4-7 it appears that at least in some circles the thought did develop into seeing the Messiah suffering as an atonement for human sin (see Justin Martyr *Dial. Tryph.* 89—90). The Messiah therefore not only fulfilled the commandments* of God but also in some way atoned for the failings of other humans by his abundance of righteousness.*

The question of major concern is what impact this thinking may have had on the NT writers. Whereas it appears that the NT accurately reflects Jewish lack of thinking of a dying, atoning Messiah (see Mt 16:22; Lk 18:34; 24:21; Jn 12:34), the NT writers themselves seem to see Jesus' suffering and death as atoning, quite possibly in terms of the messianic woes described in the Jewish literature (e.g., Mk 10:45 par. Mt 20:28; *see* Death of Christ). D. S. Russell has noted that Jesus' discourse on approaching judgment (Mk 13; Mt 24; Lk 21) is followed by the story of his suffering and death. Jesus agonizes in the garden and dies on the cross* before being resurrected as an inauguration of the day of the Lord (see Day of the Lord; Resurrection). Matthew depicts the death and resurrection with strange natural and other phenomena, such as an eclipse, the tearing of the temple* curtain, an earthquake and the splitting of rocks, tombs breaking open and the bodies of the holy* being raised (Mt 27:51-53). As Acts 2:22 (see also Acts 2:24) states through the mouth of Peter, Jesus was a man recognized by his miracles,* wonders and signs (see Signs and Wonders).

Three passages from the literature that we are discussing have primary importance in discussing the concept of the messianic woes. The first is Revelation 12, especially Revelation 12:1-6. In this chapter a woman is depicted as in the throes of birth. Just as she is about to give birth a dragon* appears from heaven* and intends to devour her child as she gives birth to it. She gives birth to a son who, the author says, is to rule all the nations with an iron scepter, and the child is snatched up to God. The result is a war in heaven, and Michael and his angels* defeat the dragon, who is Satan,* and he is hurled to earth. Even though the dragon pursues the woman, she escapes, and the dragon makes war against those obedient to God. This passage seems to reflect the Isaianic literature regarding the birth of a significant child (see Is 9:6), hence the imagery of the "birth pangs," found here only in the literature under discussion (but see Mk 13:8; Mt 24:8; cf. 1 Thess 5:3; Gal 4:19, 27; Col 1:24).

The second passage is 1 Peter 2:21-25, a possibly preformulated creedal section that appears to be an extended reflection on Isaiah 53:4-9 (including quotation of Is 53:9 in 1 Pet 2:22; see Creeds). At the end of a section of household responsibilities (see Household Codes; Household, Family), after having summarized proper obedience* in 1 Peter 2:17, the author recapitulates regarding slaves* submitting to their masters. He draws an analogy between a slave suffering for doing good with what Christ suffered. Christ suffered "for you," or on their behalf, leaving himself as an example to be followed. After quoting Isaiah 53:9, the author recapitulates Christ's suffering (cf. 1 Pet 5:1) in terms of the Suffering Servant, who does not retaliate or recriminate but entrusts himself to God. He bore their sins when he was crucified so that in his death they might live. Alluding to

Isaiah 53:5, the author says that by his wounds they have been healed, and alluding to Isaiah 53:6, he compares Christians to being sheep who have gone astray. This passage reflects the messianic suffering that is a foretaste of glorification and applies it directly to the Christian audience (see also 1 Pet 4:12-19).

A third passage is Didache 16, called by J. Lawson "an apocalyptic exhortation to faithfulness" (Lawson, 100). Didache 16 speaks of Christians maintaining readiness for the return of Christ, especially in the light of various forms of false prophets* and corrupters, including finally the deceiver of the world. At this point suffering and persecution seem to increase to their full complement until the return of the Lord. This highly apocalyptic passage is fully consonant with the imagery developed in Revelation but even more so with the apocalyptic passages in the Gospels, especially Matthew 24. It is fitting that it is the final and closing section of the Didache.*

Several other NT passages are also worth noting as possibly reflecting the language of the messianic woes in which Jesus suffers and brings atonement as a prelude to glorification. All of them seem to reflect Isaiah 53. These include Hebrews 5:8-9, which speaks of Jesus, who though being a son* learned obedience from what he suffered and, having been made perfect, became the source of eternal salvation* for all. 1 Peter 1:11 speaks of the sufferings of Christ and the glories that would follow, reflecting movement from messianic suffering to the day of the Lord. And 1 John 3:5 says that Christ appeared so that he might take away sins.

3. Conclusion.
Although there is little in the texts discussed to argue for the tribulation as conceived in systematic theological constructs, there is a noteworthy and sizeable amount of overlap between the conception of intensified tribulation before the return of Christ as depicted in some theological schemes and the concept of the messianic woes preceding the day of the Lord. The following features are worth noting. The biblical texts arguably endorse the idea that the suffering of tribulation is something that Jesus Christ himself as the Isaianic messiah underwent in his suffering and death. In that sense he was subject to the messianic woes of the expected Jewish Messiah, anticipated in a variety of biblical and

extrabiblical literature. The tribulations associated with him are seen by the biblical authors to be continued in his followers, as attested by various statements throughout the NT. There also appears to be an expectation of heightened suffering associated with following in the footsteps of the Messiah and in anticipation of his return. In this way contemporary Christians, as reflected in the NT texts, are experiencing a period of messianic woes in expectation of the future day of the Lord. Continued tribulation is seen as a necessary prelude to the return of Christ.

See also APOCALYPTIC, APOCALYPTICISM; DAY OF THE LORD; ESCHATOLOGY; PAROUSIA.

BIBLIOGRAPHY. M. Bockmuehl, *This Jesus: Martyr, Lord, Messiah* (Downers Grove, IL: InterVarsity Press, 1996); A. Chester and R. P. Martin, *The Theology of the Letters of James, Peter and Jude* (NTT; Cambridge: Cambridge University Press, 1994); J. J. Collins, *The Apocalyptic Imagination: An Introduction to the Jewish Matrix of Christianity* (New York: Crossroad, 1984); P. H. Davids, *The First Epistle of Peter* (NICNT; Grand Rapids: Eerdmans, 1990); W. Grundmann et al., "χρίω κτλ," *TDNT* 9:493-580; R. H. Gundry, *The Church and the Tribulation* (Grand Rapids: Zondervan, 1973); C. E. Hill, *Regnum Caelorum: Patterns of Future Hope in Early Christianity* (Oxford: Clarendon, 1992); G. E. Ladd, *The Last Things* (Grand Rapids: Eerdmans, 1978); J. Lawson, *A Theological and Historical Introduction to the Apostolic Fathers* (New York: Macmillan, 1961); J. B. Lightfoot, *The Apostolic Fathers* (pt. 1; 2 vols.; New York: Macmillan, 1890); D. S. Russell, *Apocalyptic: Ancient and Modern* (London: SCM, 1978); idem, *The Method and Message of Jewish Apocalyptic* (London: SCM, 1964); E. Schürer, *The History of the Jewish People in the Age of Jesus Christ (175 B.C.-A.D. 135)*, rev. and ed. G. Vermes et al. (3 vols.; Edinburgh: T & T Clark, 1973-77).

S. E. Porter

TRUMPETS

Revelation uses "trumpet" and its cognates "trumpeter" and "to sound a trumpet" in two notable contexts: to depict the character of a voice that addresses the Seer; in connection with a series of seven visions,* each of which commences with a trumpet blast. A third and minor context is the desolation of the wicked city, Babylon,* where the sound of trumpeter is no longer to be heard (Rev 18:24). In the apostolic fathers* "trumpet" denotes the clarity and forcefulness of the Word of God.

1. The Voice Like a Trumpet
2. The Trumpet Visions
3. Patristic Uses

1. The Voice Like a Trumpet.

Revelation 1:10 and Revelation 4:1 refer to a "voice like a trumpet" that addressed the Seer. The trumpet of those days was primitive and produced only a few notes with a raucous sound; it was better suited as a signaling and warning device than as a musical instrument. The Seer therefore seems to be indicating the distinctiveness or loudness of the sound of the voice—a sound that could not be ignored. Yet the use of the trumpet in the OT—to call those who were to participate in the holy war (Judg 3:27; 6:34; 1 Sam 13:3; Jer 51:27; Ezek 7:14), as the accompaniment of a theophany, to announce the Day of the Lord* and to mark the eschatological* judgment* (Joel 2:1; Zeph 1:16), the beginning of the new era of salvation* and the restoration of Israel*—cannot be overlooked. Seen against such a background, a trumpet blast is an appropriate way to introduce the Apocalypse (*see* Revelation, Book of), which announces the fulfillment of the reign of Christ* and calls on his people to engage in the holy war against the enemies of God.

2. The Trumpet Visions.

Like the preceding judgments of the seals* (Rev 6:1—8:1), the seven judgments of the trumpets in Revelation 8:2—11:19 are divided into groups of four and three, with an interlude between the sixth and seventh visions. Yet the trumpet visions provide greater detail and are of greater severity than are the seal visions: whereas the seal judgments affected one-fourth of the individual target groups, the trumpet judgments affect one-third of each group.

The seven trumpet blasts are particularly significant when they are seen against the background of the trumpet blasts accompanying the conquest of Jericho (Josh 6:4, 8, 13). In the context of the whole Apocalypse the situation is reversed: now it is Jerusalem* and the people of Israel who are defeated by their Gentile* enemies. Much of the imagery in the trumpet visions comes from the OT account of the plagues on Egypt; since Revelation 11:8 applies the name *Egypt* to Jerusalem, the implication is that these judgments are to fall on Jerusalem. The use in the individual visions of imagery drawn from prophetic denunciations of Jerusalem and Israel because of their idolatry* and apostasy* also suggests that the Seer regards Jerusalem and the Jewish people of his day as the object of God's* wrath.* But there are also allusions to OT texts proclaiming doom for Babylon, thus preparing the way for a more detailed description of the fate of the symbolic Babylon in Revelation 17—18.

2.1. The First Trumpet. The image of hail, fire and blood falling on the earth may be based on Amos 7:4, referring to a fire burning up the land of Israel.

2.2. The Second Trumpet. The image of something resembling a burning mountain plunging into the sea, killing one-third of the marine life and destroying one-third of the ships (Rev 8:8-9), could be a reference to the eruption of Vesuvius in A.D. 79. But it could also refer to Jeremiah 51:25, depicting Babylon as a mountain, fallen to earth and burned.

2.3. The Third Trumpet. The transformation of waters to wormwood and the subsequent deaths (Rev 8:10-11) are the reverse of the miracle at Marah, where bitter and undrinkable water was made drinkable (Ex 15:25). Moreover, in Jeremiah 9:15 Yahweh says that he will feed Judah with wormwood and give them poisonous water to drink because they have forsaken him and practiced idolatry (cf. Jer 9:14). Jeremiah 23:15 makes the same threat against the false prophets.*

2.4. The Fourth Trumpet. The reduction of the light of the sun, moon and stars (Rev 8:12) is a variation on Isaiah 49:10: what was to be a blessing* for the returning exiles is instead a curse. There is also an allusion to Amos 8:9, where Yahweh announces that he will darken the earth because of Israel's injustices and religious formalism. Moreover, the darkness that enabled Joshua to defeat Israel's enemies now becomes the means of Israel's defeat at the hands of her enemies (Josh 10:12-14).

2.5. The Fifth Trumpet. The plague of locusts like horses could allude to the presence of Gessius Florus's cavalry in Judea, seen as a fulfillment of Joel's prophecy of horselike locusts invading Palestine (Joel 1—2). There may also be a reference to Jeremiah 51, which warns of an attack on Babylon by "horses like bristling locusts" (Jer 51:17) and an invasion and con-

quest by an army as numerous as locusts (Jer 51:14). The Greek name of the locust plague's leader, "Apollyon," perhaps reflects the claims of Nero and Domitian to be incarnations of Apollo.

2.6. The Sixth Trumpet. Most scholars see the mention of the river Euphrates as a reference to Rome's fear of a Parthian invasion from the East under the leadership of a revived Nero—and thus as confirmation of the view that the Seer is concerned with Rome (*see* Roman Empire) as the enemy of the church.* Yet the prophets sometimes used the Euphrates (Israel's northern frontier) to signify Assyria and Babylon as the area from which Israel's punishment would come (cf. Is 7:20; 8:7; Jer 46:10), and many prophecies spoke of the invasion of Israel by a foe from the north (e.g., Is 14:31; Jer 1:14-15; 13:20: 47:2; Ezek 38:6, 15). The ability of the "horses" to wound both with their tails and with their mouths (Rev 9:19) could refer to the Parthians, whose bowmen were renowned for their skill in shooting arrows both ahead of and behind them.

2.7. The Seventh Trumpet. The vision of the ark of the covenant within "God's temple in heaven" (Rev 11:15-19) reflects the Jewish tradition that Jeremiah had hidden the ark and the altar of burnt offering so that they would not fall into the hands of the Chaldeans. Since the ark would not be restored until God regathered his people (cf. 2 Macc 2:4-8), the Seer may be hinting that the time of regathering has arrived. That the ark is seen in heaven* rather than in the temple* in Jerusalem suggests that the earthly temple has been superseded.

3. Patristic Uses.
"Trumpet" occurs in the later literature as a simile for the clarity and force with which the Word of God comes (Justin Martyr *Or. Gr.* 5), its eschatological announcement (*Did.* 16.6) or as a historical allusion to the OT (Irenaeus *Haer.* 4.18).

See also BABYLON; REVELATION, BOOK OF; VISIONS, ECSTATIC EXPERIENCE.

BIBLIOGRAPHY. A. J. Beagley, *The 'Sitz im Leben' of the Apocalypse with Particular Reference to the Role of the Enemies of the Church* (BZNW 50; Berlin: Walter de Gruyter, 1987); G. R. Beasley-Murray, *The Book of Revelation* (NCB; London: Oliphants, 1978); I. T. Beckwith, *The Apocalypse of John: Studies in Introduction with a Critical and Exegetical Com-*

mentary (Grand Rapids: Baker, 1979 [1919]);
G. B. Caird, *The Revelation of St. John the Divine*
(HNTC; New York: Harper & Row, 1966); P. Carrington, *The Meaning of the Revelation* (London:
SPCK, 1931); R. H. Charles, *A Critical and Exegetical Commentary on the Revelation of St. John* (ICC;
Edinburgh: T & T Clark, 1920); A. Y. Collins, *The Combat Myth in the Book of Revelation*
(HDR 9; Missoula, MT: Scholars Press, 1976); A.
Feuillet, *The Apocalypse* (Staten Island, NY: Alba
House, 1965); J. M. Ford, *Revelation; Introduction, Translation and Commentary* (AB; Garden
City, NY: Doubleday, 1975); G. Friedrich,
"σάλπιγξ," *TDNT* 8:71-88; S. Giet, *L'Apocalypse et
l'histoire; Étude historique sur l'Apocalypse Johannique*
(Paris: University of Paris, 1957); H. W. Günther, *Der Nah- und Enderwartungshorizont in der
Apokalypse des heiligen Johannes* (FBib 41; n.p.:
Echter, 1980); B. Malina, *On the Genre and Message of Revelation: Star Visions and Sky Journeys*
(Peabody, MA: Hendrickson, 1995); J. R.
Michaels, *Interpreting the Book of Revelation*
(GNTE; Grand Rapids: Baker, 1992); R. H.
Mounce, *The Book of Revelation* (NICNT; Grand
Rapids: Eerdmans, 1977); J. Sweet, *Revelation* (WPC; Philadelphia: Westminster, 1979);
C. van der Waal, *Openbaring van Jezus Christus:
Inleiding en Vertaling* (Groningen: De Vuurbaak,
1971); idem, *Openbaring van Jezus Christus II:
Verklaring* (Oudkarspel: De Neverheid, 1981).

A. J. Beagley

TRUTH

The English word *truth* typically translates the
Greek *alētheia* and related forms in the NT, but
one must caution against equating modern notions of truth with its functions in early Christianity. Whereas truth in Western cultures often
concerns facts that can be proven logically or
scientifically, truth in the NT may deal with genuine, dependable, faithful behavior or "things as
they really are" in contrast to something that has
been hidden or concealed (cf. Hübner, 58 and
Bultmann, 238, though etymological appeals to
lanthanō ["forget," "cover up"] as a basis for interpreting *alētheia* are suspect).

Nonetheless, as is seen especially in Acts,
alētheia can be used with reference to the truth
or reality of historical events or a speaker's
statements (see also 8 below on Ignatius). A
matter of truth is rarely defended with logical
arguments, but instead the author often appeals
to the source of revealed truth or assumes the

veracity of the claims.

Furthermore, whereas today it is commonplace to question the truth of God's existence,
this existence was typically assumed in NT contexts. Instead the authors debated which religious beliefs and behaviors were true or truthful
in contrast to those that were false or deceitful.

In addition it is important to remember that
abstract terms such as "truth," "true" or "real"—
which are extremely difficult to define out of
context—are best treated in view of closely related words. Therefore the following study attempts to understand Greek terms for "truth"
(*alētheia* and related forms) in conjunction with
terms meaning "false" (*pseudos* and related
forms) and "belief" (*pistis* and related forms),
an approach substantiated by the Septuagint
translation of the Hebrew *ˀemet* with Greek
words for righteousness* and faith.*

1. Johannine Epistles
2. Acts
3. Hebrews
4. James
5. Petrine Epistles
6. Jude
7. Revelation
8. Apostolic Fathers

1. Johannine Epistles.
Of the fifty-five uses of *alētheia* or related terminology in Acts, the General Epistles and Revelation, almost 51 percent appear in the Johannine
epistles (*see* John, Letters of): 1 John (sixteen
times), 2 John (five times) and 3 John (seven
times). Even more importantly "truth" and
"falsehood" play central roles in the thematic
structures of all three letters. Hence we start
with this corpus.

In these letters certain behavior is required
of believers who claim to "be in the truth" (1 Jn
1:8), "know the truth" (2 Jn 1-2) or "walk in the
truth" (2 Jn 4; 3 Jn 3-4). Believers must admit to
"having sin" (1 Jn 1:8). They must keep the
commands of God (1 Jn 2:4). They must not
hate their fellow believers (1 Jn 2:8-11; 4:20) but
instead love them with their actions (1 Jn 3:16-
19; 2 Jn 1; 3 Jn 1). They must not deny that Jesus
is the Messiah (1 Jn 2:20-22) and that he came
in the flesh* (1 Jn 4:1-3; cf. 2 Jn 7). They accept
as true God's* testimony that he has given them
eternal life* through his Son* (1 Jn 5:10-11).

The author assumes that truth can be known
and discerned (2 Jn 1-2; cf. 1 Jn 4:6). The basis

of truth is God (1 Jn 5:9-10), and the revealer and giver of truth is Jesus (1 Jn 5:20), who is described as the "true one" (1 Jn 5:20). But whereas God and the Spirit teach that which is true (1 Jn 2:27; 1 Jn 4:6; 1 Jn 5:6), there are also false spirits and prophets* (1 Jn 4:1-6) and idols* (1 Jn 5:21) that lead away from the truth.

2. Acts.

Despite its length Acts* uses *alētheia* only five times and *pseudos* three times; the author prefers *pistis* when speaking of one's belief or trust in the truth of something. Twice *alētheia* is used with the preposition *epi* in the sense of "indeed, truly": in Acts 4:27 to emphasize that Psalm 2:1-2 was "in fact" fulfilled in the persecution* of Jesus and in Acts 10:34 to highlight that Peter now "truly" understands God's impartiality in view of Cornelius's* encounter with a divine being (Acts 10:30-33). In Acts 12:9 Peter is not sure if his rescue from prison by an angel* was "real" *(alēthōs)* or a "vision"* *(horama);* here the author makes a clear distinction between events in time and space that happen and those that only appear to happen. When the angel leaves Peter standing in the street, Peter states in Acts 12:11 that he now "truly" *(alēthōs)* knows that the events surrounding his rescue actually occurred. Twice in Acts "truth" concerns the veracity of a person's actions or words. In Acts 5:3-4 Peter charges Ananias with lying *(pseudomai)* to the Holy Spirit* and to God after giving the church* only a portion of the proceeds from the sale of his property. In Acts 26:25 Paul responds to Festus's challenge of the truthfulness of his courtroom defense by claiming, "I speak words of truth *(alētheia)*"; that is, he is not lying.

3. Hebrews.

In Hebrews 6:18 God's promise* to Abraham* is said to be authenticated by the fact that it was confirmed with an oath, which must be true because God cannot "lie" *(pseudomai);* that is, God is the basis of truth since by his very nature he presents things as they are. Twice in Hebrews* the author contrasts an earthly religious entity with its true counterpart: the true *(alēthinos)* heavenly tabernacle* (in contrast to the earthly one), in which our high priest* Jesus now resides, has been set up by the Lord,* not humans (Heb 8:2); and similarly Christ* is said to have entered heaven,* not holy places (of the temple*) that are mere copies of the true ones

(Heb 9:24). Hebrews 10:22 uses the adjective *(alēthinos)* in a practical sense, stating that we should approach God with a true (almost in the sense of "pure, righteous") heart, one that has been cleansed from an evil conscience.* In this sense a true heart is dependent upon its moral qualities. Hebrews 10:26 speaks of truth *(alētheia)* as something that is bestowed to someone and demands certain conduct: "If we willfully sin after receiving the knowledge of truth, there no longer remains a sacrifice for sins."

4. James.

The letter of James* juxtaposes truth and wisdom* *(sophia)* with falsehood and deception *(planaō)*. God is the one who gives wisdom to individuals but only if they ask and believe (Jas 1:5-6). James 1:18 similarly treats God as the one who "brought us forth by the word of truth," probably a reference to regeneration and the gospel (Davids, 89). Those who have "wisdom" and "understanding" *(epistēmōn)* should demonstrate it by means of humble actions (Jas 3:13). Such "humble wisdom"—a wisdom that is defined as pure, peaceable, gentle, submissive, full of mercy* and good fruit, impartial and sincere—is contrasted with harsh zeal and selfish ambition, and persons who exhibit these latter characteristics are warned not to "lie against the truth" (Jas 3:14). The author still describes such conduct as "earthly, unspiritual and devilish" wisdom, yet a wisdom that is not from heaven (Jas 3:15). The verb *planaō* is used to warn the reader not to be "deceived" (Jas 1:16) and to speak of the possibility of "being led away" from the truth (Jas 5:19).

5. Petrine Epistles.

In 1 Peter* the readers are encouraged to "obey the truth" (1 Pet 1:22) with the result that they love their fellow believers (cf. the Johannine letters); in 1 Peter 5:12 the author states that "this" (= the content of the letter or perhaps the suffering* of the readers; see Michaels, 308-10) is the "true grace of God" (1 Pet 5:12; *see* Grace). Notions of truth and falsehood play a more important role in 2 Peter.* In 2 Peter 1:12 the author reminds the readers of truths in which they are already firmly established. In 2 Peter 2—3 (esp. 2 Pet 2:1-2) the author warns of false prophets and teachers who lead people astray and cause the "way of truth" to be blasphemed (2 Pet 2:2). 2 Peter 2:3 and onward then describes the punishment* and sinful conduct of these individuals and (in 2 Pet 3:3-4) possibly hints at their denial of the "Day of the Lord."* In the closing of the letter, the author again warns the readers to guard against "lawless men" but instead to "grow in the grace and knowledge of our Lord and Savior Jesus Christ" (2 Pet 3:18).

6. Jude.

It is surprising that Jude* never uses any of the common words for "truth" or "falsehood," since this brief letter is primarily an attempt to warn the readers against "godless men" who have "secretly crept in" among them (Jude 4)—a prime opportunity to make claims about truth and falsehood. However, Jude 10 does address the ability of these so-called godless men to "understand" (epistantai) by equating their minimal understanding with that of "unreasoning animals," who only have a "natural" (or instinctual) type of understanding. By implication the ability to understanding things (i.e., to know the truth about something) depends upon the level of one's understanding. According to this author, there are "natural," "logical" and perhaps even "spiritual" (see Jude 19, where the "godless men" are described as not having the Spirit) abilities to understand; these types of understanding are not further clarified.

7. Revelation.

All ten uses of truth language in Revelation (see Revelation, Book of) are with the adjective alēthinos. Often the adjective describes the activities or characteristics of Jesus or God as true. In Revelation 3:7, 14 Jesus is spoken of as the "true one" and "true witness" respectively. In Revelation 6:10 the Lord is praised as "holy and true"; in Revelation 15:3 "just and true" are the ways of the Lord God; in Revelation 16:7 and Revelation 19:2 God's judgments are "true and just." Several times in Revelation the words that John is being told to write down are declared to be "true" (Rev 19:9; 21:5; 22:6). Aside from these instances, alēthinos is used in Revelation 19:11 for the name of the rider of the white horse, namely, "Faithful and True."

As one would expect in a book with several instances of language about truth, there are various uses of terminology about falsehood: in Revelation 3:9 there are those who "lie" about being Jews but are really part of the "synagogue of Satan"; in Revelation 14:5 the 144,000 who

follow the Lamb* are said to have no "lie" in their mouths; Revelation 16:13; 19:20; 20:10 speak of the "false" prophet; and Revelation 21:27 and Revelation 22:15 describe both those who are not part of the book of life and those who are deemed "outsiders" as people who practice "falsehood" (pseudos).

8. Apostolic Fathers.

Greek words for "truth" appear approximately one hundred times in the writings of the apostolic fathers*; in several cases truth is contrasted with "falsehood" or "heresy" (Ign. Eph. 6.2; Did. 11.10; 16.3, 6). God and Christ are repeatedly described in terms of truth: God loves truth (1 Clem. 18.6); God is true or is a God "of truth" (2 Clem. 3.1; 19.1; 20.5; Mart. Pol. 14.2; Herm. Man. 3.1; Diogn. 8.8); Jesus is true life (Ign. Eph. 7.2; Ign. Smyrn. 4.1) and true love* (Pol. Phil. 1.1). Ignatius* calls his readers the "children of truth" (Ign. Phld. 2.1). The Scriptures are said to be true (1 Clem. 45.2; cf. Pol. Phil. 3.2, where Paul is said to have taught the truth to the Philippians). God is the source of truth (1 Clem. 35.2; 2 Clem. 20.5; cf. 1 Clem. 60.2; Diogn. 7.2). "Truly" is occasionally used to validate an author's claim (1 Clem. 23.6; 47.3; Ign. Eph. 17.2; Barn. 1.3; 7.9); for example, Ignatius stresses that the events of Jesus' virgin birth, persecution, death (see Death of Christ), burial and resurrection* "truly" happened (Ign. Magn. 11.1; Ign. Trall. 9.1; Ign. Smyrn. 1.1, 2; 2.1).

But in these writings truth is typically treated in relation to the behavior of people: Job was righteous, unblamable and true (1 Clem. 17.3); Abraham worked righteousness and truth through faith (1 Clem. 31.2); Christians should "live" according to the truth and "walk" or "serve God" in truth, which implies righteous behavior (1 Clem. 35.6; 62.2; Ign. Eph. 6.2; Pol. Phil. 2.1; 5.2; Herm. Man. 12.3.1; Herm. Sim. 9.25.2; cf. Barn. 20.2 and Did. 5.2, where "hating the truth" is found in a list of vices); God can be called upon in faith and truth (1 Clem. 60.4); people should speak the truth (2 Clem. 12.3; Herm. Man. 3); wives are told to cherish their husbands in all truth (Pol. Phil. 4.2); the truth of something should be investigated as to its veracity, not merely believed (Herm. Man. 10.1.4, 5, 6); truth can be abandoned (Herm. Sim. 6.2.1, 4; 8.9.1). One of the most concentrated discussions of truth is found in the third mandate of the Shepherd of Hermas,* which highlights the virtue* of speaking the truth and condemns falsehood and lying.

See also AUTHORITY; GNOSIS, GNOSTICISM; GOSPEL; KNOWLEDGE; WISDOM.

BIBLIOGRAPHY. W. Bauer, *A Greek-English Lexicon of the New Testament and Other Early Christian Literature*, rev. F. W. Gingrich and W. Danker (2d ed.; Chicago: University of Chicago Press, 1979); R. Bultmann, "ἀλήθεια κτλ," *TDNT* 1:232-51; P. H. Davids, *Commentary on James* (NIGTC; Grand Rapids: Eerdmans, 1982); H. Hübner, "ἀλήθεια κτλ," *EDNT* 1:57-60; J. R. Michaels, *1 Peter* (WBC; Waco, TX: Word, 1988);

A. C. Thiselton, "Truth," *NIDNTT* 3:874-902.

J. T. Reed

TWELVE, THE. *See* APOSTLE, APOSTLESHIP.

TWELVE TRIBES. *See* ISRAEL, TWELVE TRIBES.

TWO WAYS. *See* TEACHING, PARAENISIS; VIRTUES AND VICES.

TYPOLOGY. *See* INTERTEXTUALITY IN EARLY CHRISTIAN LITERATURE; MOSES; OLD TESTAMENT IN HEBREWS.

U

UNCLEAN. *See* PURITY AND IMPURITY.

UNIVERSALISM

Universalism is the theory that ultimately everyone will be saved. A key text for this theory as developed in the early church is found in our portion of the NT at Acts 3:21, relying heavily upon the significance of the Greek word *apokatastasis* ("restoration"). Origen (c. 185-c. 254) is the first explicit proponent of universalism, or *apokatastasis*, and draws mostly upon Romans 5:19, Romans 11:32, 1 Corinthians 15:22 and 1 Timothy 2:4 (*see DPL*, Universalism). The wording of 2 Peter 3:9 also is suggestive if it is read through a universalist lens.

    1. Acts 3:21
    2. 2 Peter 3:9
    3. Conditional Salvation in the Later
       New Testament

1. Acts 3:21.

1.1. The Restoration of All. Acts 3:17-21 can be taken one of two ways, dramatized by the differences in how the RSV and NRSV translate Acts 3:21. Jesus is to remain in heaven "until the time for establishing all that God spoke" (RSV) or "until the time of universal restoration that God announced long ago through his holy prophets" (NRSV). In the RSV's rendering, *apokatastasis pantōn* is read in the light of Luke's desire to demonstrate divine fulfillment in the unfolding events (e.g., Acts 2:23). God's purpose, as in the life and work of Christ* so in the second coming, will be established at the time he foretold through the prophets (cf. the use of the verb *apokathistanō* in Acts 1:6; Bruce). The NRSV rightly follows the RSV in rendering *pantōn* as a neuter ("all things") instead of taking it as "all people." But the NRSV's translation emphasizes the Jewish expectation that the Messiah would return all things to their original state.

1.2. Origen. Origen used Acts 3:21 as the basis for the doctrine of apokatastasis, the doctrine of the restoration of all created things. Central to his view is that the goal of God's work of salvation* is to remove all disorder in creation* that has resulted from sin, restoring all things and every person in the end to the primeval order they had in the beginning. He goes beyond the messianic expectation of the restoration of the universe to posit an anthropological effect, the reconciliation of all people to God. He reinterprets texts about judgment* in light of the absolute nature of God's dominion (Origen *De Princ.* 1.6.1-4). Since God will ultimately rule all things again, the punishment of the wicked is temporary and consists in their own internal anguish at the realization of their separation from God. The scriptural depictions of eternal punishment have value as deterrents, but they will one day come to an end. Acts 3:21, in Origen's view, hints at the time when all created things will be restored to the harmony and unity of original creation (Origen *De Princ.* 3.6.3), "when all things shall be reestablished in a state of unity and when God shall be all in all" (Origen *De Princ.* 3.6.6).

2. 2 Peter 3:9.

2.1. A Universalist Misreading of 2 Peter 3:9. The wording of 2 Peter 3:9 is suggestive along the lines of universalism: the Lord* "does not wish anyone to perish but wants all to come to repentance." The argument can be advanced that God's purpose is never thwarted, and the divine perogative will be fulfilled. Salvation for all will be fully realized because the God who wills it is omnipotent. So note the echo of 2 Peter 3:9 in *1 Clement*: "Since then he wishes all his beloved to partake of repentance, he has established it by his almighty will" (*1 Clem.* 8:5).

2.2. 2 Peter 3:9 in Context. The syntax and immediate context of 2 Peter 3:9 militate against a restorationist reading. The syntax does not address all people everywhere. Rather the author speaks of a limited sphere of concern: "but he is forebearing toward you" *(eis hymas)*, that is, 2 Peter's* auditors. The "anyone" *(tinas)* he does not wish to perish and the "all" *(pantas)* he wants to repent are those toward whom he is patient among the community addressed by the letter (Bauckham). Likewise the immediate context rules out a universalist reading as a misreading. 2 Peter 3:7 clearly delineates a conditional salvation and a "day of judgment and destruction of the godless." The discussion is not about the unconditional salvation of all human beings but about why the Parousia* delays due to God's patience, allowing an extended opportunity for repentance.* The Lord's patience and "slowness" to return are to allow more people into the kingdom (*see* Kingdom of God) but does not ensure that all will enter.

3. Conditional Salvation in the Later NT.
The dominant eschatology* of the later NT writings is unified around the judgment and permanent punishment of the godless (2 Pet 3:7). So Revelation 20:10 warns, "And the devil who had deceived them was thrown into the lake of fire and sulfur, . . . and they will be tormented day and night forever and ever" (NRSV). Judgment awaits some humans too: "anyone whose name was not found written in the book of life was thrown into the lake of fire" (Rev 20:15 NRSV). Examples need not be multiplied to demonstrate the density of language in the eschatological statements of the later NT, language that includes "destroy" *(apollymi, phtheirō)*, "destruction" *(apōleia, olethros)* and "abolish" *(katargeō)*. These terms characterize human destiny apart from Christ.

See also CREATION, COSMOLOGY; ESCHATOLOGY; EVANGELISM IN THE EARLY CHURCH; GENTILES, GENTILE MISSION; MISSION, EARLY NON-PAULINE; SALVATION; WORLD.

BIBLIOGRAPHY. R. J. Bauckham, *Jude, 2 Peter* (WBC; Waco, TX: Word, 1983); F. F. Bruce, *The Book of the Acts* (NICNT; Grand Rapids: Eerdmans, 1981); J. N. D. Kelly, *Early Christian Doctrines* (rev. ed.; San Francisco: Harper & Row, 1978 [1960]); H.-G. Link, "Apokatastasis," *NIDNTT* 3:146-48; P.-G. Müller, "ἀποκαθίστημι, ἀποκαθιστάνω," *EDNT* 1:129-30; A. F. Segal, "Conversion and Universalism: Opposites That Attract" in *Origins and Method: Toward a New Understanding of Judaism and Christianity*, ed. B. McLean (JSNTSup 86; Sheffield: JSOT, 1993) 162-89; R. J. H. Shutt, "The New Testament Doctrine of the Hereafter: Universalism or Conditional Immortality," *ExpT* 67 (1955-56) 131-35.   B. J. Dodd

V

VALENTINUS. *See* Gnosis, Gnosticism.

VIALS. *See* Bowls.

VICES. *See* Virtues and Vices.

VIRTUES AND VICES

Ethicists define a virtue as one of an integrated set of habitual inner dispositions of an ideal human life that is displayed by positive action. By contrast, a vice is a habitual inner disposition to do evil or not to do good. Yet neither virtue nor vice is to be confused with specific actions of good or evil; each holds in view inner tendencies rooted in character. Any naming or consideration of virtues and vices needs to be understood within its respective worldview, for any given term for a virtue or vice can take on different shades of meaning in the light of various and distinct moral visions.

The later NT literature, like the Pauline Epistles (*see DPL*, Virtues and Vices), exhibits several listings of virtues and vices, a feature that is also found in the apostolic fathers.* However, it should be noted that not everything that is classified as a virtue or a vice in these lists (or in this article) would be so defined by ethicists. In some cases they are simply abstentions from or addictions to sinful or evil deeds. An important consideration for interpreting these lists is the common Greco-Roman practice of listing virtues and vices as a form of moral exhortation. Nonetheless there are valuable precedents in the OT-Jewish moral traditions, as we shall observe, particularly in the wisdom traditions.

    1. Greco-Roman and Jewish Background
    2. Later New Testament Writings
    3. Apostolic Fathers

1. Greco-Roman and Jewish Background.
The NT emerged in a world in which moral thought was well developed. Aristotle's work on

the virtues was four hundred years old by the time the NT literature was written. The cataloging of virtues and vices may be traced to the Stoic philosophers, beginning with Zeno's founding of the Stoa in Athens c. 308 B.C. By the first century A.D. moral philosophy was a popular topic of instruction and discussion at various levels of Roman society. In the homes of the wealthy, in rented lecture halls and on street corners, popular philosophers of one sort or another, typically Stoics or Cynics, found a venue for their instruction, which frequently included the topics of virtue and vice. It should come as no surprise then that early Christian writers found the language and forms of moral instruction ready at hand in the popular philosophies of the day. Although transformed in its new context of the gospel, the NT's language and listing of virtues and vices is best understood with this Greco-Roman background in mind (see Kamlah, Vögtle, Wibbing, Zoeckler; for a sampling of relevant background texts, see Malherbe).

Stoic philosophers adopted the platonic fourfold division of virtue (*aretē*) into wisdom (*phronēsis*), moderation (*sōphrosynē*), justice (*dikaiosynē*) and courage (*andreia*). These four cardinal virtues the Stoics divided into various subvirtues. The four virtues were opposed by the four vices of folly (*aphrosynē*), licentiousness (*akolasia*), injustice (*adikia*) and cowardice (*deilia*), which in turn were expressed in subsidiary vices. These virtues and vices became a staple of moral discourse, and the listing of virtues and vices became an accepted and popular literary and rhetorical convention. A list could evoke a picture of an ideal good life set in contrast with a life of bad character and irrational behavior. When carefully ordered, a list of virtues could suggest a taxonomy of the ideal moral life.

The cataloging of virtues and vices is not a

feature of the OT (though cf. the "seven evils" of Prov 6:16-19 and the divine virtues of, e.g., Ex 34:6-7; Num 14:18; Ps 86:15) but the influence of this Hellenistic tradition is evident in Second-Temple Jewish writers such as Philo* of Alexandria, who developed extensive lists (e.g., Philo *Sacr.* 15-33; *Leg. All.* 86-87; *Virt.* 182). Hellenistic-Jewish writings such as Wisdom of Solomon (Wis 8:7; 14:22-27), 4 Maccabees (e.g., 4 Macc 1:2-4, 18-28; 2:15) and *Sibylline Oracles* (e.g., *Sib. Or.* 2:254-282; 3:377-80) utilized lists. And listings may also be found in the *Testaments of the Twelve Patriarchs* (e.g., *T. Reub.* 3:3-8; *T. Levi* 17:11; *T. Iss.* 7:2-6) and *3 Apocalypse of Baruch* (e.g., Apoc. Bar. 4:17; 8:5; 13:4). The rabbinic traditions of the Mishnah and Talmud barely exhibit this feature (see *m. 'Abot* 3:11; 4:21; *m. Soṭa* 9:15; *b. Soṭa* 42a; *b. Sanh.* 75a).

A related Second-Temple Jewish form is the Two Ways tradition. This is best exemplified by the Qumran* text, 1QS 4:3-14, where the two ways are aligned with the "spirit of truth [or light]," and the "spirit of perversity [or darkness]." Likewise the *Testament of Asher* utilizes this motif (*T. Asher* 1:3-9; 2:5-8), where the "two ways" are further defined as "two mind-sets, two lines of action, two models, two goals . . . everything is in pairs, the one over against the other" (*T. Asher* 1:3-4). The influence of this Two Ways tradition on the NT has been variously assessed (see Suggs, Wibbing), with Paul's listing of the works of the flesh and fruit of the Spirit in Galatians 5:19-26 being a focal point of investigation (see, e.g., Longenecker). Whatever conclusions one might draw regarding the influence of the Jewish Two Ways tradition on the NT literature, the tradition is clearly developed in the apostolic fathers (*Did.* 1—5; *Barn.* 18—20; *Herm. Man.* 6.2.1-7; see 3 below).

2. Later New Testament Writings.

Within the later NT literature outside the Pauline corpus there are several lists of virtues (Heb 7:26; Jas 3:13, 17-18; 1 Pet 3:8; 2 Pet 1:5-7) and vices (Jas 3:14-16; 1 Pet 2:1; 4:3, 15; Rev 9:21; 21:8; 22:15). These texts will be examined below. But we should recognize that within the disputed Pauline letters there are several lists of both virtues (Eph 4:2-3, 32—5:2; 5:9; Col 3:12-14; 1 Tim 3:2-4, 8-10, 11-12; 4:12; 6:11, 18; 2 Tim 2:22-25; 3:10; Tit 1:8; 2:2-10) and vices (Eph 4:25-32; 5:3-5; Col 3:5-8; 1 Tim 1:9-10; 6:4-5; 2 Tim 3:2-4; Tit 1:7; 3:3). These particular

Pauline virtue and vice lists are viewed by some scholars as partial evidence for dating these letters in the post-Pauline era, when Paul's ethical wrestling with the eschatological tension between the present and future was reduced to lists of norms, and the spiritual endowment requisite for community leadership was supplanted by civic virtues. There is a plausibility to this assessment, particularly with regard to the Pastorals, but the use of virtue and vice lists must be considered along with a number of other factors (see commentaries), including the viability of the notion of early catholicism* as a theory of early Christian development.

2.1. Virtues. In Hebrews 7:26 the focus is on the transcendent virtues of Christ* the heavenly high priest,* who is distinguished from earthly high priests by his being inherently "holy, blameless, undefiled, separated from sinners, and exalted above the heavens" (NRSV). In 1 Peter 3:8, immediately following the household code* of 1 Peter 2:13—3:7, we find a listing of five community virtues commended for these "resident aliens" who are to conduct themselves "honorably among the Gentiles" (1 Pet 2:11-12; *see* 1 Peter): unity of spirit *(homophrones);* sympathy *(sympatheis),* love for one's brother or sister *(philadelphoi),* tenderheartedness *(eusplanchnoi),* humility of mind *(tapeinophrones).* L. Goppelt has demonstrated that these virtues are a Hellenistic formulation of the virtues found in Roman 12:10, 15, 16, where they appear in a Jewish conceptual dress (Goppelt, 230-31). This suggests that both texts are reflecting a common tradition of early Christian paraenesis (cf. also 1 Pet 3:9 and Rom 12:14, 17).

In James 3:13, 17-18 we find a listing of virtues that unfold from the "wisdom from above" (Jas 3:17). The proof of wisdom* and understanding is a good life and works characterized by "gentleness of wisdom" (*en praÿtēti sophias,* Jas 3:13). In James 3:17 wisdom is first of all pure, then its subvirtues are set out in two series, the first set beginning with the Greek letter *e* (with the last two ending in -*ēs*): *eirēnikē* (*"peacable"*), *epieikēs* ("gentle"), *eupeithēs* ("deferential"), *eleous* ("merciful"); the second set beginning with the Greek letter *a* (with the last two ending in -*kritos*): *[karpōn] agathōn* ("good [fruit]"), *adiakritos* ("impartial"), *anypokritos* ("without hypocrisy"). This listing owes much to the Jewish wisdom tradition and may well be addressing the tensions that arose for Jewish

Christians* as they lived through the events leading up to the destruction of Jerusalem in A.D. 70 (see Martin, 124-38).

2 Peter 1:5-7 provides the most extensive and significant listing of virtues in the later NT (*see* Charles). This list, or chain, of virtues is presented by means of a literary device called sorites, a series, or chain, of statements that builds step by step in a logical progression to a climactic conclusion (e.g., Rom 5:3-5; Jas 1:15; *Herm. Vis.* 3.8.7; cf. Wis 6:17-20; *m. Soṭa* 9:15). Thus 2 Peter envisions eight virtues, progressing from faith* to love,* each virtue producing, or furnishing *(epichorēgō)*, the next. The eight virtues are as follows (in order): faith *(pistis)*, excellence *(aretē)*, knowledge* *(gnōsis)*, self-control *(enkrateia)*, steadfastness *(hypmonē)*, piety *(eusebeia)*, brotherly/sisterly affection *(philadelphia)*, love *(agapē)*. By framing the list with faith and love (cf. *Herm. Vis.* 3.8.1), the fundamental importance of two of the three Christian virtues of faith, hope and love is accented (see Neyrey, 155, who finds steadfastness as an equivalent to hope). The other six virtues are all found in pagan lists of virtues, and it appears that by incorporating these virtues within the framework of Christian paraenesis and its corresponding moral vision, 2 Peter lays claim to contemporary Hellenistic ethical ideals for those Christians who are experiencing moral failure in the midst of a pagan society (*see* Early Catholicism). These familiar virtues, shaped into an ethical progression from faith to love, are an antidote to blind stumbling (2 Pet 1:8-10) and a surefooted pathway to entering "the eternal kingdom of our Lord and Savior Jesus Christ" (2 Pet 1:11).

2.2. Vices. Vice lists appear in the later NT in James, 1 Peter and Revelation. In James 3:14-16 the opposite of "wisdom from above" (see 2.1 above) is spelled out: "earthly, unspiritual and devilish" wisdom is characterized by envy, selfish ambition, boastfulness and denial of the truth, and from this springs "disorder and all manner of evil." James, it would appear, has in mind a specific situation in which behavior, buttressed by persuasive ideology ("wisdom"), is seriously disrupting the well being of the community.

In 1 Peter 2:1 the readers are enjoined to rid themselves of a number of vices that destroy community: "all malice, and all guile, insincerity, envy, and all slander" (NRSV). The counterpoint is not a list of virtues but the image of

longing "like newborn infants" for "pure, spiritual milk*" so that they may "grow into salvation" (1 Pet 2:2).

1 Peter 4:3 recalls the readers' past life of pagan vices: "For you have spent enough time in the past doing what the Gentiles like to do, living in licentiousness, passions, drunkenness, revels, carousing and lawless idolatry" (NRSV). In this case behavior is viewed from a distinctly Christian perspective. Although some of these excesses were also condemned by pagan philosophers, the warning against "lawless idolatry" *(athemitoi eidōlolatriai)* is a condemnation that penetrates to the religious heart of pagan society and casts a distinct moral light on the preceding vices.

In 1 Peter 4:15, believers are warned that their suffering should not be "as a murderer, a thief, a criminal, or even as a mischief maker" (for these terms, all of which are debated as to their meaning, see commentaries). Rather their suffering* should be for the sake of Christ, a "sharing in Christ's sufferings" (1 Pet 4:13).

In Revelation* there are three instances of vice lists, each of which depicts those outside the church. Those spared from the plagues of the sixth trumpet* still do not repent of their murders, magic,* sexual immorality or thefts (Rev 9:21). In contrast with the redeemed who make up the new Jerusalem,* the cowardly, unbelieving, vile, murderers, sexually immoral, practitioners of magic, idolaters and liars will be consigned to the lake of fire (Rev 21:8). And in much the same vein, those who are granted access to the tree of life,* to enter the gates of the city, are contrasted with those outside who are "dogs," practitioners of magic, sexually immoral, murderers, idolaters and lovers of falsehood (Rev 22:15). The repeated vices of magic, murder and sexual* immorality are striking, but the total picture evokes those whose allegiance is given to the beast* and Babylon.*

3. Apostolic Fathers.

A number of virtue and vice lists of varying length have been identified in the apostolic fathers (*Barn.* 2.2-3; 18—20; *1 Clem.* 3.2; 30.1, 3, 8; 35.5; 62.2; 64.1; *2 Clem.* 4.3; *Did.* 1.1—5.2; *Herm. Man.* 5.2.4; 6.2.3-5; 8.3-5, 9-10; 11.8, 12; 12.2.1; 12.3.1; *Herm. Sim.* 6.5.5; 9.15.2-3; *Herm. Vis.* 3.8.3-7; Ign. *Eph.* 3.1; Pol. *Phil.* 2.2; 4.3; 5.2; 12.2). A few examples will serve to illustrate the nature and use of these lists in this post-canonical literature.

The *Didache** and *Barnabas** provide striking examples of the Two Ways tradition being used in Christian ethical exhortation (see Kirk). In *Barnabas* 18—20 the "two ways of teaching and power, one of light and one of darkness" are clearly set out (*see* Light and Darkness). *Barnabas*, like 1QS (see 1 above), identifies the spiritual overseers of the two ways: for the way of light, the angels* of God; for the way of darkness, the angels of Satan.* The extensive list of so-called virtues (*Barn.* 19) associated with the way of light appear in the form of commandments* reminiscent of the Decalog (e.g., "Thou shalt love thy maker . . . Thou shalt not commit fornication . . . Thou shalt not procure abortion, thou shalt not commit infanticide"). The other pathway, "the way of the black one *[tou melanos hodos]*" (*Barn.* 20), is marked by the more abbreviated language of vice lists, though its indebtedness to Jewish moral thought is clearly evident.

Didache 1.1—5.2 develops the doctrine of the Two Ways in much the same manner as *Barnabas*, but here the setting of baptismal* instruction becomes evident, with the catechumen being addressed as "my child" (*Did.* 3.1, 3, 4, 5, 6, 4.1). *Hermas Mandate* 6.2.1-7 also appears to be indebted to the Two Ways tradition when it speaks of the "two angels with man," recalling the rabbinic notion of a good and evil "tendency," or "impulse" (*yēṣer*) within humans. The angel of righteousness* enters the human heart and commends virtues; the angel of wickedness enters the heart and advises evil. The voice of the one is to be heeded, the other shunned.

In the *Shepherd of Hermas** the virtues and vices are several times portrayed in personified terms. In *Hermas Vision* 3.8.3-7 we are introduced to seven women surrounding a tower who are seven virtues surrounding the church.* These virtues are described as a generational chain of successive "daughters," seven virtues that follow one from another: faith, continence, simplicity, innocence, reverence, knowledge* and love. "Whoever serves them and has the strength to lay hold of their works, shall have his dwelling in the tower with the saints of God" (*Herm. Vis.* 3.8.8). Again in *Hermas Similitude* 9.15.2-3 the virtues are personified as twelve maidens (earlier introduced as holy spirits,* or powers of the Son* of God, *Herm. Sim.* 9.13.2) who personify the virtues of faith, temperance, power,* longsuffering, simplicity, guilessness,

holiness,* joyfulness,* truth,* understanding, concord and love. Believers must bear their names (or be clothed with their raiment, *Herm. Sim.* 9.13.3), in addition to bearing the name of the Son of God, in order to enter the kingdom* of God (*Herm. Sim.* 9.15.2). Set in contrast to these maidens of virtue are twelve women clothed in black who personify the vices of unbelief, impurity, disobedience, deceit, grief, wickedness, licentiousness, bitterness, lying, foolishness, evil-speaking and hate. Those who "bear these names shall see the kingdom of God but shall not enter into it" (*Herm. Sim.* 9.15.3).

In *Hermas Mandate* 5.2.4 a chain of vices unfolds from "ill temper": foolishness, frivolousness, silliness, bitterness, wrath, rage and fury, and from fury the "great and inexpiable sin." These vices, also depicted as evil spirits indwelling a human "vessel," crowd out the Holy Spirit* who is "delicate" and unaccustomed to dwell with evil spirits* (*Herm. Man.* 5.2.4-7).

Finally, Polycarp* in his *Letter to the Philippians* 2.2 exhorts believers to maintain a virtuous life, to "do his will, and walk in his commandments and love the things which he loved." Likewise they should refrain from the vices of "unrighteousness, covetousness, love of money, evil speaking, false witness" and vengeance. The teaching of Jesus is recalled as support for the virtues of forgiveness* and mercy* (Pol. *Phil.* 2.3; cf. Mt 7:1-2; Lk 6:36-38). This picture of Christian virtue is filled out in Polycarp's closing prayer* for the Philippians (Pol. *Phil.* 12.2). Elsewhere the desirable virtues of widows are set forth in a partial echo of 1 Timothy 5:5 (Pol. *Phil.* 4.3) and the virtues of deacons echo the wording of 1 Timothy 3:8 (Pol. *Phil.* 5.2; *see* Church Order and Government). Among the apostolic fathers, Polycarp's language of virtue bears the closest similarity to the NT letters.

Although virtue was no new thing to the world in which Christianity was born, the qualities of Christian virtues and the community, narrative and theology that undergirded them (see MacIntyre) were to have far reaching effects. The virtues, no matter how formulaic and rote in their presentation, were sufficiently nurtured, active and on display to capture the attention of pagan neighbors and onlookers. A Christian community living by the ideal of mutual love and practicing mercy (a "virtue" despised by pagan philosophers) toward needy outsiders was a compelling apology for the truth of its gospel* story and moral vision (see Stark, esp. 209-15).

See also ETHICS; FAITH, FAITHFULNESS; HOUSE-HOLD CODES; IDOLATRY; MERCY; OBEDIENCE, LAW-LESSNESS; PRIDE AND HUMILITY; PURITY AND IMPURITY; RIGHTEOUSNESS; SEXUALITY, SEXUAL ETHICS; SIN, WICKEDNESS; TEACHING, PARAENE-SIS; WISDOM.

BIBLIOGRAPHY. R. J. Bauckham, *Jude, 2 Peter* (WBC; Waco: Word, 1983); J. D. Charles, *Virtue Amidst Vice: The Function of the Catalog of Virtues in 2 Peter 1.5-7* (JSNTSup 150; Sheffield: Sheffield Academic Press, 1997); K. P. Donfried, *The Setting of Second Clement in Early Christianity* (NovTSup 38; Leiden: E. J. Brill, 1974); B. S. Easton, "New Testament Ethical Lists," *JBL* 51 (1932) 1-12; J. T. Fitzgerald, "Virtue/Vice Lists," *ABD* 6:857-59; L. Goppelt, *A Commentary on 1 Peter* (Grand Rapids: Eerdmans, 1993); E. Kamlah, *Die Form der katalogischen Paränese im Neuen Testament* (Tübingen: J. C. B. Mohr, 1964); K. E. Kirk, *The Vision of God: The Christian Doctrine of the Summum Bonum* (London: Longman, 1932); R. N. Longenecker, *Galatians* (WBC; Dallas: Word, 1990) 249-52; N. J. McEleney, "The Vice Lists of the Pastoral Epistles," *CBQ* 36 (1974) 203-19; A. MacIntyre, *After Virtue: A Study in Moral Theory* (2d ed.; Notre Dame, IN: University of Notre Dame Press, 1984); A. Malherbe, *Moral Exhortation: A Greco-Roman Sourcebook* (LEC 4; Philadelphia: Westminster, 1986); R. P. Martin, *James* (WBC; Waco, TX: Word, 1988); W. Meeks, *The Moral World of the First Christians* (LEC 6; Philadelphia: Westminster, 1986); G. Mussies, *Dio Chrysostom and the New Testament* (SCHNT 2; Leiden: E. J. Brill, 1972); J. H. Neyrey, *2 Peter, Jude* (AB; New York: Doubleday, 1993); E. Osborn, *Ethical Patterns in Early Christian Thought* (Cambridge: Cambridge University Press, 1976); R. Stark, *The Rise of Christianity: A Sociologist Reconsiders History* (Princeton, NJ: Princeton University Press, 1996); M. J. Suggs, "The Christian Two Way Tradition: Its Antiquity, Form, and Function," in *Studies in the New Testament and Early Christian Literature* (NovTSup 33; Leiden: E. J. Brill, 1972) 60-74; A. Vögtle, *Die Tugend- und Lasterkataloge im Neuen Testament* (NTAbh 16.4/5; Münster: Aschendorff, 1936); H. Währisch, H.-G. Link, A. Ringwald and R. P. Martin, "Virtue, Blameless," *NIDNTT* 3:923-32; S. Wibbing, *Die Tugend- unde Lasterkataloge im Neuen Testament und ihre Traditionsgeschichte unter besonderer Berück-sichtigung der Qumran-Texte* (BZNW 25; Berlin: Töpelmann, 1959); O. Zoeckler, *Die Tugendlehre des Christentums* (Gütersloh: C. Bertelsmann, 1904).   D. G. Reid

VISIONS, ECSTATIC EXPERIENCE

Ecstasy is the state of being removed from the awareness of the mundane perceptions of the sensory world and awakening to the perception of the extrasensory world. Those who experience *ekstasis,* and the community that has a sufficient number of members who have this experience, are confirmed in their convictions that the visible world is only the partial context in which one lives out one's life. In the early church, visions and ecstatic experience serve to confirm for its members the sense that the new community is in tune with the invisible, eternal, divine order. The presence of God's Spirit assures them of God's approval of the new community and direction of its life and mission. This confirmation allows them to deflect the criticism of and withstand hostility from those outside the community who do not have the "Spirit," who are therefore ignorant of God's perspective.

1. Acts
2. Revelation
3. Other Early Christian Literature

1. Acts.

The early Christians were vividly aware of the presence of God* in their midst. Ecstatic speech, visions and inspired utterances were commonplace. That these were manifestations of the eschatological* outpouring of God's Spirit was a common conviction of these communities (cf. Mk 1:8; Jn 7:39; Acts 2:16-21; 1 Cor 12:4-11; Gal 3:14; 4:4-7). The presence of ecstasy in the new community demonstrated to its members that God's anointing* rested upon them, while the old vessels of divine *charisma* had dried out. The Holy Spirit's* activity in the Christian movement meant that the consummation of God's plan was near, that the promises* of a restored Israel* and converted Gentile* world* were on the verge of fulfillment and that this new community would be the instrument of God's end-time purpose.

Within the narrative world of Acts,* the Christian movement derives its impetus from the initial outpouring of the Spirit at Pentecost* (Acts 2:1-21) and the visible manifestations of this divine anointing in the form of ecstatic experiences. The temple,* as former site of interaction with the divine, stands in contrast with the group forming around the apostles,* where access to God's power and presence is now enjoyed. That God's Spirit now invades the mundane sphere through this marginal group validates the very existence of the movement and offers conclusive proof of God's approval of its testimony about Jesus. The presence of *charisma,* the immediacy of access to the divine, legitimates the group's break with the traditional order and worldview of Jewish society.

Visions play a significant role in the narrative of Acts. A revelation from the Spirit prepares for and initiates each new development in the early church.* Philip's* evangelizing (Acts 8:26, 39-40), Paul's conversion and reception into the church by Ananias (Acts 9:3-17), Paul's timely departure from Jerusalem* and reorientation toward a Gentile mission (Acts 22:17-21), Peter's preaching to the household* of the Gentile Cornelius* (Acts 10:3-6, 9-16), Paul and Barnabas's commission (Acts 13:2), Paul and Barnabas's mission to Macedonia (Acts 16:6-10), Paul's preaching in Corinth (Acts 18:9-10), Paul's imprisonment and trial (Acts 20:23) and Paul's testimony in Rome* (Acts 23:11; 27:23-24) are all prompted or supported by the Spirit. The paired visions that surround Paul's conversion (Paul's in Acts 9:3-9 and Ananias's in Acts 9:10-16) and Peter's preaching to Cornelius (Cornelius's vision in Acts 10:1-6 and Peter's in Acts 10:9-16) create an especially strong sense of God's orchestration of the Christian movement.

This connection of the ethos and mission* of the Christian movement with the unmediated direction of the Spirit legitimates the group's activities, since these are grounded in the authority* of God. When the representatives of Judaism* confront Peter and the apostles, Peter can oppose submission to their authority to submission to God's authority (Acts 4:19). To the Sanhedrin this distinction was unthinkable, for they represented God's authority. For the Jesus movement, however, the experience of the Spirit's guidance through visions and ecstatic manifestations led them away from submission to traditional authorities. The charismatic experience assured them that their own existence and activity were legitimate in God's sight, since they could no longer assure

themselves of their place in God's will on the basis of the ratification of traditional authorities.

A case of central importance for Acts is the conversion of the centurion Cornelius, a Gentile. The vexed issue of how Jewish Christians and Gentile Christians were to relate in the early church is well attested (Acts 10—15; Gal; Eph 1—3; *see* Jewish Christianity). Advocates for including Gentiles in the new community on the basis of their full conversion to ethnic Israel had a ready arsenal of traditional forms of legitimation. The Hebrew Scriptures spoke clearly about membership in the people of promise (e.g., Gen 17:14; Is 52:1; Ezek 44:5-9; Jdt 14:10). In the two texts that address this issue directly (Gal; Acts), the experience of the Spirit provides the authority to move beyond traditional revelation.

Visions prepare the participants and the reader for the amazing breakthrough of ethnic boundaries and long-standing identity markers (Acts 10:1-16). Peter's vision is an essential part of his defense before the "circumcision party" (Acts 11:2-10; *see* Circumcision), clarifying for them and the reader that he was acting not on his own initiative but rather following the legitimate and unimpeachable authority of the Spirit (Haenchen, Johnson). Moreover the decisive evidence in this case (as for Paul's case in Galatia) was the ecstatic manifestation of the outpouring of the Spirit upon Cornelius's household at the hearing of Peter's message (Acts 10:44-47; 11:15-18; 15:8-9; cf. Gal 3:1-5; 4:6-7). Peter explicitly links this to Pentecost (George, Johnson): the same experience of the Spirit that constituted the Jerusalem church now demonstrates God's acceptance of the Gentile as Gentile into the new community. The awareness of God's presence and ratification of this new step alone provided the courage required for the participants to move beyond Israel's traditional understanding of its separateness and consecration to the God of Israel (cf. Johnson). Direct experience of the Spirit of holiness* assured the early church that it possessed a new mark of sanctification and dedication to the one God.

2. Revelation.

In the Revelation to John (*see* Revelation, Book of) we see visionary rhetoric in its most powerful expression. The contents of this work are explicitly ascribed to ecstasy. John was "in the Spirit" (Rev 1:10; cf. 1 Cor 14:2, 14-16), commissioned by the glorified Christ* to write down what he saw and send this message to the seven churches within which he exercised his prophetic ministry* (Rev 1:11). Every "I saw" and "I heard" serves to ground the message of the book in the ultimate, unquestionable realm. John's work is an apocalypse,* an unveiling of the true nature of the visible realities of the communities' experience as well as of unseen realities. It is debated whether the work reflects a genuine ecstatic experience or is rather a literary production that effects its message through its medium. In the climate of John's churches, ecstatic experience was not the anomaly it is for modern scholars. As a prophet, John expected to receive revelatory visions; it is natural to find these visions shaped and colored by the traditions of the Hebrew Scriptures, early church, extracanonical apocalypses and John's reflection on the social, political and religious situation of his churches.

An apocalypse as literary creation or ecstatic experience has been defined as a disclosure of "a transcendent reality" in terms of both space and time (Collins). It has the effect of placing everyday realities within a broader context that provides an interpretative lens for those experiences. John's apocalypse places the everyday world of the churches spatially between the activity around God's throne (Rev 4—5) and the bottomless pit (Rev 9:2) and in time between the triumph of Jesus (Rev 5:5-12) and the consummation of that salvation* in the new Jerusalem (Rev 21—22). The *realia* of the believers' world, such as the cult of the pagan gods, the imperial cult and the expansion of Roman power, all find a place within John's vision. The ideology of the emperors* as benefactors of humankind and Rome (*see* Roman Empire) as the bringer of peace and prosperity to the world are turned upside down in John's unveiling of Satan's* effective and final deception of the world (Rev 12—13). The Revelation stands as a complete symbolic universe (Fiorenza, building on Berger and Luckmann) in light of which Roman power loses its legitimacy and faithful witness* to Jesus becomes the only sane course of action (Rev 12:11).

As a vision, a revelation of the way things really are, Revelation accomplishes the basic goals of religion (Geertz). It formulates a picture of the cosmic order, lends credibility to this picture through anchoring it in divine revelation (ecstasy) and elicits the emotional and behavioral responses from the hearers necessary to maintain their minority culture. Roman power and the Greco-Roman people who everywhere welcomed Rome and the opportunity for prosperity it brought were in a position to exercise a great amount of social pressure on deviants. Rome was the instrument of the gods, fulfilling its eternal mission of unifying people, establishing peace and facilitating trade; the emperor was the supreme patron, able to grant such weighty benefits that any return short of worship seemed to be base ingratitude. Piety and justice demanded that Rome, its emperors and their representatives be honored as those who established order out of chaos (cf. Berger, deSilva).

Only a vision, a revelation of the bigger picture, could overturn such a powerfully supported ideology. John shows that the emperors are agents of the dragon (*see* Beasts) and that to honor them was to "make a compact with the primeval forces of darkness" (Berger). Rome was no divine agent of peace but a ravenous whore exploiting the known world. Partnership with Rome meant full participation in the judgment* God would inflict upon Rome for all its bloodshed, idolatry* and self-glorification (Rev 17—18). Only the faithful Christians—that small, marginalized, minority group—were truly in touch with the divine order, worshiping the One who alone established order out of chaos. The Christians might easily have been made to believe society's opinion of them, that they were a deviant group and a source of pollution and danger to the vast majority who rendered proper reverence to the gods and their representative on earth. John assures his readers that they are not deviants. The throne of the beast and the temples of the gods all appear marginal and vulnerable in John's alternative vision of reality (Rev 9:20; 16:10-11).

The vision of Revelation serves two purposes. For the committed believers (Smyrna and Philadelphia), it serves as encouragement that they have chosen the honorable course; for the believers who are too much at home in the Greco-Roman society, who have enjoyed a profitable partnership with the provincial economy (Laodicea, Thyatira and the Nicolaitan gospel), it serves as a warning to recognize whose interests that economy ultimately serves. John's vision looks forward in time to persecution* of all who will not worship the emperor, glorifying those who hold fast the testimony of Jesus. The vision thus corrects the notion entertained by many believers that they may be friends of the world as well as God. Ultimately the two are incompatible. The doubleminded must now break off that partnership with the world and recommit themselves to following the Lamb.* D. L. Barr notes that the hearers are enabled by the liturgical* reading of this book to share in John's ecstatic experience: they return to the world changed by this encounter, seeing their relationships and dealings with Greco-Roman society with new eyes and with a greater vigilance concerning the inviolability of their commitment to Jesus.

3. Other Early Christian Literature.

Awareness of the Spirit's activity in the life of the church continues into the postapostolic period. Alongside the growing "traditional" authority of church offices (see Church Order) that preserve the apostolic traditum, the direct experience of the Spirit still offers encouragement and direction to the believing communities.

3.1. The Martyrdom of Polycarp and the Didache. While praying shortly before his arrest, Polycarp* has a vision of his pillow bursting into flame and turning to ashes, a vision fulfilled in his sentence to be burned for his confession. The martyrdom* is recounted with a miraculous tenor: the flames do not touch Polycarp (recalling Dan 3); he is finally stabbed, with the result that the flow of blood (recalling Jn 19) extinguishes the flames. The author surrounds the execution of Polycarp with these manifestations of supernatural phenomena in order to encourage the readers that the aged bishop died a "good death," one that expressed God's sovereignty rather than the hostile governor's power over life and death. The narrative encourages believers who may face death themselves for the confession: their death signals not society's rejection so much as God's approval of their life.

The *Didache** speaks of itinerant charismatic teachers as a regular feature of life in the church at the beginning of the second century. These figures traveled from community to community, bringing words from the Spirit that they received in a state of *ecstasis*. While the *Didache* offers some guidelines for their treatment and discernment of their genuineness, these teachers enjoyed considerable carte blanche by means of their charismatic authority.

3.2. Shepherd of Hermas. Hermas is also concerned about the discernment of the true charismatic prophet and the exploiter of the office. The true prophet speaks to the assembled community: his or her visions are directed to strengthening the group's convictions and offering moral direction. The profiteer offers answers to individuals who come with questions like people consulting a pagan oracle (*Herm. Man.* 11.1-17). Visions and ecstatic utterance are not private matters but aim at the confirmation of the group.

The *Shepherd of Hermas** is a collection of revelatory discourses and is often called an apocalypse (Osiek; Hellholm). It is reminiscent of Daniel and 4 Ezra in its emphasis on the need for ascetic preparation for visions. Some scholars, following J. Donaldson, debate this generic definition on account of the abundance of paraenetic material, particularly in the last two sections (the Commands and Parables). These moral directives, however, are embedded in and legitimated by the prophet's ecstatic experiences: the commands are spoken directly by the angelic being to Hermas, and the parables are a combination of angelic revelation and the seer's participation in the visions themselves. *Hermas* is therefore very much in keeping with other early Christian apocalypses (Osiek) and is best analyzed from within that genre.

The author himself is a prophet within the circle of churches at or near Rome. L. W. Barnard finds ample evidence within the book for the activity of prophets in the Roman church, as well as echoes of Hermas's own ministry within that circle (*Herm. Vis.* 2.2.6-8; *Herm. Vis.* 3.8.9-11; *Herm. Sim.* 10.2.2-4). S. Tugwell has suggested, plausibly, that Hermas's "children" are the people of the Christian community in which he exercises this prophetic and admonitory ministry. The book functions in a manner very similar to Revelation. The seer opens for his congregation a window into the plan of God, and within this larger context he asks them to reevaluate their lives and commitments.

Hermas expresses deep concern that all believers should repent and rededicate themselves to walking in righteousness. C. Osiek and Tugwell agree that he shows special concern for those who are doubleminded, among whom the wealthy figure prominently. These believers are in danger of denying their Lord* for the sake of their property when persecution comes (*Herm. Vis.* 3.6.5-7) and are caught between dedication to the law* of God and the laws of the earthly city in which they are too much at home (*Herm. Sim.* 1.1-11). Such people suffer from placing too much value on this world and its concerns; the remedy is to set their life in the world in a larger interpretative context. Again the vision form is effective, challenging the visible world's claim to primary importance with a glimpse of the eternally significant.

Through the series of visionary revelations Hermas clarifies for his congregations the nature of the world in which they live. The primary goal of life is incorporation into the church (the tower that is being built and tested even now). All worldly business and actions must be evaluated by this one criterion: Does it lead toward cementing or jeopardizing one's place in the body of the saved? Moreover the tower is revealed as nearing completion; there can be no delay in responding to the offer of repentance* and rededication. The believers stand near the close of this age and the dawn of the next, when the righteous shall receive their inheritance and the wicked shall be exposed (*Herm. Sim.* 3—4). Hermas's vision gives considerable significance to the present moment in which repentance is offered and steadfastness to the end mandated. The commands of the Shepherd are given as a sort of end-time rule; the visions' unveiling of the demands of the moment gives these commands their binding authority.

In a manner again similar to Revelation, Hermas posits a coming period of persecution (*Herm. Vis.* 2.2.6-8; 4.1.1—4.2.6). Here Hermas seeks, in Osiek's words, "to shape heavily a community's perception of reality." The believers must not forget that the unbelieving society is hostile to Christ and therefore to Christ's true followers. We have seen Hermas's concern for the believers who have prospered in an all too comfortable relationship with that society. The word of the vision shatters this symbiosis. As the prosperous Christians in Asia Minor were most in danger of participating in Babylon's* sins and succumbing to the pressure to join the worshipers of the beast, so the wealthy in the Roman church are called to question their easy alliance with the pagan society and, when the time comes, be prepared to choose their Lord over their property and place in society. The restrictions on the term of repentance also serve to motivate the believers to fortify themselves in their commitment now, since future apostasy* will receive no pardon (*Herm. Vis.* 2.2.8).

See also HOLY SPIRIT; PROPHECY, PROPHETS, FALSE PROPHETS.

BIBLIOGRAPHY. L. W. Barnard, *Studies in the Apostolic Fathers and Their Background* (Oxford: Blackwell, 1966); D. L. Barr, "The Apocalypse as a Symbolic Transformation of the World: A Literary Analysis," *Int* 38 (1984) 39-50; P. L. Berger, *The Sacred Canopy* (Garden City, NY: Doubleday, 1967); P. L. Berger and T. Luckmann, *The Social Construction of Reality* (Garden City, NY: Doubleday, 1967); J. J. Collins, ed., *Semeia 14: Apocalypse: The Morphology of a Genre* (Missoula, MT: Scholars Press, 1979); D. A. deSilva, "The Construction and Social Function of a Counter-Cosmos in the Revelation of John," *Forum* 9 (1993) 47-61; idem, "The 'Image of the Beast' and the Christians in Asia Minor: Escalation of Sectarian Tension in Revelation 13," *TJ* n.s.12 (1991) 185-208; idem, "The Social Setting of the Revelation to John: Conflicts Within, Fears Without," *WTJ* 54 (1992) 273-302; J. Donaldson, *A Critical History of Christian Literature and Doctrine*, 1: *The Apostolical Fathers* (London: Macmillan, 1864); E. Schüssler Fiorenza, *The Book of Revelation: Justice and Judgment* (Philadelphia: Fortress, 1985); C. Geertz, *The Interpretation of Cultures* (New York: Basic Books, 1973); A. George, "L'Esprit Saint dans l'Oeuvre de Luc," *RB* 85 (1978) 500-542; E. Haenchen, *The Acts of the Apostles* (Philadelphia: Westminster, 1971); D. Hellholm, *Das Visionbuch des Hermas als Apokalypse*, Bd. 1 (ConBNT 13.1; Lund: Gleerup, 1980); L. T. Johnson, *The Acts of the Apostles* (Collegeville, MN: Liturgical Press, 1992); C. Osiek, "The Genre and Function of the Shepherd of Hermas," *Semeia* 36 (1986) 113-21; L. L. Thompson, *The Book of Revelation: Apocalypse and Empire* (Oxford: Oxford University Press, 1990); S. Tugwell, O.P., *The Apostolic Fathers* (Harrisburg, PA: Morehouse, 1989).

D. A. deSilva

VISIONS OF HERMAS. *See* HERMAS, SHEPHERD OF.

VOLUNTARY ASSOCIATIONS, GRECO-ROMAN. *See* SOCIAL SETTING OF EARLY NON-PAULINE CHRISTIANITY.

WATCHFULNESS

Most of the references in our texts use the verb *grēgoreō* ("to be awake," "to keep awake," "to watch"). This is a derivative of *egeirō* ("to rise") and means to be in a state or a condition of being awake or watchful, as distinct from being drowsy or asleep.

1. Acts
2. General Epistles and Revelation
3. Apostolic Fathers
4. Summary

1. Acts.

The guiding principle on this theme is given in the charge to the disciples in the opening verses of Acts.* Whereas in Luke 24:49 the disciples had been told to stay in Jerusalem* until the power of the Holy Spirit* came upon them, in Acts they are to wait for that no longer. Rather than speculating about when the kingdom would come (Acts 1:7; *see* Kingdom of God) or stare after the ascended Lord* (Acts 1:11; *see* Ascension; Exaltation), they are to bear witness* to the gospel to the ends of the earth. Thereafter the emphasis is on going forth with the gospel.

In Paul's farewell address to the Ephesian elders at Miletus, we see the need to be on the alert against people who will bring division and heresy (Acts 20:31). This concept probably derives from the warnings in the Gospels about false messiahs and prophets* (Mk 13:22) and warnings in the Torah against false prophets, who lead the people of God astray after false gods (Deut 13:1, 2). In this passage it is used in the context of the metaphor of the alert shepherd* protecting the flock against the incursion of wild animals. Such warnings are not untypical of the later Pauline letters (e.g., 1 Tim 4:1-3; 2 Tim 3:1-9), and they anticipate the situation of heterodoxy in the postapostolic period (see 3 below).

2. General Epistles and Revelation.

Specific references to this theme are restricted to James,* 1 Peter* and Revelation (*see* Revelation, Book of). James 5:7 refers to the need for patience in waiting for the coming of the Lord, using an agricultural analogy of a farmer waiting for his crops to receive the early and late rains. This theme of patience may have been necessary because the Parousia* seemed delayed, yet James tells his readers that it is near (*ēngiken*). P. H. Davids (39) sees this as an atmosphere of "intense apocalyptic expectancy."

In 1 Peter, the only other specific reference to being watchful in the canonical literature under review, the need to be on the alert for the devil is made clear: "Be sober, be watchful. Your adversary the devil prowls around like a roaring lion, seeking someone to devour" (1 Pet 5:8). The train of thought may be that of staying on the alert against temptation* (cf. the Gethsemane story, Mk 14:38). Sobriety (the verb used is *nēphō*) is probably used synonymously here, indicating the opposite of drowsiness or intoxication. The setting of the letter* is probably implicit opposition to and persecution of Christians, perhaps in the form of ostracism, confiscation of goods and other socially alienating and disenfranchising measures of the late first century, possibly the Domitian persecution.* Those outside the community are demonized (literally) as being in league with Satan* (see Elliott 1990; 1993, 70-86, for further discussion).

Watchfulness and wakefulness are synonymous in some texts. The antithesis of being on the alert is to be asleep (metaphorically). Thus the church at Sardis is exhorted to awaken (Rev 3:2, 3). Being awake and therefore ready for the coming of the Lord is mentioned also in Revelation 16:15, where the opposite attitude will result in being ashamed when the Lord comes.

3. Apostolic Fathers.

In the apostolic fathers* the theme of watchfulness against heresy (rather than for the Lord's coming) is continued. Thus Ignatius* urges Polycarp* to "be watchful and keep the spirit from slumbering" (Ign. *Pol.* 1.3). The context seems to be general moral exhortation, as in the surrounding passage of the same letter, although in *Polycarp* 3.1 false teachings are also mentioned. These might have taken the form of ideas that seemed immoral to Ignatius's Christian conscience.*

In the *Didache* (*Did.* 16.1), however, the advice to "watch over your life" is motivated by the unknown time of the Parousia, echoing such Gospel passages as Matthew 24:44, Mark 13:35 and Luke 12:35. This, the last section of the *Didache,** builds up to the conclusion of the tract with the theme of the return of the Lord, influenced by a number of passages in the Gospels (esp. the apocalyptic* discourse of Mk 13), as well as Pauline texts such as 1 Corinthians 15:22, 52; 16:22; 1 Thessalonians 3:13; 4:12, 16. In the *Didache* the association of false teachings or prophets and the end time is found, as in the Gospels, Paul and other apostolic fathers.

We might expect the theme of watchfulness in these texts to be more closely tied to the Parousia, but this is not wholly common. The specific theme of watchfulness itself is infrequent. The reason for this is unlikely to be given by any explanations that evoke the delay of the Parousia or early catholicism.* It is more likely that there is an indirect link between the Lord's coming and the exhortations. The Gospels, particularly the apocalyptic discourse, link the Parousia with false prophets and messiahs; in the Pauline letters this is developed into warnings against heresy and false teaching. In both groups of texts there are warnings about opposition and persecution of disciples.

In our texts the admonition against being asleep and the encouragement to watch arise precisely because the warnings in the earlier Christian literature are being experienced: false teaching, opposition, even threatened martyrdom* (which both Ignatius and Polycarp suffered). Christians are to be on the alert for those things, which are themselves the forerunners of the Parousia. *Barnabas* 4.9 exhorts the readers to avoid evil in the last days. The *Didache* stands out as having a more direct eschatological* orientation; in the other writings it is indirect.

Even in *2 Clement* 12.1, the exhortation to "wait" (*ekdechomai*) for the kingdom (which is explained as God's "appearing," *epiphaneia*) is given because its time is unknown. The discussion in the following verses in *2 Clement* 12, using traditions similar to those of the *Gospel of Thomas* 22, hardly gives the impression of the imminence of the *epiphaneia*.

4. Summary.

The exhortation to watchfulness is directly linked with the Parousia and the end times in the Gospels and Apocalypse and with that same expectation in the *Didache*. In the other texts where it is mentioned, the context seems to suggest that disciples need to be aware of the phenomena associated with the Parousia such as false teaching or persecution. It is the more immediate issues that are in mind. Vigilance is necessary in the Christian life, against temptation or trials.

See also ADVERSARIES; ESCHATOLOGY; PAROUSIA; SATAN, DEVIL.

BIBLIOGRAPHY. V. P. Cruz, "The Beatitudes of the Apocalypse: Eschatology and Ethics" in *Perspectives on Christology: Essays in Honor of Paul K. Jewett*, ed. M. Schuster and R. A. Muller (Grand Rapids: Zondervan, 1991); P. H. Davids, *The Epistle of James* (NIGTC; Grand Rapids: Eerdmans, 1982); J. H. Elliott, *A Home for the Homeless* (Minneapolis: Augsburg Fortress, 1990); idem, *What Is Social-Scientific Criticism?* (Minneapolis: Fortress, 1993); D. G. Horrell, *The Social Ethos of the Corinthian Correspondence: Interests and Ideology from 1 Corinthians to 1 Clement* (Edinburgh: T & T Clark, 1996); E. Lövestam, *Spiritual Wakefulness in the New Testament* (Lund: Gleerup, 1963); W. R. Schoedel, "Theological Norms and Social Perspectives in Ignatius of Antioch" in *Jewish and Christian Self-Definition*, ed. E. P. Sanders (3 vols.; London: SCM, 1980) 1:30-56; W. H. Wagner, *After the Apostles: Christianity in the Second Century* (Philadelphia: Fortress, 1994). D. J. Graham

WICKEDNESS. *See* SIN, WICKEDNESS.

WIDOWS. *See* SOCIAL SETTING OF EARLY NON-PAULINE CHRISTIANITY; WOMEN IN THE EARLY CHURCH.

WISDOM

The term *wisdom* has a wide variety of meanings

and applications in secular and biblical thought. The Hebrew, *ḥokmāh*, includes such cognate ideas as insight, thought and understanding. It is applied to individuals who were skilled in certain occupations, had a basic understanding of laws governing the world and were able to live wisely and successfully.

In Greek *sophia* also connotes the idea of knowledge, ability, skill and the application of wisdom to life. The NT uses *sophia* as the intellectual and/or spiritual ability of human beings, such as Jesus (Mt 13:54 par. Mk 6:12; Lk 2:40, 52), Stephen* (Acts 6:10), Joseph (Acts 7:10), Moses* (Acts 7:22) and Solomon (Mt 12:42 par. Lk 11:31), a special endowment of the Spirit (1 Cor 2:13; 12:8; Eph 1:17; Col 1:9) or gift of God (Jas 1:5; 3:17; Rev 13:18; 17:9) and a personification of God (Mt 11:19; Lk 7:35; 11:49).

1. A Brief Survey of Backgrounds and Pauline Usage
2. Wisdom in Other New Testament Literature
3. Wisdom in the Early Fathers
4. Summary

1. A Brief Survey of Backgrounds and Pauline Usage.

1.1. From the Old Testament to Paul. In the OT and intertestamental literature, wisdom is a special attribute of God* (Dan 2:20-23) that is manifest in creation* (Job 38:37; Ps 104:24; Prov 3:19; Wis 7:22; 8:1, 6; Sir 24:3-5) and may be given to certain individuals as a gift (e.g., Solomon [1 Kings 3:5-14; 10:23-24; 2 Chron 9:22-23]) and to others who ask God for it (2 Chron 1:10; 1 Esd 4:59-60) and who regulate their life by it (Prov 8:32-36). The "fear of the Lord," in the sense of reverence, submission and obedience,* is considered the beginning of wisdom (Prov 1:7; 9:10; 15:33; Ps 111:10; Job 28:28).

The so-called Wisdom Literature of postexilic Judaism* (usually understood to refer to Proverbs, Job and Ecclesiastes in the OT and Sirach and the Wisdom of Solomon from the Apocrypha) preserves many thoughts of the ancient sages. A significant development of this literature is the personification of wisdom— that is, wisdom portrayed in personal terms but not regarded as an intermediate being or an independent deity—as a preexistent* female expression of God (Prov 1:20-23; 8; Job 28; Sir 24; Wis 7:7—9:18). In some Jewish texts obedience to Torah (the Law*) is identified as a sign

of true wisdom and understanding (Sir 1:26; 6:37; 9:15; 15:1; 19:20; 21:11; 24:23-24; Bar 3:9—4:3; 4 Macc 1:16-17). In the Qumran* literature wisdom occasionally is found within the context of knowledge and insight (see 1QS 4:2-6). Wisdom is given to the elect* for teaching (1QS 4:22) and to discern God's eschatological* plan (1QS 4:18; see Wilckens, 504-5). K.-G. Sandelin's monograph focuses on the life-giving quality of wisdom through such metaphors as "hostess," "mother," "teacher," "wife," "the vine" or "tree of life" (cf. Prov 9:1-6; Sir 24; Wis 7—9).

1.2. Wisdom in Paul. There is no appreciable difference or development of wisdom in the Pauline and deutero-Pauline literature. Most of the references to wisdom in Paul are found in 1 Corinthians, where the apostle apparently is reacting to some kind of Jewish-Hellenistic speculation that emphasized human wisdom and the rhetorical skills of certain leaders (1 Cor 1—4; on Wisdom in Paul, see Ellis, Goulder, Horsley, Scroggs; *see DPL,* Wisdom). Paul derides these so-called sophists and pneumatics for their worldly wisdom (1 Cor 1:19, 20, 22; 2:1, 4), claiming that from God's perspective their wisdom is foolish and worthless because it is devoid of the gospel. True wisdom—the wisdom of God—is found in the proclamation of the gospel, is empowered by the Spirit (1 Cor 2:4, 5, 13; 12:8; 2 Cor 1:12) and focuses on the cross* of Christ* (1 Cor 1:17, 21, 30; 3:19). Those who know Christ by faith have the "power" (1 Cor 1:24) and "wisdom" (1 Cor 1:30) in its fullness.

A similar attack is made against the false teachers in Colosse who take pride in their philosophy, which Paul denounces as "human tradition" (Col 2:8) and labels counterfeit ("an appearance of wisdom," Col 2:23). In 1 Corinthians 1:30 and Colossians 1:15-20, Paul identifies Christ as God's wisdom for the believer (cf. also the confession* in 1 Cor 8:6; *see DPL,* Wisdom, 970). The Christ-hymn* in Colossians (Col 1:15-20) contains Wisdom christology* quite similar to that in the prologue in Hebrews 1:1-3.

Other references to wisdom in literature attributed to Paul are associated with "knowledge," "understanding" and "mystery" (Rom 11:33; 16:25-27; 1 Cor 2:6-10; 12:8; Col 1:9, 26-28; 2:3; Eph 1:8-9, 17; 3:4-11; 2 Tim 1:9-11; Tit 1:2-3; *see* Knowledge; Mystery), worship* (1 Cor 12:8; Col 3:16) and conduct (Rom 16:19; Eph 5:15; Col 1:10; 4:5; see lists of vices and virtues* and the household codes* in the NT, which share affinities with earlier traditions of wisdom [Prov 6:16-18; Wis 14:23-26; Sir 7:18-28; *see DPL*, Wisdom, 972]). Ephesians, with its emphasis on cosmology, defines the divine plan of salvation* as "the wisdom of God in its rich variety" *(polypoikilos sophia tou theou)*. This is understood as God's divine and wise ordering of history so that which formerly was hidden (i.e., a *mystērion)* from the eons is now made known through the church* (Eph 3:10; cf. Ign. *Eph.* 19).

2. Wisdom in Other New Testament Literature.

2.1. The Gospels. The wisdom passages (Logion sayings) in the double tradition of the Synoptics known as Q present Jesus as a teacher of wisdom (see Mt 11:16-19 par. Lk 7:31-35; Mt 11:25-27 par. Lk 10:21-22; Mt 12:42 par. Lk 11:31; Mt 23:34-36 par. Lk 11:49-51; Mt 23:37-39 par. Lk 13:34-35). The consensus among scholars is that Matthew redacts some of the material in this tradition and is the first to identify Jesus with God's divine Wisdom. Jesus is Wisdom; he is *Sophia (see DJG,* Wisdom, 875; Dunn, 204-11). John appears to go further than Jewish literature, Philo* and the Synoptics by associating Wisdom with the Logos* (Jn 1:1-18). "Jesus is presented materially and essentially as the unique Wisdom—Word of God" *(DJG,* Wisdom, 876; see also Dunn, 213-50).

2.2. Hebrews. A number of commentators suggest that the opening hymn (Heb 1:1-3) in the epistle to the Hebrews* contains christological motifs similar to those that emerged from Alexandria* through Philo. J. D. G. Dunn, although he acknowledges such possibilities, argues that the concepts in Hebrews 1:1-3 are influenced more by Wisdom christology than by Philo's concept of the Logos (Dunn, 206-9: note the similar phraseology in this passage with Wis 7:25-26: "For she [Wisdom] is a breath of the power of God, a pure emanation of the glory of the Almighty . . . a reflection of eternal light, a spotless mirror of the working of God and an image of his goodness"). According to Dunn, the thought in Hebrews "is primarily of Christ as the eschatological embodiment of the wisdom of God, as the one through whom the Creator God in all his fullness had revealed himself most clearly and definitively for man's salvation and creation's renewal" (Dunn, 211).

2.3. James. H. Conzelmann has stated that "the entire Letter of James is a wisdom docu-

ment in parenetic style" (Conzelmann, 960). This observation is confirmed in most serious studies of James,* which clearly acknowledge that the author's ideas come from Hellenistic (i.e., Diaspora) Judaism, including the conscious or unconscious adoption of Jewish wisdom traditions (Davids, Dibelius and Greeven, Martin). This is especially evident in James 1:5-8, where wisdom is a gift of God requested by the righteous within the context of "trials" or the "testing" of faith *(peirasmos),* and in James 3:13-18, where wisdom produces certain virtues of speech and conduct. Both of these passages reflect the influence of "a wisdom ideology" (Martin, xcii) from the OT, intertestamental and Qumran literature (see Davids, 51-56).

The concept of wisdom as a divine gift that is granted to those who have faith* in God while experiencing certain afflictions is a common theme in wisdom literature (see Wis 5:1-14; 7:7; 8:21; 9:4-6; 10:5). Hence James reminds his readers about the inevitability of opposition and persecution* in this life (cf. Jas 1:12-16; Wis 2—5) and summons them to seek wisdom as a way of understanding and coping with the trials they are facing.

As James 1:5-8 reminds the readers that wisdom is God's gift to believers, James 3:13-18 reminds them that genuine wisdom, "wisdom from above" (Jas 3:17), leads to a number of Christian virtues.* This passage compares two types of wisdom and could correctly be classified as "practical wisdom" (Martin, 129). The fact that the author finds it necessary to contrast earthly and divine wisdom suggests an ecclesiastical setting in which teachers and/or the entire congregation had serious misconceptions about the nature of this divine gift.

Wisdom from above (*anōthen,* i.e., from God) was a common theme of Jewish wisdom teaching (Prov 2:6; 8:22-31; Sir 1:1-4; 24:1-12; Wis 7:24-27; 9:4, 6, 9-18). Such wisdom, according to James, manifests itself as virtues of the Christian life (Jas 3:17), not unlike the fruit of the Spirit (Gal 5:22-23). Earthly wisdom, however, produces unspiritual and disruptive behavior (Jas 3:15-16). This focus on wisdom as conduct rather than knowledge or insight (see 1 above) is an important contribution by James.

A number of scholars have commented on the "wisdom pneumatology" of James. The idea of J. A. Kirk—that the concept of wisdom in James is equivalent to the Holy Spirit* in certain portions of the Bible, particularly in Paul's letters* (such as Gal 5:22-23)—is taken up and developed by P. H. Davids. Thus Davids concludes: "If some works have a wisdom Christology, James has a wisdom pneumatology, for wisdom in James functions as the Spirit does in Paul: wisdom helps one stand, delivers one from 'the flesh' . . . and produces the fruit of the Christian life" (Davids, 55-56).

2.4. 2 Peter. The reference to the "wisdom" (*sophia*) given to Paul (2 Pet 3:15) could be an early recognition of the apostolic authority* given to some of his letters that were being circulated and used by the church.

2.5. The Apocalypse of John. In Revelation (*see* Revelation, Book of) the Lamb* is praised by the heavenly choir (Rev 5:12; 7:12) who ascribe to him wisdom as an attribute of God. Sophia also is the secret knowledge* of believers by which they can interpret some of the symbols and apocalyptic* mysteries in John's vision* (Rev 13:18; 17:9). This appears to follow the pattern of earlier apocalyptic literature, in which wisdom is an eschatological gift to the faithful and righteous (*1 Enoch* 5:8; *2 Esd* 8:52; *2 Apoc. Bar.* 44:14; 59:7).

3. Wisdom in the Early Fathers.
First, Wisdom appears as the designation of the Proverbs, which are attributed to Solomon. Justin Martyr, for example, refers to the "book of Wisdom" when he quotes from Proverbs 6. Proverbs 1:23-33 is quoted by Clement (*1 Clem.* 57:3-7). And Eusebius indicates that it was common to equate Wisdom and Proverbs in the early church: "And not only he [Hegesippus] but Irenaeus also and the whole body of the ancients called the Proverbs of Solomon 'Wisdom, comprehending every virtue'" (Eusebius *Hist. Eccl.* 4.22.9; see also Eusebius *Hist. Eccl.* 4.26.14).

Second, wisdom is an attribute of God (Justin *Dial. Tryph.* 38.2; 121.2; *Barn.* 16.9), which he gives to individuals and which is manifested by intelligent choices and good deeds (*Barn.* 5.3; 6.10; 21.5; *1 Clem.* 38.2; 48.5; Ign. *Smyrn.* 1.1). The Lord* does not approve of wisdom that is selfish or arrogant (*1 Clem.* 13.1; 32.4; 38.2).

Third, wisdom as a reference to Christ. Only one passage equates Christ with Wisdom (Justin *Dial. Tryph.* 126.1). In this respect we note U. Wilckens's conclusion to his extensive study of *sophia:* "There is no further development of primitive Sophia Christology in the first half of

the 2nd cent.; only in the second half of the 2nd and in the 3rd cent. does this play a part in the working out of the early Chr. doctrine of the Trinity" (Wilckens, 525). Logos christology dominates christological discussions in the second and third centuries.

4. Summary.
From this brief account of wisdom in the later NT and early church fathers (*see* Apostolic Fathers) we are able to discern several important developments: that in a number of cases wisdom continues to be viewed as a present, divine gift that manifests itself in wise choices and virtuous behavior (especially in James); that wisdom is an eschatological gift to understand divine secrets or mysteries (Eph; Rev); that wisdom traditions that circulated in the early church as sapiential literature were influential in the composition of the letter of James, and wisdom for James functions in much the same way as the Spirit does for Paul and other authors of Scripture (Kirk); that the Wisdom christology already present in Paul (Cor) is developed further in other literature (Col; Mt; Heb; Fourth Gospel). Jesus, in other words, is considered the embodiment of divine wisdom.

See also Christology; God; Knowledge; Logos Christology; Truth.

Bibliography. H. Conzelmann, "Wisdom in the New Testament," *IDBSup* 956-60; P. H. Davids, *James* (Grand Rapids: Eerdmans, 1982); M. Dibelius and H. Greeven, *James* (Philadelphia: Fortress, 1976); J. D. G. Dunn, *Christology in the Making* (2d ed.; Grand Rapids: Eerdmans, 1989), esp. 163-212; E. E. Ellis, "Wisdom and Knowledge in 1 Corinthians," *TynB* 25 (1974) 82-98; G. D. Fee, *The First Epistle to the Corinthians* (Grand Rapids: Eerdmans, 1987); J. Goetzmann, C. Brown and H. Weigelt, "σοφία," *NIDNTT* 3:1026-38; M. D. Goulder, "Σοφία in 1 Corinthians," *NTS* 37 (1991) 516-34; R. G. Hamerton-Kelly, *Preexistence, Wisdom and the Son of Man* (Cambridge: Cambridge University Press, 1973); A. R. A. Horsley, "Wisdom of the Word and Words of Wisdom in Corinth," *CBQ* 39 (1977) 224-39; L. Hurtado, *One God, One Lord* (Philadelphia: Fortress, 1988); J. A. Kirk, "The Meaning of Wisdom in James: Examination of a Hypothesis," *NTS* 16 (1969-70) 24-38; R. P. Martin, *James* (WBC; Dallas: Word, 1988); J. M. Robinson and H. Koester, *Trajectories Through Early Christianity* (Philadelphia: Fortress, 1971), esp. 71-113; K.-G. Sandelin, *Wisdom as Nourisher: A Study of an Old Testament Theme, Its Development Within Early Judaism and Its Impact on Early Christianity* (ÅBO: ÅBO Akademi, 1986); R. Scroggs, "Paul: Σοφός and Πνευματικός," *NTS* 14 (1967-68) 33-55; G. T. Sheppard, "Wisdom," *ISBE* 4:1074-82; U. Wilckens and G. Fohrer, "σοφία," *TDNT* 7:465-528.

A. G. Patzia

WITNESS

In the NT a "witness" *(martys)* is one who testifies to either the events of Jesus' life or the message of the gospel *(see DJG, DPL,* Witness). The term becomes closely associated with persecution in some texts but takes on the meaning of "martyr" only in the postcanonical literature.

1. Acts
2. Hebrews and the General Epistles
3. Revelation
4. Apostolic Fathers

1. Acts.

The words of Jesus to the eleven disciples at his ascension* set the tone for the concept of witness in the rest of Acts*: "you shall be my witnesses in Jerusalem, in all Judea and Samaria, and to the ends of the earth" (Acts 1:8). This is the agenda of Acts and a summary of the rest of the book as well as the rest of Christian history. Being a witness—not simply in the sense of having observed Jesus in his life, death and resurrection but in bearing testimony to it—is a key qualification for the one to be elected as the twelfth disciple, a role left open after Judas's death (Acts 1:22; *see* Death of Christ). The testimony to Jesus' life is likewise mentioned in the sermons (Acts 10:39). The opening prologue of 1 John also emphasizes this.

Witness to the resurrection* is especially important in Acts, where rumors and doubts surrounding the stories of the resurrection are answered, especially in the preaching of the early church* (Acts 2:32; 3:15; 4:33; 5:32; 10:41; 13:31). In the accounts of Paul's calling, he is to be a witness (Acts 22:15, 18; 26:16; cf. Acts 9:15, where he is to bear the Lord's* name* before Jews, Gentiles* and kings). This is confirmed in a vision* or a dream after his arrest (Acts 23:11), which Acts must see taking place in Acts 28:23-31, where Paul is described as preaching and teaching in Rome.* In Paul's story, witness amounts to preaching and teaching the gospel of the king-

dom (Acts 28:23; *see* Kingdom of God).

Paul describes Stephen* as a witness (Acts 22:20) and associates this fact with Stephen's death. In contrast, Luke's own account of Stephen's death draws attention only to false witnesses (Acts 6:13; 7:58). We shall see that some of the apostolic fathers identify the two ideas of witness and martyr even more closely.

God* is also a witness in Acts, both to the gospel by confirming its message with miracles* (Acts 14:3) and in the providence of creation* (Acts 14:17).

2. Hebrews and the General Epistles.

The theme of God as witness is found also in Hebrews 2:4, where miracles corroborate the message of salvation* (cf. Acts 14:3, above). Hebrews 7:8 uses the verb *martyreō* to mean the testimony of Scripture (in this case to the person of Melchizedek*), a point reinforced in Hebrews 7:17, where the Scripture in mind (Ps 110:4) is quoted. The way in which Scripture testifies (witnesses) becomes more clear in Hebrews 10:15, where it is stated that the Holy Spirit* bears witness through Scripture (Jer 31:33-34 is used to support the author's thesis about forgiveness* and sacrifice*). The same concept, that of Scripture as a witness, can also be found in Hebrews 11:4-5, where Genesis 4:5 is alluded to in a discussion of the offering of Abel and Cain. Finally, in Hebrews 12:1 "witness(es)" is used as an equivalent to spectators at games, a different image from its other uses in the letter *(see* Hebrews).

The apostles' witness to the life of Jesus is an important qualification in 1 Peter 5:1 and 1 John 1:2 (cf. Acts 1:21), the former of these referring to his sufferings. 1 John 4:14 may make a similar point. 1 John 5:7-11 deals with the witness of God (cf. Acts 14:3, 17 above). This is complicated by textual problems, however, and the precise relationship of the witnesses mentioned. The best solution seems to be that God is the ultimate witness and that testimony reaches believers through the life and death of Jesus (the water and the blood) and is conveyed by the Spirit. Its content is the message of eternal life* in Christ.* 3 John 3, 6, 12 speaks of Christians bearing witness to fellow believers' faith* and love.*

3. Revelation.

Disciples as witnesses to the faith emerge as an

important theme in the Apocalypse (*see* Revelation, Book of). The backdrop of persecution* and martyrdom* sharpens this subject, and Revelation 1:2 sets this in the context of John's own exile and persecution because of his faith (cf. Rev 1:9, where this is understood as "testimony to Jesus"; cf. Rev 12:17).

Several other texts refer to Christian disciples as witnesses. In Revelation 19:10 witness to Jesus is described as "the spirit of prophecy" *(to pneuma tēs prophēteias)*. As with Revelation 12:17 (above), Revelation 19:10 is best understood as referring to the content of the proclaimed Christian message.

Testimony to Jesus is closely linked with martyrdom in several texts. Antipas is a faithful witness "who was killed among you" (Rev 2:13). The conclusion that this was a martyrdom seems compelling. In Revelation 6:9 there are people who had been killed for their testimony (also Rev 17:6). And in Revelation 11:3, 7, God's own two witnesses are killed. Although in these instances people are identified as "witnesses" and then face death, this close connection of witness and death for the faith serves as a bridge between Acts 22:20 and some of the texts in the apostolic fathers.

In Revelation Jesus himself (or perhaps his angel*) is called a witness (Rev 1:5; 3:14; 22:16, 18, 20).

4. Apostolic Fathers.
We find several uses of witness in the apostolic fathers.* In *Barnabas* 1.6, "love of joy and of gladness is the testimony *(martyria)* of the works of righteousness." In *1 Clement* 30.7; 38.2; 63.3 it is other people who testify to the good deeds in others rather than the good deeds themselves being the witness. In *Hermas Similitudes* 5.2.6 testimony is the reputation a believer has. *Diognetus* 12.6 links witness specifically to a lived-out evidence of the knowledge* that believers possess. In *1 Clement* 5.4-7 we read that Peter and Paul witnessed to the faith and then went to glory.* Although witness and (a martyr's) death are not specifically identified with each other here, they are mentioned within the same brief text and are thus closely related. In Ignatius* the words of the gospel can act as a witness against people who do not listen to it or obey it (Ign. *Trall.*; Ign. *Phld.* 6.3). And in Ignatius *Philadelphians* 7.2 Christ is the witness of Ignatius's words.

In the *Martyrdom of Polycarp* (*Mart. Pol.* 1.1; 14.2; 15.2; 16.2; 17.3; 19.1; 21.1; 22.1) the meaning of "witness" is specifically tied to martyrdom. It is here, more than in any other text we have considered, that the concept of testifying to the faith becomes a specific reference to dying for the faith, a connection that would be made in many other writers thereafter.

In summary, we have several uses of witness: that of God, Christ and the Spirit; of Scripture; and of Christian believers, the latter sometimes specifically associated with dying for the faith.

See also MARTYRDOM.

BIBLIOGRAPHY. J. Beutler, "μαρτυρέω κτλ," *EDNT* 2:389-91; idem, "μαρτυρία," *EDNT* 2:391-93; idem, "μάρτυς," *EDNT* 2:393-95; H. von Campenhausen, "Das Bekenntnis im Urchristentum," *ZNW* 63 (1972) 210-53; B. Dehandschutter, "The Meaning of Witness in the Apocalypse" in *L'Apocalypse johannique et l'Apocalyptique dans le Nouveau Testament,* ed. J. Lambrecht (Louvain: Louvain University Press, 1980) 283-88; S. de Diétrich, " 'You Are My Witnesses'—A Study of the Church's Witness," *Int* 8 (1954) 273-79; O. Michel, "ὁμολογέω κτλ," *TDNT* 5:199-220; T. Preiss, "The Inner Witness of the Holy Spirit," *Int* 7 (1953) 259-80; H. Strathmann, "μάρτυς κτλ," *TDNT* 4:474-514; A. A. Trites, "Μάρτυς and Martyrdom in the Apocalypse: A Semantic Study," *NovT* 15 (1973) 72-80; idem, *The New Testament Concept of Witness* (SNTSMS 31; Cambridge: Cambridge University Press, 1977); idem, *New Testament Witness in Today's World* (Valley Forge, PA: Judson, 1983); A. A. Trites and L. Coenen, "Witness," *NIDNTT* 3:1036-51.   D. J. Graham

WOES, MESSIANIC. *See* TRIBULATION, MESSIANIC WOES.

WOMAN AND MAN
The roles of women in the Roman Empire varied from place to place, according to social class and other factors. The early Christian views of role relationships between men and women at some points reflected those of their environment while at other points stood quite in contrast to that environment. This sometimes created tensions or confusion, and various Christian writers responded to this tension in different ways.

For example, examining gender relations in the book of Acts, which is largely narrative, involves a variety of ancient cultural issues that must be addressed text by text. The epistles in this discussion often reflect a specific formulation called household codes, however (for fuller discussion, see Balch 1988). From Aristotle on these household codes (German *Haustafeln*) focused especially on the relationships between the male head of the aristocratic household and his wife, children and slaves. Household codes so defined were often part of a broader set of moral instructions on relationships sometimes subsumed under the category of city management, including instructions on how to behave toward the state, parents, elders, friends, and so on. We often find only specific components of such instructions (e.g., exhortations concerning the state, slaves and parents), but even these briefer clusters of relationship instructions point to the fuller collections of moral exhortations that stand behind them. The early Christians, like other minority religions within the Roman Empire,* were eager to establish their fidelity to the Roman state against the xenophobic rumors concerning subversive Eastern cults. Thus the Christians began adapting household codes as early as Paul's letter labeled "to the Ephesians" (Keener 1992, 146-47; *see DPL,* Man and Woman) and 1 Peter (Balch 1981).

1. Women's Roles in Acts
2. Woman and Man in 1 Peter
3. Woman and Man in Revelation
4. Woman and Man in 1 Clement
5. Woman and Man in Ignatius and Polycarp
6. Woman and Man in Other Patristic Writers
7. Conclusion

1. Women's Roles in Acts.

Scholars have long recognized that Luke's Gospel shows a special interest in women's roles, amplifying a distinctive feature already found in earlier tradition (e.g., Mk 5:21-43; 7:24-30; cf. Michaels). In his Gospel, Luke typically joins stories about women to stories about men, recounts Jesus' parables about women alongside parables about men, and so forth (cf. e.g., Maly; Flanagan; Tannehill, 132-39; pagan healing reports include women but more often focus on men).

Luke continues this practice in the second volume of his history (e.g., Acts 9:32-42; 16:16-18). Tradition did not always supply women's names for Luke's Gospel accounts, but because the author's probable travels with Paul include

two years in Judea and Caesarea (Acts 21:15—27:1), Luke would have had access to the names of characters who were members of the churches there (e.g., Rhoda, Acts 12:13; cf. Acts 17:34). In Luke's view women and men are equally morally responsible (Acts 5:1-11)—that is, Luke lacks the condescension toward women's moral weakness that was typical of males in his day (e.g., Plutarch *Con. Praec.* 48, *Mor.* 145DE; Josephus *Ag. Ap.* §§200-201).

If the traditional ascription for authorship is correct, Luke's background as a physician may have increased his sensitivity to such issues; this profession was open to both men and women, although the latter often functioned as midwives (Lefkowitz and Fant, 27, 161-64; Friedländer, 1:171). Luke, whose work seems to have been sponsored by the patron Theophilus (Lk 1:3), may also address an upper class in which women tended to be more educated and influential.

Women in Acts* fulfill many of the roles assigned to the more influential women of their culture. First of all, women serve as patrons, such as Tabitha, who seems to support widows (Acts 9:36, 39; Verner, 139; cf. Safrai, 762-63), and Mary, who hosts a house church* in Jerusalem* (Acts 12:12). The gate, servant and location near the Fortress Antonia on the Temple Mount (from which Peter undoubtedly escaped) all suggest that Mary was relatively wealthy. Lydia, who showed great hospitality* to Paul and his companions, acted as a patroness (Acts 16:15). She was also undoubtedly well-to-do, as businesswomen selling purple fabrics normally were. (See Keener 1992, 243, 254-56, for further details. Inscriptions attest the prominence of women in Macedonian religion [see Abrahamsen 1986, 1987], which coincides well with the NT evidence; see Acts 16:13-16; Phil 4:2-3.) Inscriptions suggest that many women served as patrons, although they made up at most 10 percent of the total (cf. Meeks, 24; Keener 1992, 240).

Second, Luke is aware that prominent women held considerable social power, which could be used for good or for ill (the empress Livia, mother of Tiberius Caesar, was probably the early Roman Empire's most famous example). Thus one notes the powerful women of Acts 13:50 (see also Bernice in Acts 25:13, 23, 30; cf. Judge 1960 "Early Christians," 128; on local aristocracies cf. Lewis, 36-41). Although the idea of a queen ruling the Roman Empire would have been foreign to Romans, they knew of Candace, the name or the dynastic title of several queens of the African kingdom of Meroë. Luke's treatment of a male official subordinate to this queen (Acts 8:27) seems entirely positive.

Third, women also appear to have been more susceptible to "foreign" religions, including Judaism* and Christianity, than most men were (Acts 17:4, 12, 34; cf. Judge 1960 *Social Pattern*, 44). This susceptibility may have issued in part from the limitation of Jewish circumcision* to male converts but also derived from men's social status and educational background. Men's status depended more heavily on their participation in socially acceptable religious structures; hence their public status advantage often proved inversely proportional to their openness to early Christian missionaries. Even given women's greater openness, whole families usually acted together as relatively cohesive units (e.g., Acts 16:31-34), perhaps even more so when acting as Christians (cf. Acts 21:5). Nor were such conversions limited to Gentiles*; when the number of men (the term is gender-specific) came to five thousand (Acts 4:4), the counting method undoubtedly reflects Luke's source, following an ancient method of reckoning by men. Yet women were surely converted on this occasion as well; the precipitating event occurred directly outside the court of women (Acts 3:2).

Still, Acts portrays many early Christian women as enjoying some roles the culture usually, though not exclusively, applied to men. Although husband-and-wife teams are known in other professions (e.g., Gardner, 240), women rarely taught Torah (Ilan, 190-204; Keener 1992, 83-84; Swidler, 97-111). Yet Priscilla, who works alongside Aquila when Paul meets them (Acts 18:2; for more detail see Keener 1992, 240-41), joins her husband in instructing the noted Apollos (Acts 18:26). Women and men also prayed together (Acts 1:14), although this practice in Jerusalem may not be as distinctive of Christians as some writers have thought; the evidence for gender segregation in synagogues* in this period is not substantial (Brooten, 103-38).

Charismatic empowerments heighten the roles for women still more plainly, as the programmatic text for Acts makes clear: both "sons" and "daughters" will prophesy (Acts 2:17). Because "sons" in Hebrew could also include "daughters" when the term is used generically, the prophecy's* specific mention of daughters is hardly superfluous; the prophetic Spirit would break barriers of gender, age (not reserving authority for elders) and perhaps class (Joel 2:29 has "the servants" rather than "my servants"). The Holy Spirit's* function here, as it is often in the Hebrew Bible and early Judaism (e.g., *1 Enoch* 91:1; *Jub.* 31:12; Josephus *Ant.* 6.166; 1QS 8:16; *t. Pesaḥ* 2:15), is prophetic empowerment to speak under inspiration, including bearing witness* to Christ* (Acts 1:8; the prophetic "word" throughout Acts is the gospel) and tongues* (Acts 2:4).

Luke provides a specific example of this gender- and age-neutral phenomenon in Acts 21:9. Although Romans seemed to believe that perpetual virgins could acquire special favor from the gods (cf. Keener 1991, 70), Luke's point in noting that Philip's* daughters were virgins is probably the more customary sense that they were not yet of marriageable age. Neither age nor gender prevented their remarkable empowerment (the form of the term *prophesying* suggests a regular phenomenon). Prophecy marks the new era for all God's people and was the most significant ministry gift next to apostleship (1 Cor 12:28). Though different levels of prophecy existed in ancient Israel* as well as early Christianity, one of the most authoritative prophetic figures was a woman (Judg 4:4).

2. Woman and Man in 1 Peter.

The most thorough discussion of the relevant passage in 1 Peter* (1 Pet 3:1-7) is D. L. Balch's work (1981), and many insights that follow depend on his analysis. Peter addresses the role of wives in a manner analogous to the way he addresses the role of slaves* (1 Pet 2:18-25); hence he commences the relevant paragraph with the words "in the same way" (1 Pet 3:1). Peter's instructions to both groups fit the context of household codes* (and the broader *topos* of management, including a discussion of relations to civic officials [1 Pet 2:13-17]; *see* Civil Authority). The discussion also reflects the principles of submission to those in existing positions of authority* (e.g., elders in 1 Pet 5:5); while Christians should also practice mutual submission (1 Pet 5:5), Peter especially addresses wives whose husbands are not believers

(1 Pet 3:1). Nonbelievers would follow the standard patterns of society, which Peter expected these wives to uphold under normal circumstances. These patterns included the wife's quietness and obedience* to her husband (e.g., Sir 26:14-16; 30:19; see Balch 1981, 99-103); other moralists also typically attacked outward adornment (cf. Keener 1992, 103-7).

Roman men particularly resented and retaliated against non-Roman cults that drew their wives away from the family religion and so shamed the husband's authority (e.g., Rabello, 697); when those religions incited women or slaves to disobey the male head of the household* in other matters, this increased the level of hostility (e.g., Plutarch *Con. Praec.* 19, *Mor.* 140D). Many felt that foreign cults targeted well-to-do Roman women (cf. Liefeld, 239-42). Writing with the conviction that the level of persecution* existing or imminent in Rome* would soon spread to other provinces, Peter exhorts his audience to uphold appropriate family standards of Roman society. Like members of other persecuted sects and like Paul before him (Keener 1992, 139-224), Peter adapts popularly used household codes of the day to make Christian behavior less needlessly objectionable to outsiders.

Scripture provides Peter precedent for arguing that such submission can be appropriate: the Israelite women of old (like the proverbial virtuous matrons of Roman legend; e.g., Dixon, 3) submitted to their husbands (1 Pet 3:5). If the exact sense of "submit" is debatable from one context to the next, the sense of "obedience" is not: Sarah obeyed Abraham,* calling him "lord" (or "sir"; 1 Pet 3:6). Genesis does indicate that Sarah heeded or obeyed Abraham—though he labored alongside her (Gen 18:6-8)—but also points out that Abraham heeded Sarah (Gen 16:2), at least once at God's command (Gen 21:12; also *Jub.* 17:6). Peter mentions only the example that he needs to illustrate his point, however. Like others who respectfully addressed those of higher social status (Gen 33:13-14), ancient Israelite women may have regularly called their husbands "sir" (some cite Hos 2:16); in Genesis 18:12 and especially later Jewish tradition (*T. Abr.* 5—6A; 4, 6B) Sarah grants Abraham this title. Yet Isaac also grants a form of this title to Sarah (*T. Abr.* 3A, using the feminine form), and Abraham also grants it to guests (Gen 18:3-5; *T. Abr.* 2A;

cf. *T. Abr.* 15, 18A; 8, 10, 12B). Use of the title did not necessarily accompany submissive behavior (*Jos. and As.* 4:5/7, 12/16), although Peter clearly does invite such behavior. At issue is not a transcultural example of patriarchal dominance but an appropriate example of respect.

At the same time Peter reminds wives not to "fear" mortals (1 Pet 3:6, 14; except in the sense of "reverence," 1 Pet 2:17; 3:2); pagan husbands had legal authority even to discard infants, but Peter exhorts the wives to stand firm (cf. Moffatt, 133; Balch 1981, 105). While insisting on wives' and slaves' submission for the sake of witness within a hostile society, Peter's sympathy apparently lies more with the Christian wife than with the non-Christian husband. His instructions to wives follow on the analogy of his instructions to slaves, where he compares their enduring of suffering* to that of their Lord* himself (1 Pet 2:21-25); after instructing wives about submission to husbands he returns to the issue of Christians responding to persecution. Though he is not addressing the institutions of slavery or patriarchal marriage structures themselves, Peter recognizes the unjust use of such structures (1 Pet 2:19) and encourages believers in unjust situations to act strategically within them for the long-range interests of the gospel (cf. Balch 1984).

Like the instructions of other writers who are speaking in general principles (cf. 1 Cor 7:21; see Keener 1991, 22-25), Peter's words apply under general circumstances but not necessarily under circumstances he does not address. Thus he recognizes that slaves must endure beatings, often without any wrongdoing on their part (1 Pet 2:20); slaves, however, normally had little choice but to endure such beatings. By contrast Roman wives could divorce their husbands, and Christians could often flee local persecution; Peter's instructions to submit to authorities (1 Pet 2:13-17) and to husbands (1 Pet 3:1-6) involved normal and not abusive situations. The instructions to wives address what appears to be the least abusive situation in the context.

Then Peter addresses Christian husbands (1 Pet 3:7). Instead of exhorting them how to make their wives obey them, however, as would have been customary in household codes (Keener 1992, 166-70), he exhorts them to be sensitive to their wives. Other ancient writers who regarded women as the weaker gender normally meant that they were morally or mentally inferior (Apuleius *Met.* 7.8; *'Abot R. Nat.* 9, §24B; Gardner, 21, 67; Pomeroy, 150, 230; Lefkowitz, 112-32; Wegner, 159-62; less pejoratively, 4 Macc 15:4-5; 16:5, 14); this could entitle them to special consideration (*Ep. Arist.* 250; *b. B. Meṣ* 59a; Plutarch *Rom.* 108, *Mor.* 289E; Muson. Ruf. frag. 12; Chariton *Chaer.* 2.2.2; cf. 1 Cor 12:23). The rest of Peter's instructions to the husband rules out the sense of moral or mental weakness, however; Peter either thinks of the wife as weaker with regard to her societal status or because Greek men around age thirty often married women in their mid-teens, producing a disparity of social and intellectual maturation. In any case, like some of his contemporaries, Peter felt that this weakness entitled wives to special consideration and sensitivity ("according to understanding" or "knowledge"; cf. Sir 7:25).

Peter emphasizes that husbands should treat their wives with "respect" or "honor" (1 Pet 3:7), as he had exhorted wives to treat their husbands (1 Pet 3:2, using a different term). They should likewise view them as fellow heirs of the grace* of life. Whereas women's inheritance rights were normally subordinate to those of men (Num 27:8 improved their status in Israel), all God's people shared the same inheritance in the world* to come. By emphasizing the wives' spiritual equality, Peter prevents the husbands from taking his instructions to the wives as grounds for the husbands to subordinate them. The husband who failed to keep this in mind would hurt his own relationship with God in prayer* (1 Pet 3:7, 12; in a more general vein, harmony between spouses was a traditional Greco-Roman topic [Balch 1981, 88]).

Although we have focused on women's roles because most ancient literature assumes the man's status as the norm, the behavior of men toward wives in early Christianity was less culturally predictable than that of women toward husbands. In the household codes of Aristotle and later Roman ideology, a true man was a *paterfamilias* who ruled his household. Yet while Christian wives in general remained submissive, early Christians did not emphasize that husbands and fathers should express their manhood primarily by authority; rather they were to express it by service.* Thinking of a wife as a "coheir of grace" despite culturally defined power struc-

tures (1 Pet 3:7) was distinctive. A man's identity modeled after Christ contrasts not so much with womanhood as it does with boyhood; rather than being self-centered, a Christlike man must be responsible, a voluntary servant, looking out for others' interests. In contrast to Paul, who defines authority positions in terms of Christ's servanthood (Eph 5:21—6:9), Peter draws a parallel only between Jesus and those in socially weaker power roles (1 Pet 2:21-25); in either case early Christian writers summoned their hearers to imitate Christ's servanthood, not his power.

3. Woman and Man in Revelation.
Revelation portrays the city of God (new Jerusalem, Rev 12:1-2; 21:2) and the city of the world (Babylon,* Rev 17:4-5; cf. *2 Bar.* 11:1-3 for another contrast between Jerusalem and Babylon) as women—one a virtuous mother and bride and the other a prostitute, with Christ as a son and bridegroom (Rev 12:5; 19:7). The descriptions tell us little about the author's view of gender roles, however, for they reflect traditional imagery. The Hebrew Bible had long portrayed Israel and Jerusalem as God's bride and the mother of the saved remnant, and Israel's straying from God had often earned it the image of a prostitute. The images of a heavenly Jerusalem as mother of the church and of the church as Christ's bride already appeared in earlier Christian texts (Gal 4:26; 2 Cor 11:2; Eph 5:25-27). The symbols functioned within a culture whose shared assumptions conceived of women socially primarily in their sexual relation to men, but the author employs such symbols to communicate the reality the symbols represent, not to address the cultural conception from which the images draw their force.

3.1. God's People as a Virtuous Woman. Revelation 12 draws on the widespread ancient myth of a dragon seeking to destroy a divine child, who then overcomes the dragon and brings deliverance. In the early empire the myth appears most commonly in its Greek form (e.g., Aune, 112) but appears in Egyptian and other forms as well (e.g., Koester, 1:188; Beasley-Murray, 193). Many scholars argue that the emperor's propagandists from Virgil on portrayed him as the divine child and that even here Revelation is challenging the imperial cult (e.g., Knox 1939, 18-19; Caird, 148; Beasley-Murray, 193-94); second-century Christians, at least, may have applied the divine child imagery to Christ (cf. *Sib. Or.* 8:196-97). Although Revelation opposes idolatry, Jewish apocalyptic elsewhere borrows pagan imagery, and there is no reason to doubt that process was at work here (Bergmeier 1982; pace Ford, 188).

Women appeared in other visions (e.g., Plutarch *Ser. Num. Vind.* 33, *Mor.* 568A; *Herm. Vis.* 8.1) and were employed as symbolic images (e.g., *3 Bar.* 9:3, the moon in a chariot, following Greek imagery). The direct background for the woman of Revelation 12 is, however, the OT. As Ford (195) notes, the biblical tradition already portrays Zion as God's wife (Is 54:1, 5, 6; Jer 3:20; Ezek 16:8-14; Hos 2:19-20); Zion as a mother (Is 49:21; 50:1; 66:7-11; Hos 4:5; Bar 4:8-23); and in birth throes (Mic 4:9-10; cf. Is 26:16-18; Jer 4:31; 13:21; Sir 48:19[21]). (Rissi, 36-37, thinks Is 26:17—27:1 provides the closest parallel here.) The twelve stars on the woman's head represent the whole zodiac, which was popular in contemporary Judaism as a symbol for God's creation. But while a zodiacal crown was characteristic of Helios (probably echoed in *Jos. and As.* 5:5/6), the biblical background here consists of the tribes of Israel in Joseph's dream (Gen 37:9; cf. echoes in *T. Abr.* 7A, B); as elsewhere in Revelation (e.g., Rev 7:4-8; 21:12-14; elsewhere, e.g., *Ep. Arist.* 97), twelve stands for the people of God. Thus the woman here stands for the ideal Zion (e.g., Caird 1966, 149; Feuillet 1965, 115; cf. Minear 1960, 54; cf. Is 65:17-19; 66:7-13).

This image of Zion giving birth continued to be developed in subsequent Jewish tradition: thus Zion appears as a woman giving birth in 4 Ezra 10:44-46 (though in 5:50 and 10:9-14 "our mother" is earth, as in Greek story of Deucalion and Pyrrha); mourning in 4 Ezra 9:38—10:24, Zion is transformed into the heavenly Jerusalem in 4 Ezra 10:25-28 (cf. Gal 4:26). Scholars debate the precise nature of the image in 1QH 3:1-18: some think it refers to a messianic individual; probably more are skeptical, finding instead the sufferings of the community or of the psalmist himself. But in any case this passage echoes OT language about Zion giving birth in pain. In Revelation 12, Zion's birth pangs probably represent the cross (so also Caird, 149-50; cf. Jn 16:21-22).

Although most scholars concur that the woman of Revelation 12 symbolizes the people of God, many scholars have seen Mary here as well (e.g., James 1960; O'Donoghue 1960; cf.

Feuillet 1978; but note also e.g., Ford 207; Feuillet 1965: 115). Bruns goes so far in his parallel between the church and Mary* here to link the harlot of Revelation 17 with another concrete historical character, the mid-first century empress Messalina (Bruns, 462). But even early patristic exegesis of the text provides little support for Marian interpretation (so e.g., Stefaniak). Because Revelation provides no specific allusions to Mary (without recourse to parallels in John, or a new interpretation of Eve, or by a *sensus plenior* on the basis of later tradition), the text itself does not support the Marian exegesis.

The Book of Revelation also employs traditional Jewish imagery in portraying the church as Christ's bride (cf. similarly Eph 5:21-33; *2 Clem.* 14). This image itself recalls Israel as God's wife in the Hebrew Bible (e.g., Jer 3:1; Hos 2:16, 19-20) and in later Jewish texts (e.g., *Sipra Šemini Mekilta* deMiluim 99.2.2; *Sipre Deut* 43.16.1). The closing chapters of Revelation present the New Jerusalem, a traditional Jewish hope (cf. Is 65:17-18; Tobit 13:7-16; *Pss. Sol.* 11:7; 4 Ezra 7:26), as Christ's bride (Rev 21:2), employing various literary figures. One is an announcement of the impending messianic banquet of the world to come (in Jewish texts, *m. 'Abot.* 3:17; *t. Ber.* 6.21), viewed in Revelation 19:7 as Christ's wedding banquet. Another is the description of the bride, which in Revelation 21 coalesces with a literary form common in antiquity, namely an encomium on cities (e.g., Aelius Aristides on Rome; cf. Balch 1982; Ps 48). "Jerusalem" represents the people who lived in the city as well as the place (e.g., Is 3:8), and in Revelation the New Jerusalem clearly represents the saints (with e.g., Gundry).

3.2. The Prostitutes of Revelation. Scholars have proposed various solutions regarding the identity of "Jezebel" (Rev 2:20-23), for example, that she may be the leader of a competing prophetic guild (Aune, 197). The roles of women in Thyatiran society in general provide a broad context for interpreting this figure. First of all, women were involved in business guilds in Thyatira (Hemer, 121). Others have noted that the goddess Sambathe was identified with the Sibyls in Asia Minor; some have thus suggested that "Jezebel" reflects the influence of a Jewish cult associated with this syncretism in Thyatira (Ford, 405; Hemer, 119). Although this remains speculation (Ramsay, 337), we do know that second-century Christians had embraced some Sibyllism in its Jewish form (e.g., *Herm. Vis.* 8.1; Theophilus *Autol.* 2.36; Tertullian *Apol.* 19.1). Artemis Boreitene was the prominent city-goddess of Thyatira (Hemer 118), and we also know that some women were also involved in the imperial cult in first-century Asia Minor (e.g., Lalla in Lycia; Lefkowitz and Fant, 157 §159).

The nature of Jezebel's "prostitution" may be disputed. The earlier reference to "Balaam" (Rev 2:14) might suggest literal cultic prostitution (Num 25:1-3), but spiritual immorality is far more likely here (Caird, 44; cf. e.g., Jer 3:1-6; Hos 1:2; Wis 14:12; 4QpNah 3:4), given the likelihood that her "children" (Rev 2:23) represent her disciples (cf. 2 Jn 1, 13; 3 Jn 4). The "harlotries" of Jezebel in 2 Kings 9:22 represented leading Israel into the worship of Baal; here they may represent compromise with the imperial cult (Fiorenza, 195). Later in Revelation this idolatrous prophetess of compromise becomes a model for Babylon the harlot.

"Babylon the Great" represents Rome, as is usually acknowledged (Rev 17:9, 18); as the place of the new , Rome had already received the name Babylon in Jewish and Christian (1 Pet 5:13) literature. The "prostitute" image is somewhat more complex. God's unfaithful wife Israel was usually the prostitute in biblical tradition (e.g., Is 1:21; Jer 2:20; 3:1; Ezek 16:15-16; 23:5; Hos 3:3; 4:15), but Nineveh fills the role in Nahum 3:4 and Tyre in Isaiah 23:15-16; the collapse of Tyre's mercantile empire in Isaiah 23:1-14 fits the dirge of Revelation 18. Artists often portrayed a city as a goddess by their city's river (Ford, 277); *Sibylline Oracles* 3:356-59, 385-87, 469 also portray cities or regions as women; the image here especially resembles that of first-century depictions of Rome (Beauvery 1983). Babylon's reputation for harlotry (cf. the slander in Herodotus *Hist.* 1.199) may have augmented the image, but the biblical background and the contrast with the virtuous people of God from whom Christ sprang and with whom he would be united provide the primary context of the image.

4. Woman and Man in 1 Clement.

Clement (*see* Clement of Rome), probably writing about 95 or 96, maintains this Pauline and Petrine tradition of Greek and Roman household codes. As one writing within the sphere of apostolic tradition, however, he adapts those codes according to distinctive Christian emphases on mutual submission, even if his words on the subject appear less striking than those of some of his Christian predecessors.

In his first exhortation to women (*1 Clem.* 1.3), Clement may deliberately echo some of the language in Titus 2. Thus when he admonishes wives to be blameless and to show natural affection to their own husbands, he adds that wives must be "obedient" or "subordinate" to their husbands (*1 Clem.* 1.3, as in household codes; cf. Tit 2:5). With somewhat different language Clement elsewhere speaks of obedience to God (*1 Clem.* 19.1; 60.4) and to earthly rulers (*1 Clem.* 63.1). Clement also calls on the wife to "rule her house" (*1 Clem.* 1.3); Greek writers who emphasized the wife's subordination nevertheless provided for her authority in the relatively autonomous domestic sphere (see also Tit 2:5; 1 Tim 5:14). The "pure" conscience* (*1 Clem.* 1.3) might indicate undivided passion for one's husband (*1 Clem.* 38.2; cf. *2 Clem.* 8.6; Ign. *Pol.* 5.1; Tit 2:4-5), although it is not clear that Clement intends the phrase so narrowly (1 Tim 1:5; Heb 9:14; 10:22; *2 Clem.* 11.1; 16.4). Especially in times of public suspicion of Christianity, Christian women must be prudently self-controlled (Tit 2:4-5; *1 Clem.* 1.3), as must the men (Tit 2:6).

It is noteworthy that Clement interchanges between genders some exhortations from Titus 2, however, recognizing that they apply in principle to both genders: like men (Tit 2:2, 8), women are to exercise dignity (*1 Clem.* 1.3). Titus's warning that women should not slander (Tit 2:2) applies in *1 Clement* to all Christians (*1 Clem.* 30.3). But what is most noteworthy is that Clement, like some NT writers, places wifely submission in the broader context of mutual submission. Before addressing the appropriate role of Christian wives, Clement calls for submission to their leaders (*1 Clem.* 1.3; cf. *1 Clem.* 57.1-2) and older men; but this submission becomes complementary, as in 1 Peter 5:5 (*1 Clem.* 2.1).

Presumably exaggerating their virtues (as was customary in an introductory *exordium;* cf. 1 Cor 1:5-7), Clement emphasizes the Corinthians' initial humility (*1 Clem.* 2.1), introducing a central motif in his letter* (*1 Clem.* 16.1-2; 19.1; 21.8; 30.2-3, 8; 38.2; 58.2; cf. *1 Clem.* 59.4), which can also be applied to a heroic woman in *1 Clement* 55.6 (cf. 1 Pet. 5:6). Both in *1 Clement* 2.1 and elsewhere (*1 Clem.* 16.2; 21.5; 57.2; cf. *1 Clem.* 1.1; 30.8) he emphasizes lack of boastfulness; at times he follows the ancient rhetorical motif of critiquing self-boasting (*1 Clem.* 30.6; 38.2). In emphasizing submission to those in authority (*1 Clem.* 1.3; 57.1-2) he nevertheless praises those who submit rather than seek others' submission (*1 Clem.* 2.1). Clement undoubtedly emphasizes humility because of the strife among leaders (*1 Clem.* 43—50; *see* Church Order), but his dependence on this earlier Christian ethic* in the context of the *Haustafeln* affects his portrait of submission. Apparently less egalitarian than Paul, Clement is nonetheless more egalitarian than most of his contemporaries who employed household codes.

A fuller treatment of household codes and other relationships appears in *1 Clement* 21.6-9. Clement exhorts readers to reverence Christ, respect their leaders, honor their elders and educate young men in the wisdom* that begins with the fear of God (*1 Clem.* 21.6). He also exhorts men to lead their wives in the way of good (*1 Clem.* 21.6), advocating purity,* sincere meekness and silence (*1 Clem.* 21.7), all of which were cultural marks of appropriate wifely virtues* (Keener 1992, 164-66). He also exhorts Christian women to a more distinctively Christian virtue of loving all fellow Christians equally (the ancient language of "friendship") and impartially (*1 Clem.* 21.7); this final exhortation is distinctively Christian in that it treats all Christians as members of one family or social group, regardless of class or gender divisions. Then Clement provides instruction for minor children* (*1 Clem.* 21.8-9; cf. Eph 6:1-4).

Clement's Christian understanding of male-female relationships also affects his understanding of marriage.* Because marriage makes one flesh, jealousy between spouses is harmful in a marriage (*1 Clem.* 6.3; *1 Clem.* 3—6 probably focuses on jealousy largely due to the situation of jealousy over church offices attested in *1 Clem.* 43—44). Following Genesis, Clement also recognizes that God created humanity, both male and female, in his image (*1 Clem.* 33.4-6; cf. Keener 1992, 37). Yet Clement chooses a specifically masculine term to describe the messengers he has sent with the letter as its possible interpreters, possibly implying the growing preference for male leadership in the

Roman church (*1 Clem.* 63.3; contrast Rom 16:1-2; Keener 1992, 238).

Clement recognizes women heroines (*1 Clem.* 55.3-6), including apparently Christian martyrs* (*1 Clem.* 6.2). He describes their heroism as becoming "manly" not in the Philonic or gnostic* sense of "becoming male" (cf. perhaps *Herm. Vis.* 3.16.4) but in the common use of the term for "courage" (see Keener 1992, 164; Pol. *Phil.* 9.1; *Herm. Vis.* 1.4.3). Others also often viewed women taking a male role of leadership or responsibility as noble, provided a crisis forced them to do so; such writers extolled the virtue of women who acted courageously in exceptional circumstances (Plutarch *Mul. Virt., Mor.*). Like men, however, women could also constitute negative examples (cf. the sin of both Valens and his wife in Pol. *Phil.* 11.4). Thus Clement illustrates damnable apostasy* by Lot's wife (*1 Clem.* 11.1-2); immediately thereafter, however, he employs Rahab as an example of saving faith (*1 Clem.* 12.1), emphasizing her gender (*1 Clem.* 12.8). He demands moral purity from both genders (*1 Clem.* 60.2). The language of motherhood or the frailty of those "born of women" often merely reflects biblical language without indicating Clement's views relating to women's roles (*1 Clem.* 18.5; 30.5; 35.8).

5. Woman and Man in Ignatius and Polycarp.
Ignatius* provides a partial set of household duties in his letter to Polycarp. First, he exhorts Polycarp to look after the widows in his congregation (Ign. *Pol.* 4.1; cf. 1 Tim 5:3). Second, he addresses slaves, perhaps because they also might require financial help from the church. He advocates treating both male and female slaves as fellow Christians, not according to their societal status, but also warns against them becoming puffed up with pride,* urging them to serve their masters for God's honor (Ign. *Pol.* 4.3). These instructions probably presuppose a situation in which Christianity was maligned as a potentially subversive cult (Tit 2:5, 8-10; cf. Keener 1992, 139-56). That Ignatius resists the idea that the Christian community pay for their emancipation (Ign. *Pol.* 4.3) may reflect limited funds, the threat of massive slave conversions for ulterior motives and the recognition that household slaves could often save enough for their own manumission. It probably also suggests, however, that some slaves had also adopted the natural position that their Chris-

tian siblings should contribute to their efforts to purchase freedom. Some later Christian writers, such as John Chrysostom, were more sympathetic with this position (Longenecker, 65), but many free Christians were apparently too much a part of their culture to think in these terms (cf. *Mart. Pol.* 6.1; 7.1).

Finally, Ignatius turns to husband-wife relations, urging husbands and wives to love one another faithfully (Ign. *Pol.* 5.1). Rather than calling for wifely obedience, Ignatius merely exhorts "his sisters" to be content with their husbands in flesh and spirit, while reiterating Paul's demand that husbands love their wives as Christ loves the church (Ign. *Pol.* 5.1).

Polycarp,* apparently strongly influenced by Ignatius's personal exhortations to him (Pol. *Phil.* 13.2), seems to echo his household codes (Pol. *Phil.* 4.2), probably following Ignatius's instruction to offer homilies against misbehavior (Ign. *Pol.* 5.1). Ignatius's letter undoubtedly strengthened Polycarp's own position in the church (Ign. *Pol.* 6.1), a fact that may have made an enduring impression on Smyrna's bishop. Following the traditional pattern of household codes, which normally addressed only the male householder (contrast Eph 5:22—6:9), Polycarp exhorts husbands to instruct their wives in the importance of marital fidelity and of loving everyone equally in a pure way (Pol. *Phil.* 4.2; cf. the influence of Ign. *Pol.* 5.1; *1 Clem.* 21.7).

Polycarp then addresses guidance to prominent groups in the church: widows, who are to avoid slander and like offenses (Pol. *Phil.* 4.3; cf. 1 Tim 4:7; 5:13; Tit 2:3); deacons and elders (Pol. *Phil.* 5.2; 6.1; on church leadership and household codes see Verner); and younger men (Pol. *Phil.* 5.3). He instructs the young men more on sexual behavior than he does the women (Pol. *Phil.* 5.3 versus Pol. *Phil.* 4.2), perhaps because young men in the eastern Mediterranean were far more likely to be single than were the women (whom Polycarp treats as "wives" and "widows," Pol. *Phil.* 4.2-3). Just as he elsewhere continues the traditional duty of prayer for rulers (Pol. *Phil.* 12.3), Polycarp preserves the Pauline tradition of mutual submission even though he does not use it directly to qualify the household codes (Pol. *Phil.* 10.2; cf. Eph 5:21).

Ignatius's greeting to the "household of Gavia" (Ign. *Smyrn.* 13.2) could reflect her role as leader of a house church but could also

reflect merely her prominence as a hospitable mother in the faith, possibly a widow who opened her home to the church as a patroness. He also greets in Smyrna a woman named Alce (Ign. *Smyrn.* 13.2), and in his letter to Smyrna's bishop, Polycarp, he greets the same person (Ign. *Pol.* 8.3), possibly suggesting that Gavia is the unnamed "widow of Epitropus" whom Ignatius greets there with her household (Ign. *Pol.* 8.2). Finally, Ignatius recognizes Christ's deity in humanity in terms of his birth from both Mary* and God (Ign. *Eph.* 7.2; cf. Ign. *Eph.* 18.2; 19.1; Ign. *Trall.* 9; Ign. *Smyrn.* 1.1).

6. Woman and Man in Other Patristic Writers.
Like *1 Clement*, the *Didache* * preserves substantial early tradition; the *Epistle of Barnabas* * includes considerably more late material but also depends heavily on catechetical material called the Two Ways that it shares with the *Didache*. Although these texts comment little on husband-wife relations, household instructions appear in *Didache* 4.9-11, where the tradition exhorts attention to one's children (*Did.* 4.9) and prohibits speaking to slaves in anger, since masters and slaves were equals before God (*Did.* 4.10; cf. *Barn.* 19.7). Slaves were nevertheless to submit to masters respectfully as to those who by virtue of their office functioned as God's representatives (*Did.* 4.11; cf. *Barn.* 19.7). Barnabas exhorts to humility in this same context (*Barn.* 19.6).

2 Clement (perhaps c. A.D. 120) and Clement of Alexandria (Clement *Strom.* 3.13.92) cite a supposed saying of Jesus (the latter referring to the *Gos. Eg.*) that finds a parallel in *Gospel of Thomas* 22. When someone asked Jesus when his kingdom would come, he replied that when two would become one and gender distinctions would cease (*2 Clem.* 12.2). It is possible that the earliest form of the saying referred to husband and wife becoming one flesh (Mk 10:8) and that the removal of gender distinctions referred to the catastrophic reversal of the social order anticipated in the messianic woes of early Jewish expectation (e.g., *m. Soṭa* 9:15; cf. perhaps 1 Cor 7:29). *2 Clement*, however, interprets the saying positively: husband and wife share the same soul and gender would become a nonsexual issue, for one would treat fellow Christians merely as brothers and sisters in all purity (*2 Clem.* 12.3-5; cf. 1 Tim 5:1-2; there is no indication in the passage of sexual asceticism within marriage). This writer indicated that Jesus expected the kingdom to come when his followers could live so righteously; the saying thus matches less the frequent Jewish doctrine of the messianic woes and more the frequent Jewish doctrine that Israel could hasten the time of the end through good works.

Thomas naturally interprets the saying in a more gnosticizing direction, changing the question about the time of the kingdom (*2 Clem.* 12.2) to one about how to enter it (*Gos. Thom.* 22). In making male and female the same, Thomas apparently follows the lead of Philo,* for whom divinity was male and all else was female by comparison and for whom a praiseworthy woman such as the empress Livia was becoming "male in her reasoning powers" (see Baer). That *2 Clement*, which retains some traditional Palestinian Jewish motifs (e.g., possibly the Kiddush ha-Shem, *2 Clem.* 13.1-2) alongside Diaspora Jewish motifs (*see* Diaspora Judaism), may share a somewhat similar Philonic picture is suggested by his view that the humanity God created male and female refers to Christ (the male) and his church (the female, *2 Clem.* 14.2). *2 Clement* probably builds on the Pauline analogy between the church as Christ's bride, hence one "flesh" or spirit with him, and the church as Christ's body (Eph 5:29-32; cf. 1 Cor 6:17), but he reads these metaphors in a platonizing direction ("this flesh is an antitype of the Spirit," *2 Clem.* 14.3). The feminine character of the church prevailed apart from such philosophical frameworks, however; following Jewish teaching concerning Israel, Hermas envisions the church as a woman "on account of whom the world was made" (*Herm. Vis.* 2.8.1). Hermas also portrays the virtues as women (*Herm. Vis.* 3.16.3-5; virtues were feminine in Greek).

The allegorist Pseudo-Barnabas perpetuates one stream of Jewish criticism of Eve (e.g., *Life of Adam and Eve*) in emphasizing that the serpent brought about humanity's sin "by Eve" (*Barn.* 12.5). Papias preserves an account from Philip's daughters subsequent to their youthful prophetic activity in Acts 21, apparently accepting them as persons of status within the Christian community (Papias frag. 3.9, in Eusebius *Hist. Eccl.* 3.39).

7. Conclusion.
Earliest Christianity reflected the most socially progressive alternatives on women's roles in

general circulation in its day, but in time much of the church began to reflect the more conservative values of the majority culture. The step from Jesus' practices to first-century epistles containing household codes was a large one, but it was a cultural accommodation that most early Christians apparently felt necessary in order to survive in a hostile environment. Even these codes were qualified, but in time a church increasingly at home in its culture became increasingly estranged from the more radical elements in its roots, and the dominant culture of late antiquity overwhelmed the incipient egalitarianism argued by Jesus and preserved in Pauline and Petrine qualifications.

See also HOUSEHOLD CODES; HOUSEHOLD, FAMILY; MARY; MINISTRY; WOMEN IN THE EARLY CHURCH.

BIBLIOGRAPHY. V. A. Abrahamsen, "The Rock Reliefs and the Cult of Diana at Philippi" (unpublished Th.D. dissertation, Harvard Divinity School, 1986); idem, "Women at Philippi: The Pagan and Christian Evidence," *JFSR* 3 (1987) 17-30; D. E. Aune, *Prophecy in Early Christianity and the Ancient Mediterranean World* (Grand Rapids: Eerdmans, 1983); R. A. Baer, Jr., *Philo's Use of the Categories Male and Female* (ALGHJ 3; Leiden: E. J. Brill, 1970); D. L. Balch, "Early Christian Criticism of Patriarchal Authority: 1 Peter 2:11—3:12," *USQR* 39 (1984) 151-73; idem, "Household Codes" in *Greco-Roman Literature and the New Testament: Selected Forms and Genres*, ed. D. E. Aune (SBLSBS 21; Atlanta: Scholars Press, 1988) 25-50; idem, *Let Wives Be Submissive: The Domestic Code in 1 Peter* (SBLMS 26; Chico, CA: Scholars Press, 1981); idem, "Two Apologetic Encomia: Dionysius on Rome and Josephus on the Jews," *JSJ* 13 (1982) 102-22; G. R. Beasley-Murray, *The Book of Revelation* (NCBC; Grand Rapids: Eerdmans, 1974); R. Beauvery, "L'Apocalypse au risque de la numismatique: Babylone, la grande Prostituée et le sixième roi Vespasien et la déesse Rome," *RB* 90 (1983) 243-60; R. Bergmeier, "Altes und Neues zur 'Sonnenfrau am Himmel (Apk 12).' Religionsgeschichtliche und quellenkritische Beobachtungen zu Apk 12:1-17," *ZNW* 73 (1982) 97-109; B. J. Brooten, *Women Leaders in the Ancient Synagogue: Inscriptional Evidence and Background Issues* (Chico, CA: Scholars Press, 1982); J. E. Bruns, "The Contrasted Women of Apocalypse 12 and 17," *CBQ* 26 (1964) 459-63; G. B. Caird, *A Commentary on the Revelation of Saint John the Divine* (HNTC; San Francisco: Harper & Row, 1966); G. Clark, *Women in Late Antiquity: Pagan and Christian Lifestyles* (Oxford: Clarendon, 1994); P. Davids, *The First Epistle of Peter* (NICNT; Grand Rapids: Eerdmans, 1990); S. Dixon, *The Roman Mother* (Norman, OK: Oklahoma University Press, 1988); A. Feuillet, *The Apocalypse* (Staten Island: Alba House, 1965); idem, "Le chapitre XII de l'Apocalypse: Son caractère synthetique et sa richesse doctrinale," *Esprit et Vie* 88 (1978) 674-83; E. Schüssler Fiorenza, *The Book of Revelation: Justice and Judgment* (Philadelphia: Fortress, 1985); N. M. Flanagan, "The Position of Women in the Writings of St. Luke," *Marianum* 40 (1978) 288-304; J. M. Ford, *Revelation* (AB; Garden City, NY: Doubleday, 1975); L. Friedländer, *Roman Life and Manners Under the Early Empire* (4 vols; New York: Barnes & Noble, 1907) vol. 1; J. F. Gardner, *Women in Roman Law and Society* (Bloomington, IN: Indiana University Press, 1986); R. H. Gundry, "The New Jerusalem: People as Place, not Place for People," *NovT* 29 (1987) 254-64; C. J. Hemer, *The Letters to the Seven Churches of Asia in Their Local Setting* (JSNTSup 11; Sheffield: University of Sheffield, 1986); T. Ilan, *Jewish Women in Greco-Roman Palestine* (Peabody, MA: Hendrickson, 1996); P. P. James, "Mary and the Great Sign," *AER* 142 (1960) 321-29; E. A. Judge, "The Early Christians as a Scholastic Community: Part II," *JRH* 1 (1960) 125-37; idem, *The Social Pattern of the Christian Groups in the First Century: Some Prolegomena to the Study of New Testament Ideas of Social Obligation* (London: Tyndale Press, 1960); C. S. Keener, *And Marries Another: Divorce and Remarriage in the Teaching of the New Testament* (Peabody, MA: Hendrickson, 1991); idem, *Paul, Women and Wives: Marriage and Women's Ministry in the Letters of Paul* (Peabody, MA: Hendrickson, 1992); W. L. Knox, *St Paul and the Church of the Gentiles* (Cambridge: Cambridge University Press, 1939); H. Koester, *Introduction to the New Testament* (2 vols.; Philadelphia: Fortress, 1982); M. R. Lefkowitz, *Women in Greek Myth* (Baltimore: Johns Hopkins University Press, 1986); M. R. Lefkowitz and M. B. Fant, *Women's Life in Greece and Rome* (Baltimore: Johns Hopkins University Press, 1982); N. Lewis, *Life in Egypt Under Roman Rule* (Oxford: Clarendon, 1983); W. L. Liefeld, "The Wandering Preacher As a Social Figure in the Roman Empire" (unpublished Ph.D. dissertation, Columbia University, 1967); R. N.

Longenecker, *New Testament Social Ethics for Today* (Grand Rapids: Eerdmans, 1984); E. H. Maly, "Women and the Gospel of Luke," *BTB* 10 (1980) 99-104; W. A. Meeks, *The First Urban Christians: The Social World of the Apostle Paul* (New Haven, CT: Yale University Press, 1983); J. R. Michaels, "Pairs and Parallels: Jesus and Inclusive Language," *Daughters of Sarah* 11 (1985) 7-10; P. S. Minear, *Images of the Church in the New Testament* (Philadelphia: Westminster, 1960); J. Moffatt, *The General Epistles: James, Peter and Judas* (MNTC; Garden City, NY: Doubleday, Doran & Company, 1928); N.-D. O'Donoghue, "A Woman Clothed with the Sun," *Furrow* 11 (1960) 445-56; S. B. Pomeroy, *Goddesses, Whores, Wives and Slaves: Women in Classical Antiquity* (New York: Schocken, 1975); A. M. Rabello, "The Legal Condition of the Jews in the Roman Empire," *ANRW* 2.13 (1980) 662-762; W. M. Ramsay, *The Letters to the Seven Churches of Asia* (Grand Rapids: Baker, 1979 [1904]); M. Rissi, *Time and History: A Study on the Revelation* (Richmond: John Knox, 1966); S. Safrai, "Home and Family" in *The Jewish People in the First Century: Historical Geography, Political History, Social, Cultural and Religious Life and Institutions*, ed. S. Safrai, M. Stern with D. Flusser and W. C. van Unnik (2 vols.; CRINT 1.1; Assen: Van Gorcum, 1974) 728-92; E. G. Selwyn, *The First Epistle of St. Peter: The Greek Text with Introduction, Notes and Essays* (2d ed.; New York: Macmillan, 1947); L. Stefaniak, "Mulier amicta sole (Apok 12, 1-17)," *Ruch Biblijny i Liturgiczny* 9 (1956) 244-61; L. Swidler, *Women in Judaism: The Status of Women in Formative Judaism* (Metuchen, NJ: Scarecrow, 1976); R. C. Tannehill, *The Narrative Unity of Luke-Acts: A Literary Interpretation*, 1: *The Gospel According to Luke* (2 vols.; Philadelphia: Fortress, 1986); D. C. Verner, *The Household of God: The Social World of the Pastoral Epistles* (SBLDS 71; Chico, CA: Scholars Press, 1983); J. R. Wegner, *Chattel or Person? The Status of Women in the Mishnah* (New York: Oxford University Press, 1988); B. Witherington III, *Women in the Earliest Churches* (SNTSMS 59; Cambridge: Cambridge University Press, 1988).　　　C. S. Keener

WOMEN IN THE EARLY CHURCH

The vigorous participation of women in the life of the early church is attested by a considerable body of evidence, both literary and archaeological. Many of these women are nameless; frequently they are designated by the category of their ministry or by their social or marital status. Sometimes there are hints of deep involvement in leadership that cannot be demonstrated with surety. Nevertheless those possibilities deserve to be acknowledged and explored.

1. Women as Leaders in Acts and the Apostolic Fathers
2. Paul's Ministry Among Women in Acts
3. Priscilla: A Test Case
4. Women in Prophetic Ministry
5. Women in Evangelistic Traditions
6. Women as Leaders of House Churches
7. Widows and Disenfranchised Women
8. Married and Unmarried Women

1. Women as Leaders in Acts and the Apostolic Fathers.

Throughout Acts* there is a careful inclusion of women as well as men, both as believers (Acts 5:14; 8:12; 17:4, 12) and as objects of persecution* (Acts 8:3; 9:2-3; 22:4). No fewer than eleven women are specifically named, and five are involved in church-related ministries. After the ascension* of Christ,* Mary* the mother of Jesus and her female associates are included in the decision making to select Judas's replacement among the Twelve (Acts 1:14). The qualification for an apostle* is that the individual have traveled with Jesus throughout his ministry* and been a witness* for the resurrection* (Acts 2:21-22). Although a woman is not chosen for the office, Luke's record makes it clear that some of Jesus' female followers fulfill the specifications (Lk 8:1-3; 23:49, 55-56; 24:1-10). At a different level one woman, Dorcas, is specifically called a "disciple" because her ministry of social and spiritual outreach rendered her invaluable to the nascent church. And upon her untimely death, she was restored to the community who so sorely needed her services (Acts 9:36-41).

In the writings of the apostolic fathers,* greetings are sent by Ignatius to Tavia and her family, and Alce is mentioned twice (Ign. *Smyrn.* 13; Ign. *Pol.* 8.3). Alce's name occurs too in the *Martyrdom of Polycarp* 17 as a relative of the official responsible for Polycarp's arrest. Though the correspondence between Ignatius and Mary of Cassobel is generally regarded as spurious, its preservation indicates a tradition in which respect might be accorded to a female leader. In his purported reply, Ignatius gladly

accedes to her recommendation for clergy appointments and declares that her piety and command of the Scriptures have made a tremendous impression on the church at Rome* during the time that Linus was bishop.

Clement of Rome,* the successor of Linus, was well aware that women were capable of heroism, and he urged them to follow the examples of Queen Esther and of Judith, who delivered her people from the oppression of Holofernes (*1 Clem.* 55). Like James,* who commended Rahab as one whose faith* was accounted for righteousness* (Jas 2:25), Clement held her forth as a paradigm of courageous hospitality,* a woman in whom dwelt both faith and prophecy* (*1 Clem.* 12).

While the writer of the *Shepherd of Hermas** was to read its contents in the Roman congregation, Clement, as bishop, was to send copies of the document to the "cities abroad" (*Herm. Vis.* 2.8.3). A second copy was to be delivered to a female leader named Grapte in order that she might instruct the widows and children. Evidently she held a significant position in the church.

The shepherd receives much of his teaching from a succession of female figures, one of whom is certainly mother church (*Herm. Vis.* 1.1.4-5; 2.2). He reports a vision of maidens—subsequently allegorized as virtues*—building the church of Christ, represented as a tower (*Herm. Man.* 9.2-13). The scene is painted upon the ceiling of one of the chambers in the San Gennaro dei Poveri Catacomb in Naples, an indication not only of the local acceptance of the canonicity of *Hermas* but also of the strong ministry of women in southern Italy. That women should be forceful builders and teachers can be readily understood in an area that had been dominated by the Sibyl of Cumae. Here and elsewhere the sibyl was replaced in Christianity by the woman prophet.

2. Paul's Ministry Among Women in Acts.

Luke particularly noted the response of women to the apostle Paul. Upon his arrival at Antioch of Pisidia, he was welcomed into the synagogue* and encouraged to return the next sabbath (Acts 13). The congregation, composed of Jews, proselytes and God-fearers, took offense at the disruptive behavior of the Gentiles* who attended the worship* service on the succeeding sabbath. Those who were accustomed to worshiping in the orderly Hebrew fashion were angered at the *ochlos* of the heathen. (The Greek term can be used both for a crowd and for the disorderly behavior of which it is capable; see Acts 19:26; 24:12.) The well-bred women *(euschēmonai)* who participated in the sober life of the synagogue were particularly incensed, perhaps by the conduct of the heathen women, and insisted upon Paul's expulsion from the city (Acts 13:50).

Repugnance for the outrageous and abandoned worship patterns of non-Jewish women was a familiar literary and artistic theme (e.g., Juvenal *Sat.* 6; Plutarch *Mul. Virt.* 13, *Mor.;* Diodorus Siculus 4.3.2) Drunkenness, indecent and destructive conduct, obscenity, nudity, promiscuity, and ritual cries were significant components in their cults. Some of these elements are well illustrated in the famous fresco of a Dionysiac initiation at the Villa of the Mysteries in Pompeii. In certain ecstatic religions of the area (see 1 Cor 12:2), women engaged in the tearing apart of young animals and consuming of the flesh while it was still raw, warm and quivering. It would be exceedingly difficult to incorporate such individuals into a worshiping community without seriously affronting the sensibilities of others.

At the end of Paul's first missionary journey, he and Barnabas are summoned to Jerusalem* to determine how Gentiles might be integrated into faith communities composed largely of Jews and proselytes. Certain practices are proscribed, especially idolatry,* immorality and the consumption of blood (Acts 15:20, 29). Armed with these interdictions, Paul returns to all of the churches visited on the first journey and explains the decision of the Jerusalem council (Acts 15:36). Thereafter he is highly successful with the very sort of well-bred women who objected so vehemently to his missionary endeavors in Antioch of Pisidia. His first contact in Philippi is mainly feminine, and Lydia, the first convert, becomes the leader of a house church (Acts 16:12-15, 40). Although Paul has received a vision* of a man from Macedonia calling him to move in a new direction, the first objects of his ministry are women.

Prominent Hellenistic women receive Paul's message gladly in Thessalonica (Acts 17:4) and in Berea, where the response of the women is noted before that of the men (Acts 17:12). In Athens, the intellectual center of the ancient world, a woman named Damaris is converted. She was probably one of the highly cultured courtesans *(hetairai)* attached to the various schools of philosophy, but her presence in the academic circle of the Areopagus indicates that she was well equipped to follow Paul's argument and to draw her own conclusions (Acts 17:34).

3. Priscilla: A Test Case.

In Acts 18 we first encounter Priscilla, a major woman associate of the apostle Paul and a strong proponent of the gospel in her own right. Married to a Jew from Pontus in Asia Minor, she is apparently a native of Rome, from whence the couple were driven by persecution under the emperor Claudius. The name *Aquila,* though sometimes borne by citizens of Rome, was more commonly a slave name and may indicate that he was an enterprising freedman. "Priscilla" was a name more frequently given to patrician women, perhaps denoting non-Jewish birth and a higher social status.

Husband and wife received the apostle Paul into their home, their business operation (that of tent making) and into Christian fellowship* and ministry. They may well have extended their hospitality to Timothy and Silas as well (Acts 18:5). Priscilla and Aquila's mobility in missionary travel may indicate that they owned a string of family enterprises at Rome (Acts 18:2; Rom 16:3-5), Corinth (Acts 18:2), Ephesus (Acts 18:18-19) and perhaps other points as well. Such branch businesses at far-flung locations are well documented in the ancient world.

At the end of Paul's first visit to Corinth, Priscilla and Aquila accompany the apostle on his journey to Ephesus. The text here places Priscilla's name before that of her husband (Acts 18:18, as well as at Acts 18:26; Rom 16:3; 2 Tim 4:19), apparently indicating that her ministry and influence are more forceful than his. After Paul's departure, Priscilla and Aquila encounter in the synagogue Apollos, a brilliant Jewish thinker whose knowledge of the gospel is incomplete, despite a powerful command of the Scriptures. Again Priscilla's name stands first as the couple take him aside, perhaps actually into their home for a season, in order to give him the instruction he lacks. The term *expounded (exethento)* implies a careful examination of the Scriptures (compare the use of this same verb in Acts 11:4 and Acts 28:23). Though Apollos's basic understanding was adequate, a more complete level of instruction is supplied by the highly capable Priscilla and her husband.

Apparently Priscilla was possessed of a fine mind and an excellent education in order to have so impacted the learned Apollos. Thereafter he was able to "debate daily with the Jews, powerfully demonstrating from the Scriptures that Jesus was indeed the Christ" (Acts 18:28). For this reason Chrysostom dubbed Priscilla "a teacher of teachers," noting that she did the same evangelistic work as her husband (*PG* 60.281D) and recognizing in her a greater zeal (*PG* 62.658A; 51.187).

When Apollos wished to continue his evangelistic outreach in Greece, the Ephesian believers, among whom Priscilla and Aquila were foremost, furnished him with letters of recommendation. The reception that he was accorded is surely an indication of the confidence that the Christian community reposed in Priscilla and Aquila. They were apparently well known and revered throughout the Pauline world as "fellow laborers" who had risked their lives for the sake of the apostle (Rom 16:3-4).

A. von Harnack was one of the first to suggest that Priscilla and Aquila might be the authors of the epistle to the Hebrews,* a suggestion that found support from J. H. Moulton, F. M. Schiele, A. S. Peake, J. R. Harris and others. Harnack reasoned that if Priscilla were perceived as the primary author, there might be a tendency to suppress this fact. As indicative of scribal prejudice against women, he cites Codex Bezae's elimination of the conversion of Damaris in Acts 17:34 and its change of "not a few of the honorable Greek women and men" (Acts 17:12) to "of the Greeks and the honorable, many men and women." Codex Bezae also reverses the order of Acts 17:4, placing the mention of the men before that of the women. In such a climate the ascription of a woman author might well disappear from sight.

Although the letter* bears unmistakable signs of close association with Paul, it is not by the apostle himself and is a document in the NT to which no authorship is ascribed. The writer belongs to Paul's inner circle and enjoys a relationship of collegiality with Timothy (Heb 13:23). He or she had not known Jesus but rather received his teachings from others with direct experience (Heb 2:3). The apostolic tone bespeaks the level of influence and authority* wielded by the composer of the epistle (Heb 13:17-23).

The writing team or person was familiar with the persecutions that had been experienced in Rome and was demonstrably influenced by the thought of Philo* of Alexandria,* the Jewish philosopher who had visited Rome in A.D. 40. Priscilla and Aquila would be the Pauline associates most likely to have gained a familiarity with Philo.

The authors had been leaders in the community addressed by the letter and possessed an intimate knowledge of its members' lack of spiritual maturity (Heb 5:11-12). Steeped in Jewish Scriptures, they write of the ritual of the tabernacle* but give no hint of an acquaintance with temple* procedure. A Jew who had visited Jerusalem would almost inevitably have included allusions to temple practice. Priscilla and Aquila are unusual among Paul's coterie in never being recorded as traveling to Jerusalem.

Harnack observed that the author or authors move easily from a first person singular to first person plural in a manner that may suggest a team effort rather than the work of a single individual. The use of a masculine singular to refer to the writer at Hebrews 11:32 may indicate male input, while the marked sympathy for women may point toward the interests of Priscilla (Heb 11:11, 31, 35). In contrast to the reference in Genesis to Sarah's laughter of unbelief at the promise* of a son in her old age (Gen 18:11-15), the account in Hebrews emphasizes her faith as she faced the challenges of conception, gestation and birth (Heb 11:11). The record in Exodus described the activities of the mother of Moses* in concealing his birth and preserving his life (Exod 2:2-9), but here the parental action of both husband and wife is noted (Heb 11:23). Priscilla might well have empathized with the faith of a non-Jewish woman, Rahab, as she exercised the ministry of hospitality to the people of God (Heb 11:31). Harnack's theory cannot be substantiated but is worthy of respectful consideration.

4. Women in Prophetic Ministry.

Women are full recipients at the outpouring of the Holy Spirit* (Acts 2:37-38) at Pentecost* as foretold by the prophet* Joel. His promise that "your daughters shall prophesy" (Joel 2:28-32) is fulfilled in the ministry of Philip* the Evangelist's prophesying daughters as reported in the account of the apostle Paul's visit to their home (Acts 21:8-9). Later tradition maintained that Philip journeyed with his daughters to Hierapolis, where he engaged in evangelistic endeavors that led ultimately to his martyrdom.* The daughters continued in ministry, two of them being buried at Hierapolis. According to Papias, these women collected traditions about the life of Christ, and Papias maintains that his own knowledge of two Gospel events derived from these women (Eusebius *Hist. Eccl.* 3.31, 37, 39).

Besides the women prophets at Corinth (see Wire), another female prophet was based in Asia Minor, a citizen of Thyatira. Her teachings are regarded as erroneous (Rev 2:14). Significantly she was condemned not for her gender but for the harm she caused. Like the Nicolaitans of Pergamum (Rev 2:14-15), she instructed her followers to eat meat offered to idols and to practice ritual fornication (Rev 2:20). Her doctrines were regarded as "the deep things of Satan" (Rev 2:24) and were perhaps an early form of gnostic* Ophitism. She was threatened with retribution for her lack of chastity (Rev 2:22-23) and for the misleading of God's people. Perhaps as early as the mid-second century, Montanist women in Phrygian Asia Minor were to take up this tradition of prophesying. As support for their ministry, they claimed the precedent of Deborah, Huldah, Anna, the daughters of Philip and an unknown prophet named Ammia.

5. Women in Evangelistic Traditions.

Among the nonbiblical traditions preserved of the apostles, few are better attested than that of Paul's empowerment of women in ministry. Before his call to the church of Antioch,* he appears to have engaged in widespread evangelism in Asia Minor (Acts 11:25-26; 15:41). Consistent with Paul's designation of seven women as his fellow laborers (Rom 16:3, 6, 12, 16; Phil 4:2-3) are later accounts of women established in ministry. Pliny the Younger, writing from Asia Minor to the emperor Trajan in A.D. 112, tells of interrogating two leaders of the Christian community, slave women called *ministrae* ("deacons" or "ministers"; Pliny *Ep.* 96—97).

The most interesting story, however, is that of Paul's commissioning his young convert Thecla to become an apostle to Seleucia, close to his native city of Tarsus. Her story is contained in *The Acts of Paul and Thecla,* a composition usually placed in the mid-second century (MacDonald). W. M. Ramsay, however, insisted that the work "goes back ultimately to a document from the first century" (Ramsay, 375-76), though embellished with later accretions. As he saw it, at least some of the features necessitated an intimate knowledge of a first-century environment and threw "light on the character of popular Christianity in Asia Minor during the period" (Ramsey, 403).

The site of her ministry *(Aya Theckla),* one of the best attested in Christian antiquity (Festugière, 21-22), was continuously occupied as a place of pilgrimage and monastic community until the Turkish invasion in the fifteenth century. Part of the apse still stands above the great sanctuary built over the original cave where she established her ministry. The little underground chapel adjoining the cave bears evidence of masonry dating to the first century (Herzfeld and Euyer). The consistent attachment to the site of the same feminine name indicates the involvement of a strong woman leader in the early christianization of Seleucia.

6. Women as Leaders of House Churches.

From the biblical texts we know the names of female leaders more often than we know the names of male leaders of house churches. Women who exercised the grace of hospitality received into their homes both traveling missionaries and those seeking a place of Christian worship and fellowship. The mother of John Mark, a widow, opened her doors to a prayer* meeting even in the danger-filled atmosphere of Jerusalem as the execution of Peter was expected the next day. The practice of assembling there must have been a regular one, for Peter threaded his way to her house after his miraculous release from prison (Acts 12:5-17). The gatekeeper, a trusted slave woman named Rhoda, recognized his voice and ran to the others for permission to allow him to enter. Although the participants at the prayer meeting initially challenged the credibility of her story, she remained steadfast in the midst of their opposition. At Rhoda's insistence the door is opened, Peter received and the slave woman vindicated. Her critically responsible position as guardian of the gate during a time of intense persecution bespeaks her importance to the Christian community and its confidence in her. Through this house church, whose leaders are

Mary and Rhoda, Peter sends his message to the believers of Jerusalem (Acts 12:17).

The home of Lydia, the first European convert, becomes the center of the nascent Christian community in Philippi; and it is here that Paul and Silas repair after their release from prison. B. Witherington observes, "At the two points in Acts where Luke clearly tells us of a church meeting in a particular person's home, it is in the home of a woman" (Witherington 1990, 213). We read also of house churches in the homes of Chloe, Nympha, and Priscilla and Aquila (Col 4:15; 1 Cor 1:11; 16:19; Rom 16:3-5). Women with enough space in their homes (*see* Architecture) thus provided a needed function both in their hospitality and in caring for the congregational life that developed in their homes.

In the case of Lydia, her workroom as well as her house may have served the purposes of the gospel. Like Priscilla, she was involved in the textile industry and operated a business, manufacturing coveted purple cloth. We are specifically told that all of her household* were baptized (*see* Baptism), including her domestic staff. The women's workroom, as well as the house, offered prime opportunities for the propagation of the gospel in the early centuries of the church (den Boer).

The Johannine epistles (*see* John, Letters of) reveal the importance of the hospitality extended by influential Christians to traveling missionaries and evangelists who might bring both spoken and written messages (3 Jn 5-10; see also *Did.* 11—12; Rom 12:13; 1 Pet 4:9; Heb 13:2). Leaders of a house church in a community might control the purity of the gospel message by their selection of appropriate emissaries to receive into their homes (3 Jn 8). To welcome in a false teacher imperiled the spiritual life of the entire believing community (2 Jn 10-11).

Thus house churches became the fundamental bases for the furtherance of the gospel in their respective communities, with the hosts becoming "fellow laborers" (3 Jn 8). D. W. Riddle has suggested that not only did these leaders further the spread of the kingdom but also these households served as collecting stations for oral and written traditions that would later be preserved in the writings of the NT. The role of women leaders of house churches is thus far more significant than might appear at first glance.

Although the majority of biblical scholars have maintained that the "elect lady" to whom 2 John is addressed represents a church rather than an individual, a few are of the opinion that a specific woman is addressed (A. T. Robertson, A. Clarke, A. Plummer, C. C. Ryrie, A. Ross, D. W. Burdick). If that is the case, she must have been a leader of a house church somewhere near Ephesus. It is her duty to defend her children against heresy. Her appellation, *Kyria Eklektē,* is ordinarily translated "elect lady," though Kuria was a proper name attested in Asia Minor, actually a Greek rendering of the Aramaic "Martha" (Harris). The text of 2 John also contains greeting from an "elect sister" who sends greetings along with her children (2 Jn 13), either a sister congregation or another woman leader of a house church. A. Spencer points out that an entire congregation cannot be addressed as both the lady and her children (Spencer, 110-11). In 1 John and 3 John, the children represent the flock while the leaders are indicated as separate individuals.

7. Widows and Disenfranchised Women.
Throughout Luke-Acts, disadvantaged women are shown a special sympathy, so that Paul heals a deranged slave woman at the risk of his own safety (Acts 16:16-24). Several slave women are given positions of particular responsibility in the nascent church: Rhoda is doorkeeper of a house church, and two slave women of Bithynia are leaders of the Christian community and are specifically called ministers or deaconesses. As required by Roman law in the case of slaves, their testimony is obtained under torture and vindicates the harmless nature of Christian worship (Pliny *Ep.* 96).

A particular sensitivity is demonstrated toward widows or those suffering deprivation. Aware that widows of Hellenistic Jews are receiving less help than those of Palestinian background, the leaders of the early church form an order of deacons to insure an equitable distribution (Acts 6:1-6; cf. Mk 12:40; Lk 18:2-5). Dorcas's ministry is specifically said to have extended to widows, who were welded into a responsive and godly fellowship of caring (Acts 9:36-41; for the view that Dorcas was the leader of an order of widows, see Viteau; Parvey, 145).

James* the brother of Jesus enjoins upon believers a concern for widows (Jas 1:27), while the first epistle to Timothy provides these bereaved women with rules of conduct as well as legitimation and empowerment for an organized ministry of outreach and intercession (2 Tim 5:3-16). Ignatius begs Polycarp* to take special care of widows and to assume their guardianship (Ign. *Pol.* 4). Ecclesial widows were supported by the gifts of church members in return for their spiritual and social services. Polycarp recognizes their presence in the Philippian congregation (Pol. *Phil.* 6.1) and provides instructions for the proper attitude and deportment in the fulfillment of their duties. They were to be discreet, to avoid tale bearing, spite, gossip, greed and false allegations. Rather they were to give themselves to constant prayer for everyone because "they are an altar of God" (Pol. *Phil.* 4).

Ignatius* of Antioch appears to be addressing women belonging to a definite office when he writes to "virgins who are called widows" (Ign. *Smyrn.* 13.1). Witherington suggests that "widow" became a technical term for "all unmarried women dedicated to chastity and the Lord's work, including those who have never been married" (Witherington 1988, 201; see also Stählin, 9:451). Grapte was to give the widows special instruction about the message of Hermas (*Herm. Vis.* 2.8.3.), while Hermas is to give himself to the care of widows and orphans (*Herm. Man.* 8.10). Especially in the East, widows would later become a part of the ordained clergy, attached to local churches and committed to a ministry of prayer and good works.

8. Married and Unmarried Women.
The marital status of women is of considerable interest to the writers of the early Christian literature. Married women appear in Acts as fully mature persons, required to take responsibility for their own actions. Sapphira is held accountable along with her husband for the deception that they conspire to perpetrate (Acts 5:1-10). Priscilla participates equally in the leadership and exercise of the ministry that she shares with her husband. Even the Herodian queens listen to Paul's message with interest (Acts 24:24; 25:13, 23; 26:20). Though viewed in secular historical sources as concubines and oft-married pawns of power-hungry rulers, they appear in Acts as persons of power and integrity, capable of making their own moral and spiritual decisions.

As Jesus had warned (Mt 10:35-36; Lk 14:26),

embracing the new faith did not always make for harmonious family relations, though sometimes it strengthened the bonds. Domitilla, the niece of the emperor Domitian (reigned 81-96), was exiled; her husband, also apparently a Christian, was executed (Suetonius *Dom.* 10.15.17; Dio Cassius *Hist.* 67.14). Justin Martyr (Justin *Apol II* 2) tells of a woman whose profligate husband denounced her as a Christian and secured the punishment of her instructor.

Virginity in dedicated women commands a special respect. The four prophesying daughters of Philip were virgins, while the widow Anna, the sole prophet on hand to proclaim the birth of the Messiah, had lived all but seven years of her life as a celibate. Thecla, convert and follower of the apostle Paul, made celibacy a condition of her apostolic calling. Such tendencies are precursors of the asceticism that was later to pervade the early church.

The *Shepherd of Hermas* displays a knowledge of a practice known as syneisakatism, the living together of a man with a woman "as brother and not as husband" (*Herm. Sim.* 9.11.3; cf. *Herm. Vis.* 1.7.2). Though they might occupy the same bed as the man, the women (called *subintroductae* or *agapētai*) were ostensibly virgins, committed to gospel ministry. The apostle Paul may refer to this arrangement when he speaks of the virgin who is free to serve Christ rather than her husband and of the man who "keeps his virgin" (1 Cor 7:34-37). One advantage of such a "spiritual marriage" was that it afforded material security, male protection and freedom from marital responsibility to a single woman intent on Christian service (McNamara).

According to a tradition known to Clement of Alexandria, the wives of the early apostles accompanied them in their travels in order to spread the gospel more effectively (Clement of Alexandria *Strom.* 3.6; cf. Ambrosiaster *PL* 17, c496). An indication of this shared ministry may be found in the declaration of 1 Peter 5:13, "the fellow elect lady who is in Babylon greets you along with Mark my son."

While some scholars have suggested that the allusion is a personification of an entire congregation, it does not seem congruent in juxtaposition with the direct mention of Mark, who is attending Peter in Rome. It was Mark who had duly recorded the fact of the apostle's marriage in the Gospel that bears his name (Mk 1:29-31). Since "Babylon" was a widely used code name for Rome, J. A. Bengel, E. T. Mayerhoff, K. R. Jachmann, H. Alford, A. T. Robertson and others suggest that this may be a reference to Peter's wife, who is known to have journeyed with him in his missionary travels (1 Cor 9:5). Clement of Alexandria even preserved an account of the encouragement that Peter offered her as she was led to a martyr's death (Clement of Alexandria *Strom.* 7.11.63). C. Bigg observed that it would be natural for a woman who had shared in her husband's ministry to wish to send her own greeting to churches that she too had served in the gospel. He finds Peter's inclusion of a message from his wife "a noble and distinctive feature of St. Peter's character and . . . a touch of nature which speaks strongly in favour of the genuineness of the Epistle" (Bigg, 77).

Like Sarah as she forsook a settled existence for a life of wanderings (1 Pet 3:6), Peter's spouse persevered as a steadfast companion to found a new community with a new and living faith. Men and women throughout the Roman empire* faced this same challenge when they embraced Jesus Christ as Savior and Lord* of their lives and became indeed "children of Sarah."

See also WOMAN AND MAN.

BIBLIOGRAPHY. C. Bigg, *A Critical and Exegetical Commentary on the Epistles of St. Peter and St. Jude* (ICC; Edinburgh: T & T Clark, 1961); W. den Boer, "Gynaeconitis, a Center of Christian Propaganda," *VC* 4 (1950) 61-64; A. J. Festugière, *Sainte Thècle, saints Côme et Damien, saints Cyr et Jean [extraits] saint George* (Paris: A. and J. Picard, 1971); R. Gryson, *The Ministry of Women in the Early Church* (Collegeville, MN: Liturgical Press, 1976); A. von Harnack, "Probability About the Address and Author of the Epistle to the Hebrews" in *The Bible Status of Woman*, ed. L. A. Starr (New York: Revell, 1926) 394-414; R. Harris, "The Problem of the Address in the Second Epistle of John," *Expositor* (1901) 194-203; E. E. Herzfeld and S. Euyer, *Miriamlik und Korkyos: zwei christliche Ruinenstätten des Ruhen Kilikiens* (MAMA 2; Manchester: Manchester University Press, 1930); D. R. MacDonald, *The Legend and the Apostle: The Battle for Paul in Story and in Canon* (Philadelphia: Westminster, 1983); M. L. McKenna, *Women of the Church: Role and Renewal* (New York: P. J. Kennedy and Sons, 1967); J. A. McNamara, *A New Song: Celibate Women in the First Three Christian Centuries* (New York: Harrington Park Press, 1985);

W. M. Ramsay, *The Church in the Roman Empire Before A.D. 170* (London: Hodder & Stoughton, 1893); D. W. Riddle, "Early Christian Hospitality: A Factor in the Gospel Transmission," *JBL* 57 (1938) 141-54; A. B. Spencer, *Beyond the Curse: Women Called to Ministry* (Nashville: Thomas Nelson, 1985); G. Stählin, "χήρα," *TDNT* 9:40-65; J. Viteau, "L'institution des diacres et des veuves—Actes 6:1-10, 8:4-40, 21:8," *RHE* 22 (1926) 532-36; A. Wire, *The Corinthian Women Prophets: A Reconstruction Through Paul's Rhetoric* (Minneapolis: Augsburg Fortress, 1990); B. Witherington III, *Women and the Genesis of Christianity* (Cambridge: Cambridge University Press, 1990); idem, *Women in the Earliest Churches* (SNTSMS 59; Cambridge: Cambridge University Press, 1988).

C. C. Kroeger

WORKS. *See* FAITH AND WORKS.

WORLD

The "world" *(kosmos)* is used in three main ways in the later NT: spatially, temporally and anthropologically. Spatially "world" is used to refer to the created order, the earth or the earth's inhabitants. Temporally "world" refers to the inception of creation* or of the age of creation or to contrast this life with the next. Anthropologically "world" includes all people at enmity with God* and is often used in a sharp contrast between the things and people who belong to God and the things and people who belong to "this world." All of these uses are carried forward in the writings of the early church fathers.

1. Spatial Concept
2. Temporal Concept
3. Anthropological Concept

1. Spatial Concept.
As we might expect from the English use of the word, "world" is used in various places in the later NT and early church fathers (*see* Apostolic Fathers) to refer to the created order. For example, God "made the world and everything in it" (Acts 17:24; cf. *1 Clem.* 19.2; 38.3; 60.1). God's judgment* of the creation in the flood narrative is what is meant by "world" in 2 Peter 3:6 (cf. Heb 10:5; 11:7, 38; 1 Pet 5:9). Sometimes "world" is used inclusively to encompass the entire universe, or sometimes it is used in a more specific way to designate the earth and its inhabitants, a usage continued in the early

church fathers (*1 Clem.* 5.7; 7.4; 9.4; 20.8; 28.2; 59.2; *Barn.* 4.12; 5.5; 21.5).

2. Temporal Concept.
"World" can also be used temporally in one of two ways. In the commonly used phrase "foundation of the world" it refers to the time before creation began. "World" is also use eschatologically* to contrast this age with the next.

2.1. "Foundation of the World." This common phrase in the later NT refers to the completion of God's act of creation in which his "works were finished from the foundation of the world" (Heb 4:3; cf. *Barn.* 5.5). The foundation of a building determines the structure and limits of the edifice erected upon it. So it is also with the world's foundation. This was the time when God set history on its course and when the plan of salvation* through Christ* was conceived, since he was "destined" to be the redeemer "before the foundation of the world" (1 Pet 1:20; Jn 17:24). Even the elect* are somehow distinguishable from this critical moment in time, their names "written before the foundation of the world in the book of life of the Lamb that was slain" (Rev 13:8; cf. Rev 17:8; *see* Lamb).

2.2. Eschatological Usage. James* poses the rhetorical question, "Has not God chosen those who are poor in the world to be rich in faith and heirs of the kingdom that he has promised to those who love him?" (Jas 2:5). Here "the world" is synonymous with "this life" in contrast to the next, where true wealth is found. Hebrews* may contain a passage with this same sense of the term. The roll call in Hebrews 11 lists some of the faith's heroes and heroines, who are said to have achieved their eschatological reward.* Their mistreatment when they were alive shows that this age did not deserve those "of whom the world was not worthy" (Heb 11:38). 2 Peter* makes escape from the defilement of this age a goal of the Christian life, for the author prays that believers "may escape from the corruption that is in the world" (2 Pet 1:4). This eschatological usage is virtually the only employment of the term *world* found in the *Didache* (*Did.* 10.6; 16.8) and *2 Clement* (*2 Clem.* 5.1, 5; 8.2-3; 19.3; *see* Clement of Rome) and is one way "world" is used by Ignatius* (Ign. *Rom.* 2.2; 3.2; 4.2) and in the *Epistle of Barnabas** (*Barn.* 10.11; 15.8).

3. Anthropological Concept.
3.1. The World at Enmity with God. The most common usage of "world" in James, 2 Peter and 1 John is to identify people at enmity with God, those who oppose God's will and purpose: "Do you not know that friendship with the world is enmity with God?" (Jas 4:4). Therefore a Christian is "to keep oneself unstained from the world" (Jas 1:27). 2 Peter describes the world as the place where antagonism toward God dwells, incurring "defilements" that need to be escaped (2 Pet 2:20; cf. Pol. *Phil.* 5.3; Ign. *Rom.* 3.3; 7.1).

3.2. The World in Johannine Literature. In 1 John (*see* John, Letters of) and John's Gospel, where more than half of the occurrences of *kosmos* in the NT occur, the focus is no longer on the world perceived as creation, but now the emphasis lies upon the world as people who have turned away from God to deceit and delusion (*see DJG,* World). 1 John depicts a sharp dichotomy between two sides, the world's and God's. The two are diametrically opposed, and his auditors must choose between the world and God. The world is considered apostate* from God, and the whole point of John's rhetoric is to urge full loyalty to God: "We know that we are of God, and the whole world is in the power of the evil one" (1 Jn 5:19); "they are of the world, therefore what they say is of the world and the world listens to them" (1 Jn 4:5). The believer is not to "love the world or the things in the world. If anyone loves the world, love for the Father is not in him" (1 Jn 2:15). Because the things of God and the people of God are in sharp opposition with the world, believers are not to be perplexed that the world "hates" them (1 Jn 3:13). Sinfulness originates from and belongs to this world and is to be avoided (1 Jn 2:16-17; cf. 1 Jn 4:3-5, 9). Similarly Ignatius sharply exhorts, "Do not talk about Jesus Christ while you desire the world" (Ign. *Rom.* 7.1).

Even though the world is characterized in so many negative ways in the Johannine writings, there is hope for it because Christ was sent "as the savior of the world" (1 Jn 4:14), and whoever has faith* in him will be victorious in overcoming the opposition of the world (1 Jn 5:4-5). It is worthwhile to compare this distinctive emphasis with the Fourth Gospel's characterization of the world as a place under God's mercy* (e.g., Jn 3:16-17; 12:47), though still in opposition to the truth* (Jn 15:18-19), and Johannine believers are rescued "from the world"

(Jn 17:6; cf. Jn 17:11) to which they are sent back (Jn 17:18). 1 John uses "world" sometimes in a sense that encompasses the entire sphere of people outside the church. This is how false teachers can be identified: they no longer side with the church but "have gone out into the world" (1 Jn 4:1). Since they are "of the world" they no longer should be heeded or trusted (1 Jn 4:5; cf. 2 Jn 7).

See also CREATION, COSMOLOGY; ESCHATOLOGY; HEAVEN, NEW HEAVEN; JOHN, LETTERS OF; KINGDOM OF GOD; SIN, WICKEDNESS.

BIBLIOGRAPHY. R. J. Bauckham, *Jude, 2 Peter* (WBC; Waco, TX: Word, 1983); R. E. Brown, *The Epistles of John* (AB; Garden City, NY: Doubleday, 1982); R. Bultmann, *The Johannine Epistles* (Herm; Philadelphia: Fortress, 1973); idem, *Theology of the New Testament* (2 vols.; New York: Scribners, 1951, 1955); J. Schneider, *Church and World in the New Testament* (Macon, GA: Mercer University Press, 1983). B. J. Dodd

WORSHIP AND LITURGY
    1. Encouragements and Cautions
    2. Method and Approaches
    3. Paul and the Pauline Legacy
    4. Evidence from Syria-Palestine
    5. The Rome-Asia Minor Axis
    6. Johannine Patterns and their Influence
    7. Some Conclusions

1. Encouragements and Cautions.
What could be said of worship as it may be understood from the evidence of the Pauline literature (*see DPL*, Worship) is equally valid in reference to the non-Pauline literature. That is, based on the traditions of belief and praxis inherited from Judaism,* Christian understanding and praise of God* expressed itself in acknowledging him as Creator and Redeemer.* God is still hailed as the sovereign Lord whose fiat brought the world into existence (Heb 11:3; Rev 4:11) through the mediation of the cosmic Christ* (Heb 1:2; John 1:3) and by whose will the creation* is sustained (Rev 4:11; cf. Col 1:15-18). The same God has acted savingly in the coming of Christ to rescue and restore the lost creation. Revelation 5:9-14 expresses this jubilation in lyric form, while the cosmic backdrop of the new age Christ has inaugurated is seen in Ignatius's* "song of the star" (Ign. *Eph.* 19.1-3; on this text as a Christ-hymn see Lohmeyer, 64; with further comment in Martin 1997, 10-13).

In a crisp, creedal* formulary, the incarnational-redemptive tag is given in 1 Peter 1:20 in a context of Christ's sacrifice* (1 Pet 1:18-19) and victory (1 Pet 3:21-22). Praise is thus directed to Israel's God, known as the Father of Jesus Christ (1 Pet 1:3) and the Father of those whose trust is in him (1 Pet 1:17; Heb 2:10-13; 1 Jn 1:3; 2:1, 13; 3:1) and who are part of the new creation that celebrates his grace* (Jas 1:18) in hymns* and in worship speech and acts (Rev 1:12-18; 19:10; 22:8-9; for such texts that forbid worship when angelomorphic beings were regarded as rivals to the one God, see L. T. Stuckenbruch).

Just as scholars, by applying form-critical methods to the Pauline letters, have identified several passages as liturgical (*see DPL*, Liturgical Elements), so by means of these same techniques parts of 1 Peter,* Hebrews,* James* and Revelation* have been treated as embodying worship forms and fragments (*see* Liturgical Elements; Hymns). Indeed, theories that have tried to understand whole NT books as emanating from a liturgical setting and incorporating rudimentary service directives have been proposed. This has tended to bring the entire approach into disrepute, with accusations of "pan-liturgism," that is, the misplaced confidence of being able to "detect reverberations of liturgy in the New Testament even where no liturgical note was originally struck" (Moule 1961, 7; cf. Dunn, 1990, §36). One notable example will illustrate the danger. Reasoning back from the Passover celebration which may underlie Hippolytus's order in the *Apostolic Tradition* (c. A.D. 215, at Rome), M. H. Shepherd (1960) proposed that the parallel structure he perceived in Revelation contained the framework of a fully developed baptismal liturgy, made up of interrogations; preparatory fastings, leading to the initiation itself; lessons from the Law, the Prophets and Gospel, with psalmody and a baptismal Eucharist. Aside from the debated issue of whether all these elements of worship are seen in Hippolytus, it raises much skepticism to think that the entire Apocalypse is a virtual transcript of a Paschal initiation rite, composed as a running commentary on what was happening liturgically. Much the same can be said for F. L. Cross's equally imaginative reconstruction of the scenario behind 1 Peter* as a baptismal liturgy.

To remain unconvinced by these somewhat outlandish proposals, which have not withstood critical scrutiny, however, does not cast doubt on the more reasoned bids to discover snatches of hymnic and confessional forms, baptismal images and reminders, Eucharistic prayers and catechetical instructions in several places of the NT corpus (*see* Liturgical Elements). Alert to the dangers of seeing liturgical data everywhere, we are not precluded from investigating the literary, stylistic and contextual shape of the passages under review with a view to placing them in a suitable *Sitz im Leben* of the churches' worshiping life and practice, if that placement throws light on their origin and gives an extra dimension to their point.

Two other considerations, moreover, pose a warning as we seek to deduce what worship was like in the congregations reflected in our texts. One is the temptation to harmonize. In the case of the Pauline materials, the task of constructing a picture of the worshiping life of his communities was not hampered by an impossible diversity. Churches on the Pauline foundation, while different in cultural background and outlook and facing several problems, were at least kept together by their common allegiance to Paul and his colleagues and belonged together as a corpus within a manageable time frame. The biblical books under review in this article have no such unifying thread and represent a wide spectrum of diverse cultures, interests, compositions and challenges, to say nothing of the multiform nature of the literature in its genre (Acts, epistles, apocalypse) we are seeking to encompass. Given these inconcinnities, to collate the worship styles and practices with their meanings across such a wide terrain into an intelligible picture is almost an impossible venture; and to seek to harmonize the different features and findings so as to yield a common pattern is to run the risk of a false harmonization which will only distort the evidence and give a wrong impression. When we attempt a summing up, this caveat will need to be borne in mind and a question-mark will need to be reasserted against those attempts to find in too detailed a way a basic liturgical unity within the late apostolic period (see Cullmann, 7-36; Bradshaw 1992, 37).

The other pitfall is that mentioned in Bradshaw's handbook, *The Search for the Origins of Christian Worship* (1992), which by its title confesses to the tentative nature of any reconstructions of early worship and the danger of reading back from the later liturgies the evidence that all too easily we profess to find in the earlier (NT) documents. This method was the outstanding feature of H. Lietzmann's celebrated monograph, *Mass and Lord's Supper* (ET 1953, 1978), which sought to work backward from the service books and later manuals to the more fragmentary and disputed data. As a technique this may be defended, but it exposes the readers to a false impression that Christian worship developed in a linear fashion, and that we can trace the lines of development with unbounded confidence.

2. Method and Approaches.

The merit, however, of Lietzmann's approach was that it gave due respect to the origins of worship patterns in the differing geographical areas from which such service books came, using a technique that W. Bauer also employed in the same period as Lietzmann's work appeared (Bauer in 1934; Lietzmann's *Messe und Herrenmahl* in 1926). While the Bauer-Lietzmann approach is open to criticism in several of its aspects (see Turner, T. A. Robinson), there is less criticism when a similar appreciation of geographical spread is seen to underlie B. H. Streeter's works. There is no denying that early Christianity expanded across key areas of the ancient world from the Syrian Levant (*see* Syria, Syrian Christianity) to centers and hinterlands of the Greco-Roman provinces, including Rome itself (*see* Rome, Roman Christianity; Alexandria, Alexandrian Christianity; Centers of Christianity).

Equally it is true that the configurations of Christian life and worship, along with the more important aspects of belief and praxis, changed according to the places that spawned the literature emanating from such regions. Granted that in several cases the tie-in between location and literature is problematic, and we have to rest content with informed guesswork and sometimes speculation, yet it is undeniable that the pluriformity of expression of both teaching and expected life-style represented in the documents of the later NT and its developments into the so-called apostolic fathers is an attested reality. It provides a suitable framework for the evolution of worship styles and practices. The close connectedness of belief and worship, incidentally, is now an obvious datum on the principle *lex orandi, lex credendi* (how a person prays is an expression of that person's beliefs). The data will amply illustrate this linkage as we proceed to pass the evidence under review according to hypothetical geographical *stemma.*

The functionality of this approach will, we hope, be clear, and its serviceability seen in that it obviates the more simplistic way of treating the NT books *seriatim* and/or in canonical sequence. An alterative approach might have been to follow the lead of Koester and Robinson with their proposed trajectories or lines of development as we pass each aspect of worship practices under review and observe, for example, how baptism* was understood from its chronological beginnings in the post-Pentecost church(es) to the second-century congregations of Ignatius, Justin and the Marcionite* conventicles. This method might well have served the readers' interests, were it not for the possible misleading impression it would give that early liturgical observances developed in a system of end-on evolution. The truth rather is that often the local conditions that emerged in distinct and distinctive regions provided pressure points that shaped the growth or malformation of worship no less than the rise of "heresy and orthodoxy." This was the case until what emerged as "normative Christianity" (to use Hultgren's nomenclature) began to be dominant and was seen to be so in light of the embryonic creedal statements embodied in the traditions and the *regula fidei* from the mid-second or late-second century onward. In each case the items cherished as "normative" took shape within the setting of the cultural climate of the place on the map as well as under the constraints of local problems and their solutions.

3. The Pauline Legacy.

The contributions to the topic that stemmed from Paul's correspondence with his congregations have been noted elsewhere (*see DPL*, Worship). In summary, these distinctives were related to the need to regulate the use of spiritual gifts in a situation (such as Corinth) which had become chaotic and unbridled. Paul's response is given in terms of a practical reiteration of the tension between the already and the not-yet elements in Christian salvation. Believers are now in God's realm where Christ's lord-

ship is acknowledged in worship (1 Cor 12:3). Yet the fullness of their redemption is set in the future, at the Parousia when God's final kingdom will be established (1 Cor 15:28). The worship cry, "God is really here" (1 Cor 14:25) needs to be heard in this context, uniting both the reality of present salvation and its necessary futurity at the end time, which will usher in the resurrection of the dead (1 Cor 15:42). In the interim of the church's life "between the times," the emphases Paul makes are in terms of an exercise of love and thankfulness for God's acts in Christ and the altruistic call to build up the body of believers (1 Cor 14:3, 12, 17, 26; 1 Cor 12:7).

These same emphases, boldly remarked in his Corinthian correspondence, come over into Paul's later writings, whether treated as his final reflections from a Roman near the end of his days or as the legacy he bequeathed to his followers who published letters to churches that claimed to be on a Pauline foundation, at Colossae, Ephesus and its environs (*see* Pauline Legacy/School). As might well be expected, there are fresh emphases since new situations have emerged. In particular the need to consolidate the church, now dubbed "the pillar and bulwark of the truth" (1 Tim 3:15), is evident in the face of new doctrines, and its witness needs to be safeguarded against false teachers who deny the (future) resurrection. So in baptismal confessions (2 Tim 2:11-13; Tit 3:4-7), sometimes prefaced by the formula of a "trusted word," and in christological hymns (e.g., 1 Tim 3:16, introduced by "we confess") the Pauline gospel is reasserted as deserving of all acceptance (1 Tim 1:15). This is accompanied by the cardinal teachings of one God and one mediator (1 Tim 2:5-7), known to be Paul's strong conviction. Jewish-Christian prayer language is scattered through these letters (e.g., 1 Tim 1:17), partly to demonstrate the church's close ties with its roots and partly to restate the (Jewish) belief in the goodness of God's creation, which is hallowed by prayer based on Psalm 24:1 (1 Tim 4:4-5).

The baptismal teachings in Colossians-Ephesians have given rise to debate, chiefly on the issue whether they mark a divergence from Paul's careful distinction as we saw between what is true now (we are being saved) and the future hope (we shall be saved—in hope of the Parousia, Rom 5:9-10; 6:1-14). Colossians emphasizes the present possession of salvation (Col 1:12-14) and reconciliation (Col 1:21-22), with the hymn of Colossians 1:15-20 inserted to celebrate the completeness of the universe's restoration to harmony with the Creator's will and the pacification of the evil powers (Col 2:15). Believers have entered into the benefit of Christ's cosmic triumph at baptism (Col 2:12-13) with no explicit eschatological proviso of what still awaits completion at the Parousia. But the eschatological hope, while it is muted, sounds in Colossians 3:3, so it may be fairly claimed that Colossians reflects the true Pauline tradition at this point.

Less confidence is engendered, however, in the case of Ephesians. Here the implied baptismal setting of Ephesians 1:13-14, where "the seal of the Spirit" became a shorthand expression for a person's baptism (Lampe), though it does look on to the future possession of salvation, seems rather to situate the church's hope in the present (Eph 2:1-10; 5:14) and to reflect a fading of an imminent Parousia. The church is already raised to the heavenly places (Eph 2:6) where the regnant Christ has begun his rule (Eph 1:22-23, a creedal fragment, it is believed). This noble prose poem celebrates Christ's lordship in exalted, hieratic terms drawn from the worship idioms of the Asian churches. Such an eclipse of the apocalyptic* denouement, associated with Christ's return from heaven, may well be explained by the unique occasion of Ephesians, if its purpose is more doxological than edificatory or polemical. The nuances of liturgical language have given rise to the idea of the church as already triumphant and transcendent in its heavenly glory now and indeed as taking its place within the creedal confession (Eph 4:4-5), as though the church professes belief in itself—a forerunner of the sentence in the Apostles' Creed ("I believe in . . . one, holy, catholic, apostolic church")—and has its place in salvation history securely grounded on a (true) apostolic base (Eph 2:20; 3:5).

4. Evidence from Syria-Palestine.

4.1. Jerusalem. It is not easy to separate out from the data and descriptions in the book of Acts* what is objective historical reporting of church life and practice in the holy city (*see* Jerusalem; Jewish Christianity) and the holy land, with extensions to the Syrian province from Damascus to Antioch* (Acts 8:1; 9:19;

11:19-29; 13:1-3), and Luke's conscious bid to idealize the scenes in the interests of his own theological viewpoints. Perhaps the truth lies in a mediating position. Assuming that the writing of Luke is meant to have an edificatory purpose (so both Haenchen, 103-110; and Marshall, 33), it would be natural to suppose that the author recalls the early days of the church not in a nostalgic vein but in order to point up certain lessons for the church of his own day. He tells the story, based on reliable eyewitness testimony, he believed (Lk 1:1-4; Acts 1:1), of how it was in the beginning when the Spirit first came on God's new creation. He raises the cry *ad fontes*: back to the fountainhead of the church's early moments, yet he does so with a view to recapturing the past as he retells it so as to make it speak to his present. Luke's successive pictures of the church at worship are arranged to drive home a single point—that worship in his church needs to recover the emphases and features that marked the first generation, with the Holy Spirit's* power* in evidence (Acts 4:31; 13:1-3), giving rise to great freedom* and joy* (Acts 2:46, 47) and fidelity to apostolic norms (Acts 2:42).

Initiation into the community life is by baptism—based on ritual baths in distinctive Judaisms, both mainline and sectarian (Qumran, Therapeutae)—in the name of Jesus (Acts 2:38). This was a practice that spread with the expansion of the message to embrace disciples in Samaria (Acts 8:12), in Caesarea (Acts 10:47-48), in Damascus (Acts 9:18 and par.) as well as more remote, unspecified regions as the Gaza strip (Acts 8:36: v. 37 mg. in the Western reading offers a fuller account of the baptismal interrogation and response). Initiation "in the name" of Jesus (Christ) was evidently meant to confess his messianic headship of the new community and the place individuals had in this messianic group as a mark of the new age he brought. Little further theologizing of baptism is found, though Acts 19:1-7 poses the problems associated with groups that had known only John's baptism. If Acts 10 (baptism and receiving the Spirit in the home of Cornelius*) is meant to imply a Gentile* Pentecost* (cf. Lampe, chap. 5, Dunn 1970, 80-82; 1975, 154-56), then the baptism of John's disciples accompanied by the imposition of hands and gifts of tongues* and prophecy* may well indicate to Luke's readers how "disciples" become full-blown believers in Jesus as Lord.*

On face value the record in Acts gives cameo pictures of the worshiping/communal life in Jerusalem (notably at Acts 2:41-47; 4:32-35) as ideal scenes, meant to challenge and rebuke later loss of "apostolic simplicity." Features that marked out the earliest community fresh from its Pentecostal experience and radiating the Spirit's joy (Acts 2:26 based on Ps 16:8-11; cf. Acts 2:46) include above all the theme of exultant praise, whether the locale is the temple (Acts 3:1-10) or private residences (Acts 1:3; 2:46; 9:11; 9:36-43; 10:1-8, 24; 12:12). Prayers were offered for guidance (Acts 1:23-25) and for courage in the face of threats and dangers (Acts 4:23-31), though the reference to "the prayers" (Acts 2:42) suggests a continued adherence to the Jewish temple liturgy (Dugmore).

The "apostles' teaching" has been customarily regarded as a sign of early catechetical instruction, while "fellowship"* indicates either a generalized reference to common life or, more specifically, to the material contributions expected, but not demanded, of each member (Acts 4:32; 5:1-11, Jeremias once believed 2:42 referred to the offering as *koinonia*, but changed his mind; see Cullmann, 120). The "breaking of bread" is a Jewish expression for a meal occasion, presumably a communal social event in which food was shared and eaten as a sign of mutual love* (hence the name *agapē*, see Jude 12 where intruding teachers have "defiled" such convivial gatherings; and 2 Pet 2:13 if *agapais*, is read in place of *apatais*, see Bauckham, 1983; Ign. *Smyrn.* 8:2, *Acts of Paul and Thecla* 5, 25 shows how the practice persisted into later decades). If *Didache* 9—10 gives the text of prayers at the love-meal (see 4.2 below), how such meal occasions were understood may be revealed and the way the agape functioned as a prelude to the later solemn Eucharist of the Lord's sacrifice (*Didache* 14:1) is evident, perhaps explaining the link in 1 Corinthians 11:17-22 as a preparatory rite of sharing, paving the way for the solemn Pauline meal in 1 Corinthians 11:23-26.

Special mention should be made of the invocatory prayer, *maranatha* (found untranslated in its Aramaic form in 1 Cor 16:22; *Did.* 10.6). It may be claimed that here we have the oldest surviving prayer specimen, with one possible exception (an inscription on an ossuary found in Jerusalem with the wording, "Jesus (let the one who rests here) arise," thereby invoking Jesus as Lord of resurrection* (So B. Gustafsson, *NTS 3, 1956-57, 65-9.* But this interpretation of the graffito is contested, *see* J. P. Kane, *PEQ* 1971, 103-08). *Maranatha* is a composite word, almost certainly to be divided as *māranā' tā'* (Fitzmyer) and meaning, "Our Lord, come," expressing a prayer call for the Lord (i.e., Jesus) to be present either at the Eucharist (Cullmann) or the eschaton. The evidence at this point is finely balanced, *Didache* 10.6 is part of a meal liturgy while Revelation 22:20 ("even so, come, Lord Jesus") looks to be a variant of *maranatha* and is eschatological.* The setting is perhaps not exclusively one or the other; what counts is the existence of a cultus, however rudimentary, where the risen Christ is invoked in prayer as a forerunner of later, more developed invocations and hymns.

If we are safe in including as representative of early Jewish Christianity the letters of James* and Jude,* the picture may be enlarged. Jude's epistle is notable for its fulsome liturgical ending (Jude 24, 25). This feature provides a window into how Christian praying matched human need in one of the earliest NT letters emanating from Palestinian Christianity (Bauckham). The idioms in these two prayer verses correspond exactly to the felt need of the community, exposed as it was to dangers from antinomian intruders (Jude 4) and the threat of apostasy* from a common faith (Jude 3, 22; Martin 1994, 80-81). Links with Davidic heritage represented by the holy family (Jude 1; *see* Relatives of Jesus) and the catechetical apostolic traditions (Jude 17) show affinity with the situation mirrored in the *Didache*. The teaching office of prophets and leaders is the bulwark against some influences boasting of ecstatic experiences and a trust in immediate spiritual inspiration (Jude 8; Martin 1994, 83-4).

James's* letter may well embody early Judaic traditions (Davids) that go back to Palestinian communities. Such traditions and teachings may conceivably have been carried to Antioch in Syria, where an editor fashioned them into our existing letter with its excellent Greek and literary flourishes. Liturgical practices may reflect this dual setting and include a heavy emphasis on prayer in faith (Jas 1:6), especially for an individual's healing by elders at prayer (Jas 5:13-16), once confession and forgiveness* are realized and oil applied (on the possible significance of the use of oil here, see Martin 1993,

124-26). The church has an honored teaching office (Jas 3:1-12) with possible suggestions of ecstatic speech as causing problems (Martin 1988, 103, 123-24). The "excellent name" (Jas 2:7) is one invoked in baptism; and it is proposed that James 2:2, 3 conceals the presence of a church/synagogue "door-keeper," known in the later church as *ostiarius* (Cabaniss 1954, 29).

4.2. Antioch-Syria. The material associated with the northern part of Syro-Palestine (*see* Antioch; Syria, Syrian Christianity) is more plentiful—if we are permitted to base our conjecture of appropriate documents from this region on some recent findings, then the NT books will include (the redacted version of) James* and Matthew's Gospel (*see* Matthean Community), to which we may add *Didache** and Ignatius's* letters. In listing these Christian writings it is interesting that the first three are joined by at least one shared feature: they depend on and draw from the oracles/teachings of the Lord that modern research has identified as "source strand" in the Synoptic Gospels, namely Q. Antioch has been identified (since Streeter's time) as the most likely place where this collection of the Lord's sayings was assembled and used. The three main documents do not belong to the same literary category. Matthew shares the genre "gospel," or more precisely *biblos* (Mt 1:1). The *Didache* is a church order-cum- "manual of discipline" incorporating earlier and common traditions known as the "Two Ways" (*Did.* 1-6; *Barn.* 18-20). James is usually classified as paraenetic miscellany (Dibelius, 3), but it has been editorially completed to conform to the rhetorical* genre of "epistle" with both a superscription (Jas 1:1) and letter-close (Jas 5:12-20). Yet all three documents do possess common elements (cf. Shepherd 1956) and each, along with the logia source (Q; see Hartin), may be justifiably located in congregations in the same geographical region, namely around Antioch on the Orontes.

For our purposes we may note the following items in the worship life of these communities. (1) Much is made of the role of the teacher, who is to be honored (Mt 13:52; *Did.* 4:1-4; 13:2; 15:2; Jas 3), with due caution that no one should aspire to the office too hastily (Mt 23:1-12; Jas 3:1). (2) Baptism is administered in the triune name as a distinct development from initiation in the name of the (Lord) Jesus found in Acts

(see Mt 28:18-20; *Did.* 7:1-3; Jas 2:7 may allude to baptism in referring to the "worthy name" called over messianic believers). (3) Prayers couched in language and idioms directly indebted to Jewish synagogue worship (Mt 6:7-13 which incorporates the prayer "Our Father"; see Charlesworth), given in its Matthean form in *Didache* 8:2-3 with instructions to pray thus thrice daily. In James 1:13-16 the use of prayer is treated as a pastoral issue. All documents emphasize the role of corporate praying based on God's role as heavenly parent (Mt 5:16; 6:9; 16:17; *Did.* 9:1; 10:1; Jas 1:17, 27; 5:13-18), with special stress laid on the need for mutual forgiveness and confession leading to reconciliation and absolution (Mt 5:21-26; 6:12, 14-15; 18:21-22, 35; *Did.* 1:4; 2:7; 4:3-4; 14:1-3; Jas 2:8; 4:11; 5:16, 19-20). Fasting is a token of true worship, along with almsgiving (Mt 6:1-4, 16-18; *Did.* 1:5-6; 4:5-8; 7:4; 8:1-3; 13:3-7; Jas 1:27; 2:15, 16 on giving to the needy). (4) Confession of belief in the one God (a hallmark of Jewish Christianity derived from the *shema* of Judaism, Deut 6:4) runs through these documents (Mt 19:17; 22:37; 23:9; *Did.* 6:3 against idolatry; Jas 2:19).

(5) Special attention is drawn to the observance of the eucharistic service based on the Last Supper words in Matthew 26:26-29 (*see* Lord's Supper). In the main, these dominical statements conform to the Markan wording, with the important exceptions that the cup word is enlarged to connect the "blood of the covenant" represented in the cup with the forgiveness of sins ("which is poured out for many for the forgiveness of sins"). It has been surmised that for theological reasons, since remission of sins was evidently a live issue in the Matthean community, the evangelist has transferred the promise of forgiveness* from the Markan version of John the Baptist's role (Mk 1:4; cf. however, Mt 3:4-6) to his version of the Last Supper. He did so in order to relate forgiveness more intimately with the impending death* of the Lord. The sacrificial motifs expressed in Matthew's upper-room account links with *Didache* 14.1-3, which is best taken to refer to the church's Sunday Eucharist in contradistinction to the teaching expressed in the prayers of *Didache* 9—10, which are more suitably explained in reference to an agape meal. They contain no allusion to the Lord's death (unless "broken bread," *klasma*, makes this connection,

but it is more likely drawn from the non-eucharistic setting of Jn 6) and are patterned on the Jewish table prayers (*birkath hammazon*; see for these examples of grace after meals in Jasper and Cuming, 9-10) in spite of the occasion being titled as *eucharistia* in *Didache* 9.5. A convincing datum is in *Didache* 10.1 ("But after you are filled [with food]" which suggests that the meals in view in *Didache* 9—10 are taken to satisfy natural hunger, not to serve as sacramental reminders.

The issue, however, is still unresolved (see Srawley, 18-25; Bradshaw 1992, 132-37, for a conspectus of opinion). The safest conclusions are that both canonical Gospel and the *Didache* are tentative data for the deep roots of the liturgy in Jewish covenantal theology, and the patterns of table fellowship and solemn celebration have some intimate connection with both the synagogue service and the table graces of the Jewish tradition, into which the Matthean Jesus has injected overtones of his atoning sacrifice. *Didache* 14 only faintly echoes this in its allusion to sacrifice/offering (*thysia*, 3 times) which is drawn from Malachi 1:11, 14.

(6) Set in the dialogical form of the prayers in *Didache* 10.6 is the versicle/response:

Let grace come, and let this world pass away
Hosanna to the God of David.
If any one is holy, let that person come!
If any is not, let such repent.
Marana tha [our Lord, come!]
Amen.

The framework suggests a call to self-scrutinizing (already the table is "fenced" in *Didache* 9.5, citing Matt 7:6) before the congregational meal is taken, akin to the rubrics implied by Paul in 1 Corinthians 11:27-34; 16:22, 23 (see Bornkamm 1969; J. A. T. Robinson). What comes through in this dialogue is the immediacy of judgment/invitation and welcome stemming from the presence of the Lord with his people. He comes to meet them and greet the penitent with offers of his grace now as a prelude to his coming at the last day (*Did.* 16.7, 8, noting Mt 24:30), an eschatological note sounded in both Matthew 26:29 and frequent in James 5:7-11. Yet it is the awareness of the living Lord in the midst of his own that shows how these Syrian Christians had grasped the genius of early worship as an encounter with the risen Christ who comes to meet those gathered in his name (Mt 18:20; 28:20; a variant is seen in *Gos.*

Thom. 30, cf. 77) as their call to him is "Hosanna," that is, "Save now!" "Blessed is he who comes in the Lord's name. Hosanna in the highest!" (Mt 21:9).

Ignatius of Antioch picks up this last-mentioned realization exactly in his dictum: "Wherever Jesus Christ is, there is the universal church" (Ign. *Smyrn.* 8.2), as if to emphasize the unrestrictedness of the risen Lord who comes to join his people as they sing their hymns* through Christ to the Father (Ign. *Eph.* 4.2) and recognize that he is dwelling in them (Ign. *Eph.* 15.3) as members of God's Son* (Ign. *Eph.* 4.2). The earlier description (Ign. *Eph.* 4) offers the attractive picture of a Christian assembly in which "by your concord and harmonious love Jesus Christ is sung," with its suggestion that Christ is not only the mediator but also the object of hymnic praise (so Kroll, 19; Bauer 1924, 204). Granted that Ignatius is using the features of the liturgy—notably unison, harmony, the right key as in music (*eine Tonart*, so Dölger, 127)—to drive home the need for church unanimity and a closing of ranks behind and in submission to the ecclesiastical leaders (Ign. *Eph.* 5.3), it still affords some confirmation of the centrality of Christ in his depictions of worship.

Specimens of Ignatian hymnody are seen in *Ephesians* 7.2 (Kroll, 20, points to the semitic coloring, the elevated style, the antithetical sentences and their interrelatedness to suggest a snatch of creedal-hymnic material; cf. Norden, 256-57). Thus we read:

[there is] One physician,
who is both flesh and spirit,
born and yet not born.
God in man, true life in death,
both from Mary and from God,
first, subject to suffering,
then, impassible,
Jesus Christ our Lord.
(Ign. *Eph.* 7.2)

This antithetical pattern occurs also in Melito's* homily and is amplified in Ignatius's *Letter to the Ephesians* 19, expounding the "silence" of *Ephesians* 15.2, in which three mysteries were accomplished: the virginity of Mary,* her giving birth and the Lord's death. He was revealed to the "Aeons" (Bultmann, 1.177) and in the appearance of his natal star, which illumined the heavens with indescribable brightness and attracted the veneration of the constellations, including the sun and the moon, the new age was born. "When God appeared in human form to bring the newness of eternal life," all the cosmos was affected, with the ancient (demonic) astral powers overthrown and death itself defeated.

This celebration of Christ's victory and reign was evidently meant to be sung in veneration as the planetary powers too join in a chorus (Ign. *Eph.* 19.2), once we link the text with Ignatius's *Letter to the Romans* 2.2: "You form a chorus of love in singing to the Father in Christ Jesus."

A similar confession-like tribute to Christ is offered as part of Ignatius's anti-docetic polemic (*see* Docetism, for example, in *Trallians* 9.1-2 (cf. *Smyrn.* 1:1—3:3), which again may be cast in verse form (by Norden, 266). This christological text rehearses the movements of Christ's birth, earthly career, condemnation "under Pontius Pilate" (pointing to the Apostles' Creed), death on the cross (attested by all the powers, heavenly and demonic, Phil 2:10 in Paul providing the exact wording) and resurrection. All these events are connected by the adverb "truly," with the result they lay the foundation for "true" life in the church's resurrection.

Ignatius's recourse to creedal and hymnic forms obviously have a polemical thrust, yet they do throw light on how he conceived of congregational worship in the centers to which he wrote. His great fear was that of the churches' becoming fragmented and being dissipated by schism. Hence his call is to rally round the bishop and his officers (Ign. *Phil.* 3.1-3), which leads him to lift up the central role of the Eucharist as the church's focal point, with the *episkopos* as the indispensable ministrant (Ign. *Smyrn.* 8.1-2; *Pol.* 6.1-2). Moreover, the Eucharist for Ignatius now takes on a quasi-magical significance, seen most starkly in *Ephesians* 20.3, which calls it "the medicine of immortality, the antidote that we should not die, but live forever in Jesus Christ." Again, it is possible the constraints of false teaching which in turn led to rebellion against "the bishop and the presbytery" drove Ignatius to this strongly worded eucharistic teaching, since the sentence is introduced by the renewed call to unity based on "breaking one loaf" (cf. 1 Cor 10:17 in Paul).

When Ignatius writes of worship practices, mainly of baptism, confession, creedal formulas and the Eucharist, it is difficult to know whether he is describing traditions current at Antioch where he was bishop or the various centers through which he passed or to which he was headed. We may assume some common cultic practices since he makes these allusions the basis of his appeal, all set in a trinitarian frame (Ign. *Magn.* 13.1), typifying the threefold clerical ministry (bishop, elder, deacon).

5. The Rome-Asia Minor Axis.
Interestingly the parameters of this section are set by two scenes that represent an early cameo of worship in Asia Minor (Acts 20:7-12) and nearly a century later a more detailed description of how worship was understood in Rome* c. A.D. 150 (Justin Apol. *I* 67). While these two accounts are separated in time and by background, what is significant is the common elements they share. (1) The time is "the first day of the week," later to be known as "the day called Sunday" (Justin, *Dial. Tryph.* 41.4; 138.1; *see* Lord's Day). *Barnabas* 15.3-9 gives the theological reasoning behind this shift from Sabbath to the day following, "the eighth day," when Jesus rose and was made manifest and ascended to heaven,* thereby claiming the day of celebration as his own (Rev 1:10; *Did.* 14:1; *Gos. Pet.* 12.50) as the risen Lord who greeted his own people at a Sunday eucharistic meal, in accordance with the Gospel evidence (Jn 20:19; Lk 24:30, 41-43; cf. Acts 1:3-4; Rordorf 1992; McKay).

(2) The nature of the assembled company is understood as a "gathering" (*synēgmenōn* in Acts 20:7, a verbal form from which "synagogue" is derived; cf. Jas 2:2; Heb 10:25 for this verb/ noun) as people come together, with the emphasis falling more on their associating than on a consecrated building or space. At this time Christians met in house congregations. Special structures are to be dated from the third/fourth centuries, with the earliest, best-attested example at Dura-Europos in Syria, c. A.D. 256 (Hopkins; *see* Architecture, Early Church). Yet the format and ethos of synagogue worship (see Morris, with more cautious approach in McKay) carried over into the Christian synaxis (a technical term for such a gathering, as the word implied).

(3) The setting in Acts 20 suggests a two-part arrangement of public speaking (by Paul) and a meal occasion (Acts 20:11) with some more discourse to follow. This interrelation of sermon and sacrament provided the basis for the

later development of the liturgy of the Word followed by the liturgy of the upper room. One of the clearest illustrations of this dual rhythm is in fact provided in Justin, who proceeds in his description: "the memoirs of the apostles or the writings of the prophets are read. . . . When the reader has finished, the president in a discourse urges and invites [us] to imitate these noble things. . . . And, as we said before [Justin *Apol. I* 65 refers to the presenting of bread and a cup of water-and-wine, over which prayers of thanks are offered, regarded as consecrated, and then shared and distributed to those absent], when we have finished the prayer, bread is brought, and wine and water," followed by prayers and the offering. Justin sums up: "We all hold this common gathering on Sunday."

The stark simplicity of these details captures some of the basic ingredients of worship in the period c. A.D. 50-150, with suitable variations that are distinctive to each part of the Rome-Asia Minor axis.

For what developed in Asia we need to turn to the Johannine* writings. Yet the witness in the cognate epistles, Colossians-Ephesians in the Pauline corpus, must find a place in any appreciation of how worship was practiced in the churches of Paul's foundation. Colossians 3:16-17 (par. Eph 5:19-20) provides evidence of congregational assemblies who met to admonish one another in both instruction ("in all wisdom"; cf. 1 Cor 12:8 for "utterances of wisdom" as a spiritual charism) and singing of hymns (evidently christological compositions) along with psalms (perhaps drawn from the Hebrew psalter or Jewish-Christian canticles, *see DPL*, Hymns) and "songs of the Spirit" (cf. *Odes Sol.* 14:7). All such tributes were intended to express thanks to God, and so formed part of the genre *hodayah/eucharistia*, which Bradshaw (1981, 30-7; 1992, 44) maintains with some cogency, was more characteristic than the *berakah/eulogia* type in early Christianity. Expressions of praise occur in Colossians 1:3, 12-14 with the longer, more stately and measured version in Ephesians 1:3-14, which rehearses the ground-plan of salvation-history in a trinitarian frame (Martin 1992, 13-15). Indeed the first three chapters of Ephesians have been viewed as based on a transcript of praise familiar in the Asian congregations and as celebrating the characteristic themes of the success of the Pauline gospel in repelling challenges to it (cf.

1 Tim 1:15) and the pivotal role of the apostle as its chief exponent.

Hymnic specimens are clearly to be seen in these letters. Colossians 1:15-20 has evidently been subject to authorial redaction, and it is just possible (if not likely) that it incorporates a pre-Christian version in praise of gnostic redemption (Käsemann 1964: see critique in the commentaries). As it stands, it announces the universal reconciliation that both rests on Christ's redemptive work (Col 1:20) and includes his authority* as head of the ecclesial body (Col 1:18). Both these themes are important in the polemical use made of them, as seen in Ephesians 2:11-22 (incorporating, it may be, a pre-Pauline version) and in the teaching of true headship as Christ's role as heavenly bridegroom is unpacked (Eph 5:32). Moreover, Ephesians 5:14 contains one of the clearest evidences of baptismal hymnody in the Asian churches, with its swinging, trochaic rhythm and its motifs of paraenesis and application sounded in the wake-up call to move forward in Christ's light that first shone on the baptismal candidate, who is cleansed in water (Eph 5:26).

Clearly in these twin epistles we are in touch with the vibrant worshiping life that pulsated through these communities as the author(s) faced threats to Paul's apostolate and authority in Asia. The use of liturgical idioms (such as "to the praise of his glory," Eph 1:6, 12, 14), baptismal recall (in Col 1:12-14; 2:11-14; Eph 5:26) and eucharistic language (*eucharisteiō*, "to thank," is a frequent idea in Eph), along with creedal expressions (e.g., Eph 4:4-6) and samples of prayer-speech—all give indications of the letters as steeped in a liturgical atmosphere. They were meant to be read out in congregational assembly (Col 4:16) and passed on to neighboring churches, evidently at worship gatherings when their pastoral and didactic appeal would be most effective in catching the mood of praise and exultation (especially Ephesians, as in Paul's opening benedictions generally; see O'Brien) and bidding the hearers to participate in (and thereby to accept) the truth claims they make.

Ignatius, also reflecting the life-setting of the Asian churches, followed in this tradition of letter-writing habits. As we observed, many of his allusions to music, creed and adherence to the teachings are cited to repel what he regarded as error and seem to have the scenario of the churches at worship in view. Indeed, H. Schlier (48-49) regards Ignatius's *Letter to the Ephesians* 4 as showing his acquaintance with Paul's representation of the church's gathering for worship in canonical Ephesians 5:15-21.

It could also be submitted that the ordering of church life in the Pastoral Epistles, equally of Asian provenance, could have led to Ignatius's view of a strictly hierarchical government of bishop and presbyters and deacons (see 1 Tim 3:1-3; Tit 1:7-9), who are shown to be faithful in maintaining discipline* and repulsing deviance from apostolic-Pauline norms by inculcating sound teaching and promoting worship in a proper manner (1 Tim 4:11-16). False notions must be exposed and denounced by Timothy's recourse to the church's confessions of faith and creedal formulas (1 Tim 3:16, whose introductory sentence is a sign of the six-line, hymnic-poetic christological tribute that follows; 2 Tim 2:11-13). Worship functions in the pastors' congregations as a stabilizing, boundary-fixing marker (see MacDonald), whose effect is to close ranks within an inward-looking community. This body of literature evinces a trait, shared alike by Ignatius and Ephesians, of the church's assuming a role in salvation history centered on itself as an article of its faith (Eph 4:4, and often in Ignatius; cf. 1 Tim 4:15). We are here on the threshold of ecclesiastical history, where the church itself is part of God's salvific plan (Eph 3:10) and sees no incongruity—indeed it rejoices in this—that it professes to believe in itself. "I believe in . . . one, holy, catholic, apostolic church" is a sentence ready to be inserted in the creed.

If we wanted to see how the church's liturgical acts were becoming integrated into its understanding of its message and mission, the thrust conveyed in the letter to the Hebrews* would provide encouragement. By common consent, this sermon-like (Heb 13:22) document (*see* Rhetoric) reflects Roman Christianity in the post-A.D. 70 decades of the first Christian century (*see* Rome, Roman Christianity). The author's purpose is stated with clarity: it is to show the finality and superiority of the new economy brought by Christ who is both ministrant (Heb 2:10-13; 8:2) and sacrifice (Heb 9—10) in the new sanctuary. Repeatedly his arguments and appeals are punctuated with liturgical idioms, often drawn from the levitical prototypes but always suffused with and cor-

rected by Christian overtones (e.g., Heb 13:10-16). The language of offering and sacrifice is pressed into service in order to highlight the immeasurable greatness of the new covenant, based on the better sacrifice of Jesus (since it was made once-for-all) and the better effectiveness (securing a full and final forgiveness). Yet the high priestly* ministry of Jesus continues in a heavenly sanctuary (e.g., Heb 7:25; 9:24; 13:10, sometimes taken in a eucharistic sense, see Dunnill 240-42), and the implied call is made that the church is to share in this worship of God through him who is the perfect worshiper (Heb 2:11-12; 13:12-16).

This is an aspect of worship here receiving its emphasis in a unique way (in the NT) but with repercussions that were later to be enlarged and felt in the decades (e.g., *1 Clem* 36:1; 40:1-5) and centuries to come. Worship is both "through Christ" (Heb 13:15) and "in Christ," making the church one with his self-offering (Heb 7:25) so that its sacrifices of praise are joined with the one offering that is both complete (once-for-all, *eph' hapax*) and ever-renewed as it is freshly appropriated by and mediated to the believing community. Hebrews 13:17 mentions the leaders who serve the community; *1 Clement* 41—44 reflects debate over the rightful authorities in the church (at Rome?), who should succeed the apostles in presenting the church's "sacrifices and services" (*1 Clem.* 40:2); namely, the credibility of other approved persons who as overseers have "offered the sacrifices" (*1 Clem.* 44:4).

The audience of Hebrews needs both to catch this vision of itself as an eschatological people sharing in the heavenly host's triumph (Heb 12:22-24; the realized eschatology in these verses puts this part of Hebrews in touch with the "already accomplished" emphasis in Ephesians) and equally to face the stern realities of its life on earth as pilgrims and strangers (Heb 11:13-16; see Johnsson, Käsemann 1984). The way to win through, for this author and the readers, is to remain committed to early baptismal pledges (e.g., Heb 4:14; see Bornkamm 1963) and keep the lines of communication with God, established in corporate worship, open (Heb 4:16) and intact (Heb 10:19-25). The temptation to withdraw from public assembly is evidently strong in time of testing (Heb 10:32-39); so the author makes adherence to the assembly a focal point of resistance and renewal, thereby giving to worship its pragmatic value and socializing dimension.

A parallel side to the way worship is seen to provide identity markers for the new Israel and to build confidence is evident in another document also associated with Rome. In 1 Peter the addressees are facing a loss of faith but for a different set of reasons. In Hebrews, where hope plays a key role (Heb 6:9-20; 11:1), the conflicts were domestic and internal, and there was theological questioning about the imminent Parousia* (Heb 10:37-39). The call to hope in 1 Peter (1 Pet 1:3, 13, 21; 3:5; 5:20) is couched against a different background. Here the hostility is directed to the churches in Pontus-Bithynia (1 Pet 1:1) from outside (1 Pet 2:12; 4:1-6), and there seems to be no debate about their final salvation at an expected appearing of the Lord (1 Pet 1:5, 13; 4:7). The root problem faced in 1 Peter is the loss of social identity and sense of rootlessness that has come to people who, from their pagan environment, have joined the church and accepted its mores and manners. Their (physical) sufferings are raising problems to do with theodicy as they seek to understand and make sense of life's contrarieties and uncertainties when their new-found faith is tested (1 Pet 1:6; 2:19; 4:12).

The author's response in this hortatory document (1 Pet 5:12) is to impart social identity to the readers as those belonging to the "people of God," stretching back to Abraham* and Sarah (1 Pet 3:5, 6) and onward to the complete "household of faith" soon to be realized (1 Pet 2:4-10; 4:17-19) and to offer assurance that God's plans do not miscarry as the churches come to see how Christ's victory over all his enemies is one to be shared by his followers who walk in his steps (1 Pet 2:21; 3:18-22; see Martin 1994, 100, n. 26). Liturgical emphases play their role in enforcing these precise points, notably in the poetically structured passage (1 Pet 2:1-10; see commentaries, esp. Selwyn) that celebrates the church as God's new Israel* in which erstwhile strangers and alienated people find their new home as worshipers and family; and in the christological hymn* of 1 Peter 3:18-22, whose original form may well have looked like this:

Who suffered once for sins,

To bring us to God;

Put to death in the flesh,

But made alive in the spirit,

In which *he went* and preached to the spirits in prison,

[But] *having gone* into heaven he sat at the right hand of God,

Angels and authorities and powers under his control.

The intricacies of debate over this obscure passage are many (see commentaries by Reicke, Dalton, Boismard for basic treatments—all reacting to Bultmann's seminal work of 1947; for survey and bibliographical references, see Martin 1978, 335-44; 1994, 95, 110-117). For our purposes it is enough to seek to inquire how the cited lines functioned as a hymn. The key to this problem is suggestively to observe that the section encompasses a drama of Christ's odyssey, framed by two occurrences of the verb "to go" (represented in italics above). He *went* to visit the realm of the demonic; he *went* after his triumph to take his place on the universe's throne, with all cosmic powers held in subjugation. So the journey motif is the key, unlocking the chief problematic issue which is to know how relevantly such a piece of christological suprahistory would affect the lives of Peter's readers, who are also reminded of their baptism (in turn typified in the ark by which Noah's family was saved in a generation Jewish thinkers regarded as the worst imaginable and the cause of demonic influence in the world). In Christian baptism—a thought conceivably inserted by Peter into the preformed creed-hymn—there is an appropriating of Christ's identification with dark powers and his subsequent victory over them.

Here baptism receives a treatment that ostensibly links it with Paul (in Rom 6; cf. Col 2:12; 3:1). Yet it adds a dimension of considerable pictorial, even mythological, effect. It proclaims that believers share in Christ's achievement in both its horror and its glory. He made himself one with human enslavement to evil and then in his triumph over it (see Martin 1994, 114-17, referring to Rev 1:18), thus connecting its kinetic-dramatic theology with other hymns, notably Philippians 2:6-11, as well as the scenario in *Gospel of Peter* 10.41-42 and *Acts of Pilate* 5.1—8.2, in the section Christ's Descent into Hell, and of course the Apostles' Creed statement (at Rome, c. A.D. 150, as a baptismal creed; Kelly): "crucified, dead, and buried; he descended into Hades. The third day he rose again and ascended into heaven." The *Christus victor* theme reaches its zenith in the acknowledgement and proclamation that in baptism all demonic agencies that would tyrannize over the church and hold it prey are overcome, since Christ knew both their power to hurt and their being reduced to impotence. The logical and liturgical outcome of this theologoumenon will be the use of exorcistic and renunciation formulas as a prelude to the actual baptism seen in Hippolytus' *Apostolic Tradition* (Cuming).

6. Johannine Patterns and their Influence.

If we are correct in assuming the presence in the Rome-Asia axis of styles of worship that looked to Paul's and Peter's deposits of teaching to inform them, with the universally accepted practices of baptism as initiatory rite and the Lord's Supper as celebratory of Christ's resurrection victory and set in a structure that tended to respect the authority of leaders, then in the Johannine literature the emphasis falls elsewhere (*see* John, Letters of).

The powerful influences seen in the Pastorals, the *Didache*, Ignatius and *1 Clement*, with their concerns over set prayers (the permission of *Did.* 10:7, "allow the prophets to give thanks at will," needs to be read in light of *Did.* 15:1-2 which shows that itinerant prophets are on the way out and are to be succeeded by "bishops and deacons," as in Ign. *Smyrn.* 8; *1 Clem.* 44), regular ministries, orderly worship (*1 Clem.* 20) and an incipient sacramental system (Ign. *Eph.* 20) seem to brook no challenge. Yet there is another strand that mirrors a reaction in the Asian churches in which the Johannine influence is strong. This body of literature (John's Gospel, Johannine Epistles and to an extent the Apocalypse) speaks to a situation where there are competing emphases, partly christological, partly ecclesiological, in the "community of the beloved disciple" (Brown). We may even postulate a threat to worship, as John's disciples feared it. Both the Johannine Gospel and Epistles raise a warning against the trend to over-institutionalize. John senses the danger of suffocating the Spirit by placing too much emphasis on creedal orthodoxy, relying too heavily on structural forms and limiting the spontaneity that we saw to be evident in Luke's depictions. It is a moot point whether John's protest may be directed to just such a situation as that envisaged in the Pastoral

Epistles, *1 Clement* and later in Ignatius.

At all events, for John the way forward is to stress the believer's individual participation in true spirituality, as he dubbed it. (1) Worship is "in the Spirit" (1 Jn 3:24) as in reality and is largely independent of outward forms, locations and ceremonials (Jn 4:20-24). The water of Jewish purification rituals is marvelously transformed into the wine of the new age, where Jesus' glory shines out as the universal logos* (Jn 2:1-11).

(2) Love* of God and his family members is the real test of authentic spirituality (1 Jn 3:1-18; 4:7-21), over against creedal rigidity and a blind trust in sacraments. The antisacramentalism alleged in the Fourth Gospel (Bultmann 1971) is a timely, if overstressed, protest against the opposite viewpoint of Cullmann who sees baptism, unction and the Eucharist everywhere on almost every page. There is no explicit institution of the Lord's Supper in John 13, which does, however, have an upper-room meal. But the Evangelist has incorporated a discourse set in the synagogue at Capernaum (Jn 6) as though to stress that the Eucharist has an individualized, inner meaning as nothing less than a feeding on Christ the bread of life, just as John's earlier chapter (Jn 4) had depicted Jesus as the giver of living water to an individual woman of Samaria. The same note is struck in Revelation 3:20: "if any one hears my voice, I will . . . eat with that person."

(3) It cannot be fortuitous that this body of literature lacks completely the term "church"* (*ekklēsia*). (Revelation is the exception, and it is notable for its inclusion of liturgical-hymnic tributes linking the old Jewish worship [Rev 4:8, 11; 7:12; 15:3-4] to the new age of Messiah's redemption [Rev 5:9-14] and victory [Rev 12:10-12]). Yet for John believers do form a society under the imagery of a flock (Jn 10:1-16; cf. 11:52; *see* Shepherd, Flock) and the vine (Jn 15:1-11), but inevitably in such images the important thing is the personal relationship the believer sustains to the Lord. As the sheep hear the shepherd's voice when he calls each by name (Jn 10:3-5; cf. Heb 13:20; 1 Pet 5:2-4 has the chief shepherd with many under-shepherds to tend the flock, and Peter will assume such a role in Jn 21), so there is no possibility of life unless the separate branches are linked to the parent stem of the vine (Jn 15:4, 5). John's view of the church governs his concept of worship.

The church is made up of individual believers (Moule 1962) who are joined one-by-one to the Lord by the highly personal ties of baptism and new birth (Jn 3:1-6; see New Birth). The worship they offer springs from the experience of an enriched individualism: "the individual's direct and complete union with Jesus Christ sets its stamp on the ordering of the (Johannine) church" (Schweizer, 124). This is true also of its liturgy, remarkable for its absence of set forms and a Johannine passing over of much that other Christians elsewhere may have taken for granted.

7. Some Conclusions.

The above survey of worship materials and patterns, drawn from literature of a wide time span and diverse geographical and cultural spread, cannot pretend to be comprehensive. The soundings we have taken are at best, we hope, typical of the regions mentioned. Yet the picture is still incomplete, and the settings proposed conjectural. It is difficult therefore to plot a trajectory or suggest a developing pattern with any convincing coherence. The bold attempt as proposed by G. J. Cuming (SL 10 [1974] 88-105), ranging from salutation (grace* and peace*) by way of intercessions, Scripture readings to doxology, kiss of peace and dismissal is hardly convincing (see Martin 1982, 190, n. 6). A lot of the material emerges from the socially conditioned pressures on both writers and congregational addressees. The most we can hope for is to plot certain nodal points along the way. And as these are observed, we can submit that certain trends are visible.

7.1. Growing Systematization of Order. In the later Pauline/deutero-Pauline literature there is a growing move to systematization based on various factors: the squelching of charismatic fervor seems the inevitable concomitant of the growing emphasis on instruction/teaching roles (themselves in response to deviant notions that challenged the legacy of Paul's doctrine, e.g., in the Pastorals and Colossian-Ephesians). The rise of churchly concerns over order and fixity put a brake on immediacy and spontaneity in worship that we see at Corinth. Paul had sounded the caution, "let all things (in the worshiping assembly) be done in seemly fashion and in good order" (1 Cor 14:40, a phrase evidently picked up in *1 Clem.* 40, *panta taxei poiein opheilomen*); and the growing strength and

authority accorded to duly appointed leaders (in the Pastorals and Eph 4:11-16; see commentaries; Martin 1992) tended to focus the spotlight on the hierarchical controls required to ensure that unity was promoted (Ign. *Smyrn.* 8, for instance) and the episcopal office maintained (*1 Clem.* 44). Along the way from the picture of congregational egalitarianism to the recognition of a settled ministry (a transition point seen in *Did.* 9—15), we may note the recourse made to apostolic teaching (Acts 2:42; Jude 17; *Did.* incipit; Heb 13:7; cf. Heb 2:3; the Johannine letters, *1 Clem.* 42) to repel false ideas that began to rear their head.

7.2. Emerging Trinitarian Focus. The occasional nature of much of the liturgical language, called out by the contingencies of congregational problems and challenges, should not blind us to some well-attested constants. Among these we may include: (1) the appreciation of God* as the holy object of Christian adoration and praise. The legacy of the OT-Judaic traditions is not overlooked but carried forward and enriched by an emerging trinitarian faith, for example, the "thrice holy" of Isaiah 6:3 is heard in Revelation 4:8, though the history of the *Sanctus* in the eucharistic liturgy is still a complex issue (cf. *1 Clem.* 34:6; Spinks, especially 46-54). All the documents in our period highlight the transcendence and worthiness of God, without which worship (as classically understood) fails.

(2) As a counterbalance, God is praised as intimately near in Christ his Son, whose true incarnation, death for sinners and resurrection victory over all evil forces are pivotal events in salvation history (cf. creedal-hymnic forms in 1 Pet, Heb 1:1-4; 1 John 4:1-6; 5:20; Rev 5:1-14; Ign. *Eph.* 19). This prepares the ground for a doctrine of the priestly office of the exalted Christ as intercessor and participant in the church's offices (Heb 7:25; *1 Clem.* 40; 59—62.3; *1 Clem* 61.3 is an interesting specimen of prayer speech with nine pairs of parallel lines [in *1 Clem.* 59.3] consisting of divine predications and hymnic sentences [Robinson 1964] offered through "Jesus Christ the high priest and guardian of our souls through whom be glory and majesty"). The Pauline verse (Eph 2:18) is sometimes hailed as encapsulating the essence of early worship in its trinitarian format (Crichton, 18, 19) and as offering a "basic morphology that cannot be violated if liturgical theology is to be

Christian" (Hoon, 115). The data that begin with Paul's borrowing of formulas like 2 Corinthians 13:13 (14) take on this shape in Matthew 28:19,20; Acts 2:33; Hebrews 9:14; 1 Peter 1:2; *Didache* 7:1-4; and Ignatius's *Letter to the Trallians* (incipit) on the road to full-blown trinitarian creeds (in Irenaeus and beyond; see Wainwright).

7.3. Placing the Risen Lord Alongside the Father
The place of the risen Lord in early Christian worship is still hotly debated (see representative positions held in Jungmann, Harris, Bauckham, France, Hurtado, Casey). From allusions that are at best inferential (Jn 14:14 RSV mg.; cf. Jn 16:23) or incidental (Acts 7:59; *1 Clem.* 21:6) to others that precisely speak of invoking the living Christ* (1 Cor 16:22; Rev 22:20; *Did.* 10:6) or else set the exalted one at the center of a cultus on a par with Israel's covenant God (Rev 5:12-14; cf. 3:21; see Guthrie, Thompson), the line moves inexorably to a placing of Jesus alongside the Father as worthy of worship and the co-author of salvation blessings for the church and the world. The title "God," so reticently applied to Jesus in the NT literature (though see Harris for the maximum value to be extracted from such verses as Heb 1:8; 2 Pet 1:1; 1 Jn 5:20), may well have received fresh impetus from the role cast for him in the Christians' assembly when as Christians met on an appointed day (i.e., Sunday, so called in Justin *Apol I* 67 as the day after Saturday before daybreak [*stato die ante lucem*]) hymns were sung antiphonally "to Christ as to God" *carmen quasi Deo* (Pliny *Ep.* 10.96.7 for this text, c. A.D. 112; see Cabaniss 1989, 11-18).

See also BAPTISM, BAPTISMAL RITES; CENTERS OF CHRISTIANITY; GOD; HYMNS, SONGS; LITURGICAL ELEMENTS; LORD'S DAY; LORD'S SUPPER, LOVE FEAST; PRAYER; SYNAGOGUE; TEMPLE.

BIBLIOGRAPHY. R. J. Bauckham, *Jude, 2 Peter* (WBC; Waco: Word, 1983); idem, "The Worship of Jesus" *NTS* 27 (1981) 323-31; W. Bauer, *Orthodoxy and Heresy in Earliest Christianity* (Philadelphia: Fortress 1971 [1924]); idem, *Die apostolischen Väter II* (Tübingen: J. C. B. Mohr, 1924) 204; G. Bornkamm, *Early Christian Experience* (London: SCM, 1969); idem, "Das Bekenntnis im Hebräerbrief" in *Studien zu Antike und Urchristentum* (2d ed.; Munich: Kaiser, 1963) 188-203; P. F. Bradshaw, *The Search for the Origins of Christian Worship* (New York: Oxford University Press, 1992); idem, *Daily Prayer in the Early Church* (New York: Oxford University Press, 1982); R. E. Brown, *The Community of the Beloved Disciple* (New York: Paulist, 1979); R. Bultmann, *Theology of the New Testament* (2 vols.; New York: Scribner's, 1952, 1955); idem, *The Gospel of John* (Philadelphia: Fortress, 1971); A. Cabaniss, "The Epistle of Saint James," *JBR* 22 (1954) 27-9; idem, *Pattern in Early Christian Worship* (Macon, GA: Mercer University Press, 1989); M. Casey, *From Jewish Prophet to Gentile God* (Louisville: Westinster/John Knox, 1991); J. H. Charlesworth, ed., *The Lord's Prayer and Other Prayer Texts from the Greco-Roman Era* (Valley Forge: Trinity Press International, 1994); J. D. Crichton, "A Theology of Worship" in *The Study of Liturgy*, ed. C. Jones, G. Wainwright and E. Yarnold (2d. ed.; New York: Oxford University Press, 1992), 3-29; F. L. Cross, *1 Peter: A Paschal Liturgy* (London: Mowbray, 1964); O. Cullmann, *Early Christian Worship* (SBT 10; London: SCM, 1953) 7-36; P. H. Davids, *Commentary on James* (NIGTC; Grand Rapids: Eerdmans, 1982); M. Dibelius, *James* (Herm; Philadelphia: Fortress, 1976); F-J. Dölger, *Sol salutis: Gebet und Gesang im christlichen Altertum* (2d ed.; Münster: Aschendorff, 1925); C. W. Dugmore, *The Influence of the Synagogue on the Divine Office* (London: Oxford University Press, 1944); J. D. G. Dunn, *Baptism in the Holy Spirit* (Philadelphia: Westminster, 1970); idem, *Jesus and the Spirit* (Philadelphia: Westminster, 1975); idem, *Unity and Diversity in the New Testament* (2d ed.; Louisville: Westminster, 1990); J. Dunnill, *Covenant and Sacrifice in the Letters to the Hebrews* (SNTSMS 75: Cambridge: Cambridge University Press, 1992); J. A. Fitzmyer, "The Aramaic Language and the Study of the New Testament," *JBL* 99 (1980) 5-21; R. T. France, "The Worship of Jesus" in *Christ the Lord*, ed. H. H. Rowdon (Leicester/Downers Grove: InterVarsity, 1982) 17-36; D. Guthrie, "Aspects of Worship in the Book of Revelation" in *Worship, Theology and Ministry in the Early Church*, ed. M. J. Wilkins and T. Paige (Sheffield: Academic Press, 1992) 70-83; E. Haenchen, *The Acts of the Apostles* (Philadelphia: Westminster, 1971); M. J. Harris, *Jesus as God: The New Testament Use of* Theos *in Reference to Jesus* (Grand Rapids: Baker, 1992); P. J. Hartin, *James and the Sayings of Jesus* (Sheffield: JSOT Press, 1991); P. W. Hoon, *The Integrity of Worship* (Nashville: Abingdon, 1971); C. Hopkins, *The Discovery of Dura-Europos* (New Haven: Yale University Press, 1979); A. J. Hultgren, *The Rise of Normative Christianity* (Minneapolis: Augsburg/

Fortress, 1994); L. W. Hurtado, *One God, One Lord* (Philadelphia: Fortress, 1988); R. D. Jasper and G. J. Cuming, *Prayers of the Eucharist: Early and Reformed* (London: Collins, 1975); J. Jeremias, *The Eucharistic Words of Jesus* (3d ed.; Philadelphia: Fortress, 1977); W. G. Johnsson, "The Pilgrimge Motif in the Book of Hebrews" *JBL* 97 (1978) 239-51; J. A. Jungmann, *The Place of Christ in Liturgical Prayer* (New York: Alba, 1965); E. Käsemann, "A Primitive Christian Baptismal Liturgy" in *Essays on New Testament Themes* (Philadelphia: Fortress, 1982 [1964]); idem, *The Wandering People of God* (Minneapolis: Fortress, 1984); J. N. D. Kelly, *Early Christian Creeds* (5th rev. ed.; London: A. C. Black, 1977); H. Koester and J. M. Robinson, *Trajectories through Early Christianity* (Philadelphia: Fortress, 1971); J. Kroll, *Die christliche Hymnodik bis zu Klemens von Alexandreia* (Darmstadt: Wissenschaftliche Buchgesellschaft, 1968 repr.); G. W. H. Lampe, *The Seal of the Spirit* (2d ed.; London: SPCK, 1967); H. Lietzmann, *Mass and Lord's Supper: A Study in the History of the Liturgy* (Leiden: E. J. Brill, 1953-1978); E. Lohmeyer, *Kyrios Jesus: eine Untersuchung zu Phil 2.5-11* (2nd ed.; Heidelberg: Winter, 1961 [1928]); M. Y. MacDonald, *The Pauline Churches* (SNTSMS 60; Cambridge: Cambridge University Press, 1988); I. H. Marshall, *Acts* (TNTC; Grand Rapids: Eerdmans, 1980); R. P. Martin, *A Hymn of Christ* (Downers Grove, IL: InterVarsity Press, 1997 [1967, 1983]); idem and A. Chester, *The Theology of the Letters of James, Peter and Jude* (NTT, Cambridge: Cambridge University Press, 1994); idem, *James* (WBC; Waco: Word, 1988); idem, *Ephesians, Colossians, Philemon* (Int; Louisville: Westminster, 1992); idem, "New Testament Worship: Some Puzzling Practices" *AUSS* (1993) 119-26; H. A. McKay, *Sabbath and Synagogue: The Question of Sabbath in Ancient Judaism* (RGRW 122; Leiden: E. J. Brill, 1994); L. Morris, "The Saints and the Synagogue" in *Worship, Theology and Ministry in the Early Church*, ed. T. Paige and M. J. Wilkins (Sheffield: Academic Press, 1992) 39-52; C. F. D. Moule, *Worship in the New Testament* (London: Lutterworth, 1961); idem, "The Individualism of the Fourth Gospel" *NovT* 5 (1962) 171-90; E. Norden, *Agnostos Theos* (Stuttgart: Teubner, 1956); P. T. O'Brien, *Introductory Thanksgivings in the Letters of Paul* (NovTSup 49: Leiden: E. J. Brill, 1977); J. A. T. Robinson, *Twelve New Testament Studies* (SBT 34; London: 1962) 154-57; J. M. Robinson, "Die Hodajot-Formel im Gebet und Hymnus des Frühchristentums" in *Apophoreta: Festschrift für Ernst Haenchen*, ed. W. Eltester (Berlin: Töpelmann, 1964) 194-235; T. A. Robinson, *The Bauer Thesis Examined: The Geography of Heresy in the Early Christian Community* (Lewiston, NY: Mellen, 1988); W. Rordorf, *Sunday* (London: SCM, 1968); idem, "Sunday" in *Encyclopedia of the Early Church*, ed. A de Berardino (New York: Oxford University Press, 1992) 2.800-801; H. Schlier, *Die Verkündigung im Gottesdienst der Kirche* (Würzburg: Werkbung-Verlag, 1953); E. Schweizer, *Church Order in the New Testament* (SBT 32; London: SCM, 1961); E. G. Selwyn, *The First Epistle of St. Peter* (London: Macmillan, 1947); M. H. Shepherd, "The Epistle of James and the Gospel of Matthew," *JBL* 75 (1956) 40-51; idem, *The Paschal Liturgy and the Apocalypse* (Richmond: John Knox, 1960); B. D. Spinks, *The Sanctus in the Eucharistic Prayer* (Cambridge: Cambridge University Press, 1991); J. H. Srawley, *Early History of the Eucharist* (2d ed.; Cambridge: Cambridge University Press, 1947); B. H. Streeter, *The Primitive Church* (London: Macmillan, 1929); L. T. Stuckenbruch, "A Refusal of Worship of an Angel: The Tradition and its Function in the Apocalypse of John," *SBLSP* (1994); M. M. Thompson, "Worship in the Book of Revelation", *Ex Auditu* 8 (1992) 45-54; H. E. W. Turner, *The Pattern of Christian Truth* (London: Mowbray, 1954); A. W. Wainwright, *The Trinity in the New Testament* (London: SPCK, 1962).

R. P. Martin

WRATH, DESTRUCTION

The two standard words for anger or wrath, *orgē* and *thymos,* are used in these NT writings as well as those of the apostolic fathers.* Although the two words significantly overlap in meaning, there is also the distinction that *orgē* seems more characteristic of wrath or anger that leads to sin and destruction, and *thymos* denotes a kind of passion. Although there are a number of words for destruction used in these and other NT writings, the usage is more restricted in the apostolic fathers. The two most frequent words are *apollymi,* which denotes a process of perishing, and *apōleia,* the destruction that results. Next most frequent are *phtheirō* and *diaphtheirō,* words that seem to imply a corruption leading to destruction. Also used are *lyō* ("break to pieces"), *katargeō* ("render ineffective or powerless") and *olothreuō* ("complete destruction"). Context must prove decisive for determining

the meanings of these overlapping words.
1. Divine Wrath
2. Human Wrath
3. Destruction

1. Divine Wrath.

The preponderance of words for wrath or anger in these writings refers either directly or indirectly to divine wrath or anger. Indirect reference includes Hebrews 3:11 and Hebrews 4:3 (*orgē*), both quotations of Psalm 95:11. Whereas the original psalm has God* speaking (as does Heb 4:3), in Hebrews 3:11 the extended quotation of Psalm 95 in Hebrews 3:7-11 is attributed to the Holy Spirit.* In both instances the quotation is used to support the faithfulness of God despite the sinfulness of the Israelites in the desert, with a word of exhortation to readers to remain faithful so that they can enter into God's rest. Similarly in *1 Clement* 39.7, Job 4:16—5:5 is quoted, with destruction said to be the outcome of those who experience God's wrath, that is, the foolish and sinners.

The explicit language of wrath and anger is otherwise confined in the biblical writings to the book of Revelation (*see* Revelation, Book of). The language of anger and wrath is occasionally used in a context of praise and exaltation of God by those around him. Thus in Revelation 11:18 worshipers praise God for coming in his wrath (*orgē*) to judge the dead and reward* those faithful to him.

The vast majority of NT usage, however, is within the apocalyptic* context of the great final conflict between God or Christ* alongside their emissaries and the forces of the devil (*see* Satan). Thus the language is often hyperbolic, not given to fine nuances in the depiction of these warring parties. In Revelation 6:16-17 the wrath (*orgē*) is said to be the wrath of the Lamb* that is to fall upon the kings of the earth. They are unable to stand in the day of their wrath. This is consistent with the use of figurative language in Revelation, in which various characters in the divine apocalyptic drama are personified. The Lamb is the crucified and risen Christ.

In contrast is Revelation 12:12, which depicts the futile wrath (*thymos*) of the devil, passionately angry because of his knowledge that he only has a short time before his destruction. In Revelation 14:10 an angel* threatens that anyone who worships the beast* will suffer the wrath of God (*orgē*), said to be mixed in the cup

of his anger (*thymos*). Here *thymos* is probably used in distinction to *orgē*, representing its more passionate as opposed to judicial dimension.

The punishing dimension of God's wrath is developed in the apostolic fathers in *Hermas Visions* 3.6.1 and *Hermas Visions* 4.2.6, with the same sense as the biblical writers. In Revelation 14:19 an angel gathers grapes from the earth and throws them into the wine press of God's wrath (*thymos*), symbolic of his judgment* of the world.* In Revelation 15:1, 7, the author sees seven angels, the final episode in the wrath (*thymos*) of God, carrying bowls* full of God's wrath (*thymos*). In Revelation 16:1 these angels are told to go and pour out their bowls of God's wrath (*thymos*) upon the earth. In Revelation 16:19, at the fall of Babylon,* the city is remembered before God, so that he can give to it the anger (*thymos*) of his wrath (*orgē*). In Revelation 19:15 a sword comes from God's mouth, and he strikes the nations and metes out judgment of the anger (*thymos*) of his wrath (*orgē*).

Revelation 16:19 and Revelation 19:15 are the only two occasions in the NT writings where the two nouns are used together (cf. Rom 2:8). In the apostolic fathers they are used together at *1 Clement* 50.4 in a quotation of Isaiah 26:20; the reference does not have "wrath and anger" but only wrath (*orgē*). There are several possible ways that the two terms may be understood together, but this may well be a way of emphasizing the profound anger of God that results in his punishing vengeance against his enemies: "wrathful anger." The only major passage in the apostolic fathers that speaks of divine wrath in this language is Ignatius* (Ign. *Eph.* 11.1), who speaks of fearing the wrath to come or loving the grace* that is present.

Despite the views of some scholars earlier in this century (such as C. H. Dodd, who contended that anger is not a quality that is associated with God in the NT), the evidence is clear that wrath and anger are readily associated with the divine character in a number of explicit and forceful passages. This concept is present though not as thoroughly developed in the apostolic fathers.

2. Human Wrath.

In opposition to divine wrath, there are several more references to nondivine wrath in these writings. It is not entirely correct to label them instances of human wrath, since in several of the instances the context involves personification.

In two instances the writer of James* (Jas 1:19, 20) directly speaks of human anger *(orgē)*. In a word of direct exhortation, the author instructs his readers to be quick to hear, slow to speak and slow to anger. The reason for this is that human anger is not compatible with the righteousness* of God. These people are blessed for having undergone various trials (Jas 1:12), and the author instructs them not to say that God is subjecting them to such temptations.* They are said already to know that a response of anger is incongruent with accomplishing God's purpose. Although wrath or anger is not specifically defined, it seems here confined to a kind of human response to being subjected to difficulties in the course of life. It is perhaps surprising, due to the exhortative tone of James, that wording of wrath and anger does not appear more often.

The theme of exhortation against anger and wrath runs throughout the apostolic fathers. In Ignatius (Ign. *Eph.* 10.2), in language somewhat reminiscent of James 1, the author instructs his audience to respond appropriately to the wrath of others. The trait of wrath is mentioned as a characteristic to be avoided in a number of passages. In some contexts wrath is singled out as a specific trait, as in *Didache* 15.3, where wrath is opposed to peace* (the context is the appointment of church leaders; *see* Church Order). In other contexts wrath is listed as one of several characteristics to avoid, as in *1 Clement* 13.1, *1 Clement* 63.2 and *Didache* 3.2. (All of the above examples use *orgē.)*

In Hebrews 11:27 the author recounts the life of Moses,* stating that Moses did not fear Pharaoh's wrath or anger *(thymos)*. Here wrath or anger seems to be much more than simply antagonism but refers to the life-threatening anger of Pharaoh toward Moses. In *1 Clement* 45.7 the author invokes the story of the men in the furnace (Dan 3) as an example of the results of those overcome by rage and anger *(thymos)*. In Revelation 14:8 and Revelation 18:3, in two similar passages, an angel proclaims that Babylon the whore, a personification of Rome (*see* Roman Empire), has fallen. She is the one who made the nations drink the wine of the passion *(thymos)* of her immorality. There is the possibility that *thymos* here should be interpreted anger or wrath, in the light of Babylon's destructive and bloodthirsty purposes.

In a passage that in some ways reflects Romans 7 (although the level of argumentation and the concerns are more mundane) and in some ways encapsulates the moral exhortation regarding anger and wrath in the Fathers, the Shepherd traces a progression from simple ill-temper, which is foolish and silly, to bitterness, wrath *(thymos)*, anger *(orgē)* and then great sin (*Herm. Man.* 5.2.4).

3. Destruction.

The language of destruction is consonant with and even consequential to what is said of divine wrath. As Revelation 11:18 says, God's wrath came and destroyed those who were destroying the earth *(diaphtheirō)*.

Destruction is spoken of in these writings in several different ways. One of them contrasts the transience and destructibility of the world and the enduring quality of God. For example, Hebrews 1:11 contrasts the fact that heaven* and earth will perish *(apollymi)*, with God remaining. Earthly things, such as the beauty of the flower (Jas 1:11) and even gold (1 Pet 1:7) and other luxurious things (Rev 18:14), are transient and pass away *(apollymi)*, as did humanity when it was destroyed *(apollymi)* by the flood (2 Pet 3:6), even though God does not want any to be destroyed *(apollymi;* 2 Pet 3:9).

Destruction is also spoken of in more spiritual terms. This appears to be the emphasis with the use of language of destruction in the apostolic fathers, as well as the NT writings. Rejecting the faith* is said in Hebrews 10:39 to be the sure way to incur destruction *(apōleia)* and *Hermas Similitudes* 6.2.4 warns that the result of spiritual death is eternal destruction *(apōleia)*. The author of 2 John warns his readers (2 Jn 8) lest they lose what they have accomplished *(apollymi)*. For the author of 2 Peter, the ungodly face judgment and destruction *(apōleia)*, especially anyone who distorts the teaching* of Paul's letters* (2 Pet 3:7, 16). The same fate of divine destruction awaits various unbelievers, such as revilers *(phtheirō;* Jude 10), those in the rebellion of Korah *(apollymi;* Jude 5, 11), blasphemers *(phtheirō;* 2 Pet 2:12) and the whore who corrupts *(phtheirō)* the earth (Rev 19:2). This is to be contrasted with Jesus, who as God's Christ did not see destruction or corruption *(diaphthora;* Acts 2:27, 31; 13:34-35). *2 Clement* emphasizes at several places that it is Jesus Christ, who as God, is responsible for the salvation* of those who are perishing (*apollymi; 2 Clem.* 1.4; 2.5, 7; 15.1) and that it is the responsibility of believers to help to save them (*2 Clem.* 17.1-2). This balance between the work of Christ and Christian works is typical of this homily.

In some contexts destruction is spoken of in abstract fashion, as in 2 Peter 2:1, 3, where even though the author offers OT examples he says that destructive heresies such as denying the Master bring impending destruction (*apōleia*). There are also several contexts in which the agent of destruction is explicitly stated. In often apocalyptic terms, God is frequently said to be the destroyer. Thus in James 4:12 God is called a lawgiver and judge, the one who saves and destroys (*apollymi*). In Hebrews 11:28 God is depicted as the destroyer (*olothreuō*) of the first-born in Egypt. In Revelation 8:9 God's angels destroy (*diaphtheirō*) a third of the world's ships. What is said of God is also applied to Christ. In Hebrews 2:14 it is said that the death of Christ renders powerless (*katargeō*) the one with the power of death, the devil (*see* Death of Christ).

1 John 3:8 speaks of the Son of God as being able to destroy (*lyō*) the works of the devil (Rev 18:8, 11 also speaks of the beast's destruction *[apōleia]*). In the apostolic fathers it is more common to speak of the devil as the agent of destruction (*Herm. Sim.* 6.2.1, 2; *Barn.* 20.1 [not found in the parallel in *Did.* 5.1]).

See also BOWLS; DAY OF THE LORD; DEATH OF CHRIST; ESCHATOLOGY; HELL, ABYSS, ETERNAL PUNISHMENT; JUDGMENT; TRIBULATION, MESSIANIC WOES.

BIBLIOGRAPHY. A. Chester and R. P. Martin, *The Theology of the Letters of James, Peter and Jude* (NTT; Cambridge: Cambridge University Press, 1994); J. A. Kleist, *The Didache, Etc.* (ACW 6; Westminster, MD: Newman, 1948); J. Lawson, *A Theological and Historical Introduction to the Apostolic Fathers* (New York: Macmillan, 1961); J. B. Lightfoot, *The Apostolic Fathers* (pt. 1; 2 vols.; London: Macmillan, 1890); L. L. Morris, *The Apostolic Preaching of the Cross* (3d ed.; Grand Rapids: Eerdmans, 1965); S. H. Travis, "Wrath of God (NT)," *ABD* 6:996-98. S. E. Porter

Z

ZION. *See* JERUSALEM, ZION, HOLY CITY.

Scripture Index

Old Testament

Genesis
1, *342, 402, 414*
1:1, *252, 439*
1:2, *489, 492, 558, 636, 657*
1:3, *657, 785*
1:4, *657*
1:7, *785*
1:9, *785*
1:9-10, *128*
1:14, *1127*
1:16, *1127*
1:26, *485, 610, 960*
1:26-27, *793*
1:27, *831*
1:29, *6*
2:2, *266, 417, 673, 740, 844, 850*
2:7, *489, 610, 793*
2:8-9, *6*
2:9, *481, 852*
2:16, *485*
2:17, *485*
2:24, *713*
3, *278, 537*
3:1-5, *852*
3:1-7, *485*
3:8, *489*
3:14, *852*
3:14-16, *539*
3:15, *852*
3:22, *610, 852*
3:24, *852*
4, *836*
4:1, *639*
4:3, *836*
4:4, *836*
4:5, *836, 1204*
4:7-8, *42*
4:8, *718*
4:10-12, *840*
4:15-16, *840*
4:17, *639*
4:25, *639*
6, *41, 459, 538, 671*
6:1-4, *44, 63, 716, 1089, 1119*
6:1-6, *100, 538, 922*
6:2-4, *1112*
6:3-7, *41*
6:4, *1119*
6:5, *1119, 1169*
6:9, *38*
6:18, *246*
7:1, *38, 512*
7:11, *636*
8:21, *1169*
9:3-4, *162, 610*
9:8-16, *246*
10, *754, 1178*
11:1, *1178*
11:6, *1178*
11:7, *1178*
11:8-9, *1178*
12:1, *2*
12:1-2, *3, 38*
12:1-3, *390*
12:2-3, *3, 38*
12:3, *1*
12:7, *2, 40*
12:8, *3*
13:3, *3*
13:10, *341*
13:14-16, *38*
13:15, *2, 40*
14, *964, 967, 999*
14:17-20, *3, 729, 731, 843,*
849
14:18, *730, 731*
14:18-20, *45*
14:20, *3*
15:1-6, *39, 968*
15:5, *3, 38*
15:6, *88, 89, 537, 837, 1056*
15:7, *2, 3, 40*
15:9-21, *278*
15:13-14, *2, 40*
15:18-21, *643*
16:2, *1208*
17:3-8, *968*
17:4-5, *5*
17:5, *3, 38, 390*
17:7, *2*
17:7-8, *40*
17:10-14, *38, 993*
17:14, *1195*
17:15-22, *39*
17:23, *512*
18, *5, 44, 502, 538, 817*
18:1, *3*
18:1-21, *4*
18:6-8, *1208*
18:9-15, *39*
18:11-15, *1218*
18:12, *4, 538, 601, 1208*
18:16-33, *839*
18:18, *1*
18:20, *485*
18:22-32, *41*
18:25, *621*
18:27, *830*
19, *502, 1089*
19:1-11, *41*
19:1-29, *1089*
19:5, *715*
19:12-14, *715*
19:12-22, *41*
19:12-29, *538*
21:1-4, *2, 38*
21:8-14, *1*
21:12, *4, 1208*
21:15-19, *2*
22, *816, 1056*
22:1-14, *1056*
22:14, *816*
22:14-17, *729*
22:15-18, *968*
22:16, *3, 38*
22:17, *3, 130, 731*
22:18, *1*
23, *2*
25:34, *42*
26:1-5, *246*
27, *129*
27:1-40, *39*
27:30-40, *42*
27:41-45, *41*
28:12, *817*
28:13-15, *246*
28:18, *48*
31:44-54, *1141*
33:13-14, *1208*
33:18-20, *2*
37:9, *1210*
37:11, *42*
37:28, *42*
40:1—41:36, *40*
41:40, *512*
41:41, *40*
41:57, *40*
42:22, *832*
45, *512*
45:4, *42*
45:8, *40*
46:33, *1090*
47:29-31, *39*
48, *129*
48:1-22, *39*
48:4, *2, 40*
48:12-14, *121*
48:12-20, *39*
48:14-15, *828*
49:1, *331*
49:8-12, *331*
49:29-32, *2*
50:13, *2*
50:24, *265*
50:24-25, *39*

Exodus
1:15-22, *39*
2, *779*
2:1-2, *39*
2:2, *39*
2:11-12, *39*
2:11-15, *40*
2:14, *42*
2:15, *778*
2:21-22, *40*
2:22, *2, 40*
3:1, *1091*
3:1-12, *40*
3:2-6, *493*
3:5, *486*
3:5-6, *40*
3:6, *1, 43*
3:12, *2, 40*
3:14, *485*
3:20, *1094*
4:22, *1112*
4:30, *1094*
6:6-7, *939*
6:6-8, *1001*
7, *779*
7:3, *1094*
7:14, *132*
7:14-21, *132*
7:14-24, *779*
7:17-19, *854*
7:22, *930*
8:7, *930*
8:18-19, *930*
9:8-12, *132*
10:21-23, *133*
11:1—12:28, *39*
12, *280, 1160*
12:1, *644*
12:5, *174*
12:6, *196*
12:11, *642*
12:42, *779*
13:21, *1091*
14:21, *489*
15, *780*
15:1, *781*
15:1-18, *851*
15:8, *489*
15:11, *128*
15:13, *1091*
15:25, *1183*
16:23, *486*
16:31, *838*
17:1-7, *42*
17:8-13, *779*
18:1-5, *40*
18:13-27, *466*
19, *246, 445, 964*
19:4, *1080*
19:5, *270*
19:5-6, *538*
19:6, *196, 199, 200, 318, 481, 488, 838, 917*
19:8, *816*
19:16, *780*
19:20-24, *485*
20, *815, 827*
20:2, *1099*
20:3, *162, 413*
20:4-5, *528*
20:8, *130, 828*
20:13, *537*
20:13-14, *240, 645*
20:14, *537*
20:17, *715*
22:7, *825*
23:1, *718*
23:6, *962*
23:11, *962*
23:14-17, *989*
23:20-21, *666*
23:22, *538*
23:30-33, *133*
24, *279*
24:1-8, *485*
24:3-8, *199*
24:6-8, *780*
24:9-12, *439*
24:16, *396*
24:18, *673*
25:9, *439, 956*
25:22, *396*
25:40, *40, 439, 844, 956, 958*
30:26-32, *48*
31, *674*
31:10, *486*
31:13, *487*
31:18, *673, 828*
32, *674*
32:1, *40*
4, *42*
32:7-10, *830*
32:7-19, *673, 830*
32:15, *1085*
32:16, *673*
32:31-32, *830*
32:32-33, *318, 851*
33:1, *5*
33:1-3, *1158*
33:3, *5, 42*
33:7, *817*
33:11, *781*
34:1-10, *828*
34:6-7, *1054, 1191*
34:22, *492*
34:24, *268*
34:28, *239, 646, 673, 828*

Leviticus
4:3-6, *174*
4:13-17, *174*
4:20, *275, 1070*
4:26, *275, 1070*
4:31, *275, 1070*
4:35, *275, 1070*
5:5-6, *691*
7:19-21, *989*
7:22-27, *989*
8, *117*
8:15, *281*
9:3, *279*
10:1-3, *988, 989*
10:6, *838*
10:6-11, *989*
10:10, *989*
10:11, *989*
11, *989, 1104*
11:1-23, *377*
11:1-45, *647*
11:3, *673*
11:13-16, *540*
11:44, *240, 535, 838*
11:44-45, *196, 423*
13, *990*
13:12, *991*
13:13, *991*
13:15, *991*
13:45, *991*
13:46, *991*
14, *991*
14:1-8, *991*
14:5-7, *174*
14:9, *991*
14:10-20, *991*
14:21-32, *991*
15:10, *729*
16, *274, 279, 485, 487, 1165*
16:1-2, *989*
16:3, *280*
16:5, *280*
16:9, *280*
16:12-15, *607*
16:14-19, *99*
16:15-19, *274*
16:18-21, *607*
16:21-22, *828*
17, *422*
17:1-9, *989*
17:7, *716*
17:8-13, *162*
17:10-14, *989*
17:11, *1105*
17:14, *1105*
17:15-16, *989*
18:3, *989*
18:5, *365*
18:24-30, *989*
18:26, *162*
19, *484, 490, 553, 560, 649, 815*
19:1-18, *486*
19:2, *240, 485, 486, 538*
19:2-14, *488*
19:9-10, *486*
19:12-18, *480*
19:14, *486*
19:15, *480*
19:18, *240, 480, 537, 568, 827*
19:33-34, *502*
20:7, *538*
20:8, *487*
20:23, *989*
20:26, *538*
21:6, *989*
21:8, *485, 989*
21:14, *989*
21:15, *487, 989*
21:18-20, *930*
21:22, *989*
21:23, *989*
22:9, *487*
22:16, *487*
22:32, *487*
23, *989*
23:29, *673, 824*
23:43, *639*
25:23, *643*
25:55, *1099*
26, *1085*
26:1-2, *133*
26:11-12, *854*
26:18, *133*
26:21, *133*
26:23-24, *133*
26:28, *133*
26:41, *42*

Numbers
6:1-21, *1069*

6:5, *486*
6:13-18, *486*
8:4, *956*
11, *466*
11:17, *779*
11:26-30, *466*
11:29, *837*
12, *511*
12:1-15, *42*
12:3, *780, 781*
12:7, *510, 781, 782, 830,*
838
13:16-17, *779*
14, *42*
14:1-35, *1013*
14:20-23, *42*
16, *840*
16:1-35, *43*
16:5, *43*
16:13, *196*
16:17, *836*
16:22, *1118, 1121*
16:35, *836*
17, *830*
18:3, *485*
18:26-28, *3*
19, *5, 279*
20:2-13, *42*
20:29, *838*
21:9, *779*
22, *840*
22:17, *715*
22:18, *43*
22:33, *270*
23, *129*
23:7, *164*
24:13, *43*
24:14-19, *331*
24:17, *180, 605*
25:1-2, *26*
25:1-3, *43, 715, 1211*
25:12, *895*
26:9-10, *43*
27:8, *1209*
27:15-17, *270*
27:16, *1118*
27:17, *1091*
28:26, *492*
31:8, *715*
31:16, *43, 819, 836*

Deuteronomy
1:9-18, *466*
1:16, *827*
1:17, *827*
1:35, *781*
2:5, *2*
4, *861*
4:2, *675, 827*
4:2-7, *639*
4:19, *42, 704*
4:24, *419, 861*
4:25-31, *1160*
4:25-46, *825*
4:32-39, *639*
4:34, *38, 1094*
5, *815, 827*
5:6-7, *413*
5:11, *610, 673*
5:17, *537*
5:18, *537*
6, *412*
6:4, *164, 412, 413, 421,*
1229
6:4-9, *1158*
6:5, *827, 831, 1168*
6:16, *1168*
6:17-19, *1160*
6:22, *1094*
7:1-16, *1160*
7:5-6, *485*
7:6, *270, 485, 838, 1160*
7:7-16, *1160*
7:8, *1002*

7:19, *1094*
8:2, *1091*
8:3, *737*
8:5, *326*
9:12-14, *830*
9:12-17, *830*
10:3, *48*
10:14, *439*
10:16, *42, 228*
10:17, *785*
10:18, *502*
12:2, *1159*
12:3, *1159*
12:5-14, *989, 1159*
12:7, *1160*
12:12, *1160*
12:13, *1159*
12:14, *1159*
12:15-28, *989, 1160*
12:18, *1160*
12:22, *989*
12:32, *827*
13:1, *1199*
13:1-5, *1120*
13:2, *1199*
14, *1104*
14:1, *1112*
14:2, *38, 270, 838*
14:3-21, *377*
14:6, *673*
14:22-27, *1160*
15:4, *962*
15:7, *962*
15:7-9, *318*
15:11, *962*
15:17-18, *240*
16, *989, 1160*
16:9-12, *492*
17:6-7, *718*
17:12, *283*
18, *826, 999*
18:9-18, *930*
18:15, *356, 779*
18:15-16, *536, 998*
18:15-18, *780, 851*
18:15-22, *1120*
18:18, *467, 779*
18:18-19, *356, 999*
18:18-22, *51*
18:19, *536, 824*
19:15, *718*
19:19, *283*
21:9, *283*
21:22-23, *20, 272, 287*
21:23, *280*
23:1, *18, 930*
23:4, *43*
24:1-4, *713*
25:18, *838*
26:18, *270*
27:6, *174*
28, *133, 1085*
28:10, *786*
28:29, *658*
28:49, *15*
29:18, *305*
29:23, *841*
30:3, *832*
30:15-20, *47, 827*
31:6, *567, 844*
31:8, *567, 844*
31:30, *204*
32:5, *781*
32:5-6, *1116*
32:8, *537, 1112*
32:8-9, *44*
32:15, *830*
32:18, *793*
32:20, *781*
32:32, *841*
32:35, *486*
32:35-36, *850*
32:43, *252, 537, 843, 845*
33, *818, 840*

33:2, *445, 840*
33:3, *20, 196*
33:26, *396*
34, *818*
34:1, *778*
34:1-6, *778*
34:6, *778*
34:9-12, *781*
34:10, *779*

Joshua
1:5, *567*
2:1-15, *39, 41*
2:18, *830*
5:13-15, *666*
6:4, *1182*
6:8, *1182*
6:13, *1182*
8:29, *280*
10:12-14, *1183*
22:19, *643*
24:2, *2*
24:15, *512*
24:32, *2*

Judges
2:11, *676, 832*
3:12, *676*
3:27, *1182*
4:4, *1207*
4:4-16, *39*
5:4, *840*
5:19, *133*
6:33, *39*
6:34, *1182*
10:6, *39*
13:1, *39*
13:8-23, *44*
18:6, *895*
18:31, *509*
19, *502*
19:18, *509*
19:20, *897*
20:1-3, *1141*
21:1-8, *1141*

Ruth
3:3, *48*
4:9-11, *718*
4:11, *838*

1 Samuel
1:17, *895*
1:19, *639*
3:19-20, *39*
4:4, *396*
7:5-14, *39*
7:5-16, *1141*
7:15-17, *39*
10:1, *48*
10:5-6, *1177*
10:10, *1177*
13:3, *1182*
13:14, *825, 830*
16:15, *1091*
16:17-18, *490*
16:34-37, *1091*
17:26, *39*
17:32, *39*
17:34-37, *39*
17:45-47, *39*

2 Samuel
1:12, *48*
1:14, *48*
5:2, *1091*
5:7, *561*
6:2, *939*
6:6-10, *988*
6:17, *41*
7:1-2, *466*
7:1-16, *356*
7:1-17, *246*
7:5-16, *41*

7:6-16, *825*
7:11, *509*
7:14, *418, 537, 632, 845,*
854, 1112
12:20, *48*
14:2, *48*
22:3, *567*
22:11, *903*
22:16, *903*

1 Kings
3:5-14, *1201*
3:7, *1091*
4:29-34, *980*
5:3, *466*
8:27, *439, 466, 509, 537*
8:46, *485*
10:23-24, *1201*
16:24, *1075*
17:1, *779, 854*
18:12, *972*
19:10, *42*
19:14, *42*
19:16, *48*
21:8-13, *1125*
22:17, *1091*
22:19-23, *44*
22:20, *46*
22:21-22, *1120*

2 Kings
1:10-16, *779*
2:1-12, *97*
2:9-16, *972*
5:1-15, *930*
9:22, *716, 1211*
17, *1075*
19:22, *487*
23, *1147*
23:29-30, *133*

1 Chronicles
11:2, *1091*
11:5, *561*
16:13, *199*
16:36, *661*
17:13, *162, 1112*
21:1, *278*
22:6-10, *895*
22:10, *1112*
28:9, *1169*
29:18, *1169*

2 Chronicles
1:10, *1201*
5:2, *561*
9:22-23, *1201*
20:7, *837, 838*
26:16, *962*
29:15-18, *511*
35:20-24, *133*
36:22-23, *288*

Ezra
1:1-4, *288*
4, *1075*
9—10, *389*

Nehemiah
8, *979, 1142*
8:6, *661*
9:7, *2, 3, 38, 40*
9:12, *1091*
9:26, *42*
10:38-39, *3*
13:2, *43*

Esther
1:1, *754*
3:16, *707*
4:7, *968*
4:9-17, *42*
4:17, *377*
15:13, *45*

Job
1—2, *44*
1:1, *830*
1:6, *172*
1:6-8, *1077*
1:6-12, *1112*
1:9-11, *284*
1:12, *913, 1077*
2:1, *172*
2:1-6, *1112*
2:1-7, *1077*
2:6, *913*
3:5, *607*
4:1, *381*
4:16, *607, 1239*
5:11, *837*
5:12, *837*
5:17, *326, 837*
5:17-26, *674*
7:11-16, *41*
10:18, *41*
13:10, *326*
14:2, *837*
14:4-5, *830*
14:12, *440*
14:20-21, *838*
17—42, *607*
19:26, *829*
20:22, *838*
22:4, *326*
23:2, *41*
23:10, *832*
24:4-12, *838*
24:24-25, *837*
27:6, *832*
27:21, *837*
28, *1201*
28:28, *1201*
30:20-23, *41*
32:3, *708*
33, *1001*
33:19, *326*
37:9, *439, 903*
37:10, *903*
38:1, *903*
38:7, *172*
38:22, *439*
38:37, *439, 1201*
41:1-11, *128*
42:1-6, *326*
42:5, *41*
42:7, *949*

Psalms
1, *47*
1:3, *833*
2, *1112*
2:1-2, *479, 824*
2:2, *162*
2:4, *832*
2:6, *561*
2:7, *153, 162, 418, 537,*
824, 843, 845, 1112
2:8, *562*
2:8-9, *635*
2:11, *602, 832*
2:12, *832*
3:6, *829*
3:13, *538*
4:3, *827*
4:5, *832*
7:15, *838*
8:4, *418*
8:4-6, *361, 537, 1016*
9:10, *639*
9:11, *561*
10:16, *155*
11:4-6, *830*
14:1, *1169*
14:2, *831*
14:7, *561*
16:3, *196*
16:8-11, *96, 479, 1228*
16:10, *153, 537, 824, 825*

16:11, *601*
18:9, *840*
18:10, *396*
18:20, *991*
18:44, *228*
21:7-9, *830*
21:23, *510*
22:3, *485*
22:4, *829*
22:22, *510*
22:27, *562*
22:28, *155*
23, *119, 509, 680*
23:5, *48*
24:3-6, *991*
24:7-10, *396*
26:4-7, *991*
27:7, *829*
28:9, *1091*
29:1, *1112*
29:3, *396*
30:19, *830*
32:9, *832*
32:10, *735*
33:2, *522*
33:3, *522*
33:6, *439*
33:8, *602*
33:12-18, *830*
33:13-17, *538*
34:9, *196*
34:11-12, *228*
34:12-14, *481*
34:12-16, *538*
36:9, *657, 830*
36:11, *643*
36:35-37, *830*
37:2, *837*
37:11, *827*
37:14, *837*
39:1, *838*
39:7-9, *480*
40:4, *840*
41:1, *318*
41:10, *824*
41:13, *661*
41:14, *130*
42:2, *737*
44:7-8, *843*
44:22, *1092*
45, *418*
45:6, *665*
45:7, *48, 694*
46:3, *832*
46:8-9, *840*
48, *1210*
48:1-2, *561*
48:2, *561*
48:8, *3, 39*
49, *1001*
49:14-15, *830*
50:2, *561*
50:3-19, *830*
50:12, *832*
50:18-20, *716*
50:19, *830*
51, *86*
51:1, *735*
51:2, *991*
51:3, *485*
51:6, *991*
51:7, *991*
51:10, *991*
51:11, *489*
53:6, *561*
54:23, *831*
55:17, *572*
55:22, *538, 676*
56:8, *840*
61:5, *830*
61:13, *832*
63:1, *737*
64:2, *782*
64:6, *1083*

68:17, *445, 840*
68:31, *930*
68:31-33, *830*
69:22-23, *161*
69:26, *824*
69:28, *563, 624*
69:29, *840*
69:33, *318*
71:20, *460*
71:22, *487*
72:1-4, *621*
72:7, *895*
72:8, *562*
72:18-19, *130*
72:19, *396*
73:2, *270*
73:12, *837*
74:1, *1091*
74:2, *561*
74:13-14, *128*
76:2, *729*
76:9, *840*
76:11-12, *562*
77:20, *1091*
77:36-37, *830*
78:9, *1083*
78:11, *270*
78:14, *1091*
78:18-20, *837*
78:41, *487*
78:52, *270, 1091*
78:68, *561*
78:70-71, *1091*
78:70-72, *1091*
79:13, *1091*
80:1, *1091*
82, *44*
82:1, *729*
82:3-4, *318*
82:6-8, *454*
82:14-15, *838*
85:9, *831*
85:10, *895*
85:12, *831*
86:9, *541*
86:12, *541*
86:15, *1191*
87:1-3, *3, 39*
87:2, *561*
88:21, *830*
88:51-52, *778*
89, *246*
89:5, *196, 561*
89:6, *1112*
89:7, *486*
89:8, *939*
89:12, *561*
89:38, *48*
89:53, *130*
90:4, *342, 538, 739*
90:6, *425*
94:1, *1083*
94:7-11, *850*
94:8-11, *845*
94:11, *845*
95:7-11, *480*
96, *621*
96:4-5, *389*
96:7, *843*
96:10, *389*
96:11, *603*
96:12, *603*
96:13, *785, 840*
98:3, *562, 838*
98:4-5, *522*
99:2, *561*
99:3, *486, 541*
100:3, *1091*
101:2, *196*
101:5, *962*
101:26-28, *843*
102:16, *561*
102:18, *832*
102:25, *419*

103:4, *843, 1118*
104, *662*
104:4, *448, 537, 1122*
104:15, *48*
104:24, *1201*
105:6, *199*
106:9, *1091*
106:48, *130*
109:4, *845*
110:1, *43, 96, 174, 360, 416, 479, 537, 824, 1016*
110:4, *3, 360, 537, 646, 729, 730, 966, 1204*
110:10, *832*
111:9, *486*
111:10, *1201*
113:7-8, *837*
115:12, *838*
117:18, *830*
117:19-20, *830*
117:22, *199, 1126, 1127, 1128*
118, *524*
118:22, *416, 479, 480, 824, 838*
118:26, *827*
118:27, *658*
119:1-3, *196*
119:105, *658*
119:130, *657*
121:5-6, *132*
122:1, *832*
132:4-5, *41*
132:11, *247, 824*
132:13, *561*
134:6-7, *15*
135:19, *838*
136:16, *1091*
137:1-3, *561*
139:4, *838*
139:16, *563, 840*
141:3, *838*
143:6, *737*
146:10, *561*
147:7, *522*
147:12, *561*
148:2, *44*
148:4, *439*
148:5, *832*
149:3, *522*
150, *662*
150:6, *832*

Proverbs
1:1, *980*
1:7, *828, 832, 1201*
1:20-23, *1201*
1:23-33, *1203*
2:6, *1202*
2:21-22, *830*
3:4, *832*
3:5, *676*
3:8, *538*
3:9, *832*
3:11-12, *326, 419, 480, 695, 850*
3:19, *1201*
3:34, *420, 481, 537, 538, 540, 832, 837*
6, *1203*
6:16-19, *1191*
6:19, *718*
8:1, *163*
8:17-20, *541*
8:22-31, *957, 1202*
8:30, *957*
8:32-36, *1201*
9, *508*
9:1-6, *1201*
9:10, *1201*
10:12, *837*
10:23, *601*
11:12, *838*
11:13, *782*

11:27, *606*
11:30, *832*
11:31, *481, 1073*
14:21, *838*
14:27, *827*
14:29, *838*
14:31, *318*
15:10, *326*
15:32, *326*
15:33, *1201*
16:20, *602*
16:32, *838*
17:3, *832*
18:17, *540, 832*
20:19, *782*
20:27, *674*
21:6, *827*
23:3, *268*
23:6, *268*
24:12, *831*
24:21, *231*
25:9, *782*
25:14, *614*
26:5, *709*
26:11, *538, 819, 839*
26:22, *614*
27:1, *838*
28:21, *838*
29:20, *838*
29:22, *838*
29:23, *837*
30:20, *716*
31:9, *827*

Ecclesiastes
1:1, *980*
1:12, *980*
3:11, *252*
7:6, *601*
7:20, *485*
12:8-14, *980*
12:13, *831*

Song of Solomon
6:10, *539*

Isaiah
1, *980*
1:1-13, *673*
1:1-31, *621*
1:2, *228, 497, 673, 1112*
1:2-3, *639*
1:4, *487*
1:6, *48*
1:9-10, *841*
1:10, *228, 497, 673*
1:11-17, *838*
1:16-20, *674*
1:17, *838*
1:21, *716*
1:23, *827*
2:2, *561*
2:2-3, *756*
2:2-4, *226, 331, 562, 643*
2:2-5, *753*
2:3, *562, 666, 756*
2:6-22, *857, 962*
2:10, *1085*
2:13, *567*
2:19, *1085*
2:21, *1085*
3, *1019*
3:3-4, *830*
3:8, *1210*
3:9, *841*
4, *1019*
4:3, *196, 840*
4:4, *561*
5:6, *833*
5:7, *838*
5:9, *537*
5:20, *657*
6, *47, 824, 1120*
6:1-8, *486*

6:1-9, *485*
6:1-12, *956*
6:2-3, *441*
6:3, *396, 486, 524, 662, 663, 1236*
6:9-10, *479, 536, 791, 824*
7:14, *313*
7:20, *1183*
8:2, *718*
8:4, *199*
8:7, *1183*
8:9, *15*
8:12-13, *174, 487, 839*
8:13, *671*
8:14, *480, 838, 1127, 1128*
8:17-18, *849*
8:18, *1094*
8:19-22, *658*
9:1, *386*
9:6, *1181*
9:7, *895*
9:12, *326*
10:3, *265, 864*
10:12, *561*
10:12-19, *962*
11:1-2, *490*
11:1-3, *491*
11:1-10, *895*
11:2-3, *1120*
11:12, *756*
12:6, *601*
13:6, *264*
13:9, *264*
13:10, *1030*
13:13, *1030*
14:5-23, *841*
14:13, *133, 561*
14:31, *1183*
14:32, *3, 39, 561*
17:12-14, *561*
18:1-6, *561*
18:7, *562*
19:1, *840*
19:19-25, *331*
23:1-14, *1211*
23:15-16, *1211*
23:17, *232*
24, *997*
24:15, *831*
24:21-22, *841*
25, *1026*
25:6, *226*
25:6-8, *502*
25:9, *499, 601*
26:3, *1169*
26:16-18, *716, 1210*
26:17, *1210*
26:20, *844, 861*
27:1, *1033*
28:16, *161, 199, 317, 422, 480, 538, 561, 817, 838, 920, 1126, 1127, 1128*
29:1-8, *561*
29:10, *161*
29:11-12, *1085*
29:13, *830, 831, 1164*
29:19, *838*
29:23, *487*
29:24, *614*
30:19, *561*
31:4, *840*
31:4-9, *561*
31:27, *840*
32:15, *195*
32:17, *895*
33:13, *228*
34:2, *863*
34:4, *1030*
34:8, *264*
34:10, *461*
35:6, *751*
37:32, *561*
40, *752, 838, 980*
40:3, *228*

40:5, *396*
40:6, *375, 985*
40:6-7, *537, 837*
40:6-8, *480, 481, 671, 838*
40:9, *756*
40:10, *840*
40:11, *831, 1091*
40:13, *46*
40:28-31, *413*
41:4, *337*
41:8, *337, 830, 837, 838*
41:8-9, *209*
41:8-10, *2*
41:20, *639*
42:1, *491*
42:5, *537*
42:6, *247*
42:6-7, *673, 1003*
42:8, *183*
42:25, *326*
43:3-7, *1001*
43:4, *337*
43:5-6, *756*
43:6, *1112*
43:7, *786*
43:10, *164, 283*
43:20-21, *199, 538, 838, 917*
43:21, *20*
44:2, *337*
44:6, *283, 337, 413, 1017*
44:9-20, *1126*
44:28, *817*
45:1, *155*
45:2-3, *673*
45:7, *657*
45:14, *337, 481*
45:21, *247, 346, 415, 416*
45:22, *15, 562*
46:3, *838*
46:3-4, *1091*
46:13, *561*
48:2, *486*
48:12, *283, 337, 1017*
48:20, *15, 1001*
48:21, *1091*
49:1-6, *753*
49:6, *15, 251, 333, 415, 479, 486, 536, 548, 549, 562, 563, 658, 824, 886, 971*
49:6-7, *1003*
49:6-8, *247*
49:10, *132, 1092*
49:12, *756*
49:21, *1210*
49:23, *337, 481*
50:1, *485, 1210*
51:3, *341, 561*
51:11, *561*
51:17, *133*
51:22, *133*
51:22-23, *133*
52:1, *561, 1195*
52:3, *1001*
52:5, *540, 674, 831, 832, 833*
52:7, *561, 894*
52:13, *1, 271, 606*
53, *86, 115, 256, 271, 279, 280, 356, 423, 523, 524, 539, 569, 642, 826, 830, 930, 1055, 1069, 1092, 1181*
53:1-12, *180, 830, 962, 1096*
53:3-5, *1055*
53:4, *839, 1092*
53:4-6, *271*
53:4-7, *1180*
53:4-9, *1181*
53:4-12, *174, 275*
53:5, *1092, 1181*
53:6, *196, 271, 1092, 1181*

53:7, *284, 641, 642, 838, 1092*
53:7-8, *18, 271, 280, 536, 824, 930*
53:9, *481, 838, 1092, 1096, 1181*
53:10, *282*
53:10-11, *271*
53:11, *271, 1055*
53:11-12, *839*
53:12, *271, 272, 280*
54:1, *236, 574, 831, 1210*
54:5, *1210*
54:6, *1210*
54:10, *895*
55:1-6, *737*
55:3, *479, 537, 824, 825*
55:8, *485*
55:9, *485*
56, *980*
56:3-5, *18*
56:7, *832*
56:11, *1091*
57:15, *485, 542*
57:17, *196, 326*
57:19, *20*
58:4-5, *673*
58:6, *833, 1143*
58:6-10, *673*
58:8, *396*
58:9, *831*
59:1, *485*
59:2, *485*
60:1-3, *396*
60:3-16, *756*
60:5, *601*
60:14, *337*
60:17, *235, 744*
61, *490, 826*
61:1, *49, 962*
61:1-2, *271, 491, 1143*
61:2, *1143*
61:3, *48*
61:8, *246*
61:10, *601*
62:11, *15*
63:1-6, *871*
63:10, *42*
63:10-11, *489*
63:11, *1091, 1092*
63:11-14, *1092*
63:14, *1091*
64:1, *360, 439*
64:10, *486*
65:9, *199*
65:17, *331, 337, 439, 538, 854*
65:17-18, *1210*
65:17-19, *1210*
66:1-2, *414, 509, 824*
66:2, *827, 830, 962*
66:5, *831*
66:7-8, *539*
66:7-11, *1210*
66:15, *840*
66:18, *397*
66:19, *755*
66:22, *331, 337, 439*
66:24, *461, 674, 831*

Jeremiah
1:5-7, *971*
1:14-15, *1183*
2:6, *1091*
2:12-13, *828*
2:13, *120*
2:14, *1032*
2:17, *1091*
2:20, *1211*
2:26, *838*
2:30, *326*
3:1, *1211*
3:1-6, *1211*
3:1-14, *716*

3:15, *1091*
3:20, *1210*
3:22, *832, 1112*
4:3, *228*
4:4, *42, 228, 673*
4:29, *1085*
4:31, *1210*
5:3, *326*
5:4, *832*
5:15, *838*
6:8, *326, 643*
6:10, *42*
6:15, *265*
6:22-26, *1085*
7:2, *228*
7:11, *511, 674, 831*
7:28, *326*
9:15, *1183*
9:23, *497, 838*
9:23-24, *830*
9:25-26, *673*
9:26, *228, 838*
10:12, *15*
10:21, *1091*
12:3, *863*
12:15, *247, 415, 416*
13:17, *1091*
13:20, *1183*
13:21, *1210*
14, *779*
14:9, *786*
14:11-12, *1085*
15:1-2, *1085*
16:4-5, *1085*
16:19, *15*
17:13, *120*
17:24-25, *735*
18:4-6, *831*
18:11-21, *1085*
21:8, *827*
21:8-10, *1085*
22:22, *1091*
22:30, *840*
23, *1092*
23:1-2, *1091*
23:1-4, *1091*
23:1-6, *1091*
23:6, *1091*
23:14, *841*
23:15, *1183*
23:18, *782*
23:20, *331*
23:22, *782*
24:7, *832*
25:31, *840*
25:34, *863*
25:34-36, *1091*
25:38, *643*
26:20-24, *42*
28:26, *1127*
29, *896*
29:7, *896*
30:14, *326*
30:24, *331*
31, *248, 249*
31:9, *1112*
31:10, *1091*
31:31, *207, 246*
31:31-33, *247*
31:31-34, *240, 269, 331, 334, 537, 543, 564, 645, 670, 793, 844, 849, 969, 1012*
31:33, *195, 670*
31:33-34, *417, 1204*
31:34, *277*
32:20-21, *1094*
32:40, *246*
35:13, *326*
38:2, *1085*
38:31, *246*
38:31-34, *844, 845*
40, *1021*
43:6-7, *289*

44:1, *289*
44:11-14, *1085*
46:10, *1183*
46:14, *289*
47:2, *1183*
47:48, *331*
49:18, *841*
49:39, *331*
50:5, *246*
50:29-32, *962*
50:31, *264*
50:40, *841*
51, *1183*
51:8, *48*
51:14, *1183*
51:25, *1183*
51:26, *1127*
51:27, *1182*

Lamentations
1:12, *264*
2:1, *264*
2:22, *264*
4:20, *677*

Ezekiel
1, *396*
1:1-26, *956*
1:24-28, *177*
1:28, *396*
2:5, *838*
2:8-3:3, *853*
3:1, *838*
3:12, *972*
3:14, *972*
4:14, *993*
4:16, *1085*
5, *1085*
5:5, *561*
7:7-12, *264*
7:14, *1182*
7:19, *264*
7:25, *896*
9:1-11, *1031*
9:3-6, *1085*
9:4, *1085*
9:6, *511, 918*
11:19, *490, 673*
11:19-20, *793*
13:8-16, *133*
13:13, *903*
14:6, *1012*
14:14, *38, 831*
14:20, *38, 831*
14:21, *1085*
16, *112*
16:8-14, *1210*
16:9, *48*
16:15-16, *1211*
16:27-28, *326*
16:46-59, *841*
16:49-50, *962*
18:4, *485*
18:31, *490*
18:32, *829*
20:12, *487*
20:41, *487*
21:15, *863*
21:31, *837*
23:5, *1211*
23:18-20, *326*
27:13, *985*
28:1-19, *841*
28:2, *50*
33:1, *497*
33:11-27, *829*
34, *1092*
34:1-10, *1091*
34:2, *614*
34:11, *1093*
34:11-17, *1091*
34:11-22, *1091*
34:12, *264*
34:23, *1091*

34:25, *246, 895*
36:24-32, *563*
36:25-27, *793*
36:26, *490, 673*
36:27, *195*
36:35, *341*
37:1-14, *332, 793*
37:9-14, *493*
37:14, *195*
37:17, *854*
37:24, *1091*
37:26, *246*
37:27, *442, 854*
37:28, *487*
38, *561*
38:6, *1183*
38:12, *561*
38:14-16, *331*
38:14-17, *331*
38:15, *1183*
40, *770, 854, 988*
40:2, *561*
43:6-9, *988*
44:5-9, *1195*
44:9, *988*
44:10-14, *988*
44:15-16, *988*
44:19, *988*
44:20, *988*
44:21, *988*
44:22, *988*
44:23, *989*
46:10, *1091*
47:1-12, *561*
47:13, *548*
47:22, *548*

Daniel
1, *60*
1:3-17, *1104*
1:8, *377*
2, *62*
2:18, *782*
2:19, *782*
2:20-23, *1201*
2:27, *782*
29, *340*
2:28, *340, 782*
2:28-29, *340*
2:28-45, *331*
2:29, *782*
2:30, *782*
2:45, *340, 852*
2:47, *782*
3, *1240*
3:7, *831*
3:25, *45, 1112*
4:3, *1094*
4:9, *782*
5:20, *962*
6:10-12, *943*
6:27, *1094*
7, *50, 57, 61, 336, 338, 396, 539, 718, 719, 853, 959, 997, 1033, 1160, 1164, 1180*
7:1-8, *853*
7:2-7, *128*
7:3, *232*
7:3-8, *232, 988*
7:7, *539, 853*
7:7-8, *52, 342*
7:9, *47, 853, 1030*
7:9-12, *338*
7:10, *624, 840, 851*
7:13, *338, 396, 481, 853, 869, 1145*
7:13-14, *337, 360, 396*
7:14, *155, 338, 356*
7:18, *718*
7:21, *339*
7:22, *718*
7:23-27, *52*
7:24, *342*

8:10, *539*
9:24-27, *63*
9:27, *852*
10, *853*
10:5-6, *853*
10:9, *853*
10:10, *853*
10:12, *853*
10:13, *44, 666, 730*
10:14, *331*
10:18, *853*
10:21, *666, 730*
11:35, *342*
11:36, *50*
11:40-45, *331*
12:1, *44, 624, 656, 666, 840*
12:1-2, *332*
12:1-3, *730*
12:1-4, *1084, 1160*
12:1-13, *331*
12:2, *331, 776*
12:2-3, *65, 621*
12:10, *336, 342*
12:11-12, *1160*

Hosea
1:2, *1211*
1:6, *538, 735*
1:9, *538, 735*
1:9-10, *838*
1:10, *1112*
2:1, *538, 735*
2:16, *1208, 1210*
2:16-20, *246*
2:19-20, *1210*
2:19-23, *639*
2:23, *318, 538, 542, 735*
3:3, *1211*
3:4-5, *331*
4:15, *1211*
6:6, *838*
9:7, *265*
10:8, *1085*
10:12, *831*
11:1, *1112*
11:3-4, *1091*
12:13, *779*
14:2, *522*
14:2-5, *1012*

Joel
1, *1183*
1:15, *264*
2, *562, 826*
2:1, *264, 561, 562, 1182*
2:3, *341, 643*
2:11, *264*
2:12, *832*
2:15, *562*
2:17-39, *944*
2:23, *562*
2:28, *332, 562*
2:28-29, *490*
2:28-32, *21, 113, 195, 536, 824, 1178, 1218*
2:29, *1207*
2:31, *264, 859*
2:32, *160, 163, 416, 561, 562, 643, 1072*
3:1, *375*
3:1-3, *493*
3:1-5, *489, 904*
3:4, *858*
3:5, *630*
3:13, *871*
3:16, *561*
3:18, *264, 561*
3:21, *561*

Amos
1, *1030*
1:2, *561, 840*
2:10, *1091*

3:2, *621*
3:7, *782*
4:6-11, *326*
4:11, *841*
5, *826*
5:18, *658, 857*
5:18-20, *264*
5:20, *658*
5:25-27, *824*
5:27, *467*
6:1, *561*
6:6, *48*
6:8, *962*
7:4, *1183*
8:10, *838*
9:11-12, *247, 346, 415, 416, 479, 536, 824*
9:11-15, *643, 825*

Obadiah
1:1, *962*
1:17, *561*

Jonah
1:3, *244*
1:17, *244*
3:2, *244*
3:5, *244*
4:1, *244*
4:2, *1014*
4:2-11, *244*

Micah
1:3, *840*
3:12, *561*
4:1, *561*
4:1-3, *226, 331*
4:1-5, *753*
4:2, *562*
4:9-10, *1210*
5:2-4, *1091*
7:14, *1091*

Nahum
3:4, *716, 1211*

Habakkuk
1:5, *537, 824*
2:1-3, *783*
2:2-5, *873*
2:3-4, *365, 367, 844, 861, 999*
2:4, *38, 365*
3:3, *840*
7:1-8, *480*
7:4, *783*
7:8, *783*
7:13-14, *783*

Zephaniah
1:2-6, *1036*
1:7, *264*
1:7-9, *840*
1:12, *840*
1:14, *264*
1:14-15, *1030*
1:15, *658*
1:16, *1182*
2:3, *962*
3:2, *326*
3:8, *866*
3:9, *1036*
3:12-13, *962*
3:14, *561*

Haggai
2:6, *419, 843*
2:17, *326*
2:22, *840*

Zechariah
1, *62, 1030*
1:3, *838*
1:6, *326*

1:17, *561*
2:6, *827*
2:10-11, *210*
2:12, *643*
3, *818*
3:1-2, *1077*
3:1-5, *278, 778*
3:2, *459, 538*
3:8, *840*
4:4, *1120*
4:6, *1120*
4:10, *642, 1120*
4:11-14, *854*
4:14, *998*
5:3, *992*
5:4, *992*
6:14, *838*
8:20-23, *753, 756*
9, *1026*
9:1, *548*
9:9, *962, 992*
9:14, *840*
9:16, *1091*
10:3, *1091*
11:4-17, *992*
11:5, *1091*
11:15-17, *1091*
12, *264, 997*
12:1-9, *561*
12:10, *195, 338, 481, 490, 571, 869*
13:1, *992*
13:6-7, *828*
14:3, *561*
14:3-5, *857*
14:5, *827*
14:7, *659*
14:8, *833, 992*
14:9, *155*
14:10, *561*
14:12-15, *561*
14:16, *992*
14:16-19, *562, 992*
14:20, *993*
14:21, *993*

Malachi
1:11, *181, 675, 691, 827, 1072, 1230*
1:14, *181, 675, 827, 1230*
3:3, *326, 511*
3:3-5, *840*
3:5, *838*
3:12, *602*
3:16, *840*
3:17, *270, 838*
3:19, *831*
3:23, *264*
4:1, *267, 831*
4:1-6, *264*
4:5, *779*
4:5-6, *816*

New Testament

Matthew
1:1, *392, 1229*
1:1-17, *725*
1:2, *43*
1:2-17, *43*
1:5, *39, 41*
1:6, *43*
1:17, *43*
1:21, *392, 728*
1:25, *639*
2:1-12, *392, 725*
2:2, *605*
2:6, *206*
2:10, *602*
2:13-19, *35*
2:14, *659*
2:22-23, *385*
2:23, *387, 388*
3:2, *944*

3:4-6, *1229*
3:7-10, *209, 621*
3:9, *5, 43*
3:11, *113*
3:13-17, *331*
3:15, *573*
4:1, *1166*
4:1-11, *728, 1167, 1170*
4:3, *1166*
4:4, *737*
4:10, *528*
4:12, *385*
4:12-16, *385, 392, 725*
4:13, *387*
4:15, *386, 387*
4:16, *385*
4:17, *753, 944*
4:19, *752*
4:23, *386, 581, 725, 726, 1143*
4:24, *388*
4:25, *388*
5, *634, 725, 997*
5:3, *315, 568, 634*
5:5, *568, 634, 827, 963*
5:7, *735*
5:9, *896*
5:10, *574*
5:10-11, *242, 569*
5:11-12, *914*
5:12, *569*
5:13, *709*
5:13-16, *753*
5:16, *569, 817, 1136, 1229*
5:17, *854*
5:17-19, *581*
5:17-20, *728, 913*
5:17-48, *725, 728*
5:21-26, *1229*
5:23-24, *691, 946*
5:25-26, *572*
5:27-28, *995, 1088*
5:28, *715*
5:31-32, *995*
5:32, *713*
5:33-37, *992*
5:34-35, *568*
5:36, *568*
5:37, *568*
5:39-48, *572*
5:42, *710*
5:44, *576*
5:48, *838*
6:1-4, *1229*
6:1-18, *725*
6:2, *1142*
6:4, *896*
6:5, *1142*
6:5-8, *944*
6:6, *896*
6:7-13, *1229*
6:9, *487, 1229*
6:9-10, *634*
6:9-13, *181, 572*
6:10, *946*
6:12, *1229*
6:14-15, *1229*
6:16-18, *1229*
6:18, *896*
6:19-21, *1052*
6:24, *567, 634, 674*
6:29, *41*
6:31-34, *567*
6:33, *1054*
7:1, *623, 734, 735*
7:1-2, *574, 674, 1193*
7:3, *307*
7:6, *572, 675, 690*
7:7, *568*
7:7-8, *943*
7:7-12, *945*
7:12, *572*
7:15, *615*
7:15-20, *224*

7:16, *568*
7:21, *674, 699*
7:24-27, *557*
7:29, *581, 726*
8, *206*
8:1-4, *1144*
8:2-4, *990*
8:5-13, *209, 390, 392, 725, 753*
8:11, *6, 502, 643, 1162*
8:11-12, *5, 6, 389, 461, 581, 753*
8:12, *209, 658, 1162*
9:1-8, *1144*
9:9-13, *728*
9:13, *574, 733*
9:17, *725*
9:18-19, *1144*
9:20-22, *1144*
9:35, *386, 581, 725, 726, 728, 1143*
9:35-11:1, *729*
10:3, *1005*
10:5-6, *392, 581, 725*
10:6, *206, 752, 838*
10:7, *753*
10:9, *992*
10:10, *992*
10:11-14, *991*
10:12, *991*
10:13, *991*
10:15, *265, 459*
10:16, *1092*
10:17, *386*
13:54, *581*
10:17, *725, 726, 913, 1144*
10:19, *165*
10:23, *206, 467*
10:24, *913*
10:26, *1021*
10:28, *460, 1092*
10:32, *571*
10:35-36, *1221*
10:41, *728*
10:42, *1038*
11, *685, 900*
11:3, *861*
11:15, *571*
11:16-19, *1202*
11:18-19, *990*
11:19, *502, 1201*
11:20-24, *621, 1144*
11:22, *265*
11:24, *265, 581*
11:25-27, *639, 1021, 1202*
11:25-30, *162*
11:28, *685*
11:29, *962*
11:29-30, *675*
12:1-8, *728*
12:7, *733*
12:9, *386, 726*
12:9-14, *1144*
12:18-21, *577*
12:22-32, *331*
12:26, *43*
12:28, *631, 632*
12:33, *573*
12:36, *265*
12:39, *781*
12:42, *41, 1201, 1202*
12:45, *570*
13:9, *571*
13:10-15, *581*
13:11, *783*
13:16-17, *725*
13:17, *224*
13:31-32, *392*
13:35, *420*
13:44-45, *1052*
13:52, *581, 586, 913, 1229*
13:54, *386, 726, 1144, 1201*
13:55, *187, 190, 616, 617,*

1004
13:56, *1004*
15, *581*
15:3-9, *1163*
15:8, *831*
15:10-11, *990, 1144*
15:13, *573*
15:13-14, *728*
15:17-18, *378*
15:21-28, *206, 390, 392, 725*
15:24, *163, 206, 581*
15:26, *206*
16, *205*
16:1, *1166*
16:4, *781*
16:16, *417*
16:16-17, *1021*
16:17, *1229*
16:18, *728, 915, 992*
16:18-19, *223, 921*
16:19, *188, 915, 992*
16:21-27, *752*
16:22, *1180*
16:23, *915*
16:27, *396*
17:2, *658*
17:3-4, *816*
17:5, *317, 538*
17:24-27, *725, 728, 1164*
18:10, *45*
18:15, *224, 568*
18:15-16, *305*
18:15-17, *305*
18:16, *718*
18:17, *224, 728*
18:17-20, *305*
18:18, *224*
18:20, *1230*
18:21-22, *1229*
18:35, *1229*
19:3, *1166*
19:3-9, *581*
19:3-12, *995*
19:9, *713*
19:17, *1229*
19:20, *711*
19:22, *711*
19:24, *1052*
19:26, *1052*
19:27, *621*
19:28, *643, 725, 792, 913*
20:16, *320*
20:28, *1002, 1180*
21:1-9, *992*
21:5, *962*
21:9, *663, 827, 1230*
21:12, *1162, 1164*
21:12-16, *1161*
21:13, *831*
21:21-22, *945*
21:39, *567*
21:41, *581*
21:42, *838, 1127*
21:43, *207, 581, 725, 728*
22:3, *581*
22:7, *727*
22:8, *581*
22:13, *658*
22:14, *574*
22:18, *1166*
22:21, *324*
22:30, *45*
22:32, *43*
22:34-40, *634*
22:35, *1166*
22:37, *1229*
23, *161, 386, 575, 725, 726, 728*
23:1-7, *728*
23:1-12, *1229*
23:2, *581*
23:6, *1142*
23:8-12, *728*

23:9, *1229*
23:12, *568, 962*
23:16, *658*
23:24, *658*
23:34, *166, 224, 581, 726, 913, 1144*
23:34-36, *992, 1202*
23:35, *112, 718, 1085*
23:37, *718*
23:37-39, *1202*
23:38, *581*
24, *51, 301, 336, 540, 572, 1095, 1180, 1181*
24:3, *856*
24:5, *51*
24:8, *1181*
24:9, *719*
24:10-12, *570*
24:11-12, *615*
24:14, *386, 719, 753*
24:16, *912*
24:21, *1179*
24:23-24, *51*
24:27, *856*
24:30, *338, 396, 571, 1230*
24:31, *827*
24:36, *266*
24:37-39, *839*
24:42-23, *571*
24:43, *570, 866, 869*
24:43-44, *265, 266*
24:44, *266, 1200*
25:29, *709*
25:30, *658*
25:31, *396*
25:31-46, *505*
25:34, *420, 634*
25:35, *895*
26:6-13, *573*
26:14-16, *992*
26:26, *1162*
26:26-29, *686, 1229*
26:28, *245, 1162*
26:29, *1230*
26:31, *877, 880*
26:32, *385*
26:36-46, *1167*
26:39, *946*
26:41, *574*
26:42, *946*
26:52, *188, 571*
26:58, *719*
26:60, *718*
26:69-75, *719*
26:73, *387*
27:3-10, *992*
27:24, *928*
27:25, *160*
27:51, *810*
27:51-53, *1181*
27:52-53, *332*
27:54, *392*
27:56, *1005*
28:1, *680*
28:7, *385*
28:10, *385*
28:15, *581*
28:16-20, *385, 390, 392, 399, 725, 771*
28:18-20, *77, 97, 904, 1229*
28:19, *113, 115, 120, 121, 207, 258, 498, 719, 753, 754, 770*
20, *1237*
28:19-20, *492, 762, 877*
28:20, *719, 1230*

Mark
1:1, *892*
1:4, *1229*
1:8, *1194*
1:10, *489*

1:12-13, *1167, 1170*
1:13, *567, 1166*
1:14-15, *753*
1:15, *621, 864*
1:16-20, *921*
1:17, *752, 763*
1:21-28, *391, 1144*
1:23-28, *922*
1:26, *1118*
1:29, *1144*
1:29-31, *1221*
1:32-34, *922*
1:39, *1143*
1:40-44, *990*
1:40-45, *1144*
2:1-12, *1082, 1144*
2:5, *382*
2:7, *162*
2:17, *574*
3:1-6, *1144*
3:14, *77*
3:17, *1033*
3:18, *545, 1005*
3:20-21, *616*
3:21, *722*
3:28-29, *305*
3:31, *616*
3:31-33, *722*
3:35, *674*
4:9, *571*
4:11, *783*
4:14, *793*
4:22, *1021*
4:23, *571*
5:1-20, *753*
5:21-24, *1144*
5:21-43, *1206*
5:22, *609*
5:25-34, *1144*
5:34, *895*
5:35-43, *1144*
6, *49*
6:2, *1144*
6:3, *187, 190, 616, 617, 1004*
6:6, *753*
6:8, *992*
6:9, *992*
6:10, *991*
6:12, *1201*
6:13, *48, 437*
6:32, *710*
6:52-53, *1171*
6:56, *1118*
7, *575, 581, 996*
7:1-2, *996*
7:5, *996*
7:6, *831*
7:6-13, *995, 1163, 1164*
7:8-9, *1164*
7:10-12, *1164*
7:11, *1163*
7:11-12, *1164*
7:13, *1164*
7:14-15, *990, 995*
7:15, *995, 1144*
7:17, *995*
7:17-19, *995*
7:19, *378, 581*
7:20-23, *995*
7:22, *963*
7:24-30, *753, 1206*
7:27, *391*
8, *892*
8:11, *1166*
8:27, *711*
8:28, *396*
8:31-18, *752*
8:34, *921*
8:35-37, *986*
9:2-8, *175*
9:4, *816*
9:5, *816*
9:7, *317, 779*

9:42, *573*
9:42-48, *621*
9:42-49, *73*
9:48, *461, 831*
9:50, *898*
10:1-12, *1088*
10:2, *1166*
10:2-12, *995*
10:6, *831*
10:11, *713*
10:13-16, *711, 712*
10:13-45, *711*
10:17-31, *710*
10:21, *711*
10:32-34, *709*
10:34, *710*
10:35, *709*
10:41-45, *269*
10:45, *269, 282, 1002, 1092, 1180*
10:46, *709, 711*
10:52, *711*
11:1-10, *992*
11:9, *663*
11:9-10, *711*
11:15, *633, 1162, 1164*
11:15-18, *1161*
11:17, *944*
11:22-24, *945*
12:8, *567*
12:10, *838*
12:13, *1166*
12:17, *324*
12:21, *948*
12:26-27, *965*
12:30, *831*
12:31, *568*
12:35-37, *155, 667*
12:36, *964*
12:39, *1142*
12:40, *1220*
12:41-44, *1164*
13, *51, 58, 301, 336, 1030, 1036, 1164, 1180, 1200*
13:6, *51*
13:8, *1181*
13:9, *165, 913, 1144*
13:10, *753, 755, 770*
13:14, *585, 901, 912*
13:20-23, *73*
13:21-22, *51, 152*
13:22, *1199*
13:26, *338, 396*
13:32, *266*
13:35, *1200*
14:9, *770*
14:10, *992*
14:11, *992*
14:21, *573*
14:22, *269, 780, 1162*
14:22-25, *686, 793*
14:24, *245, 780, 1162*
14:27, *921*
14:27-31, *73*
14:28, *385, 904, 921*
14:29, *921*
14:36, *945*
14:38, *574, 1199*
14:50, *921*
14:51, *711*
14:51-52, *711*
14:58, *633*
14:62, *338*
14:67, *388*
14:70, *387*
15:39, *391*
15:40, *1005*
15:46, *711*
15:47, *1005*
16:1, *1005*
16:2, *680*
16:5, *711*
16:6, *388*
16:7, *385, 904*

16:9-20, *981*
16:15, *770*

Luke
1, *13, 644*
1:1, *8*
1:1-4, *7, 8, 9, 12, 13, 23, 272, 788, 877, 951, 1227*
1:2, *763*
1:3, *789, 1206*
1:4, *9*
1:5, *14, 905*
1:5-13, *244*
1:5-23, *562*
1:6, *465*
1:8-56, *243*
1:19-22, *749*
1:28, *660*
1:29, *244*
1:32, *43*
1:36, *1004*
1:38, *467, 723, 1100*
1:39, *244*
1:41, *244, 905, 972*
1:43, *669*
1:46-47, *601*
1:47, *1083*
1:48, *1100*
1:51-53, *962*
1:54, *207*
1:54-55, *209*
1:55, *38, 207*
1:67, *905, 972*
1:68, *780*
1:68-79, *20*
1:70, *346*
1:73, *43, 209*
1:75, *581*
1:76, *669*
1:76-79, *824*
1:78, *709*
1:79, *894, 1021*
2, *894*
2:1, *767*
2:8, *659*
2:11, *19, 175, 669*
2:14, *391*
2:15-20, *1021*
2:19, *426, 723*
2:22, *780*
2:29, *174*
2:29-32, *886*
2:29-35, *789*
2:30-32, *824*
2:32, *13, 391, 563*
2:34, *19*
2:35, *1021*
2:37, *658*
2:38, *40, 1002*
2:40, *1201*
2:51, *723*
2:52, *1201*
3, *14*
3:3, *269*
3:3-6, *824*
3:4-6, *391*
3:8, *5, 209*
3:10-14, *243*
3:16, *113, 566, 742, 903, 905*
3:21, *903*
3:21-22, *19, 494, 1123*
3:22, *114, 903*
3:23-38, *43*
3:31, *43*
3:34, *43, 209*
3:37, *43*
3:38, *43*
4:1, *19, 489, 1123, 1166*
4:1-2, *494*
4:1-3, *1170*
4:1-13, *1167*
4:3, *1166*
4:4, *737*

4:8, *528*
4:13, *1166*
4:14, *494*
4:14-15, *19, 1123*
4:15, *1143*
4:16-21, *1143*
4:16-30, *903, 1123*
4:18, *163, 494, 634, 1123*
4:18-19, *19, 271, 642*
4:20, *1143*
4:22, *791, 1143*
4:22-30, *1143*
4:26-27, *391*
4:27, *930*
4:33, *1118*
4:38, *1144*
4:43, *163, 753*
4:44, *14*
5:10, *752, 763*
5:11, *1051*
5:12-14, *990*
5:12-16, *1144*
5:17, *494*
5:17-26, *1144*
5:27-32, *378*
5:30-32, *687*
6, *764*
6:4, *576*
6:6-11, *1144*
6:13, *76, 77*
6:14, *929*
6:14-16, *752*
6:15-16, *1005*
6:16, *190, 616*
6:17, *211*
6:17-18, *1118*
6:20, *568, 634, 1052*
6:20-49, *634*
6:22, *569*
6:22-23, *914*
6:22-33, *569*
6:23, *42, 972*
6:24, *1052*
6:26, *42, 914*
6:27-36, *572*
6:27-38, *22*
6:28, *130*
6:31, *572*
6:32, *574*
6:35, *22, 574, 1038*
6:36-38, *574, 734, 1193*
6:39, *658*
6:40, *913*
7:1-10, *243, 391*
7:5, *1144*
7:14, *711*
7:16, *780*
7:19-20, *861*
7:31-35, *1202*
7:33-35, *990*
7:34, *502, 687*
7:35, *1201*
7:44, *504*
7:49, *162*
8:1-3, *1216*
8:3, *1051*
8:8, *571*
8:10, *783*
8:11, *793*
8:14, *930*
8:31, *460*
8:40-42, *1144*
8:43-48, *1144*
8:49-56, *1144*
9:1-6, *930*
9:3, *992*
9:4, *991*
9:10-17, *930*
9:16, *943*
9:22, *272*
9:22-26, *752*
9:23, *20, 273*
9:23-24, *1123*
9:26, *396*

9:30, *816*
9:31, *466, 467*
9:43, *272*
9:50, *576*
9:51, *211, 467, 562, 885, 1139*
9:52-55, *1033*
9:53, *562*
9:57-62, *885*
9:62, *885*
10:3, *641*
10:4, *992*
10:5, *991*
10:6, *991*
10:7, *991*
10:8, *991*
10:9, *753*
10:13-15, *1144*
10:16, *780*
10:17-21, *494*
10:18, *577*
10:21-22, *1021, 1202*
10:29-37, *391*
10:30-37, *15*
11:4, *1167*
11:9, *568*
11:13, *19, 357, 930*
11:16, *1166*
11:20, *631, 632*
11:21-22, *162*
11:26, *570*
11:28, *571*
11:31, *41, 1201*
11:34-35, *657*
11:37-54, *885*
11:40-41, *990*
11:43, *1142*
11:47-48, *42*
11:47-51, *1123*
11:48-50, *972*
11:49, *86, 1201*
11:49-51, *992, 1202*
11:50, *269*
12:8, *571, 1123*
12:8-12, *1123*
12:11, *165, 757, 1144*
12:11-12, *494, 1123*
12:12, *317*
12:27, *41*
12:29-32, *567*
12:32-45, *569*
12:33, *1051*
12:35, *1200*
12:39, *570*
12:39-40, *265, 266, 571*
12:40, *266*
13:4-12, *702*
13:10-11, *209*
13:10-17, *1144*
13:14, *609*
13:16, *43*
13:22, *562, 1139*
13:22-30, *687*
13:23, *196*
13:25, *943*
13:28, *6, 209, 1162*
13:28-29, *391, 502, 753*
13:29, *391, 643, 687, 1162*
13:33, *467*
13:33-35, *1123*
13:34, *972*
13:34-35, *466, 1202*
14:1-6, *1144*
14:1-24, *1104*
14:11, *568, 962*
14:15-24, *391*
14:26, *1221*
14:27, *273*
14:33, *1051*
14:35, *571*
15:1-2, *687*
16:9, *1051, 1052*
16:10, *574*
16:10-12, *674*

16:11-12, *574*
16:13, *674*
16:18, *713, 995*
16:19-31, *209, 624*
16:22-25, *610*
17:3, *568*
17:11, *1076, 1139*
17:11-19, *15, 391*
17:26-28, *839*
17:28-29, *41*
17:28-32, *624*
17:29, *624*
17:30, *1021*
17:33, *270*
18:1, *858*
18:2-5, *1220*
18:7, *658*
18:14, *568, 962*
18:22, *1051*
18:29-30, *1038*
18:30, *913*
18:31, *272, 1139*
18:34, *1180*
19:2-10, *391*
19:8, *1051, 1052*
19:9, *209*
19:11, *858, 1139*
19:26, *709*
19:27-28, *1123*
19:28, *12*
19:28-40, *992*
19:31, *669*
19:34, *669*
19:38, *663*
19:42-44, *1123*
19:45, *1164*
20, *563*
20:9-19, *466, 1123*
20:15, *567*
20:17, *838, 1127*
20:25, *324*
20:38, *209*
20:46, *1142*
21, *51, 336, 1180*
21:1-4, *1164*
21:5-6, *1123*
21:5-36, *1164*
21:6, *466*
21:8, *51*
21:12, *913, 1144*
21:12-15, *1123*
21:12-19, *1123*
21:13-19, *20*
21:19, *1123*
21:20-22, *900*
21:20-24, *1123*
21:21, *912*
21:24, *467*
21:27, *396*
22, *943*
22:3-6, *930*
22:15, *268*
22:16, *268*
22:17-20, *686*
22:19, *269, 271, 680, 686, 1105*
22:19-20, *20, 268, 269, 270, 272, 1162*
22:20, *245, 268, 269, 631*
22:21, *269, 272*
22:24-27, *269*
22:27, *687*
22:28-30, *273, 687*
22:29-30, *631, 686*
22:30, *76, 631, 742, 1105*
22:39-46, *1167*
22:54, *1123*
22:66, *274, 1123*
22:69, *859*
23:1-5, *1123*
23:13-25, *274*
23:28, *467*
23:28-31, *1123*
23:30, *1085*

23:42, *859*
23:43, *776*
23:46, *775*
23:47, *243, 271, 286, 487*
23:49, *137, 1216*
23:55-56, *1216*
24, *97, 101, 301, 826*
24:1, *680, 681*
24:1-10, *1216*
24:6, *904*
24:9-10, *76*
24:10, *1005*
24:13, *680*
24:13-35, *680, 931*
24:18, *1004*
24:19, *780*
24:21, *40, 780, 1180*
24:25, *137*
24:25-27, *114, 271*
24:26, *96, 281, 397*
24:26-27, *153, 272, 521, 569, 778*
24:27-35, *688*
24:30, *943, 1105, 1231*
24:30-32, *271*
24:34, *669*
24:35, *686, 1105*
24:36-43, *687*
24:37, *45*
24:39, *573*
24:41-43, *1231*
24:44, *778*
24:44-47, *628, 886*
24:44-49, *271*
24:45-49, *492*
24:46-47, *98*
24:47, *115, 269, 391, 562, 719*
24:47-48, *391, 903*
24:48, *906*
24:48-49, *496*
24:49, *19, 113, 490, 903, 904, 905, 906, 968, 1199*
24:50-51, *63, 858*
24:51, *98*
24:52, *602*

John
1, *157, 577, 597, 1114*
1:1, *163, 665, 957, 1023*
1:1-2, *665*
1:1-3, *957, 960*
1:1-14, *639*
1:1-18, *176, 356, 590, 652, 933, 957, 958, 1202*
1:3, *1224*
1:4, *425, 665*
1:5, *597*
1:5-7, *597*
1:8, *597*
1:9, *392, 425*
1:12-13, *665*
1:13, *313, 792, 793*
1:14, *163, 575, 590, 591, 639, 665, 959*
1:14-17, *665, 933*
1:17, *780*
1:17-18, *782*
1:18, *666*
1:19-20, *576*
1:21, *816*
1:23, *641*
1:29, *283, 284, 641, 1164*
1:31, *1021*
1:32-34, *119*
1:35-42, *596*
1:35-51, *589*
1:43-48, *931*
1:51, *582*
2, *810*
2:1, *723*
2:1-11, *722, 1235*
2:3, *723*
2:3-11, *597*

2:4, *723*
2:5, *723*
2:11, *1021*
2:12, *723*
2:12-17, *597*
2:13-17, *1165*
2:14-22, *1161*
2:15, *1166*
2:17-22, *1165*
2:18-27, *597*
2:21, *990, 1165*
2:28, *597*
3:1, *1131*
3:1-6, *1236*
3:1-8, *593*
3:1-21, *1131*
3:2, *1131*
3:3-5, *576*
3:3-7, *118*
3:3-8, *792*
3:3-21, *793*
3:5, *159, 540, 795*
3:11-24, *597*
3:14, *779*
3:16, *595, 1131*
3:16-17, *163, 1223*
3:16-21, *1035*
3:17, *392, 1131*
3:19, *658, 659, 1131*
3:21, *1021, 1131*
3:22—4:3, *596*
3:22-36, *589*
3:34, *163*
4, *1076, 1235*
4:1-6, *597*
4:1-42, *392, 753*
4:4, *1076*
4:6, *597*
4:7-21, *597*
4:9, *208*
4:10, *571, 833, 992*
4:14, *992*
4:20-24, *1235*
4:22, *208, 392, 582*
4:23-24, *495*
4:34, *736, 737*
4:38, *164, 931, 1077*
4:39, *1076*
4:42, *175, 392, 1074*
4:46-54, *392*
5:1-4, *597*
5:2, *188*
5:5-12, *597*
5:16-18, *164*
5:17, *582, 685*
5:19, *594*
5:21-29, *336*
5:28-29, *1016*
5:36-38, *163*
5:46, *210*
6, *233, 589, 737, 1230, 1235*
6:1, *710*
6:5-7, *931*
6:6, *1166*
6:14, *861*
6:17, *659*
6:25-59, *737*
6:29, *163*
6:52-63, *593*
6:57, *163*
7:5, *616*
7:19, *583*
7:22-23, *227*
7:23, *685*
7:29, *163*
7:35-36, *392*
7:37-39, *119*
7:38, *86, 417, 833*
7:39, *1194*
7:42, *43*
7:49, *583*
7:52, *386*
8, *161*

8:6, *1166*
8:12, *657*
8:17, *227*
8:31, *208*
8:31-39, *210*
8:33, *43*
8:38-47, *794*
8:39, *210*
8:44, *42, 582, 1079*
8:53, *210*
8:56, *210, 582*
8:58, *164*
9, *382, 589, 1091*
9:2, *381*
9:3, *1021*
9:5, *425*
9:22, *166*
9:34, *913*
9:39, *1091*
10, *541*
10:1-16, *1235*
10:1-18, *877, 880*
10:3-5, *1235*
10:8-10, *1091*
10:9, *1091*
10:10-16, *1092*
10:11-16, *1091*
10:30, *164, 1083*
10:36, *163*
11, *709, 710*
11:16, *765*
11:25, *793*
11:27, *861*
11:42, *163*
11:45, *208*
11:52, *392, 1083*
12:11, *208*
12:12-19, *992*
12:13, *663*
12:20-22, *392, 931*
12:35, *657*
12:41, *210*
12:42, *166, 853*
12:46, *425, 657*
12:47, *1223*
13, *1235*
13:3, *101*
13:14, *504*
13:16, *163, 913*
13:23, *590*
13:25, *588*
13:34, *238, 575, 594*
13:34-35, *646, 880*
14:6, *160*
14:7-10, *639*
14:8-9, *931*
14:9, *1021*
14:12, *589*
14:13-14, *589*
14:14, *1237*
14:16, *490*
14:18, *208*
14:22, *616*
14:23-24, *593*
14:25-26, *392*
14:26, *113, 490, 491, 589*
14:27, *897*
14:28, *101*
15, *640*
15:1-11, *1235*
15:4, *1235*
15:5, *1235*
15:7, *946*
15:10, *238*
15:12, *238, 594*
15:15, *1021*
15:17, *594*
15:18-19, *1223*
15:18-25, *253*
15:20, *913*
15:26, *113, 490, 491*
15:26-27, *357*
16:2, *166, 913*
16:7, *589*

16:8-11, *392*
16:10, *101*
16:13, *589, 594*
16:21-22, *1210*
16:23, *1237*
16:28, *101*
16:33, *328, 339, 897, 1180*
17, *589, 594*
17:3, *163*
17:4, *163*
17:6, *1021, 1224*
17:7-8, *639*
17:8, *163*
17:11, *1224*
17:12, *794*
17:18, *163, 164, 1224*
17:20-23, *594*
17:21, *163*
17:23, *163*
17:24, *420, 595, 1223*
17:25, *163*
17:25-26, *639*
17:26, *1021*
18:6, *164*
18:20, *1143*
18:28, *641*
18:31-34, *1171*
18:37-38, *1171*
19, *1197*
19:10-11, *913*
19:17-20, *567*
19:25, *1006*
19:25-27, *723*
19:26, *590, 723*
19:26-27, *722*
19:27, *722, 1006*
19:34, *119*
19:34-35, *914*
19:35, *588*
19:36, *641*
19, *680*
20:1, *681*
20:1-10, *224*
20:2, *590*
20:19, *681, 1231*
20:19-23, *392*
20:21, *163, 164*
20:21-23, *492*
20:22, *904*
20:23, *589*
20:24, *588*
20:26, *681*
20:28, *957, 1114*
20:30-31, *357*
20:31, *597, 723, 877, 1113*
21, *590, 925, 927, 1235*
21:2, *1005*
21:7, *590*
21:15-17, *915, 921*
21:15-19, *877, 912*
21:16, *880*
21:18, *570*
21:20, *590*
21:20-25, *590*
21:24-25, *16*

Acts
1, *14, 82, 97, 170, 171, 173, 363, 389, 562, 644, 767*
1:1, *8, 13, 23, 414, 742, 789, 1227*
1:1-2, *492*
1:1-9, *537*
1:1-12, *756*
1:2, *76, 77, 97, 98, 222, 317, 630*
1:2-3, *106*
1:3, *629, 631, 762, 859, 952, 1228*
1:3-4, *1231*
1:3-11, *332*
1:4, *19, 247, 415, 490, 562, 687, 904, 969, 1112*

1:4-5, *113, 492, 742*
1:5, *79, 360, 390, 493, 494, 630, 742*
1:5-20, *1144*
1:6, *333, 343, 416, 631, 643, 859, 1188*
1:6-7, *629, 791*
1:6-8, *21, 332, 333, 344, 766*
1:6-11, *196, 858*
1:7, *21, 251, 317, 333, 415, 859, 1112, 1199*
1:7-8, *333*
1:8, *11, 14, 15, 19, 20, 53, 79, 114, 115, 144, 243, 245, 251, 270, 333, 355, 357, 390, 391, 414, 493, 494, 562, 563, 630, 631, 661, 718, 742, 752, 753, 754, 762, 763, 766, 767, 770, 771, 774, 859, 886, 903, 906, 930, 1061, 1076, 1124, 1207*
1:9, *102*
1:9-11, *63, 96, 97, 98, 746*
1:10, *45*
1:10-11, *99*
1:11, *96, 97, 196, 333, 387, 643, 858, 859, 1199*
1:12-26, *1162*
1:13, *92, 545, 752, 756, 929, 1066*
1:13-14, *356, 743*
1:14, *357, 616, 722, 723, 903, 941, 944, 1006, 1207, 1216*
1:14-15, *20*
1:15, *752, 785*
1:15-16, *92*
1:15-17, *1086*
1:15-26, *77, 106, 467, 756, 944*
1:16, *17, 317, 467, 497, 824*
1:16-17, *137*
1:16-18, *655*
1:16-20, *930*
1:20, *824*
1:21, *17, 416, 668, 669*
1:21-22, *76, 742, 762*
1:21-26, *1086*
1:22, *76, 97, 98, 106, 171, 718, 742, 763, 1204*
1:23-25, *1228*
1:24, *20, 222, 317, 416, 941, 942*
1:24-25, *357*
1:24-26, *76*
1:25, *137, 459*
1:25-26, *756*
1:26, *76*
2, *14, 21, 113, 247, 332, 391, 437, 493, 627, 752, 764, 906, 1094, 1178*
2:1, *754, 758*
2:1-3, *492*
2:1-4, *222, 244, 390, 391, 722, 742, 903*
2:1-13, *746, 906*
2:1-21, *1194*
2:1-42, *902*
2:1-43, *332*
2:2, *508, 903*
2:4, *79, 113, 114, 357, 493, 494, 742, 971, 972, 1207*
2:4-13, *1177*
2:5, *20, 137*
2:5:31, *260*
2:5, *1066*
2:5-11, *756, 906*
2:5-12, *144*
2:7, *196, 387*
2:8, *1178*

2:9, *754, 1151*
2:9-11, *20, 288, 754, 767, 1178*
2:10, *35, 149, 150*
2:10-11, *1066*
2:11, *759, 906, 972, 1178*
2:12:12, *508*
2:12-14, *755*
2:13, *905*
2:14, *77, 106, 562, 1066*
2:14-36, *543*
2:14-40, *10, 77*
2:14-41, *944*
2:15-17, *332*
2:16, *356*
2:16-21, *1194*
2:16-36, *647, 1022*
2:16-40, *825*
2:16-41, *793*
2:17, *20, 137, 195, 251, 332, 333, 375, 562, 622, 825, 906, 970, 971, 972, 1207*
2:17-18, *390, 391, 743, 970, 971, 974*
2:17-21, *113, 479, 493, 536, 824, 904, 970*
2:18, *906, 1086, 1178*
2:18-19, *260*
2:19, *19, 906, 1094*
2:20, *668, 858, 859, 969*
2:21, *13, 20, 160, 270, 318, 416, 562, 630, 632, 786, 825, 860, 906, 942*
2:21-22, *20, 1216*
2:22, *19, 415, 466, 491, 631, 750, 906, 939, 1094, 1181*
2:22-23, *630*
2:22-24, *96, 256*
2:22-36, *96, 353*
2:23, *17, 160, 260, 274, 317, 415, 687, 904, 913, 1188*
2:23-24, *113, 655, 1069*
2:23-31, *171*
2:23-36, *19*
2:24, *137, 416, 491, 669, 939, 1181*
2:25, *668, 669*
2:25-28, *96, 479, 824*
2:25-32, *776*
2:25-36, *356*
2:26, *375, 601, 602, 860*
2:27, *375, 487, 825, 903, 1240*
2:28, *207, 601, 604, 903*
2:29, *41, 43*
2:29-31, *96*
2:29-36, *20*
2:30, *415, 631, 824, 825*
2:31, *153, 375, 825, 1240*
2:32, *96, 171, 416, 491, 718, 1204*
2:32-33, *260, 360, 490, 493*
2:32-34, *96*
2:32-35, *630*
2:32-39, *496*
2:33, *19, 96, 97, 113, 247, 273, 357, 391, 430, 490, 492, 630, 631, 825, 903, 904, 905, 969, 1237*
2:33-34, *97, 964*
2:33-35, *98*
2:33-36, *360*
2:33-39, *970*
2:34, *96, 97, 668, 670, 825, 905*
2:34-35, *97, 479, 824*
2:36, *97, 98, 106, 113, 153, 158, 171, 256, 360, 416, 508, 521, 543, 630, 661, 669, 762, 825, 860, 906, 1112*

2:36-38, *360*
2:36-39, *1012*
2:37, *21, 76*
2:37-38, *1218*
2:38, *20, 21, 113, 114, 153, 256, 260, 273, 333, 364, 380, 391, 416, 489, 493, 631, 766, 767, 785, 930, 971, 1227*
2:38-39, *271, 274, 493*
2:38-40, *382, 622*
2:38-42, *1012*
2:39, *20, 247, 318, 414, 415, 490, 668, 670, 766, 906, 1116*
2:40, *357, 749, 860, 1072*
2:41, *21, 92, 113, 144, 195, 196, 354, 364, 757, 758*
2:41-42, *114, 687*
2:41-46, *687*
2:41-47, *948*
2:42, *76, 106, 145, 271, 686, 742, 906, 942, 944, 1086, 1104, 1105, 1227, 1228, 1236*
2:42-47, *692*
2:43, *19, 76, 356, 371, 742, 747, 906, 1094*
2:43-45, *1051*
2:43-47, *373, 789, 894*
2:44, *21, 195, 196, 373, 906, 1051*
2:44-45, *20, 22, 356, 382, 476, 687, 997*
2:44-46, *378*
2:44-47, *503*
2:45, *1051*
2:46, *92, 115, 165, 197, 222, 271, 356, 508, 580, 601, 660, 683, 687, 944, 1104, 1105, 1154, 1162, 1227, 1228*
2:46-47, *521*
2:47, *195, 196, 414, 435, 521, 580, 670, 1227*
3, *1, 780, 781, 873, 949, 1126*
3:1, *20, 165, 580, 681, 755, 941, 944*
3:1-8, *357*
3:1-9, *356*
3:1-10, *78, 209, 647, 747, 751, 1010, 1228*
3:1-16, *333*
3:1-26, *398, 1162*
3:2, *346, 1207*
3:3, *580*
3:4, *755*
3:5:30, *260*
3:6, *1, 13, 20, 256, 416, 631, 786*
3:7, *207*
3:8-9, *521*
3:11-26, *77, 153, 647*
3:12, *19, 398*
3:12-21, *114*
3:13, *1, 43, 171, 274, 398, 415, 416, 751*
3:13-14, *780*
3:13-15, *243*
3:13-25, *353*
3:13-26, *19, 1022*
3:14, *171, 260, 487, 780, 942*
3:14-15, *22*
3:14-16, *260*
3:15, *1, 137, 256, 398, 399, 416, 491, 655, 718, 780, 1069, 1204*
3:16, *1, 19, 20, 21, 364, 368, 630, 631, 751*
3:17, *171, 274*
3:17-21, *1012, 1188*

3:17-26, *21, 343, 766, 793*
3:18, *153, 171, 272, 332, 356, 415*
3:18-19, *260*
3:18-21, *171, 273, 542, 824, 860*
3:19, *21, 622, 670, 1012*
3:19-20, *894*
3:19-21, *274, 333, 360, 629, 630, 859*
3:19-26, *344*
3:20, *251, 317, 398, 858*
3:20-21, *333, 440*
3:21, *17, 21, 98, 251, 317, 333, 346, 360, 487, 1188*
3:22, *40, 171, 247, 356, 415, 537, 668, 670, 779*
3:22-23, *2, 479, 779*
3:22-26, *332, 333*
3:23, *196, 197, 415, 824*
3:24, *39, 825*
3:25, *1, 38, 130, 210, 246, 247, 251, 415, 479, 906*
3:26, *1, 2, 130, 171, 415, 416, 491, 1095*
3:32, *414*
3:34, *416*
4, *581, 951*
4:1, *963*
4:1-2, *467*
4:1-21, *762*
4:1-22, *1123*
4:1-31, *355, 761*
4:1-37, *1162*
4:2, *628, 776*
4:3, *755, 1138*
4:3-21, *145*
4:4, *92, 354, 757, 758*
4:7, *416*
4:8, *79, 107, 231, 357, 494, 742, 761, 767, 906, 972*
4:8-12, *160, 972*
4:8-13, *19*
4:9, *1072*
4:10, *19, 20, 153, 171, 256, 399, 416, 491, 542, 751*
4:10-12, *172*
4:11, *414, 479, 647, 824, 838, 1126, 1128*
4:11-12, *416*
4:12, *17, 20, 160, 272, 416, 630, 786, 860, 953*
4:13, *137, 355, 382, 494, 758, 767, 916, 972*
4:16, *562, 1094*
4:17, *416, 756*
4:18, *172, 416, 907*
4:18-20, *756*
4:18-31, *972*
4:19, *137, 415, 755, 1195*
4:21, *414, 1138*
4:21-31, *521*
4:22, *1094*
4:23-28, *273*
4:23-31, *22, 273, 356, 521, 942, 1228*
4:23-33, *114*
4:24, *174, 251, 252, 414, 426, 660*
4:24-26, *526*
4:24-30, *521, 943*
4:24-31, *356*
4:25, *41, 43, 171, 479, 497*
4:25-26, *479, 824*
4:26, *152, 670*
4:27, *49, 479, 487, 542, 1185*
4:28, *17, 171, 487*
4:29, *756, 972, 1086, 1100, 1138*
4:29-30, *19*
4:29-31, *631*

4:30, *19, 20, 416, 630, 631, 1094*
4:31, *382, 390, 391, 494, 742, 761, 767, 904, 906, 941, 942, 971, 972, 1178, 1227*
4:32, *20, 22, 137, 196, 373, 1051, 1178, 1228*
4:32-35, *22, 476*
4:32-37, *1051*
4:33, *76, 77, 106, 171, 356, 416, 433, 668, 742, 940, 1204*
4:33-37, *106*
4:34, *356, 508, 680, 953*
4:35, *106*
4:36, *764, 971*
4:36-37, *22, 382*
4:37, *106*
4:42, *1053*
5, *581, 1082*
5:1, *1117*
5:1-10, *77, 1221*
5:1-11, *73, 437, 466, 747, 930, 1051, 1206, 1228*
5:2, *414*
5:3, *1077, 1079*
5:3-4, *1118, 1185*
5:5, *73, 416, 655*
5:9, *490, 1166*
5:10, *73, 655*
5:11, *195, 197, 205*
5:12, *19, 76, 356, 742, 1094*
5:12-16, *747*
5:12-33, *762*
5:13, *580*
5:14, *92, 669, 1216*
5:15, *9, 78, 436*
5:15-16, *1117*
5:15-19, *356*
5:16, *21, 333, 382, 414, 562*
5:17, *196, 747*
5:17-21, *21*
5:17-40, *1123*
5:17-41, *355, 467*
5:17-42, *160, 761*
5:19, *18, 45, 659, 668, 1012*
5:19-20, *62*
5:20, *165, 655*
5:21, *18, 231, 357, 542, 580*
5:22, *153*
5:25, *357, 580*
5:27, *1138*
5:27-32, *77*
5:28, *20, 172, 357, 416, 562, 756*
5:28-29, *756*
5:29, *17, 231*
5:29-31, *357*
5:29-32, *77, 1012*
5:30, *20, 171, 260, 280, 399, 415, 416*
5:30-31, *19, 20, 256, 273, 274, 360, 382, 491, 762, 1069*
5:30-33, *231*
5:31, *21, 40, 96, 98, 171, 260, 380, 416, 542, 630, 1072, 1082*
5:32, *171, 391, 496, 718, 742, 761, 1204*
5:33, *357, 655*
5:34, *1082*
5:37, *73, 1060*
5:38-39, *19*
5:39, *415, 878*
5:40, *20, 416, 907, 910, 1138*
5:40-41, *172*
5:41, *20, 137, 273, 356,*

416, 601, 602, 604, 913
5:41-42, *22*
5:42, *92, 165, 171, 197, 256, 353, 356, 357, 431, 580, 628, 629, 1086*
6, *273, 464, 580, 742, 1125*
6:1, *20, 463, 464, 465, 468, 580, 742, 1123, 1125*
6:1-2, *1086*
6:1-3, *742, 930, 953*
6:1-5, *465*
6:1-6, *22, 106, 137, 222, 462, 468, 549, 686, 687, 742, 929, 1051, 1104, 1123, 1124, 1220*
6:1-7, *373, 767*
6:1-15, *1125*
6:2, *106, 196, 414, 930, 1086*
6:2-3, *464*
6:2-4, *76, 742*
6:3, *106, 490, 742, 930, 971, 1123*
6:4, *106, 742, 930, 972*
6:5, *54, 196, 292, 433, 761, 764, 930, 971, 1123, 1124*
6:6, *106, 357, 942*
6:7, *20, 92, 93, 197, 364, 414, 562, 789, 963*
6:8, *19, 356, 433, 465, 631, 747, 764, 941, 971, 1094, 1123, 1124*
6:8-10, *742, 1123*
6:8-12, *743*
6:8-15, *762, 1124*
6:9, *757, 1099, 1142*
6:9-14, *1125*
6:9-15, *1123*
6:10, *107, 357, 494, 742, 1123, 1201*
6:10-11, *1123*
6:11-14, *466, 647*
6:12, *1123, 1138*
6:13, *3, 466, 487, 509, 718, 1124, 1204*
6:13-14, *2, 580, 1124*
6:14, *466, 1124*
6:15, *45*
6:20-26, *476*
6:51, *1123*
6:54-60, *743*
6:55, *1123*
7, *2, 40, 149, 270, 463, 464, 466, 479, 536, 537, 563, 644, 718, 764, 778, 780, 824, 862, 1076, 1077*
7:1, *467*
7:1-4, *42*
7:2, *2, 43, 207, 396, 479, 644*
7:2-4, *40*
7:2-8, *2, 3, 38, 40, 247, 643*
7:2-53, *10, 11, 466, 543, 972*
7:2-56, *382*
7:3, *250, 415, 479*
7:4, *2, 250*
7:5, *2, 3, 40, 479, 968*
7:5-6, *3, 207*
7:5-7, *415, 479*
7:6, *2, 3, 250*
7:6-7, *40*
7:7, *2, 3, 40, 415*
7:8, *2, 38, 39, 227, 246, 247*
7:8-10, *3*
7:9, *39, 40, 42*
7:9-10, *42, 644*
7:9-16, *40*
7:10, *40, 435, 512, 1201*
7:11-12, *40*
7:13-14, *39*
7:15-16, *39, 40*

7:16, *2*
7:16-17, *2, 40*
7:17, *247, 415, 968, 970*
7:18, *39, 479*
7:20, *39, 40*
7:20-43, *644*
7:20-44, *39, 40, 781*
7:22, *40, 778, 780, 1201*
7:23, *40, 778, 780*
7:23-25, *781*
7:23-42, *467*
7:25, *21, 778*
7:26, *894*
7:26-28, *40*
7:26-29, *781*
7:27, *42, 780*
7:27-28, *479*
7:29, *40, 250, 778*
7:30, *40*
7:31, *21, 670*
7:32, *1, 2, 40, 415*
7:32-33, *40*
7:32-35, *479*
7:33, *251*
7:34-35, *780*
7:35, *42, 778, 780*
7:35-36, *40*
7:36, *780, 1094*
7:37, *247, 356, 415, 416, 467, 479*
7:38, *40, 197, 445, 647, 1069, 1124*
7:39, *42*
7:39-41, *778*
7:39-43, *781*
7:40, *479*
7:40-41, *42*
7:41, *467, 529, 602, 604, 1069*
7:41-43, *467*
7:42, *414, 415, 508, 1069*
7:42-43, *479, 778, 824*
7:43, *111, 466, 467, 644*
7:44, *40, 467, 1070, 1154*
7:44-50, *644, 1154*
7:45, *415*
7:46, *41, 435, 466, 509*
7:46-47, *466*
7:46-48, *466*
7:47, *41, 466, 509*
7:47-50, *1124*
7:48, *161, 466, 467, 529, 633, 1124*
7:48-50, *509, 1124*
7:49, *251, 509*
7:49-50, *824*
7:50, *414*
7:51, *247, 781, 1069*
7:51-53, *231, 467, 824*
7:52, *40, 42, 137, 171, 644, 718, 1054, 1055*
7:52-53, *247*
7:53, *445, 466, 467, 647, 781, 1124*
7:54, *1124, 1125*
7:54-56, *494*
7:54-60, *762, 859, 1123, 1138*
7:55, *273, 396, 416, 495, 742, 761, 904, 971, 972*
7:55-56, *62, 332, 360, 440, 1123*
7:55-60, *1123*
7:56, *356, 630*
7:56-60, *1126*
7:57, *655*
7:57-59, *1124*
7:57-60, *718*
7:58, *166, 718, 883, 1124, 1125, 1204*
7:58-60, *907*
7:59, *360, 416, 630, 775, 943, 944, 1237*
7:59-60, *416*

7:60, *670*
8, *137, 162, 357, 364, 402, 493, 562, 743, 752, 929, 931, 1076, 1118*
8:1, *54, 76, 106, 197, 205, 222, 327, 387, 463, 467, 562, 580, 718, 755, 756, 907, 912, 1076, 1125, 1138, 1227*
8:1-3, *20, 166, 273, 467, 762, 931, 1123, 1124*
8:1-4, *22, 764, 914*
8:1-25, *114*
8:3, *92, 222, 508, 1138, 1216*
8:4, *20, 355, 431, 547, 743, 1138*
8:4-5, *114*
8:4-7, *1010*
8:4-8, *433, 742, 747*
8:4-13, *743, 1118*
8:4-17, *76*
8:4-24, *416, 1138*
8:4-25, *391, 1124*
8:4-40, *763*
8:5, *171, 521, 626, 629, 1076*
8:5-8, *930, 1076*
8:5-13, *764*
8:5-19, *631*
8:6, *1094, 1118*
8:6-7, *356*
8:6-12, *631*
8:7, *382, 414, 1117, 1118*
8:8, *602, 1076*
8:9, *114, 192, 702*
8:9-11, *529*
8:9-12, *930, 1118*
8:9-24, *73, 1076*
8:9-25, *702, 1148*
8:9-40, *537*
8:10, *414, 702*
8:11, *702, 1124*
8:12, *21, 114, 153, 172, 353, 364, 414, 416, 431, 494, 629, 786, 930, 1216, 1227*
8:12-15, *971*
8:13, *364, 930, 941, 1094, 1118*
8:14, *77, 106, 114, 414, 562, 756, 1076, 1124*
8:14-17, *76, 494, 742, 757, 767, 1076*
8:14-24, *930, 1051*
8:14-25, *78, 391, 755, 764, 1163*
8:15, *742, 942*
8:15-16, *114*
8:16, *20, 114, 256, 416, 493, 668, 785*
8:17, *114*
8:17-19, *1178*
8:18, *742, 789*
8:18-19, *115*
8:18-24, *19, 77*
8:19, *939*
8:20, *930*
8:21, *415*
8:22, *380, 942*
8:23, *357, 702, 1095*
8:24, *942*
8:25, *357, 432, 479, 562, 1076*
8:26, *44, 496, 766, 930, 972, 1195*
8:26-29, *1022*
8:26-39, *115, 743, 764, 766*
8:26-40, *18, 245, 391, 433, 754, 1124*
8:27, *754, 930, 1207*
8:27-39, *580, 754*
8:28-29, *1061*
8:29, *44, 357, 391, 496,*

630, 742, 761, 766, 972
8:31, *137*
8:32, *284, 641, 642, 1092*
8:32-33, *271, 479, 536, 642, 824, 1069, 1092, 1139*
8:32-35, *647, 930*
8:34, *356*
8:35, *353, 629*
8:35-38, *661*
8:36, *21, 256, 1227*
8:36-39, *493, 930*
8:37, *115, 354, 1112*
8:38, *115, 1061*
8:39, *44, 115, 391, 490, 493, 602, 742, 747, 761, 766, 767*
8:39-40, *1195*
8:40, *432, 758, 930*
9, *197, 790, 883, 884*
9:1, *197, 754, 1123*
9:1-2, *931, 1144*
9:1-9, *166, 747*
9:1-19, *243, 630, 718, 883, 971, 1124*
9:2, *196, 197, 291, 907, 1138*
9:2-3, *1216*
9:3, *658*
9:3-6, *78*
9:3-7, *1022*
9:3-9, *1195*
9:3-17, *1195*
9:4, *273*
9:4-5, *115, 1139*
9:4-6, *944*
9:5, *668*
9:5-6, *416*
9:6, *317*
9:7-8, *1061*
9:10, *972*
9:10-16, *107, 360, 440, 943, 944, 1195*
9:10-17, *669*
9:10-18, *357*
9:10-19, *78, 747*
9:11, *357, 508, 1228*
9:12, *115*
9:13, *196, 197, 488*
9:14, *20, 196, 197, 416, 786*
9:15, *78, 317, 324, 415, 416, 542, 562, 742, 752, 753, 764, 766, 883, 1204*
9:15-16, *1139*
9:16, *17, 20, 137, 260, 273, 317, 883*
9:17, *21, 115, 357, 391, 494, 742, 767, 905, 971, 1123*
9:17-18, *115, 631*
9:17-19, *373, 493*
9:18, *21, 115, 354, 1227*
9:18-19, *115*
9:19, *904, 1104, 1227*
9:20, *115, 171, 256, 626, 629, 630, 1112*
9:21, *13, 20, 166, 196, 416, 786*
9:22, *171, 256, 357, 521, 941, 1112*
9:23-24, *907*
9:23-25, *659, 912*
9:24, *658*
9:25, *197, 373, 758*
9:26, *197*
9:26-27, *373*
9:26-28, *106*
9:27, *416, 756*
9:28, *668*
9:28-29, *1124*
9:29, *357, 416, 972*
9:30, *197, 758*
9:31, *197, 371, 387, 390,*

496, 668, 742, 789, 894, 1076, 1077
9:32, *196, 488, 756, 758*
9:32-35, *747, 1163*
9:32-41, *1010*
9:32-42, *1206*
9:32-43, *78*
9:33-34, *333*
9:35, *669, 756, 758*
9:36, *16, 368, 758, 1051, 1206*
9:36-41, *1216, 1220*
9:36-43, *437, 747, 1163, 1228*
9:36-44, *743*
9:37, *1066*
9:37-41, *332*
9:39, *1206*
9:40-41, *655*
9:41, *196, 488*
9:43, *244, 373*
10, *49, 243, 244, 364, 378, 380, 391, 493, 566, 688, 743, 757, 886, 894, 1104, 1178, 1195, 1227*
10:1, *18, 20, 115, 243, 244, 247, 377, 382, 647, 756, 761, 764, 766, 767, 1124*
10:1-2, *1060*
10:1-4, *244*
10:1-6, *1195*
10:1-8, *1228*
10:1—11:18, *245*
10:1-16, *18, 1195*
10:1-48, *78, 930, 1144, 1163*
10:2, *116, 123, 197, 372, 414, 512, 1051*
10:2-4, *944*
10:3, *244, 659, 972*
10:3-16, *244*
10:3-22, *1022*
10:4, *244, 368, 415, 670, 1051*
10:6, *508*
10:9, *244, 357, 659, 944*
10:9-16, *943, 993, 1195*
10:10-16, *18, 1010*
10:10-20, *761*
10:13-16, *944*
10:14, *137, 244*
10:16, *244*
10:17, *244, 972*
10:19, *79, 107, 390, 391, 495, 630, 742, 972*
10:20, *244*
10:22, *356, 372, 414, 487, 1057*
10:22-33, *63*
10:23, *197, 244*
10:23-24, *1061*
10:24, *116, 123, 354, 1228*
10:25, *508*
10:27, *354*
10:28, *243, 245, 247, 761*
10:30, *659, 1061*
10:30-33, *972, 1185*
10:31, *415*
10:33, *415, 670*
10:34, *1185*
10:34-43, *11, 537, 566, 762*
10:34-47, *332*
10:35, *371, 372, 831, 1057*
10:35-36, *953*
10:36, *116, 171, 244, 256, 542, 629, 630, 668, 894*
10:36-37, *894*
10:36-38, *353, 669*
10:36-39, *567*
10:36-43, *578*
10:37, *14, 626*
10:37-39, *627*
10:38, *19, 49, 415, 491,*

631, 939, 1078
10:39, *20, 274, 280, 562, 1204*
10:39-40, *256*
10:39-41, *718*
10:40-41, *687*
10:41-42, *317*
10:42, *17, 21, 137, 318, 415, 416, 622, 623, 624, 630, 655, 749, 859, 860*
10:42-43, *171, 825*
10:43, *20, 21, 116, 244, 260, 272, 380, 382, 416, 622, 630, 766, 786*
10:44, *18, 115, 116, 493, 494, 971*
10:44-47, *742, 1195*
10:44-48, *79, 244, 247, 390, 391, 767, 930, 1178*
10:45-47, *19*
10:46, *116, 414, 669, 903, 972*
10:47, *116, 761*
10:47-48, *21, 227, 1227*
10:48, *114, 116, 123, 153, 256, 354, 416, 785*
11, *162*
11:1, *115, 197, 616, 756*
11:1-3, *243, 993*
11:1-18, *15, 77, 78, 244, 245, 391, 742, 993*
11:2, *244, 562*
11:2-3, *245, 993*
11:2-10, *1195*
11:3, *377, 508*
11:4, *1217*
11:4-10, *373*
11:5-17, *11, 767*
11:8, *106*
11:12, *391, 630*
11:12-17, *79*
11:14, *123, 197, 512, 860, 1072*
11:15-16, *494*
11:15-17, *391, 930, 1178*
11:16, *113, 364, 669*
11:17, *21, 116, 364, 416, 668, 669*
11:17-18, *18, 244*
11:18, *106, 116, 227, 244, 414, 415, 622, 688, 886, 1012*
11:19, *547, 757, 758, 764, 1138, 1180*
11:19-20, *467*
11:19-21, *144, 146, 355, 743, 1124*
11:19-24, *756*
11:19-26, *76*
11:19-29, *1227*
11:19-30, *54, 391, 1151*
11:20, *54, 256, 353, 416, 764*
11:21, *630*
11:22, *78, 222, 562*
11:22-26, *54, 764*
11:23, *434, 602*
11:24, *79, 391, 971*
11:25, *758*
11:25-26, *1219*
11:26, *196, 197, 387, 1151*
11:27, *222, 562*
11:27-28, *971*
11:27-30, *22, 78, 550, 742, 743, 953*
11:28, *251, 357, 391, 495, 630, 932, 972, 1022*
11:29, *382, 1086*
11:30, *106, 222*
12, *757*
12:1-2, *77, 145, 718, 1138*
12:1-4, *762*
12:1-11, *467*

12:1-17, *560, 757*
12:1-19, *21, 747*
12:2, *755*
12:2-4, *907*
12:3-11, *718*
12:4-10, *1060*
12:5, *414, 521, 670*
12:5-17, *1219*
12:6-11, *44, 62, 659*
12:7-11, *18*
12:9, *1185*
12:11, *45, 668, 670, 1185*
12:12, *92, 356, 508, 512, 521, 743, 765, 1206, 1228*
12:12-17, *197, 222*
12:13, *1206*
12:14, *602*
12:15, *45*
12:17, *92, 186, 197, 546, 670, 757, 764, 1066, 1220*
12:18-19, *1060*
12:19-24, *747*
12:20, *894*
12:20-23, *325, 437, 932, 1008*
12:23, *18, 45, 395, 416, 655, 668, 1060*
12:24, *789*
12:25, *562, 1086*
13, *2, 93, 378, 496, 647, 764, 767, 825, 883, 1082, 1216*
13:1, *54, 146, 197, 205, 222, 495, 496, 764, 971, 972, 973*
13:1-2, *1022*
13:1-3, *78, 107, 147, 356, 743, 1151, 1227*
13:1-4, *19, 79*
13:2, *78, 317, 357, 360, 391, 416, 630, 670, 757, 904, 1195*
13:2-3, *146*
13:2-4, *107*
13:3, *54, 78, 137, 357, 496, 942*
13:4, *391, 496, 630, 761, 1061*
13:4-5, *78*
13:4-12, *21*
13:5, *291, 758, 944*
13:6, *758, 973, 1010*
13:6-12, *78, 357, 416, 437, 747, 749, 930*
13:7, *1059*
13:8, *364, 368, 1010*
13:8-12, *78, 742*
13:9, *761, 904, 906, 972*
13:10, *1078*
13:11, *658, 659, 668*
13:12, *364, 628*
13:13, *1061*
13:13-43, *1144*
13:13-52, *1143*
13:14, *53, 291, 764, 944*
13:14-52, *758*
13:15, *293, 450, 496, 609, 1042*
13:16, *207, 288, 372, 414, 1082, 1144*
13:16-23, *536*
13:16-41, *10, 11, 450, 566, 647, 825, 972*
13:17, *250, 317, 415, 542*
13:17-18, *40*
13:17-21, *247*
13:17-25, *1082*
13:18, *415*
13:19, *250, 415*
13:20, *39*
13:22, *41, 479*
13:22-25, *2*
13:23, *207, 247, 415, 631, 1082*

13:23-32, *970*
13:24, *247*
13:24-25, *566*
13:25-41, *762*
13:26, *2, 207, 372, 414, 537, 860, 1073, 1082, 1144*
13:26-41, *537*
13:27, *272, 562*
13:27-28, *274, 566*
13:27-37, *1082*
13:27-39, *1012*
13:29, *20*
13:30, *399*
13:30-33, *543*
13:31, *562*
13:31-32, *718*
13:32, *1069*
13:32-33, *38, 415*
13:32-39, *260, 631*
13:32-41, *910*
13:33, *247, 794, 1112*
13:33-34, *491*
13:33-35, *479*
13:33-39, *969*
13:34, *479, 824, 967*
13:34-35, *825*
13:34-37, *776*
13:35, *479, 487, 824*
13:36, *17*
13:38, *21, 382*
13:38-39, *10, 260, 382, 647, 1056, 1069*
13:39, *21, 40, 248, 364*
13:40-41, *623*
13:41, *364, 479, 824*
13:43, *372, 434, 1145*
13:44, *357*
13:44-49, *20*
13:44-52, *1144*
13:45, *2, 1082, 1138*
13:45-49, *22*
13:46, *247, 347, 391, 415, 562, 623, 953*
13:46-47, *78*
13:46-48, *742*
13:47, *15, 23, 251, 271, 333, 479, 536, 562, 658, 824, 886, 1073, 1139*
13:48, *137, 318, 347, 364, 602, 604, 1082*
13:48-50, *288*
13:48-52, *1139*
13:50, *288, 372, 907, 1082, 1138, 1145, 1206, 1217*
13:50-51, *166*
13:50-52, *356*
13:52, *494, 496, 602, 1178*
14, *751*
14:1, *20, 196, 288, 291, 364, 764, 944*
14:1-3, *78*
14:1-4, *1144*
14:1-7, *137, 758*
14:1-18, *20*
14:2, *288, 355*
14:2-6, *166*
14:3, *19, 434, 631, 742, 747, 1094, 1204*
14:4, *78, 79, 107, 742, 762*
14:5, *288, 907*
14:5-6, *1139*
14:7, *432*
14:8-9, *742*
14:8-10, *78*
14:8-11, *333, 1010*
14:8-18, *437, 747*
14:8-20, *416, 762, 1148*
14:9, *21, 364, 368, 1072*
14:11, *759*
14:11-12, *414*
14:11-15, *760*

14:12, *470*
14:13, *963*
14:14, *78, 79, 107, 742, 762*
14:15, *41, 251, 354, 414, 432, 655, 718, 1012, 1148*
14:15-17, *153, 356, 627*
14:16, *415*
14:17, *354, 602, 604, 1022, 1204*
14:19, *1138, 1143*
14:19-20, *718, 747, 1139*
14:20, *769*
14:21, *432*
14:21-22, *742*
14:21-28, *1151*
14:22, *17, 20, 196, 197, 273, 317, 332, 368, 414, 629, 630, 860*
14:22-23, *373*
14:23, *78, 107, 137, 205, 222, 743*
14:23-28, *355*
14:25, *758*
14:26, *434, 1061*
14:26-28, *373*
14:27, *54, 364, 368, 767*
15, *76, 145, 162, 186, 187, 227, 247, 377, 378, 467, 546, 581, 647, 648, 670, 825, 971, 993, 994*
15:1, *40, 54, 145, 162, 647, 860, 993, 994, 1072*
15:1-12, *993*
15:1-29, *247, 503, 647*
15:1-35, *54, 391, 467, 742*
15:2, *106, 529, 562, 743*
15:2-11, *1069*
15:3, *602, 767, 1076*
15:4, *106, 373, 562, 743, 766*
15:5, *40, 162, 196, 581, 586, 647, 764, 994*
15:6, *106, 743*
15:6-11, *243*
15:7, *21, 317, 415, 432*
15:7-8, *20*
15:7-11, *78*
15:8, *415, 1178*
15:8-9, *1195*
15:9, *21*
15:10, *197, 248, 649, 994, 1166*
15:10-11, *647*
15:11, *145, 247, 416, 434, 647, 668, 860, 994, 1072*
15:12, *19, 196, 529, 631, 747, 767, 1094*
15:12-18, *196*
15:13-21, *106, 244, 546, 645, 647, 757*
15:13-29, *993*
15:13-35, *1163*
15:14, *197, 210*
15:14-18, *766*
15:15, *196*
15:15-17, *479, 824*
15:16, *631, 1154*
15:16-18, *415, 536, 824*
15:17, *13, 318, 631, 825*
15:17-18, *546*
15:18, *251, 346*
15:19, *145, 825, 994, 1163*
15:19-21, *1144*
15:20, *162, 349, 529, 883, 994, 1088, 1163, 1217*
15:21, *40, 626, 994, 1163*
15:22, *106, 222, 616, 764, 971*
15:22-23, *137, 743*
15:22-28, *106*
15:22-29, *138, 647, 994, 1163*
15:22-32, *971*

15:22-35, *1151*
15:23, *106, 153, 758, 952*
15:23-29, *26, 546*
15:26, *137, 153, 416, 668*
15:27, *616*
15:28, *145, 630, 904, 994, 1163*
15:29, *162, 529, 1217*
15:30, *196*
15:30-32, *743*
15:31, *496*
15:32, *222, 616, 971, 994, 1163*
15:33, *894, 895, 897, 994, 1163*
15:35, *628, 629*
15:36, *883, 1217*
15:39, *758, 764*
15:40, *54, 434, 764, 769*
15:41, *197, 758, 1219*
16, *14, 93, 670*
16:1, *137, 227, 764*
16:1-3, *227*
16:1-18, *930*
16:3, *227, 647, 648, 761, 1069*
16:4, *106, 529, 562, 743*
16:5, *197, 205*
16:6, *107, 357, 391, 495, 630, 904*
16:6-7, *19, 79, 496, 630*
16:6-10, *18, 630, 1022, 1195*
16:7, *107, 491, 630, 758, 904, 971*
16:7-8, *360, 440*
16:8-10, *79*
16:9, *659*
16:9-10, *44, 1010*
16:10, *317, 432, 630*
16:10-17, *16, 788*
16:11, *1009, 1061*
16:11-15, *378*
16:11-16, *922*
16:12, *961*
16:12-15, *1217*
16:12-40, *758*
16:13, *290, 944, 1143*
16:13-16, *1206*
16:14, *372, 414, 1145*
16:14-15, *123, 630, 670*
16:14-17, *493, 494*
16:15, *21, 222, 354, 356, 364, 373, 508, 760, 1104, 1206*
16:16, *668, 944, 973, 1010*
16:16-18, *356, 631, 742, 922, 941, 1206*
16:16-24, *416, 747, 886, 1220*
16:17, *196, 860, 1073, 1100*
16:18, *382, 630*
16:19, *668, 764, 1138*
16:19-31, *476*
16:19-40, *21*
16:20-21, *910*
16:22-23, *907*
16:22-24, *230, 961*
16:23, *1138*
16:24, *116, 1138*
16:25, *356, 414, 521, 526, 943*
16:25-34, *378*
16:29-32, *357*
16:30, *17, 116, 416, 1073*
16:30-31, *21, 860*
16:31, *364, 508, 512, 668, 669, 1073*
16:31-33, *364, 493, 494*
16:31-34, *1207*
16:32, *356*
16:32-34, *356*
16:33, *116, 123, 354*

16:34, *116, 196, 222, 512, 687, 760, 1104, 1178*
16:35-39, *761*
16:35-40, *953*
16:36, *894, 895*
16:37, *230*
16:37-38, *1062*
16:38, *371*
16:40, *356, 508, 512, 1217*
17, *192*
17:1, *290, 291*
17:1-2, *764, 944*
17:1-4, *758*
17:1-9, *1138, 1144*
17:2-3, *153, 256, 357, 628*
17:2-4, *628*
17:3, *17, 153, 256, 272, 317, 357, 521, 629*
17:4, *196, 354, 372, 764, 1112, 1145, 1207, 1216, 1217, 1218*
17:5, *1138*
17:5-7, *356*
17:5-9, *355, 907*
17:5-10, *761*
17:6, *251, 355*
17:6-7, *1062*
17:7, *353, 508, 629, 1138*
17:10, *291, 659, 764, 944*
17:10-12, *758*
17:10-14, *1144*
17:11-12, *628*
17:12, *1207, 1217, 1218*
17:13, *907*
17:15, *764, 1061*
17:16-34, *148, 416, 762*
17:16-35, *886*
17:17, *291, 357, 372, 944, 1145*
17:18, *353*
17:18-34, *1144*
17:19, *628*
17:19-23, *760*
17:22, *1010*
17:22-31, *153, 627*
17:23, *137, 706*
17:23-27, *627*
17:24, *251, 414, 467, 529, 670, 1154, 1222*
17:24-30, *886*
17:24-31, *1012*
17:26, *17, 43, 251, 317, 415*
17:26-27, *1012*
17:26-31, *1022*
17:28, *655, 1126*
17:29, *627, 1126, 1127*
17:30, *762*
17:30-31, *333, 622, 623, 749, 825*
17:31, *17, 251, 318, 356, 360, 415, 416, 491, 627, 766, 859, 860, 1054, 1058*
17:32, *776, 1138*
17:32-34, *758*
17:34, *886, 1206, 1207, 1217, 1218*
18, *93, 378, 1217*
18:1-2, *449*
18:1-3, *743*
18:1-4, *764, 1145*
18:1-18, *148*
18:2, *290, 291, 446, 448, 907, 1207, 1217*
18:2-3, *1062, 1066*
18:2-6, *20*
18:3, *762*
18:4, *357, 944*
18:4-7, *291*
18:5, *256, 357, 521, 1112, 1217*
18:5-8, *742*
18:5-11, *1145*
18:6, *391, 415, 562, 1138*

18:7, *222, 356, 372, 414, 508, 1145*
18:8, *21, 123, 148, 222, 364, 493, 494, 609*
18:9, *630, 659, 669, 766*
18:9-10, *972, 1022, 1195*
18:9-11, *148*
18:9-20, *18*
18:10, *197, 210*
18:11, *628, 742*
18:12, *1060*
18:12-16, *907*
18:12-17, *148, 761, 1138*
18:13, *372, 414*
18:15-16, *1062*
18:17, *293, 609, 907, 1138*
18:18, *93, 512, 581, 758, 761, 883, 1061, 1217*
18:18-19, *743, 1217*
18:18-28, *1066*
18:19, *1145*
18:19-26, *291*
18:21, *317*
18:22, *1061*
18:23, *197, 373*
18:24, *444, 765*
18:24-25, *757, 758*
18:24-26, *493*
18:25, *196, 668, 758*
18:26, *196, 356, 743, 1145, 1207, 1217*
18:27, *433, 765*
18:28, *256, 357, 940, 1218*
19, *147, 749, 883, 1118, 1178*
19:1-2, *116*
19:1-7, *116, 147, 493, 589, 596, 1178, 1227*
19:1-40, *416*
19:2-3, *116*
19:3, *116*
19:4, *116, 269*
19:5, *114, 116, 256, 668, 785*
19:5-6, *493*
19:6, *79, 116, 971*
19:8, *291, 414, 629, 944, 1145*
19:8-9, *357*
19:8-10, *147, 391, 742*
19:9, *196*
19:10, *146, 355*
19:11, *941*
19:11-12, *9, 333, 356, 436, 631, 742, 747, 1118*
19:11-20, *930, 1010*
19:12, *382*
19:13, *20, 629, 668, 785, 1010, 1118*
19:13-16, *786*
19:13-20, *147, 631*
19:15, *416, 1010*
19:16, *1118*
19:17, *416, 668*
19:17-20, *1148*
19:18, *764*
19:18-19, *354, 382, 703*
19:19, *1010, 1138*
19:20, *940*
19:21, *17, 317, 630, 1066*
19:21-41, *761*
19:22, *764, 1086*
19:23, *196*
19:23-27, *1138*
19:23-41, *21, 147, 907, 1008, 1138*
19:24, *1008, 1154*
19:24-27, *1008*
19:24-41, *528*
19:26, *529, 1217*
19:27, *372, 414*
19:31, *1008*
19:32, *197*
19:32-41, *205*

19:34, *1008*
19:35, *1008*
19:38, *1008, 1060*
19:38-39, *1008*
19:39, *197*
19:41, *197*
20, *644, 1231*
20:1, *761*
20:4, *765*
20:5-12, *758*
20:5-15, *16, 788*
20:6, *1061*
20:7, *271, 378, 680, 681, 1105, 1231*
20:7-8, *92*
20:7-12, *437, 688, 742, 747, 894, 1231*
20:7-36, *684*
20:9-12, *332*
20:10, *655*
20:11, *271, 1104, 1105*
20:13-17, *1061*
20:16, *562*
20:17, *1093*
20:17-35, *107, 883, 973*
20:18-21, *760, 762*
20:18-28, *355*
20:18-35, *10, 883*
20:19, *669, 907, 962, 1166*
20:20, *355*
20:20-21, *356*
20:21, *153, 354, 364, 669*
20:22, *562, 630, 904*
20:22-23, *79, 495, 1139*
20:22-24, *1124*
20:23, *495, 497, 630, 886, 904, 1022, 1180, 1195*
20:24, *354, 432, 434, 668, 669, 884, 1086*
20:25, *270, 629*
20:25-31, *877*
20:27, *17, 884*
20:28, *20, 107, 197, 222, 260, 269, 270, 317, 495, 518, 880, 973, 1002, 1069, 1092, 1093*
20:28-31, *743*
20:28-32, *353*
20:29, *883, 1124*
20:29-30, *25, 73*
20:30, *73, 75*
20:31, *658, 762, 1199*
20:32, *20, 196, 434, 488, 622, 623*
20:33, *884*
20:33-34, *762*
20:35, *17, 131, 137, 566, 567, 575, 668, 669, 884*
20:36-38, *894*
20:37-38, *1124*
21, *546, 883, 1163, 1214*
21:1, *15*
21:1-6, *1061*
21:1-18, *16, 788*
21:3-4, *758*
21:4, *502, 562, 630, 904, 1139*
21:5, *1116, 1207*
21:7, *502, 758*
21:8, *356, 433, 757, 763, 764, 765, 929, 972*
21:8-9, *106, 191, 743, 931, 1219*
21:8-14, *931*
21:9, *971, 1207*
21:10, *495, 971*
21:10-11, *743*
21:10-14, *1124*
21:11, *562, 630, 886, 904, 972, 1022*
21:12, *495, 562, 1139*
21:13, *20, 562, 668*
21:14, *317, 670*

21:15, *562, 1154, 1206*
21:16-17, *502*
21:17, *760*
21:17-20, *582*
21:17-26, *546, 1163*
21:18, *106, 187, 222, 757*
21:18-26, *743*
21:19, *767*
21:20, *414, 581, 757*
21:20-26, *761*
21:20-36, *1124*
21:21, *41, 73, 228, 415, 586, 1124*
21:21-26, *647, 648*
21:22, *196*
21:23, *106, 581*
21:23-26, *1069*
21:24, *228, 486, 1124*
21:25, *529*
21:26, *165, 486*
21:27, *12, 355*
21:27-36, *1124, 1163*
21:28, *389, 487*
21:30, *211*
21:30-32, *907, 1138*
21:30-40, *1062*
21:31, *1060*
21:39, *230, 293*
22, *790, 884, 887*
22:1, *207*
22:1-21, *658*
22:3, *186, 885*
22:3-5, *884*
22:3-16, *630*
22:4, *196, 1216*
22:4-5, *166, 907*
22:4-16, *971*
22:4-21, *884*
22:6, *658*
22:6-9, *1022*
22:6-11, *78, 747*
22:7-8, *115*
22:9, *658*
22:11, *394, 658*
22:12-16, *78, 562, 747*
22:14, *1054*
22:14-15, *78, 885*
22:15, *718, 885, 1204*
22:16, *21, 115, 196, 256, 364, 380, 416, 630, 766, 785, 786, 942*
22:17, *165*
22:17-21, *18, 790, 1195*
22:18, *885, 1204*
22:19, *1138, 1142, 1144*
22:20, *269, 718, 1204, 1205*
22:21, *78, 718, 885*
22:22-23, *1124*
22:22-29, *1062*
22:23-29, *1061*
22:24, *1138*
22:25, *230*
22:28, *1061*
22:29, *371*
22:30, *1062, 1124, 1138*
23, *1099*
23:1, *241, 415*
23:5, *231, 824*
23:6, *499, 776, 860, 885, 913*
23:6-8, *775*
23:8, *45*
23:9, *45*
23:10, *230, 371*
23:11, *17, 317, 357, 630, 659, 766, 886, 972, 1010, 1124, 1139, 1195, 1204*
23:12-14, *907*
23:12-22, *968*
23:12-35, *912, 1138*
23:16-22, *1061*
23:16-24, *21*
23:21, *247*

23:23, *1060*
23:23-24, *1061*
23:23-31, *659*
23:23-35, *1061*
23:24, *1060*
23:26, *1061*
23:27, *1062*
23:29, *1062*
23:33, *1061*
23:35, *1061*
24, *1138*
24:1-8, *230*
24:2, *894*
24:2-9, *907*
24:5, *196, 251, 387*
24:5-9, *1062*
24:10, *1062*
24:10-21, *10*
24:10-25, *357*
24:12, *1062, 1217*
24:13-14, *647*
24:14, *196, 415, 884, 1069*
24:14-16, *647*
24:15, *860, 1016, 1058*
24:16, *241, 415, 884*
24:18, *486, 1069*
24:22, *196, 1061, 1062*
24:23, *1061*
24:24, *153, 368, 1056, 1112, 1221*
24:24-25, *622*
24:25, *334, 356, 357, 500, 859, 1056*
24:27, *16, 435, 1060, 1061*
25:3, *16*
25:7, *1138*
25:8, *647, 1138*
25:10-12, *953, 1062*
25:11, *883*
25:12, *1139*
25:13, *184, 932, 1206, 1221*
25:19-20, *1062*
25:23, *184, 932, 1206, 1221*
25:25, *1062, 1139*
25:26, *668*
25:30, *1206*
26, *790, 884*
26:1-29, *357*
26:2, *131*
26:2-23, *10, 115, 658*
26:5, *885*
26:6, *247, 415, 500, 543, 970*
26:6-7, *38, 334, 500*
26:6-8, *969*
26:7, *542*
26:9-18, *630, 884*
26:9-19, *971*
26:10, *196, 907, 1138*
26:12-18, *78, 657*
26:13, *273, 658*
26:13-16, *1022*
26:14-15, *1139*
26:15-18, *753*
26:16, *718, 763, 885, 1204*
26:16-18, *562, 718, 1139*
26:16-20, *78*
26:17-18, *21, 764*
26:18, *20, 21, 115, 137, 196, 368, 382, 486, 488, 657, 658, 939, 1078, 1080*
26:19, *317*
26:19-20, *622, 790*
26:20, *368, 414, 1012, 1221*
26:22, *415, 825, 885*
26:22-23, *415, 766, 885*
26:23, *115, 256, 272, 356, 658*
26:25, *1185*
26:26, *467*
26:28, *196*

26:28-29, *884*
26:29, *1061, 1138*
26:30, *932*
26:31-32, *886*
26:32, *1062, 1139*
27, *15*
27:1, *16, 391, 788, 1061, 1139*
27:3, *758*
27:6, *1062*
27:9, *1157*
27:9-10, *749*
27:10, *961*
27:13, *356*
27:13-44, *747*
27:17, *371*
27:20, *197*
27:20-24, *1022*
27:21, *961*
27:21-26, *689, 749*
27:22, *1157*
27:23, *45, 659*
27:23-24, *18, 747, 1195*
27:24, *17, 317, 324, 1139*
27:26, *17*
27:29, *689*
27:31, *21, 197*
27:33-38, *688*
27:34, *689*
27:35, *414, 686, 688, 943*
27:43, *21*
28:1-6, *747*
28:1-11, *502*
28:3-6, *416*
28:4, *414*
28:5-6, *887*
28:6, *775*
28:7-10, *747*
28:8-9, *1010*
28:11, *1009, 1062*
28:13-14, *758*
28:14, *760, 1066, 1139*
28:14-15, *373*
28:15, *414, 943, 1066*
28:16, *1061, 1066, 1139*
28:16-17, *907*
28:17, *647, 1066*
28:17-19, *907*
28:17-22, *1145*
28:17-29, *20*
28:17-31, *391, 503*
28:18, *1062*
28:19, *1062*
28:20, *1138*
28:21, *197, 1066*
28:22, *196, 1066*
28:23, *41, 357, 414, 629, 766, 1066, 1069, 1204, 1217*
28:23-31, *1204*
28:24, *791*
28:24-25, *207, 1066*
28:25, *497*
28:25-28, *42, 247, 274, 479, 824, 904*
28:26-27, *536, 824*
28:26-28, *562, 791*
28:28, *391, 415, 1139*
28:28-30, *689*
28:30, *907, 1066*
28:30-31, *766, 1066*
28:31, *15, 353, 629, 668, 790*
28:34, *414*

Romans
1, *1012*
1:1, *152, 614, 668*
1:3, *43, 163, 491, 722*
1:3-4, *163, 171, 332, 492, 860, 893, 986, 1017*
1:4, *398*
1:7, *163*
1:8, *1066*

1:14, *761*
1:14-15, *354*
1:14-17, *639*
1:16, *706, 708, 752, 761*
1:16-17, *562, 802, 1021*
1:17, *1054*
1:17-18, *1021*
1:18, *1021*
1:24, *994*
1:24-32, *995*
1:29-32, *892*
2:4, *329, 622, 1073*
2:8, *1239*
2:12-16, *890*
2:15, *242*
2:22, *528*
2:24, *1015*
3, *365*
3:1-2, *913*
3:5, *1054*
3:9-20, *934*
3:19, *354*
3:20, *889*
3:21, *802*
3:21-26, *624, 934, 1021*
3:22, *4, 551, 1054*
3:23, *354, 397*
3:25, *487, 1074*
3:25-26, *1070*
3:28, *892*
4, *734, 891*
4:1, *43*
4:1-12, *354*
4:1-25, *1145*
4:3, *6, 88, 837*
4:9-10, *5*
4:9-13, *43*
4:11-12, *43*
4:16, *43*
4:16-22, *2*
4:19-21, *3, 39*
4:22, *4*
4:24, *399*
4:25, *273, 762, 891*
5:1, *163, 895*
5:3, *1180*
5:3-5, *351, 1192*
5:8, *426*
5:9-10, *1226*
5:11, *163*
5:12, *485*
5:12-17, *723*
5:12-19, *356*
5:12-21, *280*
5:15, *1055*
5:19, *1188*
5:35, *349*
6, *112, 121, 1234*
6:1-4, *354*
6:1-14, *1017, 1226*
6:1-23, *115*
6:3, *114*
6:4-5, *889*
6:8, *99*
6:19, *624*
7, *1121, 1240*
7:12-13, *890*
7:17-24, *610*
7:23, *986*
8, *376*
8:2-4, *1056*
8:9-10, *491*
8:11, *889*
8:15, *1116*
8:15-16, *495*
8:17, *99, 892, 914*
8:18, *397, 423*
8:19-23, *793*
8:23, *334, 863, 1116*
8:26-37, *495*
8:29, *794*
8:32, *270*
8:34, *96, 99, 172, 360, 398, 891, 964, 1016*

8:35-37, *339*
8:36, *913, 1092*
8:36-37, *339*
8:38-39, *44*
9, *160, 227, 391, 465, 548, 889, 891*
9:1-5, *161, 163, 218*
9:1-18, *548*
9:3, *396*
9:3-5, *913*
9:5, *163, 270, 722*
9:6, *1145*
9:9, *39*
9:10, *43*
9:13, *39, 42*
9:19-21, *831*
9:22, *329*
9:25-26, *211*
9:26, *417*
9:29, *420*
9:32, *365*
9:32-33, *161*
9:33, *838, 1127, 1128*
10:1-4, *39*
10:1-17, *161*
10:3, *1054*
10:6-8, *1092*
10:7, *460*
10:8, *626*
10:9, *114, 115, 163, 661, 667, 757*
10:9-10, *551*
10:10-12, *163*
10:12, *761*
10:13, *114, 115, 160, 163*
10:17, *639*
10:21, *161*
11, *161*
11:1, *43*
11:1-2, *161*
11:8-10, *161*
11:13-14, *217*
11:13-24, *585*
11:25-26, *205*
11:26, *1145*
11:26-29, *913*
11:26-32, *161*
11:28, *38, 161*
11:32, *1188*
11:33, *1201*
11:36, *252, 420*
12, *504*
12:1, *1158*
12:1-2, *736, 1071*
12:2, *792*
12:3-8, *892*
12:3-20, *349*
12:4-8, *888, 891*
12:6-8, *355*
12:8, *518*
12:9-13, *505*
12:9-21, *449*
12:13, *502, 504, 759, 1220*
12:14, *130, 1191*
12:17, *1191*
12:19-21, *623*
13, *230, 231, 950, 951*
13:1, *324, 919*
13:1-4, *517*
13:1-7, *324, 514, 912, 1062*
13:2, *325*
13:3-4, *230, 324, 890*
13:4, *230, 1059*
13:6-7, *517*
13:8-10, *239, 383, 449*
13:9-10, *568*
13:12-13, *715*
14, *551, 1178*
14:5, *686*
14:5-6, *675, 684*
14:10-12, *623*
14:13-23, *994*
14:14, *995*
14:14-23, *383*

14:17, *115*
14:19, *896*
14:20-21, *383*
15:7-13, *585*
15:14-29, *389*
15:16, *964*
15:18, *762*
15:18-19, *356*
15:19, *748, 755, 757, 1118*
15:19-23, *355*
15:20, *757*
15:23-24, *1066*
15:24, *754, 758*
15:26, *313, 315*
15:27, *680*
15:28, *754, 758*
15:31, *913*
15:33, *417, 895*
16, *355, 503, 512*
16:1, *758, 765*
16:1-2, *1212*
16:3, *762, 763*
16:3-4, *551, 1218*
16:3-5, *93, 378, 446, 1217, 1220*
16:3-15, *446, 447*
16:3-16, *1066*
16:4, *205, 754, 764*
16:5, *93, 220, 223, 376*
16:6, *765*
16:7, *762, 765*
16:9, *763, 765*
16:10, *446*
16:11, *446*
16:12, *765*
16:14, *446, 470*
16:15, *446*
16:17, *305*
16:19, *1201*
16:20, *417*
16:21, *763*
16:22, *220, 765*
16:23, *148, 223, 765*
16:25, *783, 1021*
16:25-27, *1201*

1 Corinthians
1, *148, 160, 761, 1201*
1:1, *152, 762, 1032*
1:2, *220, 223, 673*
1:5-7, *1211*
1:8, *265*
1:11, *512, 1021, 1220*
1:12, *78*
1:13, *114*
1:14-15, *354*
1:15, *114*
1:17, *1201*
1:17-18, *723*
1:18, *639*
1:19, *1201*
1:20, *1201*
1:20-25, *886*
1:21, *1201*
1:22, *1201*
1:23, *152, 626*
1:24, *888*
1:26, *355*
1:30, *888, 1054, 1201*
1:31, *673*
2:1, *783, 1201*
2:2, *723, 783*
2:4, *748, 1201*
2:4-5, *1118*
2:5, *761, 1201*
2:6, *1078*
2:6-7, *738*
2:6-10, *1201*
2:7, *783*
2:8, *420, 913, 1078*
2:9, *86, 674*
2:10-16, *1021*
2:11-14, *639*
2:13, *1201*

2:14, *615*
3, *637*
3:1-3, *738*
3:2, *736, 737, 738*
3:5-6, *765*
3:9, *763, 765*
3:11, *838*
3:13-15, *459*
3:16, *199, 509, 510*
3:16-17, *995, 1164*
3:19, *1201*
3:22, *78*
4:1, *763*
4:1-2, *354*
4:11-13, *503*
4:12, *762*
4:14-17, *878*
4:17, *764*
5:1-13, *305, 623*
5:5, *265, 305*
5:7, *174, 284, 503, 641*
5:10, *528*
5:11, *305, 528, 529*
6, *591*
6:1-6, *551*
6:9, *529, 715*
6:9-10, *460, 528*
6:11, *115*
6:17, *1214*
6:18-20, *995*
6:19, *510, 990, 1164*
6:20, *708, 1002*
7:1, *713*
7:10-11, *1157*
7:10-16, *995*
7:14, *356*
7:15, *713*
7:17, *1157*
7:21, *1100, 1101, 1208*
7:22, *1099*
7:23, *1002*
7:27-28, *714*
7:29, *1213*
7:34-37, *1221*
7:38-40, *540*
8, *379, 530, 994, 1163*
8:1, *529*
8:1-3, *529*
8:4, *528, 529*
8:4-6, *529, 994*
8:4-13, *383*
8:5, *668, 1102*
8:6, *270, 420, 665, 888, 889, 957*
8:7, *529*
8:7-13, *994*
8:8, *529*
8:9-13, *529*
8:10, *529*
8:10-12, *529*
8:11, *528*
8:13, *383, 994*
9:1, *667*
9:4, *355*
9:4-14, *502*
9:5, *78, 179, 616, 617, 757, 762, 1005, 1222*
9:7, *736*
9:16-17, *354*
9:19-20, *1069*
9:19-23, *648*
9:20, *383, 1110*
9:25, *327, 397*
10:1-2, *118*
10:1-14, *450*
10:1-22, *529*
10:3, *736, 738*
10:4, *491, 853*
10:7, *528*
10:7-8, *211*
10:11, *331*
10:12:28, *223*
10:14, *528*
10:14-22, *503*

10:16-17, *690*
10:16-18, *738*
10:17, *1231*
10:19, *529*
10:21, *528*
10:23, *529*
10:23-33, *383*
10:25-27, *529*
10:28-29, *529*
10:29, *529*
10:32, *220, 223, 354*
10:32-33, *383, 761*
11:1, *677*
11:1-34, *946*
11:2-16, *1105*
11:3-16, *514*
11:17-22, *1228*
11:17-34, *503, 627*
11:18, *201, 686*
11:19, *311*
11:20, *179, 679, 681, 686*
11:20-34, *378*
11:21, *686*
11:23-25, *686*
11:23-26, *680, 686, 1228*
11:24, *269, 681*
11:24-25, *780*
11:25, *245*
11:27-34, *686, 1230*
11:30, *437, 656*
12, *105, 311, 312, 355, 888, 891, 892, 1178*
12:2, *529, 1217*
12:3, *114, 179, 491, 667, 978, 1021, 1226*
12:4-11, *1194*
12:7, *1226*
12:8, *1201, 1232*
12:8-10, *892*
12:9-10, *356*
12:12-13, *112, 121*
12:13, *354, 515*
12:23, *1209*
12:28, *220, 762, 1207*
13, *839, 892*
13:4, *329*
14:1, *974*
14:2, *1196*
14:3, *1226*
14:5, *974*
14:12, *1226*
14:14, *1119*
14:14-16, *1196*
14:15, *520, 1119*
14:17, *1226*
14:19, *201*
14:22, *1178*
14:23, *905*
14:23-25, *757*
14:24-25, *357*
14:25, *1226*
14:26, *520, 526, 659, 1226*
14:28, *201*
14:29, *593*
14:31, *973*
14:32, *1120*
14:33-35, *514*
14:33-36, *1105*
14:34, *201*
14:35, *201*
14:40, *236, 1236*
15, *157, 892, 905, 1114*
15:1, *627, 1021*
15:1-5, *892*
15:1-8, *627, 628, 680*
15:2, *627*
15:3, *913*
15:3-5, *145, 762*
15:3-57, *933*
15:6, *752*
15:7, *546*
15:8, *762, 764*
15:9, *166, 220, 884*
15:10, *757*

15:12-58, *223*
15:20, *180, 673, 863, 1017*
15:20-28, *803*
15:22, *723, 1188*
15:23, *856, 863*
15:23-28, *739*
15:25, *739*
15:27-28, *420*
15:28, *1226*
15:42, *864, 1226*
15:42-44, *1017*
15:44-50, *893*
16:1-4, *356, 680*
16:2, *680*
16:9, *770*
16:10-11, *764*
16:12, *765*
16:15, *123, 892*
16:15-18, *311*
16:16, *514, 518*
16:19, *93, 376, 378, 754, 1220*
16:22, *177, 181, 305, 663, 675, 755, 870, 947, 1230, 1237*
16:23, *1230*

2 Corinthians
1:1, *223, 1032*
1:3, *660*
1:4, *1180*
1:5, *892*
1:12, *1201*
1:14, *265*
1:19, *626, 764, 915*
1:20, *662*
1:21-22, *119*
2:12, *758*
2:20-22, *334*
3, *249, 891*
3:3, *417, 1021*
3:7-18, *38*
3:16-17, *35*
3:17, *709*
3:17-18, *958*
3:18, *491, 794*
4, *1084*
4:5, *626*
4:6, *640*
4:7-12, *260*
4:10-12, *1021*
4:16, *792*
5, *343, 345*
5:1-4, *865*
5:9-11, *354*
5:10, *196, 624, 832*
5:14, *354*
5:16, *723*
5:17, *331, 792, 959*
5:18, *161*
5:21, *762, 891, 1054*
6:4, *329*
6:4-10, *503*
6:14, *450*
6:14—7:1, *1164, 1166*
6:14-18, *343*
6:16, *528*
6:16-18, *331, 854*
6:18, *426*
7:6-7, *764*
7:13-15, *764*
8:1, *754*
8:1-4, *355*
8:1-5, *356*
8:6, *764*
8:9, *958*
8:13-15, *1052*
8:23, *355, 763, 764*
9:12, *680*
10, *764, 993*
10:1, *961*
10:17, *673*
11, *764*
11:2, *1209*

11:2-4, *705*
11:3, *43*
11:13, *762, 763*
11:21-33, *503*
11:22, *913*
11:23-27, *1145*
11:24, *79, 913, 1142*
11:25, *230*
11:25-26, *1061*
11:26, *79*
11:26-27, *760, 1061*
11:28, *877*
11:30-33, *749*
11:32-33, *756*
12:1-6, *58*
12:1-10, *892*
12:2-4, *439*
12:8-9, *943*
12:12, *762, 1094, 1118*
13:1-2, *305*
13:4, *892*
13:5, *1166*
13:13, *800, 1237*
13:14, *498*

Galatians
1, *145, 161, 229*
1:1, *399, 596, 757, 764, 1032*
1:2, *754*
1:11, *883, 1021*
1:12, *921*
1:13, *161, 166*
1:16, *562*
1:17, *756*
1:18, *758*
1:19, *187, 616*
1:21, *757*
1:21-23, *758*
1:22, *754*
1:23, *166, 613*
2, *227, 229, 378, 546, 994, 995*
2:1-10, *389, 390, 467, 645, 993*
2:1-14, *1163*
2:2, *227*
2:3, *764*
2:4-5, *888*
2:6-9, *78*
2:7, *227, 551*
2:7-9, *78*
2:8, *54*
2:9, *145, 546, 764*
2:9-10, *549*
2:10, *546*
2:11, *764*
2:11-13, *54, 995*
2:11-14, *54, 467, 488, 503, 586, 754*
2:11-15, *546*
2:11-16, *888*
2:12, *581, 993*
2:12-13, *993*
2:13, *227, 884*
2:14, *227*
2:14-21, *994*
2:15, *889*
2:15-16, *4*
2:15-21, *390*
2:21, *684*
3, *262, 548, 734, 891*
3:1-3, *1055*
3:1-4, *748*
3:1-5, *888, 1195*
3:6, *88*
3:6-7, *43, 1145*
3:6-9, *4, 390, 994*
3:8, *1, 5*
3:10-14, *913*
3:12, *365*
3:13, *272, 280, 1002*
3:14, *1145, 1194*
3:15, *286*

3:17, 2, 40
3:21-4:7, 548
3:22, 551
3:23-26, 966
3:23-28, 227
3:27, 114, 119
3:27-28, 112, 1105
3:27-29, 1145
3:28, 356, 390, 515, 516, 888, 1145
4:3, 888
4:4, 331, 722
4:5, 1002, 1116
4:6, 495
4:6-7, 1195
4:8-9, 529
4:8-11, 684
4:9, 640, 888
4:10, 888
4:13, 757
4:19, 1181
4:21-31, 39, 126
4:26, 36, 1209, 1210
4:27, 831, 1181
4:28, 43
5, 376, 591
5:1, 1158
5:2, 329
5:2-6, 227
5:2-12, 993
5:5-6, 496
5:6, 351, 365, 1056
5:11, 626
5:14, 568
5:16, 1169
5:17-24, 47
5:18-23, 986
5:19, 703, 994
5:19-21, 529, 995
5:20-21, 528
5:22-23, 420, 1202, 1203
5:23, 603
6:1, 305
6:2, 877
6:13, 757
6:15, 792, 994
6:16, 548, 913, 994, 1145
6:17, 914
6:40, 365

Ephesians
1, 1027, 1195
1:1, 889, 1032
1:3, 660
1:3-14, 1232
1:4, 202, 420
1:5, 1116
1:6, 1232
1:7, 382
1:7-10, 331
1:8-9, 1201
1:9, 783, 1021, 1022
1:9-10, 783
1:12, 1232
1:13-14, 119, 334, 1121
1:13-18, 982
1:14, 889, 1232
1:15-17, 889
1:17, 1201
1:17-19, 889, 982
1:18, 889
1:19-23, 331
1:20, 96, 331, 399, 964, 1016
1:20-22, 1017
1:20-23, 46, 960
1:22, 831
1:22-23, 890, 1227
2, 206, 218
2:1-3, 354
2:5, 889, 890, 994
2:5-6, 96, 99, 1019
2:6, 741, 1227
2:8, 890

2:8-9, 889, 890
2:10, 792
2:11-22, 354, 889
2:12-13, 354
2:13-18, 889
2:14-16, 54
2:18, 1236
2:19-22, 199, 509
2:20, 311, 838, 890, 1128, 1227
2:20-22, 1129
2:22, 510
3:1, 890
3:1-11, 783
3:1-13, 890
3:2-3, 354
3:3, 783, 1022
3:3-5, 783, 889, 1021
3:4, 783
3:4-5, 639
3:4-11, 1201
3:5, 783, 1022, 1227
3:6, 889
3:7, 783
3:7-8, 354
3:8, 783, 889
3:9, 783, 889
3:10, 1202, 1233
3:14-19, 794, 889
4, 889, 891, 982, 1178
4:1, 890
4:2, 329, 982
4:2-3, 1191
4:2-5, 496
4:4, 1233
4:4-5, 1227
4:4-6, 180, 889, 1232
4:5, 311
4:7-13, 890
4:7-16, 889
4:8-10, 96, 889
4:9-10, 459
4:11, 757, 762, 763, 1093
4:11-13, 355
4:11-16, 1236
4:12, 877
4:15, 890
4:16, 889, 982
4:16-20, 311
4:18, 658
4:19, 994
4:23, 792
4:24, 792
4:25-26, 889
4:25-32, 1191
4:26, 832
4:27, 941
4:30, 119
4:32, 1191
5:1, 535
5:2, 535
5:3, 995
5:3-5, 995, 1191
5:5, 529, 889
5:5-6, 982
5:14, 115, 1027, 1232
5:15, 1201
5:15-21, 1233
5:18, 905
5:19, 520, 521, 526
5:19-20, 1232
5:21, 349, 518, 918, 1158, 1209, 1213
5:21-33, 889, 1210
5:22, 889, 982, 1213
5:22-33, 514
5:23, 1083, 1092
5:23-27, 890
5:25, 534, 714, 982
5:25-27, 1209
5:25-33, 784
5:26, 1232
5:27, 890
5:29-32, 1214

5:31, 831, 889
6:1-4, 358, 1212
6:2-3, 889
6:5, 1092
6:5-8, 1101
6:5-9, 982
6:10-17, 889
6:17, 890
6:18, 946
6:18-20, 357
6:19, 783, 889, 1022, 1023
6:21, 765
6:21-22, 889, 982

Philippians
1, 935
1:1, 224, 301, 355, 743, 758, 1093, 1099
1:2, 676
1:9, 640
1:10, 265
1:12-15, 1066
1:14, 757
1:14-16, 488
1:21, 914
1:29, 356
2:5-11, 181, 962
2:6, 163
2:6-11, 96, 163, 399, 520, 521, 566, 567, 958, 1027, 1234
2:8, 487
2:9, 96, 398
2:9-11, 325, 667
2:10, 1231
2:11, 661
2:16, 265
2:17, 641
2:25, 355
2:25-30, 765
3, 161, 764
3:2, 586, 763, 913
3:2-16, 883
3:5, 990
3:6, 166, 884
3:8, 161
3:9, 1054
3:10, 154, 892, 913
3:10-11, 914
3:17, 1157
3:20, 175, 1083
3:21, 1018
4:2-3, 1206, 1219
4:3, 84, 191, 233, 563, 624, 765
4:8, 1157
4:9, 417, 1157
4:10-18, 761
4:18, 832

Colossians
1:1, 888, 982, 1032
1:2, 888
1:3, 1232
1:3-4, 889
1:4-5, 496
1:6, 639, 754
1:7, 757, 765
1:8, 1021
1:9, 639, 1201
1:9-10, 640, 889
1:10, 639, 1201
1:12, 888
1:12-13, 657
1:12-14, 1227, 1232
1:13, 889
1:14, 382, 888
1:15, 427
1:15-16, 957, 960
1:15-18, 1224
1:15-20, 252, 520, 521, 522, 888, 891, 957, 1027, 1201, 1227, 1232
1:16, 420

1:16-17, 325
1:17-19, 890
1:18, 427, 783, 888, 1017, 1232
1:20, 1232
1:20-22, 888
1:21-22, 1227
1:22, 888
1:24, 914, 1181
1:24-28, 1022, 1023
1:26, 783
1:26-27, 888, 889
1:26-28, 1201
1:27, 783
1:28, 876
2:2, 639, 783, 888
2:3, 783, 1201
2:6-7, 1055
2:6-15, 888
2:8, 888, 1201
2:9, 665, 888
2:10, 888
2:11, 228, 354, 888
2:11-14, 1232
2:12, 889, 1234
2:12-13, 1227
2:13, 888, 889
2:14-17, 888
2:15, 46, 818, 888, 1227
2:16, 685, 888
2:18, 529, 891, 961
2:19, 888, 889, 982
2:20, 888
2:21, 888
2:23, 961, 1201
3:1, 96, 741, 889, 1016, 1234
3:1-4, 873, 1019
3:2-4, 889
3:3, 1227
3:4, 1018, 1021
3:5, 529, 888, 995
3:5-6, 982, 995
3:5-8, 1191
3:5-12, 889
3:9-10, 119
3:10, 639, 640, 792
3:11, 515, 754, 888
3:12, 329, 888, 982
3:12-14, 1191
3:16, 520, 521, 889, 1201
3:16-17, 1232
3:18, 349, 503, 514, 889, 918, 1117
3:18-19, 982
3:22, 982
3:22-23, 1101
3:22-24, 1038
4:2, 357
4:3, 783, 888, 889
4:4, 1022, 1023
4:5, 761, 1201
4:7, 765, 889, 982
4:7-9, 765
4:7-17, 888, 981
4:10-11, 765
4:11, 16, 765
4:12, 757, 765
4:14, 16, 764, 765, 915
4:15, 93, 220, 376, 1220
4:16, 659, 1232
4:18, 888, 947, 981

1 Thessalonians
1:1, 596, 758, 915
1:3, 496
1:4-6, 761
1:5, 748, 1118
1:7, 757
1:8, 757
1:9, 529, 640
1:9-10, 627, 629, 767, 1012
1:10, 399
2:1-12, 760, 761, 762, 884

2:2, 230
2:7, 355
2:9, 762
2:14-16, 168, 467, 900, 913
2:15, 42
2:19, 856
3:1-6, 764
3:2, 763
3:5, 1166
3:13, 856, 1200
4:1, 1157, 1158
4:1-2, 1157
4:3, 349
4:4, 715
4:6, 349, 715
4:7, 349
4:9, 349, 639
4:12, 349, 761, 1200
4:14-16, 160
4:15, 856
4:16, 47, 1200
4:17, 741
5:1-3, 333
5:2, 265, 266, 570, 866, 869
5:3, 235, 1181
5:5, 658, 709
5:8, 496
5:11, 614
5:12-13, 223, 514, 518
5:12-22, 349, 449
5:13, 898
5:16-18, 357
5:17, 947
5:19, 236
5:22, 349
5:23, 417, 856, 895, 933
5:27, 659

2 Thessalonians
1:1, 915
1:7, 397
1:12, 1055
2, 52, 336
2:1, 856
2:1-2, 983
2:1-12, 51
2:2, 265, 978
2:3, 73
2:3-7, 342
2:3-12, 73, 336
2:4, 530
2:7, 1033
2:8, 1021
2:8-9, 856
2:13, 793
3:7, 1157
3:8, 762
3:11, 305
3:14-15, 305
3:15, 305

1 Timothy
1:1, 891, 1083
1:2, 896
1:3, 764, 891
1:3-4, 31, 331
1:4, 707, 982
1:5, 1211
1:6, 331
1:6-7, 31
1:7, 331, 707
1:7-9, 890
1:8-11, 31
1:9-10, 1191
1:11, 534
1:11-16, 105
1:15, 891, 1226, 1232
1:15-16, 890
1:17, 891, 1226
1:19-20, 331
1:20, 305
2:1, 514, 942
2:1-2, 321, 324, 517, 947

2:1-15, *349, 1158*
2:3, *891, 1083*
2:4, *639, 1015, 1188*
2:5, *891*
2:5-7, *31, 1226*
2:7, *105, 760, 763*
2:8, *517*
2:8-15, *514, 1105*
2:9-10, *517*
2:12, *105*
2:13, *43*
3, *105*
3:1, *105, 268, 891*
3:1-3, *1233*
3:1-7, *105, 355, 891*
3:1-13, *223, 311, 518*
3:1-15, *105*
3:2, *504, 507, 759*
3:2-4, *1191*
3:2-5, *504*
3:7, *761*
3:8, *1193*
3:8-10, *1191*
3:8-13, *105, 891*
3:9, *783, 890*
3:10, *1166*
3:11, *105*
3:11-12, *1191*
3:15, *311, 504, 1226*
3:16, *46, 96, 99, 256, 332,
    520, 524, 627, 661, 783,
    890, 958, 986, 1017,
    1226, 1233*
4, *331*
4:1-3, *1199*
4:1-4, *1106*
4:3, *31, 713*
4:3-5, *890*
4:4-5, *690, 1226*
4:6, *105, 661, 891*
4:7, *331, 639, 1213*
4:7-8, *31*
4:10, *891, 1083*
4:11, *891*
4:11-16, *628, 1233*
4:12, *105, 1191*
4:14, *105, 223, 311, 891*
4:15, *1233*
4:16, *105*
5:1, *105*
5:1-2, *514, 891*
5:1-16, *891*
5:2, *967*
5:3, *1212*
5:5, *942, 1193*
5:9-10, *504*
5:10, *962, 1051*
5:11-12, *713*
5:13, *1213*
5:13-15, *331*
5:14, *714, 1211*
5:17, *105, 891*
5:17-19, *137*
5:17-22, *105*
5:19, *105, 891*
5:19-22, *891*
6, *658*
6:1-2, *514, 517*
6:4-5, *1191*
6:10, *1051*
6:11, *1191*
6:12-14, *534*
6:13, *308*
6:15-16, *657, 891*
6:17, *962*
6:17-18, *1051*
6:18, *1191*
6:20, *31, 105, 311, 400,
    628, 707, 982*
6:20-21, *331*

2 Timothy
1:2, *896*
1:3, *38, 241*

1:5, *137*
1:5-6, *534*
1:6, *105, 891*
1:9, *461, 890*
1:9-11, *1201*
1:10, *353, 658, 891, 1021,
    1083*
1:11, *105, 760*
1:12-14, *891*
1:13, *661*
1:13-14, *105, 311, 534*
1:14, *311, 661*
1:15, *31, 73, 331*
1:16-18, *765*
1:18, *1019*
2:1-2, *105*
2:2, *891, 982*
2:3:7, *639*
2:4, *397*
2:5, *327*
2:11, *99, 891*
2:11-13, *628, 661, 1226,
    1233*
2:14-17, *31*
2:15, *105, 763*
2:16-19, *331*
2:17-18, *31, 867*
2:19, *43*
2:22, *896*
2:22-25, *1191*
2:23-26, *31*
2:24-26, *32, 305*
2:25, *639*
2:25-26, *331*
3:1-9, *31, 331, 1199*
3:1-13, *305*
3:2, *963, 1051*
3:2-4, *1191*
3:2-9, *331*
3:6, *715*
3:10, *329, 1191*
3:10-15, *31*
3:10-17, *534*
3:11, *137*
3:12, *910*
3:15, *357*
4:1-8, *534*
4:3, *661*
4:5, *355, 433, 757, 763*
4:6, *641*
4:8, *354*
4:9-15, *982*
4:10, *757, 758, 765*
4:11, *16, 765, 915*
4:12, *765*
4:17, *105, 890*
4:19, *1217*
5:3-16, *1221*

Titus
1:1, *639*
1:3, *105, 891, 1083*
1:4, *764*
1:5, *105, 223, 757, 764,
    765, 891*
1:5-7, *1093*
1:6-9, *514, 518*
1:7, *504, 963, 1051, 1191*
1:7-9, *105, 891, 1233*
1:8, *504, 759, 1191*
1:9, *105, 661*
1:10-14, *32*
1:11, *32*
1:12, *819*
1:13, *661*
1:14, *32*
1:15, *32, 709, 994*
2, *519, 520, 1211*
2:1, *514*
2:1-10, *519, 889*
2:1-15, *1158*
2:2, *105, 1211*
2:3, *1213*
2:4-5, *1211*

2:4-10, *349*
2:5, *1211, 1212*
2:6, *1211*
2:6-8, *534*
2:7, *105*
2:7-8, *105*
2:8, *1211*
2:8-10, *1212*
2:9-10, *517*
2:10, *891, 1083*
3:4, *1021*
2:11-14, *515, 517*
2:13, *163, 891, 1055, 1083*
2:14, *211*
3:1, *517*
3:1-2, *514*
3:3, *1191*
3:3-8, *515, 534*
3:4, *1083*
3:4-7, *1226*
3:5, *354, 792, 795, 890*
3:5-7, *118*
3:5-8, *891*
3:6, *891*
3:9, *890*
3:9-11, *32*
3:10-11, *305*
3:12, *758*
3:13, *759, 765*

Philemon
1, *890*
2, *93, 376*
9, *890*
13, *765*
22, *503*
23, *765*
24, *16, 764, 765, 915*

Hebrews
1, *45, 88, 98, 102, 172,
    173, 363, 449, 480, 537,
    738, 948, 952, 965, 998,
    1122*
1:1, *36, 347, 447, 451,
    582, 861, 998*
1:1-2, *40, 456, 489, 521,
    665, 1022*
1:1-3, *939, 957, 1201, 1202*
1:1-4, *172, 397, 417, 444,
    450, 451, 452, 453, 477,
    670, 933, 1043, 1134,
    1236*
1:1-12, *356*
1:1-14, *1043*
1:2, *251, 252, 265, 277,
    318, 334, 347, 418, 622,
    632, 665, 860, 960, 1224*
1:2-3, *252, 957*
1:3, *96, 98, 99, 172, 252
13, 252*
1:3, *274, 275, 360, 397,
    398, 417, 521, 522, 526,
    632, 665, 957, 958, 1070,
    1096*
1:3-4, *138, 891*
1:3-5, *100, 448, 1016*
1:3-13, *456, 482*
1:4, *452, 785*
1:4-7, *360*
1:5, *96, 98, 252, 318, 398,
    399, 417, 418, 450, 451,
    452, 537, 632, 785, 793,
    794, 843, 845, 878, 1043,
    1134*
1:5-6, *45*
1:5-8, *953*
1:5-9, *399*
1:5-12, *843*
1:5-13, *334*
1:5-14, *36, 172, 417, 453,
    480, 845, 849*
1:6, *417, 665, 694*
1:6-7, *843, 845*

1:7, *100, 138, 172, 417,
    448, 1118, 1121*
1:7-9, *45*
1:8, *252, 346, 417, 430,
    563, 957, 1237*
1:8-9, *360, 632*
1:8-12, *843, 845*
1:9, *49, 360, 694, 821,
    1095*
1:10, *251, 252, 419, 670,
    957*
1:10-12, *45, 252, 276, 440,
    665*
1:11, *1240*
1:13, *98, 100, 138, 277,
    360, 418, 632, 843, 1016*
1:13-14, *45*
1:14, *172, 860, 944, 1073,
    1118*
2, *172*
2:1, *350, 444, 445, 447,
    567, 878*
2:1-3, *522*
2:1-4, *103, 252, 275, 361,
    419, 445, 453, 454, 483,
    821, 843, 845, 969*
2:1-5, *957*
2:1-18, *274, 1043*
2:2, *45, 66, 103, 418, 445,
    861, 998*
2:2-3, *261, 845, 878, 1038,
    1097*
2:2-4, *445*
2:3, *73, 417, 445, 447,
    567, 670, 767, 860, 1073,
    1218, 1236*
2:3-4, *444, 447, 632, 633*
2:4, *356, 445, 496, 941,
    1094, 1204*
2:5, *399, 451, 454, 563*
2:6, *842*
2:6-8, *632*
2:6-9, *334, 537*
2:7, *98, 418*
2:7-9, *399, 958*
2:8, *399*
2:8-9, *45, 843*
2:9, *45, 96, 98, 173, 360,
    399, 418, 434, 878*
2:10, *45, 198, 277, 334,
    361, 397, 418, 419, 499,
    567, 860*
2:10-12, *361, 1116*
2:10-13, *1224, 1233*
2:10-18, *399, 849, 1117*
2:11, *276, 487, 488*
2:11-12, *1233*
2:12, *198, 510, 522, 567*
2:12-13, *849*
2:14, *2, 261, 334, 373,
    375, 655, 878, 939, 985,
    1078, 1079, 1241*
2:14-3:6, *74*
2:14-15, *278*
2:14-16, *2*
2:14-18, *261*
2:15, *43, 371, 449, 655,
    1079*
2:15-16, *2*
2:15-18, *1038*
2:16, *1, 248, 582*
2:17, *198, 274, 275, 276,
    282, 418, 452, 453, 1096*
2:17-18, *74, 278, 451, 456,
    633*
2:18, *138, 275, 568, 1139,
    1167*
3, *36, 198, 334, 335, 475,
    509, 511, 685, 900, 998*
3:1, *138, 163, 172, 257,
    417, 450, 451, 452, 456,
    661, 878, 1043*
3:1-4:13, *452*
3:1-6, *79, 172, 445, 450,

453, 480, 537, 781, 782,
    1043, 1092*
3:1-19, *567, 878*
3:2, *418, 510, 780*
3:2-5, *456*
3:2-6, *1113*
3:3, *394, 1155*
3:3-4, *510*
3:4, *510*
3:5, *39, 456*
3:5-6, *510, 632*
3:6, *103, 153, 198, 277,
    335, 361, 418, 444, 447,
    451, 500, 510, 961, 1038*
3:7, *172, 445, 447, 453,
    497, 685, 821, 895, 1043*
3:7-4:11, *1013*
3:7-8, *445*
3:7-11, *42, 450, 453, 665,
    969, 1239*
3:7-13, *74*
3:7-19, *275, 480, 845, 850*
3:8, *985*
3:8-11, *36*
3:10, *985*
3:11, *36, 632, 861, 1239*
3:12, *74, 417, 418, 445,
    447, 453, 655, 878, 985*
3:12-13, *447*
3:12-14, *278, 327*
3:12-19, *42, 453, 623, 844*
3:13, *445, 456*
3:13-20, *209*
3:14, *153, 335, 361, 447,
    451, 461, 1038*
3:15, *985*
3:17, *1097*
3:18, *632, 861*
4:1, *66, 335, 419, 440,
    445, 447, 500, 632, 861,
    969*
4:1-2, *844*
4:1-6, *1073*
4:1-11, *850*
4:1-13, *781, 878*
4:2, *42, 364, 368, 432*
4:2-3, *365*
4:3, *251, 335, 419, 420,
    632, 861, 1223, 1239*
4:3-5, *844*
4:3-11, *647*
4:4, *417*
4:4-5, *419*
4:5, *632, 861*
4:6, *42, 335, 432*
4:7, *317, 417, 419, 985*
4:7-8, *844*
4:8, *42*
4:8-11, *480*
4:9, *198, 211, 335, 419,
    632, 633, 861, 862*
4:9-10, *42*
4:10, *335, 861*
4:11, *74, 350, 418, 419,
    440, 445, 447, 861, 878,
    969*
4:11-12, *419*
4:11-13, *418*
4:12, *418, 444, 456, 665,
    985*
4:12-13, *66, 418, 456, 623,
    665, 861*
4:13, *265, 418, 444, 623,
    665*
4:14, *36, 96, 98, 172, 248,
    257, 274, 360, 418, 440,
    452, 453, 537, 563, 661,
    734, 878, 933, 964, 1112,
    1134, 1233*
4:14-15, *958*
4:14-16, *74, 75, 107, 274,
    275, 360, 450, 633, 944,
    1012*
4:15, *274, 277, 567, 568,

734, 878, 964, 1096,
1139, 1167, 1170
4:15-16, 986
4:16, 275, 277, 361, 417,
434, 564, 632, 734, 966,
1167, 1233
5, 278, 537, 965, 998
5:1, 450, 966, 1070, 1096
5:1-6, 276
5:1-10, 248, 453, 480, 1043
5:2, 274, 275
5:2-3, 274
5:3, 1070, 1096
5:4, 317
5:4-5, 1070
5:4-10, 738
5:5, 98, 153, 318, 334,
394, 632, 793, 794
5:5-6, 98, 252, 360, 844,
845
5:5-10, 172, 1016
5:6, 172, 346, 360, 417,
456, 482, 537, 632, 730,
966, 1070, 1113
5:7, 74, 375, 418, 568,
655, 942, 944, 945, 958,
985, 1073
5:7-8, 633
5:7-9, 274, 566, 567, 878
5:7-10, 173, 261, 356, 361
5:8, 418, 958, 1112, 1139
5:8-9, 334, 1181
5:8-10, 482
5:9, 277, 461, 624, 821,
860, 944, 1073
5:10, 360, 456, 730
5:11, 117, 277, 350, 445,
447, 451, 454, 738, 1043
5:11-6:20, 849
5:11-12, 878, 1218
5:11-14, 73, 418, 445, 628,
998
5:12, 418, 445, 446, 448,
736, 737
5:12-14, 312, 1115
5:13, 418, 446, 736, 738,
1058, 1115
5:14, 334, 737, 738, 1095
5:16, 274
5:17, 942
6, 98
6:1, 153, 446, 738, 862,
878, 1012
6:1-2, 257, 622, 624, 738,
767
6:1-8, 878
6:1-12, 534
6:2, 66, 228, 335, 346,
624, 1016
6:4, 334, 658, 1022
6:4-5, 342
6:4-6, 334, 350, 381, 447,
823
6:4-8, 66, 277, 361, 419,
447, 1013
6:5, 65, 334, 445, 940
6:6, 74, 117, 381, 792,
860, 998, 1013, 1112
6:6-10, 878
6:7-8, 444, 459, 623
6:9, 74, 451, 860, 1039
6:9-11, 445
6:9-20, 1234
6:10, 107, 361, 419, 622,
696, 1086, 1139
6:10-12, 622
6:11, 445, 447
6:11-12, 335
6:12, 45, 130, 327, 350,
368, 447, 534, 969
6:13, 1, 3, 38
6:13-15, 3, 38, 327, 534,
878, 968
6:13-20, 3, 103

6:14, 130
6:15, 3, 500
6:16-17, 3, 38
6:17, 969
6:17-18, 335
6:17-20, 334
6:18, 456, 1185
6:18-20, 447
6:19, 102, 444, 500, 563,
985
6:19-20, 3, 98, 275, 276,
440, 633
6:20, 96, 98, 346, 361,
456, 567, 730, 966, 1016,
1070
7, 45, 209, 274, 730, 891,
913, 999, 1050
7:1, 1, 130, 417, 731, 738,
850
7:1-2, 456, 731, 964
7:1-3, 632
7:1-10, 3, 843, 849
7:1-25, 1043
7:1-28, 172, 248, 450, 453,
480, 878
7:2, 1, 731, 843, 895
7:2-3, 731
7:3, 655, 730, 843, 964,
965
7:4, 3, 43, 731, 964
7:4-6, 1
7:4-10, 730, 843
7:5, 240
7:6, 730, 968
7:6-7, 130
7:7, 3
7:8, 965, 1204
7:9, 1
7:10, 43
7:11, 277, 646, 862, 1016
7:11-14, 198
7:11-28, 849
7:12, 276, 646
7:13, 1113
7:13-14, 966
7:13-28, 965
7:14, 417, 567, 670
7:15, 964, 965, 966, 1016
7:15-17, 1073, 1113
7:16, 240, 360, 375, 655,
849
7:16-17, 1070
7:17, 36, 360, 482, 537,
730, 1204
7:18, 240, 646
7:18-19, 383
7:18-28, 966
7:19, 277, 500, 646
7:20, 655
7:21, 482, 537, 670
7:21-22, 646, 1070
7:22, 246, 350
7:23-24, 1070
7:23-25, 646, 655, 776
7:23-28, 172, 198, 622
7:24, 965
7:25, 99, 172, 275, 360,
418, 564, 942, 944, 946,
1013, 1016, 1073, 1233,
1236
7:26, 96, 98, 99, 360, 440,
485, 488, 1043, 1158,
1191
7:26-28, 74, 274, 275, 277,
360, 646
7:27, 35, 99, 275, 1070,
1096
7:27-28, 448
7:28, 172, 274, 418, 632,
1070
8, 35, 509, 965, 967, 1155
8:1, 96, 98, 99, 248, 334,
360, 417, 451, 453, 537,
544, 563, 632, 646, 878,

1016
8:1-2, 248, 360
8:1-6, 248, 440, 450
8:1-7, 958
8:1-11, 480
8:1-13, 172
8:2, 248, 360, 440, 563,
633, 670, 1155, 1185,
1233
8:3, 844, 1070
8:3-5, 445, 448
8:4, 248, 1043
8:5, 36, 99, 248, 274, 440,
448, 480, 482, 509, 563,
633, 958, 964, 966, 1070,
1155
8:5-6, 40
8:6, 246, 248, 350, 418
8:6-13, 198, 276, 383, 633
8:7, 138, 350
8:7-12, 277
8:7-13, 248, 450, 543, 646
8:8, 246, 350, 509
8:8-11, 670
8:8-12, 198, 248, 537, 845
8:8-13, 38
8:9, 38, 246
8:10, 198, 350, 985
8:12, 276, 277
8:13, 248, 350, 537, 844,
1070
8:19, 563
8:24-28, 74
9, 99, 243, 382, 1233
9:1, 246, 248, 334, 450,
487
9:1-7, 844
9:1-10, 448, 480
9:1-15, 276
9:1-18, 849
9:2-5, 1165
9:3, 487
9:4, 494
9:5, 396, 451
9:6, 1165
9:6-7, 248
9:7, 248, 966, 1070, 1165
9:8, 334, 497, 858, 1021,
1022, 1155
9:8-10, 844, 1165
9:9, 242, 248, 277, 1155,
1158
9:9-10, 375, 379
9:10, 228, 277, 582, 1070,
1139
9:11, 99, 153, 276, 440,
454, 633, 844, 849, 966,
1155, 1165
9:11-12, 36, 1155
9:11-14, 74, 1003
9:12, 96, 98, 99, 242, 248,
274, 275, 360, 624, 633,
966, 1070, 1165
9:12-14, 849
9:13, 261, 276, 279, 488
9:13-14, 138, 375, 456, 845
9:14, 153, 242, 248, 261,
277, 278, 346, 417, 418,
490, 491, 958, 1070,
1071, 1096, 1211, 1237
9:15, 246, 286, 335, 346
12:24, 350
9:15, 418, 1003, 1070,
1096
9:15-22, 172, 274, 278, 780
9:16, 642
9:16-17, 278, 655
9:18-22, 248
9:19, 240
9:20, 278, 780, 842
9:22, 107, 261, 275, 379
9:23, 172, 248, 274, 334,
1155
9:23-24, 482

9:23-26, 360, 1022
9:23-28, 275, 276, 933
9:24, 96, 98, 99, 153, 248,
360, 418, 440, 480, 633,
844, 1155, 1185, 1233
9:24-28, 74
9:25, 248
9:25-28, 198
9:26, 248, 251, 275, 276,
334, 858, 1070, 1096
9:26-28, 252, 860
9:27, 66, 265, 278, 657
9:27-28, 623
9:28, 153, 248, 275, 276,
335, 361, 858, 861, 944,
1073, 1096
10, 278
10:1, 248, 482, 564, 891,
964, 966
10:1-2, 248, 646
10:1-4, 1022
10:1-18, 453, 480, 850
10:2, 242, 276, 277
10:2-4, 1096
10:3, 242
10:3-4, 646
10:3-10, 537
10:4, 261, 275, 276, 487,
1070
10:5, 252, 274, 1071, 1222
10:5-6, 567
10:5-7, 958
10:5-10, 261, 418, 480,
487, 488, 646
10:5-18, 964
10:8, 1096
10:8-10, 843
10:9-10, 318
10:9-18, 74
10:10, 153, 248, 274, 275,
276, 334, 487, 488, 1070
10:11, 248, 276, 646,
1070, 1096
10:11-13, 1079
10:11-14, 261, 360, 361
10:11-15, 198
10:11-23, 944
10:12, 98, 248, 334, 360,
418, 487, 632, 1016,
1070, 1073
10:12-13, 252, 265
10:12-14, 646
10:13, 277, 360, 418, 633,
734
10:14, 248, 276, 277, 334,
487, 488
10:14-18, 277, 850
10:15, 417, 1204
10:15-18, 277
10:16, 240, 350, 670
10:16-17, 198, 248, 417
10:16-18, 383, 646
10:17, 381, 821
10:18, 275, 276, 379,
1012, 1070
10:18-19, 1013
10:19, 117, 452, 454, 966,
1043, 1134
10:19-20, 36, 456, 567
10:19-21, 450
10:19-22, 360, 361, 1155
10:19-25, 74, 117, 1233
10:19-39, 843, 1042
10:20, 375
10:21, 444, 509
10:22, 117, 242, 261, 277,
279, 419, 564, 966, 985,
1095, 1211
10:23, 117, 335, 419, 451,
500, 661, 969
10:23-25, 447
10:24, 368, 419, 696
10:24-25, 278, 877
10:24-39, 895

10:25, 38, 107, 117, 198,
252, 265, 329, 335, 445,
446, 447, 449, 622, 858,
861, 1231
10:25-27, 66
10:26, 639, 1097, 1185
10:26-27, 459, 622
10:26-29, 334
10:26-30, 278
10:26-31, 350, 381, 419,
447, 623, 878, 1013
10:27, 265, 278, 372, 419
10:28, 40, 718, 734
10:28-29, 845
10:28-31, 1038
10:29, 276, 434, 487, 488,
490, 1013, 1112
10:30, 198, 850
10:30-31, 66, 265
10:31, 278, 372, 418
10:32, 189, 658, 1062
10:32-34, 73, 189, 440,
443, 445, 446, 447, 448,
505, 718, 1012, 1038,
1062, 1067
10:32-35, 878
10:32-39, 75, 327, 718,
781, 1233
10:33-34, 1087
10:34, 356, 361, 440, 602,
604
10:34-35, 335
10:35, 38, 74, 277, 327,
335, 419, 447, 821
10:35-36, 361, 1038
10:35-37, 861
10:35-39, 447, 451, 622
10:36, 419, 969
10:36-38, 335
10:36-39, 449
10:36-41, 74
10:37, 252, 265, 861
10:37-38, 999, 1054, 1056
10:37-39, 1234
10:38, 38, 365
10:38-39, 365
10:39, 368, 459, 624, 661,
985, 1240
11, 36, 38, 327, 354, 364,
368, 480, 512, 534, 537,
538, 718, 843, 850, 891,
1050, 1223
11:1, 3, 39, 74, 103, 365,
447, 453, 878, 891, 1056,
1234
11:1-2, 1042
11:1-40, 365, 453, 969,
1073
11:2, 38
11:3, 252, 420, 958, 1224
11:3-4, 367
11:3-40, 1042
11:4, 38, 718, 719, 1056
11:4-5, 1204
11:5, 38, 138, 276, 456
11:5-7, 456
11:6, 38, 41, 419, 564,
821, 1038
11:7, 38, 512, 624, 1056,
1073, 1222
11:8, 1, 3, 38, 821, 1038
11:8-10, 1040
11:8-12, 3
11:8-16, 103
11:8-19, 968
11:9, 3, 38, 39, 40, 1158
11:9-16, 335
11:10, 39, 420, 537, 563,
632, 633, 821
11:11, 3, 39, 451, 1218
11:11-12, 3, 1038
11:12, 3, 4, 39
11:13, 440, 505, 655, 661,

861
11:13-14, *352, 419*
11:13-16, *361, 420, 1233*
11:14, *563, 632*
11:16, *335, 563, 632*
11:17, *1, 3, 4, 138, 1168*
11:17-19, *3, 39*
11:17-22, *103*
11:18, *4, 39, 43*
11:19, *1016*
11:20, *39*
11:20-21, *130*
11:21, *39, 40*
11:21-22, *40*
11:22, *39, 40*
11:23, *39, 371, 1218*
11:23-26, *821*
11:23-28, *778, 780, 781*
11:23-31, *103*
11:24, *39*
11:25, *39, 198, 1012*
11:26, *39, 153, 335, 1139*
11:27, *39, 327, 371, 1240*
11:28, *39, 537, 1241*
11:29-30, *39*
11:30, *658*
11:31, *39, 456, 895, 1218*
11:32, *39, 443, 451, 1218*
11:32-34, *1139*
11:33, *456, 563, 831*
11:33-38, *39*
11:34, *940, 1139*
11:35, *276, 335, 449, 718, 719, 1002, 1016, 1218*
11:35-38, *446, 1139*
11:36-38, *42*
11:37, *138, 448, 456, 718, 719, 1180*
11:38, *1222, 1223*
11:39, *335, 419*
11:40, *277, 1118*
12, *486, 563, 895, 899*
12:1, *138, 327, 456, 718, 719, 1095, 1204*
12:1-2, *74, 419, 540*
12:1-3, *103, 328, 361, 453*
12:1-4, *172, 719*
12:1-13, *277*
12:2, *98, 99, 275, 277, 328, 356, 360, 418, 537, 567, 602, 632, 633, 821, 862, 1038, 1073*
12:2-3, *446, 878, 913, 962*
12:3, *328, 449*
12:3-4, *419, 447*
12:4, *73, 189, 327, 328, 329, 350, 445, 446, 447, 449, 718, 907, 1012*
12:4-6, *450*
12:4-11, *277, 895*
12:4-13, *850*
12:5, *198, 419*
12:5-6, *670, 695*
12:5-11, *66, 480, 1116*
12:5-12, *1139*
12:5-13, *172*
12:6, *198, 694, 736*
12:7, *198, 419*
12:7-11, *450*
12:7-13, *327*
12:9, *375, 417, 418, 419, 459, 845, 985, 1118*
12:10, *1118*
12:10-11, *419*
12:11, *602, 895, 1057*
12:12-13, *447, 450, 895*
12:12-17, *483*
12:13, *445*
12:14, *276, 335, 457, 485, 895, 896*
12:14-17, *563*
12:14-29, *449, 453*
12:15, *222, 305, 434, 445*
12:15-17, *381*

12:15-29, *895*
12:16, *39, 42, 1088*
12:16-17, *350, 1013*
12:17, *130, 445*
12:18, *563, 564*
12:18-19, *66, 138*
12:18-21, *172, 563*
12:18-24, *65, 198, 277, 862*
12:18-29, *172, 445*
12:21, *278, 456, 842*
12:22, *36, 198, 334, 420, 537, 561, 563, 564, 632, 655, 1155*
12:22-23, *633*
12:22-24, *45, 172, 440, 505, 563, 1016, 1118, 1233*
12:23, *66, 198, 265, 279, 420, 499, 563, 776, 985, 1016, 1058, 1118*
12:24, *38, 563*
12:25, *66, 417, 419, 623, 878*
12:25-29, *335, 419, 563*
12:26, *276, 419, 843, 969*
12:26-28, *440*
12:27, *1022*
12:27-28, *335*
12:28, *419, 435, 440, 449, 563, 633, 832, 1071*
12:29, *66, 486*
13, *350, 444, 449, 715, 861, 1067*
13:1, *447, 696*
13:1-2, *4*
13:1-3, *374, 505*
13:1-6, *444*
13:1-9, *483*
13:1-19, *895*
13:1-21, *449, 451, 1043, 1157*
13:1-25, *454, 1043*
13:2, *449, 502, 504, 505, 895, 897, 1051, 1062, 1071, 1220*
13:3, *444, 449, 505, 895, 985, 1071, 1139*
13:4, *66, 335, 444, 449, 622, 623, 715, 1088*
13:4-5, *356*
13:5, *449, 567, 1051*
13:5-6, *844*
13:6, *371, 670*
13:7, *108, 311, 445, 446, 448, 534, 744, 767, 1236*
13:7-9, *447*
13:8, *153, 242, 346, 449, 767*
13:9, *327, 378, 433, 449, 522, 582, 628, 767, 879*
13:9-10, *1139*
13:10, *449, 1233*
13:10-16, *1233*
13:11, *449, 985, 1096, 1155*
13:11-12, *1070*
13:12, *198, 446, 487, 488, 567, 633, 878*
13:12-13, *446*
13:12-16, *1233*
13:13, *449, 895*
13:13-14, *327, 361, 447*
13:14, *36, 335, 352, 420, 444, 449, 632, 1067*
13:15, *449, 522, 525, 526, 943, 1233*
13:15-16, *689, 1071*
13:16, *374, 449, 1051*
13:17, *108, 444, 446, 449, 513, 514, 518, 623, 744, 985, 1233*
13:17-18, *447*
13:17-19, *447*
13:17-23, *1218*

13:18, *449, 942*
13:19, *447, 451, 454*
13:20, *98, 246, 334, 346, 417, 418, 445, 449, 670, 689, 864, 877, 1016, 1092, 1235*
13:20-21, *172, 452, 651, 660, 664, 879, 895, 942, 1016, 1038, 1134*
13:20-25, *477*
13:22, *103, 350, 444, 447, 450, 451, 453, 475, 651, 821, 860, 1042, 1157, 1233*
13:22-25, *447, 450, 451, 452, 1043, 1134*
13:23, *189, 444, 447, 449, 451, 651, 1218*
13:24, *444, 446, 447, 651, 1066*
13:25, *434, 651, 660*

James
1, *1240*
1:1, *154, 173, 198, 420, 545, 547, 551, 552, 582, 616, 670, 671, 816, 863, 913, 1043, 1086, 1099, 1229*
1:1-2, *1044*
1:1-12, *1044*
1:1-18, *1044*
1:1-21, *557*
1:2, *4, 549, 602, 815, 908, 1039, 1166*
1:2-3, *549, 556, 557, 945*
1:2-4, *327, 330, 349, 351, 356, 557, 560, 1043, 1180*
1:2-7, *879*
1:2-18, *816, 822, 1044*
1:2-21, *552*
1:2-27, *651*
1:3, *368, 421*
1:3-4, *816, 1044*
1:4, *549, 553, 556, 1039*
1:5, *253, 351, 365, 421, 556, 557, 582, 838, 945, 1039, 1167, 1169, 1201*
1:5-6, *556*
1:5-7, *670, 671*
1:5-8, *102, 420, 549, 557, 945, 1202*
1:5-11, *1043*
1:5-12, *1044*
1:6, *367, 368, 945, 1115, 1228*
1:6-8, *102, 327, 421, 557, 1170*
1:7, *420*
1:8, *139, 421, 816, 945, 986, 1168*
1:9, *421, 623, 837, 1052*
1:9-10, *962*
1:9-11, *351, 546, 549, 556, 557, 822, 879, 1051, 1139*
1:10-11, *318, 537, 837, 1051*
1:11, *655*
1:12, *4, 66, 131, 327, 328, 397, 553, 556, 557, 558, 602, 622, 655, 695, 776, 777, 815, 816, 837, 838, 862, 969, 1018, 1039, 1043, 1166, 1167, 1240*
1:12-15, *549, 815, 1180*
1:12-16, *351, 1202*
1:13, *421, 1043, 1095, 1168, 1170*
1:13-15, *74, 421, 557, 1079, 1168*
1:13-16, *253, 550, 557, 1229*
1:13-17, *556*

1:14, *1169*
1:14-15, *556, 1168, 1169*
1:15, *655, 792, 1192*
1:16, *74, 75, 556, 1185*
1:16-18, *420, 421, 557, 1044*
1:16-21, *549*
1:17, *139, 252, 253, 420, 421, 553, 556, 568, 658, 816, 945, 1229*
1:17-18, *351, 556*
1:17-21, *550*
1:18, *253, 261, 335, 351, 421, 556, 557, 582, 622, 624, 792, 793, 862, 1039, 1185, 1224*
1:19, *551, 552, 556, 816, 838, 1169, 1240*
1:19-20, *557*
1:19-21, *421*
1:19-27, *548, 879, 1044*
1:20, *422, 896, 1054, 1240*
1:20-25, *103*
1:21, *383, 421, 556, 557, 624, 941, 962, 985, 1073, 1158*
1:21-25, *645*
1:21-27, *354*
1:22, *549, 552, 557, 558, 1039, 1051*
1:22-24, *549*
1:22-25, *421, 551, 557, 558, 604, 815, 822*
1:22-27, *556*
1:24, *103*
1:25, *351, 368, 383, 553, 582, 602, 645, 1039*
1:26, *815, 838, 985*
1:26-27, *421, 558, 879, 1044, 1071*
1:27, *253, 351, 383, 420, 422, 549, 557, 734, 838, 896, 1039, 1051, 1140, 1180, 1220, 1223, 1229*
2, *561, 815, 1050*
2:1, *154, 173, 362, 368, 398, 420, 422, 547, 551, 556, 558, 582, 670, 671, 837, 953, 1018, 1044*
2:1-2, *549*
2:1-3, *420*
2:1-4, *1139*
2:1-5, *548, 556*
2:1-7, *546, 549, 816, 879, 1051, 1145, 1169*
2:1-8, *734*
2:1-9, *356*
2:1-13, *421, 422, 550, 651, 822, 879, 895, 896, 1044, 1140*
2:1-16, *734*
2:1-26, *1044*
2:2, *198, 205, 224, 549, 1139, 1145, 1229, 1231*
2:2-4, *549, 558, 560*
2:2-6, *351*
2:2-7, *822*
2:2-11, *551*
2:3, *734, 1229*
2:3-4, *549*
2:4, *623, 1095*
2:5, *318, 351, 368, 421, 548, 549, 551, 553, 556, 558, 568, 633, 634, 696, 838, 879, 969, 1039, 1223*
2:5-8, *327*
2:6, *232, 522, 734, 838, 1139*
2:6-7, *549, 550, 551, 558, 634*
2:7, *114, 173, 318, 362, 676, 786, 1139, 1229*
2:8, *240, 480, 537, 557, 558, 568, 582, 634, 645,*

697, 734, 953, 1145, 1229
2:8-10, *383*
2:8-11, *480*
2:8-12, *351, 645*
2:8-13, *421, 551, 558, 1145*
2:8-26, *556*
2:9, *623, 734, 822, 838, 1095*
2:10, *351, 480, 645, 816*
2:11, *240, 480, 537, 645, 835, 837, 1088*
2:12, *383, 582, 645*
2:12-13, *550, 551, 556, 558, 623, 624, 862*
2:12-26, *548*
2:13, *336, 623, 734, 837, 838*
2:14, *368, 421, 1073*
2:14-16, *557*
2:14-17, *4, 41, 549*
2:14-26, *88, 351, 354, 551, 558, 560, 582, 586, 624, 651, 816, 822, 1039, 1044, 1056, 1140, 1145*
2:15, *421, 734, 1139, 1229*
2:15-16, *522, 550, 894, 895*
2:15-17, *351, 383*
2:16, *421, 896, 897, 985, 1139, 1229*
2:17, *103, 365, 368, 421, 558, 655*
2:18, *103, 421, 734, 1056*
2:18-24, *892*
2:19, *257, 421, 1056, 1229*
2:20, *421, 558, 1056*
2:21, *1, 4, 43, 368, 1056*
2:21-22, *1056*
2:21-23, *816*
2:21-24, *3, 4, 39, 41, 537, 558*
2:21-25, *421*
2:21-26, *550, 734*
2:22, *351, 368, 370, 553*
2:22-24, *624*
2:23, *1, 41, 480, 537, 837, 838, 1056, 1169*
2:24, *365, 368, 1056*
2:25, *39, 41, 537, 553, 558, 895, 1056, 1216*
2:26, *41, 368, 421, 558, 655, 776, 985, 1056*
3, *951, 1229*
3:1, *107, 336, 622, 744, 837, 1044, 1229*
3:1-2, *558*
3:1-8, *551*
3:1-12, *651, 815, 822, 1044, 1050, 1229*
3:1-18, *549, 552, 557, 558*
3:2, *553, 816*
3:3-6, *558*
3:5-6, *838*
3:6, *383, 459, 624, 816, 1079*
3:6-10, *139*
3:7-8, *558*
3:8, *838*
3:9, *420, 421, 670*
3:9-10, *130, 383, 556, 558*
3:10, *816*
3:11-12, *558*
3:12, *568*
3:13, *368, 420, 558, 582, 816, 962, 1044, 1191*
3:13-16, *557*
3:13-18, *420, 421, 716, 822, 879, 896, 1044, 1202*
3:14, *985, 1185*
3:14-16, *550, 556, 1191, 1192*
3:15, *420, 558, 582, 1079, 1185*
3:15-16, *558, 1202*
3:16, *558*

3:17, *350, 351, 365, 420,*
422, 552, 556, 558, 582,
734, 895, 1039, 1191,
1201, 1202
3:17-18, *383, 488, 556,*
557, 558, 898, 1191
3:18, *351, 422, 556, 558,*
895, 896, 1057
4, *1159*
4:1, *552, 558, 601, 986*
4:1-2, *550, 716*
4:1-3, *879, 945*
4:1-4, *945, 946*
4:1-5, *549, 551*
4:1-10, *421, 557*
4:1-12, *896*
4:2, *945*
4:2-3, *558, 568, 1170*
4:3, *556, 601, 716*
4:3-4, *551*
4:3-5, *550*
4:3-6, *549*
4:3-10, *1051*
4:4, *253, 716, 717, 816,*
1088, 1223
4:4-5, *495, 558*
4:4-6, *550, 816*
4:4-10, *879*
4:5, *86, 421, 838, 1169*
4:5-6, *837*
4:6, *365, 421, 434, 480,*
537, 546, 559, 832, 961,
962
4:6-10, *351, 548, 556*
4:6-12, *550*
4:7, *383, 670, 1039, 1078,*
1080
4:7-10, *549, 556, 559, 716,*
1081
4:8, *139, 421, 488, 986,*
1013, 1039, 1080, 1168
4:8-10, *1039*
4:9, *601, 604, 838*
4:10, *420, 421, 568, 670*
4:11, *351, 383, 582, 837,*
1229
4:11-12, *422, 556, 559,*
623, 716, 862
4:12, *257, 265, 421, 1073,*
1241
4:13, *351, 541, 549, 550,*
822, 879, 1044, 1139
4:13-15, *838, 1039, 1051*
4:13-16, *421*
4:13-17, *318, 556, 559, 879*
4:14-17, *549*
4:15, *173, 420, 670*
4:16, *962, 1095*
4:17, *1095*
5, *815, 837*
5:1, *351, 549, 550, 623*
5:1-2, *838*
5:1-3, *623*
5:1-6, *103, 327, 329, 421,*
522, 546, 549, 550, 551,
560, 734, 879, 1051
5:1-8, *837*
5:1-9, *173, 253, 336, 556*
5:1-11, *863*
5:3, *335, 374, 459, 622,*
985
5:4, *351, 420, 537, 559,*
670, 671, 943, 1139
5:4-5, *863*
5:4-6, *549*
5:5, *421, 838, 1055*
5:6, *42, 559*
5:7, *420, 857, 1073, 1199*
5:7-8, *173, 351, 552, 670,*
671, 863
5:7-9, *265, 335, 553, 557,*
559, 634, 1139
5:7-11, *421, 623, 879,*
1044, 1230

5:7-12, *816, 1180*
5:7-20, *559, 1043, 1044*
5:8, *420, 857, 864*
5:9, *173, 420, 559, 623,*
863, 1039
5:9-11, *552*
5:10, *173, 671, 816, 863*
5:10-11, *327, 355, 420,*
534, 816, 863
5:10-12, *559*
5:11, *41, 173, 327, 537,*
602, 671
5:12, *74, 420, 422, 552,*
568, 863
5:12-20, *1044, 1229*
5:13, *522, 526, 942, 945*
5:13-16, *559, 1228*
5:13-18, *437, 439, 552,*
556, 945, 1145
5:13-20, *651, 1044*
5:14, *48, 107, 198, 205,*
224, 420, 786, 942, 1145
5:14-15, *437, 671, 945*
5:14-16, *356*
5:15, *368, 420, 744, 942,*
945, 1016, 1039, 1073
5:15-16, *380, 381, 437*
5:16, *139, 421, 437, 816,*
942, 945, 1013, 1057,
1229
5:16-18, *437*
5:17, *41, 537, 942*
5:17-18, *41, 550, 559, 816,*
945
5:19, *1185*
5:19-20, *305, 551, 552,*
557, 559, 568, 622, 762,
1229
5:20, *74, 655, 656, 768,*
837, 839, 985, 1013, 1073

1 Peter
1, *876*
1:1, *79, 173, 392, 422,*
476, 517, 542, 549, 569,
652, 757, 758, 764, 768,
913, 915, 917, 919, 1106,
1135, 1163, 1234
1:1-2, *224, 319, 392, 517,*
651, 822, 917
1:1-12, *1044*
1:2, *154, 173, 174, 280,*
335, 422, 434, 490, 651,
660, 821, 896, 916, 946,
1071, 1163, 1237
1:3, *118, 154, 173, 174,*
422, 499, 500, 655, 660,
671, 672, 735, 737, 776,
792, 793, 880, 917, 921,
943, 1016, 1073, 1107,
1112, 1116, 1224, 1234
1:3-4, *329, 946, 1017*
1:3-5, *130, 349, 523, 958,*
1155
1:3-7, *376, 517*
1:3-8, *526*
1:3-9, *501, 569, 623, 651,*
822, 876, 1017, 1045
1:3-12, *118, 392, 476, 522,*
523, 524, 768, 864, 917,
918
1:4, *45, 253, 336, 422,*
440, 864, 867, 921
1:4-5, *265*
1:4-8, *917*
1:5, *75, 253, 336, 368,*
422, 864, 917, 921
1:5-4, *921*
1:5, *940, 1022, 1073,*
1167, 1234
1:5-6, *941*
1:5-9, *280, 880*
1:6, *230, 281, 366, 423,*
441, 601, 602, 768, 879,

1136, 1167, 1234
1:6-7, *189, 199, 349, 351,*
908, 919, 920, 1136
1:6-8, *356*
1:6-9, *1167*
1:7, *154, 281, 368, 395,*
422, 602, 858, 864, 908,
921, 1022, 1039, 1166,
1240
1:7-8, *1136*
1:7-9, *279, 1136*
1:8, *139, 569, 601, 602,*
864, 921, 1039, 1167
1:8-9, *695*
1:9, *336, 368, 523, 864,*
921, 985, 1073
1:9-10, *917*
1:10, *768, 864, 1022*
1:10-12, *45, 356, 480, 524,*
768, 921, 1045
1:11, *100, 154, 174, 279,*
361, 397, 423, 481, 491,
523, 569, 864, 916, 958,
1181
1:11-12, *1022*
1:12, *353, 432, 768, 769,*
817, 880, 1073
1:13, *336, 349, 356, 422,*
476, 479, 499, 500, 542,
642, 651, 735, 858, 864,
921, 985, 1022, 1039,
1044, 1045, 1234
1:13-16, *917, 1158*
1:13-17, *954*
1:13-21, *118*
1:13-25, *864, 876*
1:14, *279, 328, 423, 737,*
768, 821, 822, 917, 1045,
1071, 1073
1:14-15, *500, 986*
1:14-16, *1013*
1:15, *319, 422, 423, 488,*
735, 917, 922, 1073
1:15-16, *199, 349, 486,*
488, 940
1:16, *240, 423, 480, 538,*
835, 838
1:16-17, *535*
1:17, *265, 336, 349, 422,*
476, 517, 920, 946, 1039,
1106, 1224
1:17-18, *199*
1:17-19, *623, 917*
1:18, *42, 280, 281, 328,*
392, 655, 917, 1002
1:18-21, *174, 199, 279,*
522, 523, 524, 917
1:19, *154, 279, 280, 284,*
422, 641, 642, 838, 920,
1070
1:20, *154, 173, 253, 317,*
349, 422, 523, 622, 671,
858, 864, 921, 958, 1022,
1023, 1073, 1223, 1224
1:20-21, *335*
1:21, *96, 99, 101, 118,*
256, 280, 328, 361, 365,
368, 399, 422, 491, 864,
880, 917, 920, 985, 1016,
1234
1:22, *279, 349, 374, 488,*
513, 697, 821, 822, 917,
985, 1185
1:22-23, *879, 986*
1:22-25, *118*
1:23, *118, 417, 424, 655,*
671, 737, 792, 793, 794,
864, 1073, 1116
1:23-25, *353*
1:24, *375, 394, 480, 481,*
793, 985
1:24-25, *480, 838*
1:25, *346, 422, 432, 671,*
737, 793

2, *511, 633, 738, 838*
2:1, *349, 1095, 1158,*
1191, 1192
2:1-2, *738*
2:1-3, *917*
2:1-10, *118, 211, 212, 1234*
2:2, *118, 736, 737, 793,*
864, 921, 1073, 1115,
1158, 1192
2:2-3, *119, 879, 1115, 1117*
2:3, *671, 689, 917*
2:4, *154, 199, 281, 317,*
361, 422, 538, 915, 921,
1127, 1155
2:4-5, *173, 1039, 1129*
2:4-8, *522, 524, 637, 1127,*
1128
2:4-10, *107, 174, 199, 224,*
321, 476, 480, 510, 511,
543, 633, 744, 817, 838,
1135, 1155, 1234
2:4-11, *511*
2:4-17, *817*
2:4-24, *538*
2:5, *161, 174, 362, 510,*
689, 838, 921, 1071,
1106, 1127, 1135
2:6, *199, 317, 422, 480,*
538, 561, 838, 920, 1126,
1127
2:6-8, *361, 510, 838*
2:7, *480, 916, 1127, 1128*
2:7-8, *538, 1119*
2:8, *319, 480, 915, 920,*
922, 1126, 1127
2:9, *107, 119, 174, 199,*
200, 211, 319, 422, 488,
544, 633, 658, 735, 768,
817, 913, 917, 922, 1107
2:9-10, *318, 319, 354, 510,*
542, 896, 917, 1039, 1135
2:9-12, *986*
2:9-17, *231*
2:10, *174, 544, 735, 879*
2:11, *111, 118, 199, 253,*
328, 349, 350, 352, 376,
383, 392, 422, 476, 479,
517, 915, 917, 918, 985,
986, 1044, 1045, 1106,
1135, 1158, 1214
2:11-12, *392, 423, 517,*
817, 1136, 1191
2:11-17, *233*
2:12, *139, 265, 349, 350,*
361, 388, 392, 395, 513,
517, 569, 622, 864, 879,
896, 917, 918, 919, 920,
1039, 1135, 1136, 1234
2:12-13, *231*
2:13, *230, 349, 422, 514,*
769, 919, 1106
2:13-14, *324, 1062*
2:13-15, *1045, 1062*
2:13-17, *174, 424, 514,*
517, 908, 912, 917, 951,
1066, 1207, 1208
2:14, *230, 919, 1095*
2:14-15, *1135, 1136*
2:15, *231, 350, 392, 919,*
1136
2:16, *231, 328, 383, 1086,*
1095, 1100
2:16-17, *879*
2:17, *201, 230, 231, 324,*
350, 371, 697, 917, 920,
1062, 1100, 1180, 1181
2:18, *230, 371, 423, 513,*
652, 889, 1117, 1136
2:18-23, *1100*
2:18-24, *962*
2:18-25, *350, 423, 517,*
535, 838, 918, 950, 1136,
1207
2:19, *242, 281, 879, 1136,*

1208, 1234
2:19-20, *423, 435, 1136*
2:19-21, *1100*
2:19-25, *199, 328*
2:20, *242, 281, 513, 1045,*
1135, 1136
2:21, *154, 174, 256, 278,*
280, 281, 319, 422, 423,
534, 735, 921, 1234
2:21-22, *1136*
2:21-23, *174, 350, 366, 623*
2:21-24, *118, 256, 515,*
523, 538, 627, 876
2:21-25, *174, 261, 279,*
280, 356, 481, 522, 523,
524, 538, 822, 913, 921,
1092, 1181, 1208, 1209
2:22, *480, 838, 839, 1096,*
1181
2:22-23, *918*
2:22-24, *423*
2:23, *1054, 1136*
2:23-24, *1137, 1167*
2:23-25, *569*
2:24, *174, 256, 280, 281,*
329, 655, 719, 839, 891,
1055, 1057, 1070, 1073,
1092
2:24-25, *366, 1136*
2:25, *107, 174, 199, 222,*
281, 876, 877, 915, 922,
1013, 1092
3, *818, 899*
3:1, *154, 230, 424, 517,*
768, 769, 922, 1092,
1119, 1207, 1208
3:1-2, *4, 199, 350, 513,*
517, 880, 1136
3:1-6, *350, 354, 356, 513,*
950, 1208
3:1-7, *199, 517, 518, 946,*
1088, 1207
3:2, *371, 488, 1136, 1209*
3:3-4, *985*
3:4, *424, 896, 898, 963,*
985
3:4-5, *4*
3:5, *230, 880, 1208, 1234*
3:5-6, *879*
3:6, *1, 39, 371, 538, 671,*
817, 821, 835, 1045,
1136, 1208, 1222, 1234
3:7, *350, 424, 435, 517,*
639, 655, 946, 1208, 1209
3:8, *350, 518, 696, 963,*
1191
3:8-9, *839, 918, 1136*
3:8-12, *1095*
3:8-18, *117*
3:9, *130, 319, 336, 864,*
1136, 1191
3:9-10, *281*
3:9-12, *349, 501*
3:10, *480, 698*
3:10-12, *130, 481, 538, 839*
3:11, *896*
3:11-12, *199*
3:12, *422, 671, 942, 946,*
1039, 1095, 1209
3:13, *118, 423, 476, 768,*
1044, 1045, 1136
3:13-14, *230, 879, 1057*
3:13-17, *74, 75, 361, 383,*
912, 919
3:13-22, *199, 423*
3:14, *131, 242, 281, 328,*
371, 423, 569, 602, 839,
1100, 1136, 1208
3:14-15, *174*
3:14-17, *880*
3:15, *154, 336, 355, 357,*
371, 392, 422, 499, 517,
671, 757, 768, 769, 864,
880, 963, 985, 1016, 1119

3:15-16, *423, 865, 917, 920*
3:16, *242, 350, 879, 891, 917, 918, 1136*
3:16-17, *918*
3:17, *242, 344, 423, 863, 1045, 1062, 1100, 1136*
3:17-22, *261*
3:18, *48, 96, 118, 154, 158, 174, 279, 280, 281, 329, 335, 361, 376, 422, 423, 491, 498, 523, 524, 719, 836, 919, 922, 986, 987, 1016, 1020, 1055, 1070, 1096, 1118, 1136, 1137*
3:18-4:6, *526, 923*
3:18-19, *335*
3:18-20, *286, 817*
3:18-21, *986*
3:18-22, *99, 100, 102, 256, 279, 459, 481, 515, 523, 526, 627, 671, 822, 922, 953, 1016, 1136, 1234*
3:18-25, *199*
3:19, *46, 63, 99, 376, 460, 527, 836, 1119*
3:19-20, *286, 863, 1117, 1118*
3:19-21, *1016*
3:20, *38, 41, 117, 279, 538, 655, 835, 922, 985, 1119*
3:20-21, *523*
3:21, *41, 354, 376, 538, 795, 836, 879, 1016, 1017, 1073, 1136*
3:21-22, *96, 253, 256, 335, 361, 672, 1017, 1224*
3:22, *46, 96, 99, 174, 281, 356, 422, 523, 836, 922, 964*
4, *1178*
4:1, *376, 423, 1062, 1100, 1136, 1168, 1169, 1170*
4:1-2, *423*
4:1-4, *769*
4:1-5, *383*
4:1-6, *199, 392, 538, 1234*
4:1-19, *117*
4:2, *376, 655, 985, 986, 1073*
4:2-4, *655*
4:3, *388, 424, 529, 542, 715, 917, 1088, 1158, 1191, 1192*
4:3-4, *79, 1135*
4:4, *230, 361, 818, 822, 879, 1136*
4:5, *253, 336, 424, 622, 623, 655, 656, 864, 920, 1073*
4:5-6, *265, 623, 918*
4:5-7, *66*
4:6, *279, 335, 376, 432, 459, 622, 655, 776, 920, 986, 1136*
4:7, *118, 253, 336, 349, 376, 622, 864, 880, 918, 946, 1062, 1234*
4:7-11, *118, 392, 918*
4:8, *622, 696, 699, 839, 1097*
4:8-11, *374*
4:9, *505, 759, 1051, 1062, 1220*
4:9-10, *424*
4:10, *434, 918*
4:10-11, *355, 744, 891, 1087*
4:11, *107, 174, 336, 346, 354, 392, 395, 424, 660, 661, 880, 917, 939, 946*
4:11-12, *224*
4:12, *189, 423, 879, 908,*

917, 918, 919, 1136, 1234
4:12-14, *1023, 1039*
4:12-16, *174, 230, 879*
4:12-19, *74, 75, 118, 199, 253, 328, 330, 355, 423, 822, 918, 1100, 1181*
4:13, *100, 154, 265, 281, 336, 349, 397, 422, 423, 481, 569, 601, 602, 604, 864, 892, 921, 1062, 1192*
4:13-14, *361*
4:13-16, *383*
4:14, *131, 154, 397, 490, 602, 1136*
4:14-15, *1135*
4:14-16, *281, 769, 785, 919*
4:15, *761, 769, 1191, 1192*
4:15-16, *917*
4:16, *196, 395, 513, 1039, 1136*
4:17, *242, 349, 432, 476, 511, 918, 919, 946, 1062, 1066, 1106, 1136*
4:17-18, *265, 336*
4:17-19, *253, 864, 879, 1234*
4:18, *104, 480, 481, 1057, 1058, 1073*
4:19, *281, 328, 422, 423, 623, 985, 1062, 1092, 1136*
5, *719, 1092*
5:1, *100, 265, 349, 397, 422, 423, 569, 718, 719, 760, 858, 880, 914, 915, 918, 1023, 1092, 1181*
5:1-2, *107, 1093*
5:1-4, *392, 622, 918*
5:1-5, *224, 311, 424, 513, 514, 518, 877, 880, 1066*
5:1-9, *118*
5:1-11, *818*
5:1-14, *476*
5:2, *199, 222, 880, 915, 1051*
5:2-3, *107, 818, 1092*
5:2-4, *354, 1092, 1235*
5:3, *355, 880*
5:4, *107, 265, 336, 397, 513, 655, 858, 862, 864, 880, 915, 1023, 1039, 1092*
5:5, *230, 350, 434, 480, 481, 513, 538, 880, 961, 962, 1207, 1211*
5:5-6, *962*
5:6, *336, 361, 424, 524, 864, 1212*
5:6-9, *918, 1081*
5:6-11, *253, 424, 1045*
5:7, *538, 831, 946*
5:8, *74, 75, 253, 962, 1078, 1079, 1080, 1199*
5:8-9, *719, 920, 1040, 1062, 1080, 1136*
5:8-14, *1044*
5:9, *189, 199, 201, 368, 423, 737, 910, 1066, 1222*
5:9-10, *199, 230, 879, 1039*
5:10, *118, 224, 265, 319, 336, 346, 422, 424, 434, 461, 481, 719, 880, 922, 941, 1017, 1080, 1100*
5:10-11, *918*
5:11, *118, 174, 336, 346, 660, 661, 939, 946*
5:12, *422, 434, 915, 916, 918, 1045, 1185, 1234*
5:12-13, *922, 1163*
5:12-14, *918*
5:13, *111, 186, 765, 908, 915, 919, 1062, 1066, 1135, 1211, 1221*
5:13-14, *651*

5:14, *651, 660, 697, 896, 946*
5:15, *832*
5:20, *199, 1234*

2 Peter
1, *819, 954, 1194*
1:1, *79, 154, 175, 369, 424, 430, 668, 1054, 1055, 1074, 1083, 1086, 1099, 1237*
1:1-2, *652, 923, 1045*
1:2, *175, 424, 434, 639, 660, 671, 896, 946, 1083*
1:3, *312, 319, 397, 424, 639, 940*
1:3-4, *656*
1:3-11, *652, 896, 923, 924, 926*
1:3-15, *1045*
1:4, *311, 312, 424, 716, 776, 794, 940, 968, 969, 1074, 1223*
1:4-11, *1040*
1:5, *369*
1:5-6, *639*
1:5-7, *311, 366, 926, 1191, 1192*
1:5-8, *350, 952*
1:5-9, *311, 319, 397, 1013*
1:5-11, *822*
1:6, *329*
1:7, *513, 697*
1:8, *366, 424, 639, 640, 672*
1:10, *319*
1:11, *154, 175, 337, 346, 424, 461, 624, 633, 672, 865, 1018, 1074, 1083, 1192*
1:12, *459, 1185*
1:12-15, *652, 924, 983*
1:12-16, *923*
1:12-21, *312, 760*
1:13, *475*
1:14, *154, 424, 475, 570, 655, 672, 865, 923, 1021, 1023*
1:14-15, *719, 776*
1:16, *29, 154, 424, 652, 672, 769, 865, 925, 1023, 1045*
1:16-17, *335*
1:16-18, *311, 362, 866, 915, 921, 926, 983, 1112*
1:16-19, *175*
1:16-21, *923, 924, 1045*
1:17, *318, 396, 424, 570*
1:17-18, *865*
1:18, *424, 487*
1:19, *312, 354, 424, 658, 865, 869, 973*
1:19-21, *312, 866, 926*
1:20, *983*
1:20-21, *424, 923, 925*
1:21, *424*
1:21-22, *497*
2, *305, 353, 354, 356, 538, 689, 819, 822, 896, 952, 1185*
2:1, *29, 74, 75, 76, 174, 312, 424, 459, 615, 973, 1002, 1083, 1241*
2:1-2, *1159, 1185*
2:1-3, *425, 866, 923, 924*
2:1-10, *425*
2:1-18, *424, 614, 865, 925, 983*
2:1-20, *880*
2:1-22, *335, 383*
2:2, *29, 350, 925, 1149, 1185*
2:2-3, *74*
2:3, *66, 265, 336, 459,*

715, 865, 923, 924, 925, 926, 973, 1149, 1185, 1241
2:3-10, *1045*
2:4, *46, 63, 424, 425, 534, 624, 973, 1097, 1119*
2:4-9, *253, 715, 822*
2:4-10, *839, 866*
2:5, *38, 41, 425, 459, 624, 1056, 1097*
2:6, *425, 534, 623, 624, 1088, 1097*
2:6-10, *459*
2:7, *323, 624*
2:7-8, *41, 425, 1057*
2:8, *821, 985, 1057*
2:9, *75, 265, 336, 424, 425, 623, 671, 865, 926, 973, 1013, 1101, 1167*
2:9-12, *66*
2:9-16, *1097*
2:10, *29, 30, 375, 425, 715, 923, 924, 925, 1149*
2:10-11, *46*
2:10-12, *715*
2:10-22, *1045*
2:11, *29, 424, 623, 671, 867*
2:12, *312, 715, 865, 1240*
2:13, *29, 356, 379, 601, 658, 715, 952, 1228*
2:13-14, *1149*
2:14, *658, 715, 985*
2:14-15, *715, 1051*
2:14-16, *74*
2:15, *43, 74, 312, 698, 819, 836, 1088*
2:16, *715*
2:17, *459*
2:17-22, *74*
2:18, *715, 985, 1149*
2:19, *30, 350, 383, 925, 968*
2:19-20, *312, 383*
2:19-22, *715*
2:20, *154, 570, 639, 672, 1074, 1083, 1223*
2:20-21, *640*
2:20-22, *822, 1013, 1015*
2:21, *240, 312, 1057*
2:22, *538, 570, 839*
3, *739, 819, 865, 866, 954*
3:1, *139, 312, 914, 923, 983, 985*
3:1-3, *614, 925, 983*
3:1-4, *923, 1045*
3:1-7, *1045*
3:1-10, *622, 924*
3:1-13, *873, 880*
3:2, *79, 80, 87, 240, 312, 487, 672, 744, 760, 1074, 1083*
3:3, *335, 868*
3:3-4, *29, 254, 350, 1186*
3:3-7, *822*
3:3-13, *462, 926*
3:3-14, *311, 716*
3:4, *189, 265, 425, 866, 873, 923, 924, 925, 968, 969, 1023, 1149*
3:4-6, *29*
3:5, *424, 441*
3:5-6, *253, 425*
3:5-7, *66, 622, 926*
3:5-10, *923*
3:5-14, *441, 442*
3:6, *1222, 1240*
3:7, *253, 265, 336, 354, 441, 459, 866, 908, 926, 1097, 1189, 1240*
3:7-13, *336*
3:8, *266, 424, 425, 671, 739, 740, 866*
3:8-9, *265, 880, 926*

3:8-10, *29, 175*
3:8-13, *1045*
3:9, *265, 329, 354, 424, 671, 866, 925, 968, 969, 1149, 1188, 1240*
3:10, *253, 265, 266, 337, 345, 369, 424, 425, 441, 570, 622, 671, 866, 926*
3:10-13, *46, 866*
3:10-14, *65, 312*
3:11, *350, 488, 926*
3:11-12, *337, 867, 880*
3:11-13, *253*
3:11-14, *441*
3:11-16, *923, 924*
3:11-18, *822*
3:12, *253, 265, 350, 424, 459, 671, 866, 867, 908, 1045*
3:13, *253, 337, 441, 739, 926, 968, 969, 1018, 1058*
3:14, *337, 652, 896, 926*
3:14-17, *351, 880*
3:14-18, *74, 312, 652*
3:15, *30, 329, 424, 425, 1073, 1203*
3:15-16, *30, 79, 80, 87, 311, 383, 744, 892, 983*
3:16, *312, 459, 924, 925, 1056, 1240*
3:16-17, *335*
3:17, *74, 762, 1083*
3:17-18, *354, 880, 923*
3:18, *154, 175, 265, 346, 395, 639, 652, 660, 661, 664, 672, 867, 880, 896, 946, 1074, 1083, 1186*

1 John
1:1, *593, 594, 665, 1023*
1:1-2:27, *1050*
1:1-3, *591*
1:1-4, *26, 176, 238, 282, 590, 597, 639, 652, 958, 1046, 1113*
1:2, *176, 347, 425, 665, 858, 1023, 1204*
1:2-3, *282, 1074*
1:3, *154, 155, 199, 373, 425, 591, 665, 959, 1224*
1:3-7, *819*
1:4, *652*
1:5, *425, 426, 488, 597*
1:5:13, *652*
1:5, *657, 1046, 1148*
1:5-10, *946*
1:6, *238, 425, 592*
1:6-7, *657*
1:6-10, *240, 373, 819, 823*
1:7, *27, 176, 199, 254, 281, 282, 425, 426, 539, 591, 594, 786, 1097, 1113, 1148*
1:8, *27, 282, 426, 592, 822, 1013, 1184*
1:8-10, *281, 1097*
1:9, *27, 104, 282, 381, 383, 943, 1054*
1:10, *27, 592, 1097*
1:18, *27*
1:19, *380*
2, *238*
2:1, *172, 176, 282, 351, 425, 823, 868, 881, 1013, 1055, 1097, 1115, 1224*
2:1-2, *27, 261, 282, 539, 1074*
2:2, *76, 176, 254, 257, 282, 283, 336, 351, 362, 392, 946, 1070, 1074, 1083, 1097*
2:3, *239, 351, 645*
2:3-4, *238, 239, 646*
2:3-5, *640*

2:3-6, *239, 646, 823*
2:4, *239, 351, 592, 645, 1184*
2:5, *239, 283, 426, 479, 646*
2:6, *479, 592*
2:7, *238, 239, 351, 426, 594, 645, 881, 959*
2:7-8, *880, 881, 959*
2:7-9, *239*
2:7-11, *282, 645*
2:8, *238, 336, 351, 426, 645, 659, 823, 1148*
2:8-11, *283, 1184*
2:9, *426, 592, 657, 1148*
2:9-11, *238, 479, 594, 819*
2:10, *199, 425, 426, 1148*
2:11, *425, 479, 658*
2:12, *27, 283, 380, 786, 1115*
2:12-13, *881*
2:12-14, *336, 513, 594*
2:13, *328, 425, 593, 819, 1078, 1095, 1224*
2:13-14, *254, 336, 339, 959, 1080*
2:14, *283, 328, 425, 594, 940, 941, 1078, 1081, 1095*
2:15, *199, 425, 426, 595, 1223*
2:15-16, *592*
2:15-17, *254, 282, 656*
2:16, *375, 425, 962, 985*
2:16-17, *1223*
2:17, *282, 336, 346*
2:18, *51, 74, 254, 335, 351, 589, 590, 868, 881*
2:18-19, *26, 75, 80, 199, 744, 880, 1046, 1119*
2:18-27, *108, 175, 342, 646, 1046*
2:18-29, *868*
2:19, *175, 199, 238, 257, 328, 336, 596, 868, 1024*
2:19-26, *589*
2:20, *49, 108, 119, 282, 312, 487, 490, 593, 973*
2:20-21, *495, 589, 744*
2:20-23, *592*
2:21-22, *881*
2:22, *51, 74, 155, 176, 257, 281, 328, 589, 590, 591, 661, 822*
2:22-23, *26, 80, 336, 1046*
2:22-25, *623*
2:22-27, *1113*
2:23, *176, 366, 591, 943*
2:24, *75, 200, 238, 282, 351, 594, 959, 1116*
2:25, *347, 776, 968, 969*
2:26, *80, 336*
2:26-27, *744, 973*
2:27, *49, 119, 200, 282, 312, 490, 495, 593, 597, 1185*
2:28, *66, 254, 282, 337, 354, 857, 858, 868, 897, 1024*
2:28-29, *1046*
2:29, *200, 281, 597, 792, 794, 1055, 1057*
2:29-3:3, *624*
3:1, *42, 200, 426, 597, 1116, 1224*
3:1-18, *1235*
3:1-24, *1046*
3:2, *176, 282, 337, 499, 776, 881, 1018, 1024, 1038, 1116*
3:2-3, *1013*
3:3, *283, 337, 488, 500*
3:3-6, *592*
3:4, *336, 583, 821, 823,*

1097
3:4-9, *27*
3:4-10, *823, 1013*
3:5, *176, 254, 283, 823, 1023, 1070, 1181*
3:6, *283, 1097, 1168*
3:7, *42, 74, 75, 1055, 1057*
3:7-8, *592*
3:8, *42, 199, 254, 281, 283, 336, 351, 591, 959, 1023, 1078, 1079, 1113, 1241*
3:8-10, *819, 1116*
3:9, *27, 200, 282, 283, 592, 792, 793, 794, 1170*
3:9-10, *592*
3:10, *254, 819, 1057, 1078, 1116*
3:10-11, *880*
3:11, *199, 238, 426, 513, 594, 597, 959*
3:11-12, *282, 592*
3:11-17, *699*
3:11-18, *103*
3:12, *38, 42, 534, 539, 841, 1056, 1057, 1078, 1079, 1095*
3:13, *199, 253, 819, 1223*
3:14, *254, 282, 283, 351, 426, 437, 594, 656, 776*
3:14-15, *592*
3:15, *347*
3:16, *257, 282, 351, 426, 594, 655, 656*
3:16-18, *261, 534*
3:16-19, *1184*
3:17, *366, 426, 895, 897, 1051*
3:17-18, *426, 592*
3:19, *897*
3:19-21, *985*
3:21, *103, 868, 881, 897*
3:21-22, *103, 946*
3:22, *239, 583, 597, 645, 942*
3:22-23, *104*
3:22-24, *239, 645*
3:23, *176, 199, 238, 239, 351, 369, 426, 591, 594, 645, 785, 1113*
3:24, *238, 239, 281, 336, 490, 495, 645, 1235*
4:1, *254, 592, 593, 615, 1119, 1120, 1166, 1224*
4:1-3, *108, 176, 366, 593, 596, 973, 978, 1119, 1184*
4:1-4, *1079*
4:1-6, *253, 353, 589, 593, 819, 1185, 1236*
4:1-21, *351, 1046*
4:2, *140, 155, 199, 257, 281, 328, 366, 375, 490, 495, 591, 661, 949, 959, 985, 1113*
4:2-3, *26, 52, 104, 308, 539, 973, 1119*
4:3, *26, 51, 74, 176, 199, 366, 822, 973*
4:3-5, *1223*
4:4, *75, 282, 328, 1078, 1080*
4:4-6, *75*
4:5, *283, 328, 1223, 1224*
4:6, *104, 282, 490, 495, 1184, 1185*
4:7, *426, 513, 594, 597, 792, 794*
4:7-8, *104*
4:7-12, *695, 819, 880*
4:7-19, *1083*
4:7-21, *1120, 1235*
4:8, *351, 426, 594*
4:8-10, *592*
4:9, *163, 282, 426, 591,*

594, 1023, 1116, 1223
4:9-10, *27, 254, 282*
4:9-12, *1113*
4:10, *176, 257, 261, 282, 283, 426, 591, 594, 694, 1074, 1083, 1097, 1113*
4:10-12, *354*
4:11, *283, 426*
4:11-12, *1083*
4:12, *282, 426, 595*
4:12-16, *794*
4:13, *282, 336, 490, 495*
4:13-16, *104*
4:14, *354, 392, 1074, 1083, 1204, 1223*
4:14-15, *1113*
4:15, *176, 257, 366, 591, 593, 661, 1083, 1116*
4:16, *351, 426, 593*
4:17, *66, 104, 176, 254, 265, 337, 426, 595, 622, 868, 897*
4:17-18, *282*
4:17-21, *622*
4:18, *371, 426, 590, 897*
4:19, *239, 354, 426, 594, 1083*
4:19-21, *794*
4:20, *239, 426, 592, 594, 699, 1184*
4:20-21, *104*
4:21, *238, 426, 594, 645, 1114*
5, *794*
5:1, *176, 199, 200, 281, 282, 328, 366, 369, 426, 591, 646, 792, 794, 1083*
5:1-12, *794, 1046*
5:2, *239, 645*
5:2-3, *238, 583, 645, 823*
5:3, *239, 240*
5:4, *240, 254, 281, 283, 328, 366, 369, 646, 792, 794*
5:4-5, *240, 339, 1223*
5:5, *257, 328, 369, 1113*
5:5-6, *26, 27*
5:5-8, *589*
5:5-12, *282*
5:6, *155, 281, 282, 366, 591, 1114, 1185*
5:6-8, *119, 159, 1116*
5:7, *666*
5:7-11, *1204*
5:8, *281, 282*
5:9-10, *1185*
5:9-12, *1113*
5:10, *369*
5:10-11, *1184*
5:11, *347, 591*
5:11-12, *176, 437*
5:11-13, *776*
5:13, *104, 347, 369, 539, 597, 785*
5:13-21, *597, 652, 1046*
5:14, *868, 897, 942*
5:14-15, *103, 944, 945*
5:14-17, *437, 622, 946*
5:14-21, *1046*
5:15, *942*
5:16, *305, 336*
5:16-17, *345, 656, 946*
5:17, *437*
5:18, *383, 592, 792, 793, 794, 1078, 1081, 1095, 1097, 1116*
5:18-19, *254*
5:18-21, *1113*
5:19, *199, 254, 282, 794, 1078, 1095, 1223*
5:20, *155, 176, 347, 985, 1116, 1185, 1236, 1237*
5:21, *528, 529, 596, 1185*

2 John
1, *200, 318, 595, 596, 1088, 1115, 1184, 1211*
1-2, *652, 1184*
1-3, *598, 652*
2, *346, 425*
3, *154, 155, 425, 434, 596, 652, 660, 735, 896, 946, 1113*
4, *238, 239, 425, 645, 652, 1046, 1184*
4-5, *652*
4-6, *239, 598, 644, 645, 876*
4-7, *156*
5, *238, 239, 351, 594, 596, 645, 652, 881, 1046, 1088*
6, *238, 239, 351, 426, 645*
6-11, *652, 1046*
7, *27, 51, 52, 140, 155, 199, 254, 257, 308, 375, 426, 539, 589, 591, 744, 822, 880, 959, 985, 1046, 1119, 1184, 1224*
7-8, *27*
7-9, *596*
7-11, *74, 75, 80, 239, 336, 353, 598, 615*
8, *591, 593, 652, 868, 1240*
8-9, *1046*
8-11, *596*
9, *27, 224, 257, 425, 426*
10, *200, 508, 513, 595, 652*
10-11, *140, 199, 305, 505, 506, 769, 1220*
11, *140, 373, 652, 1046, 1095*
12, *652, 1047*
12-13, *598*
13, *318, 596, 652, 1047, 1211, 1220*

3 John
1, *595, 652, 881, 1047, 1184*
1-2, *598*
2, *596, 652, 881, 897, 946*
2-4, *1047*
2-6, *652*
3-4, *652, 897, 1184*
3-8, *598, 1047*
4, *881, 1115, 1211*
5, *769, 881*
5-6, *506, 652, 1047*
5-8, *80, 374, 392, 760, 769, 894, 897, 1051*
5-10, *744, 1220*
6, *199, 200, 425, 506, 652, 769*
6-7, *355*
7, *769*
7-8, *744*
7-12, *652, 1047*
8, *596, 652, 1220*
9, *199, 200, 505*
9-10, *80, 744, 769, 881, 1047*
9-11, *305*
9-12, *598*
10, *199, 200, 513, 595*
11, *425, 426, 535, 652, 792, 793, 1095*
11-12, *1047*
12, *596, 652*
13-14, *598, 65, 10472*
14, *946*
15, *596, 653, 660, 785, 896, 897, 1047*

Jude
1, *28, 154, 174, 175, 187, 266, 319, 424, 425, 612,*

614, 616, 618, 653, 867, 1099, 1112
1-2, *612, 613, 619, 696, 1045*
2, *612, 653, 660, 735, 894, 946*
3, *74, 140, 141, 311, 369, 425, 612, 613, 617, 618, 653, 661, 760, 768, 880, 954, 1045, 1228*
3-4, *353, 425, 612, 653*
3-23, *612, 653*
4, *28, 74, 75, 76, 141, 154, 174, 266, 335, 350, 383, 424, 425, 612, 613, 615, 618, 716, 840, 867, 958, 973, 1045, 1097, 1228*
4-13, *424, 614, 925, 983, 1045*
4-16, *354*
4-19, *880*
4-23, *356*
5, *141, 175, 424, 425, 612, 614, 617, 671, 836, 880, 958, 1074, 1240*
5-7, *74, 266, 534, 613, 620, 822, 840, 867*
5-10, *613, 1045*
5-16, *175, 613, 653, 1046*
5-19, *475, 582, 612, 613*
5-23, *612*
6, *46, 63, 141, 266, 336, 425, 618, 623, 716, 836, 840, 858, 1074, 1089, 1119*
6-7, *323, 538*
6-8, *615, 1045*
7, *346, 375, 425, 459, 461, 618, 620, 624, 836, 1074, 1088*
8, *28, 29, 46, 266, 335, 375, 394, 615, 618, 836, 985, 1089, 1228*
9, *1078*
8-9, *840, 867*
8-10, *425, 613, 615, 618, 778, 973*
8-16, *74, 141*
9, *40, 66, 175, 254, 424, 538, 614, 623, 671, 836, 867, 949, 973, 1078*
10, *538, 618, 1045, 1186, 1240*
10-13, *335*
11, *38, 43, 266, 425, 613, 614, 618, 836, 840, 1088*
11-12, *29*
11-13, *613, 615, 1045*
12, *28, 29, 356, 614, 615, 618, 656, 689, 697, 973, 1228*
12-13, *613, 818, 894*
12-14, *618*
13, *254, 266, 346, 459, 618, 620, 658, 709, 840, 867*
14, *38, 43, 141, 159, 424, 425, 487, 618, 619, 620, 671, 867, 874, 958*
14-15, *46, 63, 86, 175, 266, 336, 538, 613, 614, 618, 768, 822, 840, 875, 880*
14-16, *66, 613, 867, 1045*
15, *159, 369, 425, 619, 620, 874, 1097*
16, *266, 613, 614, 615, 618, 716, 1045*
16-18, *614, 925, 983*
17, *80, 154, 174, 312, 570, 613, 617, 671, 744, 760, 880, 958, 1228, 1236*
17-18, *190, 266, 335, 425, 613, 618*

17-19, *613, 1045*
17-21, *175*
17-23, *612, 613, 653, 1046*
18, *254, 350, 425, 615, 716, 973, 1097*
18-19, *28, 305, 495, 946*
19, *613, 615, 618, 894, 973, 1186*
20, *74, 140, 141, 311, 369, 487, 495, 612, 613, 614, 619, 880, 946*
20-21, *716*
20-23, *425, 612, 613, 618, 619*
21, *74, 154, 174, 175, 337, 347, 424, 425, 618, 619, 671, 695, 735, 776, 822, 867, 880, 958, 1018*
22, *66, 735, 768, 867, 1228*
22-23, *104, 619, 620, 621, 622, 656, 880*
23, *141, 254, 375, 459, 615, 619, 1074*
24, *74, 75, 337, 397, 424, 425, 601, 623, 660, 716, 822, 1018, 1040, 1228*
24-25, *175, 257, 266, 612, 613, 615, 653, 660, 664, 867, 940, 946, 953, 1046, 1083*
25, *154, 174, 175, 346, 395, 424, 660, 661, 671, 939, 958, 1074, 1083, 1228*

Revelation
1, *25, 46, 338, 339, 345, 400, 871, 1029, 1030, 1111*
1:1, *56, 100, 155, 177, 426, 427, 441, 851, 869, 921, 974, 1024, 1047, 1086*
1:1-2, *1026*
1:1-3, *46, 653*
1:1-8, *1030, 1047*
1:2, *155, 177, 769, 770, 1026, 1137, 1205*
1:3, *60, 131, 571, 602, 851, 852, 869, 973, 1027, 1047*
1:3-8, *348*
1:4, *46, 200, 254, 426-28, 434, 490, 653, 660, 662, 869, 1032, 1120*
1:4-5, *177, 653, 897, 1026*
1:4-7, *947*
1:4-20, *539*
1:5, *100, 284, 337, 338, 362, 383, 635, 656, 694, 719, 720, 770, 776, 1002, 1009, 1017, 1071, 1096, 1205*
1:5-6, *108, 177, 338, 694, 897*
1:6, *108, 161, 200, 211, 224, 284, 337, 346, 395, 426, 428, 481, 583, 635, 653, 660, 661, 940, 963, 974, 1009, 1074*
1:6-9, *331*
1:7, *142, 338, 339, 481, 571, 623, 661, 858, 869*
1:8, *177, 232, 254, 257, 426, 427, 662, 672, 703, 869, 959, 1017*
1:9, *127, 147, 177, 200, 232, 329, 337, 342, 348, 624, 770, 823, 908, 910, 913, 915, 974, 1009, 1062, 1067, 1137, 1180, 1205*
1:9-10, *177, 682, 851*
1:9-20, *340, 1030, 1047*

1:10, *63, 266, 348, 495, 496, 675, 679, 681, 682, 685, 974, 1145, 1182, 1196, 1231*
1:10-20, *177*
1:11, *200, 340, 757, 758, 851, 1026, 1030, 1084, 1196*
1:12, *770*
1:12-16, *46, 427, 667, 1145*
1:12-17, *362*
1:12-18, *100, 340*
1:12-20, *340, 853*
1:13, *142, 337, 338, 356, 636, 853, 1145*
1:13-15, *853*
1:14, *662, 853*
1:14-20, *338*
1:16, *418, 635, 704, 1009*
1:17, *283, 372, 662, 853, 959*
1:17-18, *487, 853*
1:18, *128, 177, 283, 346, 460, 662, 776, 960, 1016, 1017, 1234*
1:19, *339, 340, 344, 366, 851, 852, 869, 959*
1:20, *46, 340, 704, 770, 783, 1009, 1120*
2, *46, 177, 205, 224, 266, 339, 340, 345, 478, 540, 571, 653, 720, 869, 947, 974, 1030, 1088, 1094*
2:1, *636, 661, 851*
2:1-7, *147*
2:2, *80, 329, 348, 353, 355, 369, 973, 1095*
2:3, *329, 348, 356, 786*
2:4, *348, 640, 698*
2:5, *75, 338, 369, 858, 869, 1014*
2:6, *75, 348, 1088*
2:7, *177, 328, 339, 481, 496, 571, 623, 776, 823, 852, 959, 1040*
2:8, *128, 283, 661, 662, 776, 851, 1016, 1017, 1074*
2:9, *75, 127, 200, 205, 228, 288, 348, 355, 583, 908, 913, 973, 1052, 1077, 1080, 1088, 1137, 1145*
2:9-10, *213, 908, 1180*
2:9-11, *283*
2:10, *46, 142, 177, 327, 329, 339, 348, 354, 356, 366, 371, 622, 623, 655, 695, 720, 823, 862, 908, 913, 914, 1017, 1029, 1035, 1040, 1078, 1080, 1137, 1138, 1167*
2:10-11, *656, 720*
2:11, *177, 328, 496, 571, 776, 823, 1026, 1074*
2:12, *418, 635, 661, 851*
2:12-17, *1010*
2:13, *46, 75, 232, 329, 348, 358, 369, 719, 720, 770, 786, 908, 973, 1017, 1029, 1077, 1078, 1080, 1137*
2:14, *348, 379, 383, 529, 542, 715, 716, 851, 1088, 1211, 1219*
2:14-15, *75, 1219*
2:14-16, *127, 353*
2:15, *348, 1088*
2:16, *338, 348, 635, 858, 869, 974, 1014*
2:17, *177, 328, 338, 496, 571, 823, 851, 1040*
2:18, *487, 661, 851, 1112*
2:19, *329, 348, 354, 369,*

698, *973, 1087*
2:19-23, *305*
2:20, *75, 305, 338, 348, 383, 400, 529, 851, 973, 974, 1086, 1088, 1149, 1219*
2:20-23, *716, 1210*
2:20-25, *176*
2:20-29, *1149*
2:21, *499, 1014*
2:22, *342, 1014*
2:22-23, *177, 1219*
2:23, *623, 908, 1211*
2:24, *232, 709, 1077, 1079, 1219*
2:25, *338, 869*
2:25-28, *362*
2:26, *328, 823, 1040*
2:26-27, *337*
2:26-28, *177, 284*
2:27, *481, 897*
2:28, *177, 339, 362, 496, 865, 1040*
2:29, *571*
2:33, *1040*
3:1, *487, 490, 636, 661, 851, 973, 1120, 1166*
3:2, *1199*
3:3, *265, 266, 338, 571, 622, 869, 1014, 1199*
3:4, *177, 348, 785, 1088*
3:5, *328, 339, 426, 563, 571, 624, 785, 823, 840, 851, 1040*
3:6, *496, 571*
3:7, *661, 770, 851, 1186*
3:8, *770, 973*
3:8-9, *166*
3:9, *75, 166, 200, 213, 228, 288, 337, 481, 583, 695, 770, 913, 1080, 1088, 1137, 1145, 1186*
3:10, *75, 142, 251, 254, 329, 337, 348, 623, 1040, 1167*
3:11, *142, 338, 858, 869, 974*
3:12, *177, 200, 328, 339, 441, 561, 823, 851, 1040, 1071, 1091, 1156*
3:13, *496, 571*
3:14, *337, 635, 661, 719, 720, 770, 851, 1186, 1205*
3:15, *348, 661, 973*
3:17, *348, 1138*
3:17-18, *437, 1052*
3:18, *1024, 1088*
3:19, *695, 1014*
3:20, *338, 420, 690, 858, 863, 943, 1235*
3:21, *47, 96, 100, 177, 328, 339, 362, 426, 427, 635, 823, 1009, 1040*
3:21-22, *284*
3:22, *496, 571*
4, *46, 63, 177, 201, 339, 340, 341, 441, 539, 634, 635, 853, 1030, 1120, 1196*
4:1, *46, 63, 339, 340, 348, 428, 441, 852, 869, 959, 1182*
4:1-5, *959*
4:1-11, *959, 1145*
4:2, *427, 495*
4:3, *427, 1127*
4:4, *108, 327, 428*
4:5, *427, 428, 490, 1120*
4:6, *46, 427, 428*
4:6-8, *662*
4:7, *487*
4:8, *254, 257, 426-428, 486, 487, 524, 526, 634, 658, 662, 663, 664, 690,*

939, *1031, 1120, 1235, 1236*
4:8-10, *775*
4:8-11, *953*
4:9, *346, 395, 427, 428, 947*
4:9-10, *283*
4:9-11, *524, 1120*
4:10, *108, 346, 427, 428, 943*
4:11, *201, 254, 257, 395, 420, 427, 428, 524, 526, 634, 660, 827, 939, 1014, 1074, 1224, 1235*
4:18, *869*
5, *634, 635, 840, 1164*
5:1, *427, 840, 851*
5:1-5, *177, 1074*
5:1-9, *770*
5:1-14, *392, 1236*
5:2, *1084*
5:2-3, *46, 362*
5:5, *43, 356, 499, 635, 642, 851, 913*
5:5-6, *261, 339, 897*
5:5-12, *1196*
5:6, *46, 100, 128, 261, 284, 428, 477, 490, 635, 642, 1034, 1071, 1120, 1122*
5:6-10, *362*
5:6-14, *871*
5:7, *427, 1074*
5:7-8, *840*
5:7-13, *1074*
5:8, *46, 108, 488, 719, 942, 974, 1071*
5:8-14, *177, 283*
5:9, *46, 428, 477, 660, 770, 1002, 1014, 1071, 1080*
5:9-10, *224, 257, 524, 635, 947*
5:9-11, *526, 635*
5:9-12, *284*
5:9-13, *201*
5:9-14, *524, 539, 627, 1224, 1235*
5:10, *108, 161, 200, 284, 337, 481, 525, 635, 974, 1009*
5:11, *428, 660*
5:11-12, *362*
5:11-13, *100*
5:11-14, *46*
5:12, *130, 257, 395, 428, 477, 660, 940, 947, 1071, 1203*
5:12-13, *399*
5:12-14, *362, 524, 1237*
5:13, *130, 251, 254, 257, 346, 395, 427, 428, 660, 939, 940, 947, 1074*
5:14, *395, 661*
5:15, *428*
6, *66, 104, 477, 870, 1030, 1179*
6:1, *132, 1030, 1179, 1182*
6:1-7, *100*
6:1-8, *348, 481*
6:1-17, *441, 636*
6:2, *327, 499*
6:3-4, *127*
6:4, *897*
6:5-6, *1085*
6:6, *908*
6:8, *460, 656, 1085*
6:9, *641, 719, 770, 974, 1137, 1205*
6:9-11, *284, 441, 622, 623, 636, 776, 908, 913, 985, 986, 1017, 1018*
6:9-17, *100*
6:10, *174, 255, 266, 348,*

426, *428, 486, 719, 870, 943, 1138, 1186*
6:10-11, *104, 337*
6:11, *142, 337, 719, 914*
6:12-17, *255, 337*
6:12-20, *1030*
6:15, *1100*
6:15-17, *1036*
6:16, *477, 871*
6:16-17, *284, 622, 869, 1239*
6:17, *266, 428, 858*
6:19, *358*
7, *119, 200, 438, 1031*
7:1, *251*
7:1-8, *108, 200*
7:1-17, *224, 477, 1085*
7:2, *417*
7:2-4, *46*
7:3, *200, 477, 641, 974, 1086*
7:4-8, *166, 542, 636, 913, 1210*
7:5-8, *851*
7:8, *40*
7:9, *428, 719, 720, 854*
7:9-17, *200, 201, 337, 441, 539, 542*
7:10, *177, 428, 947, 1074*
7:10-12, *46*
7:11, *428*
7:11-12, *177*
7:12, *130, 257, 395, 428, 660, 661, 939, 947, 1203, 1235*
7:13-14, *914*
7:13-17, *255, 622*
7:14, *75, 131, 177, 284, 337, 342, 636, 672, 720, 1071, 1179*
7:15, *177, 428, 658, 1071, 1156*
7:15-17, *119, 349, 1138*
7:16, *132*
7:17, *100, 284, 428, 1092*
8, *119*
8:1, *636, 1085*
8:1-5, *46, 1030, 1031*
8:2, *46, 428, 636, 1120, 1179*
8:2-4, *719*
8:3, *428, 974, 1071*
8:3-4, *201, 488*
8:3-5, *636*
8:4, *974, 1071*
8:5, *427, 780, 1030*
8:6, *441, 1030*
8:6-11, *636*
8:7, *780*
8:8, *780*
8:8-9, *1183*
8:9, *1241*
8:10-11, *1183*
8:10-12, *704*
8:12, *658, 1183*
9:1, *459, 704*
9:1-2, *460*
9:1-11, *127*
9:2, *459, 658, 1196*
9:3, *780*
9:6, *656, 954*
9:11, *200*
9:17-19, *127*
9:18, *428*
9:19, *1183*
9:20, *201, 428, 529, 716, 1010, 1196*
9:20-21, *177, 349, 477, 952, 1014, 1138*
9:21, *703, 1191, 1192*
10, *46, 1031*
10:1, *45, 477, 1031*
10:1-10, *770*
10:2, *1085*

10:4, *1084*
10:6, *283, 346, 427, 775*
10:7, *224, 432, 783, 851, 974, 1100*
10:8, *1085*
10:8-11, *840, 853*
10:9-10, *1085*
10:11, *208*
11, *1094*
11:1, *201, 770*
11:1-2, *108, 200, 1027, 1155*
11:1-13, *636, 644, 770, 779, 854*
11:2, *487, 561, 852*
11:3, *108, 200, 358, 719, 720, 785, 852, 1014, 1205*
11:3-6, *636*
11:3-13, *770*
11:4, *426*
11:4-6, *854*
11:5, *127, 1138*
11:6, *358, 428*
11:7, *52, 127, 232, 328, 339, 358, 459, 460, 974, 1205*
11:7-10, *337, 1035, 1137*
11:8, *112, 133, 177, 200, 426, 564, 672, 1182*
11:9-10, *720*
11:10, *561, 602, 604, 1036, 1138*
11:11, *177, 490*
11:11-12, *127*
11:11-13, *337*
11:13, *395, 564, 636*
11:14, *770*
11:14-19, *636*
11:15, *47, 155, 177, 200, 254, 255, 257, 325, 346, 362, 427, 428, 635, 947, 1009, 1074*
11:15-17, *337*
11:15-18, *201, 362, 1030*
11:15-19, *337, 1183*
11:16, *108, 127*
11:16-17, *177*
11:16-19, *622*
11:17, *254, 427, 428, 939, 943, 947*
11:17-18, *428, 943, 947*
11:18, *224, 266, 337, 372, 428, 488, 914, 974, 1086, 1100, 1239, 1240*
11:19, *246, 427, 440, 1156*
11:21:2, *561*
12, *62, 100, 127, 176, 340, 634, 723, 852, 853, 871, 1031, 1033, 1034, 1078, 1080, 1181, 1196, 1209, 1210*
12:1, *46, 141, 327, 1094*
12:1-2, *1209*
12:1-4, *539*
12:1-6, *1181*
12:1-17, *108*
12:2, *1115*
12:3, *127, 477, 853, 1078*
12:4, *704, 1078*
12:4-5, *852*
12:5, *96, 337, 362, 428, 1209*
12:5-6, *127*
12:5-12, *635*
12:6, *852*
12:7, *339, 778, 1078*
12:7-8, *46, 339*
12:7-9, *635, 730, 939*
12:7-10, *1078*
12:7-12, *254*
12:8, *939*
12:9, *75, 127, 142, 232, 251, 254, 481, 720, 852, 1078*

12:9-10, *278*
12:10, *155, 177, 200, 284, 362, 427, 939, 940, 1074, 1078, 1080*
12:10-12, *108, 201, 284*
12:11, *75, 177, 262, 339, 477, 698, 720, 770, 897, 974, 985, 1017, 1071, 1196*
12:11-12, *720*
12:12, *603, 739, 741, 869, 1078, 1239*
12:13, *636, 1078, 1080*
12:13-16, *852*
12:14, *481, 1078, 1080*
12:15, *1078*
12:17, *177, 240, 284, 583, 635, 636, 770, 852, 910, 1080, 1137, 1138, 1205*
13, *62, 128, 132, 141, 634, 853, 871, 913, 950, 951, 1034, 1078, 1198*
13:1, *128, 200, 636, 852, 1009*
13:1-2, *232, 720, 853*
13:1-8, *909*
13:1-10, *52*
13:2, *362, 852, 913*
13:2-4, *720*
13:3, *284, 656, 852, 1028, 1034*
13:3-4, *284*
13:4, *128, 201, 362, 530, 720, 913*
13:4-8, *1009*
13:5, *200, 852*
13:5-7, *349, 719*
13:5-18, *337*
13:6, *200*
13:7, *339, 488, 974, 1035, 1080*
13:7-8, *232, 362*
13:8, *201, 251, 254, 477, 530, 563, 780, 851, 1024, 1034, 1071, 1084, 1223*
13:9, *571*
13:9-10, *329, 974*
13:10, *366, 369, 488, 571, 719, 1081*
13:11, *913*
13:11-15, *1009*
13:12, *201, 284, 530, 852, 909*
13:13-14, *1094*
13:13-15, *530*
13:14, *852, 1028, 1078*
13:15, *201, 530, 909, 1137*
13:16, *232, 477, 1100*
13:16-17, *349, 908*
13:17, *1137*
13:18, *128, 909, 985, 1034, 1201, 1203*
14, *432*
14:1, *119, 426, 561, 636, 644, 851*
14:1-3, *166*
14:1-5, *100, 108, 636, 913, 1088*
14:1-17, *1137*
14:3, *284, 428, 524, 851*
14:3-5, *1002, 1074*
14:4, *75, 284, 427, 636, 793*
14:5, *1186*
14:6, *432, 719*
14:6-7, *477, 1014*
14:6-11, *974*
14:7, *201, 266, 395, 427, 428, 869*
14:8, *111, 151, 200, 564, 1027, 1067, 1088, 1240*
14:8-11, *337*
14:9, *530, 1137*
14:9-11, *284, 362, 624*

14:9-12, *240, 325, 624, 1040*
14:10, *428, 487, 1239*
14:10-12, *823*
14:11, *346, 428, 461, 530, 1137*
14:12, *240, 488, 583, 672, 1063*
14:12-13, *329, 720*
14:13, *131, 602, 672, 851, 897, 914, 954, 1040*
14:14, *338, 356, 441*
14:14-16, *770*
14:14-20, *337*
14:15, *870, 1156*
14:15-16, *636*
14:17, *441, 1156*
14:17-20, *636*
14:18, *460*
14:18:3, *1088*
14:19, *428*
14:19:2, *1088*
14:19, *1239*
14:19-20, *871*
15, *1030*
15:1, *132, 428, 636, 1179, 1239*
15:2, *339, 720, 851, 1137*
15:2-4, *362, 636*
15:3, *200, 426, 427, 428, 672, 780, 851, 939, 1054, 1186*
15:3-4, *201, 486, 524, 526, 770, 851, 1036, 1235*
15:3-5, *284*
15:4, *201, 395, 428, 870, 1024*
15:5, *636*
15:5-6, *1031*
15:5-8, *440*
15:6, *428, 1127*
15:7, *346, 427, 428, 1239*
15:8, *397, 428, 939, 1155*
15:9, *428*
15:14, *943*
16, *1033, 1074*
16:1, *132, 428, 441, 1156, 1239*
16:2, *362, 530, 1137*
16:3, *780*
16:4-6, *441*
16:5, *254, 427, 428, 486, 1054*
16:5-7, *132*
16:6, *132, 224, 488, 719, 823, 908, 974*
16:6-7, *266*
16:7, *427, 428, 1054, 1186*
16:8, *427*
16:8-9, *132*
16:9, *395, 477, 1014, 1138*
16:10, *658*
16:10-11, *133*
16:11, *477, 1014*
16:12, *133*
16:12-14, *337*
16:12-16, *52, 129*
16:13, *477, 913, 1078, 1120, 1186*
16:14, *266, 427, 858, 1010, 1094, 1117, 1120*
16:15, *131, 132, 265, 266, 337, 571, 622, 869, 1199*
16:16, *636, 997*
16:17, *428, 564, 870, 1031, 1156*
16:17-21, *337*
16:19, *111, 200, 428, 564, 1027, 1067, 1239*
16:21, *337, 428*
17, *52, 62, 111, 634, 716, 1031, 1034, 1127, 1183, 1196*
17:1, *349, 428, 564, 1031,

1067*
17:1-6, *128*
17:2, *1067*
17:3, *142, 200, 495, 564*
17:3-12, *325*
17:4, *200, 564, 1127, 1138*
17:5, *111, 232, 564, 783, 851, 1027, 1067*
17:6, *564, 635, 719, 720, 770, 908, 1017, 1067*
17:7, *63, 783*
17:7-9, *909*
17:7-18, *1034*
17:8, *128, 232, 251, 254, 318, 459, 460, 563, 851, 869, 1028, 1034*
17:9, *111, 151, 232, 908, 985, 1067, 1211*
17:9-10, *111, 128*
17:9-11, *1028*
17:10, *869*
17:11, *232*
17:12-13, *128*
17:12-14, *1035*
17:13-14, *362*
17:14, *318, 325, 337, 339, 636, 672, 785, 870, 897, 1009*
17:15, *1067*
17:15-17, *1035*
17:16, *128, 374*
17:16-17, *337, 1035*
17:18, *112, 151, 564, 1067, 1211*
18, *112, 233, 354, 1027, 1052, 1067, 1211*
18:1, *394, 1138*
18:1-24, *428*
18:2, *80, 111, 151, 564, 720, 818, 1010, 1027, 1067, 1117*
18:2-3, *151*
18:3, *232, 349, 1067, 1088, 1138, 1240*
18:4, *305, 349, 428, 564, 1052, 1067*
18:4-8, *1097*
18:5, *564*
18:6, *564, 908*
18:7, *232, 394, 395, 564, 1052, 1138*
18:8, *428, 564, 1241*
18:9, *232, 460, 1067*
18:9-10, *349*
18:9-19, *349*
18:9-20, *1138*
18:10, *111, 151, 266, 564, 870, 1027, 1067*
18:11, *112, 1241*
18:11-19, *349*
18:11-20, *564*
18:12, *1127*
18:12-13, *112*
18:13, *985, 1029, 1032*
18:14, *1240*
18:16, *1067, 1127*
18:17, *564*
18:19, *564, 1067*
18:20, *224, 488, 603, 719, 974, 1067*
18:21, *111, 151, 564, 1027, 1067*
18:23, *658, 703*
18:24, *112, 224, 488, 719, 908, 974, 1067, 1137, 1182*
19, *662*
19:1, *284, 337, 349, 395, 428, 564, 662, 664, 939, 1074*
19:1-2, *266, 719*
19:1-3, *624*
19:1-4, *622, 624*
19:1-6, *524*

19:1-8, *119*
19:1-10, *1031*
19:2, *112, 151, 428, 870, 974, 1054, 1086, 1088, 1186, 1240*
19:3, *346, 349, 461, 662, 664*
19:4, *428, 661, 662*
19:5, *1086, 1100*
19:6, *349, 362, 427, 524, 526, 601, 662, 664, 672*
19:6-7, *601*
19:6-8, *325*
19:7, *131, 395, 601, 602, 604, 1088, 1209, 1210*
19:7-9, *337*
19:7-21, *338*
19:8, *131, 428, 488*
19:9, *119, 131, 604, 690, 1088*
19:10, *46, 47, 177, 357, 490, 636, 770, 910, 915, 1026, 1036, 1120, 1137, 1205*
19:11, *635, 637, 666, 897, 1031, 1037, 1055, 1058, 1186*
19:11-13, *667*
19:11-15, *1137*
19:11-16, *46, 362, 427, 785, 870, 871, 1137*
19:11-21, *337, 872, 908, 959, 1179*
19:12, *477, 851*
19:13, *637, 666, 871*
19:14-15, *897*
19:15, *427, 635, 1239*
19:16, *155, 200, 349, 636, 672, 785, 851, 1009*
19:17-21, *636*
19:18, *374, 1100*
19:19, *636*
19:19-20, *1063*
19:20, *460, 530, 776, 1009, 1094, 1137, 1186*
19:20-21, *52*
19:21, *374, 635, 897, 1036*
19:21:2, *1088*
20, *119, 739, 740, 741, 872, 1020, 1037, 1137*
20:1-3, *460*
20:1-4, *871*
20:1-6, *108, 741, 1138*
20:1-10, *636, 644, 871*
20:2, *47, 913, 1011, 1078, 1081*
20:2-3, *739*
20:2-7, *871*
20:3, *73, 739, 1081*
20:4, *47, 155, 325, 530, 656, 720, 739, 770, 823, 985, 986, 1009, 1017, 1074, 1137*
20:4-5, *912, 1016*
20:4-6, *362, 739, 740, 741, 1017, 1018, 1031, 1036, 1137*
20:5, *739, 1018*
20:5-6, *1016*
20:6, *108, 131, 155, 161, 200, 564, 604, 656, 739, 776, 940, 963, 1009, 1074*
20:7, *739, 818*
20:7-9, *337*
20:7-10, *872, 1031*
20:9, *200, 441, 488*
20:9-15, *337*
20:10, *128, 346, 461, 1078, 1081, 1186, 1189*
20:10-15, *624*
20:11, *251, 1030*
20:11-15, *354, 1018, 1031*
20:12, *318, 428, 563, 624, 656, 739, 840, 851*

20:12-13, *656, 908*
20:13, *369, 776*
20:14, *460, 461, 656, 776, 851, 1018*
20:15, *47, 318, 460, 624, 1040, 1084, 1189*
21, *36, 65, 682, 810, 951, 1017, 1156, 1196, 1210*
21:1, *129, 200, 251, 253, 254, 255, 337, 341, 499, 636, 739, 823, 854, 908, 1137*
21:1-2, *959*
21:1-5, *349*
21:1-8, *854, 1031*
21:2, *200, 487, 561, 564, 583, 854, 1088, 1209, 1210*
21:3, *200, 564, 1040*
21:3-4, *442, 564*

21:3-8, *255*
21:4, *200, 438, 1138*
21:5, *666, 851, 1017*
21:6, *426, 427, 571, 672, 959, 1017, 1031*
21:7, *104, 328, 854, 1074, 1116*
21:8, *337, 349, 460, 528, 703, 770, 776, 1031, 1040, 1191*
21:9, *428, 1036*
21:9-14, *80*
21:10, *487, 495, 561, 564*
21:11, *397, 564, 1127*
21:11-21, *1138*
21:12, *542, 913*
21:12-14, *1210*
21:14, *108, 141, 744*
21:15-16, *564*
21:16-18, *1156*

21:17, *47*
21:18-21, *564*
21:19, *1127*
21:19-20, *1127*
21:22, *200, 442, 672, 854, 1071, 1156, 1164*
21:22-26, *564*
21:23, *397, 659, 1127*
21:24, *394*
21:24-27, *1036*
21:25, *659*
21:26, *394*
21:27, *318, 609, 637, 770, 1084, 1186*
22:1, *428, 442*
22:1-2, *656, 776*
22:1-5, *427, 441, 1156*
22:2, *438, 564, 776, 852*
22:3, *974, 1086*
22:3-5, *442, 1071*

22:4, *1014*
22:5, *337, 346, 564, 659, 1009*
22:6, *666, 869, 974, 1086, 1100, 1120*
22:6-20, *653*
22:6-21, *1027, 1031*
22:7, *60, 131, 337, 481, 672, 858, 869, 973, 974*
22:7-20, *338*
22:8-9, *46, 851*
22:9, *47, 177, 915, 974*
22:10, *60, 142, 869, 973, 1084*
22:11, *487, 488, 1057, 1058*
22:11-12, *1047*
22:12, *369, 635, 858, 869, 908, 914, 974*
22:12-13, *177*

22:13, *283, 426, 427*
22:14, *131, 852, 940*
22:15, *349, 528, 698, 703, 770, 1186, 1191, 1192*
22:16, *39, 43, 635, 704, 851, 913, 1205*
22:17, *571*
22:18, *60, 851, 973, 1205*
22:18-19, *311, 852*
22:19, *60, 200, 487, 561, 851, 973*
22:20, *177, 635, 663, 675, 703, 755, 858, 869, 870, 947, 974, 1205, 1228, 1237*
22:20-21, *672*
22:21, *155, 488, 653, 660, 661*

Subject Index

Abba, *1, 1034*
abomination of desolation, 52
Abraham, *1-6, 38-41, 43, 44,* 89, 130, 164, 169, 204, 208-210, 212-216, 218, 227, 228, 246-250, 252, 287, 327, 369, 390, 392, 396, 398, 415, 419-421, 457, 480, 481, 500, 502, 505, 507, 509, 533, 534, 536-538, 540, 551, 554, 556, 558, 560, 584, 607, 610, 620, 643, 644, 648, 671, 724, 729-731, 734, 815-817, 819, 821, 829, 830, 835, 837-839, 879, 892, 932, 963-965, 968-970, 993, 994, 999, 1004, 1039, 1056-1058, 1099, 1110, 1139, 1168, 1169, 1185, 1186, 1208, 1234
Abrahamic covenant, *209,* 227, 247, 390
abyss, *6, 128, 347, 459, 460,* 625, 636, 657, 704, 777, 988, 1034, 1081, 1241
accursed, *167*
Achaia, *123, 148, 433, 755,* 757, 764, 765, 771, 1059, 1060
Acrocorinth, *148*
Acropolis, *148*
Acts of Andrew, 6, 71, 766, 771
Acts of John, 6, 71, 308, 771, 1062
Acts of Paul, 70-72, 679, 983, 1106, 1219, 1228
Acts of Paul and Thecla, 1106, 1219, 1228
Acts of Peter, 7, 71, 72, 407, 409, 679, 757, 764, 916
Acts of Peter and the Twelve Apostles, 7, 409
Acts of Thomas, 24, 70, 72, 407, 759, 765, 771, 1005, 1151, 1153
Adam, *33, 43, 91, 124, 209,* 223, 251, 264, 273, 280, 313, 332, 334, 341, 396, 402-404, 408-410, 537, 541, 598, 667, 706, 723, 956, 978, 1016, 1214
adoption, *1, 4, 6, 15, 35, 61,* 92, 119, 219, 288, 292, 294, 297, 315, 323, 370, 376, 379, 389, 423, 447, 454, 512-513, 515, 517, 522, 615, 648, 657, 661-664, 717, 723, 740, 796, 800, 810, 822, 832, 865, 867, 872, 873, 913, 915-916, 978, 1002, 1013, 1028, 1029, 1032, 1033, 1035, 1088, 1109, 1112-1114, 1116, 1130, 1148, 1149, 1190, 1202, 1212

adoptionism, *24, 33, 306,* 586, 675, 860, 1114
adultery, *24, 112, 144, 240,* 352, 537, 645, 700, 712-717, 837, 882, 1088-1090, 1166, 1168
adversaries, opponents, *24-* 34, 45, 50, 51, 53, 76, 77, 127, 155, 158, 167, 173, 175, 196, 210, 211, 215, 227, 253, 265, 266, 281, 284, 305, 306, 311, 336, 339, 362, 370, 393, 400, 401, 403, 405, 411, 425, 426, 463, 464, 469, 470, 532, 573, 577-579, 588, 590-593, 596, 598, 612, 613, 615, 617-619, 652, 653, 702, 706, 716, 725, 728, 730, 732, 764, 775, 818, 822, 833, 836, 837, 840, 855, 865-868, 877, 914, 923, 925, 927, 953, 961, 973, 975, 976, 982, 1013, 1037, 1042, 1045, 1046, 1056, 1079, 1081, 1094, 1109, 1110, 1123, 1149, 1150, 1161, 1164, 1168, 1200
advocate, *27, 29, 31-32, 89,* 102, 282, 362, 369, 425, 539, 768, 946, 1055, 1097
Aelia, Capitolina, *185*
affliction,, *254, 308, 604,* 643, 734, 768, 781, 880, 908, 952, 1052, 1067, 1170, 1202
Agabus, *743, 971, 972*
agape, *34, 95, 379, 686, 700,* 819, 1228, 1229
age to come, *51, 63-65, 117,* 226, 264, 265, 276, 277, 320; 336, 339, 341, 556-558, 559, 695, 775, 933, 940, 1038, 1058
Agrippa, *115, 184, 186, 193,* 291, 322, 325, 382, 467, 599, 658, 718, 757, 884, 907, 932, 1008, 1060, 1061
Alexander the Great, *34,* 170, 533, 611, 760, 1008, 1011, 1075, 1146
Alexandria, *34-37, 53, 90,* 126, 135, 138-142, 144-146, 149-152, 167, 185, 186, 188, 190-193, 236, 237, 255, 289, 291-296, 298, 300, 303, 307, 308, 322, 358, 359, 389, 403, 404, 406, 444, 457, 470, 548, 576, 585, 595, 618, 665, 666, 679, 697, 708-710, 712, 723, 757, 758, 765, 766, 773, 779, 781, 783, 860, 907, 912, 916, 931, 932, 934, 966, 967, 1032, 1089, 1099, 1106, 1172, 1191, 1202, 1213,

1218, 1221, 1222, 1225
allegory, *35-37, 72, 84, 125,* 126, 214, 294, 296, 298, 480, 536, 540, 646, 706, 740, 815, 829, 830, 842, 929, 932, 933, 967, 987, 1155, 1165, 967
alms, almsgiving, *301, 476,* 699, 827, 832, 1052, 1053, 1143, 1162, 1229
altar, *50, 132, 372, 427, 441,* 528, 641, 691, 699, 719, 1007, 1008, 1027, 1126, 1137, 1170, 1183, 1221
amen, *37, 163, 427, 660,* 663, 690, 691, 960, 1230
amoraim, amoraic period, 37, 608
Ananias, *22, 73, 77, 78, 107,* 115, 243, 244, 357, 373, 466, 562, 749-751, 790, 885, 942, 944, 1054, 1118, 1166, 1185, 1195
anathema, *811, 1110, 1162*
Anatolia, *146*
ancestors, *5, 6, 37-40, 42, 43,* 134, 205, 246, 264, 317, 319, 326, 330, 417, 457, 500, 505, 508, 537, 542, 558, 599, 622, 643, 694, 730, 757, 814, 833, 850, 884, 907, 960, 969, 985, 1001, 1110
Andronicus, *762, 765*
angels, *5, 17, 18, 29, 35-37,* 44-47, 50, 51, 62, 63, 69, 74, 88, 98, 100, 108, 121, 128, 132, 133, 172, 173, 175, 177, 178, 182, 192, 198, 201, 214, 224, 244, 252-254, 266, 314, 317, 320, 339, 352, 360, 361, 381, 398, 413, 417-419, 425, 428, 431, 432, 437, 438-443, 445, 452, 453, 457, 459, 460, 462, 466, 467, 470, 480, 486, 487, 496, 503, 505, 529, 533, 537, 538, 563, 571, 603, 618, 620, 623, 624, 633, 635, 649, 663, 666-669, 671, 672, 675, 698, 701, 704, 713, 714, 716, 723, 729-731, 747, 766, 778, 782, 783, 785, 817-819, 822, 835, 836, 839-841, 843, 845, 853, 869, 870, 878, 900, 915, 922, 928, 939, 947, 948, 956, 960, 961, 965, 972, 985, 997, 998, 1009, 1014, 1022, 1026, 1030, 1031, 1036, 1043, 1078, 1081, 1085, 1089, 1093, 1097, 1100, 1112, 1113, 1117-1120, 1122, 1127, 1138, 1141, 1149, 1170, 1181, 1185, 1193, 1205, 1234, 1238-

1241
angel christology, *44, 47,* 442, 443, 457, 731, 1081, 1122
angel of the Lord, *18, 62,* 620, 666, 667, 675, 961, 972, 1170
angel worship, *998*
anger, *275, 329, 421, 428-* 430, 558, 572, 699, 815, 838, 879, 882, 1035, 1036, 1054, 1105, 1169, 1213, 1238-1240
anoint, anointing, *20, 48,* 49, 100, 107, 108, 120-122, 152, 153, 155, 158, 163, 173, 282, 409, 437, 438, 487, 490, 491, 593, 598, 605, 632, 671, 735, 742, 744, 786, 854, 939, 945, 973, 998, 1143, 1194, 1195
anthropology, *24, 27, 66,* 124, 307, 379, 462, 477, 501, 777, 800, 1053, 1084, 1104, 1132, 1188, 1222, 1223, 1134
antichrist, *27, 33, 50-53, 69,* 74, 76, 128, 129, 254, 261, 335, 343, 529, 539, 740, 920, 959, 973, 1025, 1028, 1029, 1031, 1033-1037, 1046, 1081, 1122
antinomianism, *29, 33, 89,* 231, 240, 615, 618, 716, 973, 1228, 1036
Antioch, *2, 10, 11, 15, 25,* 32, 34, 53-55, 76-79, 82, 102, 106, 107, 109, 120, 139-142, 144-147, 151, 152, 168, 169, 175, 185, 186, 191, 192, 196, 204, 205, 222, 225, 227, 229, 230, 247, 257, 263, 273, 288, 294, 301, 303, 307, 308, 355, 357, 367, 373, 382, 391, 394, 433, 434, 462-464, 467, 495, 496, 501, 507, 520, 525, 529-533, 546, 566, 585, 602, 616, 627, 630, 657, 658, 667, 672, 676, 678, 685, 686, 691, 693, 720, 721, 725-727, 729, 743, 753, 754, 756-758, 762, 764, 766, 772, 774, 777, 779, 795, 803, 832, 882, 883, 885, 886, 892, 894, 898, 912, 927, 934, 938, 971, 972, 975, 993, 994, 1009, 1048, 1050, 1061, 1067, 1082, 1086, 1100, 1101, 1109, 1111, 1114, 1124, 1125, 1143, 1144, 1150, 1151, 1153, 1157, 1163, 1216, 1217, 1219, 1221, 1227-1231
Antiochus, *50, 51, 53, 64,* 288, 533, 1029

Antipas, *720, 762, 764, 1137, 1205*

Antonia, *1061, 1099, 1206*

anxiety, *397, 457, 538, 550, 566, 761, 773, 782, 876, 1089*

Apocalypse of Paul, 408

Apocalypse of Peter, 6, 47, 55, 69, 70, 214, 243, 405, 408, 410, 411, 711

Apocalypse of Thomas, *55, 70*

apocalyptic eschatology, *56, 59-62, 64, 65, 68, 865*

apocalyptic imagery, *392, 818, 862*

apocalypticism, *47, 55, 56, 58-61, 65-68, 255, 267, 343, 424, 442, 443, 551, 617, 619, 659, 721, 741, 784, 854, 873, 1024, 1025, 1037, 1051, 1081, 1085, 1182*

apocrypha, *6, 44, 47, 68, 69, 73, 82, 85, 86, 308, 317, 667, 712, 774, 818, 827, 829, 830, 837, 889, 914, 977, 979, 1006, 1177, 1201*

apocryphal Pauline litera-ture, *68, 72*

Apollonia, *290*

Apollos, *23, 149, 444, 493, 743, 758, 765, 940, 1072, 1145, 1207, 1217, 1218*

apostasy, *42, 43, 73-76, 104, 117, 167, 168, 261, 306, 321, 330, 331, 336, 350, 368, 381, 382, 447, 453, 466, 469, 505, 532, 538, 734, 819, 821-823, 836, 838, 861, 882, 892, 912, 914, 940, 950, 1003, 1011, 1014, 1015, 1039, 1183, 1198, 1212, 1228*

Apostle's Creed, *82*

apostleship, *33, 76-79, 82, 110, 190, 742, 746, 892, 1187, 1207*

apostolic decree, *26, 647, 648, 892, 904, 996, 1088, 1149*

apostolic fathers, *1, 4, 5, 37, 43, 48, 49, 76, 80, 82-91, 96, 100-105, 109, 111, 126, 130, 131, 134, 139-143, 152, 155, 169, 184, 190, 191, 193, 194, 201, 235, 237, 238, 240-242, 246, 256-258, 263, 264, 266, 267, 284, 285, 287, 301, 303, 304, 311, 313, 329, 330, 341, 345-347, 349, 351, 352, 357, 359, 362, 364, 366, 367, 369-374, 379, 380, 384, 394, 396, 397, 399, 413, 429-436, 438, 439, 442, 459-461, 471, 481, 483, 485, 486, 488, 490, 493, 499, 500, 509, 514, 516, 518-520, 532, 533, 536, 539, 541-543, 561, 566, 571-574, 578, 579, 583, 585, 600,*

601, 603, 604, 629, 637, 638, 640, 645, 648, 653, 655, 657, 659, 662-664, 668, 672, 673, 702-704, 717, 720, 722, 732, 733, 735-738, 741, 744, 770, 775, 783, 785, 786, 792, 794, 795, 799, 803, 806, 821, 823, 826, 829, 830, 834, 876, 878, 881, 897, 936, 937, 939, 941, 947, 948, 960, 966, 967, 969, 970, 987, 1018, 1036, 1038, 1040, 1041, 1048, 1049, 1053, 1057, 1058, 1067, 1071, 1072, 1074, 1075, 1078, 1082, 1084, 1089, 1093-1098, 1121, 1122, 1128, 1140, 1148, 1154, 1156, 1158, 1169, 1178-1180, 1182, 1184, 1186, 1190-1193, 1198-1200, 1203-1205, 1216, 1222, 1225, 1238-1241

apostolic preaching, *260, 286, 359, 521, 628-630, 799, 874, 1004, 1241*

Apostolic Tradition, 10, 91, 113, 118-123, 259, 405, 618, 690, 736, 934, 1045, 1046, 1090, 1211, 1224, 1235

aqedah, *3, 4, 6, 44, 458*

Aquila, *93, 291, 313, 378, 444, 446, 448, 449, 706, 743, 757, 762-764, 900, 1066, 1207, 1217, 1218, 1220*

Arabia, *758, 759, 764, 765*

Aramaic, *60, 114, 133, 165, 166, 177, 179, 289, 313, 315, 462, 465, 468, 570, 580, 581, 585, 600, 605, 606, 608, 609, 663, 667, 675, 678, 687, 710, 759, 782, 790, 820, 870, 905, 947, 971, 974, 997, 1032, 1034, 1124, 1125, 1142, 1143, 1150, 1162, 1163, 1220, 1228, 1237*

archangels, *33, 45-47, 439, 441, 667, 730, 778, 818, 835, 839, 840, 949, 965, 1160, 1120*

architecture, *91, 92, 95, 298, 358, 377, 399, 444, 446, 507, 508, 511, 551, 1110, 1145, 1159, 1220, 1231*

Areopagus, *192, 416, 467, 537, 627, 670, 886, 1025, 1054, 1056, 1126, 1129, 1217*

aretalogy, *1147*

Aristarchus, *688, 765, 888*

Aristobulus, *287, 296, 298, 979*

army, *85, 95, 109, 128, 201, 235, 293, 295, 321, 323, 636, 1028, 1060, 1063, 1183*

Artemis, *146, 147, 416, 701, 1008, 1021, 1147, 1211*

ascension, *11, 12, 19, 20, 44-*

47, 52, 63, 69, 70, 76, 78, 95-102, 127, 260, 333, 343, 344, 359, 360, 363, 442, 459, 563, 602, 623, 629, 630, 669, 722, 723, 740, 742, 746, 756, 792, 825, 858, 859, 873, 874, 890, 904-906, 921, 922, 944, 1006, 1019, 1020, 1199, 1204, 1216

Ascension of Isaiah, 47, 52, 69, 70, 102, 740, 1006, 1019

asceticism, *30, 31, 33, 72, 192, 215, 303, 402, 405, 409, 410, 546, 585, 615, 706, 707, 713, 714, 717, 781, 987, 1019, 1088-1090, 1111, 1152, 1153, 1197, 1213, 1221*

Asia Minor, *32, 71, 126, 136, 139, 142, 144, 146, 147, 150, 151, 187, 189-191, 194, 198, 200, 224, 225, 288, 300, 308, 314, 328, 339, 348, 349, 391, 392, 434, 441, 476, 506, 529, 530, 571, 575, 582, 588, 596, 683, 691, 705, 719, 731, 732, 740, 753, 759, 764, 766, 768, 769, 869, 892, 908, 912, 916, 931, 934, 941, 959, 960, 1008-1011, 1022, 1044, 1045, 1048, 1072, 1080, 1106-1108, 1110, 1135, 1146, 1147, 1150, 1163, 1198, 1210, 1211, 1217, 1219, 1220, 1224, 1231, 1232*

assurance, *11, 59, 76, 101-104, 108, 117, 166, 272, 279, 336, 362, 365, 367, 380-382, 443, 499, 501, 517, 524, 556, 637, 719, 859, 860, 863, 864, 867, 873, 876, 881, 882, 897, 918, 946, 972, 996, 1009, 1015, 1038, 1045, 1075, 1080, 1136, 1234*

astrology, *104, 701-704, 787, 941, 1006, 1009-1011, 1081, 1147, 1150*

Athens, *148, 192, 290, 299, 303, 414, 416, 627, 754, 758, 886, 910, 1009-1011, 1126, 1144, 1190, 1217*

athlete, athletic, *85, 235, 327, 328, 721, 768, 1039*

atonement, *4, 20, 27, 36, 79, 98, 99, 104, 145, 171, 203, 261, 263, 267-276, 279, 280-287, 297, 523, 547, 592, 594, 610, 624, 633, 642, 646, 671, 694, 697, 762, 828, 861, 862, 875, 939, 966, 996, 1016, 1035, 1052, 1055, 1096, 1165, 1180, 1181, 1230*

atoning sacrifice, *79, 145, 261, 269, 281-284, 594, 694, 1016, 1230*

Augustus, *53, 148, 291-293, 325, 767, 1028, 1060,*

1065, 1076, 1142

authorities, *127, 134, 153, 174, 189, 221, 230-232, 236, 253, 293, 297, 298, 357, 361, 386, 448, 464, 466, 514, 515, 517, 605, 607, 608, 610, 699, 715, 719, 761, 786, 790, 836, 879, 884, 886, 908-911, 919, 922, 947, 953, 1005, 1007, 1008, 1029, 1035, 1062, 1123, 1126, 1128, 1142, 1144, 1163, 1195, 1208, 1233, 1234*

autobiography, *470, 600, 778, 885*

Babylon, *1, 46, 111, 112, 128, 151, 186, 232, 254, 288, 349, 422, 428, 460, 467, 564, 565, 634, 636, 644, 703, 716, 720, 783, 851, 853, 854, 870, 908, 914, 915, 1001, 1027-1029, 1037, 1047, 1052, 1066, 1067, 1075, 1127, 1135, 1138, 1179, 1182, 1183, 1192, 1209, 1211, 1221, 1239, 1240*

banquet, *5, 6, 503, 602, 604, 692, 693, 1210*

baptism, *5, 18, 20, 21, 26, 41, 49, 73, 76, 78, 84, 89, 104, 112-125, 149, 153, 173, 176, 179, 181, 191, 192, 216, 228, 229, 233, 242, 245, 247, 251, 256, 258-260, 269, 274, 282, 300, 301, 306, 330, 331, 333, 335, 349, 351, 354, 356, 357, 361, 362, 364, 367, 376, 378, 380-382, 398, 405, 409, 415, 416, 489, 491, 493, 494, 498, 508, 512, 519, 527, 540, 573, 584, 591, 624, 626, 631, 642, 656-658, 661, 664, 665, 673, 675, 676, 687, 690-693, 711, 742, 772, 784-787, 795, 817, 823, 828, 836, 903, 905, 906, 922, 930, 942, 971, 972, 993, 994, 997, 1009, 1011-1013, 1017, 1027, 1073, 1075, 1089, 1108, 1109, 1116, 1117, 1145, 1148, 1153, 1166, 1178, 1220, 1226, 1227, 1229, 1231, 1234-1237*

baptismal rites, *104, 112, 367, 382, 693, 787, 795, 1075, 1237*

Bar Kokhba, *47, 69, 125, 145, 165, 166, 185, 192, 194, 213-215, 323, 358, 605, 606, 609, 611*

barbarians, *666, 759, 761*

Basilides, *127, 146, 149, 192, 194, 400, 404*

beasts, *50, 52, 62, 127, 128, 177, 182, 191, 232, 241, 254, 309, 325, 329, 348, 349, 362, 426, 699, 715, 720, 736, 853, 854, 909,*

914, 989, 1033, 1037, 1078, 1080, 1081, 1086, 1162, 1196

Belial, Beliar, 44, 50, 52, 729, 730, 740

benediction, 121, 129, 131, 165-169, 172, 174, 398, 475, 609, 650-654, 660, 661, 663, 664, 670, 672, 673, 895, 897, 947, 952, 1026, 1083

benefactors, 20, 92, 93, 129, 288, 293, 923, 1013, 1106, 1107, 1196

Berea, 290, 758, 764, 1217

biblical theology, 55, 129, 250, 433, 473, 478, 482, 556, 796-799, 802, 804, 807-814, 876, 882, 948, 1082

binding of Isaac, 3, 837

binitarianism, 177, 178, 258, 416, 665, 1122

birth pangs, 262, 1210

bishops, 28, 32, 35, 37, 46, 55, 76, 80-82, 84, 89, 94, 105, 106-109, 120-122, 129, 135, 146, 147, 150, 151, 166, 185, 190-192, 202, 214, 222-225, 229, 233, 237, 240, 258, 259, 262, 301, 303, 307, 308, 311, 314, 320, 352, 357, 358, 363, 371, 374, 404, 405, 408, 447, 470, 507, 525, 530-532, 539, 575, 588, 654, 674, 677, 691-693, 699, 705-707, 713, 714, 721, 731, 741, 744, 745, 764, 775, 777, 832, 877, 881, 882, 891, 898, 927, 931, 934, 937, 963, 966, 974-976, 1004, 1014, 1032, 1040, 1048, 1049, 1067, 1072, 1075, 1079, 1086, 1087, 1092, 1093, 1100, 1108-1111, 1151, 1197, 1213, 1216, 1231, 1233

blaspheme, blasphemy, 355, 397, 721, 837, 963, 1063, 1097

blessing, blessedness, 1-3, 5, 6, 20, 31, 39, 41, 42, 81, 90, 95, 98, 100, 104, 118, 121, 122, 129-131, 155, 163, 165, 168, 172, 200, 208-210, 226, 246, 264, 265, 276, 281, 304, 319, 326-328, 330, 332, 337-339, 341, 342, 351, 368, 381, 396, 403, 407, 408, 410, 415, 423, 450, 469, 476, 498, 548, 549, 552, 554, 556-558, 562, 565, 566, 576, 596, 601, 609, 610, 631, 637, 648, 654, 663, 677, 680, 686, 695, 698, 720, 724, 729, 731, 733, 736, 753, 791, 816, 817, 828, 830, 839, 864, 869, 875, 889, 896, 897, 899, 943, 946, 948, 964,

968, 969, 971, 999, 1008, 1009, 1012, 1030, 1038-1041, 1055, 1092, 1136, 1138, 1153, 1160, 1163, 1183, 1237, 1240

blessing of Abraham, 130, 731

blind, blindness, 49, 70, 180, 195, 209, 236, 300, 322, 328, 381, 425, 471, 589, 658, 702, 711, 747, 790, 791, 1053, 1091, 1143, 1192, 1235, 1236

blood, 4, 26, 88, 108, 112, 117, 119, 122, 123, 131, 132, 151, 153, 155-157, 174, 176, 177, 180, 182, 199, 242, 248, 257, 258, 261, 262, 268-270, 274, 275, 278-284, 306, 308, 319, 328, 370, 373, 375, 377, 380, 393, 428, 455, 487, 503, 539, 564, 581, 603, 616, 633, 635, 641, 642, 646, 648, 657, 673, 689, 691, 692, 694, 699, 719, 720, 737, 743, 778-780, 788, 793, 830, 832, 849, 854, 870, 871, 897, 908, 928, 940, 966, 988, 989, 991, 1002-1004, 1014, 1016, 1022, 1030, 1046, 1067, 1069-1071, 1074, 1080, 1098, 1105, 1110, 1144, 1155, 1160, 1165, 1169, 1183, 1197, 1204, 1217

blood of Christ, 88, 122, 156, 174, 261, 262, 279, 280, 375, 455, 830, 940, 1002, 1070, 1071, 1080, 1169

boasting, 592, 673, 889, 890, 961, 962, 1040, 1051-52, 1171, 1212, 1228

body, 26, 32, 37, 39, 54, 65, 71, 90, 96, 97, 112, 117, 121-123, 132, 147, 153, 202, 203, 214, 221, 224, 228, 235, 242, 256, 262, 268, 269, 274, 276, 280, 289, 290, 293, 296, 304, 306, 308, 318, 319, 321, 341, 346, 362, 371, 374-376, 401, 402, 409, 462, 487, 491, 498, 500, 503, 543, 546, 552, 553, 558, 581, 586, 593, 601, 610, 612, 621, 628, 629, 650-655, 657, 686, 691, 693, 706, 708, 709, 717, 719, 730, 737, 740, 744, 755, 775-778, 783, 843, 853, 863, 866, 867, 869, 883, 888-891, 893, 899, 928, 933, 935, 946, 949, 958, 960, 970, 985-987, 990, 995, 1006, 1019, 1020, 1030, 1042, 1044, 1048, 1055, 1070, 1071, 1090, 1095, 1096, 1103-1105, 1121, 1122, 1151, 1165, 1167, 1169, 1198, 1203,

1214, 1215, 1226, 1232, 1233, 1235

body of Christ, 112, 121, 123, 783, 891, 960

bondage, 2, 3, 40, 100, 280, 321, 383, 415, 526, 694, 702, 732, 823, 939, 958, 1001, 1002, 1019, 1078-1080

book of life, 168, 254, 609, 642, 656, 851, 1034, 1186, 1189, 1223

born again, 118, 132, 258, 335, 795

boundary markers, 298, 299, 377

bowls, 46, 62, 132, 133, 340, 428, 477, 481, 942, 1030, 1031, 1037, 1179, 1190, 1239, 1241

bread, 81, 114, 123, 131, 157, 181, 201, 268, 269, 271, 285, 314, 377, 476, 502, 503, 589, 680, 681, 683, 686-688, 690-694, 720, 729, 736, 737, 942-944, 992, 993, 1007, 1104, 1105, 1162-1166, 1229, 1232, 1235

brothers of Jesus, 133, 187, 190, 983, 1005

caesar, 231, 293, 324, 325, 348, 349, 381, 478, 721, 883, 936, 948, 954, 1028, 1034, 1062, 1064, 1072, 1076, 1142, 1206

Caesar Augustus, 1076, 1142

Caesarea, 37, 135, 185, 288, 391, 433, 661, 711, 756-758, 763, 764, 790, 930, 931, 971, 1060-1062, 1163, 1206, 1227

Caiaphas, 467, 1162

Cain, 42, 134, 536, 538, 539, 614, 618, 819, 835, 836, 839, 840, 867, 1095, 1204

calendar, 96, 682, 741, 1160

Caligula, 51, 186, 289, 324, 599, 857, 932, 1008

call, calling, 2, 3, 17, 19, 26, 30, 38, 40, 43, 54, 57, 66, 77, 78, 80, 87, 89, 103, 107, 115, 132, 136, 156, 158, 177, 195-197, 201, 203, 205, 211, 213, 230, 238, 242, 255, 258, 259, 266, 273, 277, 281, 296, 307, 311, 313, 314, 318, 319, 319, 329, 349, 354, 364, 365, 368, 369, 373, 380, 383, 391, 396, 418, 422-425, 430, 446, 450, 457, 461, 475, 476, 479, 480, 485, 490-492, 500, 501, 517, 528, 529, 534, 536, 538, 539, 567, 574, 580, 581, 595, 596, 603, 617, 621, 622, 627, 630, 631, 639, 645, 653, 654, 663, 666, 692, 699, 713, 718, 747, 752, 756, 763, 764, 775, 779, 785, 786, 789, 790, 798, 806, 821,

837, 838, 841, 851, 853, 863, 864, 868, 875, 878, 880, 886, 891, 903, 908, 917, 920, 940, 942, 944, 945, 953, 954, 960, 962, 971, 979, 984, 998, 1012-1014, 1018, 1030, 1033, 1035, 1036, 1038, 1040, 1047, 1066, 1067, 1080, 1081, 1094, 1096, 1097, 1101, 1106-1108, 1110, 1120, 1131, 1143, 1167, 1173, 1182, 1204, 1208, 1213, 1217, 1219, 1221, 1223, 1226, 1228, 1230-1234

canon, canonical status, 7, 12, 13, 16, 24, 33, 44, 46, 47, 56, 69, 82, 85-87, 90, 91, 134-144, 146, 151, 156, 158, 169, 179, 184, 185, 189-191, 193, 194, 224, 228, 234, 235, 236, 245, 259, 264, 306, 311, 312, 350, 408, 410, 411, 426, 432, 443, 449, 456, 457, 459, 461, 465, 470, 471, 481, 483, 484, 497, 534, 536, 538, 539, 541, 542, 545, 546, 553-556, 559, 560, 572, 574-578, 582, 585, 613, 614, 618, 638, 655, 659, 663, 668, 673, 675-678, 684, 705-712, 722, 733, 735, 736, 752, 769, 775, 787, 796, 797, 799, 802-808, 810-812, 814, 817, 820, 827, 828, 831, 835, 867, 889, 893, 912, 914, 915, 920-922, 927, 928, 929, 934, 976-981, 983, 984, 1003, 1033, 1090, 1103, 1108, 1156, 1161, 1172-1174, 1176, 1177, 1192, 1199, 1222, 1226, 1230, 1233

canonical criticism, 245, 560

Cappadocia, 79, 757-759, 916

captive, captivity, 49, 132, 532, 759, 934, 949, 1001, 1002, 1079

catechesis, 117, 256, 257, 279, 628, 767, 1058, 1157

catechetical school, 34-36, 144, 577, 1049

celibacy, 31, 144, 315, 713, 714, 1089, 1100, 1106, 1153, 1221, 1221, 1222

Cenchreae, 758, 765

centurion, 109, 115, 209, 243, 271, 391, 392, 566, 580, 688, 928, 993, 1060-1062, 1104, 1144, 1195

Cephas, 467, 497

ceremonial law, 240, 645

Cerinthus, 152, 190, 193, 194, 308, 313, 314, 584, 591

charisma, charismata, 105, 107, 151, 891, 970, 975, 1087, 1194, 1195, 1232

child, children, 3, 5, 6, 13,

14, 20, 39, 42, 75, 79, 100,
113, 123, 124, 127, 128,
152, 192, 198, 200, 204,
208-210, 212, 216, 227,
231, 238, 239, 250, 254,
261, 274, 289, 294, 297,
323, 352, 358, 362, 366,
394, 419, 428, 498, 499,
500, 502-504, 506, 514,
518, 519, 556, 595, 597,
599, 611, 637, 638, 690,
703, 712, 714, 772, 777,
778, 793, 794, 813, 815,
817, 819, 822, 850, 852,
876, 934, 935, 946, 1002,
1004-1006, 1012-1014,
1024, 1025, 1064, 1071,
1089, 1105, 1108, 1115-
1118, 1139, 1158, 1168,
1181, 1206, 1209, 1210,
1212, 1213, 1216, 1220
childbearing, 723, 1089
children of Abraham, 5,
210, 556
children of God, 6, 42, 152,
210, 239, 254, 274, 794,
1116, 1117
Chloe, 1220
Christianity and Judaism,
34, 90, 126, 145, 157, 159,
160, 194, 204, 208, 214,
217, 218, 228, 229, 245,
249, 250, 299, 323, 379,
386, 388, 393, 394, 398,
430, 468, 501, 520, 543,
565, 585, 587, 610, 644,
649, 668, 678, 684, 724,
726, 728, 762, 775, 934,
944, 953, 1108-1110, 1141,
1145, 1159, 1165
christological monotheism,
557
chronology, 126, 150, 184,
185, 187, 189, 193, 342,
681, 883, 952, 1063, 1146
church order, government,
28, 54, 55, 75, 80, 82, 89,
105, 106, 110, 113, 118,
122, 129, 146, 181, 191,
198, 204, 219-222, 224,
225, 233, 235, 243, 267,
300, 301, 306, 311, 312,
317, 352, 358, 371, 374,
447, 465, 501, 504, 506,
519, 532, 533, 613, 653,
690, 746, 775, 882, 891,
892, 898, 934, 961, 974,
976, 1036, 1048, 1067,
1075, 1080, 1087, 1093,
1105, 1106, 1108, 1110,
1193, 1197, 1212, 1229,
1238, 1240
church of God, 107, 166,
201, 224, 270, 743, 745,
1087
Cilicia, 755, 757, 758, 764,
1060, 1150
circumcision, 5, 6, 32, 33,
38, 54, 76-79, 124, 125,
127, 145, 161, 168, 169,
189, 203, 208, 213-216,
221, 226-229, 240, 247,
249, 298, 320, 323, 354,

372, 377, 379, 383, 387,
394, 546, 580, 584, 587,
626, 642, 645, 647-649,
743, 753, 761, 764, 806,
824, 825, 828, 888, 891,
993, 1072, 1110, 1144,
1148, 1195, 1207
circumcision, party, 227, 587
citizen, citizenship, 206,
230, 233, 243, 289, 293,
294, 352, 517, 563, 599,
764, 886, 920, 953, 1060-
1062, 1064-1066, 1219
civic cult, 230, 1006-1008
civil authority, 110, 127,
174, 230-232, 236, 293,
325, 350, 352, 514, 661,
790, 884, 912, 917, 947,
1035, 1062, 1066, 1110,
1158, 1207
Claudius, 150, 192, 233,
289, 290, 325, 446, 448,
449, 529, 743, 754, 907,
911, 1061, 1062, 1065,
1066, 1100, 1217
clean cleansing, 93, 117,
131, 174, 233, 242-244,
274, 276, 277, 279, 282,
354, 375, 376, 487, 561,
726, 738, 810, 819, 928,
944, 988-992, 1013, 1104,
1144, 1166
Clement of Rome, 6, 41, 75,
83, 85, 86, 88, 91, 100,
109, 110, 138, 156, 179,
184, 190, 191, 201, 204,
216, 224, 230, 233, 234,
237, 238, 243, 246, 258,
262, 285, 291, 352, 367,
381, 435, 442, 444, 446,
448, 460, 470, 481, 485,
512, 518, 519, 532, 534,
572, 579, 658, 672, 698,
732, 795, 823, 829, 834,
899, 975, 984, 1003, 1019,
1024, 1036, 1040, 1048,
1052, 1054, 1058, 1066,
1067, 1071, 1121, 1156,
1159, 1211, 1216, 1223
Colossae, 146, 529, 1150,
1226
commandment, 26, 27, 128,
133, 162, 181, 238-241,
292, 311, 319, 336, 351,
352, 366, 371, 373, 375,
379, 397, 426, 469, 470,
492, 528, 537, 575, 583,
584, 586, 594, 598, 604,
609, 640, 644-646, 649,
652, 673, 674, 675, 683,
684, 698, 715, 815, 823,
827, 830, 831, 837, 852,
897, 991, 994, 1046, 1049,
1054, 1055, 1075, 1088,
1096, 1142, 1145, 1158-
1160, 1164, 1166, 1169,
1180, 1193
commandments of God,
128, 238, 240, 604, 1169
communion, 116-119, 121,
277, 339, 373, 374, 498,
532, 590, 686, 689-693,
697, 777, 943, 945

compassion, 4, 74, 173, 253,
274, 426, 429, 455, 671,
733, 734, 736, 745, 781,
882, 990, 1086, 1090, 1101
condemnation, 76, 100,
160, 168, 207, 230, 303,
559, 568, 612, 622, 696,
716, 736, 837, 976, 1002,
1016, 1051, 1090, 1095,
1192, 1231
confess, confession, 26, 27,
51, 74, 79, 104, 114, 117,
118, 121, 123, 153-155,
163, 164, 176, 181, 195,
199, 200, 201, 213, 216,
217, 223, 243, 251, 254-
258, 278-281, 283, 314,
344, 355, 361, 366, 368,
375, 380, 381, 382, 392,
396, 398, 399, 420, 421,
426, 437, 443, 447, 453,
454, 455, 500, 509, 522,
534, 541, 555, 571, 584,
593, 657, 661, 667, 669,
684, 689, 691, 699, 704,
739, 816, 819, 830, 833,
841, 843, 878, 889, 912,
932, 942, 943, 945, 946,
959, 973, 1012-1014, 1053-
1055, 1097, 1110, 1112,
1150, 1197, 1201, 1227-
1229, 1231
confessional forms, 82, 91,
241, 255, 256, 260, 628,
1068, 1225
conflict, 14, 17, 19, 22, 52,
72, 77, 83, 110, 127, 129,
148, 150-152, 162, 169,
175, 188, 206, 211, 215,
216, 218, 234, 236, 237,
241, 252, 255, 256, 290,
295, 309, 310, 348, 368,
386, 388-390, 393, 404,
416, 446, 462, 464-466,
471, 477, 483, 520, 547-
551, 589, 590, 592, 635,
678, 702, 706, 726-728,
751, 761, 770, 789, 805,
818, 829, 852, 854, 866,
903, 914, 918, 931, 938,
948, 954, 985, 986, 1013,
1019, 1031, 1037, 1041,
1059, 1081, 1086, 1104,
1125, 1136-1138, 1140,
1163, 1239
conflict motif, 52, 127, 241,
309, 854, 914, 1037, 1081,
1086
conscience, 117, 241-243,
261, 276-278, 322, 352,
375, 376, 529, 646, 684,
714, 884, 920, 946, 964,
985, 987, 994, 1012, 1029,
1031, 1043, 1053, 1058,
1070, 1073, 1095, 1096,
1098, 1185, 1200, 1211
contentment, 844, 1051
conversion, 45, 73, 78, 93,
103, 115, 131, 164, 166,
168, 192, 216, 226, 227,
229, 243-245, 247, 288,
292, 296, 297, 312, 316,
324, 341, 354-356, 359,

364, 376, 378, 380, 389-
391, 393, 394, 415, 416,
422, 438, 460, 476, 494,
503, 512, 534, 562, 563,
565, 580, 589, 602, 636,
642, 657, 658, 666, 702,
706, 715, 718, 719, 738,
743, 749, 753, 754, 756-
758, 761,
764-767, 769, 771, 773,
774, 789, 790, 792, 803,
822, 860, 879, 883-885,
887, 894, 907,
921, 930, 940, 953, 971,
998, 1011-1013, 1015,
1049, 1057, 1076, 1081,
1103, 1104, 1106-1109,
1111, 1136, 1138, 1140,
1144, 1149, 1152, 1152,
1159, 1194, 1207, 1217-
1221
converts, 45, 80, 93, 162,
175, 206, 226, 227, 295,
349, 354, 356, 358, 373,
374, 378, 388, 390, 391,
394, 446, 471, 503, 508,
512, 520, 521, 579, 622,
642, 645, 661, 697, 707,
715, 743, 744, 750, 756,
760, 761, 773, 894, 917,
920, 942, 1060, 1107,
1117, 1152, 1207
Coptic Apocalypse of Peter, 70,
243
Corinth, 84, 89, 90, 93, 94,
144, 147, 148, 151, 152,
193, 201, 202, 210, 220,
222, 224, 233-237, 243,
290, 355, 378, 379, 391,
446, 448, 449, 512, 529,
530, 617, 639, 678, 679,
686, 688, 698, 743, 744,
754, 755, 757, 759, 762,
764, 765, 772, 808, 829,
830, 883, 892, 910, 961,
975, 1005, 1010, 1022,
1048, 1100, 1122, 1145,
1178, 1195, 1203, 1217,
1219, 1226, 1236
Corinthian church, 75, 109,
148, 151, 179, 234, 352,
506, 1100, 1110
Cornelius, 18, 23, 45, 78, 79,
106, 107, 115, 116, 123,
227, 243-245, 332, 364,
368, 377, 378, 380, 391,
493, 494, 503, 508, 512,
566, 567, 580, 647, 688,
761, 859, 886, 903, 930,
944, 972, 993, 1022, 1060,
1104, 1124, 1144, 1178,
1195, 1227
cornerstone, 158, 183, 245,
317, 320, 361, 510, 511,
538, 633, 678, 838, 920,
1126, 1127, 1135
cosmic christology, 96, 890,
1224
cosmic powers, 232, 1234
cosmos, cosmology, 65, 66,
98, 215, 235, 245, 250,
307, 332, 343, 347, 361,
401, 427, 439-443, 499,

591, 622, 636, 638, 644, 741, 783, 956-958, 960, 1020, 1176, 1189, 1198, 1202, 1224, 1231
Council in Jerusalem, 106, 138, 186-187, 883, 1162
covenant, 1, 2, 20, 37, 38, 42, 43, 45, 74, 90, 107, 108, 117, 124-126, 144, 147, 161, 162, 168, 172, 195, 196, 198-200, 203, 207, 209-211, 213, 214, 217, 218, 226-228, 242, 245-250, 259, 262, 263, 268-270, 275, 276-279, 282, 285, 286, 299, 326, 331, 334, 336, 345, 346, 350, 375, 376, 383, 390, 413-415, 418, 443, 444, 447, 448, 453-455, 457, 458, 480, 485, 487, 492, 501, 512, 537, 540, 543, 544, 561, 563, 564, 582, 583, 600, 621, 631, 633, 637, 639, 640, 645-649, 655, 673, 679, 685, 689, 724, 733, 734, 736, 770, 780-782, 793, 795, 802, 811, 814, 821, 827-830, 834, 842, 844, 845, 849, 850, 854, 861, 862, 878, 889, 891, 899, 905, 906, 927, 930, 947, 956-969, 973, 974, 989, 990, 998, 999, 1003, 1012, 1026, 1031, 1043, 1053, 1055, 1058, 1069-1072, 1085, 1096, 1116, 1118, 1135, 1152, 1154-1156, 1160, 1183, 1230, 1233, 1237
covetousness, 715, 888, 1193
creation, 5, 45, 46, 50, 52, 57, 65, 66, 88, 98, 99, 104, 128, 183, 200, 203, 213, 215, 245, 247, 250-255, 258, 259, 266, 272, 276, 313, 318, 331-337, 341-343, 346-349, 359, 360, 363, 372, 396, 401, 405, 406, 414, 420, 421, 425, 427, 429, 440, 442, 486, 490, 499, 500, 521, 539, 540, 552, 556-558, 595, 622, 632, 635-638, 644, 657, 665, 666, 670, 674, 679, 685, 692, 706, 708, 740, 741, 748, 750, 783, 788, 793, 801, 805, 809, 811, 833, 845, 863, 866, 872, 899, 908, 926, 929, 932, 939, 952, 957-960, 974, 1003, 1012, 1017, 1019, 1020, 1022-1024, 1031, 1036, 1042, 1049, 1078, 1089, 1102, 1113, 1114, 1122, 1188, 1189, 1196, 1201, 1204, 1210, 1222-1224, 1226, 1227
creator, 5, 50, 87, 179, 211, 215, 250, 255, 256, 259, 356, 401, 402, 404, 406, 414, 421, 429, 439, 524,

525, 528, 556-558, 609, 621, 634, 655, 657, 668, 706, 776, 777, 807, 886, 939, 943, 962, 1121, 1148, 1202, 1224
creed, creedal, 82, 91, 99, 102, 117, 118, 122, 145, 164, 165, 181, 241, 255-260, 307, 308, 310, 375, 480, 491, 492, 522, 523, 573, 627, 628, 659-661, 800, 844, 887, 893, 953, 959, 973, 1018, 1020, 1027, 1068, 1111, 1114, 1118, 1181, 1224, 1226, 1227, 1230-1238
Crescens, 765
Crete, Cretans, 32, 223, 290, 757-759, 764, 765, 1059
Crispus, 148, 222, 512
cross, 20, 67, 68, 70, 71, 79, 88, 91, 99, 101, 114, 118, 119, 122, 124, 125, 144, 150, 159, 161, 182, 260-263, 267, 268, 270-287, 307, 328, 339, 351, 370, 375, 392, 397, 401, 404, 416, 423, 443, 446, 494, 495, 501, 540, 560, 573, 582, 584, 591, 592, 595, 601, 602, 610, 623, 624, 627, 632, 635, 637, 646, 648, 673, 676, 677, 685, 694, 695, 719, 722, 723, 728, 752, 753, 760, 761, 779, 795, 803, 811, 821, 833, 851, 870, 871, 885-888, 913, 915, 917, 921-923, 928, 929, 938, 950, 951, 962, 983, 985, 1000, 1004, 1016, 1038, 1039, 1047, 1050, 1072, 1077, 1079-1081, 1104, 1139, 1141, 1167, 1175, 1180, 1201, 1210, 1231, 1237, 1241
cross, theology of the, 20, 263, 286, 1175
crown, 327, 336, 622, 695, 721, 776, 777, 816, 818, 838, 862, 969, 1018, 1023, 1033, 1035, 1039, 1040, 1077, 1128, 1167, 1210
crucifixion, 20, 26, 27, 70-72, 153, 174, 177, 186, 193, 260, 272, 273, 281, 282, 306, 308, 317, 416, 446, 543, 562, 566, 567, 573, 591, 672, 687, 752, 913, 916, 928, 1105, 1161, 1162
cup, 111, 119, 121, 130, 131, 133, 157, 181, 268, 269, 428, 564, 686, 689-693, 1229, 1232, 1239
curse, curses, 20, 43, 129, 132, 168, 262, 263, 272, 280, 333, 341, 351, 469, 558, 701-704, 836, 852, 1002, 1010, 1183, 1222, 1138
Cybele, 1148
Cynic, Cynics, 357, 476, 706,

769, 1099, 1102, 1157
Cyprus, 78, 290, 291, 314, 323, 391, 416, 702, 757, 764, 765, 971, 1059, 1124
Dalmatia, 757-759, 765
Damascus, 78, 115, 117, 144, 146, 288, 314, 373, 388, 630, 658, 669, 709, 718, 747, 749, 753, 754, 756, 757, 762, 790, 803, 883, 884, 904, 941, 942, 1061, 1104, 1124, 1139, 1227
Damascus Road, 78, 669, 718, 747, 1139
dark, darkness, 6, 21, 44, 115, 118, 125, 129, 133, 146, 150, 188, 254, 264, 266, 336, 367, 384, 385, 425, 426, 438, 459, 486, 489, 519, 563, 589-592, 597, 637, 646, 657-659, 692, 730, 744, 751, 768, 780, 803, 817, 819, 823, 887, 917, 933, 939, 941, 959, 1003, 1015, 1021, 1031, 1047, 1080, 1109, 1118, 1141, 1148, 1159, 1183, 1193, 1234
daughter, daughters, 106, 191, 209, 322, 743, 765, 778, 854, 931, 932, 971, 1009, 1079, 1080, 1142, 1144, 1152, 1207, 1214, 1215, 1218, 1219, 1221
David, 39, 41, 43, 88, 152, 155, 163, 169, 171, 181, 187, 204, 208, 216, 246, 247, 264, 319, 356, 415, 435, 466, 487, 491, 497, 509, 534, 536, 537, 539, 561, 610, 631, 653, 663, 677, 690, 724, 730, 735, 776, 816, 825, 827-830, 851, 875, 963, 980, 992, 1006, 1025, 1042, 1073, 1082, 1091, 1099, 1230
David's son, 43, 155
Day of Atonement, 99, 274, 279, 297, 861, 966, 1016, 1165
day of the Lord, 63, 90, 253, 264-267, 329, 343, 425, 462, 570, 622, 625, 668, 671, 673, 679, 682, 690, 739, 779, 857-859, 863, 873, 969, 1025, 1030, 1036, 1074, 1081, 1097, 1181, 1182, 1241
day of wrath, 622
deacons, 76, 80, 81, 89, 105, 106, 109, 121, 122, 131, 146, 202, 223-225, 240, 267, 301, 405, 444, 464, 507, 519, 532, 691, 692, 741, 742, 744, 745, 759, 881, 882, 935, 975, 976, 982, 1054, 1067, 1086-1088, 1108, 1110, 1166, 1193, 1213, 1220, 1231, 1233, 1235
Dead Sea Scrolls, 44, 67, 84, 184, 188, 267, 330, 331,

411, 464, 465, 511, 541, 610, 657, 729-731, 834, 956, 997, 1000, 1122, 1160, 1164, 1165, 1170
death of Christ, 5, 27, 35, 36, 45, 74, 75, 88, 96, 98, 99, 104, 112, 114, 119, 153, 171-174, 213, 214, 240, 245, 254, 256, 257, 260, 262, 263, 267-287, 308, 317, 328, 330, 331, 335, 336, 349, 351, 359, 363, 365, 376, 382, 385, 398, 415, 435, 457, 459, 479, 487, 489, 491, 500, 524, 537, 538, 543, 547, 562, 580, 591, 610, 626, 627, 635, 637, 642, 647, 655, 667, 684, 693, 694, 719, 752, 762, 784, 802, 811, 828, 835, 871, 885, 889, 899, 913, 915, 929, 939, 962, 987, 1002, 1003, 1039, 1058, 1069, 1070, 1072, 1075, 1080, 1082, 1092, 1096, 1140, 1180, 1186, 1204, 1241
decalogue, 241, 351, 413, 480, 679, 835, 932
deconstruction, 287, 472, 473
decree, 26, 150, 297, 448, 529, 572, 647, 648, 670, 743, 892, 904, 910, 965, 971, 996, 1088, 1142, 1149, 1163
defilement, 242, 360, 377, 378, 489, 615, 690, 715, 733, 777, 840, 898, 963, 987, 989, 990, 992, 994-996, 1121, 1144, 1223
deities, 146, 417, 520, 528, 591, 655, 701, 702, 750, 965, 1007-1009, 1011, 1082, 1147, 1148
delay of Parousia, 287
deliverer, 47, 65, 415, 644, 780, 857, 1001, 1034, 1082
Demas, 765
demons, demonic, 20, 23, 44, 48, 50, 51, 128, 129, 133, 168, 232, 258, 263, 266, 287, 331, 349, 356, 362, 382, 384, 414, 416, 417, 421, 423, 438, 459, 503, 511, 529, 558, 564, 701-703, 705, 720, 730, 751, 783, 786, 787, 913, 922, 931, 938, 941, 1006, 1010, 1014, 1026, 1033, 1056, 1076, 1077, 1079, 1080, 1082, 1117, 1118, 1138, 1199, 1231-1235
Derbe, 137, 222, 758
desposynoi, 287, 387, 1005
destroy, destruction, 35, 41, 51, 64, 79, 93, 111, 126, 148, 149, 165, 166, 176, 184, 185, 187-189, 191, 192, 200, 213, 214, 216, 240, 254, 263, 267, 283, 287, 322, 332, 341, 343, 358, 362, 365, 386, 387,

441, 459-461, 466, 467, 473, 487, 492, 525, 538, 552, 561, 564, 585, 600, 601, 605, 607, 609, 610, 624, 625, 633, 636, 655, 703, 709, 727, 728, 735, 768, 821, 840, 852, 869, 879, 900-902, 911, 913, 919, 926, 989, 1019, 1023, 1027-1031, 1034-1037, 1040, 1045, 1069, 1074, 1075, 1079, 1109, 1120, 1123, 1124, 1127, 1138, 1142, 1159, 1160, 1162, 1164, 1165, 1189, 1192, 1209, 1238-1241

destruction/fall of Jerusalem, 35, 51, 93, 111, 165, 184, 187, 188, 192, 194, 214, 221, 316, 387, 546, 561, 600, 605, 607, 610, 727, 728, 861, 901, 902, 928, 1027, 1035, 1192

devil, 23, 42, 46-48, 50, 52, 104, 115, 121, 127, 129, 151, 210, 253, 254, 263, 274, 278, 281, 283-285, 287, 334, 336, 341, 351, 359, 368, 371, 460, 461, 491, 582, 592, 655, 702, 704, 705, 716, 719, 720, 732, 739, 751, 778, 794, 818, 819, 845, 852, 867, 869, 909, 931, 939-941, 1011, 1023, 1035, 1039, 1062, 1068, 1077-1082, 1094, 1098, 1116, 1122, 1149, 1166-1168, 1170, 1189, 1199, 1200, 1239, 1241

Diana, 147, 1147, 1214

diaspora, 79, 92, 144, 149, 151, 169, 170, 198, 204, 205, 215, 216, 228, 287-300, 321, 355, 372, 377, 389, 394, 431, 445, 456, 462, 521, 524, 547-550, 559, 560, 582, 585, 606, 610, 643, 651, 652, 661-663, 705, 727, 728, 743, 754, 759, 760, 764, 767, 835, 913, 917, 924, 933, 944, 1005, 1012, 1045, 1082, 1124, 1125, 1143, 1145-1147, 1149, 1150, 1202, 1214

diatribe, 161, 814

dietary laws, 54, 298, 433

Dionysus, 528, 1009, 1147

disciples, 13, 20, 22, 33, 40, 48, 49, 69, 72, 73, 76, 77, 83, 97, 113, 116, 121, 144, 163, 165, 167, 182, 188, 191, 192, 196, 197, 207, 222, 251, 262, 268, 269, 271, 273, 285, 306, 333, 373, 381, 385, 390, 392, 404, 407, 414, 415, 492, 494, 497, 501, 502, 532, 542, 546, 562, 563, 575, 580, 587, 590, 595, 598, 616, 631, 639, 646, 669, 675, 680, 681, 686-688,

692, 710, 712, 721-723, 729, 742, 743, 751, 753, 756, 757, 760, 762, 763, 765, 766, 772, 791, 794, 800, 801, 859, 871, 874, 877, 880, 882, 885, 888, 889, 892, 893, 900, 903-906, 914, 916, 921, 922, 930, 931, 940, 943, 945, 946, 953, 962, 969-971, 982, 991-993, 996, 1019, 1024, 1032, 1033, 1051, 1051, 1112, 1116, 1123-1125, 1144, 1175, 1178, 1199, 1200, 1204, 1205, 1211, 1227, 1235, 1237

discipleship, 20, 22, 118, 231, 262, 273, 281, 363, 370, 442, 443, 446, 457, 535, 560, 565, 593-595, 688, 712, 720, 722, 781, 811, 862, 877, 882, 885, 921, 944, 948, 963, 1106

discipline, 89, 109, 223, 260, 304-306, 326, 327, 330, 350, 363, 418, 419, 477, 478, 480, 519, 531, 572, 602, 623, 695, 714, 736, 797, 801, 802, 805-808, 810, 811, 818, 823, 850, 876, 882, 895, 943, 944, 947, 949, 954, 997, 1000, 1014, 1062, 1088, 1106, 1118, 1132, 1133, 1139, 1233

discourse analysis, 306, 451, 452, 458, 477, 478, 483, 484, 526, 620, 791, 1042, 1049, 1129, 1132-1135

disease 356, 747, 1144, 1160

disobedience, 5, 36, 39, 43, 63, 70, 75, 126, 172, 232, 240, 246, 248, 275, 278, 279, 282, 285, 319, 350, 377, 392, 418, 419, 425, 429, 453, 466, 511, 527, 584, 592, 621-623, 657, 723, 736, 768, 781, 790, 840, 844, 946, 1040, 1055, 1069, 1085, 1095-1097, 1123, 1124, 1136, 1140, 1160, 1193, 1208

divine presence, 211, 274, 276, 306, 336, 395-397, 399, 400, 420, 562, 971, 1055

divine warrior, 481, 870, 871

divorce, 9, 24, 33, 144, 306, 352, 700, 712-717, 882, 1033, 1084, 1088-1090, 1166, 1208, 1215

docetism, 24, 26, 27, 33, 52, 71, 75, 85, 101, 146, 152, 158, 183, 217, 239, 256, 257, 281, 285, 306-308, 401, 411, 469, 590, 591, 598, 639, 678, 929, 1018, 1019, 1049, 1114, 1140, 1150, 1231

dove, 204, 226, 746, 937, 977, 1088

doxology, 118, 125, 175, 177, 180, 256, 257, 309,

346, 395, 400, 428, 475, 498, 524, 527, 572, 612, 619, 651-654, 660, 663, 664, 672, 809, 918, 939, 940, 946, 947, 1030, 1046, 1083, 1227, 1236

dragon, 50, 52, 62, 100, 127-129, 132, 176, 177, 232, 241, 254, 309, 362, 426, 477, 634-636, 704, 720, 852-854, 913, 914, 1014, 1033, 1034, 1037, 1078, 1080, 1081, 1086, 1181, 1196, 1209

dreams, 2, 40, 244, 392, 469, 496, 550, 561, 713, 728, 853, 971, 972, 1010, 1021, 1204, 1210

drunkenness, 79, 133, 564, 686, 716, 720, 903, 905, 908, 917, 1149, 1192, 1217

dualism, 50, 51, 62, 64, 66, 67, 70, 232, 253, 276, 296, 307, 309, 375, 376, 401-403, 405, 462, 482, 590, 591, 593, 610, 615, 657, 665, 706, 707, 777, 815, 817, 880, 920, 925, 933, 939, 957, 984-987, 997, 1017, 1078, 1089, 1090, 1095, 1116, 1148, 1149

eagle, 379, 481, 634, 853, 1080, 1161

early catholicism, 89, 91, 106, 207, 226, 310, 358, 369, 532, 613, 617, 619, 893, 927, 934, 982, 1058, 1191, 1192, 1200

early church tradition, 101, 189, 633, 916

earth, 1, 14, 33, 36, 46, 47, 56, 65, 69, 95, 96, 98, 101, 104, 127-130, 132, 151, 156-158, 163, 164, 177, 196, 198, 200-204, 210, 220, 222-224, 226, 240, 250-255, 272, 276, 306, 310, 317, 329, 331, 332, 335-340, 344, 346, 348, 349, 352, 362, 375, 383, 394, 396, 401, 414, 418-420, 426-428, 438, 440-443, 459, 462, 477, 492, 505, 521, 525, 532, 552, 557, 561-564, 568, 621, 622, 624, 630, 634, 635, 637, 638, 643, 644, 656, 669, 677, 678, 690, 718, 719, 733, 739, 741, 753, 755, 756, 767, 769-771, 776, 779, 780, 811, 817, 823, 836, 840, 841, 843, 845, 851, 854, 857, 866, 870, 871, 878, 881, 897, 898, 906, 908, 922, 928, 943, 957-959, 968, 969, 977, 997, 1002, 1010, 1017, 1019, 1025, 1030, 1031, 1033, 1036, 1040, 1052, 1058, 1081, 1113, 1119, 1127, 1156, 1180, 1181, 1183, 1196, 1199, 1210, 1222, 1233, 1239,

1240

eating, 26, 33, 92, 120, 232, 240, 268, 269, 315, 316, 377-379, 383, 438, 503, 528, 529, 602, 647, 681, 686-688, 690, 693, 737, 744, 776, 853, 895, 989, 990, 991, 993, 994, 1036, 1040, 1104, 1149, 1160, 1219, 1235, 1162

Ebionism, Ebionites, 25, 33, 55, 134, 162, 168, 170, 178, 192, 193, 229, 313-316, 387, 388, 579, 584-587, 645, 648, 711, 900-902, 960, 993, 1165

ecstatic experience, 66, 317, 647, 784, 1037, 1183, 1194, 1196, 1197

Eden, 6, 304, 341, 814, 852

Edessa, 316, 317, 758, 766, 772, 774, 1150-1153

Edict of Claudius, 448

Egypt, 2, 34, 35, 38-40, 42, 48, 111, 132, 133, 144, 149, 152, 167, 175, 185, 237, 254, 280, 289-291, 295, 300, 301, 307, 321, 323, 324, 400, 415, 502, 512, 585, 618, 624, 643, 666, 712, 717, 731, 732, 757-759, 765, 771, 778-781, 822, 841, 854, 912, 916, 927, 931, 932, 1001, 1010, 1030, 1059, 1065, 1074, 1141, 1142, 1147, 1149, 1160, 1174, 1182, 1215, 1241

Egyptian, Egyptians, 34, 37, 39, 40, 60, 85, 132, 133, 147, 149, 180, 226, 236, 237, 289, 295, 298, 324, 386, 403, 407, 408, 410, 412, 415, 477, 481, 528, 621, 674, 710-712, 778, 781, 819, 839, 958, 1009, 1099, 1112, 1146, 1147, 1150, 1209

elders, 10, 27, 28, 46, 76, 78, 80, 89, 105-110, 137, 147, 148, 185, 189, 190, 198, 199, 220-225, 237, 270, 292, 305, 311, 317, 318, 355, 358, 369, 392, 428, 432, 437, 441, 447, 466, 505, 506, 511, 513, 518, 525, 529, 566, 595, 634, 635, 652, 653, 741-744, 786, 806, 818, 853, 877, 880, 883, 892, 897, 915, 918, 928, 942, 947, 973, 975, 980, 982, 1030, 1031, 1036, 1067, 1069, 1092, 1142, 1199, 1206, 1207, 1212, 1213, 1228, 1231

elect, 36, 46, 82, 106, 130, 131, 156, 161, 162, 177, 179, 180, 190, 192, 199-201, 211, 220, 221, 243, 246, 247, 249, 265, 292, 299, 317-321, 366, 400, 402, 413, 422, 423, 478, 509-511, 516, 519, 536,

538, 543, 556, 557, 562, 563, 573, 584, 624, 652, 673, 674, 688, 698, 822, 860, 876, 908, 913, 987, 1040, 1045, 1055, 1059, 1087, 1104, 1126, 1201, 1204, 1221, 1223

Eleusinian mysteries, 1009

Elijah, 41, 97, 127, 436, 437, 480, 534, 537, 539, 541, 551, 554, 559, 571, 721, 770, 779, 815, 816, 826, 830, 835, 854, 942, 945, 998, 1031

Elisha, 436, 437, 537, 539, 541, 826, 830, 930

Elkesaites, 315, 321, 584, 585, 648

emperor, 34, 50-52, 54, 75, 109, 111, 120, 128, 150, 176, 182, 184-186, 192, 193, 229-232, 240, 263, 288, 300, 321-326, 348-350, 362, 371, 438, 441, 448, 483, 526, 528-530, 535, 611, 617, 634, 636, 679, 691, 716, 734, 760, 773, 857, 869, 886, 898, 908-911, 914, 917, 919, 920, 932, 936, 1006, 1008, 1011, 1028, 1029, 1031, 1033, 1035, 1036, 1048, 1059-1065, 1067, 1074, 1076, 1082, 1083, 1099, 1109, 1110, 1112, 1137, 1140, 1196, 1197, 1217, 1219, 1221

emperor cult, 52, 176, 193, 232, 263, 321, 324, 325, 530, 535, 772, 914, 1008, 1029, 1031, 1033, 1035, 1036, 1048, 1063, 1067, 1072, 1110, 1137

end times, 51, 326, 330, 331, 334, 341, 469, 725, 860, 904, 1200

endurance, 2, 3, 25, 33, 38, 41, 45, 74, 76, 80, 98, 104, 172, 235, 240, 251, 253, 254, 262, 277, 278, 281, 296, 299, 321, 326-330, 348, 349, 351, 352, 356, 358, 361, 363, 365-370, 384, 397, 419, 422, 423, 425, 434, 435, 440, 443, 446, 453, 455, 499, 500, 501, 534, 538, 550, 558-560, 603-605, 622, 633, 719, 721, 762, 770, 786, 816, 819, 822, 823, 835, 836, 838, 845, 850, 878, 882, 897, 914, 915, 920, 940, 941, 950, 968, 969, 1013, 1015, 1023, 1038, 1062, 1063, 1067, 1100, 1121, 1136, 1138, 1140, 1167, 1168, 1170, 1180, 1208

enemies, 21, 26, 50, 51, 99, 112, 129, 130, 132, 133, 165, 191, 196, 199, 200, 263, 264, 331, 332, 338, 343, 360, 362, 374, 392,

418, 441, 459, 501, 503, 549, 589, 591, 633, 656, 677, 732, 739, 786, 792, 824, 836, 840, 919, 939, 1002, 1010, 1031, 1034, 1062, 1077, 1085, 1098, 1160, 1182, 1183, 1234, 1239

enthronement, 20, 69, 95, 100, 101, 325, 328, 330, 338, 348, 359, 360, 362, 363, 428, 442, 459, 524, 631, 635, 636, 638, 944, 1020, 1138

Epaphras, 765

Epaphroditus, 763, 765

Ephesus, 25, 71, 73, 75, 93, 116, 144, 146, 147, 151, 187, 188, 191-193, 197, 223, 317, 328-330, 355, 357, 391, 416, 495, 531, 588, 589, 591, 596, 698, 699, 702, 705, 722, 743, 754, 755, 757, 762-765, 769, 771, 772, 869, 883, 886, 903, 907, 940, 941, 1006, 1008, 1010, 1032, 1088, 1145, 1147, 1148, 1217, 1220, 1226

Epicureans, 29, 354, 356, 655, 762, 775, 776, 867, 925, 1149, 1157

Erastus, 148, 765, 1086

Esau, 39, 42, 129, 130, 249, 330, 381, 445, 829, 1013

eschatology, 21, 23, 27, 30-32, 35, 36, 47, 51, 52, 55-62, 64-68, 90, 95, 98, 125, 145, 182, 218, 255, 265-267, 277, 312, 326, 330-334, 337, 341, 343-345, 347, 348, 352, 397, 399, 423, 425, 442, 454, 462, 501, 502, 516, 560, 561, 565, 587, 595, 605, 610, 615, 620, 625, 628, 633, 638, 643, 644, 657, 659, 693, 694, 739, 741, 777, 803, 811, 854, 856-858, 860, 862, 863, 865-869, 872-875, 881, 888, 890, 925-927, 959, 970, 976, 998, 1019, 1020, 1023, 1025, 1026, 1041, 1054, 1057, 1058, 1074, 1075, 1078, 1081, 1086, 1158, 1170, 1176, 1182, 1189, 1200, 1224, 1233, 1241

Essenes, 45, 55, 60, 161, 295, 316, 345, 482, 610, 615, 775, 841, 932, 990, 997, 998, 1000, 1090, 1160, 1161, 1164, 1165, 1170

eternal destruction, 461, 821, 1074, 1240

eternal life, 27, 89, 104, 176, 241, 261, 282, 320, 327, 339, 342, 345-347, 369, 435, 517, 539, 557, 558, 592, 637, 665, 671, 690, 706, 737, 776, 777, 823, 986, 1016, 1018, 1023,

1039, 1040, 1046, 1184, 1204, 1231

eternal punishment, 6, 47, 75, 347, 429, 459, 461, 624, 625, 657, 777, 988, 1081, 1098, 1188, 1241

eternity, 88, 103, 104, 265, 276, 342, 345-347, 420, 460, 461, 673, 871, 926, 1040, 1097

ethics, 22, 25, 27, 28, 66, 67, 80, 85, 89, 90, 110, 117, 125, 144, 173, 175, 180, 181, 183, 202, 214, 232, 239, 241, 243, 261, 266, 281, 283, 300, 336, 337, 345, 347-349, 352, 354, 355, 358, 367, 370, 371, 384, 391, 397, 404, 412, 421, 422, 446, 469, 474-476, 478, 479, 480, 482, 485, 486, 488, 489, 491, 499, 500, 504, 513, 515-520, 523, 529, 533, 535, 538, 540, 541, 551, 552, 557, 558, 568, 569, 572, 576, 590-594, 615, 623, 626, 628, 638-640, 657, 699, 710, 713, 717, 733-738, 767, 775, 803, 811, 817, 819, 822, 834, 835, 837-839, 841, 862, 864, 867, 879-881, 880, 882, 889, 895, 896, 898, 918, 923-926, 940, 954, 963, 984, 987, 996, 1012, 1013, 1046, 1052-1054, 1056-1058, 1072, 1088-1090, 1097, 1103, 1107, 1110, 1116, 1145, 1149, 1157-1159, 1178, 1191-1194, 1212, 1215

Ethiopian eunuch, 18, 45, 115, 137, 271, 353, 364, 391, 493, 496, 580, 743, 767, 930, 931, 972, 1022

Eucharist, 32, 33, 55, 89, 95, 109, 118-120, 123, 130, 131, 157, 181, 201, 202, 213, 225, 262, 305, 308, 338, 352, 353, 363, 405, 409, 487, 528, 529, 572, 659, 662-664, 676, 680, 682-684, 686-694, 703, 731, 738, 745, 777, 898, 943, 973, 1072, 1108, 1224, 1228, 1229, 1231, 1235, 1238

Euodia, 765

evangelism, 23, 117, 160, 353, 355-359, 390, 392, 394, 415, 433, 578, 628, 748, 753, 755, 760, 773, 876, 929, 1118, 1189, 1219

evangelists, 9, 10, 17, 23, 35, 106, 115, 116, 163, 191, 226, 227, 353, 358, 359, 374, 378, 380, 388, 391, 468, 494, 554, 572, 575, 577, 578, 588, 598, 635, 706, 724, 743, 757, 764, 772, 877, 929-931, 944, 953, 1032, 1077, 1123,

1124, 1220, 1229, 1235

Eve, 43, 122, 264, 306, 332, 341, 396, 402, 706, 723, 1066, 1078, 1110, 1169, 1210, 1214

evil, 5, 21, 29, 33, 41, 42, 45, 47, 49-53, 62, 66, 68, 75, 80, 104, 117, 122, 125, 127-129, 151, 199-201, 214, 215, 230, 231, 241-243, 248, 253-255, 266, 267, 282, 284, 300, 317, 320, 325, 328, 336, 338, 351, 353, 357, 359, 369, 371, 373, 383, 396, 401, 402, 404, 411, 421, 426-428, 459, 470, 473, 477, 483, 486, 494, 525, 535, 538, 561, 564, 575, 601, 610, 621, 635-637, 649, 657, 659, 662, 697, 698, 701, 703, 706, 707, 715, 716, 720, 734, 735, 737-741, 752, 770, 783, 785-787, 793, 794, 852, 870, 881, 888, 898, 911, 922, 925, 932, 933, 939-941, 954, 956, 963, 970, 976, 985, 986, 997, 1003, 1010, 1029, 1035, 1036, 1047, 1052, 1074, 1077-1082, 1088, 1089, 1093-1096, 1100, 1109, 1110, 1117-1122, 1138, 1149, 1166, 1168-1170, 1180, 1185, 1190, 1192, 1193, 1200, 1223, 1227, 1234, 1236

evil age, 740, 1078

Evil One, 254, 266, 282, 359, 794, 939-941, 1078-1081, 1095

evil powers, 127, 428, 525, 561, 1227

evil spirit, 359, 701, 786, 922, 940, 985, 1079, 1118-1122, 1193

exaltation, 3, 11, 14, 18-20, 35, 46, 49, 74, 95-102, 106, 108, 158, 162-164, 171-174, 176-181, 224, 228, 239, 252, 272-274, 276, 278, 281, 312, 325, 328, 330, 332, 335, 348, 359-363, 380, 382, 396, 413, 416, 422, 430, 440, 442, 459, 479, 488, 489, 492-494, 497, 510, 521, 523, 524, 538, 539, 567, 568, 584, 626, 630-633, 637, 638, 667-671, 687, 711, 724, 726, 730, 732, 742, 780, 782, 800, 837, 841, 845, 849, 864, 904, 905, 939, 958, 960, 961, 965, 998, 1012, 1016-1018, 1020, 1025, 1035, 1072, 1082, 1096, 1113, 1128, 1191, 1199, 1227, 1236, 1237, 1239

example of Christ, 261, 350, 523, 535, 656, 822, 896

exegesis, 30, 35, 36, 84, 126, 164, 183, 256, 296, 330,

*345, 356, 376, 390, 399,
409, 410, 422, 430, 439,
444, 465, 473, 480-482,
484, 510, 511, 520, 535,
542, 554, 620, 665, 682,
732, 751, 752, 802, 805-
807, 811, 812, 815, 817,
820, 834, 835, 837, 838,
841, 842, 850, 876, 894,
923, 955, 961, 967, 974,
1000, 1102, 1106, 1111,
1130, 1134, 1135, 1152,
1166, 1170, 1210*
Exile, *1, 60, 85, 127, 188,
236, 246, 264, 288, 331,
413, 549, 609, 644, 651,
759, 778, 841, 898, 908,
919, 920, 956, 980, 1001,
1067, 1110, 1205*
Exodus, *2, 21, 40, 45, 79,
103, 118, 128, 132, 133,
149, 174, 199, 200, 207,
211, 247, 270, 279, 280,
284, 295, 296, 349, 439,
445, 466, 473, 481, 538,
539, 606, 610, 614, 635,
641, 644, 673, 674, 731,
732, 758, 778, 780, 825,
828, 838, 844, 851, 903,
932, 964, 974, 989, 1014,
1030, 1031, 1091, 1092,
1094, 1095, 1099, 1218*
exorcism, *122, 256, 258,
384, 416, 438, 631, 746,
922, 930, 1082, 1100, 1118*
expiation, *275, 282, 539,
1074, 1129*
5 Ezra, *70, 214, 363*
6 Ezra, *70, 363*
faith and works, *4, 39, 104,
138, 209, 336, 351, 352,
365, 367, 368, 383, 421,
422, 547, 551, 559, 624,
816, 822, 823, 837, 892,
951, 1003, 1040, 1044,
1056, 1058, 1073, 1222*
faith of Jesus Christ, *157, 560*
faithfulness, *1-4, 9, 11, 17,
19-22, 38-41, 50, 51, 74,
75, 79, 91, 100, 104, 105,
108, 117, 130, 131, 142,
153, 155, 172, 177, 208,
217, 218, 232, 244, 245,
249, 253-255, 264-266,
274, 282, 284, 291, 294,
299, 318-320, 327, 331,
336, 337, 339, 341, 348,
354, 358, 359, 362, 364-
368, 370, 377, 397, 414,
415, 418, 419, 421, 425,
427, 430, 441, 443, 451,
452, 454, 455, 475, 479,
483, 493, 499-501, 510,
534, 538, 539, 551, 552,
554, 556, 557, 563, 564,
574, 584, 586, 602, 621,
632, 635-637, 652, 656,
661, 669, 672, 676, 699,
717-720, 739, 741, 765,
767, 769, 770, 773, 776,
780-782, 785, 786, 814-
816, 835, 836, 839, 840,
850, 854, 860, 862, 868,*

*869, 881, 884, 891, 897,
908, 915, 920-922, 924,
925, 928, 936, 941, 949-
953, 955, 956, 960, 968-
970, 994, 1015-1018, 1035,
1038, 1043, 1045-1047,
1053, 1054, 1058, 1074,
1094, 1184, 1194, 1196,
1203, 1205, 1233, 1239*
falling away, *73, 75, 522, 563*
false apostles, *81, 82, 706*
false prophet, false prophecy, *33, 51, 52, 81, 129,
133, 254, 306, 366, 370,
425, 460, 461, 477, 505,
507, 593, 597, 636, 658,
744-746, 775, 776, 851,
881, 970, 973, 975-978,
1010, 1037, 1079, 1119-
1121, 1181, 1183, 1185,
1198-1200*
false teachers, false teaching, *29, 31, 33, 34, 41-43,
49-51, 55, 73-76, 80, 106,
108, 155, 240, 305, 331,
335, 336, 339, 342, 348,
354, 357, 364, 369, 370,
383, 401, 405, 424, 425,
459, 475, 476, 508, 513,
516, 518, 525, 532, 593,
596, 611-615, 618, 619,
652, 654, 697, 705, 707,
715, 716, 744, 768, 769,
783, 822, 874, 876, 879,
880, 896, 908, 923-925,
946, 954, 961, 968, 973,
1013, 1019, 1040, 1045,
1046, 1079, 1080, 1083,
1109, 1200, 1201, 1220,
1224, 1226, 1231*
family, *1, 2, 4, 6, 40, 93, 95,
118, 122, 124, 130, 146,
150, 195, 198, 207, 210,
217, 219, 220, 231, 233,
261, 288, 322, 354, 355,
370, 371, 374, 388, 392,
443, 446, 455-457, 466,
474, 476, 507-513, 517-
519, 534, 597, 598, 617,
640, 649, 650, 696, 697,
706, 714, 722, 723, 733,
746, 760, 762, 769, 772,
792-794, 806, 811, 836,
849, 882, 919, 920, 932,
1001, 1004-1006, 1008,
1009, 1011, 1034, 1043,
1053, 1064, 1101, 1110,
1115-1117, 1121, 1142,
1158, 1161, 1181, 1207,
1208, 1212, 1214, 1216,
1217, 1221, 1228, 1234,
1235*
famine, *40, 550, 643, 743,
757, 908, 972, 1022, 1085*
fasting, *74, 120-122, 160,
297, 300, 351, 354, 358,
361, 370, 374, 380, 441,
443, 465, 469, 476, 496,
502, 513, 583, 649, 651,
661, 699, 734, 786, 828,
857, 869, 947, 961, 1038,
1071, 1104, 1108, 1141,
1197, 1229*

fate, *41, 59, 66, 69, 127, 129,
186, 214, 255, 278, 320,
356, 357, 369, 374, 459,
461, 468, 525, 530, 538,
564, 590, 610, 618, 698,
701, 702, 752, 781, 790,
818, 836, 837, 840, 841,
874, 902, 920, 935, 972,
989, 1006, 1007, 1009-
1011, 1034, 1047, 1085,
1119, 1121, 1136, 1183,
1240*
Father (God), *1, 5, 6, 19,
21, 37, 43, 53, 74, 86, 88,
89, 99, 100, 113, 120-122,
131, 144, 153-157, 161,
163-165, 173, 174, 176,
177, 179-183, 192, 203,
209, 210, 214, 239, 251,
252, 255, 258, 259, 270,
273, 277, 282, 284, 293,
322, 333, 362, 368, 390,
397, 401, 402, 404, 405,
418, 419, 426, 428, 430,
431, 480, 486, 487, 492,
493, 495, 498, 499, 525,
539, 557, 567, 570-573,
582, 584, 589, 594, 616,
629-631, 634, 639, 665,
666, 671, 673, 675-677,
687, 689-692, 694-696,
705, 706, 723, 731, 733,
734, 745, 779, 786, 794,
795, 805, 822, 833, 843,
845, 850, 851, 854, 864,
878, 881, 899, 903, 905,
920, 931, 939, 940, 942,
944-946, 958-960, 961,
964, 965, 969, 1004, 1018,
1023, 1026, 1046, 1055,
1074, 1076, 1083, 1091,
1092, 1097, 1110, 1112-
1114, 1118, 1119, 1122,
1156, 1223, 1224, 1230,
1231, 1237*
fear, *30, 39, 43, 54, 74, 76,
109, 115, 207, 231, 241,
278, 280, 322, 325, 328,
356-358, 364, 370-372,
383, 419, 421, 426, 431,
449, 460, 502, 532, 550,
551, 590, 668, 673-675,
697, 699, 703, 714, 734,
749, 778, 787, 795, 810,
815, 832, 839, 917, 920,
922, 925, 928, 940, 990,
1027, 1033-1035, 1038,
1039, 1047, 1048, 1080,
1092, 1109, 1120, 1121,
1128, 1183, 1198, 1212,
1231, 1239, 1240*
feasts, *356, 528, 587, 606,
689, 715, 917, 989, 994,
1079, 1149, 1160*
Felix, *435, 559, 859, 884,
894, 1056, 1060, 1099*
fellowship, *18, 29, 32, 44,
46, 114, 147, 155, 161,
176, 186, 199, 245, 271,
319, 356, 373, 374, 376-
379, 386, 445, 447, 502-
505, 508, 530, 587, 589,
590, 594, 595, 640, 648,*

*649, 657, 687, 691, 693-
696, 704, 726, 746, 776,
868, 897, 899, 942-944,
946-948, 959, 984, 990,
993-996, 1013, 1017, 1036,
1038, 1039, 1046, 1081,
1104, 1105, 1110, 1156,
1162, 1163, 1217, 1219,
1220, 1230*
feminist hermeneutics, *473,
484*
festivals, *228, 297, 529, 589,
633, 888, 905, 906, 910,
1007, 1008, 1028, 1139*
final judgment, *30, 56, 90,
103, 104, 255, 264-266,
332, 335, 336, 343, 348,
354, 564, 608, 621, 622,
624, 636, 749, 770, 836,
858, 952, 1018, 1095, 1097*
finances, *112, 234, 761, 1059*
fire, *50, 52, 83, 113, 150,
184, 187, 194, 253, 254,
302, 322, 328, 419, 427,
428, 439, 441, 449, 459-
461, 486, 492, 563, 576,
624, 636, 656, 671, 677,
703, 709, 776, 779, 810,
818, 823, 840, 903, 908,
919, 926, 988, 989, 1033,
1035, 1036, 1040, 1062,
1065, 1079, 1097, 1170,
1177, 1180, 1183, 1189,
1192*
firstfruits, *109, 253, 492,
673, 745, 827, 906, 1002*
First Jewish Revolt, *387, 585*
firstborn, *39, 42, 45, 52,
129, 177, 182, 263, 337,
563, 1017, 1079, 1116,
1241*
flesh, *5, 47, 51, 80, 88, 101,
113, 122, 124, 125, 153,
155, 157, 158, 163, 176,
199, 208, 215, 218, 223,
239, 254, 257, 259, 261,
276, 281, 285, 306-308,
320, 351, 352, 366, 373-
376, 402, 491, 492, 500,
540, 566, 574, 575, 591,
615, 657, 673, 674, 676,
691, 692, 699, 703, 706,
714, 715, 737, 769, 777,
788, 833, 838, 849, 886,
888, 893, 904, 919, 933,
949, 958-960, 973, 985-
987, 991, 1016-1020, 1024,
1046, 1079, 1083, 1089,
1098, 1119, 1121, 1156,
1163, 1169, 1170, 1184,
1191, 1212-1214, 1217,
1230, 1234*
flesh and blood, *153, 261,
308, 373, 375, 692, 788,
849*
flock, *73, 156, 158, 183, 199,
201, 224, 270, 376, 424,
642, 677, 678, 743, 744,
754, 818, 828, 836, 877,
880, 882, 915, 963, 973,
1023, 1090-1093, 1199,
1220, 1235*
food, *25, 26, 29-31, 41, 54,*

115, 117, 148, 161, 162, 168, 203, 206, 226, 227, 240, 293, 300, 305, 376, 377, 379, 383, 384, 418, 433, 438, 445, 462, 502, 529, 530, 540, 580, 583, 587, 645, 648, 649, 686-693, 716, 728, 736-738, 745, 753, 761, 828, 881, 882, 888, 930, 981, 991, 994, 996, 1007, 1065, 1087, 1099, 1104, 1110, 1111, 1115, 1117, 1123, 1149, 1156, 1159, 1160, 1228

food laws, 29, 31, 54, 162, 168, 227, 240, 376, 377, 433, 530, 587, 645, 648, 649, 693, 728, 828, 888, 996, 1104, 1110, 1156

food offered to idols, 26, 377, 379, 383, 530, 994, 1149

fool, 229, 557, 816, 839

foolishness, 59, 367, 549, 555-559, 601, 715, 1071, 1193, 1201, 1239, 1240

forbearance, 424, 425, 430, 866, 1073, 1074, 1087

foreknowledge, 5, 80, 104, 317-320, 415, 744, 840, 975

forgiveness, 5, 11, 20, 21, 27, 42, 89, 98, 104, 113-116, 120-122, 124, 161, 171, 173, 236, 246, 247, 260, 261, 267, 269, 271, 273-286, 306, 333, 356, 358, 367, 376, 378-382, 384, 396, 419, 456, 469-471, 486, 572, 574, 589, 603, 622-624, 630, 631, 646, 647, 677, 692, 696, 706, 714, 718, 733-736, 766, 786, 795, 823, 830, 832, 886, 935, 939, 940, 942, 945, 969, 971, 992, 1003, 1012, 1013, 1015, 1038, 1039, 1041, 1054, 1055, 1058, 1069, 1070, 1075, 1080, 1082, 1096-1098, 1143, 1148, 1170, 1193, 1204, 1228, 1229, 1233

form criticism, 565, 748, 800, 981

fornication, 26, 112, 377, 564, 698, 716, 994, 1088-1090, 1163, 1193, 1219

freedom, 19, 30, 54, 71, 88, 116, 136, 165, 230, 231, 278, 311, 321, 352, 356, 358, 382-384, 473, 523, 529, 547, 557, 655, 664, 693, 736, 789, 862, 878, 909, 925, 951, 968, 969, 1001, 1060, 1079, 1090, 1099-1101, 1143, 1160, 1213, 1221, 1227

fruit, 5, 36, 160, 209, 277, 319, 421, 522, 541, 599, 689, 795, 796, 895, 899, 1013, 1015, 1036, 1048, 1071, 1087, 1131, 1185,

1203

fruit of the Spirit, 1121, 1191, 1202

fulfillment, 2, 3, 5, 19, 35, 37-39, 63, 84, 98, 113, 123, 153, 160, 161, 167, 171, 187, 195, 210, 215, 241, 244, 247, 251, 253, 270, 272, 331-334, 336-338, 342, 354, 356, 383, 384, 387, 415, 431, 439, 441, 454, 464, 479-481, 487, 489, 493, 494, 500, 517, 524, 525, 536, 537, 539, 541, 543, 567, 581, 585, 586, 626, 627, 630-632, 637, 647, 648, 663, 679, 685, 719, 727, 728, 738, 751, 753, 759, 767, 770, 779, 793, 799, 824-826, 837, 838, 857-860, 862, 864, 866, 872, 873, 896, 903-906, 944, 962, 966-970, 1008, 1017, 1022, 1031, 1036, 1047, 1048, 1069-1071, 1073, 1075, 1076, 1113, 1143, 1156, 1182, 1183, 1188, 1194, 1221

fullness, 14, 19, 20, 52, 183, 331, 589, 602, 637, 686, 890, 1017, 1070, 1120, 1167, 1201, 1202, 1226

funeral, 325, 329, 841, 988, 1043

Gaius, 28, 80, 83, 186, 289, 296, 324, 456, 505, 652, 769, 897, 932, 937, 1028, 1047

Galatia, 79, 146, 227, 475, 496, 680, 755, 757, 758, 764, 765, 892, 916, 1059, 1195

Galilean Christianity, 151, 385-388, 728, 902

Galilee, 94, 185, 186, 385-388, 392, 546, 570, 599, 600, 608, 611, 617, 643, 728, 752, 756, 775, 894, 900, 902, 904, 916, 922, 931, 990, 992, 1006, 1061, 1076, 1077, 1146, 1150

Gallio, 148, 193, 449, 1060

Gamaliel, 185, 186, 193, 608, 1161

genealogy, 208, 209, 315, 386, 707, 730, 731, 789, 843, 964, 966, 1103, 1172-1173

general resurrection, 636, 1074

genre, 7, 8, 12, 17, 23, 24, 56-63, 66-72, 82, 84, 112, 133, 234, 245, 295, 296, 340, 347, 408, 409, 417, 431, 443, 449, 450, 452, 469, 475, 478, 499, 539-541, 551, 555, 583, 612, 651-653, 664, 766, 802, 808, 810, 818, 842, 854, 863, 879, 923, 924, 935, 936, 951, 978-980, 995, 997, 1019, 1024, 1025,

1037, 1042, 1043, 1086, 1132, 1134, 1159, 1184, 1197, 1198, 1214, 1225, 1229, 1232

Gentile Christianity, 83, 85, 136, 145, 468, 579, 580, 587, 712, 1109

Gentile mission, 13, 18, 23, 78, 79, 145, 147, 160, 162, 169, 206, 207, 229, 244, 245, 299, 359, 387-392, 467, 479, 546, 547, 725, 753, 762, 764, 767, 792, 859, 875, 956, 977, 996, 1076, 1189, 1195

geonim, 394, 608

gift of knowledge, 490

gift of the Spirit, 19-21, 119, 124, 281, 489, 492-494, 626, 766, 767, 971

gift of tongues, 1178

glorification, 20, 98, 398, 399, 643, 890, 1181, 1196

glorify, 19, 96-98, 101, 153, 174, 178, 362, 369, 385, 392, 394, 395, 414, 416, 498, 561, 582, 609, 708, 751, 771, 817, 896, 917, 920, 943, 989, 1039, 1136, 1196, 1197

glory, 45, 47, 79, 95, 98-102, 131, 159, 163, 165, 175, 176, 183, 196, 202, 268, 275, 277, 279, 281, 282, 306, 309, 312, 317, 319, 320, 336, 337, 343, 349, 350, 361-363, 394-400, 420, 423, 424, 428, 442, 455, 458, 477, 481, 498, 499, 501, 513, 524, 525, 567, 570, 572, 597, 601, 602, 621, 623, 637, 638, 656, 659, 660, 663, 665, 671, 690, 692, 695, 744, 777, 782, 785, 810, 812, 816-818, 845, 853, 856, 865, 867, 870, 886, 891, 915, 916, 920, 921, 937-941, 956, 957, 967, 970, 1000, 1007, 1014, 1017, 1019-1023, 1025, 1039-1041, 1045, 1055, 1076, 1090, 1137, 1140, 1156, 1202, 1205, 1227, 1232, 1234-1236

glossolalia, 116, 400, 746, 905, 946, 1177-1179

gnosis, 33, 34, 36, 37, 55, 69, 127, 149, 155, 190, 192, 193, 215, 233, 249, 255, 308, 309, 328, 400, 401, 403, 406, 411, 412, 469, 592, 640, 659, 701, 704, 710, 712, 785, 898, 899, 1011, 1025, 1095, 1150, 1176, 1187, 1190

Gnostics, Gnosticism, 25-33, 36, 37, 55, 69-72, 77, 82, 85, 86, 89, 127, 134, 135, 140, 146, 149, 155, 165, 169, 183, 190, 192-194, 203, 214, 215, 236-238, 255, 259, 261, 276, 284,

285, 286, 306, 308, 309, 316, 328, 351, 353, 375, 400-412, 469, 482, 523, 525, 526, 528, 529, 531, 546, 576, 578, 582, 584, 590-592, 610, 611, 615, 617, 626, 638, 639, 640, 657, 659, 665-667, 704, 706, 707, 709, 716, 722, 730, 777, 784, 785, 798, 803, 822, 862, 866, 898-900, 912, 914, 925, 928, 931, 934, 956, 959, 961, 981, 982, 987, 1011, 1016, 1018-1020, 1025, 1036, 1077, 1078, 1089, 1095, 1106, 1112, 1116, 1122, 1146, 1148-1150, 1152, 1176, 1187, 1190, 1212, 1219, 1232

God fearers, 116, 146

God's right hand, 69, 95-101, 162, 335, 360-362, 430, 440, 459, 671, 958, 1016, 1017, 1123

God's will, 62, 173, 231, 276, 350, 363, 368, 442, 487, 549, 558, 559, 644, 663, 695, 716, 737, 766, 785, 791, 824, 950, 958, 962, 985, 986, 1038, 1195, 1223

gods, 147, 165, 192, 298, 304, 355, 358, 413, 414, 416, 430, 436, 501, 502, 528, 529, 602, 668, 701, 734, 761, 772, 773, 775, 785, 886, 910, 911, 919, 920, 961, 990, 994, 1007-1009, 1014, 1029, 1033, 1063, 1082, 1102, 1108, 1126, 1140, 1147, 1148, 1158, 1159, 1196, 1199, 1207

goodness of God, 425

Gospel of Peter, 135, 183, 306-308, 433, 679, 683, 927-929, 977, 979, 981, 983, 1005, 1019, 1234

Gospel of Thomas, 181, 183, 236, 407, 408, 410, 411, 433, 576, 584, 626, 629, 638, 722, 764, 981, 987, 1005, 1019, 1089, 1175-1177, 1200, 1213

Gospels, 7, 13, 15, 16, 22, 35, 68, 69, 86, 87, 91, 113, 119, 122, 124, 134-137, 139, 143, 152, 161, 165, 173, 180, 187, 188, 191, 194, 197, 206, 217, 218, 227, 235, 236, 256, 259, 265, 278, 302, 306, 314, 316, 317, 320, 331-334, 347, 353, 357, 378, 380, 382, 384-388, 392, 408-412, 433, 465, 467-469, 477, 479-481, 502, 503, 535, 536, 540-543, 554-556, 565, 566, 568-572, 574-579, 581, 608, 611, 621, 626, 629, 635, 638, 644, 657, 663, 665, 667, 668, 674, 686, 692, 700,

707, 708, 711, 712, 722,
723, 746, 749, 752, 759,
762, 770, 771, 792, 797,
801-803, 808, 823, 834,
856, 857, 861, 877, 904,
913, 914, 921, 922, 927-
929, 937, 948, 952, 968,
970, 977, 981, 996, 1001,
1002, 1006, 1020-1022,
1033, 1036, 1051, 1075,
1088-1090, 1117, 1143,
1144, 1161-1165, 1172,
1173, 1175-1177, 1181,
1199, 1200, 1202, 1229
gossip, 1135, 1221
government, 80, 82, 89, 106,
110, 129, 204, 219, 221,
222, 224, 230, 232, 233,
267, 291, 301, 306, 311,
312, 317, 323, 328, 350,
352, 366, 461, 473, 517,
533, 656, 661, 739, 746,
760, 775, 882, 891, 892,
908, 912, 930, 934, 950,
961, 963, 1009, 1059,
1062, 1063, 1067, 1087,
1093, 1106, 1110, 1135,
1193, 1233
governor, 185, 187, 230,
288, 289, 321, 512, 526,
599, 752, 909, 910, 1099
grace, 5, 45, 74, 89, 91, 107,
116, 120-122, 124, 145,
155, 161, 179, 202, 228,
244, 246, 247, 258, 262,
275, 278, 280, 285, 287,
311, 313, 318, 321, 365,
367, 370, 371, 379, 382,
383, 398, 417, 424, 425,
429-435, 447, 450, 498,
499, 520, 537, 538, 559,
584, 602, 603, 618, 621,
623, 647, 649-651, 660,
663, 666, 673, 688-690,
699, 716, 733-736, 775,
776, 797, 802, 822, 823,
828, 833, 837, 839, 845,
861, 867, 876, 888, 890,
896, 915, 918, 934, 938,
941, 944, 950, 953, 970,
994, 1003, 1013, 1021,
1039-1041, 1055, 1058,
1071, 1072, 1074, 1075,
1080, 1083, 1086, 1110,
1136, 1185, 1186, 1209,
1219, 1224, 1230, 1236,
1239
Greece, 71, 144, 147, 148,
194, 290, 391, 528, 753,
755, 764, 766, 772, 1006,
1007, 1011, 1043, 1215,
1218
Greeks, 34, 78, 126, 146,
147, 169, 185, 250, 289,
290, 295, 304, 320, 344,
386, 439, 475, 502, 580,
588, 611, 639, 704, 716,
721, 777, 795, 956, 961,
996, 1002, 1007, 1010,
1069, 1085, 1098, 1099,
1108, 1144, 1146, 1218
guests, 4, 209, 292, 435, 501,
502, 504, 506, 716, 792,

990, 1208
guilt, 112, 124, 241-243, 267,
270, 272-274, 276, 278,
281, 282, 285, 466, 491,
528, 543, 645, 714, 734,
909, 920, 991, 1043, 1053,
1087, 1123, 1126
Haggadah, 606, 732, 815,
1093
Halakah, 162, 226, 377, 412,
553, 606, 608, 815, 1093
hallelujah, 436, 524, 660,
662
hardness, of heart 42, 972,
1014
Hasmoneans, 290, 599, 1161
hatred, 42, 56, 90, 188, 230,
253, 282, 369, 377, 426,
592, 598, 600, 773, 819,
837, 912, 1035, 1047,
1080, 1123, 1184, 1193,
1135
Haustafel, 349-351, 436, 513,
520, 889, 890, 1117, 1158,
1206, 1212
head, 37, 39, 49, 52, 120,
122, 128, 181, 192, 292,
293, 308, 393, 426, 504,
505, 508, 512, 513, 518,
573, 647, 688, 714, 730,
853, 888, 908, 1005, 1008,
1020, 1021, 1033, 1078,
1092, 1105, 1127, 1206,
1208, 1210, 1227, 1232,
1236
healing, 1, 9, 20, 24, 48, 49,
52, 77, 78, 107, 115, 153,
164, 176, 209, 256, 322,
333, 356, 358, 368, 380,
381, 398, 416, 436-439,
491, 494, 503, 508, 513,
521, 533, 556, 559, 602,
631-633, 671, 689, 702,
746-752, 762, 786, 832,
930, 939, 942, 945, 991,
1006, 1009, 1010, 1013,
1034, 1073, 1076, 1095,
1117, 1118, 1136, 1137,
1140, 1144, 1148, 1152,
1181, 1206, 1220, 1228
heart, 5, 42, 43, 58, 64, 66,
88, 89, 98, 113, 115, 123,
154, 163, 228, 239-242,
246, 247, 259, 261-263,
274, 277, 311, 320, 363,
379, 415, 418, 433, 439,
449, 471, 480, 490, 500,
508, 525, 540, 568, 591,
596, 624, 629, 630, 645,
656, 659, 676, 677, 700,
702, 715, 736, 793-795,
797, 814, 816, 828, 879,
918, 972, 985, 986, 988,
1014, 1063, 1069, 1071,
1079, 1080, 1105, 1155,
1160, 1163-1165, 1185,
1192, 1193
heaven, 33, 36, 42, 44, 45,
47, 48, 56, 61-63, 65, 66,
68-70, 74, 95-101, 108,
112, 113, 119, 121, 123,
127, 128, 130-132, 153,
155, 156, 162-164, 169,

172, 196, 198, 201, 203,
209, 223, 230, 251-255,
258, 259, 274-276, 284,
325, 332, 343, 347, 352,
360, 362, 363, 396, 397,
400, 404, 413, 414, 418,
427, 431, 434, 435, 439-
443, 459, 460, 477, 492,
494, 502, 505, 509, 532,
543, 549, 557, 563, 564,
568, 570, 572, 591, 604,
610, 611, 625, 627, 630,
632, 634-638, 643, 644,
655, 656, 658, 666, 667,
669, 674, 677, 733, 739,
740, 756, 768, 776, 777,
779, 780, 796, 811, 817,
823, 841, 843, 851, 853,
854, 866, 870, 876, 898,
899, 903, 918, 921, 922,
940, 955-959, 969, 993,
997, 1002, 1006, 1016-
1018, 1020, 1021, 1028,
1030, 1031, 1033, 1037,
1040, 1052, 1082, 1094,
1095, 1097, 1105, 1112,
1113, 1118, 1154-1156,
1166, 1176, 1181, 1183,
1185, 1188, 1224, 1227,
1231, 1234, 1235, 1240
heavenly ascent, 63, 443, 704
heavenly beings, 44, 46,
108, 141, 215, 427, 428,
442, 443, 457, 731, 1081,
1112, 1122
heavenly Jerusalem, 36, 57,
80, 108, 198, 277, 563-565,
633, 862, 1016, 1126,
1127, 1209, 1210
heavenly places, 44, 741,
1227
Hebrew, 5, 32, 33, 35, 39,
60, 67, 114, 128, 132, 138,
152, 163, 166, 167, 186,
196, 204, 246, 252, 286,
313, 315, 316, 318, 335,
346, 347, 374, 382, 387,
401, 402, 406, 439, 440,
445, 462-467, 478, 481,
485, 487, 489, 490, 500,
502, 508, 509, 534, 543,
584, 585, 606, 609, 611,
614, 622, 643, 661-663,
676, 729, 732, 733, 736,
759, 782, 814, 815, 818,
820, 828, 830, 834-836,
838, 840, 842, 851, 852,
854, 894, 909, 932, 953,
971, 974, 980, 988, 990,
991, 997, 1002, 1004,
1032, 1034, 1077, 1082,
1091, 1099, 1110, 1111,
1117, 1118, 1125-1128,
1152, 1160, 1169, 1184,
1195, 1196, 1201, 1207,
1209, 1210, 1217, 1232
heir, 108, 247, 252, 318,
334, 479, 621, 969
hell, 6, 67, 69, 164, 177, 279,
347, 459-462, 610, 623,
625, 657, 777, 988, 1034,
1081, 1092, 1119, 1234,
1241

Hellenistic Christianity, 444,
462, 463, 468, 520, 587,
880, 956, 994, 1148
Hellenistic Judaism, 2, 68,
85, 102, 230, 232, 287,
403, 412, 440, 444, 445,
465, 515, 582, 943, 957,
1012, 1051, 1089, 1148,
1150, 1159
Hellenists, 23, 85, 149, 161,
462-465, 467, 468, 580,
587, 687, 931, 956, 1076,
1077, 1094, 1104, 1125
heresy, 25, 30, 33, 52, 101,
137, 147, 165, 167, 176,
183, 190, 234, 237, 257,
302, 304, 307, 312, 313,
315, 316, 402, 403, 412,
469, 476, 501, 533, 580,
586, 587, 595, 615, 619,
620, 705, 707, 708, 711,
716, 866, 1019, 1052,
1079, 1083, 1146, 1150,
1199, 1200, 1220, 1237,
1238
hermeneutics, 18, 56, 126,
237, 249, 287, 306, 340,
413, 416, 458, 471-474,
477-480, 482-484, 511,
524, 527, 535, 541, 620,
654, 678, 712, 791, 792,
798, 802, 804, 805, 808,
809, 811, 812, 815, 820,
824, 825, 840, 841, 842,
844, 850, 856, 874, 923,
938, 955, 976, 1001, 1042,
1049, 1103, 1111, 1132,
1134
Hermes, 414, 416, 701, 751,
752, 938, 1008, 1011, 1148
Hermogenes, 8, 142
Herods, 45, 50, 53, 77, 185,
186, 193, 273, 325, 467,
510, 599, 718, 747, 749,
750, 757, 762, 764, 894,
907, 928, 932, 1008, 1060,
1061, 1076, 1161
Herodians, 1161, 1221
Hierapolis, 52, 146, 189-
191, 575, 758, 765, 916,
931, 1219
high priest, 3, 35, 74, 79, 98-
100, 107, 108, 121, 154,
156, 172, 187, 198, 231,
248, 261, 274-278, 317,
319, 359, 361, 363, 417-
419, 431, 440, 443, 452,
455, 457, 467, 485, 498,
509, 543, 547, 567, 608,
632, 633, 655, 731, 734,
833, 844, 845, 849, 850,
861, 878, 944, 958, 963,
964, 966, 998, 999, 1016,
1022, 1070, 1072, 1073,
1096, 1110, 1123, 1156,
1160, 1161, 1163, 1165,
1167, 1185, 1191, 1236
Hillel, 186, 607, 608, 844,
990, 1161, 1162
Hippolytus, 52, 104, 113,
118-124, 164, 259, 303,
307, 314, 375, 404, 406,
407, 456, 584, 585, 590,

690, 710, 732, 775, 947, 1037, 1128, 1150, 1175, 1224

historical Jesus, 76, 79, 357, 675, 708, 710-712, 742, 797, 799, 800, 802, 803, 812, 872, 1175, 1177

history of religions, 625, 792, 797-799, 807, 1111, 1130

holiness, 88, 201, 297, 349, 350, 352, 356, 389, 419, 422-425, 430, 441, 442, 446, 457, 478, 485-488, 490, 498, 507, 510, 541, 560, 606, 634, 642, 662, 663, 771, 817, 822, 838, 895, 941, 950, 988, 989, 996, 1013, 1014, 1038, 1044, 1050, 1055, 1090, 1105, 1107, 1118, 1121, 1122, 1141, 1193, 1195

holy city, 108, 112, 151, 218, 229, 457, 467, 489, 537, 561-565, 583, 585, 587, 636, 643, 854, 1037, 1165, 1227, 1242

holy day, 587, 685

Holy Spirit, 11, 13, 14, 17-19, 21, 37, 42, 44, 47, 49, 73, 76, 78, 79, 88, 97, 101, 105-107, 113-117, 120-124, 128, 144-146, 161, 162, 164, 165, 174, 181, 195, 196, 207, 220, 222, 224, 225, 227, 243, 244, 247, 251, 258-260, 272, 303, 317, 330-334, 342, 343, 346, 348, 357, 360, 376, 381, 390, 391, 417, 420, 430, 437, 465, 470, 479, 482, 488-499, 508, 520, 536, 562, 589, 593, 598, 603, 626, 630-632, 634, 636, 637, 639, 647, 659, 669, 722, 741-743, 746, 749, 750, 757, 761, 767, 768, 777, 789, 791, 793, 795, 811, 825, 826, 828, 830, 842, 854, 859, 878, 884, 902-904, 906, 915, 930, 931, 938-942, 944, 946, 948, 950, 951, 953, 960, 968, 970-973, 975-978, 985, 990, 994, 995, 997, 1020, 1021, 1022, 1026, 1051, 1071, 1072, 1076, 1079, 1094, 1095, 1117, 1119-1122, 1125, 1155, 1156, 1166, 1174, 1177-1179, 1185, 1193, 1194, 1198, 1199, 1202, 1204, 1205, 1207, 1218, 1227, 1237, 1239

homily, 72, 81, 84, 104, 119, 124, 180, 191, 237, 256, 285, 302-304, 315, 367, 450-454, 456, 469, 475, 499, 547, 582, 584, 651, 653, 692, 710, 731-733, 764, 825, 845, 861, 876, 905, 924, 975, 1014, 1042, 1043, 1092, 1213, 1230,

1241

homosexuality, 323, 499, 710, 711, 1089, 1090

honor, 14, 28, 48, 49, 53, 68, 82, 95, 98-100, 109, 159, 167, 170, 174, 175, 184, 201, 225, 231, 267, 300, 324, 343, 344, 350, 359, 361-363, 370-372, 397, 412, 428, 438, 442, 458, 468, 501, 504, 506, 518, 529, 535, 540, 570, 608, 616, 620, 649, 678, 695, 697, 714, 721, 744, 745, 751, 782, 785, 799, 817, 826, 873, 874, 893, 917, 919, 920, 952, 970, 984, 990, 994, 1008, 1009, 1011, 1039, 1040, 1049, 1054, 1071, 1076, 1082, 1098-1101, 1104-1106, 1122, 1141, 1158, 1164, 1170, 1196, 1200, 1212

hope, 10, 14, 21, 51, 59, 61, 64, 74, 88, 90, 100, 102, 111, 117, 148, 163, 165, 168, 175, 176, 185, 199, 207, 211, 213, 216, 229, 232, 248, 252, 265, 276, 279, 285, 310, 311, 327, 330-332, 334, 335, 337, 343, 345, 354, 358, 360-363, 365, 367, 368, 370, 375, 389, 392, 396, 397, 399, 411, 413, 419, 439, 441, 442, 445, 447, 451, 453, 480, 482, 489, 496, 499-501, 515, 517, 525, 536, 537, 550, 557, 561, 564, 565, 604, 609, 610, 621-623, 651, 656, 662, 663, 671, 699, 725, 741, 751, 768, 775-777, 793, 795, 823-826, 839, 849, 856, 858-860, 862-866, 868, 871, 873-875, 879, 880, 888, 889, 917, 920, 925, 926, 933, 935, 952-954, 969, 970, 992, 1003, 1004, 1009, 1016, 1017, 1020, 1025, 1038, 1039, 1041, 1045, 1058, 1073, 1080, 1084, 1100, 1107, 1109, 1115, 1127, 1135, 1137-1140, 1166, 1182, 1192, 1210, 1223, 1226, 1227, 1234, 1236

hospitality, 4, 6, 28, 41, 80, 81, 93, 109, 245, 301, 350-352, 356, 369, 373, 374, 377, 378, 424, 435, 444, 501-508, 513, 533, 553, 595, 743-745, 759, 769, 816, 829, 895, 918, 931, 990, 1033, 1046, 1047, 1051-1053, 1057, 1058, 1062, 1066, 1067, 1071, 1087, 1089, 1104, 1111, 1129, 1142, 1143, 1156, 1206, 1216-1220, 1222

house churches, 28, 92, 94, 95, 147, 148, 150, 197, 200, 201, 221-223, 222-

226, 234, 355, 356, 358, 376, 443, 444, 446, 447, 449, 453, 476, 505, 507, 508, 512, 514, 596, 696, 755, 761, 764, 769, 911, 1066, 1067, 1100-1102, 1206, 1213, 1216, 1217, 1219, 1220

house of God, 507-511

household, 4, 14, 34, 38, 41, 79, 93, 95, 116, 123, 148, 201, 219, 220, 230, 233, 243, 244, 349, 352, 354, 356, 357, 360, 370, 371, 373, 374, 378, 436, 445, 447, 476, 478, 479, 493, 494, 503-509, 511-520, 523, 534, 628, 652, 696, 714, 760, 768, 791, 792, 806, 879, 880, 882, 889, 918-920, 922, 952, 990, 992, 1011, 1038, 1045, 1060, 1064, 1092, 1099-1102, 1105-1108, 1110, 1115-1117, 1124, 1136, 1145, 1158, 1159, 1170, 1181, 1191, 1194, 1195, 1202, 1206-1209, 1211-1215, 1220

household codes, 4, 201, 349, 352, 371, 436, 478, 479, 511, 513-519, 628, 652, 768, 806, 882, 889, 918, 922, 952, 1092, 1100, 1101, 1106, 1107, 1110, 1117, 1136, 1158, 1159, 1181, 1191, 1194, 1202, 1206-1209, 1211-1214

household of God, 34, 507, 513, 880, 1106, 1107, 1215

humility, 18, 20, 39, 43, 107, 262, 269, 278, 285, 361, 372, 421, 424, 481, 513, 518, 520, 534, 535, 735, 781, 830, 837, 880, 920, 961-963, 1014, 1051, 1081, 1191, 1194, 1211-1213

husbands, 4, 350, 356, 371, 378, 435, 504, 514, 517, 518, 534, 538, 639, 640, 699, 714, 715, 730, 743, 762, 764, 765, 768, 772, 896, 918, 946, 1100, 1107, 1108, 1117, 1136, 1158, 1186, 1207-1209, 1211, 1213, 1217, 1218, 1221

Hymenaeus, 31, 305

hymns, 69, 71, 72, 99, 102, 118, 124, 163, 181, 279, 348, 397-399, 406, 407, 409, 414, 417, 428, 478, 518, 520-527, 566, 627, 628, 634, 659-661, 664, 684, 691, 733, 783, 823, 836, 864, 888, 943, 947, 948, 952, 957, 958, 961, 964, 997, 1016, 1027, 1047, 1104, 1115, 1126, 1151, 1152, 1201, 1202, 1224-1228, 1230-1238

Iconium, 137, 222, 273, 758, 1144

idols, 26, 148, 162, 232, 354,

360, 377, 379, 383, 414, 417, 441, 528-530, 627, 634, 648, 693, 716, 778, 781, 990, 994, 1012, 1069, 1128, 1149, 1163, 1185, 1219

idolatry, 26, 40, 42, 43, 70, 126, 133, 167, 168, 232, 349, 360, 377, 379, 389, 441, 528-530, 628, 636, 642, 649, 698, 703, 704, 762, 770, 819, 836, 886, 888, 917, 988, 990, 994, 995, 1011, 1012, 1048, 1078, 1079, 1088, 1119, 1122, 1126, 1147, 1183, 1192, 1194, 1196, 1210, 1217, 1229

Ignatius of Antioch, 25, 32, 34, 55, 102, 120, 169, 204, 263, 462, 520, 525, 530, 533, 657, 667, 676, 678, 685, 686, 691, 693, 721, 777, 795, 882, 938, 1048, 1050, 1100, 1109, 1111, 1114, 1153, 1230

illness, 49, 381, 382, 436-438, 533, 751, 945, 1072, 1095, 1140

Illyricum, 755, 757

image of Christ, 177, 284, 794, 869

image of God, 372, 415, 422, 635, 990, 1091

imitate, imitation, 107, 108, 174, 273, 280, 281, 284, 285, 294, 304, 326, 352, 376, 422, 424, 532-535, 541, 551, 691, 710, 913, 914, 937, 962, 1013, 1049, 1101, 1140, 1209, 1232

imitation of Christ, 533-535, 914

immortality, 49, 70, 102, 181, 341-343, 347, 367, 376, 402, 461, 462, 535, 624, 656-658, 690, 691, 703, 721, 730, 731, 775-777, 986, 987, 1003, 1019, 1020, 1025, 1130, 1189, 1231

imperial cult, 288, 324, 325, 353, 483, 530, 535, 634, 716, 908, 1006, 1008, 1009, 1011, 1028, 1029, 1196, 1209, 1211

impurity, 233, 376, 379, 488, 535, 637, 888, 988, 989, 995, 996, 1014, 1095, 1105, 1160, 1163, 1172, 1188, 1193, 1194

in Christ, 4-6, 18, 21, 37, 38, 42, 115-118, 123, 155, 159, 162, 168, 178, 179, 183, 195, 202, 203, 211, 212, 216, 217, 220, 223, 242, 259, 273, 280, 285, 318, 321, 328, 332, 341, 342, 351, 364, 365, 367, 373, 380, 431-434, 438, 442, 454, 476, 488, 498-500, 503, 508, 513, 517, 518, 521, 526, 527, 543, 555,

579, 584, 585, 594, 597, 619, 623, 626, 637, 642, 684, 687, 694, 697, 733, 735, 738, 776, 778, 792, 793, 825, 867, 873, 874, 878, 880, 899, 920, 933, 934, 950, 951, 971, 1017, 1018, 1022, 1035, 1038, 1046, 1056, 1057, 1071, 1097, 1122, 1124, 1140, 1155, 1166, 1167, 1180, 1204, 1226, 1231, 1236, 1237

in God, 2, 38, 40, 41, 64, 122, 164, 178, 238, 239, 259, 327, 364-366, 368, 370, 399, 421, 495, 499, 500, 552, 557, 558, 592, 593, 600-602, 696, 736, 793, 795, 879, 940, 945, 994, 1001, 1013, 1021, 1038, 1039, 1110, 1167, 1169, 1202

Incarnation, 52, 55, 69, 100, 101, 155, 181, 182, 259, 261-263, 274, 281, 283, 285, 307, 361, 362, 375, 399, 478, 482, 532, 536, 567, 586, 587, 590-592, 594, 637, 639, 665, 667, 677, 691, 707, 777, 784, 803, 845, 849, 864, 933, 939, 954, 958-961, 987, 1023, 1074, 1112-1115, 1152, 1224, 1236

incest, 322, 712, 911

inheritance, 5, 6, 206, 215, 249, 262, 280, 281, 335, 339, 359, 439, 440, 549, 556, 642, 822, 823, 888, 921, 969, 988, 995, 1017, 1022, 1039, 1040, 1096, 1105, 1155, 1198, 1209

injustice, 278, 327, 328, 348, 473, 943, 1044, 1139, 1190

inner being, inner person, 985, 986

inspired utterances, 906, 1119, 1194

institution, institutionaliza-tion, 28, 107, 108, 137, 145, 204, 220, 223-226, 230, 234, 268-271, 292, 310, 311, 325, 424, 501, 513, 514, 517, 530, 686, 742, 756, 762, 791, 793, 881, 893, 899, 927, 950, 976, 1014, 1071, 1099, 1141, 1142, 1144, 1145, 1158, 1165, 1235, 1106

intercession, 39, 95, 99, 131, 360, 536, 541, 646, 689, 746, 776, 779, 942-945, 1013, 1053, 1221

intermediate state, 97, 286, 1016-1018

intertextuality, 465, 471, 479, 483, 536, 541, 553, 559, 671, 826, 834, 841, 850, 852, 854, 904, 1187

introspective conscience, 714, 1058

irony, 269, 383, 446, 686,

737, 787, 788, 790, 791, 915, 1015, 1042, 1062, 1139, 1145

Isaac, 1, 3, 4, 6, 38, 39, 41-44, 130, 209, 246, 398, 415, 419, 458, 502, 509, 537, 539, 542, 584, 709, 816, 837, 965, 1056, 1099, 1110, 1208

Isaiah, 1, 15, 18, 47, 49, 52, 69, 70, 102, 115, 133, 155, 174, 180, 183, 199, 204, 209, 210, 232, 236, 251, 256, 269, 271-272, 275, 279-281, 284, 313, 326, 331, 346, 386, 396, 397, 414, 420, 422, 441, 442, 461, 479, 481, 487, 491, 497, 499, 523, 524, 537-539, 562, 567, 569, 574, 606, 641, 642, 662, 663, 666, 671, 673, 674, 737, 740, 751, 753, 755, 791, 817, 824, 827-832, 837-839, 841, 844, 849, 852-854, 861, 864, 886, 894, 904, 930, 936, 962, 979, 980, 997, 1003, 1006, 1017, 1019, 1026, 1033, 1055, 1085, 1092, 1096, 1120, 1126-1128, 1143, 1169, 1180, 1181, 1183, 1211, 1236, 1239

Israel of God, 205, 218, 344, 488

Israelite, 8, 39, 40, 130, 157, 162, 168, 204, 208, 211, 217, 333, 434, 543, 824, 963, 978, 989, 1076, 1090, 1208

Israelites, 36, 39-41, 43, 132, 133, 161, 172, 204, 207, 211, 214, 217, 388, 389, 459, 467, 502, 509, 529, 610, 853, 989, 990, 1002, 1085, 1097, 1099, 1141, 1162, 1239

Jacob, 1, 2, 38-43, 45, 48, 129, 157, 203, 204, 209, 216, 246, 249, 398, 413, 415, 419, 438, 466, 502, 509, 537, 539, 584, 605, 611, 817, 819, 828, 829, 963, 965, 1099, 1110

James the Just, 187, 189, 190, 194, 546-548, 561, 908

jealousy, 42, 43, 168, 234, 327, 421, 557, 714, 829, 837, 898, 1138, 1144, 1212

Jerusalem apostles, 78, 145, 463, 756, 764, 767, 901

Jerusalem council, 10, 106, 145, 377, 383, 432, 434, 467, 529, 546, 581, 616, 903, 971, 1217

Jesus and Paul, 159, 317, 374, 394, 431, 468, 527, 678, 707, 733, 774, 800, 882, 1038, 1123, 1125

Jesus tradition, traditions, 86, 87, 91, 155, 173, 180, 227, 235, 236, 241, 302, 397, 411, 421, 536, 554,

565-578, 579, 588, 633, 643, 644, 674, 781, 981, 1136, 1176, 1177, 1179

Jew, 1, 14, 15, 19-21, 55, 113, 126, 164, 167, 169, 176, 192, 199, 203, 208, 218, 223, 295, 296, 299, 320, 322, 377, 378, 386, 434, 465, 508, 542, 546, 580, 584, 608, 647, 760, 764, 884, 888-890, 924, 928, 994, 1012, 1072, 1076, 1106, 1110, 1122, 1217, 1218

Jew and Gentile/Greek, 14, 15, 19, 20, 55, 113, 218, 299, 434, 542, 546, 888, 889, 1012

Jewish Christianity, 24, 25, 33, 48, 54, 69, 83, 85, 136, 145, 151, 160, 168, 169, 184, 192, 204, 228-230, 299, 315, 316, 321, 344, 378, 379, 385, 386, 388, 430, 454, 457, 462, 465, 468, 504, 529, 532, 546, 555, 559, 565, 579-587, 619, 645, 648, 649, 667, 673, 678, 683, 712, 722, 728, 761, 792, 901, 902, 926, 984, 993, 1000, 1005, 1006, 1058, 1077, 1093, 1148, 1152, 1165, 1195, 1227-1229

Jewish exegesis, interpreta-tion, 272, 339, 356, 607, 834, 835, 838

Jewish mission, 223, 389

Jewish Revolt, Jewish War, 145, 165, 184-186, 188, 189, 194, 213, 228, 229, 288, 290, 323, 387, 585, 587, 599, 600, 706, 900, 902, 1034, 1076, 1077, 1085

Johannine commu-nity/school, 26-28, 33, 51, 155, 166, 175, 587, 590, 596, 598, 868, 880, 1037, 1046, 1055, 1079, 1120, 1149

John Mark, 35, 92, 190, 743, 756, 758, 765, 1219

Joseph the Patriarch, 599

Josephus, 1-4, 7, 12, 20, 24, 34, 39, 41, 42, 53, 54, 185-187, 194, 221, 226, 231, 241, 243, 287-295, 297, 298, 321, 324, 389, 432, 445, 448, 467, 492, 528, 533, 599, 600, 605, 609, 611, 614, 641, 715, 731, 775, 778-780, 819, 857, 895, 901-903, 908, 911, 930, 932, 934, 990, 999, 1008, 1060, 1061, 1066, 1091, 1142, 1152, 1160-1164, 1206, 1207, 1214

joy, 48, 70, 174, 240, 328, 349, 351, 356, 423, 440, 477, 494, 496, 497, 549, 563, 600-605, 632, 650, 652-654, 662, 663, 687,

695, 723, 763, 821, 864, 867, 990, 1031, 1039, 1062, 1136, 1139, 1160, 1167, 1178, 1205, 1227, 1228

judaizers, 17, 31, 77, 169, 192, 213, 215, 228, 367, 581, 583-586, 593, 705, 757, 1110

Judea, 11, 14, 114, 166, 193, 194, 231, 251, 290, 294, 297, 321-323, 387, 388, 467, 496, 562, 599, 611, 631, 752, 755, 756, 759, 762, 764, 766, 857, 894, 900, 901, 903, 907, 911, 913, 931, 932, 1059-1061, 1076, 1077, 1123, 1150, 1151, 1183, 1204, 1206

judge, 30, 39, 46, 76, 88, 100, 101, 158, 164, 166, 171, 173, 178, 180, 210, 251, 253, 259, 264, 265, 272, 281, 318, 320, 327, 329, 334, 336-338, 349, 359, 360, 363, 368, 374, 392, 415, 416, 419, 422, 425, 427, 429, 472, 486, 513, 556, 557, 559, 563, 573, 574, 600, 609, 621, 623, 630, 631, 634, 719, 734, 736, 742, 766, 778, 784, 818, 859, 861, 862, 863, 864, 869, 887, 908, 920, 926, 939, 973, 1030, 1054, 1055, 1073, 1097, 1102, 1111, 1137, 1139, 1206, 1207, 1215, 1239, 1241

Junia, 762, 765

Jupiter, 294, 322, 323, 963, 1147

justice, 132, 230, 233, 351, 360, 416, 441, 442, 470, 486, 516, 519, 541, 558, 582, 621, 623, 624, 688, 734, 739, 741, 810, 818, 915, 927, 1014, 1037, 1050, 1107, 1136, 1139-1142, 1158, 1190, 1196, 1198, 1215

justification, 4, 5, 12, 88, 89, 115, 124, 143, 276, 312, 349, 351, 365, 382, 383, 390, 420, 423, 491, 555, 585, 592, 624, 625, 645, 647, 681, 792, 795, 823, 915, 950, 969, 989, 1003, 1036, 1045, 1046, 1053-1058, 1072, 1149

Justus, 93, 378, 765, 1005

kerygma, 11, 96, 98, 99, 101, 118, 160, 258, 259, 301, 302, 311, 312, 357, 359, 420, 433, 523, 527, 536, 547, 560, 620, 626-629, 632, 655, 667, 757, 770, 776, 798, 800-803, 812, 850, 874, 905, 948, 956, 1023, 1084, 1148, 1159

king of kings, 362, 672, 1035

kingdom of Christ, 36, 156,

636, 637, 776, 1030, 1031, 1037

kingdom of God, 6, 47, 50, 104, 114, 163, 197, 207, 232, 251, 273, 284, 331, 332, 339, 343, 348, 353, 432, 460, 461, 476, 502, 574, 575, 621, 629-638, 695, 718, 736, 739, 741, 753, 786, 795, 803, 811, 857, 859, 860, 872, 879, 915, 930, 946, 1004, 1009, 1021, 1025, 1030, 1031, 1035, 1036, 1095, 1118, 1121, 1180, 1189, 1193, 1199, 1204, 1224

knowledge, 31, 33, 36, 37, 39, 57, 58, 74, 85-87, 102, 108, 109, 113, 125, 150, 154, 157, 158, 166, 171, 181, 193, 232, 238, 241, 243, 277, 282, 304, 307, 333, 351, 367, 370, 381, 400-402, 404, 408-411, 425, 426, 441, 442, 444, 454, 471, 472, 484, 490, 495, 507, 521, 531, 546, 554, 565-569, 571, 572, 576, 577, 579, 591, 592, 594, 603, 618, 638-640, 642, 653, 670, 675, 690, 703, 705, 709-711, 726, 727, 748, 758, 760, 777, 782, 789, 808, 809, 819, 831, 850, 882, 890, 893, 896, 901, 914, 916, 932-934, 938, 939, 949, 954, 973, 983, 990, 1006, 1010, 1012, 1015, 1016, 1025, 1026, 1032-1034, 1078, 1080, 1083, 1088, 1098, 1102, 1125, 1131-1133, 1141, 1173, 1185-1187, 1192, 1193, 1201-1203, 1205, 1217-1219, 1221, 1239

koinonia, 22, 155, 374, 498, 640, 1228

lamb, 46, 52, 100, 104, 108, 119, 128, 131, 158, 174, 177, 183, 200, 201, 261, 262, 266, 280, 283, 284, 286, 329, 348, 362, 393, 426-428, 438, 441, 442, 477, 503, 524-526, 539, 635-637, 641, 642, 659, 672, 678, 690, 720, 731, 732, 744, 770, 780, 810, 851, 869-871, 874-876, 897, 920, 942, 947, 954, 955, 962, 991, 1002, 1024, 1030-1032, 1034, 1035, 1037, 1047, 1070-1072, 1074, 1080, 1088, 1092, 1093, 1120, 1122, 1156, 1164, 1186, 1197, 1203, 1223, 1239

Lamb of God, 642, 690, 870, 1032, 1164

lament, 112, 665, 1084, 1138

land, 2, 3, 5, 14, 15, 38-42, 112, 128, 132, 161, 162, 206, 211, 218, 246, 247,

250, 291, 297-300, 321, 335, 341, 355, 385, 387-390, 480, 502, 517, 549, 550, 557, 561, 587, 606, 634, 635, 638, 642-644, 647, 727, 728, 732, 736, 751, 753, 760, 761, 770, 778, 781, 798, 854, 900, 956, 968, 988-990, 1001, 1006, 1038, 1060, 1061, 1063, 1069, 1077, 1129, 1146, 1155, 1160, 1164, 1183, 1227

Laodicea, 49, 136, 142, 146, 329, 695, 765, 960, 1052, 1196

last days, 12, 29, 50, 51, 52, 80, 101, 113, 214, 251, 253, 277, 334, 335, 336, 341, 345, 366, 389, 509, 559, 622, 624, 639, 644, 845, 881, 959, 960, 998, 1031, 1045, 1071, 1200, 1230

Last Supper, 269, 271, 502, 588, 680, 686-688, 694, 780, 793, 794, 1105, 1229

law of Christ, 241

lawlessness, 29, 43, 51, 52, 74, 75, 79, 113, 168, 241, 336, 352, 649, 821, 823, 864, 917, 1003, 1057, 1058, 1078, 1083, 1192, 1194

leaven, 638, 1110

lectionaries, 257, 609, 1143, 1146

legalism, 383, 384, 463

legend, 41, 52, 71, 72, 77, 150, 233, 235, 257, 298, 482, 546, 643, 748, 765, 766, 779, 814, 867, 893, 1004, 1006, 1063, 1146, 1151, 1175, 1208, 1222

letter forms, 330, 474, 475, 483, 612, 649-653, 915, 952, 955, 971, 1049

Letter of Peter to Philip, 72, 408, 409, 649, 931

letter writing, 484, 654, 1159

Levites, 3, 42, 44, 50, 100, 201, 264, 389, 396, 439, 539, 575, 603, 608, 730, 731, 816, 965, 988, 1105, 1191

liberation, 2, 71, 264, 266, 348, 382, 384, 473, 474, 558, 606, 645, 804, 931, 950, 1001, 1089, 1099, 1101

liberty, 352, 382-384, 463, 529, 547, 551, 645, 655, 1101, 1172

light and darkness, 6, 264, 590, 657, 659, 817, 1193

light of the world, 659, 752, 753

Linus, 1216

literary criticism, 484, 787, 788, 792, 929, 1041, 1042, 1132

liturgical elements, 1, 37, 118, 119, 124, 129, 174,

256, 259, 309, 348, 362, 395, 396, 407, 436, 441, 478, 486, 524, 526, 627, 651, 654, 659, 662-664, 672, 678, 690, 693, 705, 917, 947, 948, 952, 1016, 1027, 1037, 1171, 1224, 1225, 1237

liturgical tradition, 181, 666, 689, 1016

liturgy, 46, 85, 118, 119, 124, 125, 132, 143, 167, 179, 183, 191, 204, 226, 228, 256, 259, 301, 370, 372, 374, 379, 388, 399, 430, 440, 456-458, 526, 527, 530, 587, 605, 606, 609, 652, 663-665, 667, 681, 685, 689, 693, 694, 707, 710, 733, 816, 832, 876, 882, 917, 923, 947, 948, 956, 976, 980, 1027, 1037, 1038, 1072, 1143, 1145, 1156, 1165, 1224, 1225, 1228, 1230, 1232, 1236-1238

Logos christology, 158, 183, 665, 666, 678, 933, 934, 960, 961, 1023, 1113, 1203

Lord of lords, 672, 682

Lord's Day, 101, 121, 177, 179, 229, 314, 344, 348, 648, 649, 675, 678, 679, 682-686, 688, 690, 693, 1069, 1110, 1231, 1237

Lord's Supper, 34, 89, 92, 114, 116, 120, 124, 131, 179, 181, 257, 285, 286, 300, 301, 353, 356, 377, 379, 398, 593, 627, 664, 679-681, 685-687, 689, 690, 693, 694, 700, 737, 777, 780, 784, 870, 943, 1072, 1162, 1165, 1178, 1225, 1229, 1235, 1237, 1238

Lot, 41, 425, 459, 502, 505, 507, 533, 538, 589, 624, 694, 771, 804, 819, 830, 835, 839, 1039, 1059, 1065, 1135, 1167, 1236

love command, 535, 540, 700

love feast, 34, 124, 286, 353, 379, 664, 685, 686, 700, 1072, 1165, 1237

lust, 141, 375, 540, 700, 712-716, 838, 917, 962, 1089, 1126, 1129

Lycus valley, 765

Lydia, 93, 123, 146, 288, 378, 503, 512, 770, 1104, 1127, 1206, 1217, 1220

Lystra, 137, 222, 273, 414, 416, 627, 718, 758, 759, 764, 1008, 1143, 1144, 1148

Maccabees, 12, 54, 60, 67, 287, 290, 296, 326, 607, 611, 816, 938, 968, 978, 1002, 1141, 1151, 1191

Macedonia, 79, 148, 290, 630, 755, 757, 759, 764,

771, 1022, 1195, 1217

magic, 23, 45, 48, 49, 104, 114, 147, 167, 192, 275, 356, 358, 382, 416, 417, 436-438, 701-705, 711, 749-752, 786, 787, 793, 806, 910, 930, 931, 941, 945, 953, 1006, 1010, 1011, 1076, 1078, 1081, 1082, 1095, 1118, 1147-1149, 1150, 1192, 1231

magicians, 115, 192, 356, 698, 702, 703, 711, 712, 749, 751, 930, 1010, 1076, 1078, 1109, 1148

male, 37, 39, 113, 203, 226, 323, 362, 428, 429, 473, 504, 518, 930, 989, 991, 1029, 1064, 1089, 1090, 1092, 1101, 1105, 1106, 1145, 1206-1208, 1212-1214, 1218, 1219, 1221

Malta, 416, 502, 759

man of lawlessness, 51

manna, 466, 737, 1040

maranatha, 619, 660, 663, 690, 705, 874, 875, 1034, 1228

Marcion, Marcionism, 5, 6, 34, 91, 137, 143, 193, 194, 214, 215, 255, 307, 308, 313, 405, 411, 431-433, 469, 585, 648, 705-708, 893, 934, 936, 1089

marriage, 24, 31, 33, 131, 144, 203, 306, 315, 322, 350, 352, 421, 444, 514, 517, 518, 528, 538, 690, 700, 706, 712-715, 717, 722, 768, 784, 882, 889, 918, 931, 995, 1004, 1006, 1071, 1088-1090, 1115, 1208, 1212, 1214, 1215, 1221

martyrdom, 32, 37, 47, 52, 54, 69, 70, 72, 81, 83, 84, 87, 89, 119, 130, 147, 156, 182, 187, 189, 191, 192, 201, 214, 225, 231, 237, 262, 263, 269, 281, 284, 285, 308, 320, 327, 329, 330, 339, 358, 359, 430, 446, 449, 460, 483, 498, 525, 532-534, 540, 600, 603, 605, 636, 637, 653, 654, 656, 657, 699, 707, 717-722, 736, 739, 740, 743, 750, 755-757, 764, 770, 777, 787, 832, 859, 871, 881, 882, 892, 893, 897, 904, 908-914, 916, 919, 920, 934, 936-938, 941, 966, 975, 1004, 1005, 1014, 1018, 1024, 1037, 1040, 1041, 1048, 1049, 1063, 1067, 1072, 1080, 1094, 1109, 1110, 1112, 1121, 1123-1125, 1128, 1135, 1138, 1140, 1141, 1151, 1179, 1180, 1197, 1200, 1205, 1216, 1219

Martyrdom of Polycarp, 83, 84, 87, 89, 156, 191, 231, 320,

329, 430, 460, 637, 653,
654, 721, 722, 777, 787,
912, 934, 936, 937, 966,
975, 1014, 1024, 1049,
1112, 1121, 1128, 1179,
1197, 1205, 1216
martyrologies, 721, 912,
962, 1141
Mary, 92, 127, 164, 187, 192,
243, 244, 257, 259, 307,
405, 407, 410, 491, 525,
663, 722-724, 743, 765,
899, 962, 1004-1006, 1206,
1210, 1213, 1214, 1216,
1220, 1230
Matthean community, 146,
151, 206, 218, 223, 378,
386-388, 578, 581, 587,
675, 724-726, 728, 729,
1229
maturity, 52, 107, 131, 277,
327, 330, 356, 383, 407,
418, 421, 445, 446, 476,
595, 738, 793, 801, 864,
890, 1039, 1095, 1111,
1132, 1166-1168, 1170,
1218, 1221
meals, 20, 25, 29, 94, 95,
115, 116, 120, 132, 181,
221, 292, 298, 304, 352,
373, 377-379, 502, 526,
627, 663, 679, 681, 684,
686-691, 693, 697, 716,
744, 976, 989, 990, 993,
995, 996, 1007, 1104,
1105, 1111, 1160, 1162-
1164, 1228-1231, 1235
mediator, 108, 172, 181,
210, 217, 246, 248, 249,
272, 275, 277, 360, 362,
396, 418, 469, 563, 665,
891, 925, 1096, 1131,
1226, 1230
mediators, 29, 198, 234,
426, 445, 701, 998, 1058
meekness, 41, 278, 279, 281,
780, 781, 827, 962, 963,
1212
Melchizedek, 3, 36, 44-48,
70, 98, 108, 130, 172, 209,
248, 346, 360, 408, 410,
413, 453, 455, 457, 537,
632, 729-731, 738, 849,
850, 878, 964-967, 997-
1000, 1043, 1050, 1070,
1073, 1113, 1204
Melito of Sardis, 91, 190,
679, 731, 733, 876, 1019,
1048
mercy, 47, 75, 103, 104, 155,
173, 175, 209, 211, 243,
244, 246, 274, 275, 320,
334, 337, 361, 396, 413,
425, 429, 430, 434, 435,
470, 488, 503, 550, 556-
558, 569, 572, 574, 596,
601, 624, 660, 696, 699,
733-737, 819, 837, 838,
863, 867, 894, 896, 962,
963, 1013-1015, 1107,
1156, 1185, 1193, 1194,
1223
mercy seat, 396

merit, 8, 207, 212, 368, 546,
558, 561, 643, 798, 1096,
1225
merkabah, 63
Messiah, 2, 14, 19, 20, 39,
42, 49-52, 69, 74, 108, 130,
144, 145, 150, 153, 155,
156, 159, 162, 165-167,
170, 171, 178, 181, 185,
192, 196, 215, 217, 218,
223, 239, 255, 256, 260,
261, 271-274, 317, 331-
332, 355, 356, 362, 375,
376, 385, 389, 392, 396,
423, 431, 479, 480, 521,
536, 539, 543, 580, 584,
586, 588, 598, 600, 602,
605, 606, 610, 611, 623,
626, 628, 631, 632, 635,
636, 641, 643, 645, 647,
669, 678, 680, 683, 706,
724, 725, 736, 742, 752,
754, 760, 762, 766, 772,
785, 824, 857, 860, 861,
864, 869, 894, 910, 932,
940, 956, 958, 960, 998,
1012, 1014, 1082, 1091,
1112, 1123, 1154, 1179-
1182, 1184, 1188, 1221,
1235
messiahs, messianism, 214,
605, 998, 999, 1000, 1179,
1199, 1200
messianic age, 626, 740,
860, 962, 1179
messianic suffering, 423,
1181
Michael, 44-47, 128, 144,
159, 226, 254, 372, 413,
638, 666, 678, 694, 698,
717, 729, 730, 778, 818,
835, 836, 839, 840, 867,
923, 937, 939, 965, 997,
998, 1037, 1078, 1160,
1181
midrash, 167, 398, 402, 419,
475, 480, 481, 510, 523,
547, 553, 559, 560, 582,
606, 608, 612, 613, 653,
670, 729, 736, 814-819,
834, 835, 837, 841-843,
849, 861, 895, 953, 980,
999, 1043, 1092, 1169
Miletus, 270, 566, 1199
military, 53, 65, 235, 288,
289, 298, 323, 348, 354,
385, 561, 635, 636, 760,
761, 897, 968, 970, 1007,
1040, 1059-1061, 1064,
1065, 1082, 1151
milk, 5, 117, 119, 121, 123,
181, 418, 445, 511, 736-
738, 793, 882, 1111, 1115,
1117, 1158, 1159, 1192
minister, 19, 114, 120-122,
258, 259, 507, 510, 614,
745, 1087
miracles, 23, 49, 52, 61, 71,
72, 128, 153, 192, 258,
298, 307, 356, 358, 398,
415, 436-438, 498, 530,
589, 630, 631, 643, 704,
710, 746-752, 760, 767,

771, 773, 801, 883, 892,
902, 903, 905, 930, 941,
951, 1008, 1010, 1011,
1076, 1093-1095, 1118,
1122, 1123, 1181, 1183,
1204
Mishnah, 130, 386, 605,
606, 608, 611, 752, 980,
991-992, 996, 1142, 1146,
1161, 1191, 1215
mission, 13-15, 17-24, 31,
53, 54, 72, 78, 79, 82, 93,
95, 98, 100, 106, 107, 114,
115, 145-147, 151, 160,
162, 169, 187, 193, 195,
204, 206, 207, 212, 223,
229, 244, 245, 251, 254,
256, 271, 292, 299, 323,
334, 350, 353, 359, 372,
378, 386-394, 412, 415,
434, 467, 479, 482, 494,
503, 505, 507, 516, 517,
519, 529, 540, 546, 547,
559, 562, 565, 604, 622,
626, 630, 631, 648, 689,
718, 721, 725, 737, 746,
747, 750-757, 759-771, 773-
775, 792, 859, 862, 875-
877, 885-888, 892, 902,
904-906, 922, 930, 931,
938, 941, 956, 972, 977,
992, 995, 996, 998, 1012,
1015, 1022, 1061, 1076,
1077, 1104, 1124, 1138,
1139, 1151, 1167, 1174,
1178, 1189, 1194-1196,
1233
mission of Jesus, 13, 206,
251, 254, 412, 1139
mission strategy, 754, 756,
771
missionaries, 2, 10, 11, 13,
15, 19, 22, 31, 32, 53, 54,
70-72, 77, 78, 79, 80, 148,
150, 169, 207, 222, 256,
303, 317, 319, 350, 368,
373, 374, 389-391, 392,
393, 394, 415, 416, 433,
463, 482, 503, 504, 516,
544, 547, 562, 563, 617,
628, 629, 647, 738, 742,
743, 748, 749, 752, 753,
754-772, 774, 781, 883,
885, 887, 892, 930, 942,
944, 991, 992, 1005, 1047,
1066, 1082, 1095, 1124,
1136, 1137, 1151-1153,
1207, 1217, 1219, 1220,
1222
missionary journeys, 2, 53,
71, 79, 222, 368, 503, 743,
748, 749, 756, 762, 883,
930, 944, 1082, 1137, 1217
Mithraism, 706, 783, 1009
money, 81, 115, 322, 506,
567, 576, 680, 687, 698,
699, 705, 716, 737, 745,
764, 881, 882, 935, 954,
963, 976, 992, 1001, 1044,
1051-1053, 1142, 1159,
1162, 1164, 1165, 1193
monotheism, 48, 70, 161-
163, 183, 184, 355, 395,

412-414, 416, 417, 421,
422, 428-431, 436, 557,
586, 609, 667, 772, 775,
890, 961, 1007, 1058
Montanism, 775, 975, 976,
1089
months, 184, 323, 564, 935
morality, 29, 30, 53, 104,
322, 351, 352, 356, 369,
402, 507, 535, 552, 564,
657, 769, 775, 920, 925,
935, 1007, 1099, 1108,
1109, 1159
mortality, 70, 284, 285, 312,
336, 343, 347, 376, 437,
462, 535, 655, 657, 716,
730, 775-777, 809, 852,
958, 987, 988, 1068, 1130
Moses, 5, 6, 14, 35, 38, 40,
42-44, 46, 50, 51, 73, 86,
127, 141, 153, 162, 171,
172, 178, 183, 186, 210,
214, 239, 246, 247, 249,
272, 295, 296, 298, 327,
350, 356, 381, 396, 410,
413, 415, 419, 445, 453,
457-459, 466, 467, 480,
481, 492, 509, 510, 524,
534, 536, 537, 539, 567,
573, 582, 607-610, 614,
623, 626, 632, 643, 644,
646, 647, 649, 698, 718,
724, 728, 743, 770, 777-
782, 816, 818, 819, 821,
829, 830, 833, 836, 838,
839, 842, 844, 845, 850,
851, 854, 867, 878, 894,
923, 930, 932, 933, 949,
956-958, 960, 963, 965,
979, 980, 989, 990, 994,
998, 999, 1031, 1043,
1045, 1091, 1092, 1094,
1099, 1100, 1110, 1113,
1123, 1124, 1144, 1154,
1155, 1163, 1180, 1187,
1201, 1218, 1240
murder, 42, 168, 240, 289,
349, 600, 645, 703, 816,
837, 840, 1012, 1079,
1109, 1192
mystery, 45, 55, 66, 262,
298, 317, 343, 356, 427,
498, 595, 639, 666, 704,
709, 712, 782-784, 792,
817, 851, 888-890, 1009,
1025, 1033, 1102, 1115,
1147, 1148, 1150, 1156,
1173, 1201
mystery cults, 55, 356, 639,
782-784, 792, 1102, 1115,
1147-1148, 1150
mysticism, 63, 67, 260, 406,
593, 665, 666, 711, 818,
1140
myth, 29, 31, 32, 44, 50, 53,
62, 72, 112, 127, 129, 133,
176, 183, 202, 214, 215,
230, 250, 264, 355, 362,
404, 406, 424, 472, 482,
523, 531, 639, 707, 724,
741, 800, 870, 871, 874,
875, 923, 956, 1007, 1009,
1028, 1035, 1037, 1047,

1086, 1115, 1130, 1140,
1148, 1151, 1184, 1209,
1215, 1234
Nag Hammadi, 33, 34, 70,
72, 73, 149, 308, 400, 402-
412, 590, 621, 638, 785,
931, 1089, 1175-1177
name of God, 38, 43, 119,
172, 258, 430, 487, 610,
634, 667, 851, 961
narrative criticism, 16, 23,
477, 482, 483, 598, 787-
790, 792, 1049, 1134
narrative theology, 8, 556,
805
nations, 5, 38, 44, 46, 62, 81,
113, 129, 132, 162, 177,
207, 208, 210, 211, 214,
216, 264, 272, 317, 338,
354, 371, 385, 386, 390,
392, 394, 396, 415, 428,
438, 485, 486, 493, 502,
503, 524, 536, 561-565,
600, 621, 634-637, 648,
666, 672, 691, 703, 719,
753-756, 766, 770, 771,
775, 792, 824, 825, 853,
903, 971, 992, 1012, 1026,
1033, 1067, 1081, 1163,
1166, 1177, 1178, 1181,
1239, 1240
natural theology, 762, 1022
Nazoreans, 33, 168, 313-316,
584, 585, 792, 900
Nero, 50-52, 128, 149, 150,
184, 185, 189, 288, 321,
324, 328, 393, 449, 478,
599, 668, 875, 908-910,
916, 918, 1027-1029, 1034,
1035, 1062, 1066, 1135,
1137, 1183
new birth, 118, 132, 173,
243, 282, 335, 341, 353,
366, 498, 500, 569, 736,
737, 792-795, 1017, 1022,
1075, 1116, 1236
new commandment, 238
new covenant, 37, 38, 42,
107, 108, 172, 195, 198-
200, 207, 211, 217, 218,
242, 245-249, 268-270,
277, 278, 285, 326, 331,
334, 350, 376, 383, 418,
447, 453, 457, 458, 487,
492, 537, 543, 563, 564,
631, 633, 645, 646, 655,
679, 780, 782, 793, 795,
811, 821, 829, 842, 844,
845, 849, 850, 854, 861,
862, 878, 891, 899, 968,
969, 998, 999, 1026, 1043,
1058, 1070-1072, 1096,
1118, 1155, 1156, 1233
new creation, 5, 200, 213,
276, 331, 333-336, 341,
342, 420, 499, 552, 557,
636, 740, 959, 1031, 1224,
1227
New Exodus, 538, 641,
1031, 1092
new heaven(s), 47, 56, 65,
66, 240, 253, 255, 332,
337, 343, 347, 363, 427,

439, 441, 443, 636, 638,
739, 796, 811, 823, 854,
866, 959, 969, 1017, 1018,
1020, 1031, 1037, 1040,
1058, 1224
new humanity, 157, 158, 735
new Israel, 108, 198, 200,
201, 203, 223, 227, 488,
542, 725, 728, 803, 1234
new moon, 330, 701
New Testament theology,
76, 129, 159, 218, 312,
330, 344, 379, 430, 478,
483, 527, 541, 628, 796,
797, 799, 802, 803, 808,
812-814, 874, 893, 961,
967, 1093
Noah, 38, 41, 46, 118, 246,
262, 279, 286, 419, 425,
481, 512, 523, 537, 538,
624, 730, 754, 795, 814,
816, 819, 822, 829, 835,
836, 839, 863, 866, 922,
1056, 1088, 1118
Nympha, 1220
oaths, 3, 38, 415, 526, 552,
568, 646, 684, 691, 710,
721, 845, 849, 863, 1070,
1109, 1126, 1185
obedience, 1, 3, 4, 6, 15, 18,
36, 38-41, 42, 75, 103, 108,
131, 173, 179, 180, 203,
208, 223, 230, 231, 240,
241, 246, 267, 268, 271,
272, 274, 279-281, 285,
286, 310, 311, 319, 320,
324, 336, 339, 350, 352,
357, 359, 361, 363, 365,
369, 370, 373, 377, 392,
432, 445, 453, 466, 467,
479, 487, 514, 518, 523,
534, 535, 558, 566, 566,
568, 584, 592, 594, 597,
603, 606, 621-624, 639,
640, 640, 646, 649, 651,
695, 697, 698, 714, 724,
735, 744, 781, 815, 817,
818, 821-823, 829, 844,
845, 852, 876, 877, 881,
882, 892, 908, 922, 933,
936, 944, 958, 969, 1012,
1015, 1039, 1040, 1047,
1051, 1053, 1055, 1058,
1071-1075, 1095, 1097,
1098, 1108, 1109, 1118,
1139, 1167, 1181, 1194,
1201, 1205, 1208, 1211,
1213
Odes of Solomon, 72, 181-183,
407, 525, 526, 590, 777,
980, 1006, 1152, 1153
offerings, 25, 36, 62, 102,
130, 198, 225, 248, 261,
274-276, 286, 310, 312,
356, 375, 394, 414, 419,
457, 491, 517, 528, 564,
594, 597, 607, 649, 660,
693, 694, 744, 823, 836,
844, 849, 850, 864, 867,
872, 902, 906, 964, 966,
985, 989, 991, 996, 1002,
1008, 1012, 1031, 1056,
1069-1072, 1079, 1096,

1104, 1120, 1129, 1141,
1155, 1156, 1157, 1161,
1162, 1165, 1183, 1197,
1204, 1228, 1230, 1232,
1233, 1236
oil, 48, 49, 119, 122, 437,
439, 490, 528, 632, 786,
908, 945, 990, 991, 1007,
1065, 1121, 1163, 1228
old covenant, 38, 74, 107,
198, 203, 228, 242, 248,
249, 275, 285, 375, 453,
487, 492, 543, 563, 646,
647, 844, 849, 965, 966,
973, 974, 1070, 1118
Old Testament in Acts, 23,
106, 152, 195, 247, 479,
483, 536, 668, 823, 904,
953, 970, 1073
Old Testament in the Apostolic Fathers, 37, 91, 126,
235, 481, 673
Old Testament in the Gen-
eral Epistles, 480, 671,
834, 953
Old Testament in Hebrews,
98, 197, 240, 248, 249,
454, 457, 479, 537, 670,
718, 841, 850, 861, 953,
999, 1156, 1187
Old Testament in Revela-
tion, 128, 132, 481, 536,
539, 571, 672, 850, 855,
974, 1037
olive, olive tree, 48, 208,
217, 327, 854, 1007, 1065
Onesimus, 147, 699, 765,
888
Onesiphorus, 765
oracles, 58, 66, 70, 111, 128,
178, 191, 264, 287, 296,
392, 542, 605, 614, 626,
653, 674, 737, 770, 779,
830, 839, 852, 855, 900,
901, 972, 980, 992, 1006,
1009, 1010, 1030, 1031,
1034, 1069, 1093, 1152,
1180, 1191, 1197, 1211,
1229
ordination, 37, 105, 137,
202, 225, 608
pagans, paganism, 36, 70,
85, 95, 98, 111, 129, 136,
169, 176, 178, 180, 183,
192, 213, 214, 216, 226,
228, 233, 279, 300, 302-
304, 326, 340, 349, 354,
356, 358, 369, 377, 378,
389-391, 393, 394, 400,
402, 403, 406, 410, 413,
416, 417, 479, 516, 517,
520, 525, 529, 530, 532,
581, 601, 603, 628, 703,
704, 707, 711, 715, 734,
750, 751, 752, 754, 760,
761, 762, 766, 768, 769,
771-774, 775, 806, 814,
817-819, 829, 834, 835,
839, 879, 880, 886, 895,
898, 925, 926, 963, 965,
973, 975, 1007, 1009-1011,
1019, 1044, 1052, 1069,
1079, 1084, 1088, 1089,

1094, 1095, 1100, 1101,
1108, 1111, 1118, 1119,
1135, 1138, 1147, 1148,
1150-1152, 1154, 1158,
1169, 1192-1194, 1196-
1198, 1206, 1208, 1210,
1214, 1215, 1234
Palestine, 33, 35, 69, 92,
146, 166, 169, 170, 184,
185, 187, 194, 211, 216,
221, 258, 287, 288, 291,
297, 298, 301, 317, 371,
377, 387, 465, 468, 521,
548-550, 580, 600, 618,
643, 644, 663, 682, 706,
758, 764, 774, 932, 956,
1005, 1006, 1045, 1066,
1099, 1141, 1142, 1146,
1183, 1215, 1224, 1227,
1229
Palestinian Christians, 114,
585, 956
Palestinian Judaism, 60,
250, 287, 294, 462, 464,
465, 580, 611, 1055, 1058,
1123
Paphos, 78, 355, 758
Papias, 83, 90, 139, 149, 189-
191, 194, 341, 342, 575,
638, 644, 740, 765, 916,
931, 934, 937, 1036, 1037,
1078, 1214, 1219
parables, 84, 96, 206, 325,
343, 363, 469, 470, 473,
502, 505, 540, 541, 567,
570, 571, 624, 676, 725,
727, 770, 793, 802, 831,
856, 858, 969, 990, 992,
1026, 1049, 1093, 1129,
1165, 1177, 1197, 1206
Paradise, 69, 344, 442, 471,
636, 730, 956
paraenesis, 30, 89, 98, 99,
110, 204, 235, 319, 350,
366, 444, 445, 449, 450,
453-455, 474, 475, 478-
483, 500, 519, 538, 540,
550, 551, 560, 567, 613,
628, 639, 651, 652, 653,
700, 715, 738, 746, 814,
816, 817, 819, 830, 834-
836, 839, 841, 856, 878,
879, 882, 891, 899, 935,
936, 981, 1023, 1043,
1044, 1051, 1052, 1095,
1156-1159, 1191, 1192,
1194, 1197, 1229, 1232
Parousia, 5, 15, 21, 29-31,
34, 44, 47, 62, 65, 66, 69,
73, 101, 189, 251, 254, 264-
267, 287, 310, 312, 332,
335, 337, 338, 343, 358,
360, 362, 363, 385, 397,
424, 442, 447, 449, 483,
557, 559, 571, 573, 605,
613, 615, 619, 622, 623,
625, 629, 632, 634, 636,
638, 663, 670, 719, 723,
739, 755, 762, 768, 769,
771, 776, 802, 822, 856-
875, 883, 904, 921, 923,
925-927, 933, 967, 1016,
1018, 1020, 1023-1025,

1037, 1045, 1051, 1055, 1081, 1149, 1179, 1182, 1189, 1199, 1200, 1226, 1227, 1234
paschal homily, 731, 732, 876, 1092
paschal lamb, 641, 642, 876
passion narrative, 160, 263, 271, 538, 567, 791, 801, 929
Passover, 39, 118, 121, 174, 178, 186, 268-270, 280, 284, 297, 492, 589, 635, 641, 642, 679, 731, 732, 778, 908, 975, 1032, 1160, 1164, 1224
Passover lamb, 174, 280, 635, 641, 642, 731, 1032
Pastoral Letters, 30-32, 86, 87, 89, 105, 137, 224, 242, 305, 310, 311, 475, 504, 507, 628, 639, 706-708, 890-893, 963, 976, 977, 979, 981, 982, 1074, 1083, 1105, 1106, 1171, 1173, 1191, 1235, 1236
pastoral theology, 352, 444, 746, 811, 835, 876, 877, 879-882, 1093, 1159, 1170
patriarchs, 1, 3, 6, 38, 42, 43, 50, 141, 205, 209, 213, 215, 413, 533, 599, 607, 610, 729, 816, 817, 851, 970, 977, 978, 1169, 1191
Pauline legacy, 87, 206, 312, 404, 444, 560, 887, 889, 890, 892, 982, 984, 1224, 1226
Pauline school, 206, 404, 555, 888, 889, 892, 893
paulinisms, 23, 537, 883, 887, 893
peace, 37, 85, 102, 121, 123, 127, 130, 151, 155, 167, 179, 234, 246, 322, 323, 326, 351, 353, 361, 387, 420, 422, 450, 477, 489, 495, 496, 516, 534, 537, 538, 558, 564, 572, 596, 601, 604, 605, 650, 653, 654, 660, 696, 716, 730, 741, 874, 886, 893-900, 918, 939, 991, 1008, 1015, 1048, 1059-1062, 1090, 1106, 1109, 1121, 1196, 1236, 1240
Pella, flight to, 127, 144, 145, 229, 387, 388, 585, 758, 900-902
Pentateuch, 45, 246, 296, 316, 449, 480, 605-607, 778-780, 824, 828, 842, 933, 979, 981, 998
Pentecost, 10, 21, 23, 77, 79, 92, 97, 113, 121, 124, 144, 149, 150, 195, 244, 247, 257, 332, 333, 380, 391, 415, 492, 493, 498, 503, 508, 543, 562, 627, 630, 631, 686, 687, 722, 743, 746, 747, 752, 755, 757, 759, 773, 782, 793, 858, 902-906, 930, 939, 970,

1026, 1066, 1072, 1151, 1177-1179, 1194, 1195, 1218, 1226, 1227
perfect, perfection, 27, 37, 85, 98, 99, 117, 128, 201, 214, 215, 242, 252, 276, 277, 283, 286, 314, 320, 335, 369, 371, 380, 400, 403, 404, 408, 409, 421, 440, 445, 458, 488, 543, 549, 551, 552, 556, 557, 560, 563, 566, 590, 592, 632, 633, 645, 646, 670, 678, 697, 710, 722, 734, 794, 816, 864, 867, 870, 874, 875, 876, 897, 941, 944, 953, 966, 967, 969, 1011, 1020, 1034, 1054, 1072, 1075, 1096, 1097, 1098, 1112, 1122, 1156, 1165, 1168, 1181, 1233
persecution, 20, 25, 34-37, 54, 58, 69, 73-76, 79, 80-82, 92, 95, 99, 100, 104, 112, 131, 134, 136, 143-146, 150, 151, 165, 166, 184-192, 194, 211, 213, 214, 216, 218, 230-232, 234, 236, 240, 256, 261, 263, 273, 279, 281, 286, 322-331, 336, 337, 339, 342, 348, 355, 356, 358, 359, 366, 368-371, 381-384, 388, 390, 392, 415, 416, 423, 433, 446, 447, 449, 460, 463, 467, 475-479, 482, 496, 500, 524, 532, 534, 562, 564, 580, 581, 589, 636, 642, 660, 662, 718-722, 735, 739-741, 743, 755-757, 761, 762, 769, 770, 772, 773, 785, 822, 823, 835, 836, 838, 860, 862-864, 878, 879, 886, 887, 894, 897, 904, 907-914, 916-919, 930, 931, 934, 938, 941, 953, 959, 962, 969, 999, 1016, 1017, 1023, 1027-1029, 1035, 1037-1039, 1044, 1047, 1062, 1063, 1066, 1067, 1076, 1080, 1088, 1107, 1110, 1123-1125, 1135, 1137-1141, 1144, 1151, 1152, 1167, 1180, 1181, 1185, 1186, 1197-1200, 1202, 1204, 1205, 1208, 1216, 1217, 1218, 1219
perseverance, 39, 42, 73-76, 82, 103, 104, 122, 130, 147, 279, 321, 326, 327, 330, 335-337, 361, 364, 365, 367, 370, 384, 419, 440, 442, 443, 455, 475, 476, 479, 480, 482, 483, 500, 501, 510, 534, 538, 563, 605, 621, 633, 655, 716, 720, 721, 776, 816, 823, 835, 836, 843, 878, 881, 882, 914, 940, 950, 952, 969, 970, 1013, 1015, 1023, 1038-1040, 1044,

1062, 1073, 1139, 1140, 1170
Persis, 765
pesher, 480, 482, 562, 904, 999
Pharisees, 45, 63, 160-162, 186, 196, 206, 207, 209, 227, 305, 378, 379, 386, 502, 573, 575, 581, 599, 600, 608, 611, 647, 725-728, 775, 792, 885, 886, 990-992, 996, 1091, 1145, 1146, 1160, 1161, 1162, 1164, 1166
Philemon, 313, 520, 560, 685, 765, 877, 882, 888, 890, 981, 1171, 1238
Philetus, 31
Philip the Evangelist, 23, 191, 353, 468, 743, 929, 931, 1077
Philippi, 116, 223, 290, 355, 373, 378, 416, 512, 521, 531, 661, 711, 759, 764, 765, 771, 832, 886, 910, 934-936, 1143, 1214, 1217, 1220
Philo, 1-4, 6, 34-37, 40, 41, 43, 126, 185, 193, 221, 226, 230, 252, 263, 286-299, 326, 378, 389, 403, 444, 445, 451, 458, 480, 482, 484, 492, 497, 515, 521, 528, 552, 600, 605, 614, 643, 644, 656, 665, 667, 715, 731, 738, 775, 778-782, 815, 816, 819, 836, 842-844, 850, 860, 874, 895, 903, 911, 930-934, 957, 967, 999, 1061, 1091, 1099, 1106, 1112, 1141, 1147, 1149, 1150, 1153, 1169, 1191, 1202, 1212, 1214, 1218
philosophy, 1, 36, 37, 64, 85, 176, 182, 183, 186, 235, 255, 295, 296, 298, 307, 324, 325, 354, 356, 379, 391, 400, 402, 410, 412, 429, 436, 458, 472, 473, 474, 482, 484, 535, 546, 552, 607, 609, 622, 657, 665, 667, 706, 708, 713, 732, 751, 752, 782, 807, 818, 867, 926, 932, 933, 978, 1009, 1010, 1012, 1033, 1042, 1049, 1064, 1105, 1109, 1113, 1114, 1140, 1147, 1149, 1150, 1157, 1190, 1201, 1214, 1217
Phoebe, 765
Phrygia, 146, 288, 758, 759, 770, 975
physical body, 32, 97, 375, 376, 401, 409, 706, 985, 987, 1020, 1104, 1105
piety, 6, 41, 71, 72, 88, 170, 183, 213, 216, 235, 236, 243, 244, 271, 301, 318, 372, 378, 391, 408, 413, 414, 421, 441, 457, 470, 476, 507, 537, 546, 551,

552, 556, 558, 591, 607, 608, 610, 693, 697, 740, 753, 762, 795, 799, 801, 1007, 1008, 1051, 1052, 1128, 1139, 1141, 1159, 1162, 1163, 1192, 1196, 1216
Pilate, 120, 164, 187, 193, 256, 258, 259, 273, 274, 566, 573, 599, 913, 928, 1162, 1234
pillar, 161, 439, 465, 504, 993, 1071, 1156, 1226
Pisidia, 2, 758, 886, 1157, 1216, 1217
Platonism, 37, 263, 276, 296, 325, 375, 400-404, 406, 410, 411, 468, 482, 655, 666, 775, 777, 860, 899, 957, 958, 966, 978, 1090, 1113, 1147, 1149, 1150, 1190
polemic, 4, 28, 29, 31, 34, 70, 85, 90, 157, 160-162, 166-170, 184, 228, 248, 249, 294, 315, 351, 481, 522, 526, 549, 575, 578, 581, 582, 584, 586, 593, 596, 599, 606, 611, 620, 661, 664, 684, 701-704, 710, 727-729, 749, 769, 781, 809, 820, 833, 839, 841, 866, 875, 888, 889, 934, 952, 998, 1019, 1023, 1046, 1126, 1147, 1149, 1150, 1231
politics, 8, 17, 23, 24, 52, 58, 59, 62, 66, 112, 128, 129, 132, 148, 160, 166, 184, 201, 204, 216, 226, 232, 233, 245, 287, 289, 292, 294, 296, 297, 299, 302, 303, 325, 348, 349, 353, 386, 388, 391, 422, 475, 507, 521, 549, 561, 605, 611, 615, 631-633, 661, 717, 749, 751, 754, 756, 773, 812, 894, 897-899, 902, 907, 911, 913, 932, 951, 955, 968, 1005, 1007-1009, 1041, 1047, 1048, 1050, 1059, 1062, 1064, 1065, 1067, 1102, 1103, 1105, 1106, 1107, 1111, 1130, 1137, 1138, 1140-1142, 1146, 1158, 1165, 1196, 1215
Pontus, 79, 193, 526, 705, 706, 752, 757-759, 771, 772, 1217, 1234
poor, poverty, 8, 14, 150, 189, 209, 222, 232, 233, 291, 313-316, 318, 323, 348, 351, 352, 356, 362, 365, 469-471, 473, 476, 480, 486, 502-504, 541, 542, 546, 548-551, 556-559, 560, 568, 574, 584, 586, 634, 687, 692, 695, 698, 699, 711, 733, 734, 743, 759, 761, 786, 816, 838, 879, 882, 905, 930, 938, 962, 991, 992, 1051-

1053, 1062, 1064, 1087,
1099, 1101, 1102, 1104,
1139, 1142, 1143, 1145,
1169, 1180, 1223
possessions, 231, 315, 442,
476, 602, 604, 656, 772,
1051-1053
postal service, 760
postmodernism, 804, 808,
809, 811, 938
poststructuralism, 472, 938,
1132
power of God, 75, 76, 330,
490, 492, 623, 631, 750,
878, 938-940, 1080, 1202
powers, 44-46, 48, 50, 52,
96, 100, 117, 127, 151,
165, 169, 232, 253, 254,
261, 277, 284, 334, 349,
356, 361, 383, 396, 397,
401, 402, 404, 416, 423,
424, 426-429, 431, 444,
525, 526, 561, 565, 589,
611, 667, 749, 777, 778,
818, 870, 879, 888, 913,
922, 941, 975, 1002, 1007,
1017, 1026, 1028, 1031,
1035, 1048, 1052, 1056,
1059, 1081, 1082, 1121,
1193, 1227, 1231, 1234
praetorium, 321, 323, 1061
praise, 46, 53, 108, 125, 129-
131, 180, 230, 244, 284,
302, 320, 374, 414, 428,
474, 475, 477, 494, 498,
520-522, 524-527, 563,
627, 635, 650, 660-662,
664, 665, 672, 689, 690,
692, 695, 780, 864, 902,
919, 936, 939, 940, 943,
945-947, 954, 964, 972,
1003, 1013, 1028, 1030,
1031, 1039, 1043, 1047,
1051, 1052, 1071, 1104,
1136, 1147, 1157, 1178,
1224, 1228, 1230, 1232,
1233, 1236, 1239
preaching, 19, 20, 45, 54,
71, 72, 76, 78, 79-82, 93,
100, 101, 109, 115, 116,
118, 124, 148, 150, 171,
188, 199, 203, 222, 241,
245, 256, 258, 260, 279,
286, 290, 328, 351, 353,
355, 356, 357, 359, 380,
381, 391, 392, 397, 414,
415, 416, 423, 445, 447,
448, 450, 451, 454, 456,
459, 465, 483, 484, 491,
493, 495-497, 503, 521,
534, 540, 562, 565, 566,
573, 579, 602, 626-630,
631, 632, 633, 635, 665,
666, 687, 688, 702, 705,
711, 718, 719, 732, 742,
745, 748, 755-757, 760-
762, 764, 766-771, 772,
786, 793, 799, 802, 818,
824, 829, 833, 836, 863,
874, 876, 884, 885, 905,
906, 923, 926, 948, 950,
951, 954, 955, 970, 972,
973, 977, 991, 992, 1004,

1017, 1054, 1056, 1073,
1076, 1114, 1119, 1123-
1125, 1143, 1144, 1195,
1204, 1241
Preaching of Peter, 72, 199,
203, 573, 665, 666, 711,
955
predestination, 317, 319-
321, 415, 587, 803, 876,
1073
preexistence, 88, 153, 154,
158, 174, 181-184, 203,
304, 314, 363, 536, 648,
667, 671, 678, 682, 777,
803, 845, 955-961, 1112-
1114, 1149, 1203
presbyters, 81, 82, 89, 109,
118, 120, 121, 146, 202,
224, 225, 233, 259, 374,
487, 532, 705, 707, 744,
745, 759, 881, 935, 961,
1014, 1023, 1048, 1067,
1086, 1087, 1092, 1110,
1163, 1233
pride, 241, 349, 464, 481,
520, 537, 876, 961-963,
1007, 1047, 1172, 1194,
1201, 1212
priest, priesthood, 3, 35, 36,
48, 52, 74, 79, 93, 98-100,
102, 106-108, 118, 121,
130, 152, 154, 155, 156,
172, 174, 177, 187, 198,
199, 200-202, 209, 225,
226, 231, 232, 240, 244,
248, 261, 274-278, 284,
293, 295, 298, 317, 318,
319, 332, 346, 359, 360,
361, 363, 417-419, 428,
431, 440, 443, 444, 452-
455, 457, 458, 467, 480,
482, 485, 488, 498, 507,
509, 510, 528, 530, 537,
538, 539, 542, 543, 544,
547, 550, 561, 567, 575,
582, 599, 605, 608, 609,
632, 633, 635, 646, 647,
655, 661, 689, 694, 720,
729-731, 734, 735, 738,
744, 776, 817, 827, 829,
833, 838, 843, 844, 845,
849, 850, 855, 861, 878,
881, 917, 928, 933, 940,
944, 958, 963-967, 974,
988-992, 998, 999, 1002,
1007, 1008, 1016, 1022,
1039, 1043, 1070-1072,
1073, 1074, 1091, 1096,
1105, 1107, 1110, 1113,
1123, 1155, 1156, 1160,
1161, 1163, 1165, 1167,
1185, 1191, 1236
principalities and powers,
44-46, 232, 401, 818
Prisca, 762-764, 975, 976
Priscilla, 93, 291, 378, 443,
444, 446-449, 743, 764,
967, 1066, 1207, 1216-
1218, 1220, 1221
prison, imprisonment, 21,
45, 46, 62, 71, 92, 100,
116, 129, 150, 186, 189,
356, 366, 374, 376, 378,

391, 415, 444, 447, 449,
459, 460, 496, 504-506,
512, 521, 535, 602, 624,
692, 721, 746, 747, 749,
750, 757, 761, 765, 808,
818, 823, 863, 883, 886,
894, 907, 982, 1003, 1017,
1067, 1080, 1087, 1100,
1101, 1119, 1123, 1137,
1138, 1139, 1185, 1195,
1219, 1220, 1234
prisoner, 54, 530, 749, 832,
883, 890, 892, 1062, 1066
proclamation, 48, 100, 101,
106, 108, 116, 146, 148,
158, 160, 161, 168, 171,
244, 249, 251, 256, 258,
263, 270, 271, 286, 348,
351, 353, 379, 432, 445,
459, 498, 526, 567, 573,
621-623, 635, 670, 719,
752, 753, 756, 757, 760,
766, 768, 770, 782, 783,
793, 800, 802, 813, 826,
838, 844, 858, 872, 877,
894, 899, 903, 906, 923,
953, 959, 971, 973, 987,
1015, 1020-1023, 1074,
1083, 1115, 1118, 1164,
1201, 1235
proconsul, 78, 147, 148,
191, 193, 323, 364, 702,
909, 910, 936, 1014
procurator, 185, 194, 764,
859, 908, 932, 1060
profane, 205, 211, 373, 377,
486, 490, 558, 639, 644,
795, 989, 1124
prophecy, 2, 17, 19, 31, 33,
40, 46, 47, 50-52, 59, 60,
66, 69, 70, 73, 101, 106,
112, 113, 115, 129, 131,
132, 151, 175, 177, 178,
183, 187, 195, 204, 235,
248, 249, 257, 262, 306,
313, 321, 331-334, 336-
338, 340, 342-345, 370,
387, 426, 437, 456, 471,
475, 478, 479, 482, 489,
495, 497, 498, 509, 521,
522, 529, 536, 537, 562,
565, 573, 589, 618, 620,
626, 628, 632, 636, 637,
638, 643, 647, 653, 677,
721, 741, 743, 746, 756,
774, 775, 780, 789, 793,
794, 820, 825, 826, 828,
829, 830, 833, 841, 850-
854, 857, 859, 874, 881,
886, 897, 899, 906, 921,
923-926, 953, 959, 970-
978, 980, 992, 998, 1003,
1010, 1019, 1020, 1022,
1024-1027, 1037, 1045-
1047, 1069, 1073, 1084,
1085, 1094, 1100, 1120,
1178, 1179, 1183, 1198,
1207, 1214, 1216, 1227
prophets, 2, 6, 14, 19, 30,
33, 36, 42, 45, 46, 48, 50-
52, 70, 78-82, 87, 106, 109,
112, 119, 120, 126, 127,
132, 133, 154, 157, 166,

173, 174, 181, 195, 196,
202, 203, 220, 222, 224,
225, 246, 247, 252, 254,
258, 264, 272, 273, 279,
281, 301, 306, 313, 317,
332, 346, 347, 366, 370,
379, 392, 393, 396, 397,
414, 415, 417, 424, 425,
434-436, 467, 479, 480,
482, 487, 489, 495-497,
499, 505-507, 510, 534,
537, 540, 542, 548, 572,
573, 576, 584, 593, 597,
607, 615, 621, 637, 643,
644, 653, 670, 683, 691,
718, 728, 741, 743-746,
762, 768, 772, 775, 779,
782-784, 815, 816, 824-
828, 830, 832-835, 837,
838, 845, 851, 852, 854,
874, 881, 884, 894, 916,
921, 958, 966, 970-978,
980, 994, 998, 999, 1022,
1024, 1026, 1036, 1037,
1045, 1054, 1067, 1072,
1075, 1085-1088, 1091,
1100, 1108, 1110, 1114,
1119-1121, 1123, 1124,
1129, 1157, 1163, 1170,
1181, 1183, 1185, 1188,
1197-1200, 1219, 1222,
1224, 1228, 1232, 1235
propitiation, 275, 278, 281,
282, 734, 1070, 1074, 1097
proselytes, 1, 54, 115, 160,
162, 165, 184, 215, 226,
227, 288, 292, 297, 316,
372, 389, 670, 742, 754,
906, 977, 1066, 1124,
1178, 1216, 1217
prostitutes, prostitution, 39,
111, 112, 128, 232, 558,
716, 851, 1029, 1067,
1088, 1090, 1209, 1210,
1211
proverbs, 231, 326, 419, 420,
480, 481, 502, 541, 556-
558, 570, 572-574, 606,
614, 670, 674, 695, 716,
781, 814, 816, 818, 819,
829, 831, 832, 837, 839,
896, 936, 957, 962, 980,
1073, 1201, 1203, 1208
providence, 39, 326, 390,
415, 422, 423, 429, 430,
773, 783, 805, 806, 886,
945, 954, 977, 1019, 1033,
1173, 1204
pseudepigrapha, 6, 44, 68,
69, 72, 85, 86, 607, 611,
783, 818, 820, 977, 979,
983, 984
pseudepigraphy, 6, 7, 24, 30,
44, 47, 55, 68, 102, 135,
142, 143, 192, 206, 234,
243, 363, 483, 489, 606-
608, 610, 616, 617, 649,
654, 766, 816, 817, 818,
823, 867, 888, 924, 927,
955, 977-984, 1086, 1159,
1175
psychology, 132, 243, 376,
439, 741, 951, 984, 985,

1117, 1170

Ptolemais, *290, 758*

punishment, *5, 6, 47, 63, 69, 75, 127, 132, 165, 213, 216, 230, 240, 246, 251, 253, 254, 272, 275, 305, 320, 326, 328, 346, 347, 357, 415, 425, 429, 438, 441, 459-461, 530, 564, 600, 621, 623-625, 657, 658, 695, 703, 715, 777, 818, 821, 841, 845, 850, 862, 902, 909, 919, 932, 956, 961, 962, 969, 988, 989, 1003, 1010, 1013, 1033, 1040, 1059, 1060-1062, 1081, 1085, 1089, 1092, 1095, 1097, 1098, 1100, 1121, 1123, 1168, 1180, 1183, 1186, 1188, 1189, 1221, 1241*

purity, *29, 32, 42, 74, 160, 233, 236, 241, 243, 261, 304, 305, 374, 376-379, 384, 386, 389, 402, 422, 423, 425, 444, 485, 486, 488, 501, 503, 518, 528, 535, 541, 546, 557, 575, 576, 592, 623, 647, 648, 699, 715, 728, 745, 822, 828, 888, 917, 925, 940, 945, 968, 988-996, 1007, 1013, 1019, 1040, 1044, 1054, 1074, 1080, 1088, 1095, 1104, 1105, 1111, 1142, 1144, 1146, 1160-1164, 1172, 1188, 1194, 1212, 1213, 1220*

Quartus, *765*

Qumran, *44-47, 60, 61, 65-67, 73, 130, 132, 192, 196, 267, 304, 305, 316, 331, 343, 345, 378, 411, 465, 480, 482, 502, 504, 510, 511, 540, 587, 607, 613, 659, 731, 782-784, 815, 817-820, 827, 834, 838, 841, 843, 864, 956, 963, 965, 980, 991, 997-1000, 1012, 1093, 1102, 1116, 1117, 1119, 1123, 1160, 1166, 1169, 1175, 1180, 1191, 1194, 1201, 1202, 1227*

rabbis, *127, 130, 164, 167, 185, 186, 293, 430, 529, 606, 608, 610, 666, 781, 842, 843, 845, 962, 994, 1112, 1142, 1145, 1146, 1161*

rabbinic tradition, *169, 608, 1157, 1161, 1191*

Rahab, *39, 41, 369, 419, 421, 480, 481, 502, 507, 537, 539, 551, 553, 554, 558, 815, 816, 830, 835, 895, 899, 1001, 1003, 1056, 1212, 1216, 1218*

realized eschatology, *27, 30-32, 51, 182, 425, 803, 868, 1233*

rebellion, *29, 35, 36, 43, 51, 109, 168, 172, 184, 185,*

214, 231, 415, 459, 538, 550, 599, 605, 635, 758, 807, 836, 840, 841, 912, 962, 1012, 1014, 1030, 1047, 1052, 1059, 1060, 1085, 1169, 1231, 1240

reconciliation, *36, 47, 161, 247, 314, 315, 343, 377, 382, 446, 485, 684, 691, 781, 792, 814, 875, 894, 896, 898, 899, 1004, 1012, 1188, 1227, 1229, 1232*

redaction, redaction criticism, *9, 468, 477, 573, 574, 614, 713, 726, 727, 800, 877, 1125, 1174*

redeem, redemption, *7, 11, 36, 40, 45, 88, 118, 124, 160, 168, 173, 174, 177, 180, 195, 200, 206, 211, 223, 252, 253, 255, 276-280, 283-286, 317, 335, 338, 347, 369, 374, 384, 401, 405, 413, 430, 433-435, 456, 498, 501, 507, 523, 532, 542, 549, 590, 601, 610, 626, 627, 633, 635, 637, 641, 660, 687, 731, 747, 770, 780, 792, 793, 801, 805, 830, 840, 898, 899, 908, 938, 939, 956-958, 1001-1004, 1014, 1035, 1036, 1070, 1072, 1074, 1075, 1080, 1083, 1086, 1098, 1114, 1118, 1148, 1150, 1160, 1165, 1192, 1226, 1232, 1235*

redeemer, *27, 172, 192, 193, 215, 306, 401, 404, 407, 410, 525, 723, 780, 888, 956, 1034, 1148, 1223, 1224*

reign of God, *232, 351, 551, 630, 1004*

relatives of Jesus, *33, 47, 133, 145, 173, 187, 229, 287, 314, 387, 467, 545, 616, 619, 723, 724, 743, 757, 1004-1006, 1098, 1228*

religions, *55, 84, 128, 146, 159, 176, 178, 212, 228, 230, 250, 287, 296, 304, 325, 389, 391, 411, 414, 436, 441, 449, 528, 530, 535, 599, 625, 639, 701, 704, 706, 760, 782-784, 792, 797-799, 807, 808, 855, 880, 911, 920, 1006, 1011, 1028, 1036, 1069, 1078, 1103, 1109, 1111, 1115, 1122, 1130, 1147, 1148, 1150, 1166, 1177, 1206-1208, 1217*

remarriage, *540, 713, 714, 717, 1089, 1215*

repentance, *6, 11, 20, 21, 32, 38, 42, 44, 46, 75, 76, 78, 89, 90, 98, 104, 109, 114, 116, 117, 120, 121, 129, 160, 167, 207, 209, 227, 236, 244, 246, 247, 258, 260, 262, 266, 269, 270, 273, 274, 305, 306,*

320, 326, 333, 334, 338, 343, 350-352, 354, 356-358, 360, 364, 367, 368, 380-382, 384, 391, 416, 417, 419, 425, 438, 442, 456, 457, 469-471, 477, 489, 500, 501, 511, 513, 518, 551, 555, 557, 583, 601, 621, 622, 626, 627, 629, 631, 656, 657, 663, 677, 687, 688, 690, 694, 713, 714, 735, 738, 744, 745, 752, 763, 766, 768, 806, 823, 829, 832, 837, 859, 866, 876, 882, 886, 887, 903, 905, 926, 940, 942, 953, 963, 1011-1015, 1040, 1052, 1054, 1055, 1058, 1074, 1075, 1081, 1082, 1086, 1100, 1101, 1118, 1119, 1123, 1138, 1149, 1159, 1168, 1170, 1180, 1188, 1189, 1192, 1197, 1198, 1230

restoration of Israel, *160, 204, 363, 885, 886, 1182*

resurrection appearances, *96, 101, 904, 905*

resurrection body, *97, 740*

retribution, *40, 129, 462, 558, 623, 625, 1219*

reveal, *33, 35, 58, 62, 66, 69, 84, 85, 134, 163, 174, 191, 232, 273, 296, 305, 335, 360, 388, 399, 416, 444, 485, 509, 510, 519, 546, 639, 640, 749, 750, 776, 784, 786, 806, 811, 825, 869, 876, 899, 932, 954, 976, 1019, 1020, 1025, 1036, 1048, 1084, 1088, 1220*

reverence, *38, 74, 172, 174, 178, 362, 370-372, 610, 632, 809, 917, 920, 943, 1032, 1038, 1053, 1071, 1090, 1101, 1120, 1193, 1196, 1201, 1212*

rewards, *38, 39, 43, 47, 69, 99, 177, 214, 251, 266, 281, 306, 320, 327, 330, 335-338, 342, 343, 352, 361, 368, 370, 419, 429, 430, 439, 507, 575, 604, 621, 623, 625, 676, 720, 735, 739, 781, 821, 821-823, 845, 862, 868, 899, 913, 914, 920, 956, 960, 970, 1018, 1038-1041, 1048, 1052, 1096, 1223, 1239*

rhetoric, *85, 179, 228, 229, 234, 302, 395, 400, 418, 427, 444, 450, 451, 457, 475, 476, 483, 529, 531, 553, 561, 599, 612, 615, 620, 650, 651, 654, 655, 707, 732, 733, 787, 788,*

791, 918, 919, 932, 955, 992, 995, 996, 1015, 1020, 1041-1050, 1056, 1105, 1132, 1134, 1158, 1159, 1195, 1222, 1223, 1233

rhetorical analysis, criticism, *34, 451, 457, 475, 483, 484, 612-614, 620, 629, 650, 654, 791, 927, 1041, 1042, 1048, 1050, 1051, 1133, 1134, 1159*

rich, riches, *14, 34, 76, 103, 153, 156, 157, 163, 173, 175, 179, 181, 189, 209, 232, 250, 291, 315, 318, 347, 349, 351, 352, 362, 365, 385, 395, 417, 444, 469-471, 476, 480, 495, 541, 542, 549-551, 553, 555, 558-560, 564, 565, 568, 606, 617, 624, 634, 654, 692, 695, 698, 709-711, 721, 732, 736, 786, 808, 816, 822, 834, 835, 837, 840, 879, 886, 938, 948, 962, 963, 1022, 1036, 1039, 1044, 1051-1054, 1061, 1064, 1087, 1102, 1104, 1126, 1145, 1202, 1223*

right hand of God, *62, 74, 164, 252, 253, 273, 275, 281, 328, 361, 479, 626, 630, 632, 633, 646, 845, 960, 1016, 1140*

Righteous One, *149, 280, 365, 956, 1053, 1054, 1058*

righteous sufferer, *271, 523, 524, 824, 839*

righteousness, *4, 5, 38, 41, 42, 66, 88-91, 117, 161, 241, 251, 253, 266, 277, 286, 310, 320, 335, 351, 360, 366, 368, 382, 413, 421, 423, 435, 442, 446, 499, 500, 537, 539, 573, 581-583, 597, 624, 625, 632, 635, 637, 655, 657, 694, 730, 735, 770, 794, 802, 803, 814, 815, 822, 824, 837, 839, 866, 876, 893, 895-897, 899, 925, 926, 935, 936, 945, 946, 951, 991, 1003, 1014, 1015, 1021, 1053-1059, 1095, 1098, 1169, 1180, 1184, 1186, 1193, 1194, 1197, 1205, 1216, 1240*

righteousness of God, *310, 802, 926, 1054, 1055, 1058*

rising with Christ, *712*

ritual purity, *261, 305, 377, 378, 386, 546, 1007*

road, *18, 53, 78, 115, 146-148, 354, 358, 658, 669, 688, 718, 747, 883, 884, 931, 990, 1014, 1061, 1139, 1237*

Roman administration, *760, 1059*

Roman Christianity, *93, 150, 151, 163, 237, 446, 457, 1059, 1063, 1065, 1225,*

1233

Roman citizenship, 230, 233, 243, 599, 764, 886, 953, 1060-1062, 1066

Roman Empire, 50, 52, 55, 59, 62, 64, 93, 95, 111, 112, 145, 184, 185, 193, 217, 222, 231, 232, 235, 240, 255, 300, 323, 325, 349, 354, 355, 359, 366, 381, 388, 389, 393, 394, 431, 483, 521, 528, 530, 550, 599, 629, 634, 636, 637, 661, 705, 707, 732, 752, 754, 757, 759, 774, 822, 898, 908, 912, 916, 918, 919, 936, 938, 1011, 1028, 1029, 1034, 1038, 1059, 1063, 1067, 1085, 1091, 1098, 1099, 1101, 1102, 1110, 1111, 1117, 1150-1152, 1179, 1183, 1196, 1205-1207, 1215, 1222, 1240

Roman religion, 792, 880, 1006, 1007, 1011, 1166

Rufus, 329, 1140

rule of faith, 256, 258, 259, 456, 457, 1068

rule of God, 790, 1009

ruler of the Synagogue, 123, 148, 223, 293

ruler of this age, 1068, 1078, 1079

rulers, 50, 107, 129, 231, 236, 284, 324, 385, 631, 636, 668, 744, 913, 947, 1008, 1012, 1014, 1029, 1033, 1074, 1075, 1082, 1091, 1120, 1158, 1211, 1213, 1221

Sabbath, 33, 35, 36, 48, 125, 130, 161, 162, 164, 203, 213, 221, 222, 226, 229, 240, 257, 292, 293, 297, 298, 314, 335, 342, 344, 455, 486, 540, 576, 580, 583, 584, 632, 633, 645, 647-649, 675, 679, 681-686, 688, 728, 735, 740, 753, 828, 844, 895, 944, 1036, 1069, 1104, 1110, 1141, 1144-1146, 1216, 1231, 1238

saboraim, 608, 1069

sacred space, 458, 565, 967, 1069

sacrifice, 3, 4, 6, 25, 26, 36, 38, 39, 41, 48, 50, 74, 79, 88, 98, 99, 145, 148, 154, 161, 172, 203, 213, 225, 240, 242, 246, 248, 261, 269, 274-278, 280-284, 286, 315, 325, 327, 334, 350, 360-362, 377, 379, 381, 383, 392, 394, 417-419, 444, 448, 450, 453, 455, 457, 458, 480, 485, 487, 510, 522, 525, 526, 528, 529, 534, 537, 567, 583, 594, 631, 641, 642, 646-649, 689-691, 693, 694, 732, 737, 744, 751,

761, 778, 780, 806, 823, 827, 828, 838, 843, 850, 861, 898, 910-912, 936, 942, 944, 958, 964, 985, 988-993, 996, 998, 1002, 1003, 1007, 1008, 1012, 1013, 1016, 1022, 1028, 1029, 1043, 1052, 1054, 1056, 1069-1073, 1079, 1096, 1097, 1100, 1108, 1140, 1141, 1149, 1155, 1156, 1159-1162, 1164-1166, 1185, 1204, 1224, 1228, 1230, 1233, 1237

Sadducees, 30, 45, 196, 209, 547, 550, 551, 775, 776, 990, 1160, 1166

saints, 45, 46, 78, 80, 95, 102, 108, 112, 126, 129, 131, 177, 196, 218, 220, 237, 238, 278, 302, 316, 330, 331, 334, 337, 339, 341, 342, 366, 468, 470, 471, 483, 488, 502, 504, 533, 540, 564, 579, 604, 619, 633, 636, 644, 658, 717-719, 730, 739, 741, 746, 776, 781, 784, 823, 838, 839, 889, 908, 927, 937, 938, 942, 974, 985, 998, 1009, 1017, 1030, 1067, 1071, 1080, 1085, 1088, 1118, 1122, 1126, 1137, 1138, 1146, 1151, 1156, 1193, 1198, 1210, 1214, 1222, 1237, 1238

Salamis, 142, 314

salvation history, 44, 45, 206, 207, 209, 212, 216, 245, 249, 632, 646, 647, 725, 746, 751, 768, 798, 799, 808, 844, 878, 904, 951, 1043, 1124, 1138, 1227, 1233, 1236

Samaria, 11, 14, 23, 73, 78, 114, 144, 151, 157, 185, 192, 211, 251, 387, 391, 416, 493, 496, 562, 631, 661, 702, 742, 752, 755, 756, 763, 764, 766, 894, 903, 930, 931, 1075-1077, 1138, 1163, 1204, 1227, 1235

sanctify, sanctification, 33, 99, 118, 276, 277, 319, 375, 485-488, 807, 895, 1195

sanctuary, 36, 53, 74, 98, 248, 274, 275, 341, 360, 440, 448, 453, 455, 457, 458, 480, 497, 511, 530, 606, 633, 816, 850, 944, 956, 958, 966, 967, 988, 1007-1010, 1016, 1027, 1072, 1077, 1085, 1141, 1145, 1154-1156, 1158, 1163, 1165, 1219, 1233

Sanhedrin, 45, 77, 185, 187, 231, 431, 743, 755, 756, 762, 767, 994, 1082, 1123-1125, 1162, 1195

Sarah, 4, 39, 419, 480, 502, 517, 538, 671, 817, 835,

879, 896, 1208, 1215, 1218, 1222, 1234

Satan, 3, 21, 26, 42, 46, 47, 50-52, 63, 74, 75, 100, 108, 115, 122, 127, 129, 166, 175, 199, 205, 210, 232, 240, 253, 254, 263, 274, 287, 331, 332, 342, 348, 359, 362, 366, 368, 371, 381, 382, 460, 477, 483, 486, 494, 528, 634-637, 640, 655, 657, 695, 698, 702-704, 718-720, 739, 751, 794, 819, 845, 852, 869, 881, 886, 898, 913, 920, 939, 941, 1011, 1015, 1023, 1028, 1031, 1034, 1035, 1039, 1040, 1047, 1048, 1062, 1068, 1077-1082, 1098, 1118, 1121, 1122, 1138, 1140, 1149, 1166, 1169, 1170, 1181, 1193, 1196, 1199, 1200, 1239

Savior, 19, 20, 23, 40, 70, 76, 79, 120, 154, 157, 159, 160, 163, 174, 175, 180, 247, 254, 282, 306, 308, 314, 330, 359, 392, 408, 411, 413, 415, 460, 521, 556, 584, 630, 633, 639, 660, 672, 677, 686, 691, 692, 706, 707, 733, 773, 813, 891, 896, 946, 961, 969, 979, 987, 1035, 1055, 1072, 1074, 1075, 1082-1084, 1112, 1128, 1186, 1192, 1222, 1223

sayings of Jesus, 87, 91, 173, 179, 180, 181, 235-237, 241, 302, 390, 411, 560, 566-570, 572-581, 584, 674, 675, 691, 693, 709, 830, 901, 948, 990, 1019, 1020, 1176, 1177, 1204, 1213, 1237, 1238

scandal, 323, 807, 887, 915, 1143

school of Tyrannus, 357

scribes, 166, 175, 268, 270, 577, 586, 676, 689, 852, 853, 908, 927, 996, 1172-1174

Scythians, 754

sea, 21, 39, 44, 52, 61, 62, 67, 84, 118, 127-129, 132, 146, 184, 188, 232, 241, 250-252, 254, 267, 296, 309, 329-331, 355, 385, 387, 388, 411, 414, 426, 427, 464, 465, 508, 511, 541, 573, 576, 610, 634, 635, 657, 688, 705, 729-731, 749, 750, 760, 780, 834, 835, 851-854, 900, 914, 927, 956, 997, 1000, 1003, 1033, 1037, 1061, 1063, 1080, 1081, 1086, 1092, 1099, 1122, 1127, 1129, 1157, 1160, 1164, 1165, 1170, 1183

sea travel, 760, 1061

seal of the Spirit, 49, 124,

1238

seals, 104, 132, 340, 441, 477, 642, 704, 851, 869, 870, 928, 1030, 1031, 1037, 1081, 1084-1086, 1162, 1179, 1182

Second Apocalypse of James, 72, 1086

Second Exodus, 200

second repentance, 76, 104, 306, 350, 352, 357, 367, 381, 382, 456, 457, 471, 882, 963, 1011, 1013, 1015, 1075, 1081, 1086

Secret Gospel of Mark, 708-710, 712, 1086

sectarian Judaism, 815, 840

sectarianism, 229, 598

seed, 1, 6, 130, 208-210, 283, 404, 491, 590, 638, 646, 720, 793, 794, 969, 1019, 1080

seed of Abraham, 209, 210

Seleucia, 53, 288, 1004, 1219

Seneca, 325, 326, 715, 718, 734, 1064-1066, 1100, 1157

Septuagint, 1, 2, 18, 34, 40, 45, 48, 49, 87, 114, 149, 164, 166, 167, 174, 196, 197, 204, 211, 221, 232, 234, 246, 251, 252, 254, 264, 268, 270, 275, 280, 283, 287, 298, 336, 337, 377, 399, 416, 439, 440, 444, 466, 479, 480, 508, 510, 521, 522, 536, 538, 540, 542, 546, 600, 601, 614, 643, 662, 677, 680, 698, 706, 708, 715, 725, 733, 754, 768, 778, 782, 786, 792, 815, 824, 826, 829-832, 829, 834, 835, 838, 839, 843-845, 849, 850, 851, 858, 886, 894, 896, 904, 905, 933, 936, 953, 957, 966, 968, 1020, 1021, 1054, 1072, 1073, 1082, 1083, 1086, 1092-1094, 1118-1120, 1126-1129, 1147, 1164, 1168, 1184

Sergius Paulus, 364, 749, 1059

sermonic genre, 450, 1086

servant, 1, 18, 46, 62, 62, 76, 95, 110, 114, 115, 132, 141, 171, 172, 177, 180, 181, 200, 209, 217, 221, 223, 242, 255, 269, 271-273, 275, 279-281, 284, 317, 356, 363, 398, 402, 423, 441, 487, 491, 507, 510, 523, 524, 545, 614, 632, 641, 642, 666, 675, 691, 697, 702, 719, 721, 739, 740, 745, 746, 750, 752, 765, 780-782, 824, 829, 833, 838, 851, 854, 881, 882, 891, 910, 915, 930, 941, 965, 969, 974, 1002, 1003, 1024, 1026, 1033, 1055, 1061, 1080, 1086-1088, 1092, 1095,

1126, 1129, 1136, 1139, 1180, 1181, 1206, 1209
Servant of the Lord/Yahweh, *491, 752*
service, *1, 9, 48, 55, 104, 106, 109, 110, 118, 122, 123, 130, 166, 171, 183, 224, 234, 274, 277, 292, 296, 348, 361, 370, 423, 424, 430, 444, 449, 452, 465, 476, 486, 487, 490, 509, 513, 521, 525, 526, 532, 541, 659, 674, 680, 684, 687, 691, 692, 696-699, 731, 744-746, 760, 763, 769, 825, 837, 860, 867, 882, 884, 885, 897, 920, 930, 931, 940, 954, 960, 966, 988, 989, 1012, 1047, 1048, 1060, 1086-1088, 1101, 1165, 1166, 1209, 1216, 1221, 1224, 1225, 1229, 1230, 1233*
sexual ethics, *144, 352, 499, 717, 882, 1088, 1090, 1110, 1194*
sexual immorality, *43, 383, 528, 703, 715, 716, 925, 1008, 1045, 1088, 1149, 1192*
sexuality, *144, 352, 499, 717, 882, 996, 1088, 1089, 1110, 1194*
Shalom, *565, 874, 1090*
shame, *99, 166, 167, 242, 280, 361, 363, 418, 446, 458, 464, 744, 749, 868, 919, 920, 1062, 1099, 1100, 1104, 1106, 1136, 1208*
sheep, *108, 188, 206, 281, 314, 473, 536, 598, 603, 638, 639, 732, 752, 828, 876, 877, 882, 915, 921, 922, 992, 1029, 1039, 1090-1093, 1181, 1235*
shekinah, *1090*
shema, *167, 412, 413, 421, 586, 889, 1158, 1229*
shepherd, *69, 91, 107, 108, 119, 125, 158, 172, 174, 183, 191, 199, 206, 208, 224, 231, 281, 286, 376, 496, 513, 554, 560, 638-639, 642, 662, 678, 694, 705, 743, 818, 828, 834, 856, 864, 876, 877, 880, 882, 915, 921, 922, 973, 1013, 1023, 1027, 1037, 1091-1091, 1095, 1096, 1180, 1199, 1224, 1229, 1235, 1238, 1240*
ships, shipping, *148, 373, 688, 689, 705, 747, 765, 972, 1061, 1063, 1183, 1241*
Sibylline Oracles, 58, 70, 111, 128, 287, 296, 1034, 1093, 1191, 1211
Sidon, *758, 894*
signs and wonders, *19, 23, 50, 51, 76, 356, 415, 437, 438, 496, 498, 630, 702,*

704, 742, 750, 751, 906, 938, 941, 1093-1095, 1181
Silas, *54, 116, 123, 356, 521, 616, 687, 743, 756, 764, 883, 886, 894, 907, 910, 971, 994, 1100, 1163, 1217, 1220*
Silvanus, *72, 323, 407, 409-411, 444, 764, 915, 916, 922, 1159, 1163*
Simon Magus, *71, 72, 146, 192, 357, 380, 381, 402-404, 529, 584, 586, 749, 750, 930, 931, 953, 1076, 1095, 1148*
Sinai, *2, 38, 40, 168, 172, 197-199, 246, 249, 396, 448, 467, 485, 561, 563-565, 610, 780, 821, 857, 861, 903, 906, 956, 958*
sinners, *4, 14, 42, 44, 49, 69, 76, 117, 160, 209, 267, 275, 378, 429, 485-488, 490, 658, 687, 694, 733, 768, 770, 823, 926, 951, 1002, 1014, 1045, 1073, 1097, 1168, 1191, 1236, 1239*
sisters of Jesus, *1004, 1006, 1098*
Sitz im Leben, 59, 521, 522, 550, 551, 554, 663, 729, 918, 1225
slander, *241, 242, 369, 558, 634, 716, 761, 778, 918-920, 1066, 1077, 1101, 1107, 1211, 1213*
slaves, slavery, *42, 113, 150, 200, 231, 278, 280, 284, 289, 291, 320, 350, 356, 371, 384, 435, 448, 500, 512-514, 517-519, 534, 668, 713, 715, 721, 735, 761, 765, 772, 835, 836, 907, 911, 917, 918, 950, 969, 973, 985, 1001-1003, 1010, 1029, 1031, 1032, 1060, 1064, 1086, 1087, 1092, 1098-1102, 1107, 1108, 1110, 1117, 1135, 1136, 1145, 1158, 1181, 1206-1208, 1212, 1213, 1215, 1217, 1219, 1220*
social institutions, *230, 231, 1102*
social setting, *58, 59, 66, 67, 129, 151, 204, 226, 237, 374, 379, 444, 445, 471, 476, 478, 483, 507, 513, 519, 533, 697, 746, 773, 882, 919, 995, 1053, 1088, 1101-1105, 1107, 1109, 1111, 1156, 1198, 1200*
sociology, *513, 547, 600, 726, 882, 1102, 1111, 1132*
soldiers, *109, 243, 291, 332, 531, 759, 913, 928, 1009, 1060, 1061, 1064, 1065*
solid food, *117, 418, 445, 736-738, 882, 1111, 1115, 1117, 1159*
Son of David, *356, 610, 1082*
Son of God, *2, 26, 27, 36,*

47, 52, 74, 88, 100, 115, 156, 158, 164, 175, 183, 192, 199, 241, 258, 259, 261, 283, 343, 363, 381, 392, 443, 445, 450, 455, 491, 509, 578, 584, 591, 597, 628, 629, 637, 668, 670, 673, 678, 704, 723, 726, 745, 779, 785, 794, 823, 845, 877, 899, 928, 944, 959-961, 964, 1003, 1023, 1024, 1046, 1057, 1073, 1074, 1079, 1083, 1111-1117, 1122, 1193, 1241
Son of man, *62, 158, 164, 206, 273, 337, 338, 356, 360, 396, 630, 704, 799, 843, 859, 956, 959-961, 1002, 1123, 1164, 1203*
songs, *21, 48, 428, 466, 520-522, 524, 525, 539, 540, 604, 662, 723, 780, 823, 851, 962, 1027, 1029, 1030, 1115, 1222, 1237*
sons of God, *100, 209*
sonship, *42, 45, 75, 108, 152-154, 172, 176, 183, 200, 238, 445, 502, 661, 785, 794, 819, 822, 1016, 1111-1116, 1118, 1139*
Sophia, *193, 395, 396, 401, 404, 406-410, 420, 931, 957, 1185, 1201-1203*
sorrow, *477, 564, 603, 949, 1121*
soul, *33, 71, 72, 122, 123, 168, 203, 239, 259, 296, 325, 367, 375, 402, 409, 410, 418, 462, 482, 610, 624, 655, 657, 706, 737, 740, 775-777, 933, 946, 985-987, 1019, 1073, 1103, 1117, 1121, 1122, 1149, 1213*
South Galatia, *146, 755, 757, 764*
Spain, *15, 71, 300, 321, 358, 446, 754, 755, 758, 762, 764, 767*
speaking in tongues, *1117, 1179*
speeches in Acts, *7, 10, 10-12, 24, 97, 269, 271, 382, 415, 450, 542, 566, 626, 627, 767, 826, 887, 905, 906, 1012, 1117, 1126*
Spirit of Christ, *154, 174, 279, 491, 499, 905, 1022*
Spirit of God, *261, 489-492, 497, 639, 702, 755, 779, 836, 905, 947, 1020, 1119, 1121, 1165*
spirits, *46-48, 100, 101, 108, 112, 129, 133, 158, 263, 266, 286, 287, 359, 376, 401, 428, 490, 498, 522, 526, 527, 563, 593, 655, 657, 701, 702, 704, 713, 776, 786, 818, 819, 836, 863, 921-923, 940, 941, 973, 985, 987, 1016, 1017, 1020, 1032, 1079, 1081,*

1117-1122, 1166, 1170, 1185, 1193
spiritual body, *96, 97*
spiritual food, *690, 738, 981*
spiritual house, *107, 507, 510, 511, 513, 519, 689, 921, 1071, 1123, 1155*
spiritual rock, *853*
spiritual songs, *520*
spirituality, *283, 458, 592, 593, 685, 1235*
Stephen, *2, 6, 11, 22, 23, 38, 40, 41, 45, 54, 62, 106, 107, 123, 146, 149, 161, 227, 247, 273, 356, 357, 360, 387, 396, 414, 416, 433, 463, 464, 466-468, 508, 509, 543, 559, 580, 586, 630, 631, 644, 647, 718, 742, 748, 750, 755-757, 762, 764, 767, 775, 824, 859, 862, 884, 904, 930, 931, 941, 943, 944, 970, 972, 1054, 1076, 1094, 1123-1126, 1180, 1201, 1204*
Stoic, Stoicism, *85, 235, 237, 311, 324, 325, 356, 370, 383, 441, 468, 515, 552, 568, 599, 655, 702, 737, 762, 772, 776, 818, 819, 866, 932, 960, 961, 1012, 1090, 1099, 1157, 1190*
stone, *37, 57, 68, 107, 158, 164, 174, 182, 183, 199, 223, 239, 245, 300, 317, 361, 422, 480, 481, 510, 538, 633, 638, 646, 678, 817, 828, 835, 838, 851, 915, 920, 1007, 1071, 1126-1128, 1155, 1162*
stone of stumbling, *915*
strangers, *4, 219, 231, 250, 253, 343, 352, 374, 388, 501, 502, 504-507, 692, 760, 883, 889, 897, 917, 919, 1129, 1136, 1233, 1234*
structuralism, *306, 452, 472, 477, 483, 791, 1049, 1129-1132*
stumbling, stumbling block, *90, 262, 319, 320, 390, 538, 644, 838, 886, 915, 920, 965, 1127, 1128, 1192*
Suffering Servant, *1, 114, 115, 180, 271, 272, 279-281, 284, 523, 641, 642, 780, 824, 838, 891, 1092, 1136, 1139, 1180, 1181*
synagogue, *2, 21, 22, 54, 78, 78, 91-93, 106, 123, 126, 130, 144, 146-148, 150, 153, 160, 165-169, 198, 204, 205, 208, 212, 218, 220-224, 226, 228, 229, 287-293, 297-300, 348, 356, 357, 377, 378, 386, 390, 391, 445, 448, 450, 454, 456, 501, 504, 512, 521, 524, 549, 558, 566, 583, 585-589, 605, 606, 609, 611, 660-662, 695,*

706, 728, 742, 743, 761, 762, 770, 774, 825, 845, 882, 885, 905, 940, 944, 947, 980, 1072, 1080, 1082, 1099, 1102, 1106, 1108, 1109, 1123, 1125, 1137, 1138, 1141-1147, 1152, 1157, 1165, 1207, 1214, 1216, 1217, 1229-1231, 1235, 1237, 1238

syncretism, 171, 299, 309, 411, 529, 703, 772, 773, 1007, 1011, 1146-1148, 1150, 1210

Syntyche, 765

Syria, 50, 53, 55, 72, 94, 126, 142, 144-146, 151, 185, 192, 194, 243, 288, 301, 307, 316, 317, 321, 323, 324, 387, 388, 404, 530, 531, 533, 548, 584, 585, 599, 618, 663, 666, 682, 683, 705, 707, 708, 726, 757, 758, 764, 766, 823, 898, 993, 1005, 1009, 1048, 1059-1061, 1089, 1150, 1151, 1175, 1224, 1225, 1227-1229, 1231

Syrian Antioch, 434, 495, 725-727, 764, 1150

Syrian Christianity, 72, 73, 151, 229, 317, 533, 766, 823, 1150-1152, 1175, 1225, 1229

tabernacle, 35, 40, 41, 98, 274, 360, 361, 396, 439, 440, 448, 453, 457, 466, 467, 480, 482, 487, 497, 508-511, 633, 646, 824, 844, 849, 850, 956, 958, 966, 967, 1003, 1016, 1022, 1070, 1072, 1077, 1154, 1155, 1165, 1185, 1218

table fellowship, 161, 186, 376-379, 502, 503, 530, 587, 649, 687, 693, 996, 1104, 1105, 1110, 1156, 1230

Talmud, 167, 507, 605, 606, 608, 609, 611, 820, 1142, 1156, 1191

tannaim, 608, 611, 1156

Tannaitic Period, 608

targums, 133, 167, 600, 605-607, 609, 656, 729, 731, 779, 817, 820, 997, 1142, 1143, 1156

Tarsus, 146, 753, 755, 758, 762, 1099, 1123, 1219

taxes, 201, 288, 289, 291, 293, 294, 297, 322, 323, 378, 385, 387, 502, 517, 549, 725, 728, 1142, 1059, 1064, 1164

teacher, teachers, 25, 28-34, 41-43, 46, 50, 51, 72-76, 78, 79, 81, 106-109, 122, 126, 142, 146, 149, 155, 158, 160, 170, 186, 194, 224, 225, 240, 255, 259, 304, 305, 308, 329, 335, 336, 342, 348, 354, 357,

368-370, 383, 392, 397, 400, 404, 405, 424, 425, 456, 459, 460, 464, 469, 475, 476, 482, 490, 504-506, 508, 513, 518, 525, 532, 549, 558, 568, 575, 589, 591, 593, 596, 603, 608, 610-613, 615, 618, 622, 628, 642, 652, 654, 697, 704, 707, 714-716, 728, 737, 741, 743-745, 752, 768, 769, 771, 772, 784, 822, 825, 833, 844, 874, 876, 879-881, 884, 894, 896, 923-925, 934, 946, 954, 961, 962, 968, 973, 978, 1007, 1013, 1019, 1044-1046, 1067, 1083, 1086, 1087, 1091, 1109, 1114, 1115, 1120, 1129, 1131, 1142, 1144-1146, 1161, 1162, 1185, 1197, 1201, 1202, 1216, 1218, 1220, 1224, 1226, 1228, 1229

teaching of Jesus, 65, 80, 81, 160, 235, 540, 565, 566, 569, 576, 645, 707, 756, 801, 803, 831, 857, 962, 1021, 1026, 1054, 1093, 1112, 1115, 1158, 1163, 1193

Teachings of Silvanus, 72, 407, 409, 411, 1159

temple of God, 51, 108, 1031, 1155

temple tax, 288, 291, 293, 294, 297, 1142

temptation, 74, 75, 253, 351, 422, 491, 604, 695, 696, 698, 703, 793, 815, 837, 879, 881, 944, 958, 986, 992, 1038, 1048, 1053, 1079, 1081, 1096, 1098, 1166-1170, 1199, 1200, 1225, 1233

Ten Commandments, 646, 827, 830, 1096

Ter Sanctus, 524, 660, 662-664, 1171

Tertius, 765

testamentary literature, 977, 1171

testimonia, 127, 479, 481, 523, 1128

testimony, 29, 30, 53, 56, 57, 77, 94, 103, 122, 123, 128, 140, 149, 150, 155, 177, 186, 240, 242, 259, 262, 282, 284, 301, 308, 312, 329, 330, 339, 342, 349, 359, 393, 409, 410, 424, 445, 467, 497, 503, 505, 506, 522, 529, 539, 569, 588, 597, 629, 635, 677, 693, 710, 717-721, 723, 769, 772, 852, 884, 897, 900, 901, 907, 908, 912, 915, 916, 918, 921, 922, 935, 959, 974, 983, 994, 1005, 1026, 1042, 1082, 1089, 1120, 1137, 1138, 1141, 1163, 1184, 1195,

1197, 1204, 1205, 1220, 1227

textual criticism, 9, 268, 483, 620, 1171, 1173

thanks, thanksgiving, 120, 130, 131, 131, 268, 407, 409, 410, 414, 428, 449, 450, 474, 522, 525, 526, 531, 607, 650-652, 671, 688-692, 733, 738, 744, 768, 864, 889, 942, 943, 947, 1030, 1053, 1226, 1232, 1235

theophany, 307, 396, 397, 419, 427, 561, 563, 818, 840, 857, 866, 867, 875, 903, 960, 1120, 1182

Thessalonica, 290, 530, 758, 764, 765, 771, 1144, 1217

thief, 266, 271, 425, 570, 571, 866, 869, 920, 1192

this age, 44, 64, 241, 348, 441, 557, 656, 913, 1013, 1038, 1068, 1078, 1079, 1155, 1198, 1223

Tiberius, 53, 148, 149, 294, 907, 911, 932, 1011, 1028, 1065, 1206

tomb, tombs, 34, 144, 186, 307, 588, 928, 1019, 1032, 1034, 1065, 1135, 1181

tongue, 130, 196, 351, 370, 459, 480, 538, 815, 822, 837, 838, 951, 974, 1054, 1079, 1110, 1178, 1179

tongues, 23, 113, 116, 124, 208, 220, 332, 351, 400, 492, 498, 905, 906, 972, 1095, 1117, 1177-1179, 1207, 1227

Torah, 30-32, 91, 158, 160-162, 218, 227-229, 241, 298, 351, 355, 368, 464, 489, 502, 508, 546, 548, 551, 558, 582, 606, 608, 610, 643, 644, 647, 666, 704, 731, 753, 764, 811, 814, 825, 893, 913, 965, 979, 980, 989, 994, 998, 1058, 1085, 1125, 1141-1143, 1145, 1157, 1160, 1179, 1199, 1201, 1207

Tosefta, 606, 608, 1142

tradition criticism, 607, 711

travel, 8, 18, 21, 70, 211, 222, 354, 393, 415, 444, 507, 528, 562, 588, 670, 688, 754, 759, 760, 762, 769, 862, 883, 986, 1059, 1061, 1063, 1120, 1139, 1179, 1217

trial, 24, 103, 187, 188, 191, 254, 327, 361, 500, 558, 622, 656, 815, 816, 862, 887, 907, 908, 927, 928, 936, 1031, 1040, 1125, 1140, 1166, 1167, 1195

trials, 12, 41, 99, 100, 102, 131, 172, 273, 327, 342, 366, 480, 483, 511, 549, 552, 557, 558, 604, 739, 781, 794, 822, 863, 879, 885, 908, 941, 945, 946,

953, 974, 1039, 1044, 1097, 1139, 1166, 1167, 1200, 1202, 1240

tribulation, 132, 273, 330-332, 335-337, 339, 340, 342-344, 348, 438, 469, 643, 871, 915, 1014, 1031, 1179-1182, 1205, 1241

tribune, 1060, 1065

Trinity, 37, 70, 88, 115, 127, 151, 159, 162, 169, 178, 180, 181, 183, 218, 235, 250, 258, 259, 388, 394, 395, 412, 430, 431, 477, 489, 490, 498, 559, 611, 628, 630, 634, 636, 666, 678, 708, 712, 728, 812, 929, 948, 976, 996, 1093, 1120, 1135, 1150, 1177, 1231, 1232, 1236-1238

triumph, 95, 96, 98-100, 159, 201, 227, 254, 260, 261, 283-285, 321, 348, 359, 362, 372, 442, 468, 480, 523, 525, 526, 539, 553, 556-559, 610, 627, 634, 635, 656, 678, 732, 733, 741, 749, 785, 807, 818, 823, 838, 922, 926, 1030, 1031, 1160, 1164, 1196, 1227, 1233, 1234

Troas, 54, 79, 191, 271, 378, 531, 681, 686, 688, 1104

trumpets, 62, 63, 132, 167, 340, 427, 477, 481, 780, 783, 870, 1030, 1031, 1035, 1037, 1085, 1179, 1182, 1183, 1192

truth, 9, 17, 36, 74, 75, 84, 98, 119, 120, 134, 135, 138, 140, 155, 183, 200, 217, 220, 239, 243, 249, 253, 258, 259, 263, 282, 296, 308, 312, 335, 351, 367, 381, 404, 407-412, 460, 466, 470, 472, 474, 484, 486, 495, 501, 510, 536, 551, 552, 580, 582, 589-591, 593-595, 597, 609, 635, 637, 639, 640, 646, 651, 652, 659, 666, 675, 692, 694, 695, 698, 699, 702, 710, 738, 751, 768-770, 782, 783, 789, 790, 793, 806, 808, 809, 814, 819, 822, 845, 852, 858, 866, 872, 876, 878, 880, 881, 884, 885, 897, 899, 922, 949-951, 954, 960, 963, 973, 987, 1023, 1024, 1028, 1031, 1045-1047, 1049, 1057, 1078, 1095, 1106, 1110, 1113, 1119, 1122, 1140, 1165, 1169, 1184-1187, 1191-1194, 1203, 1223, 1226, 1227, 1232, 1238

Tryphosa, 765

Twelve, the, 7, 38, 42, 50, 72, 73, 76-78, 80-84, 106, 108, 141, 147, 159, 166, 173, 191, 198, 206, 207, 222, 225, 300, 302, 317,

355, 407, 409, 411, 417, 425, 428, 437, 467, 469, 533, 542, 543, 545, 548, 549, 580, 588, 596, 607, 616, 628, 631, 636, 643, 675, 690, 737, 741-744, 752, 754-757, 762-764, 766, 771, 780, 784, 817, 824, 827, 851, 890, 903, 906, 921, 931, 932, 966, 972, 978, 991, 1033, 1077, 1082, 1086, 1106, 1115, 1123-1125, 1127, 1162, 1166, 1169, 1178, 1187, 1191, 1193, 1210, 1216, 1238

twelve tribes, 42, 76, 108, 166, 173, 198, 207, 542, 543, 548, 549, 631, 636, 643, 780, 1187

Two Ways, 47, 48, 129, 181, 232, 241, 300, 301, 347, 351, 352, 369, 460, 519, 572, 656, 657, 672, 823, 827, 897, 898, 963, 1108, 1109, 1157-1159, 1187, 1191, 1193, 1213

Tychicus, 765, 888

typology, 21, 214, 235, 270, 280, 436, 479-482, 479, 536, 537, 541, 631, 670, 706, 732, 737, 780-782, 811, 814, 815, 818, 819, 825, 826, 828, 830, 834-836, 839, 841, 844, 933, 953, 965, 999, 1050, 1070, 1113, 1187

Tyre, 373, 841, 894, 1211

uncircumcised, 42, 226, 227, 229, 467, 764, 993, 1109

unclean, 233, 487, 570, 647, 759, 761, 854, 988-991, 1104, 1122, 1188

unfaithfulness, 26, 112, 264, 343, 377, 712, 713, 716, 780, 798, 1043, 1211

ungodliness, 29, 41, 151, 176, 264-267, 335, 337, 356, 379, 425, 538, 570, 624, 653, 714, 816, 818, 819, 823, 836, 839, 840, 854, 1003, 1045, 1046, 1057, 1094, 1097, 1240

union with Christ, 54, 55, 262, 354, 1140

universalism, 61, 343, 359, 392, 625, 725, 1188, 1189

unleavened bread, 314

unmarried, 714, 743, 931, 1216, 1221

Urbanus, 763, 765

vanity, 279, 394, 610, 673, 972, 1015, 1028, 1031, 1164

Valentinus, 149, 193, 194, 215, 255, 400, 404, 410, 1020, 1190

vengeance, 343, 428, 486, 623, 721, 729, 837, 897, 1034, 1035, 1143, 1193, 1239

vials, 1190

vices, 157, 231, 235, 322, 349, 352, 379, 469, 478, 552, 623, 658, 710, 716, 729, 731, 735, 736, 751, 769, 771, 926, 932, 939, 940, 952, 963, 994-996, 1012, 1013, 1047, 1079, 1097, 1098, 1149, 1158, 1159, 1169, 1186, 1187, 1190-1194, 1201

victory, 39, 46, 50, 54, 96, 100, 104, 128, 133, 181, 200, 209, 240, 261, 263, 267, 283, 284, 322, 328, 336, 339, 348, 349, 353, 362, 366, 389, 423, 459, 483, 486, 499, 524, 538, 565, 627, 635, 636, 646, 662, 682, 698, 702, 720, 753, 768, 775, 776, 779, 780, 794, 823, 836, 851, 852, 863, 870, 881, 897, 899, 902, 918, 921, 922, 936, 940, 1035, 1039, 1059, 1060, 1077, 1080, 1119, 1223, 1224, 1231, 1234-1236

vine, 88, 181, 208, 212, 391, 541, 583, 629, 690, 827, 1025, 1036, 1087, 1235

violence, 127, 284, 415, 912, 1036, 1080

virgin, 33, 106, 164, 182, 187, 258, 259, 314, 315, 322, 322, 387, 573, 581, 586, 648, 663, 705, 713, 723, 724, 960, 1006, 1089, 1090, 1108, 1121, 1186, 1207, 1221, 1221

virtue, 2, 5, 85, 96, 101, 131, 210, 214, 216, 235, 242, 263, 275, 277, 280, 281, 296, 311, 319, 322, 324, 326, 329, 337, 349-352, 363, 366-370, 397, 411, 420, 469, 478, 481, 488, 501, 502, 504-506, 507, 529, 552, 599, 633, 639, 651, 658, 696, 735, 736, 742, 772, 780, 816, 818, 819, 822, 843, 844, 860, 863, 898, 899, 920, 922, 926, 932, 940, 952, 961, 963, 988, 994-996, 1012, 1014, 1017, 1049, 1062, 1073, 1098, 1104, 1121, 1157, 1158, 1159, 1161, 1187, 1190-1194, 1202, 1211-1214, 1216

virtue and vice lists, 1158, 1191, 1192

visions, 17, 18, 47, 58, 62, 66, 68, 70, 81, 84, 86, 104, 112, 132, 133, 141, 151, 155, 177, 203, 244, 317, 320, 337, 340, 344, 347, 348, 352, 415, 427, 441, 456, 469, 470, 483, 524, 525, 541, 625, 639, 659, 704, 713, 714, 719, 720, 747, 784, 790, 796, 799, 831, 851-854, 884, 898, 908, 952, 956, 959, 971,

972, 974-976, 978, 1010, 1021, 1022, 1026, 1027, 1031, 1036, 1037, 1049, 1085, 1086, 1114, 1120, 1129, 1182-1184, 1190, 1194-1198, 1210, 1239

voluntary associations, 204, 1102, 1108, 1198

vow, 383, 419, 581, 647, 648, 942, 1008, 1069, 1163

war, warfare, 3, 44, 46, 50, 51, 54, 59, 66, 67, 127, 128, 145, 165, 166, 184-186, 188, 189, 193, 194, 207, 213, 220, 229, 254, 288, 290, 291, 302, 321, 323, 332, 348, 472, 551, 599, 600, 605, 609, 635, 636, 719, 730, 798, 841, 869, 870, 889, 897, 898, 900-902, 939, 946, 986, 997, 1029, 1034, 1035, 1059, 1063, 1064, 1072, 1077, 1078, 1080, 1085, 1089, 1105, 1106, 1160, 1181, 1182

warrior, 100, 481, 785, 870, 871, 997, 1032, 1082

wash, washing, 115, 116, 118-121, 123, 131, 354, 504, 658, 692, 693, 795, 828, 928, 942, 962, 990, 996

watchfulness, 349, 424, 1170, 1199, 1200

water, 33, 41, 93, 113-123, 132, 155, 242, 253, 258, 282, 283, 354, 494, 571, 575, 591, 637, 656, 665, 691-693, 776, 795, 836, 922, 971, 991, 997, 1046, 1065, 1073, 1148, 1183, 1204, 1232, 1235

weakness, 33, 100, 104, 227, 262, 274, 284, 311, 323, 367, 375, 438, 574, 613, 615, 616, 642, 698, 745, 819, 887, 892, 918, 940, 945, 958, 961, 986, 994, 1053, 1096, 1206, 1209

wealth, 76, 93, 103, 233, 288, 291, 293, 299, 349, 351, 374, 428, 473, 503, 522, 540, 549-551, 559, 560, 564, 600, 692, 705, 711, 745, 773, 778, 879, 1035, 1051-1053, 1064, 1067, 1087, 1101, 1132, 1138, 1139, 1140, 1169, 1171, 1190, 1198, 1206, 1223

weapons, 215, 228, 294

wickedness, 47, 50-52, 63, 66, 69, 77, 90, 130, 216, 251, 253, 255, 320, 331, 337, 352, 375, 376, 382, 459-462, 490, 505, 508, 525, 526, 567, 606, 621, 624, 632, 636, 656, 658, 818, 823, 836, 880, 881, 942, 963, 976, 987, 996, 999, 1015, 1016, 1019, 1046, 1047, 1057, 1091, 1095-1097, 1119, 1122,

1170, 1182, 1188, 1193, 1194, 1198, 1200, 1224

widows, 222, 241, 462, 504, 506, 507, 518, 519, 687, 692, 713, 714, 734, 745, 759, 762, 838, 882, 930, 935, 1039, 1067, 1071, 1087, 1089, 1090, 1100, 1101, 1104, 1123, 1125, 1193, 1200, 1206, 1212, 1213, 1216, 1219, 1220, 1221

wild beasts, 329, 530, 699, 720, 736, 1080, 1199

wilderness, 40, 42, 108, 127, 247, 274, 335, 365, 415, 448, 467, 480, 489, 494, 509, 557, 567, 614, 618, 633, 737, 781, 816, 844, 850, 998, 1013, 1094, 1166, 1167

will of God, 88, 89, 134, 201, 258, 273, 320, 346, 351, 352, 365, 419, 432, 463, 488, 525, 567, 602, 638, 794, 828, 879, 946, 964-967, 986, 1038, 1062, 1166

wisdom/Wisdom, 40, 59, 60, 63, 65-69, 72, 86, 88, 102, 103, 135, 142, 143, 158, 159, 163, 172, 178, 183, 287, 296, 314, 326, 347, 350-352, 356, 365, 390, 399, 401, 409, 413, 420-422, 428, 436, 439, 445, 465, 470, 478, 480, 489, 541, 545, 548, 549, 551, 552, 556-560, 582, 591, 594, 607, 621, 638, 640, 665, 667, 678, 716, 734, 737, 738, 742, 777-779, 783, 815, 816, 819, 822, 827, 830, 832, 839, 854, 856, 876, 879, 887, 888, 891, 895, 896, 899, 932, 933, 942, 945, 952, 953, 956, 957, 960, 961, 972, 980, 995, 1012, 1039, 1044, 1055, 1079, 1123, 1145, 1157, 1158, 1167, 1169, 1176, 1177, 1185, 1187, 1190-1192, 1194, 1200-1204, 1212

Wisdom christology, 888, 891, 957, 1201-1203

witness, 5, 9, 12, 17-19, 21, 22, 24, 37, 54, 76, 79, 96, 97, 101, 106-108, 114, 119, 122, 126, 127, 139, 141, 146, 153-155, 171, 177, 191, 198, 210, 214, 217, 218, 220, 242, 259, 268, 270, 271, 273, 281, 282, 284, 292, 310, 312, 313, 317, 325, 328, 333, 338, 339, 344, 353, 356-358, 392, 411, 427, 432, 433, 439, 441, 442, 456, 457, 469, 496, 498, 503, 506, 541, 545, 546, 548, 551, 554, 555, 557, 562, 593, 622, 627, 631, 635, 636, 666, 676, 694, 717-723,

736, 740, 742, 766, 767,
770, 772, 790, 795, 806-
808, 858, 865, 884, 885,
903, 906, 915, 916, 926-
928, 930, 938, 959, 960,
981, 992, 1017, 1020,
1022, 1026, 1029, 1031-
1033, 1035, 1074, 1082,
1086, 1102, 1103, 1106,
1107, 1110, 1119, 1120,
1124, 1136, 1137, 1140,
1173, 1174, 1196, 1199,
1204, 1205, 1207, 1208,
1216, 1226, 1232
wives, 3, 4, 41, 112, 235, 325,
350, 352, 356, 371, 378,
435, 460, 504, 512-514,
517-519, 534, 599, 639,
699, 714-717, 730, 762,
764, 765, 835, 859, 896,
918, 923, 935, 946, 950,
1004, 1006, 1088, 1089,
1092, 1094, 1100, 1107,
1108, 1110, 1117, 1158,
1159, 1161, 1186, 1206-
1215, 1217, 1218, 1221,
1222
woes, 129, 343, 564, 573,
575, 614, 836, 840, 1030,
1052, 1170, 1179-1182,
1205, 1213, 1214, 1241
woman, 2, 4, 14, 31, 41, 105,
108, 111, 122, 127, 164,
195, 203, 206, 209, 221,
226, 293, 299, 313, 320,
358, 379, 386, 405, 428,
443, 451, 457, 459, 469,
473, 494, 495, 497, 502-
504, 507, 508, 512, 513,
518, 519, 537, 538, 564,
582, 603, 705, 711-717,
721, 723, 724, 743, 746,
765, 768, 772, 773, 817,
852, 853, 882, 908, 922,
935, 942, 967, 971, 975,
1006, 1033, 1034, 1064,
1070, 1076, 1080, 1089,
1090, 1100, 1101, 1104-
1106, 1108, 1110, 1111,
1116, 1117, 1140, 1144,
1166, 1176, 1181, 1193,
1200, 1205-1222, 1235
works of the Law, 277, 365,
891
wrath, 111, 132, 133, 151,
264, 266, 267, 275, 278,
282, 284, 287, 337, 343,
371, 428, 477, 538, 564,
621, 622, 625, 627, 704,
733-735, 823, 850, 869,
870, 874, 926, 1015, 1021,
1030, 1031, 1037, 1074,
1156, 1183, 1193, 1238-
1240
written code, 350
Yahoel, 44
zeal, 74, 201, 290, 463, 532,
581, 769, 772, 790, 1059,
1066, 1138, 1153, 1185,
1218
Zealot, 51, 185, 463, 551,
902, 1160
Zenas, 765

Zeus, 50, 146, 414, 416, 501,
1008, 1011, 1029, 1078,
1112, 1126, 1147, 1148
Zion, 36, 112, 151, 198, 218,
229, 334, 420, 457, 489,
537, 538, 561-565, 587,
633, 753, 851, 992, 1037,
1138, 1155, 1165, 1210,
1242
Zoroastrianism, 1152

Articles Index

Abraham, 1
Acts of the Apostles, 7
Adversaries, 24
Alexandria, Alexandrian
  Christianity, 34
Ancestors, 37
Angels, Heavenly Beings, An-
  gel Christology, 44
Anointing, 48
Antichrist, 50
Antioch on the Orontes, 53
Apocalyptic, Apocalypti-
  cism, 55
Apocryphal and Pseudepi-
  graphal Writings, 68
Apostasy, 73
Apostle, Apostleship, 76
Apostolic Fathers, 82
Architecture, Early Church,
  91
Ascension, 95
Assurance, 102
Authority, 105
Babylon, 111
Baptism, Baptismal Rites,
  112
Barnabas, Epistle of, 125
Beasts, Dragon, Sea, Con-
  flict Motif, 127
Blessing, 129
Bowls, 132
Canon, 134
Centers of Christianity, 144
Christ, 152
Christianity and Judaism:
  Partings of the Ways, 159
Christology, 170
Chronology, 184
Church, 194
Church as Israel, People of
  God, 204
Church Order, Govern-
  ment, 219
Circumcision, 226
Civil Authority, 230
Clement of Rome, 233
Commandments, 238
Conscience, 241
Cornelius, 243
Covenant, New Covenant,
  245
Creation, Cosmology, 250
Creeds, Confessional Forms,
  255
Cross, Theology of the, 260
Day of the Lord, 264
Death of Christ, 267
Diaspora Judaism, 287

Didache, The, 300
Diognetus, Epistle to, 302
Discipline, 304
Docetism, 306
Early Catholicism, 310
Ebionites, 313
Election, 317
Emperor, Emperor Cult, 321
Endurance, Perseverance,
  326
Eschatology, 330
Eternity, Eternal, 345
Ethics, 347
Evangelism in the Early
  Church, 353
Exaltation, Enthronement,
  359
Faith, Faithfulness, 364
Faith and Works, 367
Fear, 370
Fellowship, 373
Flesh, 374
Food, Food Laws, Table Fel-
  lowship, 376
Forgiveness, 379
Freedom, Liberty, 382
Galilean Christianity, 385
Gentiles, Gentile Mission,
  388
Glory, 394
Gnosis, Gnosticism, 400
God, 412
Gospel, 431
Grace, 433
Healing, Illness, 436
Heaven, New Heaven, 439
Hebrews, 443
Hell, Abyss, Eternal Punish-
  ment, 459
Hellenists, Hellenistic and
  Hellenistic-Jewish Christi-
  anity, 462
Hermas, Shepherd of, 469
Hermeneutics, 471
Holy, Holiness, 485
Holy Spirit, 489
Hope, 499
Hospitality, 501
House, Spiritual House, 507
Household, Family, 511
Household Codes, 513
Hymns, Songs, 520
Idolatry, 528
Ignatius of Antioch, 530
Imitation, 533
Intertextuality in Early Chris-
  tian Literature, 536
Israel, Twelve Tribes, 542
James, Letter of, 545
Jerusalem, Zion, Holy City,
  561
Jesus Traditions, 565
Jewish Christianity, 579
John, Letters of, 587
Josephus, 599
Joy, 600
Judaism, Post-A.D. 70, 605
Jude, 611
Judgment, 621
Kerygma and Didache, 626
Kingdom of God, 629
Knowledge, 638
Lamb, 641

Land in Early Christianity,
  642
Law, 644
Letter, Letter Form, 649
Life and Death, 655
Light and Darkness, 657
Liturgical Elements, 659
Logos Christology, 665
Lord, 667
Lord's Day, 679
Lord's Supper, Love Feast,
  686
Love, 694
Magic and Astrology, 701
Marcion, 705
Mark, Secret Gospel of, 708
Marriage, Divorce, Adultery,
  712
Martyrdom, 717
Mary, 722
Matthean Community, 724
Melchizedek, 729
Melito of Sardis, 731
Mercy, 733
Milk, Solid Food, 736
Millennium, 738
Ministry, 741
Miracles in Acts, 746
Mission, Early Non-Pauline,
  752
Mortality and Immortality,
  775
Moses, 777
Mystery, 782
Name, 785
Narrative Criticism, 787
New Birth, 792
New Testament Theology,
  796
Noncanonical Writings, Cita-
  tions in the General Epis-
  tles, 814
Obedience and Lawlessness,
  821
Old Testament in Acts, 823
Old Testament in Apostolic
  Fathers, 826
Old Testament in General
  Epistles, 834
Old Testament in Hebrews,
  841
Old Testament in Revela-
  tion, 850
Parousia, 856
Pastoral Theology, 876
Paul and Paulinisms in Acts,
  883
Pauline Legacy and School,
  887
Peace, 893
Pella, Flight to, 900
Pentecost, 902
Persecution, 907
1 Peter, 914
2 Peter, 923
Peter, Gospel of, 927
Philip the Evangelist, 929
Philo, 931
Polycarp of Smyrna, 934
Power, 938
Prayer, 941
Preaching from Acts, Gen-
  eral Epistles, Revelation,

948
Preexistence, *955*
Pride and Humility, *961*
Priest, High Priest, *963*
Promise, *967*
Prophecy, Prophets, False
    Prophets, *970*
Pseudepigraphy, *977*
Psychology, *984*
Purity and Impurity, *988*
Qumran, *997*
Redemption, *1001*
Relatives of Jesus, *1004*
Religions, Greco-Roman,
    1006
Repentance, Second Repen-
    tance, *1011*
Resurrection, *1015*
Reveal, Revelation, *1020*
Revelation, Book of, *1025*
Rewards, *1038*
Rhetoric, Rhetorical Criti-

cism, *1041*
Riches and Poverty, *1051*
Righteousness, *1053*
Roman Empire, Christian
    and the, *1059*
Rome and Roman Christian-
    ity, *1063*
Sacrifice, Offerings, Gifts,
    1069
Salvation, *1072*
Samaria, *1075*
Satan, Devil, *1077*
Savior, *1082*
Scrolls, Seals, *1084*
Servant, Service, *1086*
Sexuality, Sexual Ethics,
    1088
Shepherd, Flock, *1090*
Signs and Wonders, *1093*
Sin, Wickedness, *1095*
Slave, Slavery, *1098*

Social Setting of Early Non-
    Pauline Christianity, *1102*
Son of God, *1111*
Sonship, Child, Children,
    1115
Spirits, *1117*
Stephen, *1123*
Stone, Cornerstone, *1126*
Structuralism and Discourse
    Analysis, *1129*
Suffering, *1135*
Synagogue, *1141*
Syncretism, *1146*
Syria, Syrian Christianity,
    1150
Tabernacle, Sanctuary, *1154*
Teaching, Paraenesis, *1156*
Temple, *1159*
Temptation, *1166*
Textual Criticism, *1171*
Thomas, Gospel of, 1175

Tongues, *1177*
Tribulation, Messianic
    Woes, *1179*
Trumpets, *1182*
Truth, *1184*
Universalism, *1188*
Virtues and Vices, *1190*
Visions, Ecstatic Experience,
    1194
Watchfulness, *1199*
Wisdom, *1200*
Witness, *1204*
Woman and Man, *1205*
Women in the Early
    Church, *1215*
World, *1222*
Worship and Liturgy, *1224*
Wrath, Destruction, *1238*